THIS BIBLE BELONGS TO:

_____

_____

date

IMPACT

THE STUDENT LEADERSHIP BIBLE

IMPACT

THE STUDENT LEADERSHIP BIBLE

Dr. Jay Strack
Executive Editor

Brent Crowe, M.Div., M.A.
Associate Editor

NEW KING JAMES VERSION®

THOMAS NELSON
Since 1798

NASHVILLE   DALLAS   MEXICO CITY   RIO DE JANEIRO   BEIJING

Impact: The Student Leadership Bible
© 2008 by Jay Strack

The Holy Bible, New King James Version®
© 1982 by Thomas Nelson, Inc.

Published in Nashville, Tennessee, by Thomas Nelson. Thomas Nelson is a registered trademark of Thomas Nelson, Inc.

Thomas Nelson, Inc. titles may be purchased in bulk for educational, business, fund-raising, or sales promotional use. For information, please e-mail SpecialMarkets@ThomasNelson.com.

Printed in China
08 09 10 11 12—5 4 3 2 1

TABLE OF CONTENTS

THE OLD TESTAMENT

THE NEW TESTAMENT

INTRODUCTION TO *IMPACT*

Imagine for a moment that you are able to climb to a peak so high that you can view time from the dawn of creation to the last day before eternity and then into heaven. How amazing would that adventure be? To see the heritage of leadership, the expansion of civilizations, and the heroes and heroines who defied death to make a difference in the name of God.

Get ready—what you hold in your hands will take you there without a climb as you open the ancient Book of Books and read firsthand the words of the Creator and from the very heart of those leaders who forged forward by faith into the ends of the earth.

Waves of hope flow throughout the Scriptures from its beginning to the last book, and each and every one is available to you today. The power of these words is timeless. For example, the prophet Habakkuk earnestly sought an answer to his complaint of the prospering evildoers of 610 B.C., and the Lord replied, "*The just shall live by his faith.*"

Just a few thousand years later in A.D. 57 the apostle Paul faced great persecution and peril, but continually wrote to encourage and edify the early Christian church. So important were the words written by Habakkuk, that they are quoted three different times in the New Testament: Romans 1:17, Galatians 3:11, and Hebrews 10:38.

The wave of hope did not stop there as it flowed through the millenniums to A.D. 1517. German theologian Martin Luther began the Great Reformation, one of the most critical chapters of Christian history. The young monk had heard fragments of the Gospels and Epistles and was overjoyed to find a Latin Bible with the whole of God's Word. Diligent in the practices of the church, Luther made a pilgrimage to Rome and began the act of climbing what was known as Pilate's staircase on his knees in order to receive a special indulgence from the Pope. At each level of the staircase, the Scripture of Romans 1:17 filled his head until it exploded in his heart. He knew the truth at that moment: "*The just shall live by faith.*" He rose from his knees and walked down the steps, and the Reformation began. History shows he faced ridicule and risked death, but never wavered; and a new, uncompromising church was born in the Middle Ages of time.

Just two centuries later in 1738, John Wesley listened while Luther's commentary on Romans was read; and he reported later his heart was "strangely warmed." The call of God took him across 225,000 miles, mostly on horseback, through all kinds of weather and rough roads, to preach 40,000 times. At the heart of his preaching and writing was "*the just shall live by faith.*"

And now, less than three hundred years later, the vision of Habakkuk and an understanding of salvation by faith has impacted your life. The Word of God stands timeless and potent through the ages for every life. This book you hold in your hands demands leadership, first from God into your life and then into the lives of all in your sphere of influence. Leadership cannot impact others unless it pours forth from biblical principle that is woven into your DNA and defines your reality.

The IMPACT Bible exists as a leadership tool for students so that you can study for yourselves and be convinced in your own mind that no matter what crossroad or juncture in life, whether it is the best day or the darkest day, you can say as Luther did, "Here I stand. I can do no other."

IMPACT: The Student Leadership Bible, the serious leadership tool for students who are serious about their faith.

Throughout the Bible, you will find inspiration and information through these sections:

GC2-Relational Theology—Throughout the IMPACT Bible you will find GC2 notes in Relational Theology intended to guide you into a lifestyle of loving God, loving others and making disciples.

Inside the Influencers—Real-world examples of people who faced the obstacles and crises of life and won. Learn from those who have gone before us, how to prepare for the worst and best life has to offer. *The future belongs to those who are prepared.*

Leadership Realities—These are the 52 core realities that make up the DNA of the movement called Student Leadership University. These principles, when practiced, are the gateway to becoming a student of influence.

Leadership Issues—These are the key topics lifted from the pages of Scripture that every young leader must inherit. Because the Bible is the greatest leadership book ever written, the journey to leadership begins at the feet of Jesus.

Through the Grid—This comprehensive Christian worldview material allows you to view the most difficult and controversial questions of life through the grid of Scripture with confidence and clarity. The end result is the ability to "think Christianly" in all things.

GC2: LOVE GOD—LOVE OTHERS— MAKE DISCIPLES

Notes in Relational Theology

Jesus reduced over 1,130 commandments and traditions to the two greatest (Deut. 6:5 and Lev. 19:18), merged them into one, and gave us The Great Commandment—"Love the LORD your God and love your neighbor as yourself" (Matt. 22:37, 39). As this identity of love is lived out, it empowers fulfillment of The Great Commission: "Go therefore and make disciples of all the nations" (Matt. 28:19). With these few words Jesus gives meaning to life and relevance to all scripture. Life is about relating passionately to Jesus and being caringly involved in sharing His life and love with others that they might also follow Him.

As noted author and speaker Josh McDowell writes, "Scriptural commands and rules should not be seen as merely instructions to obey but rather as ways to relate to a person, whose name is Jesus" (*Beyond Belief to Convictions,* Tyndale House, 2002). In short, our theology or "study of God" must certainly include rational truths to believe and behavioral admonitions to obey, but most significantly these are to lead us into an ever-deepening love relationship with Jesus and those around us.

Centuries ago, the Spirit of God moved among His church in what we now call the Great Reformation. Significant and lasting changes within the church took place as its leaders sought to restore the purity of man's relationship with God, the essentials of grace and faith, and a renewed emphasis on the centrality and reliability of Scripture. Could it be that the Spirit of God longs to begin a new movement among students around the world that will be just as real, relevant, and lasting? Could it be that God is at work in you to return to the powerful simplicity of loving God and others as we go forth to make disciples? Might His Spirit be restoring His people to an identity of Great Commandment love and a lifestyle of Great Commission passion? If so, let's join Him in proclaiming and living a fresh emphasis on relationships and an accurate view of Christ by truly experiencing His Word. We need God to restore our compassion for the people around us and breathe new life into our presentation of the glorious gospel of Jesus Christ.

Life relevance might then return as we rediscover the wonder and privilege of intimately relating to the Creator. Our motivation for following Jesus would shift as feelings of duty, obligation, and the pressure to perform are replaced by joy, a sense of privilege, and a sincere desire to please Him. Righteousness would be empowered by the dread of displeasing such a loving Savior. Life significance would be found in co-laboring with Christ to love others instead of in what we acquire, accomplish, or achieve. As we join Him in loving well, we would then "love" many into His kingdom. *Let's join Him in the journey!*

Using the GC2 Notes

Twenty-four (24) different Relational Theology topics are featured in the **GC2** notes with each including six (6) scriptural studies. Used for student Bible study, small groups, or personal study, each topic can be the focus of six weeks of study.

The suggested plan below organizes the Relational Theology topics over eight (8) years of student and college ministry with a focus of three (3) six-week studies each year, possibly one each in the fall, spring, and summer. Each year there is a suggested six-week study in Relational Foundations, one in Following Jesus, and one in Relational Skills for Life. Student leaders materials are available at www.impactbible.net.

1. Loving the Real God—Gen. 2:7; Is. 30:18; Zeph. 3:17; Mark 12:29; Phil. 4:19; Heb. 4:15

2. Good News—Gen. 3:15; Is. 53:6; Rom. 5:8; Rom. 5:17; Gal. 2:20; 1 John 4:10

3. Giving First—Rom. 15:7; 1 Cor. 11:2; 1 Cor. 12:25; 2 Cor. 1:3, 4; Heb. 10:24; 1 Pet. 4:10

4. Who Am I?—Prov. 22:6; Jer. 1:5; 1 Cor. 12:6, 7; Eph. 4:4–6; 1 Thess. 2:8; 1 John 4:12

5. Skills to Relate—2 Sam. 30:6; Matt. 5:4; Acts 20:35; Eph. 4:15; Eph. 4:31, 32; James 5:16

6. Following Jesus—Gen. 18:17; Ps. 119:16; Mark 1:35; Luke 10:39; 1 Cor. 13:11; Col. 2:6

7. Defining Convictions—Ps. 19:7; Prov. 14:12; John 8:32; John 14:11; John 18:38; 2 Tim. 3:16, 17

8. Basic Training—Gen. 2:18; Matt. 18:6; Matt. 22:37–29; John 13:34; John 14:15; 2 Cor. 7:1

9. Sharing Christ—Matt. 28:19, 20; Mark 5:22–24; Acts 1:8; John 5:20; John 19:38; 2 Cor. 3:2

10. Spiritual Formation—Matt. 10:8; Mark 5:33, 34; Luke 6:40; John 14:9; 1 Thess. 5:5; 1 Tim. 4:7

PREFACE TO THE
NEW KING JAMES VERSION

Purpose

In the preface to the 1611 edition, the translators of the Authorized Version, known popularly as the King James Bible, state that it was not their purpose "to make a new translation . . . but to make a good one better." Indebted to the earlier work of William Tyndale and others, they saw their best contribution to consist in revising and enhancing the excellence of the English versions which had sprung from the Reformation of the sixteenth century. In harmony with the purpose of the King James scholars, the translators and editors of the present work have not pursued a goal of innovation. They have perceived the Holy Bible, New King James Version, as a continuation of the labors of the earlier translators, thus unlocking for today's readers the spiritual treasures found especially in the Authorized Version of the Holy Scriptures.

A Living Legacy

For nearly four hundred years, and throughout several revisions of its English form, the King James Bible has been deeply revered among the English-speaking peoples of the world. The precision of translation for which it is historically renowned, and its majesty of style, have enabled that monumental version of the Word of God to become the mainspring of the religion, language, and legal foundations of our civilization.

Although the Elizabethan period and our own era share in zeal for technical advance, the former period was more aggressively devoted to classical learning. Along with this awakened concern for the classics came a flourishing companion interest in the Scriptures, an interest that was enlivened by the conviction that the manuscripts were providentially handed down and were a trustworthy record of the inspired Word of God. The King James translators were committed to producing an English Bible that would be a precise translation, and by no means a paraphrase or a broadly approximate rendering. On the one hand, the scholars were almost as familiar with the original languages of the Bible as with their native English. On the other hand, their reverence for the divine Author and His Word assured a translation of the Scriptures in which only a principle of utmost accuracy could be accepted.

In 1786 Catholic scholar Alexander Geddes said of the King James Bible, "If accuracy and strictest attention to the letter of the text be supposed to constitute an excellent version, this is of all versions the most excellent." George Bernard

Shaw became a literary legend in our century because of his severe and often humorous criticisms of our most cherished values. Surprisingly, however, Shaw pays the following tribute to the scholars commissioned by King James: "The translation was extraordinarily well done because to the translators what they were translating was not merely a curious collection of ancient books written by different authors in different stages of culture, but the Word of God divinely revealed through His chosen and expressly inspired scribes. In this conviction they carried out their work with boundless reverence and care and achieved a beautifully artistic result." History agrees with these estimates. Therefore, while seeking to unveil the excellent *form* of the traditional English Bible, special care has also been taken in the present edition to preserve the work of *precision,* which is the legacy of the 1611 translators.

Complete Equivalence in Translation

Where new translation has been necessary in the New King James Version, the most complete representation of the original has been rendered by considering the history of usage and etymology of words in their contexts. This principle of complete equivalence seeks to preserve *all* of the information in the text, while presenting it in good literary form. Dynamic equivalence, a recent procedure in Bible translation, commonly results in paraphrasing where a more literal rendering is needed to reflect a specific and vital sense. For example, complete equivalence truly renders the original text in expressions such as "lifted her voice and wept" (Gen. 21:16); "I gave you cleanness of teeth" (Amos 4:6); "Jesus met them, saying, 'Rejoice!'" (Matt. 28:9); and "Woman, what does your concern have to do with Me?" (John 2:4). Complete equivalence translates fully, in order to provide an English text that is both accurate and readable.

In keeping with the principle of complete equivalence, it is the policy to translate interjections, which are commonly omitted in modern language renderings of the Bible. As an example, the interjection *behold,* in the older King James editions, continues to have a place in English usage, especially in dramatically calling attention to a spectacular scene, or an event of profound importance such as the Immanuel prophecy of Isaiah 7:14. Consequently, *behold* is retained for these occasions in the present edition. However, the Hebrew and Greek originals for this word can be translated variously, depending on the circumstances in the passage. Therefore, in addition to *behold,* words such as *indeed, look, see,* and *surely* are also rendered to convey the appropriate sense suggested by the context in each case.

In faithfulness to God and to our readers, it was deemed appropriate that all participating scholars sign a statement affirming their belief in the verbal and plenary inspiration of Scripture, and in the inerrancy of the original autographs.

Devotional Quality

The King James scholars readily appreciated the intrinsic beauty of divine revelation. They accordingly disciplined their talents to render well-chosen English words of their time, as well as a graceful, often musical arrangement of language, which has stirred the hearts of Bible readers through the years. The translators, the committees, and the editors of the present edition, while sensitive to the late twentieth-century English idiom, and while adhering faithfully to the Hebrew, Aramaic, and Greek texts, have sought to maintain those lyrical and devotional qualities that are so highly regarded in the Authorized Version. This devotional quality is especially apparent in the poetic and prophetic books, although even the relatively plain style of the Gospels and Epistles cannot strictly be likened, as sometimes suggested, to modern newspaper style. The Koine Greek of the New Testament is influenced by the Hebrew background of the writers, for whom even the gospel narratives were not merely flat utterance, but often song in various degrees of rhythm.

The Style

Students of the Bible applaud the timeless devotional character of our historic Bible. Yet it is also universally understood that our language, like all living languages, has undergone profound change since 1611. Subsequent revisions of the King James Bible have sought to keep abreast of changes in English speech. The present work is a further step toward this objective. Where obsolescence and other reading difficulties exist, present-day vocabulary, punctuation, and grammar have been carefully integrated. Words representing ancient objects, such as *chariot* and *phylactery,* have no modern substitutes and are therefore retained.

A special feature of the New King James Version is its conformity to the thought flow of the 1611 Bible. The reader discovers that the sequence and selection of words, phrases, and clauses of the new edition, while much clearer, are so close to the traditional that there is remarkable ease in listening to the reading of either edition while following with the other.

In the discipline of translating biblical and other ancient languages, a standard method of transliteration, that is, the English spelling of untranslated words, such as names of persons and places, has never been commonly adopted. In keeping with the design of the present work, the King James spelling of untranslated words is retained, although made uniform throughout. For example, instead of the spellings *Isaiah* and *Elijah* in the Old Testament, and *Esaias* and *Elias* in the New Testament, *Isaiah* and *Elijah* now appear in both Testaments.

King James doctrinal and theological terms, for example, *propitiation, justification,* and *sanctification,* are generally familiar to English-speaking peoples. Such terms have been retained except where the original language indicates need for a more precise translation.

Readers of the Authorized Version will immediately be struck by the absence of several pronouns: *thee, thou,* and *ye* are replaced by the simple *you,* while *your* and *yours* are substituted for *thy* and *thine* as applicable. *Thee, thou, thy,* and *thine* were once forms of address to express a special relationship to human as well as divine persons. These pronouns are no longer part of our language. However, reverence for God in the present work is preserved by capitalizing pronouns, including *You, Your,* and *Yours,* which refer to Him. Additionally, capitalization of these pronouns benefits the reader by clearly distinguishing divine and human persons referred to in a passage. Without such capitalization the distinction is often obscure, because the antecedent of a pronoun is not always clear in the English translation.

In addition to the pronoun usages of the seventeenth century, the *-eth* and *-est* verb endings, so familiar in the earlier King James editions, are now obsolete. Unless a speaker is schooled in these verb endings, there is common difficulty in selecting the correct form to be used with a given subject of the verb in vocal prayer. That is, should we use *love, loveth,* or *lovest? do, doeth, doest,* or *dost? have, hath,* or *hast?* Because these forms are obsolete, contemporary English usage has been substituted for the previous verb endings.

In older editions of the King James Version, the frequency of the connective *and* far exceeded the limits of present English usage. Also, biblical linguists agree that the Hebrew and Greek original words for this conjunction may commonly be translated otherwise, depending on the immediate context. Therefore, instead of *and,* alternatives such as *also, but, however, now, so, then,* and *thus* are accordingly rendered in the present edition, when the original language permits.

The real character of the Authorized Version does not reside in its archaic pronouns or verbs or other grammatical forms of the seventeenth century, but rather in the care taken by its scholars to impart the letter and spirit of the original text in a majestic and reverent style.

The Format

The format of the New King James Version is designed to enhance the vividness and devotional quality of the Holy Scriptures:

- Subject headings assist the reader to identify topics and transitions in the biblical content.
- Words or phrases in *italics* indicate expressions in the original language that require clarification by additional English words, as also done throughout the history of the King James Bible.

- Oblique type in the New Testament indicates a quotation from the Old Testament.
- Prose is divided into paragraphs to indicate the structure of thought.
- Poetry is structured as contemporary verse to reflect the poetic form and beauty of the passage in the original language.
- The covenant name of God was usually translated from the Hebrew as LORD or GOD (using capital letters as shown) in the King James Old Testament. This tradition is maintained. In the present edition the name is so capitalized whenever the covenant name is quoted in the New Testament from a passage in the Old Testament.

The Old Testament Text

The Hebrew Bible has come down to us through the scrupulous care of ancient scribes who copied the original text in successive generations. By the sixth century A.D. the scribes were succeeded by a group known as the Masoretes, who continued to preserve the sacred Scriptures for another five hundred years in a form known as the Masoretic Text. Babylonia, Palestine, and Tiberias were the main centers of Masoretic activity; but by the tenth century A.D. the Masoretes of Tiberias, led by the family of ben Asher, gained the ascendancy. Through subsequent editions, the ben Asher text became in the twelfth century the only recognized form of the Hebrew Scriptures.

Daniel Bomberg printed the first Rabbinic Bible in 1516–17; that work was followed in 1524–25 by a second edition prepared by Jacob ben Chayyim and also published by Bomberg. The text of ben Chayyim was adopted in most subsequent Hebrew Bibles, including those used by the King James translators. The ben Chayyim text was also used for the first two editions of Rudolph Kittel's *Biblia Hebraica* of 1906 and 1912. In 1937 Paul Kahle published a third edition of *Biblia Hebraica*. This edition was based on the oldest dated manuscript of the ben Asher text, the Leningrad Manuscript B19a (A.D. 1008), which Kahle regarded as superior to that used by ben Chayyim.

For the New King James Version the text used was the 1967/1977 Stuttgart edition of the *Biblia Hebraica,* with frequent comparisons being made with the Bomberg edition of 1524–25. The Septuagint (Greek) Version of the Old Testament and the Latin Vulgate also were consulted. In addition to referring to a variety of ancient versions of the Hebrew Scriptures, the New King James Version draws on the resources of relevant manuscripts from the Dead Sea caves. In the few places where the Hebrew was so obscure that the 1611 King James was compelled to follow one of the versions, but where information is now available to resolve the problems, the New King James Version follows the Hebrew text. Significant variations are recorded in the New King James translators' notes.

The New Testament Text

There is more manuscript support for the New Testament than for any other body of ancient literature. Over five thousand Greek, eight thousand Latin, and many more manuscripts in other languages attest the integrity of the New Testament. There is only one basic New Testament used by Protestants, Roman Catholics, and Orthodox, by conservatives and liberals. Minor variations in hand copying have appeared through the centuries, before mechanical printing began about A.D. 1450.

Some variations exist in the spelling of Greek words, in word order, and in similar details. These ordinarily do not show up in translation and do not affect the sense of the text in any way.

Other manuscript differences such as omission or inclusion of a word or a clause, and two paragraphs in the Gospels, should not overshadow the overwhelming degree of *agreement* that exists among the ancient records. Bible readers may be assured that the most important differences in English New Testaments of today are due, not to manuscript divergence, but to the way in which translators view the task of translation: How literally should the text be rendered? How does the translator view the matter of biblical inspiration? Does the translator adopt a paraphrase when a literal rendering would be quite clear and more to the point? The New King James Version follows the historic precedent of the Authorized Version in maintaining a literal approach to translation, except where the idiom of the original language cannot be translated directly into our tongue.

The King James New Testament was based on the traditional text of the Greek-speaking churches, first published in 1516, and later called the Textus Receptus or Received Text. Although based on the relatively few available manuscripts, these were representative of many more that existed at the time but only became known later. In the late nineteenth century, B. Westcott and F. Hort taught that this text had been officially edited by the fourth-century church, but a total lack of historical evidence for this event has forced a revision of the theory. It is now widely held that the Byzantine Text that largely supports the Textus Receptus has as much right as the Alexandrian or any other tradition to be weighed in determining the text of the New Testament.

Since the 1880s most contemporary translations of the New Testament have relied upon a relatively few manuscripts discovered chiefly in the late nineteenth and early twentieth centuries. Such translations depend primarily on two manuscripts, Codex Vaticanus and Codex Sinaiticus, because of their greater age. The Greek text obtained by using these sources and the related papyri (our most ancient manuscripts) is known as the Alexandrian Text. However, some scholars have grounds for doubting the faithfulness of Vaticanus and Sinaiticus, since they often disagree with one another, and Sinaiticus exhibits excessive omission.

A third viewpoint of New Testament scholarship holds that the best text is based on the consensus of the majority of existing Greek manuscripts. This text is called the Majority Text. Most of these manuscripts are in substantial agreement. Even though many are late, and none is earlier than the fifth century, usually their readings are verified by papyri, ancient versions, quotations from the early church fathers, or a combination of these. The Majority Text is similar to the Textus Receptus, but it corrects those readings that have little or no support in the Greek manuscript tradition.

Today, scholars agree that the science of New Testament textual criticism is in a state of flux. Very few scholars still favor the Textus Receptus as such, and then often for its historical prestige as the text of Luther, Calvin, Tyndale, and the King James Version. For about a century most have followed a Critical Text (so called because it is edited according to specific principles of textual criticism) which depends heavily upon the Alexandrian type of text. More recently many have abandoned this Critical Text (which is quite similar to the one edited by Westcott and Hort) for one that is more eclectic. Finally, a small but growing number of scholars prefer the Majority Text, which is close to the traditional text except in the Revelation.

In light of these facts, and also because the New King James Version is the fifth revision of a historic document translated from specific Greek texts, the editors decided to retain the traditional text in the body of the New Testament and to indicate major Critical and Majority Text variant readings in the translators' notes. Although these variations are duly indicated in the translators' notes of the present edition, it is most important to emphasize that fully eighty-five percent of the New Testament text is the same in the Textus Receptus, the Alexandrian Text, and the Majority Text.

New King James Translators' Notes

Significant textual explanations, alternate translations, and New Testament citations of Old Testament passages are supplied in the New King James translators' notes.

Important textual variants in the Old Testament are identified in a standard form.

The textual notes in the present edition of the New Testament make no evaluation of readings, but do clearly indicate the manuscript sources of readings. They objectively present the facts without such tendentious remarks as "the best manuscripts omit" or "the most reliable manuscripts read." Such notes are value judgments that differ according to varying viewpoints on the text. By giving a clearly defined set of variants the New King James Version benefits readers of all textual persuasions.

Where significant variations occur in the New Testament Greek manuscripts, textual notes are classified as follows:

NU-Text

These variations from the traditional text generally represent the Alexandrian or Egyptian type of text described previously in "The New Testament Text." They are found in the Critical Text published in the twenty-seventh edition of the Nestle-Aland Greek New Testament (N) and in the United Bible Societies' fourth edition (U), hence the acronym, "NU-Text."

M-Text

This symbol indicates points of variation in the Majority Text from the traditional text, as also previously discussed in "The New Testament Text." It should be noted that M stands for whatever reading is printed in the published *Greek New Testament According to the Majority Text,* whether supported by overwhelming, strong, or only a divided majority textual tradition.

The textual notes reflect the scholarship of the past two centuries and will assist the reader to observe the variations between the different manuscript traditions of the New Testament. Such information is generally not available in English translations of the New Testament.

CONTRIBUTORS

Leadership Realities are adapted from Leadership Rocks Student Leadership Study Guides,
Thomas Nelson Publishers, 2006.

Special thanks to the following noted leaders who have made contributions to
shaping the GC2 notes in Relational Theology:

**David Ferguson, D.Phil., D.Litt., Author, Intimate Life Ministries,
GreatCommandment.net**

**Palma Hutchinson, International Youth Dir., Church of God of
Prophecy, Cleveland, Tennessee**

**Josh McDowell, Author, speaker, Josh McDowell Ministries, True Foun-
dations.org**
Adaptations from *Beyond Belief to Convictions,* Tyndale House, 2002

**Gilbert Stafford, Th.D., Dean of Theology, Anderson University, Ander-
son, Indiana**

**Heath Thomas, Ph.D., Instructor in Theology, S.E. Baptist Seminary,
Wake Forest, North Carolina**

Terri Snead, Dir. Resource Dev., Intimate Life Ministries, Austin, Texas

**John Vining, Ph.D., Family Min. Dir., Church of God, Cleveland,
Tennessee**

**Ronald Warford, Ph.D., Relational Min. Dir., New Birth Missionary,
Decatur, Georgia**

Gen.	1:27	Ps.	19:7
Gen.	2:7	Ps.	23:6
Gen.	2:18	Ps.	24:3
Gen.	3:1	Ps.	36:9
Gen.	3:6	Ps.	50:23
Gen.	3:18	Ps.	88:1
Gen.	6:6	Ps.	103:2
Gen.	18:17	Ps.	105
Ex.	3:3	Ps.	119:16
Deut.	6:4	Prov.	14:12
Deut.	10:13	Prov.	22:6
1 Sam.	3:9	Is.	30:18
1 Sam.	18:1	Is.	53:6
2 Sam.	8:12	Jer.	1:5
2 Sam.	30:6	Ezek.	4:37

Heb.	4:12		1 Pet.	2:2
Heb.	4:15		1 Pet.	2:17
Heb.	11:1		1 Pet.	4:10
Heb.	12:1		1 John	3:17
James	1:17		1 John	4:10
James	1:19		1 John	4:12
James	1:25		Rev.	1:18
James	4:6		Rev.	19:7, 8
James	5:16			

Dr. David Adams

Prov.	18:24

Dr. Daniel Akin, President of Southeastern Baptist Theological Seminary

Gen.	1		John	14:6
Gen.	1—2		John	20
Gen.	1:26–31		Acts	4:12
Gen.	1:28		Rom.	8:28–30
Deut.	6:4–6		Rom.	13:1–7
Ps.	19		1 Cor.	6:12—11:1
Matt.	5:13–16		1 Cor.	7:2–5
Matt.	25:31–40		Eph.	2:1–10
Mark	16		Eph.	5:21—6:4
Luke	24		1 Tim.	2:5
John	1:1–18		1 Tim.	3:15–17
John	6:35			

Chuck Allen, Chief Operating Officer, Student Leadership University

Excerpt: Chuck Allen: *Extraordinary Leadership for Everyday People,* published by Insight International, 2005

Prov.	22:1
Matt.	4:21
Mark	14:3

Ryan A. Bowman, Training and Development, Chick-fil-A, Inc.

Ps.	119:11
Prov.	3:4

Dr. Bill Bright, Author and Founder, Campus Crusade for Christ

Ex.	20:1		Ex.	20:13
Ex.	20:3		Ex.	20:14
Ex.	20:4		Ex.	20:15
Ex.	20:8		Ex.	20:16
Ex.	20:8		Ex.	20:18
Ex.	20:12		Deut.	7:9

Deut.	32:4		Rom.	8:28
Ps.	18:30		Rom.	11:6
Ps.	23:4		Gal.	6:6
Ps.	119:60		Eph.	2:4
Ps.	145:17		Eph.	4:22
Is.	6:3		Phil.	1:17
Is.	40:29		1 Thess.	5:24
Jer.	29:11		Heb.	1:11
Jer.	32:7		James	1:15
Matt.	5:17		2 Pet.	3:9
Matt.	18:21		1 John	3:20
John	8:31		1 John	4:8
John	10:10		1 John	4:16
Acts	15:11		Rev.	4:11
Rom.	3:20			

Brad Bright, President, Bright Media Foundation, Orlando, Florida

Matt.	22:15
Acts	17:22

Mark Brister, Ph.D.

Rom.	12:2

Jon Brooks, Campus Pastor, Faith Christian School

John	1:35–41
John	18:10, 11

Dr. William Brown, President, Cedarville University

Excerpt: Dr. Brown: *Where Have All the Dreamers Gone*, published by Cedarville University, 2005

Gen.	2		Ps.	8:5
Gen.	2		Ps.	14:1
Gen.	2:23, 24		Ps.	19
Gen.	5:1, 2		Ps.	27:8
Gen.	18:19		Ps.	51:5
Deut.	18:10–14		Ps.	53:1
1 Sam.	16:7		Ps.	90
Job	1		Ps.	146:5, 6
Job	3		Prov.	1:8, 9
Job	4		Eccl.	2:16
Job	5		Is.	63
Job	6		Jer.	14:7–9
Job	6		Jer.	29:11
Ps.	8		Jer.	30:2

Matt.	16:13–20	1 Tim.	3:16
Matt.	28:18–20	Heb.	1:1–4
John	1:10	Heb.	11:3
John	6:32, 33	Heb.	13:4
Acts	1:16	James	1:13–15
Rom.	3:23	James	1:27
Rom.	8:16, 17	1 Pet.	2:9
1 Cor.	6:20	1 Pet.	2:22–24
1 Cor.	9:19–23	2 Pet.	1:5–8
Eph.	2:11–22	2 Pet.	1:21
Eph.	4:15, 16	Rev.	21:4
Phil.	2:2–5	Rev.	21—22
Phil.	2:9–11		

Cliff Carey, Program Manager, Hume Lake Christian Camps
Ps.   75:6

Mike Calhoun, Vice President, Word of Life Local Church Ministries
2 Kin.   2:13–15

Brent Crowe, M.Div., M.A. in Ethics, Executive Director of Training and Development, Student Leadership University; President of Leadership Rocks

Scott Dawson, Founder, Scott Dawson Evangelistic Association, Inc.
John   4:29
Acts   4:29

David Edwards, Speaker/Author, David Edwards Productions, Inc.
Ps.   15:15
What You Want to Know, but Don't Know Who to Ask: 12

Hank Hanegraaff, President, Board of Christian Research Institute International (CRI), Host, *Bible Answer Man* **broadcast**
Excerpt: *The Covering,* SLU study guide, Nelson Impact, 2006
What You Want to Know, but Don't Know Who to Ask: 2
What You Want to Know, but Don't Know Who to Ask: 5
What You Want to Know, but Don't Know Who to Ask: 6

Dr. Jairy C. Hunter, Jr., President of Charleston Southern University
Matt.   5:41

Dr. Richard Land, President, Ethics and Religious Liberty Commission
Excerpt: Richard Land, *Mercury Rising,* SLU study guide, Nelson Impact, 2006.
What You Want to Know, but Don't Know Who to Ask: 3
What You Want to Know, but Don't Know Who to Ask: 4

Ron Luce, President and Founder of Teen Mania Ministries
(Adapted from *8 Essentials for a Life of Significance,* SLU study guide, Nelson Impact, 2006)
Ps.   34:1

Troy Murphy, Launch 137
Acts   3:2

Dr. Alvin L. Reid, Professor of Evangelism, Bailey Smith Chair of Evangelism, Associate Dean for Proclamation Studies, Southeastern Baptist Theological Seminary
Acts   7:59
Acts   20:19
Acts   20:20

Dr. Jimmy Scroggins, Dean of Boyce College at Southern Baptist Theological Seminary
Rom.   13:1
Phil.   2:8

Jay L. Sedwick, Ph.D., Associate Professor of Christian Education, Dallas Theological Seminary

Gen.	4:1	1 Tim.	4:6
Gen.	4:2	1 Tim.	4:13
Gen.	6:13		

Dr. Ed Smith, President of Faith Christian School, Grapevine, Texas

Eccl.	9:1
Matt.	16:24
1 John	5:4

Dennis Steeger, Director of Student Ministries, Grace Outreach Center, Plano, Texas

Diane Strack, Founder of New Start for Single Moms

Gen.	2:18	Esth.	2:17
Gen.	16:7	Luke	1:19
Gen.	17:15	Luke	1:26
Gen.	24:15	Luke	2:6
Num.	2:11	Luke	2:36
Num.	12:3	Luke	8:2
Judg.	4:4	Luke	10:38
Ruth	1:20	Luke	10:42
Ruth	2:2	Acts	16:14
2 Sam.	11:3	1 Pet.	3:3

Dr. Jay Strack, President and Founder of Student Leadership University

Larry Taylor, Head of School, Prestonwood Christian Academy, Founder of Student Leadership Institute (SLI)

John	13:4

Kevin White, Director of 24-7 Ministries, Youth Ministry of Awana

Matt.	24:36

Pat Williams, Senior Vice President, Orlando Magic

(Adapted from *Paradox of Power,* Hachette Book Group USA, 2002)

Luke	22:24

CONTRIBUTORS xxvi

Student Leadership Alumni Contributors:
Candi Finch, Ph.D., Candidate in Systematic Theology at Southwestern Baptist Theological Seminary, Fort Worth, Texas
Luke E. Lin, M.Div., Doctoral Candidate, Princeton Seminary
Heath Thomas, Ph.D., Instructor of Old Testament and Hebrew, Southeastern Baptist Theological Seminary

Articles that are excerpt/adaptation from published work, published by permission:

Chuck Allen: Extraordinary Leadership for Everyday People, *published by Insight International, 2005.*

Dr. William Brown: Where Have All the Dreamers Gone, *published by Cedarville University, 2005.*

Richard Land, Mercury Rising, *SLU study guide, Nelson Impact, 2006.*

Ron Luce, 8 Essentials for a Life of Significance, *SLU study guide, Nelson Impact, 2006.*

Hank Hanegraaff, The Covering, *SLU study guide, Nelson Impact, 2006.*

Diane Strack, New Start for Single Moms, *Nelson Reference, 2007.*

Pat Williams, Paradox of Power, *Hachette Book Group USA, 2002.*

THE
OLD TESTAMENT

IMPACT OF THE BOOK

GENESIS

IDEA

This "book of origins" displays the sovereign God of the universe and His relationship to His people, answering the tri-lemma of life: "Who am I? Where did I come from? Where am I going?" It introduces us to the author and finisher of all that is: God Himself.

MESSAGE

The book begins with: "In the beginning, God created the heavens and the earth." Those ten words are enough to establish Him as supreme. Human beings are the crowning jewel of the creation of God; we are to act as His representatives on the earth. Man was made in the "image of God" and by the hands of God—not a chance accident or random selection. Genesis tells us the origin of family, worship, civilization, Israel, sin, sorrow, suffering, and death. Genesis tells God's plan to redeem His creation. The leadership lesson is: before one can rule over others, one must be able to rule one's self.

PEOPLE

Abraham, Adam, Enoch, Esau, Eve, Isaac, Jacob, Joseph, Lot, Noah, Rebekah, Sarah

AUTHOR

The author of Genesis is not named, but Moses is the traditionally accepted author since the Pentateuch is referred to as the "Book of the Law of Moses" and the New Testament attributes authorship to Moses (see Matt. 19:8; Luke 24:27; John 5:45–47; Acts 3:22; Rom. 10:5; Rev. 15:3).

CULTURE

The historic events in Genesis span the creation of the universe to the death of Joseph, a period of at least 2,500 years. The focus is on the nation of Israel settling in the fertile Nile Delta region of Egypt. Genesis provides the background for the rest of the Pentateuch and for the whole Bible, particularly concerning the Abrahamic covenant.

TIMELINE

between 1445 and 1405 BC

KEY SCRIPTURE MEMORY VERSES

1:1; 1:27; 2:16, 17; 2:24; 3:15; 12:1–3; 50:19, 20

THE HISTORY OF CREATION

1 In the beginning God created the heavens and the earth. ²The earth was without form, and void; and darkness *was*ᵃ on the face of the deep. And the Spirit of God was hovering over the face of the waters.

³Then God said, "Let there be light"; and there was light. ⁴And God saw the light, that *it was* good; and God divided the light from the darkness. ⁵God called the light Day, and the darkness He called Night. So the evening and the morning were the first day.

⁶Then God said, "Let there be a firmament in the midst of the waters, and let it divide the waters from the waters." ⁷Thus God made the firmament, and divided the waters which *were* under the firmament from the waters which *were* above the firmament; and it was so. ⁸And God called the firmament Heaven. So the evening and the morning were the second day.

⁹Then God said, "Let the waters under the heavens be gathered together into one place, and let the dry *land* appear"; and it was so. ¹⁰And God called the dry *land* Earth, and the gathering together of the waters He called Seas. And God saw that *it was* good.

¹¹Then God said, "Let the earth bring forth grass, the herb *that* yields seed, *and* the fruit tree *that* yields fruit according to its kind, whose seed *is* in itself, on the earth"; and it was so. ¹²And the earth brought forth grass, the herb *that* yields seed according to its kind, and the tree *that* yields fruit, whose seed *is* in itself according to its kind. And God saw that *it was* good. ¹³So the evening and the morning were the third day.

¹⁴Then God said, "Let there be lights in the firmament of the heavens to divide the day from the night; and let them be for signs and seasons, and for days and years; ¹⁵and let them be for lights in the firmament of the heavens to give light on the earth"; and it was so. ¹⁶Then God made two great lights: the greater light to rule the day, and the lesser light to rule the night. *He made* the stars also. ¹⁷God set them in the firmament of the heavens to give light on the earth, ¹⁸and to rule over the day and over the night, and to divide the light from the darkness. And God saw that *it was* good. ¹⁹So the evening and the morning were the fourth day.

²⁰Then God said, "Let the waters abound with an abundance of living creatures, and let birds fly above the earth across the face of the firmament of the heavens." ²¹So God created great sea creatures and every living thing that moves, with which the waters abounded, according to their kind, and every winged bird according to its kind. And God saw that *it was* good. ²²And God blessed them, saying, "Be fruitful and multiply, and fill the waters in the seas, and let birds multiply on

1:2 ᵃWords in italic type have been added for clarity. They are not found in the original Hebrew or Aramaic.

THROUGH THE GRID

Thinking Christianly: Different Options for the Existence of God (Gen. 1)

All beliefs about God fall under seven basic worldviews:

1. **Atheism** and **Agnosticism**. Atheism is the firm belief that there is no God, and agnosticism is the belief that perhaps God exists, but He has yet to be revealed.

2. **Theism** holds a belief in a world with an infinite God.

3. **Pantheism** is the view that the world is God.

4. **Deism** is the view that God created the world but left it on its own. This is called the "absent landlord" theory.

5. **Finitism** is a belief in a God who is not all-powerful.

6. **Panentheism** holds that the world is in God.

7. **Polytheism** is the belief in many gods.

THROUGH THE GRID
Thinking Christianly: Ten Foundational Beliefs of a Christian Worldview

Belief Three: Creation

The earth and all that exists was created by God alone through the power of His Word. All of creation testifies to His splendor and glory, and God oversees all that He has made. He governs the universe and all of creation with holiness and wisdom, and God's creation was initially created as good and to achieve moral ends (Gen. 1; 2; Ps. 19; John 1:1–5; Acts 17:22–31; Col. 1:15–17). *See Through the Grid article on page 1567.*

the earth." ²³So the evening and the morning were the fifth day.

²⁴Then God said, "Let the earth bring forth the living creature according to its kind: cattle and creeping thing and beast of the earth, *each* according to its kind"; and it was so. ²⁵And God made the beast of the earth according to its kind, cattle according to its kind, and everything that creeps on the earth according to its kind. And God saw that *it was* good.

²⁶Then God said, "Let Us make man in Our image, according to Our likeness; let them have dominion over the fish of the sea, over the birds of the air, and over the cattle, over all[a] the earth and over every creeping thing that creeps on the earth." ²⁷So God created man in His *own* image; in the image of God He created him; male and female He created them. ²⁸Then God blessed them, and God said to them, "Be fruitful and multiply; fill the earth and subdue it; have dominion over the fish of the sea, over the birds of the air, and over every living thing that moves on the earth."

²⁹And God said, "See, I have given you every

herb *that* yields seed which *is* on the face of all the earth, and every tree whose fruit yields seed; to you it shall be for food. ³⁰Also, to every beast of the earth, to every bird of the air, and to everything that creeps on the earth, in which *there is* life, *I have given* every green herb for food"; and it was so. ³¹Then God saw everything that He had made, and indeed *it was* very good. So the evening and the morning were the sixth day.

2 Thus the heavens and the earth, and all the host of them, were finished. ²And on the seventh day God ended His work which He had done, and He rested on the seventh day from all His work which He had done. ³Then God blessed the seventh day and sanctified it, because in it He rested from all His work which God had created and made.

⁴This *is* the history[a] of the heavens and the earth when they were created, in the day that the LORD God made the earth and the heavens,

1:26 [a]Syriac reads *all the wild animals of.* **2:4** [a]Hebrew *toledoth,* literally *generations*

THROUGH THE GRID
Thinking Christianly: Ten Foundational Beliefs of a Christian Worldview

Belief Four: Human Beings (*Gen. 1:26–31*)

All of humanity is created in the very image of God. Because we are created in God's image, we are set apart from the rest of creation, as nothing else in all of creation mirrors the likeness or image of God. However, we are born into this world sinful, and our inclinations are initially bent away from God. Human beings are sinners by nature and by choice (Gen. 1:26–31; 3:1–19; Ps. 51:5; 139:13–16; Rom. 3:9–20; James 3:9). *See Through the Grid article on page 1568.*

LEADERSHIP ISSUES

GC2: Male and Female

GENESIS 1:27

Importantly, maleness and femaleness preceded the introduction of sin in the world. The divine Creator sovereignly defined our gender even as He formed us in the womb (Ps. 139:13). With our gender also came our sexuality with potential for blessing or pain.

As He has in other areas of life, our creator God has defined within Scripture the boundaries for sexual expression. As with our words, thoughts, and attitudes, a good God has given us guidance that we might avoid pain and multiply blessing. He loves us and cares for us as His children. Sexuality is God's gift that calls for stewardship and accountability, not misuse, abuse, or defrauding. God calls us to place our sexuality under the lordship of Christ to maintain its purity and divine purpose (1 Cor. 6:12–20).

Pause to consider that your body is the "temple of the Holy Spirit"; ask God to teach you all that this means, and pray for His Spirit to protect and empower you to be faithful to Him.

GC2

GREAT COMMANDMENT
COMMISSION

THROUGH THE GRID

Thinking Christianly: What Does the Bible Really Say About Sex? (Gen. 1:28)

According to the Bible, sex was God's idea, not ours (Gen. 1:28). Sex belongs to God, and God ordained sex to be used within a proper context. God invented sex, so God gets to make the rules. Also, God made human beings as sexual creatures. We cannot deny our sexuality—it is the way God made us (Gen. 1:26, 27). Sex is not to be taken advantage of, but it is God's good gift to humanity to be used in the context of a marriage relationship between a man and a woman. Thus, premarital sex, extramarital sex, and unnatural sex are all wrong. We must honor God with our sexuality by using it within the context that God has prescribed. Anything else results in destruction and harm to our sexuality, so we must always guard it carefully.

[5]before any plant of the field was in the earth and before any herb of the field had grown. For the LORD God had not caused it to rain on the earth, and *there was* no man to till the ground; [6]but a mist went up from the earth and watered the whole face of the ground.

[7]And the LORD God formed man *of* the dust of the ground, and breathed into his nostrils the breath of life; and man became a living being.

LIFE IN GOD'S GARDEN

[8]The LORD God planted a garden eastward in Eden, and there He put the man whom He had formed. [9]And out of the ground the LORD God made every tree grow that is pleasant to the sight and good for food. The tree of life *was* also in the midst of the garden, and the tree of the knowledge of good and evil.

[10]Now a river went out of Eden to water the garden, and from there it parted and became four riverheads. [11]The name of the first *is* Pishon; it *is* the one which skirts the whole land of Havilah, where *there is* gold. [12]And the gold of that land *is* good. Bdellium and the onyx stone *are* there. [13]The name of the second river *is* Gihon; it *is* the

one which goes around the whole land of Cush. [14]The name of the third river *is* Hiddekel;[a] it *is* the one which goes toward the east of Assyria. The fourth river *is* the Euphrates.

[15]Then the LORD God took the man and put him in the garden of Eden to tend and keep it. [16]And the LORD God commanded the man, saying, "Of every tree of the garden you may freely eat; [17]but of the tree of the knowledge of good and evil you shall not eat, for in the day that you eat of it you shall surely die."

[18]And the LORD God said, "*It is* not good that man should be alone; I will make him a helper comparable to him." [19]Out of the ground the LORD God formed every beast of the field and every bird of the air, and brought *them* to Adam to see what he would call them. And whatever Adam called each living creature, that *was* its name. [20]So Adam gave names to all cattle, to the birds of the air, and to every beast of the field. But for Adam there was not found a helper comparable to him.

[21]And the LORD God caused a deep sleep to fall on Adam, and he slept; and He took one of

2:14 [a]Or *Tigris*

THROUGH THE GRID

Making Sense of Your World: Breaking Down Worldviews (Gen. 2)

Since so many varying worldviews exist that are held by so many people, some scholars have thought that it would be helpful to characterize the basic nature of worldviews. This approach generally breaks down worldviews to two forms: the pantheistic and the scientific. The goal is to find common ground among worldviews.

THROUGH THE GRID

Making Sense of Your World:
Pantheistic vs. Scientific (Gen. 2)

The pantheistic breakdown maintains that everyone can connect with an inner sense of spirituality or god, combined with implications of modern science. The scientific breakdown attempts to view religion as an outdated superstition that has been surpassed by modern science. Both of these appeal to many as general categories.

his ribs, and closed up the flesh in its place. ²²Then the rib which the LORD God had taken from man He made into a woman, and He brought her to the man.

²³And Adam said:

"This *is* now bone of my bones
And flesh of my flesh;
She shall be called Woman,
Because she was taken out of Man."

²⁴Therefore a man shall leave his father and mother and be joined to his wife, and they shall become one flesh.

²⁵And they were both naked, the man and his wife, and were not ashamed.

THE TEMPTATION AND FALL OF MAN

3 Now the serpent was more cunning than any beast of the field which the LORD God had made. And he said to the woman, "Has God indeed said, 'You shall not eat of every tree of the garden'?"

²And the woman said to the serpent, "We may eat the fruit of the trees of the garden; ³but of the fruit of the tree which *is* in the midst of the garden, God has said, 'You shall not eat it, nor shall you touch it, lest you die.'"

⁴Then the serpent said to the woman, "You

 the **INFLUENCERS**

EVE—Created to Love

GENESIS 2:18

Eve's name means "life-giving one." Created and fashioned by the very hand of God, she must have been extraordinarily beautiful. Created second, she was no afterthought, but a carefully planned and chosen being called "woman," so named because she was "taken out of man." She was called *helper,* a beautiful description of God's plan for her. This is not in any way an inferior term. The Holy Spirit is also called "The Helper" (John 14:26), and Hebrews says "The Lord is my Helper" (13:6). It is a term of privilege, responsibility, and joy. She was the answer to "aloneness," which God called "not good." Her creation was the beginning of human love and relationships.

When Satan saw this, his first move was sabotage. He deceived Eve, trying to disrupt the free, loving relationship she had with God, hoping she'd deceive Adam too, and damage the first marriage. He still wants to destroy marriages today by distorting the Word of Truth slightly, just enough to bring in sin, and we must be on guard. Eve began as the purest, loveliest woman on earth, living in a perfect garden of utopia; but she is remembered as the one who was deceived (2 Cor. 11:3). For all that she had, Satan was able to convince her that it wasn't enough.

LEADERSHIP ISSUES

GC2: Loving the Real God: God Relates

GENESIS 2:7   *And the LORD God formed man of the dust of the ground, and breathed into his nostrils the breath of life; and man became a living being.*

"God . . . breathed . . . and man became."

In these few words, we find the first scriptural reference to God's relationship with humankind. During the first five days of creation, the Creator simply spoke things into existence; but here, on the sixth day, He *relates*. God breathes, initiating the Spirit's activity, and man becomes. To be created in the image of God is to be created with the capacity to respond to and relate intimately with the Creator (Gen. 1:26).

Consider common elements of "relating," such as communication, apologies, sharing appreciation, hanging out together, and having common interests. Now discuss with a friend or in your small group how each of these elements of "relating" applies in your relationship with God:

- How's your communication?
- What about apologies?
- How's your appreciation? And hanging out together?
- What common interests are you and the Lord sharing?

Imagine that the real God "relates," and He's available to you! In fact, He wants a close relationship with you!

GC2
GREAT COMMANDMENT
COMMISSION

LEADERSHIP ISSUES

GC2: Basic Training: Displeasure in Paradise

GENESIS 2:18 *It is not good that man should be alone.*

God utters for the very first time this sobering phrase: "It is not good." He declared that something was missing in the Garden. Up to this point, everything in creation had been pronounced "good." Eden was a perfect paradise. So what could have been "not good" about the Garden of Eden?

At this time, Adam lived in a perfect world. There was no crime, no traffic, no pollution, no disease, and no war. It was a totally problem-free environment. Most notably, the Fall had not yet occurred, so Adam was sinless, innocent in heart and mind.

Adam also possessed everything he could possibly need or want. The Garden and everything in it (with the exception of one unique tree) was his to use and enjoy. Adam had it all. We also know that Adam had an exalted position. He had an excellent job with no competition for advancement. He was CEO over the "fish of the sea, over the birds of the air, and over the cattle, over all the earth and over every creeping thing that creeps on the earth" (Gen. 1:26).

Adam even enjoyed an intimate relationship with God. Above all the earthly benefits and blessings in the Garden, Adam walked and talked in perfect, uninterrupted fellowship with his Creator because sin had not yet come between them. What could have possibly been wrong in such an ideal setting? There was just one thing missing, but apparently this one thing troubled God's heart. In Genesis 2:18, God declared what was not good—Adam was alone. Adam needed human relationships.

A sovereign God, free to create Adam any way He desired, chose to fashion him in such a way that Adam needed to relate intimately not only with his Creator, but also with others. So it is with you, born longing to relate to God and others.

GREAT COMMANDMENT
COMMISSION

THROUGH THE GRID

Making Sense of Your World: Family as Divinely Designed (Gen. 2:23, 24)

God had a specific plan in mind when He designed the Christian home and the family. God has intended, since the beginning of creation, for man to be with woman. Relationships with other human beings is an essential part of God's plan for human relationships, and even more so is God's intentions for the relationship between husband and wife. Companionship as designed by God includes a plan both for comradeship and sexual partnership. Husbands and wives ultimately were designed to be one, as a model of Christ with the church. God indeed had an order and plan for human relationships.

will not surely die. ⁵For God knows that in the day you eat of it your eyes will be opened, and you will be like God, knowing good and evil."

⁶So when the woman saw that the tree *was* good for food, that it *was* pleasant to the eyes, and a tree desirable to make *one* wise, she took of its fruit and ate. She also gave to her husband with her, and he ate. ⁷Then the eyes of both of them were opened, and they knew that they *were* naked; and they sewed fig leaves together and made themselves coverings.

⁸And they heard the sound of the LORD God walking in the garden in the cool of the day, and Adam and his wife hid themselves from the presence of the LORD God among the trees of the garden.

⁹Then the LORD God called to Adam and said to him, "Where *are* you?"

¹⁰So he said, "I heard Your voice in the garden, and I was afraid because I was naked; and I hid myself."

¹¹And He said, "Who told you that you *were* naked? Have you eaten from the tree of which I commanded you that you should not eat?"

 the INFLUENCERS

ADAM—Genesis 2

In the book of origins is the sacred record of the great revelations of God, eternity, redemption, salvation, accounts of the world's creation, advice from heaven, and the first judgments and consequences for human sin. It is not unusual to ask: "Do I have what it takes to stay faithful to God and make a difference in the world?"

In Genesis, we learn from the first man, Adam, and from the Creator who fashioned us lovingly and tenderly, both in the dust of the earth and within the womb (Ps. 139:4).

We are made in the image of God, which means *we have the capacity and potential to lead others* (Gen. 1:26).

Both men and women have been commanded by God to act as leaders (Gen.1:27), but *leaders must demonstrate the ability to rule self* before being given the honor to lead others. Adam faced this test (Gen. 3) when he was told to obey the way, Word, and will of God in the temptation to eat from the tree.

Adam's first failure served him well with lessons for the future. Whether it was inexperience or the desire to please Eve, we don't know, but the Scripture tells us that each of us faces *temptation common to man* (1 Cor. 10:13).

LEADERSHIP ISSUES

GC2: Gratitude Lost

GENESIS 3:1

Much was lost as Eve, then Adam, sinned against their creator (Rom. 5:14). Sin and death entered human history; and intimate relationship with God was replaced with fear, shame, and blame. God's clear command was violated: "But of the tree of the knowledge of good and evil you shall not eat, for in the day that you eat of it you shall surely die" (Gen. 2:17). As we look deeper, however, we notice Satan seizing on this command; he launched a sly, cunning attack that included undermining Adam and Eve's gratitude toward God. Notice the subtlety of the serpent's approach, just slightly twisting God's words.

Notice how Satan's words implied that Adam and Eve had "needs" beyond those things which "YHWH Yireh" (Jehovah-Jireh) had committed to provide. It is as if he was saying, "Eve, you need to be able to eat from **all** the trees—you need to be like God. What kind of God would not let you eat from any tree in the Garden? What kind of God would put a tree there and then say 'Don't eat from it!'?" Taking our eyes off the blessings of God is still part of Satan's plan.

For the first time, Eve's focus shifted from all the abundance that was hers, to the one thing that was forbidden. By shifting her focus from what she had to what was prohibited, Satan was able to convince her to embrace his lies concerning God's character. This led Eve to believe her Creator was stingy and unnecessarily restrictive rather than generous and full of grace. Abandoning their gratitude, Adam and Eve selfishly took from the fruit of the tree. True to God's word, they instantly died a spiritual death, and then they progressively died in their souls; eventually, they died in their physical bodies, as well.

Important in our walk with Jesus will be restoring what the "first Adam" lost, including gratitude (1 Cor. 15:45–49). Gratitude keeps our heart focused on the Lord, which is where Adam and Eve's should have remained (Ps. 100:3; Eph. 5:20).

GC2
GREAT COMMANDMENT
COMMISSION

LEADERSHIP ISSUES

No Excuses Lifestyle

GENESIS 3:1–9

Satan is the author of deception. He chose the snake as a disguise because it was visual and intriguing. This is the first time in Scripture that Satan steps onto the stage of human history, and it is here that we see how skillful and crafty he can be.

Satan set Eve up for a fall with just the right words (v. 3). It cannot be ignored that it was a conscious act of both Adam and Eve to eat the forbidden fruit. They were given the freedom of choice, yet they seized the opportunity to betray the One who had provided that freedom. The decision to sin was theirs and could not be blamed on upbringing, family, friends, or neighborhood; they had none. It was an act of will.

Immediately following the choice to disobey God, waves of shame and guilt rushed over Adam and Eve, and the excuse was born. First, Adam said, "The woman You gave to be with me, she gave me of the tree, and I ate" (Gen. 3:12). Eve said, "The serpent deceived me" (Gen. 3:13). It is easy to laugh at Adam and Eve passing the blame and thinking that fig leaves were going to fool God; but the "fig leaf" excuses we offer to God are just as inadequate. They found themselves lying low, trying to hide from His presence, which earlier they had craved.

Hiding is the result of the darkness of sin. When we are rightly related to God, we walk in the light and have the light of life. God called Adam to come back into the light where he could be seen. To live in the light is to live a lifestyle of frequent and fresh encounters with the risen Lord Jesus. In this walk of light, there is no need for fear or guilt and no need to hide.

Excuses are usually the result of an emotional self-defense mechanism. When leaders own up to mistakes and set an example of doing the right thing with dignity, they teach a "no excuses" lifestyle and teach others to walk in truth. The leader who lives by a "no excuses" policy soars into achievement because he or she attempts to do things right the first time.

LEADERSHIP ISSUES

GC2: Lost Humility

GENESIS 3:6

At the Fall, humble dependence was abandoned. In one of the saddest moments in human history, Eve—created to receive all she needed from the hand of her loving and gracious Creator—*took* the forbidden fruit and ate it.

Never before had Adam or Eve *taken* something. They had trusted God to address their inherent neediness as humans and had freely received His provision. As they gave in to Satan's temptation, however, Adam and Eve selfishly and greedily *took* for the first time. Tragically, they discovered that taking the fruit did not fulfill their longings. Indeed, it led only to shame, guilt, fear, and an eagerness to dodge blame for their actions (Gen. 3:6–12).

Nevertheless, the damage was done: humans ceased being humble recipients and became takers. Selfish taking, though, can never truly satisfy our God-created neediness. The cry of the human heart since the Fall has consistently been, "It's not enough!" As followers of Jesus, we're called to restore what Adam lost as we clothe ourselves "with humility" (1 Pet. 5:5). It is God's desire to send us—as ambassadors for Christ—to this world full of self-focused, "taking" people, in order that we might give witness to His loving care and provision.

GC2
GREAT COMMANDMENT
COMMISSION

LEAD**ERSHIP**
REAL**ITIES**

THE EVERYDAY QUESTION: WHERE ARE YOU?   *Genesis 3:9*

God was not asking out of ignorance where Adam and Eve were, for He knew they had fallen into sin and hidden themselves from Him. The answer was in the asking: they were not in His presence. This is the question the leader has to face every day as if the Father were asking it Himself. The answer should change with the newness of each day as you grow closer to the Father and, as a result, move farther from sin. For followers of God there is the constant battle between evil and good, thus the continual need for repeating this personal question every day. Stay in the presence of God and you will find yourself staying away from sin—discerning what's right and wrong, what's black and white as clearly defined in Scripture. Sounds simple, but life is never as simple as we desire it to be. Influence is intrinsic to leadership, and the one with whom God is pleased influences out of the overflow that comes from being intimate with Him. Leaders do not need to hide in shame and defeat, for they dwell in the presence of a welcoming God.

¹²Then the man said, "The woman whom You gave *to be* with me, she gave me of the tree, and I ate."

¹³And the LORD God said to the woman, "What *is* this you have done?"

The woman said, "The serpent deceived me, and I ate."

¹⁴So the LORD God said to the serpent:

"Because you have done this,
    You *are* cursed more than all cattle,
    And more than every beast of the field;
    On your belly you shall go,
    And you shall eat dust
    All the days of your life.
¹⁵And I will put enmity
    Between you and the woman,
    And between your seed and her Seed;
    He shall bruise your head,
    And you shall bruise His heel."

¹⁶To the woman He said:

"I will greatly multiply your sorrow and your
        conception;
    In pain you shall bring forth children;
    Your desire *shall be* for your husband,
    And he shall rule over you."

¹⁷Then to Adam He said, "Because you have heeded the voice of your wife, and have eaten from the tree of which I commanded you, saying, 'You shall not eat of it':

"Cursed *is* the ground for your sake;
    In toil you shall eat *of* it
    All the days of your life.
¹⁸Both thorns and thistles it shall bring forth for
        you,
    And you shall eat the herb of the field.
¹⁹In the sweat of your face you shall eat bread
    Till you return to the ground,
    For out of it you were taken;
    For dust you *are*,
    And to dust you shall return."

²⁰And Adam called his wife's name Eve, because she was the mother of all living.

²¹Also for Adam and his wife the LORD God made tunics of skin, and clothed them.

²²Then the LORD God said, "Behold, the man has become like one of Us, to know good and evil. And now, lest he put out his hand and take also of the tree of life, and eat, and live forever"— ²³therefore the LORD God sent him out of the garden of Eden to till the ground from which he was taken. ²⁴So He drove out the man; and He placed cherubim at the east of the garden of

LEADERSHIP ISSUES

GC2: Good News: The Seed of Woman

GENESIS 3:15   *And I will put enmity between you and the woman, and between your seed and her Seed; He shall bruise your head, and you shall bruise His heel.*

The perfect and holy Creator, who knew no sin, watched as His sinful children separated from His very presence (Gen. 3:1–8). They were now disconnected from the only source that could sustain life and love and joy and peace. He watched as His children had to suffer the agony of war and hunger, disease and heartache, which would seemingly last forever. Sin separated God from the cherished family He had created, and it broke His heart (Gen. 6:6). And at that moment when His heart broke for His children, He already knew how He would respond.

God wanted so much to reconnect to His children and restore a relationship with them—with you—but God, being holy, could not relate to sin. So He devised a plan. He sent His Son into our world to become one of us—a child Himself, a human baby—for you. He who was God came to earth—in a virgin's womb, as the prophets foretold, as the shepherds learned—to cancel the curse of sin so you could know, so you could experience His love for you (Luke 1:26–38; 2:8–14).

In Genesis 3:15, the Creator addresses the Serpent of old. He declares the strife between Satan and humankind, and He foreshadows Christ's virgin birth as "her Seed." He also foreshadows Calvary through the Serpent's bruising of the woman's "Seed" and Christ's crushing of Satan. But *who* was it for?

He did it all for you! That shows you how much He wants a relationship with you!

GC2
GREAT COMMANDMENT
COMMISSION

Eden, and a flaming sword which turned every way, to guard the way to the tree of life.

CAIN MURDERS ABEL

4 Now Adam knew Eve his wife, and she conceived and bore Cain, and said, "I have acquired a man from the LORD." ²Then she bore again, this time his brother Abel. Now Abel was a keeper of sheep, but Cain was a tiller of the ground. ³And in the process of time it came to pass that Cain brought an offering of the fruit of the ground to the LORD. ⁴Abel also brought of the firstborn of his flock and of their fat. And the LORD respected Abel and his offering, ⁵but He did not respect Cain and his offering. And Cain was very angry, and his countenance fell.

⁶So the LORD said to Cain, "Why are you angry? And why has your countenance fallen? ⁷If you do well, will you not be accepted? And if you do not do well, sin lies at the door. And its desire is for you, but you should rule over it."

⁸Now Cain talked with Abel his brother;ᵃ and it came to pass, when they were in the field, that Cain rose up against Abel his brother and killed him.

⁹Then the LORD said to Cain, "Where is Abel your brother?"

He said, "I do not know. Am I my brother's keeper?"

¹⁰And He said, "What have you done? The voice of your brother's blood cries out to Me from the ground. ¹¹So now you are cursed from the earth, which has opened its mouth to receive your brother's blood from your hand. ¹²When you till the ground, it shall no longer yield its strength to you. A fugitive and a vagabond you shall be on the earth."

¹³And Cain said to the LORD, "My punishment is greater than I can bear! ¹⁴Surely You have driven me out this day from the face of the ground; I shall be hidden from Your face; I shall be a fugitive and a vagabond on the earth, and it will happen that anyone who finds me will kill me."

¹⁵And the LORD said to him, "Therefore,ᵃ whoever kills Cain, vengeance shall be taken on

4:8 ᵃSamaritan Pentateuch, Septuagint, Syriac, and Vulgate add *"Let us go out to the field."* **4:15** ᵃFollowing Masoretic Text and Targum; Septuagint, Syriac, and Vulgate read *Not so.*

INSIDE *the* INFLUENCERS

CAIN: From Arrogance to Murder

GENESIS 4:1–15

Adam and Eve had numerous children throughout their very long lives. Cain was their firstborn, followed by Abel. The story of Cain and Abel is familiar because it records the first murder (Gen. 4:1–15). Cain was a farmer, and Abel was a shepherd. Each brought offerings in gratitude for God's blessing on their work. Cain's was "the fruit of the ground." Abel brought the "fat portions" of the firstborn from his flock. God "had regard" for Abel's offering, but rejected Cain's. Cain's jealous rage was such that God warned him to control it, or he would sin. Unfortunately, Cain didn't heed the warning. He asked Abel to come out into the field, where Cain murdered his brother.

God asked Cain where his brother was. Cain's response was disrespectful and arrogant, "Am I my brother's keeper?" God condemned Cain's actions and cursed his ability to farm. In addition, there was a severing of relationship with God. In His mercy, however, God put a mark on Cain to warn people not to exact revenge on him for taking Abel's life.

Rather than repent, Cain allowed his attitude to fester and worsen to the point of murder. His jealousy overtook him. We are called to be our brother's keeper. First John 3:12 says we may not have eternal life if we do not love our brothers and sisters.

INSIDE the INFLUENCERS

ABEL: Sacrifice of Faith

GENESIS 4:2

Scripture presents Abel as the second son of Adam and Eve (Gen. 4:2). He is also the victim of the first murder. God was pleased with Abel's offering of the "fat portions" of the firstborn from his flock" (Gen. 4:1–10). Animal sacrifices weren't inherently better than grain sacrifices—the Bible allows both types—but something was different. The great "hall of faith" passage in Hebrews 11 tells us Abel's sacrifice was accepted because of his faith. We can infer from the story that God was more pleased with Abel's attitude and motivation than with Cain's. Sadly, Abel's life was cut short by Cain's murderous jealousy.

Attitude is a difficult characteristic to change. You can learn information and therefore change your knowledge. You can learn techniques and processes and therefore change your skills and abilities. But, a change of attitude is another story. The best way to improve your attitude is to let God do it through His Word and daily surrender to His will. You will be more than changed; you'll be transformed (Rom. 12:1, 2).

We often search and search for that thing we can *do* for God, but the story of Abel proves that God is more concerned about *who we are becoming*.

him sevenfold." And the LORD set a mark on Cain, lest anyone finding him should kill him.

THE FAMILY OF CAIN

[16]Then Cain went out from the presence of the LORD and dwelt in the land of Nod on the east of Eden. [17]And Cain knew his wife, and she conceived and bore Enoch. And he built a city, and called the name of the city after the name of his son—Enoch. [18]To Enoch was born Irad; and Irad begot Mehujael, and Mehujael begot Methushael, and Methushael begot Lamech.

[19]Then Lamech took for himself two wives: the name of one *was* Adah, and the name of the second *was* Zillah. [20]And Adah bore Jabal. He was the father of those who dwell in tents and have livestock. [21]His brother's name *was* Jubal. He was the father of all those who play the harp and flute. [22]And as for Zillah, she also bore Tubal-Cain, an instructor of every craftsman in bronze and iron. And the sister of Tubal-Cain *was* Naamah.

[23]Then Lamech said to his wives:

" Adah and Zillah, hear my voice;
Wives of Lamech, listen to my speech!

For I have killed a man for wounding me,
Even a young man for hurting me.
[24]If Cain shall be avenged sevenfold,
Then Lamech seventy-sevenfold."

A NEW SON

[25]And Adam knew his wife again, and she bore a son and named him Seth, "For God has appointed another seed for me instead of Abel, whom Cain killed." [26]And as for Seth, to him also a son was born; and he named him Enosh.[a] Then *men* began to call on the name of the LORD.

THE FAMILY OF ADAM

5 This is the book of the genealogy of Adam. In the day that God created man, He made him in the likeness of God. [2]He created them male and female, and blessed them and called them Mankind in the day they were created. [3]And Adam lived one hundred and thirty years, and begot *a son* in his own likeness, after his image, and named him Seth. [4]After he begot Seth, the days of Adam were eight hundred years; and he had sons and daugh-

4:26 [a]Greek *Enos*

THROUGH THE GRID

Making Sense of Your World:
Humanity's Uniqueness (Gen. 5:1, 2)

Humanity is the crowning point of all God's creation, but yet at times, humanity can seem insignificant, given the majesty and breadth of the rest of creation. We must realize our unique place as the special object of divine creation. The Bible makes clear that God created humanity especially unique—we are created *imago dei*, and we have the very breath of God in our lives. Our self-view must recognize this fact and hold the self as a highly valued part of God's creation—as one who is to reflect God's glory and will.

ters. ⁵So all the days that Adam lived were nine hundred and thirty years; and he died.

⁶Seth lived one hundred and five years, and begot Enosh. ⁷After he begot Enosh, Seth lived eight hundred and seven years, and had sons and daughters. ⁸So all the days of Seth were nine hundred and twelve years; and he died.

⁹Enosh lived ninety years, and begot Cainan.ᵃ ¹⁰After he begot Cainan, Enosh lived eight hundred and fifteen years, and had sons and daughters. ¹¹So all the days of Enosh were nine hundred and five years; and he died.

¹²Cainan lived seventy years, and begot Mahalalel. ¹³After he begot Mahalalel, Cainan lived eight hundred and forty years, and had sons and daughters. ¹⁴So all the days of Cainan were nine hundred and ten years; and he died.

¹⁵Mahalalel lived sixty-five years, and begot Jared. ¹⁶After he begot Jared, Mahalalel lived eight hundred and thirty years, and had sons and daughters. ¹⁷So all the days of Mahalalel were eight hundred and ninety-five years; and he died.

¹⁸Jared lived one hundred and sixty-two years, and begot Enoch. ¹⁹After he begot Enoch, Jared lived eight hundred years, and had sons and daughters. ²⁰So all the days of Jared were nine hundred and sixty-two years; and he died.

²¹Enoch lived sixty-five years, and begot Methuselah. ²²After he begot Methuselah, Enoch walked with God three hundred years, and had sons and daughters. ²³So all the days of Enoch were three hundred and sixty-five years. ²⁴And Enoch walked with God; and he *was* not, for God took him.

²⁵Methuselah lived one hundred and eighty-seven years, and begot Lamech. ²⁶After he begot Lamech, Methuselah lived seven hundred and eighty-two years, and had sons and daughters. ²⁷So all the days of Methuselah were nine hundred and sixty-nine years; and he died.

²⁸Lamech lived one hundred and eighty-two years, and had a son. ²⁹And he called his name Noah, saying, "This *one* will comfort us concerning our work and the toil of our hands, because of the ground which the LORD has cursed." ³⁰After he begot Noah, Lamech lived five hundred and ninety-five years, and had sons and daughters. ³¹So all the days of Lamech were seven hundred and seventy-seven years; and he died.

³²And Noah was five hundred years old, and Noah begot Shem, Ham, and Japheth.

THE WICKEDNESS AND JUDGMENT OF MAN

6 Now it came to pass, when men began to multiply on the face of the earth, and daughters were born to them, ²that the sons of God saw the daughters of men, that they *were* beautiful; and they took wives for themselves of all whom they chose.

³And the LORD said, "My Spirit shall not striveᵃ with man forever, for he *is* indeed flesh; yet his days shall be one hundred and twenty years." ⁴There were giants on the earth in those days, and also afterward, when the sons of God came in to the daughters of men and they bore *children* to them. Those *were* the mighty men who *were* of old, men of renown.

⁵Then the LORDᵃ saw that the wickedness of

5:9 ᵃHebrew *Qenan*   6:3 ᵃSeptuagint, Syriac, Targum, and Vulgate read *abide*.   6:5 ᵃFollowing Masoretic Text and Targum; Vulgate reads *God;* Septuagint reads *LORD God.*

LEADERSHIP ISSUES

GC2: God Feels!

GENESIS 6:6

The appropriateness of emotions is forever settled by realizing that God himself has emotions. Human emotionality is further confirmed in the fact that Jesus and the Holy Spirit feel and express emotions. In Mark 3:5, the Pharisees were looking for a reason to accuse Jesus, so they watched Him closely to see if He would heal on the Sabbath. When Jesus saw them, two different emotions surged through His heart: "Jesus looked around at them in **anger, deeply distressed** at their stubborn hearts." In Luke 10:21, the Scriptures record that "Jesus **rejoiced** in the Spirit." Paul taught that the Holy Spirit can feel **grieved** (Eph. 4:30).

If God expresses emotions, it must be okay for us to have emotions and do likewise. The key to healthy relationships will be how we deal with our emotions. For that, scripture must be our guide. We are created in God's image (Gen. 1:26), and we are to emulate Him.

As you consider your growing up and spiritual background, what messages did you receive relative to emotions?

_____

_____

Pause and ask God to give you His heart and truth concerning your emotions.

GC2
GREAT COMMANDMENT
COMMISSION

man *was* great in the earth, and *that* every intent of the thoughts of his heart *was* only evil continually. ⁶And the LORD was sorry that He had made man on the earth, and He was grieved in His heart. ⁷So the LORD said, "I will destroy man whom I have created from the face of the earth, both man and beast, creeping thing and birds of the air, for I am sorry that I have made them." ⁸But Noah found grace in the eyes of the LORD.

NOAH PLEASES GOD

⁹This is the genealogy of Noah. Noah was a just man, perfect in his generations. Noah walked with God. ¹⁰And Noah begot three sons: Shem, Ham, and Japheth.

¹¹The earth also was corrupt before God, and the earth was filled with violence. ¹²So God looked upon the earth, and indeed it was corrupt; for all flesh had corrupted their way on the earth.

THE ARK PREPARED

¹³And God said to Noah, "The end of all flesh has come before Me, for the earth is filled with violence through them; and behold, I will destroy them with the earth. ¹⁴Make yourself an ark of gopherwood; make rooms in the ark, and cover it inside and outside with pitch. ¹⁵And this is how you shall make it: The length of the ark *shall be* three hundred cubits, its width fifty cubits, and its height thirty cubits. ¹⁶You shall make a window for the ark, and you shall finish it to a cubit from above; and set the door of the ark in its side. You shall make it *with* lower, second, and third *decks.* ¹⁷And behold, I Myself am bringing floodwaters on the earth, to destroy from under heaven all flesh in which *is* the breath of life; everything that *is* on the earth shall die. ¹⁸But I will establish My covenant with you; and you shall go into the ark—you, your sons, your wife, and your sons' wives with you. ¹⁹And of every living thing of all flesh you shall bring two of every *sort* into the ark, to keep *them* alive with you; they shall be male and female. ²⁰Of the birds after their kind, of animals after their kind, and of every creeping thing of the earth after its kind, two of every *kind* will come to you to keep *them* alive. ²¹And you shall take for yourself of all food that is eaten, and you shall gather *it* to

---

 the **INFLUENCERS**

NOAH: A Doer of the Impossible

GENESIS 6:9

God asked Noah to build an ark which would save him, his family, and animals of every kind from a world-destroying flood. Why? The people of Noah's day were wicked to the core. The Bible says every intent of the thoughts of man "was only evil continually" (Gen. 6:5). God decided that He would no longer tolerate this blatant rebellion; He would destroy all living things.

Noah, however, "found grace in the eyes of the Lord" (6:8). In fact, he is the first biblical character to be described as righteous or "just" (6:9). In order to spare Noah, God instructed him to build the ark. Noah was 600 years old when God sent 40 days and nights of rain and opened the floodgates of the deep (7:6), but Noah and his family were saved from the destruction because of his righteous standing before God.

Ezekiel identifies Noah as a rare example of a righteous life (Ezek. 14:14, 20). The book of Hebrews includes Noah in the familiar "hall of faith" passage, indicating that he built the ark in reverent obedience (Heb. 11:7). Remember that God will not ask you to do anything that seems impossible on your own. As He did for Noah, He will provide what you need to accomplish the task.

LEADERSHIP ISSUES

Was the Flood of Genesis Real?

GENESIS 6—9

One of the best-known stories in the Old Testament is of a worldwide flood, where God destroyed all living things on the earth in judgment for the utter corruption of humankind. Only Noah was found righteous on the earth (6:13, 14). So God told Noah to build an ark that would protect him and his family, along with pairs of all the creatures of the earth, from the catastrophic flood to come.

The Bible says that the waters of the flood went twenty-two and a half feet above all the high mountains on the entire earth (7:20), killing all land-dwelling animals and living persons. God preserved humankind by saving Noah, Shem, Ham, Japheth, and their wives to repopulate the earth (9:1, 7). He promised never again to judge the earth by destroying everything with water and gave the rainbow as a frequent reminder of this pledge (9:11–17).

There is no question that the writers of Scripture believed that the story of the Flood was true and accurate, not just an allegorical tale told to teach a spiritual lesson (Is. 54:9; Heb. 11:7; 1 Pet. 3:20; 2 Pet. 2:5). Jesus used the story of Noah to illustrate what His sudden and unexpected return will be like in the future (Matt. 24:37, 38). Some people suggest that the flood was a localized event, only affecting those in the immediate vicinity; but that perspective is contrary to Scripture and geological evidence. The sedimentary rock layers ("geologic column"), which exist all around the globe, contain fossils of every manner of living thing destroyed by God in judgment—even on Mount Everest. The fossil record is strong evidence to the truth of the Flood. The layers of sedimentary rock even contain progressively more complex organisms, indicating an ability to seek higher ground before drowning. In other words, it would make sense that simpler, less advanced creatures would be buried first, then the more advanced, and finally people at the top. This is a better explanation in keeping with Scripture than that proposed by evolutionists who attempt to use the geologic column to argue for biological evolution.

yourself; and it shall be food for you and for them."

²²Thus Noah did; according to all that God commanded him, so he did.

The Great Flood

7 Then the LORD said to Noah, "Come into the ark, you and all your household, because I have seen *that* you *are* righteous before Me in this generation. ²You shall take with you seven each of every clean animal, a male and his female; two each of animals that *are* unclean, a male and his female; ³also seven each of birds of the air, male and female, to keep the species alive on the face of all the earth. ⁴For after seven more days I will cause it to rain on the earth forty days and forty nights, and I will destroy from the face of the earth all living things that I have made." ⁵And Noah did according to all that the LORD commanded him. ⁶Noah *was* six hundred years old when the floodwaters were on the earth.

⁷So Noah, with his sons, his wife, and his sons' wives, went into the ark because of the waters of the flood. ⁸Of clean animals, of animals that *are* unclean, of birds, and of everything that creeps on the earth, ⁹two by two they went into the ark to Noah, male and female, as God had commanded Noah. ¹⁰And it came to pass after seven days that the waters of the flood were on the earth. ¹¹In the six hundredth year of Noah's life, in the second month, the seventeenth day of the month, on that day all the fountains of the great deep were broken up, and the windows of heaven were opened. ¹²And the rain was on the earth forty days and forty nights.

¹³On the very same day Noah and Noah's sons, Shem, Ham, and Japheth, and Noah's wife and the three wives of his sons with them, entered the ark— ¹⁴they and every beast after its kind, all cattle after their kind, every creeping thing that creeps on the earth after its kind, and every bird after its kind, every bird of every sort. ¹⁵And they went into the ark to Noah, two by two, of all flesh in which *is* the breath of life. ¹⁶So those that entered, male and female of all flesh, went in as God had commanded him; and the LORD shut him in.

¹⁷Now the flood was on the earth forty days. The waters increased and lifted up the ark, and it rose high above the earth. ¹⁸The waters prevailed and greatly increased on the earth, and the ark moved about on the surface of the waters. ¹⁹And the waters prevailed exceedingly on the earth, and all the high hills under the whole heaven were covered. ²⁰The waters prevailed fifteen cubits upward, and the mountains were covered. ²¹And all flesh died that moved on the earth: birds and cattle and beasts and every creeping thing that creeps on the earth, and every man. ²²All in whose nostrils *was* the breath of the spirit[a] of life, all that *was* on the dry *land,* died. ²³So He destroyed all living things which were on the face of the ground: both man and cattle, creeping thing and bird of the air. They were destroyed from the earth. Only Noah and those who *were* with him in the ark remained *alive.* ²⁴And the waters prevailed on the earth one hundred and fifty days.

Noah's Deliverance

8 Then God remembered Noah, and every living thing, and all the animals that *were* with him in the ark. And God made a wind to pass over the earth, and the waters subsided. ²The fountains of the deep and the windows of heaven were also stopped, and the rain from heaven was restrained. ³And the waters receded continually from the earth. At the end of the hundred and fifty days the waters decreased. ⁴Then the ark rested in the seventh month, the seventeenth day of the month, on the mountains of Ararat. ⁵And the waters decreased continually until the tenth month. In the tenth *month,* on the first *day* of the month, the tops of the mountains were seen.

⁶So it came to pass, at the end of forty days, that Noah opened the window of the ark which he had made. ⁷Then he sent out a raven, which kept going to and fro until the waters had dried up from the earth. ⁸He also sent out from himself a dove, to see if the waters had receded from the face of the ground. ⁹But the dove found no resting place for the sole of her foot, and she returned into the ark to him, for the waters *were* on the face of the whole earth. So he put out his hand and took her, and drew her into the ark to himself. ¹⁰And he waited yet another seven days, and again he sent the dove out from the ark. ¹¹Then

7:22 ᵃSeptuagint and Vulgate omit *of the spirit.*

the dove came to him in the evening, and behold, a freshly plucked olive leaf *was* in her mouth; and Noah knew that the waters had receded from the earth. [12]So he waited yet another seven days and sent out the dove, which did not return again to him anymore.

[13]And it came to pass in the six hundred and first year, in the first *month,* the first *day* of the month, that the waters were dried up from the earth; and Noah removed the covering of the ark and looked, and indeed the surface of the ground was dry. [14]And in the second month, on the twenty-seventh day of the month, the earth was dried.

[15]Then God spoke to Noah, saying, [16]"Go out of the ark, you and your wife, and your sons and your sons' wives with you. [17]Bring out with you every living thing of all flesh that *is* with you: birds and cattle and every creeping thing that creeps on the earth, so that they may abound on the earth, and be fruitful and multiply on the earth." [18]So Noah went out, and his sons and his wife and his sons' wives with him. [19]Every animal, every creeping thing, every bird, *and* whatever creeps on the earth, according to their families, went out of the ark.

God's Covenant with Creation

[20]Then Noah built an altar to the LORD, and took of every clean animal and of every clean bird, and offered burnt offerings on the altar. [21]And the LORD smelled a soothing aroma. Then the LORD said in His heart, "I will never again curse the ground for man's sake, although the imagination of man's heart *is* evil from his youth; nor will I again destroy every living thing as I have done.

[22]"While the earth remains,
    Seedtime and harvest,
    Cold and heat,
    Winter and summer,
    And day and night
    Shall not cease."

9 So God blessed Noah and his sons, and said to them: "Be fruitful and multiply, and fill the earth.[a] [2]And the fear of you and the dread of you shall be on every beast of the earth, on every bird

of the air, on all that move *on* the earth, and on all the fish of the sea. They are given into your hand. [3]Every moving thing that lives shall be food for you. I have given you all things, even as the green herbs. [4]But you shall not eat flesh with its life, *that is,* its blood. [5]Surely for your lifeblood I will demand *a reckoning;* from the hand of every beast I will require it, and from the hand of man. From the hand of every man's brother I will require the life of man.

[6]"Whoever sheds man's blood,
    By man his blood shall be shed;
    For in the image of God
    He made man.
[7]And as for you, be fruitful and multiply;
    Bring forth abundantly in the earth
    And multiply in it."

[8]Then God spoke to Noah and to his sons with him, saying: [9]"And as for Me, behold, I establish My covenant with you and with your descendants[a] after you, [10]and with every living creature that *is* with you: the birds, the cattle, and every beast of the earth with you, of all that go out of the ark, every beast of the earth. [11]Thus I establish My covenant with you: Never again shall all flesh be cut off by the waters of the flood; never again shall there be a flood to destroy the earth."

[12]And God said: "This *is* the sign of the covenant which I make between Me and you, and every living creature that *is* with you, for perpetual generations: [13]I set My rainbow in the cloud, and it shall be for the sign of the covenant between Me and the earth. [14]It shall be, when I bring a cloud over the earth, that the rainbow shall be seen in the cloud; [15]and I will remember My covenant which *is* between Me and you and every living creature of all flesh; the waters shall never again become a flood to destroy all flesh. [16]The rainbow shall be in the cloud, and I will look on it to remember the everlasting covenant between God and every living creature of all flesh that *is* on the earth." [17]And God said to Noah, "This *is* the sign of the covenant which I have es-

9:1 [a]Compare Genesis 1:28 9:9 [a]Literally *seed*

tablished between Me and all flesh that *is* on the earth."

NOAH AND HIS SONS

[18]Now the sons of Noah who went out of the ark were Shem, Ham, and Japheth. And Ham *was* the father of Canaan. [19]These three *were* the sons of Noah, and from these the whole earth was populated.

[20]And Noah began *to be* a farmer, and he planted a vineyard. [21]Then he drank of the wine and was drunk, and became uncovered in his tent. [22]And Ham, the father of Canaan, saw the nakedness of his father, and told his two brothers outside. [23]But Shem and Japheth took a garment, laid *it* on both their shoulders, and went backward and covered the nakedness of their father. Their faces *were* turned away, and they did not see their father's nakedness.

[24]So Noah awoke from his wine, and knew what his younger son had done to him. [25]Then he said:

"Cursed *be* Canaan;
A servant of servants
He shall be to his brethren."

[26]And he said:

"Blessed *be* the LORD,
The God of Shem,
And may Canaan be his servant.
[27]May God enlarge Japheth,
And may he dwell in the tents of Shem;
And may Canaan be his servant."

[28]And Noah lived after the flood three hundred and fifty years. [29]So all the days of Noah were nine hundred and fifty years; and he died.

NATIONS DESCENDED FROM NOAH

10 Now this *is* the genealogy of the sons of Noah: Shem, Ham, and Japheth. And sons were born to them after the flood.

[2]The sons of Japheth *were* Gomer, Magog, Madai, Javan, Tubal, Meshech, and Tiras. [3]The sons of Gomer *were* Ashkenaz, Riphath,[a] and Togarmah. [4]The sons of Javan *were* Elishah, Tarshish, Kittim, and Dodanim.[a] [5]From these the coastland

peoples of the Gentiles were separated into their lands, everyone according to his language, according to their families, into their nations.

[6]The sons of Ham *were* Cush, Mizraim, Put,[a] and Canaan. [7]The sons of Cush *were* Seba, Havilah, Sabtah, Raamah, and Sabtechah; and the sons of Raamah *were* Sheba and Dedan.

[8]Cush begot Nimrod; he began to be a mighty one on the earth. [9]He was a mighty hunter before the LORD; therefore it is said, "Like Nimrod the mighty hunter before the LORD." [10]And the beginning of his kingdom was Babel, Erech, Accad, and Calneh, in the land of Shinar. [11]From that land he went to Assyria and built Nineveh, Rehoboth Ir, Calah, [12]and Resen between Nineveh and Calah (that *is* the principal city).

[13]Mizraim begot Ludim, Anamim, Lehabim, Naphtuhim, [14]Pathrusim, and Casluhim (from whom came the Philistines and Caphtorim).

[15]Canaan begot Sidon his firstborn, and Heth; [16]the Jebusite, the Amorite, and the Girgashite; [17]the Hivite, the Arkite, and the Sinite; [18]the Arvadite, the Zemarite, and the Hamathite. Afterward the families of the Canaanites were dispersed. [19]And the border of the Canaanites was from Sidon as you go toward Gerar, as far as Gaza; then as you go toward Sodom, Gomorrah, Admah, and Zeboiim, as far as Lasha. [20]These *were* the sons of Ham, according to their families, according to their languages, in their lands *and* in their nations.

[21]And *children* were born also to Shem, the father of all the children of Eber, the brother of Japheth the elder. [22]The sons of Shem *were* Elam, Asshur, Arphaxad, Lud, and Aram. [23]The sons of Aram *were* Uz, Hul, Gether, and Mash.[a] [24]Arphaxad begot Salah,[a] and Salah begot Eber. [25]To Eber were born two sons: the name of one *was* Peleg, for in his days the earth was divided; and his brother's name *was* Joktan. [26]Joktan begot Almodad, Sheleph, Hazarmaveth, Jerah, [27]Hadoram, Uzal, Diklah, [28]Obal,[a] Abimael, Sheba,

---

10:3 [a]Spelled *Diphath* in 1 Chronicles 1:6   **10:4** [a]Spelled *Rodanim* in Samaritan Pentateuch and 1 Chronicles 1:7   **10:6** [a]Or *Phut*
10:23 [a]Called *Meshech* in Septuagint and 1 Chronicles 1:17
10:24 [a]Following Masoretic Text, Vulgate, and Targum; Septuagint reads *Arphaxad begot Cainan, and Cainan begot Salah* (compare Luke 3:35, 36).   **10:28** [a]Spelled *Ebal* in 1 Chronicles 1:22

²⁹Ophir, Havilah, and Jobab. All these *were* the sons of Joktan. ³⁰And their dwelling place was from Mesha as you go toward Sephar, the mountain of the east. ³¹These *were* the sons of Shem, according to their families, according to their languages, in their lands, according to their nations.

³²These *were* the families of the sons of Noah, according to their generations, in their nations; and from these the nations were divided on the earth after the flood.

THE TOWER OF BABEL

11 Now the whole earth had one language and one speech. ²And it came to pass, as they journeyed from the east, that they found a plain in the land of Shinar, and they dwelt there. ³Then they said to one another, "Come, let us make bricks and bake *them* thoroughly." They had brick for stone, and they had asphalt for mortar. ⁴And they said, "Come, let us build ourselves a city, and a tower whose top *is* in the heavens; let us make a name for ourselves, lest we be scattered abroad over the face of the whole earth."

⁵But the LORD came down to see the city and the tower which the sons of men had built. ⁶And the LORD said, "Indeed the people *are* one and they all have one language, and this is what they begin to do; now nothing that they propose to do will be withheld from them. ⁷Come, let Us go down and there confuse their language, that they may not understand one another's speech." ⁸So the LORD scattered them abroad from there over the face of all the earth, and they ceased building the city. ⁹Therefore its name is called Babel, because there the LORD confused the language of all the earth; and from there the LORD scattered them abroad over the face of all the earth.

SHEM'S DESCENDANTS

¹⁰This *is* the genealogy of Shem: Shem *was* one hundred years old, and begot Arphaxad two years after the flood. ¹¹After he begot Arphaxad, Shem lived five hundred years, and begot sons and daughters.

¹²Arphaxad lived thirty-five years, and begot Salah. ¹³After he begot Salah, Arphaxad lived four hundred and three years, and begot sons and daughters.

¹⁴Salah lived thirty years, and begot Eber. ¹⁵After he begot Eber, Salah lived four hundred and three years, and begot sons and daughters.

¹⁶Eber lived thirty-four years, and begot Peleg. ¹⁷After he begot Peleg, Eber lived four hundred and thirty years, and begot sons and daughters.

¹⁸Peleg lived thirty years, and begot Reu. ¹⁹After he begot Reu, Peleg lived two hundred and nine years, and begot sons and daughters.

²⁰Reu lived thirty-two years, and begot Serug. ²¹After he begot Serug, Reu lived two hundred and seven years, and begot sons and daughters.

²²Serug lived thirty years, and begot Nahor. ²³After he begot Nahor, Serug lived two hundred years, and begot sons and daughters.

²⁴Nahor lived twenty-nine years, and begot Terah. ²⁵After he begot Terah, Nahor lived one hundred and nineteen years, and begot sons and daughters.

²⁶Now Terah lived seventy years, and begot Abram, Nahor, and Haran.

TERAH'S DESCENDANTS

²⁷This *is* the genealogy of Terah: Terah begot Abram, Nahor, and Haran. Haran begot Lot. ²⁸And Haran died before his father Terah in his native land, in Ur of the Chaldeans. ²⁹Then Abram and Nahor took wives: the name of Abram's wife *was* Sarai, and the name of Nahor's wife, Milcah, the daughter of Haran the father of Milcah and the father of Iscah. ³⁰But Sarai was barren; she had no child.

³¹And Terah took his son Abram and his grandson Lot, the son of Haran, and his daughter-in-law Sarai, his son Abram's wife, and they went out with them from Ur of the Chaldeans to go to the land of Canaan; and they came to Haran and dwelt there. ³²So the days of Terah were two hundred and five years, and Terah died in Haran.

PROMISES TO ABRAM

12 Now the LORD had said to Abram:

"Get out of your country,
From your family
And from your father's house,
To a land that I will show you.

²I will make you a great nation;
I will bless you
And make your name great;
And you shall be a blessing.
³I will bless those who bless you,
And I will curse him who curses you;
And in you all the families of the earth shall
    be blessed."

⁴So Abram departed as the LORD had spoken to him, and Lot went with him. And Abram *was* seventy-five years old when he departed from Haran. ⁵Then Abram took Sarai his wife and Lot his brother's son, and all their possessions that they had gathered, and the people whom they had acquired in Haran, and they departed to go to the land of Canaan. So they came to the land of Canaan. ⁶Abram passed through the land to the place of Shechem, as far as the terebinth tree of Moreh.ᵃ And the Canaanites *were* then in the land.

⁷Then the LORD appeared to Abram and said, "To your descendants I will give this land." And there he built an altar to the LORD, who had appeared to him. ⁸And he moved from there to the mountain east of Bethel, and he pitched his tent *with* Bethel on the west and Ai on the east; there he built an altar to the LORD and called on the name of the LORD. ⁹So Abram journeyed, going on still toward the South.ᵃ

ABRAM IN EGYPT

¹⁰Now there was a famine in the land, and Abram went down to Egypt to dwell there, for the famine *was* severe in the land. ¹¹And it came to pass, when he was close to entering Egypt, that he said to Sarai his wife, "Indeed I know that you *are* a woman of beautiful countenance. ¹²Therefore it will happen, when the Egyptians see you, that they will say, 'This *is* his wife'; and they will kill me, but they will let you live. ¹³Please say you *are* my sister, that it may be well with me for your sake, and that Iᵃ may live because of you."

¹⁴So it was, when Abram came into Egypt, that the Egyptians saw the woman, that she *was* very beautiful. ¹⁵The princes of Pharaoh also saw her and commended her to Pharaoh. And the woman was taken to Pharaoh's house. ¹⁶He

treated Abram well for her sake. He had sheep, oxen, male donkeys, male and female servants, female donkeys, and camels.

¹⁷But the LORD plagued Pharaoh and his house with great plagues because of Sarai, Abram's wife. ¹⁸And Pharaoh called Abram and said, "What *is* this you have done to me? Why did you not tell me that she *was* your wife? ¹⁹Why did you say, 'She *is* my sister'? I might have taken her as my wife. Now therefore, here is your wife; take *her* and go your way." ²⁰So Pharaoh commanded *his* men concerning him; and they sent him away, with his wife and all that he had.

ABRAM INHERITS CANAAN

13 Then Abram went up from Egypt, he and his wife and all that he had, and Lot with him, to the South.ᵃ ²Abram *was* very rich in livestock, in silver, and in gold. ³And he went on his journey from the South as far as Bethel, to the place where his tent had been at the beginning, between Bethel and Ai, ⁴to the place of the altar which he had made there at first. And there Abram called on the name of the LORD.

⁵Lot also, who went with Abram, had flocks and herds and tents. ⁶Now the land was not able to support them, that they might dwell together, for their possessions were so great that they could not dwell together. ⁷And there was strife between the herdsmen of Abram's livestock and the herdsmen of Lot's livestock. The Canaanites and the Perizzites then dwelt in the land.

⁸So Abram said to Lot, "Please let there be no strife between you and me, and between my herdsmen and your herdsmen; for we *are* brethren. ⁹*Is* not the whole land before you? Please separate from me. If *you take* the left, then I will go to the right; or, if *you go* to the right, then I will go to the left."

¹⁰And Lot lifted his eyes and saw all the plain of Jordan, that it *was* well watered everywhere (before the LORD destroyed Sodom and Gomorrah) like the garden of the LORD, like the land of Egypt as you go toward Zoar. ¹¹Then Lot chose for himself all the plain of Jordan, and Lot journeyed east. And they separated from each other.

12:6 ᵃHebrew *Alon Moreh*   **12:9** ᵃHebrew *Negev*   **12:13** ᵃLiterally *my soul*   **13:1** ᵃHebrew *Negev*

INSIDE *the* INFLUENCERS

LOT: The High Cost of Poor Choices

GENESIS 13:10

Lot was the nephew of Abram, who was later renamed Abraham. Lot experienced great wealth as he traveled and lived with Abraham. He was privileged to walk and live with the man called a "friend of God" (James 2:23). He had a front-row seat to God's blessing and protection; but soon, conflicts arose between Lot's and Abraham's herdsmen.

To settle their conflicts, Abraham generously allowed Lot to choose his own land. Lot selected the most fertile pasture in the Jordan valley, disregarding its sinful reputation. Not long after Lot settled in Sodom, war broke out and his entire family was taken captive. Abraham set out with all of his men to rescue Lot's family, traveling some 200–250 miles north to do so. Then Lot returned to the wicked city, drawn by its worldly influence.

Soon after, God sent angels to warn Abraham that Sodom was doomed. He begged for Lot's life and was granted his request. Lot, however, was reluctant to get out of the city as the Lord's messengers told him to do. His wife didn't heed the warnings either, and she was turned to a pillar of salt when she looked back at the city. Only Lot's daughters made it out with Lot before God rained down brimstone and fire. Lot was in the wrong place with the wrong people by his own design. In the sight of God, Sodom was wicked, but to Lot it looked appealing. Weak devotions plus worldly desires always equals wrong decisions.

In the end, Lot lost his wealth, and his wife. If he would have learned from his uncle Abraham and followed Abraham's example of devotion to God, maybe things would have turned out differently for Lot.

---

¹²Abram dwelt in the land of Canaan, and Lot dwelt in the cities of the plain and pitched *his* tent even as far as Sodom. ¹³But the men of Sodom *were* exceedingly wicked and sinful against the Lord.

¹⁴And the Lord said to Abram, after Lot had separated from him: "Lift your eyes now and look from the place where you are—northward, southward, eastward, and westward; ¹⁵for all the land which you see I give to you and your descendants[a] forever. ¹⁶And I will make your descendants as the dust of the earth; so that if a man could number the dust of the earth, *then* your descendants also could be numbered. ¹⁷Arise, walk in the land through its length and its width, for I give it to you."

¹⁸Then Abram moved *his* tent, and went and dwelt by the terebinth trees of Mamre,[a] which *are* in Hebron, and built an altar there to the Lord.

LOT'S CAPTIVITY AND RESCUE

14 And it came to pass in the days of Amraphel king of Shinar, Arioch king of Ellasar, Chedorlaomer king of Elam, and Tidal king of nations,[a] ²*that* they made war with Bera king of Sodom, Birsha king of Gomorrah, Shinab king of Admah, Shemeber king of Zeboiim, and the king of Bela (that is, Zoar). ³All these joined together in the Valley of Siddim (that is, the Salt Sea). ⁴Twelve years they served Chedorlaomer, and in the thirteenth year they rebelled.

⁵In the fourteenth year Chedorlaomer and the kings that *were* with him came and attacked the Rephaim in Ashteroth Karnaim, the Zuzim in Ham, the Emim in Shaveh Kiriathaim, ⁶and the Horites in their mountain of Seir, as far as El

13:15 [a]Literally *seed*, and so throughout the book   **13:18** [a]Hebrew *Alon Mamre*   **14:1** [a]Hebrew *goyim*

Paran, which *is* by the wilderness. ⁷Then they turned back and came to En Mishpat (that *is,* Kadesh), and attacked all the country of the Amalekites, and also the Amorites who dwelt in Hazezon Tamar.

⁸And the king of Sodom, the king of Gomorrah, the king of Admah, the king of Zeboiim, and the king of Bela (that *is,* Zoar) went out and joined together in battle in the Valley of Siddim ⁹against Chedorlaomer king of Elam, Tidal king of nations,ᵃ Amraphel king of Shinar, and Arioch king of Ellasar—four kings against five. ¹⁰Now the Valley of Siddim *was full of* asphalt pits; and the kings of Sodom and Gomorrah fled; *some* fell there, and the remainder fled to the mountains. ¹¹Then they took all the goods of Sodom and Gomorrah, and all their provisions, and went their way. ¹²They also took Lot, Abram's brother's son who dwelt in Sodom, and his goods, and departed.

¹³Then one who had escaped came and told Abram the Hebrew, for he dwelt by the terebinth trees of Mamreᵃ the Amorite, brother of Eshcol and brother of Aner; and they *were* allies with Abram. ¹⁴Now when Abram heard that his brother was taken captive, he armed his three hundred and eighteen trained *servants* who were born in his own house, and went in pursuit as far as Dan. ¹⁵He divided his forces against them by night, and he and his servants attacked them and pursued them as far as Hobah, which *is* north of Damascus. ¹⁶So he brought back all the goods, and also brought back his brother Lot and his goods, as well as the women and the people.

¹⁷And the king of Sodom went out to meet him at the Valley of Shaveh (that *is,* the King's Valley), after his return from the defeat of Chedorlaomer and the kings who *were* with him.

ABRAM AND MELCHIZEDEK

¹⁸Then Melchizedek king of Salem brought out bread and wine; he *was* the priest of God Most High. ¹⁹And he blessed him and said:

"Blessed be Abram of God Most High,
    Possessor of heaven and earth;
²⁰And blessed be God Most High,
    Who has delivered your enemies into your hand."

And he gave him a tithe of all.

²¹Now the king of Sodom said to Abram, "Give me the persons, and take the goods for yourself."

²²But Abram said to the king of Sodom, "I have raised my hand to the LORD, God Most High, the Possessor of heaven and earth, ²³that I *will take* nothing, from a thread to a sandal strap, and that I will not take anything that *is* yours, lest you should say, 'I have made Abram rich'— ²⁴except only what the young men have eaten, and the portion of the men who went with me: Aner, Eshcol, and Mamre; let them take their portion."

GOD'S COVENANT WITH ABRAM

15 After these things the word of the LORD came to Abram in a vision, saying, "Do not be afraid, Abram. I *am* your shield, your exceedingly great reward."

²But Abram said, "Lord GOD, what will You give me, seeing I go childless, and the heir of my house *is* Eliezer of Damascus?" ³Then Abram said, "Look, You have given me no offspring; indeed one born in my house is my heir!"

⁴And behold, the word of the LORD *came* to him, saying, "This one shall not be your heir, but one who will come from your own body shall be your heir." ⁵Then He brought him outside and said, "Look now toward heaven, and count the stars if you are able to number them." And He said to him, "So shall your descendants be."

⁶And he believed in the LORD, and He accounted it to him for righteousness.

⁷Then He said to him, "I *am* the LORD, who brought you out of Ur of the Chaldeans, to give you this land to inherit it."

⁸And he said, "Lord GOD, how shall I know that I will inherit it?"

⁹So He said to him, "Bring Me a three-year-old heifer, a three-year-old female goat, a three-year-old ram, a turtledove, and a young pigeon." ¹⁰Then he brought all these to Him and cut them in two, down the middle, and placed each piece opposite the other; but he did not cut the birds in two. ¹¹And when the vultures came down on the carcasses, Abram drove them away.

14:9 ᵃHebrew *goyim*   **14:13** ᵃHebrew *Alon Mamre*

¹²Now when the sun was going down, a deep sleep fell upon Abram; and behold, horror *and* great darkness fell upon him. ¹³Then He said to Abram: "Know certainly that your descendants will be strangers in a land *that is* not theirs, and will serve them, and they will afflict them four hundred years. ¹⁴And also the nation whom they serve I will judge; afterward they shall come out with great possessions. ¹⁵Now as for you, you shall go to your fathers in peace; you shall be buried at a good old age. ¹⁶But in the fourth generation they shall return here, for the iniquity of the Amorites *is* not yet complete."

¹⁷And it came to pass, when the sun went down and it was dark, that behold, there appeared a smoking oven and a burning torch that passed between those pieces. ¹⁸On the same day the LORD made a covenant with Abram, saying:

"To your descendants I have given this land, from the river of Egypt to the great river, the River Euphrates— ¹⁹the Kenites, the Kenezzites, the Kadmonites, ²⁰the Hittites, the Perizzites, the Rephaim, ²¹the Amorites, the Canaanites, the Girgashites, and the Jebusites."

HAGAR AND ISHMAEL

16 Now Sarai, Abram's wife, had borne him no *children*. And she had an Egyptian maidservant whose name was Hagar. ²So Sarai said to Abram, "See now, the LORD has restrained me from bearing *children*. Please, go in to my maid; perhaps I shall obtain children by her." And Abram heeded the voice of Sarai. ³Then Sarai, Abram's wife, took Hagar her maid, the Egyptian, and gave her to her husband Abram to be his wife, after Abram had dwelt ten years in the land of Canaan. ⁴So he went in to Hagar, and she conceived. And when she saw that she had conceived, her mistress became despised in her eyes.

⁵Then Sarai said to Abram, "My wrong *be* upon you! I gave my maid into your embrace; and when she saw that she had conceived, I became despised in her eyes. The LORD judge between you and me."

⁶So Abram said to Sarai, "Indeed your maid *is* in your hand; do to her as you please." And when Sarai dealt harshly with her, she fled from her presence.

⁷Now the Angel of the LORD found her by a spring of water in the wilderness, by the spring on the way to Shur. ⁸And He said, "Hagar, Sarai's maid, where have you come from, and where are you going?"

She said, "I am fleeing from the presence of my mistress Sarai."

⁹The Angel of the LORD said to her, "Return to your mistress, and submit yourself under her hand." ¹⁰Then the Angel of the LORD said to her, "I will multiply your descendants exceedingly, so that they shall not be counted for multitude." ¹¹And the Angel of the LORD said to her:

"Behold, you *are* with child,
    And you shall bear a son.
    You shall call his name Ishmael,
    Because the LORD has heard your affliction.
¹²He shall be a wild man;
    His hand *shall be* against every man,
    And every man's hand against him.
    And he shall dwell in the presence of all his
        brethren."

¹³Then she called the name of the LORD who spoke to her, You-Are-the-God-Who-Sees; for she said, "Have I also here seen Him who sees me?" ¹⁴Therefore the well was called Beer Lahai Roi;ᵃ observe, *it is* between Kadesh and Bered.

¹⁵So Hagar bore Abram a son; and Abram named his son, whom Hagar bore, Ishmael. ¹⁶Abram *was* eighty-six years old when Hagar bore Ishmael to Abram.

THE SIGN OF THE COVENANT

17 When Abram was ninety-nine years old, the LORD appeared to Abram and said to him, "I *am* Almighty God; walk before Me and be blameless. ²And I will make My covenant between Me and you, and will multiply you exceedingly." ³Then Abram fell on his face, and God talked with him, saying: ⁴"As for Me, behold, My covenant is with you, and you shall be a father of many nations. ⁵No longer shall your name be called Abram, but your name shall be Abraham; for I have made you a father of many nations. ⁶I will make you exceedingly fruitful; and I will make nations of you, and kings shall come from

16:14 ᵃLiterally *Well of the One Who Lives and Sees Me*

INSIDE *the* INFLUENCERS

HAGAR—Believe in Your God-Given Future

GENESIS 16; 21

There is no doubt that Hagar was a victim in this situation. Sarah's scheme to have her bear Abraham's child produced friction in the family compound. To cope with the stress, Hagar ran away to the wilderness—probably to hide, possibly to think, maybe to try and punish Abraham and Sarah (16:7, 8). God saw that she was in too great despair to believe in the future so He came looking for her personally. He asked, *"Where have you come from and where are you going?"* It wasn't that God didn't know; it was that He wanted her to think about the choice she was making. He sent an angel to minister to her with a promise: *Your son will be named Ishmael, which means "God hears."* When Hagar grasped how personal God's love was for her, she gained confidence in the future and went back home. Every time she called the name of *Ishmael*, she remembered, *"God hears me."*

Fourteen years later, Sarah's disdain for Hagar was only worse. Finally, Abraham escorted Hagar and Ishmael to the desert, leaving them with a bottle of water. In her darkest moment as they were dying, Scripture says God heard Ishmael crying. There's the promise—*God hears!* Man gave her a bottle, but *God showed Hagar a well of water* that day.

Live confidently, believing that God's love is personal and that His resources are in place before you need them.

you. ⁷And I will establish My covenant between Me and you and your descendants after you in their generations, for an everlasting covenant, to be God to you and your descendants after you. ⁸Also I give to you and your descendants after you the land in which you are a stranger, all the land of Canaan, as an everlasting possession; and I will be their God."

⁹And God said to Abraham: "As for you, you shall keep My covenant, you and your descendants after you throughout their generations. ¹⁰This *is* My covenant which you shall keep, between Me and you and your descendants after you: Every male child among you shall be circumcised; ¹¹and you shall be circumcised in the flesh of your foreskins, and it shall be a sign of the covenant between Me and you. ¹²He who is eight days old among you shall be circumcised, every male child in your generations, he who is born in your house or bought with money from any foreigner who is not your descendant. ¹³He who is

born in your house and he who is bought with your money must be circumcised, and My covenant shall be in your flesh for an everlasting covenant. ¹⁴And the uncircumcised male child, who is not circumcised in the flesh of his foreskin, that person shall be cut off from his people; he has broken My covenant."

¹⁵Then God said to Abraham, "As for Sarai your wife, you shall not call her name Sarai, but Sarah *shall be* her name. ¹⁶And I will bless her and also give you a son by her; then I will bless her, and she shall be *a mother* of nations; kings of peoples shall be from her."

¹⁷Then Abraham fell on his face and laughed, and said in his heart, "Shall *a child* be born to a man who is one hundred years old? And shall Sarah, who is ninety years old, bear *a child?*" ¹⁸And Abraham said to God, "Oh, that Ishmael might live before You!"

¹⁹Then God said: "No, Sarah your wife shall bear you a son, and you shall call his name Isaac; I

INSIDE *the* INFLUENCERS

SARAI to SARAH—Great Honor Demands Great Sacrifice

GENESIS 12:1

Abram was 75 and Sarai was 65 when the Lord uprooted them from a familiar home and took them on a wilderness trip that had no definite end in sight. They lived in tents like nomads. She had no children after all these years so when God told them He would make a great nation of Abram, they must have both smiled in wonder at the words.

Sarai's intense burden to give Abraham the child of promise caused her to sin greatly. After years of waiting, she took matters into her own hands and asked Abram to have a child by her handmaiden. This resulted in jealousy and anger. The child, Ishmael, and his mother, Hagar, ran away into the wilderness alone. It was not Sarai's finest hour. Sarai still had no children at the age of 90, so when God told them they would conceive a son, she laughed at the idea.

At the age of 99, Abram's name became Abraham, and at 90, Sarai became Sarah. Change was a constant part of her new life. They were on the move once again. The Lord called Abraham *and* Sarah. She played a vital role in the birth of a great nation—which came through their promised son Isaac. She was part of the witness to the world of the One True God through whom the Scriptures were given, the prophets arose, and eventually the Savior would come. Great honor had demanded great obedience and personal sacrifice.

will establish My covenant with him for an everlasting covenant, *and* with his descendants after him. [20]And as for Ishmael, I have heard you. Behold, I have blessed him, and will make him fruitful, and will multiply him exceedingly. He shall beget twelve princes, and I will make him a great nation. [21]But My covenant I will establish with Isaac, whom Sarah shall bear to you at this set time next year." [22]Then He finished talking with him, and God went up from Abraham.

[23]So Abraham took Ishmael his son, all who were born in his house and all who were bought with his money, every male among the men of Abraham's house, and circumcised the flesh of their foreskins that very same day, as God had said to him. [24]Abraham *was* ninety-nine years old when he was circumcised in the flesh of his foreskin. [25]And Ishmael his son *was* thirteen years old when he was circumcised in the flesh of his foreskin. [26]That very same day Abraham was circumcised, and his son Ishmael; [27]and all the men of his house, born in the house or bought with money from a foreigner, were circumcised with him.

THE SON OF PROMISE

18 Then the LORD appeared to him by the terebinth trees of Mamre,[a] as he was sitting in the tent door in the heat of the day. [2]So he lifted his eyes and looked, and behold, three men were standing by him; and when he saw *them,* he ran from the tent door to meet them, and bowed himself to the ground, [3]and said, "My Lord, if I have now found favor in Your sight, do not pass on by Your servant. [4]Please let a little water be brought, and wash your feet, and rest yourselves under the tree. [5]And I will bring a morsel of bread, that you may refresh your hearts. After that you may pass by, inasmuch as you have come to your servant."

They said, "Do as you have said."

[6]So Abraham hurried into the tent to Sarah and said, "Quickly, make ready three measures of fine meal; knead *it* and make cakes." [7]And Abraham ran to the herd, took a tender and good calf, gave *it* to a young man, and he hastened to pre-

18:1 [a]Hebrew *Alon Mamre*

pare it. [8]So he took butter and milk and the calf which he had prepared, and set *it* before them; and he stood by them under the tree as they ate.

[9]Then they said to him, "Where *is* Sarah your wife?"

So he said, "Here, in the tent."

[10]And He said, "I will certainly return to you according to the time of life, and behold, Sarah your wife shall have a son."

(Sarah was listening in the tent door which *was* behind him.) [11]Now Abraham and Sarah were old, well advanced in age; *and* Sarah had passed the age of childbearing.[a] [12]Therefore Sarah laughed within herself, saying, "After I have grown old, shall I have pleasure, my lord being old also?"

[13]And the LORD said to Abraham, "Why did Sarah laugh, saying, 'Shall I surely bear *a child,* since I am old?' [14]Is anything too hard for the LORD? At the appointed time I will return to you, according to the time of life, and Sarah shall have a son."

[15]But Sarah denied *it,* saying, "I did not laugh," for she was afraid.

And He said, "No, but you did laugh!"

ABRAHAM INTERCEDES FOR SODOM

[16]Then the men rose from there and looked toward Sodom, and Abraham went with them to send them on the way. [17]And the LORD said, "Shall I hide from Abraham what I am doing, [18]since Abraham shall surely become a great and mighty nation, and all the nations of the earth shall be blessed in him? [19]For I have known him, in order that he may command his children and his household after him, that they keep the way of the LORD, to do righteousness and justice, that the LORD may bring to Abraham what He has spoken to him." [20]And the LORD said, "Because the outcry against Sodom and Gomorrah is great, and because their sin is very grave, [21]I will go down now and see whether they have done altogether according to the outcry against it that has come to Me; and if not, I will know."

[22]Then the men turned away from there and went toward Sodom, but Abraham still stood before the LORD. [23]And Abraham came near and said, "Would You also destroy the righteous with the wicked? [24]Suppose there were fifty righteous within the city; would You also destroy the place and not spare *it* for the fifty righteous that were in it? [25]Far be it from You to do such a thing as this, to slay the righteous with the wicked, so that the righteous should be as the wicked; far be it from You! Shall not the Judge of all the earth do right?"

[26]So the LORD said, "If I find in Sodom fifty righteous within the city, then I will spare all the place for their sakes."

[27]Then Abraham answered and said, "Indeed now, I who *am but* dust and ashes have taken it upon myself to speak to the Lord: [28]Suppose there were five less than the fifty righteous; would You destroy all of the city for *lack of* five?"

So He said, "If I find there forty-five, I will not destroy *it.*"

[29]And he spoke to Him yet again and said, "Suppose there should be forty found there?"

So He said, "I will not do *it* for the sake of forty."

[30]Then he said, "Let not the Lord be angry, and I will speak: Suppose thirty should be found there?"

So He said, "I will not do *it* if I find thirty there."

[31]And he said, "Indeed now, I have taken it upon myself to speak to the Lord: Suppose twenty should be found there?"

So He said, "I will not destroy *it* for the sake of twenty."

[32]Then he said, "Let not the Lord be angry, and I will speak but once more: Suppose ten should be found there?"

And He said, "I will not destroy *it* for the sake of ten." [33]So the LORD went His way as soon as He had finished speaking with Abraham; and Abraham returned to his place.

SODOM'S DEPRAVITY

19 Now the two angels came to Sodom in the evening, and Lot was sitting in the gate of Sodom. When Lot saw *them,* he rose to meet them, and he bowed himself with his face toward the ground. [2]And he said, "Here now, my lords, please turn in to your servant's house and spend the night, and wash your feet; then you may rise early and go on your way."

18:11 [a]Literally *the manner of women had ceased to be with Sarah*

LEADERSHIP ISSUES

GC2: Divine Visitation

GENESIS 18:17

The Lord made occasional "special appearances" to His followers in the Old Testament. In fact, many Bible scholars consider this and other similar Old Testament appearances as visitations of Jesus, the Second Person of the Trinity, prior to His taking on human form in the New Testament (John 1:1–5, 14). One such appearance is to Abraham and Sarah concerning their promised son, Isaac. After spending a day with Abraham and his family, during which He affirmed that Sarah would miraculously give birth within a year, the Lord prepared to depart. Then, He paused, asking Himself if He should hide what He was about to do. Like a good friend, the Lord halted in the midst of His divine agenda to consider Abraham. He stopped to let Abraham in on what He was about to do. What if the Lord is longing to do the same for you?

What if God's heart is to let us in on what He is up to? Might our motivation to pursue Him increase if we truly believed that He longs to reveal Himself to us? Imagine living as if God, by His Spirit, might pay you a visit at any time, at any place, in any circumstance. This is a disciple's hope or "expectancy." Envision yourself approaching times of worship, prayer, Bible study, and fellowship with an eager expectation of His visitation.

As a follower of Jesus, this is our hope, anticipation, and testimony.

Pause to reflect on such a visitation in your life: "*I remember sensing Christ revealing to me* _____ *when* _____."

GREAT COMMANDMENT COMMISSION

THROUGH THE GRID

Making Sense of Your World: Family and Worldviews (Gen. 18:19)

Many today adopt a naturalist view of the family, viewing family units simply as extensions of nature with no intrinsic value. There are no absolutes, so family life can differ greatly from one context to the next. In addition, many hold to a transcendentalist worldview of the family that follows the dictates of self-expression and independent ideals with few guidelines or moral checkpoints. Families who hold a theistic worldview, however, hold the image of God as central to their lives and aim to form the family after biblical Christian ideals in order to give glory to God.

And they said, "No, but we will spend the night in the open square."

[3] But he insisted strongly; so they turned in to him and entered his house. Then he made them a feast, and baked unleavened bread, and they ate. [4] Now before they lay down, the men of the city, the men of Sodom, both old and young, all the people from every quarter, surrounded the house. [5] And they called to Lot and said to him, "Where are the men who came to you tonight? Bring them out to us that we may know them *carnally*."

[6] So Lot went out to them through the doorway, shut the door behind him, [7] and said, "Please, my brethren, do not do so wickedly! [8] See now, I have two daughters who have not known a man; please, let me bring them out to you, and you may do to them as you wish; only do nothing to these men, since this is the reason they have come under the shadow of my roof."

[9] And they said, "Stand back!" Then they said, "This one came in to stay *here,* and he keeps acting as a judge; now we will deal worse with you than with them." So they pressed hard against the man Lot, and came near to break down the door. [10] But the men reached out their hands and pulled Lot into the house with them, and shut the door. [11] And they struck the men who *were* at the doorway of the house with blindness, both small and great, so that they became weary *trying* to find the door.

Sodom and Gomorrah Destroyed

[12] Then the men said to Lot, "Have you anyone else here? Son-in-law, your sons, your daughters, and whomever you have in the city—take *them* out of this place! [13] For we will destroy this place, because the outcry against them has grown great before the face of the LORD, and the LORD has sent us to destroy it."

[14] So Lot went out and spoke to his sons-in-law, who had married his daughters, and said, "Get up, get out of this place; for the LORD will destroy this city!" But to his sons-in-law he seemed to be joking.

[15] When the morning dawned, the angels urged Lot to hurry, saying, "Arise, take your wife and your two daughters who are here, lest you be consumed in the punishment of the city." [16] And while he lingered, the men took hold of his hand, his wife's hand, and the hands of his two daughters, the LORD being merciful to him, and they brought him out and set him outside the city. [17] So it came to pass, when they had brought them outside, that he[a] said, "Escape for your life! Do not look behind you nor stay anywhere in the plain. Escape to the mountains, lest you be destroyed."

[18] Then Lot said to them, "Please, no, my lords! [19] Indeed now, your servant has found favor in your sight, and you have increased your mercy which you have shown me by saving my life; but I cannot escape to the mountains, lest some evil overtake me and I die. [20] See now, this city *is* near *enough* to flee to, and it *is* a little one; please let me escape there (*is* it not a little one?) and my soul shall live."

[21] And he said to him, "See, I have favored you concerning this thing also, in that I will not overthrow this city for which you have spoken.

19:17 [a] Septuagint, Syriac, and Vulgate read *they.*

²²Hurry, escape there. For I cannot do anything until you arrive there."

Therefore the name of the city was called Zoar.

²³The sun had risen upon the earth when Lot entered Zoar. ²⁴Then the LORD rained brimstone and fire on Sodom and Gomorrah, from the LORD out of the heavens. ²⁵So He overthrew those cities, all the plain, all the inhabitants of the cities, and what grew on the ground.

²⁶But his wife looked back behind him, and she became a pillar of salt.

²⁷And Abraham went early in the morning to the place where he had stood before the LORD. ²⁸Then he looked toward Sodom and Gomorrah, and toward all the land of the plain; and he saw, and behold, the smoke of the land which went up like the smoke of a furnace. ²⁹And it came to pass, when God destroyed the cities of the plain, that God remembered Abraham, and sent Lot out of the midst of the overthrow, when He overthrew the cities in which Lot had dwelt.

THE DESCENDANTS OF LOT

³⁰Then Lot went up out of Zoar and dwelt in the mountains, and his two daughters were with him; for he was afraid to dwell in Zoar. And he and his two daughters dwelt in a cave. ³¹Now the firstborn said to the younger, "Our father *is* old, and *there is* no man on the earth to come in to us as is the custom of all the earth. ³²Come, let us make our father drink wine, and we will lie with him, that we may preserve the lineage of our father." ³³So they made their father drink wine that night. And the firstborn went in and lay with her father, and he did not know when she lay down or when she arose.

³⁴It happened on the next day that the first-born said to the younger, "Indeed I lay with my father last night; let us make him drink wine tonight also, and you go in *and* lie with him, that we may preserve the lineage of our father." ³⁵Then they made their father drink wine that night also. And the younger arose and lay with him, and he did not know when she lay down or when she arose.

³⁶Thus both the daughters of Lot were with child by their father. ³⁷The firstborn bore a son and called his name Moab; he *is* the father of the Moabites to this day. ³⁸And the younger, she also bore a son and called his name Ben-Ammi; he *is* the father of the people of Ammon to this day.

ABRAHAM AND ABIMELECH

20 And Abraham journeyed from there to the South, and dwelt between Kadesh and Shur, and stayed in Gerar. ²Now Abraham said of Sarah his wife, "She *is* my sister." And Abimelech king of Gerar sent and took Sarah.

³But God came to Abimelech in a dream by night, and said to him, "Indeed you *are* a dead man because of the woman whom you have taken, for she *is* a man's wife."

⁴But Abimelech had not come near her; and he said, "Lord, will You slay a righteous nation also? ⁵Did he not say to me, 'She *is* my sister'? And she, even she herself said, 'He *is* my brother.' In the integrity of my heart and innocence of my hands I have done this."

⁶And God said to him in a dream, "Yes, I know that you did this in the integrity of your heart. For I also withheld you from sinning against Me; therefore I did not let you touch her. ⁷Now therefore, restore the man's wife; for he *is* a prophet, and he will pray for you and you shall live. But if you do not restore *her,* know that you shall surely die, you and all who *are* yours."

⁸So Abimelech rose early in the morning, called all his servants, and told all these things in their hearing; and the men were very much afraid. ⁹And Abimelech called Abraham and said to him, "What have you done to us? How have I offended you, that you have brought on me and on my kingdom a great sin? You have done deeds to me that ought not to be done." ¹⁰Then Abimelech said to Abraham, "What did you have in view, that you have done this thing?"

¹¹And Abraham said, "Because I thought, surely the fear of God *is* not in this place; and they will kill me on account of my wife. ¹²But indeed *she is* truly my sister. She *is* the daughter of my father, but not the daughter of my mother; and she became my wife. ¹³And it came to pass, when God caused me to wander from my father's house, that I said to her, 'This *is* your kindness that you should do for me: in every place, wherever we go, say of me, "He *is* my brother." ' "

¹⁴Then Abimelech took sheep, oxen, and male

and female servants, and gave *them* to Abraham; and he restored Sarah his wife to him. [15]And Abimelech said, "See, my land *is* before you; dwell where it pleases you." [16]Then to Sarah he said, "Behold, I have given your brother a thousand *pieces* of silver; indeed this vindicates you[a] before all who *are* with you and before everybody." Thus she was rebuked.

[17]So Abraham prayed to God; and God healed Abimelech, his wife, and his female servants. Then they bore *children;* [18]for the LORD had closed up all the wombs of the house of Abimelech because of Sarah, Abraham's wife.

ISAAC IS BORN

21 And the LORD visited Sarah as He had said, and the LORD did for Sarah as He had spoken. [2]For Sarah conceived and bore Abraham a son in his old age, at the set time of which God had spoken to him. [3]And Abraham called the name of his son who was born to him—whom Sarah bore to him—Isaac. [4]Then Abraham circumcised his son Isaac when he was eight days old, as God had commanded him. [5]Now Abraham was one hundred years old when his son Isaac was born to him. [6]And Sarah said, "God has made me laugh, *and* all who hear will laugh with me." [7]She also said, "Who would have said to Abraham that Sarah would nurse children? For I have borne *him* a son in his old age."

HAGAR AND ISHMAEL DEPART

[8]So the child grew and was weaned. And Abraham made a great feast on the same day that Isaac was weaned.

[9]And Sarah saw the son of Hagar the Egyptian, whom she had borne to Abraham, scoffing. [10]Therefore she said to Abraham, "Cast out this bondwoman and her son; for the son of this bondwoman shall not be heir with my son, *namely* with Isaac." [11]And the matter was very displeasing in Abraham's sight because of his son.

[12]But God said to Abraham, "Do not let it be displeasing in your sight because of the lad or because of your bondwoman. Whatever Sarah has said to you, listen to her voice; for in Isaac your seed shall be called. [13]Yet I will also make a nation of the son of the bondwoman, because he *is* your seed."

[14]So Abraham rose early in the morning, and took bread and a skin of water; and putting *it* on her shoulder, he gave *it* and the boy to Hagar, and sent her away. Then she departed and wandered in the Wilderness of Beersheba. [15]And the water in the skin was used up, and she placed the boy under one of the shrubs. [16]Then she went and sat down across from *him* at a distance of about a bowshot; for she said to herself, "Let me not see the death of the boy." So she sat opposite *him,* and lifted her voice and wept.

[17]And God heard the voice of the lad. Then the angel of God called to Hagar out of heaven, and said to her, "What ails you, Hagar? Fear not, for God has heard the voice of the lad where he *is.* [18]Arise, lift up the lad and hold him with your hand, for I will make him a great nation."

[19]Then God opened her eyes, and she saw a well of water. And she went and filled the skin with water, and gave the lad a drink. [20]So God was with the lad; and he grew and dwelt in the wilderness, and became an archer. [21]He dwelt in the Wilderness of Paran; and his mother took a wife for him from the land of Egypt.

A COVENANT WITH ABIMELECH

[22]And it came to pass at that time that Abimelech and Phichol, the commander of his army, spoke to Abraham, saying, "God *is* with you in all that you do. [23]Now therefore, swear to me by God that you will not deal falsely with me, with my offspring, or with my posterity; but that according to the kindness that I have done to you, you will do to me and to the land in which you have dwelt."

[24]And Abraham said, "I will swear."

[25]Then Abraham rebuked Abimelech because of a well of water which Abimelech's servants had seized. [26]And Abimelech said, "I do not know who has done this thing; you did not tell me, nor had I heard *of it* until today." [27]So Abraham took sheep and oxen and gave them to Abimelech, and the two of them made a covenant. [28]And Abraham set seven ewe lambs of the flock by themselves.

[29]Then Abimelech asked Abraham, "What *is the meaning of* these seven ewe lambs which you have set by themselves?"

20:16 [a]Literally *it is a covering of the eyes for you*

³⁰And he said, "You will take *these* seven ewe lambs from my hand, that they may be my witness that I have dug this well." ³¹Therefore he called that place Beersheba,ᵃ because the two of them swore an oath there.

³²Thus they made a covenant at Beersheba. So Abimelech rose with Phichol, the commander of his army, and they returned to the land of the Philistines. ³³Then *Abraham* planted a tamarisk tree in Beersheba, and there called on the name of the LORD, the Everlasting God. ³⁴And Abraham stayed in the land of the Philistines many days.

ABRAHAM'S FAITH CONFIRMED

22 Now it came to pass after these things that God tested Abraham, and said to him, "Abraham!"

And he said, "Here I am."

²Then He said, "Take now your son, your only *son* Isaac, whom you love, and go to the land of Moriah, and offer him there as a burnt offering on one of the mountains of which I shall tell you."

³So Abraham rose early in the morning and saddled his donkey, and took two of his young men with him, and Isaac his son; and he split the wood for the burnt offering, and arose and went to the place of which God had told him. ⁴Then on the third day Abraham lifted his eyes and saw the place afar off. ⁵And Abraham said to his young men, "Stay here with the donkey; the ladᵃ and I will go yonder and worship, and we will come back to you."

⁶So Abraham took the wood of the burnt offering and laid *it* on Isaac his son; and he took the fire in his hand, and a knife, and the two of them went together. ⁷But Isaac spoke to Abraham his father and said, "My father!"

And he said, "Here I am, my son."

Then he said, "Look, the fire and the wood, but where *is* the lamb for a burnt offering?"

⁸And Abraham said, "My son, God will provide for Himself the lamb for a burnt offering." So the two of them went together.

⁹Then they came to the place of which God had told him. And Abraham built an altar there

21:31 ᵃLiterally *Well of the Oath* or *Well of the Seven* **22:5** ᵃOr *young man*

---

the INFLUENCERS

ABRAHAM: Obedient Father . . . A Road Less Traveled

GENESIS 22:1–19

Abraham's story kicks off the lengthy epic of God's relationship to His chosen people. He lived in a time and place where his neighbors worshipped the sun, fire, moon, stars and various forces of nature. In the midst of this idolatrous culture, Abraham was called out and believed in the one true God. In Genesis 12:1–3, God made a covenant with Abraham: he must leave his homeland of Haran for an unknown new land. This covenant included promises to show him a land, make him a great nation, and use that nation to bless the whole world. First, the Lord had to bless him with a child. In Genesis 17:21, God promised Abraham that his barren wife Sarah would give birth to a son named Isaac, who would also be an ancestor of the coming Jewish messiah. Later, God tested Abraham's faith (Genesis 22), in one of the most gripping stories of the Old Testament. What an example of real obedience!

- He lived a life that stood up to rigorous testing (v. 1)
- He was faithful when things looked incredibly grim (vv. 2, 3)
- He knew God intimately and trusted Him extensively (vv. 4–10)
- He held on to God's promise and experienced God's provision (vv. 9–19)

the INFLUENCERS

ISAAC: Trusting Son . . . Child of Promise

GENESIS 22:6–9

The trust in his father that Isaac demonstrated reflects a deeper trust in his heavenly Father. His very presence was a reminder of God's covenant with Abraham (Gen.12:1–3). There is a great parallel between a Christian and Isaac, for Galatians 4:28 refers to both as "children of promise." The promise? "That God shall supply all your need according His riches in glory by Christ Jesus" (Phil. 4:19).

The theme of Isaac's life is that *identity is the great motivation to always trust God.* This is never more evident then when his father bound him and laid him upon an altar on Mount Moriah. Isaac most likely had no reservations about joining his father, and nothing suggests this was anything but a trusting son willing to please his dad.

Abraham was an old man—we know this because he was one hundred when Isaac was born (Gen. 21:5). Isaac, on the other hand, was in his prime and could have easily escaped his father's efforts. Yet at one of the most critical junctures of his life, the river of trust that ran deep in his soul rose to the surface; and he allowed his father to tie him up and place him on the altar. God would provide a sacrifice, but it would not be Abraham's son, and it would not be this day. It was the sacrifice of self, of pain, and of love that was made and accepted that day as the Lord replaced the body of Abraham's beloved Isaac with a ram.

and placed the wood in order; and he bound Isaac his son and laid him on the altar, upon the wood. [10]And Abraham stretched out his hand and took the knife to slay his son.

[11]But the Angel of the LORD called to him from heaven and said, "Abraham, Abraham!"

So he said, "Here I am."

[12]And He said, "Do not lay your hand on the lad, or do anything to him; for now I know that you fear God, since you have not withheld your son, your only *son,* from Me."

[13]Then Abraham lifted his eyes and looked, and there behind *him was* a ram caught in a thicket by its horns. So Abraham went and took the ram, and offered it up for a burnt offering instead of his son. [14]And Abraham called the name of the place, The-LORD-Will-Provide;[a] as it is said *to* this day, "In the Mount of the LORD it shall be provided."

[15]Then the Angel of the LORD called to Abraham a second time out of heaven, [16]and said: "By Myself I have sworn, says the LORD, because you have done this thing, and have not withheld your son, your only *son*— [17]blessing I will bless you, and multiplying I will multiply your descendants as the stars of the heaven and as the sand which *is* on the seashore; and your descendants shall possess the gate of their enemies. [18]In your seed all the nations of the earth shall be blessed, because you have obeyed My voice." [19]So Abraham returned to his young men, and they rose and went together to Beersheba; and Abraham dwelt at Beersheba.

THE FAMILY OF NAHOR

[20]Now it came to pass after these things that it was told Abraham, saying, "Indeed Milcah also has borne children to your brother Nahor: [21]Huz his firstborn, Buz his brother, Kemuel the father of Aram, [22]Chesed, Hazo, Pildash, Jidlaph, and Bethuel." [23]And Bethuel begot Rebekah.[a] These eight Milcah bore to Nahor, Abraham's brother. [24]His concubine, whose name was

22:14 [a]Hebrew *YHWH Yireh*   22:23 [a]Speiled *Rebecca* in Romans 9:10

Reumah, also bore Tebah, Gaham, Thahash, and Maachah.

SARAH'S DEATH AND BURIAL

23 Sarah lived one hundred and twenty-seven years; *these were* the years of the life of Sarah. ²So Sarah died in Kirjath Arba (that *is,* Hebron) in the land of Canaan, and Abraham came to mourn for Sarah and to weep for her.

³Then Abraham stood up from before his dead, and spoke to the sons of Heth, saying, ⁴"I *am* a foreigner and a visitor among you. Give me property for a burial place among you, that I may bury my dead out of my sight."

⁵And the sons of Heth answered Abraham, saying to him, ⁶"Hear us, my lord: You *are* a mighty prince among us; bury your dead in the choicest of our burial places. None of us will withhold from you his burial place, that you may bury your dead."

⁷Then Abraham stood up and bowed himself to the people of the land, the sons of Heth. ⁸And he spoke with them, saying, "If it is your wish that I bury my dead out of my sight, hear me, and meet with Ephron the son of Zohar for me, ⁹that he may give me the cave of Machpelah which he has, which *is* at the end of his field. Let him give it to me at the full price, as property for a burial place among you."

¹⁰Now Ephron dwelt among the sons of Heth; and Ephron the Hittite answered Abraham in the presence of the sons of Heth, all who entered at the gate of his city, saying, ¹¹"No, my lord, hear me: I give you the field and the cave that *is* in it; I give it to you in the presence of the sons of my people. I give it to you. Bury your dead!"

¹²Then Abraham bowed himself down before the people of the land; ¹³and he spoke to Ephron in the hearing of the people of the land, saying, "If you *will give it,* please hear me. I will give you money for the field; take *it* from me and I will bury my dead there."

¹⁴And Ephron answered Abraham, saying to him, ¹⁵"My lord, listen to me; the land *is worth* four hundred shekels of silver. What *is* that between you and me? So bury your dead." ¹⁶And Abraham listened to Ephron; and Abraham weighed out the silver for Ephron which he had named in the hearing of the sons of Heth, four hundred shekels of silver, currency of the merchants.

¹⁷So the field of Ephron which *was* in Machpelah, which *was* before Mamre, the field and the cave which *was* in it, and all the trees that *were* in the field, which *were* within all the surrounding borders, were deeded ¹⁸to Abraham as a possession in the presence of the sons of Heth, before all who went in at the gate of his city.

¹⁹And after this, Abraham buried Sarah his wife in the cave of the field of Machpelah, before Mamre (that *is,* Hebron) in the land of Canaan. ²⁰So the field and the cave that *is* in it were deeded to Abraham by the sons of Heth as property for a burial place.

A BRIDE FOR ISAAC

24 Now Abraham was old, well advanced in age; and the LORD had blessed Abraham in all things. ²So Abraham said to the oldest servant of his house, who ruled over all that he had, "Please, put your hand under my thigh, ³and I will make you swear by the LORD, the God of heaven and the God of the earth, that you will not take a wife for my son from the daughters of the Canaanites, among whom I dwell; ⁴but you shall go to my country and to my family, and take a wife for my son Isaac."

⁵And the servant said to him, "Perhaps the woman will not be willing to follow me to this land. Must I take your son back to the land from which you came?"

⁶But Abraham said to him, "Beware that you do not take my son back there. ⁷The LORD God of heaven, who took me from my father's house and from the land of my family, and who spoke to me and swore to me, saying, 'To your descendantsᵃ I give this land,' He will send His angel before you, and you shall take a wife for my son from there. ⁸And if the woman is not willing to follow you, then you will be released from this oath; only do not take my son back there." ⁹So the servant put his hand under the thigh of Abraham his master, and swore to him concerning this matter.

¹⁰Then the servant took ten of his master's camels and departed, for all his master's goods *were* in his hand. And he arose and went to

---

24:7 ᵃLiterally *seed*

Mesopotamia, to the city of Nahor. ¹¹And he made his camels kneel down outside the city by a well of water at evening time, the time when women go out to draw *water.* ¹²Then he said, "O LORD God of my master Abraham, please give me success this day, and show kindness to my master Abraham. ¹³Behold, *here* I stand by the well of water, and the daughters of the men of the city are coming out to draw water. ¹⁴Now let it be that the young woman to whom I say, 'Please let down your pitcher that I may drink,' and she says, 'Drink, and I will also give your camels a drink'—*let* her *be the one* You have appointed for Your servant Isaac. And by this I will know that You have shown kindness to my master."

¹⁵And it happened, before he had finished speaking, that behold, Rebekah, who was born to Bethuel, son of Milcah, the wife of Nahor, Abraham's brother, came out with her pitcher on her shoulder. ¹⁶Now the young woman *was* very beautiful to behold, a virgin; no man had known

her. And she went down to the well, filled her pitcher, and came up. ¹⁷And the servant ran to meet her and said, "Please let me drink a little water from your pitcher."

¹⁸So she said, "Drink, my lord." Then she quickly let her pitcher down to her hand, and gave him a drink. ¹⁹And when she had finished giving him a drink, she said, "I will draw *water* for your camels also, until they have finished drinking." ²⁰Then she quickly emptied her pitcher into the trough, ran back to the well to draw *water,* and drew for all his camels. ²¹And the man, wondering at her, remained silent so as to know whether the LORD had made his journey prosperous or not.

²²So it was, when the camels had finished drinking, that the man took a golden nose ring weighing half a shekel, and two bracelets for her wrists weighing ten *shekels* of gold, ²³and said, "Whose daughter *are* you? Tell me, please, is there room *in* your father's house for us to lodge?"

INSIDE *the* INFLUENCERS

REBEKAH: Woman of Great Initiative

GENESIS 24

Initiative can be defined as the ability to motivate oneself to act. In many ways initiative is like speech: it can be used to lift up or tear down, but the user has the choice, and Rebekah chose well.

The name Rebekah in the Hebrew means *a looped cord for tying young animals.* Like most Old Testament names, it is a clue to her family's business and her occupation; she was a shepherdess. This childhood training taught her the necessity of taking initiative as she led and protected the herd, making decisions quickly.

When Abraham's servant was sent to find Isaac a wife, he prayed that God would send a woman who showed *initiative* by watering his camels (Gen. 24:12–15). Rebekah demonstrated that she lived initiative at every turn: she ran to provide water for the servant's camels (Gen. 24:20, 28); offered the servant a place to sleep for the night (Gen. 24:25); and responded quickly to the choice to move forward into a new future (Gen. 24:53–58).

As the caravan approached her new home, they saw Isaac approaching. Informed of his presence, Rebekah immediately got off her camel and walked to meet him (Gen. 24:61–65). Since Rebekah's proactive decisions were made almost instantly, we can assume that she practiced *positive initiative* on a daily basis. It moved from a choice in her life to a habit, something every leader strives for.

LEADERSHIP
REALITIES

"AND THEN SOME" PRINCIPLE   *Genesis 24:19*

When Abraham's servant set out to find a wife for Isaac, he was looking for the woman who would go beyond what was expected of her. In this way, he knew she would be a woman of excellence, of commitment, and of mercy.

Perhaps the servant knew that it is easier to show hospitality than it is to be compassionate. The first is what's expected, the second is sent from the heart. His test would determine if the woman *talked* service or *lived* service. He chose this test carefully, for it was a big one. For a woman to offer water to a stranger was a cultural hospitality, but to offer to *also* water his camels was a great gift because a camel can drink up to 28 gallons of water at one time. This meant multiple trips to the well and carrying water up the steps one bucket at a time, a tedious and arduous task. Rebekah met the task and won her place in history.

The "and then some" principle leaves behind the "how little can I do and still get by?" state of mind. It is the attitude that transforms you from average to being set apart for leadership. Learn to cultivate the *"and then some"* attitude.

---

[24]So she said to him, "I *am* the daughter of Bethuel, Milcah's son, whom she bore to Nahor." [25]Moreover she said to him, "We have both straw and feed enough, and room to lodge."

[26]Then the man bowed down his head and worshiped the LORD. [27]And he said, "Blessed *be* the LORD God of my master Abraham, who has not forsaken His mercy and His truth toward my master. As for me, being on the way, the LORD led me to the house of my master's brethren." [28]So the young woman ran and told her mother's household these things.

[29]Now Rebekah had a brother whose name *was* Laban, and Laban ran out to the man by the well. [30]So it came to pass, when he saw the nose ring, and the bracelets on his sister's wrists, and when he heard the words of his sister Rebekah, saying, "Thus the man spoke to me," that he went to the man. And there he stood by the camels at the well. [31]And he said, "Come in, O blessed of the LORD! Why do you stand outside? For I have prepared the house, and a place for the camels."

[32]Then the man came to the house. And he unloaded the camels, and provided straw and feed for the camels, and water to wash his feet and the feet of the men who *were* with him. [33]*Food* was set before him to eat, but he said, "I will not eat until I have told about my errand."

And he said, "Speak on."

[34]So he said, "I *am* Abraham's servant. [35]The LORD has blessed my master greatly, and he has become great; and He has given him flocks and herds, silver and gold, male and female servants, and camels and donkeys. [36]And Sarah my master's wife bore a son to my master when she was old; and to him he has given all that he has. [37]Now my master made me swear, saying, 'You shall not take a wife for my son from the daughters of the Canaanites, in whose land I dwell; [38]but you shall go to my father's house and to my family, and take a wife for my son.' [39]And I said to my master, 'Perhaps the woman will not follow me.' [40]But he said to me, 'The LORD, before whom I walk, will send His angel with you and prosper your way; and you shall take a wife for my son from my family and from my father's house. [41]You will be clear from this oath when you arrive among my family; for if they will not give *her* to you, then you will be released from my oath.'

[42]"And this day I came to the well and said,

'O Lord God of my master Abraham, if You will now prosper the way in which I go, ⁴³behold, I stand by the well of water; and it shall come to pass that when the virgin comes out to draw *water,* and I say to her, "Please give me a little water from your pitcher to drink," ⁴⁴and she says to me, "Drink, and I will draw for your camels also,"— *let* her *be* the woman whom the Lord has appointed for my master's son.'

⁴⁵"But before I had finished speaking in my heart, there was Rebekah, coming out with her pitcher on her shoulder; and she went down to the well and drew *water.* And I said to her, 'Please let me drink.' ⁴⁶And she made haste and let her pitcher down from her *shoulder,* and said, 'Drink, and I will give your camels a drink also.' So I drank, and she gave the camels a drink also. ⁴⁷Then I asked her, and said, 'Whose daughter *are* you?' And she said, 'The daughter of Bethuel, Nahor's son, whom Milcah bore to him.' So I put the nose ring on her nose and the bracelets on her wrists. ⁴⁸And I bowed my head and worshiped the Lord, and blessed the Lord God of my master Abraham, who had led me in the way of truth to take the daughter of my master's brother for his son. ⁴⁹Now if you will deal kindly and truly with my master, tell me. And if not, tell me, that I may turn to the right hand or to the left."

⁵⁰Then Laban and Bethuel answered and said, "The thing comes from the Lord; we cannot speak to you either bad or good. ⁵¹Here *is* Rebekah before you; take *her* and go, and let her be your master's son's wife, as the Lord has spoken."

⁵²And it came to pass, when Abraham's servant heard their words, that he worshiped the Lord, *bowing himself* to the earth. ⁵³Then the servant brought out jewelry of silver, jewelry of gold, and clothing, and gave *them* to Rebekah. He also gave precious things to her brother and to her mother.

⁵⁴And he and the men who *were* with him ate and drank and stayed all night. Then they arose in the morning, and he said, "Send me away to my master."

⁵⁵But her brother and her mother said, "Let the young woman stay with us *a few* days, at least ten; after that she may go."

⁵⁶And he said to them, "Do not hinder me,

since the Lord has prospered my way; send me away so that I may go to my master."

⁵⁷So they said, "We will call the young woman and ask her personally." ⁵⁸Then they called Rebekah and said to her, "Will you go with this man?"

And she said, "I will go."

⁵⁹So they sent away Rebekah their sister and her nurse, and Abraham's servant and his men. ⁶⁰And they blessed Rebekah and said to her:

"Our sister, *may* you *become*
The mother of thousands of ten thousands;
And may your descendants possess
The gates of those who hate them."

⁶¹Then Rebekah and her maids arose, and they rode on the camels and followed the man. So the servant took Rebekah and departed.

⁶²Now Isaac came from the way of Beer Lahai Roi, for he dwelt in the South. ⁶³And Isaac went out to meditate in the field in the evening; and he lifted his eyes and looked, and there, the camels *were* coming. ⁶⁴Then Rebekah lifted her eyes, and when she saw Isaac she dismounted from her camel; ⁶⁵for she had said to the servant, "Who *is* this man walking in the field to meet us?"

The servant said, "It *is* my master." So she took a veil and covered herself.

⁶⁶And the servant told Isaac all the things that he had done. ⁶⁷Then Isaac brought her into his mother Sarah's tent; and he took Rebekah and she became his wife, and he loved her. So Isaac was comforted after his mother's *death.*

Abraham and Keturah

25 Abraham again took a wife, and her name *was* Keturah. ²And she bore him Zimran, Jokshan, Medan, Midian, Ishbak, and Shuah. ³Jokshan begot Sheba and Dedan. And the sons of Dedan were Asshurim, Letushim, and Leummim. ⁴And the sons of Midian *were* Ephah, Epher, Hanoch, Abidah, and Eldaah. All these *were* the children of Keturah.

⁵And Abraham gave all that he had to Isaac. ⁶But Abraham gave gifts to the sons of the concubines which Abraham had; and while he was still living he sent them eastward, away from Isaac his son, to the country of the east.

INSIDE *the* INFLUENCERS

ESAU: Moment of Weakness, Lasting Legacy

GENESIS 25:22–28

The writer of Hebrews calls Esau a "fornicator" and a "profane person who for one morsel of food sold his birthright" (Heb. 12:16). The great theme of Esau's life is that *decisions made in moments of weakness can have lasting consequences.*

Esau was the oldest of twin sons born to Isaac and Rebekah. When Esau was born, his body was reddish-brown, and he had an unusual quantity of hair. That led to his name, Esau, "the hairy one." Later he would be nicknamed "Edom," which means red. Unlike his brother, Esau was drawn to adventure; he wandered the fields and became a skillful hunter (Gen. 25:19–27).

Two events between Esau and Jacob led to their division as two nations (Esau's became Edom, and Jacob's became Israel). The first is when Esau sold his birthright to Jacob in a moment of weakness and hunger (Gen. 25:29–34). The second is when he lost his patriarchal blessing from his father Isaac to Jacob (Gen. 27:1–37). The last time the two were together was at Isaac's burial (Gen. 35:27–29). While Jacob wasn't sinless, it is important to note that Esau led a godless life with no evidence of repentance. Long after Jacob and Esau died, the Edomites took any opportunity they could to attack and annoy the Israelites (see Jer. 49:7–22; Ezek. 25:12–14; Amos 1:11, 12; Obad. 1:10–14). Leaders never sacrifice their futures on the altar of the immediate.

ABRAHAM'S DEATH AND BURIAL

[7]This *is* the sum of the years of Abraham's life which he lived: one hundred and seventy-five years. [8]Then Abraham breathed his last and died in a good old age, an old man and full *of years,* and was gathered to his people. [9]And his sons Isaac and Ishmael buried him in the cave of Machpelah, which *is* before Mamre, in the field of Ephron the son of Zohar the Hittite, [10]the field which Abraham purchased from the sons of Heth. There Abraham was buried, and Sarah his wife. [11]And it came to pass, after the death of Abraham, that God blessed his son Isaac. And Isaac dwelt at Beer Lahai Roi.

THE FAMILIES OF ISHMAEL AND ISAAC

[12]Now this *is* the genealogy of Ishmael, Abraham's son, whom Hagar the Egyptian, Sarah's maidservant, bore to Abraham. [13]And these *were* the names of the sons of Ishmael, by their names, according to their generations: The firstborn of Ishmael, Nebajoth; then Kedar, Adbeel, Mibsam, [14]Mishma, Dumah, Massa, [15]Hadar,[a] Tema, Jetur, Naphish, and Kedemah. [16]These *were* the sons of Ishmael and these *were* their names, by their towns and their settlements, twelve princes according to their nations. [17]These *were* the years of the life of Ishmael: one hundred and thirty-seven years; and he breathed his last and died, and was gathered to his people. [18](They dwelt from Havilah as far as Shur, which *is* east of Egypt as you go toward Assyria.) He died in the presence of all his brethren.

[19]This *is* the genealogy of Isaac, Abraham's son. Abraham begot Isaac. [20]Isaac was forty years old when he took Rebekah as wife, the daughter of Bethuel the Syrian of Padan Aram, the sister of Laban the Syrian. [21]Now Isaac pleaded with the LORD for his wife, because she *was* barren; and the LORD granted his plea, and Rebekah his wife conceived. [22]But the children struggled together within her; and she said, "If *all is* well, why *am I like* this?" So she went to inquire of the LORD.

[23]And the LORD said to her:

25:15 [a]Masoretic Text reads *Hadad.*

"Two nations *are* in your womb,
Two peoples shall be separated from your
     body;
One people shall be stronger than the other,
And the older shall serve the younger."

[24]So when her days were fulfilled *for her* to give birth, indeed *there were* twins in her womb. [25]And the first came out red. *He was* like a hairy garment all over; so they called his name Esau.[a] [26]Afterward his brother came out, and his hand took hold of Esau's heel; so his name was called Jacob.[a] Isaac *was* sixty years old when she bore them.

[27]So the boys grew. And Esau was a skillful hunter, a man of the field; but Jacob was a mild man, dwelling in tents. [28]And Isaac loved Esau because he ate *of his* game, but Rebekah loved Jacob.

Esau Sells His Birthright

[29]Now Jacob cooked a stew; and Esau came in from the field, and he *was* weary. [30]And Esau said to Jacob, "Please feed me with that same red stew, for I *am* weary." Therefore his name was called Edom.[a]

[31]But Jacob said, "Sell me your birthright as of this day."

[32]And Esau said, "Look, I *am* about to die; so what *is* this birthright to me?"

[33]Then Jacob said, "Swear to me as of this day."

So he swore to him, and sold his birthright to Jacob. [34]And Jacob gave Esau bread and stew of lentils; then he ate and drank, arose, and went his way. Thus Esau despised *his* birthright.

Isaac and Abimelech

26 There was a famine in the land, besides the first famine that was in the days of Abraham. And Isaac went to Abimelech king of the Philistines, in Gerar. [2]Then the LORD appeared to him and said: "Do not go down to Egypt; live in the land of which I shall tell you. [3]Dwell in this land, and I will be with you and bless you; for to you and

25:25 [a]Literally *Hairy*   25:26 [a]Literally *Supplanter*   25:30 [a]Literally *Red*

INSIDE *the* INFLUENCERS

JACOB: The Schemer Who Got Scammed and Wrestled with the Savior

Jacob is one of the most interesting and contrastive characters in all of the Old Testament. While Esau looked for adventure, Jacob preferred a milder approach to life by staying indoors (Gen. 25:27). Here is a man who swindled his brother out of his birthright (Gen. 25:29–34) and scammed him out of his patriarchal blessing (Gen. 27:1–29), yet God called Himself "the God of Jacob." God arranged for the twelve tribes of Israel to be his offspring, and met Jacob personally many times in Scripture (Gen. 28:10–17; Gen. 31:10–13; Gen. 32; Gen. 35:9–15; Gen. 46:1–4).

There is an old saying, "what goes around, comes around." Jacob learned this all too well when he journeyed to Haran and met his cousin Rachel and his uncle Laban. Jacob wanted Rachel as his wife and agreed to work for seven years, which ended in a wedding. But Laban covertly switched out Rachel for his oldest daughter Leah. The schemer got scammed! Jacob was allowed to marry Rachel, but in return, he worked another seven years (Gen. 29).

Jacob's turning point came the night he wrestled with God (Gen. 32:22–32). Jacob finally quit fighting God and started doing things God's way. John Calvin said it best, "God fights against us with His left hand, and for us with His right hand."

your descendants I give all these lands, and I will perform the oath which I swore to Abraham your father. ⁴And I will make your descendants multiply as the stars of heaven; I will give to your descendants all these lands; and in your seed all the nations of the earth shall be blessed; ⁵because Abraham obeyed My voice and kept My charge, My commandments, My statutes, and My laws."

⁶So Isaac dwelt in Gerar. ⁷And the men of the place asked about his wife. And he said, "She *is* my sister"; for he was afraid to say, "*She is* my wife," *because he thought,* "lest the men of the place kill me for Rebekah, because she *is* beautiful to behold." ⁸Now it came to pass, when he had been there a long time, that Abimelech king of the Philistines looked through a window, and saw, and there was Isaac, showing endearment to Rebekah his wife. ⁹Then Abimelech called Isaac and said, "Quite obviously she *is* your wife; so how could you say, 'She *is* my sister'?"

Isaac said to him, "Because I said, 'Lest I die on account of her.'"

¹⁰And Abimelech said, "What *is* this you have done to us? One of the people might soon have lain with your wife, and you would have brought guilt on us." ¹¹So Abimelech charged all *his* people, saying, "He who touches this man or his wife shall surely be put to death."

¹²Then Isaac sowed in that land, and reaped in the same year a hundredfold; and the LORD blessed him. ¹³The man began to prosper, and continued prospering until he became very prosperous; ¹⁴for he had possessions of flocks and possessions of herds and a great number of servants. So the Philistines envied him. ¹⁵Now the Philistines had stopped up all the wells which his father's servants had dug in the days of Abraham his father, and they had filled them with earth. ¹⁶And Abimelech said to Isaac, "Go away from us, for you are much mightier than we."

¹⁷Then Isaac departed from there and pitched his tent in the Valley of Gerar, and dwelt there. ¹⁸And Isaac dug again the wells of water which they had dug in the days of Abraham his father, for the Philistines had stopped them up after the death of Abraham. He called them by the names which his father had called them.

¹⁹Also Isaac's servants dug in the valley, and found a well of running water there. ²⁰But the herdsmen of Gerar quarreled with Isaac's herdsmen, saying, "The water *is* ours." So he called the name of the well Esek,ᵃ because they quarreled with him. ²¹Then they dug another well, and they quarreled over that *one* also. So he called its name Sitnah.ᵃ ²²And he moved from there and dug another well, and they did not quarrel over it. So he called its name Rehoboth,ᵃ because he said, "For now the LORD has made room for us, and we shall be fruitful in the land."

²³Then he went up from there to Beersheba. ²⁴And the LORD appeared to him the same night and said, "I *am* the God of your father Abraham; do not fear, for I *am* with you. I will bless you and multiply your descendants for My servant Abraham's sake." ²⁵So he built an altar there and called on the name of the LORD, and he pitched his tent there; and there Isaac's servants dug a well.

²⁶Then Abimelech came to him from Gerar with Ahuzzath, one of his friends, and Phichol the commander of his army. ²⁷And Isaac said to them, "Why have you come to me, since you hate me and have sent me away from you?"

²⁸But they said, "We have certainly seen that the LORD is with you. So we said, 'Let there now be an oath between us, between us and you; and let us make a covenant with you, ²⁹that you will do us no harm, since we have not touched you, and since we have done nothing to you but good and have sent you away in peace. You *are* now the blessed of the LORD.'"

³⁰So he made them a feast, and they ate and drank. ³¹Then they arose early in the morning and swore an oath with one another; and Isaac sent them away, and they departed from him in peace.

³²It came to pass the same day that Isaac's servants came and told him about the well which they had dug, and said to him, "We have found water." ³³So he called it Shebah.ᵃ Therefore the name of the city *is* Beershebaᵇ to this day.

³⁴When Esau was forty years old, he took as wives Judith the daughter of Beeri the Hittite, and Basemath the daughter of Elon the Hittite. ³⁵And they were a grief of mind to Isaac and Rebekah.

26:20 ᵃLiterally *Quarrel* **26:21** ᵃLiterally *Enmity* **26:22** ᵃLiterally *Spaciousness* **26:33** ᵃLiterally *Oath* or *Seven* ᵇLiterally *Well of the Oath* or *Well of the Seven*

Isaac Blesses Jacob

27 Now it came to pass, when Isaac was old and his eyes were so dim that he could not see, that he called Esau his older son and said to him, "My son."

And he answered him, "Here I am."

²Then he said, "Behold now, I am old. I do not know the day of my death. ³Now therefore, please take your weapons, your quiver and your bow, and go out to the field and hunt game for me. ⁴And make me savory food, such as I love, and bring *it* to me that I may eat, that my soul may bless you before I die."

⁵Now Rebekah was listening when Isaac spoke to Esau his son. And Esau went to the field to hunt game and to bring *it.* ⁶So Rebekah spoke to Jacob her son, saying, "Indeed I heard your father speak to Esau your brother, saying, ⁷'Bring me game and make savory food for me, that I may eat it and bless you in the presence of the LORD before my death.' ⁸Now therefore, my son, obey my voice according to what I command you. ⁹Go now to the flock and bring me from there two choice kids of the goats, and I will make savory food from them for your father, such as he loves. ¹⁰Then you shall take *it* to your father, that he may eat *it,* and that he may bless you before his death."

¹¹And Jacob said to Rebekah his mother, "Look, Esau my brother *is* a hairy man, and I *am* a smooth-*skinned* man. ¹²Perhaps my father will feel me, and I shall seem to be a deceiver to him; and I shall bring a curse on myself and not a blessing."

¹³But his mother said to him, "*Let* your curse *be* on me, my son; only obey my voice, and go, get *them* for me." ¹⁴And he went and got *them* and brought *them* to his mother, and his mother made savory food, such as his father loved. ¹⁵Then Rebekah took the choice clothes of her elder son Esau, which *were* with her in the house, and put them on Jacob her younger son. ¹⁶And she put the skins of the kids of the goats on his hands and on the smooth part of his neck. ¹⁷Then she gave the savory food and the bread, which she had prepared, into the hand of her son Jacob.

¹⁸So he went to his father and said, "My father."

And he said, "Here I am. Who *are* you, my son?"

¹⁹Jacob said to his father, "I *am* Esau your firstborn; I have done just as you told me; please arise, sit and eat of my game, that your soul may bless me."

²⁰But Isaac said to his son, "How *is it* that you have found *it* so quickly, my son?"

And he said, "Because the LORD your God brought *it* to me."

²¹Isaac said to Jacob, "Please come near, that I may feel you, my son, whether you *are* really my son Esau or not." ²²So Jacob went near to Isaac his father, and he felt him and said, "The voice *is* Jacob's voice, but the hands *are* the hands of Esau." ²³And he did not recognize him, because his hands were hairy like his brother Esau's hands; so he blessed him.

²⁴Then he said, "*Are* you really my son Esau?"

He said, "I *am.*"

²⁵He said, "Bring *it* near to me, and I will eat of my son's game, so that my soul may bless you." So he brought *it* near to him, and he ate; and he brought him wine, and he drank. ²⁶Then his father Isaac said to him, "Come near now and kiss me, my son." ²⁷And he came near and kissed him; and he smelled the smell of his clothing, and blessed him and said:

> "Surely, the smell of my son
>   *Is* like the smell of a field
>   Which the LORD has blessed.
> ²⁸Therefore may God give you
>   Of the dew of heaven,
>   Of the fatness of the earth,
>   And plenty of grain and wine.
> ²⁹Let peoples serve you,
>   And nations bow down to you.
>   Be master over your brethren,
>   And let your mother's sons bow down
>   to you.
>   Cursed *be* everyone who curses you,
>   And blessed *be* those who bless you!"

Esau's Lost Hope

³⁰Now it happened, as soon as Isaac had finished blessing Jacob, and Jacob had scarcely gone out from the presence of Isaac his father, that Esau his brother came in from his hunting. ³¹He also had made savory food, and brought it to his father, and said to his father, "Let my father arise

and eat of his son's game, that your soul may bless me."

³²And his father Isaac said to him, "Who *are* you?"

So he said, "I *am* your son, your firstborn, Esau."

³³Then Isaac trembled exceedingly, and said, "Who? Where *is* the one who hunted game and brought *it* to me? I ate all *of it* before you came, and I have blessed him—*and* indeed he shall be blessed."

³⁴When Esau heard the words of his father, he cried with an exceedingly great and bitter cry, and said to his father, "Bless me—me also, O my father!"

³⁵But he said, "Your brother came with deceit and has taken away your blessing."

³⁶And *Esau* said, "Is he not rightly named Jacob? For he has supplanted me these two times. He took away my birthright, and now look, he has taken away my blessing!" And he said, "Have you not reserved a blessing for me?"

³⁷Then Isaac answered and said to Esau, "Indeed I have made him your master, and all his brethren I have given to him as servants; with grain and wine I have sustained him. What shall I do now for you, my son?"

³⁸And Esau said to his father, "Have you only one blessing, my father? Bless me—me also, O my father!" And Esau lifted up his voice and wept.

³⁹Then Isaac his father answered and said to him:

"Behold, your dwelling shall be of the fatness of the earth,
And of the dew of heaven from above.
⁴⁰By your sword you shall live,
And you shall serve your brother;
And it shall come to pass, when you become restless,
That you shall break his yoke from your neck."

Jacob Escapes from Esau

⁴¹So Esau hated Jacob because of the blessing with which his father blessed him, and Esau said in his heart, "The days of mourning for my father are at hand; then I will kill my brother Jacob."

⁴²And the words of Esau her older son were told to Rebekah. So she sent and called Jacob her younger son, and said to him, "Surely your brother Esau comforts himself concerning you *by intending* to kill you. ⁴³Now therefore, my son, obey my voice: arise, flee to my brother Laban in Haran. ⁴⁴And stay with him a few days, until your brother's fury turns away, ⁴⁵until your brother's anger turns away from you, and he forgets what you have done to him; then I will send and bring you from there. Why should I be bereaved also of you both in one day?"

⁴⁶And Rebekah said to Isaac, "I am weary of my life because of the daughters of Heth; if Jacob takes a wife of the daughters of Heth, like these *who are* the daughters of the land, what good will my life be to me?"

28 Then Isaac called Jacob and blessed him, and charged him, and said to him: "You shall not take a wife from the daughters of Canaan. ²Arise, go to Padan Aram, to the house of Bethuel your mother's father; and take yourself a wife from there of the daughters of Laban your mother's brother.

³"May God Almighty bless you,
And make you fruitful and multiply you,
That you may be an assembly of peoples;
⁴And give you the blessing of Abraham,
To you and your descendants with you,
That you may inherit the land
In which you are a stranger,
Which God gave to Abraham."

⁵So Isaac sent Jacob away, and he went to Padan Aram, to Laban the son of Bethuel the Syrian, the brother of Rebekah, the mother of Jacob and Esau.

Esau Marries Mahalath

⁶Esau saw that Isaac had blessed Jacob and sent him away to Padan Aram to take himself a wife from there, *and that* as he blessed him he gave him a charge, saying, "You shall not take a wife from the daughters of Canaan," ⁷and that Jacob had obeyed his father and his mother and had gone to Padan Aram. ⁸Also Esau saw that the daughters of Canaan did not please his father Isaac. ⁹So Esau went to Ishmael and took Mahalath the daughter of Ishmael, Abraham's son, the

sister of Nebajoth, to be his wife in addition to the wives he had.

Jacob's Vow at Bethel

[10]Now Jacob went out from Beersheba and went toward Haran. [11]So he came to a certain place and stayed there all night, because the sun had set. And he took one of the stones of that place and put it at his head, and he lay down in that place to sleep. [12]Then he dreamed, and behold, a ladder *was* set up on the earth, and its top reached to heaven; and there the angels of God were ascending and descending on it.

[13]And behold, the LORD stood above it and said: "I *am* the LORD God of Abraham your father and the God of Isaac; the land on which you lie I will give to you and your descendants. [14]Also your descendants shall be as the dust of the earth; you shall spread abroad to the west and the east, to the north and the south; and in you and in your seed all the families of the earth shall be blessed. [15]Behold, I *am* with you and will keep you wherever you go, and will bring you back to this land; for I will not leave you until I have done what I have spoken to you."

[16]Then Jacob awoke from his sleep and said, "Surely the LORD is in this place, and I did not know *it*." [17]And he was afraid and said, "How awesome *is* this place! This *is* none other than the house of God, and this *is* the gate of heaven!"

[18]Then Jacob rose early in the morning, and took the stone that he had put at his head, set it up as a pillar, and poured oil on top of it. [19]And he called the name of that place Bethel;[a] but the name of that city had been Luz previously. [20]Then Jacob made a vow, saying, "If God will be with me, and keep me in this way that I am going, and give me bread to eat and clothing to put on, [21]so that I come back to my father's house in peace, then the LORD shall be my God. [22]And this stone which I have set as a pillar shall be God's house, and of all that You give me I will surely give a tenth to You."

Jacob Meets Rachel

29 So Jacob went on his journey and came to the land of the people of the East. [2]And he looked, and saw a well in the field; and behold, there *were* three flocks of sheep lying by it; for out of that well they watered the flocks. A large stone *was* on the well's mouth. [3]Now all the flocks would be gathered there; and they would roll the stone from the well's mouth, water the sheep, and put the stone back in its place on the well's mouth.

[4]And Jacob said to them, "My brethren, where *are* you from?"

And they said, "We *are* from Haran."

[5]Then he said to them, "Do you know Laban the son of Nahor?"

And they said, "We know him."

[6]So he said to them, "Is he well?"

And they said, "*He is* well. And look, his daughter Rachel is coming with the sheep."

[7]Then he said, "Look, *it is* still high day; *it is* not time for the cattle to be gathered together. Water the sheep, and go and feed *them*."

[8]But they said, "We cannot until all the flocks are gathered together, and they have rolled the stone from the well's mouth; then we water the sheep."

[9]Now while he was still speaking with them, Rachel came with her father's sheep, for she was a shepherdess. [10]And it came to pass, when Jacob saw Rachel the daughter of Laban his mother's brother, and the sheep of Laban his mother's brother, that Jacob went near and rolled the stone from the well's mouth, and watered the flock of Laban his mother's brother. [11]Then Jacob kissed Rachel, and lifted up his voice and wept. [12]And Jacob told Rachel that he *was* her father's relative and that he *was* Rebekah's son. So she ran and told her father.

[13]Then it came to pass, when Laban heard the report about Jacob his sister's son, that he ran to meet him, and embraced him and kissed him, and brought him to his house. So he told Laban all these things. [14]And Laban said to him, "Surely you *are* my bone and my flesh." And he stayed with him for a month.

Jacob Marries Leah and Rachel

[15]Then Laban said to Jacob, "Because you *are* my relative, should you therefore serve me for nothing? Tell me, what *should* your wages *be?*" [16]Now Laban had two daughters: the name of the

28:19 [a]Literally *House of God*

elder *was* Leah, and the name of the younger *was* Rachel. [17]Leah's eyes *were* delicate, but Rachel was beautiful of form and appearance.

[18]Now Jacob loved Rachel; so he said, "I will serve you seven years for Rachel your younger daughter."

[19]And Laban said, "*It is* better that I give her to you than that I should give her to another man. Stay with me." [20]So Jacob served seven years for Rachel, and they seemed *only* a few days to him because of the love he had for her.

[21]Then Jacob said to Laban, "Give *me* my wife, for my days are fulfilled, that I may go in to her." [22]And Laban gathered together all the men of the place and made a feast. [23]Now it came to pass in the evening, that he took Leah his daughter and brought her to Jacob; and he went in to her. [24]And Laban gave his maid Zilpah to his daughter Leah *as* a maid. [25]So it came to pass in the morning, that behold, it *was* Leah. And he said to Laban, "What is this you have done to me? Was it not for Rachel that I served you? Why then have you deceived me?"

[26]And Laban said, "It must not be done so in our country, to give the younger before the firstborn. [27]Fulfill her week, and we will give you this one also for the service which you will serve with me still another seven years."

[28]Then Jacob did so and fulfilled her week. So he gave him his daughter Rachel as wife also. [29]And Laban gave his maid Bilhah to his daughter Rachel as a maid. [30]Then *Jacob* also went in to Rachel, and he also loved Rachel more than Leah. And he served with Laban still another seven years.

The Children of Jacob

[31]When the LORD saw that Leah *was* unloved, He opened her womb; but Rachel *was* barren. [32]So Leah conceived and bore a son, and she called his name Reuben;[a] for she said, "The LORD has surely looked on my affliction. Now therefore, my husband will love me." [33]Then she conceived again and bore a son, and said, "Because the LORD has heard that I *am* unloved, He has therefore given me this *son* also." And she called his name Simeon.[a] [34]She conceived again and bore a son, and said, "Now this time my husband will become attached to me, because I have

borne him three sons." Therefore his name was called Levi.[a] [35]And she conceived again and bore a son, and said, "Now I will praise the LORD." Therefore she called his name Judah.[a] Then she stopped bearing.

30 Now when Rachel saw that she bore Jacob no children, Rachel envied her sister, and said to Jacob, "Give me children, or else I die!"

[2]And Jacob's anger was aroused against Rachel, and he said, "*Am* I in the place of God, who has withheld from you the fruit of the womb?"

[3]So she said, "Here is my maid Bilhah; go in to her, and she will bear *a child* on my knees, that I also may have children by her." [4]Then she gave him Bilhah her maid as wife, and Jacob went in to her. [5]And Bilhah conceived and bore Jacob a son. [6]Then Rachel said, "God has judged my case; and He has also heard my voice and given me a son." Therefore she called his name Dan.[a] [7]And Rachel's maid Bilhah conceived again and bore Jacob a second son. [8]Then Rachel said, "With great wrestlings I have wrestled with my sister, *and* indeed I have prevailed." So she called his name Naphtali.[a]

[9]When Leah saw that she had stopped bearing, she took Zilpah her maid and gave her to Jacob as wife. [10]And Leah's maid Zilpah bore Jacob a son. [11]Then Leah said, "A troop comes!"[a] So she called his name Gad.[b] [12]And Leah's maid Zilpah bore Jacob a second son. [13]Then Leah said, "I am happy, for the daughters will call me blessed." So she called his name Asher.[a]

[14]Now Reuben went in the days of wheat harvest and found mandrakes in the field, and brought them to his mother Leah. Then Rachel said to Leah, "Please give me *some* of your son's mandrakes."

[15]But she said to her, "*Is it* a small matter that you have taken away my husband? Would you take away my son's mandrakes also?"

And Rachel said, "Therefore he will lie with you tonight for your son's mandrakes."

29:32 [a]Literally *See, a Son*   29:33 [a]Literally *Heard*   29:34 [a]Literally *Attached*   29:35 [a]Literally *Praise*   30:6 [a]Literally *Judge*   30:8 [a]Literally *My Wrestling*   30:11 [a]Following Qere, Syriac, and Targum; Kethib, Septuagint, and Vulgate read *in fortune.* [b]Literally *Troop* or *Fortune*   30:13 [a]Literally *Happy*

¹⁶When Jacob came out of the field in the evening, Leah went out to meet him and said, "You must come in to me, for I have surely hired you with my son's mandrakes." And he lay with her that night.

¹⁷And God listened to Leah, and she conceived and bore Jacob a fifth son. ¹⁸Leah said, "God has given me my wages, because I have given my maid to my husband." So she called his name Issachar.^a ¹⁹Then Leah conceived again and bore Jacob a sixth son. ²⁰And Leah said, "God has endowed me *with* a good endowment; now my husband will dwell with me, because I have borne him six sons." So she called his name Zebulun.^a ²¹Afterward she bore a daughter, and called her name Dinah.

²²Then God remembered Rachel, and God listened to her and opened her womb. ²³And she conceived and bore a son, and said, "God has taken away my reproach." ²⁴So she called his name Joseph,^a and said, "The LORD shall add to me another son."

Jacob's Agreement with Laban

²⁵And it came to pass, when Rachel had borne Joseph, that Jacob said to Laban, "Send me away, that I may go to my own place and to my country. ²⁶Give *me* my wives and my children for whom I have served you, and let me go; for you know my service which I have done for you."

²⁷And Laban said to him, "Please *stay,* if I have found favor in your eyes, *for* I have learned by experience that the LORD has blessed me for your sake." ²⁸Then he said, "Name me your wages, and I will give *it.*"

²⁹So *Jacob* said to him, "You know how I have served you and how your livestock has been with me. ³⁰For what you had before I *came was* little, and it has increased to a great amount; the LORD has blessed you since my coming. And now, when shall I also provide for my own house?"

³¹So he said, "What shall I give you?"

And Jacob said, "You shall not give me anything. If you will do this thing for me, I will again feed and keep your flocks: ³²Let me pass through all your flock today, removing from there all the speckled and spotted sheep, and all the brown ones among the lambs, and the spotted and speckled among the goats; and *these* shall be my wages. ³³So my righteousness will answer for me in time to come, when the subject of my wages comes before you: every one that *is* not speckled and spotted among the goats, and brown among the lambs, will be considered stolen, if *it is* with me."

³⁴And Laban said, "Oh, that it were according to your word!" ³⁵So he removed that day the male goats that were speckled and spotted, all the female goats that were speckled and spotted, every one that had *some* white in it, and all the brown ones among the lambs, and gave *them* into the hand of his sons. ³⁶Then he put three days' journey between himself and Jacob, and Jacob fed the rest of Laban's flocks.

³⁷Now Jacob took for himself rods of green poplar and of the almond and chestnut trees, peeled white strips in them, and exposed the white which *was* in the rods. ³⁸And the rods which he had peeled, he set before the flocks in the gutters, in the watering troughs where the flocks came to drink, so that they should conceive when they came to drink. ³⁹So the flocks conceived before the rods, and the flocks brought forth streaked, speckled, and spotted. ⁴⁰Then Jacob separated the lambs, and made the flocks face toward the streaked and all the brown in the flock of Laban; but he put his own flocks by themselves and did not put them with Laban's flock.

⁴¹And it came to pass, whenever the stronger livestock conceived, that Jacob placed the rods before the eyes of the livestock in the gutters, that they might conceive among the rods. ⁴²But when the flocks were feeble, he did not put *them* in; so the feebler were Laban's and the stronger Jacob's. ⁴³Thus the man became exceedingly prosperous, and had large flocks, female and male servants, and camels and donkeys.

Jacob Flees from Laban

31 Now *Jacob* heard the words of Laban's sons, saying, "Jacob has taken away all that was our father's, and from what was our father's he has acquired all this wealth." ²And Jacob saw the countenance of Laban, and indeed it *was* not *favorable* toward him as before. ³Then the LORD said

30:18 ^aLiterally *Wages*   **30:20** ^aLiterally *Dwelling*   **30:24** ^aLiterally *He Will Add*

to Jacob, "Return to the land of your fathers and to your family, and I will be with you."

⁴So Jacob sent and called Rachel and Leah to the field, to his flock, ⁵and said to them, "I see your father's countenance, that it *is* not *favorable* toward me as before; but the God of my father has been with me. ⁶And you know that with all my might I have served your father. ⁷Yet your father has deceived me and changed my wages ten times, but God did not allow him to hurt me. ⁸If he said thus: 'The speckled shall be your wages,' then all the flocks bore speckled. And if he said thus: 'The streaked shall be your wages,' then all the flocks bore streaked. ⁹So God has taken away the livestock of your father and given *them* to me.

¹⁰"And it happened, at the time when the flocks conceived, that I lifted my eyes and saw in a dream, and behold, the rams which leaped upon the flocks *were* streaked, speckled, and gray-spotted. ¹¹Then the Angel of God spoke to me in a dream, saying, 'Jacob.' And I said, 'Here I am.' ¹²And He said, 'Lift your eyes now and see, all the rams which leap on the flocks *are* streaked, speckled, and gray-spotted; for I have seen all that Laban is doing to you. ¹³I *am* the God of Bethel, where you anointed the pillar *and* where you made a vow to Me. Now arise, get out of this land, and return to the land of your family.' "

¹⁴Then Rachel and Leah answered and said to him, "Is there still any portion or inheritance for us in our father's house? ¹⁵Are we not considered strangers by him? For he has sold us, and also completely consumed our money. ¹⁶For all these riches which God has taken from our father are *really* ours and our children's; now then, whatever God has said to you, do it."

¹⁷Then Jacob rose and set his sons and his wives on camels. ¹⁸And he carried away all his livestock and all his possessions which he had gained, his acquired livestock which he had gained in Padan Aram, to go to his father Isaac in the land of Canaan. ¹⁹Now Laban had gone to shear his sheep, and Rachel had stolen the household idols that were her father's. ²⁰And Jacob stole away, unknown to Laban the Syrian, in that he did not tell him that he intended to flee. ²¹So he fled with all that he had. He arose and crossed the river, and headed toward the mountains of Gilead.

Laban Pursues Jacob

²²And Laban was told on the third day that Jacob had fled. ²³Then he took his brethren with him and pursued him for seven days' journey, and he overtook him in the mountains of Gilead. ²⁴But God had come to Laban the Syrian in a dream by night, and said to him, "Be careful that you speak to Jacob neither good nor bad."

²⁵So Laban overtook Jacob. Now Jacob had pitched his tent in the mountains, and Laban with his brethren pitched in the mountains of Gilead.

²⁶And Laban said to Jacob: "What have you done, that you have stolen away unknown to me, and carried away my daughters like captives *taken* with the sword? ²⁷Why did you flee away secretly, and steal away from me, and not tell me; for I might have sent you away with joy and songs, with timbrel and harp? ²⁸And you did not allow me to kiss my sons and my daughters. Now you have done foolishly in *so* doing. ²⁹It is in my power to do you harm, but the God of your father spoke to me last night, saying, 'Be careful that you speak to Jacob neither good nor bad.' ³⁰And now you have surely gone because you greatly long for your father's house, *but* why did you steal my gods?"

³¹Then Jacob answered and said to Laban, "Because I was afraid, for I said, 'Perhaps you would take your daughters from me by force.' ³²With whomever you find your gods, do not let him live. In the presence of our brethren, identify what I have of yours and take *it* with you." For Jacob did not know that Rachel had stolen them.

³³And Laban went into Jacob's tent, into Leah's tent, and into the two maids' tents, but he did not find *them*. Then he went out of Leah's tent and entered Rachel's tent. ³⁴Now Rachel had taken the household idols, put them in the camel's saddle, and sat on them. And Laban searched all about the tent but did not find *them*. ³⁵And she said to her father, "Let it not displease my lord that I cannot rise before you, for the manner of women *is* with me." And he searched but did not find the household idols.

³⁶Then Jacob was angry and rebuked Laban, and Jacob answered and said to Laban: "What *is* my trespass? What *is* my sin, that you have so hotly pursued me? ³⁷Although you have searched

all my things, what part of your household things have you found? Set *it* here before my brethren and your brethren, that they may judge between us both! ³⁸These twenty years I *have been* with you; your ewes and your female goats have not miscarried their young, and I have not eaten the rams of your flock. ³⁹That which was torn *by beasts* I did not bring to you; I bore the loss of it. You required it from my hand, *whether* stolen by day or stolen by night. ⁴⁰*There* I was! In the day the drought consumed me, and the frost by night, and my sleep departed from my eyes. ⁴¹Thus I have been in your house twenty years; I served you fourteen years for your two daughters, and six years for your flock, and you have changed my wages ten times. ⁴²Unless the God of my father, the God of Abraham and the Fear of Isaac, had been with me, surely now you would have sent me away empty-handed. God has seen my affliction and the labor of my hands, and rebuked *you* last night."

Laban's Covenant with Jacob

⁴³And Laban answered and said to Jacob, "*These* daughters *are* my daughters, and *these* children *are* my children, and *this* flock *is* my flock; all that you see *is* mine. But what can I do this day to these my daughters or to their children whom they have borne? ⁴⁴Now therefore, come, let us make a covenant, you and I, and let it be a witness between you and me."

⁴⁵So Jacob took a stone and set it up *as* a pillar. ⁴⁶Then Jacob said to his brethren, "Gather stones." And they took stones and made a heap, and they ate there on the heap. ⁴⁷Laban called it Jegar Sahadutha,ᵃ but Jacob called it Galeed.ᵇ ⁴⁸And Laban said, "This heap *is* a witness between you and me this day." Therefore its name was called Galeed, ⁴⁹also Mizpah,ᵃ because he said, "May the LORD watch between you and me when we are absent one from another. ⁵⁰If you afflict my daughters, or if you take *other* wives besides my daughters, *although* no man *is* with us— see, God *is* witness between you and me!"

⁵¹Then Laban said to Jacob, "Here is this heap and here is *this* pillar, which I have placed between you and me. ⁵²This heap *is* a witness, and *this* pillar *is* a witness, that I will not pass beyond this heap to you, and you will not pass beyond this heap and this pillar to me, for harm. ⁵³The God of Abraham, the God of Nahor, and the God of their father judge between us." And Jacob swore by the Fear of his father Isaac. ⁵⁴Then Jacob offered a sacrifice on the mountain, and called his brethren to eat bread. And they ate bread and stayed all night on the mountain. ⁵⁵And early in the morning Laban arose, and kissed his sons and daughters and blessed them. Then Laban departed and returned to his place.

Esau Comes to Meet Jacob

32 So Jacob went on his way, and the angels of God met him. ²When Jacob saw them, he said, "This *is* God's camp." And he called the name of that place Mahanaim.ᵃ

³Then Jacob sent messengers before him to Esau his brother in the land of Seir, the country of Edom. ⁴And he commanded them, saying, "Speak thus to my lord Esau, 'Thus your servant Jacob says: "I have dwelt with Laban and stayed there until now. ⁵I have oxen, donkeys, flocks, and male and female servants; and I have sent to tell my lord, that I may find favor in your sight." ' "

⁶Then the messengers returned to Jacob, saying, "We came to your brother Esau, and he also is coming to meet you, and four hundred men *are* with him." ⁷So Jacob was greatly afraid and distressed; and he divided the people that *were* with him, and the flocks and herds and camels, into two companies. ⁸And he said, "If Esau comes to the one company and attacks it, then the other company which is left will escape."

⁹Then Jacob said, "O God of my father Abraham and God of my father Isaac, the LORD who said to me, 'Return to your country and to your family, and I will deal well with you': ¹⁰I am not worthy of the least of all the mercies and of all the truth which You have shown Your servant; for I crossed over this Jordan with my staff, and now I have become two companies. ¹¹Deliver me, I pray, from the hand of my brother, from the hand of Esau; for I fear him, lest he come and attack me *and* the mother with the children. ¹²For You said, 'I will surely treat you well, and make your

31:47 ᵃLiterally, in Aramaic, *Heap of Witness* ᵇLiterally, in Hebrew, *Heap of Witness* **31:49** ᵃLiterally *Watch* **32:2** ᵃLiterally *Double Camp*

descendants as the sand of the sea, which cannot be numbered for multitude.' "

[13]So he lodged there that same night, and took what came to his hand as a present for Esau his brother: [14]two hundred female goats and twenty male goats, two hundred ewes and twenty rams, [15]thirty milk camels with their colts, forty cows and ten bulls, twenty female donkeys and ten foals. [16]Then he delivered *them* to the hand of his servants, every drove by itself, and said to his servants, "Pass over before me, and put some distance between successive droves." [17]And he commanded the first one, saying, "When Esau my brother meets you and asks you, saying, 'To whom do you belong, and where are you going? Whose *are* these in front of you?' [18]then you shall say, 'They *are* your servant Jacob's. It *is* a present sent to my lord Esau; and behold, he also *is* behind us.' " [19]So he commanded the second, the third, and all who followed the droves, saying, "In this manner you shall speak to Esau when you find him; [20]and also say, 'Behold, your servant Jacob *is* behind us.' " For he said, "I will appease him with the present that goes before me, and afterward I will see his face; perhaps he will accept me." [21]So the present went on over before him, but he himself lodged that night in the camp.

Wrestling with God

[22]And he arose that night and took his two wives, his two female servants, and his eleven sons, and crossed over the ford of Jabbok. [23]He took them, sent them over the brook, and sent over what he had. [24]Then Jacob was left alone; and a Man wrestled with him until the breaking of day. [25]Now when He saw that He did not prevail against him, He touched the socket of his hip; and the socket of Jacob's hip was out of joint as He wrestled with him. [26]And He said, "Let Me go, for the day breaks."

But he said, "I will not let You go unless You bless me!"

[27]So He said to him, "What *is* your name?"

He said, "Jacob."

[28]And He said, "Your name shall no longer be called Jacob, but Israel;[a] for you have struggled with God and with men, and have prevailed."

[29]Then Jacob asked, saying, "Tell *me* Your name, I pray."

And He said, "Why *is* it *that* you ask about My name?" And He blessed him there.

[30]So Jacob called the name of the place Peniel:[a] "For I have seen God face to face, and my life is preserved." [31]Just as he crossed over Penuel[a] the sun rose on him, and he limped on his hip. [32]Therefore to this day the children of Israel do not eat the muscle that shrank, which *is* on the hip socket, because He touched the socket of Jacob's hip in the muscle that shrank.

Jacob and Esau Meet

33 Now Jacob lifted his eyes and looked, and there, Esau was coming, and with him were four hundred men. So he divided the children among Leah, Rachel, and the two maidservants. [2]And he put the maidservants and their children in front, Leah and her children behind, and Rachel and Joseph last. [3]Then he crossed over before them and bowed himself to the ground seven times, until he came near to his brother.

[4]But Esau ran to meet him, and embraced him, and fell on his neck and kissed him, and they wept. [5]And he lifted his eyes and saw the women and children, and said, "Who *are* these with you?"

So he said, "The children whom God has graciously given your servant." [6]Then the maidservants came near, they and their children, and bowed down. [7]And Leah also came near with her children, and they bowed down. Afterward Joseph and Rachel came near, and they bowed down.

[8]Then Esau said, "What *do* you *mean by* all this company which I met?"

And he said, "*These are* to find favor in the sight of my lord."

[9]But Esau said, "I have enough, my brother; keep what you have for yourself."

[10]And Jacob said, "No, please, if I have now found favor in your sight, then receive my present from my hand, inasmuch as I have seen your face as though I had seen the face of God, and you were pleased with me. [11]Please, take my blessing that is brought to you, because God has dealt graciously with me, and because I have enough." So he urged him, and he took *it*.

32:28 [a]Literally *Prince with God*   **32:30** [a]Literally *Face of God*
32:31 [a]Same as *Peniel*, verse 30

¹²Then Esau said, "Let us take our journey; let us go, and I will go before you."

¹³But Jacob said to him, "My lord knows that the children *are* weak, and the flocks and herds which are nursing *are* with me. And if the men should drive them hard one day, all the flock will die. ¹⁴Please let my lord go on ahead before his servant. I will lead on slowly at a pace which the livestock that go before me, and the children, are able to endure, until I come to my lord in Seir."

¹⁵And Esau said, "Now let me leave with you *some* of the people who *are* with me."

But he said, "What need is there? Let me find favor in the sight of my lord." ¹⁶So Esau returned that day on his way to Seir. ¹⁷And Jacob journeyed to Succoth, built himself a house, and made booths for his livestock. Therefore the name of the place is called Succoth.ª

Jacob Comes to Canaan

¹⁸Then Jacob came safely to the city of Shechem, which *is* in the land of Canaan, when he came from Padan Aram; and he pitched his tent before the city. ¹⁹And he bought the parcel of land, where he had pitched his tent, from the children of Hamor, Shechem's father, for one hundred pieces of money. ²⁰Then he erected an altar there and called it El Elohe Israel.ª

The Dinah Incident

34 Now Dinah the daughter of Leah, whom she had borne to Jacob, went out to see the daughters of the land. ²And when Shechem the son of Hamor the Hivite, prince of the country, saw her, he took her and lay with her, and violated her. ³His soul was strongly attracted to Dinah the daughter of Jacob, and he loved the young woman and spoke kindly to the young woman. ⁴So Shechem spoke to his father Hamor, saying, "Get me this young woman as a wife."

⁵And Jacob heard that he had defiled Dinah his daughter. Now his sons were with his livestock in the field; so Jacob held his peace until they came. ⁶Then Hamor the father of Shechem went out to Jacob to speak with him. ⁷And the sons of Jacob came in from the field when they heard *it;* and the men were grieved and very angry, because he had done a disgraceful thing in Is-

rael by lying with Jacob's daughter, a thing which ought not to be done. ⁸But Hamor spoke with them, saying, "The soul of my son Shechem longs for your daughter. Please give her to him as a wife. ⁹And make marriages with us; give your daughters to us, and take our daughters to yourselves. ¹⁰So you shall dwell with us, and the land shall be before you. Dwell and trade in it, and acquire possessions for yourselves in it."

¹¹Then Shechem said to her father and her brothers, "Let me find favor in your eyes, and whatever you say to me I will give. ¹²Ask me ever so much dowry and gift, and I will give according to what you say to me; but give me the young woman as a wife."

¹³But the sons of Jacob answered Shechem and Hamor his father, and spoke deceitfully, because he had defiled Dinah their sister. ¹⁴And they said to them, "We cannot do this thing, to give our sister to one who is uncircumcised, for that *would be* a reproach to us. ¹⁵But on this *condition* we will consent to you: If you will become as we *are,* if every male of you is circumcised, ¹⁶then we will give our daughters to you, and we will take your daughters to us; and we will dwell with you, and we will become one people. ¹⁷But if you will not heed us and be circumcised, then we will take our daughter and be gone."

¹⁸And their words pleased Hamor and Shechem, Hamor's son. ¹⁹So the young man did not delay to do the thing, because he delighted in Jacob's daughter. He *was* more honorable than all the household of his father.

²⁰And Hamor and Shechem his son came to the gate of their city, and spoke with the men of their city, saying: ²¹"These men *are* at peace with us. Therefore let them dwell in the land and trade in it. For indeed the land *is* large enough for them. Let us take their daughters to us as wives, and let us give them our daughters. ²²Only on this *condition* will the men consent to dwell with us, to be one people: if every male among us is circumcised as they *are* circumcised. ²³*Will* not their livestock, their property, and every animal of theirs *be* ours? Only let us consent to them, and they will dwell with us." ²⁴And all who went out of the gate of his city heeded Hamor and

33:17 ªLiterally *Booths* **33:20** ªLiterally *God, the God of Israel*

Shechem his son; every male was circumcised, all who went out of the gate of his city.

25Now it came to pass on the third day, when they were in pain, that two of the sons of Jacob, Simeon and Levi, Dinah's brothers, each took his sword and came boldly upon the city and killed all the males. 26And they killed Hamor and Shechem his son with the edge of the sword, and took Dinah from Shechem's house, and went out. 27The sons of Jacob came upon the slain, and plundered the city, because their sister had been defiled. 28They took their sheep, their oxen, and their donkeys, what *was* in the city and what *was* in the field, 29and all their wealth. All their little ones and their wives they took captive; and they plundered even all that *was* in the houses.

30Then Jacob said to Simeon and Levi, "You have troubled me by making me obnoxious among the inhabitants of the land, among the Canaanites and the Perizzites; and since I *am* few in number, they will gather themselves together against me and kill me. I shall be destroyed, my household and I."

31But they said, "Should he treat our sister like a harlot?"

Jacob's Return to Bethel

35 Then God said to Jacob, "Arise, go up to Bethel and dwell there; and make an altar there to God, who appeared to you when you fled from the face of Esau your brother."

2And Jacob said to his household and to all who *were* with him, "Put away the foreign gods that *are* among you, purify yourselves, and change your garments. 3Then let us arise and go up to Bethel; and I will make an altar there to God, who answered me in the day of my distress and has been with me in the way which I have gone." 4So they gave Jacob all the foreign gods which *were* in their hands, and the earrings which *were* in their ears; and Jacob hid them under the terebinth tree which *was* by Shechem.

5And they journeyed, and the terror of God was upon the cities that *were* all around them, and they did not pursue the sons of Jacob. 6So Jacob came to Luz (that *is,* Bethel), which *is* in the land of Canaan, he and all the people who *were* with him. 7And he built an altar there and called the

place El Bethel,a because there God appeared to him when he fled from the face of his brother.

8Now Deborah, Rebekah's nurse, died, and she was buried below Bethel under the terebinth tree. So the name of it was called Allon Bachuth.a

9Then God appeared to Jacob again, when he came from Padan Aram, and blessed him. 10And God said to him, "Your name *is* Jacob; your name shall not be called Jacob anymore; but Israel shall be your name." So He called his name Israel. 11Also God said to him: "I *am* God Almighty. Be fruitful and multiply; a nation and a company of nations shall proceed from you, and kings shall come from your body. 12The land which I gave Abraham and Isaac I give to you; and to your descendants after you I give this land." 13Then God went up from him in the place where He talked with him. 14So Jacob set up a pillar in the place where He talked with him, a pillar of stone; and he poured a drink offering on it, and he poured oil on it. 15And Jacob called the name of the place where God spoke with him, Bethel.

Death of Rachel

16Then they journeyed from Bethel. And when there was but a little distance to go to Ephrath, Rachel labored in *childbirth,* and she had hard labor. 17Now it came to pass, when she was in hard labor, that the midwife said to her, "Do not fear; you will have this son also." 18And so it was, as her soul was departing (for she died), that she called his name Ben-Oni;a but his father called him Benjamin.b 19So Rachel died and was buried on the way to Ephrath (that *is,* Bethlehem). 20And Jacob set a pillar on her grave, which *is* the pillar of Rachel's grave to this day.

21Then Israel journeyed and pitched his tent beyond the tower of Eder. 22And it happened, when Israel dwelt in that land, that Reuben went and lay with Bilhah his father's concubine; and Israel heard *about it.*

Jacob's Twelve Sons

Now the sons of Jacob were twelve: 23the sons of Leah *were* Reuben, Jacob's firstborn, and Simeon, Levi, Judah, Issachar, and Zebulun; 24the

35:7 aLiterally *God of the House of God*   **35:8** aLiterally *Terebinth of Weeping*   **35:18** aLiterally *Son of My Sorrow* bLiterally *Son of the Right Hand*

sons of Rachel *were* Joseph and Benjamin; ²⁵the sons of Bilhah, Rachel's maidservant, *were* Dan and Naphtali; ²⁶and the sons of Zilpah, Leah's maidservant, *were* Gad and Asher. These *were* the sons of Jacob who were born to him in Padan Aram.

DEATH OF ISAAC

²⁷Then Jacob came to his father Isaac at Mamre, or Kirjath Arbaᵃ (that *is,* Hebron), where Abraham and Isaac had dwelt. ²⁸Now the days of Isaac were one hundred and eighty years. ²⁹So Isaac breathed his last and died, and was gathered to his people, *being* old and full of days. And his sons Esau and Jacob buried him.

THE FAMILY OF ESAU

36 Now this *is* the genealogy of Esau, who is Edom. ²Esau took his wives from the daughters of Canaan: Adah the daughter of Elon the Hittite; Aholibamah the daughter of Anah, the daughter of Zibeon the Hivite; ³and Basemath, Ishmael's daughter, sister of Nebajoth. ⁴Now Adah bore Eliphaz to Esau, and Basemath bore Reuel. ⁵And Aholibamah bore Jeush, Jaalam, and Korah. These *were* the sons of Esau who were born to him in the land of Canaan.

⁶Then Esau took his wives, his sons, his daughters, and all the persons of his household, his cattle and all his animals, and all his goods which he had gained in the land of Canaan, and went to a country away from the presence of his brother Jacob. ⁷For their possessions were too great for them to dwell together, and the land where they were strangers could not support them because of their livestock. ⁸So Esau dwelt in Mount Seir. Esau *is* Edom.

⁹And this *is* the genealogy of Esau the father of the Edomites in Mount Seir. ¹⁰These *were* the names of Esau's sons: Eliphaz the son of Adah the wife of Esau, and Reuel the son of Basemath the wife of Esau. ¹¹And the sons of Eliphaz were Teman, Omar, Zepho,ᵃ Gatam, and Kenaz. ¹²Now Timna was the concubine of Eliphaz, Esau's son, and she bore Amalek to Eliphaz. These *were* the sons of Adah, Esau's wife.

¹³These *were* the sons of Reuel: Nahath, Zerah, Shammah, and Mizzah. These were the sons of Basemath, Esau's wife.

¹⁴These were the sons of Aholibamah, Esau's wife, the daughter of Anah, the daughter of Zibeon. And she bore to Esau: Jeush, Jaalam, and Korah.

THE CHIEFS OF EDOM

¹⁵These *were* the chiefs of the sons of Esau. The sons of Eliphaz, the firstborn *son* of Esau, were Chief Teman, Chief Omar, Chief Zepho, Chief Kenaz, ¹⁶Chief Korah,ᵃ Chief Gatam, *and* Chief Amalek. These *were* the chiefs of Eliphaz in the land of Edom. They *were* the sons of Adah.

¹⁷These *were* the sons of Reuel, Esau's son: Chief Nahath, Chief Zerah, Chief Shammah, and Chief Mizzah. These *were* the chiefs of Reuel in the land of Edom. These *were* the sons of Basemath, Esau's wife.

¹⁸And these *were* the sons of Aholibamah, Esau's wife: Chief Jeush, Chief Jaalam, and Chief Korah. These *were* the chiefs *who descended* from Aholibamah, Esau's wife, the daughter of Anah. ¹⁹These *were* the sons of Esau, who is Edom, and these *were* their chiefs.

THE SONS OF SEIR

²⁰These *were* the sons of Seir the Horite who inhabited the land: Lotan, Shobal, Zibeon, Anah, ²¹Dishon, Ezer, and Dishan. These *were* the chiefs of the Horites, the sons of Seir, in the land of Edom.

²²And the sons of Lotan were Hori and Hemam.ᵃ Lotan's sister *was* Timna.

²³These *were* the sons of Shobal: Alvan,ᵃ Manahath, Ebal, Shepho,ᵇ and Onam.

²⁴These *were* the sons of Zibeon: both Ajah and Anah. This *was the* Anah who found the waterᵃ in the wilderness as he pastured the donkeys of his father Zibeon. ²⁵These *were* the children of Anah: Dishon and Aholibamah the daughter of Anah.

²⁶These *were* the sons of Dishon:ᵃ Hemdan,ᵇ Eshban, Ithran, and Cheran. ²⁷These *were* the sons

---

35:27 ᵃLiterally *Town of Arba*   **36:11** ᵃSpelled *Zephi* in 1 Chronicles 1:36   **36:16** ᵃSamaritan Pentateuch omits *Chief Korah.*   **36:22** ᵃSpelled *Homam* in 1 Chronicles 1:39   **36:23** ᵃSpelled *Alian* in 1 Chronicles 1:40   ᵇSpelled *Shephi* in 1 Chronicles 1:40   **36:24** ᵃFollowing Masoretic Text and Vulgate (*hot springs*); Septuagint reads *Jamin*; Targum reads *mighty men*; Talmud interprets as *mules.*   **36:26** ᵃHebrew *Dishan* ᵇSpelled *Hamran* in 1 Chronicles 1:41

of Ezer: Bilhan, Zaavan, and Akan.[a] [28]These *were* the sons of Dishan: Uz and Aran.

[29]These *were* the chiefs of the Horites: Chief Lotan, Chief Shobal, Chief Zibeon, Chief Anah, [30]Chief Dishon, Chief Ezer, and Chief Dishan. These *were* the chiefs of the Horites, according to their chiefs in the land of Seir.

THE KINGS OF EDOM

[31]Now these *were* the kings who reigned in the land of Edom before any king reigned over the children of Israel: [32]Bela the son of Beor reigned in Edom, and the name of his city *was* Dinhabah. [33]And when Bela died, Jobab the son of Zerah of Bozrah reigned in his place. [34]When Jobab died, Husham of the land of the Temanites reigned in his place. [35]And when Husham died, Hadad the son of Bedad, who attacked Midian in the field of Moab, reigned in his place. And the name of his city *was* Avith. [36]When Hadad died, Samlah of Masrekah reigned in his place. [37]And when Samlah died, Saul of Rehoboth-*by*-the-River reigned in his place. [38]When Saul died, Baal-Hanan the son of Achbor reigned in his place. [39]And when Baal-Hanan the son of Achbor died, Hadar[a] reigned in his place; and the name of his city *was* Pau.[b] His wife's name *was* Mehetabel, the daughter of Matred, the daughter of Mezahab.

THE CHIEFS OF ESAU

[40]And these *were* the names of the chiefs of Esau, according to their families and their places, by their names: Chief Timnah, Chief Alvah,[a] Chief Jetheth, [41]Chief Aholibamah, Chief Elah, Chief Pinon, [42]Chief Kenaz, Chief Teman, Chief Mibzar, [43]Chief Magdiel, and Chief Iram. These *were* the chiefs of Edom, according to their dwelling places in the land of their possession. Esau *was* the father of the Edomites.

JOSEPH DREAMS OF GREATNESS

37 Now Jacob dwelt in the land where his father was a stranger, in the land of Canaan. [2]This *is* the history of Jacob.

Joseph, *being* seventeen years old, was feeding the flock with his brothers. And the lad *was* with the sons of Bilhah and the sons of Zilpah, his father's wives; and Joseph brought a bad report of them to his father.

[3]Now Israel loved Joseph more than all his children, because he *was* the son of his old age. Also he made him a tunic of *many* colors. [4]But when his brothers saw that their father loved him more than all his brothers, they hated him and could not speak peaceably to him.

[5]Now Joseph had a dream, and he told *it* to his brothers; and they hated him even more. [6]So he said to them, "Please hear this dream which I have dreamed: [7]There we were, binding sheaves in the field. Then behold, my sheaf arose and also stood upright; and indeed your sheaves stood all around and bowed down to my sheaf."

[8]And his brothers said to him, "Shall you indeed reign over us? Or shall you indeed have dominion over us?" So they hated him even more for his dreams and for his words.

[9]Then he dreamed still another dream and told it to his brothers, and said, "Look, I have dreamed another dream. And this time, the sun, the moon, and the eleven stars bowed down to me."

[10]So he told *it* to his father and his brothers; and his father rebuked him and said to him, "What *is* this dream that you have dreamed? Shall your mother and I and your brothers indeed come to bow down to the earth before you?" [11]And his brothers envied him, but his father kept the matter *in mind*.

JOSEPH SOLD BY HIS BROTHERS

[12]Then his brothers went to feed their father's flock in Shechem. [13]And Israel said to Joseph, "Are not your brothers feeding *the flock* in Shechem? Come, I will send you to them."

So he said to him, "Here I am."

[14]Then he said to him, "Please go and see if it is well with your brothers and well with the flocks, and bring back word to me." So he sent him out of the Valley of Hebron, and he went to Shechem.

[15]Now a certain man found him, and there he was, wandering in the field. And the man asked him, saying, "What are you seeking?"

[16]So he said, "I am seeking my brothers. Please tell me where they are feeding *their flocks*."

36:27 [a]Spelled *Jaakan* in 1 Chronicles 1:42   **36:39** [a]Spelled *Hadad* in Samaritan Pentateuch, Syriac, and 1 Chronicles 1:50   [b]Spelled *Pai* in 1 Chronicles 1:50   **36:40** [a]Spelled *Aliah* in 1 Chronicles 1:51

INSIDE *the* INFLUENCERS

JOSEPH—Don't Let the Dream Die

GENESIS 37—40

Joseph's brothers despised the young dreamer because his father showed him favor (37:3). So when Joseph bragged to them about his dream in which his brothers bowed down to him, it was the last straw.

In anger his brothers threw him in a pit, and then sold him for twenty pieces of silver, the price for a handicapped slave. He was taken to Egypt where, through faithful serving, he became successful (39:5). When his boss's wife approached him with a proposal of adultery, Joseph was careful not to trample the dream through immorality; and when he rejected her, she falsely accused him to Potiphar who banished Joseph to a dungeon.

He endured slavery, imprisonment, betrayal, and long periods of waiting, but *God taught Joseph to serve in the dungeon so he could lead in the world.* After years of faithfulness, God elevated him. Eventually, Joseph became Pharaoh's right-hand man, second in command of the world's most powerful nation (Gen. 41:40).

Joseph saved many people from starvation, including his brothers, who did—as the dream foretold—bow to him in Egypt. Instead of the common reactions of rage, resentment, and revenge, Joseph forgave them. His reward was a life of influence, leadership, and legacy. Joseph simply refused to let the dream die, regardless of circumstance or criticism.

17And the man said, "They have departed from here, for I heard them say, 'Let us go to Dothan.' " So Joseph went after his brothers and found them in Dothan.

18Now when they saw him afar off, even before he came near them, they conspired against him to kill him. 19Then they said to one another, "Look, this dreamer is coming! 20Come therefore, let us now kill him and cast him into some pit; and we shall say, 'Some wild beast has devoured him.' We shall see what will become of his dreams!"

21But Reuben heard *it,* and he delivered him out of their hands, and said, "Let us not kill him." 22And Reuben said to them, "Shed no blood, *but* cast him into this pit which *is* in the wilderness, and do not lay a hand on him"—that he might deliver him out of their hands, and bring him back to his father.

23So it came to pass, when Joseph had come to his brothers, that they stripped Joseph *of* his tunic, the tunic of *many* colors that *was* on him.

24Then they took him and cast him into a pit. And the pit *was* empty; *there was* no water in it.

25And they sat down to eat a meal. Then they lifted their eyes and looked, and there was a company of Ishmaelites, coming from Gilead with their camels, bearing spices, balm, and myrrh, on their way to carry *them* down to Egypt. 26So Judah said to his brothers, "What profit *is there* if we kill our brother and conceal his blood? 27Come and let us sell him to the Ishmaelites, and let not our hand be upon him, for he *is* our brother *and* our flesh." And his brothers listened. 28Then Midianite traders passed by; so *the brothers* pulled Joseph up and lifted him out of the pit, and sold him to the Ishmaelites for twenty *shekels* of silver. And they took Joseph to Egypt.

29Then Reuben returned to the pit, and indeed Joseph *was* not in the pit; and he tore his clothes. 30And he returned to his brothers and said, "The lad *is* no *more;* and I, where shall I go?"

31So they took Joseph's tunic, killed a kid of the goats, and dipped the tunic in the blood.

³²Then they sent the tunic of *many* colors, and they brought *it* to their father and said, "We have found this. Do you know whether it *is* your son's tunic or not?"

³³And he recognized it and said, "*It is* my son's tunic. A wild beast has devoured him. Without doubt Joseph is torn to pieces." ³⁴Then Jacob tore his clothes, put sackcloth on his waist, and mourned for his son many days. ³⁵And all his sons and all his daughters arose to comfort him; but he refused to be comforted, and he said, "For I shall go down into the grave to my son in mourning." Thus his father wept for him.

³⁶Now the Midianites[a] had sold him in Egypt to Potiphar, an officer of Pharaoh *and* captain of the guard.

JUDAH AND TAMAR

38 It came to pass at that time that Judah departed from his brothers, and visited a certain Adullamite whose name *was* Hirah. ²And Judah saw there a daughter of a certain Canaanite whose name *was* Shua, and he married her and went in to her. ³So she conceived and bore a son, and he called his name Er. ⁴She conceived again and bore a son, and she called his name Onan. ⁵And she conceived yet again and bore a son, and called his name Shelah. He was at Chezib when she bore him.

⁶Then Judah took a wife for Er his firstborn, and her name *was* Tamar. ⁷But Er, Judah's firstborn, was wicked in the sight of the LORD, and the LORD killed him. ⁸And Judah said to Onan, "Go in to your brother's wife and marry her, and raise up an heir to your brother." ⁹But Onan knew that the heir would not be his; and it came to pass, when he went in to his brother's wife, that he emitted on the ground, lest he should give an heir to his brother. ¹⁰And the thing which he did displeased the LORD; therefore He killed him also.

¹¹Then Judah said to Tamar his daughter-in-law, "Remain a widow in your father's house till my son Shelah is grown." For he said, "Lest he also die like his brothers." And Tamar went and dwelt in her father's house.

¹²Now in the process of time the daughter of Shua, Judah's wife, died; and Judah was comforted, and went up to his sheepshearers at Timnah, he and his friend Hirah the Adullamite.

¹³And it was told Tamar, saying, "Look, your father-in-law is going up to Timnah to shear his sheep." ¹⁴So she took off her widow's garments, covered *herself* with a veil and wrapped herself, and sat in an open place which *was* on the way to Timnah; for she saw that Shelah was grown, and she was not given to him as a wife. ¹⁵When Judah saw her, he thought she *was* a harlot, because she had covered her face. ¹⁶Then he turned to her by the way, and said, "Please let me come in to you"; for he did not know that she *was* his daughter-in-law.

So she said, "What will you give me, that you may come in to me?"

¹⁷And he said, "I will send a young goat from the flock."

So she said, "Will you give *me* a pledge till you send *it?*"

¹⁸Then he said, "What pledge shall I give you?"

So she said, "Your signet and cord, and your staff that *is* in your hand." Then he gave *them* to her, and went in to her, and she conceived by him. ¹⁹So she arose and went away, and laid aside her veil and put on the garments of her widowhood.

²⁰And Judah sent the young goat by the hand of his friend the Adullamite, to receive *his* pledge from the woman's hand, but he did not find her. ²¹Then he asked the men of that place, saying, "Where is the harlot who *was* openly by the roadside?"

And they said, "There was no harlot in this *place.*"

²²So he returned to Judah and said, "I cannot find her. Also, the men of the place said there was no harlot in this *place.*"

²³Then Judah said, "Let her take *them* for herself, lest we be shamed; for I sent this young goat and you have not found her."

²⁴And it came to pass, about three months after, that Judah was told, saying, "Tamar your daughter-in-law has played the harlot; furthermore she *is* with child by harlotry."

So Judah said, "Bring her out and let her be burned!"

²⁵When she *was* brought out, she sent to her

37:36 [a]Masoretic Text reads *Medanites*.

father-in-law, saying, "By the man to whom these belong, I *am* with child." And she said, "Please determine whose these *are*—the signet and cord, and staff."

²⁶So Judah acknowledged *them* and said, "She has been more righteous than I, because I did not give her to Shelah my son." And he never knew her again.

²⁷Now it came to pass, at the time for giving birth, that behold, twins *were* in her womb. ²⁸And so it was, when she was giving birth, that *the one* put out *his* hand; and the midwife took a scarlet *thread* and bound it on his hand, saying, "This one came out first." ²⁹Then it happened, as he drew back his hand, that his brother came out unexpectedly; and she said, "How did you break through? *This* breach *be* upon you!" Therefore his name was called Perez.ᵃ ³⁰Afterward his brother came out who had the scarlet *thread* on his hand. And his name was called Zerah.

Joseph a Slave in Egypt

39 Now Joseph had been taken down to Egypt. And Potiphar, an officer of Pharaoh, captain of the guard, an Egyptian, bought him from the Ishmaelites who had taken him down there. ²The LORD was with Joseph, and he was a successful man; and he was in the house of his master the Egyptian. ³And his master saw that the LORD *was* with him and that the LORD made all he did to prosper in his hand. ⁴So Joseph found favor in his sight, and served him. Then he made him overseer of his house, and all *that* he had he put under his authority. ⁵So it was, from the time *that* he had made him overseer of his house and all that he had, that the LORD blessed the Egyptian's house for Joseph's sake; and the blessing of the LORD was on all that he had in the house and in the field. ⁶Thus he left all that he had in Joseph's hand, and he did not know what he had except for the bread which he ate.

Now Joseph was handsome in form and appearance.

⁷And it came to pass after these things that his master's wife cast longing eyes on Joseph, and she said, "Lie with me."

⁸But he refused and said to his master's wife,

"Look, my master does not know what *is* with me in the house, and he has committed all that he has to my hand. ⁹*There is* no one greater in this house than I, nor has he kept back anything from me but you, because you *are* his wife. How then can I do this great wickedness, and sin against God?"

¹⁰So it was, as she spoke to Joseph day by day, that he did not heed her, to lie with her *or* to be with her.

¹¹But it happened about this time, when Joseph went into the house to do his work, and none of the men of the house *was* inside, ¹²that she caught him by his garment, saying, "Lie with me." But he left his garment in her hand, and fled and ran outside. ¹³And so it was, when she saw that he had left his garment in her hand and fled outside, ¹⁴that she called to the men of her house and spoke to them, saying, "See, he has brought in to us a Hebrew to mock us. He came in to me to lie with me, and I cried out with a loud voice. ¹⁵And it happened, when he heard that I lifted my voice and cried out, that he left his garment with me, and fled and went outside."

¹⁶So she kept his garment with her until his master came home. ¹⁷Then she spoke to him with words like these, saying, "The Hebrew servant whom you brought to us came in to me to mock me; ¹⁸so it happened, as I lifted my voice and cried out, that he left his garment with me and fled outside."

¹⁹So it was, when his master heard the words which his wife spoke to him, saying, "Your servant did to me after this manner," that his anger was aroused. ²⁰Then Joseph's master took him and put him into the prison, a place where the king's prisoners *were* confined. And he was there in the prison. ²¹But the LORD was with Joseph and showed him mercy, and He gave him favor in the sight of the keeper of the prison. ²²And the keeper of the prison committed to Joseph's hand all the prisoners who *were* in the prison; whatever they did there, it was his doing. ²³The keeper of the prison did not look into anything *that was* under *Joseph's* authority,ᵃ because the LORD was with him; and whatever he did, the LORD made *it* prosper.

38:29 ᵃLiterally *Breach* or *Breakthrough*   **39:23** ᵃLiterally *his hand*

THE PRISONERS' DREAMS

40 It came to pass after these things *that* the butler and the baker of the king of Egypt offended their lord, the king of Egypt. ²And Pharaoh was angry with his two officers, the chief butler and the chief baker. ³So he put them in custody in the house of the captain of the guard, in the prison, the place where Joseph *was* confined. ⁴And the captain of the guard charged Joseph with them, and he served them; so they were in custody for a while.

⁵Then the butler and the baker of the king of Egypt, who *were* confined in the prison, had a dream, both of them, each man's dream in one night *and* each man's dream with its *own* interpretation. ⁶And Joseph came in to them in the morning and looked at them, and saw that they *were* sad. ⁷So he asked Pharaoh's officers who *were* with him in the custody of his lord's house, saying, "Why do you look *so* sad today?"

⁸And they said to him, "We each have had a dream, and *there is* no interpreter of it."

So Joseph said to them, "Do not interpretations belong to God? Tell *them* to me, please."

⁹Then the chief butler told his dream to Joseph, and said to him, "Behold, in my dream a vine *was* before me, ¹⁰and in the vine *were* three branches; it *was* as though it budded, its blossoms shot forth, and its clusters brought forth ripe grapes. ¹¹Then Pharaoh's cup *was* in my hand; and I took the grapes and pressed them into Pharaoh's cup, and placed the cup in Pharaoh's hand."

¹²And Joseph said to him, "This *is* the interpretation of it: The three branches *are* three days. ¹³Now within three days Pharaoh will lift up your head and restore you to your place, and you will put Pharaoh's cup in his hand according to the former manner, when you were his butler. ¹⁴But remember me when it is well with you, and please show kindness to me; make mention of me to Pharaoh, and get me out of this house. ¹⁵For indeed I was stolen away from the land of the Hebrews; and also I have done nothing here that they should put me into the dungeon."

¹⁶When the chief baker saw that the interpretation was good, he said to Joseph, "I also *was* in my dream, and *there were* three white baskets on my head. ¹⁷In the uppermost basket *were* all kinds of baked goods for Pharaoh, and the birds ate them out of the basket on my head."

¹⁸So Joseph answered and said, "This *is* the interpretation of it: The three baskets *are* three days. ¹⁹Within three days Pharaoh will lift off your head from you and hang you on a tree; and the birds will eat your flesh from you."

²⁰Now it came to pass on the third day, *which was* Pharaoh's birthday, that he made a feast for all his servants; and he lifted up the head of the chief butler and of the chief baker among his servants. ²¹Then he restored the chief butler to his butlership again, and he placed the cup in Pharaoh's hand. ²²But he hanged the chief baker, as Joseph had interpreted to them. ²³Yet the chief butler did not remember Joseph, but forgot him.

PHARAOH'S DREAMS

41 Then it came to pass, at the end of two full years, that Pharaoh had a dream; and behold, he stood by the river. ²Suddenly there came up out of the river seven cows, fine looking and fat; and they fed in the meadow. ³Then behold, seven other cows came up after them out of the river, ugly and gaunt, and stood by the *other* cows on the bank of the river. ⁴And the ugly and gaunt cows ate up the seven fine looking and fat cows. So Pharaoh awoke. ⁵He slept and dreamed a second time; and suddenly seven heads of grain came up on one stalk, plump and good. ⁶Then behold, seven thin heads, blighted by the east wind, sprang up after them. ⁷And the seven thin heads devoured the seven plump and full heads. So Pharaoh awoke, and indeed, *it was* a dream. ⁸Now it came to pass in the morning that his spirit was troubled, and he sent and called for all the magicians of Egypt and all its wise men. And Pharaoh told them his dreams, but *there was* no one who could interpret them for Pharaoh.

⁹Then the chief butler spoke to Pharaoh, saying: "I remember my faults this day. ¹⁰When Pharaoh was angry with his servants, and put me in custody in the house of the captain of the guard, *both* me and the chief baker, ¹¹we each had a dream in one night, he and I. Each of us dreamed according to the interpretation of his *own* dream. ¹²Now there *was* a young Hebrew man with us there, a servant of the captain of the guard. And we told him, and he interpreted our

dreams for us; to each man he interpreted according to his *own* dream. 13And it came to pass, just as he interpreted for us, so it happened. He restored me to my office, and he hanged him."

14Then Pharaoh sent and called Joseph, and they brought him quickly out of the dungeon; and he shaved, changed his clothing, and came to Pharaoh. 15And Pharaoh said to Joseph, "I have had a dream, and *there is* no one who can interpret it. But I have heard it said of you *that* you can understand a dream, to interpret it."

16So Joseph answered Pharaoh, saying, "*It is* not in me; God will give Pharaoh an answer of peace."

17Then Pharaoh said to Joseph: "Behold, in my dream I stood on the bank of the river. 18Suddenly seven cows came up out of the river, fine looking and fat; and they fed in the meadow. 19Then behold, seven other cows came up after them, poor and very ugly and gaunt, such ugliness as I have never seen in all the land of Egypt. 20And the gaunt and ugly cows ate up the first seven, the fat cows. 21When they had eaten them up, no one would have known that they had eaten them, for they *were* just as ugly as at the beginning. So I awoke. 22Also I saw in my dream, and suddenly seven heads came up on one stalk, full and good. 23Then behold, seven heads, withered, thin, *and* blighted by the east wind, sprang up after them. 24And the thin heads devoured the seven good heads. So I told *this* to the magicians, but *there was* no one who could explain *it* to me."

25Then Joseph said to Pharaoh, "The dreams of Pharaoh *are* one; God has shown Pharaoh what He *is* about to do: 26The seven good cows *are* seven years, and the seven good heads *are* seven years; the dreams *are* one. 27And the seven thin and ugly cows which came up after them *are* seven years, and the seven empty heads blighted by the east wind are seven years of famine. 28This *is* the thing which I have spoken to Pharaoh. God has shown Pharaoh what He *is* about to do. 29Indeed seven years of great plenty will come throughout all the land of Egypt; 30but after them seven years of famine will arise, and all the plenty will be forgotten in the land of Egypt; and the famine will deplete the land. 31So the plenty will not be known in the land because of the famine following, for it *will be* very severe. 32And the

dream was repeated to Pharaoh twice because the thing *is* established by God, and God will shortly bring it to pass.

33"Now therefore, let Pharaoh select a discerning and wise man, and set him over the land of Egypt. 34Let Pharaoh do *this,* and let him appoint officers over the land, to collect one-fifth *of the produce* of the land of Egypt in the seven plentiful years. 35And let them gather all the food of those good years that are coming, and store up grain under the authority of Pharaoh, and let them keep food in the cities. 36Then that food shall be as a reserve for the land for the seven years of famine which shall be in the land of Egypt, that the land may not perish during the famine."

Joseph's Rise to Power

37So the advice was good in the eyes of Pharaoh and in the eyes of all his servants. 38And Pharaoh said to his servants, "Can we find *such a one* as this, a man in whom *is* the Spirit of God?"

39Then Pharaoh said to Joseph, "Inasmuch as God has shown you all this, *there is* no one as discerning and wise as you. 40You shall be over my house, and all my people shall be ruled according to your word; only in regard to the throne will I be greater than you." 41And Pharaoh said to Joseph, "See, I have set you over all the land of Egypt."

42Then Pharaoh took his signet ring off his hand and put it on Joseph's hand; and he clothed him in garments of fine linen and put a gold chain around his neck. 43And he had him ride in the second chariot which he had; and they cried out before him, "Bow the knee!" So he set him over all the land of Egypt. 44Pharaoh also said to Joseph, "I *am* Pharaoh, and without your consent no man may lift his hand or foot in all the land of Egypt." 45And Pharaoh called Joseph's name Zaphnath-Paaneah. And he gave him as a wife Asenath, the daughter of Poti-Pherah priest of On. So Joseph went out over *all* the land of Egypt.

46Joseph was thirty years old when he stood before Pharaoh king of Egypt. And Joseph went out from the presence of Pharaoh, and went throughout all the land of Egypt. 47Now in the seven plentiful years the ground brought forth abundantly. 48So he gathered up all the food of the seven years which were in the land of Egypt, and laid up the food in the cities; he laid up in every city the food of the fields which surrounded them. [49]Joseph gathered very much grain, as the sand of the sea, until he stopped counting, for *it was* immeasurable.

[50]And to Joseph were born two sons before the years of famine came, whom Asenath, the daughter of Poti-Pherah priest of On, bore to him. [51]Joseph called the name of the firstborn Manasseh:[a] "For God has made me forget all my toil and all my father's house." [52]And the name of the second he called Ephraim:[a] "For God has caused me to be fruitful in the land of my affliction."

[53]Then the seven years of plenty which were in the land of Egypt ended, [54]and the seven years of famine began to come, as Joseph had said. The famine was in all lands, but in all the land of Egypt there was bread. [55]So when all the land of Egypt was famished, the people cried to Pharaoh for bread. Then Pharaoh said to all the Egyptians, "Go to Joseph; whatever he says to you, do." [56]The famine was over all the face of the earth, and Joseph opened all the storehouses[a] and sold to the Egyptians. And the famine became severe in the land of Egypt. [57]So all countries came to Joseph in Egypt to buy *grain,* because the famine was severe in all lands.

JOSEPH'S BROTHERS GO TO EGYPT

42 When Jacob saw that there was grain in Egypt, Jacob said to his sons, "Why do you look at one another?" [2]And he said, "Indeed I have heard that there is grain in Egypt; go down to that place and buy for us there, that we may live and not die."

[3]So Joseph's ten brothers went down to buy grain in Egypt. [4]But Jacob did not send Joseph's brother Benjamin with his brothers, for he said, "Lest some calamity befall him." [5]And the sons of Israel went to buy *grain* among those who journeyed, for the famine was in the land of Canaan.

[6]Now Joseph *was* governor over the land; and it was he who sold to all the people of the land. And Joseph's brothers came and bowed down before him with *their* faces to the earth. [7]Joseph saw his brothers and recognized them, but he acted as a stranger to them and spoke roughly to them.

Then he said to them, "Where do you come from?"

And they said, "From the land of Canaan to buy food."

[8]So Joseph recognized his brothers, but they did not recognize him. [9]Then Joseph remembered the dreams which he had dreamed about them, and said to them, "You *are* spies! You have come to see the nakedness of the land!"

[10]And they said to him, "No, my lord, but your servants have come to buy food. [11]We *are* all one man's sons; we *are* honest *men;* your servants are not spies."

[12]But he said to them, "No, but you have come to see the nakedness of the land."

[13]And they said, "Your servants *are* twelve brothers, the sons of one man in the land of Canaan; and in fact, the youngest *is* with our father today, and one *is* no more."

[14]But Joseph said to them, "It *is* as I spoke to you, saying, 'You *are* spies!' [15]In this *manner* you shall be tested: By the life of Pharaoh, you shall not leave this place unless your youngest brother comes here. [16]Send one of you, and let him bring your brother; and you shall be kept in prison, that your words may be tested to see whether *there is* any truth in you; or else, by the life of Pharaoh, surely you *are* spies!" [17]So he put them all together in prison three days.

[18]Then Joseph said to them the third day, "Do this and live, *for* I fear God: [19]If you *are* honest *men,* let one of your brothers be confined to your prison house; but you, go and carry grain for the famine of your houses. [20]And bring your youngest brother to me; so your words will be verified, and you shall not die."

And they did so. [21]Then they said to one another, "We *are* truly guilty concerning our brother, for we saw the anguish of his soul when he pleaded with us, and we would not hear; therefore this distress has come upon us."

[22]And Reuben answered them, saying, "Did I not speak to you, saying, 'Do not sin against the boy'; and you would not listen? Therefore behold, his blood is now required of us." [23]But they did not know that Joseph understood *them,* for he spoke to them through an interpreter. [24]And he

41:51 [a]Literally *Making Forgetful* **41:52** [a]Literally *Fruitfulness*
41:56 [a]Literally *all that was in them*

turned himself away from them and wept. Then he returned to them again, and talked with them. And he took Simeon from them and bound him before their eyes.

THE BROTHERS RETURN TO CANAAN

25Then Joseph gave a command to fill their sacks with grain, to restore every man's money to his sack, and to give them provisions for the journey. Thus he did for them. 26So they loaded their donkeys with the grain and departed from there. 27But as one *of them* opened his sack to give his donkey feed at the encampment, he saw his money; and there it was, in the mouth of his sack. 28So he said to his brothers, "My money has been restored, and there it is, in my sack!" Then their hearts failed *them* and they were afraid, saying to one another, "What *is* this *that* God has done to us?"

29Then they went to Jacob their father in the land of Canaan and told him all that had happened to them, saying: 30"The man *who is* lord of the land spoke roughly to us, and took us for spies of the country. 31But we said to him, 'We *are* honest *men;* we are not spies. 32We *are* twelve brothers, sons of our father; one *is* no *more,* and the youngest *is* with our father this day in the land of Canaan.' 33Then the man, the lord of the country, said to us, 'By this I will know that you *are* honest *men:* Leave one of your brothers *here* with me, take *food for* the famine of your households, and be gone. 34And bring your youngest brother to me; so I shall know that you *are* not spies, but *that* you *are* honest *men.* I will grant your brother to you, and you may trade in the land.'"

35Then it happened as they emptied their sacks, that surprisingly each man's bundle of money *was* in his sack; and when they and their father saw the bundles of money, they were afraid. 36And Jacob their father said to them, "You have bereaved me: Joseph is no *more,* Simeon is no *more,* and you want to take Benjamin. All these things are against me."

37Then Reuben spoke to his father, saying, "Kill my two sons if I do not bring him *back* to you; put him in my hands, and I will bring him back to you."

38But he said, "My son shall not go down with you, for his brother is dead, and he is left alone. If any calamity should befall him along the way in which you go, then you would bring down my gray hair with sorrow to the grave."

JOSEPH'S BROTHERS RETURN WITH BENJAMIN

43Now the famine *was* severe in the land. 2And it came to pass, when they had eaten up the grain which they had brought from Egypt, that their father said to them, "Go back, buy us a little food."

3But Judah spoke to him, saying, "The man solemnly warned us, saying, 'You shall not see my face unless your brother *is* with you.' 4If you send our brother with us, we will go down and buy you food. 5But if you will not send *him,* we will not go down; for the man said to us, 'You shall not see my face unless your brother *is* with you.'"

6And Israel said, "Why did you deal *so* wrongfully with me *as* to tell the man whether you had still *another* brother?"

7But they said, "The man asked us pointedly about ourselves and our family, saying, 'Is your father still alive? Have you *another* brother?' And we told him according to these words. Could we possibly have known that he would say, 'Bring your brother down'?"

8Then Judah said to Israel his father, "Send the lad with me, and we will arise and go, that we may live and not die, both we and you *and* also our little ones. 9I myself will be surety for him; from my hand you shall require him. If I do not bring him *back* to you and set him before you, then let me bear the blame forever. 10For if we had not lingered, surely by now we would have returned this second time."

11And their father Israel said to them, "If *it must be* so, then do this: Take some of the best fruits of the land in your vessels and carry down a present for the man—a little balm and a little honey, spices and myrrh, pistachio nuts and almonds. 12Take double money in your hand, and take back in your hand the money that was returned in the mouth of your sacks; perhaps it was an oversight. 13Take your brother also, and arise, go back to the man. 14And may God Almighty give you mercy before the man, that he may release your other brother and Benjamin. If I am bereaved, I am bereaved!"

15So the men took that present and Benjamin,

and they took double money in their hand, and arose and went down to Egypt; and they stood before Joseph. [16]When Joseph saw Benjamin with them, he said to the steward of his house, "Take *these* men to my home, and slaughter an animal and make ready; for *these* men will dine with me at noon." [17]Then the man did as Joseph ordered, and the man brought the men into Joseph's house.

[18]Now the men were afraid because they were brought into Joseph's house; and they said, "*It is* because of the money, which was returned in our sacks the first time, that we are brought in, so that he may make a case against us and seize us, to take us as slaves with our donkeys."

[19]When they drew near to the steward of Joseph's house, they talked with him at the door of the house, [20]and said, "O sir, we indeed came down the first time to buy food; [21]but it happened, when we came to the encampment, that we opened our sacks, and there, *each* man's money *was* in the mouth of his sack, our money in full weight; so we have brought it back in our hand. [22]And we have brought down other money in our hands to buy food. We do not know who put our money in our sacks."

[23]But he said, "Peace *be* with you, do not be afraid. Your God and the God of your father has given you treasure in your sacks; I had your money." Then he brought Simeon out to them.

[24]So the man brought the men into Joseph's house and gave *them* water, and they washed their feet; and he gave their donkeys feed. [25]Then they made the present ready for Joseph's coming at noon, for they heard that they would eat bread there.

[26]And when Joseph came home, they brought him the present which *was* in their hand into the house, and bowed down before him to the earth. [27]Then he asked them about *their* well-being, and said, "*Is* your father well, the old man of whom you spoke? *Is* he still alive?"

[28]And they answered, "Your servant our father *is* in good health; he *is* still alive." And they bowed their heads down and prostrated themselves.

[29]Then he lifted his eyes and saw his brother Benjamin, his mother's son, and said, "*Is* this your younger brother of whom you spoke to me?" And he said, "God be gracious to you, my son."

[30]Now his heart yearned for his brother; so Joseph made haste and sought *somewhere* to weep. And he went into *his* chamber and wept there. [31]Then he washed his face and came out; and he restrained himself, and said, "Serve the bread."

[32]So they set him a place by himself, and them by themselves, and the Egyptians who ate with him by themselves; because the Egyptians could not eat food with the Hebrews, for that *is* an abomination to the Egyptians. [33]And they sat before him, the firstborn according to his birthright and the youngest according to his youth; and the men looked in astonishment at one another. [34]Then he took servings to them from before him, but Benjamin's serving was five times as much as any of theirs. So they drank and were merry with him.

Joseph's Cup

44 And he commanded the steward of his house, saying, "Fill the men's sacks with food, as much as they can carry, and put each man's money in the mouth of his sack. [2]Also put my cup, the silver cup, in the mouth of the sack of the youngest, and his grain money." So he did according to the word that Joseph had spoken. [3]As soon as the morning dawned, the men were sent away, they and their donkeys. [4]When they had gone out of the city, *and* were not *yet* far off, Joseph said to his steward, "Get up, follow the men; and when you overtake them, say to them, 'Why have you repaid evil for good? [5]*Is* not this *the one* from which my lord drinks, and with which he indeed practices divination? You have done evil in so doing.' "

[6]So he overtook them, and he spoke to them these same words. [7]And they said to him, "Why does my lord say these words? Far be it from us that your servants should do such a thing. [8]Look, we brought back to you from the land of Canaan the money which we found in the mouth of our sacks. How then could we steal silver or gold from your lord's house? [9]With whomever of your servants it is found, let him die, and we also will be my lord's slaves."

[10]And he said, "Now also *let* it *be* according to your words; he with whom it is found shall be my slave, and you shall be blameless." [11]Then each man speedily let down his sack to the ground, and

each opened his sack. ¹²So he searched. He began with the oldest and left off with the youngest; and the cup was found in Benjamin's sack. ¹³Then they tore their clothes, and each man loaded his donkey and returned to the city.

¹⁴So Judah and his brothers came to Joseph's house, and he *was* still there; and they fell before him on the ground. ¹⁵And Joseph said to them, "What deed *is* this you have done? Did you not know that such a man as I can certainly practice divination?"

¹⁶Then Judah said, "What shall we say to my lord? What shall we speak? Or how shall we clear ourselves? God has found out the iniquity of your servants; here we are, my lord's slaves, both we and *he* also with whom the cup was found."

¹⁷But he said, "Far be it from me that I should do so; the man in whose hand the cup was found, he shall be my slave. And as for you, go up in peace to your father."

Judah Intercedes for Benjamin

¹⁸Then Judah came near to him and said: "O my lord, please let your servant speak a word in my lord's hearing, and do not let your anger burn against your servant; for you *are* even like Pharaoh. ¹⁹My lord asked his servants, saying, 'Have you a father or a brother?' ²⁰And we said to my lord, 'We have a father, an old man, and a child of *his* old age, *who is* young; his brother is dead, and he alone is left of his mother's children, and his father loves him.' ²¹Then you said to your servants, 'Bring him down to me, that I may set my eyes on him.' ²²And we said to my lord, 'The lad cannot leave his father, for *if* he should leave his father, *his father* would die.' ²³But you said to your servants, 'Unless your youngest brother comes down with you, you shall see my face no more.'

²⁴"So it was, when we went up to your servant my father, that we told him the words of my lord. ²⁵And our father said, 'Go back *and* buy us a little food.' ²⁶But we said, 'We cannot go down; if our youngest brother is with us, then we will go down; for we may not see the man's face unless our youngest brother *is* with us.' ²⁷Then your servant my father said to us, 'You know that my wife bore me two sons; ²⁸and the one went out from me, and I said, "Surely he is torn to pieces"; and I

have not seen him since. ²⁹But if you take this one also from me, and calamity befalls him, you shall bring down my gray hair with sorrow to the grave.'

³⁰"Now therefore, when I come to your servant my father, and the lad *is* not with us, since his life is bound up in the lad's life, ³¹it will happen, when he sees that the lad *is* not *with us,* that he will die. So your servants will bring down the gray hair of your servant our father with sorrow to the grave. ³²For your servant became surety for the lad to my father, saying, 'If I do not bring him *back* to you, then I shall bear the blame before my father forever.' ³³Now therefore, please let your servant remain instead of the lad as a slave to my lord, and let the lad go up with his brothers. ³⁴For how shall I go up to my father if the lad *is* not with me, lest perhaps I see the evil that would come upon my father?"

Joseph Revealed to His Brothers

45 Then Joseph could not restrain himself before all those who stood by him, and he cried out, "Make everyone go out from me!" So no one stood with him while Joseph made himself known to his brothers. ²And he wept aloud, and the Egyptians and the house of Pharaoh heard *it.*

³Then Joseph said to his brothers, "I *am* Joseph; does my father still live?" But his brothers could not answer him, for they were dismayed in his presence. ⁴And Joseph said to his brothers, "Please come near to me." So they came near. Then he said: "I *am* Joseph your brother, whom you sold into Egypt. ⁵But now, do not therefore be grieved or angry with yourselves because you sold me here; for God sent me before you to preserve life. ⁶For these two years the famine *has been* in the land, and *there are* still five years in which *there will be* neither plowing nor harvesting. ⁷And God sent me before you to preserve a posterity for you in the earth, and to save your lives by a great deliverance. ⁸So now *it was* not you *who* sent me here, but God; and He has made me a father to Pharaoh, and lord of all his house, and a ruler throughout all the land of Egypt.

⁹"Hurry and go up to my father, and say to him, 'Thus says your son Joseph: "God has made me lord of all Egypt; come down to me, do not

tarry. [10]You shall dwell in the land of Goshen, and you shall be near to me, you and your children, your children's children, your flocks and your herds, and all that you have. [11]There I will provide for you, lest you and your household, and all that you have, come to poverty; for *there are* still five years of famine." '

[12]"And behold, your eyes and the eyes of my brother Benjamin see that *it is* my mouth that speaks to you. [13]So you shall tell my father of all my glory in Egypt, and of all that you have seen; and you shall hurry and bring my father down here."

[14]Then he fell on his brother Benjamin's neck and wept, and Benjamin wept on his neck. [15]Moreover he kissed all his brothers and wept over them, and after that his brothers talked with him.

[16]Now the report of it was heard in Pharaoh's house, saying, "Joseph's brothers have come." So it pleased Pharaoh and his servants well. [17]And Pharaoh said to Joseph, "Say to your brothers, 'Do this: Load your animals and depart; go to the land of Canaan. [18]Bring your father and your households and come to me; I will give you the best of the land of Egypt, and you will eat the fat of the land. [19]Now you are commanded—do this: Take carts out of the land of Egypt for your little ones and your wives; bring your father and come. [20]Also do not be concerned about your goods, for the best of all the land of Egypt *is* yours.' "

[21]Then the sons of Israel did so; and Joseph gave them carts, according to the command of Pharaoh, and he gave them provisions for the journey. [22]He gave to all of them, to each man, changes of garments; but to Benjamin he gave three hundred *pieces* of silver and five changes of garments. [23]And he sent to his father these *things:* ten donkeys loaded with the good things of Egypt, and ten female donkeys loaded with grain, bread, and food for his father for the journey. [24]So he sent his brothers away, and they departed; and he said to them, "See that you do not become troubled along the way."

[25]Then they went up out of Egypt, and came to the land of Canaan to Jacob their father. [26]And they told him, saying, "Joseph *is* still alive, and he *is* governor over all the land of Egypt." And Jacob's heart stood still, because he did not believe

them. [27]But when they told him all the words which Joseph had said to them, and when he saw the carts which Joseph had sent to carry him, the spirit of Jacob their father revived. [28]Then Israel said, "*It is* enough. Joseph my son *is* still alive. I will go and see him before I die."

JACOB'S JOURNEY TO EGYPT

46 So Israel took his journey with all that he had, and came to Beersheba, and offered sacrifices to the God of his father Isaac. [2]Then God spoke to Israel in the visions of the night, and said, "Jacob, Jacob!"

And he said, "Here I am."

[3]So He said, "I *am* God, the God of your father; do not fear to go down to Egypt, for I will make of you a great nation there. [4]I will go down with you to Egypt, and I will also surely bring you up *again;* and Joseph will put his hand on your eyes."

[5]Then Jacob arose from Beersheba; and the sons of Israel carried their father Jacob, their little ones, and their wives, in the carts which Pharaoh had sent to carry him. [6]So they took their livestock and their goods, which they had acquired in the land of Canaan, and went to Egypt, Jacob and all his descendants with him. [7]His sons and his sons' sons, his daughters and his sons' daughters, and all his descendants he brought with him to Egypt.

[8]Now these *were* the names of the children of Israel, Jacob and his sons, who went to Egypt: Reuben *was* Jacob's firstborn. [9]The sons of Reuben *were* Hanoch, Pallu, Hezron, and Carmi. [10]The sons of Simeon *were* Jemuel,[a] Jamin, Ohad, Jachin,[b] Zohar,[c] and Shaul, the son of a Canaanite woman. [11]The sons of Levi *were* Gershon, Kohath, and Merari. [12]The sons of Judah *were* Er, Onan, Shelah, Perez, and Zerah (but Er and Onan died in the land of Canaan). The sons of Perez were Hezron and Hamul. [13]The sons of Issachar *were* Tola, Puvah,[a] Job,[b] and Shimron. [14]The sons of Zebulun *were* Sered, Elon, and Jahleel. [15]These *were* the sons of Leah, whom she bore to Jacob in Padan Aram, with his daughter Dinah. All the

46:10 [a]Spelled *Nemuel* in 1 Chronicles 4:24 [b]Called *Jarib* in 1 Chronicles 4:24 [c]Called *Zerah* in 1 Chronicles 4:24 **46:13** [a]Spelled *Puah* in 1 Chronicles 7:1 [b]Same as *Jashub* in Numbers 26:24 and 1 Chronicles 7:1

persons, his sons and his daughters, *were* thirty-three.

[16]The sons of Gad *were* Ziphion,[a] Haggi, Shuni, Ezbon,[b] Eri, Arodi,[c] and Areli. [17]The sons of Asher *were* Jimnah, Ishuah, Isui, Beriah, and Serah, their sister. And the sons of Beriah *were* Heber and Malchiel. [18]These *were* the sons of Zilpah, whom Laban gave to Leah his daughter; and these she bore to Jacob: sixteen persons.

[19]The sons of Rachel, Jacob's wife, *were* Joseph and Benjamin. [20]And to Joseph in the land of Egypt were born Manasseh and Ephraim, whom Asenath, the daughter of Poti-Pherah priest of On, bore to him. [21]The sons of Benjamin *were* Belah, Becher, Ashbel, Gera, Naaman, Ehi, Rosh, Muppim, Huppim,[a] and Ard. [22]These *were* the sons of Rachel, who were born to Jacob: fourteen persons in all.

[23]The son of Dan *was* Hushim.[a] [24]The sons of Naphtali *were* Jahzeel,[a] Guni, Jezer, and Shillem.[b] [25]These *were* the sons of Bilhah, whom Laban gave to Rachel his daughter, and she bore these to Jacob: seven persons in all.

[26]All the persons who went with Jacob to Egypt, who came from his body, besides Jacob's sons' wives, *were* sixty-six persons in all. [27]And the sons of Joseph who were born to him in Egypt *were* two persons. All the persons of the house of Jacob who went to Egypt were seventy.

JACOB SETTLES IN GOSHEN

[28]Then he sent Judah before him to Joseph, to point out before him *the way* to Goshen. And they came to the land of Goshen. [29]So Joseph made ready his chariot and went up to Goshen to meet his father Israel; and he presented himself to him, and fell on his neck and wept on his neck a good while.

[30]And Israel said to Joseph, "Now let me die, since I have seen your face, because you *are* still alive."

[31]Then Joseph said to his brothers and to his father's household, "I will go up and tell Pharaoh, and say to him, 'My brothers and those of my father's house, who *were* in the land of Canaan, have come to me. [32]And the men *are* shepherds, for their occupation has been to feed livestock; and they have brought their flocks, their herds, and all that they have.' [33]So it shall be, when Pharaoh calls

you and says, 'What is your occupation?' [34]that you shall say, 'Your servants' occupation has been with livestock from our youth even till now, both we *and* also our fathers,' that you may dwell in the land of Goshen; for every shepherd *is* an abomination to the Egyptians."

47 Then Joseph went and told Pharaoh, and said, "My father and my brothers, their flocks and their herds and all that they possess, have come from the land of Canaan; and indeed they *are* in the land of Goshen." [2]And he took five men from among his brothers and presented them to Pharaoh. [3]Then Pharaoh said to his brothers, "What *is* your occupation?"

And they said to Pharaoh, "Your servants *are* shepherds, both we *and* also our fathers." [4]And they said to Pharaoh, "We have come to dwell in the land, because your servants have no pasture for their flocks, for the famine *is* severe in the land of Canaan. Now therefore, please let your servants dwell in the land of Goshen."

[5]Then Pharaoh spoke to Joseph, saying, "Your father and your brothers have come to you. [6]The land of Egypt *is* before you. Have your father and brothers dwell in the best of the land; let them dwell in the land of Goshen. And if you know *any* competent men among them, then make them chief herdsmen over my livestock."

[7]Then Joseph brought in his father Jacob and set him before Pharaoh; and Jacob blessed Pharaoh. [8]Pharaoh said to Jacob, "How old *are* you?"

[9]And Jacob said to Pharaoh, "The days of the years of my pilgrimage *are* one hundred and thirty years; few and evil have been the days of the years of my life, and they have not attained to the days of the years of the life of my fathers in the days of their pilgrimage." [10]So Jacob blessed Pharaoh, and went out from before Pharaoh.

[11]And Joseph situated his father and his brothers, and gave them a possession in the land of Egypt, in the best of the land, in the land of Rameses, as Pharaoh had commanded. [12]Then

---

46:16 [a]Spelled *Zephon* in Samaritan Pentateuch, Septuagint, and Numbers 26:15 [b]Called *Ozni* in Numbers 26:16 [c]Spelled *Arod* in Numbers 26:17 **46:21** [a]Called *Hupham* in Numbers 26:39 **46:23** [a]Called *Shuham* in Numbers 26:42 **46:24** [a]Spelled *Jahziel* in 1 Chronicles 7:13 [b]Spelled *Shallum* in 1 Chronicles 7:13

Joseph provided his father, his brothers, and all his father's household with bread, according to the number in *their* families.

JOSEPH DEALS WITH THE FAMINE

[13]Now *there was* no bread in all the land; for the famine *was* very severe, so that the land of Egypt and the land of Canaan languished because of the famine. [14]And Joseph gathered up all the money that was found in the land of Egypt and in the land of Canaan, for the grain which they bought; and Joseph brought the money into Pharaoh's house.

[15]So when the money failed in the land of Egypt and in the land of Canaan, all the Egyptians came to Joseph and said, "Give us bread, for why should we die in your presence? For the money has failed."

[16]Then Joseph said, "Give your livestock, and I will give you *bread* for your livestock, if the money is gone." [17]So they brought their livestock to Joseph, and Joseph gave them bread *in exchange* for the horses, the flocks, the cattle of the herds, and for the donkeys. Thus he fed them with bread *in exchange* for all their livestock that year.

[18]When that year had ended, they came to him the next year and said to him, "We will not hide from my lord that our money is gone; my lord also has our herds of livestock. There is nothing left in the sight of my lord but our bodies and our lands. [19]Why should we die before your eyes, both we and our land? Buy us and our land for bread, and we and our land will be servants of Pharaoh; give *us* seed, that we may live and not die, that the land may not be desolate."

[20]Then Joseph bought all the land of Egypt for Pharaoh; for every man of the Egyptians sold his field, because the famine was severe upon them. So the land became Pharaoh's. [21]And as for the people, he moved them into the cities,[a] from *one* end of the borders of Egypt to the *other* end. [22]Only the land of the priests he did not buy; for the priests had rations *allotted to them* by Pharaoh, and they ate their rations which Pharaoh gave them; therefore they did not sell their lands.

[23]Then Joseph said to the people, "Indeed I have bought you and your land this day for Pharaoh. Look, *here is* seed for you, and you shall sow the land. [24]And it shall come to pass in the

harvest that you shall give one-fifth to Pharaoh. Four-fifths shall be your own, as seed for the field and for your food, for those of your households and as food for your little ones."

[25]So they said, "You have saved our lives; let us find favor in the sight of my lord, and we will be Pharaoh's servants." [26]And Joseph made it a law over the land of Egypt to this day, *that* Pharaoh should have one-fifth, except for the land of the priests only, *which* did not become Pharaoh's.

JOSEPH'S VOW TO JACOB

[27]So Israel dwelt in the land of Egypt, in the country of Goshen; and they had possessions there and grew and multiplied exceedingly. [28]And Jacob lived in the land of Egypt seventeen years. So the length of Jacob's life was one hundred and forty-seven years. [29]When the time drew near that Israel must die, he called his son Joseph and said to him, "Now if I have found favor in your sight, please put your hand under my thigh, and deal kindly and truly with me. Please do not bury me in Egypt, [30]but let me lie with my fathers; you shall carry me out of Egypt and bury me in their burial place."

And he said, "I will do as you have said."

[31]Then he said, "Swear to me." And he swore to him. So Israel bowed himself on the head of the bed.

JACOB BLESSES JOSEPH'S SONS

48 Now it came to pass after these things that Joseph was told, "Indeed your father *is* sick"; and he took with him his two sons, Manasseh and Ephraim. [2]And Jacob was told, "Look, your son Joseph is coming to you"; and Israel strengthened himself and sat up on the bed. [3]Then Jacob said to Joseph: "God Almighty appeared to me at Luz in the land of Canaan and blessed me, [4]and said to me, 'Behold, I will make you fruitful and multiply you, and I will make of you a multitude of people, and give this land to your descendants after you *as* an everlasting possession.' [5]And now your two sons, Ephraim and Manasseh, who were born to you in the land of Egypt before I came to you in Egypt, *are* mine; as Reuben and Simeon, they shall be mine. [6]Your

47:21 [a]Following Masoretic Text and Targum; Samaritan Pentateuch, Septuagint, and Vulgate read *made the people virtual slaves.*

offspring whom you beget after them shall be yours; they will be called by the name of their brothers in their inheritance. ⁷But as for me, when I came from Padan, Rachel died beside me in the land of Canaan on the way, when *there was* but a little distance to go to Ephrath; and I buried her there on the way to Ephrath (that is, Bethlehem)."

⁸Then Israel saw Joseph's sons, and said, "Who *are* these?"

⁹Joseph said to his father, "They *are* my sons, whom God has given me in this *place.*"

And he said, "Please bring them to me, and I will bless them." ¹⁰Now the eyes of Israel were dim with age, *so that* he could not see. Then Joseph brought them near him, and he kissed them and embraced them. ¹¹And Israel said to Joseph, "I had not thought to see your face; but in fact, God has also shown me your offspring!"

¹²So Joseph brought them from beside his knees, and he bowed down with his face to the earth. ¹³And Joseph took them both, Ephraim with his right hand toward Israel's left hand, and Manasseh with his left hand toward Israel's right hand, and brought *them* near him. ¹⁴Then Israel stretched out his right hand and laid *it* on Ephraim's head, who *was* the younger, and his left hand on Manasseh's head, guiding his hands knowingly, for Manasseh *was* the firstborn. ¹⁵And he blessed Joseph, and said:

"God, before whom my fathers Abraham and Isaac walked,
The God who has fed me all my life long to this day,
¹⁶The Angel who has redeemed me from all evil,
Bless the lads;
Let my name be named upon them,
And the name of my fathers Abraham and Isaac;
And let them grow into a multitude in the midst of the earth."

¹⁷Now when Joseph saw that his father laid his right hand on the head of Ephraim, it displeased him; so he took hold of his father's hand to remove it from Ephraim's head to Manasseh's head. ¹⁸And Joseph said to his father, "Not so, my father, for this *one is* the firstborn; put your right hand on his head."

¹⁹But his father refused and said, "I know, my son, I know. He also shall become a people, and he also shall be great; but truly his younger brother shall be greater than he, and his descendants shall become a multitude of nations."

²⁰So he blessed them that day, saying, "By you Israel will bless, saying, 'May God make you as Ephraim and as Manasseh!' " And thus he set Ephraim before Manasseh.

²¹Then Israel said to Joseph, "Behold, I am dying, but God will be with you and bring you back to the land of your fathers. ²²Moreover I have given to you one portion above your brothers, which I took from the hand of the Amorite with my sword and my bow."

JACOB'S LAST WORDS TO HIS SONS

49 And Jacob called his sons and said, "Gather together, that I may tell you what shall befall you in the last days:

²"Gather together and hear, you sons of Jacob,
And listen to Israel your father.

³"Reuben, you are my firstborn,
My might and the beginning of my strength,
The excellency of dignity and the excellency of power.
⁴Unstable as water, you shall not excel,
Because you went up to your father's bed;
Then you defiled *it*—
He went up to my couch.

⁵"Simeon and Levi *are* brothers;
Instruments of cruelty *are in* their dwelling place.
⁶Let not my soul enter their council;
Let not my honor be united to their assembly;
For in their anger they slew a man,
And in their self-will they hamstrung an ox.
⁷Cursed *be* their anger, for *it is* fierce;
And their wrath, for it is cruel!
I will divide them in Jacob
And scatter them in Israel.

⁸"Judah, you *are he* whom your brothers shall praise;

Your hand *shall be* on the neck of your
    enemies;
Your father's children shall bow down before
    you.
⁹Judah *is* a lion's whelp;
From the prey, my son, you have gone up.
He bows down, he lies down as a lion;
And as a lion, who shall rouse him?
¹⁰The scepter shall not depart from Judah,
Nor a lawgiver from between his feet,
Until Shiloh comes;
And to Him *shall be* the obedience of the
    people.
¹¹Binding his donkey to the vine,
And his donkey's colt to the choice vine,
He washed his garments in wine,
And his clothes in the blood of grapes.
¹²His eyes *are* darker than wine,
And his teeth whiter than milk.

¹³"Zebulun shall dwell by the haven of the sea;
He *shall become* a haven for ships,
And his border shall adjoin Sidon.

¹⁴"Issachar is a strong donkey,
Lying down between two burdens;
¹⁵He saw that rest *was* good,
And that the land *was* pleasant;
He bowed his shoulder to bear *a burden,*
And became a band of slaves.

¹⁶"Dan shall judge his people
As one of the tribes of Israel.
¹⁷Dan shall be a serpent by the way,
A viper by the path,
That bites the horse's heels
So that its rider shall fall backward.
¹⁸I have waited for your salvation, O LORD!

¹⁹"Gad, a troop shall tramp upon him,
But he shall triumph at last.

²⁰"Bread from Asher *shall be* rich,
And he shall yield royal dainties.

²¹"Naphtali *is* a deer let loose;
He uses beautiful words.

²²"Joseph *is* a fruitful bough,
A fruitful bough by a well;

His branches run over the wall.
²³The archers have bitterly grieved him,
Shot *at him* and hated him.
²⁴But his bow remained in strength,
And the arms of his hands were made
    strong
By the hands of the Mighty *God* of Jacob
(From there *is* the Shepherd, the Stone of
    Israel),
²⁵By the God of your father who will help you,
And by the Almighty who will bless you
With blessings of heaven above,
Blessings of the deep that lies beneath,
Blessings of the breasts and of the womb.
²⁶The blessings of your father
Have excelled the blessings of my ancestors,
Up to the utmost bound of the everlasting
    hills.
They shall be on the head of Joseph,
And on the crown of the head of him who
    was separate from his brothers.

²⁷"Benjamin is a ravenous wolf;
In the morning he shall devour the prey,
And at night he shall divide the spoil."

²⁸All these *are* the twelve tribes of Israel, and
this *is* what their father spoke to them. And he
blessed them; he blessed each one according to his
own blessing.

JACOB'S DEATH AND BURIAL

²⁹Then he charged them and said to them: "I
am to be gathered to my people; bury me with
my fathers in the cave that *is* in the field of
Ephron the Hittite, ³⁰in the cave that *is* in the
field of Machpelah, which *is* before Mamre in the
land of Canaan, which Abraham bought with the
field of Ephron the Hittite as a possession for a
burial place. ³¹There they buried Abraham and
Sarah his wife, there they buried Isaac and Rebekah his wife, and there I buried Leah. ³²The
field and the cave that *is* there *were* purchased
from the sons of Heth." ³³And when Jacob had
finished commanding his sons, he drew his feet
up into the bed and breathed his last, and was
gathered to his people.

50 Then Joseph fell on his father's face and
wept over him, and kissed him. ²And

Joseph commanded his servants the physicians to embalm his father. So the physicians embalmed Israel. [3]Forty days were required for him, for such are the days required for those who are embalmed; and the Egyptians mourned for him seventy days.

[4]Now when the days of his mourning were past, Joseph spoke to the household of Pharaoh, saying, "If now I have found favor in your eyes, please speak in the hearing of Pharaoh, saying, [5]'My father made me swear, saying, "Behold, I am dying; in my grave which I dug for myself in the land of Canaan, there you shall bury me." Now therefore, please let me go up and bury my father, and I will come back.' "

[6]And Pharaoh said, "Go up and bury your father, as he made you swear."

[7]So Joseph went up to bury his father; and with him went up all the servants of Pharaoh, the elders of his house, and all the elders of the land of Egypt, [8]as well as all the house of Joseph, his brothers, and his father's house. Only their little ones, their flocks, and their herds they left in the land of Goshen. [9]And there went up with him both chariots and horsemen, and it was a very great gathering.

[10]Then they came to the threshing floor of Atad, which *is* beyond the Jordan, and they mourned there with a great and very solemn lamentation. He observed seven days of mourning for his father. [11]And when the inhabitants of the land, the Canaanites, saw the mourning at the threshing floor of Atad, they said, "This *is* a deep mourning of the Egyptians." Therefore its name was called Abel Mizraim,[a] which *is* beyond the Jordan.

[12]So his sons did for him just as he had commanded them. [13]For his sons carried him to the land of Canaan, and buried him in the cave of the field of Machpelah, before Mamre, which Abraham bought with the field from Ephron the Hittite as property for a burial place. [14]And after he had buried his father, Joseph returned to Egypt, he and his brothers and all who went up with him to bury his father.

JOSEPH REASSURES HIS BROTHERS

[15]When Joseph's brothers saw that their father was dead, they said, "Perhaps Joseph will hate us, and may actually repay us for all the evil which we did to him." [16]So they sent *messengers* to Joseph, saying, "Before your father died he commanded, saying, [17]'Thus you shall say to Joseph: "I beg you, please forgive the trespass of your brothers and their sin; for they did evil to you." ' Now, please, forgive the trespass of the servants of the God of your father." And Joseph wept when they spoke to him.

[18]Then his brothers also went and fell down before his face, and they said, "Behold, we *are* your servants."

[19]Joseph said to them, "Do not be afraid, for *am* I in the place of God? [20]But as for you, you meant evil against me; *but* God meant it for good, in order to bring it about as *it is* this day, to save many people alive. [21]Now therefore, do not be afraid; I will provide for you and your little ones." And he comforted them and spoke kindly to them.

DEATH OF JOSEPH

[22]So Joseph dwelt in Egypt, he and his father's household. And Joseph lived one hundred and ten years. [23]Joseph saw Ephraim's children to the third *generation.* The children of Machir, the son of Manasseh, were also brought up on Joseph's knees.

[24]And Joseph said to his brethren, "I am dying; but God will surely visit you, and bring you out of this land to the land of which He swore to Abraham, to Isaac, and to Jacob." [25]Then Joseph took an oath from the children of Israel, saying, "God will surely visit you, and you shall carry up my bones from here." [26]So Joseph died, *being* one hundred and ten years old; and they embalmed him, and he was put in a coffin in Egypt.

50:11 [a]Literally *Mourning of Egypt*

IDEA
God provides salvation or redemption for His covenant people. Humankind is unfaithful, but we see the faithfulness of God when He redeems His people for His name's sake, entering into a covenant relationship with them.

MESSAGE
There is no such thing as standing still. You are either moving forward or you are going backward. Some of the greatest moments of victory in a walk with the Lord are realized when you stop focusing on your own strengths and weaknesses and focus on God and His strength. God uses the weak, ordinary things of this world to do extraordinary things.

PEOPLE
Aaron, Jethro, Jochebed, Joshua, Miriam, Moses, Pharaoh

AUTHOR
Like Genesis, Exodus is anonymous. However, known as "the second Book of Moses," it is safe to accept Mosaic authorship. In Jewish tradition, the entire Pentateuch is called "Moses' teaching." Exodus gives great insight into Moses' life, his struggles and weaknesses, and the great things God was able to accomplish through him.

CULTURE
Egypt was the mightiest nation on earth. It was called the gift of the Nile, because the Nile nourished this desert land. The great conflict between the gods of Egypt and Yahweh Himself illustrate the religions and the times. The ten plagues were signs to Israel to assure them of His power and care. They were plagues of judgment to punish Egypt for persecuting Israel. One by one, God pushed the man-made deities off their pedestals. The two most classic being: when the Nile, which was worshipped as a god, was turned to blood, and when Ra, the sun god—who was supreme of all—was powerless when darkness covered the land.

TIMELINE
between 1445 and 1405 BC

**KEY SCRIPTURE
MEMORY VERSES**
3:14; 19:5, 6; 20:1–17

ISRAEL'S SUFFERING IN EGYPT

1 Now these *are* the names of the children of Israel who came to Egypt; each man and his household came with Jacob: ²Reuben, Simeon, Levi, and Judah; ³Issachar, Zebulun, and Benjamin; ⁴Dan, Naphtali, Gad, and Asher. ⁵All those who were descendants[a] of Jacob were seventy[b] persons (for Joseph was in Egypt *already*). ⁶And Joseph died, all his brothers, and all that generation. ⁷But the children of Israel were fruitful and increased abundantly, multiplied and grew exceedingly mighty; and the land was filled with them.

⁸Now there arose a new king over Egypt, who did not know Joseph. ⁹And he said to his people, "Look, the people of the children of Israel *are* more and mightier than we; ¹⁰come, let us deal shrewdly with them, lest they multiply, and it happen, in the event of war, that they also join our enemies and fight against us, and *so* go up out of the land." ¹¹Therefore they set taskmasters over them to afflict them with their burdens. And they built for Pharaoh supply cities, Pithom and Raamses. ¹²But the more they afflicted them, the more they multiplied and grew. And they were in dread of the children of Israel. ¹³So the Egyptians made the children of Israel serve with rigor. ¹⁴And they made their lives bitter with hard bondage—in mortar, in brick, and in all manner of service in the field. All their service in which they made them serve *was* with rigor.

¹⁵Then the king of Egypt spoke to the Hebrew midwives, of whom the name of one *was* Shiphrah and the name of the other Puah; ¹⁶and he said, "When you do the duties of a midwife for the Hebrew women, and see *them* on the birthstools, if it *is* a son, then you shall kill him; but if it *is* a daughter, then she shall live." ¹⁷But the midwives feared God, and did not do as the king of Egypt commanded them, but saved the male children alive. ¹⁸So the king of Egypt called for the midwives and said to them, "Why have you done this thing, and saved the male children alive?"

¹⁹And the midwives said to Pharaoh, "Because the Hebrew women *are* not like the Egyptian women; for they *are* lively and give birth before the midwives come to them."

²⁰Therefore God dealt well with the midwives, and the people multiplied and grew very mighty. ²¹And so it was, because the midwives feared God, that He provided households for them. ²²So Pharaoh commanded all his people, saying, "Every son who is born[a] you shall cast into the river, and every daughter you shall save alive."

MOSES IS BORN

2 And a man of the house of Levi went and took *as wife* a daughter of Levi. ²So the woman conceived and bore a son. And when she saw that he *was* a beautiful *child,* she hid him three months. ³But when she could no longer hide him, she took an ark of bulrushes for him, daubed it with asphalt and pitch, put the child in it, and laid *it* in the reeds by the river's bank. ⁴And his sister stood afar off, to know what would be done to him.

⁵Then the daughter of Pharaoh came down to bathe at the river. And her maidens walked along the riverside; and when she saw the ark among the reeds, she sent her maid to get it. ⁶And when she opened *it,* she saw the child, and behold, the baby wept. So she had compassion on him, and said, "This is one of the Hebrews' children."

⁷Then his sister said to Pharaoh's daughter, "Shall I go and call a nurse for you from the Hebrew women, that she may nurse the child for you?"

⁸And Pharaoh's daughter said to her, "Go." So the maiden went and called the child's mother. ⁹Then Pharaoh's daughter said to her, "Take this child away and nurse him for me, and I will give *you* your wages." So the woman took the child and nursed him. ¹⁰And the child grew, and she brought him to Pharaoh's daughter, and he became her son. So she called his name Moses,[a] saying, "Because I drew him out of the water."

MOSES FLEES TO MIDIAN

¹¹Now it came to pass in those days, when Moses was grown, that he went out to his brethren and looked at their burdens. And he saw an Egyptian beating a Hebrew, one of his brethren. ¹²So he looked this way and that way, and when he saw no one, he killed the Egyptian and hid him in the sand. ¹³And when he went out

1:5 a Literally *who came from the loins of* b Dead Sea Scrolls and Septuagint read *seventy-five* (compare Acts 7:14).   **1:22** a Samaritan Pentateuch, Septuagint, and Targum add *to the Hebrews.*   **2:10** a Literally *Drawn Out*

INSIDE *the* INFLUENCERS

MOSES: A Life Interrupted

EXODUS 1—3

The first three chapters of Exodus are a whirlwind adventure. Chapter one paints a picture of a paranoid Pharaoh, threatened by the Jewish people. He responded with oppression and forced labor, a command to kill all newborn males, and a ruthless totalitarian rule.

Moses was born in this context (2:1, 2), and his mother hid him to spare his life. When she could hide him no longer, she had her daughter place the baby in a tar covered, reed basket in the river. Pharaoh's daughter discovered the baby and brought him home. We know little of his childhood, except that Moses was nursed by his real mother, and the king's daughter adopted him as her own. Next, we see Moses as a man fleeing to Midian (2:11–15). Here he joined Jethro, the priest of Midian, married Jethro's daughter Zipporah, and had a son named Gershom (2:15–22).

Moses seemed happy as a desert shepherd. He traded the life of a prince for one of a refugee, and the issue was settled. However, at the age of eighty, God called to Moses from a burning bush on the back side of the desert (ch. 3). Egypt, a distant memory from his past, was about to move Moses to center stage. He would no longer lead sheep; instead, he would lead the nation of Israel out of captivity. We may never understand *how* God accomplishes His will, but He allows us to participate; and He *always* gets the job done.

the second day, behold, two Hebrew men were fighting, and he said to the one who did the wrong, "Why are you striking your companion?"

¹⁴Then he said, "Who made you a prince and a judge over us? Do you intend to kill me as you killed the Egyptian?"

So Moses feared and said, "Surely this thing is known!" ¹⁵When Pharaoh heard of this matter, he sought to kill Moses. But Moses fled from the face of Pharaoh and dwelt in the land of Midian; and he sat down by a well.

¹⁶Now the priest of Midian had seven daughters. And they came and drew water, and they filled the troughs to water their father's flock. ¹⁷Then the shepherds came and drove them away; but Moses stood up and helped them, and watered their flock.

¹⁸When they came to Reuel their father, he said, "How *is it that* you have come so soon today?"

¹⁹And they said, "An Egyptian delivered us from the hand of the shepherds, and he also drew enough water for us and watered the flock."

²⁰So he said to his daughters, "And where *is* he? Why *is it that* you have left the man? Call him, that he may eat bread."

²¹Then Moses was content to live with the man, and he gave Zipporah his daughter to Moses. ²²And she bore *him* a son. He called his name Gershom,ᵃ for he said, "I have been a stranger in a foreign land."

²³Now it happened in the process of time that the king of Egypt died. Then the children of Israel groaned because of the bondage, and they cried out; and their cry came up to God because of the bondage. ²⁴So God heard their groaning, and God remembered His covenant with Abraham, with Isaac, and with Jacob. ²⁵And God looked upon the children of Israel, and God acknowledged *them*.

MOSES AT THE BURNING BUSH

3 Now Moses was tending the flock of Jethro his father-in-law, the priest of Midian. And he led the flock to the back of the desert, and came to

2:22 ᵃLiterally *Stranger There*

LEADERSHIP ISSUES

GC2: He Calls Your Name

EXODUS 3:3

Imagine Moses tending Jethro's flock alongside Mount Horeb. As he performs the familiar routine, he catches a glimpse of a burning bush out of the corner of his eye. Moses' absentminded gaze is soon replaced by an intensifying curiosity and then perplexity as he realizes that the bush is not surrendering to the flames. As Moses draws closer to the fireproof bush, the Most High God suddenly thunders forth from within it: "Moses, Moses!" Humbly, he takes off his shoes to visit with God on holy ground (Ex. 3:4, 5).

What if the Creator is calling you, just as certainly as He called Moses? What if He has a clear divine purpose for your life just as He did for Moses? Can you feel your heart tremble with astonishment and swell with delight as you imagine the Creator is calling out *your* name? Now allow His Spirit to humble you at such a thought, just as God did with Moses.

He certainly has and is calling you, very personally just as He did Moses. Pause to allow such a truth to humble you. The same God who put His hand on Moses and Abraham, Deborah and Rahab has called *you* "out of darkness into His marvelous light" (1 Pet. 2:9).

Moses' encounter with God's glory at Mount Horeb transformed his life, his sense of purpose, his people, and human history. Encounters with Yahweh are like that. In such humbling encounters, we are never the same again!

GC2
GREAT COMMANDMENT
COMMISSION

Horeb, the mountain of God. ²And the Angel of the LORD appeared to him in a flame of fire from the midst of a bush. So he looked, and behold, the bush was burning with fire, but the bush *was* not consumed. ³Then Moses said, "I will now turn aside and see this great sight, why the bush does not burn."

⁴So when the LORD saw that he turned aside to look, God called to him from the midst of the bush and said, "Moses, Moses!"

And he said, "Here I am."

⁵Then He said, "Do not draw near this place. Take your sandals off your feet, for the place where you stand *is* holy ground." ⁶Moreover He said, "I *am* the God of your father—the God of Abraham, the God of Isaac, and the God of Jacob." And Moses hid his face, for he was afraid to look upon God.

⁷And the LORD said: "I have surely seen the oppression of My people who *are* in Egypt, and have heard their cry because of their taskmasters, for I know their sorrows. ⁸So I have come down to deliver them out of the hand of the Egyptians, and to bring them up from that land to a good and large land, to a land flowing with milk and honey, to the place of the Canaanites and the Hittites and the Amorites and the Perizzites and the Hivites and the Jebusites. ⁹Now therefore, behold, the cry of the children of Israel has come to Me, and I have also seen the oppression with which the Egyptians oppress them. ¹⁰Come now, therefore, and I will send you to Pharaoh that you may bring My people, the children of Israel, out of Egypt."

¹¹But Moses said to God, "Who *am* I that I should go to Pharaoh, and that I should bring the children of Israel out of Egypt?"

¹²So He said, "I will certainly be with you. And this *shall be* a sign to you that I have sent you: When you have brought the people out of Egypt, you shall serve God on this mountain."

¹³Then Moses said to God, "Indeed, *when* I come to the children of Israel and say to them, 'The God of your fathers has sent me to you,' and they say to me, 'What *is* His name?' what shall I say to them?"

¹⁴And God said to Moses, "I AM WHO I AM." And He said, "Thus you shall say to the children of Israel, 'I AM has sent me to you.' "

¹⁵Moreover God said to Moses, "Thus you shall say to the children of Israel: 'The LORD God of your fathers, the God of Abraham, the God of Isaac, and the God of Jacob, has sent me to you. This *is* My name forever, and this *is* My memorial to all generations.' ¹⁶Go and gather the elders of Israel together, and say to them, 'The LORD God of your fathers, the God of Abraham, of Isaac, and of Jacob, appeared to me, saying, "I have surely visited you and *seen* what is done to you in Egypt; ¹⁷and I have said I will bring you up out of the affliction of Egypt to the land of the Canaanites and the Hittites and the Amorites and the Perizzites and the Hivites and the Jebusites, to a land flowing with milk and honey." ' ¹⁸Then they will heed your voice; and you shall come, you and the elders of Israel, to the king of Egypt; and you shall say to him, 'The LORD God of the Hebrews has met with us; and now, please, let us go three days' journey into the wilderness, that we may sacrifice to the LORD our God.' ¹⁹But I am sure that the king of Egypt will not let you go, no, not even by a mighty hand. ²⁰So I will stretch out My hand and strike Egypt with all My wonders which I will do in its midst; and after that he will let you go. ²¹And I will give this people favor in the sight of the Egyptians; and it shall be, when you go, that you shall not go empty-handed. ²²But every woman shall ask of her neighbor, namely, of her who dwells near her house, articles of silver, articles of gold, and clothing; and you shall put *them* on your sons and on your daughters. So you shall plunder the Egyptians."

MIRACULOUS SIGNS FOR PHARAOH

4 Then Moses answered and said, "But suppose they will not believe me or listen to my voice; suppose they say, 'The LORD has not appeared to you.' "

²So the LORD said to him, "What *is* that in your hand?"

He said, "A rod."

³And He said, "Cast it on the ground." So he cast it on the ground, and it became a serpent; and Moses fled from it. ⁴Then the LORD said to Moses, "Reach out your hand and take *it* by the tail" (and he reached out his hand and caught it, and it became a rod in his hand), ⁵"that they may believe that the LORD God of their fathers, the

God of Abraham, the God of Isaac, and the God of Jacob, has appeared to you."

[6]Furthermore the LORD said to him, "Now put your hand in your bosom." And he put his hand in his bosom, and when he took it out, behold, his hand *was* leprous, like snow. [7]And He said, "Put your hand in your bosom again." So he put his hand in his bosom again, and drew it out of his bosom, and behold, it was restored like his *other* flesh. [8]"Then it will be, if they do not believe you, nor heed the message of the first sign, that they may believe the message of the latter sign. [9]And it shall be, if they do not believe even these two signs, or listen to your voice, that you shall take water from the river[a] and pour *it* on the dry *land*. The water which you take from the river will become blood on the dry *land*."

[10]Then Moses said to the LORD, "O my Lord, I *am* not eloquent, neither before nor since You have spoken to Your servant; but I *am* slow of speech and slow of tongue."

[11]So the LORD said to him, "Who has made man's mouth? Or who makes the mute, the deaf, the seeing, or the blind? *Have* not I, the LORD? [12]Now therefore, go, and I will be with your mouth and teach you what you shall say."

[13]But he said, "O my Lord, please send by the hand of whomever *else* You may send."

[14]So the anger of the LORD was kindled against Moses, and He said: "Is not Aaron the Levite your brother? I know that he can speak well. And look, he is also coming out to meet you. When he sees you, he will be glad in his heart. [15]Now you shall speak to him and put the words in his mouth. And I will be with your mouth and with his mouth, and I will teach you what you shall do. [16]So he shall be your spokesman to the people. And he himself shall be as a mouth for you, and you shall be to him as God. [17]And you shall take this rod in your hand, with which you shall do the signs."

Moses Goes to Egypt

[18]So Moses went and returned to Jethro his father-in-law, and said to him, "Please let me go and return to my brethren who *are* in Egypt, and see whether they are still alive."

And Jethro said to Moses, "Go in peace."

[19]Now the LORD said to Moses in Midian, "Go, return to Egypt; for all the men who sought your life are dead." [20]Then Moses took his wife and his sons and set them on a donkey, and he returned to the land of Egypt. And Moses took the rod of God in his hand.

[21]And the LORD said to Moses, "When you go back to Egypt, see that you do all those wonders before Pharaoh which I have put in your hand. But I will harden his heart, so that he will not let the people go. [22]Then you shall say to Pharaoh, 'Thus says the LORD: "Israel *is* My son, My firstborn. [23]So I say to you, let My son go that he may serve Me. But if you refuse to let him go, indeed I will kill your son, your firstborn." ' "

[24]And it came to pass on the way, at the encampment, that the LORD met him and sought to kill him. [25]Then Zipporah took a sharp stone and cut off the foreskin of her son and cast *it* at Moses'[a] feet, and said, "Surely you *are* a husband of blood to me!" [26]So He let him go. Then she said, "*You are* a husband of blood!"—because of the circumcision.

[27]And the LORD said to Aaron, "Go into the wilderness to meet Moses." So he went and met him on the mountain of God, and kissed him. [28]So Moses told Aaron all the words of the LORD who had sent him, and all the signs which He had commanded him. [29]Then Moses and Aaron went and gathered together all the elders of the children of Israel. [30]And Aaron spoke all the words which the LORD had spoken to Moses. Then he did the signs in the sight of the people. [31]So the people believed; and when they heard that the LORD had visited the children of Israel and that He had looked on their affliction, then they bowed their heads and worshiped.

First Encounter with Pharaoh

5 Afterward Moses and Aaron went in and told Pharaoh, "Thus says the LORD God of Israel: 'Let My people go, that they may hold a feast to Me in the wilderness.' "

[2]And Pharaoh said, "Who *is* the LORD, that I should obey His voice to let Israel go? I do not know the LORD, nor will I let Israel go."

4:9 [a]That is, the Nile   4:25 [a]Literally *his*

³So they said, "The God of the Hebrews has met with us. Please, let us go three days' journey into the desert and sacrifice to the LORD our God, lest He fall upon us with pestilence or with the sword."

⁴Then the king of Egypt said to them, "Moses and Aaron, why do you take the people from their work? Get *back* to your labor." ⁵And Pharaoh said, "Look, the people of the land *are* many now, and you make them rest from their labor!"

⁶So the same day Pharaoh commanded the taskmasters of the people and their officers, saying, ⁷"You shall no longer give the people straw to make brick as before. Let them go and gather straw for themselves. ⁸And you shall lay on them the quota of bricks which they made before. You shall not reduce it. For they are idle; therefore they cry out, saying, 'Let us go *and* sacrifice to our God.' ⁹Let more work be laid on the men, that they may labor in it, and let them not regard false words."

¹⁰And the taskmasters of the people and their officers went out and spoke to the people, saying, "Thus says Pharaoh: 'I will not give you straw. ¹¹Go, get yourselves straw where you can find it; yet none of your work will be reduced.' " ¹²So the people were scattered abroad throughout all the land of Egypt to gather stubble instead of straw. ¹³And the taskmasters forced *them* to hurry, saying, "Fulfill your work, *your* daily quota, as when there was straw." ¹⁴Also the officers of the children of Israel, whom Pharaoh's taskmasters had set over them, were beaten *and* were asked, "Why have you not fulfilled your task in making brick both yesterday and today, as before?"

¹⁵Then the officers of the children of Israel came and cried out to Pharaoh, saying, "Why are you dealing thus with your servants? ¹⁶There is no straw given to your servants, and they say to us, 'Make brick!' And indeed your servants *are* beaten, but the fault *is* in your *own* people."

¹⁷But he said, "You *are* idle! Idle! Therefore you say, 'Let us go *and* sacrifice to the LORD.' ¹⁸Therefore go now *and* work; for no straw shall be given you, yet you shall deliver the quota of bricks." ¹⁹And the officers of the children of Israel saw *that* they *were* in trouble after it was said, "You shall not reduce *any* bricks from your daily quota."

²⁰Then, as they came out from Pharaoh, they met Moses and Aaron who stood there to meet them. ²¹And they said to them, "Let the LORD look on you and judge, because you have made us abhorrent in the sight of Pharaoh and in the sight of his servants, to put a sword in their hand to kill us."

ISRAEL'S DELIVERANCE ASSURED

²²So Moses returned to the LORD and said, "Lord, why have You brought trouble on this people? Why *is* it You have sent me? ²³For since I came to Pharaoh to speak in Your name, he has done evil to this people; neither have You delivered Your people at all."

6 Then the LORD said to Moses, "Now you shall see what I will do to Pharaoh. For with a strong hand he will let them go, and with a strong hand he will drive them out of his land."

²And God spoke to Moses and said to him: "I *am* the LORD. ³I appeared to Abraham, to Isaac, and to Jacob, as God Almighty, but *by* My name LORDª I was not known to them. ⁴I have also established My covenant with them, to give them the land of Canaan, the land of their pilgrimage, in which they were strangers. ⁵And I have also heard the groaning of the children of Israel whom the Egyptians keep in bondage, and I have remembered My covenant. ⁶Therefore say to the children of Israel: 'I *am* the LORD; I will bring you out from under the burdens of the Egyptians, I will rescue you from their bondage, and I will redeem you with an outstretched arm and with great judgments. ⁷I will take you as My people, and I will be your God. Then you shall know that I *am* the LORD your God who brings you out from under the burdens of the Egyptians. ⁸And I will bring you into the land which I swore to give to Abraham, Isaac, and Jacob; and I will give it to you *as* a heritage: I *am* the LORD.' " ⁹So Moses spoke thus to the children of Israel; but they did not heed Moses, because of anguish of spirit and cruel bondage.

¹⁰And the LORD spoke to Moses, saying, ¹¹"Go in, tell Pharaoh king of Egypt to let the children of Israel go out of his land."

6:3 ªHebrew *YHWH,* traditionally *Jehovah*

[12]And Moses spoke before the LORD, saying, "The children of Israel have not heeded me. How then shall Pharaoh heed me, for I *am* of uncircumcised lips?"

[13]Then the LORD spoke to Moses and Aaron, and gave them a command for the children of Israel and for Pharaoh king of Egypt, to bring the children of Israel out of the land of Egypt.

THE FAMILY OF MOSES AND AARON

[14]These *are* the heads of their fathers' houses: The sons of Reuben, the firstborn of Israel, *were* Hanoch, Pallu, Hezron, and Carmi. These are the families of Reuben. [15]And the sons of Simeon *were* Jemuel,[a] Jamin, Ohad, Jachin, Zohar, and Shaul the son of a Canaanite woman. These *are* the families of Simeon. [16]These *are* the names of the sons of Levi according to their generations: Gershon, Kohath, and Merari. And the years of the life of Levi *were* one hundred and thirty-seven. [17]The sons of Gershon *were* Libni and Shimi according to their families. [18]And the sons of Kohath *were* Amram, Izhar, Hebron, and Uzziel. And the years of the life of Kohath *were* one hundred and thirty-three. [19]The sons of Merari *were* Mahli and Mushi. These *are* the families of Levi according to their generations.

[20]Now Amram took for himself Jochebed, his father's sister, as wife; and she bore him Aaron and Moses. And the years of the life of Amram *were* one hundred and thirty-seven. [21]The sons of Izhar *were* Korah, Nepheg, and Zichri. [22]And the sons of Uzziel *were* Mishael, Elzaphan, and Zithri. [23]Aaron took to himself Elisheba, daughter of Amminadab, sister of Nahshon, as wife; and she bore him Nadab, Abihu, Elemazar, and Ithamar. [24]And the sons of Korah *were* Assir, Elkanah, and Abiasaph. These are the families of the Korahites. [25]Eleazar, Aaron's son, took for himself one of the daughters of Putiel as wife; and she bore him Phinehas. These *are* the heads of the fathers' houses of the Levites according to their families.

[26]These *are the same* Aaron and Moses to whom the LORD said, "Bring out the children of Israel from the land of Egypt according to their armies." [27]These *are* the ones who spoke to Pharaoh king of Egypt, to bring out the children of Israel from Egypt. These *are the same* Moses and Aaron.

AARON IS MOSES' SPOKESMAN

[28]And it came to pass, on the day the LORD spoke to Moses in the land of Egypt, [29]that the LORD spoke to Moses, saying, "I *am* the LORD. Speak to Pharaoh king of Egypt all that I say to you."

[30]But Moses said before the LORD, "Behold, I *am* of uncircumcised lips, and how shall Pharaoh heed me?"

7 So the LORD said to Moses: "See, I have made you *as* God to Pharaoh, and Aaron your brother shall be your prophet. [2]You shall speak all that I command you. And Aaron your brother shall tell Pharaoh to send the children of Israel out of his land. [3]And I will harden Pharaoh's heart, and multiply My signs and My wonders in the land of Egypt. [4]But Pharaoh will not heed you, so that I may lay My hand on Egypt and bring My armies *and* My people, the children of Israel, out of the land of Egypt by great judgments. [5]And the Egyptians shall know that I *am* the LORD, when I stretch out My hand on Egypt and bring out the children of Israel from among them."

[6]Then Moses and Aaron did *so;* just as the LORD commanded them, so they did. [7]And Moses *was* eighty years old and Aaron eighty-three years old when they spoke to Pharaoh.

AARON'S MIRACULOUS ROD

[8]Then the LORD spoke to Moses and Aaron, saying, [9]"When Pharaoh speaks to you, saying, 'Show a miracle for yourselves,' then you shall say to Aaron, 'Take your rod and cast *it* before Pharaoh, *and* let it become a serpent.' " [10]So Moses and Aaron went in to Pharaoh, and they did so, just as the LORD commanded. And Aaron cast down his rod before Pharaoh and before his servants, and it became a serpent.

[11]But Pharaoh also called the wise men and the sorcerers; so the magicians of Egypt, they also did in like manner with their enchantments. [12]For every man threw down his rod, and they became serpents. But Aaron's rod swallowed up their rods. [13]And Pharaoh's heart grew hard, and he did not heed them, as the LORD had said.

6:15 [a]Spelled *Nemuel* in Numbers 26:12

The First Plague: Waters Become Blood

¹⁴So the LORD said to Moses: "Pharaoh's heart *is* hard; he refuses to let the people go. ¹⁵Go to Pharaoh in the morning, when he goes out to the water, and you shall stand by the river's bank to meet him; and the rod which was turned to a serpent you shall take in your hand. ¹⁶And you shall say to him, 'The LORD God of the Hebrews has sent me to you, saying, "Let My people go, that they may serve Me in the wilderness"; but indeed, until now you would not hear! ¹⁷Thus says the LORD: "By this you shall know that I *am* the LORD. Behold, I will strike the waters which *are* in the river with the rod that *is* in my hand, and they shall be turned to blood. ¹⁸And the fish that *are* in the river shall die, the river shall stink, and the Egyptians will loathe to drink the water of the river." ' "

¹⁹Then the LORD spoke to Moses, "Say to Aaron, 'Take your rod and stretch out your hand over the waters of Egypt, over their streams, over their rivers, over their ponds, and over all their pools of water, that they may become blood. And there shall be blood throughout all the land of Egypt, both in *buckets of* wood and *pitchers of* stone.' " ²⁰And Moses and Aaron did so, just as the LORD commanded. So he lifted up the rod and struck the waters that *were* in the river, in the sight of Pharaoh and in the sight of his servants. And all the waters that *were* in the river were turned to blood. ²¹The fish that *were* in the river died, the river stank, and the Egyptians could not drink the water of the river. So there was blood throughout all the land of Egypt.

²²Then the magicians of Egypt did so with their enchantments; and Pharaoh's heart grew hard, and he did not heed them, as the LORD had said. ²³And Pharaoh turned and went into his house. Neither was his heart moved by this. ²⁴So all the Egyptians dug all around the river for water to drink, because they could not drink the water of the river. ²⁵And seven days passed after the LORD had struck the river.

The Second Plague: Frogs

8And the LORD spoke to Moses, "Go to Pharaoh and say to him, 'Thus says the LORD: "Let My people go, that they may serve Me. ²But if you refuse to let *them* go, behold, I will smite all your territory with frogs. ³So the river shall bring forth frogs abundantly, which shall go up and come into your house, into your bedroom, on your bed, into the houses of your servants, on your people, into your ovens, and into your kneading bowls. ⁴And the frogs shall come up on you, on your people, and on all your servants." ' "

⁵Then the LORD spoke to Moses, "Say to Aaron, 'Stretch out your hand with your rod over the streams, over the rivers, and over the ponds, and cause frogs to come up on the land of Egypt.' " ⁶So Aaron stretched out his hand over the waters of Egypt, and the frogs came up and covered the land of Egypt. ⁷And the magicians did so with their enchantments, and brought up frogs on the land of Egypt.

⁸Then Pharaoh called for Moses and Aaron, and said, "Entreat the LORD that He may take away the frogs from me and from my people; and I will let the people go, that they may sacrifice to the LORD."

⁹And Moses said to Pharaoh, "Accept the honor of saying when I shall intercede for you, for your servants, and for your people, to destroy the frogs from you and your houses, *that* they may remain in the river only."

¹⁰So he said, "Tomorrow." And he said, "*Let it be* according to your word, that you may know that *there is* no one like the LORD our God. ¹¹And the frogs shall depart from you, from your houses, from your servants, and from your people. They shall remain in the river only."

¹²Then Moses and Aaron went out from Pharaoh. And Moses cried out to the LORD concerning the frogs which He had brought against Pharaoh. ¹³So the LORD did according to the word of Moses. And the frogs died out of the houses, out of the courtyards, and out of the fields. ¹⁴They gathered them together in heaps, and the land stank. ¹⁵But when Pharaoh saw that there was relief, he hardened his heart and did not heed them, as the LORD had said.

The Third Plague: Lice

¹⁶So the LORD said to Moses, "Say to Aaron, 'Stretch out your rod, and strike the dust of the land, so that it may become lice throughout all the land of Egypt.' " ¹⁷And they did so. For Aaron

stretched out his hand with his rod and struck the dust of the earth, and it became lice on man and beast. All the dust of the land became lice throughout all the land of Egypt.

¹⁸Now the magicians so worked with their enchantments to bring forth lice, but they could not. So there were lice on man and beast. ¹⁹Then the magicians said to Pharaoh, "This *is* the finger of God." But Pharaoh's heart grew hard, and he did not heed them, just as the LORD had said.

THE FOURTH PLAGUE: FLIES

²⁰And the LORD said to Moses, "Rise early in the morning and stand before Pharaoh as he comes out to the water. Then say to him, 'Thus says the LORD: "Let My people go, that they may serve Me. ²¹Or else, if you will not let My people go, behold, I will send swarms *of flies* on you and your servants, on your people and into your houses. The houses of the Egyptians shall be full of swarms *of flies,* and also the ground on which they *stand.* ²²And in that day I will set apart the land of Goshen, in which My people dwell, that no swarms *of flies* shall be there, in order that you may know that I *am* the LORD in the midst of the land. ²³I will make a difference[a] between My people and your people. Tomorrow this sign shall be." ' " ²⁴And the LORD did so. Thick swarms *of flies* came into the house of Pharaoh, *into* his servants' houses, and into all the land of Egypt. The land was corrupted because of the swarms *of flies.*

²⁵Then Pharaoh called for Moses and Aaron, and said, "Go, sacrifice to your God in the land."

²⁶And Moses said, "It is not right to do so, for we would be sacrificing the abomination of the Egyptians to the LORD our God. If we sacrifice the abomination of the Egyptians before their eyes, then will they not stone us? ²⁷We will go three days' journey into the wilderness and sacrifice to the LORD our God as He will command us."

²⁸So Pharaoh said, "I will let you go, that you may sacrifice to the LORD your God in the wilderness; only you shall not go very far away. Intercede for me."

²⁹Then Moses said, "Indeed I am going out from you, and I will entreat the LORD, that the swarms *of flies* may depart tomorrow from Pharaoh, from his servants, and from his people.

But let Pharaoh not deal deceitfully anymore in not letting the people go to sacrifice to the LORD."

³⁰So Moses went out from Pharaoh and entreated the LORD. ³¹And the LORD did according to the word of Moses; He removed the swarms *of flies* from Pharaoh, from his servants, and from his people. Not one remained. ³²But Pharaoh hardened his heart at this time also; neither would he let the people go.

THE FIFTH PLAGUE: LIVESTOCK DISEASED

9Then the Lord said to Moses, "Go in to Pharaoh and tell him, 'Thus says the Lord God of the Hebrews: "Let My people go, that they may serve Me. ²For if you refuse to let *them* go, and still hold them, ³behold, the hand of the Lord will be on your cattle in the field, on the horses, on the donkeys, on the camels, on the oxen, and on the sheep—a very severe pestilence. ⁴And the Lord will make a difference between the livestock of Israel and the livestock of Egypt. So nothing shall die of all *that* belongs to the children of Israel." ' " ⁵Then the Lord appointed a set time, saying, "Tomorrow the Lord will do this thing in the land."

⁶So the LORD did this thing on the next day, and all the livestock of Egypt died; but of the livestock of the children of Israel, not one died. ⁷Then Pharaoh sent, and indeed, not even one of the livestock of the Israelites was dead. But the heart of Pharaoh became hard, and he did not let the people go.

THE SIXTH PLAGUE: BOILS

⁸So the LORD said to Moses and Aaron, "Take for yourselves handfuls of ashes from a furnace, and let Moses scatter it toward the heavens in the sight of Pharaoh. ⁹And it will become fine dust in all the land of Egypt, and it will cause boils that break out in sores on man and beast throughout all the land of Egypt." ¹⁰Then they took ashes from the furnace and stood before Pharaoh, and Moses scattered *them* toward heaven. And *they* caused boils that break out in sores on man and beast. ¹¹And the magicians could not stand before Moses because of the boils, for the boils were on the magicians and on all the Egyptians. ¹²But the

8:23 [a]Literally *set a ransom* (compare Exodus 9:4 and 11:7)

LORD hardened the heart of Pharaoh; and he did not heed them, just as the LORD had spoken to Moses.

THE SEVENTH PLAGUE: HAIL

¹³Then the LORD said to Moses, "Rise early in the morning and stand before Pharaoh, and say to him, 'Thus says the LORD God of the Hebrews: "Let My people go, that they may serve Me, ¹⁴for at this time I will send all My plagues to your very heart, and on your servants and on your people, that you may know that *there is* none like Me in all the earth. ¹⁵Now if I had stretched out My hand and struck you and your people with pestilence, then you would have been cut off from the earth. ¹⁶But indeed for this *purpose* I have raised you up, that I may show My power *in* you, and that My name may be declared in all the earth. ¹⁷As yet you exalt yourself against My people in that you will not let them go. ¹⁸Behold, tomorrow about this time I will cause very heavy hail to rain down, such as has not been in Egypt since its founding until now. ¹⁹Therefore send now *and* gather your livestock and all that you have in the field, for the hail shall come down on every man and every animal which is found in the field and is not brought home; and they shall die."' "

²⁰He who feared the word of the LORD among the servants of Pharaoh made his servants and his livestock flee to the houses. ²¹But he who did not regard the word of the LORD left his servants and his livestock in the field.

²²Then the LORD said to Moses, "Stretch out your hand toward heaven, that there may be hail in all the land of Egypt—on man, on beast, and on every herb of the field, throughout the land of Egypt." ²³And Moses stretched out his rod toward heaven; and the LORD sent thunder and hail, and fire darted to the ground. And the LORD rained hail on the land of Egypt. ²⁴So there was hail, and fire mingled with the hail, so very heavy that there was none like it in all the land of Egypt since it became a nation. ²⁵And the hail struck throughout the whole land of Egypt, all that *was* in the field, both man and beast; and the hail struck every herb of the field and broke every tree of the field. ²⁶Only in the land of Goshen, where the children of Israel *were,* there was no hail.

²⁷And Pharaoh sent and called for Moses and Aaron, and said to them, "I have sinned this time. The LORD *is* righteous, and my people and I *are* wicked. ²⁸Entreat the LORD, that there may be no *more* mighty thundering and hail, for *it is* enough. I will let you go, and you shall stay no longer."

²⁹So Moses said to him, "As soon as I have gone out of the city, I will spread out my hands to the LORD; the thunder will cease, and there will be no more hail, that you may know that the earth *is* the LORD's. ³⁰But as for you and your servants, I know that you will not yet fear the LORD God."

³¹Now the flax and the barley were struck, for the barley *was* in the head and the flax *was* in bud. ³²But the wheat and the spelt were not struck, for they *are* late crops.

³³So Moses went out of the city from Pharaoh and spread out his hands to the LORD; then the thunder and the hail ceased, and the rain was not poured on the earth. ³⁴And when Pharaoh saw that the rain, the hail, and the thunder had ceased, he sinned yet more; and he hardened his heart, he and his servants. ³⁵So the heart of Pharaoh was hard; neither would he let the children of Israel go, as the LORD had spoken by Moses.

THE EIGHTH PLAGUE: LOCUSTS

10 Now the LORD said to Moses, "Go in to Pharaoh; for I have hardened his heart and the hearts of his servants, that I may show these signs of Mine before him, ²and that you may tell in the hearing of your son and your son's son the mighty things I have done in Egypt, and My signs which I have done among them, that you may know that I *am* the LORD."

³So Moses and Aaron came in to Pharaoh and said to him, "Thus says the LORD God of the Hebrews: 'How long will you refuse to humble yourself before Me? Let My people go, that they may serve Me. ⁴Or else, if you refuse to let My people go, behold, tomorrow I will bring locusts into your territory. ⁵And they shall cover the face of the earth, so that no one will be able to see the earth; and they shall eat the residue of what is left, which remains to you from the hail, and they shall eat every tree which grows up for you out of the field. ⁶They shall fill your houses, the houses of all

your servants, and the houses of all the Egyptians—which neither your fathers nor your fathers' fathers have seen, since the day that they were on the earth to this day.' " And he turned and went out from Pharaoh.

⁷Then Pharaoh's servants said to him, "How long shall this man be a snare to us? Let the men go, that they may serve the LORD their God. Do you not yet know that Egypt is destroyed?"

⁸So Moses and Aaron were brought again to Pharaoh, and he said to them, "Go, serve the LORD your God. Who *are* the ones that are going?"

⁹And Moses said, "We will go with our young and our old; with our sons and our daughters, with our flocks and our herds we will go, for we must hold a feast to the LORD."

¹⁰Then he said to them, "The LORD had better be with you when I let you and your little ones go! Beware, for evil is ahead of you. ¹¹Not so! Go now, you *who are* men, and serve the LORD, for that is what you desired." And they were driven out from Pharaoh's presence.

¹²Then the LORD said to Moses, "Stretch out your hand over the land of Egypt for the locusts, that they may come upon the land of Egypt, and eat every herb of the land—all that the hail has left." ¹³So Moses stretched out his rod over the land of Egypt, and the LORD brought an east wind on the land all that day and all *that* night. When it was morning, the east wind brought the locusts. ¹⁴And the locusts went up over all the land of Egypt and rested on all the territory of Egypt. *They were* very severe; previously there had been no such locusts as they, nor shall there be such after them. ¹⁵For they covered the face of the whole earth, so that the land was darkened; and they ate every herb of the land and all the fruit of the trees which the hail had left. So there remained nothing green on the trees or on the plants of the field throughout all the land of Egypt.

¹⁶Then Pharaoh called for Moses and Aaron in haste, and said, "I have sinned against the LORD your God and against you. ¹⁷Now therefore, please forgive my sin only this once, and entreat the LORD your God, that He may take away from me this death only." ¹⁸So he went out from Pharaoh and entreated the LORD. ¹⁹And the

LORD turned a very strong west wind, which took the locusts away and blew them into the Red Sea. There remained not one locust in all the territory of Egypt. ²⁰But the LORD hardened Pharaoh's heart, and he did not let the children of Israel go.

THE NINTH PLAGUE: DARKNESS

²¹Then the LORD said to Moses, "Stretch out your hand toward heaven, that there may be darkness over the land of Egypt, darkness *which* may even be felt." ²²So Moses stretched out his hand toward heaven, and there was thick darkness in all the land of Egypt three days. ²³They did not see one another; nor did anyone rise from his place for three days. But all the children of Israel had light in their dwellings.

²⁴Then Pharaoh called to Moses and said, "Go, serve the LORD; only let your flocks and your herds be kept back. Let your little ones also go with you."

²⁵But Moses said, "You must also give us sacrifices and burnt offerings, that we may sacrifice to the LORD our God. ²⁶Our livestock also shall go with us; not a hoof shall be left behind. For we must take some of them to serve the LORD our God, and even we do not know with what we must serve the LORD until we arrive there."

²⁷But the LORD hardened Pharaoh's heart, and he would not let them go. ²⁸Then Pharaoh said to him, "Get away from me! Take heed to yourself and see my face no more! For in the day you see my face you shall die!"

²⁹So Moses said, "You have spoken well. I will never see your face again."

DEATH OF THE FIRSTBORN ANNOUNCED

11 And the LORD said to Moses, "I will bring one more plague on Pharaoh and on Egypt. Afterward he will let you go from here. When he lets *you* go, he will surely drive you out of here altogether. ²Speak now in the hearing of the people, and let every man ask from his neighbor and every woman from her neighbor, articles of silver and articles of gold." ³And the LORD gave the people favor in the sight of the Egyptians. Moreover the man Moses *was* very great in the land of Egypt, in the sight of Pharaoh's servants and in the sight of the people.

⁴Then Moses said, "Thus says the LORD: 'About midnight I will go out into the midst of Egypt; ⁵and all the firstborn in the land of Egypt shall die, from the firstborn of Pharaoh who sits on his throne, even to the firstborn of the female servant who *is* behind the handmill, and all the firstborn of the animals. ⁶Then there shall be a great cry throughout all the land of Egypt, such as was not like it *before,* nor shall be like it again. ⁷But against none of the children of Israel shall a dog move its tongue, against man or beast, that you may know that the LORD does make a difference between the Egyptians and Israel.' ⁸And all these your servants shall come down to me and bow down to me, saying, 'Get out, and all the people who follow you!' After that I will go out." Then he went out from Pharaoh in great anger.

⁹But the LORD said to Moses, "Pharaoh will not heed you, so that My wonders may be multiplied in the land of Egypt." ¹⁰So Moses and Aaron did all these wonders before Pharaoh; and the LORD hardened Pharaoh's heart, and he did not let the children of Israel go out of his land.

THE PASSOVER INSTITUTED

12 Now the LORD spoke to Moses and Aaron in the land of Egypt, saying, ²"This month *shall be* your beginning of months; it *shall be* the first month of the year to you. ³Speak to all the congregation of Israel, saying: 'On the tenth of this month every man shall take for himself a lamb, according to the house of *his* father, a lamb for a household. ⁴And if the household is too small for the lamb, let him and his neighbor next to his house take *it* according to the number of the persons; according to each man's need you shall make your count for the lamb. ⁵Your lamb shall be without blemish, a male of the first year. You may take *it* from the sheep or from the goats. ⁶Now you shall keep it until the fourteenth day of the same month. Then the whole assembly of the congregation of Israel shall kill it at twilight. ⁷And they shall take *some* of the blood and put *it* on the two doorposts and on the lintel of the houses where they eat it. ⁸Then they shall eat the flesh on that night; roasted in fire, with unleavened bread *and* with bitter *herbs* they shall eat it. ⁹Do not eat it raw, nor boiled at all with water, but roasted in fire—its head with its legs and its entrails. ¹⁰You shall let none of it remain until morning, and what remains of it until morning you shall burn with fire. ¹¹And thus you shall eat it: *with* a belt on your waist, your sandals on your feet, and your staff in your hand. So you shall eat it in haste. It *is* the LORD's Passover.

¹²'For I will pass through the land of Egypt on that night, and will strike all the firstborn in the land of Egypt, both man and beast; and against all the gods of Egypt I will execute judgment: I *am* the LORD. ¹³Now the blood shall be a sign for you on the houses where you *are.* And when I see the blood, I will pass over you; and the plague shall not be on you to destroy *you* when I strike the land of Egypt.

¹⁴'So this day shall be to you a memorial; and you shall keep it as a feast to the LORD throughout your generations. You shall keep it as a feast by an everlasting ordinance. ¹⁵Seven days you shall eat unleavened bread. On the first day you shall remove leaven from your houses. For whoever eats leavened bread from the first day until the seventh day, that person shall be cut off from Israel. ¹⁶On the first day *there shall be* a holy convocation, and on the seventh day there shall be a holy convocation for you. No manner of work shall be done on them; but *that* which everyone must eat—that only may be prepared by you. ¹⁷So you shall observe *the Feast of* Unleavened Bread, for on this same day I will have brought your armies out of the land of Egypt. Therefore you shall observe this day throughout your generations as an everlasting ordinance. ¹⁸In the first *month,* on the fourteenth day of the month at evening, you shall eat unleavened bread, until the twenty-first day of the month at evening. ¹⁹For seven days no leaven shall be found in your houses, since whoever eats what is leavened, that same person shall be cut off from the congregation of Israel, whether *he is* a stranger or a native of the land. ²⁰You shall eat nothing leavened; in all your dwellings you shall eat unleavened bread.' "

²¹Then Moses called for all the elders of Israel and said to them, "Pick out and take lambs for yourselves according to your families, and kill the Passover *lamb.* ²²And you shall take a bunch of hyssop, dip *it* in the blood that *is* in the basin, and strike the lintel and the two doorposts with the blood that *is* in the basin. And none of you

shall go out of the door of his house until morning. ²³For the LORD will pass through to strike the Egyptians; and when He sees the blood on the lintel and on the two doorposts, the LORD will pass over the door and not allow the destroyer to come into your houses to strike *you*. ²⁴And you shall observe this thing as an ordinance for you and your sons forever. ²⁵It will come to pass when you come to the land which the LORD will give you, just as He promised, that you shall keep this service. ²⁶And it shall be, when your children say to you, 'What do you mean by this service?' ²⁷that you shall say, 'It *is* the Passover sacrifice of the LORD, who passed over the houses of the children of Israel in Egypt when He struck the Egyptians and delivered our households.' " So the people bowed their heads and worshiped. ²⁸Then the children of Israel went away and did *so*; just as the LORD had commanded Moses and Aaron, so they did.

The Tenth Plague: Death of the Firstborn

²⁹And it came to pass at midnight that the LORD struck all the firstborn in the land of Egypt, from the firstborn of Pharaoh who sat on his throne to the firstborn of the captive who *was* in the dungeon, and all the firstborn of livestock. ³⁰So Pharaoh rose in the night, he, all his servants, and all the Egyptians; and there was a great cry in Egypt, for *there was* not a house where *there was* not one dead.

The Exodus

³¹Then he called for Moses and Aaron by night, and said, "Rise, go out from among my people, both you and the children of Israel. And go, serve the LORD as you have said. ³²Also take your flocks and your herds, as you have said, and be gone; and bless me also."

³³And the Egyptians urged the people, that they might send them out of the land in haste. For they said, "We *shall* all *be* dead." ³⁴So the people took their dough before it was leavened, having their kneading bowls bound up in their clothes on their shoulders. ³⁵Now the children of Israel had done according to the word of Moses, and they had asked from the Egyptians articles of silver, articles of gold, and clothing. ³⁶And the LORD had given the people favor in the sight of the Egyptians, so that they granted them *what they requested*. Thus they plundered the Egyptians.

³⁷Then the children of Israel journeyed from Rameses to Succoth, about six hundred thousand men on foot, besides children. ³⁸A mixed multitude went up with them also, and flocks and herds—a great deal of livestock. ³⁹And they baked unleavened cakes of the dough which they had brought out of Egypt; for it was not leavened, because they were driven out of Egypt and could not wait, nor had they prepared provisions for themselves.

⁴⁰Now the sojourn of the children of Israel who lived in Egypt[a] *was* four hundred and thirty years. ⁴¹And it came to pass at the end of the four hundred and thirty years—on that very same day—it came to pass that all the armies of the LORD went out from the land of Egypt. ⁴²It *is* a night of solemn observance to the LORD for bringing them out of the land of Egypt. This *is* that night of the LORD, a solemn observance for all the children of Israel throughout their generations.

Passover Regulations

⁴³And the LORD said to Moses and Aaron, "This *is* the ordinance of the Passover: No foreigner shall eat it. ⁴⁴But every man's servant who is bought for money, when you have circumcised him, then he may eat it. ⁴⁵A sojourner and a hired servant shall not eat it. ⁴⁶In one house it shall be eaten; you shall not carry any of the flesh outside the house, nor shall you break one of its bones. ⁴⁷All the congregation of Israel shall keep it. ⁴⁸And when a stranger dwells with you *and wants* to keep the Passover to the LORD, let all his males be circumcised, and then let him come near and keep it; and he shall be as a native of the land. For no uncircumcised person shall eat it. ⁴⁹One law shall be for the native-born and for the stranger who dwells among you."

⁵⁰Thus all the children of Israel did; as the LORD commanded Moses and Aaron, so they did. ⁵¹And it came to pass, on that very same day, that the LORD brought the children of Israel out of the land of Egypt according to their armies.

12:40 [a]Samaritan Pentateuch and Septuagint read *Egypt and Canaan.*

THE FIRSTBORN CONSECRATED

13 Then the LORD spoke to Moses, saying, 2"Consecrate to Me all the firstborn, whatever opens the womb among the children of Israel, *both* of man and beast; it is Mine."

THE FEAST OF UNLEAVENED BREAD

3And Moses said to the people: "Remember this day in which you went out of Egypt, out of the house of bondage; for by strength of hand the LORD brought you out of this *place*. No leavened bread shall be eaten. 4On this day you are going out, in the month Abib. 5And it shall be, when the LORD brings you into the land of the Canaanites and the Hittites and the Amorites and the Hivites and the Jebusites, which He swore to your fathers to give you, a land flowing with milk and honey, that you shall keep this service in this month. 6Seven days you shall eat unleavened bread, and on the seventh day *there shall be* a feast to the LORD. 7Unleavened bread shall be eaten seven days. And no leavened bread shall be seen among you, nor shall leaven be seen among you in all your quarters. 8And you shall tell your son in that day, saying, '*This is done* because of what the LORD did for me when I came up from Egypt.' 9It shall be as a sign to you on your hand and as a memorial between your eyes, that the LORD's law may be in your mouth; for with a strong hand the LORD has brought you out of Egypt. 10You shall therefore keep this ordinance in its season from year to year.

THE LAW OF THE FIRSTBORN

11"And it shall be, when the LORD brings you into the land of the Canaanites, as He swore to you and your fathers, and gives it to you, 12that you shall set apart to the LORD all that open the womb, that is, every firstborn that comes from an animal which you have; the males *shall be* the LORD's. 13But every firstborn of a donkey you shall redeem with a lamb; and if you will not redeem *it*, then you shall break its neck. And all the firstborn of man among your sons you shall redeem. 14So it shall be, when your son asks you in time to come, saying, 'What *is* this?' that you shall say to him, 'By strength of hand the LORD brought us out of Egypt, out of the house of bondage. 15And it came to pass, when Pharaoh was stubborn about letting us go, that the LORD killed all the firstborn in the land of Egypt, both the firstborn of man and the firstborn of beast. Therefore I sacrifice to the LORD all males that open the womb, but all the firstborn of my sons I redeem.' 16It shall be as a sign on your hand and as frontlets between your eyes, for by strength of hand the LORD brought us out of Egypt."

THE WILDERNESS WAY

17Then it came to pass, when Pharaoh had let the people go, that God did not lead them *by* way of the land of the Philistines, although that *was* near; for God said, "Lest perhaps the people change their minds when they see war, and return to Egypt." 18So God led the people around *by* way of the wilderness of the Red Sea. And the children of Israel went up in orderly ranks out of the land of Egypt.

19And Moses took the bones of Joseph with him, for he had placed the children of Israel under solemn oath, saying, "God will surely visit you, and you shall carry up my bones from here with you."a

20So they took their journey from Succoth and camped in Etham at the edge of the wilderness. 21And the LORD went before them by day in a pillar of cloud to lead the way, and by night in a pillar of fire to give them light, so as to go by day and night. 22He did not take away the pillar of cloud by day or the pillar of fire by night *from* before the people.

THE RED SEA CROSSING

14 Now the LORD spoke to Moses, saying: 2"Speak to the children of Israel, that they turn and camp before Pi Hahiroth, between Migdol and the sea, opposite Baal Zemphon; you shall camp before it by the sea. 3For Pharaoh will say of the children of Israel, 'They *are* bewildered by the land; the wilderness has closed them in.' 4Then I will harden Pharaoh's heart, so that he will pursue them; and I will gain honor over Pharaoh and over all his army, that the Egyptians may know that I *am* the LORD." And they did so.

5Now it was told the king of Egypt that the

13:19 aGenesis 50:25

people had fled, and the heart of Pharaoh and his servants was turned against the people; and they said, "Why have we done this, that we have let Israel go from serving us?" ⁶So he made ready his chariot and took his people with him. ⁷Also, he took six hundred choice chariots, and all the chariots of Egypt with captains over every one of them. ⁸And the LORD hardened the heart of Pharaoh king of Egypt, and he pursued the children of Israel; and the children of Israel went out with boldness. ⁹So the Egyptians pursued them, all the horses *and* chariots of Pharaoh, his horsemen and his army, and overtook them camping by the sea beside Pi Hahiroth, before Baal Zephon.

¹⁰And when Pharaoh drew near, the children of Israel lifted their eyes, and behold, the Egyptians marched after them. So they were very afraid, and the children of Israel cried out to the LORD. ¹¹Then they said to Moses, "Because *there were* no graves in Egypt, have you taken us away to die in the wilderness? Why have you so dealt with us, to bring us up out of Egypt? ¹²*Is* this not the word that we told you in Egypt, saying, 'Let us alone that we may serve the Egyptians'? For *it would have been* better for us to serve the Egyptians than that we should die in the wilderness."

¹³And Moses said to the people, "Do not be afraid. Stand still, and see the salvation of the LORD, which He will accomplish for you today. For the Egyptians whom you see today, you shall see again no more forever. ¹⁴The LORD will fight for you, and you shall hold your peace."

¹⁵And the LORD said to Moses, "Why do you cry to Me? Tell the children of Israel to go forward.

LEAD**ERSHIP**
REAL**ITIES**

TENACITY—UNSTOPPABLE FORCE *Exodus 14:10–14*

The former tortured, impoverished Israelites were on their way to freedom. Once they looked back, they allowed the threat of what *might be* to overshadow God's promise. Moses said "stand still," which sounded good; but God's choice was "go forward." In every situation, there are three options: go back, stand still, or go forward.

on—**forward**—to journey, march, pull up, set out, set forward

When you feel like *going back*:

- **Don't!** Endure, persevere, and stay strong.
- **Examine your progress.** It was just as far to go back to Egypt as it was to go across the Red Sea. Why quit when you might be near the finish line?
- **Plan new goals.** Yes, right now. This is the time to plan what you will do *after* you achieve the first goal.
- **Be grateful.** What has God already done for you? Thank Him for the many answers to prayer and for the miracles of His Word.
- **Turn weakness into strength.** Identify what is stealing your confidence. Do you need to go around the weakness or grow stronger in that area?
- **Redirect your thinking.** Never let yesterday's mistakes or hurts take up too much of today. Focus on new possibilities and contacts.
- **Seek godly counsel.** There was no other leader to ask so Moses went to God who said, "Go forward." Call a godly friend or mentor to cry, laugh, think, and pray with. This will give you clarity and strength.

[16]But lift up your rod, and stretch out your hand over the sea and divide it. And the children of Israel shall go on dry *ground* through the midst of the sea. [17]And I indeed will harden the hearts of the Egyptians, and they shall follow them. So I will gain honor over Pharaoh and over all his army, his chariots, and his horsemen. [18]Then the Egyptians shall know that I *am* the LORD, when I have gained honor for Myself over Pharaoh, his chariots, and his horsemen."

[19]And the Angel of God, who went before the camp of Israel, moved and went behind them; and the pillar of cloud went from before them and stood behind them. [20]So it came between the camp of the Egyptians and the camp of Israel. Thus it was a cloud and darkness *to the one,* and it gave light by night *to the other,* so that the one did not come near the other all that night.

[21]Then Moses stretched out his hand over the sea; and the LORD caused the sea to go *back* by a strong east wind all that night, and made the sea into dry *land,* and the waters were divided. [22]So the children of Israel went into the midst of the sea on the dry *ground,* and the waters *were* a wall to them on their right hand and on their left. [23]And the Egyptians pursued and went after them into the midst of the sea, all Pharaoh's horses, his chariots, and his horsemen.

[24]Now it came to pass, in the morning watch, that the LORD looked down upon the army of the Egyptians through the pillar of fire and cloud, and He troubled the army of the Egyptians. [25]And He took off[a] their chariot wheels, so that they drove them with difficulty; and the Egyptians said, "Let us flee from the face of Israel, for the LORD fights for them against the Egyptians."

[26]Then the LORD said to Moses, "Stretch out your hand over the sea, that the waters may come back upon the Egyptians, on their chariots, and on their horsemen." [27]And Moses stretched out his hand over the sea; and when the morning appeared, the sea returned to its full depth, while the Egyptians were fleeing into it. So the LORD overthrew the Egyptians in the midst of the sea. [28]Then the waters returned and covered the chariots, the horsemen, *and* all the army of Pharaoh that came into the sea after them. Not so much as one of them remained. [29]But the children of Israel had walked on dry *land* in the midst of the sea, and the waters *were* a wall to them on their right hand and on their left.

[30]So the LORD saved Israel that day out of the hand of the Egyptians, and Israel saw the Egyptians dead on the seashore. [31]Thus Israel saw the great work which the LORD had done in Egypt; so the people feared the LORD, and believed the LORD and His servant Moses.

THE SONG OF MOSES

15 Then Moses and the children of Israel sang this song to the LORD, and spoke, saying:

"I will sing to the LORD,
    For He has triumphed gloriously!
    The horse and its rider
    He has thrown into the sea!
[2]The LORD *is* my strength and song,
    And He has become my salvation;
    He *is* my God, and I will praise Him;
    My father's God, and I will exalt Him.
[3]The LORD *is* a man of war;
    The LORD *is* His name.
[4]Pharaoh's chariots and his army He has cast
        into the sea;
    His chosen captains also are drowned in the
        Red Sea.
[5]The depths have covered them;
    They sank to the bottom like a stone.

[6]"Your right hand, O LORD, has become
        glorious in power;
    Your right hand, O LORD, has dashed the
        enemy in pieces.
[7]And in the greatness of Your excellence
    You have overthrown those who rose against
        You;
    You sent forth Your wrath;
    It consumed them like stubble.
[8]And with the blast of Your nostrils
    The waters were gathered together;
    The floods stood upright like a heap;
    The depths congealed in the heart of the sea.
[9]The enemy said, 'I will pursue,
    I will overtake,
    I will divide the spoil;
    My desire shall be satisfied on them.

14:25 [a]Samaritan Pentateuch, Septuagint, and Syriac read *bound.*

I will draw my sword,
My hand shall destroy them.'
[10]You blew with Your wind,
The sea covered them;
They sank like lead in the mighty waters.

[11]"Who *is* like You, O LORD, among the gods?
Who *is* like You, glorious in holiness,
Fearful in praises, doing wonders?
[12]You stretched out Your right hand;
The earth swallowed them.
[13]You in Your mercy have led forth
The people whom You have redeemed;
You have guided *them* in Your strength
To Your holy habitation.

[14]"The people will hear *and* be afraid;
Sorrow will take hold of the inhabitants of
Philistia.
[15]Then the chiefs of Edom will be dismayed;
The mighty men of Moab,
Trembling will take hold of them;
All the inhabitants of Canaan will melt away.
[16]Fear and dread will fall on them;
By the greatness of Your arm
They will be *as* still as a stone,
Till Your people pass over, O LORD,
Till the people pass over
Whom You have purchased.
[17]You will bring them in and plant them
In the mountain of Your inheritance,
In the place, O LORD, *which* You have made
For Your own dwelling,
The sanctuary, O Lord, *which* Your hands have
established.

[18]"The LORD shall reign forever and ever."

[19]For the horses of Pharaoh went with his
chariots and his horsemen into the sea, and the
LORD brought back the waters of the sea upon
them. But the children of Israel went on dry *land*
in the midst of the sea.

The Song of Miriam

[20]Then Miriam the prophetess, the sister of
Aaron, took the timbrel in her hand; and all the
women went out after her with timbrels and with
dances. [21]And Miriam answered them:

"Sing to the LORD,
For He has triumphed gloriously!
The horse and its rider
He has thrown into the sea!"

Bitter Waters Made Sweet

[22]So Moses brought Israel from the Red Sea;
then they went out into the Wilderness of Shur.
And they went three days in the wilderness and
found no water. [23]Now when they came to
Marah, they could not drink the waters of Marah,
for they *were* bitter. Therefore the name of it was
called Marah.[a] [24]And the people complained
against Moses, saying, "What shall we drink?" [25]So
he cried out to the LORD, and the LORD showed
him a tree. When he cast *it* into the waters, the
waters were made sweet.

There He made a statute and an ordinance
for them, and there He tested them, [26]and said, "If
you diligently heed the voice of the LORD your
God and do what is right in His sight, give ear to
His commandments and keep all His statutes, I
will put none of the diseases on you which I have
brought on the Egyptians. For I *am* the LORD
who heals you."

[27]Then they came to Elim, where there *were*
twelve wells of water and seventy palm trees; so
they camped there by the waters.

Bread from Heaven

16 And they journeyed from Elim, and all the
congregation of the children of Israel came
to the Wilderness of Sin, which is between Elim
and Sinai, on the fifteenth day of the second
month after they departed from the land of
Egypt. [2]Then the whole congregation of the children of Israel complained against Moses and
Aaron in the wilderness. [3]And the children of Israel said to them, "Oh, that we had died by the
hand of the LORD in the land of Egypt, when we
sat by the pots of meat *and* when we ate bread to
the full! For you have brought us out into this
wilderness to kill this whole assembly with
hunger."

[4]Then the LORD said to Moses, "Behold, I
will rain bread from heaven for you. And the people shall go out and gather a certain quota every

15:23 [a]Literally *Bitter*

day, that I may test them, whether they will walk in My law or not. 5And it shall be on the sixth day that they shall prepare what they bring in, and it shall be twice as much as they gather daily."

6Then Moses and Aaron said to all the children of Israel, "At evening you shall know that the LORD has brought you out of the land of Egypt. 7And in the morning you shall see the glory of the LORD; for He hears your complaints against the LORD. But what *are* we, that you complain against us?" 8Also Moses said, "*This shall be seen* when the LORD gives you meat to eat in the evening, and in the morning bread to the full; for the LORD hears your complaints which you make against Him. And what *are* we? Your complaints *are* not against us but against the LORD."

9Then Moses spoke to Aaron, "Say to all the congregation of the children of Israel, 'Come near before the LORD, for He has heard your complaints.' " 10Now it came to pass, as Aaron spoke to the whole congregation of the children of Israel, that they looked toward the wilderness, and behold, the glory of the LORD appeared in the cloud.

11And the LORD spoke to Moses, saying, 12"I have heard the complaints of the children of Israel. Speak to them, saying, 'At twilight you shall eat meat, and in the morning you shall be filled with bread. And you shall know that I *am* the LORD your God.' "

13So it was that quails came up at evening and covered the camp, and in the morning the dew lay all around the camp. 14And when the layer of dew lifted, there, on the surface of the wilderness, was a small round substance, *as* fine as frost on the ground. 15So when the children of Israel saw *it,* they said to one another, "What is it?" For they did not know what it *was.*

And Moses said to them, "This *is* the bread which the LORD has given you to eat. 16This is the thing which the LORD has commanded: 'Let every man gather it according to each one's need, one omer for each person, *according to the* number of persons; let every man take for *those* who *are* in his tent.' "

17Then the children of Israel did so and gathered, some more, some less. 18So when they measured *it* by omers, he who gathered much had nothing left over, and he who gathered little had no lack. Every man had gathered according to each one's need. 19And Moses said, "Let no one

leave any of it till morning." 20Notwithstanding they did not heed Moses. But some of them left part of it until morning, and it bred worms and stank. And Moses was angry with them. 21So they gathered it every morning, every man according to his need. And when the sun became hot, it melted.

22And so it was, on the sixth day, *that* they gathered twice as much bread, two omers for each one. And all the rulers of the congregation came and told Moses. 23Then he said to them, "This *is what* the LORD has said: 'Tomorrow *is* a Sabbath rest, a holy Sabbath to the LORD. Bake what you will bake *today,* and boil what you will boil; and lay up for yourselves all that remains, to be kept until morning.' " 24So they laid it up till morning, as Moses commanded; and it did not stink, nor were there any worms in it. 25Then Moses said, "Eat that today, for today *is* a Sabbath to the LORD; today you will not find it in the field. 26Six days you shall gather it, but on the seventh day, the Sabbath, there will be none."

27Now it happened *that some* of the people went out on the seventh day to gather, but they found none. 28And the LORD said to Moses, "How long do you refuse to keep My commandments and My laws? 29See! For the LORD has given you the Sabbath; therefore He gives you on the sixth day bread for two days. Let every man remain in his place; let no man go out of his place on the seventh day." 30So the people rested on the seventh day.

31And the house of Israel called its name Manna.a And it *was* like white coriander seed, and the taste of it *was* like wafers *made* with honey.

32Then Moses said, "This *is* the thing which the LORD has commanded: 'Fill an omer with it, to be kept for your generations, that they may see the bread with which I fed you in the wilderness, when I brought you out of the land of Egypt.' " 33And Moses said to Aaron, "Take a pot and put an omer of manna in it, and lay it up before the LORD, to be kept for your generations." 34As the LORD commanded Moses, so Aaron laid it up before the Testimony, to be kept. 35And the children of Israel ate manna forty years, until they came to an inhabited land; they ate manna until they came to the border of the land of Canaan. 36Now an omer *is* one-tenth of an ephah.

16:31 aLiterally *What?* (compare Exodus 16:15)

WATER FROM THE ROCK

17 Then all the congregation of the children of Israel set out on their journey from the Wilderness of Sin, according to the commandment of the LORD, and camped in Rephidim; but *there was* no water for the people to drink. [2]Therefore the people contended with Moses, and said, "Give us water, that we may drink."

So Moses said to them, "Why do you contend with me? Why do you tempt the LORD?"

[3]And the people thirsted there for water, and the people complained against Moses, and said, "Why *is* it you have brought us up out of Egypt, to kill us and our children and our livestock with thirst?"

[4]So Moses cried out to the LORD, saying, "What shall I do with this people? They are almost ready to stone me!"

[5]And the LORD said to Moses, "Go on before the people, and take with you some of the elders of Israel. Also take in your hand your rod with which you struck the river, and go. [6]Behold, I will stand before you there on the rock in Horeb; and you shall strike the rock, and water will come out of it, that the people may drink."

And Moses did so in the sight of the elders of Israel. [7]So he called the name of the place Massah[a] and Meribah,[b] because of the contention of the children of Israel, and because they tempted the LORD, saying, "Is the LORD among us or not?"

VICTORY OVER THE AMALEKITES

[8]Now Amalek came and fought with Israel in Rephidim. [9]And Moses said to Joshua, "Choose us some men and go out, fight with Amalek. Tomorrow I will stand on the top of the hill with the rod of God in my hand." [10]So Joshua did as Moses said to him, and fought with Amalek. And Moses, Aaron, and Hur went up to the top of the hill. [11]And so it was, when Moses held up his hand, that Israel prevailed; and when he let down his hand, Amalek prevailed. [12]But Moses' hands *became* heavy; so they took a stone and put *it* under him, and he sat on it. And Aaron and Hur supported his hands, one on one side, and the other on the other side; and his hands were steady until the going down of the sun. [13]So Joshua defeated Amalek and his people with the edge of the sword.

[14]Then the LORD said to Moses, "Write this *for* a memorial in the book and recount *it* in the hearing of Joshua, that I will utterly blot out the

17:7 [a]Literally *Tempted* [b]Literally *Contention*

LEAD**ERSHIP**
REAL**ITIES**

JOURNAL THE JOURNEY   *Exodus 17:14*

Joshua, the son of Nun, was born at a critical time in redemptive history. He was born to follow Moses and to lead the children of Israel into the land God had promised. He will forever be known for fulfilling the orders from God to "be strong and courageous." Exodus 17 introduces us to this young leader as he is baptized by fire when asked by Moses to defend Israel from the Amalekites. While this is a familiar story, with Moses making intercession on the mountain and Joshua fighting in the valley, there is an often-overlooked element that occurs following the victorious battle. When Joshua returned to Moses, the Lord directed him to record the victory in a book and recount it at a later date. This instruction is of great significance for a leader; for each must journal the journey, both victories and failures, for their own use but also for the benefit of future generations.

It is a scientific fact that 80 to 90 percent of what is heard will be forgotten within twenty-four hours if not written down. If the leader loses sight of where he came from, then he will inevitably lose sight of where he is going. Recording and recalling the journey will encourage, correct, and mature one into the leader God wants him to be.

remembrance of Amalek from under heaven."
15And Moses built an altar and called its name,
The-LORD-Is-My-Banner;a 16for he said, "Because the LORD has sworn: the LORD *will have*
war with Amalek from generation to generation."

JETHRO'S ADVICE

18And Jethro, the priest of Midian, Moses' father-in-law, heard of all that God had done
for Moses and for Israel His people—that the
LORD had brought Israel out of Egypt. 2Then
Jethro, Moses' father-in-law, took Zipporah,
Moses' wife, after he had sent her back, 3with her
two sons, of whom the name of one *was* Gershom (for he said, "I have been a stranger in a foreign land")a 4and the name of the other *was*
Eliezera (for *he said,* "The God of my father *was*
my help, and delivered me from the sword of
Pharaoh"); 5and Jethro, Moses' father-in-law, came
with his sons and his wife to Moses in the wilderness, where he was encamped at the mountain of
God. 6Now he had said to Moses, "I, your father-
in-law Jethro, am coming to you with your wife
and her two sons with her."

7So Moses went out to meet his father-in-law,
bowed down, and kissed him. And they asked each
other about *their* well-being, and they went into
the tent. 8And Moses told his father-in-law all that
the LORD had done to Pharaoh and to the Egyptians for Israel's sake, all the hardship that had come
upon them on the way, and *how* the LORD had delivered them. 9Then Jethro rejoiced for all the
good which the LORD had done for Israel, whom
He had delivered out of the hand of the Egyptians.
10And Jethro said, "Blessed *be* the LORD, who has
delivered you out of the hand of the Egyptians and
out of the hand of Pharaoh, *and* who has delivered
the people from under the hand of the Egyptians.
11Now I know that the LORD *is* greater than all
the gods; for in the very thing in which they behaved proudly, *He was* above them." 12Then Jethro,
Moses' father-in-law, tooka a burnt offering and
other sacrifices *to offer* to God. And Aaron came
with all the elders of Israel to eat bread with
Moses' father-in-law before God.

13And so it was, on the next day, that Moses
sat to judge the people; and the people stood before Moses from morning until evening. 14So
when Moses' father-in-law saw all that he did for
the people, he said, "What *is* this thing that you

are doing for the people? Why do you alone sit,
and all the people stand before you from morning
until evening?"

15And Moses said to his father-in-law, "Because the people come to me to inquire of God.
16When they have a difficulty, they come to me,
and I judge between one and another; and I make
known the statutes of God and His laws."

17So Moses' father-in-law said to him, "The
thing that you do *is* not good. 18Both you and
these people who *are* with you will surely wear
yourselves out. For this thing *is* too much for you;
you are not able to perform it by yourself. 19Lis-
ten now to my voice; I will give you counsel, and
God will be with you: Stand before God for the
people, so that you may bring the difficulties to
God. 20And you shall teach them the statutes and
the laws, and show them the way in which they
must walk and the work they must do. 21More-
over you shall select from all the people able men,
such as fear God, men of truth, hating covetousness; and place *such* over them *to be* rulers of thousands, rulers of hundreds, rulers of fifties, and
rulers of tens. 22And let them judge the people at
all times. Then it will be *that* every great matter
they shall bring to you, but every small matter
they themselves shall judge. So it will be easier for
you, for they will bear *the burden* with you. 23If
you do this thing, and God *so* commands you,
then you will be able to endure, and all this people will also go to their place in peace."

24So Moses heeded the voice of his father-
in-law and did all that he had said. 25And Moses
chose able men out of all Israel, and made them
heads over the people: rulers of thousands, rulers
of hundreds, rulers of fifties, and rulers of tens.
26So they judged the people at all times; the hard
cases they brought to Moses, but they judged
every small case themselves.

27Then Moses let his father-in-law depart,
and he went his way to his own land.

ISRAEL AT MOUNT SINAI

19In the third month after the children of Israel had gone out of the land of Egypt, on
the same day, they came *to* the Wilderness of
Sinai. 2For they had departed from Rephidim,

17:15 aHebrew *YHWH Nissi* **18:3** aCompare Exodus 2:22
18:4 aLiterally *My God Is Help* **18:12** aFollowing Masoretic Text and
Septuagint; Syriac, Targum, and Vulgate read *offered.*

LEADERSHIP ISSUES

Called to Higher Ground

EXODUS 19:3

God is always calling us to higher ground. The Old Testament often refers to God as being at the "high place," and the Lord Himself frequently called His prophets to "come up" in order to commune with Him, receive instruction, and take part in private, personal worship. "Moses went up to God, and the LORD called to him from the mountain" (Ex.19:3).

With the parting of the Red Sea, Egypt and bondage were left behind and freedom to choose a new future was ahead. The journey Moses faced was a difficult one, with many people suffering, some dying, but also with many births, marriages, and joyous celebrations. So it is in our life journey as leaders, we walk boldly toward a Promised Land of Opportunity.

As Moses led the people, he depended heavily on the direction of God. He was a beloved leader, but his next step after the great victory was to seek God's guidance on the mountain. God honored His choice and spoke personally to him with direct instruction, beginning with the Ten Commandments. Leaders need instruction, which is the foundation of life, and education, which is the gathering of information in order to achieve goals and success in the future. Instruction and education combine together to make a leader who continues to grow and excel.

One thing a leader can depend on is that God speaks clearly. While some live as though God made *Ten Suggestions*, the leader understands the truth. In Exodus 19, Moses went up to the mountain to meet with God and to receive His next instruction. This mountaintop experience was an intense one, and Moses came down from the mountain radiant with the presence of God and changed in his heart.

Unfortunately, Moses descended from the glory of that moment into chaos below. As God was laying out a plan of blessing for the people, they were experimenting with idol worship and drunkenness. What God was teaching Moses on that mountain was much more than a set of laws. He continued instruction in leadership of a people whose memories were short-lived, hearts thought only of self, and convictions were based on the moment.

had come *to* the Wilderness of Sinai, and camped in the wilderness. So Israel camped there before the mountain.

³And Moses went up to God, and the LORD called to him from the mountain, saying, "Thus you shall say to the house of Jacob, and tell the children of Israel: ⁴'You have seen what I did to the Egyptians, and *how* I bore you on eagles' wings and brought you to Myself. ⁵Now therefore, if you will indeed obey My voice and keep My covenant, then you shall be a special treasure to Me above all people; for all the earth *is* Mine. ⁶And you shall be to Me a kingdom of priests and a holy nation.' These *are* the words which you shall speak to the children of Israel."

⁷So Moses came and called for the elders of the people, and laid before them all these words which the LORD commanded him. ⁸Then all the people answered together and said, "All that the LORD has spoken we will do." So Moses brought back the words of the people to the LORD. ⁹And the LORD said to Moses, "Behold, I come to you in the thick cloud, that the people may hear when I speak with you, and believe you forever."

So Moses told the words of the people to the LORD.

¹⁰Then the LORD said to Moses, "Go to the people and consecrate them today and tomorrow, and let them wash their clothes. ¹¹And let them be ready for the third day. For on the third day the LORD will come down upon Mount Sinai in the sight of all the people. ¹²You shall set bounds for the people all around, saying, 'Take heed to yourselves *that* you do *not* go up to the mountain or touch its base. Whoever touches the mountain shall surely be put to death. ¹³Not a hand shall touch him, but he shall surely be stoned or shot *with an arrow;* whether man or beast, he shall not live.' When the trumpet sounds long, they shall come near the mountain."

¹⁴So Moses went down from the mountain to the people and sanctified the people, and they washed their clothes. ¹⁵And he said to the people, "Be ready for the third day; do not come near *your* wives."

¹⁶Then it came to pass on the third day, in the morning, that there were thunderings and lightnings, and a thick cloud on the mountain; and the sound of the trumpet was very loud, so that all

---

INSIDE *the* INFLUENCERS

AARON: Man of Conviction . . . Man of Compromise

EXODUS 19:24

Many people can relate to Aaron. On one leg of the journey he stands without compromise, while at another he falls like a house of cards. His moments of strength and conviction were followed by weakness and compromise. When the Amalekites came up against Israel, Moses called young Joshua to lead the battle and deliver the nation. During the battle, Moses stood on a hill overlooking the conflict with his staff in his outstretched hand. When his arms grew tired, Aaron and Hur held up his hands until the victory was won.

Following this victory, we see how quickly a leader can fall to cowardice and compromise. While encamped at the base of Mt. Sinai at the command of God, Moses ascended the mount to receive the tables of the law. Aaron, his two sons, and the seventy elders were permitted to go halfway up the mountain, seeing the glory of Israel's God (Ex. 19:24; 24:9–11) from far off. But then Aaron returned to the people, and because of fear, cowardice, insecurity, or any number of reasons, he made a golden calf for the people to worship (Ex. 32:4). The leader who is not constant and dependable will operate with a lid on their influence for the Kingdom.

the people who *were* in the camp trembled. [17]And Moses brought the people out of the camp to meet with God, and they stood at the foot of the mountain. [18]Now Mount Sinai *was* completely in smoke, because the LORD descended upon it in fire. Its smoke ascended like the smoke of a furnace, and the whole mountain[a] quaked greatly. [19]And when the blast of the trumpet sounded long and became louder and louder, Moses spoke, and God answered him by voice. [20]Then the LORD came down upon Mount Sinai, on the top of the mountain. And the LORD called Moses to the top of the mountain, and Moses went up.

[21]And the LORD said to Moses, "Go down and warn the people, lest they break through to gaze at the LORD, and many of them perish. [22]Also let the priests who come near the LORD consecrate themselves, lest the LORD break out against them."

[23]But Moses said to the LORD, "The people cannot come up to Mount Sinai; for You warned us, saying, 'Set bounds around the mountain and consecrate it.'"

[24]Then the LORD said to him, "Away! Get down and then come up, you and Aaron with you. But do not let the priests and the people break through to come up to the LORD, lest He break out against them." [25]So Moses went down to the people and spoke to them.

THE TEN COMMANDMENTS

20

[1]And God spoke all these words, saying:

[2]"I *am* the LORD your God, who brought you out of the land of Egypt, out of the house of bondage.

[3]"You shall have no other gods before Me.

[4]"You shall not make for yourself a carved image—any likeness of *anything that is* in heaven above, or that *is* in the earth beneath, or that *is* in the water under the earth; [5]you shall not bow down to them *nor serve them.* For I, the LORD your God, *am* a jealous God, visiting the iniquity of the fathers upon the children to the third and fourth *generations* of those who hate Me, [6]but showing mercy to thousands, to those

who love Me and keep My commandments.

[7]"You shall not take the name of the LORD your God in vain, for the LORD will not hold *him* guiltless who takes His name in vain.

[8]"Remember the Sabbath day, to keep it holy. [9]Six days you shall labor and do all your work, [10]but the seventh day *is* the Sabbath of the LORD your God. *In it* you shall do no work: you, nor your son, nor your daughter, nor your male servant, nor your female servant, nor your cattle, nor your stranger who *is* within your gates. [11]For *in* six days the LORD made the heavens and the earth, the sea, and all that *is* in them, and rested the seventh day. Therefore the LORD blessed the Sabbath day and hallowed it.

[12]"Honor your father and your mother, that your days may be long upon the land which the LORD your God is giving you.

[13]"You shall not murder.

[14]"You shall not commit adultery.

[15]"You shall not steal.

[16]"You shall not bear false witness against your neighbor.

[17]"You shall not covet your neighbor's house; you shall not covet your neighbor's wife, nor his male servant, nor his female servant, nor his ox, nor his donkey, nor anything that *is* your neighbor's."

THE PEOPLE AFRAID OF GOD'S PRESENCE

[18]Now all the people witnessed the thunderings, the lightning flashes, the sound of the trumpet, and the mountain smoking; and when the people saw *it*, they trembled and stood afar off. [19]Then they said to Moses, "You speak with us, and we will hear; but let not God speak with us, lest we die."

[20]And Moses said to the people, "Do not fear; for God has come to test you, and that His fear may be before you, so that you may not sin." [21]So the people stood afar off, but Moses drew near the thick darkness where God *was*.

19:18 [a]Septuagint reads *all the people.*

THROUGH THE GRID

In giving the Ten Commandments to humanity, God's purpose was not to limit the bounds of human expression. Rather, God has acted as any good Father would act by providing rules and guidelines that enable us to live lives of fulfillment and happiness on earth, as well as be protected from the dangers and harms that could befall us. God gave His people the Commandments in order to provide for their guidance, their encouragement, and their protection. Just as some laws are necessary to provide order and structure, the laws that God gives us help us to live optimally as members of society. They also provide a way for us to honor God through obedience, as each of the Commandments reflects part of God's identity.

The purpose of the Ten Commandments was not to assure the absence of evil but to ensure the presence of purity. Certainly, God intended the Ten Commandments to provide rules for living, but they are much more than a simple list of dos and don'ts. They are part of God's revelation to humanity, and they are to be cherished and kept. We need the Ten Commandments today because we desperately need God's love. These Commandments serve as God's divine gauge to help us discover peace and blessing for our lives.

Although the Ten Commandments have generally lost their place of authority in the context of our nation, the actual Commandments have not abated in value, worth, or authority. They are still the authoritative revelation of God to humanity, through which God reveals His will for humanity and how humanity should live in relationship to God and others. The Commandments remain timeless, relevant truths. Those who ignore the Ten Commandments ignore a vital part of the revelation of God's character, and in doing so, they live in sin. Honoring God involves obeying God and living by the rules and standards He has set forth. In the midst of an individualistic society, one of the greatest witnesses of believers is that they obey God as their ultimate source of authority.

THE LAW OF THE ALTAR

22Then the LORD said to Moses, "Thus you shall say to the children of Israel: 'You have seen that I have talked with you from heaven. 23You shall not make *anything as to be* with Me—gods of silver or gods of gold you shall not make for yourselves. 24An altar of earth you shall make for Me, and you shall sacrifice on it your burnt offerings and your peace offerings, your sheep and your oxen. In every place where I record My name I will come to you, and I will bless you. 25And if you make Me an altar of stone, you shall not build it of hewn stone; for if you use your tool on it, you have profaned it. 26Nor shall you go up by steps to My altar, that your nakedness may not be exposed on it.'

THE LAW CONCERNING SERVANTS

21 "Now these *are* the judgments which you shall set before them: 2If you buy a Hebrew servant, he shall serve six years; and in the seventh he shall go out free and pay nothing. 3If he comes in by himself, he shall go out by himself; if he *comes in* married, then his wife shall go out with him. 4If his master has given him a wife, and she has borne him sons or daughters, the wife and her children shall be her master's, and he shall go out by himself. 5But if the servant plainly says, 'I love

THROUGH THE GRID

Written by the Hand of God:
You Shall Have No Other Gods
Before Me

EXODUS 20:3 *You shall have no other gods before Me.*

The very first Commandment God gave to the people of Israel directly addressed the issue of whom the nation of Israel was to worship. Since God had laid claim to the people of Israel and delivered them out of bondage, God alone had the right to be worshipped.

The world is full of gods and idols that compete for our attention, offering some form of good or way of improving one's life. The God of the Bible, however, offers far more than one could ever hope for—a way of salvation from the darkness and brokenness of our sin, available through the Person of Jesus Christ. Through Him, we can have complete restoration, redemption, and fulfillment—more than any other god could offer!

God has a right to command our worship in the first place because God created us, along with the entire universe. Although the universe is seemingly huge, God ordained a plan for our lives before the beginning of time. God knows every detail of our lives and has promised to always be with us. Because God has created us and knows us intimately, God has a right to command our worship.

There are several ways in which we can honor God through giving Him our full worship. We can worship God by keeping Him first in our lives, in spite of all the things crying out for our attention. We can also worship God by giving to Him all the glory for the successes that we encounter. Sacrificial living is another way in which we can worship God—that is, through our full obedience. When we worship God, we can do so with a wholehearted love—one that loves God with all of our heart, soul, mind, and strength. We worship God by surrendering all of our lives to Him and allowing God to keep ultimate control of our lives. In order to do that, we must consistently walk in faith as we examine our hearts. Only God is worthy of our worship—we must worship God alone.

my master, my wife, and my children; I will not go out free,' ⁶then his master shall bring him to the judges. He shall also bring him to the door, or to the doorpost, and his master shall pierce his ear with an awl; and he shall serve him forever.

⁷"And if a man sells his daughter to be a female slave, she shall not go out as the male slaves do. ⁸If she does not please her master, who has betrothed her to himself, then he shall let her be redeemed. He shall have no right to sell her to a foreign people, since he has dealt deceitfully with

her. ⁹And if he has betrothed her to his son, he shall deal with her according to the custom of daughters. ¹⁰If he takes another *wife,* he shall not diminish her food, her clothing, and her marriage rights. ¹¹And if he does not do these three for her, then she shall go out free, without *paying* money.

THE LAW CONCERNING VIOLENCE

¹²"He who strikes a man so that he dies shall surely be put to death. ¹³However, if he did not lie in wait, but God delivered *him* into his hand,

THROUGH THE GRID

Written by the Hand of God:
Do Not Worship Idols

EXODUS 20:4 *You shall not make for yourself a carved image.*

The second Commandment deals with the issue of worshipping idols, and God forbids His people from making idols of any kind to worship. This command is related to the first one, in that the first Commandment told us *who* to worship, whereas the second Commandment tells us *how* to worship God.

This command attests to the fact that God is a jealous God who strongly desires our entire attention and focus. In order to worship God correctly, we need to follow the pattern of worship prescribed in the Scriptures. When we presume to know how to worship God, it is the sin of human presumption. We cannot fashion God in our own image nor can we worship God any way we want. We must worship God in His way.

The second Commandment addresses the heart of worship. That is, it is our attitude when worshipping God that is of utmost importance. Worshipping God with a correct attitude is not about nominal religion or "Easter Sunday attendees," but rather, the right attitude of worship emerges out of an exciting personal relationship. When we receive Christ as our Lord and Savior, we commit to turning away from the false gods in our lives, and we establish a relationship with the God of the universe!

Several idols can distract us from pure worship. When we are motivated by greed, we are practicing idolatry. We practice idolatry when we attribute Godlike characteristics to things and people other than God, such as work or a business venture or a political party. We are also idolatrous when we live by sight rather than by faith. Also, when we begin to follow the dictates of culture over the dictates of God, we are idolatrous. In response, Christians must guard their hearts and take every thought captive to the obedience of Christ. Christians must pray without ceasing, must live their lives according to God's Word and not emotions, and must share their faith actively with others.

then I will appoint for you a place where he may flee.

¹⁴"But if a man acts with premeditation against his neighbor, to kill him by treachery, you shall take him from My altar, that he may die.

¹⁵"And he who strikes his father or his mother shall surely be put to death.

¹⁶"He who kidnaps a man and sells him, or if he is found in his hand, shall surely be put to death.

¹⁷"And he who curses his father or his mother shall surely be put to death.

¹⁸"If men contend with each other, and one strikes the other with a stone or with *his* fist, and he does not die but is confined to *his* bed, ¹⁹if he rises again and walks about outside with his staff, then he who struck *him* shall be acquitted. He shall only pay *for* the loss of his time, and shall provide *for him* to be thoroughly healed.

²⁰"And if a man beats his male or female servant with a rod, so that he dies under his hand, he shall surely be punished. ²¹Notwithstanding, if he

THROUGH THE GRID

Written by the Hand of God:
Do Not Take God's Name in Vain

EXODUS 20:7 *You shall not take the name of the Lord your God in vain.*

The third Commandment addresses the issue of using God's name in vain. God prohibits the misuse of His name, because it is higher and holier than any other name. God's name is supreme among the entire universe and demands a level of dignity and respect that reflects who God is.

In the culture of the ancient Near East, the name one was given became one's identity. Your name represents who you are, your essence, your reputation, and your history. The author of Proverbs states that a "good name is to be chosen rather than great riches" (22:1). In the Lord's Prayer, Jesus taught His disciples to hallow God's name. To "hallow" is to consecrate something, or to set it apart. Thus, the language we use to address God must be done with reverence and awe. We can also take God's name in vain when we use profanity, as profanity calls into question who God is and what God has done. Profaning the name of God is to show ultimate disrespect and dishonor for the One who created us.

Although this command addresses our speech, it actually has more to do with our walk than our talk. To "take" the name of the Lord God is actually to "bear or carry" it. Thus, the Commandment addresses the ways in which we bear the name of our God. We take God's name in vain when we waste our lives on meaningless, time-consuming things that are of no eternal consequence. Having done so, we have wasted the precious time given to us.

However, it is we as finite Christians who have been entrusted with the mighty name of God. We must make sure our walk and our talk are consistent because we bear a mighty name, and we cannot permit God's name to be carried in vain. We can even more greatly come to appreciate the name of God when we stop to think of all He has done for us. Because of His faithfulness, we must bear God's name with honor and dignity.

remains alive a day or two, he shall not be punished; for he *is* his property.

²²"If men fight, and hurt a woman with child, so that she gives birth prematurely, yet no harm follows, he shall surely be punished accordingly as the woman's husband imposes on him; and he shall pay as the judges *determine.* ²³But if *any* harm follows, then you shall give life for life, ²⁴eye for eye, tooth for tooth, hand for hand, foot for foot, ²⁵burn for burn, wound for wound, stripe for stripe.

²⁶"If a man strikes the eye of his male or female servant, and destroys it, he shall let him go free for the sake of his eye. ²⁷And if he knocks out the tooth of his male or female servant, he shall let him go free for the sake of his tooth.

Animal Control Laws

²⁸"If an ox gores a man or a woman to death, then the ox shall surely be stoned, and its flesh shall not be eaten; but the owner of the ox *shall be* acquitted. ²⁹But if the ox tended to thrust with its horn in times past, and it has been made known to his owner, and he has not kept it confined, so that it has killed a man or a woman, the ox shall be stoned and its owner also shall be put to death.

THROUGH THE GRID

Written by the Hand of God:
Keep the Sabbath Holy

EXODUS 20:8 *Remember the Sabbath day, to keep it holy.*

The fourth Commandment exhorts the people of Israel to keep the Sabbath day holy. This command requires us to keep a holy day in our week for the Lord and is required for our benefit so that we can rest in the Lord. This rest is to be observed in obedience to God and for God's glory.

Although the Jewish tradition adheres to Sabbath on Saturday, Christians observe the Sabbath on Sunday because of the change of our natures when we are joined to Christ. When we become Christians, we have new natures and celebrate the Sabbath on Sunday because that is when Christ rose from the dead (John 20:1).

The ability to rest and reflect on the Sabbath has vanished. We find ourselves constantly busy, preparing for event after event or finishing that work project. The fourth Commandment has come into gross disregard. It used to be that observing the Sabbath on Sunday was a mainstream part of our culture. Stores were closed and very little was open. Nowadays, it has become a culture of convenience, and most retail stores and professional sports operate all seven days of the week. Our culture's increased focus on productivity demands that we not stop working until we finish the job; and in the professional world, taking Sunday off is looked down upon by many.

But there are several reasons why an observed Sabbath is a good thing. First, all of creation requires rest. Our bodies are designed to be productive, but they are also designed to require rest in order to recharge. Observing the Sabbath also provides a day that has been carved out to worship God. It gives an opportunity to reflect on the workings of God in our lives and to demonstrate our trust and dependence on Him. And it also becomes a great blessing to those who keep it. Finally, the Sabbath points to the rest we have in Christ. This command should be followed in order to obey God and honor Him with our bodies and with our rest.

---

³⁰If there is imposed on him a sum of money, then he shall pay to redeem his life, whatever is imposed on him. ³¹Whether it has gored a son or gored a daughter, according to this judgment it shall be done to him. ³²If the ox gores a male or female servant, he shall give to their master thirty shekels of silver, and the ox shall be stoned.

³³"And if a man opens a pit, or if a man digs a pit and does not cover it, and an ox or a donkey falls in it, ³⁴the owner of the pit shall make *it* good; he shall give money to their owner, but the dead *animal* shall be his.

³⁵"If one man's ox hurts another's, so that it dies, then they shall sell the live ox and divide the money from it; and the dead *ox* they shall also divide. ³⁶Or if it was known that the ox tended to thrust in time past, and its owner has not kept it confined, he shall surely pay ox for ox, and the dead animal shall be his own.

RESPONSIBILITY FOR PROPERTY

22 "If a man steals an ox or a sheep, and slaughters it or sells it, he shall restore five oxen for an ox and four sheep for a sheep. ²If the

THROUGH THE GRID

Written by the Hand of God:
Honor Your Parents

EXODUS 20:12   *Honor your father and your mother.*

The fifth Commandment exhorts the followers of God to honor their parents. This is the first Commandment with promise, and it is the first Commandment that instructs us how to act toward each other. God sees that the way we treat our parents is very important, as the way we treat them is a marker of how we treat all authority throughout life.

As a marker of respect for authority, God's followers are asked to honor their parents, which involves respecting them, obeying them, and treating them with care (Eph. 6:1–3). In the world today, many children grow up in homes that are anything but traditional or functional. However, respecting and honoring our parents pleases God and remains a requirement. We should treat our parents as people who are important in our lives and worthy of respect. The Bible celebrates children who honor their parents.

We are told to honor our parents because it contributes to maintaining the order God set forth for the world and society. When we obey our parents, the very first authority figures in our lives, we are modeling an honor and respect for other authorities. Societies that do not consist of order soon crumble away. Honoring parents is the foundational block of societal structure. Also, honoring our parents benefits our own well-being. Our parents know us better than anyone else, and they have years of wisdom and experience behind them. We should honor that by listening to them and obeying them. Honoring our parents also contributes to God's promise of giving us a full and long life.

However, sometimes loving our parents can be difficult, especially when our parents have wronged us. We can still honor them by forgiving them and extending Christ's love to them. We should respect their God-given authority, even if they do not deserve honor. This is a huge testament to our dependence on God and our obedience to Him. In spite of their flaws, we should give our parents our honor by loving them and respecting them.

---

thief is found breaking in, and he is struck so that he dies, *there shall be* no guilt for his bloodshed. ³If the sun has risen on him, *there shall be* guilt for his bloodshed. He should make full restitution; if he has nothing, then he shall be sold for his theft. ⁴If the theft is certainly found alive in his hand, whether it is an ox or donkey or sheep, he shall restore double.

⁵"If a man causes a field or vineyard to be grazed, and lets loose his animal, and it feeds in another man's field, he shall make restitution from the best of his own field and the best of his own vineyard.

⁶"If fire breaks out and catches in thorns, so that stacked grain, standing grain, or the field is consumed, he who kindled the fire shall surely make restitution.

⁷"If a man delivers to his neighbor money or articles to keep, and it is stolen out of the man's house, if the thief is found, he shall pay double. ⁸If the thief is not found, then the master of the house shall be brought to the judges *to see*

THROUGH THE GRID

Written by the Hand of God:
Do Not Murder

EXODUS 20:13 *You shall not murder.*

The sixth Commandment consists of God's command not to commit murder. God forbids murder because it takes away the life of another person. The murderer takes the role of God as the author of life; and when human beings attempt to play God, it never ends well.

There is a distinction between "killing" and "murder." Not all killing is murder. The narrow scope of this command focuses on the taking of innocent life by another person. Capital punishment, for example, is not murder. These deaths are administered to those who have committed heinous crimes, mostly revolving around murder. Justice is served when a guilty murderer dies for taking the sacred life of another. Also, military defense of a nation is not murder. Because of the nature of the world and its societies, it becomes necessary at times to defend one's nation against outside forces of oppression. This justifies the taking of human life. Self-defense is also not murder, as we must protect ourselves from threats. The killing of animals is also not murder, as God permits us to kill animals for food.

One of the biggest issues raised here concerns the sanctity of life. God has endowed every member of creation with His own breath and life; thus, we must consider all human life as sacred. The growing battle today is between those who hold a person's sanctity of life on one hand and their usefulness to society on the other. Our postmodern culture that is so bent on productivity tells us that disabled or elderly people can't make valuable contributions; therefore, it is okay to end their lives or to value them less.

God commands differently because God commands us to value the worth He has given them as part of creation—a worth not based on utility. That being the case, abortion, euthanasia, genocide, and suicide all break God's Commandment. However, no sin, including murder, is beyond the scope of God's forgiveness. God's bold grace knows no bounds, and so we all must be thankful for God's forgiveness of our sin.

---

whether he has put his hand into his neighbor's goods.

9"For any kind of trespass, *whether it concerns* an ox, a donkey, a sheep, or clothing, *or* for any kind of lost thing which *another* claims to be his, the cause of both parties shall come before the judges; *and* whomever the judges condemn shall pay double to his neighbor. 10If a man delivers to his neighbor a donkey, an ox, a sheep, or any animal to keep, and it dies, is hurt, or driven away, no one seeing *it,* 11*then* an oath of the LORD shall be between them both, that he has not put his hand into his neighbor's goods; and the owner of it shall accept *that,* and he shall not make *it* good. 12But if, in fact, it is stolen from him, he shall make restitution to the owner of it. 13If it is torn to pieces *by a beast, then* he shall bring it as evidence, *and* he shall not make good what was torn.

14"And if a man borrows *anything* from his neighbor, and it becomes injured or dies, the owner of it not *being* with it, he shall surely make

THROUGH THE GRID

EXODUS 20:14   *You shall not commit adultery.*

The seventh Commandment forbids God's people to commit adultery. While a very straightforward command, it is easily broken by many, including followers of Christ. This command demonstrates that God cares about our sexual purity and wants us to control the passions we have.

God prohibits adultery because He values the sexual union between husband and wife, since it mirrors Christ's relationship with the church. In a marriage relationship, two people become one flesh through sexual union. The pernicious act of adultery destroys these relationships and results in great harm to our bodies (1 Cor. 6:18). Sexual diseases are extremely rampant throughout our world, and hundreds of thousands continue to die from HIV/AIDS every year. Other STDs also have lifelong effects, and one never knows when one is contracting a disease.

Adultery destroys the model of marriage set forth between Christ and the church. Christ has made an important covenant with His church, which is something He is incapable of breaking. That is why the church is often called the bride of Christ. Christ treats the church with utmost respect because it is His body. Adultery stems from a breach in the way we view our spouses. When we treat our spouses with honor and respect, then we avoid the pitfalls of temptation. The consequences of adultery are tremendous, since it tears husband and wife apart, damaging both of them in the process. The bond of trust and intimacy is broken; and pain is the result, along with possibly divorce.

God's command to flee from adultery is for our well-being and for the unity of the marriage relationship. It is undoubtedly true that we live in an immoral culture. Marriage has become about convenience and pleasure, and there is an air of sexual exploration that invites unfaithfulness. In order to avoid adultery, we need to guard our hearts carefully. Our sexuality is a powerful force that can be used for good within the context of marriage, or misused, resulting in harm outside of marriage. We must glorify God by allowing Him to control our sexuality.

it good. ¹⁵If its owner *was* with it, he shall not make *it* good; if it *was* hired, it came for its hire.

Moral and Ceremonial Principles

¹⁶"If a man entices a virgin who is not betrothed, and lies with her, he shall surely pay the bride-price for her *to be* his wife. ¹⁷If her father utterly refuses to give her to him, he shall pay money according to the bride-price of virgins.

¹⁸"You shall not permit a sorceress to live.

¹⁹"Whoever lies with an animal shall surely be put to death.

²⁰"He who sacrifices to *any* god, except to the LORD only, he shall be utterly destroyed.

²¹"You shall neither mistreat a stranger nor oppress him, for you were strangers in the land of Egypt.

²²"You shall not afflict any widow or fatherless

THROUGH THE GRID

Written by the Hand of God:
Do Not Steal

EXODUS 20:15 *You shall not steal.*

The eighth Commandment forbids God's followers from stealing. As stealing can take a variety of forms, including any dishonesty when dealing with money or property, we must guard ourselves against any sort of stealing. In the end, this command is about our hearts and about the ways in which we treat others.

Stealing isn't just taking money from someone else's wallet; it involves dishonesty in the way we treat other people and their property. Many people, including believers, dishonestly inflate their insurance claims or file dishonest tax returns. Stealing also includes not paying our bills, not paying our tithes to God, and not working faithfully to the best of our abilities for our employers. When we steal, we are tempted by the notion that we can get something for nothing. But this always comes at a great cost in the end, and our moral compass takes a direct hit.

When we steal or defraud others, we show a fundamental lack of trust in God. Because God is our provider, He gives us all that we need. So when we defraud others and use manipulation to acquire unjust or unethical gains, we demonstrate that we do not trust God to provide for our needs. Stealing also shows a lack of respect for others. We are commanded as Christians to "love your neighbor as yourself" (Lev. 19:18). If we love our neighbors, we will not steal or cheat them out of what is theirs. Stealing also demonstrates the panic we feel in certain critical situations.

This command deals again with who we really are on the inside. If Christ has indeed changed our lives, then we should not steal or involve ourselves in dishonest or fraudulent behavior. To do so is to dishonor our God by removing our trust in His provisions, and it dishonors our neighbor by appropriating their possessions as our own. We can honor God and our neighbors by being people of integrity who turn to God and patiently wait for Him to move and to provide for our needs.

---

child. ²³If you afflict them in any way, *and* they cry at all to Me, I will surely hear their cry; ²⁴and My wrath will become hot, and I will kill you with the sword; your wives shall be widows, and your children fatherless.

²⁵"If you lend money to *any of* My people *who are* poor among you, you shall not be like a moneylender to him; you shall not charge him interest. ²⁶If you ever take your neighbor's garment as a pledge, you shall return it to him before the sun goes down. ²⁷For that *is* his only covering,

it *is* his garment for his skin. What will he sleep in? And it will be that when he cries to Me, I will hear, for I *am* gracious.

²⁸"You shall not revile God, nor curse a ruler of your people.

²⁹"You shall not delay *to offer* the first of your ripe produce and your juices. The firstborn of your sons you shall give to Me. ³⁰Likewise you shall do with your oxen *and* your sheep. It shall be with its mother seven days; on the eighth day you shall give it to Me.

THROUGH THE GRID

Written by the Hand of God:
Do Not Bear False Witness

EXODUS 20:16   *You shall not bear false witness against your neighbor.*

In the ninth Commandment, God forbids testifying falsely against one's neighbor. This command has to do with honesty, integrity, and telling the truth, which is part of God's moral fabric. We are forbidden from making false statements *about* or *to* our neighbor.

We live in a world where lying is seen as convenient in order to get out of a jam or to avoid consequences. However, lying itself can have bad consequences, as lies eventually catch up with us. God is very clear that what is true is completely true, and what is false in the least bit is entirely false.

God holds us to a high standard of morality; and anything that deviates from truth is falsehood, which God prohibits. God's very identity is linked to truth, as Jesus Himself claims to be "the way, the truth, and the life" (John 14:6). If God is truth, then He opposes all falsehood; and when we lie, we disappoint our Creator, who hears our every word and sees our every action.

Lying includes gossiping and slandering, because these activities damage others and our relationship with them by attributing untrue or destructive statements to them. We also lie when we say hurtful and harmful things about others, as truth telling involves more than just making a true statement; it also includes speaking words that edify, encourage, and build up. Falsehood is likewise more than just making a false statement; it is stating something that hurts or harms someone else.

Just as our words have the potential to tear down, they also have great potential to build up. When we say things that encourage others, we reflect the goodness of God and become a witness to God's character. Falsehood does the exact opposite by contradicting the very identity of God. Thus, as God commands, it is never right to lie. Rather, the truth sets us free. We must cling to the truth and use our words to uplift others.

[31] "And you shall be holy men to Me: you shall not eat meat torn *by beasts* in the field; you shall throw it to the dogs.

JUSTICE FOR ALL

23 "You shall not circulate a false report. Do not put your hand with the wicked to be an unrighteous witness. [2] You shall not follow a crowd to do evil; nor shall you testify in a dispute so as to turn aside after many to pervert *justice*. [3] You shall not show partiality to a poor man in his dispute.

[4] "If you meet your enemy's ox or his donkey going astray, you shall surely bring it back to him again. [5] If you see the donkey of one who hates you lying under its burden, and you would refrain from helping it, you shall surely help him with it.

[6] "You shall not pervert the judgment of your poor in his dispute. [7] Keep yourself far from a false matter; do not kill the innocent and righteous. For I will not justify the wicked. [8] And you shall take no bribe, for a bribe blinds the discerning and perverts the words of the righteous.

[9] "Also you shall not oppress a stranger, for you know the heart of a stranger, because you were strangers in the land of Egypt.

THROUGH THE GRID

Written by the Hand of God:
Do Not Covet

EXODUS 20:17 *You shall not covet . . . anything that is your neighbor's.*

The tenth and final Commandment forbids coveting the possessions or status of others. Coveting demonstrates an inappropriate desire for things that we do not have or that belong to someone else. When we crave our neighbor's possessions, we sin against God.

Coveting involves an ungodly desire for anything that could take God's place in our lives. Our principal duty and the chief concern here revolves around the priorities we give to things in our lives. We must control our desire for things, so that they never surpass our desire for God. We should desire to know and love God with all of our heart, soul, mind, and strength (Deut. 6:5).

Covetousness is like a venom that infects our minds by perpetuating the thought that we aren't truly happy until we have what others have. Of course, this undermines our trust in God, the ultimate Provider. Obsessing over others' material possessions shows dissatisfaction with what God has given to us. As all things that we have come from God, it is disrespectful to crave things that others have that we don't have. Coveting demonstrates that we are not content or happy. It is a temptation to be greedy and to always want more and more. But we should remember that there are many in the world who daily do not have nearly enough to survive. We are very rich and fortunate by the world's standards, and we should remain grateful to God for His blessings. We must learn to be content in every circumstance and thereby avoid the pitfalls of being greedy and wanting what we do not need.

In truth, the tenth Commandment actually summarizes the Law. That is, there is no way a person could break any of the other Commandments without breaking the tenth. This command lies at the root of all sin. We as Christians must be careful to avoid coveting; and we must find our contentment, not in worldly possessions, but in the Person of Jesus Christ.

THE LAW OF SABBATHS

10"Six years you shall sow your land and gather in its produce, 11but the seventh *year* you shall let it rest and lie fallow, that the poor of your people may eat; and what they leave, the beasts of the field may eat. In like manner you shall do with your vineyard *and* your olive grove. 12Six days you shall do your work, and on the seventh day you shall rest, that your ox and your donkey may rest, and the son of your female servant and the stranger may be refreshed.

13"And in all that I have said to you, be circumspect and make no mention of the name of other gods, nor let it be heard from your mouth.

THREE ANNUAL FEASTS

14"Three times you shall keep a feast to Me in the year: 15You shall keep the Feast of Unleavened Bread (you shall eat unleavened bread seven days, as I commanded you, at the time appointed in the month of Abib, for in it you came out of Egypt; none shall appear before Me empty); 16and the

Feast of Harvest, the firstfruits of your labors which you have sown in the field; and the Feast of Ingathering at the end of the year, when you have gathered in *the fruit of* your labors from the field.

17"Three times in the year all your males shall appear before the Lord GOD.ᵃ

18"You shall not offer the blood of My sacrifice with leavened bread; nor shall the fat of My sacrifice remain until morning. 19The first of the firstfruits of your land you shall bring into the house of the LORD your God. You shall not boil a young goat in its mother's milk.

The Angel and the Promises

20"Behold, I send an Angel before you to keep you in the way and to bring you into the place which I have prepared. 21Beware of Him and obey His voice; do not provoke Him, for He will not pardon your transgressions; for My name *is* in Him. 22But if you indeed obey His voice and do all that I speak, then I will be an enemy to your enemies and an adversary to your adversaries. 23For My Angel will go before you and bring you in to the Amorites and the Hittites and the Perizzites and the Canaanites and the Hivites and the Jebusites; and I will cut them off. 24You shall not bow down to their gods, nor serve them, nor do according to their works; but you shall utterly overthrow them and completely break down their *sacred* pillars.

25"So you shall serve the LORD your God, and He will bless your bread and your water. And I will take sickness away from the midst of you. 26No one shall suffer miscarriage or be barren in your land; I will fulfill the number of your days.

27"I will send My fear before you, I will cause confusion among all the people to whom you come, and will make all your enemies turn *their* backs to you. 28And I will send hornets before you, which shall drive out the Hivite, the Canaanite, and the Hittite from before you. 29I will not drive them out from before you in one year, lest the land become desolate and the beasts of the field become too numerous for you. 30Little by little I will drive them out from before you, until you have increased, and you inherit the land. 31And I will set your bounds from the Red Sea to

the sea, Philistia, and from the desert to the River.ᵃ For I will deliver the inhabitants of the land into your hand, and you shall drive them out before you. 32You shall make no covenant with them, nor with their gods. 33They shall not dwell in your land, lest they make you sin against Me. For *if* you serve their gods, it will surely be a snare to you."

Israel Affirms the Covenant

24 Now He said to Moses, "Come up to the LORD, you and Aaron, Nadab and Abihu, and seventy of the elders of Israel, and worship from afar. 2And Moses alone shall come near the LORD, but they shall not come near; nor shall the people go up with him."

3So Moses came and told the people all the words of the LORD and all the judgments. And all the people answered with one voice and said, "All the words which the LORD has said we will do." 4And Moses wrote all the words of the LORD. And he rose early in the morning, and built an altar at the foot of the mountain, and twelve pillars according to the twelve tribes of Israel. 5Then he sent young men of the children of Israel, who offered burnt offerings and sacrificed peace offerings of oxen to the LORD. 6And Moses took half the blood and put *it* in basins, and half the blood he sprinkled on the altar. 7Then he took the Book of the Covenant and read in the hearing of the people. And they said, "All that the LORD has said we will do, and be obedient." 8And Moses took the blood, sprinkled *it* on the people, and said, "This is the blood of the covenant which the LORD has made with you according to all these words."

On the Mountain with God

9Then Moses went up, also Aaron, Nadab, and Abihu, and seventy of the elders of Israel, 10and they saw the God of Israel. And *there was* under His feet as it were a paved work of sapphire stone, and it was like the very heavens in *its* clarity. 11But on the nobles of the children of Israel He did not lay His hand. So they saw God, and they ate and drank.

23:17 ᵃHebrew *YHWH*, usually translated *Lord* **23:31** ᵃHebrew *Nahar*, the Euphrates

¹²Then the LORD said to Moses, "Come up to Me on the mountain and be there; and I will give you tablets of stone, and the law and commandments which I have written, that you may teach them."

¹³So Moses arose with his assistant Joshua, and Moses went up to the mountain of God. ¹⁴And he said to the elders, "Wait here for us until we come back to you. Indeed, Aaron and Hur *are* with you. If any man has a difficulty, let him go to them." ¹⁵Then Moses went up into the mountain, and a cloud covered the mountain.

¹⁶Now the glory of the LORD rested on Mount Sinai, and the cloud covered it six days. And on the seventh day He called to Moses out of the midst of the cloud. ¹⁷The sight of the glory of the LORD *was* like a consuming fire on the top of the mountain in the eyes of the children of Israel. ¹⁸So Moses went into the midst of the cloud and went up into the mountain. And Moses was on the mountain forty days and forty nights.

Offerings for the Sanctuary

25 Then the LORD spoke to Moses, saying: ²"Speak to the children of Israel, that they bring Me an offering. From everyone who gives it willingly with his heart you shall take My offering. ³And this *is* the offering which you shall take from them: gold, silver, and bronze; ⁴blue, purple, and scarlet *thread,* fine linen, and goats' *hair;* ⁵ram skins dyed red, badger skins, and acacia wood; ⁶oil for the light, and spices for the anointing oil and for the sweet incense; ⁷onyx stones, and stones to be set in the ephod and in the breastplate. ⁸And let them make Me a sanctuary, that I may dwell among them. ⁹According to all that I show you, *that is,* the pattern of the tabernacle and the pattern of all its furnishings, just so you shall make *it.*

The Ark of the Testimony

¹⁰"And they shall make an ark of acacia wood; two and a half cubits *shall be* its length, a cubit and a half its width, and a cubit and a half its height. ¹¹And you shall overlay it with pure gold, inside and out you shall overlay it, and shall make on it a molding of gold all around. ¹²You shall cast four rings of gold for it, and put *them* in its four corners; two rings *shall be* on one side, and two rings on the other side. ¹³And you shall make poles *of* acacia wood, and overlay them with gold. ¹⁴You shall put the poles into the rings on the sides of the ark, that the ark may be carried by them. ¹⁵The poles shall be in the rings of the ark; they shall not be taken from it. ¹⁶And you shall put into the ark the Testimony which I will give you.

¹⁷"You shall make a mercy seat of pure gold; two and a half cubits *shall be* its length and a cubit and a half its width. ¹⁸And you shall make two cherubim of gold; of hammered work you shall make them at the two ends of the mercy seat. ¹⁹Make one cherub at one end, and the other cherub at the other end; you shall make the cherubim at the two ends of it *of one piece* with the mercy seat. ²⁰And the cherubim shall stretch out *their* wings above, covering the mercy seat with their wings, and they shall face one another; the faces of the cherubim *shall be* toward the mercy seat. ²¹You shall put the mercy seat on top of the ark, and in the ark you shall put the Testimony that I will give you. ²²And there I will meet with you, and I will speak with you from above the mercy seat, from between the two cherubim which *are* on the ark of the Testimony, about everything which I will give you in commandment to the children of Israel.

The Table for the Showbread

²³"You shall also make a table of acacia wood; two cubits *shall be* its length, a cubit its width, and a cubit and a half its height. ²⁴And you shall overlay it with pure gold, and make a molding of gold all around. ²⁵You shall make for it a frame of a handbreadth all around, and you shall make a gold molding for the frame all around. ²⁶And you shall make for it four rings of gold, and put the rings on the four corners that *are* at its four legs. ²⁷The rings shall be close to the frame, as holders for the poles to bear the table. ²⁸And you shall make the poles of acacia wood, and overlay them with gold, that the table may be carried with them. ²⁹You shall make its dishes, its pans, its pitchers, and its bowls for pouring. You shall make them of pure gold. ³⁰And you shall set the showbread on the table before Me always.

The Gold Lampstand

³¹"You shall also make a lampstand of pure gold; the lampstand shall be of hammered work.

Its shaft, its branches, its bowls, its *ornamental* knobs, and flowers shall be *of one piece.* ³²And six branches shall come out of its sides: three branches of the lampstand out of one side, and three branches of the lampstand out of the other side. ³³Three bowls *shall be* made like almond *blossoms* on one branch, *with* an *ornamental* knob and a flower, and three bowls made like almond *blossoms* on the other branch, *with* an *ornamental* knob and a flower—and so for the six branches that come out of the lampstand. ³⁴On the lampstand itself four bowls *shall be* made like almond *blossoms, each with* its *ornamental* knob and flower. ³⁵And *there shall be* a knob under the *first* two branches of the same, a knob under the *second* two branches of the same, and a knob under the *third* two branches of the same, according to the six branches that extend from the lampstand. ³⁶Their knobs and their branches *shall be of one piece;* all of it *shall be* one hammered piece of pure gold. ³⁷You shall make seven lamps for it, and they shall arrange its lamps so that they give light in front of it. ³⁸And its wick-trimmers and their trays *shall be* of pure gold. ³⁹It shall be made of a talent of pure gold, with all these utensils. ⁴⁰And see to it that you make *them* according to the pattern which was shown you on the mountain.

The Tabernacle

26 "Moreover you shall make the tabernacle *with* ten curtains *of* fine woven linen and blue, purple, and scarlet *thread;* with artistic designs of cherubim you shall weave them. ²The length of each curtain *shall be* twenty-eight cubits, and the width of each curtain four cubits. And every one of the curtains shall have the same measurements. ³Five curtains shall be coupled to one another, and *the other* five curtains *shall be* coupled to one another. ⁴And you shall make loops of blue *yarn* on the edge of the curtain on the selvedge of *one* set, and likewise you shall do on the outer edge of *the other* curtain of the second set. ⁵Fifty loops you shall make in the one curtain, and fifty loops you shall make on the edge of the curtain that *is* on the end of the second set, that the loops may be clasped to one another. ⁶And you shall make fifty clasps of gold, and couple the curtains together with the clasps, so that it may be one tabernacle.

⁷"You shall also make curtains of goats' *hair,* to be a tent over the tabernacle. You shall make eleven curtains. ⁸The length of each curtain *shall be* thirty cubits, and the width of each curtain four cubits; and the eleven curtains shall all have the same measurements. ⁹And you shall couple five curtains by themselves and six curtains by themselves, and you shall double over the sixth curtain at the forefront of the tent. ¹⁰You shall make fifty loops on the edge of the curtain that is outermost in *one* set, and fifty loops on the edge of the curtain of the second set. ¹¹And you shall make fifty bronze clasps, put the clasps into the loops, and couple the tent together, that it may be one. ¹²The remnant that remains of the curtains of the tent, the half curtain that remains, shall hang over the back of the tabernacle. ¹³And a cubit on one side and a cubit on the other side, of what remains of the length of the curtains of the tent, shall hang over the sides of the tabernacle, on this side and on that side, to cover it.

¹⁴"You shall also make a covering of ram skins dyed red for the tent, and a covering of badger skins above that.

¹⁵"And for the tabernacle you shall make the boards of acacia wood, standing upright. ¹⁶Ten cubits *shall be* the length of a board, and a cubit and a half *shall be* the width of each board. ¹⁷Two tenons *shall be* in each board for binding one to another. Thus you shall make for all the boards of the tabernacle. ¹⁸And you shall make the boards for the tabernacle, twenty boards for the south side. ¹⁹You shall make forty sockets of silver under the twenty boards: two sockets under each of the boards for its two tenons. ²⁰And for the second side of the tabernacle, the north side, *there shall be* twenty boards ²¹and their forty sockets of silver: two sockets under each of the boards. ²²For the far side of the tabernacle, westward, you shall make six boards. ²³And you shall also make two boards for the two back corners of the tabernacle. ²⁴They shall be coupled together at the bottom and they shall be coupled together at the top by one ring. Thus it shall be for both of them. They shall be for the two corners. ²⁵So there shall be eight boards with their sockets of silver—sixteen sockets—two sockets under each of the boards.

²⁶"And you shall make bars of acacia wood: five for the boards on one side of the tabernacle,

²⁷five bars for the boards on the other side of the tabernacle, and five bars for the boards of the side of the tabernacle, for the far side westward. ²⁸The middle bar shall pass through the midst of the boards from end to end. ²⁹You shall overlay the boards with gold, make their rings of gold *as* holders for the bars, and overlay the bars with gold. ³⁰And you shall raise up the tabernacle according to its pattern which you were shown on the mountain.

³¹"You shall make a veil woven of blue, purple, and scarlet *thread,* and fine woven linen. It shall be woven with an artistic design of cherubim. ³²You shall hang it upon the four pillars of acacia *wood* overlaid with gold. Their hooks *shall be* gold, upon four sockets of silver. ³³And you shall hang the veil from the clasps. Then you shall bring the ark of the Testimony in there, behind the veil. The veil shall be a divider for you between the holy *place* and the Most Holy. ³⁴You shall put the mercy seat upon the ark of the Testimony in the Most Holy. ³⁵You shall set the table outside the veil, and the lampstand across from the table on the side of the tabernacle toward the south; and you shall put the table on the north side.

³⁶"You shall make a screen for the door of the tabernacle, *woven of* blue, purple, and scarlet *thread,* and fine woven linen, made by a weaver. ³⁷And you shall make for the screen five pillars of acacia *wood,* and overlay them with gold; their hooks *shall be* gold, and you shall cast five sockets of bronze for them.

THE ALTAR OF BURNT OFFERING

27 "You shall make an altar of acacia wood, five cubits long and five cubits wide—the altar shall be square—and its height *shall be* three cubits. ²You shall make its horns on its four corners; its horns shall be of one piece with it. And you shall overlay it with bronze. ³Also you shall make its pans to receive its ashes, and its shovels and its basins and its forks and its firepans; you shall make all its utensils of bronze. ⁴You shall make a grate for it, a network of bronze; and on the network you shall make four bronze rings at its four corners. ⁵You shall put it under the rim of the altar beneath, that the network may be midway up the altar. ⁶And you shall make poles for the altar, poles of acacia wood, and overlay them

with bronze. ⁷The poles shall be put in the rings, and the poles shall be on the two sides of the altar to bear it. ⁸You shall make it hollow with boards; as it was shown you on the mountain, so shall they make *it.*

THE COURT OF THE TABERNACLE

⁹"You shall also make the court of the tabernacle. For the south side *there shall be* hangings for the court *made of* fine woven linen, one hundred cubits long for one side. ¹⁰And its twenty pillars and their twenty sockets *shall be* bronze. The hooks of the pillars and their bands *shall be* silver. ¹¹Likewise along the length of the north side *there shall be* hangings one hundred *cubits* long, with its twenty pillars and their twenty sockets of bronze, and the hooks of the pillars and their bands of silver.

¹²"And along the width of the court on the west side *shall be* hangings of fifty cubits, with their ten pillars and their ten sockets. ¹³The width of the court on the east side *shall be* fifty cubits. ¹⁴The hangings on *one* side *of the gate shall be* fifteen cubits, *with* their three pillars and their three sockets. ¹⁵And on the other side *shall be* hangings of fifteen *cubits, with* their three pillars and their three sockets.

¹⁶"For the gate of the court *there shall be* a screen twenty cubits long, *woven of* blue, purple, and scarlet *thread,* and fine woven linen, made by a weaver. It *shall have* four pillars and four sockets. ¹⁷All the pillars around the court shall have bands of silver; their hooks *shall be* of silver and their sockets of bronze. ¹⁸The length of the court *shall be* one hundred cubits, the width fifty throughout, and the height five cubits, *made of* fine woven linen, and its sockets of bronze. ¹⁹All the utensils of the tabernacle for all its service, all its pegs, and all the pegs of the court, *shall be* of bronze.

THE CARE OF THE LAMPSTAND

²⁰"And you shall command the children of Israel that they bring you pure oil of pressed olives for the light, to cause the lamp to burn continually. ²¹In the tabernacle of meeting, outside the veil which *is* before the Testimony, Aaron and his sons shall tend it from evening until morning before the LORD. *It shall be* a statute forever to their generations on behalf of the children of Israel.

28 "Now take Aaron your brother, and his sons with him, from among the children of Israel, that he may minister to Me as priest, Aaron *and* Aaron's sons: Nadab, Abihu, Eleazar, and Ithamar. ²And you shall make holy garments for Aaron your brother, for glory and for beauty. ³So you shall speak to all *who are* gifted artisans, whom I have filled with the spirit of wisdom, that they may make Aaron's garments, to consecrate him, that he may minister to Me as priest. ⁴And these *are* the garments which they shall make: a breastplate, an ephod,ᵃ a robe, a skillfully woven tunic, a turban, and a sash. So they shall make holy garments for Aaron your brother and his sons, that he may minister to Me as priest.

THE EPHOD

⁵"They shall take the gold, blue, purple, and scarlet *thread,* and the fine linen, ⁶and they shall make the ephod of gold, blue, purple, *and* scarlet *thread,* and fine woven linen, artistically worked. ⁷It shall have two shoulder straps joined at its two edges, and *so* it shall be joined together. ⁸And the intricately woven band of the ephod, which *is* on it, shall be of the same workmanship, *made of* gold, blue, purple, and scarlet *thread,* and fine woven linen.

⁹"Then you shall take two onyx stones and engrave on them the names of the sons of Israel: ¹⁰six of their names on one stone and six names on the other stone, in order of their birth. ¹¹With the work of an engraver in stone, *like* the engravings of a signet, you shall engrave the two stones with the names of the sons of Israel. You shall set them in settings of gold. ¹²And you shall put the two stones on the shoulders of the ephod *as* memorial stones for the sons of Israel. So Aaron shall bear their names before the LORD on his two shoulders as a memorial. ¹³You shall also make settings of gold, ¹⁴and you shall make two chains of pure gold like braided cords, and fasten the braided chains to the settings.

THE BREASTPLATE

¹⁵"You shall make the breastplate of judgment. Artistically woven according to the workmanship of the ephod you shall make it: of gold, blue, purple, and scarlet *thread,* and fine woven linen, you shall make it. ¹⁶It shall be doubled into a square: a span *shall be* its length, and a span *shall be* its width. ¹⁷And you shall put settings of stones in it, four rows of stones: *The first* row *shall be* a sardius, a topaz, and an emerald; *this shall be* the first row; ¹⁸the second row *shall be* a turquoise, a sapphire, and a diamond; ¹⁹the third row, a jacinth, an agate, and an amethyst; ²⁰and the fourth row, a beryl, an onyx, and a jasper. They shall be set in gold settings. ²¹And the stones shall have the names of the sons of Israel, twelve according to their names, *like* the engravings of a signet, each one with its own name; they shall be according to the twelve tribes.

²²"You shall make chains for the breastplate at the end, like braided cords of pure gold. ²³And you shall make two rings of gold for the breastplate, and put the two rings on the two ends of the breastplate. ²⁴Then you shall put the two braided *chains* of gold in the two rings which are on the ends of the breastplate; ²⁵and the *other* two ends of the two braided *chains* you shall fasten to the two settings, and put them on the shoulder straps of the ephod in the front.

²⁶"You shall make two rings of gold, and put them on the two ends of the breastplate, on the edge of it, which is on the inner side of the ephod. ²⁷And two *other* rings of gold you shall make, and put them on the two shoulder straps, underneath the ephod toward its front, right at the seam above the intricately woven band of the ephod. ²⁸They shall bind the breastplate by means of its rings to the rings of the ephod, using a blue cord, so that it is above the intricately woven band of the ephod, and so that the breastplate does not come loose from the ephod.

²⁹"So Aaron shall bear the names of the sons of Israel on the breastplate of judgment over his heart, when he goes into the holy *place,* as a memorial before the LORD continually. ³⁰And you shall put in the breastplate of judgment the Urim and the Thummim,ᵃ and they shall be over Aaron's heart when he goes in before the LORD. So Aaron shall bear the judgment of the children of Israel over his heart before the LORD continually.

28:4 ᵃThat is, an ornamented vest   28:30 ᵃLiterally *the Lights and the Perfections* (compare Leviticus 8:8)

Other Priestly Garments

31"You shall make the robe of the ephod all of blue. 32There shall be an opening for his head in the middle of it; it shall have a woven binding all around its opening, like the opening in a coat of mail, so that it does not tear. 33And upon its hem you shall make pomegranates of blue, purple, and scarlet, all around its hem, and bells of gold between them all around: 34a golden bell and a pomegranate, a golden bell and a pomegranate, upon the hem of the robe all around. 35And it shall be upon Aaron when he ministers, and its sound will be heard when he goes into the holy *place* before the LORD and when he comes out, that he may not die.

36"You shall also make a plate of pure gold and engrave on it, *like* the engraving of a signet:

HOLINESS TO THE LORD.

37And you shall put it on a blue cord, that it may be on the turban; it shall be on the front of the turban. 38So it shall be on Aaron's forehead, that Aaron may bear the iniquity of the holy things which the children of Israel hallow in all their holy gifts; and it shall always be on his forehead, that they may be accepted before the LORD.

39"You shall skillfully weave the tunic of fine linen *thread,* you shall make the turban of fine linen, and you shall make the sash of woven work.

40"For Aaron's sons you shall make tunics, and you shall make sashes for them. And you shall make hats for them, for glory and beauty. 41So you shall put them on Aaron your brother and on his sons with him. You shall anoint them, consecrate them, and sanctify them, that they may minister to Me as priests. 42And you shall make for them linen trousers to cover their nakedness; they shall reach from the waist to the thighs. 43They shall be on Aaron and on his sons when they come into the tabernacle of meeting, or when they come near the altar to minister in the holy *place,* that they do not incur iniquity and die. *It shall be* a statute forever to him and his descendants after him.

Aaron and His Sons Consecrated

29 "And this is what you shall do to them to hallow them for ministering to Me as priests: Take one young bull and two rams without blemish, 2and unleavened bread, unleavened cakes mixed with oil, and unleavened wafers anointed with oil (you shall make them of wheat flour). 3You shall put them in one basket and bring them in the basket, with the bull and the two rams.

4"And Aaron and his sons you shall bring to the door of the tabernacle of meeting, and you shall wash them with water. 5Then you shall take the garments, put the tunic on Aaron, and the robe of the ephod, the ephod, and the breastplate, and gird him with the intricately woven band of the ephod. 6You shall put the turban on his head, and put the holy crown on the turban. 7And you shall take the anointing oil, pour *it* on his head, and anoint him. 8Then you shall bring his sons and put tunics on them. 9And you shall gird them with sashes, Aaron and his sons, and put the hats on them. The priesthood shall be theirs for a perpetual statute. So you shall consecrate Aaron and his sons.

10"You shall also have the bull brought before the tabernacle of meeting, and Aaron and his sons shall put their hands on the head of the bull. 11Then you shall kill the bull before the LORD, *by* the door of the tabernacle of meeting. 12You shall take *some* of the blood of the bull and put *it* on the horns of the altar with your finger, and pour all the blood beside the base of the altar. 13And you shall take all the fat that covers the entrails, the fatty lobe *attached* to the liver, and the two kidneys and the fat that *is* on them, and burn *them* on the altar. 14But the flesh of the bull, with its skin and its offal, you shall burn with fire outside the camp. It *is* a sin offering.

15"You shall also take one ram, and Aaron and his sons shall put their hands on the head of the ram; 16and you shall kill the ram, and you shall take its blood and sprinkle *it* all around on the altar. 17Then you shall cut the ram in pieces, wash its entrails and its legs, and put *them* with its pieces and with its head. 18And you shall burn the whole ram on the altar. It *is* a burnt offering to the LORD; it *is* a sweet aroma, an offering made by fire to the LORD.

19"You shall also take the other ram, and Aaron and his sons shall put their hands on the head of the ram. 20Then you shall kill the ram, and take some of its blood and put *it* on the tip of the right ear of Aaron and on the tip of the right ear of his sons, on the thumb of their right hand and on the big toe of their right foot, and sprinkle the blood all around on the altar. [21]And you shall take some of the blood that is on the altar, and some of the anointing oil, and sprinkle *it* on Aaron and on his garments, on his sons and on the garments of his sons with him; and he and his garments shall be hallowed, and his sons and his sons' garments with him.

[22]"Also you shall take the fat of the ram, the fat tail, the fat that covers the entrails, the fatty lobe *attached to* the liver, the two kidneys and the fat on them, the right thigh (for it *is* a ram of consecration), [23]one loaf of bread, one cake *made with* oil, and one wafer from the basket of the unleavened bread that *is* before the LORD; [24]and you shall put all these in the hands of Aaron and in the hands of his sons, and you shall wave them *as* a wave offering before the LORD. [25]You shall receive them back from their hands and burn *them* on the altar as a burnt offering, as a sweet aroma before the LORD. It *is* an offering made by fire to the LORD.

[26]"Then you shall take the breast of the ram of Aaron's consecration and wave it *as* a wave offering before the LORD; and it shall be your portion. [27]And from the ram of the consecration you shall consecrate the breast of the wave offering which is waved, and the thigh of the heave offering which is raised, of *that* which *is* for Aaron and of *that* which is for his sons. [28]It shall be from the children of Israel *for* Aaron and his sons by a statute forever. For it is a heave offering; it shall be a heave offering from the children of Israel from the sacrifices of their peace offerings, *that is,* their heave offering to the LORD.

[29]"And the holy garments of Aaron shall be his sons' after him, to be anointed in them and to be consecrated in them. [30]That son who becomes priest in his place shall put them on for seven days, when he enters the tabernacle of meeting to minister in the holy *place.*

[31]"And you shall take the ram of the consecration and boil its flesh in the holy place. [32]Then Aaron and his sons shall eat the flesh of the ram, and the bread that *is* in the basket, *by* the door of the tabernacle of meeting. [33]They shall eat those things with which the atonement was made, to consecrate *and* to sanctify them; but an outsider shall not eat *them,* because they *are* holy. [34]And if any of the flesh of the consecration offerings, or of the bread, remains until the morning, then you shall burn the remainder with fire. It shall not be eaten, because it *is* holy.

[35]"Thus you shall do to Aaron and his sons, according to all that I have commanded you. Seven days you shall consecrate them. [36]And you shall offer a bull every day *as* a sin offering for atonement. You shall cleanse the altar when you make atonement for it, and you shall anoint it to sanctify it. [37]Seven days you shall make atonement for the altar and sanctify it. And the altar shall be most holy. Whatever touches the altar must be holy.[a]

THE DAILY OFFERINGS

[38]"Now this *is* what you shall offer on the altar: two lambs of the first year, day by day continually. [39]One lamb you shall offer in the morning, and the other lamb you shall offer at twilight. [40]With the one lamb shall be one-tenth *of an ephah* of flour mixed with one-fourth of a hin of pressed oil, and one-fourth of a hin of wine *as* a drink offering. [41]And the other lamb you shall offer at twilight; and you shall offer with it the grain offering and the drink offering, as in the morning, for a sweet aroma, an offering made by fire to the LORD. [42]*This shall be* a continual burnt offering throughout your generations *at* the door of the tabernacle of meeting before the LORD, where I will meet you to speak with you. [43]And there I will meet with the children of Israel, and *the tabernacle* shall be sanctified by My glory. [44]So I will consecrate the tabernacle of meeting and the altar. I will also consecrate both Aaron and his sons to minister to Me as priests. [45]I will dwell among the children of Israel and will be their God. [46]And they shall know that I *am* the LORD their God, who brought them up out of the land of Egypt, that I may dwell among them. I *am* the LORD their God.

THE ALTAR OF INCENSE

30 "You shall make an altar to burn incense on; you shall make it of acacia wood.

29:37 [a]Compare Numbers 4:15 and Haggai 2:11–13

²A cubit *shall be* its length and a cubit its width—it shall be square—and two cubits *shall be* its height. Its horns *shall be* of one piece with it. ³And you shall overlay its top, its sides all around, and its horns with pure gold; and you shall make for it a molding of gold all around. ⁴Two gold rings you shall make for it, under the molding on both its sides. You shall place *them* on its two sides, and they will be holders for the poles with which to bear it. ⁵You shall make the poles of acacia wood, and overlay them with gold. ⁶And you shall put it before the veil that *is* before the ark of the Testimony, before the mercy seat that *is* over the Testimony, where I will meet with you.

⁷"Aaron shall burn on it sweet incense every morning; when he tends the lamps, he shall burn incense on it. ⁸And when Aaron lights the lamps at twilight, he shall burn incense on it, a perpetual incense before the LORD throughout your generations. ⁹You shall not offer strange incense on it, or a burnt offering, or a grain offering; nor shall you pour a drink offering on it. ¹⁰And Aaron shall make atonement upon its horns once a year with the blood of the sin offering of atonement; once a year he shall make atonement upon it throughout your generations. It *is* most holy to the LORD."

The Ransom Money

¹¹Then the LORD spoke to Moses, saying: ¹²"When you take the census of the children of Israel for their number, then every man shall give a ransom for himself to the LORD, when you number them, that there may be no plague among them when *you* number them. ¹³This is what everyone among those who are numbered shall give: half a shekel according to the shekel of the sanctuary (a shekel *is* twenty gerahs). The half-shekel *shall be* an offering to the LORD. ¹⁴Everyone included among those who are numbered, from twenty years old and above, shall give an offering to the LORD. ¹⁵The rich shall not give more and the poor shall not give less than half a shekel, when *you* give an offering to the LORD, to make atonement for yourselves. ¹⁶And you shall take the atonement money of the children of Israel, and shall appoint it for the service of the tabernacle of meeting, that it may be a memorial for the children of Israel before the LORD, to make atonement for yourselves."

The Bronze Laver

¹⁷Then the LORD spoke to Moses, saying: ¹⁸"You shall also make a laver of bronze, with its base also of bronze, for washing. You shall put it between the tabernacle of meeting and the altar. And you shall put water in it, ¹⁹for Aaron and his sons shall wash their hands and their feet in water from it. ²⁰When they go into the tabernacle of meeting, or when they come near the altar to minister, to burn an offering made by fire to the LORD, they shall wash with water, lest they die. ²¹So they shall wash their hands and their feet, lest they die. And it shall be a statute forever to them—to him and his descendants throughout their generations."

The Holy Anointing Oil

²²Moreover the LORD spoke to Moses, saying: ²³"Also take for yourself quality spices—five hundred *shekels* of liquid myrrh, half as much sweet-smelling cinnamon (two hundred and fifty *shekels*), two hundred and fifty *shekels* of sweet-smelling cane, ²⁴five hundred *shekels* of cassia, according to the shekel of the sanctuary, and a hin of olive oil. ²⁵And you shall make from these a holy anointing oil, an ointment compounded according to the art of the perfumer. It shall be a holy anointing oil. ²⁶With it you shall anoint the tabernacle of meeting and the ark of the Testimony; ²⁷the table and all its utensils, the lampstand and its utensils, and the altar of incense; ²⁸the altar of burnt offering with all its utensils, and the laver and its base. ²⁹You shall consecrate them, that they may be most holy; whatever touches them must be holy.[a] ³⁰And you shall anoint Aaron and his sons, and consecrate them, that *they* may minister to Me as priests.

³¹"And you shall speak to the children of Israel, saying: 'This shall be a holy anointing oil to Me throughout your generations. ³²It shall not be poured on man's flesh; nor shall you make *any other* like it, according to its composition. It *is* holy, *and* it shall be holy to you. ³³Whoever compounds *any* like it, or whoever puts *any* of it on an outsider, shall be cut off from his people.'"

The Incense

³⁴And the LORD said to Moses: "Take sweet spices, stacte and onycha and galbanum, and pure

30:29 ªCompare Numbers 4:15 and Haggai 2:11–13

frankincense with *these* sweet spices; there shall be equal amounts of each. ³⁵You shall make of these an incense, a compound according to the art of the perfumer, salted, pure, *and* holy. ³⁶And you shall beat *some* of it very fine, and put some of it before the Testimony in the tabernacle of meeting where I will meet with you. It shall be most holy to you. ³⁷But *as for* the incense which you shall make, you shall not make any for yourselves, according to its composition. It shall be to you holy for the LORD. ³⁸Whoever makes *any* like it, to smell it, he shall be cut off from his people."

ARTISANS FOR BUILDING THE TABERNACLE

31 Then the LORD spoke to Moses, saying: ²"See, I have called by name Bezalel the son of Uri, the son of Hur, of the tribe of Judah. ³And I have filled him with the Spirit of God, in wisdom, in understanding, in knowledge, and in all *manner of* workmanship, ⁴to design artistic works, to work in gold, in silver, in bronze, ⁵in cutting jewels for setting, in carving wood, and to work in all *manner of* workmanship.

⁶"And I, indeed I, have appointed with him Aholiab the son of Ahisamach, of the tribe of Dan; and I have put wisdom in the hearts of all the gifted artisans, that they may make all that I have commanded you: ⁷the tabernacle of meeting, the ark of the Testimony and the mercy seat that *is* on it, and all the furniture of the tabernacle—⁸the table and its utensils, the pure *gold* lampstand with all its utensils, the altar of incense, ⁹the altar of burnt offering with all its utensils, and the laver and its base—¹⁰the garments of ministry,ᵃ the holy garments for Aaron the priest and the garments of his sons, to minister as priests, ¹¹and the anointing oil and sweet incense for the holy *place*. According to all that I have commanded you they shall do."

THE SABBATH LAW

¹²And the LORD spoke to Moses, saying, ¹³"Speak also to the children of Israel, saying: 'Surely My Sabbaths you shall keep, for it *is* a sign between Me and you throughout your generations, that *you* may know that I *am* the LORD who sanctifies you. ¹⁴You shall keep the Sabbath, therefore, for *it is* holy to you. Everyone who profanes it shall surely be put to death; for whoever

does *any* work on it, that person shall be cut off from among his people. ¹⁵Work shall be done for six days, but the seventh *is* the Sabbath of rest, holy to the LORD. Whoever does *any* work on the Sabbath day, he shall surely be put to death. ¹⁶Therefore the children of Israel shall keep the Sabbath, to observe the Sabbath throughout their generations *as* a perpetual covenant. ¹⁷It *is* a sign between Me and the children of Israel forever; for *in* six days the LORD made the heavens and the earth, and on the seventh day He rested and was refreshed.' "

¹⁸And when He had made an end of speaking with him on Mount Sinai, He gave Moses two tablets of the Testimony, tablets of stone, written with the finger of God.

THE GOLD CALF

32 Now when the people saw that Moses delayed coming down from the mountain, the people gathered together to Aaron, and said to him, "Come, make us gods that shall go before us; for *as for* this Moses, the man who brought us up out of the land of Egypt, we do not know what has become of him."

²And Aaron said to them, "Break off the golden earrings which *are* in the ears of your wives, your sons, and your daughters, and bring *them* to me." ³So all the people broke off the golden earrings which *were* in their ears, and brought *them* to Aaron. ⁴And he received *the gold* from their hand, and he fashioned it with an engraving tool, and made a molded calf.

Then they said, "This *is* your god, O Israel, that brought you out of the land of Egypt!"

⁵So when Aaron saw *it,* he built an altar before it. And Aaron made a proclamation and said, "Tomorrow *is* a feast to the LORD." ⁶Then they rose early on the next day, offered burnt offerings, and brought peace offerings; and the people sat down to eat and drink, and rose up to play.

⁷And the LORD said to Moses, "Go, get down! For your people whom you brought out of the land of Egypt have corrupted *themselves.* ⁸They have turned aside quickly out of the way which I commanded them. They have made themselves a molded calf, and worshiped it and

31:10 ᵃOr *woven garments*

sacrificed to it, and said, 'This *is* your god, O Israel, that brought you out of the land of Egypt!' "

⁹And the LORD said to Moses, "I have seen this people, and indeed it *is* a stiff-necked people! ¹⁰Now therefore, let Me alone, that My wrath may burn hot against them and I may consume them. And I will make of you a great nation."

¹¹Then Moses pleaded with the LORD his God, and said: "LORD, why does Your wrath burn hot against Your people whom You have brought out of the land of Egypt with great power and with a mighty hand? ¹²Why should the Egyptians speak, and say, 'He brought them out to harm them, to kill them in the mountains, and to consume them from the face of the earth'? Turn from Your fierce wrath, and relent from this harm to Your people. ¹³Remember Abraham, Isaac, and Israel, Your servants, to whom You swore by Your own self, and said to them, 'I will multiply your descendants as the stars of heaven; and all this land that I have spoken of I give to your descendants, and they shall inherit *it* forever.' "ᵃ ¹⁴So the LORD relented from the harm which He said He would do to His people.

¹⁵And Moses turned and went down from the mountain, and the two tablets of the Testimony *were* in his hand. The tablets *were* written on both sides; on the one *side* and on the other they were written. ¹⁶Now the tablets *were* the work of God, and the writing *was* the writing of God engraved on the tablets.

¹⁷And when Joshua heard the noise of the people as they shouted, he said to Moses, "*There is* a noise of war in the camp."

¹⁸But he said:

"*It is* not the noise of the shout of victory,
Nor the noise of the cry of defeat,
But the sound of singing I hear."

¹⁹So it was, as soon as he came near the camp, that he saw the calf *and* the dancing. So Moses' anger became hot, and he cast the tablets out of his hands and broke them at the foot of the mountain. ²⁰Then he took the calf which they had made, burned *it* in the fire, and ground *it* to powder; and he scattered *it* on the water and made the children of Israel drink *it*. ²¹And Moses said to Aaron, "What did this people do to

you that you have brought *so* great a sin upon them?"

²²So Aaron said, "Do not let the anger of my lord become hot. You know the people, that they *are set* on evil. ²³For they said to me, 'Make us gods that shall go before us; *as for* this Moses, the man who brought us out of the land of Egypt, we do not know what has become of him.' ²⁴And I said to them, 'Whoever has any gold, let them break *it* off.' So they gave *it* to me, and I cast *it* into the fire, and this calf came out."

²⁵Now when Moses saw that the people *were* unrestrained (for Aaron had not restrained them, to *their* shame among their enemies), ²⁶then Moses stood in the entrance of the camp, and said, "Whoever *is* on the LORD's side—*come* to me!" And all the sons of Levi gathered themselves together to him. ²⁷And he said to them, "Thus says the LORD God of Israel: 'Let every man put his sword on his side, and go in and out from entrance to entrance throughout the camp, and let every man kill his brother, every man his companion, and every man his neighbor.' " ²⁸So the sons of Levi did according to the word of Moses. And about three thousand men of the people fell that day. ²⁹Then Moses said, "Consecrate yourselves today to the LORD, that He may bestow on you a blessing this day, for every man has opposed his son and his brother."

³⁰Now it came to pass on the next day that Moses said to the people, "You have committed a great sin. So now I will go up to the LORD; perhaps I can make atonement for your sin." ³¹Then Moses returned to the LORD and said, "Oh, these people have committed a great sin, and have made for themselves a god of gold! ³²Yet now, if You will forgive their sin—but if not, I pray, blot me out of Your book which You have written."

³³And the LORD said to Moses, "Whoever has sinned against Me, I will blot him out of My book. ³⁴Now therefore, go, lead the people to *the place* of which I have spoken to you. Behold, My Angel shall go before you. Nevertheless, in the day when I visit for punishment, I will visit punishment upon them for their sin."

³⁵So the LORD plagued the people because of what they did with the calf which Aaron made.

32:13 ᵃGenesis 13:15 and 22:17

THE COMMAND TO LEAVE SINAI

33 Then the LORD said to Moses, "Depart *and* go up from here, you and the people whom you have brought out of the land of Egypt, to the land of which I swore to Abraham, Isaac, and Jacob, saying, 'To your descendants I will give it.' ²And I will send *My* Angel before you, and I will drive out the Canaanite and the Amorite and the Hittite and the Perizzite and the Hivite and the Jebusite. ³*Go up* to a land flowing with milk and honey; for I will not go up in your midst, lest I consume you on the way, for you *are* a stiff-necked people."

⁴And when the people heard this bad news, they mourned, and no one put on his ornaments. ⁵For the LORD had said to Moses, "Say to the children of Israel, 'You *are* a stiff-necked people. I could come up into your midst in one moment and consume you. Now therefore, take off your ornaments, that I may know what to do to you.' " ⁶So the children of Israel stripped themselves of their ornaments by Mount Horeb.

MOSES MEETS WITH THE LORD

⁷Moses took his tent and pitched it outside the camp, far from the camp, and called it the tabernacle of meeting. And it came to pass *that* everyone who sought the LORD went out to the tabernacle of meeting which *was* outside the camp. ⁸So it was, whenever Moses went out to the tabernacle, *that* all the people rose, and each man stood *at* his tent door and watched Moses until he had gone into the tabernacle. ⁹And it came to pass, when Moses entered the tabernacle, that the pillar of cloud descended and stood *at* the door of the tabernacle, and *the* LORD talked with Moses. ¹⁰All the people saw the pillar of cloud standing *at* the tabernacle door, and all the people rose and worshiped, each man *in* his tent door. ¹¹So the LORD spoke to Moses face to face, as a man speaks to his friend. And he would return to the camp, but his servant Joshua the son of Nun, a young man, did not depart from the tabernacle.

INSIDE *the* INFLUENCERS

MOSES: "Please, Show Me Your Glory"

EXODUS 33:18

The footsteps of God's glory and faithfulness can be traced throughout Moses' life: God in the burning bush (3); the confrontations with Pharaoh, the plagues and the deliverance of Israel (5—12); the cloud and fire in the desert (13); parting the Red Sea (14); bread from heaven (16); water from a rock (17); the ten commandments (20); meeting with God on Mount Sinai (24—33).

After all these miracles—obvious signs that prove God is omnipotent—the people still chose idols over the living God. While meeting with God on Mount Sinai, Moses left his brother Aaron in charge. Aaron listened to the people instead of obeying God, and built a golden calf for the people to worship (32).

Moses prayed to God on Israel's behalf to deal with this terrible sin and for God to continue to be with him (33). In this prayer, He asked if he could see God's glory. In chapter three, when Moses first encountered the Lord, he hid his face; yet now he prays with eyes wide open. What happened? The answer is simple: in Exodus 3 God was outside of Moses speaking from a burning bush; but in Exodus 33, Moses and God are intimate friends, and God is speaking to Moses in person. Moses sees God pass by the crack in the rock. After years of *knowing* God, Moses wants to *see* Him; and God grants that request.

The Promise of God's Presence

¹²Then Moses said to the LORD, "See, You say to me, 'Bring up this people.' But You have not let me know whom You will send with me. Yet You have said, 'I know you by name, and you have also found grace in My sight.' ¹³Now therefore, I pray, if I have found grace in Your sight, show me now Your way, that I may know You and that I may find grace in Your sight. And consider that this nation *is* Your people."

¹⁴And He said, "My Presence will go *with you,* and I will give you rest."

¹⁵Then he said to Him, "If Your Presence does not go *with us,* do not bring us up from here. ¹⁶For how then will it be known that Your people and I have found grace in Your sight, except You go with us? So we shall be separate, Your people and I, from all the people who *are* upon the face of the earth."

¹⁷So the LORD said to Moses, "I will also do this thing that you have spoken; for you have found grace in My sight, and I know you by name."

¹⁸And he said, "Please, show me Your glory."

¹⁹Then He said, "I will make all My goodness pass before you, and I will proclaim the name of the LORD before you. I will be gracious to whom I will be gracious, and I will have compassion on whom I will have compassion." ²⁰But He said, "You cannot see My face; for no man shall see Me, and live." ²¹And the LORD said, "Here is a place by Me, and you shall stand on the rock. ²²So it shall be, while My glory passes by, that I will put you in the cleft of the rock, and will cover you with My hand while I pass by. ²³Then I will take away My hand, and you shall see My back; but My face shall not be seen."

Moses Makes New Tablets

34 And the LORD said to Moses, "Cut two tablets of stone like the first *ones,* and I will write on *these* tablets the words that were on the first tablets which you broke. ²So be ready in the morning, and come up in the morning to Mount Sinai, and present yourself to Me there on the top of the mountain. ³And no man shall come up with you, and let no man be seen throughout all the mountain; let neither flocks nor herds feed before that mountain."

⁴So he cut two tablets of stone like the first *ones.* Then Moses rose early in the morning and went up Mount Sinai, as the LORD had commanded him; and he took in his hand the two tablets of stone.

⁵Now the LORD descended in the cloud and stood with him there, and proclaimed the name of the LORD. ⁶And the LORD passed before him and proclaimed, "The LORD, the LORD God, merciful and gracious, longsuffering, and abounding in goodness and truth, ⁷keeping mercy for thousands, forgiving iniquity and transgression and sin, by no means clearing *the guilty,* visiting the iniquity of the fathers upon the children and the children's children to the third and the fourth generation."

⁸So Moses made haste and bowed his head toward the earth, and worshiped. ⁹Then he said, "If now I have found grace in Your sight, O Lord, let my Lord, I pray, go among us, even though we *are* a stiff-necked people; and pardon our iniquity and our sin, and take us as Your inheritance."

The Covenant Renewed

¹⁰And He said: "Behold, I make a covenant. Before all your people I will do marvels such as have not been done in all the earth, nor in any nation; and all the people among whom you *are* shall see the work of the LORD. For it *is* an awesome thing that I will do with you. ¹¹Observe what I command you this day. Behold, I am driving out from before you the Amorite and the Canaanite and the Hittite and the Perizzite and the Hivite and the Jebusite. ¹²Take heed to yourself, lest you make a covenant with the inhabitants of the land where you are going, lest it be a snare in your midst. ¹³But you shall destroy their altars, break their *sacred* pillars, and cut down their wooden images ¹⁴(for you shall worship no other god, for the LORD, whose name *is* Jealous, *is* a jealous God), ¹⁵lest you make a covenant with the inhabitants of the land, and they play the harlot with their gods and make sacrifice to their gods, and *one of them* invites you and you eat of his sacrifice, ¹⁶and you take of his daughters for your sons, and his daughters play the harlot with their gods and make your sons play the harlot with their gods.

¹⁷"You shall make no molded gods for yourselves.

18"The Feast of Unleavened Bread you shall keep. Seven days you shall eat unleavened bread, as I commanded you, in the appointed time of the month of Abib; for in the month of Abib you came out from Egypt.

19"All that open the womb *are* Mine, and every male firstborn among your livestock, *whether* ox or sheep. 20But the firstborn of a donkey you shall redeem with a lamb. And if you will not redeem *him,* then you shall break his neck. All the firstborn of your sons you shall redeem.

"And none shall appear before Me empty-handed.

21"Six days you shall work, but on the seventh day you shall rest; in plowing time and in harvest you shall rest.

22"And you shall observe the Feast of Weeks, of the firstfruits of wheat harvest, and the Feast of Ingathering at the year's end.

23"Three times in the year all your men shall appear before the Lord, the LORD God of Israel. 24For I will cast out the nations before you and enlarge your borders; neither will any man covet your land when you go up to appear before the LORD your God three times in the year.

25"You shall not offer the blood of My sacrifice with leaven, nor shall the sacrifice of the Feast of the Passover be left until morning.

26"The first of the firstfruits of your land you shall bring to the house of the LORD your God. You shall not boil a young goat in its mother's milk."

27Then the LORD said to Moses, "Write these words, for according to the tenor of these words I have made a covenant with you and with Israel." 28So he was there with the LORD forty days and forty nights; he neither ate bread nor drank water. And He wrote on the tablets the words of the covenant, the Ten Commandments.[a]

The Shining Face of Moses

29Now it was so, when Moses came down from Mount Sinai (and the two tablets of the Testimony *were* in Moses' hand when he came down from the mountain), that Moses did not know that the skin of his face shone while he talked with Him. 30So when Aaron and all the children of Israel saw Moses, behold, the skin of his face shone, and they were afraid to come near him.

31Then Moses called to them, and Aaron and all the rulers of the congregation returned to him; and Moses talked with them. 32Afterward all the children of Israel came near, and he gave them as commandments all that the LORD had spoken with him on Mount Sinai. 33And when Moses had finished speaking with them, he put a veil on his face. 34But whenever Moses went in before the LORD to speak with Him, he would take the veil off until he came out; and he would come out and speak to the children of Israel whatever he had been commanded. 35And whenever the children of Israel saw the face of Moses, that the skin of Moses' face shone, then Moses would put the veil on his face again, until he went in to speak with Him.

Sabbath Regulations

35 Then Moses gathered all the congregation of the children of Israel together, and said to them, "These *are* the words which the LORD has commanded *you* to do: 2Work shall be done for six days, but the seventh day shall be a holy day for you, a Sabbath of rest to the LORD. Whoever does any work on it shall be put to death. 3You shall kindle no fire throughout your dwellings on the Sabbath day."

Offerings for the Tabernacle

4And Moses spoke to all the congregation of the children of Israel, saying, "This *is* the thing which the LORD commanded, saying: 5'Take from among you an offering to the LORD. Whoever *is* of a willing heart, let him bring it as an offering to the LORD: gold, silver, and bronze; 6blue, purple, and scarlet *thread,* fine linen, and goats' *hair;* 7ram skins dyed red, badger skins, and acacia wood; 8oil for the light, and spices for the anointing oil and for the sweet incense; 9onyx stones, and stones to be set in the ephod and in the breastplate.

Articles of the Tabernacle

10'All *who are* gifted artisans among you shall come and make all that the LORD has commanded: 11the tabernacle, its tent, its covering, its clasps, its boards, its bars, its pillars, and its sockets;

34:28 [a]Literally *Ten Words*

[12]the ark and its poles, *with* the mercy seat, and the veil of the covering; [13]the table and its poles, all its utensils, and the showbread; [14]also the lampstand for the light, its utensils, its lamps, and the oil for the light; [15]the incense altar, its poles, the anointing oil, the sweet incense, and the screen for the door at the entrance of the tabernacle; [16]the altar of burnt offering with its bronze grating, its poles, all its utensils, *and* the laver and its base; [17]the hangings of the court, its pillars, their sockets, and the screen for the gate of the court; [18]the pegs of the tabernacle, the pegs of the court, and their cords; [19]the garments of ministry,[a] for ministering in the holy *place*—the holy garments for Aaron the priest and the garments of his sons, to minister as priests.' "

The Tabernacle Offerings Presented

[20]And all the congregation of the children of Israel departed from the presence of Moses. [21]Then everyone came whose heart was stirred, and everyone whose spirit was willing, *and* they brought the LORD's offering for the work of the tabernacle of meeting, for all its service, and for the holy garments. [22]They came, both men and women, as many as had a willing heart, *and* brought earrings and nose rings, rings and necklaces, all jewelry of gold, that is, every man who *made* an offering of gold to the LORD. [23]And every man, with whom was found blue, purple, and scarlet *thread*, fine linen, goats' *hair,* red skins of rams, and badger skins, brought *them*. [24]Everyone who offered an offering of silver or bronze brought the LORD's offering. And everyone with whom was found acacia wood for any work of the service, brought *it*. [25]All the women *who were* gifted artisans spun yarn with their hands, and brought what they had spun, of blue, purple, *and* scarlet, and fine linen. [26]And all the women whose hearts stirred with wisdom spun yarn of goats' *hair*. [27]The rulers brought onyx stones, and the stones to be set in the ephod and in the breastplate, [28]and spices and oil for the light, for the anointing oil, and for the sweet incense. [29]The children of Israel brought a freewill offering to the LORD, all the men and women whose hearts were willing to bring *material* for all kinds of work which the LORD, by the hand of Moses, had commanded to be done.

The Artisans Called by God

[30]And Moses said to the children of Israel, "See, the LORD has called by name Bezalel the son of Uri, the son of Hur, of the tribe of Judah; [31]and He has filled him with the Spirit of God, in wisdom and understanding, in knowledge and all manner of workmanship, [32]to design artistic works, to work in gold and silver and bronze, [33]in cutting jewels for setting, in carving wood, and to work in all manner of artistic workmanship.

[34]"And He has put in his heart the ability to teach, *in* him and Aholiab the son of Ahisamach, of the tribe of Dan. [35]He has filled them with skill to do all manner of work of the engraver and the designer and the tapestry maker, in blue, purple, and scarlet *thread,* and fine linen, and of the weaver—those who do every work and those who design artistic works.

36 "And Bezalel and Aholiab, and every gifted artisan in whom the LORD has put wisdom and understanding, to know how to do all manner of work for the service of the sanctuary, shall do according to all that the LORD has commanded."

The People Give More than Enough

[2]Then Moses called Bezalel and Aholiab, and every gifted artisan in whose heart the LORD had put wisdom, everyone whose heart was stirred, to come and do the work. [3]And they received from Moses all the offering which the children of Israel had brought for the work of the service of making the sanctuary. So they continued bringing to him freewill offerings every morning. [4]Then all the craftsmen who were doing all the work of the sanctuary came, each from the work he was doing, [5]and they spoke to Moses, saying, "The people bring much more than enough for the service of the work which the LORD commanded *us* to do."

[6]So Moses gave a commandment, and they caused it to be proclaimed throughout the camp, saying, "Let neither man nor woman do any more work for the offering of the sanctuary." And the people were restrained from bringing, [7]for the

35:19 [a]Or *woven garments*

material they had was sufficient for all the work to be done—indeed too much.

Building the Tabernacle

8Then all the gifted artisans among them who worked on the tabernacle made ten curtains woven of fine linen, and of blue, purple, and scarlet *thread; with* artistic designs of cherubim they made them. 9The length of each curtain *was* twenty-eight cubits, and the width of each curtain four cubits; the curtains *were* all the same size. 10And he coupled five curtains to one another, and *the other* five curtains he coupled to one another. 11He made loops of blue *yarn* on the edge of the curtain on the selvedge of one set; likewise he did on the outer edge of *the other* curtain of the second set. 12Fifty loops he made on one curtain, and fifty loops he made on the edge of the curtain on the end of the second set; the loops held one *curtain* to another. 13And he made fifty clasps of gold, and coupled the curtains to one another with the clasps, that it might be one tabernacle.

14He made curtains of goats' *hair* for the tent over the tabernacle; he made eleven curtains. 15The length of each curtain *was* thirty cubits, and the width of each curtain four cubits; the eleven curtains *were* the same size. 16He coupled five curtains by themselves and six curtains by themselves. 17And he made fifty loops on the edge of the curtain that is outermost in one set, and fifty loops he made on the edge of the curtain of the second set. 18He also made fifty bronze clasps to couple the tent together, that it might be one. 19Then he made a covering for the tent of ram skins dyed red, and a covering of badger skins above *that.*

20For the tabernacle he made boards of acacia wood, standing upright. 21The length of each board *was* ten cubits, and the width of each board a cubit and a half. 22Each board had two tenons for binding one to another. Thus he made for all the boards of the tabernacle. 23And he made boards for the tabernacle, twenty boards for the south side. 24Forty sockets of silver he made to go under the twenty boards: two sockets under each of the boards for its two tenons. 25And for the other side of the tabernacle, the north side, he made twenty boards 26and their forty sockets of silver: two sockets under each of the boards. 27For the west side of the tabernacle

he made six boards. 28He also made two boards for the two back corners of the tabernacle. 29And they were coupled at the bottom and coupled together at the top by one ring. Thus he made both of them for the two corners. 30So there were eight boards and their sockets—sixteen sockets of silver—two sockets under each of the boards.

31And he made bars of acacia wood: five for the boards on one side of the tabernacle, 32five bars for the boards on the other side of the tabernacle, and five bars for the boards of the tabernacle on the far side westward. 33And he made the middle bar to pass through the boards from one end to the other. 34He overlaid the boards with gold, made their rings of gold *to be* holders for the bars, and overlaid the bars with gold.

35And he made a veil of blue, purple, and scarlet *thread,* and fine woven linen; it was worked *with* an artistic design of cherubim. 36He made for it four pillars of acacia *wood,* and overlaid them with gold, with their hooks of gold; and he cast four sockets of silver for them.

37He also made a screen for the tabernacle door, of blue, purple, and scarlet *thread,* and fine woven linen, made by a weaver, 38and its five pillars with their hooks. And he overlaid their capitals and their rings with gold, but their five sockets *were* bronze.

Making the Ark of the Testimony

37Then Bezalel made the ark of acacia wood; two and a half cubits *was* its length, a cubit and a half its width, and a cubit and a half its height. 2He overlaid it with pure gold inside and outside, and made a molding of gold all around it. 3And he cast for it four rings of gold *to be set* in its four corners: two rings on one side, and two rings on the other side of it. 4He made poles of acacia wood, and overlaid them with gold. 5And he put the poles into the rings at the sides of the ark, to bear the ark. 6He also made the mercy seat of pure gold; two and a half cubits *was* its length and a cubit and a half its width. 7He made two cherubim of beaten gold; he made them of one piece at the two ends of the mercy seat: 8one cherub at one end on this side, and the other cherub at the *other* end on that side. He made the cherubim at the two ends *of* *one piece* with the mercy seat. 9The cherubim spread out *their* wings above, *and* covered the mercy seat with their wings. They faced one another; the faces of the cherubim were toward the mercy seat.

MAKING THE TABLE FOR THE SHOWBREAD

10He made the table of acacia wood; two cubits *was* its length, a cubit its width, and a cubit and a half its height. 11And he overlaid it with pure gold, and made a molding of gold all around it. 12Also he made a frame of a handbreadth all around it, and made a molding of gold for the frame all around it. 13And he cast for it four rings of gold, and put the rings on the four corners that *were* at its four legs. 14The rings were close to the frame, as holders for the poles to bear the table. 15And he made the poles of acacia wood to bear the table, and overlaid them with gold. 16He made of pure gold the utensils which were on the table: its dishes, its cups, its bowls, and its pitchers for pouring.

MAKING THE GOLD LAMPSTAND

17He also made the lampstand of pure gold; of hammered work he made the lampstand. Its shaft, its branches, its bowls, its *ornamental* knobs, and its flowers were of the same piece. 18And six branches came out of its sides: three branches of the lampstand out of one side, and three branches of the lampstand out of the other side. 19There were three bowls made like almond *blossoms* on one branch, with an *ornamental* knob and a flower, and three bowls made like almond *blossoms* on the other branch, with an *ornamental* knob and a flower—and so for the six branches coming out of the lampstand. 20And on the lampstand itself *were* four bowls made like almond *blossoms, each with* its *ornamental* knob and flower. 21*There was* a knob under the *first* two branches of the same, a knob under the *second* two branches of the same, and a knob under the *third* two branches of the same, according to the six branches extending from it. 22Their knobs and their branches were of one piece; all of it *was* one hammered piece of pure gold. 23And he made its seven lamps, its wick-trimmers, and its trays of pure gold. 24Of a talent of pure gold he made it, with all its utensils.

MAKING THE ALTAR OF INCENSE

25He made the incense altar of acacia wood. Its length *was* a cubit and its width a cubit—*it was* square—and two cubits *was* its height. Its horns were *of one piece* with it. 26And he overlaid it with pure gold: its top, its sides all around, and its horns. He also made for it a molding of gold all around it. 27He made two rings of gold for it under its molding, by its two corners on both sides, as holders for the poles with which to bear it. 28And he made the poles of acacia wood, and overlaid them with gold.

MAKING THE ANOINTING OIL AND THE INCENSE

29He also made the holy anointing oil and the pure incense of sweet spices, according to the work of the perfumer.

MAKING THE ALTAR OF BURNT OFFERING

38He made the altar of burnt offering of acacia wood; five cubits *was* its length and five cubits its width—*it was* square—and its height *was* three cubits. 2He made its horns on its four corners; the horns were *of one piece* with it. And he overlaid it with bronze. 3He made all the utensils for the altar: the pans, the shovels, the basins, the forks, and the firepans; all its utensils he made of bronze. 4And he made a grate of bronze network for the altar, under its rim, midway from the bottom. 5He cast four rings for the four corners of the bronze grating, *as* holders for the poles. 6And he made the poles of acacia wood, and overlaid them with bronze. 7Then he put the poles into the rings on the sides of the altar, with which to bear it. He made the altar hollow with boards.

MAKING THE BRONZE LAVER

8He made the laver of bronze and its base of bronze, from the bronze mirrors of the serving women who assembled at the door of the tabernacle of meeting.

MAKING THE COURT OF THE TABERNACLE

9Then he made the court on the south side; the hangings of the court *were of* fine woven linen, one hundred cubits long. 10There *were* twenty pillars for them, with twenty bronze sockets. The hooks of the pillars and their bands *were* silver. [11]On the north side *the hangings were* one hundred cubits *long,* with twenty pillars and their twenty bronze sockets. The hooks of the pillars and their bands *were* silver. [12]And on the west side *there were* hangings of fifty cubits, with ten pillars and their ten sockets. The hooks of the pillars and their bands *were* silver. [13]For the east side *the hangings were* fifty cubits. [14]The hangings of one side *of the gate were* fifteen cubits *long, with* their three pillars and their three sockets, [15]and the same for the other side of the court gate; on this side and that *were* hangings of fifteen cubits, *with* their three pillars and their three sockets. [16]All the hangings of the court all around *were of* fine woven linen. [17]The sockets for the pillars *were* bronze, the hooks of the pillars and their bands *were* silver, and the overlay of their capitals *was* silver; and all the pillars of the court had bands of silver. [18]The screen for the gate of the court *was* woven of blue, purple, and scarlet *thread,* and of fine woven linen. The length *was* twenty cubits, and the height along its width *was* five cubits, corresponding to the hangings of the court. [19]And *there were* four pillars *with* their four sockets of bronze; their hooks *were* silver, and the overlay of their capitals and their bands *was* silver. [20]All the pegs of the tabernacle, and of the court all around, *were* bronze.

MATERIALS OF THE TABERNACLE

[21]This is the inventory of the tabernacle, the tabernacle of the Testimony, which was counted according to the commandment of Moses, for the service of the Levites, by the hand of Ithamar, son of Aaron the priest.

[22]Bezalel the son of Uri, the son of Hur, of the tribe of Judah, made all that the LORD had commanded Moses. [23]And with him *was* Aholiab the son of Ahisamach, of the tribe of Dan, an engraver and designer, a weaver of blue, purple, and scarlet *thread,* and of fine linen.

[24]All the gold that was used in all the work of the holy *place,* that is, the gold of the offering, was twenty-nine talents and seven hundred and thirty shekels, according to the shekel of the sanctuary. [25]And the silver from those who were numbered of the congregation *was* one hundred talents and one thousand seven hundred and seventy-five shekels, according to the shekel of the sanctuary:

[26]a bekah for each man (*that is,* half a shekel, according to the shekel of the sanctuary), for everyone included in the numbering from twenty years old and above, for six hundred and three thousand, five hundred and fifty *men.* [27]And from the hundred talents of silver were cast the sockets of the sanctuary and the bases of the veil: one hundred sockets from the hundred talents, one talent for each socket. [28]Then from the one thousand seven hundred and seventy-five *shekels* he made hooks for the pillars, overlaid their capitals, and made bands for them.

[29]The offering of bronze *was* seventy talents and two thousand four hundred shekels. [30]And with it he made the sockets for the door of the tabernacle of meeting, the bronze altar, the bronze grating for it, and all the utensils for the altar, [31]the sockets for the court all around, the bases for the court gate, all the pegs for the tabernacle, and all the pegs for the court all around.

MAKING THE GARMENTS OF THE PRIESTHOOD

39 Of the blue, purple, and scarlet *thread* they made garments of ministry,[a] for ministering in the holy *place,* and made the holy garments for Aaron, as the LORD had commanded Moses.

MAKING THE EPHOD

[2]He made the ephod of gold, blue, purple, and scarlet *thread,* and of fine woven linen. [3]And they beat the gold into thin sheets and cut *it into* threads, to work *it in with* the blue, purple, and scarlet *thread,* and the fine linen, *into* artistic designs. [4]They made shoulder straps for it to couple *it* together; it was coupled together at its two edges. [5]And the intricately woven band of his ephod that *was* on it *was* of the same workmanship, *woven of* gold, blue, purple, and scarlet *thread,* and of fine woven linen, as the LORD had commanded Moses.

[6]And they set onyx stones, enclosed in settings of gold; they were engraved, as signets are engraved, with the names of the sons of Israel. [7]He put them on the shoulders of the ephod *as* memorial stones for the sons of Israel, as the LORD had commanded Moses.

39:1 [a]Or *woven garments*

Making the Breastplate

⁸And he made the breastplate, artistically woven like the workmanship of the ephod, of gold, blue, purple, and scarlet *thread,* and of fine woven linen. ⁹They made the breastplate square by doubling it; a span *was* its length and a span its width when doubled. ¹⁰And they set in it four rows of stones: a row with a sardius, a topaz, and an emerald was the first row; ¹¹the second row, a turquoise, a sapphire, and a diamond; ¹²the third row, a jacinth, an agate, and an amethyst; ¹³the fourth row, a beryl, an onyx, and a jasper. *They were* enclosed in settings of gold in their mountings. ¹⁴*There were* twelve stones according to the names of the sons of Israel: according to their names, *engraved like* a signet, each one with its own name according to the twelve tribes. ¹⁵And they made chains for the breastplate at the ends, like braided cords of pure gold. ¹⁶They also made two settings of gold and two gold rings, and put the two rings on the two ends of the breastplate. ¹⁷And they put the two braided *chains* of gold in the two rings on the ends of the breastplate. ¹⁸The two ends of the two braided *chains* they fastened in the two settings, and put them on the shoulder straps of the ephod in the front. ¹⁹And they made two rings of gold and put *them* on the two ends of the breastplate, on the edge of it, which *was* on the inward side of the ephod. ²⁰They made two *other* gold rings and put them on the two shoulder straps, underneath the ephod toward its front, right at the seam above the intricately woven band of the ephod. ²¹And they bound the breastplate by means of its rings to the rings of the ephod with a blue cord, so that it would be above the intricately woven band of the ephod, and that the breastplate would not come loose from the ephod, as the LORD had commanded Moses.

Making the Other Priestly Garments

²²He made the robe of the ephod of woven work, all of blue. ²³And *there was* an opening in the middle of the robe, like the opening in a coat of mail, *with* a woven binding all around the opening, so that it would not tear. ²⁴They made on the hem of the robe pomegranates of blue, purple, and scarlet, and of fine woven *linen.* ²⁵And they made bells of pure gold, and put the bells between the pomegranates on the hem of the robe all around between the pomegranates: ²⁶a bell and a pomegranate, a bell and a pomegranate, all around the hem of the robe to minister in, as the LORD had commanded Moses.

²⁷They made tunics, artistically woven of fine linen, for Aaron and his sons, ²⁸a turban of fine linen, exquisite hats of fine linen, short trousers of fine woven linen, ²⁹and a sash of fine woven linen with blue, purple, and scarlet *thread,* made by a weaver, as the LORD had commanded Moses.

³⁰Then they made the plate of the holy crown of pure gold, and wrote on it an inscription *like* the engraving of a signet:

HOLINESS TO THE LORD.

³¹And they tied to it a blue cord, to fasten *it* above on the turban, as the LORD had commanded Moses.

The Work Completed

³²Thus all the work of the tabernacle of the tent of meeting was finished. And the children of Israel did according to all that the LORD had commanded Moses; so they did. ³³And they brought the tabernacle to Moses, the tent and all its furnishings: its clasps, its boards, its bars, its pillars, and its sockets; ³⁴the covering of ram skins dyed red, the covering of badger skins, and the veil of the covering; ³⁵the ark of the Testimony with its poles, and the mercy seat; ³⁶the table, all its utensils, and the showbread; ³⁷the pure *gold* lampstand with its lamps (the lamps set in order), all its utensils, and the oil for light; ³⁸the gold altar, the anointing oil, and the sweet incense; the screen for the tabernacle door; ³⁹the bronze altar, its grate of bronze, its poles, and all its utensils; the laver with its base; ⁴⁰the hangings of the court, its pillars and its sockets, the screen for the court gate, its cords, and its pegs; all the utensils for the service of the tabernacle, for the tent of meeting; ⁴¹and the garments of ministry,[a] to minister in the holy *place:* the holy garments for Aaron the priest, and his sons' garments, to minister as priests.

⁴²According to all that the LORD had commanded Moses, so the children of Israel did all the

39:41 [a]Or *woven garments*

work. [43]Then Moses looked over all the work, and indeed they had done it; as the LORD had commanded, just so they had done it. And Moses blessed them.

The Tabernacle Erected and Arranged

40 Then the LORD spoke to Moses, saying: [2]"On the first day of the first month you shall set up the tabernacle of the tent of meeting. [3]You shall put in it the ark of the Testimony, and partition off the ark with the veil. [4]You shall bring in the table and arrange the things that are to be set in order on it; and you shall bring in the lampstand and light its lamps. [5]You shall also set the altar of gold for the incense before the ark of the Testimony, and put up the screen for the door of the tabernacle. [6]Then you shall set the altar of the burnt offering before the door of the tabernacle of the tent of meeting. [7]And you shall set the laver between the tabernacle of meeting and the altar, and put water in it. [8]You shall set up the court all around, and hang up the screen at the court gate.

[9]"And you shall take the anointing oil, and anoint the tabernacle and all that *is* in it; and you shall hallow it and all its utensils, and it shall be holy. [10]You shall anoint the altar of the burnt offering and all its utensils, and consecrate the altar. The altar shall be most holy. [11]And you shall anoint the laver and its base, and consecrate it.

[12]"Then you shall bring Aaron and his sons to the door of the tabernacle of meeting and wash them with water. [13]You shall put the holy garments on Aaron, and anoint him and consecrate him, that he may minister to Me as priest. [14]And you shall bring his sons and clothe them with tunics. [15]You shall anoint them, as you anointed their father, that they may minister to Me as priests; for their anointing shall surely be an everlasting priesthood throughout their generations."

[16]Thus Moses did; according to all that the LORD had commanded him, so he did.

[17]And it came to pass in the first month of the second year, on the first *day* of the month, *that* the tabernacle was raised up. [18]So Moses raised up the tabernacle, fastened its sockets, set up its boards, put in its bars, and raised up its pillars. [19]And he spread out the tent over the tabernacle and put the covering of the tent on top of it, as the LORD had commanded Moses. [20]He took the Testimony and put *it* into the ark, inserted the poles through the rings of the ark, and put the mercy seat on top of the ark. [21]And he brought the ark into the tabernacle, hung up the veil of the covering, and partitioned off the ark of the Testimony, as the LORD had commanded Moses.

[22]He put the table in the tabernacle of meeting, on the north side of the tabernacle, outside the veil; [23]and he set the bread in order upon it before the LORD, as the LORD had commanded Moses. [24]He put the lampstand in the tabernacle of meeting, across from the table, on the south side of the tabernacle; [25]and he lit the lamps before the LORD, as the LORD had commanded Moses. [26]He put the gold altar in the tabernacle of meeting in front of the veil; [27]and he burned sweet incense on it, as the LORD had commanded Moses. [28]He hung up the screen *at* the door of the tabernacle. [29]And he put the altar of burnt offering *before* the door of the tabernacle of the tent of meeting, and offered upon it the burnt offering and the grain offering, as the LORD had commanded Moses. [30]He set the laver between the tabernacle of meeting and the altar, and put water there for washing; [31]and Moses, Aaron, and his sons would wash their hands and their feet *with water* from it. [32]Whenever they went into the tabernacle of meeting, and when they came near the altar, they washed, as the LORD had commanded Moses. [33]And he raised up the court all around the tabernacle and the altar, and hung up the screen of the court gate. So Moses finished the work.

The Cloud and the Glory

[34]Then the cloud covered the tabernacle of meeting, and the glory of the LORD filled the tabernacle. [35]And Moses was not able to enter the tabernacle of meeting, because the cloud rested above it, and the glory of the LORD filled the tabernacle. [36]Whenever the cloud was taken up from above the tabernacle, the children of Israel would go onward in all their journeys. [37]But if the cloud was not taken up, then they did not journey till the day that it was taken up. [38]For the cloud of the LORD *was* above the tabernacle by day, and fire was over it by night, in the sight of all the house of Israel, throughout all their journeys.

IMPACT OF THE BOOK

I IDEA

"Be holy because I am holy"—is the call for genuinely following God. God gave the Israelites rules and guidelines, not so their walk with Him would be reduced to a bunch of "cans and can'ts," but because a believer's lifestyle is a visual testimony to those who do not know God.

MESSAGE

To become a godly leader you must live a life worthy of imitating. Private victories will precede public victories. God took His people out of Egypt; this book is God taking the "Egypt" out of His people. His call to holiness is not easy. Daily you will face decisions to choose God's way or to settle for less than God's best. The believer who answers God's call to holy living will shine like a bright light in this dark world, pointing people to God.

PEOPLE

Aaron, Abihu, Eleazar, Moses, Nadab

AUTHOR

Leviticus's authorship is attributed to Moses by both the Hebrew tradition and the New Testament. Jesus affirms Mosaic authorship when He referred to the Levitical law of cleansing (Matt. 8:4; Lev. 14:2–32). Paul declares the Mosaic authorship of the words, "The man who does those things will live by them" (Rom. 10:5; Lev. 18:5). In the New Testament, the Pentateuch and the prophets are also repeatedly referred to as "Moses and the prophets" (Luke 16:29, 31; 24:27, 44; Acts 28:23).

CULTURE

The revelation recorded in Leviticus was given to the Israelites in the year after the Exodus as they were encamped at the foot of Mount Sinai, part of a mountain range at the southern tip of the Sinai Peninsula. This mountain has an adjacent plain that would have been able to accommodate the Israelites. God spoke to the people from the mountain (25:1) and from the "tent of meeting" (1:1).

TIMELINE

between 1445 and 1405 BC

KEY SCRIPTURE MEMORY VERSES

17:11; 19:2; 19:18; 20:7, 8; 27:30

The Burnt Offering

1 Now the LORD called to Moses, and spoke to him from the tabernacle of meeting, saying, ²"Speak to the children of Israel, and say to them: 'When any one of you brings an offering to the LORD, you shall bring your offering of the livestock—of the herd and of the flock.

³'If his offering *is* a burnt sacrifice of the herd, let him offer a male without blemish; he shall offer it of his own free will at the door of the tabernacle of meeting before the LORD. ⁴Then he shall put his hand on the head of the burnt offering, and it will be accepted on his behalf to make atonement for him. ⁵He shall kill the bull before the LORD; and the priests, Aaron's sons, shall bring the blood and sprinkle the blood all around on the altar that *is by* the door of the tabernacle of meeting. ⁶And he shall skin the burnt offering and cut it into its pieces. ⁷The sons of Aaron the priest shall put fire on the altar, and lay the wood in order on the fire. ⁸Then the priests, Aaron's sons, shall lay the parts, the head, and the fat in order on the wood that *is* on the fire upon the altar; ⁹but he shall wash its entrails and its legs with water. And the priest shall burn all on the altar as a burnt sacrifice, an offering made by fire, a sweet aroma to the LORD.

¹⁰'If his offering *is* of the flocks—of the sheep or of the goats—as a burnt sacrifice, he shall bring a male without blemish. ¹¹He shall kill it on the north side of the altar before the LORD; and the priests, Aaron's sons, shall sprinkle its blood all around on the altar. ¹²And he shall cut it into its pieces, with its head and its fat; and the priest shall lay them in order on the wood that *is* on the fire upon the altar; ¹³but he shall wash the entrails and the legs with water. Then the priest shall bring *it* all and burn *it* on the altar; it *is* a burnt sacrifice, an offering made by fire, a sweet aroma to the LORD.

¹⁴'And if the burnt sacrifice of his offering to the LORD *is* of birds, then he shall bring his offering of turtledoves or young pigeons. ¹⁵The priest shall bring it to the altar, wring off its head, and burn *it* on the altar; its blood shall be drained out at the side of the altar. ¹⁶And he shall remove its crop with its feathers and cast it beside the altar on the east side, into the place for ashes. ¹⁷Then

he shall split it at its wings, *but* shall not divide *it* completely; and the priest shall burn it on the altar, on the wood that *is* on the fire. It *is* a burnt sacrifice, an offering made by fire, a sweet aroma to the LORD.

The Grain Offering

2 'When anyone offers a grain offering to the LORD, his offering shall be *of* fine flour. And he shall pour oil on it, and put frankincense on it. ²He shall bring it to Aaron's sons, the priests, one of whom shall take from it his handful of fine flour and oil with all the frankincense. And the priest shall burn *it as* a memorial on the altar, an offering made by fire, a sweet aroma to the LORD. ³The rest of the grain offering *shall be* Aaron's and his sons'. It *is* most holy of the offerings to the LORD made by fire.

⁴'And if you bring as an offering a grain offering baked in the oven, *it shall be* unleavened cakes of fine flour mixed with oil, or unleavened wafers anointed with oil. ⁵But if your offering *is* a grain offering *baked* in a pan, *it shall be of* fine flour, unleavened, mixed with oil. ⁶You shall break it in pieces and pour oil on it; it *is* a grain offering.

⁷'If your offering *is* a grain offering *baked* in a covered pan, it shall be made *of* fine flour with oil. ⁸You shall bring the grain offering that is made of these things to the LORD. And when it is presented to the priest, he shall bring it to the altar. ⁹Then the priest shall take from the grain offering a memorial portion, and burn *it* on the altar. It *is* an offering made by fire, a sweet aroma to the LORD. ¹⁰And what is left of the grain offering *shall be* Aaron's and his sons'. It *is* most holy of the offerings to the LORD made by fire.

¹¹'No grain offering which you bring to the LORD shall be made with leaven, for you shall burn no leaven nor any honey in any offering to the LORD made by fire. ¹²As for the offering of the firstfruits, you shall offer them to the LORD, but they shall not be burned on the altar for a sweet aroma. ¹³And every offering of your grain offering you shall season with salt; you shall not allow the salt of the covenant of your God to be lacking from your grain offering. With all your offerings you shall offer salt.

¹⁴'If you offer a grain offering of your first-

fruits to the LORD, you shall offer for the grain offering of your firstfruits green heads of grain roasted on the fire, grain beaten from full heads. [15]And you shall put oil on it, and lay frankincense on it. It *is* a grain offering. [16]Then the priest shall burn the memorial portion: *part* of its beaten grain and *part* of its oil, with all the frankincense, as an offering made by fire to the LORD.

The Peace Offering

3 'When his offering *is* a sacrifice of a peace offering, if he offers *it* of the herd, whether male or female, he shall offer it without blemish before the LORD. [2]And he shall lay his hand on the head of his offering, and kill it *at* the door of the tabernacle of meeting; and Aaron's sons, the priests, shall sprinkle the blood all around on the altar. [3]Then he shall offer from the sacrifice of the peace offering an offering made by fire to the LORD. The fat that covers the entrails and all the fat that *is* on the entrails, [4]the two kidneys and the fat that *is* on them by the flanks, and the fatty lobe *attached* to the liver above the kidneys, he shall remove; [5]and Aaron's sons shall burn it on the altar upon the burnt sacrifice, which *is* on the wood that *is* on the fire, *as* an offering made by fire, a sweet aroma to the LORD.

[6]'If his offering as a sacrifice of a peace offering to the LORD *is* of the flock, *whether* male or female, he shall offer it without blemish. [7]If he offers a lamb as his offering, then he shall offer it before the LORD. [8]And he shall lay his hand on the head of his offering, and kill it before the tabernacle of meeting; and Aaron's sons shall sprinkle its blood all around on the altar.

[9]'Then he shall offer from the sacrifice of the peace offering, as an offering made by fire to the LORD, its fat *and* the whole fat tail which he shall remove close to the backbone. And the fat that covers the entrails and all the fat that *is* on the entrails, [10]the two kidneys and the fat that *is* on them by the flanks, and the fatty lobe *attached* to the liver above the kidneys, he shall remove; [11]and the priest shall burn *them* on the altar *as* food, an offering made by fire to the LORD.

[12]'And if his offering *is* a goat, then he shall offer it before the LORD. [13]He shall lay his hand on its head and kill it before the tabernacle of meeting; and the sons of Aaron shall sprinkle its blood all around on the altar. [14]Then he shall offer from it his offering, as an offering made by fire to the LORD. The fat that covers the entrails and all the fat that *is* on the entrails, [15]the two kidneys and the fat that *is* on them by the flanks, and the fatty lobe *attached* to the liver above the kidneys, he shall remove; [16]and the priest shall burn them on the altar *as* food, an offering made by fire for a sweet aroma; all the fat *is* the LORD's.

[17]'*This shall be* a perpetual statute throughout your generations in all your dwellings: you shall eat neither fat nor blood.' "

The Sin Offering

4 Now the LORD spoke to Moses, saying, [2]"Speak to the children of Israel, saying: 'If a person sins unintentionally against any of the commandments of the LORD *in anything* which ought not to be done, and does any of them, [3]if the anointed priest sins, bringing guilt on the people, then let him offer to the LORD for his sin which he has sinned a young bull without blemish as a sin offering. [4]He shall bring the bull to the door of the tabernacle of meeting before the LORD, lay his hand on the bull's head, and kill the bull before the LORD. [5]Then the anointed priest shall take some of the bull's blood and bring it to the tabernacle of meeting. [6]The priest shall dip his finger in the blood and sprinkle some of the blood seven times before the LORD, in front of the veil of the sanctuary. [7]And the priest shall put some of the blood on the horns of the altar of sweet incense before the LORD, which is in the tabernacle of meeting; and he shall pour the remaining blood of the bull at the base of the altar of the burnt offering, which is at the door of the tabernacle of meeting. [8]He shall take from it all the fat of the bull as the sin offering. The fat that covers the entrails and all the fat which *is* on the entrails, [9]the two kidneys and the fat that *is* on them by the flanks, and the fatty lobe *attached* to the liver above the kidneys, he shall remove, [10]as it was taken from the bull of the sacrifice of the peace offering; and the priest shall burn them on the altar of the burnt offering. [11]But the bull's hide and all its flesh, with its head and legs, its entrails and offal— [12]the whole bull he shall carry outside the camp to a clean place, where the ashes are poured out, and burn it on wood with fire; where the ashes are poured out it shall be burned.

¹³'Now if the whole congregation of Israel sins unintentionally, and the thing is hidden from the eyes of the assembly, and they have done *something against* any of the commandments of the LORD *in anything* which should not be done, and are guilty; ¹⁴when the sin which they have committed becomes known, then the assembly shall offer a young bull for the sin, and bring it before the tabernacle of meeting. ¹⁵And the elders of the congregation shall lay their hands on the head of the bull before the LORD. Then the bull shall be killed before the LORD. ¹⁶The anointed priest shall bring some of the bull's blood to the tabernacle of meeting. ¹⁷Then the priest shall dip his finger in the blood and sprinkle *it* seven times before the LORD, in front of the veil. ¹⁸And he shall put *some* of the blood on the horns of the altar which *is* before the LORD, which *is* in the tabernacle of meeting; and he shall pour the remaining blood at the base of the altar of burnt offering, which is at the door of the tabernacle of meeting. ¹⁹He shall take all the fat from it and burn *it* on the altar. ²⁰And he shall do with the bull as he did with the bull as a sin offering; thus he shall do with it. So the priest shall make atonement for them, and it shall be forgiven them. ²¹Then he shall carry the bull outside the camp, and burn it as he burned the first bull. It *is* a sin offering for the assembly.

²²'When a ruler has sinned, and done *something* unintentionally *against* any of the commandments of the LORD his God *in anything* which should not be done, and is guilty, ²³or if his sin which he has committed comes to his knowledge, he shall bring as his offering a kid of the goats, a male without blemish. ²⁴And he shall lay his hand on the head of the goat, and kill it at the place where they kill the burnt offering before the LORD. It *is* a sin offering. ²⁵The priest shall take some of the blood of the sin offering with his finger, put *it* on the horns of the altar of burnt offering, and pour its blood at the base of the altar of burnt offering. ²⁶And he shall burn all its fat on the altar, like the fat of the sacrifice of the peace offering. So the priest shall make atonement for him concerning his sin, and it shall be forgiven him.

²⁷'If anyone of the common people sins unintentionally by doing *something against* any of the commandments of the LORD *in anything* which ought not to be done, and is guilty, ²⁸or if his sin which he has committed comes to his knowledge, then he shall bring as his offering a kid of the goats, a female without blemish, for his sin which he has committed. ²⁹And he shall lay his hand on the head of the sin offering, and kill the sin offering at the place of the burnt offering. ³⁰Then the priest shall take *some* of its blood with his finger, put *it* on the horns of the altar of burnt offering, and pour all *the remaining* blood at the base of the altar. ³¹He shall remove all its fat, as fat is removed from the sacrifice of the peace offering; and the priest shall burn it on the altar for a sweet aroma to the LORD. So the priest shall make atonement for him, and it shall be forgiven him.

³²'If he brings a lamb as his sin offering, he shall bring a female without blemish. ³³Then he shall lay his hand on the head of the sin offering, and kill it as a sin offering at the place where they kill the burnt offering. ³⁴The priest shall take *some* of the blood of the sin offering with his finger, put *it* on the horns of the altar of burnt offering, and pour all *the remaining* blood at the base of the altar. ³⁵He shall remove all its fat, as the fat of the lamb is removed from the sacrifice of the peace offering. Then the priest shall burn it on the altar, according to the offerings made by fire to the LORD. So the priest shall make atonement for his sin that he has committed, and it shall be forgiven him.

The Trespass Offering

5 'If a person sins in hearing the utterance of an oath, and *is* a witness, whether he has seen or known *of the matter*—if he does not tell *it,* he bears guilt.

²'Or if a person touches any unclean thing, whether *it is* the carcass of an unclean beast, or the carcass of unclean livestock, or the carcass of unclean creeping things, and he is unaware of it, he also shall be unclean and guilty. ³Or if he touches human uncleanness—whatever uncleanness with which a man may be defiled, and he is unaware of it—when he realizes *it,* then he shall be guilty.

⁴'Or if a person swears, speaking thoughtlessly with *his* lips to do evil or to do good, whatever *it*

is that a man may pronounce by an oath, and he is unaware of it—when he realizes *it,* then he shall be guilty in any of these *matters.*

⁵'And it shall be, when he is guilty in any of these *matters,* that he shall confess that he has sinned in that *thing;* ⁶and he shall bring his trespass offering to the LORD for his sin which he has committed, a female from the flock, a lamb or a kid of the goats as a sin offering. So the priest shall make atonement for him concerning his sin.

⁷'If he is not able to bring a lamb, then he shall bring to the LORD, for his trespass which he has committed, two turtledoves or two young pigeons: one as a sin offering and the other as a burnt offering. ⁸And he shall bring them to the priest, who shall offer *that* which *is* for the sin offering first, and wring off its head from its neck, but shall not divide *it* completely. ⁹Then he shall sprinkle *some* of the blood of the sin offering on the side of the altar, and the rest of the blood shall be drained out at the base of the altar. It *is* a sin offering. ¹⁰And he shall offer the second *as* a burnt offering according to the prescribed manner. So the priest shall make atonement on his behalf for his sin which he has committed, and it shall be forgiven him.

¹¹'But if he is not able to bring two turtledoves or two young pigeons, then he who sinned shall bring for his offering one-tenth of an ephah of fine flour as a sin offering. He shall put no oil on it, nor shall he put frankincense on it, for it *is* a sin offering. ¹²Then he shall bring it to the priest, and the priest shall take his handful of it as a memorial portion, and burn *it* on the altar according to the offerings made by fire to the LORD. It *is* a sin offering. ¹³The priest shall make atonement for him, for his sin that he has committed in any of these matters; and it shall be forgiven him. *The rest* shall be the priest's as a grain offering.' "

OFFERINGS WITH RESTITUTION

¹⁴Then the LORD spoke to Moses, saying: ¹⁵"If a person commits a trespass, and sins unintentionally in regard to the holy things of the LORD, then he shall bring to the LORD as his trespass offering a ram without blemish from the flocks, with your valuation in shekels of silver ac-

cording to the shekel of the sanctuary, as a trespass offering. ¹⁶And he shall make restitution for the harm that he has done in regard to the holy thing, and shall add one-fifth to it and give it to the priest. So the priest shall make atonement for him with the ram of the trespass offering, and it shall be forgiven him.

¹⁷"If a person sins, and commits any of these things which are forbidden to be done by the commandments of the LORD, though he does not know *it,* yet he is guilty and shall bear his iniquity. ¹⁸And he shall bring to the priest a ram without blemish from the flock, with your valuation, as a trespass offering. So the priest shall make atonement for him regarding his ignorance in which he erred and did not know *it,* and it shall be forgiven him. ¹⁹It is a trespass offering; he has certainly trespassed against the LORD."

6 And the LORD spoke to Moses, saying: ²"If a person sins and commits a trespass against the LORD by lying to his neighbor about what was delivered to him for safekeeping, or about a pledge, or about a robbery, or if he has extorted from his neighbor, ³or if he has found what was lost and lies concerning it, and swears falsely—in any one of these things that a man may do in which he sins: ⁴then it shall be, because he has sinned and is guilty, that he shall restore what he has stolen, or the thing which he has extorted, or what was delivered to him for safekeeping, or the lost thing which he found, ⁵or all that about which he has sworn falsely. He shall restore its full value, add one-fifth more to it, *and* give it to whomever it belongs, on the day of his trespass offering. ⁶And he shall bring his trespass offering to the LORD, a ram without blemish from the flock, with your valuation, as a trespass offering, to the priest. ⁷So the priest shall make atonement for him before the LORD, and he shall be forgiven for any one of these things that he may have done in which he trespasses."

THE LAW OF THE BURNT OFFERING

⁸Then the LORD spoke to Moses, saying, ⁹"Command Aaron and his sons, saying, 'This *is* the law of the burnt offering: The burnt offering *shall be* on the hearth upon the altar all night until morning, and the fire of the altar shall be kept burning on it. ¹⁰And the priest shall put on his

LEADERSHIP ISSUES

Leadership Issues: Restoring the Right to Lead

LEVITICUS 6:2

Any one is capable of a lie, particularly when we know that a "temporary" or "white lie" could keep us out of conflict, at least until we can try to undo the sin we began with. Cover-ups never work, as seen in Genesis 1 with Adam and Eve. God, in His infinite wisdom and compassion, offers a word of judgment to admit the wrong, correct it, and then to give even more of oneself in an offering to your brother and to the Lord.

The heart of this passage is a very rare word in the Old Testament; the word *fellowship*. It appears twice—here and in Psalm 94:20. In both instances, it is plainly speaking of the wrong kind of fellowship; that which usually begins with the wrong kind of companionship, in both our private and public life. Half-faced fellowship is that which seeks its own fulfillment first without correcting the sin. Full-faced fellowship means to care about the other "fellow" in the "ship" with you. Leviticus gives a long list of trespasses against a neighbor by injury, lying, stealing, or slandering. The warning is simple: You will lose your influence if you fail to remember that if we sin against our fellow man we sin against our God. You lose the opportunity to lead others if you do not restore the fellowship, then give more from the heart, and, finally, offer repentance as a sacrifice to the Lord.

There is no perfect leader; there is, however, an influential leader, one who has seen his own heart and grown purer, more compassionate, and stronger through genuine repentance.

linen garment, and his linen trousers he shall put on his body, and take up the ashes of the burnt offering which the fire has consumed on the altar, and he shall put them beside the altar. ¹¹Then he shall take off his garments, put on other garments, and carry the ashes outside the camp to a clean place. ¹²And the fire on the altar shall be kept burning on it; it shall not be put out. And the priest shall burn wood on it every morning, and lay the burnt offering in order on it; and he shall burn on it the fat of the peace offerings. ¹³A fire shall always be burning on the altar; it shall never go out.

The Law of the Grain Offering

¹⁴"This *is* the law of the grain offering: The sons of Aaron shall offer it on the altar before the LORD. ¹⁵He shall take from it his handful of the fine flour of the grain offering, with its oil, and all the frankincense which *is* on the grain offering, and shall burn *it* on the altar *for* a sweet aroma, as a memorial to the LORD. ¹⁶And the remainder of it Aaron and his sons shall eat; with unleavened bread it shall be eaten in a holy place; in the court of the tabernacle of meeting they shall eat it. ¹⁷It shall not be baked with leaven. I have given it *as* their portion of My offerings made by fire; it *is* most holy, like the sin offering and the trespass offering. ¹⁸All the males among the children of Aaron may eat it. *It shall be* a statute forever in your generations concerning the offerings made by fire to the LORD. Everyone who touches them must be holy.' "ª

¹⁹And the LORD spoke to Moses, saying, ²⁰"This *is* the offering of Aaron and his sons, which they shall offer to the LORD, *beginning* on the day when he is anointed: one-tenth of an ephah of fine flour as a daily grain offering, half of it in the morning and half of it at night. ²¹It shall be made in a pan with oil. *When it is* mixed, you shall bring it in. The baked pieces of the grain offering you shall offer *for* a sweet aroma to the LORD. ²²The priest from among his sons, who is anointed in his place, shall offer it. *It is* a statute forever to the LORD. It shall be wholly burned. ²³For every grain offering for the priest shall be wholly burned. It shall not be eaten."

The Law of the Sin Offering

²⁴Also the LORD spoke to Moses, saying, ²⁵"Speak to Aaron and to his sons, saying, 'This *is* the law of the sin offering: In the place where the burnt offering is killed, the sin offering shall be killed before the LORD. It *is* most holy. ²⁶The priest who offers it for sin shall eat it. In a holy place it shall be eaten, in the court of the tabernacle of meeting. ²⁷Everyone who touches its flesh must be holy.ª And when its blood is sprinkled on any garment, you shall wash that on which it was sprinkled, in a holy place. ²⁸But the earthen vessel in which it is boiled shall be broken. And if it is boiled in a bronze pot, it shall be both scoured and rinsed in water. ²⁹All the males among the priests may eat it. It *is* most holy. ³⁰But no sin offering from which *any* of the blood is brought into the tabernacle of meeting, to make atonement in the holy *place,*ª shall be eaten. It shall be burned in the fire.

The Law of the Trespass Offering

7 ¹Likewise this *is* the law of the trespass offering (it *is* most holy): ²In the place where they kill the burnt offering they shall kill the trespass offering. And its blood he shall sprinkle all around on the altar. ³And he shall offer from it all its fat. The fat tail and the fat that covers the entrails, ⁴the two kidneys and the fat that *is* on them by the flanks, and the fatty lobe *attached* to the liver above the kidneys, he shall remove; ⁵and the priest shall burn them on the altar *as* an offering made by fire to the LORD. It *is* a trespass offering. ⁶Every male among the priests may eat it. It shall be eaten in a holy place. It *is* most holy. ⁷The trespass offering *is* like the sin offering; *there is* one law for them both: the priest who makes atonement with it shall have *it.* ⁸And the priest who offers anyone's burnt offering, that priest shall have for himself the skin of the burnt offering which he has offered. ⁹Also every grain offering that is baked in the oven and all that is prepared in the covered pan, or in a pan, shall be the priest's who offers it. ¹⁰Every grain offering, *whether* mixed with oil or dry, shall belong to all the sons of Aaron, to one *as much* as the other.

6:18 ªCompare Numbers 4:15 and Haggai 2:11–13   **6:27** ªCompare Numbers 4:15 and Haggai 2:11–13   **6:30** ªThe Most Holy Place when capitalized

The Law of Peace Offerings

[11]'This *is* the law of the sacrifice of peace offerings which he shall offer to the LORD: [12]If he offers it for a thanksgiving, then he shall offer, with the sacrifice of thanksgiving, unleavened cakes mixed with oil, unleavened wafers anointed with oil, or cakes of blended flour mixed with oil. [13]Besides the cakes, *as* his offering he shall offer leavened bread with the sacrifice of thanksgiving of his peace offering. [14]And from it he shall offer one cake from each offering *as* a heave offering to the LORD. It shall belong to the priest who sprinkles the blood of the peace offering.

[15]'The flesh of the sacrifice of his peace offering for thanksgiving shall be eaten the same day it is offered. He shall not leave any of it until morning. [16]But if the sacrifice of his offering *is* a vow or a voluntary offering, it shall be eaten the same day that he offers his sacrifice; but on the next day the remainder of it also may be eaten; [17]the remainder of the flesh of the sacrifice on the third day must be burned with fire. [18]And if *any* of the flesh of the sacrifice of his peace offering is eaten at all on the third day, it shall not be accepted, nor shall it be imputed to him; it shall be an abomination *to* him who offers it, and the person who eats of it shall bear guilt.

[19]'The flesh that touches any unclean thing shall not be eaten. It shall be burned with fire. And as for the *clean* flesh, all who are clean may eat of it. [20]But the person who eats the flesh of the sacrifice of the peace offering that *belongs to* the LORD, while he is unclean, that person shall be cut off from his people. [21]Moreover the person who touches any unclean thing, *such as* human uncleanness, *an* unclean animal, or any abominable unclean thing,[a] and who eats the flesh of the sacrifice of the peace offering that *belongs to* the LORD, that person shall be cut off from his people.' "

Fat and Blood May Not Be Eaten

[22]And the LORD spoke to Moses, saying, [23]"Speak to the children of Israel, saying: 'You shall not eat any fat, of ox or sheep or goat. [24]And the fat of an animal that dies *naturally,* and the fat of what is torn by wild beasts, may be used in any other way; but you shall by no means eat it. [25]For whoever eats the fat of the animal of which men offer an offering made by fire to the LORD, the person who eats *it* shall be cut off from his people. [26]Moreover you shall not eat any blood in any of your dwellings, *whether* of bird or beast. [27]Whoever eats any blood, that person shall be cut off from his people.' "

The Portion of Aaron and His Sons

[28]Then the LORD spoke to Moses, saying, [29]"Speak to the children of Israel, saying: 'He who offers the sacrifice of his peace offering to the LORD shall bring his offering to the LORD from the sacrifice of his peace offering. [30]His own hands shall bring the offerings made by fire to the LORD. The fat with the breast he shall bring, that the breast may be waved *as* a wave offering before the LORD. [31]And the priest shall burn the fat on the altar, but the breast shall be Aaron's and his sons'. [32]Also the right thigh you shall give to the priest *as* a heave offering from the sacrifices of your peace offerings. [33]He among the sons of Aaron, who offers the blood of the peace offering and the fat, shall have the right thigh for *his* part. [34]For the breast of the wave offering and the thigh of the heave offering I have taken from the children of Israel, from the sacrifices of their peace offerings, and I have given them to Aaron the priest and to his sons from the children of Israel by a statute forever.' "

[35]This *is* the consecrated portion for Aaron and his sons, from the offerings made by fire to the LORD, on the day when *Moses* presented them to minister to the LORD as priests. [36]The LORD commanded this to be given to them by the children of Israel, on the day that He anointed them, *by* a statute forever throughout their generations.

[37]This *is* the law of the burnt offering, the grain offering, the sin offering, the trespass offering, the consecrations, and the sacrifice of the peace offering, [38]which the LORD commanded Moses on Mount Sinai, on the day when He commanded the children of Israel to offer their offerings to the LORD in the Wilderness of Sinai.

7:21 [a]Following Masoretic Text, Septuagint, and Vulgate; Samaritan Pentateuch, Syriac, and Targum read *swarming thing* (compare 5:2).

AARON AND HIS SONS CONSECRATED

8 And the LORD spoke to Moses, saying: ²"Take Aaron and his sons with him, and the garments, the anointing oil, a bull as the sin offering, two rams, and a basket of unleavened bread; ³and gather all the congregation together at the door of the tabernacle of meeting."

⁴So Moses did as the LORD commanded him. And the congregation was gathered together at the door of the tabernacle of meeting. ⁵And Moses said to the congregation, "This *is* what the LORD commanded to be done."

⁶Then Moses brought Aaron and his sons and washed them with water. ⁷And he put the tunic on him, girded him with the sash, clothed him with the robe, and put the ephod on him; and he girded him with the intricately woven band of the ephod, and with it tied *the ephod* on him. ⁸Then he put the breastplate on him, and he put the Urim and the Thummim[a] in the breastplate. ⁹And he put the turban on his head. Also on the turban, on its front, he put the golden plate, the holy crown, as the LORD had commanded Moses.

¹⁰Also Moses took the anointing oil, and anointed the tabernacle and all that *was* in it, and consecrated them. ¹¹He sprinkled some of it on the altar seven times, anointed the altar and all its utensils, and the laver and its base, to consecrate them. ¹²And he poured some of the anointing oil on Aaron's head and anointed him, to consecrate him.

¹³Then Moses brought Aaron's sons and put tunics on them, girded them with sashes, and put hats on them, as the LORD had commanded Moses.

¹⁴And he brought the bull for the sin offering. Then Aaron and his sons laid their hands on the head of the bull for the sin offering, ¹⁵and Moses killed *it*. Then he took the blood, and put *some* on the horns of the altar all around with his finger, and purified the altar. And he poured the blood at the base of the altar, and consecrated it, to make atonement for it. ¹⁶Then he took all the fat that *was* on the entrails, the fatty lobe *attached to* the liver, and the two kidneys with their fat, and Moses burned *them* on the altar. ¹⁷But the bull, its hide, its flesh, and its offal, he burned with fire outside the camp, as the LORD had commanded Moses.

¹⁸Then he brought the ram as the burnt offering. And Aaron and his sons laid their hands on the head of the ram, ¹⁹and Moses killed *it*. Then he sprinkled the blood all around on the altar. ²⁰And he cut the ram into pieces; and Moses burned the head, the pieces, and the fat. ²¹Then he washed the entrails and the legs in water. And Moses burned the whole ram on the altar. It *was* a burnt sacrifice for a sweet aroma, an offering made by fire to the LORD, as the LORD had commanded Moses.

²²And he brought the second ram, the ram of consecration. Then Aaron and his sons laid their hands on the head of the ram, ²³and Moses killed *it*. Also he took *some* of its blood and put it on the tip of Aaron's right ear, on the thumb of his right hand, and on the big toe of his right foot. ²⁴Then he brought Aaron's sons. And Moses put *some* of the blood on the tips of their right ears, on the thumbs of their right hands, and on the big toes of their right feet. And Moses sprinkled the blood all around on the altar. ²⁵Then he took the fat and the fat tail, all the fat that *was* on the entrails, the fatty lobe *attached to* the liver, the two kidneys and their fat, and the right thigh; ²⁶and from the basket of unleavened bread that was before the LORD he took one unleavened cake, a cake of bread *anointed with* oil, and one wafer, and put *them* on the fat and on the right thigh; ²⁷and he put all *these* in Aaron's hands and in his sons' hands, and waved them *as* a wave offering before the LORD. ²⁸Then Moses took them from their hands and burned *them* on the altar, on the burnt offering. They *were* consecration offerings for a sweet aroma. That *was* an offering made by fire to the LORD. ²⁹And Moses took the breast and waved it *as* a wave offering before the LORD. It was Moses' part of the ram of consecration, as the LORD had commanded Moses.

³⁰Then Moses took some of the anointing oil and some of the blood which *was* on the altar, and sprinkled *it* on Aaron, on his garments, on his sons, and on the garments of his sons with him; and he consecrated Aaron, his garments, his sons, and the garments of his sons with him.

³¹And Moses said to Aaron and his sons, "Boil

8:8 ªLiterally *the Lights and the Perfections* (compare Exodus 28:30) the flesh *at* the door of the tabernacle of meeting, and eat it there with the bread that *is* in the basket of consecration offerings, as I commanded, saying, 'Aaron and his sons shall eat it.' ³²What remains of the flesh and of the bread you shall burn with fire. ³³And you shall not go outside the door of the tabernacle of meeting *for* seven days, until the days of your consecration are ended. For seven days he shall consecrate you. ³⁴As he has done this day, *so* the LORD has commanded to do, to make atonement for you. ³⁵Therefore you shall stay *at* the door of the tabernacle of meeting day and night for seven days, and keep the charge of the LORD, so that you may not die; for so I have been commanded." ³⁶So Aaron and his sons did all the things that the LORD had commanded by the hand of Moses.

The Priestly Ministry Begins

9 It came to pass on the eighth day that Moses called Aaron and his sons and the elders of Israel. ²And he said to Aaron, "Take for yourself a young bull as a sin offering and a ram as a burnt offering, without blemish, and offer *them* before the LORD. ³And to the children of Israel you shall speak, saying, 'Take a kid of the goats as a sin offering, and a calf and a lamb, *both* of the first year, without blemish, as a burnt offering, ⁴also a bull and a ram as peace offerings, to sacrifice before the LORD, and a grain offering mixed with oil; for today the LORD will appear to you.' "

⁵So they brought what Moses commanded before the tabernacle of meeting. And all the congregation drew near and stood before the LORD. ⁶Then Moses said, "This *is* the thing which the LORD commanded you to do, and the glory of the LORD will appear to you." ⁷And Moses said to Aaron, "Go to the altar, offer your sin offering and your burnt offering, and make atonement for yourself and for the people. Offer the offering of the people, and make atonement for them, as the LORD commanded."

⁸Aaron therefore went to the altar and killed the calf of the sin offering, which *was* for himself. ⁹Then the sons of Aaron brought the blood to him. And he dipped his finger in the blood, put *it* on the horns of the altar, and poured the blood at the base of the altar. ¹⁰But the fat, the kidneys, and the fatty lobe from the liver of the sin offering he

burned on the altar, as the LORD had commanded Moses. ¹¹The flesh and the hide he burned with fire outside the camp.

¹²And he killed the burnt offering; and Aaron's sons presented to him the blood, which he sprinkled all around on the altar. ¹³Then they presented the burnt offering to him, with its pieces and head, and he burned *them* on the altar. ¹⁴And he washed the entrails and the legs, and burned *them* with the burnt offering on the altar.

¹⁵Then he brought the people's offering, and took the goat, which *was* the sin offering for the people, and killed it and offered it for sin, like the first one. ¹⁶And he brought the burnt offering and offered it according to the prescribed manner. ¹⁷Then he brought the grain offering, took a handful of it, and burned *it* on the altar, besides the burnt sacrifice of the morning.

¹⁸He also killed the bull and the ram *as* sacrifices of peace offerings, which *were* for the people. And Aaron's sons presented to him the blood, which he sprinkled all around on the altar, ¹⁹and the fat from the bull and the ram—the fatty tail, what covers *the entrails* and the kidneys, and the fatty lobe *attached to* the liver; ²⁰and they put the fat on the breasts. Then he burned the fat on the altar; ²¹but the breasts and the right thigh Aaron waved *as* a wave offering before the LORD, as Moses had commanded.

²²Then Aaron lifted his hand toward the people, blessed them, and came down from offering the sin offering, the burnt offering, and peace offerings. ²³And Moses and Aaron went into the tabernacle of meeting, and came out and blessed the people. Then the glory of the LORD appeared to all the people, ²⁴and fire came out from before the LORD and consumed the burnt offering and the fat on the altar. When all the people saw *it,* they shouted and fell on their faces.

The Profane Fire of Nadab and Abihu

10 Then Nadab and Abihu, the sons of Aaron, each took his censer and put fire in it, put incense on it, and offered profane fire before the LORD, which He had not commanded them. ²So fire went out from the LORD and devoured them, and they died before the LORD. ³And Moses said to Aaron, "This is what the LORD spoke, saying:

'By those who come near Me
I must be regarded as holy;
And before all the people
I must be glorified.' ' "

So Aaron held his peace.

⁴Then Moses called Mishael and Elzaphan, the sons of Uzziel the uncle of Aaron, and said to them, "Come near, carry your brethren from before the sanctuary out of the camp." ⁵So they went near and carried them by their tunics out of the camp, as Moses had said.

⁶And Moses said to Aaron, and to Eleazar and Ithamar, his sons, "Do not uncover your heads nor tear your clothes, lest you die, and wrath come upon all the people. But let your brethren, the whole house of Israel, bewail the burning which the LORD has kindled. ⁷You shall not go out from the door of the tabernacle of meeting, lest you die, for the anointing oil of the LORD is upon you." And they did according to the word of Moses.

CONDUCT PRESCRIBED FOR PRIESTS

⁸Then the LORD spoke to Aaron, saying: ⁹"Do not drink wine or intoxicating drink, you, nor your sons with you, when you go into the tabernacle of meeting, lest you die. It shall be a statute forever throughout your generations, ¹⁰that you may distinguish between holy and unholy, and between unclean and clean, ¹¹and that you may teach the children of Israel all the statutes which the LORD has spoken to them by the hand of Moses."

¹²And Moses spoke to Aaron, and to Eleazar and Ithamar, his sons who were left: "Take the grain offering that remains of the offerings made by fire to the LORD, and eat it without leaven beside the altar; for it is most holy. ¹³You shall eat it in a holy place, because it is your due and your sons' due, of the sacrifices made by fire to the LORD; for so I have been commanded. ¹⁴The breast of the wave offering and the thigh of the heave offering you shall eat in a clean place, you, your sons, and your daughters with you; for they are your due and your sons' due, which are given from the sacrifices of peace offerings of the children of Israel. ¹⁵The thigh of the heave offering and the breast of the wave offering they shall

bring with the offerings of fat made by fire, to offer as a wave offering before the LORD. And it shall be yours and your sons' with you, by a statute forever, as the LORD has commanded."

¹⁶Then Moses made careful inquiry about the goat of the sin offering, and there it was—burned up. And he was angry with Eleazar and Ithamar, the sons of Aaron who were left, saying, ¹⁷"Why have you not eaten the sin offering in a holy place, since it is most holy, and God has given it to you to bear the guilt of the congregation, to make atonement for them before the LORD? ¹⁸See! Its blood was not brought inside the holy place,ᵃ indeed you should have eaten it in a holy place, as I commanded."

¹⁹And Aaron said to Moses, "Look, this day they have offered their sin offering and their burnt offering before the LORD, and such things have befallen me! If I had eaten the sin offering today, would it have been accepted in the sight of the LORD?" ²⁰So when Moses heard that, he was content.

FOODS PERMITTED AND FORBIDDEN

11 Now the LORD spoke to Moses and Aaron, saying to them, ²"Speak to the children of Israel, saying, 'These are the animals which you may eat among all the animals that are on the earth: ³Among the animals, whatever divides the hoof, having cloven hooves and chewing the cud—that you may eat. ⁴Nevertheless these you shall not eat among those that chew the cud or those that have cloven hooves: the camel, because it chews the cud but does not have cloven hooves, is unclean to you; ⁵the rock hyrax, because it chews the cud but does not have cloven hooves, is unclean to you; ⁶the hare, because it chews the cud but does not have cloven hooves, is unclean to you; ⁷and the swine, though it divides the hoof, having cloven hooves, yet does not chew the cud, is unclean to you. ⁸Their flesh you shall not eat, and their carcasses you shall not touch. They are unclean to you.

⁹"These you may eat of all that are in the water: whatever in the water has fins and scales, whether in the seas or in the rivers—that you may eat. ¹⁰But all in the seas or in the rivers that

10:18 ᵃThe Most Holy Place when capitalized

do not have fins and scales, all that move in the water or any living thing which *is* in the water, they *are* an abomination to you. ¹¹They shall be an abomination to you; you shall not eat their flesh, but you shall regard their carcasses as an abomination. ¹²Whatever in the water does not have fins or scales—that *shall be* an abomination to you.

¹³'And these you shall regard as an abomination among the birds; they shall not be eaten, they *are* an abomination: the eagle, the vulture, the buzzard, ¹⁴the kite, and the falcon after its kind; ¹⁵every raven after its kind, ¹⁶the ostrich, the short-eared owl, the sea gull, and the hawk after its kind; ¹⁷the little owl, the fisher owl, and the screech owl; ¹⁸the white owl, the jackdaw, and the carrion vulture; ¹⁹the stork, the heron after its kind, the hoopoe, and the bat.

²⁰'All flying insects that creep on *all* fours *shall be* an abomination to you. ²¹Yet these you may eat of every flying insect that creeps on *all* fours: those which have jointed legs above their feet with which to leap on the earth. ²²These you may eat: the locust after its kind, the destroying locust after its kind, the cricket after its kind, and the grasshopper after its kind. ²³But all *other* flying insects which have four feet *shall be* an abomination to you.

Unclean Animals

²⁴'By these you shall become unclean; whoever touches the carcass of any of them shall be unclean until evening; ²⁵whoever carries part of the carcass of any of them shall wash his clothes and be unclean until evening: ²⁶*The carcass* of any animal which divides the foot, but is not cloven-hoofed or does not chew the cud, *is* unclean to you. Everyone who touches it shall be unclean. ²⁷And whatever goes on its paws, among all kinds of animals that go on *all* fours, those *are* unclean to you. Whoever touches any such carcass shall be unclean until evening. ²⁸Whoever carries *any such* carcass shall wash his clothes and be unclean until evening. It *is* unclean to you.

²⁹'These also *shall be* unclean to you among the creeping things that creep on the earth: the mole, the mouse, and the large lizard after its kind; ³⁰the gecko, the monitor lizard, the sand reptile, the sand lizard, and the chameleon.

³¹These *are* unclean to you among all that creep. Whoever touches them when they are dead shall be unclean until evening. ³²Anything on which *any* of them falls, when they are dead shall be unclean, whether *it is* any item of wood or clothing or skin or sack, whatever item *it is,* in which *any* work is done, it must be put in water. And it shall be unclean until evening; then it shall be clean. ³³Any earthen vessel into which *any* of them falls you shall break; and whatever *is* in it shall be unclean: ³⁴in such a vessel, any edible food upon which water falls becomes unclean, and any drink that may be drunk from it becomes unclean. ³⁵And everything on which *a part* of *any such* carcass falls shall be unclean; *whether it is* an oven or cooking stove, it shall be broken down; *for* they *are* unclean, and shall be unclean to you. ³⁶Nevertheless a spring or a cistern, *in which there is* plenty of water, shall be clean, but whatever touches any such carcass becomes unclean. ³⁷And if a part of *any such* carcass falls on any planting seed which is to be sown, it *remains* clean. ³⁸But if water is put on the seed, and if *a part* of *any such* carcass falls on it, it *becomes* unclean to you.

³⁹'And if any animal which you may eat dies, he who touches its carcass shall be unclean until evening. ⁴⁰He who eats of its carcass shall wash his clothes and be unclean until evening. He also who carries its carcass shall wash his clothes and be unclean until evening.

⁴¹'And every creeping thing that creeps on the earth *shall be* an abomination. It shall not be eaten. ⁴²Whatever crawls on its belly, whatever goes on *all* fours, or whatever has many feet among all creeping things that creep on the earth—these you shall not eat, for they *are* an abomination. ⁴³You shall not make yourselves abominable with any creeping thing that creeps; nor shall you make yourselves unclean with them, lest you be defiled by them. ⁴⁴For I *am* the LORD your God. You shall therefore consecrate yourselves, and you shall be holy; for I *am* holy. Neither shall you defile yourselves with any creeping thing that creeps on the earth. ⁴⁵For I *am* the LORD who brings you up out of the land of Egypt, to be your God. You shall therefore be holy, for I *am* holy.

⁴⁶'This *is* the law of the animals and the birds and every living creature that moves in the

waters, and of every creature that creeps on the earth, [47]to distinguish between the unclean and the clean, and between the animal that may be eaten and the animal that may not be eaten.' "

THE RITUAL AFTER CHILDBIRTH

12Then the LORD spoke to Moses, saying, [2]"Speak to the children of Israel, saying: 'If a woman has conceived, and borne a male child, then she shall be unclean seven days; as in the days of her customary impurity she shall be unclean. [3]And on the eighth day the flesh of his foreskin shall be circumcised. [4]She shall then continue in the blood of *her* purification thirty-three days. She shall not touch any hallowed thing, nor come into the sanctuary until the days of her purification are fulfilled.

[5]'But if she bears a female child, then she shall be unclean two weeks, as in her customary impurity, and she shall continue in the blood of *her* purification sixty-six days.

[6]'When the days of her purification are fulfilled, whether for a son or a daughter, she shall bring to the priest a lamb of the first year as a burnt offering, and a young pigeon or a turtledove as a sin offering, to the door of the tabernacle of meeting. [7]Then he shall offer it before the LORD, and make atonement for her. And she shall be clean from the flow of her blood. This *is* the law for her who has borne a male or a female.

[8]'And if she is not able to bring a lamb, then she may bring two turtledoves or two young pigeons—one as a burnt offering and the other as a sin offering. So the priest shall make atonement for her, and she will be clean.' "

THE LAW CONCERNING LEPROSY

13And the LORD spoke to Moses and Aaron, saying: [2]"When a man has on the skin of his body a swelling, a scab, or a bright spot, and it becomes on the skin of his body *like* a leprous[a] sore, then he shall be brought to Aaron the priest or to one of his sons the priests. [3]The priest shall examine the sore on the skin of the body; and if the hair on the sore has turned white, and the sore appears *to be* deeper than the skin of his body, it *is* a leprous sore. Then the priest shall examine him, and pronounce him unclean. [4]But if the bright spot *is* white on the skin of his body,

and does not appear *to be* deeper than the skin, and its hair has not turned white, then the priest shall isolate *the one who has* the sore seven days. [5]And the priest shall examine him on the seventh day; and indeed *if* the sore appears to be as it was, *and* the sore has not spread on the skin, then the priest shall isolate him another seven days. [6]Then the priest shall examine him again on the seventh day; and indeed *if* the sore has faded, *and* the sore has not spread on the skin, then the priest shall pronounce him clean; it *is only* a scab, and he shall wash his clothes and be clean. [7]But if the scab should at all spread over the skin, after he has been seen by the priest for his cleansing, he shall be seen by the priest again. [8]And *if* the priest sees that the scab has indeed spread on the skin, then the priest shall pronounce him unclean. It *is* leprosy.

[9]"When the leprous sore is on a person, then he shall be brought to the priest. [10]And the priest shall examine *him;* and indeed *if* the swelling on the skin *is* white, and it has turned the hair white, and *there is* a spot of raw flesh in the swelling, [11]it *is* an old leprosy on the skin of his body. The priest shall pronounce him unclean, and shall not isolate him, for he *is* unclean.

[12]"And if leprosy breaks out all over the skin, and the leprosy covers all the skin of *the one who has* the sore, from his head to his foot, wherever the priest looks, [13]then the priest shall consider; and indeed *if* the leprosy has covered all his body, he shall pronounce *him* clean *who has* the sore. It has all turned white. He *is* clean. [14]But when raw flesh appears on him, he shall be unclean. [15]And the priest shall examine the raw flesh and pronounce him to be unclean; *for* the raw flesh *is* unclean. It *is* leprosy. [16]Or if the raw flesh changes and turns white again, he shall come to the priest. [17]And the priest shall examine him; and indeed *if* the sore has turned white, then the priest shall pronounce *him* clean *who has* the sore. He *is* clean.

[18]"If the body develops a boil in the skin, and it is healed, [19]and in the place of the boil there comes a white swelling or a bright spot, reddish-white, then it shall be shown to the priest; [20]and if, when the priest sees it, it indeed appears deeper

---

13:2 [a]Hebrew *saraath,* disfiguring skin diseases, including leprosy, and so in verses 2–46 and 14:1–32

than the skin, and its hair has turned white, the priest shall pronounce him unclean. It *is* a leprous sore which has broken out of the boil. ²¹But if the priest examines it, and indeed *there are* no white hairs in it, and it *is* not deeper than the skin, but has faded, then the priest shall isolate him seven days; ²²and if it should at all spread over the skin, then the priest shall pronounce him unclean. It *is* a leprous sore. ²³But if the bright spot stays in one place, *and* has not spread, it *is* the scar of the boil; and the priest shall pronounce him clean.

²⁴"Or if the body receives a burn on its skin by fire, and the raw *flesh* of the burn becomes a bright spot, reddish-white or white, ²⁵then the priest shall examine it; and indeed *if* the hair of the bright spot has turned white, and it appears deeper than the skin, it *is* leprosy broken out in the burn. Therefore the priest shall pronounce him unclean. It *is* a leprous sore. ²⁶But if the priest examines it, and indeed *there are* no white hairs in the bright spot, and it *is* not deeper than the skin, but has faded, then the priest shall isolate him seven days. ²⁷And the priest shall examine him on the seventh day. If it has at all spread over the skin, then the priest shall pronounce him unclean. It *is* a leprous sore. ²⁸But if the bright spot stays in one place, *and* has not spread on the skin, but has faded, it *is* a swelling from the burn. The priest shall pronounce him clean, for it *is* the scar from the burn.

²⁹"If a man or woman has a sore on the head or the beard, ³⁰then the priest shall examine the sore; and indeed if it appears deeper than the skin, *and there is* in it thin yellow hair, then the priest shall pronounce him unclean. It *is* a scaly leprosy of the head or beard. ³¹But if the priest examines the scaly sore, and indeed it does not appear deeper than the skin, *and there is* no black hair in it, then the priest shall isolate *the one who has* the scale seven days. ³²And on the seventh day the priest shall examine the sore; and indeed *if* the scale has not spread, and there is no yellow hair in it, and the scale does not appear deeper than the skin, ³³he shall shave himself, but the scale he shall not shave. And the priest shall isolate *the one who has* the scale another seven days. ³⁴On the seventh day the priest shall examine the scale; and indeed *if* the scale has not spread over the skin, and does not appear deeper than the skin, then the priest

shall pronounce him clean. He shall wash his clothes and be clean. ³⁵But if the scale should at all spread over the skin after his cleansing, ³⁶then the priest shall examine him; and indeed *if* the scale has spread over the skin, the priest need not seek for yellow hair. He *is* unclean. ³⁷But if the scale appears to be at a standstill, and there is black hair grown up in it, the scale has healed. He *is* clean, and the priest shall pronounce him clean.

³⁸"If a man or a woman has bright spots on the skin of the body, *specifically* white bright spots, ³⁹then the priest shall look; and indeed *if* the bright spots on the skin of the body *are* dull white, it *is* a white spot *that* grows on the skin. He *is* clean.

⁴⁰"As for the man whose hair has fallen from his head, he *is* bald, *but* he *is* clean. ⁴¹He whose hair has fallen from his forehead, he *is* bald on the forehead, *but* he *is* clean. ⁴²And if there is on the bald head or bald forehead a reddish-white sore, it *is* leprosy breaking out on his bald head or his bald forehead. ⁴³Then the priest shall examine it; and indeed *if* the swelling of the sore *is* reddish-white on his bald head or on his bald forehead, as the appearance of leprosy on the skin of the body, ⁴⁴he is a leprous man. He *is* unclean. The priest shall surely pronounce him unclean; his sore *is* on his head.

⁴⁵"Now the leper on whom the sore *is,* his clothes shall be torn and his head bare; and he shall cover his mustache, and cry, 'Unclean! Unclean!' ⁴⁶He shall be unclean. All the days he has the sore he shall be unclean. He *is* unclean, and he shall dwell alone; his dwelling *shall be* outside the camp.

THE LAW CONCERNING LEPROUS GARMENTS

⁴⁷"Also, if a garment has a leprous plagueᵃ in it, *whether it is* a woolen garment or a linen garment, ⁴⁸whether *it is* in the warp or woof of linen or wool, whether in leather or in anything made of leather, ⁴⁹and if the plague is greenish or reddish in the garment or in the leather, whether in the warp or in the woof, or in anything made of leather, it *is* a leprous plague and shall be shown to the priest. ⁵⁰The priest shall examine the

13:47 ᵃA mold, fungus, or similar infestation, and so in verses 47–59

plague and isolate *that which has* the plague seven days. ⁵¹And he shall examine the plague on the seventh day. If the plague has spread in the garment, either in the warp or in the woof, in the leather *or* in anything made of leather, the plague *is* an active leprosy. It *is* unclean. ⁵²He shall therefore burn that garment in which is the plague, whether warp or woof, in wool or in linen, or anything of leather, for it *is* an active leprosy; *the garment* shall be burned in the fire.

⁵³"But if the priest examines *it,* and indeed the plague has not spread in the garment, either in the warp or in the woof, or in anything made of leather, ⁵⁴then the priest shall command that they wash *the thing* in which *is* the plague; and he shall isolate it another seven days. ⁵⁵Then the priest shall examine the plague after it has been washed; and indeed *if* the plague has not changed its color, though the plague has not spread, it *is* unclean, and you shall burn it in the fire; it continues eating away, *whether* the damage *is* outside or inside. ⁵⁶If the priest examines *it,* and indeed the plague has faded after washing it, then he shall tear it out of the garment, whether out of the warp or out of the woof, or out of the leather. ⁵⁷But if it appears again in the garment, either in the warp or in the woof, or in anything made of leather, it *is* a spreading *plague;* you shall burn with fire that in which is the plague. ⁵⁸And if you wash the garment, either warp or woof, or whatever is made of leather, if the plague has disappeared from it, then it shall be washed a second time, and shall be clean.

⁵⁹"This *is* the law of the leprous plague in a garment of wool or linen, either in the warp or woof, or in anything made of leather, to pronounce it clean or to pronounce it unclean."

The Ritual for Cleansing Healed Lepers

14 Then the LORD spoke to Moses, saying, ²"This shall be the law of the leper for the day of his cleansing: He shall be brought to the priest. ³And the priest shall go out of the camp, and the priest shall examine *him;* and indeed, *if* the leprosy is healed in the leper, ⁴then the priest shall command to take for him who is to be cleansed two living *and* clean birds, cedar wood, scarlet, and hyssop. ⁵And the priest shall command that one of the birds be killed in an earthen vessel over running water. ⁶As for the living bird, he shall take it, the cedar wood and the scarlet and the hyssop, and dip them and the living bird in the blood of the bird *that was* killed over the running water. ⁷And he shall sprinkle it seven times on him who is to be cleansed from the leprosy, and shall pronounce him clean, and shall let the living bird loose in the open field. ⁸He who is to be cleansed shall wash his clothes, shave off all his hair, and wash himself in water, that he may be clean. After that he shall come into the camp, and shall stay outside his tent seven days. ⁹But on the seventh day he shall shave all the hair off his head and his beard and his eyebrows—all his hair he shall shave off. He shall wash his clothes and wash his body in water, and he shall be clean.

¹⁰"And on the eighth day he shall take two male lambs without blemish, one ewe lamb of the first year without blemish, three-tenths *of an ephah* of fine flour mixed with oil as a grain offering, and one log of oil. ¹¹Then the priest who makes *him* clean shall present the man who is to be made clean, and those things, before the LORD, *at* the door of the tabernacle of meeting. ¹²And the priest shall take one male lamb and offer it as a trespass offering, and the log of oil, and wave them *as* a wave offering before the LORD. ¹³Then he shall kill the lamb in the place where he kills the sin offering and the burnt offering, in a holy place; for as the sin offering *is* the priest's, so *is* the trespass offering. It *is* most holy. ¹⁴The priest shall take *some* of the blood of the trespass offering, and the priest shall put *it* on the tip of the right ear of him who is to be cleansed, on the thumb of his right hand, and on the big toe of his right foot. ¹⁵And the priest shall take *some* of the log of oil, and pour *it* into the palm of his own left hand. ¹⁶Then the priest shall dip his right finger in the oil that *is* in his left hand, and shall sprinkle some of the oil with his finger seven times before the LORD. ¹⁷And of the rest of the oil in his hand, the priest shall put *some* on the tip of the right ear of him who is to be cleansed, on the thumb of his right hand, and on the big toe of his right foot, on the blood of the trespass offering. ¹⁸The rest of the oil that *is* in the priest's hand he shall put on the head of him who is to be cleansed. So the priest shall make atonement for him before the LORD.

[19]"Then the priest shall offer the sin offering, and make atonement for him who is to be cleansed from his uncleanness. Afterward he shall kill the burnt offering. [20]And the priest shall offer the burnt offering and the grain offering on the altar. So the priest shall make atonement for him, and he shall be clean.

[21]"But if he *is* poor and cannot afford it, then he shall take one male lamb *as* a trespass offering to be waved, to make atonement for him, one-tenth *of an ephah* of fine flour mixed with oil as a grain offering, a log of oil, [22]and two turtledoves or two young pigeons, such as he is able to afford: one shall be a sin offering and the other a burnt offering. [23]He shall bring them to the priest on the eighth day for his cleansing, to the door of the tabernacle of meeting, before the LORD. [24]And the priest shall take the lamb of the trespass offering and the log of oil, and the priest shall wave them *as* a wave offering before the LORD. [25]Then he shall kill the lamb of the trespass offering, and the priest shall take *some* of the blood of the trespass offering and put *it* on the tip of the right ear of him who is to be cleansed, on the thumb of his right hand, and on the big toe of his right foot. [26]And the priest shall pour some of the oil into the palm of his own left hand. [27]Then the priest shall sprinkle with his right finger *some* of the oil that *is* in his left hand seven times before the LORD. [28]And the priest shall put *some* of the oil that *is* in his hand on the tip of the right ear of him who is to be cleansed, on the thumb of his right hand, and on the big toe of his right foot, on the place of the blood of the trespass offering. [29]The rest of the oil that *is* in the priest's hand he shall put on the head of him who is to be cleansed, to make atonement for him before the LORD. [30]And he shall offer one of the turtledoves or young pigeons, such as he can afford— [31]such as he is able to afford, the one *as* a sin offering and the other *as* a burnt offering, with the grain offering. So the priest shall make atonement for him who is to be cleansed before the LORD. [32]This *is* the law *for one* who had a leprous sore, who cannot afford the usual cleansing."

THE LAW CONCERNING LEPROUS HOUSES

[33]And the LORD spoke to Moses and Aaron, saying: [34]"When you have come into the land of Canaan, which I give you as a possession, and I put the leprous plague[a] in a house in the land of your possession, [35]and he who owns the house comes and tells the priest, saying, 'It seems to me that *there is* some plague in the house,' [36]then the priest shall command that they empty the house, before the priest goes *into it* to examine the plague, that all that *is* in the house may not be made unclean; and afterward the priest shall go in to examine the house. [37]And he shall examine the plague; and indeed *if* the plague *is* on the walls of the house with ingrained streaks, greenish or reddish, which appear to be deep in the wall, [38]then the priest shall go out of the house, to the door of the house, and shut up the house seven days. [39]And the priest shall come again on the seventh day and look; and indeed *if* the plague has spread on the walls of the house, [40]then the priest shall command that they take away the stones in which *is* the plague, and they shall cast them into an unclean place outside the city. [41]And he shall cause the house to be scraped inside, all around, and the dust that they scrape off they shall pour out in an unclean place outside the city. [42]Then they shall take other stones and put *them* in the place of *those* stones, and he shall take other mortar and plaster the house.

[43]"Now if the plague comes back and breaks out in the house, after he has taken away the stones, after he has scraped the house, and after it is plastered, [44]then the priest shall come and look; and indeed *if* the plague has spread in the house, it *is* an active leprosy in the house. It *is* unclean. [45]And he shall break down the house, its stones, its timber, and all the plaster of the house, and he shall carry *them* outside the city to an unclean place. [46]Moreover he who goes into the house at all while it is shut up shall be unclean until evening. [47]And he who lies down in the house shall wash his clothes, and he who eats in the house shall wash his clothes.

[48]"But if the priest comes in and examines *it,* and indeed the plague has not spread in the house after the house was plastered, then the priest shall pronounce the house clean, because the plague is healed. [49]And he shall take, to cleanse the house,

---

14:34 [a]Decomposition by mildew, mold, dry rot, etc., and so in verses 34–53

two birds, cedar wood, scarlet, and hyssop. ⁵⁰Then he shall kill one of the birds in an earthen vessel over running water; ⁵¹and he shall take the cedar wood, the hyssop, the scarlet, and the living bird, and dip them in the blood of the slain bird and in the running water, and sprinkle the house seven times. ⁵²And he shall cleanse the house with the blood of the bird and the running water and the living bird, with the cedar wood, the hyssop, and the scarlet. ⁵³Then he shall let the living bird loose outside the city in the open field, and make atonement for the house, and it shall be clean.

⁵⁴"This *is* the law for any leprous sore and scale, ⁵⁵for the leprosy of a garment and of a house, ⁵⁶for a swelling and a scab and a bright spot, ⁵⁷to teach when *it is* unclean and when *it is* clean. This *is* the law of leprosy."

The Law Concerning Bodily Discharges

15 And the LORD spoke to Moses and Aaron, saying, ²"Speak to the children of Israel, and say to them: 'When any man has a discharge from his body, his discharge *is* unclean. ³And this shall be his uncleanness in regard to his discharge—whether his body runs with his discharge, or his body is stopped up by his discharge, it *is* his uncleanness. ⁴Every bed is unclean on which he who has the discharge lies, and everything on which he sits shall be unclean. ⁵And whoever touches his bed shall wash his clothes and bathe in water, and be unclean until evening. ⁶He who sits on anything on which he who has the discharge sat shall wash his clothes and bathe in water, and be unclean until evening. ⁷And he who touches the body of him who has the discharge shall wash his clothes and bathe in water, and be unclean until evening. ⁸If he who has the discharge spits on him who is clean, then he shall wash his clothes and bathe in water, and be unclean until evening. ⁹Any saddle on which he who has the discharge rides shall be unclean. ¹⁰Whoever touches anything that was under him shall be unclean until evening. He who carries *any of* those things shall wash his clothes and bathe in water, and be unclean until evening. ¹¹And whomever the one who has the discharge touches, and has not rinsed his hands in water, he shall wash his clothes and bathe in water, and be unclean until evening. ¹²The vessel of earth that

he who has the discharge touches shall be broken, and every vessel of wood shall be rinsed in water.

¹³'And when he who has a discharge is cleansed of his discharge, then he shall count for himself seven days for his cleansing, wash his clothes, and bathe his body in running water; then he shall be clean. ¹⁴On the eighth day he shall take for himself two turtledoves or two young pigeons, and come before the LORD, to the door of the tabernacle of meeting, and give them to the priest. ¹⁵Then the priest shall offer them, the one *as* a sin offering and the other *as* a burnt offering. So the priest shall make atonement for him before the LORD because of his discharge.

¹⁶'If any man has an emission of semen, then he shall wash all his body in water, and be unclean until evening. ¹⁷And any garment and any leather on which there is semen, it shall be washed with water, and be unclean until evening. ¹⁸Also, when a woman lies with a man, and *there is* an emission of semen, they shall bathe in water, and be unclean until evening.

¹⁹'If a woman has a discharge, *and* the discharge from her body is blood, she shall be set apart seven days; and whoever touches her shall be unclean until evening. ²⁰Everything that she lies on during her impurity shall be unclean; also everything that she sits on shall be unclean. ²¹Whoever touches her bed shall wash his clothes and bathe in water, and be unclean until evening. ²²And whoever touches anything that she sat on shall wash his clothes and bathe in water, and be unclean until evening. ²³If *anything* is on *her* bed or on anything on which she sits, when he touches it, he shall be unclean until evening. ²⁴And if any man lies with her at all, so that her impurity is on him, he shall be unclean seven days; and every bed on which he lies shall be unclean.

²⁵'If a woman has a discharge of blood for many days, other than at the time of her *customary* impurity, or if it runs beyond her *usual time of* impurity, all the days of her unclean discharge shall be as the days of her *customary* impurity. She *shall be* unclean. ²⁶Every bed on which she lies all the days of her discharge shall be to her as the bed of her impurity; and whatever she sits on shall be unclean, as the uncleanness of her impurity. ²⁷Whoever touches those things shall be unclean;

he shall wash his clothes and bathe in water, and be unclean until evening.

²⁸"But if she is cleansed of her discharge, then she shall count for herself seven days, and after that she shall be clean. ²⁹And on the eighth day she shall take for herself two turtledoves or two young pigeons, and bring them to the priest, to the door of the tabernacle of meeting. ³⁰Then the priest shall offer the one *as* a sin offering and the other *as* a burnt offering, and the priest shall make atonement for her before the LORD for the discharge of her uncleanness.

³¹"Thus you shall separate the children of Israel from their uncleanness, lest they die in their uncleanness when they defile My tabernacle that *is* among them. ³²This *is* the law for one who has a discharge, and *for him* who emits semen and is unclean thereby, ³³and for her who is indisposed because of her *customary* impurity, and for one who has a discharge, either man or woman, and for him who lies with her who is unclean.' "

THE DAY OF ATONEMENT

16 Now the LORD spoke to Moses after the death of the two sons of Aaron, when they offered *profane fire* before the LORD, and died; ²and the LORD said to Moses: "Tell Aaron your brother not to come at *just* any time into the Holy *Place* inside the veil, before the mercy seat which *is* on the ark, lest he die; for I will appear in the cloud above the mercy seat.

³"Thus Aaron shall come into the Holy *Place:* with *the blood of* a young bull as a sin offering, and *of* a ram as a burnt offering. ⁴He shall put the holy linen tunic and the linen trousers on his body; he shall be girded with a linen sash, and with the linen turban he shall be attired. These *are* holy garments. Therefore he shall wash his body in water, and put them on. ⁵And he shall take from the congregation of the children of Israel two kids of the goats as a sin offering, and one ram as a burnt offering.

⁶"Aaron shall offer the bull as a sin offering, which *is* for himself, and make atonement for himself and for his house. ⁷He shall take the two goats and present them before the LORD *at* the door of the tabernacle of meeting. ⁸Then Aaron shall cast lots for the two goats: one lot for the LORD and the other lot for the scapegoat. ⁹And

Aaron shall bring the goat on which the LORD's lot fell, and offer it *as* a sin offering. ¹⁰But the goat on which the lot fell to be the scapegoat shall be presented alive before the LORD, to make atonement upon it, *and* to let it go as the scapegoat into the wilderness.

¹¹"And Aaron shall bring the bull of the sin offering, which is for himself, and make atonement for himself and for his house, and shall kill the bull as the sin offering which *is* for himself. ¹²Then he shall take a censer full of burning coals of fire from the altar before the LORD, with his hands full of sweet incense beaten fine, and bring *it* inside the veil. ¹³And he shall put the incense on the fire before the LORD, that the cloud of incense may cover the mercy seat that *is* on the Testimony, lest he die. ¹⁴He shall take some of the blood of the bull and sprinkle *it* with his finger on the mercy seat on the east *side;* and before the mercy seat he shall sprinkle some of the blood with his finger seven times.

¹⁵"Then he shall kill the goat of the sin offering, which *is* for the people, bring its blood inside the veil, do with that blood as he did with the blood of the bull, and sprinkle it on the mercy seat and before the mercy seat. ¹⁶So he shall make atonement for the Holy *Place,* because of the uncleanness of the children of Israel, and because of their transgressions, for all their sins; and so he shall do for the tabernacle of meeting which remains among them in the midst of their uncleanness. ¹⁷There shall be no man in the tabernacle of meeting when he goes in to make atonement in the Holy *Place,* until he comes out, that he may make atonement for himself, for his household, and for all the assembly of Israel. ¹⁸And he shall go out to the altar that *is* before the LORD, and make atonement for it, and shall take some of the blood of the bull and some of the blood of the goat, and put it on the horns of the altar all around. ¹⁹Then he shall sprinkle some of the blood on it with his finger seven times, cleanse it, and consecrate it from the uncleanness of the children of Israel.

²⁰"And when he has made an end of atoning for the Holy *Place,* the tabernacle of meeting, and the altar, he shall bring the live goat. ²¹Aaron shall lay both his hands on the head of the live goat, confess over it all the iniquities of the children of

Israel, and all their transgressions, concerning all their sins, putting them on the head of the goat, and shall send *it* away into the wilderness by the hand of a suitable man. ²²The goat shall bear on itself all their iniquities to an uninhabited land; and he shall release the goat in the wilderness.

²³"Then Aaron shall come into the tabernacle of meeting, shall take off the linen garments which he put on when he went into the Holy *Place,* and shall leave them there. ²⁴And he shall wash his body with water in a holy place, put on his garments, come out and offer his burnt offering and the burnt offering of the people, and make atonement for himself and for the people. ²⁵The fat of the sin offering he shall burn on the altar. ²⁶And he who released the goat as the scapegoat shall wash his clothes and bathe his body in water, and afterward he may come into the camp. ²⁷The bull *for* the sin offering and the goat *for* the sin offering, whose blood was brought in to make atonement in the Holy *Place,* shall be carried outside the camp. And they shall burn in the fire their skins, their flesh, and their offal. ²⁸Then he who burns them shall wash his clothes and bathe his body in water, and afterward he may come into the camp.

²⁹"*This* shall be a statute forever for you: In the seventh month, on the tenth *day* of the month, you shall afflict your souls, and do no work at all, *whether* a native of your own country or a stranger who dwells among you. ³⁰For on that day *the priest* shall make atonement for you, to cleanse you, *that* you may be clean from all your sins before the LORD. ³¹It *is* a sabbath of solemn rest for you, and you shall afflict your souls. *It is* a statute forever. ³²And the priest, who is anointed and consecrated to minister as priest in his father's place, shall make atonement, and put on the linen clothes, the holy garments; ³³then he shall make atonement for the Holy Sanctuary,ᵃ and he shall make atonement for the tabernacle of meeting and for the altar, and he shall make atonement for the priests and for all the people of the assembly. ³⁴This shall be an everlasting statute for you, to make atonement for the children of Israel, for all their sins, once a year." And he did as the LORD commanded Moses.

THE SANCTITY OF BLOOD

17 And the LORD spoke to Moses, saying, ²"Speak to Aaron, to his sons, and to all the children of Israel, and say to them, 'This *is* the thing which the LORD has commanded, saying: ³"Whatever man of the house of Israel who kills an ox or lamb or goat in the camp, or who kills *it* outside the camp, ⁴and does not bring it to the door of the tabernacle of meeting to offer an offering to the LORD before the tabernacle of the LORD, the guilt of bloodshed shall be imputed to that man. He has shed blood; and that man shall be cut off from among his people, ⁵to the end that the children of Israel may bring their sacrifices which they offer in the open field, that they may bring them to the LORD at the door of the tabernacle of meeting, to the priest, and offer them *as* peace offerings to the LORD. ⁶And the priest shall sprinkle the blood on the altar of the LORD *at* the door of the tabernacle of meeting, and burn the fat for a sweet aroma to the LORD. ⁷They shall no more offer their sacrifices to demons, after whom they have played the harlot. This shall be a statute forever for them throughout their generations." '

⁸"Also you shall say to them: 'Whatever man of the house of Israel, or of the strangers who dwell among you, who offers a burnt offering or sacrifice, ⁹and does not bring it to the door of the tabernacle of meeting, to offer it to the LORD, that man shall be cut off from among his people.

¹⁰"And whatever man of the house of Israel, or of the strangers who dwell among you, who eats any blood, I will set My face against that person who eats blood, and will cut him off from among his people. ¹¹For the life of the flesh *is* in the blood, and I have given it to you upon the altar to make atonement for your souls; for it *is* the blood *that* makes atonement for the soul.' ¹²Therefore I said to the children of Israel, 'No one among you shall eat blood, nor shall any stranger who dwells among you eat blood.'

¹³"Whatever man of the children of Israel, or of the strangers who dwell among you, who hunts and catches any animal or bird that may be eaten, he shall pour out its blood and cover it with dust; ¹⁴for *it is* the life of all flesh. Its blood

sustains its life. Therefore I said to the children of Israel, 'You shall not eat the blood of any flesh, for the life of all flesh is its blood. Whoever eats it shall be cut off.'

15"And every person who eats what died *naturally* or what was torn *by beasts, whether he is* a native of your own country or a stranger, he shall both wash his clothes and bathe in water, and be unclean until evening. Then he shall be clean. 16But if he does not wash *them* or bathe his body, then he shall bear his guilt."

Laws of Sexual Morality

18Then the LORD spoke to Moses, saying, 2"Speak to the children of Israel, and say to them: 'I am the LORD your God. 3According to the doings of the land of Egypt, where you dwelt, you shall not do; and according to the doings of the land of Canaan, where I am bringing you, you shall not do; nor shall you walk in their ordinances. 4You shall observe My judgments and keep My ordinances, to walk in them: I *am* the LORD your God. 5You shall therefore keep My statutes and My judgments, which if a man does, he shall live by them: I *am* the LORD.

6'None of you shall approach anyone who is near of kin to him, to uncover his nakedness: I *am* the LORD. 7The nakedness of your father or the nakedness of your mother you shall not uncover. She *is* your mother; you shall not uncover her nakedness. 8The nakedness of your father's wife you shall not uncover; it *is* your father's nakedness. 9The nakedness of your sister, the daughter of your father, or the daughter of your mother, *whether* born at home or elsewhere, their nakedness you shall not uncover. 10The nakedness of your son's daughter or your daughter's daughter, their nakedness you shall not uncover; for theirs *is* your own nakedness. 11The nakedness of your father's wife's daughter, begotten by your father—she *is* your sister—you shall not uncover her nakedness. 12You shall not uncover the nakedness of your father's sister; she *is* near of kin to your father. 13You shall not uncover the nakedness of your mother's sister, for she *is* near of kin to your mother. 14You shall not uncover the nakedness of your father's brother. You shall not approach his wife; she *is* your aunt. 15You shall not uncover the nakedness of your daughter-in-law—she *is* your son's wife—you

shall not uncover her nakedness. 16You shall not uncover the nakedness of your brother's wife; it *is* your brother's nakedness. 17You shall not uncover the nakedness of a woman and her daughter, nor shall you take her son's daughter or her daughter's daughter, to uncover her nakedness. They *are* near of kin to her. It *is* wickedness. 18Nor shall you take a woman as a rival to her sister, to uncover her nakedness while the other is alive.

19'Also you shall not approach a woman to uncover her nakedness as long as she is in her *customary* impurity. 20Moreover you shall not lie carnally with your neighbor's wife, to defile yourself with her. 21And you shall not let any of your descendants pass through *the fire* to Molech, nor shall you profane the name of your God: I *am* the LORD. 22You shall not lie with a male as with a woman. It *is* an abomination. 23Nor shall you mate with any animal, to defile yourself with it. Nor shall any woman stand before an animal to mate with it. It *is* perversion.

24'Do not defile yourselves with any of these things; for by all these the nations are defiled, which I am casting out before you. 25For the land is defiled; therefore I visit the punishment of its iniquity upon it, and the land vomits out its inhabitants. 26You shall therefore keep My statutes and My judgments, and shall not commit *any* of these abominations, *either* any of your own nation or any stranger who dwells among you 27(for all these abominations the men of the land have done, who *were* before you, and thus the land is defiled), 28lest the land vomit you out also when you defile it, as it vomited out the nations that *were* before you. 29For whoever commits any of these abominations, the persons who commit *them* shall be cut off from among their people.

30'Therefore you shall keep My ordinance, so that *you* do not commit *any* of these abominable customs which were committed before you, and that you do not defile yourselves by them: I *am* the LORD your God.' "

Moral and Ceremonial Laws

19And the LORD spoke to Moses, saying, 2"Speak to all the congregation of the children of Israel, and say to them: 'You shall be holy, for I the LORD your God *am* holy.

3'Every one of you shall revere his mother

and his father, and keep My Sabbaths: I *am* the LORD your God.

⁴'Do not turn to idols, nor make for yourselves molded gods: I *am* the LORD your God.

⁵'And if you offer a sacrifice of a peace offering to the LORD, you shall offer it of your own free will. ⁶It shall be eaten the same day you offer *it,* and on the next day. And if any remains until the third day, it shall be burned in the fire. ⁷And if it is eaten at all on the third day, it *is* an abomination. It shall not be accepted. ⁸Therefore *everyone* who eats it shall bear his iniquity, because he has profaned the hallowed *offering* of the LORD; and that person shall be cut off from his people.

⁹'When you reap the harvest of your land, you shall not wholly reap the corners of your field, nor shall you gather the gleanings of your harvest. ¹⁰And you shall not glean your vineyard, nor shall you gather *every* grape of your vineyard; you shall leave them for the poor and the stranger: I *am* the LORD your God.

¹¹'You shall not steal, nor deal falsely, nor lie to one another. ¹²And you shall not swear by My name falsely, nor shall you profane the name of your God: I *am* the LORD.

¹³'You shall not cheat your neighbor, nor rob *him.* The wages of him who is hired shall not remain with you all night until morning. ¹⁴You shall not curse the deaf, nor put a stumbling block before the blind, but shall fear your God: I *am* the LORD.

¹⁵'You shall do no injustice in judgment. You shall not be partial to the poor, nor honor the person of the mighty. In righteousness you shall judge your neighbor. ¹⁶You shall not go about *as* a talebearer among your people; nor shall you take a stand against the life of your neighbor: I *am* the LORD.

¹⁷'You shall not hate your brother in your heart. You shall surely rebuke your neighbor, and not bear sin because of him. ¹⁸You shall not take vengeance, nor bear any grudge against the children of your people, but you shall love your neighbor as yourself: I *am* the LORD.

¹⁹'You shall keep My statutes. You shall not let your livestock breed with another kind. You shall not sow your field with mixed seed. Nor shall a garment of mixed linen and wool come upon you.

²⁰'Whoever lies carnally with a woman who *is* betrothed to a man as a concubine, and who has not at all been redeemed nor given her freedom, for this there shall be scourging; *but* they shall not be put to death, because she was not free. ²¹And he shall bring his trespass offering to the LORD, to the door of the tabernacle of meeting, a ram as a trespass offering. ²²The priest shall make atonement for him with the ram of the trespass offering before the LORD for his sin which he has committed. And the sin which he has committed shall be forgiven him.

²³'When you come into the land, and have planted all kinds of trees for food, then you shall count their fruit as uncircumcised. Three years it shall be as uncircumcised to you. *It* shall not be eaten. ²⁴But in the fourth year all its fruit shall be holy, a praise to the LORD. ²⁵And in the fifth year you may eat its fruit, that it may yield to you its increase: I *am* the LORD your God.

²⁶'You shall not eat *anything* with the blood, nor shall you practice divination or soothsaying. ²⁷You shall not shave around the sides of your head, nor shall you disfigure the edges of your beard. ²⁸You shall not make any cuttings in your flesh for the dead, nor tattoo any marks on you: I *am* the LORD.

²⁹'Do not prostitute your daughter, to cause her to be a harlot, lest the land fall into harlotry, and the land become full of wickedness.

³⁰'You shall keep My Sabbaths and reverence My sanctuary: I *am* the LORD.

³¹'Give no regard to mediums and familiar spirits; do not seek after them, to be defiled by them: I *am* the LORD your God.

³²'You shall rise before the gray headed and honor the presence of an old man, and fear your God: I *am* the LORD.

³³'And if a stranger dwells with you in your land, you shall not mistreat him. ³⁴The stranger who dwells among you shall be to you as one born among you, and you shall love him as yourself; for you were strangers in the land of Egypt: I *am* the LORD your God.

³⁵'You shall do no injustice in judgment, in measurement of length, weight, or volume. ³⁶You shall have honest scales, honest weights, an honest ephah, and an honest hin: I *am* the LORD your God, who brought you out of the land of Egypt.

37'Therefore you shall observe all My statutes and all My judgments, and perform them: I *am* the LORD.' "

PENALTIES FOR BREAKING THE LAW

20 Then the LORD spoke to Moses, saying, 2"Again, you shall say to the children of Israel: 'Whoever of the children of Israel, or of the strangers who dwell in Israel, who gives *any* of his descendants to Molech, he shall surely be put to death. The people of the land shall stone him with stones. 3I will set My face against that man, and will cut him off from his people, because he has given *some* of his descendants to Molech, to defile My sanctuary and profane My holy name. 4And if the people of the land should in any way hide their eyes from the man, when he gives *some* of his descendants to Molech, and they do not kill him, 5then I will set My face against that man and against his family; and I will cut him off from his people, and all who prostitute themselves with him to commit harlotry with Molech.

6'And the person who turns to mediums and familiar spirits, to prostitute himself with them, I will set My face against that person and cut him off from his people. 7Consecrate yourselves therefore, and be holy, for I *am* the LORD your God. 8And you shall keep My statutes, and perform them: I *am* the LORD who sanctifies you.

9'For everyone who curses his father or his mother shall surely be put to death. He has cursed his father or his mother. His blood *shall be* upon him.

10'The man who commits adultery with *another* man's wife, *he* who commits adultery with his neighbor's wife, the adulterer and the adulteress, shall surely be put to death. 11The man who lies with his father's wife has uncovered his father's nakedness; both of them shall surely be put to death. Their blood *shall be* upon them. 12If a man lies with his daughter-in-law, both of them shall surely be put to death. They have committed perversion. Their blood *shall be* upon them. 13If a man lies with a male as he lies with a woman, both of them have committed an abomination. They shall surely be put to death. Their blood *shall be* upon them. 14If a man marries a woman and her mother, it *is* wickedness. They shall be burned with fire, both he and they, that

there may be no wickedness among you. 15If a man mates with an animal, he shall surely be put to death, and you shall kill the animal. 16If a woman approaches any animal and mates with it, you shall kill the woman and the animal. They shall surely be put to death. Their blood *is* upon them.

17'If a man takes his sister, his father's daughter or his mother's daughter, and sees her nakedness and she sees his nakedness, it *is* a wicked thing. And they shall be cut off in the sight of their people. He has uncovered his sister's nakedness. He shall bear his guilt. 18If a man lies with a woman during her sickness and uncovers her nakedness, he has exposed her flow, and she has uncovered the flow of her blood. Both of them shall be cut off from their people.

19'You shall not uncover the nakedness of your mother's sister nor of your father's sister, for that would uncover his near of kin. They shall bear their guilt. 20If a man lies with his uncle's wife, he has uncovered his uncle's nakedness. They shall bear their sin; they shall die childless. 21If a man takes his brother's wife, it *is* an unclean thing. He has uncovered his brother's nakedness. They shall be childless.

22'You shall therefore keep all My statutes and all My judgments, and perform them, that the land where I am bringing you to dwell may not vomit you out. 23And you shall not walk in the statutes of the nation which I am casting out before you; for they commit all these things, and therefore I abhor them. 24But I have said to you, "You shall inherit their land, and I will give it to you to possess, a land flowing with milk and honey." I *am* the LORD your God, who has separated you from the peoples. 25You shall therefore distinguish between clean animals and unclean, between unclean birds and clean, and you shall not make yourselves abominable by beast or by bird, or by any kind of living thing that creeps on the ground, which I have separated from you as unclean. 26And you shall be holy to Me, for I the LORD *am* holy, and have separated you from the peoples, that you should be Mine.

27'A man or a woman who is a medium, or who has familiar spirits, shall surely be put to death; they shall stone them with stones. Their blood *shall be* upon them.' "

LEADERSHIP ISSUES

GC2: Holy: Set Apart for a Purpose

LEVITICUS 20:26 *And you shall be holy to Me, for I the LORD am holy, and have separated you from the peoples, that you should be Mine.*

To live "holy" means to be "set apart," living in some ways different than the world. The children of Israel were to be "set apart" in their lifestyle, in their worship, and in how they related to others. Recall as many of the Ten Commandments as you can and consider which ones relate to lifestyle. Worship? Treatment of others? In what ways would others observe a "set apart" difference in *your* lifestyle? Worship? Relationships with others? (See Ex. 20.)

As Christ-followers, certain decisions, choices, and commitments set you apart, but what's the purpose? Because we worship on Sunday or are careful not to lie, are these choices simply to make us weird or different or to become sources of pride? Absolutely not! The children of Israel and we, as followers of Jesus, are to be set apart *from* certain things in this world in order that we would be set apart *to* a deepening relationship with the Lord.

Notice in this passage the purpose statements "be holy to Me" and "separated you from the peoples, that you should be Mine." Thus, we worship on Sunday not out of duty or obligation but out of a longing to meet together in deepened intimacy and worship of Jesus. To live a holy life includes being set apart from certain things of this world to enjoy the richness of relating intimately with Christ. Holiness is not primarily about what we "can't do" or "don't do"—it's about what we "get to do" in pursuing Jesus. Holiness is not a downer; it is a joyous and enriching journey with Jesus.

To live a holy life is not to be unplugged from the world but to be plugged into God's agenda in the world. It's not a disconnected life but a very connected life—connected to Jesus.

GC2
GREAT COMMANDMENT
COMMISSION

REGULATIONS FOR CONDUCT OF PRIESTS

21 And the LORD said to Moses, "Speak to the priests, the sons of Aaron, and say to them: 'None shall defile himself for the dead among his people, ²except for his relatives who are nearest to him: his mother, his father, his son, his daughter, and his brother; ³also his virgin sister who is near to him, who has had no husband, for her he may defile himself. ⁴*Otherwise* he shall not defile himself, *being* a chief man among his people, to profane himself.

⁵'They shall not make any bald *place* on their heads, nor shall they shave the edges of their beards nor make any cuttings in their flesh. ⁶They shall be holy to their God and not profane the name of their God, for they offer the offerings of the LORD made by fire, *and* the bread of their God; therefore they shall be holy. ⁷They shall not take a wife *who is* a harlot or a defiled woman, nor shall they take a woman divorced from her husband; for *the priest*ᵃ is holy to his God. ⁸Therefore you shall consecrate him, for he offers the bread of your God. He shall be holy to you, for I the LORD, who sanctify you, *am* holy. ⁹The daughter of any priest, if she profanes herself by playing the harlot, she profanes her father. She shall be burned with fire.

¹⁰'*He who is* the high priest among his brethren, on whose head the anointing oil was poured and who is consecrated to wear the garments, shall not uncover his head nor tear his clothes; ¹¹nor shall he go near any dead body, nor defile himself for his father or his mother; ¹²nor shall he go out of the sanctuary, nor profane the sanctuary of his God; for the consecration of the anointing oil of his God *is* upon him: I *am* the LORD. ¹³And he shall take a wife in her virginity. ¹⁴A widow or a divorced woman or a defiled woman *or* a harlot—these he shall not marry; but he shall take a virgin of his own people as wife. ¹⁵Nor shall he profane his posterity among his people, for I the LORD sanctify him.' "

¹⁶And the LORD spoke to Moses, saying, ¹⁷"Speak to Aaron, saying: 'No man of your descendants in *succeeding* generations, who has *any* defect, may approach to offer the bread of his God. ¹⁸For any man who has a defect shall not approach: a man blind or lame, who has a marred *face* or any *limb* too long, ¹⁹a man who has a broken foot or broken hand, ²⁰or is a hunchback or a dwarf, or *a man* who has a defect in his eye, or eczema or scab, or is a eunuch. ²¹No man of the descendants of Aaron the priest, who has a defect, shall come near to offer the offerings made by fire to the LORD. He has a defect; he shall not come near to offer the bread of his God. ²²He may eat the bread of his God, *both* the most holy and the holy; ²³only he shall not go near the veil or approach the altar, because he has a defect, lest he profane My sanctuaries; for I the LORD sanctify them.' "

²⁴And Moses told *it* to Aaron and his sons, and to all the children of Israel.

22 Then the LORD spoke to Moses, saying, ²"Speak to Aaron and his sons, that they separate themselves from the holy things of the children of Israel, and that they do not profane My holy name *by* what they dedicate to Me: I *am* the LORD. ³Say to them: 'Whoever of all your descendants throughout your generations, who goes near the holy things which the children of Israel dedicate to the LORD, while he has uncleanness upon him, that person shall be cut off from My presence: I *am* the LORD.

⁴'Whatever man of the descendants of Aaron, who *is* a leper or has a discharge, shall not eat the holy offerings until he is clean. And whoever touches anything made unclean *by* a corpse, or a man who has had an emission of semen, ⁵or whoever touches any creeping thing by which he would be made unclean, or any person by whom he would become unclean, whatever his uncleanness may be— ⁶the person who has touched any such thing shall be unclean until evening, and shall not eat the holy *offerings* unless he washes his body with water. ⁷And when the sun goes down he shall be clean; and afterward he may eat the holy *offerings,* because it *is* his food. ⁸Whatever dies *naturally* or is torn *by beasts* he shall not eat, to defile himself with it: I *am* the LORD.

⁹'They shall therefore keep My ordinance, lest they bear sin for it and die thereby, if they profane it: I the LORD sanctify them.

¹⁰'No outsider shall eat the holy *offering;* one

21:7 ᵃLiterally *he*

who dwells with the priest, or a hired servant, shall not eat the holy thing. ¹¹But if the priest buys a person with his money, he may eat it; and one who is born in his house may eat his food. ¹²If the priest's daughter is married to an outsider, she may not eat of the holy offerings. ¹³But if the priest's daughter is a widow or divorced, and has no child, and has returned to her father's house as in her youth, she may eat her father's food; but no outsider shall eat it.

¹⁴'And if a man eats the holy *offering* unintentionally, then he shall restore a holy *offering* to the priest, and add one-fifth to it. ¹⁵They shall not profane the holy *offerings* of the children of Israel, which they offer to the LORD, ¹⁶or allow them to bear the guilt of trespass when they eat their holy *offerings;* for I the LORD sanctify them.' "

OFFERINGS ACCEPTED AND NOT ACCEPTED

¹⁷And the LORD spoke to Moses, saying, ¹⁸"Speak to Aaron and his sons, and to all the children of Israel, and say to them:'Whatever man of the house of Israel, or of the strangers in Israel, who offers his sacrifice for any of his vows or for any of his freewill offerings, which they offer to the LORD as a burnt offering— ¹⁹*you shall offer* of your own free will a male without blemish from the cattle, from the sheep, or from the goats. ²⁰Whatever has a defect, you shall not offer, for it shall not be acceptable on your behalf. ²¹And whoever offers a sacrifice of a peace offering to the LORD, to fulfill *his* vow, or a freewill offering from the cattle or the sheep, it must be perfect to be accepted; there shall be no defect in it. ²²Those *that are* blind or broken or maimed, or have an ulcer or eczema or scabs, you shall not offer to the LORD, nor make an offering by fire of them on the altar to the LORD. ²³Either a bull or a lamb that has any limb too long or too short you may offer *as* a freewill offering, but for a vow it shall not be accepted.

²⁴'You shall not offer to the LORD what is bruised or crushed, or torn or cut; nor shall you make *any offering of them* in your land. ²⁵Nor from a foreigner's hand shall you offer any of these as the bread of your God, because their corruption *is* in them, *and* defects *are* in them. They shall not be accepted on your behalf.' "

²⁶And the LORD spoke to Moses, saying:

²⁷"When a bull or a sheep or a goat is born, it shall be seven days with its mother; and from the eighth day and thereafter it shall be accepted as an offering made by fire to the LORD. ²⁸*Whether it is* a cow or ewe, do not kill both her and her young on the same day. ²⁹And when you offer a sacrifice of thanksgiving to the LORD, offer *it* of your own free will. ³⁰On the same day it shall be eaten; you shall leave none of it until morning: I *am* the LORD.

³¹"Therefore you shall keep My commandments, and perform them: I *am* the LORD. ³²You shall not profane My holy name, but I will be hallowed among the children of Israel. I *am* the LORD who sanctifies you, ³³who brought you out of the land of Egypt, to be your God: I *am* the LORD."

FEASTS OF THE LORD

23 And the LORD spoke to Moses, saying, ²"Speak to the children of Israel, and say to them: 'The feasts of the LORD, which you shall proclaim *to be* holy convocations, these *are* My feasts.

THE SABBATH

³'Six days shall work be done, but the seventh day *is* a Sabbath of solemn rest, a holy convocation. You shall do no work *on it;* it *is* the Sabbath of the LORD in all your dwellings.

THE PASSOVER AND UNLEAVENED BREAD

⁴'These *are* the feasts of the LORD, holy convocations which you shall proclaim at their appointed times. ⁵On the fourteenth *day* of the first month at twilight *is* the LORD's Passover. ⁶And on the fifteenth day of the same month *is* the Feast of Unleavened Bread to the LORD; seven days you must eat unleavened bread. ⁷On the first day you shall have a holy convocation; you shall do no customary work on it. ⁸But you shall offer an offering made by fire to the LORD for seven days. The seventh day *shall be* a holy convocation; you shall do no customary work *on it.* ' "

THE FEAST OF FIRSTFRUITS

⁹And the LORD spoke to Moses, saying, ¹⁰"Speak to the children of Israel, and say to them: 'When you come into the land which I

give to you, and reap its harvest, then you shall bring a sheaf of the firstfruits of your harvest to the priest. [11]He shall wave the sheaf before the LORD, to be accepted on your behalf; on the day after the Sabbath the priest shall wave it. [12]And you shall offer on that day, when you wave the sheaf, a male lamb of the first year, without blemish, as a burnt offering to the LORD. [13]Its grain offering *shall be* two-tenths *of an ephah* of fine flour mixed with oil, an offering made by fire to the LORD, for a sweet aroma; and its drink offering *shall be* of wine, one-fourth of a hin. [14]You shall eat neither bread nor parched grain nor fresh grain until the same day that you have brought an offering to your God; *it shall be* a statute forever throughout your generations in all your dwellings.

The Feast of Weeks

[15]'And you shall count for yourselves from the day after the Sabbath, from the day that you brought the sheaf of the wave offering: seven Sabbaths shall be completed. [16]Count fifty days to the day after the seventh Sabbath; then you shall offer a new grain offering to the LORD. [17]You shall bring from your dwellings two wave *loaves* of two-tenths *of an ephah*. They shall be of fine flour; they shall be baked with leaven. *They are* the firstfruits to the LORD. [18]And you shall offer with the bread seven lambs of the first year, without blemish, one young bull, and two rams. They shall be *as* a burnt offering to the LORD, with their grain offering and their drink offerings, an offering made by fire for a sweet aroma to the LORD. [19]Then you shall sacrifice one kid of the goats as a sin offering, and two male lambs of the first year as a sacrifice of a peace offering. [20]The priest shall wave them with the bread of the firstfruits *as* a wave offering before the LORD, with the two lambs. They shall be holy to the LORD for the priest. [21]And you shall proclaim on the same day *that* it is a holy convocation to you. You shall do no customary work *on it. It shall be* a statute forever in all your dwellings throughout your generations.

[22]'When you reap the harvest of your land, you shall not wholly reap the corners of your field when you reap, nor shall you gather any gleaning from your harvest. You shall leave them for the poor and for the stranger: I *am* the LORD your God.' "

The Feast of Trumpets

[23]Then the LORD spoke to Moses, saying, [24]"Speak to the children of Israel, saying: 'In the seventh month, on the first *day* of the month, you shall have a sabbath-*rest,* a memorial of blowing of trumpets, a holy convocation. [25]You shall do no customary work *on it;* and you shall offer an offering made by fire to the LORD.' "

The Day of Atonement

[26]And the LORD spoke to Moses, saying: [27]"Also the tenth *day* of this seventh month *shall be* the Day of Atonement. It shall be a holy convocation for you; you shall afflict your souls, and offer an offering made by fire to the LORD. [28]And you shall do no work on that same day, for it *is* the Day of Atonement, to make atonement for you before the LORD your God. [29]For any person who is not afflicted *in soul* on that same day shall be cut off from his people. [30]And any person who does any work on that same day, that person I will destroy from among his people. [31]You shall do no manner of work; *it shall be* a statute forever throughout your generations in all your dwellings. [32]It *shall be* to you a sabbath of *solemn* rest, and you shall afflict your souls; on the ninth *day* of the month at evening, from evening to evening, you shall celebrate your sabbath."

The Feast of Tabernacles

[33]Then the LORD spoke to Moses, saying, [34]"Speak to the children of Israel, saying: 'The fifteenth day of this seventh month *shall be* the Feast of Tabernacles *for* seven days to the LORD. [35]On the first day *there shall be* a holy convocation. You shall do no customary work *on it.* [36]For seven days you shall offer an offering made by fire to the LORD. On the eighth day you shall have a holy convocation, and you shall offer an offering made by fire to the LORD. It *is* a sacred assembly, *and* you shall do no customary work *on it.*

[37]'These *are* the feasts of the LORD which you shall proclaim *to be* holy convocations, to offer an offering made by fire to the LORD, a burnt offering and a grain offering, a sacrifice and drink offerings, everything on its day— [38]besides the

Sabbaths of the LORD, besides your gifts, besides all your vows, and besides all your freewill offerings which you give to the LORD.

[39] Also on the fifteenth day of the seventh month, when you have gathered in the fruit of the land, you shall keep the feast of the LORD *for* seven days; on the first day *there shall be* a sabbath-*rest,* and on the eighth day a sabbath-*rest.* [40] And you shall take for yourselves on the first day the fruit of beautiful trees, branches of palm trees, the boughs of leafy trees, and willows of the brook; and you shall rejoice before the LORD your God for seven days. [41] You shall keep it as a feast to the LORD for seven days in the year. *It shall be* a statute forever in your generations. You shall celebrate it in the seventh month. [42] You shall dwell in booths for seven days. All who are native Israelites shall dwell in booths, [43] that your generations may know that I made the children of Israel dwell in booths when I brought them out of the land of Egypt: I *am* the LORD your God.' "

[44] So Moses declared to the children of Israel the feasts of the LORD.

CARE OF THE TABERNACLE LAMPS

24 Then the LORD spoke to Moses, saying: [2] "Command the children of Israel that they bring to you pure oil of pressed olives for the light, to make the lamps burn continually. [3] Outside the veil of the Testimony, in the tabernacle of meeting, Aaron shall be in charge of it from evening until morning before the LORD continually; *it shall be* a statute forever in your generations. [4] He shall be in charge of the lamps on the pure *gold* lampstand before the LORD continually.

THE BREAD OF THE TABERNACLE

[5] "And you shall take fine flour and bake twelve cakes with it. Two-tenths *of an ephah* shall be in each cake. [6] You shall set them in two rows, six in a row, on the pure *gold* table before the LORD. [7] And you shall put pure frankincense on *each* row, that it may be on the bread for a memorial, an offering made by fire to the LORD. [8] Every Sabbath he shall set it in order before the LORD continually, *being taken* from the children of Israel by an everlasting covenant. [9] And it shall be for Aaron and his sons, and they shall eat it in

a holy place; for it *is* most holy to him from the offerings of the LORD made by fire, by a perpetual statute."

THE PENALTY FOR BLASPHEMY

[10] Now the son of an Israelite woman, whose father *was* an Egyptian, went out among the children of Israel; and this Israelite *woman's* son and a man of Israel fought each other in the camp. [11] And the Israelite woman's son blasphemed the name *of the LORD* and cursed; and so they brought him to Moses. (His mother's name *was* Shelomith the daughter of Dibri, of the tribe of Dan.) [12] Then they put him in custody, that the mind of the LORD might be shown to them.

[13] And the LORD spoke to Moses, saying, [14] "Take outside the camp him who has cursed; then let all who heard *him* lay their hands on his head, and let all the congregation stone him.

[15] "Then you shall speak to the children of Israel, saying: 'Whoever curses his God shall bear his sin. [16] And whoever blasphemes the name of the LORD shall surely be put to death. All the congregation shall certainly stone him, the stranger as well as him who is born in the land. When he blasphemes the name *of the LORD,* he shall be put to death.

[17] "Whoever kills any man shall surely be put to death. [18] Whoever kills an animal shall make it good, animal for animal.

[19] "If a man causes disfigurement of his neighbor, as he has done, so shall it be done to him— [20] fracture for fracture, eye for eye, tooth for tooth; as he has caused disfigurement of a man, so shall it be done to him. [21] And whoever kills an animal shall restore it; but whoever kills a man shall be put to death. [22] You shall have the same law for the stranger and for one from your own country; for I *am* the LORD your God.' "

[23] Then Moses spoke to the children of Israel; and they took outside the camp him who had cursed, and stoned him with stones. So the children of Israel did as the LORD commanded Moses.

THE SABBATH OF THE SEVENTH YEAR

25 And the LORD spoke to Moses on Mount Sinai, saying, [2] "Speak to the children of Israel, and say to them: 'When you come into the land which I give you, then the land shall keep a sabbath to the LORD. ³Six years you shall sow your field, and six years you shall prune your vineyard, and gather its fruit; ⁴but in the seventh year there shall be a sabbath of solemn rest for the land, a sabbath to the LORD. You shall neither sow your field nor prune your vineyard. ⁵What grows of its own accord of your harvest you shall not reap, nor gather the grapes of your untended vine, *for* it is a year of rest for the land. ⁶And the sabbath *produce* of the land shall be food for you: for you, your male and female servants, your hired man, and the stranger who dwells with you, ⁷for your livestock and the beasts that *are* in your land—all its produce shall be for food.

THE YEAR OF JUBILEE

⁸'And you shall count seven sabbaths of years for yourself, seven times seven years; and the time of the seven sabbaths of years shall be to you forty-nine years. ⁹Then you shall cause the trumpet of the Jubilee to sound on the tenth *day* of the seventh month; on the Day of Atonement you shall make the trumpet to sound throughout all your land. ¹⁰And you shall consecrate the fiftieth year, and proclaim liberty throughout *all* the land to all its inhabitants. It shall be a Jubilee for you; and each of you shall return to his possession, and each of you shall return to his family. ¹¹That fiftieth year shall be a Jubilee to you; in it you shall neither sow nor reap what grows of its own accord, nor gather *the grapes* of your untended vine. ¹²For it *is* the Jubilee; it shall be holy to you; you shall eat its produce from the field.

¹³'In this Year of Jubilee, each of you shall return to his possession. ¹⁴And if you sell anything to your neighbor or buy from your neighbor's hand, you shall not oppress one another. ¹⁵According to the number of years after the Jubilee you shall buy from your neighbor, and according to the number of years of crops he shall sell to you. ¹⁶According to the multitude of years you shall increase its price, and according to the fewer number of years you shall diminish its price; for he sells to you *according* to the number *of the years* of the crops. ¹⁷Therefore you shall not oppress one another, but you shall fear your God; for I *am* the LORD your God.

PROVISIONS FOR THE SEVENTH YEAR

¹⁸'So you shall observe My statutes and keep My judgments, and perform them; and you will dwell in the land in safety. ¹⁹Then the land will yield its fruit, and you will eat your fill, and dwell there in safety.

²⁰'And if you say, "What shall we eat in the seventh year, since we shall not sow nor gather in our produce?" ²¹Then I will command My blessing on you in the sixth year, and it will bring forth produce enough for three years. ²²And you shall sow in the eighth year, and eat old produce until the ninth year; until its produce comes in, you shall eat *of* the old *harvest*.

REDEMPTION OF PROPERTY

²³'The land shall not be sold permanently, for the land *is* Mine; for you *are* strangers and sojourners with Me. ²⁴And in all the land of your possession you shall grant redemption of the land.

²⁵'If one of your brethren becomes poor, and has sold *some* of his possession, and if his redeeming relative comes to redeem it, then he may redeem what his brother sold. ²⁶Or if the man has no one to redeem it, but he himself becomes able to redeem it, ²⁷then let him count the years since its sale, and restore the remainder to the man to whom he sold it, that he may return to his possession. ²⁸But if he is not able to have *it* restored to himself, then what was sold shall remain in the hand of him who bought it until the Year of Jubilee; and in the Jubilee it shall be released, and he shall return to his possession.

²⁹'If a man sells a house in a walled city, then he may redeem it within a whole year after it is sold; *within* a full year he may redeem it. ³⁰But if it is not redeemed within the space of a full year, then the house in the walled city shall belong permanently to him who bought it, throughout his generations. It shall not be released in the Jubilee. ³¹However the houses of villages which have no wall around them shall be counted as the fields of the country. They may be redeemed, and they shall be released in the Jubilee. ³²Nevertheless the cities of the Levites, *and* the houses in the cities of their possession, the Levites may redeem at any time. ³³And if a man purchases a house from the Levites, then the house that was sold in

the city of his possession shall be released in the Jubilee; for the houses in the cities of the Levites *are* their possession among the children of Israel. [34]But the field of the common-land of their cities may not be sold, for it *is* their perpetual possession.

Lending to the Poor

[35]'If one of your brethren becomes poor, and falls into poverty among you, then you shall help him, like a stranger or a sojourner, that he may live with you. [36]Take no usury or interest from him; but fear your God, that your brother may live with you. [37]You shall not lend him your money for usury, nor lend him your food at a profit. [38]I *am* the LORD your God, who brought you out of the land of Egypt, to give you the land of Canaan *and* to be your God.

The Law Concerning Slavery

[39]'And if *one of* your brethren *who dwells* by you becomes poor, and sells himself to you, you shall not compel him to serve as a slave. [40]As a hired servant *and* a sojourner he shall be with you, *and* shall serve you until the Year of Jubilee. [41]And *then* he shall depart from you—he and his children with him—and shall return to his own family. He shall return to the possession of his fathers. [42]For they *are* My servants, whom I brought out of the land of Egypt; they shall not be sold as slaves. [43]You shall not rule over him with rigor, but you shall fear your God. [44]And as for your male and female slaves whom you may have—from the nations that are around you, from them you may buy male and female slaves. [45]Moreover you may buy the children of the strangers who dwell among you, and their families who are with you, which they beget in your land; and they shall become your property. [46]And you may take them as an inheritance for your children after you, to inherit *them as* a possession; they shall be your permanent slaves. But regarding your brethren, the children of Israel, you shall not rule over one another with rigor.

[47]'Now if a sojourner or stranger close to you becomes rich, and *one of* your brethren *who dwells* by him becomes poor, and sells himself to the stranger *or* sojourner close to you, or to a member of the stranger's family, [48]after he is sold he may be redeemed again. One of his brothers may redeem him; [49]or his uncle or his uncle's son may redeem him; or *anyone* who is near of kin to him in his family may redeem him; or if he is able he may redeem himself. [50]Thus he shall reckon with him who bought him: The price of his release shall be according to the number of years, from the year that he was sold to him until the Year of Jubilee; *it shall be* according to the time of a hired servant for him. [51]If *there are* still many years *remaining,* according to them he shall repay the price of his redemption from the money with which he was bought. [52]And if there remain but a few years until the Year of Jubilee, then he shall reckon with him, *and* according to his years he shall repay him the price of his redemption. [53]He shall be with him as a yearly hired servant, and he shall not rule with rigor over him in your sight. [54]And if he is not redeemed in these *years,* then he shall be released in the Year of Jubilee—he and his children with him. [55]For the children of Israel *are* servants to Me; they *are* My servants whom I brought out of the land of Egypt: I *am* the LORD your God.

Promise of Blessing and Retribution

26 'You shall not make idols for yourselves;
　　neither a carved image nor a *sacred* pillar
　　　　shall you rear up for yourselves;
　　nor shall you set up an engraved stone in
　　　　your land, to bow down to it;
　　for I *am* the LORD your God.
[2]You shall keep My Sabbaths and reverence
　　　　My sanctuary:
　　I *am* the LORD.

[3]'If you walk in My statutes and keep My
　　　　commandments, and perform them,
[4]then I will give you rain in its season, the land
　　　　shall yield its produce, and the trees of
　　　　the field shall yield their fruit.
[5]Your threshing shall last till the time of
　　　　vintage, and the vintage shall last till the
　　　　time of sowing;
　　you shall eat your bread to the full, and dwell
　　　　in your land safely.
[6]I will give peace in the land, and you shall lie
　　　　down, and none will make *you* afraid;
　　I will rid the land of evil beasts,
　　　　and the sword will not go through your land.

⁷You will chase your enemies, and they shall fall by the sword before you.

⁸Five of you shall chase a hundred, and a hundred of you shall put ten thousand to flight;

your enemies shall fall by the sword before you.

⁹For I will look on you favorably and make you fruitful, multiply you and confirm My covenant with you.

¹⁰You shall eat the old harvest, and clear out the old because of the new.

¹¹I will set My tabernacle among you, and My soul shall not abhor you.

¹²I will walk among you and be your God, and you shall be My people.

¹³I *am* the LORD your God, who brought you out of the land of Egypt, that *you* should not be their slaves;

I have broken the bands of your yoke and made you walk upright.

¹⁴'But if you do not obey Me, and do not observe all these commandments,

¹⁵and if you despise My statutes, or if your soul abhors My judgments, so that you do not perform all My commandments, *but* break My covenant,

¹⁶I also will do this to you:

I will even appoint terror over you, wasting disease and fever which shall consume the eyes and cause sorrow of heart.

And you shall sow your seed in vain, for your enemies shall eat it.

¹⁷I will set My face against you, and you shall be defeated by your enemies.

Those who hate you shall reign over you, and you shall flee when no one pursues you.

¹⁸'And after all this, if you do not obey Me, then I will punish you seven times more for your sins.

¹⁹I will break the pride of your power;

I will make your heavens like iron and your earth like bronze.

²⁰And your strength shall be spent in vain;

for your land shall not yield its produce, nor shall the trees of the land yield their fruit.

²¹'Then, if you walk contrary to Me, and are not willing to obey Me, I will bring on you seven times more plagues, according to your sins.

²²I will also send wild beasts among you, which shall rob you of your children, destroy your livestock, and make you few in number;

and your highways shall be desolate.

²³'And if by these things you are not reformed by Me, but walk contrary to Me,

²⁴then I also will walk contrary to you, and I will punish you yet seven times for your sins.

²⁵And I will bring a sword against you that will execute the vengeance of the covenant;

when you are gathered together within your cities I will send pestilence among you;

and you shall be delivered into the hand of the enemy.

²⁶When I have cut off your supply of bread, ten women shall bake your bread in one oven, and they shall bring back your bread by weight, and you shall eat and not be satisfied.

²⁷'And after all this, if you do not obey Me, but walk contrary to Me,

²⁸then I also will walk contrary to you in fury; and I, even I, will chastise you seven times for your sins.

²⁹You shall eat the flesh of your sons, and you shall eat the flesh of your daughters.

³⁰I will destroy your high places, cut down your incense altars, and cast your carcasses on the lifeless forms of your idols;

and My soul shall abhor you.

³¹I will lay your cities waste and bring your sanctuaries to desolation, and I will not smell the fragrance of your sweet aromas.

³²I will bring the land to desolation, and your enemies who dwell in it shall be astonished at it.

³³I will scatter you among the nations and draw out a sword after you;

your land shall be desolate and your cities waste.

³⁴Then the land shall enjoy its sabbaths as long as it lies desolate and you *are* in your enemies' land;

then the land shall rest and enjoy its sabbaths.
³⁵As long as *it* lies desolate it shall rest—

for the time it did not rest on your sabbaths when you dwelt in it.

³⁶'And as for those of you who are left, I will send faintness into their hearts in the lands of their enemies;

the sound of a shaken leaf shall cause them to flee;

they shall flee as though fleeing from a sword, and they shall fall when no one pursues.
³⁷They shall stumble over one another, as it were before a sword, when no one pursues;

and you shall have no *power* to stand before your enemies.
³⁸You shall perish among the nations, and the land of your enemies shall eat you up.
³⁹And those of you who are left shall waste away in their iniquity in your enemies' lands;

also in their fathers' iniquities, which are with them, they shall waste away.

⁴⁰'*But* if they confess their iniquity and the iniquity of their fathers, with their unfaithfulness in which they were unfaithful to Me, and that they also have walked contrary to Me,
⁴¹and *that* I also have walked contrary to them and have brought them into the land of their enemies;

if their uncircumcised hearts are humbled, and they accept their guilt—
⁴²then I will remember My covenant with Jacob, and My covenant with Isaac and My covenant with Abraham I will remember;

I will remember the land.
⁴³The land also shall be left empty by them, and will enjoy its sabbaths while it lies desolate without them;

they will accept their guilt, because they despised My judgments and because their soul abhorred My statutes.

⁴⁴Yet for all that, when they are in the land of their enemies, I will not cast them away, nor shall I abhor them, to utterly destroy them and break My covenant with them;

for I *am* the LORD their God.
⁴⁵But for their sake I will remember the covenant of their ancestors, whom I brought out of the land of Egypt in the sight of the nations, that I might be their God:

I *am* the LORD.' "

⁴⁶These *are* the statutes and judgments and laws which the LORD made between Himself and the children of Israel on Mount Sinai by the hand of Moses.

REDEEMING PERSONS AND PROPERTY DEDICATED TO GOD

27 Now the LORD spoke to Moses, saying, ²"Speak to the children of Israel, and say to them: 'When a man consecrates by a vow certain persons to the LORD, according to your valuation, ³if your valuation is of a male from twenty years old up to sixty years old, then your valuation shall be fifty shekels of silver, according to the shekel of the sanctuary. ⁴If it *is* a female, then your valuation shall be thirty shekels; ⁵and if from five years old up to twenty years old, then your valuation for a male shall be twenty shekels, and for a female ten shekels; ⁶and if from a month old up to five years old, then your valuation for a male shall be five shekels of silver, and for a female your valuation shall be three shekels of silver; ⁷and if from sixty years old and above, if *it is* a male, then your valuation shall be fifteen shekels, and for a female ten shekels.

⁸'But if he is too poor to pay your valuation, then he shall present himself before the priest, and the priest shall set a value for him; according to the ability of him who vowed, the priest shall value him.

⁹'If *it is* an animal that men may bring as an offering to the LORD, all that *anyone* gives to the LORD shall be holy. ¹⁰He shall not substitute it or exchange it, good for bad or bad for good; and if he at all exchanges animal for animal, then both it and the one exchanged for it shall be holy. ¹¹If *it is* an unclean animal which they do not offer as a

sacrifice to the LORD, then he shall present the animal before the priest; [12]and the priest shall set a value for it, whether it is good or bad; as you, the priest, value it, so it shall be. [13]But if he *wants* at all *to* redeem it, then he must add one-fifth to your valuation.

[14]'And when a man dedicates his house *to be* holy to the LORD, then the priest shall set a value for it, whether it is good or bad; as the priest values it, so it shall stand. [15]If he who dedicated it *wants to* redeem his house, then he must add one-fifth of the money of your valuation to it, and it shall be his.

[16]'If a man dedicates to the LORD *part* of a field of his possession, then your valuation shall be according to the seed for it. A homer of barley seed *shall be valued* at fifty shekels of silver. [17]If he dedicates his field from the Year of Jubilee, according to your valuation it shall stand. [18]But if he dedicates his field after the Jubilee, then the priest shall reckon to him the money due according to the years that remain till the Year of Jubilee, and it shall be deducted from your valuation. [19]And if he who dedicates the field ever wishes to redeem it, then he must add one-fifth of the money of your valuation to it, and it shall belong to him. [20]But if he does not want to redeem the field, or if he has sold the field to another man, it shall not be redeemed anymore; [21]but the field, when it is released in the Jubilee, shall be holy to the LORD, as a devoted field; it shall be the possession of the priest.

[22]'And if a man dedicates to the LORD a field which he has bought, which is not the field of his possession, [23]then the priest shall reckon to him the worth of your valuation, up to the Year of Jubilee, and he shall give your valuation on that day *as* a holy *offering* to the LORD. [24]In the Year of Jubilee the field shall return to him from whom it was bought, to the one who *owned* the land as a possession. [25]And all your valuations shall be according to the shekel of the sanctuary: twenty gerahs to the shekel.

[26]'But the firstborn of the animals, which should be the LORD's firstborn, no man shall dedicate; whether *it is* an ox or sheep, it *is* the LORD's. [27]And if *it is* an unclean animal, then he shall redeem *it* according to your valuation, and shall add one-fifth to it; or if it is not redeemed, then it shall be sold according to your valuation.

[28]'Nevertheless no devoted *offering* that a man may devote to the LORD of all that he has, *both* man and beast, or the field of his possession, shall be sold or redeemed; every devoted *offering is* most holy to the LORD. [29]No person under the ban, who may become doomed to destruction among men, shall be redeemed, *but* shall surely be put to death. [30]And all the tithe of the land, *whether* of the seed of the land *or* of the fruit of the tree, *is* the LORD's. It *is* holy to the LORD. [31]If a man wants at all to redeem *any* of his tithes, he shall add one-fifth to it. [32]And concerning the tithe of the herd or the flock, of whatever passes under the rod, the tenth one shall be holy to the LORD. [33]He shall not inquire whether it is good or bad, nor shall he exchange it; and if he exchanges it at all, then both it and the one exchanged for it shall be holy; it shall not be redeemed.' "

[34]These *are* the commandments which the LORD commanded Moses for the children of Israel on Mount Sinai.

IMPACT OF THE BOOK

I IDEA

God's faithfulness to His people was not dependent on their faithfulness to Him. Numbers is the Old Testament wilderness experience, which was the direct result of disobedience. This book describes their walking, wandering, warring, working, and worshipping.

MESSAGE

In Numbers, the power of a positive attitude is vividly displayed in the lives of Joshua and Caleb. Unlike the ten spies who focused on the overwhelming odds against victory, they focused on God. Your attitude is one thing that you can control. It will either lead to victory or it will defeat you before the battle has even begun.

PEOPLE

Aaron, Moses, Balaam, Caleb, Dathan, Eleazar, Joshua, Korah, Reuben

AUTHOR

The authorship of Numbers must be taken into consideration in light of the whole Pentateuch. While Numbers may have been slightly edited after Moses' death, he is the traditionally accepted author of the book.

CULTURE

At the foot of Mount Sinai, the Lord gave His people instructions, codes, and laws that would set the Israelites apart as holy, a people for Himself. These laws were not broken down into compartments; they were not intended to be religious, commercial, or government laws. The laws were to shape all aspects of Hebrew life in order to influence their neighbors and to shape the culture by their values. Instead of being conquerors as God intended, the Israelites settled for being wanderers; and their journey took them from the mountain where they had felt God's presence to the wilderness where they grumbled against the same God who led them out of Egypt.

TIMELINE

between 1445 and 1405 BC

KEY SCRIPTURE MEMORY VERSES

6:24–26; 13:30; 14:22, 23; 23:19

The First Census of Israel

1 Now the LORD spoke to Moses in the Wilderness of Sinai, in the tabernacle of meeting, on the first *day* of the second month, in the second year after they had come out of the land of Egypt, saying: [2]"Take a census of all the congregation of the children of Israel, by their families, by their fathers' houses, according to the number of names, every male individually, [3]from twenty years old and above—all who *are able to* go to war in Israel. You and Aaron shall number them by their armies. [4]And with you there shall be a man from every tribe, each one the head of his father's house.

[5]"These are the names of the men who shall stand with you: from Reuben, Elizur the son of Shedeur; [6]from Simeon, Shelumiel the son of Zurishaddai; [7]from Judah, Nahshon the son of Amminadab; [8]from Issachar, Nethanel the son of Zuar; [9]from Zebulun, Eliab the son of Helon; [10]from the sons of Joseph: from Ephraim, Elishama the son of Ammihud; from Manasseh, Gamaliel the son of Pedahzur; [11]from Benjamin, Abidan the son of Gideoni; [12]from Dan, Ahiezer the son of Ammishaddai; [13]from Asher, Pagiel the son of Ocran; [14]from Gad, Eliasaph the son of Deuel;[a] [15]from Naphtali, Ahira the son of Enan." [16]These *were* chosen from the congregation, leaders of their fathers' tribes, heads of the divisions in Israel.

[17]Then Moses and Aaron took these men who had been mentioned by name, [18]and they assembled all the congregation together on the first *day* of the second month; and they recited their ancestry by families, by their fathers' houses, according to the number of names, from twenty years old and above, each one individually. [19]As the LORD commanded Moses, so he numbered them in the Wilderness of Sinai.

[20]Now the children of Reuben, Israel's oldest son, their genealogies by their families, by their fathers' house, according to the number of names, every male individually, from twenty years old and above, all who *were able to* go to war: [21]those who were numbered of the tribe of Reuben *were* forty-six thousand five hundred.

[22]From the children of Simeon, their genealogies by their families, by their fathers' house, of those who were numbered, according to the number of names, every male individually, from twenty years old and above, all who *were able to* go to war: [23]those who were numbered of the tribe of Simeon *were* fifty-nine thousand three hundred.

[24]From the children of Gad, their genealogies by their families, by their fathers' house, according to the number of names, from twenty years old and above, all who *were able to* go to war: [25]those who were numbered of the tribe of Gad *were* forty-five thousand six hundred and fifty.

[26]From the children of Judah, their genealogies by their families, by their fathers' house, according to the number of names, from twenty years old and above, all who *were able to* go to war: [27]those who were numbered of the tribe of Judah *were* seventy-four thousand six hundred.

[28]From the children of Issachar, their genealogies by their families, by their fathers' house, according to the number of names, from twenty years old and above, all who *were able to* go to war: [29]those who were numbered of the tribe of Issachar *were* fifty-four thousand four hundred.

[30]From the children of Zebulun, their genealogies by their families, by their fathers' house, according to the number of names, from twenty years old and above, all who *were able to* go to war: [31]those who were numbered of the tribe of Zebulun *were* fifty-seven thousand four hundred.

[32]From the sons of Joseph, the children of Ephraim, their genealogies by their families, by their fathers' house, according to the number of names, from twenty years old and above, all who *were able to* go to war: [33]those who were numbered of the tribe of Ephraim *were* forty thousand five hundred.

[34]From the children of Manasseh, their genealogies by their families, by their fathers' house, according to the number of names, from twenty years old and above, all who *were able to* go to war: [35]those who were numbered of the tribe of Manasseh *were* thirty-two thousand two hundred.

[36]From the children of Benjamin, their genealogies by their families, by their fathers' house, according to the number of names, from twenty years old and above, all who *were able to* go to war:

1:14 [a]Spelled *Reuel* in 2:14

[37]those who were numbered of the tribe of Benjamin *were* thirty-five thousand four hundred.

[38]From the children of Dan, their genealogies by their families, by their fathers' house, according to the number of names, from twenty years old and above, all who *were able to* go to war: [39]those who were numbered of the tribe of Dan *were* sixty-two thousand seven hundred.

[40]From the children of Asher, their genealogies by their families, by their fathers' house, according to the number of names, from twenty years old and above, all who *were able to* go to war: [41]those who were numbered of the tribe of Asher *were* forty-one thousand five hundred.

[42]From the children of Naphtali, their genealogies by their families, by their fathers' house, according to the number of names, from twenty years old and above, all who *were able to* go to war: [43]those who were numbered of the tribe of Naphtali *were* fifty-three thousand four hundred.

[44]These are the ones who were numbered, whom Moses and Aaron numbered, with the leaders of Israel, twelve men, each one representing his father's house. [45]So all who were numbered of the children of Israel, by their fathers' houses, from twenty years old and above, all who *were able to* go to war in Israel— [46]all who were numbered were six hundred and three thousand five hundred and fifty.

[47]But the Levites were not numbered among them by their fathers' tribe; [48]for the LORD had spoken to Moses, saying: [49]"Only the tribe of Levi you shall not number, nor take a census of them among the children of Israel; [50]but you shall appoint the Levites over the tabernacle of the Testimony, over all its furnishings, and over all things that belong to it; they shall carry the tabernacle and all its furnishings; they shall attend to it and camp around the tabernacle. [51]And when the tabernacle is to go forward, the Levites shall take it down; and when the tabernacle is to be set up, the Levites shall set it up. The outsider who comes near shall be put to death. [52]The children of Israel shall pitch their tents, everyone by his own camp, everyone by his own standard, according to their armies; [53]but the Levites shall camp around the tabernacle of the Testimony, that there may be no wrath on the congregation of the children of Israel;

and the Levites shall keep charge of the tabernacle of the Testimony."

[54]Thus the children of Israel did; according to all that the LORD commanded Moses, so they did.

THE TRIBES AND LEADERS BY ARMIES

2 And the LORD spoke to Moses and Aaron, saying: [2]"Everyone of the children of Israel shall camp by his own standard, beside the emblems of his father's house; they shall camp some distance from the tabernacle of meeting. [3]On the east side, toward the rising of the sun, those of the standard of the forces with Judah shall camp according to their armies; and Nahshon the son of Amminadab *shall be* the leader of the children of Judah." [4]And his army was numbered at seventy-four thousand six hundred.

[5]"Those who camp next to him *shall be* the tribe of Issachar, and Nethanel the son of Zuar *shall be* the leader of the children of Issachar." [6]And his army was numbered at fifty-four thousand four hundred.

[7]"Then *comes* the tribe of Zebulun, and Eliab the son of Helon *shall be* the leader of the children of Zebulun." [8]And his army was numbered at fifty-seven thousand four hundred. [9]"All who were numbered according to their armies of the forces with Judah, one hundred and eighty-six thousand four hundred—these shall break camp first.

[10]"On the south side *shall be* the standard of the forces with Reuben according to their armies, and the leader of the children of Reuben *shall be* Elizur the son of Shedeur." [11]And his army was numbered at forty-six thousand five hundred.

[12]"Those who camp next to him *shall be* the tribe of Simeon, and the leader of the children of Simeon *shall be* Shelumiel the son of Zurishaddai." [13]And his army was numbered at fifty-nine thousand three hundred.

[14]"Then *comes* the tribe of Gad, and the leader of the children of Gad *shall be* Eliasaph the son of Reuel."[a] [15]And his army was numbered at forty-five thousand six hundred and fifty. [16]"All who were numbered according to their armies of the forces with Reuben, one hundred and fifty-one thousand four hundred and fifty—they shall be the second to break camp.

2:14 [a]Spelled *Deuel* in 1:14 and 7:42

¹⁷"And the tabernacle of meeting shall move out with the camp of the Levites in the middle of the camps; as they camp, so they shall move out, everyone in his place, by their standards.

¹⁸"On the west side *shall be* the standard of the forces with Ephraim according to their armies, and the leader of the children of Ephraim *shall be* Elishama the son of Ammihud." ¹⁹And his army was numbered at forty thousand five hundred.

²⁰"Next to him *comes* the tribe of Manasseh, and the leader of the children of Manasseh *shall be* Gamaliel the son of Pedahzur." ²¹And his army was numbered at thirty-two thousand two hundred.

²²"Then *comes* the tribe of Benjamin, and the leader of the children of Benjamin *shall be* Abidan the son of Gideoni." ²³And his army was numbered at thirty-five thousand four hundred. ²⁴"All who were numbered according to their armies of the forces with Ephraim, one hundred and eight thousand one hundred—they shall be the third to break camp.

²⁵"The standard of the forces with Dan *shall be* on the north side according to their armies, and the leader of the children of Dan *shall be* Ahiezer the son of Ammishaddai." ²⁶And his army was numbered at sixty-two thousand seven hundred.

²⁷"Those who camp next to him *shall be* the tribe of Asher, and the leader of the children of Asher *shall be* Pagiel the son of Ocran." ²⁸And his army was numbered at forty-one thousand five hundred.

²⁹"Then *comes* the tribe of Naphtali, and the leader of the children of Naphtali *shall be* Ahira the son of Enan." ³⁰And his army was numbered at fifty-three thousand four hundred. ³¹"All who were numbered of the forces with Dan, one hundred and fifty-seven thousand six hundred—they shall break camp last, with their standards."

³²These *are* the ones who were numbered of the children of Israel by their fathers' houses. All who were numbered according to their armies of the forces *were* six hundred and three thousand five hundred and fifty. ³³But the Levites were not numbered among the children of Israel, just as the LORD commanded Moses.

³⁴Thus the children of Israel did according to all that the LORD commanded Moses; so they camped by their standards and so they broke camp, each one by his family, according to their fathers' houses.

THE SONS OF AARON

3 Now these *are* the records of Aaron and Moses when the LORD spoke with Moses on Mount Sinai. ²And these *are* the names of the sons of Aaron: Nadab, the firstborn, and Abihu, Eleazar, and Ithamar. ³These *are* the names of the sons of Aaron, the anointed priests, whom he consecrated to minister as priests. ⁴Nadab and Abihu had died before the LORD when they offered profane fire before the LORD in the Wilderness of Sinai; and they had no children. So Eleazar and Ithamar ministered as priests in the presence of Aaron their father.

THE LEVITES SERVE IN THE TABERNACLE

⁵And the LORD spoke to Moses, saying: ⁶"Bring the tribe of Levi near, and present them before Aaron the priest, that they may serve him. ⁷And they shall attend to his needs and the needs of the whole congregation before the tabernacle of meeting, to do the work of the tabernacle. ⁸Also they shall attend to all the furnishings of the tabernacle of meeting, and to the needs of the children of Israel, to do the work of the tabernacle. ⁹And you shall give the Levites to Aaron and his sons; they *are* given entirely to him^a from among the children of Israel. ¹⁰So you shall appoint Aaron and his sons, and they shall attend to their priesthood; but the outsider who comes near shall be put to death."

¹¹Then the LORD spoke to Moses, saying: ¹²"Now behold, I Myself have taken the Levites from among the children of Israel instead of every firstborn who opens the womb among the children of Israel. Therefore the Levites shall be Mine, ¹³because all the firstborn *are* Mine. On the day that I struck all the firstborn in the land of Egypt, I sanctified to Myself all the firstborn in Israel, both man and beast. They shall be Mine: I *am* the LORD."

CENSUS OF THE LEVITES COMMANDED

¹⁴Then the LORD spoke to Moses in the Wilderness of Sinai, saying: ¹⁵"Number the

3:9 ^aSamaritan Pentateuch and Septuagint read *Me*.

children of Levi by their fathers' houses, by their families; you shall number every male from a month old and above."

¹⁶So Moses numbered them according to the word of the LORD, as he was commanded. ¹⁷These were the sons of Levi by their names: Gershon, Kohath, and Merari. ¹⁸And these *are* the names of the sons of Gershon by their families: Libni and Shimei. ¹⁹And the sons of Kohath by their families: Amram, Izehar, Hebron, and Uzziel. ²⁰And the sons of Merari by their families: Mahli and Mushi. These *are* the families of the Levites by their fathers' houses.

²¹From Gershon *came* the family of the Libnites and the family of the Shimites; these *were* the families of the Gershonites. ²²Those who were numbered, according to the number of all the males from a month old and above—of those who were numbered *there were* seven thousand five hundred. ²³The families of the Gershonites were to camp behind the tabernacle westward. ²⁴And the leader of the father's house of the Gershonites *was* Eliasaph the son of Lael. ²⁵The duties of the children of Gershon in the tabernacle of meeting *included* the tabernacle, the tent with its covering, the screen for the door of the tabernacle of meeting, ²⁶the screen for the door of the court, the hangings of the court which *are* around the tabernacle and the altar, and their cords, according to all the work relating to them.

²⁷From Kohath *came* the family of the Amramites, the family of the Izharites, the family of the Hebronites, and the family of the Uzzielites; these *were* the families of the Kohathites. ²⁸According to the number of all the males, from a month old and above, *there were* eight thousand six[a] hundred keeping charge of the sanctuary. ²⁹The families of the children of Kohath were to camp on the south side of the tabernacle. ³⁰And the leader of the fathers' house of the families of the Kohathites *was* Elizaphan the son of Uzziel. ³¹Their duty *included* the ark, the table, the lampstand, the altars, the utensils of the sanctuary with which they ministered, the screen, and all the work relating to them.

³²And Eleazar the son of Aaron the priest *was to be* chief over the leaders of the Levites, *with* oversight of those who kept charge of the sanctuary.

³³From Merari *came* the family of the Mahlites and the family of the Mushites; these *were* the families of Merari. ³⁴And those who were numbered, according to the number of all the males from a month old and above, *were* six thousand two hundred. ³⁵The leader of the fathers' house of the families of Merari *was* Zuriel the son of Abihail. These *were* to camp on the north side of the tabernacle. ³⁶And the appointed duty of the children of Merari *included* the boards of the tabernacle, its bars, its pillars, its sockets, its utensils, all the work relating to them, ³⁷and the pillars of the court all around, with their sockets, their pegs, and their cords.

³⁸Moreover those who were to camp before the tabernacle on the east, before the tabernacle of meeting, *were* Moses, Aaron, and his sons, keeping charge of the sanctuary, to meet the needs of the children of Israel; but the outsider who came near was to be put to death. ³⁹All who were numbered of the Levites, whom Moses and Aaron numbered at the commandment of the LORD, by their families, all the males from a month old and above, *were* twenty-two thousand.

LEVITES DEDICATED INSTEAD OF THE FIRSTBORN

⁴⁰Then the LORD said to Moses: "Number all the firstborn males of the children of Israel from a month old and above, and take the number of their names. ⁴¹And you shall take the Levites for Me—I *am* the LORD—instead of all the firstborn among the children of Israel, and the livestock of the Levites instead of all the firstborn among the livestock of the children of Israel." ⁴²So Moses numbered all the firstborn among the children of Israel, as the LORD commanded him. ⁴³And all the firstborn males, according to the number of names from a month old and above, of those who were numbered of them, were twenty-two thousand two hundred and seventy-three.

⁴⁴Then the LORD spoke to Moses, saying: ⁴⁵"Take the Levites instead of all the firstborn among the children of Israel, and the livestock of the Levites instead of their livestock. The Levites shall be Mine: I *am* the LORD. ⁴⁶And for the redemption of the two hundred and seventy-three of the firstborn of the children of Israel, who are

3:28 ᵃSome manuscripts of the Septuagint read *three*.

more than the number of the Levites, [47]you shall take five shekels for each one individually; you shall take *them* in the currency of the shekel of the sanctuary, the shekel of twenty gerahs. [48]And you shall give the money, with which the excess number of them is redeemed, to Aaron and his sons."

[49]So Moses took the redemption money from those who were over and above those who were redeemed by the Levites. [50]From the firstborn of the children of Israel he took the money, one thousand three hundred and sixty-five *shekels,* according to the shekel of the sanctuary. [51]And Moses gave their redemption money to Aaron and his sons, according to the word of the LORD, as the LORD commanded Moses.

DUTIES OF THE SONS OF KOHATH

4 Then the LORD spoke to Moses and Aaron, saying: [2]"Take a census of the sons of Kohath from among the children of Levi, by their families, by their fathers' house, [3]from thirty years old and above, even to fifty years old, all who enter the service to do the work in the tabernacle of meeting.

[4]"This *is* the service of the sons of Kohath in the tabernacle of meeting, *relating to* the most holy things: [5]When the camp prepares to journey, Aaron and his sons shall come, and they shall take down the covering veil and cover the ark of the Testimony with it. [6]Then they shall put on it a covering of badger skins, and spread over *that* a cloth entirely of blue; and they shall insert its poles.

[7]"On the table of showbread they shall spread a blue cloth, and put on it the dishes, the pans, the bowls, and the pitchers for pouring; and the showbread[a] shall be on it. [8]They shall spread over them a scarlet cloth, and cover the same with a covering of badger skins; and they shall insert its poles. [9]And they shall take a blue cloth and cover the lampstand of the light, with its lamps, its wick-trimmers, its trays, and all its oil vessels, with which they service it. [10]Then they shall put it with all its utensils in a covering of badger skins, and put *it* on a carrying beam.

[11]"Over the golden altar they shall spread a blue cloth, and cover it with a covering of badger skins; and they shall insert its poles. [12]Then they shall take all the utensils of service with which

they minister in the sanctuary, put *them* in a blue cloth, cover them with a covering of badger skins, and put *them* on a carrying beam. [13]Also they shall take away the ashes from the altar, and spread a purple cloth over it. [14]They shall put on it all its implements with which they minister there—the firepans, the forks, the shovels, the basins, and all the utensils of the altar—and they shall spread on it a covering of badger skins, and insert its poles. [15]And when Aaron and his sons have finished covering the sanctuary and all the furnishings of the sanctuary, when the camp is set to go, then the sons of Kohath shall come to carry *them;* but they shall not touch any holy thing, lest they die.

"These *are* the things in the tabernacle of meeting which the sons of Kohath are to carry.

[16]"The appointed duty of Eleazar the son of Aaron the priest *is* the oil for the light, the sweet incense, the daily grain offering, the anointing oil, the oversight of all the tabernacle, of all that *is* in it, with the sanctuary and its furnishings."

[17]Then the LORD spoke to Moses and Aaron, saying: [18]"Do not cut off the tribe of the families of the Kohathites from among the Levites; [19]but do this in regard to them, that they may live and not die when they approach the most holy things: Aaron and his sons shall go in and appoint each of them to his service and his task. [20]But they shall not go in to watch while the holy things are being covered, lest they die."

DUTIES OF THE SONS OF GERSHON

[21]Then the LORD spoke to Moses, saying: [22]"Also take a census of the sons of Gershon, by their fathers' house, by their families. [23]From thirty years old and above, even to fifty years old, you shall number them, all who enter to perform the service, to do the work in the tabernacle of meeting. [24]This *is* the service of the families of the Gershonites, in serving and carrying: [25]They shall carry the curtains of the tabernacle and the tabernacle of meeting *with* its covering, the covering of badger skins that *is* on it, the screen for the door of the tabernacle of meeting, [26]the screen for the door of the gate of the court, the hangings of the court which *are* around the tabernacle and altar, and their cords, all the furnishings for their

4:7 [a]Literally *the continual bread*

service and all that is made for these things: so shall they serve.

27"Aaron and his sons shall assign all the service of the sons of the Gershonites, all their tasks and all their service. And you shall appoint to them all their tasks as their duty. 28This *is* the service of the families of the sons of Gershon in the tabernacle of meeting. And their duties *shall be* under the authority[a] of Ithamar the son of Aaron the priest.

DUTIES OF THE SONS OF MERARI

29"*As for* the sons of Merari, you shall number them by their families and by their fathers' house. 30From thirty years old and above, even to fifty years old, you shall number them, everyone who enters the service to do the work of the tabernacle of meeting. 31And this *is* what they must carry as all their service for the tabernacle of meeting: the boards of the tabernacle, its bars, its pillars, its sockets, 32and the pillars around the court with their sockets, pegs, and cords, with all their furnishings and all their service; and you shall assign *to each man* by name the items he must carry. 33This *is* the service of the families of the sons of Merari, as all their service for the tabernacle of meeting, under the authority[a] of Ithamar the son of Aaron the priest."

CENSUS OF THE LEVITES

34And Moses, Aaron, and the leaders of the congregation numbered the sons of the Kohathites by their families and by their fathers' house, 35from thirty years old and above, even to fifty years old, everyone who entered the service for work in the tabernacle of meeting; 36and those who were numbered by their families were two thousand seven hundred and fifty. 37These *were* the ones who were numbered of the families of the Kohathites, all who might serve in the tabernacle of meeting, whom Moses and Aaron numbered according to the commandment of the LORD by the hand of Moses.

38And those who were numbered of the sons of Gershon, by their families and by their fathers' house, 39from thirty years old and above, even to fifty years old, everyone who entered the service for work in the tabernacle of meeting— 40those who were numbered by their families, by their fa-

thers' house, were two thousand six hundred and thirty. 41These *are* the ones who were numbered of the families of the sons of Gershon, of all who might serve in the tabernacle of meeting, whom Moses and Aaron numbered according to the commandment of the LORD.

42Those of the families of the sons of Merari who were numbered, by their families, by their fathers' house, 43from thirty years old and above, even to fifty years old, everyone who entered the service for work in the tabernacle of meeting— 44those who were numbered by their families were three thousand two hundred. 45These *are* the ones who were numbered of the families of the sons of Merari, whom Moses and Aaron numbered according to the word of the LORD by the hand of Moses.

46All who were numbered of the Levites, whom Moses, Aaron, and the leaders of Israel numbered, by their families and by their fathers' houses, 47from thirty years old and above, even to fifty years old, everyone who came to do the work of service and the work of bearing burdens in the tabernacle of meeting— 48those who were numbered were eight thousand five hundred and eighty.

49According to the commandment of the LORD they were numbered by the hand of Moses, each according to his service and according to his task; thus were they numbered by him, as the LORD commanded Moses.

CEREMONIALLY UNCLEAN PERSONS ISOLATED

5 And the LORD spoke to Moses, saying: 2"Command the children of Israel that they put out of the camp every leper, everyone who has a discharge, and whoever becomes defiled by a corpse. 3You shall put out both male and female; you shall put them outside the camp, that they may not defile their camps in the midst of which I dwell." 4And the children of Israel did so, and put them outside the camp; as the LORD spoke to Moses, so the children of Israel did.

CONFESSION AND RESTITUTION

5Then the LORD spoke to Moses, saying, 6"Speak to the children of Israel: 'When a man or

4:28 aLiterally *hand*   4:33 aLiterally *hand*

woman commits any sin that men commit in unfaithfulness against the LORD, and that person is guilty, [7]then he shall confess the sin which he has committed. He shall make restitution for his trespass in full, plus one-fifth of it, and give *it* to the one he has wronged. [8]But if the man has no relative to whom restitution may be made for the wrong, the restitution for the wrong *must go* to the LORD for the priest, in addition to the ram of the atonement with which atonement is made for him. [9]Every offering of all the holy things of the children of Israel, which they bring to the priest, shall be his. [10]And every man's holy things shall be his; whatever any man gives the priest shall be his.' "

Concerning Unfaithful Wives

[11]And the LORD spoke to Moses, saying, [12]"Speak to the children of Israel, and say to them: 'If any man's wife goes astray and behaves unfaithfully toward him, [13]and a man lies with her carnally, and it is hidden from the eyes of her husband, and it is concealed that she has defiled herself, and *there was* no witness against her, nor was she caught— [14]if the spirit of jealousy comes upon him and he becomes jealous of his wife, who has defiled herself; or if the spirit of jealousy comes upon him and he becomes jealous of his wife, although she has not defiled herself— [15]then the man shall bring his wife to the priest. He shall bring the offering required for her, one-tenth of an ephah of barley meal; he shall pour no oil on it and put no frankincense on it, because it *is* a grain offering of jealousy, an offering for remembering, for bringing iniquity to remembrance.

[16]And the priest shall bring her near, and set her before the LORD. [17]The priest shall take holy water in an earthen vessel, and take some of the dust that is on the floor of the tabernacle and put *it* into the water. [18]Then the priest shall stand the woman before the LORD, uncover the woman's head, and put the offering for remembering in her hands, which *is* the grain offering of jealousy. And the priest shall have in his hand the bitter water that brings a curse. [19]And the priest shall put her under oath, and say to the woman, "If no man has lain with you, and if you have not gone astray to uncleanness *while* under your husband's *authority,* be free from this bitter water that brings a curse. [20]But if you have gone astray *while* under your husband's *authority,* and if you have defiled yourself and some man other than your husband has lain with you"— [21]then the priest shall put the woman under the oath of the curse, and he shall say to the woman—"the LORD make you a curse and an oath among your people, when the LORD makes your thigh rot and your belly swell; [22]and may this water that causes the curse go into your stomach, and make *your* belly swell and *your* thigh rot."

'Then the woman shall say, "Amen, so be it."

[23]'Then the priest shall write these curses in a book, and he shall scrape *them* off into the bitter water. [24]And he shall make the woman drink the bitter water that brings a curse, and the water that brings the curse shall enter her *to become* bitter. [25]Then the priest shall take the grain offering of jealousy from the woman's hand, shall wave the offering before the LORD, and bring it to the altar; [26]and the priest shall take a handful of the offering, as its memorial portion, burn *it* on the altar, and afterward make the woman drink the water. [27]When he has made her drink the water, then it shall be, if she has defiled herself and behaved unfaithfully toward her husband, that the water that brings a curse will enter her *and become* bitter, and her belly will swell, her thigh will rot, and the woman will become a curse among her people. [28]But if the woman has not defiled herself, and is clean, then she shall be free and may conceive children.

[29]'This *is* the law of jealousy, when a wife, *while* under her husband's *authority,* goes astray and defiles herself, [30]or when the spirit of jealousy comes upon a man, and he becomes jealous of his wife; then he shall stand the woman before the LORD, and the priest shall execute all this law upon her. [31]Then the man shall be free from iniquity, but that woman shall bear her guilt.' "

The Law of the Nazirite

6 Then the LORD spoke to Moses, saying, [2]"Speak to the children of Israel, and say to them: 'When either a man or woman consecrates an offering to take the vow of a Nazirite, to separate himself to the LORD, [3]he shall separate himself from wine and *similar* drink; he shall drink neither vinegar made from wine nor vinegar made from *similar* drink; neither shall he drink any grape juice, nor eat fresh grapes or raisins. ⁴All the days of his separation he shall eat nothing that is produced by the grapevine, from seed to skin.

⁵"All the days of the vow of his separation no razor shall come upon his head; until the days are fulfilled for which he separated himself to the LORD, he shall be holy. *Then* he shall let the locks of the hair of his head grow. ⁶All the days that he separates himself to the LORD he shall not go near a dead body. ⁷He shall not make himself unclean even for his father or his mother, for his brother or his sister, when they die, because his separation to God *is* on his head. ⁸All the days of his separation he shall be holy to the LORD.

⁹"And if anyone dies very suddenly beside him, and he defiles his consecrated head, then he shall shave his head on the day of his cleansing; on the seventh day he shall shave it. ¹⁰Then on the eighth day he shall bring two turtledoves or two young pigeons to the priest, to the door of the tabernacle of meeting; ¹¹and the priest shall offer one as a sin offering and *the* other as a burnt offering, and make atonement for him, because he sinned in regard to the corpse; and he shall sanctify his head that same day. ¹²He shall consecrate to the LORD the days of his separation, and bring a male lamb in its first year as a trespass offering; but the former days shall be lost, because his separation was defiled.

¹³"Now this *is* the law of the Nazirite: When the days of his separation are fulfilled, he shall be brought to the door of the tabernacle of meeting. ¹⁴And he shall present his offering to the LORD: one male lamb in its first year without blemish as a burnt offering, one ewe lamb in its first year without blemish as a sin offering, one ram without blemish as a peace offering, ¹⁵a basket of unleavened bread, cakes of fine flour mixed with oil, unleavened wafers anointed with oil, and their grain offering with their drink offerings.

¹⁶"Then the priest shall bring *them* before the LORD and offer his sin offering and his burnt offering; ¹⁷and he shall offer the ram as a sacrifice of a peace offering to the LORD, with the basket of unleavened bread; the priest shall also offer its grain offering and its drink offering. ¹⁸Then the Nazirite shall shave his consecrated head *at* the door of the tabernacle of meeting, and shall take the hair from his consecrated head and put *it* on the fire which is under the sacrifice of the peace offering.

¹⁹"And the priest shall take the boiled shoulder of the ram, one unleavened cake from the basket, and one unleavened wafer, and put *them* upon the hands of the Nazirite after he has shaved his consecrated *hair,* ²⁰and the priest shall wave them as a wave offering before the LORD; they *are* holy for the priest, together with the breast of the wave offering and the thigh of the heave offering. After that the Nazirite may drink wine.'

²¹"This is the law of the Nazirite who vows to the LORD the offering for his separation, and besides that, whatever else his hand is able to provide; according to the vow which he takes, so he must do according to the law of his separation."

THE PRIESTLY BLESSING

²²And the LORD spoke to Moses, saying: ²³"Speak to Aaron and his sons, saying, 'This is the way you shall bless the children of Israel. Say to them:

²⁴"The LORD bless you and keep you;
²⁵The LORD make His face shine upon you,
And be gracious to you;
²⁶The LORD lift up His countenance upon you,
And give you peace." '

²⁷"So they shall put My name on the children of Israel, and I will bless them."

OFFERINGS OF THE LEADERS

7 Now it came to pass, when Moses had finished setting up the tabernacle, that he anointed it and consecrated it and all its furnishings, and the altar and all its utensils; so he anointed them and consecrated them. ²Then the leaders of Israel, the heads of their fathers' houses, who *were* the leaders of the tribes and over those who were numbered, made an offering. ³And they brought their offering before the LORD, six covered carts and twelve oxen, a cart for *every* two of the leaders, and for each one an ox; and they presented them before the tabernacle.

⁴Then the LORD spoke to Moses, saying, ⁵"Accept *these* from them, that they may be used in doing the work of the tabernacle of meeting;

and you shall give them to the Levites, *to* every man according to his service." ⁶So Moses took the carts and the oxen, and gave them to the Levites. ⁷Two carts and four oxen he gave to the sons of Gershon, according to their service; ⁸and four carts and eight oxen he gave to the sons of Merari, according to their service, under the authority[a] of Ithamar the son of Aaron the priest. ⁹But to the sons of Kohath he gave none, because theirs *was* the service of the holy things, *which* they carried on their shoulders.

¹⁰Now the leaders offered the dedication *offering* for the altar when it was anointed; so the leaders offered their offering before the altar. ¹¹For the LORD said to Moses, "They shall offer their offering, one leader each day, for the dedication of the altar."

¹²And the one who offered his offering on the first day *was* Nahshon the son of Amminadab, from the tribe of Judah. ¹³His offering *was* one silver platter, the weight of which *was* one hundred and thirty *shekels,* and one silver bowl of seventy shekels, according to the shekel of the sanctuary, both of them full of fine flour mixed with oil as a grain offering; ¹⁴one gold pan of ten *shekels,* full of incense; ¹⁵one young bull, one ram, and one male lamb in its first year, as a burnt offering; ⁶one kid of the goats as a sin offering; ¹⁷and for the sacrifice of peace offerings: two oxen, five rams, five male goats, and five male lambs in their first year. This *was* the offering of Nahshon the son of Amminadab.

¹⁸On the second day Nethanel the son of Zuar, leader of Issachar, presented *an offering.* ¹⁹For his offering he offered one silver platter, the weight of which *was* one hundred and thirty *shekels,* and one silver bowl of seventy shekels, according to the shekel of the sanctuary, both of them full of fine flour mixed with oil as a grain offering; ²⁰one gold pan of ten *shekels,* full of incense; ²¹one young bull, one ram, and one male lamb in its first year, as a burnt offering; ²²one kid of the goats as a sin offering; ²³and as the sacrifice of peace offerings: two oxen, five rams, five male goats, and five male lambs in their first year. This *was* the offering of Nethanel the son of Zuar.

²⁴On the third day Eliab the son of Helon, leader of the children of Zebulun, *presented an offering.* ²⁵His offering *was* one silver platter, the weight of which *was* one hundred and thirty *shekels,* and one silver bowl of seventy shekels, according to the shekel of the sanctuary, both of them full of fine flour mixed with oil as a grain offering; ²⁶one gold pan of ten *shekels,* full of incense; ²⁷one young bull, one ram, and one male lamb in its first year, as a burnt offering; ²⁸one kid of the goats as a sin offering; ²⁹and for the sacrifice of peace offerings: two oxen, five rams, five male goats, and five male lambs in their first year. This *was* the offering of Eliab the son of Helon.

³⁰On the fourth day Elizur the son of Shedeur, leader of the children of Reuben, *presented an offering.* ³¹His offering *was* one silver platter, the weight of which *was* one hundred and thirty *shekels,* and one silver bowl of seventy shekels, according to the shekel of the sanctuary, both of them full of fine flour mixed with oil as a grain offering; ³²one gold pan of ten *shekels,* full of incense; ³³one young bull, one ram, and one male lamb in its first year, as a burnt offering; ³⁴one kid of the goats as a sin offering; ³⁵and as the sacrifice of peace offerings: two oxen, five rams, five male goats, and five male lambs in their first year. This *was* the offering of Elizur the son of Shedeur.

³⁶On the fifth day Shelumiel the son of Zurishaddai, leader of the children of Simeon, *presented an offering.* ³⁷His offering *was* one silver platter, the weight of which *was* one hundred and thirty *shekels,* and one silver bowl of seventy shekels, according to the shekel of the sanctuary, both of them full of fine flour mixed with oil as a grain offering; ³⁸one gold pan of ten *shekels,* full of incense; ³⁹one young bull, one ram, and one male lamb in its first year, as a burnt offering; ⁴⁰one kid of the goats as a sin offering; ⁴¹and as the sacrifice of peace offerings: two oxen, five rams, five male goats, and five male lambs in their first year. This *was* the offering of Shelumiel the son of Zurishaddai.

⁴²On the sixth day Eliasaph the son of Deuel,[a] leader of the children of Gad, *presented an offering.* ⁴³His offering *was* one silver platter, the weight of which *was* one hundred and thirty *shekels,* and one silver bowl of seventy shekels, according to

7:8 [a]Literally *hand*   7:42 [a]Spelled *Reuel* in 2:14

the shekel of the sanctuary, both of them full of fine flour mixed with oil as a grain offering; ⁴⁴one gold pan of ten *shekels,* full of incense; ⁴⁵one young bull, one ram, and one male lamb in its first year, as a burnt offering; ⁴⁶one kid of the goats as a sin offering; ⁴⁷and as the sacrifice of peace offerings: two oxen, five rams, five male goats, and five male lambs in their first year. This *was* the offering of Eliasaph the son of Deuel.

⁴⁸On the seventh day Elishama the son of Ammihud, leader of the children of Ephraim, *presented an offering.* ⁴⁹His offering *was* one silver platter, the weight of which *was* one hundred and thirty *shekels,* and one silver bowl of seventy shekels, according to the shekel of the sanctuary, both of them full of fine flour mixed with oil as a grain offering; ⁵⁰one gold pan of ten *shekels,* full of incense; ⁵¹one young bull, one ram, and one male lamb in its first year, as a burnt offering; ⁵²one kid of the goats as a sin offering; ⁵³and as the sacrifice of peace offerings: two oxen, five rams, five male goats, and five male lambs in their first year. This *was* the offering of Elishama the son of Ammihud.

⁵⁴On the eighth day Gamaliel the son of Pedahzur, leader of the children of Manasseh, *presented an offering.* ⁵⁵His offering *was* one silver platter, the weight of which *was* one hundred and thirty *shekels,* and one silver bowl of seventy shekels, according to the shekel of the sanctuary, both of them full of fine flour mixed with oil as a grain offering; ⁵⁶one gold pan of ten *shekels,* full of incense; ⁵⁷one young bull, one ram, and one male lamb in its first year, as a burnt offering; ⁵⁸one kid of the goats as a sin offering; ⁵⁹and as the sacrifice of peace offerings: two oxen, five rams, five male goats, and five male lambs in their first year. This *was* the offering of Gamaliel the son of Pedahzur.

⁶⁰On the ninth day Abidan the son of Gideoni, leader of the children of Benjamin, *presented an offering.* ⁶¹His offering *was* one silver platter, the weight of which *was* one hundred and thirty *shekels,* and one silver bowl of seventy shekels, according to the shekel of the sanctuary, both of them full of fine flour mixed with oil as a grain offering; ⁶²one gold pan of ten *shekels,* full of incense; ⁶³one young bull, one ram, and one male lamb in its first year, as a burnt offering; ⁶⁴one kid of the goats as a sin offering; ⁶⁵and as the sacrifice

of peace offerings: two oxen, five rams, five male goats, and five male lambs in their first year. This *was* the offering of Abidan the son of Gideoni.

⁶⁶On the tenth day Ahiezer the son of Ammishaddai, leader of the children of Dan, *presented an offering.* ⁶⁷His offering *was* one silver platter, the weight of which *was* one hundred and thirty *shekels,* and one silver bowl of seventy shekels, according to the shekel of the sanctuary, both of them full of fine flour mixed with oil as a grain offering; ⁶⁸one gold pan of ten *shekels,* full of incense; ⁶⁹one young bull, one ram, and one male lamb in its first year, as a burnt offering; ⁷⁰one kid of the goats as a sin offering; ⁷¹and as the sacrifice of peace offerings: two oxen, five rams, five male goats, and five male lambs in their first year. This *was* the offering of Ahiezer the son of Ammishaddai.

⁷²On the eleventh day Pagiel the son of Ocran, leader of the children of Asher, *presented an offering.* ⁷³His offering *was* one silver platter, the weight of which *was* one hundred and thirty *shekels,* and one silver bowl of seventy shekels, according to the shekel of the sanctuary, both of them full of fine flour mixed with oil as a grain offering; ⁷⁴one gold pan of ten *shekels,* full of incense; ⁷⁵one young bull, one ram, and one male lamb in its first year, as a burnt offering; ⁷⁶one kid of the goats as a sin offering; ⁷⁷and as the sacrifice of peace offerings: two oxen, five rams, five male goats, and five male lambs in their first year. This *was* the offering of Pagiel the son of Ocran.

⁷⁸On the twelfth day Ahira the son of Enan, leader of the children of Naphtali, *presented an offering.* ⁷⁹His offering *was* one silver platter, the weight of which *was* one hundred and thirty *shekels,* and one silver bowl of seventy shekels, according to the shekel of the sanctuary, both of them full of fine flour mixed with oil as a grain offering; ⁸⁰one gold pan of ten *shekels,* full of incense; ⁸¹one young bull, one ram, and one male lamb in its first year, as a burnt offering; ⁸²one kid of the goats as a sin offering; ⁸³and as the sacrifice of peace offerings: two oxen, five rams, five male goats, and five male lambs in their first year. This *was* the offering of Ahira the son of Enan.

⁸⁴This *was* the dedication *offering* for the altar from the leaders of Israel, when it was anointed: twelve silver platters, twelve silver bowls, and

twelve gold pans. ⁸⁵Each silver platter *weighed* one hundred and thirty *shekels* and each bowl seventy *shekels.* All the silver of the vessels *weighed* two thousand four hundred *shekels,* according to the shekel of the sanctuary. ⁸⁶The twelve gold pans full of incense *weighed* ten *shekels* apiece, according to the shekel of the sanctuary; all the gold of the pans *weighed* one hundred and twenty *shekels.* ⁸⁷All the oxen for the burnt offering *were* twelve young bulls, the rams twelve, the male lambs in their first year twelve, with their grain offering, and the kids of the goats as a sin offering twelve. ⁸⁸And all the oxen for the sacrifice of peace offerings were twenty-four bulls, the rams sixty, the male goats sixty, and the lambs in their first year sixty. This *was* the dedication *offering* for the altar after it was anointed.

⁸⁹Now when Moses went into the tabernacle of meeting to speak with Him, he heard the voice of One speaking to him from above the mercy seat that *was* on the ark of the Testimony, from between the two cherubim; thus He spoke to him.

ARRANGEMENT OF THE LAMPS

8 And the LORD spoke to Moses, saying: ²"Speak to Aaron, and say to him, 'When you arrange the lamps, the seven lamps shall give light in front of the lampstand.' " ³And Aaron did so; he arranged the lamps to face toward the front of the lampstand, as the LORD commanded Moses. ⁴Now this workmanship of the lampstand *was* hammered gold; from its shaft to its flowers it *was* hammered work. According to the pattern which the LORD had shown Moses, so he made the lampstand.

CLEANSING AND DEDICATION OF THE LEVITES

⁵Then the LORD spoke to Moses, saying: ⁶"Take the Levites from among the children of Israel and cleanse them *ceremonially.* ⁷Thus you shall do to them to cleanse them: Sprinkle water of purification on them, and let them shave all their body, and let them wash their clothes, and *so* make themselves clean. ⁸Then let them take a young bull with its grain offering of fine flour mixed with oil, and you shall take another young bull as a sin offering. ⁹And you shall bring the Levites before the tabernacle of meeting, and you shall gather together the whole congregation of the children of Israel. ¹⁰So you shall bring the Levites before the LORD, and the children of Israel shall lay their hands on the Levites; ¹¹and Aaron shall offer the Levites before the LORD *like* a wave offering from the children of Israel, that they may perform the work of the LORD. ¹²Then the Levites shall lay their hands on the heads of the young bulls, and you shall offer one as a sin offering and the other as a burnt offering to the LORD, to make atonement for the Levites.

¹³"And you shall stand the Levites before Aaron and his sons, and then offer them *like* a wave offering to the LORD. ¹⁴Thus you shall separate the Levites from among the children of Israel, and the Levites shall be Mine. ¹⁵After that the Levites shall go in to service the tabernacle of meeting. So you shall cleanse them and offer them *like* a wave offering. ¹⁶For they *are* wholly given to Me from among the children of Israel; I have taken them for Myself instead of all who open the womb, the firstborn of all the children of Israel. ¹⁷For all the firstborn among the children of Israel *are* Mine, *both* man and beast; on the day that I struck all the firstborn in the land of Egypt I sanctified them to Myself. ¹⁸I have taken the Levites instead of all the firstborn of the children of Israel. ¹⁹And I have given the Levites as a gift to Aaron and his sons from among the children of Israel, to do the work for the children of Israel in the tabernacle of meeting, and to make atonement for the children of Israel, that there be no plague among the children of Israel when the children of Israel come near the sanctuary."

²⁰Thus Moses and Aaron and all the congregation of the children of Israel did to the Levites; according to all that the LORD commanded Moses concerning the Levites, so the children of Israel did to them. ²¹And the Levites purified themselves and washed their clothes; then Aaron presented them *like* a wave offering before the LORD, and Aaron made atonement for them to cleanse them. ²²After that the Levites went in to do their work in the tabernacle of meeting before Aaron and his sons; as the LORD commanded Moses concerning the Levites, so they did to them.

²³Then the LORD spoke to Moses, saying, ²⁴"This *is* what *pertains* to the Levites: From twenty-five years old and above one may enter to

perform service in the work of the tabernacle of meeting; 25and at the age of fifty years they must cease performing this work, and shall work no more. 26They may minister with their brethren in the tabernacle of meeting, to attend to needs, but they *themselves* shall do no work. Thus you shall do to the Levites regarding their duties."

The Second Passover

9 Now the LORD spoke to Moses in the Wilderness of Sinai, in the first month of the second year after they had come out of the land of Egypt, saying: 2"Let the children of Israel keep the Passover at its appointed time. 3On the fourteenth day of this month, at twilight, you shall keep it at its appointed time. According to all its rites and ceremonies you shall keep it." 4So Moses told the children of Israel that they should keep the Passover. 5And they kept the Passover on the fourteenth day of the first month, at twilight, in the Wilderness of Sinai; according to all that the LORD commanded Moses, so the children of Israel did.

6Now there were *certain* men who were defiled by a human corpse, so that they could not keep the Passover on that day; and they came before Moses and Aaron that day. 7And those men said to him, "We *became* defiled by a human corpse. Why are we kept from presenting the offering of the LORD at its appointed time among the children of Israel?"

8And Moses said to them, "Stand still, that I may hear what the LORD will command concerning you."

9Then the LORD spoke to Moses, saying, 10"Speak to the children of Israel, saying: 'If anyone of you or your posterity is unclean because of a corpse, or *is* far away on a journey, he may still keep the LORD's Passover. 11On the fourteenth day of the second month, at twilight, they may keep it. They shall eat it with unleavened bread and bitter herbs. 12They shall leave none of it until morning, nor break one of its bones. According to all the ordinances of the Passover they shall keep it. 13But the man who *is* clean and is not on a journey, and ceases to keep the Passover, that same person shall be cut off from among his people, because he did not bring the offering of the LORD at its appointed time; that man shall bear his sin.

14'And if a stranger dwells among you, and would keep the LORD's Passover, he must do so according to the rite of the Passover and according to its ceremony; you shall have one ordinance, both for the stranger and the native of the land.'"

The Cloud and the Fire

15Now on the day that the tabernacle was raised up, the cloud covered the tabernacle, the tent of the Testimony; from evening until morning it was above the tabernacle like the appearance of fire. 16So it was always: the cloud covered it *by day,* and the appearance of fire by night. 17Whenever the cloud was taken up from above the tabernacle, after that the children of Israel would journey; and in the place where the cloud settled, there the children of Israel would pitch their tents. 18At the command of the LORD the children of Israel would journey, and at the command of the LORD they would camp; as long as the cloud stayed above the tabernacle they remained encamped. 19Even when the cloud continued long, many days above the tabernacle, the children of Israel kept the charge of the LORD and did not journey. 20So it was, when the cloud was above the tabernacle a few days: according to the command of the LORD they would remain encamped, and according to the command of the LORD they would journey. 21So it was, when the cloud remained only from evening until morning: when the cloud was taken up in the morning, then they would journey; whether by day or by night, whenever the cloud was taken up, they would journey. 22*Whether it was* two days, a month, or a year that the cloud remained above the tabernacle, the children of Israel would remain encamped and not journey; but when it was taken up, they would journey. 23At the command of the LORD they remained encamped, and at the command of the LORD they journeyed; they kept the charge of the LORD, at the command of the LORD by the hand of Moses.

Two Silver Trumpets

10 And the LORD spoke to Moses, saying: 2"Make two silver trumpets for yourself; you shall make them of hammered work; you shall use them for calling the congregation and

for directing the movement of the camps. [3]When they blow both of them, all the congregation shall gather before you at the door of the tabernacle of meeting. [4]But if they blow *only* one, then the leaders, the heads of the divisions of Israel, shall gather to you. [5]When you sound the advance, the camps that lie on the east side shall then begin their journey. [6]When you sound the advance the second time, then the camps that lie on the south side shall begin their journey; they shall sound the call for them to begin their journeys. [7]And when the assembly is to be gathered together, you shall blow, but not sound the advance. [8]The sons of Aaron, the priests, shall blow the trumpets; and these shall be to you as an ordinance forever throughout your generations.

[9]"When you go to war in your land against the enemy who oppresses you, then you shall sound an alarm with the trumpets, and you will be remembered before the LORD your God, and you will be saved from your enemies. [10]Also in the day of your gladness, in your appointed feasts, and at the beginning of your months, you shall blow the trumpets over your burnt offerings and over the sacrifices of your peace offerings; and they shall be a memorial for you before your God: I *am* the LORD your God."

DEPARTURE FROM SINAI

[11]Now it came to pass on the twentieth *day* of the second month, in the second year, that the cloud was taken up from above the tabernacle of the Testimony. [12]And the children of Israel set out from the Wilderness of Sinai on their journeys; then the cloud settled down in the Wilderness of Paran. [13]So they started out for the first time according to the command of the LORD by the hand of Moses.

[14]The standard of the camp of the children of Judah set out first according to their armies; over their army was Nahshon the son of Amminadab. [15]Over the army of the tribe of the children of Issachar *was* Nethanel the son of Zuar. [16]And over the army of the tribe of the children of Zebulun *was* Eliab the son of Helon.

[17]Then the tabernacle was taken down; and the sons of Gershon and the sons of Merari set out, carrying the tabernacle.

[18]And the standard of the camp of Reuben set out according to their armies; over their army *was* Elizur the son of Shedeur. [19]Over the army of the tribe of the children of Simeon *was* Shelumiel the son of Zurishaddai. [20]And over the army of the tribe of the children of Gad *was* Eliasaph the son of Deuel.

[21]Then the Kohathites set out, carrying the holy things. (The tabernacle would be prepared for their arrival.)

[22]And the standard of the camp of the children of Ephraim set out according to their armies; over their army *was* Elishama the son of Ammihud. [23]Over the army of the tribe of the children of Manasseh *was* Gamaliel the son of Pedahzur. [24]And over the army of the tribe of the children of Benjamin *was* Abidan the son of Gideoni.

[25]Then the standard of the camp of the children of Dan (the rear guard of all the camps) set out according to their armies; over their army *was* Ahiezer the son of Ammishaddai. [26]Over the army of the tribe of the children of Asher *was* Pagiel the son of Ocran. [27]And over the army of the tribe of the children of Naphtali *was* Ahira the son of Enan.

[28]Thus *was* the order of march of the children of Israel, according to their armies, when they began their journey.

[29]Now Moses said to Hobab the son of Reuel[a] the Midianite, Moses' father-in-law, "We are setting out for the place of which the LORD said, 'I will give it to you.' Come with us, and we will treat you well; for the LORD has promised good things to Israel."

[30]And he said to him, "I will not go, but I will depart to my *own* land and to my relatives."

[31]So *Moses* said, "Please do not leave, inasmuch as you know how we are to camp in the wilderness, and you can be our eyes. [32]And it shall be, if you go with us—indeed it shall be—that whatever good the LORD will do to us, the same we will do to you."

[33]So they departed from the mountain of the LORD on a journey of three days; and the ark of the covenant of the LORD went before them for the three days' journey, to search out a resting place for them. [34]And the cloud of the LORD *was*

10:29 [a]Septuagint reads *Raguel* (compare Exodus 2:18).

above them by day when they went out from the camp.

³⁵So it was, whenever the ark set out, that Moses said:

"Rise up, O LORD!
Let Your enemies be scattered,
And let those who hate You flee before You."

³⁶And when it rested, he said:

"Return, O LORD,
To the many thousands of Israel."

THE PEOPLE COMPLAIN

11 Now *when* the people complained, it displeased the LORD; for the LORD heard *it,* and His anger was aroused. So the fire of the LORD burned among them, and consumed *some* in the outskirts of the camp. ²Then the people cried out to Moses, and when Moses prayed to the LORD, the fire was quenched. ³So he called the name of the place Taberah,ᵃ because the fire of the LORD had burned among them.

⁴Now the mixed multitude who were among them yielded to intense craving; so the children of Israel also wept again and said: "Who will give us meat to eat? ⁵We remember the fish which we ate freely in Egypt, the cucumbers, the melons, the leeks, the onions, and the garlic; ⁶but now our whole being *is* dried up; *there is* nothing at all except this manna *before* our eyes!"

⁷Now the manna *was* like coriander seed, and its color like the color of bdellium. ⁸The people went about and gathered *it,* ground *it* on millstones or beat *it* in the mortar, cooked *it* in pans, and made cakes of it; and its taste was like the taste of pastry prepared with oil. ⁹And when the dew fell on the camp in the night, the manna fell on it.

¹⁰Then Moses heard the people weeping throughout their families, everyone at the door of his tent; and the anger of the LORD was greatly aroused; Moses also was displeased. ¹¹So Moses said to the LORD, "Why have You afflicted Your servant? And why have I not found favor in Your sight, that You have laid the burden of all these people on me? ¹²Did I conceive all these people? Did I beget them, that You should say to me, 'Carry them in your bosom, as a guardian carries a nursing child,' to the land which You swore to their fathers? ¹³Where am I to get meat to give to all these people? For they weep all over me, saying, 'Give us meat, that we may eat.' ¹⁴I am not able to bear all these people alone, because the burden *is* too heavy for me. ¹⁵If You treat me like this, please kill me here and now—if I have found favor in Your sight—and do not let me see my wretchedness!"

THE SEVENTY ELDERS

¹⁶So the LORD said to Moses: "Gather to Me seventy men of the elders of Israel, whom you know to be the elders of the people and officers over them; bring them to the tabernacle of meeting, that they may stand there with you. ¹⁷Then I will come down and talk with you there. I will take of the Spirit that *is* upon you and will put *the same* upon them; and they shall bear the burden of the people with you, that you may not bear *it* yourself alone. ¹⁸Then you shall say to the people, 'Consecrate yourselves for tomorrow, and you shall eat meat; for you have wept in the hearing of the LORD, saying, "Who will give us meat to eat? For *it was* well with us in Egypt." Therefore the LORD will give you meat, and you shall eat. ¹⁹You shall eat, not one day, nor two days, nor five days, nor ten days, nor twenty days, ²⁰but *for* a whole month, until it comes out of your nostrils and becomes loathsome to you, because you have despised the LORD who is among you, and have wept before Him, saying, "Why did we ever come up out of Egypt?" ' "

²¹And Moses said, "The people whom I *am* among *are* six hundred thousand men on foot; yet You have said, 'I will give them meat, that they may eat *for* a whole month.' ²²Shall flocks and herds be slaughtered for them, to provide enough for them? Or shall all the fish of the sea be gathered together for them, to provide enough for them?"

²³And the LORD said to Moses, "Has the LORD's arm been shortened? Now you shall see whether what I say will happen to you or not."

²⁴So Moses went out and told the people the words of the LORD, and he gathered the seventy men of the elders of the people and placed them around the tabernacle. ²⁵Then the LORD came

11:3 ᵃLiterally *Burning*

down in the cloud, and spoke to him, and took of the Spirit that *was* upon him, and placed *the same* upon the seventy elders; and it happened, when the Spirit rested upon them, that they prophesied, although they never did *so* again.[a]

26But two men had remained in the camp: the name of one *was* Eldad, and the name of the other Medad. And the Spirit rested upon them. Now they *were* among those listed, but who had not gone out to the tabernacle; yet they prophesied in the camp. 27And a young man ran and told Moses, and said, "Eldad and Medad are prophesying in the camp."

28So Joshua the son of Nun, Moses' assistant, *one* of his choice men, answered and said, "Moses my lord, forbid them!"

29Then Moses said to him, "Are you zealous for my sake? Oh, that all the LORD's people were prophets *and* that the LORD would put His Spirit upon them!" 30And Moses returned to the camp, he and the elders of Israel.

The Lord Sends Quail

31Now a wind went out from the LORD, and it brought quail from the sea and left *them* fluttering near the camp, about a day's journey on this side and about a day's journey on the other side, all around the camp, and about two cubits above the surface of the ground. 32And the people stayed up all that day, all night, and all the next day, and gathered the quail (he who gathered least gathered ten homers); and they spread *them* out for themselves all around the camp. 33But while the meat *was* still between their teeth, before it was chewed, the wrath of the LORD was aroused against the people, and the LORD struck the people with a very great plague. 34So he called the name of that place Kibroth Hattaavah,[a] because there they buried the people who had yielded to craving.

35From Kibroth Hattaavah the people moved to Hazeroth, and camped at Hazeroth.

Dissension of Aaron and Miriam

12 Then Miriam and Aaron spoke against Moses because of the Ethiopian woman whom he had married; for he had married an

11:25 [a]Targum and Vulgate read *did not cease.* 11:34 [a]Literally *Graves of Craving*

INSIDE *the* INFLUENCERS

MIRIAM—Attitude Determines Behavior

NUMBERS 12

The first woman to be designated a prophetess was Miriam, the sister of Moses. She began well as we read of her leading the women of Israel in a psalm of praise about the greatness of God. Just a short time later, we read of her again, this time unfavorably. In Numbers 12, pride spread into negative speech. As people often do, she tried to put down Moses, the chosen vessel of the Lord, in an effort to elevate herself. First she criticized his choice of a wife, and then she tried to dismiss him as a leader by saying, "Aren't we just like him? Didn't God also use us?" There were some big differences. Of Moses, the Lord records, "Moses was very humble," (Num. 12:3). This could not be said of Miriam. He also spoke to Moses "face to face." She allowed pride and attitude to forfeit her privilege as a leader and to disqualify her from leadership. Maybe she just had a bad day, but we know that God dealt with her in a strong way by smiting her with leprosy. In fear, Aaron begged for Mercy and the Lord put a time limit of seven days on the illness. Because her leadership was so public, the punishment for an attitude that tore down God's leader had to be severe. God loved His man Moses and wouldn't stand for negative speech about him, but He also loved Miriam; and for that reason, He corrected her in a way she would not forget.

Ethiopian woman. ²So they said, "Has the LORD indeed spoken only through Moses? Has He not spoken through us also?" And the LORD heard *it*. ³(Now the man Moses *was* very humble, more than all men who *were* on the face of the earth.)

⁴Suddenly the LORD said to Moses, Aaron, and Miriam, "Come out, you three, to the tabernacle of meeting!" So the three came out. ⁵Then the LORD came down in the pillar of cloud and stood *in* the door of the tabernacle, and called Aaron and Miriam. And they both went forward. ⁶Then He said,

"Hear now My words:
If there is a prophet among you,
I, the LORD, make Myself known to him in a vision;
I speak to him in a dream.
⁷Not so with My servant Moses;
He *is* faithful in all My house.
⁸I speak with him face to face,
Even plainly, and not in dark sayings;
And he sees the form of the LORD.
Why then were you not afraid
To speak against My servant Moses?"

⁹So the anger of the LORD was aroused against them, and He departed. ¹⁰And when the cloud departed from above the tabernacle, suddenly Miriam *became* leprous, as *white as* snow. Then Aaron turned toward Miriam, and there she was, a leper. ¹¹So Aaron said to Moses, "Oh, my lord! Please do not lay *this* sin on us, in which we have done foolishly and in which we have sinned. ¹²Please do not let her be as one dead, whose flesh is half consumed when he comes out of his mother's womb!"

¹³So Moses cried out to the LORD, saying, "Please heal her, O God, I pray!"

¹⁴Then the LORD said to Moses, "If her father had but spit in her face, would she not be shamed seven days? Let her be shut out of the camp seven days, and afterward she may be received *again*." ¹⁵So Miriam was shut out of the camp seven days, and the people did not journey till Miriam was brought in *again*. ¹⁶And afterward the people moved from Hazeroth and camped in the Wilderness of Paran.

SPIES SENT INTO CANAAN

13 And the LORD spoke to Moses, saying, ²"Send men to spy out the land of Canaan, which I am giving to the children of Israel; from each tribe of their fathers you shall send a man, every one a leader among them."

³So Moses sent them from the Wilderness of Paran according to the command of the LORD, all of them men who *were* heads of the children of Israel. ⁴Now these *were* their names: from the tribe of Reuben, Shammua the son of Zaccur; ⁵from the tribe of Simeon, Shaphat the son of Hori; ⁶from the tribe of Judah, Caleb the son of Jephunneh; ⁷from the tribe of Issachar, Igal the son of Joseph; ⁸from the tribe of Ephraim, Hosheaᵃ the son of Nun; ⁹from the tribe of Benjamin, Palti the son of Raphu; ¹⁰from the tribe of Zebulun, Gaddiel the son of Sodi; ¹¹from the tribe of Joseph, *that is,* from the tribe of Manasseh, Gaddi the son of Susi; ¹²from the tribe of Dan, Ammiel the son of Gemalli; ¹³from the tribe of Asher, Sethur the son of Michael; ¹⁴from the tribe of Naphtali, Nahbi the son of Vophsi; ¹⁵from the tribe of Gad, Geuel the son of Machi.

¹⁶These *are* the names of the men whom Moses sent to spy out the land. And Moses called Hosheaᵃ the son of Nun, Joshua.

¹⁷Then Moses sent them to spy out the land of Canaan, and said to them, "Go up this *way* into the South, and go up to the mountains, ¹⁸and see what the land is like: whether the people who dwell in it *are* strong or weak, few or many; ¹⁹whether the land they dwell in *is* good or bad; whether the cities they inhabit *are* like camps or strongholds; ²⁰whether the land *is* rich or poor; and whether there are forests there or not. Be of good courage. And bring some of the fruit of the land." Now the time *was* the season of the first ripe grapes.

²¹So they went up and spied out the land from the Wilderness of Zin as far as Rehob, near the entrance of Hamath. ²²And they went up through the South and came to Hebron; Ahiman, Sheshai, and Talmai, the descendants of Anak, *were* there. (Now Hebron was built seven years before Zoan in Egypt.) ²³Then they came to the Valley

13:8 ᵃSeptuagint and Vulgate read *Oshea*.   13:16 ᵃSeptuagint and Vulgate read *Oshea*.

of Eshcol, and there cut down a branch with one cluster of grapes; they carried it between two of them on a pole. *They* also *brought* some of the pomegranates and figs. ²⁴The place was called the Valley of Eshcol,ᵃ because of the cluster which the men of Israel cut down there. ²⁵And they returned from spying out the land after forty days.

²⁶Now they departed and came back to Moses and Aaron and all the congregation of the children of Israel in the Wilderness of Paran, at Kadesh; they brought back word to them and to all the congregation, and showed them the fruit of the land. ²⁷Then they told him, and said: "We went to the land where you sent us. It truly flows with milk and honey, and this *is* its fruit. ²⁸Nevertheless the people who dwell in the land *are* strong; the cities *are* fortified *and* very large; moreover we saw the descendants of Anak there. ²⁹The Amalekites dwell in the land of the South; the Hittites, the Jebusites, and the Amorites dwell in the mountains; and the Canaanites dwell by the sea and along the banks of the Jordan."

³⁰Then Caleb quieted the people before Moses, and said, "Let us go up at once and take possession, for we are well able to overcome it."

³¹But the men who had gone up with him said, "We are not able to go up against the people, for they *are* stronger than we." ³²And they gave the children of Israel a bad report of the land which they had spied out, saying, "The land through which we have gone as spies *is* a land that devours its inhabitants, and all the people whom we saw in it *are* men of *great* stature. ³³There we saw the giantsᵃ (the descendants of Anak came from the giants); and we were like grasshoppers in our own sight, and so we were in their sight."

ISRAEL REFUSES TO ENTER CANAAN

14 So all the congregation lifted up their voices and cried, and the people wept that night. ²And all the children of Israel complained against Moses and Aaron, and the whole congregation said to them, "If only we had died in the land of Egypt! Or if only we had died in this wilderness! ³Why has the LORD brought us to this land to fall by the sword, that our wives and children should become victims? Would it not be better for us to return to Egypt?" ⁴So they said to one another, "Let us select a leader and return to Egypt."

13:24 ᵃLiterally *Cluster*   **13:33** ᵃHebrew *nephilim*

LEADERSHIP REALITIES

OPTIMISM   *Numbers 13; 14*

It was time to *spy out the land* to see who and what the children of Israel would face in their next adventure. The first report was overwhelmingly negative, and the entire community joined in the fear. Then, two young men, Joshua and Caleb, stepped up to the front and into history with a positive report. Caleb has been chronicled forever as a man of a *different spirit,* one who taught that **unbelief sees problems, but faith sees solutions**. Yes, it is easier to be part of the negative assembly, but leaders have been given *a different spirit* by the Lord, and with it they can step into history!

- Don't give in to the fear of the moment.
- Base your vision for any action steps on faith and truth rather than opinion and gossip.
- Believe in God's will for you—that He wants the best for your life.
- Depend on God's resources and abilities rather than your own.
- Replace fear with a declaration of genuine, personal faith in God.
- Don't settle for the natural when you have the supernatural.
- Let your first word always be your best word.

⁵Then Moses and Aaron fell on their faces before all the assembly of the congregation of the children of Israel.

⁶But Joshua the son of Nun and Caleb the son of Jephunneh, *who were* among those who had spied out the land, tore their clothes; ⁷and they spoke to all the congregation of the children of Israel, saying: "The land we passed through to spy out *is* an exceedingly good land. ⁸If the LORD delights in us, then He will bring us into this land and give it to us, 'a land which flows with milk and honey.'ᵃ ⁹Only do not rebel against the LORD, nor fear the people of the land, for they *are* our bread; their protection has departed from them, and the LORD *is* with us. Do not fear them."

¹⁰And all the congregation said to stone them with stones. Now the glory of the LORD appeared in the tabernacle of meeting before all the children of Israel.

MOSES INTERCEDES FOR THE PEOPLE

¹¹Then the LORD said to Moses: "How long will these people reject Me? And how long will they not believe Me, with all the signs which I have performed among them? ¹²I will strike them with the pestilence and disinherit them, and I will make of you a nation greater and mightier than they."

¹³And Moses said to the LORD: "Then the Egyptians will hear *it,* for by Your might You brought these people up from among them, ¹⁴and they will tell *it* to the inhabitants of this land. They have heard that You, LORD, *are* among these people; that You, LORD, are seen face to face and Your cloud stands above them, and You go before them in a pillar of cloud by day and in a pillar of fire by night. ¹⁵Now *if* You kill these people as one man, then the nations which have heard of Your fame will speak, saying, ¹⁶'Because the LORD was not able to bring this people to the land which He swore to give them, therefore He killed them in the wilderness.' ¹⁷And now, I pray, let the power of my Lord be great, just as You have spoken, saying, ¹⁸'The LORD is longsuffering and abundant in mercy, forgiving iniquity and transgression; but He by no means clears *the guilty,* visiting the iniquity of the fathers on the children to the third and fourth *generation.'*ᵃ ¹⁹Pardon the iniquity of this people, I pray, according to the greatness of Your mercy, just as You have forgiven this people, from Egypt even until now."

²⁰Then the LORD said: "I have pardoned, according to your word; ²¹but truly, as I live, all the earth shall be filled with the glory of the LORD— ²²because all these men who have seen My glory and the signs which I did in Egypt and in the wilderness, and have put Me to the test now these ten times, and have not heeded My voice, ²³they certainly shall not see the land of which I swore to their fathers, nor shall any of those who rejected Me see it. ²⁴But My servant Caleb, because he has a different spirit in him and has followed Me fully, I will bring into the land where he went, and his descendants shall inherit it. ²⁵Now the Amalekites and the Canaanites dwell in the valley; tomorrow turn and move out into the wilderness by the Way of the Red Sea."

DEATH SENTENCE ON THE REBELS

²⁶And the LORD spoke to Moses and Aaron, saying, ²⁷"How long *shall I bear with* this evil congregation who complain against Me? I have heard the complaints which the children of Israel make against Me. ²⁸Say to them, 'As I live,' says the LORD, 'just as you have spoken in My hearing, so I will do to you: ²⁹The carcasses of you who have complained against Me shall fall in this wilderness, all of you who were numbered, according to your entire number, from twenty years old and above. ³⁰Except for Caleb the son of Jephunneh and Joshua the son of Nun, you shall by no means enter the land which I swore I would make you dwell in. ³¹But your little ones, whom you said would be victims, I will bring in, and they shall know the land which you have despised. ³²But *as for* you, your carcasses shall fall in this wilderness. ³³And your sons shall be shepherds in the wilderness forty years, and bear the brunt of your infidelity, until your carcasses are consumed in the wilderness. ³⁴According to the number of the days in which you spied out the land, forty days, for each day you shall bear your guilt one year, *namely* forty years, and you shall know My rejection. ³⁵I the LORD have spoken this. I will surely

14:8 ᵃExodus 3:8   14:18 ᵃExodus 34:6, 7

do so to all this evil congregation who are gathered together against Me. In this wilderness they shall be consumed, and there they shall die.' "

³⁶Now the men whom Moses sent to spy out the land, who returned and made all the congregation complain against him by bringing a bad report of the land, ³⁷those very men who brought the evil report about the land, died by the plague before the LORD. ³⁸But Joshua the son of Nun and Caleb the son of Jephunneh remained alive, of the men who went to spy out the land.

A Futile Invasion Attempt

³⁹Then Moses told these words to all the children of Israel, and the people mourned greatly. ⁴⁰And they rose early in the morning and went up to the top of the mountain, saying, "Here we are, and we will go up to the place which the LORD has promised, for we have sinned!"

⁴¹And Moses said, "Now why do you transgress the command of the LORD? For this will not succeed. ⁴²Do not go up, lest you be defeated by your enemies, for the LORD is not among you. ⁴³For the Amalekites and the Canaanites are there before you, and you shall fall by the sword; because you have turned away from the LORD, the LORD will not be with you."

⁴⁴But they presumed to go up to the mountaintop. Nevertheless, neither the ark of the covenant of the LORD nor Moses departed from the camp. ⁴⁵Then the Amalekites and the Canaanites who dwelt in that mountain came down and attacked them, and drove them back as far as Hormah.

Laws of Grain and Drink Offerings

15 And the LORD spoke to Moses, saying, ²"Speak to the children of Israel, and say to them: 'When you have come into the land you are to inhabit, which I am giving to you, ³and you make an offering by fire to the LORD, a burnt offering or a sacrifice, to fulfill a vow or as a freewill offering or in your appointed feasts, to make a sweet aroma to the LORD, from the herd or the flock, ⁴then he who presents his offering to the LORD shall bring a grain offering of one-tenth of an ephah of fine flour mixed with one-fourth of a hin of oil; ⁵and one-fourth of a hin of wine as a drink offering you shall prepare with the burnt

offering or the sacrifice, for each lamb. ⁶Or for a ram you shall prepare as a grain offering two-tenths of an ephah of fine flour mixed with one-third of a hin of oil; ⁷and as a drink offering you shall offer one-third of a hin of wine as a sweet aroma to the LORD. ⁸And when you prepare a young bull as a burnt offering, or as a sacrifice to fulfill a vow, or as a peace offering to the LORD, ⁹then shall be offered with the young bull a grain offering of three-tenths of an ephah of fine flour mixed with half a hin of oil; ¹⁰and you shall bring as the drink offering half a hin of wine as an offering made by fire, a sweet aroma to the LORD.

¹¹'Thus it shall be done for each young bull, for each ram, or for each lamb or young goat. ¹²According to the number that you prepare, so you shall do with everyone according to their number. ¹³All who are native-born shall do these things in this manner, in presenting an offering made by fire, a sweet aroma to the LORD. ¹⁴And if a stranger dwells with you, or whoever is among you throughout your generations, and would present an offering made by fire, a sweet aroma to the LORD, just as you do, so shall he do. ¹⁵One ordinance shall be for you of the assembly and for the stranger who dwells with you, an ordinance forever throughout your generations; as you are, so shall the stranger be before the LORD. ¹⁶One law and one custom shall be for you and for the stranger who dwells with you.' "ᵃ

¹⁷Again the LORD spoke to Moses, saying, ¹⁸"Speak to the children of Israel, and say to them: 'When you come into the land to which I bring you, ¹⁹then it will be, when you eat of the bread of the land, that you shall offer up a heave offering to the LORD. ²⁰You shall offer up a cake of the first of your ground meal as a heave offering; as a heave offering of the threshing floor, so shall you offer it up. ²¹Of the first of your ground meal you shall give to the LORD a heave offering throughout your generations.

Laws Concerning Unintentional Sin

²²'If you sin unintentionally, and do not observe all these commandments which the LORD has spoken to Moses— ²³all that the LORD has commanded you by the hand of Moses, from the

15:16 ᵃCompare Exodus 12:49

day the LORD gave commandment and onward throughout your generations— ^{24}then it will be, if it is unintentionally committed, without the knowledge of the congregation, that the whole congregation shall offer one young bull as a burnt offering, as a sweet aroma to the LORD, with its grain offering and its drink offering, according to the ordinance, and one kid of the goats as a sin offering. ^{25}So the priest shall make atonement for the whole congregation of the children of Israel, and it shall be forgiven them, for it was unintentional; they shall bring their offering, an offering made by fire to the LORD, and their sin offering before the LORD, for their unintended sin. ^{26}It shall be forgiven the whole congregation of the children of Israel and the stranger who dwells among them, because all the people *did it* unintentionally.

^{27}'And if a person sins unintentionally, then he shall bring a female goat in its first year as a sin offering. ^{28}So the priest shall make atonement for the person who sins unintentionally, when he sins unintentionally before the LORD, to make atonement for him; and it shall be forgiven him. ^{29}You shall have one law for him who sins unintentionally, *for* him who is native-born among the children of Israel and for the stranger who dwells among them.

LAW CONCERNING PRESUMPTUOUS SIN

^{30}'But the person who does *anything* presumptuously, *whether he is* native-born or a stranger, that one brings reproach on the LORD, and he shall be cut off from among his people. ^{31}Because he has despised the word of the LORD, and has broken His commandment, that person shall be completely cut off; his guilt *shall be* upon him.' "

PENALTY FOR VIOLATING THE SABBATH

^{32}Now while the children of Israel were in the wilderness, they found a man gathering sticks on the Sabbath day. ^{33}And those who found him gathering sticks brought him to Moses and Aaron, and to all the congregation. ^{34}They put him under guard, because it had not been explained what should be done to him.

^{35}Then the LORD said to Moses, "The man must surely be put to death; all the congregation shall stone him with stones outside the camp."

^{36}So, as the LORD commanded Moses, all the congregation brought him outside the camp and stoned him with stones, and he died.

TASSELS ON GARMENTS

^{37}Again the LORD spoke to Moses, saying, ^{38}"Speak to the children of Israel: Tell them to make tassels on the corners of their garments throughout their generations, and to put a blue thread in the tassels of the corners. ^{39}And you shall have the tassel, that you may look upon it and remember all the commandments of the LORD and do them, and that you *may* not follow the harlotry to which your own heart and your own eyes are inclined, ^{40}and that you may remember and do all My commandments, and be holy for your God. ^{41}I *am* the LORD your God, who brought you out of the land of Egypt, to be your God: I *am* the LORD your God."

REBELLION AGAINST MOSES AND AARON

16 Now Korah the son of Izhar, the son of Kohath, the son of Levi, with Dathan and Abiram the sons of Eliab, and On the son of Peleth, sons of Reuben, took *men;* ^{2}and they rose up before Moses with some of the children of Israel, two hundred and fifty leaders of the congregation, representatives of the congregation, men of renown. ^{3}They gathered together against Moses and Aaron, and said to them, "*You take* too much upon yourselves, for all the congregation *is* holy, every one of them, and the LORD *is* among them. Why then do you exalt yourselves above the assembly of the LORD?"

^{4}So when Moses heard *it,* he fell on his face; ^{5}and he spoke to Korah and all his company, saying, "Tomorrow morning the LORD will show who *is* His and *who is* holy, and will cause *him* to come near to Him. That one whom He chooses He will cause to come near to Him. ^{6}Do this: Take censers, Korah and all your company; ^{7}put fire in them and put incense in them before the LORD tomorrow, and it shall be *that* the man whom the LORD chooses *is* the holy one. *You take* too much upon yourselves, you sons of Levi!"

^{8}Then Moses said to Korah, "Hear now, you sons of Levi: ^{9}*Is it* a small thing to you that the God of Israel has separated you from the congregation of Israel, to bring you near to Himself, to do the work of the tabernacle of the LORD, and to stand before the congregation to serve them; ¹⁰and that He has brought you near *to Himself,* you and all your brethren, the sons of Levi, with you? And are you seeking the priesthood also? ¹¹Therefore you and all your company *are* gathered together against the LORD. And what *is* Aaron that you complain against him?"

¹²And Moses sent to call Dathan and Abiram the sons of Eliab, but they said, "We will not come up! ¹³*Is it* a small thing that you have brought us up out of a land flowing with milk and honey, to kill us in the wilderness, that you should keep acting like a prince over us? ¹⁴Moreover you have not brought us into a land flowing with milk and honey, nor given us inheritance of fields and vineyards. Will you put out the eyes of these men? We will not come up!"

¹⁵Then Moses was very angry, and said to the LORD, "Do not respect their offering. I have not taken one donkey from them, nor have I hurt one of them."

¹⁶And Moses said to Korah, "Tomorrow, you and all your company be present before the LORD—you and they, as well as Aaron. ¹⁷Let each take his censer and put incense in it, and each of you bring his censer before the LORD, two hundred and fifty censers; both you and Aaron, each *with* his censer." ¹⁸So every man took his censer, put fire in it, laid incense on it, and stood at the door of the tabernacle of meeting with Moses and Aaron. ¹⁹And Korah gathered all the congregation against them at the door of the tabernacle of meeting. Then the glory of the LORD appeared to all the congregation.

²⁰And the LORD spoke to Moses and Aaron, saying, ²¹"Separate yourselves from among this congregation, that I may consume them in a moment."

²²Then they fell on their faces, and said, "O God, the God of the spirits of all flesh, shall one man sin, and You be angry with all the congregation?"

²³So the LORD spoke to Moses, saying, ²⁴"Speak to the congregation, saying, 'Get away from the tents of Korah, Dathan, and Abiram.' "

²⁵Then Moses rose and went to Dathan and Abiram, and the elders of Israel followed him. ²⁶And he spoke to the congregation, saying, "De-part now from the tents of these wicked men! Touch nothing of theirs, lest you be consumed in all their sins." ²⁷So they got away from around the tents of Korah, Dathan, and Abiram; and Dathan and Abiram came out and stood at the door of their tents, with their wives, their sons, and their little children.

²⁸And Moses said: "By this you shall know that the LORD has sent me to do all these works, for *I have* not *done them* of my own will. ²⁹If these men die naturally like all men, or if they are visited by the common fate of all men, *then* the LORD has not sent me. ³⁰But if the LORD creates a new thing, and the earth opens its mouth and swallows them up with all that belongs to them, and they go down alive into the pit, then you will understand that these men have rejected the LORD."

³¹Now it came to pass, as he finished speaking all these words, that the ground split apart under them, ³²and the earth opened its mouth and swallowed them up, with their households and all the men with Korah, with all *their* goods. ³³So they and all those with them went down alive into the pit; the earth closed over them, and they perished from among the assembly. ³⁴Then all Israel who *were* around them fled at their cry, for they said, "Lest the earth swallow us up *also!*"

³⁵And a fire came out from the LORD and consumed the two hundred and fifty men who were offering incense.

³⁶Then the LORD spoke to Moses, saying: ³⁷"Tell Eleazar, the son of Aaron the priest, to pick up the censers out of the blaze, for they are holy, and scatter the fire some distance away. ³⁸The censers of these men who sinned against their own souls, let them be made into hammered plates as a covering for the altar. Because they presented them before the LORD, therefore they are holy; and they shall be a sign to the children of Israel." ³⁹So Eleazar the priest took the bronze censers, which those who were burned up had presented, and they were hammered out as a covering on the altar, ⁴⁰*to be* a memorial to the children of Israel that no outsider, who *is* not a descendant of Aaron, should come near to offer incense before the LORD, that he might not become like Korah and his companions, just as the LORD had said to him through Moses.

COMPLAINTS OF THE PEOPLE

⁴¹On the next day all the congregation of the children of Israel complained against Moses and Aaron, saying, "You have killed the people of the LORD." ⁴²Now it happened, when the congregation had gathered against Moses and Aaron, that they turned toward the tabernacle of meeting; and suddenly the cloud covered it, and the glory of the LORD appeared. ⁴³Then Moses and Aaron came before the tabernacle of meeting.

⁴⁴And the LORD spoke to Moses, saying, ⁴⁵"Get away from among this congregation, that I may consume them in a moment."

And they fell on their faces.

⁴⁶So Moses said to Aaron, "Take a censer and put fire in it from the altar, put incense *on it,* and take it quickly to the congregation and make atonement for them; for wrath has gone out from the LORD. The plague has begun." ⁴⁷Then Aaron took *it* as Moses commanded, and ran into the midst of the assembly; and already the plague had begun among the people. So he put in the incense and made atonement for the people. ⁴⁸And he stood between the dead and the living; so the plague was stopped. ⁴⁹Now those who died in the plague were fourteen thousand seven hundred, besides those who died in the Korah incident. ⁵⁰So Aaron returned to Moses at the door of the tabernacle of meeting, for the plague had stopped.

THE BUDDING OF AARON'S ROD

17 And the LORD spoke to Moses, saying: ²"Speak to the children of Israel, and get from them a rod from each father's house, all their leaders according to their fathers' houses—twelve rods. Write each man's name on his rod. ³And you shall write Aaron's name on the rod of Levi. For there shall be one rod for the head of *each* father's house. ⁴Then you shall place them in the tabernacle of meeting before the Testimony, where I meet with you. ⁵And it shall be *that* the rod of the man whom I choose will blossom; thus I will rid Myself of the complaints of the children of Israel, which they make against you."

⁶So Moses spoke to the children of Israel, and each of their leaders gave him a rod apiece, for each leader according to their fathers' houses, twelve rods; and the rod of Aaron *was* among their rods. ⁷And Moses placed the rods before the LORD in the tabernacle of witness.

⁸Now it came to pass on the next day that Moses went into the tabernacle of witness, and behold, the rod of Aaron, of the house of Levi, had sprouted and put forth buds, had produced blossoms and yielded ripe almonds. ⁹Then Moses brought out all the rods from before the LORD to all the children of Israel; and they looked, and each man took his rod.

¹⁰And the LORD said to Moses, "Bring Aaron's rod back before the Testimony, to be kept as a sign against the rebels, that you may put their complaints away from Me, lest they die." ¹¹Thus did Moses; just as the LORD had commanded him, so he did.

¹²So the children of Israel spoke to Moses, saying, "Surely we die, we perish, we all perish! ¹³Whoever even comes near the tabernacle of the LORD must die. Shall we all utterly die?"

DUTIES OF PRIESTS AND LEVITES

18 Then the LORD said to Aaron: "You and your sons and your father's house with you shall bear the iniquity *related to* the sanctuary, and you and your sons with you shall bear the iniquity *associated with* your priesthood. ²Also bring with you your brethren of the tribe of Levi, the tribe of your father, that they may be joined with you and serve you while you and your sons *are* with you before the tabernacle of witness. ³They shall attend to your needs and all the needs of the tabernacle; but they shall not come near the articles of the sanctuary and the altar, lest they die—they and you also. ⁴They shall be joined with you and attend to the needs of the tabernacle of meeting, for all the work of the tabernacle; but an outsider shall not come near you. ⁵And you shall attend to the duties of the sanctuary and the duties of the altar, that there *may* be no more wrath on the children of Israel. ⁶Behold, I Myself have taken your brethren the Levites from among the children of Israel; *they are* a gift to you, given by the LORD, to do the work of the tabernacle of meeting. ⁷Therefore you and your sons with you shall attend to your priesthood for everything at the altar and behind the veil; and you shall serve. I give your priesthood *to you* as a gift for service, but the outsider who comes near shall be put to death."

Offerings for Support of the Priests

[8]And the LORD spoke to Aaron: "Here, I Myself have also given you charge of My heave offerings, all the holy gifts of the children of Israel; I have given them as a portion to you and your sons, as an ordinance forever. [9]This shall be yours of the most holy things *reserved* from the fire: every offering of theirs, every grain offering and every sin offering and every trespass offering which they render to Me, *shall be* most holy for you and your sons. [10]In a most holy *place* you shall eat it; every male shall eat it. It shall be holy to you.

[11]"This also *is* yours: the heave offering of their gift, with all the wave offerings of the children of Israel; I have given them to you, and your sons and daughters with you, as an ordinance forever. Everyone who is clean in your house may eat it.

[12]"All the best of the oil, all the best of the new wine and the grain, their firstfruits which they offer to the LORD, I have given them to you. [13]Whatever first ripe fruit is in their land, which they bring to the LORD, shall be yours. Everyone who is clean in your house may eat it.

[14]"Every devoted thing in Israel shall be yours.

[15]"Everything that first opens the womb of all flesh, which they bring to the LORD, whether man or beast, shall be yours; nevertheless the firstborn of man you shall surely redeem, and the firstborn of unclean animals you shall redeem. [16]And those redeemed of the devoted things you shall redeem when one month old, according to your valuation, for five shekels of silver, according to the shekel of the sanctuary, which *is* twenty gerahs. [17]But the firstborn of a cow, the firstborn of a sheep, or the firstborn of a goat you shall not redeem; they *are* holy. You shall sprinkle their blood on the altar, and burn their fat *as* an offering made by fire for a sweet aroma to the LORD. [18]And their flesh shall be yours, just as the wave breast and the right thigh are yours.

[19]"All the heave offerings of the holy things, which the children of Israel offer to the LORD, I have given to you and your sons and daughters with you as an ordinance forever; it *is* a covenant of salt forever before the LORD with you and your descendants with you."

[20]Then the LORD said to Aaron: "You shall have no inheritance in their land, nor shall you have any portion among them; I *am* your portion and your inheritance among the children of Israel.

Tithes for Support of the Levites

[21]"Behold, I have given the children of Levi all the tithes in Israel as an inheritance in return for the work which they perform, the work of the tabernacle of meeting. [22]Hereafter the children of Israel shall not come near the tabernacle of meeting, lest they bear sin and die. [23]But the Levites shall perform the work of the tabernacle of meeting, and they shall bear their iniquity; *it shall be* a statute forever, throughout your generations, that among the children of Israel they shall have no inheritance. [24]For the tithes of the children of Israel, which they offer up *as* a heave offering to the LORD, I have given to the Levites as an inheritance; therefore I have said to them, 'Among the children of Israel they shall have no inheritance.'"

The Tithe of the Levites

[25]Then the LORD spoke to Moses, saying, [26]"Speak thus to the Levites, and say to them: 'When you take from the children of Israel the tithes which I have given you from them as your inheritance, then you shall offer up a heave offering of it to the LORD, a tenth of the tithe. [27]And your heave offering shall be reckoned to you as though *it were* the grain of the threshing floor and as the fullness of the winepress. [28]Thus you shall also offer a heave offering to the LORD from all your tithes which you receive from the children of Israel, and you shall give the LORD's heave offering from it to Aaron the priest. [29]Of all your gifts you shall offer up every heave offering due to the LORD, from all the best of them, the consecrated part of them.' [30]Therefore you shall say to them: 'When you have lifted up the best of it, then *the rest* shall be accounted to the Levites as the produce of the threshing floor and as the produce of the winepress. [31]You may eat it in any place, you and your households, for it *is* your reward for your work in the tabernacle of meeting.

³²And you shall bear no sin because of it, when you have lifted up the best of it. But you shall not profane the holy gifts of the children of Israel, lest you die.' "

LAWS OF PURIFICATION

19 Now the LORD spoke to Moses and Aaron, saying, ²"This *is* the ordinance of the law which the LORD has commanded, saying: 'Speak to the children of Israel, that they bring you a red heifer without blemish, in which there *is* no defect *and* on which a yoke has never come. ³You shall give it to Eleazar the priest, that he may take it outside the camp, and it shall be slaughtered before him; ⁴and Eleazar the priest shall take some of its blood with his finger, and sprinkle some of its blood seven times directly in front of the tabernacle of meeting. ⁵Then the heifer shall be burned in his sight: its hide, its flesh, its blood, and its offal shall be burned. ⁶And the priest shall take cedar wood and hyssop and scarlet, and cast *them* into the midst of the fire burning the heifer. ⁷Then the priest shall wash his clothes, he shall bathe in water, and afterward he shall come into the camp; the priest shall be unclean until evening. ⁸And the one who burns it shall wash his clothes in water, bathe in water, and shall be unclean until evening. ⁹Then a man *who is* clean shall gather up the ashes of the heifer, and store *them* outside the camp in a clean place; and they shall be kept for the congregation of the children of Israel for the water of purification;ᵃ it *is* for purifying from sin. ¹⁰And the one who gathers the ashes of the heifer shall wash his clothes, and be unclean until evening. It shall be a statute forever to the children of Israel and to the stranger who dwells among them.

¹¹"He who touches the dead body of anyone shall be unclean seven days. ¹²He shall purify himself with the water on the third day and on the seventh day; *then* he will be clean. But if he does not purify himself on the third day and on the seventh day, he will not be clean. ¹³Whoever touches the body of anyone who has died, and does not purify himself, defiles the tabernacle of the LORD. That person shall be cut off from Israel. He shall be unclean, because the water of purification was not sprinkled on him; his uncleanness *is* still on him.

¹⁴"This *is* the law when a man dies in a tent: All who come into the tent and all who *are* in the tent shall be unclean seven days; ¹⁵and every open vessel, which has no cover fastened on it, *is* unclean. ¹⁶Whoever in the open field touches one who is slain by a sword or who has died, or a bone of a man, or a grave, shall be unclean seven days.

¹⁷"And for an unclean *person* they shall take some of the ashes of the heifer burnt for purification from sin, and running water shall be put on them in a vessel. ¹⁸A clean person shall take hyssop and dip *it* in the water, sprinkle *it* on the tent, on all the vessels, on the persons who were there, or on the one who touched a bone, the slain, the dead, or a grave. ¹⁹The clean *person* shall sprinkle the unclean on the third day and on the seventh day; and on the seventh day he shall purify himself, wash his clothes, and bathe in water; and at evening he shall be clean.

²⁰"But the man who is unclean and does not purify himself, that person shall be cut off from among the assembly, because he has defiled the sanctuary of the LORD. The water of purification has not been sprinkled on him; he *is* unclean. ²¹It shall be a perpetual statute for them. He who sprinkles the water of purification shall wash his clothes; and he who touches the water of purification shall be unclean until evening. ²²Whatever the unclean *person* touches shall be unclean; and the person who touches *it* shall be unclean until evening.' "

MOSES' ERROR AT KADESH

20 Then the children of Israel, the whole congregation, came into the Wilderness of Zin in the first month, and the people stayed in Kadesh; and Miriam died there and was buried there.

²Now there was no water for the congregation; so they gathered together against Moses and Aaron. ³And the people contended with Moses and spoke, saying: "If only we had died when our brethren died before the LORD! ⁴Why have you brought up the assembly of the LORD into this wilderness, that we and our animals should die here? ⁵And why have you made us come up out of Egypt, to bring us to this evil place? It *is* not a

19:9 ᵃLiterally *impurity*

place of grain or figs or vines or pomegranates; nor *is* there any water to drink." ⁶So Moses and Aaron went from the presence of the assembly to the door of the tabernacle of meeting, and they fell on their faces. And the glory of the LORD appeared to them.

⁷Then the LORD spoke to Moses, saying, ⁸"Take the rod; you and your brother Aaron gather the congregation together. Speak to the rock before their eyes, and it will yield its water; thus you shall bring water for them out of the rock, and give drink to the congregation and their animals." ⁹So Moses took the rod from before the LORD as He commanded him.

¹⁰And Moses and Aaron gathered the assembly together before the rock; and he said to them, "Hear now, you rebels! Must we bring water for you out of this rock?" ¹¹Then Moses lifted his hand and struck the rock twice with his rod; and water came out abundantly, and the congregation and their animals drank.

¹²Then the LORD spoke to Moses and Aaron, "Because you did not believe Me, to hallow Me in the eyes of the children of Israel, therefore you shall not bring this assembly into the land which I have given them."

¹³This *was* the water of Meribah,ᵃ because the children of Israel contended with the LORD, and He was hallowed among them.

Passage Through Edom Refused

¹⁴Now Moses sent messengers from Kadesh to the king of Edom. "Thus says your brother Israel: 'You know all the hardship that has befallen us, ¹⁵how our fathers went down to Egypt, and we dwelt in Egypt a long time, and the Egyptians afflicted us and our fathers. ¹⁶When we cried out to the LORD, He heard our voice and sent the Angel and brought us up out of Egypt; now here we are in Kadesh, a city on the edge of your border. ¹⁷Please let us pass through your country. We will not pass through fields or vineyards, nor will we drink water from wells; we will go along the King's Highway; we will not turn aside to the right hand or to the left until we have passed through your territory.' "

¹⁸Then Edom said to him, "You shall not pass through my *land,* lest I come out against you with the sword."

¹⁹So the children of Israel said to him, "We will go by the Highway, and if I or my livestock drink any of your water, then I will pay for it; let me only pass through on foot, nothing *more."*

²⁰Then he said, "You shall not pass through." So Edom came out against them with many men and with a strong hand. ²¹Thus Edom refused to give Israel passage through his territory; so Israel turned away from him.

Death of Aaron

²²Now the children of Israel, the whole congregation, journeyed from Kadesh and came to Mount Hor. ²³And the LORD spoke to Moses and Aaron in Mount Hor by the border of the land of Edom, saying: ²⁴"Aaron shall be gathered to his people, for he shall not enter the land which I have given to the children of Israel, because you rebelled against My word at the water of Meribah. ²⁵Take Aaron and Eleazar his son, and bring them up to Mount Hor; ²⁶and strip Aaron of his garments and put them on Eleazar his son; for Aaron shall be gathered *to his people* and die there." ²⁷So Moses did just as the LORD commanded, and they went up to Mount Hor in the sight of all the congregation. ²⁸Moses stripped Aaron of his garments and put them on Eleazar his son; and Aaron died there on the top of the mountain. Then Moses and Eleazar came down from the mountain. ²⁹Now when all the congregation saw that Aaron was dead, all the house of Israel mourned for Aaron thirty days.

Canaanites Defeated at Hormah

21 The king of Arad, the Canaanite, who dwelt in the South, heard that Israel was coming on the road to Atharim. Then he fought against Israel and took *some* of them prisoners. ²So Israel made a vow to the LORD, and said, "If You will indeed deliver this people into my hand, then I will utterly destroy their cities." ³And the LORD listened to the voice of Israel and delivered up the Canaanites, and they utterly destroyed them and their cities. So the name of that place was called Hormah.ᵃ

20:13 ᵃLiterally *Contention* 21:3 ᵃLiterally *Utter Destruction*

The Bronze Serpent

⁴Then they journeyed from Mount Hor by the Way of the Red Sea, to go around the land of Edom; and the soul of the people became very discouraged on the way. ⁵And the people spoke against God and against Moses: "Why have you brought us up out of Egypt to die in the wilderness? For *there is* no food and no water, and our soul loathes this worthless bread." ⁶So the Lord sent fiery serpents among the people, and they bit the people; and many of the people of Israel died.

⁷Therefore the people came to Moses, and said, "We have sinned, for we have spoken against the Lord and against you; pray to the Lord that He take away the serpents from us." So Moses prayed for the people.

⁸Then the Lord said to Moses, "Make a fiery *serpent,* and set it on a pole; and it shall be that everyone who is bitten, when he looks at it, shall live." ⁹So Moses made a bronze serpent, and put it on a pole; and so it was, if a serpent had bitten anyone, when he looked at the bronze serpent, he lived.

From Mount Hor to Moab

¹⁰Now the children of Israel moved on and camped in Oboth. ¹¹And they journeyed from Oboth and camped at Ije Abarim, in the wilderness which *is* east of Moab, toward the sunrise. ¹²From there they moved and camped in the Valley of Zered. ¹³From there they moved and camped on the other side of the Arnon, which *is* in the wilderness that extends from the border of the Amorites; for the Arnon *is* the border of Moab, between Moab and the Amorites. ¹⁴Therefore it is said in the Book of the Wars of the Lord:

> "Waheb in Suphah,ᵃ
> The brooks of the Arnon,
> ¹⁵And the slope of the brooks
> That reaches to the dwelling of Ar,
> And lies on the border of Moab."

¹⁶From there *they went* to Beer, which *is* the well where the Lord said to Moses, "Gather the people together, and I will give them water." ¹⁷Then Israel sang this song:

> "Spring up, O well!
> All of you sing to it—
> ¹⁸The well the leaders sank,
> Dug by the nation's nobles,
> By the lawgiver, with their staves."

And from the wilderness *they went* to Mattanah, ¹⁹from Mattanah to Nahaliel, from Nahaliel to Bamoth, ²⁰and from Bamoth, *in* the valley that *is* in the country of Moab, to the top of Pisgah which looks down on the wasteland.ᵃ

King Sihon Defeated

²¹Then Israel sent messengers to Sihon king of the Amorites, saying, ²²"Let me pass through your land. We will not turn aside into fields or vineyards; we will not drink water from wells. We will go by the King's Highway until we have passed through your territory." ²³But Sihon would not allow Israel to pass through his territory. So Sihon gathered all his people together and went out against Israel in the wilderness, and he came to Jahaz and fought against Israel. ²⁴Then Israel defeated him with the edge of the sword, and took possession of his land from the Arnon to the Jabbok, as far as the people of Ammon; for the border of the people of Ammon *was* fortified. ²⁵So Israel took all these cities, and Israel dwelt in all the cities of the Amorites, in Heshbon and in all its villages. ²⁶For Heshbon *was* the city of Sihon king of the Amorites, who had fought against the former king of Moab, and had taken all his land from his hand as far as the Arnon. ²⁷Therefore those who speak in proverbs say:

> "Come to Heshbon, let it be built;
> Let the city of Sihon be repaired.

> ²⁸"For fire went out from Heshbon,
> A flame from the city of Sihon;
> It consumed Ar of Moab,
> The lords of the heights of the Arnon.
> ²⁹Woe to you, Moab!
> You have perished, O people of
>   Chemosh!

21:14 ᵃAncient unknown places; Vulgate reads *What He did in the Red Sea.* **21:20** ᵃHebrew *Jeshimon*

He has given his sons as fugitives,
And his daughters into captivity,
To Sihon king of the Amorites.

30"But we have shot at them;
Heshbon has perished as far as Dibon.
Then we laid waste as far as Nophah,
Which *reaches* to Medeba."

31Thus Israel dwelt in the land of the Amorites. 32Then Moses sent to spy out Jazer; and they took its villages and drove out the Amorites who *were* there.

KING OG DEFEATED

33And they turned and went up by the way to Bashan. So Og king of Bashan went out against them, he and all his people, to battle at Edrei. 34Then the LORD said to Moses, "Do not fear him, for I have delivered him into your hand, with all his people and his land; and you shall do to him as you did to Sihon king of the Amorites, who dwelt at Heshbon." 35So they defeated him, his sons, and all his people, until there was no survivor left him; and they took possession of his land.

BALAK SENDS FOR BALAAM

22 Then the children of Israel moved, and camped in the plains of Moab on the side of the Jordan *across from* Jericho.

2Now Balak the son of Zippor saw all that Israel had done to the Amorites. 3And Moab was exceedingly afraid of the people because they *were* many, and Moab was sick with dread because of the children of Israel. 4So Moab said to the elders of Midian, "Now this company will lick up everything around us, as an ox licks up the grass of the field." And Balak the son of Zippor *was* king of the Moabites at that time. 5Then he sent messengers to Balaam the son of Beor at Pethor, which *is* near the River[a] in the land of the sons of his people,[b] to call him, saying: "Look, a people has come from Egypt. See, they cover the face of the earth, and are settling next to me! 6Therefore please come at once, curse this people for me, for they *are* too mighty for me. Perhaps I shall be able to defeat them and drive them out of the land, for I know that he whom

you bless *is* blessed, and he whom you curse is cursed."

7So the elders of Moab and the elders of Midian departed with the diviner's fee in their hand, and they came to Balaam and spoke to him the words of Balak. 8And he said to them, "Lodge here tonight, and I will bring back word to you, as the LORD speaks to me." So the princes of Moab stayed with Balaam.

9Then God came to Balaam and said, "Who *are* these men with you?"

10So Balaam said to God, "Balak the son of Zippor, king of Moab, has sent to me, *saying,* 11'Look, a people has come out of Egypt, and they cover the face of the earth. Come now, curse them for me; perhaps I shall be able to overpower them and drive them out.' "

12And God said to Balaam, "You shall not go with them; you shall not curse the people, for they *are* blessed."

13So Balaam rose in the morning and said to the princes of Balak, "Go back to your land, for the LORD has refused to give me permission to go with you."

14And the princes of Moab rose and went to Balak, and said, "Balaam refuses to come with us."

15Then Balak again sent princes, more numerous and more honorable than they. 16And they came to Balaam and said to him, "Thus says Balak the son of Zippor: 'Please let nothing hinder you from coming to me; 17for I will certainly honor you greatly, and I will do whatever you say to me. Therefore please come, curse this people for me.' "

18Then Balaam answered and said to the servants of Balak, "Though Balak were to give me his house full of silver and gold, I could not go beyond the word of the LORD my God, to do less or more. 19Now therefore, please, you also stay here tonight, that I may know what more the LORD will say to me."

20And God came to Balaam at night and said to him, "If the men come to call you, rise *and* go with them; but only the word which I speak to you—that you shall do." 21So Balaam rose in the morning, saddled his donkey, and went with the princes of Moab.

22:5 [a]That is, the Euphrates [b]Or *the people of Amau*

BALAAM, THE DONKEY, AND THE ANGEL

22Then God's anger was aroused because he went, and the Angel of the LORD took His stand in the way as an adversary against him. And he was riding on his donkey, and his two servants *were* with him. 23Now the donkey saw the Angel of the LORD standing in the way with His drawn sword in His hand, and the donkey turned aside out of the way and went into the field. So Balaam struck the donkey to turn her back onto the road. 24Then the Angel of the LORD stood in a narrow path between the vineyards, *with* a wall on this side and a wall on that side. 25And when the donkey saw the Angel of the LORD, she pushed herself against the wall and crushed Balaam's foot against the wall; so he struck her again. 26Then the Angel of the LORD went further, and stood in a narrow place where there *was* no way to turn either to the right hand or to the left. 27And when the donkey saw the Angel of the LORD, she lay down under Balaam; so Balaam's anger was aroused, and he struck the donkey with his staff.

28Then the LORD opened the mouth of the donkey, and she said to Balaam, "What have I done to you, that you have struck me these three times?"

29And Balaam said to the donkey, "Because you have abused me. I wish there were a sword in my hand, for now I would kill you!"

30So the donkey said to Balaam, "*Am* I not your donkey on which you have ridden, ever since *I became* yours, to this day? Was I ever disposed to do this to you?"

And he said, "No."

31Then the LORD opened Balaam's eyes, and he saw the Angel of the LORD standing in the way with His drawn sword in His hand; and he bowed his head and fell flat on his face. 32And the Angel of the LORD said to him, "Why have you struck your donkey these three times? Behold, I have come out to stand against you, because *your* way is perverse before Me. 33The donkey saw Me and turned aside from Me these three times. If she had not turned aside from Me, surely I would also have killed you by now, and let her live."

34And Balaam said to the Angel of the LORD, "I have sinned, for I did not know You stood in the way against me. Now therefore, if it displeases You, I will turn back."

35Then the Angel of the LORD said to Balaam, "Go with the men, but only the word that I speak to you, that you shall speak." So Balaam went with the princes of Balak.

36Now when Balak heard that Balaam was coming, he went out to meet him at the city of Moab, which *is* on the border at the Arnon, the boundary of the territory. 37Then Balak said to Balaam, "Did I not earnestly send to you, calling for you? Why did you not come to me? Am I not able to honor you?"

38And Balaam said to Balak, "Look, I have come to you! Now, have I any power at all to say anything? The word that God puts in my mouth, that I must speak." 39So Balaam went with Balak, and they came to Kirjath Huzoth. 40Then Balak offered oxen and sheep, and he sent *some* to Balaam and to the princes who *were* with him.

BALAAM'S FIRST PROPHECY

41So it was, the next day, that Balak took Balaam and brought him up to the high places of Baal, that from there he might observe the extent of the people.

23 Then Balaam said to Balak, "Build seven altars for me here, and prepare for me here seven bulls and seven rams."

2And Balak did just as Balaam had spoken, and Balak and Balaam offered a bull and a ram on *each* altar. 3Then Balaam said to Balak, "Stand by your burnt offering, and I will go; perhaps the LORD will come to meet me, and whatever He shows me I will tell you." So he went to a desolate height. 4And God met Balaam, and he said to Him, "I have prepared the seven altars, and I have offered on *each* altar a bull and a ram."

5Then the LORD put a word in Balaam's mouth, and said, "Return to Balak, and thus you shall speak." 6So he returned to him, and there he was, standing by his burnt offering, he and all the princes of Moab.

7And he took up his oracle and said:

"Balak the king of Moab has brought me from
        Aram,
    From the mountains of the east.

'Come, curse Jacob for me,
And come, denounce Israel!'

[8]"How shall I curse whom God has not
    cursed?
And how shall I denounce *whom* the LORD
    has not denounced?
[9]For from the top of the rocks I see him,
And from the hills I behold him;
There! A people dwelling alone,
Not reckoning itself among the nations.

[10]"Who can count the dust[a] of Jacob,
Or number one-fourth of Israel?
Let me die the death of the righteous,
And let my end be like his!"

[11]Then Balak said to Balaam, "What have you done to me? I took you to curse my enemies, and look, you have blessed *them* bountifully!"

[12]So he answered and said, "Must I not take heed to speak what the LORD has put in my mouth?"

Balaam's Second Prophecy

[13]Then Balak said to him, "Please come with me to another place from which you may see them; you shall see only the outer part of them, and shall not see them all; curse them for me from there." [14]So he brought him to the field of Zophim, to the top of Pisgah, and built seven altars, and offered a bull and a ram on *each* altar.

[15]And he said to Balak, "Stand here by your burnt offering while I meet[a] *the* LORD over there."

[16]Then the LORD met Balaam, and put a word in his mouth, and said, "Go back to Balak, and thus you shall speak." [17]So he came to him, and there he was, standing by his burnt offering, and the princes of Moab were with him. And Balak said to him, "What has the LORD spoken?"

[18]Then he took up his oracle and said:

"Rise up, Balak, and hear!
Listen to me, son of Zippor!

[19]"God *is* not a man, that He should lie,
Nor a son of man, that He should repent.
Has He said, and will He not do?

Or has He spoken, and will He not make it
    good?
[20]Behold, I have received *a command* to bless;
He has blessed, and I cannot reverse it.

[21]"He has not observed iniquity in Jacob,
Nor has He seen wickedness in Israel.
The LORD his God *is* with him,
And the shout of a King *is* among them.
[22]God brings them out of Egypt;
He has strength like a wild ox.

[23]"For *there is* no sorcery against Jacob,
Nor any divination against Israel.
It now must be said of Jacob
And of Israel, 'Oh, what God has done!'
[24]Look, a people rises like a lioness,
And lifts itself up like a lion;
It shall not lie down until it devours the
    prey,
And drinks the blood of the slain."

[25]Then Balak said to Balaam, "Neither curse them at all, nor bless them at all!"

[26]So Balaam answered and said to Balak, "Did I not tell you, saying, 'All that the LORD speaks, that I must do'?"

Balaam's Third Prophecy

[27]Then Balak said to Balaam, "Please come, I will take you to another place; perhaps it will please God that you may curse them for me from there." [28]So Balak took Balaam to the top of Peor, that overlooks the wasteland.[a] [29]Then Balaam said to Balak, "Build for me here seven altars, and prepare for me here seven bulls and seven rams." [30]And Balak did as Balaam had said, and offered a bull and a ram on *every* altar.

24 Now when Balaam saw that it pleased the LORD to bless Israel, he did not go as at other times, to seek to use sorcery, but he set his face toward the wilderness. [2]And Balaam raised his eyes, and saw Israel encamped according to their tribes; and the Spirit of God came upon him.

[3]Then he took up his oracle and said:

23:10 [a]Or *dust cloud*   **23:15** [a]Following Masoretic Text, Targum, and Vulgate; Syriac reads *call*; Septuagint reads *go and ask God.* **23:28** [a]Hebrew *Jeshimon*

"The utterance of Balaam the son of Beor,
  The utterance of the man whose eyes are
      opened,
⁴The utterance of him who hears the words
      of God,
  Who sees the vision of the Almighty,
  Who falls down, with eyes wide open:

⁵"How lovely are your tents, O Jacob!
  Your dwellings, O Israel!
  ⁶Like valleys that stretch out,
  Like gardens by the riverside,
  Like aloes planted by the LORD,
  Like cedars beside the waters.
⁷He shall pour water from his buckets,
  And his seed *shall be* in many waters.

"His king shall be higher than Agag,
  And his kingdom shall be exalted.

⁸"God brings him out of Egypt;
  He has strength like a wild ox;
  He shall consume the nations, his
      enemies;
  He shall break their bones
  And pierce *them* with his arrows.
⁹He bows down, he lies down as a lion;
  And as a lion, who shall rouse him?'ᵃ

"Blessed *is* he who blesses you,
  And cursed *is* he who curses you."

¹⁰Then Balak's anger was aroused against Balaam, and he struck his hands together; and Balak said to Balaam, "I called you to curse my enemies, and look, you have bountifully blessed *them* these three times! ¹¹Now therefore, flee to your place. I said I would greatly honor you, but in fact, the LORD has kept you back from honor."

¹²So Balaam said to Balak, "Did I not also speak to your messengers whom you sent to me, saying, ¹³'If Balak were to give me his house full of silver and gold, I could not go beyond the word of the LORD, to do good or bad of my own will. What the LORD says, that I must speak'? ¹⁴And now, indeed, I am going to my people. Come, I will advise you what this people will do to your people in the latter days."

BALAAM'S FOURTH PROPHECY

¹⁵So he took up his oracle and said:

"The utterance of Balaam the son of Beor,
  And the utterance of the man whose eyes are
      opened;
¹⁶The utterance of him who hears the words of
      God,
  And has the knowledge of the Most High,
  Who sees the vision of the Almighty,
  Who falls down, with eyes wide open:

¹⁷"I see Him, but not now;
  I behold Him, but not near;
  A Star shall come out of Jacob;
  A Scepter shall rise out of Israel,
  And batter the brow of Moab,
  And destroy all the sons of tumult.ᵃ

¹⁸"And Edom shall be a possession;
  Seir also, his enemies, shall be a possession,
  While Israel does valiantly.
¹⁹Out of Jacob One shall have dominion,
  And destroy the remains of the city."

²⁰Then he looked on Amalek, and he took up his oracle and said:

"Amalek *was* first among the nations,
  But *shall be* last until he perishes."

²¹Then he looked on the Kenites, and he took up his oracle and said:

"Firm is your dwelling place,
  And your nest is set in the rock;
²²Nevertheless Kain shall be burned.
  How long until Asshur carries you away
      captive?"

²³Then he took up his oracle and said:

"Alas! Who shall live when God does this?
²⁴But ships *shall come* from the coasts of Cyprus,ᵃ
  And they shall afflict Asshur and afflict Eber,
  And so shall *Amalek*,ᵇ until he perishes."

24:9 ᵃGenesis 49:9 24:17 ᵃHebrew *Sheth* (compare Jeremiah 48:45) 24:24 ᵃHebrew *Kittim* ᵇLiterally *he* or *that one*

²⁵So Balaam rose and departed and returned to his place; Balak also went his way.

ISRAEL'S HARLOTRY IN MOAB

25 Now Israel remained in Acacia Grove,^a and the people began to commit harlotry with the women of Moab. ²They invited the people to the sacrifices of their gods, and the people ate and bowed down to their gods. ³So Israel was joined to Baal of Peor, and the anger of the LORD was aroused against Israel.

⁴Then the LORD said to Moses, "Take all the leaders of the people and hang the offenders before the LORD, out in the sun, that the fierce anger of the LORD may turn away from Israel."

⁵So Moses said to the judges of Israel, "Every one of you kill his men who were joined to Baal of Peor."

⁶And indeed, one of the children of Israel came and presented to his brethren a Midianite woman in the sight of Moses and in the sight of all the congregation of the children of Israel, who *were* weeping at the door of the tabernacle of meeting. ⁷Now when Phinehas the son of Eleazar, the son of Aaron the priest, saw *it,* he rose from among the congregation and took a javelin in his hand; ⁸and he went after the man of Israel into the tent and thrust both of them through, the man of Israel, and the woman through her body. So the plague was stopped among the children of Israel. ⁹And those who died in the plague were twenty-four thousand.

¹⁰Then the LORD spoke to Moses, saying: ¹¹"Phinehas the son of Eleazar, the son of Aaron the priest, has turned back My wrath from the children of Israel, because he was zealous with My zeal among them, so that I did not consume the children of Israel in My zeal. ¹²Therefore say, 'Behold, I give to him My covenant of peace; ¹³and it shall be to him and his descendants after him a covenant of an everlasting priesthood, because he was zealous for his God, and made atonement for the children of Israel.' "

¹⁴Now the name of the Israelite who was killed, who was killed with the Midianite woman, *was* Zimri the son of Salu, a leader of a father's house among the Simeonites. ¹⁵And the name of the Midianite woman who was killed *was* Cozbi

the daughter of Zur; he *was* head of the people of a father's house in Midian.

¹⁶Then the LORD spoke to Moses, saying: ¹⁷"Harass the Midianites, and attack them; ¹⁸for they harassed you with their schemes by which they seduced you in the matter of Peor and in the matter of Cozbi, the daughter of a leader of Midian, their sister, who was killed in the day of the plague because of Peor."

THE SECOND CENSUS OF ISRAEL

26 And it came to pass, after the plague, that the LORD spoke to Moses and Eleazar the son of Aaron the priest, saying: ²"Take a census of all the congregation of the children of Israel from twenty years old and above, by their fathers' houses, all who are able to go to war in Israel." ³So Moses and Eleazar the priest spoke with them in the plains of Moab by the Jordan, *across from* Jericho, saying: ⁴"*Take a census of the people* from twenty years old and above, just as the LORD commanded Moses and the children of Israel who came out of the land of Egypt."

⁵Reuben *was* the firstborn of Israel. The children of Reuben *were: of* Hanoch, the family of the Hanochites; *of* Pallu, the family of the Palluites; ⁶*of* Hezron, the family of the Hezronites; *of* Carmi, the family of the Carmites. ⁷These *are* the families of the Reubenites: those who were numbered of them were forty-three thousand seven hundred and thirty. ⁸And the son of Pallu *was* Eliab. ⁹The sons of Eliab *were* Nemuel, Dathan, and Abiram. These *are* the Dathan and Abiram, representatives of the congregation, who contended against Moses and Aaron in the company of Korah, when they contended against the LORD; ¹⁰and the earth opened its mouth and swallowed them up together with Korah when that company died, when the fire devoured two hundred and fifty men; and they became a sign. ¹¹Nevertheless the children of Korah did not die.

¹²The sons of Simeon according to their families *were: of* Nemuel,^a the family of the Nemuelites; *of* Jamin, the family of the Jaminites; *of* Jachin,^b the family of the Jachinites; ¹³*of* Zerah,^a

25:1 ^aHebrew *Shittim*   26:12 ^aSpelled *Jemuel* in Genesis 46:10 and Exodus 6:15   ^bCalled *Jarib* in 1 Chronicles 4:24   26:13 ^aCalled *Zohar* in Genesis 46:10

the family of the Zarhites; *of* Shaul, the family of the Shaulites. [14]These *are* the families of the Simeonites: twenty-two thousand two hundred.

[15]The sons of Gad according to their families *were: of* Zephon,[a] the family of the Zephonites; *of* Haggi, the family of the Haggites; *of* Shuni, the family of the Shunites; [16]*of* Ozni,[a] the family of the Oznites; *of* Eri, the family of the Erites; [17]*of* Arod,[a] the family of the Arodites; *of* Areli, the family of the Arelites. [18]These *are* the families of the sons of Gad according to those who were numbered of them: forty thousand five hundred.

[19]The sons of Judah *were* Er and Onan; and Er and Onan died in the land of Canaan. [20]And the sons of Judah according to their families were: *of* Shelah, the family of the Shelanites; *of* Perez, the family of the Parzites; *of* Zerah, the family of the Zarhites. [21]And the sons of Perez were: *of* Hezron, the family of the Hezronites; *of* Hamul, the family of the Hamulites. [22]These *are* the families of Judah according to those who were numbered of them: seventy-six thousand five hundred.

[23]The sons of Issachar according to their families *were: of* Tola, the family of the Tolaites; of Puah,[a] the family of the Punites;[b] [24]*of* Jashub, the family of the Jashubites; *of* Shimron, the family of the Shimronites. [25]These *are* the families of Issachar according to those who were numbered of them: sixty-four thousand three hundred.

[26]The sons of Zebulun according to their families *were: of* Sered, the family of the Sardites; of Elon, the family of the Elonites; of Jahleel, the family of the Jahleelites. [27]These *are* the families of the Zebulunites according to those who were numbered of them: sixty thousand five hundred.

[28]The sons of Joseph according to their families, by Manasseh and Ephraim, *were:* [29]The sons of Manasseh: of Machir, the family of the Machirites; and Machir begot Gilead; of Gilead, the family of the Gileadites. [30]These *are* the sons of Gilead: *of* Jeezer,[a] the family of the Jeezerites; of Helek, the family of the Helekites; [31]*of* Asriel, the family of the Asrielites; *of* Shechem, the family of the Shechemites; [32]*of* Shemida, the family of the Shemidaites; *of* Hepher, the family of the Hepherites. [33]Now Zelophehad the son of Hepher had no sons, but daughters; and the names of the daughters of Zelophehad *were* Mahlah, Noah, Hoglah, Milcah, and Tirzah. [34]These *are*

the families of Manasseh; and those who were numbered of them *were* fifty-two thousand seven hundred.

[35]These *are* the sons of Ephraim according to their families: of Shuthelah, the family of the Shuthalhites; of Becher,[a] the family of the Bachrites; of Tahan, the family of the Tahanites. [36]And these *are* the sons of Shuthelah: of Eran, the family of the Eranites. [37]These *are* the families of the sons of Ephraim according to those who were numbered of them: thirty-two thousand five hundred.

These *are* the sons of Joseph according to their families.

[38]The sons of Benjamin according to their families were: of Bela, the family of the Belaites; of Ashbel, the family of the Ashbelites; of Ahiram, the family of the Ahiramites; [39]of Shupham,[a] the family of the Shuphamites; of Hupham,[b] the family of the Huphamites. [40]And the sons of Bela were Ard[a] and Naaman: *of Ard,* the family of the Ardites; of Naaman, the family of the Naamites. [41]These *are* the sons of Benjamin according to their families; and those who were numbered of them *were* forty-five thousand six hundred.

[42]These *are* the sons of Dan according to their families: of Shuham,[a] the family of the Shuhamites. These *are* the families of Dan according to their families. [43]All the families of the Shuhamites, according to those who were numbered of them, *were* sixty-four thousand four hundred.

[44]The sons of Asher according to their families *were:* of Jimna, the family of the Jimnites; of Jesui, the family of the Jesuites; of Beriah, the family of the Beriites. [45]Of the sons of Beriah: of Heber, the family of the Heberites; of Malchiel, the family of the Malchielites. [46]And the name of the daughter of Asher *was* Serah. [47]These *are* the families of the sons of Asher according to those

26:15 [a]Called *Ziphion* in Genesis 46:16   26:16 [a]Called *Ezbon* in Genesis 46:16   26:17 [a]Spelled *Arodi* in Samaritan Pentateuch, Syriac, and Genesis 46:16   26:23 [a]Hebrew *Puvah* (compare Genesis 46:13 and 1 Chronicles 7:1); Samaritan Pentateuch, Septuagint, Syriac, and Vulgate read *Puah.* [b]Samaritan Pentateuch, Septuagint, Syriac, and Vulgate read *Puaites.*   26:30 [a]Called *Abiezer* in Joshua 17:2   26:35 [a]Called *Bered* in 1 Chronicles 7:20   26:39 [a]Masoretic Text reads *Shephupham,* spelled *Shephuphan* in 1 Chronicles 8:5. [b]Called *Huppim* in Genesis 46:21   26:40 [a]Called *Addar* in 1 Chronicles 8:3   26:42 [a]Called *Hushim* in Genesis 46:23

who were numbered of them: fifty-three thousand four hundred.

⁴⁸The sons of Naphtali according to their families *were:* of Jahzeel,ᵃ the family of the Jahzeelites; of Guni, the family of the Gunites; ⁴⁹of Jezer, the family of the Jezerites; of Shillem, the family of the Shillemites. ⁵⁰These *are* the families of Naphtali according to their families; and those who were numbered of them *were* forty-five thousand four hundred.

⁵¹These *are* those who were numbered of the children of Israel: six hundred and one thousand seven hundred and thirty.

⁵²Then the LORD spoke to Moses, saying: ⁵³"To these the land shall be divided as an inheritance, according to the number of names. ⁵⁴To a large *tribe* you shall give a larger inheritance, and to a small *tribe* you shall give a smaller inheritance. Each shall be given its inheritance according to those who were numbered of them. ⁵⁵But the land shall be divided by lot; they shall inherit according to the names of the tribes of their fathers. ⁵⁶According to the lot their inheritance shall be divided between the larger and the smaller."

⁵⁷And these *are* those who were numbered of the Levites according to their families: of Gershon, the family of the Gershonites; of Kohath, the family of the Kohathites; of Merari, the family of the Merarites. ⁵⁸These *are* the families of the Levites: the family of the Libnites, the family of the Hebronites, the family of the Mahlites, the family of the Mushites, and the family of the Korathites. And Kohath begot Amram. ⁵⁹The name of Amram's wife *was* Jochebed the daughter of Levi, who was born to Levi in Egypt; and to Amram she bore Aaron and Moses and their sister Miriam. ⁶⁰To Aaron were born Nadab and Abihu, Eleazar and Ithamar. ⁶¹And Nadab and Abihu died when they offered profane fire before the LORD.

⁶²Now those who were numbered of them were twenty-three thousand, every male from a month old and above; for they were not numbered among the other children of Israel, because there was no inheritance given to them among the children of Israel.

⁶³These *are* those who were numbered by Moses and Eleazar the priest, who numbered the children of Israel in the plains of Moab by the Jordan, *across from* Jericho. ⁶⁴But among these there was not a man of those who were numbered by Moses and Aaron the priest when they numbered the children of Israel in the Wilderness of Sinai. ⁶⁵For the LORD had said of them, "They shall surely die in the wilderness." So there was not left a man of them, except Caleb the son of Jephunneh and Joshua the son of Nun.

Inheritance Laws

27 Then came the daughters of Zelophehad the son of Hepher, the son of Gilead, the son of Machir, the son of Manasseh, from the families of Manasseh the son of Joseph; and these *were* the names of his daughters: Mahlah, Noah, Hoglah, Milcah, and Tirzah. ²And they stood before Moses, before Eleazar the priest, and before the leaders and all the congregation, *by* the doorway of the tabernacle of meeting, saying: ³"Our father died in the wilderness; but he was not in the company of those who gathered together against the LORD, in company with Korah, but he died in his own sin; and he had no sons. ⁴Why should the name of our father be removed from among his family because he had no son? Give us a possession among our father's brothers."

⁵So Moses brought their case before the LORD.

⁶And the LORD spoke to Moses, saying: ⁷"The daughters of Zelophehad speak *what is* right; you shall surely give them a possession of inheritance among their father's brothers, and cause the inheritance of their father to pass to them. ⁸And you shall speak to the children of Israel, saying: 'If a man dies and has no son, then you shall cause his inheritance to pass to his daughter. ⁹If he has no daughter, then you shall give his inheritance to his brothers. ¹⁰If he has no brothers, then you shall give his inheritance to his father's brothers. ¹¹And if his father has no brothers, then you shall give his inheritance to the relative closest to him in his family, and he shall possess it.' " And it shall be to the children of Israel a statute of judgment, just as the LORD commanded Moses.

Joshua the Next Leader of Israel

¹²Now the LORD said to Moses: "Go up into this Mount Abarim, and see the land which I

26:48 ᵃSpelled *Jahziel* in 1 Chronicles 7:13

have given to the children of Israel. ¹³And when you have seen it, you also shall be gathered to your people, as Aaron your brother was gathered. ¹⁴For in the Wilderness of Zin, during the strife of the congregation, you rebelled against My command to hallow Me at the waters before their eyes." (These *are* the waters of Meribah, at Kadesh in the Wilderness of Zin.)

¹⁵Then Moses spoke to the LORD, saying: ¹⁶"Let the LORD, the God of the spirits of all flesh, set a man over the congregation, ¹⁷who may go out before them and go in before them, who may lead them out and bring them in, that the congregation of the LORD may not be like sheep which have no shepherd."

¹⁸And the LORD said to Moses: "Take Joshua the son of Nun with you, a man in whom *is* the Spirit, and lay your hand on him; ¹⁹set him before Eleazar the priest and before all the congregation, and inaugurate him in their sight. ²⁰And you shall give *some* of your authority to him, that all the congregation of the children of Israel may be obedient. ²¹He shall stand before Eleazar the priest, who shall inquire before the LORD for him by the judgment of the Urim. At his word they shall go out, and at his word they shall come in, he and all the children of Israel with him—all the congregation."

²²So Moses did as the LORD commanded him. He took Joshua and set him before Eleazar the priest and before all the congregation. ²³And he laid his hands on him and inaugurated him, just as the LORD commanded by the hand of Moses.

DAILY OFFERINGS

28 Now the LORD spoke to Moses, saying, ²"Command the children of Israel, and say to them, 'My offering, My food for My offerings made by fire as a sweet aroma to Me, you shall be careful to offer to Me at their appointed time.'

³"And you shall say to them, 'This *is* the offering made by fire which you shall offer to the LORD: two male lambs in their first year without blemish, day by day, as a regular burnt offering. ⁴The one lamb you shall offer in the morning, the other lamb you shall offer in the evening, ⁵and one-tenth of an ephah of fine flour as a grain offering mixed with one-fourth of a hin of pressed

oil. ⁶*It is* a regular burnt offering which was ordained at Mount Sinai for a sweet aroma, an offering made by fire to the LORD. ⁷And its drink offering *shall be* one-fourth of a hin for each lamb; in a holy *place* you shall pour out the drink to the LORD as an offering. ⁸The other lamb you shall offer in the evening; as the morning grain offering and its drink offering, you shall offer *it* as an offering made by fire, a sweet aroma to the LORD.

SABBATH OFFERINGS

⁹"And on the Sabbath day two lambs in their first year, without blemish, and two-tenths *of an ephah* of fine flour as a grain offering, mixed with oil, with its drink offering— ¹⁰*this is* the burnt offering for every Sabbath, besides the regular burnt offering with its drink offering.

MONTHLY OFFERINGS

¹¹"At the beginnings of your months you shall present a burnt offering to the LORD: two young bulls, one ram, and seven lambs in their first year, without blemish; ¹²three-tenths *of an ephah* of fine flour as a grain offering, mixed with oil, for each bull; two-tenths *of an ephah* of fine flour as a grain offering, mixed with oil, for the one ram; ¹³and one-tenth *of an ephah* of fine flour, mixed with oil, as a grain offering for each lamb, as a burnt offering of sweet aroma, an offering made by fire to the LORD. ¹⁴Their drink offering shall be half a hin of wine for a bull, one-third of a hin for a ram, and one-fourth of a hin for a lamb; this *is* the burnt offering for each month throughout the months of the year. ¹⁵Also one kid of the goats as a sin offering to the LORD shall be offered, besides the regular burnt offering and its drink offering.

OFFERINGS AT PASSOVER

¹⁶"On the fourteenth day of the first month *is* the Passover of the LORD. ¹⁷And on the fifteenth day of this month *is* the feast; unleavened bread shall be eaten for seven days. ¹⁸On the first day *you shall have* a holy convocation. You shall do no customary work. ¹⁹And you shall present an offering made by fire as a burnt offering to the LORD: two young bulls, one ram, and seven lambs in their first year. Be sure they are without blemish. ²⁰Their grain offering shall be of fine flour mixed

with oil: three-tenths *of an ephah* you shall offer for a bull, and two-tenths for a ram; [21]you shall offer one-tenth *of an ephah* for each of the seven lambs; [22]also one goat *as* a sin offering, to make atonement for you. [23]You shall offer these besides the burnt offering of the morning, which *is* for a regular burnt offering. [24]In this manner you shall offer the food of the offering made by fire daily for seven days, as a sweet aroma to the LORD; it shall be offered besides the regular burnt offering and its drink offering. [25]And on the seventh day you shall have a holy convocation. You shall do no customary work.

OFFERINGS AT THE FEAST OF WEEKS

[26]'Also on the day of the firstfruits, when you bring a new grain offering to the LORD at your *Feast of* Weeks, you shall have a holy convocation. You shall do no customary work. [27]You shall present a burnt offering as a sweet aroma to the LORD: two young bulls, one ram, and seven lambs in their first year, [28]with their grain offering of fine flour mixed with oil: three-tenths *of an ephah* for each bull, two-tenths for the one ram, [29]and one-tenth for each of the seven lambs; [30]*also* one kid of the goats, to make atonement for you. [31]Be sure they are without blemish. You shall present *them* with their drink offerings, besides the regular burnt offering with its grain offering.

OFFERINGS AT THE FEAST OF TRUMPETS

29 'And in the seventh month, on the first *day* of the month, you shall have a holy convocation. You shall do no customary work. For you it is a day of blowing the trumpets. [2]You shall offer a burnt offering as a sweet aroma to the LORD: one young bull, one ram, *and* seven lambs in their first year, without blemish. [3]Their grain offering *shall be* fine flour mixed with oil: three-tenths *of an ephah* for the bull, two-tenths for the ram, [4]and one-tenth for each of the seven lambs; [5]also one kid of the goats *as* a sin offering, to make atonement for you; [6]besides the burnt offering with its grain offering for the New Moon, the regular burnt offering with its grain offering, and their drink offerings, according to their ordinance, as a sweet aroma, an offering made by fire to the LORD.

OFFERINGS ON THE DAY OF ATONEMENT

[7]'On the tenth *day* of this seventh month you shall have a holy convocation. You shall afflict your souls; you shall not do any work. [8]You shall present a burnt offering to the LORD *as* a sweet aroma: one young bull, one ram, *and* seven lambs in their first year. Be sure they are without blemish. [9]Their grain offering *shall be of* fine flour mixed with oil: three-tenths *of an ephah* for the bull, two-tenths for the one ram, [10]and one-tenth for each of the seven lambs; [11]also one kid of the goats *as* a sin offering, besides the sin offering for atonement, the regular burnt offering with its grain offering, and their drink offerings.

OFFERINGS AT THE FEAST OF TABERNACLES

[12]'On the fifteenth day of the seventh month you shall have a holy convocation. You shall do no customary work, and you shall keep a feast to the LORD seven days. [13]You shall present a burnt offering, an offering made by fire as a sweet aroma to the LORD: thirteen young bulls, two rams, *and* fourteen lambs in their first year. They shall be without blemish. [14]Their grain offering *shall be of* fine flour mixed with oil: three-tenths *of an ephah* for each of the thirteen bulls, two-tenths for each of the two rams, [15]and one-tenth for each of the fourteen lambs; [16]also one kid of the goats *as* a sin offering, besides the regular burnt offering, its grain offering, and its drink offering.

[17]'On the second day *present* twelve young bulls, two rams, fourteen lambs in their first year without blemish, [18]and their grain offering and their drink offerings for the bulls, for the rams, and for the lambs, by their number, according to the ordinance; [19]also one kid of the goats *as* a sin offering, besides the regular burnt offering with its grain offering, and their drink offerings.

[20]'On the third day *present* eleven bulls, two rams, fourteen lambs in their first year without blemish, [21]and their grain offering and their drink offerings for the bulls, for the rams, and for the lambs, by their number, according to the ordinance; [22]also one goat *as* a sin offering, besides the regular burnt offering, its grain offering, and its drink offering.

[23]'On the fourth day *present* ten bulls, two

rams, *and* fourteen lambs in their first year, without blemish, 24and their grain offering and their drink offerings for the bulls, for the rams, and for the lambs, by their number, according to the ordinance; 25also one kid of the goats *as* a sin offering, besides the regular burnt offering, its grain offering, and its drink offering.

26'On the fifth day *present* nine bulls, two rams, *and* fourteen lambs in their first year without blemish, 27and their grain offering and their drink offerings for the bulls, for the rams, and for the lambs, by their number, according to the ordinance; 28also one goat *as* a sin offering, besides the regular burnt offering, its grain offering, and its drink offering.

29'On the sixth day *present* eight bulls, two rams, *and* fourteen lambs in their first year without blemish, 30and their grain offering and their drink offerings for the bulls, for the rams, and for the lambs, by their number, according to the ordinance; 31also one goat *as* a sin offering, besides the regular burnt offering, its grain offering, and its drink offering.

32'On the seventh day *present* seven bulls, two rams, *and* fourteen lambs in their first year without blemish, 33and their grain offering and their drink offerings for the bulls, for the rams, and for the lambs, by their number, according to the ordinance; 34also one goat *as* a sin offering, besides the regular burnt offering, its grain offering, and its drink offering.

35'On the eighth day you shall have a sacred assembly. You shall do no customary work. 36You shall present a burnt offering, an offering made by fire as a sweet aroma to the LORD: one bull, one ram, seven lambs in their first year without blemish, 37and their grain offering and their drink offerings for the bull, for the ram, and for the lambs, by their number, according to the ordinance; 38also one goat *as* a sin offering, besides the regular burnt offering, its grain offering, and its drink offering.

39'These you shall present to the LORD at your appointed feasts (besides your vowed offerings and your freewill offerings) as your burnt offerings and your grain offerings, as your drink offerings and your peace offerings.' "

40So Moses told the children of Israel everything, just as the LORD commanded Moses.

THE LAW CONCERNING VOWS

30 Then Moses spoke to the heads of the tribes concerning the children of Israel, saying, "This *is* the thing which the LORD has commanded: 2If a man makes a vow to the LORD, or swears an oath to bind himself by some agreement, he shall not break his word; he shall do according to all that proceeds out of his mouth.

3"Or if a woman makes a vow to the LORD, and binds *herself* by some agreement while in her father's house in her youth, 4and her father hears her vow and the agreement by which she has bound herself, and her father holds his peace, then all her vows shall stand, and every agreement with which she has bound herself shall stand. 5But if her father overrules her on the day that he hears, then none of her vows nor her agreements by which she has bound herself shall stand; and the LORD will release her, because her father overruled her.

6"If indeed she takes a husband, while bound by her vows or by a rash utterance from her lips by which she bound herself, 7and her husband hears *it,* and makes no response to her on the day that he hears, then her vows shall stand, and her agreements by which she bound herself shall stand. 8But if her husband overrules her on the day that he hears *it,* he shall make void her vow which she took and what she uttered with her lips, by which she bound herself, and the LORD will release her.

9"Also any vow of a widow or a divorced woman, by which she has bound herself, shall stand against her.

10"If she vowed in her husband's house, or bound herself by an agreement with an oath, 11and her husband heard *it,* and made no response to her *and* did not overrule her, then all her vows shall stand, and every agreement by which she bound herself shall stand. 12But if her husband truly made them void on the day he heard *them,* then whatever proceeded from her lips concerning her vows or concerning the agreement binding her, it shall not stand; her husband has made them void, and the LORD will release her. 13Every vow and every binding oath to afflict her soul, her husband may confirm it, or her husband may make it void. 14Now if her husband makes no response whatever to her from day to day, then he confirms all her vows or all the agreements that bind her; he confirms them, because he made no response to her on the day that he heard *them*. [15]But if he does make them void after he has heard *them,* then he shall bear her guilt."

[16]These *are* the statutes which the LORD commanded Moses, between a man and his wife, and between a father and his daughter in her youth in her father's house.

VENGEANCE ON THE MIDIANITES

31 And the LORD spoke to Moses, saying: [2]"Take vengeance on the Midianites for the children of Israel. Afterward you shall be gathered to your people."

[3]So Moses spoke to the people, saying, "Arm some of yourselves for war, and let them go against the Midianites to take vengeance for the LORD on Midian. [4]A thousand from each tribe of all the tribes of Israel you shall send to the war."

[5]So there were recruited from the divisions of Israel one thousand from *each* tribe, twelve thousand armed for war. [6]Then Moses sent them to the war, one thousand from *each* tribe; he sent them to the war with Phinehas the son of Eleazar the priest, with the holy articles and the signal trumpets in his hand. [7]And they warred against the Midianites, just as the LORD commanded Moses, and they killed all the males. [8]They killed the kings of Midian with *the rest of* those who were killed—Evi, Rekem, Zur, Hur, and Reba, the five kings of Midian. Balaam the son of Beor they also killed with the sword.

[9]And the children of Israel took the women of Midian captive, with their little ones, and took as spoil all their cattle, all their flocks, and all their goods. [10]They also burned with fire all the cities where they dwelt, and all their forts. [11]And they took all the spoil and all the booty—of man and beast.

RETURN FROM THE WAR

[12]Then they brought the captives, the booty, and the spoil to Moses, to Eleazar the priest, and to the congregation of the children of Israel, to the camp in the plains of Moab by the Jordan, *across from* Jericho. [13]And Moses, Eleazar the priest, and all the leaders of the congregation, went to meet them outside the camp. [14]But Moses was angry with the officers of the army, *with* the captains over thousands and captains over hundreds, who had come from the battle.

[15]And Moses said to them: "Have you kept all the women alive? [16]Look, these *women* caused the children of Israel, through the counsel of Balaam, to trespass against the LORD in the incident of Peor, and there was a plague among the congregation of the LORD. [17]Now therefore, kill every male among the little ones, and kill every woman who has known a man intimately. [18]But keep alive for yourselves all the young girls who have not known a man intimately. [19]And as for you, remain outside the camp seven days; whoever has killed any person, and whoever has touched any slain, purify yourselves and your captives on the third day and on the seventh day. [20]Purify every garment, everything made of leather, everything woven of goats' *hair,* and everything made of wood."

[21]Then Eleazar the priest said to the men of war who had gone to the battle, "This *is* the ordinance of the law which the LORD commanded Moses: [22]Only the gold, the silver, the bronze, the iron, the tin, and the lead, [23]everything that can endure fire, you shall put through the fire, and it shall be clean; and it shall be purified with the water of purification. But all that cannot endure fire you shall put through water. [24]And you shall wash your clothes on the seventh day and be clean, and afterward you may come into the camp."

DIVISION OF THE PLUNDER

[25]Now the LORD spoke to Moses, saying: [26]"Count up the plunder that was taken—of man and beast—you and Eleazar the priest and the chief fathers of the congregation; [27]and divide the plunder into two parts, between those who took part in the war, who went out to battle, and all the congregation. [28]And levy a tribute for the LORD on the men of war who went out to battle: one of every five hundred of the persons, the cattle, the donkeys, and the sheep; [29]take *it* from their half, and give *it* to Eleazar the priest as a heave offering to the LORD. [30]And from the children of Israel's half you shall take one of every fifty, drawn from the persons, the cattle, the donkeys, and the sheep, from all the livestock, and give them to the

Levites who keep charge of the tabernacle of the LORD." [31]So Moses and Eleazar the priest did as the LORD commanded Moses.

[32]The booty remaining from the plunder, which the men of war had taken, was six hundred and seventy-five thousand sheep, [33]seventy-two thousand cattle, [34]sixty-one thousand donkeys, [35]and thirty-two thousand persons in all, of women who had not known a man intimately. [36]And the half, the portion for those who had gone out to war, was in number three hundred and thirty-seven thousand five hundred sheep; [37]and the LORD's tribute of the sheep was six hundred and seventy-five. [38]The cattle *were* thirty-six thousand, of which the LORD's tribute *was* seventy-two. [39]The donkeys *were* thirty thousand five hundred, of which the LORD's tribute *was* sixty-one. [40]The persons *were* sixteen thousand, of which the LORD's tribute *was* thirty-two persons. [41]So Moses gave the tribute *which was* the LORD's heave offering to Eleazar the priest, as the LORD commanded Moses.

[42]And from the children of Israel's half, which Moses separated from the men who fought— [43]now the half belonging to the congregation was three hundred and thirty-seven thousand five hundred sheep, [44]thirty-six thousand cattle, [45]thirty thousand five hundred donkeys, [46]and sixteen thousand persons— [47]and from the children of Israel's half Moses took one of every fifty, drawn from man and beast, and gave them to the Levites, who kept charge of the tabernacle of the LORD, as the LORD commanded Moses.

[48]Then the officers who *were* over thousands of the army, the captains of thousands and captains of hundreds, came near to Moses; [49]and they said to Moses, "Your servants have taken a count of the men of war who *are* under our command, and not a man of us is missing. [50]Therefore we have brought an offering for the LORD, what every man found of ornaments of gold: armlets and bracelets and signet rings and earrings and necklaces, to make atonement for ourselves before the LORD." [51]So Moses and Eleazar the priest received the gold from them, all the fashioned ornaments. [52]And all the gold of the offering that they offered to the LORD, from the captains of thousands and captains of hundreds, was sixteen thousand seven hundred and fifty shekels. [53](The

men of war had taken spoil, every man for himself.) [54]And Moses and Eleazar the priest received the gold from the captains of thousands and of hundreds, and brought it into the tabernacle of meeting as a memorial for the children of Israel before the LORD.

THE TRIBES SETTLING EAST OF THE JORDAN

32 Now the children of Reuben and the children of Gad had a very great multitude of livestock; and when they saw the land of Jazer and the land of Gilead, that indeed the region *was* a place for livestock, [2]the children of Gad and the children of Reuben came and spoke to Moses, to Eleazar the priest, and to the leaders of the congregation, saying, [3]"Ataroth, Dibon, Jazer, Nimrah, Heshbon, Elealeh, Shebam, Nebo, and Beon, [4]the country which the LORD defeated before the congregation of Israel, *is* a land for livestock, and your servants have livestock." [5]Therefore they said, "If we have found favor in your sight, let this land be given to your servants as a possession. Do not take us over the Jordan."

[6]And Moses said to the children of Gad and to the children of Reuben: "Shall your brethren go to war while you sit here? [7]Now why will you discourage the heart of the children of Israel from going over into the land which the LORD has given them? [8]Thus your fathers did when I sent them away from Kadesh Barnea to see the land. [9]For when they went up to the Valley of Eshcol and saw the land, they discouraged the heart of the children of Israel, so that they did not go into the land which the LORD had given them. [10]So the LORD's anger was aroused on that day, and He swore an oath, saying, [11]'Surely none of the men who came up from Egypt, from twenty years old and above, shall see the land of which I swore to Abraham, Isaac, and Jacob, because they have not wholly followed Me, [12]except Caleb the son of Jephunneh, the Kenizzite, and Joshua the son of Nun, for they have wholly followed the LORD.' [13]So the LORD's anger was aroused against Israel, and He made them wander in the wilderness forty years, until all the generation that had done evil in the sight of the LORD was gone. [14]And look! You have risen in your fathers' place, a brood of sinful men, to increase still more the fierce anger of the LORD against Israel. [15]For if

you turn away from following Him, He will once again leave them in the wilderness, and you will destroy all these people."

16Then they came near to him and said: "We will build sheepfolds here for our livestock, and cities for our little ones, 17but we ourselves will be armed, ready *to go* before the children of Israel until we have brought them to their place; and our little ones will dwell in the fortified cities because of the inhabitants of the land. 18We will not return to our homes until every one of the children of Israel has received his inheritance. 19For we will not inherit with them on the other side of the Jordan and beyond, because our inheritance has fallen to us on this eastern side of the Jordan."

20Then Moses said to them: "If you do this thing, if you arm yourselves before the LORD for the war, 21and all your armed men cross over the Jordan before the LORD until He has driven out His enemies from before Him, 22and the land is subdued before the LORD, then afterward you may return and be blameless before the LORD and before Israel; and this land shall be your possession before the LORD. 23But if you do not do so, then take note, you have sinned against the LORD; and be sure your sin will find you out. 24Build cities for your little ones and folds for your sheep, and do what has proceeded out of your mouth."

25And the children of Gad and the children of Reuben spoke to Moses, saying: "Your servants will do as my lord commands. 26Our little ones, our wives, our flocks, and all our livestock will be there in the cities of Gilead; 27but your servants will cross over, every man armed for war, before the LORD to battle, just as my lord says."

28So Moses gave command concerning them to Eleazar the priest, to Joshua the son of Nun, and to the chief fathers of the tribes of the children of Israel. 29And Moses said to them: "If the children of Gad and the children of Reuben cross over the Jordan with you, every man armed for battle before the LORD, and the land is subdued before you, then you shall give them the land of Gilead as a possession. 30But if they do not cross over armed with you, they shall have possessions among you in the land of Canaan."

31Then the children of Gad and the children of Reuben answered, saying: "As the LORD has said to your servants, so we will do. 32We will cross over armed before the LORD into the land of Canaan, but the possession of our inheritance *shall remain* with us on this side of the Jordan."

33So Moses gave to the children of Gad, to the children of Reuben, and to half the tribe of Manasseh the son of Joseph, the kingdom of Sihon king of the Amorites and the kingdom of Og king of Bashan, the land with its cities within the borders, the cities of the surrounding country. 34And the children of Gad built Dibon and Ataroth and Aroer, 35Atroth and Shophan and Jazer and Jogbehah, 36Beth Nimrah and Beth Haran, fortified cities, and folds for sheep. 37And the children of Reuben built Heshbon and Elealeh and Kirjathaim, 38Nebo and Baal Meon (*their* names being changed) and Shibmah; and they gave *other* names to the cities which they built.

39And the children of Machir the son of Manasseh went to Gilead and took it, and dispossessed the Amorites who *were* in it. 40So Moses gave Gilead to Machir the son of Manasseh, and he dwelt in it. 41Also Jair the son of Manasseh went and took its small towns, and called them Havoth Jair.[a] 42Then Nobah went and took Kenath and its villages, and he called it Nobah, after his own name.

ISRAEL'S JOURNEY FROM EGYPT REVIEWED

33 These *are* the journeys of the children of Israel, who went out of the land of Egypt by their armies under the hand of Moses and Aaron. 2Now Moses wrote down the starting points of their journeys at the command of the LORD. And these *are* their journeys according to their starting points:

3They departed from Rameses in the first month, on the fifteenth day of the first month; on the day after the Passover the children of Israel went out with boldness in the sight of all the Egyptians. 4For the Egyptians were burying all *their* firstborn, whom the LORD had killed among them. Also on their gods the LORD had executed judgments.

5Then the children of Israel moved from Rameses and camped at Succoth. 6They departed

32:41 aLiterally *Towns of Jair*

from Succoth and camped at Etham, which *is* on the edge of the wilderness. [7]They moved from Etham and turned back to Pi Hahiroth, which *is* east of Baal Zephon; and they camped near Migdol. [8]They departed from before Hahiroth[a] and passed through the midst of the sea into the wilderness, went three days' journey in the Wilderness of Etham, and camped at Marah. [9]They moved from Marah and came to Elim. At Elim *were* twelve springs of water and seventy palm trees; so they camped there.

[10]They moved from Elim and camped by the Red Sea. [11]They moved from the Red Sea and camped in the Wilderness of Sin. [12]They journeyed from the Wilderness of Sin and camped at Dophkah. [13]They departed from Dophkah and camped at Alush. [14]They moved from Alush and camped at Rephidim, where there was no water for the people to drink.

[15]They departed from Rephidim and camped in the Wilderness of Sinai. [16]They moved from the Wilderness of Sinai and camped at Kibroth Hattaavah. [17]They departed from Kibroth Hattaavah and camped at Hazeroth. [18]They departed from Hazeroth and camped at Rithmah. [19]They departed from Rithmah and camped at Rimmon Perez. [20]They departed from Rimmon Perez and camped at Libnah. [21]They moved from Libnah and camped at Rissah. [22]They journeyed from Rissah and camped at Kehelathah. [23]They went from Kehelathah and camped at Mount Shepher. [24]They moved from Mount Shepher and camped at Haradah. [25]They moved from Haradah and camped at Makheloth. [26]They moved from Makheloth and camped at Tahath. [27]They departed from Tahath and camped at Terah. [28]They moved from Terah and camped at Mithkah. [29]They went from Mithkah and camped at Hashmonah. [30]They departed from Hashmonah and camped at Moseroth. [31]They departed from Moseroth and camped at Bene Jaakan. [32]They moved from Bene Jaakan and camped at Hor Hagidgad. [33]They went from Hor Hagidgad and camped at Jotbathah. [34]They moved from Jotbathah and camped at Abronah. [35]They departed from Abronah and camped at Ezion Geber. [36]They moved from Ezion Geber and camped in the Wilderness of Zin, which *is* Kadesh. [37]They moved from Kadesh and camped

at Mount Hor, on the boundary of the land of Edom.

[38]Then Aaron the priest went up to Mount Hor at the command of the LORD, and died there in the fortieth year after the children of Israel had come out of the land of Egypt, on the first *day* of the fifth month. [39]Aaron *was* one hundred and twenty-three years old when he died on Mount Hor.

[40]Now the king of Arad, the Canaanite, who dwelt in the South in the land of Canaan, heard of the coming of the children of Israel.

[41]So they departed from Mount Hor and camped at Zalmonah. [42]They departed from Zalmonah and camped at Punon. [43]They departed from Punon and camped at Oboth. [44]They departed from Oboth and camped at Ije Abarim, at the border of Moab. [45]They departed from Ijim[a] and camped at Dibon Gad. [46]They moved from Dibon Gad and camped at Almon Diblathaim. [47]They moved from Almon Diblathaim and camped in the mountains of Abarim, before Nebo. [48]They departed from the mountains of Abarim and camped in the plains of Moab by the Jordan, *across from* Jericho. [49]They camped by the Jordan, from Beth Jesimoth as far as the Abel Acacia Grove[a] in the plains of Moab.

INSTRUCTIONS FOR THE CONQUEST OF CANAAN

[50]Now the LORD spoke to Moses in the plains of Moab by the Jordan, *across from* Jericho, saying, [51]"Speak to the children of Israel, and say to them: 'When you have crossed the Jordan into the land of Canaan, [52]then you shall drive out all the inhabitants of the land from before you, destroy all their engraved stones, destroy all their molded images, and demolish all their high places; [53]you shall dispossess *the inhabitants of* the land and dwell in it, for I have given you the land to possess. [54]And you shall divide the land by lot as an inheritance among your families; to the larger you shall give a larger inheritance, and to the smaller you shall give a smaller inheritance; there everyone's *inheritance* shall be whatever falls to him by lot. You shall inherit according to the tribes of

---

33:8 [a]Many Hebrew manuscripts, Samaritan Pentateuch, Syriac, Targum, and Vulgate read *from Pi Hahiroth* (compare verse 7). **33:45** [a]Same as *Ije Abarim,* verse 44   **33:49** [a]Hebrew *Abel Shittim*

your fathers. ⁵⁵But if you do not drive out the inhabitants of the land from before you, then it shall be that those whom you let remain *shall be* irritants in your eyes and thorns in your sides, and they shall harass you in the land where you dwell. ⁵⁶Moreover it shall be *that* I will do to you as I thought to do to them.' "

THE APPOINTED BOUNDARIES OF CANAAN

34 Then the LORD spoke to Moses, saying, ²"Command the children of Israel, and say to them: 'When you come into the land of Canaan, this *is* the land that shall fall to you as an inheritance—the land of Canaan to its boundaries. ³Your southern border shall be from the Wilderness of Zin along the border of Edom; then your southern border shall extend eastward to the end of the Salt Sea; ⁴your border shall turn from the southern side of the Ascent of Akrabbim, continue to Zin, and be on the south of Kadesh Barnea; then it shall go on to Hazar Addar, and continue to Azmon; ⁵the border shall turn from Azmon to the Brook of Egypt, and it shall end at the Sea.

⁶'As for the western border, you shall have the Great Sea for a border; this shall be your western border.

⁷'And this shall be your northern border: From the Great Sea you shall mark out your *border* line to Mount Hor; ⁸from Mount Hor you shall mark out *your border* to the entrance of Hamath; then the direction of the border shall be toward Zedad; ⁹the border shall proceed to Ziphron, and it shall end at Hazar Enan. This shall be your northern border.

¹⁰'You shall mark out your eastern border from Hazar Enan to Shepham; ¹¹the border shall go down from Shepham to Riblah on the east side of Ain; the border shall go down and reach to the eastern side of the Sea of Chinnereth; ¹²the border shall go down along the Jordan, and it shall end at the Salt Sea. This shall be your land with its surrounding boundaries.' "

¹³Then Moses commanded the children of Israel, saying: "This *is* the land which you shall inherit by lot, which the LORD has commanded to give to the nine tribes and to the half-tribe. ¹⁴For the tribe of the children of Reuben according to the house of their fathers, and the tribe of the

children of Gad according to the house of their fathers, have received *their inheritance;* and the half-tribe of Manasseh has received its inheritance. ¹⁵The two tribes and the half-tribe have received their inheritance on this side of the Jordan, *across from* Jericho eastward, toward the sunrise."

THE LEADERS APPOINTED TO DIVIDE THE LAND

¹⁶And the LORD spoke to Moses, saying, ¹⁷"These *are* the names of the men who shall divide the land among you as an inheritance: Eleazar the priest and Joshua the son of Nun. ¹⁸And you shall take one leader of every tribe to divide the land for the inheritance. ¹⁹These *are* the names of the men: from the tribe of Judah, Caleb the son of Jephunneh; ²⁰from the tribe of the children of Simeon, Shemuel the son of Ammihud; ²¹from the tribe of Benjamin, Elidad the son of Chislon; ²²a leader from the tribe of the children of Dan, Bukki the son of Jogli; ²³from the sons of Joseph: a leader from the tribe of the children of Manasseh, Hanniel the son of Ephod, ²⁴and a leader from the tribe of the children of Ephraim, Kemuel the son of Shiphtan; ²⁵a leader from the tribe of the children of Zebulun, Elizaphan the son of Parnach; ²⁶a leader from the tribe of the children of Issachar, Paltiel the son of Azzan; ²⁷a leader from the tribe of the children of Asher, Ahihud the son of Shelomi; ²⁸and a leader from the tribe of the children of Naphtali, Pedahel the son of Ammihud."

²⁹These *are* the ones the LORD commanded to divide the inheritance among the children of Israel in the land of Canaan.

CITIES FOR THE LEVITES

35 And the LORD spoke to Moses in the plains of Moab by the Jordan *across from* Jericho, saying: ²"Command the children of Israel that they give the Levites cities to dwell in from the inheritance of their possession, and you shall *also* give the Levites common-land around the cities. ³They shall have the cities to dwell in; and their common-land shall be for their cattle, for their herds, and for all their animals. ⁴The common-land of the cities which you will give the Levites *shall extend* from the wall of the city outward a thousand cubits all around. ⁵And you shall measure outside the city on the east side two thousand cubits, on the south side two thousand cubits, on the west side two thousand cubits, and on the north side two thousand cubits. The city *shall be* in the middle. This shall belong to them as common-land for the cities.

6"Now among the cities which you will give to the Levites *you shall appoint* six cities of refuge, to which a manslayer may flee. And to these you shall add forty-two cities. 7So all the cities you will give to the Levites *shall be* forty-eight; these *you shall give* with their common-land. 8And the cities which you will give *shall be* from the possession of the children of Israel; from the larger *tribe* you shall give many, from the smaller you shall give few. Each shall give some of its cities to the Levites, in proportion to the inheritance that each receives."

CITIES OF REFUGE

9Then the LORD spoke to Moses, saying, 10"Speak to the children of Israel, and say to them: 'When you cross the Jordan into the land of Canaan, 11then you shall appoint cities to be cities of refuge for you, that the manslayer who kills any person accidentally may flee there. 12They shall be cities of refuge for you from the avenger, that the manslayer may not die until he stands before the congregation in judgment. 13And of the cities which you give, you shall have six cities of refuge. 14You shall appoint three cities on this side of the Jordan, and three cities you shall appoint in the land of Canaan, *which* will be cities of refuge. 15These six cities shall be for refuge for the children of Israel, for the stranger, and for the sojourner among them, that anyone who kills a person accidentally may flee there.

16"But if he strikes him with an iron implement, so that he dies, he *is* a murderer; the murderer shall surely be put to death. 17And if he strikes him with a stone in the hand, by which one could die, and he does die, he *is* a murderer; the murderer shall surely be put to death. 18Or *if* he strikes him with a wooden hand weapon, by which one could die, and he does die, he *is* a murderer; the murderer shall surely be put to death. 19The avenger of blood himself shall put the murderer to death; when he meets him, he shall put him to death. 20If he pushes him out of hatred or, while lying in wait, hurls something at him so that he dies, 21or in enmity he strikes him

with his hand so that he dies, the one who struck *him* shall surely be put to death. He *is* a murderer. The avenger of blood shall put the murderer to death when he meets him.

22"However, if he pushes him suddenly without enmity, or throws anything at him without lying in wait, 23or uses a stone, by which a man could die, throwing *it* at him without seeing *him,* so that he dies, while he was not his enemy or seeking his harm, 24then the congregation shall judge between the manslayer and the avenger of blood according to these judgments. 25So the congregation shall deliver the manslayer from the hand of the avenger of blood, and the congregation shall return him to the city of refuge where he had fled, and he shall remain there until the death of the high priest who was anointed with the holy oil. 26But if the manslayer at any time goes outside the limits of the city of refuge where he fled, 27and the avenger of blood finds him outside the limits of his city of refuge, and the avenger of blood kills the manslayer, he shall not be guilty of blood, 28because he should have remained in his city of refuge until the death of the high priest. But after the death of the high priest the manslayer may return to the land of his possession.

29"And these *things* shall be a statute of judgment to you throughout your generations in all your dwellings. 30Whoever kills a person, the murderer shall be put to death on the testimony of witnesses; but one witness is not *sufficient* testimony against a person for the death *penalty.* 31Moreover you shall take no ransom for the life of a murderer who *is* guilty of death, but he shall surely be put to death. 32And you shall take no ransom for him who has fled to his city of refuge, that he may return to dwell in the land before the death of the priest. 33So you shall not pollute the land where you *are;* for blood defiles the land, and no atonement can be made for the land, for the blood that is shed on it, except by the blood of him who shed it. 34Therefore do not defile the land which you inhabit, in the midst of which I dwell; for I the LORD dwell among the children of Israel.' "

MARRIAGE OF FEMALE HEIRS

36 Now the chief fathers of the families of the children of Gilead the son of Machir, the son of Manasseh, of the families of the sons of Joseph, came near and spoke before Moses and before the leaders, the chief fathers of the children of Israel. ²And they said: "The LORD commanded my lord *Moses* to give the land as an inheritance by lot to the children of Israel, and my lord was commanded by the LORD to give the inheritance of our brother Zelophehad to his daughters. ³Now if they are married to any of the sons of the *other* tribes of the children of Israel, then their inheritance will be taken from the inheritance of our fathers, and it will be added to the inheritance of the tribe into which they marry; so it will be taken from the lot of our inheritance. ⁴And when the Jubilee of the children of Israel comes, then their inheritance will be added to the inheritance of the tribe into which they marry; so their inheritance will be taken away from the inheritance of the tribe of our fathers."

⁵Then Moses commanded the children of Israel according to the word of the LORD, saying: "What the tribe of the sons of Joseph speaks is right. ⁶This *is* what the LORD commands concerning the daughters of Zelophehad, saying, 'Let them marry whom they think best, but they may marry only within the family of their father's tribe.' ⁷So the inheritance of the children of Israel shall not change hands from tribe to tribe, for every one of the children of Israel shall keep the inheritance of the tribe of his fathers. ⁸And every daughter who possesses an inheritance in any tribe of the children of Israel shall be the wife of one of the family of her father's tribe, so that the children of Israel each may possess the inheritance of his fathers. ⁹Thus no inheritance shall change hands from *one* tribe to another, but every tribe of the children of Israel shall keep its own inheritance."

¹⁰Just as the LORD commanded Moses, so did the daughters of Zelophehad; ¹¹for Mahlah, Tirzah, Hoglah, Milcah, and Noah, the daughters of Zelophehad, were married to the sons of their father's brothers. ¹²They were married into the families of the children of Manasseh the son of Joseph, and their inheritance remained in the tribe of their father's family.

¹³These *are* the commandments and the judgments which the LORD commanded the children of Israel by the hand of Moses in the plains of Moab by the Jordan, *across from* Jericho.

IMPACT OF THE BOOK

DEUTERONOMY

I IDEA	*Jesus quoted most often from this book in Scripture. God desires the undivided loyalty of His followers. The Greatest Commandment teaches us: "Love the LORD your God with all your heart, with all your soul, and with all your strength" (Deut. 6:1–9).*
M MESSAGE	*Moses' last words before his death prepared the Israelites to enter the Promised Land. The generation who had left Egypt with Moses had largely passed away after forty years of wandering in the wilderness. Moses gave the new generation instructions concerning the laws of God and His expectations for His people. Not simply a recitation of God's laws, it is a clear call to obedience to prepare the new generation as they moved to inhabit the land of promise.*
P PEOPLE	*Joshua and Moses*
A AUTHOR	*Mosaic authorship is indicated by several texts within the book (1:5; 31:9, 22, 24, 30), is confirmed by other passages in the Old Testament (1 Kin. 2:3; 2 Kin. 18:6), and is referenced by Jesus Himself (Matt. 19:8; John 5:46, 47).*
C CULTURE	*Since this "wilderness generation" had not experienced the miracles of Egypt, as their parents had, Moses cast the vision of their possible future: of blessing or of cursing. Israel had the choice to live confidently in God's presence (Deut. 20:1, 4). Moses compared and contrasted their past life in Egypt, their present life of wandering, and their desired future life in the Promised Land (Deut. 11:8–17). The Promised Land was not like Egypt where they had to water crops to produce food. Their land was going to be watered by God (Deut. 11:10–12). The huge doors of opportunity swung on the tiny hinges of obedience.*
T TIMELINE	*between 1445 and 1405 BC*
KEY SCRIPTURE MEMORY VERSES	5:6–21; 6:4–9; 10:12, 13; 30:19, 20

The Previous Command to Enter Canaan

1 These *are* the words which Moses spoke to all Israel on this side of the Jordan in the wilderness, in the plain[a] opposite Suph,[b] between Paran, Tophel, Laban, Hazeroth, and Dizahab. [2]*It is* eleven days' *journey* from Horeb by way of Mount Seir to Kadesh Barnea. [3]Now it came to pass in the fortieth year, in the eleventh month, on the first *day* of the month, *that* Moses spoke to the children of Israel according to all that the LORD had given him as commandments to them, [4]after he had killed Sihon king of the Amorites, who dwelt in Heshbon, and Og king of Bashan, who dwelt at Ashtaroth in[a] Edrei.

[5]On this side of the Jordan in the land of Moab, Moses began to explain this law, saying, [6]"The LORD our God spoke to us in Horeb, saying: 'You have dwelt long enough at this mountain. [7]Turn and take your journey, and go to the mountains of the Amorites, to all the neighboring *places* in the plain,[a] in the mountains and in the lowland, in the South and on the seacoast, to the land of the Canaanites and to Lebanon, as far as the great river, the River Euphrates. [8]See, I have set the land before you; go in and possess the land which the LORD swore to your fathers—to Abraham, Isaac, and Jacob—to give to them and their descendants after them.'

Tribal Leaders Appointed

[9]"And I spoke to you at that time, saying: 'I alone am not able to bear you. [10]The LORD your God has multiplied you, and here you *are* today, as the stars of heaven in multitude. [11]May the LORD God of your fathers make you a thousand times more numerous than you are, and bless you as He has promised you! [12]How can I alone bear your problems and your burdens and your complaints? [13]Choose wise, understanding, and knowledgeable men from among your tribes, and I will make them heads over you.' [14]And you answered me and said, 'The thing which you have told *us* to do *is* good.' [15]So I took the heads of your tribes, wise and knowledgeable men, and made them heads over you, leaders of thousands, leaders of hundreds, leaders of fifties, leaders of tens, and officers for your tribes.

[16]"Then I commanded your judges at that time, saying, 'Hear *the cases* between your brethren, and judge righteously between a man and his brother or the stranger who is with him. [17]You shall not show partiality in judgment; you shall hear the small as well as the great; you shall not be afraid in any man's presence, for the judgment *is* God's. The case that is too hard for you, bring to me, and I will hear it.' [18]And I commanded you at that time all the things which you should do.

Israel's Refusal to Enter the Land

[19]"So we departed from Horeb, and went through all that great and terrible wilderness which you saw on the way to the mountains of the Amorites, as the LORD our God had commanded us. Then we came to Kadesh Barnea. [20]And I said to you, 'You have come to the mountains of the Amorites, which the LORD our God is giving us. [21]Look, the LORD your God has set the land before you; go up *and* possess *it,* as the LORD God of your fathers has spoken to you; do not fear or be discouraged.'

[22]"And every one of you came near to me and said, 'Let us send men before us, and let them search out the land for us, and bring back word to us of the way by which we should go up, and of the cities into which we shall come.'

[23]"The plan pleased me well; so I took twelve of your men, one man from *each* tribe. [24]And they departed and went up into the mountains, and came to the Valley of Eshcol, and spied it out. [25]They also took *some* of the fruit of the land in their hands and brought *it* down to us; and they brought back word to us, saying, '*It is* a good land which the LORD our God is giving us.'

[26]"Nevertheless you would not go up, but rebelled against the command of the LORD your God; [27]and you complained in your tents, and said, 'Because the LORD hates us, He has brought us out of the land of Egypt to deliver us into the hand of the Amorites, to destroy us. [28]Where can we go up? Our brethren have discouraged our hearts, saying, "The people *are* greater and taller than we; the cities *are* great and fortified up to heaven; moreover we have seen the sons of the Anakim there." '

1:1 [a]Hebrew *arabah* [b]One manuscript of the Septuagint, also Targum and Vulgate, read *Red Sea.* **1:4** [a]Septuagint, Syriac, and Vulgate read *and* (compare Joshua 12:4). **1:7** [a]Hebrew *arabah*

²⁹"Then I said to you, 'Do not be terrified, or afraid of them. ³⁰The LORD your God, who goes before you, He will fight for you, according to all He did for you in Egypt before your eyes, ³¹and in the wilderness where you saw how the LORD your God carried you, as a man carries his son, in all the way that you went until you came to this place.' ³²Yet, for all that, you did not believe the LORD your God, ³³who went in the way before you to search out a place for you to pitch your tents, to show you the way you should go, in the fire by night and in the cloud by day.

The Penalty for Israel's Rebellion

³⁴"And the LORD heard the sound of your words, and was angry, and took an oath, saying, ³⁵'Surely not one of these men of this evil generation shall see that good land of which I swore to give to your fathers, ³⁶except Caleb the son of Jephunneh; he shall see it, and to him and his children I am giving the land on which he walked, because he wholly followed the LORD.' ³⁷The LORD was also angry with me for your sakes, saying, 'Even you shall not go in there. ³⁸Joshua the son of Nun, who stands before you, he shall go in there. Encourage him, for he shall cause Israel to inherit it.

³⁹'Moreover your little ones and your children, who you say will be victims, who today have no knowledge of good and evil, they shall go in there; to them I will give it, and they shall possess it. ⁴⁰But as for you, turn and take your journey into the wilderness by the Way of the Red Sea.'

⁴¹"Then you answered and said to me, 'We have sinned against the LORD; we will go up and fight, just as the LORD our God commanded us.' And when everyone of you had girded on his weapons of war, you were ready to go up into the mountain.

⁴²"And the LORD said to me, 'Tell them, "Do not go up nor fight, for I am not among you; lest you be defeated before your enemies." ' ⁴³So I spoke to you; yet you would not listen, but rebelled against the command of the LORD, and presumptuously went up into the mountain. ⁴⁴And the Amorites who dwelt in that mountain came out against you and chased you as bees do, and drove you back from Seir to Hormah. ⁴⁵Then you returned and wept before the LORD, but the LORD would not listen to your voice nor give ear to you.

⁴⁶"So you remained in Kadesh many days, according to the days that you spent there.

The Desert Years

2 "Then we turned and journeyed into the wilderness of the Way of the Red Sea, as the LORD spoke to me, and we skirted Mount Seir for many days.

²"And the LORD spoke to me, saying: ³'You have skirted this mountain long enough; turn northward. ⁴And command the people, saying, "You are about to pass through the territory of your brethren, the descendants of Esau, who live in Seir; and they will be afraid of you. Therefore watch yourselves carefully. ⁵Do not meddle with them, for I will not give you any of their land, no, not so much as one footstep, because I have given Mount Seir to Esau as a possession. ⁶You shall buy food from them with money, that you may eat; and you shall also buy water from them with money, that you may drink.

⁷"For the LORD your God has blessed you in all the work of your hand. He knows your trudging through this great wilderness. These forty years the LORD your God has been with you; you have lacked nothing." '

⁸"And when we passed beyond our brethren, the descendants of Esau who dwell in Seir, away from the road of the plain, away from Elath and Ezion Geber, we turned and passed by way of the Wilderness of Moab. ⁹Then the LORD said to me, 'Do not harass Moab, nor contend with them in battle, for I will not give you any of their land as a possession, because I have given Ar to the descendants of Lot as a possession.' "

¹⁰(The Emim had dwelt there in times past, a people as great and numerous and tall as the Anakim. ¹¹They were also regarded as giants,^a like the Anakim, but the Moabites call them Emim. ¹²The Horites formerly dwelt in Seir, but the descendants of Esau dispossessed them and destroyed them from before them, and dwelt in their place, just as Israel did to the land of their possession which the LORD gave them.)

¹³" 'Now rise and cross over the Valley of the

2:11 ^aHebrew rephaim

Zered.' So we crossed over the Valley of the Zered. ¹⁴And the time we took to come from Kadesh Barnea until we crossed over the Valley of the Zered *was* thirty-eight years, until all the generation of the men of war was consumed from the midst of the camp, just as the LORD had sworn to them. ¹⁵For indeed the hand of the LORD was against them, to destroy them from the midst of the camp until they were consumed.

¹⁶"So it was, when all the men of war had finally perished from among the people, ¹⁷that the LORD spoke to me, saying: ¹⁸'This day you are to cross over at Ar, the boundary of Moab. ¹⁹And *when* you come near the people of Ammon, do not harass them or meddle with them, for I will not give you *any* of the land of the people of Ammon *as* a possession, because I have given it to the descendants of Lot *as* a possession.' "

²⁰(That was also regarded as a land of giants;ᵃ giants formerly dwelt there. But the Ammonites call them Zamzummim, ²¹a people as great and numerous and tall as the Anakim. But the LORD destroyed them before them, and they dispossessed them and dwelt in their place, ²²just as He had done for the descendants of Esau, who dwelt in Seir, when He destroyed the Horites from before them. They dispossessed them and dwelt in their place, even to this day. ²³And the Avim, who dwelt in villages as far as Gaza—the Caphtorim, who came from Caphtor, destroyed them and dwelt in their place.)

²⁴" 'Rise, take your journey, and cross over the River Arnon. Look, I have given into your hand Sihon the Amorite, king of Heshbon, and his land. Begin to possess *it,* and engage him in battle. ²⁵This day I will begin to put the dread and fear of you upon the nations under the whole heaven, who shall hear the report of you, and shall tremble and be in anguish because of you.'

King Sihon Defeated

²⁶"And I sent messengers from the Wilderness of Kedemoth to Sihon king of Heshbon, with words of peace, saying, ²⁷'Let me pass through your land; I will keep strictly to the road, and I will turn neither to the right nor to the left. ²⁸You shall sell me food for money, that I may eat, and give me water for money, that I may drink; only let me pass through on foot, ²⁹just as the descen-

dants of Esau who dwell in Seir and the Moabites who dwell in Ar did for me, until I cross the Jordan to the land which the LORD our God is giving us.'

³⁰"But Sihon king of Heshbon would not let us pass through, for the LORD your God hardened his spirit and made his heart obstinate, that He might deliver him into your hand, as *it is* this day. ³¹And the LORD said to me, 'See, I have begun to give Sihon and his land over to you. Begin to possess *it,* that you may inherit his land.' ³²Then Sihon and all his people came out against us to fight at Jahaz. ³³And the LORD our God delivered him over to us; so we defeated him, his sons, and all his people. ³⁴We took all his cities at that time, and we utterly destroyed the men, women, and little ones of every city; we left none remaining. ³⁵We took only the livestock as plunder for ourselves, with the spoil of the cities which we took. ³⁶From Aroer, which *is* on the bank of the River Arnon, and *from* the city that *is* in the ravine, as far as Gilead, there was not one city too strong for us; the LORD our God delivered all to us. ³⁷Only you did not go near the land of the people of Ammon—anywhere along the River Jabbok, or to the cities of the mountains, or wherever the LORD our God had forbidden us.

King Og Defeated

3 "Then we turned and went up the road to Bashan; and Og king of Bashan came out against us, he and all his people, to battle at Edrei. ²And the LORD said to me, 'Do not fear him, for I have delivered him and all his people and his land into your hand; you shall do to him as you did to Sihon king of the Amorites, who dwelt at Heshbon.'

³"So the LORD our God also delivered into our hands Og king of Bashan, with all his people, and we attacked him until he had no survivors remaining. ⁴And we took all his cities at that time; there was not a city which we did not take from them: sixty cities, all the region of Argob, the kingdom of Og in Bashan. ⁵All these cities *were* fortified with high walls, gates, and bars, besides a great many rural towns. ⁶And we utterly destroyed them, as we did to Sihon king of

2:20 ªHebrew *rephaim*

Heshbon, utterly destroying the men, women, and children of every city. ⁷But all the livestock and the spoil of the cities we took as booty for ourselves.

⁸"And at that time we took the land from the hand of the two kings of the Amorites who *were* on this side of the Jordan, from the River Arnon to Mount Hermon ⁹(the Sidonians call Hermon Sirion, and the Amorites call it Senir), ¹⁰all the cities of the plain, all Gilead, and all Bashan, as far as Salcah and Edrei, cities of the kingdom of Og in Bashan.

¹¹"For only Og king of Bashan remained of the remnant of the giants.ª Indeed his bedstead *was* an iron bedstead. (*Is* it not in Rabbah of the people of Ammon?) Nine cubits *is* its length and four cubits its width, according to the standard cubit.

The Land East of the Jordan Divided

¹²"And this land, *which* we possessed at that time, from Aroer, which *is* by the River Arnon, and half the mountains of Gilead and its cities, I gave to the Reubenites and the Gadites. ¹³The rest of Gilead, and all Bashan, the kingdom of Og, I gave to half the tribe of Manasseh. (All the region of Argob, with all Bashan, was called the land of the giants.ª ¹⁴Jair the son of Manasseh took all the region of Argob, as far as the border of the Geshurites and the Maachathites, and called Bashan after his own name, Havoth Jair,ª to this day.)

¹⁵"Also I gave Gilead to Machir. ¹⁶And to the Reubenites and the Gadites I gave from Gilead as far as the River Arnon, the middle of the river as *the* border, as far as the River Jabbok, the border of the people of Ammon; ¹⁷the plain also, with the Jordan as *the* border, from Chinnereth as far as the east side of the Sea of the Arabah (the Salt Sea), below the slopes of Pisgah.

¹⁸"Then I commanded you at that time, saying: 'The Lord your God has given you this land to possess. All you men of valor shall cross over armed before your brethren, the children of Israel. ¹⁹But your wives, your little ones, and your livestock (I know that you have much livestock) shall stay in your cities which I have given you, ²⁰until the Lord has given rest to your brethren as to you, and they also possess the land which the Lord your God is giving them beyond the Jordan. Then each of you may return to his possession which I have given you.'

²¹"And I commanded Joshua at that time, saying, 'Your eyes have seen all that the Lord your God has done to these two kings; so will the Lord do to all the kingdoms through which you pass. ²²You must not fear them, for the Lord your God Himself fights for you.'

Moses Forbidden to Enter the Land

²³"Then I pleaded with the Lord at that time, saying: ²⁴'O Lord God, You have begun to show Your servant Your greatness and Your mighty hand, for what god *is there* in heaven or on earth who can do *anything* like Your works and Your mighty *deeds?* ²⁵I pray, let me cross over and see the good land beyond the Jordan, those pleasant mountains, and Lebanon.'

²⁶"But the Lord was angry with me on your account, and would not listen to me. So the Lord said to me: 'Enough of that! Speak no more to Me of this matter. ²⁷Go up to the top of Pisgah, and lift your eyes toward the west, the north, the south, and the east; behold *it* with your eyes, for you shall not cross over this Jordan. ²⁸But command Joshua, and encourage him and strengthen him; for he shall go over before this people, and he shall cause them to inherit the land which you will see.'

²⁹"So we stayed in the valley opposite Beth Peor.

Moses Commands Obedience

4 "Now, O Israel, listen to the statutes and the judgments which I teach you to observe, that you may live, and go in and possess the land which the Lord God of your fathers is giving you. ²You shall not add to the word which I command you, nor take from it, that you may keep the commandments of the Lord your God which I command you. ³Your eyes have seen what the Lord did at Baal Peor; for the Lord your God has destroyed from among you all the men who followed Baal of Peor. ⁴But you who held fast to the Lord your God *are* alive today, every one of you.

3:11 ªHebrew *rephaim*   **3:13** ªHebrew *rephaim*   **3:14** ªLiterally *Towns of Jair*

5"Surely I have taught you statutes and judgments, just as the LORD my God commanded me, that you should act according *to them* in the land which you go to possess. 6Therefore be careful to observe *them;* for this *is* your wisdom and your understanding in the sight of the peoples who will hear all these statutes, and say, 'Surely this great nation *is* a wise and understanding people.'

7"For what great nation *is there* that has God so near to it, as the LORD our God *is* to us, for whatever *reason* we may call upon Him? 8And what great nation *is there* that has *such* statutes and righteous judgments as are in all this law which I set before you this day? 9Only take heed to yourself, and diligently keep yourself, lest you forget the things your eyes have seen, and lest they depart from your heart all the days of your life. And teach them to your children and your grandchildren, 10*especially concerning* the day you stood before the LORD your God in Horeb, when the LORD said to me, 'Gather the people to Me, and I will let them hear My words, that they may learn to fear Me all the days they live on the earth, and *that* they may teach their children.'

11"Then you came near and stood at the foot of the mountain, and the mountain burned with fire to the midst of heaven, with darkness, cloud, and thick darkness. 12And the LORD spoke to you out of the midst of the fire. You heard the sound of the words, but saw no form; *you* only *heard* a voice. 13So He declared to you His covenant which He commanded you to perform, the Ten Commandments; and He wrote them on two tablets of stone. 14And the LORD commanded me at that time to teach you statutes and judgments, that you might observe them in the land which you cross over to possess.

Beware of Idolatry

15"Take careful heed to yourselves, for you saw no form when the LORD spoke to you at Horeb out of the midst of the fire, 16lest you act corruptly and make for yourselves a carved image in the form of any figure: the likeness of male or female, 17the likeness of any animal that *is* on the earth or the likeness of any winged bird that flies in the air, 18the likeness of anything that creeps on the ground or the likeness of any fish that *is* in the water beneath the earth. 19And *take heed,* lest you lift your eyes to heaven, and *when* you see the sun, the moon, and the stars, all the host of heaven, you feel driven to worship them and serve them, which the LORD your God has given to all the peoples under the whole heaven as a heritage. 20But the LORD has taken you and brought you out of the iron furnace, out of Egypt, to be His people, an inheritance, as you are this day. 21Furthermore the LORD was angry with me for your sakes, and swore that I would not cross over the Jordan, and that I would not enter the good land which the LORD your God is giving you as an inheritance. 22But I must die in this land, I must not cross over the Jordan; but you shall cross over and possess that good land. 23Take heed to yourselves, lest you forget the covenant of the LORD your God which He made with you, and make for yourselves a carved image in the form of anything which the LORD your God has forbidden you. 24For the LORD your God *is* a consuming fire, a jealous God.

25"When you beget children and grandchildren and have grown old in the land, and act corruptly and make a carved image in the form of anything, and do evil in the sight of the LORD your God to provoke Him to anger, 26I call heaven and earth to witness against you this day, that you will soon utterly perish from the land which you cross over the Jordan to possess; you will not prolong *your* days in it, but will be utterly destroyed. 27And the LORD will scatter you among the peoples, and you will be left few in number among the nations where the LORD will drive you. 28And there you will serve gods, the work of men's hands, wood and stone, which neither see nor hear nor eat nor smell. 29But from there you will seek the LORD your God, and you will find *Him* if you seek Him with all your heart and with all your soul. 30When you are in distress, and all these things come upon you in the latter days, when you turn to the LORD your God and obey His voice 31(for the LORD your God *is* a merciful God), He will not forsake you nor destroy you, nor forget the covenant of your fathers which He swore to them.

32"For ask now concerning the days that are past, which were before you, since the day that God created man on the earth, and *ask* from one end of heaven to the other, whether *any* great *thing* like this has happened, or *anything* like it has been heard. [33]Did *any* people *ever* hear the voice of God speaking out of the midst of the fire, as you have heard, and live? [34]Or did God *ever* try to go *and* take for Himself a nation from the midst of *another* nation, by trials, by signs, by wonders, by war, by a mighty hand and an outstretched arm, and by great terrors, according to all that the LORD your God did for you in Egypt before your eyes? [35]To you it was shown, that you might know that the LORD Himself *is* God; *there is* none other besides Him. [36]Out of heaven He let you hear His voice, that He might instruct you; on earth He showed you His great fire, and you heard His words out of the midst of the fire. [37]And because He loved your fathers, therefore He chose their descendants after them; and He brought you out of Egypt with His Presence, with His mighty power, [38]driving out from before you nations greater and mightier than you, to bring you in, to give you their land *as* an inheritance, as *it is* this day. [39]Therefore know this day, and consider *it* in your heart, that the LORD Himself *is* God in heaven above and on the earth beneath; *there is* no other. [40]You shall therefore keep His statutes and His commandments which I command you today, that it may go well with you and with your children after you, and that you may prolong *your* days in the land which the LORD your God is giving you for all time."

Cities of Refuge East of the Jordan

[41]Then Moses set apart three cities on this side of the Jordan, toward the rising of the sun, [42]that the manslayer might flee there, who kills his neighbor unintentionally, without having hated him in time past, and that by fleeing to one of these cities he might live: [43]Bezer in the wilderness on the plateau for the Reubenites, Ramoth in Gilead for the Gadites, and Golan in Bashan for the Manassites.

Introduction to God's Law

[44]Now this *is* the law which Moses set before the children of Israel. [45]These *are* the testimonies, the statutes, and the judgments which Moses spoke to the children of Israel after they came out of Egypt, [46]on this side of the Jordan, in the valley opposite Beth Peor, in the land of Sihon king of

the Amorites, who dwelt at Heshbon, whom Moses and the children of Israel defeated after they came out of Egypt. [47]And they took possession of his land and the land of Og king of Bashan, two kings of the Amorites, who *were* on this side of the Jordan, toward the rising of the sun, [48]from Aroer, which *is* on the bank of the River Arnon, even to Mount Sion[a] (that is, Hermon), [49]and all the plain on the east side of Jordan as far as the Sea of the Arabah, below the slopes of Pisgah.

The Ten Commandments Reviewed

5 And Moses called all Israel, and said to them: "Hear, O Israel, the statutes and judgments which I speak in your hearing today, that you may learn them and be careful to observe them. [2]The LORD our God made a covenant with us in Horeb. [3]The LORD did not make this covenant with our fathers, but with us, those who *are* here today, all of us who *are* alive. [4]The LORD talked with you face to face on the mountain from the midst of the fire. [5]I stood between the LORD and you at that time, to declare to you the word of the LORD; for you were afraid because of the fire, and you did not go up the mountain. *He* said:

> [6]'I *am* the LORD your God who brought you out of the land of Egypt, out of the house of bondage.
> [7]'You shall have no other gods before Me.
> [8]'You shall not make for yourself a carved image—any likeness *of anything* that *is* in heaven above, or that *is* in the earth beneath, or that *is* in the water under the earth; [9]you shall not bow down to them nor serve them. For I, the LORD your God, *am* a jealous God, visiting the iniquity of the fathers upon the children to the third and fourth *generations* of those who hate Me, [10]but showing mercy to thousands, to those who love Me and keep My commandments.
> [11]'You shall not take the name of the LORD your God in vain, for the LORD will not hold *him* guiltless who takes His name in vain.

4:48 [a]Syriac reads *Sirion* (compare 3:9).

¹²'Observe the Sabbath day, to keep it holy, as the LORD your God commanded you. ¹³Six days you shall labor and do all your work, ¹⁴but the seventh day *is* the Sabbath of the LORD your God. *In it* you shall do no work: you, nor your son, nor your daughter, nor your male servant, nor your female servant, nor your ox, nor your donkey, nor any of your cattle, nor your stranger who *is* within your gates, that your male servant and your female servant may rest as well as you. ¹⁵And remember that you were a slave in the land of Egypt, and the LORD your God brought you out from there by a mighty hand and by an outstretched arm; therefore the LORD your God commanded you to keep the Sabbath day.

¹⁶'Honor your father and your mother, as the LORD your God has commanded you, that your days may be long, and that it may be well with you in the land which the LORD your God is giving you.

¹⁷'You shall not murder.

¹⁸'You shall not commit adultery.

¹⁹'You shall not steal.

²⁰'You shall not bear false witness against your neighbor.

²¹'You shall not covet your neighbor's wife; and you shall not desire your neighbor's house, his field, his male servant, his female servant, his ox, his donkey, or anything that *is* your neighbor's.'

²²"These words the Lord spoke to all your assembly, in the mountain from the midst of the fire, the cloud, and the thick darkness, with a loud voice; and He added no more. And He wrote them on two tablets of stone and gave them to me.

THE PEOPLE AFRAID OF GOD'S PRESENCE

²³"So it was, when you heard the voice from the midst of the darkness, while the mountain was burning with fire, that you came near to me, all the heads of your tribes and your elders. ²⁴And you said: 'Surely the LORD our God has shown us His glory and His greatness, and we

have heard His voice from the midst of the fire. We have seen this day that God speaks with man; yet he *still* lives. ²⁵Now therefore, why should we die? For this great fire will consume us; if we hear the voice of the LORD our God anymore, then we shall die. ²⁶For who *is there* of all flesh who has heard the voice of the living God speaking from the midst of the fire, as we *have,* and lived? ²⁷You go near and hear all that the LORD our God may say, and tell us all that the LORD our God says to you, and we will hear and do *it.*'

²⁸"Then the LORD heard the voice of your words when you spoke to me, and the LORD said to me: 'I have heard the voice of the words of this people which they have spoken to you. They are right *in* all that they have spoken. ²⁹Oh, that they had such a heart in them that they would fear Me and always keep all My commandments, that it might be well with them and with their children forever! ³⁰Go and say to them, "Return to your tents." ³¹But as for you, stand here by Me, and I will speak to you all the commandments, the statutes, and the judgments which you shall teach them, that they may observe *them* in the land which I am giving them to possess.'

³²"Therefore you shall be careful to do as the LORD your God has commanded you; you shall not turn aside to the right hand or to the left. ³³You shall walk in all the ways which the LORD your God has commanded you, that you may live and *that it may be* well with you, and *that* you may prolong *your* days in the land which you shall possess.

THE GREATEST COMMANDMENT

6 "Now this *is* the commandment, *and these are* the statutes and judgments which the LORD your God has commanded to teach you, that you may observe *them* in the land which you are crossing over to possess, ²that you may fear the LORD your God, to keep all His statutes and His commandments which I command you, you and your son and your grandson, all the days of your life, and that your days may be prolonged. ³Therefore hear, O Israel, and be careful to observe *it,* that it may be well with you, and that you may multiply greatly as the LORD God of

THROUGH THE GRID
Thinking Christianly: Ten Foundational Beliefs of a Christian Worldview

Belief One: God

The Christian worldview maintains that there is only one true God, who is personal, infinite, self-revealing, omnipowerful, omniscient, omnipresent, self-existent, sovereign, and eternal. God is righteous, holy, and redemptive. God is a triune existence of three distinct and eternal Persons—the Father, the Son, and the Holy Spirit (Gen. 1:1; Deut. 6:4–6; Jon. 4:2; Matt. 28:18–20; Eph. 4:4-6; 1 Pet. 1:16–21). *See Through the Grid article on page 1565.*

your fathers has promised you—'a land flowing with milk and honey.'ᵃ

4"Hear, O Israel: The LORD our God, the LORD *is* one!ᵃ 5You shall love the LORD your God with all your heart, with all your soul, and with all your strength.

6"And these words which I command you today shall be in your heart. 7You shall teach them diligently to your children, and shall talk of them when you sit in your house, when you walk by the way, when you lie down, and when you rise up. 8You shall bind them as a sign on your hand, and they shall be as frontlets between your eyes. 9You shall write them on the doorposts of your house and on your gates.

Caution Against Disobedience

10"So it shall be, when the LORD your God brings you into the land of which He swore to your fathers, to Abraham, Isaac, and Jacob, to give you large and beautiful cities which you did not build, 11houses full of all good things, which you did not fill, hewn-out wells which you did not dig, vineyards and olive trees which you did not plant—when you have eaten and are full— 12then beware, lest you forget the LORD who brought you out of the land of Egypt, from the house of bondage. 13You shall fear the LORD your God and serve Him, and shall take oaths in His name. 14You shall not go after other gods, the gods of the peoples who *are* all around you 15(for the LORD your God *is* a jealous God among you), lest the anger of the LORD your God be aroused against you and destroy you from the face of the earth.

16"You shall not tempt the LORD your God as you tempted *Him* in Massah. 17You shall diligently keep the commandments of the LORD your God, His testimonies, and His statutes which He has commanded you. 18And you shall do *what is* right and good in the sight of the LORD, that it may be well with you, and that you may go in and possess the good land of which the LORD swore to your fathers, 19to cast out all your enemies from before you, as the LORD has spoken.

20"When your son asks you in time to come, saying, 'What *is the meaning of* the testimonies, the statutes, and the judgments which the LORD our God has commanded you?' 21then you shall say to your son: 'We were slaves of Pharaoh in Egypt, and the LORD brought us out of Egypt with a mighty hand; 22and the LORD showed signs and wonders before our eyes, great and severe, against Egypt, Pharaoh, and all his household. 23Then He brought us out from there, that He might bring us in, to give us the land of which He swore to our fathers. 24And the LORD commanded us to observe all these statutes, to fear the LORD our God, for our good always, that He might preserve us alive, as *it is* this day. 25Then it will be righteousness for us, if we are careful to observe all these commandments before the LORD our God, as He has commanded us.'

A Chosen People

7 "When the LORD your God brings you into the land which you go to possess, and has cast

6:3 ᵃExodus 3:8　6:4 ᵃOr *The Lord is our God, the Lord alone* (that is, the only one)

LEADERSHIP ISSUES

GC2: Unity: The Lord Is One!

DEUTERONOMY 6:4 *Hear, O Israel: The LORD our God, the LORD is one!*

This declaration among the children of Israel, known as the *Shema* (Hebrew for "hear"), became their call to worship and according to rabbinical law was to be recited morning and night. It stressed the uniqueness of Yahweh as the Lord *alone*. Christ would refer to this as the first and great commandment demanding our total commitment (Mark 12:29–31).

The mystery of *one* God who exists as Father, Son, and Holy Spirit speaks to the foundation of our unity in Christ. To be created in His image and after His likeness (Gen. 1:26) includes significant insights and among them is the truth that we have the capacity for unity with Christ and His body. Christ would speak of He and the Father "being one," and it was His oneness with the Father that confirmed He was God (John 10:30). In a similar way, our unity with Christ and others in His body gives witness of Him in a conflicted, divided world.

Foundational to our unity as members of His body, the church, is this question: "Does the Jesus in me love the Jesus in you?" Yes is undoubtedly the answer, but what if we don't agree on every minor detail of Bible doctrine or Christian practice? "Does the Jesus in me *still* love the Jesus in you?" Most certainly, as our unity is grounded not in the total conformity of our beliefs or practices but in the simplicity of our both being members of the same body, the church, and having the same Head, Jesus Christ.

out many nations before you, the Hittites and the Girgashites and the Amorites and the Canaanites and the Perizzites and the Hivites and the Jebusites, seven nations greater and mightier than you, [2]and when the LORD your God delivers them over to you, you shall conquer them *and* utterly destroy them. You shall make no covenant with them nor show mercy to them. [3]Nor shall you make marriages with them. You shall not give your daughter to their son, nor take their daughter for your son. [4]For they will turn your sons away from following Me, to serve other gods; so the anger of the LORD will be aroused against you and destroy you suddenly. [5]But thus you shall deal with them: you shall destroy their altars, and break down their *sacred* pillars, and cut down their wooden images,[a] and burn their carved images with fire.

[6]"For you *are* a holy people to the LORD your God; the LORD your God has chosen you to be a people for Himself, a special treasure above all the peoples on the face of the earth. [7]The LORD did not set His love on you nor choose you because you were more in number than any other people, for you were the least of all peoples; [8]but because the LORD loves you, and because He would keep the oath which He swore to your fathers, the LORD has brought you out with a mighty hand, and redeemed you from the house of bondage, from the hand of Pharaoh king of Egypt.

[9]"Therefore know that the LORD your God, He *is* God, the faithful God who keeps covenant and mercy for a thousand generations with those who love Him and keep His commandments; [10]and He repays those who hate Him to their face, to destroy them. He will not be slack with him who hates Him; He will repay him to his face. [11]Therefore you shall keep the commandment, the statutes, and the judgments which I command you today, to observe them.

BLESSINGS OF OBEDIENCE

[12]"Then it shall come to pass, because you listen to these judgments, and keep and do them, that the LORD your God will keep with you the covenant and the mercy which He swore to your fathers. [13]And He will love you and bless you and multiply you; He will also bless the fruit of your womb and the fruit of your land, your grain and your new wine and your oil, the increase of your cattle and the offspring of your flock, in the land of which He swore to your fathers to give you. [14]You shall be blessed above all peoples; there shall not be a male or female barren among you or among your livestock. [15]And the LORD will take away from you all sickness, and will afflict you with none of the terrible diseases of Egypt which you have known, but will lay *them* on all those who hate you. [16]Also you shall destroy all the peoples whom the LORD your God delivers over to you; your eye shall have no pity on them; nor

7:5 [a]Hebrew *Asherim,* Canaanite deities

THROUGH THE GRID

Discover God: God Enables Us to Be Faithful

DEUTERONOMY 7:9 *Therefore know that the LORD your God, He is God, the faithful God who keeps covenant and mercy for a thousand generations with those who love Him and keep His commandments.*

As we rely on God's faithfulness, we begin to notice that God indeed proves Himself faithful time and time again! God's faithfulness is that which enables us to be faithful as well; and through faith, we can resist temptation. But even when we fall, God's faithfulness is present, offering forgiveness to us in the midst of our most limiting weaknesses. God empowers us with gifts with which we can serve Him and others, and in so doing, enables us to be faithful as well. As we work through the power of the Holy Spirit, we strive to become more like God in His faithfulness by demonstrating to the world our faithfulness to God.

shall you serve their gods, for that *will be* a snare to you.

17"If you should say in your heart, 'These nations are greater than I; how can I dispossess them?'— 18you shall not be afraid of them, *but* you shall remember well what the LORD your God did to Pharaoh and to all Egypt: 19the great trials which your eyes saw, the signs and the wonders, the mighty hand and the outstretched arm, by which the LORD your God brought you out. So shall the LORD your God do to all the peoples of whom you are afraid. 20Moreover the LORD your God will send the hornet among them until those who are left, who hide themselves from you, are destroyed. 21You shall not be terrified of them; for the LORD your God, the great and awesome God, *is* among you. 22And the LORD your God will drive out those nations before you little by little; you will be unable to destroy them at once, lest the beasts of the field become *too* numerous for you. 23But the LORD your God will deliver them over to you, and will inflict defeat upon them until they are destroyed. 24And He will deliver their kings into your hand, and you will destroy their name from under heaven; no one shall be able to stand against you until you have destroyed them. 25You shall burn the carved images of their gods with fire; you shall not covet the silver or gold *that is on* them, nor take *it* for yourselves, lest you be snared by it; for it *is* an abomination to the LORD your God. 26Nor shall you bring an abomination into your house, lest you be doomed to destruction like it. You shall utterly detest it and utterly abhor it, for it *is* an accursed thing.

Remember the Lord Your God

8 "Every commandment which I command you today you must be careful to observe, that you may live and multiply, and go in and possess the land of which the LORD swore to your fathers. 2And you shall remember that the LORD your God led you all the way these forty years in the wilderness, to humble you *and* test you, to know what *was* in your heart, whether you would keep His commandments or not. 3So He humbled you, allowed you to hunger, and fed you with manna which you did not know nor did your fathers

know, that He might make you know that man shall not live by bread alone; but man lives by every *word* that proceeds from the mouth of the LORD. 4Your garments did not wear out on you, nor did your foot swell these forty years. 5You should know in your heart that as a man chastens his son, *so* the LORD your God chastens you.

6"Therefore you shall keep the commandments of the LORD your God, to walk in His ways and to fear Him. 7For the LORD your God is bringing you into a good land, a land of brooks of water, of fountains and springs, that flow out of valleys and hills; 8a land of wheat and barley, of vines and fig trees and pomegranates, a land of olive oil and honey; 9a land in which you will eat bread without scarcity, in which you will lack nothing; a land whose stones *are* iron and out of whose hills you can dig copper. 10When you have eaten and are full, then you shall bless the LORD your God for the good land which He has given you.

11"Beware that you do not forget the LORD your God by not keeping His commandments, His judgments, and His statutes which I command you today, 12lest—*when* you have eaten and are full, and have built beautiful houses and dwell *in them;* 13and *when* your herds and your flocks multiply, and your silver and your gold are multiplied, and all that you have is multiplied; 14when your heart is lifted up, and you forget the LORD your God who brought you out of the land of Egypt, from the house of bondage; 15who led you through that great and terrible wilderness, *in which were* fiery serpents and scorpions and thirsty land where there was no water; who brought water for you out of the flinty rock; 16who fed you in the wilderness with manna, which your fathers did not know, that He might humble you and that He might test you, to do you good in the end— 17then you say in your heart, 'My power and the might of my hand have gained me this wealth.'

18"And you shall remember the LORD your God, for *it is* He who gives you power to get wealth, that He may establish His covenant which He swore to your fathers, as *it is* this day. 19Then it shall be, if you by any means forget the LORD your God, and follow other gods, and serve them and worship them, I testify against you this day that you shall surely perish. ²⁰As the nations which the LORD destroys before you, so you shall perish, because you would not be obedient to the voice of the LORD your God.

ISRAEL'S REBELLIONS REVIEWED

9 "Hear, O Israel: You *are* to cross over the Jordan today, and go in to dispossess nations greater and mightier than yourself, cities great and fortified up to heaven, ²a people great and tall, the descendants of the Anakim, whom you know, and *of whom* you heard *it said,* 'Who can stand before the descendants of Anak?' ³Therefore understand today that the LORD your God *is* He who goes over before you *as* a consuming fire. He will destroy them and bring them down before you; so you shall drive them out and destroy them quickly, as the LORD has said to you.

⁴"Do not think in your heart, after the LORD your God has cast them out before you, saying, 'Because of my righteousness the LORD has brought me in to possess this land'; but *it is* because of the wickedness of these nations *that* the LORD is driving them out from before you. ⁵*It is* not because of your righteousness or the uprightness of your heart *that* you go in to possess their land, but because of the wickedness of these nations *that* the LORD your God drives them out from before you, and that He may fulfill the word which the LORD swore to your fathers, to Abraham, Isaac, and Jacob. ⁶Therefore understand that the LORD your God is not giving you this good land to possess because of your righteousness, for you *are* a stiff-necked people.

⁷"Remember! Do not forget how you provoked the LORD your God to wrath in the wilderness. From the day that you departed from the land of Egypt until you came to this place, you have been rebellious against the LORD. ⁸Also in Horeb you provoked the LORD to wrath, so that the LORD was angry *enough* with you to have destroyed you. ⁹When I went up into the mountain to receive the tablets of stone, the tablets of the covenant which the LORD made with you, then I stayed on the mountain forty days and forty nights. I neither ate bread nor drank water. ¹⁰Then the LORD delivered to me two tablets of stone written with the finger of God, and on them *were* all the words which the LORD had spo-

ken to you on the mountain from the midst of the fire in the day of the assembly. ¹¹And it came to pass, at the end of forty days and forty nights, *that* the LORD gave me the two tablets of stone, the tablets of the covenant.

¹²"Then the LORD said to me, 'Arise, go down quickly from here, for your people whom you brought out of Egypt have acted corruptly; they have quickly turned aside from the way which I commanded them; they have made themselves a molded image.'

¹³"Furthermore the LORD spoke to me, saying, 'I have seen this people, and indeed they are a stiff-necked people. ¹⁴Let Me alone, that I may destroy them and blot out their name from under heaven; and I will make of you a nation mightier and greater than they.'

¹⁵"So I turned and came down from the mountain, and the mountain burned with fire; and the two tablets of the covenant *were* in my two hands. ¹⁶And I looked, and behold, you had sinned against the LORD your God—had made for yourselves a molded calf! You had turned aside quickly from the way which the LORD had commanded you. ¹⁷Then I took the two tablets and threw them out of my two hands and broke them before your eyes. ¹⁸And I fell down before the LORD, as at the first, forty days and forty nights; I neither ate bread nor drank water, because of all your sin which you committed in doing wickedly in the sight of the LORD, to provoke Him to anger. ¹⁹For I was afraid of the anger and hot displeasure with which the LORD was angry with you, to destroy you. But the LORD listened to me at that time also. ²⁰And the LORD was very angry with Aaron *and* would have destroyed him; so I prayed for Aaron also at the same time. ²¹Then I took your sin, the calf which you had made, and burned it with fire and crushed it *and* ground *it* very small, until it was as fine as dust; and I threw its dust into the brook that descended from the mountain.

²²"Also at Taberah and Massah and Kibroth Hattaavah you provoked the LORD to wrath. ²³Likewise, when the LORD sent you from Kadesh Barnea, saying, 'Go up and possess the land which I have given you,' then you rebelled against the commandment of the LORD your God, and you did not believe Him nor obey His voice. ²⁴You

have been rebellious against the LORD from the day that I knew you.

25"Thus I prostrated myself before the LORD; forty days and forty nights I kept prostrating myself, because the LORD had said He would destroy you. 26Therefore I prayed to the LORD, and said: 'O Lord GOD, do not destroy Your people and Your inheritance whom You have redeemed through Your greatness, whom You have brought out of Egypt with a mighty hand. 27Remember Your servants, Abraham, Isaac, and Jacob; do not look on the stubbornness of this people, or on their wickedness or their sin, 28lest the land from which You brought us should say, "Because the LORD was not able to bring them to the land which He promised them, and because He hated them, He has brought them out to kill them in the wilderness." 29Yet they are Your people and Your inheritance, whom You brought out by Your mighty power and by Your outstretched arm.'

The Second Pair of Tablets

10 "At that time the LORD said to me, 'Hew for yourself two tablets of stone like the first, and come up to Me on the mountain and make yourself an ark of wood. 2And I will write on the tablets the words that were on the first tablets, which you broke; and you shall put them in the ark.'

3"So I made an ark of acacia wood, hewed two tablets of stone like the first, and went up the mountain, having the two tablets in my hand. 4And He wrote on the tablets according to the first writing, the Ten Commandments, which the LORD had spoken to you in the mountain from the midst of the fire in the day of the assembly; and the LORD gave them to me. 5Then I turned and came down from the mountain, and put the tablets in the ark which I had made; and there they are, just as the LORD commanded me."

6(Now the children of Israel journeyed from the wells of Bene Jaakan to Moserah, where Aaron died, and where he was buried; and Eleazar his son ministered as priest in his stead. 7From there they journeyed to Gudgodah, and from Gudgodah to Jotbathah, a land of rivers of water. 8At that time the LORD separated the tribe of Levi to bear the ark of the covenant of the LORD, to stand before the LORD to minister to Him and

to bless in His name, to this day. 9Therefore Levi has no portion nor inheritance with his brethren; the LORD is his inheritance, just as the LORD your God promised him.)

10"As at the first time, I stayed in the mountain forty days and forty nights; the LORD also heard me at that time, and the LORD chose not to destroy you. 11Then the LORD said to me, 'Arise, begin your journey before the people, that they may go in and possess the land which I swore to their fathers to give them.'

The Essence of the Law

12"And now, Israel, what does the LORD your God require of you, but to fear the LORD your God, to walk in all His ways and to love Him, to serve the LORD your God with all your heart and with all your soul, 13and to keep the commandments of the LORD and His statutes which I command you today for your good? 14Indeed heaven and the highest heavens belong to the LORD your God, also the earth with all that is in it. 15The LORD delighted only in your fathers, to love them; and He chose their descendants after them, you above all peoples, as it is this day. 16Therefore circumcise the foreskin of your heart, and be stiff-necked no longer. 17For the LORD your God is God of gods and Lord of lords, the great God, mighty and awesome, who shows no partiality nor takes a bribe. 18He administers justice for the fatherless and the widow, and loves the stranger, giving him food and clothing. 19Therefore love the stranger, for you were strangers in the land of Egypt. 20You shall fear the LORD your God; you shall serve Him, and to Him you shall hold fast, and take oaths in His name. 21He is your praise, and He is your God, who has done for you these great and awesome things which your eyes have seen. 22Your fathers went down to Egypt with seventy persons, and now the LORD your God has made you as the stars of heaven in multitude.

Love and Obedience Rewarded

11 "Therefore you shall love the LORD your God, and keep His charge, His statutes, His judgments, and His commandments always. 2Know today that I do not speak with your children, who have not known and who have not seen the chastening of the LORD your God, His

LEADERSHIP ISSUES

GC2: Nourished by the Word: God Doesn't Want You to Hurt

DEUTERONOMY 10:13

We all know that church lessons and teachers of the Word regularly emphasize the importance of the Ten Commandments (Ex. 20). From preschool classes to adult Bible Studies, we frequently revisit these instructions that are central to the Old Testament. Effective teachers explain the context in which the commandments were given, challenge us to pursue the behavioral lifestyle that the commandments exhort, and speak of the truthful insights that the commandments provide in knowing God's character and holiness.

But when we study the Ten Commandments and do not experience the heart of the compassionate Father who gave us those commandments, we cannot fully see the God who is love. We miss the relational purpose behind the Ten Commandments when we see only the "thou shalt not's" without recognizing the heart of love that lies behind them. A relational focus would lead us to ask the question, Was it to raise a standard of moral behavior and to give testimony of a righteous God? Yes. But Deuteronomy 10:13 also speaks of these commandments being given "for your good."

What good does God have in mind for us? Evidently, our loving Father gave us these commandments because He did not want to see His children hurt themselves or one another. So we ask ourselves: "What does it prompt within me when I consider that His 'thou shalt not's' were given for my good?"

Sit quietly before the Lord and consider how He has given certain commandments for your good. He loves you and does not want to see you hurt. What does that do to your heart?

"As I consider that the Lord does not want to see me hurt, my heart is touched with _____." Express your feelings to God. Tell Him about your gratefulness, humility, love, or joy. Offer your heartfelt prayers to Him.

GC2
GREAT COMMANDMENT
COMMISSION

greatness and His mighty hand and His out-stretched arm— [3]His signs and His acts which He did in the midst of Egypt, to Pharaoh king of Egypt, and to all his land; [4]what He did to the army of Egypt, to their horses and their chariots: how He made the waters of the Red Sea overflow them as they pursued you, and *how* the LORD has destroyed them to this day; [5]what He did for you in the wilderness until you came to this place; [6]and what He did to Dathan and Abiram the sons of Eliab, the son of Reuben: how the earth opened its mouth and swallowed them up, their households, their tents, and all the substance that *was* in their possession, in the midst of all Israel— [7]but your eyes have seen every great act of the LORD which He did.

[8]"Therefore you shall keep every commandment which I command you today, that you may be strong, and go in and possess the land which you cross over to possess, [9]and that you may prolong *your* days in the land which the LORD swore to give your fathers, to them and their descendants, 'a land flowing with milk and honey.'[a] [10]For the land which you go to possess *is* not like the land of Egypt from which you have come, where you sowed your seed and watered *it* by foot, as a vegetable garden; [11]but the land which you cross over to possess *is* a land of hills and valleys, which drinks water from the rain of heaven, [12]a land for which the LORD your God cares; the eyes of the LORD your God *are* always on it, from the beginning of the year to the very end of the year.

[13]"And it shall be that if you earnestly obey My commandments which I command you today, to love the LORD your God and serve Him with all your heart and with all your soul, [14]then I[a] will give *you* the rain for your land in its season, the early rain and the latter rain, that you may gather in your grain, your new wine, and your oil. [15]And I will send grass in your fields for your livestock, that you may eat and be filled.' [16]Take heed to yourselves, lest your heart be deceived, and you turn aside and serve other gods and worship them, [17]lest the LORD's anger be aroused against you, and He shut up the heavens so that there be no rain, and the land yield no produce, and you perish quickly from the good land which the LORD is giving you.

[18]"Therefore you shall lay up these words of mine in your heart and in your soul, and bind them as a sign on your hand, and they shall be as frontlets between your eyes. [19]You shall teach them to your children, speaking of them when you sit in your house, when you walk by the way, when you lie down, and when you rise up. [20]And you shall write them on the doorposts of your house and on your gates, [21]that your days and the days of your children may be multiplied in the land of which the LORD swore to your fathers to give them, like the days of the heavens above the earth.

[22]"For if you carefully keep all these commandments which I command you to do—to love the LORD your God, to walk in all His ways, and to hold fast to Him— [23]then the LORD will drive out all these nations from before you, and you will dispossess greater and mightier nations than yourselves. [24]Every place on which the sole of your foot treads shall be yours: from the wilderness and Lebanon, from the river, the River Euphrates, even to the Western Sea,[a] shall be your territory. [25]No man shall be able to stand against you; the LORD your God will put the dread of you and the fear of you upon all the land where you tread, just as He has said to you.

[26]"Behold, I set before you today a blessing and a curse: [27]the blessing, if you obey the commandments of the LORD your God which I command you today; [28]and the curse, if you do not obey the commandments of the LORD your God, but turn aside from the way which I command you today, to go after other gods which you have not known. [29]Now it shall be, when the LORD your God has brought you into the land which you go to possess, that you shall put the blessing on Mount Gerizim and the curse on Mount Ebal. [30]*Are* they not on the other side of the Jordan, toward the setting sun, in the land of the Canaanites who dwell in the plain opposite Gilgal, beside the terebinth trees of Moreh? [31]For you will cross over the Jordan and go in to possess the land which the LORD your God is giving you, and you will possess it and dwell in it. [32]And you shall be careful to observe all the

11:9 [a]Exodus 3:8   **11:14** [a]Following Masoretic Text and Targum; Samaritan Pentateuch, Septuagint, and Vulgate read *He*. **11:24** [a]That is, the Mediterranean

LEADERSHIP
REALITIES

OPPORTUNITY *Deuteronomy 11:26, 27*

This verse makes it clear that any one of us can choose to be blessed if we choose to obey the commandments of God. Now more than ever this generation needs young men and women whose hearts are set toward blessing and ready to be used as influencers in the world.

barakah—**blessing**—prosperity, gift, present

If obedience is the foundation of our blessing, then we must prepare ourselves to do so. We are given this three-point plan for our body, mind, and will in Romans 12:1, 2.

- **Present your body:** *present your bodies a living sacrifice . . .* We are to *yield* or *present* our bodies to God for His will and His service. This quickly defines some of the choices we need to make.

- **Program your mind:** *be transformed by the renewing of your mind . . .* What the Lord has in mind for us is total transformation of our thought life. This can only occur through reading, speaking, studying, and living the Word of God.

- **Prove what you are made of:** *prove what is that good and acceptable and perfect will of God.* Will you have an impact on the change being made in the world, or will you be swept up in the current of change? Set your heart toward the goal of a life that is *good, acceptable, and the perfect will of God.*

statutes and judgments which I set before you today.

A Prescribed Place of Worship

12 "These *are* the statutes and judgments which you shall be careful to observe in the land which the LORD God of your fathers is giving you to possess, all the days that you live on the earth. ²You shall utterly destroy all the places where the nations which you shall dispossess served their gods, on the high mountains and on the hills and under every green tree. ³And you shall destroy their altars, break their *sacred* pillars, and burn their wooden images with fire; you shall cut down the carved images of their gods and destroy their names from that place. ⁴You shall not worship the LORD your God *with* such *things.*

⁵"But you shall seek the place where the LORD your God chooses, out of all your tribes, to put His name for His dwelling place; and there you shall go. ⁶There you shall take your burnt of-

ferings, your sacrifices, your tithes, the heave offerings of your hand, your vowed offerings, your freewill offerings, and the firstborn of your herds and flocks. ⁷And there you shall eat before the LORD your God, and you shall rejoice in all to which you have put your hand, you and your households, in which the LORD your God has blessed you.

⁸"You shall not at all do as we are doing here today—every man doing whatever *is* right in his own eyes— ⁹for as yet you have not come to the rest and the inheritance which the LORD your God is giving you. ¹⁰But *when* you cross over the Jordan and dwell in the land which the LORD your God is giving you to inherit, and He gives you rest from all your enemies round about, so that you dwell in safety, ¹¹then there will be the place where the LORD your God chooses to make His name abide. There you shall bring all that I command you: your burnt offerings, your sacrifices, your tithes, the heave offerings of your

hand, and all your choice offerings which you vow to the LORD. ¹²And you shall rejoice before the LORD your God, you and your sons and your daughters, your male and female servants, and the Levite who *is* within your gates, since he has no portion nor inheritance with you. ¹³Take heed to yourself that you do not offer your burnt offerings in every place that you see; ¹⁴but in the place which the LORD chooses, in one of your tribes, there you shall offer your burnt offerings, and there you shall do all that I command you.

¹⁵"However, you may slaughter and eat meat within all your gates, whatever your heart desires, according to the blessing of the LORD your God which He has given you; the unclean and the clean may eat of it, of the gazelle and the deer alike. ¹⁶Only you shall not eat the blood; you shall pour it on the earth like water. ¹⁷You may not eat within your gates the tithe of your grain or your new wine or your oil, of the firstborn of your herd or your flock, of any of your offerings which you vow, of your freewill offerings, or of the heave offering of your hand. ¹⁸But you must eat them before the LORD your God in the place which the LORD your God chooses, you and your son and your daughter, your male servant and your female servant, and the Levite who *is* within your gates; and you shall rejoice before the LORD your God in all to which you put your hands. ¹⁹Take heed to yourself that you do not forsake the Levite as long as you live in your land.

²⁰"When the LORD your God enlarges your border as He has promised you, and you say, 'Let me eat meat,' because you long to eat meat, you may eat as much meat as your heart desires. ²¹If the place where the LORD your God chooses to put His name is too far from you, then you may slaughter from your herd and from your flock which the LORD has given you, just as I have commanded you, and you may eat within your gates as much as your heart desires. ²²Just as the gazelle and the deer are eaten, so you may eat them; the unclean and the clean alike may eat them. ²³Only be sure that you do not eat the blood, for the blood *is* the life; you may not eat the life with the meat. ²⁴You shall not eat it; you shall pour it on the earth like water. ²⁵You shall not eat it, that it may go well with you and your

children after you, when you do *what is* right in the sight of the LORD. ²⁶Only the holy things which you have, and your vowed offerings, you shall take and go to the place which the LORD chooses. ²⁷And you shall offer your burnt offerings, the meat and the blood, on the altar of the LORD your God; and the blood of your sacrifices shall be poured out on the altar of the LORD your God, and you shall eat the meat. ²⁸Observe and obey all these words which I command you, that it may go well with you and your children after you forever, when you do *what is* good and right in the sight of the LORD your God.

BEWARE OF FALSE GODS

²⁹"When the LORD your God cuts off from before you the nations which you go to dispossess, and you displace them and dwell in their land, ³⁰take heed to yourself that you are not ensnared to follow them, after they are destroyed from before you, and that you do not inquire after their gods, saying, 'How did these nations serve their gods? I also will do likewise.' ³¹You shall not worship the LORD your God in that way; for every abomination to the LORD which He hates they have done to their gods; for they burn even their sons and daughters in the fire to their gods.

³²"Whatever I command you, be careful to observe it; you shall not add to it nor take away from it.

PUNISHMENT OF APOSTATES

13 "If there arises among you a prophet or a dreamer of dreams, and he gives you a sign or a wonder, ²and the sign or the wonder comes to pass, of which he spoke to you, saying, 'Let us go after other gods'—which you have not known—'and let us serve them,' ³you shall not listen to the words of that prophet or that dreamer of dreams, for the LORD your God is testing you to know whether you love the LORD your God with all your heart and with all your soul. ⁴You shall walk after the LORD your God and fear Him, and keep His commandments and obey His voice; you shall serve Him and hold fast to Him. ⁵But that prophet or that dreamer of dreams shall be put to death, because he has spoken in order to turn *you* away from the LORD your God, who brought you out of the land of Egypt and redeemed you from the house of bondage, to entice you from the way in which the LORD your God commanded you to walk. So you shall put away the evil from your midst.

⁶"If your brother, the son of your mother, your son or your daughter, the wife of your bosom, or your friend who is as your own soul, secretly entices you, saying, 'Let us go and serve other gods,' which you have not known, neither you nor your fathers, ⁷of the gods of the people which *are* all around you, near to you or far off from you, from *one* end of the earth to the *other* end of the earth, ⁸you shall not consent to him or listen to him, nor shall your eye pity him, nor shall you spare him or conceal him; ⁹but you shall surely kill him; your hand shall be first against him to put him to death, and afterward the hand of all the people. ¹⁰And you shall stone him with stones until he dies, because he sought to entice you away from the LORD your God, who brought you out of the land of Egypt, from the house of bondage. ¹¹So all Israel shall hear and fear, and not again do such wickedness as this among you.

¹²"If you hear someone in one of your cities, which the LORD your God gives you to dwell in, saying, ¹³'Corrupt men have gone out from among you and enticed the inhabitants of their city, saying, "Let us go and serve other gods" '— which you have not known— ¹⁴then you shall inquire, search out, and ask diligently. And *if it is* indeed true *and* certain *that* such an abomination was committed among you, ¹⁵you shall surely strike the inhabitants of that city with the edge of the sword, utterly destroying it, all that is in it and its livestock—with the edge of the sword. ¹⁶And you shall gather all its plunder into the middle of the street, and completely burn with fire the city and all its plunder, for the LORD your God. It shall be a heap forever; it shall not be built again. ¹⁷So none of the accursed things shall remain in your hand, that the LORD may turn from the fierceness of His anger and show you mercy, have compassion on you and multiply you, just as He swore to your fathers, ¹⁸because you have listened to the voice of the LORD your God, to keep all His commandments which I command you today, to do *what is* right in the eyes of the LORD your God.

IMPROPER MOURNING

14 "You *are* the children of the LORD your God; you shall not cut yourselves nor shave the front of your head for the dead. ²For you *are* a holy people to the LORD your God, and the LORD has chosen you to be a people for Himself, a special treasure above all the peoples who *are* on the face of the earth.

CLEAN AND UNCLEAN MEAT

³"You shall not eat any detestable thing. ⁴These *are* the animals which you may eat: the ox, the sheep, the goat, ⁵the deer, the gazelle, the roe deer, the wild goat, the mountain goat,ᵃ the antelope, and the mountain sheep. ⁶And you may eat every animal with cloven hooves, having the hoof split into two parts, *and that* chews the cud, among the animals. ⁷Nevertheless, of those that chew the cud or have cloven hooves, you shall not eat, *such as* these: the camel, the hare, and the rock hyrax; for they chew the cud but do not have cloven hooves; they *are* unclean for you. ⁸Also the swine is unclean for you, because it has cloven hooves, yet *does* not *chew* the cud; you shall not eat their flesh or touch their dead carcasses.

⁹"These you may eat of all that *are* in the waters: you may eat all that have fins and scales. ¹⁰And whatever does not have fins and scales you shall not eat; it *is* unclean for you.

¹¹"All clean birds you may eat. ¹²But these you shall not eat: the eagle, the vulture, the buzzard, ¹³the red kite, the falcon, and the kite after their kinds; ¹⁴every raven after its kind; ¹⁵the ostrich, the short-eared owl, the sea gull, and the hawk after their kinds; ¹⁶the little owl, the screech owl, the white owl, ¹⁷the jackdaw, the carrion vulture, the fisher owl, ¹⁸the stork, the heron after its kind, and the hoopoe and the bat.

¹⁹"Also every creeping thing that flies is unclean for you; they shall not be eaten.

²⁰"You may eat all clean birds.

²¹"You shall not eat anything that dies *of itself;* you may give it to the alien who *is* within your gates, that he may eat it, or you may sell it to a foreigner; for you *are* a holy people to the LORD your God.

14:5 ᵃOr *addax*

"You shall not boil a young goat in its mother's milk.

Tithing Principles

22"You shall truly tithe all the increase of your grain that the field produces year by year. 23And you shall eat before the LORD your God, in the place where He chooses to make His name abide, the tithe of your grain and your new wine and your oil, of the firstborn of your herds and your flocks, that you may learn to fear the LORD your God always. 24But if the journey is too long for you, so that you are not able to carry *the tithe, or* if the place where the LORD your God chooses to put His name is too far from you, when the LORD your God has blessed you, 25then you shall exchange *it* for money, take the money in your hand, and go to the place which the LORD your God chooses. 26And you shall spend that money for whatever your heart desires: for oxen or sheep, for wine or similar drink, for whatever your heart desires; you shall eat there before the LORD your God, and you shall rejoice, you and your household. 27You shall not forsake the Levite who *is* within your gates, for he has no part nor inheritance with you.

28"At the end of *every* third year you shall bring out the tithe of your produce of that year and store *it* up within your gates. 29And the Levite, because he has no portion nor inheritance with you, and the stranger and the fatherless and the widow who *are* within your gates, may come and eat and be satisfied, that the LORD your God may bless you in all the work of your hand which you do.

Debts Canceled Every Seven Years

15 "At the end of *every* seven years you shall grant a release *of debts.* 2And this *is* the form of the release: Every creditor who has lent *anything* to his neighbor shall release *it;* he shall not require *it* of his neighbor or his brother, because it is called the LORD's release. 3Of a foreigner you may require *it;* but you shall give up your claim to what is owed by your brother, 4except when there may be no poor among you; for the LORD will greatly bless you in the land which the LORD your God is giving you to possess *as* an inheritance— 5only if you carefully obey the voice of the LORD your God, to observe with care all these commandments which I command you today. 6For the LORD your God will bless you just as He promised you; you shall lend to many nations, but you shall not borrow; you shall reign over many nations, but they shall not reign over you.

Generosity to the Poor

7"If there is among you a poor man of your brethren, within any of the gates in your land which the LORD your God is giving you, you shall not harden your heart nor shut your hand from your poor brother, 8but you shall open your hand wide to him and willingly lend him sufficient for his need, whatever he needs. 9Beware lest there be a wicked thought in your heart, saying, 'The seventh year, the year of release, is at hand,' and your eye be evil against your poor brother and you give him nothing, and he cry out to the LORD against you, and it become sin among you. 10You shall surely give to him, and your heart should not be grieved when you give to him, because for this thing the LORD your God will bless you in all your works and in all to which you put your hand. 11For the poor will never cease from the land; therefore I command you, saying, 'You shall open your hand wide to your brother, to your poor and your needy, in your land.'

The Law Concerning Bondservants

12"If your brother, a Hebrew man, or a Hebrew woman, is sold to you and serves you six years, then in the seventh year you shall let him go free from you. 13And when you send him away free from you, you shall not let him go away empty-handed; 14you shall supply him liberally from your flock, from your threshing floor, and from your winepress. *From what* the LORD your God has blessed you with, you shall give to him. 15You shall remember that you were a slave in the land of Egypt, and the LORD your God redeemed you; therefore I command you this thing today. 16And if it happens that he says to you, 'I will not go away from you,' because he loves you and your house, since he prospers with you, 17then you shall take an awl and thrust *it* through his ear to the door, and he shall be your servant forever. Also to your female servant you shall do likewise. 18It shall not seem hard to you when you send him away free from you; for he has been worth a double hired servant in serving you six years. Then the LORD your God will bless you in all that you do.

The Law Concerning Firstborn Animals

19"All the firstborn males that come from your herd and your flock you shall sanctify to the LORD your God; you shall do no work with the firstborn of your herd, nor shear the firstborn of your flock. 20You and your household shall eat *it* before the LORD your God year by year in the place which the LORD chooses. 21But if there is a defect in it, *if it is* lame or blind *or has* any serious defect, you shall not sacrifice it to the LORD your God. 22You may eat it within your gates; the unclean and the clean *person* alike *may eat it,* as *if it were* a gazelle or a deer. 23Only you shall not eat its blood; you shall pour it on the ground like water.

The Passover Reviewed

16"Observe the month of Abib, and keep the Passover to the LORD your God, for in the month of Abib the LORD your God brought you out of Egypt by night. 2Therefore you shall sacrifice the Passover to the LORD your God, from the flock and the herd, in the place where the LORD chooses to put His name. 3You shall eat no leavened bread with it; seven days you shall eat unleavened bread with it, *that is,* the bread of affliction (for you came out of the land of Egypt in haste), that you may remember the day in which you came out of the land of Egypt all the days of your life. 4And no leaven shall be seen among you in all your territory for seven days, nor shall *any* of the meat which you sacrifice the first day at twilight remain overnight until morning.

5"You may not sacrifice the Passover within any of your gates which the LORD your God gives you; 6but at the place where the LORD your God chooses to make His name abide, there you shall sacrifice the Passover at twilight, at the going down of the sun, at the time you came out of Egypt. 7And you shall roast and eat *it* in the place which the LORD your God chooses, and in the morning you shall turn and go to your tents. 8Six days you shall eat unleavened bread, and on the seventh day there *shall be* a sacred assembly to the LORD your God. You shall do no work *on it.*

The Feast of Weeks Reviewed

9"You shall count seven weeks for yourself; begin to count the seven weeks from *the time* you begin *to put* the sickle to the grain. 10Then you shall keep the Feast of Weeks to the LORD your God with the tribute of a freewill offering from your hand, which you shall give as the LORD your God blesses you. 11You shall rejoice before the LORD your God, you and your son and your daughter, your male servant and your female servant, the Levite who *is* within your gates, the stranger and the fatherless and the widow who *are* among you, at the place where the LORD your God chooses to make His name abide. 12And you shall remember that you were a slave in Egypt, and you shall be careful to observe these statutes.

The Feast of Tabernacles Reviewed

13"You shall observe the Feast of Tabernacles seven days, when you have gathered from your threshing floor and from your winepress. 14And you shall rejoice in your feast, you and your son and your daughter, your male servant and your female servant and the Levite, the stranger and the fatherless and the widow, who *are* within your gates. 15Seven days you shall keep a sacred feast to the LORD your God in the place which the LORD chooses, because the LORD your God will bless you in all your produce and in all the work of your hands, so that you surely rejoice.

16"Three times a year all your males shall appear before the LORD your God in the place which He chooses: at the Feast of Unleavened Bread, at the Feast of Weeks, and at the Feast of Tabernacles; and they shall not appear before the LORD empty-handed. 17Every man *shall give* as he is able, according to the blessing of the LORD your God which He has given you.

Justice Must Be Administered

18"You shall appoint judges and officers in all your gates, which the LORD your God gives you, according to your tribes, and they shall judge the people with just judgment. 19You shall not pervert justice; you shall not show partiality, nor take a bribe, for a bribe blinds the eyes of the wise and twists the words of the righteous. 20You shall follow what is altogether just, that you may live and inherit the land which the LORD your God is giving you.

²¹"You shall not plant for yourself any tree, as a wooden image, near the altar which you build for yourself to the LORD your God. ²²You shall not set up a *sacred* pillar, which the LORD your God hates.

17 "You shall not sacrifice to the LORD your God a bull or sheep which has any blemish *or* defect, for that *is* an abomination to the LORD your God.

²"If there is found among you, within any of your gates which the LORD your God gives you, a man or a woman who has been wicked in the sight of the LORD your God, in transgressing His covenant, ³who has gone and served other gods and worshiped them, either the sun or moon or any of the host of heaven, which I have not commanded, ⁴and it is told you, and you hear *of it,* then you shall inquire diligently. And if *it is* indeed true *and* certain that such an abomination has been committed in Israel, ⁵then you shall bring out to your gates that man or woman who has committed that wicked thing, and shall stone to death that man or woman with stones. ⁶Whoever is deserving of death shall be put to death on the testimony of two or three witnesses; he shall not be put to death on the testimony of one witness. ⁷The hands of the witnesses shall be the first against him to put him to death, and afterward the hands of all the people. So you shall put away the evil from among you.

⁸"If a matter arises which is too hard for you to judge, between degrees of guilt for bloodshed, between one judgment or another, or between one punishment or another, matters of controversy within your gates, then you shall arise and go up to the place which the LORD your God chooses. ⁹And you shall come to the priests, the Levites, and to the judge *there* in those days, and inquire *of them;* they shall pronounce upon you the sentence of judgment. ¹⁰You shall do according to the sentence which they pronounce upon you in that place which the LORD chooses. And you shall be careful to do according to all that they order you. ¹¹According to the sentence of the law in which they instruct you, according to the judgment which they tell you, you shall do; you shall not turn aside *to* the right hand or *to* the left from the sentence which they pronounce upon you. ¹²Now the man who acts presumptuously and will not heed the priest who stands to minister there before the LORD your God, or the judge, that man shall die. So you shall put away the evil from Israel. ¹³And all the people shall hear and fear, and no longer act presumptuously.

Principles Governing Kings

¹⁴"When you come to the land which the LORD your God is giving you, and possess it and dwell in it, and say, 'I will set a king over me like all the nations that *are* around me,' ¹⁵you shall surely set a king over you whom the LORD your God chooses; *one* from among your brethren you shall set as king over you; you may not set a foreigner over you, who *is* not your brother. ¹⁶But he shall not multiply horses for himself, nor cause the people to return to Egypt to multiply horses, for the LORD has said to you, 'You shall not return that way again.' ¹⁷Neither shall he multiply wives for himself, lest his heart turn away; nor shall he greatly multiply silver and gold for himself.

¹⁸"Also it shall be, when he sits on the throne of his kingdom, that he shall write for himself a copy of this law in a book, from *the one* before the priests, the Levites. ¹⁹And it shall be with him, and he shall read it all the days of his life, that he may learn to fear the LORD his God and be careful to observe all the words of this law and these statutes, ²⁰that his heart may not be lifted above his brethren, that he may not turn aside from the commandment *to* the right hand or *to* the left, and that he may prolong *his* days in his kingdom, he and his children in the midst of Israel.

The Portion of the Priests and Levites

18 "The priests, the Levites—all the tribe of Levi—shall have no part nor inheritance with Israel; they shall eat the offerings of the LORD made by fire, and His portion. ²Therefore they shall have no inheritance among their brethren; the LORD is their inheritance, as He said to them.

³"And this shall be the priest's due from the people, from those who offer a sacrifice, whether *it is* bull or sheep: they shall give to the priest the

shoulder, the cheeks, and the stomach. [4]The first-fruits of your grain and your new wine and your oil, and the first of the fleece of your sheep, you shall give him. [5]For the LORD your God has chosen him out of all your tribes to stand to minister in the name of the LORD, him and his sons forever.

[6]"So if a Levite comes from any of your gates, from where he dwells among all Israel, and comes with all the desire of his mind to the place which the LORD chooses, [7]then he may serve in the name of the LORD his God as all his brethren the Levites *do,* who stand there before the LORD. [8]They shall have equal portions to eat, besides what comes from the sale of his inheritance.

AVOID WICKED CUSTOMS

[9]"When you come into the land which the LORD your God is giving you, you shall not learn to follow the abominations of those nations. [10]There shall not be found among you *anyone* who makes his son or his daughter pass through the fire, *or one* who practices witchcraft, *or a* soothsayer, or one who interprets omens, or a sorcerer, [11]or one who conjures spells, or a medium, or a spiritist, or one who calls up the dead. [12]For all who do these things *are* an abomination to the LORD, and because of these abominations the LORD your God drives them out from before you. [13]You shall be blameless before the LORD your God. [14]For these nations which you will dispossess listened to soothsayers and diviners; but as for you, the LORD your God has not appointed such for you.

A NEW PROPHET LIKE MOSES

[15]"The LORD your God will raise up for you a Prophet like me from your midst, from your brethren. Him you shall hear, [16]according to all you desired of the LORD your God in Horeb in the day of the assembly, saying, 'Let me not hear again the voice of the LORD my God, nor let me see this great fire anymore, lest I die.'

[17]"And the LORD said to me: 'What they have spoken is good. [18]I will raise up for them a Prophet like you from among their brethren, and will put My words in His mouth, and He shall speak to them all that I command Him. [19]And it

---

THROUGH THE GRID

Where Have All the Dreamers Gone? Observations from a Biblical Worldview: Wicca (Deut. 18:10–14)

One of the fastest-growing expressions of spirituality in recent days is the Wiccan movement. The Wiccan movement takes its roots in new age spirituality and witchcraft. Those who practice Wicca are in the business of making witchcraft more appealing and popular; at the core of its beliefs is the empowerment of the individual. Wiccans affirm, along with new age mentality, the divinity of all things, and they seek to restore a respect for that divinity. As new age thought spread throughout the country, Wicca grew as a popular movement, especially within the population of teenage girls. There are plenty of movies and shows that surround witchcraft. The popularity witchcraft currently holds is due to the American emphasis on tolerance, freedom, and the empowerment of the self; and it is appealing to many who are searching for forms of spirituality without the "constraints" of organized religion.

Wiccans affirm individualized spirituality as a way of connecting with God; thus, their worldview clashes directly with the Christian worldview, which makes exclusivist claims about being the only way to salvation. Horoscopes, numerology, and psychic practices are all forms of the same new age mentality that promises to give people control, insight, and power. However, Christians must reject Wicca because truth does not come from the self or from the earth, but from God, as revealed through Christ and through the Bible.

shall be *that* whoever will not hear My words, which He speaks in My name, I will require *it* of him. 20But the prophet who presumes to speak a word in My name, which I have not commanded him to speak, or who speaks in the name of other gods, that prophet shall die.' 21And if you say in your heart, 'How shall we know the word which the LORD has not spoken?'— 22when a prophet speaks in the name of the LORD, if the thing does not happen or come to pass, that *is* the thing which the LORD has not spoken; the prophet has spoken it presumptuously; you shall not be afraid of him.

THREE CITIES OF REFUGE

19 "When the LORD your God has cut off the nations whose land the LORD your God is giving you, and you dispossess them and dwell in their cities and in their houses, 2you shall separate three cities for yourself in the midst of your land which the LORD your God is giving you to possess. 3You shall prepare roads for yourself, and divide into three parts the territory of your land which the LORD your God is giving you to inherit, that any manslayer may flee there.

4"And this *is* the case of the manslayer who flees there, that he may live: Whoever kills his neighbor unintentionally, not having hated him in time past— 5as when *a man* goes to the woods with his neighbor to cut timber, and his hand swings a stroke with the ax to cut down the tree, and the head slips from the handle and strikes his neighbor so that he dies—he shall flee to one of these cities and live; 6lest the avenger of blood, while his anger is hot, pursue the manslayer and overtake him, because the way is long, and kill him, though he *was* not deserving of death, since he had not hated the victim in time past. 7Therefore I command you, saying, 'You shall separate three cities for yourself.'

8"Now if the LORD your God enlarges your territory, as He swore to your fathers, and gives you the land which He promised to give to your fathers, 9and if you keep all these commandments and do them, which I command you today, to love the LORD your God and to walk always in His ways, then you shall add three more cities for yourself besides these three, 10lest innocent blood be shed in the midst of your land which the

LORD your God is giving you *as* an inheritance, and *thus* guilt of bloodshed be upon you.

11"But if anyone hates his neighbor, lies in wait for him, rises against him and strikes him mortally, so that he dies, and he flees to one of these cities, 12then the elders of his city shall send and bring him from there, and deliver him over to the hand of the avenger of blood, that he may die. 13Your eye shall not pity him, but you shall put away *the guilt of* innocent blood from Israel, that it may go well with you.

PROPERTY BOUNDARIES

14"You shall not remove your neighbor's landmark, which the men of old have set, in your inheritance which you will inherit in the land that the LORD your God is giving you to possess.

THE LAW CONCERNING WITNESSES

15"One witness shall not rise against a man concerning any iniquity or any sin that he commits; by the mouth of two or three witnesses the matter shall be established. 16If a false witness rises against any man to testify against him of wrongdoing, 17then both men in the controversy shall stand before the LORD, before the priests and the judges who serve in those days. 18And the judges shall make careful inquiry, and indeed, *if* the witness *is* a false witness, who has testified falsely against his brother, 19then you shall do to him as he thought to have done to his brother; so you shall put away the evil from among you. 20And those who remain shall hear and fear, and hereafter they shall not again commit such evil among you. 21Your eye shall not pity: life *shall be* for life, eye for eye, tooth for tooth, hand for hand, foot for foot.

PRINCIPLES GOVERNING WARFARE

20 "When you go out to battle against your enemies, and see horses and chariots and people more numerous than you, do not be afraid of them; for the LORD your God *is* with you, who brought you up from the land of Egypt. 2So it shall be, when you are on the verge of battle, that the priest shall approach and speak to the people. 3And he shall say to them, 'Hear, O Israel: Today you are on the verge of battle with your enemies. Do not let your heart faint, do not be

afraid, and do not tremble or be terrified because of them; [4]for the LORD your God *is* He who goes with you, to fight for you against your enemies, to save you.'

[5]"Then the officers shall speak to the people, saying: 'What man *is there* who has built a new house and has not dedicated it? Let him go and return to his house, lest he die in the battle and another man dedicate it. [6]Also what man *is there* who has planted a vineyard and has not eaten of it? Let him go and return to his house, lest he die in the battle and another man eat of it. [7]And what man *is there* who is betrothed to a woman and has not married her? Let him go and return to his house, lest he die in the battle and another man marry her.'

[8]"The officers shall speak further to the people, and say, 'What man *is there who is* fearful and fainthearted? Let him go and return to his house, lest the heart of his brethren faint[a] like his heart.' [9]And so it shall be, when the officers have finished speaking to the people, that they shall make captains of the armies to lead the people.

[10]"When you go near a city to fight against it, then proclaim an offer of peace to it. [11]And it shall be that if they accept your offer of peace, and open to you, then all the people *who are* found in it shall be placed under tribute to you, and serve you. [12]Now if they will not make peace with you, but war against you, then you shall besiege it. [13]And when the LORD your God delivers it into your hands, you shall strike every male in it with the edge of the sword. [14]But the women, the little ones, the livestock, and all that is in the city, all its spoil, you shall plunder for yourself; and you shall eat the enemies' plunder which the LORD your God gives you. [15]Thus you shall do to all the cities *which are* very far from you, which *are* not of the cities of these nations.

[16]"But of the cities of these peoples which the LORD your God gives you *as* an inheritance, you shall let nothing that breathes remain alive, [17]but you shall utterly destroy them: the Hittite and the Amorite and the Canaanite and the Perizzite and the Hivite and the Jebusite, just as the LORD your God commanded you, [18]lest they teach you to do according to all their abominations which they have done for their gods, and you sin against the LORD your God.

[19]"When you besiege a city for a long time, while making war against it to take it, you shall not destroy its trees by wielding an ax against them; if you can eat of them, do not cut them down to use in the siege, for the tree of the field *is* man's *food*. [20]Only the trees which you know *are* not trees for food you may destroy and cut down, to build siegeworks against the city that makes war with you, until it is subdued.

THE LAW CONCERNING UNSOLVED MURDER

21 "If *anyone* is found slain, lying in the field in the land which the LORD your God is giving you to possess, *and* it is not known who killed him, [2]then your elders and your judges shall go out and measure *the distance* from the slain man to the surrounding cities. [3]And it shall be *that* the elders of the city nearest to the slain man will take a heifer which has not been worked *and* which has not pulled with a yoke. [4]The elders of that city shall bring the heifer down to a valley with flowing water, which is neither plowed nor sown, and they shall break the heifer's neck there in the valley. [5]Then the priests, the sons of Levi, shall come near, for the LORD your God has chosen them to minister to Him and to bless in the name of the LORD; by their word every controversy and every assault shall be *settled*. [6]And all the elders of that city nearest to the slain *man* shall wash their hands over the heifer whose neck was broken in the valley. [7]Then they shall answer and say, 'Our hands have not shed this blood, nor have our eyes seen *it*. [8]Provide atonement, O LORD, for Your people Israel, whom You have redeemed, and do not lay innocent blood to the charge of Your people Israel.' And atonement shall be provided on their behalf for the blood. [9]So you shall put away the *guilt of* innocent blood from among you when you do *what is* right in the sight of the LORD.

FEMALE CAPTIVES

[10]"When you go out to war against your enemies, and the LORD your God delivers them into your hand, and you take them captive, [11]and you see among the captives a beautiful woman, and

20:8 [a]Following Masoretic Text and Targum; Samaritan Pentateuch, Septuagint, Syriac, and Vulgate read *lest he make his brother's heart faint.*

desire her and would take her for your wife, [12]then you shall bring her home to your house, and she shall shave her head and trim her nails. [13]She shall put off the clothes of her captivity, remain in your house, and mourn her father and her mother a full month; after that you may go in to her and be her husband, and she shall be your wife. [14]And it shall be, if you have no delight in her, then you shall set her free, but you certainly shall not sell her for money; you shall not treat her brutally, because you have humbled her.

Firstborn Inheritance Rights

[15]"If a man has two wives, one loved and the other unloved, and they have borne him children, *both* the loved and the unloved, and *if* the firstborn son is of her who is unloved, [16]then it shall be, on the day he bequeaths his possessions to his sons, *that* he must not bestow firstborn status on the son of the loved wife in preference to the son of the unloved, the *true* firstborn. [17]But he shall acknowledge the son of the unloved wife *as* the firstborn by giving him a double portion of all that he has, for he *is* the beginning of his strength; the right of the firstborn *is* his.

The Rebellious Son

[18]"If a man has a stubborn and rebellious son who will not obey the voice of his father or the voice of his mother, and *who,* when they have chastened him, will not heed them, [19]then his father and his mother shall take hold of him and bring him out to the elders of his city, to the gate of his city. [20]And they shall say to the elders of his city, 'This son of ours is stubborn and rebellious; he will not obey our voice; he is a glutton and a drunkard.' [21]Then all the men of his city shall stone him to death with stones; so you shall put away the evil from among you, and all Israel shall hear and fear.

Miscellaneous Laws

[22]"If a man has committed a sin deserving of death, and he is put to death, and you hang him on a tree, [23]his body shall not remain overnight on the tree, but you shall surely bury him that day, so that you do not defile the land which the LORD your God is giving you *as* an inheritance; for he who is hanged *is* accursed of God.

22 "You shall not see your brother's ox or his sheep going astray, and hide yourself from them; you shall certainly bring them back to your brother. [2]And if your brother *is* not near you, or if you do not know him, then you shall bring it to your own house, and it shall remain with you until your brother seeks it; then you shall restore it to him. [3]You shall do the same with his donkey, and so shall you do with his garment; with any lost thing of your brother's, which he has lost and you have found, you shall do likewise; you must not hide yourself.

[4]"You shall not see your brother's donkey or his ox fall down along the road, and hide yourself from them; you shall surely help him lift *them* up again.

[5]"A woman shall not wear anything that pertains to a man, nor shall a man put on a woman's garment, for all who do so *are* an abomination to the LORD your God.

[6]"If a bird's nest happens to be before you along the way, in any tree or on the ground, with young ones or eggs, with the mother sitting on the young or on the eggs, you shall not take the mother with the young; [7]you shall surely let the mother go, and take the young for yourself, that it may be well with you and *that* you may prolong *your* days.

[8]"When you build a new house, then you shall make a parapet for your roof, that you may not bring guilt of bloodshed on your household if anyone falls from it.

[9]"You shall not sow your vineyard with different kinds of seed, lest the yield of the seed which you have sown and the fruit of your vineyard be defiled.

[10]"You shall not plow with an ox and a donkey together.

[11]"You shall not wear a garment of different sorts, *such as* wool and linen mixed together.

[12]"You shall make tassels on the four corners of the clothing with which you cover *yourself.*

Laws of Sexual Morality

[13]"If any man takes a wife, and goes in to her, and detests her, [14]and charges her with shameful conduct, and brings a bad name on her, and says, 'I took this woman, and when I came to her I found she *was* not a virgin,' [15]then the father and

mother of the young woman shall take and bring out *the evidence of* the young woman's virginity to the elders of the city at the gate. [16]And the young woman's father shall say to the elders, 'I gave my daughter to this man as wife, and he detests her. [17]Now he has charged her with shameful conduct, saying, "I found your daughter *was* not a virgin," and yet these *are the evidences of* my daughter's virginity.' And they shall spread the cloth before the elders of the city. [18]Then the elders of that city shall take that man and punish him; [19]and they shall fine him one hundred *shekels* of silver and give *them* to the father of the young woman, because he has brought a bad name on a virgin of Israel. And she shall be his wife; he cannot divorce her all his days.

[20]"But if the thing is true, *and evidences of* virginity are not found for the young woman, [21]then they shall bring out the young woman to the door of her father's house, and the men of her city shall stone her to death with stones, because she has done a disgraceful thing in Israel, to play the harlot in her father's house. So you shall put away the evil from among you.

[22]"If a man is found lying with a woman married to a husband, then both of them shall die—the man that lay with the woman, and the woman; so you shall put away the evil from Israel.

[23]"If a young woman *who is* a virgin is betrothed to a husband, and a man finds her in the city and lies with her, [24]then you shall bring them both out to the gate of that city, and you shall stone them to death with stones, the young woman because she did not cry out in the city, and the man because he humbled his neighbor's wife; so you shall put away the evil from among you.

[25]"But if a man finds a betrothed young woman in the countryside, and the man forces her and lies with her, then only the man who lay with her shall die. [26]But you shall do nothing to the young woman; *there is* in the young woman no sin *deserving* of death, for just as when a man rises against his neighbor and kills him, even so *is* this matter. [27]For he found her in the countryside, *and* the betrothed young woman cried out, but *there was* no one to save her.

[28]"If a man finds a young woman *who is* a virgin, who is not betrothed, and he seizes her and lies with her, and they are found out, [29]then the man who lay with her shall give to the young woman's father fifty *shekels* of silver, and she shall be his wife because he has humbled her; he shall not be permitted to divorce her all his days.

[30]"A man shall not take his father's wife, nor uncover his father's bed.

Those Excluded from the Congregation

23 "He who is emasculated by crushing or mutilation shall not enter the assembly of the LORD.

[2]"One of illegitimate birth shall not enter the assembly of the LORD; even to the tenth generation none of his *descendants* shall enter the assembly of the LORD.

[3]"An Ammonite or Moabite shall not enter the assembly of the LORD; even to the tenth generation none of his *descendants* shall enter the assembly of the LORD forever, [4]because they did not meet you with bread and water on the road when you came out of Egypt, and because they hired against you Balaam the son of Beor from Pethor of Mesopotamia,[a] to curse you. [5]Nevertheless the LORD your God would not listen to Balaam, but the LORD your God turned the curse into a blessing for you, because the LORD your God loves you. [6]You shall not seek their peace nor their prosperity all your days forever.

[7]"You shall not abhor an Edomite, for he *is* your brother. You shall not abhor an Egyptian, because you were an alien in his land. [8]The children of the third generation born to them may enter the assembly of the LORD.

Cleanliness of the Campsite

[9]"When the army goes out against your enemies, then keep yourself from every wicked thing. [10]If there is any man among you who becomes unclean by some occurrence in the night, then he shall go outside the camp; he shall not come inside the camp. [11]But it shall be, when evening comes, that he shall wash with water; and when the sun sets, he may come into the camp.

[12]"Also you shall have a place outside the camp, where you may go out; [13]and you shall have an implement among your equipment, and when

23:4 [a]Hebrew *Aram Naharaim*

you sit down outside, you shall dig with it and turn and cover your refuse. ¹⁴For the LORD your God walks in the midst of your camp, to deliver you and give your enemies over to you; therefore your camp shall be holy, that He may see no unclean thing among you, and turn away from you.

MISCELLANEOUS LAWS

¹⁵"You shall not give back to his master the slave who has escaped from his master to you. ¹⁶He may dwell with you in your midst, in the place which he chooses within one of your gates, where it seems best to him; you shall not oppress him.

¹⁷"There shall be no *ritual* harlot[a] of the daughters of Israel, or a perverted[b] one of the sons of Israel. ¹⁸You shall not bring the wages of a harlot or the price of a dog to the house of the LORD your God for any vowed offering, for both of these *are* an abomination to the LORD your God.

¹⁹"You shall not charge interest to your brother—interest on money *or* food *or* anything that is lent out at interest. ²⁰To a foreigner you may charge interest, but to your brother you shall not charge interest, that the LORD your God may bless you in all to which you set your hand in the land which you are entering to possess.

²¹"When you make a vow to the LORD your God, you shall not delay to pay it; for the LORD your God will surely require it of you, and it would be sin to you. ²²But if you abstain from vowing, it shall not be sin to you. ²³That which has gone from your lips you shall keep and perform, for you voluntarily vowed to the LORD your God what you have promised with your mouth.

²⁴"When you come into your neighbor's vineyard, you may eat your fill of grapes at your pleasure, but you shall not put *any* in your container. ²⁵When you come into your neighbor's standing grain, you may pluck the heads with your hand, but you shall not use a sickle on your neighbor's standing grain.

LAW CONCERNING DIVORCE

24 "When a man takes a wife and marries her, and it happens that she finds no favor in his eyes because he has found some uncleanness in her, and he writes her a certificate of divorce, puts *it* in her hand, and sends her out of his house,

²when she has departed from his house, and goes and becomes another man's *wife,* ³if the latter husband detests her and writes her a certificate of divorce, puts *it* in her hand, and sends her out of his house, or if the latter husband dies who took her as his wife, ⁴*then* her former husband who divorced her must not take her back to be his wife after she has been defiled; for that *is* an abomination before the LORD, and you shall not bring sin on the land which the LORD your God is giving you *as* an inheritance.

MISCELLANEOUS LAWS

⁵"When a man has taken a new wife, he shall not go out to war or be charged with any business; he shall be free at home one year, and bring happiness to his wife whom he has taken.

⁶"No man shall take the lower or the upper millstone in pledge, for he takes *one's* living in pledge.

⁷"If a man is found kidnapping any of his brethren of the children of Israel, and mistreats him or sells him, then that kidnapper shall die; and you shall put away the evil from among you.

⁸"Take heed in an outbreak of leprosy, that you carefully observe and do according to all that the priests, the Levites, shall teach you; just as I commanded them, *so* you shall be careful to do. ⁹Remember what the LORD your God did to Miriam on the way when you came out of Egypt!

¹⁰"When you lend your brother anything, you shall not go into his house to get his pledge. ¹¹You shall stand outside, and the man to whom you lend shall bring the pledge out to you. ¹²And if the man *is* poor, you shall not keep his pledge overnight. ¹³You shall in any case return the pledge to him again when the sun goes down, that he may sleep in his own garment and bless you; and it shall be righteousness to you before the LORD your God.

¹⁴"You shall not oppress a hired servant *who is* poor and needy, *whether* one of your brethren or one of the aliens who *is* in your land within your gates. ¹⁵Each day you shall give *him* his wages, and not let the sun go down on it, for he *is* poor and

23:17 ᵃHebrew *qedeshah,* feminine of *qadesh* (see note b) ᵇHebrew *qadesh,* that is, one practicing sodomy and prostitution in religious rituals has set his heart on it; lest he cry out against you to the LORD, and it be sin to you.

¹⁶"Fathers shall not be put to death for *their* children, nor shall children be put to death for *their* fathers; a person shall be put to death for his own sin.

¹⁷"You shall not pervert justice due the stranger or the fatherless, nor take a widow's garment as a pledge. ¹⁸But you shall remember that you were a slave in Egypt, and the LORD your God redeemed you from there; therefore I command you to do this thing.

¹⁹"When you reap your harvest in your field, and forget a sheaf in the field, you shall not go back to get it; it shall be for the stranger, the fatherless, and the widow, that the LORD your God may bless you in all the work of your hands. ²⁰When you beat your olive trees, you shall not go over the boughs again; it shall be for the stranger, the fatherless, and the widow. ²¹When you gather the grapes of your vineyard, you shall not glean *it* afterward; it shall be for the stranger, the fatherless, and the widow. ²²And you shall remember that you were a slave in the land of Egypt; therefore I command you to do this thing.

25 "If there is a dispute between men, and they come to court, that *the judges* may judge them, and they justify the righteous and condemn the wicked, ²then it shall be, if the wicked man deserves to be beaten, that the judge will cause him to lie down and be beaten in his presence, according to his guilt, with a certain number of blows. ³Forty blows he may give him *and* no more, lest he should exceed this and beat him with many blows above these, and your brother be humiliated in your sight.

⁴"You shall not muzzle an ox while it treads out *the grain*.

MARRIAGE DUTY OF THE SURVIVING BROTHER

⁵"If brothers dwell together, and one of them dies and has no son, the widow of the dead man shall not be *married* to a stranger outside *the family;* her husband's brother shall go in to her, take her as his wife, and perform the duty of a husband's brother to her. ⁶And it shall be *that* the firstborn son which she bears will succeed to the name of his dead brother, that his name may not

be blotted out of Israel. ⁷But if the man does not want to take his brother's wife, then let his brother's wife go up to the gate to the elders, and say, 'My husband's brother refuses to raise up a name to his brother in Israel; he will not perform the duty of my husband's brother.' ⁸Then the elders of his city shall call him and speak to him. But *if* he stands firm and says, 'I do not want to take her,' ⁹then his brother's wife shall come to him in the presence of the elders, remove his sandal from his foot, spit in his face, and answer and say, 'So shall it be done to the man who will not build up his brother's house.' ¹⁰And his name shall be called in Israel, 'The house of him who had his sandal removed.'

MISCELLANEOUS LAWS

¹¹"If *two* men fight together, and the wife of one draws near to rescue her husband from the hand of the one attacking him, and puts out her hand and seizes him by the genitals, ¹²then you shall cut off her hand; your eye shall not pity *her.*

¹³"You shall not have in your bag differing weights, a heavy and a light. ¹⁴You shall not have in your house differing measures, a large and a small. ¹⁵You shall have a perfect and just weight, a perfect and just measure, that your days may be lengthened in the land which the LORD your God is giving you. ¹⁶For all who do such things, all who behave unrighteously, *are* an abomination to the LORD your God.

DESTROY THE AMALEKITES

¹⁷"Remember what Amalek did to you on the way as you were coming out of Egypt, ¹⁸how he met you on the way and attacked your rear ranks, all the stragglers at your rear, when you *were* tired and weary; and he did not fear God. ¹⁹Therefore it shall be, when the LORD your God has given you rest from your enemies all around, in the land which the LORD your God is giving you to possess *as* an inheritance, *that* you will blot out the remembrance of Amalek from under heaven. You shall not forget.

OFFERINGS OF FIRSTFRUITS AND TITHES

26 "And it shall be, when you come into the land which the LORD your God is giving you *as* an inheritance, and you possess it and dwell

in it, [2]that you shall take some of the first of all the produce of the ground, which you shall bring from your land that the LORD your God is giving you, and put *it* in a basket and go to the place where the LORD your God chooses to make His name abide. [3]And you shall go to the one who is priest in those days, and say to him, 'I declare today to the LORD your[a] God that I have come to the country which the LORD swore to our fathers to give us.'

[4]"Then the priest shall take the basket out of your hand and set it down before the altar of the LORD your God. [5]And you shall answer and say before the LORD your God: 'My father *was* a Syrian,[a] about to perish, and he went down to Egypt and dwelt there, few in number; and there he became a nation, great, mighty, and populous. [6]But the Egyptians mistreated us, afflicted us, and laid hard bondage on us. [7]Then we cried out to the LORD God of our fathers, and the LORD heard our voice and looked on our affliction and our labor and our oppression. [8]So the LORD brought us out of Egypt with a mighty hand and with an outstretched arm, with great terror and with signs and wonders. [9]He has brought us to this place and has given us this land, "a land flowing with milk and honey"; [10]and now, behold, I have brought the firstfruits of the land which you, O LORD, have given me.'

"Then you shall set it before the LORD your God, and worship before the LORD your God. [11]So you shall rejoice in every good *thing* which the LORD your God has given to you and your house, you and the Levite and the stranger who *is* among you.

[12]"When you have finished laying aside all the tithe of your increase in the third year—the year of tithing—and have given *it* to the Levite, the stranger, the fatherless, and the widow, so that they may eat within your gates and be filled, [13]then you shall say before the LORD your God: 'I have removed the holy *tithe* from *my* house, and also have given them to the Levite, the stranger, the fatherless, and the widow, according to all Your commandments which You have commanded me; I have not transgressed Your commandments, nor have I forgotten *them.* [14]I have not eaten any of it when in mourning, nor have I removed *any* of it for an unclean *use,* nor given

any of it for the dead. I have obeyed the voice of the LORD my God, and have done according to all that You have commanded me. [15]Look down from Your holy habitation, from heaven, and bless Your people Israel and the land which You have given us, just as You swore to our fathers, "a land flowing with milk and honey." '[a]

A Special People of God

[16]"This day the LORD your God commands you to observe these statutes and judgments; therefore you shall be careful to observe them with all your heart and with all your soul. [17]Today you have proclaimed the LORD to be your God, and that you will walk in His ways and keep His statutes, His commandments, and His judgments, and that you will obey His voice. [18]Also today the LORD has proclaimed you to be His special people, just as He promised you, that *you* should keep all His commandments, [19]and that He will set you high above all nations which He has made, in praise, in name, and in honor, and that you may be a holy people to the LORD your God, just as He has spoken."

The Law Inscribed on Stones

27 Now Moses, with the elders of Israel, commanded the people, saying: "Keep all the commandments which I command you today. [2]And it shall be, on the day when you cross over the Jordan to the land which the LORD your God is giving you, that you shall set up for yourselves large stones, and whitewash them with lime. [3]You shall write on them all the words of this law, when you have crossed over, that you may enter the land which the LORD your God is giving you, 'a land flowing with milk and honey,'[a] just as the LORD God of your fathers promised you. [4]Therefore it shall be, when you have crossed over the Jordan, *that* on Mount Ebal you shall set up these stones, which I command you today, and you shall whitewash them with lime. [5]And there you shall build an altar to the LORD your God, an altar of stones; you shall not use an iron *tool* on them. [6]You shall build with whole stones the altar of the LORD your God, and offer burnt offerings

26:3 [a]Septuagint reads *my.*   **26:5** [a]Or *Aramean*   **26:9** [a]Exodus 3:8   **26:15** [a]Exodus 3:8   **27:3** [a]Exodus 3:8

on it to the LORD your God. [7]You shall offer peace offerings, and shall eat there, and rejoice before the LORD your God. [8]And you shall write very plainly on the stones all the words of this law."

[9]Then Moses and the priests, the Levites, spoke to all Israel, saying, "Take heed and listen, O Israel: This day you have become the people of the LORD your God. [10]Therefore you shall obey the voice of the LORD your God, and observe His commandments and His statutes which I command you today."

CURSES PRONOUNCED FROM MOUNT EBAL

[11]And Moses commanded the people on the same day, saying, [12]"These shall stand on Mount Gerizim to bless the people, when you have crossed over the Jordan: Simeon, Levi, Judah, Issachar, Joseph, and Benjamin; [13]and these shall stand on Mount Ebal to curse: Reuben, Gad, Asher, Zebulun, Dan, and Naphtali.

[14]"And the Levites shall speak with a loud voice and say to all the men of Israel: [15]'Cursed *is* the one who makes a carved or molded image, an abomination to the LORD, the work of the hands of the craftsman, and sets *it* up in secret.'

"And all the people shall answer and say, 'Amen!'

[16]'Cursed *is* the one who treats his father or his mother with contempt.'

"And all the people shall say, 'Amen!'

[17]'Cursed *is* the one who moves his neighbor's landmark.'

"And all the people shall say, 'Amen!'

[18]'Cursed *is* the one who makes the blind to wander off the road.'

"And all the people shall say, 'Amen!'

[19]'Cursed *is* the one who perverts the justice due the stranger, the fatherless, and widow.'

"And all the people shall say, 'Amen!'

[20]'Cursed *is* the one who lies with his father's wife, because he has uncovered his father's bed.'

"And all the people shall say, 'Amen!'

[21]'Cursed *is* the one who lies with any kind of animal.'

"And all the people shall say, 'Amen!'

[22]'Cursed *is* the one who lies with his sister, the daughter of his father or the daughter of his mother.'

"And all the people shall say, 'Amen!'

[23]'Cursed *is* the one who lies with his mother-in-law.'

"And all the people shall say, 'Amen!'

[24]'Cursed *is* the one who attacks his neighbor secretly.'

"And all the people shall say, 'Amen!'

[25]'Cursed *is* the one who takes a bribe to slay an innocent person.'

"And all the people shall say, 'Amen!'

[26]'Cursed *is* the one who does not confirm *all* the words of this law by observing them.'

"And all the people shall say, 'Amen!' "

BLESSINGS ON OBEDIENCE

28 "Now it shall come to pass, if you diligently obey the voice of the LORD your God, to observe carefully all His commandments which I command you today, that the LORD your God will set you high above all nations of the earth. [2]And all these blessings shall come upon you and overtake you, because you obey the voice of the LORD your God:

[3]"Blessed *shall* you *be* in the city, and blessed *shall* you *be* in the country.

[4]"Blessed *shall be* the fruit of your body, the produce of your ground and the increase of your herds, the increase of your cattle and the offspring of your flocks.

[5]"Blessed *shall be* your basket and your kneading bowl.

[6]"Blessed *shall* you *be* when you come in, and blessed *shall* you *be* when you go out.

[7]"The LORD will cause your enemies who rise against you to be defeated before your face; they shall come out against you one way and flee before you seven ways.

[8]"The LORD will command the blessing on you in your storehouses and in all to which you set your hand, and He will bless you in the land which the LORD your God is giving you.

[9]"The LORD will establish you as a holy people to Himself, just as He has sworn to you, if you keep the commandments of the LORD your God and walk in His ways. [10]Then all peoples of the earth shall see that you are called by the name of the LORD, and they shall be afraid of you. [11]And the LORD will grant you plenty of goods, in the fruit of your body, in the increase of your live-

stock, and in the produce of your ground, in the land of which the LORD swore to your fathers to give you. ¹²The LORD will open to you His good treasure, the heavens, to give the rain to your land in its season, and to bless all the work of your hand. You shall lend to many nations, but you shall not borrow. ¹³And the LORD will make you the head and not the tail; you shall be above only, and not be beneath, if you heed the commandments of the LORD your God, which I command you today, and are careful to observe *them.* ¹⁴So you shall not turn aside from any of the words which I command you this day, *to* the right or the left, to go after other gods to serve them.

CURSES ON DISOBEDIENCE

¹⁵"But it shall come to pass, if you do not obey the voice of the LORD your God, to observe carefully all His commandments and His statutes which I command you today, that all these curses will come upon you and overtake you:

¹⁶"Cursed *shall* you *be* in the city, and cursed *shall* you *be* in the country.

¹⁷"Cursed *shall be* your basket and your kneading bowl.

¹⁸"Cursed *shall be* the fruit of your body and the produce of your land, the increase of your cattle and the offspring of your flocks.

¹⁹"Cursed *shall* you *be* when you come in, and cursed *shall* you *be* when you go out.

²⁰"The LORD will send on you cursing, confusion, and rebuke in all that you set your hand to do, until you are destroyed and until you perish quickly, because of the wickedness of your doings in which you have forsaken Me. ²¹The LORD will make the plague cling to you until He has consumed you from the land which you are going to possess. ²²The LORD will strike you with consumption, with fever, with inflammation, with severe burning fever, with the sword, with scorching, and with mildew; they shall pursue you until you perish. ²³And your heavens which *are* over your head shall be bronze, and the earth which is under you *shall be* iron. ²⁴The LORD will change the rain of your land to powder and dust; from the heaven it shall come down on you until you are destroyed.

²⁵"The LORD will cause you to be defeated before your enemies; you shall go out one way

against them and flee seven ways before them; and you shall become troublesome to all the kingdoms of the earth. ²⁶Your carcasses shall be food for all the birds of the air and the beasts of the earth, and no one shall frighten *them* away. ²⁷The LORD will strike you with the boils of Egypt, with tumors, with the scab, and with the itch, from which you cannot be healed. ²⁸The LORD will strike you with madness and blindness and confusion of heart. ²⁹And you shall grope at noonday, as a blind man gropes in darkness; you shall not prosper in your ways; you shall be only oppressed and plundered continually, and no one shall save *you.*

³⁰"You shall betroth a wife, but another man shall lie with her; you shall build a house, but you shall not dwell in it; you shall plant a vineyard, but shall not gather its grapes. ³¹Your ox *shall be* slaughtered before your eyes, but you shall not eat of it; your donkey *shall be* violently taken away from before you, and shall not be restored to you; your sheep *shall be* given to your enemies, and you shall have no one to rescue *them.* ³²Your sons and your daughters *shall be* given to another people, and your eyes shall look and fail *with longing* for them all day long; and *there shall be* no strength in your hand. ³³A nation whom you have not known shall eat the fruit of your land and the produce of your labor, and you shall be only oppressed and crushed continually. ³⁴So you shall be driven mad because of the sight which your eyes see. ³⁵The LORD will strike you in the knees and on the legs with severe boils which cannot be healed, and from the sole of your foot to the top of your head.

³⁶"The LORD will bring you and the king whom you set over you to a nation which neither you nor your fathers have known, and there you shall serve other gods—wood and stone. ³⁷And you shall become an astonishment, a proverb, and a byword among all nations where the LORD will drive you.

³⁸"You shall carry much seed out to the field but gather little in, for the locust shall consume it. ³⁹You shall plant vineyards and tend *them,* but you shall neither drink *of* the wine nor gather the *grapes;* for the worms shall eat them. ⁴⁰You shall have olive trees throughout all your territory, but you shall not anoint *yourself* with the oil; for your

olives shall drop off. [41]You shall beget sons and daughters, but they shall not be yours; for they shall go into captivity. [42]Locusts shall consume all your trees and the produce of your land.

[43]"The alien who *is* among you shall rise higher and higher above you, and you shall come down lower and lower. [44]He shall lend to you, but you shall not lend to him; he shall be the head, and you shall be the tail.

[45]"Moreover all these curses shall come upon you and pursue and overtake you, until you are destroyed, because you did not obey the voice of the LORD your God, to keep His commandments and His statutes which He commanded you. [46]And they shall be upon you for a sign and a wonder, and on your descendants forever.

[47]"Because you did not serve the LORD your God with joy and gladness of heart, for the abundance of everything, [48]therefore you shall serve your enemies, whom the LORD will send against you, in hunger, in thirst, in nakedness, and in need of everything; and He will put a yoke of iron on your neck until He has destroyed you. [49]The LORD will bring a nation against you from afar, from the end of the earth, *as swift* as the eagle flies, a nation whose language you will not understand, [50]a nation of fierce countenance, which does not respect the elderly nor show favor to the young. [51]And they shall eat the increase of your livestock and the produce of your land, until you are destroyed; they shall not leave you grain or new wine or oil, *or* the increase of your cattle or the offspring of your flocks, until they have destroyed you.

[52]"They shall besiege you at all your gates until your high and fortified walls, in which you trust, come down throughout all your land; and they shall besiege you at all your gates throughout all your land which the LORD your God has given you. [53]You shall eat the fruit of your own body, the flesh of your sons and your daughters whom the LORD your God has given you, in the siege and desperate straits in which your enemy shall distress you. [54]The sensitive and very refined man among you will be hostile toward his brother, toward the wife of his bosom, and toward the rest of his children whom he leaves behind, [55]so that he will not give any of them the flesh of his children whom he will eat, because he has nothing left in the siege and desperate straits in

which your enemy shall distress you at all your gates. [56]The tender and delicate woman among you, who would not venture to set the sole of her foot on the ground because of her delicateness and sensitivity, will refuse[a] to the husband of her bosom, and to her son and her daughter, [57]her placenta which comes out from between her feet and her children whom she bears; for she will eat them secretly for lack of everything in the siege and desperate straits in which your enemy shall distress you at all your gates.

[58]"If you do not carefully observe all the words of this law that are written in this book, that you may fear this glorious and awesome name, THE LORD YOUR GOD, [59]then the LORD will bring upon you and your descendants extraordinary plagues—great and prolonged plagues—and serious and prolonged sicknesses. [60]Moreover He will bring back on you all the diseases of Egypt, of which you were afraid, and they shall cling to you. [61]Also every sickness and every plague, which *is* not written in this Book of the Law, will the LORD bring upon you until you are destroyed. [62]You shall be left few in number, whereas you were as the stars of heaven in multitude, because you would not obey the voice of the LORD your God. [63]And it shall be, *that* just as the LORD rejoiced over you to do you good and multiply you, so the LORD will rejoice over you to destroy you and bring you to nothing; and you shall be plucked from off the land which you go to possess.

[64]"Then the LORD will scatter you among all peoples, from one end of the earth to the other, and there you shall serve other gods, which neither you nor your fathers have known—wood and stone. [65]And among those nations you shall find no rest, nor shall the sole of your foot have a resting place; but there the LORD will give you a trembling heart, failing eyes, and anguish of soul. [66]Your life shall hang in doubt before you; you shall fear day and night, and have no assurance of life. [67]In the morning you shall say, 'Oh, that it were evening!' And at evening you shall say, 'Oh, that it were morning!' because of the fear which terrifies your heart, and because of the sight which your eyes see.

28:56 [a]Literally *her eye shall be evil toward*

[68]"And the LORD will take you back to Egypt in ships, by the way of which I said to you, 'You shall never see it again.' And there you shall be offered for sale to your enemies as male and female slaves, but no one will buy *you*."

THE COVENANT RENEWED IN MOAB

29 These *are* the words of the covenant which the LORD commanded Moses to make with the children of Israel in the land of Moab, besides the covenant which He made with them in Horeb.

[2]Now Moses called all Israel and said to them: "You have seen all that the LORD did before your eyes in the land of Egypt, to Pharaoh and to all his servants and to all his land— [3]the great trials which your eyes have seen, the signs, and those great wonders. [4]Yet the LORD has not given you a heart to perceive and eyes to see and ears to hear, to this *very* day. [5]And I have led you forty years in the wilderness. Your clothes have not worn out on you, and your sandals have not worn out on your feet. [6]You have not eaten bread, nor have you drunk wine or *similar* drink, that you may know that I *am* the LORD your God. [7]And when you came to this place, Sihon king of Heshbon and Og king of Bashan came out against us to battle, and we conquered them. [8]We took their land and gave it as an inheritance to the Reubenites, to the Gadites, and to half the tribe of Manasseh. [9]Therefore keep the words of this covenant, and do them, that you may prosper in all that you do.

[10]"All of you stand today before the LORD your God: your leaders and your tribes and your elders and your officers, all the men of Israel, [11]your little ones and your wives—also the stranger who *is* in your camp, from the one who cuts your wood to the one who draws your water— [12]that you may enter into covenant with the LORD your God, and into His oath, which the LORD your God makes with you today, [13]that He may establish you today as a people for Himself, and *that* He may be God to you, just as He has spoken to you, and just as He has sworn to your fathers, to Abraham, Isaac, and Jacob.

[14]"I make this covenant and this oath, not with you alone, [15]but with *him* who stands here with us today before the LORD our God, as well

as with *him* who *is* not here with us today [16](for you know that we dwelt in the land of Egypt and that we came through the nations which you passed by, [17]and you saw their abominations and their idols which *were* among them—wood and stone and silver and gold); [18]so that there may not be among you man or woman or family or tribe, whose heart turns away today from the LORD our God, to go *and* serve the gods of these nations, and that there may not be among you a root bearing bitterness or wormwood; [19]and so it may not happen, when he hears the words of this curse, that he blesses himself in his heart, saying, 'I shall have peace, even though I follow the dictates[a] of my heart'—as though the drunkard could be included with the sober.

[20]"The LORD would not spare him; for then the anger of the LORD and His jealousy would burn against that man, and every curse that is written in this book would settle on him, and the LORD would blot out his name from under heaven. [21]And the LORD would separate him from all the tribes of Israel for adversity, according to all the curses of the covenant that are written in this Book of the Law, [22]so that the coming generation of your children who rise up after you, and the foreigner who comes from a far land, would say, when they see the plagues of that land and the sicknesses which the LORD has laid on it:

[23]'The whole land *is* brimstone, salt, and burning; it is not sown, nor does it bear, nor does any grass grow there, like the overthrow of Sodom and Gomorrah, Admah, and Zeboiim, which the LORD overthrew in His anger and His wrath.' [24]All nations would say, 'Why has the LORD done so to this land? What does the heat of this great anger mean?' [25]Then *people* would say: 'Because they have forsaken the covenant of the LORD God of their fathers, which He made with them when He brought them out of the land of Egypt; [26]for they went and served other gods and worshiped them, gods that they did not know and that He had not given to them. [27]Then the anger of the LORD was aroused against this land, to bring on it every curse that is written in this book. [28]And the LORD uprooted

29:19 [a]Or *stubbornness*

them from their land in anger, in wrath, and in great indignation, and cast them into another land, as *it is* this day.'

²⁹"The secret *things belong* to the LORD our God, but those *things which are* revealed *belong* to us and to our children forever, that *we* may do all the words of this law.

THE BLESSING OF RETURNING TO GOD

30 "Now it shall come to pass, when all these things come upon you, the blessing and the curse which I have set before you, and you call *them* to mind among all the nations where the LORD your God drives you, ²and you return to the LORD your God and obey His voice, according to all that I command you today, you and your children, with all your heart and with all your soul, ³that the LORD your God will bring you back from captivity, and have compassion on you, and gather you again from all the nations where the LORD your God has scattered you. ⁴If *any* of you are driven out to the farthest *parts* under heaven, from there the LORD your God will gather you, and from there He will bring you. ⁵Then the LORD your God will bring you to the land which your fathers possessed, and you shall possess it. He will prosper you and multiply you more than your fathers. ⁶And the LORD your God will circumcise your heart and the heart of your descendants, to love the LORD your God with all your heart and with all your soul, that you may live.

⁷"Also the LORD your God will put all these curses on your enemies and on those who hate you, who persecuted you. ⁸And you will again obey the voice of the LORD and do all His commandments which I command you today. ⁹The LORD your God will make you abound in all the work of your hand, in the fruit of your body, in the increase of your livestock, and in the produce of your land for good. For the LORD will again rejoice over you for good as He rejoiced over your fathers, ¹⁰if you obey the voice of the LORD your God, to keep His commandments and His statutes which are written in this Book of the Law, *and* if you turn to the LORD your God with all your heart and with all your soul.

THE CHOICE OF LIFE OR DEATH

¹¹"For this commandment which I command you today *is* not *too* mysterious for you, nor *is* it far off. ¹²It *is* not in heaven, that you should say, 'Who will ascend into heaven for us and bring it to us, that we may hear it and do it?' ¹³Nor *is* it beyond the sea, that you should say, 'Who will go over the sea for us and bring it to us, that we may hear it and do it?' ¹⁴But the word *is* very near you, in your mouth and in your heart, that you may do it.

¹⁵"See, I have set before you today life and good, death and evil, ¹⁶in that I command you today to love the LORD your God, to walk in His ways, and to keep His commandments, His statutes, and His judgments, that you may live and multiply; and the LORD your God will bless you in the land which you go to possess. ¹⁷But if your heart turns away so that you do not hear, and are drawn away, and worship other gods and serve them, ¹⁸I announce to you today that you shall surely perish; you shall not prolong *your* days in the land which you cross over the Jordan to go in and possess. ¹⁹I call heaven and earth as witnesses today against you, *that* I have set before you life and death, blessing and cursing; therefore choose life, that both you and your descendants may live; ²⁰that you may love the LORD your God, that you may obey His voice, and that you may cling to Him, for He *is* your life and the length of your days; and that you may dwell in the land which the LORD swore to your fathers, to Abraham, Isaac, and Jacob, to give them."

JOSHUA THE NEW LEADER OF ISRAEL

31 Then Moses went and spoke these words to all Israel. ²And he said to them: "I *am* one hundred and twenty years old today. I can no longer go out and come in. Also the LORD has said to me, 'You shall not cross over this Jordan.' ³The LORD your God Himself crosses over before you; He will destroy these nations from before you, and you shall dispossess them. Joshua himself crosses over before you, just as the LORD has said. ⁴And the LORD will do to them as He did to Sihon and Og, the kings of the Amorites and their land, when He destroyed them. ⁵The LORD will give them over to you, that you may do to them

according to every commandment which I have commanded you. [6]Be strong and of good courage, do not fear nor be afraid of them; for the LORD your God, He *is* the One who goes with you. He will not leave you nor forsake you."

[7]Then Moses called Joshua and said to him in the sight of all Israel, "Be strong and of good courage, for you must go with this people to the land which the LORD has sworn to their fathers to give them, and you shall cause them to inherit it. [8]And the LORD, He *is* the One who goes before you. He will be with you, He will not leave you nor forsake you; do not fear nor be dismayed."

The Law to Be Read Every Seven Years

[9]So Moses wrote this law and delivered it to the priests, the sons of Levi, who bore the ark of the covenant of the LORD, and to all the elders of Israel. [10]And Moses commanded them, saying: "At the end of *every* seven years, at the appointed time in the year of release, at the Feast of Tabernacles, [11]when all Israel comes to appear before the LORD your God in the place which He chooses, you shall read this law before all Israel in their hearing. [12]Gather the people together, men and women and little ones, and the stranger who *is* within your gates, that they may hear and that they may learn to fear the LORD your God and carefully observe all the words of this law, [13]and *that* their children, who have not known it, may hear and learn to fear the LORD your God as long as you live in the land which you cross the Jordan to possess."

Prediction of Israel's Rebellion

[14]Then the LORD said to Moses, "Behold, the days approach when you must die; call Joshua, and present yourselves in the tabernacle of meeting, that I may inaugurate him."

So Moses and Joshua went and presented themselves in the tabernacle of meeting. [15]Now the LORD appeared at the tabernacle in a pillar of cloud, and the pillar of cloud stood above the door of the tabernacle.

[16]And the LORD said to Moses: "Behold, you will rest with your fathers; and this people will rise and play the harlot with the gods of the foreigners of the land, where they go *to be* among them, and they will forsake Me and break My covenant which I have made with them. [17]Then My anger shall be aroused against them in that day, and I will forsake them, and I will hide My face from them, and they shall be devoured. And many evils and troubles shall befall them, so that they will say in that day, 'Have not these evils come upon us because our God *is* not among us?' [18]And I will surely hide My face in that day because of all the evil which they have done, in that they have turned to other gods.

[19]"Now therefore, write down this song for yourselves, and teach it to the children of Israel; put it in their mouths, that this song may be a witness for Me against the children of Israel. [20]When I have brought them to the land flowing with milk and honey, of which I swore to their fathers, and they have eaten and filled themselves and grown fat, then they will turn to other gods and serve them; and they will provoke Me and break My covenant. [21]Then it shall be, when many evils and troubles have come upon them, that this song will testify against them as a witness; for it will not be forgotten in the mouths of their descendants, for I know the inclination of their behavior today, even before I have brought them to the land of which I swore *to give them*."

[22]Therefore Moses wrote this song the same day, and taught it to the children of Israel. [23]Then He inaugurated Joshua the son of Nun, and said, "Be strong and of good courage; for you shall bring the children of Israel into the land of which I swore to them, and I will be with you."

[24]So it was, when Moses had completed writing the words of this law in a book, when they were finished, [25]that Moses commanded the Levites, who bore the ark of the covenant of the LORD, saying: [26]"Take this Book of the Law, and put it beside the ark of the covenant of the LORD your God, that it may be there as a witness against you; [27]for I know your rebellion and your stiff neck. *If* today, while I am yet alive with you, you have been rebellious against the LORD, then how much more after my death? [28]Gather to me all the elders of your tribes, and your officers, that I may speak these words in their hearing and call heaven and earth to witness against them. [29]For I know that after my death you will become utterly corrupt, and turn aside from the way which I

have commanded you. And evil will befall you in the latter days, because you will do evil in the sight of the LORD, to provoke Him to anger through the work of your hands."

THE SONG OF MOSES

³⁰Then Moses spoke in the hearing of all the assembly of Israel the words of this song until they were ended:

32 "Give ear, O heavens, and I will speak;
And hear, O earth, the words of my mouth.
²Let my teaching drop as the rain,
My speech distill as the dew,
As raindrops on the tender herb,
And as showers on the grass.
³For I proclaim the name of
the LORD:
Ascribe greatness to our God.
⁴*He is* the Rock, His work *is* perfect;
For all His ways *are* justice,
A God of truth and without injustice;
Righteous and upright *is* He.

⁵"They have corrupted themselves;
They are not His children,
Because of their blemish:

A perverse and crooked generation.
⁶Do you thus deal with the LORD,
O foolish and unwise people?
Is He not your Father, *who* bought you?
Has He not made you and established you?

⁷"Remember the days of old,
Consider the years of many generations.
Ask your father, and he will show you;
Your elders, and they will tell you:
⁸When the Most High divided their
inheritance to the nations,
When He separated the sons of Adam,
He set the boundaries of the peoples
According to the number of the children of
Israel.
⁹For the LORD's portion *is* His people;
Jacob *is* the place of His inheritance.

¹⁰"He found him in a desert land
And in the wasteland, a howling wilderness;
He encircled him, He instructed him,
He kept him as the apple of His eye.
¹¹As an eagle stirs up its nest,
Hovers over its young,
Spreading out its wings, taking them up,
Carrying them on its wings,

THROUGH THE GRID   *Discover God: God Is Just*

DEUTERONOMY 32:4   *For all His ways are justice, a God of truth and without injustice; righteous and upright is He.*

God is the standard of what is just, since God always acts in accordance with what is morally upright or good. God is a perfect judge who knows true justice; and as such, our only response before God is confession. God's understanding of justice is perfect, transcending our limited understandings, and God can never be fooled. God's judgments are absolute, and God's standard is the ultimate one against which all human actions are judged. Since God is a perfect judge, God has these characteristics: He has authority, the power to execute His authority, He knows and understands the law, and He has the highest moral qualities. Besides these, God hates sin as the opposite of righteousness, and God eventually will punish all sin. In the end, God will bring the final judgment down on sin because a righteous, holy, and just God cannot coexist with sin. Thankfully, the faithfulness of Christ has provided for and covered all of humanity.

¹²*So* the LORD alone led him,
And *there was* no foreign god with him.

¹³"He made him ride in the heights of the earth,
That he might eat the produce of the fields;
He made him draw honey from the rock,
And oil from the flinty rock;
¹⁴Curds from the cattle, and milk of the flock,
With fat of lambs;
And rams of the breed of Bashan, and goats,
With the choicest wheat;
And you drank wine, the blood of the grapes.

¹⁵"But Jeshurun grew fat and kicked;
You grew fat, you grew thick,
You are obese!
Then he forsook God *who* made him,
And scornfully esteemed the Rock of his
salvation.
¹⁶They provoked Him to jealousy with foreign
gods;
With abominations they provoked Him to
anger.
¹⁷They sacrificed to demons, not to God,
To gods they did not know,
To new *gods,* new arrivals
That your fathers did not fear.
¹⁸Of the Rock *who* begot you, you are
unmindful,
And have forgotten the God who fathered
you.

¹⁹"And when the LORD saw *it,* He spurned
them,
Because of the provocation of His sons and
His daughters.
²⁰And He said: 'I will hide My face from them,
I will see what their end *will be,*
For they *are* a perverse generation,
Children in whom *is* no faith.
²¹They have provoked Me to jealousy by *what*
is not God;
They have moved Me to anger by their
foolish idols.
But I will provoke them to jealousy by *those*
who are not a nation;
I will move them to anger by a foolish
nation.
²²For a fire is kindled in My anger,

And shall burn to the lowest hell;
It shall consume the earth with her increase,
And set on fire the foundations of the
mountains.

²³'I will heap disasters on them;
I will spend My arrows on them.
²⁴*They shall be* wasted with hunger,
Devoured by pestilence and bitter
destruction;
I will also send against them the teeth of
beasts,
With the poison of serpents of the dust.
²⁵The sword shall destroy outside;
There shall be terror within
For the young man and virgin,
The nursing child with the man of gray
hairs.
²⁶I would have said, "I will dash them in pieces,
I will make the memory of them to cease
from among men,"
²⁷Had I not feared the wrath of the enemy,
Lest their adversaries should misunderstand,
Lest they should say, "Our hand *is* high;
And it is not the LORD who has done all
this." '

²⁸"For they *are* a nation void of counsel,
Nor *is there any* understanding in them.
²⁹Oh, that they were wise, *that* they understood
this,
That they would consider their latter end!
³⁰How could one chase a thousand,
And two put ten thousand to flight,
Unless their Rock had sold them,
And the LORD had surrendered them?
³¹For their rock *is* not like our Rock,
Even our enemies themselves *being* judges.
³²For their vine *is* of the vine of Sodom
And of the fields of Gomorrah;
Their grapes *are* grapes of gall,
Their clusters *are* bitter.
³³Their wine *is* the poison of serpents,
And the cruel venom of cobras.

³⁴'*Is* this not laid up in store with Me,
Sealed up among My treasures?
³⁵Vengeance is Mine, and recompense;
Their foot shall slip in *due* time;

> For the day of their calamity *is* at hand,
> And the things to come hasten upon them.'

³⁶"For the LORD will judge His people
> And have compassion on His servants,
> When He sees that *their* power is gone,
> And *there is* no one *remaining,* bond or free.
³⁷He will say: 'Where *are* their gods,
> The rock in which they sought refuge?
³⁸Who ate the fat of their sacrifices,
> *And* drank the wine of their drink offering?
> Let them rise and help you,
> *And* be your refuge.

³⁹'Now see that I, *even* I, *am* He,
> And *there is* no God besides Me;
> I kill and I make alive;
> I wound and I heal;
> Nor *is there any* who can deliver from My
> hand.
⁴⁰For I raise My hand to heaven,
> And say, "*As* I live forever,
⁴¹If I whet My glittering sword,
> And My hand takes hold on judgment,
> I will render vengeance to My enemies,
> And repay those who hate Me.
⁴²I will make My arrows drunk with blood,
> And My sword shall devour flesh,
> With the blood of the slain and the captives,
> From the heads of the leaders of the
> enemy." '

⁴³"Rejoice, O Gentiles, *with* His people;^a
> For He will avenge the blood of His servants,
> And render vengeance to His adversaries;
> He will provide atonement for His land *and*
> His people."

⁴⁴So Moses came with Joshua^a the son of Nun and spoke all the words of this song in the hearing of the people. ⁴⁵Moses finished speaking all these words to all Israel, ⁴⁶and he said to them: "Set your hearts on all the words which I testify among you today, which you shall command your children to be careful to observe—all the words of this law. ⁴⁷For it *is* not a futile thing for you, because it *is* your life, and by this word you shall prolong *your* days in the land which you cross over the Jordan to possess."

MOSES TO DIE ON MOUNT NEBO

⁴⁸Then the LORD spoke to Moses that very same day, saying: ⁴⁹"Go up this mountain of the Abarim, Mount Nebo, which *is* in the land of Moab, across from Jericho; view the land of Canaan, which I give to the children of Israel as a possession; ⁵⁰and die on the mountain which you ascend, and be gathered to your people, just as Aaron your brother died on Mount Hor and was gathered to his people; ⁵¹because you trespassed against Me among the children of Israel at the waters of Meribah Kadesh, in the Wilderness of Zin, because you did not hallow Me in the midst of the children of Israel. ⁵²Yet you shall see the land before *you,* though you shall not go there, into the land which I am giving to the children of Israel."

MOSES' FINAL BLESSING ON ISRAEL

33 Now this *is* the blessing with which Moses the man of God blessed the children of Israel before his death. ²And he said:

> "The LORD came from Sinai,
> And dawned on them from Seir;
> He shone forth from Mount Paran,
> And He came with ten thousands of saints;
> From His right hand
> *Came* a fiery law for them.
³Yes, He loves the people;
> All His saints *are* in Your hand;
> They sit down at Your feet;
> *Everyone* receives Your words.
⁴Moses commanded a law for us,
> A heritage of the congregation of Jacob.
⁵And He was King in Jeshurun,
> When the leaders of the people were gathered,
> All the tribes of Israel together.

⁶"Let Reuben live, and not die,
> *Nor* let his men be few."

⁷And this he said of Judah:

> "Hear, LORD, the voice of Judah,
> And bring him to his people;

32:43 ^aA Dead Sea Scroll fragment adds *And let all the gods (angels) worship Him* (compare Septuagint and Hebrews 1:6).
32:44 ^aHebrew *Hoshea* (compare Numbers 13:8, 16)

Let his hands be sufficient for him,
And may You be a help against his enemies."

⁸And of Levi he said:

"*Let* Your Thummim and Your Urim *be* with
Your holy one,
Whom You tested at Massah,
And with whom You contended at the waters
of Meribah,
⁹Who says of his father and mother,
'I have not seen them';
Nor did he acknowledge his brothers,
Or know his own children;
For they have observed Your word
And kept Your covenant.
¹⁰They shall teach Jacob Your judgments,
And Israel Your law.
They shall put incense before You,
And a whole burnt sacrifice on Your altar.
¹¹Bless his substance, LORD,
And accept the work of his hands;
Strike the loins of those who rise against him,
And of those who hate him, that they rise not
again."

¹²Of Benjamin he said:

"The beloved of the LORD shall dwell in safety
by Him,
Who shelters him all the day long;
And he shall dwell between His shoulders."

¹³And of Joseph he said:

"Blessed of the LORD *is* his land,
With the precious things of heaven, with the
dew,
And the deep lying beneath,
¹⁴With the precious fruits of the sun,
With the precious produce of the months,
¹⁵With the best things of the ancient mountains,
With the precious things of the everlasting
hills,
¹⁶With the precious things of the earth and its
fullness,
And the favor of Him who dwelt in the bush.
Let *the blessing* come 'on the head of Joseph,
And on the crown of the head of him *who
was* separate from his brothers.'ᵃ

¹⁷His glory *is like* a firstborn bull,
And his horns *like* the horns of the wild ox;
Together with them
He shall push the peoples
To the ends of the earth;
They *are* the ten thousands of Ephraim,
And they *are* the thousands of Manasseh."

¹⁸And of Zebulun he said:

"Rejoice, Zebulun, in your going out,
And Issachar in your tents!
¹⁹They shall call the peoples *to* the mountain;
There they shall offer sacrifices of
righteousness;
For they shall partake *of* the abundance of the
seas
And *of* treasures hidden in the sand."

²⁰And of Gad he said:

"Blessed *is* he who enlarges Gad;
He dwells as a lion,
And tears the arm and the crown of his
head.
²¹He provided the first *part* for himself,
Because a lawgiver's portion was reserved
there.
He came *with* the heads of the people;
He administered the justice of the LORD,
And His judgments with Israel."

²²And of Dan he said:

"Dan *is* a lion's whelp;
He shall leap from Bashan."

²³And of Naphtali he said:

"O Naphtali, satisfied with favor,
And full of the blessing of the LORD,
Possess the west and the south."

²⁴And of Asher he said:

"Asher *is* most blessed of sons;
Let him be favored by his brothers,

33:16 ᵃGenesis 49:26

And let him dip his foot in oil.
25Your sandals *shall be* iron and bronze;
    As your days, *so shall* your strength *be*.

26"*There is* no one like the God of Jeshurun,
    Who rides the heavens to help you,
    And in His excellency on the clouds.
27The eternal God *is your* refuge,
    And underneath *are* the everlasting arms;
    He will thrust out the enemy from before
        you,
    And will say, 'Destroy!'
28Then Israel shall dwell in safety,
    The fountain of Jacob alone,
    In a land of grain and new wine;
    His heavens shall also drop dew.
29Happy *are* you, O Israel!
    Who *is* like you, a people saved by the LORD,
    The shield of your help
    And the sword of your majesty!
    Your enemies shall submit to you,
    And you shall tread down their high places."

MOSES DIES ON MOUNT NEBO

34 Then Moses went up from the plains of Moab to Mount Nebo, to the top of Pisgah, which is across from Jericho. And the LORD showed him all the land of Gilead as far as Dan, 2all Naphtali and the land of Ephraim and Manasseh, all the land of Judah as far as the Western Sea,a 3the South, and the plain of the Valley of Jericho, the city of palm trees, as far as Zoar. 4Then the LORD said to him, "This *is* the land of which I swore to give Abraham, Isaac, and Jacob, saying, 'I will give it to your descendants.' I have caused you to see *it* with your eyes, but you shall not cross over there."

5So Moses the servant of the LORD died there in the land of Moab, according to the word of the LORD. 6And He buried him in a valley in the land of Moab, opposite Beth Peor; but no one knows his grave to this day. 7Moses *was* one hundred and twenty years old when he died. His eyes were not

34:2 aThat is, the Mediterranean

INSIDE *the* INFLUENCERS

NATION OF ISRAEL—Adversity Gives Birth to Strength

DEUTERONOMY 34:5

When Moses died, he was succeeded by Joshua, who led the Israelites to victory over the Canaanites. They experienced times of great prosperity until Joshua died, but then they fell back into a cycle of sin: neglecting God, God sending judgment, bringing about repentance and restoration. This cycle repeated seven times. It was not a pretty picture in the history of Israel as they gave in to the worship of idols and pagan practices for about 400 years.

God raised up Samuel, the prophet, who led them to walk with God and to prosper once again. But, he neglected his own sons who tragically went astray. The people rejected them, asking for a king like their neighboring countries. Saul was the first king of Israel.

Then David, the greatest king, helped form Israel into a mighty nation. Solomon, his son, built the great temple. When he died, the nation split, and Israel faltered. When it was conquered, many of its people were taken into bondage.

Throughout Israel's history, God called prophets to warn, instruct, and comfort the people. The four Major Prophets were Isaiah, Jeremiah, Ezekiel, and Daniel. There were twelve others, called Minor Prophets, who had more limited ministries. The prophets predicted the Messiah's arrival, leading Israel to anticipate the fulfillment of that promise.

dim nor his natural vigor diminished. [8]And the children of Israel wept for Moses in the plains of Moab thirty days. So the days of weeping *and* mourning for Moses ended.

[9]Now Joshua the son of Nun was full of the spirit of wisdom, for Moses had laid his hands on him; so the children of Israel heeded him, and did as the LORD had commanded Moses.

[10]But since then there has not arisen in Israel a prophet like Moses, whom the LORD knew face to face, [11]in all the signs and wonders which the LORD sent him to do in the land of Egypt, before Pharaoh, before all his servants, and in all his land, [12]and by all that mighty power and all the great terror which Moses performed in the sight of all Israel.

IMPACT OF THE BOOK

IDEA | *God fulfilled His promise to the Israelite nation and gave them the Promised Land.*

MESSAGE | *The main characters in this narrative teach widely different lessons: Caleb demonstrated the power of a courageous spirit; Joshua modeled the importance of daily reliance upon God; Rahab's life testified that God desires to use any willing heart; Achan showed how one sin can have tragic consequences in many people's lives. This book illustrates that everything rises and falls on leadership.*

PEOPLE | *Achan, Caleb, Eleazar, Joshua, Rahab*

AUTHOR | *Even though parts of this book appear to occur after his death, Joshua—whose name means "the Lord saves"—is the primary author of this work. As one of the two spies who placed their confidence in God's ability to give them the Promised Land, Joshua was chosen to take up the mantle of leadership after Moses' death.*

CULTURE | *The events in this book take place over a thirty-year period as the Israelites take possession of Canaan—a small, strategic country connecting Africa with Asia and the site of so much international struggle. The people of Canaan worshipped pagan gods and goddesses and practiced child sacrifices and cult prostitution. At the time, people viewed each nation as a testimony to the power of their deity. So, as the Israelites claimed victory after victory in their conquest of Canaan, the pagan people viewed it as a demonstration of the power of the Israelites' God.*

TIMELINE | *c. 1380 BC*

KEY SCRIPTURE
MEMORY VERSES | 1:8; 24:15

GOD'S COMMISSION TO JOSHUA

1 After the death of Moses the servant of the LORD, it came to pass that the LORD spoke to Joshua the son of Nun, Moses' assistant, saying: [2]"Moses My servant is dead. Now therefore, arise, go over this Jordan, you and all this people, to the land which I am giving to them—the children of Israel. [3]Every place that the sole of your foot will tread upon I have given you, as I said to Moses. [4]From the wilderness and this Lebanon as far as the great river, the River Euphrates, all the land of the Hittites, and to the Great Sea toward the going down of the sun, shall be your territory. [5]No man shall *be able to* stand before you all the days of your life; as I was with Moses, *so* I will be with you. I will not leave you nor forsake you. [6]Be strong and of good courage, for to this people you shall divide as an inheritance the land which I swore to their fathers to give them. [7]Only be strong and very courageous, that you may observe to do according to all the law which Moses My servant com-manded you; do not turn from it to the right hand or to the left, that you may prosper wherever you go. [8]This Book of the Law shall not depart from your mouth, but you shall meditate in it day and night, that you may observe to do according to all that is written in it. For then you will make your way prosperous, and then you will have good success. [9]Have I not commanded you? Be strong and of good courage; do not be afraid, nor be dismayed, for the LORD your God *is* with you wherever you go."

THE ORDER TO CROSS THE JORDAN

[10]Then Joshua commanded the officers of the people, saying, [11]"Pass through the camp and command the people, saying, 'Prepare provisions for yourselves, for within three days you will cross over this Jordan, to go in to possess the land which the LORD your God is giving you to possess.'"

[12]And to the Reubenites, the Gadites, and half the tribe of Manasseh Joshua spoke, saying,

 the **INFLUENCERS**

JOSHUA: The Over-comer that Could

JOSHUA 1:6

Joshua was born to lead Israel into the Promised Land and will forever be known for fulfilling God's orders to "be strong and of good courage" (Josh. 1:6). Joshua appears on the scene in Exodus 17, and prior to that, not much is known of his life or family, except he was from the tribe of Ephraim (Num. 13:8, 16), the son of Nun, and grandson of Elishama, chief of Ephraim (1 Chr. 7:20–27).

The name Joshua means "Yahweh is our help." He received this name at the time he entered into Moses' service, around the time of the battle with the Amalekites where Moses chose him to lead a group of men. Joshua's entire life was preparing him for the moment he would succeed Moses as the leader of Israel.

Joshua's leadership was influenced strongly by Moses. He served Moses until his death in Deuteronomy 34, and they overcame numerous obstacles together. Young Joshua watched Moses lead, and he learned through both Moses' teaching and example. Obstacles are inevitable for those who lead others, but Joshua became *the overcomer that could* lead Israel after the passing of their beloved Moses. He was the humble, yet effective, #2 man until the day the Lord called and said, "arise, and go over this Jordan, you and all this people to the land which I am giving to them—the children of Israel" (Josh. 1:2).

13"Remember the word which Moses the servant of the LORD commanded you, saying, 'The LORD your God is giving you rest and is giving you this land.' 14Your wives, your little ones, and your livestock shall remain in the land which Moses gave you on this side of the Jordan. But you shall pass before your brethren armed, all your mighty men of valor, and help them, 15until the LORD has given your brethren rest, as He *gave* you, and they also have taken possession of the land which the LORD your God is giving them. Then you shall return to the land of your possession and enjoy it, which Moses the LORD's servant gave you on this side of the Jordan toward the sunrise."

16So they answered Joshua, saying, "All that you command us we will do, and wherever you send us we will go. 17Just as we heeded Moses in all things, so we will heed you. Only the LORD your God be with you, as He was with Moses. 18Whoever rebels against your command and does not heed your words, in all that you command him, shall be put to death. Only be strong and of good courage."

RAHAB HIDES THE SPIES

2 Now Joshua the son of Nun sent out two men from Acacia Grove[a] to spy secretly, saying, "Go, view the land, especially Jericho."

So they went, and came to the house of a harlot named Rahab, and lodged there. 2And it was told the king of Jericho, saying, "Behold, men have come here tonight from the children of Israel to search out the country."

3So the king of Jericho sent to Rahab, saying, "Bring out the men who have come to you, who have entered your house, for they have come to search out all the country."

4Then the woman took the two men and hid them. So she said, "Yes, the men came to me, but I did not know where they *were* from. 5And it happened as the gate was being shut, when it was dark, that the men went out. Where the men went I do not know; pursue them quickly, for you may overtake them." 6(But she had brought them up to the roof and hidden them with the stalks of flax, which she had laid in order on the roof.)

2:1 aHebrew *Shittim*

INSIDE *the* INFLUENCERS

RAHAB—It Doesn't Matter Where You Start

JOSHUA 2, 6

Rahab was a young woman whose life didn't start off well. She was a prostitute, a common occupation for a woman in her environment. The spies sent by Joshua came to her inn, and she helped them. Her story shows the power of speaking the truth about who God is. She said, "We have heard," and the conclusion she came to was, "the LORD your God, He *is* God in heaven above and on earth beneath" (Josh. 2:10,11).

Rahab risked everything by trusting God and helping the spies. In return, they saved her and her family. The most important aspect of this dramatic story is that it doesn't matter where you start or what you've done; God wants to bless your life, starting from this very moment.

Rahab started out a prostitute, but her decision to live by faith changed everything. So much so, that God placed her in the lineage of Jesus, the Messiah (Matt. 1:5). She is a reflection of God's unconditional love, forgiveness, and mercy.

If you know someone whose past didn't start out well or whose present looks bleak, read or give them this chapter of Scripture. It just might be the encouragement they need to start over.

7Then the men pursued them by the road to the Jordan, to the fords. And as soon as those who pursued them had gone out, they shut the gate.

8Now before they lay down, she came up to them on the roof, 9and said to the men: "I know that the LORD has given you the land, that the terror of you has fallen on us, and that all the inhabitants of the land are fainthearted because of you. 10For we have heard how the LORD dried up the water of the Red Sea for you when you came out of Egypt, and what you did to the two kings of the Amorites who *were* on the other side of the Jordan, Sihon and Og, whom you utterly destroyed. 11And as soon as we heard *these things,* our hearts melted; neither did there remain any more courage in anyone because of you, for the LORD your God, He *is* God in heaven above and on earth beneath. 12Now therefore, I beg you, swear to me by the LORD, since I have shown you kindness, that you also will show kindness to my father's house, and give me a true token, 13and spare my father, my mother, my brothers, my sisters, and all that they have, and deliver our lives from death."

14So the men answered her, "Our lives for yours, if none of you tell this business of ours. And it shall be, when the LORD has given us the land, that we will deal kindly and truly with you."

15Then she let them down by a rope through the window, for her house *was* on the city wall; she dwelt on the wall. 16And she said to them, "Get to the mountain, lest the pursuers meet you. Hide there three days, until the pursuers have returned. Afterward you may go your way."

17So the men said to her: "We *will be* blameless of this oath of yours which you have made us swear, 18unless, *when* we come into the land, you bind this line of scarlet cord in the window through which you let us down, and unless you bring your father, your mother, your brothers, and all your father's household to your own home. 19So it shall be *that* whoever goes outside the doors of your house into the street, his blood *shall be* on his own head, and we *will be* guiltless. And whoever is with you in the house, his blood *shall be* on our head if a hand is laid on him. 20And if you tell this business of ours, then we will be free from your oath which you made us swear."

21Then she said, "According to your words, so

be it." And she sent them away, and they departed. And she bound the scarlet cord in the window.

22They departed and went to the mountain, and stayed there three days until the pursuers returned. The pursuers sought *them* all along the way, but did not find *them.* 23So the two men returned, descended from the mountain, and crossed over; and they came to Joshua the son of Nun, and told him all that had befallen them. 24And they said to Joshua, "Truly the LORD has delivered all the land into our hands, for indeed all the inhabitants of the country are fainthearted because of us."

ISRAEL CROSSES THE JORDAN

3 Then Joshua rose early in the morning; and they set out from Acacia Grove[a] and came to the Jordan, he and all the children of Israel, and lodged there before they crossed over. 2So it was, after three days, that the officers went through the camp; 3and they commanded the people, saying, "When you see the ark of the covenant of the LORD your God, and the priests, the Levites, bearing it, then you shall set out from your place and go after it. 4Yet there shall be a space between you and it, about two thousand cubits by measure. Do not come near it, that you may know the way by which you must go, for you have not passed *this* way before."

5And Joshua said to the people, "Sanctify yourselves, for tomorrow the LORD will do wonders among you." 6Then Joshua spoke to the priests, saying, "Take up the ark of the covenant and cross over before the people."

So they took up the ark of the covenant and went before the people.

7And the LORD said to Joshua, "This day I will begin to exalt you in the sight of all Israel, that they may know that, as I was with Moses, *so* I will be with you. 8You shall command the priests who bear the ark of the covenant, saying, 'When you have come to the edge of the water of the Jordan, you shall stand in the Jordan.' "

9So Joshua said to the children of Israel, "Come here, and hear the words of the LORD your God." 10And Joshua said, "By this you shall know that the living God *is* among you, and *that*

3:1 aHebrew *Shittim*

LEADERSHIP
REALITIES

BECOME TODAY WHAT YOU
WANT TO BE TOMORROW *Joshua 3*

This chapter is a defining moment in Joshua's evolution as a leader. Moses was dead and God had already commissioned him to lead the people of Israel. His first task was to take the nation across the Jordan. For most of the year the Jordan River was about 100 feet wide, but during the spring flood time, the overflowing banks could stretch to a mile wide in places. God had chosen this place and this time to demonstrate the power of His presence to both Joshua and the nation. Joshua was called to cross the flooding river by faith; to lead Israel in the campaigns on the other side of it (ch. 6); to win victory against the Amorite kings; to secure cities in the northern and southern regions (chs. 9—12); and to divide the land among the tribes (chs. 13—17). Opportunities for leadership were abundant, but Joshua could not lead tomorrow unless he accepted the call to be a leader *today*.

The English word *opportunity* is from the Latin *opportunus,* meaning favorable or prosperous. It is a word picture of favorable winds blowing a ship in the right direction. If you want the favor of God on your tomorrow, *set yourself apart for God's service today.*

He will without fail drive out from before you the Canaanites and the Hittites and the Hivites and the Perizzites and the Girgashites and the Amorites and the Jebusites: ¹¹Behold, the ark of the covenant of the Lord of all the earth is crossing over before you into the Jordan. ¹²Now therefore, take for yourselves twelve men from the tribes of Israel, one man from every tribe. ¹³And it shall come to pass, as soon as the soles of the feet of the priests who bear the ark of the LORD, the Lord of all the earth, shall rest in the waters of the Jordan, *that* the waters of the Jordan shall be cut off, the waters that come down from upstream, and they shall stand as a heap."

¹⁴So it was, when the people set out from their camp to cross over the Jordan, with the priests bearing the ark of the covenant before the people, ¹⁵and as those who bore the ark came to the Jordan, and the feet of the priests who bore the ark dipped in the edge of the water (for the Jordan overflows all its banks during the whole time of harvest), ¹⁶that the waters which came down from upstream stood *still, and* rose in a heap very far away at Adam, the city that *is* beside Zaretan. So the waters that went down into the Sea of the Arabah, the Salt Sea, failed, *and* were cut off; and the people crossed over opposite Jericho. ¹⁷Then the priests who bore the ark of the covenant of the LORD stood firm on dry ground in the midst of the Jordan; and all Israel crossed over on dry ground, until all the people had crossed completely over the Jordan.

THE MEMORIAL STONES

4 And it came to pass, when all the people had completely crossed over the Jordan, that the LORD spoke to Joshua, saying: ²"Take for yourselves twelve men from the people, one man from every tribe, ³and command them, saying, 'Take for yourselves twelve stones from here, out of the midst of the Jordan, from the place where the priests' feet stood firm. You shall carry them over with you and leave them in the lodging place where you lodge tonight.'"

⁴Then Joshua called the twelve men whom he had appointed from the children of Israel, one man from every tribe; ⁵and Joshua said to them: "Cross over before the ark of the LORD your God

into the midst of the Jordan, and each one of you take up a stone on his shoulder, according to the number of the tribes of the children of Israel, [6]that this may be a sign among you when your children ask in time to come, saying, 'What do these stones *mean* to you?' [7]Then you shall answer them that the waters of the Jordan were cut off before the ark of the covenant of the LORD; when it crossed over the Jordan, the waters of the Jordan were cut off. And these stones shall be for a memorial to the children of Israel forever."

[8]And the children of Israel did so, just as Joshua commanded, and took up twelve stones from the midst of the Jordan, as the LORD had spoken to Joshua, according to the number of the tribes of the children of Israel, and carried them over with them to the place where they lodged, and laid them down there. [9]Then Joshua set up twelve stones in the midst of the Jordan, in the place where the feet of the priests who bore the ark of the covenant stood; and they are there to this day.

[10]So the priests who bore the ark stood in the midst of the Jordan until everything was finished that the LORD had commanded Joshua to speak to the people, according to all that Moses had commanded Joshua; and the people hurried and crossed over. [11]Then it came to pass, when all the people had completely crossed over, that the ark of the LORD and the priests crossed over in the presence of the people. [12]And the men of Reuben, the men of Gad, and half the tribe of Manasseh crossed over armed before the children of Israel, as Moses had spoken to them. [13]About forty thousand prepared for war crossed over before the LORD for battle, to the plains of Jericho. [14]On that day the LORD exalted Joshua in the sight of all Israel; and they feared him, as they had feared Moses, all the days of his life.

[15]Then the LORD spoke to Joshua, saying, [16]"Command the priests who bear the ark of the Testimony to come up from the Jordan." [17]Joshua therefore commanded the priests, saying, "Come up from the Jordan." [18]And it came to pass, when the priests who bore the ark of the covenant of the LORD had come from the midst of the Jordan, *and* the soles of the priests' feet touched the dry land, that the waters of the Jordan returned to their place and overflowed all its banks as before.

[19]Now the people came up from the Jordan on the tenth *day* of the first month, and they camped in Gilgal on the east border of Jericho. [20]And those twelve stones which they took out of the Jordan, Joshua set up in Gilgal. [21]Then he spoke to the children of Israel, saying: "When your children ask their fathers in time to come, saying, 'What *are* these stones?' [22]then you shall let your children know, saying, 'Israel crossed over this Jordan on dry land'; [23]for the LORD your God dried up the waters of the Jordan before you until you had crossed over, as the LORD your God did to the Red Sea, which He dried up before us until we had crossed over, [24]that all the peoples of the earth may know the hand of the LORD, that it *is* mighty, that you may fear the LORD your God forever."

The Second Generation Circumcised

5 So it was, when all the kings of the Amorites who *were* on the west side of the Jordan, and all the kings of the Canaanites who *were* by the sea, heard that the LORD had dried up the waters of the Jordan from before the children of Israel until we[a] had crossed over, that their heart melted; and there was no spirit in them any longer because of the children of Israel.

[2]At that time the LORD said to Joshua, "Make flint knives for yourself, and circumcise the sons of Israel again the second time." [3]So Joshua made flint knives for himself, and circumcised the sons of Israel at the hill of the foreskins.[a] [4]And this *is* the reason why Joshua circumcised them: All the people who came out of Egypt *who were* males, all the men of war, had died in the wilderness on the way, after they had come out of Egypt. [5]For all the people who came out had been circumcised, but all the people born in the wilderness, on the way as they came out of Egypt, had not been circumcised. [6]For the children of Israel walked forty years in the wilderness, till all the people *who were* men of war, who came out of Egypt, were consumed, because they did not obey the voice of the LORD—to whom the LORD swore that He would not show them the land which the LORD had sworn to their fathers that He would give us,

5:1 [a]Following Kethib; Qere, some Hebrew manuscripts and editions, Septuagint, Syriac, Targum, and Vulgate read *they.*   **5:3** [a]Hebrew *Gibeath Haaraloth*

"a land flowing with milk and honey."[a] [7]Then Joshua circumcised their sons *whom* He raised up in their place; for they were uncircumcised, because they had not been circumcised on the way.

[8]So it was, when they had finished circumcising all the people, that they stayed in their places in the camp till they were healed. [9]Then the LORD said to Joshua, "This day I have rolled away the reproach of Egypt from you." Therefore the name of the place is called Gilgal[a] to this day.

[10]Now the children of Israel camped in Gilgal, and kept the Passover on the fourteenth day of the month at twilight on the plains of Jericho. [11]And they ate of the produce of the land on the day after the Passover, unleavened bread and parched grain, on the very same day. [12]Then the manna ceased on the day after they had eaten the produce of the land; and the children of Israel no longer had manna, but they ate the food of the land of Canaan that year.

THE COMMANDER OF THE ARMY OF THE LORD

[13]And it came to pass, when Joshua was by Jericho, that he lifted his eyes and looked, and behold, a Man stood opposite him with His sword drawn in His hand. And Joshua went to Him and said to Him, "*Are* You for us or for our adversaries?"

[14]So He said, "No, but *as* Commander of the army of the LORD I have now come."

And Joshua fell on his face to the earth and worshiped, and said to Him, "What does my Lord say to His servant?"

[15]Then the Commander of the LORD's army said to Joshua, "Take your sandal off your foot, for the place where you stand *is* holy." And Joshua did so.

THE DESTRUCTION OF JERICHO

6 Now Jericho was securely shut up because of the children of Israel; none went out, and none came in. [2]And the LORD said to Joshua: "See! I have given Jericho into your hand, its king, *and* the mighty men of valor. [3]You shall march around the city, all *you* men of war; you shall go all around the city once. This you shall do six days. [4]And seven priests shall bear seven trumpets of rams' horns before the ark. But the seventh day you shall march around the city seven times,

and the priests shall blow the trumpets. [5]It shall come to pass, when they make a long *blast* with the ram's horn, *and* when you hear the sound of the trumpet, that all the people shall shout with a great shout; then the wall of the city will fall down flat. And the people shall go up every man straight before him."

[6]Then Joshua the son of Nun called the priests and said to them, "Take up the ark of the covenant, and let seven priests bear seven trumpets of rams' horns before the ark of the LORD." [7]And he said to the people, "Proceed, and march around the city, and let him who is armed advance before the ark of the LORD."

[8]So it was, when Joshua had spoken to the people, that the seven priests bearing the seven trumpets of rams' horns before the LORD advanced and blew the trumpets, and the ark of the covenant of the LORD followed them. [9]The armed men went before the priests who blew the trumpets, and the rear guard came after the ark, while *the priests* continued blowing the trumpets. [10]Now Joshua had commanded the people, saying, "You shall not shout or make any noise with your voice, nor shall a word proceed out of your mouth, until the day I say to you, 'Shout!' Then you shall shout." [11]So he had the ark of the LORD circle the city, going around *it* once. Then they came into the camp and lodged in the camp.

[12]And Joshua rose early in the morning, and the priests took up the ark of the LORD. [13]Then seven priests bearing seven trumpets of rams' horns before the ark of the LORD went on continually and blew with the trumpets. And the armed men went before them. But the rear guard came after the ark of the LORD, while *the priests* continued blowing the trumpets. [14]And the second day they marched around the city once and returned to the camp. So they did six days.

[15]But it came to pass on the seventh day that they rose early, about the dawning of the day, and marched around the city seven times in the same manner. On that day only they marched around the city seven times. [16]And the seventh time it happened, when the priests blew the trumpets, that Joshua said to the people: "Shout, for the LORD has given you the city! [17]Now the city shall

5:6 [a]Exodus 3:8 5:9 [a]Literally *Rolling*

be doomed by the LORD to destruction, it and all who *are* in it. Only Rahab the harlot shall live, she and all who *are* with her in the house, because she hid the messengers that we sent. ¹⁸And you, by all means abstain from the accursed things, lest you become accursed when you take of the accursed things, and make the camp of Israel a curse, and trouble it. ¹⁹But all the silver and gold, and vessels of bronze and iron, *are* consecrated to the LORD; they shall come into the treasury of the LORD."

²⁰So the people shouted when *the priests* blew the trumpets. And it happened when the people heard the sound of the trumpet, and the people shouted with a great shout, that the wall fell down flat. Then the people went up into the city, every man straight before him, and they took the city. ²¹And they utterly destroyed all that *was* in the city, both man and woman, young and old, ox and sheep and donkey, with the edge of the sword.

²²But Joshua had said to the two men who had spied out the country, "Go into the harlot's house, and from there bring out the woman and all that she has, as you swore to her." ²³And the young men who had been spies went in and brought out Rahab, her father, her mother, her brothers, and all that she had. So they brought out all her relatives and left them outside the camp of Israel. ²⁴But they burned the city and all that *was* in it with fire. Only the silver and gold, and the vessels of bronze and iron, they put into the treasury of the house of the LORD. ²⁵And Joshua spared Rahab the harlot, her father's household, and all that she had. So she dwells in Israel to this day, because she hid the messengers whom Joshua sent to spy out Jericho.

²⁶Then Joshua charged *them* at that time, saying, "Cursed *be* the man before the LORD who rises up and builds this city Jericho; he shall lay its foundation with his firstborn, and with his youngest he shall set up its gates."

²⁷So the LORD was with Joshua, and his fame spread throughout all the country.

Defeat at Ai

7 But the children of Israel committed a trespass regarding the accursed things, for Achan the son of Carmi, the son of Zabdi,ª the son of Zerah, of the tribe of Judah, took of the accursed things;

so the anger of the LORD burned against the children of Israel.

²Now Joshua sent men from Jericho to Ai, which *is* beside Beth Aven, on the east side of Bethel, and spoke to them, saying, "Go up and spy out the country." So the men went up and spied out Ai. ³And they returned to Joshua and said to him, "Do not let all the people go up, but let about two or three thousand men go up and attack Ai. Do not weary all the people there, for *the people of Ai are* few." ⁴So about three thousand men went up there from the people, but they fled before the men of Ai. ⁵And the men of Ai struck down about thirty-six men, for they chased them *from* before the gate as far as Shebarim, and struck them down on the descent; therefore the hearts of the people melted and became like water.

⁶Then Joshua tore his clothes, and fell to the earth on his face before the ark of the LORD until evening, he and the elders of Israel; and they put dust on their heads. ⁷And Joshua said, "Alas, Lord GOD, why have You brought this people over the Jordan at all—to deliver us into the hand of the Amorites, to destroy us? Oh, that we had been content, and dwelt on the other side of the Jordan! ⁸O Lord, what shall I say when Israel turns its back before its enemies? ⁹For the Canaanites and all the inhabitants of the land will hear *it,* and surround us, and cut off our name from the earth. Then what will You do for Your great name?"

The Sin of Achan

¹⁰So the LORD said to Joshua: "Get up! Why do you lie thus on your face? ¹¹Israel has sinned, and they have also transgressed My covenant which I commanded them. For they have even taken some of the accursed things, and have both stolen and deceived; and they have also put *it* among their own stuff. ¹²Therefore the children of Israel could not stand before their enemies, *but* turned *their* backs before their enemies, because they have become doomed to destruction. Neither will I be with you anymore, unless you destroy the accursed from among you. ¹³Get up, sanctify the people, and say, 'Sanctify yourselves for tomorrow, because thus says the LORD God of Israel: "*There is* an accursed thing in your midst,

7:1 ªCalled *Zimri* in 1 Chronicles 2:6

O Israel; you cannot stand before your enemies until you take away the accursed thing from among you." [14]In the morning therefore you shall be brought according to your tribes. And it shall be *that* the tribe which the LORD takes shall come according to families; and the family which the LORD takes shall come by households; and the household which the LORD takes shall come man by man. [15]Then it shall be *that* he who is taken with the accursed thing shall be burned with fire, he and all that he has, because he has transgressed the covenant of the LORD, and because he has done a disgraceful thing in Israel.' "

[16]So Joshua rose early in the morning and brought Israel by their tribes, and the tribe of Judah was taken. [17]He brought the clan of Judah, and he took the family of the Zarhites; and he brought the family of the Zarhites man by man, and Zabdi was taken. [18]Then he brought his household man by man, and Achan the son of Carmi, the son of Zabdi, the son of Zerah, of the tribe of Judah, was taken.

[19]Now Joshua said to Achan, "My son, I beg you, give glory to the LORD God of Israel, and make confession to Him, and tell me now what you have done; do not hide *it* from me."

[20]And Achan answered Joshua and said, "Indeed I have sinned against the LORD God of Israel, and this is what I have done: [21]When I saw among the spoils a beautiful Babylonian garment, two hundred shekels of silver, and a wedge of gold weighing fifty shekels, I coveted them and took them. And there they are, hidden in the earth in the midst of my tent, with the silver under it."

[22]So Joshua sent messengers, and they ran to the tent; and there it was, hidden in his tent, with the silver under it. [23]And they took them from the midst of the tent, brought them to Joshua and to all the children of Israel, and laid them out before the LORD. [24]Then Joshua, and all Israel with him, took Achan the son of Zerah, the silver, the garment, the wedge of gold, his sons, his daughters, his oxen, his donkeys, his sheep, his tent, and all that he had, and they brought them to the Valley of Achor. [25]And Joshua said, "Why have you troubled us? The LORD will trouble you this day." So all Israel stoned him with stones; and they burned them with fire after they had stoned them with stones.

[26]Then they raised over him a great heap of stones, still there to this day. So the LORD turned from the fierceness of His anger. Therefore the name of that place has been called the Valley of Achor[a] to this day.

The Fall of Ai

8 Now the LORD said to Joshua: "Do not be afraid, nor be dismayed; take all the people of war with you, and arise, go up to Ai. See, I have given into your hand the king of Ai, his people, his city, and his land. [2]And you shall do to Ai and its king as you did to Jericho and its king. Only its spoil and its cattle you shall take as booty for yourselves. Lay an ambush for the city behind it."

[3]So Joshua arose, and all the people of war, to go up against Ai; and Joshua chose thirty thousand mighty men of valor and sent them away by night. [4]And he commanded them, saying: "Behold, you shall lie in ambush against the city, behind the city. Do not go very far from the city, but all of you be ready. [5]Then I and all the people who *are* with me will approach the city; and it will come about, when they come out against us as at the first, that we shall flee before them. [6]For they will come out after us till we have drawn them from the city, for they will say, 'They are fleeing before us as at the first.' Therefore we will flee before them. [7]Then you shall rise from the ambush and seize the city, for the LORD your God will deliver it into your hand. [8]And it will be, when you have taken the city, *that* you shall set the city on fire. According to the commandment of the LORD you shall do. See, I have commanded you."

[9]Joshua therefore sent them out; and they went to lie in ambush, and stayed between Bethel and Ai, on the west side of Ai; but Joshua lodged that night among the people. [10]Then Joshua rose up early in the morning and mustered the people, and went up, he and the elders of Israel, before the people to Ai. [11]And all the people of war who *were* with him went up and drew near; and they came before the city and camped on the north side of Ai. Now a valley *lay* between them and Ai. [12]So he took about five thousand men and set them in ambush between Bethel and Ai, on the

7:26 [a]Literally *Trouble*

west side of the city. [13]And when they had set the people, all the army that *was* on the north of the city, and its rear guard on the west of the city, Joshua went that night into the midst of the valley.

[14]Now it happened, when the king of Ai saw *it,* that the men of the city hurried and rose early and went out against Israel to battle, he and all his people, at an appointed place before the plain. But he did not know that *there was* an ambush against him behind the city. [15]And Joshua and all Israel made as if they were beaten before them, and fled by the way of the wilderness. [16]So all the people who *were* in Ai were called together to pursue them. And they pursued Joshua and were drawn away from the city. [17]There was not a man left in Ai or Bethel who did not go out after Israel. So they left the city open and pursued Israel.

[18]Then the LORD said to Joshua, "Stretch out the spear that *is* in your hand toward Ai, for I will give it into your hand." And Joshua stretched out the spear that *was* in his hand toward the city. [19]So *those in* ambush arose quickly out of their place; they ran as soon as he had stretched out his hand, and they entered the city and took it, and hurried to set the city on fire. [20]And when the men of Ai looked behind them, they saw, and behold, the smoke of the city ascended to heaven. So they had no power to flee this way or that way, and the people who had fled to the wilderness turned back on the pursuers.

[21]Now when Joshua and all Israel saw that the ambush had taken the city and that the smoke of the city ascended, they turned back and struck down the men of Ai. [22]Then the others came out of the city against them; so they were *caught* in the midst of Israel, some on this side and some on that side. And they struck them down, so that they let none of them remain or escape. [23]But the king of Ai they took alive, and brought him to Joshua.

[24]And it came to pass when Israel had made an end of slaying all the inhabitants of Ai in the field, in the wilderness where they pursued them, and when they all had fallen by the edge of the sword until they were consumed, that all the Israelites returned to Ai and struck it with the edge of the sword. [25]So it was *that* all who fell that day, both men and women, *were* twelve thousand—all

the people of Ai. [26]For Joshua did not draw back his hand, with which he stretched out the spear, until he had utterly destroyed all the inhabitants of Ai. [27]Only the livestock and the spoil of that city Israel took as booty for themselves, according to the word of the LORD which He had commanded Joshua. [28]So Joshua burned Ai and made it a heap forever, a desolation to this day. [29]And the king of Ai he hanged on a tree until evening. And as soon as the sun was down, Joshua commanded that they should take his corpse down from the tree, cast it at the entrance of the gate of the city, and raise over it a great heap of stones *that remains* to this day.

JOSHUA RENEWS THE COVENANT

[30]Now Joshua built an altar to the LORD God of Israel in Mount Ebal, [31]as Moses the servant of the LORD had commanded the children of Israel, as it is written in the Book of the Law of Moses: "an altar of whole stones over which no man has wielded an iron *tool*."[a] And they offered on it burnt offerings to the LORD, and sacrificed peace offerings. [32]And there, in the presence of the children of Israel, he wrote on the stones a copy of the law of Moses, which he had written. [33]Then all Israel, with their elders and officers and judges, stood on either side of the ark before the priests, the Levites, who bore the ark of the covenant of the LORD, the stranger as well as he who was born among them. Half of them *were* in front of Mount Gerizim and half of them in front of Mount Ebal, as Moses the servant of the LORD had commanded before, that they should bless the people of Israel. [34]And afterward he read all the words of the law, the blessings and the cursings, according to all that is written in the Book of the Law. [35]There was not a word of all that Moses had commanded which Joshua did not read before all the assembly of Israel, with the women, the little ones, and the strangers who were living among them.

THE TREATY WITH THE GIBEONITES

9 And it came to pass when all the kings who *were* on this side of the Jordan, in the hills and in the lowland and in all the coasts of the Great

8:31 [a]Deuteronomy 27:5, 6

Sea toward Lebanon—the Hittite, the Amorite, the Canaanite, the Perizzite, the Hivite, and the Jebusite—heard *about it,* ²that they gathered together to fight with Joshua and Israel with one accord.

³But when the inhabitants of Gibeon heard what Joshua had done to Jericho and Ai, ⁴they worked craftily, and went and pretended to be ambassadors. And they took old sacks on their donkeys, old wineskins torn and mended, ⁵old and patched sandals on their feet, and old garments on themselves; and all the bread of their provision was dry *and* moldy. ⁶And they went to Joshua, to the camp at Gilgal, and said to him and to the men of Israel, "We have come from a far country; now therefore, make a covenant with us."

⁷Then the men of Israel said to the Hivites, "Perhaps you dwell among us; so how can we make a covenant with you?"

⁸But they said to Joshua, "We *are* your servants."

And Joshua said to them, "Who *are* you, and where do you come from?"

⁹So they said to him: "From a very far country your servants have come, because of the name of the LORD your God; for we have heard of His fame, and all that He did in Egypt, ¹⁰and all that He did to the two kings of the Amorites who *were* beyond the Jordan—to Sihon king of Heshbon, and Og king of Bashan, who was at Ashtaroth. ¹¹Therefore our elders and all the inhabitants of our country spoke to us, saying, 'Take provisions with you for the journey, and go to meet them, and say to them, "We *are* your servants; now therefore, make a covenant with us." ' ¹²This bread of ours we took hot *for* our provision from our houses on the day we departed to come to you. But now look, it is dry and moldy. ¹³And these wineskins which we filled *were* new, and see, they are torn; and these our garments and our sandals have become old because of the very long journey."

¹⁴Then the men of Israel took some of their provisions; but they did not ask counsel of the LORD. ¹⁵So Joshua made peace with them, and made a covenant with them to let them live; and the rulers of the congregation swore to them.

¹⁶And it happened at the end of three days,

after they had made a covenant with them, that they heard that they *were* their neighbors who dwelt near them. ¹⁷Then the children of Israel journeyed and came to their cities on the third day. Now their cities *were* Gibeon, Chephirah, Beeroth, and Kirjath Jearim. ¹⁸But the children of Israel did not attack them, because the rulers of the congregation had sworn to them by the LORD God of Israel. And all the congregation complained against the rulers.

¹⁹Then all the rulers said to all the congregation, "We have sworn to them by the LORD God of Israel; now therefore, we may not touch them. ²⁰This we will do to them: We will let them live, lest wrath be upon us because of the oath which we swore to them." ²¹And the rulers said to them, "Let them live, but let them be woodcutters and water carriers for all the congregation, as the rulers had promised them."

²²Then Joshua called for them, and he spoke to them, saying, "Why have you deceived us, saying, 'We *are* very far from you,' when you dwell near us? ²³Now therefore, you *are* cursed, and none of you shall be freed from being slaves—woodcutters and water carriers for the house of my God."

²⁴So they answered Joshua and said, "Because your servants were clearly told that the LORD your God commanded His servant Moses to give you all the land, and to destroy all the inhabitants of the land from before you; therefore we were very much afraid for our lives because of you, and have done this thing. ²⁵And now, here we are, in your hands; do with us as it seems good and right to do to us." ²⁶So he did to them, and delivered them out of the hand of the children of Israel, so that they did not kill them. ²⁷And that day Joshua made them woodcutters and water carriers for the congregation and for the altar of the LORD, in the place which He would choose, even to this day.

THE SUN STANDS STILL

10 Now it came to pass when Adoni-Zedek king of Jerusalem heard how Joshua had taken Ai and had utterly destroyed it—as he had done to Jericho and its king, so he had done to Ai and its king—and how the inhabitants of Gibeon had made peace with Israel and were among them, ²that they feared greatly, because Gibeon *was* a great city, like one of the royal cities, and because it *was* greater than Ai, and all its men *were* mighty. ³Therefore Adoni-Zedek king of Jerusalem sent to Hoham king of Hebron, Piram king of Jarmuth, Japhia king of Lachish, and Debir king of Eglon, saying, ⁴"Come up to me and help me, that we may attack Gibeon, for it has made peace with Joshua and with the children of Israel." ⁵Therefore the five kings of the Amorites, the king of Jerusalem, the king of Hebron, the king of Jarmuth, the king of Lachish, *and* the king of Eglon, gathered together and went up, they and all their armies, and camped before Gibeon and made war against it.

⁶And the men of Gibeon sent to Joshua at the camp at Gilgal, saying, "Do not forsake your servants; come up to us quickly, save us and help us, for all the kings of the Amorites who dwell in the mountains have gathered together against us."

⁷So Joshua ascended from Gilgal, he and all the people of war with him, and all the mighty men of valor. ⁸And the LORD said to Joshua, "Do not fear them, for I have delivered them into your hand; not a man of them shall stand before you." ⁹Joshua therefore came upon them suddenly, having marched all night from Gilgal. ¹⁰So the LORD routed them before Israel, killed them with a great slaughter at Gibeon, chased them along the road that goes to Beth Horon, and struck them down as far as Azekah and Makkedah. ¹¹And it happened, as they fled before Israel *and* were on the descent of Beth Horon, that the LORD cast down large hailstones from heaven on them as far as Azekah, and they died. *There were* more who died from the hailstones than the children of Israel killed with the sword.

¹²Then Joshua spoke to the LORD in the day when the LORD delivered up the Amorites before the children of Israel, and he said in the sight of Israel:

"Sun, stand still over Gibeon;
  And Moon, in the Valley of Aijalon."
¹³So the sun stood still,
  And the moon stopped,
  Till the people had revenge
  Upon their enemies.

Is this not written in the Book of Jasher? So the sun stood still in the midst of heaven, and did not hasten to go *down* for about a whole day. ¹⁴And there has been no day like that, before it or after it, that the LORD heeded the voice of a man; for the LORD fought for Israel.

¹⁵Then Joshua returned, and all Israel with him, to the camp at Gilgal.

THE AMORITE KINGS EXECUTED

¹⁶But these five kings had fled and hidden themselves in a cave at Makkedah. ¹⁷And it was told Joshua, saying, "The five kings have been found hidden in the cave at Makkedah."

¹⁸So Joshua said, "Roll large stones against the mouth of the cave, and set men by it to guard them. ¹⁹And do not stay *there* yourselves, *but* pursue your enemies, and attack their rear *guard*. Do not allow them to enter their cities, for the LORD your God has delivered them into your hand." ²⁰Then it happened, while Joshua and the children of Israel made an end of slaying them with a very great slaughter, till they had finished, that those who escaped entered fortified cities. ²¹And all the people returned to the camp, to Joshua at Makkedah, in peace.

No one moved his tongue against any of the children of Israel.

²²Then Joshua said, "Open the mouth of the cave, and bring out those five kings to me from the cave." ²³And they did so, and brought out those five kings to him from the cave: the king of Jerusalem, the king of Hebron, the king of Jarmuth, the king of Lachish, *and* the king of Eglon.

²⁴So it was, when they brought out those kings to Joshua, that Joshua called for all the men of Israel, and said to the captains of the men of war who went with him, "Come near, put your feet on the necks of these kings." And they drew near and put their feet on their necks. ²⁵Then Joshua said to them, "Do not be afraid, nor be dismayed; be strong and of good courage, for thus the LORD will do to all your enemies against whom you fight." ²⁶And afterward Joshua struck them and killed them, and hanged them on five trees; and they were hanging on the trees until evening. ²⁷So it was at the time of the going down of the sun *that* Joshua commanded, and they took them down from the trees, cast them

into the cave where they had been hidden, and laid large stones against the cave's mouth, *which remain* until this very day.

Conquest of the Southland

²⁸On that day Joshua took Makkedah, and struck it and its king with the edge of the sword. He utterly destroyed them[a]—all the people who *were* in it. He let none remain. He also did to the king of Makkedah as he had done to the king of Jericho.

²⁹Then Joshua passed from Makkedah, and all Israel with him, to Libnah; and they fought against Libnah. ³⁰And the LORD also delivered it and its king into the hand of Israel; he struck it and all the people who *were* in it with the edge of the sword. He let none remain in it, but did to its king as he had done to the king of Jericho.

³¹Then Joshua passed from Libnah, and all Israel with him, to Lachish; and they encamped against it and fought against it. ³²And the LORD delivered Lachish into the hand of Israel, who took it on the second day, and struck it and all the people who *were* in it with the edge of the sword, according to all that he had done to Libnah. ³³Then Horam king of Gezer came up to help Lachish; and Joshua struck him and his people, until he left him none remaining.

³⁴From Lachish Joshua passed to Eglon, and all Israel with him; and they encamped against it and fought against it. ³⁵They took it on that day and struck it with the edge of the sword; all the people who *were* in it he utterly destroyed that day, according to all that he had done to Lachish.

³⁶So Joshua went up from Eglon, and all Israel with him, to Hebron; and they fought against it. ³⁷And they took it and struck it with the edge of the sword—its king, all its cities, and all the people who *were* in it; he left none remaining, according to all that he had done to Eglon, but utterly destroyed it and all the people who *were* in it.

³⁸Then Joshua returned, and all Israel with him, to Debir; and they fought against it. ³⁹And he took it and its king and all its cities; they struck them with the edge of the sword and utterly destroyed all the people who *were* in it. He left none remaining; as he had done to Hebron, so he did to Debir and its king, as he had done also to Libnah and its king.

⁴⁰So Joshua conquered all the land: the mountain country and the South[a] and the lowland and the wilderness slopes, and all their kings; he left none remaining, but utterly destroyed all that breathed, as the LORD God of Israel had commanded. ⁴¹And Joshua conquered them from Kadesh Barnea as far as Gaza, and all the country of Goshen, even as far as Gibeon. ⁴²All these kings and their land Joshua took at one time, because the LORD God of Israel fought for Israel. ⁴³Then Joshua returned, and all Israel with him, to the camp at Gilgal.

The Northern Conquest

11 And it came to pass, when Jabin king of Hazor heard *these things,* that he sent to Jobab king of Madon, to the king of Shimron, to the king of Achshaph, ²and to the kings who *were* from the north, in the mountains, in the plain south of Chinneroth, in the lowland, and in the heights of Dor on the west, ³to the Canaanites in the east and in the west, the Amorite, the Hittite, the Perizzite, the Jebusite in the mountains, and the Hivite below Hermon in the land of Mizpah. ⁴So they went out, they and all their armies with them, *as* many people *as* the sand that *is* on the seashore in multitude, with very many horses and chariots. ⁵And when all these kings had met together, they came and camped together at the waters of Merom to fight against Israel.

⁶But the LORD said to Joshua, "Do not be afraid because of them, for tomorrow about this time I will deliver all of them slain before Israel. You shall hamstring their horses and burn their chariots with fire." ⁷So Joshua and all the people of war with him came against them suddenly by the waters of Merom, and they attacked them. ⁸And the LORD delivered them into the hand of Israel, who defeated them and chased them to Greater Sidon, to the Brook Misrephoth,[a] and to the Valley of Mizpah eastward; they attacked them until they left none of them remaining. ⁹So Joshua did to them as the LORD had told him: he hamstrung their horses and burned their chariots with fire.

10:28 [a]Following Masoretic Text and most authorities; many Hebrew manuscripts, some manuscripts of the Septuagint, and some manuscripts of the Targum read *it.* **10:40** [a]Hebrew *Negev,* and so throughout this book **11:8** [a]Hebrew *Misrephoth Maim*

¹⁰Joshua turned back at that time and took Hazor, and struck its king with the sword; for Hazor was formerly the head of all those kingdoms. ¹¹And they struck all the people who *were* in it with the edge of the sword, utterly destroying *them*. There was none left breathing. Then he burned Hazor with fire.

¹²So all the cities of those kings, and all their kings, Joshua took and struck with the edge of the sword. He utterly destroyed them, as Moses the servant of the LORD had commanded. ¹³But *as for* the cities that stood on their mounds,ª Israel burned none of them, except Hazor only, *which* Joshua burned. ¹⁴And all the spoil of these cities and the livestock, the children of Israel took as booty for themselves; but they struck every man with the edge of the sword until they had destroyed them, and they left none breathing. ¹⁵As the LORD had commanded Moses his servant, so Moses commanded Joshua, and so Joshua did. He left nothing undone of all that the LORD had commanded Moses.

Summary of Joshua's Conquests

¹⁶Thus Joshua took all this land: the mountain country, all the South, all the land of Goshen, the lowland, and the Jordan plainª—the mountains of Israel and its lowlands, ¹⁷from Mount Halak and the ascent to Seir, even as far as Baal Gad in the Valley of Lebanon below Mount Hermon. He captured all their kings, and struck them down and killed them. ¹⁸Joshua made war a long time with all those kings. ¹⁹There was not a city that made peace with the children of Israel, except the Hivites, the inhabitants of Gibeon. All *the others* they took in battle. ²⁰For it was of the LORD to harden their hearts, that they should come against Israel in battle, that He might utterly destroy them, *and* that they might receive no mercy, but that He might destroy them, as the LORD had commanded Moses.

²¹And at that time Joshua came and cut off the Anakim from the mountains: from Hebron, from Debir, from Anab, from all the mountains of Judah, and from all the mountains of Israel; Joshua utterly destroyed them with their cities. ²²None of the Anakim were left in the land of the children of Israel; they remained only in Gaza, in Gath, and in Ashdod.

²³So Joshua took the whole land, according to all that the LORD had said to Moses; and Joshua gave it as an inheritance to Israel according to their divisions by their tribes. Then the land rested from war.

The Kings Conquered by Moses

12 These *are* the kings of the land whom the children of Israel defeated, and whose land they possessed on the other side of the Jordan toward the rising of the sun, from the River Arnon to Mount Hermon, and all the eastern Jordan plain: ²*One king was* Sihon king of the Amorites, who dwelt in Heshbon *and* ruled half of Gilead, from Aroer, which is on the bank of the River Arnon, from the middle of that river, even as far as the River Jabbok, *which is* the border of the Ammonites, ³and the eastern Jordan plain from the Sea of Chinneroth as far as the Sea of the Arabah (the Salt Sea), the road to Beth Jeshimoth, and southward below the slopes of Pisgah. ⁴*The other king was* Og king of Bashan and his territory, *who was* of the remnant of the giants, who dwelt at Ashtaroth and at Edrei, ⁵and reigned over Mount Hermon, over Salcah, over all Bashan, as far as the border of the Geshurites and the Maachathites, and over half of Gilead *to* the border of Sihon king of Heshbon.

⁶These Moses the servant of the LORD and the children of Israel had conquered; and Moses the servant of the LORD had given it *as* a possession to the Reubenites, the Gadites, and half the tribe of Manasseh.

The Kings Conquered by Joshua

⁷And these *are* the kings of the country which Joshua and the children of Israel conquered on this side of the Jordan, on the west, from Baal Gad in the Valley of Lebanon as far as Mount Halak and the ascent to Seir, which Joshua gave to the tribes of Israel *as* a possession according to their divisions, ⁸in the mountain country, in the lowlands, in the *Jordan* plain, in the slopes, in the wilderness, and in the South—the Hittites, the Amorites, the Canaanites, the Perizzites, the Hivites, and the Jebusites: ⁹the king of Jericho, one; the king of Ai, which *is* beside Bethel, one; ¹⁰the

11:13 ªHebrew *tel,* a heap of successive city ruins **11:16** ªHebrew *arabah*

king of Jerusalem, one; the king of Hebron, one; [11]the king of Jarmuth, one; the king of Lachish, one; [12]the king of Eglon, one; the king of Gezer, one; [13]the king of Debir, one; the king of Geder, one; [14]the king of Hormah, one; the king of Arad, one; [15]the king of Libnah, one; the king of Adullam, one; [16]the king of Makkedah, one; the king of Bethel, one; [17]the king of Tappuah, one; the king of Hepher, one; [18]the king of Aphek, one; the king of Lasharon, one; [19]the king of Madon, one; the king of Hazor, one; [20]the king of Shimron Meron, one; the king of Achshaph, one; [21]the king of Taanach, one; the king of Megiddo, one; [22]the king of Kedesh, one; the king of Jokneam in Carmel, one; [23]the king of Dor in the heights of Dor, one; the king of the people of Gilgal, one; [24]the king of Tirzah, one—all the kings, thirty-one.

Remaining Land to Be Conquered

13 Now Joshua was old, advanced in years. And the LORD said to him: "You are old, advanced in years, and there remains very much land yet to be possessed. [2]This is the land that yet remains: all the territory of the Philistines and all *that of* the Geshurites, [3]from Sihor, which *is* east of Egypt, as far as the border of Ekron northward (*which* is counted as Canaanite); the five lords of the Philistines—the Gazites, the Ashdodites, the Ashkelonites, the Gittites, and the Ekronites; also the Avites; [4]from the south, all the land of the Canaanites, and Mearah that belongs to the Sidonians as far as Aphek, to the border of the Amorites; [5]the land of the Gebalites,[a] and all Lebanon, toward the sunrise, from Baal Gad below Mount Hermon as far as the entrance to Hamath; [6]all the inhabitants of the mountains from Lebanon as far as the Brook Misrephoth,[a] *and* all the Sidonians—them I will drive out before the children of Israel; only divide it by lot to Israel as an inheritance, as I have commanded you. [7]Now therefore, divide this land as an inheritance to the nine tribes and half the tribe of Manasseh."

The Land Divided East of the Jordan

[8]With the other half-tribe the Reubenites and the Gadites received their inheritance, which Moses had given them, beyond the Jordan eastward, as Moses the servant of the LORD had given them: [9]from Aroer which *is* on the bank of the

River Arnon, and the town that *is* in the midst of the ravine, and all the plain of Medeba as far as Dibon; [10]all the cities of Sihon king of the Amorites, who reigned in Heshbon, as far as the border of the children of Ammon; [11]Gilead, and the border of the Geshurites and Maachathites, all Mount Hermon, and all Bashan as far as Salcah; [12]all the kingdom of Og in Bashan, who reigned in Ashtaroth and Edrei, who remained of the remnant of the giants; for Moses had defeated and cast out these.

[13]Nevertheless the children of Israel did not drive out the Geshurites or the Maachathites, but the Geshurites and the Maachathites dwell among the Israelites until this day.

[14]Only to the tribe of Levi he had given no inheritance; the sacrifices of the LORD God of Israel made by fire *are* their inheritance, as He said to them.

The Land of Reuben

[15]And Moses had given to the tribe of the children of Reuben *an inheritance* according to their families. [16]Their territory was from Aroer, which *is* on the bank of the River Arnon, and the city that *is* in the midst of the ravine, and all the plain by Medeba; [17]Heshbon and all its cities that *are* in the plain: Dibon, Bamoth Baal, Beth Baal Meon, [18]Jahaza, Kedemoth, Mephaath, [19]Kirjathaim, Sibmah, Zereth Shahar on the mountain of the valley, [20]Beth Peor, the slopes of Pisgah, and Beth Jeshimoth— [21]all the cities of the plain and all the kingdom of Sihon king of the Amorites, who reigned in Heshbon, whom Moses had struck with the princes of Midian: Evi, Rekem, Zur, Hur, and Reba, who *were* princes of Sihon dwelling in the country. [22]The children of Israel also killed with the sword Balaam the son of Beor, the soothsayer, among those who were killed by them. [23]And the border of the children of Reuben was the bank of the Jordan. This *was* the inheritance of the children of Reuben according to their families, the cities and their villages.

The Land of Gad

[24]Moses also had given *an inheritance* to the tribe of Gad, to the children of Gad according to

13:5 [a]Or *Giblites*   13:6 [a]Hebrew *Misrephoth Maim*

their families. 25Their territory was Jazer, and all the cities of Gilead, and half the land of the Ammonites as far as Aroer, which *is* before Rabbah, 26and from Heshbon to Ramath Mizpah and Betonim, and from Mahanaim to the border of Debir, 27and in the valley Beth Haram, Beth Nimrah, Succoth, and Zaphon, the rest of the kingdom of Sihon king of Heshbon, with the Jordan as *its* border, as far as the edge of the Sea of Chinnereth, on the other side of the Jordan eastward. 28This *is* the inheritance of the children of Gad according to their families, the cities and their villages.

Half the Tribe of Manasseh (East)

29Moses also had given *an inheritance* to half the tribe of Manasseh; it was for half the tribe of the children of Manasseh according to their families: 30Their territory was from Mahanaim, all Bashan, all the kingdom of Og king of Bashan, and all the towns of Jair which are in Bashan, sixty cities; 31half of Gilead, and Ashtaroth and Edrei, cities of the kingdom of Og in Bashan, *were* for the children of Machir the son of Manasseh, for half of the children of Machir according to their families.

32These *are the areas* which Moses had distributed as an inheritance in the plains of Moab on the other side of the Jordan, by Jericho eastward. 33But to the tribe of Levi Moses had given no inheritance; the LORD God of Israel *was* their inheritance, as He had said to them.

The Land Divided West of the Jordan

14 These *are the areas* which the children of Israel inherited in the land of Canaan, which Eleazar the priest, Joshua the son of Nun, and the heads of the fathers of the tribes of the children of Israel distributed as an inheritance to them. 2Their inheritance *was* by lot, as the LORD had commanded by the hand of Moses, for the nine tribes and the half-tribe. 3For Moses had given the inheritance of the two tribes and the half-tribe on the other side of the Jordan; but to the Levites he had given no inheritance among them. 4For the children of Joseph were two tribes: Manasseh and Ephraim. And they gave no part to the Levites in the land, except cities to dwell *in,* with their common-lands for their livestock and their

property. 5As the LORD had commanded Moses, so the children of Israel did; and they divided the land.

Caleb Inherits Hebron

6Then the children of Judah came to Joshua in Gilgal. And Caleb the son of Jephunneh the Kenizzite said to him: "You know the word which the LORD said to Moses the man of God concerning you and me in Kadesh Barnea. 7I *was* forty years old when Moses the servant of the LORD sent me from Kadesh Barnea to spy out the land, and I brought back word to him as *it was* in my heart. 8Nevertheless my brethren who went up with me made the heart of the people melt, but I wholly followed the LORD my God. 9So Moses swore on that day, saying, 'Surely the land where your foot has trodden shall be your inheritance and your children's forever, because you have wholly followed the LORD my God.' 10And now, behold, the LORD has kept me alive, as He said, these forty-five years, ever since the LORD spoke this word to Moses while Israel wandered in the wilderness; and now, here I am this day, eighty-five years old. 11As yet I *am as* strong this day as on the day that Moses sent me; just as my strength *was* then, so now *is* my strength for war, both for going out and for coming in. 12Now therefore, give me this mountain of which the LORD spoke in that day; for you heard in that day how the Anakim *were* there, and *that* the cities *were* great *and* fortified. It may be that the LORD *will be* with me, and I shall be able to drive them out as the LORD said."

13And Joshua blessed him, and gave Hebron to Caleb the son of Jephunneh as an inheritance. 14Hebron therefore became the inheritance of Caleb the son of Jephunneh the Kenizzite to this day, because he wholly followed the LORD God of Israel. 15And the name of Hebron formerly was Kirjath Arba (*Arba was* the greatest man among the Anakim).

Then the land had rest from war.

The Land of Judah

15 So *this* was the lot of the tribe of the children of Judah according to their families:

The border of Edom at the Wilderness of Zin southward *was* the extreme southern boundary.

²And their southern border began at the shore of the Salt Sea, from the bay that faces southward. ³Then it went out to the southern side of the Ascent of Akrabbim, passed along to Zin, ascended on the south side of Kadesh Barnea, passed along to Hezron, went up to Adar, and went around to Karkaa. ⁴*From there* it passed toward Azmon and went out to the Brook of Egypt; and the border ended at the sea. This shall be your southern border.

⁵The east border *was* the Salt Sea as far as the mouth of the Jordan.

And the border on the northern quarter *began* at the bay of the sea at the mouth of the Jordan. ⁶The border went up to Beth Hoglah and passed north of Beth Arabah; and the border went up to the stone of Bohan the son of Reuben. ⁷Then the border went up toward Debir from the Valley of Achor, and it turned northward toward Gilgal, which *is* before the Ascent of Adummim, which *is* on the south side of the valley. The border continued toward the waters of En Shemesh and ended at En Rogel. ⁸And the border went up by the Valley of the Son of Hinnom to the southern slope of the Jebusite *city* (which *is* Jerusalem). The border went up to the top of the mountain that *lies* before the Valley of Hinnom westward, which *is* at the end of the Valley of Rephaimᵃ northward. ⁹Then the border went around from the top of the hill to the fountain of the water of Nephtoah, and extended to the cities of Mount Ephron. And the border went around to Baalah (which *is* Kirjath Jearim). ¹⁰Then the border turned westward from Baalah to Mount Seir, passed along to the side of Mount Jearim on the north (which *is* Chesalon), went down to Beth Shemesh, and passed on to Timnah. ¹¹And the border went out to the side of Ekron northward. Then the border went around to Shicron, passed along to Mount Baalah, and extended to Jabneel; and the border ended at the sea.

¹²The west border *was* the coastline of the Great Sea. This *is* the boundary of the children of Judah all around according to their families.

CALEB OCCUPIES HEBRON AND DEBIR

¹³Now to Caleb the son of Jephunneh he gave a share among the children of Judah, according to the commandment of the LORD to Joshua, *namely,* Kirjath Arba, which *is* Hebron (*Arba was* the father of Anak). ¹⁴Caleb drove out the three sons of Anak from there: Sheshai, Ahiman, and Talmai, the children of Anak. ¹⁵Then he went up from there to the inhabitants of Debir (formerly the name of Debir *was* Kirjath Sepher).

¹⁶And Caleb said, "He who attacks Kirjath Sepher and takes it, to him I will give Achsah my daughter as wife." ¹⁷So Othniel the son of Kenaz, the brother of Caleb, took it; and he gave him Achsah his daughter as wife. ¹⁸Now it was so, when she came *to him,* that she persuaded him to ask her father for a field. So she dismounted from *her* donkey, and Caleb said to her, "What do you wish?" ¹⁹She answered, "Give me a blessing; since you have given me land in the South, give me also springs of water." So he gave her the upper springs and the lower springs.

THE CITIES OF JUDAH

²⁰This *was* the inheritance of the tribe of the children of Judah according to their families:

²¹The cities at the limits of the tribe of the children of Judah, toward the border of Edom in the South, were Kabzeel, Eder, Jagur, ²²Kinah, Dimonah, Adadah, ²³Kedesh, Hazor, Ithnan, ²⁴Ziph, Telem, Bealoth, ²⁵Hazor, Hadattah, Kerioth, Hezron (which *is* Hazor), ²⁶Amam, Shema, Moladah, ²⁷Hazar Gaddah, Heshmon, Beth Pelet, ²⁸Hazar Shual, Beersheba, Bizjothjah, ²⁹Baalah, Ijim, Ezem, ³⁰Eltolad, Chesil, Hormah, ³¹Ziklag, Madmannah, Sansannah, ³²Lebaoth, Shilhim, Ain, and Rimmon: all the cities *are* twenty-nine, with their villages.

³³In the lowland: Eshtaol, Zorah, Ashnah, ³⁴Zanoah, En Gannim, Tappuah, Enam, ³⁵Jarmuth, Adullam, Socoh, Azekah, ³⁶Sharaim, Adithaim, Gederah, and Gederothaim: fourteen cities with their villages; ³⁷Zenan, Hadashah, Migdal Gad, ³⁸Dilean, Mizpah, Joktheel, ³⁹Lachish, Bozkath, Eglon, ⁴⁰Cabbon, Lahmas,ᵃ Kithlish, ⁴¹Gederoth, Beth Dagon, Naamah, and Makkedah: sixteen cities with their villages; ⁴²Libnah, Ether, Ashan, ⁴³Jiphtah, Ashnah, Nezib, ⁴⁴Keilah, Achzib, and Mareshah: nine cities with their villages; ⁴⁵Ekron, with its towns and villages; ⁴⁶from Ekron to the

15:8 ᵃLiterally *Giants* 15:40 ᵃOr *Lahmam*

sea, all that *lay* near Ashdod, with their villages; [47]Ashdod with its towns and villages, Gaza with its towns and villages—as far as the Brook of Egypt and the Great Sea with *its* coastline.

[48]And in the mountain country: Shamir, Jattir, Sochoh, [49]Dannah, Kirjath Sannah (which *is* Debir), [50]Anab, Eshtemoh, Anim, [51]Goshen, Holon, and Giloh: eleven cities with their villages; [52]Arab, Dumah, Eshean, [53]Janum, Beth Tappuah, Aphekah, [54]Humtah, Kirjath Arba (which *is* Hebron), and Zior: nine cities with their villages; [55]Maon, Carmel, Ziph, Juttah, [56]Jezreel, Jokdeam, Zanoah, [57]Kain, Gibeah, and Timnah: ten cities with their villages; [58]Halhul, Beth Zur, Gedor, [59]Maarath, Beth Anoth, and Eltekon: six cities with their villages; [60]Kirjath Baal (which *is* Kirjath Jearim) and Rabbah: two cities with their villages.

[61]In the wilderness: Beth Arabah, Middin, Secacah, [62]Nibshan, the City of Salt, and En Gedi: six cities with their villages.

[63]As for the Jebusites, the inhabitants of Jerusalem, the children of Judah could not drive them out; but the Jebusites dwell with the children of Judah at Jerusalem to this day.

Ephraim and West Manasseh

16 The lot fell to the children of Joseph from the Jordan, by Jericho, to the waters of Jericho on the east, to the wilderness that goes up from Jericho through the mountains to Bethel, [2]then went out from Bethel to Luz,[a] passed along to the border of the Archites at Ataroth, [3]and went down westward to the boundary of the Japhletites, as far as the boundary of Lower Beth Horon to Gezer; and it ended at the sea.

[4]So the children of Joseph, Manasseh and Ephraim, took their inheritance.

The Land of Ephraim

[5]The border of the children of Ephraim, according to their families, was *thus:* The border of their inheritance on the east side was Ataroth Addar as far as Upper Beth Horon.

[6]And the border went out toward the sea on the north side of Michmethath; then the border went around eastward to Taanath Shiloh, and passed by it on the east of Janohah. [7]Then it went down from Janohah to Ataroth and Naarah,[a] reached to Jericho, and came out at the Jordan.

[8]The border went out from Tappuah westward to the Brook Kanah, and it ended at the sea. This *was* the inheritance of the tribe of the children of Ephraim according to their families. [9]The separate cities for the children of Ephraim *were* among the inheritance of the children of Manasseh, all the cities with their villages.

[10]And they did not drive out the Canaanites who dwelt in Gezer; but the Canaanites dwell among the Ephraimites to this day and have become forced laborers.

The Other Half-Tribe of Manasseh (West)

17 There was also a lot for the tribe of Manasseh, for he *was* the firstborn of Joseph: *namely* for Machir the firstborn of Manasseh, the father of Gilead, because he was a man of war; therefore he was given Gilead and Bashan. [2]And there was *a lot* for the rest of the children of Manasseh according to their families: for the children of Abiezer,[a] the children of Helek, the children of Asriel, the children of Shechem, the children of Hepher, and the children of Shemida; these *were* the male children of Manasseh the son of Joseph according to their families.

[3]But Zelophehad the son of Hepher, the son of Gilead, the son of Machir, the son of Manasseh, had no sons, but only daughters. And these *are* the names of his daughters: Mahlah, Noah, Hoglah, Milcah, and Tirzah. [4]And they came near before Eleazar the priest, before Joshua the son of Nun, and before the rulers, saying, "The LORD commanded Moses to give us an inheritance among our brothers." Therefore, according to the commandment of the LORD, he gave them an inheritance among their father's brothers. [5]Ten shares fell to Manasseh, besides the land of Gilead and Bashan, which *were* on the other side of the Jordan, [6]because the daughters of Manasseh received an inheritance among his sons; and the rest of Manasseh's sons had the land of Gilead.

[7]And the territory of Manasseh was from Asher to Michmethath, that *lies* east of Shechem; and the border went along south to the inhabitants of En Tappuah. [8]Manasseh had the land of

16:2 [a]Septuagint reads *Bethel* (that is, Luz).   **16:7** [a]Or *Naaran* (compare 1 Chronicles 7:28)   **17:2** [a]Called *Jeezer* in Numbers 26:30

Tappuah, but Tappuah on the border of Manasseh *belonged* to the children of Ephraim. ⁹And the border descended to the Brook Kanah, southward to the brook. These cities of Ephraim *are* among the cities of Manasseh. The border of Manasseh *was* on the north side of the brook; and it ended at the sea.

¹⁰Southward *it was* Ephraim's, northward *it was* Manasseh's, and the sea was its border. Manasseh's territory was adjoining Asher on the north and Issachar on the east. ¹¹And in Issachar and in Asher, Manasseh had Beth Shean and its towns, Ibleam and its towns, the inhabitants of Dor and its towns, the inhabitants of En Dor and its towns, the inhabitants of Taanach and its towns, and the inhabitants of Megiddo and its towns—three hilly regions. ¹²Yet the children of Manasseh could not drive out *the inhabitants of* those cities, but the Canaanites were determined to dwell in that land. ¹³And it happened, when the children of Israel grew strong, that they put the Canaanites to forced labor, but did not utterly drive them out.

MORE LAND FOR EPHRAIM AND MANASSEH

¹⁴Then the children of Joseph spoke to Joshua, saying, "Why have you given us *only* one lot and one share to inherit, since we *are* a great people, inasmuch as the LORD has blessed us until now?"

¹⁵So Joshua answered them, "If you *are* a great people, *then* go up to the forest *country* and clear a place for yourself there in the land of the Perizzites and the giants, since the mountains of Ephraim are too confined for you."

¹⁶But the children of Joseph said, "The mountain country is not enough for us; and all the Canaanites who dwell in the land of the valley have chariots of iron, *both those* who *are* of Beth Shean and its towns and *those* who *are* of the Valley of Jezreel."

¹⁷And Joshua spoke to the house of Joseph—to Ephraim and Manasseh—saying, "You *are* a great people and have great power; you shall not have *only* one lot, ¹⁸but the mountain country shall be yours. Although it *is* wooded, you shall cut it down, and its farthest extent shall be yours; for you shall drive out the Canaanites, though they have iron chariots *and* are strong."

THE REMAINDER OF THE LAND DIVIDED

18 Now the whole congregation of the children of Israel assembled together at Shiloh, and set up the tabernacle of meeting there. And the land was subdued before them. ²But there remained among the children of Israel seven tribes which had not yet received their inheritance.

³Then Joshua said to the children of Israel: "How long will you neglect to go and possess the land which the LORD God of your fathers has given you? ⁴Pick out from among you three men for *each* tribe, and I will send them; they shall rise and go through the land, survey it according to their inheritance, and come *back* to me. ⁵And they shall divide it into seven parts. Judah shall remain in their territory on the south, and the house of Joseph shall remain in their territory on the north. ⁶You shall therefore survey the land in seven parts and bring *the survey* here to me, that I may cast lots for you here before the LORD our God. ⁷But the Levites have no part among you, for the priesthood of the LORD *is* their inheritance. And Gad, Reuben, and half the tribe of Manasseh have received their inheritance beyond the Jordan on the east, which Moses the servant of the LORD gave them."

⁸Then the men arose to go away; and Joshua charged those who went to survey the land, saying, "Go, walk through the land, survey it, and come back to me, that I may cast lots for you here before the LORD in Shiloh." ⁹So the men went, passed through the land, and wrote the survey in a book in seven parts by cities; and they came to Joshua at the camp in Shiloh. ¹⁰Then Joshua cast lots for them in Shiloh before the LORD, and there Joshua divided the land to the children of Israel according to their divisions.

THE LAND OF BENJAMIN

¹¹Now the lot of the tribe of the children of Benjamin came up according to their families, and the territory of their lot came out between the children of Judah and the children of Joseph. ¹²Their border on the north side began at the Jordan, and the border went up to the side of Jericho on the north, and went up through the mountains westward; it ended at the Wilderness of Beth Aven. ¹³The border went over from there toward

Luz, to the side of Luz (which *is* Bethel) southward; and the border descended to Ataroth Addar, near the hill that *lies* on the south side of Lower Beth Horon.

[14]Then the border extended around the west side to the south, from the hill that *lies* before Beth Horon southward; and it ended at Kirjath Baal (which *is* Kirjath Jearim), a city of the children of Judah. This *was* the west side.

[15]The south side *began* at the end of Kirjath Jearim, and the border extended on the west and went out to the spring of the waters of Nephtoah. [16]Then the border came down to the end of the mountain that *lies* before the Valley of the Son of Hinnom, which *is* in the Valley of the Rephaim[a] on the north, descended to the Valley of Hinnom, to the side of the Jebusite *city* on the south, and descended to En Rogel. [17]And it went around from the north, went out to En Shemesh, and extended toward Geliloth, which is before the Ascent of Adummim, and descended to the stone of Bohan the son of Reuben. [18]Then it passed along toward the north side of Arabah,[a] and went down to Arabah. [19]And the border passed along to the north side of Beth Hoglah; then the border ended at the north bay at the Salt Sea, at the south end of the Jordan. This *was* the southern boundary.

[20]The Jordan was its border on the east side. This *was* the inheritance of the children of Benjamin, according to its boundaries all around, according to their families.

[21]Now the cities of the tribe of the children of Benjamin, according to their families, were Jericho, Beth Hoglah, Emek Keziz, [22]Beth Arabah, Zemaraim, Bethel, [23]Avim, Parah, Ophrah, [24]Chephar Haammoni, Ophni, and Gaba: twelve cities with their villages; [25]Gibeon, Ramah, Beeroth, [26]Mizpah, Chephirah, Mozah, [27]Rekem, Irpeel, Taralah, [28]Zelah, Eleph, Jebus (which *is* Jerusalem), Gibeath, *and* Kirjath: fourteen cities with their villages. This was the inheritance of the children of Benjamin according to their families.

SIMEON'S INHERITANCE WITH JUDAH

19 The second lot came out for Simeon, for the tribe of the children of Simeon according to their families. And their inheritance was within the inheritance of the children of Judah.

[2]They had in their inheritance Beersheba (Sheba), Moladah, [3]Hazar Shual, Balah, Ezem, [4]Eltolad, Bethul, Hormah, [5]Ziklag, Beth Marcaboth, Hazar Susah, [6]Beth Lebaoth, and Sharuhen: thirteen cities and their villages; [7]Ain, Rimmon, Ether, and Ashan: four cities and their villages; [8]and all the villages that *were* all around these cities as far as Baalath Beer, Ramah of the South. This *was* the inheritance of the tribe of the children of Simeon according to their families.

[9]The inheritance of the children of Simeon *was included* in the share of the children of Judah, for the share of the children of Judah was too much for them. Therefore the children of Simeon had *their* inheritance within the inheritance of that people.

THE LAND OF ZEBULUN

[10]The third lot came out for the children of Zebulun according to their families, and the border of their inheritance was as far as Sarid. [11]Their border went toward the west and to Maralah, went to Dabbasheth, and extended along the brook that is east of Jokneam. [12]Then from Sarid it went eastward toward the sunrise along the border of Chisloth Tabor, and went out toward Daberath, bypassing Japhia. [13]And from there it passed along on the east of Gath Hepher, toward Eth Kazin, and extended to Rimmon, which borders on Neah. [14]Then the border went around it on the north side of Hannathon, and it ended in the Valley of Jiphthah El. [15]Included were Kattath, Nahallal, Shimron, Idalah, and Bethlehem: twelve cities with their villages. [16]This *was* the inheritance of the children of Zebulun according to their families, these cities with their villages.

THE LAND OF ISSACHAR

[17]The fourth lot came out to Issachar, for the children of Issachar according to their families. [18]And their territory went to Jezreel, and *included* Chesulloth, Shunem, [19]Haphraim, Shion, Anaharath, [20]Rabbith, Kishion, Abez, [21]Remeth, En Gannim, En Haddah, and Beth Pazzez. [22]And the border reached to Tabor, Shahazimah, and Beth Shemesh; their border ended at the Jordan: sixteen cities with their villages. [23]This *was* the

18:16 [a]Literally *Giants* **18:18** [a]Or *Beth Arabah* (compare 15:6 and 18:22)

inheritance of the tribe of the children of Issachar according to their families, the cities and their villages.

The Land of Asher

[24]The fifth lot came out for the tribe of the children of Asher according to their families. [25]And their territory included Helkath, Hali, Beten, Achshaph, [26]Alammelech, Amad, and Mishal; it reached to Mount Carmel westward, along the Brook Shihor Libnath. [27]It turned toward the sunrise to Beth Dagon; and it reached to Zebulun and to the Valley of Jiphthah El, then northward beyond Beth Emek and Neiel, bypassing Cabul which was on the left, [28]including Ebron,[a] Rehob, Hammon, and Kanah, as far as Greater Sidon. [29]And the border turned to Ramah and to the fortified city of Tyre; then the border turned to Hosah, and ended at the sea by the region of Achzib. [30]Also Ummah, Aphek, and Rehob were included: twenty-two cities with their villages. [31]This was the inheritance of the tribe of the children of Asher according to their families, these cities with their villages.

The Land of Naphtali

[32]The sixth lot came out to the children of Naphtali, for the children of Naphtali according to their families. [33]And their border began at Heleph, enclosing the territory from the terebinth tree in Zaanannim, Adami Nekeb, and Jabneel, as far as Lakkum; it ended at the Jordan. [34]From Heleph the border extended westward to Aznoth Tabor, and went out from there toward Hukkok; it adjoined Zebulun on the south side and Asher on the west side, and ended at Judah by the Jordan toward the sunrise. [35]And the fortified cities are Ziddim, Zer, Hammath, Rakkath, Chinnereth, [36]Adamah, Ramah, Hazor, [37]Kedesh, Edrei, En Hazor, [38]Iron, Migdal El, Horem, Beth Anath, and Beth Shemesh: nineteen cities with their villages. [39]This was the inheritance of the tribe of the children of Naphtali according to their families, the cities and their villages.

The Land of Dan

[40]The seventh lot came out for the tribe of the children of Dan according to their families. [41]And the territory of their inheritance was Zo-

rah, Eshtaol, Ir Shemesh, [42]Shaalabbin, Aijalon, Jethlah, [43]Elon, Timnah, Ekron, [44]Eltekeh, Gibbethon, Baalath, [45]Jehud, Bene Berak, Gath Rimmon, [46]Me Jarkon, and Rakkon, with the region near Joppa. [47]And the border of the children of Dan went beyond these, because the children of Dan went up to fight against Leshem and took it; and they struck it with the edge of the sword, took possession of it, and dwelt in it. They called Leshem, Dan, after the name of Dan their father. [48]This is the inheritance of the tribe of the children of Dan according to their families, these cities with their villages.

Joshua's Inheritance

[49]When they had made an end of dividing the land as an inheritance according to their borders, the children of Israel gave an inheritance among them to Joshua the son of Nun. [50]According to the word of the LORD they gave him the city which he asked for, Timnath Serah in the mountains of Ephraim; and he built the city and dwelt in it.

[51]These were the inheritances which Eleazar the priest, Joshua the son of Nun, and the heads of the fathers of the tribes of the children of Israel divided as an inheritance by lot in Shiloh before the LORD, at the door of the tabernacle of meeting. So they made an end of dividing the country.

The Cities of Refuge

20 The LORD also spoke to Joshua, saying, [2]"Speak to the children of Israel, saying: 'Appoint for yourselves cities of refuge, of which I spoke to you through Moses, [3]that the slayer who kills a person accidentally or unintentionally may flee there; and they shall be your refuge from the avenger of blood. [4]And when he flees to one of those cities, and stands at the entrance of the gate of the city, and declares his case in the hearing of the elders of that city, they shall take him into the city as one of them, and give him a place, that he may dwell among them. [5]Then if the avenger of blood pursues him, they shall not deliver the slayer into his hand, because he struck his neighbor unintentionally, but did not hate him before-

19:28 [a]Following Masoretic Text, Targum, and Vulgate; a few Hebrew manuscripts read Abdon (compare 21:30 and 1 Chronicles 6:74).

hand. ⁶And he shall dwell in that city until he stands before the congregation for judgment, *and* until the death of the one who is high priest in those days. Then the slayer may return and come to his own city and his own house, to the city from which he fled.' "

⁷So they appointed Kedesh in Galilee, in the mountains of Naphtali, Shechem in the mountains of Ephraim, and Kirjath Arba (which *is* Hebron) in the mountains of Judah. ⁸And on the other side of the Jordan, by Jericho eastward, they assigned Bezer in the wilderness on the plain, from the tribe of Reuben, Ramoth in Gilead, from the tribe of Gad, and Golan in Bashan, from the tribe of Manasseh. ⁹These were the cities appointed for all the children of Israel and for the stranger who dwelt among them, that whoever killed a person accidentally might flee there, and not die by the hand of the avenger of blood until he stood before the congregation.

CITIES OF THE LEVITES

21 Then the heads of the fathers' *houses* of the Levites came near to Eleazar the priest, to Joshua the son of Nun, and to the heads of the fathers' *houses* of the tribes of the children of Israel. ²And they spoke to them at Shiloh in the land of Canaan, saying, "The LORD commanded through Moses to give us cities to dwell in, with their common-lands for our livestock." ³So the children of Israel gave to the Levites from their inheritance, at the commandment of the LORD, these cities and their common-lands:

⁴Now the lot came out for the families of the Kohathites. And the children of Aaron the priest, *who were* of the Levites, had thirteen cities by lot from the tribe of Judah, from the tribe of Simeon, and from the tribe of Benjamin. ⁵The rest of the children of Kohath had ten cities by lot from the families of the tribe of Ephraim, from the tribe of Dan, and from the half-tribe of Manasseh.

⁶And the children of Gershon had thirteen cities by lot from the families of the tribe of Issachar, from the tribe of Asher, from the tribe of Naphtali, and from the half-tribe of Manasseh in Bashan.

⁷The children of Merari according to their families had twelve cities from the tribe of Reuben, from the tribe of Gad, and from the tribe of Zebulun.

⁸And the children of Israel gave these cities with their common-lands by lot to the Levites, as the LORD had commanded by the hand of Moses.

⁹So they gave from the tribe of the children of Judah and from the tribe of the children of Simeon these cities which are designated by name, ¹⁰which were for the children of Aaron, one of the families of the Kohathites, *who were* of the children of Levi; for the lot was theirs first. ¹¹And they gave them Kirjath Arba (*Arba was* the father of Anak), which *is* Hebron, in the mountains of Judah, with the common-land surrounding it. ¹²But the fields of the city and its villages they gave to Caleb the son of Jephunneh as his possession.

¹³Thus to the children of Aaron the priest they gave Hebron with its common-land (a city of refuge for the slayer), Libnah with its common-land, ¹⁴Jattir with its common-land, Eshtemoa with its common-land, ¹⁵Holon with its common-land, Debir with its common-land, ¹⁶Ain with its common-land, Juttah with its common-land, and Beth Shemesh with its common-land: nine cities from those two tribes; ¹⁷and from the tribe of Benjamin, Gibeon with its common-land, Geba with its common-land, ¹⁸Anathoth with its common-land, and Almon with its common-land: four cities. ¹⁹All the cities of the children of Aaron, the priests, *were* thirteen cities with their common-lands.

²⁰And the families of the children of Kohath, the Levites, the rest of the children of Kohath, even they had the cities of their lot from the tribe of Ephraim. ²¹For they gave them Shechem with its common-land in the mountains of Ephraim (a city of refuge for the slayer), Gezer with its common-land, ²²Kibzaim with its common-land, and Beth Horon with its common-land: four cities; ²³and from the tribe of Dan, Eltekeh with its common-land, Gibbethon with its common-land, ²⁴Aijalon with its common-land, *and* Gath Rimmon with its common-land: four cities; ²⁵and from the half-tribe of Manasseh, Tanach with its common-land and Gath Rimmon with its common-land: two cities. ²⁶All the ten cities

with their common-lands were for the rest of the families of the children of Kohath.

27Also to the children of Gershon, of the families of the Levites, from the *other* half-tribe of Manasseh, *they gave* Golan in Bashan with its common-land (a city of refuge for the slayer), and Be Eshterah with its common-land: two cities; 28and from the tribe of Issachar, Kishion with its common-land, Daberath with its common-land, 29Jarmuth with its common-land, *and* En Gannim with its common-land: four cities; 30and from the tribe of Asher, Mishal with its common-land, Abdon with its common-land, 31Helkath with its common-land, and Rehob with its common-land: four cities; 32and from the tribe of Naphtali, Kedesh in Galilee with its common-land (a city of refuge for the slayer), Hammoth Dor with its common-land, and Kartan with its common-land: three cities. 33All the cities of the Gershonites according to their families *were* thirteen cities with their common-lands.

34And to the families of the children of Merari, the rest of the Levites, from the tribe of Zebulun, Jokneam with its common-land, Kartah with its common-land, 35Dimnah with its common-land, *and* Nahalal with its common-land: four cities; 36and from the tribe of Reuben, Bezer with its common-land, Jahaz with its common-land, 37Kedemoth with its common-land, and Mephaath with its common-land: four cities;[a] 38and from the tribe of Gad, Ramoth in Gilead with its common-land (a city of refuge for the slayer), Mahanaim with its common-land, 39Heshbon with its common-land, *and* Jazer with its common-land: four cities in all. 40So all the cities for the children of Merari according to their families, the rest of the families of the Levites, were *by* their lot twelve cities.

41All the cities of the Levites within the possession of the children of Israel *were* forty-eight cities with their common-lands. 42Every one of these cities had its common-land surrounding it; thus *were* all these cities.

The Promise Fulfilled

43So the LORD gave to Israel all the land of which He had sworn to give to their fathers, and they took possession of it and dwelt in it. 44The

LORD gave them rest all around, according to all that He had sworn to their fathers. And not a man of all their enemies stood against them; the LORD delivered all their enemies into their hand. 45Not a word failed of any good thing which the LORD had spoken to the house of Israel. All came to pass.

Eastern Tribes Return to Their Lands

22 Then Joshua called the Reubenites, the Gadites, and half the tribe of Manasseh, 2and said to them: "You have kept all that Moses the servant of the LORD commanded you, and have obeyed my voice in all that I commanded you. 3You have not left your brethren these many days, up to this day, but have kept the charge of the commandment of the LORD your God. 4And now the LORD your God has given rest to your brethren, as He promised them; now therefore, return and go to your tents *and* to the land of your possession, which Moses the servant of the LORD gave you on the other side of the Jordan. 5But take careful heed to do the commandment and the law which Moses the servant of the LORD commanded you, to love the LORD your God, to walk in all His ways, to keep His commandments, to hold fast to Him, and to serve Him with all your heart and with all your soul." 6So Joshua blessed them and sent them away, and they went to their tents.

7Now to half the tribe of Manasseh Moses had given a possession in Bashan, but to the *other* half of it Joshua gave *a possession* among their brethren on this side of the Jordan, westward. And indeed, when Joshua sent them away to their tents, he blessed them, 8and spoke to them, saying, "Return with much riches to your tents, with very much livestock, with silver, with gold, with bronze, with iron, and with very much clothing. Divide the spoil of your enemies with your brethren."

9So the children of Reuben, the children of Gad, and half the tribe of Manasseh returned, and departed from the children of Israel at Shiloh, which *is* in the land of Canaan, to go to the country of Gilead, to the land of their possession,

21:37 aFollowing Septuagint and Vulgate (compare 1 Chronicles 6:78, 79); Masoretic Text, Bomberg, and Targum omit verses 36 and 37.

which they had obtained according to the word of the LORD by the hand of Moses.

AN ALTAR BY THE JORDAN

¹⁰And when they came to the region of the Jordan which *is* in the land of Canaan, the children of Reuben, the children of Gad, and half the tribe of Manasseh built an altar there by the Jordan—a great, impressive altar. ¹¹Now the children of Israel heard *someone* say, "Behold, the children of Reuben, the children of Gad, and half the tribe of Manasseh have built an altar on the frontier of the land of Canaan, in the region of the Jordan—on the children of Israel's side." ¹²And when the children of Israel heard *of it,* the whole congregation of the children of Israel gathered together at Shiloh to go to war against them.

¹³Then the children of Israel sent Phinehas the son of Eleazar the priest to the children of Reuben, to the children of Gad, and to half the tribe of Manasseh, into the land of Gilead, ¹⁴and with him ten rulers, one ruler each from the chief house of every tribe of Israel; and each one *was* the head of the house of his father among the divisionsᵃ of Israel. ¹⁵Then they came to the children of Reuben, to the children of Gad, and to half the tribe of Manasseh, to the land of Gilead, and they spoke with them, saying, ¹⁶"Thus says the whole congregation of the LORD: 'What treachery *is* this that you have committed against the God of Israel, to turn away this day from following the LORD, in that you have built for yourselves an altar, that you might rebel this day against the LORD? ¹⁷*Is* the iniquity of Peor not enough for us, from which we are not cleansed till this day, although there was a plague in the congregation of the LORD, ¹⁸but that you must turn away this day from following the LORD? And it shall be, if you rebel today against the LORD, that tomorrow He will be angry with the whole congregation of Israel. ¹⁹Nevertheless, if the land of your possession *is* unclean, *then* cross over to the land of the possession of the LORD, where the LORD's tabernacle stands, and take possession among us; but do not rebel against the LORD, nor rebel against us, by building yourselves an altar besides the altar of the LORD our God. ²⁰Did not Achan the son of Zerah commit a trespass in the accursed thing, and wrath fell on all the congregation of Israel? And that man did not perish alone in his iniquity.' "

²¹Then the children of Reuben, the children of Gad, and half the tribe of Manasseh answered and said to the heads of the divisionsᵃ of Israel: ²²"The LORD God of gods, the LORD God of gods, He knows, and let Israel itself know—if *it is* in rebellion, or if in treachery against the LORD, do not save us this day. ²³If we have built ourselves an altar to turn from following the LORD, or if to offer on it burnt offerings or grain offerings, or if to offer peace offerings on it, let the LORD Himself require *an account.* ²⁴But in fact we have done it for fear, for a reason, saying, 'In time to come your descendants may speak to our descendants, saying, "What have you to do with the LORD God of Israel? ²⁵For the LORD has made the Jordan a border between you and us, *you* children of Reuben and children of Gad. You have no part in the LORD." So your descendants would make our descendants cease fearing the LORD.' ²⁶Therefore we said, 'Let us now prepare to build ourselves an altar, not for burnt offering nor for sacrifice, ²⁷but *that* it *may be* a witness between you and us and our generations after us, that we may perform the service of the LORD before Him with our burnt offerings, with our sacrifices, and with our peace offerings; that your descendants may not say to our descendants in time to come, "You have no part in the LORD." ' ²⁸Therefore we said that it will be, when they say *this* to us or to our generations in time to come, that we may say, 'Here is the replica of the altar of the LORD which our fathers made, though not for burnt offerings nor for sacrifices; but it *is* a witness between you and us.' ²⁹Far be it from us that we should rebel against the LORD, and turn from following the LORD this day, to build an altar for burnt offerings, for grain offerings, or for sacrifices, besides the altar of the LORD our God which *is* before His tabernacle."

³⁰Now when Phinehas the priest and the rulers of the congregation, the heads of the divisionsᵃ of Israel who *were* with him, heard the words that the children of Reuben, the children of Gad, and the children of Manasseh spoke, it pleased them. ³¹Then Phinehas the son of Eleazar the priest said to the children of Reuben, the

22:14 ᵃLiterally *thousands* 22:21 ᵃLiterally *thousands* 22:30 ᵃLiterally *thousands* children of Gad, and the children of Manasseh, "This day we perceive that the LORD *is* among us, because you have not committed this treachery against the LORD. Now you have delivered the children of Israel out of the hand of the LORD."

³²And Phinehas the son of Eleazar the priest, and the rulers, returned from the children of Reuben and the children of Gad, from the land of Gilead to the land of Canaan, to the children of Israel, and brought back word to them. ³³So the thing pleased the children of Israel, and the children of Israel blessed God; they spoke no more of going against them in battle, to destroy the land where the children of Reuben and Gad dwelt.

³⁴The children of Reuben and the children of Gadª called the altar, *Witness,* "For *it is* a witness between us that the LORD *is* God."

JOSHUA'S FAREWELL ADDRESS

23 Now it came to pass, a long time after the LORD had given rest to Israel from all their enemies round about, that Joshua was old, advanced in age. ²And Joshua called for all Israel, for their elders, for their heads, for their judges, and for their officers, and said to them:

"I am old, advanced in age. ³You have seen all that the LORD your God has done to all these nations because of you, for the LORD your God *is* He who has fought for you. ⁴See, I have divided to you by lot these nations that remain, to be an inheritance for your tribes, from the Jordan, with all the nations that I have cut off, as far as the Great Sea westward. ⁵And the LORD your God will expel them from before you and drive them out of your sight. So you shall possess their land, as the LORD your God promised you. ⁶Therefore be very courageous to keep and to do all that is written in the Book of the Law of Moses, lest you turn aside from it to the right hand or to the left, ⁷*and* lest you go among these nations, these who remain among you. You shall not make mention of the name of their gods, nor cause *anyone* to swear *by them;* you shall not serve them nor bow down to them, ⁸but you shall hold fast to the LORD your God, as you have done to this day. ⁹For the LORD has driven out from before you great and strong nations; but *as for* you, no one has been able to stand against you to this day. ¹⁰One

man of you shall chase a thousand, for the LORD your God *is* He who fights for you, as He promised you. ¹¹Therefore take careful heed to yourselves, that you love the LORD your God. ¹²Or else, if indeed you do go back, and cling to the remnant of these nations—these that remain among you—and make marriages with them, and go in to them and they to you, ¹³know for certain that the LORD your God will no longer drive out these nations from before you. But they shall be snares and traps to you, and scourges on your sides and thorns in your eyes, until you perish from this good land which the LORD your God has given you.

¹⁴"Behold, this day I *am* going the way of all the earth. And you know in all your hearts and in all your souls that not one thing has failed of all the good things which the LORD your God spoke concerning you. All have come to pass for you; not one word of them has failed. ¹⁵Therefore it shall come to pass, that as all the good things have come upon you which the LORD your God promised you, so the LORD will bring upon you all harmful things, until He has destroyed you from this good land which the LORD your God has given you. ¹⁶When you have transgressed the covenant of the LORD your God, which He commanded you, and have gone and served other gods, and bowed down to them, then the anger of the LORD will burn against you, and you shall perish quickly from the good land which He has given you."

THE COVENANT AT SHECHEM

24 Then Joshua gathered all the tribes of Israel to Shechem and called for the elders of Israel, for their heads, for their judges, and for their officers; and they presented themselves before God. ²And Joshua said to all the people, "Thus says the LORD God of Israel: 'Your fathers, *including* Terah, the father of Abraham and the father of Nahor, dwelt on the other side of the Riverª in old times; and they served other gods. ³Then I took your father Abraham from the other side of the River, led him throughout all the land of Canaan, and multiplied his descendants and gave him Isaac. ⁴To Isaac I gave Jacob and Esau. To

22:34 ªSeptuagint adds *and half the tribe of Manasseh.* 24:2 ªHebrew *Nahar,* the Euphrates, and so in verses 3, 14, and 15

Esau I gave the mountains of Seir to possess, but Jacob and his children went down to Egypt. ⁵Also I sent Moses and Aaron, and I plagued Egypt, according to what I did among them. Afterward I brought you out.

⁶'Then I brought your fathers out of Egypt, and you came to the sea; and the Egyptians pursued your fathers with chariots and horsemen to the Red Sea. ⁷So they cried out to the LORD; and He put darkness between you and the Egyptians, brought the sea upon them, and covered them. And your eyes saw what I did in Egypt. Then you dwelt in the wilderness a long time. ⁸And I brought you into the land of the Amorites, who dwelt on the other side of the Jordan, and they fought with you. But I gave them into your hand, that you might possess their land, and I destroyed them from before you. ⁹Then Balak the son of Zippor, king of Moab, arose to make war against Israel, and sent and called Balaam the son of Beor to curse you. ¹⁰But I would not listen to Balaam; therefore he continued to bless you. So I delivered you out of his hand. ¹¹Then you went over the Jordan and came to Jericho. And the men of Jericho fought against you—also the Amorites, the Perizzites, the Canaanites, the Hittites, the Girgashites, the Hivites, and the Jebusites. But I delivered them into your hand. ¹²I sent the hornet before you which drove them out from before you, also the two kings of the Amorites, but not with your sword or with your bow. ¹³I have given you a land for which you did not labor, and cities which you did not build, and you dwell in them; you eat of the vineyards and olive groves which you did not plant.'

¹⁴"Now therefore, fear the LORD, serve Him in sincerity and in truth, and put away the gods which your fathers served on the other side of the River and in Egypt. Serve the LORD! ¹⁵And if it seems evil to you to serve the LORD, choose for yourselves this day whom you will serve, whether the gods which your fathers served that *were* on the other side of the River, or the gods of the Amorites, in whose land you dwell. But as for me and my house, we will serve the LORD."

¹⁶So the people answered and said: "Far be it from us that we should forsake the LORD to serve other gods; ¹⁷for the LORD our God *is* He who brought us and our fathers up out of the land of Egypt, from the house of bondage, who did those great signs in our sight, and preserved us in all the way that we went and among all the people through whom we passed. ¹⁸And the LORD drove out from before us all the people, including the Amorites who dwelt in the land. We also will serve the LORD, for He *is* our God."

¹⁹But Joshua said to the people, "You cannot serve the LORD, for He *is* a holy God. He *is* a jealous God; He will not forgive your transgressions nor your sins. ²⁰If you forsake the LORD and serve foreign gods, then He will turn and do you harm and consume you, after He has done you good."

²¹And the people said to Joshua, "No, but we will serve the LORD!"

²²So Joshua said to the people, "You *are* witnesses against yourselves that you have chosen LORD for yourselves, to serve Him."

And they said, "*We are* witnesses!"

²³"Now therefore," *he said,* "put away the foreign gods which *are* among you, and incline your heart to the LORD God of Israel."

²⁴And the people said to Joshua, "The LORD our God we will serve, and His voice we will obey!"

²⁵So Joshua made a covenant with the people that day, and made for them a statute and an ordinance in Shechem.

²⁶Then Joshua wrote these words in the Book of the Law of God. And he took a large stone, and set it up there under the oak that *was* by the sanctuary of the LORD. ²⁷And Joshua said to all the people, "Behold, this stone shall be a witness to us, for it has heard all the words of the LORD which He spoke to us. It shall therefore be a witness to you, lest you deny your God." ²⁸So Joshua let the people depart, each to his own inheritance.

DEATH OF JOSHUA AND ELEAZAR

²⁹Now it came to pass after these things that Joshua the son of Nun, the servant of the LORD, died, *being* one hundred and ten years old. ³⁰And they buried him within the border of his inheritance at Timnath Serah, which *is* in the mountains of Ephraim, on the north side of Mount Gaash.

³¹Israel served the LORD all the days of

Joshua, and all the days of the elders who outlived Joshua, who had known all the works of the LORD which He had done for Israel.

³²The bones of Joseph, which the children of Israel had brought up out of Egypt, they buried at Shechem, in the plot of ground which Jacob had bought from the sons of Hamor the father of Shechem for one hundred pieces of silver, and which had become an inheritance of the children of Joseph.

³³And Eleazar the son of Aaron died. They buried him in a hill *belonging to* Phinehas his son, which was given to him in the mountains of Ephraim.

IMPACT OF THE BOOK

JUDGES

IDEA
As God's people wandered away from Him, God repeatedly brought leaders to draw them back to Him.

MESSAGE
Compromise wreaks havoc and leads to sin in the believer's life. Unless a person is willing to learn from his or her mistakes and from the mistakes of past generations, the sin cycle will remain unbroken. This book teaches how evil influences can be disastrous for a whole nation. When the Israelites allowed the pagan nations to have influence on them, they started to compromise God's standards for their lives. However, God teaches His people that all it takes is one voice willing to stand for the truth to turn an entire generation back to Him.

PEOPLE
Abdon, Abimelech, Barak, Deborah, Ehud, Elon, Gideon, Ibzan, Jael, Jair, Jepththah, Michah, Othniel, Samson, Shamgar, Tola

AUTHOR
While this book has no stated author, Samuel has traditionally been understood as the author.

CULTURE
This book records the events from Joshua's death until Samson's death (1380–1060 BC). During this time, the ancient Near East was transitioning from the Bronze Age to the Iron Age, yet this time happens to be one of the darkest periods in Israel's history as a cycle of sin, oppression, and deliverance recurred in the history of Israel. God's people had short memories. As God would bring deliverance in their lives, they would soon forget and turn to the wicked practices of the surrounding pagan nations again. They forgot God's call to holiness for His people.

TIMELINE
1050 BC

KEY SCRIPTURE MEMORY VERSES
2:10; 21:25

The Continuing Conquest of Canaan

1 Now after the death of Joshua it came to pass that the children of Israel asked the LORD, saying, "Who shall be first to go up for us against the Canaanites to fight against them?"

2And the LORD said, "Judah shall go up. Indeed I have delivered the land into his hand."

3So Judah said to Simeon his brother, "Come up with me to my allotted territory, that we may fight against the Canaanites; and I will likewise go with you to your allotted territory." And Simeon went with him. 4Then Judah went up, and the LORD delivered the Canaanites and the Perizzites into their hand; and they killed ten thousand men at Bezek. 5And they found Adoni-Bezek in Bezek, and fought against him; and they defeated the Canaanites and the Perizzites. 6Then Adoni-Bezek fled, and they pursued him and caught him and cut off his thumbs and big toes. 7And Adoni-Bezek said, "Seventy kings with their thumbs and big toes cut off used to gather *scraps* under my table; as I have done, so God has repaid me." Then they brought him to Jerusalem, and there he died.

8Now the children of Judah fought against Jerusalem and took it; they struck it with the edge of the sword and set the city on fire. 9And afterward the children of Judah went down to fight against the Canaanites who dwelt in the mountains, in the South,a and in the lowland. 10Then Judah went against the Canaanites who dwelt in Hebron. (Now the name of Hebron *was* formerly Kirjath Arba.) And they killed Sheshai, Ahiman, and Talmai.

11From there they went against the inhabitants of Debir. (The name of Debir *was* formerly Kirjath Sepher.)

12Then Caleb said, "Whoever attacks Kirjath Sepher and takes it, to him I will give my daughter Achsah as wife." 13And Othniel the son of Kenaz, Caleb's younger brother, took it; so he gave him his daughter Achsah as wife. 14Now it happened, when she came *to him,* that she urged hima to ask her father for a field. And she dismounted from *her* donkey, and Caleb said to her, "What do you wish?" 15So she said to him, "Give me a blessing; since you have given me land in the South, give me also springs of water."

And Caleb gave her the upper springs and the lower springs.

16Now the children of the Kenite, Moses' father-in-law, went up from the City of Palms with the children of Judah into the Wilderness of Judah, which *lies* in the South *near* Arad; and they went and dwelt among the people. 17And Judah went with his brother Simeon, and they attacked the Canaanites who inhabited Zephath, and utterly destroyed it. So the name of the city was called Hormah. 18Also Judah took Gaza with its territory, Ashkelon with its territory, and Ekron with its territory. 19So the LORD was with Judah. And they drove out the mountaineers, but they could not drive out the inhabitants of the lowland, because they had chariots of iron. 20And they gave Hebron to Caleb, as Moses had said. Then he expelled from there the three sons of Anak. 21But the children of Benjamin did not drive out the Jebusites who inhabited Jerusalem; so the Jebusites dwell with the children of Benjamin in Jerusalem to this day.

22And the house of Joseph also went up against Bethel, and the LORD *was* with them. 23So the house of Joseph sent men to spy out Bethel. (The name of the city *was* formerly Luz.) 24And when the spies saw a man coming out of the city, they said to him, "Please show us the entrance to the city, and we will show you mercy." 25So he showed them the entrance to the city, and they struck the city with the edge of the sword; but they let the man and all his family go. 26And the man went to the land of the Hittites, built a city, and called its name Luz, which *is* its name to this day.

Incomplete Conquest of the Land

27However, Manasseh did not drive out *the inhabitants of* Beth Shean and its villages, or Taanach and its villages, or the inhabitants of Dor and its villages, or the inhabitants of Ibleam and its villages, or the inhabitants of Megiddo and its villages; for the Canaanites were determined to dwell in that land. 28And it came to pass, when Israel was strong, that they put the Canaanites under tribute, but did not completely drive them out.

1:9 aHebrew *Negev,* and so throughout this book   **1:14** aSeptuagint and Vulgate read *he urged her.*

²⁹Nor did Ephraim drive out the Canaanites who dwelt in Gezer; so the Canaanites dwelt in Gezer among them.

³⁰Nor did Zebulun drive out the inhabitants of Kitron or the inhabitants of Nahalol; so the Canaanites dwelt among them, and were put under tribute.

³¹Nor did Asher drive out the inhabitants of Acco or the inhabitants of Sidon, or of Ahlab, Achzib, Helbah, Aphik, or Rehob. ³²So the Asherites dwelt among the Canaanites, the inhabitants of the land; for they did not drive them out.

³³Nor did Naphtali drive out the inhabitants of Beth Shemesh or the inhabitants of Beth Anath; but they dwelt among the Canaanites, the inhabitants of the land. Nevertheless the inhabitants of Beth Shemesh and Beth Anath were put under tribute to them.

³⁴And the Amorites forced the children of Dan into the mountains, for they would not allow them to come down to the valley; ³⁵and the Amorites were determined to dwell in Mount Heres, in Aijalon, and in Shaalbim;ᵃ yet when the strength of the house of Joseph became greater, they were put under tribute.

³⁶Now the boundary of the Amorites *was* from the Ascent of Akrabbim, from Sela, and upward.

Israel's Disobedience

2 Then the Angel of the LORD came up from Gilgal to Bochim, and said: "I led you up from Egypt and brought you to the land of which I swore to your fathers; and I said, 'I will never break My covenant with you. ²And you shall make no covenant with the inhabitants of this land; you shall tear down their altars.' But you have not obeyed My voice. Why have you done this? ³Therefore I also said, 'I will not drive them out before you; but they shall be *thorns* in your side,ᵃ and their gods shall be a snare to you.' " ⁴So it was, when the Angel of the LORD spoke these words to all the children of Israel, that the people lifted up their voices and wept.

⁵Then they called the name of that place Bochim;ᵃ and they sacrificed there to the LORD. ⁶And when Joshua had dismissed the people, the children of Israel went each to his own inheritance to possess the land.

Death of Joshua

⁷So the people served the LORD all the days of Joshua, and all the days of the elders who outlived Joshua, who had seen all the great works of the LORD which He had done for Israel. ⁸Now Joshua the son of Nun, the servant of the LORD, died *when he was* one hundred and ten years old. ⁹And they buried him within the border of his inheritance at Timnath Heres, in the mountains of Ephraim, on the north side of Mount Gaash. ¹⁰When all that generation had been gathered to their fathers, another generation arose after them who did not know the LORD nor the work which He had done for Israel.

Israel's Unfaithfulness

¹¹Then the children of Israel did evil in the sight of the LORD, and served the Baals; ¹²and they forsook the LORD God of their fathers, who had brought them out of the land of Egypt; and they followed other gods from *among* the gods of the people who *were* all around them, and they bowed down to them; and they provoked the LORD to anger. ¹³They forsook the LORD and served Baal and the Ashtoreths.ᵃ ¹⁴And the anger of the LORD was hot against Israel. So He delivered them into the hands of plunderers who despoiled them; and He sold them into the hands of their enemies all around, so that they could no longer stand before their enemies. ¹⁵Wherever they went out, the hand of the LORD was against them for calamity, as the LORD had said, and as the LORD had sworn to them. And they were greatly distressed.

¹⁶Nevertheless, the LORD raised up judges who delivered them out of the hand of those who plundered them. ¹⁷Yet they would not listen to their judges, but they played the harlot with other gods, and bowed down to them. They turned quickly from the way in which their fathers walked, in obeying the commandments of the LORD; they did not do so. ¹⁸And when the LORD raised up judges for them, the LORD was with the judge and delivered them out of the hand of their enemies all the days of the judge; for

1:35 ᵃSpelled *Shaalabbin* in Joshua 19:42   **2:3** ᵃSeptuagint, Targum, and Vulgate read *enemies to you.*   **2:5** ᵃLiterally *Weeping* **2:13** ᵃCanaanite goddesses the LORD was moved to pity by their groaning because of those who oppressed them and harassed them. [19]And it came to pass, when the judge was dead, that they reverted and behaved more corruptly than their fathers, by following other gods, to serve them and bow down to them. They did not cease from their own doings nor from their stubborn way.

[20]Then the anger of the LORD was hot against Israel; and He said, "Because this nation has transgressed My covenant which I commanded their fathers, and has not heeded My voice, [21]I also will no longer drive out before them any of the nations which Joshua left when he died, [22]so that through them I may test Israel, whether they will keep the ways of the LORD, to walk in them as their fathers kept *them,* or not." [23]Therefore the LORD left those nations, without driving them out immediately; nor did He deliver them into the hand of Joshua.

THE NATIONS REMAINING IN THE LAND

3 Now these *are* the nations which the LORD left, that He might test Israel by them, *that is,* all who had not known any of the wars in Canaan [2](*this was* only so that the generations of the children of Israel might be taught to know war, at least those who had not formerly known it), [3]*namely,* five lords of the Philistines, all the Canaanites, the Sidonians, and the Hivites who dwelt in Mount Lebanon, from Mount Baal Hermon to the entrance of Hamath. [4]And they were *left, that He might* test Israel by them, to know whether they would obey the commandments of the LORD, which He had commanded their fathers by the hand of Moses.

[5]Thus the children of Israel dwelt among the Canaanites, the Hittites, the Amorites, the Perizzites, the Hivites, and the Jebusites. [6]And they took their daughters to be their wives, and gave their daughters to their sons; and they served their gods.

OTHNIEL

[7]So the children of Israel did evil in the sight of the LORD. They forgot the LORD their God, and served the Baals and Asherahs.[a] [8]Therefore the anger of the LORD was hot against Israel, and He sold them into the hand of Cushan-

Rishathaim king of Mesopotamia; and the children of Israel served Cushan-Rishathaim eight years. [9]When the children of Israel cried out to the LORD, the LORD raised up a deliverer for the children of Israel, who delivered them: Othniel the son of Kenaz, Caleb's younger brother. [10]The Spirit of the LORD came upon him, and he judged Israel. He went out to war, and the LORD delivered Cushan-Rishathaim king of Mesopotamia into his hand; and his hand prevailed over Cushan-Rishathaim. [11]So the land had rest for forty years. Then Othniel the son of Kenaz died.

EHUD

[12]And the children of Israel again did evil in the sight of the LORD. So the LORD strengthened Eglon king of Moab against Israel, because they had done evil in the sight of the LORD. [13]Then he gathered to himself the people of Ammon and Amalek, went and defeated Israel, and took possession of the City of Palms. [14]So the children of Israel served Eglon king of Moab eighteen years.

[15]But when the children of Israel cried out to the LORD, the LORD raised up a deliverer for them: Ehud the son of Gera, the Benjamite, a left-handed man. By him the children of Israel sent tribute to Eglon king of Moab. [16]Now Ehud made himself a dagger (it was double-edged and a cubit in length) and fastened it under his clothes on his right thigh. [17]So he brought the tribute to Eglon king of Moab. (Now Eglon *was* a very fat man.) [18]And when he had finished presenting the tribute, he sent away the people who had carried the tribute. [19]But he himself turned back from the stone images that *were* at Gilgal, and said, "I have a secret message for you, O king."

He said, "Keep silence!" And all who attended him went out from him.

[20]So Ehud came to him (now he was sitting upstairs in his cool private chamber). Then Ehud said, "I have a message from God for you." So he arose from *his* seat. [21]Then Ehud reached with his left hand, took the dagger from his right thigh, and thrust it into his belly. [22]Even the hilt went in after the blade, and the fat closed over the blade, for he did not draw the dagger out of his belly;

3:7 [a]Name or symbol for Canaanite goddesses

and his entrails came out. ²³Then Ehud went out through the porch and shut the doors of the upper room behind him and locked them.

²⁴When he had gone out, *Eglon's*ᵃ servants came to look, and *to their* surprise, the doors of the upper room were locked. So they said, "He is probably attending to his needs in the cool chamber." ²⁵So they waited till they were embarrassed, and still he had not opened the doors of the upper room. Therefore they took the key and opened *them*. And there was their master, fallen dead on the floor.

²⁶But Ehud had escaped while they delayed, and passed beyond the stone images and escaped to Seirah. ²⁷And it happened, when he arrived, that he blew the trumpet in the mountains of Ephraim, and the children of Israel went down with him from the mountains; and he led them. ²⁸Then he said to them, "Follow *me,* for the LORD has delivered your enemies the Moabites into your hand." So they went down after him, seized the fords of the Jordan leading to Moab, and did not allow anyone to cross over. ²⁹And at that time they killed about ten thousand men of Moab, all stout men of valor; not a man escaped. ³⁰So Moab was subdued that day under the hand of Israel. And the land had rest for eighty years.

SHAMGAR

³¹After him was Shamgar the son of Anath, who killed six hundred men of the Philistines with an ox goad; and he also delivered Israel.

DEBORAH

4 When Ehud was dead, the children of Israel again did evil in the sight of the LORD. ²So the LORD sold them into the hand of Jabin king of Canaan, who reigned in Hazor. The commander of his army *was* Sisera, who dwelt in Harosheth Hagoyim. ³And the children of Israel cried out to the LORD; for Jabin had nine hundred chariots of iron, and for twenty years he had harshly oppressed the children of Israel.

⁴Now Deborah, a prophetess, the wife of Lapidoth, was judging Israel at that time. ⁵And she would sit under the palm tree of Deborah between Ramah and Bethel in the mountains of Ephraim. And the children of Israel came up to her for judgment. ⁶Then she sent and called for

3:24 ªLiterally *his*

the INFLUENCERS

SHAMGAR—Start Where You Are, Use What You Have

JUDGES 3:31

Shamgar's story takes one verse: He saved Israel with an ox goad. By the time Shamgar was born, the great Hebrew leaders, Moses and Joshua, were long dead. The Hebrews had no king, and times were evil and dangerous. After Joshua died, Israel was repeatedly overrun by foreign invaders. The people avoided main highways for fear of the bandits and terrorists, such as the Philistines, who were the gangsters of their day. With no central government or army, Israel was leaderless and defenseless, vulnerable on every side.

Shamgar was probably a farmer, which explains why he had an ox goad, a long wooden pole tipped with a sharp, iron point at one end, and a flattened chisel-like iron blade at the other. One man killed 600 Philistines, a barbarous, violent race of people who occupied the southern coastal area of Palestine now known as the Gaza Strip. How did he do it? Probably he killed them one, two, or at the most, a few at a time. However it happened, he saved Israel. The Shamgar Principle is to: Start where you are. Use what you have. Do what you can.

the INFLUENCERS

DEBORAH—Leadership Against the Odds

JUDGES 4, 5

Each time the people of Israel lived in peace, they forgot God. He allowed them to fall under the judgment of a pagan king until they cried out with genuine repentance seven times in the book of Judges.

Deborah was called to save Israel from the enemy, but there were a few obstacles, including the fact that she appears to be the first female leader in Israel. The land was in a severe economic recession, spiritual bankruptcy, and emotional oppression. The Israelites lacked resources of any kind as they made the 50 mile hike through crime-ridden paths. In this setting, Deborah was called to command 10,000 untrained, unarmed, hungry men against 100,000 armed, trained, well-fed warriors.

Her resume looks ordinary: a wife, a mother, a judge who *sat under the palm tree*. But Deborah the prophetess spoke the word of God with confidence. She called nervous leader Barak for help, but predicted God would use a woman to get the victory (4:6, 17, 21). She was a team player. She wholeheartedly believed in God's plans for the lives of those He loved. God's part was to provide a miraculous victory. Deborah simply had to have faith and lead with confidence. As a result, the people willingly followed (5:2).

Barak the son of Abinoam from Kedesh in Naphtali, and said to him, "Has not the LORD God of Israel commanded, 'Go and deploy *troops* at Mount Tabor; take with you ten thousand men of the sons of Naphtali and of the sons of Zebulun; 7and against you I will deploy Sisera, the commander of Jabin's army, with his chariots and his multitude at the River Kishon; and I will deliver him into your hand'?"

8And Barak said to her, "If you will go with me, then I will go; but if you will not go with me, I will not go!"

9So she said, "I will surely go with you; nevertheless there will be no glory for you in the journey you are taking, for the LORD will sell Sisera into the hand of a woman." Then Deborah arose and went with Barak to Kedesh. 10And Barak called Zebulun and Naphtali to Kedesh; he went up with ten thousand men under his command,a and Deborah went up with him.

11Now Heber the Kenite, of the children of Hobab the father-in-law of Moses, had separated himself from the Kenites and pitched his tent near the terebinth tree at Zaanaim, which *is* beside Kedesh.

12And they reported to Sisera that Barak the son of Abinoam had gone up to Mount Tabor. 13So Sisera gathered together all his chariots, nine hundred chariots of iron, and all the people who *were* with him, from Harosheth Hagoyim to the River Kishon.

14Then Deborah said to Barak, "Up! For this *is* the day in which the LORD has delivered Sisera into your hand. Has not the LORD gone out before you?" So Barak went down from Mount Tabor with ten thousand men following him. 15And the LORD routed Sisera and all *his* chariots and all *his* army with the edge of the sword before Barak; and Sisera alighted from *his* chariot and fled away on foot. 16But Barak pursued the chariots and the army as far as Harosheth Hagoyim, and all the army of Sisera fell by the edge of the sword; not a man was left.

17However, Sisera had fled away on foot to the tent of Jael, the wife of Heber the Kenite; for *there was* peace between Jabin king of Hazor and the house of Heber the Kenite. 18And Jael went out to meet Sisera, and said to him, "Turn aside,

4:10 aLiterally *at his feet*

my lord, turn aside to me; do not fear." And when he had turned aside with her into the tent, she covered him with a blanket.

¹⁹Then he said to her, "Please give me a little water to drink, for I am thirsty." So she opened a jug of milk, gave him a drink, and covered him. ²⁰And he said to her, "Stand at the door of the tent, and if any man comes and inquires of you, and says, 'Is there any man here?' you shall say, 'No.' "

²¹Then Jael, Heber's wife, took a tent peg and took a hammer in her hand, and went softly to him, and drove the peg into his temple, and it went down into the ground; for he was fast asleep and weary. So he died. ²²And then, as Barak pursued Sisera, Jael came out to meet him, and said to him, "Come, I will show you the man whom you seek." And when he went into her *tent,* there lay Sisera, dead with the peg in his temple.

²³So on that day God subdued Jabin king of Canaan in the presence of the children of Israel. ²⁴And the hand of the children of Israel grew stronger and stronger against Jabin king of Canaan, until they had destroyed Jabin king of Canaan.

The Song of Deborah

5 Then Deborah and Barak the son of Abinoam sang on that day, saying:

²"When leaders lead in Israel,
   When the people willingly offer themselves,
   Bless the LORD!

³"Hear, O kings! Give ear, O princes!
   I, *even* I, will sing to the LORD;
   I will sing praise to the LORD God of Israel.

⁴"LORD, when You went out from Seir,
   When You marched from the field of Edom,
   The earth trembled and the heavens poured,
   The clouds also poured water;
⁵The mountains gushed before the LORD,
   This Sinai, before the LORD God of Israel.

⁶"In the days of Shamgar, son of Anath,
   In the days of Jael,
   The highways were deserted,
   And the travelers walked along the byways.

⁷Village life ceased, it ceased in Israel,
   Until I, Deborah, arose,
   Arose a mother in Israel.
⁸They chose new gods;
   Then *there was* war in the gates;
   Not a shield or spear was seen among forty
      thousand in Israel.
⁹My heart *is* with the rulers of Israel
   Who offered themselves willingly with the
      people.
   Bless the LORD!

¹⁰"Speak, you who ride on white donkeys,
   Who sit in judges' attire,
   And who walk along the road.
¹¹Far from the noise of the archers, among the
      watering places,
   There they shall recount the righteous acts of
      the LORD,
   The righteous acts *for* His villagers in
      Israel;
   Then the people of the LORD shall go down
      to the gates.

¹²"Awake, awake, Deborah!
   Awake, awake, sing a song!
   Arise, Barak, and lead your captives away,
   O son of Abinoam!

¹³"Then the survivors came down, the people
      against the nobles;
   The LORD came down for me against the
      mighty.
¹⁴From Ephraim *were* those whose roots were
      in Amalek.
   After you, Benjamin, with your peoples,
   From Machir rulers came down,
   And from Zebulun those who bear the
      recruiter's staff.
¹⁵And the princes of Issacharᵃ *were* with
      Deborah;
   As Issachar, so *was* Barak
   Sent into the valley under his command;ᵇ
   Among the divisions of Reuben
   There were great resolves of heart.
¹⁶Why did you sit among the sheepfolds,
   To hear the pipings for the flocks?

5:15 ᵃFollowing Septuagint, Syriac, Targum, and Vulgate; Masoretic Text reads *And my princes in Issachar.* ᵇLiterally *at his feet*

The divisions of Reuben have great
searchings of heart.
¹⁷Gilead stayed beyond the Jordan,
And why did Dan remain on ships?ª
Asher continued at the seashore,
And stayed by his inlets.
¹⁸Zebulun *is* a people *who* jeopardized their
lives to the point of death,
Naphtali also, on the heights of the
battlefield.

¹⁹"The kings came *and* fought,
Then the kings of Canaan fought
In Taanach, by the waters of Megiddo;
They took no spoils of silver.
²⁰They fought from the heavens;
The stars from their courses fought against
Sisera.
²¹The torrent of Kishon swept them away,
That ancient torrent, the torrent of Kishon.
O my soul, march on in strength!
²²Then the horses' hooves pounded,
The galloping, galloping of his steeds.
²³'Curse Meroz,' said the angelª of the LORD,
'Curse its inhabitants bitterly,
Because they did not come to the help of the
LORD,
To the help of the LORD against the mighty.'

²⁴"Most blessed among women is Jael,
The wife of Heber the Kenite;
Blessed is she among women in tents.
²⁵He asked for water, she gave milk;
She brought out cream in a lordly bowl.
²⁶She stretched her hand to the tent peg,
Her right hand to the workmen's hammer;
She pounded Sisera, she pierced his head,
She split and struck through his temple.
²⁷At her feet he sank, he fell, he lay still;
At her feet he sank, he fell;
Where he sank, there he fell dead.

²⁸"The mother of Sisera looked through the
window,
And cried out through the lattice,
'Why is his chariot *so* long in coming?
Why tarries the clatter of his chariots?'
²⁹Her wisest ladies answered her,
Yes, she answered herself,

³⁰'Are they not finding and dividing the spoil:
To every man a girl *or* two;
For Sisera, plunder of dyed garments,
Plunder of garments embroidered and
dyed,
Two pieces of dyed embroidery for the
neck of the looter?'

³¹"Thus let all Your enemies perish,
O LORD!
But *let* those who love Him *be* like the sun
When it comes out in full strength."

So the land had rest for forty years.

MIDIANITES OPPRESS ISRAEL

6 Then the children of Israel did evil in the
sight of the LORD. So the LORD delivered
them into the hand of Midian for seven years,
²and the hand of Midian prevailed against Israel.
Because of the Midianites, the children of Israel
made for themselves the dens, the caves, and the
strongholds which *are* in the mountains. ³So it
was, whenever Israel had sown, Midianites would
come up; also Amalekites and the people of the
East would come up against them. ⁴Then they
would encamp against them and destroy the produce of the earth as far as Gaza, and leave no sustenance for Israel, neither sheep nor ox nor donkey. ⁵For they would come up with their
livestock and their tents, coming in as numerous
as locusts; both they and their camels were without number; and they would enter the land to
destroy it. ⁶So Israel was greatly impoverished because of the Midianites, and the children of Israel
cried out to the LORD.

⁷And it came to pass, when the children of Israel cried out to the LORD because of the Midianites, ⁸that the LORD sent a prophet to the children of Israel, who said to them, "Thus says the
LORD God of Israel: 'I brought you up from
Egypt and brought you out of the house of
bondage; ⁹and I delivered you out of the hand of
the Egyptians and out of the hand of all who oppressed you, and drove them out before you and
gave you their land. ¹⁰Also I said to you, "I *am* the
LORD your God; do not fear the gods of the

5:17 ªOr *at ease* 5:23 ªOr *Angel*

Amorites, in whose land you dwell.' But you have not obeyed My voice.' "

GIDEON

¹¹Now the Angel of the LORD came and sat under the terebinth tree which *was* in Ophrah, which *belonged* to Joash the Abiezrite, while his son Gideon threshed wheat in the winepress, in order to hide *it* from the Midianites. ¹²And the Angel of the LORD appeared to him, and said to him, "The LORD *is* with you, you mighty man of valor!"

¹³Gideon said to Him, "O my lord,ᵃ if the LORD is with us, why then has all this happened to us? And where *are* all His miracles which our fathers told us about, saying, 'Did not the LORD bring us up from Egypt?' But now the LORD has forsaken us and delivered us into the hands of the Midianites."

¹⁴Then the LORD turned to him and said, "Go in this might of yours, and you shall save Israel from the hand of the Midianites. Have I not sent you?"

¹⁵So he said to Him, "O my Lord,ᵃ how can I save Israel? Indeed my clan *is* the weakest in Manasseh, and I *am* the least in my father's house."

¹⁶And the LORD said to him, "Surely I will be with you, and you shall defeat the Midianites as one man."

¹⁷Then he said to Him, "If now I have found favor in Your sight, then show me a sign that it is You who talk with me. ¹⁸Do not depart from here, I pray, until I come to You and bring out my offering and set *it* before You."

And He said, "I will wait until you come back."

¹⁹So Gideon went in and prepared a young goat, and unleavened bread from an ephah of flour. The meat he put in a basket, and he put the broth in a pot; and he brought *them* out to Him under the terebinth tree and presented *them*. ²⁰The Angel of God said to him, "Take the meat and the unleavened bread and lay *them* on this rock, and pour out the broth." And he did so.

²¹Then the Angel of the LORD put out the end of the staff that *was* in His hand, and touched the meat and the unleavened bread; and fire rose out of the rock and consumed the meat and the

unleavened bread. And the Angel of the LORD departed out of his sight.

²²Now Gideon perceived that He *was* the Angel of the LORD. So Gideon said, "Alas, O Lord GOD! For I have seen the Angel of the LORD face to face."

²³Then the LORD said to him, "Peace *be* with you; do not fear, you shall not die." ²⁴So Gideon built an altar there to the LORD, and called it The-LORD-*Is*-Peace.ᵃ To this day it *is* still in Ophrah of the Abiezrites.

²⁵Now it came to pass the same night that the LORD said to him, "Take your father's young bull, the second bull of seven years old, and tear down the altar of Baal that your father has, and cut down the wooden imageᵃ that *is* beside it; ²⁶and build an altar to the LORD your God on top of this rock in the proper arrangement, and take the second bull and offer a burnt sacrifice with the wood of the image which you shall cut down." ²⁷So Gideon took ten men from among his servants and did as the LORD had said to him. But because he feared his father's household and the men of the city too much to do *it* by day, he did *it* by night.

GIDEON DESTROYS THE ALTAR OF BAAL

²⁸And when the men of the city arose early in the morning, there was the altar of Baal, torn down; and the wooden image that *was* beside it was cut down, and the second bull was being offered on the altar *which had been* built. ²⁹So they said to one another, "Who has done this thing?" And when they had inquired and asked, they said, "Gideon the son of Joash has done this thing." ³⁰Then the men of the city said to Joash, "Bring out your son, that he may die, because he has torn down the altar of Baal, and because he has cut down the wooden image that *was* beside it."

³¹But Joash said to all who stood against him, "Would you plead for Baal? Would you save him? Let the one who would plead for him be put to death by morning! If he *is* a god, let him plead for himself, because his altar has been torn down!" ³²Therefore on that day he called him Jerubbaal,ᵃ saying, "Let Baal plead against him, because he has torn down his altar."

6:13 ᵃHebrew *adoni,* used of man   **6:15** ᵃHebrew *Adonai,* used of God   **6:24** ᵃHebrew *YHWH Shalom*   **6:25** ᵃHebrew *Asherah,* a Canaanite goddess   **6:32** ᵃLiterally *Let Baal Plead*

the INFLUENCERS

GIDEON: A Legacy of Faith, Not Passed On . . .

JUDGES 6:11—9:6

Gideon was hiding from the enemy on his own farm. Not only was he a coward, but he was from the weakest clan in his area, and the most insignificant member of that family. Does that sound like the rescuer of a nation? Gideon wasn't at the top of the list of probable heroes, but he was exactly who God wanted to use. "Man looks at the outward appearance, but the Lord looks at the heart" (1 Sam. 16:7). When God looked at Gideon, He saw a mighty warrior waiting for a call.

When God called Gideon to deliver Israel from the Midianites, Gideon found his new identity in this powerful God. He grew from a coward to a careful planner who didn't make a move unless he was completely confident that he was in God's will and walking in His way. Gideon traded his inferiority complex for faith and humility, but he wasn't perfect.

This chosen warrior struggled with fear (6:27), doubt (6:36–40), and even idolatry (8:25–27) during his lifetime. The greatest tragedy occurred after he had died. He had worked to influence an entire nation, yet didn't pass on that influence or his own faith to his family (9:1–6). Leadership is successful when those who know you best are drawn to seek the will of God.

---

³³Then all the Midianites and Amalekites, the people of the East, gathered together; and they crossed over and encamped in the Valley of Jezreel. ³⁴But the Spirit of the LORD came upon Gideon; then he blew the trumpet, and the Abiezrites gathered behind him. ³⁵And he sent messengers throughout all Manasseh, who also gathered behind him. He also sent messengers to Asher, Zebulun, and Naphtali; and they came up to meet them.

THE SIGN OF THE FLEECE

³⁶So Gideon said to God, "If You will save Israel by my hand as You have said— ³⁷look, I shall put a fleece of wool on the threshing floor; if there is dew on the fleece only, and *it is* dry on all the ground, then I shall know that You will save Israel by my hand, as You have said." ³⁸And it was so. When he rose early the next morning and squeezed the fleece together, he wrung the dew out of the fleece, a bowlful of water. ³⁹Then Gideon said to God, "Do not be angry with me, but let me speak just once more: Let me test, I pray, just once more with the fleece; let it now be

dry only on the fleece, but on all the ground let there be dew." ⁴⁰And God did so that night. It was dry on the fleece only, but there was dew on all the ground.

GIDEON'S VALIANT THREE HUNDRED

7 Then Jerubbaal (that *is*, Gideon) and all the people who *were* with him rose early and encamped beside the well of Harod, so that the camp of the Midianites was on the north side of them by the hill of Moreh in the valley.

²And the LORD said to Gideon, "The people who *are* with you *are* too many for Me to give the Midianites into their hands, lest Israel claim glory for itself against Me, saying, 'My own hand has saved me.' ³Now therefore, proclaim in the hearing of the people, saying, 'Whoever *is* fearful and afraid, let him turn and depart at once from Mount Gilead.' " And twenty-two thousand of the people returned, and ten thousand remained.

⁴But the LORD said to Gideon, "The people *are* still *too* many; bring them down to the water, and I will test them for you there. Then it will be, *that* of whom I say to you, 'This one shall go with

you,' the same shall go with you; and of whomever I say to you, 'This one shall not go with you,' the same shall not go." ⁵So he brought the people down to the water. And the LORD said to Gideon, "Everyone who laps from the water with his tongue, as a dog laps, you shall set apart by himself; likewise everyone who gets down on his knees to drink." ⁶And the number of those who lapped, *putting* their hand to their mouth, was three hundred men; but all the rest of the people got down on their knees to drink water. ⁷Then the LORD said to Gideon, "By the three hundred men who lapped I will save you, and deliver the Midianites into your hand. Let all the *other* people go, every man to his place." ⁸So the people took provisions and their trumpets in their hands. And he sent away all *the rest of* Israel, every man to his tent, and retained those three hundred men. Now the camp of Midian was below him in the valley.

⁹It happened on the same night that the LORD said to him, "Arise, go down against the camp, for I have delivered it into your hand. ¹⁰But if you are afraid to go down, go down to the camp with Purah your servant, ¹¹and you shall hear what they say; and afterward your hands shall be strengthened to go down against the camp." Then he went down with Purah his servant to the outpost of the armed men who *were* in the camp. ¹²Now the Midianites and Amalekites, all the people of the East, were lying in the valley as numerous as locusts; and their camels *were* without number, as the sand by the seashore in multitude.

¹³And when Gideon had come, there was a man telling a dream to his companion. He said, "I have had a dream: *To my* surprise, a loaf of barley bread tumbled into the camp of Midian; it came to a tent and struck it so that it fell and overturned, and the tent collapsed."

¹⁴Then his companion answered and said, "This *is* nothing else but the sword of Gideon the son of Joash, a man of Israel! Into his hand God has delivered Midian and the whole camp."

¹⁵And so it was, when Gideon heard the telling of the dream and its interpretation, that he worshiped. He returned to the camp of Israel, and said, "Arise, for the LORD has delivered the camp of Midian into your hand." ¹⁶Then he divided the three hundred men *into* three companies, and he put a trumpet into every man's hand, with empty pitchers, and torches inside the pitchers. ¹⁷And he said to them, "Look at me and do likewise; watch, and when I come to the edge of the camp you shall do as I do: ¹⁸When I blow the trumpet, I and all who *are* with me, then you also blow the trumpets on every side of the whole camp, and say, '*The sword of* the LORD and of Gideon!' "

¹⁹So Gideon and the hundred men who *were* with him came to the outpost of the camp at the beginning of the middle watch, just as they had posted the watch; and they blew the trumpets and broke the pitchers that *were* in their hands. ²⁰Then the three companies blew the trumpets and broke the pitchers—they held the torches in their left hands and the trumpets in their right hands for blowing—and they cried, "The sword of the LORD and of Gideon!" ²¹And every man stood in his place all around the camp; and the whole army ran and cried out and fled. ²²When the three hundred blew the trumpets, the LORD set every man's sword against his companion throughout the whole camp; and the army fled to Beth Acacia,ᵃ toward Zererah, as far as the border of Abel Meholah, by Tabbath.

²³And the men of Israel gathered together from Naphtali, Asher, and all Manasseh, and pursued the Midianites.

²⁴Then Gideon sent messengers throughout all the mountains of Ephraim, saying, "Come down against the Midianites, and seize from them the watering places as far as Beth Barah and the Jordan." Then all the men of Ephraim gathered together and seized the watering places as far as Beth Barah and the Jordan. ²⁵And they captured two princes of the Midianites, Oreb and Zeeb. They killed Oreb at the rock of Oreb, and Zeeb they killed at the winepress of Zeeb. They pursued Midian and brought the heads of Oreb and Zeeb to Gideon on the other side of the Jordan.

Gideon Subdues the Midianites

8 Now the men of Ephraim said to him, "Why have you done this to us by not calling us when you went to fight with the Midianites?" And they reprimanded him sharply.

²So he said to them, "What have I done now in comparison with you? *Is* not the gleaning *of the*

grapes of Ephraim better than the vintage of Abiezer? ³God has delivered into your hands the princes of Midian, Oreb and Zeeb. And what was I able to do in comparison with you?" Then their anger toward him subsided when he said that.

⁴When Gideon came to the Jordan, he and the three hundred men who *were* with him crossed over, exhausted but still in pursuit. ⁵Then he said to the men of Succoth, "Please give loaves of bread to the people who follow me, for they are exhausted, and I am pursuing Zebah and Zalmunna, kings of Midian."

⁶And the leaders of Succoth said, "*Are* the hands of Zebah and Zalmunna now in your hand, that we should give bread to your army?"

⁷So Gideon said, "For this cause, when the LORD has delivered Zebah and Zalmunna into my hand, then I will tear your flesh with the thorns of the wilderness and with briers!" ⁸Then he went up from there to Penuel and spoke to them in the same way. And the men of Penuel answered him as the men of Succoth had answered. ⁹So he also spoke to the men of Penuel, saying, "When I come back in peace, I will tear down this tower!"

¹⁰Now Zebah and Zalmunna *were* at Karkor, and their armies with them, about fifteen thousand, all who were left of all the army of the people of the East; for one hundred and twenty thousand men who drew the sword had fallen. ¹¹Then Gideon went up by the road of those who dwell in tents on the east of Nobah and Jogbehah; and he attacked the army while the camp felt secure. ¹²When Zebah and Zalmunna fled, he pursued them; and he took the two kings of Midian, Zebah and Zalmunna, and routed the whole army.

¹³Then Gideon the son of Joash returned from battle, from the Ascent of Heres. ¹⁴And he caught a young man of the men of Succoth and interrogated him; and he wrote down for him the leaders of Succoth and its elders, seventy-seven men. ¹⁵Then he came to the men of Succoth and said, "Here are Zebah and Zalmunna, about whom you ridiculed me, saying, '*Are* the hands of Zebah and Zalmunna now in your hand, that we should give bread to your weary men?' " ¹⁶And he took the elders of the city, and thorns of the wilderness and briers, and with them he taught the men of Succoth. ¹⁷Then he tore down the tower of Penuel and killed the men of the city.

¹⁸And he said to Zebah and Zalmunna, "What kind of men *were they* whom you killed at Tabor?"

So they answered, "As you *are,* so *were* they; each one resembled the son of a king."

¹⁹Then he said, "They *were* my brothers, the sons of my mother. *As* the LORD lives, if you had let them live, I would not kill you." ²⁰And he said to Jether his firstborn, "Rise, kill them!" But the youth would not draw his sword; for he was afraid, because he *was* still a youth.

²¹So Zebah and Zalmunna said, "Rise yourself, and kill us; for as a man *is, so is* his strength." So Gideon arose and killed Zebah and Zalmunna, and took the crescent ornaments that *were* on their camels' necks.

GIDEON'S EPHOD

²²Then the men of Israel said to Gideon, "Rule over us, both you and your son, and your grandson also; for you have delivered us from the hand of Midian."

²³But Gideon said to them, "I will not rule over you, nor shall my son rule over you; the LORD shall rule over you." ²⁴Then Gideon said to them, "I would like to make a request of you, that each of you would give me the earrings from his plunder." For they had golden earrings, because they *were* Ishmaelites.

²⁵So they answered, "We will gladly give *them.*" And they spread out a garment, and each man threw into it the earrings from his plunder. ²⁶Now the weight of the gold earrings that he requested was one thousand seven hundred *shekels* of gold, besides the crescent ornaments, pendants, and purple robes which *were* on the kings of Midian, and besides the chains that *were* around their camels' necks. ²⁷Then Gideon made it into an ephod and set it up in his city, Ophrah. And all Israel played the harlot with it there. It became a snare to Gideon and to his house.

²⁸Thus Midian was subdued before the children of Israel, so that they lifted their heads no more. And the country was quiet for forty years in the days of Gideon.

DEATH OF GIDEON

²⁹Then Jerubbaal the son of Joash went and dwelt in his own house. ³⁰Gideon had seventy sons who were his own offspring, for he had

many wives. ³¹And his concubine who *was* in Shechem also bore him a son, whose name he called Abimelech. ³²Now Gideon the son of Joash died at a good old age, and was buried in the tomb of Joash his father, in Ophrah of the Abiezrites.

³³So it was, as soon as Gideon was dead, that the children of Israel again played the harlot with the Baals, and made Baal-Berith their god. ³⁴Thus the children of Israel did not remember the Lᴏʀᴅ their God, who had delivered them from the hands of all their enemies on every side; ³⁵nor did they show kindness to the house of Jerubbaal (Gideon) in accordance with the good he had done for Israel.

Abimelech's Conspiracy

9 Then Abimelech the son of Jerubbaal went to Shechem, to his mother's brothers, and spoke with them and with all the family of the house of his mother's father, saying, ²"Please speak in the hearing of all the men of Shechem: 'Which is better for you, that all seventy of the sons of Jerubbaal reign over you, or that one reign over you?' Remember that I *am* your own flesh and bone."

³And his mother's brothers spoke all these words concerning him in the hearing of all the men of Shechem; and their heart was inclined to follow Abimelech, for they said, "He is our brother." ⁴So they gave him seventy *shekels* of silver from the temple of Baal-Berith, with which Abimelech hired worthless and reckless men; and they followed him. ⁵Then he went to his father's house at Ophrah and killed his brothers, the seventy sons of Jerubbaal, on one stone. But Jotham the youngest son of Jerubbaal was left, because he hid himself. ⁶And all the men of Shechem gathered together, all of Beth Millo, and they went and made Abimelech king beside the terebinth tree at the pillar that *was* in Shechem.

The Parable of the Trees

⁷Now when they told Jotham, he went and stood on top of Mount Gerizim, and lifted his voice and cried out. And he said to them:

"Listen to me, you men of Shechem,
That God may listen to you!

⁸"The trees once went forth to anoint a king
    over them.
And they said to the olive tree,
'Reign over us!'
⁹But the olive tree said to them,
'Should I cease giving my oil,
With which they honor God and men,
And go to sway over trees?'

¹⁰"Then the trees said to the fig tree,
'You come *and* reign over us!'
¹¹But the fig tree said to them,
'Should I cease my sweetness and my good
    fruit,
And go to sway over trees?'

¹²"Then the trees said to the vine,
'You come *and* reign over us!'
¹³But the vine said to them,
'Should I cease my new wine,
Which cheers *both* God and men,
And go to sway over trees?'

¹⁴"Then all the trees said to the bramble,
'You come *and* reign over us!'
¹⁵And the bramble said to the trees,
'If in truth you anoint me as king over you,
Then come *and* take shelter in my shade;
But if not, let fire come out of the bramble
And devour the cedars of Lebanon!'

¹⁶"Now therefore, if you have acted in truth and sincerity in making Abimelech king, and if you have dealt well with Jerubbaal and his house, and have done to him as he deserves— ¹⁷for my father fought for you, risked his life, and delivered you out of the hand of Midian; ¹⁸but you have risen up against my father's house this day, and killed his seventy sons on one stone, and made Abimelech, the son of his female servant, king over the men of Shechem, because he is your brother— ¹⁹if then you have acted in truth and sincerity with Jerubbaal and with his house this day, *then* rejoice in Abimelech, and let him also rejoice in you. ²⁰But if not, let fire come from Abimelech and devour the men of Shechem and Beth Millo; and let fire come from the men of Shechem and from Beth Millo and devour Abimelech!" ²¹And Jotham ran away and fled; and he

went to Beer and dwelt there, for fear of Abimelech his brother.

DOWNFALL OF ABIMELECH

²²After Abimelech had reigned over Israel three years, ²³God sent a spirit of ill will between Abimelech and the men of Shechem; and the men of Shechem dealt treacherously with Abimelech, ²⁴that the crime *done* to the seventy sons of Jerubbaal might be settled and their blood be laid on Abimelech their brother, who killed them, and on the men of Shechem, who aided him in the killing of his brothers. ²⁵And the men of Shechem set men in ambush against him on the tops of the mountains, and they robbed all who passed by them along that way; and it was told Abimelech.

²⁶Now Gaal the son of Ebed came with his brothers and went over to Shechem; and the men of Shechem put their confidence in him. ²⁷So they went out into the fields, and gathered *grapes* from their vineyards and trod *them,* and made merry. And they went into the house of their god, and ate and drank, and cursed Abimelech. ²⁸Then Gaal the son of Ebed said, "Who *is* Abimelech, and who *is* Shechem, that we should serve him? *Is he* not the son of Jerubbaal, and *is not* Zebul his officer? Serve the men of Hamor the father of Shechem; but why should we serve him? ²⁹If only this people were under my authority!ᵃ Then I would remove Abimelech." So heᵇ said to Abimelech, "Increase your army and come out!"

³⁰When Zebul, the ruler of the city, heard the words of Gaal the son of Ebed, his anger was aroused. ³¹And he sent messengers to Abimelech secretly, saying, "Take note! Gaal the son of Ebed and his brothers have come to Shechem; and here they are, fortifying the city against you. ³²Now therefore, get up by night, you and the people who *are* with you, and lie in wait in the field. ³³And it shall be, as soon as the sun is up in the morning, *that* you shall rise early and rush upon the city; and *when* he and the people who are with him come out against you, you may then do to them as you find opportunity."

³⁴So Abimelech and all the people who *were* with him rose by night, and lay in wait against Shechem in four companies. ³⁵When Gaal the son of Ebed went out and stood in the entrance to the city gate, Abimelech and the people who *were* with him rose from lying in wait. ³⁶And when Gaal saw the people, he said to Zebul, "Look, people are coming down from the tops of the mountains!"

But Zebul said to him, "You see the shadows of the mountains as *if they were* men."

³⁷So Gaal spoke again and said, "See, people are coming down from the center of the land, and another company is coming from the Diviners'ᵃ Terebinth Tree."

³⁸Then Zebul said to him, "Where indeed *is* your mouth now, with which you said, 'Who is Abimelech, that we should serve him?' *Are* not these the people whom you despised? Go out, if you will, and fight with them now."

³⁹So Gaal went out, leading the men of Shechem, and fought with Abimelech. ⁴⁰And Abimelech chased him, and he fled from him; and many fell wounded, to the *very* entrance of the gate. ⁴¹Then Abimelech dwelt at Arumah, and Zebul drove out Gaal and his brothers, so that they would not dwell in Shechem.

⁴²And it came about on the next day that the people went out into the field, and they told Abimelech. ⁴³So he took his people, divided them into three companies, and lay in wait in the field. And he looked, and there were the people, coming out of the city; and he rose against them and attacked them. ⁴⁴Then Abimelech and the company that *was* with him rushed forward and stood at the entrance of the gate of the city; and the *other* two companies rushed upon all who *were* in the fields and killed them. ⁴⁵So Abimelech fought against the city all that day; he took the city and killed the people who *were* in it; and he demolished the city and sowed it with salt.

⁴⁶Now when all the men of the tower of Shechem had heard *that,* they entered the stronghold of the temple of the god Berith. ⁴⁷And it was told Abimelech that all the men of the tower of Shechem were gathered together. ⁴⁸Then Abimelech went up to Mount Zalmon, he and all the people who *were* with him. And Abimelech took an ax in his hand and cut down a bough from the trees, and took it and laid *it* on his shoulder; then he said to the people who were

9:29 ᵃLiterally *hand* ᵇFollowing Masoretic Text and Targum; Dead Sea Scrolls read *they;* Septuagint reads *I.* **9:37** ᵃHebrew *Meonenim*

with him, "What you have seen me do, make haste *and* do as I *have done*." ⁴⁹So each of the people likewise cut down his own bough and followed Abimelech, put *them* against the stronghold, and set the stronghold on fire above them, so that all the people of the tower of Shechem died, about a thousand men and women.

⁵⁰Then Abimelech went to Thebez, and he encamped against Thebez and took it. ⁵¹But there was a strong tower in the city, and all the men and women—all the people of the city—fled there and shut themselves in; then they went up to the top of the tower. ⁵²So Abimelech came as far as the tower and fought against it; and he drew near the door of the tower to burn it with fire. ⁵³But a certain woman dropped an upper millstone on Abimelech's head and crushed his skull. ⁵⁴Then he called quickly to the young man, his armorbearer, and said to him, "Draw your sword and kill me, lest men say of me, 'A woman killed him.'" So his young man thrust him through, and he died. ⁵⁵And when the men of Israel saw that Abimelech was dead, they departed, every man to his place.

⁵⁶Thus God repaid the wickedness of Abimelech, which he had done to his father by killing his seventy brothers. ⁵⁷And all the evil of the men of Shechem God returned on their own heads, and on them came the curse of Jotham the son of Jerubbaal.

Tola

10 After Abimelech there arose to save Israel Tola the son of Puah, the son of Dodo, a man of Issachar; and he dwelt in Shamir in the mountains of Ephraim. ²He judged Israel twenty-three years; and he died and was buried in Shamir.

Jair

³After him arose Jair, a Gileadite; and he judged Israel twenty-two years. ⁴Now he had thirty sons who rode on thirty donkeys; they also had thirty towns, which are called "Havoth Jair"[a] to this day, which *are* in the land of Gilead. ⁵And Jair died and was buried in Camon.

Israel Oppressed Again

⁶Then the children of Israel again did evil in the sight of the LORD, and served the Baals and the Ashtoreths, the gods of Syria, the gods of

Sidon, the gods of Moab, the gods of the people of Ammon, and the gods of the Philistines; and they forsook the LORD and did not serve Him. ⁷So the anger of the LORD was hot against Israel; and He sold them into the hands of the Philistines and into the hands of the people of Ammon. ⁸From that year they harassed and oppressed the children of Israel for eighteen years—all the children of Israel who *were* on the other side of the Jordan in the land of the Amorites, in Gilead. ⁹Moreover the people of Ammon crossed over the Jordan to fight against Judah also, against Benjamin, and against the house of Ephraim, so that Israel was severely distressed.

¹⁰And the children of Israel cried out to the LORD, saying, "We have sinned against You, because we have both forsaken our God and served the Baals!"

¹¹So the LORD said to the children of Israel, "*Did I* not *deliver you* from the Egyptians and from the Amorites and from the people of Ammon and from the Philistines? ¹²Also the Sidonians and Amalekites and Maonites[a] oppressed you; and you cried out to Me, and I delivered you from their hand. ¹³Yet you have forsaken Me and served other gods. Therefore I will deliver you no more. ¹⁴Go and cry out to the gods which you have chosen; let them deliver you in your time of distress."

¹⁵And the children of Israel said to the LORD, "We have sinned! Do to us whatever seems best to You; only deliver us this day, we pray." ¹⁶So they put away the foreign gods from among them and served the LORD. And His soul could no longer endure the misery of Israel.

¹⁷Then the people of Ammon gathered together and encamped in Gilead. And the children of Israel assembled together and encamped in Mizpah. ¹⁸And the people, the leaders of Gilead, said to one another, "Who *is* the man who will begin the fight against the people of Ammon? He shall be head over all the inhabitants of Gilead."

Jephthah

11 Now Jephthah the Gileadite was a mighty man of valor, but he *was* the son of a harlot; and Gilead begot Jephthah. ²Gilead's wife

10:4 [a]Literally *Towns of Jair* (compare Numbers 32:41 and Deuteronomy 3:14)   **10:12** [a]Some Septuagint manuscripts read *Midianites.*

bore sons; and when his wife's sons grew up, they drove Jephthah out, and said to him, "You shall have no inheritance in our father's house, for you *are* the son of another woman." ³Then Jephthah fled from his brothers and dwelt in the land of Tob; and worthless men banded together with Jephthah and went out *raiding* with him.

⁴It came to pass after a time that the people of Ammon made war against Israel. ⁵And so it was, when the people of Ammon made war against Israel, that the elders of Gilead went to get Jephthah from the land of Tob. ⁶Then they said to Jephthah, "Come and be our commander, that we may fight against the people of Ammon."

⁷So Jephthah said to the elders of Gilead, "Did you not hate me, and expel me from my father's house? Why have you come to me now when you are in distress?"

⁸And the elders of Gilead said to Jephthah, "That is why we have turned again to you now, that you may go with us and fight against the people of Ammon, and be our head over all the inhabitants of Gilead."

⁹So Jephthah said to the elders of Gilead, "If you take me back home to fight against the people of Ammon, and the LORD delivers them to me, shall I be your head?"

¹⁰And the elders of Gilead said to Jephthah, "The LORD will be a witness between us, if we do not do according to your words." ¹¹Then Jephthah went with the elders of Gilead, and the people made him head and commander over them; and Jephthah spoke all his words before the LORD in Mizpah.

¹²Now Jephthah sent messengers to the king of the people of Ammon, saying, "What do you have against me, that you have come to fight against me in my land?"

¹³And the king of the people of Ammon answered the messengers of Jephthah, "Because Israel took away my land when they came up out of Egypt, from the Arnon as far as the Jabbok, and to the Jordan. Now therefore, restore those *lands* peaceably."

¹⁴So Jephthah again sent messengers to the king of the people of Ammon, ¹⁵and said to him, "Thus says Jephthah: 'Israel did not take away the land of Moab, nor the land of the people of Ammon; ¹⁶for when Israel came up from Egypt, they walked through the wilderness as far as the Red Sea and came to Kadesh. ¹⁷Then Israel sent messengers to the king of Edom, saying, 'Please let me pass through your land.' But the king of Edom would not heed. And in like manner they sent to the king of Moab, but he would not *consent.* So Israel remained in Kadesh. ¹⁸And they went along through the wilderness and bypassed the land of Edom and the land of Moab, came to the east side of the land of Moab, and encamped on the other side of the Arnon. But they did not enter the border of Moab, for the Arnon *was* the border of Moab. ¹⁹Then Israel sent messengers to Sihon king of the Amorites, king of Heshbon; and Israel said to him, "Please let us pass through your land into our place." ²⁰But Sihon did not trust Israel to pass through his territory. So Sihon gathered all his people together, encamped in Jahaz, and fought against Israel. ²¹And the LORD God of Israel delivered Sihon and all his people into the hand of Israel, and they defeated them. Thus Israel gained possession of all the land of the Amorites, who inhabited that country. ²²They took possession of all the territory of the Amorites, from the Arnon to the Jabbok and from the wilderness to the Jordan.

²³'And now the LORD God of Israel has dispossessed the Amorites from before His people Israel; should you then possess it? ²⁴Will you not possess whatever Chemosh your god gives you to possess? So whatever the LORD our God takes possession of before us, we will possess. ²⁵And now, *are* you any better than Balak the son of Zippor, king of Moab? Did he ever strive against Israel? Did he ever fight against them? ²⁶While Israel dwelt in Heshbon and its villages, in Aroer and its villages, and in all the cities along the banks of the Arnon, for three hundred years, why did you not recover *them* within that time? ²⁷Therefore I have not sinned against you, but you wronged me by fighting against me. May the LORD, the Judge, render judgment this day between the children of Israel and the people of Ammon.' " ²⁸However, the king of the people of Ammon did not heed the words which Jephthah sent him.

JEPHTHAH'S VOW AND VICTORY

²⁹Then the Spirit of the LORD came upon Jephthah, and he passed through Gilead and Manasseh, and passed through Mizpah of Gilead; and

from Mizpah of Gilead he advanced *toward* the people of Ammon. ³⁰And Jephthah made a vow to the LORD, and said, "If You will indeed deliver the people of Ammon into my hands, ³¹then it will be that whatever comes out of the doors of my house to meet me, when I return in peace from the people of Ammon, shall surely be the LORD's, and I will offer it up as a burnt offering."

³²So Jephthah advanced toward the people of Ammon to fight against them, and the LORD delivered them into his hands. ³³And he defeated them from Aroer as far as Minnith—twenty cities—and to Abel Keramim,ᵃ with a very great slaughter. Thus the people of Ammon were subdued before the children of Israel.

Jephthah's Daughter

³⁴When Jephthah came to his house at Mizpah, there was his daughter, coming out to meet him with timbrels and dancing; and she *was his* only child. Besides her he had neither son nor daughter. ³⁵And it came to pass, when he saw her, that he tore his clothes, and said, "Alas, my daughter! You have brought me very low! You are among those who trouble me! For I have given my word to the LORD, and I cannot go back on it."

³⁶So she said to him, "My father, *if* you have given your word to the LORD, do to me according to what has gone out of your mouth, because the LORD has avenged you of your enemies, the people of Ammon." ³⁷Then she said to her father, "Let this thing be done for me: let me alone for two months, that I may go and wander on the mountains and bewail my virginity, my friends and I."

³⁸So he said, "Go." And he sent her away *for* two months; and she went with her friends, and bewailed her virginity on the mountains. ³⁹And it was so at the end of two months that she returned to her father, and he carried out his vow with her which he had vowed. She knew no man.

And it became a custom in Israel ⁴⁰*that* the daughters of Israel went four days each year to lament the daughter of Jephthah the Gileadite.

Jephthah's Conflict with Ephraim

12 Then the men of Ephraim gathered together, crossed over toward Zaphon, and said to Jephthah, "Why did you cross over to fight against the people of Ammon, and did not call us

to go with you? We will burn your house down on you with fire!"

²And Jephthah said to them, "My people and I were in a great struggle with the people of Ammon; and when I called you, you did not deliver me out of their hands. ³So when I saw that you would not deliver *me,* I took my life in my hands and crossed over against the people of Ammon; and the LORD delivered them into my hand. Why then have you come up to me this day to fight against me?" ⁴Now Jephthah gathered together all the men of Gilead and fought against Ephraim. And the men of Gilead defeated Ephraim, because they said, "You Gileadites *are* fugitives of Ephraim among the Ephraimites *and* among the Manassites." ⁵The Gileadites seized the fords of the Jordan before the Ephraimites *arrived.* And when *any* Ephraimite who escaped said, "Let me cross over," the men of Gilead would say to him, "*Are* you an Ephraimite?" If he said, "No," ⁶then they would say to him, "Then say, 'Shibboleth'!" And he would say, "Sibboleth," for he could not pronounce *it* right. Then they would take him and kill him at the fords of the Jordan. There fell at that time forty-two thousand Ephraimites.

⁷And Jephthah judged Israel six years. Then Jephthah the Gileadite died and was buried among the cities of Gilead.

Ibzan, Elon, and Abdon

⁸After him, Ibzan of Bethlehem judged Israel. ⁹He had thirty sons. And he gave away thirty daughters in marriage, and brought in thirty daughters from elsewhere for his sons. He judged Israel seven years. ¹⁰Then Ibzan died and was buried at Bethlehem.

¹¹After him, Elon the Zebulunite judged Israel. He judged Israel ten years. ¹²And Elon the Zebulunite died and was buried at Aijalon in the country of Zebulun.

¹³After him, Abdon the son of Hillel the Pirathonite judged Israel. ¹⁴He had forty sons and thirty grandsons, who rode on seventy young donkeys. He judged Israel eight years. ¹⁵Then Abdon the son of Hillel the Pirathonite died and was buried in Pirathon in the land of Ephraim, in the mountains of the Amalekites.

11:33 ᵃLiterally *Plain of Vineyards*

The Birth of Samson

13 Again the children of Israel did evil in the sight of the LORD, and the LORD delivered them into the hand of the Philistines for forty years.

²Now there was a certain man from Zorah, of the family of the Danites, whose name *was* Manoah; and his wife *was* barren and had no children. ³And the Angel of the LORD appeared to the woman and said to her, "Indeed now, you are barren and have borne no children, but you shall conceive and bear a son. ⁴Now therefore, please be careful not to drink wine or *similar* drink, and not to eat anything unclean. ⁵For behold, you shall conceive and bear a son. And no razor shall come upon his head, for the child shall be a Nazirite to God from the womb; and he shall begin to deliver Israel out of the hand of the Philistines."

⁶So the woman came and told her husband, saying, "A Man of God came to me, and His countenance *was* like the countenance of the Angel of God, very awesome; but I did not ask Him where He *was* from, and He did not tell me His name. ⁷And He said to me, 'Behold, you shall conceive and bear a son. Now drink no wine or *similar* drink, nor eat anything unclean, for the child shall be a Nazirite to God from the womb to the day of his death.' "

⁸Then Manoah prayed to the LORD, and said, "O my Lord, please let the Man of God whom You sent come to us again and teach us what we shall do for the child who will be born."

⁹And God listened to the voice of Manoah, and the Angel of God came to the woman again as she was sitting in the field; but Manoah her husband *was* not with her. ¹⁰Then the woman ran in haste and told her husband, and said to him, "Look, the Man who came to me the *other* day has just now appeared to me!"

¹¹So Manoah arose and followed his wife. When he came to the Man, he said to Him, "Are You the Man who spoke to this woman?"

And He said, "I *am*."

¹²Manoah said, "Now let Your words come *to pass!* What will be the boy's rule of life, and his work?"

¹³So the Angel of the LORD said to Manoah, "Of all that I said to the woman let her be care-

ful. ¹⁴She may not eat anything that comes from the vine, nor may she drink wine or *similar* drink, nor eat anything unclean. All that I commanded her let her observe."

¹⁵Then Manoah said to the Angel of the LORD, "Please let us detain You, and we will prepare a young goat for You."

¹⁶And the Angel of the LORD said to Manoah, "Though you detain Me, I will not eat your food. But if you offer a burnt offering, you must offer it to the LORD." (For Manoah did not know He *was* the Angel of the LORD.)

¹⁷Then Manoah said to the Angel of the LORD, "What *is* Your name, that when Your words come *to pass* we may honor You?"

¹⁸And the Angel of the LORD said to him, "Why do you ask My name, seeing it *is* wonderful?"

¹⁹So Manoah took the young goat with the grain offering, and offered it upon the rock to the LORD. And He did a wondrous thing while Manoah and his wife looked on— ²⁰it happened as the flame went up toward heaven from the altar—the Angel of the LORD ascended in the flame of the altar! When Manoah and his wife saw *this,* they fell on their faces to the ground. ²¹When the Angel of the LORD appeared no more to Manoah and his wife, then Manoah knew that He *was* the Angel of the LORD.

²²And Manoah said to his wife, "We shall surely die, because we have seen God!"

²³But his wife said to him, "If the LORD had desired to kill us, He would not have accepted a burnt offering and a grain offering from our hands, nor would He have shown us all these *things,* nor would He have told us *such things* as these at this time."

²⁴So the woman bore a son and called his name Samson; and the child grew, and the LORD blessed him. ²⁵And the Spirit of the LORD began to move upon him at Mahaneh Danᵃ between Zorah and Eshtaol.

Samson's Philistine Wife

14 Now Samson went down to Timnah, and saw a woman in Timnah of the daughters of the Philistines. ²So he went up and told his fa-

13:25 ᵃLiterally *Camp of Dan* (compare 18:12)

ther and mother, saying, "I have seen a woman in Timnah of the daughters of the Philistines; now therefore, get her for me as a wife."

[3]Then his father and mother said to him, "*Is there* no woman among the daughters of your brethren, or among all my people, that you must go and get a wife from the uncircumcised Philistines?"

And Samson said to his father, "Get her for me, for she pleases me well."

[4]But his father and mother did not know that it was of the LORD—that He was seeking an occasion to move against the Philistines. For at that time the Philistines had dominion over Israel.

[5]So Samson went down to Timnah with his father and mother, and came to the vineyards of Timnah.

Now *to his* surprise, a young lion *came* roaring against him. [6]And the Spirit of the LORD came mightily upon him, and he tore the lion apart as one would have torn apart a young goat, though *he had* nothing in his hand. But he did not tell his father or his mother what he had done.

[7]Then he went down and talked with the woman; and she pleased Samson well. [8]After some time, when he returned to get her, he turned aside to see the carcass of the lion. And behold, a swarm of bees and honey *were* in the carcass of the lion. [9]He took some of it in his hands and went along, eating. When he came to his father and mother, he gave *some* to them, and they also ate. But he did not tell them that he had taken the honey out of the carcass of the lion.

[10]So his father went down to the woman. And Samson gave a feast there, for young men used to do so. [11]And it happened, when they saw him, that they brought thirty companions to be with him.

[12]Then Samson said to them, "Let me pose a riddle to you. If you can correctly solve and explain it to me within the seven days of the feast, then I will give you thirty linen garments and thirty changes of clothing. [13]But if you cannot explain *it* to me, then you shall give me thirty linen garments and thirty changes of clothing."

And they said to him, "Pose your riddle, that we may hear it."

[14]So he said to them:

"Out of the eater came something to eat,
    And out of the strong came something
        sweet."

Now for three days they could not explain the riddle.

[15]But it came to pass on the seventh[a] day that they said to Samson's wife, "Entice your husband, that he may explain the riddle to us, or else we will burn you and your father's house with fire. Have you invited us in order to take what is ours? *Is that* not *so?*"

[16]Then Samson's wife wept on him, and said, "You only hate me! You do not love me! You have posed a riddle to the sons of my people, but you have not explained *it* to me."

And he said to her, "Look, I have not explained *it* to my father or my mother; so should I explain *it* to you?" [17]Now she had wept on him the seven days while their feast lasted. And it happened on the seventh day that he told her, because she pressed him so much. Then she explained the riddle to the sons of her people. [18]So the men of the city said to him on the seventh day before the sun went down:

"What *is* sweeter than honey?
    And what *is* stronger than a lion?"

And he said to them:

"If you had not plowed with my heifer,
    You would not have solved my riddle!"

[19]Then the Spirit of the LORD came upon him mightily, and he went down to Ashkelon and killed thirty of their men, took their apparel, and gave the changes *of clothing* to those who had explained the riddle. So his anger was aroused, and he went back up to his father's house. [20]And Samson's wife was *given* to his companion, who had been his best man.

SAMSON DEFEATS THE PHILISTINES

15 After a while, in the time of wheat harvest, it happened that Samson visited his wife with a young goat. And he said, "Let me go in to

14:15 [a]Following Masoretic Text, Targum, and Vulgate; Septuagint and Syriac read *fourth*.

my wife, into *her* room." But her father would not permit him to go in.

²Her father said, "I really thought that you thoroughly hated her; therefore I gave her to your companion. *Is* not her younger sister better than she? Please, take her instead."

³And Samson said to them, "This time I shall be blameless regarding the Philistines if I harm them!" ⁴Then Samson went and caught three hundred foxes; and he took torches, turned *the foxes* tail to tail, and put a torch between each pair of tails. ⁵When he had set the torches on fire, he let *the foxes* go into the standing grain of the Philistines, and burned up both the shocks and the standing grain, as well as the vineyards *and* olive groves.

⁶Then the Philistines said, "Who has done this?"

And they answered, "Samson, the son-in-law of the Timnite, because he has taken his wife and given her to his companion." So the Philistines came up and burned her and her father with fire.

⁷Samson said to them, "Since you would do a thing like this, I will surely take revenge on you, and after that I will cease." ⁸So he attacked them hip and thigh with a great slaughter; then he went down and dwelt in the cleft of the rock of Etam.

⁹Now the Philistines went up, encamped in Judah, and deployed themselves against Lehi. ¹⁰And the men of Judah said, "Why have you come up against us?"

So they answered, "We have come up to arrest Samson, to do to him as he has done to us."

¹¹Then three thousand men of Judah went down to the cleft of the rock of Etam, and said to Samson, "Do you not know that the Philistines rule over us? What *is* this you have done to us?"

And he said to them, "As they did to me, so I have done to them."

¹²But they said to him, "We have come down to arrest you, that we may deliver you into the hand of the Philistines."

Then Samson said to them, "Swear to me that you will not kill me yourselves."

¹³So they spoke to him, saying, "No, but we will tie you securely and deliver you into their hand; but we will surely not kill you." And they bound him with two new ropes and brought him up from the rock.

¹⁴When he came to Lehi, the Philistines came shouting against him. Then the Spirit of the LORD came mightily upon him; and the ropes that *were* on his arms became like flax that is burned with fire, and his bonds broke loose from his hands. ¹⁵He found a fresh jawbone of a donkey, reached out his hand and took it, and killed a thousand men with it. ¹⁶Then Samson said:

"With the jawbone of a donkey,
  Heaps upon heaps,
  With the jawbone of a donkey
  I have slain a thousand men!"

¹⁷And so it was, when he had finished speaking, that he threw the jawbone from his hand, and called that place Ramath Lehi.ᵃ

¹⁸Then he became very thirsty; so he cried out to the LORD and said, "You have given this great deliverance by the hand of Your servant; and now shall I die of thirst and fall into the hand of the uncircumcised?" ¹⁹So God split the hollow place that *is* in Lehi,ᵃ and water came out, and he drank; and his spirit returned, and he revived. Therefore he called its name En Hakkore,ᵇ which is in Lehi to this day. ²⁰And he judged Israel twenty years in the days of the Philistines.

SAMSON AND DELILAH

16 Now Samson went to Gaza and saw a harlot there, and went in to her. ²*When the* Gazites *were told,* "Samson has come here!" they surrounded *the place* and lay in wait for him all night at the gate of the city. They were quiet all night, saying, "In the morning, when it is daylight, we will kill him." ³And Samson lay *low* till midnight; then he arose at midnight, took hold of the doors of the gate of the city and the two gateposts, pulled them up, bar and all, put *them* on his shoulders, and carried them to the top of the hill that faces Hebron.

⁴Afterward it happened that he loved a woman in the Valley of Sorek, whose name *was* Delilah. ⁵And the lords of the Philistines came up to her and said to her, "Entice him, and find out where his great strength *lies,* and by what *means* we may overpower him, that we may bind him to

15:17 ᵃLiterally *Jawbone Height*   **15:19** ᵃLiterally *Jawbone* (compare verse 14) ᵇLiterally *Spring of the Caller*

INSIDE *the* INFLUENCERS

SAMSON: Incredible Strength and Glaring Weakness

JUDGES 13—16

The life of Samson says a lot about strength, and even more about weakness.

Samson was set apart by God even before his birth. In spite of the fantastic feats that God accomplished through Samson, he allowed his character flaws to rule his life. Samson did not take his calling to heart. Called to be different, he frequently participated in ungodly acts. Ultimately, his downfall came through his inability to maintain the boundaries God had set for him. Samson didn't control his desires; his desires controlled him.

Three times in the narrative of Samson's life, this strong man fell to his weakness for women: he married a Philistine woman (14:1–3); he slept with a Philistine prostitute (16:1); and he fell in love with the infamous Delilah, a woman of the Valley of Sorek (16:4).

Samson paid dearly for the lack of regard for God's calling in his life and his inability to tame his desires. Leaders should note that the two go hand in hand.

He was deceived by Delilah and blinded by his Philistine captors. He was humiliated for years and forced to do the work of a farm animal (16:21). Samson eventually reached a place of brokenness; God restored his strength and allowed him to die with dignity. In spite of Samson's obvious weakness, God was faithful to him and allowed him to finish well.

---

afflict him; and every one of us will give you eleven hundred *pieces* of silver."

⁶So Delilah said to Samson, "Please tell me where your great strength *lies,* and with what you may be bound to afflict you."

⁷And Samson said to her, "If they bind me with seven fresh bowstrings, not yet dried, then I shall become weak, and be like any *other* man."

⁸So the lords of the Philistines brought up to her seven fresh bowstrings, not yet dried, and she bound him with them. ⁹Now *men were* lying in wait, staying with her in the room. And she said to him, "The Philistines *are* upon you, Samson!" But he broke the bowstrings as a strand of yarn breaks when it touches fire. So the secret of his strength was not known.

¹⁰Then Delilah said to Samson, "Look, you have mocked me and told me lies. Now, please tell me what you may be bound with."

¹¹So he said to her, "If they bind me securely with new ropes that have never been used, then I shall become weak, and be like any *other* man."

¹²Therefore Delilah took new ropes and bound him with them, and said to him, "The Philistines *are* upon you, Samson!" And *men were* lying in wait, staying in the room. But he broke them off his arms like a thread.

¹³Delilah said to Samson, "Until now you have mocked me and told me lies. Tell me what you may be bound with."

And he said to her, "If you weave the seven locks of my head into the web of the loom"—

¹⁴So she wove *it* tightly with the batten of the loom, and said to him, "The Philistines *are* upon you, Samson!" But he awoke from his sleep, and pulled out the batten and the web from the loom.

¹⁵Then she said to him, "How can you say, 'I love you,' when your heart *is* not with me? You have mocked me these three times, and have not told me where your great strength *lies."* ¹⁶And it came to pass, when she pestered him daily with her words and pressed him, *so* that his soul was vexed to death, ¹⁷that he told her all his heart, and said to her, "No razor has ever come upon my head, for I *have been* a Nazirite to God from my mother's womb. If I am shaven, then my strength will leave me, and I shall become weak, and be like any *other* man."

¹⁸When Delilah saw that he had told her all his heart, she sent and called for the lords of the Philistines, saying, "Come up once more, for he has told me all his heart." So the lords of the Philistines came up to her and brought the money in their hand. ¹⁹Then she lulled him to sleep on her knees, and called for a man and had him shave off the seven locks of his head. Then she began to torment him,^a and his strength left him. ²⁰And she said, "The Philistines *are* upon you, Samson!" So he awoke from his sleep, and said, "I will go out as before, at other times, and shake myself free!" But he did not know that the LORD had departed from him.

²¹Then the Philistines took him and put out his eyes, and brought him down to Gaza. They bound him with bronze fetters, and he became a grinder in the prison. ²²However, the hair of his head began to grow again after it had been shaven.

SAMSON DIES WITH THE PHILISTINES

²³Now the lords of the Philistines gathered together to offer a great sacrifice to Dagon their god, and to rejoice. And they said:

"Our god has delivered into our hands
Samson our enemy!"

²⁴When the people saw him, they praised their god; for they said:

"Our god has delivered into our hands our
    enemy,
The destroyer of our land,
And the one who multiplied our dead."

²⁵So it happened, when their hearts were merry, that they said, "Call for Samson, that he may perform for us." So they called for Samson from the prison, and he performed for them. And they stationed him between the pillars. ²⁶Then Samson said to the lad who held him by the hand, "Let me feel the pillars which support the temple, so that I can lean on them." ²⁷Now the temple was full of men and women. All the lords of the Philistines *were* there—about three thousand men and women on the roof watching while Samson performed.

²⁸Then Samson called to the LORD, saying, "O Lord GOD, remember me, I pray! Strengthen me, I pray, just this once, O God, that I may with one *blow* take vengeance on the Philistines for my two eyes!" ²⁹And Samson took hold of the two middle pillars which supported the temple, and he braced himself against them, one on his right and the other on his left. ³⁰Then Samson said, "Let me die with the Philistines!" And he pushed with *all his* might, and the temple fell on the lords and all the people who *were* in it. So the dead that he killed at his death were more than he had killed in his life.

³¹And his brothers and all his father's household came down and took him, and brought *him* up and buried him between Zorah and Eshtaol in the tomb of his father Manoah. He had judged Israel twenty years.

MICAH'S IDOLATRY

17 Now there was a man from the mountains of Ephraim, whose name *was* Micah. ²And he said to his mother, "The eleven hundred *shekels* of silver that were taken from you, and on which you put a curse, even saying it in my ears—here *is* the silver with me; I took it."

And his mother said, "*May you be* blessed by the LORD, my son!" ³So when he had returned the eleven hundred *shekels* of silver to his mother, his mother said, "I had wholly dedicated the silver from my hand to the LORD for my son, to make a carved image and a molded image; now therefore, I will return it to you." ⁴Thus he returned the silver to his mother. Then his mother took two hundred *shekels* of silver and gave them to the silversmith, and he made it into a carved image and a molded image; and they were in the house of Micah.

⁵The man Micah had a shrine, and made an ephod and household idols;^a and he consecrated one of his sons, who became his priest. ⁶In those days *there was* no king in Israel; everyone did *what was* right in his own eyes.

⁷Now there was a young man from Bethlehem in Judah, of the family of Judah; he *was* a Levite, and was staying there. ⁸The man departed from the city of Bethlehem in Judah to stay

^{16:19} ^aFollowing Masoretic Text, Targum, and Vulgate; Septuagint reads *he began to be weak*.   **17:5** ^aHebrew *teraphim*

wherever he could find *a place*. Then he came to the mountains of Ephraim, to the house of Micah, as he journeyed. ⁹And Micah said to him, "Where do you come from?"

So he said to him, "I *am* a Levite from Bethlehem in Judah, and I am on my way to find *a place* to stay."

¹⁰Micah said to him, "Dwell with me, and be a father and a priest to me, and I will give you ten *shekels* of silver per year, a suit of clothes, and your sustenance." So the Levite went in. ¹¹Then the Levite was content to dwell with the man; and the young man became like one of his sons to him. ¹²So Micah consecrated the Levite, and the young man became his priest, and lived in the house of Micah. ¹³Then Micah said, "Now I know that the Lord will be good to me, since I have a Levite as priest!"

The Danites Adopt Micah's Idolatry

18 In those days *there was* no king in Israel. And in those days the tribe of the Danites was seeking an inheritance for itself to dwell in; for until that day *their* inheritance among the tribes of Israel had not fallen to them. ²So the children of Dan sent five men of their family from their territory, men of valor from Zorah and Eshtaol, to spy out the land and search it. They said to them, "Go, search the land." So they went to the mountains of Ephraim, to the house of Micah, and lodged there. ³While they *were* at the house of Micah, they recognized the voice of the young Levite. They turned aside and said to him, "Who brought you here? What are you doing in this *place?* What do you have here?"

⁴He said to them, "Thus and so Micah did for me. He has hired me, and I have become his priest."

⁵So they said to him, "Please inquire of God, that we may know whether the journey on which we go will be prosperous."

⁶And the priest said to them, "Go in peace. The presence of the Lord *be* with you on your way."

⁷So the five men departed and went to Laish. They saw the people who *were* there, how they dwelt safely, in the manner of the Sidonians, quiet and secure. *There were* no rulers in the land who might put *them* to shame for anything. They *were*

far from the Sidonians, and they had no ties with anyone.ᵃ

⁸Then *the spies* came back to their brethren at Zorah and Eshtaol, and their brethren said to them, "What *is* your *report?*"

⁹So they said, "Arise, let us go up against them. For we have seen the land, and indeed it *is* very good. *Would* you *do* nothing? Do not hesitate to go, *and* enter to possess the land. ¹⁰When you go, you will come to a secure people and a large land. For God has given it into your hands, a place where *there is* no lack of anything that *is* on the earth."

¹¹And six hundred men of the family of the Danites went from there, from Zorah and Eshtaol, armed with weapons of war. ¹²Then they went up and encamped in Kirjath Jearim in Judah. (Therefore they call that place Mahaneh Danᵃ to this day. There *it is,* west of Kirjath Jearim.) ¹³And they passed from there to the mountains of Ephraim, and came to the house of Micah.

¹⁴Then the five men who had gone to spy out the country of Laish answered and said to their brethren, "Do you know that there are in these houses an ephod, household idols, a carved image, and a molded image? Now therefore, consider what you should do." ¹⁵So they turned aside there, and came to the house of the young Levite man—to the house of Micah—and greeted him. ¹⁶The six hundred men armed with their weapons of war, who *were* of the children of Dan, stood by the entrance of the gate. ¹⁷Then the five men who had gone to spy out the land went up. Entering there, they took the carved image, the ephod, the household idols, and the molded image. The priest stood at the entrance of the gate with the six hundred men *who were* armed with weapons of war.

¹⁸When these went into Micah's house and took the carved image, the ephod, the household idols, and the molded image, the priest said to them, "What are you doing?"

¹⁹And they said to him, "Be quiet, put your hand over your mouth, and come with us; be a father and a priest to us. *Is it* better for you to be a priest to the household of one man, or that you be a priest to a tribe and a family in Israel?" ²⁰So

18:7 ᵃFollowing Masoretic Text, Targum, and Vulgate; Septuagint reads *with Syria.* **18:12** ᵃLiterally *Camp of Dan*

the priest's heart was glad; and he took the ephod, the household idols, and the carved image, and took his place among the people.

²¹Then they turned and departed, and put the little ones, the livestock, and the goods in front of them. ²²When they were a good way from the house of Micah, the men who *were* in the houses near Micah's house gathered together and overtook the children of Dan. ²³And they called out to the children of Dan. So they turned around and said to Micah, "What ails you, that you have gathered such a company?"

²⁴So he said, "You have taken away my gods which I made, and the priest, and you have gone away. Now what more do I have? How can you say to me, 'What ails you?' "

²⁵And the children of Dan said to him, "Do not let your voice be heard among us, lest angry men fall upon you, and you lose your life, with the lives of your household!" ²⁶Then the children of Dan went their way. And when Micah saw that they *were* too strong for him, he turned and went back to his house.

DANITES SETTLE IN LAISH

²⁷So they took *the things* Micah had made, and the priest who had belonged to him, and went to Laish, to a people quiet and secure; and they struck them with the edge of the sword and burned the city with fire. ²⁸*There was* no deliverer, because it *was* far from Sidon, and they had no ties with anyone. It was in the valley that belongs to Beth Rehob. So they rebuilt the city and dwelt there. ²⁹And they called the name of the city Dan, after the name of Dan their father, who was born to Israel. However, the name of the city formerly *was* Laish.

³⁰Then the children of Dan set up for themselves the carved image; and Jonathan the son of Gershom, the son of Manasseh,ᵃ and his sons were priests to the tribe of Dan until the day of the captivity of the land. ³¹So they set up for themselves Micah's carved image which he made, all the time that the house of God was in Shiloh.

THE LEVITE'S CONCUBINE

19 And it came to pass in those days, when *there was* no king in Israel, that there was a certain Levite staying in the remote mountains of Ephraim. He took for himself a concubine from Bethlehem in Judah. ²But his concubine played the harlot against him, and went away from him to her father's house at Bethlehem in Judah, and was there four whole months. ³Then her husband arose and went after her, to speak kindly to her *and* bring her back, having his servant and a couple of donkeys with him. So she brought him into her father's house; and when the father of the young woman saw him, he was glad to meet him. ⁴Now his father-in-law, the young woman's father, detained him; and he stayed with him three days. So they ate and drank and lodged there.

⁵Then it came to pass on the fourth day that they arose early in the morning, and he stood to depart; but the young woman's father said to his son-in-law, "Refresh your heart with a morsel of bread, and afterward go your way."

⁶So they sat down, and the two of them ate and drank together. Then the young woman's father said to the man, "Please be content to stay all night, and let your heart be merry." ⁷And when the man stood to depart, his father-in-law urged him; so he lodged there again. ⁸Then he arose early in the morning on the fifth day to depart, but the young woman's father said, "Please refresh your heart." So they delayed until afternoon; and both of them ate.

⁹And when the man stood to depart—he and his concubine and his servant—his father-in-law, the young woman's father, said to him, "Look, the day is now drawing toward evening; please spend the night. See, the day is coming to an end; lodge here, that your heart may be merry. Tomorrow go your way early, so that you may get home."

¹⁰However, the man was not willing to spend that night; so he rose and departed, and came opposite Jebus (that *is,* Jerusalem). With him were the two saddled donkeys; his concubine *was* also with him. ¹¹They *were* near Jebus, and the day was far spent; and the servant said to his master, "Come, please, and let us turn aside into this city of the Jebusites and lodge in it."

¹²But his master said to him, "We will not turn aside here into a city of foreigners, who *are* not of the children of Israel; we will go on to Gibeah." ¹³So he said to his servant, "Come, let us

18:30 ᵃSeptuagint and Vulgate read *Moses.*

draw near to one of these places, and spend the night in Gibeah or in Ramah." ¹⁴And they passed by and went their way; and the sun went down on them near Gibeah, which belongs to Benjamin. ¹⁵They turned aside there to go in to lodge in Gibeah. And when he went in, he sat down in the open square of the city, for no one would take them into *his* house to spend the night.

¹⁶Just then an old man came in from his work in the field at evening, who also *was* from the mountains of Ephraim; he was staying in Gibeah, whereas the men of the place *were* Benjamites. ¹⁷And when he raised his eyes, he saw the traveler in the open square of the city; and the old man said, "Where are you going, and where do you come from?"

¹⁸So he said to him, "We *are* passing from Bethlehem in Judah toward the remote mountains of Ephraim; I *am* from there. I went to Bethlehem in Judah; *now* I am going to the house of the LORD. But there *is* no one who will take me into his house, ¹⁹although we have both straw and fodder for our donkeys, and bread and wine for myself, for your female servant, and for the young man *who is* with your servant; *there is* no lack of anything."

²⁰And the old man said, "Peace *be* with you! However, *let* all your needs *be* my responsibility; only do not spend the night in the open square." ²¹So he brought him into his house, and gave fodder to the donkeys. And they washed their feet, and ate and drank.

Gibeah's Crime

²²As they were enjoying themselves, suddenly certain men of the city, perverted men,ᵃ surrounded the house *and* beat on the door. They spoke to the master of the house, the old man, saying, "Bring out the man who came to your house, that we may know him *carnally!*"

²³But the man, the master of the house, went out to them and said to them, "No, my brethren! I beg you, do not act *so* wickedly! Seeing this man has come into my house, do not commit this outrage. ²⁴Look, *here is* my virgin daughter and *the man'sᵃ* concubine; let me bring them out now. Humble them, and do with them as you please; but to this man do not do such a vile thing!"

²⁵But the men would not heed him. So the man took his concubine and brought *her* out to them. And they knew her and abused her all night until morning; and when the day began to break, they let her go.

²⁶Then the woman came as the day was dawning, and fell down at the door of the man's house where her master *was,* till it was light.

²⁷When her master arose in the morning, and opened the doors of the house and went out to go his way, there was his concubine, fallen *at* the door of the house with her hands on the threshold. ²⁸And he said to her, "Get up and let us be going." But there was no answer. So the man lifted her onto the donkey; and the man got up and went to his place.

²⁹When he entered his house he took a knife, laid hold of his concubine, and divided her into twelve pieces, limb by limb,ᵃ and sent her throughout all the territory of Israel. ³⁰And so it was that all who saw it said, "No such deed has been done or seen from the day that the children of Israel came up from the land of Egypt until this day. Consider it, confer, and speak up!"

Israel's War with the Benjamites

20 So all the children of Israel came out, from Dan to Beersheba, as well as from the land of Gilead, and the congregation gathered together as one man before the LORD at Mizpah. ²And the leaders of all the people, all the tribes of Israel, presented themselves in the assembly of the people of God, four hundred thousand foot soldiers who drew the sword. ³(Now the children of Benjamin heard that the children of Israel had gone up to Mizpah.)

Then the children of Israel said, "Tell *us,* how did this wicked deed happen?"

⁴So the Levite, the husband of the woman who was murdered, answered and said, "My concubine and I went into Gibeah, which belongs to Benjamin, to spend the night. ⁵And the men of Gibeah rose against me, and surrounded the house at night because of me. They intended to kill me, but instead they ravished my concubine so that she died. ⁶So I took hold of my concubine, cut her in pieces, and sent her throughout all the territory of the inheritance of Israel, because

19:22 ᵃLiterally *sons of Belial*   **19:24** ᵃLiterally *his*   **19:29** ᵃLiterally *with her bones*

they committed lewdness and outrage in Israel. ⁷Look! All of you *are* children of Israel; give your advice and counsel here and now!"

⁸So all the people arose as one man, saying, "None *of us* will go to his tent, nor will any turn back to his house; ⁹but now this *is* the thing which we will do to Gibeah: *We will go up* against it by lot. ¹⁰We will take ten men out of *every* hundred throughout all the tribes of Israel, a hundred out of *every* thousand, and a thousand out of *every* ten thousand, to make provisions for the people, that when they come to Gibeah in Benjamin, they may repay all the vileness that they have done in Israel." ¹¹So all the men of Israel were gathered against the city, united together as one man.

¹²Then the tribes of Israel sent men through all the tribe of Benjamin, saying, "What *is* this wickedness that has occurred among you? ¹³Now therefore, deliver up the men, the perverted menᵃ who *are* in Gibeah, that we may put them to death and remove the evil from Israel!" But the children of Benjamin would not listen to the voice of their brethren, the children of Israel. ¹⁴Instead, the children of Benjamin gathered together from their cities to Gibeah, to go to battle against the children of Israel. ¹⁵And from their cities at that time the children of Benjamin numbered twenty-six thousand men who drew the sword, besides the inhabitants of Gibeah, who numbered seven hundred select men. ¹⁶Among all this people *were* seven hundred select men *who were* left-handed; every one could sling a stone at a hair's *breadth* and not miss. ¹⁷Now besides Benjamin, the men of Israel numbered four hundred thousand men who drew the sword; all of these *were* men of war.

¹⁸Then the children of Israel arose and went up to the house of Godᵃ to inquire of God. They said, "Which of us shall go up first to battle against the children of Benjamin?"

The LORD said, "Judah first!"

¹⁹So the children of Israel rose in the morning and encamped against Gibeah. ²⁰And the men of Israel went out to battle against Benjamin, and the men of Israel put themselves in battle array to fight against them at Gibeah. ²¹Then the children of Benjamin came out of Gibeah, and on that day cut down to the ground twenty-two thousand

men of the Israelites. ²²And the people, that is, the men of Israel, encouraged themselves and again formed the battle line at the place where they had put themselves in array on the first day. ²³Then the children of Israel went up and wept before the LORD until evening, and asked counsel of the LORD, saying, "Shall I again draw near for battle against the children of my brother Benjamin?"

And the LORD said, "Go up against him."

²⁴So the children of Israel approached the children of Benjamin on the second day. ²⁵And Benjamin went out against them from Gibeah on the second day, and cut down to the ground eighteen thousand more of the children of Israel; all these drew the sword.

²⁶Then all the children of Israel, that is, all the people, went up and came to the house of Godᵃ and wept. They sat there before the LORD and fasted that day until evening; and they offered burnt offerings and peace offerings before the LORD. ²⁷So the children of Israel inquired of the LORD (the ark of the covenant of God *was* there in those days, ²⁸and Phinehas the son of Eleazar, the son of Aaron, stood before it in those days), saying, "Shall I yet again go out to battle against the children of my brother Benjamin, or shall I cease?"

And the LORD said, "Go up, for tomorrow I will deliver them into your hand."

²⁹Then Israel set men in ambush all around Gibeah. ³⁰And the children of Israel went up against the children of Benjamin on the third day, and put themselves in battle array against Gibeah as at the other times. ³¹So the children of Benjamin went out against the people, *and* were drawn away from the city. They began to strike down *and* kill some of the people, as at the other times, in the highways (one of which goes up to Bethel and the other to Gibeah) and in the field, about thirty men of Israel. ³²And the children of Benjamin said, "They *are* defeated before us, as at first."

But the children of Israel said, "Let us flee and draw them away from the city to the highways." ³³So all the men of Israel rose from their place and put themselves in battle array at Baal Tamar. Then Israel's men in ambush burst forth from

20:13 ᵃLiterally *sons of Belial*   20:18 ᵃOr *Bethel*   20:26 ᵃOr *Bethel* their position in the plain of Geba. ³⁴And ten thousand select men from all Israel came against Gibeah, and the battle was fierce. But *the Benjamites*ᵃ did not know that disaster *was* upon them. ³⁵The LORD defeated Benjamin before Israel. And the children of Israel destroyed that day twenty-five thousand one hundred Benjamites; all these drew the sword.

³⁶So the children of Benjamin saw that they were defeated. The men of Israel had given ground to the Benjamites, because they relied on the men in ambush whom they had set against Gibeah. ³⁷And the men in ambush quickly rushed upon Gibeah; the men in ambush spread out and struck the whole city with the edge of the sword. ³⁸Now the appointed signal between the men of Israel and the men in ambush was that they would make a great cloud of smoke rise up from the city, ³⁹whereupon the men of Israel would turn in battle. Now Benjamin had begun to strike *and* kill about thirty of the men of Israel. For they said, "Surely they are defeated before us, as *in* the first battle." ⁴⁰But when the cloud began to rise from the city in a column of smoke, the Benjamites looked behind them, and there was the whole city going up *in smoke* to heaven. ⁴¹And when the men of Israel turned back, the men of Benjamin panicked, for they saw that disaster had come upon them. ⁴²Therefore they turned *their backs* before the men of Israel in the direction of the wilderness; but the battle overtook them, and whoever *came* out of the cities they destroyed in their midst. ⁴³They surrounded the Benjamites, chased them, *and* easily trampled them down as far as the front of Gibeah toward the east. ⁴⁴And eighteen thousand men of Benjamin fell; all these *were* men of valor. ⁴⁵Then theyᵃ turned and fled toward the wilderness to the rock of Rimmon; and they cut down five thousand of them on the highways. Then they pursued them relentlessly up to Gidom, and killed two thousand of them. ⁴⁶So all who fell of Benjamin that day were twenty-five thousand men who drew the sword; all these *were* men of valor.

⁴⁷But six hundred men turned and fled toward the wilderness to the rock of Rimmon, and they stayed at the rock of Rimmon for four months. ⁴⁸And the men of Israel turned back against the children of Benjamin, and struck them down with the edge of the sword—from *every* city, men and beasts, all who were found. They also set fire to all the cities they came to.

WIVES PROVIDED FOR THE BENJAMITES

21 Now the men of Israel had sworn an oath at Mizpah, saying, "None of us shall give his daughter to Benjamin as a wife." ²Then the people came to the house of God,ᵃ and remained there before God till evening. They lifted up their voices and wept bitterly, ³and said, "O LORD God of Israel, why has this come to pass in Israel, that today there should be one tribe *missing* in Israel?"

⁴So it was, on the next morning, that the people rose early and built an altar there, and offered burnt offerings and peace offerings. ⁵The children of Israel said, "Who *is there* among all the tribes of Israel who did not come up with the assembly to the LORD?" For they had made a great oath concerning anyone who had not come up to the LORD at Mizpah, saying, "He shall surely be put to death." ⁶And the children of Israel grieved for Benjamin their brother, and said, "One tribe is cut off from Israel today. ⁷What shall we do for wives for those who remain, seeing we have sworn by the LORD that we will not give them our daughters as wives?"

⁸And they said, "What one *is there* from the tribes of Israel who did not come up to Mizpah to the LORD?" And, in fact, no one had come to the camp from Jabesh Gilead to the assembly. ⁹For when the people were counted, indeed, not one of the inhabitants of Jabesh Gilead *was* there. ¹⁰So the congregation sent out there twelve thousand of their most valiant men, and commanded them, saying, "Go and strike the inhabitants of Jabesh Gilead with the edge of the sword, including the women and children. ¹¹And this *is* the thing that you shall do: You shall utterly destroy every male, and every woman who has known a man intimately." ¹²So they found among the inhabitants of Jabesh Gilead four hundred young virgins who had not known a man intimately; and they brought them to the camp at Shiloh, which is in the land of Canaan.

¹³Then the whole congregation sent *word* to the children of Benjamin who *were* at the rock of

20:34 ᵃLiterally *they*   **20:45** ᵃSeptuagint reads *the rest.*   **21:2** ᵃOr *Bethel*

Rimmon, and announced peace to them. [14]So Benjamin came back at that time, and they gave them the women whom they had saved alive of the women of Jabesh Gilead; and yet they had not found enough for them.

[15]And the people grieved for Benjamin, because the LORD had made a void in the tribes of Israel.

[16]Then the elders of the congregation said, "What shall we do for wives for those who remain, since the women of Benjamin have been destroyed?" [17]And they said, "*There must be* an inheritance for the survivors of Benjamin, that a tribe may not be destroyed from Israel. [18]However, we cannot give them wives from our daughters, for the children of Israel have sworn an oath, saying, 'Cursed *be* the one who gives a wife to Benjamin.' " [19]Then they said, "In fact, *there is* a yearly feast of the LORD in Shiloh, which *is* north of Bethel, on the east side of the highway that goes up from Bethel to Shechem, and south of Lebonah."

[20]Therefore they instructed the children of Benjamin, saying, "Go, lie in wait in the vineyards, [21]and watch; and just when the daughters of Shiloh come out to perform their dances, then come out from the vineyards, and every man catch a wife for himself from the daughters of Shiloh; then go to the land of Benjamin. [22]Then it shall be, when their fathers or their brothers come to us to complain, that we will say to them, 'Be kind to them for our sakes, because we did not take a wife for any of them in the war; for *it is* not *as though* you have given the *women* to them at this time, making yourselves guilty of your oath.' "

[23]And the children of Benjamin did so; they took enough wives for their number from those who danced, whom they caught. Then they went and returned to their inheritance, and they rebuilt the cities and dwelt in them. [24]So the children of Israel departed from there at that time, every man to his tribe and family; they went out from there, every man to his inheritance.

[25]In those days *there was* no king in Israel; everyone did *what was* right in his own eyes.

IMPACT OF THE BOOK

RUTH

IDEA
God is the ultimate Kinsman-Redeemer who desires to rescue His people and protect them.

MESSAGE
Two beautiful pictures are powerfully displayed in the Book of Ruth: Ruth's devotion to Naomi and her devotion to the God of Israel, despite the dire circumstances. These pictures remind believers how our devotion to Him should sustain us through the deepest valleys. Leaders rise above discouragement and disappointment to trust God for a hopeful future. Boaz, as the kinsman-redeemer, foreshadows Jesus' role as the Kinsman-Redeemer for all humanity. God uses the worst times of our lives to bring us the best and to accomplish His purpose through us.

PEOPLE
Boaz, Chilion, Elimelech, Mahlon, Naomi, Orpah, Ruth

AUTHOR
Though no author is listed, the similarities between this book and Judges, 1 Samuel, and 2 Samuel suggest Samuel as the possible author, which is also supported by Jewish tradition.

CULTURE
During the time of the Judges, Elimelech took his family to the land of Moab, the nation that resulted from the incestuous relationship between Lot and his oldest daughter. Elimelech's sons took pagan wives, a practice forbidden by God. When the men in the family died, the widows were left desperate because they had no means of providing for themselves. Instead of returning to her own family, Ruth pledged her allegiance to Naomi and to the God of Israel. God used the faithfulness of the young Moabitess to accomplish His plan of redemption. Through the line of Boaz and Ruth, King David was born and ultimately, so was Jesus.

TIMELINE
c. 1010–970 BC (during the reign of David)

KEY SCRIPTURE MEMORY VERSES
1:16; 3:11

ELIMELECH'S FAMILY GOES TO MOAB

1 Now it came to pass, in the days when the judges ruled, that there was a famine in the land. And a certain man of Bethlehem, Judah, went to dwell in the country of Moab, he and his wife and his two sons. ²The name of the man *was* Elimelech, the name of his wife *was* Naomi, and the names of his two sons *were* Mahlon and Chilion—Ephrathites of Bethlehem, Judah. And they went to the country of Moab and remained there. ³Then Elimelech, Naomi's husband, died; and she was left, and her two sons. ⁴Now they took wives of the women of Moab: the name of the one *was* Orpah, and the name of the other Ruth. And they dwelt there about ten years. ⁵Then both Mahlon and Chilion also died; so the woman survived her two sons and her husband.

NAOMI RETURNS WITH RUTH

⁶Then she arose with her daughters-in-law that she might return from the country of Moab, for she had heard in the country of Moab that the LORD had visited His people by giving them bread. ⁷Therefore she went out from the place where she was, and her two daughters-in-law with her; and they went on the way to return to the land of Judah. ⁸And Naomi said to her two daughters-in-law, "Go, return each to her mother's house. The LORD deal kindly with you, as you have dealt with the dead and with me. ⁹The LORD grant that you may find rest, each in the house of her husband."

So she kissed them, and they lifted up their voices and wept. ¹⁰And they said to her, "Surely we will return with you to your people."

¹¹But Naomi said, "Turn back, my daughters; why will you go with me? *Are* there still sons in my womb, that they may be your husbands? ¹²Turn back, my daughters, go—for I am too old to have a husband. If I should say I have hope, *if* I should have a husband tonight and should also bear sons, ¹³would you wait for them till they were grown? Would you restrain yourselves from having husbands? No, my daughters; for it grieves me very much for your sakes that the hand of the LORD has gone out against me!"

¹⁴Then they lifted up their voices and wept again; and Orpah kissed her mother-in-law, but Ruth clung to her.

¹⁵And she said, "Look, your sister-in-law has gone back to her people and to her gods; return after your sister-in-law."

¹⁶But Ruth said:

"Entreat me not to leave you,
  Or to turn back from following after you;
  For wherever you go, I will go;
  And wherever you lodge, I will lodge;
  Your people *shall be* my people,
  And your God, my God.
¹⁷Where you die, I will die,
  And there will I be buried.
  The LORD do so to me, and more also,
  If *anything but* death parts you and me."

¹⁸When she saw that she was determined to go with her, she stopped speaking to her.

¹⁹Now the two of them went until they came to Bethlehem. And it happened, when they had come to Bethlehem, that all the city was excited because of them; and the women said, "*Is* this Naomi?"

²⁰But she said to them, "Do not call me Naomi;ᵃ call me Mara,ᵇ for the Almighty has dealt very bitterly with me. ²¹I went out full, and the LORD has brought me home again empty. Why do you call me Naomi, since the LORD has testified against me, and the Almighty has afflicted me?"

²²So Naomi returned, and Ruth the Moabitess her daughter-in-law with her, who returned from the country of Moab. Now they came to Bethlehem at the beginning of barley harvest.

RUTH MEETS BOAZ

2 There was a relative of Naomi's husband, a man of great wealth, of the family of Elimelech. His name *was* Boaz. ²So Ruth the Moabitess said to Naomi, "Please let me go to the field, and glean heads of grain after *him* in whose sight I may find favor."

And she said to her, "Go, my daughter."

³Then she left, and went and gleaned in the

the INFLUENCERS

NAOMI—Virtue in the Face of Adversity

RUTH 1

She began life as *Naomi*, meaning *lovely, my delight,* but she changed her name to *Mara,* meaning *bitterness* when she became a widow and both sons died. She found herself in a strange land and without protector or provider. She chose to go back to her homeland, and she begged her daughters-in-law, Ruth and Orpah, to go back to their respective homelands, as well.

Ruth was willing to give up all she knew from childhood to stay with Naomi, and this causes us to look closely at Naomi's life. Maybe Ruth wasn't *just* drawn to Naomi as her mother-in-law, but to the God Naomi so fervently worshipped. What unfolds is a mentoring relationship and friendship.

Naomi had nothing left to give except love and the wisdom of a godly woman; that was enough for Ruth to follow her to a new home. Naomi's wisdom wasn't based on superstition or stone idols. She talked plainly of the true God; she taught Ruth how to be a virtuous woman. She is an example of how taking care of other peoples' needs can help us through our own pain.

Wise Naomi, led Ruth to the Lord, and was blessed when God provided a husband to Ruth and gave them a son. She was once again *Naomi*. She is a woman whose faith—during years of adversity—and careful teachings exemplify a virtuous woman.

field after the reapers. And she happened to come to the part of the field *belonging* to Boaz, who *was* of the family of Elimelech.

⁴Now behold, Boaz came from Bethlehem, and said to the reapers, "The LORD *be* with you!"

And they answered him, "The LORD bless you!"

⁵Then Boaz said to his servant who was in charge of the reapers, "Whose young woman *is* this?"

⁶So the servant who was in charge of the reapers answered and said, "It *is* the young Moabite woman who came back with Naomi from the country of Moab. ⁷And she said, 'Please let me glean and gather after the reapers among the sheaves.' So she came and has continued from morning until now, though she rested a little in the house."

⁸Then Boaz said to Ruth, "You will listen, my daughter, will you not? Do not go to glean in another field, nor go from here, but stay close by my young women. ⁹*Let* your eyes *be* on the field which they reap, and go after them. Have I not commanded the young men not to touch you? And when you are thirsty, go to the vessels and drink from what the young men have drawn."

¹⁰So she fell on her face, bowed down to the ground, and said to him, "Why have I found favor in your eyes, that you should take notice of me, since I *am* a foreigner?"

¹¹And Boaz answered and said to her, "It has been fully reported to me, all that you have done for your mother-in-law since the death of your husband, and *how* you have left your father and your mother and the land of your birth, and have come to a people whom you did not know before. ¹²The LORD repay your work, and a full reward be given you by the LORD God of Israel, under whose wings you have come for refuge."

¹³Then she said, "Let me find favor in your sight, my lord; for you have comforted me, and have spoken kindly to your maidservant, though I am not like one of your maidservants."

¹⁴Now Boaz said to her at mealtime, "Come

INSIDE *the* INFLUENCERS

RUTH—Virtue and Commitment Above All

RUTH 1:16

Ruth shows us how God uses people to help each other heal and move on. Three deaths left three women without husbands. Naomi urged her daughters-in-law, Ruth and Orpah, to return to their people and their gods. Ruth's famous declaration of "Wherever you go, I will go" (1:16) has been used in wedding ceremonies for centuries as a picture of love's commitment in the midst of difficult circumstances. In that moment, Ruth accepted the God of Israel as her own. This Gentile woman, from the enemy land of Moab, shows us that everyone—regardless of where they grew up, what they believe, or what they did in the past—can come into God's family.

As He did with Rahab, God took a Gentile, called her to faith in Him, and then elevated her to a privileged status in the Messiah's bloodline (Matt. 1:5). What a detailed and powerful picture of His grace and unconditional love.

Boaz was drawn to Ruth because of her reputation as a virtuous woman (3:11). She married Boaz and had a child, Obed. In her love for Naomi, Ruth is described as "better than seven sons"—a high compliment in a culture where sons were highly esteemed (4:15). Ruth was committed to Naomi and Naomi's God; and because of this, their grief was exchanged for joy.

---

here, and eat of the bread, and dip your piece of bread in the vinegar." So she sat beside the reapers, and he passed parched *grain* to her; and she ate and was satisfied, and kept some back. ¹⁵And when she rose up to glean, Boaz commanded his young men, saying, "Let her glean even among the sheaves, and do not reproach her. ¹⁶Also let *grain* from the bundles fall purposely for her; leave *it* that she may glean, and do not rebuke her."

¹⁷So she gleaned in the field until evening, and beat out what she had gleaned, and it was about an ephah of barley. ¹⁸Then she took *it* up and went into the city, and her mother-in-law saw what she had gleaned. So she brought out and gave to her what she had kept back after she had been satisfied.

¹⁹And her mother-in-law said to her, "Where have you gleaned today? And where did you work? Blessed be the one who took notice of you."

So she told her mother-in-law with whom she had worked, and said, "The man's name with whom I worked today *is* Boaz."

²⁰Then Naomi said to her daughter-in-law, "Blessed *be* he of the LORD, who has not forsaken His kindness to the living and the dead!" And Naomi said to her, "This man *is* a relation of ours, one of our close relatives."

²¹Ruth the Moabitess said, "He also said to me, 'You shall stay close by my young men until they have finished all my harvest.'"

²²And Naomi said to Ruth her daughter-in-law, "*It is* good, my daughter, that you go out with his young women, and that people do not meet you in any other field." ²³So she stayed close by the young women of Boaz, to glean until the end of barley harvest and wheat harvest; and she dwelt with her mother-in-law.

RUTH'S REDEMPTION ASSURED

3 Then Naomi her mother-in-law said to her, "My daughter, shall I not seek security for you that it may be well with you? ²Now Boaz, whose young women you were with, *is he* not our relative? In fact, he is winnowing barley tonight at the threshing floor. ³Therefore wash yourself and anoint yourself, put on your *best* garment and go

INSIDE *the* INFLUENCERS

BOAZ—The Definition of a Successful Man

RUTH 2, 3, 4

The Book of Ruth furnishes a panorama of God's sovereignty in everyday life. Boaz, through the providence of God, was Ruth's kinsman redeemer. The kinsman redeemer was the nearest of kin who had the responsibility of redeeming his kinsman's lost opportunities. Although he was not the first in line, he did become her husband. The Lord uses this true story to show us that He is providential in His care of us and that He overcomes obstacles to accomplish His will. Boaz was a godly man who appeared to live his life to bless others, and he is an excellent example of true success. Boaz:

- Was respected by those he worked for and treated them well (2:4)
- Spoke openly of the Lord in his every day speech (2:12)
- Had compassion for those in need (2:14–25)
- Chose a virtuous woman to be his wife. (3:11)
- Was known in the city and respected (4:11)

The gentle, compassionate Boaz is a picture to us of a kind and benevolent God Who personally cares for us and of Christ, our kinsman redeemer Who has bought us out of sin and redeemed us into eternal life: *"In Him we have redemption through His blood, the forgiveness of sins, according to the riches of His grace"* (Eph. 1:7).

down to the threshing floor; *but* do not make yourself known to the man until he has finished eating and drinking. ⁴Then it shall be, when he lies down, that you shall notice the place where he lies; and you shall go in, uncover his feet, and lie down; and he will tell you what you should do."

⁵And she said to her, "All that you say to me I will do."

⁶So she went down to the threshing floor and did according to all that her mother-in-law instructed her. ⁷And after Boaz had eaten and drunk, and his heart was cheerful, he went to lie down at the end of the heap of grain; and she came softly, uncovered his feet, and lay down.

⁸Now it happened at midnight that the man was startled, and turned himself; and there, a woman was lying at his feet. ⁹And he said, "Who are you?"

So she answered, "I *am* Ruth, your maidservant. Take your maidservant under your wing,ᵃ for you are a close relative."

¹⁰Then he said, "Blessed *are* you of the LORD, my daughter! For you have shown more kindness

at the end than at the beginning, in that you did not go after young men, whether poor or rich. ¹¹And now, my daughter, do not fear. I will do for you all that you request, for all the people of my town know that you *are* a virtuous woman. ¹²Now it is true that I *am* a close relative; however, there is a relative closer than I. ¹³Stay this night, and in the morning it shall be *that* if he will perform the duty of a close relative for you—good; let him do it. But if he does not want to perform the duty for you, then I will perform the duty for you, *as* the LORD lives! Lie down until morning."

¹⁴So she lay at his feet until morning, and she arose before one could recognize another. Then he said, "Do not let it be known that the woman came to the threshing floor." ¹⁵Also he said, "Bring the shawl that *is* on you and hold it." And when she held it, he measured six *ephahs* of barley, and laid *it* on her. Then sheᵃ went into the city.

3:9 ᵃOr *Spread the corner of your garment over your maidservant*
3:15 ᵃMany Hebrew manuscripts, Syriac, and Vulgate read *she;* Masoretic Text, Septuagint, and Targum read *he.*

¹⁶When she came to her mother-in-law, she said, "*Is* that you, my daughter?"

Then she told her all that the man had done for her. ¹⁷And she said, "These six *ephahs* of barley he gave me; for he said to me, 'Do not go empty-handed to your mother-in-law.' "

¹⁸Then she said, "Sit still, my daughter, until you know how the matter will turn out; for the man will not rest until he has concluded the matter this day."

Boaz Redeems Ruth

4 Now Boaz went up to the gate and sat down there; and behold, the close relative of whom Boaz had spoken came by. So Boaz said, "Come aside, friend,^a sit down here." So he came aside and sat down. ²And he took ten men of the elders of the city, and said, "Sit down here." So they sat down. ³Then he said to the close relative, "Naomi, who has come back from the country of Moab, sold the piece of land which *belonged* to our brother Elimelech. ⁴And I thought to inform you, saying, 'Buy *it* back in the presence of the inhabitants and the elders of my people. If you will redeem *it*, redeem *it*; but if you^a will not redeem *it, then* tell me, that I may know; for *there is* no one but you to redeem *it*, and I *am* next after you.' "

And he said, "I will redeem *it*."

⁵Then Boaz said, "On the day you buy the field from the hand of Naomi, you must also buy *it* from Ruth the Moabitess, the wife of the dead, to perpetuate^a the name of the dead through his inheritance."

⁶And the close relative said, "I cannot redeem *it* for myself, lest I ruin my own inheritance. You redeem my right of redemption for yourself, for I cannot redeem *it*."

⁷Now this *was the custom* in former times in Israel concerning redeeming and exchanging, to confirm anything: one man took off his sandal and gave *it* to the other, and this *was* a confirmation in Israel.

⁸Therefore the close relative said to Boaz, "Buy *it* for yourself." So he took off his sandal.

⁹And Boaz said to the elders and all the people,

"You *are* witnesses this day that I have bought all that was Elimelech's, and all that *was* Chilion's and Mahlon's, from the hand of Naomi. ¹⁰Moreover, Ruth the Moabitess, the widow of Mahlon, I have acquired as my wife, to perpetuate the name of the dead through his inheritance, that the name of the dead may not be cut off from among his brethren and from his position at the gate.^a You *are* witnesses this day."

¹¹And all the people who *were* at the gate, and the elders, said, "*We are* witnesses. The LORD make the woman who is coming to your house like Rachel and Leah, the two who built the house of Israel; and may you prosper in Ephrathah and be famous in Bethlehem. ¹²May your house be like the house of Perez, whom Tamar bore to Judah, because of the offspring which the LORD will give you from this young woman."

Descendants of Boaz and Ruth

¹³So Boaz took Ruth and she became his wife; and when he went in to her, the LORD gave her conception, and she bore a son. ¹⁴Then the women said to Naomi, "Blessed *be* the LORD, who has not left you this day without a close relative; and may his name be famous in Israel! ¹⁵And may he be to you a restorer of life and a nourisher of your old age; for your daughter-in-law, who loves you, who is better to you than seven sons, has borne him." ¹⁶Then Naomi took the child and laid him on her bosom, and became a nurse to him. ¹⁷Also the neighbor women gave him a name, saying, "There is a son born to Naomi." And they called his name Obed. He *is* the father of Jesse, the father of David.

¹⁸Now this *is* the genealogy of Perez: Perez begot Hezron; ¹⁹Hezron begot Ram, and Ram begot Amminadab; ²⁰Amminadab begot Nahshon, and Nahshon begot Salmon;^a ²¹Salmon begot Boaz, and Boaz begot Obed; ²²Obed begot Jesse, and Jesse begot David.

4:1 ^aHebrew *peloni almoni;* literally *so and so*   **4:4** ^aFollowing many Hebrew manuscripts, Septuagint, Syriac, Targum, and Vulgate; Masoretic Text reads *he.*   **4:5** ^aLiterally *raise up*   **4:10** ^aProbably his civic office   **4:20** ^aHebrew *Salmah*

IMPACT OF THE BOOK

IDEA | *Human ability can never serve as a substitute for the power of God in a person's life.*

MESSAGE | *Saul sacrificed his leadership when he let the voice of the people become louder than the voice of God. His life illustrates that it's not how you start, but how you finish that counts. Two sins cost him the kingdom: presumption and incomplete obedience. Social position, physical stature, religious notoriety, and age will never guarantee the success of a leader. Leadership lessons: spiritual leadership is to be preferred over cunning and cleverness; it must never be used for personal gain or for power or fame.*

PEOPLE | *Abigail, David, David's mighty men, Eli, Goliath, Hannah, Jonathan, Samuel, Saul*

AUTHOR | *Originally one book in the Hebrew tradition, the authorship of 1 and 2 Samuel is attributed to the prophet Samuel. It is more likely that a later historian or editor used written records from Samuel and Nathan to compile 1 and 2 Samuel.*

CULTURE | *First Samuel spans over one hundred years, recording the events from the end of the time of the judges to the death of King Saul. Israel's weakened state, the weak leadership of Saul, and war with the Philistines set off a chain of events that revealed David's character and prepared him for the throne. Three interesting men (Samuel, Saul, and David) are the focus of the Book, but the story of Hannah testifies that one person's persistence can change the course of an entire people.*

TIMELINE | *c. 970–722 BC (sometime between the death of David and the Assyrian captivity)*

EY SCRIPTURE **MORY VERSES** | 15:22; 16:7; 17:45

FIRST SAMUEL

The Family of Elkanah

1 Now there was a certain man of Ramathaim Zophim, of the mountains of Ephraim, and his name *was* Elkanah the son of Jeroham, the son of Elihu,[a] the son of Tohu,[b] the son of Zuph, an Ephraimite. ²And he had two wives: the name of one *was* Hannah, and the name of the other Peninnah. Peninnah had children, but Hannah had no children. ³This man went up from his city yearly to worship and sacrifice to the LORD of hosts in Shiloh. Also the two sons of Eli, Hophni and Phinehas, the priests of the LORD, *were* there. ⁴And whenever the time came for Elkanah to make an offering, he would give portions to Peninnah his wife and to all her sons and daughters. ⁵But to Hannah he would give a double portion, for he loved Hannah, although the LORD had closed her womb. ⁶And her rival also provoked her severely, to make her miserable, because the LORD had closed her womb. ⁷So it was, year by year, when she went up to the house of the LORD, that she provoked her; therefore she wept and did not eat.

Hannah's Vow

⁸Then Elkanah her husband said to her, "Hannah, why do you weep? Why do you not eat? And why is your heart grieved? *Am* I not better to you than ten sons?"

⁹So Hannah arose after they had finished eating and drinking in Shiloh. Now Eli the priest was sitting on the seat by the doorpost of the tabernacle[a] of the LORD. ¹⁰And she *was* in bitterness of soul, and prayed to the LORD and wept in anguish. ¹¹Then she made a vow and said, "O LORD of hosts, if You will indeed look on the affliction of Your maidservant and remember me, and not forget Your maidservant, but will give Your maidservant a male child, then I will give him to the LORD all the days of his life, and no razor shall come upon his head."

¹²And it happened, as she continued praying before the LORD, that Eli watched her mouth. ¹³Now Hannah spoke in her heart; only her lips moved, but her voice was not heard. Therefore Eli thought she was drunk. ¹⁴So Eli said to her, "How long will you be drunk? Put your wine away from you!"

¹⁵But Hannah answered and said, "No, my lord, I *am* a woman of sorrowful spirit. I have drunk neither wine nor intoxicating drink, but have poured out my soul before the LORD. ¹⁶Do not consider your maidservant a wicked woman,[a] for out of the abundance of my complaint and grief I have spoken until now."

¹⁷Then Eli answered and said, "Go in peace, and the God of Israel grant your petition which you have asked of Him."

¹⁸And she said, "Let your maidservant find favor in your sight." So the woman went her way and ate, and her face was no longer *sad*.

Samuel Is Born and Dedicated

¹⁹Then they rose early in the morning and worshiped before the LORD, and returned and came to their house at Ramah. And Elkanah knew Hannah his wife, and the LORD remembered her. ²⁰So it came to pass in the process of time that Hannah conceived and bore a son, and called his name Samuel,[a] *saying*, "Because I have asked for him from the LORD."

²¹Now the man Elkanah and all his house went up to offer to the LORD the yearly sacrifice and his vow. ²²But Hannah did not go up, for she said to her husband, "*Not* until the child is weaned; then I will take him, that he may appear before the LORD and remain there forever."

²³So Elkanah her husband said to her, "Do what seems best to you; wait until you have weaned him. Only let the LORD establish His[ʳ] word." Then the woman stayed and nursed her son until she had weaned him.

²⁴Now when she had weaned him, she took him up with her, with three bulls,[a] one ephah of flour, and a skin of wine, and brought him to the house of the LORD in Shiloh. And the child *was* young. ²⁵Then they slaughtered a bull, and brought the child to Eli. ²⁶And she said, "O my lord! As your soul lives, my lord, I *am* the woman who stood by you here, praying to the LORD. ²⁷For this child I prayed, and the LORD has

1:1 ᵃSpelled *Eliel* in 1 Chronicles 6:34 ᵇSpelled *Toah* in 1 Chronicles 6:34   1:9 ᵃHebrew *heykal*, palace or temple   1:16 ᵃLiterally *daughter of Belial*   1:20 ᵃLiterally *Heard by God*   1:23 ᵃFollowing Masoretic Text, Targum, and Vulgate; Dead Sea Scrolls, Septuagint, and Syriac read *your*.   1:24 ᵃDead Sea Scrolls, Septuagint, and Syriac read *a three-year-old bull.*   —

granted me my petition which I asked of Him. [28]Therefore I also have lent him to the LORD; as long as he lives he shall be lent to the LORD." So they worshiped the LORD there.

HANNAH'S PRAYER

2 And Hannah prayed and said:

"My heart rejoices in the LORD;
My horn[a] is exalted in the LORD.
I smile at my enemies,
Because I rejoice in Your salvation.

[2]"No one is holy like the LORD,
For *there is* none besides You,
Nor *is there* any rock like our God.

[3]"Talk no more so very proudly;
Let no arrogance come from your mouth,
For the LORD *is* the God of knowledge;
And by Him actions are weighed.

[4]"The bows of the mighty men *are* broken,
And those who stumbled are girded with
strength.
[5]*Those who were* full have hired themselves out
for bread,
And the hungry have ceased *to hunger.*
Even the barren has borne seven,
And she who has many children has become
feeble.

[6]"The LORD kills and makes alive;
He brings down to the grave and brings up.
[7]The LORD makes poor and makes rich;
He brings low and lifts up.
[8]He raises the poor from the dust
And lifts the beggar from the ash heap,
To set *them* among princes
And make them inherit the throne of glory.

"For the pillars of the earth *are* the LORD's,
And He has set the world upon them.
[9]He will guard the feet of His saints,
But the wicked shall be silent in darkness.

"For by strength no man shall prevail.
[10]The adversaries of the LORD shall be broken
in pieces;

From heaven He will thunder against them.
The LORD will judge the ends of the earth.

"He will give strength to His king,
And exalt the horn of His anointed."

[11]Then Elkanah went to his house at Ramah. But the child ministered to the LORD before Eli the priest.

THE WICKED SONS OF ELI

[12]Now the sons of Eli *were* corrupt;[a] they did not know the LORD. [13]And the priests' custom with the people *was that* when any man offered a sacrifice, the priest's servant would come with a three-pronged fleshhook in his hand while the meat was boiling. [14]Then he would thrust *it* into the pan, or kettle, or caldron, or pot; and the priest would take for himself all that the fleshhook brought up. So they did in Shiloh to all the Israelites who came there. [15]Also, before they burned the fat, the priest's servant would come and say to the man who sacrificed, "Give meat for roasting to the priest, for he will not take boiled meat from you, but raw."

[16]And *if* the man said to him, "They should really burn the fat first; *then* you may take *as much* as your heart desires," he would then answer him, "*No,* but you must give *it* now; and if not, I will take *it* by force."

[17]Therefore the sin of the young men was very great before the LORD, for men abhorred the offering of the LORD.

SAMUEL'S CHILDHOOD MINISTRY

[18]But Samuel ministered before the LORD, *even as* a child, wearing a linen ephod. [19]Moreover his mother used to make him a little robe, and bring *it* to him year by year when she came up with her husband to offer the yearly sacrifice. [20]And Eli would bless Elkanah and his wife, and say, "The LORD give you descendants from this woman for the loan that was given to the LORD." Then they would go to their own home.

[21]And the LORD visited Hannah, so that she conceived and bore three sons and two daughters. Meanwhile the child Samuel grew before the LORD.

2:1 [a]That is, strength   **2:12** [a]Literally *sons of Belial*

the INFLUENCERS

HANNAH: Abandon Your Will to His

1 SAMUEL 1

In Hannah's day, a woman's worth was measured by her ability to have children, most especially sons. Hannah's husband loved her dearly in spite of her barrenness, but he allowed her rival, Peninnah, who was already a mother, to belittle her. Hannah felt cursed and rejected, which wasn't true; but she still became deeply depressed.

After years of praying at the temple, Hannah finally surrendered the terms of her life to God. God gave her peace before she even knew He was about to answer her in a better way than she could have imagined. She **worshipped** the Lord (1:7), abandoned her own will (11), and changed her thinking patterns, which changed her life (1:18). The Lord answered her prayer with the birth of Samuel; and Hannah brought him to Eli the priest, giving him back to God just the way she promised.

As a child, Samuel heard God speak to him at the shrine in Shiloh. As an adult, he helped unite Israel against the growing threat of the *Philistines*. Samuel anointed Saul as king of Israel (1 Sam. 10:1–8), and later went to Bethlehem to anoint *David* as Saul's successor (1 Sam. 16:1–13). The Lord continued to bless Hannah, who conceived and bore three sons and two daughters (1 Sam. 2:21).

PROPHECY AGAINST ELI'S HOUSEHOLD

22Now Eli was very old; and he heard everything his sons did to all Israel,[a] and how they lay with the women who assembled at the door of the tabernacle of meeting. 23So he said to them, "Why do you do such things? For I hear of your evil dealings from all the people. 24No, my sons! For *it is* not a good report that I hear. You make the LORD's people transgress. 25If one man sins against another, God will judge him. But if a man sins against the LORD, who will intercede for him?" Nevertheless they did not heed the voice of their father, because the LORD desired to kill them.

26And the child Samuel grew in stature, and in favor both with the LORD and men.

27Then a man of God came to Eli and said to him, "Thus says the LORD: 'Did I not clearly reveal Myself to the house of your father when they were in Egypt in Pharaoh's house? 28Did I not choose him out of all the tribes of Israel *to be* My priest, to offer upon My altar, to burn incense, and to wear an ephod before Me? And did I not give to the house of your father all the offerings of the children of Israel made by fire? 29Why do you kick at My sacrifice and My offering which I have commanded *in My* dwelling place, and honor your sons more than Me, to make yourselves fat with the best of all the offerings of Israel My people?' 30Therefore the LORD God of Israel says: 'I said indeed *that* your house and the house of your father would walk before Me forever.' But now the LORD says: 'Far be it from Me; for those who honor Me I will honor, and those who despise Me shall be lightly esteemed. 31Behold, the days are coming that I will cut off your arm and the arm of your father's house, so that there will not be an old man in your house. 32And you will see an enemy *in My* dwelling place, *despite* all the good which God does for Israel. And there shall not be an old man in your house forever. 33But any of your men *whom* I do not cut off from My altar shall consume your eyes and grieve your heart. And all the descendants of your house shall die in the flower of their age. 34Now this *shall be* a sign to you that

2:22 aFollowing Masoretic Text, Targum, and Vulgate; Dead Sea Scrolls and Septuagint omit the rest of this verse.

will come upon your two sons, on Hophni and Phinehas: in one day they shall die, both of them. [35]Then I will raise up for Myself a faithful priest *who* shall do according to what *is* in My heart and in My mind. I will build him a sure house, and he shall walk before My anointed forever. [36]And it shall come to pass that everyone who is left in your house will come *and* bow down to him for a piece of silver and a morsel of bread, and say, "Please, put me in one of the priestly positions, that I may eat a piece of bread." ' "

Samuel's First Prophecy

3 Now the boy Samuel ministered to the LORD before Eli. And the word of the LORD was rare in those days; *there was* no widespread revelation. [2]And it came to pass at that time, while Eli *was* lying down in his place, and when his eyes had begun to grow so dim that he could not see, [3]and before the lamp of God went out in the tabernacle[a] of the LORD where the ark of God *was,* and while Samuel was lying down, [4]that the LORD called Samuel. And he answered, "Here I am!" [5]So he ran to Eli and said, "Here I am, for you called me."

And he said, "I did not call; lie down again." And he went and lay down.

[6]Then the LORD called yet again, "Samuel!"

So Samuel arose and went to Eli, and said, "Here I am, for you called me." He answered, "I did not call, my son; lie down again." [7](Now Samuel did not yet know the LORD, nor was the word of the LORD yet revealed to him.)

[8]And the LORD called Samuel again the third time. So he arose and went to Eli, and said, "Here I am, for you did call me."

Then Eli perceived that the LORD had called the boy. [9]Therefore Eli said to Samuel, "Go, lie down; and it shall be, if He calls you, that you must say, 'Speak, LORD, for Your servant hears.' " So Samuel went and lay down in his place.

[10]Now the LORD came and stood and called as at other times, "Samuel! Samuel!"

And Samuel answered, "Speak, for Your servant hears."

[11]Then the LORD said to Samuel: "Behold, I will do something in Israel at which both ears of everyone who hears it will tingle. [12]In that day I will perform against Eli all that I have spoken concerning his house, from beginning to end.

[13]For I have told him that I will judge his house forever for the iniquity which he knows, because his sons made themselves vile, and he did not restrain them. [14]And therefore I have sworn to the house of Eli that the iniquity of Eli's house shall not be atoned for by sacrifice or offering forever."

[15]So Samuel lay down until morning,[a] and opened the doors of the house of the LORD. And Samuel was afraid to tell Eli the vision. [16]Then Eli called Samuel and said, "Samuel, my son!"

He answered, "Here I am."

[17]And he said, "What *is* the word that *the LORD* spoke to you? Please do not hide *it* from me. God do so to you, and more also, if you hide anything from me of all the things that He said to you." [18]Then Samuel told him everything, and hid nothing from him. And he said, "It *is* the LORD. Let Him do what seems good to Him."

[19]So Samuel grew, and the LORD was with him and let none of his words fall to the ground. [20]And all Israel from Dan to Beersheba knew that Samuel *had been* established as a prophet of the LORD. [21]Then the LORD appeared again in Shiloh. For the LORD revealed Himself to Samuel in Shiloh by the word of the LORD.

4 And the word of Samuel came to all Israel.[a]

The Ark of God Captured

Now Israel went out to battle against the Philistines, and encamped beside Ebenezer; and the Philistines encamped in Aphek. [2]Then the Philistines put themselves in battle array against Israel. And when they joined battle, Israel was defeated by the Philistines, who killed about four thousand men of the army in the field. [3]And when the people had come into the camp, the elders of Israel said, "Why has the LORD defeated us today before the Philistines? Let us bring the ark of the covenant of the LORD from Shiloh to us, that when it comes among us it may save us from the hand of our enemies." [4]So the people sent to Shiloh, that they might bring from there

3:3 [a]Hebrew *heykal,* palace or temple   **3:15** [a]Following Masoretic Text, Targum, and Vulgate; Septuagint adds *and he arose in the morning.*   **4:1** [a]Following Masoretic Text and Targum; Septuagint and Vulgate add *And it came to pass in those days that the Philistines gathered themselves together to fight;* Septuagint adds further *against Israel.*

LEADERSHIP ISSUES

GC2: Listening: Listening for the Lord

1 SAMUEL 3:10

Imagine you show up at your parents' house and say to mom or dad, "I've realized I have not been listening to you as much as I need to—could we plan some time where I just listen to your advice?" No really, imagine it! After your parents recovered from the shock, I'm sure they would be grateful and blessed that you wanted to listen to them.

This human "fantasy" helps us understand how our listening to the Lord "serves" or "ministers" to Him. God is blessed that we want to hear from Him. Setting aside time to listen as part of our Bible reading, prayer, and meditation gives Jesus opportunity to speak to us (see John 10:1–5). It's during such "vertical" times of listening to the Lord that we learn the critical principles for listening "horizontally" to others—friends, family, loved ones, etc.

Listening requires:

- humility, admitting we're needful of others;
- thinking of someone else;
- giving undivided attention.

Christ's followers give priority to the "ministry" of listening!

GC2
GREAT COMMANDMENT
COMMISSION

the ark of the covenant of the LORD of hosts, who dwells *between* the cherubim. And the two sons of Eli, Hophni and Phinehas, *were* there with the ark of the covenant of God.

⁵And when the ark of the covenant of the LORD came into the camp, all Israel shouted so loudly that the earth shook. ⁶Now when the Philistines heard the noise of the shout, they said, "What *does* the sound of this great shout in the camp of the Hebrews *mean?*" Then they understood that the ark of the LORD had come into the camp. ⁷So the Philistines were afraid, for they said, "God has come into the camp!" And they said, "Woe to us! For such a thing has never happened before. ⁸Woe to us! Who will deliver us from the hand of these mighty gods? These *are* the gods who struck the Egyptians with all the plagues in the wilderness. ⁹Be strong and conduct yourselves like men, you Philistines, that you do not become servants of the Hebrews, as they have been to you. Conduct yourselves like men, and fight!"

¹⁰So the Philistines fought, and Israel was defeated, and every man fled to his tent. There was a very great slaughter, and there fell of Israel thirty thousand foot soldiers. ¹¹Also the ark of God was captured; and the two sons of Eli, Hophni and Phinehas, died.

Death of Eli

¹²Then a man of Benjamin ran from the battle line the same day, and came to Shiloh with his clothes torn and dirt on his head. ¹³Now when he came, there was Eli, sitting on a seat by the wayside watching,ᵃ for his heart trembled for the ark of God. And when the man came into the city and told *it,* all the city cried out. ¹⁴When Eli heard the noise of the outcry, he said, "What *does* the sound of this tumult *mean?*" And the man came quickly and told Eli. ¹⁵Eli was ninety-eight years old, and his eyes were so dim that he could not see.

¹⁶Then the man said to Eli, "I *am* he who came from the battle. And I fled today from the battle line."

And he said, "What happened, my son?"

¹⁷So the messenger answered and said, "Israel has fled before the Philistines, and there has been a great slaughter among the people. Also your two sons, Hophni and Phinehas, are dead; and the ark of God has been captured."

¹⁸Then it happened, when he made mention of the ark of God, that Eli fell off the seat backward by the side of the gate; and his neck was broken and he died, for the man was old and heavy. And he had judged Israel forty years.

Ichabod

¹⁹Now his daughter-in-law, Phinehas' wife, was with child, *due* to be delivered; and when she heard the news that the ark of God was captured, and that her father-in-law and her husband were dead, she bowed herself and gave birth, for her labor pains came upon her. ²⁰And about the time of her death the women who stood by her said to her, "Do not fear, for you have borne a son." But she did not answer, nor did she regard *it.* ²¹Then she named the child Ichabod,ᵃ saying, "The glory has departed from Israel!" because the ark of God had been captured and because of her father-in-law and her husband. ²²And she said, "The glory has departed from Israel, for the ark of God has been captured."

The Philistines and the Ark

5 Then the Philistines took the ark of God and brought it from Ebenezer to Ashdod. ²When the Philistines took the ark of God, they brought it into the house of Dagonᵃ and set it by Dagon. ³And when the people of Ashdod arose early in the morning, there was Dagon, fallen on its face to the earth before the ark of the LORD. So they took Dagon and set it in its place again. ⁴And when they arose early the next morning, there was Dagon, fallen on its face to the ground before the ark of the LORD. The head of Dagon and both the palms of its hands *were* broken off on the threshold; only Dagon's torsoᵃ was left of it. ⁵Therefore neither the priests of Dagon nor any who come into Dagon's house tread on the threshold of Dagon in Ashdod to this day.

⁶But the hand of the LORD was heavy on the people of Ashdod, and He ravaged them and struck them with tumors,ᵃ *both* Ashdod and its territory. ⁷And when the men of Ashdod saw

4:13 ᵃFollowing Masoretic Text and Vulgate; Septuagint reads *beside the gate watching the road.* **4:21** ᵃLiterally *Inglorious* **5:2** ᵃA Philistine idol **5:4** ᵃFollowing Septuagint, Syriac, Targum, and Vulgate; Masoretic Text reads *Dagon.* **5:6** ᵃProbably bubonic plague. Septuagint and Vulgate add here *And in the midst of their land rats sprang up, and there was a great death panic in the city.*

how *it was,* they said, "The ark of the God of Israel must not remain with us, for His hand is harsh toward us and Dagon our god." [8]Therefore they sent and gathered to themselves all the lords of the Philistines, and said, "What shall we do with the ark of the God of Israel?"

And they answered, "Let the ark of the God of Israel be carried away to Gath." So they carried the ark of the God of Israel away. [9]So it was, after they had carried it away, that the hand of the LORD was against the city with a very great destruction; and He struck the men of the city, both small and great, and tumors broke out on them.

[10]Therefore they sent the ark of God to Ekron. So it was, as the ark of God came to Ekron, that the Ekronites cried out, saying, "They have brought the ark of the God of Israel to us, to kill us and our people!" [11]So they sent and gathered together all the lords of the Philistines, and said, "Send away the ark of the God of Israel, and let it go back to its own place, so that it does not kill us and our people." For there was a deadly destruction throughout all the city; the hand of God was very heavy there. [12]And the men who did not die were stricken with the tumors, and the cry of the city went up to heaven.

THE ARK RETURNED TO ISRAEL

6 Now the ark of the LORD was in the country of the Philistines seven months. [2]And the Philistines called for the priests and the diviners, saying, "What shall we do with the ark of the LORD? Tell us how we should send it to its place."

[3]So they said, "If you send away the ark of the God of Israel, do not send it empty; but by all means return *it* to Him *with* a trespass offering. Then you will be healed, and it will be known to you why His hand is not removed from you."

[4]Then they said, "What *is* the trespass offering which we shall return to Him?"

They answered, "Five golden tumors and five golden rats, *according to* the number of the lords of the Philistines. For the same plague *was* on all of you and on your lords. [5]Therefore you shall make images of your tumors and images of your rats that ravage the land, and you shall give glory to the God of Israel; perhaps He will lighten His hand from you, from your gods, and

from your land. [6]Why then do you harden your hearts as the Egyptians and Pharaoh hardened their hearts? When He did mighty things among them, did they not let the people go, that they might depart? [7]Now therefore, make a new cart, take two milk cows which have never been yoked, and hitch the cows to the cart; and take their calves home, away from them. [8]Then take the ark of the LORD and set it on the cart; and put the articles of gold which you are returning to Him *as* a trespass offering in a chest by its side. Then send it away, and let it go. [9]And watch: if it goes up the road to its own territory, to Beth Shemesh, *then* He has done us this great evil. But if not, then we shall know that *it is* not His hand *that* struck us—it happened to us by chance."

[10]Then the men did so; they took two milk cows and hitched them to the cart, and shut up their calves at home. [11]And they set the ark of the LORD on the cart, and the chest with the gold rats and the images of their tumors. [12]Then the cows headed straight for the road to Beth Shemesh, *and* went along the highway, lowing as they went, and did not turn aside to the right hand or the left. And the lords of the Philistines went after them to the border of Beth Shemesh.

[13]Now *the people of* Beth Shemesh *were* reaping their wheat harvest in the valley; and they lifted their eyes and saw the ark, and rejoiced to see *it.* [14]Then the cart came into the field of Joshua of Beth Shemesh, and stood there; a large stone *was* there. So they split the wood of the cart and offered the cows as a burnt offering to the LORD. [15]The Levites took down the ark of the LORD and the chest that *was* with it, in which *were* the articles of gold, and put *them* on the large stone. Then the men of Beth Shemesh offered burnt offerings and made sacrifices the same day to the LORD. [16]So when the five lords of the Philistines had seen *it,* they returned to Ekron same day.

[17]These *are* the golden tumors which the Philistines returned *as* a trespass offering to the LORD: one for Ashdod, one for Gaza, one for Ashkelon, one for Gath, one for Ekron; [18]and the golden rats, *according to* the number of all the cities of the Philistines *belonging* to the five lords, *both* fortified cities and country villages, even as far as

the large *stone of* Abel on which they set the ark of the LORD, *which stone remains* to this day in the field of Joshua of Beth Shemesh.

[19]Then He struck the men of Beth Shemesh, because they had looked into the ark of the LORD. He struck fifty thousand and seventy men[a] of the people, and the people lamented because the LORD had struck the people with a great slaughter.

The Ark at Kirjath Jearim

[20]And the men of Beth Shemesh said, "Who is able to stand before this holy LORD God? And to whom shall it go up from us?" [21]So they sent messengers to the inhabitants of Kirjath Jearim, saying, "The Philistines have brought back the ark of the LORD; come down *and* take it up with you."

7Then the men of Kirjath Jearim came and took the ark of the LORD, and brought it into the house of Abinadab on the hill, and consecrated Eleazar his son to keep the ark of the LORD.

Samuel Judges Israel

[2]So it was that the ark remained in Kirjath Jearim a long time; it was there twenty years. And all the house of Israel lamented after the LORD.

[3]Then Samuel spoke to all the house of Israel, saying, "If you return to the LORD with all your hearts, *then* put away the foreign gods and the Ashtoreths[a] from among you, and prepare your hearts for the LORD, and serve Him only; and He will deliver you from the hand of the Philistines." [4]So the children of Israel put away the Baals and the Ashtoreths,[a] and served LORD only.

[5]And Samuel said, "Gather all Israel to Mizpah, and I will pray to the LORD for you." [6]So they gathered together at Mizpah, drew water, and poured *it* out before the LORD. And they fasted that day, and said there, "We have sinned against the LORD." And Samuel judged the children of Israel at Mizpah.

[7]Now when the Philistines heard that the children of Israel had gathered together at Mizpah, the lords of the Philistines went up against Israel. And when the children of Israel heard *of it,* they were afraid of the Philistines. [8]So the children of Israel said to Samuel, "Do not cease to cry

out to the LORD our God for us, that He may save us from the hand of the Philistines."

[9]And Samuel took a suckling lamb and offered *it as* a whole burnt offering to the LORD. Then Samuel cried out to the LORD for Israel, and the LORD answered him. [10]Now as Samuel was offering up the burnt offering, the Philistines drew near to battle against Israel. But the LORD thundered with a loud thunder upon the Philistines that day, and so confused them that they were overcome before Israel. [11]And the men of Israel went out of Mizpah and pursued the Philistines, and drove them back as far as below Beth Car. [12]Then Samuel took a stone and set *it* up between Mizpah and Shen, and called its name Ebenezer,[a] saying, "Thus far the LORD has helped us."

[13]So the Philistines were subdued, and they did not come anymore into the territory of Israel. And the hand of the LORD was against the Philistines all the days of Samuel. [14]Then the cities which the Philistines had taken from Israel were restored to Israel, from Ekron to Gath; and Israel recovered its territory from the hands of the Philistines. Also there was peace between Israel and the Amorites.

[15]And Samuel judged Israel all the days of his life. [16]He went from year to year on a circuit to Bethel, Gilgal, and Mizpah, and judged Israel in all those places. [17]But he always returned to Ramah, for his home *was* there. There he judged Israel, and there he built an altar to the LORD.

Israel Demands a King

8Now it came to pass when Samuel was old that he made his sons judges over Israel. [2]The name of his firstborn was Joel, and the name of his second, Abijah; *they were* judges in Beersheba. [3]But his sons did not walk in his ways; they turned aside after dishonest gain, took bribes, and perverted justice.

[4]Then all the elders of Israel gathered together and came to Samuel at Ramah, [5]and said to him, "Look, you are old, and your sons do not walk in your ways. Now make us a king to judge us like all the nations."

6:19 [a]Or *He struck seventy men of the people and fifty oxen of a man*   **7:3** [a]Canaanite goddesses   **7:4** [a]Canaanite goddesses   **7:12** [a]Literally *Stone of Help*

the INFLUENCERS

SAMUEL: Success vs. Obedience

1 SAMUEL 8:1–3

Samuel is an important figure in Christian history. He lived in a time of great transition in the nation of Israel. He was the last of the judges and the first of the prophets; he was a priest, a military leader, a "seer," a counselor to the king, and a father. His leadership is best defined by one word: obedience.

Samuel served the Lord faithfully for his entire life, and in his old age, the people began to clamor for a king. The prophet knew that Israel did NOT need a king, but he was obedient when God told him to appoint Saul as their new leader. Sometimes the Lord allows us to see that the thing we so desperately want is inferior next to His chosen blessing.

But as king, Saul proved to be more interested in success than faithfulness, and God allowed the obedient and humble Samuel to inform him that his rule would not last (13:13, 14). Instead, God chose David, the son of Jesse, to lead Israel. Samuel had the dangerous task of anointing David as God's chosen while Saul still occupied the throne.

Unlike Saul, Samuel was more interested in honoring God than building a reputation for himself. He demonstrated consistent obedience, regardless of his circumstances.

⁶But the thing displeased Samuel when they said, "Give us a king to judge us." So Samuel prayed to the LORD. ⁷And the LORD said to Samuel, "Heed the voice of the people in all that they say to you; for they have not rejected you, but they have rejected Me, that I should not reign over them. ⁸According to all the works which they have done since the day that I brought them up out of Egypt, even to this day—with which they have forsaken Me and served other gods—so they are doing to you also. ⁹Now therefore, heed their voice. However, you shall solemnly forewarn them, and show them the behavior of the king who will reign over them."

¹⁰So Samuel told all the words of the LORD to the people who asked him for a king. ¹¹And he said, "This will be the behavior of the king who will reign over you: He will take your sons and appoint *them* for his own chariots and *to be* his horsemen, and *some* will run before his chariots. ¹²He will appoint captains over his thousands and captains over his fifties, *will set some* to plow his ground and reap his harvest, and *some* to make his weapons of war and equipment for his chariots. ¹³He will take your daughters *to be* perfumers,

cooks, and bakers. ¹⁴And he will take the best of your fields, your vineyards, and your olive groves, and give *them* to his servants. ¹⁵He will take a tenth of your grain and your vintage, and give it to his officers and servants. ¹⁶And he will take your male servants, your female servants, your finest young men,ª and your donkeys, and put *them* to his work. ¹⁷He will take a tenth of your sheep. And you will be his servants. ¹⁸And you will cry out in that day because of your king whom you have chosen for yourselves, and the LORD will not hear you in that day."

¹⁹Nevertheless the people refused to obey the voice of Samuel; and they said, "No, but we will have a king over us, ²⁰that we also may be like all the nations, and that our king may judge us and go out before us and fight our battles."

²¹And Samuel heard all the words of the people, and he repeated them in the hearing of the LORD. ²²So the LORD said to Samuel, "Heed their voice, and make them a king."

And Samuel said to the men of Israel, "Every man go to his city."

8:16 ªSeptuagint reads *cattle.*

SAUL CHOSEN TO BE KING

9 There was a man of Benjamin whose name *was* Kish the son of Abiel, the son of Zeror, the son of Bechorath, the son of Aphiah, a Benjamite, a mighty man of power. ²And he had a choice and handsome son whose name *was* Saul. *There was* not a more handsome person than he among the children of Israel. From his shoulders upward *he was* taller than any of the people.

³Now the donkeys of Kish, Saul's father, were lost. And Kish said to his son Saul, "Please take one of the servants with you, and arise, go and look for the donkeys." ⁴So he passed through the mountains of Ephraim and through the land of Shalisha, but they did not find *them.* Then they passed through the land of Shaalim, and *they were* not *there.* Then he passed through the land of the Benjamites, but they did not find *them.*

⁵When they had come to the land of Zuph, Saul said to his servant who *was* with him, "Come, let us return, lest my father cease *caring* about the donkeys and become worried about us."

⁶And he said to him, "Look now, *there is* in this city a man of God, and *he is* an honorable man; all that he says surely comes to pass. So let us go there; perhaps he can show us the way that we should go."

⁷Then Saul said to his servant, "But look, *if* we go, what shall we bring the man? For the bread in our vessels is all gone, and *there is* no present to bring to the man of God. What do we have?"

⁸And the servant answered Saul again and said, "Look, I have here at hand one-fourth of a shekel of silver. I will give *that* to the man of God, to tell us our way." ⁹(Formerly in Israel, when a man went to inquire of God, he spoke thus: "Come, let us go to the seer"; for *he who is* now *called* a prophet was formerly called a seer.)

¹⁰Then Saul said to his servant, "Well said; come, let us go." So they went to the city where the man of God *was.*

¹¹As they went up the hill to the city, they met some young women going out to draw water, and said to them, "Is the seer here?"

the INFLUENCERS

KING SAUL—Disqualified from Leadership

1 SAMUEL 9:2

Politically, choosing a king for Israel was a wise move, but spiritually it was a huge mistake. The people seemed to be smitten by the superstitious fact that Saul was the tallest man in Israel. Saul, born of the tribe of Benjamin, was chosen by the people and not by the Lord. At first a God-fearing servant, he developed a poisonous attitude over the years.

Saul made many mistakes that caused him to fail as a leader. He traded confidence in God for self-sufficiency. He refused to wait for the prophet and turned the worship of God through sacrifice into a ritual ceremony of show. While he was outwardly attractive, Saul was inwardly flawed. The Lord said of His chosen king, David, "man looks at the outward appearance, but the LORD looks at the heart" (1 Sam. 16:7). Soon Saul's ego wasn't enough and anxiety attacks occurred. He often made excuses for his own disobedience.

In spite of David's efforts to honor him as king, Saul grew increasingly angry and jealous and even tried to have David killed. Perhaps the lowest point in Saul's life was when the paranoia drove him to consult a witch in order to see the future (1 Sam. 28). His lack of courage is reflected in his own statements: "I fear the people and I obey their voice" (1 Sam. 15:24). Lack of courage and a self-serving lifestyle disqualified Saul from leading others.

[12]And they answered them and said, "Yes, there he is, just ahead of you. Hurry now; for today he came to this city, because there is a sacrifice of the people today on the high place. [13]As soon as you come into the city, you will surely find him before he goes up to the high place to eat. For the people will not eat until he comes, because he must bless the sacrifice; afterward those who are invited will eat. Now therefore, go up, for about this time you will find him." [14]So they went up to the city. As they were coming into the city, there was Samuel, coming out toward them on his way up to the high place.

[15]Now the LORD had told Samuel in his ear the day before Saul came, saying, [16]"Tomorrow about this time I will send you a man from the land of Benjamin, and you shall anoint him commander over My people Israel, that he may save My people from the hand of the Philistines; for I have looked upon My people, because their cry has come to Me."

[17]So when Samuel saw Saul, the LORD said to him, "There he is, the man of whom I spoke to you. This one shall reign over My people." [18]Then Saul drew near to Samuel in the gate, and said, "Please tell me, where is the seer's house?"

[19]Samuel answered Saul and said, "I am the seer. Go up before me to the high place, for you shall eat with me today; and tomorrow I will let you go and will tell you all that is in your heart. [20]But as for your donkeys that were lost three days ago, do not be anxious about them, for they have been found. And on whom is all the desire of Israel? Is it not on you and on all your father's house?"

[21]And Saul answered and said, "Am I not a Benjamite, of the smallest of the tribes of Israel, and my family the least of all the families of the tribe[a] of Benjamin? Why then do you speak like this to me?"

[22]Now Samuel took Saul and his servant and brought them into the hall, and had them sit in the place of honor among those who were invited; there were about thirty persons. [23]And Samuel said to the cook, "Bring the portion which I gave you, of which I said to you, 'Set it apart.' " [24]So the cook took up the thigh with its upper part and set it before Saul. And Samuel said, "Here it is, what was kept back. It was set apart for

you. Eat; for until this time it has been kept for you, since I said I invited the people." So Saul ate with Samuel that day.

[25]When they had come down from the high place into the city, Samuel spoke with Saul on the top of the house.[a] [26]They arose early; and it was about the dawning of the day that Samuel called to Saul on the top of the house, saying, "Get up, that I may send you on your way." And Saul arose, and both of them went outside, he and Samuel.

SAUL ANOINTED KING

[27]As they were going down to the outskirts of the city, Samuel said to Saul, "Tell the servant to go on ahead of us." And he went on. "But you stand here awhile, that I may announce to you the word of God."

10 Then Samuel took a flask of oil and poured it on his head, and kissed him and said: "Is it not because the LORD has anointed you commander over His inheritance?[a] [2]When you have departed from me today, you will find two men by Rachel's tomb in the territory of Benjamin at Zelzah; and they will say to you, 'The donkeys which you went to look for have been found. And now your father has ceased caring about the donkeys and is worrying about you, saying, "What shall I do about my son?" ' [3]Then you shall go on forward from there and come to the terebinth tree of Tabor. There three men going up to God at Bethel will meet you, one carrying three young goats, another carrying three loaves of bread, and another carrying a skin of wine. [4]And they will greet you and give you two loaves of bread, which you shall receive from their hands. [5]After that you shall come to the hill of God where the Philistine garrison is. And it will happen, when you have come there to the city, that you will meet a group of prophets coming down from the high place with a stringed instrument, a tambourine, a flute, and a harp before them; and they will be prophesying. [6]Then the

9:21 [a]Literally tribes   9:25 [a]Following Masoretic Text and Targum; Septuagint omits He spoke with Saul on the top of the house; Septuagint and Vulgate add And he prepared a bed for Saul on the top of the house, and he slept.   10:1 [a]Following Masoretic Text, Targum, and Vulgate; Septuagint reads His people Israel; and you shall rule the people of the Lord; Septuagint and Vulgate add And you shall deliver His people from the hands of their enemies all around them. And this shall be a sign to you, that God has anointed you to be a prince.

Spirit of the LORD will come upon you, and you will prophesy with them and be turned into another man. ⁷And let it be, when these signs come to you, *that* you do as the occasion demands; for God *is* with you. ⁸You shall go down before me to Gilgal; and surely I will come down to you to offer burnt offerings *and* make sacrifices of peace offerings. Seven days you shall wait, till I come to you and show you what you should do."

⁹So it was, when he had turned his back to go from Samuel, that God gave him another heart; and all those signs came to pass that day. ¹⁰When they came there to the hill, there was a group of prophets to meet him; then the Spirit of God came upon him, and he prophesied among them. ¹¹And it happened, when all who knew him formerly saw that he indeed prophesied among the prophets, that the people said to one another, "What *is* this *that* has come upon the son of Kish? *Is* Saul also among the prophets?" ¹²Then a man from there answered and said, "But who *is* their father?" Therefore it became a proverb: "*Is* Saul also among the prophets?" ¹³And when he had finished prophesying, he went to the high place.

¹⁴Then Saul's uncle said to him and his servant, "Where did you go?"

So he said, "To look for the donkeys. When we saw that *they were* nowhere *to be found,* we went to Samuel."

¹⁵And Saul's uncle said, "Tell me, please, what Samuel said to you."

¹⁶So Saul said to his uncle, "He told us plainly that the donkeys had been found." But about the matter of the kingdom, he did not tell him what Samuel had said.

SAUL PROCLAIMED KING

¹⁷Then Samuel called the people together to the LORD at Mizpah, ¹⁸and said to the children of Israel, "Thus says the LORD God of Israel: 'I brought up Israel out of Egypt, and delivered you from the hand of the Egyptians *and* from the hand of all kingdoms and from those who oppressed you.' ¹⁹But you have today rejected your God, who Himself saved you from all your adversities and your tribulations; and you have said to Him, 'No, set a king over us!' Now therefore, present yourselves before the LORD by your tribes and by your clans."ᵃ

²⁰And when Samuel had caused all the tribes of Israel to come near, the tribe of Benjamin was chosen. ²¹When he had caused the tribe of Benjamin to come near by their families, the family of Matri was chosen. And Saul the son of Kish was chosen. But when they sought him, he could not be found. ²²Therefore they inquired of the LORD further, "Has the man come here yet?"

And the LORD answered, "There he is, hidden among the equipment."

²³So they ran and brought him from there; and when he stood among the people, he was taller than any of the people from his shoulders upward. ²⁴And Samuel said to all the people, "Do you see him whom the LORD has chosen, that *there is* no one like him among all the people?"

So all the people shouted and said, "Long live the king!"

²⁵Then Samuel explained to the people the behavior of royalty, and wrote *it* in a book and laid *it* up before the LORD. And Samuel sent all the people away, every man to his house. ²⁶And Saul also went home to Gibeah; and valiant *men* went with him, whose hearts God had touched. ²⁷But some rebels said, "How can this man save us?" So they despised him, and brought him no presents. But he held his peace.

SAUL SAVES JABESH GILEAD

11 Then Nahash the Ammonite came up and encamped against Jabesh Gilead; and all the men of Jabesh said to Nahash, "Make a covenant with us, and we will serve you."

²And Nahash the Ammonite answered them, "On this *condition* I will make *a covenant* with you, that I may put out all your right eyes, and bring reproach on all Israel."

³Then the elders of Jabesh said to him, "Hold off for seven days, that we may send messengers to all the territory of Israel. And then, if *there is* no one to save us, we will come out to you."

⁴So the messengers came to Gibeah of Saul and told the news in the hearing of the people. And all the people lifted up their voices and wept. ⁵Now there was Saul, coming behind the herd from the field; and Saul said, "What *troubles* the people, that they weep?" And they told him the words of the men of Jabesh. ⁶Then the Spirit of

10:19 ᵃLiterally *thousands*

God came upon Saul when he heard this news, and his anger was greatly aroused. [7]So he took a yoke of oxen and cut them in pieces, and sent *them* throughout all the territory of Israel by the hands of messengers, saying, "Whoever does not go out with Saul and Samuel to battle, so it shall be done to his oxen."

And the fear of the LORD fell on the people, and they came out with one consent. [8]When he numbered them in Bezek, the children of Israel were three hundred thousand, and the men of Judah thirty thousand. [9]And they said to the messengers who came, "Thus you shall say to the men of Jabesh Gilead: 'Tomorrow, by *the time* the sun is hot, you shall have help.'" Then the messengers came and reported *it* to the men of Jabesh, and they were glad. [10]Therefore the men of Jabesh said, "Tomorrow we will come out to you, and you may do with us whatever seems good to you."

[11]So it was, on the next day, that Saul put the people in three companies; and they came into the midst of the camp in the morning watch, and killed Ammonites until the heat of the day. And it happened that those who survived were scattered, so that no two of them were left together.

[12]Then the people said to Samuel, "Who *is* he who said, 'Shall Saul reign over us?' Bring the men, that we may put them to death."

[13]But Saul said, "Not a man shall be put to death this day, for today the LORD has accomplished salvation in Israel."

[14]Then Samuel said to the people, "Come, let us go to Gilgal and renew the kingdom there." [15]So all the people went to Gilgal, and there they made Saul king before the LORD in Gilgal. There they made sacrifices of peace offerings before the LORD, and there Saul and all the men of Israel rejoiced greatly.

SAMUEL'S ADDRESS AT SAUL'S CORONATION

12 Now Samuel said to all Israel: "Indeed I have heeded your voice in all that you said to me, and have made a king over you. [2]And now here is the king, walking before you; and I am old and grayheaded, and look, my sons *are* with you. I have walked before you from my childhood to this day. [3]Here I am. Witness against me before the LORD and before His anointed: Whose ox have I taken, or whose donkey have I taken, or whom

have I cheated? Whom have I oppressed, or from whose hand have I received *any* bribe with which to blind my eyes? I will restore *it* to you."

[4]And they said, "You have not cheated us or oppressed us, nor have you taken anything from any man's hand."

[5]Then he said to them, "The LORD *is* witness against you, and His anointed *is* witness this day, that you have not found anything in my hand."

And they answered, "*He is* witness."

[6]Then Samuel said to the people, "*It is* the LORD who raised up Moses and Aaron, and who brought your fathers up from the land of Egypt. [7]Now therefore, stand still, that I may reason with you before the LORD concerning all the righteous acts of the LORD which He did to you and your fathers: [8]When Jacob had gone into Egypt,[a] and your fathers cried out to the LORD, then the LORD sent Moses and Aaron, who brought your fathers out of Egypt and made them dwell in this place. [9]And when they forgot the LORD their God, He sold them into the hand of Sisera, commander of the army of Hazor, into the hand of the Philistines, and into the hand of the king of Moab; and they fought against them. [10]Then they cried out to the LORD, and said, 'We have sinned, because we have forsaken the LORD and served the Baals and Ashtoreths;[a] but now deliver us from the hand of our enemies, and we will serve You.' [11]And the LORD sent Jerubbaal,[a] Bedan,[b] Jephthah, and Samuel,[c] and delivered you out of the hand of your enemies on every side; and you dwelt in safety. [12]And when you saw that Nahash king of the Ammonites came against you, you said to me, 'No, but a king shall reign over us,' when the LORD your God *was* your king.

[13]"Now therefore, here is the king whom you have chosen *and* whom you have desired. And take note, the LORD has set a king over you. [14]If you fear the LORD and serve Him and obey His voice, and do not rebel against the commandment of the LORD, then both you and the king who reigns over you will continue following the LORD your God. [15]However, if you do not obey the voice of the LORD, but rebel against the commandment of

12:8 [a]Following Masoretic Text, Targum, and Vulgate; Septuagint adds *and the Egyptians afflicted them.* **12:10** [a]Canaanite goddesses **12:11** [a]Syriac reads *Deborah;* Targum reads *Gideon.* [b]Septuagint and Syriac read *Barak;* Targum reads *Simson.* [c]Syriac reads *Simson.*

the LORD, then the hand of the LORD will be against you, as *it was* against your fathers.

¹⁶"Now therefore, stand and see this great thing which the LORD will do before your eyes: ¹⁷*Is* today not the wheat harvest? I will call to the LORD, and He will send thunder and rain, that you may perceive and see that your wickedness *is* great, which you have done in the sight of the LORD, in asking a king for yourselves."

¹⁸So Samuel called to the LORD, and the LORD sent thunder and rain that day; and all the people greatly feared the LORD and Samuel.

¹⁹And all the people said to Samuel, "Pray for your servants to the LORD your God, that we may not die; for we have added to all our sins the evil of asking a king for ourselves."

²⁰Then Samuel said to the people, "Do not fear. You have done all this wickedness; yet do not turn aside from following the LORD, but serve the LORD with all your heart. ²¹And do not turn aside; for *then you would go* after empty things which cannot profit or deliver, for they *are* nothing. ²²For the LORD will not forsake His people, for His great name's sake, because it has pleased the LORD to make you His people. ²³Moreover, as for me, far be it from me that I should sin against the LORD in ceasing to pray for you; but I will teach you the good and the right way. ²⁴Only fear the LORD, and serve Him in truth with all your heart; for consider what great things He has done for you. ²⁵But if you still do wickedly, you shall be swept away, both you and your king."

SAUL'S UNLAWFUL SACRIFICE

13 Saul reigned one year; and when he had reigned two years over Israel,ᵃ ²Saul chose for himself three thousand *men* of Israel. Two thousand were with Saul in Michmash and in the mountains of Bethel, and a thousand were with Jonathan in Gibeah of Benjamin. The rest of the people he sent away, every man to his tent.

³And Jonathan attacked the garrison of the Philistines that *was* in Geba, and the Philistines heard *of it.* Then Saul blew the trumpet throughout all the land, saying, "Let the Hebrews hear!" ⁴Now all Israel heard it said *that* Saul had attacked a garrison of the Philistines, and *that* Israel had also become an abomination to the Philistines. And the people were called together to Saul at Gilgal.

⁵Then the Philistines gathered together to fight with Israel, thirtyᵃ thousand chariots and six thousand horsemen, and people as the sand which *is* on the seashore in multitude. And they came up and encamped in Michmash, to the east of Beth Aven. ⁶When the men of Israel saw that they were in danger (for the people were distressed), then the people hid in caves, in thickets, in rocks, in holes, and in pits. ⁷And *some of* the Hebrews crossed over the Jordan to the land of Gad and Gilead.

As for Saul, he *was* still in Gilgal, and all the people followed him trembling. ⁸Then he waited seven days, according to the time set by Samuel. But Samuel did not come to Gilgal; and the people were scattered from him. ⁹So Saul said, "Bring a burnt offering and peace offerings here to me." And he offered the burnt offering. ¹⁰Now it happened, as soon as he had finished presenting the burnt offering, that Samuel came; and Saul went out to meet him, that he might greet him.

¹¹And Samuel said, "What have you done?"

Saul said, "When I saw that the people were scattered from me, and *that* you did not come within the days appointed, and *that* the Philistines gathered together at Michmash, ¹²then I said, 'The Philistines will now come down on me at Gilgal, and I have not made supplication to the LORD.' Therefore I felt compelled, and offered a burnt offering."

¹³And Samuel said to Saul, "You have done foolishly. You have not kept the commandment of the LORD your God, which He commanded you. For now the LORD would have established your kingdom over Israel forever. ¹⁴But now your kingdom shall not continue. The LORD has sought for Himself a man after His own heart, and the LORD has commanded him *to be* commander over His people, because you have not kept what the LORD commanded you."

¹⁵Then Samuel arose and went up from Gilgal to Gibeah of Benjamin.ᵃ And Saul numbered the people present with him, about six hundred men.

13:1 ᵃThe Hebrew is difficult (compare 2 Samuel 5:4; 2 Kings 14:2; see also 2 Samuel 2:10; Acts 13:21). **13:5** ᵃFollowing Masoretic Text, Septuagint, Targum, and Vulgate; Syriac and some manuscripts of the Septuagint read *three.* **13:15** ᵃFollowing Masoretic Text and Targum; Septuagint and Vulgate add *And the rest of the people went up after Saul to meet the people who fought against them, going from Gilgal to Gibeah in the hill of Benjamin.*

No Weapons for the Army

[16]Saul, Jonathan his son, and the people present with them remained in Gibeah of Benjamin. But the Philistines encamped in Michmash. [17]Then raiders came out of the camp of the Philistines in three companies. One company turned onto the road to Ophrah, to the land of Shual, [18]another company turned to the road *to* Beth Horon, and another company turned *to* the road of the border that overlooks the Valley of Zeboim toward the wilderness.

[19]Now there was no blacksmith to be found throughout all the land of Israel, for the Philistines said, "Lest the Hebrews make swords or spears." [20]But all the Israelites would go down to the Philistines to sharpen each man's plowshare, his mattock, his ax, and his sickle; [21]and the charge for a sharpening was a pim[a] for the plowshares, the mattocks, the forks, and the axes, and to set the points of the goads. [22]So it came about, on the day of battle, that there was neither sword nor spear found in the hand of any of the people who *were* with Saul and Jonathan. But they were found with Saul and Jonathan his son.

[23]And the garrison of the Philistines went out to the pass of Michmash.

Jonathan Defeats the Philistines

14 Now it happened one day that Jonathan the son of Saul said to the young man who bore his armor, "Come, let us go over to the Philistines' garrison that *is* on the other side." But he did not tell his father. [2]And Saul was sitting in the outskirts of Gibeah under a pomegranate tree which *is* in Migron. The people who *were* with him *were* about six hundred men. [3]Ahijah the son of Ahitub, Ichabod's brother, the son of Phinehas, the son of Eli, the LORD's priest in Shiloh, was wearing an ephod. But the people did not know that Jonathan had gone.

[4]Between the passes, by which Jonathan sought to go over to the Philistines' garrison, *there was* a sharp rock on one side and a sharp rock on the other side. And the name of one *was* Bozez, and the name of the other Seneh. [5]The front of one faced northward opposite Michmash, and the other southward opposite Gibeah.

[6]Then Jonathan said to the young man who bore his armor, "Come, let us go over to the garrison of these uncircumcised; it may be that the LORD will work for us. For nothing restrains the LORD from saving by many or by few."

[7]So his armorbearer said to him, "Do all that is in your heart. Go then; here I am with you, according to your heart."

[8]Then Jonathan said, "Very well, let us cross over to *these* men, and we will show ourselves to them. [9]If they say thus to us, 'Wait until we come to you,' then we will stand still in our place and not go up to them. [10]But if they say thus, 'Come up to us,' then we will go up. For the LORD has delivered them into our hand, and this *will be* a sign to us."

[11]So both of them showed themselves to the garrison of the Philistines. And the Philistines said, "Look, the Hebrews are coming out of the holes where they have hidden." [12]Then the men of the garrison called to Jonathan and his armorbearer, and said, "Come up to us, and we will show you something."

Jonathan said to his armorbearer, "Come up after me, for the LORD has delivered them into the hand of Israel." [13]And Jonathan climbed up on his hands and knees with his armorbearer after him; and they fell before Jonathan. And as he came after him, his armorbearer killed them. [14]That first slaughter which Jonathan and his armorbearer made was about twenty men within about half an acre of land.[a]

[15]And there was trembling in the camp, in the field, and among all the people. The garrison and the raiders also trembled; and the earth quaked, so that it was a very great trembling. [16]Now the watchmen of Saul in Gibeah of Benjamin looked, and *there* was the multitude, melting away; and they went here and there. [17]Then Saul said to the people who *were* with him, "Now call the roll and see who has gone from us." And when they had called the roll, surprisingly, Jonathan and his armorbearer *were* not *there.* [18]And Saul said to Ahijah, "Bring the ark[a] of God here" (for at that time the ark[b] of God was with the children of Israel). [19]Now it happened, while Saul talked to the

13:21 [a]About two-thirds shekel weight   **14:14** [a]Literally *half the area plowed by a yoke* (of oxen in a day)   **14:18** [a]Following Masoretic Text, Targum, and Vulgate; Septuagint reads *ephod.* [b]Following Masoretic Text, Targum, and Vulgate; Septuagint reads *ephod.*

priest, that the noise which *was* in the camp of the Philistines continued to increase; so Saul said to the priest, "Withdraw your hand." ²⁰Then Saul and all the people who *were* with him assembled, and they went to the battle; and indeed every man's sword was against his neighbor, *and there was* very great confusion. ²¹Moreover the Hebrews *who* were with the Philistines before that time, who went up with them into the camp *from the* surrounding *country,* they also joined the Israelites who *were* with Saul and Jonathan. ²²Likewise all the men of Israel who had hidden in the mountains of Ephraim, *when* they heard that the Philistines fled, they also followed hard after them in the battle. ²³So the LORD saved Israel that day, and the battle shifted to Beth Aven.

Saul's Rash Oath

²⁴And the men of Israel were distressed that day, for Saul had placed the people under oath, saying, "Cursed *is* the man who eats *any* food until evening, before I have taken vengeance on my enemies." So none of the people tasted food. ²⁵Now all *the people* of the land came to a forest; and there was honey on the ground. ²⁶And when the people had come into the woods, there was the honey, dripping; but no one put his hand to his mouth, for the people feared the oath. ²⁷But Jonathan had not heard his father charge the people with the oath; therefore he stretched out the end of the rod that *was* in his hand and dipped it in a honeycomb, and put his hand to his mouth; and his countenance brightened. ²⁸Then one of the people said, "Your father strictly charged the people with an oath, saying, 'Cursed *is* the man who eats food this day.' " And the people were faint.

²⁹But Jonathan said, "My father has troubled the land. Look now, how my countenance has brightened because I tasted a little of this honey. ³⁰How much better if the people had eaten freely today of the spoil of their enemies which they found! For now would there not have been a much greater slaughter among the Philistines?"

³¹Now they had driven back the Philistines that day from Michmash to Aijalon. So the people were very faint. ³²And the people rushed on the spoil, and took sheep, oxen, and calves, and slaughtered *them* on the ground; and the people

ate *them* with the blood. ³³Then they told Saul, saying, "Look, the people are sinning against the LORD by eating with the blood!"

So he said, "You have dealt treacherously; roll a large stone to me this day." ³⁴Then Saul said, "Disperse yourselves among the people, and say to them, 'Bring me here every man's ox and every man's sheep, slaughter *them* here, and eat; and do not sin against the LORD by eating with the blood.' " So every one of the people brought his ox with him that night, and slaughtered *it* there. ³⁵Then Saul built an altar to the LORD. This was the first altar that he built to the LORD.

³⁶Now Saul said, "Let us go down after the Philistines by night, and plunder them until the morning light; and let us not leave a man of them."

And they said, "Do whatever seems good to you."

Then the priest said, "Let us draw near to God here."

³⁷So Saul asked counsel of God, "Shall I go down after the Philistines? Will You deliver them into the hand of Israel?" But He did not answer him that day. ³⁸And Saul said, "Come over here, all you chiefs of the people, and know and see what this sin was today. ³⁹For *as* the LORD lives, who saves Israel, though it be in Jonathan my son, he shall surely die." But not a man among all the people answered him. ⁴⁰Then he said to all Israel, "You be on one side, and my son Jonathan and I will be on the other side."

And the people said to Saul, "Do what seems good to you."

⁴¹Therefore Saul said to the LORD God of Israel, "Give a perfect *lot*."ᵃ So Saul and Jonathan were taken, but the people escaped. ⁴²And Saul said, "Cast *lots* between my son Jonathan and me." So Jonathan was taken. ⁴³Then Saul said to Jonathan, "Tell me what you have done."

And Jonathan told him, and said, "I only tasted a little honey with the end of the rod that *was* in my hand. So now I must die!"

⁴⁴Saul answered, "God do so and more also; for you shall surely die, Jonathan."

14:41 ᵃFollowing Masoretic Text and Targum; Septuagint and Vulgate read *Why do You not answer Your servant today? If the injustice is with me or Jonathan my son, O LORD God of Israel, give proof; and if You say it is with Your people Israel, give holiness.*

45But the people said to Saul, "Shall Jonathan die, who has accomplished this great deliverance in Israel? Certainly not! *As* the LORD lives, not one hair of his head shall fall to the ground, for he has worked with God this day." So the people rescued Jonathan, and he did not die.

46Then Saul returned from pursuing the Philistines, and the Philistines went to their own place.

SAUL'S CONTINUING WARS

47So Saul established his sovereignty over Israel, and fought against all his enemies on every side, against Moab, against the people of Ammon, against Edom, against the kings of Zobah, and against the Philistines. Wherever he turned, he harassed *them.*a 48And he gathered an army and attacked the Amalekites, and delivered Israel from the hands of those who plundered them.

49The sons of Saul were Jonathan, Jishui,a and Malchishua. And the names of his two daughters *were these:* the name of the firstborn Merab, and the name of the younger Michal. 50The name of Saul's wife *was* Ahinoam the daughter of Ahimaaz. And the name of the commander of his army *was* Abner the son of Ner, Saul's uncle. 51Kish *was* the father of Saul, and Ner the father of Abner *was* the son of Abiel.

52Now there was fierce war with the Philistines all the days of Saul. And when Saul saw any strong man or any valiant man, he took him for himself.

SAUL SPARES KING AGAG

15 Samuel also said to Saul, "The LORD sent me to anoint you king over His people, over Israel. Now therefore, heed the voice of the words of the LORD. 2Thus says the LORD of hosts: 'I will punish Amalek *for* what he did to Israel, how he ambushed him on the way when he came up from Egypt. 3Now go and attack Amalek, and utterly destroy all that they have, and do not spare them. But kill both man and woman, infant and nursing child, ox and sheep, camel and donkey.' "

4So Saul gathered the people together and numbered them in Telaim, two hundred thousand foot soldiers and ten thousand men of Judah.

5And Saul came to a city of Amalek, and lay in wait in the valley.

6Then Saul said to the Kenites, "Go, depart, get down from among the Amalekites, lest I destroy you with them. For you showed kindness to all the children of Israel when they came up out of Egypt." So the Kenites departed from among the Amalekites. 7And Saul attacked the Amalekites, from Havilah all the way to Shur, which is east of Egypt. 8He also took Agag king of the Amalekites alive, and utterly destroyed all the people with the edge of the sword. 9But Saul and the people spared Agag and the best of the sheep, the oxen, the fatlings, the lambs, and all *that was* good, and were unwilling to utterly destroy them. But everything despised and worthless, that they utterly destroyed.

SAUL REJECTED AS KING

10Now the word of the LORD came to Samuel, saying, 11"I greatly regret that I have set up Saul *as* king, for he has turned back from following Me, and has not performed My commandments." And it grieved Samuel, and he cried out to the LORD all night. 12So when Samuel rose early in the morning to meet Saul, it was told Samuel, saying, "Saul went to Carmel, and indeed, he set up a monument for himself; and he has gone on around, passed by, and gone down to Gilgal." 13Then Samuel went to Saul, and Saul said to him, "Blessed *are* you of the LORD! I have performed the commandment of the LORD."

14But Samuel said, "What then *is* this bleating of the sheep in my ears, and the lowing of the oxen which I hear?"

15And Saul said, "They have brought them from the Amalekites; for the people spared the best of the sheep and the oxen, to sacrifice to the LORD your God; and the rest we have utterly destroyed."

16Then Samuel said to Saul, "Be quiet! And I will tell you what the LORD said to me last night."

And he said to him, "Speak on."

17So Samuel said, "When you *were* little in your own eyes, *were* you not head of the tribes of Israel? And did not the LORD anoint you king over Israel? 18Now the LORD sent you on a mis-

14:47 aSeptuagint and Vulgate read *prospered.*   **14:49** aCalled *Abinadab* in 1 Chronicles 8:33 and 9:39

sion, and said, 'Go, and utterly destroy the sinners, the Amalekites, and fight against them until they are consumed.' ¹⁹Why then did you not obey the voice of the LORD? Why did you swoop down on the spoil, and do evil in the sight of the LORD?"

²⁰And Saul said to Samuel, "But I have obeyed the voice of the LORD, and gone on the mission on which the LORD sent me, and brought back Agag king of Amalek; I have utterly destroyed the Amalekites. ²¹But the people took of the plunder, sheep and oxen, the best of the things which should have been utterly destroyed, to sacrifice to the LORD your God in Gilgal."

²²So Samuel said:

"Has the LORD *as great* delight in burnt
        offerings and sacrifices,
    As in obeying the voice of the LORD?
    Behold, to obey is better than sacrifice,
    And to heed than the fat of rams.
²³For rebellion *is as* the sin of witchcraft,
    And stubbornness *is as* iniquity and idolatry.
    Because you have rejected the word of the
        LORD,
    He also has rejected you from *being* king."

²⁴Then Saul said to Samuel, "I have sinned, for I have transgressed the commandment of the LORD and your words, because I feared the people and obeyed their voice. ²⁵Now therefore, please pardon my sin, and return with me, that I may worship the LORD."

²⁶But Samuel said to Saul, "I will not return with you, for you have rejected the word of the LORD, and the LORD has rejected you from being king over Israel."

²⁷And as Samuel turned around to go away, *Saul* seized the edge of his robe, and it tore. ²⁸So Samuel said to him, "The LORD has torn the kingdom of Israel from you today, and has given it to a neighbor of yours, *who is* better than you. ²⁹And also the Strength of Israel will not lie nor relent. For He *is* not a man, that He should relent."

³⁰Then he said, "I have sinned; *yet* honor me now, please, before the elders of my people and before Israel, and return with me, that I may worship the LORD your God." ³¹So Samuel turned back after Saul, and Saul worshiped the LORD.

³²Then Samuel said, "Bring Agag king of the Amalekites here to me." So Agag came to him cautiously.

And Agag said, "Surely the bitterness of death is past."

³³But Samuel said, "As your sword has made women childless, so shall your mother be childless among women." And Samuel hacked Agag in pieces before the LORD in Gilgal.

³⁴Then Samuel went to Ramah, and Saul went up to his house at Gibeah of Saul. ³⁵And Samuel went no more to see Saul until the day of his death. Nevertheless Samuel mourned for Saul, and the LORD regretted that He had made Saul king over Israel.

DAVID ANOINTED KING

16 Now the LORD said to Samuel, "How long will you mourn for Saul, seeing I have rejected him from reigning over Israel? Fill your horn with oil, and go; I am sending you to Jesse the Bethlehemite. For I have provided Myself a king among his sons."

²And Samuel said, "How can I go? If Saul hears *it,* he will kill me."

But the LORD said, "Take a heifer with you, and say, 'I have come to sacrifice to the LORD.' ³Then invite Jesse to the sacrifice, and I will show you what you shall do; you shall anoint for Me the one I name to you."

⁴So Samuel did what the LORD said, and went to Bethlehem. And the elders of the town trembled at his coming, and said, "Do you come peaceably?"

⁵And he said, "Peaceably; I have come to sacrifice to the LORD. Sanctify yourselves, and come with me to the sacrifice." Then he consecrated Jesse and his sons, and invited them to the sacrifice.

⁶So it was, when they came, that he looked at Eliab and said, "Surely the LORD's anointed *is* before Him!"

⁷But the LORD said to Samuel, "Do not look at his appearance or at his physical stature, because I have refused him. For *the LORD does* not *see* as man sees;[a] for man looks at the outward appearance, but the LORD looks at the heart."

16:7 [a]Septuagint reads *For God does not see as man sees;* Targum reads *It is not by the appearance of a man;* Vulgate reads *Nor do I judge according to the looks of a man.*

THROUGH THE GRID

*Where Have All the Dreamers Gone?
Observations from a Biblical
Worldview: Liberation from Morality
(1 Sam. 16:7)*

Much of our culture despises morality and accountability, and it seeks to promote the "what I do in private is my own business" mentality. However, the biblical Christian worldview says that "the LORD does not see as man sees . . . the LORD looks at the heart" (1 Sam. 16:7); that is, He sees all.

⁸So Jesse called Abinadab, and made him pass before Samuel. And he said, "Neither has the LORD chosen this one." ⁹Then Jesse made Shammah pass by. And he said, "Neither has the LORD chosen this one." ¹⁰Thus Jesse made seven of his sons pass before Samuel. And Samuel said to Jesse, "The LORD has not chosen these." ¹¹And Samuel said to Jesse, "Are all the young men here?" Then he said, "There remains yet the youngest, and there he is, keeping the sheep."

And Samuel said to Jesse, "Send and bring him. For we will not sit down[a] till he comes here." ¹²So he sent and brought him in. Now he *was* ruddy, with bright eyes, and good-looking. And the LORD said, "Arise, anoint him; for this *is* the one!" ¹³Then Samuel took the horn of oil and anointed him in the midst of his brothers; and the Spirit of the LORD came upon David from that day forward. So Samuel arose and went to Ramah.

A DISTRESSING SPIRIT TROUBLES SAUL

¹⁴But the Spirit of the LORD departed from Saul, and a distressing spirit from the LORD troubled him. ¹⁵And Saul's servants said to him, "Surely, a distressing spirit from God is troubling you. ¹⁶Let our master now command your servants, *who are* before you, to seek out a man *who is* a skillful player on the harp. And it shall be that he will play it with his hand when the distressing spirit from God is upon you, and you shall be well."

¹⁷So Saul said to his servants, "Provide me now a man who can play well, and bring *him* to me."

¹⁸Then one of the servants answered and said, "Look, I have seen a son of Jesse the Bethle-

hemite, *who is* skillful in playing, a mighty man of valor, a man of war, prudent in speech, and a handsome person; and the LORD *is* with him."

¹⁹Therefore Saul sent messengers to Jesse, and said, "Send me your son David, who *is* with the sheep." ²⁰And Jesse took a donkey *loaded with* bread, a skin of wine, and a young goat, and sent *them* by his son David to Saul. ²¹So David came to Saul and stood before him. And he loved him greatly, and he became his armorbearer. ²²Then Saul sent to Jesse, saying, "Please let David stand before me, for he has found favor in my sight." ²³And so it was, whenever the spirit from God was upon Saul, that David would take a harp and play *it* with his hand. Then Saul would become refreshed and well, and the distressing spirit would depart from him.

DAVID AND GOLIATH

17 Now the Philistines gathered their armies together to battle, and were gathered at Sochoh, which *belongs* to Judah; they encamped between Sochoh and Azekah, in Ephes Dammim. ²And Saul and the men of Israel were gathered together, and they encamped in the Valley of Elah, and drew up in battle array against the Philistines. ³The Philistines stood on a mountain on one side, and Israel stood on a mountain on the other side, with a valley between them.

⁴And a champion went out from the camp of the Philistines, named Goliath, from Gath, whose height *was* six cubits and a span. ⁵*He had* a bronze helmet on his head, and he *was* armed with a coat of mail, and the weight of the coat *was* five thousand shekels of bronze. ⁶And *he had* bronze armor

16:11 ªFollowing Septuagint and Vulgate; Masoretic Text reads *turn around;* Targum and Syriac read *turn away.*

on his legs and a bronze javelin between his shoulders. ⁷Now the staff of his spear *was* like a weaver's beam, and his iron spearhead *weighed* six hundred shekels; and a shield-bearer went before him. ⁸Then he stood and cried out to the armies of Israel, and said to them, "Why have you come out to line up for battle? *Am* I not a Philistine, and you the servants of Saul? Choose a man for yourselves, and let him come down to me. ⁹If he is able to fight with me and kill me, then we will be your servants. But if I prevail against him and kill him, then you shall be our servants and serve us." ¹⁰And the Philistine said, "I defy the armies of Israel this day; give me a man, that we may fight together." ¹¹When Saul and all Israel heard these words of the Philistine, they were dismayed and greatly afraid.

¹²Now David *was* the son of that Ephrathite of Bethlehem Judah, whose name *was* Jesse, and who had eight sons. And the man was old, advanced *in years,* in the days of Saul. ¹³The three oldest sons of Jesse had gone to follow Saul to the battle. The names of his three sons who went to the battle *were* Eliab the firstborn, next to him Abinadab, and the third Shammah. ¹⁴David *was* the youngest. And the three oldest followed Saul. ¹⁵But David occasionally went and returned from Saul to feed his father's sheep at Bethlehem.

¹⁶And the Philistine drew near and presented himself forty days, morning and evening.

¹⁷Then Jesse said to his son David, "Take now for your brothers an ephah of this dried *grain* and these ten loaves, and run to your brothers at the camp. ¹⁸And carry these ten cheeses to the captain of *their* thousand, and see how your brothers fare, and bring back news of them." ¹⁹Now Saul and they and all the men of Israel *were* in the Valley of Elah, fighting with the Philistines.

²⁰So David rose early in the morning, left the sheep with a keeper, and took *the things* and went as Jesse had commanded him. And he came to the camp as the army was going out to the fight and shouting for the battle. ²¹For Israel and the Philistines had drawn up in battle array, army against army. ²²And David left his supplies in the hand of the supply keeper, ran to the army, and came and greeted his brothers. ²³Then as he talked with them, there was the champion, the Philistine of Gath, Goliath by name, coming up from the armies of the Philistines; and he spoke according to the same words. So David heard *them.* ²⁴And all the men of Israel, when they saw the man, fled from him and were dreadfully afraid. ²⁵So the men of Israel said, "Have you seen this man who has come up? Surely he has come up to defy Israel; and it shall be *that* the man who kills him the king will enrich with great riches, will give him his daughter, and give his father's house exemption *from taxes* in Israel."

²⁶Then David spoke to the men who stood by him, saying, "What shall be done for the man who kills this Philistine and takes away the reproach from Israel? For who *is* this uncircumcised Philistine, that he should defy the armies of the living God?"

²⁷And the people answered him in this manner, saying, "So shall it be done for the man who kills him."

²⁸Now Eliab his oldest brother heard when he spoke to the men; and Eliab's anger was aroused against David, and he said, "Why did you come down here? And with whom have you left those few sheep in the wilderness? I know your pride and the insolence of your heart, for you have come down to see the battle."

²⁹And David said, "What have I done now? *Is there* not a cause?" ³⁰Then he turned from him toward another and said the same thing; and these people answered him as the first ones *did.*

³¹Now when the words which David spoke were heard, they reported *them* to Saul; and he sent for him. ³²Then David said to Saul, "Let no man's heart fail because of him; your servant will go and fight with this Philistine."

³³And Saul said to David, "You are not able to go against this Philistine to fight with him; for you *are* a youth, and he a man of war from his youth."

³⁴But David said to Saul, "Your servant used to keep his father's sheep, and when a lion or a bear came and took a lamb out of the flock, ³⁵I went out after it and struck it, and delivered *the lamb* from its mouth; and when it arose against me, I caught *it* by its beard, and struck and killed it. ³⁶Your servant has killed both lion and bear; and this uncircumcised Philistine will be like one of them, seeing he has defied the armies of the living God." ³⁷Moreover David said, "The LORD,

LEADERSHIP
REALITIES

INSPIRATION: LEAD WITH YOUR LIFE, NOT WITH YOUR MOUTH *1 Samuel 17*

One of the greatest life lessons of all time is that leadership begins at the feet of the Father. Once the believer understands this truth, then, and only then can he or she truly inspire others with a lasting impact. If what comes out of a leader's mouth is not first birthed and exemplified in a life lived for the glory of God, then it is best not to speak at all. When Saul disqualified himself as king of Israel, the Lord raised up young David, whose courage inspired a nation to follow him. In 1 Samuel 18 the people sang and danced in celebration of David's victory over the Philistines. The joy began in chapter 17 where David faced Goliath and it erupted as they beheld the continued courage and faithfulness of the young warrior. Though much of what David said is recorded in this chapter, it is obvious that it was his actions that moved others. The words he spoke were simply a preview of the coming attractions. David *led with his life, not his mouth*:

- because of his unwavering belief that God was on his side (vv. 26, 37, 46, 47).
- because of his commitment to preparation (vv. 34–36).
- because of his courage demonstrated in his reckless abandonment to the mission (vv. 38–54).

who delivered me from the paw of the lion and from the paw of the bear, He will deliver me from the hand of this Philistine."

And Saul said to David, "Go, and the LORD be with you!"

[38]So Saul clothed David with his armor, and he put a bronze helmet on his head; he also clothed him with a coat of mail. [39]David fastened his sword to his armor and tried to walk, for he had not tested *them*. And David said to Saul, "I cannot walk with these, for I have not tested *them*." So David took them off.

[40]Then he took his staff in his hand; and he chose for himself five smooth stones from the brook, and put them in a shepherd's bag, in a pouch which he had, and his sling was in his hand. And he drew near to the Philistine. [41]So the Philistine came, and began drawing near to David, and the man who bore the shield *went* before him. [42]And when the Philistine looked about and saw David, he disdained him; for he was *only* a youth, ruddy and good-looking. [43]So the Philistine said to David, "*Am* I a dog, that you come to me with sticks?" And the Philistine cursed David

by his gods. [44]And the Philistine said to David, "Come to me, and I will give your flesh to the birds of the air and the beasts of the field!"

[45]Then David said to the Philistine, "You come to me with a sword, with a spear, and with a javelin. But I come to you in the name of the LORD of hosts, the God of the armies of Israel, whom you have defied. [46]This day the LORD will deliver you into my hand, and I will strike you and take your head from you. And this day I will give the carcasses of the camp of the Philistines to the birds of the air and the wild beasts of the earth, that all the earth may know that there is a God in Israel. [47]Then all this assembly shall know that the LORD does not save with sword and spear; for the battle *is* the LORD's, and He will give you into our hands."

[48]So it was, when the Philistine arose and came and drew near to meet David, that David hurried and ran toward the army to meet the Philistine. [49]Then David put his hand in his bag and took out a stone; and he slung *it* and struck the Philistine in his forehead, so that the stone sank into his forehead, and he fell on his face to

INSIDE _the_ INFLUENCERS

DAVID—Live a Life of Worship

1 SAMUEL 17:34–37

Most people think of David as the guy who killed Goliath. He was an incredible warrior, but David also wasn't shy about where his strength came from, proudly telling Saul his courage and skill was from God.

David poured his heart out when he wrote many of the Psalms. He was a worshipper from his childhood. David grew up taking care of his father's sheep. He was in the fields most days and probably many nights. Taking care of sheep sounds like a boring job, but David made the most of it.

In his free time, David learned to play the harp. He wrote original songs. He watched the glory of creation alone in the quiet, and the worship songs flowed from his heart. David and God met one on one, and this personal worship made David who he became. _If you want to live a life of significance, then you need to have the heart of a worshipper._

Later in his life, David ran from Saul, who wanted to kill him, only to find himself in front of another king, Abimelech, who thought he was a spy. David escaped through the hand of God and wisdom, and the genuine worship that followed caused him to write psalms of praise to God and encouragement to others.

---

the earth. ⁵⁰So David prevailed over the Philistine with a sling and a stone, and struck the Philistine and killed him. But _there was_ no sword in the hand of David. ⁵¹Therefore David ran and stood over the Philistine, took his sword and drew it out of its sheath and killed him, and cut off his head with it.

And when the Philistines saw that their champion was dead, they fled. ⁵²Now the men of Israel and Judah arose and shouted, and pursued the Philistines as far as the entrance of the valley[a] and to the gates of Ekron. And the wounded of the Philistines fell along the road to Shaaraim, even as far as Gath and Ekron. ⁵³Then the children of Israel returned from chasing the Philistines, and they plundered their tents. ⁵⁴And David took the head of the Philistine and brought it to Jerusalem, but he put his armor in his tent.

⁵⁵When Saul saw David going out against the Philistine, he said to Abner, the commander of the army, "Abner, whose son _is_ this youth?"

And Abner said, "As your soul lives, O king, I do not know."

⁵⁶So the king said, "Inquire whose son this young man _is._"

⁵⁷Then, as David returned from the slaughter of the Philistine, Abner took him and brought him before Saul with the head of the Philistine in his hand. ⁵⁸And Saul said to him, "Whose son _are_ you, young man?"

So David answered, "_I am_ the son of your servant Jesse the Bethlehemite."

SAUL RESENTS DAVID

18 Now when he had finished speaking to Saul, the soul of Jonathan was knit to the soul of David, and Jonathan loved him as his own soul. ²Saul took him that day, and would not let him go home to his father's house anymore. ³Then Jonathan and David made a covenant, because he loved him as his own soul. ⁴And Jonathan took off the robe that _was_ on him and gave it to David, with his armor, even to his sword and his bow and his belt.

⁵So David went out wherever Saul sent him, _and_ behaved wisely. And Saul set him over the men of war, and he was accepted in the sight of

17:52 ᵃFollowing Masoretic Text, Syriac, Targum, and Vulgate; Septuagint reads _Gath._

LEADERSHIP REALITIES

ORGANIZE OR AGONIZE   *1 Samuel 17*

Shepherd boys were as common as flies, but this one dared to expect life to be extraordinary. David organized his every day skills into a brilliant scheme. As the giant lowered his guard, the teen aimed his slingshot into the one unprotected area of Goliath's body. David won.

In order to prevail, the leader must first prepare. No doubt young David used his free time to learn to play the harp, commune with his God, and to practice the slingshot. If you are facing a larger than life obstacle, get organized.

- Write down your goal. As you do so, you can visualize the project in measurable steps.
- Identify the stages of your plan. Within the long-term goal will be short-term goals or "steps" toward the end result. As you accomplish the steps, you'll be pumped about taking the next one.
- Set a target completion date for each step and an estimate for the overall goal. This can be and probably will be adjusted, but it takes you out of the land of "someday."
- Organize at the outset to avoid disappointments later. What do I need; where are those things; who do I need to see or talk to; what are my obstacles; what are my resources?
- Ask for help. Most successful people are more than happy to assist you, for they themselves were once (and probably will be again) on the asking side. Make a list of contact people who can help you achieve your goal.

all the people and also in the sight of Saul's servants. ⁶Now it had happened as they were coming *home,* when David was returning from the slaughter of the Philistine, that the women had come out of all the cities of Israel, singing and dancing, to meet King Saul, with tambourines, with joy, and with musical instruments. ⁷So the women sang as they danced, and said:

"Saul has slain his thousands,
And David his ten thousands."

⁸Then Saul was very angry, and the saying displeased him; and he said, "They have ascribed to David ten thousands, and to me they have ascribed only thousands. Now what more can he have but the kingdom?" ⁹So Saul eyed David from that day forward.

¹⁰And it happened on the next day that the distressing spirit from God came upon Saul, and he prophesied inside the house. So David played *music* with his hand, as at other times; but *there was* a spear in Saul's hand. ¹¹And Saul cast the spear, for he said, "I will pin David to the wall!" But David escaped his presence twice.

¹²Now Saul was afraid of David, because the LORD was with him, but had departed from Saul. ¹³Therefore Saul removed him from his presence, and made him his captain over a thousand; and he went out and came in before the people. ¹⁴And David behaved wisely in all his ways, and the LORD *was* with him. ¹⁵Therefore, when Saul saw that he behaved very wisely, he was afraid of him. ¹⁶But all Israel and Judah loved David, because he went out and came in before them.

DAVID MARRIES MICHAL

¹⁷Then Saul said to David, "Here is my older daughter Merab; I will give her to you as a wife. Only be valiant for me, and fight the LORD's

LEADERSHIP ISSUES

GC2: Be a Good Friend

1 SAMUEL 18:1

Healthy, God-honoring friendships are to be pursued, developed, and valued. Even from the first "not good" pronouncement of aloneness (Gen. 2:18), God has declared the significance of caring relationships. In addition to the blessing of our friendship with God, for our abundance He has provided families, marriage, and friendships within the body of Christ. Eve was brought to Adam so that aloneness was removed through the first marriage (Gen. 2:22, 24). God removes aloneness through children who are gifts or "rewards" from the Lord. They are to be cherished and loved within families as God intended (Ps. 127:1–5; Is. 49:15, 16). Close friendships within God's family are also for the removal of aloneness.

As with Jonathan and David, having our hearts knit together in caring friendship, is where we develop lifelong relational skills. These skills, developed in our youth, will serve us well throughout life as a single adult, a husband or wife, and parent.

The writer of Proverbs gives several important friendship principles, such as:

- Love a friend at all times, even in tough times (Prov. 17:17).
- Avoid those given to anger (Prov. 22:24).
- Receive a reproof from a friend (Prov. 27:6).
- Gossip and slander separate friends (Prov. 16:28).

Pause to consider these scriptures and your friends; thank the Lord for God-honoring friendships in your life; ask Him to make you a good friend.

GC2
GREAT COMMANDMENT
COMMISSION

LEAD**ERSHIP**
REAL**ITIES**

LEADERS HAVE FOLLOWERS   *1 Samuel 18:7*

This is a critical time in the leadership journey of David. It is here that the influence pendulum begins to shift from King Saul's favor toward David's. Female citizens in their celebration attributed more success to the rising leader than the failing one as the news of David's successes spread. While David had great favor with the Lord and his popularity with the people was growing, Saul's life was spiraling out of control. Saul was clearly a man after the people's heart and David a man after God's heart. Saul's disbelief and disobedience was the direct cause of his failing influence. He lost his influence because:

- He was afraid to lose what only God could provide and preserve (13:7–14).
- He had fallen in love with his own title thinking himself wiser than God (15:1–35).
- He sought to please an audience of many rather than an audience of one (15:24).
- He was consumed with jealousy over what God was doing in someone else's life (18:1—20:42).

Leaders have followers may seem like an obvious principle, but many people don't get it. Without followers, one is simply living in a state of self-delusion.

---

battles." For Saul thought, "Let my hand not be against him, but let the hand of the Philistines be against him."

¹⁸So David said to Saul, "Who *am* I, and what *is* my life *or* my father's family in Israel, that I should be son-in-law to the king?" ¹⁹But it happened at the time when Merab, Saul's daughter, should have been given to David, that she was given to Adriel the Meholathite as a wife.

²⁰Now Michal, Saul's daughter, loved David. And they told Saul, and the thing pleased him. ²¹So Saul said, "I will give her to him, that she may be a snare to him, and that the hand of the Philistines may be against him." Therefore Saul said to David a second time, "You shall be my son-in-law today."

²²And Saul commanded his servants, "Communicate with David secretly, and say, 'Look, the king has delight in you, and all his servants love you. Now therefore, become the king's son-in-law.' "

²³So Saul's servants spoke those words in the hearing of David. And David said, "Does it seem to you *a* light *thing* to be a king's son-in-law, seeing I *am* a poor and lightly esteemed man?" ²⁴And the servants of Saul told him, saying, "In this manner David spoke."

²⁵Then Saul said, "Thus you shall say to David: 'The king does not desire any dowry but one hundred foreskins of the Philistines, to take vengeance on the king's enemies.' " But Saul thought to make David fall by the hand of the Philistines. ²⁶So when his servants told David these words, it pleased David well to become the king's son-in-law. Now the days had not expired; ²⁷therefore David arose and went, he and his men, and killed two hundred men of the Philistines. And David brought their foreskins, and they gave them in full count to the king, that he might become the king's son-in-law. Then Saul gave him Michal his daughter as a wife.

²⁸Thus Saul saw and knew that the LORD *was* with David, and *that* Michal, Saul's daughter, loved him; ²⁹and Saul was still more afraid of David. So Saul became David's enemy continually. ³⁰Then the princes of the Philistines went out *to war*. And so it was, whenever they went out, *that* David behaved more wisely than all the servants of Saul, so that his name became highly esteemed.

SAUL PERSECUTES DAVID

19 Now Saul spoke to Jonathan his son and to all his servants, that they should kill David; but Jonathan, Saul's son, delighted greatly in David. ²So Jonathan told David, saying, "My father Saul seeks to kill you. Therefore please be on your guard until morning, and stay in a secret *place* and hide. ³And I will go out and stand beside my father in the field where you *are,* and I will speak with my father about you. Then what I observe, I will tell you."

⁴Thus Jonathan spoke well of David to Saul his father, and said to him, "Let not the king sin against his servant, against David, because he has not sinned against you, and because his works *have been* very good toward you. ⁵For he took his life in his hands and killed the Philistine, and the LORD brought about a great deliverance for all Israel. You saw *it* and rejoiced. Why then will you sin against innocent blood, to kill David without a cause?"

⁶So Saul heeded the voice of Jonathan, and Saul swore, "*As* the LORD lives, he shall not be killed." ⁷Then Jonathan called David, and Jonathan told him all these things. So Jonathan brought David to Saul, and he was in his presence as in times past.

⁸And there was war again; and David went out and fought with the Philistines, and struck them with a mighty blow, and they fled from him.

⁹Now the distressing spirit from the LORD came upon Saul as he sat in his house with his spear in his hand. And David was playing *music* with *his* hand. ¹⁰Then Saul sought to pin David to the wall with the spear, but he slipped away from Saul's presence; and he drove the spear into the wall. So David fled and escaped that night.

¹¹Saul also sent messengers to David's house to watch him and to kill him in the morning. And Michal, David's wife, told him, saying, "If you do not save your life tonight, tomorrow you will be killed." ¹²So Michal let David down through a window. And he went and fled and escaped. ¹³And Michal took an image and laid *it* in the bed, put a cover of goats' *hair* for his head, and covered *it* with clothes. ¹⁴So when Saul sent messengers to take David, she said, "He *is* sick."

¹⁵Then Saul sent the messengers *back* to see David, saying, "Bring him up to me in the bed, that I may kill him." ¹⁶And when the messengers had come in, there was the image in the bed, with a cover of goats' *hair* for his head. ¹⁷Then Saul said to Michal, "Why have you deceived me like this, and sent my enemy away, so that he has escaped?"

LEADERSHIP REALITIES

CULTIVATE A WIN-WIN LIFESTYLE *1 Samuel 19:4–7*

Jonathan will forever be remembered for his friendship and loyalty to David. At first glance, the friendship forged between them seems both odd and unlikely. Saul, Jonathan's father, wanted to destroy David. But, realizing his father had lost favor with God and was daily growing more insanely jealous of David, Jonathan made the decision to trust God's choice for the next king, even though he was the natural, rightful successor to the throne as Saul's firstborn son. Instead of despising David or seeing him as competition, he blessed and befriended him. Jonathan knew the leadership reality of *cultivating a win-win lifestyle*.

dabar towb—**spoke good**—to declare excellence about a person, event, or thing

He understood that as he helped others become successful, God would also give him success. It was clear to him that a band of brothers is always more powerful than a lone ranger, and history never records Jonathan accompanying his father in the campaigns to hunt David down. If you are afraid to let others succeed, you place a lid on the opportunity to represent the purposes of God and limit His blessings on your future.

And Michal answered Saul, "He said to me, 'Let me go! Why should I kill you?' "

[18]So David fled and escaped, and went to Samuel at Ramah, and told him all that Saul had done to him. And he and Samuel went and stayed in Naioth. [19]Now it was told Saul, saying, "Take note, David is at Naioth in Ramah!" [20]Then Saul sent messengers to take David. And when they saw the group of prophets prophesying, and Samuel standing as leader over them, the Spirit of God came upon the messengers of Saul, and they also prophesied. [21]And when Saul was told, he sent other messengers, and they prophesied likewise. Then Saul sent messengers again the third time, and they prophesied also. [22]Then he also went to Ramah, and came to the great well that is at Sechu. So he asked, and said, "Where are Samuel and David?"

And someone said, "Indeed they are at Naioth in Ramah." [23]So he went there to Naioth in Ramah. Then the Spirit of God was upon him also, and he went on and prophesied until he came to Naioth in Ramah. [24]And he also stripped off his clothes and prophesied before Samuel in like manner, and lay down naked all that day and all that night. Therefore they say, "Is Saul also among the prophets?"[a]

20Then David fled from Naioth in Ramah, and went and said to Jonathan, "What have I done? What is my iniquity, and what is my sin before your father, that he seeks my life?"

[2]So Jonathan said to him, "By no means! You shall not die! Indeed, my father will do nothing either great or small without first telling me. And why should my father hide this thing from me? It is not so!"

[3]Then David took an oath again, and said, "Your father certainly knows that I have found favor in your eyes, and he has said, 'Do not let Jonathan know this, lest he be grieved.' But truly, as the LORD lives and as your soul lives, there is but a step between me and death."

[4]So Jonathan said to David, "Whatever you yourself desire, I will do it for you."

[5]And David said to Jonathan, "Indeed tomorrow is the New Moon, and I should not fail to sit with the king to eat. But let me go, that I may hide in the field until the third day at evening. [6]If your father misses me at all, then say, 'David earnestly asked permission of me that he might run over to Bethlehem, his city, for there is a yearly sacrifice there for all the family.' [7]If he says thus: 'It is well,' your servant will be safe. But if he is very angry, be sure that evil is determined by him. [8]Therefore you shall deal kindly with your servant, for you have brought your servant into a covenant of the LORD with you. Nevertheless, if there is iniquity in me, kill me yourself, for why should you bring me to your father?"

[9]But Jonathan said, "Far be it from you! For if I knew certainly that evil was determined by my father to come upon you, then would I not tell you?"

[10]Then David said to Jonathan, "Who will tell me, or what if your father answers you roughly?"

[11]And Jonathan said to David, "Come, let us go out into the field." So both of them went out into the field. [12]Then Jonathan said to David: "The LORD God of Israel is witness! When I have sounded out my father sometime tomorrow, or the third day, and indeed there is good toward David, and I do not send to you and tell you, [13]may the LORD do so and much more to Jonathan. But if it pleases my father to do you evil, then I will report it to you and send you away, that you may go in safety. And the LORD be with you as He has been with my father. [14]And you shall not only show me the kindness of the LORD while I still live, that I may not die; [15]but you shall not cut off your kindness from my house forever, no, not when the LORD has cut off every one of the enemies of David from the face of the earth." [16]So Jonathan made a covenant with the house of David, saying, "Let the LORD require it at the hand of David's enemies."

[17]Now Jonathan again caused David to vow, because he loved him; for he loved him as he loved his own soul. [18]Then Jonathan said to David, "Tomorrow is the New Moon; and you will be missed, because your seat will be empty. [19]And when you have stayed three days, go down quickly and come to the place where you hid on the day of the deed; and remain by the stone Ezel. [20]Then I will shoot three arrows to the side, as

though I shot at a target; [21]and there I will send a lad, *saying,* 'Go, find the arrows.' If I expressly say to the lad, 'Look, the arrows *are* on this side of you; get them and come'—then, as the LORD lives, *there is* safety for you and no harm. [22]But if I say thus to the young man, 'Look, the arrows *are* beyond you'—go your way, for the LORD has sent you away. [23]And as for the matter which you and I have spoken of, indeed the LORD *be* between you and me forever."

[24]Then David hid in the field. And when the New Moon had come, the king sat down to eat the feast. [25]Now the king sat on his seat, as at other times, on a seat by the wall. And Jonathan arose,[a] and Abner sat by Saul's side, but David's place was empty. [26]Nevertheless Saul did not say anything that day, for he thought, "Something has happened to him; he *is* unclean, surely he *is* unclean." [27]And it happened the next day, the second *day* of the month, that David's place was empty. And Saul said to Jonathan his son, "Why has the son of Jesse not come to eat, either yesterday or today?"

[28]So Jonathan answered Saul, "David earnestly asked *permission* of me *to go* to Bethlehem. [29]And he said, 'Please let me go, for our family has a sacrifice in the city, and my brother has commanded me *to be there.* And now, if I have found favor in your eyes, please let me get away and see my brothers.' Therefore he has not come to the king's table."

[30]Then Saul's anger was aroused against Jonathan, and he said to him, "You son of a perverse, rebellious *woman!* Do I not know that you have chosen the son of Jesse to your own shame and to the shame of your mother's nakedness? [31]For as long as the son of Jesse lives on the earth, you shall not be established, nor your kingdom. Now therefore, send and bring him to me, for he shall surely die."

[32]And Jonathan answered Saul his father, and said to him, "Why should he be killed? What has he done?" [33]Then Saul cast a spear at him to kill him, by which Jonathan knew that it was determined by his father to kill David.

[34]So Jonathan arose from the table in fierce anger, and ate no food the second day of the month, for he was grieved for David, because his father had treated him shamefully.

[35]And so it was, in the morning, that Jonathan went out into the field at the time appointed with David, and a little lad *was* with him. [36]Then he said to his lad, "Now run, find the arrows which I shoot." As the lad ran, he shot an arrow beyond him. [37]When the lad had come to the place where the arrow was which Jonathan had shot, Jonathan cried out after the lad and said, "*Is* not the arrow beyond you?" [38]And Jonathan cried out after the lad, "Make haste, hurry, do not delay!" So Jonathan's lad gathered up the arrows and came back to his master. [39]But the lad did not know anything. Only Jonathan and David knew of the matter. [40]Then Jonathan gave his weapons to his lad, and said to him, "Go, carry *them* to the city."

[41]As soon as the lad had gone, David arose from *a place* toward the south, fell on his face to the ground, and bowed down three times. And they kissed one another; and they wept together, but David more so. [42]Then Jonathan said to David, "Go in peace, since we have both sworn in the name of the LORD, saying, 'May the LORD be between you and me, and between your descendants and my descendants, forever.' " So he arose and departed, and Jonathan went into the city.

DAVID AND THE HOLY BREAD

21 Now David came to Nob, to Ahimelech the priest. And Ahimelech was afraid when he met David, and said to him, "Why *are* you alone, and no one is with you?"

[2]So David said to Ahimelech the priest, "The king has ordered me on some business, and said to me, 'Do not let anyone know anything about the business on which I send you, or what I have commanded you.' And I have directed *my* young men to such and such a place. [3]Now therefore, what have you on hand? Give *me* five *loaves of* bread in my hand, or whatever can be found."

[4]And the priest answered David and said, "*There is* no common bread on hand; but there is holy bread, if the young men have at least kept themselves from women."

[5]Then David answered the priest, and said to him, "Truly, women *have been* kept from us about three days since I came out. And the vessels of the young men are holy, and *the bread is* in effect

20:25 [a]Following Masoretic Text, Syriac, Targum, and Vulgate; Septuagint reads *he sat across from Jonathan.*

common, even though it was consecrated in the vessel this day."

⁶So the priest gave him holy *bread;* for there was no bread there but the showbread which had been taken from before the LORD, in order to put hot bread *in its place* on the day when it was taken away.

⁷Now a certain man of the servants of Saul *was* there that day, detained before the LORD. And his name *was* Doeg, an Edomite, the chief of the herdsmen who *belonged* to Saul.

⁸And David said to Ahimelech, "Is there not here on hand a spear or a sword? For I have brought neither my sword nor my weapons with me, because the king's business required haste."

⁹So the priest said, "The sword of Goliath the Philistine, whom you killed in the Valley of Elah, there it is, wrapped in a cloth behind the ephod. If you will take that, take *it.* For *there is* no other except that one here."

And David said, "*There is* none like it; give it to me."

David Flees to Gath

¹⁰Then David arose and fled that day from before Saul, and went to Achish the king of Gath. ¹¹And the servants of Achish said to him, "*Is* this not David the king of the land? Did they not sing of him to one another in dances, saying:

'Saul has slain his thousands,
And David his ten thousands'?"ᵃ

¹²Now David took these words to heart, and was very much afraid of Achish the king of Gath. ¹³So he changed his behavior before them, pretended madness in their hands, scratched on the doors of the gate, and let his saliva fall down on his beard. ¹⁴Then Achish said to his servants, "Look, you see the man is insane. Why have you brought him to me? ¹⁵Have I need of madmen, that you have brought this *fellow* to play the madman in my presence? Shall this *fellow* come into my house?"

David's Four Hundred Men

22 David therefore departed from there and escaped to the cave of Adullam. So when his brothers and all his father's house heard *it,*

they went down there to him. ²And everyone *who was* in distress, everyone who *was* in debt, and everyone *who was* discontented gathered to him. So he became captain over them. And there were about four hundred men with him.

³Then David went from there to Mizpah of Moab; and he said to the king of Moab, "Please let my father and mother come here with you, till I know what God will do for me." ⁴So he brought them before the king of Moab, and they dwelt with him all the time that David was in the stronghold.

⁵Now the prophet Gad said to David, "Do not stay in the stronghold; depart, and go to the land of Judah." So David departed and went into the forest of Hereth.

Saul Murders the Priests

⁶When Saul heard that David and the men who *were* with him had been discovered—now Saul was staying in Gibeah under a tamarisk tree in Ramah, with his spear in his hand, and all his servants standing about him— ⁷then Saul said to his servants who stood about him, "Hear now, you Benjamites! Will the son of Jesse give every one of you fields and vineyards, *and* make you all captains of thousands and captains of hundreds? ⁸All of you have conspired against me, and *there is* no one who reveals to me that my son has made a covenant with the son of Jesse; and *there is* not one of you who is sorry for me or reveals to me that my son has stirred up my servant against me, to lie in wait, as *it is* this day."

⁹Then answered Doeg the Edomite, who was set over the servants of Saul, and said, "I saw the son of Jesse going to Nob, to Ahimelech the son of Ahitub. ¹⁰And he inquired of the LORD for him, gave him provisions, and gave him the sword of Goliath the Philistine."

¹¹So the king sent to call Ahimelech the priest, the son of Ahitub, and all his father's house, the priests who *were* in Nob. And they all came to the king. ¹²And Saul said, "Hear now, son of Ahitub!"

He answered, "Here I am, my lord."

¹³Then Saul said to him, "Why have you conspired against me, you and the son of Jesse, in that

you have given him bread and a sword, and have inquired of God for him, that he should rise against me, to lie in wait, as it is this day?"

[14]So Ahimelech answered the king and said, "And who among all your servants *is as* faithful as David, who is the king's son-in-law, who goes at your bidding, and is honorable in your house? [15]Did I then begin to inquire of God for him? Far be it from me! Let not the king impute anything to his servant, *or* to any in the house of my father. For your servant knew nothing of all this, little or much."

[16]And the king said, "You shall surely die, Ahimelech, you and all your father's house!" [17]Then the king said to the guards who stood about him, "Turn and kill the priests of the LORD, because their hand also *is* with David, and because they knew when he fled and did not tell it to me." But the servants of the king would not lift their hands to strike the priests of the LORD. [18]And the king said to Doeg, "You turn and kill the priests!" So Doeg the Edomite turned and struck the priests, and killed on that day eighty-five men who wore a linen ephod. [19]Also Nob, the city of the priests, he struck with the edge of the sword, both men and women, children and nursing infants, oxen and donkeys and sheep—with the edge of the sword.

[20]Now one of the sons of Ahimelech the son of Ahitub, named Abiathar, escaped and fled after David. [21]And Abiathar told David that Saul had killed the LORD's priests. [22]So David said to Abiathar, "I knew that day, when Doeg the Edomite *was* there, that he would surely tell Saul. I have caused *the death* of all the persons of your father's house. [23]Stay with me; do not fear. For he who seeks my life seeks your life, but with me you *shall be* safe."

DAVID SAVES THE CITY OF KEILAH

23 Then they told David, saying, "Look, the Philistines are fighting against Keilah, and they are robbing the threshing floors."

[2]Therefore David inquired of the LORD, saying, "Shall I go and attack these Philistines?"

And the LORD said to David, "Go and attack the Philistines, and save Keilah."

[3]But David's men said to him, "Look, we are afraid here in Judah. How much more then if we go to Keilah against the armies of the Philistines?" [4]Then David inquired of the LORD once again.

And the LORD answered him and said, "Arise, go down to Keilah. For I will deliver the Philistines into your hand." [5]And David and his men went to Keilah and fought with the Philistines, struck them with a mighty blow, and took away their livestock. So David saved the inhabitants of Keilah.

[6]Now it happened, when Abiathar the son of Ahimelech fled to David at Keilah, *that* he went down *with* an ephod in his hand.

[7]And Saul was told that David had gone to Keilah. So Saul said, "God has delivered him into my hand, for he has shut himself in by entering a town that has gates and bars." [8]Then Saul called all the people together for war, to go down to Keilah to besiege David and his men.

[9]When David knew that Saul plotted evil against him, he said to Abiathar the priest, "Bring the ephod here." [10]Then David said, "O LORD God of Israel, Your servant has certainly heard that Saul seeks to come to Keilah to destroy the city for my sake. [11]Will the men of Keilah deliver me into his hand? Will Saul come down, as Your servant has heard? O LORD God of Israel, I pray, tell Your servant."

And the LORD said, "He will come down."

[12]Then David said, "Will the men of Keilah deliver me and my men into the hand of Saul?"

And the LORD said, "They will deliver *you*."

[13]So David and his men, about six hundred, arose and departed from Keilah and went wherever they could go. Then it was told Saul that David had escaped from Keilah; so he halted the expedition.

DAVID IN WILDERNESS STRONGHOLDS

[14]And David stayed in strongholds in the wilderness, and remained in the mountains in the Wilderness of Ziph. Saul sought him every day, but God did not deliver him into his hand. [15]So David saw that Saul had come out to seek his life. And David *was* in the Wilderness of Ziph in a forest.[a] [16]Then Jonathan, Saul's son, arose and went to David in the woods and strengthened his

23:15 [a]Or *in Horesh*

hand in God. [17]And he said to him, "Do not fear, for the hand of Saul my father shall not find you. You shall be king over Israel, and I shall be next to you. Even my father Saul knows that." [18]So the two of them made a covenant before the LORD. And David stayed in the woods, and Jonathan went to his own house.

[19]Then the Ziphites came up to Saul at Gibeah, saying, "Is David not hiding with us in strongholds in the woods, in the hill of Hachilah, which is on the south of Jeshimon? [20]Now therefore, O king, come down according to all the desire of your soul to come down; and our part shall be to deliver him into the king's hand."

[21]And Saul said, "Blessed are you of the LORD, for you have compassion on me. [22]Please go and find out for sure, and see the place where his hideout is, and who has seen him there. For I am told he is very crafty. [23]See therefore, and take knowledge of all the lurking places where he hides; and come back to me with certainty, and I will go with you. And it shall be, if he is in the land, that I will search for him throughout all the clans[a] of Judah."

[24]So they arose and went to Ziph before Saul. But David and his men were in the Wilderness of Maon, in the plain on the south of Jeshimon. [25]When Saul and his men went to seek him, they told David. Therefore he went down to the rock, and stayed in the Wilderness of Maon. And when Saul heard that, he pursued David in the Wilderness of Maon. [26]Then Saul went on one side of the mountain, and David and his men on the other side of the mountain. So David made haste to get away from Saul, for Saul and his men were encircling David and his men to take them.

[27]But a messenger came to Saul, saying, "Hurry and come, for the Philistines have invaded the land!" [28]Therefore Saul returned from pursuing David, and went against the Philistines; so they called that place the Rock of Escape.[a] [29]Then David went up from there and dwelt in strongholds at En Gedi.

DAVID SPARES SAUL

24 Now it happened, when Saul had returned from following the Philistines, that it was told him, saying, "Take note! David is in the Wilderness of En Gedi." [2]Then Saul took three thousand chosen men from all Israel, and went to seek David and his men on the Rocks of the Wild Goats. [3]So he came to the sheepfolds by the road, where there was a cave; and Saul went in to attend to his needs. (David and his men were staying in the recesses of the cave.) [4]Then the men of David said to him, "This is the day of which the LORD said to you, 'Behold, I will deliver your enemy into your hand, that you may do to him as it seems good to you.' " And David arose and secretly cut off a corner of Saul's robe. [5]Now it happened afterward that David's heart troubled him because he had cut Saul's robe. [6]And he said to his men, "The LORD forbid that I should do this thing to my master, the LORD's anointed, to stretch out my hand against him, seeing he is the anointed of the LORD." [7]So David restrained his servants with these words, and did not allow them to rise against Saul. And Saul got up from the cave and went on his way.

[8]David also arose afterward, went out of the cave, and called out to Saul, saying, "My lord the king!" And when Saul looked behind him, David stooped with his face to the earth, and bowed down. [9]And David said to Saul: "Why do you listen to the words of men who say, 'Indeed David seeks your harm'? [10]Look, this day your eyes have seen that the LORD delivered you today into my hand in the cave, and someone urged me to kill you. But my eye spared you, and I said, 'I will not stretch out my hand against my lord, for he is the LORD's anointed.' [11]Moreover, my father, see! Yes, see the corner of your robe in my hand! For in that I cut off the corner of your robe, and did not kill you, know and see that there is neither evil nor rebellion in my hand, and I have not sinned against you. Yet you hunt my life to take it. [12]Let the LORD judge between you and me, and let the LORD avenge me on you. But my hand shall not be against you. [13]As the proverb of the ancients says, 'Wickedness proceeds from the wicked.' But my hand shall not be against you. [14]After whom has the king of Israel come out? Whom do you pursue? A dead dog? A flea? [15]Therefore let the LORD be judge, and judge between you and me, and see and plead my case, and deliver me out of your hand."

23:23 [a]Literally thousands **23:28** [a]Hebrew Sela Hammahlekoth

16So it was, when David had finished speaking these words to Saul, that Saul said, "Is this your voice, my son David?" And Saul lifted up his voice and wept. 17Then he said to David: "You are more righteous than I; for you have rewarded me with good, whereas I have rewarded you with evil. 18And you have shown this day how you have dealt well with me; for when the LORD delivered me into your hand, you did not kill me. 19For if a man finds his enemy, will he let him get away safely? Therefore may the LORD reward you with good for what you have done to me this day. 20And now I know indeed that you shall surely be king, and that the kingdom of Israel shall be established in your hand. 21Therefore swear now to me by the LORD that you will not cut off my descendants after me, and that you will not destroy my name from my father's house."

22So David swore to Saul. And Saul went home, but David and his men went up to the stronghold.

DEATH OF SAMUEL

25 Then Samuel died; and the Israelites gathered together and lamented for him, and buried him at his home in Ramah. And David arose and went down to the Wilderness of Paran.ᵃ

DAVID AND THE WIFE OF NABAL

2Now there was a man in Maon whose business was in Carmel, and the man was very rich. He had three thousand sheep and a thousand goats. And he was shearing his sheep in Carmel. 3The name of the man was Nabal, and the name of his wife Abigail. And she was a woman of good understanding and beautiful appearance; but the man was harsh and evil in his doings. He was of the house of Caleb.

4When David heard in the wilderness that Nabal was shearing his sheep, 5David sent ten young men; and David said to the young men, "Go up to Carmel, go to Nabal, and greet him in my name. 6And thus you shall say to him who lives in prosperity: 'Peace be to you, peace to your house, and peace to all that you have! 7Now I have heard that you have shearers. Your shepherds were with us, and we did not hurt them, nor was there anything missing from them all the while they were in Carmel. 8Ask your young men, and

they will tell you. Therefore let my young men find favor in your eyes, for we come on a feast day. Please give whatever comes to your hand to your servants and to your son David.' "

9So when David's young men came, they spoke to Nabal according to all these words in the name of David, and waited.

10Then Nabal answered David's servants, and said, "Who is David, and who is the son of Jesse? There are many servants nowadays who break away each one from his master. 11Shall I then take my bread and my water and my meat that I have killed for my shearers, and give it to men when I do not know where they are from?"

12So David's young men turned on their heels and went back; and they came and told him all these words. 13Then David said to his men, "Every man gird on his sword." So every man girded on his sword, and David also girded on his sword. And about four hundred men went with David, and two hundred stayed with the supplies.

14Now one of the young men told Abigail, Nabal's wife, saying, "Look, David sent messengers from the wilderness to greet our master; and he reviled them. 15But the men were very good to us, and we were not hurt, nor did we miss anything as long as we accompanied them, when we were in the fields. 16They were a wall to us both by night and day, all the time we were with them keeping the sheep. 17Now therefore, know and consider what you will do, for harm is determined against our master and against all his household. For he is such a scoundrelᵃ that one cannot speak to him."

18Then Abigail made haste and took two hundred loaves of bread, two skins of wine, five sheep already dressed, five seahs of roasted grain, one hundred clusters of raisins, and two hundred cakes of figs, and loaded them on donkeys. 19And she said to her servants, "Go on before me; see, I am coming after you." But she did not tell her husband Nabal.

20So it was, as she rode on the donkey, that she went down under cover of the hill; and there were David and his men, coming down toward her, and she met them. 21Now David had said, "Surely in vain I have protected all that this fellow

25:1 ᵃFollowing Masoretic Text, Syriac, Targum, and Vulgate; Septuagint reads Maon.   25:17 ᵃLiterally son of Belial has in the wilderness, so that nothing was missed of all that *belongs* to him. And he has repaid me evil for good. [22]May God do so, and more also, to the enemies of David, if I leave one male of all who *belong* to him by morning light."

[23]Now when Abigail saw David, she dismounted quickly from the donkey, fell on her face before David, and bowed down to the ground. [24]So she fell at his feet and said: "On me, my lord, *on me let* this iniquity *be!* And please let your maidservant speak in your ears, and hear the words of your maidservant. [25]Please, let not my lord regard this scoundrel Nabal. For as his name *is,* so *is* he: Nabal[a] *is* his name, and folly *is* with him! But I, your maidservant, did not see the young men of my lord whom you sent. [26]Now therefore, my lord, *as* the LORD lives and *as* your soul lives, since the LORD has held you back from coming to bloodshed and from avenging yourself with your own hand, now then, let your enemies and those who seek harm for my lord be as Nabal. [27]And now this present which your maidservant has brought to my lord, let it be given to the young men who follow my lord. [28]Please forgive the trespass of your maidservant. For the LORD will certainly make for my lord an enduring house, because my lord fights the battles of the LORD, and evil is not found in you throughout your days. [29]Yet a man has risen to pursue you and seek your life, but the life of my lord shall be bound in the bundle of the living with the LORD your God; and the lives of your enemies He shall sling out, *as from* the pocket of a sling. [30]And it shall come to pass, when the LORD has done for my lord according to all the good that He has spoken concerning you, and has appointed you ruler over Israel, [31]that this will be no grief to you, nor offense of heart to my lord, either that you have shed blood without cause, or that my lord has avenged himself. But when the LORD has dealt well with my lord, then remember your maidservant."

[32]Then David said to Abigail: "Blessed *is* the LORD God of Israel, who sent you this day to meet me! [33]And blessed *is* your advice and blessed *are* you, because you have kept me this day from coming to bloodshed and from avenging myself with my own hand. [34]For indeed, *as* the LORD God of Israel lives, who has kept me back from hurting you, unless you had hurried and come to meet me, surely by morning light no males would have been left to Nabal!" [35]So David received from her hand what she had brought him, and said to her, "Go up in peace to your house. See, I have heeded your voice and respected your person."

[36]Now Abigail went to Nabal, and there he was, holding a feast in his house, like the feast of a king. And Nabal's heart *was* merry within him, for he *was* very drunk; therefore she told him nothing, little or much, until morning light. [37]So it was, in the morning, when the wine had gone from Nabal, and his wife had told him these things, that his heart died within him, and he became *like* a stone. [38]Then it happened, *after* about ten days, that the LORD struck Nabal, and he died.

[39]So when David heard that Nabal was dead, he said, "Blessed *be* the LORD, who has pleaded the cause of my reproach from the hand of Nabal, and has kept His servant from evil! For the LORD has returned the wickedness of Nabal on his own head."

And David sent and proposed to Abigail, to take her as his wife. [40]When the servants of David had come to Abigail at Carmel, they spoke to her saying, "David sent us to you, to ask you to become his wife."

[41]Then she arose, bowed her face to the earth, and said, "Here is your maidservant, a servant to wash the feet of the servants of my lord." [42]So Abigail rose in haste and rode on a donkey, attended by five of her maidens; and she followed the messengers of David, and became his wife. [43]David also took Ahinoam of Jezreel, and so both of them were his wives.

[44]But Saul had given Michal his daughter, David's wife, to Palti[a] the son of Laish, who *was* from Gallim.

DAVID SPARES SAUL A SECOND TIME

26Now the Ziphites came to Saul at Gibeah, saying, "Is David not hiding in the hill of Hachilah, opposite Jeshimon?" [2]Then Saul arose and went down to the Wilderness of Ziph, having three thousand chosen men of Israel with him, to

25:25 [a]Literally *Fool* 25:44 [a]Spelled *Paltiel* in 2 Samuel 3:15

seek David in the Wilderness of Ziph. ³And Saul encamped in the hill of Hachilah, which *is* opposite Jeshimon, by the road. But David stayed in the wilderness, and he saw that Saul came after him into the wilderness. ⁴David therefore sent out spies, and understood that Saul had indeed come.

⁵So David arose and came to the place where Saul had encamped. And David saw the place where Saul lay, and Abner the son of Ner, the commander of his army. Now Saul lay within the camp, with the people encamped all around him. ⁶Then David answered, and said to Ahimelech the Hittite and to Abishai the son of Zeruiah, brother of Joab, saying, "Who will go down with me to Saul in the camp?"

And Abishai said, "I will go down with you."

⁷So David and Abishai came to the people by night; and there Saul lay sleeping within the camp, with his spear stuck in the ground by his head. And Abner and the people lay all around him. ⁸Then Abishai said to David, "God has delivered your enemy into your hand this day. Now therefore, please, let me strike him at once with the spear, right to the earth; and I will not *have to strike* him a second time!"

⁹But David said to Abishai, "Do not destroy him; for who can stretch out his hand against the LORD's anointed, and be guiltless?" ¹⁰David said furthermore, "*As* the LORD lives, the LORD shall strike him, or his day shall come to die, or he shall go out to battle and perish. ¹¹The LORD forbid that I should stretch out my hand against the LORD's anointed. But please, take now the spear and the jug of water that *are* by his head, and let us go." ¹²So David took the spear and the jug of water *by* Saul's head, and they got away; and no man saw or knew *it* or awoke. For they *were* all asleep, because a deep sleep from the LORD had fallen on them.

¹³Now David went over to the other side, and stood on the top of a hill afar off, a great distance *being* between them. ¹⁴And David called out to the people and to Abner the son of Ner, saying, "Do you not answer, Abner?"

Then Abner answered and said, "Who *are* you, calling out to the king?"

¹⁵So David said to Abner, "*Are* you not a man? And who *is* like you in Israel? Why then have you not guarded your lord the king? For one

of the people came in to destroy your lord the king. ¹⁶This thing that you have done *is* not good. *As* the LORD lives, you deserve to die, because you have not guarded your master, the LORD's anointed. And now see where the king's spear *is,* and the jug of water that *was* by his head."

¹⁷Then Saul knew David's voice, and said, "*Is* that your voice, my son David?"

David said, "*It is* my voice, my lord, O king." ¹⁸And he said, "Why does my lord thus pursue his servant? For what have I done, or what evil *is* in my hand? ¹⁹Now therefore, please, let my lord the king hear the words of his servant: If the LORD has stirred you up against me, let Him accept an offering. But if *it is* the children of men, *may* they *be* cursed before the LORD, for they have driven me out this day from sharing in the inheritance of the LORD, saying, 'Go, serve other gods.' ²⁰So now, do not let my blood fall to the earth before the face of the LORD. For the king of Israel has come out to seek a flea, as when one hunts a partridge in the mountains."

²¹Then Saul said, "I have sinned. Return, my son David. For I will harm you no more, because my life was precious in your eyes this day. Indeed I have played the fool and erred exceedingly."

²²And David answered and said, "Here is the king's spear. Let one of the young men come over and get it. ²³May the LORD repay every man *for* his righteousness and his faithfulness; for the LORD delivered you into *my* hand today, but I would not stretch out my hand against the LORD's anointed. ²⁴And indeed, as your life was valued much this day in my eyes, so let my life be valued much in the eyes of the LORD, and let Him deliver me out of all tribulation."

²⁵Then Saul said to David, "*May* you *be* blessed, my son David! You shall both do great things and also still prevail."

So David went on his way, and Saul returned to his place.

David Allied with the Philistines

27 And David said in his heart, "Now I shall perish someday by the hand of Saul. *There is* nothing better for me than that I should speedily escape to the land of the Philistines; and Saul will despair of me, to seek me anymore in any part of Israel. So I shall escape out of his hand." [2]Then David arose and went over with the six hundred men who *were* with him to Achish the son of Maoch, king of Gath. [3]So David dwelt with Achish at Gath, he and his men, each man with his household, *and* David with his two wives, Ahinoam the Jezreelitess, and Abigail the Carmelitess, Nabal's widow. [4]And it was told Saul that David had fled to Gath; so he sought him no more.

[5]Then David said to Achish, "If I have now found favor in your eyes, let them give me a place in some town in the country, that I may dwell there. For why should your servant dwell in the royal city with you?" [6]So Achish gave him Ziklag that day. Therefore Ziklag has belonged to the kings of Judah to this day. [7]Now the time that David dwelt in the country of the Philistines was one full year and four months.

[8]And David and his men went up and raided the Geshurites, the Girzites,[a] and the Amalekites. For those *nations* were the inhabitants of the land from of old, as you go to Shur, even as far as the land of Egypt. [9]Whenever David attacked the land, he left neither man nor woman alive, but took away the sheep, the oxen, the donkeys, the camels, and the apparel, and returned and came to Achish. [10]Then Achish would say, "Where have you made a raid today?" And David would say, "Against the southern *area* of Judah, or against the southern *area* of the Jerahmeelites, or against the southern *area* of the Kenites." [11]David would save neither man nor woman alive, to bring *news* to Gath, saying, "Lest they should inform on us, saying, 'Thus David did.' " And thus *was* his behavior all the time he dwelt in the country of the Philistines. [12]So Achish believed David, saying, "He has made his people Israel utterly abhor him; therefore he will be my servant forever."

28 Now it happened in those days that the Philistines gathered their armies together for war, to fight with Israel. And Achish said to David, "You assuredly know that you will go out with me to battle, you and your men."

[2]So David said to Achish, "Surely you know what your servant can do."

And Achish said to David, "Therefore I will make you one of my chief guardians forever."

SAUL CONSULTS A MEDIUM

[3]Now Samuel had died, and all Israel had lamented for him and buried him in Ramah, in his own city. And Saul had put the mediums and the spiritists out of the land.

[4]Then the Philistines gathered together, and came and encamped at Shunem. So Saul gathered all Israel together, and they encamped at Gilboa. [5]When Saul saw the army of the Philistines, he was afraid, and his heart trembled greatly. [6]And when Saul inquired of the LORD, the LORD did not answer him, either by dreams or by Urim or by the prophets.

[7]Then Saul said to his servants, "Find me a woman who is a medium, that I may go to her and inquire of her."

And his servants said to him, "In fact, *there is* a woman who is a medium at En Dor."

[8]So Saul disguised himself and put on other clothes, and he went, and two men with him; and they came to the woman by night. And he said, "Please conduct a séance for me, and bring up for me the one I shall name to you."

[9]Then the woman said to him, "Look, you know what Saul has done, how he has cut off the mediums and the spiritists from the land. Why then do you lay a snare for my life, to cause me to die?"

[10]And Saul swore to her by the LORD, saying, "*As* the LORD lives, no punishment shall come upon you for this thing."

[11]Then the woman said, "Whom shall I bring up for you?"

And he said, "Bring up Samuel for me."

[12]When the woman saw Samuel, she cried out with a loud voice. And the woman spoke to Saul, saying, "Why have you deceived me? For you *are* Saul!"

[13]And the king said to her, "Do not be afraid. What did you see?"

And the woman said to Saul, "I saw a spirit[a] ascending out of the earth."

[14]So he said to her, "What *is* his form?"

And she said, "An old man is coming up, and he *is* covered with a mantle." And Saul perceived that it *was* Samuel, and he stooped with *his* face to the ground and bowed down.

27:8 [a]Or *Gezrites*   28:13 [a]Hebrew *elohim*

¹⁵Now Samuel said to Saul, "Why have you disturbed me by bringing me up?"

And Saul answered, "I am deeply distressed; for the Philistines make war against me, and God has departed from me and does not answer me anymore, neither by prophets nor by dreams. Therefore I have called you, that you may reveal to me what I should do."

¹⁶Then Samuel said: "So why do you ask me, seeing the LORD has departed from you and has become your enemy? ¹⁷And the LORD has done for Himself[a] as He spoke by me. For the LORD has torn the kingdom out of your hand and given it to your neighbor, David. ¹⁸Because you did not obey the voice of the LORD nor execute His fierce wrath upon Amalek, therefore the LORD has done this thing to you this day. ¹⁹Moreover the LORD will also deliver Israel with you into the hand of the Philistines. And tomorrow you and your sons *will be* with me. The LORD will also deliver the army of Israel into the hand of the Philistines."

²⁰Immediately Saul fell full length on the ground, and was dreadfully afraid because of the words of Samuel. And there was no strength in him, for he had eaten no food all day or all night.

²¹And the woman came to Saul and saw that he was severely troubled, and said to him, "Look, your maidservant has obeyed your voice, and I have put my life in my hands and heeded the words which you spoke to me. ²²Now therefore, please, heed also the voice of your maidservant, and let me set a piece of bread before you; and eat, that you may have strength when you go on *your* way."

²³But he refused and said, "I will not eat."

So his servants, together with the woman, urged him; and he heeded their voice. Then he arose from the ground and sat on the bed. ²⁴Now the woman had a fatted calf in the house, and she hastened to kill it. And she took flour and kneaded *it,* and baked unleavened bread from it. ²⁵So she brought *it* before Saul and his servants, and they ate. Then they rose and went away that night.

The Philistines Reject David

29 Then the Philistines gathered together all their armies at Aphek, and the Israelites encamped by a fountain which *is* in Jezreel. ²And the lords of the Philistines passed in review by

hundreds and by thousands, but David and his men passed in review at the rear with Achish. ³Then the princes of the Philistines said, "What *are* these Hebrews *doing here?"*

And Achish said to the princes of the Philistines, "*Is* this not David, the servant of Saul king of Israel, who has been with me these days, or these years? And to this day I have found no fault in him since he defected *to me.*"

⁴But the princes of the Philistines were angry with him; so the princes of the Philistines said to him, "Make this fellow return, that he may go back to the place which you have appointed for him, and do not let him go down with us to battle, lest in the battle he become our adversary. For with what could he reconcile himself to his master, if not with the heads of these men? ⁵*Is* this not David, of whom they sang to one another in dances, saying:

'Saul has slain his thousands,
And David his ten thousands'?"[a]

⁶Then Achish called David and said to him, "Surely, *as* the LORD lives, you have been upright, and your going out and your coming in with me in the army *is* good in my sight. For to this day I have not found evil in you since the day of your coming to me. Nevertheless the lords do not favor you. ⁷Therefore return now, and go in peace, that you may not displease the lords of the Philistines."

⁸So David said to Achish, "But what have I done? And to this day what have you found in your servant as long as I have been with you, that I may not go and fight against the enemies of my lord the king?"

⁹Then Achish answered and said to David, "I know that you *are* as good in my sight as an angel of God; nevertheless the princes of the Philistines have said, 'He shall not go up with us to the battle.' ¹⁰Now therefore, rise early in the morning with your master's servants who have come with you.[a] And as soon as you are up early in the morning and have light, depart."

28:17 ᵃOr *him,* that is, David   **29:5** ᵃCompare 1 Samuel 18:7   **29:10** ᵃFollowing Masoretic Text, Targum, and Vulgate; Septuagint adds *and go to the place which I have selected for you there; and set no bothersome word in your heart, for you are good before me. And rise on your way.*

[11]So David and his men rose early to depart in the morning, to return to the land of the Philistines. And the Philistines went up to Jezreel.

DAVID'S CONFLICT WITH THE AMALEKITES

30 Now it happened, when David and his men came to Ziklag, on the third day, that the Amalekites had invaded the South and Ziklag, attacked Ziklag and burned it with fire, [2]and had taken captive the women and those who *were* there, from small to great; they did not kill anyone, but carried *them* away and went their way. [3]So David and his men came to the city, and there it was, burned with fire; and their wives, their sons, and their daughters had been taken captive. [4]Then David and the people who *were* with him lifted up their voices and wept, until they had no more power to weep. [5]And David's two wives, Ahinoam the Jezreelitess, and Abigail the widow of Nabal the Carmelite, had been taken captive. [6]Now David was greatly distressed, for the people spoke of stoning him, because the soul of all the people was grieved, every man for his sons and his daughters. But David strengthened himself in the LORD his God.

[7]Then David said to Abiathar the priest, Ahimelech's son, "Please bring the ephod here to me." And Abiathar brought the ephod to David. [8]So David inquired of the LORD, saying, "Shall I pursue this troop? Shall I overtake them?"

And He answered him, "Pursue, for you shall surely overtake *them* and without fail recover *all.*"

[9]So David went, he and the six hundred men who *were* with him, and came to the Brook Besor, where those stayed who were left behind. [10]But David pursued, he and four hundred men; for two hundred stayed *behind,* who were so weary that they could not cross the Brook Besor.

[11]Then they found an Egyptian in the field, and brought him to David; and they gave him bread and he ate, and they let him drink water. [12]And they gave him a piece of a cake of figs and two clusters of raisins. So when he had eaten, his strength came back to him; for he had eaten no bread nor drunk water for three days and three nights. [13]Then David said to him, "To whom do you *belong,* and where *are* you from?"

And he said, "I *am* a young man from Egypt, servant of an Amalekite; and my master left me behind, because three days ago I fell sick. [14]We made an invasion of the southern *area* of the Cherethites, in the *territory* which *belongs* to Judah, and of the southern *area* of Caleb; and we burned Ziklag with fire."

[15]And David said to him, "Can you take me down to this troop?"

So he said, "Swear to me by God that you will neither kill me nor deliver me into the hands of my master, and I will take you down to this troop."

[16]And when he had brought him down, there they were, spread out over all the land, eating and drinking and dancing, because of all the great spoil which they had taken from the land of the Philistines and from the land of Judah. [17]Then David attacked them from twilight until the evening of the next day. Not a man of them escaped, except four hundred young men who rode on camels and fled. [18]So David recovered all that the Amalekites had carried away, and David rescued his two wives. [19]And nothing of theirs was lacking, either small or great, sons or daughters, spoil or anything which they had taken from them; David recovered all. [20]Then David took all the flocks and herds they had driven before those *other* livestock, and said, "This *is* David's spoil."

[21]Now David came to the two hundred men who had been so weary that they could not follow David, whom they also had made to stay at the Brook Besor. So they went out to meet David and to meet the people who *were* with him. And when David came near the people, he greeted them. [22]Then all the wicked and worthless men[a] of those who went with David answered and said, "Because they did not go with us, we will not give them *any* of the spoil that we have recovered, except for every man's wife and children, that they may lead *them* away and depart."

[23]But David said, "My brethren, you shall not do so with what the LORD has given us, who has preserved us and delivered into our hand the troop that came against us. [24]For who will heed you in this matter? But as his part *is* who goes down to the battle, so *shall* his part *be* who stays by the supplies; they shall share alike." [25]So it was, from that day forward; he made it a statute and an ordinance for Israel to this day.

30:22 [a]Literally *men of Belial*

LEADERSHIP ISSUES

GC2: Trusting Our Needs to God

1 SAMUEL 30:6

God's intended design for relationships is that He will meet many of our needs through family, friends and the church. This is His way of building our inter-dependency with one another. In the midst of giving to each other's needs, love and intimacy are developed, and we experience part of the "oneness" Christ prayed for (John 17:20–23); but what happens when our families fail us and friends let us down?

Our expectancy and faith must always be directed toward God, realizing that He may involve others in care for us, but He will never fail us! We must remember that when others fail us, He remains faithful. "He will not leave you nor forsake you," (Deut. 31:8). "My God shall supply all your need," (Phil. 4:19).

David, the king of Israel, often received what he needed directly from the hand of the Lord. In 1 Samuel 30:6, David didn't have his friend Jonathan or his wife to talk to; he was alone. What did David do? "David strengthened himself in the LORD his God."

Hours before His death, when Jesus was in agony in the Garden of Gethsemane, He looked to His disciples for comfort and encouragement (Matt. 26:38); but they neglected Him. He came back to them and "found them sleeping" (Matt. 26:40). His closest friends on earth had failed him. God the Father, however, did not leave Him without help: "An angel appeared to Him from heaven, strengthening Him" (Luke 22:43).

God knows our needs, and He is committed to seeing that they are met (Matt. 6:25–34). If others miss the opportunity to care for you, don't despair. God will provide according to His will and promise! Without us trusting Him, we might feel: unworthy of love, angry at others, overly sensitive, disappointed, and fearful. This might lead us to avoid the relationships He wants for us. Trusting Him to love us and provide for our needs brings freedom!

GC2
GREAT COMMANDMENT
COMMISSION

[26]Now when David came to Ziklag, he sent *some* of the spoil to the elders of Judah, to his friends, saying, "Here is a present for you from the spoil of the enemies of the LORD"— [27]to *those* who *were* in Bethel, *those* who *were* in Ramoth of the South, *those* who *were* in Jattir, [28]*those* who *were* in Aroer, *those* who *were* in Siphmoth, *those* who *were* in Eshtemoa, [29]*those* who *were* in Rachal, *those* who *were* in the cities of the Jerahmeelites, *those* who *were* in the cities of the Kenites, [30]*those* who *were* in Hormah, *those* who *were* in Chorashan,[a] *those* who *were* in Athach, [31]*those* who *were* in Hebron, and to all the places where David himself and his men were accustomed to rove.

THE TRAGIC END OF SAUL AND HIS SONS

31 Now the Philistines fought against Israel; and the men of Israel fled from before the Philistines, and fell slain on Mount Gilboa. [2]Then the Philistines followed hard after Saul and his sons. And the Philistines killed Jonathan, Abinadab, and Malchishua, Saul's sons. [3]The battle became fierce against Saul. The archers hit him, and he was severely wounded by the archers.

[4]Then Saul said to his armorbearer, "Draw your sword, and thrust me through with it, lest these uncircumcised men come and thrust me through and abuse me."

But his armorbearer would not, for he was greatly afraid. Therefore Saul took a sword and fell on it. [5]And when his armorbearer saw that Saul was dead, he also fell on his sword, and died with him. [6]So Saul, his three sons, his armorbearer, and all his men died together that same day.

[7]And when the men of Israel who *were* on the other side of the valley, and *those* who *were* on the other side of the Jordan, saw that the men of Israel had fled and that Saul and his sons were dead, they forsook the cities and fled; and the Philistines came and dwelt in them. [8]So it happened the next day, when the Philistines came to strip the slain, that they found Saul and his three sons fallen on Mount Gilboa. [9]And they cut off his head and stripped off his armor, and sent *word* throughout the land of the Philistines, to proclaim *it in* the temple of their idols and among the people. [10]Then they put his armor in the temple of the Ashtoreths, and they fastened his body to the wall of Beth Shan.[a]

[11]Now when the inhabitants of Jabesh Gilead heard what the Philistines had done to Saul, [12]all the valiant men arose and traveled all night, and took the body of Saul and the bodies of his sons from the wall of Beth Shan; and they came to Jabesh and burned them there. [13]Then they took their bones and buried *them* under the tamarisk tree at Jabesh, and fasted seven days.

30:30 [a]Or *Borashan*   **31:10** [a]Spelled *Beth Shean* in Joshua 17:11 and elsewhere

IMPACT OF THE BOOK

I IDEA *Second Samuel describes the establishment of the "house of David" through which the Messiah would later come. Painful detail is also given to the truth that while sin turns triumphs into tragedy, repentance restores relationships.*

M MESSAGE *Leaders cannot live off of past victories. David, who had coura-geously faced the giant Goliath as a young teenager, irrevocably tar-nished his testimony when he succumbed to temptation with Bath-sheba. Instead of giving up after his failure, David repented and was restored. He would have to live with the consequences of his sin, but leaders must learn from their mistakes. Don't quit the race after the first misstep or hurdle, thinking you can't have an impact for God.*

P PEOPLE *Abner, Absalom, Bathsheba, David, Ishbosheth, Joab, Michal, Nathan, Samuel, Tamar, Uriah*

A AUTHOR *While the authorship of 1 and 2 Samuel (which is one book in the Hebrew tradition) is sometimes attributed to the prophet Samuel, who anointed both Saul and David, it is more likely that a later historian or editor used written records from Samuel and Nathan to compile 1 and 2 Samuel.*

C CULTURE *Second Samuel covers the forty-year period of David's reign. David ruled over Judah in Hebron for seven years, united Judah with Israel, and established Jerusalem as his capital city after seven years of civil war. David cleared from Jerusalem the rem-nants of the Jebusites who had held that stronghold in defiance of Israel for centuries. God entered into a covenant with David to establish his house forever. David began preparations for build-ing the temple, which for centuries was the center of Jewish na-tional and religious life.*

T TIMELINE *c. 970–722 BC (sometime between the death of David and the Assyrian captivity)*

KEY SCRIPTURE
MEMORY VERSES 7:12, 13; 7:16; 12:13; 22:2–4

The Report of Saul's Death

1 Now it came to pass after the death of Saul, when David had returned from the slaughter of the Amalekites, and David had stayed two days in Ziklag, ²on the third day, behold, it happened that a man came from Saul's camp with his clothes torn and dust on his head. So it was, when he came to David, that he fell to the ground and prostrated himself.

³And David said to him, "Where have you come from?"

So he said to him, "I have escaped from the camp of Israel."

⁴Then David said to him, "How did the matter go? Please tell me."

And he answered, "The people have fled from the battle, many of the people are fallen and dead, and Saul and Jonathan his son are dead also."

⁵So David said to the young man who told him, "How do you know that Saul and Jonathan his son are dead?"

⁶Then the young man who told him said, "As I happened by chance *to be* on Mount Gilboa, there was Saul, leaning on his spear; and indeed the chariots and horsemen followed hard after him. ⁷Now when he looked behind him, he saw me and called to me. And I answered, 'Here I am.' ⁸And he said to me, 'Who *are* you?' So I answered him, 'I *am* an Amalekite.' ⁹He said to me again, 'Please stand over me and kill me, for anguish has come upon me, but my life still *remains* in me.' ¹⁰So I stood over him and killed him, because I was sure that he could not live after he had fallen. And I took the crown that *was* on his head and the bracelet that *was* on his arm, and have brought them here to my lord."

¹¹Therefore David took hold of his own clothes and tore them, and *so did* all the men who *were* with him. ¹²And they mourned and wept and fasted until evening for Saul and for Jonathan his son, for the people of the LORD and for the house of Israel, because they had fallen by the sword.

¹³Then David said to the young man who told him, "Where *are* you from?"

And he answered, "I *am* the son of an alien, an Amalekite."

¹⁴So David said to him, "How was it you were not afraid to put forth your hand to destroy the LORD's anointed?" ¹⁵Then David called one of the young men and said, "Go near, *and* execute him!" And he struck him so that he died. ¹⁶So David said to him, "Your blood *is* on your own head, for your own mouth has testified against you, saying, 'I have killed the LORD's anointed.' "

The Song of the Bow

¹⁷Then David lamented with this lamentation over Saul and over Jonathan his son, ¹⁸and he told *them* to teach the children of Judah *the Song of* the Bow; indeed *it is* written in the Book of Jasher:

¹⁹"The beauty of Israel is slain on your high
        places!
    How the mighty have fallen!
²⁰Tell *it* not in Gath,
    Proclaim *it* not in the streets of Ashkelon—
    Lest the daughters of the Philistines rejoice,
    Lest the daughters of the uncircumcised
        triumph.

²¹"O mountains of Gilboa,
    Let there be no dew nor rain upon you,
    Nor fields of offerings.
    For the shield of the mighty is cast away
        there!
    The shield of Saul, not anointed with oil.
²²From the blood of the slain,
    From the fat of the mighty,
    The bow of Jonathan did not turn back,
    And the sword of Saul did not return empty.

²³"Saul and Jonathan *were* beloved and pleasant
        in their lives,
    And in their death they were not divided;
    They were swifter than eagles,
    They were stronger than lions.

²⁴"O daughters of Israel, weep over Saul,
    Who clothed you in scarlet, with luxury;
    Who put ornaments of gold on your apparel.

²⁵"How the mighty have fallen in the midst of
        the battle!
    Jonathan *was* slain in your high places.
²⁶I am distressed for you, my brother
        Jonathan;
    You have been very pleasant to me;

Your love to me was wonderful,
Surpassing the love of women.

²⁷"How the mighty have fallen,
And the weapons of war perished!"

David Anointed King of Judah

2 It happened after this that David inquired of the LORD, saying, "Shall I go up to any of the cities of Judah?"

And the LORD said to him, "Go up."

David said, "Where shall I go up?"

And He said, "To Hebron."

²So David went up there, and his two wives also, Ahinoam the Jezreelitess, and Abigail the widow of Nabal the Carmelite. ³And David brought up the men who *were* with him, every man with his household. So they dwelt in the cities of Hebron.

⁴Then the men of Judah came, and there they anointed David king over the house of Judah. And they told David, saying, "The men of Jabesh Gilead *were the ones* who buried Saul." ⁵So David sent messengers to the men of Jabesh Gilead, and said to them, "You *are* blessed of the LORD, for you have shown this kindness to your lord, to Saul, and have buried him. ⁶And now may the LORD show kindness and truth to you. I also will repay you this kindness, because you have done this thing. ⁷Now therefore, let your hands be strengthened, and be valiant; for your master Saul is dead, and also the house of Judah has anointed me king over them."

Ishbosheth Made King of Israel

⁸But Abner the son of Ner, commander of Saul's army, took Ishbosheth^a the son of Saul and brought him over to Mahanaim; ⁹and he made him king over Gilead, over the Ashurites, over Jezreel, over Ephraim, over Benjamin, and over all Israel. ¹⁰Ishbosheth, Saul's son, *was* forty years old when he began to reign over Israel, and he reigned two years. Only the house of Judah followed David. ¹¹And the time that David was king in Hebron over the house of Judah was seven years and six months.

Israel and Judah at War

¹²Now Abner the son of Ner, and the servants of Ishbosheth the son of Saul, went out from Ma-

hanaim to Gibeon. ¹³And Joab the son of Zeruiah, and the servants of David, went out and met them by the pool of Gibeon. So they sat down, one on one side of the pool and the other on the other side of the pool. ¹⁴Then Abner said to Joab, "Let the young men now arise and compete before us."

And Joab said, "Let them arise."

¹⁵So they arose and went over by number, twelve from Benjamin, *followers* of Ishbosheth the son of Saul, and twelve from the servants of David. ¹⁶And each one grasped his opponent by the head and *thrust* his sword in his opponent's side; so they fell down together. Therefore that place was called the Field of Sharp Swords,^a which *is* in Gibeon. ¹⁷So there was a very fierce battle that day, and Abner and the men of Israel were beaten before the servants of David.

¹⁸Now the three sons of Zeruiah were there: Joab and Abishai and Asahel. And Asahel *was as* fleet of foot as a wild gazelle. ¹⁹So Asahel pursued Abner, and in going he did not turn to the right hand or to the left from following Abner.

²⁰Then Abner looked behind him and said, "*Are* you Asahel?"

He answered, "I *am.*"

²¹And Abner said to him, "Turn aside to your right hand or to your left, and lay hold on one of the young men and take his armor for yourself." But Asahel would not turn aside from following him. ²²So Abner said again to Asahel, "Turn aside from following me. Why should I strike you to the ground? How then could I face your brother Joab?" ²³However, he refused to turn aside. Therefore Abner struck him in the stomach with the blunt end of the spear, so that the spear came out of his back; and he fell down there and died on the spot. So it was *that* as many as came to the place where Asahel fell down and died, stood still.

²⁴Joab and Abishai also pursued Abner. And the sun was going down when they came to the hill of Ammah, which *is* before Giah by the road to the Wilderness of Gibeon. ²⁵Now the children of Benjamin gathered together behind Abner and became a unit, and took their stand on top of a hill. ²⁶Then Abner called to Joab and said, "Shall the sword devour forever? Do you not know that

it will be bitter in the latter end? How long will it be then until you tell the people to return from pursuing their brethren?"

²⁷And Joab said, "*As* God lives, unless you had spoken, surely then by morning all the people would have given up pursuing their brethren." ²⁸So Joab blew a trumpet; and all the people stood still and did not pursue Israel anymore, nor did they fight anymore. ²⁹Then Abner and his men went on all that night through the plain, crossed over the Jordan, and went through all Bithron; and they came to Mahanaim.

³⁰So Joab returned from pursuing Abner. And when he had gathered all the people together, there were missing of David's servants nineteen men and Asahel. ³¹But the servants of David had struck down, of Benjamin and Abner's men, three hundred and sixty men who died. ³²Then they took up Asahel and buried him in his father's tomb, which *was in* Bethlehem. And Joab and his men went all night, and they came to Hebron at daybreak.

3 Now there was a long war between the house of Saul and the house of David. But David grew stronger and stronger, and the house of Saul grew weaker and weaker.

Sons of David

²Sons were born to David in Hebron: His firstborn was Amnon by Ahinoam the Jezreelitess; ³his second, Chileab, by Abigail the widow of Nabal the Carmelite; the third, Absalom the son of Maacah, the daughter of Talmai, king of Geshur; ⁴the fourth, Adonijah the son of Haggith; the fifth, Shephatiah the son of Abital; ⁵and the sixth, Ithream, by David's wife Eglah. These were born to David in Hebron.

Abner Joins Forces with David

⁶Now it was so, while there was war between the house of Saul and the house of David, that Abner was strengthening *his hold* on the house of Saul.

⁷And Saul had a concubine, whose name *was* Rizpah, the daughter of Aiah. So *Ishbosheth* said to Abner, "Why have you gone in to my father's concubine?"

⁸Then Abner became very angry at the words of Ishbosheth, and said, "*Am* I a dog's head that belongs to Judah? Today I show loyalty to the house of Saul your father, to his brothers, and to his friends, and have not delivered you into the hand of David; and you charge me today with a fault concerning this woman? ⁹May God do so to Abner, and more also, if I do not do for David as the LORD has sworn to him— ¹⁰to transfer the kingdom from the house of Saul, and set up the throne of David over Israel and over Judah, from Dan to Beersheba." ¹¹And he could not answer Abner another word, because he feared him.

¹²Then Abner sent messengers on his behalf to David, saying, "Whose *is* the land?" saying *also,* "Make your covenant with me, and indeed my hand *shall be* with you to bring all Israel to you."

¹³And *David* said, "Good, I will make a covenant with you. But one thing I require of you: you shall not see my face unless you first bring Michal, Saul's daughter, when you come to see my face." ¹⁴So David sent messengers to Ishbosheth, Saul's son, saying, "Give *me* my wife Michal, whom I betrothed to myself for a hundred foreskins of the Philistines." ¹⁵And Ishbosheth sent and took her from *her* husband, from Paltiel^a the son of Laish. ¹⁶Then her husband went along with her to Bahurim, weeping behind her. So Abner said to him, "Go, return!" And he returned.

¹⁷Now Abner had communicated with the elders of Israel, saying, "In time past you were seeking for David *to be* king over you. ¹⁸Now then, do *it!* For the LORD has spoken of David, saying, 'By the hand of My servant David, I^a will save My people Israel from the hand of the Philistines and the hand of all their enemies.'"

¹⁹And Abner also spoke in the hearing of Benjamin. Then Abner also went to speak in the hearing of David in Hebron all that seemed good to Israel and the whole house of Benjamin.

²⁰So Abner and twenty men with him came to David at Hebron. And David made a feast for Abner and the men who *were* with him. ²¹Then Abner said to David, "I will arise and go, and gather all Israel to my lord the king, that they may make a covenant with you, and that you may

3:15 ^aSpelled *Palti* in 1 Samuel 25:44 **3:18** ^aFollowing many Hebrew manuscripts, Septuagint, Syriac, and Targum; Masoretic Text reads *he.*

reign over all that your heart desires." So David sent Abner away, and he went in peace.

JOAB MURDERS ABNER

22At that moment the servants of David and Joab came from a raid and brought much spoil with them. But Abner *was* not with David in Hebron, for he had sent him away, and he had gone in peace. 23When Joab and all the troops that *were* with him had come, they told Joab, saying, "Abner the son of Ner came to the king, and he sent him away, and he has gone in peace." 24Then Joab came to the king and said, "What have you done? Look, Abner came to you; why *is* it *that* you sent him away, and he has already gone? 25Surely you realize that Abner the son of Ner came to deceive you, to know your going out and your coming in, and to know all that you are doing."

26And when Joab had gone from David's presence, he sent messengers after Abner, who brought him back from the well of Sirah. But David did not know *it.* 27Now when Abner had returned to Hebron, Joab took him aside in the gate to speak with him privately, and there stabbed him in the stomach, so that he died for the blood of Asahel his brother.

28Afterward, when David heard *it,* he said, "My kingdom and I *are* guiltless before the LORD forever of the blood of Abner the son of Ner. 29Let it rest on the head of Joab and on all his father's house; and let there never fail to be in the house of Joab one who has a discharge or is a leper, who leans on a staff or falls by the sword, or who lacks bread." 30So Joab and Abishai his brother killed Abner, because he had killed their brother Asahel at Gibeon in the battle.

DAVID'S MOURNING FOR ABNER

31Then David said to Joab and to all the people who were with him, "Tear your clothes, gird yourselves with sackcloth, and mourn for Abner." And King David followed the coffin. 32So they buried Abner in Hebron; and the king lifted up his voice and wept at the grave of Abner, and all the people wept. 33And the king sang *a lament* over Abner and said:

"Should Abner die as a fool dies?
34Your hands were not bound

Nor your feet put into fetters;
As a man falls before wicked men, *so* you
    fell."

Then all the people wept over him again. 35And when all the people came to persuade David to eat food while it was still day, David took an oath, saying, "God do so to me, and more also, if I taste bread or anything else till the sun goes down!" 36Now all the people took note *of it,* and it pleased them, since whatever the king did pleased all the people. 37For all the people and all Israel understood that day that it had not been the king's *intent* to kill Abner the son of Ner. 38Then the king said to his servants, "Do you not know that a prince and a great man has fallen this day in Israel? 39And I *am* weak today, though anointed king; and these men, the sons of Zeruiah, *are* too harsh for me. The LORD shall repay the evildoer according to his wickedness."

ISHBOSHETH IS MURDERED

4 When Saul's son[a] heard that Abner had died in Hebron, he lost heart, and all Israel was troubled. 2Now Saul's son *had* two men *who were* captains of troops. The name of one *was* Baanah and the name of the other Rechab, the sons of Rimmon the Beerothite, of the children of Benjamin. (For Beeroth also was *part* of Benjamin, 3because the Beerothites fled to Gittaim and have been sojourners there until this day.)

4Jonathan, Saul's son, had a son *who was* lame in *his* feet. He was five years old when the news about Saul and Jonathan came from Jezreel; and his nurse took him up and fled. And it happened, as she made haste to flee, that he fell and became lame. His name *was* Mephibosheth.[a]

5Then the sons of Rimmon the Beerothite, Rechab and Baanah, set out and came at about the heat of the day to the house of Ishbosheth, who was lying on his bed at noon. 6And they came there, all the way into the house, *as though* to get wheat, and they stabbed him in the stomach. Then Rechab and Baanah his brother escaped. 7For when they came into the house, he was lying on his bed in his bedroom; then they struck him and killed him, beheaded him and

4:1 [a]That is, Ishbosheth   **4:4** [a]Called *Merib-Baal* in 1 Chronicles 8:34 and 9:40

took his head, and were all night escaping through the plain. [8]And they brought the head of Ishbosheth to David at Hebron, and said to the king, "Here is the head of Ishbosheth, the son of Saul your enemy, who sought your life; and the LORD has avenged my lord the king this day of Saul and his descendants."

[9]But David answered Rechab and Baanah his brother, the sons of Rimmon the Beerothite, and said to them, "*As* the LORD lives, who has redeemed my life from all adversity, [10]when someone told me, saying, 'Look, Saul is dead,' thinking to have brought good news, I arrested him and had him executed in Ziklag—the one who *thought* I would give him a reward for *his* news. [11]How much more, when wicked men have killed a righteous person in his own house on his bed? Therefore, shall I not now require his blood at your hand and remove you from the earth?" [12]So David commanded his young men, and they executed them, cut off their hands and feet, and hanged *them* by the pool in Hebron. But they took the head of Ishbosheth and buried *it* in the tomb of Abner in Hebron.

DAVID REIGNS OVER ALL ISRAEL

5 Then all the tribes of Israel came to David at Hebron and spoke, saying, "Indeed we *are* your bone and your flesh. [2]Also, in time past, when Saul was king over us, you were the one who led Israel out and brought them in; and the LORD said to you, 'You shall shepherd My people Israel, and be ruler over Israel.' " [3]Therefore all the elders of Israel came to the king at Hebron, and King David made a covenant with them at Hebron before the LORD. And they anointed David king over Israel. [4]David *was* thirty years old when he began to reign, *and* he reigned forty years. [5]In Hebron he reigned over Judah seven years and six months, and in Jerusalem he reigned thirty-three years over all Israel and Judah.

THE CONQUEST OF JERUSALEM

[6]And the king and his men went to Jerusalem against the Jebusites, the inhabitants of the land, who spoke to David, saying, "You shall not come in here; but the blind and the lame will repel you," thinking, "David cannot come in here." [7]Nevertheless David took the stronghold of Zion (that *is,* the City of David).

[8]Now David said on that day, "Whoever climbs up by way of the water shaft and defeats the Jebusites (the lame and the blind, *who are* hated by David's soul), *he shall be chief and captain*."[a] Therefore they say, "The blind and the lame shall not come into the house."

[9]Then David dwelt in the stronghold, and called it the City of David. And David built all around from the Millo[a] and inward. [10]So David went on and became great, and the LORD God of hosts *was* with him.

[11]Then Hiram king of Tyre sent messengers to David, and cedar trees, and carpenters and masons. And they built David a house. [12]So David knew that the LORD had established him as king over Israel, and that He had exalted His kingdom for the sake of His people Israel.

[13]And David took more concubines and wives from Jerusalem, after he had come from Hebron. Also more sons and daughters were born to David. [14]Now these *are* the names of those who were born to him in Jerusalem: Shammua,[a] Shobab, Nathan, Solomon, [15]Ibhar, Elishua,[a] Nepheg, Japhia, [16]Elishama, Eliada, and Eliphelet.

THE PHILISTINES DEFEATED

[17]Now when the Philistines heard that they had anointed David king over Israel, all the Philistines went up to search for David. And David heard *of it* and went down to the stronghold. [18]The Philistines also went and deployed themselves in the Valley of Rephaim. [19]So David inquired of the LORD, saying, "Shall I go up against the Philistines? Will You deliver them into my hand?"

And the LORD said to David, "Go up, for I will doubtless deliver the Philistines into your hand."

[20]So David went to Baal Perazim, and David defeated them there; and he said, "The LORD has broken through my enemies before me, like a breakthrough of water." Therefore he called the name of that place Baal Perazim.[a] [21]And they left their images there, and David and his men carried them away.

[22]Then the Philistines went up once again and deployed themselves in the Valley of

---

5:8 [a]Compare 1 Chronicles 11:6   **5:9** [a]Literally *The Landfill*
5:14 [a]Spelled *Shimea* in 1 Chronicles 3:5   **5:15** [a]Spelled *Elishama* in 1 Chronicles 3:6   **5:20** [a]Literally *Master of Breakthroughs*

LEAD**ERSHIP**
REAL**ITIES**

SPIRIT OF NEVERTHELESS   *2 Samuel 5:7*

David went from the pasture to the palace, from sheepherder to sovereign. His journey to success was accompanied by voices of criticism, negative reports, anger, and betrayal. *Nevertheless,* David managed to take the strongholds of life one by one.

ak—**nevertheless**—surely, truly, certainly, notwithstanding

There are four voices that will accompany you in life. Only one will encourage you to *the spirit of nevertheless.*

Failers are those who never quite make their goal, for some reason or another. They try to attach their past failures and current excuses to your life. Don't listen.

Figurers have based the outcome of your dream on their own ability and reason. These told David: "The fortress is too strong. The hill is too high." Just say "thanks," smile, and walk away. (When told the giant was too big to fight, David replied that he was too big to miss!)

Feelers say, "This sounds like a good idea, but we just don't *feel right* about it." They want you to take part in their fear and try to alter your courage. Every circumstance in life affects their mood so that they are either elated or depressed—seldom in between.

Faithers are few, but potent in their friendship and advice. David was a forerunner in this group. He believed in the Lord and in himself and never contemplated defeat, only God's timing.

Rephaim. ²³Therefore David inquired of the LORD, and He said, "You shall not go up; circle around behind them, and come upon them in front of the mulberry trees. ²⁴And it shall be, when you hear the sound of marching in the tops of the mulberry trees, then you shall advance quickly. For then the LORD will go out before you to strike the camp of the Philistines." ²⁵And David did so, as the LORD commanded him; and he drove back the Philistines from Gebaᵃ as far as Gezer.

THE ARK BROUGHT TO JERUSALEM

6 Again David gathered all *the* choice *men* of Israel, thirty thousand. ²And David arose and went with all the people who *were* with him from Baale Judah to bring up from there the ark of God, whose name is called by the Name,ᵃ the LORD of Hosts, who dwells *between* the cherubim. ³So they set the ark of God on a new cart, and

brought it out of the house of Abinadab, which *was* on the hill; and Uzzah and Ahio, the sons of Abinadab, drove the new cart.ᵃ ⁴And they brought it out of the house of Abinadab, which *was* on the hill, accompanying the ark of God; and Ahio went before the ark. ⁵Then David and all the house of Israel played *music* before the LORD on all kinds of *instruments of* fir wood, on harps, on stringed instruments, on tambourines, on sistrums, and on cymbals.

⁶And when they came to Nachon's threshing floor, Uzzah put out *his* hand to the ark of God and took hold of it, for the oxen stumbled. ⁷Then the anger of the LORD was aroused against Uzzah, and God struck him there for *his* error; and he died there by the ark of God. ⁸And David

5:25 ᵃFollowing Masoretic Text, Targum, and Vulgate; Septuagint reads *Gibeon.* **6:2** ᵃSeptuagint, Targum, and Vulgate omit *by the Name;* many Hebrew manuscripts and Syriac read *there.* **6:3** ᵃSeptuagint adds *with the ark.*

became angry because of the LORD's outbreak against Uzzah; and he called the name of the place Perez Uzzah[a] to this day.

⁹David was afraid of the LORD that day; and he said, "How can the ark of the LORD come to me?" ¹⁰So David would not move the ark of the LORD with him into the City of David; but David took it aside into the house of Obed-Edom the Gittite. ¹¹The ark of the LORD remained in the house of Obed-Edom the Gittite three months. And the LORD blessed Obed-Edom and all his household.

¹²Now it was told King David, saying, "The LORD has blessed the house of Obed-Edom and all that *belongs* to him, because of the ark of God." So David went and brought up the ark of God from the house of Obed-Edom to the City of David with gladness. ¹³And so it was, when those bearing the ark of the LORD had gone six paces, that he sacrificed oxen and fatted sheep. ¹⁴Then David danced before the LORD with all *his* might; and David *was* wearing a linen ephod. ¹⁵So David and all the house of Israel brought up the ark of the LORD with shouting and with the sound of the trumpet.

¹⁶Now as the ark of the LORD came into the City of David, Michal, Saul's daughter, looked through a window and saw King David leaping and whirling before the LORD; and she despised him in her heart. ¹⁷So they brought the ark of the LORD, and set it in its place in the midst of the tabernacle that David had erected for it. Then David offered burnt offerings and peace offerings before the LORD. ¹⁸And when David had finished offering burnt offerings and peace offerings, he blessed the people in the name of the LORD of hosts. ¹⁹Then he distributed among all the people, among the whole multitude of Israel, both the women and the men, to everyone a loaf of bread, a piece *of meat,* and a cake of raisins. So all the people departed, everyone to his house.

²⁰Then David returned to bless his household. And Michal the daughter of Saul came out to meet David, and said, "How glorious was the king of Israel today, uncovering himself today in the eyes of the maids of his servants, as one of the base fellows shamelessly uncovers himself!"

²¹So David said to Michal, "*It was* before the LORD, who chose me instead of your father and

all his house, to appoint me ruler over the people of the LORD, over Israel. Therefore I will play *music* before the LORD. ²²And I will be even more undignified than this, and will be humble in my own sight. But as for the maidservants of whom you have spoken, by them I will be held in honor."

²³Therefore Michal the daughter of Saul had no children to the day of her death.

GOD'S COVENANT WITH DAVID

7 Now it came to pass when the king was dwelling in his house, and the LORD had given him rest from all his enemies all around, ²that the king said to Nathan the prophet, "See now, I dwell in a house of cedar, but the ark of God dwells inside tent curtains."

³Then Nathan said to the king, "Go, do all that *is* in your heart, for the LORD *is* with you."

⁴But it happened that night that the word of the LORD came to Nathan, saying, ⁵"Go and tell My servant David, 'Thus says the LORD: "Would you build a house for Me to dwell in? ⁶For I have not dwelt in a house since the time that I brought the children of Israel up from Egypt, even to this day, but have moved about in a tent and in a tabernacle. ⁷Wherever I have moved about with all the children of Israel, have I ever spoken a word to anyone from the tribes of Israel, whom I commanded to shepherd My people Israel, saying, 'Why have you not built Me a house of cedar?' " ' ⁸Now therefore, thus shall you say to My servant David, 'Thus says the LORD of hosts: "I took you from the sheepfold, from following the sheep, to be ruler over My people, over Israel. ⁹And I have been with you wherever you have gone, and have cut off all your enemies from before you, and have made you a great name, like the name of the great men who *are* on the earth. ¹⁰Moreover I will appoint a place for My people Israel, and will plant them, that they may dwell in a place of their own and move no more; nor shall the sons of wickedness oppress them anymore, as previously, ¹¹since the time that I commanded judges *to be* over My people Israel, and have caused you to rest from all your enemies. Also the LORD tells you that He will make you a house.[a]

6:8 [a]Literally *Outburst Against Uzzah* **7:11** [a]That is, a royal dynasty

¹²"When your days are fulfilled and you rest with your fathers, I will set up your seed after you, who will come from your body, and I will establish his kingdom. ¹³He shall build a house for My name, and I will establish the throne of his kingdom forever. ¹⁴I will be his Father, and he shall be My son. If he commits iniquity, I will chasten him with the rod of men and with the blows of the sons of men. ¹⁵But My mercy shall not depart from him, as I took it from Saul, whom I removed from before you. ¹⁶And your house and your kingdom shall be established forever before you.[a] Your throne shall be established forever." ' "

¹⁷According to all these words and according to all this vision, so Nathan spoke to David.

David's Thanksgiving to God

¹⁸Then King David went in and sat before the Lord; and he said: "Who am I, O Lord God? And what is my house, that You have brought me this far? ¹⁹And yet this was a small thing in Your sight, O Lord God; and You have also spoken of Your servant's house for a great while to come. Is this the manner of man, O Lord God? ²⁰Now what more can David say to You? For You, Lord God, know Your servant. ²¹For Your word's sake, and according to Your own heart, You have done all these great things, to make Your servant know them. ²²Therefore You are great, O Lord God.[a] For there is none like You, nor is there any God besides You, according to all that we have heard with our ears. ²³And who is like Your people, like Israel, the one nation on the earth whom God went to redeem for Himself as a people, to make for Himself a name—and to do for Yourself great and awesome deeds for Your land—before Your people whom You redeemed for Yourself from Egypt, the nations, and their gods? ²⁴For You have made Your people Israel Your very own people forever; and You, Lord, have become their God.

²⁵"Now, O Lord God, the word which You have spoken concerning Your servant and concerning his house, establish it forever and do as You have said. ²⁶So let Your name be magnified forever, saying, 'The Lord of hosts is the God over Israel.' And let the house of Your servant David be established before You. ²⁷For You, O Lord of hosts, God of Israel, have revealed this to Your servant, saying, 'I will build you a house.' Therefore Your servant has found it in his heart to pray this prayer to You.

²⁸"And now, O Lord God, You are God, and Your words are true, and You have promised this goodness to Your servant. ²⁹Now therefore, let it please You to bless the house of Your servant, that it may continue before You forever; for You, O Lord God, have spoken it, and with Your blessing let the house of Your servant be blessed forever."

David's Further Conquests

8 After this it came to pass that David attacked the Philistines and subdued them. And David took Metheg Ammah from the hand of the Philistines.

²Then he defeated Moab. Forcing them down to the ground, he measured them off with a line. With two lines he measured off those to be put to death, and with one full line those to be kept alive. So the Moabites became David's servants, and brought tribute.

³David also defeated Hadadezer the son of Rehob, king of Zobah, as he went to recover his territory at the River Euphrates. ⁴David took from him one thousand chariots, seven hundred[a] horsemen, and twenty thousand foot soldiers. Also David hamstrung all the chariot horses, except that he spared enough of them for one hundred chariots.

⁵When the Syrians of Damascus came to help Hadadezer king of Zobah, David killed twenty-two thousand of the Syrians. ⁶Then David put garrisons in Syria of Damascus; and the Syrians became David's servants, and brought tribute. So the Lord preserved David wherever he went. ⁷And David took the shields of gold that had belonged to the servants of Hadadezer, and brought them to Jerusalem. ⁸Also from Betah[a] and from Berothai, cities of Hadadezer, King David took a large amount of bronze.

⁹When Toi[a] king of Hamath heard that David had defeated all the army of Hadadezer, ¹⁰then Toi sent Joram[a] his son to King David, to greet him and bless him, because he had fought against

Hadadezer and defeated him (for Hadadezer had been at war with Toi); and *Joram* brought with him articles of silver, articles of gold, and articles of bronze. ¹¹King David also dedicated these to the LORD, along with the silver and gold that he had dedicated from all the nations which he had subdued— ¹²from Syria,ᵃ from Moab, from the people of Ammon, from the Philistines, from Amalek, and from the spoil of Hadadezer the son of Rehob, king of Zobah.

¹³And David made *himself* a name when he returned from killing eighteen thousand Syriansᵃ in the Valley of Salt. ¹⁴He also put garrisons in Edom; throughout all Edom he put garrisons, and all the Edomites became David's servants. And the LORD preserved David wherever he went.

David's Administration

¹⁵So David reigned over all Israel; and David administered judgment and justice to all his people. ¹⁶Joab the son of Zeruiah *was* over the army; Jehoshaphat the son of Ahilud *was* recorder; ¹⁷Zadok the son of Ahitub and Ahimelech the son of Abiathar *were* the priests; Seraiahᵃ *was* the scribe; ¹⁸Benaiah the son of Jehoiada *was over* both the Cherethites and the Pelethites; and David's sons were chief ministers.

David's Kindness to Mephibosheth

9 Now David said, "Is there still anyone who is left of the house of Saul, that I may show him kindness for Jonathan's sake?"

²And *there was* a servant of the house of Saul whose name *was* Ziba. So when they had called him to David, the king said to him, "*Are* you Ziba?"

He said, "At your service!"

³Then the king said, "*Is* there not still someone of the house of Saul, to whom I may show the kindness of God?"

And Ziba said to the king, "There is still a son of Jonathan *who is* lame in *his* feet."

⁴So the king said to him, "Where *is* he?"

And Ziba said to the king, "Indeed he *is* in the house of Machir the son of Ammiel, in Lo Debar."

⁵Then King David sent and brought him out of the house of Machir the son of Ammiel, from Lo Debar.

⁶Now when Mephibosheth the son of Jonathan, the son of Saul, had come to David, he fell on his face and prostrated himself. Then David said, "Mephibosheth?"

And he answered, "Here is your servant!"

⁷So David said to him, "Do not fear, for I will surely show you kindness for Jonathan your father's sake, and will restore to you all the land of Saul your grandfather; and you shall eat bread at my table continually."

⁸Then he bowed himself, and said, "What *is* your servant, that you should look upon such a dead dog as I?"

⁹And the king called to Ziba, Saul's servant, and said to him, "I have given to your master's son all that belonged to Saul and to all his house. ¹⁰You therefore, and your sons and your servants, shall work the land for him, and you shall bring in *the harvest,* that your master's son may have food to eat. But Mephibosheth your master's son shall eat bread at my table always." Now Ziba had fifteen sons and twenty servants.

¹¹Then Ziba said to the king, "According to all that my lord the king has commanded his servant, so will your servant do."

"As for Mephibosheth," *said the king,* "he shall eat at my tableᵃ like one of the king's sons." ¹²Mephibosheth had a young son whose name *was* Micha. And all who dwelt in the house of Ziba *were* servants of Mephibosheth. ¹³So Mephibosheth dwelt in Jerusalem, for he ate continually at the king's table. And he was lame in both his feet.

The Ammonites and Syrians Defeated

10 It happened after this that the king of the people of Ammon died, and Hanun his son reigned in his place. ²Then David said, "I will show kindness to Hanun the son of Nahash, as his father showed kindness to me."

So David sent by the hand of his servants to comfort him concerning his father. And David's servants came into the land of the people of Ammon. ³And the princes of the people of Ammon said to Hanun their lord, "Do you think that

8:12 ᵃSeptuagint, Syriac, and some Hebrew manuscripts read *Edom.*   8:13 ᵃSeptuagint, Syriac, and some Hebrew manuscripts read *Edomites* (compare 1 Chronicles 18:12).   8:17 ᵃSpelled *Shavsha* in 1 Chronicles 18:16   9:11 ᵃSeptuagint reads *David's table.*

David really honors your father because he has sent comforters to you? Has David not *rather* sent his servants to you to search the city, to spy it out, and to overthrow it?"

[4]Therefore Hanun took David's servants, shaved off half of their beards, cut off their garments in the middle, at their buttocks, and sent them away. [5]When they told David, he sent to meet them, because the men were greatly ashamed. And the king said, "Wait at Jericho until your beards have grown, and *then* return."

[6]When the people of Ammon saw that they had made themselves repulsive to David, the people of Ammon sent and hired the Syrians of Beth Rehob and the Syrians of Zoba, twenty thousand foot soldiers; and from the king of Maacah one thousand men, and from Ish-Tob twelve thousand men. [7]Now when David heard *of it,* he sent Joab and all the army of the mighty men. [8]Then the people of Ammon came out and put themselves in battle array at the entrance of the gate. And the Syrians of Zoba, Beth Rehob, Ish-Tob, and Maacah *were* by themselves in the field.

[9]When Joab saw that the battle line was against him before and behind, he chose some of Israel's best and put *them* in battle array against the Syrians. [10]And the rest of the people he put under the command of Abishai his brother, that he might set *them* in battle array against the people of Ammon. [11]Then he said, "If the Syrians are too strong for me, then you shall help me; but if the people of Ammon are too strong for you, then I will come and help you. [12]Be of good courage, and let us be strong for our people and for the cities of our God. And may the Lord do *what is* good in His sight."

[13]So Joab and the people who *were* with him drew near for the battle against the Syrians, and they fled before him. [14]When the people of Ammon saw that the Syrians were fleeing, they also fled before Abishai, and entered the city. So Joab returned from the people of Ammon and went to Jerusalem.

[15]When the Syrians saw that they had been defeated by Israel, they gathered together. [16]Then Hadadezer[a] sent and brought out the Syrians who *were* beyond the River,[b] and they came to Helam. And Shobach the commander of Hadadezer's army *went* before them. [17]When it was told

David, he gathered all Israel, crossed over the Jordan, and came to Helam. And the Syrians set themselves in battle array against David and fought with him. [18]Then the Syrians fled before Israel; and David killed seven hundred charioteers and forty thousand horsemen of the Syrians, and struck Shobach the commander of their army, who died there. [19]And when all the kings *who were* servants to Hadadezer[a] saw that they were defeated by Israel, they made peace with Israel and served them. So the Syrians were afraid to help the people of Ammon anymore.

DAVID, BATHSHEBA, AND URIAH

11 It happened in the spring of the year, at the time when kings go out *to battle,* that David sent Joab and his servants with him, and all Israel; and they destroyed the people of Ammon and besieged Rabbah. But David remained at Jerusalem.

[2]Then it happened one evening that David arose from his bed and walked on the roof of the king's house. And from the roof he saw a woman bathing, and the woman *was* very beautiful to behold. [3]So David sent and inquired about the woman. And *someone* said, "*Is* this not Bathsheba, the daughter of Eliam, the wife of Uriah the Hittite?" [4]Then David sent messengers, and took her; and she came to him, and he lay with her, for she was cleansed from her impurity; and she returned to her house. [5]And the woman conceived; so she sent and told David, and said, "I *am* with child."

[6]Then David sent to Joab, *saying,* "Send me Uriah the Hittite." And Joab sent Uriah to David. [7]When Uriah had come to him, David asked how Joab was doing, and how the people were doing, and how the war prospered. [8]And David said to Uriah, "Go down to your house and wash your feet." So Uriah departed from the king's house, and a gift *of food* from the king followed him. [9]But Uriah slept at the door of the king's house with all the servants of his lord, and did not go down to his house. [10]So when they told David, saying, "Uriah did not go down to his house," David said to Uriah, "Did you not come from a journey? Why did you not go down to your house?"

[11]And Uriah said to David, "The ark and

10:16 [a]Hebrew *Hadarezer* [b]That is, the Euphrates 10:19 [a]Hebrew *Hadarezer*

LEAD**ERSHIP**
REAL**ITIES**

NEVER SACRIFICE YOUR FUTURE ON THE ALTAR
OF THE IMMEDIATE   *2 Samuel 11:2–4a*

David is described in Scripture as a man who *"walked in integrity of heart and in upright-ness."* That is a strong statement and specific in the measure of a man. But, this same man, earnest in his faith, his worship, and his commitment to holiness, suddenly made a move that brought grave consequences for David, for Bathsheba, and for their children's future. In a moment, David made a choice that marked his testimony for hundreds, even thousands of years.

Leaders have to consider this possibility in their own lives. Because of the carnal nature of man and the pervasiveness of evil in the world, every person experiences temptation. These, in and of themselves, are not sin. It is acting on those thoughts and lusts that causes people to worship the immediate and sacrifice the future. No matter how strong one thinks he or she is, every believer must beware lest he fall. If it can happen to David, it can happen to anyone.

Consider the progression of temptation to sin as defined in James: *But each one is tempted when he is drawn away by his own desires and enticed. Then, when desire has conceived, it gives birth to sin; and sin, when it is full-grown, brings forth death (James 1:14, 15).*

Israel and Judah are dwelling in tents, and my lord Joab and the servants of my lord are encamped in the open fields. Shall I then go to my house to eat and drink, and to lie with my wife? *As* you live, and *as* your soul lives, I will not do this thing." [12]Then David said to Uriah, "Wait here today also, and tomorrow I will let you depart." So Uriah remained in Jerusalem that day and the next. [13]Now when David called him, he ate and drank before him; and he made him drunk. And at evening he went out to lie on his bed with the servants of his lord, but he did not go down to his house.

[14]In the morning it happened that David wrote a letter to Joab and sent *it* by the hand of Uriah. [15]And he wrote in the letter, saying, "Set Uriah in the forefront of the hottest battle, and retreat from him, that he may be struck down and die." [16]So it was, while Joab besieged the city, that he assigned Uriah to a place where he knew there *were* valiant men. [17]Then the men of the city came out and fought with Joab. And *some* of the people of the servants of David fell; and Uriah the Hittite died also.

[18]Then Joab sent and told David all the things concerning the war, [19]and charged the messenger, saying, "When you have finished telling the matters of the war to the king, [20]if it happens that the king's wrath rises, and he says to you: 'Why did you approach so near to the city when you fought? Did you not know that they would shoot from the wall? [21]Who struck Abimelech the son of Jerubbesheth?[a] Was it not a woman who cast a piece of a millstone on him from the wall, so that he died in Thebez? Why did you go near the wall?'—then you shall say, 'Your servant Uriah the Hittite is dead also.'"

[22]So the messenger went, and came and told David all that Joab had sent by him. [23]And the messenger said to David, "Surely the men prevailed against us and came out to us in the field; then we drove them back as far as the entrance of the gate. [24]The archers shot from the wall at your servants; and *some* of the king's servants are dead, and your servant Uriah the Hittite is dead also."

[25]Then David said to the messenger, "Thus you shall say to Joab: 'Do not let this thing dis-

11:21 [a]Same as *Jerubbaal* (Gideon), Judges 6:32ff

INSIDE the INFLUENCERS

BATHSHEBA—The Danger of an Unguarded Heart

2 SAMUEL 11

Bathsheba had it all. She was beautiful, the daughter of one of David's mighty men (1 Chr. 3:5), and the wife of Uriah. Uriah in Hebrew means "YHWH is my light," and from the looks of it, Uriah was an honest, faithful man. The close proximity of their home to the palace illustrates how much David honored him, and his position as an officer explains why he stayed at the front battle lines when David tried to use him to cover his sin. Summoned to the palace by King David's messenger, Bathsheba's entire life changed. It was common for kings of the east to see a woman and take her on a whim, but this wasn't yet common to David. Sadly, this moment of passion became a lifetime of pain.

To cover their sin, David sent Uriah to the front lines to die; and the child they had together died shortly after birth. We will never know how much she contributed to the sin of adultery, but it appears Bathsheba adapted quickly to life as a queen. She gave birth to another son, Solomon, and became the favored wife. With the aid of Nathan the prophet, she was able to secure succession-rights for her son Solomon.

please you, for the sword devours one as well as another. Strengthen your attack against the city, and overthrow it.' So encourage him."

²⁶When the wife of Uriah heard that Uriah her husband was dead, she mourned for her husband. ²⁷And when her mourning was over, David sent and brought her to his house, and she became his wife and bore him a son. But the thing that David had done displeased the LORD.

NATHAN'S PARABLE AND DAVID'S CONFESSION

12 Then the LORD sent Nathan to David. And he came to him, and said to him: "There were two men in one city, one rich and the other poor. ²The rich *man* had exceedingly many flocks and herds. ³But the poor *man* had nothing, except one little ewe lamb which he had bought and nourished; and it grew up together with him and with his children. It ate of his own food and drank from his own cup and lay in his bosom; and it was like a daughter to him. ⁴And a traveler came to the rich man, who refused to take from his own flock and from his own herd to prepare one for the wayfaring man who had come to him; but he took the poor man's lamb and prepared it for the man who had come to him."

⁵So David's anger was greatly aroused against the man, and he said to Nathan, "*As* the LORD lives, the man who has done this shall surely die! ⁶And he shall restore fourfold for the lamb, because he did this thing and because he had no pity."

⁷Then Nathan said to David, "You *are* the man! Thus says the LORD God of Israel: 'I anointed you king over Israel, and I delivered you from the hand of Saul. ⁸I gave you your master's house and your master's wives into your keeping, and gave you the house of Israel and Judah. And if *that had been* too little, I also would have given you much more! ⁹Why have you despised the commandment of the LORD, to do evil in His sight? You have killed Uriah the Hittite with the sword; you have taken his wife *to be* your wife, and have killed him with the sword of the people of Ammon. ¹⁰Now therefore, the sword shall never depart from your house, because you have despised Me, and have taken the wife of Uriah the Hittite to be your wife.' ¹¹Thus says the LORD: 'Behold, I will raise up adversity against you from your own house; and I will take your wives before your eyes and give *them* to your neighbor, and he shall lie with your wives in the sight of this sun. ¹²For you did *it* secretly, but I will do this thing before all Israel, before the sun.' "

[13]So David said to Nathan, "I have sinned against the LORD."

And Nathan said to David, "The LORD also has put away your sin; you shall not die. [14]However, because by this deed you have given great occasion to the enemies of the LORD to blaspheme, the child also *who is* born to you shall surely die." [15]Then Nathan departed to his house.

The Death of David's Son

And the LORD struck the child that Uriah's wife bore to David, and it became ill. [16]David therefore pleaded with God for the child, and David fasted and went in and lay all night on the ground. [17]So the elders of his house arose *and went* to him, to raise him up from the ground. But he would not, nor did he eat food with them. [18]Then on the seventh day it came to pass that the child died. And the servants of David were afraid to tell him that the child was dead. For they said, "Indeed, while the child was alive, we spoke to him, and he would not heed our voice. How can we tell him that the child is dead? He may do some harm!"

[19]When David saw that his servants were whispering, David perceived that the child was dead. Therefore David said to his servants, "Is the child dead?"

And they said, "He is dead."

[20]So David arose from the ground, washed and anointed himself, and changed his clothes; and he went into the house of the LORD and worshiped. Then he went to his own house; and when he requested, they set food before him, and he ate. [21]Then his servants said to him, "What *is* this that you have done? You fasted and wept for the child *while he was* alive, but when the child died, you arose and ate food."

[22]And he said, "While the child was alive, I fasted and wept; for I said, 'Who can tell *whether* the LORD[a] will be gracious to me, that the child may live?' [23]But now he is dead; why should I fast? Can I bring him back again? I shall go to him, but he shall not return to me."

Solomon Is Born

[24]Then David comforted Bathsheba his wife, and went in to her and lay with her. So she bore a son, and he[a] called his name Solomon. Now the LORD loved him, [25]and He sent *word* by the hand of Nathan the prophet: So he[a] called his name Jedidiah,[b] because of the LORD.

Rabbah Is Captured

[26]Now Joab fought against Rabbah of the people of Ammon, and took the royal city. [27]And Joab sent messengers to David, and said, "I have fought against Rabbah, and I have taken the city's water *supply.* [28]Now therefore, gather the rest of the people together and encamp against the city and take it, lest I take the city and it be called after my name." [29]So David gathered all the people together and went to Rabbah, fought against it, and took it. [30]Then he took their king's crown from his head. Its weight *was* a talent of gold, with precious stones. And it was *set* on David's head. Also he brought out the spoil of the city in great abundance. [31]And he brought out the people who *were* in it, and put *them to work* with saws and iron picks and iron axes, and made them cross over to the brick works. So he did to all the cities of the people of Ammon. Then David and all the people returned to Jerusalem.

Amnon and Tamar

13 After this Absalom the son of David had a lovely sister, whose name *was* Tamar; and Amnon the son of David loved her. [2]Amnon was so distressed over his sister Tamar that he became sick; for she *was* a virgin. And it was improper for Amnon to do anything to her. [3]But Amnon had a friend whose name *was* Jonadab the son of Shimeah, David's brother. Now Jonadab *was* a very crafty man. [4]And he said to him, "Why *are* you, the king's son, becoming thinner day after day? Will you not tell me?"

Amnon said to him, "I love Tamar, my brother Absalom's sister."

[5]So Jonadab said to him, "Lie down on your bed and pretend to be ill. And when your father comes to see you, say to him, 'Please let my sister Tamar come and give me food, and prepare the food in my sight, that I may see *it* and eat it from

12:22 [a]A few Hebrew manuscripts and Syriac read *God.*
12:24 [a]Following Kethib, Septuagint, and Vulgate; Qere, a few Hebrew manuscripts, Syriac, and Targum read *she.*   12:25 [a]Qere, some Hebrew manuscripts, Syriac, and Targum read *she.*   [b]Literally *Beloved of the LORD*

her hand.' " ⁶Then Amnon lay down and pretended to be ill; and when the king came to see him, Amnon said to the king, "Please let Tamar my sister come and make a couple of cakes for me in my sight, that I may eat from her hand."

⁷And David sent home to Tamar, saying, "Now go to your brother Amnon's house, and prepare food for him." ⁸So Tamar went to her brother Amnon's house; and he was lying down. Then she took flour and kneaded *it,* made cakes in his sight, and baked the cakes. ⁹And she took the pan and placed *them* out before him, but he refused to eat. Then Amnon said, "Have everyone go out from me." And they all went out from him. ¹⁰Then Amnon said to Tamar, "Bring the food into the bedroom, that I may eat from your hand." And Tamar took the cakes which she had made, and brought *them* to Amnon her brother in the bedroom. ¹¹Now when she had brought *them* to him to eat, he took hold of her and said to her, "Come, lie with me, my sister."

¹²But she answered him, "No, my brother, do not force me, for no such thing should be done in Israel. Do not do this disgraceful thing! ¹³And I, where could I take my shame? And as for you, you would be like one of the fools in Israel. Now therefore, please speak to the king; for he will not withhold me from you." ¹⁴However, he would not heed her voice; and being stronger than she, he forced her and lay with her.

¹⁵Then Amnon hated her exceedingly, so that the hatred with which he hated her *was* greater than the love with which he had loved her. And Amnon said to her, "Arise, be gone!"

¹⁶So she said to him, "No, indeed! This evil of sending me away *is* worse than the other that you did to me."

But he would not listen to her. ¹⁷Then he called his servant who attended him, and said, "Here! Put this *woman* out, away from me, and bolt the door behind her." ¹⁸Now she had on a robe of many colors, for the king's virgin daughters wore such apparel. And his servant put her out and bolted the door behind her.

¹⁹Then Tamar put ashes on her head, and tore her robe of many colors that *was* on her, and laid her hand on her head and went away crying bitterly. ²⁰And Absalom her brother said to her, "Has Amnon your brother been with you? But now

hold your peace, my sister. He *is* your brother; do not take this thing to heart." So Tamar remained desolate in her brother Absalom's house.

²¹But when King David heard of all these things, he was very angry. ²²And Absalom spoke to his brother Amnon neither good nor bad. For Absalom hated Amnon, because he had forced his sister Tamar.

Absalom Murders Amnon

²³And it came to pass, after two full years, that Absalom had sheepshearers in Baal Hazor, which *is* near Ephraim; so Absalom invited all the king's sons. ²⁴Then Absalom came to the king and said, "Kindly note, your servant has sheepshearers; please, let the king and his servants go with your servant."

²⁵But the king said to Absalom, "No, my son, let us not all go now, lest we be a burden to you." Then he urged him, but he would not go; and he blessed him.

²⁶Then Absalom said, "If not, please let my brother Amnon go with us."

And the king said to him, "Why should he go with you?" ²⁷But Absalom urged him; so he let Amnon and all the king's sons go with him.

²⁸Now Absalom had commanded his servants, saying, "Watch now, when Amnon's heart is merry with wine, and when I say to you, 'Strike Amnon!' then kill him. Do not be afraid. Have I not commanded you? Be courageous and valiant." ²⁹So the servants of Absalom did to Amnon as Absalom had commanded. Then all the king's sons arose, and each one got on his mule and fled.

³⁰And it came to pass, while they were on the way, that news came to David, saying, "Absalom has killed all the king's sons, and not one of them is left!" ³¹So the king arose and tore his garments and lay on the ground, and all his servants stood by with their clothes torn. ³²Then Jonadab the son of Shimeah, David's brother, answered and said, "Let not my lord suppose they have killed all the young men, the king's sons, for only Amnon is dead. For by the command of Absalom this has been determined from the day that he forced his sister Tamar. ³³Now therefore, let not my lord the king take the thing to his heart, to think that all the king's sons are dead. For only Amnon is dead."

Absalom Flees to Geshur

34Then Absalom fled. And the young man who was keeping watch lifted his eyes and looked, and there, many people were coming from the road on the hillside behind him.ᵃ 35And Jonadab said to the king, "Look, the king's sons are coming; as your servant said, so it is." 36So it was, as soon as he had finished speaking, that the king's sons indeed came, and they lifted up their voice and wept. Also the king and all his servants wept very bitterly.

37But Absalom fled and went to Talmai the son of Ammihud, king of Geshur. And *David* mourned for his son every day. 38So Absalom fled and went to Geshur, and was there three years. 39And King Davidᵃ longed to go toᵇ Absalom. For he had been comforted concerning Amnon, because he was dead.

Absalom Returns to Jerusalem

14 So Joab the son of Zeruiah perceived that the king's heart *was* concerned about Absalom. 2And Joab sent to Tekoa and brought from there a wise woman, and said to her, "Please pretend to be a mourner, and put on mourning apparel; do not anoint yourself with oil, but act like a woman who has been mourning a long time for the dead. 3Go to the king and speak to him in this manner." So Joab put the words in her mouth.

4And when the woman of Tekoa spokeᵃ to the king, she fell on her face to the ground and prostrated herself, and said, "Help, O king!"

5Then the king said to her, "What troubles you?"

And she answered, "Indeed I *am* a widow, my husband is dead. 6Now your maidservant had two sons; and the two fought with each other in the field, and *there was* no one to part them, but the one struck the other and killed him. 7And now the whole family has risen up against your maidservant, and they said, 'Deliver him who struck his brother, that we may execute him for the life of his brother whom he killed; and we will destroy the heir also.' So they would extinguish my ember that is left, and leave to my husband *neither* name nor remnant on the earth."

8Then the king said to the woman, "Go to your house, and I will give orders concerning you."

9And the woman of Tekoa said to the king, "My lord, O king, *let* the iniquity *be* on me and on my father's house, and the king and his throne *be* guiltless."

10So the king said, "Whoever says *anything* to you, bring him to me, and he shall not touch you anymore."

11Then she said, "Please let the king remember the LORD your God, and do not permit the avenger of blood to destroy anymore, lest they destroy my son."

And he said, "*As* the LORD lives, not one hair of your son shall fall to the ground."

12Therefore the woman said, "Please, let your maidservant speak *another* word to my lord the king."

And he said, "Say on."

13So the woman said: "Why then have you schemed such a thing against the people of God? For the king speaks this thing as one who is guilty, *in that* the king does not bring his banished one home again. 14For we will surely die and *become* like water spilled on the ground, which cannot be gathered up again. Yet God does not take away a life; but He devises means, so that His banished ones are not expelled from Him. 15Now therefore, I have come to speak of this thing to my lord the king because the people have made me afraid. And your maidservant said, 'I will now speak to the king; it may be that the king will perform the request of his maidservant. 16For the king will hear and deliver his maidservant from the hand of the man *who would* destroy me and my son together from the inheritance of God.' 17Your maidservant said, 'The word of my lord the king will now be comforting; for as the angel of God, so *is* my lord the king in discerning good and evil. And may the LORD your God be with you.'"

18Then the king answered and said to the woman, "Please do not hide from me anything that I ask you."

And the woman said, "Please, let my lord the king speak."

13:34 ᵃSeptuagint adds *And the watchman went and told the king and said, "I see men from the way of Horonaim, from the regions of the mountains."* **13:39** ᵃFollowing Masoretic Text, Syriac, and Vulgate; Septuagint reads *the spirit of the king;* Targum reads *the soul of King David.* ᵇFollowing Masoretic Text and Targum; Septuagint and Vulgate read *ceased to pursue after.* **14:4** ᵃMany Hebrew manuscripts, Septuagint, Syriac, and Vulgate read *came.*

¹⁹So the king said, "Is the hand of Joab with you in all this?" And the woman answered and said, "As you live, my lord the king, no one can turn to the right hand or to the left from anything that my lord the king has spoken. For your servant Joab commanded me, and he put all these words in the mouth of your maidservant. ²⁰To bring about this change of affairs your servant Joab has done this thing; but my lord is wise, according to the wisdom of the angel of God, to know everything that is in the earth."

²¹And the king said to Joab, "All right, I have granted this thing. Go therefore, bring back the young man Absalom."

²²Then Joab fell to the ground on his face and bowed himself, and thanked the king. And Joab said, "Today your servant knows that I have found favor in your sight, my lord, O king, in that the king has fulfilled the request of his servant." ²³So Joab arose and went to Geshur, and brought Absalom to Jerusalem. ²⁴And the king said, "Let him return to his own house, but do not let him see my face." So Absalom returned to his own house, but did not see the king's face.

David Forgives Absalom

²⁵Now in all Israel there was no one who was praised as much as Absalom for his good looks. From the sole of his foot to the crown of his head there was no blemish in him. ²⁶And when he cut the hair of his head—at the end of every year he cut it because it was heavy on him—when he cut it, he weighed the hair of his head at two hundred shekels according to the king's standard. ²⁷To Absalom were born three sons, and one daughter whose name was Tamar. She was a woman of beautiful appearance.

²⁸And Absalom dwelt two full years in Jerusalem, but did not see the king's face. ²⁹Therefore Absalom sent for Joab, to send him to the king, but he would not come to him. And when he sent again the second time, he would not come. ³⁰So he said to his servants, "See, Joab's field is near mine, and he has barley there; go and set it on fire." And Absalom's servants set the field on fire.

³¹Then Joab arose and came to Absalom's house, and said to him, "Why have your servants set my field on fire?"

³²And Absalom answered Joab, "Look, I sent to you, saying, 'Come here, so that I may send you to the king, to say, "Why have I come from Geshur? It would be better for me to be there still." ' Now therefore, let me see the king's face; but if there is iniquity in me, let him execute me."

³³So Joab went to the king and told him. And when he had called for Absalom, he came to the king and bowed himself on his face to the ground before the king. Then the king kissed Absalom.

Absalom's Treason

15 After this it happened that Absalom provided himself with chariots and horses, and fifty men to run before him. ²Now Absalom would rise early and stand beside the way to the gate. So it was, whenever anyone who had a lawsuit came to the king for a decision, that Absalom would call to him and say, "What city are you from?" And he would say, "Your servant is from such and such a tribe of Israel." ³Then Absalom would say to him, "Look, your case is good and right; but there is no deputy of the king to hear you." ⁴Moreover Absalom would say, "Oh, that I were made judge in the land, and everyone who has any suit or cause would come to me; then I would give him justice." ⁵And so it was, whenever anyone came near to bow down to him, that he would put out his hand and take him and kiss him. ⁶In this manner Absalom acted toward all Israel who came to the king for judgment. So Absalom stole the hearts of the men of Israel.

⁷Now it came to pass after forty[a] years that Absalom said to the king, "Please, let me go to Hebron and pay the vow which I made to the LORD. ⁸For your servant took a vow while I dwelt at Geshur in Syria, saying, 'If the LORD indeed brings me back to Jerusalem, then I will serve the LORD.' "

⁹And the king said to him, "Go in peace." So he arose and went to Hebron.

¹⁰Then Absalom sent spies throughout all the tribes of Israel, saying, "As soon as you hear the sound of the trumpet, then you shall say, 'Absalom reigns in Hebron!' " ¹¹And with Absalom

15:7 ªSeptuagint manuscripts, Syriac, and Josephus read *four*.

went two hundred men invited from Jerusalem, and they went along innocently and did not know anything. ¹²Then Absalom sent for Ahithophel the Gilonite, David's counselor, from his city—from Giloh—while he offered sacrifices. And the conspiracy grew strong, for the people with Absalom continually increased in number.

DAVID ESCAPES FROM JERUSALEM

¹³Now a messenger came to David, saying, "The hearts of the men of Israel are with Absalom."

¹⁴So David said to all his servants who *were* with him at Jerusalem, "Arise, and let us flee, or we shall not escape from Absalom. Make haste to depart, lest he overtake us suddenly and bring disaster upon us, and strike the city with the edge of the sword."

¹⁵And the king's servants said to the king, "We *are* your servants, *ready to do* whatever my lord the king commands." ¹⁶Then the king went out with all his household after him. But the king left ten women, concubines, to keep the house. ¹⁷And the king went out with all the people after him, and stopped at the outskirts. ¹⁸Then all his servants passed before him; and all the Cherethites, all the Pelethites, and all the Gittites, six hundred men who had followed him from Gath, passed before the king.

¹⁹Then the king said to Ittai the Gittite, "Why are you also going with us? Return and remain with the king. For you *are* a foreigner and also an exile from your own place. ²⁰In fact, you came *only* yesterday. Should I make you wander up and down with us today, since I go I know not where? Return, and take your brethren back. Mercy and truth *be* with you."

²¹But Ittai answered the king and said, "*As* the LORD lives, and *as* my lord the king lives, surely in whatever place my lord the king shall be, whether in death or life, even there also your servant will be."

²²So David said to Ittai, "Go, and cross over." Then Ittai the Gittite and all his men and all the little ones who *were* with him crossed over. ²³And all the country wept with a loud voice, and all the people crossed over. The king himself also crossed over the Brook Kidron, and all the

people crossed over toward the way of the wilderness.

²⁴There was Zadok also, and all the Levites with him, bearing the ark of the covenant of God. And they set down the ark of God, and Abiathar went up until all the people had finished crossing over from the city. ²⁵Then the king said to Zadok, "Carry the ark of God back into the city. If I find favor in the eyes of the LORD, He will bring me back and show me *both* it and His dwelling place. ²⁶But if He says thus: 'I have no delight in you,' here I am, let Him do to me as seems good to Him." ²⁷The king also said to Zadok the priest, "*Are* you *not* a seer? Return to the city in peace, and your two sons with you, Ahimaaz your son, and Jonathan the son of Abiathar. ²⁸See, I will wait in the plains of the wilderness until word comes from you to inform me." ²⁹Therefore Zadok and Abiathar carried the ark of God back to Jerusalem. And they remained there.

³⁰So David went up by the Ascent of the *Mount of* Olives, and wept as he went up; and he had his head covered and went barefoot. And all the people who *were* with him covered their heads and went up, weeping as they went up. ³¹Then *someone* told David, saying, "Ahithophel is among the conspirators with Absalom." And David said, "O LORD, I pray, turn the counsel of Ahithophel into foolishness!"

³²Now it happened when David had come to the top *of the mountain,* where he worshiped God—there was Hushai the Archite coming to meet him with his robe torn and dust on his head. ³³David said to him, "If you go on with me, then you will become a burden to me. ³⁴But if you return to the city, and say to Absalom, 'I will be your servant, O king; *as* I *was* your father's servant previously, so I *will* now also *be* your servant,' then you may defeat the counsel of Ahithophel for me. ³⁵And *do* you not *have* Zadok and Abiathar the priests with you there? Therefore it will be *that* whatever you hear from the king's house you shall tell to Zadok and Abiathar the priests. ³⁶Indeed *they have* there with them their two sons, Ahimaaz, Zadok's *son,* and Jonathan, Abiathar's *son;* and by them you shall send me everything you hear."

³⁷So Hushai, David's friend, went into the city. And Absalom came into Jerusalem.

MEPHIBOSHETH'S SERVANT

16 When David was a little past the top *of the mountain,* there was Ziba the servant of Mephibosheth, who met him with a couple of saddled donkeys, and on them two hundred *loaves* of bread, one hundred clusters of raisins, one hundred summer fruits, and a skin of wine. [2]And the king said to Ziba, "What do you mean to do with these?"

So Ziba said, "The donkeys *are* for the king's household to ride on, the bread and summer fruit for the young men to eat, and the wine for those who are faint in the wilderness to drink."

[3]Then the king said, "And where *is* your master's son?"

And Ziba said to the king, "Indeed he is staying in Jerusalem, for he said, 'Today the house of Israel will restore the kingdom of my father to me.' "

[4]So the king said to Ziba, "Here, all that *belongs* to Mephibosheth *is* yours."

And Ziba said, "I humbly bow before you, *that* I may find favor in your sight, my lord, O king!"

SHIMEI CURSES DAVID

[5]Now when King David came to Bahurim, there was a man from the family of the house of Saul, whose name *was* Shimei the son of Gera, coming from there. He came out, cursing continuously as he came. [6]And he threw stones at David and at all the servants of King David. And all the people and all the mighty men *were* on his right hand and on his left. [7]Also Shimei said thus when he cursed: "Come out! Come out! You bloodthirsty man, you rogue! [8]The LORD has brought upon you all the blood of the house of Saul, in whose place you have reigned; and the LORD has delivered the kingdom into the hand of Absalom your son. So now you *are caught* in your own evil, because you are a bloodthirsty man!"

[9]Then Abishai the son of Zeruiah said to the king, "Why should this dead dog curse my lord the king? Please, let me go over and take off his head!"

[10]But the king said, "What have I to do with you, you sons of Zeruiah? So let him curse, be-cause the LORD has said to him, 'Curse David.' Who then shall say, 'Why have you done so?' "

[11]And David said to Abishai and all his servants, "See how my son who came from my own body seeks my life. How much more now *may this* Benjamite? Let him alone, and let him curse; for so the LORD has ordered him. [12]It may be that the LORD will look on my affliction,[a] and that the LORD will repay me with good for his cursing this day." [13]And as David and his men went along the road, Shimei went along the hillside opposite him and cursed as he went, threw stones at him and kicked up dust. [14]Now the king and all the people who *were* with him became weary; so they refreshed themselves there.

THE ADVICE OF AHITHOPHEL

[15]Meanwhile Absalom and all the people, the men of Israel, came to Jerusalem; and Ahithophel *was* with him. [16]And so it was, when Hushai the Archite, David's friend, came to Absalom, that Hushai said to Absalom, "*Long* live the king! *Long* live the king!"

[17]So Absalom said to Hushai, "*Is* this your loyalty to your friend? Why did you not go with your friend?"

[18]And Hushai said to Absalom, "No, but whom the LORD and this people and all the men of Israel choose, his I will be, and with him I will remain. [19]Furthermore, whom should I serve? *Should I* not *serve* in the presence of his son? As I have served in your father's presence, so will I be in your presence."

[20]Then Absalom said to Ahithophel, "Give advice as to what we should do."

[21]And Ahithophel said to Absalom, "Go in to your father's concubines, whom he has left to keep the house; and all Israel will hear that you are abhorred by your father. Then the hands of all who are with you will be strong." [22]So they pitched a tent for Absalom on the top of the house, and Absalom went in to his father's concubines in the sight of all Israel.

[23]Now the advice of Ahithophel, which he gave in those days, *was* as if one had inquired at the oracle of God. So *was* all the advice of Ahithophel both with David and with Absalom.

16:12 [a]Following Kethib, Septuagint, Syriac, and Vulgate; Qere reads *my eyes;* Targum reads *tears of my eyes.*

17 Moreover Ahithophel said to Absalom, "Now let me choose twelve thousand men, and I will arise and pursue David tonight. 2I will come upon him while he *is* weary and weak, and make him afraid. And all the people who *are* with him will flee, and I will strike only the king. 3Then I will bring back all the people to you. When all return except the man whom you seek, all the people will be at peace." 4And the saying pleased Absalom and all the elders of Israel.

The Advice of Hushai

5Then Absalom said, "Now call Hushai the Archite also, and let us hear what he says too." 6And when Hushai came to Absalom, Absalom spoke to him, saying, "Ahithophel has spoken in this manner. Shall we do as he says? If not, speak up."

7So Hushai said to Absalom: "The advice that Ahithophel has given *is* not good at this time. 8For," said Hushai, "you know your father and his men, that they *are* mighty men, and they *are* enraged in their minds, like a bear robbed of her cubs in the field; and your father *is* a man of war, and will not camp with the people. 9Surely by now he is hidden in some pit, or in some *other* place. And it will be, when some of them are overthrown at the first, that whoever hears *it* will say, 'There is a slaughter among the people who follow Absalom.' 10And even he *who is* valiant, whose heart *is* like the heart of a lion, will melt completely. For all Israel knows that your father *is* a mighty man, and *those* who *are* with him *are* valiant men. 11Therefore I advise that all Israel be fully gathered to you, from Dan to Beersheba, like the sand that *is* by the sea for multitude, and that you go to battle in person. 12So we will come upon him in some place where he may be found, and we will fall on him as the dew falls on the ground. And of him and all the men who *are* with him there shall not be left so much as one. 13Moreover, if he has withdrawn into a city, then all Israel shall bring ropes to that city; and we will pull it into the river, until there is not one small stone found there."

14So Absalom and all the men of Israel said, "The advice of Hushai the Archite *is* better than the advice of Ahithophel." For the LORD had purposed to defeat the good advice of Ahithophel, to the intent that the LORD might bring disaster on Absalom.

Hushai Warns David to Escape

15Then Hushai said to Zadok and Abiathar the priests, "Thus and so Ahithophel advised Absalom and the elders of Israel, and thus and so I have advised. 16Now therefore, send quickly and tell David, saying, 'Do not spend this night in the plains of the wilderness, but speedily cross over, lest the king and all the people who *are* with him be swallowed up.' " 17Now Jonathan and Ahimaaz stayed at En Rogel, for they dared not be seen coming into the city; so a female servant would come and tell them, and they would go and tell King David. 18Nevertheless a lad saw them, and told Absalom. But both of them went away quickly and came to a man's house in Bahurim, who had a well in his court; and they went down into it. 19Then the woman took and spread a covering over the well's mouth, and spread ground grain on it; and the thing was not known. 20And when Absalom's servants came to the woman at the house, they said, "Where *are* Ahimaaz and Jonathan?"

So the woman said to them, "They have gone over the water brook."

And when they had searched and could not find *them,* they returned to Jerusalem. 21Now it came to pass, after they had departed, that they came up out of the well and went and told King David, and said to David, "Arise and cross over the water quickly. For thus has Ahithophel advised against you." 22So David and all the people who *were* with him arose and crossed over the Jordan. By morning light not one of them was left who had not gone over the Jordan.

23Now when Ahithophel saw that his advice was not followed, he saddled a donkey, and arose and went home to his house, to his city. Then he put his household in order, and hanged himself and died; and he was buried in his father's tomb.

24Then David went to Mahanaim. And Absalom crossed over the Jordan, he and all the men of Israel with him. 25And Absalom made Amasa captain of the army instead of Joab. This Amasa *was* the son of a man whose name *was* Jithra,[a] an Israelite,

17:25 [a]Spelled *Jether* in 1 Chronicles 2:17 and elsewhere [b]Following Masoretic Text, some manuscripts of the Septuagint, and Targum; some manuscripts of the Septuagint read *Ishmaelite* (compare 1 Chronicles 2:17); Vulgate reads *of Jezreal.*

who had gone in to Abigail the daughter of Nahash, sister of Zeruiah, Joab's mother. ²⁶So Israel and Absalom encamped in the land of Gilead.

²⁷Now it happened, when David had come to Mahanaim, that Shobi the son of Nahash from Rabbah of the people of Ammon, Machir the son of Ammiel from Lo Debar, and Barzillai the Gileadite from Rogelim, ²⁸brought beds and basins, earthen vessels and wheat, barley and flour, parched *grain* and beans, lentils and parched *seeds,* ²⁹honey and curds, sheep and cheese of the herd, for David and the people who *were* with him to eat. For they said, "The people are hungry and weary and thirsty in the wilderness."

ABSALOM'S DEFEAT AND DEATH

18 And David numbered the people who *were* with him, and set captains of thousands and captains of hundreds over them. ²Then David sent out one third of the people under the hand of Joab, one third under the hand of Abishai the son of Zeruiah, Joab's brother, and one third under the hand of Ittai the Gittite. And the king said to the people, "I also will surely go out with you myself."

³But the people answered, "You shall not go out! For if we flee away, they will not care about us; nor if half of us die, will they care about us. But *you* are worth ten thousand of us now. For you are now more help to us in the city."

⁴Then the king said to them, "Whatever seems best to you I will do." So the king stood beside the gate, and all the people went out by hundreds and by thousands. ⁵Now the king had commanded Joab, Abishai, and Ittai, saying, "*Deal gently* for my sake with the young man Absalom." And all the people heard when the king gave all the captains orders concerning Absalom.

⁶So the people went out into the field of battle against Israel. And the battle was in the woods of Ephraim. ⁷The people of Israel were overthrown there before the servants of David, and a great slaughter of twenty thousand took place there that day. ⁸For the battle there was scattered over the face of the whole countryside, and the woods devoured more people that day than the sword devoured.

⁹Then Absalom met the servants of David. Absalom rode on a mule. The mule went under the thick boughs of a great terebinth tree, and his head caught in the terebinth; so he was left hanging between heaven and earth. And the mule which *was* under him went on. ¹⁰Now a certain man saw *it* and told Joab, and said, "I just saw Absalom hanging in a terebinth tree!"

¹¹So Joab said to the man who told him, "You just saw *him!* And why did you not strike him there to the ground? I would have given you ten *shekels* of silver and a belt."

¹²But the man said to Joab, "Though I were to receive a thousand *shekels* of silver in my hand, I would not raise my hand against the king's son. For in our hearing the king commanded you and Abishai and Ittai, saying, 'Beware lest anyone *touch* the young man Absalom!'ᵃ ¹³Otherwise I would have dealt falsely against my own life. For there is nothing hidden from the king, and you yourself would have set yourself against *me.*"

¹⁴Then Joab said, "I cannot linger with you." And he took three spears in his hand and thrust them through Absalom's heart, while he was *still* alive in the midst of the terebinth tree. ¹⁵And ten young men who bore Joab's armor surrounded Absalom, and struck and killed him.

¹⁶So Joab blew the trumpet, and the people returned from pursuing Israel. For Joab held back the people. ¹⁷And they took Absalom and cast him into a large pit in the woods, and laid a very large heap of stones over him. Then all Israel fled, everyone to his tent.

¹⁸Now Absalom in his lifetime had taken and set up a pillar for himself, which *is* in the King's Valley. For he said, "I have no son to keep my name in remembrance." He called the pillar after his own name. And to this day it is called Absalom's Monument.

DAVID HEARS OF ABSALOM'S DEATH

¹⁹Then Ahimaaz the son of Zadok said, "Let me run now and take the news to the king, how the LORD has avenged him of his enemies."

²⁰And Joab said to him, "You shall not take the news this day, for you shall take the news another day. But today you shall take no news, because the king's son is dead." ²¹Then Joab said to the Cushite, "Go, tell the king what you have

---

18:12 ᵃThe ancient versions read *'Protect the young man Absalom for me!'*

seen." So the Cushite bowed himself to Joab and ran.

22And Ahimaaz the son of Zadok said again to Joab, "But whatever happens, please let me also run after the Cushite."

So Joab said, "Why will you run, my son, since you have no news ready?"

23"But whatever happens," he said, "let me run."

So he said to him, "Run." Then Ahimaaz ran by way of the plain, and outran the Cushite.

24Now David was sitting between the two gates. And the watchman went up to the roof over the gate, to the wall, lifted his eyes and looked, and there was a man, running alone. 25Then the watchman cried out and told the king. And the king said, "If he is alone, there is news in his mouth." And he came rapidly and drew near.

26Then the watchman saw another man running, and the watchman called to the gatekeeper and said, "There is another man, running alone!"

And the king said, "He also brings news."

27So the watchman said, "I think the running of the first is like the running of Ahimaaz the son of Zadok."

And the king said, "He is a good man, and comes with good news."

28So Ahimaaz called out and said to the king, "All is well!" Then he bowed down with his face to the earth before the king, and said, "Blessed be the LORD your God, who has delivered up the men who raised their hand against my lord the king!"

29The king said, "Is the young man Absalom safe?"

Ahimaaz answered, "When Joab sent the king's servant and me your servant, I saw a great tumult, but I did not know what it was about."

30And the king said, "Turn aside and stand here." So he turned aside and stood still.

31Just then the Cushite came, and the Cushite said, "There is good news, my lord the king! For the LORD has avenged you this day of all those who rose against you."

32And the king said to the Cushite, "Is the young man Absalom safe?"

So the Cushite answered, "May the enemies of my lord the king, and all who rise against you to do harm, be like that young man!"

DAVID'S MOURNING FOR ABSALOM

33Then the king was deeply moved, and went up to the chamber over the gate, and wept. And as he went, he said thus: "O my son Absalom—my son, my son Absalom—if only I had died in your place! O Absalom my son, my son!"

19 And Joab was told, "Behold, the king is weeping and mourning for Absalom." 2So the victory that day was turned into mourning for all the people. For the people heard it said that day, "The king is grieved for his son." 3And the people stole back into the city that day, as people who are ashamed steal away when they flee in battle. 4But the king covered his face, and the king cried out with a loud voice, "O my son Absalom! O Absalom, my son, my son!"

5Then Joab came into the house to the king, and said, "Today you have disgraced all your servants who today have saved your life, the lives of your sons and daughters, the lives of your wives and the lives of your concubines, 6in that you love your enemies and hate your friends. For you have declared today that you regard neither princes nor servants; for today I perceive that if Absalom had lived and all of us had died today, then it would have pleased you well. 7Now therefore, arise, go out and speak comfort to your servants. For I swear by the LORD, if you do not go out, not one will stay with you this night. And that will be worse for you than all the evil that has befallen you from your youth until now." 8Then the king arose and sat in the gate. And they told all the people, saying, "There is the king, sitting in the gate." So all the people came before the king.

For everyone of Israel had fled to his tent.

DAVID RETURNS TO JERUSALEM

9Now all the people were in a dispute throughout all the tribes of Israel, saying, "The king saved us from the hand of our enemies, he delivered us from the hand of the Philistines, and now he has fled from the land because of Absalom. 10But Absalom, whom we anointed over us, has died in battle. Now therefore, why do you say nothing about bringing back the king?"

11So King David sent to Zadok and Abi

athar the priests, saying, "Speak to the elders of Judah, saying, 'Why are you the last to bring the king back to his house, since the words of all Israel have come to the king, to his *very* house? ¹²You *are* my brethren, you *are* my bone and my flesh. Why then are you the last to bring back the king?' ¹³And say to Amasa, '*Are* you not my bone and my flesh? God do so to me, and more also, if you are not commander of the army before me continually in place of Joab.' " ¹⁴So he swayed the hearts of all the men of Judah, just as *the heart of* one man, so that they sent *this word* to the king: "Return, you and all your servants!"

¹⁵Then the king returned and came to the Jordan. And Judah came to Gilgal, to go to meet the king, to escort the king across the Jordan. ¹⁶And Shimei the son of Gera, a Benjamite, who *was* from Bahurim, hurried and came down with the men of Judah to meet King David. ¹⁷*There were* a thousand men of Benjamin with him, and Ziba the servant of the house of Saul, and his fifteen sons and his twenty servants with him; and they went over the Jordan before the king. ¹⁸Then a ferryboat went across to carry over the king's household, and to do what he thought good.

David's Mercy to Shimei

Now Shimei the son of Gera fell down before the king when he had crossed the Jordan. ⁹Then he said to the king, "Do not let my lord impute iniquity to me, or remember what wrong your servant did on the day that my lord the king left Jerusalem, that the king should take *it* to heart. ²⁰For I, your servant, know that I have sinned. Therefore here I am, the first to come today of all the house of Joseph to go down to meet my lord the king."

²¹But Abishai the son of Zeruiah answered and said, "Shall not Shimei be put to death for this, because he cursed the LORD's anointed?"

²²And David said, "What have I to do with you, you sons of Zeruiah, that you should be adversaries to me today? Shall any man be put to death today in Israel? For do I not know that today I *am* king over Israel?" ²³Therefore the king said to Shimei, "You shall not die." And the king swore to him.

David and Mephibosheth Meet

²⁴Now Mephibosheth the son of Saul came down to meet the king. And he had not cared for his feet, nor trimmed his mustache, nor washed his clothes, from the day the king departed until the day he returned in peace. ²⁵So it was, when he had come to Jerusalem to meet the king, that the king said to him, "Why did you not go with me, Mephibosheth?"

²⁶And he answered, "My lord, O king, my servant deceived me. For your servant said, 'I will saddle a donkey for myself, that I may ride on it and go to the king,' because your servant *is* lame. ²⁷And he has slandered your servant to my lord the king, but my lord the king *is* like the angel of God. Therefore do *what is* good in your eyes. ²⁸For all my father's house were but dead men before my lord the king. Yet you set your servant among those who eat at your own table. Therefore what right have I still to cry out anymore to the king?"

²⁹So the king said to him, "Why do you speak anymore of your matters? I have said, 'You and Ziba divide the land.' "

³⁰Then Mephibosheth said to the king, "Rather, let him take it all, inasmuch as my lord the king has come back in peace to his own house."

David's Kindness to Barzillai

³¹And Barzillai the Gileadite came down from Rogelim and went across the Jordan with the king, to escort him across the Jordan. ³²Now Barzillai was a very aged man, eighty years old. And he had provided the king with supplies while he stayed at Mahanaim, for he *was* a very rich man. ³³And the king said to Barzillai, "Come across with me, and I will provide for you while you are with me in Jerusalem."

³⁴But Barzillai said to the king, "How long have I to live, that I should go up with the king to Jerusalem? ³⁵I *am* today eighty years old. Can I discern between the good and bad? Can your servant taste what I eat or what I drink? Can I hear any longer the voice of singing men and singing women? Why then should your servant be a further burden to my lord the king? ³⁶Your servant will go a little way across the Jordan with the king. And why should the king repay me *with* such a

reward? ³⁷Please let your servant turn back again, that I may die in my own city, near the grave of my father and mother. But here is your servant Chimham; let him cross over with my lord the king, and do for him what seems good to you."

³⁸And the king answered, "Chimham shall cross over with me, and I will do for him what seems good to you. Now whatever you request of me, I will do for you." ³⁹Then all the people went over the Jordan. And when the king had crossed over, the king kissed Barzillai and blessed him, and he returned to his own place.

The Quarrel About the King

⁴⁰Now the king went on to Gilgal, and Chimham[a] went on with him. And all the people of Judah escorted the king, and also half the people of Israel. ⁴¹Just then all the men of Israel came to the king, and said to the king, "Why have our brethren, the men of Judah, stolen you away and brought the king, his household, and all David's men with him across the Jordan?"

⁴²So all the men of Judah answered the men of Israel, "Because the king *is* a close relative of ours. Why then are you angry over this matter? Have we ever eaten at the king's *expense?* Or has he given us any gift?"

⁴³And the men of Israel answered the men of Judah, and said, "We have ten shares in the king; therefore we also have more *right* to David than you. Why then do you despise us—were we not the first to advise bringing back our king?"

Yet the words of the men of Judah were fiercer than the words of the men of Israel.

The Rebellion of Sheba

20 And there happened to be there a rebel,[a] whose name *was* Sheba the son of Bichri, a Benjamite. And he blew a trumpet, and said:

"We have no share in David,
    Nor do we have inheritance in the son of
        Jesse;
    Every man to his tents, O Israel!"

²So every man of Israel deserted David, *and* followed Sheba the son of Bichri. But the men of Judah, from the Jordan as far as Jerusalem, remained loyal to their king.

³Now David came to his house at Jerusalem. And the king took the ten women, his concubines whom he had left to keep the house, and put them in seclusion and supported them, but did not go in to them. So they were shut up to the day of their death, living in widowhood.

⁴And the king said to Amasa, "Assemble the men of Judah for me within three days, and be present here yourself." ⁵So Amasa went to assemble *the men of* Judah. But he delayed longer than the set time which David had appointed him. ⁶And David said to Abishai, "Now Sheba the son of Bichri will do us more harm than Absalom. Take your lord's servants and pursue him, lest he find for himself fortified cities, and escape us." ⁷So Joab's men, with the Cherethites, the Pelethites, and all the mighty men, went out after him. And they went out of Jerusalem to pursue Sheba the son of Bichri. ⁸When they *were* at the large stone which *is* in Gibeon, Amasa came before them. Now Joab was dressed in battle armor; on it was a belt *with* a sword fastened in its sheath at his hips; and as he was going forward, it fell out. ⁹Then Joab said to Amasa, "*Are* you in health, my brother?" And Joab took Amasa by the beard with his right hand to kiss him. ¹⁰But Amasa did not notice the sword that *was* in Joab's hand. And he struck him with it in the stomach, and his entrails poured out on the ground; and he did not *strike* him again. Thus he died.

Then Joab and Abishai his brother pursued Sheba the son of Bichri. ¹¹Meanwhile one of Joab's men stood near Amasa, and said, "Whoever favors Joab and whoever *is* for David—follow Joab!" ¹²But Amasa wallowed in *his* blood in the middle of the highway. And when the man saw that all the people stood still, he moved Amasa from the highway to the field and threw a garment over him, when he saw that everyone who came upon him halted. ¹³When he was removed from the highway, all the people went on after Joab to pursue Sheba the son of Bichri.

¹⁴And he went through all the tribes of Israel to Abel and Beth Maachah and all the Berites. So they were gathered together and also went after Sheba.[a] ¹⁵Then they came and besieged him in Abel of Beth Maachah; and they cast up a siege

19:40 ᵃMasoretic Text reads *Chimhan.*   20:1 ᵃLiterally *man of Belial*
20:14 ᵃLiterally *him*

mound against the city, and it stood by the rampart. And all the people who *were* with Joab battered the wall to throw it down.

16Then a wise woman cried out from the city, "Hear, hear! Please say to Joab, 'Come nearby, that I may speak with you.' " 17When he had come near to her, the woman said, "*Are* you Joab?"

He answered, "I *am*."

Then she said to him, "Hear the words of your maidservant."

And he answered, "I am listening."

18So she spoke, saying, "They used to talk in former times, saying, 'They shall surely seek *guidance* at Abel,' and so they would end *disputes*. 19I *am among the* peaceable *and* faithful in Israel. You seek to destroy a city and a mother in Israel. Why would you swallow up the inheritance of the LORD?"

20And Joab answered and said, "Far be it, far be it from me, that I should swallow up or destroy! 21That *is* not so. But a man from the mountains of Ephraim, Sheba the son of Bichri by name, has raised his hand against the king, against David. Deliver him only, and I will depart from the city."

So the woman said to Joab, "Watch, his head will be thrown to you over the wall." 22Then the woman in her wisdom went to all the people. And they cut off the head of Sheba the son of Bichri, and threw *it* out to Joab. Then he blew a trumpet, and they withdrew from the city, every man to his tent. So Joab returned to the king at Jerusalem.

DAVID'S GOVERNMENT OFFICERS

23And Joab *was* over all the army of Israel; Benaiah the son of Jehoiada *was* over the Cherethites and the Pelethites; 24Adoram *was* in charge of revenue; Jehoshaphat the son of Ahilud *was* recorder; 25Sheva *was* scribe; Zadok and Abiathar *were* the priests; 26and Ira the Jairite was a chief minister under David.

DAVID AVENGES THE GIBEONITES

21 Now there was a famine in the days of David for three years, year after year; and David inquired of the LORD. And the LORD answered, "*It is* because of Saul and *his* bloodthirsty house, because he killed the Gibeonites." 2So the

king called the Gibeonites and spoke to them. Now the Gibeonites *were* not of the children of Israel, but of the remnant of the Amorites; the children of Israel had sworn protection to them, but Saul had sought to kill them in his zeal for the children of Israel and Judah.

3Therefore David said to the Gibeonites, "What shall I do for you? And with what shall I make atonement, that you may bless the inheritance of the LORD?"

4And the Gibeonites said to him, "We will have no silver or gold from Saul or from his house, nor shall you kill any man in Israel for us."

So he said, "Whatever you say, I will do for you."

5Then they answered the king, "As for the man who consumed us and plotted against us, *that* we should be destroyed from remaining in any of the territories of Israel, 6let seven men of his descendants be delivered to us, and we will hang them before the LORD in Gibeah of Saul, *whom* the LORD chose."

And the king said, "I will give *them*."

7But the king spared Mephibosheth the son of Jonathan, the son of Saul, because of the LORD's oath that *was* between them, between David and Jonathan the son of Saul. 8So the king took Armoni and Mephibosheth, the two sons of Rizpah the daughter of Aiah, whom she bore to Saul, and the five sons of Michala the daughter of Saul, whom she brought up for Adriel the son of Barzillai the Meholathite; 9and he delivered them into the hands of the Gibeonites, and they hanged them on the hill before the LORD. So they fell, *all* seven together, and were put to death in the days of harvest, in the first *days,* in the beginning of barley harvest.

10Now Rizpah the daughter of Aiah took sackcloth and spread it for herself on the rock, from the beginning of harvest until the late rains poured on them from heaven. And she did not allow the birds of the air to rest on them by day nor the beasts of the field by night.

11And David was told what Rizpah the daughter of Aiah, the concubine of Saul, had done. 12Then David went and took the bones of Saul, and the bones of Jonathan his son, from the

21:8 aOr *Merab* (compare 1 Samuel 18:19 and 25:44; 2 Samuel 3:14 and 6:23)

men of Jabesh Gilead who had stolen them from the street of Beth Shan,[a] where the Philistines had hung them up, after the Philistines had struck down Saul in Gilboa. [13]So he brought up the bones of Saul and the bones of Jonathan his son from there; and they gathered the bones of those who had been hanged. [14]They buried the bones of Saul and Jonathan his son in the country of Benjamin in Zelah, in the tomb of Kish his father. So they performed all that the king commanded. And after that God heeded the prayer for the land.

PHILISTINE GIANTS DESTROYED

[15]When the Philistines were at war again with Israel, David and his servants with him went down and fought against the Philistines; and David grew faint. [16]Then Ishbi-Benob, who *was* one of the sons of the giant, the weight of whose bronze spear *was* three hundred *shekels,* who was bearing a new *sword,* thought he could kill David. [17]But Abishai the son of Zeruiah came to his aid, and struck the Philistine and killed him. Then the men of David swore to him, saying, "You shall go out no more with us to battle, lest you quench the lamp of Israel."

[18]Now it happened afterward that there was again a battle with the Philistines at Gob. Then Sibbechai the Hushathite killed Saph,[a] who *was* one of the sons of the giant. [19]Again there was war at Gob with the Philistines, where Elhanan the son of Jaare-Oregim[a] the Bethlehemite killed *the brother of* Goliath the Gittite, the shaft of whose spear *was* like a weaver's beam.

[20]Yet again there was war at Gath, where there was a man of *great* stature, who had six fingers on each hand and six toes on each foot, twenty-four in number; and he also was born to the giant. [21]So when he defied Israel, Jonathan the son of Shimea,[a] David's brother, killed him.

[22]These four were born to the giant in Gath, and fell by the hand of David and by the hand of his servants.

PRAISE FOR GOD'S DELIVERANCE

22 Then David spoke to the LORD the words of this song, on the day when the LORD had delivered him from the hand of all his enemies, and from the hand of Saul. [2]And he said:[a]

"The LORD *is* my rock and my fortress and my deliverer;
[3]The God of my strength, in whom I will trust;
My shield and the horn of my salvation,
My stronghold and my refuge;
My Savior, You save me from violence.
[4]I will call upon the LORD, *who is worthy* to be praised;
So shall I be saved from my enemies.

[5]"When the waves of death surrounded me,
The floods of ungodliness made me afraid.
[6]The sorrows of Sheol surrounded me;
The snares of death confronted me.
[7]In my distress I called upon the LORD,
And cried out to my God;
He heard my voice from His temple,
And my cry *entered* His ears.

[8]"Then the earth shook and trembled;
The foundations of heaven[a] quaked and were shaken,
Because He was angry.
[9]Smoke went up from His nostrils,
And devouring fire from His mouth;
Coals were kindled by it.
[10]He bowed the heavens also, and came down
With darkness under His feet.
[11]He rode upon a cherub, and flew;
And He was seen[a] upon the wings of the wind.
[12]He made darkness canopies around Him,
Dark waters *and* thick clouds of the skies.
[13]From the brightness before Him
Coals of fire were kindled.

[14]"The LORD thundered from heaven,
And the Most High uttered His voice.
[15]He sent out arrows and scattered them;
Lightning bolts, and He vanquished them.
[16]Then the channels of the sea were seen,

21:12 [a]Spelled *Beth Shean* in Joshua 17:11 and elsewhere **21:18** [a]Spelled *Sippai* in 1 Chronicles 20:4 **21:19** [a]Spelled *Jair* i 1 Chronicles 20:5 **21:21** [a]Spelled *Shammah* in 1 Samuel 16:9 an elsewhere **22:2** [a]Compare Psalm 18 **22:8** [a]Following Masoreti Text, Septuagint, and Targum; Syriac and Vulgate read *hills* (com pare Psalm 18:7). **22:11** [a]Following Masoretic Text and Septu agint; many Hebrew manuscripts, Syriac, and Vulgate read *He flev* (compare Psalm 18:10); Targum reads *He spoke with power.*

The foundations of the world were
    uncovered,
At the rebuke of the LORD,
At the blast of the breath of His nostrils.

¹⁷"He sent from above, He took me,
    He drew me out of many waters.
¹⁸He delivered me from my strong enemy,
    From those who hated me;
    For they were too strong for me.
¹⁹They confronted me in the day of my
    calamity,
    But the LORD was my support.
²⁰He also brought me out into a broad place;
    He delivered me because He delighted in me.

²¹"The LORD rewarded me according to my
    righteousness;
    According to the cleanness of my hands
    He has recompensed me.
²²For I have kept the ways of the LORD,
    And have not wickedly departed from my
    God.
²³For all His judgments *were* before me;
    And *as for* His statutes, I did not depart from
    them.
²⁴I was also blameless before Him,
    And I kept myself from my iniquity.
²⁵Therefore the LORD has recompensed me
    according to my righteousness,
    According to my cleanness in His eyes.^a

²⁶"With the merciful You will show Yourself
    merciful;
    With a blameless man You will show Yourself
    blameless;
²⁷With the pure You will show Yourself pure;
    And with the devious You will show Yourself
    shrewd.
²⁸You will save the humble people;
    But Your eyes *are* on the haughty, *that* You
    may bring *them* down.

²⁹"For You *are* my lamp, O LORD;
    The LORD shall enlighten my darkness.
³⁰For by You I can run against a troop;
    By my God I can leap over a wall.
³¹*As for* God, His way *is* perfect;

The word of the LORD *is* proven;
    He *is* a shield to all who trust in Him.

³²"For who *is* God, except the LORD?
    And who *is* a rock, except our God?
³³God *is* my strength *and* power,^a
    And He makes my^b way perfect.
³⁴He makes my^a feet like the *feet* of deer,
    And sets me on my high places.
³⁵He teaches my hands to make war,
    So that my arms can bend a bow of
    bronze.

³⁶"You have also given me the shield of Your
    salvation;
    Your gentleness has made me great.
³⁷You enlarged my path under me;
    So my feet did not slip.

³⁸"I have pursued my enemies and destroyed
    them;
    Neither did I turn back again till they were
    destroyed.
³⁹And I have destroyed them and wounded
    them,
    So that they could not rise;
    They have fallen under my feet.
⁴⁰For You have armed me with strength for the
    battle;
    You have subdued under me those who rose
    against me.
⁴¹You have also given me the necks of my
    enemies,
    So that I destroyed those who hated me.
⁴²They looked, but *there was* none to save;
    Even to the LORD, but He did not answer
    them.
⁴³Then I beat them as fine as the dust of the
    earth;
    I trod them like dirt in the streets,
    And I spread them out.

22:25 ^aSeptuagint, Syriac, and Vulgate read *the cleanness of my hands in His sight* (compare Psalm 18:24); Targum reads *my cleanness before His word.* **22:33** ^aDead Sea Scrolls, Septuagint, Syriac, and Vulgate read *It is God who arms me with strength* (compare Psalm 18:32); Targum reads *It is God who sustains me with strength.* ^bFollowing Qere, Septuagint, Syriac, Targum, and Vulgate (compare Psalm 18:32); Kethib reads *His.* **22:34** ^aFollowing Qere, Septuagint, Syriac, Targum, and Vulgate (compare Psalm 18:33); Kethib reads *His.*

⁴⁴"You have also delivered me from the strivings
of my people;
You have kept me as the head of the nations.
A people I have not known shall serve me.
⁴⁵The foreigners submit to me;
As soon as they hear, they obey me.
⁴⁶The foreigners fade away,
And come frightened^a from their hideouts.

⁴⁷"The LORD lives!
Blessed *be* my Rock!
Let God be exalted,
The Rock of my salvation!
⁴⁸*It is* God who avenges me,
And subdues the peoples under me;
⁴⁹He delivers me from my enemies.
You also lift me up above those who rise
against me;
You have delivered me from the violent
man.
⁵⁰Therefore I will give thanks to You, O LORD,
among the Gentiles,
And sing praises to Your name.

⁵¹*He is* the tower of salvation to His king,
And shows mercy to His anointed,
To David and his descendants forevermore."

David's Last Words

23 Now these *are* the last words of David.

Thus says David the son of Jesse;
Thus says the man raised up on high,
The anointed of the God of Jacob,
And the sweet psalmist of Israel:

²"The Spirit of the LORD spoke by me,
And His word *was* on my tongue.
³The God of Israel said,
The Rock of Israel spoke to me:
'He who rules over men *must be* just,
Ruling in the fear of God.
⁴And *he shall be* like the light of the morning
when the sun rises,
A morning without clouds,
Like the tender grass *springing* out of the
earth,
By clear shining after rain.'

⁵"Although my house *is* not so with God,
Yet He has made with me an everlasting
covenant,
Ordered in all *things* and secure.
For *this is* all my salvation and all *my* desire;
Will He not make *it* increase?
⁶But *the sons* of rebellion *shall* all *be* as thorns
thrust away,
Because they cannot be taken with hands.
⁷But the man *who* touches them
Must be armed with iron and the shaft of a
spear,
And they shall be utterly burned with fire in
their place."

David's Mighty Men

⁸These *are* the names of the mighty men
whom David had: Josheb-Basshebeth^a the Tach-
monite, chief among the captains.^b He was called
Adino the Eznite, because he had killed eight
hundred men at one time. ⁹And after him *was*
Eleazar the son of Dodo,^a the Ahohite, *one* of the
three mighty men with David when they defied
the Philistines *who* were gathered there for battle,
and the men of Israel had retreated. ¹⁰He arose
and attacked the Philistines until his hand was
weary, and his hand stuck to the sword. The LORD
brought about a great victory that day; and the
people returned after him only to plunder. ¹¹And
after him *was* Shammah the son of Agee the
Hararite. The Philistines had gathered together
into a troop where there was a piece of ground
full of lentils. So the people fled from the
Philistines. ¹²But he stationed himself in the middle of the field, defended it, and killed the
Philistines. So the LORD brought about a great
victory.

¹³Then three of the thirty chief men went
down at harvest time and came to David at the
cave of Adullam. And the troop of Philistines encamped in the Valley of Rephaim. ¹⁴David *was*
then in the stronghold, and the garrison of the
Philistines *was* then *in* Bethlehem. ¹⁵And David
said with longing, "Oh, that someone would give
me a drink of the water from the well of Bethle-

22:46 ^aFollowing Septuagint, Targum, and Vulgate (compare Psalm
18:45); Masoretic Text reads *gird themselves.* **23:8** ^aLiterally *On
Who Sits in the Seat* (compare 1 Chronicles 11:11) ^bFollowing Masoretic Text and Targum; Septuagint and Vulgate read *the three*
23:9 ^aSpelled *Dodai* in 1 Chronicles 27:4

INSIDE *the* INFLUENCERS

DAVID'S MIGHTY MEN—Losers or Heroes?

2 SAMUEL 23:8–39

David's mighty men weren't always so mighty. In fact, they started out as a bunch of losers; definitely not the best group of people. The Bible says they were discontent, distressed, and in debt. These men didn't appear as potential heroes when they joined David at his cave in Adullam (1 Sam. 22:1, 2). They lost their will, their peace, and even their money. They were the very definition of "losers." But that was just the beginning of their story, because this distressed and weak group went on to become "mighty."

God used a strong leader to transform them from men in hiding to the greatest warriors the world had ever seen. When they had no courage, David gave them his courage (1 Sam. 23:3, 4); and through his example, they traded in their discontent for devotion, their distress for determination, and their debt for duty. David poured his life into these men by mentoring them into heroes.

Because of this, David's mighty men were devoted to their leader even at the risk of losing their own lives (2 Sam. 23:16, 17). They were grateful that David had seen something great in them when no one else could. True leaders, like David, have a different view of people and look beyond circumstance to potential.

hem, which *is* by the gate!" [16]So the three mighty men broke through the camp of the Philistines, drew water from the well of Bethlehem that *was* by the gate, and took it and brought *it* to David. Nevertheless he would not drink it, but poured it out to the LORD. [17]And he said, "Far be it from me, O LORD, that I should do this! Is *this not* the blood of the men who went in *jeopardy of* their lives?" Therefore he would not drink it.

These things were done by the three mighty men.

[18]Now Abishai the brother of Joab, the son of Zeruiah, was chief of *another* three.[a] He lifted his spear against three hundred *men*, killed *them*, and won a name among *these* three. [19]Was he not the most honored of three? Therefore he became their captain. However, he did not attain to the *first* three.

[20]Benaiah *was* the son of Jehoiada, the son of a valiant man from Kabzeel, who had done many deeds. He had killed two lion-like heroes of Moab. He also had gone down and killed a lion in the midst of a pit on a snowy day. [21]And he killed an Egyptian, a spectacular man. The Egyptian *had* a spear in his hand; so he went down to

him with a staff, wrested the spear out of the Egyptian's hand, and killed him with his own spear. [22]These *things* Benaiah the son of Jehoiada did, and won a name among three mighty men. [23]He was more honored than the thirty, but he did not attain to the *first* three. And David appointed him over his guard.

[24]Asahel the brother of Joab *was* one of the thirty; Elhanan the son of Dodo of Bethlehem, [25]Shammah the Harodite, Elika the Harodite, [26]Helez the Paltite, Ira the son of Ikkesh the Tekoite, [27]Abiezer the Anathothite, Mebunnai the Hushathite, [28]Zalmon the Ahohite, Maharai the Netophathite, [29]Heleb the son of Baanah (the Netophathite), Ittai the son of Ribai from Gibeah of the children of Benjamin, [30]Benaiah a Pirathonite, Hiddai from the brooks of Gaash, [31]Abi-Albon the Arbathite, Azmaveth the Barhumite, [32]Eliahba the Shaalbonite (of the sons of Jashen), Jonathan, [33]Shammah the Hararite, Ahiam the son of Sharar the Hararite, [34]Eliphelet the son

23:18 [a]Following Masoretic Text, Septuagint, and Vulgate; some Hebrew manuscripts and Syriac read *thirty;* Targum reads *the mighty men.*

of Ahasbai, the son of the Maachathite, Eliam the son of Ahithophel the Gilonite, [35]Hezrai[a] the Carmelite, Paarai the Arbite, [36]Igal the son of Nathan of Zobah, Bani the Gadite, [37]Zelek the Ammonite, Naharai the Beerothite (armorbearer of Joab the son of Zeruiah), [38]Ira the Ithrite, Gareb the Ithrite, [39]*and* Uriah the Hittite: thirty-seven in all.

DAVID'S CENSUS OF ISRAEL AND JUDAH

24 Again the anger of the LORD was aroused against Israel, and He moved David against them to say, "Go, number Israel and Judah."

[2]So the king said to Joab the commander of the army who *was* with him, "Now go throughout all the tribes of Israel, from Dan to Beersheba, and count the people, that I may know the number of the people."

[3]And Joab said to the king, "Now may the LORD your God add to the people a hundred times more than there are, and may the eyes of my lord the king see *it*. But why does my lord the king desire this thing?" [4]Nevertheless the king's word prevailed against Joab and against the captains of the army. Therefore Joab and the captains of the army went out from the presence of the king to count the people of Israel.

[5]And they crossed over the Jordan and camped in Aroer, on the right side of the town which *is* in the midst of the ravine of Gad, and toward Jazer. [6]Then they came to Gilead and to the land of Tahtim Hodshi; they came to Dan Jaan and around to Sidon; [7]and they came to the stronghold of Tyre and to all the cities of the Hivites and the Canaanites. Then they went out to South Judah *as far as* Beersheba. [8]So when they had gone through all the land, they came to Jerusalem at the end of nine months and twenty days. [9]Then Joab gave the sum of the number of the people to the king. And there were in Israel eight hundred thousand valiant men who drew the sword, and the men of Judah were five hundred thousand men.

THE JUDGMENT ON DAVID'S SIN

[10]And David's heart condemned him after he had numbered the people. So David said to the LORD, "I have sinned greatly in what I have done; but now, I pray, O LORD, take away the in-

iquity of Your servant, for I have done very foolishly."

[11]Now when David arose in the morning, the word of the LORD came to the prophet Gad, David's seer, saying, [12]"Go and tell David, 'Thus says the LORD: "I offer you three *things;* choose one of them for yourself, that I may do *it* to you." ' " [13]So Gad came to David and told him; and he said to him, "Shall seven[a] years of famine come to you in your land? Or shall you flee three months before your enemies, while they pursue you? Or shall there be three days' plague in your land? Now consider and see what answer I should take back to Him who sent me."

[14]And David said to Gad, "I am in great distress. Please let us fall into the hand of the LORD, for His mercies *are* great; but do not let me fall into the hand of man."

[15]So the LORD sent a plague upon Israel from the morning till the appointed time. From Dan to Beersheba seventy thousand men of the people died. [16]And when the angel[a] stretched out His hand over Jerusalem to destroy it, the LORD relented from the destruction, and said to the angel who was destroying the people, "It is enough; now restrain your hand." And the angel of the LORD was by the threshing floor of Araunah[b] the Jebusite.

[17]Then David spoke to the LORD when he saw the angel who was striking the people, and said, "Surely I have sinned, and I have done wickedly; but these sheep, what have they done? Let Your hand, I pray, be against me and against my father's house."

THE ALTAR ON THE THRESHING FLOOR

[18]And Gad came that day to David and said to him, "Go up, erect an altar to the LORD on the threshing floor of Araunah the Jebusite." [19]So David, according to the word of Gad, went up as the LORD commanded. [20]Now Araunah looked, and saw the king and his servants coming toward him. So Araunah went out and bowed before the king with his face to the ground.

[21]Then Araunah said, "Why has my lord the king come to his servant?"

23:35 [a]Spelled *Hezro* in 1 Chronicles 11:37   **24:13** [a]Following Masoretic Text, Syriac, Targum, and Vulgate; Septuagint reads *three* (compare 1 Chronicles 21:12).   **24:16** [a]Or *Angel* [b]Spelled *Ornan* in 1 Chronicles 21:15

And David said, "To buy the threshing floor from you, to build an altar to the LORD, that the plague may be withdrawn from the people."

22Now Araunah said to David, "Let my lord the king take and offer up whatever *seems* good to him. Look, *here are* oxen for burnt sacrifice, and threshing implements and the yokes of the oxen for wood. 23All these, O king, Araunah has given to the king."

And Araunah said to the king, "May the LORD your God accept you."

24Then the king said to Araunah, "No, but I will surely buy *it* from you for a price; nor will I offer burnt offerings to the LORD my God with that which costs me nothing." So David bought the threshing floor and the oxen for fifty shekels of silver. 25And David built there an altar to the LORD, and offered burnt offerings and peace offerings. So the LORD heeded the prayers for the land, and the plague was withdrawn from Israel.

IMPACT OF THE BOOK

IDEA	*The key principle of wisdom is the simple truth that "the fear of the LORD is the beginning of wisdom" (Ps. 111:10). The leader sets the tone for a nation and can point its people to God or quickly lead them astray.*
MESSAGE	*The Lord visited Solomon, the son of David, early in his reign; the Lord gave him permission to ask anything. Solomon's request was for wisdom. Delighted, the Lord gave him wisdom and great understanding and largeness of heart "like sand on the seashore." The second visit near the end of his reign came with a warning to avoid the idolatry of his many wives. His heart was not loyal to the Lord his God (11:4). Under Solomon's leadership, Israel experienced great success; however, the world's wisest man failed miserably in one key area—he did not invest in the next generation by training a successor, which led to the splintering of the nation.*
PEOPLE	*Ahab, Ahaziah, Ahijah, Asa, Baasha, David, Elijah, Jehoshaphat, Jehu, Jeroboam, Jezebel, Micaiah, Nathan, Obadiah, Rehoboam, Shemiah, Solomon*
AUTHOR	*First and 2 Kings were originally one book. No author is listed, although Jeremiah has traditionally been credited. Whoever the author was, he drew from earlier historical sources for his writing.*
CULTURE	*The events in this book span from David's death (c. 970 BC) to Jehoshaphat's death (c. 848 BC). Israel reached its zenith in national influence; however, after the death of Solomon, the Davidic kingdom was split into the northern (centered in Israel) and southern kingdoms (centered in Judah). The kings led the people in pagan worship practices. God punished their disobedience by sending pagan kingdoms to conquer them.*
TIMELINE	*c. 560 BC*
KEY SCRIPTURE MEMORY VERSES	3:9; 8:27; 9:4, 5; 11:11

ADONIJAH PRESUMES TO BE KING

1 Now King David was old, advanced in years; and they put covers on him, but he could not get warm. ²Therefore his servants said to him, "Let a young woman, a virgin, be sought for our lord the king, and let her stand before the king, and let her care for him; and let her lie in your bosom, that our lord the king may be warm." ³So they sought for a lovely young woman throughout all the territory of Israel, and found Abishag the Shunammite, and brought her to the king. ⁴The young woman *was* very lovely; and she cared for the king, and served him; but the king did not know her.

⁵Then Adonijah the son of Haggith exalted himself, saying, "I will be king"; and he prepared for himself chariots and horsemen, and fifty men to run before him. ⁶(And his father had not rebuked him at any time by saying, "Why have you done so?" He *was* also very good-looking. *His mother* had borne him after Absalom.) ⁷Then he conferred with Joab the son of Zeruiah and with Abiathar the priest, and they followed and helped Adonijah. ⁸But Zadok the priest, Benaiah the son of Jehoiada, Nathan the prophet, Shimei, Rei, and the mighty men who *belonged* to David were not with Adonijah.

⁹And Adonijah sacrificed sheep and oxen and fattened cattle by the stone of Zoheleth, which *is* by En Rogel; he also invited all his brothers, the king's sons, and all the men of Judah, the king's servants. ¹⁰But he did not invite Nathan the prophet, Benaiah, the mighty men, or Solomon his brother.

¹¹So Nathan spoke to Bathsheba the mother of Solomon, saying, "Have you not heard that Adonijah the son of Haggith has become king, and David our lord does not know *it?* ¹²Come, please, let me now give you advice, that you may save your own life and the life of your son Solomon. ¹³Go immediately to King David and say to him, 'Did you not, my lord, O king, swear to your maidservant, saying, "Assuredly your son Solomon shall reign after me, and he shall sit on my throne"? Why then has Adonijah become king?' ¹⁴Then, while you are still talking there with the king, I also will come in after you and confirm your words."

¹⁵So Bathsheba went into the chamber to the king. (Now the king was very old, and Abishag the Shunammite was serving the king.) ¹⁶And Bathsheba bowed and did homage to the king. Then the king said, "What is your wish?"

¹⁷Then she said to him, "My lord, you swore by the LORD your God to your maidservant, *saying,* 'Assuredly Solomon your son shall reign after me, and he shall sit on my throne.' ¹⁸So now, look! Adonijah has become king; and now, my lord the king, you do not know about *it.* ¹⁹He has sacrificed oxen and fattened cattle and sheep in abundance, and has invited all the sons of the king, Abiathar the priest, and Joab the commander of the army; but Solomon your servant he has not invited. ²⁰And as for you, my lord, O king, the eyes of all Israel *are* on you, that you should tell them who will sit on the throne of my lord the king after him. ²¹Otherwise it will happen, when my lord the king rests with his fathers, that I and my son Solomon will be counted as offenders."

²²And just then, while she was still talking with the king, Nathan the prophet also came in. ²³So they told the king, saying, "Here is Nathan the prophet." And when he came in before the king, he bowed down before the king with his face to the ground. ²⁴And Nathan said, "My lord, O king, have you said, 'Adonijah shall reign after me, and he shall sit on my throne'? ²⁵For he has gone down today, and has sacrificed oxen and fattened cattle and sheep in abundance, and has invited all the king's sons, and the commanders of the army, and Abiathar the priest; and look! They are eating and drinking before him; and they say, '*Long* live King Adonijah!' ²⁶But he has not invited me—me your servant—nor Zadok the priest, nor Benaiah the son of Jehoiada, nor your servant Solomon. ²⁷Has this thing been done by my lord the king, and you have not told your servant who should sit on the throne of my lord the king after him?"

DAVID PROCLAIMS SOLOMON KING

²⁸Then King David answered and said, "Call Bathsheba to me." So she came into the king's presence and stood before the king. ²⁹And the king took an oath and said, "*As* the LORD lives, who has redeemed my life from every distress, ³⁰just as I swore to you by the LORD God of Israel, saying, 'Assuredly Solomon your son shall be

king after me, and he shall sit on my throne in my place,' so I certainly will do this day."

31Then Bathsheba bowed with *her* face to the earth, and paid homage to the king, and said, "Let my lord King David live forever!"

32And King David said, "Call to me Zadok the priest, Nathan the prophet, and Benaiah the son of Jehoiada." So they came before the king. 33The king also said to them, "Take with you the servants of your lord, and have Solomon my son ride on my own mule, and take him down to Gihon. 34There let Zadok the priest and Nathan the prophet anoint him king over Israel; and blow the horn, and say, 'Long live King Solomon!' 35Then you shall come up after him, and he shall come and sit on my throne, and he shall be king in my place. For I have appointed him to be ruler over Israel and Judah."

36Benaiah the son of Jehoiada answered the king and said, "Amen! May the LORD God of my lord the king say so *too.* 37As the LORD has been with my lord the king, even so may He be with Solomon, and make his throne greater than the throne of my lord King David."

38So Zadok the priest, Nathan the prophet, Benaiah the son of Jehoiada, the Cherethites, and the Pelethites went down and had Solomon ride on King David's mule, and took him to Gihon. 39Then Zadok the priest took a horn of oil from the tabernacle and anointed Solomon. And they blew the horn, and all the people said, *"Long* live King Solomon!" 40And all the people went up after him; and the people played the flutes and rejoiced with great joy, so that the earth *seemed to* split with their sound.

41Now Adonijah and all the guests who *were* with him heard *it* as they finished eating. And when Joab heard the sound of the horn, he said, "Why *is* the city in such a noisy uproar?" 42While he was still speaking, there came Jonathan, the son of Abiathar the priest. And Adonijah said to him, "Come in, for you *are* a prominent man, and bring good news."

43Then Jonathan answered and said to Adonijah, "No! Our lord King David has made Solomon king. 44The king has sent with him Zadok the priest, Nathan the prophet, Benaiah the son of Jehoiada, the Cherethites, and the Pelethites; and they have made him ride on the king's mule. 45So Zadok the priest and Nathan the prophet have anointed him king at Gihon; and they have gone up from there rejoicing, so that the city is in an uproar. This *is* the noise that you have heard. 46Also Solomon sits on the throne of the kingdom. 47And moreover the king's servants have gone to bless our lord King David, saying, 'May God make the name of Solomon better than your name, and may He make his throne greater than your throne.' Then the king bowed himself on the bed. 48Also the king said thus, 'Blessed *be* the LORD God of Israel, who has given *one* to sit on my throne this day, while my eyes see *it!*' "

49So all the guests who were with Adonijah were afraid, and arose, and each one went his way.

50Now Adonijah was afraid of Solomon; so he arose, and went and took hold of the horns of the altar. 51And it was told Solomon, saying, "Indeed Adonijah is afraid of King Solomon; for look, he has taken hold of the horns of the altar, saying, 'Let King Solomon swear to me today that he will not put his servant to death with the sword.' "

52Then Solomon said, "If he proves himself a worthy man, not one hair of him shall fall to the earth; but if wickedness is found in him, he shall die." 53So King Solomon sent them to bring him down from the altar. And he came and fell down before King Solomon; and Solomon said to him, "Go to your house."

DAVID'S INSTRUCTIONS TO SOLOMON

2 Now the days of David drew near that he should die, and he charged Solomon his son, saying: 2"I go the way of all the earth; be strong, therefore, and prove yourself a man. 3And keep the charge of the LORD your God: to walk in His ways, to keep His statutes, His commandments, His judgments, and His testimonies, as it is written in the Law of Moses, that you may prosper in all that you do and wherever you turn; 4that the LORD may fulfill His word which He spoke concerning me, saying, 'If your sons take heed to their way, to walk before Me in truth with all their heart and with all their soul,' He said, 'you shall not lack a man on the throne of Israel.'

5"Moreover you know also what Joab the son of Zeruiah did to me, *and* what he did to the two commanders of the armies of Israel, to Abner the son of Ner and Amasa the son of Jether, whom he killed. And he shed the blood of war in peacetime, and put the blood of war on his belt that *was* around his waist, and on his sandals that *were* on his feet. [6]Therefore do according to your wisdom, and do not let his gray hair go down to the grave in peace.

[7]"But show kindness to the sons of Barzillai the Gileadite, and let them be among those who eat at your table, for so they came to me when I fled from Absalom your brother.

[8]"And see, *you have* with you Shimei the son of Gera, a Benjamite from Bahurim, who cursed me with a malicious curse in the day when I went to Mahanaim. But he came down to meet me at the Jordan, and I swore to him by the LORD, saying, 'I will not put you to death with the sword.' [9]Now therefore, do not hold him guiltless, for you *are* a wise man and know what you ought to do to him; but bring his gray hair down to the grave with blood."

DEATH OF DAVID

[10]So David rested with his fathers, and was buried in the City of David. [11]The period that David reigned over Israel *was* forty years; seven years he reigned in Hebron, and in Jerusalem he reigned thirty-three years. [12]Then Solomon sat on the throne of his father David; and his kingdom was firmly established.

SOLOMON EXECUTES ADONIJAH

[13]Now Adonijah the son of Haggith came to Bathsheba the mother of Solomon. So she said, "Do you come peaceably?"

And he said, "Peaceably." [14]Moreover he said, "I have something *to say* to you."

And she said, "Say it."

[15]Then he said, "You know that the kingdom was mine, and all Israel had set their expectations on me, that I should reign. However, the kingdom has been turned over, and has become my brother's; for it was his from the LORD. [16]Now I ask one petition of you; do not deny me."

And she said to him, "Say it."

[17]Then he said, "Please speak to King Solomon, for he will not refuse you, that he may give me Abishag the Shunammite as wife."

[18]So Bathsheba said, "Very well, I will speak for you to the king."

[19]Bathsheba therefore went to King Solomon, to speak to him for Adonijah. And the king rose up to meet her and bowed down to her, and sat down on his throne and had a throne set for the king's mother; so she sat at his right hand. [20]Then she said, "I desire one small petition of you; do not refuse me."

And the king said to her, "Ask it, my mother, for I will not refuse you."

[21]So she said, "Let Abishag the Shunammite be given to Adonijah your brother as wife."

[22]And King Solomon answered and said to his mother, "Now why do you ask Abishag the Shunammite for Adonijah? Ask for him the kingdom also—for he *is* my older brother—for him, and for Abiathar the priest, and for Joab the son of Zeruiah." [23]Then King Solomon swore by the LORD, saying, "May God do so to me, and more also, if Adonijah has not spoken this word against his own life! [24]Now therefore, *as* the LORD lives, who has confirmed me and set me on the throne of David my father, and who has established a house[a] for me, as He promised, Adonijah shall be put to death today!"

[25]So King Solomon sent by the hand of Benaiah the son of Jehoiada; and he struck him down, and he died.

ABIATHAR EXILED, JOAB EXECUTED

[26]And to Abiathar the priest the king said, "Go to Anathoth, to your own fields, for you *are* deserving of death; but I will not put you to death at this time, because you carried the ark of the Lord GOD before my father David, and because you were afflicted every time my father was afflicted." [27]So Solomon removed Abiathar from being priest to the LORD, that he might fulfill the word of the LORD which He spoke concerning the house of Eli at Shiloh.

[28]Then news came to Joab, for Joab had defected to Adonijah, though he had not defected to Absalom. So Joab fled to the tabernacle of the LORD, and took hold of the horns of the altar. [29]And King Solomon was told, "Joab has fled to the tabernacle of the LORD; there *he is,* by the

2:24 [a]That is, a royal dynasty

altar." Then Solomon sent Benaiah the son of Je-hoiada, saying, "Go, strike him down." ³⁰So Bena-iah went to the tabernacle of the LORD, and said to him, "Thus says the king, 'Come out!' "

And he said, "No, but I will die here." And Benaiah brought back word to the king, saying, "Thus said Joab, and thus he answered me."

³¹Then the king said to him, "Do as he has said, and strike him down and bury him, that you may take away from me and from the house of my father the innocent blood which Joab shed. ³²So the LORD will return his blood on his head, because he struck down two men more righteous and better than he, and killed them with the sword—Abner the son of Ner, the commander of the army of Israel, and Amasa the son of Jether, the commander of the army of Judah—though my father David did not know *it*. ³³Their blood shall therefore return upon the head of Joab and upon the head of his descendants forever. But upon David and his descendants, upon his house and his throne, there shall be peace forever from the LORD."

³⁴So Benaiah the son of Jehoiada went up and struck and killed him; and he was buried in his own house in the wilderness. ³⁵The king put Be-naiah the son of Jehoiada in his place over the army, and the king put Zadok the priest in the place of Abiathar.

SHIMEI EXECUTED

³⁶Then the king sent and called for Shimei, and said to him, "Build yourself a house in Jerusalem and dwell there, and do not go out from there anywhere. ³⁷For it shall be, on the day you go out and cross the Brook Kidron, know for certain you shall surely die; your blood shall be on your own head."

³⁸And Shimei said to the king, "The saying *is* good. As my lord the king has said, so your ser-vant will do." So Shimei dwelt in Jerusalem many days.

³⁹Now it happened at the end of three years, that two slaves of Shimei ran away to Achish the son of Maachah, king of Gath. And they told Shimei, saying, "Look, your slaves *are* in Gath!" ⁴⁰So Shimei arose, saddled his donkey, and went to Achish at Gath to seek his slaves. And Shimei went and brought his slaves from Gath. ⁴¹And

Solomon was told that Shimei had gone from Jerusalem to Gath and had come back. ⁴²Then the king sent and called for Shimei, and said to him, "Did I not make you swear by the LORD, and warn you, saying, 'Know for certain that on the day you go out and travel anywhere, you shall surely die'? And you said to me, 'The word I have heard *is* good.' ⁴³Why then have you not kept the oath of the LORD and the commandment that I gave you?" ⁴⁴The king said moreover to Shimei, "You know, as your heart acknowledges, all the wickedness that you did to my father David; therefore the LORD will return your wickedness on your own head. ⁴⁵But King Solomon *shall be* blessed, and the throne of David shall be estab-lished before the LORD forever."

⁴⁶So the king commanded Benaiah the son of Jehoiada; and he went out and struck him down, and he died. Thus the kingdom was established in the hand of Solomon.

SOLOMON REQUESTS WISDOM

3 Now Solomon made a treaty with Pharaoh king of Egypt, and married Pharaoh's daughter; then he brought her to the City of David until he had finished building his own house, and the house of the LORD, and the wall all around Jeru-salem. ²Meanwhile the people sacrificed at the high places, because there was no house built for the name of the LORD until those days. ³And Solomon loved the LORD, walking in the statutes of his father David, except that he sacrificed and burned incense at the high places.

⁴Now the king went to Gibeon to sacrifice there, for that *was* the great high place: Solomon offered a thousand burnt offerings on that altar. ⁵At Gibeon the LORD appeared to Solomon in a dream by night; and God said, "Ask! What shall I give you?"

⁶And Solomon said: "You have shown great mercy to Your servant David my father, because he walked before You in truth, in righteousness, and in uprightness of heart with You; You have continued this great kindness for him, and You have given him a son to sit on his throne, as *it is* this day. ⁷Now, O LORD my God, You have made Your servant king instead of my father David, but I *am* a little child; I do not know *how* to go out or come in. ⁸And Your servant *is* in the midst of Your

the INFLUENCERS

SOLOMON: How Much Wisdom Does It Take?

1 KINGS 3:1–28

Solomon, whose name means "peaceful," was a ruler because he chose to serve the one true King (v. 7, 8). Because of his servant's heart and love of peace, David's son was chosen to build God's first earthly temple.

While in Gibeon—sacrificing to the Lord—the Lord appeared to him in a dream. God allowed Solomon to ask for anything. Solomon asked for wisdom—"an understanding heart . . . that I may discern between good and evil" (v. 9). Leading God's people was beyond his human efforts. God granted his request because it "pleased the LORD" (v. 10), so much so, He gave Solomon everything he _didn't_ ask for, as well. When Solomon woke up, the dream became a reality: he became the wisest, wealthiest, most powerful ruler on earth.

Israel experienced its greatest heights during Solomon's reign. His wisdom extended to every area of life except one: his father's sin of adultery became his own. He married over 700 women, and had 300 concubines. One weakness lead Solomon's heart astray, to the point where he no longer walked completely with God (1 Kin. 11:6). His great wisdom extended throughout the known world yet failed to keep his heart where it belonged.

Jesus said, "But seek first the kingdom of God and His righteousness, and all these things shall be added to you" (Matt. 6:33). If you are seeking God's will, you too, can ask for wisdom. Then all the other things you need will be added to you.

---

people whom You have chosen, a great people, too numerous to be numbered or counted. ⁹Therefore give to Your servant an understanding heart to judge Your people, that I may discern between good and evil. For who is able to judge this great people of Yours?"

¹⁰The speech pleased the Lord, that Solomon had asked this thing. ¹¹Then God said to him: "Because you have asked this thing, and have not asked long life for yourself, nor have asked riches for yourself, nor have asked the life of your enemies, but have asked for yourself understanding to discern justice, ¹²behold, I have done according to your words; see, I have given you a wise and understanding heart, so that there has not been anyone like you before you, nor shall any like you arise after you. ¹³And I have also given you what you have not asked: both riches and honor, so that there shall not be anyone like you among the kings all your days. ¹⁴So if you walk in My ways, to keep My statutes and My

commandments, as your father David walked, then I will lengthen your days."

¹⁵Then Solomon awoke; and indeed it had been a dream. And he came to Jerusalem and stood before the ark of the covenant of the LORD, offered up burnt offerings, offered peace offerings, and made a feast for all his servants.

SOLOMON'S WISE JUDGMENT

¹⁶Now two women _who were_ harlots came to the king, and stood before him. ¹⁷And one woman said, "O my lord, this woman and I dwell in the same house; and I gave birth while she _was_ in the house. ¹⁸Then it happened, the third day after I had given birth, that this woman also gave birth. And we _were_ together; no one _was_ with us in the house, except the two of us in the house. ¹⁹And this woman's son died in the night, because she lay on him. ²⁰So she arose in the middle of the night and took my son from my side, while your maidservant slept, and laid him in her

bosom, and laid her dead child in my bosom. 21And when I rose in the morning to nurse my son, there he was, dead. But when I had examined him in the morning, indeed, he was not my son whom I had borne."

22Then the other woman said, "No! But the living one *is* my son, and the dead one *is* your son." And the first woman said, "No! But the dead one *is* your son, and the living one *is* my son."

Thus they spoke before the king.

23And the king said, "The one says, 'This *is* my son, who lives, and your son *is* the dead one'; and the other says, 'No! But your son *is* the dead one, and my son *is* the living one.' " 24Then the king said, "Bring me a sword." So they brought a sword before the king. 25And the king said, "Divide the living child in two, and give half to one, and half to the other."

26Then the woman whose son *was* living spoke to the king, for she yearned with compassion for her son; and she said, "O my lord, give her the living child, and by no means kill him!" But the other said, "Let him be neither mine nor yours, *but* divide *him*."

27So the king answered and said, "Give the first woman the living child, and by no means kill him; she *is* his mother."

28And all Israel heard of the judgment which the king had rendered; and they feared the king, for they saw that the wisdom of God *was* in him to administer justice.

Solomon's Administration

4 So King Solomon was king over all Israel. 2And these *were* his officials: Azariah the son of Zadok, the priest; 3Elihoreph and Ahijah, the sons of Shisha, scribes; Jehoshaphat the son of Ahilud, the recorder; 4Benaiah the son of Jehoiada, over the army; Zadok and Abiathar, the priests; 5Azariah the son of Nathan, over the officers; Zabud the son of Nathan, a priest *and* the king's friend; 6Ahishar, over the household; and Adoniram the son of Abda, over the labor force.

7And Solomon had twelve governors over all Israel, who provided food for the king and his household; each one made provision for one month of the year. 8These *are* their names: Ben-Hur,a in the mountains of Ephraim; 9Ben-Deker,a in Makaz, Shaalbim, Beth Shemesh, and Elon

Beth Hanan; 10Ben-Hesed,a in Arubboth; to him *belonged* Sochoh and all the land of Hepher; 11Ben-Abinadab,a *in* all the regions of Dor; he had Taphath the daughter of Solomon as wife; 12Baana the son of Ahilud, *in* Taanach, Megiddo, and all Beth Shean, which *is* beside Zaretan below Jezreel, from Beth Shean to Abel Meholah, as far as the other side of Jokneam; 13Ben-Geber,a in Ramoth Gilead; to him *belonged* the towns of Jair the son of Manasseh, in Gilead; to him *also belonged* the region of Argob in Bashan—sixty large cities with walls and bronze gate-bars; 14Ahinadab the son of Iddo, *in* Mahanaim; 15Ahimaaz, in Naphtali; he also took Basemath the daughter of Solomon as wife; 16Baanah the son of Hushai, in Asher and Aloth; 17Jehoshaphat the son of Paruah, in Issachar; 18Shimei the son of Elah, in Benjamin; 19Geber the son of Uri, in the land of Gilead, *in* the country of Sihon king of the Amorites, and of Og king of Bashan. *He was* the only governor who *was* in the land.

Prosperity and Wisdom of Solomon's Reign

20Judah and Israel *were* as numerous as the sand by the sea in multitude, eating and drinking and rejoicing. 21So Solomon reigned over all kingdoms from the Rivera *to* the land of the Philistines, as far as the border of Egypt. *They* brought tribute and served Solomon all the days of his life.

22Now Solomon's provision for one day was thirty kors of fine flour, sixty kors of meal, 23ten fatted oxen, twenty oxen from the pastures, and one hundred sheep, besides deer, gazelles, roebucks, and fatted fowl.

24For he had dominion over all *the region* on this side of the Rivera from Tiphsah even to Gaza, namely over all the kings on this side of the River; and he had peace on every side all around him. 25And Judah and Israel dwelt safely, each man under his vine and his fig tree, from Dan as far as Beersheba, all the days of Solomon.

26Solomon had fortya thousand stalls of horses for his chariots, and twelve thousand horsemen.

4:8 aLiterally *Son of Hur*   4:9 aLiterally *Son of Deker*   4:10 aLiterally *Son of Hesed*   4:11 aLiterally *Son of Abinadab*   4:13 aLiterally *Son of Geber*   4:21 aThat is, the Euphrates   4:24 aThat is, the Euphrates   4:26 aFollowing Masoretic Text and most other authorities; some manuscripts of the Septuagint read *four* (compare 2 Chronicles 9:25).

²⁷And these governors, each man in his month, provided food for King Solomon and for all who came to King Solomon's table. There was no lack in their supply. ²⁸They also brought barley and straw to the proper place, for the horses and steeds, each man according to his charge.

²⁹And God gave Solomon wisdom and exceedingly great understanding, and largeness of heart like the sand on the seashore. ³⁰Thus Solomon's wisdom excelled the wisdom of all the men of the East and all the wisdom of Egypt. ³¹For he was wiser than all men—than Ethan the Ezrahite, and Heman, Chalcol, and Darda, the sons of Mahol; and his fame was in all the surrounding nations. ³²He spoke three thousand proverbs, and his songs were one thousand five. ³³Also he spoke of trees, from the cedar tree of Lebanon even to the hyssop that springs out of the wall; he spoke also of animals, of birds, of creeping things, and of fish. ³⁴And men of all nations, from all the kings of the earth who had heard of his wisdom, came to hear the wisdom of Solomon.

SOLOMON PREPARES TO BUILD THE TEMPLE

5 Now Hiram king of Tyre sent his servants to Solomon, because he heard that they had anointed him king in place of his father, for Hiram had always loved David. ²Then Solomon sent to Hiram, saying:

³You know how my father David could not build a house for the name of the LORD his God because of the wars which were fought against him on every side, until the LORD put *his foes*ᵃ under the soles of his feet.
⁴But now the LORD my God has given me rest on every side; *there is* neither adversary nor evil occurrence.
⁵And behold, I propose to build a house for the name of the LORD my God, as the LORD spoke to my father David, saying, "Your son, whom I will set on your throne in your place, he shall build the house for My name."
⁶Now therefore, command that they cut down cedars for me from Lebanon; and my servants will be with your servants, and I will pay you wages for your servants according to whatever you say. For you know *there is* none

among us who has skill to cut timber like the Sidonians.

⁷So it was, when Hiram heard the words of Solomon, that he rejoiced greatly and said,

Blessed *be* the LORD this day, for He has given David a wise son over this great people!

⁸Then Hiram sent to Solomon, saying:

I have considered *the message* which you sent me, *and* I will do all you desire concerning the cedar and cypress logs.
⁹My servants shall bring *them* down from Lebanon to the sea; I will float them in rafts by sea to the place you indicate to me, and will have them broken apart there; then you can take *them* away. And you shall fulfill my desire by giving food for my household.

¹⁰Then Hiram gave Solomon cedar and cypress logs *according to* all his desire. ¹¹And Solomon gave Hiram twenty thousand kors of wheat *as* food for his household, and twentyᵃ kors of pressed oil. Thus Solomon gave to Hiram year by year.

¹²So the LORD gave Solomon wisdom, as He had promised him; and there was peace between Hiram and Solomon, and the two of them made a treaty together.

¹³Then King Solomon raised up a labor force out of all Israel; and the labor force was thirty thousand men. ¹⁴And he sent them to Lebanon, ten thousand a month in shifts: they were one month in Lebanon *and* two months at home; Adoniram *was* in charge of the labor force. ¹⁵Solomon had seventy thousand who carried burdens, and eighty thousand who quarried *stone* in the mountains, ¹⁶besides three thousand three hundredᵃ from the chiefs of Solomon's deputies, who supervised the people who labored in the work. ¹⁷And the king commanded them to quarry large stones, costly stones, *and* hewn stones, to lay the foundation of the temple.ᵃ ¹⁸So

5:3 ᵃLiterally *them*   **5:11** ᵃFollowing Masoretic Text, Targum, and Vulgate; Septuagint and Syriac read *twenty thousand.*   **5:16** ᵃFollowing Masoretic Text, Targum, and Vulgate; Septuagint reads *three thousand six hundred.*   **5:17** ᵃLiterally *house*, and so frequently throughout this book

Solomon's builders, Hiram's builders, and the Gebalites quarried *them;* and they prepared timber and stones to build the temple.

SOLOMON BUILDS THE TEMPLE

6 And it came to pass in the four hundred and eightieth[a] year after the children of Israel had come out of the land of Egypt, in the fourth year of Solomon's reign over Israel, in the month of Ziv, which *is* the second month, that he began to build the house of the LORD. ²Now the house which King Solomon built for the LORD, its length *was* sixty cubits, its width twenty, and its height thirty cubits. ³The vestibule in front of the sanctuary[a] of the house *was* twenty cubits long across the width of the house, *and* the width of *the vestibule*[b] *extended* ten cubits from the front of the house. ⁴And he made for the house windows with beveled frames.

⁵Against the wall of the temple he built chambers all around, *against* the walls of the temple, all around the sanctuary and the inner sanctuary.[a] Thus he made side chambers all around it. ⁶The lowest chamber *was* five cubits wide, the middle *was* six cubits wide, and the third *was* seven cubits wide; for he made narrow ledges around the outside of the temple, so that *the support beams* would not be fastened into the walls of the temple. ⁷And the temple, when it was being built, was built with stone finished at the quarry, so that no hammer or chisel *or* any iron tool was heard in the temple while it was being built. ⁸The doorway for the middle story[a] *was* on the right side of the temple. They went up by stairs to the middle *story,* and from the middle to the third.

⁹So he built the temple and finished it, and he paneled the temple with beams and boards of cedar. ¹⁰And he built side chambers against the entire temple, each five cubits high; they were attached to the temple with cedar beams.

¹¹Then the word of the LORD came to Solomon, saying: ¹²"Concerning this temple which you are building, if you walk in My statutes, execute My judgments, keep all My commandments, and walk in them, then I will perform My word with you, which I spoke to your father David. ¹³And I will dwell among the children of Israel, and will not forsake My people Israel."

¹⁴So Solomon built the temple and finished it. ¹⁵And he built the inside walls of the temple with cedar boards; from the floor of the temple to the ceiling he paneled the inside with wood; and he covered the floor of the temple with planks of cypress. ¹⁶Then he built the twenty-cubit room at the rear of the temple, from floor to ceiling, with cedar boards; he built *it* inside as the inner sanctuary, as the Most Holy *Place.* ¹⁷And in front of it the temple sanctuary was forty cubits *long.* ¹⁸The inside of the temple was cedar, carved with ornamental buds and open flowers. All *was* cedar; there was no stone *to be* seen.

¹⁹And he prepared the inner sanctuary inside the temple, to set the ark of the covenant of the LORD there. ²⁰The inner sanctuary *was* twenty cubits long, twenty cubits wide, and twenty cubits high. He overlaid it with pure gold, and overlaid the altar of cedar. ²¹So Solomon overlaid the inside of the temple with pure gold. He stretched gold chains across the front of the inner sanctuary, and overlaid it with gold. ²²The whole temple he overlaid with gold, until he had finished all the temple; also he overlaid with gold the entire altar that *was* by the inner sanctuary.

²³Inside the inner sanctuary he made two cherubim *of* olive wood, *each* ten cubits high. ²⁴One wing of the cherub *was* five cubits, and the other wing of the cherub five cubits: ten cubits from the tip of one wing to the tip of the other. ²⁵And the other cherub *was* ten cubits; both cherubim *were* of the same size and shape. ²⁶The height of one cherub *was* ten cubits, and so *was* the other cherub. ²⁷Then he set the cherubim inside the inner room;[a] and they stretched out the wings of the cherubim so that the wing of the one touched *one* wall, and the wing of the other cherub touched the other wall. And their wings touched each other in the middle of the room. ²⁸Also he overlaid the cherubim with gold.

²⁹Then he carved all the walls of the temple all around, both the inner and outer *sanctuaries,* with carved figures of cherubim, palm trees, and open flowers. ³⁰And the floor of the temple he

6:1 aFollowing Masoretic Text, Targum, and Vulgate; Septuagint reads *fortieth.* 6:3 aHebrew *heykal;* here the main room of the temple, elsewhere called the holy place (compare Exodus 26:33 and Ezekiel 41:1) bLiterally *it* 6:5 aHebrew *debir;* here the inner room of the temple, elsewhere called the Most Holy Place (compare verse 16). 6:8 aFollowing Masoretic Text and Vulgate; Septuagint reads *upper story;* Targum reads *ground story.* 6:27 aLiterally *house* overlaid with gold, both the inner and outer *sanctuaries.*

31For the entrance of the inner sanctuary he made doors *of* olive wood; the lintel *and* doorposts *were* one-fifth *of the wall.* 32The two doors *were of* olive wood; and he carved on them figures of cherubim, palm trees, and open flowers, and overlaid *them* with gold; and he spread gold on the cherubim and on the palm trees. 33So for the door of the sanctuary he also made doorposts *of* olive wood, one-fourth *of the wall.* 34And the two doors *were of* cypress wood; two panels *comprised* one folding door, and two panels *comprised* the other folding door. 35Then he carved cherubim, palm trees, and open flowers *on them,* and overlaid *them* with gold applied evenly on the carved work.

36And he built the inner court with three rows of hewn stone and a row of cedar beams.

37In the fourth year the foundation of the house of the LORD was laid, in the month of Ziv. 38And in the eleventh year, in the month of Bul, which is the eighth month, the house was finished in all its details and according to all its plans. So he was seven years in building it.

Solomon's Other Buildings

7But Solomon took thirteen years to build his own house; so he finished all his house.

2He also built the House of the Forest of Lebanon; its length *was* one hundred cubits, its width fifty cubits, and its height thirty cubits, with four rows of cedar pillars, and cedar beams on the pillars. 3And *it was* paneled with cedar above the beams that *were* on forty-five pillars, fifteen *to* a row. 4*There were* windows *with beveled frames in* three rows, and window *was* opposite window *in* three tiers. 5And all the doorways and doorposts *had* rectangular frames; and window *was* opposite window *in* three tiers.

6He also made the Hall of Pillars: its length *was* fifty cubits, and its width thirty cubits; and in front of them *was* a portico with pillars, and a canopy *was* in front of them.

7Then he made a hall for the throne, the Hall of Judgment, where he might judge; and *it was* paneled with cedar from floor to ceiling.a

8And the house where he dwelt *had* another court inside the hall, of like workmanship.

Solomon also made a house like this hall for Pharaoh's daughter, whom he had taken *as wife.*

9All these *were of* costly stones cut to size, trimmed with saws, inside and out, from the foundation to the eaves, and also on the outside to the great court. 10The foundation *was of* costly stones, large stones, some ten cubits and some eight cubits. 11And above *were* costly stones, hewn to size, and cedar wood. 12The great court *was* enclosed with three rows of hewn stones and a row of cedar beams. So were the inner court of the house of the LORD and the vestibule of the temple.

Hiram the Craftsman

13Now King Solomon sent and brought Hurama from Tyre. 14He *was* the son of a widow from the tribe of Naphtali, and his father *was* a man of Tyre, a bronze worker; he was filled with wisdom and understanding and skill in working with all kinds of bronze work. So he came to King Solomon and did all his work.

The Bronze Pillars for the Temple

15And he cast two pillars of bronze, each one eighteen cubits high, and a line of twelve cubits measured the circumference of each. 16Then he made two capitals *of* cast bronze, to set on the tops of the pillars. The height of one capital *was* five cubits, and the height of the other capital *was* five cubits. 17*He made* a lattice network, with wreaths of chainwork, for the capitals which *were* on top of the pillars: seven chains for one capital and seven for the other capital. 18So he made the pillars, and two rows of pomegranates above the network all around to cover the capitals that *were* on top; and thus he did for the other capital.

19The capitals which *were* on top of the pillars in the hall *were* in the shape of lilies, four cubits. 20The capitals on the two pillars also *had pomegranates* above, by the convex surface which *was* next to the network; and there *were* two hundred such pomegranates in rows on each of the capitals all around.

21Then he set up the pillars by the vestibule of the temple; he set up the pillar on the right and called its name Jachin, and he set up the pillar on the left and called its name Boaz. 22The tops of

7:7 aLiterally *floor,* that is, of the upper level   7:13 aHebrew *Hiram* (compare 2 Chronicles 2:13, 14)

the pillars were in the shape of lilies. So the work of the pillars was finished.

The Sea and the Oxen

²³And he made the Sea of cast bronze, ten cubits from one brim to the other; *it was* completely round. Its height *was* five cubits, and a line of thirty cubits measured its circumference. ²⁴Below its brim *were* ornamental buds encircling it all around, ten to a cubit, all the way around the Sea. The ornamental buds *were* cast in two rows when it was cast. ²⁵It stood on twelve oxen: three looking toward the north, three looking toward the west, three looking toward the south, and three looking toward the east; the Sea *was set* upon them, and all their back parts *pointed* inward. ²⁶It *was* a handbreadth thick; and its brim was shaped like the brim of a cup, *like* a lily blossom. It contained two thousandᵃ baths.

The Carts and the Lavers

²⁷He also made ten carts of bronze; four cubits *was* the length of each cart, four cubits its width, and three cubits its height. ²⁸And this *was* the design of the carts: They had panels, and the panels *were* between frames; ²⁹on the panels that *were* between the frames *were* lions, oxen, and cherubim. And on the frames *was* a pedestal on top. Below the lions and oxen *were* wreaths of plaited work. ³⁰Every cart had four bronze wheels and axles of bronze, and its four feet had supports. Under the laver *were* supports of cast *bronze* beside each wreath. ³¹Its opening inside the crown at the top *was* one cubit in diameter; and the opening *was* round, shaped *like* a pedestal, one and a half cubits in outside diameter; and also on the opening *were* engravings, but the panels were square, not round. ³²Under the panels *were* the four wheels, and the axles of the wheels *were joined* to the cart. The height of a wheel *was* one and a half cubits. ³³The workmanship of the wheels *was* like the workmanship of a chariot wheel; their axle pins, their rims, their spokes, and their hubs *were* all of cast *bronze*. ³⁴And *there were* four supports at the four corners of each cart; its supports *were* part of the cart itself. ³⁵On the top of the cart, at the height of half a cubit, *it was* perfectly round. And on the top of the cart, its flanges and its panels *were* of the same casting. ³⁶On the plates of its flanges and on its panels he engraved cherubim, lions, and palm trees, wherever there was a clear space on each, with wreaths all around. ³⁷Thus he made the ten carts. All of them were of the same mold, one measure, *and* one shape.

³⁸Then he made ten lavers of bronze; each laver contained forty baths, *and* each laver *was* four cubits. On each of the ten carts *was* a laver. ³⁹And he put five carts on the right side of the house, and five on the left side of the house. He set the Sea on the right side of the house, toward the southeast.

Furnishings of the Temple

⁴⁰Huramᵃ made the lavers and the shovels and the bowls. So Huram finished doing all the work that he was to do for King Solomon *for* the house of the LORD: ⁴¹the two pillars, the *two* bowl-shaped capitals that *were* on top of the two pillars; the two networks covering the two bowl-shaped capitals which *were* on top of the pillars; ⁴²four hundred pomegranates for the two networks (two rows of pomegranates for each network, to cover the two bowl-shaped capitals that *were* on top of the pillars); ⁴³the ten carts, and ten lavers on the carts; ⁴⁴one Sea, and twelve oxen under the Sea; ⁴⁵the pots, the shovels, and the bowls.

All these articles which Huramᵃ made for King Solomon *for* the house of the LORD *were of* burnished bronze. ⁴⁶In the plain of Jordan the king had them cast in clay molds, between Succoth and Zaretan. ⁴⁷And Solomon did not weigh all the articles, because *there were* so many; the weight of the bronze was not determined.

⁴⁸Thus Solomon had all the furnishings made for the house of the LORD: the altar of gold, and the table of gold on which *was* the showbread; ⁴⁹the lampstands of pure gold, five on the right *side* and five on the left in front of the inner sanctuary, with the flowers and the lamps and the wick-trimmers of gold; ⁵⁰the basins, the trimmers, the bowls, the ladles, and the censers of pure gold; and the hinges of gold, *both* for the doors of the inner room (the Most Holy *Place*) *and* for the doors of the main hall of the temple.

⁵¹So all the work that King Solomon had

7:26 ᵃOr *three thousand* (compare 2 Chronicles 4:5)   7:40 ᵃHebrew *Hiram* (compare 2 Chronicles 2:13, 14)   7:45 ᵃHebrew *Hiram* (compare 2 Chronicles 2:13, 14) done for the house of the LORD was finished; and Solomon brought in the things which his father David had dedicated: the silver and the gold and the furnishings. He put them in the treasuries of the house of the LORD.

The Ark Brought into the Temple

8 Now Solomon assembled the elders of Israel and all the heads of the tribes, the chief fathers of the children of Israel, to King Solomon in Jerusalem, that they might bring up the ark of the covenant of the LORD from the City of David, which *is* Zion. ²Therefore all the men of Israel assembled with King Solomon at the feast in the month of Ethanim, which *is* the seventh month. ³So all the elders of Israel came, and the priests took up the ark. ⁴Then they brought up the ark of the LORD, the tabernacle of meeting, and all the holy furnishings that *were* in the tabernacle. The priests and the Levites brought them up. ⁵Also King Solomon, and all the congregation of Israel who were assembled with him, *were* with him before the ark, sacrificing sheep and oxen that could not be counted or numbered for multitude. ⁶Then the priests brought in the ark of the covenant of the LORD to its place, into the inner sanctuary of the temple, to the Most Holy *Place,* under the wings of the cherubim. ⁷For the cherubim spread *their* two wings over the place of the ark, and the cherubim overshadowed the ark and its poles. ⁸The poles extended so that the ends of the poles could be seen from the holy *place,* in front of the inner sanctuary; but they could not be seen from outside. And they are there to this day. ⁹Nothing *was* in the ark except the two tablets of stone which Moses put there at Horeb, when the LORD made *a covenant* with the children of Israel, when they came out of the land of Egypt.

¹⁰And it came to pass, when the priests came out of the holy *place,* that the cloud filled the house of the LORD, ¹¹so that the priests could not continue ministering because of the cloud; for the glory of the LORD filled the house of the LORD.

¹²Then Solomon spoke:

"The LORD said He would dwell in the dark cloud.
¹³I have surely built You an exalted house,
And a place for You to dwell in forever."

Solomon's Speech at Completion of the Work

¹⁴Then the king turned around and blessed the whole assembly of Israel, while all the assembly of Israel was standing. ¹⁵And he said: "Blessed *be* the LORD God of Israel, who spoke with His mouth to my father David, and with His hand has fulfilled *it,* saying, ¹⁶'Since the day that I brought My people Israel out of Egypt, I have chosen no city from any tribe of Israel *in which* to build a house, that My name might be there; but I chose David to be over My people Israel.' ¹⁷Now it was in the heart of my father David to build a temple[a] for the name of the LORD God of Israel. ¹⁸But the LORD said to my father David, 'Whereas it was in your heart to build a temple for My name, you did well that it was in your heart. ¹⁹Nevertheless you shall not build the temple, but your son who will come from your body, he shall build the temple for My name.' ²⁰So the LORD has fulfilled His word which He spoke; and I have filled the position of my father David, and sit on the throne of Israel, as the LORD promised; and I have built a temple for the name of the LORD God of Israel. ²¹And there I have made a place for the ark, in which *is* the covenant of the LORD which He made with our fathers, when He brought them out of the land of Egypt."

Solomon's Prayer of Dedication

²²Then Solomon stood before the altar of the LORD in the presence of all the assembly of Israel, and spread out his hands toward heaven; ²³and he said: "LORD God of Israel, *there is* no God in heaven above or on earth below like You, who keep *Your* covenant and mercy with Your servants who walk before You with all their hearts. ²⁴You have kept what You promised Your servant David my father; You have both spoken with Your mouth and fulfilled *it* with Your hand, as *it is* this day. ²⁵Therefore, LORD God of Israel, now keep what You promised Your servant David my father, saying, 'You shall not fail to have a man sit before Me on the throne of Israel, only if your sons take heed to their way, that they walk before Me as you have walked before Me.' ²⁶And now I pray, O God of Israel, let Your word come true, which You have spoken to Your servant David my father.

8:17 ªLiterally *house,* and so in verses 18–20

27"But will God indeed dwell on the earth? Behold, heaven and the heaven of heavens cannot contain You. How much less this temple which I have built! 28Yet regard the prayer of Your servant and his supplication, O LORD my God, and listen to the cry and the prayer which Your servant is praying before You today: 29that Your eyes may be open toward this temple night and day, toward the place of which You said, 'My name shall be there,' that You may hear the prayer which Your servant makes toward this place. 30And may You hear the supplication of Your servant and of Your people Israel, when they pray toward this place. Hear in heaven Your dwelling place; and when You hear, forgive.

31"When anyone sins against his neighbor, and is forced to take an oath, and comes and takes an oath before Your altar in this temple, 32then hear in heaven, and act, and judge Your servants, condemning the wicked, bringing his way on his head, and justifying the righteous by giving him according to his righteousness.

33"When Your people Israel are defeated before an enemy because they have sinned against You, and when they turn back to You and confess Your name, and pray and make supplication to You in this temple, 34then hear in heaven, and forgive the sin of Your people Israel, and bring them back to the land which You gave to their fathers.

35"When the heavens are shut up and there is no rain because they have sinned against You, when they pray toward this place and confess Your name, and turn from their sin because You afflict them, 36then hear in heaven, and forgive the sin of Your servants, Your people Israel, that You may teach them the good way in which they should walk; and send rain on Your land which You have given to Your people as an inheritance.

37"When there is famine in the land, pestilence or blight or mildew, locusts or grasshoppers; when their enemy besieges them in the land of their cities; whatever plague or whatever sickness there is; 38whatever prayer, whatever supplication is made by anyone, or by all Your people Israel, when each one knows the plague of his own heart, and spreads out his hands toward this temple: 39then hear in heaven Your dwelling place, and forgive, and act, and give to everyone according to all his ways, whose heart You know (for You alone know the hearts of all the sons of men), 40that they may fear You all the days that they live in the land which You gave to our fathers.

41"Moreover, concerning a foreigner, who is not of Your people Israel, but has come from a far country for Your name's sake 42(for they will hear of Your great name and Your strong hand and Your outstretched arm), when he comes and prays toward this temple, 43hear in heaven Your dwelling place, and do according to all for which the foreigner calls to You, that all peoples of the earth may know Your name and fear You, as do Your people Israel, and that they may know that this temple which I have built is called by Your name.

44"When Your people go out to battle against their enemy, wherever You send them, and when they pray to the LORD toward the city which You have chosen and the temple which I have built for Your name, 45then hear in heaven their prayer and their supplication, and maintain their cause.

46"When they sin against You (for there is no one who does not sin), and You become angry with them and deliver them to the enemy, and they take them captive to the land of the enemy, far or near; 47yet when they come to themselves in the land where they were carried captive, and repent, and make supplication to You in the land of those who took them captive, saying, 'We have sinned and done wrong, we have committed wickedness'; 48and when they return to You with all their heart and with all their soul in the land of their enemies who led them away captive, and pray to You toward their land which You gave to their fathers, the city which You have chosen and the temple which I have built for Your name: 49then hear in heaven Your dwelling place their prayer and their supplication, and maintain their cause, 50and forgive Your people who have sinned against You, and all their transgressions which they have transgressed against You; and grant them compassion before those who took them captive, that they may have compassion on them 51(for they are Your people and Your inheritance, whom You brought out of Egypt, out of the iron furnace), 52that Your eyes may be open to the supplication of Your servant and the supplication of Your people Israel, to listen to them whenever they call to You. 53For You separated them from among all the peoples of the earth *to be* Your inheritance, as You spoke by Your servant Moses, when You brought our fathers out of Egypt, O Lord GOD."

SOLOMON BLESSES THE ASSEMBLY

⁵⁴And so it was, when Solomon had finished praying all this prayer and supplication to the LORD, that he arose from before the altar of the LORD, from kneeling on his knees with his hands spread up to heaven. ⁵⁵Then he stood and blessed all the assembly of Israel with a loud voice, saying: ⁵⁶"Blessed *be* the LORD, who has given rest to His people Israel, according to all that He promised. There has not failed one word of all His good promise, which He promised through His servant Moses. ⁵⁷May the LORD our God be with us, as He was with our fathers. May He not leave us nor forsake us, ⁵⁸that He may incline our hearts to Himself, to walk in all His ways, and to keep His commandments and His statutes and His judgments, which He commanded our fathers. ⁵⁹And may these words of mine, with which I have made supplication before the LORD, be near the LORD our God day and night, that He may maintain the cause of His servant and the cause of His people Israel, as each day may require, ⁶⁰that all the peoples of the earth may know that the LORD *is* God; *there is* no other. ⁶¹Let your heart therefore be loyal to the LORD our God, to walk in His statutes and keep His commandments, as at this day."

SOLOMON DEDICATES THE TEMPLE

⁶²Then the king and all Israel with him offered sacrifices before the LORD. ⁶³And Solomon offered a sacrifice of peace offerings, which he offered to the LORD, twenty-two thousand bulls and one hundred and twenty thousand sheep. So the king and all the children of Israel dedicated the house of the LORD. ⁶⁴On the same day the king consecrated the middle of the court that *was* in front of the house of the LORD; for there he offered burnt offerings, grain offerings, and the fat of the peace offerings, because the bronze altar that *was* before the LORD *was* too small to receive the burnt offerings, the grain offerings, and the fat of the peace offerings.

⁶⁵At that time Solomon held a feast, and all Israel with him, a great assembly from the entrance of Hamath to the Brook of Egypt, before the LORD our God, seven days and seven *more* days—fourteen days. ⁶⁶On the eighth day he sent the people away; and they blessed the king, and went to their tents joyful and glad of heart for all the good that the LORD had done for His servant David, and for Israel His people.

GOD'S SECOND APPEARANCE TO SOLOMON

9 And it came to pass, when Solomon had finished building the house of the LORD and the king's house, and all Solomon's desire which he wanted to do, ²that the LORD appeared to Solomon the second time, as He had appeared to him at Gibeon. ³And the LORD said to him: "I have heard your prayer and your supplication that you have made before Me; I have consecrated this house which you have built to put My name there forever, and My eyes and My heart will be there perpetually. ⁴Now if you walk before Me as your father David walked, in integrity of heart and in uprightness, to do according to all that I have commanded you, *and* if you keep My statutes and My judgments, ⁵then I will establish the throne of your kingdom over Israel forever, as I promised David your father, saying, 'You shall not fail to have a man on the throne of Israel.' ⁶But if you or your sons at all turn from following Me, and do not keep My commandments *and* My statutes which I have set before you, but go and serve other gods and worship them, ⁷then I will cut off Israel from the land which I have given them; and this house which I have consecrated for My name I will cast out of My sight. Israel will be a proverb and a byword among all peoples. ⁸And *as for* this house, *which* is exalted, everyone who passes by it will be astonished and will hiss, and say, 'Why has the LORD done thus to this land and to this house?' ⁹Then they will answer, 'Because they forsook the LORD their God, who brought their fathers out of the land of Egypt, and have embraced other gods, and worshiped them and served them; therefore the LORD has brought all this calamity on them.' "

SOLOMON AND HIRAM EXCHANGE GIFTS

¹⁰Now it happened at the end of twenty years, when Solomon had built the two houses, the house of the LORD and the king's house ¹¹(Hiram the king of Tyre had supplied Solomon

with cedar and cypress and gold, as much as he desired), *that* King Solomon then gave Hiram twenty cities in the land of Galilee. ¹²Then Hiram went from Tyre to see the cities which Solomon had given him, but they did not please him. ¹³So he said, "What *kind of* cities *are* these which you have given me, my brother?" And he called them the land of Cabul,ᵃ as they are to this day. ¹⁴Then Hiram sent the king one hundred and twenty talents of gold.

SOLOMON'S ADDITIONAL ACHIEVEMENTS

¹⁵And this *is* the reason for the labor force which King Solomon raised: to build the house of the LORD, his own house, the Millo,ᵃ the wall of Jerusalem, Hazor, Megiddo, and Gezer. ¹⁶(Pharaoh king of Egypt had gone up and taken Gezer and burned it with fire, had killed the Canaanites who dwelt in the city, and had given it *as* a dowry to his daughter, Solomon's wife.) ¹⁷And Solomon built Gezer, Lower Beth Horon, ¹⁸Baalath, and Tadmor in the wilderness, in the land *of Judah,* ¹⁹all the storage cities that Solomon had, cities for his chariots and cities for his cavalry, and whatever Solomon desired to build in Jerusalem, in Lebanon, and in all the land of his dominion.

²⁰All the people *who were* left of the Amorites, Hittites, Perizzites, Hivites, and Jebusites, who *were* not of the children of Israel— ²¹that is, their descendants who were left in the land after them, whom the children of Israel had not been able to destroy completely—from these Solomon raised forced labor, as it is to this day. ²²But of the children of Israel Solomon made no forced laborers, because they *were* men of war and his servants: his officers, his captains, commanders of his chariots, and his cavalry.

²³Others *were* chiefs of the officials who *were* over Solomon's work: five hundred and fifty, who ruled over the people who did the work.

²⁴But Pharaoh's daughter came up from the City of David to her house which *Solomon*ᵃ had built for her. Then he built the Millo.

²⁵Now three times a year Solomon offered burnt offerings and peace offerings on the altar which he had built for the LORD, and he burned incense with them *on the altar* that *was* before the LORD. So he finished the temple.

²⁶King Solomon also built a fleet of ships at Ezion Geber, which *is* near Elathᵃ on the shore of the Red Sea, in the land of Edom. ²⁷Then Hiram sent his servants with the fleet, seamen who knew the sea, to work with the servants of Solomon. ²⁸And they went to Ophir, and acquired four hundred and twenty talents of gold from there, and brought *it* to King Solomon.

THE QUEEN OF SHEBA'S PRAISE OF SOLOMON

10 Now when the queen of Sheba heard of the fame of Solomon concerning the name of the LORD, she came to test him with hard questions. ²She came to Jerusalem with a very great retinue, with camels that bore spices, very much gold, and precious stones; and when she came to Solomon, she spoke with him about all that was in her heart. ³So Solomon answered all her questions; there was nothing so difficult for the king that he could not explain *it* to her. ⁴And when the queen of Sheba had seen all the wisdom of Solomon, the house that he had built, ⁵the food on his table, the seating of his servants, the service of his waiters and their apparel, his cupbearers, and his entryway by which he went up to the house of the LORD, there was no more spirit in her. ⁶Then she said to the king: "It was a true report which I heard in my own land about your words and your wisdom. ⁷However I did not believe the words until I came and saw with my own eyes; and indeed the half was not told me. Your wisdom and prosperity exceed the fame of which I heard. ⁸Happy *are* your men and happy *are* these your servants, who stand continually before you *and* hear your wisdom! ⁹Blessed be the LORD your God, who delighted in you, setting you on the throne of Israel! Because the LORD has loved Israel forever, therefore He made you king, to do justice and righteousness."

¹⁰Then she gave the king one hundred and twenty talents of gold, spices in great quantity, and precious stones. There never again came such abundance of spices as the queen of Sheba gave to King Solomon. ¹¹Also, the ships of Hiram, which brought gold from Ophir, brought great quantities of almugᵃ wood and precious stones from

9:13 ᵃLiterally *Good for Nothing*   9:15 ᵃLiterally *The Landfill* 9:24 ᵃLiterally *he* (compare 2 Chronicles 8:11)   9:26 ᵃHebrew *Eloth* (compare 2 Kings 14:22)   10:11 ᵃOr *algum* (compare 2 Chronicles 9:10, 11)

Ophir. [12]And the king made steps of the almug wood for the house of the LORD and for the king's house, also harps and stringed instruments for singers. There never again came such almug wood, nor has the like been seen to this day.

[13]Now King Solomon gave the queen of Sheba all she desired, whatever she asked, besides what Solomon had given her according to the royal generosity. So she turned and went to her own country, she and her servants.

SOLOMON'S GREAT WEALTH

[14]The weight of gold that came to Solomon yearly was six hundred and sixty-six talents of gold, [15]besides *that* from the traveling merchants, from the income of traders, from all the kings of Arabia, and from the governors of the country.

[16]And King Solomon made two hundred large shields *of* hammered gold; six hundred *shekels* of gold went into each shield. [17]He also *made* three hundred shields *of* hammered gold; three minas of gold went into each shield. The king put them in the House of the Forest of Lebanon.

[18]Moreover the king made a great throne of ivory, and overlaid it with pure gold. [19]The throne had six steps, and the top of the throne *was* round at the back; *there were* armrests on either side of the place of the seat, and two lions stood beside the armrests. [20]Twelve lions stood there, one on each side of the six steps; nothing like *this* had been made for any *other* kingdom.

[21]All King Solomon's drinking vessels *were* gold, and all the vessels of the House of the Forest of Lebanon *were* pure gold. Not *one was* silver, for this was accounted as nothing in the days of Solomon. [22]For the king had merchant ships[a] at sea with the fleet of Hiram. Once every three years the merchant ships came bringing gold, silver, ivory, apes, and monkeys.[b] [23]So King Solomon surpassed all the kings of the earth in riches and wisdom.

[24]Now all the earth sought the presence of Solomon to hear his wisdom, which God had put in his heart. [25]Each man brought his present: articles of silver and gold, garments, armor, spices, horses, and mules, at a set rate year by year.

[26]And Solomon gathered chariots and horsemen; he had one thousand four hundred chariots and twelve thousand horsemen, whom he stationed[a] in the chariot cities and with the king at Jerusalem. [27]The king made silver *as common* in Jerusalem as stones, and he made cedar trees as abundant as the sycamores which *are* in the lowland.

[28]Also Solomon had horses imported from Egypt and Keveh; the king's merchants bought them in Keveh at the *current* price. [29]Now a chariot that was imported from Egypt cost six hundred *shekels* of silver, and a horse one hundred and fifty; and thus, through their agents,[a] they exported *them* to all the kings of the Hittites and the kings of Syria.

SOLOMON'S HEART TURNS FROM THE LORD

11 But King Solomon loved many foreign women, as well as the daughter of Pharaoh: women of the Moabites, Ammonites, Edomites, Sidonians, *and* Hittites— [2]from the nations of whom the LORD had said to the children of Israel, "You shall not intermarry with them, nor they with you. Surely they will turn away your hearts after their gods." Solomon clung to these in love. [3]And he had seven hundred wives, princesses, and three hundred concubines; and his wives turned away his heart. [4]For it was so, when Solomon was old, that his wives turned his heart after other gods; and his heart was not loyal to the LORD his God, as *was* the heart of his father David. [5]For Solomon went after Ashtoreth the goddess of the Sidonians, and after Milcom the abomination of the Ammonites. [6]Solomon did evil in the sight of the LORD, and did not fully follow the LORD, as *did* his father David. [7]Then Solomon built a high place for Chemosh the abomination of Moab, on the hill that *is* east of Jerusalem, and for Molech the abomination of the people of Ammon. [8]And he did likewise for all his foreign wives, who burned incense and sacrificed to their gods.

[9]So the LORD became angry with Solomon, because his heart had turned from the LORD God of Israel, who had appeared to him twice, [10]and had commanded him concerning this thing, that

10:22 [a]Literally *ships of Tarshish,* deep-sea vessels [b]Or *peacocks*
10:26 [a]Following Septuagint, Syriac, Targum, and Vulgate (compare 2 Chronicles 9:25); Masoretic Text reads *led.* **10:29** [a]Literally *by their hands*

the**INFLUENCERS**

"FOREIGN WOMEN": Self-Destruction through Bad Choices

1 KINGS 11:1

At first glance, the phrase "foreign women" seems to be a prejudiced statement, but look closer. 1 Kings 11 warns Israel that foreigners would *turn away your hearts after their gods.* Clearly, this isn't about friendship or animosity; it's about allowing others to control your spiritual life by inviting their morals to impact your own. Solomon brought foreign women into his home, but thought their pagan gods could sit in the background. The wisest man in the world still lacked self-control.

These are the factors that cause us to make bad decisions in relationships:

- **Lust.** The Israelite women dressed modestly and believed in moral purity, but the foreign women were loose in morals, speech, and dress.
- **Pride.** Many of Solomon's foreign wives were the daughters of tributary chiefs, given as gifts to Solomon, like "trophies" for his pride.
- **Overconfidence.** He may have been so confident in himself that he thought he could control anyone by treating them as a possession.
- **Power.** Solomon was king. Everyone in Israel bowed to him, catered to him, and he didn't want to abide by rules when it came to his own pleasure.

The "missionary marriages" didn't work any better than today's "evangelistic dating."

he should not go after other gods; but he did not keep what the LORD had commanded. [11]Therefore the LORD said to Solomon, "Because you have done this, and have not kept My covenant and My statutes, which I have commanded you, I will surely tear the kingdom away from you and give it to your servant. [12]Nevertheless I will not do it in your days, for the sake of your father David; I will tear it out of the hand of your son. [13]However I will not tear away the whole kingdom; I will give one tribe to your son for the sake of My servant David, and for the sake of Jerusalem which I have chosen."

ADVERSARIES OF SOLOMON

[14]Now the LORD raised up an adversary against Solomon, Hadad the Edomite; he *was* a descendant of the king in Edom. [15]For it happened, when David was in Edom, and Joab the commander of the army had gone up to bury the slain, after he had killed every male in Edom [16](because for six months Joab remained there with all Israel, until he had cut down every male

in Edom), [17]that Hadad fled to go to Egypt, he and certain Edomites of his father's servants with him. Hadad *was* still a little child. [18]Then they arose from Midian and came to Paran; and they took men with them from Paran and came to Egypt, to Pharaoh king of Egypt, who gave him a house, apportioned food for him, and gave him land. [19]And Hadad found great favor in the sight of Pharaoh, so that he gave him as wife the sister of his own wife, that is, the sister of Queen Tahpenes. [20]Then the sister of Tahpenes bore him Genubath his son, whom Tahpenes weaned in Pharaoh's house. And Genubath was in Pharaoh's household among the sons of Pharaoh.

[21]So when Hadad heard in Egypt that David rested with his fathers, and that Joab the commander of the army was dead, Hadad said to Pharaoh, "Let me depart, that I may go to my own country."

[22]Then Pharaoh said to him, "But what have you lacked with me, that suddenly you seek to go to your own country?"

So he answered, "Nothing, but do let me go anyway."

²³And God raised up *another* adversary against him, Rezon the son of Eliadah, who had fled from his lord, Hadadezer king of Zobah. ²⁴So he gathered men to him and became captain over a band *of raiders,* when David killed those *of Zobah.* And they went to Damascus and dwelt there, and reigned in Damascus. ²⁵He was an adversary of Israel all the days of Solomon (besides the trouble that Hadad *caused*); and he abhorred Israel, and reigned over Syria.

Jeroboam's Rebellion

²⁶Then Solomon's servant, Jeroboam the son of Nebat, an Ephraimite from Zereda, whose mother's name *was* Zeruah, a widow, also rebelled against the king.

²⁷And this *is* what caused him to rebel against the king: Solomon had built the Millo *and* repaired the damages to the City of David his father. ²⁸The man Jeroboam *was* a mighty man of valor; and Solomon, seeing that the young man was industrious, made him the officer over all the labor force of the house of Joseph.

²⁹Now it happened at that time, when Jeroboam went out of Jerusalem, that the prophet Ahijah the Shilonite met him on the way; and he had clothed himself with a new garment, and the two *were* alone in the field. ³⁰Then Ahijah took hold of the new garment that *was* on him, and tore it *into* twelve pieces. ³¹And he said to Jeroboam, "Take for yourself ten pieces, for thus says the LORD, the God of Israel: 'Behold, I will tear the kingdom out of the hand of Solomon and will give ten tribes to you ³²(but he shall have one tribe for the sake of My servant David, and for the sake of Jerusalem, the city which I have chosen out of all the tribes of Israel), ³³because they have[a] forsaken Me, and worshiped Ashtoreth the goddess of the Sidonians, Chemosh the god of the Moabites, and Milcom the god of the people of Ammon, and have not walked in My ways to do *what is* right in My eyes and *keep* My statutes and My judgments, as *did* his father David. ³⁴However I will not take the whole kingdom out of his hand, because I have made him ruler all the days of his life for the sake of My servant David, whom I chose because he kept My com-

mandments and My statutes. ³⁵But I will take the kingdom out of his son's hand and give it to you—ten tribes. ³⁶And to his son I will give one tribe, that My servant David may always have a lamp before Me in Jerusalem, the city which I have chosen for Myself, to put My name there. ³⁷So I will take you, and you shall reign over all your heart desires, and you shall be king over Israel. ³⁸Then it shall be, if you heed all that I command you, walk in My ways, and do *what is* right in My sight, to keep My statutes and My commandments, as My servant David did, then I will be with you and build for you an enduring house, as I built for David, and will give Israel to you. ³⁹And I will afflict the descendants of David because of this, but not forever.' "

⁴⁰Solomon therefore sought to kill Jeroboam. But Jeroboam arose and fled to Egypt, to Shishak king of Egypt, and was in Egypt until the death of Solomon.

Death of Solomon

⁴¹Now the rest of the acts of Solomon, all that he did, and his wisdom, *are* they not written in the book of the acts of Solomon? ⁴²And the period that Solomon reigned in Jerusalem over all Israel *was* forty years. ⁴³Then Solomon rested with his fathers, and was buried in the City of David his father. And Rehoboam his son reigned in his place.

The Revolt Against Rehoboam

12 And Rehoboam went to Shechem, for all Israel had gone to Shechem to make him king. ²So it happened, when Jeroboam the son of Nebat heard *it* (he was still in Egypt, for he had fled from the presence of King Solomon and had been dwelling in Egypt), ³that they sent and called him. Then Jeroboam and the whole assembly of Israel came and spoke to Rehoboam, saying, ⁴"Your father made our yoke heavy; now therefore, lighten the burdensome service of your father, and his heavy yoke which he put on us, and we will serve you."

⁵So he said to them, "Depart *for* three days, then come back to me." And the people departed.

⁶Then King Rehoboam consulted the elders who stood before his father Solomon while he

11:33 [a]Following Masoretic Text and Targum; Septuagint, Syriac, and Vulgate read *he has.*

still lived, and he said, "How do you advise *me* to answer these people?"

⁷And they spoke to him, saying, "If you will be a servant to these people today, and serve them, and answer them, and speak good words to them, then they will be your servants forever."

⁸But he rejected the advice which the elders had given him, and consulted the young men who had grown up with him, who stood before him. ⁹And he said to them, "What advice do you give? How should we answer this people who have spoken to me, saying, 'Lighten the yoke which your father put on us'?"

¹⁰Then the young men who had grown up with him spoke to him, saying, "Thus you should speak to this people who have spoken to you, saying, 'Your father made our yoke heavy, but you make it lighter on us'—thus you shall say to them: 'My little *finger* shall be thicker than my father's waist! ¹¹And now, whereas my father put a heavy yoke on you, I will add to your yoke; my father chastised you with whips, but I will chastise you with scourges!' "ᵃ

¹²So Jeroboam and all the people came to Rehoboam the third day, as the king had directed, saying, "Come back to me the third day." ¹³Then the king answered the people roughly, and rejected the advice which the elders had given him; ¹⁴and he spoke to them according to the advice of the young men, saying, "My father made your yoke heavy, but I will add to your yoke; my father chastised you with whips, but I will chastise you with scourges!"ᵃ ¹⁵So the king did not listen to the people; for the turn *of events* was from the LORD, that He might fulfill His word, which the LORD had spoken by Ahijah the Shilonite to Jeroboam the son of Nebat.

¹⁶Now when all Israel saw that the king did not listen to them, the people answered the king, saying:

"What share have we in David?
We have no inheritance in the son of Jesse.
To your tents, O Israel!
Now, see to your own house, O David!"

So Israel departed to their tents. ¹⁷But Rehoboam reigned over the children of Israel who dwelt in the cities of Judah.

¹⁸Then King Rehoboam sent Adoram, who *was* in charge of the revenue; but all Israel stoned him with stones, and he died. Therefore King Rehoboam mounted his chariot in haste to flee to Jerusalem. ¹⁹So Israel has been in rebellion against the house of David to this day.

²⁰Now it came to pass when all Israel heard that Jeroboam had come back, they sent for him and called him to the congregation, and made him king over all Israel. There was none who followed the house of David, but the tribe of Judah only.

²¹And when Rehoboam came to Jerusalem, he assembled all the house of Judah with the tribe of Benjamin, one hundred and eighty thousand chosen *men* who were warriors, to fight against the house of Israel, that he might restore the kingdom to Rehoboam the son of Solomon. ²²But the word of God came to Shemaiah the man of God, saying, ²³"Speak to Rehoboam the son of Solomon, king of Judah, to all the house of Judah and Benjamin, and to the rest of the people, saying, ²⁴'Thus says the LORD: "You shall not go up nor fight against your brethren the children of Israel. Let every man return to his house, for this thing is from Me." ' " Therefore they obeyed the word of the LORD, and turned back, according to the word of the LORD.

JEROBOAM'S GOLD CALVES

²⁵Then Jeroboam built Shechem in the mountains of Ephraim, and dwelt there. Also he went out from there and built Penuel. ²⁶And Jeroboam said in his heart, "Now the kingdom may return to the house of David: ²⁷If these people go up to offer sacrifices in the house of the LORD at Jerusalem, then the heart of this people will turn back to their lord, Rehoboam king of Judah, and they will kill me and go back to Rehoboam king of Judah."

²⁸Therefore the king asked advice, made two calves of gold, and said to the people, "It is too much for you to go up to Jerusalem. Here are your gods, O Israel, which brought you up from the land of Egypt!" ²⁹And he set up one in Bethel, and the other he put in Dan. ³⁰Now this thing became a sin, for the people went *to worship* before the one as far as Dan. ³¹He made

12:11 ᵃLiterally *scorpions*   12:14 ᵃLiterally *scorpions* shrines[a] on the high places, and made priests from every class of people, who were not of the sons of Levi.

[32]Jeroboam ordained a feast on the fifteenth day of the eighth month, like the feast that *was* in Judah, and offered sacrifices on the altar. So he did at Bethel, sacrificing to the calves that he had made. And at Bethel he installed the priests of the high places which he had made. [33]So he made offerings on the altar which he had made at Bethel on the fifteenth day of the eighth month, in the month which he had devised in his own heart. And he ordained a feast for the children of Israel, and offered sacrifices on the altar and burned incense.

The Message of the Man of God

13 And behold, a man of God went from Judah to Bethel by the word of the LORD, and Jeroboam stood by the altar to burn incense. [2]Then he cried out against the altar by the word of the LORD, and said, "O altar, altar! Thus says the LORD: 'Behold, a child, Josiah by name, shall be born to the house of David; and on you he shall sacrifice the priests of the high places who burn incense on you, and men's bones shall be burned on you.' " [3]And he gave a sign the same day, saying, "This *is* the sign which the LORD has spoken: Surely the altar shall split apart, and the ashes on it shall be poured out."

[4]So it came to pass when King Jeroboam heard the saying of the man of God, who cried out against the altar in Bethel, that he stretched out his hand from the altar, saying, "Arrest him!" Then his hand, which he stretched out toward him, withered, so that he could not pull it back to himself. [5]The altar also was split apart, and the ashes poured out from the altar, according to the sign which the man of God had given by the word of the LORD. [6]Then the king answered and said to the man of God, "Please entreat the favor of the LORD your God, and pray for me, that my hand may be restored to me."

So the man of God entreated the LORD, and the king's hand was restored to him, and became as before. [7]Then the king said to the man of God, "Come home with me and refresh yourself, and I will give you a reward."

[8]But the man of God said to the king, "If you

were to give me half your house, I would not go in with you; nor would I eat bread nor drink water in this place. [9]For so it was commanded me by the word of the LORD, saying, 'You shall not eat bread, nor drink water, nor return by the same way you came.' " [10]So he went another way and did not return by the way he came to Bethel.

Death of the Man of God

[11]Now an old prophet dwelt in Bethel, and his sons came and told him all the works that the man of God had done that day in Bethel; they also told their father the words which he had spoken to the king. [12]And their father said to them, "Which way did he go?" For his sons had seen[a] which way the man of God went who came from Judah. [13]Then he said to his sons, "Saddle the donkey for me." So they saddled the donkey for him; and he rode on it, [14]and went after the man of God, and found him sitting under an oak. Then he said to him, "*Are* you the man of God who came from Judah?"

And he said, "I *am*."

[15]Then he said to him, "Come home with me and eat bread."

[16]And he said, "I cannot return with you nor go in with you; neither can I eat bread nor drink water with you in this place. [17]For I have been told by the word of the LORD, 'You shall not eat bread nor drink water there, nor return by going the way you came.' "

[18]He said to him, "I too *am* a prophet as you *are,* and an angel spoke to me by the word of the LORD, saying, 'Bring him back with you to your house, that he may eat bread and drink water.' " (He was lying to him.)

[19]So he went back with him, and ate bread in his house, and drank water.

[20]Now it happened, as they sat at the table, that the word of the LORD came to the prophet who had brought him back; [21]and he cried out to the man of God who came from Judah, saying, "Thus says the LORD: 'Because you have disobeyed the word of the LORD, and have not kept the commandment which the LORD your God commanded you, [22]but you came back, ate bread, and drank water in the place of which *the LORD*

12:31 [a]Literally *a house* **13:12** [a]Septuagint, Syriac, Targum, and Vulgate read *showed him.*

said to you, "Eat no bread and drink no water," your corpse shall not come to the tomb of your fathers.' "

²³So it was, after he had eaten bread and after he had drunk, that he saddled the donkey for him, the prophet whom he had brought back. ²⁴When he was gone, a lion met him on the road and killed him. And his corpse was thrown on the road, and the donkey stood by it. The lion also stood by the corpse. ²⁵And there, men passed by and saw the corpse thrown on the road, and the lion standing by the corpse. Then they went and told *it* in the city where the old prophet dwelt.

²⁶Now when the prophet who had brought him back from the way heard *it,* he said, "It *is* the man of God who was disobedient to the word of the LORD. Therefore the LORD has delivered him to the lion, which has torn him and killed him, according to the word of the LORD which He spoke to him." ²⁷And he spoke to his sons, saying, "Saddle the donkey for me." So they saddled *it.* ²⁸Then he went and found his corpse thrown on the road, and the donkey and the lion standing by the corpse. The lion had not eaten the corpse nor torn the donkey. ²⁹And the prophet took up the corpse of the man of God, laid it on the donkey, and brought it back. So the old prophet came to the city to mourn, and to bury him. ³⁰Then he laid the corpse in his own tomb; and they mourned over him, *saying,* "Alas, my brother!" ³¹So it was, after he had buried him, that he spoke to his sons, saying, "When I am dead, then bury me in the tomb where the man of God *is* buried; lay my bones beside his bones. ³²For the saying which he cried out by the word of the LORD against the altar in Bethel, and against all the shrinesᵃ on the high places which *are* in the cities of Samaria, will surely come to pass."

³³After this event Jeroboam did not turn from his evil way, but again he made priests from every class of people for the high places; whoever wished, he consecrated him, and he became *one* of the priests of the high places. ³⁴And this thing was the sin of the house of Jeroboam, so as to exterminate and destroy *it* from the face of the earth.

JUDGMENT ON THE HOUSE OF JEROBOAM

14 At that time Abijah the son of Jeroboam became sick. ²And Jeroboam said to his wife,

"Please arise, and disguise yourself, that they may not recognize you as the wife of Jeroboam, and go to Shiloh. Indeed, Ahijah the prophet *is* there, who told me that *I would be* king over this people. ³Also take with you ten loaves, *some* cakes, and a jar of honey, and go to him; he will tell you what will become of the child." ⁴And Jeroboam's wife did so; she arose and went to Shiloh, and came to the house of Ahijah. But Ahijah could not see, for his eyes were glazed by reason of his age.

⁵Now the LORD had said to Ahijah, "Here is the wife of Jeroboam, coming to ask you something about her son, for he *is* sick. Thus and thus you shall say to her; for it will be, when she comes in, that she will pretend *to be* another *woman.*"

⁶And so it was, when Ahijah heard the sound of her footsteps as she came through the door, he said, "Come in, wife of Jeroboam. Why do you pretend *to be* another *person?* For I *have been* sent to you *with* bad *news.* ⁷Go, tell Jeroboam, 'Thus says the LORD God of Israel: "Because I exalted you from among the people, and made you ruler over My people Israel, ⁸and tore the kingdom away from the house of David, and gave it to you; and *yet* you have not been as My servant David, who kept My commandments and who followed Me with all his heart, to do only *what was* right in My eyes; ⁹but you have done more evil than all who were before you, for you have gone and made for yourself other gods and molded images to provoke Me to anger, and have cast Me behind your back— ¹⁰therefore behold! I will bring disaster on the house of Jeroboam, and will cut off from Jeroboam every male in Israel, bond and free; I will take away the remnant of the house of Jeroboam, as one takes away refuse until it is all gone. ¹¹The dogs shall eat whoever belongs to Jeroboam and dies in the city, and the birds of the air shall eat whoever dies in the field; for the LORD has spoken!" ' ¹²Arise therefore, go to your own house. When your feet enter the city, the child shall die. ¹³And all Israel shall mourn for him and bury him, for he is the only one of Jeroboam who shall come to the grave, because in him there is found something good toward the LORD God of Israel in the house of Jeroboam.

¹⁴"Moreover the LORD will raise up for Him-

13:32 ᵃLiterally *houses*

self a king over Israel who shall cut off the house of Jeroboam; this is the day. What? Even now! [15]For the LORD will strike Israel, as a reed is shaken in the water. He will uproot Israel from this good land which He gave to their fathers, and will scatter them beyond the River,[a] because they have made their wooden images,[b] provoking the LORD to anger. [16]And He will give Israel up because of the sins of Jeroboam, who sinned and who made Israel sin."

[17]Then Jeroboam's wife arose and departed, and came to Tirzah. When she came to the threshold of the house, the child died. [18]And they buried him; and all Israel mourned for him, according to the word of the LORD which He spoke through His servant Ahijah the prophet.

DEATH OF JEROBOAM

[19]Now the rest of the acts of Jeroboam, how he made war and how he reigned, indeed they *are* written in the book of the chronicles of the kings of Israel. [20]The period that Jeroboam reigned *was* twenty-two years. So he rested with his fathers. Then Nadab his son reigned in his place.

REHOBOAM REIGNS IN JUDAH

[21]And Rehoboam the son of Solomon reigned in Judah. Rehoboam *was* forty-one years old when he became king. He reigned seventeen years in Jerusalem, the city which the LORD had chosen out of all the tribes of Israel, to put His name there. His mother's name *was* Naamah, an Ammonitess. [22]Now Judah did evil in the sight of the LORD, and they provoked Him to jealousy with their sins which they committed, more than all that their fathers had done. [23]For they also built for themselves high places, *sacred* pillars, and wooden images on every high hill and under every green tree. [24]And there were also perverted persons[a] in the land. They did according to all the abominations of the nations which the LORD had cast out before the children of Israel.

[25]It happened in the fifth year of King Rehoboam *that* Shishak king of Egypt came up against Jerusalem. [26]And he took away the treasures of the house of the LORD and the treasures of the king's house; he took away everything. He also took away all the gold shields which Solomon had made. [27]Then King Rehoboam

made bronze shields in their place, and committed *them* to the hands of the captains of the guard, who guarded the doorway of the king's house. [28]And whenever the king entered the house of the LORD, the guards carried them, then brought them back into the guardroom.

[29]Now the rest of the acts of Rehoboam, and all that he did, *are* they not written in the book of the chronicles of the kings of Judah? [30]And there was war between Rehoboam and Jeroboam all *their* days. [31]So Rehoboam rested with his fathers, and was buried with his fathers in the City of David. His mother's name *was* Naamah, an Ammonitess. Then Abijam[a] his son reigned in his place.

ABIJAM REIGNS IN JUDAH

15 In the eighteenth year of King Jeroboam the son of Nebat, Abijam became king over Judah. [2]He reigned three years in Jerusalem. His mother's name *was* Maachah the granddaughter of Abishalom. [3]And he walked in all the sins of his father, which he had done before him; his heart was not loyal to the LORD his God, as was the heart of his father David. [4]Nevertheless for David's sake the LORD his God gave him a lamp in Jerusalem, by setting up his son after him and by establishing Jerusalem; [5]because David did *what was* right in the eyes of the LORD, and had not turned aside from anything that He commanded him all the days of his life, except in the matter of Uriah the Hittite. [6]And there was war between Rehoboam[a] and Jeroboam all the days of his life. [7]Now the rest of the acts of Abijam, and all that he did, *are* they not written in the book of the chronicles of the kings of Judah? And there was war between Abijam and Jeroboam.

[8]So Abijam rested with his fathers, and they buried him in the City of David. Then Asa his son reigned in his place.

ASA REIGNS IN JUDAH

[9]In the twentieth year of Jeroboam king of Israel, Asa became king over Judah. [10]And he reigned forty-one years in Jerusalem. His

14:15 [a]That is, the Euphrates [b]Hebrew *Asherim*, Canaanite deities **14:24** [a]Hebrew *qadesh*, that is, one practicing sodomy and prostitution in religious rituals **14:31** [a]Spelled *Abijah* in 2 Chronicles 12:16ff **15:6** [a]Following Masoretic Text, Septuagint, Targum, and Vulgate; some Hebrew manuscripts and Syriac read *Abijam*.

grandmother's name *was* Maachah the grand-daughter of Abishalom. ¹¹Asa did *what was* right in the eyes of the LORD, as *did* his father David. ¹²And he banished the perverted persons[a] from the land, and removed all the idols that his fathers had made. ¹³Also he removed Maachah his grandmother from *being* queen mother, because she had made an obscene image of Asherah.[a] And Asa cut down her obscene image and burned *it* by the Brook Kidron. ¹⁴But the high places were not removed. Nevertheless Asa's heart was loyal to the LORD all his days. ¹⁵He also brought into the house of the LORD the things which his father had dedicated, and the things which he himself had dedicated: silver and gold and utensils.

¹⁶Now there was war between Asa and Baasha king of Israel all their days. ¹⁷And Baasha king of Israel came up against Judah, and built Ramah, that he might let none go out or come in to Asa king of Judah. ¹⁸Then Asa took all the silver and gold *that was* left in the treasuries of the house of the LORD and the treasuries of the king's house, and delivered them into the hand of his servants. And King Asa sent them to Ben-Hadad the son of Tabrimmon, the son of Hezion, king of Syria, who dwelt in Damascus, saying, ¹⁹"*Let there be* a treaty between you and me, as there was between my father and your father. See, I have sent you a present of silver and gold. Come and break your treaty with Baasha king of Israel, so that he will withdraw from me."

²⁰So Ben-Hadad heeded King Asa, and sent the captains of his armies against the cities of Israel. He attacked Ijon, Dan, Abel Beth Maachah, and all Chinneroth, with all the land of Naphtali. ²¹Now it happened, when Baasha heard *it,* that he stopped building Ramah, and remained in Tirzah.

²²Then King Asa made a proclamation throughout all Judah; none *was* exempted. And they took away the stones and timber of Ramah, which Baasha had used for building; and with them King Asa built Geba of Benjamin, and Mizpah.

²³The rest of all the acts of Asa, all his might, all that he did, and the cities which he built, *are* they not written in the book of the chronicles of the kings of Judah? But in the time of his old age he was diseased in his feet. ²⁴So Asa rested with his fathers, and was buried with his fathers in the City of David his father. Then Jehoshaphat his son reigned in his place.

NADAB REIGNS IN ISRAEL

²⁵Now Nadab the son of Jeroboam became king over Israel in the second year of Asa king of Judah, and he reigned over Israel two years. ²⁶And he did evil in the sight of the LORD, and walked in the way of his father, and in his sin by which he had made Israel sin.

²⁷Then Baasha the son of Ahijah, of the house of Issachar, conspired against him. And Baasha killed him at Gibbethon, which *belonged* to the Philistines, while Nadab and all Israel laid siege to Gibbethon. ²⁸Baasha killed him in the third year of Asa king of Judah, and reigned in his place. ²⁹And it was so, when he became king, *that* he killed all the house of Jeroboam. He did not leave to Jeroboam anyone that breathed, until he had destroyed him, according to the word of the LORD which He had spoken by His servant Ahijah the Shilonite, ³⁰because of the sins of Jeroboam, which he had sinned and by which he had made Israel sin, because of his provocation with which he had provoked the LORD God of Israel to anger.

³¹Now the rest of the acts of Nadab, and all that he did, *are* they not written in the book of the chronicles of the kings of Israel? ³²And there was war between Asa and Baasha king of Israel all their days.

BAASHA REIGNS IN ISRAEL

³³In the third year of Asa king of Judah, Baasha the son of Ahijah became king over all Israel in Tirzah, and *reigned* twenty-four years. ³⁴He did evil in the sight of the LORD, and walked in the way of Jeroboam, and in his sin by which he had made Israel sin.

16 Then the word of the LORD came to Jehu the son of Hanani, against Baasha, saying: ²"Inasmuch as I lifted you out of the dust and made you ruler over My people Israel, and you have walked in the way of Jeroboam, and have made My people Israel sin, to provoke Me to anger with their sins, ³surely I will take away the posterity of Baasha and the posterity of his house,

15:12 ªHebrew *qedeshim,* that is, those practicing sodomy and prostitution in religious rituals   **15:13** ªA Canaanite goddess and I will make your house like the house of Jeroboam the son of Nebat. ⁴The dogs shall eat whoever belongs to Baasha and dies in the city, and the birds of the air shall eat whoever dies in the fields."

⁵Now the rest of the acts of Baasha, what he did, and his might, *are* they not written in the book of the chronicles of the kings of Israel? ⁶So Baasha rested with his fathers and was buried in Tirzah. Then Elah his son reigned in his place.

⁷And also the word of the LORD came by the prophet Jehu the son of Hanani against Baasha and his house, because of all the evil that he did in the sight of the LORD in provoking Him to anger with the work of his hands, in being like the house of Jeroboam, and because he killed them.

Elah Reigns in Israel

⁸In the twenty-sixth year of Asa king of Judah, Elah the son of Baasha became king over Israel, *and reigned* two years in Tirzah. ⁹Now his servant Zimri, commander of half *his* chariots, conspired against him as he was in Tirzah drinking himself drunk in the house of Arza, steward of *his* house in Tirzah. ¹⁰And Zimri went in and struck him and killed him in the twenty-seventh year of Asa king of Judah, and reigned in his place.

¹¹Then it came to pass, when he began to reign, as soon as he was seated on his throne, *that* he killed all the household of Baasha; he did not leave him one male, neither of his relatives nor of his friends. ¹²Thus Zimri destroyed all the household of Baasha, according to the word of the LORD, which He spoke against Baasha by Jehu the prophet, ¹³for all the sins of Baasha and the sins of Elah his son, by which they had sinned and by which they had made Israel sin, in provoking the LORD God of Israel to anger with their idols.

¹⁴Now the rest of the acts of Elah, and all that he did, *are* they not written in the book of the chronicles of the kings of Israel?

Zimri Reigns in Israel

¹⁵In the twenty-seventh year of Asa king of Judah, Zimri had reigned in Tirzah seven days. And the people *were* encamped against Gibbethon, which *belonged* to the Philistines. ¹⁶Now the people *who were* encamped heard it said, "Zimri has conspired and also has killed the

king." So all Israel made Omri, the commander of the army, king over Israel that day in the camp. ¹⁷Then Omri and all Israel with him went up from Gibbethon, and they besieged Tirzah. ¹⁸And it happened, when Zimri saw that the city was taken, that he went into the citadel of the king's house and burned the king's house down upon himself with fire, and died, ¹⁹because of the sins which he had committed in doing evil in the sight of the LORD, in walking in the way of Jeroboam, and in his sin which he had committed to make Israel sin.

²⁰Now the rest of the acts of Zimri, and the treason he committed, *are* they not written in the book of the chronicles of the kings of Israel?

Omri Reigns in Israel

²¹Then the people of Israel were divided into two parts: half of the people followed Tibni the son of Ginath, to make him king, and half followed Omri. ²²But the people who followed Omri prevailed over the people who followed Tibni the son of Ginath. So Tibni died and Omri reigned. ²³In the thirty-first year of Asa king of Judah, Omri became king over Israel, *and reigned* twelve years. Six years he reigned in Tirzah. ²⁴And he bought the hill of Samaria from Shemer for two talents of silver; then he built on the hill, and called the name of the city which he built, Samaria, after the name of Shemer, owner of the hill. ²⁵Omri did evil in the eyes of the LORD, and did worse than all who *were* before him. ²⁶For he walked in all the ways of Jeroboam the son of Nebat, and in his sin by which he had made Israel sin, provoking the LORD God of Israel to anger with their idols.

²⁷Now the rest of the acts of Omri which he did, and the might that he showed, *are* they not written in the book of the chronicles of the kings of Israel?

²⁸So Omri rested with his fathers and was buried in Samaria. Then Ahab his son reigned in his place.

Ahab Reigns in Israel

²⁹In the thirty-eighth year of Asa king of Judah, Ahab the son of Omri became king over Israel; and Ahab the son of Omri reigned over Israel in Samaria twenty-two years. ³⁰Now Ahab the

son of Omri did evil in the sight of the LORD, more than all who *were* before him. [31]And it came to pass, as though it had been a trivial thing for him to walk in the sins of Jeroboam the son of Nebat, that he took as wife Jezebel the daughter of Ethbaal, king of the Sidonians; and he went and served Baal and worshiped him. [32]Then he set up an altar for Baal in the temple of Baal, which he had built in Samaria. [33]And Ahab made a wooden image.[a] Ahab did more to provoke the LORD God of Israel to anger than all the kings of Israel who were before him. [34]In his days Hiel of Bethel built Jericho. He laid its foundation with Abiram his firstborn, and with his youngest *son* Segub he set up its gates, according to the word of the LORD, which He had spoken through Joshua the son of Nun.[a]

Elijah Proclaims a Drought

17And Elijah the Tishbite, of the inhabitants of Gilead, said to Ahab, "*As* the LORD God of Israel lives, before whom I stand, there shall not be dew nor rain these years, except at my word."

[2]Then the word of the LORD came to him, saying, [3]"Get away from here and turn eastward, and hide by the Brook Cherith, which flows into the Jordan. [4]And it will be *that* you shall drink from the brook, and I have commanded the ravens to feed you there."

[5]So he went and did according to the word of the LORD, for he went and stayed by the Brook Cherith, which flows into the Jordan. [6]The ravens brought him bread and meat in the morning, and bread and meat in the evening; and he drank from the brook. [7]And it happened after a while that the brook dried up, because there had been no rain in the land.

Elijah and the Widow

[8]Then the word of the LORD came to him, saying, [9]"Arise, go to Zarephath, which *belongs* to Sidon, and dwell there. See, I have commanded a widow there to provide for you." [10]So he arose and went to Zarephath. And when he came to the gate of the city, indeed a widow *was* there gathering sticks. And he called to her and said, "Please bring me a little water in a cup, that I may drink." [11]And as she was going to get *it,* he called to her and said, "Please bring me a morsel of bread in your hand."

[12]So she said, "As the LORD your God lives, I do not have bread, only a handful of flour in a bin, and a little oil in a jar; and see, I *am* gathering a couple of sticks that I may go in and prepare it for myself and my son, that we may eat it, and die."

[13]And Elijah said to her, "Do not fear; go *and* do as you have said, but make me a small cake from it first, and bring *it* to me; and afterward make *some* for yourself and your son. [14]For thus says the LORD God of Israel: 'The bin of flour shall not be used up, nor shall the jar of oil run dry, until the day the LORD sends rain on the earth.' "

[15]So she went away and did according to the word of Elijah; and she and he and her household ate for *many* days. [16]The bin of flour was not used up, nor did the jar of oil run dry, according to the word of the LORD which He spoke by Elijah.

Elijah Revives the Widow's Son

[17]Now it happened after these things *that* the son of the woman who owned the house became sick. And his sickness was so serious that there was no breath left in him. [18]So she said to Elijah, "What have I to do with you, O man of God? Have you come to me to bring my sin to remembrance, and to kill my son?"

[19]And he said to her, "Give me your son." So he took him out of her arms and carried him to the upper room where he was staying, and laid him on his own bed. [20]Then he cried out to the LORD and said, "O LORD my God, have You also brought tragedy on the widow with whom I lodge, by killing her son?" [21]And he stretched himself out on the child three times, and cried out to the LORD and said, "O LORD my God, I pray, let this child's soul come back to him." [22]Then the LORD heard the voice of Elijah; and the soul of the child came back to him, and he revived.

[23]And Elijah took the child and brought him down from the upper room into the house, and gave him to his mother. And Elijah said, "See, your son lives!"

[24]Then the woman said to Elijah, "Now by this I know that you *are* a man of God, *and* that the word of the LORD in your mouth *is* the truth."

16:33 [a]Hebrew *Asherah,* a Canaanite goddess   **16:34** [a]Compare Joshua 6:26

Elijah's Message to Ahab

18 And it came to pass *after* many days that the word of the LORD came to Elijah, in the third year, saying, "Go, present yourself to Ahab, and I will send rain on the earth."

²So Elijah went to present himself to Ahab; and *there was* a severe famine in Samaria. ³And Ahab had called Obadiah, who *was* in charge of *his* house. (Now Obadiah feared the LORD greatly. ⁴For so it was, while Jezebel massacred the prophets of the LORD, that Obadiah had taken one hundred prophets and hidden them, fifty in a cave, and had fed them with bread and water.) ⁵And Ahab had said to Obadiah, "Go into the land to all the springs of water and to all the brooks; perhaps we may find grass to keep the horses and mules alive, so that we will not have to kill any livestock." ⁶So they divided the land between them to explore it; Ahab went one way by himself, and Obadiah went another way by himself.

⁷Now as Obadiah was on his way, suddenly Elijah met him; and he recognized him, and fell on his face, and said, "*Is* that you, my lord Elijah?"

⁸And he answered him, "*It is* I. Go, tell your master, 'Elijah *is here.*'"

⁹So he said, "How have I sinned, that you are delivering your servant into the hand of Ahab, to kill me? ¹⁰*As* the LORD your God lives, there is no nation or kingdom where my master has not sent someone to hunt for you; and when they said, '*He is* not *here,*' he took an oath from the kingdom or nation that they could not find you. ¹¹And now you say, 'Go, tell your master, "Elijah *is here*" '! ¹²And it shall come to pass, *as soon as* I am gone from you, that the Spirit of the LORD will carry you to a place I do not know; so when I go and tell Ahab, and he cannot find you, he will kill me. But I your servant have feared the LORD from my youth. ¹³Was it not reported to my lord what I did when Jezebel killed the prophets of the LORD, how I hid one hundred men of the LORD's prophets, fifty to a cave, and fed them with bread and water? ¹⁴And now you say, 'Go, tell your master, "Elijah *is here.*" ' He will kill me!"

¹⁵Then Elijah said, "*As* the LORD of hosts lives, before whom I stand, I will surely present myself to him today."

¹⁶So Obadiah went to meet Ahab, and told him; and Ahab went to meet Elijah.

¹⁷Then it happened, when Ahab saw Elijah, that Ahab said to him, "*Is that* you, O troubler of Israel?"

¹⁸And he answered, "I have not troubled Israel, but you and your father's house *have,* in that you have forsaken the commandments of the LORD and have followed the Baals. ¹⁹Now therefore, send *and* gather all Israel to me on Mount Carmel, the four hundred and fifty prophets of Baal, and the four hundred prophets of Asherah,ᵃ who eat at Jezebel's table."

Elijah's Mount Carmel Victory

²⁰So Ahab sent for all the children of Israel, and gathered the prophets together on Mount Carmel. ²¹And Elijah came to all the people, and said, "How long will you falter between two opinions? If the LORD *is* God, follow Him; but if Baal, follow him." But the people answered him not a word. ²²Then Elijah said to the people, "I alone am left a prophet of the LORD; but Baal's prophets *are* four hundred and fifty men. ²³Therefore let them give us two bulls; and let them choose one bull for themselves, cut it in pieces, and lay *it* on the wood, but put no fire *under it;* and I will prepare the other bull, and lay *it* on the wood, but put no fire *under it.* ²⁴Then you call on the name of your gods, and I will call on the name of the LORD; and the God who answers by fire, He is God."

So all the people answered and said, "It is well spoken."

²⁵Now Elijah said to the prophets of Baal, "Choose one bull for yourselves and prepare *it* first, for you *are* many; and call on the name of your god, but put no fire *under it.*"

²⁶So they took the bull which was given them, and they prepared *it,* and called on the name of Baal from morning even till noon, saying, "O Baal, hear us!" But *there was* no voice; no one answered. Then they leaped about the altar which they had made.

²⁷And so it was, at noon, that Elijah mocked them and said, "Cry aloud, for he *is* a god; either he is meditating, or he is busy, or he is on a journey, *or* perhaps he is sleeping and must be awakened." ²⁸So they cried aloud, and cut themselves, as was their custom, with knives and lances, until

18:19 ᵃA Canaanite goddess

the blood gushed out on them. ²⁹And when midday was past, they prophesied until the *time* of the offering of the *evening* sacrifice. But *there was* no voice; no one answered, no one paid attention.

³⁰Then Elijah said to all the people, "Come near to me." So all the people came near to him. And he repaired the altar of the LORD *that was* broken down. ³¹And Elijah took twelve stones, according to the number of the tribes of the sons of Jacob, to whom the word of the LORD had come, saying, "Israel shall be your name."ᵃ ³²Then with the stones he built an altar in the name of the LORD; and he made a trench around the altar large enough to hold two seahs of seed. ³³And he put the wood in order, cut the bull in pieces, and laid *it* on the wood, and said, "Fill four waterpots with water, and pour *it* on the burnt sacrifice and on the wood." ³⁴Then he said, "Do *it* a second time," and they did *it* a second time; and he said, "Do *it* a third time," and they did *it* a third time. ³⁵So the water ran all around the altar; and he also filled the trench with water.

³⁶And it came to pass, at *the time of* the offering of the *evening* sacrifice, that Elijah the prophet came near and said, "LORD God of Abraham, Isaac, and Israel, let it be known this day that You *are* God in Israel and I *am* Your servant, and *that* I have done all these things at Your word. ³⁷Hear me, O LORD, hear me, that this people may know that You *are* the LORD God, and *that* You have turned their hearts back *to You* again."

³⁸Then the fire of the LORD fell and consumed the burnt sacrifice, and the wood and the stones and the dust, and it licked up the water that *was* in the trench. ³⁹Now when all the people saw *it,* they fell on their faces; and they said, "The LORD, He *is* God! The LORD, He *is* God!"

⁴⁰And Elijah said to them, "Seize the prophets of Baal! Do not let one of them escape!" So they seized them; and Elijah brought them down to the Brook Kishon and executed them there.

THE DROUGHT ENDS

⁴¹Then Elijah said to Ahab, "Go up, eat and drink; for *there is* the sound of abundance of rain." ⁴²So Ahab went up to eat and drink. And Elijah went up to the top of Carmel; then he bowed down on the ground, and put his face between his knees, ⁴³and said to his servant, "Go up now, look toward the sea."

So he went up and looked, and said, "*There is* nothing." And seven times he said, "Go again."

⁴⁴Then it came to pass the seventh *time,* that he said, "There is a cloud, as small as a man's hand, rising out of the sea!" So he said, "Go up, say to Ahab, 'Prepare *your chariot,* and go down before the rain stops you.'"

⁴⁵Now it happened in the meantime that the sky became black with clouds and wind, and there was a heavy rain. So Ahab rode away and went to Jezreel. ⁴⁶Then the hand of the LORD came upon Elijah; and he girded up his loins and ran ahead of Ahab to the entrance of Jezreel.

ELIJAH ESCAPES FROM JEZEBEL

19 And Ahab told Jezebel all that Elijah had done, also how he had executed all the prophets with the sword. ²Then Jezebel sent a messenger to Elijah, saying, "So let the gods do *to me,* and more also, if I do not make your life as the life of one of them by tomorrow about this time." ³And when he saw *that,* he arose and ran for his life, and went to Beersheba, which *belongs* to Judah, and left his servant there.

⁴But he himself went a day's journey into the wilderness, and came and sat down under a broom tree. And he prayed that he might die, and said, "It is enough! Now, LORD, take my life, for I *am* no better than my fathers!"

⁵Then as he lay and slept under a broom tree, suddenly an angelᵃ touched him, and said to him, "Arise *and* eat." ⁶Then he looked, and there by his head *was* a cake baked on coals, and a jar of water. So he ate and drank, and lay down again. ⁷And the angelᵃ of the LORD came back the second time, and touched him, and said, "Arise *and* eat, because the journey *is* too great for you." ⁸So he arose, and ate and drank; and he went in the strength of that food forty days and forty nights as far as Horeb, the mountain of God.

⁹And there he went into a cave, and spent the night in that place; and behold, the word of the LORD *came* to him, and He said to him, "What are you doing here, Elijah?"

¹⁰So he said, "I have been very zealous for the LORD God of hosts; for the children of Israel have

18:31 ªGenesis 32:28   **19:5** ªOr *Angel*   **19:7** ªOr *Angel*

forsaken Your covenant, torn down Your altars, and killed Your prophets with the sword. I alone am left; and they seek to take my life."

God's Revelation to Elijah

¹¹Then He said, "Go out, and stand on the mountain before the LORD." And behold, the LORD passed by, and a great and strong wind tore into the mountains and broke the rocks in pieces before the LORD, *but* the LORD *was* not in the wind; and after the wind an earthquake, *but* the LORD *was* not in the earthquake; ¹²and after the earthquake a fire, *but* the LORD *was* not in the fire; and after the fire a still small voice.

¹³So it was, when Elijah heard *it,* that he wrapped his face in his mantle and went out and stood in the entrance of the cave. Suddenly a voice *came* to him, and said, "What are you doing here, Elijah?"

¹⁴And he said, "I have been very zealous for the LORD God of hosts; because the children of Israel have forsaken Your covenant, torn down Your altars, and killed Your prophets with the sword. I alone am left; and they seek to take my life."

¹⁵Then the LORD said to him: "Go, return on your way to the Wilderness of Damascus; and when you arrive, anoint Hazael *as* king over Syria. ¹⁶Also you shall anoint Jehu the son of Nimshi *as* king over Israel. And Elisha the son of Shaphat of Abel Meholah you shall anoint *as* prophet in your place. ¹⁷It shall be *that* whoever escapes the sword of Hazael, Jehu will kill; and whoever escapes the sword of Jehu, Elisha will kill. ¹⁸Yet I have reserved seven thousand in Israel, all whose knees have not bowed to Baal, and every mouth that has not kissed him."

Elisha Follows Elijah

¹⁹So he departed from there, and found Elisha the son of Shaphat, who *was* plowing *with* twelve yoke *of* oxen before him, and he was with the twelfth. Then Elijah passed by him and threw his mantle on him. ²⁰And he left the oxen and ran after Elijah, and said, "Please let me kiss my father and my mother, and *then* I will follow you."

And he said to him, "Go back again, for what have I done to you?"

²¹So *Elisha* turned back from him, and took a yoke of oxen and slaughtered them and boiled their flesh, using the oxen's equipment, and gave it to the people, and they ate. Then he arose and followed Elijah, and became his servant.

Ahab Defeats the Syrians

20 Now Ben-Hadad the king of Syria gathered all his forces together; thirty-two kings *were* with him, with horses and chariots. And he went up and besieged Samaria, and made war against it. ²Then he sent messengers into the city to Ahab king of Israel, and said to him, "Thus says Ben-Hadad: ³'Your silver and your gold *are* mine; your loveliest wives and children are mine.'"

⁴And the king of Israel answered and said, "My lord, O king, just as you say, I and all that I have *are* yours."

⁵Then the messengers came back and said, "Thus speaks Ben-Hadad, saying, 'Indeed I have sent to you, saying, "You shall deliver to me your silver and your gold, your wives and your children"; ⁶but I will send my servants to you tomorrow about this time, and they shall search your house and the houses of your servants. And it shall be, *that* whatever is pleasant in your eyes, they will put *it* in their hands and take *it.*'"

⁷So the king of Israel called all the elders of the land, and said, "Notice, please, and see how this *man* seeks trouble, for he sent to me for my wives, my children, my silver, and my gold; and I did not deny him."

⁸And all the elders and all the people said to him, "Do not listen or consent."

⁹Therefore he said to the messengers of Ben-Hadad, "Tell my lord the king, 'All that you sent for to your servant the first time I will do, but this thing I cannot do.'"

And the messengers departed and brought back word to him.

¹⁰Then Ben-Hadad sent to him and said, "The gods do so to me, and more also, if enough dust is left of Samaria for a handful for each of the people who follow me."

¹¹So the king of Israel answered and said, "Tell *him,* 'Let not the one who puts on *his armor* boast like the one who takes *it off.*'"

¹²And it happened when *Ben-Hadad* heard this message, as he and the kings *were* drinking at the command post, that he said to his servants,

"Get ready." And they got ready to attack the city.

¹³Suddenly a prophet approached Ahab king of Israel, saying, "Thus says the LORD: 'Have you seen all this great multitude? Behold, I will deliver it into your hand today, and you shall know that I *am* the LORD.'"

¹⁴So Ahab said, "By whom?"

And he said, "Thus says the LORD: 'By the young leaders of the provinces.'"

Then he said, "Who will set the battle in order?"

And he answered, "You."

¹⁵Then he mustered the young leaders of the provinces, and there were two hundred and thirty-two; and after them he mustered all the people, all the children of Israel—seven thousand.

¹⁶So they went out at noon. Meanwhile Ben-Hadad and the thirty-two kings helping him were getting drunk at the command post. ¹⁷The young leaders of the provinces went out first. And Ben-Hadad sent out *a patrol,* and they told him, saying, "Men are coming out of Samaria!" ¹⁸So he said, "If they have come out for peace, take them alive; and if they have come out for war, take them alive."

¹⁹Then these young leaders of the provinces went out of the city with the army which followed them. ²⁰And each one killed his man; so the Syrians fled, and Israel pursued them; and Ben-Hadad the king of Syria escaped on a horse with the cavalry. ²¹Then the king of Israel went out and attacked the horses and chariots, and killed the Syrians with a great slaughter.

²²And the prophet came to the king of Israel and said to him, "Go, strengthen yourself; take note, and see what you should do, for in the spring of the year the king of Syria will come up against you."

The Syrians Again Defeated

²³Then the servants of the king of Syria said to him, "Their gods *are* gods of the hills. Therefore they were stronger than we; but if we fight against them in the plain, surely we will be stronger than they. ²⁴So do this thing: Dismiss the kings, each from his position, and put captains in their places; ²⁵and you shall muster an army like the army that you have lost, horse for horse and chariot for

chariot. Then we will fight against them in the plain; surely we will be stronger than they."

And he listened to their voice and did so.

²⁶So it was, in the spring of the year, that Ben-Hadad mustered the Syrians and went up to Aphek to fight against Israel. ²⁷And the children of Israel were mustered and given provisions, and they went against them. Now the children of Israel encamped before them like two little flocks of goats, while the Syrians filled the countryside.

²⁸Then a man of God came and spoke to the king of Israel, and said, "Thus says the LORD: 'Because the Syrians have said, "The LORD *is* God of the hills, but He *is* not God of the valleys," therefore I will deliver all this great multitude into your hand, and you shall know that I *am* the LORD.'" ²⁹And they encamped opposite each other for seven days. So it was that on the seventh day the battle was joined; and the children of Israel killed one hundred thousand foot soldiers *of* the Syrians in one day. ³⁰But the rest fled to Aphek, into the city; then a wall fell on twenty-seven thousand of the men *who were* left.

And Ben-Hadad fled and went into the city, into an inner chamber.

Ahab's Treaty with Ben-Hadad

³¹Then his servants said to him, "Look now, we have heard that the kings of the house of Israel *are* merciful kings. Please, let us put sackcloth around our waists and ropes around our heads, and go out to the king of Israel; perhaps he will spare your life." ³²So they wore sackcloth around their waists and *put* ropes around their heads, and came to the king of Israel and said, "Your servant Ben-Hadad says, 'Please let me live.'"

And he said, "*Is* he still alive? He *is* my brother."

³³Now the men were watching closely to see whether *any sign of mercy would come* from him; and they quickly grasped *at this word* and said, "Your brother Ben-Hadad."

So he said, "Go, bring him." Then Ben-Hadad came out to him; and he had him come up into the chariot.

³⁴So *Ben-Hadad* said to him, "The cities which my father took from your father I will restore; and you may set up marketplaces for yourself in Damascus, as my father did in Samaria."

Then *Ahab said,* "I will send you away with this treaty." So he made a treaty with him and sent him away.

AHAB CONDEMNED

³⁵Now a certain man of the sons of the prophets said to his neighbor by the word of the LORD, "Strike me, please." And the man refused to strike him. ³⁶Then he said to him, "Because you have not obeyed the voice of the LORD, surely, as soon as you depart from me, a lion shall kill you." And as soon as he left him, a lion found him and killed him.

³⁷And he found another man, and said, "Strike me, please." So the man struck him, inflicting a wound. ³⁸Then the prophet departed and waited for the king by the road, and disguised himself with a bandage over his eyes. ³⁹Now as the king passed by, he cried out to the king and said, "Your servant went out into the midst of the battle; and there, a man came over and brought a man to me, and said, 'Guard this man; if by any means he is missing, your life shall be for his life, or else you shall pay a talent of silver.' ⁴⁰While your servant was busy here and there, he was gone."

Then the king of Israel said to him, "So *shall* your judgment *be;* you yourself have decided *it.*" ⁴¹And he hastened to take the bandage away from his eyes; and the king of Israel recognized him as one of the prophets. ⁴²Then he said to him, "Thus says the LORD: 'Because you have let slip out of *your* hand a man whom I appointed to utter destruction, therefore your life shall go for his life, and your people for his people.' "

⁴³So the king of Israel went to his house sullen and displeased, and came to Samaria.

NABOTH IS MURDERED FOR HIS VINEYARD

21 And it came to pass after these things *that* Naboth the Jezreelite had a vineyard which *was* in Jezreel, next to the palace of Ahab king of Samaria. ²So Ahab spoke to Naboth, saying, "Give me your vineyard, that I may have it for a vegetable garden, because it *is* near, next to my house; and for it I will give you a vineyard better than it. *Or,* if it seems good to you, I will give you its worth in money."

³But Naboth said to Ahab, "The LORD forbid that I should give the inheritance of my fathers to you!"

⁴So Ahab went into his house sullen and displeased because of the word which Naboth the Jezreelite had spoken to him; for he had said, "I will not give you the inheritance of my fathers." And he lay down on his bed, and turned away his face, and would eat no food. ⁵But Jezebel his wife came to him, and said to him, "Why is your spirit so sullen that you eat no food?"

⁶He said to her, "Because I spoke to Naboth the Jezreelite, and said to him, 'Give me your vineyard for money; or else, if it pleases you, I will give you *another* vineyard for it.' And he answered, 'I will not give you my vineyard.' "

⁷Then Jezebel his wife said to him, "You now exercise authority over Israel! Arise, eat food, and let your heart be cheerful; I will give you the vineyard of Naboth the Jezreelite."

⁸And she wrote letters in Ahab's name, sealed *them* with his seal, and sent the letters to the elders and the nobles who *were* dwelling in the city with Naboth. ⁹She wrote in the letters, saying,

> Proclaim a fast, and seat Naboth with high honor among the people; ¹⁰and seat two men, scoundrels, before him to bear witness against him, saying, "You have blasphemed God and the king." *Then* take him out, and stone him, that he may die.

¹¹So the men of his city, the elders and nobles who were inhabitants of his city, did as Jezebel had sent to them, as it *was* written in the letters which she had sent to them. ¹²They proclaimed a fast, and seated Naboth with high honor among the people. ¹³And two men, scoundrels, came in and sat before him; and the scoundrels witnessed against him, against Naboth, in the presence of the people, saying, "Naboth has blasphemed God and the king!" Then they took him outside the city and stoned him with stones, so that he died. ¹⁴Then they sent to Jezebel, saying, "Naboth has been stoned and is dead."

¹⁵And it came to pass, when Jezebel heard that Naboth had been stoned and was dead, that Jezebel said to Ahab, "Arise, take possession of the vineyard of Naboth the Jezreelite, which he refused to give you for money; for Naboth is not

alive, but dead." [16]So it was, when Ahab heard that Naboth was dead, that Ahab got up and went down to take possession of the vineyard of Naboth the Jezreelite.

The Lord Condemns Ahab

[17]Then the word of the LORD came to Elijah the Tishbite, saying, [18]"Arise, go down to meet Ahab king of Israel, who *lives* in Samaria. There *he is,* in the vineyard of Naboth, where he has gone down to take possession of it. [19]You shall speak to him, saying, 'Thus says the LORD: "Have you murdered and also taken possession?" ' And you shall speak to him, saying, 'Thus says the LORD: "In the place where dogs licked the blood of Naboth, dogs shall lick your blood, even yours." ' "

[20]So Ahab said to Elijah, "Have you found me, O my enemy?"

And he answered, "I have found *you,* because you have sold yourself to do evil in the sight of the LORD: [21]Behold, I will bring calamity on you. I will take away your posterity, and will cut off from Ahab every male in Israel, both bond and free. [22]I will make your house like the house of Jeroboam the son of Nebat, and like the house of Baasha the son of Ahijah, because of the provocation with which you have provoked *Me* to anger, and made Israel sin.' [23]And concerning Jezebel the LORD also spoke, saying, 'The dogs shall eat Jezebel by the wall[a] of Jezreel.' [24]The dogs shall eat whoever belongs to Ahab and dies in the city, and the birds of the air shall eat whoever dies in the field."

[25]But there was no one like Ahab who sold himself to do wickedness in the sight of the LORD, because Jezebel his wife stirred him up. [26]And he behaved very abominably in following idols, according to all *that* the Amorites had done, whom the LORD had cast out before the children of Israel.

[27]So it was, when Ahab heard those words, that he tore his clothes and put sackcloth on his body, and fasted and lay in sackcloth, and went about mourning.

[28]And the word of the LORD came to Elijah the Tishbite, saying, [29]"See how Ahab has humbled himself before Me? Because he has humbled himself before Me, I will not bring the calamity in his days. In the days of his son I will bring the calamity on his house."

Micaiah Warns Ahab

22Now three years passed without war between Syria and Israel. [2]Then it came to pass, in the third year, that Jehoshaphat the king of Judah went down to *visit* the king of Israel.

[3]And the king of Israel said to his servants, "Do you know that Ramoth in Gilead *is* ours, but we hesitate to take it out of the hand of the king of Syria?" [4]So he said to Jehoshaphat, "Will you go with me to fight at Ramoth Gilead?"

Jehoshaphat said to the king of Israel, "I *am* as you *are,* my people as your people, my horses as your horses." [5]Also Jehoshaphat said to the king of Israel, "Please inquire for the word of the LORD today."

[6]Then the king of Israel gathered the prophets together, about four hundred men, and said to them, "Shall I go against Ramoth Gilead to fight, or shall I refrain?"

So they said, "Go up, for the Lord will deliver *it* into the hand of the king."

[7]And Jehoshaphat said, "*Is there* not still a prophet of the LORD here, that we may inquire of Him?"[a]

[8]So the king of Israel said to Jehoshaphat, "*There is* still one man, Micaiah the son of Imlah, by whom we may inquire of the LORD; but I hate him, because he does not prophesy good concerning me, but evil."

And Jehoshaphat said, "Let not the king say such things!"

[9]Then the king of Israel called an officer and said, "Bring Micaiah the son of Imlah quickly!"

[10]The king of Israel and Jehoshaphat the king of Judah, having put on *their* robes, sat each on his throne, at a threshing floor at the entrance of the gate of Samaria; and all the prophets prophesied before them. [11]Now Zedekiah the son of Chenaanah had made horns of iron for himself; and he said, "Thus says the LORD: 'With these you shall gore the Syrians until they are destroyed.' "

[12]And all the prophets prophesied so, saying, "Go up to Ramoth Gilead and prosper, for the LORD will deliver *it* into the king's hand."

[13]Then the messenger who had gone to call

21:23 [a]Following Masoretic Text and Septuagint; some Hebrew manuscripts, Syriac, Targum, and Vulgate read *plot of ground* (compare 2 Kings 9:36). 22:7 [a]Or *him*

Micaiah spoke to him, saying, "Now listen, the words of the prophets with one accord encourage the king. Please, let your word be like the word of one of them, and speak encouragement."

[14]And Micaiah said, "*As* the LORD lives, whatever the LORD says to me, that I will speak."

[15]Then he came to the king; and the king said to him, "Micaiah, shall we go to war against Ramoth Gilead, or shall we refrain?"

And he answered him, "Go and prosper, for the LORD will deliver *it* into the hand of the king!"

[16]So the king said to him, "How many times shall I make you swear that you tell me nothing but the truth in the name of the LORD?"

[17]Then he said, "I saw all Israel scattered on the mountains, as sheep that have no shepherd. And the LORD said, 'These have no master. Let each return to his house in peace.' "

[18]And the king of Israel said to Jehoshaphat, "Did I not tell you he would not prophesy good concerning me, but evil?"

[19]Then *Micaiah* said, "Therefore hear the word of the LORD: I saw the LORD sitting on His throne, and all the host of heaven standing by, on His right hand and on His left. [20]And the LORD said, 'Who will persuade Ahab to go up, that he may fall at Ramoth Gilead?' So one spoke in this manner, and another spoke in that manner. [21]Then a spirit came forward and stood before the LORD, and said, 'I will persuade him.' [22]The LORD said to him, 'In what way?' So he said, 'I will go out and be a lying spirit in the mouth of all his prophets.' And the LORD said, 'You shall persuade *him,* and also prevail. Go out and do so.' [23]Therefore look! The LORD has put a lying spirit in the mouth of all these prophets of yours, and the LORD has declared disaster against you."

[24]Now Zedekiah the son of Chenaanah went near and struck Micaiah on the cheek, and said, "Which way did the spirit from the LORD go from me to speak to you?"

[25]And Micaiah said, "Indeed, you shall see on that day when you go into an inner chamber to hide!"

[26]So the king of Israel said, "Take Micaiah, and return him to Amon the governor of the city and to Joash the king's son; [27]and say, 'Thus says the king: "Put this *fellow* in prison, and feed him with bread of affliction and water of affliction, until I come in peace." ' "

[28]But Micaiah said, "If you ever return in peace, the LORD has not spoken by me." And he said, "Take heed, all you people!"

AHAB DIES IN BATTLE

[29]So the king of Israel and Jehoshaphat the king of Judah went up to Ramoth Gilead. [30]And the king of Israel said to Jehoshaphat, "I will disguise myself and go into battle; but you put on your robes." So the king of Israel disguised himself and went into battle.

[31]Now the king of Syria had commanded the thirty-two captains of his chariots, saying, "Fight with no one small or great, but only with the king of Israel." [32]So it was, when the captains of the chariots saw Jehoshaphat, that they said, "Surely it *is* the king of Israel!" Therefore they turned aside to fight against him, and Jehoshaphat cried out. [33]And it happened, when the captains of the chariots saw that it *was* not the king of Israel, that they turned back from pursuing him. [34]Now a *certain* man drew a bow at random, and struck the king of Israel between the joints of his armor. So he said to the driver of his chariot, "Turn around and take me out of the battle, for I am wounded."

[35]The battle increased that day; and the king was propped up in his chariot, facing the Syrians, and died at evening. The blood ran out from the wound onto the floor of the chariot. [36]Then, as the sun was going down, a shout went throughout the army, saying, "Every man to his city, and every man to his own country!"

[37]So the king died, and was brought to Samaria. And they buried the king in Samaria. [38]Then *someone* washed the chariot at a pool in Samaria, and the dogs licked up his blood while the harlots bathed,[a] according to the word of the LORD which He had spoken.

[39]Now the rest of the acts of Ahab, and all that he did, the ivory house which he built and all the cities that he built, *are* they not written in the book of the chronicles of the kings of Israel? [40]So Ahab rested with his fathers. Then Ahaziah his son reigned in his place.

22:38 [a]Syriac and Targum read *they washed his armor.*

Jehoshaphat Reigns in Judah

⁴¹Jehoshaphat the son of Asa had become king over Judah in the fourth year of Ahab king of Israel. ⁴²Jehoshaphat *was* thirty-five years old when he became king, and he reigned twenty-five years in Jerusalem. His mother's name *was* Azubah the daughter of Shilhi. ⁴³And he walked in all the ways of his father Asa. He did not turn aside from them, doing *what was* right in the eyes of the LORD. Nevertheless the high places were not taken away, *for* the people offered sacrifices and burned incense on the high places. ⁴⁴Also Jehoshaphat made peace with the king of Israel.

⁴⁵Now the rest of the acts of Jehoshaphat, the might that he showed, and how he made war, *are* they not written in the book of the chronicles of the kings of Judah? ⁴⁶And the rest of the perverted persons,ᵃ who remained in the days of his father Asa, he banished from the land. ⁴⁷*There was* then no king in Edom, only a deputy of the king.

⁴⁸Jehoshaphat made merchant shipsᵃ to go to Ophir for gold; but they never sailed, for the ships were wrecked at Ezion Geber. ⁴⁹Then Ahaziah the son of Ahab said to Jehoshaphat, "Let my servants go with your servants in the ships." But Jehoshaphat would not.

⁵⁰And Jehoshaphat rested with his fathers, and was buried with his fathers in the City of David his father. Then Jehoram his son reigned in his place.

Ahaziah Reigns in Israel

⁵¹Ahaziah the son of Ahab became king over Israel in Samaria in the seventeenth year of Jehoshaphat king of Judah, and reigned two years over Israel. ⁵²He did evil in the sight of the LORD, and walked in the way of his father and in the way of his mother and in the way of Jeroboam the son of Nebat, who had made Israel sin; ⁵³for he served Baal and worshiped him, and provoked the LORD God of Israel to anger, according to all that his father had done.

22:46 ᵃHebrew *qadesh*, that is, one practicing sodomy and prostitution in religious rituals　　**22:48** ᵃOr *ships of Tarshish*

IMPACT OF THE BOOK

I IDEA *The decline and fall of Israel and Judea is detailed through the decline and fall of its leaders. No matter how dark the times, God still spoke through His faithful prophets to warn both the nation and its leaders. History has proved that the people consistently received the leadership they deserved, and the leadership they chose resulted in judgment.*

M MESSAGE *Several key individuals in 2 Kings stand out for the leadership traits they modeled. Elijah modeled the importance of finishing well, while Elisha demonstrated how valuable a mentor can be. Hezekiah, the most godly king since David, exemplified the value of removing wicked influence from one's life. King Josiah illustrated that true leaders begin by focusing on revival in their own lives so they can lead others to revival.*

P PEOPLE *Ahab, Ahaz, Ahaziah, Elijah, Elisha, Hazael, Hezekiah, Isaiah, Jehoram, Jehu, Jezebel, Joash, Josiah, Naaman, Nebuchadnez-zar*

A AUTHOR *First and 2 Kings were originally one book. No author is listed, although Jeremiah has traditionally been credited with author-ship. Whoever the author was, he drew from earlier historical sources for his writing.*

C CULTURE *The events in this book record the time from King Ahab's death (c. 853 BC) to King Jehoiachin's exile in Babylon (c. 561 BC). The northern kingdom was taken captive in 722 BC by the Assyrian king Sargon II. In 586 BC, the Babylonian king Nebuchadnezzar carried the southern kingdom into captivity. At the close of this book, the Promised Land had been conquered, and the great temple built by Solomon lay in ruins.*

TIMELINE *c. 560 BC*

KEY SCRIPTURE MEMORY VERSES 17:22, 23; 22:11; 23:25; 23:27

God Judges Ahaziah

1 Moab rebelled against Israel after the death of Ahab.

2 Now Ahaziah fell through the lattice of his upper room in Samaria, and was injured; so he sent messengers and said to them, "Go, inquire of Baal-Zebub, the god of Ekron, whether I shall recover from this injury." 3 But the angel[a] of the LORD said to Elijah the Tishbite, "Arise, go up to meet the messengers of the king of Samaria, and say to them, 'Is it because there is no God in Israel that you are going to inquire of Baal-Zebub, the god of Ekron?' 4 Now therefore, thus says the LORD: 'You shall not come down from the bed to which you have gone up, but you shall surely die.'" So Elijah departed.

5 And when the messengers returned to him, he said to them, "Why have you come back?"

6 So they said to him, "A man came up to meet us, and said to us, 'Go, return to the king who sent you, and say to him, "Thus says the LORD: 'Is it because there is no God in Israel that you are sending to inquire of Baal-Zebub, the god of Ekron? Therefore you shall not come down from the bed to which you have gone up, but you shall surely die.'" '"

7 Then he said to them, "What kind of man was it who came up to meet you and told you these words?"

8 So they answered him, "A hairy man wearing a leather belt around his waist."

And he said, "It is Elijah the Tishbite."

9 Then the king sent to him a captain of fifty with his fifty men. So he went up to him; and there he was, sitting on the top of a hill. And he spoke to him: "Man of God, the king has said, 'Come down!'"

10 So Elijah answered and said to the captain of fifty, "If I am a man of God, then let fire come down from heaven and consume you and your fifty men." And fire came down from heaven and consumed him and his fifty. 11 Then he sent to him another captain of fifty with his fifty men.

And he answered and said to him: "Man of God, thus has the king said, 'Come down quickly!'"

12 So Elijah answered and said to them, "If I am a man of God, let fire come down from heaven and consume you and your fifty men." And the fire of God came down from heaven and consumed him and his fifty.

13 Again, he sent a third captain of fifty with his fifty men. And the third captain of fifty went up, and came and fell on his knees before Elijah, and pleaded with him, and said to him: "Man of God, please let my life and the life of these fifty servants of yours be precious in your sight. 14 Look, fire has come down from heaven and burned up the first two captains of fifties with their fifties. But let my life now be precious in your sight."

15 And the angel[a] of the LORD said to Elijah, "Go down with him; do not be afraid of him." So he arose and went down with him to the king. 16 Then he said to him, "Thus says the LORD: 'Because you have sent messengers to inquire of Baal-Zebub, the god of Ekron, is it because there is no God in Israel to inquire of His word? Therefore you shall not come down from the bed to which you have gone up, but you shall surely die.'"

17 So Ahaziah died according to the word of the LORD which Elijah had spoken. Because he had no son, Jehoram[a] became king in his place, in the second year of Jehoram the son of Jehoshaphat, king of Judah.

18 Now the rest of the acts of Ahaziah which he did, are they not written in the book of the chronicles of the kings of Israel?

Elijah Ascends to Heaven

2 And it came to pass, when the LORD was about to take up Elijah into heaven by a whirlwind, that Elijah went with Elisha from Gilgal. 2 Then Elijah said to Elisha, "Stay here, please, for the LORD has sent me on to Bethel."

But Elisha said, "As the LORD lives, and as your soul lives, I will not leave you!" So they went down to Bethel.

3 Now the sons of the prophets who were at Bethel came out to Elisha, and said to him, "Do you know that the LORD will take away your master from over you today?"

And he said, "Yes, I know; keep silent!"

1:3 [a]Or Angel　**1:15** [a]Or Angel　**1:17** [a]The son of Ahab king of Israel (compare 3:1)

INSIDE *the* INFLUENCERS

ELISHA's Leadership Formula

2 KINGS 2:13–15

We were first introduced to Elisha in 1 Kings 19:19–21. He was plowing a field with oxen and Elijah invited him to follow. He made the right decision and left everything else in order to accompany Elijah and to learn. Over the next eight years he ministered to the prophet, and, in return, Elijah mentored him.

Elisha became an effective leader because he embraced a Biblical model for leadership; that is the pattern to learn, practice, and then, teach leadership. He was mentored and befriended by the prophet Elijah for eight years as he "learned" leadership lessons. Elisha learned the meaning of godliness as a man and the purity of ministering to others by serving. He is not mentioned again until 2 Kings 2 where we are privileged to be the audience for his final leadership lessons.

Once again we are reminded of Elisha's loyalty and commitment to Elijah as he refuses to leave him. Elisha's final request of Elijah is not for possessions, popularity, or position. Instead, he asked for the power of God on his life—power that was represented by Elijah's mantle. He was an eye witness to the rapture of Elijah into heaven on a chariot of fire, and at that moment picked up Elijah's mantle (cloak or prophet's garment) and began immediately to serve in the name of the Lord. After Elijah was taxied away by the fiery chariot, Elisha inaugurated the "practice" stage of his leadership by an awesome display of God's power, the first of many in his 50 year ministry.

Once across the Jordan River, he immediately began "teaching" the younger prophets what he had been "learning" and "practicing" for eight years. Elisha demonstrates for us the valuable and successful act of leadership through preparation (learning), application (practicing) and implementation (teaching).

---

⁴Then Elijah said to him, "Elisha, stay here, please, for the LORD has sent me on to Jericho."

But he said, "*As* the LORD lives, and *as* your soul lives, I will not leave you!" So they came to Jericho.

⁵Now the sons of the prophets who *were* at Jericho came to Elisha and said to him, "Do you know that the LORD will take away your master from over you today?"

So he answered, "Yes, I know; keep silent!"

⁶Then Elijah said to him, "Stay here, please, for the LORD has sent me on to the Jordan."

But he said, "*As* the LORD lives, and *as* your soul lives, I will not leave you!" So the two of them went on. ⁷And fifty men of the sons of the prophets went and stood facing *them* at a distance, while the two of them stood by the Jordan. ⁸Now Elijah took his mantle, rolled *it* up, and struck the water; and it was divided this way and that, so that the two of them crossed over on dry ground.

⁹And so it was, when they had crossed over, that Elijah said to Elisha, "Ask! What may I do for you, before I am taken away from you?"

Elisha said, "Please let a double portion of your spirit be upon me."

¹⁰So he said, "You have asked a hard thing. *Nevertheless,* if you see me *when I am* taken from you, it shall be so for you; but if not, it shall not be *so.*" ¹¹Then it happened, as they continued on and talked, that suddenly a chariot of fire *appeared* with horses of fire, and separated the two of them; and Elijah went up by a whirlwind into heaven.

¹²And Elisha saw *it,* and he cried out, "My father, my father, the chariot of Israel and its horsemen!" So he saw him no more. And he took hold

of his own clothes and tore them into two pieces. ¹³He also took up the mantle of Elijah that had fallen from him, and went back and stood by the bank of the Jordan. ¹⁴Then he took the mantle of Elijah that had fallen from him, and struck the water, and said, "Where *is* the LORD God of Elijah?" And when he also had struck the water, it was divided this way and that; and Elisha crossed over.

¹⁵Now when the sons of the prophets who *were* from Jericho saw him, they said, "The spirit of Elijah rests on Elisha." And they came to meet him, and bowed to the ground before him. ¹⁶Then they said to him, "Look now, there are fifty strong men with your servants. Please let them go and search for your master, lest perhaps the Spirit of the LORD has taken him up and cast him upon some mountain or into some valley."

And he said, "You shall not send anyone."

¹⁷But when they urged him till he was ashamed, he said, "Send *them!*" Therefore they sent fifty men, and they searched for three days but did not find him. ¹⁸And when they came back to him, for he had stayed in Jericho, he said to them, "Did I not say to you, 'Do not go'?"

Elisha Performs Miracles

¹⁹Then the men of the city said to Elisha, "Please notice, the situation of this city *is* pleasant, as my lord sees; but the water *is* bad, and the ground barren." ²⁰And he said, "Bring me a new bowl, and put salt in it." So they brought *it* to him. ²¹Then he went out to the source of the water, and cast in the salt there, and said, "Thus says the LORD: 'I have healed this water; from it there shall be no more death or barrenness.' " ²²So the water remains healed to this day, according to the word of Elisha which he spoke.

²³Then he went up from there to Bethel; and as he was going up the road, some youths came from the city and mocked him, and said to him, "Go up, you baldhead! Go up, you baldhead!" ²⁴So he turned around and looked at them, and pronounced a curse on them in the name of the LORD. And two female bears came out of the woods and mauled forty-two of the youths.

²⁵Then he went from there to Mount Carmel, and from there he returned to Samaria.

Moab Rebels Against Israel

3Now Jehoram the son of Ahab became king over Israel at Samaria in the eighteenth year of Jehoshaphat king of Judah, and reigned twelve years. ²And he did evil in the sight of the LORD, but not like his father and mother; for he put away the *sacred* pillar of Baal that his father had made. ³Nevertheless he persisted in the sins of Jeroboam the son of Nebat, who had made Israel sin; he did not depart from them.

⁴Now Mesha king of Moab was a sheepbreeder, and he regularly paid the king of Israel one hundred thousand lambs and the wool of one hundred thousand rams. ⁵But it happened, when Ahab died, that the king of Moab rebelled against the king of Israel.

⁶So King Jehoram went out of Samaria at that time and mustered all Israel. ⁷Then he went and sent to Jehoshaphat king of Judah, saying, "The king of Moab has rebelled against me. Will you go with me to fight against Moab?"

And he said, "I will go up; I *am* as you *are,* my people as your people, my horses as your horses." ⁸Then he said, "Which way shall we go up?"

And he answered, "By way of the Wilderness of Edom."

⁹So the king of Israel went with the king of Judah and the king of Edom, and they marched on that roundabout route seven days; and there was no water for the army, nor for the animals that followed them. ¹⁰And the king of Israel said, "Alas! For the LORD has called these three kings together to deliver them into the hand of Moab."

¹¹But Jehoshaphat said, "*Is there* no prophet of the LORD here, that we may inquire of the LORD by him?"

So one of the servants of the king of Israel answered and said, "Elisha the son of Shaphat *is* here, who poured water on the hands of Elijah."

¹²And Jehoshaphat said, "The word of the LORD is with him." So the king of Israel and Jehoshaphat and the king of Edom went down to him.

¹³Then Elisha said to the king of Israel, "What have I to do with you? Go to the prophets of your father and the prophets of your mother."

But the king of Israel said to him, "No, for

the LORD has called these three kings *together* to deliver them into the hand of Moab."

¹⁴And Elisha said, "*As* the LORD of hosts lives, before whom I stand, surely were it not that I regard the presence of Jehoshaphat king of Judah, I would not look at you, nor see you. ¹⁵But now bring me a musician."

Then it happened, when the musician played, that the hand of the LORD came upon him. ¹⁶And he said, "Thus says the LORD: 'Make this valley full of ditches.' ¹⁷For thus says the LORD: 'You shall not see wind, nor shall you see rain; yet that valley shall be filled with water, so that you, your cattle, and your animals may drink.' ¹⁸And this is a simple matter in the sight of the LORD; He will also deliver the Moabites into your hand. ¹⁹Also you shall attack every fortified city and every choice city, and shall cut down every good tree, and stop up every spring of water, and ruin every good piece of land with stones."

²⁰Now it happened in the morning, when the grain offering was offered, that suddenly water came by way of Edom, and the land was filled with water.

²¹And when all the Moabites heard that the kings had come up to fight against them, all who were able to bear arms and older were gathered; and they stood at the border. ²²Then they rose up early in the morning, and the sun was shining on the water; and the Moabites saw the water on the other side *as* red as blood. ²³And they said, "This *is* blood; the kings have surely struck swords and have killed one another; now therefore, Moab, to the spoil!"

²⁴So when they came to the camp of Israel, Israel rose up and attacked the Moabites, so that they fled before them; and they entered *their* land, killing the Moabites. ²⁵Then they destroyed the cities, and each man threw a stone on every good piece of land and filled it; and they stopped up all the springs of water and cut down all the good trees. But they left the stones of Kir Haraseth *intact*. However the slingers surrounded and attacked it.

²⁶And when the king of Moab saw that the battle was too fierce for him, he took with him seven hundred men who drew swords, to break through to the king of Edom, but they could not. ²⁷Then he took his eldest son who would have

reigned in his place, and offered him *as* a burnt offering upon the wall; and there was great indignation against Israel. So they departed from him and returned to *their own* land.

ELISHA AND THE WIDOW'S OIL

4 A certain woman of the wives of the sons of the prophets cried out to Elisha, saying, "Your servant my husband is dead, and you know that your servant feared the LORD. And the creditor is coming to take my two sons to be his slaves."

²So Elisha said to her, "What shall I do for you? Tell me, what do you have in the house?" And she said, "Your maidservant has nothing in the house but a jar of oil."

³Then he said, "Go, borrow vessels from everywhere, from all your neighbors—empty vessels; do not gather just a few. ⁴And when you have come in, you shall shut the door behind you and your sons; then pour it into all those vessels, and set aside the full ones."

⁵So she went from him and shut the door behind her and her sons, who brought *the vessels* to her; and she poured *it* out. ⁶Now it came to pass, when the vessels were full, that she said to her son, "Bring me another vessel."

And he said to her, "*There is* not another vessel." So the oil ceased. ⁷Then she came and told the man of God. And he said, "Go, sell the oil and pay your debt; and you *and* your sons live on the rest."

ELISHA RAISES THE SHUNAMMITE'S SON

⁸Now it happened one day that Elisha went to Shunem, where there *was* a notable woman, and she persuaded him to eat some food. So it was, as often as he passed by, he would turn in there to eat some food. ⁹And she said to her husband, "Look now, I know that this *is* a holy man of God, who passes by us regularly. ¹⁰Please, let us make a small upper room on the wall; and let us put a bed for him there, and a table and a chair and a lampstand; so it will be, whenever he comes to us, he can turn in there."

¹¹And it happened one day that he came there, and he turned in to the upper room and lay down there. ¹²Then he said to Gehazi his servant, "Call this Shunammite woman." When he had called her, she stood before him. ¹³And he said to

him, "Say now to her, 'Look, you have been concerned for us with all this care. What *can I* do for you? Do you want me to speak on your behalf to the king or to the commander of the army?' "

She answered, "I dwell among my own people."

[14]So he said, "What then *is* to be done for her?"

And Gehazi answered, "Actually, she has no son, and her husband is old."

[15]So he said, "Call her." When he had called her, she stood in the doorway. [16]Then he said, "About this time next year you shall embrace a son."

And she said, "No, my lord. Man of God, do not lie to your maidservant!"

[17]But the woman conceived, and bore a son when the appointed time had come, of which Elisha had told her.

[18]And the child grew. Now it happened one day that he went out to his father, to the reapers. [19]And he said to his father, "My head, my head!"

So he said to a servant, "Carry him to his mother." [20]When he had taken him and brought him to his mother, he sat on her knees till noon, and *then* died. [21]And she went up and laid him on the bed of the man of God, shut *the door* upon him, and went out. [22]Then she called to her husband, and said, "Please send me one of the young men and one of the donkeys, that I may run to the man of God and come back."

[23]So he said, "Why are you going to him today? *It is* neither the New Moon nor the Sabbath."

And she said, "*It is* well." [24]Then she saddled a donkey, and said to her servant, "Drive, and go forward; do not slacken the pace for me unless I tell you." [25]And so she departed, and went to the man of God at Mount Carmel.

So it was, when the man of God saw her afar off, that he said to his servant Gehazi, "Look, the Shunammite woman! [26]Please run now to meet her, and say to her, '*Is it* well with you? *Is it* well with your husband? *Is it* well with the child?' "

And she answered, "*It is* well." [27]Now when she came to the man of God at the hill, she caught him by the feet, but Gehazi came near to push her away. But the man of God said, "Let her alone; for her soul *is* in deep distress, and the

LORD has hidden *it* from me, and has not told me."

[28]So she said, "Did I ask a son of my lord? Did I not say, 'Do not deceive me'?"

[29]Then he said to Gehazi, "Get yourself ready, and take my staff in your hand, and be on your way. If you meet anyone, do not greet him; and if anyone greets you, do not answer him; but lay my staff on the face of the child."

[30]And the mother of the child said, "*As* the LORD lives, and *as* your soul lives, I will not leave you." So he arose and followed her. [31]Now Gehazi went on ahead of them, and laid the staff on the face of the child; but *there was* neither voice nor hearing. Therefore he went back to meet him, and told him, saying, "The child has not awakened."

[32]When Elisha came into the house, there was the child, lying dead on his bed. [33]He went in therefore, shut the door behind the two of them, and prayed to the LORD. [34]And he went up and lay on the child, and put his mouth on his mouth, his eyes on his eyes, and his hands on his hands; and he stretched himself out on the child, and the flesh of the child became warm. [35]He returned and walked back and forth in the house, and again went up and stretched himself out on him; then the child sneezed seven times, and the child opened his eyes. [36]And he called Gehazi and said, "Call this Shunammite woman." So he called her. And when she came in to him, he said, "Pick up your son." [37]So she went in, fell at his feet, and bowed to the ground; then she picked up her son and went out.

ELISHA PURIFIES THE POT OF STEW

[38]And Elisha returned to Gilgal, and *there was* a famine in the land. Now the sons of the prophets *were* sitting before him; and he said to his servant, "Put on the large pot, and boil stew for the sons of the prophets." [39]So one went out into the field to gather herbs, and found a wild vine, and gathered from it a lapful of wild gourds, and came and sliced *them* into the pot of stew, though they did not know *what they were*. [40]Then they served it to the men to eat. Now it happened, as they were eating the stew, that they cried out and said, "Man of God, *there is* death in the pot!" And they could not eat *it*.

⁴¹So he said, "Then bring some flour." And he put *it* into the pot, and said, "Serve *it* to the people, that they may eat." And there was nothing harmful in the pot.

ELISHA FEEDS ONE HUNDRED MEN

⁴²Then a man came from Baal Shalisha, and brought the man of God bread of the firstfruits, twenty loaves of barley bread, and newly ripened grain in his knapsack. And he said, "Give *it* to the people, that they may eat."

⁴³But his servant said, "What? Shall I set this before one hundred men?"

He said again, "Give it to the people, that they may eat; for thus says the LORD: 'They shall eat and have *some* left over.' " ⁴⁴So he set *it* before them; and they ate and had *some* left over, according to the word of the LORD.

NAAMAN'S LEPROSY HEALED

5 Now Naaman, commander of the army of the king of Syria, was a great and honorable man in the eyes of his master, because by him the LORD had given victory to Syria. He was also a mighty man of valor, *but* a leper. ²And the Syrians had gone out on raids, and had brought back captive a young girl from the land of Israel. She waited on Naaman's wife. ³Then she said to her mistress, "If only my master *were* with the prophet who *is* in Samaria! For he would heal him of his leprosy." ⁴And *Naaman* went in and told his master, saying, "Thus and thus said the girl who *is* from the land of Israel."

⁵Then the king of Syria said, "Go now, and I will send a letter to the king of Israel."

So he departed and took with him ten talents of silver, six thousand *shekels* of gold, and ten changes of clothing. ⁶Then he brought the letter to the king of Israel, which said,

Now be advised, when this letter comes to you, that I have sent Naaman my servant to you, that you may heal him of his leprosy.

⁷And it happened, when the king of Israel read the letter, that he tore his clothes and said, "Am I God, to kill and make alive, that this man sends a man to me to heal him of his leprosy? Therefore please consider, and see how he seeks a quarrel with me."

⁸So it was, when Elisha the man of God heard that the king of Israel had torn his clothes, that he sent to the king, saying, "Why have you torn your clothes? Please let him come to me, and he shall know that there is a prophet in Israel."

⁹Then Naaman went with his horses and chariot, and he stood at the door of Elisha's house. ¹⁰And Elisha sent a messenger to him, saying, "Go and wash in the Jordan seven times, and your flesh shall be restored to you, and *you shall* be clean." ¹¹But Naaman became furious, and went away and said, "Indeed, I said to myself, 'He will surely come out *to me,* and stand and call on the name of the LORD his God, and wave his hand over the place, and heal the leprosy.' ¹²*Are* not the Abanah[a] and the Pharpar, the rivers of Damascus, better than all the waters of Israel? Could I not wash in them and be clean?" So he turned and went away in a rage. ¹³And his servants came near and spoke to him, and said, "My father, *if* the prophet had told you *to do* something great, would you not have done *it?* How much more then, when he says to you, 'Wash, and be clean'?" ¹⁴So he went down and dipped seven times in the Jordan, according to the saying of the man of God; and his flesh was restored like the flesh of a little child, and he was clean.

¹⁵And he returned to the man of God, he and all his aides, and came and stood before him; and he said, "Indeed, now I know that *there is* no God in all the earth, except in Israel; now therefore, please take a gift from your servant."

¹⁶But he said, "*As* the LORD lives, before whom I stand, I will receive nothing." And he urged him to take *it,* but he refused.

¹⁷So Naaman said, "Then, if not, please let your servant be given two mule-loads of earth; for your servant will no longer offer either burnt offering or sacrifice to other gods, but to the LORD. ¹⁸Yet in this thing may the LORD pardon your servant: when my master goes into the temple of Rimmon to worship there, and he leans on my hand, and I bow down in the temple of Rimmon—when I bow down in the temple of Rimmon, may the LORD please pardon your servant in this thing."

5:12 ªFollowing Kethib, Septuagint, and Vulgate; Qere, Syriac, and Targum read *Amanah.*

[19]Then he said to him, "Go in peace." So he departed from him a short distance.

GEHAZI'S GREED

[20]But Gehazi, the servant of Elisha the man of God, said, "Look, my master has spared Naaman this Syrian, while not receiving from his hands what he brought; but as the LORD lives, I will run after him and take something from him." [21]So Gehazi pursued Naaman. When Naaman saw him running after him, he got down from the chariot to meet him, and said, "Is all well?"

[22]And he said, "All is well. My master has sent me, saying, 'Indeed, just now two young men of the sons of the prophets have come to me from the mountains of Ephraim. Please give them a talent of silver and two changes of garments.' "

[23]So Naaman said, "Please, take two talents." And he urged him, and bound two talents of silver in two bags, with two changes of garments, and handed them to two of his servants; and they carried them on ahead of him. [24]When he came to the citadel, he took them from their hand, and stored them away in the house; then he let the men go, and they departed. [25]Now he went in and stood before his master. Elisha said to him, "Where did you go, Gehazi?"

And he said, "Your servant did not go anywhere."

[26]Then he said to him, "Did not my heart go with you when the man turned back from his chariot to meet you? Is it time to receive money and to receive clothing, olive groves and vineyards, sheep and oxen, male and female servants? [27]Therefore the leprosy of Naaman shall cling to you and your descendants forever." And he went out from his presence leprous, as white as snow.

THE FLOATING AX HEAD

6 And the sons of the prophets said to Elisha, "See now, the place where we dwell with you is too small for us. [2]Please, let us go to the Jordan, and let every man take a beam from there, and let us make there a place where we may dwell."

So he answered, "Go."

[3]Then one said, "Please consent to go with your servants."

And he answered, "I will go." [4]So he went with them. And when they came to the Jordan, they cut down trees. [5]But as one was cutting down a tree, the iron ax head fell into the water; and he cried out and said, "Alas, master! For it was borrowed."

[6]So the man of God said, "Where did it fall?" And he showed him the place. So he cut off a stick, and threw it in there; and he made the iron float. [7]Therefore he said, "Pick it up for yourself." So he reached out his hand and took it.

THE BLINDED SYRIANS CAPTURED

[8]Now the king of Syria was making war against Israel; and he consulted with his servants, saying, "My camp will be in such and such a place." [9]And the man of God sent to the king of Israel, saying, "Beware that you do not pass this place, for the Syrians are coming down there." [10]Then the king of Israel sent someone to the place of which the man of God had told him. Thus he warned him, and he was watchful there, not just once or twice.

[11]Therefore the heart of the king of Syria was greatly troubled by this thing; and he called his servants and said to them, "Will you not show me which of us is for the king of Israel?"

[12]And one of his servants said, "None, my lord, O king; but Elisha, the prophet who is in Israel, tells the king of Israel the words that you speak in your bedroom."

[13]So he said, "Go and see where he is, that I may send and get him."

And it was told him, saying, "Surely he is in Dothan."

[14]Therefore he sent horses and chariots and a great army there, and they came by night and surrounded the city. [15]And when the servant of the man of God arose early and went out, there was an army, surrounding the city with horses and chariots. And his servant said to him, "Alas, my master! What shall we do?"

[16]So he answered, "Do not fear, for those who are with us are more than those who are with them." [17]And Elisha prayed, and said, "LORD, I pray, open his eyes that he may see." Then the LORD opened the eyes of the young man, and he saw. And behold, the mountain was full of horses and chariots of fire all around Elisha. [18]So when the Syrians came down to him, Elisha prayed to the LORD, and said, "Strike this people, I pray,

with blindness." And He struck them with blindness according to the word of Elisha.

¹⁹Now Elisha said to them, "This *is* not the way, nor *is* this the city. Follow me, and I will bring you to the man whom you seek." But he led them to Samaria.

²⁰So it was, when they had come to Samaria, that Elisha said, "LORD, open the eyes of these *men,* that they may see." And the LORD opened their eyes, and they saw; and there *they were,* inside Samaria!

²¹Now when the king of Israel saw them, he said to Elisha, "My father, shall I kill *them?* Shall I kill *them?*"

²²But he answered, "You shall not kill *them.* Would you kill those whom you have taken captive with your sword and your bow? Set food and water before them, that they may eat and drink and go to their master." ²³Then he prepared a great feast for them; and after they ate and drank, he sent them away and they went to their master. So the bands of Syrian *raiders* came no more into the land of Israel.

Syria Besieges Samaria in Famine

²⁴And it happened after this that Ben-Hadad king of Syria gathered all his army, and went up and besieged Samaria. ²⁵And there was a great famine in Samaria; and indeed they besieged it until a donkey's head was *sold* for eighty *shekels* of silver, and one-fourth of a kab of dove droppings for five *shekels* of silver.

²⁶Then, as the king of Israel was passing by on the wall, a woman cried out to him, saying, "Help, my lord, O king!"

²⁷And he said, "If the LORD does not help you, where can I find help for you? From the threshing floor or from the winepress?" ²⁸Then the king said to her, "What is troubling you?"

And she answered, "This woman said to me, 'Give your son, that we may eat him today, and we will eat my son tomorrow.' ²⁹So we boiled my son, and ate him. And I said to her on the next day, 'Give your son, that we may eat him'; but she has hidden her son."

³⁰Now it happened, when the king heard the words of the woman, that he tore his clothes; and as he passed by on the wall, the people looked, and there underneath *he had* sackcloth on his

body. ³¹Then he said, "God do so to me and more also, if the head of Elisha the son of Shaphat remains on him today!"

³²But Elisha was sitting in his house, and the elders were sitting with him. And *the king* sent a man ahead of him, but before the messenger came to him, he said to the elders, "Do you see how this son of a murderer has sent someone to take away my head? Look, when the messenger comes, shut the door, and hold him fast at the door. *Is* not the sound of his master's feet behind him?" ³³And while he was still talking with them, there was the messenger, coming down to him; and then *the king* said, "Surely this calamity *is* from the LORD; why should I wait for the LORD any longer?"

7 Then Elisha said, "Hear the word of the LORD. Thus says the LORD: 'Tomorrow about this time a seah of fine flour *shall be sold* for a shekel, and two seahs of barley for a shekel, at the gate of Samaria.' "

²So an officer on whose hand the king leaned answered the man of God and said, "Look, *if* the LORD would make windows in heaven, could this thing be?"

And he said, "In fact, you shall see *it* with your eyes, but you shall not eat of it."

The Syrians Flee

³Now there were four leprous men at the entrance of the gate; and they said to one another, "Why are we sitting here until we die? ⁴If we say, 'We will enter the city,' the famine *is* in the city, and we shall die there. And if we sit here, we die also. Now therefore, come, let us surrender to the army of the Syrians. If they keep us alive, we shall live; and if they kill us, we shall only die." ⁵And they rose at twilight to go to the camp of the Syrians; and when they had come to the outskirts of the Syrian camp, to their surprise no one *was* there. ⁶For the Lord had caused the army of the Syrians to hear the noise of chariots and the noise of horses—the noise of a great army; so they said to one another, "Look, the king of Israel has hired against us the kings of the Hittites and the kings of the Egyptians to attack us!" ⁷Therefore they arose and fled at twilight, and left the camp intact—their tents, their horses, and their donkeys—and they fled for their lives. ⁸And when

these lepers came to the outskirts of the camp, they went into one tent and ate and drank, and carried from it silver and gold and clothing, and went and hid *them;* then they came back and entered another tent, and carried *some* from there *also,* and went and hid *it.*

9Then they said to one another, "We are not doing right. This day *is* a day of good news, and we remain silent. If we wait until morning light, some punishment will come upon us. Now therefore, come, let us go and tell the king's household." 10So they went and called to the gatekeepers of the city, and told them, saying, "We went to the Syrian camp, and surprisingly no one *was* there, not a human sound—only horses and donkeys tied, and the tents intact." 11And the gatekeepers called out, and they told *it* to the king's household inside.

12So the king arose in the night and said to his servants, "Let me now tell you what the Syrians have done to us. They know that we *are* hungry; therefore they have gone out of the camp to hide themselves in the field, saying, 'When they come out of the city, we shall catch them alive, and get into the city.'"

13And one of his servants answered and said, "Please, let several *men* take five of the remaining horses which are left in the city. Look, they *may either become* like all the multitude of Israel that are left in it; or indeed, *I say,* they *may become* like all the multitude of Israel left from those who are consumed; so let us send them and see." 14Therefore they took two chariots with horses; and the king sent them in the direction of the Syrian army, saying, "Go and see." 15And they went after them to the Jordan; and indeed all the road *was* full of garments and weapons which the Syrians had thrown away in their haste. So the messengers returned and told the king. 16Then the people went out and plundered the tents of the Syrians. So a seah of fine flour was *sold* for a shekel, and two seahs of barley for a shekel, according to the word of the LORD.

17Now the king had appointed the officer on whose hand he leaned to have charge of the gate. But the people trampled him in the gate, and he died, just as the man of God had said, who spoke when the king came down to him. 18So it happened just as the man of God had spoken to the king, saying, "Two seahs of barley for a shekel, and a seah of fine flour for a shekel, shall be *sold* tomorrow about this time in the gate of Samaria."

19Then that officer had answered the man of God, and said, "Now look, *if* the LORD would make windows in heaven, could such a thing be?"

And he had said, "In fact, you shall see *it* with your eyes, but you shall not eat of it." 20And so it happened to him, for the people trampled him in the gate, and he died.

THE KING RESTORES THE SHUNAMMITE'S LAND

8 Then Elisha spoke to the woman whose son he had restored to life, saying, "Arise and go, you and your household, and stay wherever you can; for the LORD has called for a famine, and furthermore, it will come upon the land for seven years." 2So the woman arose and did according to the saying of the man of God, and she went with her household and dwelt in the land of the Philistines seven years.

3It came to pass, at the end of seven years, that the woman returned from the land of the Philistines; and she went to make an appeal to the king for her house and for her land. 4Then the king talked with Gehazi, the servant of the man of God, saying, "Tell me, please, all the great things Elisha has done." 5Now it happened, as he was telling the king how he had restored the dead to life, that there was the woman whose son he had restored to life, appealing to the king for her house and for her land. And Gehazi said, "My lord, O king, this *is* the woman, and this *is* her son whom Elisha restored to life." 6And when the king asked the woman, she told him.

So the king appointed a certain officer for her, saying, "Restore all that *was* hers, and all the proceeds of the field from the day that she left the land until now."

DEATH OF BEN-HADAD

7Then Elisha went to Damascus, and Ben-Hadad king of Syria was sick; and it was told him, saying, "The man of God has come here." 8And the king said to Hazael, "Take a present in your hand, and go to meet the man of God, and inquire of the LORD by him, saying, 'Shall I recover from this disease?'" 9So Hazael went to meet him and took a present with him, of every good thing of Damascus, forty camel-loads; and he came and stood before him, and said, "Your son Ben-Hadad king of Syria has sent me to you, saying, 'Shall I recover from this disease?' "

[10]And Elisha said to him, "Go, say to him, 'You shall certainly recover.' However the LORD has shown me that he will really die." [11]Then he set his countenance in a stare until he was ashamed; and the man of God wept. [12]And Hazael said, "Why is my lord weeping?"

He answered, "Because I know the evil that you will do to the children of Israel: Their strongholds you will set on fire, and their young men you will kill with the sword; and you will dash their children, and rip open their women with child."

[13]So Hazael said, "But what is your servant—a dog, that he should do this gross thing?"

And Elisha answered, "The LORD has shown me that you will become king over Syria."

[14]Then he departed from Elisha, and came to his master, who said to him, "What did Elisha say to you?" And he answered, "He told me you would surely recover." [15]But it happened on the next day that he took a thick cloth and dipped it in water, and spread it over his face so that he died; and Hazael reigned in his place.

Jehoram Reigns in Judah

[16]Now in the fifth year of Joram the son of Ahab, king of Israel, Jehoshaphat having been king of Judah, Jehoram the son of Jehoshaphat began to reign as king of Judah. [17]He was thirty-two years old when he became king, and he reigned eight years in Jerusalem. [18]And he walked in the way of the kings of Israel, just as the house of Ahab had done, for the daughter of Ahab was his wife; and he did evil in the sight of the LORD. [19]Yet the LORD would not destroy Judah, for the sake of His servant David, as He promised him to give a lamp to him and his sons forever.

[20]In his days Edom revolted against Judah's authority, and made a king over themselves. [21]So Joram[a] went to Zair, and all his chariots with him. Then he rose by night and attacked the Edomites who had surrounded him and the captains of the chariots; and the troops fled to their tents. [22]Thus Edom has been in revolt against Judah's authority to this day. And Libnah revolted at that time.

[23]Now the rest of the acts of Joram, and all that he did, are they not written in the book of the chronicles of the kings of Judah? [24]So Joram rested with his fathers, and was buried with his fathers in the City of David. Then Ahaziah his son reigned in his place.

Ahaziah Reigns in Judah

[25]In the twelfth year of Joram the son of Ahab, king of Israel, Ahaziah the son of Jehoram, king of Judah, began to reign. [26]Ahaziah was twenty-two years old when he became king, and he reigned one year in Jerusalem. His mother's name was Athaliah the granddaughter of Omri, king of Israel. [27]And he walked in the way of the house of Ahab, and did evil in the sight of the LORD, like the house of Ahab, for he was the son-in-law of the house of Ahab.

[28]Now he went with Joram the son of Ahab to war against Hazael king of Syria at Ramoth Gilead; and the Syrians wounded Joram. [29]Then King Joram went back to Jezreel to recover from the wounds which the Syrians had inflicted on him at Ramah, when he fought against Hazael king of Syria. And Ahaziah the son of Jehoram, king of Judah, went down to see Joram the son of Ahab in Jezreel, because he was sick.

Jehu Anointed King of Israel

9 And Elisha the prophet called one of the sons of the prophets, and said to him, "Get yourself ready, take this flask of oil in your hand, and go to Ramoth Gilead. [2]Now when you arrive at that place, look there for Jehu the son of Jehoshaphat, the son of Nimshi, and go in and make him rise up from among his associates, and take him to an inner room. [3]Then take the flask of oil, and pour it on his head, and say, 'Thus says the LORD: "I have anointed you king over Israel." ' Then open the door and flee, and do not delay."

[4]So the young man, the servant of the prophet, went to Ramoth Gilead. [5]And when he arrived, there were the captains of the army sitting; and he said, "I have a message for you, Commander."

Jehu said, "For which one of us?"

And he said, "For you, Commander." [6]Then

8:21 [a]Spelled Jehoram in verse 16

he arose and went into the house. And he poured the oil on his head, and said to him, "Thus says the LORD God of Israel:'I have anointed you king over the people of the LORD, over Israel. [7]You shall strike down the house of Ahab your master, that I may avenge the blood of My servants the prophets, and the blood of all the servants of the LORD, at the hand of Jezebel. [8]For the whole house of Ahab shall perish; and I will cut off from Ahab all the males in Israel, both bond and free. [9]So I will make the house of Ahab like the house of Jeroboam the son of Nebat, and like the house of Baasha the son of Ahijah. [10]The dogs shall eat Jezebel on the plot *of ground* at Jezreel, and *there shall be* none to bury *her.*' " And he opened the door and fled.

[11]Then Jehu came out to the servants of his master, and *one* said to him, "*Is* all well? Why did this madman come to you?"

And he said to them, "You know the man and his babble."

[12]And they said, "A lie! Tell us now."

So he said, "Thus and thus he spoke to me, saying, 'Thus says the LORD: "I have anointed you king over Israel." ' "

[13]Then each man hastened to take his garment and put *it* under him on the top of the steps; and they blew trumpets, saying, "Jehu is king!"

JORAM OF ISRAEL KILLED

[14]So Jehu the son of Jehoshaphat, the son of Nimshi, conspired against Joram. (Now Joram had been defending Ramoth Gilead, he and all Israel, against Hazael king of Syria. [15]But King Joram had returned to Jezreel to recover from the wounds which the Syrians had inflicted on him when he fought with Hazael king of Syria.) And Jehu said, "If you are so minded, let no one leave *or* escape from the city to go and tell *it* in Jezreel." [16]So Jehu rode in a chariot and went to Jezreel, for Joram was laid up there; and Ahaziah king of Judah had come down to see Joram.

[17]Now a watchman stood on the tower in Jezreel, and he saw the company of Jehu as he came, and said, "I see a company of men."

And Joram said, "Get a horseman and send him to meet them, and let him say, '*Is it* peace?' "

[18]So the horseman went to meet him, and said, "Thus says the king:'*Is it* peace?' "

And Jehu said, "What have you to do with peace? Turn around and follow me."

So the watchman reported, saying, "The messenger went to them, but is not coming back."

[19]Then he sent out a second horseman who came to them, and said, "Thus says the king:'*Is it* peace?' "

And Jehu answered, "What have you to do with peace? Turn around and follow me."

[20]So the watchman reported, saying, "He went up to them and is not coming back; and the driving *is* like the driving of Jehu the son of Nimshi, for he drives furiously!"

[21]Then Joram said, "Make ready." And his chariot was made ready. Then Joram king of Israel and Ahaziah king of Judah went out, each in his chariot; and they went out to meet Jehu, and met him on the property of Naboth the Jezreelite. [22]Now it happened, when Joram saw Jehu, that he said, "*Is it* peace, Jehu?"

So he answered, "What peace, as long as the harlotries of your mother Jezebel and her witchcraft *are so* many?"

[23]Then Joram turned around and fled, and said to Ahaziah, "Treachery, Ahaziah!" [24]Now Jehu drew his bow with full strength and shot Jehoram between his arms; and the arrow came out at his heart, and he sank down in his chariot. [25]Then *Jehu* said to Bidkar his captain, "Pick *him* up, *and* throw him into the tract of the field of Naboth the Jezreelite; for remember, when you and I were riding together behind Ahab his father, that the LORD laid this burden upon him: [26]'Surely I saw yesterday the blood of Naboth and the blood of his sons,' says the LORD, 'and I will repay you in this plot,' says the LORD. Now therefore, take *and* throw him on the plot *of ground,* according to the word of the LORD."

AHAZIAH OF JUDAH KILLED

[27]But when Ahaziah king of Judah saw *this,* he fled by the road to Beth Haggan.[a] So Jehu pursued him, and said, "Shoot him also in the chariot." *And they shot him* at the Ascent of Gur, which is by Ibleam. Then he fled to Megiddo, and died there. [28]And his servants carried him in the chariot to Jerusalem, and buried him in his tomb

9:27 [a]Literally *The Garden House*

with his fathers in the City of David. ²⁹In the eleventh year of Joram the son of Ahab, Ahaziah had become king over Judah.

JEZEBEL'S VIOLENT DEATH

³⁰Now when Jehu had come to Jezreel, Jezebel heard *of it;* and she put paint on her eyes and adorned her head, and looked through a window. ³¹Then, as Jehu entered at the gate, she said, "*Is it* peace, Zimri, murderer of your master?"

³²And he looked up at the window, and said, "Who *is* on my side? Who?" So two *or* three eunuchs looked out at him. ³³Then he said, "Throw her down." So they threw her down, and *some* of her blood spattered on the wall and on the horses; and he trampled her underfoot. ³⁴And when he had gone in, he ate and drank. Then he said, "Go now, see to this accursed *woman,* and bury her, for she was a king's daughter." ³⁵So they went to bury her, but they found no more of her than the skull and the feet and the palms of *her* hands. ³⁶Therefore they came back and told him. And he said, "This *is* the word of the LORD, which He spoke by His servant Elijah the Tishbite, saying, 'On the plot *of ground* at Jezreel dogs shall eat the flesh of Jezebel;ᵃ ³⁷and the corpse of Jezebel shall be as refuse on the surface of the field, in the plot at Jezreel, so that they shall not say, "Here *lies* Jezebel."' "

AHAB'S SEVENTY SONS KILLED

10 Now Ahab had seventy sons in Samaria. And Jehu wrote and sent letters to Samaria, to the rulers of Jezreel,ᵃ to the elders, and to those who reared Ahab's *sons,* saying:

²Now as soon as this letter comes to you, since your master's sons *are* with you, and you have chariots and horses, a fortified city also, and weapons, ³choose the best qualified of your master's sons, set *him* on his father's throne, and fight for your master's house.

⁴But they were exceedingly afraid, and said, Look, two kings could not stand up to him; how then can we stand?" ⁵And he who *was* in charge of the house, and he who *was* in charge of the city, the elders also, and those who reared *the sons,*

sent to Jehu, saying, "We *are* your servants, we will do all you tell us; but we will not make anyone king. Do *what is* good in your sight." ⁶Then he wrote a second letter to them, saying:

> If you *are* for me and will obey my voice, take the heads of the men, your master's sons, and come to me at Jezreel by this time tomorrow.

Now the king's sons, seventy persons, *were* with the great men of the city, *who* were rearing them. ⁷So it was, when the letter came to them, that they took the king's sons and slaughtered seventy persons, put their heads in baskets and sent *them* to him at Jezreel.

⁸Then a messenger came and told him, saying, "They have brought the heads of the king's sons."

And he said, "Lay them in two heaps at the entrance of the gate until morning."

⁹So it was, in the morning, that he went out and stood, and said to all the people, "You *are* righteous. Indeed I conspired against my master and killed him; but who killed all these? ¹⁰Know now that nothing shall fall to the earth of the word of the LORD which the LORD spoke concerning the house of Ahab; for the LORD has done what He spoke by His servant Elijah." ¹¹So Jehu killed all who remained of the house of Ahab in Jezreel, and all his great men and his close acquaintances and his priests, until he left him none remaining.

AHAZIAH'S FORTY-TWO BROTHERS KILLED

¹²And he arose and departed and went to Samaria. On the way, at Beth Ekedᵃ of the Shepherds, ¹³Jehu met with the brothers of Ahaziah king of Judah, and said, "Who *are* you?"

So they answered, "We *are* the brothers of Ahaziah; we have come down to greet the sons of the king and the sons of the queen mother."

¹⁴And he said, "Take them alive!" So they took them alive, and killed them at the well of Beth Eked, forty-two men; and he left none of them.

9:36 ᵃ1 Kings 21:23   **10:1** ᵃFollowing Masoretic Text, Syriac, and Targum; Septuagint reads *Samaria;* Vulgate reads *city.*   **10:12** ᵃOr *The Shearing House*

THE REST OF AHAB'S FAMILY KILLED

[15]Now when he departed from there, he met Jehonadab the son of Rechab, *coming* to meet him; and he greeted him and said to him, "Is your heart right, as my heart *is* toward your heart?"

And Jehonadab answered, "It is."

Jehu said, "If it is, give *me* your hand." So he gave *him* his hand, and he took him up to him into the chariot. [16]Then he said, "Come with me, and see my zeal for the LORD." So they had him ride in his chariot. [17]And when he came to Samaria, he killed all who remained to Ahab in Samaria, till he had destroyed them, according to the word of the LORD which He spoke to Elijah.

WORSHIPERS OF BAAL KILLED

[18]Then Jehu gathered all the people together, and said to them, "Ahab served Baal a little, Jehu will serve him much. [19]Now therefore, call to me all the prophets of Baal, all his servants, and all his priests. Let no one be missing, for I have a great sacrifice for Baal. Whoever is missing shall not live." But Jehu acted deceptively, with the intent of destroying the worshipers of Baal. [20]And Jehu said, "Proclaim a solemn assembly for Baal." So they proclaimed *it.* [21]Then Jehu sent throughout all Israel; and all the worshipers of Baal came, so that there was not a man left who did not come. So they came into the temple[a] of Baal, and the temple of Baal was full from one end to the other. [22]And he said to the one in charge of the wardrobe, "Bring out vestments for all the worshipers of Baal." So he brought out vestments for them. [23]Then Jehu and Jehonadab the son of Rechab went into the temple of Baal, and said to the worshipers of Baal, "Search and see that no servants of the LORD are here with you, but only the worshipers of Baal." [24]So they went in to offer sacrifices and burnt offerings. Now Jehu had appointed for himself eighty men on the outside, and had said, "*If* any of the men whom I have brought into your hands escapes, *whoever lets him escape, it shall be* his life for the life of the other."

[25]Now it happened, as soon as he had made an end of offering the burnt offering, that Jehu said to the guard and to the captains, "Go in *and* kill them; let no one come out!" And they killed them with the edge of the sword; then the guards and the officers threw *them* out, and went into the inner room of the temple of Baal. [26]And they brought the *sacred* pillars out of the temple of Baal and burned them. [27]Then they broke down the *sacred* pillar of Baal, and tore down the temple of Baal and made it a refuse dump to this day. [28]Thus Jehu destroyed Baal from Israel.

[29]However Jehu did not turn away from the sins of Jeroboam the son of Nebat, who had made Israel sin, *that is,* from the golden calves that *were* at Bethel and Dan. [30]And the LORD said to Jehu, "Because you have done well in doing *what is* right in My sight, *and* have done to the house of Ahab all that *was* in My heart, your sons shall sit on the throne of Israel to the fourth *generation.*" [31]But Jehu took no heed to walk in the law of the LORD God of Israel with all his heart; for he did not depart from the sins of Jeroboam, who had made Israel sin.

DEATH OF JEHU

[32]In those days the LORD began to cut off *parts* of Israel; and Hazael conquered them in all the territory of Israel [33]from the Jordan eastward all the land of Gilead—Gad, Reuben, and Manasseh—from Aroer, which *is* by the River Arnon, including Gilead and Bashan.

[34]Now the rest of the acts of Jehu, all that he did, and all his might, *are* they not written in the book of the chronicles of the kings of Israel? [35]So Jehu rested with his fathers, and they buried him in Samaria. Then Jehoahaz his son reigned in his place. [36]And the period that Jehu reigned over Israel in Samaria *was* twenty-eight years.

ATHALIAH REIGNS IN JUDAH

11 When Athaliah the mother of Ahaziah saw that her son was dead, she arose and destroyed all the royal heirs. [2]But Jehosheba, the daughter of King Joram, sister of Ahaziah, took Joash the son of Ahaziah, and stole him away from among the king's sons *who were* being murdered; and they hid him and his nurse in the bedroom, from Athaliah, so that he was not killed. [3]So he was hidden with her in the house of the LORD for six years, while Athaliah reigned over the land.

10:21 [a]Literally *house,* and so elsewhere in this chapter

JOASH CROWNED KING OF JUDAH

4In the seventh year Jehoiada sent and brought the captains of hundreds—of the bodyguards and the escorts—and brought them into the house of the LORD to him. And he made a covenant with them and took an oath from them in the house of the LORD, and showed them the king's son. 5Then he commanded them, saying, "This *is* what you shall do: One-third of you who come on duty on the Sabbath shall be keeping watch over the king's house, 6one-third *shall be* at the gate of Sur, and one-third at the gate behind the escorts. You shall keep the watch of the house, lest it be broken down. 7The two contingents of you who go off duty on the Sabbath shall keep the watch of the house of the LORD for the king. 8But you shall surround the king on all sides, every man with his weapons in his hand; and whoever comes within range, let him be put to death. You are to be with the king as he goes out and as he comes in."

9So the captains of the hundreds did according to all that Jehoiada the priest commanded. Each of them took his men who were to be on duty on the Sabbath, with those who were going off duty on the Sabbath, and came to Jehoiada the priest. 10And the priest gave the captains of hundreds the spears and shields which *had belonged* to King David, that were in the temple of the LORD. 11Then the escorts stood, every man with his weapons in his hand, all around the king, from the right side of the temple to the left side of the temple, by the altar and the house. 12And he brought out the king's son, put the crown on him, and *gave him* the Testimony;a they made him king and anointed him, and they clapped their hands and said, "Long live the king!"

DEATH OF ATHALIAH

13Now when Athaliah heard the noise of the escorts *and* the people, she came to the people *in* the temple of the LORD. 14When she looked, there was the king standing by a pillar according to custom; and the leaders and the trumpeters were by the king. All the people of the land were rejoicing and blowing trumpets. So Athaliah tore her clothes and cried out, "Treason! Treason!"

15And Jehoiada the priest commanded the captains of the hundreds, the officers of the army, and said to them, "Take her outside under guard, and slay with the sword whoever follows her." For the priest had said, "Do not let her be killed in the house of the LORD." 16So they seized her; and she went by way of the horses' entrance *into* the king's house, and there she was killed.

17Then Jehoiada made a covenant between the LORD, the king, and the people, that they should be the LORD's people, and *also* between the king and the people. 18And all the people of the land went to the temple of Baal, and tore it down. They thoroughly broke in pieces its altars and images, and killed Mattan the priest of Baal before the altars. And the priest appointed officers over the house of the LORD. 19Then he took the captains of hundreds, the bodyguards, the escorts, and all the people of the land; and they brought the king down from the house of the LORD, and went by way of the gate of the escorts to the king's house. Then he sat on the throne of the kings. 20So all the people of the land rejoiced; and the city was quiet, for they had slain Athaliah with the sword *in* the king's house. 21Jehoash *was* seven years old when he became king.

JEHOASH REPAIRS THE TEMPLE

12 In the seventh year of Jehu, Jehoasha became king, and he reigned forty years in Jerusalem. His mother's name *was* Zibiah of Beersheba. 2Jehoash did *what was* right in the sight of the LORD all the days in which Jehoiada the priest instructed him. 3But the high places were not taken away; the people still sacrificed and burned incense on the high places.

4And Jehoash said to the priests, "All the money of the dedicated gifts that are brought into the house of the LORD—each man's census money, each man's assessment moneya—*and* all the money that a man purposes in his heart to bring into the house of the LORD, 5let the priests take *it* themselves, each from his constituency; and let them repair the damages of the temple, wherever any dilapidation is found."

6Now it was so, by the twenty-third year of King Jehoash, *that* the priests had not repaired the

11:12 aThat is, the Law (compare Exodus 25:16, 21 and Deuteronomy 31:9) 12:1 aSpelled *Joash* in 11:2ff 12:4 aCompare Leviticus 27:2ff damages of the temple. 7So King Jehoash called Jehoiada the priest and the *other* priests, and said to them, "Why have you not repaired the damages of the temple? Now therefore, do not take *more* money from your constituency, but deliver it for repairing the damages of the temple." 8And the priests agreed that they would neither receive *more* money from the people, nor repair the damages of the temple.

9Then Jehoiada the priest took a chest, bored a hole in its lid, and set it beside the altar, on the right side as one comes into the house of the LORD; and the priests who kept the door put there all the money brought into the house of the LORD. 10So it was, whenever they saw that *there was* much money in the chest, that the king's scribe and the high priest came up and put it in bags, and counted the money that was found in the house of the LORD. 11Then they gave the money, which had been apportioned, into the hands of those who did the work, who had the oversight of the house of the LORD; and they paid it out to the carpenters and builders who worked on the house of the LORD, 12and to masons and stonecutters, and for buying timber and hewn stone, to repair the damage of the house of the LORD, and for all that was paid out to repair the temple. 13However there were not made for the house of the LORD basins of silver, trimmers, sprinkling-bowls, trumpets, any articles of gold or articles of silver, from the money brought into the house of the LORD. 14But they gave that to the workmen, and they repaired the house of the LORD with it. 15Moreover they did not require an account from the men into whose hand they delivered the money to be paid to workmen, for they dealt faithfully. 16The money from the trespass offerings and the money from the sin offerings was not brought into the house of the LORD. It belonged to the priests.

Hazael Threatens Jerusalem

17Hazael king of Syria went up and fought against Gath, and took it; then Hazael set his face to go up to Jerusalem. 18And Jehoash king of Judah took all the sacred things that his fathers, Jehoshaphat and Jehoram and Ahaziah, kings of Judah, had dedicated, and his own sacred things, and all the gold found in the treasuries of the house of the LORD and in the king's house, and sent *them* to Hazael king of Syria. Then he went away from Jerusalem.

Death of Joash

19Now the rest of the acts of Joash,a and all that he did, *are* they not written in the book of the chronicles of the kings of Judah?

20And his servants arose and formed a conspiracy, and killed Joash in the house of the Millo,a which goes down to Silla. 21For Jozachara the son of Shimeath and Jehozabad the son of Shomer,b his servants, struck him. So he died, and they buried him with his fathers in the City of David. Then Amaziah his son reigned in his place.

Jehoahaz Reigns in Israel

13 In the twenty-third year of Joasha the son of Ahaziah, king of Judah, Jehoahaz the son of Jehu became king over Israel in Samaria, *and reigned* seventeen years. 2And he did evil in the sight of the LORD, and followed the sins of Jeroboam the son of Nebat, who had made Israel sin. He did not depart from them.

3Then the anger of the LORD was aroused against Israel, and He delivered them into the hand of Hazael king of Syria, and into the hand of Ben-Hadad the son of Hazael, all *their* days. 4So Jehoahaz pleaded with the LORD, and the LORD listened to him; for He saw the oppression of Israel, because the king of Syria oppressed them. 5Then the LORD gave Israel a deliverer, so that they escaped from under the hand of the Syrians, and the children of Israel dwelt in their tents as before. 6Nevertheless they did not depart from the sins of the house of Jeroboam, who had made Israel sin, *but* walked in them; and the wooden imagea also remained in Samaria. 7For He left of the army of Jehoahaz only fifty horsemen, ten chariots, and ten thousand foot soldiers; for the king of Syria had destroyed them and made them like the dust at threshing.

8Now the rest of the acts of Jehoahaz, all that he did, and his might, *are* they not written in the book of the chronicles of the kings of Israel? 9So

12:19 aSpelled *Jehoash* in 12:1ff   **12:20** aLiterally *The Landfill*   **12:21** aCalled *Zabad* in 2 Chronicles 24:26   bCalled *Shimrith* in 2 Chronicles 24:26   **13:1** aSpelled *Jehoash* in 12:1ff   **13:6** aHebrew *Asherah*, a Canaanite goddess

Jehoahaz rested with his fathers, and they buried him in Samaria. Then Joash his son reigned in his place.

Jehoash Reigns in Israel

[10]In the thirty-seventh year of Joash king of Judah, Jehoash[a] the son of Jehoahaz became king over Israel in Samaria, *and reigned* sixteen years. [11]And he did evil in the sight of the LORD. He did not depart from all the sins of Jeroboam the son of Nebat, who made Israel sin, *but* walked in them.

[12]Now the rest of the acts of Joash, all that he did, and his might with which he fought against Amaziah king of Judah, *are* they not written in the book of the chronicles of the kings of Israel? [13]So Joash rested with his fathers. Then Jeroboam sat on his throne. And Joash was buried in Samaria with the kings of Israel.

Death of Elisha

[14]Elisha had become sick with the illness of which he would die. Then Joash the king of Israel came down to him, and wept over his face, and said, "O my father, my father, the chariots of Israel and their horsemen!"

[15]And Elisha said to him, "Take a bow and some arrows." So he took himself a bow and some arrows. [16]Then he said to the king of Israel, "Put your hand on the bow." So he put his hand *on it,* and Elisha put his hands on the king's hands. [17]And he said, "Open the east window"; and he opened it. Then Elisha said, "Shoot"; and he shot. And he said, "The arrow of the LORD's deliverance and the arrow of deliverance from Syria; for you must strike the Syrians at Aphek till you have destroyed *them.*" [18]Then he said, "Take the arrows"; so he took *them.* And he said to the king of Israel, "Strike the ground"; so he struck three times, and stopped. [19]And the man of God was angry with him, and said, "You should have struck five or six times; then you would have struck Syria till you had destroyed *it!* But now you will strike Syria *only* three times."

[20]Then Elisha died, and they buried him. And the *raiding* bands from Moab invaded the land in the spring of the year. [21]So it was, as they were burying a man, that suddenly they spied a band *of raiders;* and they put the man in the tomb of Elisha; and when the man was let down and touched the bones of Elisha, he revived and stood on his feet.

Israel Recaptures Cities from Syria

[22]And Hazael king of Syria oppressed Israel all the days of Jehoahaz. [23]But the LORD was gracious to them, had compassion on them, and regarded them, because of His covenant with Abraham, Isaac, and Jacob, and would not yet destroy them or cast them from His presence.

[24]Now Hazael king of Syria died. Then Ben-Hadad his son reigned in his place. [25]And Jehoash[a] the son of Jehoahaz recaptured from the hand of Ben-Hadad, the son of Hazael, the cities which he had taken out of the hand of Jehoahaz his father by war. Three times Joash defeated him and recaptured the cities of Israel.

Amaziah Reigns in Judah

14 In the second year of Joash the son of Jehoahaz, king of Israel, Amaziah the son of Joash, king of Judah, became king. [2]He was twenty-five years old when he became king, and he reigned twenty-nine years in Jerusalem. His mother's name was Jehoaddan of Jerusalem. [3]And he did *what was* right in the sight of the LORD, yet not like his father David; he did everything as his father Joash had done. [4]However the high places were not taken away, and the people still sacrificed and burned incense on the high places.

[5]Now it happened, as soon as the kingdom was established in his hand, that he executed his servants who had murdered his father the king. [6]But the children of the murderers he did not execute, according to what is written in the Book of the Law of Moses, in which the LORD commanded, saying, "Fathers shall not be put to death for their children, nor shall children be put to death for their fathers; but a person shall be put to death for his own sin."[a]

[7]He killed ten thousand Edomites in the Valley of Salt, and took Sela by war, and called its name Joktheel to this day.

[8]Then Amaziah sent messengers to Jehoash[a] the son of Jehoahaz, the son of Jehu, king of Israel, saying, "Come, let us face one another *in battle.*"

13:10 [a]Spelled *Joash* in verse 9   **13:25** [a]Spelled *Joash* in verses 12–14, 25   **14:6** [a]Deuteronomy 24:16   **14:8** [a]Spelled *Joash* in 13:12ff and 2 Chronicles 25:17ff

⁹And Jehoash king of Israel sent to Amaziah king of Judah, saying, "The thistle that *was* in Lebanon sent to the cedar that *was* in Lebanon, saying, 'Give your daughter to my son as wife'; and a wild beast that *was* in Lebanon passed by and trampled the thistle. ¹⁰You have indeed defeated Edom, and your heart has lifted you up. Glory *in that,* and stay at home; for why should you meddle with trouble so that you fall—you and Judah with you?"

¹¹But Amaziah would not heed. Therefore Jehoash king of Israel went out; so he and Amaziah king of Judah faced one another at Beth Shemesh, which *belongs* to Judah. ¹²And Judah was defeated by Israel, and every man fled to his tent. ¹³Then Jehoash king of Israel captured Amaziah king of Judah, the son of Jehoash, the son of Ahaziah, at Beth Shemesh; and he went to Jerusalem, and broke down the wall of Jerusalem from the Gate of Ephraim to the Corner Gate—four hundred cubits. ¹⁴And he took all the gold and silver, all the articles that were found in the house of the LORD and in the treasuries of the king's house, and hostages, and returned to Samaria.

¹⁵Now the rest of the acts of Jehoash which he did—his might, and how he fought with Amaziah king of Judah—*are* they not written in the book of the chronicles of the kings of Israel? ¹⁶So Jehoash rested with his fathers, and was buried in Samaria with the kings of Israel. Then Jeroboam his son reigned in his place.

¹⁷Amaziah the son of Joash, king of Judah, lived fifteen years after the death of Jehoash the son of Jehoahaz, king of Israel. ¹⁸Now the rest of the acts of Amaziah, *are* they not written in the book of the chronicles of the kings of Judah? ¹⁹And they formed a conspiracy against him in Jerusalem, and he fled to Lachish; but they sent after him to Lachish and killed him there. ²⁰Then they brought him on horses, and he was buried at Jerusalem with his fathers in the City of David.

²¹And all the people of Judah took Azariah,ᵃ who *was* sixteen years old, and made him king instead of his father Amaziah. ²²He built Elath and restored it to Judah, after the king rested with his fathers.

Jeroboam II Reigns in Israel

²³In the fifteenth year of Amaziah the son of Joash, king of Judah, Jeroboam the son of Joash, king of Israel, became king in Samaria, *and reigned* forty-one years. ²⁴And he did evil in the sight of the LORD; he did not depart from all the sins of Jeroboam the son of Nebat, who had made Israel sin. ²⁵He restored the territory of Israel from the entrance of Hamath to the Sea of the Arabah, according to the word of the LORD God of Israel, which He had spoken through His servant Jonah the son of Amittai, the prophet who *was* from Gath Hepher. ²⁶For the LORD saw *that* the affliction of Israel *was* very bitter; and whether bond or free, there was no helper for Israel. ²⁷And the LORD did not say that He would blot out the name of Israel from under heaven; but He saved them by the hand of Jeroboam the son of Joash.

²⁸Now the rest of the acts of Jeroboam, and all that he did—his might, how he made war, and how he recaptured for Israel, from Damascus and Hamath, *what had belonged* to Judah—*are* they not written in the book of the chronicles of the kings of Israel? ²⁹So Jeroboam rested with his fathers, the kings of Israel. Then Zechariah his son reigned in his place.

Azariah Reigns in Judah

15 In the twenty-seventh year of Jeroboam king of Israel, Azariah the son of Amaziah, king of Judah, became king. ²He was sixteen years old when he became king, and he reigned fifty-two years in Jerusalem. His mother's name *was* Jecholiah of Jerusalem. ³And he did *what was* right in the sight of the LORD, according to all that his father Amaziah had done, ⁴except that the high places were not removed; the people still sacrificed and burned incense on the high places. ⁵Then the LORD struck the king, so that he was a leper until the day of his death; so he dwelt in an isolated house. And Jotham the king's son *was* over the *royal* house, judging the people of the land.

⁶Now the rest of the acts of Azariah, and all that he did, *are* they not written in the book of the chronicles of the kings of Judah? ⁷So Azariah rested with his fathers, and they buried him with his fathers in the City of David. Then Jotham his son reigned in his place.

14:21 ᵃCalled *Uzziah* in 2 Chronicles 26:1ff, Isaiah 6:1, and elsewhere

ZECHARIAH REIGNS IN ISRAEL

8In the thirty-eighth year of Azariah king of Judah, Zechariah the son of Jeroboam reigned over Israel in Samaria six months. 9And he did evil in the sight of the LORD, as his fathers had done; he did not depart from the sins of Jeroboam the son of Nebat, who had made Israel sin. 10Then Shallum the son of Jabesh conspired against him, and struck and killed him in front of the people; and he reigned in his place.

11Now the rest of the acts of Zechariah, indeed they *are* written in the book of the chronicles of the kings of Israel.

12This *was* the word of the LORD which He spoke to Jehu, saying, "Your sons shall sit on the throne of Israel to the fourth *generation*."a And so it was.

SHALLUM REIGNS IN ISRAEL

13Shallum the son of Jabesh became king in the thirty-ninth year of Uzziaha king of Judah; and he reigned a full month in Samaria. 14For Menahem the son of Gadi went up from Tirzah, came to Samaria, and struck Shallum the son of Jabesh in Samaria and killed him; and he reigned in his place.

15Now the rest of the acts of Shallum, and the conspiracy which he led, indeed they *are* written in the book of the chronicles of the kings of Israel. 16Then from Tirzah, Menahem attacked Tiphsah, all who *were* there, and its territory. Because they did not surrender, therefore he attacked *it*. All the women there who were with child he ripped open.

MENAHEM REIGNS IN ISRAEL

17In the thirty-ninth year of Azariah king of Judah, Menahem the son of Gadi became king over Israel, *and reigned* ten years in Samaria. 18And he did evil in the sight of the LORD; he did not depart all his days from the sins of Jeroboam the son of Nebat, who had made Israel sin. 19Pula king of Assyria came against the land; and Menahem gave Pul a thousand talents of silver, that his hand might be with him to strengthen the kingdom under his control. 20And Menahem exacted the money from Israel, from all the very wealthy, from each man fifty shekels of silver, to give to the king of Assyria. So the king of Assyria turned back, and did not stay there in the land.

21Now the rest of the acts of Menahem, and all that he did, *are* they not written in the book of the chronicles of the kings of Israel? 22So Menahem rested with his fathers. Then Pekahiah his son reigned in his place.

PEKAHIAH REIGNS IN ISRAEL

23In the fiftieth year of Azariah king of Judah, Pekahiah the son of Menahem became king over Israel in Samaria, *and reigned* two years. 24And he did evil in the sight of the LORD; he did not depart from the sins of Jeroboam the son of Nebat, who had made Israel sin. 25Then Pekah the son of Remaliah, an officer of his, conspired against him and killed him in Samaria, in the citadel of the king's house, along with Argob and Arieh; and with him were fifty men of Gilead. He killed him and reigned in his place.

26Now the rest of the acts of Pekahiah, and all that he did, indeed they *are* written in the book of the chronicles of the kings of Israel.

PEKAH REIGNS IN ISRAEL

27In the fifty-second year of Azariah king of Judah, Pekah the son of Remaliah became king over Israel in Samaria, *and reigned* twenty years. 28And he did evil in the sight of the LORD; he did not depart from the sins of Jeroboam the son of Nebat, who had made Israel sin. 29In the days of Pekah king of Israel, Tiglath-Pileser king of Assyria came and took Ijon, Abel Beth Maachah, Janoah, Kedesh, Hazor, Gilead, and Galilee, all the land of Naphtali; and he carried them captive to Assyria. 30Then Hoshea the son of Elah led a conspiracy against Pekah the son of Remaliah, and struck and killed him; so he reigned in his place in the twentieth year of Jotham the son of Uzziah.

31Now the rest of the acts of Pekah, and all that he did, indeed they *are* written in the book of the chronicles of the kings of Israel.

JOTHAM REIGNS IN JUDAH

32In the second year of Pekah the son of Remaliah, king of Israel, Jotham the son of Uzziah,

15:12 a2 Kings 10:30   15:13 aCalled *Azariah* in 14:21ff and 15:1ff
15:19 aThat is, Tiglath-Pileser III (compare verse 29)

king of Judah, began to reign. [33]He was twenty-five years old when he became king, and he reigned sixteen years in Jerusalem. His mother's name *was* Jerusha[a] the daughter of Zadok. [34]And he did *what was* right in the sight of the LORD; he did according to all that his father Uzziah had done. [35]However the high places were not removed; the people still sacrificed and burned incense on the high places. He built the Upper Gate of the house of the LORD.

[36]Now the rest of the acts of Jotham, and all that he did, *are* they not written in the book of the chronicles of the kings of Judah? [37]In those days the LORD began to send Rezin king of Syria and Pekah the son of Remaliah against Judah. [38]So Jotham rested with his fathers, and was buried with his fathers in the City of David his father. Then Ahaz his son reigned in his place.

AHAZ REIGNS IN JUDAH

16 In the seventeenth year of Pekah the son of Remaliah, Ahaz the son of Jotham, king of Judah, began to reign. [2]Ahaz *was* twenty years old when he became king, and he reigned sixteen years in Jerusalem; and he did not do *what was* right in the sight of the LORD his God, as his father David *had done.* [3]But he walked in the way of the kings of Israel; indeed he made his son pass through the fire, according to the abominations of the nations whom the LORD had cast out from before the children of Israel. [4]And he sacrificed and burned incense on the high places, on the hills, and under every green tree.

[5]Then Rezin king of Syria and Pekah the son of Remaliah, king of Israel, came up to Jerusalem to *make* war; and they besieged Ahaz but could not overcome *him.* [6]At that time Rezin king of Syria captured Elath for Syria, and drove the men of Judah from Elath. Then the Edomites[a] went to Elath, and dwell there to this day.

[7]So Ahaz sent messengers to Tiglath-Pileser king of Assyria, saying, "I *am* your servant and your son. Come up and save me from the hand of the king of Syria and from the hand of the king of Israel, who rise up against me." [8]And Ahaz took the silver and gold that was found in the house of the LORD, and in the treasuries of the king's house, and sent *it as* a present to the king of As-

syria. [9]So the king of Assyria heeded him; for the king of Assyria went up against Damascus and took it, carried *its people* captive to Kir, and killed Rezin.

[10]Now King Ahaz went to Damascus to meet Tiglath-Pileser king of Assyria, and saw an altar that *was* at Damascus; and King Ahaz sent to Urijah the priest the design of the altar and its pattern, according to all its workmanship. [11]Then Urijah the priest built an altar according to all that King Ahaz had sent from Damascus. So Urijah the priest made *it* before King Ahaz came back from Damascus. [12]And when the king came back from Damascus, the king saw the altar; and the king approached the altar and made offerings on it. [13]So he burned his burnt offering and his grain offering; and he poured his drink offering and sprinkled the blood of his peace offerings on the altar. [14]He also brought the bronze altar which *was* before the LORD, from the front of the temple—from between the *new* altar and the house of the LORD—and put it on the north side of the *new* altar. [15]Then King Ahaz commanded Urijah the priest, saying, "On the great *new* altar burn the morning burnt offering, the evening grain offering, the king's burnt sacrifice, and his grain offering, with the burnt offering of all the people of the land, their grain offering, and their drink offerings; and sprinkle on it all the blood of the burnt offering and all the blood of the sacrifice. And the bronze altar shall be for me to inquire *by.*" [16]Thus did Urijah the priest, according to all that King Ahaz commanded.

[17]And King Ahaz cut off the panels of the carts, and removed the lavers from them; and he took down the Sea from the bronze oxen that *were* under it, and put it on a pavement of stones. [18]Also he removed the Sabbath pavilion which they had built in the temple, and he removed the king's outer entrance from the house of the LORD, on account of the king of Assyria.

[19]Now the rest of the acts of Ahaz which he did, *are* they not written in the book of the chronicles of the kings of Judah? [20]So Ahaz rested with his fathers, and was buried with his fathers in the City of David. Then Hezekiah his son reigned in his place.

15:33 [a]Spelled *Jerushah* in 2 Chronicles 27:1 **16:6** [a]Some ancient authorities read *Syrians.*

Hoshea Reigns in Israel

17 In the twelfth year of Ahaz king of Judah, Hoshea the son of Elah became king of Israel in Samaria, *and he reigned* nine years. ²And he did evil in the sight of the LORD, but not as the kings of Israel who were before him. ³Shalmaneser king of Assyria came up against him; and Hoshea became his vassal, and paid him tribute money. ⁴And the king of Assyria uncovered a conspiracy by Hoshea; for he had sent messengers to So, king of Egypt, and brought no tribute to the king of Assyria, as *he had done* year by year. Therefore the king of Assyria shut him up, and bound him in prison.

Israel Carried Captive to Assyria

⁵Now the king of Assyria went throughout all the land, and went up to Samaria and besieged it for three years. ⁶In the ninth year of Hoshea, the king of Assyria took Samaria and carried Israel away to Assyria, and placed them in Halah and by the Habor, the River of Gozan, and in the cities of the Medes.

⁷For so it was that the children of Israel had sinned against the LORD their God, who had brought them up out of the land of Egypt, from under the hand of Pharaoh king of Egypt; and they had feared other gods, ⁸and had walked in the statutes of the nations whom the LORD had cast out from before the children of Israel, and of the kings of Israel, which they had made. ⁹Also the children of Israel secretly did against the LORD their God things that *were* not right, and they built for themselves high places in all their cities, from watchtower to fortified city. ¹⁰They set up for themselves *sacred* pillars and wooden images[a] on every high hill and under every green tree. ¹¹There they burned incense on all the high places, like the nations whom the LORD had carried away before them; and they did wicked things to provoke the LORD to anger, ¹²for they served idols, of which the LORD had said to them, "You shall not do this thing."

¹³Yet the LORD testified against Israel and against Judah, by all of His prophets, every seer, saying, "Turn from your evil ways, and keep My commandments *and* My statutes, according to all the law which I commanded your fathers, and

which I sent to you by My servants the prophets." ¹⁴Nevertheless they would not hear, but stiffened their necks, like the necks of their fathers, who did not believe in the LORD their God. ¹⁵And they rejected His statutes and His covenant that He had made with their fathers, and His testimonies which He had testified against them; they followed idols, became idolaters, and *went* after the nations who *were* all around them, *concerning* whom the LORD had charged them that they should not do like them. ¹⁶So they left all the commandments of the LORD their God, made for themselves a molded image *and* two calves, made a wooden image and worshiped all the host of heaven, and served Baal. ¹⁷And they caused their sons and daughters to pass through the fire, practiced witchcraft and soothsaying, and sold themselves to do evil in the sight of the LORD, to provoke Him to anger. ¹⁸Therefore the LORD was very angry with Israel, and removed them from His sight; there was none left but the tribe of Judah alone.

¹⁹Also Judah did not keep the commandments of the LORD their God, but walked in the statutes of Israel which they made. ²⁰And the LORD rejected all the descendants of Israel, afflicted them, and delivered them into the hand of plunderers, until He had cast them from His sight. ²¹For He tore Israel from the house of David, and they made Jeroboam the son of Nebat king. Then Jeroboam drove Israel from following the LORD, and made them commit a great sin. ²²For the children of Israel walked in all the sins of Jeroboam which he did; they did not depart from them, ²³until the LORD removed Israel out of His sight, as He had said by all His servants the prophets. So Israel was carried away from their own land to Assyria, *as it is* to this day.

Assyria Resettles Samaria

²⁴Then the king of Assyria brought *people* from Babylon, Cuthah, Ava, Hamath, and from Sepharvaim, and placed *them* in the cities of Samaria instead of the children of Israel; and they took possession of Samaria and dwelt in its cities. ²⁵And it was so, at the beginning of their dwelling there, *that* they did not fear the LORD; therefore

17:10 ᵃHebrew *Asherim*, Canaanite deities

the LORD sent lions among them, which killed *some* of them. ²⁶So they spoke to the king of Assyria, saying, "The nations whom you have removed and placed in the cities of Samaria do not know the rituals of the God of the land; therefore He has sent lions among them, and indeed, they are killing them because they do not know the rituals of the God of the land." ²⁷Then the king of Assyria commanded, saying, "Send there one of the priests whom you brought from there; let him go and dwell there, and let him teach them the rituals of the God of the land." ²⁸Then one of the priests whom they had carried away from Samaria came and dwelt in Bethel, and taught them how they should fear the LORD.

²⁹However every nation continued to make gods of its own, and put *them* in the shrines on the high places which the Samaritans had made, *every* nation in the cities where they dwelt. ³⁰The men of Babylon made Succoth Benoth, the men of Cuth made Nergal, the men of Hamath made Ashima, ³¹and the Avites made Nibhaz and Tartak; and the Sepharvites burned their children in fire to Adrammelech and Anammelech, the gods of Sepharvaim. ³²So they feared the LORD, and from every class they appointed for themselves priests of the high places, who sacrificed for them in the shrines of the high places. ³³They feared the LORD, yet served their own gods—according to the rituals of the nations from among whom they were carried away.

³⁴To this day they continue practicing the former rituals; they do not fear the LORD, nor do they follow their statutes or their ordinances, or the law and commandment which the LORD had commanded the children of Jacob, whom He named Israel, ³⁵with whom the LORD had made a covenant and charged them, saying: "You shall not fear other gods, nor bow down to them nor serve them nor sacrifice to them; ³⁶but the LORD, who brought you up from the land of Egypt with great power and an outstretched arm, Him you shall fear, Him you shall worship, and to Him you shall offer sacrifice. ³⁷And the statutes, the ordinances, the law, and the commandment which He wrote for you, you shall be careful to observe forever; you shall not fear other gods. ³⁸And the covenant that I have made with you, you shall not forget, nor shall you fear other gods. ³⁹But the LORD

your God you shall fear; and He will deliver you from the hand of all your enemies." ⁴⁰However they did not obey, but they followed their former rituals. ⁴¹So these nations feared the LORD, yet served their carved images; also their children and their children's children have continued doing as their fathers did, even to this day.

HEZEKIAH REIGNS IN JUDAH

18 Now it came to pass in the third year of Hoshea the son of Elah, king of Israel, *that* Hezekiah the son of Ahaz, king of Judah, began to reign. ²He was twenty-five years old when he became king, and he reigned twenty-nine years in Jerusalem. His mother's name *was* Abi^a the daughter of Zechariah. ³And he did *what was* right in the sight of the LORD, according to all that his father David had done.

⁴He removed the high places and broke the *sacred* pillars, cut down the wooden image^a and broke in pieces the bronze serpent that Moses had made; for until those days the children of Israel burned incense to it, and called it Nehushtan.^b ⁵He trusted in the LORD God of Israel, so that after him was none like him among all the kings of Judah, nor who were before him. ⁶For he held fast to the LORD; he did not depart from following Him, but kept His commandments, which the LORD had commanded Moses. ⁷The LORD was with him; he prospered wherever he went. And he rebelled against the king of Assyria and did not serve him. ⁸He subdued the Philistines, as far as Gaza and its territory, from watchtower to fortified city.

⁹Now it came to pass in the fourth year of King Hezekiah, which *was* the seventh year of Hoshea the son of Elah, king of Israel, *that* Shalmaneser king of Assyria came up against Samaria and besieged it. ¹⁰And at the end of three years they took it. In the sixth year of Hezekiah, that *is* the ninth year of Hoshea king of Israel, Samaria was taken. ¹¹Then the king of Assyria carried Israel away captive to Assyria, and put them in Halah and by the Habor, the River of Gozan, and in the cities of the Medes, ¹²because they did not obey the voice of the LORD their God, but transgressed His covenant *and* all that Moses the ser-

18:2 ^aCalled *Abijah* in 2 Chronicles 29:1ff **18:4** ^aHebrew *Asherah*, Canaanite goddess ^bLiterally *Bronze Thing* vant of the LORD had commanded; and they would neither hear nor do *them.*

¹³And in the fourteenth year of King Hezekiah, Sennacherib king of Assyria came up against all the fortified cities of Judah and took them. ¹⁴Then Hezekiah king of Judah sent to the king of Assyria at Lachish, saying, "I have done wrong; turn away from me; whatever you impose on me I will pay." And the king of Assyria assessed Hezekiah king of Judah three hundred talents of silver and thirty talents of gold. ¹⁵So Hezekiah gave *him* all the silver that was found in the house of the LORD and in the treasuries of the king's house. ¹⁶At that time Hezekiah stripped *the gold from* the doors of the temple of the LORD, and *from* the pillars which Hezekiah king of Judah had overlaid, and gave it to the king of Assyria.

Sennacherib Boasts Against the Lord

¹⁷Then the king of Assyria sent *the* Tartan,ᵃ *the* Rabsaris,ᵇ *and the* Rabshakehᶜ from Lachish, with a great army against Jerusalem, to King Hezekiah. And they went up and came to Jerusalem. When they had come up, they went and stood by the aqueduct from the upper pool, which *was* on the highway to the Fuller's Field. ¹⁸And when they had called to the king, Eliakim the son of Hilkiah, who *was* over the household, Shebna the scribe, and Joah the son of Asaph, the recorder, came out to them. ¹⁹Then *the* Rabshakeh said to them, "Say now to Hezekiah, 'Thus says the great king, the king of Assyria: "What confidence *is* this in which you trust? ²⁰You speak of *having* plans and power for war; but *they are* mere words. And in whom do you trust, that you rebel against me? ²¹Now look! You are trusting in the staff of this broken reed, Egypt, on which if a man leans, it will go into his hand and pierce it. So *is* Pharaoh king of Egypt to all who trust in him. ²²But if you say to me, 'We trust in the LORD our God,' *is* it not He whose high places and whose altars Hezekiah has taken away, and said to Judah and Jerusalem, 'You shall worship before this altar in Jerusalem'?' ' ²³Now therefore, I urge you, give a pledge to my master the king of Assyria, and I will give you two thousand horses—if you are able on your part to put riders on them! ²⁴How then will you repel one captain of the least of my master's servants, and put your trust in Egypt for chariots and horsemen?

²⁵Have I now come up without the LORD against this place to destroy it? The LORD said to me, 'Go up against this land, and destroy it.' "

²⁶Then Eliakim the son of Hilkiah, Shebna, and Joah said to *the* Rabshakeh, "Please speak to your servants in Aramaic, for we understand *it;* and do not speak to us in Hebrewᵃ in the hearing of the people who *are* on the wall."

²⁷But *the* Rabshakeh said to them, "Has my master sent me to your master and to you to speak these words, and not to the men who sit on the wall, who will eat and drink their own waste with you?"

²⁸Then *the* Rabshakeh stood and called out with a loud voice in Hebrew, and spoke, saying, "Hear the word of the great king, the king of Assyria! ²⁹Thus says the king: 'Do not let Hezekiah deceive you, for he shall not be able to deliver you from his hand; ³⁰nor let Hezekiah make you trust in the LORD, saying, "The LORD will surely deliver us; this city shall not be given into the hand of the king of Assyria." ' ³¹Do not listen to Hezekiah; for thus says the king of Assyria: 'Make *peace* with me by a present and come out to me; and every one of you eat from his own vine and every one from his own fig tree, and every one of you drink the waters of his own cistern; ³²until I come and take you away to a land like your own land, a land of grain and new wine, a land of bread and vineyards, a land of olive groves and honey, that you may live and not die. But do not listen to Hezekiah, lest he persuade you, saying, "The LORD will deliver us." ³³Has any of the gods of the nations at all delivered its land from the hand of the king of Assyria? ³⁴Where *are* the gods of Hamath and Arpad? Where *are* the gods of Sepharvaim and Hena and Ivah? Indeed, have they delivered Samaria from my hand? ³⁵Who among all the gods of the lands have delivered their countries from my hand, that the LORD should deliver Jerusalem from my hand?' "

³⁶But the people held their peace and answered him not a word; for the king's commandment was, "Do not answer him." ³⁷Then Eliakim the son of Hilkiah, who *was* over the household, Shebna the scribe, and Joah the son of Asaph, the

18:17 ᵃA title, probably *Commander in Chief* ᵇA title, probably *Chief Officer* ᶜA title, probably *Chief of Staff* or *Governor* **18:26** ᵃLiterally *Judean*

recorder, came to Hezekiah with *their* clothes torn, and told him the words of *the* Rabshakeh.

ISAIAH ASSURES DELIVERANCE

19 And so it was, when King Hezekiah heard *it,* that he tore his clothes, covered himself with sackcloth, and went into the house of the LORD. ²Then he sent Eliakim, who *was* over the household, Shebna the scribe, and the elders of the priests, covered with sackcloth, to Isaiah the prophet, the son of Amoz. ³And they said to him, "Thus says Hezekiah: 'This day *is* a day of trouble, and rebuke, and blasphemy; for the children have come to birth, but *there is* no strength to bring them forth. ⁴It may be that the LORD your God will hear all the words of *the* Rabshakeh, whom his master the king of Assyria has sent to reproach the living God, and will rebuke the words which the LORD your God has heard. Therefore lift up *your* prayer for the remnant that is left.' "

⁵So the servants of King Hezekiah came to Isaiah. ⁶And Isaiah said to them, "Thus you shall say to your master, 'Thus says the LORD: "Do not be afraid of the words which you have heard, with which the servants of the king of Assyria have blasphemed Me. ⁷Surely I will send a spirit upon him, and he shall hear a rumor and return to his own land; and I will cause him to fall by the sword in his own land." ' "

SENNACHERIB'S THREAT AND HEZEKIAH'S PRAYER

⁸Then *the* Rabshakeh returned and found the king of Assyria warring against Libnah, for he heard that he had departed from Lachish. ⁹And the king heard concerning Tirhakah king of Ethiopia, "Look, he has come out to make war with you." So he again sent messengers to Hezekiah, saying, ¹⁰"Thus you shall speak to Hezekiah king of Judah, saying: 'Do not let your God in whom you trust deceive you, saying, "Jerusalem shall not be given into the hand of the king of Assyria." ¹¹Look! You have heard what the kings of Assyria have done to all lands by utterly destroying them; and shall you be delivered? ¹²Have the gods of the nations delivered those whom my fathers have destroyed, Gozan and Haran and Rezeph, and the people of Eden who *were* in Telassar? ¹³Where *is* the king of Hamath,

the king of Arpad, and the king of the city of Sepharvaim, Hena, and Ivah?' "

¹⁴And Hezekiah received the letter from the hand of the messengers, and read it; and Hezekiah went up to the house of the LORD, and spread it before the LORD. ¹⁵Then Hezekiah prayed before the LORD, and said: "O LORD God of Israel, *the* One who dwells *between* the cherubim, You are God, You alone, of all the kingdoms of the earth. You have made heaven and earth. ¹⁶Incline Your ear, O LORD, and hear; open Your eyes, O LORD, and see; and hear the words of Sennacherib, which he has sent to reproach the living God. ¹⁷Truly, LORD, the kings of Assyria have laid waste the nations and their lands, ¹⁸and have cast their gods into the fire; for they *were* not gods, but the work of men's hands—wood and stone. Therefore they destroyed them. ¹⁹Now therefore, O LORD our God, I pray, save us from his hand, that all the kingdoms of the earth may know that You *are* the LORD God, You alone."

THE WORD OF THE LORD CONCERNING SENNACHERIB

²⁰Then Isaiah the son of Amoz sent to Hezekiah, saying, "Thus says the LORD God of Israel: 'Because you have prayed to Me against Sennacherib king of Assyria, I have heard.' ²¹This *is* the word which the LORD has spoken concerning him:

'The virgin, the daughter of Zion,
　Has despised you, laughed you to scorn;
　The daughter of Jerusalem
　Has shaken *her* head behind your back!

²²'Whom have you reproached and
　　blasphemed?
　Against whom have you raised *your* voice,
　And lifted up your eyes on high?
　Against the Holy *One* of Israel.
²³By your messengers you have reproached the
　　Lord,
　And said: "By the multitude of my
　　chariots
　I have come up to the height of the
　　mountains,
　To the limits of Lebanon;
　I will cut down its tall cedars
　And its choice cypress trees;

I will enter the extremity of its borders,
    To its fruitful forest.
²⁴I have dug and drunk strange water,
    And with the soles of my feet I have dried up
    All the brooks of defense."

²⁵'Did you not hear long ago
    How I made it,
    From ancient times that I formed it?
    Now I have brought it to pass,
    That you should be
    For crushing fortified cities *into* heaps of
        ruins.
²⁶Therefore their inhabitants had little power;
    They were dismayed and confounded;
    They were *as* the grass of the field
    And the green herb,
    As the grass on the housetops
    And *grain* blighted before it is grown.

²⁷'But I know your dwelling place,
    Your going out and your coming in,
    And your rage against Me.
²⁸Because your rage against Me and your
        tumult
    Have come up to My ears,
    Therefore I will put My hook in your nose
    And My bridle in your lips,
    And I will turn you back
    By the way which you came.

²⁹'This *shall be* a sign to you:

    You shall eat this year such as grows of
        itself,
    And in the second year what springs from
        the same;
    Also in the third year sow and reap,
    Plant vineyards and eat the fruit of them.
³⁰And the remnant who have escaped of the
        house of Judah
    Shall again take root downward,
    And bear fruit upward.
³¹For out of Jerusalem shall go a remnant,
    And those who escape from Mount Zion.
    The zeal of the LORD of hosts^a will do this.'

³²"Therefore thus says the LORD concerning
the king of Assyria:

'He shall not come into this city,
    Nor shoot an arrow there,
    Nor come before it with shield,
    Nor build a siege mound against it.
³³By the way that he came,
    By the same shall he return;
    And he shall not come into this city,'
    Says the LORD.
³⁴'For I will defend this city, to save it
    For My own sake and for My servant David's
        sake.' "

SENNACHERIB'S DEFEAT AND DEATH

³⁵And it came to pass on a certain night that the angel^a of the LORD went out, and killed in the camp of the Assyrians one hundred and eighty-five thousand; and when *people* arose early in the morning, there were the corpses—all dead. ³⁶So Sennacherib king of Assyria departed and went away, returned *home,* and remained at Nineveh. ³⁷Now it came to pass, as he was worshiping in the temple of Nisroch his god, that his sons Adrammelech and Sharezer struck him down with the sword; and they escaped into the land of Ararat. Then Esarhaddon his son reigned in his place.

HEZEKIAH'S LIFE EXTENDED

20 In those days Hezekiah was sick and near death. And Isaiah the prophet, the son of Amoz, went to him and said to him, "Thus says the LORD: 'Set your house in order, for you shall die, and not live.' "

²Then he turned his face toward the wall, and prayed to the LORD, saying, ³"Remember now, O LORD, I pray, how I have walked before You in truth and with a loyal heart, and have done *what was* good in Your sight." And Hezekiah wept bitterly.

⁴And it happened, before Isaiah had gone out into the middle court, that the word of the LORD came to him, saying, ⁵"Return and tell Hezekiah the leader of My people, 'Thus says the LORD, the God of David your father: "I have heard your prayer, I have seen your tears; surely I will heal you. On the third day you shall go up to the

19:31 aFollowing many Hebrew manuscripts and ancient versions (compare Isaiah 37:32); Masoretic Text omits *of hosts.* **19:35** aOr *Angel* house of the LORD. [6]And I will add to your days fifteen years. I will deliver you and this city from the hand of the king of Assyria; and I will defend this city for My own sake, and for the sake of My servant David." ' "

[7]Then Isaiah said, "Take a lump of figs." So they took and laid *it* on the boil, and he recovered.

[8]And Hezekiah said to Isaiah, "What *is* the sign that the LORD will heal me, and that I shall go up to the house of the LORD the third day?"

[9]Then Isaiah said, "This is the sign to you from the LORD, that the LORD will do the thing which He has spoken: *shall* the shadow go forward ten degrees or go backward ten degrees?"

[10]And Hezekiah answered, "It is an easy thing for the shadow to go down ten degrees; no, but let the shadow go backward ten degrees."

[11]So Isaiah the prophet cried out to the LORD, and He brought the shadow ten degrees backward, by which it had gone down on the sundial of Ahaz.

THE BABYLONIAN ENVOYS

[12]At that time Berodach-Baladan[a] the son of Baladan, king of Babylon, sent letters and a present to Hezekiah, for he heard that Hezekiah had been sick. [13]And Hezekiah was attentive to them, and showed them all the house of his treasures— the silver and gold, the spices and precious ointment, and all[a] his armory—all that was found among his treasures. There was nothing in his house or in all his dominion that Hezekiah did not show them.

[14]Then Isaiah the prophet went to King Hezekiah, and said to him, "What did these men say, and from where did they come to you?"

So Hezekiah said, "They came from a far country, from Babylon."

[15]And he said, "What have they seen in your house?"

So Hezekiah answered, "They have seen all that *is* in my house; there is nothing among my treasures that I have not shown them."

[16]Then Isaiah said to Hezekiah, "Hear the word of the LORD: [17]'Behold, the days are coming when all that *is* in your house, and what your fathers have accumulated until this day, shall be carried to Babylon; nothing shall be left,' says the LORD. [18]'And they shall take away some of your sons who will descend from you, whom you will beget; and they shall be eunuchs in the palace of the king of Babylon.' "

[19]So Hezekiah said to Isaiah, "The word of the LORD which you have spoken *is* good!" For he said, "Will there not be peace and truth at least in my days?"

DEATH OF HEZEKIAH

[20]Now the rest of the acts of Hezekiah—all his might, and how he made a pool and a tunnel and brought water into the city—*are* they not written in the book of the chronicles of the kings of Judah? [21]So Hezekiah rested with his fathers. Then Manasseh his son reigned in his place.

MANASSEH REIGNS IN JUDAH

21 Manasseh *was* twelve years old when he became king, and he reigned fifty-five years in Jerusalem. His mother's name *was* Hephzibah. [2]And he did evil in the sight of the LORD, according to the abominations of the nations whom the LORD had cast out before the children of Israel. [3]For he rebuilt the high places which Hezekiah his father had destroyed; he raised up altars for Baal, and made a wooden image,[a] as Ahab king of Israel had done; and he worshiped all the host of heaven[b] and served them. [4]He also built altars in the house of the LORD, of which the LORD had said, "In Jerusalem I will put My name." [5]And he built altars for all the host of heaven in the two courts of the house of the LORD. [6]Also he made his son pass through the fire, practiced soothsaying, used witchcraft, and consulted spiritists and mediums. He did much evil in the sight of the LORD, to provoke *Him* to anger. [7]He even set a carved image of Asherah that he had made, in the house of which the LORD had said to David and to Solomon his son, "In this house and in Jerusalem, which I have chosen out of all the tribes of Israel, I will put My name forever; [8]and I will not make the feet of Israel wander anymore from the land which I gave their fathers—only if they are careful to do ac-

20:12 [a]Spelled *Merodach-Baladan* in Isaiah 39:1   **20:13** [a]Following many Hebrew manuscripts, Syriac, and Targum; Masoretic Text omits *all.*   **21:3** [a]Hebrew *Asherah,* a Canaanite goddess   [b]The gods of the Assyrians   **21:7** [a]A Canaanite goddess cording to all that I have commanded them, and according to all the law that My servant Moses commanded them." ⁹But they paid no attention, and Manasseh seduced them to do more evil than the nations whom the LORD had destroyed before the children of Israel.

¹⁰And the LORD spoke by His servants the prophets, saying, ¹¹"Because Manasseh king of Judah has done these abominations (he has acted more wickedly than all the Amorites who *were* before him, and has also made Judah sin with his idols), ¹²therefore thus says the LORD God of Israel: 'Behold, *I* am bringing *such* calamity upon Jerusalem and Judah, that whoever hears of it, both his ears will tingle. ¹³And I will stretch over Jerusalem the measuring line of Samaria and the plummet of the house of Ahab; I will wipe Jerusalem as *one* wipes a dish, wiping *it* and turning *it* upside down. ¹⁴So I will forsake the remnant of My inheritance and deliver them into the hand of their enemies; and they shall become victims of plunder to all their enemies, ¹⁵because they have done evil in My sight, and have provoked Me to anger since the day their fathers came out of Egypt, even to this day.' "

¹⁶Moreover Manasseh shed very much innocent blood, till he had filled Jerusalem from one end to another, besides his sin by which he made Judah sin, in doing evil in the sight of the LORD. ¹⁷Now the rest of the acts of Manasseh—all that he did, and the sin that he committed—*are* they not written in the book of the chronicles of the kings of Judah? ¹⁸So Manasseh rested with his fathers, and was buried in the garden of his own house, in the garden of Uzza. Then his son Amon reigned in his place.

Amon's Reign and Death

¹⁹Amon *was* twenty-two years old when he became king, and he reigned two years in Jerusalem. His mother's name *was* Meshullemeth the daughter of Haruz of Jotbah. ²⁰And he did evil in the sight of the LORD, as his father Manasseh had done. ²¹So he walked in all the ways that his father had walked; and he served the idols that his father had served, and worshiped them. ²²He forsook the LORD God of his fathers, and did not walk in the way of the LORD.

²³Then the servants of Amon conspired against him, and killed the king in his own house. ²⁴But the people of the land executed all those who had conspired against King Amon. Then the people of the land made his son Josiah king in his place.

²⁵Now the rest of the acts of Amon which he did, *are* they not written in the book of the chronicles of the kings of Judah? ²⁶And he was buried in his tomb in the garden of Uzza. Then Josiah his son reigned in his place.

Josiah Reigns in Judah

22 Josiah *was* eight years old when he became king, and he reigned thirty-one years in Jerusalem. His mother's name *was* Jedidah the daughter of Adaiah of Bozkath. ²And he did *what was* right in the sight of the LORD, and walked in all the ways of his father David; he did not turn aside to the right hand or to the left.

Hilkiah Finds the Book of the Law

³Now it came to pass, in the eighteenth year of King Josiah, *that* the king sent Shaphan the scribe, the son of Azaliah, the son of Meshullam, to the house of the LORD, saying: ⁴"Go up to Hilkiah the high priest, that he may count the money which has been brought into the house of the LORD, which the doorkeepers have gathered from the people. ⁵And let them deliver it into the hand of those doing the work, who are the overseers in the house of the LORD; let them give it to those who *are* in the house of the LORD doing the work, to repair the damages of the house— ⁶to carpenters and builders and masons—and to buy timber and hewn stone to repair the house. ⁷However there need be no accounting made with them of the money delivered into their hand, because they deal faithfully."

⁸Then Hilkiah the high priest said to Shaphan the scribe, "I have found the Book of the Law in the house of the LORD." And Hilkiah gave the book to Shaphan, and he read it. ⁹So Shaphan the scribe went to the king, bringing the king word, saying, "Your servants have gathered the money that was found in the house, and have delivered it into the hand of those who do the work, who oversee the house of the LORD." ¹⁰Then Shaphan the scribe showed the king, saying, "Hilkiah the priest has given me a book." And Shaphan read it before the king.

[11]Now it happened, when the king heard the words of the Book of the Law, that he tore his clothes. [12]Then the king commanded Hilkiah the priest, Ahikam the son of Shaphan, Achbor[a] the son of Michaiah, Shaphan the scribe, and Asaiah a servant of the king, saying, [13]"Go, inquire of the LORD for me, for the people and for all Judah, concerning the words of this book that has been found; for great *is* the wrath of the LORD that is aroused against us, because our fathers have not obeyed the words of this book, to do according to all that is written concerning us."

[14]So Hilkiah the priest, Ahikam, Achbor, Shaphan, and Asaiah went to Huldah the prophetess, the wife of Shallum the son of Tikvah, the son of Harhas, keeper of the wardrobe. (She dwelt in Jerusalem in the Second Quarter.) And they spoke with her. [15]Then she said to them, "Thus says the LORD God of Israel, 'Tell the man who sent you to Me, [16]"Thus says the LORD: 'Behold, I will bring calamity on this place and on its inhabitants—all the words of the book which the king of Judah has read— [17]because they have forsaken Me and burned incense to other gods, that they might provoke Me to anger with all the works of their hands. Therefore My wrath shall be aroused against this place and shall not be quenched.' " ' [18]But as for the king of Judah, who sent you to inquire of the LORD, in this manner you shall speak to him, 'Thus says the LORD God of Israel: "*Concerning* the words which you have heard— [19]because your heart was tender, and you humbled yourself before the LORD when you heard what I spoke against this place and against its inhabitants, that they would become a desolation and a curse, and you tore your clothes and wept before Me, I also have heard *you*," says the LORD. [20]"Surely, therefore, I will gather you to your fathers, and you shall be gathered to your grave in peace; and your eyes shall not see all the calamity which I will bring on this place." ' " So they brought back word to the king.

JOSIAH RESTORES TRUE WORSHIP

23 Now the king sent them to gather all the elders of Judah and Jerusalem to him. [2]The king went up to the house of the LORD with all the men of Judah, and with him all the inhabitants of Jerusalem—the priests and the prophets and all the people, both small and great. And he read in their hearing all the words of the Book of the Covenant which had been found in the house of the LORD.

[3]Then the king stood by a pillar and made a covenant before the LORD, to follow the LORD and to keep His commandments and His testimonies and His statutes, with all *his* heart and all *his* soul, to perform the words of this covenant that were written in this book. And all the people took a stand for the covenant. [4]And the king commanded Hilkiah the high priest, the priests of the second order, and the doorkeepers, to bring out of the temple of the LORD all the articles that were made for Baal, for Asherah,[a] and for all the host of heaven;[b] and he burned them outside Jerusalem in the fields of Kidron, and carried their ashes to Bethel. [5]Then he removed the idolatrous priests whom the kings of Judah had ordained to burn incense on the high places in the cities of Judah and in the places all around Jerusalem, and those who burned incense to Baal, to the sun, to the moon, to the constellations, and to all the host of heaven. [6]And he brought out the wooden image[a] from the house of the LORD, to the Brook Kidron outside Jerusalem, burned it at the Brook Kidron and ground *it* to ashes, and threw its ashes on the graves of the common people. [7]Then he tore down the *ritual* booths of the perverted persons[a] that *were* in the house of the LORD, where the women wove hangings for the wooden image. [8]And he brought all the priests from the cities of Judah, and defiled the high places where the priests had burned incense, from Geba to Beersheba; also he broke down the high places at the gates which *were* at the entrance of the Gate of Joshua the governor of the city, which *were* to the left of the city gate. [9]Nevertheless the priests of the high places did not come up to the altar of the LORD in Jerusalem, but they ate unleavened bread among their brethren.

[10]And he defiled Topheth, which *is* in the Valley of the Son[a] of Hinnom, that no man might

22:12 [a]*Abdon the son of Micah* in 2 Chronicles 34:20 **23:4** [a]Canaanite goddess [b]The gods of the Assyrians **23:6** [a]Hebrew *Asherah*, a Canaanite goddess **23:7** [a]Hebrew *qedeshim*, those practicing sodomy and prostitution in religious ritual **23:10** [a]Kethib reads *Sons*.

make his son or his daughter pass through the fire to Molech. [11]Then he removed the horses that the kings of Judah had dedicated to the sun, at the entrance to the house of the LORD, by the chamber of Nathan-Melech, the officer who *was* in the court; and he burned the chariots of the sun with fire. [12]The altars that *were* on the roof, the upper chamber of Ahaz, which the kings of Judah had made, and the altars which Manasseh had made in the two courts of the house of the LORD, the king broke down and pulverized there, and threw their dust into the Brook Kidron. [13]Then the king defiled the high places that *were* east of Jerusalem, which *were* on the south of the Mount of Corruption, which Solomon king of Israel had built for Ashtoreth the abomination of the Sidonians, for Chemosh the abomination of the Moabites, and for Milcom the abomination of the people of Ammon. [14]And he broke in pieces the *sacred* pillars and cut down the wooden images, and filled their places with the bones of men.

[15]Moreover the altar that *was* at Bethel, *and* the high place which Jeroboam the son of Nebat, who made Israel sin, had made, both that altar and the high place he broke down; and he burned the high place *and* crushed *it* to powder, and burned the wooden image. [16]As Josiah turned, he saw the tombs that *were* there on the mountain. And he sent and took the bones out of the tombs and burned *them* on the altar, and defiled it according to the word of the LORD which the man of God proclaimed, who proclaimed these words. [17]Then he said, "What gravestone *is* this that I see?"

So the men of the city told him, "*It is* the tomb of the man of God who came from Judah and proclaimed these things which you have done against the altar of Bethel."

[18]And he said, "Let him alone; let no one move his bones." So they let his bones alone, with the bones of the prophet who came from Samaria.

[19]Now Josiah also took away all the shrines of the high places that *were* in the cities of Samaria, which the kings of Israel had made to provoke the LORD[a] to anger; and he did to them according to all the deeds he had done in Bethel. [20]He executed all the priests of the high places who *were* there, on the altars, and burned men's bones on them; and he returned to Jerusalem.

[21]Then the king commanded all the people,

saying, "Keep the Passover to the LORD your God, as *it is* written in this Book of the Covenant." [22]Such a Passover surely had never been held since the days of the judges who judged Israel, nor in all the days of the kings of Israel and the kings of Judah. [23]But in the eighteenth year of King Josiah this Passover was held before the LORD in Jerusalem. [24]Moreover Josiah put away those who consulted mediums and spiritists, the household gods and idols, all the abominations that were seen in the land of Judah and in Jerusalem, that he might perform the words of the law which were written in the book that Hilkiah the priest found in the house of the LORD. [25]Now before him there was no king like him, who turned to the LORD with all his heart, with all his soul, and with all his might, according to all the Law of Moses; nor after him did *any* arise like him.

IMPENDING JUDGMENT ON JUDAH

[26]Nevertheless the LORD did not turn from the fierceness of His great wrath, with which His anger was aroused against Judah, because of all the provocations with which Manasseh had provoked Him. [27]And the LORD said, "I will also remove Judah from My sight, as I have removed Israel, and will cast off this city Jerusalem which I have chosen, and the house of which I said, 'My name shall be there.' "[a]

JOSIAH DIES IN BATTLE

[28]Now the rest of the acts of Josiah, and all that he did, *are* they not written in the book of the chronicles of the kings of Judah? [29]In his days Pharaoh Necho king of Egypt went to the aid of the king of Assyria, to the River Euphrates; and King Josiah went against him. And *Pharaoh Necho* killed him at Megiddo when he confronted him. [30]Then his servants moved his body in a chariot from Megiddo, brought him to Jerusalem, and buried him in his own tomb. And the people of the land took Jehoahaz the son of Josiah, anointed him, and made him king in his father's place.

THE REIGN AND CAPTIVITY OF JEHOAHAZ

[31]Jehoahaz *was* twenty-three years old when he became king, and he reigned three months in

23:19 [a]Following Septuagint, Syriac, and Vulgate; Masoretic Text and Targum omit *the LORD*.   23:27 [a]1 Kings 8:29

Jerusalem. His mother's name *was* Hamutal the daughter of Jeremiah of Libnah. ³²And he did evil in the sight of the LORD, according to all that his fathers had done. ³³Now Pharaoh Necho put him in prison at Riblah in the land of Hamath, that he might not reign in Jerusalem; and he imposed on the land a tribute of one hundred talents of silver and a talent of gold. ³⁴Then Pharaoh Necho made Eliakim the son of Josiah king in place of his father Josiah, and changed his name to Jehoiakim. And *Pharaoh* took Jehoahaz and went to Egypt, and heᵃ died there.

JEHOIAKIM REIGNS IN JUDAH

³⁵So Jehoiakim gave the silver and gold to Pharaoh; but he taxed the land to give money according to the command of Pharaoh; he exacted the silver and gold from the people of the land, from every one according to his assessment, to give *it* to Pharaoh Necho. ³⁶Jehoiakim *was* twenty-five years old when he became king, and he reigned eleven years in Jerusalem. His mother's name *was* Zebudah the daughter of Pedaiah of Rumah. ³⁷And he did evil in the sight of the LORD, according to all that his fathers had done.

JUDAH OVERRUN BY ENEMIES

24 In his days Nebuchadnezzar king of Babylon came up, and Jehoiakim became his vassal *for* three years. Then he turned and rebelled against him. ²And the LORD sent against him *raiding* bands of Chaldeans, bands of Syrians, bands of Moabites, and bands of the people of Ammon; He sent them against Judah to destroy it, according to the word of the LORD which He had spoken by His servants the prophets. ³Surely at the commandment of the LORD *this* came upon Judah, to remove *them* from His sight because of the sins of Manasseh, according to all that he had done, ⁴and also because of the innocent blood that he had shed; for he had filled Jerusalem with innocent blood, which the LORD would not pardon.

⁵Now the rest of the acts of Jehoiakim, and all that he did, *are* they not written in the book of the chronicles of the kings of Judah? ⁶So Jehoiakim rested with his fathers. Then Jehoiachin his son reigned in his place.

⁷And the king of Egypt did not come out of his land anymore, for the king of Babylon had taken all that belonged to the king of Egypt from the Brook of Egypt to the River Euphrates.

THE REIGN AND CAPTIVITY OF JEHOIACHIN

⁸Jehoiachin *was* eighteen years old when he became king, and he reigned in Jerusalem three months. His mother's name *was* Nehushta the daughter of Elnathan of Jerusalem. ⁹And he did evil in the sight of the LORD, according to all that his father had done.

¹⁰At that time the servants of Nebuchadnezzar king of Babylon came up against Jerusalem, and the city was besieged. ¹¹And Nebuchadnezzar king of Babylon came against the city, as his servants were besieging it. ¹²Then Jehoiachin king of Judah, his mother, his servants, his princes, and his officers went out to the king of Babylon; and the king of Babylon, in the eighth year of his reign, took him prisoner.

THE CAPTIVITY OF JERUSALEM

¹³And he carried out from there all the treasures of the house of the LORD and the treasures of the king's house, and he cut in pieces all the articles of gold which Solomon king of Israel had made in the temple of the LORD, as the LORD had said. ¹⁴Also he carried into captivity all Jerusalem: all the captains and all the mighty men of valor, ten thousand captives, and all the craftsmen and smiths. None remained except the poorest people of the land. ¹⁵And he carried Jehoiachin captive to Babylon. The king's mother, the king's wives, his officers, and the mighty of the land he carried into captivity from Jerusalem to Babylon. ¹⁶All the valiant men, seven thousand, and craftsmen and smiths, one thousand, all *who were* strong *and* fit for war, these the king of Babylon brought captive to Babylon.

ZEDEKIAH REIGNS IN JUDAH

¹⁷Then the king of Babylon made Mattaniah, *Jehoiachin's*ᵃ uncle, king in his place, and changed his name to Zedekiah.

¹⁸Zedekiah *was* twenty-one years old when he became king, and he reigned eleven years in Jerusalem. His mother's name *was* Hamutal the daughter of Jeremiah of Libnah. ¹⁹He also did

23:34 ᵃThat is, Jehoahaz 24:17 ᵃLiterally *his*

evil in the sight of the LORD, according to all that Jehoiakim had done. [20]For because of the anger of the LORD *this* happened in Jerusalem and Judah, that He finally cast them out from His presence. Then Zedekiah rebelled against the king of Babylon.

THE FALL AND CAPTIVITY OF JUDAH

25 Now it came to pass in the ninth year of his reign, in the tenth month, on the tenth *day* of the month, *that* Nebuchadnezzar king of Babylon and all his army came against Jerusalem and encamped against it; and they built a siege wall against it all around. [2]So the city was besieged until the eleventh year of King Zedekiah. [3]By the ninth *day* of the *fourth* month the famine had become so severe in the city that there was no food for the people of the land.

[4]Then the city wall was broken through, and all the men of war *fled* at night by way of the gate between two walls, which was by the king's garden, even though the Chaldeans *were* still encamped all around against the city. And *the king*[a] went by way of the plain.[b] [5]But the army of the Chaldeans pursued the king, and they overtook him in the plains of Jericho. All his army was scattered from him. [6]So they took the king and brought him up to the king of Babylon at Riblah, and they pronounced judgment on him. [7]Then they killed the sons of Zedekiah before his eyes, put out the eyes of Zedekiah, bound him with bronze fetters, and took him to Babylon.

[8]And in the fifth month, on the seventh *day* of the month (which *was* the nineteenth year of King Nebuchadnezzar king of Babylon), Nebuzaradan the captain of the guard, a servant of the king of Babylon, came to Jerusalem. [9]He burned the house of the LORD and the king's house; all the houses of Jerusalem, that is, all the houses of the great, he burned with fire. [10]And all the army of the Chaldeans who *were with* the captain of the guard broke down the walls of Jerusalem all around.

[11]Then Nebuzaradan the captain of the guard carried away captive the rest of the people *who* remained in the city and the defectors who had deserted to the king of Babylon, with the rest of the multitude. [12]But the captain of the guard left *some* of the poor of the land as vinedressers and farm-

ers. [13]The bronze pillars that *were* in the house of the LORD, and the carts and the bronze Sea that *were* in the house of the LORD, the Chaldeans broke in pieces, and carried their bronze to Babylon. [14]They also took away the pots, the shovels, the trimmers, the spoons, and all the bronze utensils with which the priests ministered. [15]The firepans and the basins, the things of solid gold and solid silver, the captain of the guard took away. [16]The two pillars, one Sea, and the carts, which Solomon had made for the house of the LORD, the bronze of all these articles was beyond measure. [17]The height of one pillar *was* eighteen cubits, and the capital on it *was* of bronze. The height of the capital was three cubits, and the network and pomegranates all around the capital were all of bronze. The second pillar was the same, with a network.

[18]And the captain of the guard took Seraiah the chief priest, Zephaniah the second priest, and the three doorkeepers. [19]He also took out of the city an officer who had charge of the men of war, five men of the king's close associates who were found in the city, the chief recruiting officer of the army, who mustered the people of the land, and sixty men of the people of the land *who were* found in the city. [20]So Nebuzaradan, captain of the guard, took these and brought them to the king of Babylon at Riblah. [21]Then the king of Babylon struck them and put them to death at Riblah in the land of Hamath. Thus Judah was carried away captive from its own land.

GEDALIAH MADE GOVERNOR OF JUDAH

[22]Then he made Gedaliah the son of Ahikam, the son of Shaphan, governor over the people who remained in the land of Judah, whom Nebuchadnezzar king of Babylon had left. [23]Now when all the captains of the armies, they and *their* men, heard that the king of Babylon had made Gedaliah governor, they came to Gedaliah at Mizpah—Ishmael the son of Nethaniah, Johanan the son of Careah, Seraiah the son of Tanhumeth the Netophathite, and Jaazaniah[a] the son of a Maachathite, they and their men. [24]And Gedaliah took an oath before them and their men, and said to them, "Do not be afraid of the servants of the

25:4 [a]Literally *he* [b]Or *Arabah*, that is, the Jordan Valley
25:23 [a]Spelled *Jezaniah* in Jeremiah 40:8

Chaldeans. Dwell in the land and serve the king of Babylon, and it shall be well with you."

25But it happened in the seventh month that Ishmael the son of Nethaniah, the son of Elishama, of the royal family, came with ten men and struck and killed Gedaliah, the Jews, as well as the Chaldeans who were with him at Mizpah. 26And all the people, small and great, and the captains of the armies, arose and went to Egypt; for they were afraid of the Chaldeans.

Jehoiachin Released from Prison

27Now it came to pass in the thirty-seventh year of the captivity of Jehoiachin king of Judah, in the twelfth month, on the twenty-seventh *day* of the month, *that* Evil-Merodach[a] king of Babylon, in the year that he began to reign, released Jehoiachin king of Judah from prison. 28He spoke kindly to him, and gave him a more prominent seat than those of the kings who *were* with him in Babylon. 29So Jehoiachin changed from his prison garments, and he ate bread regularly before the king all the days of his life. 30And as for his provisions, *there was* a regular ration given him by the king, a portion for each day, all the days of his life.

25:27 aLiterally *Man of Marduk*

IMPACT OF THE BOOK

FIRST CHRONICLES

IDEA

David's life, though not perfect, plainly reveals that the seeds he planted blessed Israel. His great legacy is reflected in his religious and military achievements.

MESSAGE

In the life of David, we find many timeless leadership principles. First and foremost, every leader's potential will be determined by those he chooses to have closest to him. Second, the key to being successful is to enable others to be successful. David began investing in a group of friends, later called "the mighty men." Third, David's legacy is loyalty: to God in spite of personal weakness, to the nation of Israel, to his mighty men, and to his son, whom he prepared through the vision of the building of the temple. Leaders hopefully see further down the road than anyone else. David's careful preparations for potential—beyond himself and his own time—show his understanding of vision.

PEOPLE

David, Eleazar, Gad, Jashobeam, Joab, Nathan, Saul, Solomon

AUTHOR

The anonymous author of 1 and 2 Chronicles is referred to as the "the Chronicler" by some scholars, but Jewish tradition assigns authorship to Ezra, though that cannot be proved.

CULTURE

This book "chronicles" the story of God's people from the generations of Adam to the return from the Babylonian exile, focusing on the forty-year reign of King David (c. 1010–970 BC). This account was written for the exiles who had returned from Babylon (beginning in 538 BC) to remind them of their history before they were taken into captivity. The genealogies included offer evidence that God had preserved a remnant of His people throughout the generations.

TIMELINE

c. 450 BC

KEY SCRIPTURE MEMORY VERSES

4:10; 17:11–14; 28:9; 29:11

The Family of Adam—Seth to Abraham

1 Adam, Seth, Enosh, [2]Cainan,[a] Mahalalel, Jared, [3]Enoch, Methuselah, Lamech, [4]Noah,[a] Shem, Ham, and Japheth.

[5]The sons of Japheth *were* Gomer, Magog, Madai, Javan, Tubal, Meshech, and Tiras. [6]The sons of Gomer *were* Ashkenaz, Diphath,[a] and Togarmah. [7]The sons of Javan *were* Elishah, Tarshishah,[a] Kittim, and Rodanim.[b]

[8]The sons of Ham *were* Cush, Mizraim, Put, and Canaan. [9]The sons of Cush *were* Seba, Havilah, Sabta,[a] Raama,[b] and Sabtecha. The sons of Raama *were* Sheba and Dedan. [10]Cush begot Nimrod; he began to be a mighty one on the earth. [11]Mizraim begot Ludim, Anamim, Lehabim, Naphtuhim, [12]Pathrusim, Casluhim (from whom came the Philistines and the Caphtorim). [13]Canaan begot Sidon, his firstborn, and Heth; [14]the Jebusite, the Amorite, and the Girgashite; [15]the Hivite, the Arkite, and the Sinite; [16]the Arvadite, the Zemarite, and the Hamathite.

[17]The sons of Shem *were* Elam, Asshur, Arphaxad, Lud, Aram, Uz, Hul, Gether, and Meshech.[a] [18]Arphaxad begot Shelah, and Shelah begot Eber. [19]To Eber were born two sons: the name of one *was* Peleg,[a] for in his days the earth was divided; and his brother's name *was* Joktan. [20]Joktan begot Almodad, Sheleph, Hazarmaveth, Jerah, [21]Hadoram, Uzal, Diklah, [22]Ebal,[a] Abimael, Sheba, [23]Ophir, Havilah, and Jobab. All these *were* the sons of Joktan.

[24]Shem, Arphaxad, Shelah, [25]Eber, Peleg, Reu, [26]Serug, Nahor, Terah, [27]and Abram, who *is* Abraham. [28]The sons of Abraham *were* Isaac and Ishmael.

The Family of Ishmael

[29]These *are* their genealogies: The firstborn of Ishmael *was* Nebajoth; then Kedar, Adbeel, Mibsam, [30]Mishma, Dumah, Massa, Hadad,[a] Tema, [31]Jetur, Naphish, and Kedemah. These *were* the sons of Ishmael.

The Family of Keturah

[32]Now the sons born to Keturah, Abraham's concubine, *were* Zimran, Jokshan, Medan, Midian, Ishbak, and Shuah. The sons of Jokshan *were* Sheba and Dedan. [33]The sons of Midian *were*

Ephah, Epher, Hanoch, Abida, and Eldaah. All these were the children of Keturah.

The Family of Isaac

[34]And Abraham begot Isaac. The sons of Isaac *were* Esau and Israel. [35]The sons of Esau *were* Eliphaz, Reuel, Jeush, Jaalam, and Korah. [36]And the sons of Eliphaz *were* Teman, Omar, Zephi,[a] Gatam, *and* Kenaz; and *by* Timna,[b] Amalek. [37]The sons of Reuel *were* Nahath, Zerah, Shammah, and Mizzah.

The Family of Seir

[38]The sons of Seir *were* Lotan, Shobal, Zibeon, Anah, Dishon, Ezer, and Dishan. [39]And the sons of Lotan *were* Hori and Homam; Lotan's sister *was* Timna. [40]The sons of Shobal *were* Alian,[a] Manahath, Ebal, Shephi,[b] and Onam. The sons of Zibeon *were* Ajah and Anah. [41]The son of Anah *was* Dishon. The sons of Dishon *were* Hamran,[a] Eshban, Ithran, and Cheran. [42]The sons of Ezer *were* Bilhan, Zaavan, *and* Jaakan.[a] The sons of Dishan *were* Uz and Aran.

The Kings of Edom

[43]Now these *were* the kings who reigned in the land of Edom before a king reigned over the children of Israel: Bela the son of Beor, and the name of his city *was* Dinhabah. [44]And when Bela died, Jobab the son of Zerah of Bozrah reigned in his place. [45]When Jobab died, Husham of the land of the Temanites reigned in his place. [46]And when Husham died, Hadad the son of Bedad, who attacked Midian in the field of Moab, reigned in his place. The name of his city *was* Avith. [47]When Hadad died, Samlah of Masrekah reigned in his place. [48]And when Samlah died, Saul of Rehoboth-by-the-River reigned in his place. [49]When Saul died, Baal-Hanan the son of Achbor reigned in his place. [50]And when Baal-Hanan died, Hadad[a] reigned in his place; and the name of his city was Pai.[b] His wife's name was Mehetabel

1:2 [a]Hebrew *Qenan*   1:4 [a]Following Masoretic Text and Vulgate Septuagint adds *the sons of Noah.*   1:6 [a]Spelled *Riphath* in Genesis 10:3   1:7 [a]Spelled *Tarshish* in Genesis 10:4   [b]Spelled *Dodanim* in Genesis 10:4   1:9 [a]Spelled *Sabtah* in Genesis 10:7   [b]Spelled *Raamah* in Genesis 10:7   1:17 [a]Spelled *Mash* in Genesis 10:2   1:19 [a]Literally *Division*   1:22 [a]Spelled *Obal* in Genesis 10:2   1:30 [a]Spelled *Hadar* in Genesis 25:15   1:36 [a]Spelled *Zepho* in Genesis 36:11   [b]Compare Genesis 36:12   1:40 [a]Spelled *Alvan* in Genesis 36:23   [b]Spelled *Shepho* in Genesis 36:23   1:41 [a]Spelled *Hemdan* in Genesis 36:26   1:42 [a]Spelled *Akan* in Genesis 36:27   1:50 [a]Spelled *Hadar* in Genesis 36:39   [b]Spelled *Pau* in Genesis 36:39

the daughter of Matred, the daughter of Mezahab. [51]Hadad died also. And the chiefs of Edom were Chief Timnah, Chief Aliah,[a] Chief Jetheth, [52]Chief Aholibamah, Chief Elah, Chief Pinon, [53]Chief Kenaz, Chief Teman, Chief Mibzar, [54]Chief Magdiel, and Chief Iram. These were the chiefs of Edom.

THE FAMILY OF ISRAEL

2 These were the sons of Israel: Reuben, Simeon, Levi, Judah, Issachar, Zebulun, [2]Dan, Joseph, Benjamin, Naphtali, Gad, and Asher.

FROM JUDAH TO DAVID

[3]The sons of Judah were Er, Onan, and Shelah. These three were born to him by the daughter of Shua, the Canaanitess. Er, the firstborn of Judah, was wicked in the sight of the LORD; so He killed him. [4]And Tamar, his daughter-in-law, bore him Perez and Zerah. All the sons of Judah were five.

[5]The sons of Perez were Hezron and Hamul. [6]The sons of Zerah were Zimri, Ethan, Heman, Calcol, and Dara—five of them in all.

[7]The son of Carmi was Achar,[a] the troubler of Israel, who transgressed in the accursed thing.

[8]The son of Ethan was Azariah.

[9]Also the sons of Hezron who were born to him were Jerahmeel, Ram, and Chelubai.[a] [10]Ram begot Amminadab, and Amminadab begot Nahshon, leader of the children of Judah; [11]Nahshon begot Salma,[a] and Salma begot Boaz; [12]Boaz begot Obed, and Obed begot Jesse; [13]Jesse begot Eliab his firstborn, Abinadab the second, Shimea[a] the third, [14]Nethanel the fourth, Raddai the fifth, [15]Ozem the sixth, and David the seventh.

[16]Now their sisters were Zeruiah and Abigail. And the sons of Zeruiah were Abishai, Joab, and Asahel—three. [17]Abigail bore Amasa; and the father of Amasa was Jether the Ishmaelite.[a]

THE FAMILY OF HEZRON

[18]Caleb the son of Hezron had children by Azubah, his wife, and by Jerioth. Now these were her sons: Jesher, Shobab, and Ardon. [19]When Azubah died, Caleb took Ephrath[a] as his wife, who bore him Hur. [20]And Hur begot Uri, and Uri begot Bezalel.

[21]Now afterward Hezron went in to the daughter of Machir the father of Gilead, whom he married when he was sixty years old; and she bore him Segub. [22]Segub begot Jair, who had twenty-three cities in the land of Gilead. [23](Geshur and Syria took from them the towns of Jair, with Kenath and its towns—sixty towns.) All these belonged to the sons of Machir the father of Gilead. [24]After Hezron died in Caleb Ephrathah, Hezron's wife Abijah bore him Ashhur the father of Tekoa.

THE FAMILY OF JERAHMEEL

[25]The sons of Jerahmeel, the firstborn of Hezron, were Ram, the firstborn, and Bunah, Oren, Ozem, and Ahijah. [26]Jerahmeel had another wife, whose name was Atarah; she was the mother of Onam. [27]The sons of Ram, the firstborn of Jerahmeel, were Maaz, Jamin, and Eker. [28]The sons of Onam were Shammai and Jada. The sons of Shammai were Nadab and Abishur.

[29]And the name of the wife of Abishur was Abihail, and she bore him Ahban and Molid. [30]The sons of Nadab were Seled and Appaim; Seled died without children. [31]The son of Appaim was Ishi, the son of Ishi was Sheshan, and Sheshan's son was Ahlai. [32]The sons of Jada, the brother of Shammai, were Jether and Jonathan; Jether died without children. [33]The sons of Jonathan were Peleth and Zaza. These were the sons of Jerahmeel.

[34]Now Sheshan had no sons, only daughters. And Sheshan had an Egyptian servant whose name was Jarha. [35]Sheshan gave his daughter to Jarha his servant as wife, and she bore him Attai. [36]Attai begot Nathan, and Nathan begot Zabad; [37]Zabad begot Ephlal, and Ephlal begot Obed; [38]Obed begot Jehu, and Jehu begot Azariah; [39]Azariah begot Helez, and Helez begot Eleasah; [40]Eleasah begot Sismai, and Sismai begot Shallum; [41]Shallum begot Jekamiah, and Jekamiah begot Elishama.

THE FAMILY OF CALEB

[42]The descendants of Caleb the brother of Jerahmeel were Mesha, his firstborn, who was the father of Ziph, and the sons of Mareshah the

1:51 [a]Spelled *Alvah* in Genesis 36:40   **2:7** [a]Spelled *Achan* in Joshua 7:1 and elsewhere   **2:9** [a]Spelled *Caleb* in 2:18, 42   **2:11** [a]Spelled *Salmon* in Ruth 4:21 and Luke 3:32   **2:13** [a]Spelled *Shammah* in 1 Samuel 16:9 and elsewhere   **2:17** [a]Compare 2 Samuel 17:25 **2:19** [a]Spelled *Ephrathah* elsewhere father of Hebron. ⁴³The sons of Hebron *were* Korah, Tappuah, Rekem, and Shema. ⁴⁴Shema begot Raham the father of Jorkoam, and Rekem begot Shammai. ⁴⁵And the son of Shammai *was* Maon, and Maon *was* the father of Beth Zur.

⁴⁶Ephah, Caleb's concubine, bore Haran, Moza, and Gazez; and Haran begot Gazez. ⁴⁷And the sons of Jahdai *were* Regem, Jotham, Geshan, Pelet, Ephah, and Shaaph.

⁴⁸Maachah, Caleb's concubine, bore Sheber and Tirhanah. ⁴⁹She also bore Shaaph the father of Madmannah, Sheva the father of Machbenah and the father of Gibea. And the daughter of Caleb *was* Achsah.

⁵⁰These were the descendants of Caleb: The sons of Hur, the firstborn of Ephrathah, *were* Shobal the father of Kirjath Jearim, ⁵¹Salma the father of Bethlehem, *and* Hareph the father of Beth Gader.

⁵²And Shobal the father of Kirjath Jearim had descendants: Haroeh, *and* half of the *families of Manuhoth.*ᵃ ⁵³The families of Kirjath Jearim *were* the Ithrites, the Puthites, the Shumathites, and the Mishraites. From these came the Zorathites and the Eshtaolites.

⁵⁴The sons of Salma *were* Bethlehem, the Netophathites, Atroth Beth Joab, half of the Manahethites, and the Zorites.

⁵⁵And the families of the scribes who dwelt at Jabez *were* the Tirathites, the Shimeathites, *and* the Suchathites. These *were* the Kenites who came from Hammath, the father of the house of Rechab.

The Family of David

3 Now these were the sons of David who were born to him in Hebron: The firstborn *was* Amnon, by Ahinoam the Jezreelitess; the second, Daniel,ᵃ by Abigail the Carmelitess; ²the third, Absalom the son of Maacah, the daughter of Talmai, king of Geshur; the fourth, Adonijah the son of Haggith; ³the fifth, Shephatiah, by Abital; the sixth, Ithream, by his wife Eglah.

⁴*These* six were born to him in Hebron. There he reigned seven years and six months, and in Jerusalem he reigned thirty-three years. ⁵And these were born to him in Jerusalem: Shimea,ᵃ Shobab, Nathan, and Solomon—four by Bathshuaᵇ the daughter of Ammiel.ᶜ ⁶Also *there* were Ibhar,

Elishama,ᵃ Eliphelet,ᵇ ⁷Nogah, Nepheg, Japhia, ⁸Elishama, Eliada,ᵃ and Eliphelet—nine *in all.* ⁹*These were* all the sons of David, besides the sons of the concubines, and Tamar their sister.

The Family of Solomon

¹⁰Solomon's son *was* Rehoboam; Abijahᵃ his son, Asa his son, Jehoshaphat his son, ¹¹Joramᵃ his son, Ahaziah his son, Joashᵇ his son, ¹²Amaziah his son, Azariahᵃ his son, Jotham his son, ¹³Ahaz his son, Hezekiah his son, Manasseh his son, ¹⁴Amon his son, *and* Josiah his son. ¹⁵The sons of Josiah *were* Johanan the firstborn, the second Jehoiakim, the third Zedekiah, and the fourth Shallum.ᵃ ¹⁶The sons of Jehoiakim *were* Jeconiah his son *and* Zedekiahᵃ his son.

The Family of Jeconiah

¹⁷And the sons of Jeconiahᵃ *were* Assir,ᵇ Shealtiel his son, ¹⁸*and* Malchiram, Pedaiah, Shenazzar, Jecamiah, Hoshama, and Nedabiah. ¹⁹The sons of Pedaiah *were* Zerubbabel and Shimei. The sons of Zerubbabel *were* Meshullam, Hananiah, Shelomith their sister, ²⁰and Hashubah, Ohel, Berechiah, Hasadiah, and Jushab-Hesed—five *in all.* ²¹The sons of Hananiah *were* Pelatiah and Jeshaiah, the sons of Rephaiah, the sons of Arnan, the sons of Obadiah, and the sons of Shechaniah. ²²The son of Shechaniah was Shemaiah. The sons of Shemaiah *were* Hattush, Igal, Bariah, Neariah, and Shaphat—six *in all.* ²³The sons of Neariah *were* Elioenai, Hezekiah, and Azrikam—three *in all.* ²⁴The sons of Elioenai *were* Hodaviah, Eliashib, Pelaiah, Akkub, Johanan, Delaiah, and Anani—seven *in all.*

The Family of Judah

4 The sons of Judah *were* Perez, Hezron, Carmi, Hur, and Shobal. ²And Reaiah the son of Shobal begot Jahath, and Jahath begot Ahumai and

2:52 ᵃSame as the *Manahethites,* verse 54   **3:1** ᵃCalled *Chileab* in 2 Samuel 3:3   **3:5** ᵃSpelled *Shammua* in 14:4 and 2 Samuel 5:14   ᵇSpelled *Bathsheba* in 2 Samuel 11:3   ᶜCalled *Eliam* in 2 Samuel 11:3   **3:6** ᵃSpelled *Elishua* in 14:5 and 2 Samuel 5:15   ᵇSpelled *Elpelet* in 14:5   **3:8** ᵃSpelled *Beeliada* in 14:7   **3:10** ᵃSpelled *Abijam* in 1 Kings 15:1   **3:11** ᵃSpelled *Jehoram* in 2 Kings 1:17 and 8:16   ᵇSpelled *Jehoash* in 2 Kings 12:1   **3:12** ᵃCalled *Uzziah* in Isaiah 6:1   **3:15** ᵃCalled *Jehoahaz* in 2 Kings 23:31   **3:16** ᵃCompare 2 Kings 24:17   **3:17** ᵃAlso called *Coniah* in Jeremiah 22:24 and *Jehoiachin* in 2 Kings 24:8   ᵇOr *Jeconiah the captive were*

Lahad. These *were* the families of the Zorathites. [3]These *were the sons of* the father of Etam: Jezreel, Ishma, and Idbash; and the name of their sister *was* Hazelelponi; [4]and Penuel *was* the father of Gedor, and Ezer *was the* father of Hushah.

These *were* the sons of Hur, the firstborn of Ephrathah the father of Bethlehem.

[5]And Ashhur the father of Tekoa had two wives, Helah and Naarah. [6]Naarah bore him Ahuzzam, Hepher, Temeni, and Haahashtari. These *were* the sons of Naarah. [7]The sons of Helah *were* Zereth, Zohar, and Ethnan; [8]and Koz begot Anub, Zobebah, and the families of Aharhel the son of Harum.

[9]Now Jabez was more honorable than his brothers, and his mother called his name Jabez,[a] saying, "Because I bore *him* in pain." [10]And Jabez called on the God of Israel saying, "Oh, that You would bless me indeed, and enlarge my territory, that Your hand would be with me, and that You would keep *me* from evil, that I may not cause pain!" So God granted him what he requested.

[11]Chelub the brother of Shuhah begot Mehir, who *was* the father of Eshton. [12]And Eshton begot Beth-Rapha, Paseah, and Tehinnah the father of Ir-Nahash. These *were* the men of Rechab.

[13]The sons of Kenaz *were* Othniel and Seraiah. The sons of Othniel *were* Hathath,[a] [14]and Meonothai *who* begot Ophrah. Seraiah begot Joab the father of Ge Harashim,[a] for they were craftsmen. [15]The sons of Caleb the son of Jephunneh *were* Iru, Elah, and Naam. The son of Elah *was* Kenaz. [16]The sons of Jehallelel *were* Ziph, Ziphah, Tiria, and Asarel. [17]The sons of Ezrah *were* Jether, Mered, Epher, and Jalon. And *Mered's wife*[a] bore Miriam, Shammai, and Ishbah the father of Eshtemoa. [18](His wife Jehudijah[a] bore Jered the father of Gedor, Heber the father of Sochoh, and Jekuthiel the father of Zanoah.) And these were the sons of Bithiah the daughter of Pharaoh, whom Mered took.

[19]The sons of Hodiah's wife, the sister of Naham, *were* the fathers of Keilah the Garmite and of Eshtemoa the Maachathite. [20]And the sons of Shimon *were* Amnon, Rinnah, Ben-Hanan, and Tilon. And the sons of Ishi *were* Zoheth and Ben-Zoheth.

[21]The sons of Shelah the son of Judah *were* Er the father of Lecah, Laadah the father of Mare-shah, and the families of the house of the linen workers of the house of Ashbea; [22]also Jokim, the men of Chozeba, and Joash; Saraph, who ruled in Moab, and Jashubi-Lehem. Now the records are ancient. [23]These *were* the potters and those who dwell at Netaim[a] and Gederah;[b] there they dwelt with the king for his work.

THE FAMILY OF SIMEON

[24]The sons of Simeon *were* Nemuel, Jamin, Jarib,[a] Zerah,[b] *and* Shaul, [25]Shallum his son, Mibsam his son, and Mishma his son. [26]And the sons of Mishma *were* Hamuel his son, Zacchur his son, and Shimei his son. [27]Shimei had sixteen sons and six daughters; but his brothers did not have many children, nor did any of their families multiply as much as the children of Judah.

[28]They dwelt at Beersheba, Moladah, Hazar Shual, [29]Bilhah, Ezem, Tolad, [30]Bethuel, Hormah, Ziklag, [31]Beth Marcaboth, Hazar Susim, Beth Biri, and at Shaaraim. These *were* their cities until the reign of David. [32]And their villages *were* Etam, Ain, Rimmon, Tochen, and Ashan—five cities— [33]and all the villages that *were* around these cities as far as Baal.[a] These *were* their dwelling places, and they maintained their genealogy: [34]Meshobab, Jamlech, and Joshah the son of Amaziah; [35]Joel, and Jehu the son of Joshibiah, the son of Seraiah, the son of Asiel; [36]Elioenai, Jaakobah, Jeshohaiah, Asaiah, Adiel, Jesimiel, and Benaiah; [37]Ziza the son of Shiphi, the son of Allon, the son of Jedaiah, the son of Shimri, the son of Shemaiah— [38]these mentioned by name *were* leaders in their families, and their father's house increased greatly.

[39]So they went to the entrance of Gedor, as far as the east side of the valley, to seek pasture for their flocks. [40]And they found rich, good pasture, and the land *was* broad, quiet, and peaceful; for some Hamites formerly lived there.

[41]These recorded by name came in the days of Hezekiah king of Judah; and they attacked their tents and the Meunites who were found there, and utterly destroyed them, as it is to this day. So they dwelt in their place, because *there was* pasture for their flocks there. [42]Now *some* of

4:9 [a]Literally *He Will Cause Pain*   **4:13** [a]Septuagint and Vulgate add *and Meonothai.*   **4:14** [a]Literally *Valley of Craftsmen*   **4:17** [a]Literally *she*   **4:18** [a]Or *His Judean wife*   **4:23** [a]Literally *Plants* [b]Literally *Hedges*   **4:24** [a]Called *Jachin* in Genesis 46:10 [b]Called *Zohar* in Genesis 46:10   **4:33** [a]Or *Baalath Beer* (compare Joshua 19:8) them, five hundred men of the sons of Simeon, went to Mount Seir, having as their captains Pelatiah, Neariah, Rephaiah, and Uzziel, the sons of Ishi. ⁴³And they defeated the rest of the Amalekites who had escaped. They have dwelt there to this day.

THE FAMILY OF REUBEN

5 Now the sons of Reuben the firstborn of Israel—he *was* indeed the firstborn, but because he defiled his father's bed, his birthright was given to the sons of Joseph, the son of Israel, so that the genealogy is not listed according to the birthright; ²yet Judah prevailed over his brothers, and from him *came* a ruler, although the birthright was Joseph's— ³the sons of Reuben the firstborn of Israel were Hanoch, Pallu, Hezron, and Carmi.

⁴The sons of Joel *were* Shemaiah his son, Gog his son, Shimei his son, ⁵Micah his son, Reaiah his son, Baal his son, ⁶and Beerah his son, whom Tiglath-Pileser[a] king of Assyria carried into captivity. He *was* leader of the Reubenites. ⁷And his brethren by their families, when the genealogy of their generations was registered: the chief, Jeiel, and Zechariah, ⁸and Bela the son of Azaz, the son of Shema, the son of Joel, who dwelt in Aroer, as far as Nebo and Baal Meon. ⁹Eastward they settled as far as the entrance of the wilderness this side of the River Euphrates, because their cattle had multiplied in the land of Gilead.

¹⁰Now in the days of Saul they made war with the Hagrites, who fell by their hand; and they dwelt in their tents throughout the entire *area* east of Gilead.

THE FAMILY OF GAD

¹¹And the children of Gad dwelt next to them in the land of Bashan as far as Salcah: ¹²Joel *was* the chief, Shapham the next, then Jaanai and Shaphat in Bashan, ¹³and their brethren of their father's house: Michael, Meshullam, Sheba, Jorai, Jachan, Zia, and Eber—seven *in all.* ¹⁴These *were* the children of Abihail the son of Huri, the son of Jaroah, the son of Gilead, the son of Michael, the son of Jeshishai, the son of Jahdo, the son of Buz; ¹⁵Ahi the son of Abdiel, the son of Guni, *was* chief of their father's house. ¹⁶And *the* Gadites dwelt in Gilead, in Bashan and in its villages, and in all the common-lands of Sharon within their borders.

¹⁷All these were registered by genealogies in the days of Jotham king of Judah, and in the days of Jeroboam king of Israel.

¹⁸The sons of Reuben, the Gadites, and half the tribe of Manasseh *had* forty-four thousand seven hundred and sixty valiant men, men able to bear shield and sword, to shoot with the bow, and skillful in war, who went to war. ¹⁹They made war with the Hagrites, Jetur, Naphish, and Nodab. ²⁰And they were helped against them, and the Hagrites were delivered into their hand, and all who *were* with them, for they cried out to God in the battle. He heeded their prayer, because they put their trust in Him. ²¹Then they took away their livestock—fifty thousand of their camels, two hundred and fifty thousand of their sheep, and two thousand of their donkeys—also one hundred thousand of their men; ²²for many fell dead, because the war *was* God's. And they dwelt in their place until the captivity.

THE FAMILY OF MANASSEH (EAST)

²³So the children of the half-tribe of Manasseh dwelt in the land. Their *numbers* increased from Bashan to Baal Hermon, that is, to Senir, or Mount Hermon. ²⁴These *were* the heads of their fathers' houses: Epher, Ishi, Eliel, Azriel, Jeremiah, Hodaviah, and Jahdiel. They were mighty men of valor, famous men, *and* heads of their fathers' houses.

²⁵And they were unfaithful to the God of their fathers, and played the harlot after the gods of the peoples of the land, whom God had destroyed before them. ²⁶So the God of Israel stirred up the spirit of Pul king of Assyria, that is, Tiglath-Pileser[a] king of Assyria. He carried the Reubenites, the Gadites, and the half-tribe of Manasseh into captivity. He took them to Halah, Habor, Hara, and the river of Gozan to this day.

THE FAMILY OF LEVI

6 The sons of Levi *were* Gershon, Kohath, and Merari. ²The sons of Kohath *were* Amram, Izhar, Hebron, and Uzziel. ³The children of Amram *were* Aaron, Moses, and Miriam. And the sons of Aaron *were* Nadab, Abihu, Eleazar, and Ithamar. ⁴Eleazar begot Phinehas, *and* Phinehas begot

5:6 ªHebrew *Tilgath-Pileser* **5:26** ªHebrew *Tilgath-Pilneser*

Abishua; [5]Abishua begot Bukki, and Bukki begot Uzzi; [6]Uzzi begot Zerahiah, and Zerahiah begot Meraioth; [7]Meraioth begot Amariah, and Amariah begot Ahitub; [8]Ahitub begot Zadok, and Zadok begot Ahimaaz; [9]Ahimaaz begot Azariah, and Azariah begot Johanan; [10]Johanan begot Azariah (it was he who ministered as priest in the temple that Solomon built in Jerusalem); [11]Azariah begot Amariah, and Amariah begot Ahitub; [12]Ahitub begot Zadok, and Zadok begot Shallum; [13]Shallum begot Hilkiah, and Hilkiah begot Azariah; [14]Azariah begot Seraiah, and Seraiah begot Jehozadak. [15]Jehozadak went *into captivity* when the LORD carried Judah and Jerusalem into captivity by the hand of Nebuchadnezzar.

[16]The sons of Levi *were* Gershon,[a] Kohath, and Merari. [17]These are the names of the sons of Gershon: Libni and Shimei. [18]The sons of Kohath *were* Amram, Izhar, Hebron, and Uzziel. [19]The sons of Merari *were* Mahli and Mushi. Now these *are* the families of the Levites according to their fathers: [20]Of Gershon *were* Libni his son, Jahath his son, Zimmah his son, [21]Joah his son, Iddo his son, Zerah his son, *and* Jeatherai his son. [22]The sons of Kohath *were* Amminadab his son, Korah his son, Assir his son, [23]Elkanah his son, Ebiasaph his son, Assir his son, [24]Tahath his son, Uriel his son, Uzziah his son, and Shaul his son. [25]The sons of Elkanah *were* Amasai and Ahimoth. [26]*As for* Elkanah,[a] the sons of Elkanah *were* Zophai[b] his son, Nahath[c] his son, [27]Eliab[a] his son, Jeroham his son, *and* Elkanah his son. [28]The sons of Samuel *were* Joel[a] the firstborn, and Abijah the second.[b] [29]The sons of Merari *were* Mahli, Libni his son, Shimei his son, Uzzah his son, [30]Shimea his son, Haggiah his son, *and* Asaiah his son.

Musicians in the House of the Lord

[31]Now these are the men whom David appointed over the service of song in the house of the LORD, after the ark came to rest. [32]They were ministering with music before the dwelling place of the tabernacle of meeting, until Solomon had built the house of the LORD in Jerusalem, and they served in their office according to their order.

[33]And these *are* the ones who ministered with their sons: Of the sons of the Kohathites *were* Heman the singer, the son of Joel, the son of Samuel,

[34]the son of Elkanah, the son of Jeroham, the son of Eliel,[a] the son of Toah,[b] [35]the son of Zuph, the son of Elkanah, the son of Mahath, the son of Amasai, [36]the son of Elkanah, the son of Joel, the son of Azariah, the son of Zephaniah, [37]the son of Tahath, the son of Assir, the son of Ebiasaph, the son of Korah, [38]the son of Izhar, the son of Kohath, the son of Levi, the son of Israel. [39]And his brother Asaph, who stood at his right hand, *was* Asaph the son of Berachiah, the son of Shimea, [40]the son of Michael, the son of Baaseiah, the son of Malchijah, [41]the son of Ethni, the son of Zerah, the son of Adaiah, [42]the son of Ethan, the son of Zimmah, the son of Shimei, [43]the son of Jahath, the son of Gershon, the son of Levi.

[44]Their brethren, the sons of Merari, on the left hand, *were* Ethan the son of Kishi, the son of Abdi, the son of Malluch, [45]the son of Hashabiah, the son of Amaziah, the son of Hilkiah, [46]the son of Amzi, the son of Bani, the son of Shamer, [47]the son of Mahli, the son of Mushi, the son of Merari, the son of Levi.

[48]And their brethren, the Levites, *were* appointed to every kind of service of the tabernacle of the house of God.

The Family of Aaron

[49]But Aaron and his sons offered sacrifices on the altar of burnt offering and on the altar of incense, for all the work of the Most Holy *Place,* and to make atonement for Israel, according to all that Moses the servant of God had commanded. [50]Now these *are* the sons of Aaron: Eleazar his son, Phinehas his son, Abishua his son, [51]Bukki his son, Uzzi his son, Zerahiah his son, [52]Meraioth his son, Amariah his son, Ahitub his son, [53]Zadok his son, *and* Ahimaaz his son.

Dwelling Places of the Levites

[54]Now these *are* their dwelling places throughout their settlements in their territory, for they were *given* by lot to the sons of Aaron, of the family of the Kohathites: [55]They gave them Hebron in the land of Judah, with its surrounding

---

6:16 [a]Hebrew *Gershom* (alternate spelling of *Gershon,* as in verses 1, 17, 20, 43, 62, and 71) **6:26** [a]Compare verse 35 [b]Spelled *Zuph* in verse 35 and 1 Samuel 1:1 [c]Compare verse 34 **6:27** [a]Compare verse 34 **6:28** [a]Following Septuagint, Syriac, and Arabic (compare verse 33 and 1 Samuel 8:2) [b]Hebrew *Vasheni* **6:34** [a]Spelled *Elihu* in 1 Samuel 1:1 [b]Spelled *Tohu* in 1 Samuel 1:1

common-lands. [56]But the fields of the city and its villages they gave to Caleb the son of Jephunneh. [57]And to the sons of Aaron they gave *one of* the cities of refuge, Hebron; also Libnah with its common-lands, Jattir, Eshtemoa with its common-lands, [58]Hilen[a] with its common-lands, Debir with its common-lands, [59]Ashan[a] with its common-lands, and Beth Shemesh with its common-lands. [60]And from the tribe of Benjamin: Geba with its common-lands, Alemeth[a] with its common-lands, and Anathoth with its common-lands. All their cities among their families *were* thirteen.

[61]To the rest of the family of the tribe of the Kohathites *they gave* by lot ten cities from half the tribe of Manasseh. [62]And to the sons of Gershon, throughout their families, *they gave* thirteen cities from the tribe of Issachar, from the tribe of Asher, from the tribe of Naphtali, and from the tribe of Manasseh in Bashan. [63]To the sons of Merari, throughout their families, *they gave* twelve cities from the tribe of Reuben, from the tribe of Gad, and from the tribe of Zebulun. [64]So the children of Israel gave *these* cities with their common-lands to the Levites. [65]And they gave by lot from the tribe of the children of Judah, from the tribe of the children of Simeon, and from the tribe of the children of Benjamin these cities which are called by *their* names.

[66]Now some of the families of the sons of Kohath *were given* cities as their territory from the tribe of Ephraim. [67]And they gave them *one of* the cities of refuge, Shechem with its common-lands, in the mountains of Ephraim, also Gezer with its common-lands, [68]Jokmeam with its common-lands, Beth Horon with its common-lands, [69]Aijalon with its common-lands, and Gath Rimmon with its common-lands. [70]And from the half-tribe of Manasseh: Aner with its common-lands and Bileam with its common-lands, for the rest of the family of the sons of Kohath.

[71]From the family of the half-tribe of Manasseh the sons of Gershon *were given* Golan in Bashan with its common-lands and Ashtaroth with its common-lands. [72]And from the tribe of Issachar: Kedesh with its common-lands, Daberath with its common-lands, [73]Ramoth with its common-lands, and Anem with its common-lands. [74]And from the tribe of Asher: Mashal with its common-lands, Abdon with its common-

lands, [75]Hukok with its common-lands, and Rehob with its common-lands. [76]And from the tribe of Naphtali: Kedesh in Galilee with its common-lands, Hammon with its common-lands, and Kirjathaim with its common-lands.

[77]From the tribe of Zebulun the rest of the children of Merari *were given* Rimmon[a] with its common-lands and Tabor with its common-lands. [78]And on the other side of the Jordan, across from Jericho, on the east side of the Jordan, *they were given* from the tribe of Reuben: Bezer in the wilderness with its common-lands, Jahzah with its common-lands, [79]Kedemoth with its common-lands, and Mephaath with its common-lands. [80]And from the tribe of Gad: Ramoth in Gilead with its common-lands, Mahanaim with its common-lands, [81]Heshbon with its common-lands, and Jazer with its common-lands.

THE FAMILY OF ISSACHAR

7 The sons of Issachar *were* Tola, Puah,[a] Jashub, and Shimron—four *in all*. [2]The sons of Tola *were* Uzzi, Rephaiah, Jeriel, Jahmai, Jibsam, and Shemuel, heads of their father's house. *The sons* of Tola *were* mighty men of valor in their generations; their number in the days of David *was* twenty-two thousand six hundred. [3]The son of Uzzi *was* Izrahiah, and the sons of Izrahiah *were* Michael, Obadiah, Joel, and Ishiah. All five of them *were* chief men. [4]And with them, by their generations, according to their fathers' houses, *were* thirty-six thousand troops ready for war; for they had many wives and sons.

[5]Now their brethren among all the families of Issachar *were* mighty men of valor, listed by their genealogies, eighty-seven thousand in all.

THE FAMILY OF BENJAMIN

[6]*The sons* of Benjamin *were* Bela, Becher, and Jediael—three *in all*. [7]The sons of Bela were Ezbon, Uzzi, Uzziel, Jerimoth, and Iri—five *in all*. They *were* heads of *their* fathers' houses, and they were listed by their genealogies, twenty-two thousand and thirty-four mighty men of valor.

[8]The sons of Becher *were* Zemirah, Joash,

6:58 [a]Spelled *Holon* in Joshua 21:15 **6:59** [a]Spelled *Ain* in Joshua 21:16 **6:60** [a]Spelled *Almon* in Joshua 21:18 **6:77** [a]Hebrew *Rimmono,* alternate spelling of *Rimmon;* see 4:32 **7:1** [a]Spelled *Puvah* in Genesis 46:13

Eliezer, Elioenai, Omri, Jerimoth, Abijah, Anathoth, and Alemeth. All these *are* the sons of Becher. ⁹And they were recorded by genealogy according to their generations, heads of their fathers' houses, twenty thousand two hundred mighty men of valor. ¹⁰The son of Jediael *was* Bilhan, and the sons of Bilhan *were* Jeush, Benjamin, Ehud, Chenaanah, Zethan, Tharshish, and Ahishahar.

¹¹All these sons of Jediael *were* heads of their fathers' houses; *there were* seventeen thousand two hundred mighty men of valor fit to go out for war *and* battle. ¹²Shuppim and Huppimᵃ *were* the sons of Ir, *and* Hushim *was* the son of Aher.

The Family of Naphtali

¹³The sons of Naphtali *were* Jahziel,ᵃ Guni, Jezer, and Shallum,ᵇ the sons of Bilhah.

The Family of Manasseh (West)

¹⁴The descendants of Manasseh: his Syrian concubine bore him Machir the father of Gilead, the father of Asriel.ᵃ ¹⁵Machir took as his wife *the sister* of Huppim and Shuppim,ᵃ whose name *was* Maachah. The name of *Gilead's* grandsonᵇ *was* Zelophehad,ᶜ but Zelophehad begot only daughters. ¹⁶(Maachah the wife of Machir bore a son, and she called his name Peresh. The name of his brother *was* Sheresh, and his sons *were* Ulam and Rakem. ¹⁷The son of Ulam *was* Bedan.) These *were* the descendants of Gilead the son of Machir, the son of Manasseh.

¹⁸His sister Hammoleketh bore Ishhod, Abiezer, and Mahlah.

¹⁹And the sons of Shemida were Ahian, Shechem, Likhi, and Aniam.

The Family of Ephraim

²⁰The sons of Ephraim *were* Shuthelah, Bered his son, Tahath his son, Eladah his son, Tahath his son, ²¹Zabad his son, Shuthelah his son, and Ezer and Elead. The men of Gath who were born in *that* land killed *them* because they came down to take away their cattle. ²²Then Ephraim their father mourned many days, and his brethren came to comfort him.

²³And when he went in to his wife, she conceived and bore a son; and he called his name Beriah,ᵃ because tragedy had come upon his house.

²⁴Now his daughter *was* Sheerah, who built Lower and Upper Beth Horon and Uzzen Sheerah; ²⁵and Rephah *was* his son, *as well as* Resheph, and Telah his son, Tahan his son, ²⁶Laadan his son, Ammihud his son, Elishama his son, ²⁷Nunᵃ his son, and Joshua his son.

²⁸Now their possessions and dwelling places *were* Bethel and its towns: to the east Naaran, to the west Gezer and its towns, and Shechem and its towns, as far as Ayyahᵃ and its towns; ²⁹and by the borders of the children of Manasseh *were* Beth Shean and its towns, Taanach and its towns, Megiddo and its towns, Dor and its towns. In these dwelt the children of Joseph, the son of Israel.

The Family of Asher

³⁰The sons of Asher *were* Imnah, Ishvah, Ishvi, Beriah, and their sister Serah. ³¹The sons of Beriah *were* Heber and Malchiel, who was the father of Birzaith.ᵃ ³²And Heber begot Japhlet, Shomer,ᵃ Hotham,ᵇ and their sister Shua. ³³The sons of Japhlet *were* Pasach, Bimhal, and Ashvath. These *were* the children of Japhlet. ³⁴The sons of Shemer *were* Ahi, Rohgah, Jehubbah, and Aram. ³⁵And the sons of his brother Helem *were* Zophah, Imna, Shelesh, and Amal. ³⁶The sons of Zophah *were* Suah, Harnepher, Shual, Beri, Imrah, ³⁷Bezer, Hod, Shamma, Shilshah, Jithran,ᵃ and Beera. ³⁸The sons of Jether *were* Jephunneh, Pispah, and Ara. ³⁹The sons of Ulla *were* Arah, Haniel, and Rizia.

⁴⁰All these *were* the children of Asher, heads of *their* fathers' houses, choice men, mighty men of valor, chief leaders. And they were recorded by genealogies among the army fit for battle; their number *was* twenty-six thousand.

The Family Tree of King Saul of Benjamin

8 Now Benjamin begot Bela his firstborn, Ashbel the second, Aharahᵃ the third, ²Nohah the fourth, and Rapha the fifth. ³The sons of Bela *were* Addar,ᵃ Gera, Abihud, ⁴Abishua, Naaman, Ahoah, ⁵Gera, Shephuphan, and Huram.

7:12 ªCalled *Hupham* in Numbers 26:39 7:13 ªSpelled *Jahzeel* in Genesis 46:24 ᵇSpelled *Shillem* in Genesis 46:24 7:14 ªThe son of Gilead (compare Numbers 26:30, 31) 7:15 ªCompare verse 12 ᵇLiterally *the second* ᶜCompare Numbers 26:30–33 7:23 ªLiterally *In Tragedy* 7:27 ªHebrew *Non* 7:28 ªMany Hebrew manuscripts, Bomberg, Septuagint, Targum, and Vulgate read *Gazza.* 7:31 ªOr *Birzavith* or *Birzoth* 7:32 ªSpelled *Shemer* in verse 34 ᵇSpelled *Helem* in verse 35 7:37 ªSpelled *Jether* in verse 38 8:1 ªSpelled *Ahiram* in Numbers 26:38 8:3 ªCalled *Ard* in Numbers 26:40

⁶These *are* the sons of Ehud, who were the heads of the fathers' *houses* of the inhabitants of Geba, and who forced them to move to Manahath: ⁷Naaman, Ahijah, and Gera who forced them to move. He begot Uzza and Ahihud.

⁸Also Shaharaim had children in the country of Moab, after he had sent away Hushim and Baara his wives. ⁹By Hodesh his wife he begot Jobab, Zibia, Mesha, Malcam, ¹⁰Jeuz, Sachiah, and Mirmah. These *were* his sons, heads of their fathers' *houses.*

¹¹And by Hushim he begot Abitub and Elpaal. ¹²The sons of Elpaal *were* Eber, Misham, and Shemed, who built Ono and Lod with its towns; ¹³and Beriah and Shema, who *were* heads of their fathers' *houses* of the inhabitants of Aijalon, who drove out the inhabitants of Gath. ¹⁴Ahio, Shashak, Jeremoth, ¹⁵Zebadiah, Arad, Eder, ¹⁶Michael, Ispah, and Joha *were* the sons of Beriah. ¹⁷Zebadiah, Meshullam, Hizki, Heber, ¹⁸Ishmerai, Jizliah, and Jobab *were* the sons of Elpaal. ¹⁹Jakim, Zichri, Zabdi, ²⁰Elienai, Zillethai, Eliel, ²¹Adaiah, Beraiah, and Shimrath *were* the sons of Shimei. ²²Ishpan, Eber, Eliel, ²³Abdon, Zichri, Hanan, ²⁴Hananiah, Elam, Antothijah, ²⁵Iphdeiah, and Penuel *were* the sons of Shashak. ²⁶Shamsherai, Shehariah, Athaliah, ²⁷Jaareshiah, Elijah, and Zichri *were* the sons of Jeroham.

²⁸These *were* heads of the fathers' *houses* by their generations, chief men. These dwelt in Jerusalem.

²⁹Now the father of Gibeon, whose wife's name *was* Maacah, dwelt at Gibeon. ³⁰And his firstborn son *was* Abdon, then Zur, Kish, Baal, Nadab, ³¹Gedor, Ahio, Zecher, ³²and Mikloth, *who* begot Shimeah.ᵃ They also dwelt alongside their relatives in Jerusalem, with their brethren. ³³Nerᵃ begot Kish, Kish begot Saul, and Saul begot Jonathan, Malchishua, Abinadab,ᵇ and Esh-Baal.ᶜ ³⁴The son of Jonathan *was* Merib-Baal,ᵃ and Merib-Baal begot Micah. ³⁵The sons of Micah *were* Pithon, Melech, Tarea, and Ahaz. ³⁶And Ahaz begot Jehoaddah;ᵃ Jehoaddah begot Alemeth, Azmaveth, and Zimri; and Zimri begot Moza. ³⁷Moza begot Binea, Raphahᵃ his son, Eleasah his son, *and* Azel his son.

³⁸Azel had six sons whose names *were* these: Azrikam, Bocheru, Ishmael, Sheariah, Obadiah, and Hanan. All these *were* the sons of Azel. ³⁹And the sons of Eshek his brother *were* Ulam his firstborn, Jeush the second, and Eliphelet the third.

⁴⁰The sons of Ulam were mighty men of valor—archers. *They* had many sons and grandsons, one hundred and fifty *in all.* These *were* all sons of Benjamin.

9 So all Israel was recorded by genealogies, and indeed, they *were* inscribed in the book of the kings of Israel. But Judah was carried away captive to Babylon because of their unfaithfulness. ²And the first inhabitants who *dwelt* in their possessions in their cities *were* Israelites, priests, Levites, and the Nethinim.

DWELLERS IN JERUSALEM

³Now in Jerusalem the children of Judah dwelt, and some of the children of Benjamin, and of the children of Ephraim and Manasseh: ⁴Uthai the son of Ammihud, the son of Omri, the son of Imri, the son of Bani, of the descendants of Perez, the son of Judah. ⁵Of the Shilonites: Asaiah the firstborn and his sons. ⁶Of the sons of Zerah: Jeuel, and their brethren—six hundred and ninety. ⁷Of the sons of Benjamin: Sallu the son of Meshullam, the son of Hodaviah, the son of Hassenuah; ⁸Ibneiah the son of Jeroham; Elah the son of Uzzi, the son of Michri; Meshullam the son of Shephatiah, the son of Reuel, the son of Ibnijah; ⁹and their brethren, according to their generations—nine hundred and fifty-six. All these men *were* heads of a father's *house* in their fathers' houses.

THE PRIESTS AT JERUSALEM

¹⁰Of the priests: Jedaiah, Jehoiarib, and Jachin; ¹¹Azariah the son of Hilkiah, the son of Meshullam, the son of Zadok, the son of Meraioth, the son of Ahitub, the officer over the house of God; ¹²Adaiah the son of Jeroham, the son of Pashur, the son of Malchijah; Maasai the son of Adiel, the son of Jahzerah, the son of Meshullam, the son of Meshillemith, the son of Immer; ¹³and their brethren, heads of their fathers' houses—one thousand seven hundred and sixty. *They were* very able men for the work of the service of the house of God.

8:32 ᵃSpelled *Shimeam* in 9:38 **8:33** ᵃAlso the son of Gibeon (compare 9:36, 39) ᵇCalled *Jishui* in 1 Samuel 14:49 ᶜCalled *Ishbosheth* in 2 Samuel 2:8 and elsewhere **8:34** ᵃCalled *Mephibosheth* in 2 Samuel 4:4 **8:36** ᵃSpelled *Jarah* in 9:42 **8:37** ᵃSpelled *Rephaiah* in 9:43

The Levites at Jerusalem

[14]Of the Levites: Shemaiah the son of Hasshub, the son of Azrikam, the son of Hashabiah, of the sons of Merari; [15]Bakbakkar, Heresh, Galal, and Mattaniah the son of Micah, the son of Zichri, the son of Asaph; [16]Obadiah the son of Shemaiah, the son of Galal, the son of Jeduthun; and Berechiah the son of Asa, the son of Elkanah, who lived in the villages of the Netophathites.

The Levite Gatekeepers

[17]And the gatekeepers *were* Shallum, Akkub, Talmon, Ahiman, and their brethren. Shallum *was* the chief. [18]Until then *they had been* gatekeepers for the camps of the children of Levi at the King's Gate on the east.

[19]Shallum the son of Kore, the son of Ebiasaph, the son of Korah, and his brethren, from his father's house, the Korahites, *were* in charge of the work of the service, gatekeepers of the tabernacle. Their fathers had been keepers of the entrance to the camp of the LORD. [20]And Phinehas the son of Eleazar had been the officer over them in time past; the LORD *was* with him. [21]Zechariah the son of Meshelemiah *was* keeper of the door of the tabernacle of meeting.

[22]All those chosen as gatekeepers *were* two hundred and twelve. They were recorded by their genealogy, in their villages. David and Samuel the seer had appointed them to their trusted office. [23]So they and their children *were* in charge of the gates of the house of the LORD, the house of the tabernacle, by assignment. [24]The gatekeepers were assigned to the four directions: the east, west, north, and south. [25]And their brethren in their villages *had* to come with them from time to time for seven days. [26]For in this trusted office *were* four chief gatekeepers; they were Levites. And they had charge over the chambers and treasuries of the house of God. [27]And they lodged *all* around the house of God because they *had* the responsibility, and they *were* in charge of opening *it* every morning.

Other Levite Responsibilities

[28]Now *some* of them were in charge of the serving vessels, for they brought them in and took them out by count. [29]*Some* of them *were* ap-pointed over the furnishings and over all the implements of the sanctuary, and over the fine flour and the wine and the oil and the incense and the spices. [30]And *some* of the sons of the priests made the ointment of the spices.

[31]Mattithiah of the Levites, the firstborn of Shallum the Korahite, had the trusted office over the things that were baked in the pans. [32]And some of their brethren of the sons of the Kohathites *were* in charge of preparing the showbread for every Sabbath.

[33]These are the singers, heads of the fathers' *houses* of the Levites, *who* lodged in the chambers, *and were* free *from other duties;* for they were employed in *that* work day and night. [34]These heads of the fathers' *houses* of the Levites *were* heads throughout their generations. They dwelt at Jerusalem.

The Family of King Saul

[35]Jeiel the father of Gibeon, whose wife's name *was* Maacah, dwelt at Gibeon. [36]His firstborn son *was* Abdon, then Zur, Kish, Baal, Ner, Nadab, [37]Gedor, Ahio, Zechariah,[a] and Mikloth. [38]And Mikloth begot Shimeam.[a] They also dwelt alongside their relatives in Jerusalem, with their brethren. [39]Ner begot Kish, Kish begot Saul, and Saul begot Jonathan, Malchishua, Abinadab, and Esh-Baal. [40]The son of Jonathan *was* Merib-Baal, and Merib-Baal begot Micah. [41]The sons of Micah *were* Pithon, Melech, Tahrea,[a] and Ahaz.[b] [42]And Ahaz begot Jarah;[a] Jarah begot Alemeth, Azmaveth, and Zimri; and Zimri begot Moza; [43]Moza begot Binea, Rephaiah[a] his son, Eleasah his son, and Azel his son.

[44]And Azel had six sons whose names *were* these: Azrikam, Bocheru, Ishmael, Sheariah, Obadiah, and Hanan; these *were* the sons of Azel.

Tragic End of Saul and His Sons

10 Now the Philistines fought against Israel; and the men of Israel fled from before the Philistines, and fell slain on Mount Gilboa. [2]Then the Philistines followed hard after Saul and his sons. And the Philistines killed Jonathan, Abinadab,

---

9:37 [a]Called *Zecher* in 8:31   **9:38** [a]Spelled *Shimeah* in 8:32
9:41 [a]Spelled *Tarea* in 8:35 [b]Following Arabic, Syriac, Targum, and Vulgate (compare 8:35); Masoretic Text and Septuagint omit *and Ahaz.*
9:42 [a]Spelled *Jehoaddah* in 8:36   **9:43** [a]Spelled *Raphah* in 8:37

and Malchishua, Saul's sons. ³The battle became fierce against Saul. The archers hit him, and he was wounded by the archers. ⁴Then Saul said to his armorbearer, "Draw your sword, and thrust me through with it, lest these uncircumcised men come and abuse me." But his armorbearer would not, for he was greatly afraid. Therefore Saul took a sword and fell on it. ⁵And when his armorbearer saw that Saul was dead, he also fell on his sword and died. ⁶So Saul and his three sons died, and all his house died together. ⁷And when all the men of Israel who *were* in the valley saw that they had fled and that Saul and his sons were dead, they forsook their cities and fled; then the Philistines came and dwelt in them.

⁸So it happened the next day, when the Philistines came to strip the slain, that they found Saul and his sons fallen on Mount Gilboa. ⁹And they stripped him and took his head and his armor, and sent word throughout the land of the Philistines to proclaim the news *in the temple* of their idols and among the people. ¹⁰Then they put his armor in the temple of their gods, and fastened his head in the temple of Dagon.

¹¹And when all Jabesh Gilead heard all that the Philistines had done to Saul, ¹²all the valiant men arose and took the body of Saul and the bodies of his sons; and they brought them to Jabesh, and buried their bones under the tamarisk tree at Jabesh, and fasted seven days.

¹³So Saul died for his unfaithfulness which he had committed against the LORD, because he did not keep the word of the LORD, and also because he consulted a medium for guidance. ¹⁴But *he* did not inquire of the LORD; therefore He killed him, and turned the kingdom over to David the son of Jesse.

DAVID MADE KING OVER ALL ISRAEL

11 Then all Israel came together to David at Hebron, saying, "Indeed we *are* your bone and your flesh. ²Also, in time past, even when Saul was king, you *were* the one who led Israel out and brought them in; and the LORD your God said to you, 'You shall shepherd My people Israel, and be ruler over My people Israel.' " ³Therefore all the elders of Israel came to the king at Hebron, and David made a covenant with them at Hebron before the LORD. And they anointed David king

over Israel, according to the word of the LORD by Samuel.

THE CITY OF DAVID

⁴And David and all Israel went to Jerusalem, which is Jebus, where the Jebusites *were,* the inhabitants of the land. ⁵But the inhabitants of Jebus said to David, "You shall not come in here!" Nevertheless David took the stronghold of Zion (that is, the City of David). ⁶Now David said, "Whoever attacks the Jebusites first shall be chief and captain." And Joab the son of Zeruiah went up first, and became chief. ⁷Then David dwelt in the stronghold; therefore they called it the City of David. ⁸And he built the city around it, from the Milloᵃ to the surrounding area. Joab repaired the rest of the city. ⁹So David went on and became great, and the LORD of hosts *was* with him.

THE MIGHTY MEN OF DAVID

¹⁰Now these *were* the heads of the mighty men whom David had, who strengthened themselves with him in his kingdom, with all Israel, to make him king, according to the word of the LORD concerning Israel.

¹¹And this *is* the number of the mighty men whom David had: Jashobeam the son of a Hachmonite, chief of the captains;ᵃ he had lifted up his spear against three hundred, killed *by him* at one time.

¹²After him *was* Eleazar the son of Dodo, the Ahohite, who *was one* of the three mighty men. ¹³He was with David at Pasdammim. Now there the Philistines were gathered for battle, and there was a piece of ground full of barley. So the people fled from the Philistines. ¹⁴But they stationed themselves in the middle of *that* field, defended it, and killed the Philistines. So the LORD brought about a great victory.

¹⁵Now three of the thirty chief men went down to the rock to David, into the cave of Adullam; and the army of the Philistines encamped in the Valley of Rephaim. ¹⁶David *was* then in the stronghold, and the garrison of the Philistines *was* then in Bethlehem. ¹⁷And David said with longing, "Oh, that someone would give me a drink of water from the well of Bethlehem, which is by

11:8 ᵃLiterally *The Landfill* 11:11 ᵃFollowing Qere; Kethib, Septuagint, and Vulgate read *the thirty* (compare 2 Samuel 23:8).

the gate!" ¹⁸So the three broke through the camp of the Philistines, drew water from the well of Bethlehem that *was* by the gate, and took *it* and brought *it* to David. Nevertheless David would not drink it, but poured it out to the LORD. ¹⁹And he said, "Far be it from me, O my God, that I should do this! Shall I drink the blood of these men *who have put* their lives *in jeopardy?* For at the risk of their lives they brought it." Therefore he would not drink it. These things were done by the three mighty men.

²⁰Abishai the brother of Joab was chief of *another* three.ª He had lifted up his spear against three hundred *men,* killed *them,* and won a name among *these* three. ²¹Of the three he was more honored than the other two men. Therefore he became their captain. However he did not attain to the *first* three.

²²Benaiah was the son of Jehoiada, the son of a valiant man from Kabzeel, who had done many deeds. He had killed two lion-like heroes of Moab. He also had gone down and killed a lion in the midst of a pit on a snowy day. ²³And he killed an Egyptian, a man of *great* height, five cubits tall. In the Egyptian's hand *there was* a spear like a weaver's beam; and he went down to him with a staff, wrested the spear out of the Egyptian's hand, and killed him with his own spear. ²⁴These *things* Benaiah the son of Jehoiada did, and won a name among three mighty men. ²⁵Indeed he was more honored than the thirty, but he did not attain to the *first* three. And David appointed him over his guard.

²⁶Also the mighty warriors *were* Asahel the brother of Joab, Elhanan the son of Dodo of Bethlehem, ²⁷Shammoth the Harorite,ª Helez the Pelonite,ᵇ ²⁸Ira the son of Ikkesh the Tekoite, Abiezer the Anathothite, ²⁹Sibbechai the Hushathite, Ilai the Ahohite, ³⁰Maharai the Netophathite, Heledª the son of Baanah the Netophathite, ³¹Ithaiª the son of Ribai of Gibeah, of the sons of Benjamin, Benaiah the Pirathonite, ³²Huraiª of the brooks of Gaash, Abielᵇ the Arbathite, ³³Azmaveth the Baharumite,ª Eliahba the Shaalbonite, ³⁴the sons of Hashem the Gizonite, Jonathan the son of Shagee the Hararite, ³⁵Ahiam the son of Sacar the Hararite, Eliphal the son of Ur, ³⁶Hepher the Mecherathite, Ahijah the Pelonite, ³⁷Hezro the Carmelite, Naarai the son of

Ezbai, ³⁸Joel the brother of Nathan, Mibhar the son of Hagri, ³⁹Zelek the Ammonite, Naharai the Berothiteª (the armorbearer of Joab the son of Zeruiah), ⁴⁰Ira the Ithrite, Gareb the Ithrite, ⁴¹Uriah the Hittite, Zabad the son of Ahlai, ⁴²Adina the son of Shiza the Reubenite (a chief of the Reubenites) and thirty with him, ⁴³Hanan the son of Maachah, Joshaphat the Mithnite, ⁴⁴Uzzia the Ashterathite, Shama and Jeiel the sons of Hotham the Aroerite, ⁴⁵Jediael the son of Shimri, and Joha his brother, the Tizite, ⁴⁶Eliel the Mahavite, Jeribai and Joshaviah the sons of Elnaam, Ithmah the Moabite, ⁴⁷Eliel, Obed, and Jaasiel the Mezobaite.

THE GROWTH OF DAVID'S ARMY

12 Now these *were* the men who came to David at Ziklag while he was still a fugitive from Saul the son of Kish; and they *were* among the mighty men, helpers in the war, ²armed with bows, using both the right hand and the left in *hurling* stones and *shooting* arrows with the bow. *They were* of Benjamin, Saul's brethren.

³The chief *was* Ahiezer, then Joash, the sons of Shemaah the Gibeathite; Jeziel and Pelet the sons of Azmaveth; Berachah, and Jehu the Anathothite; ⁴Ishmaiah the Gibeonite, a mighty man among the thirty, and over the thirty; Jeremiah, Jahaziel, Johanan, and Jozabad the Gederathite; ⁵Eluzai, Jerimoth, Bealiah, Shemariah, and Shephatiah the Haruphite; ⁶Elkanah, Jisshiah, Azarel, Joezer, and Jashobeam, the Korahites; ⁷and Joelah and Zebadiah the sons of Jeroham of Gedor.

⁸*Some* Gadites joined David at the stronghold in the wilderness, mighty men of valor, men trained for battle, who could handle shield and spear, whose faces *were* like the faces of lions, and *were* as swift as gazelles on the mountains: ⁹Ezer the first, Obadiah the second, Eliab the third, ¹⁰Mishmannah the fourth, Jeremiah the fifth, ¹¹Attai the sixth, Eliel the seventh, ¹²Johanan the eighth, Elzabad the ninth, ¹³Jeremiah the tenth, and Machbanai the eleventh. ¹⁴These *were* from the sons of Gad, captains of the army; the least

11:20 ªFollowing Masoretic Text, Septuagint, and Vulgate; Syriac reads *thirty.* **11:27** ªSpelled *Harodite* in 2 Samuel 23:25 ᵇCalled *Paltite* in 2 Samuel 23:26 **11:30** ªSpelled *Heleb* in 2 Samuel 23:29 and *Heldai* in 1 Chronicles 27:15 **11:31** ªSpelled *Ittai* in 2 Samuel 23:29 **11:32** ªSpelled *Hiddai* in 2 Samuel 23:30 ᵇSpelled *Abi-Albon* in 2 Samuel 23:31 **11:33** ªSpelled *Barhumite* in 2 Samuel 23:31 **11:39** ªSpelled *Beerothite* in 2 Samuel 23:37

was over a hundred, and the greatest was over a thousand. ¹⁵These *are* the ones who crossed the Jordan in the first month, when it had overflowed all its banks; and they put to flight all *those* in the valleys, to the east and to the west.

¹⁶Then some of the sons of Benjamin and Judah came to David at the stronghold. ¹⁷And David went out to meet them, and answered and said to them, "If you have come peaceably to me to help me, my heart will be united with you; but if to betray me to my enemies, since *there is* no wrong in my hands, may the God of our fathers look and bring judgment." ¹⁸Then the Spirit came upon Amasai, chief of the captains, *and he said:*

"*We are* yours, O David;
 We *are* on your side, O son of Jesse!
 Peace, peace to you,
 And peace to your helpers!
 For your God helps you."

So David received them, and made them captains of the troop.

¹⁹And *some* from Manasseh defected to David when he was going with the Philistines to battle against Saul; but they did not help them, for the lords of the Philistines sent him away by agreement, saying, "He may defect to his master Saul *and endanger* our heads." ²⁰When he went to Ziklag, those of Manasseh who defected to him were Adnah, Jozabad, Jediael, Michael, Jozabad, Elihu, and Zillethai, captains of the thousands who *were* from Manasseh. ²¹And they helped David against the bands *of raiders,* for they *were* all mighty men of valor, and they were captains in the army. ²²For at *that* time they came to David day by day to help him, until *it was* a great army, like the army of God.

DAVID'S ARMY AT HEBRON

²³Now these *were* the numbers of the divisions *that were* equipped for war, *and* came to David at Hebron to turn *over* the kingdom of Saul to him, according to the word of the LORD: ²⁴of the sons of Judah bearing shield and spear, six thousand eight hundred armed for war; ²⁵of the sons of Simeon, mighty men of valor fit for war, seven thousand one hundred; ²⁶of the sons of Levi

four thousand six hundred; ²⁷Jehoiada, the leader of the Aaronites, and with him three thousand seven hundred; ²⁸Zadok, a young man, a valiant warrior, and from his father's house twenty-two captains; ²⁹of the sons of Benjamin, relatives of Saul, three thousand (until then the greatest part of them had remained loyal to the house of Saul); ³⁰of the sons of Ephraim twenty thousand eight hundred, mighty men of valor, famous men throughout their father's house; ³¹of the half-tribe of Manasseh eighteen thousand, who were designated by name to come and make David king; ³²of the sons of Issachar who had understanding of the times, to know what Israel ought to do, their chiefs were two hundred; and all their brethren were at their command; ³³of Zebulun there were fifty thousand who went out to battle, expert in war with all weapons of war, stouthearted men who could keep ranks; ³⁴of Naphtali one thousand captains, and with them thirty-seven thousand with shield and spear; ³⁵of the Danites who could keep battle formation, twenty-eight thousand six hundred; ³⁶of Asher, those who could go out to war, able to keep battle formation, forty thousand; ³⁷of the Reubenites and the Gadites and the half-tribe of Manasseh, from the other side of the Jordan, one hundred and twenty thousand armed for battle with every *kind* of weapon of war.

³⁸All these men of war, who could keep ranks, came to Hebron with a loyal heart, to make David king over all Israel; and all the rest of Israel *were* of one mind to make David king. ³⁹And they were there with David three days, eating and drinking, for their brethren had prepared for them. ⁴⁰Moreover those who were near to them, from as far away as Issachar and Zebulun and Naphtali, were bringing food on donkeys and camels, on mules and oxen—provisions of flour and cakes of figs and cakes of raisins, wine and oil and oxen and sheep abundantly, for *there was* joy in Israel.

THE ARK BROUGHT FROM KIRJATH JEARIM

13 Then David consulted with the captains of thousands and hundreds, *and* with every leader. ²And David said to all the assembly of Israel, "If *it seems* good to you, and if it is of the LORD our God, let us send out to our brethren everywhere *who are* left in all the land of Israel, and with them to the priests and Levites *who are* in their cities *and* their common-lands, that they may gather together to us; ³and let us bring the ark of our God back to us, for we have not inquired at it since the days of Saul." ⁴Then all the assembly said that they would do so, for the thing was right in the eyes of all the people.

⁵So David gathered all Israel together, from Shihor in Egypt to as far as the entrance of Hamath, to bring the ark of God from Kirjath Jearim. ⁶And David and all Israel went up to Baalah,ᵃ to Kirjath Jearim, which belonged to Judah, to bring up from there the ark of God the LORD, who dwells *between* the cherubim, where *His* name is proclaimed. ⁷So they carried the ark of God on a new cart from the house of Abinadab, and Uzza and Ahio drove the cart. ⁸Then David and all Israel played *music* before God with all *their* might, with singing, on harps, on stringed instruments, on tambourines, on cymbals, and with trumpets.

⁹And when they came to Chidon'sᵃ threshing floor, Uzza put out his hand to hold the ark, for the oxen stumbled. ¹⁰Then the anger of the LORD was aroused against Uzza, and He struck him because he put his hand to the ark; and he died there before God. ¹¹And David became angry because of the LORD's outbreak against Uzza; therefore that place is called Perez Uzzaᵃ to this day. ¹²David was afraid of God that day, saying, "How can I bring the ark of God to me?"

¹³So David would not move the ark with him into the City of David, but took it aside into the house of Obed-Edom the Gittite. ¹⁴The ark of God remained with the family of Obed-Edom in his house three months. And the LORD blessed the house of Obed-Edom and all that he had.

DAVID ESTABLISHED AT JERUSALEM

14 Now Hiram king of Tyre sent messengers to David, and cedar trees, with masons and carpenters, to build him a house. ²So David knew that the LORD had established him as king over Israel, for his kingdom was highly exalted for the sake of His people Israel.

³Then David took more wives in Jerusalem, and David begot more sons and daughters. ⁴And these are the names of his children whom he had

in Jerusalem: Shammua,ᵃ Shobab, Nathan, Solomon, ⁵Ibhar, Elishua,ᵃ Elpelet,ᵇ ⁶Nogah, Nepheg, Japhia, ⁷Elishama, Beeliada,ᵃ and Eliphelet.

THE PHILISTINES DEFEATED

⁸Now when the Philistines heard that David had been anointed king over all Israel, all the Philistines went up to search for David. And David heard *of it* and went out against them. ⁹Then the Philistines went and made a raid on the Valley of Rephaim. ¹⁰And David inquired of God, saying, "Shall I go up against the Philistines? Will You deliver them into my hand?"

The LORD said to him, "Go up, for I will deliver them into your hand."

¹¹So they went up to Baal Perazim, and David defeated them there. Then David said, "God has broken through my enemies by my hand like a breakthrough of water." Therefore they called the name of that place Baal Perazim.ᵃ ¹²And when they left their gods there, David gave a commandment, and they were burned with fire.

¹³Then the Philistines once again made a raid on the valley. ¹⁴Therefore David inquired again of God, and God said to him, "You shall not go up after them; circle around them, and come upon them in front of the mulberry trees. ¹⁵And it shall be, when you hear a sound of marching in the tops of the mulberry trees, then you shall go out to battle, for God has gone out before you to strike the camp of the Philistines." ¹⁶So David did as God commanded him, and they drove back the army of the Philistines from Gibeon as far as Gezer. ¹⁷Then the fame of David went out into all lands, and the LORD brought the fear of him upon all nations.

THE ARK BROUGHT TO JERUSALEM

15 *David* built houses for himself in the City of David; and he prepared a place for the ark of God, and pitched a tent for it. ²Then David said, "No one may carry the ark of God but the Levites, for the LORD has chosen them to carry the ark of God and to minister before Him

---

13:6 ᵃCalled *Baale Judah* in 2 Samuel 6:2   13:9 ᵃCalled *Nachon* in 2 Samuel 6:6   13:11 ᵃLiterally *Outburst Against Uzza*   14:4 ᵃSpelled *Shimea* in 3:5   14:5 ᵃSpelled *Elishama* in 3:6   ᵇSpelled *Eliphelet* in 3:6   14:7 ᵃSpelled *Eliada* in 3:8   14:11 ᵃLiterally *Master of Breakthroughs* forever." ³And David gathered all Israel together at Jerusalem, to bring up the ark of the LORD to its place, which he had prepared for it. ⁴Then David assembled the children of Aaron and the Levites: ⁵of the sons of Kohath, Uriel the chief, and one hundred and twenty of his brethren; ⁶of the sons of Merari, Asaiah the chief, and two hundred and twenty of his brethren; ⁷of the sons of Gershom, Joel the chief, and one hundred and thirty of his brethren; ⁸of the sons of Elizaphan, Shemaiah the chief, and two hundred of his brethren; ⁹of the sons of Hebron, Eliel the chief, and eighty of his brethren; ¹⁰of the sons of Uzziel, Amminadab the chief, and one hundred and twelve of his brethren.

¹¹And David called for Zadok and Abiathar the priests, and for the Levites: for Uriel, Asaiah, Joel, Shemaiah, Eliel, and Amminadab. ¹²He said to them, "You *are* the heads of the fathers' *houses* of the Levites; sanctify yourselves, you and your brethren, that you may bring up the ark of the LORD God of Israel to *the place* I have prepared for it. ¹³For because you *did* not *do it* the first *time,* the LORD our God broke out against us, because we did not consult Him about the proper order."

¹⁴So the priests and the Levites sanctified themselves to bring up the ark of the LORD God of Israel. ¹⁵And the children of the Levites bore the ark of God on their shoulders, by its poles, as Moses had commanded according to the word of the LORD.

¹⁶Then David spoke to the leaders of the Levites to appoint their brethren *to be* the singers accompanied by instruments of music, stringed instruments, harps, and cymbals, by raising the voice with resounding joy. ¹⁷So the Levites appointed Heman the son of Joel; and of his brethren, Asaph the son of Berechiah; and of their brethren, the sons of Merari, Ethan the son of Kushaiah; ¹⁸and with them their brethren of the second *rank:* Zechariah, Ben,ᵃ Jaaziel, Shemiramoth, Jehiel, Unni, Eliab, Benaiah, Maaseiah, Mattithiah, Elipheleh, Mikneiah, Obed-Edom, and Jeiel, the gatekeepers; ¹⁹the singers, Heman, Asaph, and Ethan, *were* to sound the cymbals of bronze; ²⁰Zechariah, Aziel, Shemiramoth, Jehiel, Unni, Eliab, Maaseiah, and Benaiah, with strings according to Alamoth; ²¹Mattithiah, Elipheleh, Mikneiah, Obed-Edom, Jeiel, and Azaziah, to di-

rect with harps on the Sheminith; ²²Chenaniah, leader of the Levites, was instructor *in charge of* the music, because he *was* skillful; ²³Berechiah and Elkanah *were* doorkeepers for the ark; ²⁴Shebaniah, Joshaphat, Nethanel, Amasai, Zechariah, Benaiah, and Eliezer, the priests, were to blow the trumpets before the ark of God; and Obed-Edom and Jehiah, doorkeepers for the ark.

²⁵So David, the elders of Israel, and the captains over thousands went to bring up the ark of the covenant of the LORD from the house of Obed-Edom with joy. ²⁶And so it was, when God helped the Levites who bore the ark of the covenant of the LORD, that they offered seven bulls and seven rams. ²⁷David was clothed with a robe of fine linen, as were all the Levites who bore the ark, the singers, and Chenaniah the music master *with* the singers. David also wore a linen ephod. ²⁸Thus all Israel brought up the ark of the covenant of the LORD with shouting and with the sound of the horn, with trumpets and with cymbals, making music with stringed instruments and harps.

²⁹And it happened, *as* the ark of the covenant of the LORD came to the City of David, that Michal, Saul's daughter, looked through a window and saw King David whirling and playing music; and she despised him in her heart.

THE ARK PLACED IN THE TABERNACLE

16 So they brought the ark of God, and set it in the midst of the tabernacle that David had erected for it. Then they offered burnt offerings and peace offerings before God. ²And when David had finished offering the burnt offerings and the peace offerings, he blessed the people in the name of the LORD. ³Then he distributed to everyone of Israel, both man and woman, to everyone a loaf of bread, a piece *of meat,* and a cake of raisins.

⁴And he appointed some of the Levites to minister before the ark of the LORD, to commemorate, to thank, and to praise the LORD God of Israel: ⁵Asaph the chief, and next to him Zechariah, *then* Jeiel, Shemiramoth, Jehiel, Mattithiah, Eliab, Benaiah, and Obed-Edom: Jeiel with stringed instruments and harps, but Asaph

made music with cymbals; [6]Benaiah and Jahaziel the priests regularly *blew* the trumpets before the ark of the covenant of God.

DAVID'S SONG OF THANKSGIVING

[7]On that day David first delivered *this psalm* into the hand of Asaph and his brethren, to thank the LORD:

[8]Oh, give thanks to the LORD!
Call upon His name;
Make known His deeds among the peoples!
[9]Sing to Him, sing psalms to Him;
Talk of all His wondrous works!
[10]Glory in His holy name;
Let the hearts of those rejoice who seek the LORD!
[11]Seek the LORD and His strength;
Seek His face evermore!
[12]Remember His marvelous works which He has done,
His wonders, and the judgments of His mouth,
[13]O seed of Israel His servant,
You children of Jacob, His chosen ones!

[14]He *is* the LORD our God;
His judgments *are* in all the earth.
[15]Remember His covenant forever,
The word which He commanded, for a thousand generations,
[16]*The covenant which* He made with Abraham,
And His oath to Isaac,
[17]And confirmed it to Jacob for a statute,
To Israel *for* an everlasting covenant,
[18]Saying, "To you I will give the land of Canaan
As the allotment of your inheritance,"
[19]When you were few in number,
Indeed very few, and strangers in it.

[20]When they went from one nation to another,
And from *one* kingdom to another people,
[21]He permitted no man to do them wrong;
Yes, He rebuked kings for their sakes,
[22]*Saying,* "Do not touch My anointed ones,
And do My prophets no harm."[a]

[23]Sing to the LORD, all the earth;
Proclaim the good news of His salvation from day to day.
[24]Declare His glory among the nations,
His wonders among all peoples.

[25]For the LORD *is* great and greatly to be praised;
He *is* also to be feared above all gods.
[26]For all the gods of the peoples *are* idols,
But the LORD made the heavens.
[27]Honor and majesty *are* before Him;
Strength and gladness are in His place.

[28]Give to the LORD, O families of the peoples,
Give to the LORD glory and strength.
[29]Give to the LORD the glory *due* His name;
Bring an offering, and come before Him.
Oh, worship the LORD in the beauty of holiness!
[30]Tremble before Him, all the earth.
The world also is firmly established,
It shall not be moved.

[31]Let the heavens rejoice, and let the earth be glad;
And let them say among the nations, "The LORD reigns."
[32]Let the sea roar, and all its fullness;
Let the field rejoice, and all that *is* in it.
[33]Then the trees of the woods shall rejoice before the LORD,
For He is coming to judge the earth.[a]

[34]Oh, give thanks to the LORD, for *He is* good!
For His mercy *endures* forever.[a]
[35]And say, "Save us, O God of our salvation;
Gather us together, and deliver us from the Gentiles,
To give thanks to Your holy name,
To triumph in Your praise."

[36]Blessed *be* the LORD God of Israel
From everlasting to everlasting![a]

16:22 [a]Compare verses 8–22 with Psalm 105:1–15   **16:33** [a]Compare verses 23–33 with Psalm 96:1–13   **16:34** [a]Compare verse 34 with Psalm 106:1   **16:36** [a]Compare verses 35, 36 with Psalm 106:47, 48

And all the people said, "Amen!" and praised the LORD.

REGULAR WORSHIP MAINTAINED

[37]So he left Asaph and his brothers there before the ark of the covenant of the LORD to minister before the ark regularly, as every day's work required; [38]and Obed-Edom with his sixty-eight brethren, including Obed-Edom the son of Jeduthun, and Hosah, *to be* gatekeepers; [39]and Zadok the priest and his brethren the priests, before the tabernacle of the LORD at the high place that *was* at Gibeon, [40]to offer burnt offerings to the LORD on the altar of burnt offering regularly morning and evening, and *to do* according to all that is written in the Law of the LORD which He commanded Israel; [41]and with them Heman and Jeduthun and the rest who were chosen, who were designated by name, to give thanks to the LORD, because His mercy *endures* forever; [42]and with them Heman and Jeduthun, to sound aloud with trumpets and cymbals and the musical instruments of God. Now the sons of Jeduthun *were* gatekeepers.

[43]Then all the people departed, every man to his house; and David returned to bless his house.

GOD'S COVENANT WITH DAVID

17 Now it came to pass, when David was dwelling in his house, that David said to Nathan the prophet, "See now, I dwell in a house of cedar, but the ark of the covenant of the LORD *is* under tent curtains."

[2]Then Nathan said to David, "Do all that *is* in your heart, for God *is* with you."

[3]But it happened that night that the word of God came to Nathan, saying, [4]"Go and tell My servant David, 'Thus says the LORD: "You shall not build Me a house to dwell in. [5]For I have not dwelt in a house since the time that I brought up Israel, even to this day, but have gone from tent to tent, and from *one* tabernacle *to another.* [6]Wherever I have moved about with all Israel, have I ever spoken a word to any of the judges of Israel, whom I commanded to shepherd My people, saying, 'Why have you not built Me a house of cedar?' " ' [7]Now therefore, thus shall you say to My servant David, 'Thus says the LORD of hosts: "I took you from the sheepfold, from following

the sheep, to be ruler over My people Israel. [8]And I have been with you wherever you have gone, and have cut off all your enemies from before you, and have made you a name like the name of the great men who *are* on the earth. [9]Moreover I will appoint a place for My people Israel, and will plant them, that they may dwell in a place of their own and move no more; nor shall the sons of wickedness oppress them anymore, as previously, [10]since the time that I commanded judges *to be* over My people Israel. Also I will subdue all your enemies. Furthermore I tell you that the LORD will build you a house.[a] [11]And it shall be, when your days are fulfilled, when you must go *to be* with your fathers, that I will set up your seed after you, who will be of your sons; and I will establish his kingdom. [12]He shall build Me a house, and I will establish his throne forever. [13]I will be his Father, and he shall be My son; and I will not take My mercy away from him, as I took *it* from *him* who was before you. [14]And I will establish him in My house and in My kingdom forever; and his throne shall be established forever." ' "

[15]According to all these words and according to all this vision, so Nathan spoke to David.

[16]Then King David went in and sat before the LORD; and he said: "Who *am* I, O LORD God? And what is my house, that You have brought me this far? [17]And *yet* this was a small thing in Your sight, O God; and You have *also* spoken of Your servant's house for a great while to come, and have regarded me according to the rank of a man of high degree, O LORD God. [18]What more can David *say* to You for the honor of Your servant? For You know Your servant. [19]O LORD, for Your servant's sake, and according to Your own heart, You have done all this greatness, in making known all these great things. [20]O LORD, *there is* none like You, nor *is there any* God besides You, according to all that we have heard with our ears. [21]And who *is* like Your people Israel, the one nation on the earth whom God went to redeem for Himself *as* a people—to make for Yourself a name by great and awesome deeds, by driving out nations from before Your people whom You redeemed from Egypt? [22]For You have made Your people Israel Your very own

17:10 [a]That is, a royal dynasty

people forever; and You, LORD, have become their God.

²³"And now, O LORD, the word which You have spoken concerning Your servant and concerning his house, *let it* be established forever, and do as You have said. ²⁴So let it be established, that Your name may be magnified forever, saying, 'The LORD of hosts, the God of Israel, *is* Israel's God.' And let the house of Your servant David be established before You. ²⁵For You, O my God, have revealed to Your servant that You will build him a house. Therefore Your servant has found it *in his heart* to pray before You. ²⁶And now, LORD, You are God, and have promised this goodness to Your servant. ²⁷Now You have been pleased to bless the house of Your servant, that it may continue before You forever; for You have blessed it, O LORD, and *it shall be* blessed forever."

David's Further Conquests

18 After this it came to pass that David attacked the Philistines, subdued them, and took Gath and its towns from the hand of the Philistines. ²Then he defeated Moab, and the Moabites became David's servants, *and* brought tribute.

³And David defeated Hadadezerᵃ king of Zobah *as far as* Hamath, as he went to establish his power by the River Euphrates. ⁴David took from him one thousand chariots, seven thousandᵃ horsemen, and twenty thousand foot soldiers. Also David hamstrung all the chariot *horses,* except that he spared enough of them for one hundred chariots.

⁵When the Syrians of Damascus came to help Hadadezer king of Zobah, David killed twenty-two thousand of the Syrians. ⁶Then David put *garrisons* in Syria of Damascus; and the Syrians became David's servants, *and* brought tribute. So the LORD preserved David wherever he went. ⁷And David took the shields of gold that were on the servants of Hadadezer, and brought them to Jerusalem. ⁸Also from Tibhathᵃ and from Chun, cities of Hadadezer, David brought a large amount of bronze, with which Solomon made the bronze Sea, the pillars, and the articles of bronze.

⁹Now when Touᵃ king of Hamath heard that David had defeated all the army of Hadadezer

king of Zobah, ¹⁰he sent Hadoramᵃ his son to King David, to greet him and bless him, because he had fought against Hadadezer and defeated him (for Hadadezer had been at war with Tou); and *Hadoram brought with him* all kinds of articles of gold, silver, and bronze. ¹¹King David also dedicated these to the LORD, along with the silver and gold that he had brought from all *these* nations—from Edom, from Moab, from the people of Ammon, from the Philistines, and from Amalek.

¹²Moreover Abishai the son of Zeruiah killed eighteen thousand Edomitesᵃ in the Valley of Salt. ¹³He also put garrisons in Edom, and all the Edomites became David's servants. And the LORD preserved David wherever he went.

David's Administration

¹⁴So David reigned over all Israel, and administered judgment and justice to all his people. ¹⁵Joab the son of Zeruiah *was* over the army; Jehoshaphat the son of Ahilud *was* recorder; ¹⁶Zadok the son of Ahitub and Abimelech the son of Abiathar *were* the priests; Shavshaᵃ *was* the scribe; ¹⁷Benaiah the son of Jehoiada *was* over the Cherethites and the Pelethites; and David's sons *were* chief ministers at the king's side.

The Ammonites and Syrians Defeated

19 It happened after this that Nahash the king of the people of Ammon died, and his son reigned in his place. ²Then David said, "I will show kindness to Hanun the son of Nahash, because his father showed kindness to me." So David sent messengers to comfort him concerning his father. And David's servants came to Hanun in the land of the people of Ammon to comfort him.

³And the princes of the people of Ammon said to Hanun, "Do you think that David really honors your father because he has sent comforters to you? Did his servants not come to you to search and to overthrow and to spy out the land?"

⁴Therefore Hanun took David's servants, shaved them, and cut off their garments in the middle, at their buttocks, and sent them away.

18:3 ᵃHebrew *Hadarezer,* and so throughout chapters 18 and 19 **18:4** ᵃOr *seven hundred* (compare 2 Samuel 8:4) **18:8** ᵃSpelled *Betah* in 2 Samuel 8:8 **18:9** ᵃSpelled *Toi* in 2 Samuel 8:9, 10 **18:10** ᵃSpelled *Joram* in 2 Samuel 8:10 **18:12** ᵃOr *Syrians* (compare 2 Samuel 8:13) **18:16** ᵃSpelled *Seraiah* in 2 Samuel 8:17

⁵Then *some* went and told David about the men; and he sent to meet them, because the men were greatly ashamed. And the king said, "Wait at Jericho until your beards have grown, and *then* return."

⁶When the people of Ammon saw that they had made themselves repulsive to David, Hanun and the people of Ammon sent a thousand talents of silver to hire for themselves chariots and horsemen from Mesopotamia,ᵃ from Syrian Maacah, and from Zobah.ᵇ ⁷So they hired for themselves thirty-two thousand chariots, with the king of Maacah and his people, who came and encamped before Medeba. Also the people of Ammon gathered together from their cities, and came to battle.

⁸Now when David heard *of it,* he sent Joab and all the army of the mighty men. ⁹Then the people of Ammon came out and put themselves in battle array before the gate of the city, and the kings who had come *were* by themselves in the field.

¹⁰When Joab saw that the battle line was against him before and behind, he chose some of Israel's best, and put *them* in battle array against the Syrians. ¹¹And the rest of the people he put under the command of Abishai his brother, and they set *themselves* in battle array against the people of Ammon. ¹²Then he said, "If the Syrians are too strong for me, then you shall help me; but if the people of Ammon are too strong for you, then I will help you. ¹³Be of good courage, and let us be strong for our people and for the cities of our God. And may the LORD do *what is* good in His sight."

¹⁴So Joab and the people who *were* with him drew near for the battle against the Syrians, and they fled before him. ¹⁵When the people of Ammon saw that the Syrians were fleeing, they also fled before Abishai his brother, and entered the city. So Joab went to Jerusalem.

¹⁶Now when the Syrians saw that they had been defeated by Israel, they sent messengers and brought the Syrians who were beyond the River,ᵃ and Shophachᵇ the commander of Hadadezer's army *went* before them. ¹⁷When it was told David, he gathered all Israel, crossed over the Jordan and came upon them, and set up in *battle* array against them. So when David had set up in battle array against the Syrians, they fought with

him. ¹⁸Then the Syrians fled before Israel; and David killed seven thousandᵃ charioteers and forty thousand foot soldiersᵇ of the Syrians, and killed Shophach the commander of the army. ¹⁹And when the servants of Hadadezer saw that they were defeated by Israel, they made peace with David and became his servants. So the Syrians were not willing to help the people of Ammon anymore.

RABBAH IS CONQUERED

20 It happened in the spring of the year, at the time kings go out *to battle,* that Joab led out the armed forces and ravaged the country of the people of Ammon, and came and besieged Rabbah. But David stayed at Jerusalem. And Joab defeated Rabbah and overthrew it. ²Then David took their king's crown from his head, and found it to weigh a talent of gold, and *there were* precious stones in it. And it was set on David's head. Also he brought out the spoil of the city in great abundance. ³And he brought out the people who *were* in it, and put *them* to workᵃ with saws, with iron picks, and with axes. So David did to all the cities of the people of Ammon. Then David and all the people returned *to* Jerusalem.

PHILISTINE GIANTS DESTROYED

⁴Now it happened afterward that war broke out at Gezer with the Philistines, at which time Sibbechai the Hushathite killed Sippai,ᵃ *who was one* of the sons of the giant. And they were subdued.

⁵Again there was war with the Philistines, and Elhanan the son of Jairᵃ killed Lahmi the brother of Goliath the Gittite, the shaft of whose spear *was* like a weaver's beam.

⁶Yet again there was war at Gath, where there was a man of *great* stature, with twenty-four fingers and toes, six *on each hand* and six *on each foot;* and he also was born to the giant. ⁷So when he defied Israel, Jonathan the son of Shimea,ᵃ David's brother, killed him.

19:6 ᵃHebrew *Aram Naharaim* ᵇSpelled *Zoba* in 2 Samuel 10:6 **19:16** ᵃThat is, the Euphrates ᵇSpelled *Shobach* in 2 Samuel 10:16 **19:18** ᵃOr *seven hundred* (compare 2 Samuel 10:18) ᵇOr *horsemen* (compare 2 Samuel 10:18) **20:3** ᵃSeptuagint reads *cut them.* **20:4** ᵃSpelled *Saph* in 2 Samuel 21:18 **20:5** ᵃSpelled *Jaare-Oregim* in 2 Samuel 21:19 **20:7** ᵃSpelled *Shimeah* in 2 Samuel 21:21 and *Shammah* in 1 Samuel 16:9

⁸These were born to the giant in Gath, and they fell by the hand of David and by the hand of his servants.

The Census of Israel and Judah

21 Now Satan stood up against Israel, and moved David to number Israel. ²So David said to Joab and to the leaders of the people, "Go, number Israel from Beersheba to Dan, and bring the number of them to me that I may know *it.*"

³And Joab answered, "May the LORD make His people a hundred times more than they are. But, my lord the king, *are* they not all my lord's servants? Why then does my lord require this thing? Why should he be a cause of guilt in Israel?"

⁴Nevertheless the king's word prevailed against Joab. Therefore Joab departed and went throughout all Israel and came to Jerusalem. ⁵Then Joab gave the sum of the number of the people to David. All Israel *had* one million one hundred thousand men who drew the sword, and Judah *had* four hundred and seventy thousand men who drew the sword. ⁶But he did not count Levi and Benjamin among them, for the king's word was abominable to Joab.

⁷And God was displeased with this thing; therefore He struck Israel. ⁸So David said to God, "I have sinned greatly, because I have done this thing; but now, I pray, take away the iniquity of Your servant, for I have done very foolishly."

⁹Then the LORD spoke to Gad, David's seer, saying, ¹⁰"Go and tell David, saying, 'Thus says the LORD: "I offer you three *things;* choose one of them for yourself, that I may do *it* to you." ' "

¹¹So Gad came to David and said to him, "Thus says the LORD: 'Choose for yourself, ¹²either threeᵃ years of famine, or three months to be defeated by your foes with the sword of your enemies overtaking *you,* or else for three days the sword of the LORD—the plague in the land, with the angelᵇ of the LORD destroying throughout all the territory of Israel.' Now consider what answer I should take back to Him who sent me."

¹³And David said to Gad, "I am in great distress. Please let me fall into the hand of the LORD, for His mercies *are* very great; but do not let me fall into the hand of man."

¹⁴So the LORD sent a plague upon Israel, and seventy thousand men of Israel fell. ¹⁵And God sent an angel to Jerusalem to destroy it. As heᵃ was destroying, the LORD looked and relented of the disaster, and said to the angel who was destroying, "It is enough; now restrain yourᵇ hand." And the angel of the LORD stood by the threshing floor of Ornanᶜ the Jebusite.

¹⁶Then David lifted his eyes and saw the angel of the LORD standing between earth and heaven, having in his hand a drawn sword stretched out over Jerusalem. So David and the elders, clothed in sackcloth, fell on their faces. ¹⁷And David said to God, "Was it not I who commanded the people to be numbered? I am the one who has sinned and done evil indeed; but these sheep, what have they done? Let Your hand, I pray, O LORD my God, be against me and my father's house, but not against Your people that they should be plagued."

¹⁸Therefore, the angel of the LORD commanded Gad to say to David that David should go and erect an altar to the LORD on the threshing floor of Ornan the Jebusite. ¹⁹So David went up at the word of Gad, which he had spoken in the name of the LORD. ²⁰Now Ornan turned and saw the angel; and his four sons *who were* with him hid themselves, but Ornan continued threshing wheat. ²¹So David came to Ornan, and Ornan looked and saw David. And he went out from the threshing floor, and bowed before David with *his* face to the ground. ²²Then David said to Ornan, "Grant me the place of *this* threshing floor, that I may build an altar on it to the LORD. You shall grant it to me at the full price, that the plague may be withdrawn from the people."

²³But Ornan said to David, "Take *it* to yourself, and let my lord the king do *what is* good in his eyes. Look, I *also* give *you* the oxen for burnt offerings, the threshing implements for wood, and the wheat for the grain offering; I give *it* all."

²⁴Then King David said to Ornan, "No, but I will surely buy *it* for the full price, for I will not take what is yours for the LORD, nor offer burnt offerings with *that which* costs *me* nothing." ²⁵So David gave Ornan six hundred shekels of gold by weight for the place. ²⁶And David built there an

21:12 ᵃOr *seven* (compare 2 Samuel 24:13)   ᵇOr *Angel,* and so elsewhere in this chapter   **21:15** ᵃOr *He*   ᵇOr *Your*   ᶜSpelled *Araunah* in 2 Samuel 24:16

altar to the LORD, and offered burnt offerings and peace offerings, and called on the LORD; and He answered him from heaven by fire on the altar of burnt offering.

27So the LORD commanded the angel, and he returned his sword to its sheath.

28At that time, when David saw that the LORD had answered him on the threshing floor of Ornan the Jebusite, he sacrificed there. 29For the tabernacle of the LORD and the altar of the burnt offering, which Moses had made in the wilderness, *were* at that time at the high place in Gibeon. 30But David could not go before it to inquire of God, for he was afraid of the sword of the angel of the LORD.

DAVID PREPARES TO BUILD THE TEMPLE

22 Then David said, "This *is* the house of the LORD God, and this *is* the altar of burnt offering for Israel." 2So David commanded to gather the aliens who *were* in the land of Israel; and he appointed masons to cut hewn stones to build the house of God. 3And David prepared iron in abundance for the nails of the doors of the gates and for the joints, and bronze in abundance beyond measure, 4and cedar trees in abundance; for the Sidonians and those from Tyre brought much cedar wood to David.

5Now David said, "Solomon my son *is* young and inexperienced, and the house to be built for the LORD *must be* exceedingly magnificent, famous and glorious throughout all countries. I will now make preparation for it." So David made abundant preparations before his death.

6Then he called for his son Solomon, and charged him to build a house for the LORD God of Israel. 7And David said to Solomon: "My son, as for me, it was in my mind to build a house to the name of the LORD my God; 8but the word of the LORD came to me, saying, 'You have shed much blood and have made great wars; you shall not build a house for My name, because you have shed much blood on the earth in My sight. 9Behold, a son shall be born to you, who shall be a man of rest; and I will give him rest from all his enemies all around. His name shall be Solomon,a for I will give peace and quietness to Israel in his days. 10He shall build a house for My name, and he shall be My son, and I *will be* his Father; and I

will establish the throne of his kingdom over Israel forever.' 11Now, my son, may the LORD be with you; and may you prosper, and build the house of the LORD your God, as He has said to you. 12Only may the LORD give you wisdom and understanding, and give you charge concerning Israel, that you may keep the law of the LORD your God. 13Then you will prosper, if you take care to fulfill the statutes and judgments with which the LORD charged Moses concerning Israel. Be strong and of good courage; do not fear nor be dismayed. 14Indeed I have taken much trouble to prepare for the house of the LORD one hundred thousand talents of gold and one million talents of silver, and bronze and iron beyond measure, for it is so abundant. I have prepared timber and stone also, and you may add to them. 15Moreover *there are* workmen with you in abundance: woodsmen and stonecutters, and all types of skillful men for every kind of work. 16Of gold and silver and bronze and iron *there is* no limit. Arise and begin working, and the LORD be with you."

17David also commanded all the leaders of Israel to help Solomon his son, *saying,* 18"*Is* not the LORD your God with you? And has He *not* given you rest on every side? For He has given the inhabitants of the land into my hand, and the land is subdued before the LORD and before His people. 19Now set your heart and your soul to seek the LORD your God. Therefore arise and build the sanctuary of the LORD God, to bring the ark of the covenant of the LORD and the holy articles of God into the house that is to be built for the name of the LORD."

THE DIVISIONS OF THE LEVITES

23 So when David was old and full of days, he made his son Solomon king over Israel.

2And he gathered together all the leaders of Israel, with the priests and the Levites. 3Now the Levites were numbered from the age of thirty years and above; and the number of individual males was thirty-eight thousand. 4Of these, twenty-four thousand *were* to look after the work of the house of the LORD, six thousand *were* officers and judges, 5four thousand *were* gatekeepers,

22:9 aLiterally *Peaceful*

and four thousand praised the LORD with *musical* instruments, "which I made," *said David,* "for giving praise."

⁶Also David separated them into divisions among the sons of Levi: Gershon, Kohath, and Merari.

⁷Of the Gershonites: Laadanᵃ and Shimei. ⁸The sons of Laadan: the first Jehiel, then Zetham and Joel—three *in all.* ⁹The sons of Shimei: Shelomith, Haziel, and Haran—three *in all.* These were the heads of the fathers' *houses* of Laadan. ¹⁰And the sons of Shimei: Jahath, Zina,ᵃ Jeush, and Beriah. These *were* the four sons of Shimei. ¹¹Jahath was the first and Zizah the second. But Jeush and Beriah did not have many sons; therefore they were assigned as one father's house.

¹²The sons of Kohath: Amram, Izhar, Hebron, and Uzziel—four *in all.* ¹³The sons of Amram: Aaron and Moses; and Aaron was set apart, he and his sons forever, that he should sanctify the most holy things, to burn incense before the LORD, to minister to Him, and to give the blessing in His name forever. ¹⁴Now the sons of Moses the man of God were reckoned to the tribe of Levi. ¹⁵The sons of Moses *were* Gershonᵃ and Eliezer. ¹⁶Of the sons of Gershon, Shebuelᵃ *was* the first. ¹⁷Of the descendants of Eliezer, Rehabiah was the first. And Eliezer had no other sons, but the sons of Rehabiah were very many. ¹⁸Of the sons of Izhar, Shelomith *was* the first. ¹⁹Of the sons of Hebron, Jeriah *was* the first, Amariah the second, Jahaziel the third, and Jekameam the fourth. ²⁰Of the sons of Uzziel, Michah *was* the first and Jesshiah the second.

²¹The sons of Merari *were* Mahli and Mushi. The sons of Mahli *were* Eleazar and Kish. ²²And Eleazar died, and had no sons, but only daughters; and their brethren, the sons of Kish, took them *as wives.* ²³The sons of Mushi *were* Mahli, Eder, and Jeremoth—three *in all.*

²⁴These *were* the sons of Levi by their fathers' houses—the heads of the fathers' *houses* as they were counted individually by the number of their names, who did the work for the service of the house of the LORD, from the age of twenty years and above.

²⁵For David said, "The LORD God of Israel has given rest to His people, that they may dwell in Jerusalem forever"; ²⁶and also to the Levites,

"They shall no longer carry the tabernacle, or any of the articles for its service." ²⁷For by the last words of David the Levites *were* numbered from twenty years old and above; ²⁸because their duty *was* to help the sons of Aaron in the service of the house of the LORD, in the courts and in the chambers, in the purifying of all holy things and the work of the service of the house of God, ²⁹both with the showbread and the fine flour for the grain offering, with the unleavened cakes and *what is baked in* the pan, with what is mixed and with all kinds of measures and sizes; ³⁰to stand every morning to thank and praise the LORD, and likewise at evening; ³¹and at every presentation of a burnt offering to the LORD on the Sabbaths and on the New Moons and on the set feasts, by number according to the ordinance governing them, regularly before the LORD; ³²and that they should attend to the needs of the tabernacle of meeting, the needs of the holy *place,* and the needs of the sons of Aaron their brethren in the work of the house of the LORD.

THE DIVISIONS OF THE PRIESTS

24 Now *these are* the divisions of the sons of Aaron. The sons of Aaron *were* Nadab, Abihu, Eleazar, and Ithamar. ²And Nadab and Abihu died before their father, and had no children; therefore Eleazar and Ithamar ministered as priests. ³Then David with Zadok of the sons of Eleazar, and Ahimelech of the sons of Ithamar, divided them according to the schedule of their service.

⁴There were more leaders found of the sons of Eleazar than of the sons of Ithamar, and *thus* they were divided. Among the sons of Eleazar *were* sixteen heads of *their* fathers' houses, and eight heads of their fathers' houses among the sons of Ithamar. ⁵Thus they were divided by lot, one group as another, for there were officials of the sanctuary and officials *of the house* of God, from the sons of Eleazar and from the sons of Ithamar. ⁶And the scribe, Shemaiah the son of Nethanel, *one of* the Levites, wrote them down before the king, the leaders, Zadok the priest, Ahimelech the son of Abiathar, and the heads of the fathers' *houses* of the

---

23:7 ᵃSpelled *Libni* in Exodus 6:17   **23:10** ᵃSeptuagint and Vulgate read *Zizah* (compare verse 11).   **23:15** ᵃHebrew *Gershom* (compare 6:16)   **23:16** ᵃSpelled *Shubael* in 24:20

priests and Levites, one father's house taken for Eleazar and *one* for Ithamar.

[7]Now the first lot fell to Jehoiarib, the second to Jedaiah, [8]the third to Harim, the fourth to Seorim, [9]the fifth to Malchijah, the sixth to Mijamin, [10]the seventh to Hakkoz, the eighth to Abijah, [11]the ninth to Jeshua, the tenth to Shecaniah, [12]the eleventh to Eliashib, the twelfth to Jakim, [13]the thirteenth to Huppah, the fourteenth to Jeshebeab, [14]the fifteenth to Bilgah, the sixteenth to Immer, [15]the seventeenth to Hezir, the eighteenth to Happizzez,[a] [16]the nineteenth to Pethahiah, the twentieth to Jehezekel,[a] [17]the twenty-first to Jachin, the twenty-second to Gamul, [18]the twenty-third to Delaiah, the twenty-fourth to Maaziah.

[19]This *was* the schedule of their service for coming into the house of the LORD according to their ordinance by the hand of Aaron their father, as the LORD God of Israel had commanded him.

OTHER LEVITES

[20]And the rest of the sons of Levi: of the sons of Amram, Shubael;[a] of the sons of Shubael, Jehdeiah. [21]Concerning Rehabiah, of the sons of Rehabiah, the first *was* Isshiah. [22]Of the Izharites, Shelomoth;[a] of the sons of Shelomoth, Jahath. [23]Of the sons *of Hebron,*[a] Jeriah *was the first,*[b] Amariah the second, Jahaziel the third, *and* Jekameam the fourth. [24]*Of* the sons of Uzziel, Micah; of the sons of Michah, Shamir. [25]The brother of Michah, Isshiah; of the sons of Isshiah, Zechariah. [26]The sons of Merari *were* Mahli and Mushi; the son of Jaaziah, Beno. [27]The sons of Merari by Jaaziah *were* Beno, Shoham, Zaccur, and Ibri. [28]Of Mahli: Eleazar, who had no sons. [29]Of Kish: the son of Kish, Jerahmeel.

[30]Also the sons of Mushi *were* Mahli, Eder, and Jerimoth. These *were* the sons of the Levites according to their fathers' houses.

[31]These also cast lots just as their brothers the sons of Aaron did, in the presence of King David, Zadok, Ahimelech, and the heads of the fathers' *houses* of the priests and Levites. The chief fathers *did* just as their younger brethren.

THE MUSICIANS

25 Moreover David and the captains of the army separated for the service *some* of the sons of Asaph, of Heman, and of Jeduthun, who *should* prophesy with harps, stringed instruments, and cymbals. And the number of the skilled men performing their service was: [2]Of the sons of Asaph: Zaccur, Joseph, Nethaniah, and Asharelah;[a] the sons of Asaph *were* under the direction of Asaph, who prophesied according to the order of the king. [3]Of Jeduthun, the sons of Jeduthun: Gedaliah, Zeri,[a] Jeshaiah, *Shimei,* Hashabiah, and Mattithiah, six,[b] under the direction of their father Jeduthun, who prophesied with a harp to give thanks and to praise the LORD. [4]Of Heman, the sons of Heman: Bukkiah, Mattaniah, Uzziel,[a] Shebuel,[b] Jerimoth,[c] Hananiah, Hanani, Eliathah, Giddalti, Romamti-Ezer, Joshbekashah, Mallothi, Hothir, *and* Mahazioth. [5]All these *were* the sons of Heman the king's seer in the words of God, to exalt his horn.[a] For God gave Heman fourteen sons and three daughters.

[6]All these *were* under the direction of their father for the music *in* the house of the LORD, with cymbals, stringed instruments, and harps, for the service of the house of God. Asaph, Jeduthun, and Heman *were* under the authority of the king. [7]So the number of them, with their brethren who were instructed in the songs of the LORD, all who were skillful, *was* two hundred and eighty-eight.

[8]And they cast lots for their duty, the small as well as the great, the teacher with the student.

[9]Now the first lot for Asaph came out for Joseph; the second for Gedaliah, him with his brethren and sons, twelve; [10]the third for Zaccur, his sons and his brethren, twelve; [11]the fourth for Jizri,[a] his sons and his brethren, twelve; [12]the fifth for Nethaniah, his sons and his brethren, twelve; [13]the sixth for Bukkiah, his sons and his brethren, twelve; [14]the seventh for Jesharelah,[a] his sons and his brethren, twelve; [15]the eighth for Jeshaiah, his sons and his brethren, twelve; [16]the ninth for Mattaniah, his sons and his brethren, twelve; [17]the

24:15 [a]Septuagint and Vulgate read *Aphses.* **24:16** [a]Masoretic Text reads *Jehezkel.* **24:20** [a]Spelled *Shebuel* in 23:16 **24:22** [a]Spelled *Shelomith* in 23:18 **24:23** [a]Supplied from 23:19 (following some Hebrew manuscripts and Septuagint manuscripts) [b]Supplied from 23:19 (following some Hebrew manuscripts and Septuagint manuscripts) **25:2** [a]Spelled *Jesharelah* in verse 14 **25:3** [a]Spelled *Jizri* in verse 11 [b]*Shimei,* appearing in one Hebrew and several Septuagint manuscripts, completes the total of six sons (compare verse 17). **25:4** [a]Spelled *Azarel* in verse 18 [b]Spelled *Shubael* in verse 20 [c]Spelled *Jeremoth* in verse 22 **25:5** [a]That is, to increase his power or influence **25:11** [a]Spelled *Zeri* in verse 3 **25:14** [a]Spelled *Asharelah* in verse 2 tenth for Shimei, his sons and his brethren, twelve; [18]the eleventh for Azarel,[a] his sons and his brethren, twelve; [19]the twelfth for Hashabiah, his sons and his brethren, twelve; [20]the thirteenth for Shubael,[a] his sons and his brethren, twelve; [21]the fourteenth for Mattithiah, his sons and his brethren, twelve; [22]the fifteenth for Jeremoth,[a] his sons and his brethren, twelve; [23]the sixteenth for Hananiah, his sons and his brethren, twelve; [24]the seventeenth for Joshbekashah, his sons and his brethren, twelve; [25]the eighteenth for Hanani, his sons and his brethren, twelve; [26]the nineteenth for Mallothi, his sons and his brethren, twelve; [27]the twentieth for Eliathah, his sons and his brethren, twelve; [28]the twenty-first for Hothir, his sons and his brethren, twelve; [29]the twenty-second for Giddalti, his sons and his brethren, twelve; [30]the twenty-third for Mahazioth, his sons and his brethren, twelve; [31]the twenty-fourth for Romamti-Ezer, his sons and his brethren, twelve.

The Gatekeepers

26 Concerning the divisions of the gatekeepers: of the Korahites, Meshelemiah the son of Kore, of the sons of Asaph. [2]And the sons of Meshelemiah *were* Zechariah the firstborn, Jediael the second, Zebadiah the third, Jathniel the fourth, [3]Elam the fifth, Jehohanan the sixth, Eliehoenai the seventh.

[4]Moreover the sons of Obed-Edom *were* Shemaiah the firstborn, Jehozabad the second, Joah the third, Sacar the fourth, Nethanel the fifth, [5]Ammiel the sixth, Issachar the seventh, Peulthai the eighth; for God blessed him.

[6]Also to Shemaiah his son were sons born who governed their fathers' houses, because they *were* men of great ability. [7]The sons of Shemaiah *were* Othni, Rephael, Obed, and Elzabad, whose brothers Elihu and Semachiah *were* able men.

[8]All these *were* of the sons of Obed-Edom, they and their sons and their brethren, able men with strength for the work: sixty-two of Obed-Edom.

[9]And Meshelemiah had sons and brethren, eighteen able men.

[10]Also Hosah, of the children of Merari, had sons: Shimri the first (for *though* he was not the firstborn, his father made him the first), [11]Hilkiah the second, Tebaliah the third, Zechariah the

fourth; all the sons and brethren of Hosah *were* thirteen.

[12]Among these *were* the divisions of the gatekeepers, among the chief men, *having* duties just like their brethren, to serve in the house of the LORD. [13]And they cast lots for each gate, the small as well as the great, according to their father's house. [14]The lot for the East *Gate* fell to Shelemiah. Then they cast lots *for* his son Zechariah, a wise counselor, and his lot came out for the North Gate; [15]to Obed-Edom the South Gate, and to his sons the storehouse.[a] [16]To Shuppim and Hosah *the lot came out* for the West Gate, with the Shallecheth Gate on the ascending highway—watchman opposite watchman. [17]On the east *were* six Levites, on the north four each day, on the south four each day, and for the storehouse[a] two by two. [18]As for the Parbar[a] on the west, *there were* four on the highway *and* two at the Parbar. [19]These were the divisions of the gatekeepers among the sons of Korah and among the sons of Merari.

The Treasuries and Other Duties

[20]Of the Levites, Ahijah *was* over the treasuries of the house of God and over the treasuries of the dedicated things. [21]The sons of Laadan, the descendants of the Gershonites of Laadan, heads of their fathers' *houses,* of Laadan the Gershonite: Jehieli. [22]The sons of Jehieli, Zetham and Joel his brother, *were* over the treasuries of the house of the LORD. [23]Of the Amramites, the Izharites, the Hebronites, and the Uzzielites: [24]Shebuel the son of Gershom, the son of Moses, *was* overseer of the treasuries. [25]And his brethren by Eliezer *were* Rehabiah his son, Jeshaiah his son, Joram his son, Zichri his son, and Shelomith his son.

[26]This Shelomith and his brethren *were* over all the treasuries of the dedicated things which King David and the heads of fathers' *houses,* the captains over thousands and hundreds, and the captains of the army, had dedicated. [27]Some of the spoils won in battles they dedicated to maintain the house of the LORD. [28]And all that Samuel the seer, Saul the son of Kish, Abner the son of Ner,

25:18 [a]Spelled *Uzziel* in verse 4   25:20 [a]Spelled *Shebuel* in verse 4   25:22 [a]Spelled *Jerimoth* in verse 4   26:15 [a]Hebrew *asuppim*
26:17 [a]Hebrew *asuppim*   26:18 [a]Probably a court or colonnade extending west of the temple

and Joab the son of Zeruiah had dedicated, every dedicated *thing,* was under the hand of Shelomith and his brethren.

²⁹Of the Izharites, Chenaniah and his sons *performed* duties as officials and judges over Israel outside Jerusalem.

³⁰Of the Hebronites, Hashabiah and his brethren, one thousand seven hundred able men, had the oversight of Israel on the west side of the Jordan for all the business of the LORD, and in the service of the king. ³¹Among the Hebronites, Jerijah *was* head of the Hebronites according to his genealogy of the fathers. In the fortieth year of the reign of David they were sought, and there were found among them capable men at Jazer of Gilead. ³²And his brethren *were* two thousand seven hundred able men, heads of fathers' *houses,* whom King David made officials over the Reubenites, the Gadites, and the half-tribe of Manasseh, for every matter pertaining to God and the affairs of the king.

THE MILITARY DIVISIONS

27 And the children of Israel, according to their number, the heads of fathers' *houses,* the captains of thousands and hundreds and their officers, served the king in every matter of the *military* divisions. *These divisions* came in and went out month by month throughout all the months of the year, each division *having* twenty-four thousand.

²Over the first division for the first month *was* Jashobeam the son of Zabdiel, and in his division *were* twenty-four thousand; ³he *was* of the children of Perez, and the chief of all the captains of the army for the first month. ⁴Over the division of the second month *was* Dodai* an Ahohite, and of his division Mikloth also *was* the leader; in his division *were* twenty-four thousand. ⁵The third captain of the army for the third month *was* Benaiah, the son of Jehoiada the priest, who was chief; in his division *were* twenty-four thousand. ⁶This was the Benaiah *who was* mighty *among* the thirty, and was over the thirty; in his division *was* Ammizabad his son. ⁷The fourth *captain* for the fourth month *was* Asahel the brother of Joab, and Zebadiah his son after him; in his division *were* twenty-four thousand. ⁸The fifth captain for the fifth month *was* Shamhuth* the Izrahite; in his di-

vision were twenty-four thousand. ⁹The sixth *captain* for the sixth month *was* Ira the son of Ikkesh the Tekoite; in his division *were* twenty-four thousand. ¹⁰The seventh *captain* for the seventh month *was* Helez the Pelonite, of the children of Ephraim; in his division *were* twenty-four thousand. ¹¹The eighth *captain* for the eighth month *was* Sibbechai the Hushathite, of the Zarhites; in his division *were* twenty-four thousand. ¹²The ninth *captain* for the ninth month *was* Abiezer the Anathothite, of the Benjamites; in his division *were* twenty-four thousand. ¹³The tenth *captain* for the tenth month *was* Maharai the Netophathite, of the Zarhites; in his division *were* twenty-four thousand. ¹⁴The eleventh *captain* for the eleventh month *was* Benaiah the Pirathonite, of the children of Ephraim; in his division *were* twenty-four thousand. ¹⁵The twelfth *captain* for the twelfth month *was* Heldai* the Netophathite, of Othniel; in his division *were* twenty-four thousand.

LEADERS OF TRIBES

¹⁶Furthermore, over the tribes of Israel: the officer over the Reubenites *was* Eliezer the son of Zichri; over the Simeonites, Shephatiah the son of Maachah; ¹⁷over the Levites, Hashabiah the son of Kemuel; over the Aaronites, Zadok; ¹⁸over Judah, Elihu, *one* of David's brothers; *over* Issachar, Omri the son of Michael; ¹⁹*over* Zebulun, Ishmaiah the son of Obadiah; *over* Naphtali, Jerimoth the son of Azriel; ²⁰*over* the children of Ephraim, Hoshea the son of Azaziah; *over* the half-tribe of Manasseh, Joel the son of Pedaiah; ²¹*over* the half-*tribe* of Manasseh in Gilead, Iddo the son of Zechariah; *over* Benjamin, Jaasiel the son of Abner; ²²*over* Dan, Azarel the son of Jeroham. These *were* the leaders of the tribes of Israel.

²³But David did not take the number of those twenty years old and under, because the LORD had said He would multiply Israel like the stars of the heavens. ²⁴Joab the son of Zeruiah began a census, but he did not finish, for wrath came upon Israel because of this census; nor was the number recorded in the account of the chronicles of King David.

27:4 ªHebrew *Dodai,* usually spelled *Dodo* (compare 2 Samuel 23:9)
27:8 ªSpelled *Shammoth* in 11:27 and *Shammah* in 2 Samuel 23:11
27:15 ªSpelled *Heled* in 11:30 and *Heleb* in 2 Samuel 23:29

OTHER STATE OFFICIALS

²⁵And Azmaveth the son of Adiel *was* over the king's treasuries; and Jehonathan the son of Uzziah was over the storehouses in the field, in the cities, in the villages, and in the fortresses. ²⁶Ezri the son of Chelub was over those who did the work of the field for tilling the ground. ²⁷And Shimei the Ramathite *was* over the vineyards, and Zabdi the Shiphmite was over the produce of the vineyards for the supply of wine. ²⁸Baal-Hanan the Gederite was over the olive trees and the sycamore trees that *were* in the lowlands, and Joash *was* over the store of oil. ²⁹And Shitrai the Sharonite *was* over the herds that fed in Sharon, and Shaphat the son of Adlai was over the herds *that were* in the valleys. ³⁰Obil the Ishmaelite *was* over the camels, Jehdeiah the Meronothite *was* over the donkeys, ³¹and Jaziz the Hagrite *was* over the flocks. All these *were* the officials over King David's property.

³²Also Jehonathan, David's uncle, *was* a counselor, a wise man, and a scribe; and Jehiel the son of Hachmoni *was* with the king's sons. ³³Ahithophel *was* the king's counselor, and Hushai the Archite *was* the king's companion. ³⁴After Ahithophel *was* Jehoiada the son of Benaiah, then Abiathar. And the general of the king's army *was* Joab.

SOLOMON INSTRUCTED TO BUILD THE TEMPLE

28 Now David assembled at Jerusalem all the leaders of Israel: the officers of the tribes and the captains of the divisions who served the king, the captains over thousands and captains over hundreds, and the stewards over all the substance and possessions of the king and of his sons, with the officials, the valiant men, and all the mighty men of valor.

²Then King David rose to his feet and said, "Hear me, my brethren and my people: I *had* it in my heart to build a house of rest for the ark of the covenant of the LORD, and for the footstool of our God, and had made preparations to build it. ³But God said to me, 'You shall not build a house for My name, because you *have been* a man of war and have shed blood.' ⁴However the LORD God of Israel chose me above all the house of my father to be king over Israel forever, for He has

chosen Judah *to be* the ruler. And of the house of Judah, the house of my father, and among the sons of my father, He was pleased with me to make *me* king over all Israel. ⁵And of all my sons (for the LORD has given me many sons) He has chosen my son Solomon to sit on the throne of the kingdom of the LORD over Israel. ⁶Now He said to me, 'It is your son Solomon *who* shall build My house and My courts; for I have chosen him *to be* My son, and I will be his Father. ⁷Moreover I will establish his kingdom forever, if he is steadfast to observe My commandments and My judgments, as it is this day.' ⁸Now therefore, in the sight of all Israel, the assembly of the LORD, and in the hearing of our God, be careful to seek out all the commandments of the LORD your God, that you may possess this good land, and leave *it* as an inheritance for your children after you forever.

⁹"As for you, my son Solomon, know the God of your father, and serve Him with a loyal heart and with a willing mind; for the LORD searches all hearts and understands all the intent of the thoughts. If you seek Him, He will be found by you; but if you forsake Him, He will cast you off forever. ¹⁰Consider now, for the LORD has chosen you to build a house for the sanctuary; be strong, and do it."

¹¹Then David gave his son Solomon the plans for the vestibule, its houses, its treasuries, its upper chambers, its inner chambers, and the place of the mercy seat; ¹²and the plans for all that he had by the Spirit, of the courts of the house of the LORD, of all the chambers all around, of the treasuries of the house of God, and of the treasuries for the dedicated things; ¹³also for the division of the priests and the Levites, for all the work of the service of the house of the LORD, and for all the articles of service in the house of the LORD. ¹⁴*He gave* gold by weight for *things* of gold, for all articles used in every kind of service; also *silver* for all articles of silver by weight, for all articles used in every kind of service; ¹⁵the weight for the lampstands of gold, and their lamps of gold, by weight for each lampstand and its lamps; for the lampstands of silver by weight, for the lampstand and its lamps, according to the use of each lampstand. ¹⁶And by weight *he gave* gold for the tables of the showbread, for each table, and silver for the tables of silver; ¹⁷also pure gold for the forks, the basins,

the pitchers of pure gold, and the golden bowls— *he gave gold* by weight for every bowl; and for the silver bowls, *silver* by weight for every bowl; [18]and refined gold by weight for the altar of incense, and for the construction of the chariot, that is, the gold cherubim that spread *their wings* and overshadowed the ark of the covenant of the LORD. [19]"All *this,*" said David, "the LORD made me understand in writing, by *His* hand upon me, all the works of these plans."

[20]And David said to his son Solomon, "Be strong and of good courage, and do *it;* do not fear nor be dismayed, for the LORD God—my God— *will be* with you. He will not leave you nor forsake you, until you have finished all the work for the service of the house of the LORD. [21]*Here are* the divisions of the priests and the Levites for all the service of the house of God; and every willing craftsman *will be* with you for all manner of workmanship, for every kind of service; also the leaders and all the people *will be* completely at your command."

Offerings for Building the Temple

29 Furthermore King David said to all the assembly: "My son Solomon, whom alone God has chosen, *is* young and inexperienced; and the work *is* great, because the temple[a] *is* not for man but for the LORD God. [2]Now for the house of my God I have prepared with all my might: gold for *things to be made of* gold, silver for *things of* silver, bronze for *things of* bronze, iron for *things of* iron, wood for *things of* wood, onyx stones, *stones* to be set, glistening stones of various colors, all kinds of precious stones, and marble slabs in abundance. [3]Moreover, because I have set my affection on the house of my God, I have given to the house of my God, over and above all that I have prepared for the holy house, my own special treasure of gold and silver: [4]three thousand talents of gold, of the gold of Ophir, and seven thousand talents of refined silver, to overlay the walls of the houses; [5]the gold for *things of* gold and the silver for *things of* silver, and for all kinds of work *to be done* by the hands of craftsmen. Who *then* is willing to consecrate himself this day to the LORD?"

[6]Then the leaders of the fathers' *houses,* leaders of the tribes of Israel, the captains of thousands and of hundreds, with the officers over the king's

work, offered willingly. [7]They gave for the work of the house of God five thousand talents and ten thousand darics of gold, ten thousand talents of silver, eighteen thousand talents of bronze, and one hundred thousand talents of iron. [8]And whoever had *precious* stones gave *them* to the treasury of the house of the LORD, into the hand of Jehiel[a] the Gershonite. [9]Then the people rejoiced, for they had offered willingly, because with a loyal heart they had offered willingly to the LORD; and King David also rejoiced greatly.

David's Praise to God

[10]Therefore David blessed the LORD before all the assembly; and David said:

"Blessed are You, LORD God of Israel, our
Father, forever and ever.
[11]Yours, O LORD, *is* the greatness,
The power and the glory,
The victory and the majesty;
For all *that is* in heaven and in earth *is Yours;*
Yours *is* the kingdom, O LORD,
And You are exalted as head over all.
[12]Both riches and honor *come* from You,
And You reign over all.
In Your hand *is* power and might;
In Your hand *it is* to make great
And to give strength to all.

[13]"Now therefore, our God,
We thank You
And praise Your glorious name.
[14]But who *am* I, and who *are* my people,
That we should be able to offer so willingly
as this?
For all things *come* from You,
And of Your own we have given You.
[15]For we *are* aliens and pilgrims before You,
As *were* all our fathers;
Our days on earth *are* as a shadow,
And without hope.

[16]"O LORD our God, all this abundance that we have prepared to build You a house for Your holy name is from Your hand, and *is* all Your own. [17]I know also, my God, that You test the heart and

29:1 [a]Literally *palace* **29:8** [a]Possibly the same as *Jehieli* (compare 26:21, 22)

have pleasure in uprightness. As for me, in the uprightness of my heart I have willingly offered all these *things;* and now with joy I have seen Your people, who are present here to offer willingly to You. [18]O LORD God of Abraham, Isaac, and Israel, our fathers, keep this forever in the intent of the thoughts of the heart of Your people, and fix their heart toward You. [19]And give my son Solomon a loyal heart to keep Your commandments and Your testimonies and Your statutes, to do all *these things,* and to build the temple[a] for which I have made provision."

[20]Then David said to all the assembly, "Now bless the LORD your God." So all the assembly blessed the LORD God of their fathers, and bowed their heads and prostrated themselves before the LORD and the king.

Solomon Anointed King

[21]And they made sacrifices to the LORD and offered burnt offerings to the LORD on the next day: a thousand bulls, a thousand rams, a thousand lambs, with their drink offerings, and sacrifices in abundance for all Israel. [22]So they ate and drank before the LORD with great gladness on that day. And they made Solomon the son of David king the second time, and anointed *him* before the LORD *to be* the leader, and Zadok *to be* priest. [23]Then Solomon sat on the throne of the LORD as king instead of David his father, and prospered; and all Israel obeyed him. [24]All the leaders and the mighty men, and also all the sons of King David, submitted themselves to King Solomon. [25]So the LORD exalted Solomon exceedingly in the sight of all Israel, and bestowed on him *such* royal majesty as had not been on any king before him in Israel.

The Close of David's Reign

[26]Thus David the son of Jesse reigned over all Israel. [27]And the period that he reigned over Israel *was* forty years; seven years he reigned in Hebron, and thirty-three *years* he reigned in Jerusalem. [28]So he died in a good old age, full of days and riches and honor; and Solomon his son reigned in his place. [29]Now the acts of King David, first and last, indeed they *are* written in the book of Samuel the seer, in the book of Nathan the prophet, and in the book of Gad the seer, [30]with all his reign and his might, and the events that happened to him, to Israel, and to all the kingdoms of the lands.

29:19 [a]Literally *palace*

IMPACT OF THE BOOK

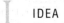

SECOND CHRONICLES

I IDEA

Leaders need to finish well. All four kings: Solomon, Asa, Uzziah, and Jehoshaphat began their reigns with humility and success. All four failed to finish strong. The easiest way to be defeated is to be distracted, relying on your own understanding and self-sufficiency rather than on God. Successful leadership cannot be separated from one's spiritual condition.

MESSAGE

Like the rudder of a ship, a leader can chart the course with even the smallest decisions. Rehoboam listened to the wrong counselors, Jehoshaphat forged poor alliances, Asa made hasty decisions in anger—each bringing judgment upon the nation of Israel. The measure of any good leader, is the extent to which he or she does evil or right in the sight of the Lord.

PEOPLE

Abijah, Ahaz, Ahaziah, Amaziah, Asa, Hezekiah, Jehoshaphat, Joash, Josiah, Manasseh, Micaiah, Obed, Rehoboam, Shemaiah, Solomon, Uzziah

AUTHOR

The anonymous author of 1 and 2 Chronicles is referred to as the "the Chronicler" by some scholars. Jewish tradition, however, assigns authorship to Ezra, although that cannot be proved.

CULTURE

The events in this book occur from the beginning of Solomon's reign (c. 970 BC) until the decree of King Cyrus of Persia for the Israelite exiles to return to Jerusalem (c. 538 BC). Under Solomon's leadership, the nation of Israel expanded its geographical boundaries. However, three successful foreign powers dominated Israel after Solomon's reign: Assyria, which conquered the northern kingdom in 722 BC; Babylon, which conquered the southern kingdom in 586 BC; and finally Persia, which remained in power until Alexander the Great conquered the land in 331 BC.

TIMELINE

c. 450 BC

KEY SCRIPTURE MEMORY VERSES

7:14; 16:9

SOLOMON REQUESTS WISDOM

1 Now Solomon the son of David was strengthened in his kingdom, and the LORD his God *was* with him and exalted him exceedingly.

2 And Solomon spoke to all Israel, to the captains of thousands and of hundreds, to the judges, and to every leader in all Israel, the heads of the fathers' *houses.* 3 Then Solomon, and all the assembly with him, went to the high place that *was* at Gibeon; for the tabernacle of meeting with God was there, which Moses the servant of the LORD had made in the wilderness. 4 But David had brought up the ark of God from Kirjath Jearim to *the place* David had prepared for it, for he had pitched a tent for it at Jerusalem. 5 Now the bronze altar that Bezalel the son of Uri, the son of Hur, had made, he put[a] before the tabernacle of the LORD; Solomon and the assembly sought Him *there.* 6 And Solomon went up there to the bronze altar before the LORD, which *was* at the tabernacle of meeting, and offered a thousand burnt offerings on it.

7 On that night God appeared to Solomon, and said to him, "Ask! What shall I give you?"

8 And Solomon said to God: "You have shown great mercy to David my father, and have made me king in his place. 9 Now, O LORD God, let Your promise to David my father be established, for You have made me king over a people like the dust of the earth in multitude. 10 Now give me wisdom and knowledge, that I may go out and come in before this people; for who can judge this great people of Yours?"

11 Then God said to Solomon: "Because this was in your heart, and you have not asked riches or wealth or honor or the life of your enemies, nor have you asked long life—but have asked wisdom and knowledge for yourself, that you may judge My people over whom I have made you king— 12 wisdom and knowledge *are* granted to you; and I will give you riches and wealth and honor, such as none of the kings have had who *were* before you, nor shall any after you have the like."

SOLOMON'S MILITARY AND ECONOMIC POWER

13 So Solomon came to Jerusalem from the high place that *was* at Gibeon, from before the tabernacle of meeting, and reigned over Israel.

14 And Solomon gathered chariots and horsemen; he had one thousand four hundred chariots and twelve thousand horsemen, whom he stationed in the chariot cities and with the king in Jerusalem. 15 Also the king made silver and gold as common in Jerusalem as stones, and he made cedars as abundant as the sycamores which *are* in the lowland. 16 And Solomon had horses imported from Egypt and Keveh; the king's merchants bought them in Keveh at the *current* price. 17 They also acquired and imported from Egypt a chariot for six hundred *shekels* of silver, and a horse for one hundred and fifty; thus, through their agents,[a] they exported them to all the kings of the Hittites and the kings of Syria.

SOLOMON PREPARES TO BUILD THE TEMPLE

2 Then Solomon determined to build a temple for the name of the LORD, and a royal house for himself. 2 Solomon selected seventy thousand men to bear burdens, eighty thousand to quarry *stone* in the mountains, and three thousand six hundred to oversee them.

3 Then Solomon sent to Hiram[a] king of Tyre, saying:

> As you have dealt with David my father, and sent him cedars to build himself a house to dwell in, *so deal with me.* 4 Behold, I am building a temple for the name of the LORD my God, to dedicate *it* to Him, to burn before Him sweet incense, for the continual showbread, for the burnt offerings morning and evening, on the Sabbaths, on the New Moons, and on the set feasts of the LORD our God. This *is an ordinance* forever to Israel.
>
> 5 And the temple which I build *will be* great, for our God is greater than all gods. 6 But who is able to build Him a temple, since heaven and the heaven of heavens cannot contain Him? Who *am* I then, that I should build Him a temple, except to burn sacrifice before Him?
>
> 7 Therefore send me at once a man skillful to work in gold and silver, in bronze and iron,

1:5 [a]Some authorities read *it was there.*   1:17 [a]Literally *by their hands*   2:3 [a]Hebrew *Huram* (compare 1 Kings 5:1) in purple and crimson and blue, who has skill to engrave with the skillful men who are with me in Judah and Jerusalem, whom David my father provided. [8]Also send me cedar and cypress and algum logs from Lebanon, for I know that your servants have skill to cut timber in Lebanon; and indeed my servants *will be* with your servants, [9]to prepare timber for me in abundance, for the temple which I am about to build *shall be* great and wonderful.

[10]And indeed I will give to your servants, the woodsmen who cut timber, twenty thousand kors of ground wheat, twenty thousand kors of barley, twenty thousand baths of wine, and twenty thousand baths of oil.

[11]Then Hiram king of Tyre answered in writing, which he sent to Solomon:

Because the LORD loves His people, He has made you king over them.

[12]Hiram[a] also said:

Blessed *be* the LORD God of Israel, who made heaven and earth, for He has given King David a wise son, endowed with prudence and understanding, who will build a temple for the LORD and a royal house for himself!

[13]And now I have sent a skillful man, endowed with understanding, Huram[a] my master[b] *craftsman* [14](the son of a woman of the daughters of Dan, and his father was a man of Tyre), skilled to work in gold and silver, bronze and iron, stone and wood, purple and blue, fine linen and crimson, and to make any engraving and to accomplish any plan which may be given to him, with your skillful men and with the skillful men of my lord David your father.

[15]Now therefore, the wheat, the barley, the oil, and the wine which my lord has spoken of, let him send to his servants. [16]And we will cut wood from Lebanon, as much as you need; we will bring it to you in rafts by sea to Joppa, and you will carry it up to Jerusalem.

[17]Then Solomon numbered all the aliens who *were* in the land of Israel, after the census in which David his father had numbered them; and there were found to be one hundred and fifty-three thousand six hundred. [18]And he made seventy thousand of them bearers of burdens, eighty thousand stonecutters in the mountain, and three thousand six hundred overseers to make the people work.

SOLOMON BUILDS THE TEMPLE

3 Now Solomon began to build the house of the LORD at Jerusalem on Mount Moriah, where *the LORD*[a] had appeared to his father David, at the place that David had prepared on the threshing floor of Ornan[b] the Jebusite. [2]And he began to build on the second *day* of the second month in the fourth year of his reign.

[3]This is the foundation which Solomon laid for building the house of God: The length *was* sixty cubits (by cubits according to the former measure) and the width twenty cubits. [4]And the vestibule that *was* in front *of the sanctuary*[a] was twenty cubits long across the width of the house, and the height *was* one hundred and[b] twenty. He overlaid the inside with pure gold. [5]The larger room[a] he paneled with cypress which he overlaid with fine gold, and he carved palm trees and chainwork on it. [6]And he decorated the house with precious stones for beauty, and the gold *was* gold from Parvaim. [7]He also overlaid the house— the beams and doorposts, its walls and doors— with gold; and he carved cherubim on the walls.

[8]And he made the Most Holy Place. Its length was according to the width of the house, twenty cubits, and its width twenty cubits. He overlaid it with six hundred talents of fine gold. [9]The weight of the nails *was* fifty shekels of gold; and he overlaid the upper area with gold. [10]In the

2:12 [a]Hebrew *Huram* (compare 1 Kings 5:1)   **2:13** [a]Spelled *Hiram* in 1 Kings 7:13   [b]Literally *father* (compare 1 Kings 7:13, 14)   **3:1** [a]Literally *He,* following Masoretic Text and Vulgate; Septuagint reads *the LORD;* Targum reads *the Angel of the LORD.* [b]Spelled *Araunah* in 2 Samuel 24:16ff   **3:4** [a]The main room of the temple; elsewhere called the holy place (compare 1 Kings 6:3) [b]Following Masoretic Text, Septuagint, and Vulgate; Arabic, some manuscripts of the Septuagint, and Syriac omit *one hundred and.* **3:5** [a]Literally *house*

Most Holy Place he made two cherubim, fashioned by carving, and overlaid them with gold. [11]The wings of the cherubim *were* twenty cubits in *overall* length: one wing *of the one cherub was* five cubits, touching the wall of the room, and the other wing *was* five cubits, touching the wing of the other cherub; [12]*one* wing of the other cherub *was* five cubits, touching the wall of the room, and the other wing *also was* five cubits, touching the wing of the other cherub. [13]The wings of these cherubim spanned twenty cubits overall. They stood on their feet, and they faced inward. [14]And he made the veil of blue, purple, crimson, and fine linen, and wove cherubim into it.

[15]Also he made in front of the temple[a] two pillars thirty-five[b] cubits high, and the capital that *was* on the top of each of *them* was five cubits. [16]He made wreaths of chainwork, as in the inner sanctuary, and put *them* on top of the pillars; and he made one hundred pomegranates, and put *them* on the wreaths of chainwork. [17]Then he set up the pillars before the temple, one on the right hand and the other on the left; he called the name of the one on the right hand Jachin, and the name of the one on the left Boaz.

Furnishings of the Temple

4 Moreover he made a bronze altar: twenty cubits was its length, twenty cubits its width, and ten cubits its height.

[2]Then he made the Sea of cast *bronze,* ten cubits from one brim to the other; *it was* completely round. Its height *was* five cubits, and a line of thirty cubits measured its circumference. [3]And under it *was* the likeness of oxen encircling it all around, ten to a cubit, all the way around the Sea. The oxen *were* cast in two rows, when it was cast. [4]It stood on twelve oxen: three looking toward the north, three looking toward the west, three looking toward the south, and three looking toward the east; the Sea *was set* upon them, and all their back parts *pointed* inward. [5]It *was* a handbreadth thick; and its brim was shaped like the brim of a cup, *like* a lily blossom. It contained three thousand[a] baths.

[6]He also made ten lavers, and put five on the right side and five on the left, to wash in them; such things as they offered for the burnt offering they would wash in them, but the Sea *was* for the priests to wash in. [7]And he made ten lampstands of gold according to their design, and set *them* in the temple, five on the right side and five on the left. [8]He also made ten tables, and placed *them* in the temple, five on the right side and five on the left. And he made one hundred bowls of gold.

[9]Furthermore he made the court of the priests, and the great court and doors for the court; and he overlaid these doors with bronze. [10]He set the Sea on the right side, toward the southeast.

[11]Then Huram made the pots and the shovels and the bowls. So Huram finished doing the work that he was to do for King Solomon for the house of God: [12]the two pillars and the bowl-shaped capitals *that were* on top of the two pillars; the two networks covering the two bowl-shaped capitals which *were* on top of the pillars; [13]four hundred pomegranates for the two networks (two rows of pomegranates for each network, to cover the two bowl-shaped capitals that *were* on the pillars); [14]he also made carts and the lavers on the carts; [15]one Sea and twelve oxen under it; [16]also the pots, the shovels, the forks—and all their articles Huram his master[a] *craftsman* made of burnished bronze for King Solomon for the house of the LORD.

[17]In the plain of Jordan the king had them cast in clay molds, between Succoth and Zeredah.[a] [18]And Solomon had all these articles made in such great abundance that the weight of the bronze was not determined.

[19]Thus Solomon had all the furnishings made for the house of God: the altar of gold and the tables on which *was* the showbread; [20]the lampstands with their lamps of pure gold, to burn in the prescribed manner in front of the inner sanctuary, [21]with the flowers and the lamps and the wick-trimmers of gold, of purest gold; [22]the trimmers, the bowls, the ladles, and the censers of pure gold. As for the entry of the sanctuary, its inner doors to the Most Holy *Place,* and the doors of the main hall of the temple, *were* gold.

5 So all the work that Solomon had done for the house of the LORD was finished; and Solomon brought in the things which his father David had

---

3:15 [a]Literally *house* [b]Or *eighteen* (compare 1 Kings 7:15; 2 Kings 25:17; and Jeremiah 52:21)   **4:5** [a]Or *two thousand* (compare 1 Kings 7:26)   **4:16** [a]Literally *father*   **4:17** [a]Spelled *Zaretan* in 1 Kings 7:46

dedicated: the silver and the gold and all the furnishings. And he put *them* in the treasuries of the house of God.

The Ark Brought into the Temple

[2]Now Solomon assembled the elders of Israel and all the heads of the tribes, the chief fathers of the children of Israel, in Jerusalem, that they might bring the ark of the covenant of the LORD up from the City of David, which *is* Zion. [3]Therefore all the men of Israel assembled with the king at the feast, which *was* in the seventh month. [4]So all the elders of Israel came, and the Levites took up the ark. [5]Then they brought up the ark, the tabernacle of meeting, and all the holy furnishings that *were* in the tabernacle. The priests and the Levites brought them up. [6]Also King Solomon, and all the congregation of Israel who were assembled with him before the ark, were sacrificing sheep and oxen that could not be counted or numbered for multitude. [7]Then the priests brought in the ark of the covenant of the LORD to its place, into the inner sanctuary of the temple,[a] to the Most Holy *Place,* under the wings of the cherubim. [8]For the cherubim spread *their* wings over the place of the ark, and the cherubim overshadowed the ark and its poles. [9]The poles extended so that the ends of the poles of the ark could be seen from *the holy place,* in front of the inner sanctuary; but they could not be seen from outside. And they are there to this day. [10]Nothing was in the ark except the two tablets which Moses put *there* at Horeb, when the LORD made *a covenant* with the children of Israel, when they had come out of Egypt.

[11]And it came to pass when the priests came out of the *Most* Holy *Place* (for all the priests who *were* present had sanctified themselves, without keeping to their divisions), [12]and the Levites *who were* the singers, all those of Asaph and Heman and Jeduthun, with their sons and their brethren, stood at the east end of the altar, clothed in white linen, having cymbals, stringed instruments and harps, and with them one hundred and twenty priests sounding with trumpets— [13]indeed it came to pass, when the trumpeters and singers *were* as one, to make one sound to be heard in praising and thanking the LORD, and when they

lifted up their voice with the trumpets and cymbals and instruments of music, and praised the LORD, *saying:*

"*For He is* good,
For His mercy *endures* forever,"[a]

that the house, the house of the LORD, was filled with a cloud, [14]so that the priests could not continue ministering because of the cloud; for the glory of the LORD filled the house of God.

6 Then Solomon spoke:

"The LORD said He would dwell in the dark cloud.
[2]I have surely built You an exalted house,
And a place for You to dwell in forever."

Solomon's Speech upon Completion of the Work

[3]Then the king turned around and blessed the whole assembly of Israel, while all the assembly of Israel was standing. [4]And he said: "Blessed *be* the LORD God of Israel, who has fulfilled with His hands *what* He spoke with His mouth to my father David, saying, [5]'Since the day that I brought My people out of the land of Egypt, I have chosen no city from any tribe of Israel *in which* to build a house, that My name might be there, nor did I choose any man to be a ruler over My people Israel. [6]Yet I have chosen Jerusalem, that My name may be there, and I have chosen David to be over My people Israel.' [7]Now it was in the heart of my father David to build a temple[a] for the name of the LORD God of Israel. [8]But the LORD said to my father David, 'Whereas it was in your heart to build a temple for My name, you did well in that it was in your heart. [9]Nevertheless you shall not build the temple, but your son who will come from your body, he shall build the temple for My name.' [10]So the LORD has fulfilled His word which He spoke, and I have filled the position of my father David, and sit on the throne of Israel, as the LORD promised; and I have built the temple for the name of the LORD God of Israel. [11]And there I have put the ark, in which *is* the covenant of the LORD which He made with the children of Israel."

5:7 [a]Literally *house* **5:13** [a]Compare Psalm 106:1 **6:7** [a]Literally *house,* and so in verses 8–10

Solomon's Prayer of Dedication

[12]Then *Solomon*[a] stood before the altar of the LORD in the presence of all the assembly of Israel, and spread out his hands [13](for Solomon had made a bronze platform five cubits long, five cubits wide, and three cubits high, and had set it in the midst of the court; and he stood on it, knelt down on his knees before all the assembly of Israel, and spread out his hands toward heaven); [14]and he said: "LORD God of Israel, *there is* no God in heaven or on earth like You, who keep *Your* covenant and mercy with Your servants who walk before You with all their hearts. [15]You have kept what You promised Your servant David my father; You have both spoken with Your mouth and fulfilled *it* with Your hand, as *it is* this day. [16]Therefore, LORD God of Israel, now keep what You promised Your servant David my father, saying, 'You shall not fail to have a man sit before Me on the throne of Israel, only if your sons take heed to their way, that they walk in My law as you have walked before Me.' [17]And now, O LORD God of Israel, let Your word come true, which You have spoken to Your servant David.

[18]"But will God indeed dwell with men on the earth? Behold, heaven and the heaven of heavens cannot contain You. How much less this temple[a] which I have built! [19]Yet regard the prayer of Your servant and his supplication, O LORD my God, and listen to the cry and the prayer which Your servant is praying before You: [20]that Your eyes may be open toward this temple day and night, toward the place where *You* said *You would* put Your name, that You may hear the prayer which Your servant makes toward this place. [21]And may You hear the supplications of Your servant and of Your people Israel, when they pray toward this place. Hear from heaven Your dwelling place, and when You hear, forgive.

[22]"If anyone sins against his neighbor, and is forced to take an oath, and comes *and* takes an oath before Your altar in this temple, [23]then hear from heaven, and act, and judge Your servants, bringing retribution on the wicked by bringing his way on his own head, and justifying the righteous by giving him according to his righteousness.

[24]"Or if Your people Israel are defeated before an enemy because they have sinned against You, and return and confess Your name, and pray and make supplication before You in this temple, [25]then hear from heaven and forgive the sin of Your people Israel, and bring them back to the land which You gave to them and their fathers.

[26]"When the heavens are shut up and there is no rain because they have sinned against You, when they pray toward this place and confess Your name, and turn from their sin because You afflict them, [27]then hear *in* heaven, and forgive the sin of Your servants, Your people Israel, that You may teach them the good way in which they should walk; and send rain on Your land which You have given to Your people as an inheritance.

[28]"When there is famine in the land, pestilence or blight or mildew, locusts or grasshoppers; when their enemies besiege them in the land of their cities; whatever plague or whatever sickness *there is;* [29]whatever prayer, whatever supplication is *made* by anyone, or by all Your people Israel, when each one knows his own burden and his own grief, and spreads out his hands to this temple: [30]then hear from heaven Your dwelling place, and forgive, and give to everyone according to all his ways, whose heart You know (for You alone know the hearts of the sons of men), [31]that they may fear You, to walk in Your ways as long as they live in the land which You gave to our fathers.

[32]"Moreover, concerning a foreigner, who is not of Your people Israel, but has come from a far country for the sake of Your great name and Your mighty hand and Your outstretched arm, when they come and pray in this temple; [33]then hear from heaven Your dwelling place, and do according to all for which the foreigner calls to You, that all peoples of the earth may know Your name and fear You, as *do* Your people Israel, and that they may know that this temple which I have built is called by Your name.

[34]"When Your people go out to battle against their enemies, wherever You send them, and when they pray to You toward this city which You have chosen and the temple which I have built for Your name, [35]then hear from heaven their prayer and their supplication, and maintain their cause.

[36]"When they sin against You (for *there is* no one who does not sin), and You become angry

6:12 [a]Literally *he* (compare 1 Kings 8:22)　6:18 [a]Literally *house* with them and deliver them to the enemy, and they take them captive to a land far or near; [37]yet when they come to themselves in the land where they were carried captive, and repent, and make supplication to You in the land of their captivity, saying, 'We have sinned, we have done wrong, and have committed wickedness'; [38]and *when* they return to You with all their heart and with all their soul in the land of their captivity, where they have been carried captive, and pray toward their land which You gave to their fathers, the city which You have chosen, and toward the temple which I have built for Your name: [39]then hear from heaven Your dwelling place their prayer and their supplications, and maintain their cause, and forgive Your people who have sinned against You. [40]Now, my God, I pray, let Your eyes be open and *let* Your ears *be* attentive to the prayer *made* in this place.

[41]"Now therefore,
Arise, O LORD God, to Your resting place,
You and the ark of Your strength.
Let Your priests, O LORD God, be clothed
    with salvation,
And let Your saints rejoice in goodness.

[42]"O LORD God, do not turn away the face of
    Your Anointed;
Remember the mercies of Your servant
    David."[a]

SOLOMON DEDICATES THE TEMPLE

7 When Solomon had finished praying, fire came down from heaven and consumed the burnt offering and the sacrifices; and the glory of the LORD filled the temple.[a] [2]And the priests could not enter the house of the LORD, because the glory of the LORD had filled the LORD's house. [3]When all the children of Israel saw how the fire came down, and the glory of the LORD on the temple, they bowed their faces to the ground on the pavement, and worshiped and praised the LORD, *saying:*

"For *He is* good,
For His mercy *endures* forever."[a]

[4]Then the king and all the people offered sacrifices before the LORD. [5]King Solomon offered a sacrifice of twenty-two thousand bulls and one hundred and twenty thousand sheep. So the king and all the people dedicated the house of God. [6]And the priests attended to their services; the Levites also with instruments of the music of the LORD, which King David had made to praise the LORD, saying, "For His mercy *endures* forever,"[a] whenever David offered praise by their ministry. The priests sounded trumpets opposite them, while all Israel stood.

[7]Furthermore Solomon consecrated the middle of the court that *was* in front of the house of the LORD; for there he offered burnt offerings and the fat of the peace offerings, because the bronze altar which Solomon had made was not able to receive the burnt offerings, the grain offerings, and the fat.

[8]At that time Solomon kept the feast seven days, and all Israel with him, a very great assembly from the entrance of Hamath to the Brook of Egypt.[a] [9]And on the eighth day they held a sacred assembly, for they observed the dedication of the altar seven days, and the feast seven days. [10]On the twenty-third day of the seventh month he sent the people away to their tents, joyful and glad of heart for the good that the LORD had done for David, for Solomon, and for His people Israel. [11]Thus Solomon finished the house of the LORD and the king's house; and Solomon successfully accomplished all that came into his heart to make in the house of the LORD and in his own house.

GOD'S SECOND APPEARANCE TO SOLOMON

[12]Then the LORD appeared to Solomon by night, and said to him: "I have heard your prayer, and have chosen this place for Myself as a house of sacrifice. [13]When I shut up heaven and there is no rain, or command the locusts to devour the land, or send pestilence among My people, [14]if My people who are called by My name will humble themselves, and pray and seek My face, and turn from their wicked ways, then I will hear from heaven, and will forgive their sin and heal their land. [15]Now My eyes will be open and My ears attentive to prayer *made* in this place. [16]For now I have chosen and sanctified this house, that

6:42 [a]Compare Psalm 132:8–10 **7:1** [a]Literally *house* **7:3** [a]Compare Psalm 106:1 **7:6** [a]Compare Psalm 106:1 **7:8** [a]That is, the Shihor (compare 1 Chronicles 13:5)

My name may be there forever; and My eyes and My heart will be there perpetually. ¹⁷As for you, if you walk before Me as your father David walked, and do according to all that I have commanded you, and if you keep My statutes and My judgments, ¹⁸then I will establish the throne of your kingdom, as I covenanted with David your father, saying, 'You shall not fail *to have* a man as ruler in Israel.'

¹⁹"But if you turn away and forsake My statutes and My commandments which I have set before you, and go and serve other gods, and worship them, ²⁰then I will uproot them from My land which I have given them; and this house which I have sanctified for My name I will cast out of My sight, and will make it a proverb and a byword among all peoples.

²¹"And *as for* this house, which is exalted, everyone who passes by it will be astonished and say, 'Why has the LORD done thus to this land and this house?' ²²Then they will answer, 'Because they forsook the LORD God of their fathers, who brought them out of the land of Egypt, and embraced other gods, and worshiped them and served them; therefore He has brought all this calamity on them.' "

SOLOMON'S ADDITIONAL ACHIEVEMENTS

8 It came to pass at the end of twenty years, when Solomon had built the house of the LORD and his own house, ²that the cities which Hiram[a] had given to Solomon, Solomon built them; and he settled the children of Israel there. ³And Solomon went to Hamath Zobah and seized it. ⁴He also built Tadmor in the wilderness, and all the storage cities which he built in Hamath. ⁵He built Upper Beth Horon and Lower Beth Horon, fortified cities *with* walls, gates, and bars, ⁶also Baalath and all the storage cities that Solomon had, and all the chariot cities and the cities of the cavalry, and all that Solomon desired to build in Jerusalem, in Lebanon, and in all the land of his dominion.

⁷All the people *who were* left of the Hittites, Amorites, Perizzites, Hivites, and Jebusites, who *were* not of Israel— ⁸that is, their descendants who were left in the land after them, whom the children of Israel did not destroy—from these Solomon raised forced labor, as it is to this day.

⁹But Solomon did not make the children of Israel servants for his work. Some *were* men of war, captains of his officers, captains of his chariots, and his cavalry. ¹⁰And others *were* chiefs of the officials of King Solomon: two hundred and fifty, who ruled over the people.

¹¹Now Solomon brought the daughter of Pharaoh up from the City of David to the house he had built for her, for he said, "My wife shall not dwell in the house of David king of Israel, because *the places* to which the ark of the LORD has come are holy."

¹²Then Solomon offered burnt offerings to the LORD on the altar of the LORD which he had built before the vestibule, ¹³according to the daily rate, offering according to the commandment of Moses, for the Sabbaths, the New Moons, and the three appointed yearly feasts—the Feast of Unleavened Bread, the Feast of Weeks, and the Feast of Tabernacles. ¹⁴And, according to the order of David his father, he appointed the divisions of the priests for their service, the Levites for their duties (to praise and serve before the priests) as the duty of each day required, and the gatekeepers by their divisions at each gate; for so David the man of God had commanded. ¹⁵They did not depart from the command of the king to the priests and Levites concerning any matter or concerning the treasuries.

¹⁶Now all the work of Solomon was well-ordered from[a] the day of the foundation of the house of the LORD until it was finished. So the house of the LORD was completed.

¹⁷Then Solomon went to Ezion Geber and Elath[a] on the seacoast, in the land of Edom. ¹⁸And Hiram sent him ships by the hand of his servants, and servants who knew the sea. They went with the servants of Solomon to Ophir, and acquired four hundred and fifty talents of gold from there, and brought it to King Solomon.

THE QUEEN OF SHEBA'S PRAISE OF SOLOMON

9 Now when the queen of Sheba heard of the fame of Solomon, she came to Jerusalem to test Solomon with hard questions, *having* a very great retinue, camels that bore spices, gold in abundance, and precious stones; and when she came to

8:2 ªHebrew *Huram* (compare 2 Chronicles 2:3)   **8:16** ªFollowing Septuagint, Syriac, and Vulgate; Masoretic Text reads *as far as.*
8:17 ªHebrew *Eloth* (compare 2 Kings 14:22)

Solomon, she spoke with him about all that was in her heart. [2]So Solomon answered all her questions; there was nothing so difficult for Solomon that he could not explain it to her. [3]And when the queen of Sheba had seen the wisdom of Solomon, the house that he had built, [4]the food on his table, the seating of his servants, the service of his waiters and their apparel, his cupbearers and their apparel, and his entryway by which he went up to the house of the LORD, there was no more spirit in her.

[5]Then she said to the king: "*It was* a true report which I heard in my own land about your words and your wisdom. [6]However I did not believe their words until I came and saw with my own eyes; and indeed the half of the greatness of your wisdom was not told me. You exceed the fame of which I heard. [7]Happy *are* your men and happy *are* these your servants, who stand continually before you and hear your wisdom! [8]Blessed be the LORD your God, who delighted in you, setting you on His throne *to be* king for the LORD your God! Because your God has loved Israel, to establish them forever, therefore He made you king over them, to do justice and righteousness."

[9]And she gave the king one hundred and twenty talents of gold, spices in great abundance, and precious stones; there never were any spices such as those the queen of Sheba gave to King Solomon.

[10]Also, the servants of Hiram and the servants of Solomon, who brought gold from Ophir, brought algum[a] wood and precious stones. [11]And the king made walkways *of* the algum[a] wood for the house of the LORD and for the king's house, also harps and stringed instruments for singers; and there were none such *as these* seen before in the land of Judah.

[12]Now King Solomon gave to the queen of Sheba all she desired, whatever she asked, *much more* than she had brought to the king. So she turned and went to her own country, she and her servants.

SOLOMON'S GREAT WEALTH

[13]The weight of gold that came to Solomon yearly was six hundred and sixty-six talents of gold, [14]besides *what* the traveling merchants and traders brought. And all the kings of Arabia and governors of the country brought gold and silver

to Solomon. [15]And King Solomon made two hundred large shields of hammered gold; six hundred *shekels* of hammered gold went into each shield. [16]*He* also *made* three hundred shields of hammered gold; three hundred *shekels*[a] of gold went into each shield. The king put them in the House of the Forest of Lebanon.

[17]Moreover the king made a great throne of ivory, and overlaid it with pure gold. [18]The throne *had* six steps, with a footstool of gold, *which were* fastened to the throne; there were armrests on either side of the place of the seat, and two lions stood beside the armrests. [19]Twelve lions stood there, one on each side of the six steps; nothing like *this* had been made for any *other* kingdom.

[20]All King Solomon's drinking vessels *were* gold, and all the vessels of the House of the Forest of Lebanon *were* pure gold. Not *one was* silver, for this was accounted as nothing in the days of Solomon. [21]For the king's ships went to Tarshish with the servants of Hiram.[a] Once every three years the merchant ships[b] came, bringing gold, silver, ivory, apes, and monkeys.[c]

[22]So King Solomon surpassed all the kings of the earth in riches and wisdom. [23]And all the kings of the earth sought the presence of Solomon to hear his wisdom, which God had put in his heart. [24]Each man brought his present: articles of silver and gold, garments, armor, spices, horses, and mules, at a set rate year by year.

[25]Solomon had four thousand stalls for horses and chariots, and twelve thousand horsemen whom he stationed in the chariot cities and with the king at Jerusalem.

[26]So he reigned over all the kings from the River[a] to the land of the Philistines, as far as the border of Egypt. [27]The king made silver *as common* in Jerusalem as stones, and he made cedar trees as abundant as the sycamores which *are* in the lowland. [28]And they brought horses to Solomon from Egypt and from all lands.

DEATH OF SOLOMON

[29]Now the rest of the acts of Solomon, first and last, *are* they not written in the book of

9:10 [a]Or *almug* (compare 1 Kings 10:11, 12)   **9:11** [a]Or *almug* (compare 1 Kings 10:11, 12)   **9:16** [a]Or *three minas* (compare 1 Kings 10:17)   **9:21** [a]Hebrew *Huram* (compare 1 Kings 10:22) [b]Literally *ships of Tarshish* (deep-sea vessels) [c]Or *peacocks* **9:26** [a]That is, the Euphrates

Nathan the prophet, in the prophecy of Ahijah the Shilonite, and in the visions of Iddo the seer concerning Jeroboam the son of Nebat? ³⁰Solomon reigned in Jerusalem over all Israel forty years. ³¹Then Solomon rested with his fathers, and was buried in the City of David his father. And Rehoboam his son reigned in his place.

The Revolt Against Rehoboam

10And Rehoboam went to Shechem, for all Israel had gone to Shechem to make him king. ²So it happened, when Jeroboam the son of Nebat heard *it* (he was in Egypt, where he had fled from the presence of King Solomon), that Jeroboam returned from Egypt. ³Then they sent for him and called him. And Jeroboam and all Israel came and spoke to Rehoboam, saying, ⁴"Your father made our yoke heavy; now therefore, lighten the burdensome service of your father and his heavy yoke which he put on us, and we will serve you."

⁵So he said to them, "Come back to me after three days." And the people departed.

⁶Then King Rehoboam consulted the elders who stood before his father Solomon while he still lived, saying, "How do you advise *me* to answer these people?"

⁷And they spoke to him, saying, "If you are kind to these people, and please them, and speak good words to them, they will be your servants forever."

⁸But he rejected the advice which the elders had given him, and consulted the young men who had grown up with him, who stood before him. ⁹And he said to them, "What advice do you give? How should we answer this people who have spoken to me, saying, 'Lighten the yoke which your father put on us'?"

¹⁰Then the young men who had grown up with him spoke to him, saying, "Thus you should speak to the people who have spoken to you, saying, 'Your father made our yoke heavy, but you make *it* lighter on us'—thus you shall say to them: 'My little *finger* shall be thicker than my father's waist! ¹¹And now, whereas my father put a heavy yoke on you, I will add to your yoke; my father chastised you with whips, but I *will chastise you* with scourges!' "ᵃ

¹²So Jeroboam and all the people came to Rehoboam on the third day, as the king had directed, saying, "Come back to me the third day." ¹³Then the king answered them roughly. King Rehoboam rejected the advice of the elders, ¹⁴and he spoke to them according to the advice of the young men, saying, "My fatherᵃ made your yoke heavy, but I will add to it; my father chastised you with whips, but I *will chastise you* with scourges!"ᵇ ¹⁵So the king did not listen to the people; for the turn *of events* was from God, that the LORD might fulfill His word, which He had spoken by the hand of Ahijah the Shilonite to Jeroboam the son of Nebat.

¹⁶Now when all Israel *saw* that the king did not listen to them, the people answered the king, saying:

"What share have we in David?
    We have no inheritance in the son of Jesse.
    Every man to your tents, O Israel!
    Now see to your own house, O David!"

So all Israel departed to their tents. ¹⁷But Rehoboam reigned over the children of Israel who dwelt in the cities of Judah.

¹⁸Then King Rehoboam sent Hadoram, who *was* in charge of revenue; but the children of Israel stoned him with stones, and he died. Therefore King Rehoboam mounted *his* chariot in haste to flee to Jerusalem. ¹⁹So Israel has been in rebellion against the house of David to this day.

11Now when Rehoboam came to Jerusalem, he assembled from the house of Judah and Benjamin one hundred and eighty thousand chosen *men* who were warriors, to fight against Israel, that he might restore the kingdom to Rehoboam.

²But the word of the LORD came to Shemaiah the man of God, saying, ³"Speak to Rehoboam the son of Solomon, king of Judah, and to all Israel in Judah and Benjamin, saying, ⁴'Thus says the LORD: "You shall not go up or fight against your brethren! Let every man return to his house, for this thing is from Me." ' " Therefore they obeyed the words of the LORD, and turned back from attacking Jeroboam.

10:11 ᵃLiterally *scorpions* **10:14** ᵃFollowing many Hebrew manuscripts, Septuagint, Syriac, and Vulgate (compare verse 10 and 1 Kings 12:14); Masoretic Text reads *I.* ᵇLiterally *scorpions*

Rehoboam Fortifies the Cities

[5]So Rehoboam dwelt in Jerusalem, and built cities for defense in Judah. [6]And he built Bethlehem, Etam, Tekoa, [7]Beth Zur, Sochoh, Adullam, [8]Gath, Mareshah, Ziph, [9]Adoraim, Lachish, Azekah, [10]Zorah, Aijalon, and Hebron, which are in Judah and Benjamin, fortified cities. [11]And he fortified the strongholds, and put captains in them, and stores of food, oil, and wine. [12]Also in every city *he put* shields and spears, and made them very strong, having Judah and Benjamin on his side.

Priests and Levites Move to Judah

[13]And from all their territories the priests and the Levites who *were* in all Israel took their stand with him. [14]For the Levites left their commonlands and their possessions and came to Judah and Jerusalem, for Jeroboam and his sons had rejected them from serving as priests to the LORD. [15]Then he appointed for himself priests for the high places, for the demons, and the calf idols which he had made. [16]And after *the Levites left*,[a] those from all the tribes of Israel, such as set their heart to seek the LORD God of Israel, came to Jerusalem to sacrifice to the LORD God of their fathers. [17]So they strengthened the kingdom of Judah, and made Rehoboam the son of Solomon strong for three years, because they walked in the way of David and Solomon for three years.

The Family of Rehoboam

[18]Then Rehoboam took for himself as wife Mahalath the daughter of Jerimoth the son of David, *and of* Abihail the daughter of Eliah the son of Jesse. [19]And she bore him children: Jeush, Shamariah, and Zaham. [20]After her he took Maachah the granddaughter[a] of Absalom; and she bore him Abijah, Attai, Ziza, and Shelomith. [21]Now Rehoboam loved Maachah the granddaughter of Absalom more than all his wives and his concubines; for he took eighteen wives and sixty concubines, and begot twenty-eight sons and sixty daughters. [22]And Rehoboam appointed Abijah the son of Maachah as chief, *to be* leader among his brothers; for he *intended* to make him king. [23]He dealt wisely, and dispersed some of his sons throughout all the territories of Judah and Benjamin, to every fortified city; and he gave them provisions in abundance. He also sought many wives *for them.*

Egypt Attacks Judah

12 Now it came to pass, when Rehoboam had established the kingdom and had strengthened himself, that he forsook the law of the LORD, and all Israel along with him. [2]And it happened in the fifth year of King Rehoboam *that* Shishak king of Egypt came up against Jerusalem, because they had transgressed against the LORD, [3]with twelve hundred chariots, sixty thousand horsemen, and people without number who came with him out of Egypt—the Lubim and the Sukkiim and the Ethiopians. [4]And he took the fortified cities of Judah and came to Jerusalem.

[5]Then Shemaiah the prophet came to Rehoboam and the leaders of Judah, who were gathered together in Jerusalem because of Shishak, and said to them, "Thus says the LORD: 'You have forsaken Me, and therefore I also have left you in the hand of Shishak.' "

[6]So the leaders of Israel and the king humbled themselves; and they said, "The LORD *is* righteous."

[7]Now when the LORD saw that they humbled themselves, the word of the LORD came to Shemaiah, saying, "They have humbled themselves; *therefore* I will not destroy them, but I will grant them some deliverance. My wrath shall not be poured out on Jerusalem by the hand of Shishak. [8]Nevertheless they will be his servants, that they may distinguish My service from the service of the kingdoms of the nations."

[9]So Shishak king of Egypt came up against Jerusalem, and took away the treasures of the house of the LORD and the treasures of the king's house; he took everything. He also carried away the gold shields which Solomon had made. [10]Then King Rehoboam made bronze shields in their place, and committed *them* to the hands of the captains of the guard, who guarded the doorway of the king's house. [11]And whenever the king entered the house of the LORD, the guard would go and bring them out; then they would take

11:16 [a]Literally *after them* **11:20** [a]Literally *daughter,* but in the broader sense of granddaughter (compare 2 Chronicles 13:2)

them back into the guardroom. [12]When he humbled himself, the wrath of the LORD turned from him, so as not to destroy *him* completely; and things also went well in Judah.

THE END OF REHOBOAM'S REIGN

[13]Thus King Rehoboam strengthened himself in Jerusalem and reigned. Now Rehoboam *was* forty-one years old when he became king; and he reigned seventeen years in Jerusalem, the city which the LORD had chosen out of all the tribes of Israel, to put His name there. His mother's name *was* Naamah, an Ammonitess. [14]And he did evil, because he did not prepare his heart to seek the LORD.

[15]The acts of Rehoboam, first and last, *are* they not written in the book of Shemaiah the prophet, and of Iddo the seer concerning genealogies? And *there were* wars between Rehoboam and Jeroboam all their days. [16]So Rehoboam rested with his fathers, and was buried in the City of David. Then Abijah[a] his son reigned in his place.

ABIJAH REIGNS IN JUDAH

13 In the eighteenth year of King Jeroboam, Abijah became king over Judah. [2]He reigned three years in Jerusalem. His mother's name *was* Michaiah[a] the daughter of Uriel of Gibeah.

And there was war between Abijah and Jeroboam. [3]Abijah set the battle in order with an army of valiant warriors, four hundred thousand choice men. Jeroboam also drew up in battle formation against him with eight hundred thousand choice men, mighty men of valor.

[4]Then Abijah stood on Mount Zemaraim, which *is* in the mountains of Ephraim, and said, "Hear me, Jeroboam and all Israel: [5]Should you not know that the LORD God of Israel gave the dominion over Israel to David forever, to him and his sons, by a covenant of salt? [6]Yet Jeroboam the son of Nebat, the servant of Solomon the son of David, rose up and rebelled against his lord. [7]Then worthless rogues gathered to him, and strengthened themselves against Rehoboam the son of Solomon, when Rehoboam was young and inexperienced and could not withstand them. [8]And now you think to withstand the kingdom of the LORD, which is in the hand of the sons of David; and you *are* a great multitude, and with you are the gold calves which Jeroboam made for you as gods. [9]Have you not cast out the priests of the LORD, the sons of Aaron, and the Levites, and made for yourselves priests, like the peoples of *other* lands, so that whoever comes to consecrate himself with a young bull and seven rams may be a priest of *things that are* not gods? [10]But as for us, the LORD *is* our God, and we have not forsaken Him; and the priests who minister to the LORD *are* the sons of Aaron, and the Levites *attend* to *their* duties. [11]And they burn to the LORD every morning and every evening burnt sacrifices and sweet incense; *they* also *set* the showbread *in order* on the pure *gold* table, and the lampstand of gold with its lamps to burn every evening; for we keep the command of the LORD our God, but you have forsaken Him. [12]Now look, God Himself is with us as *our* head, and His priests with sounding trumpets to sound the alarm against you. O children of Israel, do not fight against the LORD God of your fathers, for you shall not prosper!"

[13]But Jeroboam caused an ambush to go around behind them; so they were in front of Judah, and the ambush *was* behind them. [14]And when Judah looked around, to their surprise the battle line *was* at both front and rear; and they cried out to the LORD, and the priests sounded the trumpets. [15]Then the men of Judah gave a shout; and as the men of Judah shouted, it happened that God struck Jeroboam and all Israel before Abijah and Judah. [16]And the children of Israel fled before Judah, and God delivered them into their hand. [17]Then Abijah and his people struck them with a great slaughter; so five hundred thousand choice men of Israel fell slain. [18]Thus the children of Israel were subdued at that time; and the children of Judah prevailed, because they relied on the LORD God of their fathers.

[19]And Abijah pursued Jeroboam and took cities from him: Bethel with its villages, Jeshanah with its villages, and Ephrain[a] with its villages. [20]So Jeroboam did not recover strength again in the days of Abijah; and the LORD struck him, and he died.

[21]But Abijah grew mighty, married fourteen

12:16 [a]Spelled *Abijam* in 1 Kings 14:31　**13:2** [a]Spelled *Maachah* in 11:20, 21 and 1 Kings 15:2　**13:19** [a]Or *Ephron* wives, and begot twenty-two sons and sixteen daughters. ²²Now the rest of the acts of Abijah, his ways, and his sayings *are* written in the annals of the prophet Iddo.

14 So Abijah rested with his fathers, and they buried him in the City of David. Then Asa his son reigned in his place. In his days the land was quiet for ten years.

ASA REIGNS IN JUDAH

²Asa did *what was* good and right in the eyes of the LORD his God, ³for he removed the altars of the foreign *gods* and the high places, and broke down the *sacred* pillars and cut down the wooden images. ⁴He commanded Judah to seek the LORD God of their fathers, and to observe the law and the commandment. ⁵He also removed the high places and the incense altars from all the cities of Judah, and the kingdom was quiet under him. ⁶And he built fortified cities in Judah, for the land had rest; he had no war in those years, because the LORD had given him rest. ⁷Therefore he said to Judah, "Let us build these cities and make walls around *them,* and towers, gates, and bars, *while* the land *is* yet before us, because we have sought the LORD our God; we have sought *Him,* and He has given us rest on every side." So they built and prospered. ⁸And Asa had an army of three hundred thousand from Judah who carried shields and spears, and from Benjamin two hundred and eighty thousand men who carried shields and drew bows; all these *were* mighty men of valor.

⁹Then Zerah the Ethiopian came out against them with an army of a million men and three hundred chariots, and he came to Mareshah. ¹⁰So Asa went out against him, and they set the troops in battle array in the Valley of Zephathah at Mareshah. ¹¹And Asa cried out to the LORD his God, and said, "LORD, *it is* nothing for You to help, whether with many or with those who have no power; help us, O LORD our God, for we rest on You, and in Your name we go against this multitude. O LORD, You *are* our God; do not let man prevail against You!"

¹²So the LORD struck the Ethiopians before Asa and Judah, and the Ethiopians fled. ¹³And Asa and the people who *were* with him pursued them to Gerar. So the Ethiopians were overthrown, and they could not recover, for they were broken be-

fore the LORD and His army. And they carried away very much spoil. ¹⁴Then they defeated all the cities around Gerar, for the fear of the LORD came upon them; and they plundered all the cities, for there was exceedingly much spoil in them. ¹⁵They also attacked the livestock enclosures, and carried off sheep and camels in abundance, and returned to Jerusalem.

THE REFORMS OF ASA

15 Now the Spirit of God came upon Azariah the son of Oded. ²And he went out to meet Asa, and said to him: "Hear me, Asa, and all Judah and Benjamin. The LORD *is* with you while you are with Him. If you seek Him, He will be found by you; but if you forsake Him, He will forsake you. ³For a long time Israel *has been* without the true God, without a teaching priest, and without law; ⁴but when in their trouble they turned to the LORD God of Israel, and sought Him, He was found by them. ⁵And in those times *there was* no peace to the one who went out, nor to the one who came in, but great turmoil *was* on all the inhabitants of the lands. ⁶So nation was destroyed by nation, and city by city, for God troubled them with every adversity. ⁷But you, be strong and do not let your hands be weak, for your work shall be rewarded!"

⁸And when Asa heard these words and the prophecy of Oded[a] the prophet, he took courage, and removed the abominable idols from all the land of Judah and Benjamin and from the cities which he had taken in the mountains of Ephraim; and he restored the altar of the LORD that *was* before the vestibule of the LORD. ⁹Then he gathered all Judah and Benjamin, and those who dwelt with them from Ephraim, Manasseh, and Simeon, for they came over to him in great numbers from Israel when they saw that the LORD his God was with him.

¹⁰So they gathered together at Jerusalem in the third month, in the fifteenth year of the reign of Asa. ¹¹And they offered to the LORD at that time seven hundred bulls and seven thousand sheep from the spoil they had brought. ¹²Then they entered into a covenant to seek the LORD God of their fathers with all their heart and with

---

15:8 [a]Following Masoretic Text and Septuagint; Syriac and Vulgate read *Azariah the son of Oded* (compare verse 1).

all their soul; [13]and whoever would not seek the LORD God of Israel was to be put to death, whether small or great, whether man or woman. [14]Then they took an oath before the LORD with a loud voice, with shouting and trumpets and rams' horns. [15]And all Judah rejoiced at the oath, for they had sworn with all their heart and sought Him with all their soul; and He was found by them, and the LORD gave them rest all around.

[16]Also he removed Maachah, the mother of Asa the king, from *being* queen mother, because she had made an obscene image of Asherah;[a] and Asa cut down her obscene image, then crushed and burned *it* by the Brook Kidron. [17]But the high places were not removed from Israel. Nevertheless the heart of Asa was loyal all his days.

[18]He also brought into the house of God the things that his father had dedicated and that he himself had dedicated: silver and gold and utensils. [19]And there was no war until the thirty-fifth year of the reign of Asa.

Asa's Treaty with Syria

16 In the thirty-sixth year of the reign of Asa, Baasha king of Israel came up against Judah and built Ramah, that he might let none go out or come in to Asa king of Judah. [2]Then Asa brought silver and gold from the treasuries of the house of the LORD and of the king's house, and sent to Ben-Hadad king of Syria, who dwelt in Damascus, saying, [3]*"Let there be* a treaty between you and me, as there was between my father and your father. See, I have sent you silver and gold; come, break your treaty with Baasha king of Israel, so that he will withdraw from me."

[4]So Ben-Hadad heeded King Asa, and sent the captains of his armies against the cities of Israel. They attacked Ijon, Dan, Abel Maim, and all the storage cities of Naphtali. [5]Now it happened, when Baasha heard *it,* that he stopped building Ramah and ceased his work. [6]Then King Asa took all Judah, and they carried away the stones and timber of Ramah, which Baasha had used for building; and with them he built Geba and Mizpah.

Hanani's Message to Asa

[7]And at that time Hanani the seer came to Asa king of Judah, and said to him: "Because you have relied on the king of Syria, and have not relied on the LORD your God, therefore the army of the king of Syria has escaped from your hand. [8]Were the Ethiopians and the Lubim not a huge army with very many chariots and horsemen? Yet, because you relied on the LORD, He delivered them into your hand. [9]For the eyes of the LORD run to and fro throughout the whole earth, to show Himself strong on behalf of *those* whose heart *is* loyal to Him. In this you have done foolishly; therefore from now on you shall have wars." [10]Then Asa was angry with the seer, and put him in prison, for *he was* enraged at him because of this. And Asa oppressed *some* of the people at that time.

Illness and Death of Asa

[11]Note that the acts of Asa, first and last, are indeed written in the book of the kings of Judah and Israel. [12]And in the thirty-ninth year of his reign, Asa became diseased in his feet, and his malady was severe; yet in his disease he did not seek the LORD, but the physicians.

[13]So Asa rested with his fathers; he died in the forty-first year of his reign. [14]They buried him in his own tomb, which he had made for himself in the City of David; and they laid him in the bed which was filled with spices and various ingredients prepared in a mixture of ointments. They made a very great burning for him.

Jehoshaphat Reigns in Judah

17 Then Jehoshaphat his son reigned in his place, and strengthened himself against Israel. [2]And he placed troops in all the fortified cities of Judah, and set garrisons in the land of Judah and in the cities of Ephraim which Asa his father had taken. [3]Now the LORD was with Jehoshaphat, because he walked in the former ways of his father David; he did not seek the Baals, [4]but sought the God[a] of his father, and walked in His commandments and not according to the acts of Israel. [5]Therefore the LORD established the kingdom in his hand; and all Judah gave presents to Jehoshaphat, and he had riches and honor in abundance. [6]And his heart took delight in the ways of the LORD; moreover he removed the high places and wooden images from Judah.

15:16 [a]A Canaanite deity   **17:4** [a]Septuagint reads *LORD God.*

⁷Also in the third year of his reign he sent his leaders, Ben-Hail, Obadiah, Zechariah, Nethanel, and Michaiah, to teach in the cities of Judah. ⁸And with them *he sent* Levites: Shemaiah, Nethaniah, Zebadiah, Asahel, Shemiramoth, Jehonathan, Adonijah, Tobijah, and Tobadonijah—the Levites; and with them Elishama and Jehoram, the priests. ⁹So they taught in Judah, and *had* the Book of the Law of the LORD with them; they went throughout all the cities of Judah and taught the people.

¹⁰And the fear of the LORD fell on all the kingdoms of the lands that *were* around Judah, so that they did not make war against Jehoshaphat. ¹¹Also *some* of the Philistines brought Jehoshaphat presents and silver as tribute; and the Arabians brought him flocks, seven thousand seven hundred rams and seven thousand seven hundred male goats.

¹²So Jehoshaphat became increasingly powerful, and he built fortresses and storage cities in Judah. ¹³He had much property in the cities of Judah; and the men of war, mighty men of valor, *were* in Jerusalem.

¹⁴These *are* their numbers, according to their fathers' houses. Of Judah, the captains of thousands: Adnah the captain, and with him three hundred thousand mighty men of valor; ¹⁵and next to him *was* Jehohanan the captain, and with him two hundred and eighty thousand; ¹⁶and next to him *was* Amasiah the son of Zichri, who willingly offered himself to the LORD, and with him two hundred thousand mighty men of valor. ¹⁷Of Benjamin: Eliada a mighty man of valor, and with him two hundred thousand men armed with bow and shield; ¹⁸and next to him *was* Jehozabad, and with him one hundred and eighty thousand prepared for war. ¹⁹These served the king, besides those the king put in the fortified cities throughout all Judah.

Micaiah Warns Ahab

18 Jehoshaphat had riches and honor in abundance; and by marriage he allied himself with Ahab. ²After some years he went down to *visit* Ahab in Samaria; and Ahab killed sheep and oxen in abundance for him and the people who were with him, and persuaded him to go up *with him* to Ramoth Gilead. ³So Ahab king of Israel said to Jehoshaphat king of Judah, "Will you go with me *against* Ramoth Gilead?"

And he answered him, "I *am* as you *are,* and my people as your people; *we will be* with you in the war."

⁴Also Jehoshaphat said to the king of Israel, "Please inquire for the word of the LORD today."

⁵Then the king of Israel gathered the prophets together, four hundred men, and said to them, "Shall we go to war against Ramoth Gilead, or shall I refrain?"

So they said, "Go up, for God will deliver it into the king's hand."

⁶But Jehoshaphat said, "*Is there* not still a prophet of the LORD here, that we may inquire of Him?"[a]

⁷So the king of Israel said to Jehoshaphat, "*There is* still one man by whom we may inquire of the LORD; but I hate him, because he never prophesies good concerning me, but always evil. He *is* Micaiah the son of Imla."

And Jehoshaphat said, "Let not the king say such things!"

⁸Then the king of Israel called one *of his* officers and said, "Bring Micaiah the son of Imla quickly!"

⁹The king of Israel and Jehoshaphat king of Judah, clothed in *their* robes, sat each on his throne; and they sat at a threshing floor at the entrance of the gate of Samaria; and all the prophets prophesied before them. ¹⁰Now Zedekiah the son of Chenaanah had made horns of iron for himself; and he said, "Thus says the LORD: 'With these you shall gore the Syrians until they are destroyed.' "

¹¹And all the prophets prophesied so, saying, "Go up to Ramoth Gilead and prosper, for the LORD will deliver *it* into the king's hand."

¹²Then the messenger who had gone to call Micaiah spoke to him, saying, "Now listen, the words of the prophets with one accord encourage the king. Therefore please let your word be like *the word of* one of them, and speak encouragement."

¹³And Micaiah said, "*As* the LORD lives, whatever my God says, that I will speak."

¹⁴Then he came to the king; and the king said to him, "Micaiah, shall we go to war against Ramoth Gilead, or shall I refrain?"

And he said, "Go and prosper, and they shall be delivered into your hand!"

18:6 [a]Or *him*

¹⁵So the king said to him, "How many times shall I make you swear that you tell me nothing but the truth in the name of the LORD?"

¹⁶Then he said, "I saw all Israel scattered on the mountains, as sheep that have no shepherd. And the LORD said, 'These have no master. Let each return to his house in peace.'"

¹⁷And the king of Israel said to Jehoshaphat, "Did I not tell you he would not prophesy good concerning me, but evil?"

¹⁸Then *Micaiah* said, "Therefore hear the word of the LORD: I saw the LORD sitting on His throne, and all the host of heaven standing on His right hand and His left. ¹⁹And the LORD said, 'Who will persuade Ahab king of Israel to go up, that he may fall at Ramoth Gilead?' So one spoke in this manner, and another spoke in that manner. ²⁰Then a spirit came forward and stood before the LORD, and said, 'I will persuade him.' The LORD said to him, 'In what way?' ²¹So he said, 'I will go out and be a lying spirit in the mouth of all his prophets.' And *the* LORD said, 'You shall persuade *him* and also prevail; go out and do so.' ²²Therefore look! The LORD has put a lying spirit in the mouth of these prophets of yours, and the LORD has declared disaster against you."

²³Then Zedekiah the son of Chenaanah went near and struck Micaiah on the cheek, and said, "Which way did the spirit from the LORD go from me to speak to you?"

²⁴And Micaiah said, "Indeed you shall see on that day when you go into an inner chamber to hide!"

²⁵Then the king of Israel said, "Take Micaiah, and return him to Amon the governor of the city and to Joash the king's son; ²⁶and say, 'Thus says the king: "Put this *fellow* in prison, and feed him with bread of affliction and water of affliction, until I return in peace."'"

²⁷But Micaiah said, "If you ever return in peace, the LORD has not spoken by me." And he said, "Take heed, all you people!"

Ahab Dies in Battle

²⁸So the king of Israel and Jehoshaphat the king of Judah went up to Ramoth Gilead. ²⁹And the king of Israel said to Jehoshaphat, "I will disguise myself and go into battle; but you put on your robes." So the king of Israel disguised himself, and they went into battle.

³⁰Now the king of Syria had commanded the captains of the chariots who *were* with him, saying, "Fight with no one small or great, but only with the king of Israel."

³¹So it was, when the captains of the chariots saw Jehoshaphat, that they said, "It *is* the king of Israel!" Therefore they surrounded him to attack; but Jehoshaphat cried out, and the LORD helped him, and God diverted them from him. ³²For so it was, when the captains of the chariots saw that it was not the king of Israel, that they turned back from pursuing him. ³³Now a certain man drew a bow at random, and struck the king of Israel between the joints of his armor. So he said to the driver of his chariot, "Turn around and take me out of the battle, for I am wounded." ³⁴The battle increased that day, and the king of Israel propped *himself* up in *his* chariot facing the Syrians until evening; and about the time of sunset he died.

19 Then Jehoshaphat the king of Judah returned safely to his house in Jerusalem. ²And Jehu the son of Hanani the seer went out to meet him, and said to King Jehoshaphat, "Should you help the wicked and love those who hate the LORD? Therefore the wrath of the LORD *is* upon you. ³Nevertheless good things are found in you, in that you have removed the wooden images from the land, and have prepared your heart to seek God."

The Reforms of Jehoshaphat

⁴So Jehoshaphat dwelt at Jerusalem; and he went out again among the people from Beersheba to the mountains of Ephraim, and brought them back to the LORD God of their fathers. ⁵Then he set judges in the land throughout all the fortified cities of Judah, city by city, ⁶and said to the judges, "Take heed to what you are doing, for you do not judge for man but for the LORD, who *is* with you in the judgment. ⁷Now therefore, let the fear of the LORD be upon you; take care and do *it,* for *there is* no iniquity with the LORD our God, no partiality, nor taking of bribes."

⁸Moreover in Jerusalem, for the judgment of the LORD and for controversies, Jehoshaphat appointed some of the Levites and priests, and some of the chief fathers of Israel, when they returned

to Jerusalem.ᵃ ⁹And he commanded them, saying, "Thus you shall act in the fear of the LORD, faithfully and with a loyal heart: ¹⁰Whatever case comes to you from your brethren who dwell in their cities, whether of bloodshed or offenses against law or commandment, against statutes or ordinances, you shall warn them, lest they trespass against the LORD and wrath come upon you and your brethren. Do this, and you will not be guilty. ¹¹And take notice: Amariah the chief priest *is* over you in all matters of the LORD; and Zebadiah the son of Ishmael, the ruler of the house of Judah, for all the king's matters; also the Levites *will be* officials before you. Behave courageously, and the LORD will be with the good."

AMMON, MOAB, AND MOUNT SEIR DEFEATED

20 It happened after this *that* the people of Moab with the people of Ammon, and *others* with them besides the Ammonites,ᵃ came to battle against Jehoshaphat. ²Then some came and told Jehoshaphat, saying, "A great multitude is coming against you from beyond the sea, from Syria;ᵃ and they are in Hazazon Tamar" (which *is* En Gedi). ³And Jehoshaphat feared, and set himself to seek the LORD, and proclaimed a fast throughout all Judah. ⁴So Judah gathered together to ask *help* from the LORD; and from all the cities of Judah they came to seek the LORD.

⁵Then Jehoshaphat stood in the assembly of Judah and Jerusalem, in the house of the LORD, before the new court, ⁶and said: "O LORD God of our fathers, *are* You not God in heaven, and do You *not* rule over all the kingdoms of the nations, and in Your hand *is there not* power and might, so that no one is able to withstand You? ⁷*Are* You not our God, *who* drove out the inhabitants of this land before Your people Israel, and gave it to the descendants of Abraham Your friend forever? ⁸And they dwell in it, and have built You a sanctuary in it for Your name, saying, ⁹'If disaster comes upon us—sword, judgment, pestilence, or famine—we will stand before this temple and in Your presence (for Your name *is* in this temple), and cry out to You in our affliction, and You will hear and save.' ¹⁰And now, here are the people of Ammon, Moab, and Mount Seir—whom You would not let Israel invade when they came out of the land of Egypt, but they turned from them

and did not destroy them— ¹¹here they are, rewarding us by coming to throw us out of Your possession which You have given us to inherit. ¹²O our God, will You not judge them? For we have no power against this great multitude that is coming against us; nor do we know what to do, but our eyes *are* upon You."

¹³Now all Judah, with their little ones, their wives, and their children, stood before the LORD.

¹⁴Then the Spirit of the LORD came upon Jahaziel the son of Zechariah, the son of Benaiah, the son of Jeiel, the son of Mattaniah, a Levite of the sons of Asaph, in the midst of the assembly. ¹⁵And he said, "Listen, all you of Judah and you inhabitants of Jerusalem, and you, King Jehoshaphat! Thus says the LORD to you: 'Do not be afraid nor dismayed because of this great multitude, for the battle *is* not yours, but God's. ¹⁶Tomorrow go down against them. They will surely come up by the Ascent of Ziz, and you will find them at the end of the brook before the Wilderness of Jeruel. ¹⁷You will not *need* to fight in this *battle.* Position yourselves, stand still and see the salvation of the LORD, who is with you, O Judah and Jerusalem!' Do not fear or be dismayed; tomorrow go out against them, for the LORD *is* with you."

¹⁸And Jehoshaphat bowed his head with *his* face to the ground, and all Judah and the inhabitants of Jerusalem bowed before the LORD, worshiping the LORD. ¹⁹Then the Levites of the children of the Kohathites and of the children of the Korahites stood up to praise the LORD God of Israel with voices loud and high.

²⁰So they rose early in the morning and went out into the Wilderness of Tekoa; and as they went out, Jehoshaphat stood and said, "Hear me, O Judah and you inhabitants of Jerusalem: Believe in the LORD your God, and you shall be established; believe His prophets, and you shall prosper." ²¹And when he had consulted with the people, he appointed those who should sing to the LORD, and who should praise the beauty of holiness, as they went out before the army and were saying:

19:8 ᵃSeptuagint and Vulgate read *for the inhabitants of Jerusalem* **20:1** ᵃFollowing Masoretic Text and Vulgate; Septuagint reads *Meunites* (compare 26:7). **20:2** ᵃFollowing Masoretic Text, Septuagint and Vulgate; some Hebrew manuscripts and Old Latin read *Edom.*

LEADERSHIP ISSUES

GC2: Our Eyes Are Upon You

2 CHRONICLES 20:12

Has there ever been a time when you, like King Jehoshaphat, were surrounded by obstacles and humbled yourself in utter dependence? Can you remember an occasion when, not knowing what to do or where to go, you turned your eyes toward Him? Maybe it was a time when you:

- needed provision,
- suffered a tragic loss,
- faced great uncertainty about the future,
- needed clear direction,
- felt helpless.

Perhaps you are even going through a time like this right now. Allow such times to humble you, and then look up! Put your eyes upon Him! *David Ferguson*

Complete whichever of the two following sentences is most appropriate for you at this time:

I remember when _____,
and I was completely dependent upon God. (For example: I remember when I first moved here and had no friends, and I was completely dependent on God.)

Right now, I need to depend completely on God concerning _____
_____.

(For example: Right now, I need to depend completely on God concerning my youngest sister. She is very sick, but the doctors cannot seem to determine what the illness is.)

GC2
GREAT COMMANDMENT
COMMISSION

"Praise the LORD,
For His mercy *endures* forever."[a]

²²Now when they began to sing and to praise, the LORD set ambushes against the people of Ammon, Moab, and Mount Seir, who had come against Judah; and they were defeated. ²³For the people of Ammon and Moab stood up against the inhabitants of Mount Seir to utterly kill and destroy *them*. And when they had made an end of the inhabitants of Seir, they helped to destroy one another.

²⁴So when Judah came to a place overlooking the wilderness, they looked toward the multitude; and there *were* their dead bodies, fallen on the earth. No one had escaped.

²⁵When Jehoshaphat and his people came to take away their spoil, they found among them an abundance of valuables on the dead bodies,[a] and precious jewelry, which they stripped off for themselves, more than they could carry away; and they were three days gathering the spoil because there was so much. ²⁶And on the fourth day they assembled in the Valley of Berachah, for there they blessed the LORD; therefore the name of that place was called The Valley of Berachah[a] until this day. ²⁷Then they returned, every man of Judah and Jerusalem, with Jehoshaphat in front of them, to go back to Jerusalem with joy, for the LORD had made them rejoice over their enemies. ²⁸So they came to Jerusalem, with stringed instruments and harps and trumpets, to the house of the LORD. ²⁹And the fear of God was on all the kingdoms of *those* countries when they heard that the LORD had fought against the enemies of Israel. ³⁰Then the realm of Jehoshaphat was quiet, for his God gave him rest all around.

THE END OF JEHOSHAPHAT'S REIGN

³¹So Jehoshaphat was king over Judah. *He was* thirty-five years old when he became king, and he reigned twenty-five years in Jerusalem. His mother's name *was* Azubah the daughter of Shilhi. ³²And he walked in the way of his father Asa, and did not turn aside from it, doing *what was* right in the sight of the LORD. ³³Nevertheless the high places were not taken away, for as yet the people had not directed their hearts to the God of their fathers.

³⁴Now the rest of the acts of Jehoshaphat, first and last, indeed they *are* written in the book of Jehu the son of Hanani, which *is* mentioned in the book of the kings of Israel.

³⁵After this Jehoshaphat king of Judah allied himself with Ahaziah king of Israel, who acted very wickedly. ³⁶And he allied himself with him to make ships to go to Tarshish, and they made the ships in Ezion Geber. ³⁷But Eliezer the son of Dodavah of Mareshah prophesied against Jehoshaphat, saying, "Because you have allied yourself with Ahaziah, the LORD has destroyed your works." Then the ships were wrecked, so that they were not able to go to Tarshish.

JEHORAM REIGNS IN JUDAH

21 And Jehoshaphat rested with his fathers, and was buried with his fathers in the City of David. Then Jehoram his son reigned in his place. ²He had brothers, the sons of Jehoshaphat: Azariah, Jehiel, Zechariah, Azaryahu, Michael, and Shephatiah; all these *were* the sons of Jehoshaphat king of Israel. ³Their father gave them great gifts of silver and gold and precious things, with fortified cities in Judah; but he gave the kingdom to Jehoram, because he *was* the firstborn.

⁴Now when Jehoram was established over the kingdom of his father, he strengthened himself and killed all his brothers with the sword, and also *others* of the princes of Israel.

⁵Jehoram *was* thirty-two years old when he became king, and he reigned eight years in Jerusalem. ⁶And he walked in the way of the kings of Israel, just as the house of Ahab had done, for he had the daughter of Ahab as a wife; and he did evil in the sight of the LORD. ⁷Yet the LORD would not destroy the house of David, because of the covenant that He had made with David, and since He had promised to give a lamp to him and to his sons forever.

⁸In his days Edom revolted against Judah's authority, and made a king over themselves. ⁹So Jehoram went out with his officers, and all his chariots with him. And he rose by night and attacked the Edomites who had surrounded him and the

20:21 ªCompare Psalm 106:1　20:25 ªA few Hebrew manuscripts, Old Latin, and Vulgate read *garments;* Septuagint reads *armor.* 20:26 ªLiterally *Blessing* captains of the chariots. [10]Thus Edom has been in revolt against Judah's authority to this day. At that time Libnah revolted against his rule, because he had forsaken the LORD God of his fathers. [11]Moreover he made high places in the mountains of Judah, and caused the inhabitants of Jerusalem to commit harlotry, and led Judah astray.

[12]And a letter came to him from Elijah the prophet, saying,

Thus says the LORD God of your father David:
Because you have not walked in the ways of Jehoshaphat your father, or in the ways of Asa king of Judah, [13]but have walked in the way of the kings of Israel, and have made Judah and the inhabitants of Jerusalem to play the harlot like the harlotry of the house of Ahab, and also have killed your brothers, those of your father's household, *who were* better than yourself, [14]behold, the LORD will strike your people with a serious affliction—your children, your wives, and all your possessions; [15]and you *will become* very sick with a disease of your intestines, until your intestines come out by reason of the sickness, day by day.

[16]Moreover the LORD stirred up against Jehoram the spirit of the Philistines and the Arabians who *were* near the Ethiopians. [17]And they came up into Judah and invaded it, and carried away all the possessions that were found in the king's house, and also his sons and his wives, so that there was not a son left to him except Jehoahaz,[a] the youngest of his sons.

[18]After all this the LORD struck him in his intestines with an incurable disease. [19]Then it happened in the course of time, after the end of two years, that his intestines came out because of his sickness; so he died in severe pain. And his people made no burning for him, like the burning for his fathers.

[20]He was thirty-two years old when he became king. He reigned in Jerusalem eight years and, to no one's sorrow, departed. However they buried him in the City of David, but not in the tombs of the kings.

AHAZIAH REIGNS IN JUDAH

22Then the inhabitants of Jerusalem made Ahaziah his youngest son king in his place, for the raiders who came with the Arabians into the camp had killed all the older *sons.* So Ahaziah the son of Jehoram, king of Judah, reigned. [2]Ahaziah *was* forty-two[a] years old when he became king, and he reigned one year in Jerusalem. His mother's name *was* Athaliah the granddaughter of Omri. [3]He also walked in the ways of the house of Ahab, for his mother advised him to do wickedly. [4]Therefore he did evil in the sight of the LORD, like the house of Ahab; for they were his counselors after the death of his father, to his destruction. [5]He also followed their advice, and went with Jehoram[a] the son of Ahab king of Israel to war against Hazael king of Syria at Ramoth Gilead; and the Syrians wounded Joram. [6]Then he returned to Jezreel to recover from the wounds which he had received at Ramah, when he fought against Hazael king of Syria. And Azariah[a] the son of Jehoram, king of Judah, went down to see Jehoram the son of Ahab in Jezreel, because he was sick.

[7]His going to Joram was God's occasion for Ahaziah's downfall; for when he arrived, he went out with Jehoram against Jehu the son of Nimshi, whom the LORD had anointed to cut off the house of Ahab. [8]And it happened, when Jehu was executing judgment on the house of Ahab, and found the princes of Judah and the sons of Ahaziah's brothers who served Ahaziah, that he killed them. [9]Then he searched for Ahaziah; and they caught him (he was hiding in Samaria), and brought him to Jehu. When they had killed him, they buried him, "because," they said, "he is the son of Jehoshaphat, who sought the LORD with all his heart."

So the house of Ahaziah had no one to assume power over the kingdom.

ATHALIAH REIGNS IN JUDAH

[10]Now when Athaliah the mother of Ahaziah saw that her son was dead, she arose and destroyed

21:17 [a]Elsewhere called *Ahaziah* (compare 2 Chronicles 22:1) **22:2** [a]Or *twenty-two* (compare 2 Kings 8:26) **22:5** [a]Also spelled *Joram* (compare verses 5 and 7; 2 Kings 8:28; and elsewhere) **22:6** [a]Some Hebrew manuscripts, Septuagint, Syriac, Vulgate, and 2 Kings 8:29 read *Ahaziah.*

all the royal heirs of the house of Judah. ¹¹But Jehoshabeath,ª the daughter of the king, took Joash the son of Ahaziah, and stole him away from among the king's sons who were being murdered, and put him and his nurse in a bedroom. So Jehoshabeath, the daughter of King Jehoram, the wife of Jehoiada the priest (for she was the sister of Ahaziah), hid him from Athaliah so that she did not kill him. ¹²And he was hidden with them in the house of God for six years, while Athaliah reigned over the land.

JOASH CROWNED KING OF JUDAH

23 In the seventh year Jehoiada strengthened himself, *and made a* covenant with the captains of hundreds: Azariah the son of Jeroham, Ishmael the son of Jehohanan, Azariah the son of Obed, Maaseiah the son of Adaiah, and Elishaphat the son of Zichri. ²And they went throughout Judah and gathered the Levites from all the cities of Judah, and the chief fathers of Israel, and they came to Jerusalem.

³Then all the assembly made a covenant with the king in the house of God. And he said to them, "Behold, the king's son shall reign, as the LORD has said of the sons of David. ⁴This *is* what you shall do: One-third of you entering on the Sabbath, of the priests and the Levites, *shall be* keeping watch over the doors; ⁵one-third *shall be* at the king's house; and one-third at the Gate of the Foundation. All the people *shall be* in the courts of the house of the LORD. ⁶But let no one come into the house of the LORD except the priests and those of the Levites who serve. They may go in, for they *are* holy; but all the people shall keep the watch of the LORD. ⁷And the Levites shall surround the king on all sides, every man with his weapons in his hand; and whoever comes into the house, let him be put to death. You are to be with the king when he comes in and when he goes out."

⁸So the Levites and all Judah did according to all that Jehoiada the priest commanded. And each man took his men who were to be on duty on the Sabbath, with those who were going *off duty* on the Sabbath; for Jehoiada the priest had not dismissed the divisions. ⁹And Jehoiada the priest gave to the captains of hundreds the spears and the large and small shields which *had belonged* to King David, that *were* in the temple of God. ¹⁰Then he set all the people, every man with his weapon in his hand, from the right side of the temple to the left side of the temple, along by the altar and by the temple, all around the king. ¹¹And they brought out the king's son, put the crown on him, *gave him* the Testimony,ª and made him king. Then Jehoiada and his sons anointed him, and said, "*Long* live the king!"

DEATH OF ATHALIAH

¹²Now when Athaliah heard the noise of the people running and praising the king, she came to the people *in* the temple of the LORD. ¹³*When* she looked, there was the king standing by his pillar at the entrance; and the leaders and the trumpeters *were* by the king. All the people of the land were rejoicing and blowing trumpets, also the singers with musical instruments, and those who led in praise. So Athaliah tore her clothes and said, "Treason! Treason!"

¹⁴And Jehoiada the priest brought out the captains of hundreds who were set over the army, and said to them, "Take her outside under guard, and slay with the sword whoever follows her." For the priest had said, "Do not kill her in the house of the LORD."

¹⁵So they seized her; and she went by way of the entrance of the Horse Gate *into* the king's house, and they killed her there.

¹⁶Then Jehoiada made a covenant between himself, the people, and the king, that they should be the LORD's people. ¹⁷And all the people went to the templeª of Baal, and tore it down. They broke in pieces its altars and images, and killed Mattan the priest of Baal before the altars. ¹⁸Also Jehoiada appointed the oversight of the house of the LORD to the hand of the priests, the Levites, whom David had assigned in the house of the LORD, to offer the burnt offerings of the LORD, as *it is* written in the Law of Moses, with rejoicing and with singing, *as it was established* by David. ¹⁹And he set the gatekeepers at the gates of the house of the LORD, so that no one *who was* in any way unclean should enter.

²⁰Then he took the captains of hundreds, the nobles, the governors of the people, and all the

22:11 ªSpelled *Jehosheba* in 2 Kings 11:2   **23:11** ªThat is, the Law (compare Exodus 25:16, 21; 31:18)   **23:17** ªLiterally *house*

people of the land, and brought the king down from the house of the LORD; and they went through the Upper Gate to the king's house, and set the king on the throne of the kingdom. ²¹So all the people of the land rejoiced; and the city was quiet, for they had slain Athaliah with the sword.

Joash Repairs the Temple

24 Joash *was* seven years old when he became king, and he reigned forty years in Jerusalem. His mother's name *was* Zibiah of Beersheba. ²Joash did *what was* right in the sight of the LORD all the days of Jehoiada the priest. ³And Jehoiada took two wives for him, and he had sons and daughters.

⁴Now it happened after this *that* Joash set his heart on repairing the house of the LORD. ⁵Then he gathered the priests and the Levites, and said to them, "Go out to the cities of Judah, and gather from all Israel money to repair the house of your God from year to year, and see that you do it quickly."

However the Levites did not do it quickly. ⁶So the king called Jehoiada the chief *priest,* and said to him, "Why have you not required the Levites to bring in from Judah and from Jerusalem the collection, *according to the commandment* of Moses the servant of the LORD and of the assembly of Israel, for the tabernacle of witness?" For the sons of Athaliah, that wicked woman, had broken into the house of God, and had also presented all the dedicated things of the house of the LORD to the Baals.

⁸Then at the king's command they made a chest, and set it outside at the gate of the house of the LORD. ⁹And they made a proclamation throughout Judah and Jerusalem to bring to the LORD the collection *that* Moses the servant of God *had imposed* on Israel in the wilderness. ¹⁰Then all the leaders and all the people rejoiced, brought their contributions, and put *them* into the chest until all had given. ¹¹So it was, at that time, when the chest was brought to the king's official by the hand of the Levites, and when they saw that *there was* much money, that the king's scribe and the high priest's officer came and emptied the chest, and took it and returned it to its place. Thus they did day by day, and gathered money in abundance.

¹²The king and Jehoiada gave it to those who did the work of the service of the house of the LORD; and they hired masons and carpenters to repair the house of the LORD, and also those who worked in iron and bronze to restore the house of the LORD. ¹³So the workmen labored, and the work was completed by them; they restored the house of God to its original condition and reinforced it. ¹⁴When they had finished, they brought the rest of the money before the king and Jehoiada; they made from it articles for the house of the LORD, articles for serving and offering, spoons and vessels of gold and silver. And they offered burnt offerings in the house of the LORD continually all the days of Jehoiada.

Apostasy of Joash

¹⁵But Jehoiada grew old and was full of days, and he died; *he was* one hundred and thirty years old when he died. ¹⁶And they buried him in the City of David among the kings, because he had done good in Israel, both toward God and His house.

¹⁷Now after the death of Jehoiada the leaders of Judah came and bowed down to the king. And the king listened to them. ¹⁸Therefore they left the house of the LORD God of their fathers, and served wooden images and idols; and wrath came upon Judah and Jerusalem because of their trespass. ¹⁹Yet He sent prophets to them, to bring them back to the LORD; and they testified against them, but they would not listen.

²⁰Then the Spirit of God came upon Zechariah the son of Jehoiada the priest, who stood above the people, and said to them, "Thus says God: 'Why do you transgress the commandments of the LORD, so that you cannot prosper? Because you have forsaken the LORD, He also has forsaken you.' " ²¹So they conspired against him, and at the command of the king they stoned him with stones in the court of the house of the LORD. ²²Thus Joash the king did not remember the kindness which Jehoiada his father had done to him, but killed his son; and as he died, he said, "The LORD look on *it,* and repay!"

Death of Joash

²³So it happened in the spring of the year *that* the army of Syria came up against him; and they

came to Judah and Jerusalem, and destroyed all the leaders of the people from among the people, and sent all their spoil to the king of Damascus. [24]For the army of the Syrians came with a small company of men; but the LORD delivered a very great army into their hand, because they had forsaken the LORD God of their fathers. So they executed judgment against Joash. [25]And when they had withdrawn from him (for they left him severely wounded), his own servants conspired against him because of the blood of the sons[a] of Jehoiada the priest, and killed him on his bed. So he died. And they buried him in the City of David, but they did not bury him in the tombs of the kings.

[26]These are the ones who conspired against him: Zabad[a] the son of Shimeath the Ammonitess, and Jehozabad the son of Shimrith[b] the Moabitess. [27]Now *concerning* his sons, and the many oracles about him, and the repairing of the house of God, indeed they *are* written in the annals of the book of the kings. Then Amaziah his son reigned in his place.

Amaziah Reigns in Judah

25 Amaziah *was* twenty-five years old *when* he became king, and he reigned twenty-nine years in Jerusalem. His mother's name *was* Jehoaddan of Jerusalem. [2]And he did *what was* right in the sight of the LORD, but not with a loyal heart.

[3]Now it happened, as soon as the kingdom was established for him, that he executed his servants who had murdered his father the king. [4]However he did not execute their children, but *did* as *it is* written in the Law in the Book of Moses, where the LORD commanded, saying, "The fathers shall not be put to death for their children, nor shall the children be put to death for their fathers; but a person shall die for his own sin."[a]

The War Against Edom

[5]Moreover Amaziah gathered Judah together and set over them captains of thousands and captains of hundreds, according to *their* fathers' houses, throughout all Judah and Benjamin; and he numbered them from twenty years old and

above, and found them to be three hundred thousand choice *men, able* to go to war, who could handle spear and shield. [6]He also hired one hundred thousand mighty men of valor from Israel for one hundred talents of silver. [7]But a man of God came to him, saying, "O king, do not let the army of Israel go with you, for the LORD *is* not with Israel—*not with* any of the children of Ephraim. [8]But if you go, be gone! Be strong in battle! *Even so,* God shall make you fall before the enemy; for God has power to help and to overthrow."

[9]Then Amaziah said to the man of God, "But what *shall we* do about the hundred talents which I have given to the troops of Israel?"

And the man of God answered, "The LORD is able to give you much more than this." [10]So Amaziah discharged the troops that had come to him from Ephraim, to go back home. Therefore their anger was greatly aroused against Judah, and they returned home in great anger.

[11]Then Amaziah strengthened himself, and leading his people, he went to the Valley of Salt and killed ten thousand of the people of Seir. [12]Also the children of Judah took captive ten thousand alive, brought them to the top of the rock, and cast them down from the top of the rock, so that they all were dashed in pieces.

[13]But as for the soldiers of the army which Amaziah had discharged, so that they would no go with him to battle, they raided the cities of Judah from Samaria to Beth Horon, killed three thousand in them, and took much spoil.

[14]Now it was so, after Amaziah came from the slaughter of the Edomites, that he brought the gods of the people of Seir, set them up *to b* his gods, and bowed down before them and burned incense to them. [15]Therefore the anger of the LORD was aroused against Amaziah and He sent him a prophet who said to him "Why have you sought the gods of the people which could not rescue their own people from your hand?"

[16]So it was, as he talked with him, that *the kin* said to him, "Have we made you the king's counselor? Cease! Why should you be killed?"

24:25 [a]Septuagint and Vulgate read *son* (compare verses 20–22
24:26 [a]Or *Jozachar* (compare 2 Kings 12:21) [b]Or *Shomer* (compa
2 Kings 12:21) 25:4 [a]Deuteronomy 24:16

Then the prophet ceased, and said, "I know that God has determined to destroy you, because you have done this and have not heeded my advice."

ISRAEL DEFEATS JUDAH

[17]Now Amaziah king of Judah asked advice and sent to Joash[a] the son of Jehoahaz, the son of Jehu, king of Israel, saying, "Come, let us face one another *in battle.*"

[18]And Joash king of Israel sent to Amaziah king of Judah, saying, "The thistle that *was* in Lebanon sent to the cedar that was in Lebanon, saying, 'Give your daughter to my son as wife'; and a wild beast that *was* in Lebanon passed by and trampled the thistle. [19]Indeed you say that you have defeated the Edomites, and your heart is lifted up to boast. Stay at home now; why should you meddle with trouble, that you should fall— you and Judah with you?"

[20]But Amaziah would not heed, for it *came* from God, that He might give them into the hand *of their enemies,* because they sought the gods of Edom. [21]So Joash king of Israel went out; and he and Amaziah king of Judah faced one another at Beth Shemesh, which *belongs* to Judah. [22]And Judah was defeated by Israel, and every man fled to his tent. [23]Then Joash the king of Israel captured Amaziah king of Judah, the son of Joash, the son of Jehoahaz, at Beth Shemesh; and he brought him to Jerusalem, and broke down the wall of Jerusalem from the Gate of Ephraim to the Corner Gate—four hundred cubits. [24]And *he took* all the gold and silver, all the articles that were found in the house of God with Obed-Edom, the treasures of the king's house, and hostages, and returned to Samaria.

DEATH OF AMAZIAH

[25]Amaziah the son of Joash, king of Judah, lived fifteen years after the death of Joash the son of Jehoahaz, king of Israel. [26]Now the rest of the acts of Amaziah, from first to last, indeed *are* they not written in the book of the kings of Judah and Israel? [27]After the time that Amaziah turned away from following the LORD, they made a conspiracy against him in Jerusalem, and he fled to Lachish; but they sent after him to Lachish and killed him there. [28]Then they brought him on horses and buried him with his fathers in the City of Judah.

UZZIAH REIGNS IN JUDAH

26 Now all the people of Judah took Uzziah,[a] who *was* sixteen years old, and made him king instead of his father Amaziah. [2]He built Elath[a] and restored it to Judah, after the king rested with his fathers.

[3]Uzziah *was* sixteen years old when he became king, and he reigned fifty-two years in Jerusalem. His mother's name was Jecholiah of Jerusalem. [4]And he did *what was* right in the sight of the LORD, according to all that his father Amaziah had done. [5]He sought God in the days of Zechariah, who had understanding in the visions[a] of God; and as long as he sought the LORD, God made him prosper.

[6]Now he went out and made war against the Philistines, and broke down the wall of Gath, the wall of Jabneh, and the wall of Ashdod; and he built cities *around* Ashdod and among the Philistines. [7]God helped him against the Philistines, against the Arabians who lived in Gur Baal, and against the Meunites. [8]Also the Ammonites brought tribute to Uzziah. His fame spread as far as the entrance of Egypt, for he became exceedingly strong.

[9]And Uzziah built towers in Jerusalem at the Corner Gate, at the Valley Gate, and at the corner buttress of the wall; then he fortified them. [10]Also he built towers in the desert. He dug many wells, for he had much livestock, both in the lowlands and in the plains; *he also had* farmers and vinedressers in the mountains and in Carmel, for he loved the soil.

[11]Moreover Uzziah had an army of fighting men who went out to war by companies, according to the number on their roll as prepared by Jeiel the scribe and Maaseiah the officer, under the hand of Hananiah, *one* of the king's captains. [12]The total number of chief officers[a] of the mighty men of valor *was* two thousand six hundred. [13]And under their authority *was* an army of three hundred and seven thousand five hundred,

25:17 [a]Spelled *Jehoash* in 2 Kings 14:8ff   **26:1** [a]Called *Azariah* in 2 Kings 14:21ff   **26:2** [a]Hebrew *Eloth*   **26:5** [a]Several Hebrew manuscripts, Septuagint, Syriac, Targum, and Arabic read *fear.* **26:12** [a]Literally *chief fathers*

that made war with mighty power, to help the king against the enemy. [14]Then Uzziah prepared for them, for the entire army, shields, spears, helmets, body armor, bows, and slings *to cast* stones. [15]And he made devices in Jerusalem, invented by skillful men, to be on the towers and the corners, to shoot arrows and large stones. So his fame spread far and wide, for he was marvelously helped till he became strong.

THE PENALTY FOR UZZIAH'S PRIDE

[16]But when he was strong his heart was lifted up, to *his* destruction, for he transgressed against the LORD his God by entering the temple of the LORD to burn incense on the altar of incense. [17]So Azariah the priest went in after him, and with him were eighty priests of the LORD— valiant men. [18]And they withstood King Uzziah, and said to him, "*It is* not for you, Uzziah, to burn incense to the LORD, but for the priests, the sons of Aaron, who are consecrated to burn incense. Get out of the sanctuary, for you have trespassed! You *shall have* no honor from the LORD God." [19]Then Uzziah became furious; and he *had* a censer in his hand to burn incense. And while he was angry with the priests, leprosy broke out on his forehead, before the priests in the house of the LORD, beside the incense altar. [20]And Azariah the chief priest and all the priests looked at him, and there, on his forehead, he *was* leprous; so they thrust him out of that place. Indeed he also hurried to get out, because the LORD had struck him. [21]King Uzziah was a leper until the day of his death. He dwelt in an isolated house, because he was a leper; for he was cut off from the house of the LORD. Then Jotham his son *was* over the king's house, judging the people of the land. [22]Now the rest of the acts of Uzziah, from first to last, the prophet Isaiah the son of Amoz wrote. [23]So Uzziah rested with his fathers, and they buried him with his fathers in the field of burial which *belonged* to the kings, for they said, "He is a leper." Then Jotham his son reigned in his place.

JOTHAM REIGNS IN JUDAH

27 Jotham *was* twenty-five years old when he became king, and he reigned sixteen years in Jerusalem. His mother's name *was* Jerushah[a] the daughter of Zadok. [2]And he did *what was* right in the sight of the LORD, according to all that his father Uzziah had done (although he did not enter the temple of the LORD). But still the people acted corruptly.

[3]He built the Upper Gate of the house of the LORD, and he built extensively on the wall of Ophel. [4]Moreover he built cities in the mountains of Judah, and in the forests he built fortresses and towers. [5]He also fought with the king of the Ammonites and defeated them. And the people of Ammon gave him in that year one hundred talents of silver, ten thousand kors of wheat, and ten thousand of barley. The people of Ammon paid this to him in the second and third years also. [6]So Jotham became mighty, because he prepared his ways before the LORD his God.

[7]Now the rest of the acts of Jotham, and all his wars and his ways, indeed they *are* written in the book of the kings of Israel and Judah. [8]He was twenty-five years old when he became king, and he reigned sixteen years in Jerusalem. [9]So Jotham rested with his fathers, and they buried him in the City of David. Then Ahaz his son reigned in his place.

AHAZ REIGNS IN JUDAH

28 Ahaz *was* twenty years old when he became king, and he reigned sixteen years in Jerusalem; and he did not do *what was* right in the sight of the LORD, as his father David *had done.* [2]For he walked in the ways of the kings of Israel, and made molded images for the Baals. [3]He burned incense in the Valley of the Son of Hinnom, and burned his children in the fire, according to the abominations of the nations whom the LORD had cast out before the children of Israel. [4]And he sacrificed and burned incense on the high places, on the hills, and under every green tree.

SYRIA AND ISRAEL DEFEAT JUDAH

[5]Therefore the LORD his God delivered him into the hand of the king of Syria. They defeated him, and carried away a great multitude of them as captives, and brought *them* to Damascus. Then he was also delivered into the hand of the king of Israel, who defeated him with a great slaughter

27:1 [a]Spelled *Jerusha* in 2 Kings 15:33

For Pekah the son of Remaliah killed one hundred and twenty thousand in Judah in one day, all valiant men, because they had forsaken the LORD God of their fathers. [7]Zichri, a mighty man of Ephraim, killed Maaseiah the king's son, Azrikam the officer over the house, and Elkanah *who was* second to the king. [8]And the children of Israel carried away captive of their brethren two hundred thousand women, sons, and daughters; and they also took away much spoil from them, and brought the spoil to Samaria.

ISRAEL RETURNS THE CAPTIVES

[9]But a prophet of the LORD was there, whose name *was* Oded; and he went out before the army that came to Samaria, and said to them: "Look, because the LORD God of your fathers was angry with Judah, He has delivered them into your hand; but you have killed them in a rage *that* reaches up to heaven. [10]And now you propose to force the children of Judah and Jerusalem to be your male and female slaves; *but are* you not also guilty before the LORD your God? [11]Now hear me, therefore, and return the captives, whom you have taken captive from your brethren, for the fierce wrath of the LORD *is* upon you."

[12]Then some of the heads of the children of Ephraim, Azariah the son of Johanan, Berechiah the son of Meshillemoth, Jehizkiah the son of Shallum, and Amasa the son of Hadlai, stood up against those who came from the war, [13]and said to them, "You shall not bring the captives here, for we *already* have offended the LORD. You intend to add to our sins and to our guilt; for our guilt is great, and *there is* fierce wrath against Israel." [14]So the armed men left the captives and the spoil before the leaders and all the assembly. [15]Then the men who were designated by name rose up and took the captives, and from the spoil they clothed all who were naked among them, dressed them and gave them sandals, gave them food and drink, and anointed them; and they let all the feeble ones ride on donkeys. So they brought them to their brethren at Jericho, the city of palm trees. Then they returned to Samaria.

ASSYRIA REFUSES TO HELP JUDAH

[16]At the same time King Ahaz sent to the kings[a] of Assyria to help him. [17]For again the Edomites had come, attacked Judah, and carried away captives. [18]The Philistines also had invaded the cities of the lowland and of the South of Judah, and had taken Beth Shemesh, Aijalon, Gederoth, Sochoh with its villages, Timnah with its villages, and Gimzo with its villages; and they dwelt there. [19]For the LORD brought Judah low because of Ahaz king of Israel, for he had encouraged moral decline in Judah and had been continually unfaithful to the LORD. [20]Also Tiglath-Pileser[a] king of Assyria came to him and distressed him, and did not assist him. [21]For Ahaz took part *of the treasures* from the house of the LORD, from the house of the king, and from the leaders, and he gave *it* to the king of Assyria; but he did not help him.

APOSTASY AND DEATH OF AHAZ

[22]Now in the time of his distress King Ahaz became increasingly unfaithful to the LORD. This *is that* King Ahaz. [23]For he sacrificed to the gods of Damascus which had defeated him, saying, "Because the gods of the kings of Syria help them, I will sacrifice to them that they may help me." But they were the ruin of him and of all Israel. [24]So Ahaz gathered the articles of the house of God, cut in pieces the articles of the house of God, shut up the doors of the house of the LORD, and made for himself altars in every corner of Jerusalem. [25]And in every single city of Judah he made high places to burn incense to other gods, and provoked to anger the LORD God of his fathers.

[26]Now the rest of his acts and all his ways, from first to last, indeed they *are* written in the book of the kings of Judah and Israel. [27]So Ahaz rested with his fathers, and they buried him in the city, in Jerusalem; but they did not bring him into the tombs of the kings of Israel. Then Hezekiah his son reigned in his place.

HEZEKIAH REIGNS IN JUDAH

29 Hezekiah became king *when he was* twenty-five years old, and he reigned twenty-nine years in Jerusalem. His mother's name *was* Abijah[a] the daughter of Zechariah.

28:16 [a]Septuagint, Syriac, and Vulgate read *king* (compare verse 20). **28:20** [a]Hebrew *Tilgath-Pilneser* **29:1** [a]Spelled *Abi* in 2 Kings 18:2

[2]And he did *what was* right in the sight of the LORD, according to all that his father David had done.

HEZEKIAH CLEANSES THE TEMPLE

[3]In the first year of his reign, in the first month, he opened the doors of the house of the LORD and repaired them. [4]Then he brought in the priests and the Levites, and gathered them in the East Square, [5]and said to them: "Hear me, Levites! Now sanctify yourselves, sanctify the house of the LORD God of your fathers, and carry out the rubbish from the holy *place*. [6]For our fathers have trespassed and done evil in the eyes of the LORD our God; they have forsaken Him, have turned their faces away from the dwelling place of the LORD, and turned *their* backs *on* Him. [7]They have also shut up the doors of the vestibule, put out the lamps, and have not burned incense or offered burnt offerings in the holy *place* to the God of Israel. [8]Therefore the wrath of the LORD fell upon Judah and Jerusalem, and He has given them up to trouble, to desolation, and to jeering, as you see with your eyes. [9]For indeed, because of this our fathers have fallen by the sword; and our sons, our daughters, and our wives *are* in captivity.

[10]"Now *it is* in my heart to make a covenant with the LORD God of Israel, that His fierce wrath may turn away from us. [11]My sons, do not be negligent now, for the LORD has chosen you to stand before Him, to serve Him, and that you should minister to Him and burn incense."

[12]Then these Levites arose: Mahath the son of Amasai and Joel the son of Azariah, of the sons of the Kohathites; of the sons of Merari, Kish the son of Abdi and Azariah the son of Jehallelel; of the Gershonites, Joah the son of Zimmah and Eden the son of Joah; [13]of the sons of Elizaphan, Shimri and Jeiel; of the sons of Asaph, Zechariah and Mattaniah; [14]of the sons of Heman, Jehiel and Shimei; and of the sons of Jeduthun, Shemaiah and Uzziel.

[15]And they gathered their brethren, sanctified themselves, and went according to the commandment of the king, at the words of the LORD, to cleanse the house of the LORD. [16]Then the priests went into the inner part of the house of the LORD to cleanse *it,* and brought out all the debris that they found in the temple of the LORD to the court of the house of the LORD. And the Levites took *it* out and carried *it* to the Brook Kidron.

[17]Now they began to sanctify on the first *day* of the first month, and on the eighth day of the month they came to the vestibule of the LORD. So they sanctified the house of the LORD in eight days, and on the sixteenth day of the first month they finished.

[18]Then they went in to King Hezekiah and said, "We have cleansed all the house of the LORD, the altar of burnt offerings with all its articles, and the table of the showbread with all its articles. [19]Moreover all the articles which King Ahaz in his reign had cast aside in his transgression we have prepared and sanctified; and there they *are* before the altar of the LORD."

HEZEKIAH RESTORES TEMPLE WORSHIP

[20]Then King Hezekiah rose early, gathered the rulers of the city, and went up to the house of the LORD. [21]And they brought seven bulls, seven rams, seven lambs, and seven male goats for a sin offering for the kingdom, for the sanctuary, and for Judah. Then he commanded the priests, the sons of Aaron, to offer *them* on the altar of the LORD. [22]So they killed the bulls, and the priests received the blood and sprinkled *it* on the altar. Likewise they killed the rams and sprinkled the blood on the altar. They also killed the lambs and sprinkled the blood on the altar. [23]Then they brought out the male goats *for* the sin offering before the king and the assembly, and they laid their hands on them. [24]And the priests killed them; and they presented their blood on the altar as a sin offering to make an atonement for all Israel, for the king commanded *that* the burnt offering and the sin offering *be made* for all Israel.

[25]And he stationed the Levites in the house of the LORD with cymbals, with stringed instruments, and with harps, according to the commandment of David, of Gad the king's seer, and of Nathan the prophet; for thus *was* the commandment of the LORD by His prophets. [26]The Levites stood with the instruments of David, and the priests with the trumpets. [27]Then Hezekiah commanded *them* to offer the burnt offering on the altar. And when the burnt offering began, the song of the LORD *also* began, with the trumpets and with the instruments of David king of Israel.

28So all the assembly worshiped, the singers sang, and the trumpeters sounded; all *this continued* until the burnt offering was finished. 29And when they had finished offering, the king and all who were present with him bowed and worshiped. 30Moreover King Hezekiah and the leaders commanded the Levites to sing praise to the LORD with the words of David and of Asaph the seer. So they sang praises with gladness, and they bowed their heads and worshiped.

31Then Hezekiah answered and said, "Now *that* you have consecrated yourselves to the LORD, come near, and bring sacrifices and thank offerings into the house of the LORD." So the assembly brought in sacrifices and thank offerings, and as many as were of a willing heart *brought* burnt offerings. 32And the number of the burnt offerings which the assembly brought was seventy bulls, one hundred rams, *and* two hundred lambs; all these *were* for a burnt offering to the LORD. 33The consecrated things *were* six hundred bulls and three thousand sheep. 34But the priests were too few, so that they could not skin all the burnt offerings; therefore their brethren the Levites helped them until the work was ended and until the *other* priests had sanctified themselves, for the Levites were more diligent in sanctifying themselves than the priests. 35Also the burnt offerings *were* in abundance, with the fat of the peace offerings and *with* the drink offerings for *every* burnt offering.

So the service of the house of the LORD was set in order. 36Then Hezekiah and all the people rejoiced that God had prepared the people, since the events took place so suddenly.

HEZEKIAH KEEPS THE PASSOVER

30 And Hezekiah sent to all Israel and Judah, and also wrote letters to Ephraim and Manasseh, that they should come to the house of the LORD at Jerusalem, to keep the Passover to the LORD God of Israel. 2For the king and his leaders and all the assembly in Jerusalem had agreed to keep the Passover in the second month. 3For they could not keep it at the regular time,a because a sufficient number of priests had not consecrated themselves, nor had the people gathered together at Jerusalem. 4And the matter pleased the king and all the assembly. 5So they resolved to make a proclamation throughout all Israel, from Beer-sheba to Dan, that they should come to keep the Passover to the LORD God of Israel at Jerusalem, since they had not done *it* for a long *time* in the *prescribed* manner.

6Then the runners went throughout all Israel and Judah with the letters from the king and his leaders, and spoke according to the command of the king: "Children of Israel, return to the LORD God of Abraham, Isaac, and Israel; then He will return to the remnant of you who have escaped from the hand of the kings of Assyria. 7And do not be like your fathers and your brethren, who trespassed against the LORD God of their fathers, so that He gave them up to desolation, as you see. 8Now do not be stiff-necked, as your fathers *were, but* yield yourselves to the LORD; and enter His sanctuary, which He has sanctified forever, and serve the LORD your God, that the fierceness of His wrath may turn away from you. 9For if you return to the LORD, your brethren and your children *will be treated* with compassion by those who lead them captive, so that they may come back to this land; for the LORD your God *is* gracious and merciful, and will not turn *His* face from you if you return to Him."

10So the runners passed from city to city through the country of Ephraim and Manasseh, as far as Zebulun; but they laughed at them and mocked them. 11Nevertheless some from Asher, Manasseh, and Zebulun humbled themselves and came to Jerusalem. 12Also the hand of God was on Judah to give them singleness of heart to obey the command of the king and the leaders, at the word of the LORD.

13Now many people, a very great assembly, gathered at Jerusalem to keep the Feast of Unleavened Bread in the second month. 14They arose and took away the altars that *were* in Jerusalem, and they took away all the incense altars and cast *them* into the Brook Kidron. 15Then they slaughtered the Passover *lambs* on the fourteenth *day* of the second month. The priests and the Levites were ashamed, and sanctified themselves, and brought the burnt offerings to the house of the LORD. 16They stood in their place according to their custom, according to the Law of Moses the man of God; the priests sprinkled

30:3 aThat is, the first month (compare Leviticus 23:5); literally *at that time*

the blood *received* from the hand of the Levites. [17]For *there were* many in the assembly who had not sanctified themselves; therefore the Levites had charge of the slaughter of the Passover *lambs* for everyone *who was* not clean, to sanctify *them* to the LORD. [18]For a multitude of the people, many from Ephraim, Manasseh, Issachar, and Zebulun, had not cleansed themselves, yet they ate the Passover contrary to what was written. But Hezekiah prayed for them, saying, "May the good LORD provide atonement for everyone [19]*who* prepares his heart to seek God, the LORD God of his fathers, though *he is* not *cleansed* according to the purification of the sanctuary." [20]And the LORD listened to Hezekiah and healed the people.

[21]So the children of Israel who were present at Jerusalem kept the Feast of Unleavened Bread seven days with great gladness; and the Levites and the priests praised the LORD day by day, *singing* to the LORD, accompanied by loud instruments. [22]And Hezekiah gave encouragement to all the Levites who taught the good knowledge of the LORD; and they ate throughout the feast seven days, offering peace offerings and making confession to the LORD God of their fathers.

[23]Then the whole assembly agreed to keep *the feast* another seven days, and they kept it *another* seven days with gladness. [24]For Hezekiah king of Judah gave to the assembly a thousand bulls and seven thousand sheep, and the leaders gave to the assembly a thousand bulls and ten thousand sheep; and a great number of priests sanctified themselves. [25]The whole assembly of Judah rejoiced, also the priests and Levites, all the assembly that came from Israel, the sojourners who came from the land of Israel, and those who dwelt in Judah. [26]So there was great joy in Jerusalem, for since the time of Solomon the son of David, king of Israel, *there had* been nothing like this in Jerusalem. [27]Then the priests, the Levites, arose and blessed the people, and their voice was heard; and their prayer came *up* to His holy dwelling place, to heaven.

THE REFORMS OF HEZEKIAH

31 Now when all this was finished, all Israel who were present went out to the cities of Judah and broke the *sacred* pillars in pieces, cut down the wooden images, and threw down the high places and the altars—from all Judah, Benjamin, Ephraim, and Manasseh—until they had utterly destroyed them all. Then all the children of Israel returned to their own cities, every man to his possession.

[2]And Hezekiah appointed the divisions of the priests and the Levites according to their divisions, each man according to his service, the priests and Levites for burnt offerings and peace offerings, to serve, to give thanks, and to praise in the gates of the camp[a] of the LORD. [3]The king also *appointed* a portion of his possessions for the burnt offerings: for the morning and evening burnt offerings, the burnt offerings for the Sabbaths and the New Moons and the set feasts, as *is* written in the Law of the LORD.

[4]Moreover he commanded the people who dwelt in Jerusalem to contribute support for the priests and the Levites, that they might devote themselves to the Law of the LORD.

[5]As soon as the commandment was circulated, the children of Israel brought in abundance the firstfruits of grain and wine, oil and honey and of all the produce of the field; and they brought in abundantly the tithe of everything. [6]And the children of Israel and Judah, who dwelt in the cities of Judah, brought the tithe of oxen and sheep; also the tithe of holy things which were consecrated to the LORD their God they laid in heaps.

[7]In the third month they began laying them in heaps, and they finished in the seventh month. [8]And when Hezekiah and the leaders came and saw the heaps, they blessed the LORD and His people Israel. [9]Then Hezekiah questioned the priests and the Levites concerning the heaps. [10]And Azariah the chief priest, from the house of Zadok, answered him and said, "Since *the people* began to bring the offerings into the house of the LORD, we have had enough to eat and have plenty left, for the LORD has blessed His people, and what is left *is* this great abundance."

[11]Now Hezekiah commanded *them* to prepare rooms in the house of the LORD, and they prepared them. [12]Then they faithfully brought in the offerings, the tithes, and the dedicated things; Cononiah the Levite had charge of them, and Shimei his brother *was* the next. [13]Jehiel, Azazia

31:2 [a]That is, the temple

Nahath, Asahel, Jerimoth, Jozabad, Eliel, Ismachiah, Mahath, and Benaiah *were* overseers under the hand of Cononiah and Shimei his brother, at the commandment of Hezekiah the king and Azariah the ruler of the house of God. ¹⁴Kore the son of Imnah the Levite, the keeper of the East Gate, *was* over the freewill offerings to God, to distribute the offerings of the LORD and the most holy things. ¹⁵And under him *were* Eden, Miniamin, Jeshua, Shemaiah, Amariah, and Shecaniah, *his* faithful assistants in the cities of the priests, to distribute allotments to their brethren by divisions, to the great as well as the small.

¹⁶Besides those males from three years old and up who were written in the genealogy, they distributed to everyone who entered the house of the LORD his daily portion for the work of his service, by his division, ¹⁷and to the priests who were written in the genealogy according to their father's house, and to the Levites from twenty years old and up according to their work, by their divisions, ¹⁸and to all who were written in the genealogy—their little ones and their wives, their sons and daughters, the whole company of them—for in their faithfulness they sanctified themselves in holiness.

¹⁹Also for the sons of Aaron the priests, *who were* in the fields of the common-lands of their cities, in every single city, *there were* men who were designated by name to distribute portions to all the males among the priests and to all who were listed by genealogies among the Levites.

²⁰Thus Hezekiah did throughout all Judah, and he did what *was* good and right and true before the LORD his God. ²¹And in every work that he began in the service of the house of God, in the law and in the commandment, to seek his God, he did *it* with all his heart. So he prospered.

SENNACHERIB BOASTS AGAINST THE LORD

32 After these deeds of faithfulness, Sennacherib king of Assyria came and entered Judah; he encamped against the fortified cities, thinking to win them over to himself. ²And when Hezekiah saw that Sennacherib had come, and that his purpose *was* to make war against Jerusalem, ³he consulted with his leaders and commandersª to stop the water from the springs which *were* outside the city; and they helped him.

⁴Thus many people gathered together who stopped all the springs and the brook that ran through the land, saying, "Why should the kingsª of Assyria come and find much water?" ⁵And he strengthened himself, built up all the wall that was broken, raised *it* up to the towers, and *built* another wall outside; also he repaired the Milloª *in* the City of David, and made weapons and shields in abundance. ⁶Then he set military captains over the people, gathered them together to him in the open square of the city gate, and gave them encouragement, saying, ⁷"Be strong and courageous; do not be afraid nor dismayed before the king of Assyria, nor before all the multitude that *is* with him; for *there are* more with us than with him. ⁸With him *is* an arm of flesh; but with us *is* the LORD our God, to help us and to fight our battles." And the people were strengthened by the words of Hezekiah king of Judah.

⁹After this Sennacherib king of Assyria sent his servants to Jerusalem (but he and all the forces with him *laid siege* against Lachish), to Hezekiah king of Judah, and to all Judah who *were* in Jerusalem, saying, ¹⁰"Thus says Sennacherib king of Assyria: 'In what do you trust, that you remain under siege in Jerusalem? ¹¹Does not Hezekiah persuade you to give yourselves over to die by famine and by thirst, saying, "The LORD our God will deliver us from the hand of the king of Assyria"? ¹²Has not the same Hezekiah taken away His high places and His altars, and commanded Judah and Jerusalem, saying, "You shall worship before one altar and burn incense on it"? ¹³Do you not know what I and my fathers have done to all the peoples of *other* lands? Were the gods of the nations of those lands in any way able to deliver their lands out of my hand? ¹⁴Who *was there* among all the gods of those nations that my fathers utterly destroyed that could deliver his people from my hand, that your God should be able to deliver you from my hand? ¹⁵Now therefore, do not let Hezekiah deceive you or persuade you like this, and do not believe him; for no god of any nation or kingdom was able to deliver his people from my hand or the hand of my fathers. How much less will your God deliver you from my hand?' "

32:3 ªLiterally *mighty men*   **32:4** ªFollowing Masoretic Text and Vulgate; Arabic, Septuagint, and Syriac read *king*.   **32:5** ªLiterally *The Landfill*

[16]Furthermore, his servants spoke against the LORD God and against His servant Hezekiah.

[17]He also wrote letters to revile the LORD God of Israel, and to speak against Him, saying, "As the gods of the nations of *other* lands have not delivered their people from my hand, so the God of Hezekiah will not deliver His people from my hand." [18]Then they called out with a loud voice in Hebrew[a] to the people of Jerusalem who *were* on the wall, to frighten them and trouble them, that they might take the city. [19]And they spoke against the God of Jerusalem, as against the gods of the people of the earth—the work of men's hands.

SENNACHERIB'S DEFEAT AND DEATH

[20]Now because of this King Hezekiah and the prophet Isaiah, the son of Amoz, prayed and cried out to heaven. [21]Then the LORD sent an angel who cut down every mighty man of valor, leader, and captain in the camp of the king of Assyria. So he returned shamefaced to his own land. And when he had gone into the temple of his god, some of his own offspring struck him down with the sword there.

[22]Thus the LORD saved Hezekiah and the inhabitants of Jerusalem from the hand of Sennacherib the king of Assyria, and from the hand of all *others,* and guided them[a] on every side. [23]And many brought gifts to the LORD at Jerusalem, and presents to Hezekiah king of Judah, so that he was exalted in the sight of all nations thereafter.

HEZEKIAH HUMBLES HIMSELF

[24]In those days Hezekiah was sick and near death, and he prayed to the LORD; and He spoke to him and gave him a sign. [25]But Hezekiah did not repay according to the favor *shown* him, for his heart was lifted up; therefore wrath was looming over him and over Judah and Jerusalem. [26]Then Hezekiah humbled himself for the pride of his heart, he and the inhabitants of Jerusalem, so that the wrath of the LORD did not come upon them in the days of Hezekiah.

HEZEKIAH'S WEALTH AND HONOR

[27]Hezekiah had very great riches and honor. And he made himself treasuries for silver, for gold, for precious stones, for spices, for shields, and for all kinds of desirable items; [28]storehouses for the harvest of grain, wine, and oil; and stalls for all kinds of livestock, and folds for flocks.[a] [29]Moreover he provided cities for himself, and possessions of flocks and herds in abundance; for God had given him very much property. [30]This same Hezekiah also stopped the water outlet of Upper Gihon, and brought the water by tunnel[a] to the west side of the City of David. Hezekiah prospered in all his works.

[31]However, *regarding* the ambassadors of the princes of Babylon, whom they sent to him to inquire about the wonder that was *done* in the land, God withdrew from him, in order to test him, that He might know all *that was* in his heart.

DEATH OF HEZEKIAH

[32]Now the rest of the acts of Hezekiah, and his goodness, indeed they *are* written in the vision of Isaiah the prophet, the son of Amoz, *and* in the book of the kings of Judah and Israel. [33]So Hezekiah rested with his fathers, and they buried him in the upper tombs of the sons of David; and all Judah and the inhabitants of Jerusalem honored him at his death. Then Manasseh his son reigned in his place.

MANASSEH REIGNS IN JUDAH

33 Manasseh *was* twelve years old when he became king, and he reigned fifty-five years in Jerusalem. [2]But he did evil in the sight of the LORD, according to the abominations of the nations whom the LORD had cast out before the children of Israel. [3]For he rebuilt the high places which Hezekiah his father had broken down; he raised up altars for the Baals, and made wooden images; and he worshiped all the host of heaven[a] and served them. [4]He also built altars in the house of the LORD, of which the LORD had said, "In Jerusalem shall My name be forever." [5]And he built altars for all the host of heaven in the two courts of the house of the LORD. [6]Also he caused his sons to pass through the fire in the Valley of the Son of Hinnom; he practiced soothsaying, used witchcraft and sorcery, and consulted mediums and spiritists. He did much evil in the sight

32:18 [a]Literally *Judean* 32:22 [a]Septuagint reads *gave them rest* Vulgate reads *gave them treasures.* 32:28 [a]Following Septuagint and Vulgate; Arabic and Syriac omit *folds for flocks;* Masoretic Text reads *flocks for sheepfolds.* 32:30 [a]Literally *brought it straight* (compare 2 Kings 20:20) 33:3 [a]The gods of the Assyrians of the LORD, to provoke Him to anger. [7]He even set a carved image, the idol which he had made, in the house of God, of which God had said to David and to Solomon his son, "In this house and in Jerusalem, which I have chosen out of all the tribes of Israel, I will put My name forever; [8]and I will not again remove the foot of Israel from the land which I have appointed for your fathers— only if they are careful to do all that I have commanded them, according to the whole law and the statutes and the ordinances by the hand of Moses." [9]So Manasseh seduced Judah and the inhabitants of Jerusalem to do more evil than the nations whom the LORD had destroyed before the children of Israel.

MANASSEH RESTORED AFTER REPENTANCE

[10]And the LORD spoke to Manasseh and his people, but they would not listen. [11]Therefore the LORD brought upon them the captains of the army of the king of Assyria, who took Manasseh with hooks,[a] bound him with bronze *fetters,* and carried him off to Babylon. [12]Now when he was in affliction, he implored the LORD his God, and humbled himself greatly before the God of his fathers, [13]and prayed to Him; and He received his entreaty, heard his supplication, and brought him back to Jerusalem into his kingdom. Then Manasseh knew that the LORD *was* God.

[14]After this he built a wall outside the City of David on the west side of Gihon, in the valley, as far as the entrance of the Fish Gate; and *it* enclosed Ophel, and he raised it to a very great height. Then he put military captains in all the fortified cities of Judah. [15]He took away the foreign gods and the idol from the house of the LORD, and all the altars that he had built in the mount of the house of the LORD and in Jerusalem; and he cast *them* out of the city. [16]He also repaired the altar of the LORD, sacrificed peace offerings and thank offerings on it, and commanded Judah to serve the LORD God of Israel. [17]Nevertheless the people still sacrificed on the high places, *but* only to the LORD their God.

DEATH OF MANASSEH

[18]Now the rest of the acts of Manasseh, his prayer to his God, and the words of the seers who spoke to him in the name of the LORD God of Israel, indeed they *are written* in the book[a] of the kings of Israel. [19]Also his prayer and *how God* received his entreaty, and all his sin and trespass, and the sites where he built high places and set up wooden images and carved images, before he was humbled, indeed they *are* written among the sayings of Hozai.[a] [20]So Manasseh rested with his fathers, and they buried him in his own house. Then his son Amon reigned in his place.

AMON'S REIGN AND DEATH

[21]Amon *was* twenty-two years old when he became king, and he reigned two years in Jerusalem. [22]But he did evil in the sight of the LORD, as his father Manasseh had done; for Amon sacrificed to all the carved images which his father Manasseh had made, and served them. [23]And he did not humble himself before the LORD, as his father Manasseh had humbled himself; but Amon trespassed more and more.

[24]Then his servants conspired against him, and killed him in his own house. [25]But the people of the land executed all those who had conspired against King Amon. Then the people of the land made his son Josiah king in his place.

JOSIAH REIGNS IN JUDAH

34 Josiah *was* eight years old when he became king, and he reigned thirty-one years in Jerusalem. [2]And he did *what was* right in the sight of the LORD, and walked in the ways of his father David; he did *not* turn aside to the right hand or to the left.

[3]For in the eighth year of his reign, while he was still young, he began to seek the God of his father David; and in the twelfth year he began to purge Judah and Jerusalem of the high places, the wooden images, the carved images, and the molded images. [4]They broke down the altars of the Baals in his presence, and the incense altars which *were* above them he cut down; and the wooden images, the carved images, and the molded images he broke in pieces, and made dust of them and scattered *it* on the graves of those who had sacrificed to them. [5]He also burned the bones of the priests on their altars, and cleansed Judah and Jerusalem. [6]And *so he did* in the cities of

33:11 [a]That is, nose hooks (compare 2 Kings 19:28)   **33:18** [a]Literally *words*   **33:19** [a]Septuagint reads *the seers.*

INSIDE *the* INFLUENCERS

JOSIAH

2 KINGS 22—23 & 2 CHRONICLES 34—35

Josiah became king of Judah when he was only eight years old. His country was in a state of moral and spiritual decay. Many evil kings before him offended God, and the people followed in each kings' footsteps. Even to an experienced ruler, reformation seemed all but impossible, but Josiah stepped forward to lead. Four events during Josiah's thirty-one year reign are of great significance:

- His religious experience at the age of sixteen (632 BC) (2 Chr. 34:3)

Josiah demonstrates a timeless principle of leadership: *you cannot lead others where you're not willing to go.*

- The reform movement he launched at the age of twenty (628 BC) (2 Chr. 34:3)

Four years after his spiritual transformation, Josiah abolished idolatry in Judah and all of Israel. He purged the temple of all the wicked and idolatrous practices, and destroyed pagan places of worship.

- The restoration of the temple (2 Chr. 34:8–21)

He allotted funds to repair and restore the House of the Lord. During this time the lost scrolls containing the Mosaic Law were found.

- The revival (622 BC) (2 Chr. 34:29–33)

God's Word brought revival into Josiah's heart and the hearts of Israel's inhabitants. The effects of this revival would last for the rest of Josiah's life—until he was killed in the battle with Pharaoh Neco in 609 BC at Megiddo (2 Chr. 35:20–27).

Manasseh, Ephraim, and Simeon, as far as Naphtali and all around, with axes.ᵃ ⁷When he had broken down the altars and the wooden images, had beaten the carved images into powder, and cut down all the incense altars throughout all the land of Israel, he returned to Jerusalem.

HILKIAH FINDS THE BOOK OF THE LAW

⁸In the eighteenth year of his reign, when he had purged the land and the temple,ᵃ he sent Shaphan the son of Azaliah, Maaseiah the governor of the city, and Joah the son of Joahaz the recorder, to repair the house of the LORD his God. ⁹When they came to Hilkiah the high priest, they delivered the money that was brought into the house of God, which the Levites who kept the doors had gathered from the hand of Manasseh and Ephraim, from all the remnant of Israel, from all Judah and Benjamin, and *which*

they had brought back to Jerusalem. ¹⁰Then they put *it* in the hand of the foremen who had the oversight of the house of the LORD; and they gave it to the workmen who worked in the house of the LORD, to repair and restore the house. ¹¹They gave *it* to the craftsmen and builders to buy hewn stone and timber for beams, and to floor the houses which the kings of Judah had destroyed. ¹²And the men did the work faithfully. Their overseers *were* Jahath and Obadiah the Levites, of the sons of Merari, and Zechariah and Meshullam, of the sons of the Kohathites, to supervise. *Others of* the Levites, all of whom were skillful with instruments of music, ¹³*were* over the burden bearers and *were* overseers of all who did work in any kind of service. And *some* of the Levites *were* scribes, officers, and gatekeepers.

¹⁴Now when they brought out the money

34:6 ᵃLiterally *swords*   34:8 ᵃLiterally *house*

that was brought into the house of the LORD, Hilkiah the priest found the Book of the Law of the LORD *given* by Moses. [15]Then Hilkiah answered and said to Shaphan the scribe, "I have found the Book of the Law in the house of the LORD." And Hilkiah gave the book to Shaphan. [16]So Shaphan carried the book to the king, bringing the king word, saying, "All that was committed to your servants they are doing. [17]And they have gathered the money that was found in the house of the LORD, and have delivered it into the hand of the overseers and the workmen." [18]Then Shaphan the scribe told the king, saying, "Hilkiah the priest has given me a book." And Shaphan read it before the king.

[19]Thus it happened, when the king heard the words of the Law, that he tore his clothes. [20]Then the king commanded Hilkiah, Ahikam the son of Shaphan, Abdon[a] the son of Micah, Shaphan the scribe, and Asaiah a servant of the king, saying, [21]"Go, inquire of the LORD for me, and for those who are left in Israel and Judah, concerning the words of the book that is found; for great *is* the wrath of the LORD that is poured out on us, because our fathers have not kept the word of the LORD, to do according to all that is written in this book."

[22]So Hilkiah and those the king *had appointed* went to Huldah the prophetess, the wife of Shallum the son of Tokhath,[a] the son of Hasrah,[b] keeper of the wardrobe. (She dwelt in Jerusalem in the Second Quarter.) And they spoke to her to that *effect*.

[23]Then she answered them, "Thus says the LORD God of Israel, 'Tell the man who sent you to Me, [24]"Thus says the LORD: 'Behold, I will bring calamity on this place and on its inhabitants, all the curses that are written in the book which they have read before the king of Judah, [25]because they have forsaken Me and burned incense to other gods, that they might provoke Me to anger with all the works of their hands. Therefore My wrath will be poured out on this place, and not be quenched.' " ' [26]But as for the king of Judah, who sent you to inquire of the LORD, in this manner you shall speak to him, 'Thus says the LORD God of Israel: "*Concerning* the words which you have heard— [27]because your heart was tender, and you humbled yourself before God when

you heard His words against this place and against its inhabitants, and you humbled yourself before Me, and you tore your clothes and wept before Me, I also have heard *you*," says the LORD. [28]"Surely I will gather you to your fathers, and you shall be gathered to your grave in peace; and your eyes shall not see all the calamity which I will bring on this place and its inhabitants." ' " So they brought back word to the king.

Josiah Restores True Worship

[29]Then the king sent and gathered all the elders of Judah and Jerusalem. [30]The king went up to the house of the LORD, with all the men of Judah and the inhabitants of Jerusalem—the priests and the Levites, and all the people, great and small. And he read in their hearing all the words of the Book of the Covenant which had been found in the house of the LORD. [31]Then the king stood in his place and made a covenant before the LORD, to follow the LORD, and to keep His commandments and His testimonies and His statutes with all his heart and all his soul, to perform the words of the covenant that were written in this book. [32]And he made all who were present in Jerusalem and Benjamin take a stand. So the inhabitants of Jerusalem did according to the covenant of God, the God of their fathers. [33]Thus Josiah removed all the abominations from all the country that *belonged* to the children of Israel, and made all who were present in Israel diligently serve the LORD their God. All his days they did not depart from following the LORD God of their fathers.

Josiah Keeps the Passover

35 Now Josiah kept a Passover to the LORD in Jerusalem, and they slaughtered the Passover *lambs* on the fourteenth *day* of the first month. [2]And he set the priests in their duties and encouraged them for the service of the house of the LORD. [3]Then he said to the Levites who taught all Israel, who were holy to the LORD: "Put the holy ark in the house which Solomon the son of David, king of Israel, built. *It shall* no longer *be* a burden on *your* shoulders. Now serve the LORD your God and His people

34:20 [a]*Achbor the son of Michaiah* in 2 Kings 22:12 **34:22** [a]Spelled *Tikvah* in 2 Kings 22:14 [b]Spelled *Harhas* in 2 Kings 22:14

Israel. [4]Prepare *yourselves* according to your fathers' houses, according to your divisions, following the written instruction of David king of Israel and the written instruction of Solomon his son. [5]And stand in the holy *place* according to the divisions of the fathers' houses of your brethren the *lay* people, and *according to* the division of the father's house of the Levites. [6]So slaughter the Passover *offerings,* consecrate yourselves, and prepare *them* for your brethren, that *they* may do according to the word of the LORD by the hand of Moses."

[7]Then Josiah gave the *lay* people lambs and young goats from the flock, all for Passover *offerings* for all who were present, to the number of thirty thousand, as well as three thousand cattle; these *were* from the king's possessions. [8]And his leaders gave willingly to the people, to the priests, and to the Levites. Hilkiah, Zechariah, and Jehiel, rulers of the house of God, gave to the priests for the Passover *offerings* two thousand six hundred *from the flock,* and three hundred cattle. [9]Also Conaniah, his brothers Shemaiah and Nethanel, and Hashabiah and Jeiel and Jozabad, chief of the Levites, gave to the Levites for Passover *offerings* five thousand *from the flock* and five hundred cattle.

[10]So the service was prepared, and the priests stood in their places, and the Levites in their divisions, according to the king's command. [11]And they slaughtered the Passover *offerings;* and the priests sprinkled *the blood* with their hands, while the Levites skinned *the animals.* [12]Then they removed the burnt offerings that *they* might give them to the divisions of the fathers' houses of the *lay* people, to offer to the LORD, as *it is* written in the Book of Moses. And so *they did* with the cattle. [13]Also they roasted the Passover *offerings* with fire according to the ordinance; but the *other* holy *offerings* they boiled in pots, in caldrons, and in pans, and divided *them* quickly among all the *lay* people. [14]Then afterward they prepared portions for themselves and for the priests, because the priests, the sons of Aaron, *were busy* in offering burnt offerings and fat until night; therefore the Levites prepared portions for themselves and for the priests, the sons of Aaron. [15]And the singers, the sons of Asaph, *were* in their places, according to the command of David, Asaph, Heman, and Je-

duthun the king's seer. Also the gatekeepers were at each gate; they did not have to leave their position, because their brethren the Levites prepared portions for them.

[16]So all the service of the LORD was prepared the same day, to keep the Passover and to offer burnt offerings on the altar of the LORD, according to the command of King Josiah. [17]And the children of Israel who were present kept the Passover at that time, and the Feast of Unleavened Bread for seven days. [18]There had been no Passover kept in Israel like that since the days of Samuel the prophet; and none of the kings of Israel had kept such a Passover as Josiah kept, with the priests and the Levites, all Judah and Israel who were present, and the inhabitants of Jerusalem. [19]In the eighteenth year of the reign of Josiah this Passover was kept.

JOSIAH DIES IN BATTLE

[20]After all this, when Josiah had prepared the temple, Necho king of Egypt came up to fight against Carchemish by the Euphrates; and Josiah went out against him. [21]But he sent messengers to him, saying, "What have I to do with you, king of Judah? *I have* not *come* against you this day, but against the house with which I have war; for God commanded me to make haste. Refrain *from meddling with* God, who *is* with me, lest He destroy you." [22]Nevertheless Josiah would not turn his face from him, but disguised himself so that he might fight with him, and did not heed the words of Necho from the mouth of God. So he came to fight in the Valley of Megiddo.

[23]And the archers shot King Josiah; and the king said to his servants, "Take me away, for I am severely wounded." [24]His servants therefore took him out of that chariot and put him in the second chariot that he had, and they brought him to Jerusalem. So he died, and was buried in *one of* the tombs of his fathers. And all Judah and Jerusalem mourned for Josiah.

[25]Jeremiah also lamented for Josiah. And to this day all the singing men and the singing women speak of Josiah in their lamentations. They made it a custom in Israel; and indeed they *are* written in the Laments.

[26]Now the rest of the acts of Josiah and his goodness, according to *what was* written in the

Law of the LORD, ²⁷and his deeds from first to last, indeed they *are* written in the book of the kings of Israel and Judah.

THE REIGN AND CAPTIVITY OF JEHOAHAZ

36 Then the people of the land took Jehoahaz the son of Josiah, and made him king in his father's place in Jerusalem. ²Jehoahaz^a *was* twenty-three years old when he became king, and he reigned three months in Jerusalem. ³Now the king of Egypt deposed him at Jerusalem; and he imposed on the land a tribute of one hundred talents of silver and a talent of gold. ⁴Then the king of Egypt made *Jehoahaz's*^a brother Eliakim king over Judah and Jerusalem, and changed his name to Jehoiakim. And Necho took Jehoahaz^b his brother and carried him off to Egypt.

THE REIGN AND CAPTIVITY OF JEHOIAKIM

⁵Jehoiakim *was* twenty-five years old when he became king, and he reigned eleven years in Jerusalem. And he did evil in the sight of the LORD his God. ⁶Nebuchadnezzar king of Babylon came up against him, and bound him in bronze *fetters* to carry him off to Babylon. ⁷Nebuchadnezzar also carried off *some* of the articles from the house of the LORD to Babylon, and put them in his temple at Babylon. ⁸Now the rest of the acts of Jehoiakim, the abominations which he did, and what was found against him, indeed they *are* written in the book of the kings of Israel and Judah. Then Jehoiachin his son reigned in his place.

THE REIGN AND CAPTIVITY OF JEHOIACHIN

⁹Jehoiachin *was* eight^a years old when he became king, and he reigned in Jerusalem three months and ten days. And he did evil in the sight of the LORD. ¹⁰At the turn of the year King Nebuchadnezzar summoned *him* and took him to Babylon, with the costly articles from the house of the LORD, and made Zedekiah, *Jehoiakim's*^a brother, king over Judah and Jerusalem.

ZEDEKIAH REIGNS IN JUDAH

¹¹Zedekiah *was* twenty-one years old when he became king, and he reigned eleven years in Jerusalem. ¹²He did evil in the sight of the LORD his God, *and* did not humble himself before Jere-

miah the prophet, *who spoke* from the mouth of the LORD. ¹³And he also rebelled against King Nebuchadnezzar, who had made him swear *an oath* by God; but he stiffened his neck and hardened his heart against turning to the LORD God of Israel. ¹⁴Moreover all the leaders of the priests and the people transgressed more and more, *according* to all the abominations of the nations, and defiled the house of the LORD which He had consecrated in Jerusalem.

THE FALL OF JERUSALEM

¹⁵And the LORD God of their fathers sent *warnings* to them by His messengers, rising up early and sending *them,* because He had compassion on His people and on His dwelling place. ¹⁶But they mocked the messengers of God, despised His words, and scoffed at His prophets, until the wrath of the LORD arose against His people, till *there was* no remedy.

¹⁷Therefore He brought against them the king of the Chaldeans, who killed their young men with the sword in the house of their sanctuary, and had no compassion on young man or virgin, on the aged or the weak; He gave *them* all into his hand. ¹⁸And all the articles from the house of God, great and small, the treasures of the house of the LORD, and the treasures of the king and of his leaders, all *these* he took to Babylon. ¹⁹Then they burned the house of God, broke down the wall of Jerusalem, burned all its palaces with fire, and destroyed all its precious possessions. ²⁰And those who escaped from the sword he carried away to Babylon, where they became servants to him and his sons until the rule of the kingdom of Persia, ²¹to fulfill the word of the LORD by the mouth of Jeremiah, until the land had enjoyed her Sabbaths. As long as she lay desolate she kept Sabbath, to fulfill seventy years.

THE PROCLAMATION OF CYRUS

²²Now in the first year of Cyrus king of Persia, that the word of the LORD by the mouth of Jeremiah might be fulfilled, the LORD stirred up the spirit of Cyrus king of Persia, so that he made

---

36:2 ^aMasoretic Text reads *Joahaz.* **36:4** ^aLiterally *his* ^bMasoretic Text reads *Joahaz.* **36:9** ^aSome Hebrew manuscripts, Septuagint, Syriac, and 2 Kings 24:8 read *eighteen.* **36:10** ^aLiterally *his* (compare 2 Kings 24:17)

a proclamation throughout all his kingdom, and also *put it* in writing, saying,

²³Thus says Cyrus king of Persia:
All the kingdoms of the earth the LORD

God of heaven has given me. And He has commanded me to build Him a house at Jerusalem which is in Judah. Who *is* among you of all His people? May the LORD his God *be* with him, and let him go up!

IMPACT OF THE BOOK

EZRA

IDEA | *God fulfills His promises. He is able to restore the rubble of a broken city or a broken relationship.*

MESSAGE | *Ezra reflects the significance of being faithful in difficult circumstances hundreds of miles from home in exile. He shows that doing small things well for many years may prepare you for prominent roles, and true change requires commitment. As God was restoring the Israelite nation and reestablishing their presence in Jerusalem, He used a passionate priest named Ezra, who was on-fire for God's Word and who was committed to hearing and doing what it said. God's Word brings conviction, and as a catalyst for change among God's people, Ezra courageously acted on that conviction. His courage was contagious as it strengthened the people.*

PEOPLE | *Artaxerxes, Cyrus, Darius, Ezra, Haggai, Zechariah, Zerubbabel*

AUTHOR | *The author of this book is not directly mentioned in the text, although Jewish tradition ascribes the book to Ezra. Some scholars have suggested that the same person, known as the "chronicler," wrote 1 and 2 Chronicles, Ezra, and Nehemiah. They base this on theological similarities in these books.*

CULTURE | *The Book of Ezra is a record of the events of the return of the Jewish people from exile and the restoration of the temple. Beginning in 605 BC, the Jewish people were taken from Jerusalem, the temple was destroyed, and the riches were plundered by King Nebuchadnezzar of Babylon (see Jer. 52:28–30). However, in 538 BC, when King Cyrus of Persia took over rule of Babylon, he allowed his subjects to resume worship of their own gods for political reasons, thus enabling the Jewish people to resume worship of the one, true God.*

TIMELINE | *Composed after 458 BC*

Y SCRIPTURE MORY VERSES | 1:3; 7:10

END OF THE BABYLONIAN CAPTIVITY

1 Now in the first year of Cyrus king of Persia, that the word of the LORD by the mouth of Jeremiah might be fulfilled, the LORD stirred up the spirit of Cyrus king of Persia, so that he made a proclamation throughout all his kingdom, and also *put it* in writing, saying,

> ²Thus says Cyrus king of Persia:
> All the kingdoms of the earth the LORD God of heaven has given me. And He has commanded me to build Him a house at Jerusalem which *is* in Judah. ³Who *is* among you of all His people? May his God be with him, and let him go up to Jerusalem which *is* in Judah, and build the house of the LORD God of Israel (He *is* God), which *is* in Jerusalem. ⁴And whoever is left in any place where he dwells, let the men of his place help him with silver and gold, with goods and livestock, besides the freewill offerings for the house of God which *is* in Jerusalem.

⁵Then the heads of the fathers' *houses* of Judah and Benjamin, and the priests and the Levites, with all whose spirits God had moved, arose to go up and build the house of the LORD which *is* in Jerusalem. ⁶And all those who *were* around them encouraged them with articles of silver and gold, with goods and livestock, and with precious things, besides all *that* was willingly offered.

⁷King Cyrus also brought out the articles of the house of the LORD, which Nebuchadnezzar had taken from Jerusalem and put in the temple of his gods; ⁸and Cyrus king of Persia brought them out by the hand of Mithredath the treasurer, and counted them out to Sheshbazzar the prince of Judah. ⁹This *is* the number of them: thirty gold platters, one thousand silver platters, twenty-nine knives, ¹⁰thirty gold basins, four hundred and ten silver basins of a similar *kind, and* one thousand other articles. ¹¹All the articles of gold and silver *were* five thousand four hundred. All *these* Sheshbazzar took with the captives who were brought from Babylon to Jerusalem.

THE CAPTIVES WHO RETURNED TO JERUSALEM

2 Now[a] these *are* the people of the province who came back from the captivity, of those who had been carried away, whom Nebuchadnezzar the king of Babylon had carried away to Babylon, and who returned to Jerusalem and Judah, everyone to his *own* city.

²*Those* who came with Zerubbabel *were* Jeshua, Nehemiah, Seraiah, Reelaiah, Mordecai, Bilshan, Mispar,[a] Bigvai, Rehum,[b] *and* Baanah. The number of the men of the people of Israel: ³the people of Parosh, two thousand one hundred and seventy-two; ⁴the people of Shephatiah, three hundred and seventy-two; ⁵the people of Arah, seven hundred and seventy-five; ⁶the people of Pahath-Moab, of the people of Jeshua *and* Joab, two thousand eight hundred and twelve; ⁷the people of Elam, one thousand two hundred and fifty-four; ⁸the people of Zattu, nine hundred and forty-five; ⁹the people of Zaccai, seven hundred and sixty; ¹⁰the people of Bani,[a] six hundred and forty-two; ¹¹the people of Bebai, six hundred and twenty-three; ¹²the people of Azgad, one thousand two hundred and twenty-two; ¹³the people of Adonikam, six hundred and sixty-six; ¹⁴the people of Bigvai, two thousand and fifty-six; ¹⁵the people of Adin, four hundred and fifty-four; ¹⁶the people of Ater of Hezekiah, ninety-eight; ¹⁷the people of Bezai, three hundred and twenty-three; ¹⁸the people of Jorah,[a] one hundred and twelve; ¹⁹the people of Hashum, two hundred and twenty-three; ²⁰the people of Gibbar,[a] ninety-five; ²¹the people of Bethlehem, one hundred and twenty-three; ²²the men of Netophah, fifty-six; ²³the men of Anathoth, one hundred and twenty-eight; ²⁴the people of Azmaveth,[a] forty-two; ²⁵the people of Kirjath Arim,[a] Chephirah, and Beeroth, seven hundred and forty-three; ²⁶the people of Ramah and Geba, six hundred and twenty-one; ²⁷the men of Michmas, one hundred and twenty-two; ²⁸the men of Bethel and Ai, two hundred and twenty-three; ²⁹the people of Nebo, fifty-two; ³⁰the people of Magbish, one hundred and fifty-

2:1 ªCompare this chapter with Nehemiah 7:6–73.   2:2 ªSpelle Mispereth in Nehemiah 7:7 ᵇSpelled Nehum in Nehemiah 7:   2:10 ªSpelled Binnui in Nehemiah 7:15   2:18 ªCalled Hariph in Ne hemiah 7:24   2:20 ªCalled Gibeon in Nehemiah 7:25   2:24 ªCalle Beth Azmaveth in Nehemiah 7:28   2:25 ªCalled Kirjath Jearim i Nehemiah 7:29

six; [31]the people of the other Elam, one thousand two hundred and fifty-four; [32]the people of Harim, three hundred and twenty; [33]the people of Lod, Hadid, and Ono, seven hundred and twenty-five; [34]the people of Jericho, three hundred and forty-five; [35]the people of Senaah, three thousand six hundred and thirty.

[36]The priests: the sons of Jedaiah, of the house of Jeshua, nine hundred and seventy-three; [37]the sons of Immer, one thousand and fifty-two; [38]the sons of Pashhur, one thousand two hundred and forty-seven; [39]the sons of Harim, one thousand and seventeen.

[40]The Levites: the sons of Jeshua and Kadmiel, of the sons of Hodaviah,[a] seventy-four.

[41]The singers: the sons of Asaph, one hundred and twenty-eight.

[42]The sons of the gatekeepers: the sons of Shallum, the sons of Ater, the sons of Talmon, the sons of Akkub, the sons of Hatita, and the sons of Shobai, one hundred and thirty-nine *in* all.

[43]The Nethinim: the sons of Ziha, the sons of Hasupha, the sons of Tabbaoth, [44]the sons of Keros, the sons of Siaha,[a] the sons of Padon, [45]the sons of Lebanah, the sons of Hagabah, the sons of Akkub, [46]the sons of Hagab, the sons of Shalmai, the sons of Hanan, [47]the sons of Giddel, the sons of Gahar, the sons of Reaiah, [48]the sons of Rezin, the sons of Nekoda, the sons of Gazzam, [49]the sons of Uzza, the sons of Paseah, the sons of Besai, [50]the sons of Asnah, the sons of Meunim, the sons of Nephusim,[a] [51]the sons of Bakbuk, the sons of Hakupha, the sons of Harhur, [52]the sons of Bazluth,[a] the sons of Mehida, the sons of Harsha, [53]the sons of Barkos, the sons of Sisera, the sons of Tamah, [54]the sons of Neziah, and the sons of Hatipha.

[55]The sons of Solomon's servants: the sons of Sotai, the sons of Sophereth, the sons of Peruda,[a] [56]the sons of Jaala, the sons of Darkon, the sons of Giddel, [57]the sons of Shephatiah, the sons of Hattil, the sons of Pochereth of Zebaim, and the sons of Ami.[a] [58]All the Nethinim and the children of Solomon's servants were three hundred and ninety-two.

[59]And these *were* the ones who came up from Tel Melah, Tel Harsha, Cherub, Addan,[a] and Immer; but they could not identify their father's house or their genealogy,[b] whether they *were* of Israel: [60]the sons of Delaiah, the sons of Tobiah, and the sons of Nekoda, six hundred and fifty-two; [61]and of the sons of the priests: the sons of Habaiah, the sons of Koz,[a] and the sons of Barzillai, who took a wife of the daughters of Barzillai the Gileadite, and was called by their name. [62]These sought their listing *among* those who were registered by genealogy, but they were not found; therefore they *were excluded* from the priesthood as defiled. [63]And the governor[a] said to them that they should not eat of the most holy things till a priest could consult with the Urim and Thummim.

[64]The whole assembly together *was* forty-two thousand three hundred *and* sixty, [65]besides their male and female servants, of whom *there were* seven thousand three hundred and thirty-seven; and they had two hundred men and women singers. [66]Their horses *were* seven hundred and thirty-six, their mules two hundred and forty-five, [67]their camels four hundred and thirty-five, and *their* donkeys six thousand seven hundred and twenty.

[68]*Some* of the heads of the fathers' *houses,* when they came to the house of the LORD which *is* in Jerusalem, offered freely for the house of God, to erect it in its place: [69]According to their ability, they gave to the treasury for the work sixty-one thousand gold drachmas, five thousand minas of silver, and one hundred priestly garments.

[70]So the priests and the Levites, *some* of the people, the singers, the gatekeepers, and the Nethinim, dwelt in their cities, and all Israel in their cities.

WORSHIP RESTORED AT JERUSALEM

3 And when the seventh month had come, and the children of Israel *were* in the cities, the people gathered together as one man to Jerusalem. [2]Then Jeshua the son of Jozadak[a] and his brethren the priests, and Zerubbabel the son of Shealtiel and his brethren, arose and built the altar of the God of Israel, to offer burnt offerings on it, as *it is* written in the Law of Moses the man of God.

2:40 [a]Spelled *Hodevah* in Nehemiah 7:43 **2:44** [a]Spelled *Sia* in Nehemiah 7:47 **2:50** [a]Spelled *Nephishesim* in Nehemiah 7:52 **2:52** [a]Spelled *Bazlith* in Nehemiah 7:54 **2:55** [a]Spelled *Perida* in Nehemiah 7:57 **2:57** [a]Spelled *Amon* in Nehemiah 7:59 **2:59** [a]Spelled *Addon* in Nehemiah 7:61 [b]Literally *seed* **2:61** [a]Or *Hakkoz* **2:63** [a]Hebrew *Tirshatha* **3:2** [a]Spelled *Jehozadak* in 1 Chronicles 6:14

³Though fear *had come* upon them because of the people of those countries, they set the altar on its bases; and they offered burnt offerings on it to the LORD, *both* the morning and evening burnt offerings. ⁴They also kept the Feast of Tabernacles, as *it is* written, and *offered* the daily burnt offerings in the number required by ordinance for each day. ⁵Afterwards *they offered* the regular burnt offering, and *those* for New Moons and for all the appointed feasts of the LORD that were consecrated, and *those* of everyone who willingly offered a freewill offering to the LORD. ⁶From the first day of the seventh month they began to offer burnt offerings to the LORD, although the foundation of the temple of the LORD had not been laid. ⁷They also gave money to the masons and the carpenters, and food, drink, and oil to the people of Sidon and Tyre to bring cedar logs from Lebanon to the sea, to Joppa, according to the permission which they had from Cyrus king of Persia.

RESTORATION OF THE TEMPLE BEGINS

⁸Now in the second month of the second year of their coming to the house of God at Jerusalem, Zerubbabel the son of Shealtiel, Jeshua the son of Jozadak,ᵃ and the rest of their brethren the priests and the Levites, and all those who had come out of the captivity to Jerusalem, began *work* and appointed the Levites from twenty years old and above to oversee the work of the house of the LORD. ⁹Then Jeshua *with* his sons and brothers, Kadmiel *with* his sons, and the sons of Judah,ᵃ arose as one to oversee those working on the house of God: the sons of Henadad *with* their sons and their brethren the Levites.

¹⁰When the builders laid the foundation of the temple of the LORD, the priests stoodᵃ in their apparel with trumpets, and the Levites, the sons of Asaph, with cymbals, to praise the LORD, according to the ordinance of David king of Israel. ¹¹And they sang responsively, praising and giving thanks to the LORD:

"For *He is* good,
For His mercy *endures* forever toward Israel."ᵃ

Then all the people shouted with a great shout, when they praised the LORD, because the foundation of the house of the LORD was laid.

¹²But many of the priests and Levites and heads of the fathers' *houses,* old men who had seen the first temple, wept with a loud voice when the foundation of this temple was laid before their eyes. Yet many shouted aloud for joy, ¹³so that the people could not discern the noise of the shout of joy from the noise of the weeping of the people, for the people shouted with a loud shout, and the sound was heard afar off.

RESISTANCE TO REBUILDING THE TEMPLE

4 Now when the adversaries of Judah and Benjamin heard that the descendants of the captivity were building the temple of the LORD God of Israel, ²they came to Zerubbabel and the heads of the fathers' *houses,* and said to them, "Let us build with you, for we seek your God as you *do;* and we have sacrificed to Him since the days of Esarhaddon king of Assyria, who brought us here." ³But Zerubbabel and Jeshua and the rest of the heads of the fathers' *houses* of Israel said to them, "You may do nothing with us to build a house for our God; but we alone will build to the LORD God of Israel, as King Cyrus the king of Persia has commanded us." ⁴Then the people of the land tried to discourage the people of Judah. They troubled them in building, ⁵and hired counselors against them to frustrate their purpose all the days of Cyrus king of Persia, even until the reign of Darius king of Persia.

REBUILDING OF JERUSALEM OPPOSED

⁶In the reign of Ahasuerus, in the beginning of his reign, they wrote an accusation against the inhabitants of Judah and Jerusalem.

⁷In the days of Artaxerxes also, Bishlam, Mithredath, Tabel, and the rest of their companions wrote to Artaxerxes king of Persia; and the letter *was* written in Aramaic script, and translated into the Aramaic language. ⁸Rehumᵃ the commander and Shimshai the scribe wrote a letter against Jerusalem to King Artaxerxes in this fashion:

⁹Fromᵃ Rehum the commander, Shimshai the scribe, and the rest of their

3:8 ᵃSpelled *Jehozadak* in 1 Chronicles 6:14   3:9 ᵃOr *Hodaviah* (compare 2:40)   3:10 ᵃFollowing Septuagint, Syriac, and Vulgate, Masoretic Text reads *they stationed the priests.*   3:11 ᵃCompare Psalm 136:1   4:8 ᵃThe original language of Ezra 4:8 through 6:18 is Aramaic.   4:9 ᵃLiterally *Then* companions—*representatives* of the Dinaites, the Apharsathchites, the Tarpelites, the people of Persia and Erech and Babylon and Shushan,[b] the Dehavites, the Elamites, [10]and the rest of the nations whom the great and noble Osnapper took captive and settled in the cities of Samaria and the remainder beyond the River[a]—and so forth.[b]

[11](This *is* a copy of the letter that they sent him)

To King Artaxerxes from your servants, the men *of the region* beyond the River, and so forth:[a]

[12]Let it be known to the king that the Jews who came up from you have come to us at Jerusalem, and are building the rebellious and evil city, and are finishing *its* walls and repairing the foundations. [13]Let it now be known to the king that, if this city is built and the walls completed, they will not pay tax, tribute, or custom, and the king's treasury will be diminished. [14]Now because we receive support from the palace, it was not proper for us to see the king's dishonor; therefore we have sent and informed the king, [15]that search may be made in the book of the records of your fathers. And you will find in the book of the records and know that this city *is* a rebellious city, harmful to kings and provinces, and that they have incited sedition within the city in former times, for which cause this city was destroyed.

[16]We inform the king that if this city is rebuilt and its walls are completed, the result will be that you will have no dominion beyond the River.

[17]The king sent an answer:

To Rehum the commander, *to* Shimshai the scribe, *to* the rest of their companions who dwell in Samaria, and *to* the remainder beyond the River:

Peace, and so forth.[a]

[18]The letter which you sent to us has been clearly read before me. [19]And I gave the command, and a search has been made, and it was found that this city in former times has revolted against kings, and rebellion and sedition have been fostered in it. [20]There have also been mighty kings over Jerusalem, who have ruled over all *the region* beyond the River; and tax, tribute, and custom were paid to them. [21]Now give the command to make these men cease, that this city may not be built until the command is given by me.

[22]Take heed now that you do not fail to do this. Why should damage increase to the hurt of the kings?

[23]Now when the copy of King Artaxerxes' letter *was* read before Rehum, Shimshai the scribe, and their companions, they went up in haste to Jerusalem against the Jews, and by force of arms made them cease. [24]Thus the work of the house of God which *is* at Jerusalem ceased, and it was discontinued until the second year of the reign of Darius king of Persia.

RESTORATION OF THE TEMPLE RESUMED

5 Then the prophet Haggai and Zechariah the son of Iddo, prophets, prophesied to the Jews who *were* in Judah and Jerusalem, in the name of the God of Israel, *who was* over them. [2]So Zerubbabel the son of Shealtiel and Jeshua the son of Jozadak[a] rose up and began to build the house of God which *is* in Jerusalem; and the prophets of God *were* with them, helping them.

[3]At the same time Tattenai the governor of *the region* beyond the River[a] and Shethar-Boznai and their companions came to them and spoke thus to them: "Who has commanded you to build this temple and finish this wall?" [4]Then, accordingly, we told them the names of the men who were constructing this building. [5]But the eye of their God was upon the elders of the Jews, so that they could not make them cease till a report could go

---

4:9 [b]Or *Susa*   4:10 [a]That is, the Euphrates   [b]Literally *and now*
4:11 [a]Literally *and now*   4:17 [a]Literally *and now*   5:2 [a]Spelled *Jehozadak* in 1 Chronicles 6:14   5:3 [a]That is, the Euphrates

to Darius. Then a written answer was returned concerning this *matter.* ⁶This is a copy of the letter that Tattenai sent:

> The governor of *the region* beyond the River, and Shethar-Boznai, and his companions, the Persians who *were in the region* beyond the River, to Darius the king.

⁷(They sent a letter to him, in which was written thus)

> To Darius the king:
>
> All peace.

⁸Let it be known to the king that we went into the province of Judea, to the temple of the great God, which is being built with heavy stones, and timber is being laid in the walls; and this work goes on diligently and prospers in their hands.

⁹Then we asked those elders, *and* spoke thus to them: "Who commanded you to build this temple and to finish these walls?" ¹⁰We also asked them their names to inform you, that we might write the names of the men who *were* chief among them.

¹¹And thus they returned us an answer, saying: "We are the servants of the God of heaven and earth, and we are rebuilding the temple that was built many years ago, which a great king of Israel built and completed. ¹²But because our fathers provoked the God of heaven to wrath, He gave them into the hand of Nebuchadnezzar king of Babylon, the Chaldean, *who* destroyed this temple and carried the people away to Babylon. ¹³However, in the first year of Cyrus king of Babylon, King Cyrus issued a decree to build this house of God. ¹⁴Also, the gold and silver articles of the house of God, which Nebuchadnezzar had taken from the temple that *was* in Jerusalem and carried into the temple of Babylon—those King

Cyrus took from the temple of Babylon, and they were given to one named Sheshbazzar, whom he had made governor. ¹⁵And he said to him, 'Take these articles; go, carry them to the temple *site* that *is* in Jerusalem, and let the house of God be rebuilt on its former site.' ¹⁶Then the same Sheshbazzar came *and* laid the foundation of the house of God which *is* in Jerusalem; but from that time even until now it has been under construction, and it is not finished."

¹⁷Now therefore, if *it seems* good to the king, let a search be made in the king's treasure house, which *is* there in Babylon, whether it is *so* that a decree was issued by King Cyrus to build this house of God at Jerusalem, and let the king send us his pleasure concerning this *matter.*

The Decree of Darius

6 Then King Darius issued a decree, and a search was made in the archives,ᵃ where the treasures were stored in Babylon. ²And at Achmetha,ᵃ in the palace that *is* in the province of Media, a scroll was found, and in it a record *was* written thus:

> ³In the first year of King Cyrus, King Cyrus issued a decree *concerning* the house of God at Jerusalem: "Let the house be rebuilt, the place where they offered sacrifices; and let the foundations of it be firmly laid, its height sixty cubits *and* its width sixty cubits, ⁴*with* three rows of heavy stones and one row of new timber. Let the expenses be paid from the king's treasury. ⁵Also let the gold and silver articles of the house of God, which Nebuchadnezzar took from the temple which *is* in Jerusalem and brought to Babylon, be restored and taken back to the temple which *is* in Jerusalem, *each* to its place; and deposit *them* in the house of God"—

⁶Now *therefore,* Tattenai, governor of *the region* beyond the River, and Shethar-

6:1 ᵃLiterally *house of the scrolls* **6:2** ᵃProbably *Ecbatana,* the ancient capital of Media

Boznai, and your companions the Persians who *are* beyond the River, keep yourselves far from there. [7]Let the work of this house of God alone; let the governor of the Jews and the elders of the Jews build this house of God on its site.

[8]Moreover I issue a decree *as to* what you shall do for the elders of these Jews, for the building of this house of God: Let the cost be paid at the king's expense from taxes *on the region* beyond the River; this is to be given immediately to these men, so that they are not hindered. [9]And whatever they need—young bulls, rams, and lambs for the burnt offerings of the God of heaven, wheat, salt, wine, and oil, according to the request of the priests who *are* in Jerusalem—let it be given them day by day without fail, [10]that they may offer sacrifices of sweet aroma to the God of heaven, and pray for the life of the king and his sons.

[11]Also I issue a decree that whoever alters this edict, let a timber be pulled from his house and erected, and let him be hanged on it; and let his house be made a refuse heap because of this. [12]And may the God who causes His name to dwell there destroy any king or people who put their hand to alter it, or to destroy this house of God which is in Jerusalem. I Darius issue a decree; let it be done diligently.

The Temple Completed and Dedicated

[13]Then Tattenai, governor of *the region* beyond the River, Shethar-Boznai, and their companions diligently did according to what King Darius had sent. [14]So the elders of the Jews built, and they prospered through the prophesying of Haggai the prophet and Zechariah the son of Iddo. And they built and finished *it,* according to the commandment of the God of Israel, and according to the command of Cyrus, Darius, and Artaxerxes king of Persia. [15]Now the temple was finished on the third day of the month of Adar, which was in the sixth year of the reign of King Darius. [16]Then the children of Israel, the priests and the Levites and the rest of the descendants of the captivity, celebrated the dedication of this house of God with joy. [17]And they offered sacrifices at the dedication of this house of God, one hundred bulls, two hundred rams, four hundred lambs, and as a sin offering for all Israel twelve male goats, according to the number of the tribes of Israel. [18]They assigned the priests to their divisions and the Levites to their divisions, over the service of God in Jerusalem, as it is written in the Book of Moses.

The Passover Celebrated

[19]And the descendants of the captivity kept the Passover on the fourteenth *day* of the first month. [20]For the priests and the Levites had purified themselves; all of them *were ritually* clean. And they slaughtered the Passover *lambs* for all the descendants of the captivity, for their brethren the priests, and for themselves. [21]Then the children of Israel who had returned from the captivity ate together with all who had separated themselves from the filth of the nations of the land in order to seek the LORD God of Israel. [22]And they kept the Feast of Unleavened Bread seven days with joy; for the LORD made them joyful, and turned the heart of the king of Assyria toward them, to strengthen their hands in the work of the house of God, the God of Israel.

The Arrival of Ezra

7 Now after these things, in the reign of Artaxerxes king of Persia, Ezra the son of Seraiah, the son of Azariah, the son of Hilkiah, [2]the son of Shallum, the son of Zadok, the son of Ahitub, [3]the son of Amariah, the son of Azariah, the son of Meraioth, [4]the son of Zerahiah, the son of Uzzi, the son of Bukki, [5]the son of Abishua, the son of Phinehas, the son of Eleazar, the son of Aaron the chief priest— [6]this Ezra came up from Babylon; and he *was* a skilled scribe in the Law of Moses, which the LORD God of Israel had given. The king granted him all his request, according to the hand of the LORD his God upon him. [7]*Some* of the children of Israel, the priests, the Levites, the singers, the gatekeepers, and the Nethinim came up to Jerusalem in the seventh year of King Artaxerxes. [8]And Ezra came to Jerusalem in the fifth month,

which *was* in the seventh year of the king. ⁹On the first *day* of the first month he began *his* journey from Babylon, and on the first *day* of the fifth month he came to Jerusalem, according to the good hand of his God upon him. ¹⁰For Ezra had prepared his heart to seek the Law of the LORD, and to do *it,* and to teach statutes and ordinances in Israel.

THE LETTER OF ARTAXERXES TO EZRA

¹¹This *is* a copy of the letter that King Artaxerxes gave Ezra the priest, the scribe, expert in the words of the commandments of the LORD, and of His statutes to Israel:

¹²Artaxerxes,ᵃ king of kings,

To Ezra the priest, a scribe of the Law of the God of heaven:

Perfect *peace,* and so forth.ᵇ

¹³I issue a decree that all those of the people of Israel and the priests and Levites in my realm, who volunteer to go up to Jerusalem, may go with you. ¹⁴And whereas you are being sent by the king and his seven counselors to inquire concerning Judah and Jerusalem, with regard to the Law of your God which *is* in your hand; ¹⁵and *whereas you are* to carry the silver and gold which the king and his counselors have freely offered to the God of Israel, whose dwelling *is* in Jerusalem; ¹⁶and *whereas* all the silver and gold that you may find in all the province of Babylon, along with the freewill offering of the people and the priests, *are to be* freely offered for the house of their God in Jerusalem— ¹⁷now therefore, be careful to buy with this money bulls, rams, and lambs, with their grain offerings and their drink offerings, and offer them on the altar of the house of your God in Jerusalem.

¹⁸And whatever seems good to you and your brethren to do with the rest of the silver and the gold, do it according to the will of your God. ¹⁹Also the articles that are given to you for the service of the house of your God, deliver in full before the God of Jerusalem. ²⁰And whatever more may be needed for the house of your God, which you may have occasion to provide, pay *for it* from the king's treasury.

²¹And I, *even* I, Artaxerxes the king, issue a decree to all the treasurers who *are in the region* beyond the River, that whatever Ezra the priest, the scribe of the Law of the God of heaven, may require of you, let it be done diligently, ²²up to one hundred talents of silver, one hundred kors of wheat, one hundred baths of wine, one hundred baths of oil, and salt without prescribed limit. ²³Whatever is commanded by the God of heaven, let it diligently be done for the house of the God of heaven. For why should there be wrath against the realm of the king and his sons?

²⁴Also we inform you that it shall not be lawful to impose tax, tribute, or custom on any of the priests, Levites, singers, gatekeepers, Nethinim, or servants of this house of God. ²⁵And you, Ezra, according to your God-given wisdom, set magistrates and judges who may judge all the people who *are in the region* beyond the River, all such as know the laws of your God; and teach those who do not know *them.* ²⁶Whoever will not observe the law of your God and the law of the king, let judgment be executed speedily on him, whether *it be* death, or banishment, or confiscation of goods, or imprisonment.

²⁷Blessed *be* the LORD God of our fathers, who has put *such a thing* as this in the king's heart, to beautify the house of the LORD which *is* in Jerusalem, ²⁸and has extended mercy to me before the king and his counselors, and before all the king's mighty princes.

So I was encouraged, as the hand of the LORD my God *was* upon me; and I gathered leading men of Israel to go up with me.

7:12 ᵃThe original language of Ezra 7:12–26 is Aramaic. ᵇLiterally *and now*

HEADS OF FAMILIES WHO RETURNED WITH EZRA

8 These *are* the heads of their fathers' *houses,* and *this is* the genealogy of those who went up with me from Babylon, in the reign of King Artaxerxes: ²of the sons of Phinehas, Gershom; of the sons of Ithamar, Daniel; of the sons of David, Hattush; ³of the sons of Shecaniah, of the sons of Parosh, Zechariah; and registered with him *were* one hundred and fifty males; ⁴of the sons of Pahath-Moab, Eliehoenai the son of Zerahiah, and with him two hundred males; ⁵of the sons of Shechaniah,ᵃ Ben-Jahaziel, and with him three hundred males; ⁶of the sons of Adin, Ebed the son of Jonathan, and with him fifty males; ⁷of the sons of Elam, Jeshaiah the son of Athaliah, and with him seventy males; ⁸of the sons of Shephatiah, Zebadiah the son of Michael, and with him eighty males; ⁹of the sons of Joab, Obadiah the son of Jehiel, and with him two hundred and eighteen males; ¹⁰of the sons of Shelomith,ᵃ Ben-Josiphiah, and with him one hundred and sixty males; ¹¹of the sons of Bebai, Zechariah the son of Bebai, and with him twenty-eight males; ¹²of the sons of Azgad, Johanan the son of Hakkatan, and with him one hundred and ten males; ¹³of the last sons of Adonikam, whose names *are* these—Eliphelet, Jeiel, and Shemaiah—and with them sixty males; ¹⁴also of the sons of Bigvai, Uthai and Zabbud, and with them seventy males.

SERVANTS FOR THE TEMPLE

¹⁵Now I gathered them by the river that flows to Ahava, and we camped there three days. And I looked among the people and the priests, and found none of the sons of Levi there. ¹⁶Then I sent for Eliezer, Ariel, Shemaiah, Elnathan, Jarib, Elnathan, Nathan, Zechariah, and Meshullam, leaders; also for Joiarib and Elnathan, men of understanding. ¹⁷And I gave them a command for Iddo the chief man at the place Casiphia, and I told them what they should say to Iddo *and* his brethrenᵃ the Nethinim at the place Casiphia— that they should bring us servants for the house of our God. ¹⁸Then, by the good hand of our God upon us, they brought us a man of understanding, of the sons of Mahli the son of Levi, the son of Israel, namely Sherebiah, with his sons and brothers, eighteen men; ¹⁹and Hashabiah, and with him

Jeshaiah of the sons of Merari, his brothers and their sons, twenty men; ²⁰also of the Nethinim, whom David and the leaders had appointed for the service of the Levites, two hundred and twenty Nethinim. All of them were designated by name.

FASTING AND PRAYER FOR PROTECTION

²¹Then I proclaimed a fast there at the river of Ahava, that we might humble ourselves before our God, to seek from Him the right way for us and our little ones and all our possessions. ²²For I was ashamed to request of the king an escort of soldiers and horsemen to help us against the enemy on the road, because we had spoken to the king, saying, "The hand of our God *is* upon all those for good who seek Him, but His power and His wrath *are* against all those who forsake Him." ²³So we fasted and entreated our God for this, and He answered our prayer.

GIFTS FOR THE TEMPLE

²⁴And I separated twelve of the leaders of the priests—Sherebiah, Hashabiah, and ten of their brethren with them— ²⁵and weighed out to them the silver, the gold, and the articles, the offering for the house of our God which the king and his counselors and his princes, and all Israel *who were* present, had offered. ²⁶I weighed into their hand six hundred and fifty talents of silver, silver articles *weighing* one hundred talents, one hundred talents of gold, ²⁷twenty gold basins *worth* a thousand drachmas, and two vessels of fine polished bronze, precious as gold. ²⁸And I said to them, "You *are* holy to the LORD; the articles *are* holy also; and the silver and the gold *are* a freewill offering to the LORD God of your fathers. ²⁹Watch and keep *them* until you weigh *them* before the leaders of the priests and the Levites and heads of the fathers' *houses* of Israel in Jerusalem, *in* the chambers of the house of the LORD." ³⁰So the priests and the Levites received the silver and the gold and the articles by weight, to bring *them* to Jerusalem to the house of our God.

8:5 ᵃFollowing Masoretic Text and Vulgate; Septuagint reads *the sons of Zatho, Shechaniah.* **8:10** ᵃFollowing Masoretic Text and Vulgate; Septuagint reads *the sons of Banni, Shelomith.* **8:17** ᵃFollowing Vulgate; Masoretic Text reads *to Iddo his brother;* Septuagint reads *to their brethren.*

The Return to Jerusalem

³¹Then we departed from the river of Ahava on the twelfth *day* of the first month, to go to Jerusalem. And the hand of our God was upon us, and He delivered us from the hand of the enemy and from ambush along the road. ³²So we came to Jerusalem, and stayed there three days.

³³Now on the fourth day the silver and the gold and the articles were weighed in the house of our God by the hand of Meremoth the son of Uriah the priest, and with him *was* Eleazar the son of Phinehas; with them *were* the Levites, Jozabad the son of Jeshua and Noadiah the son of Binnui, ³⁴with the number *and* weight of everything. All the weight was written down at that time.

³⁵The children of those who had been carried away captive, who had come from the captivity, offered burnt offerings to the God of Israel: twelve bulls for all Israel, ninety-six rams, seventy-seven lambs, and twelve male goats *as* a sin offering. All *this was* a burnt offering to the LORD.

³⁶And they delivered the king's orders to the king's satraps and the governors *in the region* beyond the River. So they gave support to the people and the house of God.

Intermarriage with Pagans

9 When these things were done, the leaders came to me, saying, "The people of Israel and the priests and the Levites have not separated themselves from the peoples of the lands, with respect to the abominations of the Canaanites, the Hittites, the Perizzites, the Jebusites, the Ammonites, the Moabites, the Egyptians, and the Amorites. ²For they have taken some of their daughters *as wives* for themselves and their sons, so that the holy seed is mixed with the peoples of *those* lands. Indeed, the hand of the leaders and rulers has been foremost in this trespass." ³So when I heard this thing, I tore my garment and my robe, and plucked out some of the hair of my head and beard, and sat down astonished. ⁴Then everyone who trembled at the words of the God of Israel assembled to me, because of the transgression of those who had been carried away captive, and I sat astonished until the evening sacrifice.

⁵At the evening sacrifice I arose from my fasting; and having torn my garment and my robe, I fell on my knees and spread out my hands to the LORD my God. ⁶And I said: "O my God, I am too ashamed and humiliated to lift up my face to You, my God; for our iniquities have risen higher than *our* heads, and our guilt has grown up to the heavens. ⁷Since the days of our fathers to this day we *have been* very guilty, and for our iniquities we, our kings, *and* our priests have been delivered into the hand of the kings of the lands, to the sword, to captivity, to plunder, and to humiliation, as *it is* this day. ⁸And now for a little while grace has been *shown* from the LORD our God, to leave us a remnant to escape, and to give us a peg in His holy place, that our God may enlighten our eyes and give us a measure of revival in our bondage. ⁹For we *were* slaves. Yet our God did not forsake us in our bondage; but He extended mercy to us in the sight of the kings of Persia, to revive us, to repair the house of our God, to rebuild its ruins, and to give us a wall in Judah and Jerusalem. ¹⁰And now, O our God, what shall we say after this? For we have forsaken Your commandments, ¹¹which You commanded by Your servants the prophets, saying, 'The land which you are entering to possess is an unclean land, with the uncleanness of the peoples of the lands, with their abominations which have filled it from one end to another with their impurity. ¹²Now therefore, do not give your daughters as wives for their sons, nor take their daughters to your sons; and never seek their peace or prosperity, that you may be strong and eat the good of the land, and leave *it* as an inheritance to your children forever.' ¹³And after all that has come upon us for our evil deeds and for our great guilt, since You our God have punished us less than our iniquities *deserve,* and have given us *such* deliverance as this, ¹⁴should we again break Your commandments, and join in marriage with the people *committing* these abominations? Would You not be angry with us until You had consumed *us,* so that *there would be* no remnant or survivor? ¹⁵O LORD God of Israel, You *are* righteous, for we are left as a remnant, as *it is* this day. Here we *are* before You, in our guilt, though no one can stand before You because of this!"

Confession of Improper Marriages

10 Now while Ezra was praying, and while he was confessing, weeping, and bowing down before the house of God, a very large assembly of

Inside the INFLUENCERS

EZRA: Scholar and Catalyst

EZRA 9, 10

Ezra was a priest in a time when the Jewish people were in captivity. He led the second group of exiles back to their homeland as Nehemiah had done before him when he reconstructed the wall. Scripture records that Ezra "devoted himself to the study and observance of the Law of the LORD and to teaching its decrees and laws in Israel" (7:10). Ezra was a biblical scholar who was addicted to the Words of Scripture. He feasted on God's Word, and this led to a greater and deeper relationship with the Author of Scripture, God Himself.

Perhaps the study of God's Word is what allowed him to become a catalyst for change. When Ezra arrived in Jerusalem with the group of exiles, he learned that even while the people were rebuilding the great wall they were being unfaithful in their relationship with God. They intermarried with people who worshiped other gods, and, as a result, their convictions became diluted. Ezra was so brokenhearted that he cried out to God (ch. 9). His genuine fervor and repentant heart was talked about throughout Jerusalem and became so contagious (10:1) that revival broke out among the people. God used the example of this great leader to draw His people back into a right relationship with Himself.

men, women, and children gathered to him from Israel; for the people wept very bitterly. ²And Shechaniah the son of Jehiel, *one* of the sons of Elam, spoke up and said to Ezra, "We have trespassed against our God, and have taken pagan wives from the peoples of the land; yet now there is hope in Israel in spite of this. ³Now therefore, let us make a covenant with our God to put away all these wives and those who have been born to them, according to the advice of my master and of those who tremble at the commandment of our God; and let it be done according to the law. ⁴Arise, for *this* matter *is* your *responsibility.* We also *are* with you. Be of good courage, and do *it.*"

⁵Then Ezra arose, and made the leaders of the priests, the Levites, and all Israel swear an oath that they would do according to this word. So they swore an oath. ⁶Then Ezra rose up from before the house of God, and went into the chamber of Jehohanan the son of Eliashib; and *when* he came there, he ate no bread and drank no water, for he mourned because of the guilt of those from the captivity.

⁷And they issued a proclamation throughout Judah and Jerusalem to all the descendants of the captivity, that they must gather at Jerusalem, ⁸and

that whoever would not come within three days, according to the instructions of the leaders and elders, all his property would be confiscated, and he himself would be separated from the assembly of those from the captivity.

⁹So all the men of Judah and Benjamin gathered at Jerusalem within three days. It *was* the ninth month, on the twentieth of the month; and all the people sat in the open square of the house of God, trembling because of *this* matter and because of heavy rain. ¹⁰Then Ezra the priest stood up and said to them, "You have transgressed and have taken pagan wives, adding to the guilt of Israel. ¹¹Now therefore, make confession to the LORD God of your fathers, and do His will; separate yourselves from the peoples of the land, and from the pagan wives."

¹²Then all the assembly answered and said with a loud voice, "Yes! As you have said, so we must do. ¹³But *there are* many people; *it is* the season for heavy rain, and we are not able to stand outside. Nor *is this* the work of one or two days, for *there are* many of us who have transgressed in this matter. ¹⁴Please, let the leaders of our entire assembly stand; and let all those in our cities who have taken pagan wives come at appointed times,

together with the elders and judges of their cities, until the fierce wrath of our God is turned away from us in this matter." [15]Only Jonathan the son of Asahel and Jahaziah the son of Tikvah opposed this, and Meshullam and Shabbethai the Levite gave them support.

[16]Then the descendants of the captivity did so. And Ezra the priest, *with* certain heads of the fathers' *households,* were set apart by the fathers' households, each of them by name; and they sat down on the first day of the tenth month to examine the matter. [17]By the first day of the first month they finished *questioning* all the men who had taken pagan wives.

Pagan Wives Put Away

[18]And among the sons of the priests who had taken pagan wives *the following* were found of the sons of Jeshua the son of Jozadak,[a] and his brothers: Maaseiah, Eliezer, Jarib, and Gedaliah. [19]And they gave their promise that they would put away their wives; and *being* guilty, *they presented* a ram of the flock as their trespass offering.

[20]Also of the sons of Immer: Hanani and Zebadiah; [21]of the sons of Harim: Maaseiah, Elijah, Shemaiah, Jehiel, and Uzziah; [22]of the sons of Pashhur: Elioenai, Maaseiah, Ishmael, Nethanel, Jozabad, and Elasah.

[23]Also of the Levites: Jozabad, Shimei, Kelaiah (the same *is* Kelita), Pethahiah, Judah, and Eliezer.

[24]Also of the singers: Eliashib; and of the gatekeepers: Shallum, Telem, and Uri.

[25]And others of Israel: of the sons of Parosh: Ramiah, Jeziah, Malchiah, Mijamin, Eleazar, Malchijah, and Benaiah; [26]of the sons of Elam: Mattaniah, Zechariah, Jehiel, Abdi, Jeremoth, and Eliah; [27]of the sons of Zattu: Elioenai, Eliashib, Mattaniah, Jeremoth, Zabad, and Aziza; [28]of the sons of Bebai: Jehohanan, Hananiah, Zabbai, *and* Athlai; [29]of the sons of Bani: Meshullam, Malluch, Adaiah, Jashub, Sheal, *and* Ramoth;[a] [30]of the sons of Pahath-Moab: Adna, Chelal, Benaiah, Maaseiah, Mattaniah, Bezalel, Binnui, and Manasseh; [31]*of* the sons of Harim: Eliezer, Ishijah, Malchijah, Shemaiah, Shimeon, [32]Benjamin, Malluch, *and* Shemariah; [33]of the sons of Hashum: Mattenai, Mattattah, Zabad, Eliphelet, Jeremai, Manasseh, *and* Shimei; [34]of the sons of Bani: Maadai, Amram, Uel, [35]Benaiah, Bedeiah, Cheluh,[a] [36]Vaniah, Meremoth, Eliashib, [37]Mattaniah, Mattenai, Jaasai,[a] [38]Bani, Binnui, Shimei, [39]Shelemiah, Nathan, Adaiah, [40]Machnadebai, Shashai, Sharai, [41]Azarel, Shelemiah, Shemariah, [42]Shallum, Amariah, *and* Joseph; [43]of the sons of Nebo: Jeiel, Mattithiah, Zabad, Zebina, Jaddai,[a] Joel, *and* Benaiah.

[44]All these had taken pagan wives, and *some* of them had wives *by whom* they had children.

10:18 aSpelled *Jehozadak* in 1 Chronicles 6:14   10:29 aOr *Jeremoth*
10:35 aOr *Cheluhi,* or *Cheluhu*   10:37 aOr *Jaasu*   10:43 aOr *Jaddu*

IMPACT OF THE BOOK

NEHEMIAH

IDEA   *God uses ordinary people to accomplish extraordinary tasks, one brick at a time. Nehemiah saw a need, prayed earnestly, felt deeply, and then envisioned what God wanted.*

MESSAGE   *Put people first and the project second. Nehemiah inquired about his countrymen in his homeland. After hearing of their condition—that the Lord's name was mocked and the walls were broken down—he wept, prayed, and enlisted the help of others. He proved that every task is a divine appointment. His trusted reputation as cupbearer to the king gave him the ability to influence from a strategic position. He was able to motivate, unite, and inspire—as only a truly gifted leader can. He united a nation to accomplish one of the greatest tasks in the Bible.*

PEOPLE   *Artaxerxes, Ezra, Geshem, Nehemiah, Sanballat, Tobiah*

AUTHOR   *The author is unnamed, but the similarities in Ezra, Nehemiah, and 1 and 2 Chronicles lead people to believe that they were compiled by Ezra or even the anonymous writer known as the "chronicler."*

CULTURE   *The Book of Nehemiah records the rebuilding of the walls around Jerusalem up to Nehemiah's second term as governor (c. 446 – 430 BC). The first of three exile groups returned in 538 BC under the leadership of Zerubbabel; the second group returned in 458 BC, led by Ezra. The final group returned in 445 BC, led by Nehemiah. The temple had been completed in 516 BC, but the walls around Jerusalem were in shambles. Nehemiah's group built the wall. Nehemiah's efforts restored the walls and helped preserve and challenge the spiritual condition of the people. This is the last recorded history of Israel before the intertestamental period.*

TIMELINE   *c. 430–424 BC*

KEY SCRIPTURE MEMORY VERSES   2:20; 6:15, 16; 8:3, 8

Nehemiah Prays for His People

1 The words of Nehemiah the son of Hachaliah.
It came to pass in the month of Chislev, *in* the twentieth year, as I was in Shushan[a] the citadel, [2]that Hanani one of my brethren came with men from Judah; and I asked them concerning the Jews who had escaped, who had survived the captivity, and concerning Jerusalem. [3]And they said to me, "The survivors who are left from the captivity in the province *are* there in great distress and reproach. The wall of Jerusalem *is* also broken down, and its gates are burned with fire."

[4]So it was, when I heard these words, that I sat down and wept, and mourned *for many* days; I was fasting and praying before the God of heaven.

[5]And I said: "I pray, LORD God of heaven, O great and awesome God, *You* who keep *Your* covenant and mercy with those who love You[a] and observe Your[b] commandments, [6]please let Your ear be attentive and Your eyes open, that You may hear the prayer of Your servant which I pray before You now, day and night, for the children of Israel Your servants, and confess the sins of the children of Israel which we have sinned against You. Both my father's house and I have sinned. [7]We have acted very corruptly against You, and have not kept the commandments, the statutes, nor the ordinances which You commanded Your servant Moses. [8]Remember, I pray, the word that You commanded Your servant Moses, saying, '*If* you are unfaithful, I will scatter you among the nations;[a] [9]but *if* you return to Me, and keep My commandments and do them, though some of you were cast out to the farthest part of the heavens, *yet* I will gather them from there, and bring them to the place which I have chosen as a dwelling for My name.'[a] [10]Now these *are* Your servants and Your people, whom You have redeemed by Your great power, and by Your strong hand. [11]O Lord, I pray, please let Your ear be attentive to the prayer of Your servant, and to the prayer of Your servants who desire to fear Your name; and let Your servant prosper this day, I pray, and grant him mercy in the sight of this man."

For I was the king's cupbearer.

Nehemiah Sent to Judah

2 And it came to pass in the month of Nisan, in the twentieth year of King Artaxerxes, *when* wine *was* before him, that I took the wine and gave it to the king. Now I had never been sad in his presence before. [2]Therefore the king said to me, "Why *is* your face sad, since you *are* not sick? This *is* nothing but sorrow of heart."

So I became dreadfully afraid, [3]and said to the king, "May the king live forever! Why should my face not be sad, when the city, the place of my fathers' tombs, *lies* waste, and its gates are burned with fire?"

[4]Then the king said to me, "What do you request?"

So I prayed to the God of heaven. [5]And I said to the king, "If it pleases the king, and if your servant has found favor in your sight, I ask that you send me to Judah, to the city of my fathers' tombs, that I may rebuild it."

[6]Then the king said to me (the queen also sitting beside him), "How long will your journey be? And when will you return?" So it pleased the king to send me; and I set him a time.

[7]Furthermore I said to the king, "If it pleases the king, let letters be given to me for the governors *of the region* beyond the River,[a] that they must permit me to pass through till I come to Judah, [8]and a letter to Asaph the keeper of the king's forest, that he must give me timber to make beams for the gates of the citadel which *pertains* to the temple,[a] for the city wall, and for the house that I will occupy." And the king granted *them* to me according to the good hand of my God upon me.

[9]Then I went to the governors *in the region* beyond the River, and gave them the king's letters. Now the king had sent captains of the army and horsemen with me. [10]When Sanballat the Horonite and Tobiah the Ammonite official[a] heard *of it,* they were deeply disturbed that a man had come to seek the well-being of the children of Israel.

Nehemiah Views the Wall of Jerusalem

[11]So I came to Jerusalem and was there three days. [12]Then I arose in the night, I and a few men

1:1 [a]Or *Susa*   **1:5** [a]Literally *Him* [b]Literally *His*   **1:8** [a]Leviticus 26:33   **1:9** [a]Deuteronomy 30:2–5   **2:7** [a]That is, the Euphrates, and so elsewhere in this book   **2:8** [a]Literally *house*   **2:10** [a]Literally *servant,* and so elsewhere in this book with me; I told no one what my God had put in my heart to do at Jerusalem; nor was there any animal with me, except the one on which I rode. ¹³And I went out by night through the Valley Gate to the Serpent Well and the Refuse Gate, and viewed the walls of Jerusalem which were broken down and its gates which were burned with fire. ¹⁴Then I went on to the Fountain Gate and to the King's Pool, but *there was* no room for the animal under me to pass. ¹⁵So I went up in the night by the valley, and viewed the wall; then I turned back and entered by the Valley Gate, and so returned. ¹⁶And the officials did not know where I had gone or what I had done; I had not yet told the Jews, the priests, the nobles, the officials, or the others who did the work.

¹⁷Then I said to them, "You see the distress that we *are* in, how Jerusalem *lies* waste, and its gates are burned with fire. Come and let us build the wall of Jerusalem, that we may no longer be a reproach." ¹⁸And I told them of the hand of my God which had been good upon me, and also of the king's words that he had spoken to me.

So they said, "Let us rise up and build." Then they set their hands to *this* good *work*.

¹⁹But when Sanballat the Horonite, Tobiah the Ammonite official, and Geshem the Arab heard *of it,* they laughed at us and despised us, and said, "What *is* this thing that you are doing? Will you rebel against the king?"

²⁰So I answered them, and said to them, "The God of heaven Himself will prosper us; therefore we His servants will arise and build, but you have no heritage or right or memorial in Jerusalem."

Rebuilding the Wall

3 Then Eliashib the high priest rose up with his brethren the priests and built the Sheep Gate; they consecrated it and hung its doors. They built as far as the Tower of the Hundred,ᵃ *and* consecrated it, then as far as the Tower of Hananel. ²Next to *Eliashib*ᵃ the men of Jericho built. And next to them Zaccur the son of Imri built.

³Also the sons of Hassenaah built the Fish Gate; they laid its beams and hung its doors with its bolts and bars. ⁴And next to them Meremoth the son of Urijah, the son of Koz,ᵃ made repairs. Next to them Meshullam the son of Berechiah, the son of Meshezabel, made repairs. Next to

them Zadok the son of Baana made repairs. ⁵Next to them the Tekoites made repairs; but their nobles did not put their shouldersᵃ to the work of their Lord.

⁶Moreover Jehoiada the son of Paseah and Meshullam the son of Besodeiah repaired the Old Gate; they laid its beams and hung its doors, with its bolts and bars. ⁷And next to them Melatiah the Gibeonite, Jadon the Meronothite, the men of Gibeon and Mizpah, repaired the residenceᵃ of the governor *of the region* beyond the River. ⁸Next to him Uzziel the son of Harhaiah, one of the goldsmiths, made repairs. Also next to him Hananiah, oneᵃ of the perfumers, made repairs; and they fortified Jerusalem as far as the Broad Wall. ⁹And next to them Rephaiah the son of Hur, leader of half the district of Jerusalem, made repairs. ¹⁰Next to them Jedaiah the son of Harumaph made repairs in front of his house. And next to him Hattush the son of Hashabniah made repairs.

¹¹Malchijah the son of Harim and Hashub the son of Pahath-Moab repaired another section, as well as the Tower of the Ovens. ¹²And next to him was Shallum the son of Hallohesh, leader of half the district of Jerusalem; he and his daughters made repairs.

¹³Hanun and the inhabitants of Zanoah repaired the Valley Gate. They built it, hung its doors with its bolts and bars, and *repaired* a thousand cubits of the wall as far as the Refuse Gate.

¹⁴Malchijah the son of Rechab, leader of the district of Beth Haccerem, repaired the Refuse Gate; he built it and hung its doors with its bolts and bars.

¹⁵Shallun the son of Col-Hozeh, leader of the district of Mizpah, repaired the Fountain Gate; he built it, covered it, hung its doors with its bolts and bars, and repaired the wall of the Pool of Shelah by the King's Garden, as far as the stairs that go down from the City of David. ¹⁶After him Nehemiah the son of Azbuk, leader of half the district of Beth Zur, made repairs as far as *the place* in front of the tombsᵃ of David, to the man-made pool, and as far as the House of the Mighty.

¹⁷After him the Levites, *under* Rehum the son

3:1 ᵃHebrew *Hammeah,* also at 12:39   **3:2** ᵃLiterally *On his hand*   **3:4** ᵃOr *Hakkoz*   **3:5** ᵃLiterally *necks*   **3:7** ᵃLiterally *throne*   **3:8** ᵃLiterally *the son*   **3:16** ᵃSeptuagint, Syriac, and Vulgate read *tomb.*

of Bani, made repairs. Next to him Hashabiah, leader of half the district of Keilah, made repairs for his district. [18]After him their brethren, *under* Bavai[a] the son of Henadad, leader of the *other* half of the district of Keilah, made repairs. [19]And next to him Ezer the son of Jeshua, the leader of Mizpah, repaired another section from the Ascent to the Armory at the buttress. [20]After him Baruch the son of Zabbai[a] carefully repaired the other section, from the buttress to the door of the house of Eliashib the high priest. [21]After him Meremoth the son of Urijah, the son of Koz,[a] repaired another section, from the door of the house of Eliashib to the end of the house of Eliashib.

[22]And after him the priests, the men of the plain, made repairs. [23]After him Benjamin and Hasshub made repairs opposite their house. After them Azariah the son of Maaseiah, the son of Ananiah, made repairs by his house. [24]After him Binnui the son of Henadad repaired another section, from the house of Azariah to the buttress, even as far as the corner. [25]Palal the son of Uzai *made repairs* opposite the buttress, and on the tower which projects from the king's upper house that *was* by the court of the prison. After him Pedaiah the son of Parosh *made repairs.*

[26]Moreover the Nethinim who dwelt in Ophel *made repairs* as far as *the place* in front of the Water Gate toward the east, and on the projecting tower. [27]After them the Tekoites repaired another section, next to the great projecting tower, and as far as the wall of Ophel.

[28]Beyond the Horse Gate the priests made repairs, each in front of his *own* house. [29]After them Zadok the son of Immer made repairs in front of his *own* house. After him Shemaiah the son of Shechaniah, the keeper of the East Gate, made repairs. [30]After him Hananiah the son of Shelemiah, and Hanun, the sixth son of Zalaph, repaired another section. After him Meshullam the son of Berechiah made repairs in front of his dwelling. [31]After him Malchijah, one of the goldsmiths, made repairs as far as the house of the Nethinim and of the merchants, in front of the Miphkad[a] Gate, and as far as the upper room at the corner. [32]And between the upper room at the corner, as far as the Sheep Gate, the goldsmiths and the merchants made repairs.

THE WALL DEFENDED AGAINST ENEMIES

4 But it so happened, when Sanballat heard that we were rebuilding the wall, that he was furious and very indignant, and mocked the Jews. [2]And he spoke before his brethren and the army of Samaria, and said, "What are these feeble Jews doing? Will they fortify themselves? Will they offer sacrifices? Will they complete it in a day? Will they revive the stones from the heaps of rubbish—*stones* that are burned?"

[3]Now Tobiah the Ammonite *was* beside him, and he said, "Whatever they build, if even a fox goes up *on it,* he will break down their stone wall."

[4]Hear, O our God, for we are despised; turn their reproach on their own heads, and give them as plunder to a land of captivity! [5]Do not cover their iniquity, and do not let their sin be blotted out from before You; for they have provoked *You* to anger before the builders.

[6]So we built the wall, and the entire wall was joined together up to half its *height,* for the people had a mind to work.

[7]Now it happened, when Sanballat, Tobiah, the Arabs, the Ammonites, and the Ashdodites heard that the walls of Jerusalem were being restored and the gaps were beginning to be closed, that they became very angry, [8]and all of them conspired together to come *and* attack Jerusalem and create confusion. [9]Nevertheless we made our prayer to our God, and because of them we set a watch against them day and night.

[10]Then Judah said, "The strength of the laborers is failing, and *there is* so much rubbish that we are not able to build the wall."

[11]And our adversaries said, "They will neither know nor see anything, till we come into their midst and kill them and cause the work to cease."

[12]So it was, when the Jews who dwelt near them came, that they told us ten times, "From whatever place you turn, *they will be* upon us."

[13]Therefore I positioned *men* behind the lower parts of the wall, at the openings; and I set the people according to their families, with their swords, their spears, and their bows. [14]And I

3:18 [a]Following Masoretic Text and Vulgate; some Hebrew manuscripts, Septuagint, and Syriac read *Binnui* (compare verse 24). **3:20** [a]A few Hebrew manuscripts, Syriac, and Vulgate read *Zaccai.* **3:21** [a]Or *Hakkoz* **3:31** [a]Literally *Inspection* or *Recruiting*

looked, and arose and said to the nobles, to the leaders, and to the rest of the people, "Do not be afraid of them. Remember the Lord, great and awesome, and fight for your brethren, your sons, your daughters, your wives, and your houses."

[15]And it happened, when our enemies heard that it was known to us, and *that* God had brought their plot to nothing, that all of us returned to the wall, everyone to his work. [16]So it was, from that time on, *that* half of my servants worked at construction, while the other half held the spears, the shields, the bows, and *wore* armor; and the leaders *were* behind all the house of Judah. [17]Those who built on the wall, and those who carried burdens, loaded themselves so that with one hand they worked at construction, and with the other held a weapon. [18]Every one of the builders had his sword girded at his side as he built. And the one who sounded the trumpet *was* beside me.

[19]Then I said to the nobles, the rulers, and the rest of the people, "The work *is* great and extensive, and we are separated far from one another on the wall. [20]Wherever you hear the sound of the trumpet, rally to us there. Our God will fight for us."

[21]So we labored in the work, and half of *the men*[a] held the spears from daybreak until the stars appeared. [22]At the same time I also said to the people, "Let each man and his servant stay at night in Jerusalem, that they may be our guard by night and a working party by day." [23]So neither I, my brethren, my servants, nor the men of the guard who followed me took off our clothes, *except* that everyone took them off for washing.

NEHEMIAH DEALS WITH OPPRESSION

5 And there was a great outcry of the people and their wives against their Jewish brethren. [2]For there were those who said, "We, our sons, and our daughters *are* many; therefore let us get grain, that we may eat and live."

[3]There were also *some* who said, "We have mortgaged our lands and vineyards and houses, that we might buy grain because of the famine."

[4]There were also those who said, "We have borrowed money for the king's tax *on* our lands and vineyards. [5]Yet now our flesh *is* as the flesh of our brethren, our children as their children; and

indeed we are forcing our sons and our daughters to be slaves, and *some* of our daughters have been brought into slavery. *It is* not in our power *to redeem them,* for other men have our lands and vineyards."

[6]And I became very angry when I heard their outcry and these words. [7]After serious thought, I rebuked the nobles and rulers, and said to them, "Each of you is exacting usury from his brother." So I called a great assembly against them. [8]And I said to them, "According to our ability we have redeemed our Jewish brethren who were sold to the nations. Now indeed, will you even sell your brethren? Or should they be sold to us?"

Then they were silenced and found nothing *to say.* [9]Then I said, "What you are doing *is* not good. Should you not walk in the fear of our God because of the reproach of the nations, our enemies? [10]I also, *with* my brethren and my servants, am lending them money and grain. Please, let us stop this usury! [11]Restore now to them, even this day, their lands, their vineyards, their olive groves, and their houses, also a hundredth of the money and the grain, the new wine and the oil, that you have charged them."

[12]So they said, "We will restore *it,* and will require nothing from them; we will do as you say."

Then I called the priests, and required an oath from them that they would do according to this promise. [13]Then I shook out the fold of my garment[a] and said, "So may God shake out each man from his house, and from his property, who does not perform this promise. Even thus may he be shaken out and emptied."

And all the assembly said, "Amen!" and praised the LORD. Then the people did according to this promise.

THE GENEROSITY OF NEHEMIAH

[14]Moreover, from the time that I was appointed to be their governor in the land of Judah, from the twentieth year until the thirty-second year of King Artaxerxes, twelve years, neither I nor my brothers ate the governor's provisions. [15]But the former governors who *were* before me laid burdens on the people, and took from them bread and wine, besides forty shekels of silver. Yes,

4:21 [a]Literally *them*   5:13 [a]Literally *my lap*

even their servants bore rule over the people, but I did not do so, because of the fear of God. [16]Indeed, I also continued the work on this wall, and we[a] did not buy any land. All my servants *were* gathered there for the work.

[17]And at my table *were* one hundred and fifty Jews and rulers, besides those who came to us from the nations around us. [18]Now *that* which was prepared daily *was* one ox *and* six choice sheep. Also fowl were prepared for me, and once every ten days an abundance of all kinds of wine. Yet in spite of this I did not demand the governor's provisions, because the bondage was heavy on this people.

[19]Remember me, my God, for good, *according to* all that I have done for this people.

CONSPIRACY AGAINST NEHEMIAH

6 Now it happened when Sanballat, Tobiah, Geshem the Arab, and the rest of our enemies heard that I had rebuilt the wall, and *that* there were no breaks left in it (though at that time I had not hung the doors in the gates), [2]that Sanballat and Geshem sent to me, saying, "Come, let us meet together among the villages in the plain of Ono." But they thought to do me harm.

[3]So I sent messengers to them, saying, "I *am* doing a great work, so that I cannot come down. Why should the work cease while I leave it and go down to you?"

[4]But they sent me this message four times, and I answered them in the same manner.

[5]Then Sanballat sent his servant to me as before, the fifth time, with an open letter in his hand. [6]In it *was* written:

> It is reported among the nations, and Geshem[a] says, *that* you and the Jews plan to rebel; therefore, according to these rumors, you are rebuilding the wall, that you may be their king. [7]And you have also appointed prophets to proclaim concerning you at Jerusalem, saying, "*There is* a king in Judah!" Now these matters will be reported to the king. So come, therefore, and let us consult together.

5:16 [a]Following Masoretic Text; Septuagint, Syriac, and Vulgate read *I.*   6:6 [a]Hebrew *Gashmu*

INSIDE *the* INFLUENCERS

NEHEMIAH—Never Stoop—Stay Focused

NEHEMIAH 6

Nehemiah is legendary. As a young man, he was the royal cup-bearer at the palace of Shushan for King Artaxerxes. For many days Nehemiah fasted, grieved, and prayed for wisdom concerning his beloved homeland of Jerusalem; and when the king asked why he was sad, he was ready with an answer.

Suddenly, every barrier was dispelled by the king's favor, and Nehemiah set out to rebuild. He went with a strong escort, letters of reference for safe passage, and permission to use resources of the royal forests; all of this was from the king, but set in motion by the One True God. He completed the restoration through leadership and vision.

When the enemy asked him to come talk things over, Nehemiah replied, "I am doing a great work, so that I cannot come down" (Neh. 6:3). There are two keys here to staying motivated as leaders. First, believe that the work you are doing is significant. Second, Nehemiah resisted distractions. No diversion would make him lower his standard. Many of the best intentions have fallen to "reasonable" diversions such as this.

If Nehemiah had measured his work daily and evaluated the difficulties, he might have quit. He was able to finish the work because he stayed focused on the higher call.

⁸Then I sent to him, saying, "No such things as you say are being done, but you invent them in your own heart."

⁹For they all *were trying to* make us afraid, saying, "Their hands will be weakened in the work, and it will not be done."

Now therefore, O God, strengthen my hands.

¹⁰Afterward I came to the house of Shemaiah the son of Delaiah, the son of Mehetabel, who *was* a secret informer; and he said, "Let us meet together in the house of God, within the temple, and let us close the doors of the temple, for they are coming to kill you; indeed, at night they will come to kill you."

¹¹And I said, "Should such a man as I flee? And who *is there* such as I who would go into the temple to save his life? I will not go in!" ¹²Then I perceived that God had not sent him at all, but that he pronounced *this* prophecy against me because Tobiah and Sanballat had hired him. ¹³For this reason he *was* hired, that I should be afraid and act that way and sin, so *that* they might have *cause* for an evil report, that they might reproach me.

¹⁴My God, remember Tobiah and Sanballat, according to these their works, and the prophetess Noadiah and the rest of the prophets who would have made me afraid.

The Wall Completed

¹⁵So the wall was finished on the twenty-fifth *day* of Elul, in fifty-two days. ¹⁶And it happened, when all our enemies heard *of it,* and all the nations around us saw *these things,* that they were very disheartened in their own eyes; for they perceived that this work was done by our God.

¹⁷Also in those days the nobles of Judah sent many letters to Tobiah, and *the letters* of Tobiah came to them. ¹⁸For many in Judah were pledged to him, because he was the son-in-law of Shechaniah the son of Arah, and his son Jehohanan had married the daughter of Meshullam the son of Berechiah. ¹⁹Also they reported his good deeds before me, and reported my words to him. Tobiah sent letters to frighten me.

7 Then it was, when the wall was built and I had hung the doors, when the gatekeepers, the singers, and the Levites had been appointed, ²that I gave the charge of Jerusalem to my brother

Hanani, and Hananiah the leader of the citadel, for he *was* a faithful man and feared God more than many.

³And I said to them, "Do not let the gates of Jerusalem be opened until the sun is hot; and while they stand *guard,* let them shut and bar the doors; and appoint guards from among the inhabitants of Jerusalem, one at his watch station and another in front of his own house."

The Captives Who Returned to Jerusalem

⁴Now the city *was* large and spacious, but the people in it *were* few, and the houses *were* not rebuilt. ⁵Then my God put it into my heart to gather the nobles, the rulers, and the people, that they might be registered by genealogy. And I found a register of the genealogy of those who had come up in the first *return,* and found written in it:

⁶These[a] *are* the people of the province who came back from the captivity, of those who had been carried away, whom Nebuchadnezzar the king of Babylon had carried away, and who returned to Jerusalem and Judah, everyone to his city.

⁷Those who came with Zerubbabel *were* Jeshua, Nehemiah, Azariah, Raamiah, Nahamani, Mordecai, Bilshan, Mispereth,[a] Bigvai, Nehum, and Baanah.

The number of the men of the people of Israel: ⁸the sons of Parosh, two thousand one hundred and seventy-two;
⁹the sons of Shephatiah, three hundred and seventy-two;
¹⁰the sons of Arah, six hundred and fifty-two;
¹¹the sons of Pahath-Moab, of the sons of Jeshua and Joab, two thousand eight hundred and eighteen;
¹²the sons of Elam, one thousand two hundred and fifty-four;
¹³the sons of Zattu, eight hundred and forty-five;
¹⁴the sons of Zaccai, seven hundred and sixty;

7:6 [a]Compare verses 6–72 with Ezra 2:1–70   **7:7** [a]Spelled *Mispar* in Ezra 2:2

¹⁵the sons of Binnui,ᵃ six hundred and forty-eight;

¹⁶the sons of Bebai, six hundred and twenty-eight;

¹⁷the sons of Azgad, two thousand three hundred and twenty-two;

¹⁸the sons of Adonikam, six hundred and sixty-seven;

¹⁹the sons of Bigvai, two thousand and sixty-seven;

²⁰the sons of Adin, six hundred and fifty-five;

²¹the sons of Ater of Hezekiah, ninety-eight;

²²the sons of Hashum, three hundred and twenty-eight;

²³the sons of Bezai, three hundred and twenty-four;

²⁴the sons of Hariph,ᵃ one hundred and twelve;

²⁵the sons of Gibeon,ᵃ ninety-five;

²⁶the men of Bethlehem and Netophah, one hundred and eighty-eight;

²⁷the men of Anathoth, one hundred and twenty-eight;

²⁸the men of Beth Azmaveth,ᵃ forty-two;

²⁹the men of Kirjath Jearim, Chephirah, and Beeroth, seven hundred and forty-three;

³⁰the men of Ramah and Geba, six hundred and twenty-one;

³¹the men of Michmas, one hundred and twenty-two;

³²the men of Bethel and Ai, one hundred and twenty-three;

³³the men of the other Nebo, fifty-two;

³⁴the sons of the other Elam, one thousand two hundred and fifty-four;

³⁵the sons of Harim, three hundred and twenty;

³⁶the sons of Jericho, three hundred and forty-five;

³⁷the sons of Lod, Hadid, and Ono, seven hundred and twenty-one;

³⁸the sons of Senaah, three thousand nine hundred and thirty.

³⁹The priests: the sons of Jedaiah, of the house of Jeshua, nine hundred and seventy-three;

⁴⁰the sons of Immer, one thousand and fifty-two;

⁴¹the sons of Pashhur, one thousand two hundred and forty-seven;

⁴²the sons of Harim, one thousand and seventeen.

⁴³The Levites: the sons of Jeshua, of Kadmiel, *and* of the sons of Hodevah,ᵃ seventy-four.

⁴⁴The singers: the sons of Asaph, one hundred and forty-eight.

⁴⁵The gatekeepers: the sons of Shallum, the sons of Ater, the sons of Talmon, the sons of Akkub, the sons of Hatita, the sons of Shobai, one hundred and thirty-eight.

⁴⁶The Nethinim: the sons of Ziha, the sons of Hasupha, the sons of Tabbaoth, ⁴⁷the sons of Keros, the sons of Sia,ᵃ the sons of Padon, ⁴⁸the sons of Lebana,ᵃ the sons of Hagaba,ᵇ the sons of Salmai,ᶜ ⁴⁹the sons of Hanan, the sons of Giddel, the sons of Gahar, ⁵⁰the sons of Reaiah, the sons of Rezin, the sons of Nekoda, ⁵¹the sons of Gazzam, the sons of Uzza, the sons of Paseah, ⁵²the sons of Besai, the sons of Meunim, the sons of Nephishesim,ᵃ ⁵³the sons of Bakbuk, the sons of Hakupha, the sons of Harhur, ⁵⁴the sons of Bazlith,ᵃ

7:15 ᵃSpelled *Bani* in Ezra 2:10   **7:24** ᵃCalled *Jorah* in Ezra 2:18   **7:25** ᵃCalled *Gibbar* in Ezra 2:20   **7:28** ᵃCalled *Azmaveth* in Ezra 2:24   **7:43** ᵃSpelled *Hodaviah* in Ezra 2:40   **7:47** ᵃSpelled *Siaha* in Ezra 2:44   **7:48** ᵃMasoretic Text reads *Lebanah.* ᵇMasoretic Text reads *Hogabah.* ᶜOr *Shalmai*, or *Shamlai*   **7:52** ᵃSpelled *Nephusim* in Ezra 2:50   **7:54** ᵃSpelled *Bazluth* in Ezra 2:52

the sons of Mehida,
the sons of Harsha,
[55]the sons of Barkos,
the sons of Sisera,
the sons of Tamah,
[56]the sons of Neziah,
and the sons of Hatipha.

[57]The sons of Solomon's servants: the sons
of Sotai,
the sons of Sophereth,
the sons of Perida,[a]
[58]the sons of Jaala,
the sons of Darkon,
the sons of Giddel,
[59]the sons of Shephatiah,
the sons of Hattil,
the sons of Pochereth of Zebaim,
and the sons of Amon.[a]
[60]All the Nethinim, and the sons of
Solomon's servants, *were* three hundred and
ninety-two.

[61]And these *were* the ones who came up from
Tel Melah, Tel Harsha, Cherub, Addon,[a] and
Immer, but they could not identify their
father's house nor their lineage, whether they
were of Israel: [62]the sons of Delaiah,
the sons of Tobiah,
the sons of Nekoda, six hundred and
forty-two;
[63]and of the priests: the sons of Habaiah,
the sons of Koz,[a]
the sons of Barzillai, who took a wife of the
daughters of Barzillai the Gileadite, and was
called by their name.
[64]These sought their listing *among* those
who were registered by genealogy, but it
was not found; therefore they were
excluded from the priesthood as defiled.
[65]And the governor[a] said to them that they
should not eat of the most holy things till a
priest could consult with the Urim and
Thummim.

[66]Altogether the whole assembly *was* forty-two
thousand three hundred and sixty, [67]besides
their male and female servants, of whom *there
were* seven thousand three hundred and

thirty-seven; and they had two hundred and
forty-five men and women singers. [68]Their
horses were seven hundred and thirty-six,
their mules two hundred and forty-five,
[69]*their* camels four hundred and thirty-five,
and donkeys six thousand seven hundred and
twenty.

[70]And some of the heads of the fathers' *houses*
gave to the work. The governor[a] gave to the
treasury one thousand gold drachmas, fifty
basins, and five hundred and thirty priestly
garments. [71]Some of the heads of the fathers'
houses gave to the treasury of the work
twenty thousand gold drachmas, and two
thousand two hundred silver minas. [72]And
that which the rest of the people gave *was*
twenty thousand gold drachmas, two
thousand silver minas, and sixty-seven
priestly garments.

[73]So the priests, the Levites, the gatekeepers,
the singers, *some* of the people, the Nethinim, and
all Israel dwelt in their cities.

Ezra Reads the Law

When the seventh month came, the children
of Israel *were* in their cities.

8 Now all the people gathered together as one
man in the open square that *was* in front of the
Water Gate; and they told Ezra the scribe to bring
the Book of the Law of Moses, which the LORD
had commanded Israel. [2]So Ezra the priest brought
the Law before the assembly of men and women
and all who *could* hear with understanding on the
first day of the seventh month. [3]Then he read from
it in the open square that *was* in front of the Water
Gate from morning until midday, before the men
and women and those who could understand; and
the ears of all the people *were attentive* to the Book
of the Law.

[4]So Ezra the scribe stood on a platform of
wood which they had made for the purpose; and
beside him, at his right hand, stood Mattithiah,
Shema, Anaiah, Urijah, Hilkiah, and Maaseiah;
and at his left hand Pedaiah, Mishael, Malchijah,

7:57 [a]Spelled *Peruda* in Ezra 2:55   7:59 [a]Spelled *Ami* in Ezra 2:57
7:61 [a]Spelled *Addan* in Ezra 2:59   7:63 [a]Or *Hakkoz*   7:65 [a]Hebrew
Tirshatha   7:70 [a]Hebrew *Tirshatha*

Hashum, Hashbadana, Zechariah, *and* Meshullam. ⁵And Ezra opened the book in the sight of all the people, for he was *standing* above all the people; and when he opened it, all the people stood up. ⁶And Ezra blessed the LORD, the great God.

Then all the people answered, "Amen, Amen!" while lifting up their hands. And they bowed their heads and worshiped the LORD with *their* faces to the ground.

⁷Also Jeshua, Bani, Sherebiah, Jamin, Akkub, Shabbethai, Hodijah, Maaseiah, Kelita, Azariah, Jozabad, Hanan, Pelaiah, and the Levites, helped the people to understand the Law; and the people *stood* in their place. ⁸So they read distinctly from the book, in the Law of God; and they gave the sense, and helped *them* to understand the reading.

⁹And Nehemiah, who *was* the governor,ᵃ Ezra the priest *and* scribe, and the Levites who taught the people said to all the people, "This day *is* holy to the LORD your God; do not mourn nor weep." For all the people wept, when they heard the words of the Law.

¹⁰Then he said to them, "Go your way, eat the fat, drink the sweet, and send portions to those for whom nothing is prepared; for *this* day *is* holy to our Lord. Do not sorrow, for the joy of the LORD is your strength."

¹¹So the Levites quieted all the people, saying, "Be still, for the day *is* holy; do not be grieved." ¹²And all the people went their way to eat and drink, to send portions and rejoice greatly, because they understood the words that were declared to them.

The Feast of Tabernacles

¹³Now on the second day the heads of the fathers' *houses* of all the people, with the priests and Levites, were gathered to Ezra the scribe, in order to understand the words of the Law. ¹⁴And they found written in the Law, which the LORD had commanded by Moses, that the children of Israel should dwell in booths during the feast of the seventh month, ¹⁵and that they should announce and proclaim in all their cities and in Jerusalem, saying, "Go out to the mountain, and bring olive branches, branches of oil trees, myrtle branches, palm branches, and branches of leafy trees, to make booths, as *it is* written."

¹⁶Then the people went out and brought

them and made themselves booths, each one on the roof of his house, or in their courtyards or the courts of the house of God, and in the open square of the Water Gate and in the open square of the Gate of Ephraim. ¹⁷So the whole assembly of those who had returned from the captivity made booths and sat under the booths; for since the days of Joshua the son of Nun until that day the children of Israel had not done so. And there was very great gladness. ¹⁸Also day by day, from the first day until the last day, he read from the Book of the Law of God. And they kept the feast seven days; and on the eighth day *there was* a sacred assembly, according to the *prescribed* manner.

The People Confess Their Sins

9 Now on the twenty-fourth day of this month the children of Israel were assembled with fasting, in sackcloth, and with dust on their heads.ᵃ ²Then those of Israelite lineage separated themselves from all foreigners; and they stood and confessed their sins and the iniquities of their fathers. ³And they stood up in their place and read from the Book of the Law of the LORD their God *for one*-fourth of the day; and *for another* fourth they confessed and worshiped the LORD their God.

⁴Then Jeshua, Bani, Kadmiel, Shebaniah, Bunni, Sherebiah, Bani, *and* Chenani stood on the stairs of the Levites and cried out with a loud voice to the LORD their God. ⁵And the Levites, Jeshua, Kadmiel, Bani, Hashabniah, Sherebiah, Hodijah, Shebaniah, *and* Pethahiah, said:

"Stand up and bless the LORD your God
   Forever and ever!

"Blessed be Your glorious name,
   Which is exalted above all blessing and
      praise!
⁶You alone *are* the LORD;
   You have made heaven,
   The heaven of heavens, with all their host,
   The earth and everything on it,
   The seas and all that is in them,
   And You preserve them all.
   The host of heaven worships You.

8:9 ᵃHebrew *Tirshatha*   **9:1** ᵃLiterally *earth on them*

⁷"You *are* the LORD God,
  Who chose Abram,
  And brought him out of Ur of the
        Chaldeans,
  And gave him the name Abraham;
⁸You found his heart faithful before You,
  And made a covenant with him
  To give the land of the Canaanites,
  The Hittites, the Amorites,
  The Perizzites, the Jebusites,
  And the Girgashites—
  To give *it* to his descendants.
  You have performed Your words,
  For You *are* righteous.

⁹"You saw the affliction of our fathers in Egypt,
  And heard their cry by the Red Sea.
¹⁰You showed signs and wonders against
        Pharaoh,
  Against all his servants,
  And against all the people of his land.
  For You knew that they acted proudly against
        them.
  So You made a name for Yourself, as *it is* this
        day.
¹¹And You divided the sea before them,
  So that they went through the midst of the
        sea on the dry land;
  And their persecutors You threw into the
        deep,
  As a stone into the mighty waters.
¹²Moreover You led them by day with a cloudy
        pillar,
  And by night with a pillar of fire,
  To give them light on the road
  Which they should travel.

¹³"You came down also on Mount Sinai,
  And spoke with them from heaven,
  And gave them just ordinances and true laws,
  Good statutes and commandments.
¹⁴You made known to them Your holy Sabbath,
  And commanded them precepts, statutes and
        laws,
  By the hand of Moses Your servant.
¹⁵You gave them bread from heaven for their
        hunger,
  And brought them water out of the rock for
        their thirst,

And told them to go in to possess the land
  Which You had sworn to give them.

¹⁶"But they and our fathers acted proudly,
  Hardened their necks,
  And did not heed Your commandments.
¹⁷They refused to obey,
  And they were not mindful of Your wonders
  That You did among them.
  But they hardened their necks,
  And in their rebellionᵃ
  They appointed a leader
  To return to their bondage.
  But You *are* God,
  Ready to pardon,
  Gracious and merciful,
  Slow to anger,
  Abundant in kindness,
  And did not forsake them.

¹⁸"Even when they made a molded calf for
        themselves,
  And said, 'This *is* your god
  That brought you up out of Egypt,'
  And worked great provocations,
¹⁹Yet in Your manifold mercies
  You did not forsake them in the wilderness.
  The pillar of the cloud did not depart from
        them by day,
  To lead them on the road;
  Nor the pillar of fire by night,
  To show them light,
  And the way they should go.
²⁰You also gave Your good Spirit to instruct
        them,
  And did not withhold Your manna from their
        mouth,
  And gave them water for their thirst.
²¹Forty years You sustained them in the
        wilderness;
  They lacked nothing;
  Their clothes did not wear outᵃ
  And their feet did not swell.

²²"Moreover You gave them kingdoms and
        nations,
  And divided them into districts.ᵃ
  So they took possession of the land of Sihon,

9:17 ᵃFollowing Masoretic Text and Vulgate; Septuagint reads *in Egypt.* **9:21** ᵃCompare Deuteronomy 29:5 **9:22** ᵃLiterally *corners*

The land of[b] the king of Heshbon,
And the land of Og king of Bashan.
[23]You also multiplied their children as the stars
of heaven,
And brought them into the land
Which You had told their fathers
To go in and possess.
[24]So the people went in
And possessed the land;
You subdued before them the inhabitants of
the land,
The Canaanites,
And gave them into their hands,
With their kings
And the people of the land,
That they might do with them as they
wished.
[25]And they took strong cities and a rich land,
And possessed houses full of all goods,
Cisterns *already* dug, vineyards, olive groves,
And fruit trees in abundance.
So they ate and were filled and grew fat,
And delighted themselves in Your great
goodness.

[26]"Nevertheless they were disobedient
And rebelled against You,
Cast Your law behind their backs
And killed Your prophets, who testified
against them
To turn them to Yourself;
And they worked great provocations.
[27]Therefore You delivered them into the hand
of their enemies,
Who oppressed them;
And in the time of their trouble,
When they cried to You,
You heard from heaven;
And according to Your abundant mercies
You gave them deliverers who saved them
From the hand of their enemies.

[28]"But after they had rest,
They again did evil before You.
Therefore You left them in the hand of their
enemies,
So that they had dominion over them;
Yet when they returned and cried out to You,
You heard from heaven;

And many times You delivered them
according to Your mercies,
[29]And testified against them,
That You might bring them back to Your
law.
Yet they acted proudly,
And did not heed Your commandments,
But sinned against Your judgments,
'Which if a man does, he shall live by them.'[a]
And they shrugged their shoulders,
Stiffened their necks,
And would not hear.
[30]Yet for many years You had patience with
them,
And testified against them by Your Spirit in
Your prophets.
Yet they would not listen;
Therefore You gave them into the hand of the
peoples of the lands.
[31]Nevertheless in Your great mercy
You did not utterly consume them nor
forsake them;
For You *are* God, gracious and merciful.

[32]"Now therefore, our God,
The great, the mighty, and awesome God,
Who keeps covenant and mercy:
Do not let all the trouble seem small before
You
That has come upon us,
Our kings and our princes,
Our priests and our prophets,
Our fathers and on all Your people,
From the days of the kings of Assyria until
this day.
[33]However You *are* just in all that has befallen
us;
For You have dealt faithfully,
But we have done wickedly.
[34]Neither our kings nor our princes,
Our priests nor our fathers,
Have kept Your law,
Nor heeded Your commandments and Your
testimonies,
With which You testified against them.
[35]For they have not served You in their
kingdom,

9:22 [b]Following Masoretic Text and Vulgate; Septuagint omits *The land of.* **9:29** [a]Leviticus 18:5

Or in the many good *things* that You gave
  them,
Or in the large and rich land which You set
  before them;
Nor did they turn from their wicked works.

³⁶"Here we *are,* servants today!
And the land that You gave to our fathers,
  To eat its fruit and its bounty,
Here we *are,* servants in it!
³⁷And it yields much increase to the kings
  You have set over us,
Because of our sins;
Also they have dominion over our bodies and
  our cattle
At their pleasure;
And we *are* in great distress.

³⁸"And because of all this,
We make a sure *covenant* and write *it;*
Our leaders, our Levites, *and* our priests
  seal *it.*"

The People Who Sealed the Covenant

10 Now those who placed *their* seal on *the document* were:

Nehemiah the governor, the son of Hacaliah,
and Zedekiah, ²Seraiah, Azariah, Jeremiah,
³Pashhur, Amariah, Malchijah, ⁴Hattush,
Shebaniah, Malluch, ⁵Harim, Meremoth,
Obadiah, ⁶Daniel, Ginnethon, Baruch,
⁷Meshullam, Abijah, Mijamin, ⁸Maaziah,
Bilgai, *and* Shemaiah. These *were* the priests.

⁹The Levites: Jeshua the son of Azaniah,
Binnui of the sons of Henadad, *and* Kadmiel.

¹⁰Their brethren: Shebaniah, Hodijah, Kelita,
Pelaiah, Hanan, ¹¹Micha, Rehob, Hashabiah,
¹²Zaccur, Sherebiah, Shebaniah, ¹³Hodijah,
Bani, *and* Beninu.

¹⁴The leaders of the people: Parosh, Pahath-
Moab, Elam, Zattu, Bani, ¹⁵Bunni, Azgad,
Bebai, ¹⁶Adonijah, Bigvai, Adin, ¹⁷Ater,
Hezekiah, Azzur, ¹⁸Hodijah, Hashum, Bezai,
¹⁹Hariph, Anathoth, Nebai, ²⁰Magpiash,
Meshullam, Hezir, ²¹Meshezabel, Zadok,

Jaddua, ²²Pelatiah, Hanan, Anaiah, ²³Hoshea,
Hananiah, Hasshub, ²⁴Hallohesh, Pilha,
Shobek, ²⁵Rehum, Hashabnah, Maaseiah,
²⁶Ahijah, Hanan, Anan, ²⁷Malluch, Harim, *and*
Baanah.

The Covenant That Was Sealed

²⁸Now the rest of the people—the priests, the
Levites, the gatekeepers, the singers, the
Nethinim, and all those who had separated themselves from the peoples of the lands to the Law of
God, their wives, their sons, and their daughters,
everyone who had knowledge and understand-
ing— ²⁹these joined with their brethren, their nobles, and entered into a curse and an oath to walk
in God's Law, which was given by Moses the servant of God, and to observe and do all the commandments of the LORD our Lord, and His ordinances and His statutes: ³⁰We would not give our
daughters as wives to the peoples of the land, nor
take their daughters for our sons; ³¹*if* the peoples
of the land brought wares or any grain to sell on
the Sabbath day, we would not buy it from them
on the Sabbath, or on a holy day; and we would
forego the seventh year's *produce* and the exacting
of every debt.

³²Also we made ordinances for ourselves, to
exact from ourselves yearly one-third of a shekel
for the service of the house of our God: ³³for the
showbread, for the regular grain offering, for the
regular burnt offering of the Sabbaths, the New
Moons, and the set feasts; for the holy things, for
the sin offerings to make atonement for Israel,
and all the work of the house of our God. ³⁴We
cast lots among the priests, the Levites, and the
people, for bringing the wood offering into the
house of our God, according to our fathers'
houses, at the appointed times year by year, to
burn on the altar of the LORD our God as *it is*
written in the Law.

³⁵And *we made ordinances* to bring the first-
fruits of our ground and the firstfruits of all fruit
of all trees, year by year, to the house of the
LORD; ³⁶to bring the firstborn of our sons and
our cattle, as *it is* written in the Law, and the firstborn of our herds and our flocks, to the house of
our God, to the priests who minister in the house
of our God; ³⁷to bring the firstfruits of our
dough, our offerings, the fruit from all kinds of

trees, *the* new wine and oil, to the priests, to the storerooms of the house of our God; and to bring the tithes of our land to the Levites, for the Levites should receive the tithes in all our farming communities. [38]And the priest, the descendant of Aaron, shall be with the Levites when the Levites receive tithes; and the Levites shall bring up a tenth of the tithes to the house of our God, to the rooms of the storehouse.

[39]For the children of Israel and the children of Levi shall bring the offering of the grain, of the new wine and the oil, to the storerooms where the articles of the sanctuary *are, where* the priests who minister and the gatekeepers and the singers *are;* and we will not neglect the house of our God.

THE PEOPLE DWELLING IN JERUSALEM

11 Now the leaders of the people dwelt at Jerusalem; the rest of the people cast lots to bring one out of ten to dwell in Jerusalem, the holy city, and nine-tenths *were to dwell in other* cities. [2]And the people blessed all the men who willingly offered themselves to dwell at Jerusalem.

[3]These *are* the heads of the province who dwelt in Jerusalem. (But in the cities of Judah everyone dwelt in his own possession in their cities—Israelites, priests, Levites, Nethinim, and descendants of Solomon's servants.) [4]Also in Jerusalem dwelt *some* of the children of Judah and of the children of Benjamin.

The children of Judah: Athaiah the son of Uzziah, the son of Zechariah, the son of Amariah, the son of Shephatiah, the son of Mahalalel, of the children of Perez; [5]and Maaseiah the son of Baruch, the son of Col-Hozeh, the son of Hazaiah, the son of Adaiah, the son of Joiarib, the son of Zechariah, the son of Shiloni. [6]All the sons of Perez who dwelt at Jerusalem *were* four hundred and sixty-eight valiant men.

[7]And these are the sons of Benjamin: Sallu the son of Meshullam, the son of Joed, the son of Pedaiah, the son of Kolaiah, the son of Maaseiah, the son of Ithiel, the son of Jeshaiah; [8]and after him Gabbai *and* Sallai, nine hundred and twenty-eight. [9]Joel the son of Zichri *was* their overseer, and Judah the son of Senuah[a] *was* second over the city.

[10]Of the priests: Jedaiah the son of Joiarib, and Jachin; [11]Seraiah the son of Hilkiah, the son of Meshullam, the son of Zadok, the son of Meraioth, the son of Ahitub, *was* the leader of the house of God. [12]Their brethren who did the work of the house *were* eight hundred and twenty-two; and Adaiah the son of Jeroham, the son of Pelaliah, the son of Amzi, the son of Zechariah, the son of Pashhur, the son of Malchijah, [13]and his brethren, heads of the fathers' *houses, were* two hundred and forty-two; and Amashai the son of Azarel, the son of Ahzai, the son of Meshillemoth, the son of Immer, [14]and their brethren, mighty men of valor, *were* one hundred and twenty-eight. Their overseer *was* Zabdiel son of *one of* the great men.[a]

[15]Also of the Levites: Shemaiah the son of Hasshub, the son of Azrikam, the son of Hashabiah, the son of Bunni; [16]Shabbethai and Jozabad, of the heads of the Levites, *had* the oversight of the business outside of the house of God; [17]Mattaniah the son of Micha,[a] the son of Zabdi, the son of Asaph, the leader *who* began the thanksgiving with prayer; Bakbukiah, the second among his brethren; and Abda the son of Shammua, the son of Galal, the son of Jeduthun. [18]All the Levites in the holy city *were* two hundred and eighty-four.

[19]Moreover the gatekeepers, Akkub, Talmon, and their brethren who kept the gates, *were* one hundred and seventy-two.

[20]And the rest of Israel, of the priests *and* Levites, *were* in all the cities of Judah, everyone in his inheritance. [21]But the Nethinim dwelt in Ophel. And Ziha and Gishpa *were* over the Nethinim.

[22]Also the overseer of the Levites at Jerusalem *was* Uzzi the son of Bani, the son of Hashabiah, the son of Mattaniah, the son of Micha, of the sons of Asaph, the singers in charge of the service of the house of God. [23]For *it was* the king's command concerning them that a certain portion should be for the singers, a quota day by day. [24]Pethahiah the son of Meshezabel, of the children of Zerah the son of Judah, *was* the king's deputy[a] in all matters concerning the people.

THE PEOPLE DWELLING OUTSIDE JERUSALEM

[25]And as for the villages with their fields, *some* of the children of Judah dwelt in Kirjath Arba and

11:9 [a]Or *Hassenuah*   **11:14** [a]Or *the son of Haggedolim*   **11:17** [a]Or *Michah*   **11:24** [a]Literally *at the king's hand*

its villages, Dibon and its villages, Jekabzeel and its villages; [26]in Jeshua, Moladah, Beth Pelet, [27]Hazar Shual, and Beersheba and its villages; [28]in Ziklag and Meconah and its villages; [29]in En Rimmon, Zorah, Jarmuth, [30]Zanoah, Adullam, and their villages; in Lachish and its fields; in Azekah and its villages. They dwelt from Beersheba to the Valley of Hinnom.

[31]Also the children of Benjamin from Geba *dwelt* in Michmash, Aija, and Bethel, and their villages; [32]in Anathoth, Nob, Ananiah; [33]in Hazor, Ramah, Gittaim; [34]in Hadid, Zeboim, Neballat; [35]in Lod, Ono, *and* the Valley of Craftsmen. [36]Some of the Judean divisions of Levites *were* in Benjamin.

THE PRIESTS AND LEVITES

12 Now these *are* the priests and the Levites who came up with Zerubbabel the son of Shealtiel, and Jeshua: Seraiah, Jeremiah, Ezra, [2]Amariah, Malluch, Hattush, [3]Shechaniah, Rehum, Meremoth, [4]Iddo, Ginnethoi,[a] Abijah, [5]Mijamin, Maadiah, Bilgah, [6]Shemaiah, Joiarib, Jedaiah, [7]Sallu, Amok, Hilkiah, *and* Jedaiah.

These *were* the heads of the priests and their brethren in the days of Jeshua.

[8]Moreover the Levites *were* Jeshua, Binnui, Kadmiel, Sherebiah, Judah, *and* Mattaniah *who led* the thanksgiving *psalms,* he and his brethren. [9]Also Bakbukiah and Unni, their brethren, *stood* across from them in *their* duties.

[10]Jeshua begot Joiakim, Joiakim begot Eliashib, Eliashib begot Joiada, [11]Joiada begot Jonathan, and Jonathan begot Jaddua.

[12]Now in the days of Joiakim, the priests, the heads of the fathers' *houses were:* of Seraiah, Meraiah; of Jeremiah, Hananiah; [13]of Ezra, Meshullam; of Amariah, Jehohanan; [14]of Melichu,[a] Jonathan; of Shebaniah,[b] Joseph; [15]of Harim,[a] Adna; of Meraioth,[b] Helkai; [16]of Iddo, Zechariah; of Ginnethon, Meshullam; [17]of Abijah, Zichri; *the son* of Minjamin;[a] of Moadiah,[b] Piltai; [18]of Bilgah, Shammua; of Shemaiah, Jehonathan; [19]of Joiarib, Mattenai; of Jedaiah, Uzzi; [20]of Sallai,[a] Kallai; of Amok, Eber; [21]of Hilkiah, Hashabiah; *and* of Jedaiah, Nethanel.

[22]During the reign of Darius the Persian, a record *was* also *kept* of the Levites and priests *who had been* heads of their fathers' *houses* in the days of Eliashib, Joiada, Johanan, and Jaddua. [23]The sons of Levi, the heads of the fathers' *houses* until the days of Johanan the son of Eliashib, *were* written in the book of the chronicles.

[24]And the heads of the Levites *were* Hashabiah, Sherebiah, and Jeshua the son of Kadmiel, with their brothers across from them, to praise *and* give thanks, group alternating with group, according to the command of David the man of God. [25]Mattaniah, Bakbukiah, Obadiah, Meshullam, Talmon, and Akkub *were* gatekeepers keeping the watch at the storerooms of the gates. [26]These *lived* in the days of Joiakim the son of Jeshua, the son of Jozadak,[a] and in the days of Nehemiah the governor, and of Ezra the priest, the scribe.

NEHEMIAH DEDICATES THE WALL

[27]Now at the dedication of the wall of Jerusalem they sought out the Levites in all their places, to bring them to Jerusalem to celebrate the dedication with gladness, both with thanksgivings and singing, *with* cymbals and stringed instruments and harps. [28]And the sons of the singers gathered together from the countryside around Jerusalem, from the villages of the Netophathites, [29]from the house of Gilgal, and from the fields of Geba and Azmaveth; for the singers had built themselves villages all around Jerusalem. [30]Then the priests and Levites purified themselves, and purified the people, the gates, and the wall.

[31]So I brought the leaders of Judah up on the wall, and appointed two large thanksgiving choirs. *One* went to the right hand on the wall toward the Refuse Gate. [32]After them went Hoshaiah and half of the leaders of Judah, [33]and Azariah, Ezra, Meshullam, [34]Judah, Benjamin, Shemaiah, Jeremiah, [35]and some of the priests' sons with trumpets—Zechariah the son of Jonathan, the son of Shemaiah, the son of Mattaniah, the son of Michaiah, the son of Zaccur, the son of Asaph, [36]and his brethren, Shemaiah, Azarel, Milalai, Gilalai, Maai, Nethanel, Judah, *and* Hanani, with the musical instruments of David the man of God. And Ezra the scribe *went* before them. [37]By the

12:4 [a]Or *Ginnethon* (compare verse 16)   12:14 [a]Or *Malluch* (compare verse 2)   [b]Or *Shechaniah* (compare verse 3)   12:15 [a]Or *Rehum* (compare verse 3)   [b]Or *Meremoth* (compare verse 3)   12:17 [a]Or *Mijamin* (compare verse 5)   [b]Or *Maadiah* (compare verse 5)   12:20 [a]Or *Sallu* (compare verse 7)   12:26 [a]Spelled *Jehozadak* in 1 Chronicles 6:14

Fountain Gate, in front of them, they went up the stairs of the City of David, on the stairway of the wall, beyond the house of David, as far as the Water Gate eastward.

[38]The other thanksgiving choir went the opposite *way,* and I *was* behind them with half of the people on the wall, going past the Tower of the Ovens as far as the Broad Wall, [39]and above the Gate of Ephraim, above the Old Gate, above the Fish Gate, the Tower of Hananel, the Tower of the Hundred, as far as the Sheep Gate; and they stopped by the Gate of the Prison.

[40]So the two thanksgiving choirs stood in the house of God, likewise I and the half of the rulers with me; [41]and the priests, Eliakim, Maaseiah, Minjamin,[a] Michaiah, Elioenai, Zechariah, *and* Hananiah, with trumpets; [42]also Maaseiah, Shemaiah, Eleazar, Uzzi, Jehohanan, Malchijah, Elam, and Ezer. The singers sang loudly with Jezrahiah the director.

[43]Also that day they offered great sacrifices, and rejoiced, for God had made them rejoice with great joy; the women and the children also rejoiced, so that the joy of Jerusalem was heard afar off.

Temple Responsibilities

[44]And at the same time some were appointed over the rooms of the storehouse for the offerings, the firstfruits, and the tithes, to gather into them from the fields of the cities the portions specified by the Law for the priests and Levites; for Judah rejoiced over the priests and Levites who ministered. [45]Both the singers and the gatekeepers kept the charge of their God and the charge of the purification, according to the command of David *and* Solomon his son. [46]For in the days of David and Asaph of old *there were* chiefs of the singers, and songs of praise and thanksgiving to God. [47]In the days of Zerubbabel and in the days of Nehemiah all Israel gave the portions for the singers and the gatekeepers, a portion for each day. They also consecrated *holy things* for the Levites, and the Levites consecrated *them* for the children of Aaron.

Principles of Separation

13 On that day they read from the Book of Moses in the hearing of the people, and in it was found written that no Ammonite or Moabite should ever come into the assembly of God, [2]because they had not met the children of Israel with bread and water, but hired Balaam against them to curse them. However, our God turned the curse into a blessing. [3]So it was, when they had heard the Law, that they separated all the mixed multitude from Israel.

The Reforms of Nehemiah

[4]Now before this, Eliashib the priest, having authority over the storerooms of the house of our God, *was* allied with Tobiah. [5]And he had prepared for him a large room, where previously they had stored the grain offerings, the frankincense, the articles, the tithes of grain, the new wine and oil, which were commanded *to be given* to the Levites and singers and gatekeepers, and the offerings for the priests. [6]But during all this I was not in Jerusalem, for in the thirty-second year of Artaxerxes king of Babylon I had returned to the king. Then after certain days I obtained leave from the king, [7]and I came to Jerusalem and discovered the evil that Eliashib had done for Tobiah, in preparing a room for him in the courts of the house of God. [8]And it grieved me bitterly; therefore I threw all the household goods of Tobiah out of the room. [9]Then I commanded them to cleanse the rooms; and I brought back into them the articles of the house of God, with the grain offering and the frankincense.

[10]I also realized that the portions for the Levites had not been given *them;* for each of the Levites and the singers who did the work had gone back to his field. [11]So I contended with the rulers, and said, "Why is the house of God forsaken?" And I gathered them together and set them in their place. [12]Then all Judah brought the tithe of the grain and the new wine and the oil to the storehouse. [13]And I appointed as treasurers over the storehouse Shelemiah the priest and Zadok the scribe, and of the Levites, Pedaiah; and next to them *was* Hanan the son of Zaccur, the son of Mattaniah; for they were considered faithful, and their task *was* to distribute to their brethren.

[14]Remember me, O my God, concerning this, and do not wipe out my good deeds that I

LEAD**ERSHIP**
REAL**ITIES**

INTEGRITY: THE POWER OF REPUTATION *Nehemiah 13:11–13*

An inseparable quality to leadership is to possess a reputation of integrity (Matt. 22:16). Only then will others follow. Nehemiah risked hardship, danger, ridicule, and status to lead the people to rebuild Jerusalem. The city was now fortified with gates and walls, a civil authority to protect and govern was in place, and revival had broken out in the hearts of God's people. Upon completion of the vision God had given, he returned to the king who had granted him leave, just as Nehemiah said he would do. This, it seems, would be the time to rejoice.

But in the final chapter of this book, Nehemiah learns that leadership can never be a one-man show. His homecoming back to his beloved Jerusalem was met with compromised covenants. Once again, the Sabbath was dishonored, and the people chose to do whatever pleased them. Nehemiah stepped forward as a consistent, trustworthy leader to establish certain reforms that would ensure future success. He did so by selecting those who were considered *faithful* or *reliable*. A reputation of integrity is built over a lifetime, but can be destroyed in a moment.

'aman—**faithful**—confirmed, established, pillars, supporters of the door

---

have done for the house of my God, and for its services!

¹⁵In those days I saw *people* in Judah treading wine presses on the Sabbath, and bringing in sheaves, and loading donkeys with wine, grapes, figs, and all *kinds of* burdens, which they brought into Jerusalem on the Sabbath day. And I warned *them* about the day on which they were selling provisions. ¹⁶Men of Tyre dwelt there also, who brought in fish and all kinds of goods, and sold *them* on the Sabbath to the children of Judah, and in Jerusalem.

¹⁷Then I contended with the nobles of Judah, and said to them, "What evil thing *is* this that you do, by which you profane the Sabbath day? ¹⁸Did not your fathers do thus, and did not our God bring all this disaster on us and on this city? Yet you bring added wrath on Israel by profaning the Sabbath."

¹⁹So it was, at the gates of Jerusalem, as it began to be dark before the Sabbath, that I commanded the gates to be shut, and charged that they must not be opened till after the Sabbath. Then I posted *some* of my servants at the gates, *so that* no burdens would be brought in on the Sabbath day. ²⁰Now the merchants and sellers of all kinds of wares lodged outside Jerusalem once or twice.

²¹Then I warned them, and said to them, "Why do you spend the night around the wall? If you do *so* again, I will lay hands on you!" From that time on they came no *more* on the Sabbath. ²²And I commanded the Levites that they should cleanse themselves, and that they should go and guard the gates, to sanctify the Sabbath day.

Remember me, O my God, *concerning* this also, and spare me according to the greatness of Your mercy!

²³In those days I also saw Jews *who* had married women of Ashdod, Ammon, *and* Moab. ²⁴And half of their children spoke the language of Ashdod, and could not speak the language of Judah, but spoke according to the language of one or the other people.

²⁵So I contended with them and cursed them, struck some of them and pulled out their hair, and made them swear by God, *saying,* "You shall not give your daughters as wives to their sons, nor take their daughters for your sons or yourselves. ²⁶Did not Solomon king of Israel sin by these things? Yet among many nations there was no king like him, who was beloved of his

God; and God made him king over all Israel. Nevertheless pagan women caused even him to sin. ²⁷Should we then hear of your doing all this great evil, transgressing against our God by marrying pagan women?"

²⁸And *one* of the sons of Joiada, the son of Eliashib the high priest, *was* a son-in-law of Sanballat the Horonite; therefore I drove him from me.

²⁹Remember them, O my God, because they have defiled the priesthood and the covenant of the priesthood and the Levites.

³⁰Thus I cleansed them of everything pagan. I also assigned duties to the priests and the Levites, each to his service, ³¹and *to bringing* the wood offering and the firstfruits at appointed times.

Remember me, O my God, for good!

IMPACT OF THE BOOK

E S T H E R

I IDEA

Although we may not always be able to see God at work, His providence—pro means "before" + video means "to see"—assures us that He sees beforehand. He is the One orchestrating our "for such a time as this" moments.

M MESSAGE

Great leaders always consider the big picture. Esther's road to the palace, where she was put into a position to be a voice for her people, testifies to the fact that God was weaving the tapestry of her life. As she stood at the crossroads of whether she should speak for her people, she realized that God had brought her to the position she was in "for such a time as this," even though it meant she could lose her life. Esther's sacrifice of risking her life saved the lives of thousands.

P PEOPLE

Esther, Haman, Hathach, Mordecai, Xerxes

A AUTHOR

The author of the Book of Esther is not named, although who-ever he was, he displayed intimate knowledge of Susa and Per-sian customs. This has historically led some to believe that the writer was Mordecai, Esther's uncle, a scribe who later become Xerxes' highest ranking official.

C CULTURE

The story of Esther takes place during the reign of Xerxes I—also known as Ahasuerus of Persia—who ruled from 486 to 465 BC. Esther became queen during the seventh year of his reign when Queen Vashti was banished from the throne. They lived in Susa, one of the capital cities that served as a strategically important cultural, religious, and political center.

T TIMELINE

Possibly late fifth century BC (c. 465 BC)

**KEY SCRIPTURE
MEMORY VERSES**

4:14; 8:17

THE KING DETHRONES QUEEN VASHTI

1 Now it came to pass in the days of Ahasuerus[a] (this *was* the Ahasuerus who reigned over one hundred and twenty-seven provinces, from India to Ethiopia), [2]in those days when King Ahasuerus sat on the throne of his kingdom, which *was* in Shushan[a] the citadel, [3]*that* in the third year of his reign he made a feast for all his officials and servants—the powers of Persia and Media, the nobles, and the princes of the provinces *being* before him— [4]when he showed the riches of his glorious kingdom and the splendor of his excellent majesty for many days, one hundred and eighty days *in all*.

[5]And when these days were completed, the king made a feast lasting seven days for all the people who were present in Shushan the citadel, from great to small, in the court of the garden of the king's palace. [6]*There were* white and blue linen *curtains* fastened with cords of fine linen and purple on silver rods and marble pillars; *and the* couches *were* of gold and silver on a *mosaic* pavement of alabaster, turquoise, and white and black marble. [7]And they served drinks in golden vessels, each vessel being different from the other, with royal wine in abundance, according to the generosity of the king. [8]In accordance with the law, the drinking was not compulsory; for so the king had ordered all the officers of his household, that they should do according to each man's pleasure.

[9]Queen Vashti also made a feast for the women *in* the royal palace which *belonged* to King Ahasuerus.

[10]On the seventh day, when the heart of the king was merry with wine, he commanded Mehuman, Biztha, Harbona, Bigtha, Abagtha, Zethar, and Carcas, seven eunuchs who served in the presence of King Ahasuerus, [11]to bring Queen Vashti before the king, *wearing* her royal crown, in order to show her beauty to the people and the officials, for she *was* beautiful to behold. [12]But Queen Vashti refused to come at the king's command *brought* by *his* eunuchs; therefore the king was furious, and his anger burned within him.

[13]Then the king said to the wise men who understood the times (for this *was* the king's manner toward all who knew law and justice, [14]those closest to him *being* Carshena, Shethar, Admatha, Tarshish, Meres, Marsena, and Memucan, the seven princes of Persia and Media, who had access to the king's presence, *and* who ranked highest in the kingdom): [15]"What *shall we* do to Queen Vashti, according to law, because she did not obey the command of King Ahasuerus *brought to her* by the eunuchs?"

[16]And Memucan answered before the king and the princes: "Queen Vashti has not only wronged the king, but also all the princes, and all the people who *are* in all the provinces of King Ahasuerus. [17]For the queen's behavior will become known to all women, so that they will despise their husbands in their eyes, when they report, 'King Ahasuerus commanded Queen Vashti to be brought in before him, but she did not come.' [18]This very day the *noble* ladies of Persia and Media will say to all the king's officials that they have heard of the behavior of the queen. Thus *there will be* excessive contempt and wrath. [19]If it pleases the king, let a royal decree go out from him, and let it be recorded in the laws of the Persians and the Medes, so that it will not be altered, that Vashti shall come no more before King Ahasuerus; and let the king give her royal position to another who is better than she. [20]When the king's decree which he will make is proclaimed throughout all his empire (for it is great), all wives will honor their husbands, both great and small."

[21]And the reply pleased the king and the princes, and the king did according to the word of Memucan. [22]Then he sent letters to all the king's provinces, to each province in its own script, and to every people in their own language, that each man should be master in his own house, and speak in the language of his own people.

ESTHER BECOMES QUEEN

2 After these things, when the wrath of King Ahasuerus subsided, he remembered Vashti, what she had done, and what had been decreed against her. [2]Then the king's servants who attended him said: "Let beautiful young virgins be sought for the king; [3]and let the king appoint officers in all the provinces of his kingdom, that they may gather all the beautiful young virgins to Shushan the citadel, into the women's quarters, under the custody of Hegai[a] the king's eu-

1:1 [a]Generally identified with Xerxes I (485–464 B.C.)   1:2 [a]Or *Susa*, and so throughout this book   2:3 [a]Hebrew *Hege* nuch, custodian of the women. And let beauty preparations be given *them*. ⁴Then let the young woman who pleases the king be queen instead of Vashti."

This thing pleased the king, and he did so.

⁵In Shushan the citadel there was a certain Jew whose name *was* Mordecai the son of Jair, the son of Shimei, the son of Kish, a Benjamite. ⁶*Kish*ᵃ had been carried away from Jerusalem with the captives who had been captured with Jeconiahᵇ king of Judah, whom Nebuchadnezzar the king of Babylon had carried away. ⁷And *Mordecai* had brought up Hadassah, that *is,* Esther, his uncle's daughter, for she had neither father nor mother. The young woman *was* lovely and beautiful. When her father and mother died, Mordecai took her as his own daughter.

⁸So it was, when the king's command and decree were heard, and when many young women were gathered at Shushan the citadel, *under* the custody of Hegai, that Esther also was taken to the king's palace, into the care of Hegai the custodian of the women. ⁹Now the young woman pleased him, and she obtained his favor; so he readily gave beauty preparations to her, besides her allowance. Then seven choice maidservants were provided for her from the king's palace, and he moved her and her maidservants to the best *place* in the house of the women.

¹⁰Esther had not revealed her people or family, for Mordecai had charged her not to reveal *it.* ¹¹And every day Mordecai paced in front of the court of the women's quarters, to learn of Esther's welfare and what was happening to her.

¹²Each young woman's turn came to go in to King Ahasuerus after she had completed twelve months' preparation, according to the regulations for the women, for thus were the days of their preparation apportioned: six

2:6 ᵃLiterally *Who* ᵇSame as *Jehoiachin,* 2 Kings 24:6 and elsewhere

INSIDE *the* INFLUENCERS

ESTHER—From Orphan to Influence

BOOK OF ESTHER

Esther wasn't bitter—though she could have been—about her status as an orphan. Having little material possessions, Esther learned to value courage, resolve, and kindness. She competed against many beautiful women for the throne, but the powerful king chose Esther because she found "grace and favor in his sight."

The king uses two Hebrew words for "favor." The first is the same "favor" that Esther's chief advisor used. But then he adds a second word, the Hebrew *checed,* implying a piety—that is, a modest goodness.

So different was this modest spirit of kindness and goodness in Esther that it caused her to stand out above all other women, and it invoked a love for her spirit in this otherwise selfish king. All of the moments of Esther's life worked together to make her who she was and bring her into a position of prestige.

When her people were endangered, she approached the king and risked his anger, even though she knew of his volatile temper.

- God blessed Esther's faith and *favored* her.
- God softened Xerxes' heart so that he listened to her request and worked to bring peace.

A life of significance is centered on a unique purpose planned by God *for such a time as this.* Every event in life works toward this purpose.

months with oil of myrrh, and six months with perfumes and preparations for beautifying women. ¹³Thus *prepared, each* young woman went to the king, and she was given whatever she desired to take with her from the women's quarters to the king's palace. ¹⁴In the evening she went, and in the morning she returned to the second house of the women, to the custody of Shaashgaz, the king's eunuch who kept the concubines. She would not go in to the king again unless the king delighted in her and called for her by name.

¹⁵Now when the turn came for Esther the daughter of Abihail the uncle of Mordecai, who had taken her as his daughter, to go in to the king, she requested nothing but what Hegai the king's eunuch, the custodian of the women, advised. And Esther obtained favor in the sight of all who saw her. ¹⁶So Esther was taken to King Ahasuerus, into his royal palace, in the tenth month, which *is* the month of Tebeth, in the seventh year of his reign. ¹⁷The king loved Esther more than all the *other* women, and she obtained grace and favor in his sight more than all the virgins; so he set the royal crown upon her head and made her queen instead of Vashti. ¹⁸Then the king made a great feast, the Feast of Esther, for all his officials and servants; and he proclaimed a holiday in the provinces and gave gifts according to the generosity of a king.

Mordecai Discovers a Plot

¹⁹When virgins were gathered together a second time, Mordecai sat within the king's gate. ²⁰*Now* Esther had not revealed her family and her people, just as Mordecai had charged her, for Esther obeyed the command of Mordecai as when she was brought up by him.

²¹In those days, while Mordecai sat within the king's gate, two of the king's eunuchs, Bigthan and Teresh, doorkeepers, became furious and sought to lay hands on King Ahasuerus. ²²So the matter became known to Mordecai, who told Queen Esther, and Esther informed the king in Mordecai's name. ²³And when an inquiry was made into the matter, it was confirmed, and both were hanged on a gallows; and it was written in the book of the chronicles in the presence of the king.

Haman's Conspiracy Against the Jews

3 After these things King Ahasuerus promoted Haman, the son of Hammedatha the Agagite, and advanced him and set his seat above all the princes who *were* with him. ²And all the king's servants who *were* within the king's gate bowed and paid homage to Haman, for so the king had commanded concerning him. But Mordecai would not bow or pay homage. ³Then the king's servants who *were* within the king's gate said to Mordecai, "Why do you transgress the king's command?" ⁴Now it happened, when they spoke to him daily and he would not listen to them, that they told *it* to Haman, to see whether Mordecai's words would stand; for *Mordecai* had told them that he *was* a Jew. ⁵When Haman saw that Mordecai did not bow or pay him homage, Haman was filled with wrath. ⁶But he disdained to lay hands on Mordecai alone, for they had told him of the people of Mordecai. Instead, Haman sought to destroy all the Jews who *were* throughout the whole kingdom of Ahasuerus—the people of Mordecai.

⁷In the first month, which is the month of Nisan, in the twelfth year of King Ahasuerus, they cast Pur (that *is,* the lot), before Haman to determine the day and the month,ᵃ until *it fell on the* twelfth *month,*ᵇ which *is* the month of Adar.

⁸Then Haman said to King Ahasuerus, "There is a certain people scattered and dispersed among the people in all the provinces of your kingdom; their laws *are* different from all *other* people's, and they do not keep the king's laws. Therefore it *is* not fitting for the king to let them remain. ⁹If it pleases the king, let *a decree* be written that they be destroyed, and I will pay ten thousand talents of silver into the hands of those who do the work, to bring *it* into the king's treasuries."

¹⁰So the king took his signet ring from his hand and gave it to Haman, the son of Hammedatha the Agagite, the enemy of the Jews. ¹¹And the king said to Haman, "The money and the people *are* given to you, to do with them as seems good to you."

¹²Then the king's scribes were called on the thirteenth day of the first month, and *a decree* was

3:7 ᵃSeptuagint adds *to destroy the people of Mordecai in one day,* Vulgate adds *the nation of the Jews should be destroyed.* ᵇFollowing Masoretic Text and Vulgate; Septuagint reads *and the lot fell on the fourteenth of the month.*

written according to all that Haman commanded—to the king's satraps, to the governors who *were* over each province, to the officials of all people, to every province according to its script, and to every people in their language. In the name of King Ahasuerus it was written, and sealed with the king's signet ring. [13]And the letters were sent by couriers into all the king's provinces, to destroy, to kill, and to annihilate all the Jews, both young and old, little children and women, in one day, on the thirteenth *day* of the twelfth month, which *is* the month of Adar, and to plunder their possessions.[a] [14]A copy of the document was to be issued as law in every province, being published for all people, that they should be ready for that day. [15]The couriers went out, hastened by the king's command; and the decree was proclaimed in Shushan the citadel. So the king and Haman sat down to drink, but the city of Shushan was perplexed.

ESTHER AGREES TO HELP THE JEWS

4 When Mordecai learned all that had happened, he tore his clothes and put on sackcloth and ashes, and went out into the midst of the city. He cried out with a loud and bitter cry. [2]He went as far as the front of the king's gate, for no one *might* enter the king's gate clothed with sackcloth. [3]And in every province where the king's command and decree arrived, *there was* great mourning among the Jews, with fasting, weeping, and wailing; and many lay in sackcloth and ashes.

[4]So Esther's maids and eunuchs came and told her, and the queen was deeply distressed. Then she sent garments to clothe Mordecai and take his sackcloth away from him, but he would not accept *them*. [5]Then Esther called Hathach, *one* of the king's eunuchs whom he had appointed to attend her, and she gave him a command concerning Mordecai, to learn what and why this *was*. [6]So Hathach went out to Mordecai in the city square that *was* in front of the king's gate. [7]And Mordecai told him all that had happened to him, and the sum of money that Haman had promised to pay into the king's treasuries to destroy the Jews. [8]He also gave him a copy of the written decree for their destruction, which was given at Shushan, that he might show it to Esther and explain it to her, and that he might command her to go in to

the king to make supplication to him and plead before him for her people. [9]So Hathach returned and told Esther the words of Mordecai.

[10]Then Esther spoke to Hathach, and gave him a command for Mordecai: [11]"All the king's servants and the people of the king's provinces know that any man or woman who goes into the inner court to the king, who has not been called, *he has* but one law: put *all* to death, except the one to whom the king holds out the golden scepter, that he may live. Yet I myself have not been called to go in to the king these thirty days." [12]So they told Mordecai Esther's words.

[13]And Mordecai told *them* to answer Esther: "Do not think in your heart that you will escape in the king's palace any more than all the other Jews. [14]For if you remain completely silent at this time, relief and deliverance will arise for the Jews from another place, but you and your father's house will perish. Yet who knows whether you have come to the kingdom for *such* a time as this?"

[15]Then Esther told *them* to reply to Mordecai: [16]"Go, gather all the Jews who are present in Shushan, and fast for me; neither eat nor drink for three days, night or day. My maids and I will fast likewise. And so I will go to the king, which *is* against the law; and if I perish, I perish!"

[17]So Mordecai went his way and did according to all that Esther commanded him.[a]

ESTHER'S BANQUET

5 Now it happened on the third day that Esther put on *her* royal *robes* and stood in the inner court of the king's palace, across from the king's house, while the king sat on his royal throne in the royal house, facing the entrance of the house.[a] [2]So it was, when the king saw Queen Esther standing in the court, *that* she found favor in his sight, and the king held out to Esther the golden scepter that *was* in his hand. Then Esther went near and touched the top of the scepter.

[3]And the king said to her, "What do you wish, Queen Esther? What *is* your request? It shall be given to you—up to half the kingdom!"

[4]So Esther answered, "If it pleases the king, let

3:13 [a]Septuagint adds the text of the letter here. **4:17** [a]Septuagint adds a prayer of Mordecai here. **5:1** [a]Septuagint adds many extra details in verses 1 and 2.

the king and Haman come today to the banquet that I have prepared for him."

⁵Then the king said, "Bring Haman quickly, that he may do as Esther has said." So the king and Haman went to the banquet that Esther had prepared.

⁶At the banquet of wine the king said to Esther, "What *is* your petition? It shall be granted you. What *is* your request, up to half the kingdom? It shall be done!"

⁷Then Esther answered and said, "My petition and request *is this:* ⁸If I have found favor in the sight of the king, and if it pleases the king to grant my petition and fulfill my request, then let the king and Haman come to the banquet which I will prepare for them, and tomorrow I will do as the king has said."

HAMAN'S PLOT AGAINST MORDECAI

⁹So Haman went out that day joyful and with a glad heart; but when Haman saw Mordecai in the king's gate, and that he did not stand or tremble before him, he was filled with indignation against Mordecai. ¹⁰Nevertheless Haman restrained himself and went home, and he sent and called for his friends and his wife Zeresh. ¹¹Then Haman told them of his great riches, the multitude of his children, everything in which the king had promoted him, and how he had advanced him above the officials and servants of the king.

¹²Moreover Haman said, "Besides, Queen Esther invited no one but me to come in with the king to the banquet that she prepared; and tomorrow I am again invited by her, along with the king. ¹³Yet all this avails me nothing, so long as I see Mordecai the Jew sitting at the king's gate."

¹⁴Then his wife Zeresh and all his friends said to him, "Let a gallows be made, fifty cubits high, and in the morning suggest to the king that Mordecai be hanged on it; then go merrily with the king to the banquet." And the thing pleased Haman; so he had the gallows made.

THE KING HONORS MORDECAI

6 That night the king could not sleep. So one was commanded to bring the book of the records of the chronicles; and they were read before the king. ²And it was found written that Mordecai had told of Bigthana and Teresh, two of the king's eunuchs, the doorkeepers who had sought to lay hands on King Ahasuerus. ³Then the king said, "What honor or dignity has been bestowed on Mordecai for this?"

And the king's servants who attended him said, "Nothing has been done for him."

⁴So the king said, "Who *is* in the court?" Now Haman had *just* entered the outer court of the king's palace to suggest that the king hang Mordecai on the gallows that he had prepared for him.

⁵The king's servants said to him, "Haman is there, standing in the court."

And the king said, "Let him come in."

⁶So Haman came in, and the king asked him, "What shall be done for the man whom the king delights to honor?"

Now Haman thought in his heart, "Whom would the king delight to honor more than me?" ⁷And Haman answered the king, "*For* the man whom the king delights to honor, ⁸let a royal robe be brought which the king has worn, and a horse on which the king has ridden, which has a royal crest placed on its head. ⁹Then let this robe and horse be delivered to the hand of one of the king's most noble princes, that he may array the man whom the king delights to honor. Then parade him on horseback through the city square, and proclaim before him: 'Thus shall it be done to the man whom the king delights to honor!'"

¹⁰Then the king said to Haman, "Hurry, take the robe and the horse, as you have suggested, and do so for Mordecai the Jew who sits within the king's gate! Leave nothing undone of all that you have spoken."

¹¹So Haman took the robe and the horse, arrayed Mordecai and led him on horseback through the city square, and proclaimed before him, "Thus shall it be done to the man whom the king delights to honor!"

¹²Afterward Mordecai went back to the king's gate. But Haman hurried to his house, mourning and with his head covered. ¹³When Haman told his wife Zeresh and all his friends everything that had happened to him, his wise men and his wife Zeresh said to him, "If Mordecai, before whom you have begun to fall, is of Jewish descent, you will not prevail against him but will surely fall before him."

¹⁴While they *were* still talking with him, the king's eunuchs came, and hastened to bring Haman to the banquet which Esther had prepared.

Haman Hanged Instead of Mordecai

7So the king and Haman went to dine with Queen Esther. ²And on the second day, at the banquet of wine, the king again said to Esther, "What *is* your petition, Queen Esther? It shall be granted *you*. And what *is* your request, up to half the kingdom? It shall be done!"

³Then Queen Esther answered and said, "If I have found favor in your sight, O king, and if it pleases the king, let my life be given me at my petition, and my people at my request. ⁴For we have been sold, my people and I, to be destroyed, to be killed, and to be annihilated. Had we been sold as male and female slaves, I would have held my tongue, although the enemy could never compensate for the king's loss."

⁵So King Ahasuerus answered and said to Queen Esther, "Who is he, and where is he, who would dare presume in his heart to do such a thing?"

⁶And Esther said, "The adversary and enemy *is* this wicked Haman!"

So Haman was terrified before the king and queen.

⁷Then the king arose in his wrath from the banquet of wine *and went* into the palace garden; but Haman stood before Queen Esther, pleading for his life, for he saw that evil was determined against him by the king. ⁸When the king returned from the palace garden to the place of the banquet of wine, Haman had fallen across the couch where Esther *was*. Then the king said, 'Will he also assault the queen while I *am* in the house?"

As the word left the king's mouth, they covered Haman's face. ⁹Now Harbonah, one of the eunuchs, said to the king, "Look! The gallows, fifty cubits high, which Haman made for Mordecai, who spoke good on the king's behalf, is standing at the house of Haman."

Then the king said, "Hang him on it!"

¹⁰So they hanged Haman on the gallows that he had prepared for Mordecai. Then the king's wrath subsided.

Esther Saves the Jews

8On that day King Ahasuerus gave Queen Esther the house of Haman, the enemy of the Jews. And Mordecai came before the king, for Esther had told how he *was related* to her. ²So the king took off his signet ring, which he had taken from Haman, and gave it to Mordecai; and Esther appointed Mordecai over the house of Haman.

³Now Esther spoke again to the king, fell down at his feet, and implored him with tears to counteract the evil of Haman the Agagite, and the scheme which he had devised against the Jews. ⁴And the king held out the golden scepter toward Esther. So Esther arose and stood before the king, ⁵and said, "If it pleases the king, and if I have found favor in his sight and the thing *seems* right to the king and I am pleasing in his eyes, let it be written to revoke the letters devised by Haman, the son of Hammedatha the Agagite, which he wrote to annihilate the Jews who *are* in all the king's provinces. ⁶For how can I endure to see the evil that will come to my people? Or how can I endure to see the destruction of my countrymen?"

⁷Then King Ahasuerus said to Queen Esther and Mordecai the Jew, "Indeed, I have given Esther the house of Haman, and they have hanged him on the gallows because he *tried to* lay his hand on the Jews. ⁸You yourselves write *a decree* concerning the Jews, as you please, in the king's name, and seal *it* with the king's signet ring; for whatever is written in the king's name and sealed with the king's signet ring no one can revoke."

⁹So the king's scribes were called at that time, in the third month, which *is* the month of Sivan, on the twenty-third *day;* and it was written, according to all that Mordecai commanded, to the Jews, the satraps, the governors, and the princes of the provinces from India to Ethiopia, one hundred and twenty-seven provinces *in all,* to every province in its own script, to every people in their own language, and to the Jews in their own script and language. ¹⁰And he wrote in the name of King Ahasuerus, sealed *it* with the king's signet ring, and sent letters by couriers on horseback, riding on royal horses bred from swift steeds.^a

¹¹By these letters the king permitted the Jews

8:10 ^aLiterally *sons of the swift horses*

who *were* in every city to gather together and protect their lives—to destroy, kill, and annihilate all the forces of any people or province that would assault them, *both* little children and women, and to plunder their possessions, ¹²on one day in all the provinces of King Ahasuerus, on the thirteenth *day* of the twelfth month, which *is* the month of Adar.ᵃ ¹³A copy of the document was to be issued as a decree in every province and published for all people, so that the Jews would be ready on that day to avenge themselves on their enemies. ¹⁴The couriers who rode on royal horses went out, hastened and pressed on by the king's command. And the decree was issued in Shushan the citadel.

¹⁵So Mordecai went out from the presence of the king in royal apparel of blue and white, with a great crown of gold and a garment of fine linen and purple; and the city of Shushan rejoiced and was glad. ¹⁶The Jews had light and gladness, joy and honor. ¹⁷And in every province and city, wherever the king's command and decree came, the Jews had joy and gladness, a feast and a holiday. Then many of the people of the land became Jews, because fear of the Jews fell upon them.

THE JEWS DESTROY THEIR TORMENTORS

9 Now in the twelfth month, that *is,* the month of Adar, on the thirteenth day, *the time* came for the king's command and his decree to be executed. On the day that the enemies of the Jews had hoped to overpower them, the opposite occurred, in that the Jews themselves overpowered those who hated them. ²The Jews gathered together in their cities throughout all the provinces of King Ahasuerus to lay hands on those who sought their harm. And no one could withstand them, because fear of them fell upon all people. ³And all the officials of the provinces, the satraps, the governors, and all those doing the king's work, helped the Jews, because the fear of Mordecai fell upon them. ⁴For Mordecai *was* great in the king's palace, and his fame spread throughout all the provinces; for this man Mordecai became increasingly prominent. ⁵Thus the Jews defeated all their enemies with the stroke of the sword, with slaughter and destruction, and did what they pleased with those who hated them.

⁶And in Shushan the citadel the Jews killed and destroyed five hundred men. ⁷Also Parshandatha, Dalphon, Aspatha, ⁸Poratha, Adalia, Aridatha, ⁹Parmashta, Arisai, Aridai, and Vajezatha—¹⁰the ten sons of Haman the son of Hammedatha, the enemy of the Jews—they killed; but they did not lay a hand on the plunder.

¹¹On that day the number of those who were killed in Shushan the citadel was brought to the king. ¹²And the king said to Queen Esther, "The Jews have killed and destroyed five hundred men in Shushan the citadel, and the ten sons of Haman. What have they done in the rest of the king's provinces? Now what *is* your petition? It shall be granted to you. Or what *is* your further request? It shall be done."

¹³Then Esther said, "If it pleases the king, let it be granted to the Jews who *are* in Shushan to do again tomorrow according to today's decree, and let Haman's ten sons be hanged on the gallows."

¹⁴So the king commanded this to be done; the decree was issued in Shushan, and they hanged Haman's ten sons.

¹⁵And the Jews who *were* in Shushan gathered together again on the fourteenth day of the month of Adar and killed three hundred men at Shushan; but they did not lay a hand on the plunder.

¹⁶The remainder of the Jews in the king's provinces gathered together and protected their lives, had rest from their enemies, and killed seventy-five thousand of their enemies; but they did not lay a hand on the plunder. ¹⁷This *was* on the thirteenth day of the month of Adar. And on the fourteenth of *the month*ᵃ they rested and made it a day of feasting and gladness.

THE FEAST OF PURIM

¹⁸But the Jews who *were* at Shushan assembled together on the thirteenth *day,* as well as on the fourteenth; and on the fifteenth of *the month*ᵃ they rested, and made it a day of feasting and gladness. ¹⁹Therefore the Jews of the villages who dwelt in the unwalled towns celebrated the fourteenth day of the month of Adar *with* gladness and feasting, as a holiday, and for sending presents to one another.

²⁰And Mordecai wrote these things and sent

8:12 ᵃSeptuagint adds the text of the letter here.   9:17 ᵃLiterally *i*
9:18 ᵃLiterally *it*

letters to all the Jews, near and far, who *were* in all the provinces of King Ahasuerus, [21]to establish among them that they should celebrate yearly the fourteenth and fifteenth days of the month of Adar, [22]as the days on which the Jews had rest from their enemies, as the month which was turned from sorrow to joy for them, and from mourning to a holiday; that they should make them days of feasting and joy, of sending presents to one another and gifts to the poor. [23]So the Jews accepted the custom which they had begun, as Mordecai had written to them, [24]because Haman, the son of Hammedatha the Agagite, the enemy of all the Jews, had plotted against the Jews to annihilate them, and had cast Pur (that *is,* the lot), to consume them and destroy them; [25]but when *Esther*[a] came before the king, he commanded by letter that this[b] wicked plot which *Haman* had devised against the Jews should return on his own head, and that he and his sons should be hanged on the gallows.

[26]So they called these days Purim, after the name Pur. Therefore, because of all the words of this letter, what they had seen concerning this matter, and what had happened to them, [27]the Jews established and imposed it upon themselves and their descendants and all who would join them, that without fail they should celebrate these two days every year, according to the written *instructions* and according to the *prescribed* time, [28]*that* these days *should be* remembered and kept throughout every generation, every family, every province, and every city, that these days of Purim should not fail *to be observed* among the Jews, and *that* the memory of them should not perish among their descendants.

[29]Then Queen Esther, the daughter of Abihail, with Mordecai the Jew, wrote with full authority to confirm this second letter about Purim. [30]And *Mordecai* sent letters to all the Jews, to the one hundred and twenty-seven provinces of the kingdom of Ahasuerus, *with* words of peace and truth, [31]to confirm these days of Purim at their *appointed* time, as Mordecai the Jew and Queen Esther had prescribed for them, and as they had decreed for themselves and their descendants concerning matters of their fasting and lamenting. [32]So the decree of Esther confirmed these matters of Purim, and it was written in the book.

MORDECAI'S ADVANCEMENT

10And King Ahasuerus imposed tribute on the land and *on* the islands of the sea. [2]Now all the acts of his power and his might, and the account of the greatness of Mordecai, to which the king advanced him, *are* they not written in the book of the chronicles of the kings of Media and Persia? [3]For Mordecai the Jew *was* second to King Ahasuerus, and was great among the Jews and well received by the multitude of his brethren, seeking the good of his people and speaking peace to all his countrymen.[a]

9:25 [a]Literally *she* or *it* [b]Literally *his*   **10:3** [a]Literally *seed*. Septuagint and Vulgate add a dream of Mordecai here; Vulgate adds six more chapters.

IMPACT OF THE BOOK

JOB

IDEA

Suffering is not a sign of God's judgment on a person's life but can serve to strengthen a person's faith. The phrase "the patience of Job" is known around the world. The character and faith Job demonstrated proves he had real faith which held up in the worst of times.

MESSAGE

Integrity is not something that is developed overnight; it is cultivated over a lifetime. Integrity means "wholeness." When the storms raged, Job's friends questioned his integrity. He was able to point to his unblemished walk with the Lord. Each decision we make, even when no one else—except God—is looking determines our integrity. Job, even in the midst of his struggles, chose to trust God instead of the counsel of men. No other book in the Bible does more to dispel the false belief that your life circumstances are an indication of your standing before God.

PEOPLE

Bildad, Elihu, Eliphaz, Job, Zophar

AUTHOR

As with many of the Old Testament books, Job's author is anonymous. The use of the term "Lord" (Heb. Yahweh) to refer to God suggests the writer was an Israelite, possibly Job himself, or even Solomon, Hezekiah, Isaiah, or Ezra, as some scholars have suggested.

CULTURE

The descriptions of Job's wealth, his long life (42:16), and the fact that he acted as priest for his family indicates that this story happened during the time of the patriarchs (between 2000 and 1500 BC), making it the oldest book in the Bible. Job lived in Uz, a city that was located either east or southeast of Palestine (between Edom and northern Arabia).

TIMELINE

Date unknown; possibly during the time of the patriarchs

KEY SCRIPTURE MEMORY VERSES

1:8; 13:15; 19:25, 26; 38:4–7

Job and His Family in Uz

1 There was a man in the land of Uz, whose name *was* Job; and that man was blameless and upright, and one who feared God and shunned evil. [2]And seven sons and three daughters were born to him. [3]Also, his possessions were seven thousand sheep, three thousand camels, five hundred yoke of oxen, five hundred female donkeys, and a very large household, so that this man was the greatest of all the people of the East.

[4]And his sons would go and feast *in their* houses, each on his *appointed* day, and would send and invite their three sisters to eat and drink with them. [5]So it was, when the days of feasting had run their course, that Job would send and sanctify them, and he would rise early in the morning and offer burnt offerings *according to* the number of them all. For Job said, "It may be that my sons have sinned and cursed[a] God in their hearts." Thus Job did regularly.

Satan Attacks Job's Character

[6]Now there was a day when the sons of God came to present themselves before the LORD, and Satan[a] also came among them. [7]And the LORD said to Satan, "From where do you come?"

So Satan answered the LORD and said, "From going to and fro on the earth, and from walking back and forth on it."

[8]Then the LORD said to Satan, "Have you considered My servant Job, that *there is* none like him on the earth, a blameless and upright man, one who fears God and shuns evil?"

[9]So Satan answered the LORD and said, "Does Job fear God for nothing? [10]Have You not made a hedge around him, around his household, and around all that he has on every side? You have blessed the work of his hands, and his possessions have increased in the land. [11]But now, stretch out Your hand and touch all that he has, and he will surely curse You to Your face!"

[12]And the LORD said to Satan, "Behold, all that he has *is* in your power; only do not lay a hand on his *person*."

So Satan went out from the presence of the LORD.

Job Loses His Property and Children

[13]Now there was a day when his sons and daughters *were* eating and drinking wine in their oldest brother's house; [14]and a messenger came to Job and said, "The oxen were plowing and the donkeys feeding beside them, [15]when the Sabeans[a] raided *them* and took them away—indeed they have killed the servants with the edge of the sword; and I alone have escaped to tell you!"

[16]While he *was* still speaking, another also came and said, "The fire of God fell from heaven and burned up the sheep and the servants, and consumed them; and I alone have escaped to tell you!"

[17]While he *was* still speaking, another also came and said, "The Chaldeans formed three bands, raided the camels and took them away, yes, and killed the servants with the edge of the sword; and I alone have escaped to tell you!"

[18]While he *was* still speaking, another also came and said, "Your sons and daughters *were* eating and drinking wine in their oldest brother's house, [19]and suddenly a great wind came from across[a] the wilderness and struck the four corners of the house, and it fell on the young people, and they are dead; and I alone have escaped to tell you!"

1:5 [a]Literally *blessed*, but used here in the evil sense, and so in verse 11 and 2:5, 9   **1:6** [a]Literally *the Adversary*, and so throughout this book   **1:15** [a]Literally *Sheba* (compare 6:19)   **1:19** [a]Septuagint omits *across*.

THROUGH THE GRID   *Making Sense of Your World: The Aspects of Evil (Job)*

There are two aspects to the problem of evil—the logical problem and the emotional problem. The logical problem attempts to account for evil, given a God who is all-good and all-powerful. The emotional problem of evil deals with why God would allow suffering and pain to come to an individual who doesn't "deserve" it.

²⁰Then Job arose, tore his robe, and shaved his head; and he fell to the ground and worshiped. ²¹And he said:

"Naked I came from my mother's womb,
And naked shall I return there.
The LORD gave, and the LORD has taken
        away;
Blessed be the name of the LORD."

²²In all this Job did not sin nor charge God with wrong.

SATAN ATTACKS JOB'S HEALTH

2 Again there was a day when the sons of God came to present themselves before the LORD, and Satan came also among them to present himself before the LORD. ²And the LORD said to Satan, "From where do you come?"

Satan answered the LORD and said, "From going to and fro on the earth, and from walking back and forth on it."

³Then the LORD said to Satan, "Have you considered My servant Job, that *there is* none like him on the earth, a blameless and upright man, one who fears God and shuns evil? And still he holds fast to his integrity, although you incited Me against him, to destroy him without cause."

⁴So Satan answered the LORD and said, "Skin for skin! Yes, all that a man has he will give for his life. ⁵But stretch out Your hand now, and touch his bone and his flesh, and he will surely curse You to Your face!"

⁶And the LORD said to Satan, "Behold, he *is* in your hand, but spare his life."

⁷So Satan went out from the presence of the LORD, and struck Job with painful boils from the sole of his foot to the crown of his head. ⁸And he took for himself a potsherd with which to scrape himself while he sat in the midst of the ashes.

⁹Then his wife said to him, "Do you still hold fast to your integrity? Curse God and die!"

¹⁰But he said to her, "You speak as one of the foolish women speaks. Shall we indeed accept good from God, and shall we not accept adversity?" In all this Job did not sin with his lips.

 the INFLUENCERS

JOB: Irrepressible Attitude of Gratitude

CHAPTERS 1—2

In the span of a few minutes, Job lost almost everything he loved in life. His job as a farmer and rancher was destroyed when all his livestock died (1:13–17); then all but four of his servants were killed, and all ten of his children died in a freak windstorm (1:18, 19).

To make matters worse, Job came down with a horrible skin disease (2:7). He went from being the richest, most respected man in the land to a broken down, miserable outcast who wasn't welcome in the city. If ever a man needed the support and encouragement of family and friends, it was Job; but he did not receive it.

Everyone important to Job either died or turned their backs on him. His wife told him to "curse God and die!" (2:9). His friends spent all of their time telling Job that his suffering was his own fault. Everyone was convinced that God didn't care about this righteous man (19:7).

In spite of all the tragedy, Job demonstrated an *irrepressible attitude of gratitude.* In his darkest hours, he refused to blame God for his pain or stop believing in His goodness (1:21). Even in his worst moment, we read that "Job prayed for his friends" (42:10). God rewarded his faithfulness with a double restoration of all that he had.

JOB'S THREE FRIENDS

[11]Now when Job's three friends heard of all this adversity that had come upon him, each one came from his own place—Eliphaz the Temanite, Bildad the Shuhite, and Zophar the Naamathite. For they had made an appointment together to come and mourn with him, and to comfort him. [12]And when they raised their eyes from afar, and did not recognize him, they lifted their voices and wept; and each one tore his robe and sprinkled dust on his head toward heaven. [13]So they sat down with him on the ground seven days and seven nights, and no one spoke a word to him, for they saw that *his* grief was very great.

JOB DEPLORES HIS BIRTH

3 After this Job opened his mouth and cursed the day of his *birth*. [2]And Job spoke, and said:

[3]"May the day perish on which I was born,
   And the night *in which* it was said,
   'A male child is conceived.'
[4]May that day be darkness;
   May God above not seek it,
   Nor the light shine upon it.
[5]May darkness and the shadow of death claim it;
   May a cloud settle on it;
   May the blackness of the day terrify it.
[6]*As for* that night, may darkness seize it;
   May it not rejoice[a] among the days of the year,
   May it not come into the number of the months.
[7]Oh, may that night be barren!
   May no joyful shout come into it!

[8]May those curse it who curse the day,
   Those who are ready to arouse Leviathan.
[9]May the stars of its morning be dark;
   May it look for light, but *have* none,
   And not see the dawning of the day;
[10]Because it did not shut up the doors of my *mother's* womb,
   Nor hide sorrow from my eyes.

[11]"Why did I not die at birth?
   Why did I *not* perish when I came from the womb?
[12]Why did the knees receive me?
   Or why the breasts, that I should nurse?
[13]For now I would have lain still and been quiet,
   I would have been asleep;
   Then I would have been at rest
[14]With kings and counselors of the earth,
   Who built ruins for themselves,
[15]Or with princes who had gold,
   Who filled their houses *with* silver;
[16]Or *why* was I not hidden like a stillborn child,
   Like infants who never saw light?
[17]There the wicked cease *from* troubling,
   And there the weary are at rest.
[18]*There* the prisoners rest together;
   They do not hear the voice of the oppressor.
[19]The small and great are there,
   And the servant *is* free from his master.

[20]"Why is light given to him who is in misery,
   And life to the bitter of soul,
[21]Who long for death, but it does not *come,*
   And search for it more than hidden treasures;

3:6 [a]Septuagint, Syriac, Targum, and Vulgate read *be joined.*

THROUGH THE GRID

Making Sense of Your World:
Four Postures to Answering Evil (Job)

There are four main postures that have been adopted over the years in an attempt to account for the evil and the injustices in our world. These include fideism, illusionism, finitism, and transmoralism. Fideism is the position of "blind faith"—a view that trusts God blindly and explains evil away as part of God's mysterious ways of dealing with creation. Illusionism claims that evil is not real and that the evil that appears to be manifest is merely an illusion. Finitism claims that God is not all-powerful, but rather that God also is attempting to overcome evil. Transmoralism retains the power of God but claims that God's power and goodness actually work differently than we expect.

²²Who rejoice exceedingly,
And are glad when they can find the grave?
²³*Why is light given* to a man whose way is
hidden,
And whom God has hedged in?
²⁴For my sighing comes before I eat,[a]
And my groanings pour out like water.
²⁵For the thing I greatly feared has come upon
me,
And what I dreaded has happened to me.
²⁶I am not at ease, nor am I quiet;
I have no rest, for trouble comes."

Eliphaz: Job Has Sinned

4 Then Eliphaz the Temanite answered and said:

²"If one attempts a word with you, will you
become weary?
But who can withhold himself from
speaking?
³Surely you have instructed many,
And you have strengthened weak hands.
⁴Your words have upheld him who was
stumbling,
And you have strengthened the feeble knees;
⁵But now it comes upon you, and you are
weary;
It touches you, and you are troubled.
⁶*Is* not your reverence your confidence?
And the integrity of your ways your hope?

⁷"Remember now, who *ever* perished being
innocent?
Or where were the upright *ever* cut off?

⁸Even as I have seen,
Those who plow iniquity
And sow trouble reap the same.
⁹By the blast of God they perish,
And by the breath of His anger they are
consumed.
¹⁰The roaring of the lion,
The voice of the fierce lion,
And the teeth of the young lions are broken.
¹¹The old lion perishes for lack of prey,
And the cubs of the lioness are scattered.

¹²"Now a word was secretly brought to me,
And my ear received a whisper of it.
¹³In disquieting thoughts from the visions of
the night,
When deep sleep falls on men,
¹⁴Fear came upon me, and trembling,
Which made all my bones shake.
¹⁵Then a spirit passed before my face;
The hair on my body stood up.
¹⁶It stood still,
But I could not discern its appearance.
A form *was* before my eyes;
There was silence;
Then I heard a voice *saying:*
¹⁷"Can a mortal be more righteous than God?
Can a man be more pure than his Maker?
¹⁸If He puts no trust in His servants,
If He charges His angels with error,
¹⁹How much more those who dwell in houses
of clay,

3:24 [a]Literally *my bread*

THROUGH THE GRID

*Making Sense of Your World:
The Limitations of Fideism
and Illusionism (Job)*

Fideism may sound appealing to some theists; but at the end of the day, it ignores the most pressing problems confronting one's faith. Fideism "gives up" too quickly on the problem and does not attempt to seek a solution to the existence of evil. Adherents of a biblical worldview will seek instead to search out meaning and to attempt to arrive at an adequate answer, given God's revelation to us of His plan and will. Illusionism, likewise, denies evil and avoids dealing with the real problem. Evil is redefined in ways that are not biblical, and this view does not fit one's pragmatic experience with real evil in the world. This view provides no satisfactory answer to evil.

Whose foundation is in the dust,
Who are crushed before a moth?
[20]They are broken in pieces from morning till
    evening;
They perish forever, with no one regarding.
[21]Does not their own excellence go away?
They die, even without wisdom.'

ELIPHAZ: JOB IS CHASTENED BY GOD

5 "Call out now;
  Is there anyone who will answer you?
  And to which of the holy ones will you
      turn?
[2]For wrath kills a foolish man,
  And envy slays a simple one.
[3]I have seen the foolish taking root,
  But suddenly I cursed his dwelling place.
[4]His sons are far from safety,
  They are crushed in the gate,
  And *there is* no deliverer.
[5]Because the hungry eat up his harvest,
  Taking it even from the thorns,[a]
  And a snare snatches their substance.[b]
[6]For affliction does not come from the dust,
  Nor does trouble spring from the ground;
[7]Yet man is born to trouble,
  As the sparks fly upward.

[8]"But as for me, I would seek God,
  And to God I would commit my cause—
[9]Who does great things, and unsearchable,
  Marvelous things without number.
[10]He gives rain on the earth,

And sends waters on the fields.
[11]He sets on high those who are lowly,
  And those who mourn are lifted to safety.
[12]He frustrates the devices of the crafty,
  So that their hands cannot carry out their plans.
[13]He catches the wise in their own craftiness,
  And the counsel of the cunning comes
      quickly upon them.
[14]They meet with darkness in the daytime,
  And grope at noontime as in the night.
[15]But He saves the needy from the sword,
  From the mouth of the mighty,
  And from their hand.
[16]So the poor have hope,
  And injustice shuts her mouth.

[17]"Behold, happy *is* the man whom God corrects;
  Therefore do not despise the chastening of
      the Almighty.
[18]For He bruises, but He binds up;
  He wounds, but His hands make whole.
[19]He shall deliver you in six troubles,
  Yes, in seven no evil shall touch you.
[20]In famine He shall redeem you from death,
  And in war from the power of the sword.
[21]You shall be hidden from the scourge of the
      tongue,
  And you shall not be afraid of destruction
      when it comes.

5:5 [a]Septuagint reads *They shall not be taken from evil men;* Vulgate reads *And the armed man shall take him by violence.* [b]Septuagint reads *The might shall draw them off;* Vulgate reads *And the thirsty shall drink up their riches.*

THROUGH THE GRID

Making Sense of Your World:
The Limitations of Finitism
and Transmoralism (Job)

Finitism attempts to solve the problem by changing the definition of God's sovereignty in ways that ultimately limit God's power and entire identity. Adherents of finitism believe that God exists but that He is just incapable of solving the problems of evil. This clashes with the biblical worldview, which affirms God's complete and total power over all of creation. Finitism cannot be part of a biblical worldview. Transmoralism also redefines God's sovereignty by claiming that whatever God does or allows to happen is good and moral, since God is good and whatever happens is caused by God. Thus, evil must also be good. This view is inadequate to account for the extant evil in our world as well as pragmatic dealings with evil.

²²You shall laugh at destruction and famine,
  And you shall not be afraid of the beasts of
    the earth.
²³For you shall have a covenant with the stones
    of the field,
  And the beasts of the field shall be at peace
    with you.
²⁴You shall know that your tent *is* in peace;
  You shall visit your dwelling and find
    nothing amiss.
²⁵You shall also know that your descendants
    shall be many,
  And your offspring like the grass of the
    earth.
²⁶You shall come to the grave at a full age,
  As a sheaf of grain ripens in its season.
²⁷Behold, this we have searched out;
  It *is* true.
  Hear it, and know for yourself."

JOB: MY COMPLAINT IS JUST

6 Then Job answered and said:

²"Oh, that my grief were fully weighed,
  And my calamity laid with it on the scales!

³For then it would be heavier than the sand of
    the sea—
  Therefore my words have been rash.
⁴For the arrows of the Almighty *are* within
    me;
  My spirit drinks in their poison;
  The terrors of God are arrayed against me.
⁵Does the wild donkey bray when it has grass,
  Or does the ox low over its fodder?
⁶Can flavorless food be eaten without salt?
  Or is there *any* taste in the white of an egg?
⁷My soul refuses to touch them;
  They *are* as loathsome food to me.

⁸"Oh, that I might have my request,
  That God would grant *me* the thing that I
    long for!
⁹That it would please God to crush me,
  That He would loose His hand and cut me
    off!
¹⁰Then I would still have comfort;
  Though in anguish I would exult,
  He will not spare;
  For I have not concealed the words of the
    Holy One.

THROUGH THE GRID

*Making Sense of Your World: Finding
an Adequate Solution to Evil (Job)*

The previous postures listed in regard to evil cannot adequately solve the problem of evil. The problem of evil, however, has no easy formulaic or quick-fix answer because it takes on so many extensions and forms. One can approach a response to the problem of suffering by viewing suffering as a direct result of a moral choice to sin. That is, because we are beings who sin, suffering comes to us as a part of human existence. Suffering can also be explained as that which can cause a greater good, Paul's "thorn in the flesh" or Joseph's enslavement and imprisonment in Egypt. Developing a biblical worldview demands that we look at three other factors: free will, time, and the suffering of Jesus. Free will is a property of human existence, in that we have the ability to make choices. Thus, humanity always has the capacity to choose between good and evil. Accordingly, evil arises because human beings sometimes use their free will to choose evil. God cannot take away free will, so we are left with the evil. Time is another factor because the Bible does promise that evil will one day be eradicated. Thus, we live in an age of the "already but not yet." We must wait patiently for time to be fulfilled. The suffering of Jesus also provides a keen perspective, since Jesus Himself experienced evil and suffering. Following His lead, those developing a biblical worldview must learn to respond to pain and suffering as Jesus did, by trusting the will and sovereignty of God and obeying God in spite of suffering.

¹¹"What strength do I have, that I should hope?
  And what *is* my end, that I should prolong
    my life?
¹²*Is* my strength the strength of stones?
  Or is my flesh bronze?
¹³*Is* my help not within me?
  And is success driven from me?

¹⁴"To him who is afflicted, kindness *should be
    shown* by his friend,
  Even though he forsakes the fear of the
    Almighty.
¹⁵My brothers have dealt deceitfully like a
    brook,
  Like the streams of the brooks that pass
    away,
¹⁶Which are dark because of the ice,
  And into which the snow vanishes.
¹⁷When it is warm, they cease to flow;
  When it is hot, they vanish from their place.
¹⁸The paths of their way turn aside,
  They go nowhere and perish.
¹⁹The caravans of Tema look,
  The travelers of Sheba hope for them.
²⁰They are disappointed because they were
    confident;

They come there and are confused.
²¹For now you are nothing,
  You see terror and are afraid.
²²Did I ever say, 'Bring *something* to me'?
  Or, 'Offer a bribe for me from your
    wealth'?
²³Or, 'Deliver me from the enemy's hand'?
  Or, 'Redeem me from the hand of
    oppressors'?

²⁴"Teach me, and I will hold my tongue;
  Cause me to understand wherein I have
    erred.
²⁵How forceful are right words!
  But what does your arguing prove?
²⁶Do you intend to rebuke *my* words,
  And the speeches of a desperate one, *which are*
    as wind?
²⁷Yes, you overwhelm the fatherless,
  And you undermine your friend.
²⁸Now therefore, be pleased to look at me;
  For I would never lie to your face.
²⁹Yield now, let there be no injustice!
  Yes, concede, my righteousness still stands!
³⁰Is there injustice on my tongue?
  Cannot my taste discern the unsavory?

THROUGH THE GRID

Making Sense of Your World:
The Christian Response to Evil (Job)

No doubt, we all recognize how prevalent evil is in our world. The response of Christians is to see that human beings are free agents with moral choice. But with this recognition comes a huge responsibility to act positively to overcome the evil in our world. It is true that we cannot eliminate evil in a world full of people who all can make free choices. Evil will not be completely eradicated until Christ's return when God will usher in a new heaven and a new earth, removing sin and evil from the midst of reality. However, until then, those who are developing a Christian worldview have a great responsibility to their neighbor in terms of social ethics. Though we cannot stop or prevent evil at times, we can, however, be agents of good in a world of evil. When horrible tragedies strike and people undergo pain and suffering, Christians have the responsibility to become agents of Christ, coming alongside of people in their suffering and in their encounters with evil. The evil extant in our world gives Christians multiple opportunities to practice their faith and to demonstrate their belief in a God who has all things under control. By helping others in their time of need, we become the hands and feet of Christ. We don't eliminate evil, but we contribute to the good that can be done. The responsibility is ours as biblical Christians, who have been created in the very image of God, to do good in the midst of a world that is encompassed by evil, suffering, and injustice.

Job: My Suffering Is Comfortless

7 "*Is there* not a time of hard service for man
  on earth?
  Are not his days also like the days of a hired
  man?
  ²Like a servant who earnestly desires the shade,
  And like a hired man who eagerly looks for
  his wages,
  ³So I have been allotted months of futility,
  And wearisome nights have been appointed
  to me.
  ⁴When I lie down, I say, 'When shall I arise,
  And the night be ended?'
  For I have had my fill of tossing till dawn.
  ⁵My flesh is caked with worms and dust,
  My skin is cracked and breaks out afresh.

  ⁶"My days are swifter than a weaver's shuttle,
  And are spent without hope.
  ⁷Oh, remember that my life *is* a breath!
  My eye will never again see good.
  ⁸The eye of him who sees me will see me no
  more;
  While your eyes *are* upon me, I shall no
  longer *be.*
  ⁹*As* the cloud disappears and vanishes away,
  So he who goes down to the grave does not
  come up.
  ¹⁰He shall never return to his house,
  Nor shall his place know him anymore.

  ¹¹"Therefore I will not restrain my mouth;
  I will speak in the anguish of my spirit;
  I will complain in the bitterness of my soul.
  ¹²*Am* I a sea, or a sea serpent,
  That You set a guard over me?
  ¹³When I say, 'My bed will comfort me,
  My couch will ease my complaint,'
  ¹⁴Then You scare me with dreams
  And terrify me with visions,
  ¹⁵So that my soul chooses strangling
  And death rather than my body.ᵃ
  ¹⁶I loathe *my life;*
  I would not live forever.
  Let me alone,
  For my days *are but* a breath.

  ¹⁷"What *is* man, that You should exalt him,
  That You should set Your heart on him,

¹⁸That You should visit him every morning,
  And test him every moment?
¹⁹How long?
  Will You not look away from me,
  And let me alone till I swallow my saliva?
²⁰Have I sinned?
  What have I done to You, O watcher of men?
  Why have You set me as Your target,
  So that I am a burden to myself?ᵃ
²¹Why then do You not pardon my
    transgression,
  And take away my iniquity?
  For now I will lie down in the dust,
  And You will seek me diligently,
  But I *will* no longer *be.*"

Bildad: Job Should Repent

8 Then Bildad the Shuhite answered and said:

²"How long will you speak these *things,*
  And the words of your mouth *be like* a strong
  wind?
³Does God subvert judgment?
  Or does the Almighty pervert justice?
⁴If your sons have sinned against Him,
  He has cast them away for their transgression.
⁵If you would earnestly seek God
  And make your supplication to the Almighty,
⁶If you *were* pure and upright,
  Surely now He would awake for you,
  And prosper your rightful dwelling place.
⁷Though your beginning was small,
  Yet your latter end would increase
    abundantly.

⁸"For inquire, please, of the former age,
  And consider the things discovered by their
    fathers;
⁹For we *were born* yesterday, and know nothing,
  Because our days on earth *are* a shadow.
¹⁰Will they not teach you and tell you,
  And utter words from their heart?

¹¹"Can the papyrus grow up without a marsh?
  Can the reeds flourish without water?
¹²While it *is* yet green *and* not cut down,
  It withers before any *other* plant.

7:15 ᵃLiterally *my bones*   **7:20** ᵃFollowing Masoretic Text, Targum
and Vulgate; Septuagint and Jewish tradition read *to You.*

¹³So *are* the paths of all who forget God;
  And the hope of the hypocrite shall perish,
¹⁴Whose confidence shall be cut off,
  And whose trust *is* a spider's web.
¹⁵He leans on his house, but it does not stand.
  He holds it fast, but it does not endure.
¹⁶He grows green in the sun,
  And his branches spread out in his garden.
¹⁷His roots wrap around the rock heap,
  And look for a place in the stones.
¹⁸If he is destroyed from his place,
  Then *it* will deny him, *saying,* 'I have not seen
  you.'

¹⁹"Behold, this is the joy of His way,
  And out of the earth others will grow.
²⁰Behold, God will not cast away the blameless,
  Nor will He uphold the evildoers.
²¹He will yet fill your mouth with laughing,
  And your lips with rejoicing.
²²Those who hate you will be clothed with
  shame,
  And the dwelling place of the wicked will
  come to nothing."ᵃ

JOB: THERE IS NO MEDIATOR

9 Then Job answered and said:

²"Truly I know *it is* so,
  But how can a man be righteous before God?
³If one wished to contend with Him,
  He could not answer Him one time out of a
  thousand.
⁴*God is* wise in heart and mighty in strength.
  Who has hardened *himself* against Him and
  prospered?
⁵He removes the mountains, and they do not
  know
  When He overturns them in His anger;
⁶He shakes the earth out of its place,
  And its pillars tremble;
⁷He commands the sun, and it does not rise;
  He seals off the stars;
⁸He alone spreads out the heavens,
  And treads on the waves of the sea;
⁹He made the Bear, Orion, and the Pleiades,
  And the chambers of the south;
¹⁰He does great things past finding out,
  Yes, wonders without number.

¹¹If He goes by me, I do not see *Him;*
  If He moves past, I do not perceive Him;
¹²If He takes away, who can hinder Him?
  Who can say to Him, 'What are You doing?'
¹³God will not withdraw His anger,
  The allies of the proudᵃ lie prostrate beneath
  Him.

¹⁴"How then can I answer Him,
  And choose my words *to reason* with Him?
¹⁵For though I were righteous, I could not
  answer Him;
  I would beg mercy of my Judge.
¹⁶If I called and He answered me,
  I would not believe that He was listening to
  my voice.
¹⁷For He crushes me with a tempest,
  And multiplies my wounds without cause.
¹⁸He will not allow me to catch my breath,
  But fills me with bitterness.
¹⁹If *it is a matter* of strength, indeed *He is* strong;
  And if of justice, who will appoint my day *in
  court?*
²⁰Though I were righteous, my own mouth
  would condemn me;
  Though I *were* blameless, it would prove me
  perverse.

²¹"I am blameless, yet I do not know myself;
  I despise my life.
²²It *is all one thing;*
  Therefore I say, 'He destroys the blameless and
  the wicked.'
²³If the scourge slays suddenly,
  He laughs at the plight of the innocent.
²⁴The earth is given into the hand of the
  wicked.
  He covers the faces of its judges.
  If it is not *He,* who else could it be?

²⁵"Now my days are swifter than a runner;
  They flee away, they see no good.
²⁶They pass by like swift ships,
  Like an eagle swooping on its prey.
²⁷If I say, 'I will forget my complaint,
  I will put off my sad face and wear a smile,'
²⁸I am afraid of all my sufferings;

8:22 ᵃLiterally *will not be*   9:13 ᵃHebrew *rahab*

I know that You will not hold me innocent.
²⁹*If* I am condemned,
  Why then do I labor in vain?
³⁰If I wash myself with snow water,
  And cleanse my hands with soap,
³¹Yet You will plunge me into the pit,
  And my own clothes will abhor me.

³²"For *He is* not a man, as I *am,*
  That I may answer Him,
  And that we should go to court together.
³³Nor is there any mediator between us,
  Who may lay his hand on us both.
³⁴Let Him take His rod away from me,
  And do not let dread of Him terrify me.
³⁵*Then* I would speak and not fear Him,
  But it is not so with me.

JOB: I WOULD PLEAD WITH GOD

10 "My soul loathes my life;
  I will give free course to my complaint,
  I will speak in the bitterness of my soul.
²I will say to God, 'Do not condemn me;
  Show me why You contend with me.
³*Does it* seem good to You that You should
    oppress,
  That You should despise the work of Your
    hands,
  And smile on the counsel of the wicked?
⁴Do You have eyes of flesh?
  Or do You see as man sees?
⁵*Are* Your days like the days of a mortal man?
  Are Your years like the days of a mighty man,
⁶That You should seek for my iniquity
  And search out my sin,
⁷Although You know that I am not wicked,
  And *there is* no one who can deliver from
    Your hand?

⁸'Your hands have made me and fashioned me,
  An intricate unity;
  Yet You would destroy me.
⁹Remember, I pray, that You have made me
    like clay.
  And will You turn me into dust again?
¹⁰Did You not pour me out like milk,
  And curdle me like cheese,
¹¹Clothe me with skin and flesh,
  And knit me together with bones and sinews?

¹²You have granted me life and favor,
  And Your care has preserved my spirit.

¹³'And these *things* You have hidden in Your
    heart;
  I know that this *was* with You:
¹⁴If I sin, then You mark me,
  And will not acquit me of my iniquity.
¹⁵If I am wicked, woe to me;
  Even *if* I am righteous, I cannot lift up my
    head.
  I am full of disgrace;
  See my misery!
¹⁶If *my head* is exalted,
  You hunt me like a fierce lion,
  And again You show Yourself awesome against
    me.
¹⁷You renew Your witnesses against me,
  And increase Your indignation toward me;
  Changes and war are *ever* with me.

¹⁸'Why then have You brought me out of the
    womb?
  Oh, that I had perished and no eye had seen
    me!
¹⁹I would have been as though I had not
    been.
  I would have been carried from the womb to
    the grave.
²⁰Are not my days few?
  Cease! Leave me alone, that I may take a little
    comfort,
²¹Before I go *to the place from which* I shall not
    return,
  To the land of darkness and the shadow of
    death,
²²A land as dark as darkness *itself,*
  As the shadow of death, without any order,
  Where even the light *is* like darkness.' "

ZOPHAR URGES JOB TO REPENT

11 Then Zophar the Naamathite answered
  and said:

²"Should not the multitude of words be
    answered?
  And should a man full of talk be vindicated?
³Should your empty talk make men hold their
    peace?

And when you mock, should no one rebuke
  you?
[4]For you have said,
'My doctrine *is* pure,
  And I am clean in your eyes.'
[5]But oh, that God would speak,
  And open His lips against you,
[6]That He would show you the secrets of
  wisdom!
For *they would* double *your* prudence.
Know therefore that God exacts from you
Less than your iniquity *deserves.*

[7]"Can you search out the deep things of God?
  Can you find out the limits of the Almighty?
[8]*They are* higher than heaven— what can you
  do?
Deeper than Sheol— what can you know?
[9]Their measure *is* longer than the earth
  And broader than the sea.

[10]"If He passes by, imprisons, and gathers *to*
  judgment,
Then who can hinder Him?
[11]For He knows deceitful men;
  He sees wickedness also.
Will He not then consider *it?*
[12]For an empty-headed man will be wise,
  When a wild donkey's colt is born a man.

[13]"If you would prepare your heart,
  And stretch out your hands toward Him;
[14]If iniquity *were* in your hand, *and you* put it far
  away,
And would not let wickedness dwell in your
  tents;
[15]Then surely you could lift up your face
  without spot;
Yes, you could be steadfast, and not fear;
[16]Because you would forget *your* misery,
  And remember *it* as waters *that have* passed
  away,
[17]And *your* life would be brighter than noonday.
Though you were dark, you would be like the
  morning.
[18]And you would be secure, because there is
  hope;
Yes, you would dig *around you, and* take your
  rest in safety.

[19]You would also lie down, and no one would
  make *you* afraid;
Yes, many would court your favor.
[20]But the eyes of the wicked will fail,
  And they shall not escape,
  And their hope—loss of life!"

Job Answers His Critics

12 Then Job answered and said:

[2]"No doubt you *are* the people,
  And wisdom will die with you!
[3]But I have understanding as well as you;
  I *am* not inferior to you.
  Indeed, who does not *know* such things as
  these?

[4]"I am one mocked by his friends,
  Who called on God, and He answered him,
  The just and blameless *who is* ridiculed.
[5]A lamp[a] is despised in the thought of one
  who is at ease;
It is made ready for those whose feet slip.
[6]The tents of robbers prosper,
  And those who provoke God are secure—
  In what God provides by His hand.

[7]"But now ask the beasts, and they will teach
  you;
And the birds of the air, and they will tell
  you;
[8]Or speak to the earth, and it will teach you;
  And the fish of the sea will explain to you.
[9]Who among all these does not know
  That the hand of the LORD has done this,
[10]In whose hand *is* the life of every living
  thing,
  And the breath of all mankind?
[11]Does not the ear test words
  And the mouth taste its food?
[12]Wisdom *is* with aged men,
  And with length of days, understanding.

[13]"With Him *are* wisdom and strength,
  He has counsel and understanding.
[14]If He breaks *a thing* down, it cannot be
  rebuilt;

12:5 [a]Or *disaster*

If He imprisons a man, there can be no release.

¹⁵If He withholds the waters, they dry up;
If He sends them out, they overwhelm the earth.

¹⁶With Him *are* strength and prudence.
The deceived and the deceiver *are* His.

¹⁷He leads counselors away plundered,
And makes fools of the judges.

¹⁸He loosens the bonds of kings,
And binds their waist with a belt.

¹⁹He leads princes[a] away plundered,
And overthrows the mighty.

²⁰He deprives the trusted ones of speech,
And takes away the discernment of the elders.

²¹He pours contempt on princes,
And disarms the mighty.

²²He uncovers deep things out of darkness,
And brings the shadow of death to light.

²³He makes nations great, and destroys them;
He enlarges nations, and guides them.

²⁴He takes away the understanding[a] of the chiefs of the people of the earth,
And makes them wander in a pathless wilderness.

²⁵They grope in the dark without light,
And He makes them stagger like a drunken *man*.

13 "Behold, my eye has seen all *this,*
My ear has heard and understood it.

²What you know, I also know;
I *am* not inferior to you.

³But I would speak to the Almighty,
And I desire to reason with God.

⁴But you forgers of lies,
You *are* all worthless physicians.

⁵Oh, that you would be silent,
And it would be your wisdom!

⁶Now hear my reasoning,
And heed the pleadings of my lips.

⁷Will you speak wickedly for God,
And talk deceitfully for Him?

⁸Will you show partiality for Him?
Will you contend for God?

⁹Will it be well when He searches you out?
Or can you mock Him as one mocks a man?

¹⁰He will surely rebuke you
If you secretly show partiality.

¹¹Will not His excellence make you afraid,
And the dread of Him fall upon you?

¹²Your platitudes *are* proverbs of ashes,
Your defenses are defenses of clay.

¹³"Hold your peace with me, and let me speak,
Then let come on me what *may!*

¹⁴Why do I take my flesh in my teeth,
And put my life in my hands?

¹⁵Though He slay me, yet will I trust Him.
Even so, I will defend my own ways before Him.

¹⁶He also *shall* be my salvation,
For a hypocrite could not come before Him.

¹⁷Listen carefully to my speech,
And to my declaration with your ears.

¹⁸See now, I have prepared *my* case,
I know that I shall be vindicated.

¹⁹Who *is* he *who* will contend with me?
If now I hold my tongue, I perish.

Job's Despondent Prayer

²⁰"Only two *things* do not do to me,
Then I will not hide myself from You:

²¹Withdraw Your hand far from me,
And let not the dread of You make me afraid.

²²Then call, and I will answer;
Or let me speak, then You respond to me.

²³How many *are* my iniquities and sins?
Make me know my transgression and my sin.

²⁴Why do You hide Your face,
And regard me as Your enemy?

²⁵Will You frighten a leaf driven to and fro?
And will You pursue dry stubble?

²⁶For You write bitter things against me,
And make me inherit the iniquities of my youth.

²⁷You put my feet in the stocks,
And watch closely all my paths.
You set a limit[a] for the soles of my feet.

²⁸"*Man*[a] decays like a rotten thing,
Like a garment that is moth-eaten.

14 "Man *who is* born of woman
Is of few days and full of trouble.

²He comes forth like a flower and fades away;

12:19 aLiterally *priests*, but not in a technical sense 12:24 aLiterally
heart 13:27 aLiterally *inscribe a print* 13:28 aLiterally *He*

He flees like a shadow and does not continue.
³And do You open Your eyes on such a one,
And bring me^a to judgment with Yourself?
⁴Who can bring a clean *thing* out of an
unclean?
No one!
⁵Since his days *are* determined,
The number of his months *is* with You;
You have appointed his limits, so that he
cannot pass.
⁶Look away from him that he may rest,
Till like a hired man he finishes his day.

⁷"For there is hope for a tree,
If it is cut down, that it will sprout again,
And that its tender shoots will not cease.
⁸Though its root may grow old in the earth,
And its stump may die in the ground,
⁹*Yet* at the scent of water it will bud
And bring forth branches like a plant.
¹⁰But man dies and is laid away;
Indeed he breathes his last
And where *is* he?
¹¹*As* water disappears from the sea,
And a river becomes parched and dries up,
¹²So man lies down and does not rise.
Till the heavens *are* no more,
They will not awake
Nor be roused from their sleep.

¹³"Oh, that You would hide me in the grave,
That You would conceal me until Your wrath
is past,
That You would appoint me a set time, and
remember me!
¹⁴If a man dies, shall he live *again?*
All the days of my hard service I will wait,
Till my change comes.
¹⁵You shall call, and I will answer You;
You shall desire the work of Your hands.
¹⁶For now You number my steps,
But do not watch over my sin.
¹⁷My transgression *is* sealed up in a bag,
And You cover^a my iniquity.

¹⁸"But *as* a mountain falls *and* crumbles away,
And *as* a rock is moved from its place;
¹⁹*As* water wears away stones,
And as torrents wash away the soil of the earth;

So You destroy the hope of man.
²⁰You prevail forever against him, and he passes
on;
You change his countenance and send him
away.
²¹His sons come to honor, and he does not
know *it;*
They are brought low, and he does not
perceive *it.*
²²But his flesh will be in pain over it,
And his soul will mourn over it."

ELIPHAZ ACCUSES JOB OF FOLLY

15 Then Eliphaz the Temanite answered and
said:

²"Should a wise man answer with empty
knowledge,
And fill himself with the east wind?
³Should he reason with unprofitable talk,
Or by speeches with which he can do no
good?
⁴Yes, you cast off fear,
And restrain prayer before God.
⁵For your iniquity teaches your mouth,
And you choose the tongue of the crafty.
⁶Your own mouth condemns you, and not I;
Yes, your own lips testify against you.

⁷"*Are* you the first man *who* was born?
Or were you made before the hills?
⁸Have you heard the counsel of God?
Do you limit wisdom to yourself?
⁹What do you know that we do not know?
What do you understand that *is* not in us?
¹⁰Both the gray-haired and the aged *are* among
us,
Much older than your father.
¹¹*Are* the consolations of God too small for you,
And the word *spoken* gently^a with you?
¹²Why does your heart carry you away,
And what do your eyes wink at,
¹³That you turn your spirit against God,
And let *such* words go out of your mouth?

¹⁴"What *is* man, that he could be pure?
And *he who is* born of a woman, that he could
be righteous?

14:3 ^aSeptuagint, Syriac, and Vulgate read *him.*   14:17 ^aLiterally
plaster over   15:11 ^aSeptuagint reads *a secret thing.*

¹⁵If *God* puts no trust in His saints,
  And the heavens are not pure in His sight,
¹⁶How much less man, *who is* abominable and
    filthy,
  Who drinks iniquity like water!

¹⁷"I will tell you, hear me;
  What I have seen I will declare,
¹⁸What wise men have told,
  Not hiding *anything received* from their fathers,
¹⁹To whom alone the land was given,
  And no alien passed among them:
²⁰The wicked man writhes with pain all *his*
    days,
  And the number of years is hidden from the
    oppressor.
²¹Dreadful sounds *are* in his ears;
  In prosperity the destroyer comes upon him.
²²He does not believe that he will return from
    darkness,
  For a sword is waiting for him.
²³He wanders about for bread, *saying,* 'Where *is*
    it?'
  He knows that a day of darkness is ready at
    his hand.
²⁴Trouble and anguish make him afraid;
  They overpower him, like a king ready for
    battle.
²⁵For he stretches out his hand against God,
  And acts defiantly against the Almighty,
²⁶Running stubbornly against Him
  With his strong, embossed shield.

²⁷"Though he has covered his face with his
    fatness,
  And made *his* waist heavy with fat,
²⁸He dwells in desolate cities,
  In houses which no one inhabits,
  Which are destined to become ruins.
²⁹He will not be rich,
  Nor will his wealth continue,
  Nor will his possessions overspread the earth.
³⁰He will not depart from darkness;
  The flame will dry out his branches,
  And by the breath of His mouth he will go
    away.
³¹Let him not trust in futile *things,* deceiving
    himself,
  For futility will be his reward.

³²It will be accomplished before his time,
  And his branch will not be green.
³³He will shake off his unripe grape like a vine,
  And cast off his blossom like an olive tree.
³⁴For the company of hypocrites *will be* barren,
  And fire will consume the tents of bribery.
³⁵They conceive trouble and bring forth
    futility;
  Their womb prepares deceit."

JOB REPROACHES HIS PITILESS FRIENDS

16 Then Job answered and said:

²"I have heard many such things;
  Miserable comforters *are* you all!
³Shall words of wind have an end?
  Or what provokes you that you answer?
⁴I also could speak as you *do,*
  If your soul were in my soul's place.
  I could heap up words against you,
  And shake my head at you;
⁵*But* I would strengthen you with my mouth,
  And the comfort of my lips would relieve
    your grief.

⁶"Though I speak, my grief is not relieved;
  And *if* I remain silent, how am I eased?
⁷But now He has worn me out;
  You have made desolate all my company.
⁸You have shriveled me up,
  And it is a witness *against me;*
  My leanness rises up against me
  And bears witness to my face.
⁹He tears *me* in His wrath, and hates me;
  He gnashes at me with His teeth;
  My adversary sharpens His gaze on me.
¹⁰They gape at me with their mouth,
  They strike me reproachfully on the cheek,
  They gather together against me.
¹¹God has delivered me to the ungodly,
  And turned me over to the hands of the
    wicked.
¹²I was at ease, but He has shattered me;
  He also has taken *me* by my neck, and shaken
    me to pieces;
  He has set me up for His target,
¹³His archers surround me.
  He pierces my heart[a] and does not pity;

16:13 [a]Literally *kidneys*

He pours out my gall on the ground.
[14]He breaks me with wound upon wound;
He runs at me like a warrior.[a]

[15]"I have sewn sackcloth over my skin,
And laid my head[a] in the dust.
[16]My face is flushed from weeping,
And on my eyelids *is* the shadow of death;
[17]Although no violence *is* in my hands,
And my prayer *is* pure.

[18]"O earth, do not cover my blood,
And let my cry have no *resting* place!
[19]Surely even now my witness *is* in heaven,
And my evidence *is* on high.
[20]My friends scorn me;
My eyes pour out *tears* to God.
[21]Oh, that one might plead for a man with God,
As a man *pleads* for his neighbor!
[22]For when a few years are finished,
I shall go the way of no return.

JOB PRAYS FOR RELIEF

17"My spirit is broken,
My days are extinguished,
The grave *is ready* for me.
[2]*Are* not mockers with me?
And does not my eye dwell on their provocation?

[3]"Now put down a pledge for me with Yourself.
Who *is* he *who* will shake hands with me?
[4]For You have hidden their heart from understanding;
Therefore You will not exalt *them*.
[5]He who speaks flattery to *his* friends,
Even the eyes of his children will fail.

[6]"But He has made me a byword of the people,
And I have become one in whose face men spit.
[7]My eye has also grown dim because of sorrow,
And all my members *are* like shadows.
[8]Upright *men* are astonished at this,
And the innocent stirs himself up against the hypocrite.
[9]Yet the righteous will hold to his way,

And he who has clean hands will be stronger and stronger.

[10]"But please, come back again, all of you,[a]
For I shall not find *one* wise *man* among you.
[11]My days are past,
My purposes are broken off,
Even the thoughts of my heart.
[12]They change the night into day;
'The light *is* near,' *they say,* in the face of darkness.
[13]If I wait *for* the grave *as* my house,
If I make my bed in the darkness,
[14]If I say to corruption, 'You *are* my father,'
And to the worm, 'You *are* my mother and my sister,'
[15]Where then *is* my hope?
As for my hope, who can see it?
[16]*Will* they go down to the gates of Sheol?
Shall *we have* rest together in the dust?"

BILDAD: THE WICKED ARE PUNISHED

18Then Bildad the Shuhite answered and said:

[2]"How long *till* you put an end to words?
Gain understanding, and afterward we will speak.
[3]Why are we counted as beasts,
And regarded as stupid in your sight?
[4]You who tear yourself in anger,
Shall the earth be forsaken for you?
Or shall the rock be removed from its place?

[5]"The light of the wicked indeed goes out,
And the flame of his fire does not shine.
[6]The light is dark in his tent,
And his lamp beside him is put out.
[7]The steps of his strength are shortened,
And his own counsel casts him down.
[8]For he is cast into a net by his own feet,
And he walks into a snare.
[9]The net takes *him* by the heel,
And a snare lays hold of him.
[10]A noose *is* hidden for him on the ground,
And a trap for him in the road.
[11]Terrors frighten him on every side,

16:14 [a]Vulgate reads *giant.* **16:15** [a]Literally *horn* **17:10** [a]Following some Hebrew manuscripts, Septuagint, Syriac, and Vulgate; Masoretic Text and Targum read *all of them.*

And drive him to his feet.
¹²His strength is starved,
  And destruction *is* ready at his side.
¹³It devours patches of his skin;
  The firstborn of death devours his limbs.
¹⁴He is uprooted from the shelter of his tent,
  And they parade him before the king of
    terrors.
¹⁵They dwell in his tent *who are* none of his;
  Brimstone is scattered on his dwelling.
¹⁶His roots are dried out below,
  And his branch withers above.
¹⁷The memory of him perishes from the earth,
  And he has no name among the renowned.ᵃ
¹⁸He is driven from light into darkness,
  And chased out of the world.
¹⁹He has neither son nor posterity among his
    people,
  Nor any remaining in his dwellings.
²⁰Those in the west are astonished at his day,
  As those in the east are frightened.
²¹Surely such *are* the dwellings of the wicked,
  And this *is* the place *of him who* does not
    know God."

Job Trusts in His Redeemer

19 Then Job answered and said:

²"How long will you torment my soul,
  And break me in pieces with words?
³These ten times you have reproached me;
  You are not ashamed *that* you have wronged
    me.ᵃ
⁴And if indeed I have erred,
  My error remains with me.
⁵If indeed you exalt *yourselves* against me,
  And plead my disgrace against me,
⁶Know then that God has wronged me,
  And has surrounded me with His net.

⁷"If I cry out concerning wrong, I am not
    heard.
  If I cry aloud, *there is* no justice.
⁸He has fenced up my way, so that I cannot
    pass;
  And He has set darkness in my paths.
⁹He has stripped me of my glory,
  And taken the crown *from* my head.
¹⁰He breaks me down on every side,

And I am gone;
  My hope He has uprooted like a tree.
¹¹He has also kindled His wrath against me,
  And He counts me as *one of* His enemies.
¹²His troops come together
  And build up their road against me;
  They encamp all around my tent.

¹³"He has removed my brothers far from me,
  And my acquaintances are completely
    estranged from me.
¹⁴My relatives have failed,
  And my close friends have forgotten me.
¹⁵Those who dwell in my house, and my
    maidservants,
  Count me as a stranger;
  I am an alien in their sight.
¹⁶I call my servant, but he gives no answer;
  I beg him with my mouth.
¹⁷My breath is offensive to my wife,
  And I am repulsive to the children of my
    own body.
¹⁸Even young children despise me;
  I arise, and they speak against me.
¹⁹All my close friends abhor me,
  And those whom I love have turned against
    me.
²⁰My bone clings to my skin and to my flesh,
  And I have escaped by the skin of my teeth.

²¹"Have pity on me, have pity on me, O you my
    friends,
  For the hand of God has struck me!
²²Why do you persecute me as God *does,*
  And are not satisfied with my flesh?

²³"Oh, that my words were written!
  Oh, that they were inscribed in a book!
²⁴That they were engraved on a rock
  With an iron pen and lead, forever!
²⁵For I know *that* my Redeemer lives,
  And He shall stand at last on the earth;
²⁶And after my skin is destroyed, this *I know,*
  That in my flesh I shall see God,
²⁷Whom I shall see for myself,
  And my eyes shall behold, and not another.
  How my heart yearns within me!

18:17 ᵃLiterally *before the outside,* meaning distinguished, famous
19:3 ᵃA Jewish tradition reads *make yourselves strange to me.*

²⁸If you should say, 'How shall we persecute
    him?'—
  Since the root of the matter is found in me,
²⁹Be afraid of the sword for yourselves;
  For wrath *brings* the punishment of the sword,
  That you may know *there is* a judgment."

ZOPHAR'S SERMON ON THE WICKED MAN

20 Then Zophar the Naamathite answered
    and said:

²"Therefore my anxious thoughts make me
      answer,
  Because of the turmoil within me.
³I have heard the rebuke that reproaches me,
  And the spirit of my understanding causes me
      to answer.

⁴"Do you *not* know this of old,
  Since man was placed on earth,
⁵That the triumphing of the wicked is short,
  And the joy of the hypocrite is *but* for a
      moment?
⁶Though his haughtiness mounts up to the
      heavens,
  And his head reaches to the clouds,
⁷*Yet* he will perish forever like his own refuse;
  Those who have seen him will say, 'Where is
      he?'
⁸He will fly away like a dream, and not be
      found;
  Yes, he will be chased away like a vision of
      the night.
⁹The eye *that* saw him will *see him* no more,
  Nor will his place behold him anymore.
¹⁰His children will seek the favor of the poor,
  And his hands will restore his wealth.
¹¹His bones are full of his youthful vigor,
  But it will lie down with him in the dust.

¹²"Though evil is sweet in his mouth,
  And he hides it under his tongue,
¹³*Though* he spares it and does not forsake it,
  But still keeps it in his mouth,
¹⁴*Yet* his food in his stomach turns sour;
  It becomes cobra venom within him.
¹⁵He swallows down riches
  And vomits them up again;
  God casts them out of his belly.

¹⁶He will suck the poison of cobras;
  The viper's tongue will slay him.
¹⁷He will not see the streams,
  The rivers flowing with honey and cream.
¹⁸He will restore that for which he labored,
  And will not swallow *it* down;
  From the proceeds of business
  He will get no enjoyment.
¹⁹For he has oppressed *and* forsaken the poor,
  He has violently seized a house which he did
      not build.

²⁰"Because he knows no quietness in his heart,ᵃ
  He will not save anything he desires.
²¹Nothing is left for him to eat;
  Therefore his well-being will not last.
²²In his self-sufficiency he will be in distress;
  Every hand of misery will come against him.
²³*When* he is about to fill his stomach,
  God will cast on him the fury of His wrath,
  And will rain *it* on him while he is eating.
²⁴He will flee from the iron weapon;
  A bronze bow will pierce him through.
²⁵It is drawn, and comes out of the body;
  Yes, the glittering *point comes* out of his gall.
  Terrors *come* upon him;
²⁶Total darkness *is* reserved for his treasures.
  An unfanned fire will consume him;
  It shall go ill with him who is left in his tent.
²⁷The heavens will reveal his iniquity,
  And the earth will rise up against him.
²⁸The increase of his house will depart,
  And his goods will flow away in the day of His
      wrath.
²⁹This *is* the portion from God for a wicked
      man,
  The heritage appointed to him by God."

JOB'S DISCOURSE ON THE WICKED

21 Then Job answered and said:

²"Listen carefully to my speech,
  And let this be your consolation.
³Bear with me that I may speak,
  And after I have spoken, keep mocking.

⁴"As for me, *is* my complaint against man?
  And if *it were,* why should I not be impatient?

20:20 ᵃLiterally *belly*

5Look at me and be astonished;
  Put *your* hand over *your* mouth.
6Even when I remember I am terrified,
  And trembling takes hold of my flesh.
7Why do the wicked live *and* become old,
  Yes, become mighty in power?
8Their descendants are established with them
      in their sight,
  And their offspring before their eyes.
9Their houses *are* safe from fear,
  Neither *is* the rod of God upon them.
10Their bull breeds without failure;
  Their cow calves without miscarriage.
11They send forth their little ones like a flock,
  And their children dance.
12They sing to the tambourine and harp,
  And rejoice to the sound of the flute.
13They spend their days in wealth,
  And in a moment go down to the grave.ᵃ
14Yet they say to God, 'Depart from us,
  For we do not desire the knowledge of Your
      ways.
15Who *is* the Almighty, that we should serve
      Him?
  And what profit do we have if we pray to
      Him?'
16Indeed their prosperity *is* not in their hand;
  The counsel of the wicked is far from me.

17"How often is the lamp of the wicked put out?
  How often does their destruction come upon
      them,
  The sorrows *God* distributes in His anger?
18They are like straw before the wind,
  And like chaff that a storm carries away.
19*They say,* 'God lays up one'sᵃ iniquity for his
      children';
  Let Him recompense him, that he may
      know *it.*
20Let his eyes see his destruction,
  And let him drink of the wrath of the
      Almighty.
21For what does he care about his household
      after him,
  When the number of his months is cut in
      half?

22"Can *anyone* teach God knowledge,
  Since He judges those on high?

23One dies in his full strength,
  Being wholly at ease and secure;
24His pailsᵃ are full of milk,
  And the marrow of his bones is moist.
25Another man dies in the bitterness of his soul,
  Never having eaten with pleasure.
26They lie down alike in the dust,
  And worms cover them.

27"Look, I know your thoughts,
  And the schemes *with which* you would
      wrong me.
28For you say,
  'Where *is* the house of the prince?
  And where *is* the tent,ᵃ
  The dwelling place of the wicked?'
29Have you not asked those who travel the road?
  And do you not know their signs?
30For the wicked are reserved for the day of
      doom;
  They shall be brought out on the day of wrath.
31Who condemns his way to his face?
  And who repays him *for what* he has done?
32Yet he shall be brought to the grave,
  And a vigil kept over the tomb.
33The clods of the valley shall be sweet to him;
  Everyone shall follow him,
  As countless *have gone* before him.
34How then can you comfort me with empty
      words,
  Since falsehood remains in your answers?"

ELIPHAZ ACCUSES JOB OF WICKEDNESS

22 Then Eliphaz the Temanite answered and
  said:

2"Can a man be profitable to God,
  Though he who is wise may be profitable to
      himself?
3*Is it* any pleasure to the Almighty that you are
      righteous?
  Or *is it* gain *to Him* that you make your ways
      blameless?

4"Is it because of your fear of Him that He
      corrects you,

21:13 ᵃOr *Sheol* **21:19** ᵃLiterally *his* **21:24** ᵃSeptuagint and
Vulgate read *bowels;* Syriac reads *sides;* Targum reads *breasts*
21:28 ᵃVulgate omits *the tent.*

And enters into judgment with you?
⁵*Is* not your wickedness great,
And your iniquity without end?
⁶For you have taken pledges from your brother
for no reason,
And stripped the naked of their clothing.
⁷You have not given the weary water to drink,
And you have withheld bread from the
hungry.
⁸But the mighty man possessed the land,
And the honorable man dwelt in it.
⁹You have sent widows away empty,
And the strength of the fatherless was
crushed.
¹⁰Therefore snares *are* all around you,
And sudden fear troubles you,
¹¹Or darkness *so that* you cannot see;
And an abundance of water covers you.

¹²"Is not God in the height of heaven?
And see the highest stars, how lofty they are!
¹³And you say, 'What does God know?
Can He judge through the deep darkness?
¹⁴Thick clouds cover Him, so that He cannot
see,
And He walks above the circle of heaven.'
¹⁵Will you keep to the old way
Which wicked men have trod,
¹⁶Who were cut down before their time,
Whose foundations were swept away by a
flood?
¹⁷They said to God, 'Depart from us!
What can the Almighty do to them?'ᵃ
¹⁸Yet He filled their houses with good *things;*
But the counsel of the wicked is far from me.

¹⁹"The righteous see *it* and are glad,
And the innocent laugh at them:
²⁰'Surely our adversariesᵃ are cut down,
And the fire consumes their remnant.'

²¹"Now acquaint yourself with Him, and be at
peace;
Thereby good will come to you.
²²Receive, please, instruction from His mouth,
And lay up His words in your heart.
²³If you return to the Almighty, you will be
built up;
You will remove iniquity far from your tents.

²⁴Then you will lay your gold in the dust,
And the *gold* of Ophir among the stones of
the brooks.
²⁵Yes, the Almighty will be your goldᵃ
And your precious silver;
²⁶For then you will have your delight in the
Almighty,
And lift up your face to God.
²⁷You will make your prayer to Him,
He will hear you,
And you will pay your vows.
²⁸You will also declare a thing,
And it will be established for you;
So light will shine on your ways.
²⁹When they cast *you* down, and you say,
'Exaltation *will come!*'
Then He will save the humble *person.*
³⁰He will *even* deliver one who is not innocent;
Yes, he will be delivered by the purity of your
hands."

JOB PROCLAIMS GOD'S RIGHTEOUS JUDGMENTS

23 Then Job answered and said:

²"Even today my complaint is bitter;
Myᵃ hand is listless because of my groaning.
³Oh, that I knew where I might find Him,
That I might come to His seat!
⁴I would present *my* case before Him,
And fill my mouth with arguments.
⁵I would know the words *which* He would
answer me,
And understand what He would say to me.
⁶Would He contend with me in His great
power?
No! But He would take *note* of me.
⁷There the upright could reason with Him,
And I would be delivered forever from my
Judge.

⁸"Look, I go forward, but He is not *there,*
And backward, but I cannot perceive Him;
⁹When He works on the left hand, I cannot
behold *Him;*
When He turns to the right hand, I cannot
see *Him.*

22:17 ᵃSeptuagint and Syriac read *us.* 22:20 ᵃSeptuagint reads
substance. 22:25 ᵃThe ancient versions suggest *defense;* Hebrew
reads *gold* as in verse 24. 23:2 ᵃFollowing Masoretic Text, Targum,
and Vulgate; Septuagint and Syriac read *His.*

[10]But He knows the way that I take;
When He has tested me, I shall come forth as
gold.
[11]My foot has held fast to His steps;
I have kept His way and not turned aside.
[12]I have not departed from the commandment
of His lips;
I have treasured the words of His mouth
More than my necessary *food*.

[13]"But He *is* unique, and who can make Him
change?
And *whatever* His soul desires, *that* He does.
[14]For He performs *what is* appointed for me,
And many such *things are* with Him.
[15]Therefore I am terrified at His presence;
When I consider *this,* I am afraid of Him.
[16]For God made my heart weak,
And the Almighty terrifies me;
[17]Because I was not cut off from the presence
of darkness,
And He did *not* hide deep darkness from my
face.

Job Complains of Violence on the Earth

24 "*Since* times are not hidden from the
Almighty,
Why do those who know Him see not His
days?

[2]" *Some* remove landmarks;
They seize flocks violently and feed *on them;*
[3]They drive away the donkey of the
fatherless;
They take the widow's ox as a pledge.
[4]They push the needy off the road;
All the poor of the land are forced to hide.
[5]Indeed, *like* wild donkeys in the desert,
They go out to their work, searching for
food.
The wilderness *yields* food for them *and* for
their children.
[6]They gather their fodder in the field
And glean in the vineyard of the wicked.
[7]They spend the night naked, without
clothing,
And have no covering in the cold.
[8]They are wet with the showers of the
mountains,

And huddle around the rock for want of
shelter.
[9]" *Some* snatch the fatherless from the breast,
And take a pledge from the poor.
[10]They cause *the poor* to go naked, without
clothing;
And they take away the sheaves from the
hungry.
[11]They press out oil within their walls,
And tread winepresses, yet suffer thirst.
[12]The dying groan in the city,
And the souls of the wounded cry out;
Yet God does not charge *them* with wrong.

[13]"There are those who rebel against the light;
They do not know its ways
Nor abide in its paths.
[14]The murderer rises with the light;
He kills the poor and needy;
And in the night he is like a thief.
[15]The eye of the adulterer waits for the
twilight,
Saying, 'No eye will see me';
And he disguises *his* face.
[16]In the dark they break into houses
Which they marked for themselves in the
daytime;
They do not know the light.
[17]For the morning is the same to them as the
shadow of death;
If *someone* recognizes *them,*
They are in the terrors of the shadow of death.

[18]"They *should be* swift on the face of the
waters,
Their portion *should be* cursed in the earth,
So that no *one would* turn into the way of their
vineyards.
[19]As drought and heat consume the snow
waters,
So the grave[a] *consumes those who* have sinned.
[20]The womb *should* forget him,
The worm *should* feed sweetly on him;
He *should* be remembered no more,
And wickedness *should* be broken like a tree.
[21]For he preys on the barren *who* do not bear,
And does no good for the widow.

24:19 [a]Or *Sheol*

²²"But *God* draws the mighty away with His
  power;
  He rises up, but no *man* is sure of life.
²³He gives them security, and they rely *on it;*
  Yet His eyes *are* on their ways.
²⁴They are exalted for a little while,
  Then they are gone.
  They are brought low;
  They are taken out of the way like all *others;*
  They dry out like the heads of grain.

²⁵"Now if *it is* not *so,* who will prove me a liar,
  And make my speech worth nothing?"

BILDAD: HOW CAN MAN BE RIGHTEOUS?

25 Then Bildad the Shuhite answered and
  said:

²"Dominion and fear *belong* to Him;
  He makes peace in His high places.
³Is there any number to His armies?
  Upon whom does His light not rise?
⁴How then can man be righteous before God?
  Or how can he be pure *who is* born of a
  woman?
⁵If even the moon does not shine,
  And the stars are not pure in His sight,
⁶How much less man, *who is* a maggot,
  And a son of man, *who is* a worm?"

JOB: MAN'S FRAILTY AND GOD'S MAJESTY

26 But Job answered and said:

²"How have you helped *him who is* without
  power?
  How have you saved the arm *that has* no
  strength?
³How have you counseled *one who has* no
  wisdom?
  And *how* have you declared sound advice to
  many?
⁴To whom have you uttered words?
  And whose spirit came from you?

⁵"The dead tremble,
  Those under the waters and those inhabiting
  them.
⁶Sheol *is* naked before Him,
  And Destruction has no covering.
⁷He stretches out the north over empty space;

He hangs the earth on nothing.
⁸He binds up the water in His thick clouds,
  Yet the clouds are not broken under it.
⁹He covers the face of *His* throne,
  And spreads His cloud over it.
¹⁰He drew a circular horizon on the face of the
  waters,
  At the boundary of light and darkness.
¹¹The pillars of heaven tremble,
  And are astonished at His rebuke.
¹²He stirs up the sea with His power,
  And by His understanding He breaks up the
  storm.
¹³By His Spirit He adorned the heavens;
  His hand pierced the fleeing serpent.
¹⁴Indeed these *are* the mere edges of His ways,
  And how small a whisper we hear of Him!
  But the thunder of His power who can
  understand?"

JOB MAINTAINS HIS INTEGRITY

27 Moreover Job continued his discourse, and
  said:

²"*As* God lives, *who* has taken away my justice,
  And the Almighty, *who* has made my soul
  bitter,
³As long as my breath *is* in me,
  And the breath of God in my nostrils,
⁴My lips will not speak wickedness,
  Nor my tongue utter deceit.
⁵Far be it from me
  That I should say you are right;
  Till I die I will not put away my integrity
  from me.
⁶My righteousness I hold fast, and will not let
  it go;
  My heart shall not reproach *me* as long as I live.

⁷"May my enemy be like the wicked,
  And he who rises up against me like the
  unrighteous.
⁸For what is the hope of the hypocrite,
  Though he may gain *much,*
  If God takes away his life?
⁹Will God hear his cry
  When trouble comes upon him?
¹⁰Will he delight himself in the Almighty?
  Will he always call on God?

11"I will teach you about the hand of God;
What *is* with the Almighty I will not
  conceal.
12Surely all of you have seen *it;*
Why then do you behave with complete
  nonsense?

13"This is the portion of a wicked man with
  God,
And the heritage of oppressors, received from
  the Almighty:
14If his children are multiplied, *it is* for the
  sword;
And his offspring shall not be satisfied with
  bread.
15Those who survive him shall be buried in
  death,
And their[a] widows shall not weep,
16Though he heaps up silver like dust,
And piles up clothing like clay—
17He may pile *it* up, but the just will wear *it,*
And the innocent will divide the silver.
18He builds his house like a moth,[a]
Like a booth *which* a watchman makes.
19The rich man will lie down,
But not be gathered *up;*[a]
He opens his eyes,
And he *is* no more.
20Terrors overtake him like a flood;
A tempest steals him away in the night.
21The east wind carries him away, and he is
  gone;
It sweeps him out of his place.
22It hurls against him and does not spare;
He flees desperately from its power.
23*Men* shall clap their hands at him,
And shall hiss him out of his place.

JOB'S DISCOURSE ON WISDOM

28

"Surely there is a mine for silver,
And a place *where* gold is refined.
2Iron is taken from the earth,
And copper *is* smelted *from* ore.
3*Man* puts an end to darkness,
And searches every recess
For ore in the darkness and the shadow of
  death.
4He breaks open a shaft away from people;
In places forgotten by feet

They hang far away from men;
They swing to and fro.
5*As for* the earth, from it comes bread,
But underneath it is turned up as by fire;
6Its stones *are* the source of sapphires,
And it contains gold dust.
7*That* path no bird knows,
Nor has the falcon's eye seen it.
8The proud lions[a] have not trodden it,
Nor has the fierce lion passed over it.
9He puts his hand on the flint;
He overturns the mountains at the roots.
10He cuts out channels in the rocks,
And his eye sees every precious thing.
11He dams up the streams from trickling;
What is hidden he brings forth to light.

12"But where can wisdom be found?
And where *is* the place of understanding?
13Man does not know its value,
Nor is it found in the land of the living.
14The deep says, 'It *is* not in me';
And the sea says, '*It is* not with me.'
15It cannot be purchased for gold,
Nor can silver be weighed *for* its price.
16It cannot be valued in the gold of Ophir,
In precious onyx or sapphire.
17Neither gold nor crystal can equal it,
Nor can it be exchanged for jewelry of fine
  gold.
18No mention shall be made of coral or quartz,
For the price of wisdom *is* above rubies.
19The topaz of Ethiopia cannot equal it,
Nor can it be valued in pure gold.

20"From where then does wisdom come?
And where *is* the place of understanding?
21It is hidden from the eyes of all living,
And concealed from the birds of the air.
22Destruction and Death say,
'We have heard a report about it with our
  ears.'
23God understands its way,
And He knows its place.

27:15 [a]Literally *his*   **27:18** [a]Following Masoretic Text and Vulgate
Septuagint and Syriac read *spider* (compare 8:14); Targum reads
decay.   **27:19** [a]Following Masoretic Text and Targum; Septuagint
and Syriac read *But shall not add* (that is, do it again); Vulgate reads
But take away nothing.   **28:8** [a]Literally *sons of pride,* figurative o
the great lions

²⁴For He looks to the ends of the earth,
And sees under the whole heavens,
²⁵To establish a weight for the wind,
And apportion the waters by measure.
²⁶When He made a law for the rain,
And a path for the thunderbolt,
²⁷Then He saw *wisdom*^a and declared it;
He prepared it, indeed, He searched it out.
²⁸And to man He said,
'Behold, the fear of the Lord, that *is* wisdom,
And to depart from evil *is* understanding.' "

Job's Summary Defense

29 Job further continued his discourse, and said:

²"Oh, that I were as *in* months past,
As *in* the days *when* God watched over me;
³When His lamp shone upon my head,
And when by His light I walked *through* darkness;
⁴Just as I was in the days of my prime,
When the friendly counsel of God *was* over my tent;
⁵When the Almighty *was* yet with me,
When my children *were* around me;
⁶When my steps were bathed with cream,^a
And the rock poured out rivers of oil for me!

⁷"When I went out to the gate by the city,
When I took my seat in the open square,
⁸The young men saw me and hid,
And the aged arose *and* stood;
⁹The princes refrained from talking,
And put *their* hand on their mouth;
¹⁰The voice of nobles was hushed,
And their tongue stuck to the roof of their mouth.
¹¹When the ear heard, then it blessed me,
And when the eye saw, then it approved me;
¹²Because I delivered the poor who cried out,
The fatherless and *the one who* had no helper.
¹³The blessing of a perishing *man* came upon me,
And I caused the widow's heart to sing for joy.
¹⁴I put on righteousness, and it clothed me;
My justice *was* like a robe and a turban.

¹⁵I *was* eyes to the blind,
And I *was* feet to the lame.
¹⁶I *was* a father to the poor,
And I searched out the case *that* I did not know.
¹⁷I broke the fangs of the wicked,
And plucked the victim from his teeth.

¹⁸"Then I said, 'I shall die in my nest,
And multiply *my* days as the sand.
¹⁹My root *is* spread out to the waters,
And the dew lies all night on my branch.
²⁰My glory *is* fresh within me,
And my bow is renewed in my hand.'

²¹"*Men* listened to me and waited,
And kept silence for my counsel.
²²After my words they did not speak again,
And my speech settled on them *as dew.*
²³They waited for me *as* for the rain,
And they opened their mouth wide *as* for the spring rain.
²⁴*If* I mocked at them, they did not believe *it,*
And the light of my countenance they did not cast down.
²⁵I chose the way for them, and sat as chief;
So I dwelt as a king in the army,
As one *who* comforts mourners.

30 "But now they mock at me, *men* younger than I,
Whose fathers I disdained to put with the dogs of my flock.
²Indeed, what *profit* is the strength of their hands to me?
Their vigor has perished.
³*They are* gaunt from want and famine,
Fleeing late to the wilderness, desolate and waste,
⁴Who pluck mallow by the bushes,
And broom tree roots *for* their food.
⁵They were driven out from among *men,*
They shouted at them as *at* a thief.
⁶*They had* to live in the clefts of the valleys,
In caves of the earth and the rocks.
⁷Among the bushes they brayed,
Under the nettles they nestled.

28:27 ^aLiterally *it* **29:6** ^aMasoretic Text reads *wrath;* ancient versions and some Hebrew manuscripts read *cream* (compare 20:17).

8*They were* sons of fools,
Yes, sons of vile men;
They were scourged from the land.

9"And now I am their taunting song;
Yes, I am their byword.
10They abhor me, they keep far from me;
They do not hesitate to spit in my face.
11Because He has loosed my[a] bowstring and
afflicted me,
They have cast off restraint before me.
12At *my* right *hand* the rabble arises;
They push away my feet,
And they raise against me their ways of
destruction.
13They break up my path,
They promote my calamity;
They have no helper.
14They come as broad breakers;
Under the ruinous storm they roll along.
15Terrors are turned upon me;
They pursue my honor as the wind,
And my prosperity has passed like a cloud.

16"And now my soul is poured out because of
my *plight;*
The days of affliction take hold of me.
17My bones are pierced in me at night,
And my gnawing pains take no rest.
18By great force my garment is disfigured;
It binds me about as the collar of my coat.
19He has cast me into the mire,
And I have become like dust and ashes.

20"I cry out to You, but You do not answer me;
I stand up, and You regard me.
21*But* You have become cruel to me;
With the strength of Your hand You oppose
me.
22You lift me up to the wind and cause me to
ride *on it;*
You spoil my success.
23For I know *that* You will bring me *to* death,
And *to* the house appointed for all living.

24"Surely He would not stretch out *His* hand
against a heap of ruins,
If they cry out when He destroys *it.*
25Have I not wept for him who was in trouble?

Has *not* my soul grieved for the poor?
26But when I looked for good, evil came *to me;*
And when I waited for light, then came
darkness.
27My heart is in turmoil and cannot rest;
Days of affliction confront me.
28I go about mourning, but not in the sun;
I stand up in the assembly *and* cry out for
help.
29I am a brother of jackals,
And a companion of ostriches.
30My skin grows black and falls from me;
My bones burn with fever.
31My harp is *turned* to mourning,
And my flute to the voice of those who
weep.

31 "I have made a covenant with my eyes;
Why then should I look upon a young
woman?
2For what *is* the allotment of God from above,
And the inheritance of the Almighty from on
high?
3*Is* it not destruction for the wicked,
And disaster for the workers of iniquity?
4Does He not see my ways,
And count all my steps?

5"If I have walked with falsehood,
Or if my foot has hastened to deceit,
6Let me be weighed on honest scales,
That God may know my integrity.
7If my step has turned from the way,
Or my heart walked after my eyes,
Or if any spot adheres to my hands,
8*Then* let me sow, and another eat;
Yes, let my harvest be rooted out.

9"If my heart has been enticed by a woman,
Or *if* I have lurked at my neighbor's door,
10*Then* let my wife grind for another,
And let others bow down over her.
11For that *would be* wickedness;
Yes, it *would be* iniquity *deserving of* judgment.
12For that *would be* a fire *that* consumes to
destruction,
And would root out all my increase.

30:11 [a]Following Masoretic Text, Syriac, and Targum; Septuagint and Vulgate read *His.*

¹³"If I have despised the cause of my male or
female servant
When they complained against me,
¹⁴What then shall I do when God rises up?
When He punishes, how shall I answer
Him?
¹⁵Did not He who made me in the womb
make them?
Did not the same One fashion us in the
womb?

¹⁶"If I have kept the poor from *their* desire,
Or caused the eyes of the widow to fail,
¹⁷Or eaten my morsel by myself,
So that the fatherless could not eat of it
¹⁸(But from my youth I reared him as a father,
And from my mother's womb I guided *the
widow*^a);
¹⁹If I have seen anyone perish for lack of
clothing,
Or any poor *man* without covering;
²⁰If his heart^a has not blessed me,
And *if* he was *not* warmed with the fleece of
my sheep;
²¹If I have raised my hand against the
fatherless,
When I saw I had help in the gate;
²²*Then* let my arm fall from my shoulder,
Let my arm be torn from the socket.
²³For destruction *from* God *is* a terror to me,
And because of His magnificence I cannot
endure.

²⁴"If I have made gold my hope,
Or said to fine gold,'*You are* my confidence';
²⁵If I have rejoiced because my wealth *was*
great,
And because my hand had gained much;
²⁶If I have observed the sun^a when it shines,
Or the moon moving *in* brightness,
²⁷So that my heart has been secretly enticed,
And my mouth has kissed my hand;
²⁸This also *would be* an iniquity *deserving of*
judgment,
For I would have denied God *who is* above.

²⁹"If I have rejoiced at the destruction of him
who hated me,
Or lifted myself up when evil found him

³⁰(Indeed I have not allowed my mouth to sin
By asking for a curse on his soul);
³¹If the men of my tent have not said,
'Who is there that has not been satisfied with
his meat?'
³²(*But* no sojourner had to lodge in the street,
For I have opened my doors to the traveler^a);
³³If I have covered my transgressions as Adam,
By hiding my iniquity in my bosom,
³⁴Because I feared the great multitude,
And dreaded the contempt of families,
So that I kept silence
And did not go out of the door—
³⁵Oh, that I had one to hear me!
Here is my mark.
Oh, that the Almighty would answer me,
That my Prosecutor had written a book!
³⁶Surely I would carry it on my shoulder,
And bind it on me *like* a crown;
³⁷I would declare to Him the number of my
steps;
Like a prince I would approach Him.

³⁸"If my land cries out against me,
And its furrows weep together;
³⁹If I have eaten its fruit^a without money,
Or caused its owners to lose their lives;
⁴⁰*Then* let thistles grow instead of wheat,
And weeds instead of barley."

The words of Job are ended.

Elihu Contradicts Job's Friends

32 So these three men ceased answering Job,
because he *was* righteous in his own eyes.
²Then the wrath of Elihu, the son of Barachel the
Buzite, of the family of Ram, was aroused against
Job; his wrath was aroused because he justified
himself rather than God. ³Also against his three
friends his wrath was aroused, because they had
found no answer, and *yet* had condemned Job.

⁴Now because they *were* years older than he,
Elihu had waited to speak to Job.^a ⁵When Elihu
saw that *there was* no answer in the mouth of
these three men, his wrath was aroused.

31:18 ^aLiterally *her* (compare verse 16)   **31:20** ^aLiterally *loins*
31:26 ^aLiterally *light*   **31:32** ^aFollowing Septuagint, Syriac, Targum,
and Vulgate; Masoretic Text reads *road.*   **31:39** ^aLiterally *its
strength*   **32:4** ^aVulgate reads *till Job had spoken.*

⁶So Elihu, the son of Barachel the Buzite, answered and said:

"I *am* young in years, and you *are* very old;
Therefore I was afraid,
And dared not declare my opinion to you.
⁷I said, 'Ageᵃ should speak,
And multitude of years should teach
    wisdom.'
⁸But *there is* a spirit in man,
And the breath of the Almighty gives him
    understanding.
⁹Great menᵃ are not *always* wise,
Nor do the aged *always* understand justice.

¹⁰"Therefore I say, 'Listen to me,
I also will declare my opinion.'
¹¹Indeed I waited for your words,
I listened to your reasonings, while you
    searched out what to say.
¹²I paid close attention to you;
And surely not one of you convinced Job,
Or answered his words—
¹³Lest you say,
'We have found wisdom';
God will vanquish him, not man.
¹⁴Now he has not directed *his* words against
    me;
So I will not answer him with your words.

¹⁵"They are dismayed and answer no more;
Words escape them.
¹⁶And I have waited, because they did not
    speak,
Because they stood still *and* answered no
    more.
¹⁷I also will answer my part,
I too will declare my opinion.
¹⁸For I am full of words;
The spirit within me compels me.
¹⁹Indeed my belly *is* like wine *that* has no vent;
It is ready to burst like new wineskins.
²⁰I will speak, that I may find relief;
I must open my lips and answer.
²¹Let me not, I pray, show partiality to
    anyone;
Nor let me flatter any man.
²²For I do not know how to flatter,
Else my Maker would soon take me away.

ELIHU CONTRADICTS JOB

33 "But please, Job, hear my speech,
And listen to all my words.
²Now, I open my mouth;
My tongue speaks in my mouth.
³My words *come* from my upright heart;
My lips utter pure knowledge.
⁴The Spirit of God has made me,
And the breath of the Almighty gives me
    life.
⁵If you can answer me,
Set *your words* in order before me;
Take your stand.
⁶Truly I *am* as your spokesmanᵃ before God;
I also have been formed out of clay.
⁷Surely no fear of me will terrify you,
Nor will my hand be heavy on you.

⁸"Surely you have spoken in my hearing,
And I have heard the sound of *your* words,
    saying,
⁹'I *am* pure, without transgression;
I *am* innocent, and *there is* no iniquity in me.
¹⁰Yet He finds occasions against me,
He counts me as His enemy;
¹¹He puts my feet in the stocks,
He watches all my paths.'

¹²"Look, *in* this you are not righteous.
I will answer you,
For God is greater than man.
¹³Why do you contend with Him?
For He does not give an accounting of any of
    His words.
¹⁴For God may speak in one way, or in
    another,
Yet man does not perceive it.
¹⁵In a dream, in a vision of the night,
When deep sleep falls upon men,
While slumbering on their beds,
¹⁶Then He opens the ears of men,
And seals their instruction.
¹⁷In order to turn man *from his* deed,
And conceal pride from man,
¹⁸He keeps back his soul from the Pit,
And his life from perishing by the sword.

32:7 ᵃLiterally *Days,* that is, years   **32:9** ᵃOr *Men of many years*
33:6 ᵃLiterally *as your mouth*

19"*Man* is also chastened with pain on his bed,
And with strong *pain* in many of his bones,
20So that his life abhors bread,
And his soul succulent food.
21His flesh wastes away from sight,
And his bones stick out *which once* were not seen.
22Yes, his soul draws near the Pit,
And his life to the executioners.

23"If there is a messenger for him,
A mediator, one among a thousand,
To show man His uprightness,
24Then He is gracious to him, and says,
'Deliver him from going down to the Pit;
I have found a ransom';
25His flesh shall be young like a child's,
He shall return to the days of his youth.
26He shall pray to God, and He will delight in him,
He shall see His face with joy,
For He restores to man His righteousness.
27Then he looks at men and says,
'I have sinned, and perverted *what was* right,
And it did not profit me.'
28He will redeem his^a soul from going down to the Pit,
And his^b life shall see the light.

29"Behold, God works all these *things,*
Twice, *in fact,* three *times* with a man,
30To bring back his soul from the Pit,
That he may be enlightened with the light of life.

31"Give ear, Job, listen to me;
Hold your peace, and I will speak.
32If you have anything to say, answer me;
Speak, for I desire to justify you.
33If not, listen to me;
Hold your peace, and I will teach you wisdom."

ELIHU PROCLAIMS GOD'S JUSTICE

34 Elihu further answered and said:

2"Hear my words, you wise *men;*
Give ear to me, you who have knowledge.
3For the ear tests words

As the palate tastes food.
4Let us choose justice for ourselves;
Let us know among ourselves what *is* good.

5"For Job has said, 'I am righteous,
But God has taken away my justice;
6Should I lie concerning my right?
My wound *is* incurable, *though I am* without transgression.'
7What man *is* like Job,
Who drinks scorn like water,
8Who goes in company with the workers of iniquity,
And walks with wicked men?
9For he has said, 'It profits a man nothing
That he should delight in God.'

10"Therefore listen to me, you men of understanding:
Far be it from God *to do* wickedness,
And *from* the Almighty to *commit* iniquity.
11For He repays man *according to* his work,
And makes man to find a reward according to *his* way.
12Surely God will never do wickedly,
Nor will the Almighty pervert justice.
13Who gave Him charge over the earth?
Or who appointed *Him over* the whole world?
14If He should set His heart on it,
If He should gather to Himself His Spirit and His breath,
15All flesh would perish together,
And man would return to dust.

16"If *you have* understanding, hear this;
Listen to the sound of my words:
17Should one who hates justice govern?
Will you condemn *Him who is* most just?
18*Is it fitting* to say to a king, 'You are worthless,'
And to nobles, 'You are wicked'?
19Yet He is not partial to princes,
Nor does He regard the rich more than the poor;
For they *are* all the work of His hands.
20In a moment they die, in the middle of the night;

The people are shaken and pass away;
  The mighty are taken away without a hand.

21"For His eyes *are* on the ways of man,
  And He sees all his steps.
22There is no darkness nor shadow of death
  Where the workers of iniquity may hide
    themselves.
23For He need not further consider a man,
  That he should go before God in judgment.
24He breaks in pieces mighty men without
    inquiry,
  And sets others in their place.
25Therefore He knows their works;
  He overthrows *them* in the night,
  And they are crushed.
26He strikes them as wicked *men*
  In the open sight of others,
27Because they turned back from Him,
  And would not consider any of His ways,
28So that they caused the cry of the poor to
    come to Him;
  For He hears the cry of the afflicted.
29When He gives quietness, who then can
    make trouble?
  And when He hides *His* face, who then can
    see Him,
  Whether *it is* against a nation or a man
    alone?—
30That the hypocrite should not reign,
  Lest the people be ensnared.
31"For has *anyone* said to God,
  'I have borne *chastening;*
  I will offend no more;
32Teach me *what* I do not see;
  If I have done iniquity, I will do no more'?
33Should He repay *it* according to your *terms,*
  Just because you disavow it?
  You must choose, and not I;
  Therefore speak what you know.

34"Men of understanding say to me,
  Wise men who listen to me:
35'Job speaks without knowledge,
  His words *are* without wisdom.'
36Oh, that Job were tried to the utmost,
  Because *his* answers *are like* those of wicked
    men!
37For he adds rebellion to his sin;

He claps *his hands* among us,
  And multiplies his words against God."

ELIHU CONDEMNS SELF-RIGHTEOUSNESS

35 Moreover Elihu answered and said:

2"Do you think this is right?
  Do you say,
  'My righteousness is more than God's'?
3For you say,
  'What advantage will it be to You?
  What profit shall I have, more than *if* I had
    sinned?'

4"I will answer you,
  And your companions with you.
5Look to the heavens and see;
  And behold the clouds—
  They are higher than you.
6If you sin, what do you accomplish against
    Him?
  Or, *if* your transgressions are multiplied, what
    do you do to Him?
7If you are righteous, what do you give Him?
  Or what does He receive from your hand?
8Your wickedness affects a man such as you,
  And your righteousness a son of man.

9"Because of the multitude of oppressions they
    cry out;
  They cry out for help because of the arm of
    the mighty.
10But no one says, 'Where *is* God my Maker,
  Who gives songs in the night,
11Who teaches us more than the beasts of the
    earth,
  And makes us wiser than the birds of
    heaven?'
12There they cry out, but He does not
    answer,
  Because of the pride of evil men.
13Surely God will not listen to empty *talk,*
  Nor will the Almighty regard it.
14Although you say you do not see Him,
  Yet justice *is* before Him, and you must wait
    for Him.
15And now, because He has not punished in
    His anger,
  Nor taken much notice of folly,

¹⁶Therefore Job opens his mouth in vain;
He multiplies words without knowledge."

Elihu Proclaims God's Goodness

36 Elihu also proceeded and said:

²"Bear with me a little, and I will show you
That *there are* yet words to speak on God's
behalf.
³I will fetch my knowledge from afar;
I will ascribe righteousness to my Maker.
⁴For truly my words *are* not false;
One who is perfect in knowledge *is* with you.

⁵"Behold, God *is* mighty, but despises *no one;*
He is mighty in strength of understanding.
⁶He does not preserve the life of the wicked,
But gives justice to the oppressed.
⁷He does not withdraw His eyes from the
righteous;
But *they are* on the throne with kings,
For He has seated them forever,
And they are exalted.
⁸And if *they are* bound in fetters,
Held in the cords of affliction,
⁹Then He tells them their work and their
transgressions—
That they have acted defiantly.
¹⁰He also opens their ear to instruction,
And commands that they turn from iniquity.
¹¹If they obey and serve *Him,*
They shall spend their days in prosperity,
And their years in pleasures.
¹²But if they do not obey,
They shall perish by the sword,
And they shall die without knowledge.^a

¹³"But the hypocrites in heart store up wrath;
They do not cry for help when He binds
them.
¹⁴They die in youth,
And their life *ends* among the perverted
persons.^a
¹⁵He delivers the poor in their affliction,
And opens their ears in oppression.

¹⁶"Indeed He would have brought you out of
dire distress,
Into a broad place where *there is* no restraint;

And what is set on your table *would be* full of
richness.
¹⁷But you are filled with the judgment due the
wicked;
Judgment and justice take hold *of you.*
¹⁸Because *there is* wrath, *beware* lest He take you
away with *one* blow;
For a large ransom would not help you avoid
it.
¹⁹Will your riches,
Or all the mighty forces,
Keep you from distress?
²⁰Do not desire the night,
When people are cut off in their place.
²¹Take heed, do not turn to iniquity,
For you have chosen this rather than
affliction.

²²"Behold, God is exalted by His power;
Who teaches like Him?
²³Who has assigned Him His way,
Or who has said, 'You have done wrong'?

Elihu Proclaims God's Majesty

²⁴"Remember to magnify His work,
Of which men have sung.
²⁵Everyone has seen it;
Man looks on *it* from afar.

²⁶"Behold, God *is* great, and we do not know
Him;
Nor can the number of His years *be*
discovered.
²⁷For He draws up drops of water,
Which distill as rain from the mist,
²⁸Which the clouds drop down
And pour abundantly on man.
²⁹Indeed, can *anyone* understand the spreading
of clouds,
The thunder from His canopy?
³⁰Look, He scatters His light upon it,
And covers the depths of the sea.
³¹For by these He judges the peoples;
He gives food in abundance.
³²He covers *His* hands with lightning,
And commands it to strike.

36:12 ^aMasoretic Text reads *as one without knowledge.* **36:14** ^aHebrew *qedeshim,* that is, those practicing sodomy and prostitution in religious rituals

³³His thunder declares it,
　　The cattle also, concerning the rising *storm*.

37

"At this also my heart trembles,
　　And leaps from its place.
²Hear attentively the thunder of His voice,
　　And the rumbling *that* comes from His
　　　mouth.
³He sends it forth under the whole heaven,
　　His lightning to the ends of the earth.
⁴After it a voice roars;
　　He thunders with His majestic voice,
　　And He does not restrain them when His
　　　voice is heard.
⁵God thunders marvelously with His voice;
　　He does great things which we cannot
　　　comprehend.
⁶For He says to the snow, 'Fall *on* the earth';
　　Likewise to the gentle rain and the heavy rain
　　　of His strength.
⁷He seals the hand of every man,
　　That all men may know His work.
⁸The beasts go into dens,
　　And remain in their lairs.
⁹From the chamber *of the south* comes the
　　　whirlwind,
　　And cold from the scattering winds *of the
　　　north*.
¹⁰By the breath of God ice is given,
　　And the broad waters are frozen.
¹¹Also with moisture He saturates the thick
　　　clouds;
　　He scatters His bright clouds.
¹²And they swirl about, being turned by His
　　　guidance,
　　That they may do whatever He commands
　　　them
　　On the face of the whole earth.ᵃ
¹³He causes it to come,
　　Whether for correction,
　　Or for His land,
　　Or for mercy.

¹⁴"Listen to this, O Job;
　　Stand still and consider the wondrous works
　　　of God.
¹⁵Do you know when God dispatches them,
　　And causes the light of His cloud to shine?
¹⁶Do you know how the clouds are balanced,

Those wondrous works of Him who is
　　perfect in knowledge?
¹⁷Why *are* your garments hot,
　　When He quiets the earth by the south
　　　wind?
¹⁸With Him, have you spread out the skies,
　　Strong as a cast metal mirror?

¹⁹"Teach us what we should say to Him,
　　For we can prepare nothing because of the
　　　darkness.
²⁰Should He be told that I *wish to* speak?
　　If a man were to speak, surely he would be
　　　swallowed up.
²¹Even now *men* cannot look at the light *when
　　it is* bright in the skies,
　　When the wind has passed and cleared
　　　them.
²²He comes from the north *as* golden *splendor;*
　　With God *is* awesome majesty.
²³*As for* the Almighty, we cannot find Him;
　　He is excellent in power,
　　In judgment and abundant justice;
　　He does not oppress.
²⁴Therefore men fear Him;
　　He shows no partiality to any *who are* wise of
　　　heart."

THE LORD REVEALS HIS OMNIPOTENCE TO JOB

38

Then the LORD answered Job out of the
whirlwind, and said:

²"Who *is* this who darkens counsel
　　By words without knowledge?
³Now prepare yourself like a man;
　　I will question you, and you shall answer Me.

⁴"Where were you when I laid the foundations
　　　of the earth?
　　Tell *Me,* if you have understanding.
⁵Who determined its measurements?
　　Surely you know!
　　Or who stretched the line upon it?
⁶To what were its foundations fastened?
　　Or who laid its cornerstone,
⁷When the morning stars sang together,
　　And all the sons of God shouted for joy?

37:12 ᵃLiterally *the world of the earth*

⁸"Or *who* shut in the sea with doors,
　When it burst forth *and* issued from the
　　womb;
⁹When I made the clouds its garment,
　And thick darkness its swaddling band;
¹⁰When I fixed My limit for it,
　And set bars and doors;
¹¹When I said,
　'This far you may come, but no farther,
　And here your proud waves must stop!'

¹²"Have you commanded the morning since
　　your days *began,*
　And caused the dawn to know its place,
¹³That it might take hold of the ends of the
　earth,
　And the wicked be shaken out of it?
¹⁴It takes on form like clay *under* a seal,
　And stands out like a garment.
¹⁵From the wicked their light is withheld,
　And the uplifted arm is broken.

¹⁶"Have you entered the springs of the sea?
　Or have you walked in search of the depths?
¹⁷Have the gates of death been revealed to you?
　Or have you seen the doors of the shadow of
　　death?
¹⁸Have you comprehended the breadth of the
　earth?
　Tell *Me,* if you know all this.

¹⁹"Where *is* the way *to* the dwelling of light?
　And darkness, where *is* its place,
²⁰That you may take it to its territory,
　That you may know the paths *to* its home?
²¹Do you know *it,* because you were born
　then,
　Or *because* the number of your days *is* great?

²²"Have you entered the treasury of snow,
　Or have you seen the treasury of hail,
²³Which I have reserved for the time of trouble,
　For the day of battle and war?
²⁴By what way is light diffused,
　Or the east wind scattered over the earth?

²⁵"Who has divided a channel for the
　　overflowing *water,*
　Or a path for the thunderbolt,

²⁶To cause it to rain on a land *where there is* no
　　one,
　A wilderness in which *there is* no man;
²⁷To satisfy the desolate waste,
　And cause to spring forth the growth of
　　tender grass?
²⁸Has the rain a father?
　Or who has begotten the drops of dew?
²⁹From whose womb comes the ice?
　And the frost of heaven, who gives it birth?
³⁰The waters harden like stone,
　And the surface of the deep is frozen.

³¹"Can you bind the cluster of the Pleiades,
　Or loose the belt of Orion?
³²Can you bring out Mazzaroth[a] in its season?
　Or can you guide the Great Bear with its
　　cubs?
³³Do you know the ordinances of the heavens?
　Can you set their dominion over the earth?

³⁴"Can you lift up your voice to the clouds,
　That an abundance of water may cover you?
³⁵Can you send out lightnings, that they may
　go,
　And say to you, 'Here we *are!*'?
³⁶Who has put wisdom in the mind?[a]
　Or who has given understanding to the
　　heart?
³⁷Who can number the clouds by wisdom?
　Or who can pour out the bottles of heaven,
³⁸When the dust hardens in clumps,
　And the clods cling together?

³⁹"Can you hunt the prey for the lion,
　Or satisfy the appetite of the young lions,
⁴⁰When they crouch in *their* dens,
　Or lurk in their lairs to lie in wait?
⁴¹Who provides food for the raven,
　When its young ones cry to God,
　And wander about for lack of food?

39

"Do you know the time when the wild
　　mountain goats bear young?
　Or can you mark when the deer gives birth?
²Can you number the months *that* they fulfill?
　Or do you know the time when they bear
　　young?

38:32 ᵃLiterally *Constellations*　38:36 ᵃLiterally *inward parts*

³They bow down,
They bring forth their young,
They deliver their offspring.ᵃ
⁴Their young ones are healthy,
They grow strong with grain;
They depart and do not return to them.

⁵"Who set the wild donkey free?
Who loosed the bonds of the onager,
⁶Whose home I have made the wilderness,
And the barren land his dwelling?
⁷He scorns the tumult of the city;
He does not heed the shouts of the driver.
⁸The range of the mountains *is* his pasture,
And he searches after every green thing.

⁹"Will the wild ox be willing to serve you?
Will he bed by your manger?
¹⁰Can you bind the wild ox in the furrow with
ropes?
Or will he plow the valleys behind you?
¹¹Will you trust him because his strength *is*
great?
Or will you leave your labor to him?
¹²Will you trust him to bring home your
grain,
And gather it to your threshing floor?

¹³"The wings of the ostrich wave proudly,
But are her wings and pinions *like the* kindly
stork's?
¹⁴For she leaves her eggs on the ground,
And warms them in the dust;
¹⁵She forgets that a foot may crush them,
Or that a wild beast may break them.
¹⁶She treats her young harshly, as though *they
were* not hers;
Her labor is in vain, without concern,
¹⁷Because God deprived her of wisdom,
And did not endow her with understanding.
¹⁸When she lifts herself on high,
She scorns the horse and its rider.

¹⁹"Have you given the horse strength?
Have you clothed his neck with thunder?ᵃ
²⁰Can you frighten him like a locust?
His majestic snorting strikes terror.
²¹He paws in the valley, and rejoices in *his*
strength;

He gallops into the clash of arms.
²²He mocks at fear, and is not frightened;
Nor does he turn back from the sword.
²³The quiver rattles against him,
The glittering spear and javelin.
²⁴He devours the distance with fierceness and
rage;
Nor does he come to a halt because the
trumpet *has* sounded.
²⁵At *the blast of* the trumpet he says, 'Aha!'
He smells the battle from afar,
The thunder of captains and shouting.

²⁶"Does the hawk fly by your wisdom,
And spread its wings toward the south?
²⁷Does the eagle mount up at your
command,
And make its nest on high?
²⁸On the rock it dwells and resides,
On the crag of the rock and the stronghold.
²⁹From there it spies out the prey;
Its eyes observe from afar.
³⁰Its young ones suck up blood;
And where the slain *are,* there it *is.*"

40

Moreover the LORD answered Job, and
said:

²"Shall the one who contends with the
Almighty correct *Him?*
He who rebukes God, let him answer it."

JOB'S RESPONSE TO GOD

³Then Job answered the LORD and said:

⁴"Behold, I am vile;
What shall I answer You?
I lay my hand over my mouth.
⁵Once I have spoken, but I will not answer;
Yes, twice, but I will proceed no further."

GOD'S CHALLENGE TO JOB

⁶Then the LORD answered Job out of the
whirlwind, and said:

⁷"Now prepare yourself like a man;
I will question you, and you shall answer Me:

39:3 ᵃLiterally *pangs,* figurative of offspring   39:19 ᵃOr *a mane*

⁸"Would you indeed annul My judgment?
  Would you condemn Me that you may be
    justified?
⁹Have you an arm like God?
  Or can you thunder with a voice like His?
¹⁰Then adorn yourself *with* majesty and
    splendor,
  And array yourself with glory and beauty.
¹¹Disperse the rage of your wrath;
  Look on everyone *who is* proud, and humble
    him.
¹²Look on everyone *who is* proud, *and* bring
    him low;
  Tread down the wicked in their place.
¹³Hide them in the dust together,
  Bind their faces in hidden *darkness.*
¹⁴Then I will also confess to you
  That your own right hand can save you.
¹⁵"Look now at the behemoth,ᵃ which I made
    along with you;
  He eats grass like an ox.
¹⁶See now, his strength *is* in his hips,
  And his power *is* in his stomach muscles.
¹⁷He moves his tail like a cedar;
  The sinews of his thighs are tightly knit.
¹⁸His bones *are like* beams of bronze,
  His ribs like bars of iron.
¹⁹He *is* the first of the ways of God;
  Only He who made him can bring near His
    sword.
²⁰Surely the mountains yield food for him,
  And all the beasts of the field play there.
²¹He lies under the lotus trees,
  In a covert of reeds and marsh.
²²The lotus trees cover him *with* their shade;
  The willows by the brook surround him.
²³Indeed the river may rage,
  Yet he is not disturbed;
  He is confident, though the Jordan gushes
    into his mouth,
²⁴*Though* he takes it in his eyes,
  Or one pierces *his* nose with a snare.

41 "Can you draw out Leviathanᵃ with a
    hook,
  Or *snare* his tongue with a line *which* you
    lower?
²Can you put a reed through his nose,
  Or pierce his jaw with a hook?

³Will he make many supplications to you?
  Will he speak softly to you?
⁴Will he make a covenant with you?
  Will you take him as a servant forever?
⁵Will you play with him as *with* a bird,
  Or will you leash him for your maidens?
⁶Will *your* companions make a banquetᵃ of
    him?
  Will they apportion him among the
    merchants?
⁷Can you fill his skin with harpoons,
  Or his head with fishing spears?
⁸Lay your hand on him;
  Remember the battle—
  Never do it again!
⁹Indeed, *any* hope of *overcoming* him is false;
  Shall *one not* be overwhelmed at the sight of
    him?
¹⁰No one *is so* fierce that he would dare stir
    him up.
  Who then is able to stand against Me?
¹¹Who has preceded Me, that I should pay *him?*
  Everything under heaven is Mine.

¹²"I will not concealᵃ his limbs,
  His mighty power, or his graceful
    proportions.
¹³Who can remove his outer coat?
  Who can approach *him* with a double bridle?
¹⁴Who can open the doors of his face,
  With his terrible teeth all around?
¹⁵*His* rows of scales are *his* pride,
  Shut up tightly *as with* a seal;
¹⁶One is so near another
  That no air can come between them;
¹⁷They are joined one to another,
  They stick together and cannot be parted.
¹⁸His sneezings flash forth light,
  And his eyes *are* like the eyelids of the
    morning.
¹⁹Out of his mouth go burning lights;
  Sparks of fire shoot out.
²⁰Smoke goes out of his nostrils,
  As *from* a boiling pot and burning rushes.
²¹His breath kindles coals,
  And a flame goes out of his mouth.

40:15 ᵃA large animal, exact identity unknown   **41:1** ᵃA large sea
creature, exact identity unknown   **41:6** ᵃOr *bargain over him*
41:12 ᵃLiterally *keep silent about*

²²Strength dwells in his neck,
  And sorrow dances before him.
²³The folds of his flesh are joined together;
  They are firm on him and cannot be moved.
²⁴His heart is as hard as stone,
  Even as hard as the lower *millstone.*
²⁵When he raises himself up, the mighty are
    afraid;
  Because of his crashings they are beside[a]
    themselves.
²⁶*Though* the sword reaches him, it cannot avail;
  Nor does spear, dart, or javelin.
²⁷He regards iron as straw,
  And bronze as rotten wood.
²⁸The arrow cannot make him flee;
  Slingstones become like stubble to him.
²⁹Darts are regarded as straw;
  He laughs at the threat of javelins.
³⁰His undersides *are* like sharp potsherds;
  He spreads pointed *marks* in the mire.
³¹He makes the deep boil like a pot;
  He makes the sea like a pot of ointment.
³²He leaves a shining wake behind him;
  One would think the deep had white hair.
³³On earth there is nothing like him,

  Which is made without fear.
³⁴He beholds every high *thing;*
  He *is* king over all the children of pride."

Job's Repentance and Restoration

42 Then Job answered the Lord and said:

²"I know that You can do everything,
  And that no purpose *of Yours* can be withheld
    from You.
³*You asked,* 'Who *is* this who hides counsel
    without knowledge?'
  Therefore I have uttered what I did not
    understand,
  Things too wonderful for me, which I did
    not know.
⁴Listen, please, and let me speak;
  You said, 'I will question you, and you shall
    answer Me.'

⁵"I have heard of You by the hearing of the ear,
  But now my eye sees You.
⁶Therefore I abhor *myself,*
  And repent in dust and ashes."

41:25 [a]*Or purify themselves*

INSIDE *the* INFLUENCERS

JOB: Positioned for Blessing

JOB 42:10–17

Most readers find some events in Job's life disturbing. Why should a "blameless" man have to endure such torture? If not for the final verses in the Book of Job, there would be no answers to this dilemma. Job's life is a testament to his righteousness, and even more so to God's greatness.

Job endured horrible circumstances, but only because God knew what the outcome would be. In the end He would bless Job in ways that he could never even imagine.

Job's suffering taught him an important lesson. It is human nature to question God when things go wrong. There's nothing wrong with asking God "Why?" (3:20–24). On the other hand, it's important to remember that God is not obligated to explain Himself to us. His ways and reasons are above and beyond our human understanding. God's obligation is to remain true to who He is. For Job, this resulted in a greater blessing than he'd ever experienced. Job honored God when things were good in his life (1:1–3). Job continued to honor God when things turned awful in his life (1:21, 22). He refused to "Curse God and die!" as his wife had suggested (2:9). Job positioned himself for the blessing of God by consistently honoring God in all of his circumstances.

[7]And so it was, after the LORD had spoken these words to Job, that the LORD said to Eliphaz the Temanite, "My wrath is aroused against you and your two friends, for you have not spoken of Me *what is* right, as My servant Job *has.* [8]Now therefore, take for yourselves seven bulls and seven rams, go to My servant Job, and offer up for yourselves a burnt offering; and My servant Job shall pray for you. For I will accept him, lest I deal with you *according to your* folly; because you have not spoken of Me *what is* right, as My servant Job *has.*"

[9]So Eliphaz the Temanite and Bildad the Shuhite *and* Zophar the Naamathite went and did as the LORD commanded them; for the LORD had accepted Job. [10]And the LORD restored Job's losses[a] when he prayed for his friends. Indeed the LORD gave Job twice as much as he had before. [11]Then all his brothers, all his sisters, and all those who had been his acquaintances before, came to him and ate food with him in his house; and they consoled him and comforted him for all the adversity that the LORD had brought upon him. Each one gave him a piece of silver and each a ring of gold.

[12]Now the LORD blessed the latter *days* of Job more than his beginning; for he had fourteen thousand sheep, six thousand camels, one thousand yoke of oxen, and one thousand female donkeys. [13]He also had seven sons and three daughters. [14]And he called the name of the first Jemimah, the name of the second Keziah, and the name of the third Keren-Happuch. [15]In all the land were found no women *so* beautiful as the daughters of Job; and their father gave them an inheritance among their brothers.

[16]After this Job lived one hundred and forty years, and saw his children and grandchildren *for* four generations. [17]So Job died, old and full of days.

42:10 [a]Literally *Job's captivity,* that is, what was captured from Job

IMPACT OF THE BOOK

PSALMS

I IDEA | *Let everything that has breath praise the Lord in all circumstances!*

m MESSAGE | *Each psalm contains great wisdom for daily living. The emphasis is clear: God matters, you matter, and today matters. Throughout this book of devotion, the importance of godly friends and God's Word in a leader's life are stressed. A leader must learn not to walk "in the counsel of the ungodly" (Ps.1:1). The 150 psalms proclaim the role God's Word should play in our lives: it is to be our delight, a light for our paths, our meditation, our food, and our map for navigating life. In times of joy and pain, David was driven into the presence of God. This book is a must-read for every leader. Renowned preacher and statesman, Billy Graham, advised young leaders to read five psalms and one proverb every day as a devotional.*

P PEOPLE | *Asaph, David, Ethan, Heman, sons of Korah, Moses, Solomon*

A AUTHOR | *Psalms is a collection of worship songs written by a variety of authors.*

C CULTURE | *These collections of songs were written over a long period of time, yet each one reflects a worshiper's response to God. The honesty of emotions displayed through psalms of joy, praise, lament, confession, thanksgiving, and distress suggest the authenticity that each worshiper desired to have before God. This book later became known as the Psalter and functioned as a hymnbook. It can be divided into five smaller books: Book 1 (Pss. 1—41), Book 2 (Pss. 42—72), Book 3 (Pss. 73—89), Book 4 (Pss. 90—106), and Book 5 (Pss. 107—150).*

T TIMELINE | *finally composed c. 400 BC*

KEY SCRIPTURE MEMORY VERSES | 1:1–3; 2:8; 8:4, 5, 9; 22:18; 23; 24:1; 37:4–6; 42:1; 46:1, 10; 51:10–12, 16, 17; 100:1–5; 101:2, 3; 119:9, 11, 105; 121:1, 2; 139:13–16; 150:6

Book One: Psalms 1—41

PSALM 1

THE WAY OF THE RIGHTEOUS AND THE END
OF THE UNGODLY

¹Blessed *is* the man
   Who walks not in the counsel of the ungodly,
      Nor stands in the path of sinners,
      Nor sits in the seat of the scornful;
²But his delight *is* in the law of the LORD,
      And in His law he meditates day and night.
³He shall be like a tree
      Planted by the rivers of water,
      That brings forth its fruit in its season,
      Whose leaf also shall not wither;
   And whatever he does shall prosper.

⁴The ungodly *are* not so,
   But *are* like the chaff which the wind drives
      away.
⁵Therefore the ungodly shall not stand in the
      judgment,
   Nor sinners in the congregation of the
      righteous.

⁶For the LORD knows the way of the righteous,
   But the way of the ungodly shall perish.

PSALM 2

THE MESSIAH'S TRIUMPH AND KINGDOM

¹Why do the nations rage,
   And the people plot a vain thing?
²The kings of the earth set themselves,
   And the rulers take counsel together,
   Against the LORD and against His Anointed,
      saying,
³"Let us break Their bonds in pieces
   And cast away Their cords from us."

⁴He who sits in the heavens shall laugh;
   The Lord shall hold them in derision.
⁵Then He shall speak to them in His wrath,
   And distress them in His deep displeasure:
⁶"Yet I have set My King
   On My holy hill of Zion."

⁷"I will declare the decree:
   The LORD has said to Me,
   'You *are* My Son,

Today I have begotten You.
⁸Ask of Me, and I will give *You*
   The nations *for* Your inheritance,
   And the ends of the earth *for* Your possession.
⁹You shall break[a] them with a rod of iron;
   You shall dash them to pieces like a potter's
      vessel.' "

¹⁰Now therefore, be wise, O kings;
   Be instructed, you judges of the earth.
¹¹Serve the LORD with fear,
   And rejoice with trembling.
¹²Kiss the Son,[a] lest He[b] be angry,
   And you perish *in* the way,
   When His wrath is kindled but a little.
   Blessed *are* all those who put their trust in Him.

PSALM 3

THE LORD HELPS HIS TROUBLED PEOPLE
A Psalm of David when he fled from Absalom
his son.

¹LORD, how they have increased who trouble
      me!
   Many *are* they who rise up against me.
²Many *are* they who say of me,
   "*There is* no help for him in God."   *Selah*

³But You, O LORD, *are* a shield for me,
   My glory and the One who lifts up my head.
⁴I cried to the LORD with my voice,
   And He heard me from His holy hill.   *Selah*

⁵I lay down and slept;
   I awoke, for the LORD sustained me.
⁶I will not be afraid of ten thousands of people
   Who have set *themselves* against me all around.

⁷Arise, O LORD;
   Save me, O my God!
   For You have struck all my enemies on the
      cheekbone;
   You have broken the teeth of the ungodly.
⁸Salvation *belongs* to the LORD.
   Your blessing *is* upon Your people.   *Selah*

2:9 [a]Following Masoretic Text and Targum; Septuagint, Syriac, and
Vulgate read *rule* (compare Revelation 2:27).   **2:12** [a]Septuagint and
Vulgate read *Embrace discipline;* Targum reads *Receive instruction.*
[b]Septuagint reads *the LORD.*

PSALM 4

THE SAFETY OF THE FAITHFUL
To the Chief Musician. With stringed
instruments. A Psalm of David.

[1]Hear me when I call, O God of my
righteousness!
You have relieved me in *my* distress;
Have mercy on me, and hear my prayer.

[2]How long, O you sons of men,
Will you turn my glory to shame?
How long will you love worthlessness
And seek falsehood?   *Selah*
[3]But know that the LORD has set apart[a] for
Himself him who is godly;
The LORD will hear when I call to Him.

[4]Be angry, and do not sin.
Meditate within your heart on your bed, and
be still.   *Selah*
[5]Offer the sacrifices of righteousness,
And put your trust in the LORD.

[6]*There are* many who say,
"Who will show us *any* good?"
LORD, lift up the light of Your countenance
upon us.
[7]You have put gladness in my heart,
More than in the season that their grain and
wine increased.
[8]I will both lie down in peace, and sleep;
For You alone, O LORD, make me dwell in
safety.

PSALM 5

A PRAYER FOR GUIDANCE
To the Chief Musician. With flutes.[a] A Psalm
of David.

[1]Give ear to my words, O LORD,
Consider my meditation.
[2]Give heed to the voice of my cry,
My King and my God,
For to You I will pray.
[3]My voice You shall hear in the morning,
O LORD;
In the morning I will direct *it* to You,
And I will look up.

[4]For You *are* not a God who takes pleasure in
wickedness,
Nor shall evil dwell with You.
[5]The boastful shall not stand in Your sight;
You hate all workers of iniquity.
[6]You shall destroy those who speak falsehood;
The LORD abhors the bloodthirsty and
deceitful man.

[7]But as for me, I will come into Your house in
the multitude of Your mercy;
In fear of You I will worship toward Your holy
temple.
[8]Lead me, O LORD, in Your righteousness
because of my enemies;
Make Your way straight before my face.

[9]For *there is* no faithfulness in their mouth;
Their inward part *is* destruction;
Their throat *is* an open tomb;
They flatter with their tongue.
[10]Pronounce them guilty, O God!
Let them fall by their own counsels;
Cast them out in the multitude of their
transgressions,
For they have rebelled against You.

[11]But let all those rejoice who put their trust in
You;
Let them ever shout for joy, because You
defend them;
Let those also who love Your name
Be joyful in You.
[12]For You, O LORD, will bless the righteous;
With favor You will surround him as *with* a
shield.

PSALM 6

A PRAYER OF FAITH IN TIME OF DISTRESS
To the Chief Musician. With stringed
instruments. On an eight-stringed harp.[a] A Psalm
of David.

[1]O LORD, do not rebuke me in Your anger,
Nor chasten me in Your hot displeasure.
[2]Have mercy on me, O LORD, for I *am* weak;
O LORD, heal me, for my bones are troubled.

4:3 [a]Many Hebrew manuscripts, Septuagint, Targum, and Vulgate
read *made wonderful.*   **5:title** [a]Hebrew *nehiloth*   **6:title** [a]Hebrew
sheminith

³My soul also is greatly troubled;
  But You, O LORD—how long?

⁴Return, O LORD, deliver me!
  Oh, save me for Your mercies' sake!
⁵For in death *there is* no remembrance of You;
  In the grave who will give You thanks?

⁶I am weary with my groaning;
  All night I make my bed swim;
  I drench my couch with my tears.
⁷My eye wastes away because of grief;
  It grows old because of all my enemies.

⁸Depart from me, all you workers of iniquity;
  For the LORD has heard the voice of my
    weeping.
⁹The LORD has heard my supplication;
  The LORD will receive my prayer.
¹⁰Let all my enemies be ashamed and greatly
    troubled;
  Let them turn back *and* be ashamed suddenly.

PSALM 7

PRAYER AND PRAISE FOR DELIVERANCE
FROM ENEMIES

A Meditation[a] of David, which he sang to the
  LORD concerning the words of Cush, a
  Benjamite.

¹O LORD my God, in You I put my trust;
  Save me from all those who persecute me;
  And deliver me,
²Lest they tear me like a lion,
  Rending *me* in pieces, while *there is* none to
    deliver.

³O LORD my God, if I have done this:
  If there is iniquity in my hands,
⁴If I have repaid evil to him who was at peace
    with me,
  Or have plundered my enemy without cause,
⁵Let the enemy pursue me and overtake *me;*
  Yes, let him trample my life to the earth,
  And lay my honor in the dust.   *Selah*

⁶Arise, O LORD, in Your anger;
  Lift Yourself up because of the rage of my
    enemies;
  Rise up for me[a] *to* the judgment You have
    commanded!

⁷So the congregation of the peoples shall
    surround You;
  For their sakes, therefore, return on high.
⁸The LORD shall judge the peoples;
  Judge me, O LORD, according to my
    righteousness,
  And according to my integrity within me.

⁹Oh, let the wickedness of the wicked come
    to an end,
  But establish the just;
  For the righteous God tests the hearts and
    minds.
¹⁰My defense *is* of God,
  Who saves the upright in heart.

¹¹God *is* a just judge,
  And God is angry *with the wicked* every day.
¹²If he does not turn back,
  He will sharpen His sword;
  He bends His bow and makes it ready.
¹³He also prepares for Himself instruments of
    death;
  He makes His arrows into fiery shafts.

¹⁴Behold, *the wicked* brings forth iniquity;
  Yes, he conceives trouble and brings forth
    falsehood.
¹⁵He made a pit and dug it out,
  And has fallen into the ditch *which* he made.
¹⁶His trouble shall return upon his own head,
  And his violent dealing shall come down on
    his own crown.

¹⁷I will praise the LORD according to His
    righteousness,
  And will sing praise to the name of the LORD
    Most High.

PSALM 8

THE GLORY OF THE LORD IN CREATION

To the Chief Musician. On the instrument of
  Gath.[a] A Psalm of David.

¹O LORD, our Lord,
  How excellent *is* Your name in all the earth,
  Who have set Your glory above the heavens!

7:title [a]Hebrew *Shiggaion*   **7:6** [a]Following Masoretic Text, Targum,
and Vulgate; Septuagint reads *O LORD my God.*   **8:title** [a]Hebrew *Al
Gittith*

THROUGH THE GRID

*Making Sense of Your World:
The Church's Slow Response (Ps. 8)*

The church has largely been sluggish in responding to issues of environmental or ecological importance. Believers must remember that their relationship with nature is one of good stewardship. The church has often been concerned more with doctrinal issues than with care of the environment. We must take care of the earth.

²Out of the mouth of babes and nursing
    infants
You have ordained strength,
Because of Your enemies,
That You may silence the enemy and the
    avenger.

³When I consider Your heavens, the work of
    Your fingers,
The moon and the stars, which You have
    ordained,
⁴What is man that You are mindful of him,
And the son of man that You visit him?
⁵For You have made him a little lower than the
    angels,[a]
And You have crowned him with glory and
    honor.

⁶You have made him to have dominion over
    the works of Your hands;
You have put all *things* under his feet,
⁷All sheep and oxen—
Even the beasts of the field,
⁸The birds of the air,

And the fish of the sea
That pass through the paths of the seas.

⁹O LORD, our Lord,
How excellent *is* Your name in all the earth!

PSALM 9

PRAYER AND THANKSGIVING FOR THE LORD'S
RIGHTEOUS JUDGMENTS
To the Chief Musician. To the *tune* of "Death of
the Son."[a] A Psalm of David.

¹I will praise *You,* O LORD, with my whole
    heart;
I will tell of all Your marvelous works.
²I will be glad and rejoice in You;
I will sing praise to Your name, O Most High.

³When my enemies turn back,
They shall fall and perish at Your presence.
⁴For You have maintained my right and my
    cause;

8:5 [a]Hebrew *Elohim, God;* Septuagint, Syriac, Targum, and Jewish tradition translate as *angels.*   **9:title** [a]Hebrew *Muth Labben*

THROUGH THE GRID

*Making Sense of Your World:
Confronting Humanity (Ps. 8:5)*

The way we view our own selves and our fellow humanity forms an integral part of our worldview because a worldview by nature involves the person and the person in relation to other people. Everyone must confront the concerns of their own humanity and existence as they seek answers to why they exist, how they must live, and even the matter of death. The way in which we answer these questions about humanity shapes our worldview and likewise shapes how we live our lives. How we shape our worldview defines how we live our lives—if we reason that our existence has meaning, then we live our lives with purpose.

You sat on the throne judging in
 righteousness.
[5]You have rebuked the nations,
 You have destroyed the wicked;
 You have blotted out their name forever and
 ever.

[6]O enemy, destructions are finished forever!
 And you have destroyed cities;
 Even their memory has perished.
[7]But the LORD shall endure forever;
 He has prepared His throne for judgment.
[8]He shall judge the world in righteousness,
 And He shall administer judgment for the
 peoples in uprightness.

[9]The LORD also will be a refuge for the
 oppressed,
 A refuge in times of trouble.
[10]And those who know Your name will put
 their trust in You;
 For You, LORD, have not forsaken those who
 seek You.

[11]Sing praises to the LORD, who dwells in
 Zion!
 Declare His deeds among the people.
[12]When He avenges blood, He remembers
 them;
 He does not forget the cry of the humble.

[13]Have mercy on me, O LORD!
 Consider my trouble from those who hate
 me,
 You who lift me up from the gates of
 death,
[14]That I may tell of all Your praise
 In the gates of the daughter of Zion.
 I will rejoice in Your salvation.

[15]The nations have sunk down in the pit *which*
 they made;
 In the net which they hid, their own foot is
 caught.
[16]The LORD is known *by* the judgment He
 executes;
 The wicked is snared in the work of his own
 hands.
  Meditation.[a]   *Selah*

[17]The wicked shall be turned into hell,
 And all the nations that forget God.
[18]For the needy shall not always be forgotten;
 The expectation of the poor shall *not* perish
 forever.

[19]Arise, O LORD,
 Do not let man prevail;
 Let the nations be judged in Your sight.
[20]Put them in fear, O LORD,
 That the nations may know themselves *to be*
 but men.   *Selah*

PSALM 10

A SONG OF CONFIDENCE IN GOD'S TRIUMPH OVER EVIL

[1]Why do You stand afar off, O LORD?
 Why do You hide in times of trouble?
[2]The wicked in *his* pride persecutes the poor;
 Let them be caught in the plots which they
 have devised.

[3]For the wicked boasts of his heart's desire;
 He blesses the greedy *and* renounces the
 LORD.
[4]The wicked in his proud countenance does
 not seek *God;*
 God *is* in none of his thoughts.

[5]His ways are always prospering;
 Your judgments *are* far above, out of his sight;
 As for all his enemies, he sneers at them.
[6]He has said in his heart, "I shall not be
 moved;
 I shall never be in adversity."
[7]His mouth is full of cursing and deceit and
 oppression;
 Under his tongue *is* trouble and iniquity.

[8]He sits in the lurking places of the villages;
 In the secret places he murders the innocent;
 His eyes are secretly fixed on the helpless.
[9]He lies in wait secretly, as a lion in his den;
 He lies in wait to catch the poor;
 He catches the poor when he draws him into
 his net.
[10]So he crouches, he lies low,

9:16 [a]Hebrew *Higgaion*

That the helpless may fall by his strength.
[11]He has said in his heart,
"God has forgotten;
He hides His face;
He will never see."

[12]Arise, O LORD!
O God, lift up Your hand!
Do not forget the humble.
[13]Why do the wicked renounce God?
He has said in his heart,
"You will not require *an account*."

[14]But You have seen, for You observe trouble
and grief,
To repay *it* by Your hand.
The helpless commits himself to You;
You are the helper of the fatherless.
[15]Break the arm of the wicked and the evil
man;
Seek out his wickedness *until* You find none.

[16]The LORD *is* King forever and ever;
The nations have perished out of His land.
[17]LORD, You have heard the desire of the
humble;
You will prepare their heart;
You will cause Your ear to hear,
[18]To do justice to the fatherless and the
oppressed,
That the man of the earth may oppress no
more.

PSALM 11

FAITH IN THE LORD'S RIGHTEOUSNESS
To the Chief Musician. *A Psalm* of David.

[1]In the LORD I put my trust;
How can you say to my soul,
"Flee *as* a bird to your mountain"?
[2]For look! The wicked bend *their* bow,
They make ready their arrow on the string,
That they may shoot secretly at the upright in
heart.
[3]If the foundations are destroyed,
What can the righteous do?

[4]The LORD *is* in His holy temple,
The LORD'S throne *is* in heaven;
His eyes behold,

His eyelids test the sons of men.
[5]The LORD tests the righteous,
But the wicked and the one who loves
violence His soul hates.
[6]Upon the wicked He will rain coals;
Fire and brimstone and a burning wind
Shall be the portion of their cup.

[7]For the LORD *is* righteous,
He loves righteousness;
His countenance beholds the upright.[a]

PSALM 12

MAN'S TREACHERY AND GOD'S CONSTANCY
To the Chief Musician. On an eight-stringed
harp.[a] A Psalm of David.

[1]Help, LORD, for the godly man ceases!
For the faithful disappear from among the
sons of men.
[2]They speak idly everyone with his neighbor;
With flattering lips *and* a double heart they
speak.

[3]May the LORD cut off all flattering lips,
And the tongue that speaks proud things,
[4]Who have said,
"With our tongue we will prevail;
Our lips *are* our own;
Who *is* lord over us?"

[5]"For the oppression of the poor, for the
sighing of the needy,
Now I will arise," says the LORD;
"I will set *him* in the safety for which he
yearns."

[6]The words of the LORD *are* pure words,
Like silver tried in a furnace of earth,
Purified seven times.
[7]You shall keep them, O LORD,
You shall preserve them from this generation
forever.

[8]The wicked prowl on every side,
When vileness is exalted among the sons of
men.

11:7 [a]Or *The upright beholds His countenance* 12:title [a]Hebrew
sheminith

PSALM 13

TRUST IN THE SALVATION OF THE LORD
To the Chief Musician. A Psalm of David.

[1]How long, O LORD? Will You forget me
     forever?
How long will You hide Your face from me?
[2]How long shall I take counsel in my soul,
Having sorrow in my heart daily?
How long will my enemy be exalted over
     me?

[3]Consider *and* hear me, O LORD my God;
Enlighten my eyes,
Lest I sleep the *sleep of* death;
[4]Lest my enemy say,
"I have prevailed against him";
Lest those who trouble me rejoice when I am
     moved.

[5]But I have trusted in Your mercy;
My heart shall rejoice in Your salvation.
[6]I will sing to the LORD,
Because He has dealt bountifully with me.

PSALM 14

FOLLY OF THE GODLESS, AND GOD'S FINAL
TRIUMPH
To the Chief Musician. *A Psalm* of David.

[1]The fool has said in his heart,
"*There is* no God."
They are corrupt,
They have done abominable works,
There is none who does good.

[2]The LORD looks down from heaven upon
     the children of men,
To see if there are any who understand, who
     seek God.
[3]They have all turned aside,
They have together become corrupt;
There is none who does good,
No, not one.

[4]Have all the workers of iniquity no
     knowledge,
Who eat up my people *as* they eat bread,
And do not call on the LORD?
[5]There they are in great fear,
For God *is* with the generation of the
     righteous.
[6]You shame the counsel of the poor,
But the LORD *is* his refuge.

[7]Oh, that the salvation of Israel *would come* out
     of Zion!
When the LORD brings back the captivity of
     His people,
Let Jacob rejoice *and* Israel be glad.

PSALM 15

THE CHARACTER OF THOSE WHO MAY DWELL
WITH THE LORD
A Psalm of David.

[1]LORD, who may abide in Your tabernacle?
Who may dwell in Your holy hill?

[2]He who walks uprightly,
     And works righteousness,

THROUGH THE GRID

Where Have All the Dreamers Gone?
Observations from a Biblical
Worldview: Making Sense of the World
(Ps. 14:1)

The complaint of Christians against the transcendentalist and their claims is not so much that they believe in nothing; but rather, they believe in everything. This is a kind of mix-and-match pluralism that uses the self as the means by which objective and absolute truth is measured. Because people have rejected the existence of God, it has had an extreme effect on morality; and it has, in fact, demolished the very base and foundation of morality and truth. Christians must stand against this tide of counter-cultural by pointing to the truth of Christ.

And speaks the truth in his heart;
³He *who* does not backbite with his tongue,
Nor does evil to his neighbor,
Nor does he take up a reproach against his
friend;
⁴In whose eyes a vile person is despised,
But he honors those who fear the LORD;
He *who* swears to his own hurt and does not
change;
⁵He *who* does not put out his money at usury,
Nor does he take a bribe against the
innocent.

He who does these *things* shall never be
moved.

PSALM 16

THE HOPE OF THE FAITHFUL, AND THE
MESSIAH'S VICTORY
A Michtam of David.

¹Preserve me, O God, for in You I put my trust.

²*O my soul,* you have said to the LORD,
"You *are* my Lord,
My goodness is nothing apart from You."
³As for the saints who *are* on the earth,
"They are the excellent ones, in whom is all
my delight."

⁴Their sorrows shall be multiplied who hasten
after another *god;*
Their drink offerings of blood I will not
offer,
Nor take up their names on my lips.

⁵O LORD, *You are* the portion of my
inheritance and my cup;
You maintain my lot.
⁶The lines have fallen to me in pleasant *places;*
Yes, I have a good inheritance.

⁷I will bless the LORD who has given me
counsel;
My heart also instructs me in the night
seasons.
⁸I have set the LORD always before me;
Because *He is* at my right hand I shall not be
moved.

⁹Therefore my heart is glad, and my glory
rejoices;
My flesh also will rest in hope.
¹⁰For You will not leave my soul in Sheol,
Nor will You allow Your Holy One to see
corruption.
¹¹You will show me the path of life;
In Your presence *is* fullness of joy;
At Your right hand *are* pleasures forevermore.

PSALM 17

PRAYER WITH CONFIDENCE IN FINAL SALVATION
A Prayer of David.

¹Hear a just cause, O LORD,
Attend to my cry;
Give ear to my prayer *which is* not from
deceitful lips.
²Let my vindication come from Your presence;
Let Your eyes look on the things that are
upright.

³You have tested my heart;
You have visited *me* in the night;
You have tried me and have found nothing;
I have purposed that my mouth shall not
transgress.
⁴Concerning the works of men,
By the word of Your lips,
I have kept away from the paths of the
destroyer.
⁵Uphold my steps in Your paths,
That my footsteps may not slip.

⁶I have called upon You, for You will hear me,
O God;
Incline Your ear to me, *and* hear my speech.
⁷Show Your marvelous lovingkindness by Your
right hand,
O You who save those who trust *in You*
From those who rise up *against them.*
⁸Keep me as the apple of Your eye;
Hide me under the shadow of Your wings,
⁹From the wicked who oppress me,
From my deadly enemies who surround me.

¹⁰They have closed up their fat *hearts;*
With their mouths they speak proudly.
¹¹They have now surrounded us in our steps;

LEADERSHIP ISSUES

What Is Character?

PSALM 15

David lays out eight core values of a person of character. These give us predetermined responses to life situations, according to God's Word.

A person of character:

1. "works righteousness" (v. 2); a leader does the right thing, that is, "God's thing," no matter how great the cost.

2. "walks uprightly" (v. 2); a leader deals with personal mistakes with integrity. A person of integrity admits mistakes and makes corrections and restitutions.

3. "speaks truth in his heart" (v. 2); a leader delights in honesty, guards the honesty of his heart, and takes delight in what is honest and genuine.

4. "does not backbite with his tongue" (v. 3); a leader uses disciplined words and does not slander. Leaders speak truth, bring life, strength, and joy to others by their words.

5. "honors those who fear the LORD" (v. 4); a leader defends others who are righteous, whether a friend or not. Leaders go to their aid, regardless of the cost.

6. "swears to his own hurt and does not change" (v. 4); when a leader says "Yes," they mean "Yes." When they say "No," they mean "No."

7. "does not put out his money at usury" (v. 5); usury means charging interest on money loaned. Leaders don't use money to gain at the expense of others. They understand that what they have is a gift of God and needs to be used to accomplish God's purposes.

8. does not "take a bribe against the innocent" (v. 5); leaders do not use people to meet emotional, physical, or financial needs. A leader treats everyone as the sons and daughters of God they are.

When we serve and honor others, view others as children of God, and treat them respectfully, we help them come closer to knowing Jesus Christ.

They have set their eyes, crouching down to
the earth,
[12]As a lion is eager to tear his prey,
And like a young lion lurking in secret places.

[13]Arise, O LORD,
Confront him, cast him down;
Deliver my life from the wicked with Your
sword,
[14]With Your hand from men, O LORD,
From men of the world *who have* their
portion in *this* life,
And whose belly You fill with Your hidden
treasure.
They are satisfied with children,
And leave the rest of their *possession* for their
babes.

[15]As for me, I will see Your face in
righteousness;
I shall be satisfied when I awake in Your
likeness.

PSALM 18

GOD THE SOVEREIGN SAVIOR

To the Chief Musician. *A Psalm* of David the
servant of the LORD, who spoke to the LORD the
words of this song on the day that the LORD
delivered him from the hand of all his enemies
and from the hand of Saul. And he said:

[1]I will love You, O LORD, my strength.
[2]The LORD is my rock and my fortress and my
deliverer;
My God, my strength, in whom I will trust;
My shield and the horn of my salvation, my
stronghold.
[3]I will call upon the LORD, *who is worthy* to be
praised;
So shall I be saved from my enemies.

[4]The pangs of death surrounded me,
And the floods of ungodliness made me
afraid.
[5]The sorrows of Sheol surrounded me;
The snares of death confronted me.
[6]In my distress I called upon the LORD,
And cried out to my God;
He heard my voice from His temple,

And my cry came before Him, *even* to His
ears.

[7]Then the earth shook and trembled;
The foundations of the hills also quaked and
were shaken,
Because He was angry.
[8]Smoke went up from His nostrils,
And devouring fire from His mouth;
Coals were kindled by it.
[9]He bowed the heavens also, and came down
With darkness under His feet.
[10]And He rode upon a cherub, and flew;
He flew upon the wings of the wind.
[11]He made darkness His secret place;
His canopy around Him *was* dark waters
And thick clouds of the skies.
[12]From the brightness before Him,
His thick clouds passed with hailstones and
coals of fire.

[13]The LORD thundered from heaven,
And the Most High uttered His voice,
Hailstones and coals of fire.[a]
[14]He sent out His arrows and scattered the foe,
Lightnings in abundance, and He vanquished
them.
[15]Then the channels of the sea were seen,
The foundations of the world were
uncovered
At Your rebuke, O LORD,
At the blast of the breath of Your nostrils.

[16]He sent from above, He took me;
He drew me out of many waters.
[17]He delivered me from my strong enemy,
From those who hated me,
For they were too strong for me.
[18]They confronted me in the day of my
calamity,
But the LORD was my support.
[19]He also brought me out into a broad place;
He delivered me because He delighted in me.

[20]The LORD rewarded me according to my
righteousness;
According to the cleanness of my hands

18:13 [a]Following Masoretic Text, Targum, and Vulgate; a few Hebrew manuscripts and Septuagint omit *Hailstones and coals of fire.*

He has recompensed me.
²¹For I have kept the ways of the LORD,
And have not wickedly departed from my
    God.
²²For all His judgments *were* before me,
And I did not put away His statutes from me.
²³I was also blameless before Him,
And I kept myself from my iniquity.
²⁴Therefore the LORD has recompensed me
    according to my righteousness,
According to the cleanness of my hands in
    His sight.

²⁵With the merciful You will show Yourself
    merciful;
With a blameless man You will show Yourself
    blameless;
²⁶With the pure You will show Yourself pure;
And with the devious You will show Yourself
    shrewd.
²⁷For You will save the humble people,
But will bring down haughty looks.

²⁸For You will light my lamp;
The LORD my God will enlighten my
    darkness.
²⁹For by You I can run against a troop,
By my God I can leap over a wall.
³⁰*As for* God, His way *is* perfect;

The word of the LORD is proven;
He *is* a shield to all who trust in Him.

³¹For who *is* God, except the LORD?
And who *is* a rock, except our God?
³²*It is* God who arms me with strength,
And makes my way perfect.
³³He makes my feet like the *feet of* deer,
And sets me on my high places.
³⁴He teaches my hands to make war,
So that my arms can bend a bow of bronze.

³⁵You have also given me the shield of Your
    salvation;
Your right hand has held me up,
Your gentleness has made me great.
³⁶You enlarged my path under me,
So my feet did not slip.

³⁷I have pursued my enemies and overtaken
    them;
Neither did I turn back again till they were
    destroyed.
³⁸I have wounded them,
So that they could not rise;
They have fallen under my feet.
³⁹For You have armed me with strength for the
    battle;
You have subdued under me those who rose
    up against me.

THROUGH THE GRID

Discover God: God Gives Us Rest in Him

PSALM 18:30 *As for God, His way is perfect; the word of the LORD is proven; He is a shield to all who trust in Him.*

Because God never changes, we can rest safely in His promises and in His character. All of God's attributes attest to His greatness and His love for all humanity. What God has started, God will finish; and all that God has promised, God will accomplish. What an incredible promise for us to rely on, especially in our toughest moments. We can be led securely through the storms of life by God's guidance, knowing that God will never lead us away from His perfect plan and that He only has the best in store for us. God loves us unconditionally and is ready to give us all we need and more through the Holy Spirit when we depend fully on Him.

⁴⁰You have also given me the necks of my enemies,

So that I destroyed those who hated me.

⁴¹They cried out, but *there was* none to save;

Even to the LORD, but He did not answer them.

⁴²Then I beat them as fine as the dust before the wind;

I cast them out like dirt in the streets.

⁴³You have delivered me from the strivings of the people;

You have made me the head of the nations;

A people I have not known shall serve me.

⁴⁴As soon as they hear of me they obey me;

The foreigners submit to me.

⁴⁵The foreigners fade away,

And come frightened from their hideouts.

⁴⁶The LORD lives!

Blessed *be* my Rock!

Let the God of my salvation be exalted.

⁴⁷*It is* God who avenges me,

And subdues the peoples under me;

⁴⁸He delivers me from my enemies.

You also lift me up above those who rise against me;

You have delivered me from the violent man.

⁴⁹Therefore I will give thanks to You, O LORD, among the Gentiles,

And sing praises to Your name.

⁵⁰Great deliverance He gives to His king,

And shows mercy to His anointed,

To David and his descendants forevermore.

PSALM 19

THE PERFECT REVELATION OF THE LORD

To the Chief Musician. A Psalm of David.

¹The heavens declare the glory of God;

And the firmament shows His handiwork.

²Day unto day utters speech,

And night unto night reveals knowledge.

³*There is* no speech nor language

Where their voice is not heard.

⁴Their line[a] has gone out through all the earth,

And their words to the end of the world.

In them He has set a tabernacle for the sun,

⁵Which *is* like a bridegroom coming out of his chamber,

And rejoices like a strong man to run its race.

⁶Its rising *is* from one end of heaven,

And its circuit to the other end;

And there is nothing hidden from its heat.

⁷The law of the LORD *is* perfect, converting the soul;

The testimony of the LORD *is* sure, making wise the simple;

19:4 ᵃSeptuagint, Syriac, and Vulgate read *sound;* Targum reads *business.*

THROUGH THE GRID

Thinking Christianly: Evidences for God's Existence (Ps. 19)

Several evidences and arguments mark God's reality and existence in the world:

1. The cosmological argument says that since the world exists, there must be a Creator.

2. The teleological argument says that since the world is full of design, there must be an intelligent Designer.

3. The moral argument for God bases God's existence on the existence of morality.

4. The ontological argument holds that God necessarily exists since God is the greatest being.

5. The historical argument holds that we can see God through His works in history.

6. And finally, the existence of Jesus points to God.

LEADERSHIP ISSUES

GC2: Convictions: Choices Shaped by the Word

PSALM 19:7   *The law of the LORD is perfect, converting the soul; the testimony of the LORD is sure, making wise the simple.*

The laws and commands of God's Word are perfect, trustworthy, right, clear, and true, because those are qualities of the Lawgiver—God—Himself. The Word of God doesn't possess those qualities or powers in and of itself; it derives them from God as the Author of Scripture (2 Tim. 3:16, 17; 1 Pet. 1:10–12).

Living according to God's ways simply reflects the way God is, which in turn brings clear and certain benefits. King David references Scripture as reviving our soul, making us wise, bringing us joy, and giving us wisdom; it doesn't get much better than that!

As we know and actually live or experience God's Word, we come to know the benefits that King David writes about: the benefits of knowing God and His peace, a clear conscience and close relationships, a secure sense of who we are and why we're here!

Living out God's Word also helps protect us from guilt, shame, loneliness, and destructive relationships. Our convictions concerning decisions, actions, thoughts, and attitudes are then to be based in God's Word, empowered by the Holy Spirit (Gal. 5:16–25).

GC2
GREAT COMMANDMENT
COMMISSION

THROUGH THE GRID

Making Sense of Your World: Christian Response to the Environment (Ps. 19)

Several principles guide the biblical worldview of Christians toward the environment. Although humanity is the crowning point of creation, we cannot neglect the environmental problems mounting today, as a result of humanity's sin. Also, our importance as human beings does not negate the importance of the environment. God values nature also, and we must care for it. Science and technology cannot fully answer today's environmental problems, and we must work toward making changes. We must ground our response to nature in the Bible.

⁸The statutes of the LORD *are* right, rejoicing
    the heart;
The commandment of the LORD *is* pure,
    enlightening the eyes;
⁹The fear of the LORD *is* clean, enduring
    forever;
The judgments of the LORD *are* true *and*
    righteous altogether.
¹⁰More to be desired *are they* than gold,
Yea, than much fine gold;
Sweeter also than honey and the honeycomb.
¹¹Moreover by them Your servant is warned,
And in keeping them *there is* great reward.

¹²Who can understand *his* errors?
Cleanse me from secret *faults.*
¹³Keep back Your servant also from
    presumptuous *sins;*
Let them not have dominion over me.
Then I shall be blameless,
And I shall be innocent of great
    transgression.

¹⁴Let the words of my mouth and the
    meditation of my heart
Be acceptable in Your sight,
O LORD, my strength and my Redeemer.

PSALM 20

THE ASSURANCE OF GOD'S SAVING WORK
To the Chief Musician. A Psalm of David.

¹May the LORD answer you in the day of
    trouble;
May the name of the God of Jacob defend
    you;

²May He send you help from the sanctuary,
And strengthen you out of Zion;
³May He remember all your offerings,
And accept your burnt sacrifice.   *Selah*

⁴May He grant you according to your heart's
    desire,
And fulfill all your purpose.
⁵We will rejoice in your salvation,
And in the name of our God we will set up
    our banners!
May the LORD fulfill all your petitions.

⁶Now I know that the LORD saves His
    anointed;
He will answer him from His holy heaven
With the saving strength of His right hand.

⁷Some *trust* in chariots, and some in horses;
But we will remember the name of the LORD
    our God.
⁸They have bowed down and fallen;
But we have risen and stand upright.

⁹Save, LORD!
May the King answer us when we call.

PSALM 21

JOY IN THE SALVATION OF THE LORD
To the Chief Musician. A Psalm of David.

¹The king shall have joy in Your strength,
    O LORD;
And in Your salvation how greatly shall he
    rejoice!
²You have given him his heart's desire,

And have not withheld the request of his
    lips.   *Selah*

³For You meet him with the blessings of
    goodness;
You set a crown of pure gold upon his head.
⁴He asked life from You, *and* You gave *it* to
    him—
Length of days forever and ever.
⁵His glory *is* great in Your salvation;
Honor and majesty You have placed upon
    him.
⁶For You have made him most blessed forever;
You have made him exceedingly glad with
    Your presence.
⁷For the king trusts in the LORD,
And through the mercy of the Most High he
    shall not be moved.

⁸Your hand will find all Your enemies;
Your right hand will find those who hate You.
⁹You shall make them as a fiery oven in the
    time of Your anger;
The LORD shall swallow them up in His
    wrath,
And the fire shall devour them.
¹⁰Their offspring You shall destroy from the
    earth,
And their descendants from among the sons
    of men.
¹¹For they intended evil against You;
They devised a plot *which* they are not able *to
    perform.*
¹²Therefore You will make them turn their
    back;
You will make ready *Your arrows* on Your
    string toward their faces.

¹³Be exalted, O LORD, in Your own strength!
We will sing and praise Your power.

PSALM 22

THE SUFFERING, PRAISE, AND POSTERITY
OF THE MESSIAH
To the Chief Musician. Set to "The Deer of the
Dawn."[a] A Psalm of David.

¹My God, My God, why have You forsaken
    Me?

Why are You so far from helping Me,
And from the words of My groaning?
²O My God, I cry in the daytime, but You do
    not hear;
And in the night season, and am not silent.

³But You *are* holy,
Enthroned in the praises of Israel.
⁴Our fathers trusted in You;
They trusted, and You delivered them.
⁵They cried to You, and were delivered;
They trusted in You, and were not ashamed.

⁶But I *am* a worm, and no man;
A reproach of men, and despised by the
    people.
⁷All those who see Me ridicule Me;
They shoot out the lip, they shake the head,
    saying,
⁸"He trusted[a] in the LORD, let Him rescue
    Him;
Let Him deliver Him, since He delights in
    Him!"

⁹But You *are* He who took Me out of the
    womb;
You made Me trust *while* on My mother's
    breasts.
¹⁰I was cast upon You from birth.
From My mother's womb
You *have been* My God.
¹¹Be not far from Me,
For trouble *is* near;
For *there is* none to help.

¹²Many bulls have surrounded Me;
Strong *bulls* of Bashan have encircled Me.
¹³They gape at Me *with* their mouths,
Like a raging and roaring lion.

¹⁴I am poured out like water,
And all My bones are out of joint;
My heart is like wax;
It has melted within Me.
¹⁵My strength is dried up like a potsherd,
And My tongue clings to My jaws;
You have brought Me to the dust of death.

22:title [a]Hebrew *Aijeleth Hashahar* **22:8** [a]Septuagint, Syriac, and
Vulgate read *hoped;* Targum reads *praised.*

[16]For dogs have surrounded Me;
The congregation of the wicked has
enclosed Me.
They pierced[a] My hands and My feet;
[17]I can count all My bones.
They look *and* stare at Me.
[18]They divide My garments among them,
And for My clothing they cast lots.

[19]But You, O LORD, do not be far from Me;
O My Strength, hasten to help Me!
[20]Deliver Me from the sword,
My precious *life* from the power of the dog.
[21]Save Me from the lion's mouth
And from the horns of the wild oxen!

You have answered Me.

[22]I will declare Your name to My brethren;
In the midst of the assembly I will praise
You.
[23]You who fear the LORD, praise Him!
All you descendants of Jacob, glorify Him,
And fear Him, all you offspring of Israel!

[24]For He has not despised nor abhorred the
affliction of the afflicted;
Nor has He hidden His face from Him;
But when He cried to Him, He heard.

[25]My praise *shall be* of You in the great
assembly;
I will pay My vows before those who fear
Him.
[26]The poor shall eat and be satisfied;
Those who seek Him will praise the
LORD.
Let your heart live forever!

[27]All the ends of the world
Shall remember and turn to the LORD,
And all the families of the nations
Shall worship before You.[a]
[28]For the kingdom *is* the LORD's,
And He rules over the nations.

22:16 [a]Following some Hebrew manuscripts, Septuagint, Syriac, Vulgate; Masoretic Text reads *Like a lion.* **22:27** [a]Following Masoretic Text, Septuagint, and Targum; Arabic, Syriac, and Vulgate read *Him.*

THROUGH THE GRID

Discover God: God Is Always with Us

PSALM 23:4 *Yea, though I walk through the valley of the shadow of death, I will fear no evil; for You are with me; Your rod and Your staff, they comfort me.*

We never have to work to merit God's presence in our lives—God is always with us, no matter where we are. We can always rely on the close presence of God in our lives by praying, for it is through prayer that we begin to recognize and accept the omnipresent and infinite power of God. God remains with us at the heights of our joys and in the depths of our sorrows and troubles—there is no pit so deep that God cannot reach us. God's infinite presence with us can give us strength and hope in times of despair; and even when we have nowhere else to turn, God stands with us, present in our times of crisis or need. It is God's constant presence with us that gives us power to witness. In response, each believer should practice living consciously in the presence of God by relying on God at all times and through prayer. Here are several truths we can derive from the omnipresence of God for our lives: God will guide us when we are confused, when we are afraid, when we are tempted, when we are hurting, when we are discouraged, and when we are lonely. God is always there with us and for us, and we can always count on God.

LEADERSHIP ISSUES

GC2: Becoming a Good Samaritan: Jesus the Good Shepherd

PSALM 23:6

Making the Shepherd's attentive care for you personal is what prompts the gratitude and compassion to care for others. The Good Shepherd means for us to become a person who receives and gives from His divine care (see John 10:11; Matt. 10:8).

Reread Psalm 23, and put special emphasis on the words "my," "me," and "I" as you make His care personal. Then pause to consider a time when you were needy and alone. Maybe it was a time of disappointment or rejection. Imagine that at your point of need—your point of aloneness—the Lord quiets your spirit, causing you to pause and be still. Now, imagine looking over your shoulder—and goodness and mercy are chasing you. Picture also, the Lord Jesus in all of His abundance and love, pursuing you. Then, pray something like this:

Heavenly Father, it is abundantly clear and true that I have been cared for by You, Father. I have been touched by You. At my points of aloneness and neediness, I have been blessed abundantly by You. Father, might the wonder of such care prompt me to touch other people with the care with which I've been touched. Thank You that I have freely received and out of the wonder and gratitude for those gifts of care, may I freely give. Thank You for the privilege of doing that. In Christ's name, I pray.

GC2
GREAT COMMANDMENT
COMMISSION

²⁹All the prosperous of the earth
Shall eat and worship;
All those who go down to the dust
Shall bow before Him,
Even he who cannot keep himself alive.

³⁰A posterity shall serve Him.
It will be recounted of the Lord to the *next*
    generation,
³¹They will come and declare His
    righteousness to a people who will be
    born,
That He has done *this*.

PSALM 23

THE LORD THE SHEPHERD OF HIS PEOPLE
A Psalm of David.

¹The LORD *is* my shepherd;
I shall not want.
²He makes me to lie down in green pastures;
He leads me beside the still waters.
³He restores my soul;
He leads me in the paths of righteousness
For His name's sake.

⁴Yea, though I walk through the valley of the
    shadow of death,
I will fear no evil;
For You *are* with me;
Your rod and Your staff, they comfort me.

⁵You prepare a table before me in the presence
    of my enemies;
You anoint my head with oil;
My cup runs over.
⁶Surely goodness and mercy shall follow me
All the days of my life;
And I will dwell^a in the house of the LORD
Forever.

PSALM 24

THE KING OF GLORY AND HIS KINGDOM
A Psalm of David.

¹The earth *is* the LORD's, and all its fullness,
The world and those who dwell therein.
²For He has founded it upon the seas,
And established it upon the waters.

³Who may ascend into the hill of the LORD?
Or who may stand in His holy place?
⁴He who has clean hands and a pure heart,
Who has not lifted up his soul to an idol,
Nor sworn deceitfully.
⁵He shall receive blessing from the LORD,
And righteousness from the God of his
    salvation.
⁶This *is* Jacob, the generation of those who
    seek Him,
Who seek Your face.   *Selah*

⁷Lift up your heads, O you gates!
And be lifted up, you everlasting doors!
And the King of glory shall come in.
⁸Who *is* this King of glory?
The LORD strong and mighty,
The LORD mighty in battle.
⁹Lift up your heads, O you gates!
Lift up, you everlasting doors!
And the King of glory shall come in.
¹⁰Who is this King of glory?
The LORD of hosts,
He *is* the King of glory.   *Selah*

PSALM 25

A PLEA FOR DELIVERANCE AND FORGIVENESS
A Psalm of David.

¹To You, O LORD, I lift up my soul.
²O my God, I trust in You;
Let me not be ashamed;
Let not my enemies triumph over me.
³Indeed, let no one who waits on You be
    ashamed;
Let those be ashamed who deal treacherously
    without cause.

⁴Show me Your ways, O LORD;
Teach me Your paths.
⁵Lead me in Your truth and teach me,
For You *are* the God of my salvation;
On You I wait all the day.

⁶Remember, O LORD, Your tender mercies
        and Your lovingkindnesses,
For they *are* from of old.

23:6 ^aFollowing Septuagint, Syriac, Targum, and Vulgate; Masoretic
Text reads *return*.

LEADERSHIP ISSUES

GC2: Holy: Who Can Ascend to the Holy Place?

PSALM 24:3

Imagine the wonder of a God who is approachable. Unlike the false gods of the day, the children of Israel's God could be approached. Moses would ascend to Sinai and meet with God as one does face-to-face with a friend. In both the wilderness tabernacle and King Solomon's temple in Jerusalem, God met in the Most Holy Place with the appointed priests on behalf of the people.

But who is it that can "ascend" into His holy presence, asks the psalmist? Is it the rich, the privileged, or the super religious? No, it is those with clean hands and a pure heart. Beyond the Old Testament ceremony or our modern-day choruses and hand raising, God still searches for those with clean hands and pure hearts.

"Clean hands" speaks to the holiness of lifestyle in our decisions and choices, words and deeds—literally the person we are when we think no one notices (Eph. 5:1–4). "Pure heart" speaks to the holiness of thought and attitude that takes every thought captive in purity of devotion to Christ, that thinks of others more highly than self, and is constrained by Christ's love to a life of giving first to Him and the needs of others (2 Cor. 10:5; Eph. 4:1–3; Phil. 2:3, 4). God's priorities are purity, truth, and selfless love. These priorities bring about genuineness, transparency, and intimacy with Christ.

Christ has offered Himself as the final sacrifice; and now, God is approachable to all who embrace Christ's sacrifice (Heb. 4:16; 9:11, 12). Pause quietly to ask Him:

- What cleansing of "hand" might You, Lord, desire for my life?
- What purity of "heart" might You desire?

Now as you sense His response, yield to the sanctifying, "setting apart" work of the One within you who is holy, even the Holy Spirit.

GC2
GREAT COMMANDMENT
COMMISSION

[7]Do not remember the sins of my youth, nor
my transgressions;
According to Your mercy remember me,
For Your goodness' sake, O LORD.

[8]Good and upright *is* the LORD;
Therefore He teaches sinners in the way.
[9]The humble He guides in justice,
And the humble He teaches His way.
[10]All the paths of the LORD *are* mercy and truth,
To such as keep His covenant and His
testimonies.
[11]For Your name's sake, O LORD,
Pardon my iniquity, for it *is* great.

[12]Who *is* the man that fears the LORD?
Him shall He[a] teach in the way He[b] chooses.
[13]He himself shall dwell in prosperity,
And his descendants shall inherit the earth.
[14]The secret of the LORD *is* with those who
fear Him,
And He will show them His covenant.
[15]My eyes *are* ever toward the LORD,
For He shall pluck my feet out of the net.

[16]Turn Yourself to me, and have mercy on me,
For I *am* desolate and afflicted.
[17]The troubles of my heart have enlarged;
Bring me out of my distresses!
[18]Look on my affliction and my pain,
And forgive all my sins.
[19]Consider my enemies, for they are many;
And they hate me with cruel hatred.
[20]Keep my soul, and deliver me;
Let me not be ashamed, for I put my trust in
You.
[21]Let integrity and uprightness preserve me,
For I wait for You.

[22]Redeem Israel, O God,
Out of all their troubles!

PSALM 26

A PRAYER FOR DIVINE SCRUTINY AND
REDEMPTION
A Psalm of David.

[1]Vindicate me, O LORD,
For I have walked in my integrity.
I have also trusted in the LORD;

I shall not slip.
[2]Examine me, O LORD, and prove me;
Try my mind and my heart.
[3]For Your lovingkindness *is* before my eyes,
And I have walked in Your truth.
[4]I have not sat with idolatrous mortals,
Nor will I go in with hypocrites.
[5]I have hated the assembly of evildoers,
And will not sit with the wicked.

[6]I will wash my hands in innocence;
So I will go about Your altar, O LORD,
[7]That I may proclaim with the voice of
thanksgiving,
And tell of all Your wondrous works.
[8]LORD, I have loved the habitation of Your
house,
And the place where Your glory dwells.

[9]Do not gather my soul with sinners,
Nor my life with bloodthirsty men,
[10]In whose hands *is* a sinister scheme,
And whose right hand is full of bribes.
[11]But as for me, I will walk in my integrity;
Redeem me and be merciful to me.
[12]My foot stands in an even place;
In the congregations I will bless the LORD.

PSALM 27

AN EXUBERANT DECLARATION OF FAITH
A Psalm of David.

[1]The LORD *is* my light and my salvation;
Whom shall I fear?
The LORD *is* the strength of my life;
Of whom shall I be afraid?
[2]When the wicked came against me
To eat up my flesh,
My enemies and foes,
They stumbled and fell.
[3]Though an army may encamp against me,
My heart shall not fear;
Though war may rise against me,
In this I *will be* confident.

[4]One *thing* I have desired of the LORD,
That will I seek:

25:12 [a]Or *he* [b]Or *he*

That I may dwell in the house of the LORD
All the days of my life,
To behold the beauty of the LORD,
And to inquire in His temple.
⁵For in the time of trouble
He shall hide me in His pavilion;
In the secret place of His tabernacle
He shall hide me;
He shall set me high upon a rock.

⁶And now my head shall be lifted up above my
enemies all around me;
Therefore I will offer sacrifices of joy in His
tabernacle;
I will sing, yes, I will sing praises to the LORD.

⁷Hear, O LORD, *when* I cry with my voice!
Have mercy also upon me, and answer me.
⁸*When You said,* "Seek My face,"
My heart said to You, "Your face, LORD, I will
seek."
⁹Do not hide Your face from me;
Do not turn Your servant away in anger;
You have been my help;
Do not leave me nor forsake me,
O God of my salvation.
¹⁰When my father and my mother forsake me,
Then the LORD will take care of me.

¹¹Teach me Your way, O LORD,
And lead me in a smooth path, because of my
enemies.
¹²Do not deliver me to the will of my
adversaries;
For false witnesses have risen against me,

And such as breathe out violence.
¹³*I would have lost heart,* unless I had believed
That I would see the goodness of the LORD
In the land of the living.

¹⁴Wait on the LORD;
Be of good courage,
And He shall strengthen your heart;
Wait, I say, on the LORD!

PSALM 28

REJOICING IN ANSWERED PRAYER
A Psalm of David.

¹To You I will cry, O LORD my Rock:
Do not be silent to me,
Lest, if You *are* silent to me,
I become like those who go down to the pit.
²Hear the voice of my supplications
When I cry to You,
When I lift up my hands toward Your holy
sanctuary.

³Do not take me away with the wicked
And with the workers of iniquity,
Who speak peace to their neighbors,
But evil *is* in their hearts.
⁴Give them according to their deeds,
And according to the wickedness of their
endeavors;
Give them according to the work of their
hands;
Render to them what they deserve.
⁵Because they do not regard the works of the
LORD,

THROUGH THE GRID

Making Sense of Your World: Another Dimension to the World (Ps. 27:8)

Besides the physical world that we can see, hear, smell, taste, and touch, our worldview also encompasses our posture toward the unseen sphere of existence. Is there a reality that our physical bodies cannot directly encounter? Is there a viable world of spirits around us? Although we have been conditioned by our existence in a modern world to dismiss that which cannot be objectively proven, the nonphysical world cannot be so easily dismissed. Thousands of years of history, as well as personal narratives and a rising interest in the field, demand that the spiritual realm be reckoned with alongside of the scientific.

Nor the operation of His hands,
He shall destroy them
And not build them up.

[6]Blessed *be* the LORD,
Because He has heard the voice of my
    supplications!
[7]The LORD *is* my strength and my shield;
My heart trusted in Him, and I am helped;
Therefore my heart greatly rejoices,
And with my song I will praise Him.

[8]The LORD *is* their strength,[a]
And He *is* the saving refuge of His anointed.
[9]Save Your people,
And bless Your inheritance;
Shepherd them also,
And bear them up forever.

PSALM 29

PRAISE TO GOD IN HIS HOLINESS AND MAJESTY
A Psalm of David.

[1]Give unto the LORD, O you mighty ones,
Give unto the LORD glory and strength.
[2]Give unto the LORD the glory due to His
    name;
Worship the LORD in the beauty of holiness.

[3]The voice of the LORD *is* over the waters;
The God of glory thunders;
The LORD *is* over many waters.
[4]The voice of the LORD *is* powerful;
The voice of the LORD *is* full of majesty.

[5]The voice of the LORD breaks the cedars,
Yes, the LORD splinters the cedars of
    Lebanon.
[6]He makes them also skip like a calf,
Lebanon and Sirion like a young wild ox.
[7]The voice of the LORD divides the flames of
    fire.

[8]The voice of the LORD shakes the wilderness;
The LORD shakes the Wilderness of Kadesh.
[9]The voice of the LORD makes the deer give
    birth,
And strips the forests bare;
And in His temple everyone says, "Glory!"

[10]The LORD sat *enthroned* at the Flood,
And the LORD sits as King forever.
[11]The LORD will give strength to His people;
The LORD will bless His people with peace.

PSALM 30

THE BLESSEDNESS OF ANSWERED PRAYER
A Psalm. A Song at the dedication of the house
of David.

[1]I will extol You, O LORD, for You have lifted
    me up,
And have not let my foes rejoice over me.
[2]O LORD my God, I cried out to You,
And You healed me.
[3]O LORD, You brought my soul up from the
    grave;
You have kept me alive, that I should not go
    down to the pit.[a]

[4]Sing praise to the LORD, you saints of His,
And give thanks at the remembrance of His
    holy name.[a]
[5]For His anger *is but for* a moment,
His favor *is for* life;
Weeping may endure for a night,
But joy *comes* in the morning.

[6]Now in my prosperity I said,
"I shall never be moved."
[7]LORD, by Your favor You have made my
    mountain stand strong;
You hid Your face, *and* I was troubled.

[8]I cried out to You, O LORD;
And to the LORD I made supplication:
[9]"What profit *is there* in my blood,
When I go down to the pit?
Will the dust praise You?
Will it declare Your truth?
[10]Hear, O LORD, and have mercy on me;
LORD, be my helper!"

[11]You have turned for me my mourning into
    dancing;

28:8 [a]Following Masoretic Text and Targum; Septuagint, Syriac, and
Vulgate read *the strength of His people.* **30:3** [a]Following Qere and
Targum; Kethib, Septuagint, Syriac, and Vulgate read *from those
who descend to the pit.* **30:4** [a]Or *His holiness*

You have put off my sackcloth and clothed
  me with gladness,
¹²To the end that *my* glory may sing praise to
  You and not be silent.
O LORD my God, I will give thanks to You
  forever.

PSALM 31

THE LORD A FORTRESS IN ADVERSITY
To the Chief Musician. A Psalm of David.

¹In You, O LORD, I put my trust;
  Let me never be ashamed;
  Deliver me in Your righteousness.
²Bow down Your ear to me,
  Deliver me speedily;
  Be my rock of refuge,
  A fortress of defense to save me.

³For You *are* my rock and my fortress;
  Therefore, for Your name's sake,
  Lead me and guide me.
⁴Pull me out of the net which they have
  secretly laid for me,
  For You *are* my strength.
⁵Into Your hand I commit my spirit;
  You have redeemed me, O LORD God of
  truth.

⁶I have hated those who regard useless idols;
  But I trust in the LORD.
⁷I will be glad and rejoice in Your mercy,
  For You have considered my trouble;
  You have known my soul in adversities,
⁸And have not shut me up into the hand of
  the enemy;
  You have set my feet in a wide place.

⁹Have mercy on me, O LORD, for I am in
  trouble;
  My eye wastes away with grief,
  Yes, my soul and my body!
¹⁰For my life is spent with grief,
  And my years with sighing;
  My strength fails because of my iniquity,
  And my bones waste away.
¹¹I am a reproach among all my enemies,
  But especially among my neighbors,
  And *am* repulsive to my acquaintances;
  Those who see me outside flee from me.

¹²I am forgotten like a dead man, out of mind;
  I am like a broken vessel.
¹³For I hear the slander of many;
  Fear *is* on every side;
  While they take counsel together against me,
  They scheme to take away my life.

¹⁴But as for me, I trust in You, O LORD;
  I say, "You *are* my God."
¹⁵My times *are* in Your hand;
  Deliver me from the hand of my enemies,
  And from those who persecute me.
¹⁶Make Your face shine upon Your servant;
  Save me for Your mercies' sake.
¹⁷Do not let me be ashamed, O LORD, for I
  have called upon You;
  Let the wicked be ashamed;
  Let them be silent in the grave.
¹⁸Let the lying lips be put to silence,
  Which speak insolent things proudly and
  contemptuously against the righteous.

¹⁹Oh, how great *is* Your goodness,
  Which You have laid up for those who fear
  You,
  Which You have prepared for those who trust
  in You
  In the presence of the sons of men!
²⁰You shall hide them in the secret place of
  Your presence
  From the plots of man;
  You shall keep them secretly in a pavilion
  From the strife of tongues.

²¹Blessed *be* the LORD,
  For He has shown me His marvelous
  kindness in a strong city!
²²For I said in my haste,
  "I am cut off from before Your eyes";
  Nevertheless You heard the voice of my
  supplications
  When I cried out to You.

²³Oh, love the LORD, all you His saints!
  For the LORD preserves the faithful,
  And fully repays the proud person.
²⁴Be of good courage,
  And He shall strengthen your heart,
  All you who hope in the LORD.

PSALM 32

THE JOY OF FORGIVENESS
A Psalm of David. A Contemplation.[a]

[1]Blessed *is he whose* transgression *is* forgiven,
  Whose sin *is* covered.
[2]Blessed *is* the man to whom the LORD does
    not impute iniquity,
  And in whose spirit *there is* no deceit.

[3]When I kept silent, my bones grew old
  Through my groaning all the day long.
[4]For day and night Your hand was heavy upon
    me;
  My vitality was turned into the drought of
    summer.   *Selah*
[5]I acknowledged my sin to You,
  And my iniquity I have not hidden.
  I said, "I will confess my transgressions to the
    LORD,"
  And You forgave the iniquity of my
    sin.   *Selah*

[6]For this cause everyone who is godly shall
    pray to You
  In a time when You may be found;
  Surely in a flood of great waters
  They shall not come near him.
[7]You *are* my hiding place;
  You shall preserve me from trouble;
  You shall surround me with songs of
    deliverance.   *Selah*

[8]I will instruct you and teach you in the way
    you should go;
  I will guide you with My eye.
[9]Do not be like the horse *or* like the mule,
  Which have no understanding,
  Which must be harnessed with bit and
    bridle,
  Else they will not come near you.

[10]Many sorrows *shall be* to the wicked;
  But he who trusts in the LORD, mercy shall
    surround him.
[11]Be glad in the LORD and rejoice, you
    righteous;
  And shout for joy, all *you* upright in heart!

PSALM 33

THE SOVEREIGNTY OF THE LORD IN CREATION AND HISTORY

[1]Rejoice in the LORD, O you righteous!
  For praise from the upright is beautiful.
[2]Praise the LORD with the harp;
  Make melody to Him with an instrument of
    ten strings.
[3]Sing to Him a new song;
  Play skillfully with a shout of joy.

[4]For the word of the LORD *is* right,
  And all His work *is done* in truth.
[5]He loves righteousness and justice;
  The earth is full of the goodness of the
    LORD.

[6]By the word of the LORD the heavens were
    made,
  And all the host of them by the breath of His
    mouth.
[7]He gathers the waters of the sea together as a
    heap;[a]
  He lays up the deep in storehouses.

[8]Let all the earth fear the LORD;
  Let all the inhabitants of the world stand in
    awe of Him.
[9]For He spoke, and it was *done;*
  He commanded, and it stood fast.

[10]The LORD brings the counsel of the nations
    to nothing;
  He makes the plans of the peoples of no
    effect.
[11]The counsel of the LORD stands forever,
  The plans of His heart to all generations.
[12]Blessed *is* the nation whose God *is* the
    LORD,
  The people He has chosen as His own
    inheritance.

[13]The LORD looks from heaven;
  He sees all the sons of men.
[14]From the place of His dwelling He looks
  On all the inhabitants of the earth;

32:title [a]Hebrew *Maschil* **33:7** [a]Septuagint, Targum, and Vulgate
read *in a vessel.*

¹⁵He fashions their hearts individually;
He considers all their works.

¹⁶No king *is* saved by the multitude of an army;
A mighty man is not delivered by great
strength.
¹⁷A horse *is* a vain hope for safety;
Neither shall it deliver *any* by its great
strength.

¹⁸Behold, the eye of the LORD *is* on those who
fear Him,
On those who hope in His mercy,
¹⁹To deliver their soul from death,
And to keep them alive in famine.

²⁰Our soul waits for the LORD;
He *is* our help and our shield.
²¹For our heart shall rejoice in Him,
Because we have trusted in His holy name.
²²Let Your mercy, O LORD, be upon us,
Just as we hope in You.

PSALM 34

THE HAPPINESS OF THOSE WHO TRUST IN GOD
A Psalm of David when he pretended madness
before Abimelech, who drove him away, and
he departed.

¹I will bless the LORD at all times;
His praise *shall* continually *be* in my mouth.
²My soul shall make its boast in the LORD;
The humble shall hear *of it* and be glad.
³Oh, magnify the LORD with me,
And let us exalt His name together.

⁴I sought the LORD, and He heard me,
And delivered me from all my fears.
⁵They looked to Him and were radiant,
And their faces were not ashamed.
⁶This poor man cried out, and the LORD
heard *him,*
And saved him out of all his troubles.
⁷The angel[a] of the LORD encamps all around
those who fear Him,
And delivers them.

34:7 [a]Or *Angel*

INSIDE *the* INFLUENCERS

DAVID—Psalm 34—Worship Makes Us a World-Changer

The psalms David wrote are beautiful, powerful, and encouraging. David understood that when he worshiped, the presence of God helped David conquer many enemies, both public and private.

Psalm 34, which was written in a tough time in David's life, contains five things needed to be a WORLD-CHANGER:

1. Resolve to praise God at all times.
2. Point others to your source of joy.
3. Invite others to join in the worship.
4. Tell your unique story.
5. Proclaim God's goodness.

David said, "I will bless the LORD at all times" (v. 1). He was quick to tell everyone he had resolved to live by praise. Even when circumstances were bad (like being chased by two murderous kings), if no one else praised God, David said "I will praise God at all times."

To make sure he didn't get the praise God deserved, he directed people to the source of his joy. Psalm 34:2 says, "My soul shall make its boast in the LORD." David invited others to experience God's goodness: "Magnify the LORD with me!" (v. 3). "Oh, taste and see that the LORD is good!" (v. 8). He wrote of his personal worship, and he enthusiastically told others about it.

LEADERSHIP ISSUES

Tapping the Leader's Secret Source of Power

PSALM 34

As a young, maturing believer and a developing leader, you must be able to find opportunity and success in everyday circumstances. To do so, you will have to be able to tap into a power greater than yourself to overcome the stress, resentment, pettiness, confrontations, and challenges that lie ahead.

Throughout the Old and New Testament, we see a source of power in the influencers chosen by God to impact generations through the stories of their lives. The Bible allows us to peak into the private lives of these servant leaders and to see where they found a source of power to face various challenges with faith, courage, and joy. Abram faced new situations by building an altar to worship (Gen. 12:7). Deborah took 10,000 untrained men to the top of a mountain to face 100,000 trained warriors and then wrote one of the greatest songs of praise ever. Hannah faced criticism, remained faithful, and was blessed to give birth to the prophet Samuel (1 Sam. 2:1–10). Her song of praise was mirrored by one written by the Virgin Mary, mother of Jesus (Luke 1:46).

David wrote, "I will bless the LORD at all times" (Ps. 34:1). David is quick here to pronounce to God and man that he has resolved in his heart to live by praise. So that no one should give David praise, he directed them to the source of his joy: "My soul shall make its boast in the LORD" (Ps. 34:2). David brings everyone in because this joy is too good to keep to himself: "Magnify the LORD with me!" (v. 3), and then, "Oh, taste and see that the LORD is good!" (v. 8).

The Apostle Paul, a man who was transformed through a personal encounter with Christ and shook the world with passionate, uncompromising preaching, wrote of giving praise to the God *who is able* (Eph. 3:20). No doubt this was the source of his tenacity, even unto death.

Jude, the half brother of Jesus, went from critic to apostle and tapped into that secret power by giving praise (Jude 24, 25).

When you worship in praise, the presence of God comes and joins you in all that you do, and, together, you change the world.

[8]Oh, taste and see that the LORD *is* good;
   Blessed *is* the man *who* trusts in Him!
[9]Oh, fear the LORD, you His saints!
   There is no want to those who fear Him.
[10]The young lions lack and suffer hunger;
   But those who seek the LORD shall not lack
      any good *thing*.

[11]Come, you children, listen to me;
   I will teach you the fear of the LORD.
[12]Who *is* the man *who* desires life,
   And loves *many* days, that he may see good?
[13]Keep your tongue from evil,
   And your lips from speaking deceit.
[14]Depart from evil and do good;
   Seek peace and pursue it.

[15]The eyes of the LORD *are* on the righteous,
   And His ears *are* open to their cry.
[16]The face of the LORD *is* against those who do
      evil,
   To cut off the remembrance of them from
      the earth.

[17]*The righteous* cry out, and the LORD hears,
   And delivers them out of all their troubles.
[18]The LORD *is* near to those who have a
      broken heart,
   And saves such as have a contrite spirit.

[19]Many *are* the afflictions of the righteous,
   But the LORD delivers him out of them all.
[20]He guards all his bones;
   Not one of them is broken.
[21]Evil shall slay the wicked,
   And those who hate the righteous shall be
      condemned.
[22]The LORD redeems the soul of His servants,
   And none of those who trust in Him shall be
      condemned.

PSALM 35

THE LORD THE AVENGER OF HIS PEOPLE
A Psalm of David.

[1]Plead *my cause,* O LORD, with those who
      strive with me;
   Fight against those who fight against me.
[2]Take hold of shield and buckler,

And stand up for my help.
[3]Also draw out the spear,
   And stop those who pursue me.
   Say to my soul,
   "I *am* your salvation."

[4]Let those be put to shame and brought to
      dishonor
   Who seek after my life;
   Let those be turned back and brought to
      confusion
   Who plot my hurt.
[5]Let them be like chaff before the wind,
   And let the angel[a] of the LORD chase *them.*
[6]Let their way be dark and slippery,
   And let the angel of the LORD pursue them.
[7]For without cause they have hidden their net
      for me *in* a pit,
   Which they have dug without cause for my
      life.
[8]Let destruction come upon him
      unexpectedly,
   And let his net that he has hidden catch
      himself;
   Into that very destruction let him fall.

[9]And my soul shall be joyful in the LORD;
   It shall rejoice in His salvation.
[10]All my bones shall say,
   "LORD, who *is* like You,
   Delivering the poor from him who is too
      strong for him,
   Yes, the poor and the needy from him who
      plunders him?"

[11]Fierce witnesses rise up;
   They ask me *things* that I do not know.
[12]They reward me evil for good,
   To the sorrow of my soul.
[13]But as for me, when they were sick,
   My clothing *was* sackcloth;
   I humbled myself with fasting;
   And my prayer would return to my own
      heart.
[14]I paced about as though *he were* my friend *or*
      brother;
   I bowed down heavily, as one who mourns *for*
      his mother.

35:5 [a]Or *Angel*

¹⁵But in my adversity they rejoiced
And gathered together;
Attackers gathered against me,
And I did not know *it;*
They tore *at me* and did not cease;
¹⁶With ungodly mockers at feasts
They gnashed at me with their teeth.

¹⁷Lord, how long will You look on?
Rescue me from their destructions,
My precious *life* from the lions.
¹⁸I will give You thanks in the great assembly;
I will praise You among many people.

¹⁹Let them not rejoice over me who are
wrongfully my enemies;
Nor let them wink with the eye who hate
me without a cause.
²⁰For they do not speak peace,
But they devise deceitful matters
Against *the* quiet ones in the land.
²¹They also opened their mouth wide against
me,
And said, "Aha, aha!
Our eyes have seen *it.*"

²²*This* You have seen, O LORD;
Do not keep silence.
O Lord, do not be far from me.
²³Stir up Yourself, and awake to my vindication,
To my cause, my God and my Lord.
²⁴Vindicate me, O LORD my God, according to
Your righteousness;
And let them not rejoice over me.
²⁵Let them not say in their hearts, "Ah, so we
would have it!"
Let them not say, "We have swallowed him
up."

²⁶Let them be ashamed and brought to mutual
confusion
Who rejoice at my hurt;
Let them be clothed with shame and
dishonor
Who exalt themselves against me.

²⁷Let them shout for joy and be glad,
Who favor my righteous cause;
And let them say continually,

"Let the LORD be magnified,
Who has pleasure in the prosperity of His
servant."
²⁸And my tongue shall speak of Your
righteousness
And of Your praise all the day long.

PSALM 36

MAN'S WICKEDNESS AND GOD'S PERFECTIONS
To the Chief Musician. *A Psalm* of David the
servant of the LORD.

¹An oracle within my heart concerning the
transgression of the wicked:
There is no fear of God before his eyes.
²For he flatters himself in his own eyes,
When he finds out his iniquity *and* when he
hates.
³The words of his mouth *are* wickedness and
deceit;
He has ceased to be wise *and* to do good.
⁴He devises wickedness on his bed;
He sets himself in a way *that is* not good;
He does not abhor evil.

⁵Your mercy, O LORD, *is* in the heavens;
Your faithfulness *reaches* to the clouds.
⁶Your righteousness *is* like the great
mountains;
Your judgments *are* a great deep;
O LORD, You preserve man and beast.

⁷How precious *is* Your lovingkindness, O God!
Therefore the children of men put their trust
under the shadow of Your wings.
⁸They are abundantly satisfied with the fullness
of Your house,
And You give them drink from the river of
Your pleasures.
⁹For with You *is* the fountain of life;
In Your light we see light.

¹⁰Oh, continue Your lovingkindness to those
who know You,
And Your righteousness to the upright in
heart.
¹¹Let not the foot of pride come against me,
And let not the hand of the wicked drive me
away.

LEADERSHIP ISSUES

GC2: God's Light

PSALM 36:9

Scripture gives us insight into the loving and abundant provision of God as the psalmist declares. Our view of Him is reshaped as we look beyond our human experience and life events toward the light that only He can give. It is God's light that reveals who He really is, who we are, and why we're here on the planet! While God certainly reveals Himself in creation and circumstances, much of His "light" comes through relationships. God reveals Himself through the testimony of His Son, through the revelation of His Word, and through the love of His people.

These three sources of light have been graciously provided that they might guide us into abundant life (John 10:10). Consider *your schedule*; look for times of encountering Jesus, experiencing His Word, and enjoying fellowship with His people. Hopefully, you're walking in the light this week.

¹²There the workers of iniquity have fallen;
They have been cast down and are not able to
rise.

PSALM 37

THE HERITAGE OF THE RIGHTEOUS AND THE
CALAMITY OF THE WICKED
A Psalm of David.

¹Do not fret because of evildoers,
Nor be envious of the workers of iniquity.
²For they shall soon be cut down like the grass,
And wither as the green herb.

³Trust in the LORD, and do good;
Dwell in the land, and feed on His
faithfulness.
⁴Delight yourself also in the LORD,
And He shall give you the desires of your
heart.

⁵Commit your way to the LORD,
Trust also in Him,
And He shall bring *it* to pass.
⁶He shall bring forth your righteousness as the
light,
And your justice as the noonday.

⁷Rest in the LORD, and wait patiently for Him;
Do not fret because of him who prospers in
his way,
Because of the man who brings wicked
schemes to pass.
⁸Cease from anger, and forsake wrath;
Do not fret—*it* only *causes* harm.

⁹For evildoers shall be cut off;
But those who wait on the LORD,
They shall inherit the earth.
¹⁰For yet a little while and the wicked *shall be*
no *more;*
Indeed, you will look carefully for his place,
But it *shall be* no *more.*
¹¹But the meek shall inherit the earth,
And shall delight themselves in the
abundance of peace.

¹²The wicked plots against the just,
And gnashes at him with his teeth.

¹³The Lord laughs at him,
For He sees that his day is coming.
¹⁴The wicked have drawn the sword
And have bent their bow,
To cast down the poor and needy,
To slay those who are of upright conduct.
¹⁵Their sword shall enter their own heart,
And their bows shall be broken.

¹⁶A little that a righteous man has
Is better than the riches of many wicked.
¹⁷For the arms of the wicked shall be broken,
But the LORD upholds the righteous.

¹⁸The LORD knows the days of the upright,
And their inheritance shall be forever.
¹⁹They shall not be ashamed in the evil time,
And in the days of famine they shall be
satisfied.
²⁰But the wicked shall perish;
And the enemies of the LORD,
Like the splendor of the meadows, shall
vanish.
Into smoke they shall vanish away.

²¹The wicked borrows and does not repay,
But the righteous shows mercy and gives.
²²For *those* blessed by Him shall inherit the
earth,
But *those* cursed by Him shall be cut off.

²³The steps of a *good* man are ordered by the
LORD,
And He delights in his way.
²⁴Though he fall, he shall not be utterly cast
down;
For the LORD upholds *him with* His hand.

²⁵I have been young, and *now* am old;
Yet I have not seen the righteous forsaken,
Nor his descendants begging bread.
²⁶*He is* ever merciful, and lends;
And his descendants *are* blessed.

²⁷Depart from evil, and do good;
And dwell forevermore.
²⁸For the LORD loves justice,
And does not forsake His saints;
They are preserved forever,

But the descendants of the wicked shall be
cut off.
²⁹The righteous shall inherit the land,
And dwell in it forever.

³⁰The mouth of the righteous speaks wisdom,
And his tongue talks of justice.
³¹The law of his God *is* in his heart;
None of his steps shall slide.

³²The wicked watches the righteous,
And seeks to slay him.
³³The LORD will not leave him in his hand,
Nor condemn him when he is judged.

³⁴Wait on the LORD,
And keep His way,
And He shall exalt you to inherit the land;
When the wicked are cut off, you shall see *it.*
³⁵I have seen the wicked in great power,
And spreading himself like a native green
tree.
³⁶Yet he passed away,ᵃ and behold, he *was* no
more;
Indeed I sought him, but he could not be
found.

³⁷Mark the blameless *man,* and observe the
upright;
For the future of *that* man *is* peace.
³⁸But the transgressors shall be destroyed
together;
The future of the wicked shall be cut off.

³⁹But the salvation of the righteous *is* from the
LORD;
He is their strength in the time of trouble.
⁴⁰And the LORD shall help them and deliver
them;
He shall deliver them from the wicked,
And save them,
Because they trust in Him.

PSALM 38

PRAYER IN TIME OF CHASTENING
A Psalm of David. To bring to remembrance.

¹O LORD, do not rebuke me in Your wrath,
Nor chasten me in Your hot displeasure!

²For Your arrows pierce me deeply,
And Your hand presses me down.

³*There is* no soundness in my flesh
Because of Your anger,
Nor *any* health in my bones
Because of my sin.
⁴For my iniquities have gone over my head;
Like a heavy burden they are too heavy for
me.
⁵My wounds are foul *and* festering
Because of my foolishness.

⁶I am troubled, I am bowed down greatly;
I go mourning all the day long.
⁷For my loins are full of inflammation,
And *there is* no soundness in my flesh.
⁸I am feeble and severely broken;
I groan because of the turmoil of my heart.

⁹Lord, all my desire *is* before You;
And my sighing is not hidden from You.
¹⁰My heart pants, my strength fails me;
As for the light of my eyes, it also has gone
from me.

¹¹My loved ones and my friends stand aloof
from my plague,
And my relatives stand afar off.
¹²Those also who seek my life lay snares *for me;*
Those who seek my hurt speak of
destruction,
And plan deception all the day long.

¹³But I, like a deaf *man,* do not hear;
And *I am* like a mute *who* does not open his
mouth.
¹⁴Thus I am like a man who does not hear,
And in whose mouth *is* no response.

¹⁵For in You, O LORD, I hope;
You will hear, O Lord my God.
¹⁶For I said, *"Hear me,* lest they rejoice over me,
Lest, when my foot slips, they exalt *themselves*
against me."

¹⁷For I *am* ready to fall,
And my sorrow *is* continually before me.

37:36 ᵃFollowing Masoretic Text, Septuagint, and Targum; Syriac
and Vulgate read *I passed by.*

¹⁸For I will declare my iniquity;
I will be in anguish over my sin.
¹⁹But my enemies *are* vigorous, *and* they are
strong;
And those who hate me wrongfully have
multiplied.
²⁰Those also who render evil for good,
They are my adversaries, because I follow
what is good.

²¹Do not forsake me, O LORD;
O my God, be not far from me!
²²Make haste to help me,
O Lord, my salvation!

PSALM 39

PRAYER FOR WISDOM AND FORGIVENESS
To the Chief Musician. To Jeduthun. A Psalm
of David.

¹I said, "I will guard my ways,
Lest I sin with my tongue;
I will restrain my mouth with a muzzle,
While the wicked are before me."
²I was mute with silence,
I held my peace *even* from good;
And my sorrow was stirred up.
³My heart was hot within me;
While I was musing, the fire burned.
Then I spoke with my tongue:

⁴"LORD, make me to know my end,
And what *is* the measure of my days,
That I may know how frail I *am*.
⁵Indeed, You have made my days *as*
handbreadths,
And my age *is* as nothing before You;
Certainly every man at his best state *is* but
vapor.   *Selah*
⁶Surely every man walks about like a shadow;
Surely they busy themselves in vain;
He heaps up *riches,*
And does not know who will gather them.

⁷"And now, Lord, what do I wait for?
My hope *is* in You.
⁸Deliver me from all my transgressions;
Do not make me the reproach of the foolish.
⁹I was mute, I did not open my mouth,

Because it was You who did *it*.
¹⁰Remove Your plague from me;
I am consumed by the blow of Your hand.
¹¹When with rebukes You correct man for
iniquity,
You make his beauty melt away like a moth;
Surely every man *is* vapor.   *Selah*

¹²"Hear my prayer, O LORD,
And give ear to my cry;
Do not be silent at my tears;
For I *am* a stranger with You,
A sojourner, as all my fathers *were.*
¹³Remove Your gaze from me, that I may regain
strength,
Before I go away and am no more."

PSALM 40

FAITH PERSEVERING IN TRIAL
To the Chief Musician. A Psalm of David.

¹I waited patiently for the LORD;
And He inclined to me,
And heard my cry.
²He also brought me up out of a horrible pit,
Out of the miry clay,
And set my feet upon a rock,
And established my steps.
³He has put a new song in my mouth—
Praise to our God;
Many will see *it* and fear,
And will trust in the LORD.

⁴Blessed *is* that man who makes the LORD his
trust,
And does not respect the proud, nor such as
turn aside to lies.
⁵Many, O LORD my God, *are* Your wonderful
works
Which You have done;
And Your thoughts toward us
Cannot be recounted to You in order;
If I would declare and speak *of them,*
They are more than can be numbered.

⁶Sacrifice and offering You did not desire;
My ears You have opened.
Burnt offering and sin offering You did not
require.

⁷Then I said, "Behold, I come;
  In the scroll of the book *it is* written of me.
⁸I delight to do Your will, O my God,
  And Your law *is* within my heart."

⁹I have proclaimed the good news of
    righteousness
  In the great assembly;
  Indeed, I do not restrain my lips,
  O Lord, You Yourself know.
¹⁰I have not hidden Your righteousness within
    my heart;
  I have declared Your faithfulness and Your
    salvation;
  I have not concealed Your lovingkindness and
    Your truth
  From the great assembly.

¹¹Do not withhold Your tender mercies from
    me, O Lord;
  Let Your lovingkindness and Your truth
    continually preserve me.
¹²For innumerable evils have surrounded me;
  My iniquities have overtaken me, so that I am
    not able to look up;
  They are more than the hairs of my head;
  Therefore my heart fails me.

¹³Be pleased, O Lord, to deliver me;
  O Lord, make haste to help me!
¹⁴Let them be ashamed and brought to mutual
    confusion
  Who seek to destroy my life;
  Let them be driven backward and brought to
    dishonor
  Who wish me evil.
¹⁵Let them be confounded because of their
    shame,
  Who say to me, "Aha, aha!"

¹⁶Let all those who seek You rejoice and be
    glad in You;
  Let such as love Your salvation say
    continually,
  "The Lord be magnified!"
¹⁷But I *am* poor and needy;
  Yet the Lord thinks upon me.
  You *are* my help and my deliverer;
  Do not delay, O my God.

PSALM 41

The Blessing and Suffering of the Godly
To the Chief Musician. A Psalm of David.

¹Blessed *is* he who considers the poor;
  The Lord will deliver him in time of
    trouble.
²The Lord will preserve him and keep him
    alive,
  And he will be blessed on the earth;
  You will not deliver him to the will of his
    enemies.
³The Lord will strengthen him on his bed of
    illness;
  You will sustain him on his sickbed.

⁴I said, "Lord, be merciful to me;
  Heal my soul, for I have sinned against You."
⁵My enemies speak evil of me:
  "When will he die, and his name perish?"
⁶And if he comes to see *me,* he speaks lies;
  His heart gathers iniquity to itself;
  When he goes out, he tells *it.*

⁷All who hate me whisper together against
    me;
  Against me they devise my hurt.
⁸"An evil disease," *they say,* "clings to him.
  And *now* that he lies down, he will rise up no
    more."
⁹Even my own familiar friend in whom I
    trusted,
  Who ate my bread,
  Has lifted up *his* heel against me.

¹⁰But You, O Lord, be merciful to me, and
    raise me up,
  That I may repay them.
¹¹By this I know that You are well pleased with
    me,
  Because my enemy does not triumph over
    me.
¹²As for me, You uphold me in my
    integrity,
  And set me before Your face forever.

¹³Blessed *be* the Lord God of Israel
  From everlasting to everlasting!
  Amen and Amen.

Book Two: Psalms 42—72

PSALM 42

YEARNING FOR GOD IN THE MIDST OF
DISTRESSES

To the Chief Musician. A Contemplation[a] of the
sons of Korah.

[1]As the deer pants for the water brooks,
So pants my soul for You, O God.
[2]My soul thirsts for God, for the living God.
When shall I come and appear before God?[a]
[3]My tears have been my food day and night,
While they continually say to me,
"Where *is* your God?"

[4]When I remember these *things,*
I pour out my soul within me.
For I used to go with the multitude;
I went with them to the house of God,
With the voice of joy and praise,
With a multitude that kept a pilgrim feast.

[5]Why are you cast down, O my soul?
And *why* are you disquieted within me?
Hope in God, for I shall yet praise Him
For the help of His countenance.[a]

[6]O my God,[a] my soul is cast down within me;
Therefore I will remember You from the land
of the Jordan,
And from the heights of Hermon,
From the Hill Mizar.
[7]Deep calls unto deep at the noise of Your
waterfalls;
All Your waves and billows have gone over
me.
[8]The LORD will command His lovingkindness
in the daytime,
And in the night His song *shall be* with me—
A prayer to the God of my life.

[9]I will say to God my Rock,
"Why have You forgotten me?
Why do I go mourning because of the
oppression of the enemy?"
[10]*As* with a breaking of my bones,
My enemies reproach me,
While they say to me all day long,
"Where *is* your God?"

[11]Why are you cast down, O my soul?
And why are you disquieted within me?
Hope in God;
For I shall yet praise Him,
The help of my countenance and my God.

PSALM 43

PRAYER TO GOD IN TIME OF TROUBLE

[1]Vindicate me, O God,
And plead my cause against an ungodly
nation;
Oh, deliver me from the deceitful and unjust
man!
[2]For You *are* the God of my strength;
Why do You cast me off?
Why do I go mourning because of the
oppression of the enemy?

[3]Oh, send out Your light and Your truth!
Let them lead me;
Let them bring me to Your holy hill
And to Your tabernacle.
[4]Then I will go to the altar of God,
To God my exceeding joy;
And on the harp I will praise You,
O God, my God.

[5]Why are you cast down, O my soul?
And why are you disquieted within me?
Hope in God;
For I shall yet praise Him,
The help of my countenance and my God.

PSALM 44

REDEMPTION REMEMBERED IN PRESENT
DISHONOR

To the Chief Musician. A Contemplation[a] of the
sons of Korah.

[1]We have heard with our ears, O God,
Our fathers have told us,
The deeds You did in their days,

42:title [a]Hebrew *Maschil* **42:2** [a]Following Masoretic Text and Vulgate; some Hebrew manuscripts, Septuagint, Syriac, and Targum read *I see the face of God.* **42:5** [a]Following Masoretic Text and Targum; a few Hebrew manuscripts, Septuagint, Syriac, and Vulgate read *The help of my countenance, my God.* **42:6** [a]Following Masoretic Text and Targum; a few Hebrew manuscripts, Septuagint, Syriac, and Vulgate put *my God* at the end of verse 5. **44:title** [a]Hebrew *Maschil*

In days of old:

²You drove out the nations with Your hand,
But them You planted;
You afflicted the peoples, and cast them out.
³For they did not gain possession of the land
by their own sword,
Nor did their own arm save them;
But it was Your right hand, Your arm, and the
light of Your countenance,
Because You favored them.

⁴You are my King, O God;ª
Commandᵇ victories for Jacob.
⁵Through You we will push down our enemies;
Through Your name we will trample those
who rise up against us.
⁶For I will not trust in my bow,
Nor shall my sword save me.
⁷But You have saved us from our enemies,
And have put to shame those who hated us.
⁸In God we boast all day long,
And praise Your name forever.   Selah

⁹But You have cast us off and put us to shame,
And You do not go out with our armies.
¹⁰You make us turn back from the enemy,
And those who hate us have taken spoil for
themselves.
¹¹You have given us up like sheep *intended* for
food,
And have scattered us among the nations.
¹²You sell Your people for *next to* nothing,
And are not enriched by selling them.

¹³You make us a reproach to our neighbors,
A scorn and a derision to those all around us.
¹⁴You make us a byword among the nations,
A shaking of the head among the peoples.
¹⁵My dishonor *is* continually before me,
And the shame of my face has covered me,
¹⁶Because of the voice of him who reproaches
and reviles,
Because of the enemy and the avenger.

¹⁷All this has come upon us;
But we have not forgotten You,
Nor have we dealt falsely with Your covenant.
¹⁸Our heart has not turned back,
Nor have our steps departed from Your way;

¹⁹But You have severely broken us in the place
of jackals,
And covered us with the shadow of death.

²⁰If we had forgotten the name of our God,
Or stretched out our hands to a foreign god,
²¹Would not God search this out?
For He knows the secrets of the heart.
²²Yet for Your sake we are killed all day long;
We are accounted as sheep for the slaughter.

²³Awake! Why do You sleep, O Lord?
Arise! Do not cast *us* off forever.
²⁴Why do You hide Your face,
And forget our affliction and our oppression?
²⁵For our soul is bowed down to the dust;
Our body clings to the ground.
²⁶Arise for our help,
And redeem us for Your mercies' sake.

PSALM 45

THE GLORIES OF THE MESSIAH AND HIS BRIDE
To the Chief Musician. Set to "The Lilies."ª
A Contemplationᵇ of the sons of Korah.
A Song of Love.

¹My heart is overflowing with a good theme;
I recite my composition concerning the King;
My tongue *is* the pen of a ready writer.

²You are fairer than the sons of men;
Grace is poured upon Your lips;
Therefore God has blessed You forever.
³Gird Your sword upon *Your* thigh, O Mighty
One,
With Your glory and Your majesty.
⁴And in Your majesty ride prosperously because
of truth, humility, *and* righteousness;
And Your right hand shall teach You awesome
things.
⁵Your arrows *are* sharp in the heart of the
King's enemies;
The peoples fall under You.

⁶Your throne, O God, *is* forever and ever;
A scepter of righteousness *is* the scepter of
Your kingdom.

44:4 ªFollowing Masoretic Text and Targum; Septuagint and Vulgate
read *and my God.* ᵇFollowing Masoretic Text and Targum; Septuagint, Syriac, and Vulgate read *Who commands.* **45:title** ªHebrew
Shoshannim ᵇHebrew *Maschil*

⁷You love righteousness and hate wickedness;
Therefore God, Your God, has anointed You
With the oil of gladness more than Your
companions.
⁸All Your garments *are scented* with myrrh and
aloes *and* cassia,
Out of the ivory palaces, by which they have
made You glad.
⁹Kings' daughters *are* among Your honorable
women;
At Your right hand stands the queen in gold
from Ophir.

¹⁰Listen, O daughter,
Consider and incline your ear;
Forget your own people also, and your
father's house;
¹¹So the King will greatly desire your beauty;
Because He *is* your Lord, worship Him.
¹²And the daughter of Tyre *will come* with a gift;
The rich among the people will seek your
favor.

¹³The royal daughter *is* all glorious within *the
palace;*
Her clothing *is* woven with gold.
¹⁴She shall be brought to the King in robes of
many colors;
The virgins, her companions who follow her,
shall be brought to You.
¹⁵With gladness and rejoicing they shall be
brought;
They shall enter the King's palace.

¹⁶Instead of Your fathers shall be Your sons,
Whom You shall make princes in all the
earth.
¹⁷I will make Your name to be remembered in
all generations;
Therefore the people shall praise You forever
and ever.

PSALM 46

GOD THE REFUGE OF HIS PEOPLE AND
CONQUEROR OF THE NATIONS
To the Chief Musician. *A Psalm* of the sons of
Korah. A Song for Alamoth.

¹God *is* our refuge and strength,
A very present help in trouble.

²Therefore we will not fear,
Even though the earth be removed,
And though the mountains be carried into
the midst of the sea;
³*Though* its waters roar *and* be troubled,
Though the mountains shake with its
swelling. *Selah*

⁴*There is* a river whose streams shall make glad
the city of God,
The holy *place* of the tabernacle of the Most
High.
⁵God *is* in the midst of her, she shall not be
moved;
God shall help her, just at the break of dawn.
⁶The nations raged, the kingdoms were
moved;
He uttered His voice, the earth melted.

⁷The LORD of hosts *is* with us;
The God of Jacob *is* our refuge. *Selah*

⁸Come, behold the works of the LORD,
Who has made desolations in the earth.
⁹He makes wars cease to the end of the earth;
He breaks the bow and cuts the spear in two;
He burns the chariot in the fire.

¹⁰Be still, and know that I *am* God;
I will be exalted among the nations,
I will be exalted in the earth!

¹¹The LORD of hosts *is* with us;
The God of Jacob *is* our refuge. *Selah*

PSALM 47

PRAISE TO GOD, THE RULER OF THE EARTH
To the Chief Musician. A Psalm of the sons
of Korah.

¹Oh, clap your hands, all you peoples!
Shout to God with the voice of triumph!
²For the LORD Most High *is* awesome;
He is a great King over all the earth.
³He will subdue the peoples under us,
And the nations under our feet.
⁴He will choose our inheritance for us,
The excellence of Jacob whom He
loves. *Selah*

⁵God has gone up with a shout,
  The LORD with the sound of a trumpet.
⁶Sing praises to God, sing praises!
  Sing praises to our King, sing praises!
⁷For God *is* the King of all the earth;
  Sing praises with understanding.

⁸God reigns over the nations;
  God sits on His holy throne.
⁹The princes of the people have gathered
      together,
  The people of the God of Abraham.
  For the shields of the earth *belong* to God;
  He is greatly exalted.

PSALM 48

THE GLORY OF GOD IN ZION
A Song. A Psalm of the sons of Korah.

¹Great *is* the LORD, and greatly to be praised
  In the city of our God,
  In His holy mountain.
²Beautiful in elevation,
  The joy of the whole earth,
  Is Mount Zion *on* the sides of the north,
  The city of the great King.
³God *is* in her palaces;
  He is known as her refuge.

⁴For behold, the kings assembled,
  They passed by together.
⁵They saw *it, and* so they marveled;
  They were troubled, they hastened away.
⁶Fear took hold of them there,
  And pain, as of a woman in birth pangs,
⁷*As when* You break the ships of Tarshish
  With an east wind.

⁸As we have heard,
  So we have seen
  In the city of the LORD of hosts,
  In the city of our God:
  God will establish it forever.   *Selah*

⁹We have thought, O God, on Your
      lovingkindness,
  In the midst of Your temple.
¹⁰According to Your name, O God,
  So *is* Your praise to the ends of the earth;

  Your right hand is full of righteousness.
¹¹Let Mount Zion rejoice,
  Let the daughters of Judah be glad,
  Because of Your judgments.

¹²Walk about Zion,
  And go all around her.
  Count her towers;
¹³Mark well her bulwarks;
  Consider her palaces;
  That you may tell *it* to the generation
      following.
¹⁴For this *is* God,
  Our God forever and ever;
  He will be our guide
  Even to death.ᵃ

PSALM 49

THE CONFIDENCE OF THE FOOLISH
To the Chief Musician. A Psalm of the sons
of Korah.

¹Hear this, all peoples;
  Give ear, all inhabitants of the world,
²Both low and high,
  Rich and poor together.
³My mouth shall speak wisdom,
  And the meditation of my heart *shall give*
      understanding.
⁴I will incline my ear to a proverb;
  I will disclose my dark saying on the harp.

⁵Why should I fear in the days of evil,
  When the iniquity at my heels surrounds me?
⁶Those who trust in their wealth
  And boast in the multitude of their riches,
⁷None *of them* can by any means redeem *his*
      brother,
  Nor give to God a ransom for him—
⁸For the redemption of their souls *is* costly,
  And it shall cease forever—
⁹That he should continue to live eternally,
  And not see the Pit.

¹⁰For he sees wise men die;
  Likewise the fool and the senseless person
      perish,

48:14 ᵃFollowing Masoretic Text and Syriac; Septuagint and Vulgate
read *Forever.*

And leave their wealth to others.
[11]Their inner thought *is that* their houses *will
last* forever,[a]
Their dwelling places to all generations;
They call *their* lands after their own names.
[12]Nevertheless man, *though* in honor, does not
remain;[a]
He is like the beasts *that* perish.

[13]This is the way of those who *are* foolish,
And of their posterity who approve their
sayings.   *Selah*
[14]Like sheep they are laid in the grave;
Death shall feed on them;
The upright shall have dominion over them
in the morning;
And their beauty shall be consumed in the
grave, far from their dwelling.
[15]But God will redeem my soul from the
power of the grave,
For He shall receive me.   *Selah*

[16]Do not be afraid when one becomes rich,
When the glory of his house is increased;
[17]For when he dies he shall carry nothing
away;
His glory shall not descend after him.
[18]Though while he lives he blesses himself
(For *men* will praise you when you do well
for yourself),
[19]He shall go to the generation of his fathers;
They shall never see light.
[20]A man *who is* in honor, yet does not
understand,
Is like the beasts *that* perish.

PSALM 50

GOD THE RIGHTEOUS JUDGE
A Psalm of Asaph.

[1]The Mighty One, God the LORD,
Has spoken and called the earth
From the rising of the sun to its going down.
[2]Out of Zion, the perfection of beauty,
God will shine forth.
[3]Our God shall come, and shall not keep silent;
A fire shall devour before Him,
And it shall be very tempestuous all around
Him.

[4]He shall call to the heavens from above,
And to the earth, that He may judge His
people:
[5]"Gather My saints together to Me,
Those who have made a covenant with Me
by sacrifice."
[6]Let the heavens declare His righteousness,
For God Himself *is* Judge.   *Selah*

[7]"Hear, O My people, and I will speak,
O Israel, and I will testify against you;
I *am* God, your God!
[8]I will not rebuke you for your sacrifices
Or your burnt offerings,
Which are continually before Me.
[9]I will not take a bull from your house,
Nor goats out of your folds.
[10]For every beast of the forest *is* Mine,
And the cattle on a thousand hills.
[11]I know all the birds of the mountains,
And the wild beasts of the field *are* Mine.

[12]"If I were hungry, I would not tell you;
For the world *is* Mine, and all its fullness.
[13]Will I eat the flesh of bulls,
Or drink the blood of goats?
[14]Offer to God thanksgiving,
And pay your vows to the Most High.
[15]Call upon Me in the day of trouble;
I will deliver you, and you shall glorify Me."

[16]But to the wicked God says:
"What *right* have you to declare My statutes,
Or take My covenant in your mouth,
[17]Seeing you hate instruction
And cast My words behind you?
[18]When you saw a thief, you consented[a] with
him,
And have been a partaker with adulterers.
[19]You give your mouth to evil,
And your tongue frames deceit.
[20]You sit *and* speak against your brother;
You slander your own mother's son.
[21]These *things* you have done, and I kept silent;
You thought that I was altogether like you;

49:11 [a]Septuagint, Syriac, Targum, and Vulgate read *Their graves
shall be their houses forever.* **49:12** [a]Following Masoretic Text and
Targum; Septuagint, Syriac, and Vulgate read *understand* (compare
verse 20). **50:18** [a]Septuagint, Syriac, Targum, and Vulgate read
ran.

LEADERSHIP ISSUES

GC2: Gratitude for the Journey

PSALM 50:23

The children of Israel were on countless journeys through the wilderness, in and out of captivity; but they often missed seeing God's hand in them. We also are on a journey. Christlikeness is the destination, and it's important for us to bless Him with our gratitude along the journey, as God's Spirit works through all things to perfect in us Jesus (Rom. 8:28, 29).

Pause to consider that God's ultimate purpose for your life—transforming you into the likeness of Christ to express His glory—also:

- allows you to receive of God's abundant blessings (John 10:10),
- enables you to bless others with His love (1 John 4:12),
- blesses God and brings Him pleasure (Ps. 100:2; Rev. 4:11).

What do these truths do to your heart? Might you be touched to offer a sacrifice of thanksgiving to God, confident that such an offering honors and glorifies Him?

Share with Him your response to the following:

Jesus, as I consider the wonder that Your transforming purpose in my life actually blesses You and others around me, and that Your calling on my life also serves as one of the avenues through which You bless and provide for me, my heart is filled with _____

(For example: *my heart is filled with praise, awe, wonder, gratitude, love, joy. I cannot get over how much You love me, and I hope I never do!*)

Pause to pray with a friend or small group, giving God honor through your praise and thanksgiving.

But I will rebuke you,
And set *them* in order before your eyes.

22"Now consider this, you who forget God,
Lest I tear *you* in pieces,
And *there be* none to deliver:
23Whoever offers praise glorifies Me;
And to him who orders *his* conduct *aright*
I will show the salvation of God."

PSALM 51

A PRAYER OF REPENTANCE

To the Chief Musician. A Psalm of David when
Nathan the prophet went to him, after he had
gone in to Bathsheba.

1Have mercy upon me, O God,
According to Your lovingkindness;
According to the multitude of Your tender
mercies,
Blot out my transgressions.
2Wash me thoroughly from my iniquity,
And cleanse me from my sin.

3For I acknowledge my transgressions,
And my sin *is* always before me.
4Against You, You only, have I sinned,
And done *this* evil in Your sight—
That You may be found just when You speak,[a]
And blameless when You judge.

5Behold, I was brought forth in iniquity,
And in sin my mother conceived me.
6Behold, You desire truth in the inward parts,
And in the hidden *part* You will make me to
know wisdom.

7Purge me with hyssop, and I shall be clean;
Wash me, and I shall be whiter than snow.
8Make me hear joy and gladness,
That the bones You have broken may rejoice.
9Hide Your face from my sins,
And blot out all my iniquities.

10Create in me a clean heart, O God,
And renew a steadfast spirit within me.

51:4 aSeptuagint, Targum, and Vulgate read *in Your words.*

LEADERSHIP
REALITIES

PRIVATE VICTORIES PRECEDE PUBLIC VICTORIES   *Psalm 51*

Shortly after he committed adultery with Bathsheba, David was confronted by the prophet
Nathan about his sin. Godly sorrow and repentance followed, and David poured out his heart
through this psalm with intensity and emotion. As David writes, he confesses the severity of
his sin and the inability to have victory in the private areas of his life. The pain of his heart
saturates his writing as he realizes that the consequences of his sin will impact future generations and his ability to lead the nation of Israel. The beauty of this text is that it shows that
true repentance can serve as a gateway to forgiveness and restoration. Even in the midst of
man's moral failure and defeat, the journey to restoration is always just around the corner because the *lovingkindness of God* is never far from us. David outlines his journey from failure
to forgiveness with humility:

- Recognition (vv. 1–4): accepting the guilt
- Resentment (vv. 1, 2): understanding the sinfulness of sin
- Repentance (vv. 1–4, 9): possessing a godly sorrow (2 Cor. 7:10)
- Renewal (vv. 10, 11): receiving the gift of a clean heart, a steadfast spirit and enjoying
  the presence of the Holy Spirit
- Restoration (vv. 12–17): living in such a way that leads others to God

LEADERSHIP ISSUES

Repentance: The Road to Redemption

PSALM 51

David was a man of both significant victories and major defeats. He was able to rise from the defeat and experience great victory because, first, he got on his knees. One of the great evidences that the Bible is God's Book, and not the result of man's work alone, is that it highlights both the successes and failures of the characters found scattered across its pages. This psalm is the climactic moment of worshipful repentance for the sin of immorality and murder (2 Sam. 11). Although this prayer was written by one individual in response to his sin, its message is one for every heart in need of repentance.

1. **Recognition** (vv. 1–4) of the act as sin was a long time coming. For a year, David hid the sin, rationalized his actions, and lived in entitlement as king. That ended when his sin against God was exposed and the conviction consumed him.

2. **Resentment** (vv. 1, 2): In the opening lines, it is obvious that the stench of David's sin was something he could tolerate no more. The rationalizations died and his own sin became a stain on his heart.

   a. He had destroyed relationships: "blot out" is a phrase that refers to human records that can be erased.

   b. He had destroyed appearance: "wash away" is a phrase that was used in connection with getting clothes clean.

   c. He had destroyed worship: "cleanse" speaks of purification for temple participation.

3. **Repentance** (vv. 4, 5, 7, 9–11): David became conscious of the sin that had polluted every area of his life; He was rendered helpless and desperate for something only God could provide.

4. **Renewal** (v. 10): David's life was littered with and stagnant from the spiritual decay. He cried out for God to give him the chance to start over.

5. **Restoration** (v. 12): David's ultimate goal was to have victory over sin and the joy of salvation restored to his life. The loneliness of separation from God overtook him as he understood that he could no longer operate in his own power.

It is only through genuine repentance that we can receive a restored relationship with the holy God.

THROUGH THE GRID

Making Sense of Your World:
Human Sin (Ps. 51:5)

Through Scripture, we know that humanity was originally created good. All of God's creation was initially good; and in humanity, one could see the highlight of all that God had created. However, God's good creation became marred by sin with the Fall of man. This sin has given rise to many atrocities throughout history; and the individual's relationship with nature, with God, and with others stands broken. As a result of the Fall, everyone's initial disposition when they are born stands in the realm of sinfulness. We are sinful beings by nature because of the Fall. Some hold that all evil and sin has been predestined to happen. However, this takes away free choice and human responsibility, and this view is ultimately not biblical, since God both gives us free choice and holds us accountable for our actions. We are rebellious against God by nature, and we are prone to sin, as we see from our own selfish ambitions and those in the world around us. The biblical worldview maintains that all humans are personally depraved and in need of salvation from that depravity. We are responsible for our actions and for their consequences. Recognizing our sinfulness is the only way that we can recognize our need for salvation. To deny sin is to deny our human depravity, as well as to deny the need for a Savior to save us from our condition. Ultimately, such a view alienates us from ourselves, others, and from God.

¹¹Do not cast me away from Your presence,
  And do not take Your Holy Spirit from me.

¹²Restore to me the joy of Your salvation,
  And uphold me *by Your* generous Spirit.
¹³*Then* I will teach transgressors Your ways,
  And sinners shall be converted to You.

¹⁴Deliver me from the guilt of bloodshed,
    O God,
  The God of my salvation,
  And my tongue shall sing aloud of Your
    righteousness.
¹⁵O Lord, open my lips,
  And my mouth shall show forth Your
    praise.
¹⁶For You do not desire sacrifice, or else I
    would give *it;*
  You do not delight in burnt offering.
¹⁷The sacrifices of God *are* a broken spirit,
  A broken and a contrite heart—
  These, O God, You will not despise.

¹⁸Do good in Your good pleasure to Zion;
  Build the walls of Jerusalem.

¹⁹Then You shall be pleased with the sacrifices
    of righteousness,
  With burnt offering and whole burnt
    offering;
  Then they shall offer bulls on Your altar.

PSALM 52

THE END OF THE WICKED AND THE PEACE
OF THE GODLY

To the Chief Musician. A Contemplation[a] of
David when Doeg the Edomite went and told
Saul, and said to him, "David has gone to the
house of Ahimelech."

¹Why do you boast in evil, O mighty man?
  The goodness of God *endures* continually.
²Your tongue devises destruction,
  Like a sharp razor, working deceitfully.
³You love evil more than good,
  Lying rather than speaking
    righteousness.   *Selah*
⁴You love all devouring words,
  You deceitful tongue.

52:title ªHebrew *Maschil*

[5]God shall likewise destroy you forever;
He shall take you away, and pluck you out of
your dwelling place,
And uproot you from the land of the
living.   *Selah*
[6]The righteous also shall see and fear,
And shall laugh at him, *saying,*
[7]"Here is the man *who* did not make God his
strength,
But trusted in the abundance of his riches,
And strengthened himself in his
wickedness."

[8]But I *am* like a green olive tree in the house
of God;
I trust in the mercy of God forever and ever.
[9]I will praise You forever,
Because You have done *it;*
And in the presence of Your saints
I will wait on Your name, for *it is* good.

PSALM 53

Folly of the Godless, and the Restoration
of Israel

To the Chief Musician. Set to "Mahalath." A
Contemplation[a] of David.

[1]The fool has said in his heart,
"*There is* no God."
They are corrupt, and have done abominable
iniquity;
There is none who does good.

[2]God looks down from heaven upon the
children of men,
To see if there are *any* who understand, who
seek God.
[3]Every one of them has turned aside;

They have together become corrupt;
There is none who does good,
No, not one.

[4]Have the workers of iniquity no
knowledge,
Who eat up my people *as* they eat bread,
And do not call upon God?
[5]There they are in great fear
Where no fear was,
For God has scattered the bones of him who
encamps against you;
You have put *them* to shame,
Because God has despised them.

[6]Oh, that the salvation of Israel would come
out of Zion!
When God brings back the captivity of His
people,
Let Jacob rejoice *and* Israel be glad.

PSALM 54

Answered Prayer for Deliverance from
Adversaries

To the Chief Musician. With stringed
instruments.[a] A Contemplation[b] of David when
the Ziphites went and said to Saul, "Is David not
hiding with us?"

[1]Save me, O God, by Your name,
And vindicate me by Your strength.
[2]Hear my prayer, O God;
Give ear to the words of my mouth.
[3]For strangers have risen up against me,
And oppressors have sought after my life;
They have not set God before them.   *Selah*

53:title [a]Hebrew *Maschil* **54:title** [a]Hebrew *neginoth* [b]Hebrew
Maschil

THROUGH THE GRID

*Where Have All the Dreamers Gone?
Observations from a Biblical
Worldview: No God? (Ps. 53:1)*

One who claims there is no God also single-handedly removes any basis for morality and ultimate truth, other than that of one's own self. Without a God, the development of truth and morality is hard-pressed to find a source, since Christians claim that God is the only author of morality and truth. Without God, there is no moral compass.

4Behold, God *is* my helper;
  The Lord *is* with those who uphold my life.
5He will repay my enemies for their evil.
  Cut them off in Your truth.

6I will freely sacrifice to You;
  I will praise Your name, O LORD, for *it is*
    good.
7For He has delivered me out of all trouble;
  And my eye has seen *its desire* upon my
    enemies.

PSALM 55

TRUST IN GOD CONCERNING THE TREACHERY OF FRIENDS

  To the Chief Musician. With stringed
instruments.[a] A Contemplation[b] of David.

1Give ear to my prayer, O God,
  And do not hide Yourself from my
    supplication.
2Attend to me, and hear me;
  I am restless in my complaint, and moan
    noisily,
3Because of the voice of the enemy,
  Because of the oppression of the wicked;
  For they bring down trouble upon me,
  And in wrath they hate me.

4My heart is severely pained within me,
  And the terrors of death have fallen upon
    me.
5Fearfulness and trembling have come upon
    me,
  And horror has overwhelmed me.
6So I said, "Oh, that I had wings like a dove!
  I would fly away and be at rest.
7Indeed, I would wander far off,
  And remain in the wilderness.   *Selah*
8I would hasten my escape
  From the windy storm *and* tempest."

9Destroy, O Lord, *and* divide their tongues,
  For I have seen violence and strife in the city.
10Day and night they go around it on its walls;
  Iniquity and trouble *are* also in the midst of it.
11Destruction *is* in its midst;
  Oppression and deceit do not depart from its
    streets.

12For *it is* not an enemy *who* reproaches me;
  Then I could bear *it.*
  Nor *is it* one *who* hates me who has exalted
    himself against me;
  Then I could hide from him.
13But *it was* you, a man my equal,
  My companion and my acquaintance.
14We took sweet counsel together,
  And walked to the house of God in the
    throng.

15Let death seize them;
  Let them go down alive into hell,
  For wickedness *is* in their dwellings *and*
    among them.

16As for me, I will call upon God,
  And the LORD shall save me.
17Evening and morning and at noon
  I will pray, and cry aloud,
  And He shall hear my voice.
18He has redeemed my soul in peace from the
    battle *that was* against me,
  For there were many against me.
19God will hear, and afflict them,
  Even He who abides from of old.   *Selah*
  Because they do not change,
  Therefore they do not fear God.

20He has put forth his hands against those who
    were at peace with him;
  He has broken his covenant.
21*The words* of his mouth were smoother than
    butter,
  But war *was* in his heart;
  His words were softer than oil,
  Yet they *were* drawn swords.

22Cast your burden on the LORD,
  And He shall sustain you;
  He shall never permit the righteous to be
    moved.

23But You, O God, shall bring them down to
    the pit of destruction;
  Bloodthirsty and deceitful men shall not live
    out half their days;
  But I will trust in You.

55:title [a]Hebrew *neginoth* [b]Hebrew *Maschil*

PSALM 56

PRAYER FOR RELIEF FROM TORMENTORS
To the Chief Musician. Set to "The Silent Dove
in Distant Lands."[a] A Michtam of David when
the Philistines captured him in Gath.

¹Be merciful to me, O God, for man would
swallow me up;
Fighting all day he oppresses me.
²My enemies would hound *me* all day,
For *there are* many who fight against me,
O Most High.

³Whenever I am afraid,
I will trust in You.
⁴In God (I will praise His word),
In God I have put my trust;
I will not fear.
What can flesh do to me?

⁵All day they twist my words;
All their thoughts *are* against me for evil.
⁶They gather together,
They hide, they mark my steps,
When they lie in wait for my life.
⁷Shall they escape by iniquity?
In anger cast down the peoples, O God!

⁸You number my wanderings;
Put my tears into Your bottle;
Are they not in Your book?
⁹When I cry out *to You,*
Then my enemies will turn back;
This I know, because God *is* for me.
¹⁰In God (I will praise *His* word),
In the LORD (I will praise *His* word),
¹¹In God I have put my trust;
I will not be afraid.
What can man do to me?

¹²Vows *made* to You *are binding* upon me, O God;
I will render praises to You,
¹³For You have delivered my soul from death.
Have You not *kept* my feet from falling,
That I may walk before God
In the light of the living?

PSALM 57

PRAYER FOR SAFETY FROM ENEMIES
To the Chief Musician. Set to "Do Not Destroy."[a]
A Michtam of David when he fled from Saul into
the cave.

¹Be merciful to me, O God, be merciful to me!
For my soul trusts in You;

56:title [a]Hebrew *Jonath Elem Rechokim*   **57:title** [a]Hebrew *Al Tashcheth*

LEADERSHIP REALITIES

HOW TO GET ALONG WITH DIFFICULT PEOPLE: SWIMMING WITH SHARKS IN THE SEA OF LIFE   *Psalm 57*

Difficult people are an inevitable part of life. David recorded this psalm while hiding in a cave from King Saul and his men (1 Sam. 22; 24). He described those hunting him as *lions . . . whose teeth are spears and arrows, and their tongue a sharp sword*. David took comfort in the reality that God would protect and deliver him. So genuine was his belief in God's protection that he did not retaliate when the opportunity presented itself, but trusted in God's timing for his life. His choices show that unshakable confidence in God is the only way to face life's adversaries. David refers to God twenty-one times in this psalm either by name or by personal pronoun. His bold statement, "*My soul trusts in You*" is a short, but powerful statement. John Calvin commented thus: "This is a form of expression, the force of which is not to be overlooked: for it implies that the trust which he exercised proceeded from the very innermost affections—that it was of no volatile character, but deeply and strongly rooted." As one's soul trusts wholly in God and refuge is found in the shadow of His wings, one can find the strength and tenacity to swim alongside any "sharks" in life.

And in the shadow of Your wings I will make
  my refuge,
Until *these* calamities have passed by.

²I will cry out to God Most High,
  To God who performs *all things* for me.
³He shall send from heaven and save me;
  He reproaches the one who would swallow
    me up.   *Selah*
  God shall send forth His mercy and His
    truth.

⁴My soul *is* among lions;
  I lie *among* the sons of men
  Who are set on fire,
  Whose teeth *are* spears and arrows,
  And their tongue a sharp sword.
⁵Be exalted, O God, above the heavens;
  Let Your glory *be* above all the earth.

⁶They have prepared a net for my steps;
  My soul is bowed down;
  They have dug a pit before me;
  Into the midst of it they *themselves* have
    fallen.   *Selah*

⁷My heart is steadfast, O God, my heart is
    steadfast;
  I will sing and give praise.
⁸Awake, my glory!
  Awake, lute and harp!
  I will awaken the dawn.

⁹I will praise You, O Lord, among the peoples;
  I will sing to You among the nations.
¹⁰For Your mercy reaches unto the heavens,
  And Your truth unto the clouds.

¹¹Be exalted, O God, above the heavens;
  Let Your glory *be* above all the earth.

PSALM 58

THE JUST JUDGMENT OF THE WICKED
To the Chief Musician. Set to "Do Not Destroy."ᵃ
A Michtam of David.

¹Do you indeed speak righteousness, you silent
    ones?
  Do you judge uprightly, you sons of men?

²No, in heart you work wickedness;
  You weigh out the violence of your hands in
    the earth.

³The wicked are estranged from the womb;
  They go astray as soon as they are born,
    speaking lies.
⁴Their poison *is* like the poison of a serpent;
  They are like the deaf cobra *that* stops its ear,
⁵Which will not heed the voice of charmers,
  Charming ever so skillfully.

⁶Break their teeth in their mouth, O God!
  Break out the fangs of the young lions,
    O LORD!
⁷Let them flow away as waters *which* run
    continually;
  When he bends *his bow,*
  Let his arrows be as if cut in pieces.
⁸*Let them be* like a snail which melts away as it
    goes,
  Like a stillborn child of a woman, that they
    may not see the sun.

⁹Before your pots can feel *the burning* thorns,
  He shall take them away as with a
    whirlwind,
  As in His living and burning wrath.
¹⁰The righteous shall rejoice when he sees the
    vengeance;
  He shall wash his feet in the blood of the
    wicked,
¹¹So that men will say,
  "Surely *there is* a reward for the righteous;
  Surely He is God who judges in the earth."

PSALM 59

THE ASSURED JUDGMENT OF THE WICKED
To the Chief Musician. Set to "Do Not Destroy."ᵃ
A Michtam of David when Saul sent men, and
they watched the house in order to kill him.

¹Deliver me from my enemies, O my God;
  Defend me from those who rise up against
    me.
²Deliver me from the workers of iniquity,
  And save me from bloodthirsty men.

58:title ᵃHebrew *Al Tashcheth*   59:title ᵃHebrew *Al Tashcheth*

³For look, they lie in wait for my life;
 The mighty gather against me,
 Not *for* my transgression nor *for* my sin,
  O LORD.
⁴They run and prepare themselves through no
  fault *of mine.*

Awake to help me, and behold!
⁵You therefore, O LORD God of hosts, the
  God of Israel,
Awake to punish all the nations;
Do not be merciful to any wicked
  transgressors.   *Selah*

⁶At evening they return,
 They growl like a dog,
 And go all around the city.
⁷Indeed, they belch with their mouth;
 Swords *are* in their lips;
 For *they say,* "Who hears?"

⁸But You, O LORD, shall laugh at them;
 You shall have all the nations in derision.
⁹I will wait for You, O You his Strength;ᵃ
 For God *is* my defense.
¹⁰My God of mercyᵃ shall come to meet me;
 God shall let me see *my desire* on my
  enemies.

¹¹Do not slay them, lest my people forget;
 Scatter them by Your power,
 And bring them down,
 O Lord our shield.
¹²*For* the sin of their mouth *and* the words of
  their lips,
 Let them even be taken in their pride,
 And for the cursing and lying *which* they
  speak.
¹³Consume *them* in wrath, consume *them,*
 That they *may* not *be;*
 And let them know that God rules in
  Jacob
 To the ends of the earth.   *Selah*

¹⁴And at evening they return,
 They growl like a dog,
 And go all around the city.
¹⁵They wander up and down for food,
 And howlᵃ if they are not satisfied.

¹⁶But I will sing of Your power;
 Yes, I will sing aloud of Your mercy in the
  morning;
 For You have been my defense
 And refuge in the day of my trouble.
¹⁷To You, O my Strength, I will sing praises;
 For God *is* my defense,
 My God of mercy.

PSALM 60

URGENT PRAYER FOR THE RESTORED FAVOR
OF GOD

To the Chief Musician. Set to "Lily of the
Testimony."ᵃ A Michtam of David. For teaching.
When he fought against Mesopotamia and Syria
of Zobah, and Joab returned and killed twelve
thousand Edomites in the Valley of Salt.

¹O God, You have cast us off;
 You have broken us down;
 You have been displeased;
 Oh, restore us again!
²You have made the earth tremble;
 You have broken it;
 Heal its breaches, for it is shaking.
³You have shown Your people hard things;
 You have made us drink the wine of
  confusion.

⁴You have given a banner to those who fear
  You,
 That it may be displayed because of the
  truth.   *Selah*
⁵That Your beloved may be delivered,
 Save *with* Your right hand, and hear me.

⁶God has spoken in His holiness:
"I will rejoice;
 I will divide Shechem
 And measure out the Valley of Succoth.
⁷Gilead *is* Mine, and Manasseh *is* Mine;
 Ephraim also *is* the helmet for My head;
 Judah *is* My lawgiver.

59:9 ᵃFollowing Masoretic Text and Syriac; some Hebrew manuscripts, Septuagint, Targum, and Vulgate read *my Strength.*
59:10 ᵃFollowing Qere; some Hebrew manuscripts, Septuagint, and
Vulgate read *My God, His mercy;* Kethib, some Hebrew manuscripts
and Targum read *O God, my mercy;* Syriac reads *O God, Your
mercy.*   **59:15** ᵃFollowing Septuagint and Vulgate; Masoretic Text,
Syriac, and Targum read *spend the night.* **60:title** ᵃHebrew
Shushan Eduth

⁸Moab *is* My washpot;
 Over Edom I will cast My shoe;
 Philistia, shout in triumph because of Me."

⁹Who will bring me *to* the strong city?
 Who will lead me to Edom?
¹⁰*Is it* not You, O God, *who* cast us off?
 And You, O God, *who* did not go out with
  our armies?
¹¹Give us help from trouble,
 For the help of man *is* useless.
¹²Through God we will do valiantly,
 For *it is* He *who* shall tread down our enemies.ª

PSALM 61

ASSURANCE OF GOD'S ETERNAL PROTECTION
  To the Chief Musician. On a stringed
   instrument.ª *A Psalm* of David.

¹Hear my cry, O God;
 Attend to my prayer.
²From the end of the earth I will cry to You,
 When my heart is overwhelmed;
 Lead me to the rock that is higher than I.

³For You have been a shelter for me,
 A strong tower from the enemy.
⁴I will abide in Your tabernacle forever;
 I will trust in the shelter of Your wings.   *Selah*

⁵For You, O God, have heard my vows;
 You have given *me* the heritage of those who
  fear Your name.
⁶You will prolong the king's life,
 His years as many generations.
⁷He shall abide before God forever.
 Oh, prepare mercy and truth, *which* may
  preserve him!

⁸So I will sing praise to Your name forever,
 That I may daily perform my vows.

PSALM 62

A CALM RESOLVE TO WAIT FOR THE SALVATION
  OF GOD
 To the Chief Musician. To Jeduthun. A Psalm
  of David.

¹Truly my soul silently *waits* for God;
 From Him *comes* my salvation.

²He only *is* my rock and my salvation;
 He is my defense;
 I shall not be greatly moved.

³How long will you attack a man?
 You shall be slain, all of you,
 Like a leaning wall and a tottering fence.
⁴They only consult to cast *him* down from his
  high position;
 They delight in lies;
 They bless with their mouth,
 But they curse inwardly.   *Selah*

⁵My soul, wait silently for God alone,
 For my expectation *is* from Him.
⁶He only *is* my rock and my salvation;
 He is my defense;
 I shall not be moved.
⁷In God *is* my salvation and my glory;
 The rock of my strength,
 And my refuge, *is* in God.

⁸Trust in Him at all times, you people;
 Pour out your heart before Him;
 God *is* a refuge for us.   *Selah*

⁹Surely men of low degree *are* a vapor,
 Men of high degree *are* a lie;
 If they are weighed on the scales,
 They *are* altogether *lighter* than vapor.
¹⁰Do not trust in oppression,
 Nor vainly hope in robbery;
 If riches increase,
 Do not set *your* heart *on them.*

¹¹God has spoken once,
 Twice I have heard this:
 That power *belongs* to God.
¹²Also to You, O Lord, *belongs* mercy;
 For You render to each one according to his
  work.

PSALM 63

JOY IN THE FELLOWSHIP OF GOD
A Psalm of David when he was in the wilderness
  of Judah.

¹O God, You *are* my God;
 Early will I seek You;

60:12 ªCompare verses 5–12 with 108:6–13   **61:title** ªHebrew
neginah

My soul thirsts for You;
My flesh longs for You
In a dry and thirsty land
Where there is no water.
²So I have looked for You in the sanctuary,
To see Your power and Your glory.

³Because Your lovingkindness *is* better than life,
My lips shall praise You.
⁴Thus I will bless You while I live;
I will lift up my hands in Your name.
⁵My soul shall be satisfied as with marrow and
fatness,
And my mouth shall praise *You* with joyful
lips.

⁶When I remember You on my bed,
I meditate on You in the *night* watches.
⁷Because You have been my help,
Therefore in the shadow of Your wings I will
rejoice.
⁸My soul follows close behind You;
Your right hand upholds me.

⁹But those *who* seek my life, to destroy *it,*
Shall go into the lower parts of the earth.
¹⁰They shall fall by the sword;
They shall be a portion for jackals.

¹¹But the king shall rejoice in God;
Everyone who swears by Him shall glory;
But the mouth of those who speak lies shall
be stopped.

PSALM 64

OPPRESSED BY THE WICKED BUT REJOICING IN
THE LORD
To the Chief Musician. A Psalm of David.

¹Hear my voice, O God, in my meditation;
Preserve my life from fear of the enemy.
²Hide me from the secret plots of the wicked,
From the rebellion of the workers of iniquity,
³Who sharpen their tongue like a sword,
And bend *their bows to shoot* their arrows—
bitter words,
⁴That they may shoot in secret at the
blameless;
Suddenly they shoot at him and do not fear.

⁵They encourage themselves *in* an evil
matter;
They talk of laying snares secretly;
They say, "Who will see them?"
⁶They devise iniquities:
"We have perfected a shrewd scheme."
Both the inward thought and the heart of
man are deep.

⁷But God shall shoot at them *with* an arrow;
Suddenly they shall be wounded.
⁸So He will make them stumble over their
own tongue;
All who see them shall flee away.
⁹All men shall fear,
And shall declare the work of God;
For they shall wisely consider His doing.

¹⁰The righteous shall be glad in the LORD, and
trust in Him.
And all the upright in heart shall glory.

PSALM 65

PRAISE TO GOD FOR HIS SALVATION AND
PROVIDENCE
To the Chief Musician. A Psalm of David.
A Song.

¹Praise is awaiting You, O God, in Zion;
And to You the vow shall be performed.
²O You who hear prayer,
To You all flesh will come.
³Iniquities prevail against me;
As for our transgressions,
You will provide atonement for them.

⁴Blessed *is the man* You choose,
And cause to approach *You,*
That he may dwell in Your courts.
We shall be satisfied with the goodness of
Your house,
Of Your holy temple.

⁵*By* awesome deeds in righteousness You will
answer us,
O God of our salvation,
You who are the confidence of all the ends of
the earth,
And of the far-off seas;

⁶Who established the mountains by His
   strength,
Being clothed with power;
⁷You who still the noise of the seas,
The noise of their waves,
And the tumult of the peoples.
⁸They also who dwell in the farthest parts are
   afraid of Your signs;
You make the outgoings of the morning and
   evening rejoice.

⁹You visit the earth and water it,
You greatly enrich it;
The river of God is full of water;
You provide their grain,
For so You have prepared it.
¹⁰You water its ridges abundantly,
You settle its furrows;
You make it soft with showers,
You bless its growth.

¹¹You crown the year with Your goodness,
And Your paths drip *with* abundance.
¹²They drop *on* the pastures of the wilderness,
And the little hills rejoice on every side.
¹³The pastures are clothed with flocks;
The valleys also are covered with grain;
They shout for joy, they also sing.

PSALM 66

PRAISE TO GOD FOR HIS AWESOME WORKS
To the Chief Musician. A Song. A Psalm.

¹Make a joyful shout to God, all the earth!
²Sing out the honor of His name;
Make His praise glorious.
³Say to God,
"How awesome are Your works!
Through the greatness of Your power
Your enemies shall submit themselves to You.
⁴All the earth shall worship You
And sing praises to You;
They shall sing praises *to* Your name."   *Selah*

⁵Come and see the works of God;
He is awesome *in His* doing toward the sons
   of men.
⁶He turned the sea into dry *land;*
They went through the river on foot.
There we will rejoice in Him.

⁷He rules by His power forever;
His eyes observe the nations;
Do not let the rebellious exalt
   themselves.   *Selah*

⁸Oh, bless our God, you peoples!
And make the voice of His praise to be heard,
⁹Who keeps our soul among the living,
And does not allow our feet to be moved.
¹⁰For You, O God, have tested us;
You have refined us as silver is refined.
¹¹You brought us into the net;
You laid affliction on our backs.
¹²You have caused men to ride over our heads;
We went through fire and through water;
But You brought us out to rich *fulfillment.*

¹³I will go into Your house with burnt
   offerings;
I will pay You my vows,
¹⁴Which my lips have uttered
And my mouth has spoken when I was in
   trouble.
¹⁵I will offer You burnt sacrifices of fat animals,
With the sweet aroma of rams;
I will offer bulls with goats.   *Selah*

¹⁶Come *and* hear, all you who fear God,
And I will declare what He has done for my
   soul.
¹⁷I cried to Him with my mouth,
And He was extolled with my tongue.
¹⁸If I regard iniquity in my heart,
The Lord will not hear.
¹⁹*But* certainly God has heard *me;*
He has attended to the voice of my prayer.

²⁰Blessed *be* God,
Who has not turned away my prayer,
Nor His mercy from me!

PSALM 67

AN INVOCATION AND A DOXOLOGY
To the Chief Musician. On stringed instruments.[a]
A Psalm. A Song.

¹God be merciful to us and bless us,
And cause His face to shine upon us,   *Selah*

67:title [a]Hebrew *neginoth*

²That Your way may be known on earth,
 Your salvation among all nations.

³Let the peoples praise You, O God;
 Let all the peoples praise You.
⁴Oh, let the nations be glad and sing for joy!
 For You shall judge the people righteously,
 And govern the nations on earth.   *Selah*

⁵Let the peoples praise You, O God;
 Let all the peoples praise You.
⁶*Then* the earth shall yield her increase;
 God, our own God, shall bless us.
⁷God shall bless us,
 And all the ends of the earth shall fear Him.

PSALM 68

THE GLORY OF GOD IN HIS GOODNESS TO ISRAEL
To the Chief Musician. A Psalm of David.
A Song.

¹Let God arise,
 Let His enemies be scattered;
 Let those also who hate Him flee before Him.
²As smoke is driven away,
 So drive *them* away;
 As wax melts before the fire,
 So let the wicked perish at the presence of
  God.
³But let the righteous be glad;
 Let them rejoice before God;
 Yes, let them rejoice exceedingly.

⁴Sing to God, sing praises to His name;
 Extol Him who rides on the clouds,ᵃ
 By His name YAH,
 And rejoice before Him.

⁵A father of the fatherless, a defender of
  widows,
 Is God in His holy habitation.
⁶God sets the solitary in families;
 He brings out those who are bound into
  prosperity;
 But the rebellious dwell in a dry *land.*

⁷O God, when You went out before Your
  people,

When You marched through the
  wilderness,   *Selah*
⁸The earth shook;
 The heavens also dropped *rain* at the presence
  of God;
 Sinai itself *was moved* at the presence of God,
  the God of Israel.
⁹You, O God, sent a plentiful rain,
 Whereby You confirmed Your inheritance,
 When it was weary.
¹⁰Your congregation dwelt in it;
 You, O God, provided from Your goodness
  for the poor.

¹¹The Lord gave the word;
 Great *was* the company of those who
  proclaimed *it:*
¹²"Kings of armies flee, they flee,
 And she who remains at home divides the
  spoil.
¹³Though you lie down among the
  sheepfolds,
 You will be like the wings of a dove covered
  with silver,
 And her feathers with yellow gold."
¹⁴When the Almighty scattered kings in it,
 It was *white* as snow in Zalmon.

¹⁵A mountain of God *is* the mountain of
  Bashan;
 A mountain *of many* peaks *is* the mountain of
  Bashan.
¹⁶Why do you fume with envy, you mountains
  of *many* peaks?
 This is the mountain *which* God desires to
  dwell in;
 Yes, the LORD will dwell *in it* forever.

¹⁷The chariots of God *are* twenty thousand,
 Even thousands of thousands;
 The Lord is among them *as in* Sinai, in the
  Holy *Place.*
¹⁸You have ascended on high,
 You have led captivity captive;
 You have received gifts among men,
 Even *from* the rebellious,
 That the LORD God might dwell *there.*

68:4 ᵃMasoretic Text reads *deserts;* Targum reads *heavens* (compare verse 34 and Isaiah 19:1).

¹⁹Blessed *be* the Lord,
Who daily loads us *with benefits,*
The God of our salvation! *Selah*
²⁰Our God *is* the God of salvation;
And to GOD the Lord *belong* escapes from
death.

²¹But God will wound the head of His enemies,
The hairy scalp of the one who still goes on
in his trespasses.
²²The Lord said, "I will bring back from
Bashan,
I will bring *them* back from the depths of the
sea,
²³That your foot may crush *them*ᵃ in blood,
And the tongues of your dogs *may have* their
portion from *your* enemies."

²⁴They have seen Your procession, O God,
The procession of my God, my King, into the
sanctuary.
²⁵The singers went before, the players on
instruments *followed* after;
Among *them were* the maidens playing
timbrels.
²⁶Bless God in the congregations,
The Lord, from the fountain of Israel.
²⁷There *is* little Benjamin, their leader,
The princes of Judah *and* their company,
The princes of Zebulun *and* the princes of
Naphtali.

²⁸Your God has commandedᵃ your strength;
Strengthen, O God, what You have done for
us.
²⁹Because of Your temple at Jerusalem,
Kings will bring presents to You.
³⁰Rebuke the beasts of the reeds,
The herd of bulls with the calves of the
peoples,
Till everyone submits himself with pieces of
silver.
Scatter the peoples *who* delight in war.
³¹Envoys will come out of Egypt;
Ethiopia will quickly stretch out her hands to
God.

³²Sing to God, you kingdoms of the earth;
Oh, sing praises to the Lord, *Selah*

³³To Him who rides on the heaven of heavens,
which were of old!
Indeed, He sends out His voice, a mighty
voice.
³⁴Ascribe strength to God;
His excellence *is* over Israel,
And His strength *is* in the clouds.
³⁵O God, *You are* more awesome than Your
holy places.
The God of Israel *is* He who gives strength
and power to *His* people.

Blessed *be* God!

PSALM 69

AN URGENT PLEA FOR HELP IN TROUBLE
To the Chief Musician. Set to "The Lilies."ᵃ
A Psalm of David.

¹Save me, O God!
For the waters have come up to *my* neck.
²I sink in deep mire,
Where *there is* no standing;
I have come into deep waters,
Where the floods overflow me.
³I am weary with my crying;
My throat is dry;
My eyes fail while I wait for my God.

⁴Those who hate me without a cause
Are more than the hairs of my head;
They are mighty who would destroy me,
Being my enemies wrongfully;
Though I have stolen nothing,
I *still* must restore *it.*

⁵O God, You know my foolishness;
And my sins are not hidden from You.
⁶Let not those who wait for You, O Lord GOD
of hosts, be ashamed because of me;
Let not those who seek You be confounded
because of me, O God of Israel.
⁷Because for Your sake I have borne reproach;
Shame has covered my face.
⁸I have become a stranger to my brothers,
And an alien to my mother's children;

68:23 ᵃSeptuagint, Syriac, Targum, and Vulgate read *you may dip your foot.* **68:28** ᵃSeptuagint, Syriac, Targum, and Vulgate read *Command, O God.* **69:title** ᵃHebrew *Shoshannim*

⁹Because zeal for Your house has eaten me up,
And the reproaches of those who reproach
You have fallen on me.
¹⁰When I wept *and chastened* my soul with
fasting,
That became my reproach.
¹¹I also made sackcloth my garment;
I became a byword to them.
¹²Those who sit in the gate speak against me,
And I *am* the song of the drunkards.

¹³But as for me, my prayer *is* to You,
O LORD, *in* the acceptable time;
O God, in the multitude of Your mercy,
Hear me in the truth of Your salvation.
¹⁴Deliver me out of the mire,
And let me not sink;
Let me be delivered from those who hate me,
And out of the deep waters.
¹⁵Let not the floodwater overflow me,
Nor let the deep swallow me up;
And let not the pit shut its mouth on me.

¹⁶Hear me, O LORD, for Your lovingkindness *is*
good;
Turn to me according to the multitude of
Your tender mercies.
¹⁷And do not hide Your face from Your servant,
For I am in trouble;
Hear me speedily.
¹⁸Draw near to my soul, *and* redeem it;
Deliver me because of my enemies.

¹⁹You know my reproach, my shame, and my
dishonor;
My adversaries *are* all before You.
²⁰Reproach has broken my heart,
And I am full of heaviness;
I looked *for someone* to take pity, but *there was*
none;
And for comforters, but I found none.
²¹They also gave me gall for my food,
And for my thirst they gave me vinegar to
drink.

²²Let their table become a snare before them,
And their well-being a trap.
²³Let their eyes be darkened, so that they do
not see;

And make their loins shake continually.
²⁴Pour out Your indignation upon them,
And let Your wrathful anger take hold of
them.
²⁵Let their dwelling place be desolate;
Let no one live in their tents.
²⁶For they persecute the *ones* You have struck,
And talk of the grief of those You have
wounded.
²⁷Add iniquity to their iniquity,
And let them not come into Your
righteousness.
²⁸Let them be blotted out of the book of the
living,
And not be written with the righteous.

²⁹But I *am* poor and sorrowful;
Let Your salvation, O God, set me up on high.
³⁰I will praise the name of God with a song,
And will magnify Him with thanksgiving.
³¹*This* also shall please the LORD better than an
ox *or* bull,
Which has horns and hooves.
³²The humble shall see *this and* be glad;
And you who seek God, your hearts shall
live.
³³For the LORD hears the poor,
And does not despise His prisoners.

³⁴Let heaven and earth praise Him,
The seas and everything that moves in them.
³⁵For God will save Zion
And build the cities of Judah,
That they may dwell there and possess it.
³⁶Also, the descendants of His servants shall
inherit it,
And those who love His name shall dwell
in it.

PSALM 70

PRAYER FOR RELIEF FROM ADVERSARIES

To the Chief Musician. *A Psalm* of David. To bring
to remembrance.

¹*Make haste,* O God, to deliver me!
Make haste to help me, O LORD!

²Let them be ashamed and confounded
Who seek my life;

Let them be turned back[a] and confused
Who desire my hurt.
3Let them be turned back because of their
        shame,
Who say, "Aha, aha!"

4Let all those who seek You rejoice and be
        glad in You;
And let those who love Your salvation say
        continually,
"Let God be magnified!"

5But I *am* poor and needy;
Make haste to me, O God!
You *are* my help and my deliverer;
O LORD, do not delay.

PSALM 71

GOD THE ROCK OF SALVATION

1In You, O LORD, I put my trust;
Let me never be put to shame.
2Deliver me in Your righteousness, and cause
        me to escape;
Incline Your ear to me, and save me.
3Be my strong refuge,
To which I may resort continually;
You have given the commandment to
        save me,
For You *are* my rock and my fortress.

4Deliver me, O my God, out of the hand of
        the wicked,
Out of the hand of the unrighteous and cruel
        man.
5For You are my hope, O Lord GOD;
You are my trust from my youth.
6By You I have been upheld from birth;
You are He who took me out of my mother's
        womb.
My praise *shall be* continually of You.

7I have become as a wonder to many,
But You *are* my strong refuge.
8Let my mouth be filled *with* Your praise
And with Your glory all the day.

9Do not cast me off in the time of old age;
Do not forsake me when my strength fails.

10For my enemies speak against me;
And those who lie in wait for my life take
        counsel together,
11Saying, "God has forsaken him;
Pursue and take him, for *there is* none to
        deliver *him."*

12O God, do not be far from me;
O my God, make haste to help me!
13Let them be confounded *and* consumed
Who are adversaries of my life;
Let them be covered *with* reproach and
        dishonor
Who seek my hurt.

14But I will hope continually,
And will praise You yet more and more.
15My mouth shall tell of Your righteousness
And Your salvation all the day,
For I do not know *their* limits.
16I will go in the strength of the Lord GOD;
I will make mention of Your righteousness, of
        Yours only.

17O God, You have taught me from my youth;
And to this *day* I declare Your wondrous
        works.
18Now also when *I am* old and grayheaded,
O God, do not forsake me,
Until I declare Your strength to *this*
        generation,
Your power to everyone *who* is to come.

19Also Your righteousness, O God, *is* very high,
You who have done great things;
O God, who *is* like You?
20*You,* who have shown me great and severe
        troubles,
Shall revive me again,
And bring me up again from the depths of
        the earth.
21You shall increase my greatness,
And comfort me on every side.

22Also with the lute I will praise You—
And Your faithfulness, O my God!

70:2 aFollowing Masoretic Text, Septuagint, Targum, and Vulgate;
some Hebrew manuscripts and Syriac read *be appalled* (compare
40:15).

To You I will sing with the harp,
O Holy One of Israel.
²³My lips shall greatly rejoice when I sing to
You,
And my soul, which You have redeemed.
²⁴My tongue also shall talk of Your
righteousness all the day long;
For they are confounded,
For they are brought to shame
Who seek my hurt.

PSALM 72

Glory and Universality of the Messiah's
Reign
A Psalm of Solomon.

¹Give the king Your judgments, O God,
And Your righteousness to the king's Son.
²He will judge Your people with
righteousness,
And Your poor with justice.
³The mountains will bring peace to the
people,
And the little hills, by righteousness.
⁴He will bring justice to the poor of the
people;
He will save the children of the needy,
And will break in pieces the oppressor.

⁵They shall fear You[a]
As long as the sun and moon endure,
Throughout all generations.
⁶He shall come down like rain upon the grass
before mowing,
Like showers *that* water the earth.
⁷In His days the righteous shall flourish,
And abundance of peace,
Until the moon is no more.

⁸He shall have dominion also from sea to sea,
And from the River to the ends of the
earth.
⁹Those who dwell in the wilderness will bow
before Him,
And His enemies will lick the dust.
¹⁰The kings of Tarshish and of the isles
Will bring presents;
The kings of Sheba and Seba
Will offer gifts.

¹¹Yes, all kings shall fall down before Him;
All nations shall serve Him.

¹²For He will deliver the needy when he cries,
The poor also, and *him* who has no helper.
¹³He will spare the poor and needy,
And will save the souls of the needy.
¹⁴He will redeem their life from oppression and
violence;
And precious shall be their blood in His sight.

¹⁵And He shall live;
And the gold of Sheba will be given to Him;
Prayer also will be made for Him continually,
And daily He shall be praised.

¹⁶There will be an abundance of grain in the
earth,
On the top of the mountains;
Its fruit shall wave like Lebanon;
And *those* of the city shall flourish like grass of
the earth.

¹⁷His name shall endure forever;
His name shall continue as long as the sun.
And *men* shall be blessed in Him;
All nations shall call Him blessed.

¹⁸Blessed *be* the Lord God, the God of Israel,
Who only does wondrous things!
¹⁹And blessed *be* His glorious name forever!
And let the whole earth be filled *with* His
glory.
Amen and Amen.

²⁰The prayers of David the son of Jesse are
ended.

Book Three: Psalms 73—89

PSALM 73

The Tragedy of the Wicked, and the
Blessedness of Trust in God
A Psalm of Asaph.

¹Truly God *is* good to Israel,
To such as are pure in heart.

72:5 [a]Following Masoretic Text and Targum; Septuagint and Vulgate
read *They shall continue.*

²But as for me, my feet had almost stumbled;
  My steps had nearly slipped.
³For I *was* envious of the boastful,
  When I saw the prosperity of the wicked.

⁴For *there are* no pangs in their death,
  But their strength *is* firm.
⁵They *are* not in trouble *as other* men,
  Nor are they plagued like *other* men.
⁶Therefore pride serves as their necklace;
  Violence covers them *like* a garment.
⁷Their eyes bulge[a] with abundance;
  They have more than heart could wish.
⁸They scoff and speak wickedly *concerning*
    oppression;
  They speak loftily.
⁹They set their mouth against the heavens,
  And their tongue walks through the earth.

¹⁰Therefore his people return here,
  And waters of a full *cup* are drained by them.
¹¹And they say, "How does God know?
  And is there knowledge in the Most High?"
¹²Behold, these *are* the ungodly,
  Who are always at ease;
  They increase *in* riches.
¹³Surely I have cleansed my heart *in* vain,
  And washed my hands in innocence.
¹⁴For all day long I have been plagued,
  And chastened every morning.

¹⁵If I had said, "I will speak thus,"
  Behold, I would have been untrue to the
    generation of Your children.
¹⁶When I thought *how* to understand this,
  It *was* too painful for me—
¹⁷Until I went into the sanctuary of God;
  Then I understood their end.

¹⁸Surely You set them in slippery places;
  You cast them down to destruction.
¹⁹Oh, how they are *brought* to desolation, as in a
    moment!
  They are utterly consumed with terrors.
²⁰As a dream when *one* awakes,
  So, Lord, when You awake,
  You shall despise their image.

²¹Thus my heart was grieved,
  And I was vexed in my mind.

²²I *was* so foolish and ignorant;
  I was *like* a beast before You.
²³Nevertheless I *am* continually with You;
  You hold *me* by my right hand.
²⁴You will guide me with Your counsel,
  And afterward receive me *to* glory.

²⁵Whom have I in heaven *but You?*
  And *there is* none upon earth *that* I desire
    besides You.
²⁶My flesh and my heart fail;
  But God *is* the strength of my heart and my
    portion forever.

²⁷For indeed, those who are far from You shall
    perish;
  You have destroyed all those who desert You
    for harlotry.
²⁸But *it is* good for me to draw near to God;
  I have put my trust in the Lord GOD,
  That I may declare all Your works.

PSALM 74

A PLEA FOR RELIEF FROM OPPRESSORS
A Contemplation[a] of Asaph.

¹O God, why have You cast *us* off forever?
  Why does Your anger smoke against the sheep
    of Your pasture?
²Remember Your congregation, *which* You
    have purchased of old,
  The tribe of Your inheritance, *which* You have
    redeemed—
  This Mount Zion where You have dwelt.
³Lift up Your feet to the perpetual
    desolations.
  The enemy has damaged everything in the
    sanctuary.
⁴Your enemies roar in the midst of Your
    meeting place;
  They set up their banners *for* signs.
⁵They seem like men who lift up
  Axes among the thick trees.
⁶And now they break down its carved work,
    all at once,
  With axes and hammers.

73:7 ᵃTargum reads *face bulges;* Septuagint, Syriac, and Vulgate
read *iniquity bulges.*   **74:title** ᵃHebrew *Maschil*

⁷They have set fire to Your sanctuary;
They have defiled the dwelling place of Your
    name to the ground.
⁸They said in their hearts,
"Let us destroy them altogether."
They have burned up all the meeting places
    of God in the land.

⁹We do not see our signs;
There is no longer any prophet;
Nor *is there* any among us who knows how
    long.
¹⁰O God, how long will the adversary
    reproach?
Will the enemy blaspheme Your name
    forever?
¹¹Why do You withdraw Your hand, even Your
    right hand?
Take it out of Your bosom and destroy *them*.
¹²For God *is* my King from of old,
Working salvation in the midst of the earth.
¹³You divided the sea by Your strength;
You broke the heads of the sea serpents in
    the waters.
¹⁴You broke the heads of Leviathan in
    pieces,
And gave him *as* food to the people
    inhabiting the wilderness.
¹⁵You broke open the fountain and the
    flood;
You dried up mighty rivers.
¹⁶The day *is* Yours, the night also *is* Yours;
You have prepared the light and the sun.
¹⁷You have set all the borders of the earth;
You have made summer and winter.

¹⁸Remember this, *that* the enemy has
    reproached, O LORD,
And *that* a foolish people has blasphemed
    Your name.
¹⁹Oh, do not deliver the life of Your turtledove
    to the wild beast!
Do not forget the life of Your poor forever.
²⁰Have respect to the covenant;
For the dark places of the earth are full of the
    haunts of cruelty.
²¹Oh, do not let the oppressed return
    ashamed!
Let the poor and needy praise Your name.

²²Arise, O God, plead Your own cause;
Remember how the foolish man reproaches
    You daily.
²³Do not forget the voice of Your enemies;
The tumult of those who rise up against You
    increases continually.

PSALM 75

THANKSGIVING FOR GOD'S RIGHTEOUS
JUDGMENT
To the Chief Musician. Set to "Do Not Destroy."[a]
A Psalm of Asaph. A Song.

¹We give thanks to You, O God, we give
    thanks!
For Your wondrous works declare *that* Your
    name is near.

²"When I choose the proper time,
I will judge uprightly.
³The earth and all its inhabitants are dissolved;
I set up its pillars firmly.   *Selah*

⁴"I said to the boastful, 'Do not deal boastfully,'
And to the wicked, 'Do not lift up the horn.
⁵Do not lift up your horn on high;
Do *not* speak with a stiff neck.' "

⁶For exaltation *comes* neither from the east
Nor from the west nor from the south.
⁷But God *is* the Judge:
He puts down one,
And exalts another.
⁸For in the hand of the LORD *there is* a cup,
And the wine is red;
It is fully mixed, and He pours it out;
Surely its dregs shall all the wicked of the
    earth
Drain *and* drink down.

⁹But I will declare forever,
I will sing praises to the God of Jacob.

¹⁰"All the horns of the wicked I will also cut
    off,
But the horns of the righteous shall be
    exalted."

75:title [a]Hebrew *Al Tashcheth*

LEADERSHIP ISSUES

Promotion Comes from Above

PSALM 75:6, 7

Just mention the word "leadership" and images come to mind of dynamic personalities who give great speeches and motivate others. The people we envision may have great followings and fame, but this is not the picture we see of the Old Testament prophets or the New Testament apostles. To be a leader in biblical times meant persecution, trials, and potentially, death. The biblical leader is one who is compelled or burdened to lead—out of necessity and calling—rather than out of desire to achieve prestige or power. Just look at Jesus and the apostles to see the treatment afforded them by the leaders of the early church.

Consider the ultimate Servant who was not humbled by humankind, but who humbled Himself by choice. That is the key to effective leadership, and Jesus *chose* it. Paul's description of Christ in Philippians 2 tells of the King of creation who became lowly and allowed Himself to be beaten and tortured like a criminal. His crucifixion is the ultimate example of genuine humbling—born out of burden.

If we are to be truly Christlike, our attitude toward leading others should proceed from a heart that longs to minister to others; and that ministering should lead them to be Christ-followers. Any position of authority is one that has been ordained by God Himself (Ps. 75:6, 7; Rom. 13:1–7). He can remove you from leadership at His whim or promote you to influence. As you serve, be aware of pride that creeps in, and try to remove all efforts for position and achievement. If you find that pride, rather than service and sacrifice, has become your motivation for leadership, remove yourself from that position. Through prayer and reflection, keep your priorities in check. God will place you in the right position of leadership at the appropriate time, not a moment sooner. Remember Jeremiah's words to Baruch in Jeremiah 45:5, "And do you seek great things for yourself? Do not seek them."

PSALM 76

THE MAJESTY OF GOD IN JUDGMENT
To the Chief Musician. On stringed instruments.[a]
A Psalm of Asaph. A Song.

[1] In Judah God *is* known;
His name *is* great in Israel.
[2] In Salem[a] also is His tabernacle,
And His dwelling place in Zion.
[3] There He broke the arrows of the bow,
The shield and sword of battle.   *Selah*

[4] You *are* more glorious and excellent
Than the mountains of prey.
[5] The stouthearted were plundered;
They have sunk into their sleep;
And none of the mighty men have found the
use of their hands.
[6] At Your rebuke, O God of Jacob,
Both the chariot and horse were cast into a
dead sleep.

[7] You, Yourself, *are* to be feared;
And who may stand in Your presence
When once You are angry?
[8] You caused judgment to be heard from
heaven;
The earth feared and was still,
[9] When God arose to judgment,
To deliver all the oppressed of the earth. *Selah*

[10] Surely the wrath of man shall praise You;
With the remainder of wrath You shall gird
Yourself.

[11] Make vows to the LORD your God, and pay
them;
Let all who are around Him bring presents to
Him who ought to be feared.
[12] He shall cut off the spirit of princes;
He is awesome to the kings of the earth.

PSALM 77

THE CONSOLING MEMORY OF GOD'S
REDEMPTIVE WORKS
To the Chief Musician. To Jeduthun. A Psalm
of Asaph.

[1] I cried out to God with my voice—
To God with my voice;

And He gave ear to me.
[2] In the day of my trouble I sought the Lord;
My hand was stretched out in the night
without ceasing;
My soul refused to be comforted.
[3] I remembered God, and was troubled;
I complained, and my spirit was
overwhelmed.   *Selah*

[4] You hold my eyelids *open;*
I am so troubled that I cannot speak.
[5] I have considered the days of old,
The years of ancient times.
[6] I call to remembrance my song in the night;
I meditate within my heart,
And my spirit makes diligent search.

[7] Will the Lord cast off forever?
And will He be favorable no more?
[8] Has His mercy ceased forever?
Has *His* promise failed forevermore?
[9] Has God forgotten to be gracious?
Has He in anger shut up His tender
mercies?   *Selah*

[10] And I said, "This *is* my anguish;
But I will remember the years of the right hand
of the Most High."
[11] I will remember the works of the LORD;
Surely I will remember Your wonders of old.
[12] I will also meditate on all Your work,
And talk of Your deeds.
[13] Your way, O God, *is* in the sanctuary;
Who *is* so great a God as *our* God?
[14] You *are* the God who does wonders;
You have declared Your strength among the
peoples.
[15] You have with *Your* arm redeemed Your
people,
The sons of Jacob and Joseph.   *Selah*

[16] The waters saw You, O God;
The waters saw You, they were afraid;
The depths also trembled.
[17] The clouds poured out water;
The skies sent out a sound;
Your arrows also flashed about.

76:title [a]Hebrew *neginoth*   **76:2** [a]That is, Jerusalem

¹⁸The voice of Your thunder *was* in the
    whirlwind;
  The lightnings lit up the world;
  The earth trembled and shook.
¹⁹Your way *was* in the sea,
  Your path in the great waters,
  And Your footsteps were not known.
²⁰You led Your people like a flock
  By the hand of Moses and Aaron.

PSALM 78

<small>GOD'S KINDNESS TO REBELLIOUS ISRAEL</small>
A Contemplation[a] of Asaph.

¹Give ear, O my people, *to* my law;
  Incline your ears to the words of my mouth.
²I will open my mouth in a parable;
  I will utter dark sayings of old,
³Which we have heard and known,
  And our fathers have told us.
⁴We will not hide *them* from their children,
  Telling to the generation to come the praises
    of the LORD,
  And His strength and His wonderful works
    that He has done.

⁵For He established a testimony in Jacob,
  And appointed a law in Israel,
  Which He commanded our fathers,
  That they should make them known to their
    children;
⁶That the generation to come might know
    them,
  The children *who* would be born,
  That they may arise and declare *them* to their
    children,
⁷That they may set their hope in God,
  And not forget the works of God,
  But keep His commandments;
⁸And may not be like their fathers,
  A stubborn and rebellious generation,
  A generation *that* did not set its heart aright,
  And whose spirit was not faithful to God.

⁹The children of Ephraim, *being* armed *and*
    carrying bows,
  Turned back in the day of battle.
¹⁰They did not keep the covenant of God;
  They refused to walk in His law,

¹¹And forgot His works
  And His wonders that He had shown them.

¹²Marvelous things He did in the sight of their
    fathers,
  In the land of Egypt, *in* the field of Zoan.
¹³He divided the sea and caused them to pass
    through;
  And He made the waters stand up like a
    heap.
¹⁴In the daytime also He led them with the
    cloud,
  And all the night with a light of fire.
¹⁵He split the rocks in the wilderness,
  And gave *them* drink in abundance like the
    depths.
¹⁶He also brought streams out of the rock,
  And caused waters to run down like rivers.

¹⁷But they sinned even more against Him
  By rebelling against the Most High in the
    wilderness.
¹⁸And they tested God in their heart
  By asking for the food of their fancy.
¹⁹Yes, they spoke against God:
  They said, "Can God prepare a table in the
    wilderness?
²⁰Behold, He struck the rock,
  So that the waters gushed out,
  And the streams overflowed.
  Can He give bread also?
  Can He provide meat for His people?"

²¹Therefore the LORD heard *this* and was
    furious;
  So a fire was kindled against Jacob,
  And anger also came up against Israel,
²²Because they did not believe in God,
  And did not trust in His salvation.
²³Yet He had commanded the clouds above,
  And opened the doors of heaven,
²⁴Had rained down manna on them to eat,
  And given them of the bread of heaven.
²⁵Men ate angels' food;
  He sent them food to the full.

²⁶He caused an east wind to blow in the
    heavens;

78:title [a]Hebrew *Maschil*

And by His power He brought in the south
wind.
27He also rained meat on them like the dust,
Feathered fowl like the sand of the seas;
28And He let *them* fall in the midst of their
camp,
All around their dwellings.
29So they ate and were well filled,
For He gave them their own desire.
30They were not deprived of their craving;
But while their food *was* still in their mouths,
31The wrath of God came against them,
And slew the stoutest of them,
And struck down the choice *men* of Israel.

32In spite of this they still sinned,
And did not believe in His wondrous works.
33Therefore their days He consumed in futility,
And their years in fear.

34When He slew them, then they sought Him;
And they returned and sought earnestly for
God.
35Then they remembered that God *was* their
rock,
And the Most High God their Redeemer.
36Nevertheless they flattered Him with their
mouth,
And they lied to Him with their tongue;
37For their heart was not steadfast with Him,
Nor were they faithful in His covenant.
38But He, *being* full of compassion, forgave *their*
iniquity,
And did not destroy *them*.
Yes, many a time He turned His anger away,
And did not stir up all His wrath;
39For He remembered that they *were but* flesh,
A breath that passes away and does not come
again.

40How often they provoked Him in the
wilderness,
And grieved Him in the desert!
41Yes, again and again they tempted God,
And limited the Holy One of Israel.
42They did not remember His power:
The day when He redeemed them from the
enemy,
43When He worked His signs in Egypt,

And His wonders in the field of Zoan;
44Turned their rivers into blood,
And their streams, that they could not drink.
45He sent swarms of flies among them, which
devoured them,
And frogs, which destroyed them.
46He also gave their crops to the caterpillar,
And their labor to the locust.
47He destroyed their vines with hail,
And their sycamore trees with frost.
48He also gave up their cattle to the hail,
And their flocks to fiery lightning.
49He cast on them the fierceness of His anger,
Wrath, indignation, and trouble,
By sending angels of destruction *among them*.
50He made a path for His anger;
He did not spare their soul from death,
But gave their life over to the plague;
51And destroyed all the firstborn in Egypt,
The first of *their* strength in the tents of
Ham.
52But He made His own people go forth like
sheep,
And guided them in the wilderness like a
flock;
53And He led them on safely, so that they did
not fear;
But the sea overwhelmed their enemies.
54And He brought them to His holy border,
This mountain *which* His right hand had
acquired.
55He also drove out the nations before them,
Allotted them an inheritance by survey,
And made the tribes of Israel dwell in their
tents.

56Yet they tested and provoked the Most High
God,
And did not keep His testimonies,
57But turned back and acted unfaithfully like
their fathers;
They were turned aside like a deceitful bow.
58For they provoked Him to anger with their
high places,
And moved Him to jealousy with their
carved images.
59When God heard *this*, He was furious,
And greatly abhorred Israel,
60So that He forsook the tabernacle of Shiloh,

The tent He had placed among men,
⁶¹And delivered His strength into captivity,
And His glory into the enemy's hand.
⁶²He also gave His people over to the sword,
And was furious with His inheritance.
⁶³The fire consumed their young men,
And their maidens were not given in
marriage.
⁶⁴Their priests fell by the sword,
And their widows made no lamentation.

⁶⁵Then the Lord awoke as *from* sleep,
Like a mighty man who shouts because of
wine.
⁶⁶And He beat back His enemies;
He put them to a perpetual reproach.

⁶⁷Moreover He rejected the tent of Joseph,
And did not choose the tribe of Ephraim,
⁶⁸But chose the tribe of Judah,
Mount Zion which He loved.
⁶⁹And He built His sanctuary like the heights,
Like the earth which He has established
forever.
⁷⁰He also chose David His servant,
And took him from the sheepfolds;
⁷¹From following the ewes that had young He
brought him,
To shepherd Jacob His people,
And Israel His inheritance.
⁷²So he shepherded them according to the
integrity of his heart,
And guided them by the skillfulness of his
hands.

PSALM 79

A Dirge and a Prayer for Israel, Destroyed
by Enemies
A Psalm of Asaph.

¹O God, the nations have come into Your
inheritance;
Your holy temple they have defiled;
They have laid Jerusalem in heaps.
²The dead bodies of Your servants
They have given *as* food for the birds of the
heavens,
The flesh of Your saints to the beasts of the
earth.

³Their blood they have shed like water all
around Jerusalem,
And *there was* no one to bury *them*.
⁴We have become a reproach to our
neighbors,
A scorn and derision to those who are
around us.

⁵How long, LORD?
Will You be angry forever?
Will Your jealousy burn like fire?
⁶Pour out Your wrath on the nations that do
not know You,
And on the kingdoms that do not call on
Your name.
⁷For they have devoured Jacob,
And laid waste his dwelling place.

⁸Oh, do not remember former iniquities
against us!
Let Your tender mercies come speedily to
meet us,
For we have been brought very low.
⁹Help us, O God of our salvation,
For the glory of Your name;
And deliver us, and provide atonement for
our sins,
For Your name's sake!
¹⁰Why should the nations say,
"Where *is* their God?"
Let there be known among the nations in our
sight
The avenging of the blood of Your servants
which has been shed.

¹¹Let the groaning of the prisoner come before
You;
According to the greatness of Your power
Preserve those who are appointed to die;
¹²And return to our neighbors sevenfold into
their bosom
Their reproach with which they have
reproached You, O Lord.

¹³So we, Your people and sheep of Your
pasture,
Will give You thanks forever;
We will show forth Your praise to all
generations.

PSALM 80

PRAYER FOR ISRAEL'S RESTORATION
To the Chief Musician. Set to "The Lilies."[a]
A Testimony[b] of Asaph. A Psalm.

[1] Give ear, O Shepherd of Israel,
You who lead Joseph like a flock;
You who dwell *between* the cherubim, shine
    forth!
[2] Before Ephraim, Benjamin, and Manasseh,
Stir up Your strength,
And come *and* save us!

[3] Restore us, O God;
Cause Your face to shine,
And we shall be saved!

[4] O LORD God of hosts,
How long will You be angry
Against the prayer of Your people?
[5] You have fed them with the bread of tears,
And given them tears to drink in great
    measure.
[6] You have made us a strife to our neighbors,
And our enemies laugh among themselves.

[7] Restore us, O God of hosts;
Cause Your face to shine,
And we shall be saved!

[8] You have brought a vine out of Egypt;
You have cast out the nations, and planted it.
[9] You prepared *room* for it,
And caused it to take deep root,
And it filled the land.
[10] The hills were covered with its shadow,
And the mighty cedars with its boughs.
[11] She sent out her boughs to the Sea,[a]
And her branches to the River.[b]

[12] Why have You broken down her hedges,
So that all who pass by the way pluck her
    fruit?
[13] The boar out of the woods uproots it,
And the wild beast of the field devours it.

[14] Return, we beseech You, O God of hosts;
Look down from heaven and see,
And visit this vine

[15] And the vineyard which Your right hand has
    planted,
And the branch *that* You made strong for
    Yourself.
[16] *It is* burned with fire, *it is* cut down;
They perish at the rebuke of Your
    countenance.
[17] Let Your hand be upon the man of Your right
    hand,
Upon the son of man *whom* You made strong
    for Yourself.
[18] Then we will not turn back from You;
Revive us, and we will call upon Your name.

[19] Restore us, O LORD God of hosts;
Cause Your face to shine,
And we shall be saved!

PSALM 81

AN APPEAL FOR ISRAEL'S REPENTANCE
To the Chief Musician. On an instrument of
Gath.[a] *A Psalm* of Asaph.

[1] Sing aloud to God our strength;
Make a joyful shout to the God of Jacob.
[2] Raise a song and strike the timbrel,
The pleasant harp with the lute.

[3] Blow the trumpet at the time of the New
    Moon,
At the full moon, on our solemn feast day.
[4] For this *is* a statute for Israel,
A law of the God of Jacob.
[5] This He established in Joseph *as* a testimony,
When He went throughout the land of
    Egypt,
Where I heard a language I did not
    understand.

[6] "I removed his shoulder from the burden;
His hands were freed from the baskets.
[7] You called in trouble, and I delivered you;
I answered you in the secret place of thunder;
I tested you at the waters of Meribah.   *Selah*

[8] "Hear, O My people, and I will admonish you!
O Israel, if you will listen to Me!

80:title [a]Hebrew *Shoshannim* [b]Hebrew *Eduth*   80:11 [a]That is, the Mediterranean [b]That is, the Euphrates   81:title [a]Hebrew *Al Gittith*

9There shall be no foreign god among you;
Nor shall you worship any foreign god.
10I *am* the LORD your God,
Who brought you out of the land of Egypt;
Open your mouth wide, and I will fill it.

11"But My people would not heed My voice,
And Israel would *have* none of Me.
12So I gave them over to their own stubborn
heart,
To walk in their own counsels.

13"Oh, that My people would listen to Me,
That Israel would walk in My ways!
14I would soon subdue their enemies,
And turn My hand against their adversaries.
15The haters of the LORD would pretend
submission to Him,
But their fate would endure forever.
16He would have fed them also with the finest
of wheat;
And with honey from the rock I would have
satisfied you."

PSALM 82

A PLEA FOR JUSTICE
A Psalm of Asaph.

1God stands in the congregation of the
mighty;
He judges among the gods.a
2How long will you judge unjustly,
And show partiality to the wicked?   *Selah*
3Defend the poor and fatherless;
Do justice to the afflicted and needy.
4Deliver the poor and needy;
Free *them* from the hand of the wicked.

5They do not know, nor do they understand;
They walk about in darkness;
All the foundations of the earth are unstable.

6I said, "You *are* gods,a
And all of you *are* children of the Most High.
7But you shall die like men,
And fall like one of the princes."

8Arise, O God, judge the earth;
For You shall inherit all nations.

PSALM 83

PRAYER TO FRUSTRATE CONSPIRACY
AGAINST ISRAEL
A Song. A Psalm of Asaph.

1Do not keep silent, O God!
Do not hold Your peace,
And do not be still, O God!
2For behold, Your enemies make a tumult;
And those who hate You have lifted up their
head.
3They have taken crafty counsel against Your
people,
And consulted together against Your sheltered
ones.
4They have said, "Come, and let us cut them
off from *being* a nation,
That the name of Israel may be remembered
no more."

5For they have consulted together with one
consent;
They form a confederacy against You:
6The tents of Edom and the Ishmaelites;
Moab and the Hagrites;
7Gebal, Ammon, and Amalek;
Philistia with the inhabitants of Tyre;
8Assyria also has joined with them;
They have helped the children of Lot.   *Selah*

9Deal with them as *with* Midian,
As *with* Sisera,
As *with* Jabin at the Brook Kishon,
10Who perished at En Dor,
Who became *as* refuse on the earth.
11Make their nobles like Oreb and like Zeeb,
Yes, all their princes like Zebah and
Zalmunna,
12Who said, "Let us take for ourselves
The pastures of God for a possession."

13O my God, make them like the whirling
dust,
Like the chaff before the wind!
14As the fire burns the woods,
And as the flame sets the mountains on fire,
15So pursue them with Your tempest,

82:1 aHebrew *elohim, mighty ones;* that is, the judges   **82:6** aHebrew *elohim, mighty ones;* that is, the judges

And frighten them with Your storm.
16Fill their faces with shame,
That they may seek Your name, O LORD.
17Let them be confounded and dismayed
forever;
Yes, let them be put to shame and perish,
18That they may know that You, whose name
alone *is* the LORD,
Are the Most High over all the earth.

PSALM 84

THE BLESSEDNESS OF DWELLING IN THE HOUSE
OF GOD

To the Chief Musician. On an instrument of
Gath.ᵃ A Psalm of the sons of Korah.

1How lovely *is* Your tabernacle,
O LORD of hosts!
2My soul longs, yes, even faints
For the courts of the LORD;
My heart and my flesh cry out for the living
God.

3Even the sparrow has found a home,
And the swallow a nest for herself,
Where she may lay her young—
Even Your altars, O LORD of hosts,
My King and my God.
4Blessed *are* those who dwell in Your house;
They will still be praising You.   *Selah*

5Blessed *is* the man whose strength *is* in You,
Whose heart *is* set on pilgrimage.
6*As they* pass through the Valley of Baca,
They make it a spring;
The rain also covers it with pools.
7They go from strength to strength;
Each one appears before God in Zion.ᵃ

8O LORD God of hosts, hear my prayer;
Give ear, O God of Jacob!   *Selah*
9O God, behold our shield,
And look upon the face of Your anointed.

10For a day in Your courts *is* better than a
thousand.
I would rather be a doorkeeper in the house
of my God
Than dwell in the tents of wickedness.

11For the LORD God *is* a sun and shield;
The LORD will give grace and glory;
No good *thing* will He withhold
From those who walk uprightly.

12O LORD of hosts,
Blessed *is* the man who trusts in You!

PSALM 85

PRAYER THAT THE LORD WILL RESTORE FAVOR
TO THE LAND

To the Chief Musician. A Psalm of the sons
of Korah.

1LORD, You have been favorable to Your land;
You have brought back the captivity of Jacob.
2You have forgiven the iniquity of Your
people;
You have covered all their sin.   *Selah*
3You have taken away all Your wrath;
You have turned from the fierceness of Your
anger.

4Restore us, O God of our salvation,
And cause Your anger toward us to cease.
5Will You be angry with us forever?
Will You prolong Your anger to all
generations?
6Will You not revive us again,
That Your people may rejoice in You?
7Show us Your mercy, LORD,
And grant us Your salvation.

8I will hear what God the LORD will speak,
For He will speak peace
To His people and to His saints;
But let them not turn back to folly.
9Surely His salvation *is* near to those who fear
Him,
That glory may dwell in our land.

10Mercy and truth have met together;
Righteousness and peace have kissed.
11Truth shall spring out of the earth,
And righteousness shall look down from
heaven.
12Yes, the LORD will give *what is* good;

84:title ᵃHebrew *Al Gittith* **84:7** ᵃSeptuagint, Syriac, and Vulgate
read *The God of gods shall be seen.*

And our land will yield its increase.
¹³Righteousness will go before Him,
And shall make His footsteps *our* pathway.

PSALM 86

PRAYER FOR MERCY, WITH MEDITATION ON THE
EXCELLENCIES OF THE LORD
A Prayer of David.

¹Bow down Your ear, O LORD, hear me;
For I *am* poor and needy.
²Preserve my life, for I *am* holy;
You are my God;
Save Your servant who trusts in You!
³Be merciful to me, O Lord,
For I cry to You all day long.
⁴Rejoice the soul of Your servant,
For to You, O Lord, I lift up my soul.
⁵For You, Lord, *are* good, and ready to forgive,
And abundant in mercy to all those who call
upon You.

⁶Give ear, O LORD, to my prayer;
And attend to the voice of my supplications.
⁷In the day of my trouble I will call upon You,
For You will answer me.

⁸Among the gods *there is* none like You,
O Lord;
Nor *are there any works* like Your works.
⁹All nations whom You have made
Shall come and worship before You, O Lord,
And shall glorify Your name.
¹⁰For You *are* great, and do wondrous things;
You alone *are* God.

¹¹Teach me Your way, O LORD;
I will walk in Your truth;
Unite my heart to fear Your name.
¹²I will praise You, O Lord my God, with all my
heart,
And I will glorify Your name forevermore.
¹³For great *is* Your mercy toward me,
And You have delivered my soul from the
depths of Sheol.

¹⁴O God, the proud have risen against me,
And a mob of violent *men* have sought my life,
And have not set You before them.

¹⁵But You, O Lord, *are* a God full of
compassion, and gracious,
Longsuffering and abundant in mercy and
truth.

¹⁶Oh, turn to me, and have mercy on me!
Give Your strength to Your servant,
And save the son of Your maidservant.
¹⁷Show me a sign for good,
That those who hate me may see *it* and be
ashamed,
Because You, LORD, have helped me and
comforted me.

PSALM 87

THE GLORIES OF THE CITY OF GOD
A Psalm of the sons of Korah. A Song.

¹His foundation *is* in the holy mountains.
²The LORD loves the gates of Zion
More than all the dwellings of Jacob.
³Glorious things are spoken of you,
O city of God!   *Selah*

⁴"I will make mention of Rahab and Babylon
to those who know Me;
Behold, O Philistia and Tyre, with Ethiopia:
'This *one* was born there.' "

⁵And of Zion it will be said,
"This *one* and that *one* were born in her;
And the Most High Himself shall establish
her."
⁶The LORD will record,
When He registers the peoples:
"This *one* was born there."   *Selah*

⁷Both the singers and the players on
instruments *say,*
"All my springs *are* in you."

PSALM 88

A PRAYER FOR HELP IN DESPONDENCY
A Song. A Psalm of the sons of Korah. To the
Chief Musician. Set to "Mahalath Leannoth."
A Contemplation[a] of Heman the Ezrahite.

¹O LORD, God of my salvation,
I have cried out day and night before You.

88:title [a]Hebrew *Maschil*

LEADERSHIP ISSUES

GC2: Openness with Emotion

PSALM 88:1, 2

As you read this entire Psalm, notice how vulnerable the psalmist is with the Lord. We should be honest and vulnerable with God about our joys, anxieties, fears, and hurts. Our emotions are not a surprise to God, so why not share with Him how we are feeling?

We also need to share our emotions with other people. We all need friends with whom we can share our emotions—people with whom we can be open, transparent, and vulnerable and who will care about how we feel and respond appropriately.

A great place to start in sharing our heartfelt emotions with God and others is to develop a "feeling vocabulary." Review the six scenes below and consider what emotions you might experience in each.

- *Today when I left school, it was raining. When I reached the sidewalk, I slipped and fell right in front of everyone. I felt* _____.

- *I went to lunch with three friends from school that I haven't seen since summer break. Not once in the conversation did anyone ask about me. I felt* _____.

- *As I think about my growing up, I've always known my mom and dad love each other and are committed to each other for life. I feel* _____.

- *I worked for days on the school auction. I never heard a "good job" or even a "we appreciate you." I feel* _____.

- *My mother passed away a year ago today. I really miss her. I feel* _____.

- *I worked hard to get a part in the school play. I found out today I got the lead role. I feel* _____.

Begin sharing your heart and emotions openly with the Lord and with those close to you. Being vulnerable and biblical with your emotions will help prepare you for healthy, God-honoring relationships.

GC2
GREAT COMMANDMENT
COMMISSION

²Let my prayer come before You;
  Incline Your ear to my cry.

³For my soul is full of troubles,
  And my life draws near to the grave.
⁴I am counted with those who go down to
    the pit;
  I am like a man *who has* no strength,
⁵Adrift among the dead,
  Like the slain who lie in the grave,
  Whom You remember no more,
  And who are cut off from Your hand.

⁶You have laid me in the lowest pit,
  In darkness, in the depths.
⁷Your wrath lies heavy upon me,
  And You have afflicted *me* with all Your
    waves.   *Selah*
⁸You have put away my acquaintances far from
    me;
  You have made me an abomination to them;
  I am shut up, and I cannot get out;
⁹My eye wastes away because of affliction.

LORD, I have called daily upon You;
  I have stretched out my hands to You.
¹⁰Will You work wonders for the dead?
  Shall the dead arise *and* praise You?   *Selah*
¹¹Shall Your lovingkindness be declared in the
    grave?
  Or Your faithfulness in the place of
    destruction?
¹²Shall Your wonders be known in the dark?
  And Your righteousness in the land of
    forgetfulness?

¹³But to You I have cried out, O LORD,
  And in the morning my prayer comes before
    You.
¹⁴LORD, why do You cast off my soul?
  Why do You hide Your face from me?
¹⁵I *have been* afflicted and ready to die from *my*
    youth;
  I suffer Your terrors;
  I am distraught.
¹⁶Your fierce wrath has gone over me;
  Your terrors have cut me off.
¹⁷They came around me all day long like water;
  They engulfed me altogether.

¹⁸Loved one and friend You have put far from
    me,
  And my acquaintances into darkness.

PSALM 89

REMEMBERING THE COVENANT WITH DAVID, AND
SORROW FOR LOST BLESSINGS
A Contemplation[a] of Ethan the Ezrahite.

¹I will sing of the mercies of the LORD forever;
  With my mouth will I make known Your
    faithfulness to all generations.
²For I have said, "Mercy shall be built up
    forever;
  Your faithfulness You shall establish in the
    very heavens."

³"I have made a covenant with My chosen,
  I have sworn to My servant David:
⁴'Your seed I will establish forever,
  And build up your throne to all
    generations.' "   *Selah*

⁵And the heavens will praise Your wonders,
    O LORD;
  Your faithfulness also in the assembly of the
    saints.
⁶For who in the heavens can be compared to
    the LORD?
  Who among the sons of the mighty can be
    likened to the LORD?
⁷God is greatly to be feared in the assembly of
    the saints,
  And to be held in reverence by all *those*
    around Him.
⁸O LORD God of hosts,
  Who *is* mighty like You, O LORD?
  Your faithfulness also surrounds You.
⁹You rule the raging of the sea;
  When its waves rise, You still them.
¹⁰You have broken Rahab in pieces, as one
    who is slain;
  You have scattered Your enemies with Your
    mighty arm.

¹¹The heavens *are* Yours, the earth also *is* Yours;
  The world and all its fullness, You have
    founded them.

89:title ªHebrew *Maschil*

¹²The north and the south, You have created
   them;
   Tabor and Hermon rejoice in Your name.
¹³You have a mighty arm;
   Strong is Your hand, *and* high is Your right
   hand.
¹⁴Righteousness and justice *are* the foundation
   of Your throne;
   Mercy and truth go before Your face.
¹⁵Blessed *are* the people who know the joyful
   sound!
   They walk, O LORD, in the light of Your
   countenance.
¹⁶In Your name they rejoice all day long,
   And in Your righteousness they are exalted.
¹⁷For You *are* the glory of their strength,
   And in Your favor our horn is exalted.
¹⁸For our shield *belongs* to the LORD,
   And our king to the Holy One of Israel.

¹⁹Then You spoke in a vision to Your holy one,ª
   And said: "I have given help to *one who is*
   mighty;
   I have exalted one chosen from the people.
²⁰I have found My servant David;
   With My holy oil I have anointed him,
²¹With whom My hand shall be established;
   Also My arm shall strengthen him.
²²The enemy shall not outwit him,
   Nor the son of wickedness afflict him.
²³I will beat down his foes before his face,
   And plague those who hate him.

²⁴"But My faithfulness and My mercy *shall be*
   with him,
   And in My name his horn shall be exalted.
²⁵Also I will set his hand over the sea,
   And his right hand over the rivers.
²⁶He shall cry to Me, 'You *are* my Father,
   My God, and the rock of my salvation.'
²⁷Also I will make him *My* firstborn,
   The highest of the kings of the earth.
²⁸My mercy I will keep for him forever,
   And My covenant shall stand firm with him.
²⁹His seed also I will make to *endure* forever,
   And his throne as the days of heaven.

³⁰"If his sons forsake My law
   And do not walk in My judgments,

³¹If they break My statutes
   And do not keep My commandments,
³²Then I will punish their transgression with
   the rod,
   And their iniquity with stripes.
³³Nevertheless My lovingkindness I will not
   utterly take from him,
   Nor allow My faithfulness to fail.
³⁴My covenant I will not break,
   Nor alter the word that has gone out of My
   lips.
³⁵Once I have sworn by My holiness;
   I will not lie to David:
³⁶His seed shall endure forever,
   And his throne as the sun before Me;
³⁷It shall be established forever like the moon,
   Even *like* the faithful witness in the
   sky."   *Selah*

³⁸But You have cast off and abhorred,
   You have been furious with Your anointed.
³⁹You have renounced the covenant of Your
   servant;
   You have profaned his crown *by casting it* to
   the ground.
⁴⁰You have broken down all his hedges;
   You have brought his strongholds to ruin.
⁴¹All who pass by the way plunder him;
   He is a reproach to his neighbors.
⁴²You have exalted the right hand of his
   adversaries;
   You have made all his enemies rejoice.
⁴³You have also turned back the edge of his
   sword,
   And have not sustained him in the battle.
⁴⁴You have made his glory cease,
   And cast his throne down to the ground.
⁴⁵The days of his youth You have shortened;
   You have covered him with shame.   *Selah*

⁴⁶How long, LORD?
   Will You hide Yourself forever?
   Will Your wrath burn like fire?
⁴⁷Remember how short my time is;
   For what futility have You created all the
   children of men?
⁴⁸What man can live and not see death?

89:19 ªFollowing many Hebrew manuscripts; Masoretic Text, Septuagint, Targum, and Vulgate read *holy ones.*

Can he deliver his life from the power of the
  grave?   *Selah*

⁴⁹Lord, where *are* Your former lovingkindnesses,
  Which You swore to David in Your truth?
⁵⁰Remember, Lord, the reproach of Your
  servants—
  How I bear in my bosom *the reproach of* all the
  many peoples,
⁵¹With which Your enemies have reproached,
  O LORD,
  With which they have reproached the
  footsteps of Your anointed.

⁵²Blessed *be* the LORD forevermore!
  Amen and Amen.

Book Four: Psalms 90—106

PSALM 90

THE ETERNITY OF GOD, AND MAN'S FRAILTY
  A Prayer of Moses the man of God.

¹Lord, You have been our dwelling placeᵃ in all
  generations.
²Before the mountains were brought forth,
  Or ever You had formed the earth and the
  world,
  Even from everlasting to everlasting, You *are*
  God.

³You turn man to destruction,
  And say, "Return, O children of men."

⁴For a thousand years in Your sight
  Are like yesterday when it is past,
  And *like* a watch in the night.
⁵You carry them away *like* a flood;
  They are like a sleep.
  In the morning they are like grass *which*
  grows up:
⁶In the morning it flourishes and grows up;
  In the evening it is cut down and withers.

⁷For we have been consumed by Your anger,
  And by Your wrath we are terrified.
⁸You have set our iniquities before You,
  Our secret *sins* in the light of Your
  countenance.
⁹For all our days have passed away in Your
  wrath;
  We finish our years like a sigh.
¹⁰The days of our lives *are* seventy years;
  And if by reason of strength *they are* eighty
  years,
  Yet their boast *is* only labor and sorrow;
  For it is soon cut off, and we fly away.
¹¹Who knows the power of Your anger?
  For as the fear of You, *so is* Your wrath.
¹²So teach *us* to number our days,
  That we may gain a heart of wisdom.

¹³Return, O LORD!
  How long?

90:1 ᵃSeptuagint, Targum, and Vulgate read *refuge*.

THROUGH THE GRID

*Making Sense of Your World:
Confronting God and Ultimate Reality
(Ps. 90)*

The matter of "ultimate reality" is at the core of our existence. This is the question of what is really real and why anything matters. Everyone must deal with this question at some point in their lives. Atheists must still grapple with whether there is a God, and they must decide for themselves why or why not. An atheist must still answer questions concerning how the universe came into being and about what their purpose in the universe must be, along with questions of morality. Christians not only acknowledge the existence of God but also develop their worldview by coming to know about the God in whom they believe; thus, they, too, must answer questions regarding the existence of God and God's involvement in the universe and in their lives.

And have compassion on Your servants.
¹⁴Oh, satisfy us early with Your mercy,
  That we may rejoice and be glad all our days!
¹⁵Make us glad according to the days *in which*
      You have afflicted us,
  The years *in which* we have seen evil.
¹⁶Let Your work appear to Your servants,
  And Your glory to their children.
¹⁷And let the beauty of the Lᴏʀᴅ our God be
      upon us,
  And establish the work of our hands for us;
  Yes, establish the work of our hands.

PSALM 91

Sᴀғᴇᴛʏ ᴏғ Aʙɪᴅɪɴɢ ɪɴ ᴛʜᴇ Pʀᴇsᴇɴᴄᴇ ᴏғ Gᴏᴅ

¹He who dwells in the secret place of the
      Most High
  Shall abide under the shadow of the
      Almighty.
²I will say of the Lᴏʀᴅ, "*He is* my refuge and
      my fortress;
  My God, in Him I will trust."

³Surely He shall deliver you from the snare of
      the fowlerᵃ
  And from the perilous pestilence.
⁴He shall cover you with His feathers,
  And under His wings you shall take refuge;
  His truth *shall be your* shield and buckler.
⁵You shall not be afraid of the terror by night,
  Nor of the arrow *that* flies by day,
⁶*Nor* of the pestilence *that* walks in darkness,
  Nor of the destruction *that* lays waste at
      noonday.

⁷A thousand may fall at your side,
  And ten thousand at your right hand;
  But it shall not come near you.
⁸Only with your eyes shall you look,
  And see the reward of the wicked.

⁹Because you have made the Lᴏʀᴅ, *who is* my
      refuge,
  Even the Most High, your dwelling place,
¹⁰No evil shall befall you,
  Nor shall any plague come near your
      dwelling;
¹¹For He shall give His angels charge over you,

To keep you in all your ways.
¹²In *their* hands they shall bear you up,
  Lest you dash your foot against a stone.
¹³You shall tread upon the lion and the cobra,
  The young lion and the serpent you shall
      trample underfoot.

¹⁴"Because he has set his love upon Me,
      therefore I will deliver him;
  I will set him on high, because he has known
      My name.
¹⁵He shall call upon Me, and I will answer him;
  I *will be* with him in trouble;
  I will deliver him and honor him.
¹⁶With long life I will satisfy him,
  And show him My salvation."

PSALM 92

Pʀᴀɪsᴇ ᴛᴏ ᴛʜᴇ Lᴏʀᴅ ғᴏʀ Hɪs Lᴏᴠᴇ ᴀɴᴅ
Fᴀɪᴛʜғᴜʟɴᴇss
A Psalm. A Song for the Sabbath day.

¹*It is* good to give thanks to the Lᴏʀᴅ,
  And to sing praises to Your name, O Most
      High;
²To declare Your lovingkindness in the
      morning,
  And Your faithfulness every night,
³On an instrument of ten strings,
  On the lute,
  And on the harp,
  With harmonious sound.
⁴For You, Lᴏʀᴅ, have made me glad through
      Your work;
  I will triumph in the works of Your hands.

⁵O Lᴏʀᴅ, how great are Your works!
  Your thoughts are very deep.
⁶A senseless man does not know,
  Nor does a fool understand this.
⁷When the wicked spring up like grass,
  And when all the workers of iniquity
      flourish,
  It is that they may be destroyed forever.

⁸But You, Lᴏʀᴅ, *are* on high forevermore.
⁹For behold, Your enemies, O Lᴏʀᴅ,

91:3 ᵃThat is, one who catches birds in a trap or snare

For behold, Your enemies shall perish;
All the workers of iniquity shall be scattered.

[10]But my horn You have exalted like a wild ox;
I have been anointed with fresh oil.
[11]My eye also has seen *my desire* on my
enemies;
My ears hear *my desire* on the wicked
Who rise up against me.

[12]The righteous shall flourish like a palm tree,
He shall grow like a cedar in Lebanon.
[13]Those who are planted in the house of the
LORD
Shall flourish in the courts of our God.
[14]They shall still bear fruit in old age;
They shall be fresh and flourishing,
[15]To declare that the LORD is upright;
He is my rock, and *there is* no unrighteousness
in Him.

PSALM 93

THE ETERNAL REIGN OF THE LORD

[1]The LORD reigns, He is clothed with
majesty;
The LORD is clothed,
He has girded Himself with strength.
Surely the world is established, so that it
cannot be moved.
[2]Your throne *is* established from of old;
You *are* from everlasting.

[3]The floods have lifted up, O LORD,
The floods have lifted up their voice;
The floods lift up their waves.
[4]The LORD on high *is* mightier
Than the noise of many waters,
Than the mighty waves of the sea.

[5]Your testimonies are very sure;
Holiness adorns Your house,
O LORD, forever.

PSALM 94

GOD THE REFUGE OF THE RIGHTEOUS

[1]O LORD God, to whom vengeance
belongs—

O God, to whom vengeance belongs, shine
forth!
[2]Rise up, O Judge of the earth;
Render punishment to the proud.
[3]LORD, how long will the wicked,
How long will the wicked triumph?

[4]They utter speech, *and* speak insolent things;
All the workers of iniquity boast in
themselves.
[5]They break in pieces Your people, O LORD,
And afflict Your heritage.
[6]They slay the widow and the stranger,
And murder the fatherless.
[7]Yet they say, "The LORD does not see,
Nor does the God of Jacob understand."

[8]Understand, you senseless among the
people;
And *you* fools, when will you be wise?
[9]He who planted the ear, shall He not hear?
He who formed the eye, shall He not see?
[10]He who instructs the nations, shall He not
correct,
He who teaches man knowledge?
[11]The LORD knows the thoughts of man,
That they *are* futile.

[12]Blessed *is* the man whom You instruct,
O LORD,
And teach out of Your law,
[13]That You may give him rest from the days of
adversity,
Until the pit is dug for the wicked.
[14]For the LORD will not cast off His people,
Nor will He forsake His inheritance.
[15]But judgment will return to righteousness,
And all the upright in heart will follow it.

[16]Who will rise up for me against the
evildoers?
Who will stand up for me against the workers
of iniquity?
[17]Unless the LORD *had been* my help,
My soul would soon have settled in silence.
[18]If I say, "My foot slips,"
Your mercy, O LORD, will hold me up.
[19]In the multitude of my anxieties within me,
Your comforts delight my soul.

²⁰Shall the throne of iniquity, which devises evil by law,
Have fellowship with You?
²¹They gather together against the life of the righteous,
And condemn innocent blood.
²²But the LORD has been my defense,
And my God the rock of my refuge.
²³He has brought on them their own iniquity,
And shall cut them off in their own wickedness;
The LORD our God shall cut them off.

PSALM 95

A CALL TO WORSHIP AND OBEDIENCE

¹Oh come, let us sing to the LORD!
Let us shout joyfully to the Rock of our salvation.
²Let us come before His presence with thanksgiving;
Let us shout joyfully to Him with psalms.
³For the LORD *is* the great God,
And the great King above all gods.
⁴In His hand *are* the deep places of the earth;
The heights of the hills *are* His also.
⁵The sea *is* His, for He made it;
And His hands formed the dry *land*.

⁶Oh come, let us worship and bow down;
Let us kneel before the LORD our Maker.
⁷For He *is* our God,
And we *are* the people of His pasture,
And the sheep of His hand.

Today, if you will hear His voice:
⁸"Do not harden your hearts, as in the rebellion,^a
As *in* the day of trial^b in the wilderness,
⁹When your fathers tested Me;
They tried Me, though they saw My work.
¹⁰For forty years I was grieved with *that* generation,
And said, 'It *is* a people who go astray in their hearts,
And they do not know My ways.'
¹¹So I swore in My wrath,
'They shall not enter My rest.' "

PSALM 96

A SONG OF PRAISE TO GOD COMING IN JUDGMENT

¹Oh, sing to the LORD a new song!
Sing to the LORD, all the earth.
²Sing to the LORD, bless His name;
Proclaim the good news of His salvation from day to day.
³Declare His glory among the nations,
His wonders among all peoples.

⁴For the LORD *is* great and greatly to be praised;
He *is* to be feared above all gods.
⁵For all the gods of the peoples *are* idols,
But the LORD made the heavens.
⁶Honor and majesty *are* before Him;
Strength and beauty *are* in His sanctuary.

⁷Give to the LORD, O families of the peoples,
Give to the LORD glory and strength.
⁸Give to the LORD the glory *due* His name;
Bring an offering, and come into His courts.
⁹Oh, worship the LORD in the beauty of holiness!
Tremble before Him, all the earth.

¹⁰Say among the nations, "The LORD reigns;
The world also is firmly established,
It shall not be moved;
He shall judge the peoples righteously."

¹¹Let the heavens rejoice, and let the earth be glad;
Let the sea roar, and all its fullness;
¹²Let the field be joyful, and all that *is* in it.
Then all the trees of the woods will rejoice
¹³before the LORD.
For He is coming, for He is coming to judge the earth.
He shall judge the world with righteousness,
And the peoples with His truth.

PSALM 97

A SONG OF PRAISE TO THE SOVEREIGN LORD

¹The LORD reigns;
Let the earth rejoice;
Let the multitude of isles be glad!

95:8 ^aOr *Meribah* ^bOr *Massah*

²Clouds and darkness surround Him;
Righteousness and justice *are* the foundation
of His throne.
³A fire goes before Him,
And burns up His enemies round about.
⁴His lightnings light the world;
The earth sees and trembles.
⁵The mountains melt like wax at the presence
of the LORD,
At the presence of the Lord of the whole
earth.
⁶The heavens declare His righteousness,
And all the peoples see His glory.

⁷Let all be put to shame who serve carved
images,
Who boast of idols.
Worship Him, all *you* gods.
⁸Zion hears and is glad,
And the daughters of Judah rejoice
Because of Your judgments, O LORD.
⁹For You, LORD, *are* most high above all the
earth;
You are exalted far above all gods.

¹⁰You who love the LORD, hate evil!
He preserves the souls of His saints;
He delivers them out of the hand of the
wicked.
¹¹Light is sown for the righteous,
And gladness for the upright in heart.
¹²Rejoice in the LORD, you righteous,
And give thanks at the remembrance of His
holy name.ª

PSALM 98

A SONG OF PRAISE TO THE LORD FOR HIS
SALVATION AND JUDGMENT
A Psalm.

¹Oh, sing to the LORD a new song!
For He has done marvelous things;
His right hand and His holy arm have gained
Him the victory.
²The LORD has made known His salvation;
His righteousness He has revealed in the sight
of the nations.
³He has remembered His mercy and His
faithfulness to the house of Israel;

All the ends of the earth have seen the
salvation of our God.

⁴Shout joyfully to the LORD, all the earth;
Break forth in song, rejoice, and sing praises.
⁵Sing to the LORD with the harp,
With the harp and the sound of a psalm,
⁶With trumpets and the sound of a horn;
Shout joyfully before the LORD, the King.

⁷Let the sea roar, and all its fullness,
The world and those who dwell in it;
⁸Let the rivers clap *their* hands;
Let the hills be joyful together
⁹before the LORD,
For He is coming to judge the earth.
With righteousness He shall judge the world,
And the peoples with equity.

PSALM 99

PRAISE TO THE LORD FOR HIS HOLINESS

¹The LORD reigns;
Let the peoples tremble!
He dwells *between* the cherubim;
Let the earth be moved!
²The LORD *is* great in Zion,
And He *is* high above all the peoples.
³Let them praise Your great and awesome
name—
He *is* holy.

⁴The King's strength also loves justice;
You have established equity;
You have executed justice and righteousness
in Jacob.
⁵Exalt the LORD our God,
And worship at His footstool—
He *is* holy.

⁶Moses and Aaron were among His priests,
And Samuel was among those who called
upon His name;
They called upon the LORD, and He
answered them.
⁷He spoke to them in the cloudy pillar;
They kept His testimonies and the ordinance
He gave them.

97:12 ªOr *His holiness*

[8]You answered them, O LORD our God;
You were to them God-Who-Forgives,
Though You took vengeance on their deeds.
[9]Exalt the LORD our God,
And worship at His holy hill;
For the LORD our God *is* holy.

PSALM 100

A SONG OF PRAISE FOR THE FAITHFULNESS TO
HIS PEOPLE
A Psalm of Thanksgiving.

[1]Make a joyful shout to the LORD, all you
lands!
[2]Serve the LORD with gladness;
Come before His presence with singing.
[3]Know that the LORD, He *is* God;
It is He *who* has made us, and not we
ourselves;[a]
We are His people and the sheep of His
pasture.

[4]Enter into His gates with thanksgiving,
And into His courts with praise.
Be thankful to Him, *and* bless His name.
[5]For the LORD *is* good;
His mercy *is* everlasting,
And His truth *endures* to all generations.

PSALM 101

PROMISED FAITHFULNESS TO THE LORD
A Psalm of David.

[1]I will sing of mercy and justice;
To You, O LORD, I will sing praises.

[2]I will behave wisely in a perfect way.
Oh, when will You come to me?
I will walk within my house with a perfect
heart.

[3]I will set nothing wicked before my eyes;
I hate the work of those who fall away;
It shall not cling to me.
[4]A perverse heart shall depart from me;
I will not know wickedness.

[5]Whoever secretly slanders his neighbor,
Him I will destroy;

The one who has a haughty look and a proud
heart,
Him I will not endure.

[6]My eyes *shall be* on the faithful of the land,
That they may dwell with me;
He who walks in a perfect way,
He shall serve me.
[7]He who works deceit shall not dwell within
my house;
He who tells lies shall not continue in my
presence.
[8]Early I will destroy all the wicked of the land,
That I may cut off all the evildoers from the
city of the LORD.

PSALM 102

THE LORD'S ETERNAL LOVE
A Prayer of the afflicted, when he is overwhelmed
and pours out his complaint before the LORD.

[1]Hear my prayer, O LORD,
And let my cry come to You.
[2]Do not hide Your face from me in the day of
my trouble;
Incline Your ear to me;
In the day that I call, answer me speedily.

[3]For my days are consumed like smoke,
And my bones are burned like a hearth.
[4]My heart is stricken and withered like grass,
So that I forget to eat my bread.
[5]Because of the sound of my groaning
My bones cling to my skin.
[6]I am like a pelican of the wilderness;
I am like an owl of the desert.
[7]I lie awake,
And am like a sparrow alone on the
housetop.

[8]My enemies reproach me all day long;
Those who deride me swear an oath against
me.
[9]For I have eaten ashes like bread,
And mingled my drink with weeping,
[10]Because of Your indignation and Your wrath;
For You have lifted me up and cast me away.

100:3 [a]Following Kethib, Septuagint, and Vulgate; Qere, many Hebrew manuscripts, and Targum read *we are His.*

¹¹My days *are* like a shadow that lengthens,
And I wither away like grass.

¹²But You, O LORD, shall endure forever,
And the remembrance of Your name to all
generations.
¹³You will arise *and* have mercy on Zion;
For the time to favor her,
Yes, the set time, has come.
¹⁴For Your servants take pleasure in her stones,
And show favor to her dust.
¹⁵So the nations shall fear the name of the
LORD,
And all the kings of the earth Your glory.
¹⁶For the LORD shall build up Zion;
He shall appear in His glory.
¹⁷He shall regard the prayer of the destitute,
And shall not despise their prayer.

¹⁸This will be written for the generation to
come,
That a people yet to be created may praise
the LORD.
¹⁹For He looked down from the height of His
sanctuary;
From heaven the LORD viewed the earth,
²⁰To hear the groaning of the prisoner,
To release those appointed to death,
²¹To declare the name of the LORD in Zion,
And His praise in Jerusalem,
²²When the peoples are gathered together,
And the kingdoms, to serve the LORD.

²³He weakened my strength in the way;
He shortened my days.
²⁴I said, "O my God,
Do not take me away in the midst of my days;
Your years *are* throughout all generations.
²⁵Of old You laid the foundation of the earth,
And the heavens *are* the work of Your hands.
²⁶They will perish, but You will endure;
Yes, they will all grow old like a garment;
Like a cloak You will change them,
And they will be changed.
²⁷But You *are* the same,
And Your years will have no end.
²⁸The children of Your servants will continue,
And their descendants will be established
before You."

PSALM 103

PRAISE FOR THE LORD'S MERCIES
A Psalm of David.

¹Bless the LORD, O my soul;
And all that is within me, *bless* His holy name!
²Bless the LORD, O my soul,
And forget not all His benefits:
³Who forgives all your iniquities,
Who heals all your diseases,
⁴Who redeems your life from destruction,
Who crowns you with lovingkindness and
tender mercies,
⁵Who satisfies your mouth with good *things,*
So *that* your youth is renewed like the eagle's.

⁶The LORD executes righteousness
And justice for all who are oppressed.
⁷He made known His ways to Moses,
His acts to the children of Israel.
⁸The LORD *is* merciful and gracious,
Slow to anger, and abounding in mercy.
⁹He will not always strive *with us,*
Nor will He keep *His anger* forever.
¹⁰He has not dealt with us according to our
sins,
Nor punished us according to our iniquities.

¹¹For as the heavens are high above the earth,
So great is His mercy toward those who fear
Him;
¹²As far as the east is from the west,
So far has He removed our transgressions
from us.
¹³As a father pities *his* children,
So the LORD pities those who fear Him.
¹⁴For He knows our frame;
He remembers that we *are* dust.

¹⁵*As for* man, his days *are* like grass;
As a flower of the field, so he flourishes.
¹⁶For the wind passes over it, and it is gone,
And its place remembers it no more.ᵃ
¹⁷But the mercy of the LORD *is* from
everlasting to everlasting
On those who fear Him,
And His righteousness to children's children,
¹⁸To such as keep His covenant,

103:16 ᵃCompare Job 7:10

LEADERSHIP ISSUES

GC2: Faith Is Expectant

PSALM 103:2

Faithful followers of God fully expect Him to "show up." They remain mindful of the ways in which He has provided and intervened in the past. Faith-filled disciples declare what *can* happen and what God *can* do, rather than focusing on all the reasons why things will not work out. In short, they are looking for God's "benefits"!

Recall Christ's gathering with His followers in the Upper Room (John 13). It was only hours before His betrayal, torment, and death. He would soon "become sin" at Calvary (John 18, 19; 2 Cor. 5:21), but notice Christ's **expectant** faith: "Jesus, knowing that the Father had given all things into His hands, and that He had come from God and was going to God . . . " (John 13:3).

- Notice where His focus is **not:** He is not focused on self, circumstances, or what He does *not* have.
- Notice where His focus **is:** He is focused on His Father and what the Father has given Him and promised Him.

How might your own focus need to change in order to encourage the development of mature faith?

It will be important for my focus to move from _____ *to* _____
_____ *as the Spirit reminds me of* _____
_____.

(For example: *It will be important for my focus to move from what I wish I had—such as more money or a better job—to gratefulness for all God has provided as the Spirit reminds me of God's total faithfulness to meet all my needs.*)

Pause to celebrate His many benefits in your life and then expectantly look for His next blessing!

GC2
GREAT COMMANDMENT
COMMISSION

And to those who remember His
   commandments to do them.

19The LORD has established His throne in
   heaven,
And His kingdom rules over all.

20Bless the LORD, you His angels,
   Who excel in strength, who do His word,
   Heeding the voice of His word.
21Bless the LORD, all *you* His hosts,
   You ministers of His, who do His pleasure.
22Bless the LORD, all His works,
   In all places of His dominion.

Bless the LORD, O my soul!

PSALM 104

PRAISE TO THE SOVEREIGN LORD FOR HIS
CREATION AND PROVIDENCE

1Bless the LORD, O my soul!

O LORD my God, You are very great:
   You are clothed with honor and majesty,
2Who cover *Yourself* with light as *with* a
   garment,
Who stretch out the heavens like a curtain.

3He lays the beams of His upper chambers in
   the waters,
Who makes the clouds His chariot,
Who walks on the wings of the wind,
4Who makes His angels spirits,
   His ministers a flame of fire.

5*You who* laid the foundations of the earth,
   So *that* it should not be moved forever,
6You covered it with the deep as *with* a
   garment;
The waters stood above the mountains.
7At Your rebuke they fled;
   At the voice of Your thunder they hastened
   away.
8They went up over the mountains;
   They went down into the valleys,
   To the place which You founded for them.
9You have set a boundary that they may not
   pass over,
   That they may not return to cover the earth.

10He sends the springs into the valleys;
   They flow among the hills.
11They give drink to every beast of the field;
   The wild donkeys quench their thirst.
12By them the birds of the heavens have their
   home;
   They sing among the branches.
13He waters the hills from His upper chambers;
   The earth is satisfied with the fruit of Your
   works.

14He causes the grass to grow for the cattle,
   And vegetation for the service of man,
   That he may bring forth food from the earth,
15And wine *that* makes glad the heart of man,
   Oil to make *his* face shine,
   And bread *which* strengthens man's heart.
16The trees of the LORD are full *of sap,*
   The cedars of Lebanon which He planted,
17Where the birds make their nests;
   The stork has her home in the fir trees.
18The high hills *are* for the wild goats;
   The cliffs are a refuge for the rock badgers.[a]

19He appointed the moon for seasons;
   The sun knows its going down.
20You make darkness, and it is night,
   In which all the beasts of the forest creep
   about.
21The young lions roar after their prey,
   And seek their food from God.
22*When* the sun rises, they gather together
   And lie down in their dens.
23Man goes out to his work
   And to his labor until the evening.

24O LORD, how manifold are Your works!
   In wisdom You have made them all.
   The earth is full of Your possessions—
25This great and wide sea,
   In which *are* innumerable teeming things,
   Living things both small and great.
26There the ships sail about;
   There is that Leviathan
   Which You have made to play there.

27These all wait for You,
   That You may give *them* their food in due
   season.

104:18 aOr *rock hyrax* (compare Leviticus 11:5)

²⁸*What* You give them they gather in;
   You open Your hand, they are filled with
      good.
²⁹You hide Your face, they are troubled;
   You take away their breath, they die and
      return to their dust.
³⁰You send forth Your Spirit, they are created;
   And You renew the face of the earth.

³¹May the glory of the LORD endure forever;
   May the LORD rejoice in His works.
³²He looks on the earth, and it trembles;
   He touches the hills, and they smoke.

³³I will sing to the LORD as long as I live;
   I will sing praise to my God while I have my
      being.
³⁴May my meditation be sweet to Him;
   I will be glad in the LORD.
³⁵May sinners be consumed from the earth,
   And the wicked be no more.

Bless the LORD, O my soul!
Praise the LORD!

PSALM 105

THE ETERNAL FAITHFULNESS OF THE LORD

¹Oh, give thanks to the LORD!
   Call upon His name;
   Make known His deeds among the peoples!
²Sing to Him, sing psalms to Him;
   Talk of all His wondrous works!
³Glory in His holy name;
   Let the hearts of those rejoice who seek the
      LORD!
⁴Seek the LORD and His strength;
   Seek His face evermore!
⁵Remember His marvelous works which He
      has done,
   His wonders, and the judgments of His mouth,
⁶O seed of Abraham His servant,
   You children of Jacob, His chosen ones!

⁷He *is* the LORD our God;
   His judgments *are* in all the earth.
⁸He remembers His covenant forever,
   The word *which* He commanded, for a
      thousand generations,

⁹*The covenant* which He made with Abraham,
   And His oath to Isaac,
¹⁰And confirmed it to Jacob for a statute,
   To Israel *as* an everlasting covenant,
¹¹Saying, "To you I will give the land of
      Canaan
   As the allotment of your inheritance,"
¹²When they were few in number,
   Indeed very few, and strangers in it.

¹³When they went from one nation to another,
   From *one* kingdom to another people,
¹⁴He permitted no one to do them wrong;
   Yes, He rebuked kings for their sakes,
¹⁵*Saying,* "Do not touch My anointed ones,
   And do My prophets no harm."

¹⁶Moreover He called for a famine in the land;
   He destroyed all the provision of bread.
¹⁷He sent a man before them—
   Joseph—*who* was sold as a slave.
¹⁸They hurt his feet with fetters,
   He was laid in irons.
¹⁹Until the time that his word came to pass,
   The word of the LORD tested him.
²⁰The king sent and released him,
   The ruler of the people let him go free.
²¹He made him lord of his house,
   And ruler of all his possessions,
²²To bind his princes at his pleasure,
   And teach his elders wisdom.

²³Israel also came into Egypt,
   And Jacob dwelt in the land of Ham.
²⁴He increased His people greatly,
   And made them stronger than their enemies.
²⁵He turned their heart to hate His people,
   To deal craftily with His servants.

²⁶He sent Moses His servant,
   And Aaron whom He had chosen.
²⁷They performed His signs among them,
   And wonders in the land of Ham.
²⁸He sent darkness, and made *it* dark;
   And they did not rebel against His word.
²⁹He turned their waters into blood,
   And killed their fish.
³⁰Their land abounded with frogs,
   Even in the chambers of their kings.

³¹He spoke, and there came swarms of flies,
And lice in all their territory.
³²He gave them hail for rain,
And flaming fire in their land.
³³He struck their vines also, and their fig trees,
And splintered the trees of their territory.
³⁴He spoke, and locusts came,
Young locusts without number,
³⁵And ate up all the vegetation in their land,
And devoured the fruit of their ground.
³⁶He also destroyed all the firstborn in their land,
The first of all their strength.

³⁷He also brought them out with silver and gold,
And *there was* none feeble among His tribes.
³⁸Egypt was glad when they departed,
For the fear of them had fallen upon them.
³⁹He spread a cloud for a covering,
And fire to give light in the night.
⁴⁰*The people* asked, and He brought quail,
And satisfied them with the bread of heaven.
⁴¹He opened the rock, and water gushed out;
It ran in the dry places *like* a river.

⁴²For He remembered His holy promise,
And Abraham His servant.
⁴³He brought out His people with joy,
His chosen ones with gladness.
⁴⁴He gave them the lands of the Gentiles,
And they inherited the labor of the nations,
⁴⁵That they might observe His statutes
And keep His laws.

Praise the LORD!

PSALM 106

JOY IN FORGIVENESS OF ISRAEL'S SINS

¹Praise the LORD!

Oh, give thanks to the LORD, for *He is* good!
For His mercy *endures* forever.

²Who can utter the mighty acts of the LORD?
Who can declare all His praise?

³Blessed *are* those who keep justice,
And he who does[a] righteousness at all times!

⁴Remember me, O LORD, with the favor *You have toward* Your people.
Oh, visit me with Your salvation,
⁵That I may see the benefit of Your chosen ones,
That I may rejoice in the gladness of Your nation,
That I may glory with Your inheritance.

⁶We have sinned with our fathers,
We have committed iniquity,
We have done wickedly.
⁷Our fathers in Egypt did not understand Your wonders;
They did not remember the multitude of Your mercies,
But rebelled by the sea—the Red Sea.

⁸Nevertheless He saved them for His name's sake,
That He might make His mighty power known.
⁹He rebuked the Red Sea also, and it dried up;
So He led them through the depths,
As through the wilderness.
¹⁰He saved them from the hand of him who hated *them,*
And redeemed them from the hand of the enemy.
¹¹The waters covered their enemies;
There was not one of them left.
¹²Then they believed His words;
They sang His praise.

¹³They soon forgot His works;
They did not wait for His counsel,
¹⁴But lusted exceedingly in the wilderness,
And tested God in the desert.
¹⁵And He gave them their request,
But sent leanness into their soul.

¹⁶When they envied Moses in the camp,
And Aaron the saint of the LORD,

106:3 ªSeptuagint, Syriac, Targum, and Vulgate read *those who do.*

¹⁷The earth opened up and swallowed
Dathan,
And covered the faction of Abiram.
¹⁸A fire was kindled in their company;
The flame burned up the wicked.

¹⁹They made a calf in Horeb,
And worshiped the molded image.
²⁰Thus they changed their glory
Into the image of an ox that eats grass.
²¹They forgot God their Savior,
Who had done great things in Egypt,
²²Wondrous works in the land of Ham,
Awesome things by the Red Sea.
²³Therefore He said that He would destroy
them,
Had not Moses His chosen one stood before
Him in the breach,
To turn away His wrath, lest He destroy
them.

²⁴Then they despised the pleasant land;
They did not believe His word,
²⁵But complained in their tents,
And did not heed the voice of the LORD.
²⁶Therefore He raised His hand *in an oath*
against them,
To overthrow them in the wilderness,
²⁷To overthrow their descendants among the
nations,
And to scatter them in the lands.

²⁸They joined themselves also to Baal of Peor,
And ate sacrifices made to the dead.
²⁹Thus they provoked *Him* to anger with their
deeds,
And the plague broke out among them.
³⁰Then Phinehas stood up and intervened,
And the plague was stopped.
³¹And that was accounted to him for
righteousness
To all generations forevermore.

³²They angered *Him* also at the waters of
strife,[a]
So that it went ill with Moses on account of
them;
³³Because they rebelled against His Spirit,
So that he spoke rashly with his lips.

³⁴They did not destroy the peoples,
Concerning whom the LORD had
commanded them,
³⁵But they mingled with the Gentiles
And learned their works;
³⁶They served their idols,
Which became a snare to them.
³⁷They even sacrificed their sons
And their daughters to demons,
³⁸And shed innocent blood,
The blood of their sons and daughters,
Whom they sacrificed to the idols of Canaan;
And the land was polluted with blood.
³⁹Thus they were defiled by their own works,
And played the harlot by their own deeds.

⁴⁰Therefore the wrath of the LORD was kindled
against His people,
So that He abhorred His own inheritance.
⁴¹And He gave them into the hand of the
Gentiles,
And those who hated them ruled over them.
⁴²Their enemies also oppressed them,
And they were brought into subjection under
their hand.
⁴³Many times He delivered them;
But they rebelled in their counsel,
And were brought low for their iniquity.

⁴⁴Nevertheless He regarded their affliction,
When He heard their cry;
⁴⁵And for their sake He remembered His
covenant,
And relented according to the multitude of
His mercies.
⁴⁶He also made them to be pitied
By all those who carried them away captive.

⁴⁷Save us, O LORD our God,
And gather us from among the Gentiles,
To give thanks to Your holy name,
To triumph in Your praise.

⁴⁸Blessed *be* the LORD God of Israel
From everlasting to everlasting!
And let all the people say, "Amen!"

Praise the LORD!

106:32 [a]Or *Meribah*

Book Five: Psalms 107—150

PSALM 107

THANKSGIVING TO THE LORD FOR HIS GREAT
WORKS OF DELIVERANCE

¹Oh, give thanks to the LORD, for *He is* good!
For His mercy *endures* forever.
²Let the redeemed of the LORD say *so,*
Whom He has redeemed from the hand of
the enemy,
³And gathered out of the lands,
From the east and from the west,
From the north and from the south.

⁴They wandered in the wilderness in a
desolate way;
They found no city to dwell in.
⁵Hungry and thirsty,
Their soul fainted in them.
⁶Then they cried out to the LORD in their
trouble,
And He delivered them out of their distresses.
⁷And He led them forth by the right way,
That they might go to a city for a dwelling
place.
⁸Oh, that *men* would give thanks to the LORD
for His goodness,
And *for* His wonderful works to the children
of men!
⁹For He satisfies the longing soul,
And fills the hungry soul with goodness.

¹⁰Those who sat in darkness and in the shadow
of death,
Bound in affliction and irons—
¹¹Because they rebelled against the words of
God,
And despised the counsel of the Most High,
¹²Therefore He brought down their heart with
labor;
They fell down, and *there was* none to help.
¹³Then they cried out to the LORD in their
trouble,
And He saved them out of their distresses.
¹⁴He brought them out of darkness and the
shadow of death,
And broke their chains in pieces.
¹⁵Oh, that *men* would give thanks to the LORD
for His goodness,

And *for* His wonderful works to the children
of men!
¹⁶For He has broken the gates of bronze,
And cut the bars of iron in two.

¹⁷Fools, because of their transgression,
And because of their iniquities, were afflicted.
¹⁸Their soul abhorred all manner of food,
And they drew near to the gates of death.
¹⁹Then they cried out to the LORD in their
trouble,
And He saved them out of their distresses.
²⁰He sent His word and healed them,
And delivered *them* from their destructions.
²¹Oh, that *men* would give thanks to the LORD
for His goodness,
And *for* His wonderful works to the children
of men!
²²Let them sacrifice the sacrifices of
thanksgiving,
And declare His works with rejoicing.

²³Those who go down to the sea in ships,
Who do business on great waters,
²⁴They see the works of the LORD,
And His wonders in the deep.
²⁵For He commands and raises the stormy wind,
Which lifts up the waves of the sea.
²⁶They mount up to the heavens,
They go down again to the depths;
Their soul melts because of trouble.
²⁷They reel to and fro, and stagger like a
drunken man,
And are at their wits' end.
²⁸Then they cry out to the LORD in their
trouble,
And He brings them out of their distresses.
²⁹He calms the storm,
So that its waves are still.
³⁰Then they are glad because they are quiet;
So He guides them to their desired haven.
³¹Oh, that *men* would give thanks to the LORD
for His goodness,
And *for* His wonderful works to the children
of men!
³²Let them exalt Him also in the assembly of
the people,
And praise Him in the company of the
elders.

³³He turns rivers into a wilderness,
And the watersprings into dry ground;
³⁴A fruitful land into barrenness,
For the wickedness of those who dwell in it.
³⁵He turns a wilderness into pools of water,
And dry land into watersprings.
³⁶There He makes the hungry dwell,
That they may establish a city for a dwelling
place,
³⁷And sow fields and plant vineyards,
That they may yield a fruitful harvest.
³⁸He also blesses them, and they multiply greatly;
And He does not let their cattle decrease.

³⁹When they are diminished and brought low
Through oppression, affliction, and sorrow,
⁴⁰He pours contempt on princes,
And causes them to wander in the wilderness
where there is no way;
⁴¹Yet He sets the poor on high, far from
affliction,
And makes *their* families like a flock.
⁴²The righteous see *it* and rejoice,
And all iniquity stops its mouth.

⁴³Whoever *is* wise will observe these *things,*
And they will understand the lovingkindness
of the LORD.

PSALM 108

ASSURANCE OF GOD'S VICTORY OVER ENEMIES
A Song. A Psalm of David.

¹O God, my heart is steadfast;
I will sing and give praise, even with my
glory.
²Awake, lute and harp!
I will awaken the dawn.
³I will praise You, O LORD, among the
peoples,
And I will sing praises to You among the
nations.
⁴For Your mercy *is* great above the heavens,
And Your truth *reaches* to the clouds.

⁵Be exalted, O God, above the heavens,
And Your glory above all the earth;
⁶That Your beloved may be delivered,
Save *with* Your right hand, and hear me.

⁷God has spoken in His holiness:
"I will rejoice;
I will divide Shechem
And measure out the Valley of Succoth.
⁸Gilead *is* Mine; Manasseh *is* Mine;
Ephraim also *is* the helmet for My head;
Judah *is* My lawgiver.
⁹Moab *is* My washpot;
Over Edom I will cast My shoe;
Over Philistia I will triumph."

¹⁰Who will bring me *into* the strong city?
Who will lead me to Edom?
¹¹*Is it* not *You,* O God, *who* cast us off?
And *You,* O God, *who* did not go out with
our armies?
¹²Give us help from trouble,
For the help of man is useless.
¹³Through God we will do valiantly,
For *it is* He *who* shall tread down our
enemies.ᵃ

PSALM 109

PLEA FOR JUDGMENT OF FALSE ACCUSERS
To the Chief Musician. A Psalm of David.

¹Do not keep silent,
O God of my praise!
²For the mouth of the wicked and the mouth
of the deceitful
Have opened against me;
They have spoken against me with a lying
tongue.
³They have also surrounded me with words of
hatred,
And fought against me without a cause.
⁴In return for my love they are my accusers,
But I *give myself to* prayer.
⁵Thus they have rewarded me evil for good,
And hatred for my love.

⁶Set a wicked man over him,
And let an accuserᵃ stand at his right hand.
⁷When he is judged, let him be found guilty,
And let his prayer become sin.
⁸Let his days be few,
And let another take his office.

108:13 ᵃCompare verses 6–13 with 60:5–12   109:6 ᵃHebrew *satan*

9Let his children be fatherless,
And his wife a widow.
10Let his children continually be vagabonds,
    and beg;
Let them seek *their bread*ᵃ also from their
    desolate places.
11Let the creditor seize all that he has,
And let strangers plunder his labor.
12Let there be none to extend mercy to him,
Nor let there be any to favor his fatherless
    children.
13Let his posterity be cut off,
And in the generation following let their
    name be blotted out.

14Let the iniquity of his fathers be remembered
    before the LORD,
And let not the sin of his mother be blotted
    out.
15Let them be continually before the LORD,
That He may cut off the memory of them
    from the earth;
16Because he did not remember to show mercy,
But persecuted the poor and needy man,
That he might even slay the broken in heart.
17As he loved cursing, so let it come to him;
As he did not delight in blessing, so let it be
    far from him.
18As he clothed himself with cursing as with his
    garment,
So let it enter his body like water,
And like oil into his bones.
19Let it be to him like the garment which
    covers him,
And for a belt with which he girds himself
    continually.
20*Let* this *be* the LORD's reward to my accusers,
And to those who speak evil against my
    person.

21But You, O GOD the Lord,
Deal with me for Your name's sake;
Because Your mercy *is* good, deliver me.
22For I *am* poor and needy,
And my heart is wounded within me.
23I am gone like a shadow when it lengthens;
I am shaken off like a locust.
24My knees are weak through fasting,
And my flesh is feeble from lack of fatness.

25I also have become a reproach to them;
When they look at me, they shake their heads.

26Help me, O LORD my God!
Oh, save me according to Your mercy,
27That they may know that this *is* Your hand—
That You, LORD, have done it!
28Let them curse, but You bless;
When they arise, let them be ashamed,
But let Your servant rejoice.
29Let my accusers be clothed with shame,
And let them cover themselves with their
    own disgrace as with a mantle.

30I will greatly praise the LORD with my
    mouth;
Yes, I will praise Him among the multitude.
31For He shall stand at the right hand of the
    poor,
To save *him* from those who condemn him.

PSALM 110

ANNOUNCEMENT OF THE MESSIAH'S REIGN
A Psalm of David.

1The LORD said to my Lord,
"Sit at My right hand,
Till I make Your enemies Your footstool."
2The LORD shall send the rod of Your strength
    out of Zion.
Rule in the midst of Your enemies!

3Your people *shall be* volunteers
In the day of Your power;
In the beauties of holiness, from the womb of
    the morning,
You have the dew of Your youth.
4The LORD has sworn
And will not relent,
"You *are* a priest forever
According to the order of Melchizedek."

5The Lord *is* at Your right hand;
He shall execute kings in the day of His wrath.
6He shall judge among the nations,
He shall fill *the places* with dead bodies,
He shall execute the heads of many countries.

109:10 ᵃFollowing Masoretic Text and Targum; Septuagint and Vulgate read *be cast out.*

7He shall drink of the brook by the wayside;
Therefore He shall lift up the head.

PSALM 111

PRAISE TO GOD FOR HIS FAITHFULNESS AND JUSTICE

1Praise the LORD!

I will praise the LORD with *my* whole heart,
In the assembly of the upright and *in* the
congregation.

2The works of the LORD *are* great,
Studied by all who have pleasure in them.
3His work *is* honorable and glorious,
And His righteousness endures forever.
4He has made His wonderful works to be
remembered;
The LORD *is* gracious and full of compassion.
5He has given food to those who fear Him;
He will ever be mindful of His covenant.
6He has declared to His people the power of
His works,
In giving them the heritage of the nations.

7The works of His hands *are* verity and justice;
All His precepts *are* sure.
8They stand fast forever and ever,
And are done in truth and uprightness.
9He has sent redemption to His people;
He has commanded His covenant forever:
Holy and awesome *is* His name.

10The fear of the LORD *is* the beginning of
wisdom;
A good understanding have all those who do
His commandments.
His praise endures forever.

PSALM 112

THE BLESSED STATE OF THE RIGHTEOUS

1Praise the LORD!

Blessed *is* the man *who* fears the LORD,
Who delights greatly in His commandments.

2His descendants will be mighty on earth;
The generation of the upright will be blessed.

3Wealth and riches *will be* in his house,
And his righteousness endures forever.
4Unto the upright there arises light in the
darkness;
He is gracious, and full of compassion, and
righteous.
5A good man deals graciously and lends;
He will guide his affairs with discretion.
6Surely he will never be shaken;
The righteous will be in everlasting
remembrance.
7He will not be afraid of evil tidings;
His heart is steadfast, trusting in the LORD.
8His heart *is* established;
He will not be afraid,
Until he sees *his desire* upon his enemies.

9He has dispersed abroad,
He has given to the poor;
His righteousness endures forever;
His horn will be exalted with honor.
10The wicked will see *it* and be grieved;
He will gnash his teeth and melt away;
The desire of the wicked shall perish.

PSALM 113

THE MAJESTY AND CONDESCENSION OF GOD

1Praise the LORD!

Praise, O servants of the LORD,
Praise the name of the LORD!
2Blessed be the name of the LORD
From this time forth and forevermore!
3From the rising of the sun to its going down
The LORD's name *is* to be praised.

4The LORD *is* high above all nations,
His glory above the heavens.
5Who *is* like the LORD our God,
Who dwells on high,
6Who humbles Himself to behold
The things that are in the heavens and in the
earth?

7He raises the poor out of the dust,
And lifts the needy out of the ash heap,
8That He may seat *him* with princes—
With the princes of His people.

⁹He grants the barren woman a home,
Like a joyful mother of children.

Praise the LORD!

PSALM 114

THE POWER OF GOD IN HIS DELIVERANCE
OF ISRAEL

¹When Israel went out of Egypt,
The house of Jacob from a people of strange
language,
²Judah became His sanctuary,
And Israel His dominion.

³The sea saw *it* and fled;
Jordan turned back.
⁴The mountains skipped like rams,
The little hills like lambs.
⁵What ails you, O sea, that you fled?
O Jordan, *that* you turned back?
⁶O mountains, *that* you skipped like rams?
O little hills, like lambs?

⁷Tremble, O earth, at the presence of the
Lord,
At the presence of the God of Jacob,
⁸Who turned the rock *into* a pool of water,
The flint into a fountain of waters.

PSALM 115

THE FUTILITY OF IDOLS AND THE
TRUSTWORTHINESS OF GOD

¹Not unto us, O LORD, not unto us,
But to Your name give glory,
Because of Your mercy,
Because of Your truth.
²Why should the Gentiles say,
"So where *is* their God?"

³But our God *is* in heaven;
He does whatever He pleases.
⁴Their idols *are* silver and gold,
The work of men's hands.
⁵They have mouths, but they do not speak;
Eyes they have, but they do not see;
⁶They have ears, but they do not hear;
Noses they have, but they do not smell;
⁷They have hands, but they do not handle;

Feet they have, but they do not walk;
Nor do they mutter through their throat.
⁸Those who make them are like them;
So is everyone who trusts in them.

⁹O Israel, trust in the LORD;
He *is* their help and their shield.
¹⁰O house of Aaron, trust in the LORD;
He *is* their help and their shield.
¹¹You who fear the LORD, trust in the LORD;
He *is* their help and their shield.

¹²The LORD has been mindful of *us;*
He will bless us;
He will bless the house of Israel;
He will bless the house of Aaron.
¹³He will bless those who fear the LORD,
Both small and great.

¹⁴May the LORD give you increase more and
more,
You and your children.
¹⁵*May* you *be* blessed by the LORD,
Who made heaven and earth.

¹⁶The heaven, *even* the heavens, *are* the LORD's;
But the earth He has given to the children of
men.
¹⁷The dead do not praise the LORD,
Nor any who go down into silence.
¹⁸But we will bless the LORD
From this time forth and forevermore.

Praise the LORD!

PSALM 116

THANKSGIVING FOR DELIVERANCE FROM DEATH

¹I love the LORD, because He has heard
My voice *and* my supplications.
²Because He has inclined His ear to me,
Therefore I will call *upon Him* as long as I
live.

³The pains of death surrounded me,
And the pangs of Sheol laid hold of me;
I found trouble and sorrow.
⁴Then I called upon the name of the LORD:
"O LORD, I implore You, deliver my soul!"

⁵Gracious *is* the LORD, and righteous;
Yes, our God *is* merciful.
⁶The LORD preserves the simple;
I was brought low, and He saved me.
⁷Return to your rest, O my soul,
For the LORD has dealt bountifully with you.

⁸For You have delivered my soul from death,
My eyes from tears,
And my feet from falling.
⁹I will walk before the LORD
In the land of the living.
¹⁰I believed, therefore I spoke,
"I am greatly afflicted."
¹¹I said in my haste,
"All men *are* liars."

¹²What shall I render to the LORD
For all His benefits toward me?
¹³I will take up the cup of salvation,
And call upon the name of the LORD.
¹⁴I will pay my vows to the LORD
Now in the presence of all His people.

¹⁵Precious in the sight of the LORD
Is the death of His saints.

¹⁶O LORD, truly I *am* Your servant;
I *am* Your servant, the son of Your maidservant;
You have loosed my bonds.
¹⁷I will offer to You the sacrifice of
thanksgiving,
And will call upon the name of the LORD.

¹⁸I will pay my vows to the LORD
Now in the presence of all His people,
¹⁹In the courts of the LORD's house,
In the midst of you, O Jerusalem.

Praise the LORD!

PSALM 117

LET ALL PEOPLES PRAISE THE LORD

¹Praise the LORD, all you Gentiles!
Laud Him, all you peoples!
²For His merciful kindness is great toward us,
And the truth of the LORD *endures* forever.

Praise the LORD!

PSALM 118

PRAISE TO GOD FOR HIS EVERLASTING MERCY

¹Oh, give thanks to the LORD, for *He is* good!
For His mercy *endures* forever.

²Let Israel now say,
"His mercy *endures* forever."
³Let the house of Aaron now say,
"His mercy *endures* forever."
⁴Let those who fear the LORD now say,
"His mercy *endures* forever."

⁵I called on the LORD in distress;
The LORD answered me *and set me* in a broad
place.
⁶The LORD *is* on my side;
I will not fear.
What can man do to me?
⁷The LORD is for me among those who help
me;
Therefore I shall see *my desire* on those who
hate me.
⁸*It is* better to trust in the LORD
Than to put confidence in man.
⁹*It is* better to trust in the LORD
Than to put confidence in princes.

¹⁰All nations surrounded me,
But in the name of the LORD I will destroy
them.
¹¹They surrounded me,
Yes, they surrounded me;
But in the name of the LORD I will destroy
them.
¹²They surrounded me like bees;
They were quenched like a fire of thorns;
For in the name of the LORD I will destroy
them.
¹³You pushed me violently, that I might fall,
But the LORD helped me.
¹⁴The LORD *is* my strength and song,
And He has become my salvation.[a]

¹⁵The voice of rejoicing and salvation
Is in the tents of the righteous;
The right hand of the LORD does valiantly.
¹⁶The right hand of the LORD is exalted;

118:14 [a]Compare Exodus 15:2

LEADERSHIP ISSUES

Quiet Time that Rocks

PSALM 119

A lot of people talk about the importance of a quiet time, but not many actually have a plan to make it a significant part of personal worship.

- **Honor God.** Leaders know that something amazing happens when you drop to your knees and come humbly and quietly before our majestic Lord. When I humble myself before God, I am ready to serve other people.

- **Get into the Word.** Try reading five psalms for praise and worship every day and one chapter in Proverbs for wisdom. This gives you the ability to rightly relate to God and the wisdom to live skillfully with those around you.

- **Quote the Scripture.** Say it often; say it aloud. When you read the Word out loud, you see it and hear it. When you write it, you have a triple advantage to making it your own.

- **Journal your thoughts.** Write out the verse, and then think about what it says. Journal thoughts about: changes that need to be made, encouragement you find, instruction on serving, loving, praying, the character of God, and thoughts of gratitude.

- **Meditate on the Word.** Continue to think about the verse's meaning and how it applies to you throughout the day when you face temptations or decisions.

- **Memorize it.** There is no greater force for a leader than knowing the Word of God. Write Scripture on note cards and carry them with you.

- **Pray it.** If you are having trouble praying aloud to God, try writing your thoughts to Him or praying through Bible verses. To pray is literally "to think about." Use your daily scripture in a prayer by inserting your name or the name of someone you care about.

- **Give God thanks.** There is great power in rehearsing what God has already done.

- **Resolve to live the Word.** Make a decision to live out a part of the Word that you have read today.

The best time to have a quiet time is anytime you can sit still and *be quiet!* Schedule your appointment with God, and determine in your heart that no one and nothing will interfere.

The right hand of the LORD does valiantly.
¹⁷I shall not die, but live,
And declare the works of the LORD.
¹⁸The LORD has chastened me severely,
But He has not given me over to death.

¹⁹Open to me the gates of righteousness;
I will go through them,
And I will praise the LORD.
²⁰This is the gate of the LORD,
Through which the righteous shall enter.

²¹I will praise You,
For You have answered me,
And have become my salvation.

²²The stone *which* the builders rejected
Has become the chief cornerstone.
²³This was the LORD's doing;
It *is* marvelous in our eyes.
²⁴This *is* the day the LORD has made;
We will rejoice and be glad in it.

²⁵Save now, I pray, O LORD;
O LORD, I pray, send now prosperity.
²⁶Blessed *is* he who comes in the name of the
LORD!
We have blessed you from the house of the
LORD.
²⁷God *is* the LORD,
And He has given us light;
Bind the sacrifice with cords to the horns of
the altar.
²⁸You *are* my God, and I will praise You;
You are my God, I will exalt You.

²⁹Oh, give thanks to the LORD, for *He is* good!
For His mercy *endures* forever.

PSALM 119

MEDITATIONS ON THE EXCELLENCIES OF THE
WORD OF GOD

א ALEPH
¹Blessed *are* the undefiled in the way,
Who walk in the law of the LORD!
²Blessed *are* those who keep His testimonies,
Who seek Him with the whole heart!
³They also do no iniquity;

They walk in His ways.
⁴You have commanded *us*
To keep Your precepts diligently.
⁵Oh, that my ways were directed
To keep Your statutes!
⁶Then I would not be ashamed,
When I look into all Your commandments.
⁷I will praise You with uprightness of heart,
When I learn Your righteous judgments.
⁸I will keep Your statutes;
Oh, do not forsake me utterly!

ב BETH
⁹How can a young man cleanse his way?
By taking heed according to Your word.
¹⁰With my whole heart I have sought You;
Oh, let me not wander from Your
commandments!
¹¹Your word I have hidden in my heart,
That I might not sin against You.
¹²Blessed *are* You, O LORD!
Teach me Your statutes.
¹³With my lips I have declared
All the judgments of Your mouth.
¹⁴I have rejoiced in the way of Your
testimonies,
As *much as* in all riches.
¹⁵I will meditate on Your precepts,
And contemplate Your ways.
¹⁶I will delight myself in Your statutes;
I will not forget Your word.

ג GIMEL
¹⁷Deal bountifully with Your servant,
That I may live and keep Your word.
¹⁸Open my eyes, that I may see
Wondrous things from Your law.
¹⁹I *am* a stranger in the earth;
Do not hide Your commandments from me.
²⁰My soul breaks with longing
For Your judgments at all times.
²¹You rebuke the proud—the cursed,
Who stray from Your commandments.
²²Remove from me reproach and contempt,
For I have kept Your testimonies.
²³Princes also sit *and* speak against me,
But Your servant meditates on Your statutes.
²⁴Your testimonies also *are* my delight
And my counselors.

LEADERSHIP ISSUES

It Can Happen in a Moment: Finishing Well

PSALM 119:11

Many Christian leaders begin well in their life journey to follow God's personal will. They serve in the local church and are compassionate to those in need. These disciplines are evident for most of a leader's life as God uses them mightily; and then, in a moment, sin can take over, causing a testimony to be darkened. Temptation turns to lust, decisions are compromised, or trust is breached; and the pattern of inconsistency with the Word of God turns to tragedy in the life of the believer.

King David was considered a man after God's own heart (Acts 13:22). After being anointed as Israel's next king, he patiently waited for his time. He boldly fought Goliath. The Bible states, as a leader to God's people, David "shepherded them according to the integrity of his heart, and guided them by the skillfulness of his hands" (Ps. 78:72). He was a man of God and a mighty warrior; but with one choice, his influence was tainted. It started with being in the wrong place at the wrong time. The king should have been at war with his troops, not at home. It continued when one glance led to a stare, which led to adultery (2 Sam.11). He indulged when he should have disengaged immediately. An unwanted pregnancy, murder, family discourse, and a troubled nation were the results because of one moment in which he could have, and should have, gone the other way.

Although David was reconciled to God before his death, the effects of David not finishing well had an impact on his own and future generations. What David looked at as a momentary pleasure had consequences forever. The key to finishing well is a commitment to leadership that is not built on moments, but on a lifetime. The influence of that will go on for multiple generations. Psalm 119:11 states, "Your word I have hidden in my heart, that I might not sin against You." Leaders hold themselves accountable to a higher standard—the Word of God; they memorize it, letting it fill their minds and hearts. Surround yourself with godly men and women who are not afraid to ask you the tough questions, address your obvious sins in love, and pray for you. The goal is to finish well.

ד DALETH

25My soul clings to the dust;
 Revive me according to Your word.
26I have declared my ways, and You answered me;
 Teach me Your statutes.
27Make me understand the way of Your precepts;
 So shall I meditate on Your wonderful works.
28My soul melts from heaviness;
 Strengthen me according to Your word.
29Remove from me the way of lying,
 And grant me Your law graciously.
30I have chosen the way of truth;
 Your judgments I have laid *before me.*
31I cling to Your testimonies;
 O Lord, do not put me to shame!
32I will run the course of Your commandments,
 For You shall enlarge my heart.

ה HE

33Teach me, O Lord, the way of Your statutes,
 And I shall keep it *to* the end.
34Give me understanding, and I shall keep Your law;
 Indeed, I shall observe it with *my* whole heart.
35Make me walk in the path of Your commandments,
 For I delight in it.
36Incline my heart to Your testimonies,
 And not to covetousness.
37Turn away my eyes from looking at worthless things,
 And revive me in Your way.a
38Establish Your word to Your servant,
 Who *is devoted* to fearing You.
39Turn away my reproach which I dread,
 For Your judgments *are* good.
40Behold, I long for Your precepts;
 Revive me in Your righteousness.

ו WAW

41Let Your mercies come also to me,
  O Lord—
 Your salvation according to Your word.
42So shall I have an answer for him who reproaches me,
 For I trust in Your word.

43And take not the word of truth utterly out of my mouth,
 For I have hoped in Your ordinances.
44So shall I keep Your law continually,
 Forever and ever.
45And I will walk at liberty,
 For I seek Your precepts.
46I will speak of Your testimonies also before kings,
 And will not be ashamed.
47And I will delight myself in Your commandments,
 Which I love.
48My hands also I will lift up to Your commandments,
 Which I love,
 And I will meditate on Your statutes.

ז ZAYIN

49Remember the word to Your servant,
 Upon which You have caused me to hope.
50This *is* my comfort in my affliction,
 For Your word has given me life.
51The proud have me in great derision,
 Yet I do not turn aside from Your law.
52I remembered Your judgments of old,
  O Lord,
 And have comforted myself.
53Indignation has taken hold of me
 Because of the wicked, who forsake Your law.
54Your statutes have been my songs
 In the house of my pilgrimage.
55I remember Your name in the night, O Lord,
 And I keep Your law.
56This has become mine,
 Because I kept Your precepts.

ח HETH

57*You are* my portion, O Lord;
 I have said that I would keep Your words.
58I entreated Your favor with *my* whole heart;
 Be merciful to me according to Your word.
59I thought about my ways,
 And turned my feet to Your testimonies.
60I made haste, and did not delay
 To keep Your commandments.
61The cords of the wicked have bound me,

119:37 aFollowing Masoretic Text, Septuagint, and Vulgate; Targum reads *Your words.*

LEADERSHIP ISSUES

GC2: Delight in the Word

PSALM 119:16

Disciples delight in God's Word, not forgetting how His truth has blessed them. Consider a specific Bible verse that has become especially meaningful to you. Then reflect on how God made it alive for you, leading you out of darkness into light (1 Pet. 2:9, 10). Maybe God used a particular Bible verse—such as John 3:16—to draw you into a new-birth encounter with Christ.

Maybe God used a particular Bible promise—such as Psalm 23—to lead you out of a valley of despair into "green pastures." Maybe God used a specific Bible admonition—such as Ephesians 4:31—to challenge you to rid yourself of some area of bitterness so that you could walk with Him and hear His voice.

I'm grateful to God for using (insert your Bible verse) *in my life in order to lead me out of _____ and into the light of _____.*

After sharing your responses with your partner or small group, pray together and express gratitude for the power, promise, and potential of the light of God's Word.

GC2

GREAT COMMANDMENT
COMMISSION

THROUGH THE GRID

Discover God:
God Is Absolute Truth

PSALM 119:160 *The entirety of Your word is truth, and every one of Your righteous judgments endures forever.*

God is the author of everything that is true, and all of what God says or promises is absolute truth. In a day and age when it can be difficult to determine what is really true, we can rely on God as the only real source of truth. God is always consistent, and God's constancy has been a sure foundation that has lasted since the beginning of time and will last until the end of time. God reveals truth to us through the Bible; through the life, obedient death, and resurrection of Christ; and through the workings of the Holy Spirit.

But I have not forgotten Your law.
⁶²At midnight I will rise to give thanks to You,
Because of Your righteous judgments.
⁶³I *am* a companion of all who fear You,
And of those who keep Your precepts.
⁶⁴The earth, O LORD, is full of Your mercy;
Teach me Your statutes.

ב TETH
⁶⁵You have dealt well with Your servant,
O LORD, according to Your word.
⁶⁶Teach me good judgment and knowledge,
For I believe Your commandments.
⁶⁷Before I was afflicted I went astray,
But now I keep Your word.
⁶⁸You *are* good, and do good;
Teach me Your statutes.
⁶⁹The proud have forged a lie against me,
But I will keep Your precepts with *my* whole heart.
⁷⁰Their heart is as fat as grease,
But I delight in Your law.
⁷¹*It is* good for me that I have been afflicted,
That I may learn Your statutes.
⁷²The law of Your mouth *is* better to me
Than thousands of *coins of* gold and silver.

י YOD
⁷³Your hands have made me and fashioned me;
Give me understanding, that I may learn Your commandments.
⁷⁴Those who fear You will be glad when they see me,

Because I have hoped in Your word.
⁷⁵I know, O LORD, that Your judgments *are* right,
And *that* in faithfulness You have afflicted me.
⁷⁶Let, I pray, Your merciful kindness be for my comfort,
According to Your word to Your servant.
⁷⁷Let Your tender mercies come to me, that I may live;
For Your law *is* my delight.
⁷⁸Let the proud be ashamed,
For they treated me wrongfully with falsehood;
But I will meditate on Your precepts.
⁷⁹Let those who fear You turn to me,
Those who know Your testimonies.
⁸⁰Let my heart be blameless regarding Your statutes,
That I may not be ashamed.

כ KAPH
⁸¹My soul faints for Your salvation,
But I hope in Your word.
⁸²My eyes fail *from searching* Your word,
Saying, "When will You comfort me?"
⁸³For I have become like a wineskin in smoke,
Yet I do not forget Your statutes.
⁸⁴How many *are* the days of Your servant?
When will You execute judgment on those who persecute me?
⁸⁵The proud have dug pits for me,
Which *is* not according to Your law.
⁸⁶All Your commandments *are* faithful;

They persecute me wrongfully;
Help me!
[87]They almost made an end of me on earth,
But I did not forsake Your precepts.
[88]Revive me according to Your lovingkindness,
So that I may keep the testimony of Your
mouth.

ל LAMED
[89]Forever, O LORD,
Your word is settled in heaven.
[90]Your faithfulness *endures* to all generations;
You established the earth, and it abides.
[91]They continue this day according to Your
ordinances,
For all *are* Your servants.
[92]Unless Your law *had been* my delight,
I would then have perished in my affliction.
[93]I will never forget Your precepts,
For by them You have given me life.
[94]I *am* Yours, save me;
For I have sought Your precepts.
[95]The wicked wait for me to destroy me,
But I will consider Your testimonies.
[96]I have seen the consummation of all
perfection,
But Your commandment *is* exceedingly
broad.

מ MEM
[97]Oh, how I love Your law!
It *is* my meditation all the day.
[98]You, through Your commandments, make me
wiser than my enemies;
For they *are* ever with me.
[99]I have more understanding than all my
teachers,
For Your testimonies *are* my meditation.
[100]I understand more than the ancients,
Because I keep Your precepts.
[101]I have restrained my feet from every evil
way,
That I may keep Your word.
[102]I have not departed from Your judgments,
For You Yourself have taught me.
[103]How sweet are Your words to my taste,
Sweeter than honey to my mouth!
[104]Through Your precepts I get understanding;
Therefore I hate every false way.

נ NUN
[105]Your word *is* a lamp to my feet
And a light to my path.
[106]I have sworn and confirmed
That I will keep Your righteous judgments.
[107]I am afflicted very much;
Revive me, O LORD, according to Your
word.
[108]Accept, I pray, the freewill offerings of my
mouth, O LORD,
And teach me Your judgments.
[109]My life *is* continually in my hand,
Yet I do not forget Your law.
[110]The wicked have laid a snare for me,
Yet I have not strayed from Your precepts.
[111]Your testimonies I have taken as a heritage
forever,
For they *are* the rejoicing of my heart.
[112]I have inclined my heart to perform Your
statutes
Forever, to the very end.

ס SAMEK
[113]I hate the double-minded,
But I love Your law.
[114]You *are* my hiding place and my shield;
I hope in Your word.
[115]Depart from me, you evildoers,
For I will keep the commandments of my
God!
[116]Uphold me according to Your word, that I
may live;
And do not let me be ashamed of my hope.
[117]Hold me up, and I shall be safe,
And I shall observe Your statutes continually.
[118]You reject all those who stray from Your
statutes,
For their deceit *is* falsehood.
[119]You put away all the wicked of the earth *like*
dross;
Therefore I love Your testimonies.
[120]My flesh trembles for fear of You,
And I am afraid of Your judgments.

ע AYIN
[121]I have done justice and righteousness;
Do not leave me to my oppressors.
[122]Be surety for Your servant for good;
Do not let the proud oppress me.

LEADERSHIP ISSUES

GC2: The Light of God's Word

PSALM 119:105

When we walk in the light of God's Word, we experience a source of His transforming power. Psalm 119 makes it known that His Word is a source of insight, truth, wisdom, and encouragement. As we experience God's Book and are drawn into a deepening relationship with Him, we see Him for who He really is. Our concept of God is reshaped as the Holy Spirit leads us into an expanding love relationship with the God of Scripture. We also come to find that His Word is "living and powerful," bringing transformation as we encounter Him in His Word (Heb. 4:12).

Consider these verses:

Proverbs 15:1—"A soft answer turns away wrath."

Romans 15:7—"Receive one another, just as Christ also received us."

James 5:16—"Confess your trespasses to one another."

Ephesians 4:32—"Forgiving one another, even as God in Christ God forgave you."

How might experiencing these verses add blessing and relevance in your life and relationships?

_____

_____

How might failing to experience these verses contribute to the lack of meaning in our lives and pain in our relationships?

_____

_____

Pray a prayer declaring your openness to God and His work as He leads you into experiencing more of His Word.

Father, lead us beyond mere knowledge of truth to a genuine experience of it.
Replace knowledge with love that builds up as Your truth is lived out (1 Cor. 8:1–3).

GC2
GREAT COMMANDMENT
COMMISSION

¹²³My eyes fail *from seeking* Your salvation
 And Your righteous word.
¹²⁴Deal with Your servant according to Your
    mercy,
 And teach me Your statutes.
¹²⁵I *am* Your servant;
 Give me understanding,
 That I may know Your testimonies.
¹²⁶*It is* time for *You* to act, O LORD,
 For they have regarded Your law as void.
¹²⁷Therefore I love Your commandments
 More than gold, yes, than fine gold!
¹²⁸Therefore all *Your* precepts *concerning* all
    things
 I consider *to be* right;
 I hate every false way.

 פ PE
¹²⁹Your testimonies are wonderful;
 Therefore my soul keeps them.
¹³⁰The entrance of Your words gives light;
 It gives understanding to the simple.
¹³¹I opened my mouth and panted,
 For I longed for Your commandments.
¹³²Look upon me and be merciful to me,
 As Your custom *is* toward those who love
    Your name.
¹³³Direct my steps by Your word,
 And let no iniquity have dominion over me.
¹³⁴Redeem me from the oppression of man,
 That I may keep Your precepts.
¹³⁵Make Your face shine upon Your servant,
 And teach me Your statutes.
¹³⁶Rivers of water run down from my eyes,
 Because *men* do not keep Your law.

צ TSADDE
¹³⁷Righteous *are* You, O LORD,
 And upright *are* Your judgments.
¹³⁸Your testimonies, *which* You have
    commanded,
 Are righteous and very faithful.
¹³⁹My zeal has consumed me,
 Because my enemies have forgotten Your
    words.
¹⁴⁰Your word *is* very pure;
 Therefore Your servant loves it.
¹⁴¹I *am* small and despised,
 Yet I do not forget Your precepts.

¹⁴²Your righteousness *is* an everlasting
    righteousness,
 And Your law *is* truth.
¹⁴³Trouble and anguish have overtaken me,
 Yet Your commandments *are* my delights.
¹⁴⁴The righteousness of Your testimonies *is*
    everlasting;
 Give me understanding, and I shall live.

ק QOPH
¹⁴⁵I cry out with *my* whole heart;
 Hear me, O LORD!
 I will keep Your statutes.
¹⁴⁶I cry out to You;
 Save me, and I will keep Your testimonies.
¹⁴⁷I rise before the dawning of the morning,
 And cry for help;
 I hope in Your word.
¹⁴⁸My eyes are awake through the *night* watches,
 That I may meditate on Your word.
¹⁴⁹Hear my voice according to Your
    lovingkindness;
 O LORD, revive me according to Your
    justice.
¹⁵⁰They draw near who follow after
    wickedness;
 They are far from Your law.
¹⁵¹You *are* near, O LORD,
 And all Your commandments *are* truth.
¹⁵²Concerning Your testimonies,
 I have known of old that You have founded
    them forever.

ר RESH
¹⁵³Consider my affliction and deliver me,
 For I do not forget Your law.
¹⁵⁴Plead my cause and redeem me;
 Revive me according to Your word.
¹⁵⁵Salvation *is* far from the wicked,
 For they do not seek Your statutes.
¹⁵⁶Great *are* Your tender mercies, O LORD;
 Revive me according to Your judgments.
¹⁵⁷Many *are* my persecutors and my enemies,
 Yet I do not turn from Your testimonies.
¹⁵⁸I see the treacherous, and am disgusted,
 Because they do not keep Your word.
¹⁵⁹Consider how I love Your precepts;
 Revive me, O LORD, according to Your
    lovingkindness.

160The entirety of Your word *is* truth,
And every one of Your righteous judgments
    endures forever.

ש SHIN

161Princes persecute me without a cause,
But my heart stands in awe of Your word.
162I rejoice at Your word
As one who finds great treasure.
163I hate and abhor lying,
But I love Your law.
164Seven times a day I praise You,
Because of Your righteous judgments.
165Great peace have those who love Your law,
And nothing causes them to stumble.
166LORD, I hope for Your salvation,
And I do Your commandments.
167My soul keeps Your testimonies,
And I love them exceedingly.
168I keep Your precepts and Your testimonies,
For all my ways *are* before You.

ת TAU

169Let my cry come before You, O LORD;
Give me understanding according to Your
    word.
170Let my supplication come before You;
Deliver me according to Your word.
171My lips shall utter praise,
For You teach me Your statutes.
172My tongue shall speak of Your word,
For all Your commandments *are*
    righteousness.
173Let Your hand become my help,
For I have chosen Your precepts.
174I long for Your salvation, O LORD,
And Your law *is* my delight.
175Let my soul live, and it shall praise You;
And let Your judgments help me.
176I have gone astray like a lost sheep;
Seek Your servant,
For I do not forget Your commandments.

PSALM 120

PLEA FOR RELIEF FROM BITTER FOES
A Song of Ascents.

1In my distress I cried to the LORD,
And He heard me.

2Deliver my soul, O LORD, from lying lips
And from a deceitful tongue.

3What shall be given to you,
Or what shall be done to you,
You false tongue?
4Sharp arrows of the warrior,
With coals of the broom tree!

5Woe is me, that I dwell in Meshech,
That I dwell among the tents of Kedar!
6My soul has dwelt too long
With one who hates peace.
7I *am for* peace;
But when I speak, they *are* for war.

PSALM 121

GOD THE HELP OF THOSE WHO SEEK HIM
A Song of Ascents.

1I will lift up my eyes to the hills—
From whence comes my help?
2My help *comes* from the LORD,
Who made heaven and earth.

3He will not allow your foot to be moved;
He who keeps you will not slumber.
4Behold, He who keeps Israel
Shall neither slumber nor sleep.

5The LORD *is* your keeper;
The LORD *is* your shade at your right hand.
6The sun shall not strike you by day,
Nor the moon by night.

7The LORD shall preserve you from all evil;
He shall preserve your soul.
8The LORD shall preserve your going out and
    your coming in
From this time forth, and even forevermore.

PSALM 122

THE JOY OF GOING TO THE HOUSE OF THE LORD
A Song of Ascents. Of David.

1I was glad when they said to me,
"Let us go into the house of the LORD."
2Our feet have been standing
Within your gates, O Jerusalem!

³Jerusalem is built
 As a city that is compact together,
⁴Where the tribes go up,
 The tribes of the LORD,
 To the Testimony of Israel,
 To give thanks to the name of the LORD.
⁵For thrones are set there for judgment,
 The thrones of the house of David.

⁶Pray for the peace of Jerusalem:
"May they prosper who love you.
⁷Peace be within your walls,
 Prosperity within your palaces."
⁸For the sake of my brethren and companions,
 I will now say, "Peace *be* within you."
⁹Because of the house of the LORD our God
 I will seek your good.

PSALM 123

PRAYER FOR RELIEF FROM CONTEMPT
A Song of Ascents.

¹Unto You I lift up my eyes,
 O You who dwell in the heavens.
²Behold, as the eyes of servants *look* to the
  hand of their masters,
 As the eyes of a maid to the hand of her
  mistress,
 So our eyes *look* to the LORD our God,
 Until He has mercy on us.

³Have mercy on us, O LORD, have mercy
  on us!
 For we are exceedingly filled with contempt.
⁴Our soul is exceedingly filled
 With the scorn of those who are at ease,
 With the contempt of the proud.

PSALM 124

THE LORD THE DEFENSE OF HIS PEOPLE
A Song of Ascents. Of David.

¹"If it had not been the LORD who was on our
  side,"
 Let Israel now say—
²"If it had not been the LORD who was on our
  side,
 When men rose up against us,
³Then they would have swallowed us alive,

 When their wrath was kindled against us;
⁴Then the waters would have overwhelmed
  us,
 The stream would have gone over our soul;
⁵Then the swollen waters
 Would have gone over our soul."

⁶Blessed *be* the LORD,
 Who has not given us *as* prey to their teeth.
⁷Our soul has escaped as a bird from the snare
  of the fowlers;ᵃ
 The snare is broken, and we have escaped.
⁸Our help *is* in the name of the LORD,
 Who made heaven and earth.

PSALM 125

THE LORD THE STRENGTH OF HIS PEOPLE
A Song of Ascents.

¹Those who trust in the LORD
 Are like Mount Zion,
 Which cannot be moved, *but* abides forever.
²As the mountains surround Jerusalem,
 So the LORD surrounds His people
 From this time forth and forever.

³For the scepter of wickedness shall not rest
 On the land allotted to the righteous,
 Lest the righteous reach out their hands to
  iniquity.

⁴Do good, O LORD, to *those who are* good,
 And to *those who are* upright in their hearts.

⁵As for such as turn aside to their crooked
  ways,
 The LORD shall lead them away
 With the workers of iniquity.

Peace *be* upon Israel!

PSALM 126

A JOYFUL RETURN TO ZION
A Song of Ascents.

¹When the LORD brought back the captivity
  of Zion,
 We were like those who dream.

124:7 ᵃThat is, persons who catch birds in a trap or snare

²Then our mouth was filled with laughter,
　And our tongue with singing.
　Then they said among the nations,
"The LORD has done great things for them."
³The LORD has done great things for us,
　And we are glad.

⁴Bring back our captivity, O LORD,
　As the streams in the South.

⁵Those who sow in tears
　Shall reap in joy.
⁶He who continually goes forth weeping,
　Bearing seed for sowing,
　Shall doubtless come again with rejoicing,
　Bringing his sheaves *with him.*

PSALM 127

Laboring and Prospering with the Lord
A Song of Ascents. Of Solomon.

¹Unless the LORD builds the house,
　They labor in vain who build it;
　Unless the LORD guards the city,
　The watchman stays awake in vain.
²*It is* vain for you to rise up early,
　To sit up late,
　To eat the bread of sorrows;
　For so He gives His beloved sleep.

³Behold, children *are* a heritage from the
　LORD,
　The fruit of the womb *is* a reward.
⁴Like arrows in the hand of a warrior,
　So *are* the children of one's youth.
⁵Happy *is* the man who has his quiver full of
　them;
　They shall not be ashamed,
　But shall speak with their enemies in the gate.

PSALM 128

Blessings of Those Who Fear the Lord
A Song of Ascents.

¹Blessed *is* every one who fears the LORD,
　Who walks in His ways.

²When you eat the labor of your hands,
　You *shall be* happy, and *it shall be* well with you.

³Your wife *shall be* like a fruitful vine
　In the very heart of your house,
　Your children like olive plants
　All around your table.
⁴Behold, thus shall the man be blessed
　Who fears the LORD.

⁵The LORD bless you out of Zion,
　And may you see the good of Jerusalem
　All the days of your life.
⁶Yes, may you see your children's children.

Peace *be* upon Israel!

PSALM 129

Song of Victory over Zion's Enemies
A Song of Ascents.

¹"Many a time they have afflicted me from my
　youth,"
　Let Israel now say—
²"Many a time they have afflicted me from my
　youth;
　Yet they have not prevailed against me.
³The plowers plowed on my back;
　They made their furrows long."
⁴The LORD *is* righteous;
　He has cut in pieces the cords of the
　wicked.

⁵Let all those who hate Zion
　Be put to shame and turned back.
⁶Let them be as the grass *on* the housetops,
　Which withers before it grows up,
⁷With which the reaper does not fill his hand,
　Nor he who binds sheaves, his arms.
⁸Neither let those who pass by them say,
"The blessing of the LORD *be* upon you;
　We bless you in the name of the LORD!"

PSALM 130

Waiting for the Redemption of the Lord
A Song of Ascents.

¹Out of the depths I have cried to You,
　O LORD;
²Lord, hear my voice!
　Let Your ears be attentive
　To the voice of my supplications.

³If You, LORD, should mark iniquities,
O Lord, who could stand?
⁴But *there is* forgiveness with You,
That You may be feared.

⁵I wait for the LORD, my soul waits,
And in His word I do hope.
⁶My soul *waits* for the Lord
More than those who watch for the
morning—
Yes, more than those who watch for the
morning.

⁷O Israel, hope in the LORD;
For with the LORD *there is* mercy,
And with Him *is* abundant redemption.
⁸And He shall redeem Israel
From all his iniquities.

PSALM 131

SIMPLE TRUST IN THE LORD
A Song of Ascents. Of David.

¹LORD, my heart is not haughty,
Nor my eyes lofty.
Neither do I concern myself with great
matters,
Nor with things too profound for me.

²Surely I have calmed and quieted my soul,
Like a weaned child with his mother;
Like a weaned child *is* my soul within me.

³O Israel, hope in the LORD
From this time forth and forever.

PSALM 132

THE ETERNAL DWELLING OF GOD IN ZION
A Song of Ascents.

¹LORD, remember David
And all his afflictions;
²How he swore to the LORD,
And vowed to the Mighty One of Jacob:
³"Surely I will not go into the chamber of my
house,
Or go up to the comfort of my bed;
⁴I will not give sleep to my eyes
Or slumber to my eyelids,

⁵Until I find a place for the LORD,
A dwelling place for the Mighty One of
Jacob."

⁶Behold, we heard of it in Ephrathah;
We found it in the fields of the woods.ª
⁷Let us go into His tabernacle;
Let us worship at His footstool.
⁸Arise, O LORD, to Your resting place,
You and the ark of Your strength.
⁹Let Your priests be clothed with righteousness,
And let Your saints shout for joy.

¹⁰For Your servant David's sake,
Do not turn away the face of Your Anointed.

¹¹The LORD has sworn *in* truth to David;
He will not turn from it:
"I will set upon your throne the fruit of your
body.
¹²If your sons will keep My covenant
And My testimony which I shall teach them,
Their sons also shall sit upon your throne
forevermore."

¹³For the LORD has chosen Zion;
He has desired *it* for His dwelling place:
¹⁴"This *is* My resting place forever;
Here I will dwell, for I have desired it.
¹⁵I will abundantly bless her provision;
I will satisfy her poor with bread.
¹⁶I will also clothe her priests with salvation,
And her saints shall shout aloud for joy.
¹⁷There I will make the horn of David grow;
I will prepare a lamp for My Anointed.
¹⁸His enemies I will clothe with shame,
But upon Himself His crown shall flourish."

PSALM 133

BLESSED UNITY OF THE PEOPLE OF GOD
A Song of Ascents. Of David.

¹Behold, how good and how pleasant *it is*
For brethren to dwell together in unity!

²*It is* like the precious oil upon the head,
Running down on the beard,
The beard of Aaron,

132:6 ªHebrew *Jaar*

Running down on the edge of his garments.
³*It is* like the dew of Hermon,
Descending upon the mountains of Zion;
For there the LORD commanded the
      blessing—
Life forevermore.

PSALM 134

PRAISING THE LORD IN HIS HOUSE AT NIGHT
A Song of Ascents.

¹Behold, bless the LORD,
All *you* servants of the LORD,
Who by night stand in the house of the
   LORD!
²Lift up your hands *in* the sanctuary,
And bless the LORD.
³The LORD who made heaven and earth
Bless you from Zion!

PSALM 135

PRAISE TO GOD IN CREATION AND REDEMPTION

¹Praise the LORD!

Praise the name of the LORD;
Praise *Him,* O you servants of the LORD!
²You who stand in the house of the LORD,
In the courts of the house of our God,
³Praise the LORD, for the LORD *is* good;
Sing praises to His name, for *it is* pleasant.
⁴For the LORD has chosen Jacob for Himself,
Israel for His special treasure.

⁵For I know that the LORD *is* great,
And our Lord *is* above all gods.
⁶Whatever the LORD pleases He does,
In heaven and in earth,
In the seas and in all deep places.
⁷He causes the vapors to ascend from the ends
    of the earth;
He makes lightning for the rain;
He brings the wind out of His treasuries.

⁸He destroyed the firstborn of Egypt,
Both of man and beast.
⁹He sent signs and wonders into the midst of
    you, O Egypt,
Upon Pharaoh and all his servants.

¹⁰He defeated many nations
And slew mighty kings—
¹¹Sihon king of the Amorites,
Og king of Bashan,
And all the kingdoms of Canaan—
¹²And gave their land *as* a heritage,
A heritage to Israel His people.

¹³Your name, O LORD, *endures* forever,
Your fame, O LORD, throughout all
   generations.
¹⁴For the LORD will judge His people,
And He will have compassion on His
   servants.

¹⁵The idols of the nations *are* silver and gold,
The work of men's hands.
¹⁶They have mouths, but they do not speak;
Eyes they have, but they do not see;
¹⁷They have ears, but they do not hear;
Nor is there *any* breath in their mouths.
¹⁸Those who make them are like them;
So is everyone who trusts in them.

¹⁹Bless the LORD, O house of Israel!
Bless the LORD, O house of Aaron!
²⁰Bless the LORD, O house of Levi!
You who fear the LORD, bless the LORD!
²¹Blessed be the LORD out of Zion,
Who dwells in Jerusalem!

Praise the LORD!

PSALM 136

THANKSGIVING TO GOD FOR HIS
ENDURING MERCY

¹Oh, give thanks to the LORD, for *He is*
   good!
For His mercy *endures* forever.
²Oh, give thanks to the God of gods!
For His mercy *endures* forever.
³Oh, give thanks to the Lord of lords!
For His mercy *endures* forever:

⁴To Him who alone does great wonders,
For His mercy *endures* forever;
⁵To Him who by wisdom made the heavens,
For His mercy *endures* forever;

⁶To Him who laid out the earth above the
       waters,
    For His mercy *endures* forever;
⁷To Him who made great lights,
    For His mercy *endures* forever—
⁸The sun to rule by day,
    For His mercy *endures* forever;
⁹The moon and stars to rule by night,
    For His mercy *endures* forever.

¹⁰To Him who struck Egypt in their firstborn,
    For His mercy *endures* forever;
¹¹And brought out Israel from among them,
    For His mercy *endures* forever;
¹²With a strong hand, and with an outstretched
       arm,
    For His mercy *endures* forever;
¹³To Him who divided the Red Sea in two,
    For His mercy *endures* forever;
¹⁴And made Israel pass through the midst of it,
    For His mercy *endures* forever;
¹⁵But overthrew Pharaoh and his army in the
       Red Sea,
    For His mercy *endures* forever;
¹⁶To Him who led His people through the
       wilderness,
    For His mercy *endures* forever;
¹⁷To Him who struck down great kings,
    For His mercy *endures* forever;
¹⁸And slew famous kings,
    For His mercy *endures* forever—
¹⁹Sihon king of the Amorites,
    For His mercy *endures* forever;
²⁰And Og king of Bashan,
    For His mercy *endures* forever—
²¹And gave their land as a heritage,
    For His mercy *endures* forever;
²²A heritage to Israel His servant,
    For His mercy *endures* forever.

²³Who remembered us in our lowly state,
    For His mercy *endures* forever;
²⁴And rescued us from our enemies,
    For His mercy *endures* forever;
²⁵Who gives food to all flesh,
    For His mercy *endures* forever.

²⁶Oh, give thanks to the God of heaven!
    For His mercy *endures* forever.

PSALM 137

LONGING FOR ZION IN A FOREIGN LAND

¹By the rivers of Babylon,
    There we sat down, yea, we wept
    When we remembered Zion.
²We hung our harps
    Upon the willows in the midst of it.
³For there those who carried us away captive
       asked of us a song,
    And those who plundered us *requested* mirth,
    Saying, "Sing us *one* of the songs of Zion!"

⁴How shall we sing the LORD's song
    In a foreign land?
⁵If I forget you, O Jerusalem,
    Let my right hand forget *its skill!*
⁶If I do not remember you,
    Let my tongue cling to the roof of my
       mouth—
    If I do not exalt Jerusalem
    Above my chief joy.

⁷Remember, O LORD, against the sons of
       Edom
    The day of Jerusalem,
    Who said, "Raze *it,* raze *it,*
    To its very foundation!"

⁸O daughter of Babylon, who are to be
       destroyed,
    Happy the one who repays you as you have
       served us!
⁹Happy the one who takes and dashes
    Your little ones against the rock!

PSALM 138

THE LORD'S GOODNESS TO THE FAITHFUL
A Psalm of David.

¹I will praise You with my whole heart;
    Before the gods I will sing praises to You.
²I will worship toward Your holy temple,
    And praise Your name
    For Your lovingkindness and Your truth;
    For You have magnified Your word above all
       Your name.
³In the day when I cried out, You answered me,
    And made me bold *with* strength in my soul.

⁴All the kings of the earth shall praise You,
  O LORD,
When they hear the words of Your mouth.
⁵Yes, they shall sing of the ways of the LORD,
For great *is* the glory of the LORD.
⁶Though the LORD *is* on high,
Yet He regards the lowly;
But the proud He knows from afar.

⁷Though I walk in the midst of trouble, You
    will revive me;
You will stretch out Your hand
Against the wrath of my enemies,
And Your right hand will save me.
⁸The LORD will perfect *that which* concerns
    me;
Your mercy, O LORD, *endures* forever;
Do not forsake the works of Your hands.

PSALM 139

GOD'S PERFECT KNOWLEDGE OF MAN
For the Chief Musician. A Psalm of David.

¹O LORD, You have searched me and known
    me.
²You know my sitting down and my rising up;
You understand my thought afar off.
³You comprehend my path and my lying
    down,
And are acquainted with all my ways.
⁴For *there is* not a word on my tongue,
But behold, O LORD, You know it altogether.
⁵You have hedged me behind and before,
And laid Your hand upon me.
⁶*Such* knowledge *is* too wonderful for me;
It is high, I cannot *attain* it.

⁷Where can I go from Your Spirit?
Or where can I flee from Your presence?
⁸If I ascend into heaven, You *are* there;
If I make my bed in hell, behold, You *are*
    there.
⁹*If* I take the wings of the morning,
And dwell in the uttermost parts of the sea,
¹⁰Even there Your hand shall lead me,
And Your right hand shall hold me.
¹¹If I say, "Surely the darkness shall fallᵃ on
    me,"
Even the night shall be light about me;

¹²Indeed, the darkness shall not hide from
    You,
But the night shines as the day;
The darkness and the light *are* both alike *to
    You.*

¹³For You formed my inward parts;
You covered me in my mother's womb.
¹⁴I will praise You, for I am fearfully *and*
    wonderfully made;ᵃ
Marvelous are Your works,
And *that* my soul knows very well.
¹⁵My frame was not hidden from You,
When I was made in secret,
And skillfully wrought in the lowest parts of
    the earth.
¹⁶Your eyes saw my substance, being yet
    unformed.
And in Your book they all were written,
The days fashioned for me,
When *as yet there were* none of them.

¹⁷How precious also are Your thoughts to me,
    O God!
How great is the sum of them!
¹⁸*If* I should count them, they would be more
    in number than the sand;
When I awake, I am still with You.

¹⁹Oh, that You would slay the wicked, O God!
Depart from me, therefore, you bloodthirsty
    men.
²⁰For they speak against You wickedly;
Your enemies take *Your name* in vain.ᵃ
²¹Do I not hate them, O LORD, who hate
    You?
And do I not loathe those who rise up
    against You?
²²I hate them with perfect hatred;
I count them my enemies.

²³Search me, O God, and know my heart;
Try me, and know my anxieties;
²⁴And see if *there is any* wicked way in me,
And lead me in the way everlasting.

139:11 ᵃVulgate and Symmachus read *cover.* **139:14** ᵃFollowing
Masoretic Text and Targum; Septuagint, Syriac, and Vulgate read
You are fearfully wonderful. **139:20** ᵃSeptuagint and Vulgate read
They take your cities in vain.

PSALM 140

PRAYER FOR DELIVERANCE FROM EVIL MEN
To the Chief Musician. A Psalm of David.

¹Deliver me, O LORD, from evil men;
Preserve me from violent men,
²Who plan evil things in *their* hearts;
They continually gather together *for* war.
³They sharpen their tongues like a serpent;
The poison of asps *is* under their lips.   *Selah*

⁴Keep me, O LORD, from the hands of the
wicked;
Preserve me from violent men,
Who have purposed to make my steps
stumble.
⁵The proud have hidden a snare for me, and
cords;
They have spread a net by the wayside;
They have set traps for me.   *Selah*

⁶I said to the LORD: "You *are* my God;
Hear the voice of my supplications,
O LORD.
⁷O GOD the Lord, the strength of my
salvation,
You have covered my head in the day of
battle.
⁸Do not grant, O LORD, the desires of the
wicked;
Do not further his *wicked* scheme,
Lest they be exalted.   *Selah*

⁹"*As for* the head of those who surround me,
Let the evil of their lips cover them;
¹⁰Let burning coals fall upon them;
Let them be cast into the fire,
Into deep pits, that they rise not up again.
¹¹Let not a slanderer be established in the
earth;
Let evil hunt the violent man to overthrow
him."

¹²I know that the LORD will maintain
The cause of the afflicted,
And justice for the poor.
¹³Surely the righteous shall give thanks to Your
name;
The upright shall dwell in Your presence.

PSALM 141

PRAYER FOR SAFEKEEPING FROM WICKEDNESS
A Psalm of David.

¹LORD, I cry out to You;
Make haste to me!
Give ear to my voice when I cry out to You.
²Let my prayer be set before You *as* incense,
The lifting up of my hands *as* the evening
sacrifice.

³Set a guard, O LORD, over my mouth;
Keep watch over the door of my lips.
⁴Do not incline my heart to any evil thing,
To practice wicked works
With men who work iniquity;
And do not let me eat of their delicacies.

⁵Let the righteous strike me;
It shall be a kindness.
And let him rebuke me;
It shall be as excellent oil;
Let my head not refuse it.

For still my prayer *is* against the deeds of the
wicked.
⁶Their judges are overthrown by the sides of
the cliff,
And they hear my words, for they are sweet.
⁷Our bones are scattered at the mouth of the
grave,
As when one plows and breaks up the earth.

⁸But my eyes *are* upon You, O GOD the Lord;
In You I take refuge;
Do not leave my soul destitute.
⁹Keep me from the snares they have laid for m
And from the traps of the workers of iniquit
¹⁰Let the wicked fall into their own nets,
While I escape safely.

PSALM 142

A PLEA FOR RELIEF FROM PERSECUTORS
A Contemplationª of David. A Prayer when he
was in the cave.

¹I cry out to the LORD with my voice;
With my voice to the LORD I make my
supplication.

142:title ªHebrew *Maschil*

²I pour out my complaint before Him;
I declare before Him my trouble.

³When my spirit was overwhelmed within
me,
Then You knew my path.
In the way in which I walk
They have secretly set a snare for me.
⁴Look on *my* right hand and see,
For *there is* no one who acknowledges me;
Refuge has failed me;
No one cares for my soul.

⁵I cried out to You, O LORD:
I said, "You *are* my refuge,
My portion in the land of the living.
⁶Attend to my cry,
For I am brought very low;
Deliver me from my persecutors,
For they are stronger than I.
⁷Bring my soul out of prison,
That I may praise Your name;
The righteous shall surround me,
For You shall deal bountifully with me."

PSALM 143

AN EARNEST APPEAL FOR GUIDANCE
AND DELIVERANCE
A Psalm of David.

¹Hear my prayer, O LORD,
Give ear to my supplications!
In Your faithfulness answer me,
And in Your righteousness.
²Do not enter into judgment with Your
servant,
For in Your sight no one living is righteous.

³For the enemy has persecuted my soul;
He has crushed my life to the ground;
He has made me dwell in darkness,
Like those who have long been dead.
⁴Therefore my spirit is overwhelmed within
me;
My heart within me is distressed.

⁵I remember the days of old;
I meditate on all Your works;
I muse on the work of Your hands.

⁶I spread out my hands to You;
My soul *longs* for You like a thirsty land. *Selah*

⁷Answer me speedily, O LORD;
My spirit fails!
Do not hide Your face from me,
Lest I be like those who go down into the pit.
⁸Cause me to hear Your lovingkindness in the
morning,
For in You do I trust;
Cause me to know the way in which I should
walk,
For I lift up my soul to You.

⁹Deliver me, O LORD, from my enemies;
In You I take shelter.ᵃ
¹⁰Teach me to do Your will,
For You *are* my God;
Your Spirit *is* good.
Lead me in the land of uprightness.

¹¹Revive me, O LORD, for Your name's sake!
For Your righteousness' sake bring my soul
out of trouble.
¹²In Your mercy cut off my enemies,
And destroy all those who afflict my soul;
For I *am* Your servant.

PSALM 144

A SONG TO THE LORD WHO PRESERVES AND
PROSPERS HIS PEOPLE
A *Psalm* of David.

¹Blessed *be* the LORD my Rock,
Who trains my hands for war,
And my fingers for battle—
²My lovingkindness and my fortress,
My high tower and my deliverer,
My shield and *the One* in whom I take
refuge,
Who subdues my peopleᵃ under me.

³LORD, what *is* man, that You take knowledge
of him?
Or the son of man, that You are mindful of
him?

143:9 ᵃSeptuagint and Vulgate read *To You I flee.* **144:2** ᵃFollowing
Masoretic Text, Septuagint, and Vulgate; Syriac and Targum read
the peoples (compare 18:47).

⁴Man is like a breath;
His days *are* like a passing shadow.

⁵Bow down Your heavens, O Lord, and come down;
Touch the mountains, and they shall smoke.
⁶Flash forth lightning and scatter them;
Shoot out Your arrows and destroy them.
⁷Stretch out Your hand from above;
Rescue me and deliver me out of great waters,
From the hand of foreigners,
⁸Whose mouth speaks lying words,
And whose right hand *is* a right hand of falsehood.

⁹I will sing a new song to You, O God;
On a harp of ten strings I will sing praises to You,
¹⁰*The One* who gives salvation to kings,
Who delivers David His servant
From the deadly sword.

¹¹Rescue me and deliver me from the hand of foreigners,
Whose mouth speaks lying words,
And whose right hand *is* a right hand of falsehood—
¹²That our sons *may be* as plants grown up in their youth;
That our daughters *may be* as pillars,
Sculptured in palace style;
¹³*That* our barns *may be* full,
Supplying all kinds of produce;
That our sheep may bring forth thousands
And ten thousands in our fields;
¹⁴*That* our oxen *may be* well laden;
That there be no breaking in or going out;
That there be no outcry in our streets.
¹⁵Happy *are* the people who are in such a state;
Happy *are* the people whose God *is* the Lord!

PSALM 145

A Song of God's Majesty and Love
A Praise of David.

¹I will extol You, my God, O King;
And I will bless Your name forever and ever.

²Every day I will bless You,
And I will praise Your name forever and ever
³Great *is* the Lord, and greatly to be praised;
And His greatness *is* unsearchable.

⁴One generation shall praise Your works to another,
And shall declare Your mighty acts.
⁵I[a] will meditate on the glorious splendor of Your majesty,
And on Your wondrous works.[b]
⁶*Men* shall speak of the might of Your awesome acts,
And I will declare Your greatness.
⁷They shall utter the memory of Your great goodness,
And shall sing of Your righteousness.

⁸The Lord *is* gracious and full of compassion,
Slow to anger and great in mercy.
⁹The Lord *is* good to all,
And His tender mercies *are* over all His works.

¹⁰All Your works shall praise You, O Lord,
And Your saints shall bless You.
¹¹They shall speak of the glory of Your kingdom,
And talk of Your power,
¹²To make known to the sons of men His mighty acts,
And the glorious majesty of His kingdom.
¹³Your kingdom *is* an everlasting kingdom,
And Your dominion *endures* throughout all generations.[a]

¹⁴The Lord upholds all who fall,
And raises up all *who are* bowed down.
¹⁵The eyes of all look expectantly to You,
And You give them their food in due season.
¹⁶You open Your hand
And satisfy the desire of every living thing.

¹⁷The Lord *is* righteous in all His ways,
Gracious in all His works.

145:5 [a]Following Masoretic Text and Targum; Dead Sea Scrolls, Septuagint, Syriac, and Vulgate read *They.* [b]Literally *on the words of Your wondrous works* **145:13** [a]Following Masoretic Text and Targum; Dead Sea Scrolls, Septuagint, Syriac, and Vulgate add *The Lord is faithful in all His words, And holy in all His works.*

THROUGH THE GRID　　*Discover God: God Is Righteous*

PSALM 145:17　*The L*ORD *is righteous in all His ways, gracious in all His works.*

The only One who can be considered wholly righteous is God, since God is the only One who is holy. Because God is holy, He can be characterized as righteous—meaning that God always does that which is right and in accordance with God's own will. While holiness describes God's nature, righteousness describes God's actions, in accordance with God's holiness. Because God is righteous, God desires for all of creation to be righteous as well. One of the chief applications of God's righteousness is in the role of Righteous Judge. That is, God is the standard upon which every measure of righteousness must be based. It is God's righteousness that establishes the foundation of justice and morality. We cannot truly become righteous on our own; rather, it is our participation in Christ as the faithful One who bridges the gap between humanity and God.

18The LORD *is* near to all who call upon Him,
　To all who call upon Him in truth.
19He will fulfill the desire of those who fear
　　Him;
　He also will hear their cry and save them.
20The LORD preserves all who love Him,
　But all the wicked He will destroy.
21My mouth shall speak the praise of the LORD,
　And all flesh shall bless His holy name
　　Forever and ever.

PSALM 146

THE HAPPINESS OF THOSE WHOSE HELP
IS THE LORD

1Praise the LORD!

Praise the LORD, O my soul!
2While I live I will praise the LORD;
　I will sing praises to my God while I have my
　　being.

3Do not put your trust in princes,
　Nor in a son of man, in whom *there is* no help.
4His spirit departs, he returns to his earth;
　In that very day his plans perish.

5Happy *is he* who *has* the God of Jacob for his
　　help,
　Whose hope *is* in the LORD his God,

6Who made heaven and earth,
　The sea, and all that *is* in them;
　Who keeps truth forever,
7Who executes justice for the oppressed,
　Who gives food to the hungry.
　The LORD gives freedom to the prisoners.

8The LORD opens *the eyes of* the blind;
　The LORD raises those who are bowed down;
　The LORD loves the righteous.
9The LORD watches over the strangers;
　He relieves the fatherless and widow;
　But the way of the wicked He turns upside
　　down.

10The LORD shall reign forever—
　Your God, O Zion, to all generations.

Praise the LORD!

PSALM 147

PRAISE TO GOD FOR HIS WORD AND
PROVIDENCE

1Praise the LORD!
　For *it is* good to sing praises to our God;
　For *it is* pleasant, *and* praise is beautiful.

2The LORD builds up Jerusalem;
　He gathers together the outcasts of Israel.

THROUGH THE GRID

Making Sense of Your World:
A Biblical Perspective
on the Environment (Ps. 146:5, 6)

Many exhibit a display of apathy toward issues concerning the environment. This selfish view of the world does not coincide with the biblical worldview, which calls for us to protect and to preserve nature. The earth belongs to the Lord, and we are the guardians of the earth. Instead of being the last to respond to environmental issues, Christians should be the first to respond, providing a witness that demonstrates that we care for the earth with which we have been entrusted. All of creation is important to God, and we must demonstrate that we value God's creation by caring for it.

³He heals the brokenhearted
And binds up their wounds.
⁴He counts the number of the stars;
He calls them all by name.
⁵Great *is* our Lord, and mighty in power;
His understanding *is* infinite.
⁶The LORD lifts up the humble;
He casts the wicked down to the ground.

⁷Sing to the LORD with thanksgiving;
Sing praises on the harp to our God,
⁸Who covers the heavens with clouds,
Who prepares rain for the earth,
Who makes grass to grow on the mountains.
⁹He gives to the beast its food,
And to the young ravens that cry.

¹⁰He does not delight in the strength of the
horse;
He takes no pleasure in the legs of a man.
¹¹The LORD takes pleasure in those who fear
Him,
In those who hope in His mercy.

¹²Praise the LORD, O Jerusalem!
Praise your God, O Zion!
¹³For He has strengthened the bars of your
gates;
He has blessed your children within you.
¹⁴He makes peace *in* your borders,
And fills you with the finest wheat.

¹⁵He sends out His command *to the* earth;
His word runs very swiftly.

¹⁶He gives snow like wool;
He scatters the frost like ashes;
¹⁷He casts out His hail like morsels;
Who can stand before His cold?
¹⁸He sends out His word and melts them;
He causes His wind to blow, *and* the waters
flow.

¹⁹He declares His word to Jacob,
His statutes and His judgments to Israel.
²⁰He has not dealt thus with any nation;
And *as for His* judgments, they have not
known them.

Praise the LORD!

PSALM 148

PRAISE TO THE LORD FROM CREATION

¹Praise the LORD!

Praise the LORD from the heavens;
Praise Him in the heights!
²Praise Him, all His angels;
Praise Him, all His hosts!
³Praise Him, sun and moon;
Praise Him, all you stars of light!
⁴Praise Him, you heavens of heavens,
And you waters above the heavens!

⁵Let them praise the name of the LORD,
For He commanded and they were created.
⁶He also established them forever and ever;
He made a decree which shall not pass away.

7Praise the LORD from the earth,
  You great sea creatures and all the depths;
8Fire and hail, snow and clouds;
  Stormy wind, fulfilling His word;
9Mountains and all hills;
  Fruitful trees and all cedars;
10Beasts and all cattle;
  Creeping things and flying fowl;
11Kings of the earth and all peoples;
  Princes and all judges of the earth;
12Both young men and maidens;
  Old men and children.

13Let them praise the name of the LORD,
  For His name alone is exalted;
  His glory *is* above the earth and heaven.
14And He has exalted the horn of His
      people,
  The praise of all His saints—
  Of the children of Israel,
  A people near to Him.

Praise the LORD!

PSALM 149

PRAISE TO GOD FOR HIS SALVATION
AND JUDGMENT

1Praise the LORD!

  Sing to the LORD a new song,
  And His praise in the assembly of saints.

2Let Israel rejoice in their Maker;
  Let the children of Zion be joyful in their
      King.
3Let them praise His name with the dance;
  Let them sing praises to Him with the
      timbrel and harp.

4For the LORD takes pleasure in His people;
  He will beautify the humble with salvation.

5Let the saints be joyful in glory;
  Let them sing aloud on their beds.
6Let the high praises of God *be* in their mouth,
  And a two-edged sword in their hand,
7To execute vengeance on the nations,
  And punishments on the peoples;
8To bind their kings with chains,
  And their nobles with fetters of iron;
9To execute on them the written judgment—
  This honor have all His saints.

Praise the LORD!

PSALM 150

LET ALL THINGS PRAISE THE LORD

1Praise the LORD!

  Praise God in His sanctuary;
  Praise Him in His mighty firmament!

2Praise Him for His mighty acts;
  Praise Him according to His excellent
      greatness!

3Praise Him with the sound of the trumpet;
  Praise Him with the lute and harp!
4Praise Him with the timbrel and dance;
  Praise Him with stringed instruments and
      flutes!
5Praise Him with loud cymbals;
  Praise Him with clashing cymbals!

6Let everything that has breath praise the LORD.

  Praise the LORD!

IMPACT OF THE BOOK

I IDEA	*True wisdom begins with the fear (or reverence) of the Lord.*
MESSAGE	*The power of personal choice means you can determine to make good choices or suffer the consequences of evil choices. Leaders learn to **think** rightly according to God's wisdom—not worldly wisdom—before they **do** anything. By allowing God's Word to be a guide to direct them and a guard to protect them, they learn true wisdom. Proverbs also proclaims the dangers of laziness, making the most of each day, learning how to manage time effectively, and having the maximum impact for the Lord.*
PEOPLE	*Agur, Lemuel, Solomon*
AUTHOR	*Aside from sections of Proverbs 22—24, Proverbs 30 (which was written by Agur—of whom nothing is known), and Proverbs 31 (which is credited to King Lemuel), this book was penned by Solomon, the son of King David and Bathsheba, who ruled Israel from c. 970 to 931 BC.*
CULTURE	*There are several forms of teaching in this book: proverbs, admonitions, numerical sayings, rhetorical questions, poems, and stories or lessons. Each form was meant to drive home truth and cause the reader to contemplate his own life in light of God's wisdom. Proverbs often refer to a "path" hearers should take, pointing them to the "goal" of godly living. However, while wisdom is available to all who are willing to hear, few choose the right path.*
TIMELINE	*The proverbs of Solomon were composed before his death c. 931 BC, with the final compilation probably occurring at a later date.*
KEY SCRIPTURE MEMORY VERSES	1:7; 3:5, 6; 15:1; 16:18, 25; 22:6; 27:17; 31:10, 28–30

THE BEGINNING OF KNOWLEDGE

1 The proverbs of Solomon the son of David,
king of Israel:

[2]To know wisdom and instruction,
To perceive the words of understanding,
[3]To receive the instruction of wisdom,
Justice, judgment, and equity;
[4]To give prudence to the simple,
To the young man knowledge and
discretion—
[5]A wise *man* will hear and increase learning,
And a man of understanding will attain wise
counsel,
[6]To understand a proverb and an enigma,
The words of the wise and their riddles.

[7]The fear of the LORD *is* the beginning of
knowledge,
But fools despise wisdom and instruction.

SHUN EVIL COUNSEL

[8]My son, hear the instruction of your father,
And do not forsake the law of your mother;
[9]For they *will be* a graceful ornament on your
head,
And chains about your neck.

[10]My son, if sinners entice you,
Do not consent.
[11]If they say, "Come with us,
Let us lie in wait to *shed* blood;
Let us lurk secretly for the innocent without
cause;
[12]Let us swallow them alive like Sheol,[a]

And whole, like those who go down to the
Pit;
[13]We shall find all *kinds* of precious possessions,
We shall fill our houses with spoil;
[14]Cast in your lot among us,
Let us all have one purse"—
[15]My son, do not walk in the way with them,
Keep your foot from their path;
[16]For their feet run to evil,
And they make haste to shed blood.
[17]Surely, in vain the net is spread
In the sight of any bird;
[18]But they lie in wait for their *own* blood,
They lurk secretly for their *own* lives.
[19]So *are* the ways of everyone who is greedy for
gain;
It takes away the life of its owners.

THE CALL OF WISDOM

[20]Wisdom calls aloud outside;
She raises her voice in the open squares.
[21]She cries out in the chief concourses,[a]
At the openings of the gates in the city
She speaks her words:
[22]"How long, you simple ones, will you love
simplicity?
For scorners delight in their scorning,
And fools hate knowledge.
[23]Turn at my rebuke;
Surely I will pour out my spirit on you;
I will make my words known to you.
[24]Because I have called and you refused,
I have stretched out my hand and no one
regarded,

1:12 [a]Or *the grave* **1:21** [a]Septuagint, Syriac, and Targum read *top
of the walls;* Vulgate reads *the head of multitudes.*

THROUGH THE GRID

*Making Sense of Your World:
Obtaining a Worldview (Prov. 1:8, 9)*

Our views of ultimate reality, humanity, and nature comprise the bulk of the basic information upon which our worldview rests. However, there is also the realization that we do not arrive at these answers to our worldview questions by a conscious scientific process most of the time. Of course, there are decisive moments and experiences in our lives that occur and shape the way we think, but most of the time, our worldview is determined from the lives into which we have been immersed. Our culture and our development therein play a crucial role in forming the shape and extent of our worldview.

²⁵Because you disdained all my counsel,
  And would have none of my rebuke,
²⁶I also will laugh at your calamity;
  I will mock when your terror comes,
²⁷When your terror comes like a storm,
  And your destruction comes like a whirlwind,
  When distress and anguish come upon you.

²⁸"Then they will call on me, but I will not answer;
  They will seek me diligently, but they will not find me.
²⁹Because they hated knowledge
  And did not choose the fear of the LORD,
³⁰They would have none of my counsel
  And despised my every rebuke.
³¹Therefore they shall eat the fruit of their own way,
  And be filled to the full with their own fancies.
³²For the turning away of the simple will slay them,
  And the complacency of fools will destroy them;
³³But whoever listens to me will dwell safely,
  And will be secure, without fear of evil."

THE VALUE OF WISDOM

2 My son, if you receive my words,
  And treasure my commands within you,
²So that you incline your ear to wisdom,
  And apply your heart to understanding;
³Yes, if you cry out for discernment,
  And lift up your voice for understanding,
⁴If you seek her as silver,
  And search for her as for hidden treasures;
⁵Then you will understand the fear of the LORD,
  And find the knowledge of God.
⁶For the LORD gives wisdom;
  From His mouth come knowledge and understanding;
⁷He stores up sound wisdom for the upright;
  He is a shield to those who walk uprightly;
⁸He guards the paths of justice,
  And preserves the way of His saints.
⁹Then you will understand righteousness and justice,
  Equity and every good path.

¹⁰When wisdom enters your heart,
  And knowledge is pleasant to your soul,
¹¹Discretion will preserve you;
  Understanding will keep you,
¹²To deliver you from the way of evil,
  From the man who speaks perverse things,
¹³From those who leave the paths of uprightness
  To walk in the ways of darkness;
¹⁴Who rejoice in doing evil,
  And delight in the perversity of the wicked;
¹⁵Whose ways are crooked,
  And who are devious in their paths;
¹⁶To deliver you from the immoral woman,
  From the seductress who flatters with her words,
¹⁷Who forsakes the companion of her youth,
  And forgets the covenant of her God.
¹⁸For her house leads down to death,
  And her paths to the dead;
¹⁹None who go to her return,
  Nor do they regain the paths of life—
²⁰So you may walk in the way of goodness,
  And keep to the paths of righteousness.
²¹For the upright will dwell in the land,
  And the blameless will remain in it;
²²But the wicked will be cut off from the earth,
  And the unfaithful will be uprooted from it.

GUIDANCE FOR THE YOUNG

3 My son, do not forget my law,
  But let your heart keep my commands;
²For length of days and long life
  And peace they will add to you.

³Let not mercy and truth forsake you;
  Bind them around your neck,
  Write them on the tablet of your heart,
⁴And so find favor and high esteem
  In the sight of God and man.

⁵Trust in the LORD with all your heart,
  And lean not on your own understanding;
⁶In all your ways acknowledge Him,
  And He shall directᵃ your paths.

⁷Do not be wise in your own eyes;
  Fear the LORD and depart from evil.

3:6 ᵃOr make smooth or straight

LEADERSHIP ISSUES

Character and Skill: Pillars of Leadership

PROVERBS 3:4–6

Two pillars of leadership are character and skill. Skills can be acquired, such as the ability to present oneself through speech or the written word or to think critically, but character comes from knowing Christ and being filled with His Spirit. The two can be separate, but work powerfully when combined.

Leaders who demonstrated tremendous skill dominate pages of the Bible and history. Several biblical examples come to mind: Samson had skill as a warrior, Balaam as a prophet, and Judas Iscariot as a treasurer. In more recent history, Adolf Hitler was a great orator and Osama Bin Laden an effective strategist. Each of these leaders demonstrated tremendous skill, but as leadership expert Peter Drucker says, "Character in itself does not make a leader, but the absence of it flaws the entire process."

Although the skills displayed by a leader initially earn recognition, compromising on character will eventually lead to a tainted legacy. Protect yourself:

First, leaders must solidify their belief system. Know assuredly which core beliefs determine any course of action. This belief system must be rooted in a relationship with Christ and grounded in the Word.

Second, leaders must surround themselves with people of integrity. These individuals should know Christ, be rooted in the Word of God, and willing to speak candidly even if they might offend. Consider Paul's letters to the churches at Corinth and Galatia. Although Paul loves the church dearly, he is not afraid to address false witnesses and dissension.

Third, leaders must volunteer to have measures of accountability in place. Satan attacks each leader differently based on his or her individual weaknesses. Leaders must self-administer filters that prevent Satan from obtaining a stronghold. Some filters might include blocking certain Internet sites, patronizing only family-oriented businesses, or having an accountability partner who will regularly ask questions of your activities—particularly those away from the protection of family or friends. Live your life so that even if your skills fade over time the content of your character will remain.

⁸It will be health to your flesh,ᵃ
  And strengthᵇ to your bones.

⁹Honor the LORD with your possessions,
  And with the firstfruits of all your increase;
¹⁰So your barns will be filled with plenty,
  And your vats will overflow with new wine.

¹¹My son, do not despise the chastening of the
      LORD,
  Nor detest His correction;
¹²For whom the LORD loves He corrects,
  Just as a father the son *in whom* he delights.

¹³Happy *is* the man *who* finds wisdom,
  And the man *who* gains understanding;
¹⁴For her proceeds *are* better than the profits of
      silver,
  And her gain than fine gold.
¹⁵She *is* more precious than rubies,
  And all the things you may desire cannot
      compare with her.
¹⁶Length of days *is* in her right hand,
  In her left hand riches and honor.
¹⁷Her ways *are* ways of pleasantness,
  And all her paths *are* peace.
¹⁸She *is* a tree of life to those who take hold of
      her,
  And happy *are all* who retain her.

¹⁹The LORD by wisdom founded the earth;
  By understanding He established the heavens;
²⁰By His knowledge the depths were broken
      up,
  And clouds drop down the dew.

²¹My son, let them not depart from your
      eyes—
  Keep sound wisdom and discretion;
²²So they will be life to your soul
  And grace to your neck.
²³Then you will walk safely in your way,
  And your foot will not stumble.
²⁴When you lie down, you will not be afraid;
  Yes, you will lie down and your sleep will be
      sweet.
²⁵Do not be afraid of sudden terror,
  Nor of trouble from the wicked when it
      comes;

²⁶For the LORD will be your confidence,
  And will keep your foot from being caught.

²⁷Do not withhold good from those to whom
      it is due,
  When it is in the power of your hand to do
      so.
²⁸Do not say to your neighbor,
 "Go, and come back,
  And tomorrow I will give *it,"*
  When you have it with you.
²⁹Do not devise evil against your neighbor,
  For he dwells by you for safety's sake.
³⁰Do not strive with a man without cause,
  If he has done you no harm.

³¹Do not envy the oppressor,
  And choose none of his ways;
³²For the perverse *person is* an abomination to
      the LORD,
  But His secret counsel *is* with the upright.
³³The curse of the LORD *is* on the house of the
      wicked,
  But He blesses the home of the just.
³⁴Surely He scorns the scornful,
  But gives grace to the humble.
³⁵The wise shall inherit glory,
  But shame shall be the legacy of fools.

SECURITY IN WISDOM

4 Hear, my children, the instruction of a father,
  And give attention to know understanding;
²For I give you good doctrine:
  Do not forsake my law.
³When I was my father's son,
  Tender and the only one in the sight of my
      mother,
⁴He also taught me, and said to me:
 "Let your heart retain my words;
  Keep my commands, and live.
⁵Get wisdom! Get understanding!
  Do not forget, nor turn away from the words
      of my mouth.
⁶Do not forsake her, and she will preserve you;
  Love her, and she will keep you.
⁷Wisdom *is* the principal thing;
  Therefore get wisdom.

3:8 ᵃLiterally *navel,* figurative of the body ᵇLiterally *drink* or *refreshment*

And in all your getting, get understanding.
⁸Exalt her, and she will promote you;
She will bring you honor, when you embrace her.
⁹She will place on your head an ornament of grace;
A crown of glory she will deliver to you."

¹⁰Hear, my son, and receive my sayings,
And the years of your life will be many.
¹¹I have taught you in the way of wisdom;
I have led you in right paths.
¹²When you walk, your steps will not be hindered,
And when you run, you will not stumble.
¹³Take firm hold of instruction, do not let go;
Keep her, for she *is* your life.

¹⁴Do not enter the path of the wicked,
And do not walk in the way of evil.
¹⁵Avoid it, do not travel on it;
Turn away from it and pass on.
¹⁶For they do not sleep unless they have done evil;
And their sleep is taken away unless they make *someone* fall.
¹⁷For they eat the bread of wickedness,
And drink the wine of violence.

¹⁸But the path of the just *is* like the shining sun,ᵃ
That shines ever brighter unto the perfect day.
¹⁹The way of the wicked *is* like darkness;
They do not know what makes them stumble.

²⁰My son, give attention to my words;
Incline your ear to my sayings.
²¹Do not let them depart from your eyes;
Keep them in the midst of your heart;
²²For they *are* life to those who find them,
And health to all their flesh.

²³Keep your heart with all diligence,
For out of it *spring* the issues of life.
²⁴Put away from you a deceitful mouth,
And put perverse lips far from you.
²⁵Let your eyes look straight ahead,

And your eyelids look right before you.
²⁶Ponder the path of your feet,
And let all your ways be established.
²⁷Do not turn to the right or the left;
Remove your foot from evil.

The Peril of Adultery

5 My son, pay attention to my wisdom;
Lend your ear to my understanding,
²That you may preserve discretion,
And your lips may keep knowledge.
³For the lips of an immoral woman drip honey,
And her mouth *is* smoother than oil;
⁴But in the end she is bitter as wormwood,
Sharp as a two-edged sword.
⁵Her feet go down to death,
Her steps lay hold of hell.ᵃ
⁶Lest you ponder *her* path of life—
Her ways are unstable;
You do not know *them*.

⁷Therefore hear me now, *my* children,
And do not depart from the words of my mouth.
⁸Remove your way far from her,
And do not go near the door of her house,
⁹Lest you give your honor to others,
And your years to the cruel *one;*
¹⁰Lest aliens be filled with your wealth,
And your labors *go* to the house of a foreigner;
¹¹And you mourn at last,
When your flesh and your body are consumed,
¹²And say:
"How I have hated instruction,
And my heart despised correction!
¹³I have not obeyed the voice of my teachers,
Nor inclined my ear to those who instructed me!
¹⁴I was on the verge of total ruin,
In the midst of the assembly and congregation."

¹⁵Drink water from your own cistern,
And running water from your own well.

4:18 ᵃLiterally *light*   **5:5** ᵃOr *Sheol*

¹⁶Should your fountains be dispersed abroad,
Streams of water in the streets?
¹⁷Let them be only your own,
And not for strangers with you.
¹⁸Let your fountain be blessed,
And rejoice with the wife of your youth.
¹⁹*As a* loving deer and a graceful doe,
Let her breasts satisfy you at all times;
And always be enraptured with her love.
²⁰For why should you, my son, be enraptured
by an immoral woman,
And be embraced in the arms of a seductress?

²¹For the ways of man *are* before the eyes of the
LORD,
And He ponders all his paths.
²²His own iniquities entrap the wicked *man,*
And he is caught in the cords of his sin.
²³He shall die for lack of instruction,
And in the greatness of his folly he shall go
astray.

DANGEROUS PROMISES

6 My son, if you become surety for your friend,
If you have shaken hands in pledge for a
stranger,
²You are snared by the words of your mouth;
You are taken by the words of your mouth.
³So do this, my son, and deliver yourself;
For you have come into the hand of your
friend:
Go and humble yourself;
Plead with your friend.
⁴Give no sleep to your eyes,
Nor slumber to your eyelids.
⁵Deliver yourself like a gazelle from the hand
of the hunter,
And like a bird from the hand of the fowler.ᵃ

THE FOLLY OF INDOLENCE

⁶Go to the ant, you sluggard!
Consider her ways and be wise,
⁷Which, having no captain,
Overseer or ruler,
⁸Provides her supplies in the summer,
And gathers her food in the harvest.
⁹How long will you slumber, O sluggard?
When will you rise from your sleep?
¹⁰A little sleep, a little slumber,

A little folding of the hands to sleep—
¹¹So shall your poverty come on you like a
prowler,
And your need like an armed man.

THE WICKED MAN

¹²A worthless person, a wicked man,
Walks with a perverse mouth;
¹³He winks with his eyes,
He shuffles his feet,
He points with his fingers;
¹⁴Perversity *is* in his heart,
He devises evil continually,
He sows discord.
¹⁵Therefore his calamity shall come suddenly;
Suddenly he shall be broken without remedy.

¹⁶These six *things* the LORD hates,
Yes, seven *are* an abomination to Him:
¹⁷A proud look,
A lying tongue,
Hands that shed innocent blood,
¹⁸A heart that devises wicked plans,
Feet that are swift in running to evil,
¹⁹A false witness *who* speaks lies,
And one who sows discord among brethren.

BEWARE OF ADULTERY

²⁰My son, keep your father's command,
And do not forsake the law of your mother.
²¹Bind them continually upon your heart;
Tie them around your neck.
²²When you roam, theyᵃ will lead you;
When you sleep, they will keep you;
And *when* you awake, they will speak with
you.
²³For the commandment *is* a lamp,
And the law a light;
Reproofs of instruction *are* the way of life,
²⁴To keep you from the evil woman,
From the flattering tongue of a seductress.
²⁵Do not lust after her beauty in your heart,
Nor let her allure you with her eyelids.
²⁶For by means of a harlot
A man is reduced to a crust of bread;
And an adulteressᵃ will prey upon his precious
life.

6:5 ᵃThat is, one who catches birds in a trap or snare   **6:22** ᵃLiterally *it*   **6:26** ᵃLiterally *a man's wife,* that is, of another

²⁷Can a man take fire to his bosom,
And his clothes not be burned?
²⁸Can one walk on hot coals,
And his feet not be seared?
²⁹So *is* he who goes in to his neighbor's wife;
Whoever touches her shall not be innocent.

³⁰*People* do not despise a thief
If he steals to satisfy himself when he is
starving.
³¹Yet *when* he is found, he must restore
sevenfold;
He may have to give up all the substance of
his house.
³²Whoever commits adultery with a woman
lacks understanding;
He *who* does so destroys his own soul.
³³Wounds and dishonor he will get,
And his reproach will not be wiped away.
³⁴For jealousy *is* a husband's fury;
Therefore he will not spare in the day of
vengeance.
³⁵He will accept no recompense,
Nor will he be appeased though you give
many gifts.

7 My son, keep my words,
And treasure my commands within you.
²Keep my commands and live,
And my law as the apple of your eye.
³Bind them on your fingers;
Write them on the tablet of your heart.
⁴Say to wisdom, "You *are* my sister,"
And call understanding *your* nearest kin,
⁵That they may keep you from the immoral
woman,
From the seductress *who* flatters with her
words.

THE CRAFTY HARLOT

⁶For at the window of my house
I looked through my lattice,
⁷And saw among the simple,
I perceived among the youths,
A young man devoid of understanding,
⁸Passing along the street near her corner;
And he took the path to her house
⁹In the twilight, in the evening,
In the black and dark night.

¹⁰And there a woman met him,
With the attire of a harlot, and a crafty
heart.
¹¹She *was* loud and rebellious,
Her feet would not stay at home.
¹²At times *she was* outside, at times in the open
square,
Lurking at every corner.
¹³So she caught him and kissed him;
With an impudent face she said to him:
¹⁴"*I have* peace offerings with me;
Today I have paid my vows.
¹⁵So I came out to meet you,
Diligently to seek your face,
And I have found you.
¹⁶I have spread my bed with tapestry,
Colored coverings of Egyptian linen.
¹⁷I have perfumed my bed
With myrrh, aloes, and cinnamon.
¹⁸Come, let us take our fill of love until
morning;
Let us delight ourselves with love.
¹⁹For my husband *is* not at home;
He has gone on a long journey;
²⁰He has taken a bag of money with him,
And will come home on the appointed day."

²¹With her enticing speech she caused him to
yield,
With her flattering lips she seduced him.
²²Immediately he went after her, as an ox goes
to the slaughter,
Or as a fool to the correction of the stocks,ª
²³Till an arrow struck his liver.
As a bird hastens to the snare,
He did not know it *would cost* his life.

²⁴Now therefore, listen to me, *my* children;
Pay attention to the words of my mouth:
²⁵Do not let your heart turn aside to her
ways,
Do not stray into her paths;
²⁶For she has cast down many wounded,
And all who were slain by her were strong
men.
²⁷Her house *is* the way to hell,ª
Descending to the chambers of death.

7:22 ªSeptuagint, Syriac, and Targum read *as a dog to bonds*; Vulgate reads *as a lamb . . . to bonds.*   **7:27** ªOr *Sheol*

The Excellence of Wisdom

8 Does not wisdom cry out,
And understanding lift up her voice?
²She takes her stand on the top of the high hill,
Beside the way, where the paths meet.
³She cries out by the gates, at the entry of the city,
At the entrance of the doors:
⁴"To you, O men, I call,
And my voice *is* to the sons of men.
⁵O you simple ones, understand prudence,
And you fools, be of an understanding heart.
⁶Listen, for I will speak of excellent things,
And from the opening of my lips *will come* right things;
⁷For my mouth will speak truth;
Wickedness *is* an abomination to my lips.
⁸All the words of my mouth *are* with righteousness;
Nothing crooked or perverse *is* in them.
⁹They *are* all plain to him who understands,
And right to those who find knowledge.
¹⁰Receive my instruction, and not silver,
And knowledge rather than choice gold;
¹¹For wisdom *is* better than rubies,
And all the things one may desire cannot be compared with her.

¹²"I, wisdom, dwell with prudence,
And find out knowledge *and* discretion.
¹³The fear of the LORD *is* to hate evil;
Pride and arrogance and the evil way
And the perverse mouth I hate.
¹⁴Counsel *is* mine, and sound wisdom;
I *am* understanding, I have strength.
¹⁵By me kings reign,
And rulers decree justice.
¹⁶By me princes rule, and nobles,
All the judges of the earth.ᵃ
¹⁷I love those who love me,
And those who seek me diligently will find me.
¹⁸Riches and honor *are* with me,
Enduring riches and righteousness.
¹⁹My fruit *is* better than gold, yes, than fine gold,
And my revenue than choice silver.

²⁰I traverse the way of righteousness,
In the midst of the paths of justice,
²¹That I may cause those who love me to inherit wealth,
That I may fill their treasuries.

²²"The LORD possessed me at the beginning of His way,
Before His works of old.
²³I have been established from everlasting,
From the beginning, before there was ever an earth.
²⁴When *there were* no depths I was brought forth,
When *there were* no fountains abounding with water.
²⁵Before the mountains were settled,
Before the hills, I was brought forth;
²⁶While as yet He had not made the earth or the fields,
Or the primal dust of the world.
²⁷When He prepared the heavens, I *was* there,
When He drew a circle on the face of the deep,
²⁸When He established the clouds above,
When He strengthened the fountains of the deep,
²⁹When He assigned to the sea its limit,
So that the waters would not transgress His command,
When He marked out the foundations of the earth,
³⁰Then I was beside Him *as* a master craftsman;ᵃ
And I was daily *His* delight,
Rejoicing always before Him,
³¹Rejoicing in His inhabited world,
And my delight *was* with the sons of men.

³²"Now therefore, listen to me, *my* children,
For blessed *are those who* keep my ways.
³³Hear instruction and be wise,
And do not disdain *it*.
³⁴Blessed is the man who listens to me,
Watching daily at my gates,
Waiting at the posts of my doors.

8:16 ᵃMasoretic Text, Syriac, Targum, and Vulgate read *righteousness;* Septuagint, Bomberg, and some manuscripts and editions read *earth.* **8:30** ᵃA Jewish tradition reads *one brought up.*

³⁵For whoever finds me finds life,
And obtains favor from the LORD;
³⁶But he who sins against me wrongs his own
soul;
All those who hate me love death."

THE WAY OF WISDOM

9 Wisdom has built her house,
She has hewn out her seven pillars;
²She has slaughtered her meat,
She has mixed her wine,
She has also furnished her table.
³She has sent out her maidens,
She cries out from the highest places of the
city,
⁴"Whoever *is* simple, let him turn in here!"
As for him who lacks understanding, she says
to him,
⁵"Come, eat of my bread
And drink of the wine I have mixed.
⁶Forsake foolishness and live,
And go in the way of understanding.

⁷"He who corrects a scoffer gets shame for
himself,
And he who rebukes a wicked *man only*
harms himself.
⁸Do not correct a scoffer, lest he hate you;
Rebuke a wise *man,* and he will love you.
⁹Give *instruction* to a wise *man,* and he will be
still wiser;
Teach a just *man,* and he will increase in
learning.

¹⁰"The fear of the LORD *is* the beginning of
wisdom,
And the knowledge of the Holy One *is*
understanding.
¹¹For by me your days will be multiplied,
And years of life will be added to you.
¹²If you are wise, you are wise for yourself,
And *if* you scoff, you will bear *it* alone."

THE WAY OF FOLLY

¹³A foolish woman is clamorous;
She is simple, and knows nothing.
¹⁴For she sits at the door of her house,
On a seat *by* the highest places of the city,
¹⁵To call to those who pass by,

Who go straight on their way:
¹⁶"Whoever *is* simple, let him turn in here";
And *as for* him who lacks understanding, she
says to him,
¹⁷"Stolen water is sweet,
And bread *eaten* in secret is pleasant."
¹⁸But he does not know that the dead *are* there,
That her guests *are* in the depths of hell.ᵃ

WISE SAYINGS OF SOLOMON

10 The proverbs of Solomon:

A wise son makes a glad father,
But a foolish son *is* the grief of his mother.

²Treasures of wickedness profit nothing,
But righteousness delivers from death.
³The LORD will not allow the righteous soul
to famish,
But He casts away the desire of the wicked.

⁴He who has a slack hand becomes poor,
But the hand of the diligent makes rich.
⁵He who gathers in summer *is* a wise son;
He who sleeps in harvest *is* a son who causes
shame.

⁶Blessings *are* on the head of the righteous,
But violence covers the mouth of the wicked.
⁷The memory of the righteous *is* blessed,
But the name of the wicked will rot.

⁸The wise in heart will receive commands,
But a prating fool will fall.

⁹He who walks with integrity walks securely,
But he who perverts his ways will become
known.

¹⁰He who winks with the eye causes trouble,
But a prating fool will fall.

¹¹The mouth of the righteous *is* a well of life,
But violence covers the mouth of the
wicked.

¹²Hatred stirs up strife,
But love covers all sins.

9:18 ᵃOr *Sheol*

13Wisdom is found on the lips of him who has
  understanding,
But a rod *is* for the back of him who is
  devoid of understanding.

14Wise *people* store up knowledge,
But the mouth of the foolish *is* near
  destruction.

15The rich man's wealth *is* his strong city;
The destruction of the poor *is* their poverty.

16The labor of the righteous *leads* to life,
The wages of the wicked to sin.

17He who keeps instruction *is in* the way of
  life,
But he who refuses correction goes astray.

18Whoever hides hatred *has* lying lips,
And whoever spreads slander *is* a fool.

19In the multitude of words sin is not lacking,
But he who restrains his lips *is* wise.
20The tongue of the righteous *is* choice silver;
The heart of the wicked *is worth* little.
21The lips of the righteous feed many,
But fools die for lack of wisdom.ª

22The blessing of the LORD makes *one* rich,
And He adds no sorrow with it.

23To do evil *is* like sport to a fool,
But a man of understanding has wisdom.
24The fear of the wicked will come upon him,
And the desire of the righteous will be
  granted.
25When the whirlwind passes by, the wicked *is*
  no *more,*
But the righteous *has* an everlasting
  foundation.

26As vinegar to the teeth and smoke to the
  eyes,
So *is* the lazy *man* to those who send him.

27The fear of the LORD prolongs days,
But the years of the wicked will be
  shortened.

28The hope of the righteous *will be* gladness,
But the expectation of the wicked will
  perish.
29The way of the LORD *is* strength for the
  upright,
But destruction *will come* to the workers of
  iniquity.

30The righteous will never be removed,
But the wicked will not inhabit the earth.
31The mouth of the righteous brings forth
  wisdom,
But the perverse tongue will be cut out.
32The lips of the righteous know what is
  acceptable,
But the mouth of the wicked *what is*
  perverse.

11 Dishonest scales *are* an abomination to the
  LORD,
But a just weight *is* His delight.

2When pride comes, then comes shame;
But with the humble *is* wisdom.

3The integrity of the upright will guide them,
But the perversity of the unfaithful will
  destroy them.
4Riches do not profit in the day of wrath,
But righteousness delivers from death.
5The righteousness of the blameless will directª
  his way aright,
But the wicked will fall by his own
  wickedness.
6The righteousness of the upright will deliver
  them,
But the unfaithful will be caught by *their* lust.

7When a wicked man dies, *his* expectation
  will perish,
And the hope of the unjust perishes.
8The righteous is delivered from trouble,
And it comes to the wicked instead.
9The hypocrite with *his* mouth destroys his
  neighbor,
But through knowledge the righteous will be
  delivered.

10:21 ªLiterally *heart*   **11:5** ªOr *make smooth* or *straight*

10When it goes well with the righteous, the
city rejoices;
And when the wicked perish, *there is*
jubilation.
11By the blessing of the upright the city is
exalted,
But it is overthrown by the mouth of the
wicked.

12He who is devoid of wisdom despises his
neighbor,
But a man of understanding holds his peace.

13A talebearer reveals secrets,
But he who is of a faithful spirit conceals a
matter.

14Where *there is* no counsel, the people fall;
But in the multitude of counselors *there is*
safety.

15He who is surety for a stranger will suffer,
But one who hates being surety is secure.

16A gracious woman retains honor,
But ruthless *men* retain riches.
17The merciful man does good for his own
soul,
But *he who is* cruel troubles his own flesh.
18The wicked *man* does deceptive work,
But he who sows righteousness *will have* a
sure reward.
19As righteousness *leads* to life,
So he who pursues evil *pursues it* to his own
death.
20Those who are of a perverse heart *are* an
abomination to the LORD,
But *the* blameless in their ways *are* His
delight.
21*Though they join* forces,[a] the wicked will not
go unpunished;
But the posterity of the righteous will be
delivered.

22*As* a ring of gold in a swine's snout,
So is a lovely woman who lacks discretion.

23The desire of the righteous *is* only good,
But the expectation of the wicked *is* wrath.

24There is *one* who scatters, yet increases more;
And there is *one* who withholds more than is
right,
But it *leads* to poverty.
25The generous soul will be made rich,
And he who waters will also be watered
himself.
26The people will curse him who withholds
grain,
But blessing *will be* on the head of him who
sells *it*.

27He who earnestly seeks good finds favor,
But trouble will come to him who seeks *evil*.

28He who trusts in his riches will fall,
But the righteous will flourish like foliage.

29He who troubles his own house will inherit
the wind,
And the fool *will be* servant to the wise of
heart.

30The fruit of the righteous *is a* tree of life,
And he who wins souls *is* wise.

31If the righteous will be recompensed on the
earth,
How much more the ungodly and the
sinner.

12 Whoever loves instruction loves
knowledge,
But he who hates correction *is* stupid.

2A good *man* obtains favor from the LORD,
But a man of wicked intentions He will
condemn.

3A man is not established by wickedness,
But the root of the righteous cannot be
moved.

4An excellent[a] wife *is* the crown of her
husband,
But she who causes shame *is* like rottenness
in his bones.

⁵The thoughts of the righteous *are* right,
But the counsels of the wicked *are* deceitful.
⁶The words of the wicked *are,* "Lie in wait for
blood,"
But the mouth of the upright will deliver
them.

⁷The wicked are overthrown and *are* no more,
But the house of the righteous will stand.

⁸A man will be commended according to his
wisdom,
But he who is of a perverse heart will be
despised.

⁹Better *is the one* who is slighted but has a
servant,
Than he who honors himself but lacks bread.

¹⁰A righteous *man* regards the life of his animal,
But the tender mercies of the wicked *are*
cruel.

¹¹He who tills his land will be satisfied with
bread,
But he who follows frivolity *is* devoid of
understanding.ᵃ

¹²The wicked covet the catch of evil *men,*
But the root of the righteous yields *fruit.*
¹³The wicked is ensnared by the transgression
of *his* lips,
But the righteous will come through trouble.
¹⁴A man will be satisfied with good by the fruit
of *his* mouth,
And the recompense of a man's hands will be
rendered to him.

¹⁵The way of a fool *is* right in his own eyes,
But he who heeds counsel *is* wise.
¹⁶A fool's wrath is known at once,
But a prudent *man* covers shame.

¹⁷He *who* speaks truth declares righteousness,
But a false witness, deceit.
¹⁸There is one who speaks like the piercings of
a sword,
But the tongue of the wise *promotes* health.
¹⁹The truthful lip shall be established forever,

But a lying tongue *is* but for a moment.
²⁰Deceit is in the heart of those who devise evil,
But counselors of peace have joy.
²¹No grave trouble will overtake the righteous,
But the wicked shall be filled with evil.
²²Lying lips *are* an abomination to the LORD,
But those who deal truthfully *are* His delight.

²³A prudent man conceals knowledge,
But the heart of fools proclaims foolishness.

²⁴The hand of the diligent will rule,
But the lazy *man* will be put to forced labor.

²⁵Anxiety in the heart of man causes
depression,
But a good word makes it glad.

²⁶The righteous should choose his friends
carefully,
For the way of the wicked leads them astray.

²⁷The lazy *man* does not roast what he took in
hunting,
But diligence *is* man's precious possession.

²⁸In the way of righteousness *is* life,
And in *its* pathway *there is* no death.

13 A wise son *heeds* his father's instruction,
But a scoffer does not listen to rebuke.

²A man shall eat well by the fruit of *his* mouth,
But the soul of the unfaithful feeds on
violence.
³He who guards his mouth preserves his life,
But he who opens wide his lips shall have
destruction.

⁴The soul of a lazy *man* desires, and *has*
nothing;
But the soul of the diligent shall be made
rich.

⁵A righteous *man* hates lying,
But a wicked *man* is loathsome and comes to
shame.

12:11 ᵃLiterally *heart*

⁶Righteousness guards *him whose* way is
    blameless,
But wickedness overthrows the sinner.

⁷There is one who makes himself rich, yet *has*
    nothing;
And one who makes himself poor, yet *has*
    great riches.

⁸The ransom of a man's life *is* his riches,
But the poor does not hear rebuke.

⁹The light of the righteous rejoices,
But the lamp of the wicked will be put out.

¹⁰By pride comes nothing but strife,
But with the well-advised *is* wisdom.

¹¹Wealth *gained by* dishonesty will be
    diminished,
But he who gathers by labor will increase.

¹²Hope deferred makes the heart sick,
But *when* the desire comes, *it is* a tree of life.

¹³He who despises the word will be destroyed,
But he who fears the commandment will be
    rewarded.
¹⁴The law of the wise *is* a fountain of life,
To turn *one* away from the snares of death.

¹⁵Good understanding gains favor,
But the way of the unfaithful *is* hard.
¹⁶Every prudent *man* acts with knowledge,
But a fool lays open *his* folly.

¹⁷A wicked messenger falls into trouble,
But a faithful ambassador *brings* health.

¹⁸Poverty and shame *will come* to him who
    disdains correction,
But he who regards a rebuke will be honored.

¹⁹A desire accomplished is sweet to the soul,
But *it is* an abomination to fools to depart
    from evil.

²⁰He who walks with wise *men* will be wise,
But the companion of fools will be destroyed.

²¹Evil pursues sinners,
But to the righteous, good shall be repaid.

²²A good *man* leaves an inheritance to his
    children's children,
But the wealth of the sinner is stored up for
    the righteous.

²³Much food *is in* the fallow *ground* of the poor,
And for lack of justice there is waste.ᵃ

²⁴He who spares his rod hates his son,
But he who loves him disciplines him
    promptly.

²⁵The righteous eats to the satisfying of his
    soul,
But the stomach of the wicked shall be in
    want.

14 The wise woman builds her house,
    But the foolish pulls it down with her
    hands.

²He who walks in his uprightness fears the
    Lᴏʀᴅ,
But *he who is* perverse in his ways despises
    Him.

³In the mouth of a fool *is* a rod of pride,
But the lips of the wise will preserve them.

⁴Where no oxen *are,* the trough *is* clean;
But much increase *comes* by the strength of
    an ox.

⁵A faithful witness does not lie,
But a false witness will utter lies.

⁶A scoffer seeks wisdom and does not *find it,*
But knowledge *is* easy to him who
    understands.
⁷Go from the presence of a foolish man,
When you do not perceive *in him* the lips of
    knowledge.
⁸The wisdom of the prudent *is* to understand
    his way,
But the folly of fools *is* deceit.

13:23 ᵃLiterally *what is swept away*

⁹Fools mock at sin,
But among the upright *there is* favor.

¹⁰The heart knows its own bitterness,
And a stranger does not share its joy.

¹¹The house of the wicked will be overthrown,
But the tent of the upright will flourish.

¹²There is a way *that seems* right to a man,
But its end *is* the way of death.

¹³Even in laughter the heart may sorrow,
And the end of mirth *may be* grief.

¹⁴The backslider in heart will be filled with his
own ways,
But a good man *will be satisfied* from above.[a]

¹⁵The simple believes every word,
But the prudent considers well his steps.

¹⁶A wise *man* fears and departs from evil,
But a fool rages and is self-confident.

¹⁷A quick-tempered *man* acts foolishly,
And a man of wicked intentions is hated.

¹⁸The simple inherit folly,
But the prudent are crowned with
knowledge.

¹⁹The evil will bow before the good,
And the wicked at the gates of the righteous.

²⁰The poor *man* is hated even by his own
neighbor,
But the rich *has* many friends.

²¹He who despises his neighbor sins;
But he who has mercy on the poor, happy *is*
he.

²²Do they not go astray who devise evil?
But mercy and truth *belong* to those who
devise good.

²³In all labor there is profit,
But idle chatter[a] *leads* only to poverty.

²⁴The crown of the wise is their riches,
But the foolishness of fools *is* folly.

²⁵A true witness delivers souls,
But a deceitful *witness* speaks lies.

²⁶In the fear of the LORD *there is* strong
confidence,
And His children will have a place of refuge.

²⁷The fear of the LORD *is* a fountain of life,
To turn *one* away from the snares of death.

²⁸In a multitude of people *is* a king's honor,
But in the lack of people *is* the downfall of a
prince.

²⁹*He who is* slow to wrath has great
understanding,
But *he who is* impulsive[a] exalts folly.

³⁰A sound heart *is* life to the body,
But envy *is* rottenness to the bones.

³¹He who oppresses the poor reproaches his
Maker,
But he who honors Him has mercy on the
needy.

³²The wicked is banished in his wickedness,
But the righteous has a refuge in his death.

³³Wisdom rests in the heart of him who has
understanding,
But *what is* in the heart of fools is made
known.

³⁴Righteousness exalts a nation,
But sin *is* a reproach to *any* people.

³⁵The king's favor *is* toward a wise servant,
But his wrath *is against* him who causes shame.

15 A soft answer turns away wrath,
But a harsh word stirs up anger.

²The tongue of the wise uses knowledge
rightly,
But the mouth of fools pours forth
foolishness.

³The eyes of the LORD *are* in every place,
Keeping watch on the evil and the good.

⁴A wholesome tongue *is* a tree of life,
But perverseness in it breaks the spirit.

14:14 [a]Literally *from above himself*   14:23 [a]Literally *talk of the lips*
14:29 [a]Literally *short of spirit*

LEADERSHIP ISSUES

GC2: Convictions: Shift from "What" to "Who"

PROVERBS 14:12 *There is a way that seems right to a man, but its end is the way of death.*

No doubt we live in a world where everyone wants to determine what's "right" for them. Truth, many say, is not absolute but relative to the situation (Rom. 1:18–23).

To counter our world's faulty thinking about truth—that all moral and spiritual truth is subjective and equal—we must shift the emphasis. What we believe about God or the Bible, or about what is right or wrong, is important. But "what we believe" must be seen in the context of "who we believe." Believing in Christ is about forming a relationship with a real Person. Therefore, how we relate to the Person of Truth must become the central issue.

This change from "what" to "who" will mean a major shift in how we think as we follow Jesus. How we relate to moral and spiritual truth should no longer be thought of merely as a philosophical concept or an abstract idea but rather as how we relate to Christ. Scriptural commands and rules should not be seen as merely instructions to obey but rather as ways to relate to our Lord.

As we embrace the realization that Jesus is the embodiment of truth and explain the gospel as a life lived in relationship with God through Christ, we can counter our world's faulty perceptions of God, truth, and reality. Our convictions concerning right and wrong are to be grounded in our relationship with Jesus; we live out our convictions as we long to please Him, not wanting to grieve His Holy Spirit (Mark 3:5; Eph. 4:30).

GC2
GREAT COMMANDMENT
COMMISSION

⁵A fool despises his father's instruction,
But he who receives correction is prudent.

⁶*In* the house of the righteous *there is* much
treasure,
But in the revenue of the wicked is trouble.

⁷The lips of the wise disperse knowledge,
But the heart of the fool *does* not *do* so.

⁸The sacrifice of the wicked *is* an abomination
to the LORD,
But the prayer of the upright *is* His delight.
⁹The way of the wicked *is* an abomination to
the LORD,
But He loves him who follows righteousness.

¹⁰Harsh discipline *is* for him who forsakes the
way,
And he who hates correction will die.

¹¹Hellᵃ and Destructionᵇ *are* before the LORD;
So how much more the hearts of the sons of
men.

¹²A scoffer does not love one who corrects
him,
Nor will he go to the wise.

¹³A merry heart makes a cheerful
countenance,
But by sorrow of the heart the spirit is
broken.

¹⁴The heart of him who has understanding
seeks knowledge,
But the mouth of fools feeds on foolishness.

¹⁵All the days of the afflicted *are* evil,
But he who is of a merry heart *has* a
continual feast.

¹⁶Better *is* a little with the fear of the LORD,
Than great treasure with trouble.
¹⁷Better *is* a dinner of herbsᵃ where love is,
Than a fatted calf with hatred.

¹⁸A wrathful man stirs up strife,
But *he who is* slow to anger allays contention.

¹⁹The way of the lazy *man is* like a hedge of
thorns,
But the way of the upright *is* a highway.

²⁰A wise son makes a father glad,
But a foolish man despises his mother.

²¹Folly *is* joy *to him who is* destitute of
discernment,
But a man of understanding walks
uprightly.

²²Without counsel, plans go awry,
But in the multitude of counselors they are
established.

²³A man has joy by the answer of his mouth,
And a word *spoken* in due season, how good
it is!

²⁴The way of life *winds* upward for the wise,
That he may turn away from hellᵃ below.

²⁵The LORD will destroy the house of the
proud,
But He will establish the boundary of the
widow.

²⁶The thoughts of the wicked *are* an
abomination to the LORD,
But the words of the pure *are* pleasant.

²⁷He who is greedy for gain troubles his own
house,
But he who hates bribes will live.

²⁸The heart of the righteous studies how to
answer,
But the mouth of the wicked pours forth
evil.

²⁹The LORD *is* far from the wicked,
But He hears the prayer of the righteous.

³⁰The light of the eyes rejoices the heart,
And a good report makes the bones
healthy.ᵃ

15:11 ᵃOr *Sheol* ᵇHebrew *Abaddon*   **15:17** ᵃOr *vegetables*
15:24 ᵃOr *Sheol*   **15:30** ᵃLiterally *fat*

³¹The ear that hears the rebukes of life
  Will abide among the wise.
³²He who disdains instruction despises his own
    soul,
  But he who heeds rebuke gets understanding.
³³The fear of the LORD *is* the instruction of
    wisdom,
  And before honor *is* humility.

16 The preparations of the heart *belong* to
    man,
  But the answer of the tongue *is* from the
    LORD.

²All the ways of a man *are* pure in his own
    eyes,
  But the LORD weighs the spirits.

³Commit your works to the LORD,
  And your thoughts will be established.

⁴The LORD has made all for Himself,
  Yes, even the wicked for the day of doom.

⁵Everyone proud in heart *is* an abomination to
    the LORD;
  Though they join forces,ᵃ none will go
    unpunished.

⁶In mercy and truth
  Atonement is provided for iniquity;
  And by the fear of the LORD *one* departs from
    evil.

⁷When a man's ways please the LORD,
  He makes even his enemies to be at peace
    with him.

⁸Better *is* a little with righteousness,
  Than vast revenues without justice.

⁹A man's heart plans his way,
  But the LORD directs his steps.

¹⁰Divination *is* on the lips of the king;
  His mouth must not transgress in judgment.
¹¹Honest weights and scales *are* the LORD's;
  All the weights in the bag *are* His work.
¹²*It is* an abomination for kings to commit
    wickedness,

For a throne is established by righteousness.
¹³Righteous lips *are* the delight of kings,
  And they love him who speaks *what is* right.
¹⁴As messengers of death *is* the king's wrath,
  But a wise man will appease it.
¹⁵In the light of the king's face *is* life,
  And his favor *is* like a cloud of the latter rain.

¹⁶How much better to get wisdom than gold!
  And to get understanding is to be chosen
    rather than silver.

¹⁷The highway of the upright *is* to depart from
    evil;
  He who keeps his way preserves his soul.

¹⁸Pride *goes* before destruction,
  And a haughty spirit before a fall.
¹⁹Better *to be* of a humble spirit with the lowly,
  Than to divide the spoil with the proud.

²⁰He who heeds the word wisely will find
    good,
  And whoever trusts in the LORD, happy *is* he.

²¹The wise in heart will be called prudent,
  And sweetness of the lips increases learning.

²²Understanding *is* a wellspring of life to him
    who has it.
  But the correction of fools *is* folly.

²³The heart of the wise teaches his mouth,
  And adds learning to his lips.

²⁴Pleasant words *are like* a honeycomb,
  Sweetness to the soul and health to the
    bones.

²⁵There is a way *that seems* right to a man,
  But its end *is* the way of death.

²⁶The person who labors, labors for himself,
  For his *hungry* mouth drives him *on.*

²⁷An ungodly man digs up evil,
  And *it is* on his lips like a burning fire.

16:5 ᵃLiterally *hand to hand*

²⁸A perverse man sows strife,
And a whisperer separates the best of
friends.
²⁹A violent man entices his neighbor,
And leads him in a way *that is* not good.
³⁰He winks his eye to devise perverse things;
He purses his lips *and* brings about evil.

³¹The silver-haired head *is* a crown of glory,
If it is found in the way of righteousness.

³²*He who is* slow to anger *is* better than the
mighty,
And he who rules his spirit than he who
takes a city.

³³The lot is cast into the lap,
But its every decision *is* from the LORD.

17 Better *is* a dry morsel with quietness,
Than a house full of feasting^a *with* strife.

²A wise servant will rule over a son who
causes shame,
And will share an inheritance among the
brothers.

³The refining pot *is* for silver and the furnace
for gold,
But the LORD tests the hearts.

⁴An evildoer gives heed to false lips;
A liar listens eagerly to a spiteful tongue.

⁵He who mocks the poor reproaches his
Maker;
He who is glad at calamity will not go
unpunished.

⁶Children's children *are* the crown of old
men,
And the glory of children *is* their father.

⁷Excellent speech is not becoming to a fool,
Much less lying lips to a prince.

⁸A present *is* a precious stone in the eyes of its
possessor;
Wherever he turns, he prospers.

⁹He who covers a transgression seeks love,
But he who repeats a matter separates friends.

¹⁰Rebuke is more effective for a wise *man*
Than a hundred blows on a fool.

¹¹An evil *man* seeks only rebellion;
Therefore a cruel messenger will be sent
against him.

¹²Let a man meet a bear robbed of her cubs,
Rather than a fool in his folly.

¹³Whoever rewards evil for good,
Evil will not depart from his house.

¹⁴The beginning of strife *is like* releasing
water;
Therefore stop contention before a quarrel
starts.

¹⁵He who justifies the wicked, and he who
condemns the just,
Both of them alike *are* an abomination to the
LORD.

¹⁶Why *is there* in the hand of a fool the
purchase price of wisdom,
Since *he has* no heart *for it?*

¹⁷A friend loves at all times,
And a brother is born for adversity.

¹⁸A man devoid of understanding shakes hands
in a pledge,
And becomes surety for his friend.

¹⁹He who loves transgression loves strife,
And he who exalts his gate seeks
destruction.

²⁰He who has a deceitful heart finds no good,
And he who has a perverse tongue falls into
evil.

²¹He who begets a scoffer *does so* to his
sorrow,
And the father of a fool has no joy.

17:1 ^aOr *sacrificial meals*

LEADERSHIP REALITIES

LEARN TO LISTEN:
TWO EARS AND ONE MOUTH! *Proverbs 17:27, 28*

Proverbs is a book dedicated to wisdom. On more than one occasion, Solomon writes concerning the great wisdom found in simply listening. One of the biggest challenges that young leaders face is the willingness and discipline to close their mouths and open their ears. The art of listening demonstrates the heart of leadership because:

- It is more important to understand than to be understood.
- When caution precedes words, advice is not loosely (and sometimes incorrectly) given.
- Listening intently shows control over impulse.
- One is not enticed by worthless words but hears the truth in the conversation.
- Silence on the front end leaves channels of communication open on the back end.
- One can never learn while talking, but the student of life is anxious to hear.
- Verbal domination does not demonstrate true power.
- To be in love with the sound of ones own voice demonstrates a selfish attitude.
- The more one talks the less others want to listen.
- Every conversation does not need your input.

22A merry heart does good, *like* medicine,[a]
   But a broken spirit dries the bones.

23A wicked *man* accepts a bribe behind the back[a]
   To pervert the ways of justice.

24Wisdom *is* in the sight of him who has understanding,
   But the eyes of a fool *are* on the ends of the earth.

25A foolish son *is* a grief to his father,
   And bitterness to her who bore him.

26Also, to punish the righteous *is* not good,
   Nor to strike princes for *their* uprightness.

27He who has knowledge spares his words,
   And a man of understanding is of a calm spirit.

28Even a fool is counted wise when he holds his peace;

When he shuts his lips, *he is considered* perceptive.

18 A man who isolates himself seeks his own desire;
   He rages against all wise judgment.

2A fool has no delight in understanding,
   But in expressing his own heart.

3When the wicked comes, contempt comes also;
   And with dishonor *comes* reproach.

4The words of a man's mouth *are* deep waters;
   The wellspring of wisdom *is* a flowing brook.

5*It is* not good to show partiality to the wicked,
   Or to overthrow the righteous in judgment.

17:22 [a]Or *makes medicine even better*   **17:23** [a]Literally *from the bosom*

⁶A fool's lips enter into contention,
And his mouth calls for blows.
⁷A fool's mouth *is* his destruction,
And his lips *are* the snare of his soul.
⁸The words of a talebearer *are* like tasty trifles,ᵃ
And they go down into the inmost body.

⁹He who is slothful in his work
Is a brother to him who is a great destroyer.

¹⁰The name of the LORD *is* a strong tower;
The righteous run to it and are safe.
¹¹The rich man's wealth *is* his strong city,
And like a high wall in his own esteem.

¹²Before destruction the heart of a man is
haughty,
And before honor *is* humility.

¹³He who answers a matter before he hears *it,*
It *is* folly and shame to him.

¹⁴The spirit of a man will sustain him in
sickness,
But who can bear a broken spirit?

¹⁵The heart of the prudent acquires
knowledge,
And the ear of the wise seeks knowledge.

¹⁶A man's gift makes room for him,
And brings him before great men.

¹⁷The first *one* to plead his cause *seems* right,
Until his neighbor comes and examines him.

¹⁸Casting lots causes contentions to cease,
And keeps the mighty apart.

¹⁹A brother offended *is harder to win* than a
strong city,
And contentions *are* like the bars of a castle.

²⁰A man's stomach shall be satisfied from the
fruit of his mouth;
From the produce of his lips he shall be filled.

²¹Death and life *are* in the power of the tongue,
And those who love it will eat its fruit.

²²*He who* finds a wife finds a good *thing,*
And obtains favor from the LORD.

²³The poor *man* uses entreaties,
But the rich answers roughly.

²⁴A man *who has* friends must himself be
friendly,ᵃ
But there is a friend *who* sticks closer than a
brother.

19 Better *is* the poor who walks in his
integrity
Than *one who is* perverse in his lips, and is a
fool.

²Also it is not good *for* a soul *to be* without
knowledge,
And he sins who hastens with *his* feet.

³The foolishness of a man twists his way,
And his heart frets against the LORD.

⁴Wealth makes many friends,
But the poor is separated from his friend.

⁵A false witness will not go unpunished,
And *he who* speaks lies will not escape.

⁶Many entreat the favor of the nobility,
And every man *is* a friend to one who gives
gifts.
⁷All the brothers of the poor hate him;
How much more do his friends go far from
him!
He may pursue *them with* words, *yet* they
abandon *him.*

⁸He who gets wisdom loves his own soul;
He who keeps understanding will find good.

⁹A false witness will not go unpunished,
And *he who* speaks lies shall perish.

¹⁰Luxury is not fitting for a fool,
Much less for a servant to rule over princes.

18:8 ᵃA Jewish tradition reads *wounds.* **18:24** ᵃFollowing Greek
manuscripts, Syriac, Targum, and Vulgate; Masoretic Text reads
may come to ruin.

¹¹The discretion of a man makes him slow to
  anger,
  And his glory *is* to overlook a transgression.

¹²The king's wrath *is* like the roaring of a lion,
  But his favor *is* like dew on the grass.

¹³A foolish son *is* the ruin of his father,
  And the contentions of a wife *are* a continual
  dripping.

¹⁴Houses and riches *are* an inheritance from
  fathers,
  But a prudent wife *is* from the LORD.

¹⁵Laziness casts *one* into a deep sleep,
  And an idle person will suffer hunger.

¹⁶He who keeps the commandment keeps his
  soul,
  But he who is careless[a] of his ways will die.

¹⁷He who has pity on the poor lends to the
  LORD,
  And He will pay back what he has given.

¹⁸Chasten your son while there is hope,
  And do not set your heart on his destruction.[a]

¹⁹*A man of* great wrath will suffer punishment;
  For if you rescue *him,* you will have to do it
  again.

²⁰Listen to counsel and receive instruction,
  That you may be wise in your latter days.

²¹There are many plans in a man's heart,
  Nevertheless the LORD's counsel—that will
  stand.

²²What is desired in a man is kindness,
  And a poor man is better than a liar.

²³The fear of the LORD *leads* to life,
  And *he who has it* will abide in satisfaction;
  He will not be visited with evil.

²⁴A lazy *man* buries his hand in the bowl,[a]
  And will not so much as bring it to his
  mouth again.

²⁵Strike a scoffer, and the simple will become
  wary;
  Rebuke one who has understanding, *and* he
  will discern knowledge.

²⁶He who mistreats *his* father *and* chases away
  his mother
  Is a son who causes shame and brings
  reproach.

²⁷Cease listening to instruction, my son,
  And you will stray from the words of
  knowledge.

²⁸A disreputable witness scorns justice,
  And the mouth of the wicked devours
  iniquity.

²⁹Judgments are prepared for scoffers,
  And beatings for the backs of fools.

20 Wine *is* a mocker,
  Strong drink *is* a brawler,
  And whoever is led astray by it is not wise.

²The wrath[a] of a king *is* like the roaring of a
  lion;
  Whoever provokes him to anger sins *against* his
  own life.

³*It is* honorable for a man to stop striving,
  Since any fool can start a quarrel.

⁴The lazy *man* will not plow because of
  winter;
  He will beg during harvest and *have*
  nothing.

⁵Counsel in the heart of man *is like* deep
  water,
  But a man of understanding will draw it out.

⁶Most men will proclaim each his own
  goodness,
  But who can find a faithful man?

19:16 [a]Literally *despises,* figurative of recklessness or carelessness
19:18 [a]Literally *to put him to death;* a Jewish tradition reads *on his
crying.*   19:24 [a]Septuagint and Syriac read *bosom;* Targum and
Vulgate read *armpit.*   20:2 [a]Literally *fear* or *terror* which is produced by the king's wrath

7The righteous *man* walks in his integrity;
His children *are* blessed after him.

8A king who sits on the throne of judgment
Scatters all evil with his eyes.

9Who can say, "I have made my heart clean,
I am pure from my sin"?

10Diverse weights *and* diverse measures,
They *are* both alike, an abomination to the
LORD.

11Even a child is known by his deeds,
Whether what he does *is* pure and right.

12The hearing ear and the seeing eye,
The LORD has made them both.

13Do not love sleep, lest you come to poverty;
Open your eyes, *and* you will be satisfied with
bread.

14"*It is* good for nothing,"a cries the buyer;
But when he has gone his way, then he boasts.

15There is gold and a multitude of rubies,
But the lips of knowledge *are* a precious
jewel.

16Take the garment of one who is surety *for* a
stranger,
And hold it as a pledge *when it* is for a
seductress.

17Bread gained by deceit *is* sweet to a man,
But afterward his mouth will be filled with
gravel.

18Plans are established by counsel;
By wise counsel wage war.

19He who goes about *as* a talebearer reveals
secrets;
Therefore do not associate with one who
flatters with his lips.

20Whoever curses his father or his mother,
His lamp will be put out in deep darkness.

21An inheritance gained hastily at the
beginning
Will not be blessed at the end.

22Do not say, "I will recompense evil";
Wait for the LORD, and He will save you.

23Diverse weights *are* an abomination to the
LORD,
And dishonest scales *are* not good.

24A man's steps *are* of the LORD;
How then can a man understand his own way?

25*It is* a snare for a man to devote rashly
something as holy,
And afterward to reconsider *his* vows.

26A wise king sifts out the wicked,
And brings the threshing wheel over them.

27The spirit of a man *is* the lamp of the LORD,
Searching all the inner depths of his heart.a

28Mercy and truth preserve the king,
And by lovingkindness he upholds his throne.

29The glory of young men *is* their strength,
And the splendor of old men *is* their gray
head.

30Blows that hurt cleanse away evil,
As *do* stripes the inner depths of the heart.a

21 The king's heart *is* in the hand of the
LORD,
Like the rivers of water;
He turns it wherever He wishes.

2Every way of a man *is* right in his own eyes,
But the LORD weighs the hearts.

3To do righteousness and justice
Is more acceptable to the LORD than sacrifice.

4A haughty look, a proud heart,
And the plowinga of the wicked *are* sin.

20:14 aLiterally *evil, evil*   **20:27** aLiterally *the rooms of the belly*
20:30 aLiterally *the rooms of the belly*   **21:4** aOr *lamp*

[5]The plans of the diligent *lead* surely to plenty,
But *those* of everyone *who is* hasty, surely to
poverty.

[6]Getting treasures by a lying tongue
Is the fleeting fantasy of those who seek
death.[a]

[7]The violence of the wicked will destroy
them,[a]
Because they refuse to do justice.

[8]The way of a guilty man *is* perverse;[a]
But *as for* the pure, his work *is* right.

[9]Better to dwell in a corner of a housetop,
Than in a house shared with a contentious
woman.

[10]The soul of the wicked desires evil;
His neighbor finds no favor in his eyes.

[11]When the scoffer is punished, the simple is
made wise;
But when the wise is instructed, he receives
knowledge.

[12]The righteous *God* wisely considers the
house of the wicked,
Overthrowing the wicked for *their*
wickedness.

[13]Whoever shuts his ears to the cry of the
poor
Will also cry himself and not be heard.

[14]A gift in secret pacifies anger,
And a bribe behind the back,[a] strong wrath.

[15]*It is* a joy for the just to do justice,
But destruction *will come* to the workers of
iniquity.

[16]A man who wanders from the way of
understanding
Will rest in the assembly of the dead.

[17]He who loves pleasure *will be* a poor man;
He who loves wine and oil will not be rich.

[18]The wicked *shall be* a ransom for the
righteous,
And the unfaithful for the upright.

[19]Better to dwell in the wilderness,
Than with a contentious and angry woman.

[20]*There is* desirable treasure,
And oil in the dwelling of the wise,
But a foolish man squanders it.

[21]He who follows righteousness and mercy
Finds life, righteousness, and honor.

[22]A wise *man* scales the city of the mighty,
And brings down the trusted stronghold.

[23]Whoever guards his mouth and tongue
Keeps his soul from troubles.

[24]A proud *and* haughty *man*—"Scoffer" *is* his
name;
He acts with arrogant pride.

[25]The desire of the lazy *man* kills him,
For his hands refuse to labor.
[26]He covets greedily all day long,
But the righteous gives and does not spare.

[27]The sacrifice of the wicked *is* an
abomination;
How much more *when* he brings it with
wicked intent!

[28]A false witness shall perish,
But the man who hears *him* will speak
endlessly.

[29]A wicked man hardens his face,
But *as for* the upright, he establishes[a] his
way.

[30]*There is* no wisdom or understanding
Or counsel against the LORD.

21:6 [a]Septuagint reads *Pursue vanity on the snares of death;* Vulgate reads *Is vain and foolish, and shall stumble on the snares of death;* Targum reads *They shall be destroyed, and they shall fall who seek death.* **21:7** [a]Literally *drag them away* **21:8** [a]Or *The way of a man is perverse and strange* **21:14** [a]Literally *in the bosom* **21:29** [a]Qere and Septuagint read *understands.*

³¹The horse *is* prepared for the day of battle,
But deliverance *is* of the LORD.

22 A *good* name is to be chosen rather than
       great riches,
Loving favor rather than silver and gold.

²The rich and the poor have this in common,
The LORD *is* the maker of them all.

³A prudent *man* foresees evil and hides
       himself,
But the simple pass on and are punished.

⁴By humility *and* the fear of the LORD
Are riches and honor and life.

⁵Thorns *and* snares *are* in the way of the
       perverse;
He who guards his soul will be far from
       them.

⁶Train up a child in the way he should go,
And when he is old he will not depart
       from it.

⁷The rich rules over the poor,
And the borrower *is* servant to the lender.

⁸He who sows iniquity will reap sorrow,
And the rod of his anger will fail.

⁹He who has a generous eye will be blessed,
For he gives of his bread to the poor.

¹⁰Cast out the scoffer, and contention will
       leave;
Yes, strife and reproach will cease.

¹¹He who loves purity of heart
And has grace on his lips,
The king *will be* his friend.

¹²The eyes of the LORD preserve knowledge,
But He overthrows the words of the
       faithless.

¹³The lazy *man* says, "*There is* a lion outside!
I shall be slain in the streets!"

¹⁴The mouth of an immoral woman *is* a deep
       pit;
He who is abhorred by the LORD will fall
       there.

¹⁵Foolishness *is* bound up in the heart of a child;
The rod of correction will drive it far from
       him.

¹⁶He who oppresses the poor to increase his
       riches,
And he who gives to the rich, *will* surely *come*
       to poverty.

SAYINGS OF THE WISE

¹⁷Incline your ear and hear the words of the
       wise,
And apply your heart to my knowledge;
¹⁸For *it is* a pleasant thing if you keep them
       within you;
Let them all be fixed upon your lips,
¹⁹So that your trust may be in the LORD;
I have instructed you today, even you.
²⁰Have I not written to you excellent things
Of counsels and knowledge,
²¹That I may make you know the certainty of
       the words of truth,
That you may answer words of truth
To those who send to you?

²²Do not rob the poor because he *is* poor,
Nor oppress the afflicted at the gate;
²³For the LORD will plead their cause,
And plunder the soul of those who plunder
       them.

²⁴Make no friendship with an angry man,
And with a furious man do not go,
²⁵Lest you learn his ways
And set a snare for your soul.

²⁶Do not be one of those who shakes hands in
       a pledge,
One of those who is surety for debts;
²⁷If you have nothing *with which* to pay,
Why should he take away your bed from
       under you?

²⁸Do not remove the ancient landmark
Which your fathers have set.

LEADERSHIP ISSUES

The "Character-Based" Leader

PROVERBS 22:1

As leaders, one of our primary directives is to constantly allow God's character to be reflected in our leadership. We are deciding how much of God's character is allowed to fill our hearts and how much is ultimately reflected in our words and actions. Not only is the Bible the most effective leadership Book ever written, it is the only authority which demonstrates how God like character is to be embodied in our lives.

Every leader has an obligation to paint a self-portrait of God's character. This is revealed one stroke of the paint brush (action) at a time. Our character is defined by our behaviors over time, but the face of it can change with just one stroke or action. The portrait is under our control and may take years to paint in order for our circle of friends to recognize God's character within our own.

Proverbs 22:1 states: "A good name is to be chosen rather than great riches." The Bible paints portraits of many effective leaders. It defines them as choosing reputation over riches or relationships—such as Job, who is defined as "upright" (Job 1:1). We also read of others who chose poorly, such as Balaam, and were rebuked (2 Pet. 2:13–15). When we lead like Job, God honors us; when we lead like Balaam, God humbles and rebukes us.

The level of God's character in our life is reflected through four cornerstones: *relationship, purity, integrity,* and *humility.* These supply the foundational strength for leadership.

LEADERSHIP ISSUES

GC2: Who Am I? Your Natural "Bent"

PROVERBS 22:6 *Train up a child in the way he should go, and when he is old he will not depart from it.*

Unfortunately, this verse is often misunderstood, and misapplied by those who are responsible for the training of young people. Many parents and church leaders think it means, "Have family devotions, make sure kids attend church and youth group and Christian camps; and when they are grown up, they will not depart from the faith."

The real emphasis of this verse, however, centers on the phrase "the way he should go." The writer is referring to the child's way, his or her leaning or bent. The root meanings of these words suggest stimulating a desire for guidance according to each child's own uniqueness.

The same Hebrew word that is used in Proverbs 22 is translated "bend" in two psalms and refers to the bending of the archer's bow (Ps. 11:2; 64:3). All archers made their own bows and had to know the unique characteristics of that bow if they hoped to hit anything with it. God's Word is telling us that you have an inborn uniqueness that needs to be identified and trained accordingly. You have a unique "bent," and the Creator knows all about you.

Jesus, eternally existing as God, came to earth miraculously through a virgin birth that He might show us the way to a fulfilling life. (See John 1:14; Luke 1:26–35.) His "bent" was to be a perfect sacrifice on our behalf that we might become all that He intended (John 10:10).

Jesus came to provide a means to adopt you into the family of God. He has made you His special, one-of-a-kind child by giving you various skills. He has given you certain talents as well. And He has also placed within you certain personal preferences with a distinct personality that makes you a one-of-a-kind individual, a person designed to do things in ways that only you can do.

GC2
GREAT COMMANDMENT
COMMISSION

²⁹Do you see a man *who* excels in his work?
  He will stand before kings;
  He will not stand before unknown *men*.

23
¹When you sit down to eat with a ruler,
  Consider carefully what *is* before you;
²And put a knife to your throat
  If you *are* a man given to appetite.
³Do not desire his delicacies,
  For they *are* deceptive food.

⁴Do not overwork to be rich;
  Because of your own understanding, cease!
⁵Will you set your eyes on that which is
    not?
  For *riches* certainly make themselves wings;
  They fly away like an eagle *toward* heaven.

⁶Do not eat the bread of a miser,ᵃ
  Nor desire his delicacies;
⁷For as he thinks in his heart, so *is* he.
  "Eat and drink!" he says to you,
  But his heart is not with you.
⁸The morsel you have eaten, you will
    vomit up,
  And waste your pleasant words.

⁹Do not speak in the hearing of a fool,
  For he will despise the wisdom of your
    words.

¹⁰Do not remove the ancient landmark,
  Nor enter the fields of the fatherless;
¹¹For their Redeemer *is* mighty;
  He will plead their cause against you.

¹²Apply your heart to instruction,
  And your ears to words of knowledge.

¹³Do not withhold correction from a child,
  For *if* you beat him with a rod, he will not
    die.
¹⁴You shall beat him with a rod,
  And deliver his soul from hell.ᵃ

¹⁵My son, if your heart is wise,
  My heart will rejoice—indeed, I myself;
¹⁶Yes, my inmost being will rejoice
  When your lips speak right things.

¹⁷Do not let your heart envy sinners,
  But *be zealous* for the fear of the LORD all the
    day;
¹⁸For surely there is a hereafter,
  And your hope will not be cut off.

¹⁹Hear, my son, and be wise;
  And guide your heart in the way.
²⁰Do not mix with winebibbers,
  Or with gluttonous eaters of meat;
²¹For the drunkard and the glutton will come
    to poverty,
  And drowsiness will clothe *a man* with rags.

²²Listen to your father who begot you,
  And do not despise your mother when she is
    old.

²³Buy the truth, and do not sell *it,*
  Also wisdom and instruction and
    understanding.

²⁴The father of the righteous will greatly
    rejoice,
  And he who begets a wise *child* will delight in
    him.
²⁵Let your father and your mother be glad,
  And let her who bore you rejoice.

²⁶My son, give me your heart,
  And let your eyes observe my ways.
²⁷For a harlot *is* a deep pit,
  And a seductress *is* a narrow well.
²⁸She also lies in wait as *for* a victim,
  And increases the unfaithful among men.

²⁹Who has woe?
  Who has sorrow?
  Who has contentions?
  Who has complaints?
  Who has wounds without cause?
  Who has redness of eyes?
³⁰Those who linger long at the wine,
  Those who go in search of mixed wine.
³¹Do not look on the wine when it is red,
  When it sparkles in the cup,
  When it swirls around smoothly;

23:6 ᵃLiterally *one who has an evil eye* **23:14** ᵃOr *Sheol*

³²At the last it bites like a serpent,
  And stings like a viper.
³³Your eyes will see strange things,
  And your heart will utter perverse things.
³⁴Yes, you will be like one who lies down in
    the midst of the sea,
  Or like one who lies at the top of the mast,
    saying:
³⁵"They have struck me, *but* I was not hurt;
  They have beaten me, but I did not feel *it.*
  When shall I awake, that I may seek another
    drink?"

24
Do not be envious of evil men,
  Nor desire to be with them;
²For their heart devises violence,
  And their lips talk of troublemaking.

³Through wisdom a house is built,
  And by understanding it is established;
⁴By knowledge the rooms are filled
  With all precious and pleasant riches.

⁵A wise man *is* strong,
  Yes, a man of knowledge increases strength;
⁶For by wise counsel you will wage your
    own war,
  And in a multitude of counselors *there is*
    safety.

⁷Wisdom *is* too lofty for a fool;
  He does not open his mouth in the gate.

⁸He who plots to do evil
  Will be called a schemer.
⁹The devising of foolishness *is* sin,
  And the scoffer *is* an abomination to men.

¹⁰*If* you faint in the day of adversity,
  Your strength *is* small.

¹¹Deliver *those who* are drawn toward death,
  And hold back *those* stumbling to the
    slaughter.
¹²If you say, "Surely we did not know this,"
  Does not He who weighs the hearts
    consider *it?*
  He who keeps your soul, does He *not*
    know *it?*

And will He *not* render to *each* man according
    to his deeds?

¹³My son, eat honey because *it is* good,
  And the honeycomb *which is* sweet to your
    taste;
¹⁴So *shall* the knowledge of wisdom *be* to your
    soul;
  If you have found *it,* there is a prospect,
  And your hope will not be cut off.

¹⁵Do not lie in wait, O wicked *man,* against the
    dwelling of the righteous;
  Do not plunder his resting place;
¹⁶For a righteous *man* may fall seven times
  And rise again,
  But the wicked shall fall by calamity.

¹⁷Do not rejoice when your enemy falls,
  And do not let your heart be glad when he
    stumbles;
¹⁸Lest the LORD see *it,* and it displease Him,
  And He turn away His wrath from him.

¹⁹Do not fret because of evildoers,
  Nor be envious of the wicked;
²⁰For there will be no prospect for the evil
    man;
  The lamp of the wicked will be put out.

²¹My son, fear the LORD and the king;
  Do not associate with those given to change;
²²For their calamity will rise suddenly,
  And who knows the ruin those two can
    bring?

FURTHER SAYINGS OF THE WISE

²³These *things* also *belong* to the wise:

It is *not* good to show partiality in judgment.
²⁴He who says to the wicked, "You *are*
    righteous,"
  Him the people will curse;
  Nations will abhor him.
²⁵But those who rebuke *the wicked* will have
    delight,
  And a good blessing will come upon them.

²⁶He who gives a right answer kisses the lips.

27Prepare your outside work,
  Make it fit for yourself in the field;
  And afterward build your house.

28Do not be a witness against your neighbor
    without cause,
  For would you deceive[a] with your lips?
29Do not say, "I will do to him just as he has
    done to me;
  I will render to the man according to his
    work."

30I went by the field of the lazy *man,*
  And by the vineyard of the man devoid of
    understanding;
31And there it was, all overgrown with thorns;
  Its surface was covered with nettles;
  Its stone wall was broken down.
32When I saw *it,* I considered *it* well;
  I looked on *it and* received instruction:
33A little sleep, a little slumber,
  A little folding of the hands to rest;
34So shall your poverty come *like* a prowler,
  And your need like an armed man.

Further Wise Sayings of Solomon

25 These also *are* proverbs of Solomon which
the men of Hezekiah king of Judah copied:

2*It is* the glory of God to conceal a matter,
  But the glory of kings *is* to search out a
    matter.

3*As* the heavens for height and the earth for
    depth,
  So the heart of kings *is* unsearchable.

4Take away the dross from silver,
  And it will go to the silversmith *for* jewelry.
5Take away the wicked from before the
    king,
  And his throne will be established in
    righteousness.

6Do not exalt yourself in the presence of the
    king,
  And do not stand in the place of the great;
7For *it is* better that he say to you,
  "Come up here,"

Than that you should be put lower in the
    presence of the prince,
  Whom your eyes have seen.

8Do not go hastily to court;
  For what will you do in the end,
  When your neighbor has put you to shame?
9Debate your case with your neighbor,
  And do not disclose the secret to another;
10Lest he who hears *it* expose your shame,
  And your reputation be ruined.

11A word fitly spoken *is like* apples of gold
  In settings of silver.
12*Like* an earring of gold and an ornament of
    fine gold
  Is a wise rebuker to an obedient ear.

13Like the cold of snow in time of harvest
  Is a faithful messenger to those who send
    him,
  For he refreshes the soul of his masters.

14Whoever falsely boasts of giving
  Is like clouds and wind without rain.

15By long forbearance a ruler is persuaded,
  And a gentle tongue breaks a bone.

16Have you found honey?
  Eat only as much as you need,
  Lest you be filled with it and vomit.

17Seldom set foot in your neighbor's house,
  Lest he become weary of you and hate you.

18A man who bears false witness against his
    neighbor
  Is like a club, a sword, and a sharp arrow.

19Confidence in an unfaithful *man* in time of
    trouble
  Is like a bad tooth and a foot out of joint.

20*Like* one who takes away a garment in cold
    weather,
  And like vinegar on soda,
  Is one who sings songs to a heavy heart.

24:28 [a]Septuagint and Vulgate read *Do not deceive.*

²¹If your enemy is hungry, give him bread to
    eat;
  And if he is thirsty, give him water to drink;
²²For *so* you will heap coals of fire on his head,
  And the LORD will reward you.

²³The north wind brings forth rain,
  And a backbiting tongue an angry
    countenance.

²⁴*It is* better to dwell in a corner of a housetop,
  Than in a house shared with a contentious
    woman.

²⁵*As* cold water to a weary soul,
  So *is* good news from a far country.

²⁶A righteous *man* who falters before the wicked
  Is like a murky spring and a polluted well.

²⁷*It is* not good to eat much honey;
  So to seek one's own glory *is not* glory.

²⁸Whoever *has* no rule over his own spirit
  Is like a city broken down, without walls.

26 As snow in summer and rain in harvest,
    So honor is not fitting for a fool.

²Like a flitting sparrow, like a flying swallow,
  So a curse without cause shall not alight.

³A whip for the horse,
  A bridle for the donkey,
  And a rod for the fool's back.
⁴Do not answer a fool according to his folly,
  Lest you also be like him.
⁵Answer a fool according to his folly,
  Lest he be wise in his own eyes.
⁶He who sends a message by the hand of a fool
  Cuts off *his own* feet *and* drinks violence.
⁷*Like* the legs of the lame that hang limp
  Is a proverb in the mouth of fools.
⁸Like one who binds a stone in a sling
  Is he who gives honor to a fool.
⁹*Like* a thorn *that* goes into the hand of a
    drunkard
  Is a proverb in the mouth of fools.
¹⁰The great *God* who formed everything

Gives the fool *his* hire and the transgressor *his*
    wages.ᵃ
¹¹As a dog returns to his own vomit,
  So a fool repeats his folly.
¹²Do you see a man wise in his own eyes?
  There is more hope for a fool than for him.

¹³The lazy *man* says, "*There is* a lion in the road!
  A fierce lion *is* in the streets!"
¹⁴*As* a door turns on its hinges,
  So *does* the lazy *man* on his bed.
¹⁵The lazy *man* buries his hand in the bowl;ᵃ
  It wearies him to bring it back to his mouth.
¹⁶The lazy *man is* wiser in his own eyes
  Than seven men who can answer sensibly.

¹⁷He who passes by *and* meddles in a quarrel
    not his own
  Is like one who takes a dog by the ears.

¹⁸Like a madman who throws firebrands,
    arrows, and death,
¹⁹*Is* the man *who* deceives his neighbor,
  And says, "I was only joking!"

²⁰Where *there is* no wood, the fire goes out;
  And where *there is* no talebearer, strife ceases.
²¹*As* charcoal *is* to burning coals, and wood to
    fire,
  So *is* a contentious man to kindle strife.
²²The words of a talebearer *are* like tasty trifles,
  And they go down into the inmost body.

²³Fervent lips with a wicked heart
  Are like earthenware covered with silver dross.

²⁴He who hates, disguises *it* with his lips,
  And lays up deceit within himself;
²⁵When he speaks kindly, do not believe him,
  For *there are* seven abominations in his heart;
²⁶*Though his* hatred is covered by deceit,
  His wickedness will be revealed before the
    assembly.

²⁷Whoever digs a pit will fall into it,
  And he who rolls a stone will have it roll
    back on him.

26:10 ᵃThe Hebrew is difficult; ancient and modern translators differ
greatly. **26:15** ᵃCompare 19:24

²⁸A lying tongue hates *those who are* crushed
    by it,
And a flattering mouth works ruin.

27

Do not boast about tomorrow,
    For you do not know what a day may
    bring forth.

²Let another man praise you, and not your
    own mouth;
A stranger, and not your own lips.

³A stone *is* heavy and sand *is* weighty,
But a fool's wrath *is* heavier than both of
    them.

⁴Wrath *is* cruel and anger a torrent,
But who *is* able to stand before jealousy?

⁵Open rebuke *is* better
Than love carefully concealed.

⁶Faithful *are* the wounds of a friend,
But the kisses of an enemy *are* deceitful.

⁷A satisfied soul loathes the honeycomb,
But to a hungry soul every bitter thing *is*
    sweet.

⁸Like a bird that wanders from its nest
Is a man who wanders from his place.

⁹Ointment and perfume delight the heart,
And the sweetness of a man's friend *gives
delight* by hearty counsel.

¹⁰Do not forsake your own friend or your
    father's friend,
Nor go to your brother's house in the day of
    your calamity;
Better *is* a neighbor nearby than a brother far
    away.

¹¹My son, be wise, and make my heart glad,
That I may answer him who reproaches me.

¹²A prudent *man* foresees evil *and* hides
    himself;
The simple pass on *and* are punished.

¹³Take the garment of him who is surety for a
    stranger,
And hold it in pledge *when* he is surety for a
    seductress.

¹⁴He who blesses his friend with a loud voice,
    rising early in the morning,
It will be counted a curse to him.

¹⁵A continual dripping on a very rainy day
And a contentious woman are alike;
¹⁶Whoever restrains her restrains the wind,
And grasps oil with his right hand.

¹⁷*As* iron sharpens iron,
So a man sharpens the countenance of his
    friend.

¹⁸Whoever keeps the fig tree will eat its fruit;
So he who waits on his master will be
    honored.

¹⁹As in water face *reflects* face,
So a man's heart *reveals* the man.

²⁰Hell[a] and Destruction[b] are never full;
So the eyes of man are never satisfied.

²¹The refining pot *is* for silver and the furnace
    for gold,
And a man *is valued* by what others say
    of him.

²²Though you grind a fool in a mortar with a
    pestle along with crushed grain,
Yet his foolishness will not depart from him.

²³Be diligent to know the state of your flocks,
    And attend to your herds;
²⁴For riches *are* not forever,
Nor does a crown *endure* to all generations.
²⁵*When* the hay is removed, and the tender grass
    shows itself,
And the herbs of the mountains are
    gathered in,
²⁶The lambs *will provide* your clothing,
And the goats the price of a field;

27:20 [a]Or *Sheol* [b]Hebrew *Abaddon*

²⁷*You shall have* enough goats' milk for your
   food,
For the food of your household,
And the nourishment of your maidservants.

28 The wicked flee when no one pursues,
   But the righteous are bold as a lion.

²Because of the transgression of a land, many
   are its princes;
But by a man of understanding *and* knowledge
Right will be prolonged.

³A poor man who oppresses the poor
Is like a driving rain which leaves no food.

⁴Those who forsake the law praise the
   wicked,
But such as keep the law contend with
   them.

⁵Evil men do not understand justice,
But those who seek the LORD
   understand all.

⁶Better *is* the poor who walks in his integrity
Than one perverse *in his* ways, though he *be*
   rich.

⁷Whoever keeps the law *is* a discerning son,
But a companion of gluttons shames his
   father.

⁸One who increases his possessions by usury
   and extortion
Gathers it for him who will pity the poor.

⁹One who turns away his ear from hearing
   the law,
Even his prayer *is* an abomination.

¹⁰Whoever causes the upright to go astray in
   an evil way,
He himself will fall into his own pit;
But the blameless will inherit good.

¹¹The rich man *is* wise in his own eyes,
But the poor who has understanding
   searches him out.

¹²When the righteous rejoice, *there is* great
   glory;
But when the wicked arise, men hide
   themselves.

¹³He who covers his sins will not prosper,
But whoever confesses and forsakes *them*
   will have mercy.

¹⁴Happy *is* the man who is always reverent,
But he who hardens his heart will fall into
   calamity.

¹⁵*Like* a roaring lion and a charging bear
Is a wicked ruler over poor people.

¹⁶A ruler who lacks understanding *is* a great
   oppressor,
But he who hates covetousness will prolong
   his days.

¹⁷A man burdened with bloodshed will flee
   into a pit;
Let no one help him.

¹⁸Whoever walks blamelessly will be saved,
But *he who is* perverse *in his* ways will
   suddenly fall.

¹⁹He who tills his land will have plenty of
   bread,
But he who follows frivolity will have
   poverty enough!

²⁰A faithful man will abound with blessings,
But he who hastens to be rich will not go
   unpunished.

²¹To show partiality *is* not good,
Because for a piece of bread a man will
   transgress.

²²A man with an evil eye hastens after riches,
And does not consider that poverty will
   come upon him.

²³He who rebukes a man will find more favor
   afterward
Than he who flatters with the tongue.

²⁴Whoever robs his father or his mother,
And says, "It is no transgression,"
The same is companion to a destroyer.

²⁵He who is of a proud heart stirs up strife,
But he who trusts in the LORD will be
prospered.

²⁶He who trusts in his own heart is a fool,
But whoever walks wisely will be delivered.

²⁷He who gives to the poor will not lack,
But he who hides his eyes will have many
curses.

²⁸When the wicked arise, men hide
themselves;
But when they perish, the righteous increase.

29 He who is often rebuked, and hardens his
neck,
Will suddenly be destroyed, and that without
remedy.

²When the righteous are in authority, the
people rejoice;
But when a wicked man rules, the people
groan.

³Whoever loves wisdom makes his father
rejoice,
But a companion of harlots wastes his wealth.

⁴The king establishes the land by justice,
But he who receives bribes overthrows it.

⁵A man who flatters his neighbor
Spreads a net for his feet.

⁶By transgression an evil man is snared,
But the righteous sings and rejoices.

⁷The righteous considers the cause of the
poor,
But the wicked does not understand such
knowledge.

⁸Scoffers set a city aflame,
But wise men turn away wrath.

⁹If a wise man contends with a foolish man,
Whether the fool rages or laughs, there is no
peace.

¹⁰The bloodthirsty hate the blameless,
But the upright seek his well-being.ᵃ

¹¹A fool vents all his feelings,ᵃ
But a wise man holds them back.

¹²If a ruler pays attention to lies,
All his servants become wicked.

¹³The poor man and the oppressor have this in
common:
The LORD gives light to the eyes of both.

¹⁴The king who judges the poor with truth,
His throne will be established forever.

¹⁵The rod and rebuke give wisdom,
But a child left to himself brings shame to his
mother.

¹⁶When the wicked are multiplied,
transgression increases;
But the righteous will see their fall.

¹⁷Correct your son, and he will give you rest;
Yes, he will give delight to your soul.

¹⁸Where there is no revelation,ᵃ the people cast
off restraint;
But happy is he who keeps the law.

¹⁹A servant will not be corrected by mere words;
For though he understands, he will not
respond.

²⁰Do you see a man hasty in his words?
There is more hope for a fool than for him.

²¹He who pampers his servant from childhood
Will have him as a son in the end.

²²An angry man stirs up strife,
And a furious man abounds in transgression.

29:10 ᵃLiterally soul   **29:11** ᵃLiterally spirit   **29:18** ᵃOr prophetic
vision

²³A man's pride will bring him low,
   But the humble in spirit will retain honor.

²⁴Whoever is a partner with a thief hates his
      own life;
   He swears to tell the truth,[a] but reveals
      nothing.

²⁵The fear of man brings a snare,
   But whoever trusts in the LORD shall be safe.

²⁶Many seek the ruler's favor,
   But justice for man *comes* from the LORD.

²⁷An unjust man *is* an abomination to the
      righteous,
   And *he who is* upright in the way *is* an
      abomination to the wicked.

THE WISDOM OF AGUR

30 The words of Agur the son of Jakeh, *his*
   utterance. This man declared to Ithiel—to
Ithiel and Ucal:

²Surely I *am* more stupid than *any* man,
   And do not have the understanding of a man.
³I neither learned wisdom
   Nor have knowledge of the Holy One.

⁴Who has ascended into heaven, or
      descended?
   Who has gathered the wind in His fists?
   Who has bound the waters in a garment?
   Who has established all the ends of the earth?
   What *is* His name, and what *is* His Son's
      name,
   If you know?

⁵Every word of God *is* pure;
   He *is* a shield to those who put their trust in
      Him.
⁶Do not add to His words,
   Lest He rebuke you, and you be found a liar.

⁷Two *things* I request of You
   (Deprive me not before I die):
⁸Remove falsehood and lies far from me;
   Give me neither poverty nor riches—
   Feed me with the food allotted to me;

⁹Lest I be full and deny *You,*
   And say, "Who *is* the LORD?"
   Or lest I be poor and steal,
   And profane the name of my God.

¹⁰Do not malign a servant to his master,
   Lest he curse you, and you be found guilty.

¹¹*There is* a generation *that* curses its father,
   And does not bless its mother.
¹²*There is* a generation *that is* pure in its own
      eyes,
   Yet is not washed from its filthiness.
¹³*There is* a generation—oh, how lofty are their
      eyes!
   And their eyelids are lifted up.
¹⁴*There is* a generation whose teeth *are like*
      swords,
   And whose fangs *are like* knives,
   To devour the poor from off the earth,
   And the needy from *among* men.

¹⁵The leech has two daughters—
   Give *and* Give!

   There are three *things that* are never satisfied,
   Four never say, "Enough!":
¹⁶The grave,[a]
   The barren womb,
   The earth *that* is not satisfied with water—
   And the fire never says, "Enough!"

¹⁷The eye *that* mocks *his* father,
   And scorns obedience to *his* mother,
   The ravens of the valley will pick it out,
   And the young eagles will eat it.

¹⁸There are three *things which* are too wonderful
      for me,
   Yes, four *which* I do not understand:
¹⁹The way of an eagle in the air,
   The way of a serpent on a rock,
   The way of a ship in the midst of the sea,
   And the way of a man with a virgin.

²⁰This *is* the way of an adulterous woman:
   She eats and wipes her mouth,
   And says, "I have done no wickedness."

29:24 [a]Literally *hears the adjuration*   **30:16** [a]Or *Sheol*

²¹For three *things* the earth is perturbed,
  Yes, for four it cannot bear up:
²²For a servant when he reigns,
  A fool when he is filled with food,
²³A hateful *woman* when she is married,
  And a maidservant who succeeds her mistress.

²⁴There are four *things which* are little on the earth,
  But they *are* exceedingly wise:
²⁵The ants *are* a people not strong,
  Yet they prepare their food in the summer;
²⁶The rock badgers[a] are a feeble folk,
  Yet they make their homes in the crags;
²⁷The locusts have no king,
  Yet they all advance in ranks;
²⁸The spider[a] skillfully grasps with its hands,
  And it is in kings' palaces.

²⁹There are three *things which* are majestic in pace,
  Yes, four *which* are stately in walk:
³⁰A lion, *which is* mighty among beasts
  And does not turn away from any;
³¹A greyhound,[a]
  A male goat also,
  And a king *whose* troops *are* with him.[b]

³²If you have been foolish in exalting yourself,
  Or if you have devised evil, *put your* hand on *your* mouth.
³³For *as* the churning of milk produces butter,
  And wringing the nose produces blood,
  So the forcing of wrath produces strife.

The Words of King Lemuel's Mother

31 The words of King Lemuel, the utterance which his mother taught him:

²What, my son?
  And what, son of my womb?
  And what, son of my vows?
³Do not give your strength to women,
  Nor your ways to that which destroys kings.

⁴*It is* not for kings, O Lemuel,
  It is not for kings to drink wine,
  Nor for princes intoxicating drink;
⁵Lest they drink and forget the law,

And pervert the justice of all the afflicted.
⁶Give strong drink to him who is perishing,
  And wine to those who are bitter of heart.
⁷Let him drink and forget his poverty,
  And remember his misery no more.

⁸Open your mouth for the speechless,
  In the cause of all *who are* appointed to die.[a]
⁹Open your mouth, judge righteously,
  And plead the cause of the poor and needy.

The Virtuous Wife

¹⁰Who[a] can find a virtuous[b] wife?
  For her worth *is* far above rubies.
¹¹The heart of her husband safely trusts her;
  So he will have no lack of gain.
¹²She does him good and not evil
  All the days of her life.
¹³She seeks wool and flax,
  And willingly works with her hands.
¹⁴She is like the merchant ships,
  She brings her food from afar.
¹⁵She also rises while it is yet night,
  And provides food for her household,
  And a portion for her maidservants.
¹⁶She considers a field and buys it;
  From her profits she plants a vineyard.
¹⁷She girds herself with strength,
  And strengthens her arms.
¹⁸She perceives that her merchandise *is* good,
  And her lamp does not go out by night.
¹⁹She stretches out her hands to the distaff,
  And her hand holds the spindle.
²⁰She extends her hand to the poor,
  Yes, she reaches out her hands to the needy.
²¹She is not afraid of snow for her household,
  For all her household *is* clothed with scarlet.
²²She makes tapestry for herself;
  Her clothing *is* fine linen and purple.
²³Her husband is known in the gates,
  When he sits among the elders of the land.
²⁴She makes linen garments and sells *them,*
  And supplies sashes for the merchants.
²⁵Strength and honor *are* her clothing;
  She shall rejoice in time to come.

30:26 [a]Or *hyraxes* **30:28** [a]Or *lizard* **30:31** [a]Exact identity unknown [b]A Jewish tradition reads *a king against whom there is no uprising.* **31:8** [a]Literally *sons of passing away* **31:10** [a]Verses 10 through 31 are an alphabetic acrostic in Hebrew (compare Psalm 119). [b]Literally *a wife of valor,* in the sense of all forms of excellence

[26]She opens her mouth with wisdom,
  And on her tongue *is* the law of kindness.
[27]She watches over the ways of her
      household,
  And does not eat the bread of idleness.
[28]Her children rise up and call her blessed;
  Her husband *also,* and he praises her:

[29]"Many daughters have done well,
  But you excel them all."
[30]Charm *is* deceitful and beauty *is* passing,
  But a woman *who* fears the LORD, she shall be
      praised.
[31]Give her of the fruit of her hands,
  And let her own works praise her in the gates.

IMPACT OF THE BOOK

E CCLESIASTES

I IDEA	*A life lived for personal pleasure, pain, or experience is ultimately useless or "vanity." Vanity is complete emptiness apart from God—a life that has no meaning or purpose. Only the life lived in obedience to God will have eternal significance. Foolish pride leads nowhere.*
M MESSAGE	*"What is the purpose of life?" Pursuits after material possessions, sensual pleasure, or worldly wisdom may bring temporary satisfaction, but a person will never find true fulfillment apart from God. People who desire to have a life of lasting impact are motivated by things of eternal significance. Solomon, the wisest man who has ever lived, sought earthly pleasures, but he realized that all those pursuits were useless.*
P PEOPLE	*The Teacher*
A AUTHOR	*The author calls himself the "Qoheleth," meaning "teacher" or "preacher," who was also the "son of David." This has lead to the conclusion that Solomon wrote the book, probably toward the end of his life after he had allowed himself to be distracted by worldly temptations. Solomon tasted all of the so-called "good life," and he wrote to young people to allow them to benefit from his mistakes.*
C CULTURE	*Ecclesiastes, along with Proverbs and Song of Solomon, belongs to the biblical wisdom books. Wisdom books approach reality differently from other biblical books. Instead of focusing on Israel's history, they center on daily life and present human experience. Their intent is not to reflect how God has worked in the lives of His people so much as it is to teach people how to navigate through life by living wisely according to godly principles.*
T TIMELINE	*c. 935 BC*
KEY SCRIPTURE MEMORY VERSES	1:2; 3:1; 4:9–12; 12:1, 13, 14

The Vanity of Life

1 The words of the Preacher, the son of David, king in Jerusalem.

[2] "Vanity[a] of vanities," says the Preacher;
"Vanity of vanities, all *is* vanity."

[3] What profit has a man from all his labor
In which he toils under the sun?
[4] *One* generation passes away, and *another*
generation comes;
But the earth abides forever.
[5] The sun also rises, and the sun goes down,
And hastens to the place where it arose.
[6] The wind goes toward the south,
And turns around to the north;
The wind whirls about continually,
And comes again on its circuit.
[7] All the rivers run into the sea,
Yet the sea *is* not full;
To the place from which the rivers come,
There they return again.
[8] All things *are* full of labor;
Man cannot express *it*.
The eye is not satisfied with seeing,
Nor the ear filled with hearing.

[9] That which has been *is* what will be,
That which *is* done is what will be done,
And *there is* nothing new under the sun.
[10] Is there anything of which it may be said,
"See, this *is* new"?
It has already been in ancient times
before us.
[11] *There is* no remembrance of former *things,*
Nor will there be any remembrance of *things*
that are to come
By *those* who will come after.

The Grief of Wisdom

[12] I, the Preacher, was king over Israel in Jerusalem. [13] And I set my heart to seek and search out by wisdom concerning all that is done under heaven; this burdensome task God has given to the sons of man, by which they may be exercised. [14] I have seen all the works that are done under the sun; and indeed, all *is* vanity and grasping for the wind.

[15] *What is* crooked cannot be made straight,
And what is lacking cannot be numbered.

[16] I communed with my heart, saying, "Look, I have attained greatness, and have gained more wisdom than all who were before me in Jerusalem. My heart has understood great wisdom and knowledge." [17] And I set my heart to know wisdom and to know madness and folly. I perceived that this also is grasping for the wind.

[18] For in much wisdom *is* much grief,
And he who increases knowledge increases
sorrow.

The Vanity of Pleasure

2 I said in my heart, "Come now, I will test you with mirth; therefore enjoy pleasure"; but surely, this also *was* vanity. [2] I said of laughter— "Madness!"; and of mirth, "What does it accomplish?" [3] I searched in my heart *how* to gratify my flesh with wine, while guiding my heart with wisdom, and how to lay hold on folly, till I might see what *was* good for the sons of men to do under heaven all the days of their lives.

[4] I made my works great, I built myself houses, and planted myself vineyards. [5] I made myself gardens and orchards, and I planted all *kinds* of fruit trees in them. [6] I made myself water pools from which to water the growing trees of the grove. [7] I acquired male and female servants, and had servants born in my house. Yes, I had greater possessions of herds and flocks than all who were in Jerusalem before me. [8] I also gathered for myself silver and gold and the special treasures of kings and of the provinces. I acquired male and female singers, the delights of the sons of men, *and* musical instruments[a] of all kinds.

[9] So I became great and excelled more than all who were before me in Jerusalem. Also my wisdom remained with me.

[10] Whatever my eyes desired I did not keep
from them.
I did not withhold my heart from any pleasure,
For my heart rejoiced in all my labor;
And this was my reward from all my labor.

1:2 [a]Or *Absurdity, Frustration, Futility, Nonsense;* and so throughout this book   **2:8** [a]Exact meaning unknown

[11]Then I looked on all the works that my hands
had done
And on the labor in which I had toiled;
And indeed all *was* vanity and grasping for
the wind.
There was no profit under the sun.

THE END OF THE WISE AND THE FOOL

[12]Then I turned myself to consider wisdom
and madness and folly;
For what *can* the man *do* who succeeds the
king?—
Only what he has already done.
[13]Then I saw that wisdom excels folly
As light excels darkness.
[14]The wise man's eyes *are* in his head,
But the fool walks in darkness.
Yet I myself perceived
That the same event happens to them all.

[15]So I said in my heart,
"As it happens to the fool,
It also happens to me,
And why was I then more wise?"
Then I said in my heart,
"This also *is* vanity."
[16]For *there* is no more remembrance of the wise
than of the fool forever,
Since all that now *is* will be forgotten in the
days to come.
And how does a wise *man* die?
As the fool!

[17]Therefore I hated life because the work that was
done under the sun *was* distressing to me, for all *is*
vanity and grasping for the wind.

[18]Then I hated all my labor in which I had
toiled under the sun, because I must leave it to
the man who will come after me. [19]And who
knows whether he will be wise or a fool? Yet he
will rule over all my labor in which I toiled and
in which I have shown myself wise under the
sun. This also *is* vanity. [20]Therefore I turned my
heart and despaired of all the labor in which I had
toiled under the sun. [21]For there is a man whose
labor *is* with wisdom, knowledge, and skill; yet he
must leave his heritage to a man who has not labored for it. This also *is* vanity and a great evil.
[22]For what has man for all his labor, and for the
striving of his heart with which he has toiled under the sun? [23]For all his days *are* sorrowful, and
his work burdensome; even in the night his heart
takes no rest. This also is vanity.

[24]Nothing *is* better for a man *than* that he
should eat and drink, and *that* his soul should enjoy good in his labor. This also, I saw, was from the
hand of God. [25]For who can eat, or who can have
enjoyment, more than I?[a] [26]For *God* gives wisdom
and knowledge and joy to a man who *is* good in
His sight; but to the sinner He gives the work of
gathering and collecting, that he may give to *him
who is* good before God. This also *is* vanity and
grasping for the wind.

EVERYTHING HAS ITS TIME

3 To everything *there is* a season,
A time for every purpose under heaven:

[2]A time to be born,
And a time to die;

2:25 [a]Following Masoretic Text, Targum, and Vulgate; some Hebrew
manuscripts, Septuagint, and Syriac read *without Him.*

THROUGH THE GRID

*Where Have All the Dreamers Gone?
Observations from a Biblical
Worldview: Nihilism (Eccl. 2:15)*

As an alternative worldview, some have embraced the principles of nihilism; it argues
that there is no meaning or point to life, since there is no God. Nihilists do not care about
the meaning of life, because accordingly, it all amounts to nothing anyway. At death, we
decompose and that's life. We are born, we live, and we die. No afterlife, no salvation,
no hope. Self-destruction is the logical extension of nihilism because, for the nihilist,
nothing matters anyway. Nihilism goes against every Christian tenet that claims God exists and that our lives indeed do have meaning.

A time to plant,
   And a time to pluck *what is* planted;
³A time to kill,
   And a time to heal;
A time to break down,
   And a time to build up;
⁴A time to weep,
   And a time to laugh;
A time to mourn,
   And a time to dance;
⁵A time to cast away stones,
   And a time to gather stones;
A time to embrace,
   And a time to refrain from embracing;
⁶A time to gain,
   And a time to lose;
A time to keep,
   And a time to throw away;
⁷A time to tear,
   And a time to sew;
A time to keep silence,
   And a time to speak;
⁸A time to love,
   And a time to hate;
A time of war,
   And a time of peace.

The God-Given Task

⁹What profit has the worker from that in which he labors? ¹⁰I have seen the God-given task with which the sons of men are to be occupied. ¹¹He has made everything beautiful in its time. Also He has put eternity in their hearts, except that no one can find out the work that God does from beginning to end.

¹²I know that nothing *is* better for them than to rejoice, and to do good in their lives, ¹³and also that every man should eat and drink and enjoy the good of all his labor—it *is* the gift of God.

¹⁴I know that whatever God does,
   It shall be forever.
Nothing can be added to it,
   And nothing taken from it.
God does *it,* that men should fear before
      Him.
¹⁵That which is has already been,
   And what is to be has already been;
And God requires an account of what is past.

Injustice Seems to Prevail

¹⁶Moreover I saw under the sun:

In the place of judgment,
Wickedness *was* there;
And *in* the place of righteousness,
Iniquity *was* there.

¹⁷I said in my heart,

"God shall judge the righteous and the
      wicked,
For *there is* a time there for every purpose
      and for every work."

¹⁸I said in my heart, "Concerning the condition of the sons of men, God tests them, that they may see that they themselves are *like* animals." ¹⁹For what happens to the sons of men also happens to animals; one thing befalls them: as one dies, so dies the other. Surely, they all have one breath; man has no advantage over animals, for all *is* vanity. ²⁰All go to one place: all are from the dust, and all return to dust. ²¹Who knows the spirit of the sons of men, which goes upward, and the spirit of the animal, which goes down to the earth?ᵃ ²²So I perceived that nothing *is* better than that a man should rejoice in his own works, for that *is* his heritage. For who can bring him to see what will happen after him?

4 Then I returned and considered all the oppression that is done under the sun:

And look! The tears of the oppressed,
   But they have no comforter—
On the side of their oppressors *there is*
      power,
   But they have no comforter.
²Therefore I praised the dead who were
      already dead,
   More than the living who are still alive.
³Yet, better than both *is he* who has never
      existed,
   Who has not seen the evil work that is done
      under the sun.

3:21 ᵃSeptuagint, Syriac, Targum, and Vulgate read *Who knows whether the spirit . . . goes upward, and whether . . . goes downward to the earth?*

The Vanity of Selfish Toil

[4]Again, I saw that for all toil and every skillful work a man is envied by his neighbor. This also *is* vanity and grasping for the wind.

[5]The fool folds his hands
And consumes his own flesh.
[6]Better a handful *with* quietness
Than both hands full, *together with* toil and
grasping for the wind.

[7]Then I returned, and I saw vanity under the sun:

[8]There is one alone, without companion:
He has neither son nor brother.
Yet *there is* no end to all his labors,
Nor is his eye satisfied with riches.
But he never asks,
"For whom do I toil and deprive myself of
good?"
This also *is* vanity and a grave misfortune.

The Value of a Friend

[9]Two *are* better than one,
Because they have a good reward for their
labor.
[10]For if they fall, one will lift up his
companion.
But woe to him *who is* alone when he falls,
For *he has* no one to help him up.
[11]Again, if two lie down together, they will
keep warm;
But how can one be warm *alone*?
[12]Though one may be overpowered by
another, two can withstand him.
And a threefold cord is not quickly broken.

Popularity Passes Away

[13]Better a poor and wise youth
Than an old and foolish king who will be
admonished no more.
[14]For he comes out of prison to be king,
Although he was born poor in his kingdom.
[15]I saw all the living who walk under the sun;
They were with the second youth who stands
in his place.
[16]*There was* no end of all the people over whom
he was made king;

Yet those who come afterward will not
rejoice in him.
Surely this also *is* vanity and grasping for the
wind.

Fear God, Keep Your Vows

5 Walk prudently when you go to the house of God; and draw near to hear rather than to give the sacrifice of fools, for they do not know that they do evil.

[2]Do not be rash with your mouth,
And let not your heart utter anything hastily
before God.
For God *is* in heaven, and you on earth;
Therefore let your words be few.
[3]For a dream comes through much activity,
And a fool's voice *is known* by *his* many words.

[4]When you make a vow to God, do not delay
to pay it;
For *He has* no pleasure in fools.
Pay what you have vowed—
[5]Better not to vow than to vow and not pay.

[6]Do not let your mouth cause your flesh to sin, nor say before the messenger *of God* that it *was* an error. Why should God be angry at your excuse[a] and destroy the work of your hands? [7]For in the multitude of dreams and many words *there is* also vanity. But fear God.

The Vanity of Gain and Honor

[8]If you see the oppression of the poor, and the violent perversion of justice and righteousness in a province, do not marvel at the matter; for high official watches over high official, and higher officials are over them. [9]Moreover the profit of the land is for all; *even* the king is served from the field.

[10]He who loves silver will not be satisfied with
silver;
Nor he who loves abundance, with increase.
This also *is* vanity.

[11]When goods increase,
They increase who eat them;

5:6 [a]Literally *voice*

So what profit have the owners
Except to see *them* with their eyes?

¹²The sleep of a laboring man *is* sweet,
  Whether he eats little or much;
But the abundance of the rich will not
    permit him to sleep.

¹³There is a severe evil *which* I have seen under
    the sun:
Riches kept for their owner to his hurt.
¹⁴But those riches perish through misfortune;
  When he begets a son, *there is* nothing in his
    hand.
¹⁵As he came from his mother's womb, naked
    shall he return,
To go as he came;
And he shall take nothing from his labor
Which he may carry away in his hand.

¹⁶And this also *is* a severe evil—
  Just exactly as he came, so shall he go.
And what profit has he who has labored for
    the wind?
¹⁷All his days he also eats in darkness,
  And *he has* much sorrow and sickness and
    anger.

¹⁸Here is what I have seen: *It is* good and fitting *for one* to eat and drink, and to enjoy the good of all his labor in which he toils under the sun all the days of his life which God gives him; for it *is* his heritage. ¹⁹As for every man to whom God has given riches and wealth, and given him power to eat of it, to receive his heritage and rejoice in his labor—this *is* the gift of God. ²⁰For he will not dwell unduly on the days of his life, because God keeps *him* busy with the joy of his heart.

6 There is an evil which I have seen under the sun, and it *is* common among men: ²A man to whom God has given riches and wealth and honor, so that he lacks nothing for himself of all he desires; yet God does not give him power to eat of it, but a foreigner consumes it. This *is* vanity, and it *is* an evil affliction.

³If a man begets a hundred *children* and lives many years, so that the days of his years are many, but his soul is not satisfied with goodness, or indeed he has no burial, I say *that* a stillborn child *is*

better than he— ⁴for it comes in vanity and departs in darkness, and its name is covered with darkness. ⁵Though it has not seen the sun or known *anything*, this has more rest than that man, ⁶even if he lives a thousand years twice—but has not seen goodness. Do not all go to one place?

⁷All the labor of man *is* for his mouth,
  And yet the soul is not satisfied.
⁸For what more has the wise *man* than the
    fool?
What does the poor man have,
Who knows *how* to walk before the living?
⁹Better *is* the sight of the eyes than the
    wandering of desire.
This also *is* vanity and grasping for the wind.

¹⁰Whatever one is, he has been named already,
  For it is known that he *is* man;
And he cannot contend with Him who is
    mightier than he.
¹¹Since there are many things that increase
    vanity,
How *is* man the better?

¹²For who knows what *is* good for man in life, all the days of his vain life which he passes like a shadow? Who can tell a man what will happen after him under the sun?

The Value of Practical Wisdom

7 A good name is better than precious
    ointment,
And the day of death than the day of one's
    birth;
²Better to go to the house of mourning
  Than to go to the house of feasting,
For that *is* the end of all men;
And the living will take *it* to heart.
³Sorrow *is* better than laughter,
  For by a sad countenance the heart is made
    better.
⁴The heart of the wise *is* in the house of
    mourning,
But the heart of fools *is* in the house of mirth.

⁵*It is* better to hear the rebuke of the wise
  Than for a man to hear the song of fools.
⁶For like the crackling of thorns under a pot,

So *is* the laughter of the fool.
This also is vanity.
[7]Surely oppression destroys a wise *man's* reason,
And a bribe debases the heart.

[8]The end of a thing *is* better than its beginning;
The patient in spirit *is* better than the proud in spirit.
[9]Do not hasten in your spirit to be angry,
For anger rests in the bosom of fools.
[10]Do not say,
"Why were the former days better than these?"
For you do not inquire wisely concerning this.

[11]Wisdom *is* good with an inheritance,
And profitable to those who see the sun.
[12]For wisdom *is* a defense *as* money *is* a defense,
But the excellence of knowledge *is that* wisdom gives life to those who have it.

[13]Consider the work of God;
For who can make straight what He has made crooked?
[14]In the day of prosperity be joyful,
But in the day of adversity consider:
Surely God has appointed the one as well as the other,
So that man can find out nothing *that will come* after him.

[15]I have seen everything in my days of vanity:

There is a just *man* who perishes in his righteousness,
And there is a wicked *man* who prolongs *life* in his wickedness.

[16]Do not be overly righteous,
Nor be overly wise:
Why should you destroy yourself?
[17]Do not be overly wicked,
Nor be foolish:
Why should you die before your time?
[18]*It is* good that you grasp this,

And also not remove your hand from the other;
For he who fears God will escape them all.

[19]Wisdom strengthens the wise
More than ten rulers of the city.

[20]For *there is* not a just man on earth who does good
And does not sin.

[21]Also do not take to heart everything people say,
Lest you hear your servant cursing you.
[22]For many times, also, your own heart has known
That even you have cursed others.

[23]All this I have proved by wisdom.
I said, "I will be wise";
But it *was* far from me.
[24]As for that which is far off and exceedingly deep,
Who can find it out?
[25]I applied my heart to know,
To search and seek out wisdom and the reason *of things,*
To know the wickedness of folly,
Even of foolishness *and* madness.
[26]And I find more bitter than death
The woman whose heart *is* snares and nets,
Whose hands *are* fetters.
He who pleases God shall escape from her,
But the sinner shall be trapped by her.

[27]"Here is what I have found," says the Preacher,
"*Adding* one thing to the other to find out the reason,
[28]Which my soul still seeks but I cannot find:
One man among a thousand I have found,
But a woman among all these I have not found.
[29]Truly, this only I have found:
That God made man upright,
But they have sought out many schemes."

8 Who *is* like a wise *man?*
And who knows the interpretation of a thing?

A man's wisdom makes his face shine,
And the sternness of his face is changed.

OBEY AUTHORITIES FOR GOD'S SAKE

[2]I *say,* "Keep the king's commandment for the sake of your oath to God. [3]Do not be hasty to go from his presence. Do not take your stand for an evil thing, for he does whatever pleases him."

[4]Where the word of a king *is, there is* power;
And who may say to him, "What are you doing?"
[5]He who keeps his command will experience nothing harmful;
And a wise man's heart discerns both time and judgment,
[6]Because for every matter there is a time and judgment,
Though the misery of man increases greatly.
[7]For he does not know what will happen;
So who can tell him when it will occur?
[8]No one has power over the spirit to retain the spirit,
And no one has power in the day of death.
There is no release from that war,
And wickedness will not deliver those who are given to it.

[9]All this I have seen, and applied my heart to every work that is done under the sun: *There is* a time in which one man rules over another to his own hurt.

DEATH COMES TO ALL

[10]Then I saw the wicked buried, who had come and gone from the place of holiness, and they were forgotten[a] in the city where they had so done. This also *is* vanity. [11]Because the sentence against an evil work is not executed speedily, therefore the heart of the sons of men is fully set in them to do evil. [12]Though a sinner does evil a hundred *times,* and his *days* are prolonged, yet I surely know that it will be well with those who fear God, who fear before Him. [13]But it will not be well with the wicked; nor will he prolong *his* days, *which are* as a shadow, because he does not fear before God.

[14]There is a vanity which occurs on earth, that there are just *men* to whom it happens ac-cording to the work of the wicked; again, there are wicked *men* to whom it happens according to the work of the righteous. I said that this also *is* vanity.

[15]So I commended enjoyment, because a man has nothing better under the sun than to eat, drink, and be merry; for this will remain with him in his labor *all* the days of his life which God gives him under the sun.

[16]When I applied my heart to know wisdom and to see the business that is done on earth, even though one sees no sleep day or night, [17]then I saw all the work of God, that a man cannot find out the work that is done under the sun. For though a man labors to discover *it,* yet he will not find *it;* moreover, though a wise *man* attempts to know *it,* he will not be able to find *it.*

9 For I considered all this in my heart, so that I could declare it all: that the righteous and the wise and their works *are* in the hand of God. People know neither love nor hatred *by* anything *they see* before them. [2]All things *come* alike to all:

One event *happens* to the righteous and the wicked;
To the good,[a] the clean, and the unclean;
To him who sacrifices and him who does not sacrifice.
As is the good, so *is* the sinner;
He who takes an oath as *he* who fears an oath.

[3]This *is* an evil in all that is done under the sun: that one thing *happens* to all. Truly the hearts of the sons of men are full of evil; madness *is* in their hearts while they live, and after that *they go* to the dead. [4]But for him who is joined to all the living there is hope, for a living dog is better than a dead lion.

[5]For the living know that they will die;
But the dead know nothing,
And they have no more reward,
For the memory of them is forgotten.
[6]Also their love, their hatred, and their envy have now perished;
Nevermore will they have a share
In anything done under the sun.

8:10 [a]Some Hebrew manuscripts, Septuagint, and Vulgate read *praised.* **9:2** [a]Septuagint, Syriac, and Vulgate read *good and bad.*

LEADERSHIP ISSUES

The Hand of God

ECCLESIASTES 9:1

God's all-powerful hand, molding matter into humanity, is vividly symbolized in Rodin's sculpture *The Hand of God*. This masterpiece compels the Christ-follower to ponder the works of His hand in perspective. When the hand of God positions one to receive instruction, it should be accepted. When the hand of God pushes one out of luxurious gardens and into wilderness, it is an opportunity to develop one's potential. When He places leaders in the pathways of kingly influencers, the ripple effect should be far reaching.

Consider that the same hand that created man was pierced to hang upon a cross to pay for man's sin. The Shepherd's tender hand that guides, provides, and protects is the same one that often must chastise "the righteous and the wise." Casual Christians love to embrace the provision and protection of His hand, but authentic Christian leaders separate themselves by submitting appropriately both to God's hand of love and discipline.

The same Hand of God that created Adam and Eve later pushed them from the garden. The Hand of God set Moses in position to receive the Ten Commandments and also held him back from going into the Promised Land. The hand that protected Noah's family by closing the Ark's door released judgment on every other living thing. The same hand that knocked Saul of Tarsus in the dirt, raised Paul up to preach before magistrates and kept him from dying in shipwrecks and stonings. The same hand that pushed Vashti off the throne placed Esther in a position of influence to save a nation.

Future world-changers should consider the Hand of God in every area of life. As an emerging leader, remember that God disciplines with His loving hand to instill self-discipline. His consistent application of the rod leads obedient Christ-followers to His Word, and discipline in the Word increases wisdom. Leadership, therefore, becomes authentically Christian only when it is filled with the Word of God. Christian men and women who desire to have a timeless impact upon the world must not only find refuge in God's righteous hand, but they must also seek wisdom from His Holy Word.

7Go, eat your bread with joy,
  And drink your wine with a merry heart;
  For God has already accepted your works.
8Let your garments always be white,
  And let your head lack no oil.

9Live joyfully with the wife whom you love all the days of your vain life which He has given you under the sun, all your days of vanity; for that *is* your portion in life, and in the labor which you perform under the sun.
10Whatever your hand finds to do, do *it* with your might; for *there is* no work or device or knowledge or wisdom in the grave where you are going.
11I returned and saw under the sun that—

  The race *is* not to the swift,
  Nor the battle to the strong,
  Nor bread to the wise,
  Nor riches to men of understanding,
  Nor favor to men of skill;
  But time and chance happen to them all.
12For man also does not know his time:
  Like fish taken in a cruel net,
  Like birds caught in a snare,
  So the sons of men *are* snared in an evil time,
  When it falls suddenly upon them.

Wisdom Superior to Folly

13This wisdom I have also seen under the sun, and it *seemed* great to me: 14*There was* a little city with few men in it; and a great king came against it, besieged it, and built great snares[a] around it. 15Now there was found in it a poor wise man, and he by his wisdom delivered the city. Yet no one remembered that same poor man.
16Then I said:

  "Wisdom *is* better than strength.
  Nevertheless the poor man's wisdom *is* despised,
  And his words are not heard.
17Words of the wise, *spoken* quietly, *should be* heard
  Rather than the shout of a ruler of fools.
18Wisdom *is* better than weapons of war;
  But one sinner destroys much good."

10 Dead flies putrefy[a] the perfumer's ointment,
  And cause it to give off a foul odor;
  So does a little folly to one respected for wisdom *and* honor.
2A wise man's heart *is* at his right hand,
  But a fool's heart at his left.
3Even when a fool walks along the way,
  He lacks wisdom,
  And he shows everyone *that* he *is* a fool.
4If the spirit of the ruler rises against you,
  Do not leave your post;
  For conciliation pacifies great offenses.

5There is an evil I have seen under the sun,
  As an error proceeding from the ruler:
6Folly is set in great dignity,
  While the rich sit in a lowly place.
7I have seen servants on horses,
  While princes walk on the ground like servants.

8He who digs a pit will fall into it,
  And whoever breaks through a wall will be bitten by a serpent.
9He who quarries stones may be hurt by them,
  And he who splits wood may be endangered by it.
10If the ax is dull,
  And one does not sharpen the edge,
  Then he must use more strength;
  But wisdom brings success.

11A serpent may bite when *it is* not charmed;
  The babbler is no different.
12The words of a wise man's mouth *are* gracious,
  But the lips of a fool shall swallow him up;
13The words of his mouth begin with foolishness,
  And the end of his talk *is* raving madness.
14A fool also multiplies words.
  No man knows what is to be;
  Who can tell him what will be after him?
15The labor of fools wearies them,
  For they do not even know how to go to the city!

9:14 [a]Septuagint, Syriac, and Vulgate read *bulwarks*. **10:1** [a]Targum and Vulgate omit *putrefy*.

[16]Woe to you, O land, when your king *is* a
      child,
And your princes feast in the morning!
[17]Blessed *are* you, O land, when your king *is*
      the son of nobles,
And your princes feast at the proper time—
For strength and not for drunkenness!
[18]Because of laziness the building decays,
And through idleness of hands the house leaks.
[19]A feast is made for laughter,
And wine makes merry;
But money answers everything.

[20]Do not curse the king, even in your thought;
Do not curse the rich, even in your bedroom;
For a bird of the air may carry your voice,
And a bird in flight may tell the matter.

The Value of Diligence

11 Cast your bread upon the waters,
      For you will find it after many days.
[2]Give a serving to seven, and also to eight,
For you do not know what evil will be on
      the earth.

[3]If the clouds are full of rain,
They empty *themselves* upon the earth;
And if a tree falls to the south or the north,
In the place where the tree falls, there it
      shall lie.
[4]He who observes the wind will not sow,
And he who regards the clouds will not reap.

[5]As you do not know what *is* the way of the
      wind,[a]
Or how the bones *grow* in the womb of her
      who is with child,
So you do not know the works of God who
      makes everything.
[6]In the morning sow your seed,
And in the evening do not withhold your
      hand;
For you do not know which will prosper,
Either this or that,
Or whether both alike *will be* good.

[7]Truly the light is sweet,
And *it is* pleasant for the eyes to behold
      the sun;

[8]But if a man lives many years
And rejoices in them all,
Yet let him remember the days of darkness,
For they will be many.
All that is coming *is* vanity.

Seek God in Early Life

[9]Rejoice, O young man, in your youth,
And let your heart cheer you in the days of
      your youth;
Walk in the ways of your heart,
And in the sight of your eyes;
But know that for all these
God will bring you into judgment.
[10]Therefore remove sorrow from your heart,
And put away evil from your flesh,
For childhood and youth *are* vanity.

12 Remember now your Creator in the days
      of your youth,
Before the difficult days come,
And the years draw near when you say,
"I have no pleasure in them":
[2]While the sun and the light,
The moon and the stars,
Are not darkened,
And the clouds do not return after the
      rain;
[3]In the day when the keepers of the house
      tremble,
And the strong men bow down;
When the grinders cease because they are
      few,
And those that look through the windows
      grow dim;
[4]When the doors are shut in the streets,
And the sound of grinding is low;
When one rises up at the sound of a bird,
And all the daughters of music are brought
      low.
[5]Also they are afraid of height,
And of terrors in the way;
When the almond tree blossoms,
The grasshopper is a burden,
And desire fails.
For man goes to his eternal home,
And the mourners go about the streets.

11:5 [a]Or *spirit*

[6]*Remember your Creator* before the silver cord is
    loosed,[a]
Or the golden bowl is broken,
Or the pitcher shattered at the fountain,
Or the wheel broken at the well.
[7]Then the dust will return to the earth as it
    was,
And the spirit will return to God who
    gave it.

[8]"Vanity of vanities," says the Preacher,
"All *is* vanity."

THE WHOLE DUTY OF MAN

[9]And moreover, because the Preacher was
wise, he still taught the people knowledge; yes, he
pondered and sought out *and* set in order many
proverbs. [10]The Preacher sought to find acceptable words; and *what was* written *was* upright—

words of truth. [11]The words of the wise are like
goads, and the words of scholars[a] are like well-
driven nails, given by one Shepherd. [12]And further, my son, be admonished by these. Of making
many books *there is* no end, and much study *is*
wearisome to the flesh.

[13]Let us hear the conclusion of the whole
matter:

Fear God and keep His commandments,
For this is man's all.
[14]For God will bring every work into
    judgment,
Including every secret thing,
Whether good or evil.

12:6 [a]Following Qere and Targum; Kethib reads *removed;* Septuagint
and Vulgate read *broken.* **12:11** [a]Literally *masters of the assemblies*

IMPACT OF THE BOOK

IDEA

Just as a committed husband loves his wife, so, too, does the Lord love His people.

MESSAGE

The couple in this book express sincerity in their love for one another, their commitment, and the importance of exclusivity in their relationship. This is an indication of the kind of commitment God expects and desires from His bride, the church. Every leader must learn to love the people under his or her care just like God loves His people.

PEOPLE

Solomon (or the husband) and "Shulamite" (or the wife)

AUTHOR

Solomon, son of David and Bathsheba and wisest man on earth, penned this book probably during the early years of his reign.

CULTURE

This book is a nuptial song, a form of romantic poetry, expressing love between a bride and a bridegroom. Solomon spent most of his time in the large city of Jerusalem learning the ways of a king in the palace filled with finery and elegance. He was accustomed to festivities, feasts, and crowds. The Shulamite, by contrast, was raised southeast of the Sea of Galilee in a land rich with plants, animals, and many fragrances. She was not pampered or privileged, but lived in a slower, quieter way among the simple pleasures of nature. Both were able to enjoy and appreciate the environments of the other, and their varied backgrounds fill the song with interest. Throughout, both the outdoors and the opulence of palace life were employed to describe the love of the couple.

TIMELINE

Between 971 and 931 BC (during Solomon's reign)

EY SCRIPTURE MORY VERSES

7:10; 8:7

ONG OF SOLOMON

SONG OF SOLOMON

1
The song of songs, which *is* Solomon's.

THE BANQUET

THE SHULAMITE[a]
2Let him kiss me with the kisses of his
        mouth—
    For your[b] love *is* better than wine.
3Because of the fragrance of your good
        ointments,
    Your name *is* ointment poured forth;
    Therefore the virgins love you.
4Draw me away!

THE DAUGHTERS OF JERUSALEM
    We will run after you.[a]

THE SHULAMITE
    The king has brought me into his chambers.

THE DAUGHTERS OF JERUSALEM
    We will be glad and rejoice in you.[b]

    We will remember your[c] love more than
        wine.

THE SHULAMITE
    Rightly do they love you.[d]

5I *am* dark, but lovely,
    O daughters of Jerusalem,
    Like the tents of Kedar,
    Like the curtains of Solomon.
6Do not look upon me, because I *am* dark,
    Because the sun has tanned me.
    My mother's sons were angry with me;
    They made me the keeper of the vineyards,
    But my own vineyard I have not kept.

(TO HER BELOVED)
7Tell me, O you whom I love,
    Where you feed *your flock,*
    Where you make *it* rest at noon.
    For why should I be as one who veils herself[a]
    By the flocks of your companions?

THE BELOVED
8If you do not know, O fairest among women,
    Follow in the footsteps of the flock,

    And feed your little goats
        Beside the shepherds' tents.
9I have compared you, my love,
    To my filly among Pharaoh's chariots.
10Your cheeks are lovely with ornaments,
    Your neck with chains *of gold.*

THE DAUGHTERS OF JERUSALEM
11We will make you[a] ornaments of gold
    With studs of silver.

THE SHULAMITE
12While the king *is* at his table,
    My spikenard sends forth its fragrance.
13A bundle of myrrh *is* my beloved to me,
    That lies all night between my breasts.
14My beloved *is* to me a cluster of henna
        blooms
    In the vineyards of En Gedi.

THE BELOVED
15Behold, you *are* fair, my love!
    Behold, you *are* fair!
    You *have* dove's eyes.

THE SHULAMITE
16Behold, you *are* handsome, my beloved!
    Yes, pleasant!
    Also our bed *is* green.
17The beams of our houses *are* cedar,
    And our rafters of fir.

2
I *am* the rose of Sharon,
    And the lily of the valleys.

THE BELOVED
2Like a lily among thorns,
    So is my love among the daughters.

THE SHULAMITE
3Like an apple tree among the trees of the
        woods,

1:2 [a]A young woman from the town of Shulam or Shunem (compare 6:13). The speaker and audience are identified according to the number, gender, and person of the Hebrew words. Occasionally the identity is not certain. [b]Masculine singular, that is, the Beloved **1:4** [a]Masculine singular, that is, the Beloved [b]Feminine singular, that is, the Shulamite [c]Masculine singular, that is, the Beloved [d]Masculine singular, that is, the Beloved **1:7** [a]Septuagint, Syriac, and Vulgate read *wanders.* **1:11** [a]Feminine singular, that is, the Shulamite

So *is* my beloved among the sons.
I sat down in his shade with great delight,
And his fruit *was* sweet to my taste.

THE SHULAMITE TO THE DAUGHTERS OF JERUSALEM

4He brought me to the banqueting house,
And his banner over me *was* love.
5Sustain me with cakes of raisins,
Refresh me with apples,
For I *am* lovesick.

6His left hand *is* under my head,
And his right hand embraces me.
7I charge you, O daughters of Jerusalem,
By the gazelles or by the does of the field,
Do not stir up nor awaken love
Until it pleases.

THE BELOVED'S REQUEST

THE SHULAMITE

8The voice of my beloved!
Behold, he comes
Leaping upon the mountains,
Skipping upon the hills.
9My beloved is like a gazelle or a young
     stag.
Behold, he stands behind our wall;
He is looking through the windows,
Gazing through the lattice.

10My beloved spoke, and said to me:
"Rise up, my love, my fair one,
And come away.
11For lo, the winter is past,
The rain is over *and* gone.
12The flowers appear on the earth;
The time of singing has come,
And the voice of the turtledove
Is heard in our land.
13The fig tree puts forth her green figs,
And the vines *with* the tender grapes
Give a *good* smell.
Rise up, my love, my fair one,
And come away!

14"O my dove, in the clefts of the rock,
In the secret *places* of the cliff,
Let me see your face,

Let me hear your voice;
For your voice *is* sweet,
And your face *is* lovely."

HER BROTHERS

15Catch us the foxes,
The little foxes that spoil the vines,
For our vines *have* tender grapes.

THE SHULAMITE

16My beloved *is* mine, and I *am* his.
He feeds *his flock* among the lilies.

(TO HER BELOVED)

17Until the day breaks
And the shadows flee away,
Turn, my beloved,
And be like a gazelle
Or a young stag
Upon the mountains of Bether.[a]

A TROUBLED NIGHT

THE SHULAMITE

3 By night on my bed I sought the one I love;
I sought him, but I did not find him.
2"I will rise now," I *said,*
"And go about the city;
In the streets and in the squares
I will seek the one I love."
I sought him, but I did not find him.
3The watchmen who go about the city found
     me;
I said,
"Have you seen the one I love?"

4Scarcely had I passed by them,
When I found the one I love.
I held him and would not let him go,
Until I had brought him to the house of my
     mother,
And into the chamber of her who conceived
     me.

5I charge you, O daughters of Jerusalem,
By the gazelles or by the does of the field,
Do not stir up nor awaken love
Until it pleases.

2:17 aLiterally *Separation*

The Coming of Solomon

The Shulamite

⁶Who *is* this coming out of the wilderness
  Like pillars of smoke,
  Perfumed with myrrh and frankincense,
  With all the merchant's fragrant powders?
⁷Behold, it *is* Solomon's couch,
  With sixty valiant men around it,
  Of the valiant of Israel.
⁸They all hold swords,
  Being expert in war.
  Every man *has* his sword on his thigh
  Because of fear in the night.

⁹Of the wood of Lebanon
  Solomon the King
  Made himself a palanquin:ᵃ
¹⁰He made its pillars *of* silver,
  Its support *of* gold,
  Its seat *of* purple,
  Its interior paved *with* love
  By the daughters of Jerusalem.
¹¹Go forth, O daughters of Zion,
  And see King Solomon with the crown
  With which his mother crowned him
  On the day of his wedding,
  The day of the gladness of his heart.

The Bridegroom Praises the Bride

The Beloved

4 Behold, you *are* fair, my love!
  Behold, you *are* fair!
  You *have* dove's eyes behind your veil.
  Your hair *is* like a flock of goats,
  Going down from Mount Gilead.
²Your teeth *are* like a flock of shorn *sheep*
  Which have come up from the washing,
  Every one of which bears twins,
  And none *is* barren among them.
³Your lips *are* like a strand of scarlet,
  And your mouth is lovely.
  Your temples behind your veil
  Are like a piece of pomegranate.
⁴Your neck *is* like the tower of David,
  Built for an armory,
  On which hang a thousand bucklers,
  All shields of mighty men.
⁵Your two breasts *are* like two fawns,

  Twins of a gazelle,
  Which feed among the lilies.

⁶Until the day breaks
  And the shadows flee away,
  I will go my way to the mountain of myrrh
  And to the hill of frankincense.

⁷You *are* all fair, my love,
  And *there is* no spot in you.
⁸Come with me from Lebanon, *my* spouse,
  With me from Lebanon.
  Look from the top of Amana,
  From the top of Senir and Hermon,
  From the lions' dens,
  From the mountains of the leopards.

⁹You have ravished my heart,
  My sister, *my* spouse;
  You have ravished my heart
  With one *look* of your eyes,
  With one link of your necklace.
¹⁰How fair is your love,
  My sister, *my* spouse!
  How much better than wine is your love,
  And the scent of your perfumes
  Than all spices!
¹¹Your lips, O *my* spouse,
  Drip as the honeycomb;
  Honey and milk *are* under your tongue;
  And the fragrance of your garments
  Is like the fragrance of Lebanon.

¹²A garden enclosed
  Is my sister, *my* spouse,
  A spring shut up,
  A fountain sealed.
¹³Your plants *are* an orchard of pomegranates
  With pleasant fruits,
  Fragrant henna with spikenard,
¹⁴Spikenard and saffron,
  Calamus and cinnamon,
  With all trees of frankincense,
  Myrrh and aloes,
  With all the chief spices—
¹⁵A fountain of gardens,
  A well of living waters,
  And streams from Lebanon.

3:9 ᵃA portable enclosed chair

THE SHULAMITE

16Awake, O north *wind,*
And come, O south!
Blow upon my garden,
That its spices may flow out.
Let my beloved come to his garden
And eat its pleasant fruits.

THE BELOVED

5 I have come to my garden, my sister, *my*
    spouse;
I have gathered my myrrh with my spice;
I have eaten my honeycomb with my honey;
I have drunk my wine with my milk.

(TO HIS FRIENDS)

Eat, O friends!
Drink, yes, drink deeply,
O beloved ones!

THE SHULAMITE'S TROUBLED EVENING

THE SHULAMITE

2I sleep, but my heart is awake;
It is the voice of my beloved!
He knocks, *saying,*
"Open for me, my sister, my love,
My dove, my perfect one;
For my head is covered with dew,
My locks with the drops of the night."

3I have taken off my robe;
How can I put it on *again?*
I have washed my feet;
How can I defile them?
4My beloved put his hand
By the latch *of the door,*
And my heart yearned for him.
5I arose to open for my beloved,
And my hands dripped *with* myrrh,
My fingers with liquid myrrh,
On the handles of the lock.

6I opened for my beloved,
But my beloved had turned away *and* was gone.
My heart leaped up when he spoke.
I sought him, but I could not find him;
I called him, but he gave me no answer.
7The watchmen who went about the city
    found me.

They struck me, they wounded me;
The keepers of the walls
Took my veil away from me.
8I charge you, O daughters of Jerusalem,
If you find my beloved,
That you tell him I *am* lovesick!

THE DAUGHTERS OF JERUSALEM

9What *is* your beloved
More than *another* beloved,
O fairest among women?
What *is* your beloved
More than *another* beloved,
That you so charge us?

THE SHULAMITE

10My beloved *is* white and ruddy,
Chief among ten thousand.
11His head *is like* the finest gold;
His locks *are* wavy,
And black as a raven.
12His eyes *are* like doves
By the rivers of waters,
Washed with milk,
And fitly set.
13His cheeks *are* like a bed of spices,
Banks of scented herbs.
His lips *are* lilies,
Dripping liquid myrrh.

14His hands *are* rods of gold
Set with beryl.
His body *is* carved ivory
Inlaid *with* sapphires.
15His legs *are* pillars of marble
Set on bases of fine gold.
His countenance *is* like Lebanon,
Excellent as the cedars.
16His mouth *is* most sweet,
Yes, he *is* altogether lovely.
This *is* my beloved,
And this *is* my friend,
O daughters of Jerusalem!

THE DAUGHTERS OF JERUSALEM

6 Where has your beloved gone,
    O fairest among women?
Where has your beloved turned aside,
That we may seek him with you?

THE SHULAMITE

²My beloved has gone to his garden,
To the beds of spices,
To feed *his flock* in the gardens,
And to gather lilies.
³I *am* my beloved's,
And my beloved *is* mine.
He feeds *his flock* among the lilies.

PRAISE OF THE SHULAMITE'S BEAUTY

THE BELOVED

⁴O my love, you *are as* beautiful as Tirzah,
Lovely as Jerusalem,
Awesome as *an army* with banners!
⁵Turn your eyes away from me,
For they have overcome me.
Your hair *is* like a flock of goats
Going down from Gilead.
⁶Your teeth *are* like a flock of sheep
Which have come up from the washing;
Every one bears twins,
And none *is* barren among them.
⁷Like a piece of pomegranate
Are your temples behind your veil.

⁸There are sixty queens
And eighty concubines,
And virgins without number.
⁹My dove, my perfect one,
Is the only one,
The only one of her mother,
The favorite of the one who bore her.
The daughters saw her
And called her blessed,
The queens and the concubines,
And they praised her.

¹⁰Who is she who looks forth as the morning,
Fair as the moon,
Clear as the sun,
Awesome as *an army* with banners?

THE SHULAMITE

¹¹I went down to the garden of nuts
To see the verdure of the valley,
To see whether the vine had budded
And the pomegranates had bloomed.
¹²Before I was even aware,

My soul had made me
As the chariots of my noble people.ᵃ

THE BELOVED AND HIS FRIENDS

¹³Return, return, O Shulamite;
Return, return, that we may look upon you!

THE SHULAMITE

What would you see in the Shulamite—
As it were, the dance of the two camps?ᵃ

EXPRESSIONS OF PRAISE

THE BELOVED

7 How beautiful are your feet in sandals,
O prince's daughter!
The curves of your thighs *are* like jewels,
The work of the hands of a skillful workman.
²Your navel *is* a rounded goblet;
It lacks no blended beverage.
Your waist *is* a heap of wheat
Set about with lilies.
³Your two breasts *are* like two fawns,
Twins of a gazelle.
⁴Your neck *is* like an ivory tower,
Your eyes *like* the pools in Heshbon
By the gate of Bath Rabbim.
Your nose *is* like the tower of Lebanon
Which looks toward Damascus.
⁵Your head *crowns* you like *Mount* Carmel,
And the hair of your head *is* like purple;
A king *is* held captive by *your* tresses.

⁶How fair and how pleasant you are,
O love, with your delights!
⁷This stature of yours is like a palm tree,
And your breasts *like* its clusters.
⁸I said, "I will go up to the palm tree,
I will take hold of its branches."
Let now your breasts be like clusters of the
vine,
The fragrance of your breath like apples,
⁹And the roof of your mouth like the best
wine.

THE SHULAMITE

The wine goes *down* smoothly for my beloved,
Moving gently the lips of sleepers.ᵃ

6:12 ᵃHebrew *Ammi Nadib* **6:13** ᵃHebrew *Mahanaim* **7:9** ᵃSeptuagint, Syriac, and Vulgate read *lips and teeth.*

¹⁰I *am* my beloved's,
And his desire *is* toward me.

¹¹Come, my beloved,
Let us go forth to the field;
Let us lodge in the villages.
¹²Let us get up early to the vineyards;
Let us see if the vine has budded,
Whether the grape blossoms are open,
And the pomegranates are in bloom.
There I will give you my love.
¹³The mandrakes give off a fragrance,
And at our gates *are* pleasant *fruits,*
All manner, new and old,
Which I have laid up for you, my beloved.

8 Oh, that you were like my brother,
Who nursed at my mother's breasts!
If I should find you outside,
I would kiss you;
I would not be despised.
²I would lead you *and* bring you
Into the house of my mother,
She *who* used to instruct me.
I would cause you to drink of spiced wine,
Of the juice of my pomegranate.

(TO THE DAUGHTERS OF JERUSALEM)
³His left hand *is* under my head,
And his right hand embraces me.
⁴I charge you, O daughters of Jerusalem,
Do not stir up nor awaken love
Until it pleases.

LOVE RENEWED IN LEBANON

A RELATIVE
⁵Who *is* this coming up from the
    wilderness,
Leaning upon her beloved?

I awakened you under the apple tree.
There your mother brought you forth;
There she *who* bore you brought *you* forth.

THE SHULAMITE TO HER BELOVED
⁶Set me as a seal upon your heart,
As a seal upon your arm;
For love *is as* strong as death,
Jealousy *as* cruel as the grave;^a

Its flames *are* flames of fire,
A most vehement flame.^b

⁷Many waters cannot quench love,
Nor can the floods drown it.
If a man would give for love
All the wealth of his house,
It would be utterly despised.

THE SHULAMITE'S BROTHERS
⁸We have a little sister,
And she has no breasts.
What shall we do for our sister
In the day when she is spoken for?
⁹If she *is* a wall,
We will build upon her
A battlement of silver;
And if she *is* a door,
We will enclose her
With boards of cedar.

THE SHULAMITE
¹⁰I *am* a wall,
And my breasts like towers;
Then I became in his eyes
As one who found peace.
¹¹Solomon had a vineyard at Baal Hamon;
He leased the vineyard to keepers;
Everyone was to bring for its fruit
A thousand silver *coins.*

(TO SOLOMON)
¹²My own vineyard *is* before me.
You, O Solomon, *may have* a thousand,
And those who tend its fruit two hundred.

THE BELOVED
¹³You who dwell in the gardens,
The companions listen for your voice—
Let me hear it!

THE SHULAMITE
¹⁴Make haste, my beloved,
And be like a gazelle
Or a young stag
On the mountains of spices.

8:6 ^aOr *Sheol* ^bLiterally *A flame of Yah* (a poetic form of YHWH, *the* LORD)

IMPACT OF THE BOOK

IDEA | *Religious activity is never a substitute for moral and ethical living. One must have a fresh view of God. Isaiah reveals God as the One who will most certainly save, help, and restore.*

MESSAGE | *God is the ultimate example of the Servant Leader. In the messianic chapters in Isaiah, we see the coming Messiah as the "suffering servant." Jesus Christ sacrificed His life to lead the way of salvation for His people. A true leader must be willing to put the well-being of the people first, so they can see how much you care.*

PEOPLE | *Hezekiah, Isaiah, the Messiah*

AUTHOR | *Isaiah lived in Jerusalem, came from a noble family, was married, and had at least two sons. It is possible that he was martyred by being sawed in half. (See Heb. 11:37.) He is remarkable for the way he answered the call of God on his life, "Here am I! Send me," (Is. 6:8). He is described by commentators as the "eagle" among the prophets because of his great vision and detail about the Messiah. He is also called the golden prophet and the evangelist.*

CULTURE | *Isaiah prophesied during the reigns of Uzziah, Jotham, Ahaz, and Hezekiah. Hebrew prophecy not only told of future events, but it also often called for a course of action for its hearers. This book can be divided into two sections: chapters 1—39 describe judgment and chapters 40—66 offer comfort. Isaiah's prophecies concerned the coming of the Messiah: He would be born of a virgin (7:14), He would be the Prince of Peace (9:6), and He would suffer for His people (ch. 53). Isaiah prophesied about the coming judgment against Judah and the surrounding nations.*

TIMELINE | *c. 680 BC*

KEY SCRIPTURE MEMORY VERSES | 1:18; 6:3, 5, 8; 7:14; 9:6; 40:31; 53:1–9; 59:1, 2; 61:1; 66:2

1 The vision of Isaiah the son of Amoz, which he saw concerning Judah and Jerusalem in the days of Uzziah, Jotham, Ahaz, *and* Hezekiah, kings of Judah.

The Wickedness of Judah

2Hear, O heavens, and give ear, O earth!
  For the LORD has spoken:
"I have nourished and brought up children,
  And they have rebelled against Me;
3The ox knows its owner
  And the donkey its master's crib;
But Israel does not know,
  My people do not consider."

4Alas, sinful nation,
  A people laden with iniquity,
  A brood of evildoers,
  Children who are corrupters!
They have forsaken the LORD,
  They have provoked to anger
  The Holy One of Israel,
  They have turned away backward.

5Why should you be stricken again?
  You will revolt more and more.
  The whole head is sick,
  And the whole heart faints.
6From the sole of the foot even to the head,
  There is no soundness in it,
But wounds and bruises and putrefying sores;
  They have not been closed or bound up,
  Or soothed with ointment.

7Your country *is* desolate,
  Your cities *are* burned with fire;
  Strangers devour your land in your presence;
  And *it is* desolate, as overthrown by strangers.
8So the daughter of Zion is left as a booth in a
    vineyard,
  As a hut in a garden of cucumbers,
  As a besieged city.
9Unless the LORD of hosts
  Had left to us a very small remnant,
  We would have become like Sodom,
  We would have been made like Gomorrah.

10Hear the word of the LORD,
  You rulers of Sodom;

Give ear to the law of our God,
  You people of Gomorrah:
11"To what purpose *is* the multitude of your
    sacrifices to Me?"
  Says the LORD.
"I have had enough of burnt offerings of rams
  And the fat of fed cattle.
I do not delight in the blood of bulls,
  Or of lambs or goats.

12"When you come to appear before Me,
  Who has required this from your hand,
  To trample My courts?
13Bring no more futile sacrifices;
  Incense is an abomination to Me.
The New Moons, the Sabbaths, and the
    calling of assemblies—
  I cannot endure iniquity and the sacred
    meeting.
14Your New Moons and your appointed feasts
  My soul hates;
  They are a trouble to Me,
  I am weary of bearing *them*.
15When you spread out your hands,
  I will hide My eyes from you;
  Even though you make many prayers,
  I will not hear.
  Your hands are full of blood.

16"Wash yourselves, make yourselves clean;
  Put away the evil of your doings from before
    My eyes.
  Cease to do evil,
17Learn to do good;
  Seek justice,
  Rebuke the oppressor;[a]
  Defend the fatherless,
  Plead for the widow.

18"Come now, and let us reason together,"
  Says the LORD,
"Though your sins are like scarlet,
  They shall be as white as snow;
  Though they are red like crimson,
  They shall be as wool.
19If you are willing and obedient,
  You shall eat the good of the land;

1:17 [a]Some ancient versions read *the oppressed.*

²⁰But if you refuse and rebel,
  You shall be devoured by the sword";
  For the mouth of the LORD has spoken.

THE DEGENERATE CITY

²¹How the faithful city has become a harlot!
  It was full of justice;
  Righteousness lodged in it,
  But now murderers.
²²Your silver has become dross,
  Your wine mixed with water.
²³Your princes *are* rebellious,
  And companions of thieves;
  Everyone loves bribes,
  And follows after rewards.
  They do not defend the fatherless,
  Nor does the cause of the widow come
    before them.

²⁴Therefore the Lord says,
  The LORD of hosts, the Mighty One of
    Israel,
  " Ah, I will rid Myself of My adversaries,
  And take vengeance on My enemies.
²⁵I will turn My hand against you,
  And thoroughly purge away your dross,
  And take away all your alloy.
²⁶I will restore your judges as at the first,
  And your counselors as at the beginning.
  Afterward you shall be called the city of
    righteousness, the faithful city."

²⁷Zion shall be redeemed with justice,
  And her penitents with righteousness.
²⁸The destruction of transgressors and of
    sinners *shall be* together,
  And those who forsake the LORD shall be
    consumed.
²⁹For theyᵃ shall be ashamed of the terebinth
    trees
  Which you have desired;
  And you shall be embarrassed because of the
    gardens
  Which you have chosen.
³⁰For you shall be as a terebinth whose leaf
    fades,
  And as a garden that has no water.
³¹The strong shall be as tinder,
  And the work of it as a spark;

Both will burn together,
  And no one shall quench *them*.

THE FUTURE HOUSE OF GOD

2 The word that Isaiah the son of Amoz saw
  concerning Judah and Jerusalem.

²Now it shall come to pass in the latter days
  That the mountain of the LORD's house
  Shall be established on the top of the
    mountains,
  And shall be exalted above the hills;
  And all nations shall flow to it.
³Many people shall come and say,
  "Come, and let us go up to the mountain of
    the LORD,
  To the house of the God of Jacob;
  He will teach us His ways,
  And we shall walk in His paths."
  For out of Zion shall go forth the law,
  And the word of the LORD from Jerusalem.
⁴He shall judge between the nations,
  And rebuke many people;
  They shall beat their swords into plowshares,
  And their spears into pruning hooks;
  Nation shall not lift up sword against
    nation,
  Neither shall they learn war anymore.

THE DAY OF THE LORD

⁵O house of Jacob, come and let us walk
  In the light of the LORD.

⁶For You have forsaken Your people, the house
    of Jacob,
  Because they are filled with eastern ways;
  They *are* soothsayers like the Philistines,
  And they are pleased with the children of
    foreigners.
⁷Their land is also full of silver and gold,
  And there is no end to their treasures;
  Their land is also full of horses,
  And there is no end to their chariots.
⁸Their land is also full of idols;
  They worship the work of their own hands,
  That which their own fingers have made.
⁹People bow down,

1:29 ᵃFollowing Masoretic Text, Septuagint, and Vulgate; some Hebrew manuscripts and Targum read *you*.

And each man humbles himself;
Therefore do not forgive them.

¹⁰Enter into the rock, and hide in the dust,
From the terror of the LORD
And the glory of His majesty.
¹¹The lofty looks of man shall be humbled,
The haughtiness of men shall be bowed
down,
And the LORD alone shall be exalted in that
day.

¹²For the day of the LORD of hosts
Shall come upon everything proud and lofty,
Upon everything lifted up—
And it shall be brought low—
¹³Upon all the cedars of Lebanon *that are* high
and lifted up,
And upon all the oaks of Bashan;
¹⁴Upon all the high mountains,
And upon all the hills *that are* lifted up;
¹⁵Upon every high tower,
And upon every fortified wall;
¹⁶Upon all the ships of Tarshish,
And upon all the beautiful sloops.
¹⁷The loftiness of man shall be bowed down,
And the haughtiness of men shall be
brought low;
The LORD alone will be exalted in that day,
¹⁸But the idols He shall utterly abolish.

¹⁹They shall go into the holes of the rocks,
And into the caves of the earth,
From the terror of the LORD
And the glory of His majesty,
When He arises to shake the earth mightily.

²⁰In that day a man will cast away his idols of
silver
And his idols of gold,
Which they made, *each* for himself to
worship,
To the moles and bats,
²¹To go into the clefts of the rocks,
And into the crags of the rugged rocks,
From the terror of the LORD
And the glory of His majesty,
When He arises to shake the earth
mightily.

²²Sever yourselves from such a man,
Whose breath *is* in his nostrils;
For of what account is he?

JUDGMENT ON JUDAH AND JERUSALEM

3 For behold, the Lord, the LORD of hosts,
Takes away from Jerusalem and from Judah
The stock and the store,
The whole supply of bread and the whole
supply of water;
²The mighty man and the man of war,
The judge and the prophet,
And the diviner and the elder;
³The captain of fifty and the honorable man,
The counselor and the skillful artisan,
And the expert enchanter.

⁴"I will give children *to be* their princes,
And babes shall rule over them.
⁵The people will be oppressed,
Every one by another and every one by his
neighbor;
The child will be insolent toward the elder,
And the base toward the honorable."

⁶When a man takes hold of his brother
In the house of his father, *saying,*
"You have clothing;
You be our ruler,
And *let* these ruins *be* under your power,"^a
⁷In that day he will protest, saying,
"I cannot cure *your* ills,
For in my house *is* neither food nor
clothing;
Do not make me a ruler of the people."

⁸For Jerusalem stumbled,
And Judah is fallen,
Because their tongue and their doings
Are against the LORD,
To provoke the eyes of His glory.
⁹The look on their countenance witnesses
against them,
And they declare their sin as Sodom;
They do not hide *it.*
Woe to their soul!
For they have brought evil upon
themselves.

3:6 ^aLiterally *hand*

¹⁰"Say to the righteous that *it shall be* well *with them,*
For they shall eat the fruit of their doings.
¹¹Woe to the wicked! *It shall be* ill *with him,*
For the reward of his hands shall be given him.
¹²*As for* My people, children *are* their oppressors,
And women rule over them.
O My people! Those who lead you cause *you* to err,
And destroy the way of your paths."

OPPRESSION AND LUXURY CONDEMNED

¹³The LORD stands up to plead,
And stands to judge the people.
¹⁴The LORD will enter into judgment
With the elders of His people
And His princes:
"For you have eaten up the vineyard;
The plunder of the poor *is* in your houses.
¹⁵What do you mean by crushing My people
And grinding the faces of the poor?"
Says the Lord GOD of hosts.

¹⁶Moreover the LORD says:

"Because the daughters of Zion are haughty,
And walk with outstretched necks
And wanton eyes,
Walking and mincing *as* they go,
Making a jingling with their feet,
¹⁷Therefore the Lord will strike with a scab
The crown of the head of the daughters of Zion,
And the LORD will uncover their secret parts."

¹⁸In that day the Lord will take away the finery:
The jingling anklets, the scarves, and the crescents;
¹⁹The pendants, the bracelets, and the veils;
²⁰The headdresses, the leg ornaments, and the headbands;
The perfume boxes, the charms,
²¹and the rings;
The nose jewels,
²²the festal apparel, and the mantles;

The outer garments, the purses,
²³and the mirrors;
The fine linen, the turbans, and the robes.

²⁴And so it shall be:

Instead of a sweet smell there will be a stench;
Instead of a sash, a rope;
Instead of well-set hair, baldness;
Instead of a rich robe, a girding of sackcloth;
And branding instead of beauty.
²⁵Your men shall fall by the sword,
And your mighty in the war.

²⁶Her gates shall lament and mourn,
And she *being* desolate shall sit on the ground.

4 And in that day seven women shall take hold of one man, saying,
"We will eat our own food and wear our own apparel;
Only let us be called by your name,
To take away our reproach."

THE RENEWAL OF ZION

²In that day the Branch of the LORD shall be beautiful and glorious;
And the fruit of the earth *shall be* excellent and appealing
For those of Israel who have escaped.

³And it shall come to pass that *he who is* left in Zion and remains in Jerusalem will be called holy—everyone who is recorded among the living in Jerusalem. ⁴When the Lord has washed away the filth of the daughters of Zion, and purged the blood of Jerusalem from her midst, by the spirit of judgment and by the spirit of burning, ⁵then the LORD will create above every dwelling place of Mount Zion, and above her assemblies, a cloud and smoke by day and the shining of a flaming fire by night. For over all the glory there *will be* a covering. ⁶And there will be a tabernacle for shade in the daytime from the heat, for a place of refuge, and for a shelter from storm and rain.

God's Disappointing Vineyard

5 Now let me sing to my Well-beloved
A song of my Beloved regarding His
vineyard:

My Well-beloved has a vineyard
On a very fruitful hill.
²He dug it up and cleared out its stones,
And planted it with the choicest vine.
He built a tower in its midst,
And also made a winepress in it;
So He expected *it* to bring forth *good* grapes,
But it brought forth wild grapes.

³"And now, O inhabitants of Jerusalem and
men of Judah,
Judge, please, between Me and My vineyard.
⁴What more could have been done to My
vineyard
That I have not done in it?
Why then, when I expected *it* to bring forth
good grapes,
Did it bring forth wild grapes?
⁵And now, please let Me tell you what I will
do to My vineyard:
I will take away its hedge, and it shall be
burned;
And break down its wall, and it shall be
trampled down.
⁶I will lay it waste;
It shall not be pruned or dug,
But there shall come up briers and thorns.
I will also command the clouds
That they rain no rain on it."

⁷For the vineyard of the LORD of hosts *is* the
house of Israel,
And the men of Judah are His pleasant plant.
He looked for justice, but behold, oppression;
For righteousness, but behold, a cry *for help*.

Impending Judgment on Excesses

⁸Woe to those who join house to house;
They add field to field,
Till *there is* no place
Where they may dwell alone in the midst of
the land!
⁹In my hearing the LORD of hosts *said*,

"Truly, many houses shall be desolate,
Great and beautiful ones, without inhabitant.
¹⁰For ten acres of vineyard shall yield one bath,
And a homer of seed shall yield one ephah."

¹¹Woe to those who rise early in the morning,
That they may follow intoxicating drink;
Who continue until night, *till* wine inflames
them!
¹²The harp and the strings,
The tambourine and flute,
And wine are in their feasts;
But they do not regard the work of the LORD,
Nor consider the operation of His hands.

¹³Therefore my people have gone into captivity,
Because *they have* no knowledge;
Their honorable men *are* famished,
And their multitude dried up with thirst.
¹⁴Therefore Sheol has enlarged itself
And opened its mouth beyond measure;
Their glory and their multitude and their
pomp,
And he who is jubilant, shall descend into it.
¹⁵People shall be brought down,
Each man shall be humbled,
And the eyes of the lofty shall be humbled.
¹⁶But the LORD of hosts shall be exalted in
judgment,
And God who is holy shall be hallowed in
righteousness.
¹⁷Then the lambs shall feed in their pasture,
And in the waste places of the fat ones
strangers shall eat.

¹⁸Woe to those who draw iniquity with cords
of vanity,
And sin as if with a cart rope;
¹⁹That say, "Let Him make speed *and* hasten
His work,
That we may see *it;*
And let the counsel of the Holy One of Israel
draw near and come,
That we may know *it.*"

²⁰Woe to those who call evil good, and good
evil;
Who put darkness for light, and light for
darkness;

Who put bitter for sweet, and sweet for
  bitter!

²¹Woe to *those who are* wise in their own eyes,
  And prudent in their own sight!

²²Woe to men mighty at drinking wine,
  Woe to men valiant for mixing intoxicating
    drink,
²³Who justify the wicked for a bribe,
  And take away justice from the righteous
    man!

²⁴Therefore, as the fire devours the stubble,
  And the flame consumes the chaff,
  So their root will be as rottenness,
  And their blossom will ascend like dust;
  Because they have rejected the law of the
    Lord of hosts,
  And despised the word of the Holy One of
    Israel.
²⁵Therefore the anger of the Lord is aroused
    against His people;
  He has stretched out His hand against them
  And stricken them,
  And the hills trembled.
  Their carcasses *were* as refuse in the midst of
    the streets.

  For all this His anger is not turned away,
  But His hand *is* stretched out still.

²⁶He will lift up a banner to the nations from
    afar,
  And will whistle to them from the end of the
    earth;
  Surely they shall come with speed, swiftly.
²⁷No one will be weary or stumble among
    them,
  No one will slumber or sleep;
  Nor will the belt on their loins be loosed,
  Nor the strap of their sandals be broken;
²⁸Whose arrows *are* sharp,
  And all their bows bent;
  Their horses' hooves will seem like flint,
  And their wheels like a whirlwind.
²⁹Their roaring *will be* like a lion,
  They will roar like young lions;
  Yes, they will roar

And lay hold of the prey;
  They will carry *it* away safely,
  And no one will deliver.
³⁰In that day they will roar against them
  Like the roaring of the sea.
  And if *one* looks to the land,
  Behold, darkness *and* sorrow;
  And the light is darkened by the clouds.

ISAIAH CALLED TO BE A PROPHET

6 In the year that King Uzziah died, I saw the
  Lord sitting on a throne, high and lifted up,
and the train of His *robe* filled the temple. ²Above
it stood seraphim; each one had six wings: with
two he covered his face, with two he covered his
feet, and with two he flew. ³And one cried to another and said:

  "Holy, holy, holy *is* the Lord of hosts;
  The whole earth *is* full of His glory!"

⁴And the posts of the door were shaken by
the voice of him who cried out, and the house
was filled with smoke.
⁵So I said:

  "Woe *is* me, for I am undone!
  Because I *am* a man of unclean lips,
  And I dwell in the midst of a people of
    unclean lips;
  For my eyes have seen the King,
  The Lord of hosts."

⁶Then one of the seraphim flew to me, having in his hand a live coal *which* he had taken with
the tongs from the altar. ⁷And he touched my
mouth *with it,* and said:

  "Behold, this has touched your lips;
  Your iniquity is taken away,
  And your sin purged."

⁸Also I heard the voice of the Lord, saying:

  "Whom shall I send,
  And who will go for Us?"

  Then I said, "Here *am* I! Send me."
⁹And He said, "Go, and tell this people:

LEADERSHIP
REALITIES

VISION—A 360-DEGREE VIEW   Isaiah 6:1–4

After a setback or discouragement, we are often ready for a breakthrough and in need of a fresh understanding. Isaiah was in this situation, and he ran to the temple for a fresh vision of the Lord. There he knelt and understood that the throne of heaven is still occupied. There may be confusion and unrest on earth, but there is perfect peace in heaven. The **upward look** is to see God seated in power and glory.

har—**see**—perceive, have vision

The natural progression from seeing the holiness of God is the **inward look** into our own sin. Isaiah's new view of God immediately banished any thoughts of pride and indifference as he cried out in confession of his sin. A true spiritual experience humbles you and awakens a renewal within you.

A genuine **inward look** leads us to the **outward look** of pure motives and banished selfishness. When Isaiah was convicted of his sin, it moved him to compassion for others. His next thought was, *"These people have the same problem. I can help."* A fresh cleansing of the heart immediately causes us to look for ways to pray for, to encourage, and to share with those around us.

'Keep on hearing, but do not understand;
Keep on seeing, but do not perceive.'

10"Make the heart of this people dull,
And their ears heavy,
And shut their eyes;
Lest they see with their eyes,
And hear with their ears,
And understand with their heart,
And return and be healed."

11Then I said, "Lord, how long?"
And He answered:

"Until the cities are laid waste and without
    inhabitant,
The houses are without a man,
The land is utterly desolate,
12The LORD has removed men far away,
And the forsaken places *are* many in the midst
    of the land.
13But yet a tenth *will be* in it,
And will return and be for consuming,
As a terebinth tree or as an oak,

Whose stump *remains* when it is cut down.
So the holy seed *shall be* its stump."

ISAIAH SENT TO KING AHAZ

7 Now it came to pass in the days of Ahaz the son of Jotham, the son of Uzziah, king of Judah, *that* Rezin king of Syria and Pekah the son of Remaliah, king of Israel, went up to Jerusalem to *make* war against it, but could not prevail against it. 2And it was told to the house of David, saying, "Syria's forces are deployed in Ephraim." So his heart and the heart of his people were moved as the trees of the woods are moved with the wind.

3Then the LORD said to Isaiah, "Go out now to meet Ahaz, you and Shear-Jashub[a] your son, at the end of the aqueduct from the upper pool, on the highway to the Fuller's Field, 4and say to him: 'Take heed, and be quiet; do not fear or be fainthearted for these two stubs of smoking firebrands, for the fierce anger of Rezin and Syria, and the son of Remaliah. 5Because Syria, Ephraim, and the son of Remaliah have plotted evil against you,

7:3 [a]Literally *A Remnant Shall Return*

THROUGH THE GRID

Discover God: God Is Holy

ISAIAH 6:3   *Holy, Holy, Holy is the LORD of hosts; the whole earth is full of His glory!*

God's holiness is one of God's chief characteristics, as nothing can compare to the splendor of God's holiness. God is holy because God is completely pure, completely infinite, and completely exalted. In fact, God cannot compare with anything else in all of creation—God is separate and set apart in infinite majesty. God's description as holy also exists because God is wholly set apart from sin. Nothing else has such an attribute, as God exists in a purity that is perfect and unblemished. God is the standard of all perfection, unity, integrity, and wholeness. God has demanded holiness from us as well; and the only acceptable sacrifice for our sin is the sacrifice of the pure, innocent blood of Christ. Our response to God's holiness, to God's moral perfection and absolute purity, is modeled in humble adoration and worship.

saying, [6]"Let us go up against Judah and trouble it, and let us make a gap in its wall for ourselves, and set a king over them, the son of Tabel"—[7]thus says the Lord GOD:

"It shall not stand,
   Nor shall it come to pass.
[8]For the head of Syria *is* Damascus,
   And the head of Damascus *is* Rezin.
Within sixty-five years Ephraim will be broken,
   So that it will not *be* a people.
[9]The head of Ephraim *is* Samaria,
   And the head of Samaria *is* Remaliah's son.
If you will not believe,
   Surely you shall not be established." ' "

THE IMMANUEL PROPHECY

[10]Moreover the LORD spoke again to Ahaz, saying, [11]"Ask a sign for yourself from the LORD your God; ask it either in the depth or in the height above."

[12]But Ahaz said, "I will not ask, nor will I test the LORD!"

[13]Then he said, "Hear now, O house of David! *Is it* a small thing for you to weary men, but will you weary my God also? [14]Therefore the Lord Himself will give you a sign: Behold, the virgin shall conceive and bear a Son, and shall call His name Immanuel.[a] [15]Curds and honey He shall eat, that He may know to refuse the evil and choose the good. [16]For before the Child shall know to refuse the evil and choose the good, the land that you dread will be forsaken by both her kings. [17]The LORD will bring the king of Assyria upon you and your people and your father's house—days that have not come since the day that Ephraim departed from Judah."

[18]And it shall come to pass in that day
   That the LORD will whistle for the fly
   That *is* in the farthest part of the rivers of Egypt,
   And for the bee that *is* in the land of Assyria.
[19]They will come, and all of them will rest
   In the desolate valleys and in the clefts of the rocks,
   And on all thorns and in all pastures.

[20]In the same day the Lord will shave with a hired razor,
   With those from beyond the River,[a] with the king of Assyria,
   The head and the hair of the legs,
   And will also remove the beard.

7:14 [a]Literally *God-With-Us*   7:20 [a]That is, the Euphrates

²¹It shall be in that day
  That a man will keep alive a young cow and
    two sheep;
²²So it shall be, from the abundance of milk
    they give,
  That he will eat curds;
  For curds and honey everyone will eat who is
    left in the land.

²³It shall happen in that day,
  That wherever there could be a thousand
    vines
  Worth a thousand *shekels* of silver,
  It will be for briers and thorns.
²⁴With arrows and bows *men* will come there,
  Because all the land will become briers and
    thorns.

²⁵And to any hill which could be dug with the
    hoe,
  You will not go there for fear of briers and
thorns;
  But it will become a range for oxen
  And a place for sheep to roam.

Assyria Will Invade the Land

8 Moreover the LORD said to me, "Take a large
scroll, and write on it with a man's pen concerning Maher-Shalal-Hash-Baz.ª ²And I will
take for Myself faithful witnesses to record, Uriah
the priest and Zechariah the son of Jeberechiah."

³Then I went to the prophetess, and she conceived and bore a son. Then the LORD said to me,
"Call his name Maher-Shalal-Hash-Baz; ⁴for before the child shall have knowledge to cry 'My father' and 'My mother,' the riches of Damascus and
the spoil of Samaria will be taken away before the
king of Assyria."

⁵The LORD also spoke to me again, saying:

⁶"Inasmuch as these people refused
  The waters of Shiloah that flow softly,
  And rejoice in Rezin and in Remaliah's son;
⁷Now therefore, behold, the Lord brings up
    over them
  The waters of the River,ª strong and
    mighty—
  The king of Assyria and all his glory;
  He will go up over all his channels

And go over all his banks.
⁸He will pass through Judah,
  He will overflow and pass over,
  He will reach up to the neck;
  And the stretching out of his wings
  Will fill the breadth of Your land,
    O Immanuel.ª

⁹"Be shattered, O you peoples, and be broken
    in pieces!
  Give ear, all you from far countries.
  Gird yourselves, but be broken in pieces;
  Gird yourselves, but be broken in pieces.
¹⁰Take counsel together, but it will come to
    nothing;
  Speak the word, but it will not stand,
  For God *is* with us."ª

Fear God, Heed His Word

¹¹For the LORD spoke thus to me with a
strong hand, and instructed me that I should not
walk in the way of this people, saying:

¹²"Do not say, 'A conspiracy,'
  Concerning all that this people call a
    conspiracy,
  Nor be afraid of their threats, nor be troubled.
¹³The LORD of hosts, Him you shall hallow;
  Let Him *be* your fear,
  And *let* Him *be* your dread.
¹⁴He will be as a sanctuary,
  But a stone of stumbling and a rock of
    offense
  To both the houses of Israel,
  As a trap and a snare to the inhabitants of
    Jerusalem.
¹⁵And many among them shall stumble;
  They shall fall and be broken,
  Be snared and taken."

¹⁶Bind up the testimony,
  Seal the law among my disciples.
¹⁷And I will wait on the LORD,
  Who hides His face from the house of Jacob;
  And I will hope in Him.
¹⁸Here am I and the children whom the LORD
    has given me!

8:1 ªLiterally *Speed the Spoil, Hasten the Booty* **8:7** ªThat is, the
Euphrates **8:8** ªLiterally *God-With-Us* **8:10** ªHebrew *Immanuel*

We are for signs and wonders in Israel
From the LORD of hosts,
Who dwells in Mount Zion.

¹⁹And when they say to you, "Seek those who are mediums and wizards, who whisper and mutter," should not a people seek their God? *Should they seek* the dead on behalf of the living? ²⁰To the law and to the testimony! If they do not speak according to this word, *it is* because *there is* no light in them.

²¹They will pass through it hard-pressed and hungry; and it shall happen, when they are hungry, that they will be enraged and curse their king and their God, and look upward. ²²Then they will look to the earth, and see trouble and darkness, gloom of anguish; and *they will be* driven into darkness.

THE GOVERNMENT OF THE PROMISED SON

9 Nevertheless the gloom *will* not *be* upon her who *is* distressed,
As when at first He lightly esteemed
The land of Zebulun and the land of Naphtali,
And afterward more heavily oppressed *her,*
By the way of the sea, beyond the Jordan,
In Galilee of the Gentiles.
²The people who walked in darkness
Have seen a great light;
Those who dwelt in the land of the shadow of death,
Upon them a light has shined.

³You have multiplied the nation
And increased its joy;^a
They rejoice before You
According to the joy of harvest,
As *men* rejoice when they divide the spoil.
⁴For You have broken the yoke of his burden
And the staff of his shoulder,
The rod of his oppressor,
As in the day of Midian.
⁵For every warrior's sandal from the noisy battle,
And garments rolled in blood,
Will be used for burning *and* fuel of fire.

⁶For unto us a Child is born,
Unto us a Son is given;

And the government will be upon His shoulder.
And His name will be called
Wonderful, Counselor, Mighty God,
Everlasting Father, Prince of Peace.
⁷Of the increase of *His* government and peace
There will be no end,
Upon the throne of David and over His kingdom,
To order it and establish it with judgment and justice
From that time forward, even forever.
The zeal of the Lord of hosts will perform this.

THE PUNISHMENT OF SAMARIA

⁸The Lord sent a word against Jacob,
And it has fallen on Israel.
⁹All the people will know—
Ephraim and the inhabitant of Samaria—
Who say in pride and arrogance of heart:
¹⁰"The bricks have fallen down,
But we will rebuild with hewn stones;
The sycamores are cut down,
But we will replace *them* with cedars."
¹¹Therefore the LORD shall set up
The adversaries of Rezin against him,
And spur his enemies on,
¹²The Syrians before and the Philistines behind;
And they shall devour Israel with an open mouth.

For all this His anger is not turned away,
But His hand *is* stretched out still.

¹³For the people do not turn to Him who strikes them,
Nor do they seek the LORD of hosts.
¹⁴Therefore the LORD will cut off head and tail from Israel,
Palm branch and bulrush in one day.
¹⁵The elder and honorable, he *is* the head;
The prophet who teaches lies, he *is* the tail.
¹⁶For the leaders of this people cause *them* to err,

9:3 ^aFollowing Qere and Targum; Kethib and Vulgate read *not increased joy;* Septuagint reads *Most of the people You brought down in Your joy.*

And *those who are* led by them are destroyed.
¹⁷Therefore the Lord will have no joy in their
young men,
Nor have mercy on their fatherless and
widows;
For everyone *is* a hypocrite and an evildoer,
And every mouth speaks folly.

For all this His anger is not turned away,
But His hand *is* stretched out still.

¹⁸For wickedness burns as the fire;
It shall devour the briers and thorns,
And kindle in the thickets of the forest;
They shall mount up *like* rising smoke.
¹⁹Through the wrath of the LORD of hosts
The land is burned up,
And the people shall be as fuel for the fire;
No man shall spare his brother.
²⁰And he shall snatch on the right hand
And be hungry;
He shall devour on the left hand
And not be satisfied;
Every man shall eat the flesh of his own
arm.
²¹Manasseh *shall devour* Ephraim, and Ephraim
Manasseh;
Together they *shall be* against Judah.

For all this His anger is not turned away,
But His hand *is* stretched out still.

10

"Woe to those who decree unrighteous
decrees,
Who write misfortune,
Which they have prescribed
²To rob the needy of justice,
And to take what is right from the poor of
My people,
That widows may be their prey,
And *that* they may rob the fatherless.
³What will you do in the day of punishment,
And in the desolation *which* will come from
afar?
To whom will you flee for help?
And where will you leave your glory?
⁴Without Me they shall bow down among the
prisoners,
And they shall fall among the slain."

For all this His anger is not turned away,
But His hand *is* stretched out still.

ARROGANT ASSYRIA ALSO JUDGED

⁵"Woe to Assyria, the rod of My anger
And the staff in whose hand is My
indignation.
⁶I will send him against an ungodly
nation,
And against the people of My wrath
I will give him charge,
To seize the spoil, to take the prey,
And to tread them down like the mire of
the streets.
⁷Yet he does not mean so,
Nor does his heart think so;
But *it is* in his heart to destroy,
And cut off not a few nations.
⁸For he says,
'*Are* not my princes altogether kings?
⁹*Is* not Calno like Carchemish?
Is not Hamath like Arpad?
Is not Samaria like Damascus?
¹⁰As my hand has found the kingdoms of the
idols,
Whose carved images excelled those of
Jerusalem and Samaria,
¹¹As I have done to Samaria and her idols,
Shall I not do also to Jerusalem and her
idols?' "

¹²Therefore it shall come to pass, when the
Lord has performed all His work on Mount Zion
and on Jerusalem, *that He will say,* "I will punish
the fruit of the arrogant heart of the king of Assyria, and the glory of his haughty looks."

¹³For he says:

"By the strength of my hand I have done *it,*
And by my wisdom, for I am prudent;
Also I have removed the boundaries of the
people,
And have robbed their treasuries;
So I have put down the inhabitants like a
valiant *man.*
¹⁴My hand has found like a nest the riches of
the people,
And as one gathers eggs *that are* left,
I have gathered all the earth;

And there was no one who moved *his* wing,
Nor opened *his* mouth with even a peep."

[15]Shall the ax boast itself against him who
chops with it?
Or shall the saw exalt itself against him who
saws with it?
As if a rod could wield *itself* against those who
lift it up,
Or as if a staff could lift up, *as if it were* not
wood!

[16]Therefore the Lord, the Lord[a] of hosts,
Will send leanness among his fat ones;
And under his glory
He will kindle a burning
Like the burning of a fire.

[17]So the Light of Israel will be for a fire,
And his Holy One for a flame;
It will burn and devour
His thorns and his briers in one day.

[18]And it will consume the glory of his forest
and of his fruitful field,
Both soul and body;
And they will be as when a sick man wastes
away.

[19]Then the rest of the trees of his forest
Will be so few in number
That a child may write them.

The Returning Remnant of Israel

[20]And it shall come to pass in that day
That the remnant of Israel,
And such as have escaped of the house of
Jacob,
Will never again depend on him who
defeated them,
But will depend on the LORD, the Holy One
of Israel, in truth.

[21]The remnant will return, the remnant of
Jacob,
To the Mighty God.

[22]For though your people, O Israel, be as the
sand of the sea,
A remnant of them will return;
The destruction decreed shall overflow with
righteousness.

[23]For the Lord GOD of hosts
Will make a determined end
In the midst of all the land.

[24]Therefore thus says the Lord GOD of hosts:
"O My people, who dwell in Zion, do not be
afraid of the Assyrian. He shall strike you with a
rod and lift up his staff against you, in the manner
of Egypt. [25]For yet a very little while and the indignation will cease, as will My anger in their destruction." [26]And the LORD of hosts will stir up a
scourge for him like the slaughter of Midian at
the rock of Oreb; *as* His rod was on the sea, so
will He lift it up in the manner of Egypt.

[27]It shall come to pass in that day
That his burden will be taken away from your
shoulder,
And his yoke from your neck,
And the yoke will be destroyed because of
the anointing oil.

[28]He has come to Aiath,
He has passed Migron;
At Michmash he has attended to his
equipment.

[29]They have gone along the ridge,
They have taken up lodging at Geba.
Ramah is afraid,
Gibeah of Saul has fled.

[30]Lift up your voice,
O daughter of Gallim!
Cause it to be heard as far as Laish—
O poor Anathoth![a]

[31]Madmenah has fled,
The inhabitants of Gebim seek refuge.

[32]As yet he will remain at Nob that day;
He will shake his fist at the mount of the
daughter of Zion,
The hill of Jerusalem.

[33]Behold, the Lord,
The LORD of hosts,
Will lop off the bough with terror;
Those of high stature *will be* hewn down,
And the haughty will be humbled.

[34]He will cut down the thickets of the forest
with iron,
And Lebanon will fall by the Mighty
One.

10:16 [a]Following Bomberg; Masoretic Text and Dead Sea Scrolls
read *YHWH (the LORD).* **10:30** [a]Following Masoretic Text, Targum,
and Vulgate; Septuagint and Syriac read *Listen to her, O Anathoth.*

The Reign of Jesse's Offspring

11 There shall come forth a Rod from the stem of Jesse,
And a Branch shall grow out of his roots.
[2]The Spirit of the LORD shall rest upon Him,
The Spirit of wisdom and understanding,
The Spirit of counsel and might,
The Spirit of knowledge and of the fear of the LORD.

[3]His delight *is* in the fear of the LORD,
And He shall not judge by the sight of His eyes,
Nor decide by the hearing of His ears;
[4]But with righteousness He shall judge the poor,
And decide with equity for the meek of the earth;
He shall strike the earth with the rod of His mouth,
And with the breath of His lips He shall slay the wicked.
[5]Righteousness shall be the belt of His loins,
And faithfulness the belt of His waist.

[6]"The wolf also shall dwell with the lamb,
The leopard shall lie down with the young goat,
The calf and the young lion and the fatling together;
And a little child shall lead them.
[7]The cow and the bear shall graze;
Their young ones shall lie down together;
And the lion shall eat straw like the ox.
[8]The nursing child shall play by the cobra's hole,
And the weaned child shall put his hand in the viper's den.
[9]They shall not hurt nor destroy in all My holy mountain,
For the earth shall be full of the knowledge of the LORD
As the waters cover the sea.

[10]"And in that day there shall be a Root of Jesse,
Who shall stand as a banner to the people;
For the Gentiles shall seek Him,
And His resting place shall be glorious."

[11]It shall come to pass in that day
That the Lord shall set His hand again the second time
To recover the remnant of His people who are left,
From Assyria and Egypt,
From Pathros and Cush,
From Elam and Shinar,
From Hamath and the islands of the sea.

[12]He will set up a banner for the nations,
And will assemble the outcasts of Israel,
And gather together the dispersed of Judah
From the four corners of the earth.
[13]Also the envy of Ephraim shall depart,
And the adversaries of Judah shall be cut off;
Ephraim shall not envy Judah,
And Judah shall not harass Ephraim.
[14]But they shall fly down upon the shoulder of the Philistines toward the west;
Together they shall plunder the people of the East;
They shall lay their hand on Edom and Moab;
And the people of Ammon shall obey them.
[15]The LORD will utterly destroy[a] the tongue of the Sea of Egypt;
With His mighty wind He will shake His fist over the River,[b]
And strike it in the seven streams,
And make *men* cross over dryshod.
[16]There will be a highway for the remnant of His people
Who will be left from Assyria,
As it was for Israel
In the day that he came up from the land of Egypt.

A Hymn of Praise

12 And in that day you will say:

"O LORD, I will praise You;
Though You were angry with me,
Your anger is turned away, and You comfort me.
[2]Behold, God *is* my salvation,
I will trust and not be afraid;

11:15 [a]Following Masoretic Text and Vulgate; Septuagint, Syriac, and Targum read *dry up.* [b]That is, the Euphrates

'For YAH, the LORD, *is* my strength and song;
He also has become my salvation.' "[a]

[3]Therefore with joy you will draw water
From the wells of salvation.

[4]And in that day you will say:

"Praise the LORD, call upon His name;
Declare His deeds among the peoples,
Make mention that His name is exalted.
[5]Sing to the LORD,
For He has done excellent things;
This *is* known in all the earth.
[6]Cry out and shout, O inhabitant of Zion,
For great *is* the Holy One of Israel in your
midst!"

PROCLAMATION AGAINST BABYLON

13 The burden against Babylon which Isaiah
the son of Amoz saw.

[2]"Lift up a banner on the high mountain,
Raise your voice to them;
Wave your hand, that they may enter the
gates of the nobles.
[3]I have commanded My sanctified ones;
I have also called My mighty ones for My
anger—
Those who rejoice in My exaltation."

[4]The noise of a multitude in the mountains,
Like that of many people!
A tumultuous noise of the kingdoms of
nations gathered together!
The LORD of hosts musters
The army for battle.
[5]They come from a far country,
From the end of heaven—
The LORD and His weapons of indignation,
To destroy the whole land.

[6]Wail, for the day of the LORD *is* at hand!
It will come as destruction from the
Almighty.
[7]Therefore all hands will be limp,
Every man's heart will melt,
[8]And they will be afraid.
Pangs and sorrows will take hold of *them;*

They will be in pain as a woman in
childbirth;
They will be amazed at one another;
Their faces *will be like* flames.

[9]Behold, the day of the LORD comes,
Cruel, with both wrath and fierce anger,
To lay the land desolate;
And He will destroy its sinners from it.
[10]For the stars of heaven and their
constellations
Will not give their light;
The sun will be darkened in its going forth,
And the moon will not cause its light to
shine.

[11]"I will punish the world for *its* evil,
And the wicked for their iniquity;
I will halt the arrogance of the proud,
And will lay low the haughtiness of the
terrible.
[12]I will make a mortal more rare than fine gold,
A man more than the golden wedge of
Ophir.
[13]Therefore I will shake the heavens,
And the earth will move out of her place,
In the wrath of the LORD of hosts
And in the day of His fierce anger.
[14]It shall be as the hunted gazelle,
And as a sheep that no man takes up;
Every man will turn to his own people,
And everyone will flee to his own land.
[15]Everyone who is found will be thrust
through,
And everyone who is captured will fall by the
sword.
[16]Their children also will be dashed to pieces
before their eyes;
Their houses will be plundered
And their wives ravished.

[17]"Behold, I will stir up the Medes against them,
Who will not regard silver;
And *as for* gold, they will not delight in it.
[18]Also *their* bows will dash the young men to
pieces,
And they will have no pity on the fruit of the
womb;

12:2 [a]Exodus 15:2

Their eye will not spare children.
¹⁹And Babylon, the glory of kingdoms,
The beauty of the Chaldeans' pride,
Will be as when God overthrew Sodom and
    Gomorrah.
²⁰It will never be inhabited,
Nor will it be settled from generation to
    generation;
Nor will the Arabian pitch tents there,
Nor will the shepherds make their sheepfolds
    there.
²¹But wild beasts of the desert will lie there,
And their houses will be full of owls;
Ostriches will dwell there,
And wild goats will caper there.
²²The hyenas will howl in their citadels,
And jackals in their pleasant palaces.
Her time *is* near to come,
And her days will not be prolonged."

MERCY ON JACOB

14 For the LORD will have mercy on Jacob,
and will still choose Israel, and settle them
in their own land. The strangers will be joined
with them, and they will cling to the house of Jacob. ²Then people will take them and bring them
to their place, and the house of Israel will possess
them for servants and maids in the land of the
LORD; they will take them captive whose captives
they were, and rule over their oppressors.

FALL OF THE KING OF BABYLON

³It shall come to pass in the day the LORD
gives you rest from your sorrow, and from your
fear and the hard bondage in which you were
made to serve, ⁴that you will take up this proverb
against the king of Babylon, and say:

"How the oppressor has ceased,
The golden^a city ceased!
⁵The LORD has broken the staff of the wicked,
The scepter of the rulers;
⁶He who struck the people in wrath with a
    continual stroke,
He who ruled the nations in anger,
Is persecuted *and* no one hinders.
⁷The whole earth is at rest *and* quiet;
They break forth into singing.
⁸Indeed the cypress trees rejoice over you,

And the cedars of Lebanon,
Saying, 'Since you were cut down,
No woodsman has come up against us.'

⁹"Hell from beneath is excited about you,
To meet *you* at your coming;
It stirs up the dead for you,
All the chief ones of the earth;
It has raised up from their thrones
All the kings of the nations.
¹⁰They all shall speak and say to you:
'Have you also become as weak as we?
Have you become like us?
¹¹Your pomp is brought down to Sheol,
And the sound of your stringed instruments;
The maggot is spread under you,
And worms cover you.'

THE FALL OF LUCIFER

¹²"How you are fallen from heaven,
O Lucifer,^a son of the morning!
How you are cut down to the ground,
You who weakened the nations!
¹³For you have said in your heart:
'I will ascend into heaven,
I will exalt my throne above the stars of God;
I will also sit on the mount of the
    congregation
On the farthest sides of the north;
¹⁴I will ascend above the heights of the clouds,
I will be like the Most High.'
¹⁵Yet you shall be brought down to Sheol,
To the lowest depths of the Pit.

¹⁶"Those who see you will gaze at you,
And consider you, *saying:*
'*Is* this the man who made the earth tremble,
Who shook kingdoms,
¹⁷Who made the world as a wilderness
And destroyed its cities,
Who did not open the house of his
    prisoners?'

¹⁸"All the kings of the nations,
All of them, sleep in glory,
Everyone in his own house;
¹⁹But you are cast out of your grave
Like an abominable branch,

14:4 ^aOr *insolent*   14:12 ^aLiterally *Day Star*

Like the garment of those who are slain,
Thrust through with a sword,
Who go down to the stones of the pit,
Like a corpse trodden underfoot.
²⁰You will not be joined with them in burial,
Because you have destroyed your land
And slain your people.
The brood of evildoers shall never be named.
²¹Prepare slaughter for his children
Because of the iniquity of their fathers,
Lest they rise up and possess the land,
And fill the face of the world with cities."

BABYLON DESTROYED

²²"For I will rise up against them," says the
   LORD of hosts,
"And cut off from Babylon the name and
   remnant,
And offspring and posterity," says the LORD.
²³"I will also make it a possession for the
   porcupine,
And marshes of muddy water;
I will sweep it with the broom of
   destruction," says the LORD of hosts.

ASSYRIA DESTROYED

²⁴The LORD of hosts has sworn, saying,
"Surely, as I have thought, so it shall come to
   pass,
And as I have purposed, *so* it shall stand:
²⁵That I will break the Assyrian in My land,
And on My mountains tread him underfoot.
Then his yoke shall be removed from them,
And his burden removed from their shoulders.
²⁶This *is* the purpose that is purposed against
   the whole earth,
And this *is* the hand that is stretched out over
   all the nations."
²⁷For the LORD of hosts has purposed,
And who will annul *it?*
His hand *is* stretched out,
And who will turn it back?"

PHILISTIA DESTROYED

²⁸This is the burden which came in the year
that King Ahaz died.

²⁹"Do not rejoice, all you of Philistia,
Because the rod that struck you is broken;

For out of the serpent's roots will come forth
   a viper,
And its offspring *will be* a fiery flying serpent.
³⁰The firstborn of the poor will feed,
And the needy will lie down in safety;
I will kill your roots with famine,
And it will slay your remnant.
³¹Wail, O gate! Cry, O city!
All you of Philistia *are* dissolved;
For smoke will come from the north,
And no one *will be* alone in his appointed
   times."

³²What will they answer the messengers of the
   nation?
That the LORD has founded Zion,
And the poor of His people shall take refuge
   in it.

PROCLAMATION AGAINST MOAB

15 The burden against Moab.

Because in the night Ar of Moab is laid waste
And destroyed,
Because in the night Kir of Moab is laid
   waste
And destroyed,
²He has gone up to the templeᵃ and Dibon,
To the high places to weep.
Moab will wail over Nebo and over Medeba;
On all their heads *will be* baldness,
And every beard cut off.
³In their streets they will clothe themselves
   with sackcloth;
On the tops of their houses
And in their streets
Everyone will wail, weeping bitterly.
⁴Heshbon and Elealeh will cry out,
Their voice shall be heard as far as Jahaz;
Therefore the armed soldiersᵃ of Moab will
   cry out;
His life will be burdensome to him.

⁵"My heart will cry out for Moab;
His fugitives *shall flee* to Zoar,
Like a three-year-old heifer.ᵃ

15:2 ᵃHebrew *bayith,* literally *house*   **15:4** ᵃFollowing Masoretic
Text, Targum, and Vulgate; Septuagint and Syriac read *loins.*
15:5 ᵃOr *The Third Eglath,* an unknown city (compare Jeremiah
48:34)

For by the Ascent of Luhith
They will go up with weeping;
For in the way of Horonaim
They will raise up a cry of destruction,
⁶For the waters of Nimrim will be desolate,
For the green grass has withered away;
The grass fails, there is nothing green.
⁷Therefore the abundance they have gained,
And what they have laid up,
They will carry away to the Brook of the
    Willows.
⁸For the cry has gone all around the borders of
    Moab,
Its wailing to Eglaim
And its wailing to Beer Elim.
⁹For the waters of Dimonᵃ will be full of blood;
Because I will bring more upon Dimon,ᵇ
Lions upon him who escapes from Moab,
And on the remnant of the land."

Moab Destroyed

16 Send the lamb to the ruler of the land,
From Sela to the wilderness,
To the mount of the daughter of Zion.
²For it shall be as a wandering bird thrown out
    of the nest;
So shall be the daughters of Moab at the fords
    of the Arnon.

³"Take counsel, execute judgment;
Make your shadow like the night in the
    middle of the day;
Hide the outcasts,
Do not betray him who escapes.
⁴Let My outcasts dwell with you, O Moab;
Be a shelter to them from the face of the
    spoiler.
For the extortioner is at an end,
Devastation ceases,
The oppressors are consumed out of the
    land.
⁵In mercy the throne will be established;
And One will sit on it in truth, in the
    tabernacle of David,
Judging and seeking justice and hastening
    righteousness."

⁶We have heard of the pride of Moab—
He is very proud—

Of his haughtiness and his pride and his
    wrath;
But his lies *shall* not *be* so.
⁷Therefore Moab shall wail for Moab;
Everyone shall wail.
For the foundations of Kir Hareseth you shall
    mourn;
Surely *they are* stricken.

⁸For the fields of Heshbon languish,
And the vine of Sibmah;
The lords of the nations have broken down
    its choice plants,
Which have reached to Jazer
And wandered through the wilderness.
Her branches are stretched out,
They are gone over the sea.
⁹Therefore I will bewail the vine of Sibmah,
With the weeping of Jazer;
I will drench you with my tears,
O Heshbon and Elealeh;
For battle cries have fallen
Over your summer fruits and your harvest.

¹⁰Gladness is taken away,
And joy from the plentiful field;
In the vineyards there will be no singing,
Nor will there be shouting;
No treaders will tread out wine in the
    presses;
I have made their shouting cease.
¹¹Therefore my heart shall resound like a harp
    for Moab,
And my inner being for Kir Heres.

¹²And it shall come to pass,
When it is seen that Moab is weary on the
    high place,
That he will come to his sanctuary to pray;
But he will not prevail.

¹³This *is* the word which the Lord has spoken concerning Moab since that time. ¹⁴But now the Lord has spoken, saying, "Within three years, as the years of a hired man, the glory of Moab

15:9 ᵃFollowing Masoretic Text and Targum; Dead Sea Scrolls and Vulgate read *Dibon;* Septuagint reads *Rimon.* ᵇFollowing Masoretic Text and Targum; Dead Sea Scrolls and Vulgate read *Dibon;* Septuagint reads *Rimon.*

will be despised with all that great multitude, and the remnant *will be* very small *and* feeble."

Proclamation Against Syria and Israel

17 The burden against Damascus.

"Behold, Damascus will cease from *being* a city,
And it will be a ruinous heap.
²The cities of Aroer *are* forsaken;ª
They will be for flocks
Which lie down, and no one will make *them* afraid.
³The fortress also will cease from Ephraim,
The kingdom from Damascus,
And the remnant of Syria;
They will be as the glory of the children of Israel,"
Says the LORD of hosts.
⁴"In that day it shall come to pass
That the glory of Jacob will wane,
And the fatness of his flesh grow lean.
⁵It shall be as when the harvester gathers the grain,
And reaps the heads with his arm;
It shall be as he who gathers heads of grain
In the Valley of Rephaim.
⁶Yet gleaning grapes will be left in it,
Like the shaking of an olive tree,
Two *or* three olives at the top of the uppermost bough,
Four *or* five in its most fruitful branches,"
Says the LORD God of Israel.

⁷In that day a man will look to his Maker,
And his eyes will have respect for the Holy One of Israel.
⁸He will not look to the altars,
The work of his hands;
He will not respect what his fingers have made,
Nor the wooden imagesª nor the incense altars.

⁹In that day his strong cities will be as a forsaken boughª
And an uppermost branch,ᵇ
Which they left because of the children of Israel;
And there will be desolation.

¹⁰Because you have forgotten the God of your salvation,
And have not been mindful of the Rock of your stronghold,
Therefore you will plant pleasant plants
And set out foreign seedlings;
¹¹In the day you will make your plant to grow,
And in the morning you will make your seed to flourish;
But the harvest *will be* a heap of ruins
In the day of grief and desperate sorrow.

¹²Woe to the multitude of many people
Who make a noise like the roar of the seas,
And to the rushing of nations
That make a rushing like the rushing of mighty waters!
¹³The nations will rush like the rushing of many waters;
But *God* will rebuke them and they will flee far away,
And be chased like the chaff of the mountains before the wind,
Like a rolling thing before the whirlwind.
¹⁴Then behold, at eventide, trouble!
And before the morning, he *is* no more.
This *is* the portion of those who plunder us,
And the lot of those who rob us.

Proclamation Against Ethiopia

18 Woe to the land shadowed with buzzing wings,
Which *is* beyond the rivers of Ethiopia,
²Which sends ambassadors by sea,
Even in vessels of reed on the waters, *saying,*
"Go, swift messengers, to a nation tall and smooth *of skin,*
To a people terrible from their beginning onward,
A nation powerful and treading down,
Whose land the rivers divide."

³All inhabitants of the world and dwellers on the earth:

17:2 ªFollowing Masoretic Text and Vulgate; Septuagint reads *It shall be forsaken forever;* Targum reads *Its cities shall be forsaken and desolate.* **17:8** ªHebrew *Asherim,* Canaanite deities **17:9** ªSeptuagint reads *Hivites;* Targum reads *laid waste;* Vulgate reads *as the plows.* ᵇSeptuagint reads *Amorites;* Targum reads *in ruins;* Vulgate reads *corn.*

When he lifts up a banner on the mountains,
    you see *it;*
And when he blows a trumpet, you hear *it.*
⁴For so the LORD said to me,
"I will take My rest,
    And I will look from My dwelling place
    Like clear heat in sunshine,
    Like a cloud of dew in the heat of harvest."
⁵For before the harvest, when the bud is
    perfect
And the sour grape is ripening in the flower,
He will both cut off the sprigs with pruning
    hooks
And take away *and* cut down the branches.
⁶They will be left together for the mountain
    birds of prey
And for the beasts of the earth;
    The birds of prey will summer on them,
    And all the beasts of the earth will winter on
    them.

⁷In that time a present will be brought to the
    LORD of hosts
From* a people tall and smooth *of skin,*
And from a people terrible from their
    beginning onward,
A nation powerful and treading down,
Whose land the rivers divide—
To the place of the name of the LORD of hosts,
To Mount Zion.

Proclamation Against Egypt

19 The burden against Egypt.

Behold, the LORD rides on a swift cloud,
And will come into Egypt;
The idols of Egypt will totter at His
    presence,
And the heart of Egypt will melt in its midst.

²"I will set Egyptians against Egyptians;
Everyone will fight against his brother,
And everyone against his neighbor,
City against city, kingdom against kingdom.
³The spirit of Egypt will fail in its midst;
I will destroy their counsel,
And they will consult the idols and the
    charmers,
The mediums and the sorcerers.

⁴And the Egyptians I will give
Into the hand of a cruel master,
And a fierce king will rule over them,"
Says the Lord, the LORD of hosts.

⁵The waters will fail from the sea,
And the river will be wasted and dried up.
⁶The rivers will turn foul;
The brooks of defense will be emptied and
    dried up;
The reeds and rushes will wither.
⁷The papyrus reeds by the River,* by the
    mouth of the River,
And everything sown by the River,
Will wither, be driven away, and be no more.
⁸The fishermen also will mourn;
All those will lament who cast hooks into the
    River,
And they will languish who spread nets on
    the waters.
⁹Moreover those who work in fine flax
And those who weave fine fabric will be
    ashamed;
¹⁰And its foundations will be broken.
All who make wages *will be* troubled of soul.

¹¹Surely the princes of Zoan *are* fools;
Pharaoh's wise counselors give foolish counsel.
How do you say to Pharaoh, "I *am* the son of
    the wise,
The son of ancient kings?"
¹²Where *are* they?
Where are your wise men?
Let them tell you now,
And let them know what the LORD of hosts
    has purposed against Egypt.
¹³The princes of Zoan have become fools;
The princes of Noph* are deceived;
They have also deluded Egypt,
Those who are the mainstay of its tribes.
¹⁴The LORD has mingled a perverse spirit in
    her midst;
And they have caused Egypt to err in all her
    work,
As a drunken man staggers in his vomit.
¹⁵Neither will there be *any* work for Egypt,

18:7 *Following Dead Sea Scrolls, Septuagint, and Vulgate; Masoretic Text omits *From;* Targum reads *To.* **19:7** *That is, the Nile **19:13** *That is, ancient Memphis

Which the head or tail,
Palm branch or bulrush, may do.ᵃ

¹⁶In that day Egypt will be like women, and will be afraid and fear because of the waving of the hand of the LORD of hosts, which He waves over it. ¹⁷And the land of Judah will be a terror to Egypt; everyone who makes mention of it will be afraid in himself, because of the counsel of the LORD of hosts which He has determined against it.

EGYPT, ASSYRIA, AND ISRAEL BLESSED

¹⁸In that day five cities in the land of Egypt will speak the language of Canaan and swear by the LORD of hosts; one will be called the City of Destruction.ᵃ

¹⁹In that day there will be an altar to the LORD in the midst of the land of Egypt, and a pillar to the LORD at its border. ²⁰And it will be for a sign and for a witness to the LORD of hosts in the land of Egypt; for they will cry to the LORD because of the oppressors, and He will send them a Savior and a Mighty One, and He will deliver them. ²¹Then the LORD will be known to Egypt, and the Egyptians will know the LORD in that day, and will make sacrifice and offering; yes, they will make a vow to the LORD and perform *it.* ²²And the LORD will strike Egypt, He will strike and heal *it;* they will return to the LORD, and He will be entreated by them and heal them.

²³In that day there will be a highway from Egypt to Assyria, and the Assyrian will come into Egypt and the Egyptian into Assyria, and the Egyptians will serve with the Assyrians.

²⁴In that day Israel will be one of three with Egypt and Assyria—a blessing in the midst of the land, ²⁵whom the LORD of hosts shall bless, saying, "Blessed *is* Egypt My people, and Assyria the work of My hands, and Israel My inheritance."

THE SIGN AGAINST EGYPT AND ETHIOPIA

20 In the year that Tartanᵃ came to Ashdod, when Sargon the king of Assyria sent him, and he fought against Ashdod and took it, ²at the same time the LORD spoke by Isaiah the son of Amoz, saying, "Go, and remove the sackcloth from your body, and take your sandals off your feet." And he did so, walking naked and barefoot.

³Then the LORD said, "Just as My servant Isaiah has walked naked and barefoot three years *for* a sign and a wonder against Egypt and Ethiopia, ⁴so shall the king of Assyria lead away the Egyptians as prisoners and the Ethiopians as captives, young and old, naked and barefoot, with their buttocks uncovered, to the shame of Egypt. ⁵Then they shall be afraid and ashamed of Ethiopia their expectation and Egypt their glory. ⁶And the inhabitant of this territory will say in that day, 'Surely such *is* our expectation, wherever we flee for help to be delivered from the king of Assyria; and how shall we escape?' "

THE FALL OF BABYLON PROCLAIMED

21 The burden against the Wilderness of the Sea.

As whirlwinds in the South pass through,
So it comes from the desert, from a terrible
    land.
²A distressing vision is declared to me;
The treacherous dealer deals treacherously,
And the plunderer plunders.
Go up, O Elam!
Besiege, O Media!
All its sighing I have made to cease.

³Therefore my loins are filled with pain;
Pangs have taken hold of me, like the pangs of
    a woman in labor.
I was distressed when *I* heard *it;*
I was dismayed when *I* saw *it.*
⁴My heart wavered, fearfulness frightened
    me;
The night for which I longed He turned into
    fear for me.
⁵Prepare the table,
Set a watchman in the tower,
Eat and drink.
Arise, you princes,
Anoint the shield!

⁶For thus has the Lord said to me:
"Go, set a watchman,

19:15 ᵃCompare Isaiah 9:14–16   19:18 ᵃSome Hebrew manuscripts, Arabic, Dead Sea Scrolls, Targum, and Vulgate read *Sun;* Septuagint reads *Asedek* (literally *Righteousness*).   20:1 ᵃOr *the Commander in Chief*

Let him declare what he sees."
⁷And he saw a chariot *with* a pair of horsemen,
A chariot of donkeys, *and* a chariot of camels,
And he listened earnestly with great care.
⁸Then he cried, "A lion,ᵃ my Lord!
I stand continually on the watchtower in the daytime;
I have sat at my post every night.
⁹And look, here comes a chariot of men *with* a pair of horsemen!"
Then he answered and said,
"Babylon is fallen, is fallen!
And all the carved images of her gods
He has broken to the ground."

¹⁰Oh, my threshing and the grain of my floor!
That which I have heard from the LORD of hosts,
The God of Israel,
I have declared to you.

PROCLAMATION AGAINST EDOM

¹¹The burden against Dumah.

He calls to me out of Seir,
"Watchman, what of the night?
Watchman, what of the night?"
¹²The watchman said,
"The morning comes, and also the night.
If you will inquire, inquire;
Return! Come back!"

PROCLAMATION AGAINST ARABIA

¹³The burden against Arabia.

In the forest in Arabia you will lodge,
O you traveling companies of Dedanites.
¹⁴O inhabitants of the land of Tema,
Bring water to him who is thirsty;
With their bread they met him who fled.
¹⁵For they fled from the swords, from the drawn sword,
From the bent bow, and from the distress of war.

¹⁶For thus the LORD has said to me: "Within a year, according to the year of a hired man, all the glory of Kedar will fail; ¹⁷and the remainder of the number of archers, the mighty men of the

people of Kedar, will be diminished; for the LORD God of Israel has spoken *it.*"

PROCLAMATION AGAINST JERUSALEM

22 The burden against the Valley of Vision.

What ails you now, that you have all gone up to the housetops,
²You who are full of noise,
A tumultuous city, a joyous city?
Your slain *men are* not slain with the sword,
Nor dead in battle.
³All your rulers have fled together;
They are captured by the archers.
All who are found in you are bound together;
They have fled from afar.
⁴Therefore I said, "Look away from me,
I will weep bitterly;
Do not labor to comfort me
Because of the plundering of the daughter of my people."

⁵For *it is* a day of trouble and treading down and perplexity
By the Lord GOD of hosts
In the Valley of Vision—
Breaking down the walls
And of crying to the mountain.
⁶Elam bore the quiver
With chariots of men *and* horsemen,
And Kir uncovered the shield.
⁷It shall come to pass *that* your choicest valleys
Shall be full of chariots,
And the horsemen shall set themselves in array at the gate.

⁸He removed the protection of Judah.
You looked in that day to the armor of the House of the Forest;
⁹You also saw the damage to the city of David,
That it was great;
And you gathered together the waters of the lower pool.
¹⁰You numbered the houses of Jerusalem,
And the houses you broke down
To fortify the wall.

21:8 ᵃDead Sea Scrolls read *Then the observer cried.*

[11]You also made a reservoir between the two walls
For the water of the old pool.
But you did not look to its Maker,
Nor did you have respect for Him who fashioned it long ago.

[12]And in that day the Lord GOD of hosts
Called for weeping and for mourning,
For baldness and for girding with sackcloth.
[13]But instead, joy and gladness,
Slaying oxen and killing sheep,
Eating meat and drinking wine:
"Let us eat and drink, for tomorrow we die!"

[14]Then it was revealed in my hearing by the LORD of hosts,
"Surely for this iniquity there will be no atonement for you,
Even to your death," says the Lord GOD of hosts.

The Judgment on Shebna

[15]Thus says the Lord GOD of hosts:

"Go, proceed to this steward,
To Shebna, who *is* over the house, *and say:*
[16]'What have you here, and whom have you here,
That you have hewn a sepulcher here,
As he who hews himself a sepulcher on high,
Who carves a tomb for himself in a rock?
[17]Indeed, the LORD will throw you away violently,
O mighty man,
And will surely seize you.
[18]He will surely turn violently and toss you like a ball
Into a large country;
There you shall die, and there your glorious chariots
Shall be the shame of your master's house.
[19]So I will drive you out of your office,
And from your position he will pull you down.[a]

[20]'Then it shall be in that day,
That I will call My servant Eliakim the son of Hilkiah;

[21]I will clothe him with your robe
And strengthen him with your belt;
I will commit your responsibility into his hand.
He shall be a father to the inhabitants of Jerusalem
And to the house of Judah.
[22]The key of the house of David
I will lay on his shoulder;
So he shall open, and no one shall shut;
And he shall shut, and no one shall open.
[23]I will fasten him *as* a peg in a secure place,
And he will become a glorious throne to his father's house.

[24]'They will hang on him all the glory of his father's house, the offspring and the posterity, all vessels of small quantity, from the cups to all the pitchers. [25]In that day,' says the LORD of hosts, 'the peg that is fastened in the secure place will be removed and be cut down and fall, and the burden that *was* on it will be cut off; for the LORD has spoken.'"

Proclamation Against Tyre

23 The burden against Tyre.

Wail, you ships of Tarshish!
For it is laid waste,
So that there is no house, no harbor;
From the land of Cyprus[a] it is revealed to them.

[2]Be still, you inhabitants of the coastland,
You merchants of Sidon,
Whom those who cross the sea have filled.[a]
[3]And on great waters the grain of Shihor,
The harvest of the River,[a] *is* her revenue;
And she is a marketplace for the nations.

[4]Be ashamed, O Sidon;
For the sea has spoken,
The strength of the sea, saying,
"I do not labor, nor bring forth children;

22:19 [a]Septuagint omits *he will pull you down;* Syriac, Targum, and Vulgate read *I will pull you down.*   23:1 [a]Hebrew *Kittim,* western lands, especially Cyprus   23:2 [a]Following Masoretic Text and Vulgate; Septuagint and Targum read *Passing over the water;* Dead Sea Scrolls read *Your messengers passing over the sea.*   23:3 [a]That is, the Nile

Neither do I rear young men,
Nor bring up virgins."
[5]When the report *reaches* Egypt,
They also will be in agony at the report of Tyre.

[6]Cross over to Tarshish;
Wail, you inhabitants of the coastland!
[7]*Is* this your joyous *city,*
Whose antiquity *is* from ancient days,
Whose feet carried her far off to dwell?
[8]Who has taken this counsel against Tyre, the crowning *city,*
Whose merchants *are* princes,
Whose traders *are* the honorable of the earth?
[9]The LORD of hosts has purposed it,
To bring to dishonor the pride of all glory,
To bring into contempt all the honorable of the earth.

[10]Overflow through your land like the River,[a]
O daughter of Tarshish;
There is no more strength.
[11]He stretched out His hand over the sea,
He shook the kingdoms;
The LORD has given a commandment against Canaan
To destroy its strongholds.
[12]And He said, "You will rejoice no more,
O you oppressed virgin daughter of Sidon.
Arise, cross over to Cyprus;
There also you will have no rest."

[13]Behold, the land of the Chaldeans,
This people *which* was not;
Assyria founded it for wild beasts of the desert.
They set up its towers,
They raised up its palaces,
And brought it to ruin.

[14]Wail, you ships of Tarshish!
For your strength is laid waste.

[15]Now it shall come to pass in that day that Tyre will be forgotten seventy years, according to the days of one king. At the end of seventy years it will happen to Tyre as *in* the song of the harlot:

[16]"Take a harp, go about the city,
You forgotten harlot;
Make sweet melody, sing many songs,
That you may be remembered."

[17]And it shall be, at the end of seventy years, that the LORD will deal with Tyre. She will return to her hire, and commit fornication with all the kingdoms of the world on the face of the earth. [18]Her gain and her pay will be set apart for the LORD; it will not be treasured nor laid up, for her gain will be for those who dwell before the LORD, to eat sufficiently, and for fine clothing.

IMPENDING JUDGMENT ON THE EARTH

24 Behold, the LORD makes the earth empty
and makes it waste,
Distorts its surface
And scatters abroad its inhabitants.
[2]And it shall be:
As with the people, so with the priest;
As with the servant, so with his master;
As with the maid, so with her mistress;
As with the buyer, so with the seller;
As with the lender, so with the borrower;
As with the creditor, so with the debtor.
[3]The land shall be entirely emptied and utterly plundered,
For the LORD has spoken this word.

[4]The earth mourns *and* fades away,
The world languishes *and* fades away;
The haughty people of the earth languish.
[5]The earth is also defiled under its inhabitants,
Because they have transgressed the laws,
Changed the ordinance,
Broken the everlasting covenant.
[6]Therefore the curse has devoured the earth,
And those who dwell in it are desolate.
Therefore the inhabitants of the earth are burned,
And few men *are* left.

[7]The new wine fails, the vine languishes,
All the merry-hearted sigh.
[8]The mirth of the tambourine ceases,
The noise of the jubilant ends,
The joy of the harp ceases.

23:10 [a]That is, the Nile

⁹They shall not drink wine with a song;
  Strong drink is bitter to those who drink it.
¹⁰The city of confusion is broken down;
  Every house is shut up, so that none may
    go in.
¹¹*There is* a cry for wine in the streets,
  All joy is darkened,
  The mirth of the land is gone.
¹²In the city desolation is left,
  And the gate is stricken with destruction.
¹³When it shall be thus in the midst of the land
    among the people,
  It shall be like the shaking of an olive tree,
  Like the gleaning of grapes when the vintage
    is done.

¹⁴They shall lift up their voice, they shall sing;
  For the majesty of the LORD
  They shall cry aloud from the sea.
¹⁵Therefore glorify the LORD in the dawning
    light,
  The name of the LORD God of Israel in the
    coastlands of the sea.
¹⁶From the ends of the earth we have heard
    songs:
  "Glory to the righteous!"
  But I said, "I am ruined, ruined!
  Woe to me!
  The treacherous dealers have dealt
    treacherously,
  Indeed, the treacherous dealers have dealt
    very treacherously."

¹⁷Fear and the pit and the snare
  Are upon you, O inhabitant of the earth.
¹⁸And it shall be
  That he who flees from the noise of the fear
  Shall fall into the pit,
  And he who comes up from the midst of
    the pit
  Shall be caught in the snare;
  For the windows from on high are open,
  And the foundations of the earth are shaken.

¹⁹The earth is violently broken,
  The earth is split open,
  The earth is shaken exceedingly.
²⁰The earth shall reel to and fro like a
    drunkard,

And shall totter like a hut;
  Its transgression shall be heavy upon it,
  And it will fall, and not rise again.

²¹It shall come to pass in that day
  That the LORD will punish on high the host
    of exalted ones,
  And on the earth the kings of the earth.
²²They will be gathered together,
  As prisoners are gathered in the pit,
  And will be shut up in the prison;
  After many days they will be punished.
²³Then the moon will be disgraced
  And the sun ashamed;
  For the LORD of hosts will reign
  On Mount Zion and in Jerusalem
  And before His elders, gloriously.

PRAISE TO GOD

25 O LORD, You *are* my God.
  I will exalt You,
  I will praise Your name,
  For You have done wonderful *things;*
  Your counsels of old *are* faithfulness *and*
    truth.
²For You have made a city a ruin,
  A fortified city a ruin,
  A palace of foreigners to be a city no more;
  It will never be rebuilt.
³Therefore the strong people will glorify You;
  The city of the terrible nations will fear You.
⁴For You have been a strength to the poor,
  A strength to the needy in his distress,
  A refuge from the storm,
  A shade from the heat;
  For the blast of the terrible ones *is* as a storm
    against the wall.
⁵You will reduce the noise of aliens,
  As heat in a dry place;
  As heat in the shadow of a cloud,
  The song of the terrible ones will be
    diminished.

⁶And in this mountain
  The LORD of hosts will make for all people
  A feast of choice pieces,
  A feast of wines on the lees,
  Of fat things full of marrow,
  Of well-refined wines on the lees.

[7]And He will destroy on this mountain
The surface of the covering cast over all
    people,
And the veil that is spread over all nations.
[8]He will swallow up death forever,
And the Lord GOD will wipe away tears from
    all faces;
The rebuke of His people
He will take away from all the earth;
For the LORD has spoken.

[9]And it will be said in that day:
"Behold, this *is* our God;
We have waited for Him, and He will save us.
This *is* the LORD;
We have waited for Him;
We will be glad and rejoice in His salvation."

[10]For on this mountain the hand of the LORD
    will rest,
And Moab shall be trampled down under
    Him,
As straw is trampled down for the refuse
    heap.
[11]And He will spread out His hands in their
    midst
As a swimmer reaches out to swim,
And He will bring down their pride
Together with the trickery of their hands.
[12]The fortress of the high fort of your walls
He will bring down, lay low,
And bring to the ground, down to the dust.

A Song of Salvation

26 In that day this song will be sung in the
    land of Judah:

"We have a strong city;
God will appoint salvation *for* walls and
    bulwarks.
[2]Open the gates,
That the righteous nation which keeps the
    truth may enter in.
[3]You will keep *him* in perfect peace,
Whose mind *is* stayed *on* You,
Because he trusts in You.
[4]Trust in the LORD forever,
For in YAH, the LORD, *is* everlasting
    strength.[a]

[5]For He brings down those who dwell on
    high,
The lofty city;
He lays it low,
He lays it low to the ground,
He brings it down to the dust.
[6]The foot shall tread it down—
The feet of the poor
And the steps of the needy."

[7]The way of the just *is* uprightness;
O Most Upright,
You weigh the path of the just.
[8]Yes, in the way of Your judgments,
O LORD, we have waited for You;
The desire of *our* soul *is* for Your name
And for the remembrance of You.
[9]With my soul I have desired You in the night,
Yes, by my spirit within me I will seek You
    early;
For when Your judgments *are* in the earth,
The inhabitants of the world will learn
    righteousness.

[10]Let grace be shown to the wicked,
Yet he will not learn righteousness;
In the land of uprightness he will deal
    unjustly,
And will not behold the majesty of the
    LORD.
[11]LORD, *when* Your hand is lifted up, they will
    not see.
But they will see and be ashamed
For *their* envy of people;
Yes, the fire of Your enemies shall devour
    them.

[12]LORD, You will establish peace for us,
For You have also done all our works in us.
[13]O LORD our God, masters besides You
Have had dominion over us;
But by You only we make mention of Your
    name.
[14]*They are* dead, they will not live;
They are deceased, they will not rise.
Therefore You have punished and destroyed
    them,
And made all their memory to perish.

26:4 [a]Or *Rock of Ages*

[15]You have increased the nation, O LORD,
You have increased the nation;
You are glorified;
You have expanded all the borders of the
land.

[16]LORD, in trouble they have visited You,
They poured out a prayer *when* Your
chastening *was* upon them.
[17]As a woman with child
Is in pain and cries out in her pangs,
When she draws near the time of her
delivery,
So have we been in Your sight, O LORD.
[18]We have been with child, we have been in
pain;
We have, as it were, brought forth wind;
We have not accomplished any deliverance in
the earth,
Nor have the inhabitants of the world fallen.

[19]Your dead shall live;
Together with my dead body[a] they shall arise.
Awake and sing, you who dwell in dust;
For your dew *is like* the dew of herbs,
And the earth shall cast out the dead.

Take Refuge from the Coming Judgment

[20]Come, my people, enter your chambers,
And shut your doors behind you;
Hide yourself, as it were, for a little moment,
Until the indignation is past.
[21]For behold, the LORD comes out of His place
To punish the inhabitants of the earth for
their iniquity;
The earth will also disclose her blood,
And will no more cover her slain.

27 In that day the LORD with His severe
sword, great and strong,
Will punish Leviathan the fleeing serpent,
Leviathan that twisted serpent;
And He will slay the reptile that *is* in the sea.

The Restoration of Israel

[2]In that day sing to her,
"A vineyard of red wine![a]
[3]I, the LORD, keep it,
I water it every moment;

Lest any hurt it,
I keep it night and day.
[4]Fury *is* not in Me.
Who would set briers *and* thorns
Against Me in battle?
I would go through them,
I would burn them together.
[5]Or let him take hold of My strength,
That he may make peace with Me;
And he shall make peace with Me."

[6]Those who come He shall cause to take root
in Jacob;
Israel shall blossom and bud,
And fill the face of the world with fruit.

[7]Has He struck Israel as He struck those who
struck him?
Or has He been slain according to the
slaughter of those who were slain by
Him?
[8]In measure, by sending it away,
You contended with it.
He removes *it* by His rough wind
In the day of the east wind.
[9]Therefore by this the iniquity of Jacob will be
covered;
And this *is* all the fruit of taking away
his sin:
When he makes all the stones of the altar
Like chalkstones that are beaten to dust,
Wooden images[a] and incense altars shall not
stand.

[10]Yet the fortified city *will be* desolate,
The habitation forsaken and left like a
wilderness;
There the calf will feed, and there it will lie
down
And consume its branches.
[11]When its boughs are withered, they will be
broken off;
The women come *and* set them on fire.
For it *is* a people of no understanding;

26:19 [a]Following Masoretic Text and Vulgate; Syriac and Targum read *their dead bodies;* Septuagint reads *those in the tombs.* **27:2** [a]Following Masoretic Text (Kittel's *Biblia Hebraica*), Bomberg, and Vulgate; Masoretic Text (*Biblia Hebraica Stuttgartensia*), some Hebrew manuscripts, and Septuagint read *delight;* Targum reads *choice vineyard.* **27:9** [a]Hebrew *Asherim,* Canaanite deities

Therefore He who made them will not have
    mercy on them,
And He who formed them will show them
    no favor.

12And it shall come to pass in that day
    That the LORD will thresh,
From the channel of the River[a] to the Brook
    of Egypt;
And you will be gathered one by one,
O you children of Israel.

13So it shall be in that day:
    The great trumpet will be blown;
They will come, who are about to perish in
    the land of Assyria,
And they who are outcasts in the land of
    Egypt,
And shall worship the LORD in the holy
    mount at Jerusalem.

WOE TO EPHRAIM AND JERUSALEM

28 Woe to the crown of pride, to the
drunkards of Ephraim,
Whose glorious beauty *is* a fading flower
Which *is* at the head of the verdant valleys,
To those who are overcome with wine!
2Behold, the Lord has a mighty and strong
    one,
Like a tempest of hail and a destroying storm,
Like a flood of mighty waters overflowing,
Who will bring *them* down to the earth with
    His hand.
3The crown of pride, the drunkards of
    Ephraim,
Will be trampled underfoot;
4And the glorious beauty is a fading flower
Which *is* at the head of the verdant valley,
Like the first fruit before the summer,
Which an observer sees;
He eats it up while it is still in his hand.

5In that day the LORD of hosts will be
For a crown of glory and a diadem of beauty
To the remnant of His people,
6For a spirit of justice to him who sits in
    judgment,
And for strength to those who turn back the
    battle at the gate.

7But they also have erred through wine,
And through intoxicating drink are out of the
    way;
The priest and the prophet have erred
    through intoxicating drink,
They are swallowed up by wine,
They are out of the way through intoxicating
    drink;
They err in vision, they stumble *in* judgment.
8For all tables are full of vomit *and* filth;
    No place *is* clean.

9"Whom will he teach knowledge?
And whom will he make to understand the
    message?
Those *just* weaned from milk?
Those *just* drawn from the breasts?
10For precept *must be* upon precept, precept
    upon precept,
Line upon line, line upon line,
Here a little, there a little."

11For with stammering lips and another tongue
He will speak to this people,
12To whom He said, "This *is* the rest *with which*
You may cause the weary to rest,"
And, "This *is* the refreshing";
Yet they would not hear.
13But the word of the LORD was to them,
"Precept upon precept, precept upon precept,
Line upon line, line upon line,
Here a little, there a little,"
That they might go and fall backward, and be
    broken
And snared and caught.

14Therefore hear the word of the LORD, you
    scornful men,
Who rule this people who *are* in Jerusalem,
15Because you have said, "We have made a
    covenant with death,
And with Sheol we are in agreement.
When the overflowing scourge passes
    through,
It will not come to us,
For we have made lies our refuge,
And under falsehood we have hidden
    ourselves."

27:12 [a]That is, the Euphrates

A Cornerstone in Zion

¹⁶Therefore thus says the Lord GOD:

"Behold, I lay in Zion a stone for a
foundation,
A tried stone, a precious cornerstone, a sure
foundation;
Whoever believes will not act hastily.
¹⁷Also I will make justice the measuring line,
And righteousness the plummet;
The hail will sweep away the refuge of lies,
And the waters will overflow the hiding
place.
¹⁸Your covenant with death will be annulled,
And your agreement with Sheol will not
stand;
When the overflowing scourge passes
through,
Then you will be trampled down by it.
¹⁹As often as it goes out it will take you;
For morning by morning it will pass over,
And by day and by night;
It will be a terror just to understand the
report."

²⁰For the bed is too short to stretch out *on*,
And the covering so narrow that one cannot
wrap himself *in it*.
²¹For the LORD will rise up as *at* Mount
Perazim,
He will be angry as in the Valley of
Gibeon—
That He may do His work, His awesome
work,
And bring to pass His act, His unusual act.
²²Now therefore, do not be mockers,
Lest your bonds be made strong;
For I have heard from the Lord GOD of
hosts,
A destruction determined even upon the
whole earth.

Listen to the Teaching of God

²³Give ear and hear my voice,
Listen and hear my speech.
²⁴Does the plowman keep plowing all day to
sow?
Does he keep turning his soil and breaking
the clods?

²⁵When he has leveled its surface,
Does he not sow the black cummin
And scatter the cummin,
Plant the wheat in rows,
The barley in the appointed place,
And the spelt in its place?
²⁶For He instructs him in right judgment,
His God teaches him.

²⁷For the black cummin is not threshed with a
threshing sledge,
Nor is a cartwheel rolled over the
cummin;
But the black cummin is beaten out with a
stick,
And the cummin with a rod.
²⁸Bread *flour* must be ground;
Therefore he does not thresh it forever,
Break *it with* his cartwheel,
Or crush it *with* his horsemen.
²⁹This also comes from the LORD of hosts,
Who is wonderful in counsel *and* excellent in
guidance.

Woe to Jerusalem

29 "Woe to Ariel,[a] to Ariel, the city *where*
David dwelt!
Add year to year;
Let feasts come around.
²Yet I will distress Ariel;
There shall be heaviness and sorrow,
And it shall be to Me as Ariel.
³I will encamp against you all around,
I will lay siege against you with a mound,
And I will raise siegeworks against you.
⁴You shall be brought down,
You shall speak out of the ground;
Your speech shall be low, out of the dust;
Your voice shall be like a medium's, out of
the ground;
And your speech shall whisper out of the
dust.

⁵"Moreover the multitude of your foes
Shall be like fine dust,
And the multitude of the terrible ones
Like chaff that passes away;
Yes, it shall be in an instant, suddenly.

29:1 [a]That is, Jerusalem

⁶You will be punished by the LORD of hosts
With thunder and earthquake and great
        noise,
With storm and tempest
And the flame of devouring fire.
⁷The multitude of all the nations who fight
        against Ariel,
Even all who fight against her and her
        fortress,
And distress her,
Shall be as a dream of a night vision.
⁸It shall even be as when a hungry man
        dreams,
And look—he eats;
But he awakes, and his soul is still empty;
Or as when a thirsty man dreams,
And look—he drinks;
But he awakes, and indeed *he is* faint,
And his soul still craves:
So the multitude of all the nations shall be,
Who fight against Mount Zion."

THE BLINDNESS OF DISOBEDIENCE

⁹Pause and wonder!
Blind yourselves and be blind!
They are drunk, but not with wine;
They stagger, but not with intoxicating
        drink.
¹⁰For the LORD has poured out on you
The spirit of deep sleep,
And has closed your eyes, namely, the
        prophets;
And He has covered your heads, *namely,* the
        seers.

¹¹The whole vision has become to you like
the words of a book that is sealed, which *men* deliver to one who is literate, saying, "Read this,
please."

And he says, "I cannot, for it *is* sealed."
¹²Then the book is delivered to one who is
illiterate, saying, "Read this, please."

And he says, "I am not literate."
¹³Therefore the Lord said:

"Inasmuch as these people draw near with
        their mouths
And honor Me with their lips,
But have removed their hearts far from Me,

And their fear toward Me is taught by the
        commandment of men,
¹⁴Therefore, behold, I will again do a marvelous
        work
Among this people,
A marvelous work and a wonder;
For the wisdom of their wise *men* shall
        perish,
And the understanding of their prudent *men*
        shall be hidden."

¹⁵Woe to those who seek deep to hide their
        counsel far from the LORD,
And their works are in the dark;
They say, "Who sees us?" and, "Who knows
        us?"
¹⁶Surely you have things turned around!
Shall the potter be esteemed as the clay;
For shall the thing made say of him who
        made it,
"He did not make me"?
Or shall the thing formed say of him who
        formed it,
"He has no understanding"?

FUTURE RECOVERY OF WISDOM

¹⁷*Is* it not yet a very little while
Till Lebanon shall be turned into a fruitful
        field,
And the fruitful field be esteemed as a
        forest?
¹⁸In that day the deaf shall hear the words of
        the book,
And the eyes of the blind shall see out of
        obscurity and out of darkness.
¹⁹The humble also shall increase *their* joy in the
        LORD,
And the poor among men shall rejoice
In the Holy One of Israel.
²⁰For the terrible one is brought to nothing,
The scornful one is consumed,
And all who watch for iniquity are cut off—
²¹Who make a man an offender by a word,
And lay a snare for him who reproves in the
        gate,
And turn aside the just by empty words.

²²Therefore thus says the LORD, who redeemed Abraham, concerning the house of Jacob:

"Jacob shall not now be ashamed,
Nor shall his face now grow pale;
²³But when he sees his children,
The work of My hands, in his midst,
They will hallow My name,
And hallow the Holy One of Jacob,
And fear the God of Israel.
²⁴These also who erred in spirit will come to understanding,
And those who complained will learn doctrine."

Futile Confidence in Egypt

30 "Woe to the rebellious children," says the LORD,
"Who take counsel, but not of Me,
And who devise plans, but not of My Spirit,
That they may add sin to sin;
²Who walk to go down to Egypt,
And have not asked My advice,
To strengthen themselves in the strength of Pharaoh,
And to trust in the shadow of Egypt!
³Therefore the strength of Pharaoh
Shall be your shame,
And trust in the shadow of Egypt
Shall be your humiliation.
⁴For his princes were at Zoan,
And his ambassadors came to Hanes.
⁵They were all ashamed of a people who could not benefit them,
Or be help or benefit,
But a shame and also a reproach."

⁶The burden against the beasts of the South.

Through a land of trouble and anguish,
From which came the lioness and lion,
The viper and fiery flying serpent,
They will carry their riches on the backs of young donkeys,
And their treasures on the humps of camels,
To a people who shall not profit;
⁷For the Egyptians shall help in vain and to no purpose.
Therefore I have called her
Rahab-Hem-Shebeth.^a

A Rebellious People

⁸Now go, write it before them on a tablet,
And note it on a scroll,
That it may be for time to come,
Forever and ever:
⁹That this is a rebellious people,
Lying children,
Children who will not hear the law of the LORD;
¹⁰Who say to the seers, "Do not see,"
And to the prophets, "Do not prophesy to us right things;
Speak to us smooth things, prophesy deceits.
¹¹Get out of the way,
Turn aside from the path,
Cause the Holy One of Israel
To cease from before us."

¹²Therefore thus says the Holy One of Israel:

"Because you despise this word,
And trust in oppression and perversity,
And rely on them,
¹³Therefore this iniquity shall be to you
Like a breach ready to fall,
A bulge in a high wall,
Whose breaking comes suddenly, in an instant.
¹⁴And He shall break it like the breaking of the potter's vessel,
Which is broken in pieces;
He shall not spare.
So there shall not be found among its fragments
A shard to take fire from the hearth,
Or to take water from the cistern."

¹⁵For thus says the Lord GOD, the Holy One of Israel:

"In returning and rest you shall be saved;
In quietness and confidence shall be your strength."
But you would not,
¹⁶And you said, "No, for we will flee on horses"—
Therefore you shall flee!

LEADERSHIP ISSUES

GC2: Loving the Real God: A God of Grace and Mercy

ISAIAH 30:18 *Therefore the LORD will wait, that He may be gracious to you; and therefore He will be exalted, that He may have mercy on you. For the LORD is a God of justice; blessed are all those who wait for Him.*

What is the Lord's heart toward us? From His place at the right hand of the Father, is Christ longing to prove us wrong? Does He hope to expose our error? Does He want to embarrass us before others?

May it never be!

Pause and consider the truth that Christ longs to show you grace. He is excited to show you favor and mercy. He earnestly desires to shower you with undeserved, unexpected blessings.

Use your imagination to paint the scene in the throne room of heaven. God the Father sits on His throne. God the Son sits to the right, the place of power and of honor. Picture it now: Christ rises from His seat in the throne room. Jesus invites you close and welcomes you to Himself. With excitement in His eyes and graciousness in His voice, the Savior speaks a blessing over you.

Meditate on the Person of Christ, who, with outstretched arms and nail-pierced hands, welcomes you into His presence and is excited to bless you. As certainly as the prodigal son was welcomed with compassion and excitedly embraced by the father (Luke 15), we have a Savior who longs to show us grace and rises to show us mercy.

Pray now with a friend or one of the members of your small group. Share with them what it does to your heart to encounter such a Savior.

"As I imagine Christ and think about how He is excited to welcome and bless me, how He rises to show me mercy, my heart is filled with
_____."

(For example: gratitude and joy, humility and confidence, or reassurance and security)

GC2
GREAT COMMANDMENT
COMMISSION

And, "We will ride on swift *horses*"—
Therefore those who pursue you shall be
    swift!

¹⁷One thousand *shall flee* at the threat of one,
At the threat of five you shall flee,
Till you are left as a pole on top of a
    mountain
And as a banner on a hill.

God Will Be Gracious

¹⁸Therefore the LORD will wait, that He may
    be gracious to you;
And therefore He will be exalted, that He
    may have mercy on you.
For the LORD *is* a God of justice;
Blessed *are* all those who wait for Him.

¹⁹For the people shall dwell in Zion at
    Jerusalem;
You shall weep no more.
He will be very gracious to you at the sound
    of your cry;
When He hears it, He will answer you.
²⁰And *though* the Lord gives you
The bread of adversity and the water of
    affliction,
Yet your teachers will not be moved into a
    corner anymore,
But your eyes shall see your teachers.
²¹Your ears shall hear a word behind you,
    saying,
"This *is* the way, walk in it,"
Whenever you turn to the right hand
Or whenever you turn to the left.
²²You will also defile the covering of your
    images of silver,
And the ornament of your molded images of
    gold.
You will throw them away as an unclean
    thing;
You will say to them, "Get away!"

²³Then He will give the rain for your seed
With which you sow the ground,
And bread of the increase of the earth;
It will be fat and plentiful.
In that day your cattle will feed
In large pastures.

²⁴Likewise the oxen and the young donkeys
    that work the ground
Will eat cured fodder,
Which has been winnowed with the shovel
    and fan.
²⁵There will be on every high mountain
And on every high hill
Rivers *and* streams of waters,
In the day of the great slaughter,
When the towers fall.
²⁶Moreover the light of the moon will be as the
    light of the sun,
And the light of the sun will be sevenfold,
As the light of seven days,
In the day that the LORD binds up the bruise
    of His people
And heals the stroke of their wound.

Judgment on Assyria

²⁷Behold, the name of the LORD comes from
    afar,
Burning *with* His anger,
And *His* burden *is* heavy;
His lips are full of indignation,
And His tongue like a devouring fire.
²⁸His breath is like an overflowing stream,
Which reaches up to the neck,
To sift the nations with the sieve of futility;
And *there shall be* a bridle in the jaws of the
    people,
Causing *them* to err.

²⁹You shall have a song
As in the night *when* a holy festival is kept,
And gladness of heart as when one goes with
    a flute,
To come into the mountain of the LORD,
To the Mighty One of Israel.
³⁰The LORD will cause His glorious voice to be
    heard,
And show the descent of His arm,
With the indignation of *His* anger
And the flame of a devouring fire,
With scattering, tempest, and hailstones.
³¹For through the voice of the LORD
Assyria will be beaten down,
As He strikes with the rod.
³²And *in* every place where the staff of
    punishment passes,

Which the LORD lays on him,
It will be with tambourines and harps;
And in battles of brandishing He will fight
    with it.
33For Tophet *was* established of old,
Yes, for the king it is prepared.
He has made *it* deep and large;
Its pyre *is* fire with much wood;
The breath of the LORD, like a stream of
    brimstone,
Kindles it.

THE FOLLY OF NOT TRUSTING GOD

31 Woe to those who go down to Egypt for
    help,
And rely on horses,
Who trust in chariots because *they are* many,
And in horsemen because they are very
    strong,
But who do not look to the Holy One of
    Israel,
Nor seek the LORD!
2Yet He also *is* wise and will bring disaster,
And will not call back His words,
But will arise against the house of evildoers,
And against the help of those who work
    iniquity.
3Now the Egyptians *are* men, and not God;
And their horses are flesh, and not spirit.
When the LORD stretches out His hand,
Both he who helps will fall,
And he who is helped will fall down;
They all will perish together.

GOD WILL DELIVER JERUSALEM

4For thus the LORD has spoken to me:

"As a lion roars,
And a young lion over his prey
(When a multitude of shepherds is
    summoned against him,
He will not be afraid of their voice
Nor be disturbed by their noise),
So the LORD of hosts will come down
To fight for Mount Zion and for its hill.
5Like birds flying about,
So will the LORD of hosts defend Jerusalem.
Defending, He will also deliver *it;*
Passing over, He will preserve *it.*"

6Return *to Him* against whom the children of
Israel have deeply revolted. 7For in that day every
man shall throw away his idols of silver and his
idols of gold—sin, which your own hands have
made for yourselves.

8"Then Assyria shall fall by a sword not of man,
And a sword not of mankind shall devour
    him.
But he shall flee from the sword,
And his young men shall become forced
    labor.
9He shall cross over to his stronghold for fear,
And his princes shall be afraid of the banner,"
Says the LORD,
Whose fire *is* in Zion
And whose furnace *is* in Jerusalem.

A REIGN OF RIGHTEOUSNESS

32 Behold, a king will reign in righteousness,
And princes will rule with justice.
2A man will be as a hiding place from the
    wind,
And a cover from the tempest,
As rivers of water in a dry place,
As the shadow of a great rock in a weary land.
3The eyes of those who see will not be dim,
And the ears of those who hear will listen.
4Also the heart of the rash will understand
    knowledge,
And the tongue of the stammerers will be
    ready to speak plainly.

5The foolish person will no longer be called
    generous,
Nor the miser said *to be* bountiful;
6For the foolish person will speak foolishness,
And his heart will work iniquity:
To practice ungodliness,
To utter error against the LORD,
To keep the hungry unsatisfied,
And he will cause the drink of the thirsty to
    fail.
7Also the schemes of the schemer *are* evil;
He devises wicked plans
To destroy the poor with lying words,
Even when the needy speaks justice.
8But a generous man devises generous things,
And by generosity he shall stand.

Consequences of Complacency

⁹Rise up, you women who are at ease,
Hear my voice;
You complacent daughters,
Give ear to my speech.
¹⁰In a year and *some* days
You will be troubled, you complacent
women;
For the vintage will fail,
The gathering will not come.
¹¹Tremble, you *women* who are at ease;
Be troubled, you complacent ones;
Strip yourselves, make yourselves bare,
And gird *sackcloth* on *your* waists.

¹²People shall mourn upon their breasts
For the pleasant fields, for the fruitful vine.
¹³On the land of my people will come up
thorns *and* briers,
Yes, on all the happy homes *in* the joyous
city;
¹⁴Because the palaces will be forsaken,
The bustling city will be deserted.
The forts and towers will become lairs
forever,
A joy of wild donkeys, a pasture of flocks—
¹⁵Until the Spirit is poured upon us from on
high,
And the wilderness becomes a fruitful field,
And the fruitful field is counted as a forest.

The Peace of God's Reign

¹⁶Then justice will dwell in the wilderness,
And righteousness remain in the fruitful
field.
¹⁷The work of righteousness will be peace,
And the effect of righteousness, quietness
and assurance forever.
¹⁸My people will dwell in a peaceful
habitation,
In secure dwellings, and in quiet resting
places,
¹⁹Though hail comes down on the forest,
And the city is brought low in humiliation.

²⁰Blessed *are* you who sow beside all waters,
Who send out freely the feet of the ox and
the donkey.

A Prayer in Deep Distress

33 Woe to you who plunder, though you *have*
not *been* plundered;
And you who deal treacherously, though they
have not dealt treacherously with you!
When you cease plundering,
You will be plundered;
When you make an end of dealing
treacherously,
They will deal treacherously with you.

²O Lord, be gracious to us;
We have waited for You.
Be their[a] arm every morning,
Our salvation also in the time of trouble.
³At the noise of the tumult the people shall
flee;
When You lift Yourself up, the nations shall be
scattered;
⁴And Your plunder shall be gathered
Like the gathering of the caterpillar;
As the running to and fro of locusts,
He shall run upon them.

⁵The Lord is exalted, for He dwells on high;
He has filled Zion with justice and
righteousness.
⁶Wisdom and knowledge will be the stability
of your times,
And the strength of salvation;
The fear of the Lord *is* His treasure.

⁷Surely their valiant ones shall cry outside,
The ambassadors of peace shall weep
bitterly.
⁸The highways lie waste,
The traveling man ceases.
He has broken the covenant,
He has despised the cities,[a]
He regards no man.
⁹The earth mourns *and* languishes,
Lebanon is shamed *and* shriveled;
Sharon is like a wilderness,
And Bashan and Carmel shake off *their fruits.*

33:2 [a]Septuagint omits *their;* Syriac, Targum, and Vulgate read *our.*
33:8 [a]Following Masoretic Text and Vulgate; Dead Sea Scrolls read
witnesses; Septuagint omits *cities;* Targum reads *They have been
removed from their cities.*

Impending Judgment on Zion

¹⁰"Now I will rise," says the LORD;
"Now I will be exalted,
Now I will lift Myself up.
¹¹You shall conceive chaff,
You shall bring forth stubble;
Your breath, *as* fire, shall devour you.
¹²And the people shall be *like* the burnings of
lime;
Like thorns cut up they shall be burned in the
fire.
¹³Hear, you *who are* afar off, what I have done;
And you *who are* near, acknowledge My
might."

¹⁴The sinners in Zion are afraid;
Fearfulness has seized the hypocrites:
"Who among us shall dwell with the
devouring fire?
Who among us shall dwell with everlasting
burnings?"
¹⁵He who walks righteously and speaks
uprightly,
He who despises the gain of oppressions,
Who gestures with his hands, refusing bribes,
Who stops his ears from hearing of
bloodshed,
And shuts his eyes from seeing evil:
¹⁶He will dwell on high;
His place of defense *will be* the fortress of
rocks;
Bread will be given him,
His water *will be* sure.

The Land of the Majestic King

¹⁷Your eyes will see the King in His beauty;
They will see the land that is very far off.
¹⁸Your heart will meditate on terror:
"Where *is* the scribe?
Where *is* he who weighs?
Where *is* he who counts the towers?"
¹⁹You will not see a fierce people,
A people of obscure speech, beyond
perception,
Of a stammering tongue *that you* cannot
understand.

²⁰Look upon Zion, the city of our appointed
feasts;

Your eyes will see Jerusalem, a quiet home,
A tabernacle *that* will not be taken down;
Not one of its stakes will ever be removed,
Nor will any of its cords be broken.
²¹But there the majestic LORD *will be* for us
A place of broad rivers *and* streams,
In which no galley with oars will sail,
Nor majestic ships pass by
²²(For the LORD *is* our Judge,
The LORD *is* our Lawgiver,
The LORD *is* our King;
He will save us);
²³Your tackle is loosed,
They could not strengthen their mast,
They could not spread the sail.

Then the prey of great plunder is divided;
The lame take the prey.
²⁴And the inhabitant will not say, "I am sick";
The people who dwell in it *will be* forgiven
their iniquity.

Judgment on the Nations

34 Come near, you nations, to hear;
And heed, you people!
Let the earth hear, and all that is in it,
The world and all things that come forth
from it.
²For the indignation of the LORD *is* against all
nations,
And *His* fury against all their armies;
He has utterly destroyed them,
He has given them over to the slaughter.
³Also their slain shall be thrown out;
Their stench shall rise from their corpses,
And the mountains shall be melted with their
blood.
⁴All the host of heaven shall be dissolved,
And the heavens shall be rolled up like a
scroll;
All their host shall fall down
As the leaf falls from the vine,
And as *fruit* falling from a fig tree.

⁵"For My sword shall be bathed in heaven;
Indeed it shall come down on Edom,
And on the people of My curse, for
judgment.
⁶The sword of the LORD is filled with blood,

It is made overflowing with fatness,
With the blood of lambs and goats,
With the fat of the kidneys of rams.
For the LORD has a sacrifice in Bozrah,
And a great slaughter in the land of Edom.
⁷The wild oxen shall come down with them,
And the young bulls with the mighty bulls;
Their land shall be soaked with blood,
And their dust saturated with fatness."

⁸For *it is* the day of the LORD's vengeance,
The year of recompense for the cause of
    Zion.
⁹Its streams shall be turned into pitch,
And its dust into brimstone;
Its land shall become burning pitch.
¹⁰It shall not be quenched night or day;
Its smoke shall ascend forever.
From generation to generation it shall lie
    waste;
No one shall pass through it forever and ever.
¹¹But the pelican and the porcupine shall
    possess it,
Also the owl and the raven shall dwell in it.
And He shall stretch out over it
The line of confusion and the stones of
    emptiness.
¹²They shall call its nobles to the kingdom,
But none *shall be* there, and all its princes shall
    be nothing.

¹³And thorns shall come up in its palaces,
Nettles and brambles in its fortresses;
It shall be a habitation of jackals,
A courtyard for ostriches.
¹⁴The wild beasts of the desert shall also meet
    with the jackals,
And the wild goat shall bleat to its
    companion;
Also the night creature shall rest there,
And find for herself a place of rest.
¹⁵There the arrow snake shall make her nest
    and lay *eggs*
And hatch, and gather *them* under her shadow;
There also shall the hawks be gathered,
Every one with her mate.

¹⁶"Search from the book of the LORD, and read:
Not one of these shall fail;

Not one shall lack her mate.
For My mouth has commanded it, and His
    Spirit has gathered them.
¹⁷He has cast the lot for them,
And His hand has divided it among them
    with a measuring line.
They shall possess it forever;
From generation to generation they shall
    dwell in it."

THE FUTURE GLORY OF ZION

35 The wilderness and the wasteland shall be
    glad for them,
And the desert shall rejoice and blossom as
    the rose;
²It shall blossom abundantly and rejoice,
Even with joy and singing.
The glory of Lebanon shall be given to it,
The excellence of Carmel and Sharon.
They shall see the glory of the LORD,
The excellency of our God.

³Strengthen the weak hands,
And make firm the feeble knees.
⁴Say to those *who are* fearful-hearted,
"Be strong, do not fear!
Behold, your God will come *with* vengeance,
With the recompense of God;
He will come and save you."

⁵Then the eyes of the blind shall be opened,
And the ears of the deaf shall be unstopped.
⁶Then the lame shall leap like a deer,
And the tongue of the dumb sing.
For waters shall burst forth in the wilderness,
And streams in the desert.
⁷The parched ground shall become a pool,
And the thirsty land springs of water;
In the habitation of jackals, where each lay,
There shall be grass with reeds and rushes.

⁸A highway shall be there, and a road,
And it shall be called the Highway of
    Holiness.
The unclean shall not pass over it,
But it *shall be* for others.
Whoever walks the road, although a fool,
Shall not go astray.
⁹No lion shall be there,

Nor shall *any* ravenous beast go up on it;
It shall not be found there.
But the redeemed shall walk *there,*
¹⁰And the ransomed of the LORD shall return,
And come to Zion with singing,
With everlasting joy on their heads.
They shall obtain joy and gladness,
And sorrow and sighing shall flee away.

SENNACHERIB BOASTS AGAINST THE LORD

36Now it came to pass in the fourteenth year of King Hezekiah *that* Sennacherib king of Assyria came up against all the fortified cities of Judah and took them. ²Then the king of Assyria sent *the* Rabshakehᵃ with a great army from Lachish to King Hezekiah at Jerusalem. And he stood by the aqueduct from the upper pool, on the highway to the Fuller's Field. ³And Eliakim the son of Hilkiah, who was over the household, Shebna the scribe, and Joah the son of Asaph, the recorder, came out to him.

⁴Then *the* Rabshakeh said to them, "Say now to Hezekiah, 'Thus says the great king, the king of Assyria: "What confidence is this in which you trust? ⁵I say you speak of having plans and power for war; but *they are* mere words. Now in whom do you trust, that you rebel against me? ⁶Look! You are trusting in the staff of this broken reed, Egypt, on which if a man leans, it will go into his hand and pierce it. So *is* Pharaoh king of Egypt to all who trust in him.

⁷"But if you say to me, 'We trust in the LORD our God,' *is it* not He whose high places and whose altars Hezekiah has taken away, and said to Judah and Jerusalem, 'You shall worship before this altar'?' ' ⁸Now therefore, I urge you, give a pledge to my master the king of Assyria, and I will give you two thousand horses—if you are able on your part to put riders on them! ⁹How then will you repel one captain of the least of my master's servants, and put your trust in Egypt for chariots and horsemen? ¹⁰Have I now come up without the LORD against this land to destroy it? The LORD said to me, 'Go up against this land, and destroy it.' "

¹¹Then Eliakim, Shebna, and Joah said to *the* Rabshakeh, "Please speak to your servants in Aramaic, for we understand *it;* and do not speak to us in Hebrewᵃ in the hearing of the people who *are* on the wall."

¹²But *the* Rabshakeh said, "Has my master sent me to your master and to you to speak these words, and not to the men who sit on the wall, who will eat and drink their own waste with you?"

¹³Then *the* Rabshakeh stood and called out with a loud voice in Hebrew, and said, "Hear the words of the great king, the king of Assyria! ¹⁴Thus says the king: 'Do not let Hezekiah deceive you, for he will not be able to deliver you; ¹⁵nor let Hezekiah make you trust in the LORD, saying, "The LORD will surely deliver us; this city will not be given into the hand of the king of Assyria." ' ¹⁶Do not listen to Hezekiah; for thus says the king of Assyria: 'Make *peace* with me *by a* present and come out to me; and every one of you eat from his own vine and every one from his own fig tree, and every one of you drink the waters of his own cistern; ¹⁷until I come and take you away to a land like your own land, a land of grain and new wine, a land of bread and vineyards. ¹⁸*Beware* lest Hezekiah persuade you, saying, "The LORD will deliver us." Has any one of the gods of the nations delivered its land from the hand of the king of Assyria? ¹⁹Where *are* the gods of Hamath and Arpad? Where *are* the gods of Sepharvaim? Indeed, have they delivered Samaria from my hand? ²⁰Who among all the gods of these lands have delivered their countries from my hand, that the LORD should deliver Jerusalem from my hand?' "

²¹But they held their peace and answered him not a word; for the king's commandment was, "Do not answer him." ²²Then Eliakim the son of Hilkiah, who *was* over the household, Shebna the scribe, and Joah the son of Asaph, the recorder, came to Hezekiah with *their* clothes torn, and told him the words of *the* Rabshakeh.

ISAIAH ASSURES DELIVERANCE

37And so it was, when King Hezekiah heard *it,* that he tore his clothes, covered himself with sackcloth, and went into the house of the LORD. ²Then he sent Eliakim, who *was* over the household, Shebna the scribe, and the elders of the priests, covered with sackcloth, to Isaiah the prophet, the son of Amoz. ³And they said to him,

36:2 ᵃA title, probably *Chief of Staff* or *Governor*   **36:11** ᵃLiterally *Judean*

"Thus says Hezekiah: 'This day *is* a day of trouble and rebuke and blasphemy; for the children have come to birth, but *there is* no strength to bring them forth. 4It may be that the LORD your God will hear the words of *the* Rabshakeh, whom his master the king of Assyria has sent to reproach the living God, and will rebuke the words which the LORD your God has heard. Therefore lift up *your* prayer for the remnant that is left.' "

5So the servants of King Hezekiah came to Isaiah. 6And Isaiah said to them, "Thus you shall say to your master, 'Thus says the LORD: "Do not be afraid of the words which you have heard, with which the servants of the king of Assyria have blasphemed Me. 7Surely I will send a spirit upon him, and he shall hear a rumor and return to his own land; and I will cause him to fall by the sword in his own land." ' "

Sennacherib's Threat and Hezekiah's Prayer

8Then *the* Rabshakeh returned, and found the king of Assyria warring against Libnah, for he heard that he had departed from Lachish. 9And the king heard concerning Tirhakah king of Ethiopia, "He has come out to make war with you." So when he heard *it,* he sent messengers to Hezekiah, saying, 10"Thus you shall speak to Hezekiah king of Judah, saying: 'Do not let your God in whom you trust deceive you, saying, "Jerusalem shall not be given into the hand of the king of Assyria." 11Look! You have heard what the kings of Assyria have done to all lands by utterly destroying them; and shall you be delivered? 12Have the gods of the nations delivered those whom my fathers have destroyed, Gozan and Haran and Rezeph, and the people of Eden who *were* in Telassar? 13Where *is* the king of Hamath, the king of Arpad, and the king of the city of Sepharvaim, Hena, and Ivah?' "

14And Hezekiah received the letter from the hand of the messengers, and read it; and Hezekiah went up to the house of the LORD, and spread it before the LORD. 15Then Hezekiah prayed to the LORD, saying: 16"O LORD of hosts, God of Israel, *the One* who dwells *between* the cherubim, You *are* God, You alone, of all the kingdoms of the earth. You have made heaven and earth. 17Incline Your ear, O LORD, and hear; open Your eyes, O LORD, and see; and hear all the words of Sennacherib,

which he has sent to reproach the living God. 18Truly, LORD, the kings of Assyria have laid waste all the nations and their lands, 19and have cast their gods into the fire; for they *were* not gods, but the work of men's hands—wood and stone. Therefore they destroyed them. 20Now therefore, O LORD our God, save us from his hand, that all the kingdoms of the earth may know that You *are* the LORD, You alone."

The Word of the Lord Concerning Sennacherib

21Then Isaiah the son of Amoz sent to Hezekiah, saying, "Thus says the LORD God of Israel, 'Because you have prayed to Me against Sennacherib king of Assyria, 22this *is* the word which the LORD has spoken concerning him:

"The virgin, the daughter of Zion,
Has despised you, laughed you to scorn;
The daughter of Jerusalem
Has shaken *her* head behind your back!

23"Whom have you reproached and
 blasphemed?
Against whom have you raised *your* voice,
And lifted up your eyes on high?
Against the Holy One of Israel.
24By your servants you have reproached the
 Lord,
And said, 'By the multitude of my chariots
I have come up to the height of the
 mountains,
To the limits of Lebanon;
I will cut down its tall cedars
And its choice cypress trees;
I will enter its farthest height,
To its fruitful forest.
25I have dug and drunk water,
And with the soles of my feet I have dried up
All the brooks of defense.'

26"Did you not hear long ago
How I made it,
From ancient times that I formed it?
Now I have brought it to pass,
That you should be
For crushing fortified cities *into* heaps of ruins.
27Therefore their inhabitants *had* little power;
They were dismayed and confounded;

They were *as* the grass of the field
And the green herb,
As the grass on the housetops
And grain blighted before it is grown.

28"But I know your dwelling place,
Your going out and your coming in,
And your rage against Me.
29Because your rage against Me and your tumult
Have come up to My ears,
Therefore I will put My hook in your nose
And My bridle in your lips,
And I will turn you back
By the way which you came." '

30"This *shall be* a sign to you:

You shall eat this year such as grows of itself,
And the second year what springs from the same;
Also in the third year sow and reap,
Plant vineyards and eat the fruit of them.
31And the remnant who have escaped of the house of Judah
Shall again take root downward,
And bear fruit upward.
32For out of Jerusalem shall go a remnant,
And those who escape from Mount Zion.
The zeal of the LORD of hosts will do this.

33"Therefore thus says the LORD concerning the king of Assyria:

'He shall not come into this city,
Nor shoot an arrow there,
Nor come before it with shield,
Nor build a siege mound against it.
34By the way that he came,
By the same shall he return;
And he shall not come into this city,'
Says the LORD.
35'For I will defend this city, to save it
For My own sake and for My servant David's sake.' "

SENNACHERIB'S DEFEAT AND DEATH

36Then the angel[a] of the LORD went out, and killed in the camp of the Assyrians one hundred and eighty-five thousand; and when *people* arose early in the morning, there were the corpses—all

dead. 37So Sennacherib king of Assyria departed and went away, returned *home,* and remained at Nineveh. 38Now it came to pass, as he was worshiping in the house of Nisroch his god, that his sons Adrammelech and Sharezer struck him down with the sword; and they escaped into the land of Ararat. Then Esarhaddon his son reigned in his place.

HEZEKIAH'S LIFE EXTENDED

38 In those days Hezekiah was sick and near death. And Isaiah the prophet, the son of Amoz, went to him and said to him, "Thus says the LORD: 'Set your house in order, for you shall die and not live.' "

2Then Hezekiah turned his face toward the wall, and prayed to the LORD, 3and said, "Remember now, O LORD, I pray, how I have walked before You in truth and with a loyal heart, and have done *what is* good in Your sight." And Hezekiah wept bitterly.

4And the word of the LORD came to Isaiah, saying, 5"Go and tell Hezekiah, 'Thus says the LORD, the God of David your father: "I have heard your prayer, I have seen your tears; surely I will add to your days fifteen years. 6I will deliver you and this city from the hand of the king of Assyria, and I will defend this city." ' 7And this *is* the sign to you from the LORD, that the LORD will do this thing which He has spoken: 8Behold, I will bring the shadow on the sundial, which has gone down with the sun on the sundial of Ahaz, ten degrees backward." So the sun returned ten degrees on the dial by which it had gone down.

9This is the writing of Hezekiah king of Judah, when he had been sick and had recovered from his sickness:

10I said,
"In the prime of my life
I shall go to the gates of Sheol;
I am deprived of the remainder of my years."
11I said,
"I shall not see YAH,
The LORD[a] in the land of the living;
I shall observe man no more among the inhabitants of the world.[b]

37:36 [a]Or *Angel* 38:11 [a]Hebrew *YAH, YAH* [b]Following some Hebrew manuscripts; Masoretic Text and Vulgate read *rest*; Septuagint omits *among the inhabitants of the world*; Targum reads *land.*

¹²My life span is gone,
Taken from me like a shepherd's tent;
I have cut off my life like a weaver.
He cuts me off from the loom;
From day until night You make an end of me.
¹³I have considered until morning—
Like a lion,
So He breaks all my bones;
From day until night You make an end of me.
¹⁴Like a crane *or* a swallow, so I chattered;
I mourned like a dove;
My eyes fail *from looking* upward.
O Lord,^a I am oppressed;
Undertake for me!

¹⁵"What shall I say?
He has both spoken to me,^a
And He Himself has done *it*.
I shall walk carefully all my years
In the bitterness of my soul.
¹⁶O Lord, by these *things men* live;
And in all these *things is* the life of my
    spirit;
So You will restore me and make me live.
¹⁷Indeed *it was* for *my own* peace
That I had great bitterness;
But You have lovingly *delivered* my soul from
    the pit of corruption,
For You have cast all my sins behind Your
    back.
¹⁸For Sheol cannot thank You,
Death cannot praise You;
Those who go down to the pit cannot hope
    for Your truth.
¹⁹The living, the living man, he shall
    praise You,
As I *do* this day;
The father shall make known Your truth to
    the children.

²⁰"The Lord *was ready* to save me;
Therefore we will sing my songs with
    stringed instruments
All the days of our life, in the house of the
    Lord."

²¹Now Isaiah had said, "Let them take a lump
of figs, and apply *it* as a poultice on the boil, and
he shall recover."

²²And Hezekiah had said, "What *is* the sign
that I shall go up to the house of the Lord?"

THE BABYLONIAN ENVOYS

39 At that time Merodach-Baladan^a the son of
Baladan, king of Babylon, sent letters and a
present to Hezekiah, for he heard that he had
been sick and had recovered. ²And Hezekiah was
pleased with them, and showed them the house
of his treasures—the silver and gold, the spices
and precious ointment, and all his armory—all
that was found among his treasures. There was
nothing in his house or in all his dominion that
Hezekiah did not show them.

³Then Isaiah the prophet went to King
Hezekiah, and said to him, "What did these men
say, and from where did they come to you?"

So Hezekiah said, "They came to me from a
far country, from Babylon."

⁴And he said, "What have they seen in your
house?"

So Hezekiah answered, "They have seen all
that *is* in my house; there is nothing among my
treasures that I have not shown them."

⁵Then Isaiah said to Hezekiah, "Hear the
word of the Lord of hosts: ⁶'Behold, the days are
coming when all that *is* in your house, and what
your fathers have accumulated until this day, shall
be carried to Babylon; nothing shall be left,' says
the Lord. ⁷'And they shall take away *some* of your
sons who will descend from you, whom you will
beget; and they shall be eunuchs in the palace of
the king of Babylon.' "

⁸So Hezekiah said to Isaiah, "The word of the
Lord which you have spoken *is* good!" For he
said, "At least there will be peace and truth in my
days."

GOD'S PEOPLE ARE COMFORTED

40 "Comfort, yes, comfort My people!"
Says your God.
²"Speak comfort to Jerusalem, and cry out to
    her,
That her warfare is ended,
That her iniquity is pardoned;

38:14 ^aFollowing Bomberg; Masoretic Text and Dead Sea Scrolls
read *Lord.*   38:15 ^aFollowing Masoretic Text and Vulgate; Dead Sea
Scrolls and Targum read *And shall I say to Him;* Septuagint omits
first half of this verse.   39:1 ^aSpelled *Berodach-Baladan* in 2 Kings
20:12

For she has received from the LORD's hand
Double for all her sins."

³The voice of one crying in the wilderness:
"Prepare the way of the LORD;
Make straight in the desert^a
A highway for our God.
⁴Every valley shall be exalted
And every mountain and hill brought low;
The crooked places shall be made straight
And the rough places smooth;
⁵The glory of the LORD shall be revealed,
And all flesh shall see it together;
For the mouth of the LORD has spoken."

⁶The voice said, "Cry out!"
And he^a said, "What shall I cry?"

"All flesh is grass,
And all its loveliness is like the flower of the
field.
⁷The grass withers, the flower fades,
Because the breath of the LORD blows
upon it;
Surely the people are grass.
⁸The grass withers, the flower fades,
But the word of our God stands forever."

⁹O Zion,
You who bring good tidings,
Get up into the high mountain;
O Jerusalem,
You who bring good tidings,
Lift up your voice with strength,
Lift it up, be not afraid;
Say to the cities of Judah, "Behold your God!"

¹⁰Behold, the Lord GOD shall come with a
strong hand,
And His arm shall rule for Him;
Behold, His reward is with Him,
And His work before Him.
¹¹He will feed His flock like a shepherd;
He will gather the lambs with His arm,
And carry them in His bosom,
And gently lead those who are with young.

¹²Who has measured the waters^a in the hollow
of His hand,

Measured heaven with a span
And calculated the dust of the earth in a
measure?
Weighed the mountains in scales
And the hills in a balance?
¹³Who has directed the Spirit of the LORD,
Or as His counselor has taught Him?
¹⁴With whom did He take counsel, and who
instructed Him,
And taught Him in the path of justice?
Who taught Him knowledge,
And showed Him the way of understanding?

¹⁵Behold, the nations are as a drop in a bucket,
And are counted as the small dust on the
scales;
Look, He lifts up the isles as a very little
thing.
¹⁶And Lebanon is not sufficient to burn,
Nor its beasts sufficient for a burnt offering.
¹⁷All nations before Him are as nothing,
And they are counted by Him less than
nothing and worthless.

¹⁸To whom then will you liken God?
Or what likeness will you compare to Him?
¹⁹The workman molds an image,
The goldsmith overspreads it with gold,
And the silversmith casts silver chains.
²⁰Whoever is too impoverished for such a
contribution
Chooses a tree that will not rot;
He seeks for himself a skillful workman
To prepare a carved image that will not
totter.

²¹Have you not known?
Have you not heard?
Has it not been told you from the
beginning?
Have you not understood from the
foundations of the earth?
²²It is He who sits above the circle of the earth,
And its inhabitants are like grasshoppers,
Who stretches out the heavens like a curtain,

40:3 ^aFollowing Masoretic Text, Targum, and Vulgate; Septuagint omits in the desert. **40:6** ^aFollowing Masoretic Text and Targum; Dead Sea Scrolls, Septuagint, and Vulgate read I. **40:12** ^aFollowing Masoretic Text, Septuagint, and Vulgate; Dead Sea Scrolls read waters of the sea; Targum reads waters of the world.

And spreads them out like a tent to dwell in.
²³He brings the princes to nothing;
He makes the judges of the earth useless.

²⁴Scarcely shall they be planted,
Scarcely shall they be sown,
Scarcely shall their stock take root in the
earth,
When He will also blow on them,
And they will wither,
And the whirlwind will take them away like
stubble.

²⁵"To whom then will you liken Me,
Or *to whom* shall I be equal?" says the Holy
One.

²⁶Lift up your eyes on high,
And see who has created these *things,*
Who brings out their host by number;
He calls them all by name,
By the greatness of His might
And the strength of *His* power;
Not one is missing.

²⁷Why do you say, O Jacob,
And speak, O Israel:
"My way is hidden from the LORD,
And my just claim is passed over by my
God"?
²⁸Have you not known?
Have you not heard?
The everlasting God, the LORD,

LEADERSHIP
REALITIES

ENDURANCE *Isaiah 40:29, 31*

All of us can be characterized as *weak* at some points of our lives. Not only do we have a sin nature, but we are constantly surrounded by evil in the world. We get assaulted with temptation and sometimes with discouragement. It is important for us to focus on God's unchanging, faithful love and power and to believe that He is willing to impart or freely share this power with anyone who will *wait* for it.

qavah—**wait**—look for, hope, expect, look eagerly for

Wait on the Lord: Expect Him to come through;

Have confidence in both His power and His love;

Believe God will be there when you need Him to be;

Know that He is worth the wait.

God promises that when you wait, He will *renew* your strength; that is, He will **make the exchange** of His power for your weakness and His endurance for your weariness.

The result of the exchange is that we:

- *mount up* over **circumstance.** We can fly higher and stronger, above adversity, disappointment, betrayal, or failure.
- *run* from **carnal** self with victory over laziness, procrastination, and lack of focus. We are able to accomplish goals with a strong heart.
- *walk every day* through the **crowd** without giving in to the attitude of "whatever."
- *faint not,* but we endure as faithful servants of purpose, passion, and moral purity. Do not allow yourself to be weary in the good works of life (2 Thess. 3:13).

The Creator of the ends of the earth,
Neither faints nor is weary.
His understanding is unsearchable.
²⁹He gives power to the weak,
    And to *those who have* no might He increases
        strength.
³⁰Even the youths shall faint and be weary,
    And the young men shall utterly fall,
³¹But those who wait on the LORD
    Shall renew *their* strength;
They shall mount up with wings like eagles,
    They shall run and not be weary,
    They shall walk and not faint.

ISRAEL ASSURED OF GOD'S HELP

41 "Keep silence before Me, O coastlands,
    And let the people renew *their* strength!
Let them come near, then let them speak;
Let us come near together for judgment.

²"Who raised up one from the east?
    Who in righteousness called him to His
        feet?
Who gave the nations before him,
    And made *him* rule over kings?
Who gave *them* as the dust *to* his sword,
    As driven stubble to his bow?
³Who pursued them, *and* passed safely

By the way *that* he had not gone with his
    feet?
⁴Who has performed and done *it,*
    Calling the generations from the beginning?
'I, the LORD, am the first;
    And with the last I *am* He.' "

⁵The coastlands saw *it* and feared,
    The ends of the earth were afraid;
    They drew near and came.
⁶Everyone helped his neighbor,
    And said to his brother,
    "Be of good courage!"
⁷So the craftsman encouraged the goldsmith;
    He who smooths *with* the hammer *inspired*
        him who strikes the anvil,
    Saying, "It *is* ready for the soldering";
    Then he fastened it with pegs,
    That it might not totter.

⁸"But you, Israel, *are* My servant,
    Jacob whom I have chosen,
    The descendants of Abraham My friend.
⁹*You* whom I have taken from the ends of the
        earth,
    And called from its farthest regions,
    And said to you,
    'You *are* My servant,

THROUGH THE GRID

Discover God: God Uses His Power on Our Behalf

ISAIAH 40:29 *He gives power to the weak, and to those who have no might He increases strength.*

How does God use power? Although one could imagine all the different ways in which God could demonstrate power, God chooses to use power on behalf of those who follow Him. This means that the power of God is available to believers who allow God to work through their lives. Central to this understanding is the notion that God, indeed, has a plan for the world and for all the individuals therein, and that God remains in control of all that happens. God's infinite power is never used to bring about evil, nor do God's powers correspond to the magic of a genie in a bottle. God uses His power to bring His will about in our lives. The most significant demonstration of this centers on the life, ministry, and total obedience of Jesus Christ. Through God's power, we ourselves have the ability to do the following: conquer evil forces, live a holy life, proclaim the gospel, and fulfill God's plan for our own lives.

I have chosen you and have not cast you
away:
¹⁰Fear not, for I *am* with you;
Be not dismayed, for I *am* your God.
I will strengthen you,
Yes, I will help you,
I will uphold you with My righteous right
hand.'

¹¹"Behold, all those who were incensed against
you
Shall be ashamed and disgraced;
They shall be as nothing,
And those who strive with you shall perish.
¹²You shall seek them and not find them—
Those who contended with you.
Those who war against you
Shall be as nothing,
As a nonexistent thing.
¹³For I, the LORD your God, will hold your
right hand,
Saying to you, 'Fear not, I will help you.'

¹⁴"Fear not, you worm Jacob,
You men of Israel!
I will help you," says the LORD
And your Redeemer, the Holy One of Israel.
¹⁵"Behold, I will make you into a new threshing
sledge with sharp teeth;
You shall thresh the mountains and beat *them*
small,
And make the hills like chaff.
¹⁶You shall winnow them, the wind shall carry
them away,
And the whirlwind shall scatter them;
You shall rejoice in the LORD,
And glory in the Holy One of Israel.

¹⁷"The poor and needy seek water, but *there is*
none,
Their tongues fail for thirst.
I, the LORD, will hear them;
I, the God of Israel, will not forsake them.
¹⁸I will open rivers in desolate heights,
And fountains in the midst of the valleys;
I will make the wilderness a pool of water,
And the dry land springs of water.
¹⁹I will plant in the wilderness the cedar and
the acacia tree,

The myrtle and the oil tree;
I will set in the desert the cypress tree *and* the
pine
And the box tree together,
²⁰That they may see and know,
And consider and understand together,
That the hand of the LORD has done this,
And the Holy One of Israel has created it.

THE FUTILITY OF IDOLS

²¹"Present your case," says the LORD.
"Bring forth your strong *reasons,*" says the King
of Jacob.
²²"Let them bring forth and show us what will
happen;
Let them show the former things, what they
were,
That we may consider them,
And know the latter end of them;
Or declare to us things to come.
²³Show the things that are to come hereafter,
That we may know that you *are* gods;
Yes, do good or do evil,
That we may be dismayed and see *it*
together.
²⁴Indeed you *are* nothing,
And your work *is* nothing;
He who chooses you *is* an abomination.

²⁵"I have raised up one from the north,
And he shall come;
From the rising of the sun he shall call on
My name;
And he shall come against princes as *though*
mortar,
As the potter treads clay.
²⁶Who has declared from the beginning, that
we may know?
And former times, that we may say, '*He is*
righteous'?
Surely *there is* no one who shows,
Surely *there is* no one who declares,
Surely *there is* no one who hears your
words.
²⁷The first time *I said* to Zion,
'Look, there they are!'
And I will give to Jerusalem one who brings
good tidings.
²⁸For I looked, and *there was* no man;

I looked among them, but *there was* no
  counselor,
Who, when I asked of them, could answer a
  word.
[29]Indeed they *are* all worthless;[a]
  Their works *are* nothing;
  Their molded images *are* wind and
    confusion.

THE SERVANT OF THE LORD

42 "Behold! My Servant whom I uphold,
  My Elect One *in whom* My soul delights!
I have put My Spirit upon Him;
  He will bring forth justice to the Gentiles.
[2]He will not cry out, nor raise *His voice,*
  Nor cause His voice to be heard in the street.
[3]A bruised reed He will not break,
  And smoking flax He will not quench;
  He will bring forth justice for truth.
[4]He will not fail nor be discouraged,
  Till He has established justice in the earth;
  And the coastlands shall wait for His law."

[5]Thus says God the LORD,
  Who created the heavens and stretched them
    out,
  Who spread forth the earth and that which
    comes from it,
  Who gives breath to the people on it,
  And spirit to those who walk on it:
[6]"I, the LORD, have called You in righteousness,
  And will hold Your hand;
  I will keep You and give You as a covenant to
    the people,
  As a light to the Gentiles,
[7]To open blind eyes,
  To bring out prisoners from the prison,
  Those who sit in darkness from the prison
    house.
[8]I *am* the LORD, that *is* My name;
  And My glory I will not give to another,
  Nor My praise to carved images.
[9]Behold, the former things have come to pass,
  And new things I declare;
  Before they spring forth I tell you of them."

PRAISE TO THE LORD

[10]Sing to the LORD a new song,
  And His praise from the ends of the earth,

You who go down to the sea, and all that is in
  it,
You coastlands and you inhabitants of them!
[11]Let the wilderness and its cities lift up *their
  voice,*
  The villages *that* Kedar inhabits.
  Let the inhabitants of Sela sing,
  Let them shout from the top of the
    mountains.
[12]Let them give glory to the LORD,
  And declare His praise in the coastlands.
[13]The LORD shall go forth like a mighty man;
  He shall stir up *His* zeal like a man of war.
  He shall cry out, yes, shout aloud;
  He shall prevail against His enemies.

PROMISE OF THE LORD'S HELP

[14]"I have held My peace a long time,
  I have been still and restrained Myself.
  Now I will cry like a woman in labor,
  I will pant and gasp at once.
[15]I will lay waste the mountains and hills,
  And dry up all their vegetation;
  I will make the rivers coastlands,
  And I will dry up the pools.
[16]I will bring the blind by a way they did not
    know;
  I will lead them in paths they have not
    known.
  I will make darkness light before them,
  And crooked places straight.
  These things I will do for them,
  And not forsake them.
[17]They shall be turned back,
  They shall be greatly ashamed,
  Who trust in carved images,
  Who say to the molded images,
  'You *are* our gods.'

[18]"Hear, you deaf;
  And look, you blind, that you may see.
[19]Who *is* blind but My servant,
  Or deaf as My messenger *whom* I send?
  Who *is* blind as *he who is* perfect,
  And blind as the LORD's servant?
[20]Seeing many things, but you do not observe;
  Opening the ears, but he does not hear."

41:29 [a]Following Masoretic Text and Vulgate; Dead Sea Scrolls, Syriac, and Targum read *nothing;* Septuagint omits the first line.

ISRAEL'S OBSTINATE DISOBEDIENCE

21The LORD is well pleased for His
 righteousness' sake;
He will exalt the law and make *it* honorable.
22But this *is* a people robbed and plundered;
All of them are snared in holes,
And they are hidden in prison houses;
They are for prey, and no one delivers;
For plunder, and no one says, "Restore!"

23Who among you will give ear to this?
Who will listen and hear for the time to
 come?
24Who gave Jacob for plunder, and Israel to the
 robbers?
Was it not the LORD,
He against whom we have sinned?
For they would not walk in His ways,
Nor were they obedient to His law.
25Therefore He has poured on him the fury of
 His anger
And the strength of battle;
It has set him on fire all around,
Yet he did not know;
And it burned him,
Yet he did not take *it* to heart.

THE REDEEMER OF ISRAEL

43 But now, thus says the LORD, who created
 you, O Jacob,
And He who formed you, O Israel:
"Fear not, for I have redeemed you;
I have called *you* by your name;
You *are* Mine.
2When you pass through the waters, I *will be*
 with you;
And through the rivers, they shall not
 overflow you.
When you walk through the fire, you shall
 not be burned,
Nor shall the flame scorch you.
3For I *am* the LORD your God,
The Holy One of Israel, your Savior;
I gave Egypt for your ransom,
Ethiopia and Seba in your place.
4Since you were precious in My sight,
You have been honored,
And I have loved you;

Therefore I will give men for you,
And people for your life.
5Fear not, for I *am* with you;
I will bring your descendants from the east,
And gather you from the west;
6I will say to the north, 'Give them up!'
And to the south, 'Do not keep them
 back!'
Bring My sons from afar,
And My daughters from the ends of the
 earth—
7Everyone who is called by My name,
Whom I have created for My glory;
I have formed him, yes, I have made him."

8Bring out the blind people who have eyes,
And the deaf who have ears.
9Let all the nations be gathered together,
And let the people be assembled.
Who among them can declare this,
And show us former things?
Let them bring out their witnesses, that they
 may be justified;
Or let them hear and say, "*It is* truth."
10"You *are* My witnesses," says the LORD,
"And My servant whom I have chosen,
That you may know and believe Me,
And understand that I *am* He.
Before Me there was no God formed,
Nor shall there be after Me.
11I, *even* I, *am* the LORD,
And besides Me *there is* no savior.
12I have declared and saved,
I have proclaimed,
And *there was* no foreign *god* among you;
Therefore you *are* My witnesses,"
Says the LORD, "that I *am* God.
13Indeed before the day *was,* I *am* He;
And *there is* no one who can deliver out of
 My hand;
I work, and who will reverse it?"

14Thus says the LORD, your Redeemer,
The Holy One of Israel:
"For your sake I will send to Babylon,
And bring them all down as fugitives—
The Chaldeans, who rejoice in their ships.
15I *am* the LORD, your Holy One,
The Creator of Israel, your King."

THROUGH THE GRID

Making Sense of Your World:
Confronting God in Theism (Is. 43:10)

Transcendentalists view the term "god" as the life force shared by all things. However, theism sees God differently by conceiving of God as One who is separate from the natural world. Most theists agree to a creation of matter, the universe, and humanity by God; and so God differs because God is uncreated. Theism, in part, attempts to prove the existence of God. That is, it attempts to demonstrate that God exists, not so much by finite examples, but through argumentation that utilizes the natural world as well as personal experiences. The three major proofs for God's existence include the cosmological argument (that the universe exists), the teleological argument (design within creation), and the moral argument (humanity's morality must originate from a source).

¹⁶Thus says the LORD, who makes a way in the
  sea
  And a path through the mighty waters,
¹⁷Who brings forth the chariot and horse,
  The army and the power
  (They shall lie down together, they shall not
    rise;
  They are extinguished, they are quenched like
    a wick):
¹⁸"Do not remember the former things,
  Nor consider the things of old.
¹⁹Behold, I will do a new thing,
  Now it shall spring forth;
  Shall you not know it?
  I will even make a road in the wilderness
  And rivers in the desert.
²⁰The beast of the field will honor Me,
  The jackals and the ostriches,
  Because I give waters in the wilderness
  And rivers in the desert,
  To give drink to My people, My chosen.
²¹This people I have formed for Myself;
  They shall declare My praise.

Pleading with Unfaithful Israel

²²"But you have not called upon Me, O Jacob;
  And you have been weary of Me, O Israel.
²³You have not brought Me the sheep for your
    burnt offerings,
  Nor have you honored Me with your
    sacrifices.
  I have not caused you to serve with grain
    offerings,
  Nor wearied you with incense.

²⁴You have bought Me no sweet cane with
    money,
  Nor have you satisfied Me with the fat of
    your sacrifices;
  But you have burdened Me with your sins,
  You have wearied Me with your iniquities.

²⁵"I, *even* I, *am* He who blots out your
    transgressions for My own sake;
  And I will not remember your sins.
²⁶Put Me in remembrance;
  Let us contend together;
  State your *case*, that you may be acquitted.
²⁷Your first father sinned,
  And your mediators have transgressed against
    Me.
²⁸Therefore I will profane the princes of the
    sanctuary;
  I will give Jacob to the curse,
  And Israel to reproaches.

God's Blessing on Israel

44 "Yet hear now, O Jacob My servant,
  And Israel whom I have chosen.
²Thus says the LORD who made you
  And formed you from the womb, *who* will
    help you:
  'Fear not, O Jacob My servant;
  And you, Jeshurun, whom I have chosen.
³For I will pour water on him who is thirsty,
  And floods on the dry ground;
  I will pour My Spirit on your descendants,
  And My blessing on your offspring;
⁴They will spring up among the grass

Like willows by the watercourses.'
⁵One will say, 'I *am* the LORD's';
Another will call *himself* by the name of Jacob;
Another will write *with* his hand, 'The
LORD's,'
And name *himself* by the name of Israel.

THERE IS NO OTHER GOD

⁶"Thus says the LORD, the King of Israel,
And his Redeemer, the LORD of hosts:
"I *am* the First and I *am* the Last;
Besides Me *there is* no God.
⁷And who can proclaim as I do?
Then let him declare it and set it in order for
Me,
Since I appointed the ancient people.
And the things that are coming and shall
come,
Let them show these to them.
⁸Do not fear, nor be afraid;
Have I not told you from that time, and
declared *it?*
You *are* My witnesses.
Is there a God besides Me?
Indeed *there is* no other Rock;
I know not *one.*' "

IDOLATRY IS FOOLISHNESS

⁹Those who make an image, all of them *are*
useless,
And their precious things shall not profit;
They *are* their own witnesses;
They neither see nor know, that they may be
ashamed.
¹⁰Who would form a god or mold an image
That profits him nothing?
¹¹Surely all his companions would be ashamed;
And the workmen, they *are* mere men.
Let them all be gathered together,
Let them stand up;
Yet they shall fear,
They shall be ashamed together.

¹²The blacksmith with the tongs works one in
the coals,
Fashions it with hammers,
And works it with the strength of his arms.
Even so, he is hungry, and his strength fails;
He drinks no water and is faint.

¹³The craftsman stretches out *his* rule,
He marks one out with chalk;
He fashions it with a plane,
He marks it out with the compass,
And makes it like the figure of a man,
According to the beauty of a man, that it may
remain in the house.
¹⁴He cuts down cedars for himself,
And takes the cypress and the oak;
He secures *it* for himself among the trees of
the forest.
He plants a pine, and the rain nourishes *it.*

¹⁵Then it shall be for a man to burn,
For he will take some of it and warm himself;
Yes, he kindles *it* and bakes bread;
Indeed he makes a god and worships *it;*
He makes it a carved image, and falls down to
it.
¹⁶He burns half of it in the fire;
With this half he eats meat;
He roasts a roast, and is satisfied.
He even warms *himself* and says,
"Ah! I am warm,
I have seen the fire."
¹⁷And the rest of it he makes into a god,
His carved image.
He falls down before it and worships *it,*
Prays to it and says,
"Deliver me, for you *are* my god!"

¹⁸They do not know nor understand;
For He has shut their eyes, so that they
cannot see,
And their hearts, so that they cannot
understand.
¹⁹And no one considers in his heart,
Nor *is there* knowledge nor understanding to
say,
"I have burned half of it in the fire,
Yes, I have also baked bread on its coals;
I have roasted meat and eaten *it;*
And shall I make the rest of it an
abomination?
Shall I fall down before a block of wood?"
²⁰He feeds on ashes;
A deceived heart has turned him aside;
And he cannot deliver his soul,
Nor say, "*Is there* not a lie in my right hand?"

ISRAEL IS NOT FORGOTTEN

21"Remember these, O Jacob,
And Israel, for you *are* My servant;
I have formed you, you *are* My servant;
O Israel, you will not be forgotten by Me!
22I have blotted out, like a thick cloud, your
transgressions,
And like a cloud, your sins.
Return to Me, for I have redeemed you."

23Sing, O heavens, for the LORD has done *it!*
Shout, you lower parts of the earth;
Break forth into singing, you mountains,
O forest, and every tree in it!
For the LORD has redeemed Jacob,
And glorified Himself in Israel.

JUDAH WILL BE RESTORED

24Thus says the LORD, your Redeemer,
And He who formed you from the womb:
"I *am* the LORD, who makes all *things,*
Who stretches out the heavens all alone,
Who spreads abroad the earth by Myself;
25Who frustrates the signs of the babblers,
And drives diviners mad;
Who turns wise men backward,
And makes their knowledge foolishness;
26Who confirms the word of His servant,
And performs the counsel of His messengers;
Who says to Jerusalem, 'You shall be
inhabited,'
To the cities of Judah, 'You shall be built,'
And I will raise up her waste places;
27Who says to the deep, 'Be dry!
And I will dry up your rivers';
28Who says of Cyrus, '*He is* My shepherd,
And he shall perform all My pleasure,
Saying to Jerusalem, "You shall be built,"
And to the temple, "Your foundation shall be
laid." '

CYRUS, GOD'S INSTRUMENT

45 "Thus says the LORD to His anointed,
To Cyrus, whose right hand I have
held—
To subdue nations before him
And loose the armor of kings,
To open before him the double doors,

So that the gates will not be shut:
2'I will go before you
And make the crooked places[a] straight;
I will break in pieces the gates of bronze
And cut the bars of iron.
3I will give you the treasures of darkness
And hidden riches of secret places,
That you may know that I, the LORD,
Who call *you* by your name,
Am the God of Israel.
4For Jacob My servant's sake,
And Israel My elect,
I have even called you by your name;
I have named you, though you have not
known Me.
5I *am* the LORD, and *there is* no other;
There is no God besides Me.
I will gird you, though you have not known
Me,
6That they may know from the rising of the
sun to its setting
That *there is* none besides Me.
I *am* the LORD, and *there is* no other;
7I form the light and create darkness,
I make peace and create calamity;
I, the LORD, do all these *things.'*

8"Rain down, you heavens, from above,
And let the skies pour down
righteousness;
Let the earth open, let them bring forth
salvation,
And let righteousness spring up together.
I, the LORD, have created it.

9"Woe to him who strives with his Maker!
Let the potsherd *strive* with the potsherds of
the earth!
Shall the clay say to him who forms it, 'What
are you making?'
Or shall your handiwork *say,* 'He has no
hands'?
10Woe to him who says to *his* father, 'What are
you begetting?'
Or to the woman, 'What have you brought
forth?' "

45:2 [a]Dead Sea Scrolls and Septuagint read *mountains;* Targum
reads *I will trample down the walls;* Vulgate reads *I will humble the
great ones of the earth.*

[11]Thus says the LORD,
The Holy One of Israel, and his Maker:
"Ask Me of things to come concerning My
   sons;
And concerning the work of My hands, you
   command Me.
[12]I have made the earth,
And created man on it.
I—My hands—stretched out the heavens,
And all their host I have commanded.
[13]I have raised him up in righteousness,
And I will direct all his ways;
He shall build My city
And let My exiles go free,
Not for price nor reward,"
Says the LORD of hosts.

THE LORD, THE ONLY SAVIOR

[14]Thus says the LORD:

"The labor of Egypt and merchandise of Cush
And of the Sabeans, men of stature,
Shall come over to you, and they shall be
   yours;
They shall walk behind you,
They shall come over in chains;
And they shall bow down to you.
They will make supplication to you, *saying,*
   'Surely God *is* in you,
And *there is* no other;
There is no other God.' "

[15]Truly You *are* God, who hide Yourself,
O God of Israel, the Savior!
[16]They shall be ashamed
And also disgraced, all of them;
They shall go in confusion together,
Who are makers of idols.
[17]*But* Israel shall be saved by the LORD
With an everlasting salvation;
You shall not be ashamed or disgraced
Forever and ever.

[18]For thus says the LORD,
Who created the heavens,
Who is God,
Who formed the earth and made it,
Who has established it,
Who did not create it in vain,
Who formed it to be inhabited:
"I *am* the LORD, and *there is* no other.
[19]I have not spoken in secret,
In a dark place of the earth;
I did not say to the seed of Jacob,
'Seek Me in vain';
I, the LORD, speak righteousness,
I declare things that are right.

[20]"Assemble yourselves and come;
Draw near together,
You *who have* escaped from the nations.
They have no knowledge,
Who carry the wood of their carved image,

THROUGH THE GRID

*Making Sense of Your World:
Confronting Humanity in Theism
(Is. 45:12)*

Theistic understandings of humanity center on questions of human existence. Why do we exist? For what purpose were we created? How are we to live as created beings? The answers to such deep questions cannot be answered in the human realm, but they require answers from beyond our own abilities and thoughts. Theists believe that they have been brought into existence by a creator God, who has a purpose for every living being. Our existence as human beings centers on dependence, dignity, and dominion. Theists maintain that they are not independent, but rather, that they are dependent on God, that their dignity is based in God as part of creation, and that they are to have a protective dominion over nature. While the naturalist claims that there is no God and the transcendentalist claims that all are god, the theist insists that each person *belongs* to God.

And pray to a god *that* cannot save.
²¹Tell and bring forth *your case;*
Yes, let them take counsel together.
Who has declared this from ancient time?
Who has told it from that time?
Have not I, the LORD?
And *there is* no other God besides Me,
A just God and a Savior;
There is none besides Me.

²²"Look to Me, and be saved,
All you ends of the earth!
For I *am* God, and *there is* no other.
²³I have sworn by Myself;
The word has gone out of My mouth *in*
righteousness,
And shall not return,
That to Me every knee shall bow,
Every tongue shall take an oath.
²⁴He shall say,
"Surely in the LORD I have righteousness and
strength.
To Him *men* shall come,
And all shall be ashamed
Who are incensed against Him.
²⁵In the LORD all the descendants of Israel
Shall be justified, and shall glory.' "

Dead Idols and the Living God

46 Bel bows down, Nebo stoops;
Their idols were on the beasts and on the
cattle.
Your carriages *were* heavily loaded,
A burden to the weary *beast.*
²They stoop, they bow down together;
They could not deliver the burden,
But have themselves gone into captivity.

³"Listen to Me, O house of Jacob,
And all the remnant of the house of Israel,
Who have been upheld *by Me* from birth,
Who have been carried from the womb:
⁴Even to *your* old age, I *am* He,
And *even* to gray hairs I will carry *you!*
I have made, and I will bear;
Even I will carry, and will deliver *you.*

⁵"To whom will you liken Me, and make *Me*
equal

And compare Me, that we should be alike?
⁶They lavish gold out of the bag,
And weigh silver on the scales;
They hire a goldsmith, and he makes it a
god;
They prostrate themselves, yes, they worship.
⁷They bear it on the shoulder, they carry it
And set it in its place, and it stands;
From its place it shall not move.
Though *one* cries out to it, yet it cannot
answer
Nor save him out of his trouble.

⁸"Remember this, and show yourselves men;
Recall to mind, O you transgressors.
⁹Remember the former things of old,
For I *am* God, and *there is* no other;
I am God, and *there is* none like Me,
¹⁰Declaring the end from the beginning,
And from ancient times *things* that are not *yet*
done,
Saying, 'My counsel shall stand,
And I will do all My pleasure,'
¹¹Calling a bird of prey from the east,
The man who executes My counsel, from a
far country.
Indeed I have spoken *it;*
I will also bring it to pass.
I have purposed *it;*
I will also do it.

¹²"Listen to Me, you stubborn-hearted,
Who *are* far from righteousness:
¹³I bring My righteousness near, it shall not be
far off;
My salvation shall not linger.
And I will place salvation in Zion,
For Israel My glory.

The Humiliation of Babylon

47 "Come down and sit in the dust,
O virgin daughter of Babylon;
Sit on the ground without a throne,
O daughter of the Chaldeans!
For you shall no more be called
Tender and delicate.
²Take the millstones and grind meal.
Remove your veil,
Take off the skirt,

Uncover the thigh,
Pass through the rivers.
³Your nakedness shall be uncovered,
Yes, your shame will be seen;
I will take vengeance,
And I will not arbitrate with a man."

⁴*As for* our Redeemer, the LORD of hosts *is*
     His name,
The Holy One of Israel.

⁵"Sit in silence, and go into darkness,
O daughter of the Chaldeans;
For you shall no longer be called
The Lady of Kingdoms.
⁶I was angry with My people;
I have profaned My inheritance,
And given them into your hand.
You showed them no mercy;
On the elderly you laid your yoke very
     heavily.
⁷And you said, 'I shall be a lady forever,'
So that you did not take these *things* to heart,
Nor remember the latter end of them.

⁸"Therefore hear this now, *you who are* given to
     pleasures,
Who dwell securely,
Who say in your heart, 'I *am*, and *there is* no
     one else besides me;
I shall not sit *as* a widow,
Nor shall I know the loss of children';
⁹But these two *things* shall come to you
In a moment, in one day:
The loss of children, and widowhood.
They shall come upon you in their fullness
Because of the multitude of your sorceries,
For the great abundance of your
     enchantments.

¹⁰"For you have trusted in your wickedness;
You have said, 'No one sees me';
Your wisdom and your knowledge have
     warped you;
And you have said in your heart,
"I *am*, and *there is* no one else besides me.'
¹¹Therefore evil shall come upon you;
You shall not know from where it arises.
And trouble shall fall upon you;

You will not be able to put it off.
And desolation shall come upon you
     suddenly,
Which you shall not know.

¹²"Stand now with your enchantments
And the multitude of your sorceries,
In which you have labored from your
     youth—
Perhaps you will be able to profit,
Perhaps you will prevail.
¹³You are wearied in the multitude of your
     counsels;
Let now the astrologers, the stargazers,
And the monthly prognosticators
Stand up and save you
From what shall come upon you.
¹⁴Behold, they shall be as stubble,
The fire shall burn them;
They shall not deliver themselves
From the power of the flame;
It shall not *be* a coal to be warmed by,
Nor a fire to sit before!
¹⁵Thus shall they be to you
With whom you have labored,
Your merchants from your youth;
They shall wander each one to his quarter.
No one shall save you.

ISRAEL REFINED FOR GOD'S GLORY

48 "Hear this, O house of Jacob,
Who are called by the name of Israel,
And have come forth from the wellsprings of
     Judah;
Who swear by the name of the LORD,
And make mention of the God of Israel,
But not in truth or in righteousness;
²For they call themselves after the holy city,
And lean on the God of Israel;
The LORD of hosts *is* His name:

³"I have declared the former things from the
     beginning;
They went forth from My mouth, and I
     caused them to hear it.
Suddenly I did *them,* and they came to pass.
⁴Because I knew that you *were* obstinate,
And your neck *was* an iron sinew,
And your brow bronze,

⁵Even from the beginning I have declared *it* to
  you;
Before it came to pass I proclaimed *it* to you,
Lest you should say, 'My idol has done them,
And my carved image and my molded image
Have commanded them.'

⁶"You have heard;
  See all this.
  And will you not declare *it?*
  I have made you hear new things from this
    time,
  Even hidden things, and you did not know
    them.
⁷They are created now and not from the
    beginning;
  And before this day you have not heard
    them,
  Lest you should say, 'Of course I knew them.'
⁸Surely you did not hear,
  Surely you did not know;
  Surely from long ago your ear was not
    opened.
  For I knew that you would deal very
    treacherously,
  And were called a transgressor from the
    womb.

⁹"For My name's sake I will defer My anger,
  And *for* My praise I will restrain it from you,
  So that I do not cut you off.
¹⁰Behold, I have refined you, but not as silver;
  I have tested you in the furnace of affliction.
¹¹For My own sake, for My own sake, I will do
    it;
  For how should *My name* be profaned?
  And I will not give My glory to another.

God's Ancient Plan to Redeem Israel

¹²"Listen to Me, O Jacob,
  And Israel, My called:
  I *am* He, I *am* the First,
  I *am* also the Last.
¹³Indeed My hand has laid the foundation of
    the earth,
  And My right hand has stretched out the
    heavens;
  When I call to them,
  They stand up together.

¹⁴"All of you, assemble yourselves, and hear!
  Who among them has declared these *things?*
  The LORD loves him;
  He shall do His pleasure on Babylon,
  And His arm *shall be against* the Chaldeans.
¹⁵I, *even* I, have spoken;
  Yes, I have called him,
  I have brought him, and his way will prosper.

¹⁶"Come near to Me, hear this:
  I have not spoken in secret from the
    beginning;
  From the time that it was, I *was* there.
  And now the Lord GOD and His Spirit
  Have[a] sent Me."

¹⁷Thus says the LORD, your Redeemer,
  The Holy One of Israel:
  "I *am* the LORD your God,
  Who teaches you to profit,
  Who leads you by the way you should go.
¹⁸Oh, that you had heeded My
    commandments!
  Then your peace would have been like a
    river,
  And your righteousness like the waves of
    the sea.
¹⁹Your descendants also would have been like
    the sand,
  And the offspring of your body like the
    grains of sand;
  His name would not have been cut off
  Nor destroyed from before Me."

²⁰Go forth from Babylon!
  Flee from the Chaldeans!
  With a voice of singing,
  Declare, proclaim this,
  Utter it to the end of the earth;
  Say, "The LORD has redeemed
  His servant Jacob!"
²¹And they did not thirst
  When He led them through the deserts;
  He caused the waters to flow from the rock
    for them;
  He also split the rock, and the waters gushed
    out.

48:16 aThe Hebrew verb is singular.

²²"*There is* no peace," says the LORD, "for the
    wicked."

THE SERVANT, THE LIGHT TO THE GENTILES

49 "Listen, O coastlands, to Me,
    And take heed, you peoples from afar!
The LORD has called Me from the womb;
    From the matrix of My mother He has made
        mention of My name.
²And He has made My mouth like a sharp
        sword;
    In the shadow of His hand He has hidden
        Me,
    And made Me a polished shaft;
    In His quiver He has hidden Me."

³"And He said to me,
    'You *are* My servant, O Israel,
    In whom I will be glorified.'
⁴Then I said, 'I have labored in vain,
    I have spent my strength for nothing and in
        vain;
    Yet surely my just reward *is* with the LORD,
    And my work with my God.' "

⁵"And now the LORD says,
    Who formed Me from the womb *to be* His
        Servant,
    To bring Jacob back to Him,
    So that Israel is gathered to Him^a
    (For I shall be glorious in the eyes of the
        LORD,
    And My God shall be My strength),

⁶Indeed He says,
    'It is too small a thing that You should be My
        Servant
    To raise up the tribes of Jacob,
    And to restore the preserved ones of Israel;
    I will also give You as a light to the Gentiles,
    That You should be My salvation to the ends
        of the earth.' "

⁷Thus says the LORD,
    The Redeemer of Israel, their Holy One,
    To Him whom man despises,
    To Him whom the nation abhors,
    To the Servant of rulers:
    "Kings shall see and arise,

Princes also shall worship,
    Because of the LORD who is faithful,
    The Holy One of Israel;
    And He has chosen You."

⁸Thus says the LORD:

"In an acceptable time I have heard You,
    And in the day of salvation I have helped
        You;
    I will preserve You and give You
    As a covenant to the people,
    To restore the earth,
    To cause them to inherit the desolate
        heritages;
⁹That You may say to the prisoners, 'Go forth,'
    To those who *are* in darkness, 'Show
        yourselves.'

"They shall feed along the roads,
    And their pastures *shall be* on all desolate
        heights.
¹⁰They shall neither hunger nor thirst,
    Neither heat nor sun shall strike them;
    For He who has mercy on them will lead
        them,
    Even by the springs of water He will guide
        them.
¹¹I will make each of My mountains a road,
    And My highways shall be elevated.
¹²Surely these shall come from afar;
    Look! Those from the north and the west,
    And these from the land of Sinim."

¹³Sing, O heavens!
    Be joyful, O earth!
    And break out in singing, O mountains!
    For the LORD has comforted His people,
    And will have mercy on His afflicted.

GOD WILL REMEMBER ZION

¹⁴But Zion said, "The LORD has forsaken me,
    And my Lord has forgotten me."

¹⁵"Can a woman forget her nursing child,
    And not have compassion on the son of her
        womb?

49:5 ^aQere, Dead Sea Scrolls, and Septuagint read *is gathered to
Him;* Kethib reads *is not gathered.*

Surely they may forget,
Yet I will not forget you.

[16]See, I have inscribed you on the palms *of My hands;*
Your walls *are* continually before Me.
[17]Your sons[a] shall make haste;
Your destroyers and those who laid you waste
Shall go away from you.
[18]Lift up your eyes, look around and see;
All these gather together *and* come to you.
As I live," says the LORD,
"You shall surely clothe yourselves with them all as an ornament,
And bind them *on you* as a bride *does.*

[19]"For your waste and desolate places,
And the land of your destruction,
Will even now be too small for the inhabitants;
And those who swallowed you up will be far away.
[20]The children you will have,
After you have lost the others,
Will say again in your ears,
'The place *is* too small for me;
Give me a place where I may dwell.'
[21]Then you will say in your heart,
'Who has begotten these for me,
Since I have lost my children and am desolate,
A captive, and wandering to and fro?
And who has brought these up?
There I was, left alone;
But these, where *were* they?' "

[22]Thus says the Lord GOD:

"Behold, I will lift My hand in an oath to the nations,
And set up My standard for the peoples;
They shall bring your sons in *their* arms,
And your daughters shall be carried on *their* shoulders;
[23]Kings shall be your foster fathers,
And their queens your nursing mothers;
They shall bow down to you with *their* faces to the earth,
And lick up the dust of your feet.
Then you will know that I *am* the LORD,

For they shall not be ashamed who wait for Me."

[24]Shall the prey be taken from the mighty,
Or the captives of the righteous[a] be delivered?

[25]But thus says the LORD:

"Even the captives of the mighty shall be taken away,
And the prey of the terrible be delivered;
For I will contend with him who contends with you,
And I will save your children.
[26]I will feed those who oppress you with their own flesh,
And they shall be drunk with their own blood as with sweet wine.
All flesh shall know
That I, the LORD, *am* your Savior,
And your Redeemer, the Mighty One of Jacob."

The Servant, Israel's Hope

50 Thus says the LORD:

"Where *is* the certificate of your mother's divorce,
Whom I have put away?
Or which of My creditors *is it* to whom I have sold you?
For your iniquities you have sold yourselves,
And for your transgressions your mother has been put away.
[2]Why, when I came, *was there* no man?
Why, when I called, *was there* none to answer?
Is My hand shortened at all that it cannot redeem?
Or have I no power to deliver?
Indeed with My rebuke I dry up the sea,
I make the rivers a wilderness;
Their fish stink because *there is* no water,
And die of thirst.
[3]I clothe the heavens with blackness,
And I make sackcloth their covering."

49:17 [a]Dead Sea Scrolls, Septuagint, Targum, and Vulgate read *builders.* 49:24 [a]Following Masoretic Text and Targum; Dead Sea Scrolls, Syriac, and Vulgate read *the mighty;* Septuagint reads *unjustly.*

⁴"The Lord GOD has given Me
The tongue of the learned,
That I should know how to speak
A word in season to *him who is* weary.
He awakens Me morning by morning,
He awakens My ear
To hear as the learned.
⁵The Lord GOD has opened My ear;
And I was not rebellious,
Nor did I turn away.
⁶I gave My back to those who struck *Me,*
And My cheeks to those who plucked out
    the beard;
I did not hide My face from shame and
    spitting.

⁷"For the Lord GOD will help Me;
Therefore I will not be disgraced;
Therefore I have set My face like a flint,
And I know that I will not be ashamed.
⁸*He is* near who justifies Me;
Who will contend with Me?
Let us stand together.
Who *is* My adversary?
Let him come near Me.
⁹Surely the Lord GOD will help Me;
Who *is* he *who* will condemn Me?
Indeed they will all grow old like a
    garment;
The moth will eat them up.

¹⁰"Who among you fears the LORD?
Who obeys the voice of His Servant?
Who walks in darkness
And has no light?
Let him trust in the name of the LORD
And rely upon his God.
¹¹Look, all you who kindle a fire,
Who encircle *yourselves* with sparks:
Walk in the light of your fire and in the
    sparks you have kindled—
This you shall have from My hand:
You shall lie down in torment.

THE LORD COMFORTS ZION

51 "Listen to Me, you who follow after
      righteousness,
You who seek the LORD:
Look to the rock *from which* you were hewn,

And to the hole of the pit *from which* you
    were dug.
²Look to Abraham your father,
And to Sarah *who* bore you;
For I called him alone,
And blessed him and increased him."

³For the LORD will comfort Zion,
He will comfort all her waste places;
He will make her wilderness like Eden,
And her desert like the garden of the LORD;
Joy and gladness will be found in it,
Thanksgiving and the voice of melody.

⁴"Listen to Me, My people;
And give ear to Me, O My nation:
For law will proceed from Me,
And I will make My justice rest
As a light of the peoples.
⁵My righteousness *is* near,
My salvation has gone forth,
And My arms will judge the peoples;
The coastlands will wait upon Me,
And on My arm they will trust.
⁶Lift up your eyes to the heavens,
And look on the earth beneath.
For the heavens will vanish away like smoke,
The earth will grow old like a garment,
And those who dwell in it will die in like
    manner;
But My salvation will be forever,
And My righteousness will not be
    abolished.

⁷"Listen to Me, you who know righteousness,
You people in whose heart *is* My law:
Do not fear the reproach of men,
Nor be afraid of their insults.
⁸For the moth will eat them up like a
    garment,
And the worm will eat them like wool;
But My righteousness will be forever,
And My salvation from generation to
    generation."

⁹Awake, awake, put on strength,
O arm of the LORD!
Awake as in the ancient days,
In the generations of old.

INSIDE *the* INFLUENCERS

THE HEBREW PEOPLE—Leadership Is Influence

ISAIAH 51:2

The Old Testament is the story of God choosing, calling, and setting apart His chosen people, the Israelites. It began with Abram, whose obedient response birthed a nation which would bless the entire world. These people declared the one true God to a culture of pantheism and idol worship. Through them would come the 10 commandments, the Law, and the Messiah.

Abram left Ur to embark on this journey of faith; and by faith, Sarai, his wife, conceived Isaac in her old age (Gen.15). Jacob, Isaac's son, was renamed "Israel" and had 12 sons. Joseph, the favorite, was sold as a slave to traders and ended up in Egypt.

Through years of trials, he eventually became the governor of Egypt. In a forgiving gesture, he saved his father and brothers from famine. Jacob and his sons died in Egypt, but their children, now known as the Hebrews or Israelites, greatly multiplied. Their numbers became a threat to Pharaoh, who ordered the deaths of every male baby.

Moses, a Hebrew baby, was placed in a basket in the Nile. He was found and adopted by Pharaoh's daughter. He grew mighty and trained in the arts and science of an Egyptian prince before being called by God to deliver the Hebrews through a series of miracles. This event, Passover, is celebrated to this day by Jewish people around the world.

Are You not *the arm* that cut Rahab apart,
And wounded the serpent?

¹⁰ *Are* You not *the One* who dried up the sea,
The waters of the great deep;
That made the depths of the sea a road
For the redeemed to cross over?
¹¹ So the ransomed of the LORD shall return,
And come to Zion with singing,
With everlasting joy on their heads.
They shall obtain joy and gladness;
Sorrow and sighing shall flee away.

¹² "I, *even* I, *am* He who comforts you.
Who *are* you that you should be afraid
Of a man *who* will die,
And of the son of a man *who* will be made
like grass?
¹³ And you forget the LORD your Maker,
Who stretched out the heavens
And laid the foundations of the earth;
You have feared continually every day
Because of the fury of the oppressor,
When *he has* prepared to destroy.

And where *is* the fury of the oppressor?
¹⁴ The captive exile hastens, that he may be
loosed,
That he should not die in the pit,
And that his bread should not fail.
¹⁵ But I *am* the LORD your God,
Who divided the sea whose waves roared—
The LORD of hosts *is* His name.
¹⁶ And I have put My words in your mouth;
I have covered you with the shadow of My
hand,
That I may plant the heavens,
Lay the foundations of the earth,
And say to Zion, 'You *are* My people.' "

GOD'S FURY REMOVED

¹⁷ Awake, awake!
Stand up, O Jerusalem,
You who have drunk at the hand of the
LORD
The cup of His fury;
You have drunk the dregs of the cup of
trembling,
And drained *it* out.

¹⁸*There is* no one to guide her
   Among all the sons she has brought forth;
   Nor *is there any* who takes her by the hand
   Among all the sons she has brought up.
¹⁹These two *things* have come to you;
   Who will be sorry for you?—
   Desolation and destruction, famine and
      sword—
   By whom will I comfort you?
²⁰Your sons have fainted,
   They lie at the head of all the streets,
   Like an antelope in a net;
   They are full of the fury of the LORD,
   The rebuke of your God.

²¹Therefore please hear this, you afflicted,
   And drunk but not with wine.
²²Thus says your Lord,
   The LORD and your God,
   Who pleads the cause of His people:
"See, I have taken out of your hand
   The cup of trembling,
   The dregs of the cup of My fury;
   You shall no longer drink it.
²³But I will put it into the hand of those who
      afflict you,
   Who have said to you,^a
   'Lie down, that we may walk over you.'
   And you have laid your body like the
      ground,
   And as the street, for those who walk over."

GOD REDEEMS JERUSALEM

52 Awake, awake!
   Put on your strength, O Zion;
   Put on your beautiful garments,
   O Jerusalem, the holy city!
   For the uncircumcised and the unclean
   Shall no longer come to you.
²Shake yourself from the dust, arise;
   Sit down, O Jerusalem!
   Loose yourself from the bonds of your neck,
   O captive daughter of Zion!

³For thus says the LORD:

"You have sold yourselves for nothing,
   And you shall be redeemed without
      money."

⁴For thus says the Lord GOD:

"My people went down at first
   Into Egypt to dwell there;
   Then the Assyrian oppressed them without
      cause.
⁵Now therefore, what have I here," says the
      LORD,
"That My people are taken away for nothing?
   Those who rule over them
   Make them wail,"^a says the LORD,
"And My name *is* blasphemed continually
      every day.
⁶Therefore My people shall know My name;
   Therefore *they shall know* in that day
   That I *am* He who speaks:
   'Behold, *it is* I.'"

⁷How beautiful upon the mountains
   Are the feet of him who brings good news,
   Who proclaims peace,
   Who brings glad tidings of good *things*,
   Who proclaims salvation,
   Who says to Zion,
"Your God reigns!"
⁸Your watchmen shall lift up *their* voices,
   With their voices they shall sing together;
   For they shall see eye to eye
   When the LORD brings back Zion.
⁹Break forth into joy, sing together,
   You waste places of Jerusalem!
   For the LORD has comforted His people,
   He has redeemed Jerusalem.
¹⁰The LORD has made bare His holy arm
   In the eyes of all the nations;
   And all the ends of the earth shall see
   The salvation of our God.

¹¹Depart! Depart! Go out from there,
   Touch no unclean *thing*;
   Go out from the midst of her,
   Be clean,
   You who bear the vessels of the LORD.
¹²For you shall not go out with haste,
   Nor go by flight;
   For the LORD will go before you,

51:23 [a]Literally *your soul*   52:5 [a]Dead Sea Scrolls read *Mock;* Septuagint reads *Marvel and wail;* Targum reads *Boast themselves;* Vulgate reads *Treat them unjustly.*

And the God of Israel *will be* your rear
   guard.

The Sin-Bearing Servant

[13]Behold, My Servant shall deal prudently;
   He shall be exalted and extolled and be very
     high.
[14]Just as many were astonished at you,
   So His visage was marred more than any
     man,
   And His form more than the sons of men;
[15]So shall He sprinkle[a] many nations.
   Kings shall shut their mouths at Him;
   For what had not been told them they shall
     see,
   And what they had not heard they shall
     consider.

53 Who has believed our report?
   And to whom has the arm of the LORD
     been revealed?
[2]For He shall grow up before Him as a tender
     plant,
   And as a root out of dry ground.
   He has no form or comeliness;
   And when we see Him,
   There is no beauty that we should desire
     Him.
[3]He is despised and rejected by men,
   A Man of sorrows and acquainted with grief.

And we hid, as it were, *our* faces from Him;
   He was despised, and we did not esteem
     Him.

[4]Surely He has borne our griefs
   And carried our sorrows;
   Yet we esteemed Him stricken,
   Smitten by God, and afflicted.
[5]But He *was* wounded for our transgressions,
   He was bruised for our iniquities;
   The chastisement for our peace *was* upon
     Him,
   And by His stripes we are healed.
[6]All we like sheep have gone astray;
   We have turned, every one, to his own way;
   And the LORD has laid on Him the iniquity
     of us all.

[7]He was oppressed and He was afflicted,
   Yet He opened not His mouth;
   He was led as a lamb to the slaughter,
   And as a sheep before its shearers is silent,
   So He opened not His mouth.
[8]He was taken from prison and from
     judgment,
   And who will declare His generation?
   For He was cut off from the land of the
     living;

52:15 [a]Or *startle*

LEADERSHIP REALITIES

SEE FURTHER DOWN THE ROAD *Isaiah 53*

Old Testament prophets can be described as people who stood on a peak in the mountain range of history and saw and proclaimed another peak, sometimes hundreds of years away. While often misunderstood, the prophets demonstrated the leadership principle *to see further down the road*, to see tomorrow while others concentrate on the present or even the past. No one lived this principle more than the prophet Isaiah when in chapter 53 he describes Jesus as the Servant who would come to suffer and die. His description of Christ is so vivid that it is difficult to believe that he was not present at the crucifixion of Christ. He actually lived and wrote some 500 years earlier, but his God-given vision was as accurate as that of an eyewitness. This quality is a gift and requires the mental discipline that will take the leader on a lonely, but amazing venture that few will experience. The future belongs to those who are prepared, to those who dig a well now, before they are thirsty.

LEADERSHIP ISSUES

GC2: Good News: God Loves You Sacrificially

ISAIAH 53:6 *All we like sheep have gone astray; we have turned, every one, to his own way; and the LORD has laid on Him the iniquity of us all.*

God has demonstrated that He is willing to go to extraordinary lengths to connect with you. He passionately desires a relationship with you. The significance of Christ's life and love go even further and deeper than that.

Yes, God accepts us without condition (Rom. 5:8). That unconditional acceptance is demonstrated in His willingness to take the initiative and enter our world in order to reclaim and restore our relationship with Him, "even when we were dead in trespasses" (Eph. 2:5).

God is not only a God who is "rich in mercy" (Eph. 2:4)—He is also holy. The Bible says of God, "You are of purer eyes than to behold evil, and cannot look on wickedness" (Hab. 1:13). God is so holy that He cannot relate to sin in any form. Since each of us was born with a sinful human nature, tainted by sin, we are totally unsuitable for a relationship with a holy God. When Adam sinned, "sin entered the world, and . . . death spread to all men" (Rom. 5:12). The apostle Paul said, "We all once conducted ourselves in the lusts of our flesh . . . and were by nature children of wrath, just as the others" (Eph. 2:3).

And, if that were not enough, we even further ruined our chances to relate to God by adding our own sins to original sin. Romans 3:23 says it clearly: "For all have sinned and fall short of the glory of God."

Despite your sin, Jesus valued you enough to die for you. His love for you is so great, He spread His arms the width of a cross and said, "I lay down My life for you."

GREAT COMMANDMENT
COMMISSION

For the transgressions of My people He was
stricken.

[9]And they[a] made His grave with the wicked—
But with the rich at His death,
Because He had done no violence,
Nor *was any* deceit in His mouth.

[10]Yet it pleased the LORD to bruise Him;
He has put *Him* to grief.
When You make His soul an offering for sin,
He shall see *His* seed, He shall prolong *His*
days,
And the pleasure of the LORD shall prosper in
His hand.
[11]He shall see the labor of His soul,[a] *and* be
satisfied.
By His knowledge My righteous Servant
shall justify many,
For He shall bear their iniquities.
[12]Therefore I will divide Him a portion with
the great,
And He shall divide the spoil with the
strong,
Because He poured out His soul unto
death,
And He was numbered with the
transgressors,
And He bore the sin of many,
And made intercession for the transgressors.

A PERPETUAL COVENANT OF PEACE

54 "Sing, O barren,
You *who* have not borne!
Break forth into singing, and cry aloud,
You *who* have not labored with child!
For more *are* the children of the desolate
Than the children of the married woman,"
says the LORD.
[2]"Enlarge the place of your tent,
And let them stretch out the curtains of your
dwellings;
Do not spare;
Lengthen your cords,
And strengthen your stakes.
[3]For you shall expand to the right and to the
left,
And your descendants will inherit the
nations,
And make the desolate cities inhabited.

[4]"Do not fear, for you will not be ashamed;
Neither be disgraced, for you will not be put
to shame;
For you will forget the shame of your youth,
And will not remember the reproach of your
widowhood anymore.
[5]For your Maker *is* your husband,
The LORD of hosts *is* His name;
And your Redeemer *is* the Holy One of
Israel;
He is called the God of the whole earth.
[6]For the LORD has called you
Like a woman forsaken and grieved in spirit,
Like a youthful wife when you were
refused,"
Says your God.
[7]"For a mere moment I have forsaken you,
But with great mercies I will gather you.
[8]With a little wrath I hid My face from you
for a moment;
But with everlasting kindness I will have
mercy on you,"
Says the LORD, your Redeemer.

[9]"For this *is* like the waters of Noah to Me;
For as I have sworn
That the waters of Noah would no longer
cover the earth,
So have I sworn
That I would not be angry with you, nor
rebuke you.
[10]For the mountains shall depart
And the hills be removed,
But My kindness shall not depart from you,
Nor shall My covenant of peace be
removed,"
Says the LORD, who has mercy on you.

[11]"O you afflicted one,
Tossed with tempest, *and* not comforted,
Behold, I will lay your stones with colorful
gems,
And lay your foundations with sapphires.
[12]I will make your pinnacles of rubies,
Your gates of crystal,
And all your walls of precious stones.

53:9 [a]Literally *he* or *He* 53:11 [a]Following Masoretic Text, Targum,
and Vulgate; Dead Sea Scrolls and Septuagint read *From the labor
of His soul He shall see light.*

¹³All your children *shall be* taught by the LORD,
  And great *shall be* the peace of your children.
¹⁴In righteousness you shall be established;
  You shall be far from oppression, for you shall
    not fear;
  And from terror, for it shall not come near
    you.
¹⁵Indeed they shall surely assemble, *but* not
    because of Me.
  Whoever assembles against you shall fall for
    your sake.

¹⁶"Behold, I have created the blacksmith
  Who blows the coals in the fire,
  Who brings forth an instrument for his
    work;
  And I have created the spoiler to destroy.
¹⁷No weapon formed against you shall prosper,
  And every tongue *which* rises against you in
    judgment
  You shall condemn.
  This *is* the heritage of the servants of the
    LORD,
  And their righteousness *is* from Me,"
  Says the LORD.

AN INVITATION TO ABUNDANT LIFE

55 "Ho! Everyone who thirsts,
    Come to the waters;
  And you who have no money,
    Come, buy and eat.
  Yes, come, buy wine and milk
    Without money and without price.
²Why do you spend money for *what is* not
    bread,
  And your wages for *what* does not satisfy?
  Listen carefully to Me, and eat *what is* good,
  And let your soul delight itself in
    abundance.
³Incline your ear, and come to Me.
  Hear, and your soul shall live;
  And I will make an everlasting covenant with
    you—
  The sure mercies of David.
⁴Indeed I have given him *as* a witness to the
    people,
  A leader and commander for the people.
⁵Surely you shall call a nation you do not
    know,

And nations *who* do not know you shall run
    to you,
  Because of the LORD your God,
  And the Holy One of Israel;
  For He has glorified you."

⁶Seek the LORD while He may be found,
  Call upon Him while He is near.
⁷Let the wicked forsake his way,
  And the unrighteous man his thoughts;
  Let him return to the LORD,
  And He will have mercy on him;
  And to our God,
  For He will abundantly pardon.

⁸"For My thoughts *are* not your thoughts,
  Nor *are* your ways My ways," says the
    LORD.
⁹"For *as* the heavens are higher than the earth,
  So are My ways higher than your ways,
  And My thoughts than your thoughts.

¹⁰"For as the rain comes down, and the snow
    from heaven,
  And do not return there,
  But water the earth,
  And make it bring forth and bud,
  That it may give seed to the sower
  And bread to the eater,
¹¹So shall My word be that goes forth from My
    mouth;
  It shall not return to Me void,
  But it shall accomplish what I please,
  And it shall prosper *in the thing* for which I
    sent it.

¹²"For you shall go out with joy,
  And be led out with peace;
  The mountains and the hills
  Shall break forth into singing before you,
  And all the trees of the field shall clap *their*
    hands.
¹³Instead of the thorn shall come up the cypress
    tree,
  And instead of the brier shall come up the
    myrtle tree;
  And it shall be to the LORD for a name,
  For an everlasting sign *that* shall not be cut
    off."

LEADERSHIP ISSUES

Why Do Bad Things Happen to Good People?

JOB 55:8

The question of why God allows adversity may never be answered in this life, but we will understand it in eternity (Is. 55:8, 9). The believer comes to an understanding of that. To intensify this faith, a leader focuses on what he or she *knows*: God is good, His character and majesty are clearly told in His Word, and the leader has experienced answered prayers. The one who impacts the lives of others believes that God always desires the best for us and that He can be trusted. We see this every day in creation (Ps. 19:1–11).

The question "Does God care?" has already been answered. We never need ask it again, for God proved His love for us by sending His Son, Jesus, who willingly endured the pain of the cross (Is. 53:5). The word "suffering" comes from the Latin word that means "to bear up under work or illness." Christ has indeed suffered for us. When we understand the scope of His love, then we get to know Him and understand the power of His love.

Because God is described as loving, good, and compassionate (Rom. 5:8; Titus 3:4; 1 John 3:1; 4:8), we are tempted to ask the question "Why is there evil in the world?" God did not create evil, but He did allow free choice and the potential for evil. Individuals have the right every day to love or hate, to do good or to choose evil.

The apostle Paul—who endured imprisonment, illness, and beatings—gives his best advice for answering the "whys" of life in Hebrews 12:3: "For consider Him who endured such hostility from sinners against Himself, lest you become weary and discouraged in your souls." In other words, focus on what Christ has done for us, knowing that He also hates evil; and that will keep you from becoming discouraged about the evil in the world. Leaders look back at what God has already done in order to look forward, with anticipation, to what He will continue to do.

Salvation for the Gentiles

56 Thus says the LORD:

"Keep justice, and do righteousness,
For My salvation *is* about to come,
And My righteousness to be revealed.
[2]Blessed *is* the man *who* does this,
And the son of man *who* lays hold on it;
Who keeps from defiling the Sabbath,
And keeps his hand from doing any evil."

[3]Do not let the son of the foreigner
Who has joined himself to the LORD
Speak, saying,
"The LORD has utterly separated me from His
people";
Nor let the eunuch say,
"Here I am, a dry tree."
[4]For thus says the LORD:
"To the eunuchs who keep My Sabbaths,
And choose what pleases Me,
And hold fast My covenant,
[5]Even to them I will give in My house
And within My walls a place and a name
Better than that of sons and daughters;
I will give them[a] an everlasting name
That shall not be cut off.

[6]"Also the sons of the foreigner
Who join themselves to the LORD, to serve
Him,
And to love the name of the LORD, to be His
servants—
Everyone who keeps from defiling the
Sabbath,
And holds fast My covenant—
[7]Even them I will bring to My holy
mountain,
And make them joyful in My house of
prayer.
Their burnt offerings and their sacrifices
Will be accepted on My altar;
For My house shall be called a house of
prayer for all nations."
[8]The Lord GOD, who gathers the outcasts of
Israel, says,
"Yet I will gather to him
Others besides those who are gathered to
him."

Israel's Irresponsible Leaders

[9]All you beasts of the field, come to devour,
All you beasts in the forest.
[10]His watchmen *are* blind,
They are all ignorant;
They *are* all dumb dogs,
They cannot bark;
Sleeping, lying down, loving to slumber.
[11]Yes, *they are* greedy dogs
Which never have enough.
And they *are* shepherds
Who cannot understand;
They all look to their own way,
Every one for his own gain,
From his *own* territory.
[12]"Come," *one says,* "I will bring wine,
And we will fill ourselves with intoxicating
drink;
Tomorrow will be as today,
And much more abundant."

Israel's Futile Idolatry

57 The righteous perishes,
And no man takes *it* to heart;
Merciful men *are* taken away,
While no one considers
That the righteous is taken away from evil.
[2]He shall enter into peace;
They shall rest in their beds,
Each one walking *in* his uprightness.

[3]"But come here,
You sons of the sorceress,
You offspring of the adulterer and the
harlot!
[4]Whom do you ridicule?
Against whom do you make a wide mouth
And stick out the tongue?
Are you not children of transgression,
Offspring of falsehood,
[5]Inflaming yourselves with gods under every
green tree,
Slaying the children in the valleys,
Under the clefts of the rocks?
[6]Among the smooth *stones* of the stream
Is your portion;
They, they, *are* your lot!

56:5 [a]Literally *him*

Even to them you have poured a drink
    offering,
You have offered a grain offering.
Should I receive comfort in these?

7"On a lofty and high mountain
    You have set your bed;
    Even there you went up
    To offer sacrifice.
8Also behind the doors and their posts
    You have set up your remembrance;
    For you have uncovered yourself *to those other*
        than Me,
    And have gone up to them;
    You have enlarged your bed
    And made *a covenant* with them;
    You have loved their bed,
    Where you saw *their* nudity.ᵃ
9You went to the king with ointment,
    And increased your perfumes;
    You sent your messengers far off,
    And *even* descended to Sheol.
10You are wearied in the length of your way;
    Yet you did not say, 'There is no hope.'
    You have found the life of your hand;
    Therefore you were not grieved.

11"And of whom have you been afraid, or feared,
    That you have lied
    And not remembered Me,
    Nor taken *it* to your heart?
    Is it not because I have held My peace from
        of old
    That you do not fear Me?
12I will declare your righteousness
    And your works,
    For they will not profit you.
13When you cry out,
    Let your collection *of idols* deliver you.
    But the wind will carry them all away,
    A breath will take *them.*
    But he who puts his trust in Me shall possess
        the land,
    And shall inherit My holy mountain."

Healing for the Backslider

14And one shall say,
    "Heap it up! Heap it up!
    Prepare the way,

Take the stumbling block out of the way of
    My people."

15For thus says the High and Lofty One
    Who inhabits eternity, whose name *is* Holy:
"I dwell in the high and holy *place,*
    With him *who* has a contrite and humble
        spirit,
    To revive the spirit of the humble,
    And to revive the heart of the contrite ones.
16For I will not contend forever,
    Nor will I always be angry;
    For the spirit would fail before Me,
    And the souls *which* I have made.
17For the iniquity of his covetousness
    I was angry and struck him;
    I hid and was angry,
    And he went on backsliding in the way of his
        heart.
18I have seen his ways, and will heal him;
    I will also lead him,
    And restore comforts to him
    And to his mourners.

19"I create the fruit of the lips:
    Peace, peace to *him who is* far off and to *him
        who is* near,"
    Says the LORD,
    "And I will heal him."
20But the wicked *are* like the troubled sea,
    When it cannot rest,
    Whose waters cast up mire and dirt.

21"*There is* no peace,"
    Says my God, "for the wicked."

Fasting that Pleases God

58 "Cry aloud, spare not;
    Lift up your voice like a trumpet;
    Tell My people their transgression,
    And the house of Jacob their sins.
2Yet they seek Me daily,
    And delight to know My ways,
    As a nation that did righteousness,
    And did not forsake the ordinance of their
        God.
    They ask of Me the ordinances of justice;
    They take delight in approaching God.

57:8 ᵃLiterally *hand,* a euphemism

³'Why have we fasted,' *they say,* 'and You have
       not seen?
  Why have we afflicted our souls, and You take
       no notice?'

"In fact, in the day of your fast you find
       pleasure,
  And exploit all your laborers.
⁴Indeed you fast for strife and debate,
  And to strike with the fist of wickedness.
  You will not fast as *you do* this day,
  To make your voice heard on high.
⁵Is it a fast that I have chosen,
  A day for a man to afflict his soul?
  Is it to bow down his head like a bulrush,
  And to spread out sackcloth and ashes?
  Would you call this a fast,
  And an acceptable day to the LORD?

⁶"*Is* this not the fast that I have chosen:
  To loose the bonds of wickedness,
  To undo the heavy burdens,
  To let the oppressed go free,
  And that you break every yoke?
⁷*Is it* not to share your bread with the hungry,
  And that you bring to your house the poor
       who are cast out;
  When you see the naked, that you cover
       him,
  And not hide yourself from your own flesh?
⁸Then your light shall break forth like the
       morning,
  Your healing shall spring forth speedily,
  And your righteousness shall go before you;
  The glory of the LORD shall be your rear
       guard.
⁹Then you shall call, and the LORD will
       answer;
  You shall cry, and He will say, 'Here I *am.*'

"If you take away the yoke from your midst,
  The pointing of the finger, and speaking
       wickedness,
¹⁰*If* you extend your soul to the hungry
  And satisfy the afflicted soul,
  Then your light shall dawn in the darkness,
  And your darkness shall *be* as the noonday.
¹¹The LORD will guide you continually,
  And satisfy your soul in drought,

And strengthen your bones;
  You shall be like a watered garden,
  And like a spring of water, whose waters do
       not fail.
¹²Those from among you
  Shall build the old waste places;
  You shall raise up the foundations of many
       generations;
  And you shall be called the Repairer of the
       Breach,
  The Restorer of Streets to Dwell In.

¹³"If you turn away your foot from the Sabbath,
  From doing your pleasure on My holy day,
  And call the Sabbath a delight,
  The holy *day* of the LORD honorable,
  And shall honor Him, not doing your own
       ways,
  Nor finding your own pleasure,
  Nor speaking *your own* words,
¹⁴Then you shall delight yourself in the LORD;
  And I will cause you to ride on the high hills
       of the earth,
  And feed you with the heritage of Jacob your
       father.
  The mouth of the LORD has spoken."

SEPARATED FROM GOD

59 Behold, the LORD'S hand is not shortened,
     That it cannot save;
  Nor His ear heavy,
  That it cannot hear.
²But your iniquities have separated you from
       your God;
  And your sins have hidden *His* face from
       you,
  So that He will not hear.
³For your hands are defiled with blood,
  And your fingers with iniquity;
  Your lips have spoken lies,
  Your tongue has muttered perversity.

⁴No one calls for justice,
  Nor does *any* plead for truth.
  They trust in empty words and speak lies;
  They conceive evil and bring forth iniquity.
⁵They hatch vipers' eggs and weave the spider's
       web;
  He who eats of their eggs dies,

And *from* that which is crushed a viper breaks
out.

[6]Their webs will not become garments,
Nor will they cover themselves with their
works;
Their works *are* works of iniquity,
And the act of violence *is* in their hands.
[7]Their feet run to evil,
And they make haste to shed innocent
blood;
Their thoughts *are* thoughts of iniquity;
Wasting and destruction *are* in their paths.
[8]The way of peace they have not known,
And *there is* no justice in their ways;
They have made themselves crooked paths;
Whoever takes that way shall not know
peace.

Sin Confessed

[9]Therefore justice is far from us,
Nor does righteousness overtake us;
We look for light, but there is darkness!
For brightness, *but* we walk in blackness!
[10]We grope for the wall like the blind,
And we grope as if *we had* no eyes;
We stumble at noonday as at twilight;
We are as dead *men* in desolate places.
[11]We all growl like bears,
And moan sadly like doves;
We look for justice, but *there is* none;
For salvation, *but* it is far from us.
[12]For our transgressions are multiplied before
You,
And our sins testify against us;
For our transgressions *are* with us,
And *as for* our iniquities, we know them:
[13]In transgressing and lying against the LORD,
And departing from our God,
Speaking oppression and revolt,
Conceiving and uttering from the heart
words of falsehood.
[14]Justice is turned back,
And righteousness stands afar off;
For truth is fallen in the street,
And equity cannot enter.
[15]So truth fails,
And he *who* departs from evil makes himself
a prey.

The Redeemer of Zion

Then the LORD saw *it*, and it displeased Him
That *there was* no justice.
[16]He saw that *there was* no man,
And wondered that *there was* no intercessor;
Therefore His own arm brought salvation for
Him;
And His own righteousness, it sustained
Him.
[17]For He put on righteousness as a breastplate,
And a helmet of salvation on His head;
He put on the garments of vengeance for
clothing,
And was clad with zeal as a cloak.
[18]According to *their* deeds, accordingly He will
repay,
Fury to His adversaries,
Recompense to His enemies;
The coastlands He will fully repay.
[19]So shall they fear
The name of the LORD from the west,
And His glory from the rising of the sun;
When the enemy comes in like a flood,
The Spirit of the LORD will lift up a standard
against him.

[20]"The Redeemer will come to Zion,
And to those who turn from transgression in
Jacob,"
Says the LORD.

[21]"As for Me," says the LORD, "this *is* My
covenant with them: My Spirit who *is* upon you,
and My words which I have put in your mouth,
shall not depart from your mouth, nor from the
mouth of your descendants, nor from the mouth
of your descendants' descendants," says the LORD,
"from this time and forevermore."

The Gentiles Bless Zion

60 Arise, shine;
For your light has come!
And the glory of the LORD is risen upon
you.
[2]For behold, the darkness shall cover the earth,
And deep darkness the people;
But the LORD will arise over you,
And His glory will be seen upon you.

³The Gentiles shall come to your light,
  And kings to the brightness of your rising.

⁴"Lift up your eyes all around, and see:
  They all gather together, they come to you;
  Your sons shall come from afar,
  And your daughters shall be nursed at *your*
    side.
⁵Then you shall see and become radiant,
  And your heart shall swell with joy;
  Because the abundance of the sea shall be
    turned to you,
  The wealth of the Gentiles shall come to
    you.
⁶The multitude of camels shall cover your
    land,
  The dromedaries of Midian and Ephah;
  All those from Sheba shall come;
  They shall bring gold and incense,
  And they shall proclaim the praises of the
    LORD.
⁷All the flocks of Kedar shall be gathered
    together to you,
  The rams of Nebaioth shall minister to you;
  They shall ascend with acceptance on My
    altar,
  And I will glorify the house of My glory.

⁸"Who *are* these *who* fly like a cloud,
  And like doves to their roosts?
⁹Surely the coastlands shall wait for Me;
  And the ships of Tarshish *will come* first,
  To bring your sons from afar,
  Their silver and their gold with them,
  To the name of the LORD your God,
  And to the Holy One of Israel,
  Because He has glorified you.

¹⁰"The sons of foreigners shall build up your
    walls,
  And their kings shall minister to you;
  For in My wrath I struck you,
  But in My favor I have had mercy on you.
¹¹Therefore your gates shall be open
    continually;
  They shall not be shut day or night,
  That *men* may bring to you the wealth of the
    Gentiles,
  And their kings in procession.

¹²For the nation and kingdom which will not
    serve you shall perish,
  And *those* nations shall be utterly ruined.

¹³"The glory of Lebanon shall come to you,
  The cypress, the pine, and the box tree
    together,
  To beautify the place of My sanctuary;
  And I will make the place of My feet
    glorious.
¹⁴Also the sons of those who afflicted you
  Shall come bowing to you,
  And all those who despised you shall fall
    prostrate at the soles of your feet;
  And they shall call you The City of the
    LORD,
  Zion of the Holy One of Israel.

¹⁵"Whereas you have been forsaken and hated,
  So that no one went through *you,*
  I will make you an eternal excellence,
  A joy of many generations.
¹⁶You shall drink the milk of the Gentiles,
  And milk the breast of kings;
  You shall know that I, the LORD, *am* your
    Savior
  And your Redeemer, the Mighty One of
    Jacob.

¹⁷"Instead of bronze I will bring gold,
  Instead of iron I will bring silver,
  Instead of wood, bronze,
  And instead of stones, iron.
  I will also make your officers peace,
  And your magistrates righteousness.
¹⁸Violence shall no longer be heard in your
    land,
  Neither wasting nor destruction within your
    borders;
  But you shall call your walls Salvation,
  And your gates Praise.

GOD THE GLORY OF HIS PEOPLE

¹⁹"The sun shall no longer be your light by day,
  Nor for brightness shall the moon give light
    to you;
  But the LORD will be to you an everlasting
    light,
  And your God your glory.

²⁰Your sun shall no longer go down,
Nor shall your moon withdraw itself;
For the LORD will be your everlasting light,
And the days of your mourning shall be
    ended.
²¹Also your people *shall* all *be* righteous;
They shall inherit the land forever,
The branch of My planting,
The work of My hands,
That I may be glorified.
²²A little one shall become a thousand,
And a small one a strong nation.
I, the LORD, will hasten it in its time."

THE GOOD NEWS OF SALVATION

61 "The Spirit of the Lord GOD *is* upon Me,
Because the LORD has anointed Me
To preach good tidings to the poor;
He has sent Me to heal the brokenhearted,
To proclaim liberty to the captives,
And the opening of the prison to *those who
    are* bound;
²To proclaim the acceptable year of the LORD,
And the day of vengeance of our God;
To comfort all who mourn,
³To console those who mourn in Zion,
To give them beauty for ashes,
The oil of joy for mourning,
The garment of praise for the spirit of
    heaviness;
That they may be called trees of
    righteousness,
The planting of the LORD, that He may be
    glorified."

⁴And they shall rebuild the old ruins,
They shall raise up the former desolations,
And they shall repair the ruined cities,
The desolations of many generations.
⁵Strangers shall stand and feed your flocks,
And the sons of the foreigner
Shall be your plowmen and your vinedressers.
⁶But you shall be named the priests of the
    LORD,
They shall call you the servants of our God.
You shall eat the riches of the Gentiles,
And in their glory you shall boast.
⁷Instead of your shame *you shall have* double
    honor,

And *instead of* confusion they shall rejoice in
    their portion.
Therefore in their land they shall possess
    double;
Everlasting joy shall be theirs.

⁸"For I, the LORD, love justice;
I hate robbery for burnt offering;
I will direct their work in truth,
And will make with them an everlasting
    covenant.
⁹Their descendants shall be known among the
    Gentiles,
And their offspring among the people.
All who see them shall acknowledge them,
That they *are* the posterity *whom* the LORD
    has blessed."

¹⁰I will greatly rejoice in the LORD,
My soul shall be joyful in my God;
For He has clothed me with the garments of
    salvation,
He has covered me with the robe of
    righteousness,
As a bridegroom decks *himself* with
    ornaments,
And as a bride adorns *herself* with her jewels.
¹¹For as the earth brings forth its bud,
As the garden causes the things that are sown
    in it to spring forth,
So the Lord GOD will cause righteousness
    and praise to spring forth before all the
    nations.

ASSURANCE OF ZION'S SALVATION

62 For Zion's sake I will not hold My peace,
And for Jerusalem's sake I will not rest,
Until her righteousness goes forth as
    brightness,
And her salvation as a lamp *that* burns.
²The Gentiles shall see your righteousness,
And all kings your glory.
You shall be called by a new name,
Which the mouth of the LORD will name.
³You shall also be a crown of glory
In the hand of the LORD,
And a royal diadem
In the hand of your God.
⁴You shall no longer be termed Forsaken,

Nor shall your land any more be termed
 Desolate;
But you shall be called Hephzibah,[a] and your
 land Beulah;[b]
For the LORD delights in you,
And your land shall be married.
⁵For *as* a young man marries a virgin,
 So shall your sons marry you;
And *as* the bridegroom rejoices over the
 bride,
 So shall your God rejoice over you.

⁶I have set watchmen on your walls,
 O Jerusalem;
They shall never hold their peace day or
 night.
You who make mention of the LORD, do not
 keep silent,
⁷And give Him no rest till He establishes
And till He makes Jerusalem a praise in the
 earth.

⁸The LORD has sworn by His right hand
And by the arm of His strength:
"Surely I will no longer give your grain
 As food for your enemies;
And the sons of the foreigner shall not drink
 your new wine,
For which you have labored.
⁹But those who have gathered it shall eat it,
And praise the LORD;
Those who have brought it together shall
 drink it in My holy courts."

¹⁰Go through,
 Go through the gates!
Prepare the way for the people;
Build up,
Build up the highway!
Take out the stones,
Lift up a banner for the peoples!

¹¹Indeed the LORD has proclaimed
To the end of the world:
"Say to the daughter of Zion,
"Surely your salvation is coming;
 Behold, His reward *is* with Him,
And His work before Him.'"
¹²And they shall call them The Holy People,

The Redeemed of the LORD;
And you shall be called Sought Out,
A City Not Forsaken.

THE LORD IN JUDGMENT AND SALVATION

63 Who *is* this who comes from Edom,
 With dyed garments from Bozrah,
This *One who is* glorious in His apparel,
Traveling in the greatness of His strength?—

"I who speak in righteousness, mighty to save."

²Why *is* Your apparel red,
And Your garments like one who treads in
 the winepress?

³"I have trodden the winepress alone,
And from the peoples no one *was* with Me.
For I have trodden them in My anger,
And trampled them in My fury;
Their blood is sprinkled upon My garments,
And I have stained all My robes.
⁴For the day of vengeance *is* in My heart,
And the year of My redeemed has come.
⁵I looked, but *there was* no one to help,
And I wondered
That *there was* no one to uphold;
Therefore My own arm brought salvation for
 Me;
And My own fury, it sustained Me.
⁶I have trodden down the peoples in My
 anger,
Made them drunk in My fury,
And brought down their strength to the
 earth."

GOD'S MERCY REMEMBERED

⁷I will mention the lovingkindnesses of the
 LORD
And the praises of the LORD,
According to all that the LORD has bestowed
 on us,
And the great goodness toward the house of
 Israel,
Which He has bestowed on them according
 to His mercies,
According to the multitude of His
 lovingkindnesses.

62:4 [a]Literally *My Delight Is in Her* [b]Literally *Married*

THROUGH THE GRID

*Where Have All the Dreamers Gone?
Observations from a Biblical
Worldview: God Communicates
Through Suffering (Is. 53)*

God can use the suffering of human individuals to communicate truth to those who are listening and watching. Although many claim that suffering and evil drive people away from God, it often happens the exact opposite way, in that the presence of suffering and evil turn people toward God as they seek answers and meaning to the incomprehensibility of evil. Christian believers recognize that living a life filled with meaning and purpose does not mean that life will be free of problems or from the presence of evil. God makes no such claims. In fact, God can use suffering to get our attention or to revamp our perspectives on life and existence.

Unfortunately, no definitive or easy answer can be given to those who ask why an all-good and all-powerful God allowed evil to transpire. However, an answer does exist in the Person of Jesus Christ. God speaks to human beings through their pain; and in the midst of their suffering, He communicates love, assurance, and comfort. Ultimately, suffering should not prevent the Christian believer from engaging the culture in a way that allows the Christian's identity as "salt and light" to be emphasized (Matt. 5:13–16). The ways in which we respond to suffering give us many opportunities to demonstrate our trust in God, as well as our love for those who may be suffering. May we be observed as faithful as we live out our identities as salt and light in the midst of a dark and broken world.

8For He said, "Surely they *are* My people,
   Children *who* will not lie."
So He became their Savior.
9In all their affliction He was afflicted,
   And the Angel of His Presence saved them;
   In His love and in His pity He redeemed
      them;
   And He bore them and carried them
   All the days of old.
10But they rebelled and grieved His Holy
      Spirit;
   So He turned Himself against them as an
      enemy,
   And He fought against them.

11Then he remembered the days of old,
   Moses *and* his people, *saying:*
"Where *is* He who brought them up out of
      the sea
   With the shepherd of His flock?
   Where *is* He who put His Holy Spirit within
      them,

12Who led *them* by the right hand of Moses,
   With His glorious arm,
   Dividing the water before them
   To make for Himself an everlasting name,
13Who led them through the deep,
   As a horse in the wilderness,
   That they might not stumble?"

14As a beast goes down into the valley,
   And the Spirit of the LORD causes him to
      rest,
   So You lead Your people,
   To make Yourself a glorious name.

A PRAYER OF PENITENCE

15Look down from heaven,
   And see from Your habitation, holy and
      glorious.
   Where *are* Your zeal and Your strength,
   The yearning of Your heart and Your mercies
      toward me?
   Are they restrained?

¹⁶Doubtless You *are* our Father,
 Though Abraham was ignorant of us,
 And Israel does not acknowledge us.
 You, O LORD, *are* our Father;
 Our Redeemer from Everlasting *is* Your
  name.
¹⁷O LORD, why have You made us stray from
  Your ways,
 And hardened our heart from Your fear?
 Return for Your servants' sake,
 The tribes of Your inheritance.
¹⁸Your holy people have possessed *it* but a little
  while;
 Our adversaries have trodden down Your
  sanctuary.
¹⁹We have become *like* those of old, over
  whom You never ruled,
 Those who were never called by Your name.

64 Oh, that You would rend the heavens!
  That You would come down!
 That the mountains might shake at Your
  presence—
²As fire burns brushwood,
 As fire causes water to boil—
 To make Your name known to Your
  adversaries,
 That the nations may tremble at Your
  presence!
³When You did awesome things *for which* we
  did not look,
 You came down,
 The mountains shook at Your presence.
⁴For since the beginning of the world
 Men have not heard nor perceived by the ear,
 Nor has the eye seen any God besides You,
 Who acts for the one who waits for Him.
⁵You meet him who rejoices and does
  righteousness,
 Who remembers You in Your ways.
 You are indeed angry, for we have sinned—
 In these ways we continue;
 And we need to be saved.

⁶But we are all like an unclean *thing,*
 And all our righteousnesses *are* like filthy rags;
 We all fade as a leaf,
 And our iniquities, like the wind,
 Have taken us away.

⁷And *there is* no one who calls on Your name,
 Who stirs himself up to take hold of You;
 For You have hidden Your face from us,
 And have consumed us because of our
  iniquities.

⁸But now, O LORD,
 You *are* our Father;
 We *are* the clay, and You our potter;
 And all we *are* the work of Your hand.
⁹Do not be furious, O LORD,
 Nor remember iniquity forever;
 Indeed, please look—we all *are* Your people!
¹⁰Your holy cities are a wilderness,
 Zion is a wilderness,
 Jerusalem a desolation.
¹¹Our holy and beautiful temple,
 Where our fathers praised You,
 Is burned up with fire;
 And all our pleasant things are laid waste.
¹²Will You restrain Yourself because of these
  things, O LORD?
 Will You hold Your peace, and afflict us very
  severely?

THE RIGHTEOUSNESS OF GOD'S JUDGMENT

65 "I was sought by *those who* did not ask
  for Me;
 I was found by *those who* did not seek Me.
 I said, 'Here I am, here I am,'
 To a nation *that* was not called by My name.
²I have stretched out My hands all day long to
  a rebellious people,
 Who walk in a way *that is* not good,
 According to their own thoughts;
³A people who provoke Me to anger
  continually to My face;
 Who sacrifice in gardens,
 And burn incense on altars of brick;
⁴Who sit among the graves,
 And spend the night in the tombs;
 Who eat swine's flesh,
 And the broth of abominable things is *in* their
  vessels;
⁵Who say, 'Keep to yourself,
 Do not come near me,
 For I am holier than you!'
 These *are* smoke in My nostrils,
 A fire that burns all the day.

⁶"Behold, *it is* written before Me:
I will not keep silence, but will repay—
Even repay into their bosom—
⁷Your iniquities and the iniquities of your
fathers together,"
Says the LORD,
"Who have burned incense on the mountains
And blasphemed Me on the hills;
Therefore I will measure their former work
into their bosom."

⁸Thus says the LORD:

"As the new wine is found in the cluster,
And *one* says, 'Do not destroy it,
For a blessing *is* in it,'
So will I do for My servants' sake,
That I may not destroy them all.
⁹I will bring forth descendants from Jacob,
And from Judah an heir of My mountains;
My elect shall inherit it,
And My servants shall dwell there.
¹⁰Sharon shall be a fold of flocks,
And the Valley of Achor a place for herds to
lie down,
For My people who have sought Me.

¹¹"But you *are* those who forsake the LORD,
Who forget My holy mountain,
Who prepare a table for Gad,ᵃ
And who furnish a drink offering for Meni.ᵇ
¹²Therefore I will number you for the sword,
And you shall all bow down to the slaughter;
Because, when I called, you did not answer;
When I spoke, you did not hear,
But did evil before My eyes,
And chose *that* in which I do not delight."

¹³Therefore thus says the Lord GOD:

"Behold, My servants shall eat,
But you shall be hungry;
Behold, My servants shall drink,
But you shall be thirsty;
Behold, My servants shall rejoice,
But you shall be ashamed;
¹⁴Behold, My servants shall sing for joy of
heart,
But you shall cry for sorrow of heart,

And wail for grief of spirit.
¹⁵You shall leave your name as a curse to My
chosen;
For the Lord GOD will slay you,
And call His servants by another name;
¹⁶So that he who blesses himself in the earth
Shall bless himself in the God of truth;
And he who swears in the earth
Shall swear by the God of truth;
Because the former troubles are forgotten,
And because they are hidden from My eyes.

THE GLORIOUS NEW CREATION

¹⁷"For behold, I create new heavens and a new
earth;
And the former shall not be remembered or
come to mind.
¹⁸But be glad and rejoice forever in what I
create;
For behold, I create Jerusalem *as* a rejoicing,
And her people a joy.
¹⁹I will rejoice in Jerusalem,
And joy in My people;
The voice of weeping shall no longer be
heard in her,
Nor the voice of crying.

²⁰"No more shall an infant from there *live but a
few* days,
Nor an old man who has not fulfilled his
days;
For the child shall die one hundred years old,
But the sinner *being* one hundred years old
shall be accursed.
²¹They shall build houses and inhabit *them;*
They shall plant vineyards and eat their fruit.
²²They shall not build and another inhabit;
They shall not plant and another eat;
For as the days of a tree, *so shall be* the days of
My people,
And My elect shall long enjoy the work of
their hands.
²³They shall not labor in vain,
Nor bring forth children for trouble;
For they *shall be* the descendants of the
blessed of the LORD,
And their offspring with them.

65:11 ᵃLiterally *Troop* or *Fortune,* a pagan deity ᵇLiterally *Number* or
Destiny, a pagan deity

²⁴"It shall come to pass
That before they call, I will answer;
And while they are still speaking, I will hear.
²⁵The wolf and the lamb shall feed together,
The lion shall eat straw like the ox,
And dust *shall be* the serpent's food.
They shall not hurt nor destroy in all My
    holy mountain,"
Says the LORD.

TRUE WORSHIP AND FALSE

66 Thus says the LORD:

"Heaven is My throne,
And earth *is* My footstool.
Where *is* the house that you will build Me?
And where *is* the place of My rest?
²For all those *things* My hand has made,
And all those *things* exist,"
Says the LORD.
"But on this *one* will I look:
On *him who is* poor and of a contrite spirit,
And who trembles at My word.

³"He who kills a bull *is as if* he slays a man;
He who sacrifices a lamb, *as if* he breaks a
    dog's neck;
He who offers a grain offering, *as if he offers*
    swine's blood;
He who burns incense, *as if* he blesses an
    idol.
Just as they have chosen their own ways,
And their soul delights in their
    abominations,
⁴So will I choose their delusions,
And bring their fears on them;
Because, when I called, no one answered,
When I spoke they did not hear;
But they did evil before My eyes,
And chose *that* in which I do not delight."

THE LORD VINDICATES ZION

⁵Hear the word of the LORD,
You who tremble at His word:
"Your brethren who hated you,
Who cast you out for My name's sake, said,
"Let the LORD be glorified,
That we may see your joy.'
But they shall be ashamed."

⁶The sound of noise from the city!
A voice from the temple!
The voice of the LORD,
Who fully repays His enemies!

⁷"Before she was in labor, she gave birth;
Before her pain came,
She delivered a male child.
⁸Who has heard such a thing?
Who has seen such things?
Shall the earth be made to give birth in one
    day?
Or shall a nation be born at once?
For as soon as Zion was in labor,
She gave birth to her children.
⁹Shall I bring to the time of birth, and not
    cause delivery?" says the LORD.
"Shall I who cause delivery shut up *the womb?*"
    says your God.
¹⁰"Rejoice with Jerusalem,
And be glad with her, all you who love her;
Rejoice for joy with her, all you who mourn
    for her;
¹¹That you may feed and be satisfied
With the consolation of her bosom,
That you may drink deeply and be delighted
With the abundance of her glory."

¹²For thus says the LORD:

"Behold, I will extend peace to her like a river,
And the glory of the Gentiles like a flowing
    stream.
Then you shall feed;
On *her* sides shall you be carried,
And be dandled on *her* knees.
¹³As one whom his mother comforts,
So I will comfort you;
And you shall be comforted in Jerusalem."

THE REIGN AND INDIGNATION OF GOD

¹⁴When you see *this,* your heart shall rejoice,
And your bones shall flourish like grass;
The hand of the LORD shall be known to His
    servants,
And *His* indignation to His enemies.
¹⁵For behold, the LORD will come with fire
And with His chariots, like a whirlwind,
To render His anger with fury,

And His rebuke with flames of fire.
¹⁶For by fire and by His sword
    The LORD will judge all flesh;
    And the slain of the LORD shall be many.

¹⁷"Those who sanctify themselves and purify
       themselves,
    To go to the gardens
    After an *idol* in the midst,
    Eating swine's flesh and the abomination
       and the mouse,
    Shall be consumed together," says the
       LORD.

¹⁸"For I *know* their works and their thoughts. It shall be that I will gather all nations and tongues; and they shall come and see My glory. ¹⁹I will set a sign among them; and those among them who escape I will send to the nations: *to* Tarshish and Pul[a] and Lud, who draw the bow, and Tubal and Javan, *to* the coastlands afar off who have not heard My fame nor seen My glory. And they shall declare My glory among the Gentiles. ²⁰Then they shall bring all your brethren for an offering to the LORD out of all nations, on horses and in chariots and in litters, on mules and on camels, to My holy mountain Jerusalem," says the LORD, "as the children of Israel bring an offering in a clean vessel into the house of the LORD. ²¹And I will also take some of them for priests *and* Levites," says the LORD.

²²"For as the new heavens and the new earth
    Which I will make shall remain before Me,"
       says the LORD,
   "So shall your descendants and your name
       remain.
²³And it shall come to pass
    That from one New Moon to another,
    And from one Sabbath to another,
    All flesh shall come to worship before Me,"
       says the LORD.

²⁴"And they shall go forth and look
    Upon the corpses of the men
    Who have transgressed against Me.
    For their worm does not die,
    And their fire is not quenched.
    They shall be an abhorrence to all flesh."

66:19 [a]Following Masoretic Text and Targum; Septuagint reads *Put* (compare Jeremiah 46:9).

IMPACT OF THE BOOK

IDEA | *Our sins and their consequences will always catch up to us. God keeps His promise and works His plan for His people.*

MESSAGE | *God has a plan for each one of our lives; even before Jeremiah was born, God set him apart to prophesy to His people. Jeremiah's calling was not an easy one. He brought bad news to the people because of their sin, and the people rejected his message. Although he wanted to quit several times, Jeremiah determined to stay faithful to God's task for his life. Our calling may mean some hardships in our own lives, but we must determine to stay true to God—even through the difficult assignments.*

PEOPLE | *Baruch, Hananiah, Jehoiakim, Jeremiah, Pashhur*

AUTHOR | *Jeremiah, known as "The Weeping Prophet," penned this book near the end of his ministry. He never married, and his ministry began when he was still in his teens. He prophesied for over forty years and died in Egypt.*

CULTURE | *Jeremiah prophesied during the reigns of the last five kings of Judah and during the early days of the Exile (c. 626–585 BC). During this time, Egypt, Assyria, and Babylon were vying for world domination. Although Judah was a small country, it signified a strategic land bridge. By the end of Jeremiah's life, Babylon had become supreme, and the land of Judah had been decimated. In this book, though, Jeremiah foretells the ultimate destruction of Babylon and proclaims God's promise to restore His people.*

TIMELINE | *c. 585 BC*

KEY SCRIPTURE MEMORY VERSES | 1:5; 9:23, 24; 17:9; 29:11–13; 31:31–33; 32:17

JEREMIAH

1 The words of Jeremiah the son of Hilkiah, of the priests who *were* in Anathoth in the land of Benjamin, ²to whom the word of the LORD came in the days of Josiah the son of Amon, king of Judah, in the thirteenth year of his reign. ³It came also in the days of Jehoiakim the son of Josiah, king of Judah, until the end of the eleventh year of Zedekiah the son of Josiah, king of Judah, until the carrying away of Jerusalem captive in the fifth month.

THE PROPHET IS CALLED

⁴Then the word of the LORD came to me, saying:

⁵"Before I formed you in the womb I knew you;
Before you were born I sanctified you;
I ordained you a prophet to the nations."

⁶Then said I:

"Ah, Lord GOD!
Behold, I cannot speak, for I *am* a youth."

⁷But the LORD said to me:

"Do not say, 'I *am* a youth,'
For you shall go to all to whom I send you,
And whatever I command you, you shall speak.
⁸Do not be afraid of their faces,
For I *am* with you to deliver you," says the LORD.

⁹Then the LORD put forth His hand and touched my mouth, and the LORD said to me:

"Behold, I have put My words in your mouth.
¹⁰See, I have this day set you over the nations and over the kingdoms,
To root out and to pull down,
To destroy and to throw down,
To build and to plant."

¹¹Moreover the word of the LORD came to me, saying, "Jeremiah, what do you see?"
And I said, "I see a branch of an almond tree."
¹²Then the LORD said to me, "You have seen well, for I am ready to perform My word."

¹³And the word of the LORD came to me the second time, saying, "What do you see?"
And I said, "I see a boiling pot, and it is facing away from the north."
¹⁴Then the LORD said to me:

"Out of the north calamity shall break forth
On all the inhabitants of the land.
¹⁵For behold, I am calling
All the families of the kingdoms of the north," says the LORD;
"They shall come and each one set his throne
At the entrance of the gates of Jerusalem,
Against all its walls all around,
And against all the cities of Judah.
¹⁶I will utter My judgments
Against them concerning all their wickedness,
Because they have forsaken Me,
Burned incense to other gods,
And worshiped the works of their own hands.

¹⁷"Therefore prepare yourself and arise,
And speak to them all that I command you.
Do not be dismayed before their faces,
Lest I dismay you before them.
¹⁸For behold, I have made you this day
A fortified city and an iron pillar,
And bronze walls against the whole land—
Against the kings of Judah,
Against its princes,
Against its priests,
And against the people of the land.
¹⁹They will fight against you,
But they shall not prevail against you.
For I *am* with you," says the LORD, "to deliver you."

GOD'S CASE AGAINST ISRAEL

2 Moreover the word of the LORD came to me, saying, ²"Go and cry in the hearing of Jerusalem, saying, 'Thus says the LORD:

"I remember you,
The kindness of your youth,
The love of your betrothal,
When you went after Me in the wilderness,
In a land not sown.

LEADERSHIP ISSUES

GC2: Who Am I? One-of-a-Kind Original

JEREMIAH 1:5 *Before I formed you in the womb I knew you; before you were born I sanctified you; I ordained you a prophet to the nations.*

Have you ever stepped outside on a winter's morning as the soft flakes of snow drifted slowly to the ground? If you could inspect the microscopic details of these tiny snowflakes landing on your sleeve, you would see, of course, that each has a distinct shape. You've probably seen a photograph or video that magnifies a snowflake; if so, you've certainly marveled at the intricate shape, structure, and beauty of that single flake. And undoubtedly you've heard scientists claim that no two snowflakes are alike. They are all one-of-a-kind originals.

You and I and other people in our lives are one-of-a-kind originals as well. We have been given distinct and special identities that make each of us unique. Created for relationships, we unfortunately try to relate in all the wrong ways because of sin. The prophet Jeremiah gave another example in his writings when he referred to the potter remaking the clay vessel after it had been marred (Jer. 18:1–6). Coming into relationship with God through the miracle of being born again allows His Spirit to lead each one of us to discover the person He created each of us to be.

Born alienated and disconnected from God, we have all lost the sense of who we really are. But it is through the relational atmosphere of God's love, acceptance, understanding, and continuous involvement in our lives that we can discover the unique people God made us to be, that one-of-a-kind original designed to relate to God and others.

Pause to celebrate that the Creator knows you, formed you, and longs to love you as a one-of-a-kind original!

GC2
GREAT COMMANDMENT
COMMISSION

³Israel *was* holiness to the LORD,
The firstfruits of His increase.
All that devour him will offend;
Disaster will come upon them," says the
    LORD.' "

⁴Hear the word of the LORD, O house of Jacob and all the families of the house of Israel.
⁵Thus says the LORD:

"What injustice have your fathers found in
    Me,
That they have gone far from Me,
Have followed idols,
And have become idolaters?
⁶Neither did they say, 'Where *is* the LORD,
Who brought us up out of the land of Egypt,
Who led us through the wilderness,
Through a land of deserts and pits,
Through a land of drought and the shadow of
    death,
Through a land that no one crossed
And where no one dwelt?'
⁷I brought you into a bountiful country,
To eat its fruit and its goodness.
But when you entered, you defiled My land
And made My heritage an abomination.
⁸The priests did not say, 'Where *is* the LORD?'
And those who handle the law did not know
    Me;
The rulers also transgressed against Me;
The prophets prophesied by Baal,
And walked after *things that* do not profit.

⁹"Therefore I will yet bring charges against
    you," says the LORD,
"And against your children's children I will
    bring charges.
¹⁰For pass beyond the coasts of Cyprusᵃ and
    see,
Send to Kedarᵇ and consider diligently,
And see if there has been such *a thing*.
¹¹Has a nation changed *its* gods,
Which *are* not gods?
But My people have changed their Glory
For *what* does not profit.
¹²Be astonished, O heavens, at this,
And be horribly afraid;
Be very desolate," says the LORD.

¹³"For My people have committed two evils:
They have forsaken Me, the fountain of living
    waters,
And hewn themselves cisterns—broken
    cisterns that can hold no water.

¹⁴"*Is* Israel a servant?
Is he a homeborn *slave?*
Why is he plundered?
¹⁵The young lions roared at him, *and* growled;
They made his land waste;
His cities are burned, without inhabitant.
¹⁶Also the people of Nophᵃ and Tahpanhes
Have broken the crown of your head.
¹⁷Have you not brought this on yourself,
In that you have forsaken the LORD your
    God
When He led you in the way?
¹⁸And now why take the road to Egypt,
To drink the waters of Sihor?
Or why take the road to Assyria,
To drink the waters of the River?ᵃ
¹⁹Your own wickedness will correct you,
And your backslidings will rebuke you.
Know therefore and see that *it is* an evil and
    bitter *thing*
That you have forsaken the LORD your
    God,
And the fear of Me *is* not in you,"
Says the Lord GOD of hosts.

²⁰"For of old I have broken your yoke *and* burst
    your bonds;
And you said, 'I will not transgress,'
When on every high hill and under every
    green tree
You lay down, playing the harlot.
²¹Yet I had planted you a noble vine, a seed of
    highest quality.
How then have you turned before Me
Into the degenerate plant of an alien vine?
²²For though you wash yourself with lye, and
    use much soap,
Yet your iniquity is marked before Me," says
    the Lord GOD.

2:10 ᵃHebrew *Kittim*, western lands, especially Cyprus ᵇIn the northern Arabian desert, representative of the eastern cultures
2:16 ᵃThat is, Memphis in ancient Egypt **2:18** ᵃThat is, the Euphrates

²³"How can you say, 'I am not polluted,
  I have not gone after the Baals'?
  See your way in the valley;
  Know what you have done:
  You are a swift dromedary breaking loose in
    her ways,
²⁴A wild donkey used to the wilderness,
  That sniffs at the wind in her desire;
  In her time of mating, who can turn her
    away?
  All those who seek her will not weary
    themselves;
  In her month they will find her.
²⁵Withhold your foot from being unshod, and
    your throat from thirst.
  But you said, 'There is no hope.
  No! For I have loved aliens, and after them I
    will go.'

²⁶"As the thief is ashamed when he is found out,
  So is the house of Israel ashamed;
  They and their kings and their princes, and
    their priests and their prophets,
²⁷Saying to a tree, 'You *are* my father,'
  And to a stone, 'You gave birth to me.'
  For they have turned *their* back to Me, and
    not *their* face.
  But in the time of their trouble
  They will say, 'Arise and save us.'
²⁸But where *are* your gods that you have made
    for yourselves?
  Let them arise,
  If they can save you in the time of your
    trouble;
  For *according to* the number of your cities
  Are your gods, O Judah.

²⁹"Why will you plead with Me?
  You all have transgressed against Me," says the
    LORD.
³⁰"In vain I have chastened your children;
  They received no correction.
  Your sword has devoured your prophets
  Like a destroying lion.

³¹"O generation, see the word of the LORD!
  Have I been a wilderness to Israel,
  Or a land of darkness?
  Why do My people say, 'We are lords;

We will come no more to You'?
³²Can a virgin forget her ornaments,
  Or a bride her attire?
  Yet My people have forgotten Me days
    without number.

³³"Why do you beautify your way to seek love?
  Therefore you have also taught
  The wicked women your ways.
³⁴Also on your skirts is found
  The blood of the lives of the poor innocents.
  I have not found it by secret search,
  But plainly on all these things.
³⁵Yet you say, 'Because I am innocent,
  Surely His anger shall turn from me.'
  Behold, I will plead My case against you,
  Because you say, 'I have not sinned.'
³⁶Why do you gad about so much to change
    your way?
  Also you shall be ashamed of Egypt as you
    were ashamed of Assyria.
³⁷Indeed you will go forth from him
  With your hands on your head;
  For the LORD has rejected your trusted allies,
  And you will not prosper by them.

ISRAEL IS SHAMELESS

3 "They say, 'If a man divorces his wife,
  And she goes from him
  And becomes another man's,
  May he return to her again?'
  Would not that land be greatly polluted?
  But you have played the harlot with many
    lovers;
  Yet return to Me," says the LORD.

²"Lift up your eyes to the desolate heights and
    see:
  Where have you not lain *with men*?
  By the road you have sat for them
  Like an Arabian in the wilderness;
  And you have polluted the land
  With your harlotries and your wickedness.
³Therefore the showers have been withheld,
  And there has been no latter rain.
  You have had a harlot's forehead;
  You refuse to be ashamed.
⁴Will you not from this time cry to Me,
  'My Father, You *are* the guide of my youth?

⁵Will He remain angry forever?
  Will He keep it to the end?'
  Behold, you have spoken and done evil
      things,
  As you were able."

A CALL TO REPENTANCE

⁶The LORD said also to me in the days of Josiah the king: "Have you seen what backsliding Israel has done? She has gone up on every high mountain and under every green tree, and there played the harlot. ⁷And I said, after she had done all these *things,* 'Return to Me.' But she did not return. And her treacherous sister Judah saw it. ⁸Then I saw that for all the causes for which backsliding Israel had committed adultery, I had put her away and given her a certificate of divorce; yet her treacherous sister Judah did not fear, but went and played the harlot also. ⁹So it came to pass, through her casual harlotry, that she defiled the land and committed adultery with stones and trees. ¹⁰And yet for all this her treacherous sister Judah has not turned to Me with her whole heart, but in pretense," says the LORD.

¹¹Then the LORD said to me, "Backsliding Israel has shown herself more righteous than treacherous Judah. ¹²Go and proclaim these words toward the north, and say:

'Return, backsliding Israel,' says the LORD;
'I will not cause My anger to fall on you.
For I *am* merciful,' says the LORD;
'I will not remain angry forever.
¹³Only acknowledge your iniquity,
  That you have transgressed against the LORD
    your God,
  And have scattered your charms
  To alien deities under every green tree,
  And you have not obeyed My voice,' says the
    LORD.

¹⁴"Return, O backsliding children," says the LORD; "for I am married to you. I will take you, one from a city and two from a family, and I will bring you to Zion. ¹⁵And I will give you shepherds according to My heart, who will feed you with knowledge and understanding. ¹⁶"Then it shall come to pass, when you are multiplied and increased in the land in those days," says the LORD, "that they will say no more, 'The ark of the covenant of the LORD.' It shall not come to mind, nor shall they remember it, nor shall they visit *it,* nor shall it be made anymore.

¹⁷"At that time Jerusalem shall be called The Throne of the LORD, and all the nations shall be gathered to it, to the name of the LORD, to Jerusalem. No more shall they follow the dictates of their evil hearts.

¹⁸"In those days the house of Judah shall walk with the house of Israel, and they shall come together out of the land of the north to the land that I have given as an inheritance to your fathers.

¹⁹"But I said:

'How can I put you among the children
  And give you a pleasant land,
  A beautiful heritage of the hosts of
    nations?'

"And I said:

'You shall call Me, "My Father,"
  And not turn away from Me.'
²⁰Surely, *as* a wife treacherously departs from
    her husband,
So have you dealt treacherously with Me,
  O house of Israel," says the LORD.

²¹A voice was heard on the desolate heights,
  Weeping *and* supplications of the children of
    Israel.
For they have perverted their way;
  They have forgotten the LORD their God.

²²"Return, you backsliding children,
  And I will heal your backslidings."

"Indeed we do come to You,
  For You are the LORD our God.
²³Truly, in vain *is salvation hoped for* from the
    hills,
  And from the multitude of mountains;
Truly, in the LORD our God
  Is the salvation of Israel.
²⁴For shame has devoured
  The labor of our fathers from our youth—
  Their flocks and their herds,
  Their sons and their daughters.

²⁵We lie down in our shame,
And our reproach covers us.
For we have sinned against the LORD our
God,
We and our fathers,
From our youth even to this day,
And have not obeyed the voice of the LORD
our God."

4 "If you will return, O Israel," says the LORD,
"Return to Me;
And if you will put away your abominations
out of My sight,
Then you shall not be moved.
²And you shall swear, 'The LORD lives,'
In truth, in judgment, and in righteousness;
The nations shall bless themselves in Him,
And in Him they shall glory."

³For thus says the LORD to the men of Judah
and Jerusalem:

"Break up your fallow ground,
And do not sow among thorns.
⁴Circumcise yourselves to the LORD,
And take away the foreskins of your hearts,
You men of Judah and inhabitants of
Jerusalem,
Lest My fury come forth like fire,
And burn so that no one can quench it,
Because of the evil of your doings."

An Imminent Invasion

⁵Declare in Judah and proclaim in Jerusalem,
and say:

"Blow the trumpet in the land;
Cry, 'Gather together,'
And say, 'Assemble yourselves,
And let us go into the fortified cities.'
⁶Set up the standard toward Zion.
Take refuge! Do not delay!
For I will bring disaster from the north,
And great destruction."

⁷The lion has come up from his thicket,
And the destroyer of nations is on his way.
He has gone forth from his place
To make your land desolate.

Your cities will be laid waste,
Without inhabitant.
⁸For this, clothe yourself with sackcloth,
Lament and wail.
For the fierce anger of the LORD
Has not turned back from us.

⁹"And it shall come to pass in that day," says the
LORD,
"That the heart of the king shall perish,
And the heart of the princes;
The priests shall be astonished,
And the prophets shall wonder."

¹⁰Then I said, "Ah, Lord GOD!
Surely You have greatly deceived this people
and Jerusalem,
Saying, 'You shall have peace,'
Whereas the sword reaches to the heart."

¹¹At that time it will be said
To this people and to Jerusalem,
"A dry wind of the desolate heights blows in
the wilderness
Toward the daughter of My people—
Not to fan or to cleanse—
¹²A wind too strong for these will come for Me;
Now I will also speak judgment against
them."

¹³"Behold, he shall come up like clouds,
And his chariots like a whirlwind.
His horses are swifter than eagles.
Woe to us, for we are plundered!"

¹⁴O Jerusalem, wash your heart from
wickedness,
That you may be saved.
How long shall your evil thoughts lodge
within you?
¹⁵For a voice declares from Dan
And proclaims affliction from Mount
Ephraim:
¹⁶"Make mention to the nations,
Yes, proclaim against Jerusalem,
That watchers come from a far country
And raise their voice against the cities of Judah.
¹⁷Like keepers of a field they are against her all
around,

Because she has been rebellious against Me,"
    says the LORD.
18"Your ways and your doings
    Have procured these *things* for you.
    This *is* your wickedness,
    Because it is bitter,
    Because it reaches to your heart."

SORROW FOR THE DOOMED NATION

19O my soul, my soul!
    I am pained in my very heart!
    My heart makes a noise in me;
    I cannot hold my peace,
    Because you have heard, O my soul,
    The sound of the trumpet,
    The alarm of war.
20Destruction upon destruction is cried,
    For the whole land is plundered.
    Suddenly my tents are plundered,
    And my curtains in a moment.
21How long will I see the standard,
    And hear the sound of the trumpet?

22"For My people *are* foolish,
    They have not known Me.
    They *are* silly children,
    And they have no understanding.
    They *are* wise to do evil,
    But to do good they have no
        knowledge."

23I beheld the earth, and indeed *it was* without
        form, and void;
    And the heavens, they *had* no light.
24I beheld the mountains, and indeed they
        trembled,
    And all the hills moved back and forth.
25I beheld, and indeed *there was* no man,
    And all the birds of the heavens had fled.
26I beheld, and indeed the fruitful land *was* a
        wilderness,
    And all its cities were broken down
    At the presence of the LORD,
    By His fierce anger.

27For thus says the LORD:

"The whole land shall be desolate;
    Yet I will not make a full end.

28For this shall the earth mourn,
    And the heavens above be black,
    Because I have spoken.
    I have purposed and will not relent,
    Nor will I turn back from it.
29The whole city shall flee from the noise of
        the horsemen and bowmen.
    They shall go into thickets and climb up on
        the rocks.
    Every city *shall be* forsaken,
    And not a man shall dwell in it.

30"And *when* you *are* plundered,
    What will you do?
    Though you clothe yourself with crimson,
    Though you adorn *yourself* with ornaments of
        gold,
    Though you enlarge your eyes with paint,
    In vain you will make yourself fair;
    Your lovers will despise you;
    They will seek your life.

31"For I have heard a voice as of a woman in
        labor,
    The anguish as of her who brings forth her
        first child,
    The voice of the daughter of Zion bewailing
        herself;
    She spreads her hands, *saying,*
    'Woe *is* me now, for my soul is weary
    Because of murderers!'

THE JUSTICE OF GOD'S JUDGMENT

5 "Run to and fro through the streets of
        Jerusalem;
    See now and know;
    And seek in her open places
    If you can find a man,
    If there is *anyone* who executes judgment,
    Who seeks the truth,
    And I will pardon her.
2Though they say, 'As the LORD lives,'
    Surely they swear falsely."

3O LORD, *are* not Your eyes on the truth?
    You have stricken them,
    But they have not grieved;
    You have consumed them,
    But they have refused to receive correction.

They have made their faces harder than rock;
They have refused to return.

4Therefore I said, "Surely these *are* poor.
They are foolish;
For they do not know the way of the LORD,
The judgment of their God.
5I will go to the great men and speak to them,
For they have known the way of the LORD,
The judgment of their God."

But these have altogether broken the yoke
And burst the bonds.
6Therefore a lion from the forest shall slay
them,
A wolf of the deserts shall destroy them;
A leopard will watch over their cities.
Everyone who goes out from there shall be
torn in pieces,
Because their transgressions are many;
Their backslidings have increased.

7"How shall I pardon you for this?
Your children have forsaken Me
And sworn by *those that are* not gods.
When I had fed them to the full,
Then they committed adultery
And assembled themselves by troops in the
harlots' houses.
8They were *like* well-fed lusty stallions;
Every one neighed after his neighbor's wife.
9Shall I not punish *them* for these *things?*" says
the LORD.
"And shall I not avenge Myself on such a
nation as this?

10"Go up on her walls and destroy,
But do not make a complete end.
Take away her branches,
For they *are* not the LORD's.
11For the house of Israel and the house of
Judah
Have dealt very treacherously with Me," says
the LORD.

12They have lied about the LORD,
And said, "*It is* not He.
Neither will evil come upon us,
Nor shall we see sword or famine.

13And the prophets become wind,
For the word *is* not in them.
Thus shall it be done to them."

14Therefore thus says the LORD God of hosts:

"Because you speak this word,
Behold, I will make My words in your mouth
fire,
And this people wood,
And it shall devour them.
15Behold, I will bring a nation against you from
afar,
O house of Israel," says the LORD.
"It *is* a mighty nation,
It *is* an ancient nation,
A nation whose language you do not know,
Nor can you understand what they say.
16Their quiver *is* like an open tomb;
They *are* all mighty men.
17And they shall eat up your harvest and your
bread,
Which your sons and daughters should eat.
They shall eat up your flocks and your herds;
They shall eat up your vines and your fig
trees;
They shall destroy your fortified cities,
In which you trust, with the sword.

18"Nevertheless in those days," says the LORD,
"I will not make a complete end of you. 19And it
will be when you say, 'Why does the LORD our
God do all these *things* to us?' then you shall answer them, 'Just as you have forsaken Me and
served foreign gods in your land, so you shall
serve aliens in a land *that is* not yours.'

20"Declare this in the house of Jacob
And proclaim it in Judah, saying,
21'Hear this now, O foolish people,
Without understanding,
Who have eyes and see not,
And who have ears and hear not:
22Do you not fear Me?' says the LORD.
'Will you not tremble at My presence,
Who have placed the sand as the bound of
the sea,
By a perpetual decree, that it cannot pass
beyond it?

And though its waves toss to and fro,
Yet they cannot prevail;
Though they roar, yet they cannot pass over
  it.
²³But this people has a defiant and rebellious
  heart;
They have revolted and departed.
²⁴They do not say in their heart,
"Let us now fear the LORD our God,
Who gives rain, both the former and the
  latter, in its season.
He reserves for us the appointed weeks of the
  harvest."
²⁵Your iniquities have turned these *things* away,
And your sins have withheld good from you.

²⁶'For among My people are found wicked *men;*
They lie in wait as one who sets snares;
They set a trap;
They catch men.
²⁷As a cage is full of birds,
So their houses *are* full of deceit.
Therefore they have become great and grown
  rich.
²⁸They have grown fat, they are sleek;
Yes, they surpass the deeds of the wicked;
They do not plead the cause,
The cause of the fatherless;
Yet they prosper,
And the right of the needy they do not
  defend.
²⁹Shall I not punish *them* for these *things?*' says
  the LORD.
'Shall I not avenge Myself on such a nation as
  this?'

³⁰"An astonishing and horrible thing
Has been committed in the land:
³¹The prophets prophesy falsely,
And the priests rule by their *own* power;
And My people love *to have* it so.
But what will you do in the end?

Impending Destruction from the North

6 "O you children of Benjamin,
Gather yourselves to flee from the midst of
  Jerusalem!
Blow the trumpet in Tekoa,
And set up a signal-fire in Beth Haccerem;

For disaster appears out of the north,
And great destruction.
²I have likened the daughter of Zion
To a lovely and delicate woman.
³The shepherds with their flocks shall come to
  her.
They shall pitch *their* tents against her all
  around.
Each one shall pasture in his own place."

⁴"Prepare war against her;
Arise, and let us go up at noon.
Woe to us, for the day goes away,
For the shadows of the evening are
  lengthening.
⁵Arise, and let us go by night,
And let us destroy her palaces."

⁶For thus has the LORD of hosts said:

"Cut down trees,
And build a mound against Jerusalem.
This *is* the city to be punished.
She *is* full of oppression in her midst.
⁷As a fountain wells up with water,
So she wells up with her wickedness.
Violence and plundering are heard in her.
Before Me continually *are* grief and wounds.
⁸Be instructed, O Jerusalem,
Lest My soul depart from you;
Lest I make you desolate,
A land not inhabited."

⁹Thus says the LORD of hosts:

"They shall thoroughly glean as a vine the
  remnant of Israel;
As a grape-gatherer, put your hand back into
  the branches."

¹⁰To whom shall I speak and give warning,
That they may hear?
Indeed their ear *is* uncircumcised,
And they cannot give heed.
Behold, the word of the LORD is a reproach
  to them;
They have no delight in it.
¹¹Therefore I am full of the fury of the LORD.
I am weary of holding *it* in.

"I will pour it out on the children outside,
And on the assembly of young men together;
For even the husband shall be taken with the wife,
The aged with *him who is* full of days.
¹²And their houses shall be turned over to others,
Fields and wives together;
For I will stretch out My hand
Against the inhabitants of the land," says the LORD.
¹³"Because from the least of them even to the greatest of them,
Everyone *is* given to covetousness;
And from the prophet even to the priest,
Everyone deals falsely.
¹⁴They have also healed the hurt of My people slightly,
Saying, 'Peace, peace!'
When *there is* no peace.
¹⁵Were they ashamed when they had committed abomination?
No! They were not at all ashamed;
Nor did they know how to blush.
Therefore they shall fall among those who fall;
At the time I punish them,
They shall be cast down," says the LORD.

¹⁶Thus says the LORD:

"Stand in the ways and see,
And ask for the old paths, where the good way *is*,
And walk in it;
Then you will find rest for your souls.
But they said, 'We will not walk *in it.*'
¹⁷Also, I set watchmen over you, *saying,*
'Listen to the sound of the trumpet!'
But they said, 'We will not listen.'
¹⁸Therefore hear, you nations,
And know, O congregation, what *is* among them.
¹⁹Hear, O earth!
Behold, I will certainly bring calamity on this people—
The fruit of their thoughts,
Because they have not heeded My words
Nor My law, but rejected it.

²⁰For what purpose to Me
Comes frankincense from Sheba,
And sweet cane from a far country?
Your burnt offerings *are* not acceptable,
Nor your sacrifices sweet to Me."

²¹Therefore thus says the LORD:

"Behold, I will lay stumbling blocks before this people,
And the fathers and the sons together shall fall on them.
The neighbor and his friend shall perish."

²²Thus says the LORD:

"Behold, a people comes from the north country,
And a great nation will be raised from the farthest parts of the earth.
²³They will lay hold on bow and spear;
They *are* cruel and have no mercy;
Their voice roars like the sea;
And they ride on horses,
As men of war set in array against you,
O daughter of Zion."

²⁴We have heard the report of it;
Our hands grow feeble.
Anguish has taken hold of us,
Pain as of a woman in labor.
²⁵Do not go out into the field,
Nor walk by the way.
Because of the sword of the enemy,
Fear *is* on every side.
²⁶O daughter of my people,
Dress in sackcloth
And roll about in ashes!
Make mourning *as for* an only son, most bitter lamentation;
For the plunderer will suddenly come upon us.

²⁷"I have set you *as* an assayer *and* a fortress among My people,
That you may know and test their way.
²⁸They *are* all stubborn rebels, walking as slanderers.
They are bronze and iron,

They *are* all corrupters;
²⁹The bellows blow fiercely,
The lead is consumed by the fire;
The smelter refines in vain,
For the wicked are not drawn off.
³⁰*People* will call them rejected silver,
Because the LORD has rejected them."

TRUSTING IN LYING WORDS

7 The word that came to Jeremiah from the LORD, saying, ²"Stand in the gate of the LORD's house, and proclaim there this word, and say, 'Hear the word of the LORD, all *you of* Judah who enter in at these gates to worship the LORD!' " ³Thus says the LORD of hosts, the God of Israel: "Amend your ways and your doings, and I will cause you to dwell in this place. ⁴Do not trust in these lying words, saying, 'The temple of the LORD, the temple of the LORD, the temple of the LORD *are* these.'

⁵"For if you thoroughly amend your ways and your doings, if you thoroughly execute judgment between a man and his neighbor, ⁶*if* you do not oppress the stranger, the fatherless, and the widow, and do not shed innocent blood in this place, or walk after other gods to your hurt, ⁷then I will cause you to dwell in this place, in the land that I gave to your fathers forever and ever.

⁸"Behold, you trust in lying words that cannot profit. ⁹Will you steal, murder, commit adultery, swear falsely, burn incense to Baal, and walk after other gods whom you do not know, ¹⁰and *then* come and stand before Me in this house which is called by My name, and say, 'We are delivered to do all these abominations'? ¹¹Has this house, which is called by My name, become a den of thieves in your eyes? Behold, I, even I, have seen *it*," says the LORD.

¹²"But go now to My place which *was* in Shiloh, where I set My name at the first, and see what I did to it because of the wickedness of My people Israel. ¹³And now, because you have done all these works," says the LORD, "and I spoke to you, rising up early and speaking, but you did not hear, and I called you, but you did not answer, ¹⁴therefore I will do to the house which is called by My name, in which you trust, and to this place which I gave to you and your fathers, as I have done to Shiloh. ¹⁵And I will cast you out of My sight, as I have cast out all your brethren—the whole posterity of Ephraim.

¹⁶"Therefore do not pray for this people, nor lift up a cry or prayer for them, nor make intercession to Me; for I will not hear you. ¹⁷Do you not see what they do in the cities of Judah and in the streets of Jerusalem? ¹⁸The children gather wood, the fathers kindle the fire, and the women knead dough, to make cakes for the queen of heaven; and *they* pour out drink offerings to other gods, that they may provoke Me to anger. ¹⁹Do they provoke Me to anger?" says the LORD. "*Do they* not *provoke* themselves, to the shame of their own faces?"

²⁰Therefore thus says the Lord GOD: "Behold, My anger and My fury will be poured out on this place—on man and on beast, on the trees of the field and on the fruit of the ground. And it will burn and not be quenched."

²¹Thus says the LORD of hosts, the God of Israel: "Add your burnt offerings to your sacrifices and eat meat. ²²For I did not speak to your fathers, or command them in the day that I brought them out of the land of Egypt, concerning burnt offerings or sacrifices. ²³But this is what I commanded them, saying, 'Obey My voice, and I will be your God, and you shall be My people. And walk in all the ways that I have commanded you, that it may be well with you.' ²⁴Yet they did not obey or incline their ear, but followed the counsels *and* the dictates of their evil hearts, and went backward and not forward. ²⁵Since the day that your fathers came out of the land of Egypt until this day, I have even sent to you all My servants the prophets, daily rising up early and sending *them*. ²⁶Yet they did not obey Me or incline their ear, but stiffened their neck. They did worse than their fathers.

²⁷"Therefore you shall speak all these words to them, but they will not obey you. You shall also call to them, but they will not answer you.

JUDGMENT ON OBSCENE RELIGION

²⁸"So you shall say to them, 'This *is* a nation that does not obey the voice of the LORD their God nor receive correction. Truth has perished and has been cut off from their mouth. ²⁹Cut off your hair and cast *it* away, and take up a lamentation on the desolate heights; for the LORD has

rejected and forsaken the generation of His wrath.' ³⁰For the children of Judah have done evil in My sight," says the LORD. "They have set their abominations in the house which is called by My name, to pollute it. ³¹And they have built the high places of Tophet, which *is* in the Valley of the Son of Hinnom, to burn their sons and their daughters in the fire, which I did not command, nor did it come into My heart.

³²"Therefore behold, the days are coming," says the LORD, "when it will no more be called Tophet, or the Valley of the Son of Hinnom, but the Valley of Slaughter; for they will bury in Tophet until there is no room. ³³The corpses of this people will be food for the birds of the heaven and for the beasts of the earth. And no one will frighten *them away.* ³⁴Then I will cause to cease from the cities of Judah and from the streets of Jerusalem the voice of mirth and the voice of gladness, the voice of the bridegroom and the voice of the bride. For the land shall be desolate.

8 "At that time," says the LORD, "they shall bring out the bones of the kings of Judah, and the bones of its princes, and the bones of the priests, and the bones of the prophets, and the bones of the inhabitants of Jerusalem, out of their graves. ²They shall spread them before the sun and the moon and all the host of heaven, which they have loved and which they have served and after which they have walked, which they have sought and which they have worshiped. They shall not be gathered nor buried; they shall be like refuse on the face of the earth. ³Then death shall be chosen rather than life by all the residue of those who remain of this evil family, who remain in all the places where I have driven them," says the LORD of hosts.

THE PERIL OF FALSE TEACHING

⁴"Moreover you shall say to them, 'Thus says the LORD:

"Will they fall and not rise?
Will one turn away and not return?
⁵Why has this people slidden back,
Jerusalem, in a perpetual backsliding?
They hold fast to deceit,
They refuse to return.

⁶I listened and heard,
But they do not speak aright.
No man repented of his wickedness,
Saying, 'What have I done?'
Everyone turned to his own course,
As the horse rushes into the battle.

⁷"Even the stork in the heavens
Knows her appointed times;
And the turtledove, the swift, and the swallow
Observe the time of their coming.
But My people do not know the judgment of the LORD.

⁸"How can you say, 'We *are* wise,
And the law of the LORD *is* with us'?
Look, the false pen of the scribe certainly works falsehood.
⁹The wise men are ashamed,
They are dismayed and taken.
Behold, they have rejected the word of the LORD;
So what wisdom do they have?
¹⁰Therefore I will give their wives to others,
And their fields to those who will inherit *them;*
Because from the least even to the greatest
Everyone is given to covetousness;
From the prophet even to the priest
Everyone deals falsely.
¹¹For they have healed the hurt of the daughter of My people slightly,
Saying, 'Peace, peace!'
When *there is* no peace.
¹²Were they ashamed when they had committed abomination?
No! They were not at all ashamed,
Nor did they know how to blush.
Therefore they shall fall among those who fall;
In the time of their punishment
They shall be cast down," says the LORD.

¹³"I will surely consume them," says the LORD.
"No grapes *shall be* on the vine,
Nor figs on the fig tree,
And the leaf shall fade;
And *the things* I have given them shall pass away from them." ' "

¹⁴"Why do we sit still?
Assemble yourselves,
And let us enter the fortified cities,
And let us be silent there.
For the LORD our God has put us to silence
And given us water of gall to drink,
Because we have sinned against the LORD.

¹⁵"*We* looked for peace, but no good *came;*
And for a time of health, and there was
trouble!
¹⁶The snorting of His horses was heard from
Dan.
The whole land trembled at the sound of the
neighing of His strong ones;
For they have come and devoured the land
and all that is in it,
The city and those who dwell in it."

¹⁷"For behold, I will send serpents among you,
Vipers which cannot be charmed,
And they shall bite you," says the LORD.

THE PROPHET MOURNS FOR THE PEOPLE

¹⁸I would comfort myself in sorrow;
My heart *is* faint in me.
¹⁹Listen! The voice,
The cry of the daughter of my people
From a far country:
"*Is* not the LORD in Zion?
Is not her King in her?"

"Why have they provoked Me to anger
With their carved images—
With foreign idols?"

²⁰"The harvest is past,
The summer is ended,
And we are not saved!"

²¹For the hurt of the daughter of my people I
am hurt.
I am mourning;
Astonishment has taken hold of me.
²²*Is there* no balm in Gilead,
Is there no physician there?
Why then is there no recovery
For the health of the daughter of my
people?

9 Oh, that my head were waters,
And my eyes a fountain of tears,
That I might weep day and night
For the slain of the daughter of my people!
²Oh, that I had in the wilderness
A lodging place for travelers;
That I might leave my people,
And go from them!
For they *are* all adulterers,
An assembly of treacherous men.

³"And *like* their bow they have bent their
tongues *for* lies.
They are not valiant for the truth on the
earth.
For they proceed from evil to evil,
And they do not know Me," says the LORD.
⁴"Everyone take heed to his neighbor,
And do not trust any brother;
For every brother will utterly supplant,
And every neighbor will walk with
slanderers.
⁵Everyone will deceive his neighbor,
And will not speak the truth;
They have taught their tongue to speak lies;
They weary themselves to commit iniquity.
⁶Your dwelling place *is* in the midst of deceit;
Through deceit they refuse to know Me," says
the LORD.

⁷Therefore thus says the LORD of hosts:

"Behold, I will refine them and try them;
For how shall I deal with the daughter of My
people?
⁸Their tongue *is* an arrow shot out;
It speaks deceit;
One speaks peaceably to his neighbor with his
mouth,
But in his heart he lies in wait.
⁹Shall I not punish them for these *things?*" says
the LORD.
"Shall I not avenge Myself on such a nation as
this?"

¹⁰I will take up a weeping and wailing for the
mountains,
And for the dwelling places of the wilderness
a lamentation,

Because they are burned up,
So that no one can pass through;
Nor can *men* hear the voice of the cattle.
Both the birds of the heavens and the beasts
    have fled;
They are gone.

11"I will make Jerusalem a heap of ruins, a den
    of jackals.
I will make the cities of Judah desolate,
    without an inhabitant."

12Who *is* the wise man who may understand this? And *who is he* to whom the mouth of the LORD has spoken, that he may declare it? Why does the land perish *and* burn up like a wilderness, so that no one can pass through?

13And the LORD said, "Because they have forsaken My law which I set before them, and have not obeyed My voice, nor walked according to it, 14but they have walked according to the dictates of their own hearts and after the Baals, which their fathers taught them," 15therefore thus says the LORD of hosts, the God of Israel: "Behold, I will feed them, this people, with wormwood, and give them water of gall to drink. 16I will scatter them also among the Gentiles, whom neither they nor their fathers have known. And I will send a sword after them until I have consumed them."

THE PEOPLE MOURN IN JUDGMENT

17Thus says the LORD of hosts:

"Consider and call for the mourning
    women,
That they may come;
And send for skillful *wailing* women,
That they may come.
18Let them make haste
And take up a wailing for us,
That our eyes may run with tears,
And our eyelids gush with water.
19For a voice of wailing is heard from Zion:
"How we are plundered!
We are greatly ashamed,
Because we have forsaken the land,
Because we have been cast out of our
    dwellings.' "

20Yet hear the word of the LORD, O women,
And let your ear receive the word of His
    mouth;
Teach your daughters wailing,
And everyone her neighbor a lamentation.
21For death has come through our windows,
Has entered our palaces,
To kill off the children—*no longer to be* outside!
And the young men—*no longer* on the streets!

22Speak, "Thus says the LORD:

'Even the carcasses of men shall fall as refuse
    on the open field,
Like cuttings after the harvester,
And no one shall gather *them*.' "

23Thus says the LORD:

"Let not the wise *man* glory in his wisdom,
Let not the mighty *man* glory in his might,
Nor let the rich *man* glory in his riches;
24But let him who glories glory in this,
That he understands and knows Me,
That I *am* the LORD, exercising
    lovingkindness, judgment, and
    righteousness in the earth.
For in these I delight," says the LORD.

25"Behold, the days are coming," says the LORD, "that I will punish all *who are* circumcised with the uncircumcised— 26Egypt, Judah, Edom, the people of Ammon, Moab, and all *who are* in the farthest corners, who dwell in the wilderness. For all *these* nations *are* uncircumcised, and all the house of Israel *are* uncircumcised in the heart."

IDOLS AND THE TRUE GOD

10 Hear the word which the LORD speaks to you, O house of Israel. 2Thus says the LORD:

"Do not learn the way of the Gentiles;
Do not be dismayed at the signs of heaven,
For the Gentiles are dismayed at them.
3For the customs of the peoples *are* futile;
For *one* cuts a tree from the forest,
The work of the hands of the workman, with
    the ax.

[4]They decorate it with silver and gold;
They fasten it with nails and hammers
So that it will not topple.
[5]They *are* upright, like a palm tree,
And they cannot speak;
They must be carried,
Because they cannot go *by themselves.*
Do not be afraid of them,
For they cannot do evil,
Nor can they do any good."

[6]Inasmuch as *there is* none like You, O LORD
(You *are* great, and Your name *is* great in
    might),
[7]Who would not fear You, O King of the
    nations?
For this is Your rightful due.
For among all the wise *men* of the nations,
And in all their kingdoms,
There is none like You.
[8]But they are altogether dull-hearted and
    foolish;
A wooden idol *is* a worthless doctrine.
[9]Silver is beaten into plates;
It is brought from Tarshish,
And gold from Uphaz,
The work of the craftsman
And of the hands of the metalsmith;
Blue and purple *are* their clothing;
They *are* all the work of skillful *men.*
[10]But the LORD *is* the true God;
He *is* the living God and the everlasting King.
At His wrath the earth will tremble,
And the nations will not be able to endure
    His indignation.

[11]Thus you shall say to them: "The gods that
have not made the heavens and the earth shall
perish from the earth and from under these heavens."

[12]He has made the earth by His power,
He has established the world by His wisdom,
And has stretched out the heavens at His
    discretion.
[13]When He utters His voice,
There is a multitude of waters in the heavens:
"And He causes the vapors to ascend from the
    ends of the earth.

He makes lightning for the rain,
He brings the wind out of His treasuries."[a]

[14]Everyone is dull-hearted, without knowledge;
Every metalsmith is put to shame by an
    image;
For his molded image *is* falsehood,
And *there is* no breath in them.
[15]They *are* futile, a work of errors;
In the time of their punishment they shall
    perish.
[16]The Portion of Jacob *is* not like them,
For He *is* the Maker of all *things,*
And Israel *is* the tribe of His inheritance;
The LORD of hosts *is* His name.

THE COMING CAPTIVITY OF JUDAH

[17]Gather up your wares from the land,
O inhabitant of the fortress!

[18]For thus says the LORD:

"Behold, I will throw out at this time
The inhabitants of the land,
And will distress them,
That they may find *it so.*"

[19]Woe is me for my hurt!
My wound is severe.
But I say, "Truly this *is* an infirmity,
And I must bear it."
[20]My tent is plundered,
And all my cords are broken;
My children have gone from me,
And they *are* no more.
There is no one to pitch my tent anymore,
Or set up my curtains.

[21]For the shepherds have become dull-hearted,
And have not sought the LORD;
Therefore they shall not prosper,
And all their flocks shall be scattered.
[22]Behold, the noise of the report has come,
And a great commotion out of the north
    country,
To make the cities of Judah desolate, a den of
    jackals.

10:13 [a]Psalm 135:7

²³O Lord, I know the way of man *is* not in
  himself;
  It is not in man who walks to direct his own
  steps.
²⁴O Lord, correct me, but with justice;
  Not in Your anger, lest You bring me to
  nothing.
²⁵Pour out Your fury on the Gentiles, who do
  not know You,
  And on the families who do not call on Your
  name;
  For they have eaten up Jacob,
  Devoured him and consumed him,
  And made his dwelling place desolate.

The Broken Covenant

11 The word that came to Jeremiah from the
Lord, saying, ²"Hear the words of this
covenant, and speak to the men of Judah and to
the inhabitants of Jerusalem; ³and say to them,
'Thus says the Lord God of Israel: "Cursed *is* the
man who does not obey the words of this
covenant ⁴which I commanded your fathers in
the day I brought them out of the land of Egypt,
from the iron furnace, saying, 'Obey My voice,
and do according to all that I command you; so
shall you be My people, and I will be your God,'
⁵that I may establish the oath which I have sworn
to your fathers, to give them 'a land flowing with
milk and honey,'ᵃ as *it is* this day." ' "

And I answered and said, "So be it, Lord."

⁶Then the Lord said to me, "Proclaim all
these words in the cities of Judah and in the
streets of Jerusalem, saying: 'Hear the words of this
covenant and do them. ⁷For I earnestly exhorted
your fathers in the day I brought them up out of
the land of Egypt, until this day, rising early and
exhorting, saying, "Obey My voice." ⁸Yet they did
not obey or incline their ear, but everyone followed the dictates of his evil heart; therefore I will
bring upon them all the words of this covenant,
which I commanded *them* to do, but *which* they
have not done.' "

⁹And the Lord said to me, "A conspiracy has
been found among the men of Judah and among
the inhabitants of Jerusalem. ¹⁰They have turned
back to the iniquities of their forefathers who refused to hear My words, and they have gone after
other gods to serve them; the house of Israel and

the house of Judah have broken My covenant
which I made with their fathers."

¹¹Therefore thus says the Lord: "Behold, I
will surely bring calamity on them which they
will not be able to escape; and though they cry
out to Me, I will not listen to them. ¹²Then the
cities of Judah and the inhabitants of Jerusalem
will go and cry out to the gods to whom they offer incense, but they will not save them at all in
the time of their trouble. ¹³For *according to* the
number of your cities were your gods, O Judah;
and *according to* the number of the streets of
Jerusalem you have set up altars to *that* shameful
thing, altars to burn incense to Baal.

¹⁴"So do not pray for this people, or lift up a
cry or prayer for them; for I will not hear *them* in
the time that they cry out to Me because of their
trouble.

¹⁵"What has My beloved to do in My house,
  Having done lewd deeds with many?
  And the holy flesh has passed from you.
  When you do evil, then you rejoice.
¹⁶The Lord called your name,
  Green Olive Tree, Lovely *and* of Good Fruit.
  With the noise of a great tumult
  He has kindled fire on it,
  And its branches are broken.

¹⁷"For the Lord of hosts, who planted you,
has pronounced doom against you for the evil of
the house of Israel and of the house of Judah,
which they have done against themselves to provoke Me to anger in offering incense to Baal."

Jeremiah's Life Threatened

¹⁸Now the Lord gave me knowledge *of it,*
and I know *it;* for You showed me their doings.
¹⁹But I *was* like a docile lamb brought to the
slaughter; and I did not know that they had devised schemes against me, *saying,* "Let us destroy
the tree with its fruit, and let us cut him off from
the land of the living, that his name may be remembered no more."

²⁰But, O Lord of hosts,
  You who judge righteously,

11:5 ᵃExodus 3:8

Testing the mind and the heart,
Let me see Your vengeance on them,
For to You I have revealed my cause.

21"Therefore thus says the LORD concerning the men of Anathoth who seek your life, saying, 'Do not prophesy in the name of the LORD, lest you die by our hand'— 22therefore thus says the LORD of hosts: 'Behold, I will punish them. The young men shall die by the sword, their sons and their daughters shall die by famine; 23and there shall be no remnant of them, for I will bring catastrophe on the men of Anathoth, *even* the year of their punishment.' "

JEREMIAH'S QUESTION

12 Righteous *are* You, O LORD, when I plead with You;
Yet let me talk with You about *Your* judgments.
Why does the way of the wicked prosper?
Why are those happy who deal so treacherously?
2You have planted them, yes, they have taken root;
They grow, yes, they bear fruit.
You *are* near in their mouth
But far from their mind.

3But You, O LORD, know me;
You have seen me,
And You have tested my heart toward You.
Pull them out like sheep for the slaughter,
And prepare them for the day of slaughter.
4How long will the land mourn,
And the herbs of every field wither?
The beasts and birds are consumed,
For the wickedness of those who dwell there,
Because they said, "He will not see our final end."

THE LORD ANSWERS JEREMIAH

5"If you have run with the footmen, and they have wearied you,
Then how can you contend with horses?
And *if* in the land of peace,
In which you trusted, *they wearied you,*
Then how will you do in the floodplain[a] of the Jordan?

6For even your brothers, the house of your father,
Even they have dealt treacherously with you;
Yes, they have called a multitude after you.
Do not believe them,
Even though they speak smooth words to you.

7"I have forsaken My house, I have left My heritage;
I have given the dearly beloved of My soul into the hand of her enemies.
8My heritage is to Me like a lion in the forest;
It cries out against Me;
Therefore I have hated it.
9My heritage *is* to Me *like* a speckled vulture;
The vultures all around *are* against her.
Come, assemble all the beasts of the field,
Bring them to devour!

10"Many rulers[a] have destroyed My vineyard,
They have trodden My portion underfoot;
They have made My pleasant portion a desolate wilderness.
11They have made it desolate;
Desolate, it mourns to Me;
The whole land is made desolate,
Because no one takes *it* to heart.
12The plunderers have come
On all the desolate heights in the wilderness,
For the sword of the LORD shall devour
From *one* end of the land to the *other* end of the land;
No flesh shall have peace.
13They have sown wheat but reaped thorns;
They have put themselves to pain *but* do not profit.
But be ashamed of your harvest
Because of the fierce anger of the LORD."

14Thus says the LORD: "Against all My evil neighbors who touch the inheritance which I have caused My people Israel to inherit—behold, I will pluck them out of their land and pluck out the house of Judah from among them. 15Then it shall be, after I have plucked them out, that I will return and have compassion on them and bring

12:5 aOr *thicket* **12:10** aLiterally *shepherds* or *pastors*

them back, everyone to his heritage and everyone to his land. ¹⁶And it shall be, if they will learn carefully the ways of My people, to swear by My name, 'As the LORD lives,' as they taught My people to swear by Baal, then they shall be established in the midst of My people. ¹⁷But if they do not obey, I will utterly pluck up and destroy that nation," says the LORD.

SYMBOL OF THE LINEN SASH

13 Thus the LORD said to me: "Go and get yourself a linen sash, and put it around your waist, but do not put it in water." ²So I got a sash according to the word of the LORD, and put *it* around my waist.

³And the word of the LORD came to me the second time, saying, ⁴"Take the sash that you acquired, which *is* around your waist, and arise, go to the Euphrates,ᵃ and hide it there in a hole in the rock." ⁵So I went and hid it by the Euphrates, as the LORD commanded me.

⁶Now it came to pass after many days that the LORD said to me, "Arise, go to the Euphrates, and take from there the sash which I commanded you to hide there." ⁷Then I went to the Euphrates and dug, and I took the sash from the place where I had hidden it; and there was the sash, ruined. It was profitable for nothing.

⁸Then the word of the LORD came to me, saying, ⁹"Thus says the LORD: 'In this manner I will ruin the pride of Judah and the great pride of Jerusalem. ¹⁰This evil people, who refuse to hear My words, who follow the dictates of their hearts, and walk after other gods to serve them and worship them, shall be just like this sash which is profitable for nothing. ¹¹For as the sash clings to the waist of a man, so I have caused the whole house of Israel and the whole house of Judah to cling to Me,' says the LORD, 'that they may become My people, for renown, for praise, and for glory; but they would not hear.'

SYMBOL OF THE WINE BOTTLES

¹²"Therefore you shall speak to them this word: 'Thus says the LORD God of Israel: "Every bottle shall be filled with wine." '

"And they will say to you, 'Do we not certainly know that every bottle will be filled with wine?'

¹³"Then you shall say to them, 'Thus says the LORD: "Behold, I will fill all the inhabitants of this land—even the kings who sit on David's throne, the priests, the prophets, and all the inhabitants of Jerusalem—with drunkenness! ¹⁴And I will dash them one against another, even the fathers and the sons together," says the LORD. "I will not pity nor spare nor have mercy, but will destroy them." ' "

PRIDE PRECEDES CAPTIVITY

¹⁵Hear and give ear:
    Do not be proud,
    For the LORD has spoken.
¹⁶Give glory to the LORD your God
    Before He causes darkness,
    And before your feet stumble
    On the dark mountains,
    And while you are looking for light,
    He turns it into the shadow of death
    And makes *it* dense darkness.
¹⁷But if you will not hear it,
    My soul will weep in secret for *your* pride;
    My eyes will weep bitterly
    And run down with tears,
    Because the LORD's flock has been taken
        captive.

¹⁸Say to the king and to the queen mother,
    "Humble yourselves;
    Sit down,
    For your rule shall collapse, the crown of your
        glory."
¹⁹The cities of the South shall be shut up,
    And no one shall open *them;*
    Judah shall be carried away captive, all of it;
    It shall be wholly carried away captive.

²⁰Lift up your eyes and see
    Those who come from the north.
    Where *is* the flock *that* was given to you,
    Your beautiful sheep?
²¹What will you say when He punishes you?
    For you have taught them
    To be chieftains, to be head over you.
    Will not pangs seize you,
    Like a woman in labor?

13:4 ᵃHebrew *Perath*

²²And if you say in your heart,
"Why have these things come upon me?"
For the greatness of your iniquity
Your skirts have been uncovered,
Your heels made bare.
²³Can the Ethiopian change his skin or the
leopard its spots?
Then may you also do good who are
accustomed to do evil.

²⁴"Therefore I will scatter them like stubble
That passes away by the wind of the
wilderness.
²⁵This is your lot,
The portion of your measures from Me," says
the LORD,
"Because you have forgotten Me
And trusted in falsehood.
²⁶Therefore I will uncover your skirts over your
face,
That your shame may appear.
²⁷I have seen your adulteries
And your *lustful* neighings,
The lewdness of your harlotry,
Your abominations on the hills in the
fields.
Woe to you, O Jerusalem!
Will you still not be made clean?"

SWORD, FAMINE, AND PESTILENCE

14 The word of the LORD that came to Jeremiah concerning the droughts.

²"Judah mourns,
And her gates languish;
They mourn for the land,
And the cry of Jerusalem has gone up.
³Their nobles have sent their lads for water;
They went to the cisterns *and* found no
water.
They returned with their vessels empty;
They were ashamed and confounded
And covered their heads.
⁴Because the ground is parched,
For there was no rain in the land,
The plowmen were ashamed;
They covered their heads.
⁵Yes, the deer also gave birth in the field,
But left because there was no grass.

⁶And the wild donkeys stood in the desolate
heights;
They sniffed at the wind like jackals;
Their eyes failed because *there was* no grass."

⁷O LORD, though our iniquities testify against
us,
Do it for Your name's sake;
For our backslidings are many,
We have sinned against You.
⁸O the Hope of Israel, his Savior in time of
trouble,
Why should You be like a stranger in the
land,
And like a traveler *who* turns aside to tarry for
a night?
⁹Why should You be like a man astonished,
Like a mighty one *who* cannot save?
Yet You, O LORD, *are* in our midst,
And we are called by Your name;
Do not leave us!

¹⁰Thus says the LORD to this people:

"Thus they have loved to wander;
They have not restrained their feet.
Therefore the LORD does not accept them;
He will remember their iniquity now,
And punish their sins."

¹¹Then the LORD said to me, "Do not pray
for this people, for *their* good. ¹²When they fast, I
will not hear their cry; and when they offer burnt
offering and grain offering, I will not accept
them. But I will consume them by the sword, by
the famine, and by the pestilence."

¹³Then I said, "Ah, Lord GOD! Behold, the
prophets say to them, 'You shall not see the sword,
nor shall you have famine, but I will give you assured peace in this place.'"

¹⁴And the LORD said to me, "The prophets
prophesy lies in My name. I have not sent them,
commanded them, nor spoken to them; they
prophesy to you a false vision, divination, a
worthless thing, and the deceit of their heart.
¹⁵Therefore thus says the LORD concerning the
prophets who prophesy in My name, whom I did
not send, and who say, 'Sword and famine shall
not be in this land'—'By sword and famine those

| **THROUGH THE GRID** | *Where Have All the Dreamers Gone?*
Observations from a Biblical
Worldview: Admitting Sin (Jer. 14:7–9) |

It is often difficult—especially in our culture that avoids responsibility and blames fault on other people—to consider oneself as the one to blame. Yet one of the keystones of Christianity involves admitting that we are inadequate in and of ourselves and that we are the ones at fault. Acknowledging one's own sin is the first step to acquiring a biblical worldview of society and culture, since it allows us to take responsibility for our actions and adds a dimension of accountability. To be sure, it definitely takes courage to admit one's sin, ask for forgiveness, and accept the grace of God.

prophets shall be consumed! [16]And the people to whom they prophesy shall be cast out in the streets of Jerusalem because of the famine and the sword; they will have no one to bury them—them nor their wives, their sons nor their daughters—for I will pour their wickedness on them.'

[17]"Therefore you shall say this word to them:

'Let my eyes flow with tears night and day,
And let them not cease;
For the virgin daughter of my people
Has been broken with a mighty stroke, with a very severe blow.
[18]If I go out to the field,
Then behold, those slain with the sword!
And if I enter the city,
Then behold, those sick from famine!
Yes, both prophet and priest go about in a land they do not know.' "

The People Plead for Mercy

[19]Have You utterly rejected Judah?
Has Your soul loathed Zion?
Why have You stricken us so that *there is* no healing for us?
We looked for peace, but *there was* no good;
And for the time of healing, and there was trouble.
[20]We acknowledge, O LORD, our wickedness
And the iniquity of our fathers,
For we have sinned against You.
[21]Do not abhor *us,* for Your name's sake;
Do not disgrace the throne of Your glory.
Remember, do not break Your covenant with us.

[22]Are there any among the idols of the nations that can cause rain?
Or can the heavens give showers?
Are You not He, O LORD our God?
Therefore we will wait for You,
Since You have made all these.

The Lord Will Not Relent

15 Then the LORD said to me, "*Even* if Moses and Samuel stood before Me, My mind *would* not *be* favorable toward this people. Cast *them* out of My sight, and let them go forth. [2]And it shall be, if they say to you, 'Where should we go?' then you shall tell them, 'Thus says the LORD:

"Such as *are* for death, to death;
And such as *are* for the sword, to the sword;
And such as *are* for the famine, to the famine;
And such as *are* for the captivity, to the captivity." '

[3]"And I will appoint over them four forms *of destruction,*" says the LORD: "the sword to slay, the dogs to drag, the birds of the heavens and the beasts of the earth to devour and destroy. [4]I will hand them over to trouble, to all kingdoms of the earth, because of Manasseh the son of Hezekiah, king of Judah, for what he did in Jerusalem.

[5]"For who will have pity on you, O Jerusalem?
Or who will bemoan you?
Or who will turn aside to ask how you are doing?

⁶"You have forsaken Me," says the LORD,
"You have gone backward.
Therefore I will stretch out My hand against
     you and destroy you;
I am weary of relenting!
⁷And I will winnow them with a winnowing
     fan in the gates of the land;
I will bereave *them* of children;
I will destroy My people,
Since they do not return from their ways.
⁸Their widows will be increased to Me more
     than the sand of the seas;
I will bring against them,
Against the mother of the young men,
A plunderer at noonday;
I will cause anguish and terror to fall on them
     suddenly.

⁹"She languishes who has borne seven;
She has breathed her last;
Her sun has gone down
While *it was* yet day;
She has been ashamed and confounded.
And the remnant of them I will deliver to the
     sword
Before their enemies," says the LORD.

JEREMIAH'S DEJECTION

¹⁰Woe is me, my mother,
That you have borne me,
A man of strife and a man of contention to
     the whole earth!
I have neither lent for interest,
Nor have men lent to me for interest.
Every one of them curses me.

¹¹The LORD said:

"Surely it will be well with your remnant;
Surely I will cause the enemy to intercede
     with you
In the time of adversity and in the time of
     affliction.
¹²Can anyone break iron,
The northern iron and the bronze?
¹³Your wealth and your treasures
I will give as plunder without price,
Because of all your sins,
Throughout your territories.

¹⁴And I will make *you* cross over with[a] your
     enemies
Into a land *which* you do not know;
For a fire is kindled in My anger,
Which shall burn upon you."

¹⁵O LORD, You know;
Remember me and visit me,
And take vengeance for me on my
     persecutors.
In Your enduring patience, do not take me
     away.
Know that for Your sake I have suffered
     rebuke.
¹⁶Your words were found, and I ate them,
And Your word was to me the joy and
     rejoicing of my heart;
For I am called by Your name,
O LORD God of hosts.
¹⁷I did not sit in the assembly of the
     mockers,
Nor did I rejoice;
I sat alone because of Your hand,
For You have filled me with indignation.
¹⁸Why is my pain perpetual
And my wound incurable,
Which refuses to be healed?
Will You surely be to me like an unreliable
     stream,
As waters *that* fail?

THE LORD REASSURES JEREMIAH

¹⁹Therefore thus says the LORD:

"If you return,
Then I will bring you back;
You shall stand before Me;
If you take out the precious from the vile,
You shall be as My mouth.
Let them return to you,
But you must not return to them.
²⁰And I will make you to this people a fortified
     bronze wall;
And they will fight against you,
But they shall not prevail against you;
For I *am* with you to save you
And deliver you," says the LORD.

15:14 ªFollowing Masoretic Text and Vulgate; Septuagint, Syriac,
and Targum read *cause you to serve* (compare 17:4).

²¹"I will deliver you from the hand of the
wicked,
And I will redeem you from the grip of the
terrible."

JEREMIAH'S LIFE-STYLE AND MESSAGE

16The word of the LORD also came to me,
saying, ²"You shall not take a wife, nor shall
you have sons or daughters in this place." ³For
thus says the LORD concerning the sons and
daughters who are born in this place, and concerning their mothers who bore them and their
fathers who begot them in this land: ⁴"They shall
die gruesome deaths; they shall not be lamented
nor shall they be buried, *but* they shall be like refuse on the face of the earth. They shall be consumed by the sword and by famine, and their
corpses shall be meat for the birds of heaven and
for the beasts of the earth."

⁵For thus says the LORD: "Do not enter the
house of mourning, nor go to lament or bemoan
them; for I have taken away My peace from this
people," says the LORD, "lovingkindness and mercies. ⁶Both the great and the small shall die in this
land. They shall not be buried; neither shall men
lament for them, cut themselves, nor make themselves bald for them. ⁷Nor shall *men* break *bread* in
mourning for them, to comfort them for the
dead; nor shall *men* give them the cup of consolation to drink for their father or their mother.
⁸Also you shall not go into the house of feasting
to sit with them, to eat and drink."

⁹For thus says the LORD of hosts, the God of
Israel: "Behold, I will cause to cease from this
place, before your eyes and in your days, the voice
of mirth and the voice of gladness, the voice of
the bridegroom and the voice of the bride.

¹⁰"And it shall be, when you show this people
all these words, and they say to you, 'Why has the
LORD pronounced all this great disaster against
us? Or what *is* our iniquity? Or what *is* our sin
that we have committed against the LORD our
God?' ¹¹then you shall say to them, 'Because your
fathers have forsaken Me,' says the LORD; 'they
have walked after other gods and have served
them and worshiped them, and have forsaken Me
and not kept My law. ¹²And you have done worse
than your fathers, for behold, each one follows
the dictates of his own evil heart, so that no one

listens to Me. ¹³Therefore I will cast you out of
this land into a land that you do not know, neither you nor your fathers; and there you shall
serve other gods day and night, where I will not
show you favor.'

GOD WILL RESTORE ISRAEL

¹⁴"Therefore behold, the days are coming,"
says the LORD, "that it shall no more be said, 'The
LORD lives who brought up the children of Israel
from the land of Egypt,' ¹⁵but, 'The LORD lives
who brought up the children of Israel from the
land of the north and from all the lands where He
had driven them.' For I will bring them back into
their land which I gave to their fathers.

¹⁶"Behold, I will send for many fishermen,"
says the LORD, "and they shall fish them; and afterward I will send for many hunters, and they
shall hunt them from every mountain and every
hill, and out of the holes of the rocks. ¹⁷For My
eyes *are* on all their ways; they are not hidden
from My face, nor is their iniquity hidden from
My eyes. ¹⁸And first I will repay double for their
iniquity and their sin, because they have defiled
My land; they have filled My inheritance with the
carcasses of their detestable and abominable idols."

¹⁹O LORD, my strength and my fortress,
My refuge in the day of affliction,
The Gentiles shall come to You
From the ends of the earth and say,
"Surely our fathers have inherited lies,
Worthlessness and unprofitable *things.*"
²⁰Will a man make gods for himself,
Which *are* not gods?

²¹"Therefore behold, I will this once cause them
to know,
I will cause them to know
My hand and My might;
And they shall know that My name *is* the
LORD.

JUDAH'S SIN AND PUNISHMENT

17"The sin of Judah *is* written with a pen of
iron;
With the point of a diamond *it is*
engraved
On the tablet of their heart,

And on the horns of your altars,
²While their children remember
Their altars and their wooden images[a]
By the green trees on the high hills.
³O My mountain in the field,
I will give as plunder your wealth, all your
        treasures,
And your high places of sin within all your
        borders.
⁴And you, even yourself,
Shall let go of your heritage which I gave
        you;
And I will cause you to serve your enemies
In the land which you do not know;
For you have kindled a fire in My anger *which*
        shall burn forever."

⁵Thus says the LORD:

"Cursed *is* the man who trusts in man
And makes flesh his strength,
Whose heart departs from the LORD.

⁶For he shall be like a shrub in the desert,
And shall not see when good comes,
But shall inhabit the parched places in the
        wilderness,
In a salt land *which is* not inhabited.

⁷"Blessed *is* the man who trusts in the LORD,
And whose hope is the LORD.
⁸For he shall be like a tree planted by the
        waters,
Which spreads out its roots by the river,
And will not fear[a] when heat comes;
But its leaf will be green,
And will not be anxious in the year of
        drought,
Nor will cease from yielding fruit.

⁹"The heart *is* deceitful above all *things,*
And desperately wicked;
Who can know it?

17:2 ªHebrew *Asherim,* Canaanite deities   **17:8** ªQere and Targum
read *see.*

INSIDE *the* INFLUENCERS

JEREMIAH: Stand Alone if You Must, but Stand

JEREMIAH 17:9

The ever increasing pressure of living in turbulent times only clarified things for Jeremiah. On a daily basis he witnessed how evil and twisted the human heart could be. His culture, which once loved the One True God, now worshiped idols. The northern kingdom (Israel) and much of Judah (the southern kingdom) had fallen to foreign control. The once great city of Jerusalem was all that remained of a free Israel and Judah.

Jeremiah, a young man at the time he was called by God, spent nearly forty years warning the people of Jerusalem to repent, or suffer the same fate as the northern kingdom. Jeremiah begged the people to repent so God could bless them; but they ignored him, and rejected God.

Jeremiah watched five different kings occupy David's throne. He watched through a veil of tears when Israel desperately needed strong leaders but was denied. He wept as he saw the children slaughtered, the famine spreading, the chains of captivity shackled, his messages torn to shreds, and the Word of God cast into the fire. Jeremiah represented the loving God who was broken over the degradation of his people. When God was trying to do something new in the lives of his people (31:1–4), Jeremiah stood alone in faithfulness and obedience. When Jerusalem fell to Babylon, who was the only one still standing proclaiming the message of God? It was, of course, Jeremiah.

¹⁰I, the LORD, search the heart,
I test the mind,
Even to give every man according to his
ways,
According to the fruit of his doings.

¹¹"*As* a partridge that broods but does not hatch,
So is he who gets riches, but not by right;
It will leave him in the midst of his days,
And at his end he will be a fool."

¹²A glorious high throne from the beginning
Is the place of our sanctuary.
¹³O LORD, the hope of Israel,
All who forsake You shall be ashamed.

"Those who depart from Me
Shall be written in the earth,
Because they have forsaken the LORD,
The fountain of living waters."

JEREMIAH PRAYS FOR DELIVERANCE

¹⁴Heal me, O LORD, and I shall be healed;
Save me, and I shall be saved,
For You *are* my praise.
¹⁵Indeed they say to me,
"Where *is* the word of the LORD?
Let it come now!"
¹⁶As for me, I have not hurried away from *being*
a shepherd *who* follows You,
Nor have I desired the woeful day;
You know what came out of my lips;
It was right there before You.
¹⁷Do not be a terror to me;
You *are* my hope in the day of doom.
¹⁸Let them be ashamed who persecute me,
But do not let me be put to shame;
Let them be dismayed,
But do not let me be dismayed.
Bring on them the day of doom,
And destroy them with double destruction!

HALLOW THE SABBATH DAY

¹⁹Thus the LORD said to me: "Go and stand in the gate of the children of the people, by which the kings of Judah come in and by which they go out, and in all the gates of Jerusalem; ²⁰and say to them, 'Hear the word of the LORD, you kings of Judah, and all Judah, and all the in-

habitants of Jerusalem, who enter by these gates. ²¹Thus says the LORD: "Take heed to yourselves, and bear no burden on the Sabbath day, nor bring *it* in by the gates of Jerusalem; ²²nor carry a burden out of your houses on the Sabbath day, nor do any work, but hallow the Sabbath day, as I commanded your fathers. ²³But they did not obey nor incline their ear, but made their neck stiff, that they might not hear nor receive instruction.

²⁴"And it shall be, if you heed Me carefully," says the LORD, "to bring no burden through the gates of this city on the Sabbath day, but hallow the Sabbath day, to do no work in it, ²⁵then shall enter the gates of this city kings and princes sitting on the throne of David, riding in chariots and on horses, they and their princes, accompanied by the men of Judah and the inhabitants of Jerusalem; and this city shall remain forever. ²⁶And they shall come from the cities of Judah and from the places around Jerusalem, from the land of Benjamin and from the lowland, from the mountains and from the South, bringing burnt offerings and sacrifices, grain offerings and incense, bringing sacrifices of praise to the house of the LORD.

²⁷"But if you will not heed Me to hallow the Sabbath day, such as not carrying a burden when entering the gates of Jerusalem on the Sabbath day, then I will kindle a fire in its gates, and it shall devour the palaces of Jerusalem, and it shall not be quenched." ' "

THE POTTER AND THE CLAY

18 The word which came to Jeremiah from the LORD, saying: ²"Arise and go down to the potter's house, and there I will cause you to hear My words." ³Then I went down to the potter's house, and there he was, making something at the wheel. ⁴And the vessel that he made of clay was marred in the hand of the potter; so he made it again into another vessel, as it seemed good to the potter to make.

⁵Then the word of the LORD came to me, saying: ⁶"O house of Israel, can I not do with you as this potter?" says the LORD. "Look, as the clay *is* in the potter's hand, so *are* you in My hand, O house of Israel! ⁷The instant I speak concerning a nation and concerning a kingdom, to pluck up, to pull down, and to destroy *it*, ⁸if that nation against whom I have spoken turns from its evil, I will re-

lent of the disaster that I thought to bring upon it. ⁹And the instant I speak concerning a nation and concerning a kingdom, to build and to plant *it,* ¹⁰if it does evil in My sight so that it does not obey My voice, then I will relent concerning the good with which I said I would benefit it.

¹¹"Now therefore, speak to the men of Judah and to the inhabitants of Jerusalem, saying, 'Thus says the LORD: "Behold, I am fashioning a disaster and devising a plan against you. Return now every one from his evil way, and make your ways and your doings good." ' "

God's Warning Rejected

¹²And they said, "That is hopeless! So we will walk according to our own plans, and we will every one obey the dictates of his evil heart."

¹³Therefore thus says the LORD:

"Ask now among the Gentiles,
    Who has heard such things?
    The virgin of Israel has done a very horrible
        thing.
¹⁴Will *a man* leave the snow water of Lebanon,
    Which comes from the rock of the field?
    Will the cold flowing waters be forsaken for
        strange waters?

¹⁵"Because My people have forgotten Me,
    They have burned incense to worthless
        idols.
    And they have caused themselves to stumble
        in their ways,
    From the ancient paths,
    To walk in pathways and not on a highway,
¹⁶To make their land desolate *and* a perpetual
        hissing;
    Everyone who passes by it will be
        astonished
    And shake his head.
¹⁷I will scatter them as with an east wind before
        the enemy;
    I will show themᵃ the back and not the face
    In the day of their calamity."

Jeremiah Persecuted

¹⁸Then they said, "Come and let us devise plans against Jeremiah; for the law shall not perish from the priest, nor counsel from the wise, nor

the word from the prophet. Come and let us attack him with the tongue, and let us not give heed to any of his words."

¹⁹Give heed to me, O LORD,
    And listen to the voice of those who contend
        with me!
²⁰Shall evil be repaid for good?
    For they have dug a pit for my life.
    Remember that I stood before You
    To speak good for them,
    To turn away Your wrath from them.
²¹Therefore deliver up their children to the
        famine,
    And pour out their *blood*
    By the force of the sword;
    Let their wives *become* widows
    And bereaved of their children.
    Let their men be put to death,
    Their young men *be* slain
    By the sword in battle.
²²Let a cry be heard from their houses,
    When You bring a troop suddenly upon
        them;
    For they have dug a pit to take me,
    And hidden snares for my feet.
²³Yet, LORD, You know all their counsel
    Which is against me, to slay *me.*
    Provide no atonement for their iniquity,
    Nor blot out their sin from Your sight;
    But let them be overthrown before You.
    Deal *thus* with them
    In the time of Your anger.

The Sign of the Broken Flask

19 Thus says the LORD: "Go and get a potter's earthen flask, and *take* some of the elders of the people and some of the elders of the priests. ²And go out to the Valley of the Son of Hinnom, which *is* by the entry of the Potsherd Gate; and proclaim there the words that I will tell you, ³and say, 'Hear the word of the LORD, O kings of Judah and inhabitants of Jerusalem. Thus says the LORD of hosts, the God of Israel: "Behold, I will bring such a catastrophe on this place, that whoever hears of it, his ears will tingle.

18:17 ᵃFollowing Septuagint, Syriac, Targum, and Vulgate; Masoretic Text reads *look them in.*

4"Because they have forsaken Me and made this an alien place, because they have burned incense in it to other gods whom neither they, their fathers, nor the kings of Judah have known, and have filled this place with the blood of the innocents 5(they have also built the high places of Baal, to burn their sons with fire *for* burnt offerings to Baal, which I did not command or speak, nor did it come into My mind), 6therefore behold, the days are coming," says the LORD, "that this place shall no more be called Tophet or the Valley of the Son of Hinnom, but the Valley of Slaughter. 7And I will make void the counsel of Judah and Jerusalem in this place, and I will cause them to fall by the sword before their enemies and by the hands of those who seek their lives; their corpses I will give as meat for the birds of the heaven and for the beasts of the earth. 8I will make this city desolate and a hissing; everyone who passes by it will be astonished and hiss because of all its plagues. 9And I will cause them to eat the flesh of their sons and the flesh of their daughters, and everyone shall eat the flesh of his friend in the siege and in the desperation with which their enemies and those who seek their lives shall drive them to despair." '

10"Then you shall break the flask in the sight of the men who go with you, 11and say to them, 'Thus says the LORD of hosts: "Even so I will break this people and this city, as *one* breaks a potter's vessel, which cannot be made whole again; and they shall bury *them* in Tophet till *there is* no place to bury. 12Thus I will do to this place," says the LORD, "and to its inhabitants, and make this city like Tophet. 13And the houses of Jerusalem and the houses of the kings of Judah shall be defiled like the place of Tophet, because of all the houses on whose roofs they have burned incense to all the host of heaven, and poured out drink offerings to other gods." ' "

14Then Jeremiah came from Tophet, where the LORD had sent him to prophesy; and he stood in the court of the Lord's house and said to all the people, 15"Thus says the LORD of hosts, the God of Israel: 'Behold, I will bring on this city and on all her towns all the doom that I have pronounced against it, because they have stiffened their necks that they might not hear My words.' "

THE WORD OF GOD TO PASHHUR

20 Now Pashhur the son of Immer, the priest who *was* also chief governor in the house of the LORD, heard that Jeremiah prophesied these things. 2Then Pashhur struck Jeremiah the prophet, and put him in the stocks that *were* in the high gate of Benjamin, which *was* by the house of the LORD.

3And it happened on the next day that Pashhur brought Jeremiah out of the stocks. Then Jeremiah said to him, "The LORD has not called your name Pashhur, but Magor-Missabib.[a] 4For thus says the LORD: 'Behold, I will make you a terror to yourself and to all your friends; and they shall fall by the sword of their enemies, and your eyes shall see *it*. I will give all Judah into the hand of the king of Babylon, and he shall carry them captive to Babylon and slay them with the sword. 5Moreover I will deliver all the wealth of this city, all its produce, and all its precious things; all the treasures of the kings of Judah I will give into the hand of their enemies, who will plunder them, seize them, and carry them to Babylon. 6And you, Pashhur, and all who dwell in your house, shall go into captivity. You shall go to Babylon, and there you shall die, and be buried there, you and all your friends, to whom you have prophesied lies.' "

JEREMIAH'S UNPOPULAR MINISTRY

7O LORD, You induced me, and I was persuaded;
You are stronger than I, and have prevailed.
I am in derision daily;
Everyone mocks me.
8For when I spoke, I cried out;
I shouted, "Violence and plunder!"
Because the word of the LORD was made to me
A reproach and a derision daily.
9Then I said, "I will not make mention of Him,
Nor speak anymore in His name."
But *His word* was in my heart like a burning fire
Shut up in my bones;

20:3 aLiterally *Fear on Every Side*

I was weary of holding *it* back,
And I could not.
[10]For I heard many mocking:
"Fear on every side!"
"Report," *they say,* "and we will report it!"
All my acquaintances watched for my
stumbling, *saying,*
"Perhaps he can be induced;
Then we will prevail against him,
And we will take our revenge on him."

[11]But the LORD *is* with me as a mighty,
awesome One.
Therefore my persecutors will stumble, and
will not prevail.
They will be greatly ashamed, for they will
not prosper.
Their everlasting confusion will never be
forgotten.
[12]But, O LORD of hosts,
You who test the righteous,
And see the mind and heart,
Let me see Your vengeance on them;
For I have pleaded my cause before You.

[13]Sing to the LORD! Praise the LORD!
For He has delivered the life of the poor
From the hand of evildoers.

[14]Cursed *be* the day in which I was born!
Let the day not be blessed in which my
mother bore me!
[15]Let the man *be* cursed
Who brought news to my father, saying,
"A male child has been born to you!"
Making him very glad.
[16]And let that man be like the cities
Which the LORD overthrew, and did not
relent;
Let him hear the cry in the morning
And the shouting at noon,
[17]Because he did not kill me from the womb,
That my mother might have been my
grave,
And her womb always enlarged *with* me.
[18]Why did I come forth from the womb to see
labor and sorrow,
That my days should be consumed with
shame?

JERUSALEM'S DOOM IS SEALED

21 The word which came to Jeremiah from the LORD when King Zedekiah sent to him Pashhur the son of Melchiah, and Zephaniah the son of Maaseiah, the priest, saying, [2]"Please inquire of the LORD for us, for Nebuchadnezzar[a] king of Babylon makes war against us. Perhaps the LORD will deal with us according to all His wonderful works, that *the king* may go away from us."

[3]Then Jeremiah said to them, "Thus you shall say to Zedekiah, [4]"Thus says the LORD God of Israel: "Behold, I will turn back the weapons of war that *are* in your hands, with which you fight against the king of Babylon and the Chaldeans[a] who besiege you outside the walls; and I will assemble them in the midst of this city. [5]I Myself will fight against you with an outstretched hand and with a strong arm, even in anger and fury and great wrath. [6]I will strike the inhabitants of this city, both man and beast; they shall die of a great pestilence. [7]And afterward," says the LORD, "I will deliver Zedekiah king of Judah, his servants and the people, and such as are left in this city from the pestilence and the sword and the famine, into the hand of Nebuchadnezzar king of Babylon, into the hand of their enemies, and into the hand of those who seek their life; and he shall strike them with the edge of the sword. He shall not spare them, or have pity or mercy." '

[8]"Now you shall say to this people, 'Thus says the LORD: "Behold, I set before you the way of life and the way of death. [9]He who remains in this city shall die by the sword, by famine, and by pestilence; but he who goes out and defects to the Chaldeans who besiege you, he shall live, and his life shall be as a prize to him. [10]For I have set My face against this city for adversity and not for good," says the LORD. "It shall be given into the hand of the king of Babylon, and he shall burn it with fire." '

MESSAGE TO THE HOUSE OF DAVID

[11]"And concerning the house of the king of Judah, *say,* 'Hear the word of the LORD, [12]O house of David! Thus says the LORD:

21:2 [a]Hebrew *Nebuchadrezzar,* and so elsewhere 21:4 [a]Or *Babylonians*

"Execute judgment in the morning;
  And deliver *him who is* plundered
  Out of the hand of the oppressor,
  Lest My fury go forth like fire
  And burn so that no one can quench *it,*
  Because of the evil of your doings.

¹³"Behold, I *am* against you, O inhabitant of the
      valley,
  And rock of the plain," says the LORD,
"Who say, 'Who shall come down against us?
  Or who shall enter our dwellings?'
¹⁴But I will punish you according to the fruit
      of your doings," says the LORD;
"I will kindle a fire in its forest,
  And it shall devour all things around it." ' "

22 Thus says the LORD: "Go down to the house of the king of Judah, and there speak this word, ²and say, 'Hear the word of the LORD, O king of Judah, you who sit on the throne of David, you and your servants and your people who enter these gates! ³Thus says the LORD: "Execute judgment and righteousness, and deliver the plundered out of the hand of the oppressor. Do no wrong and do no violence to the stranger, the fatherless, or the widow, nor shed innocent blood in this place. ⁴For if you indeed do this thing, then shall enter the gates of this house, riding on horses and in chariots, accompanied by servants and people, kings who sit on the throne of David. ⁵But if you will not hear these words, I swear by Myself," says the LORD, "that this house shall become a desolation." ' "

⁶For thus says the LORD to the house of the king of Judah:

"You *are* Gilead to Me,
  The head of Lebanon;
  Yet I surely will make you a wilderness,
  Cities *which* are not inhabited.
⁷I will prepare destroyers against you,
  Everyone with his weapons;
  They shall cut down your choice cedars
  And cast *them* into the fire.

⁸And many nations will pass by this city; and everyone will say to his neighbor, 'Why has the LORD done so to this great city?' ⁹Then they will answer, 'Because they have forsaken the covenant of the LORD their God, and worshiped other gods and served them.' "

¹⁰Weep not for the dead, nor bemoan him;
  Weep bitterly for him who goes away,
  For he shall return no more,
  Nor see his native country.

MESSAGE TO THE SONS OF JOSIAH

¹¹For thus says the LORD concerning Shallum[a] the son of Josiah, king of Judah, who reigned instead of Josiah his father, who went from this place: "He shall not return here anymore, ¹²but he shall die in the place where they have led him captive, and shall see this land no more.

¹³"Woe to him who builds his house by
      unrighteousness
  And his chambers by injustice,
  Who uses his neighbor's service without
      wages
  And gives him nothing for his work,
¹⁴Who says, 'I will build myself a wide house
      with spacious chambers,
  And cut out windows for it,
  Paneling *it* with cedar
  And painting *it* with vermilion.'

¹⁵"Shall you reign because you enclose *yourself* in
      cedar?
  Did not your father eat and drink,
  And do justice and righteousness?
  Then *it was* well with him.
¹⁶He judged the cause of the poor and needy;
  Then *it was* well.
  Was not this knowing Me?" says the LORD.
¹⁷"Yet your eyes and your heart *are* for nothing
      but your covetousness,
  For shedding innocent blood,
  And practicing oppression and violence."

¹⁸Therefore thus says the LORD concerning Jehoiakim the son of Josiah, king of Judah:

"They shall not lament for him,
  Saying, 'Alas, my brother!' or 'Alas, my sister!'

22:11 [a]Also called *Jehoahaz*

They shall not lament for him,
Saying, 'Alas, master!' or 'Alas, his glory!'
¹⁹He shall be buried with the burial of a
donkey,
Dragged and cast out beyond the gates of
Jerusalem.

²⁰"Go up to Lebanon, and cry out,
And lift up your voice in Bashan;
Cry from Abarim,
For all your lovers are destroyed.
²¹I spoke to you in your prosperity,
But you said, 'I will not hear.'
This *has been* your manner from your youth,
That you did not obey My voice.
²²The wind shall eat up all your rulers,
And your lovers shall go into captivity;
Surely then you will be ashamed and
humiliated
For all your wickedness.
²³O inhabitant of Lebanon,
Making your nest in the cedars,
How gracious will you be when pangs come
upon you,
Like the pain of a woman in labor?

MESSAGE TO CONIAH

²⁴"*As* I live," says the LORD, "though Coniah[a]
the son of Jehoiakim, king of Judah, were the
signet on My right hand, yet I would pluck you
off; ²⁵and I will give you into the hand of those
who seek your life, and into the hand *of those*
whose face you fear—the hand of Nebuchadnezzar king of Babylon and the hand of the
Chaldeans. ²⁶So I will cast you out, and your
mother who bore you, into another country
where you were not born; and there you shall die.
²⁷But to the land to which they desire to return,
there they shall not return.

²⁸"Is this man Coniah a despised, broken idol—
A vessel in which *is* no pleasure?
Why are they cast out, he and his
descendants,
And cast into a land which they do not know?
²⁹O earth, earth, earth,
Hear the word of the LORD!
³⁰Thus says the LORD:
'Write this man down as childless,

A man *who* shall not prosper in his days;
For none of his descendants shall prosper,
Sitting on the throne of David,
And ruling anymore in Judah.' "

THE BRANCH OF RIGHTEOUSNESS

23 "Woe to the shepherds who destroy and
scatter the sheep of My pasture!" says the
LORD. ²Therefore thus says the LORD God of Israel against the shepherds who feed My people:
"You have scattered My flock, driven them away,
and not attended to them. Behold, I will attend to
you for the evil of your doings," says the LORD.
³"But I will gather the remnant of My flock out
of all countries where I have driven them, and
bring them back to their folds; and they shall be
fruitful and increase. ⁴I will set up shepherds over
them who will feed them; and they shall fear no
more, nor be dismayed, nor shall they be lacking,"
says the LORD.

⁵"Behold, *the* days are coming," says the LORD,
"That I will raise to David a Branch of
righteousness;
A King shall reign and prosper,
And execute judgment and righteousness in
the earth.
⁶In His days Judah will be saved,
And Israel will dwell safely;
Now this *is* His name by which He will be
called:

THE LORD OUR RIGHTEOUSNESS.[a]

⁷"Therefore, behold, *the* days are coming," says
the LORD, "that they shall no longer say, 'As the
LORD lives who brought up the children of Israel
from the land of Egypt,' ⁸but, 'As the LORD lives
who brought up and led the descendants of the
house of Israel from the north country and from
all the countries where I had driven them.' And
they shall dwell in their own land."

FALSE PROPHETS AND EMPTY ORACLES

⁹My heart within me is broken
Because of the prophets;
All my bones shake.

22:24 [a]Also called *Jeconiah* and *Jehoiachin*   **23:6** [a]Hebrew *YHWH Tsidkenu*

I am like a drunken man,
And like a man whom wine has overcome,
Because of the LORD,
And because of His holy words.
¹⁰For the land is full of adulterers;
For because of a curse the land mourns.
The pleasant places of the wilderness are
    dried up.
Their course of life is evil,
And their might is not right.

¹¹"For both prophet and priest are profane;
    Yes, in My house I have found their
        wickedness," says the LORD.
¹²"Therefore their way shall be to them
    Like slippery ways;
    In the darkness they shall be driven on
    And fall in them;
    For I will bring disaster on them,
    The year of their punishment," says the
        LORD.
¹³"And I have seen folly in the prophets of
    Samaria:
    They prophesied by Baal
    And caused My people Israel to err.
¹⁴Also I have seen a horrible thing in the
    prophets of Jerusalem:
    They commit adultery and walk in lies;
    They also strengthen the hands of
        evildoers,
    So that no one turns back from his
        wickedness.
    All of them are like Sodom to Me,
    And her inhabitants like Gomorrah.

¹⁵"Therefore thus says the LORD of hosts
concerning the prophets:

'Behold, I will feed them with wormwood,
    And make them drink the water of gall;
    For from the prophets of Jerusalem
    Profaneness has gone out into all the
        land.'"

¹⁶Thus says the LORD of hosts:

"Do not listen to the words of the prophets
    who prophesy to you.
    They make you worthless;

They speak a vision of their own heart,
    Not from the mouth of the LORD.
¹⁷They continually say to those who despise
    Me,
    'The LORD has said, "You shall have
        peace" ';
    And to everyone who walks according to the
        dictates of his own heart, they say,
    'No evil shall come upon you.' "

¹⁸For who has stood in the counsel of the
    LORD,
    And has perceived and heard His word?
    Who has marked His word and heard it?
¹⁹Behold, a whirlwind of the LORD has gone
    forth in fury—
    A violent whirlwind!
    It will fall violently on the head of the
        wicked.
²⁰The anger of the LORD will not turn back
    Until He has executed and performed the
        thoughts of His heart.
    In the latter days you will understand it
        perfectly.

²¹"I have not sent these prophets, yet they ran.
    I have not spoken to them, yet they
        prophesied.
²²But if they had stood in My counsel,
    And had caused My people to hear My
        words,
    Then they would have turned them from
        their evil way
    And from the evil of their doings.

²³"Am I a God near at hand," says the LORD,
    "And not a God afar off?
²⁴Can anyone hide himself in secret places,
    So I shall not see him?" says the LORD;
    "Do I not fill heaven and earth?" says the
        LORD.

²⁵"I have heard what the prophets have said
who prophesy lies in My name, saying, 'I have
dreamed, I have dreamed!' ²⁶How long will this
be in the heart of the prophets who prophesy
lies? Indeed they are prophets of the deceit of
their own heart, ²⁷who try to make My people
forget My name by their dreams which everyone

tells his neighbor, as their fathers forgot My name for Baal.

28"The prophet who has a dream, let him tell a
    dream;
And he who has My word, let him speak My
    word faithfully.
What *is* the chaff to the wheat?" says the
    LORD.
29"*Is* not My word like a fire?" says the LORD,
"And like a hammer *that* breaks the rock in
    pieces?

30"Therefore behold, I *am* against the prophets," says the LORD, "who steal My words every one from his neighbor. 31Behold, I *am* against the prophets," says the LORD, "who use their tongues and say, 'He says.' 32Behold, I *am* against those who prophesy false dreams," says the LORD, "and tell them, and cause My people to err by their lies and by their recklessness. Yet I did not send them or command them; therefore they shall not profit this people at all," says the LORD.

33"So when these people or the prophet or the priest ask you, saying, 'What is the oracle of the LORD?' you shall then say to them, 'What oracle?'ª I will even forsake you," says the LORD. 34"And *as for* the prophet and the priest and the people who say, 'The oracle of the LORD!' I will even punish that man and his house. 35Thus every one of you shall say to his neighbor, and every one to his brother, 'What has the LORD answered?' and, 'What has the LORD spoken?' 36And the oracle of the LORD you shall mention no more. For every man's word will be his oracle, for you have perverted the words of the living God, the LORD of hosts, our God. 37Thus you shall say to the prophet, 'What has the LORD answered you?' and, 'What has the LORD spoken?' 38But since you say, 'The oracle of the LORD!' therefore thus says the LORD: 'Because you say this word, "The oracle of the LORD!" and I have sent to you, saying, "Do not say, 'The oracle of the LORD!' " 39therefore behold, I, even I, will utterly forget you and forsake you, and the city that I gave you and your fathers, and *will cast you* out of My presence. 40And I will bring an everlasting reproach upon you, and a perpetual shame, which shall not be forgotten.' "

THE SIGN OF TWO BASKETS OF FIGS

24 The LORD showed me, and there were two baskets of figs set before the temple of the LORD, after Nebuchadnezzar king of Babylon had carried away captive Jeconiah the son of Jehoiakim, king of Judah, and the princes of Judah with the craftsmen and smiths, from Jerusalem, and had brought them to Babylon. 2One basket *had* very good figs, like the figs *that are* first ripe; and the other basket *had* very bad figs which could not be eaten, they were so bad. 3Then the LORD said to me, "What do you see, Jeremiah?"

And I said, "Figs, the good figs, very good; and the bad, very bad, which cannot be eaten, they are so bad."

4Again the word of the LORD came to me, saying, 5"Thus says the LORD, the God of Israel: 'Like these good figs, so will I acknowledge those who are carried away captive from Judah, whom I have sent out of this place for *their own* good, into the land of the Chaldeans. 6For I will set My eyes on them for good, and I will bring them back to this land; I will build them and not pull *them* down, and I will plant them and not pluck *them* up. 7Then I will give them a heart to know Me, that I *am* the LORD; and they shall be My people, and I will be their God, for they shall return to Me with their whole heart.

8'And as the bad figs which cannot be eaten, they are so bad'—surely thus says the LORD—'so will I give up Zedekiah the king of Judah, his princes, the residue of Jerusalem who remain in this land, and those who dwell in the land of Egypt. 9I will deliver them to trouble into all the kingdoms of the earth, for *their* harm, *to be* a reproach and a byword, a taunt and a curse, in all places where I shall drive them. 10And I will send the sword, the famine, and the pestilence among them, till they are consumed from the land that I gave to them and their fathers.' "

SEVENTY YEARS OF DESOLATION

25 The word that came to Jeremiah concerning all the people of Judah, in the fourth year of Jehoiakim the son of Josiah, king of Judah (which *was* the first year of Nebuchadnezzar king of Babylon), 2which Jeremiah the prophet spoke to all the people of Judah and to all the inhabitants

23:33 ªSeptuagint, Targum, and Vulgate read '*You are the burden.*'

of Jerusalem, saying: [3]"From the thirteenth year of Josiah the son of Amon, king of Judah, even to this day, this *is* the twenty-third year in which the word of the LORD has come to me; and I have spoken to you, rising early and speaking, but you have not listened. [4]And the LORD has sent to you all His servants the prophets, rising early and sending *them,* but you have not listened nor inclined your ear to hear. [5]They said, 'Repent now everyone of his evil way and his evil doings, and dwell in the land that the LORD has given to you and your fathers forever and ever. [6]Do not go after other gods to serve them and worship them, and do not provoke Me to anger with the works of your hands; and I will not harm you.' [7]Yet you have not listened to Me," says the LORD, "that you might provoke Me to anger with the works of your hands to your own hurt.

[8]"Therefore thus says the LORD of hosts: 'Because you have not heard My words, [9]behold, I will send and take all the families of the north,' says the LORD, 'and Nebuchadnezzar the king of Babylon, My servant, and will bring them against this land, against its inhabitants, and against these nations all around, and will utterly destroy them, and make them an astonishment, a hissing, and perpetual desolations. [10]Moreover I will take from them the voice of mirth and the voice of gladness, the voice of the bridegroom and the voice of the bride, the sound of the millstones and the light of the lamp. [11]And this whole land shall be a desolation *and* an astonishment, and these nations shall serve the king of Babylon seventy years.

[12]"Then it will come to pass, when seventy years are completed, *that* I will punish the king of Babylon and that nation, the land of the Chaldeans, for their iniquity,' says the LORD; 'and I will make it a perpetual desolation. [13]So I will bring on that land all My words which I have pronounced against it, all that is written in this book, which Jeremiah has prophesied concerning all the nations. [14](For many nations and great kings shall be served by them also; and I will repay them according to their deeds and according to the works of their own hands.)' "

JUDGMENT ON THE NATIONS

[15]For thus says the LORD God of Israel to me: "Take this wine cup of fury from My hand, and cause all the nations, to whom I send you, to drink it. [16]And they will drink and stagger and go mad because of the sword that I will send among them."

[17]Then I took the cup from the LORD's hand, and made all the nations drink, to whom the LORD had sent me: [18]Jerusalem and the cities of Judah, its kings and its princes, to make them a desolation, an astonishment, a hissing, and a curse, as *it is* this day; [19]Pharaoh king of Egypt, his servants, his princes, and all his people; [20]all the mixed multitude, all the kings of the land of Uz, all the kings of the land of the Philistines (namely, Ashkelon, Gaza, Ekron, and the remnant of Ashdod); [21]Edom, Moab, and the people of Ammon; [22]all the kings of Tyre, all the kings of Sidon, and the kings of the coastlands which *are* across the sea; [23]Dedan, Tema, Buz, and all *who are* in the farthest corners; [24]all the kings of Arabia and all the kings of the mixed multitude who dwell in the desert; [25]all the kings of Zimri, all the kings of Elam, and all the kings of the Medes; [26]all the kings of the north, far and near, one with another; and all the kingdoms of the world which *are* on the face of the earth. Also the king of Sheshach[a] shall drink after them.

[27]"Therefore you shall say to them, 'Thus says the LORD of hosts, the God of Israel: "Drink, be drunk, and vomit! Fall and rise no more, because of the sword which I will send among you." ' [28]And it shall be, if they refuse to take the cup from your hand to drink, then you shall say to them, 'Thus says the LORD of hosts: "You shall certainly drink! [29]For behold, I begin to bring calamity on the city which is called by My name, and should you be utterly unpunished? You shall not be unpunished, for I will call for a sword on all the inhabitants of the earth," says the LORD of hosts.'

[30]"Therefore prophesy against them all these words, and say to them:

'The LORD will roar from on high,
　　And utter His voice from His holy
　　　　habitation;
　　He will roar mightily against His fold.
　　He will give a shout, as those who tread *the
　　　　grapes,*

25:26 [a]A code word for Babylon (compare 51:41)

Against all the inhabitants of the earth.
³¹A noise will come to the ends of the earth—
For the LORD has a controversy with the
    nations;
He will plead His case with all flesh.
He will give those *who are* wicked to the
    sword,' says the LORD."

³²Thus says the LORD of hosts:

"Behold, disaster shall go forth
From nation to nation,
And a great whirlwind shall be raised up
From the farthest parts of the earth.

³³"And at that day the slain of the LORD shall
be from *one* end of the earth even to the *other* end
of the earth. They shall not be lamented, or gathered, or buried; they shall become refuse on the
ground.

³⁴"Wail, shepherds, and cry!
Roll about *in the ashes,*
You leaders of the flock!
For the days of your slaughter and your
    dispersions are fulfilled;
You shall fall like a precious vessel.
³⁵And the shepherds will have no way to flee,
Nor the leaders of the flock to escape.
³⁶A voice of the cry of the shepherds,
And a wailing of the leaders of the flock *will
    be heard.*
For the LORD has plundered their pasture,
³⁷And the peaceful dwellings are cut down
Because of the fierce anger of the LORD.
³⁸He has left His lair like the lion;
For their land is desolate
Because of the fierceness of the Oppressor,
And because of His fierce anger."

JEREMIAH SAVED FROM DEATH

26 In the beginning of the reign of Jehoiakim
the son of Josiah, king of Judah, this word
came from the LORD, saying, ²"Thus says the
LORD: 'Stand in the court of the LORD's house,
and speak to all the cities of Judah, which come
to worship *in* the LORD's house, all the words that
I command you to speak to them. Do not diminish a word. ³Perhaps everyone will listen and turn

from his evil way, that I may relent concerning
the calamity which I purpose to bring on them
because of the evil of their doings.' ⁴And you shall
say to them, 'Thus says the LORD: "If you will not
listen to Me, to walk in My law which I have set
before you, ⁵to heed the words of My servants the
prophets whom I sent to you, both rising up early
and sending *them* (but you have not heeded),
⁶then I will make this house like Shiloh, and will
make this city a curse to all the nations of the
earth." ' "

⁷So the priests and the prophets and all the
people heard Jeremiah speaking these words in
the house of the LORD. ⁸Now it happened, when
Jeremiah had made an end of speaking all that the
LORD had commanded *him* to speak to all the
people, that the priests and the prophets and all
the people seized him, saying, "You will surely
die! ⁹Why have you prophesied in the name of
the LORD, saying, 'This house shall be like Shiloh,
and this city shall be desolate, without an inhabitant'?" And all the people were gathered against
Jeremiah in the house of the LORD.

¹⁰When the princes of Judah heard these
things, they came up from the king's house to the
house of the LORD and sat down in the entry of
the New Gate of the LORD's *house.* ¹¹And the
priests and the prophets spoke to the princes and
all the people, saying, "This man deserves to die!
For he has prophesied against this city, as you have
heard with your ears."

¹²Then Jeremiah spoke to all the princes and
all the people, saying: "The LORD sent me to
prophesy against this house and against this city
with all the words that you have heard. ¹³Now
therefore, amend your ways and your doings, and
obey the voice of the LORD your God; then the
LORD will relent concerning the doom that He
has pronounced against you. ¹⁴As for me, here I
am, in your hand; do with me as seems good and
proper to you. ¹⁵But know for certain that if you
put me to death, you will surely bring innocent
blood on yourselves, on this city, and on its inhabitants; for truly the LORD has sent me to you to
speak all these words in your hearing."

¹⁶So the princes and all the people said to the
priests and the prophets, "This man does not deserve to die. For he has spoken to us in the name
of the LORD our God."

¹⁷Then certain of the elders of the land rose up and spoke to all the assembly of the people, saying: ¹⁸"Micah of Moresheth prophesied in the days of Hezekiah king of Judah, and spoke to all the people of Judah, saying, 'Thus says the LORD of hosts:

"Zion shall be plowed *like* a field,
Jerusalem shall become heaps of ruins,
And the mountain of the temple^a
Like the bare hills of the forest." '^b

¹⁹Did Hezekiah king of Judah and all Judah ever put him to death? Did he not fear the LORD and seek the LORD's favor? And the LORD relented concerning the doom which He had pronounced against them. But we are doing great evil against ourselves."

²⁰Now there was also a man who prophesied in the name of the LORD, Urijah the son of Shemaiah of Kirjath Jearim, who prophesied against this city and against this land according to all the words of Jeremiah. ²¹And when Jehoiakim the king, with all his mighty men and all the princes, heard his words, the king sought to put him to death; but when Urijah heard *it,* he was afraid and fled, and went to Egypt. ²²Then Jehoiakim the king sent men to Egypt: Elnathan the son of Achbor, and *other* men *who went* with him to Egypt. ²³And they brought Urijah from Egypt and brought him to Jehoiakim the king, who killed him with the sword and cast his dead body into the graves of the common people.

²⁴Nevertheless the hand of Ahikam the son of Shaphan was with Jeremiah, so that they should not give him into the hand of the people to put him to death.

SYMBOL OF THE BONDS AND YOKES

27 In the beginning of the reign of Jehoiakim^a the son of Josiah, king of Judah, this word came to Jeremiah from the LORD, saying,^b ²"Thus says the LORD to me: 'Make for yourselves bonds and yokes, and put them on your neck, ³and send them to the king of Edom, the king of Moab, the king of the Ammonites, the king of Tyre, and the king of Sidon, by the hand of the messengers who come to Jerusalem to Zedekiah king of Judah. ⁴And command them to say to their masters,

"Thus says the LORD of hosts, the God of Israel—thus you shall say to your masters: ⁵'I have made the earth, the man and the beast that *are* on the ground, by My great power and by My outstretched arm, and have given it to whom it seemed proper to Me. ⁶And now I have given all these lands into the hand of Nebuchadnezzar the king of Babylon, My servant; and the beasts of the field I have also given him to serve him. ⁷So all nations shall serve him and his son and his son's son, until the time of his land comes; and then many nations and great kings shall make him serve them. ⁸And it shall be, *that* the nation and kingdom which will not serve Nebuchadnezzar the king of Babylon, and which will not put its neck under the yoke of the king of Babylon, that nation I will punish,' says the LORD, 'with the sword, the famine, and the pestilence, until I have consumed them by his hand. ⁹Therefore do not listen to your prophets, your diviners, your dreamers, your soothsayers, or your sorcerers, who speak to you, saying, "You shall not serve the king of Babylon." ¹⁰For they prophesy a lie to you, to remove you far from your land; and I will drive you out, and you will perish. ¹¹But the nations that bring their necks under the yoke of the king of Babylon and serve him, I will let them remain in their own land,' says the LORD, 'and they shall till it and dwell in it.' " ' "

¹²I also spoke to Zedekiah king of Judah according to all these words, saying, "Bring your necks under the yoke of the king of Babylon, and serve him and his people, and live! ¹³Why will you die, you and your people, by the sword, by the famine, and by the pestilence, as the LORD has spoken against the nation that will not serve the king of Babylon? ¹⁴Therefore do not listen to the words of the prophets who speak to you, saying, 'You shall not serve the king of Babylon,' for they prophesy a lie to you; ¹⁵for I have not sent them," says the LORD, "yet they prophesy a lie in My name, that I may drive you out, and that you may perish, you and the prophets who prophesy to you."

¹⁶Also I spoke to the priests and to all this people, saying, "Thus says the LORD: 'Do not listen to the words of your prophets who prophesy

26:18 ^aLiterally *house* ^bCompare Micah 3:12 **27:1** ^aFollowing Masoretic Text, Targum, and Vulgate; some Hebrew manuscripts, Arabic, and Syriac read *Zedekiah* (compare 27:3, 12; 28:1). ^bSeptuagint omits verse 1.

to you, saying, "Behold, the vessels of the LORD's house will now shortly be brought back from Babylon"; for they prophesy a lie to you. [17]Do not listen to them; serve the king of Babylon, and live! Why should this city be laid waste? [18]But if they *are* prophets, and if the word of the LORD is with them, let them now make intercession to the LORD of hosts, that the vessels which are left in the house of the LORD, *in* the house of the king of Judah, and at Jerusalem, do not go to Babylon.'

[19]"For thus says the LORD of hosts concerning the pillars, concerning the Sea, concerning the carts, and concerning the remainder of the vessels that remain in this city, [20]which Nebuchadnezzar king of Babylon did not take, when he carried away captive Jeconiah the son of Jehoiakim, king of Judah, from Jerusalem to Babylon, and all the nobles of Judah and Jerusalem— [21]yes, thus says the LORD of hosts, the God of Israel, concerning the vessels that remain in the house of the LORD, and in the house of the king of Judah and of Jerusalem: [22]'They shall be carried to Babylon, and there they shall be until the day that I visit them,' says the LORD. 'Then I will bring them up and restore them to this place.' "

Hananiah's Falsehood and Doom

28 And it happened in the same year, at the beginning of the reign of Zedekiah king of Judah, in the fourth year *and* in the fifth month, *that* Hananiah the son of Azur the prophet, who *was* from Gibeon, spoke to me in the house of the LORD in the presence of the priests and of all the people, saying, [2]"Thus speaks the LORD of hosts, the God of Israel, saying: 'I have broken the yoke of the king of Babylon. [3]Within two full years I will bring back to this place all the vessels of the LORD's house, that Nebuchadnezzar king of Babylon took away from this place and carried to Babylon. [4]And I will bring back to this place Jeconiah the son of Jehoiakim, king of Judah, with all the captives of Judah who went to Babylon,' says the LORD, 'for I will break the yoke of the king of Babylon.' "

[5]Then the prophet Jeremiah spoke to the prophet Hananiah in the presence of the priests and in the presence of all the people who stood in the house of the LORD, [6]and the prophet Jeremiah said, "Amen! The LORD do so; the LORD perform your words which you have prophesied, to bring back the vessels of the LORD's house and all who were carried away captive, from Babylon to this place. [7]Nevertheless hear now this word that I speak in your hearing and in the hearing of all the people: [8]The prophets who have been before me and before you of old prophesied against many countries and great kingdoms—of war and disaster and pestilence. [9]As for the prophet who prophesies of peace, when the word of the prophet comes to pass, the prophet will be known *as* one whom the LORD has truly sent."

[10]Then Hananiah the prophet took the yoke off the prophet Jeremiah's neck and broke it. [11]And Hananiah spoke in the presence of all the people, saying, "Thus says the LORD: 'Even so I will break the yoke of Nebuchadnezzar king of Babylon from the neck of all nations within the space of two full years.' " And the prophet Jeremiah went his way.

[12]Now the word of the LORD came to Jeremiah, after Hananiah the prophet had broken the yoke from the neck of the prophet Jeremiah, saying, [13]"Go and tell Hananiah, saying, 'Thus says the LORD: "You have broken the yokes of wood, but you have made in their place yokes of iron." [14]For thus says the LORD of hosts, the God of Israel: "I have put a yoke of iron on the neck of all these nations, that they may serve Nebuchadnezzar king of Babylon; and they shall serve him. I have given him the beasts of the field also." ' "

[15]Then the prophet Jeremiah said to Hananiah the prophet, "Hear now, Hananiah, the LORD has not sent you, but you make this people trust in a lie. [16]Therefore thus says the LORD: 'Behold, I will cast you from the face of the earth. This year you shall die, because you have taught rebellion against the LORD.' "

[17]So Hananiah the prophet died the same year in the seventh month.

Jeremiah's Letter to the Captives

29 Now these *are* the words of the letter that Jeremiah the prophet sent from Jerusalem to the remainder of the elders who were carried away captive—to the priests, the prophets, and all the people whom Nebuchadnezzar had carried away captive from Jerusalem to Babylon. [2](This happened after Jeconiah the king, the queen mother, the eunuchs, the princes of Judah and Jerusalem, the craftsmen, and the smiths had departed from Jerusalem.) ³*The letter was sent* by the hand of Elasah the son of Shaphan, and Gemariah the son of Hilkiah, whom Zedekiah king of Judah sent to Babylon, to Nebuchadnezzar king of Babylon, saying,

⁴Thus says the LORD of hosts, the God of Israel, to all who were carried away captive, whom I have caused to be carried away from Jerusalem to Babylon:

⁵Build houses and dwell *in them;* plant gardens and eat their fruit. ⁶Take wives and beget sons and daughters; and take wives for your sons and give your daughters to husbands, so that they may bear sons and daughters—that you may be increased there, and not diminished. ⁷And seek the peace of the city where I have caused you to be carried away captive, and pray to the LORD for it; for in its peace you will have peace. ⁸For thus says the LORD of hosts, the God of Israel: Do not let your prophets and your diviners who are in your midst deceive you, nor listen to your dreams which you cause to be dreamed. ⁹For they prophesy falsely to you in My name; I have not sent them, says the LORD.

¹⁰For thus says the LORD: After seventy years are completed at Babylon, I will visit you and perform My good word toward you, and cause you to return to this place. ¹¹For I know the thoughts that I think toward you, says the LORD, thoughts of peace and not of evil, to give you a future and a hope. ¹²Then you will call upon Me and go and pray to Me, and I will listen to you. ¹³And you will seek Me and find *Me,* when you search for Me with all your heart. ¹⁴I will be found by you, says the LORD, and I will bring you back from your captivity; I will gather you from all the nations and from all the places where I have driven you, says the LORD, and I will bring you to the place from which I cause you to be carried away captive.

¹⁵Because you have said, "The LORD has raised up prophets for us in Babylon"— ¹⁶therefore thus says the LORD concerning the king who sits on the throne of David, concerning all the people who dwell in this city, and concerning your brethren who have not gone out with you into captivity— ¹⁷thus says the LORD of hosts: Behold, I will send on them the sword, the famine, and the pestilence, and will make them like rotten figs that cannot be eaten,

THROUGH THE GRID

Where Have All the Dreamers Gone? Observations from a Biblical Worldview: A Culture of Nothingness (Jer. 29:11)

Nihilism has infected many aspects of our culture and society, so that one could say that we belong to a culture of nothingness. Nihilism is simply the by-product of a naturalistic worldview, which denies the existence of God as well as ultimate purpose for all that exists. According to a naturalist or nihilist view of life, one cannot possibly have any meaning in life; and if one happens to find meaning, then one is ultimately deluded. Nihilists place no value in human accomplishments or efforts, as it all means nothing in the end. Many nihilists do not start there, but they begin by searching for meaning and purpose. Most never fully consider the Christian worldview; and as a result, they never find ultimate meaning and purpose. If nothing at all matters, then it doesn't matter what one does, and one does not live by any sort of moral code. One can do whatever one pleases since ultimately it all means nothing.

they are so bad. ¹⁸And I will pursue them
with the sword, with famine, and with
pestilence; and I will deliver them to
trouble among all the kingdoms of the
earth—to be a curse, an astonishment, a
hissing, and a reproach among all the
nations where I have driven them,
¹⁹because they have not heeded My words,
says the LORD, which I sent to them by
My servants the prophets, rising up early
and sending *them;* neither would you
heed, says the LORD. ²⁰Therefore hear the
word of the LORD, all you of the captivity,
whom I have sent from Jerusalem to
Babylon.

²¹Thus says the LORD of hosts, the God of
Israel, concerning Ahab the son of Kolaiah,
and Zedekiah the son of Maaseiah, who
prophesy a lie to you in My name: Behold,
I will deliver them into the hand of
Nebuchadnezzar king of Babylon, and he
shall slay them before your eyes. ²²And
because of them a curse shall be taken up
by all the captivity of Judah who *are* in
Babylon, saying, "The LORD make you like
Zedekiah and Ahab, whom the king of
Babylon roasted in the fire"; ²³because they
have done disgraceful things in Israel, have
committed adultery with their neighbors'
wives, and have spoken lying words in My
name, which I have not commanded them.
Indeed I know, and *am* a witness, says the
LORD.

²⁴You shall also speak to Shemaiah the
Nehelamite, saying, ²⁵Thus speaks the
LORD of hosts, the God of Israel, saying:
You have sent letters in your name to all
the people who *are* at Jerusalem, to
Zephaniah the son of Maaseiah the priest,
and to all the priests, saying, ²⁶"The LORD
has made you priest instead of Jehoiada the
priest, so that there should be officers *in*
the house of the LORD over every man
who is demented and considers himself a
prophet, that you should put him in prison
and in the stocks. ²⁷Now therefore, why
have you not rebuked Jeremiah of

Anathoth who makes himself a prophet to
you? ²⁸For he has sent to us *in* Babylon,
saying, 'This *captivity is* long; build houses
and dwell *in them,* and plant gardens and
eat their fruit.' "

²⁹Now Zephaniah the priest read this letter
in the hearing of Jeremiah the prophet.
³⁰Then the word of the LORD came to
Jeremiah, saying: ³¹Send to all those in
captivity, saying, Thus says the LORD
concerning Shemaiah the Nehelamite:
Because Shemaiah has prophesied to you,
and I have not sent him, and he has
caused you to trust in a lie— ³²therefore
thus says the LORD: Behold, I will punish
Shemaiah the Nehelamite and his family:
he shall not have anyone to dwell among
this people, nor shall he see the good that
I will do for My people, says the LORD,
because he has taught rebellion against the
LORD.

RESTORATION OF ISRAEL AND JUDAH

30 The word that came to Jeremiah from the
LORD, saying, ²"Thus speaks the LORD
God of Israel, saying: 'Write in a book for yourself
all the words that I have spoken to you. ³For behold, the days are coming,' says the LORD, 'that I
will bring back from captivity My people Israel
and Judah,' says the LORD. 'And I will cause them
to return to the land that I gave to their fathers,
and they shall possess it.' "

⁴Now these *are* the words that the LORD
spoke concerning Israel and Judah.

⁵"For thus says the LORD:

'We have heard a voice of trembling,
    Of fear, and not of peace.
⁶Ask now, and see,
    Whether a man is ever in labor with child?
    So why do I see every man *with* his hands on
        his loins
    Like a woman in labor,
    And all faces turned pale?
⁷Alas! For that day *is* great,
    So that none *is* like it;
    And it *is* the time of Jacob's trouble,
    But he shall be saved out of it.

THROUGH THE GRID

Making Sense of Your World: An Understanding of Revelation (Jer. 30:2)

Those who hold a biblical worldview hold that human beings and the cosmos have been created by God, who reveals Himself through Scripture. This is the hinge statement for Christian theology and theism, but it cannot absolutely be proven true because of the nature of proving the existence of God. All worldviews carry certain assumptions and presuppositions about the order of the universe and about humanity, but the Christian worldview cannot be proven without appealing to the spiritual realm. The biblical worldview relies on the revelation of God through creation, and this revelation is animated by the Holy Spirit.

8'For it shall come to pass in that day,'
   Says the LORD of hosts,
 '*That* I will break his yoke from your neck,
   And will burst your bonds;
   Foreigners shall no more enslave them.
9But they shall serve the LORD their God,
   And David their king,
   Whom I will raise up for them.

10'Therefore do not fear, O My servant Jacob,'
      says the LORD,
 'Nor be dismayed, O Israel;
   For behold, I will save you from afar,
   And your seed from the land of their
      captivity.
   Jacob shall return, have rest and be quiet,
   And no one shall make *him* afraid.
11For I *am* with you,' says the LORD, 'to save
      you;
   Though I make a full end of all nations
      where I have scattered you,
   Yet I will not make a complete end of you.
   But I will correct you in justice,
   And will not let you go altogether
      unpunished.'

12"For thus says the LORD:

 'Your affliction *is* incurable,
   Your wound *is* severe.
13*There is* no one to plead your cause,
   That you may be bound up;
   You have no healing medicines.
14All your lovers have forgotten you;
   They do not seek you;

   For I have wounded you with the wound of
      an enemy,
   With the chastisement of a cruel one,
   For the multitude of your iniquities,
   Because your sins have increased.
15Why do you cry about your affliction?
   Your sorrow *is* incurable.
   Because of the multitude of your iniquities,
   Because your sins have increased,
   I have done these things to you.

16'Therefore all those who devour you shall be
      devoured;
   And all your adversaries, every one of them,
      shall go into captivity;
   Those who plunder you shall become
      plunder,
   And all who prey upon you I will make a
      prey.
17For I will restore health to you
   And heal you of your wounds,' says the
      LORD,
 'Because they called you an outcast *saying:*
   "This *is* Zion;
   No one seeks her." '

18"Thus says the LORD:

 'Behold, I will bring back the captivity of
      Jacob's tents,
   And have mercy on his dwelling places;
   The city shall be built upon its own mound,
   And the palace shall remain according to its
      own plan.
19Then out of them shall proceed thanksgiving

And the voice of those who make merry;
I will multiply them, and they shall not
    diminish;
I will also glorify them, and they shall not be
    small.
²⁰Their children also shall be as before,
And their congregation shall be established
    before Me;
And I will punish all who oppress them.
²¹Their nobles shall be from among them,
And their governor shall come from their
    midst;
Then I will cause him to draw near,
And he shall approach Me;
For who is this who pledged his heart to
    approach Me?' says the LORD.
²²'You shall be My people,
And I will be your God.' "

²³Behold, the whirlwind of the LORD
Goes forth with fury,
A continuing whirlwind;
It will fall violently on the head of the
    wicked.
²⁴The fierce anger of the LORD will not return
    until He has done it,
And until He has performed the intents of
    His heart.

In the latter days you will consider it.

THE REMNANT OF ISRAEL SAVED

31 "At the same time," says the LORD, "I will
be the God of all the families of Israel, and
they shall be My people."
²Thus says the LORD:

"The people who survived the sword
Found grace in the wilderness—
Israel, when I went to give him rest."

³The LORD has appeared of old to me, saying:
"Yes, I have loved you with an everlasting
    love;
Therefore with lovingkindness I have drawn
    you.
⁴Again I will build you, and you shall be
    rebuilt,
O virgin of Israel!

You shall again be adorned with your
    tambourines,
And shall go forth in the dances of those who
    rejoice.
⁵You shall yet plant vines on the mountains of
    Samaria;
The planters shall plant and eat them as
    ordinary food.
⁶For there shall be a day
When the watchmen will cry on Mount
    Ephraim,
'Arise, and let us go up to Zion,
To the LORD our God.' "

⁷For thus says the LORD:

"Sing with gladness for Jacob,
And shout among the chief of the nations;
Proclaim, give praise, and say,
'O LORD, save Your people,
The remnant of Israel!'
⁸Behold, I will bring them from the north
    country,
And gather them from the ends of the earth,
Among them the blind and the lame,
The woman with child
And the one who labors with child, together;
A great throng shall return there.
⁹They shall come with weeping,
And with supplications I will lead them.
I will cause them to walk by the rivers of
    waters,
In a straight way in which they shall not
    stumble;
For I am a Father to Israel,
And Ephraim is My firstborn.

¹⁰"Hear the word of the LORD, O nations,
And declare it in the isles afar off, and say,
'He who scattered Israel will gather him,
And keep him as a shepherd does his flock.'
¹¹For the LORD has redeemed Jacob,
And ransomed him from the hand of one
    stronger than he.
¹²Therefore they shall come and sing in the
    height of Zion,
Streaming to the goodness of the LORD—
For wheat and new wine and oil,
For the young of the flock and the herd;

Their souls shall be like a well-watered
garden,
And they shall sorrow no more at all.

¹³"Then shall the virgin rejoice in the dance,
And the young men and the old, together;
For I will turn their mourning to joy,
Will comfort them,
And make them rejoice rather than sorrow.
¹⁴I will satiate the soul of the priests with
abundance,
And My people shall be satisfied with My
goodness, says the LORD."

MERCY ON EPHRAIM

¹⁵Thus says the LORD:

"A voice was heard in Ramah,
Lamentation *and* bitter weeping,
Rachel weeping for her children,
Refusing to be comforted for her children,
Because they *are* no more."

¹⁶Thus says the LORD:

"Refrain your voice from weeping,
And your eyes from tears;
For your work shall be rewarded, says the
LORD,
And they shall come back from the land of
the enemy.
¹⁷There is hope in your future, says the LORD,
That *your* children shall come back to their
own border.

¹⁸"I have surely heard Ephraim bemoaning
himself:
'You have chastised me, and I was chastised,
Like an untrained bull;
Restore me, and I will return,
For You *are* the LORD my God.
¹⁹Surely, after my turning, I repented;
And after I was instructed, I struck myself on
the thigh;
I was ashamed, yes, even humiliated,
Because I bore the reproach of my youth.'
²⁰*Is* Ephraim My dear son?
Is he a pleasant child?
For though I spoke against him,

I earnestly remember him still;
Therefore My heart yearns for him;
I will surely have mercy on him, says the
LORD.

²¹"Set up signposts,
Make landmarks;
Set your heart toward the highway,
The way in *which* you went.
Turn back, O virgin of Israel,
Turn back to these your cities.
²²How long will you gad about,
O you backsliding daughter?
For the LORD has created a new thing in the
earth—
A woman shall encompass a man."

FUTURE PROSPERITY OF JUDAH

²³Thus says the LORD of hosts, the God of Israel: "They shall again use this speech in the land
of Judah and in its cities, when I bring back their
captivity: 'The LORD bless you, O home of justice, *and* mountain of holiness!' ²⁴And there shall
dwell in Judah itself, and in all its cities together,
farmers and those going out with flocks. ²⁵For I
have satiated the weary soul, and I have replen-
ished every sorrowful soul."

²⁶After this I awoke and looked around, and
my sleep was sweet to me.

²⁷"Behold, the days are coming, says the
LORD, that I will sow the house of Israel and the
house of Judah with the seed of man and the seed
of beast. ²⁸And it shall come to pass, *that* as I have
watched over them to pluck up, to break down,
to throw down, to destroy, and to afflict, so I will
watch over them to build and to plant, says the
LORD. ²⁹In those days they shall say no more:

'The fathers have eaten sour grapes,
And the children's teeth are set on edge.'

³⁰But every one shall die for his own iniquity;
every man who eats the sour grapes, his teeth
shall be set on edge.

A NEW COVENANT

³¹"Behold, the days are coming, says the
LORD, when I will make a new covenant with
the house of Israel and with the house of Judah—

[32]not according to the covenant that I made with their fathers in the day *that* I took them by the hand to lead them out of the land of Egypt, My covenant which they broke, though I was a husband to them,[a] says the LORD. [33]But this *is* the covenant that I will make with the house of Israel after those days, says the LORD: I will put My law in their minds, and write it on their hearts; and I will be their God, and they shall be My people. [34]No more shall every man teach his neighbor, and every man his brother, saying, 'Know the LORD,' for they all shall know Me, from the least of them to the greatest of them, says the LORD. For I will forgive their iniquity, and their sin I will remember no more."

[35]Thus says the LORD,
   Who gives the sun for a light by day,
   The ordinances of the moon and the stars
      for a light by night,
   Who disturbs the sea,
   And its waves roar
   (The LORD of hosts *is* His name):

[36]"If those ordinances depart
   From before Me, says the LORD,
   Then the seed of Israel shall also cease
   From being a nation before Me forever."

[37]Thus says the LORD:

"If heaven above can be measured,
   And the foundations of the earth searched
      out beneath,
   I will also cast off all the seed of Israel
   For all that they have done, says the
      LORD.

[38]"Behold, the days are coming, says the LORD, that the city shall be built for the LORD from the Tower of Hananel to the Corner Gate. [39]The surveyor's line shall again extend straight forward over the hill Gareb; then it shall turn toward Goath. [40]And the whole valley of the dead bodies and of the ashes, and all the fields as far as the Brook Kidron, to the corner of the Horse Gate toward the east, *shall be* holy to the LORD. It shall not be plucked up or thrown down anymore forever."

JEREMIAH BUYS A FIELD

32 The word that came to Jeremiah from the LORD in the tenth year of Zedekiah king of Judah, which was the eighteenth year of Nebuchadnezzar. [2]For then the king of Babylon's army besieged Jerusalem, and Jeremiah the prophet was shut up in the court of the prison, which *was in* the king of Judah's house. [3]For Zedekiah king of Judah had shut him up, saying, "Why do you prophesy and say, 'Thus says the LORD: "Behold, I will give this city into the hand of the king of Babylon, and he shall take it; [4]and Zedekiah king of Judah shall not escape from the hand of the Chaldeans, but shall surely be delivered into the hand of the king of Babylon, and shall speak with him face to face,[a] and see him eye to eye; [5]then he shall lead Zedekiah to Babylon, and there he shall be until I visit him," says the LORD; "though you fight with the Chaldeans, you shall not succeed" '?"

[6]And Jeremiah said, "The word of the LORD came to me, saying, [7]'Behold, Hanamel the son of Shallum your uncle will come to you, saying, "Buy my field which *is* in Anathoth, for the right of redemption *is* yours to buy *it*." ' [8]Then Hanamel my uncle's son came to me in the court of the prison according to the word of the LORD, and said to me, 'Please buy my field that *is* in Anathoth, which *is* in the country of Benjamin; for the right of inheritance *is* yours, and the redemption yours; buy *it* for yourself.' Then I knew that this was the word of the LORD. [9]So I bought the field from Hanamel, the son of my uncle who *was* in Anathoth, and weighed *out to* him the money—seventeen shekels of silver. [10]And I signed the deed and sealed *it,* took witnesses, and weighed the money on the scales. [11]So I took the purchase deed, *both* that which was sealed *according* to the law and custom, and that which was open; [12]and I gave the purchase deed to Baruch the son of Neriah, son of Mahseiah, in the presence of Hanamel my uncle's *son,* and in the presence of the witnesses who signed the purchase deed, before all the Jews who sat in the court of the prison.

31:32 [a]Following Masoretic Text, Targum, and Vulgate; Septuagint and Syriac read *and I turned away from them.*   **32:4** [a]Literally *mouth to mouth*

¹³"Then I charged Baruch before them, saying, ¹⁴'Thus says the LORD of hosts, the God of Israel: "Take these deeds, both this purchase deed which is sealed and this deed which is open, and put them in an earthen vessel, that they may last many days." ¹⁵For thus says the LORD of hosts, the God of Israel: "Houses and fields and vineyards shall be possessed again in this land." '

JEREMIAH PRAYS FOR UNDERSTANDING

¹⁶"Now when I had delivered the purchase deed to Baruch the son of Neriah, I prayed to the LORD, saying: ¹⁷'Ah, Lord GOD! Behold, You have made the heavens and the earth by Your great power and outstretched arm. There is nothing too hard for You. ¹⁸You show lovingkindness to thousands, and repay the iniquity of the fathers into the bosom of their children after them—the Great, the Mighty God, whose name is the LORD of hosts. ¹⁹You are great in counsel and mighty in work, for Your eyes are open to all the ways of the sons of men, to give everyone according to his ways and according to the fruit of his doings. ²⁰You have set signs and wonders in the land of Egypt, to this day, and in Israel and among other men; and You have made Yourself a name, as it is this day. ²¹You have brought Your people Israel out of the land of Egypt with signs and wonders, with a strong hand and an outstretched arm, and with great terror; ²²You have given them this land, of which You swore to their fathers to give them—"a land flowing with milk and honey."ᵃ ²³And they came in and took possession of it, but they have not obeyed Your voice or walked in Your law. They have done nothing of all that You commanded them to do; therefore You have caused all this calamity to come upon them.

²⁴'Look, the siege mounds! They have come to the city to take it; and the city has been given into the hand of the Chaldeans who fight against it, because of the sword and famine and pestilence. What You have spoken has happened; there You see it! ²⁵And You have said to me, O Lord GOD, "Buy the field for money, and take witnesses"!—yet the city has been given into the hand of the Chaldeans.' "

GOD'S ASSURANCE OF THE PEOPLE'S RETURN

²⁶Then the word of the LORD came to Jeremiah, saying, ²⁷"Behold, I am the LORD, the God of all flesh. Is there anything too hard for Me?

²⁸Therefore thus says the LORD: 'Behold, I will give this city into the hand of the Chaldeans, into the hand of Nebuchadnezzar king of Babylon, and he shall take it. ²⁹And the Chaldeans who fight against this city shall come and set fire to this city and burn it, with the houses on whose roofs they have offered incense to Baal and poured out drink offerings to other gods, to provoke Me to anger; ³⁰because the children of Israel and the children of Judah have done only evil before Me from their youth. For the children of Israel have provoked Me only to anger with the work of their hands,' says the LORD. ³¹'For this city has been to Me a provocation of My anger and My fury from the day that they built it, even to this day; so I will remove it from before My face ³²because of all the evil of the children of Israel and the children of Judah, which they have done to provoke Me to anger—they, their kings, their princes, their priests, their prophets, the men of Judah, and the inhabitants of Jerusalem. ³³And they have turned to Me the back, and not the face; though I taught them, rising up early and teaching them, yet they have not listened to receive instruction. ³⁴But they set their abominations in the house which is called by My name, to defile it. ³⁵And they built the high places of Baal which are in the Valley of the Son of Hinnom, to cause their sons and their daughters to pass through the fire to Molech, which I did not command them, nor did it come into My mind that they should do this abomination, to cause Judah to sin.'

³⁶"Now therefore, thus says the LORD, the God of Israel, concerning this city of which you say, 'It shall be delivered into the hand of the king of Babylon by the sword, by the famine, and by the pestilence: ³⁷Behold, I will gather them out of all countries where I have driven them in My anger, in My fury, and in great wrath; I will bring them back to this place, and I will cause them to dwell safely. ³⁸They shall be My people, and I will be their God; ³⁹then I will give them one heart and one way, that they may fear Me forever, for the good of them and their children after them. ⁴⁰And I will make an everlasting covenant with them, that I will not turn away from doing them good; but I will put My fear in their hearts so that they will not depart from Me. ⁴¹Yes, I will rejoice

32:22 ᵃExodus 3:8

THROUGH THE GRID

Discover God: God Is All-Powerful

JEREMIAH 32:27   *Behold, I am the LORD, the God of all flesh. Is there anything too hard for Me?*

As you gaze at the stars at night, there's a sense of wonder that permeates your view as you perceive of how enormously expansive the universe really is. The One who placed all of this before us must certainly be infinitely bigger! One of the most primary attributes of God is God's ability to do anything, as long as it does not violate any other of God's attributes. This attribute is known as *God's omnipotence*—the all-extensive power of God. God's power comprises the act of creating the universe, through which humanity can fundamentally observe the extent of God's creative abilities. God is the One who set the universe in place; thus, God is the Prime Mover and Source of all power. Several important characteristics of God's power include the following: God has the power to create something from nothing; God has the power to sustain all that has been created; and God has the power to judge sin and rebellion. As we grasp the infinite extent of God's power, our response as finite human beings is to bow in awe and to offer our praise to the mighty Creator of the universe.

over them to do them good, and I will assuredly plant them in this land, with all My heart and with all My soul.'

⁴²"For thus says the LORD: 'Just as I have brought all this great calamity on this people, so I will bring on them all the good that I have promised them. ⁴³And fields will be bought in this land of which you say, "*It is* desolate, without man or beast; it has been given into the hand of the Chaldeans." ⁴⁴Men will buy fields for money, sign deeds and seal *them,* and take witnesses, in the land of Benjamin, in the places around Jerusalem, in the cities of Judah, in the cities of the mountains, in the cities of the lowland, and in the cities of the South; for I will cause their captives to return,' says the LORD."

EXCELLENCE OF THE RESTORED NATION

33 Moreover the word of the LORD came to Jeremiah a second time, while he was still shut up in the court of the prison, saying, ²"Thus says the LORD who made it, the LORD who formed it to establish it (the LORD *is* His name): ³'Call to Me, and I will answer you, and show you great and mighty things, which you do not know.'

⁴"For thus says the LORD, the God of Israel,

concerning the houses of this city and the houses of the kings of Judah, which have been pulled down *to fortify*ᵃ against the siege mounds and the sword: ⁵'They come to fight with the Chaldeans, but *only* to fill their placesᵃ with the dead bodies of men whom I will slay in My anger and My fury, all for whose wickedness I have hidden My face from this city. ⁶Behold, I will bring it health and healing; I will heal them and reveal to them the abundance of peace and truth. ⁷And I will cause the captives of Judah and the captives of Israel to return, and will rebuild those places as at the first. ⁸I will cleanse them from all their iniquity by which they have sinned against Me, and I will pardon all their iniquities by which they have sinned and by which they have transgressed against Me. ⁹Then it shall be to Me a name of joy, a praise, and an honor before all nations of the earth, who shall hear all the good that I do to them; they shall fear and tremble for all the goodness and all the prosperity that I provide for it.'

¹⁰"Thus says the LORD: 'Again there shall be heard in this place—of which you say, "It *is* desolate, without man and without beast"—in the cities of Judah, in the streets of Jerusalem that are

33:4 ᵃCompare Isaiah 22:10   **33:5** ᵃCompare 2 Kings 23:14

desolate, without man and without inhabitant and without beast, ¹¹the voice of joy and the voice of gladness, the voice of the bridegroom and the voice of the bride, the voice of those who will say:

"Praise the LORD of hosts,
For the LORD *is* good,
For His mercy *endures* forever"—

and of those *who will* bring the sacrifice of praise into the house of the LORD. For I will cause the captives of the land to return as at the first,' says the LORD.

¹²"Thus says the LORD of hosts: 'In this place which is desolate, without man and without beast, and in all its cities, there shall again be a dwelling place of shepherds causing *their* flocks to lie down. ¹³In the cities of the mountains, in the cities of the lowland, in the cities of the South, in the land of Benjamin, in the places around Jerusalem, and in the cities of Judah, the flocks shall again pass under the hands of him who counts *them*,' says the LORD.

¹⁴"Behold, the days are coming,' says the LORD, 'that I will perform that good thing which I have promised to the house of Israel and to the house of Judah:

¹⁵'In those days and at that time
I will cause to grow up to David
A Branch of righteousness;
He shall execute judgment and righteousness
     in the earth.
¹⁶In those days Judah will be saved,
And Jerusalem will dwell safely.
And this *is the name* by which she will be
     called:

THE LORD OUR RIGHTEOUSNESS.'ᵃ

¹⁷"For thus says the LORD: 'David shall never lack a man to sit on the throne of the house of Israel; ¹⁸nor shall the priests, the Levites, lack a man to offer burnt offerings before Me, to kindle grain offerings, and to sacrifice continually.' "

The Permanence of God's Covenant

¹⁹And the word of the LORD came to Jeremiah, saying, ²⁰"Thus says the LORD: 'If you can break My covenant with the day and My covenant with the night, so that there will not be day and night in their season, ²¹then My covenant may also be broken with David My servant, so that he shall not have a son to reign on his throne, and with the Levites, the priests, My ministers. ²²As the host of heaven cannot be numbered, nor the sand of the sea measured, so will I multiply the descendants of David My servant and the Levites who minister to Me.' "

²³Moreover the word of the LORD came to Jeremiah, saying, ²⁴"Have you not considered what these people have spoken, saying, 'The two families which the LORD has chosen, He has also cast them off'? Thus they have despised My people, as if they should no more be a nation before them.

²⁵"Thus says the LORD: 'If My covenant *is* not with day and night, *and if* I have not appointed the ordinances of heaven and earth, ²⁶then I will cast away the descendants of Jacob and David My servant, *so* that I will not take *any* of his descendants *to be* rulers over the descendants of Abraham, Isaac, and Jacob. For I will cause their captives to return, and will have mercy on them.' "

Zedekiah Warned by God

34 The word which came to Jeremiah from the LORD, when Nebuchadnezzar king of Babylon and all his army, all the kingdoms of the earth under his dominion, and all the people, fought against Jerusalem and all its cities, saying, ²"Thus says the LORD, the God of Israel: 'Go and speak to Zedekiah king of Judah and tell him, "Thus says the LORD: 'Behold, I will give this city into the hand of the king of Babylon, and he shall burn it with fire. ³And you shall not escape from his hand, but shall surely be taken and delivered into his hand; your eyes shall see the eyes of the king of Babylon, he shall speak with you face to face,ᵃ and you shall go to Babylon.' " ' ⁴Yet hear the word of the LORD, O Zedekiah king of Judah! Thus says the LORD concerning you: 'You shall not die by the sword. ⁵You shall die in peace; as in the ceremonies of your fathers, the former kings who were before you, so they shall burn *incense* for you and lament for you, *saying*, "Alas, lord!" For I have pronounced the word, says the LORD.' "

33:16 ᵃCompare 23:5, 6   **34:3** ᵃLiterally *mouth to mouth*

⁶Then Jeremiah the prophet spoke all these words to Zedekiah king of Judah in Jerusalem, ⁷when the king of Babylon's army fought against Jerusalem and all the cities of Judah that were left, against Lachish and Azekah; for *only* these fortified cities remained of the cities of Judah.

Treacherous Treatment of Slaves

⁸*This is* the word that came to Jeremiah from the LORD, after King Zedekiah had made a covenant with all the people who *were* at Jerusalem to proclaim liberty to them: ⁹that every man should set free his male and female slave—a Hebrew man or woman—that no one should keep a Jewish brother in bondage. ¹⁰Now when all the princes and all the people, who had entered into the covenant, heard that everyone should set free his male and female slaves, that no one should keep them in bondage anymore, they obeyed and let *them* go. ¹¹But afterward they changed their minds and made the male and female slaves return, whom they had set free, and brought them into subjection as male and female slaves.

¹²Therefore the word of the LORD came to Jeremiah from the LORD, saying, ¹³"Thus says the LORD, the God of Israel: 'I made a covenant with your fathers in the day that I brought them out of the land of Egypt, out of the house of bondage, saying, ¹⁴"At the end of seven years let every man set free his Hebrew brother, who has been sold to him; and when he has served you six years, you shall let him go free from you." But your fathers did not obey Me nor incline their ear. ¹⁵Then you recently turned and did what was right in My sight—every man proclaiming liberty to his neighbor; and you made a covenant before Me in the house which is called by My name. ¹⁶Then you turned around and profaned My name, and every one of you brought back his male and female slaves, whom you had set at liberty, at their pleasure, and brought them back into subjection, to be your male and female slaves.'

¹⁷"Therefore thus says the LORD: 'You have not obeyed Me in proclaiming liberty, every one to his brother and every one to his neighbor. Behold, I proclaim liberty to you,' says the LORD— 'to the sword, to pestilence, and to famine! And I will deliver you to trouble among all the king-doms of the earth. ¹⁸And I will give the men who have transgressed My covenant, who have not performed the words of the covenant which they made before Me, when they cut the calf in two and passed between the parts of it— ¹⁹the princes of Judah, the princes of Jerusalem, the eunuchs, the priests, and all the people of the land who passed between the parts of the calf— ²⁰I will give them into the hand of their enemies and into the hand of those who seek their life. Their dead bodies shall be for meat for the birds of the heaven and the beasts of the earth. ²¹And I will give Zedekiah king of Judah and his princes into the hand of their enemies, into the hand of those who seek their life, and into the hand of the king of Babylon's army which has gone back from you. ²²Behold, I will command,' says the LORD, 'and cause them to return to this city. They will fight against it and take it and burn it with fire; and I will make the cities of Judah a desolation without inhabitant.'"

The Obedient Rechabites

35 The word which came to Jeremiah from the LORD in the days of Jehoiakim the son of Josiah, king of Judah, saying, ²"Go to the house of the Rechabites, speak to them, and bring them into the house of the LORD, into one of the chambers, and give them wine to drink."

³Then I took Jaazaniah the son of Jeremiah, the son of Habazziniah, his brothers and all his sons, and the whole house of the Rechabites, ⁴and I brought them into the house of the LORD, into the chamber of the sons of Hanan the son of Igdaliah, a man of God, which *was* by the chamber of the princes, above the chamber of Maaseiah the son of Shallum, the keeper of the door. ⁵Then I set before the sons of the house of the Rechabites bowls full of wine, and cups; and I said to them, "Drink wine."

⁶But they said, "We will drink no wine, for Jonadab the son of Rechab, our father, commanded us, saying, 'You shall drink no wine, you nor your sons, forever. ⁷You shall not build a house, sow seed, plant a vineyard, nor have *any of these;* but all your days you shall dwell in tents, that you may live many days in the land where you are sojourners.' ⁸Thus we have obeyed the voice of Jonadab the son of Rechab, our father, in

all that he charged us, to drink no wine all our days, we, our wives, our sons, or our daughters, [9]nor to build ourselves houses to dwell in; nor do we have vineyard, field, or seed. [10]But we have dwelt in tents, and have obeyed and done according to all that Jonadab our father commanded us. [11]But it came to pass, when Nebuchadnezzar king of Babylon came up into the land, that we said, 'Come, let us go to Jerusalem for fear of the army of the Chaldeans and for fear of the army of the Syrians.' So we dwell at Jerusalem."

[12]Then came the word of the LORD to Jeremiah, saying, [13]"Thus says the LORD of hosts, the God of Israel: 'Go and tell the men of Judah and the inhabitants of Jerusalem, "Will you not receive instruction to obey My words?" says the LORD. [14]"The words of Jonadab the son of Rechab, which he commanded his sons, not to drink wine, are performed; for to this day they drink none, and obey their father's commandment. But although I have spoken to you, rising early and speaking, you did not obey Me. [15]I have also sent to you all My servants the prophets, rising up early and sending *them,* saying, 'Turn now everyone from his evil way, amend your doings, and do not go after other gods to serve them; then you will dwell in the land which I have given you and your fathers.' But you have not inclined your ear, nor obeyed Me. [16]Surely the sons of Jonadab the son of Rechab have performed the commandment of their father, which he commanded them, but this people has not obeyed Me."'

[17]"Therefore thus says the LORD God of hosts, the God of Israel: 'Behold, I will bring on Judah and on all the inhabitants of Jerusalem all the doom that I have pronounced against them; because I have spoken to them but they have not heard, and I have called to them but they have not answered.'"

[18]And Jeremiah said to the house of the Rechabites, "Thus says the LORD of hosts, the God of Israel: 'Because you have obeyed the commandment of Jonadab your father, and kept all his precepts and done according to all that he commanded you, [19]therefore thus says the LORD of hosts, the God of Israel: "Jonadab the son of Rechab shall not lack a man to stand before Me forever."'"

THE SCROLL READ IN THE TEMPLE

36 Now it came to pass in the fourth year of Jehoiakim the son of Josiah, king of Judah, *that* this word came to Jeremiah from the LORD, saying: [2]"Take a scroll of a book and write on it all the words that I have spoken to you against Israel, against Judah, and against all the nations, from the day I spoke to you, from the days of Josiah even to this day. [3]It may be that the house of Judah will hear all the adversities which I purpose to bring upon them, that everyone may turn from his evil way, that I may forgive their iniquity and their sin."

[4]Then Jeremiah called Baruch the son of Neriah; and Baruch wrote on a scroll of a book, at the instruction of Jeremiah,[a] all the words of the LORD which He had spoken to him. [5]And Jeremiah commanded Baruch, saying, "I *am* confined, I cannot go into the house of the LORD. [6]You go, therefore, and read from the scroll which you have written at my instruction,[a] the words of the LORD, in the hearing of the people in the LORD's house on the day of fasting. And you shall also read them in the hearing of all Judah who come from their cities. [7]It may be that they will present their supplication before the LORD, and everyone will turn from his evil way. For great *is* the anger and the fury that the LORD has pronounced against this people." [8]And Baruch the son of Neriah did according to all that Jeremiah the prophet commanded him, reading from the book the words of the LORD in the LORD's house.

[9]Now it came to pass in the fifth year of Jehoiakim the son of Josiah, king of Judah, in the ninth month, *that* they proclaimed a fast before the LORD to all the people in Jerusalem, and to all the people who came from the cities of Judah to Jerusalem. [10]Then Baruch read from the book the words of Jeremiah in the house of the LORD, in the chamber of Gemariah the son of Shaphan the scribe, in the upper court at the entry of the New Gate of the LORD's house, in the hearing of all the people.

THE SCROLL READ IN THE PALACE

[11]When Michaiah the son of Gemariah, the son of Shaphan, heard all the words of the LORD

36:4 [a]Literally *from Jeremiah's mouth*   36:6 [a]Literally *from my mouth* from the book, [12]he then went down to the king's house, into the scribe's chamber; and there all the princes were sitting—Elishama the scribe, Delaiah the son of Shemaiah, Elnathan the son of Achbor, Gemariah the son of Shaphan, Zedekiah the son of Hananiah, and all the princes. [13]Then Michaiah declared to them all the words that he had heard when Baruch read the book in the hearing of the people. [14]Therefore all the princes sent Jehudi the son of Nethaniah, the son of Shelemiah, the son of Cushi, to Baruch, saying, "Take in your hand the scroll from which you have read in the hearing of the people, and come." So Baruch the son of Neriah took the scroll in his hand and came to them. [15]And they said to him, "Sit down now, and read it in our hearing." So Baruch read *it* in their hearing.

[16]Now it happened, when they had heard all the words, that they looked in fear from one to another, and said to Baruch, "We will surely tell the king of all these words." [17]And they asked Baruch, saying, "Tell us now, how did you write all these words—at his instruction?"[a]

[18]So Baruch answered them, "He proclaimed with his mouth all these words to me, and I wrote *them* with ink in the book."

[19]Then the princes said to Baruch, "Go and hide, you and Jeremiah; and let no one know where you are."

The King Destroys Jeremiah's Scroll

[20]And they went to the king, into the court; but they stored the scroll in the chamber of Elishama the scribe, and told all the words in the hearing of the king. [21]So the king sent Jehudi to bring the scroll, and he took it from Elishama the scribe's chamber. And Jehudi read it in the hearing of the king and in the hearing of all the princes who stood beside the king. [22]Now the king was sitting in the winter house in the ninth month, with *a fire* burning on the hearth before him. [23]And it happened, when Jehudi had read three or four columns, *that the king* cut it with the scribe's knife and cast *it* into the fire that *was* on the hearth, until all the scroll was consumed in the fire that *was* on the hearth. [24]Yet they were not afraid, nor did they tear their garments, the king nor any of his servants who heard all these words. [25]Nevertheless Elnathan, Delaiah, and

Gemariah implored the king not to burn the scroll; but he would not listen to them. [26]And the king commanded Jerahmeel the king's[a] son, Seraiah the son of Azriel, and Shelemiah the son of Abdeel, to seize Baruch the scribe and Jeremiah the prophet, but the LORD hid them.

Jeremiah Rewrites the Scroll

[27]Now after the king had burned the scroll with the words which Baruch had written at the instruction of Jeremiah,[a] the word of the LORD came to Jeremiah, saying: [28]"Take yet another scroll, and write on it all the former words that were in the first scroll which Jehoiakim the king of Judah has burned. [29]And you shall say to Jehoiakim king of Judah, 'Thus says the LORD: "You have burned this scroll, saying, 'Why have you written in it that the king of Babylon will certainly come and destroy this land, and cause man and beast to cease from here?' " [30]Therefore thus says the LORD concerning Jehoiakim king of Judah: "He shall have no one to sit on the throne of David, and his dead body shall be cast out to the heat of the day and the frost of the night. [31]I will punish him, his family, and his servants for their iniquity; and I will bring on them, on the inhabitants of Jerusalem, and on the men of Judah all the doom that I have pronounced against them; but they did not heed." ' "

[32]Then Jeremiah took another scroll and gave it to Baruch the scribe, the son of Neriah, who wrote on it at the instruction of Jeremiah[a] all the words of the book which Jehoiakim king of Judah had burned in the fire. And besides, there were added to them many similar words.

Zedekiah's Vain Hope

37 Now King Zedekiah the son of Josiah reigned instead of Coniah the son of Jehoiakim, whom Nebuchadnezzar king of Babylon made king in the land of Judah. [2]But neither he nor his servants nor the people of the land gave heed to the words of the LORD which He spoke by the prophet Jeremiah.

[3]And Zedekiah the king sent Jehucal the son of Shelemiah, and Zephaniah the son of Maaseiah,

36:17 [a]Literally *with his mouth* **36:26** [a]Hebrew *Hammelech*
36:27 [a]Literally *from Jeremiah's mouth* **36:32** [a]Literally *from Jeremiah's mouth*

the priest, to the prophet Jeremiah, saying, "Pray now to the LORD our God for us." 4Now Jeremiah was coming and going among the people, for they had not *yet* put him in prison. 5Then Pharaoh's army came up from Egypt; and when the Chaldeans who were besieging Jerusalem heard news of them, they departed from Jerusalem.

6Then the word of the LORD came to the prophet Jeremiah, saying, 7"Thus says the LORD, the God of Israel, 'Thus you shall say to the king of Judah, who sent you to Me to inquire of Me: "Behold, Pharaoh's army which has come up to help you will return to Egypt, to their own land. 8And the Chaldeans shall come back and fight against this city, and take it and burn it with fire." ' 9Thus says the LORD: 'Do not deceive yourselves, saying, "The Chaldeans will surely depart from us," for they will not depart. 10For though you had defeated the whole army of the Chaldeans who fight against you, and there remained *only* wounded men among them, they would rise up, every man in his tent, and burn the city with fire.' "

JEREMIAH IMPRISONED

11And it happened, when the army of the Chaldeans left *the siege* of Jerusalem for fear of Pharaoh's army, 12that Jeremiah went out of Jerusalem to go into the land of Benjamin to claim his property there among the people. 13And when he was in the Gate of Benjamin, a captain of the guard *was* there whose name *was* Irijah the son of Shelemiah, the son of Hananiah; and he seized Jeremiah the prophet, saying, "You are defecting to the Chaldeans!"

14Then Jeremiah said, "False! I am not defecting to the Chaldeans." But he did not listen to him.

So Irijah seized Jeremiah and brought him to the princes. 15Therefore the princes were angry with Jeremiah, and they struck him and put him in prison in the house of Jonathan the scribe. For they had made that the prison.

16When Jeremiah entered the dungeon and the cells, and Jeremiah had remained there many days, 17then Zedekiah the king sent and took him *out*. The king asked him secretly in his house, and said, "Is there *any* word from the LORD?"

And Jeremiah said, "There is." Then he said, "You shall be delivered into the hand of the king of Babylon!"

18Moreover Jeremiah said to King Zedekiah, "What offense have I committed against you, against your servants, or against this people, that you have put me in prison? 19Where now *are* your prophets who prophesied to you, saying, 'The king of Babylon will not come against you or against this land'? 20Therefore please hear now, O my lord the king. Please, let my petition be accepted before you, and do not make me return to the house of Jonathan the scribe, lest I die there."

21Then Zedekiah the king commanded that they should commit Jeremiah to the court of the prison, and that they should give him daily a piece of bread from the bakers' street, until all the bread in the city was gone. Thus Jeremiah remained in the court of the prison.

JEREMIAH IN THE DUNGEON

38 Now Shephatiah the son of Mattan, Gedaliah the son of Pashhur, Jucal[a] the son of Shelemiah, and Pashhur the son of Malchiah heard the words that Jeremiah had spoken to all the people, saying, 2"Thus says the LORD: 'He who remains in this city shall die by the sword, by famine, and by pestilence; but he who goes over to the Chaldeans shall live; his life shall be as a prize to him, and he shall live.'[a] 3Thus says the LORD: 'This city shall surely be given into the hand of the king of Babylon's army, which shall take it.' "

4Therefore the princes said to the king, "Please, let this man be put to death, for thus he weakens the hands of the men of war who remain in this city, and the hands of all the people, by speaking such words to them. For this man does not seek the welfare of this people, but their harm."

5Then Zedekiah the king said, "Look, he *is* in your hand. For the king can *do* nothing against you." 6So they took Jeremiah and cast him into the dungeon of Malchiah the king's[a] son, which *was* in the court of the prison, and they let Jeremiah down with ropes. And in the dungeon *there was* no water, but mire. So Jeremiah sank in the mire.

38:1 aSame as *Jehucal* (compare 37:3)   **38:2** aCompare 21:9
38:6 aHebrew *Hammelech*

[7]Now Ebed-Melech the Ethiopian, one of the eunuchs, who was in the king's house, heard that they had put Jeremiah in the dungeon. When the king was sitting at the Gate of Benjamin, [8]Ebed-Melech went out of the king's house and spoke to the king, saying: [9]"My lord the king, these men have done evil in all that they have done to Jeremiah the prophet, whom they have cast into the dungeon, and he is likely to die from hunger in the place where he is. For *there is* no more bread in the city." [10]Then the king commanded Ebed-Melech the Ethiopian, saying, "Take from here thirty men with you, and lift Jeremiah the prophet out of the dungeon before he dies." [11]So Ebed-Melech took the men with him and went into the house of the king under the treasury, and took from there old clothes and old rags, and let them down by ropes into the dungeon to Jeremiah. [12]Then Ebed-Melech the Ethiopian said to Jeremiah, "Please put these old clothes and rags under your armpits, under the ropes." And Jeremiah did so. [13]So they pulled Jeremiah up with ropes and lifted him out of the dungeon. And Jeremiah remained in the court of the prison.

Zedekiah's Fears and Jeremiah's Advice

[14]Then Zedekiah the king sent and had Jeremiah the prophet brought to him at the third entrance of the house of the LORD. And the king said to Jeremiah, "I will ask you something. Hide nothing from me."

[15]Jeremiah said to Zedekiah, "If I declare *it* to you, will you not surely put me to death? And if I give you advice, you will not listen to me."

[16]So Zedekiah the king swore secretly to Jeremiah, saying, "*As* the LORD lives, who made our very souls, I will not put you to death, nor will I give you into the hand of these men who seek your life."

[17]Then Jeremiah said to Zedekiah, "Thus says the LORD, the God of hosts, the God of Israel: 'If you surely surrender to the king of Babylon's princes, then your soul shall live; this city shall not be burned with fire, and you and your house shall live. [18]But if you do not surrender to the king of Babylon's princes, then this city shall be given into the hand of the Chaldeans; they shall burn it with fire, and you shall not escape from their hand.' "

[19]And Zedekiah the king said to Jeremiah, "I am afraid of the Jews who have defected to the Chaldeans, lest they deliver me into their hand, and they abuse me."

[20]But Jeremiah said, "They shall not deliver *you.* Please, obey the voice of the LORD which I speak to you. So it shall be well with you, and your soul shall live. [21]But if you refuse to surrender, this *is* the word that the LORD has shown me: [22]Now behold, all the women who are left in the king of Judah's house *shall be* surrendered to the king of Babylon's princes, and those *women* shall say:

"Your close friends have set upon you
      And prevailed against you;
   Your feet have sunk in the mire,
      And they have turned away again."

[23]"So they shall surrender all your wives and children to the Chaldeans. You shall not escape from their hand, but shall be taken by the hand of the king of Babylon. And you shall cause this city to be burned with fire.' "

[24]Then Zedekiah said to Jeremiah, "Let no one know of these words, and you shall not die. [25]But if the princes hear that I have talked with you, and they come to you and say to you, 'Declare to us now what you have said to the king, and also what the king said to you; do not hide *it* from us, and we will not put you to death,' [26]then you shall say to them, 'I presented my request before the king, that he would not make me return to Jonathan's house to die there.' "

[27]Then all the princes came to Jeremiah and asked him. And he told them according to all these words that the king had commanded. So they stopped speaking with him, for the conversation had not been heard. [28]Now Jeremiah remained in the court of the prison until the day that Jerusalem was taken. And he was *there* when Jerusalem was taken.

The Fall of Jerusalem

39 In the ninth year of Zedekiah king of Judah, in the tenth month, Nebuchadnezzar king of Babylon and all his army came against Jerusalem, and besieged it. [2]In the eleventh year of Zedekiah, in the fourth month, on the ninth *day* of the month, the city was penetrated.

³Then all the princes of the king of Babylon came in and sat in the Middle Gate: Nergal-Sharezer, Samgar-Nebo, Sarsechim, Rabsaris,ᵃ Nergal-Sarezer, Rabmag,ᵇ with the rest of the princes of the king of Babylon.

⁴So it was, when Zedekiah the king of Judah and all the men of war saw them, that they fled and went out of the city by night, by way of the king's garden, by the gate between the two walls. And he went out by way of the plain.ᵃ ⁵But the Chaldean army pursued them and overtook Zedekiah in the plains of Jericho. And when they had captured him, they brought him up to Nebuchadnezzar king of Babylon, to Riblah in the land of Hamath, where he pronounced judgment on him. ⁶Then the king of Babylon killed the sons of Zedekiah before his eyes in Riblah; the king of Babylon also killed all the nobles of Judah. ⁷Moreover he put out Zedekiah's eyes, and bound him with bronze fetters to carry him off to Babylon. ⁸And the Chaldeans burned the king's house and the houses of the people with fire, and broke down the walls of Jerusalem. ⁹Then Nebuzaradan the captain of the guard carried away captive to Babylon the remnant of the people who remained in the city and those who defected to him, with the rest of the people who remained. ¹⁰But Nebuzaradan the captain of the guard left in the land of Judah the poor people, who had nothing, and gave them vineyards and fields at the same time.

JEREMIAH GOES FREE

¹¹Now Nebuchadnezzar king of Babylon gave charge concerning Jeremiah to Nebuzaradan the captain of the guard, saying, ¹²"Take him and look after him, and do him no harm; but do to him just as he says to you." ¹³So Nebuzaradan the captain of the guard sent Nebushasban, Rabsaris, Nergal-Sharezer, Rabmag, and all the king of Babylon's chief officers; ¹⁴then they sent *someone* to take Jeremiah from the court of the prison, and committed him to Gedaliah the son of Ahikam, the son of Shaphan, that he should take him home. So he dwelt among the people.

¹⁵Meanwhile the word of the LORD had come to Jeremiah while he was shut up in the court of the prison, saying, ¹⁶"Go and speak to Ebed-Melech the Ethiopian, saying, 'Thus says the LORD of hosts, the God of Israel: "Behold, I will bring My words upon this city for adversity and not for good, and they shall be *performed* in that day before you. ¹⁷But I will deliver you in that day," says the LORD, "and you shall not be given into the hand of the men of whom you *are* afraid. ¹⁸For I will surely deliver you, and you shall not fall by the sword; but your life shall be as a prize to you, because you have put your trust in Me," says the LORD.'"

JEREMIAH WITH GEDALIAH THE GOVERNOR

40 The word that came to Jeremiah from the LORD after Nebuzaradan the captain of the guard had let him go from Ramah, when he had taken him bound in chains among all who were carried away captive from Jerusalem and Judah, who were carried away captive to Babylon.

²And the captain of the guard took Jeremiah and said to him: "The LORD your God has pronounced this doom on this place. ³Now the LORD has brought *it,* and has done just as He said. Because you *people* have sinned against the LORD, and not obeyed His voice, therefore this thing has come upon you. ⁴And now look, I free you this day from the chains that *were* on your hand. If it seems good to you to come with me to Babylon, come, and I will look after you. But if it seems wrong for you to come with me to Babylon, remain here. See, all the land *is* before you; wherever it seems good and convenient for you to go, go there."

⁵Now while Jeremiah had not yet gone back, *Nebuzaradan said,* "Go back to Gedaliah the son of Ahikam, the son of Shaphan, whom the king of Babylon has made governor over the cities of Judah, and dwell with him among the people. Or go wherever it seems convenient for you to go." So the captain of the guard gave him rations and a gift and let him go. ⁶Then Jeremiah went to Gedaliah the son of Ahikam, to Mizpah, and dwelt with him among the people who were left in the land.

⁷And when all the captains of the armies who *were* in the fields, they and their men, heard that the king of Babylon had made Gedaliah the son of

39:3 ᵃA title, probably *Chief Officer;* also verse 13 ᵇA title, probably *Troop Commander;* also verse 13 **39:4** ᵃOr *the Arabah,* that is, the Jordan Valley

Ahikam governor in the land, and had committed to him men, women, children, and the poorest of the land who had not been carried away captive to Babylon, [8]then they came to Gedaliah at Mizpah—Ishmael the son of Nethaniah, Johanan and Jonathan the sons of Kareah, Seraiah the son of Tanhumeth, the sons of Ephai the Netophathite, and Jezaniah[a] the son of a Maachathite, they and their men. [9]And Gedaliah the son of Ahikam, the son of Shaphan, took an oath before them and their men, saying, "Do not be afraid to serve the Chaldeans. Dwell in the land and serve the king of Babylon, and it shall be well with you. [10]As for me, I will indeed dwell at Mizpah and serve the Chaldeans who come to us. But you, gather wine and summer fruit and oil, put *them* in your vessels, and dwell in your cities that you have taken."

[11]Likewise, when all the Jews who *were* in Moab, among the Ammonites, in Edom, and who *were* in all the countries, heard that the king of Babylon had left a remnant of Judah, and that he had set over them Gedaliah the son of Ahikam, the son of Shaphan, [12]then all the Jews returned out of all places where they had been driven, and came to the land of Judah, to Gedaliah at Mizpah, and gathered wine and summer fruit in abundance.

[13]Moreover Johanan the son of Kareah and all the captains of the forces that *were* in the fields came to Gedaliah at Mizpah, [14]and said to him, "Do you certainly know that Baalis the king of the Ammonites has sent Ishmael the son of Nethaniah to murder you?" But Gedaliah the son of Ahikam did not believe them.

[15]Then Johanan the son of Kareah spoke secretly to Gedaliah in Mizpah, saying, "Let me go, please, and I will kill Ishmael the son of Nethaniah, and no one will know *it*. Why should he murder you, so that all the Jews who are gathered to you would be scattered, and the remnant in Judah perish?"

[16]But Gedaliah the son of Ahikam said to Johanan the son of Kareah, "You shall not do this thing, for you speak falsely concerning Ishmael."

INSURRECTION AGAINST GEDALIAH

41 Now it came to pass in the seventh month *that* Ishmael the son of Nethaniah, the son of Elishama, of the royal family and of the officers of the king, came with ten men to Gedaliah the son of Ahikam, at Mizpah. And there they ate bread together in Mizpah. [2]Then Ishmael the son of Nethaniah, and the ten men who were with him, arose and struck Gedaliah the son of Ahikam, the son of Shaphan, with the sword, and killed him whom the king of Babylon had made governor over the land. [3]Ishmael also struck down all the Jews who were with him, *that is,* with Gedaliah at Mizpah, and the Chaldeans who were found there, the men of war.

[4]And it happened, on the second day after he had killed Gedaliah, when as yet no one knew *it,* [5]that certain men came from Shechem, from Shiloh, and from Samaria, eighty men with their beards shaved and their clothes torn, having cut themselves, with offerings and incense in their hand, to bring *them* to the house of the LORD. [6]Now Ishmael the son of Nethaniah went out from Mizpah to meet them, weeping as he went along; and it happened as he met them that he said to them, "Come to Gedaliah the son of Ahikam!" [7]So it was, when they came into the midst of the city, that Ishmael the son of Nethaniah killed them *and cast them* into the midst of a pit, he and the men who were with him. [8]But ten men were found among them who said to Ishmael, "Do not kill us, for we have treasures of wheat, barley, oil, and honey in the field." So he desisted and did not kill them among their brethren. [9]Now the pit into which Ishmael had cast all the dead bodies of the men whom he had slain, because of Gedaliah, *was* the same one Asa the king had made for fear of Baasha king of Israel. Ishmael the son of Nethaniah filled it with *the* slain. [10]Then Ishmael carried away captive all the rest of the people who *were* in Mizpah, the king's daughters and all the people who remained in Mizpah, whom Nebuzaradan the captain of the guard had committed to Gedaliah the son of Ahikam. And Ishmael the son of Nethaniah carried them away captive and departed to go over to the Ammonites.

[11]But when Johanan the son of Kareah and all the captains of the forces that *were* with him heard of all the evil that Ishmael the son of Nethaniah had done, [12]they took all the men and went to fight with Ishmael the son of Nethaniah; and they found him by the great pool that *is* in Gibeon.

40:8 [a]Spelled *Jaazaniah* in 2 Kings 25:23

¹³So it was, when all the people who *were* with Ishmael saw Johanan the son of Kareah, and all the captains of the forces who *were* with him, that they were glad. ¹⁴Then all the people whom Ishmael had carried away captive from Mizpah turned around and came back, and went to Johanan the son of Kareah. ¹⁵But Ishmael the son of Nethaniah escaped from Johanan with eight men and went to the Ammonites.

¹⁶Then Johanan the son of Kareah, and all the captains of the forces that were with him, took from Mizpah all the rest of the people whom he had recovered from Ishmael the son of Nethaniah after he had murdered Gedaliah the son of Ahikam—the mighty men of war and the women and the children and the eunuchs, whom he had brought back from Gibeon. ¹⁷And they departed and dwelt in the habitation of Chimham, which is near Bethlehem, as they went on their way to Egypt, ¹⁸because of the Chaldeans; for they were afraid of them, because Ishmael the son of Nethaniah had murdered Gedaliah the son of Ahikam, whom the king of Babylon had made governor in the land.

The Flight to Egypt Forbidden

42 Now all the captains of the forces, Johanan the son of Kareah, Jezaniah the son of Hoshaiah, and all the people, from the least to the greatest, came near ²and said to Jeremiah the prophet, "Please, let our petition be acceptable to you, and pray for us to the LORD your God, for all this remnant (since we are left *but* a few of many, as you can see), ³that the LORD your God may show us the way in which we should walk and the thing we should do."

⁴Then Jeremiah the prophet said to them, "I have heard. Indeed, I will pray to the LORD your God according to your words, and it shall be, *that* whatever the LORD answers you, I will declare *it* to you. I will keep nothing back from you."

⁵So they said to Jeremiah, "Let the LORD be a true and faithful witness between us, if we do not do according to everything which the LORD your God sends us by you. ⁶Whether *it is* pleasing or displeasing, we will obey the voice of the LORD our God to whom we send you, that it may be well with us when we obey the voice of the LORD our God."

⁷And it happened after ten days that the word of the LORD came to Jeremiah. ⁸Then he called Johanan the son of Kareah, all the captains of the forces which *were* with him, and all the people from the least even to the greatest, ⁹and said to them, "Thus says the LORD, the God of Israel, to whom you sent me to present your petition before Him: ¹⁰'If you will still remain in this land, then I will build you and not pull *you* down, and I will plant you and not pluck *you* up. For I relent concerning the disaster that I have brought upon you. ¹¹Do not be afraid of the king of Babylon, of whom you are afraid; do not be afraid of him,' says the LORD, 'for I *am* with you, to save you and deliver you from his hand. ¹²And I will show you mercy, that he may have mercy on you and cause you to return to your own land.'

¹³"But if you say, 'We will not dwell in this land,' disobeying the voice of the LORD your God, ¹⁴saying, 'No, but we will go to the land of Egypt where we shall see no war, nor hear the sound of the trumpet, nor be hungry for bread, and there we will dwell'— ¹⁵Then hear now the word of the LORD, O remnant of Judah! Thus says the LORD of hosts, the God of Israel: 'If you wholly set your faces to enter Egypt, and go to dwell there, ¹⁶then it shall be *that* the sword which you feared shall overtake you there in the land of Egypt; the famine of which you were afraid shall follow close after you there *in* Egypt; and there you shall die. ¹⁷So shall it be with all the men who set their faces to go to Egypt to dwell there. They shall die by the sword, by famine, and by pestilence. And none of them shall remain or escape from the disaster that I will bring upon them.'

¹⁸"For thus says the LORD of hosts, the God of Israel: 'As My anger and My fury have been poured out on the inhabitants of Jerusalem, so will My fury be poured out on you when you enter Egypt. And you shall be an oath, an astonishment, a curse, and a reproach; and you shall see this place no more.'

¹⁹"The LORD has said concerning you, O remnant of Judah, 'Do not go to Egypt!' Know certainly that I have admonished you this day. ²⁰For you were hypocrites in your hearts when you sent me to the LORD your God, saying, 'Pray for us to the LORD our God, and according to all

that the LORD your God says, so declare to us and we will do *it.*' ²¹And I have this day declared *it* to you, but you have not obeyed the voice of the LORD your God, or anything which He has sent you by me. ²²Now therefore, know certainly that you shall die by the sword, by famine, and by pestilence in the place where you desire to go to dwell."

JEREMIAH TAKEN TO EGYPT

43Now it happened, when Jeremiah had stopped speaking to all the people all the words of the LORD their God, for which the LORD their God had sent him to them, all these words, ²that Azariah the son of Hoshaiah, Johanan the son of Kareah, and all the proud men spoke, saying to Jeremiah, "You speak falsely! The LORD our God has not sent you to say, 'Do not go to Egypt to dwell there.' ³But Baruch the son of Neriah has set you against us, to deliver us into the hand of the Chaldeans, that they may put us to death or carry us away captive to Babylon." ⁴So Johanan the son of Kareah, all the captains of the forces, and all the people would not obey the voice of the LORD, to remain in the land of Judah. ⁵But Johanan the son of Kareah and all the captains of the forces took all the remnant of Judah who had returned to dwell in the land of Judah, from all nations where they had been driven— ⁶men, women, children, the king's daughters, and every person whom Nebuzaradan the captain of the guard had left with Gedaliah the son of Ahikam, the son of Shaphan, and Jeremiah the prophet and Baruch the son of Neriah. ⁷So they went to the land of Egypt, for they did not obey the voice of the LORD. And they went as far as Tahpanhes.

⁸Then the word of the LORD came to Jeremiah in Tahpanhes, saying, ⁹"Take large stones in your hand, and hide them in the sight of the men of Judah, in the clay in the brick courtyard which *is* at the entrance to Pharaoh's house in Tahpanhes; ¹⁰and say to them, 'Thus says the LORD of hosts, the God of Israel: "Behold, I will send and bring Nebuchadnezzar the king of Babylon, My servant, and will set his throne above these stones that I have hidden. And he will spread his royal pavilion over them. ¹¹When he comes, he shall strike the land of Egypt *and deliver* to death *those*

appointed for death, and to captivity *those appointed* for captivity, and to the sword *those appointed* for the sword. ¹²Iª will kindle a fire in the houses of the gods of Egypt, and he shall burn them and carry them away captive. And he shall array himself with the land of Egypt, as a shepherd puts on his garment, and he shall go out from there in peace. ¹³He shall also break the *sacred* pillars of Beth Shemeshª that *are* in the land of Egypt; and the houses of the gods of the Egyptians he shall burn with fire." ' "

ISRAELITES WILL BE PUNISHED IN EGYPT

44The word that came to Jeremiah concerning all the Jews who dwell in the land of Egypt, who dwell at Migdol, at Tahpanhes, at Noph,ª and in the country of Pathros, saying, ²"Thus says the LORD of hosts, the God of Israel: 'You have seen all the calamity that I have brought on Jerusalem and on all the cities of Judah; and behold, this day they *are* a desolation, and no one dwells in them, ³because of their wickedness which they have committed to provoke Me to anger, in that they went to burn incense *and* to serve other gods whom they did not know, they nor you nor your fathers. ⁴However I have sent to you all My servants the prophets, rising early and sending *them,* saying, "Oh, do not do this abominable thing that I hate!" ⁵But they did not listen or incline their ear to turn from their wickedness, to burn no incense to other gods. ⁶So My fury and My anger were poured out and kindled in the cities of Judah and in the streets of Jerusalem; and they are wasted *and* desolate, as it is this day.'

⁷"Now therefore, thus says the LORD, the God of hosts, the God of Israel: 'Why do you commit *this* great evil against yourselves, to cut off from you man and woman, child and infant, out of Judah, leaving none to remain, ⁸in that you provoke Me to wrath with the works of your hands, burning incense to other gods in the land of Egypt where you have gone to dwell, that you may cut yourselves off and be a curse and a reproach among all the nations of the earth? ⁹Have you forgotten the wickedness of your fathers, the wickedness of the kings of Judah, the wickedness

43:12 ªFollowing Masoretic Text and Targum; Septuagint, Syriac, and Vulgate read *He.* **43:13** ªLiterally *House of the Sun,* ancient On; later called Heliopolis **44:1** ªThat is, ancient Memphis of their wives, your own wickedness, and the wickedness of your wives, which they committed in the land of Judah and in the streets of Jerusalem? [10]They have not been humbled, to this day, nor have they feared; they have not walked in My law or in My statutes that I set before you and your fathers.'

[11]"Therefore thus says the LORD of hosts, the God of Israel: 'Behold, I will set My face against you for catastrophe and for cutting off all Judah. [12]And I will take the remnant of Judah who have set their faces to go into the land of Egypt to dwell there, and they shall all be consumed *and* fall in the land of Egypt. They shall be consumed by the sword *and* by famine. They shall die, from the least to the greatest, by the sword and by famine; and they shall be an oath, an astonishment, a curse and a reproach! [13]For I will punish those who dwell in the land of Egypt, as I have punished Jerusalem, by the sword, by famine, and by pestilence, [14]so that none of the remnant of Judah who have gone into the land of Egypt to dwell there shall escape or survive, lest they return to the land of Judah, to which they desire to return and dwell. For none shall return except those who escape.' "

[15]Then all the men who knew that their wives had burned incense to other gods, with all the women who stood by, a great multitude, and all the people who dwelt in the land of Egypt, in Pathros, answered Jeremiah, saying: [16]"*As for* the word that you have spoken to us in the name of the LORD, we will not listen to you! [17]But we will certainly do whatever has gone out of our own mouth, to burn incense to the queen of heaven and pour out drink offerings to her, as we have done, we and our fathers, our kings and our princes, in the cities of Judah and in the streets of Jerusalem. For *then* we had plenty of food, were well-off, and saw no trouble. [18]But since we stopped burning incense to the queen of heaven and pouring out drink offerings to her, we have lacked everything and have been consumed by the sword and by famine."

[19]*The women also said,* "And when we burned incense to the queen of heaven and poured out drink offerings to her, did we make cakes for her, to worship her, and pour out drink offerings to her without our husbands' *permission?*"

[20]Then Jeremiah spoke to all the people—the men, the women, and all the people who had given him *that* answer—saying: [21]"The incense that you burned in the cities of Judah and in the streets of Jerusalem, you and your fathers, your kings and your princes, and the people of the land, did not the LORD remember them, and did it *not* come into His mind? [22]So the LORD could no longer bear *it,* because of the evil of your doings *and* because of the abominations which you committed. Therefore your land is a desolation, an astonishment, a curse, and without an inhabitant, as *it is* this day. [23]Because you have burned incense and because you have sinned against the LORD, and have not obeyed the voice of the LORD or walked in His law, in His statutes or in His testimonies, therefore this calamity has happened to you, as *at* this day."

[24]Moreover Jeremiah said to all the people and to all the women, "Hear the word of the LORD, all Judah who *are* in the land of Egypt! [25]Thus says the LORD of hosts, the God of Israel, saying: 'You and your wives have spoken with your mouths and fulfilled with your hands, saying, "We will surely keep our vows that we have made, to burn incense to the queen of heaven and pour out drink offerings to her." You will surely keep your vows and perform your vows!' [26]Therefore hear the word of the LORD, all Judah who dwell in the land of Egypt: 'Behold, I have sworn by My great name,' says the LORD, 'that My name shall no more be named in the mouth of any man of Judah in all the land of Egypt, saying, "The Lord GOD lives." [27]Behold, I will watch over them for adversity and not for good. And all the men of Judah who *are* in the land of Egypt shall be consumed by the sword and by famine, until there is an end to them. [28]Yet a small number who escape the sword shall return from the land of Egypt to the land of Judah; and all the remnant of Judah, who have gone to the land of Egypt to dwell there, shall know whose words will stand, Mine or theirs. [29]And this *shall be* a sign to you,' says the LORD, 'that I will punish you in this place, that you may know that My words will surely stand against you for adversity.'

[30]"Thus says the LORD: 'Behold, I will give Pharaoh Hophra king of Egypt into the hand of

his enemies and into the hand of those who seek his life, as I gave Zedekiah king of Judah into the hand of Nebuchadnezzar king of Babylon, his enemy who sought his life.' "

Assurance to Baruch

45 The word that Jeremiah the prophet spoke to Baruch the son of Neriah, when he had written these words in a book at the instruction of Jeremiah,[a] in the fourth year of Jehoiakim the son of Josiah, king of Judah, saying, ²"Thus says the LORD, the God of Israel, to you, O Baruch: ³You said, "Woe is me now! For the LORD has added grief to my sorrow. I fainted in my sighing, and I find no rest." '

⁴"Thus you shall say to him, 'Thus says the LORD: "Behold, what I have built I will break down, and what I have planted I will pluck up, that is, this whole land. ⁵And do you seek great things for yourself? Do not seek *them;* for behold, I will bring adversity on all flesh," says the LORD. "But I will give your life to you as a prize in all places, wherever you go." ' "

Judgment on Egypt

46 The word of the LORD which came to Jeremiah the prophet against the nations. ²Against Egypt.

Concerning the army of Pharaoh Necho, king of Egypt, which was by the River Euphrates in Carchemish, and which Nebuchadnezzar king of Babylon defeated in the fourth year of Jehoiakim the son of Josiah, king of Judah:

³"Order the buckler and shield,
  And draw near to battle!
⁴Harness the horses,
  And mount up, you horsemen!
  Stand forth with *your* helmets,
  Polish the spears,
  Put on the armor!
⁵Why have I seen them dismayed *and* turned
    back?
  Their mighty ones are beaten down;
  They have speedily fled,
  And did not look back,
  For fear *was* all around," says the LORD.
⁶"Do not let the swift flee away,
  Nor the mighty man escape;

They will stumble and fall
  Toward the north, by the River Euphrates.

⁷"Who *is* this coming up like a flood,
  Whose waters move like the rivers?
⁸Egypt rises up like a flood,
  And *its* waters move like the rivers;
  And he says, 'I will go up *and* cover the earth,
  I will destroy the city and its inhabitants.'
⁹Come up, O horses, and rage, O chariots!
  And let the mighty men come forth:
  The Ethiopians and the Libyans who handle
    the shield,
  And the Lydians who handle *and* bend the
    bow.
¹⁰For this *is* the day of the Lord GOD of hosts,
  A day of vengeance,
  That He may avenge Himself on His
    adversaries.
  The sword shall devour;
  It shall be satiated and made drunk with their
    blood;
  For the Lord GOD of hosts has a sacrifice
  In the north country by the River Euphrates.

¹¹"Go up to Gilead and take balm,
  O virgin, the daughter of Egypt;
  In vain you will use many medicines;
  You shall not be cured.
¹²The nations have heard of your shame,
  And your cry has filled the land;
  For the mighty man has stumbled against the
    mighty;
  They both have fallen together."

Babylonia Will Strike Egypt

¹³The word that the LORD spoke to Jeremiah the prophet, how Nebuchadnezzar king of Babylon would come *and* strike the land of Egypt.

¹⁴"Declare in Egypt, and proclaim in Migdol;
  Proclaim in Noph[a] and in Tahpanhes;
  Say, 'Stand fast and prepare yourselves,
  For the sword devours all around you.'
¹⁵Why are your valiant *men* swept away?
  They did not stand
  Because the LORD drove them away.

45:1 [a]Literally *from Jeremiah's mouth* **46:14** [a]That is, ancient Memphis

¹⁶He made many fall;
Yes, one fell upon another.
And they said, 'Arise!
Let us go back to our own people
And to the land of our nativity
From the oppressing sword.'
¹⁷They cried there,
'Pharaoh, king of Egypt, *is but* a noise.
He has passed by the appointed time!'

¹⁸"*As* I live," says the King,
Whose name *is* the LORD of hosts,
"Surely as Tabor *is* among the mountains
And as Carmel by the sea, *so* he shall come.
¹⁹O you daughter dwelling in Egypt,
Prepare yourself to go into captivity!
For Noph^a shall be waste and desolate,
without inhabitant.

²⁰"Egypt *is* a very pretty heifer,
But destruction comes, it comes from the
north.
²¹Also her mercenaries are in her midst like fat
bulls,
For they also are turned back,
They have fled away together.
They did not stand,
For the day of their calamity had come upon
them,
The time of their punishment.
²²Her noise shall go like a serpent,
For they shall march with an army
And come against her with axes,
Like those who chop wood.

²³"They shall cut down her forest," says the
LORD,
"Though it cannot be searched,
Because they *are* innumerable,
And more numerous than grasshoppers.
²⁴The daughter of Egypt shall be ashamed;
She shall be delivered into the hand
Of the people of the north."

²⁵The LORD of hosts, the God of Israel, says:
"Behold, I will bring punishment on Amon^a of
No,^b and Pharaoh and Egypt, with their gods and
their kings—Pharaoh and those who trust in him.
²⁶And I will deliver them into the hand of those

who seek their lives, into the hand of Nebuchadnezzar king of Babylon and the hand of his servants. Afterward it shall be inhabited as in the days
of old," says the LORD.

GOD WILL PRESERVE ISRAEL

²⁷"But do not fear, O My servant Jacob,
And do not be dismayed, O Israel!
For behold, I will save you from afar,
And your offspring from the land of their
captivity;
Jacob shall return, have rest and be at ease;
No one shall make *him* afraid.
²⁸Do not fear, O Jacob My servant," says the
LORD,
"For I *am* with you;
For I will make a complete end of all the
nations
To which I have driven you,
But I will not make a complete end of you.
I will rightly correct you,
For I will not leave you wholly unpunished."

JUDGMENT ON PHILISTIA

47 The word of the LORD that came to Jeremiah the prophet against the Philistines,
before Pharaoh attacked Gaza.
²Thus says the LORD:

"Behold, waters rise out of the north,
And shall be an overflowing flood;
They shall overflow the land and all that
is in it,
The city and those who dwell within;
Then the men shall cry,
And all the inhabitants of the land shall wail.
³At the noise of the stamping hooves of his
strong horses,
At the rushing of his chariots,
At the rumbling of his wheels,
The fathers will not look back for *their*
children,
Lacking courage,
⁴Because of the day that comes to plunder all
the Philistines,
To cut off from Tyre and Sidon every helper
who remains;

46:19 ^aThat is, ancient Memphis   **46:25** ^aA sun god   ^bThat is, ancient Thebes

For the L ord shall plunder the Philistines,
The remnant of the country of Caphtor.
⁵Baldness has come upon Gaza,
Ashkelon is cut off
With the remnant of their valley.
How long will you cut yourself?

⁶"O you sword of the L ord,
How long until you are quiet?
Put yourself up into your scabbard,
Rest and be still!
⁷How can it be quiet,
Seeing the L ord has given it a charge
Against Ashkelon and against the seashore?
There He has appointed it."

Judgment on Moab

48 Against Moab.
Thus says the L ord of hosts, the God of
Israel:

"Woe to Nebo!
For it is plundered,
Kirjathaim is shamed *and* taken;
The high stronghold[a] is shamed and
dismayed—
²No more praise of Moab.
In Heshbon they have devised evil against
her:
'Come, and let us cut her off as a nation.'
You also shall be cut down, O Madmen![a]
The sword shall pursue you;
³A voice of crying *shall be* from Horonaim:
'Plundering and great destruction!'

⁴"Moab is destroyed;
Her little ones have caused a cry to be
heard;[a]
⁵For in the Ascent of Luhith they ascend with
continual weeping;
For in the descent of Horonaim the enemies
have heard a cry of destruction.

⁶"Flee, save your lives!
And be like the juniper[a] in the wilderness.
⁷For because you have trusted in your works
and your treasures,
You also shall be taken.
And Chemosh shall go forth into captivity,

His priests and his princes together.
⁸And the plunderer shall come against every
city;
No one shall escape.
The valley also shall perish,
And the plain shall be destroyed,
As the L ord has spoken.

⁹"Give wings to Moab,
That she may flee and get away;
For her cities shall be desolate,
Without any to dwell in them.
¹⁰Cursed *is* he who does the work of the L ord
deceitfully,
And cursed *is* he who keeps back his sword
from blood.

¹¹"Moab has been at ease from his[a] youth;
He has settled on his dregs,
And has not been emptied from vessel to
vessel,
Nor has he gone into captivity.
Therefore his taste remained in him,
And his scent has not changed.

¹²"Therefore behold, the days are coming," says
the L ord,
"That I shall send him wine-workers
Who will tip him over
And empty his vessels
And break the bottles.
¹³Moab shall be ashamed of Chemosh,
As the house of Israel was ashamed of Bethel,
their confidence.

¹⁴"How can you say, 'We *are* mighty
And strong men for the war'?
¹⁵Moab is plundered and gone up *from* her
cities;
Her chosen young men have gone down to
the slaughter," says the King,
Whose name *is* the L ord of hosts.

¹⁶"The calamity of Moab *is* near at hand,
And his affliction comes quickly.

48:1 ᵃHebrew *Misgab* **48:2** ᵃA city of Moab **48:4** ᵃFollowing Masoretic Text, Targum, and Vulgate; Septuagint reads *Proclaim it in Zoar.* **48:6** ᵃOr *Aroer,* a city of Moab **48:11** ᵃThe Hebrew uses masculine and feminine pronouns interchangeably in this chapter.

17Bemoan him, all you who are around him;
And all you who know his name,
Say, 'How the strong staff is broken,
The beautiful rod!'

18"O daughter inhabiting Dibon,
Come down from *your* glory,
And sit in thirst;
For the plunderer of Moab has come against you,
He has destroyed your strongholds.
19O inhabitant of Aroer,
Stand by the way and watch;
Ask him who flees
And her who escapes;
Say, 'What has happened?'
20Moab is shamed, for he is broken down.
Wail and cry!
Tell it in Arnon, that Moab is plundered.

21"And judgment has come on the plain country:
On Holon and Jahzah and Mephaath,
22On Dibon and Nebo and Beth Diblathaim,
23On Kirjathaim and Beth Gamul and Beth Meon,
24On Kerioth and Bozrah,
On all the cities of the land of Moab,
Far or near.
25The horn of Moab is cut off,
And his arm is broken," says the LORD.

26"Make him drunk,
Because he exalted *himself* against the LORD.
Moab shall wallow in his vomit,
And he shall also be in derision.
27For was not Israel a derision to you?
Was he found among thieves?
For whenever you speak of him,
You shake *your head in scorn.*
28You who dwell in Moab,
Leave the cities and dwell in the rock,
And be like the dove *which* makes her nest
In the sides of the cave's mouth.

29"We have heard the pride of Moab
(He *is* exceedingly proud),
Of his loftiness and arrogance and pride,
And of the haughtiness of his heart."

30"I know his wrath," says the LORD,
"But it *is* not right;
His lies have made nothing right.
31Therefore I will wail for Moab,
And I will cry out for all Moab;
Ia will mourn for the men of Kir Heres.
32O vine of Sibmah! I will weep for you with the weeping of Jazer.
Your plants have gone over the sea,
They reach to the sea of Jazer.
The plunderer has fallen on your summer fruit and your vintage.
33Joy and gladness are taken
From the plentiful field
And from the land of Moab;
I have caused wine to fail from the winepresses;
No one will tread with joyous shouting—
Not joyous shouting!

34"From the cry of Heshbon to Elealeh and to Jahaz
They have uttered their voice,
From Zoar to Horonaim,
Like a three-year-old heifer;a
For the waters of Nimrim also shall be desolate.

35"Moreover," says the LORD,
"I will cause to cease in Moab
The one who offers *sacrifices* in the high places
And burns incense to his gods.
36Therefore My heart shall wail like flutes for Moab,
And like flutes My heart shall wail
For the men of Kir Heres.
Therefore the riches they have acquired have perished.

37"For every head *shall be* bald, and every beard clipped;
On all the hands *shall be* cuts, and on the loins sackcloth—
38A general lamentation
On all the housetops of Moab,

48:31 aFollowing Dead Sea Scrolls, Septuagint, and Vulgate; Masoretic Text reads *He.*   48:34 aOr *The Third Eglath,* an unknown city (compare Isaiah 15:5)

And in its streets;
For I have broken Moab like a vessel in
    which *is* no pleasure," says the LORD.
³⁹"They shall wail:
  "How she is broken down!
  How Moab has turned her back with
    shame!'
  So Moab shall be a derision
  And a dismay to all those about her."

⁴⁰For thus says the LORD:

  "Behold, one shall fly like an eagle,
  And spread his wings over Moab.
⁴¹Kerioth is taken,
  And the strongholds are surprised;
  The mighty men's hearts in Moab on that
    day shall be
  Like the heart of a woman in birth pangs.
⁴²And Moab shall be destroyed as a people,
  Because he exalted *himself* against the LORD.
⁴³Fear and the pit and the snare *shall be* upon
    you,
  O inhabitant of Moab," says the LORD.
⁴⁴"He who flees from the fear shall fall into the
    pit,
  And he who gets out of the pit shall be
    caught in the snare.
  For upon Moab, upon it I will bring
  The year of their punishment," says the
    LORD.

⁴⁵"Those who fled stood under the shadow of
    Heshbon
  Because of exhaustion.
  But a fire shall come out of Heshbon,
  A flame from the midst of Sihon,
  And shall devour the brow of Moab,
  The crown of the head of the sons of
    tumult.
⁴⁶Woe to you, O Moab!
  The people of Chemosh perish;
  For your sons have been taken captive,
  And your daughters captive.

⁴⁷"Yet I will bring back the captives of Moab
  In the latter days," says the LORD.

Thus far *is* the judgment of Moab.

JUDGMENT ON AMMON

49 Against the Ammonites.
Thus says the LORD:

  "Has Israel no sons?
  Has he no heir?
  Why *then* does Milcomª inherit Gad,
  And his people dwell in its cities?
²Therefore behold, the days are coming," says
    the LORD,
  "That I will cause to be heard an alarm of war
  In Rabbah of the Ammonites;
  It shall be a desolate mound,
  And her villages shall be burned with fire.
  Then Israel shall take possession of his
    inheritance," says the LORD.

³"Wail, O Heshbon, for Ai is plundered!
  Cry, you daughters of Rabbah,
  Gird yourselves with sackcloth!
  Lament and run to and fro by the walls;
  For Milcom shall go into captivity
  With his priests and his princes together.
⁴Why do you boast in the valleys,
  Your flowing valley, O backsliding daughter?
  Who trusted in her treasures, *saying,*
  'Who will come against me?'
⁵Behold, I will bring fear upon you,"
  Says the Lord GOD of hosts,
  "From all those who are around you;
  You shall be driven out, everyone headlong,
  And no one will gather those who wander
    off.
⁶But afterward I will bring back
  The captives of the people of Ammon," says
    the LORD.

JUDGMENT ON EDOM

⁷Against Edom.
Thus says the LORD of hosts:

  "*Is* wisdom no more in Teman?
  Has counsel perished from the prudent?
  Has their wisdom vanished?
⁸Flee, turn back, dwell in the depths,
  O inhabitants of Dedan!

49:1 ªHebrew *Malcam,* literally *their king,* a god of the Ammonites;
also called *Molech* (compare verse 3)

For I will bring the calamity of Esau upon
him,
The time *that* I will punish him.
⁹If grape-gatherers came to you,
Would they not leave *some* gleaning grapes?
If thieves by night,
Would they not destroy until they have
enough?
¹⁰But I have made Esau bare;
I have uncovered his secret places,ᵃ
And he shall not be able to hide himself.
His descendants are plundered,
His brethren and his neighbors,
And he *is* no more.
¹¹Leave your fatherless children,
I will preserve *them* alive;
And let your widows trust in Me."

¹²For thus says the LORD: "Behold, those
whose judgment *was* not to drink of the cup
have assuredly drunk. And *are* you the one who
will altogether go unpunished? You shall not go
unpunished, but you shall surely drink *of it*. ¹³For
I have sworn by Myself," says the LORD, "that
Bozrah shall become a desolation, a reproach, a
waste, and a curse. And all its cities shall be perpetual wastes."

¹⁴I have heard a message from the LORD,
And an ambassador has been sent to the
nations:
"Gather together, come against her,
And rise up to battle!

¹⁵"For indeed, I will make you small among
nations,
Despised among men.
¹⁶Your fierceness has deceived you,
The pride of your heart,
O you who dwell in the clefts of the rock,
Who hold the height of the hill!
Though you make your nest as high as the
eagle,
I will bring you down from there," says the
LORD.ᵃ

¹⁷"Edom also shall be an astonishment;
Everyone who goes by it will be astonished
And will hiss at all its plagues.

¹⁸As in the overthrow of Sodom and
Gomorrah
And their neighbors," says the LORD,
"No one shall remain there,
Nor shall a son of man dwell in it.

¹⁹"Behold, he shall come up like a lion from the
floodplainᵃ of the Jordan
Against the dwelling place of the strong;
But I will suddenly make him run away from
her.
And who *is* a chosen *man that* I may appoint
over her?
For who *is* like Me?
Who will arraign Me?
And who *is* that shepherd
Who will withstand Me?"

²⁰Therefore hear the counsel of the LORD that
He has taken against Edom,
And His purposes that He has proposed
against the inhabitants of Teman:
Surely the least of the flock shall draw them
out;
Surely He shall make their dwelling places
desolate with them.
²¹The earth shakes at the noise of their fall;
At the cry its noise is heard at the Red Sea.
²²Behold, He shall come up and fly like the
eagle,
And spread His wings over Bozrah;
The heart of the mighty men of Edom in
that day shall be
Like the heart of a woman in birth pangs.

JUDGMENT ON DAMASCUS

²³Against Damascus.

"Hamath and Arpad are shamed,
For they have heard bad news.
They are fainthearted;
There is trouble on the sea;
It cannot be quiet.
²⁴Damascus has grown feeble;
She turns to flee,
And fear has seized *her*.

49:10 ᵃCompare Obadiah 5, 6   49:16 ᵃCompare Obadiah 3, 4
49:19 ᵃOr *thicket*

Anguish and sorrows have taken her like a
    woman in labor.
²⁵Why is the city of praise not deserted, the city
    of My joy?
²⁶Therefore her young men shall fall in her
    streets,
And all the men of war shall be cut off in that
    day," says the LORD of hosts.
²⁷"I will kindle a fire in the wall of Damascus,
And it shall consume the palaces of
    Ben-Hadad."ᵃ

JUDGMENT ON KEDAR AND HAZOR

²⁸Against Kedar and against the kingdoms of
Hazor, which Nebuchadnezzar king of Babylon
shall strike.

Thus says the LORD:

"Arise, go up to Kedar,
And devastate the men of the East!
²⁹Their tents and their flocks they shall take
    away.
They shall take for themselves their
    curtains,
All their vessels and their camels;
And they shall cry out to them,
'Fear *is* on every side!'

³⁰"Flee, get far away! Dwell in the depths,
O inhabitants of Hazor!" says the LORD.
"For Nebuchadnezzar king of Babylon has
    taken counsel against you,
And has conceived a plan against you.

³¹"Arise, go up to the wealthy nation that dwells
    securely," says the LORD,
"Which has neither gates nor bars,
Dwelling alone.
³²Their camels shall be for booty,
And the multitude of their cattle for
    plunder.
I will scatter to all winds those in the farthest
    corners,
And I will bring their calamity from all its
    sides," says the LORD.
³³"Hazor shall be a dwelling for jackals, a
    desolation forever;
No one shall reside there,
Nor son of man dwell in it."

JUDGMENT ON ELAM

³⁴The word of the LORD that came to Jeremiah the prophet against Elam, in the beginning
of the reign of Zedekiah king of Judah, saying,
³⁵"Thus says the LORD of hosts:

'Behold, I will break the bow of Elam,
The foremost of their might.
³⁶Against Elam I will bring the four winds
From the four quarters of heaven,
And scatter them toward all those winds;
There shall be no nations where the outcasts
    of Elam will not go.
³⁷For I will cause Elam to be dismayed before
    their enemies
And before those who seek their life.
I will bring disaster upon them,
My fierce anger,' says the LORD;
'And I will send the sword after them
Until I have consumed them.
³⁸I will set My throne in Elam,
And will destroy from there the king and the
    princes,' says the LORD.

³⁹'But it shall come to pass in the latter days:
I will bring back the captives of Elam,' says
    the LORD."

JUDGMENT ON BABYLON AND BABYLONIA

50 The word that the LORD spoke against
Babylon *and* against the land of the
Chaldeans by Jeremiah the prophet.

²"Declare among the nations,
Proclaim, and set up a standard;
Proclaim—do not conceal *it*—
Say, 'Babylon is taken, Bel is shamed.
Merodachᵃ is broken in pieces;
Her idols are humiliated,
Her images are broken in pieces.'
³For out of the north a nation comes up
    against her,
Which shall make her land desolate,
And no one shall dwell therein.
They shall move, they shall depart,
Both man and beast.

49:27 ᵃCompare Amos 1:4 **50:2** ᵃA Babylonian god; sometimes
spelled *Marduk*

⁴"In those days and in that time," says the
        LORD,
  "The children of Israel shall come,
    They and the children of Judah together;
    With continual weeping they shall come,
    And seek the LORD their God.
⁵They shall ask the way to Zion,
    With their faces toward it, *saying,*
  'Come and let us join ourselves to the LORD
    In a perpetual covenant
    That will not be forgotten.'

⁶"My people have been lost sheep.
    Their shepherds have led them astray;
    They have turned them away *on* the
        mountains.
    They have gone from mountain to hill;
    They have forgotten their resting place.
⁷All who found them have devoured them;
    And their adversaries said, 'We have not
        offended,
    Because they have sinned against the LORD,
        the habitation of justice,
    The LORD, the hope of their fathers.'

⁸"Move from the midst of Babylon,
    Go out of the land of the Chaldeans;
    And be like the rams before the flocks.
⁹For behold, I will raise and cause to come up
        against Babylon
    An assembly of great nations from the north
        country,
    And they shall array themselves against her;
    From there she shall be captured.
    Their arrows *shall be* like *those* of an expert
        warrior;ᵃ
    None shall return in vain.
¹⁰And Chaldea shall become plunder;
    All who plunder her shall be satisfied," says
        the LORD.

¹¹"Because you were glad, because you
        rejoiced,
    You destroyers of My heritage,
    Because you have grown fat like a heifer
        threshing grain,
    And you bellow like bulls,
¹²Your mother shall be deeply ashamed;
    She who bore you shall be ashamed.

Behold, the least of the nations *shall be* a
        wilderness,
    A dry land and a desert.
¹³Because of the wrath of the LORD
    She shall not be inhabited,
    But she shall be wholly desolate.
    Everyone who goes by Babylon shall be
        horrified
    And hiss at all her plagues.

¹⁴"Put yourselves in array against Babylon all
        around,
    All you who bend the bow;
    Shoot at her, spare no arrows,
    For she has sinned against the LORD.
¹⁵Shout against her all around;
    She has given her hand,
    Her foundations have fallen,
    Her walls are thrown down;
    For it *is* the vengeance of the LORD.
    Take vengeance on her.
    As she has done, so do to her.
¹⁶Cut off the sower from Babylon,
    And him who handles the sickle at harvest
        time.
    For fear of the oppressing sword
    Everyone shall turn to his own people,
    And everyone shall flee to his own land.

¹⁷"Israel *is* like scattered sheep;
    The lions have driven *him* away.
    First the king of Assyria devoured him;
    Now at last this Nebuchadnezzar king of
        Babylon has broken his bones."

¹⁸Therefore thus says the LORD of hosts, the
God of Israel:

  "Behold, I will punish the king of Babylon and
        his land,
    As I have punished the king of Assyria.
¹⁹But I will bring back Israel to his home,
    And he shall feed on Carmel and Bashan;
    His soul shall be satisfied on Mount Ephraim
        and Gilead.
²⁰In those days and in that time," says the
        LORD,

50:9 ᵃFollowing some Hebrew manuscripts, Septuagint, and Syriac;
Masoretic Text, Targum, and Vulgate read *a warrior who makes
childless.*

"The iniquity of Israel shall be sought, but *there
    shall be* none;
And the sins of Judah, but they shall not be
    found;
For I will pardon those whom I preserve.

21"Go up against the land of Merathaim,
        against it,
    And against the inhabitants of Pekod.
    Waste and utterly destroy them," says the
        LORD,
    "And do according to all that I have
        commanded you.
22A sound of battle *is* in the land,
    And of great destruction.
23How the hammer of the whole earth has
        been cut apart and broken!
    How Babylon has become a desolation
        among the nations!
24I have laid a snare for you;
    You have indeed been trapped, O Babylon,
    And you were not aware;
    You have been found and also caught,
    Because you have contended against the
        LORD.
25The LORD has opened His armory,
    And has brought out the weapons of His
        indignation;
    For this *is* the work of the Lord GOD of hosts
    In the land of the Chaldeans.
26Come against her from the farthest border;
    Open her storehouses;
    Cast her up as heaps of ruins,
    And destroy her utterly;
    Let nothing of her be left.
27Slay all her bulls,
    Let them go down to the slaughter.
    Woe to them!
    For their day has come, the time of their
        punishment.
28The voice of those who flee and escape from
        the land of Babylon
    Declares in Zion the vengeance of the LORD
        our God,
    The vengeance of His temple.

29"Call together the archers against Babylon.
    All you who bend the bow, encamp against it
        all around;

    Let none of them escape.a
    Repay her according to her work;
    According to all she has done, do to her;
    For she has been proud against the LORD,
    Against the Holy One of Israel.
30Therefore her young men shall fall in the
        streets,
    And all her men of war shall be cut off in that
        day," says the LORD.
31"Behold, I *am* against you,
    O most haughty one!" says the Lord GOD of
        hosts;
    "For your day has come,
    The time *that* I will punish you.a
32The most proud shall stumble and fall,
    And no one will raise him up;
    I will kindle a fire in his cities,
    And it will devour all around him."

33Thus says the LORD of hosts:

"The children of Israel *were* oppressed,
    Along with the children of Judah;
    All who took them captive have held them
        fast;
    They have refused to let them go.
34Their Redeemer *is* strong;
    The LORD of hosts *is* His name.
    He will thoroughly plead their case,
    That He may give rest to the land,
    And disquiet the inhabitants of Babylon.

35"A sword *is* against the Chaldeans," says the
        LORD,
    "Against the inhabitants of Babylon,
    And against her princes and her wise men.
36A sword *is* against the soothsayers, and they
        will be fools.
    A sword *is* against her mighty men, and they
        will be dismayed.
37A sword *is* against their horses,
    Against their chariots,
    And against all the mixed peoples who *are* in
        her midst;
    And they will become like women.

50:29 aQere, some Hebrew manuscripts, Septuagint, and Targum
add *to her.* **50:31** aFollowing Masoretic Text and Targum; Septuagint and Vulgate read *The time of your punishment.*

A sword *is* against her treasures, and they will
be robbed.
[38]A drought[a] *is* against her waters, and they will
be dried up.
For it *is* the land of carved images,
And they are insane with *their* idols.

[39]"Therefore the wild desert beasts shall dwell
there with the jackals,
And the ostriches shall dwell in it.
It shall be inhabited no more forever,
Nor shall it be dwelt in from generation to
generation.
[40]As God overthrew Sodom and Gomorrah
And their neighbors," says the LORD,
"*So* no one shall reside there,
Nor son of man dwell in it.

[41]"Behold, a people shall come from the north,
And a great nation and many kings
Shall be raised up from the ends of the
earth.
[42]They shall hold the bow and the lance;
They *are* cruel and shall not show mercy.
Their voice shall roar like the sea;
They shall ride on horses,
Set in array, like a man for the battle,
Against you, O daughter of Babylon.

[43]"The king of Babylon has heard the report
about them,
And his hands grow feeble;
Anguish has taken hold of him,
Pangs as of a woman in childbirth.

[44]"Behold, he shall come up like a lion from the
floodplain[a] of the Jordan
Against the dwelling place of the strong;
But I will make them suddenly run away
from her.
And who *is* a chosen *man that* I may appoint
over her?
For who *is* like Me?
Who will arraign Me?
And who *is* that shepherd
Who will withstand Me?"

[45]Therefore hear the counsel of the LORD that
He has taken against Babylon,

And His purposes that He has proposed
against the land of the Chaldeans:
Surely the least of the flock shall draw
them out;
Surely He will make their dwelling place
desolate with them.
[46]At the noise of the taking of Babylon
The earth trembles,
And the cry is heard among the nations.

THE UTTER DESTRUCTION OF BABYLON

51

Thus says the LORD:

"Behold, I will raise up against Babylon,
Against those who dwell in Leb Kamai,[a]
A destroying wind.
[2]And I will send winnowers to Babylon,
Who shall winnow her and empty her land.
For in the day of doom
They shall be against her all around.
[3]Against *her* let the archer bend his bow,
And lift himself up against *her* in his armor.
Do not spare her young men;
Utterly destroy all her army.
[4]Thus the slain shall fall in the land of the
Chaldeans,
And *those* thrust through in her streets.
[5]For Israel is not forsaken, nor Judah,
By his God, the LORD of hosts,
Though their land was filled with sin against
the Holy One of Israel."

[6]Flee from the midst of Babylon,
And every one save his life!
Do not be cut off in her iniquity,
For this *is* the time of the LORD's vengeance;
He shall recompense her.
[7]Babylon *was* a golden cup in the LORD's
hand,
That made all the earth drunk.
The nations drank her wine;
Therefore the nations are deranged.
[8]Babylon has suddenly fallen and been
destroyed.
Wail for her!

50:38 [a]Following Masoretic Text, Targum, and Vulgate; Syriac reads
sword; Septuagint omits *A drought is.*   **50:44** [a]Or *thicket*   **51:1** [a]A
code word for Chaldea (Babylonia); may be translated *The Midst of
Those Who Rise Up Against Me*

Take balm for her pain;
Perhaps she may be healed.

⁹We would have healed Babylon,
But she is not healed.
Forsake her, and let us go everyone to his
own country;
For her judgment reaches to heaven and is
lifted up to the skies.
¹⁰The LORD has revealed our righteousness.
Come and let us declare in Zion the work of
the LORD our God.

¹¹Make the arrows bright!
Gather the shields!
The LORD has raised up the spirit of the
kings of the Medes.
For His plan *is* against Babylon to destroy it,
Because it *is* the vengeance of the LORD,
The vengeance for His temple.
¹²Set up the standard on the walls of Babylon;
Make the guard strong,
Set up the watchmen,
Prepare the ambushes.
For the LORD has both devised and done
What He spoke against the inhabitants of
Babylon.
¹³O you who dwell by many waters,
Abundant in treasures,
Your end has come,
The measure of your covetousness.
¹⁴The LORD of hosts has sworn by Himself:
"Surely I will fill you with men, as with locusts,
And they shall lift up a shout against you."

¹⁵He has made the earth by His power;
He has established the world by His wisdom,
And stretched out the heaven by His
understanding.
¹⁶When He utters *His* voice—
There is a multitude of waters in the heavens:
"He causes the vapors to ascend from the ends
of the earth;
He makes lightnings for the rain;
He brings the wind out of His treasuries."ᵃ

¹⁷Everyone is dull-hearted, without knowledge;
Every metalsmith is put to shame by the
carved image;

For his molded image *is* falsehood,
And *there is* no breath in them.
¹⁸They *are* futile, a work of errors;
In the time of their punishment they shall
perish.
¹⁹The Portion of Jacob *is* not like them,
For He *is* the Maker of all things;
And *Israel is* the tribe of His inheritance.
The LORD of hosts *is* His name.

²⁰"You *are* My battle-ax *and* weapons of war:
For with you I will break the nation in
pieces;
With you I will destroy kingdoms;
²¹With you I will break in pieces the horse and
its rider;
With you I will break in pieces the chariot
and its rider;
²²With you also I will break in pieces man and
woman;
With you I will break in pieces old and
young;
With you I will break in pieces the young
man and the maiden;
²³With you also I will break in pieces the
shepherd and his flock;
With you I will break in pieces the farmer
and his yoke of oxen;
And with you I will break in pieces
governors and rulers.

²⁴"And I will repay Babylon
And all the inhabitants of Chaldea
For all the evil they have done
In Zion in your sight," says the LORD.

²⁵"Behold, I *am* against you, O destroying
mountain,
Who destroys all the earth," says the LORD.
"And I will stretch out My hand against you,
Roll you down from the rocks,
And make you a burnt mountain.
²⁶They shall not take from you a stone for a
corner
Nor a stone for a foundation,
But you shall be desolate forever," says the
LORD.

51:16 ᵃPsalm 135:7

²⁷Set up a banner in the land,
Blow the trumpet among the nations!
Prepare the nations against her,
Call the kingdoms together against her:
Ararat, Minni, and Ashkenaz.
Appoint a general against her;
Cause the horses to come up like the bristling
locusts.
²⁸Prepare against her the nations,
With the kings of the Medes,
Its governors and all its rulers,
All the land of his dominion.
²⁹And the land will tremble and sorrow;
For every purpose of the LORD shall be
performed against Babylon,
To make the land of Babylon a desolation
without inhabitant.
³⁰The mighty men of Babylon have ceased
fighting,
They have remained in their strongholds;
Their might has failed,
They became *like* women;
They have burned her dwelling places,
The bars of her *gate* are broken.
³¹One runner will run to meet another,
And one messenger to meet another,
To show the king of Babylon that his city is
taken on *all* sides;
³²The passages are blocked,
The reeds they have burned with fire,
And the men of war are terrified.

³³For thus says the LORD of hosts, the God of
Israel:

"The daughter of Babylon *is* like a threshing
floor
When it is time to thresh her;
Yet a little while
And the time of her harvest will come."

³⁴"Nebuchadnezzar the king of Babylon
Has devoured me, he has crushed me;
He has made me an empty vessel,
He has swallowed me up like a monster,
He has filled his stomach with my delicacies,
He has spit me out.
³⁵Let the violence *done* to me and my flesh *be*
upon Babylon,"

The inhabitant of Zion will say;
"And my blood be upon the inhabitants of
Chaldea!"
Jerusalem will say.

³⁶Therefore thus says the LORD:

"Behold, I will plead your case and take
vengeance for you.
I will dry up her sea and make her
springs dry.
³⁷Babylon shall become a heap,
A dwelling place for jackals,
An astonishment and a hissing,
Without an inhabitant.
³⁸They shall roar together like lions,
They shall growl like lions' whelps.
³⁹In their excitement I will prepare their feasts;
I will make them drunk,
That they may rejoice,
And sleep a perpetual sleep
And not awake," says the LORD.
⁴⁰"I will bring them down
Like lambs to the slaughter,
Like rams with male goats.

⁴¹"Oh, how Sheshachᵃ is taken!
Oh, how the praise of the whole earth is
seized!
How Babylon has become desolate among
the nations!
⁴²The sea has come up over Babylon;
She is covered with the multitude of its
waves.
⁴³Her cities are a desolation,
A dry land and a wilderness,
A land where no one dwells,
Through which no son of man passes.
⁴⁴I will punish Bel in Babylon,
And I will bring out of his mouth what he
has swallowed;
And the nations shall not stream to him
anymore.
Yes, the wall of Babylon shall fall.

⁴⁵"My people, go out of the midst of her!
And let everyone deliver himself from the
fierce anger of the LORD.

51:41 ᵃA code word for Babylon (compare Jeremiah 25:26)

⁴⁶And lest your heart faint,
And you fear for the rumor that *will be* heard
   in the land
(A rumor will come *one* year,
And after that, in *another* year
A rumor *will come,*
And violence in the land,
Ruler against ruler),
⁴⁷Therefore behold, the days are coming
That I will bring judgment on the carved
   images of Babylon;
Her whole land shall be ashamed,
And all her slain shall fall in her midst.
⁴⁸Then the heavens and the earth and all that *is*
   in them
Shall sing joyously over Babylon;
For the plunderers shall come to her from the
   north," says the LORD.

⁴⁹As Babylon *has caused* the slain of Israel to fall,
So at Babylon the slain of all the earth shall
   fall.
⁵⁰You who have escaped the sword,
Get away! Do not stand still!
Remember the LORD afar off,
And let Jerusalem come to your mind.

⁵¹We are ashamed because we have heard
   reproach.
Shame has covered our faces,
For strangers have come into the sanctuaries
   of the LORD's house.

⁵²"Therefore behold, the days are coming," says
   the LORD,
"That I will bring judgment on her carved
   images,
And throughout all her land the wounded
   shall groan.
⁵³Though Babylon were to mount up to
   heaven,
And though she were to fortify the height of
   her strength,
Yet from Me plunderers would come to her,"
   says the LORD.

⁵⁴The sound of a cry *comes* from Babylon,
And great destruction from the land of the
   Chaldeans,

⁵⁵Because the LORD is plundering Babylon
And silencing her loud voice,
Though her waves roar like great waters,
And the noise of their voice is uttered,
⁵⁶Because the plunderer comes against her,
   against Babylon,
And her mighty men are taken.
Every one of their bows is broken;
For the LORD *is* the God of recompense,
He will surely repay.

⁵⁷"And I will make drunk
Her princes and wise men,
Her governors, her deputies, and her mighty
   men.
And they shall sleep a perpetual sleep
And not awake," says the King,
Whose name *is* the LORD of hosts.

⁵⁸Thus says the LORD of hosts:

"The broad walls of Babylon shall be utterly
   broken,
And her high gates shall be burned with fire;
The people will labor in vain,
And the nations, because of the fire;
And they shall be weary."

JEREMIAH'S COMMAND TO SERAIAH

⁵⁹The word which Jeremiah the prophet commanded Seraiah the son of Neriah, the son of Mahseiah, when he went with Zedekiah the king of Judah to Babylon in the fourth year of his reign. And Seraiah *was* the quartermaster. ⁶⁰So Jeremiah wrote in a book all the evil that would come upon Babylon, all these words that are written against Babylon. ⁶¹And Jeremiah said to Seraiah, "When you arrive in Babylon and see it, and read all these words, ⁶²then you shall say, 'O LORD, You have spoken against this place to cut it off, so that none shall remain in it, neither man nor beast, but it shall be desolate forever.' ⁶³Now it shall be, when you have finished reading this book, *that* you shall tie a stone to it and throw it out into the Euphrates. ⁶⁴Then you shall say, 'Thus Babylon shall sink and not rise from the catastrophe that I will bring upon her. And they shall be weary.' "
Thus far *are* the words of Jeremiah.

The Fall of Jerusalem Reviewed

52 Zedekiah *was* twenty-one years old when he became king, and he reigned eleven years in Jerusalem. His mother's name *was* Hamutal the daughter of Jeremiah of Libnah. [2]He also did evil in the sight of the LORD, according to all that Jehoiakim had done. [3]For because of the anger of the LORD *this* happened in Jerusalem and Judah, till He finally cast them out from His presence. Then Zedekiah rebelled against the king of Babylon.

[4]Now it came to pass in the ninth year of his reign, in the tenth month, on the tenth *day* of the month, *that* Nebuchadnezzar king of Babylon and all his army came against Jerusalem and encamped against it; and *they* built a siege wall against it all around. [5]So the city was besieged until the eleventh year of King Zedekiah. [6]By the fourth month, on the ninth day of the month, the famine had become so severe in the city that there was no food for the people of the land. [7]Then the city *wall* was broken through, and all the men of war fled and went out of the city at night by way of the gate between the two walls, which *was* by the king's garden, even though the Chaldeans *were* near the city all around. And they went by way of the plain.[a]

[8]But the army of the Chaldeans pursued the king, and they overtook Zedekiah in the plains of Jericho. All his army was scattered from him. [9]So they took the king and brought him up to the king of Babylon at Riblah in the land of Hamath, and he pronounced judgment on him. [10]Then the king of Babylon killed the sons of Zedekiah before his eyes. And he killed all the princes of Judah in Riblah. [11]He also put out the eyes of Zedekiah; and the king of Babylon bound him in bronze fetters, took him to Babylon, and put him in prison till the day of his death.

The Temple and City Plundered and Burned

[12]Now in the fifth month, on the tenth *day* of the month (which *was* the nineteenth year of King Nebuchadnezzar king of Babylon), Nebuzaradan, the captain of the guard, *who* served the king of Babylon, came to Jerusalem. [13]He burned the house of the LORD and the king's house; all

the houses of Jerusalem, that is, all the houses of the great, he burned with fire. [14]And all the army of the Chaldeans who *were* with the captain of the guard broke down all the walls of Jerusalem all around. [15]Then Nebuzaradan the captain of the guard carried away captive *some* of the poor people, the rest of the people who remained in the city, the defectors who had deserted to the king of Babylon, and the rest of the craftsmen. [16]But Nebuzaradan the captain of the guard left *some* of the poor of the land as vinedressers and farmers.

[17]The bronze pillars that *were* in the house of the LORD, and the carts and the bronze Sea that *were* in the house of the LORD, the Chaldeans broke in pieces, and carried all their bronze to Babylon. [18]They also took away the pots, the shovels, the trimmers, the bowls, the spoons, and all the bronze utensils with which the *priests* ministered. [19]The basins, the firepans, the bowls, the pots, the lampstands, the spoons, and the cups, whatever *was* solid gold and whatever *was* solid silver, the captain of the guard took away. [20]The two pillars, one Sea, the twelve bronze bulls which *were* under *it, and* the carts, which King Solomon had made for the house of the LORD— the bronze of all these articles was beyond measure. [21]Now *concerning* the pillars: the height of one pillar *was* eighteen cubits, a measuring line of twelve cubits could measure its circumference, and its thickness *was* four fingers; *it was* hollow. [22]A capital of bronze *was* on it; and the height of one capital *was* five cubits, with a network and pomegranates all around the capital, all of bronze. The second pillar, with pomegranates was the same. [23]There were ninety-six pomegranates on the sides; all the pomegranates, all around on the network, *were* one hundred.

The People Taken Captive to Babylonia

[24]The captain of the guard took Seraiah the chief priest, Zephaniah the second priest, and the three doorkeepers. [25]He also took out of the city an officer who had charge of the men of war, seven men of the king's close associates who were found in the city, the principal scribe of the army who mustered the people of the land, and

52:7 [a]Or *the Arabah,* that is, the Jordan Valley

sixty men of the people of the land who were found in the midst of the city. ²⁶And Nebuzaradan the captain of the guard took these and brought them to the king of Babylon at Riblah. ²⁷Then the king of Babylon struck them and put them to death at Riblah in the land of Hamath. Thus Judah was carried away captive from its own land.

²⁸These *are* the people whom Nebuchadnezzar carried away captive: in the seventh year, three thousand and twenty-three Jews; ²⁹in the eighteenth year of Nebuchadnezzar he carried away captive from Jerusalem eight hundred and thirty-two persons; ³⁰in the twenty-third year of Nebuchadnezzar, Nebuzaradan the captain of the guard carried away captive of the Jews seven hundred and forty-five persons. All the persons *were* four thousand six hundred.

Jehoiachin Released from Prison

³¹Now it came to pass in the thirty-seventh year of the captivity of Jehoiachin king of Judah, in the twelfth month, on the twenty-fifth *day* of the month, *that* Evil-Merodach[a] king of Babylon, in the *first* year of his reign, lifted up the head of Jehoiachin king of Judah and brought him out of prison. ³²And he spoke kindly to him and gave him a more prominent seat than those of the kings who *were* with him in Babylon. ³³So Jehoiachin changed from his prison garments, and he ate bread regularly before the *king* all the days of his life. ³⁴And as for his provisions, there was a regular ration given him by the king of Babylon, a portion for each day until the day of his death, all the days of his life.

52:31 [a]Or *Awil-Marduk*

IMPACT OF THE BOOK

I   **IDEA** | *This book answers the question, "How can you keep your faith in God in the midst of tribulation?"*

M   **MESSAGE** | *There is hope in the midst of trouble; and the wise person learns to trust God in the midst of calamity, allowing God to use those times to strengthen him or her. Because God is just and holy, He must punish sin. However, He is also merciful, so He never allows His people to suffer more than they can bear. His compassions are new every morning; His faithfulness is great! Leaders must cling to this truth if they are to keep their faith in the midst of storms.*

P   **PEOPLE** | *Jeremiah, Zedekiah*

A   **AUTHOR** | *Although not stated in the text, traditionally Jeremiah has been ascribed authorship. He wrote this small book at the end of his ministry, after prophesying forty years to the Jewish people.*

C   **CULTURE** | *A "lament" or "lamentation" is a formal expression of sorrow over loss or death, and this book is a lament over the fall of Jerusalem at the hands of Nebuchadnezzar. During Jeremiah's ministry, three different deportations of Jews to Babylon took place. In each case, the strongest and brightest of the Jewish people were taken, leaving Judah without any leadership. The poorest of the people were allowed to remain; they experienced starvation, disease, and death because they were unable to defend themselves against any invaders.*

T   **TIMELINE** | *c. 585 BC*

KEY SCRIPTURE MEMORY VERSES | 3:22, 23

JERUSALEM IN AFFLICTION

1 How lonely sits the city
That was full of people!
How like a widow is she,
Who *was* great among the nations!
The princess among the provinces
Has become a slave!

²She weeps bitterly in the night,
Her tears *are* on her cheeks;
Among all her lovers
She has none to comfort *her.*
All her friends have dealt treacherously with
    her;
They have become her enemies.

³Judah has gone into captivity,
Under affliction and hard servitude;
She dwells among the nations,
She finds no rest;
All her persecutors overtake her in dire
    straits.

⁴The roads to Zion mourn
Because no one comes to the set feasts.
All her gates are desolate;
Her priests sigh,
Her virgins are afflicted,
And she *is* in bitterness.

⁵Her adversaries have become the master,
Her enemies prosper;
For the LORD has afflicted her
Because of the multitude of her
    transgressions.
Her children have gone into captivity before
    the enemy.

⁶And from the daughter of Zion
All her splendor has departed.
Her princes have become like deer
That find no pasture,
That flee without strength
Before the pursuer.

⁷In the days of her affliction and roaming,
Jerusalem remembers all her pleasant
    things

That she had in the days of old.
When her people fell into the hand of the
    enemy,
With no one to help her,
The adversaries saw her
And mocked at her downfall.ᵃ

⁸Jerusalem has sinned gravely,
Therefore she has become vile.ᵃ
All who honored her despise her
Because they have seen her nakedness;
Yes, she sighs and turns away.

⁹Her uncleanness *is* in her skirts;
She did not consider her destiny;
Therefore her collapse was awesome;
She had no comforter.
"O LORD, behold my affliction,
For *the* enemy is exalted!"

¹⁰The adversary has spread his hand
Over all her pleasant things;
For she has seen the nations enter her
    sanctuary,
Those whom You commanded
Not to enter Your assembly.

¹¹All her people sigh,
They seek bread;
They have given their valuables for food to
    restore life.
"See, O LORD, and consider,
For I am scorned."

¹²"*Is it* nothing to you, all you who pass by?
Behold and see
If there is any sorrow like my sorrow,
Which has been brought on me,
Which the LORD has inflicted
In the day of His fierce anger.

¹³"From above He has sent fire into my
    bones,
And it overpowered them;
He has spread a net for my feet
And turned me back;

1:7 ᵃVulgate reads *her Sabbaths.* 1:8 ᵃSeptuagint and Vulgate read *moved* or *removed.*

INSIDE *the* INFLUENCERS

JEREMIAH: The Consequence of Sin

LAMENTATIONS 1:8, 9

Lamentations is a supplement to the book of Jeremiah. It is kind of like the journal of Jeremiah, The Weeping Prophet. It is a tragic example of what happens when God's people turn their backs on Him. God warned the people of Jerusalem constantly through his prophet Jeremiah, but they refused to stop their idol worship. Sin may look appealing in its glorious façade, but it always carries with it a great price. The people of Judah may not have concerned themselves with the consequences of their idolatry, but the holy God did.

The Babylonian army surrounded Jerusalem, and it was only a matter of time before it fell. The situation grew so dire that starving mothers even ate their own children. (2:20; 4:10). Jeremiah witnessed the fall of the great city (5:16). The Babylonian King, Nebuchadnezzar, took everything valuable, leaving the rest in pieces (2 Kings 25:8–10).

Jerusalem was corrupt and wicked, but watching God deliver justice didn't make Jeremiah feel any better. He knew Jerusalem got what she deserved, yet Jeremiah mourned. He longed to see her restored (5:19–22). Out of a heart of compassion and brokenness the prophet interceded on her behalf. This book commemorates the death of the holy city, but it also reveals the heart of God. Jeremiah knew God's heart and understood that He was weeping over His people.

He has made me desolate
And faint all the day.

14"The yoke of my transgressions was bound;[a]
They were woven together by His hands,
And thrust upon my neck.
He made my strength fail;
The Lord delivered me into the hands of *those*
    whom I am not able to
        withstand.

15"The Lord has trampled underfoot all my
        mighty *men* in my midst;
He has called an assembly against me
To crush my young men;
The Lord trampled *as* in a winepress
The virgin daughter of Judah.

16"For these *things* I weep;
My eye, my eye overflows with water;
Because the comforter, who should restore
    my life,
Is far from me.

My children are desolate
Because the enemy prevailed."

17Zion spreads out her hands,
But no one comforts her;
The LORD has commanded concerning
        Jacob
That those around him *become* his adversaries;
Jerusalem has become an unclean thing
        among them.

18"The LORD is righteous,
For I rebelled against His commandment.
Hear now, all peoples,
And behold my sorrow;
My virgins and my young men
Have gone into captivity.

19"I called for my lovers,
But they deceived me;
My priests and my elders

1:14 aFollowing Masoretic Text and Targum; Septuagint, Syriac, and Vulgate read *watched over.*

Breathed their last in the city,
While they sought food
To restore their life.

20"See, O LORD, that I *am* in distress;
My soul is troubled;
My heart is overturned within me,
For I have been very rebellious.
Outside the sword bereaves,
At home *it is* like death.

21"They have heard that I sigh,
But no one comforts me.
All my enemies have heard of my trouble;
They are glad that You have done *it*.
Bring on the day You have announced,
That they may become like me.

22"Let all their wickedness come before You,
And do to them as You have done to me
For all my transgressions;
For my sighs *are* many,
And my heart *is* faint."

GOD'S ANGER WITH JERUSALEM

2 How the Lord has covered the daughter of
Zion
With a cloud in His anger!
He cast down from heaven to the earth
The beauty of Israel,
And did not remember His footstool
In the day of His anger.

2The Lord has swallowed up and has not
pitied
All the dwelling places of Jacob.
He has thrown down in His wrath
The strongholds of the daughter of Judah;
He has brought *them* down to the ground;
He has profaned the kingdom and its
princes.

3He has cut off in fierce anger
Every horn of Israel;
He has drawn back His right hand
From before the enemy.
He has blazed against Jacob like a flaming
fire
Devouring all around.

4Standing like an enemy, He has bent His bow;
With His right hand, like an adversary,
He has slain all *who were* pleasing to His eye;
On the tent of the daughter of Zion,
He has poured out His fury like fire.

5The Lord was like an enemy.
He has swallowed up Israel,
He has swallowed up all her palaces;
He has destroyed her strongholds,
And has increased mourning and lamentation
In the daughter of Judah.

6He has done violence to His tabernacle,
As if it were a garden;
He has destroyed His place of assembly;
The LORD has caused
The appointed feasts and Sabbaths to be
forgotten in Zion.
In His burning indignation He has spurned
the king and the priest.

7The Lord has spurned His altar,
He has abandoned His sanctuary;
He has given up the walls of her palaces
Into the hand of the enemy.
They have made a noise in the house of the
LORD
As on the day of a set feast.

8The LORD has purposed to destroy
The wall of the daughter of Zion.
He has stretched out a line;
He has not withdrawn His hand from
destroying;
Therefore He has caused the rampart and
wall to lament;
They languished together.

9Her gates have sunk into the ground;
He has destroyed and broken her bars.
Her king and her princes *are* among the
nations;
The Law *is* no *more*,
And her prophets find no vision from the
LORD.

10The elders of the daughter of Zion
Sit on the ground *and* keep silence;

They throw dust on their heads
And gird themselves with sackcloth.
The virgins of Jerusalem
Bow their heads to the ground.

11My eyes fail with tears,
My heart is troubled;
My bile is poured on the ground
Because of the destruction of the daughter of
    my people,
Because the children and the infants
Faint in the streets of the city.

12They say to their mothers,
"Where *is* grain and wine?"
As they swoon like the wounded
In the streets of the city,
As their life is poured out
In their mothers' bosom.

13How shall I console you?
To what shall I liken you,
O daughter of Jerusalem?
What shall I compare with you, that I may
    comfort you,
O virgin daughter of Zion?
For your ruin *is* spread wide as the sea;
Who can heal you?

14Your prophets have seen for you
False and deceptive visions;
They have not uncovered your iniquity,
To bring back your captives,
But have envisioned for you false prophecies
    and delusions.

15All who pass by clap *their* hands at you;
They hiss and shake their heads
At the daughter of Jerusalem:
"*Is* this the city that is called
'The perfection of beauty,
The joy of the whole earth'?"

16All your enemies have opened their mouth
    against you;
They hiss and gnash *their* teeth.
They say, "We have swallowed *her* up!
Surely this *is* the day we have waited for;
We have found *it*, we have seen *it!*"

17The LORD has done what He purposed;
He has fulfilled His word
Which He commanded in days of old.
He has thrown down and has not pitied,
And He has caused an enemy to rejoice over
    you;
He has exalted the horn of your adversaries.

18Their heart cried out to the Lord,
"O wall of the daughter of Zion,
Let tears run down like a river day and night;
Give yourself no relief;
Give your eyes no rest.

19"Arise, cry out in the night,
At the beginning of the watches;
Pour out your heart like water before the face
    of the Lord.
Lift your hands toward Him
For the life of your young children,
Who faint from hunger at the head of every
    street."

20"See, O LORD, and consider!
To whom have You done this?
Should the women eat their offspring,
The children they have cuddled?a
Should the priest and prophet be slain
In the sanctuary of the Lord?

21"Young and old lie
On the ground in the streets;
My virgins and my young men
Have fallen by the sword;
You have slain *them* in the day of Your anger,
You have slaughtered *and* not pitied.

22"You have invited as to a feast day
The terrors that surround me.
In the day of the LORD's anger
There was no refugee or survivor.
Those whom I have borne and brought up
My enemies have destroyed."

THE PROPHET'S ANGUISH AND HOPE

3 I *am* the man *who* has seen affliction by the
    rod of His wrath.
2He has led me and made *me* walk

2:20 aVulgate reads *a span long.*

In darkness and not *in* light.
³Surely He has turned His hand against me
Time and time again throughout the day.

⁴He has aged my flesh and my skin,
And broken my bones.
⁵He has besieged me
And surrounded *me* with bitterness and
woe.
⁶He has set me in dark places
Like the dead of long ago.

⁷He has hedged me in so that I cannot get
out;
He has made my chain heavy.
⁸Even when I cry and shout,
He shuts out my prayer.
⁹He has blocked my ways with hewn stone;
He has made my paths crooked.

¹⁰He *has been* to me a bear lying in wait,
Like a lion in ambush.
¹¹He has turned aside my ways and torn me in
pieces;
He has made me desolate.
¹²He has bent His bow
And set me up as a target for the arrow.

¹³He has caused the arrows of His quiver
To pierce my loins.ᵃ
¹⁴I have become the ridicule of all my
people—
Their taunting song all the day.
¹⁵He has filled me with bitterness,
He has made me drink wormwood.

¹⁶He has also broken my teeth with gravel,
And covered me with ashes.
¹⁷You have moved my soul far from peace;
I have forgotten prosperity.
¹⁸And I said, "My strength and my hope
Have perished from the LORD."

¹⁹Remember my affliction and roaming,
The wormwood and the gall.
²⁰My soul still remembers
And sinks within me.
²¹This I recall to my mind,
Therefore I have hope.

²²*Through* the LORD's mercies we are not
consumed,
Because His compassions fail not.
²³*They are* new every morning;
Great *is* Your faithfulness.
²⁴"The LORD *is* my portion," says my soul,
"Therefore I hope in Him!"

²⁵The LORD *is* good to those who wait for
Him,
To the soul *who* seeks Him.
²⁶*It is* good that *one* should hope and wait
quietly
For the salvation of the LORD.
²⁷*It is* good for a man to bear
The yoke in his youth.

²⁸Let him sit alone and keep silent,
Because *God* has laid *it* on him;
²⁹Let him put his mouth in the dust—
There may yet be hope.
³⁰Let him give *his* cheek to the one who strikes
him,
And be full of reproach.

³¹For the Lord will not cast off forever.
³²Though He causes grief,
Yet He will show compassion
According to the multitude of His mercies.
³³For He does not afflict willingly,
Nor grieve the children of men.

³⁴To crush under one's feet
All the prisoners of the earth,
³⁵To turn aside the justice *due* a man
Before the face of the Most High,
³⁶Or subvert a man in his cause—
The Lord does not approve.

³⁷Who *is* he *who* speaks and it comes to pass,
When the Lord has not commanded *it*?
³⁸*Is it* not from the mouth of the Most High
That woe and well-being proceed?
³⁹Why should a living man complain,
A man for the punishment of his sins?

⁴⁰Let us search out and examine our ways,
And turn back to the LORD;

3:13 ᵃLiterally *kidneys*

⁴¹Let us lift our hearts and hands
  To God in heaven.
⁴²We have transgressed and rebelled;
  You have not pardoned.

⁴³You have covered *Yourself* with anger
  And pursued us;
  You have slain *and* not pitied.
⁴⁴You have covered Yourself with a cloud,
  That prayer should not pass through.
⁴⁵You have made us an offscouring and refuse
  In the midst of the peoples.

⁴⁶All our enemies
  Have opened their mouths against us.
⁴⁷Fear and a snare have come upon us,
  Desolation and destruction.
⁴⁸My eyes overflow with rivers of water
  For the destruction of the daughter of my
    people.

⁴⁹My eyes flow and do not cease,
  Without interruption,
⁵⁰Till the LORD from heaven
  Looks down and sees.
⁵¹My eyes bring suffering to my soul
  Because of all the daughters of my city.

⁵²My enemies without cause
  Hunted me down like a bird.
⁵³They silenced[a] my life in the pit
  And threw stones at me.
⁵⁴The waters flowed over my head;
  I said, "I am cut off!"

⁵⁵I called on Your name, O LORD,
  From the lowest pit.
⁵⁶You have heard my voice:
  "Do not hide Your ear
  From my sighing, from my cry for help."
⁵⁷You drew near on the day I called on You,
  And said, "Do not fear!"

⁵⁸O Lord, You have pleaded the case for my soul;
  You have redeemed my life.
⁵⁹O LORD, You have seen *how* I am wronged;
  Judge my case.
⁶⁰You have seen all their vengeance,
  All their schemes against me.

⁶¹You have heard their reproach, O LORD,
  All their schemes against me,
⁶²The lips of my enemies
  And their whispering against me all the day.
⁶³Look at their sitting down and their rising up;
  I *am* their taunting song.

⁶⁴Repay them, O LORD,
  According to the work of their hands.
⁶⁵Give them a veiled[a] heart;
  Your curse *be* upon them!
⁶⁶In Your anger,
  Pursue and destroy them
  From under the heavens of the LORD.

THE DEGRADATION OF ZION

4 How the gold has become dim!
  How changed the fine gold!
  The stones of the sanctuary are scattered
  At the head of every street.

²The precious sons of Zion,
  Valuable as fine gold,
  How they are regarded as clay pots,
  The work of the hands of the potter!

³Even the jackals present their breasts
  To nurse their young;
  But the daughter of my people *is* cruel,
  Like ostriches in the wilderness.

⁴The tongue of the infant clings
  To the roof of its mouth for thirst;
  The young children ask for bread,
  But no one breaks *it* for them.

⁵Those who ate delicacies
  Are desolate in the streets;
  Those who were brought up in scarlet
  Embrace ash heaps.

⁶The punishment of the iniquity of the
    daughter of my people
  Is greater than the punishment of the sin of
    Sodom,
  Which was overthrown in a moment,
  With no hand to help her!

3:53 [a]Septuagint reads *put to death.* **3:65** [a]A Jewish tradition reads *sorrow of.*

7Her Nazirites[a] were brighter than snow
And whiter than milk;
They were more ruddy in body than rubies,
Like sapphire in their appearance.

8*Now* their appearance is blacker than soot;
They go unrecognized in the streets;
Their skin clings to their bones,
It has become as dry as wood.

9*Those* slain by the sword are better off
Than *those* who die of hunger;
For these pine away,
Stricken *for lack* of the fruits of the field.

10The hands of the compassionate women
Have cooked their own children;
They became food for them
In the destruction of the daughter of my
people.

11The LORD has fulfilled His fury,
He has poured out His fierce anger.
He kindled a fire in Zion,
And it has devoured its foundations.

12The kings of the earth,
And all inhabitants of the world,
Would not have believed
That the adversary and the enemy
Could enter the gates of Jerusalem—

13Because of the sins of her prophets
And the iniquities of her priests,
Who shed in her midst
The blood of the just.

14They wandered blind in the streets;
They have defiled themselves with blood,
So that no one would touch their
garments.

15They cried out to them,
"Go away, unclean!
Go away, go away,
Do not touch us!"
When they fled and wandered,
Those among the nations said,
"They shall no longer dwell *here*."

16The face[a] of the LORD scattered them;
He no longer regards them.
The people do not respect the priests
Nor show favor to the elders.

17Still our eyes failed us,
Watching vainly for our help;
In our watching we watched
For a nation *that* could not save *us*.

18They tracked our steps
So that we could not walk in our streets.
Our end was near;
Our days were over,
For our end had come.

19Our pursuers were swifter
Than the eagles of the heavens.
They pursued us on the mountains
And lay in wait for us in the wilderness.

20The breath of our nostrils, the anointed of the
LORD,
Was caught in their pits,
Of whom we said, "Under his shadow
We shall live among the nations."

21Rejoice and be glad, O daughter of Edom,
You who dwell in the land of Uz!
The cup shall also pass over to you
And you shall become drunk and make
yourself naked.

22*The punishment of* your iniquity is
accomplished,
O daughter of Zion;
He will no longer send you into captivity.
He will punish your iniquity,
O daughter of Edom;
He will uncover your sins!

A Prayer for Restoration

5 Remember, O LORD, what has come
upon us;
Look, and behold our reproach!
2Our inheritance has been turned over to
aliens,
And our houses to foreigners.

4:7 [a]Or *nobles* 4:16 [a]Targum reads *anger.*

³We have become orphans and waifs,
Our mothers *are* like widows.

⁴We pay for the water we drink,
And our wood comes at a price.
⁵*They* pursue at our heels;ᵃ
We labor *and* have no rest.
⁶We have given our hand *to* the Egyptians
And the Assyrians, to be satisfied with bread.

⁷Our fathers sinned *and are* no more,
But we bear their iniquities.
⁸Servants rule over us;
There is none to deliver *us* from their hand.
⁹We get our bread *at the risk* of our lives,
Because of the sword in the wilderness.

¹⁰Our skin is hot as an oven,
Because of the fever of famine.
¹¹They ravished the women in Zion,
The maidens in the cities of Judah.
¹²Princes were hung up by their hands,
And elders were not respected.
¹³Young men ground at the millstones;

Boys staggered under *loads of* wood.
¹⁴The elders have ceased *gathering at* the gate,
And the young men from their music.

¹⁵The joy of our heart has ceased;
Our dance has turned into mourning.
¹⁶The crown has fallen *from* our head.
Woe to us, for we have sinned!
¹⁷Because of this our heart is faint;
Because of these *things* our eyes grow dim;
¹⁸Because of Mount Zion which is desolate,
With foxes walking about on it.

¹⁹You, O LORD, remain forever;
Your throne from generation to generation.
²⁰Why do You forget us forever,
And forsake us for so long a time?
²¹Turn us back to You, O LORD, and we will be
restored;
Renew our days as of old,
²²Unless You have utterly rejected us,
And are very angry with us!

5:5 ᵃLiterally *necks*

IMPACT OF THE BOOK

EZEKIEL

I IDEA · *People must take responsibility for their own actions.*

M MESSAGE · *God told Ezekiel that the people would not want to heed his message, yet God still called him to be faithful to proclaim the truth. Ezekiel's ministry was a sign to the people that God had not forsaken them because even in the midst of their rebellion and judgment, God sent one of His prophets to remind them of His mercy and their future restoration. The difficulty Ezekiel faced was not letting the despair or hard-heartedness of the people to whom he ministered cause him to lose faith. Leaders must keep their focus on God and not on circumstances if they desire to stand strong during difficult challenges.*

P PEOPLE · *Ezekiel, Jaazaniah, Nebuchadnezzar, Pelatiah, Pharaoh*

A AUTHOR · *Ezekiel, the son of Buzi, was born into a priestly family and lived in Judah. As a young adult he was taken captive by the Babylonians in 597 BC. While in captivity at the age of 30, he was called by God to prohpesy.*

C CULTURE · *Ezekiel ministered to the Israelites who had been taken into captivity. By the time his ministry began, the people had already been in exile for several years. During his ministry, the exiles learned of the fall of Jerusalem in 586 BC, causing them despair and hopelessness. Ezekiel's message was two-pronged: he spoke of the righteous judgment of God but also of the hope of a coming restoration. God gave visions to Ezekiel to make His message clear—a practice common in the Old Testament.*

T TIMELINE · *c. 570 BC*

KEY SCRIPTURE MEMORY VERSES · 28:11–19; 36:24–28

Ezekiel's Vision of God

1 Now it came to pass in the thirtieth year, in the fourth *month,* on the fifth *day* of the month, as I *was* among the captives by the River Chebar, *that* the heavens were opened and I saw visions[a] of God. ²On the fifth *day* of the month, which *was* in the fifth year of King Jehoiachin's captivity, ³the word of the LORD came expressly to Ezekiel the priest, the son of Buzi, in the land of the Chaldeans[a] by the River Chebar; and the hand of the LORD was upon him there.

⁴Then I looked, and behold, a whirlwind was coming out of the north, a great cloud with raging fire engulfing itself; and brightness *was* all around it and radiating out of its midst like the color of amber, out of the midst of the fire. ⁵Also from within it *came* the likeness of four living creatures. And this *was* their appearance: they had the likeness of a man. ⁶Each one had four faces, and each one had four wings. ⁷Their legs *were* straight, and the soles of their feet *were* like the soles of calves' feet. They sparkled like the color of burnished bronze. ⁸The hands of a man *were* under their wings on their four sides; and each of the four had faces and wings. ⁹Their wings touched one another. *The creatures* did not turn when they went, but each one went straight forward.

¹⁰As for the likeness of their faces, *each* had the face of a man; each of the four had the face of a lion on the right side, each of the four had the face of an ox on the left side, and each of the four had the face of an eagle. ¹¹Thus *were* their faces. Their wings stretched upward; two *wings* of each one touched one another, and two covered their bodies. ¹²And each one went straight forward; they went wherever the spirit wanted to go, and they did not turn when they went.

¹³As for the likeness of the living creatures, their appearance *was* like burning coals of fire, like the appearance of torches going back and forth among the living creatures. The fire was bright, and out of the fire went lightning. ¹⁴And the living creatures ran back and forth, in appearance like a flash of lightning.

¹⁵Now as I looked at the living creatures, behold, a wheel *was* on the earth beside each living creature with its four faces. ¹⁶The appearance of the wheels and their workings *was* like the color of beryl, and all four had the same likeness. The appearance of their workings *was,* as it were, a wheel in the middle of a wheel. ¹⁷When they moved, they went toward any one of four directions; they did not turn aside when they went. ¹⁸As for their rims, they were so high they were awesome; and their rims *were* full of eyes, all around the four of them. ¹⁹When the living creatures went, the wheels went beside them; and when the living creatures were lifted up from the earth, the wheels were lifted up. ²⁰Wherever the spirit wanted to go, they went, *because* there the spirit went; and the wheels were lifted together with them, for the spirit of the living creatures[a] *was* in the wheels. ²¹When those went, *these* went; when those stood, *these* stood; and when those were lifted up from the earth, the wheels were lifted up together with them, for the spirit of the living creatures[a] *was* in the wheels.

²²The likeness of the firmament above the heads of the living creatures[a] *was* like the color of an awesome crystal, stretched out over their heads. ²³And under the firmament their wings *spread out* straight, one toward another. Each one had two which covered one side, and each one had two which covered the other side of the body. ²⁴When they went, I heard the noise of their wings, like the noise of many waters, like the voice of the Almighty, a tumult like the noise of an army; and when they stood still, they let down their wings. ²⁵A voice came from above the firmament that *was* over their heads; whenever they stood, they let down their wings.

²⁶And above the firmament over their heads *was* the likeness of a throne, in appearance like a sapphire stone; on the likeness of the throne *was* a likeness with the appearance of a man high above it. ²⁷Also from the appearance of His waist and upward I saw, as it were, the color of amber with the appearance of fire all around within it; and from the appearance of His waist and downward I saw, as it were, the appearance of fire with bright-

---

1:1 ᵃFollowing Masoretic Text, Septuagint, and Vulgate; Syriac and Targum read *a vision.* **1:3** ᵃOr *Babylonians,* and so elsewhere in this book **1:20** ᵃLiterally *living creature;* Septuagint and Vulgate read *spirit of life;* Targum reads *creatures.* **1:21** ᵃLiterally *living creature;* Septuagint and Vulgate read *spirit of life;* Targum reads *creatures.* **1:22** ᵃFollowing Septuagint, Targum, and Vulgate; Masoretic Text reads *living creature.*

ness all around. 28Like the appearance of a rainbow in a cloud on a rainy day, so *was* the appearance of the brightness all around it. This *was* the appearance of the likeness of the glory of the Lord.

Ezekiel Sent to Rebellious Israel

So when I saw *it,* I fell on my face, and I heard a voice of One speaking.

2And He said to me, "Son of man, stand on your feet, and I will speak to you." 2Then the Spirit entered me when He spoke to me, and set me on my feet; and I heard Him who spoke to me. 3And He said to me: "Son of man, I am sending you to the children of Israel, to a rebellious nation that has rebelled against Me; they and their fathers have transgressed against Me to this very day. 4For *they are* impudent and stubborn children. I am sending you to them, and you shall say to them, 'Thus says the Lord God.' 5As for them, whether they hear or whether they refuse—for they *are* a rebellious house—yet they will know that a prophet has been among them.

6"And you, son of man, do not be afraid of them nor be afraid of their words, though briers and thorns *are* with you and you dwell among scorpions; do not be afraid of their words or dismayed by their looks, though they *are* a rebellious house. 7You shall speak My words to them, whether they hear or whether they refuse, for they *are* rebellious. 8But you, son of man, hear what I say to you. Do not be rebellious like that rebellious house; open your mouth and eat what I give you."

9Now when I looked, there was a hand stretched out to me; and behold, a scroll of a book *was* in it. 10Then He spread it before me; and *there was* writing on the inside and on the outside, and written on it *were* lamentations and mourning and woe.

3Moreover He said to me, "Son of man, eat what you find; eat this scroll, and go, speak to the house of Israel." 2So I opened my mouth, and He caused me to eat that scroll.

3And He said to me, "Son of man, feed your belly, and fill your stomach with this scroll that I give you." So I ate, and it was in my mouth like honey in sweetness.

4Then He said to me: "Son of man, go to the house of Israel and speak with My words to them. 5For you *are* not sent to a people of unfamiliar speech and of hard language, *but* to the house of Israel, 6not to many people of unfamiliar speech and of hard language, whose words you cannot understand. Surely, had I sent you to them, they would have listened to you. 7But the house of Israel will not listen to you, because they will not listen to Me; for all the house of Israel *are* impudent and hard-hearted. 8Behold, I have made your face strong against their faces, and your forehead strong against their foreheads. 9Like adamant stone, harder than flint, I have made your forehead; do not be afraid of them, nor be dismayed at their looks, though they *are* a rebellious house."

10Moreover He said to me: "Son of man, receive into your heart all My words that I speak to you, and hear with your ears. 11And go, get to the captives, to the children of your people, and speak to them and tell them, 'Thus says the Lord God,' whether they hear, or whether they refuse."

12Then the Spirit lifted me up, and I heard behind me a great thunderous voice: "Blessed *is* the glory of the Lord from His place!" 13I also *heard* the noise of the wings of the living creatures that touched one another, and the noise of the wheels beside them, and a great thunderous noise. 14So the Spirit lifted me up and took me away, and I went in bitterness, in the heat of my spirit; but the hand of the Lord was strong upon me. 15Then I came to the captives at Tel Abib, who dwelt by the River Chebar; and I sat where they sat, and remained there astonished among them seven days.

Ezekiel Is a Watchman

16Now it came to pass at the end of seven days that the word of the Lord came to me, saying, 17"Son of man, I have made you a watchman for the house of Israel; therefore hear a word from My mouth, and give them warning from Me: 18When I say to the wicked, 'You shall surely die,' and you give him no warning, nor speak to warn the wicked from his wicked way, to save his life, that same wicked *man* shall die in his iniquity; but his blood I will require at your hand. 19Yet, if you warn the wicked, and he does not turn from his wickedness, nor from his wicked way, he shall die in his iniquity; but you have delivered your soul.

20"Again, when a righteous *man* turns from his righteousness and commits iniquity, and I lay a stumbling block before him, he shall die; because you did not give him warning, he shall die in his sin, and his righteousness which he has done shall not be remembered; but his blood I will require at your hand. 21Nevertheless if you warn the righteous *man* that the righteous should not sin, and he does not sin, he shall surely live because he took warning; also you will have delivered your soul."

22Then the hand of the LORD was upon me there, and He said to me, "Arise, go out into the plain, and there I shall talk with you."

23So I arose and went out into the plain, and behold, the glory of the LORD stood there, like the glory which I saw by the River Chebar; and I fell on my face. 24Then the Spirit entered me and set me on my feet, and spoke with me and said to me: "Go, shut yourself inside your house. 25And you, O son of man, surely they will put ropes on you and bind you with them, so that you cannot go out among them. 26I will make your tongue cling to the roof of your mouth, so that you shall be mute and not be one to rebuke them, for they *are* a rebellious house. 27But when I speak with you, I will open your mouth, and you shall say to them, 'Thus says the Lord GOD.' He who hears, let him hear; and he who refuses, let him refuse; for they *are* a rebellious house.

The Siege of Jerusalem Portrayed

4 "You also, son of man, take a clay tablet and lay it before you, and portray on it a city, Jerusalem. 2Lay siege against it, build a siege wall against it, and heap up a mound against it; set camps against it also, and place battering rams against it all around. 3Moreover take for yourself an iron plate, and set it *as* an iron wall between you and the city. Set your face against it, and it shall be besieged, and you shall lay siege against it. This *will be* a sign to the house of Israel.

4"Lie also on your left side, and lay the iniquity of the house of Israel upon it. *According* to the number of the days that you lie on it, you shall bear their iniquity. 5For I have laid on you the years of their iniquity, according to the number of the days, three hundred and ninety days; so you shall bear the iniquity of the house of Israel. 6And

when you have completed them, lie again on your right side; then you shall bear the iniquity of the house of Judah forty days. I have laid on you a day for each year.

7"Therefore you shall set your face toward the siege of Jerusalem; your arm *shall be* uncovered, and you shall prophesy against it. 8And surely I will restrain you so that you cannot turn from one side to another till you have ended the days of your siege.

9"Also take for yourself wheat, barley, beans, lentils, millet, and spelt; put them into one vessel, and make bread of them for yourself. *During* the number of days that you lie on your side, three hundred and ninety days, you shall eat it. 10And your food which you eat *shall be* by weight, twenty shekels a day; from time to time you shall eat it. 11You shall also drink water by measure, one-sixth of a hin; from time to time you shall drink. 12And you shall eat it *as* barley cakes; and bake it using fuel of human waste in their sight."

13Then the LORD said, "So shall the children of Israel eat their defiled bread among the Gentiles, where I will drive them."

14So I said, "Ah, Lord GOD! Indeed I have never defiled myself from my youth till now; I have never eaten what died of itself or was torn by beasts, nor has abominable flesh ever come into my mouth."

15Then He said to me, "See, I am giving you cow dung instead of human waste, and you shall prepare your bread over it."

16Moreover He said to me, "Son of man, surely I will cut off the supply of bread in Jerusalem; they shall eat bread by weight and with anxiety, and shall drink water by measure and with dread, 17that they may lack bread and water, and be dismayed with one another, and waste away because of their iniquity.

A Sword Against Jerusalem

5 "And you, son of man, take a sharp sword, take it as a barber's razor, and pass *it* over your head and your beard; then take scales to weigh and divide the *hair.* 2You shall burn with fire one-third in the midst of the city, when the days of the siege are finished; then you shall take one-third and strike around *it* with the sword, and one-third you shall scatter in the wind: I will draw out a sword

after them. ³You shall also take a small number of them and bind them in the edge of your *garment.* ⁴Then take some of them again and throw them into the midst of the fire, and burn them in the fire. From there a fire will go out into all the house of Israel.

⁵"Thus says the Lord GOD: 'This *is* Jerusalem; I have set her in the midst of the nations and the countries all around her. ⁶She has rebelled against My judgments by doing wickedness more than the nations, and against My statutes more than the countries that *are* all around her; for they have refused My judgments, and they have not walked in My statutes.' ⁷Therefore thus says the Lord GOD: 'Because you have multiplied *disobedience* more than the nations that *are* all around you, have not walked in My statutes nor kept My judgments, nor even doneª according to the judgments of the nations that *are* all around you'— ⁸therefore thus says the Lord GOD: 'Indeed I, even I, *am* against you and will execute judgments in your midst in the sight of the nations. ⁹And I will do among you what I have never done, and the like of which I will never do again, because of all your abominations. ¹⁰Therefore fathers shall eat *their* sons in your midst, and sons shall eat their fathers; and I will execute judgments among you, and all of you who remain I will scatter to all the winds.

¹¹'Therefore, *as* I live,' says the Lord GOD, 'surely, because you have defiled My sanctuary with all your detestable things and with all your abominations, therefore I will also diminish *you;* My eye will not spare, nor will I have any pity. ¹²One-third of you shall die of the pestilence, and be consumed with famine in your midst; and one-third shall fall by the sword all around you; and I will scatter another third to all the winds, and I will draw out a sword after them.

¹³'Thus shall My anger be spent, and I will cause My fury to rest upon them, and I will be avenged; and they shall know that I, the LORD, have spoken *it* in My zeal, when I have spent My fury upon them. ¹⁴Moreover I will make you a waste and a reproach among the nations that *are* all around you, in the sight of all who pass by.

¹⁵'So it ª shall be a reproach, a taunt, a lesson, and an astonishment to the nations that *are* all around you, when I execute judgments among you in anger and in fury and in furious rebukes. I,

the LORD, have spoken. ¹⁶When I send against them the terrible arrows of famine which shall be for destruction, which I will send to destroy you, I will increase the famine upon you and cut off your supply of bread. ¹⁷So I will send against you famine and wild beasts, and they will bereave you. Pestilence and blood shall pass through you, and I will bring the sword against you. I, the LORD, have spoken.' "

JUDGMENT ON IDOLATROUS ISRAEL

6 Now the word of the LORD came to me, saying: ²"Son of man, set your face toward the mountains of Israel, and prophesy against them, ³and say, 'O mountains of Israel, hear the word of the Lord GOD! Thus says the Lord GOD to the mountains, to the hills, to the ravines, and to the valleys: "Indeed I, *even* I, will bring a sword against you, and I will destroy your high places. ⁴Then your altars shall be desolate, your incense altars shall be broken, and I will cast down your slain *men* before your idols. ⁵And I will lay the corpses of the children of Israel before their idols, and I will scatter your bones all around your altars. ⁶In all your dwelling places the cities shall be laid waste, and the high places shall be desolate, so that your altars may be laid waste and made desolate, your idols may be broken and made to cease, your incense altars may be cut down, and your works may be abolished. ⁷The slain shall fall in your midst, and you shall know that I *am* the LORD.

⁸"Yet I will leave a remnant, so that you may have *some* who escape the sword among the nations, when you are scattered through the countries. ⁹Then those of you who escape will remember Me among the nations where they are carried captive, because I was crushed by their adulterous heart which has departed from Me, and by their eyes which play the harlot after their idols; they will loathe themselves for the evils which they committed in all their abominations. ¹⁰And they shall know that I *am* the LORD; I have not said in vain that I would bring this calamity upon them."

¹¹'Thus says the Lord GOD: "Pound your fists and stamp your feet, and say, 'Alas, for all the evil

---

5:7 ªFollowing Masoretic Text, Septuagint, Targum, and Vulgate; many Hebrew manuscripts and Syriac read *but have done* (compare 11:12). **5:15** ªSeptuagint, Syriac, Targum, and Vulgate read *you.*

abominations of the house of Israel! For they shall fall by the sword, by famine, and by pestilence. [12]He who is far off shall die by the pestilence, he who is near shall fall by the sword, and he who remains and is besieged shall die by the famine. Thus will I spend My fury upon them. [13]Then you shall know that I *am* the LORD, when their slain are among their idols all around their altars, on every high hill, on all the mountaintops, under every green tree, and under every thick oak, wherever they offered sweet incense to all their idols. [14]So I will stretch out My hand against them and make the land desolate, yes, more desolate than the wilderness toward Diblah, in all their dwelling places. Then they shall know that I *am* the LORD.' " ' "

JUDGMENT ON ISRAEL IS NEAR

7 Moreover the word of the LORD came to me, saying, [2]"And you, son of man, thus says the Lord GOD to the land of Israel:

'An end! The end has come upon the four
corners of the land.
[3]Now the end *has come* upon you,
And I will send My anger against you;
I will judge you according to your ways,
And I will repay you for all your
abominations.
[4]My eye will not spare you,
Nor will I have pity;
But I will repay your ways,
And your abominations will be in your midst;
Then you shall know that I *am* the LORD!'

[5]"Thus says the Lord GOD:

'A disaster, a singular disaster;
Behold, it has come!
[6]An end has come,
The end has come;
It has dawned for you;
Behold, it has come!
[7]Doom has come to you, you who dwell in
the land;
The time has come,
A day of trouble *is* near,
And not of rejoicing on the mountains.
[8]Now upon you I will soon pour out My fury,

And spend My anger upon you;
I will judge you according to your ways,
And I will repay you for all your abominations.

[9]'My eye will not spare,
Nor will I have pity;
I will repay you according to your ways,
And your abominations will be in your midst.
Then you shall know that I *am* the LORD
who strikes.

[10]'Behold, the day!
Behold, it has come!
Doom has gone out;
The rod has blossomed,
Pride has budded.
[11]Violence has risen up into a rod of
wickedness;
None of them *shall remain,*
None of their multitude,
None of them;
Nor *shall there be* wailing for them.
[12]The time has come,
The day draws near.

'Let not the buyer rejoice,
Nor the seller mourn,
For wrath *is* on their whole multitude.
[13]For the seller shall not return to what has
been sold,
Though he may still be alive;
For the vision concerns the whole multitude,
And it shall not turn back;
No one will strengthen himself
Who lives in iniquity.

[14]'They have blown the trumpet and made
everyone ready,
But no one goes to battle;
For My wrath *is* on all their multitude.
[15]The sword *is* outside,
And the pestilence and famine within.
Whoever *is* in the field
Will die by the sword;
And whoever *is* in the city,
Famine and pestilence will devour him.

[16]'Those who survive will escape and be on the
mountains

Like doves of the valleys,
All of them mourning,
Each for his iniquity.
¹⁷Every hand will be feeble,
And every knee will be *as* weak *as* water.
¹⁸They will also be girded with sackcloth;
Horror will cover them;
Shame *will be* on every face,
Baldness on all their heads.

¹⁹"They will throw their silver into the streets,
And their gold will be like refuse;
Their silver and their gold will not be able to
deliver them
In the day of the wrath of the LORD;
They will not satisfy their souls,
Nor fill their stomachs,
Because it became their stumbling block of
iniquity.

²⁰'As for the beauty of his ornaments,
He set it in majesty;
But they made from it
The images of their abominations—
Their detestable things;
Therefore I have made it
Like refuse to them.
²¹I will give it as plunder
Into the hands of strangers,
And to the wicked of the earth as spoil;
And they shall defile it.
²²I will turn My face from them,
And they will defile My secret place;
For robbers shall enter it and defile it.

²³'Make a chain,
For the land is filled with crimes of blood,
And the city is full of violence.
²⁴Therefore I will bring the worst of the
Gentiles,
And they will possess their houses;
I will cause the pomp of the strong to cease,
And their holy places shall be defiled.
²⁵Destruction comes;
They will seek peace, but *there shall be* none.
²⁶Disaster will come upon disaster,
And rumor will be upon rumor.
Then they will seek a vision from a
prophet;

But the law will perish from the priest,
And counsel from the elders.

²⁷'The king will mourn,
The prince will be clothed with desolation,
And the hands of the common people will
tremble.
I will do to them according to their way,
And according to what they deserve I will
judge them;
Then they shall know that I *am* the LORD!' "

ABOMINATIONS IN THE TEMPLE

8And it came to pass in the sixth year, in the sixth *month,* on the fifth *day* of the month, as I sat in my house with the elders of Judah sitting before me, that the hand of the Lord GOD fell upon me there. ²Then I looked, and there was a likeness, like the appearance of fire—from the appearance of His waist and downward, fire; and from His waist and upward, like the appearance of brightness, like the color of amber. ³He stretched out the form of a hand, and took me by a lock of my hair; and the Spirit lifted me up between earth and heaven, and brought me in visions of God to Jerusalem, to the door of the north gate of the inner *court,* where the seat of the image of jealousy *was,* which provokes to jealousy. ⁴And behold, the glory of the God of Israel *was* there, like the vision that I saw in the plain.

⁵Then He said to me, "Son of man, lift your eyes now toward the north." So I lifted my eyes toward the north, and there, north of the altar gate, was this image of jealousy in the entrance.

⁶Furthermore He said to me, "Son of man, do you see what they are doing, the great abominations that the house of Israel commits here, to make Me go far away from My sanctuary? Now turn again, you will see greater abominations." ⁷So He brought me to the door of the court; and when I looked, there was a hole in the wall. ⁸Then He said to me, "Son of man, dig into the wall"; and when I dug into the wall, there was a door.

⁹And He said to me, "Go in, and see the wicked abominations which they are doing there." ¹⁰So I went in and saw, and there—every sort of creeping thing, abominable beasts, and all the idols of the house of Israel, portrayed all

around on the walls. ¹¹And there stood before them seventy men of the elders of the house of Israel, and in their midst stood Jaazaniah the son of Shaphan. Each man had a censer in his hand, and a thick cloud of incense went up. ¹²Then He said to me, "Son of man, have you seen what the elders of the house of Israel do in the dark, every man in the room of his idols? For they say, 'The LORD does not see us, the LORD has forsaken the land.' "

¹³And He said to me, "Turn again, *and* you will see greater abominations that they are doing." ¹⁴So He brought me to the door of the north gate of the LORD's house; and to my dismay, women were sitting there weeping for Tammuz.

¹⁵Then He said to me, "Have you seen *this,* O son of man? Turn again, you will see greater abominations than these." ¹⁶So He brought me into the inner court of the LORD's house; and there, at the door of the temple of the LORD, between the porch and the altar, *were* about twenty-five men with their backs toward the temple of the LORD and their faces toward the east, and they were worshiping the sun toward the east.

¹⁷And He said to me, "Have you seen *this,* O son of man? Is it a trivial thing to the house of Judah to commit the abominations which they commit here? For they have filled the land with violence; then they have returned to provoke Me to anger. Indeed they put the branch to their nose. ¹⁸Therefore I also will act in fury. My eye will not spare nor will I have pity; and though they cry in My ears with a loud voice, I will not hear them."

The Wicked Are Slain

9 Then He called out in my hearing with a loud voice, saying, "Let those who have charge over the city draw near, each *with* a deadly weapon in his hand." ²And suddenly six men came from the direction of the upper gate, which faces north, each with his battle-ax in his hand. One man among them *was* clothed with linen and had a writer's inkhorn at his side. They went in and stood beside the bronze altar.

³Now the glory of the God of Israel had gone up from the cherub, where it had been, to the threshold of the temple.ᵃ And He called to the man clothed with linen, who *had* the writer's

inkhorn at his side; ⁴and the LORD said to him, "Go through the midst of the city, through the midst of Jerusalem, and put a mark on the foreheads of the men who sigh and cry over all the abominations that are done within it."

⁵To the others He said in my hearing, "Go after him through the city and kill; do not let your eye spare, nor have any pity. ⁶Utterly slay old *and* young men, maidens and little children and women; but do not come near anyone on whom *is* the mark; and begin at My sanctuary." So they began with the elders who *were* before the temple. ⁷Then He said to them, "Defile the temple, and fill the courts with the slain. Go out!" And they went out and killed in the city.

⁸So it was, that while they were killing them, I was left *alone;* and I fell on my face and cried out, and said, "Ah, Lord GOD! Will You destroy all the remnant of Israel in pouring out Your fury on Jerusalem?"

⁹Then He said to me, "The iniquity of the house of Israel and Judah *is* exceedingly great, and the land is full of bloodshed, and the city full of perversity; for they say, 'The LORD has forsaken the land, and the LORD does not see!' ¹⁰And as for Me also, My eye will neither spare, nor will I have pity, *but* I will recompense their deeds on their own head."

¹¹Just then, the man clothed with linen, who *had* the inkhorn at his side, reported back and said, "I have done as You commanded me."

The Glory Departs from the Temple

10 And I looked, and there in the firmament that was above the head of the cherubim, there appeared something like a sapphire stone, having the appearance of the likeness of a throne. ²Then He spoke to the man clothed with linen, and said, "Go in among the wheels, under the cherub, fill your hands with coals of fire from among the cherubim, and scatter *them* over the city." And he went in as I watched.

³Now the cherubim were standing on the south side of the templeᵃ when the man went in, and the cloud filled the inner court. ⁴Then the glory of the LORD went up from the cherub, *and paused* over the threshold of the temple; and the house was filled with the cloud, and the court was

9:3 ᵃLiterally *house* **10:3** ᵃLiterally *house,* also in verses 4 and 18

full of the brightness of the LORD's glory. ⁵And the sound of the wings of the cherubim was heard *even* in the outer court, like the voice of Almighty God when He speaks.

⁶Then it happened, when He commanded the man clothed in linen, saying, "Take fire from among the wheels, from among the cherubim," that he went in and stood beside the wheels. ⁷And the cherub stretched out his hand from among the cherubim to the fire that *was* among the cherubim, and took *some of it* and put *it* into the hands of the *man* clothed with linen, who took *it* and went out. ⁸The cherubim appeared to have the form of a man's hand under their wings.

⁹And when I looked, there were four wheels by the cherubim, one wheel by one cherub and another wheel by each other cherub; the wheels appeared *to have* the color of a beryl stone. ¹⁰*As for* their appearance, all four looked alike—as it were, a wheel in the middle of a wheel. ¹¹When they went, they went toward *any of* their four directions; they did not turn aside when they went, but followed in the direction the head was facing. They did not turn aside when they went. ¹²And their whole body, with their back, their hands, their wings, and the wheels that the four had, *were* full of eyes all around. ¹³As for the wheels, they were called in my hearing, "Wheel."

¹⁴Each one had four faces: the first face *was* the face of a cherub, the second face the face of a man, the third the face of a lion, and the fourth the face of an eagle. ¹⁵And the cherubim were lifted up. This *was* the living creature I saw by the River Chebar. ¹⁶When the cherubim went, the wheels went beside them; and when the cherubim lifted their wings to mount up from the earth, the same wheels also did not turn from beside them. ¹⁷When *the cherubim*ᵃ stood still, *the wheels* stood still, and when *one*ᵇ was lifted up, *the other*ᶜ lifted itself up, for the spirit of the living creature *was* in them.

¹⁸Then the glory of the LORD departed from the threshold of the temple and stood over the cherubim. ¹⁹And the cherubim lifted their wings and mounted up from the earth in my sight. When they went out, the wheels *were* beside them; and they stood at the door of the east gate of the LORD's house, and the glory of the God of Israel *was* above them.

²⁰This *is* the living creature I saw under the God of Israel by the River Chebar, and I knew they *were* cherubim. ²¹Each one had four faces and each one four wings, and the likeness of the hands of a man *was* under their wings. ²²And the likeness of their faces *was* the same *as* the faces which I had seen by the River Chebar, their appearance and their persons. They each went straight forward.

JUDGMENT ON WICKED COUNSELORS

11 Then the Spirit lifted me up and brought me to the East Gate of the LORD's house, which faces eastward; and there at the door of the gate were twenty-five men, among whom I saw Jaazaniah the son of Azzur, and Pelatiah the son of Benaiah, princes of the people. ²And He said to me: "Son of man, these *are* the men who devise iniquity and give wicked counsel in this city, ³who say, 'The time is not near to build houses; this *city is* the caldron, and we *are* the meat.' ⁴Therefore prophesy against them, prophesy, O son of man!"

⁵Then the Spirit of the LORD fell upon me, and said to me, "Speak! 'Thus says the LORD: "Thus you have said, O house of Israel; for I know the things that come into your mind. ⁶You have multiplied your slain in this city, and you have filled its streets with the slain." ⁷Therefore thus says the Lord GOD: "Your slain whom you have laid in its midst, they *are* the meat, and this *city is* the caldron; but I shall bring you out of the midst of it. ⁸You have feared the sword; and I will bring a sword upon you," says the Lord GOD. ⁹"And I will bring you out of its midst, and deliver you into the hands of strangers, and execute judgments on you. ¹⁰You shall fall by the sword. I will judge you at the border of Israel. Then you shall know that I *am* the LORD. ¹¹This *city* shall not be your caldron, nor shall you be the meat in its midst. I will judge you at the border of Israel. ¹²And you shall know that I *am* the LORD; for you have not walked in My statutes nor executed My judgments, but have done according to the customs of the Gentiles which *are* all around you.' " "

¹³Now it happened, while I was prophesying, that Pelatiah the son of Benaiah died. Then I fell

10:17 ªLiterally *they* ᵇLiterally *they* ᶜLiterally *they*

on my face and cried with a loud voice, and said, "Ah, Lord GOD! Will You make a complete end of the remnant of Israel?"

GOD WILL RESTORE ISRAEL

[14]Again the word of the LORD came to me, saying, [15]"Son of man, your brethren, your relatives, your countrymen, and all the house of Israel in its entirety, *are* those about whom the inhabitants of Jerusalem have said, 'Get far away from the LORD; this land has been given to us as a possession.' [16]Therefore say, 'Thus says the Lord GOD: "Although I have cast them far off among the Gentiles, and although I have scattered them among the countries, yet I shall be a little sanctuary for them in the countries where they have gone." ' [17]Therefore say, 'Thus says the Lord GOD: "I will gather you from the peoples, assemble you from the countries where you have been scattered, and I will give you the land of Israel." ' [18]And they will go there, and they will take away all its detestable things and all its abominations from there. [19]Then I will give them one heart, and I will put a new spirit within them,[a] and take the stony heart out of their flesh, and give them a heart of flesh, [20]that they may walk in My statutes and keep My judgments and do them; and they shall be My people, and I will be their God. [21]But *as for those* whose hearts follow the desire for their detestable things and their abominations, I will recompense their deeds on their own heads," says the Lord GOD.

[22]So the cherubim lifted up their wings, with the wheels beside them, and the glory of the God of Israel *was* high above them. [23]And the glory of the LORD went up from the midst of the city and stood on the mountain, which *is* on the east side of the city.

[24]Then the Spirit took me up and brought me in a vision by the Spirit of God into Chaldea,[a] to those in captivity. And the vision that I had seen went up from me. [25]So I spoke to those in captivity of all the things the LORD had shown me.

JUDAH'S CAPTIVITY PORTRAYED

12 Now the word of the LORD came to me, saying: [2]"Son of man, you dwell in the midst of a rebellious house, which has eyes to see but does not see, and ears to hear but does not hear; for they *are* a rebellious house.

[3]"Therefore, son of man, prepare your belongings for captivity, and go into captivity by day in their sight. You shall go from your place into captivity to another place in their sight. It may be that they will consider, though they *are* a rebellious house. [4]By day you shall bring out your belongings in their sight, as though going into captivity; and at evening you shall go in their sight, like those who go into captivity. [5]Dig through the wall in their sight, and carry *your belongings* out through it. [6]In their sight you shall bear *them* on *your* shoulders *and* carry *them* out at twilight; you shall cover your face, so that you cannot see the ground, for I have made you a sign to the house of Israel."

[7]So I did as I was commanded. I brought out my belongings by day, as though going into captivity, and at evening I dug through the wall with my hand. I brought *them* out at twilight, *and* I bore *them* on *my* shoulder in their sight.

[8]And in the morning the word of the LORD came to me, saying, [9]"Son of man, has not the house of Israel, the rebellious house, said to you, 'What are you doing?' [10]Say to them, 'Thus says the Lord GOD: "This burden *concerns* the prince in Jerusalem and all the house of Israel who are among them." ' [11]Say, 'I *am* a sign to you. As I have done, so shall it be done to them; they shall be carried away into captivity.' [12]And the prince who *is* among them shall bear *his belongings* on *his* shoulder at twilight and go out. They shall dig through the wall to carry *them* out through it. He shall cover his face, so that he cannot see the ground with *his* eyes. [13]I will also spread My net over him, and he shall be caught in My snare. I will bring him to Babylon, *to* the land of the Chaldeans; yet he shall not see it, though he shall die there. [14]I will scatter to every wind all who *are* around him to help him, and all his troops; and I will draw out the sword after them.

[15]"Then they shall know that I *am* the LORD, when I scatter them among the nations and disperse them throughout the countries. [16]But I will spare a few of their men from the sword, from famine, and from pestilence, that they may declare

11:19 [a]Literally *you*   **11:24** [a]Or *Babylon,* and so elsewhere in this book all their abominations among the Gentiles wherever they go. Then they shall know that I *am* the LORD."

JUDGMENT NOT POSTPONED

17Moreover the word of the LORD came to me, saying, 18"Son of man, eat your bread with quaking, and drink your water with trembling and anxiety. 19And say to the people of the land, 'Thus says the Lord GOD to the inhabitants of Jerusalem *and* to the land of Israel: "They shall eat their bread with anxiety, and drink their water with dread, so that her land may be emptied of all who are in it, because of the violence of all those who dwell in it. 20Then the cities that are inhabited shall be laid waste, and the land shall become desolate; and you shall know that I *am* the LORD." ' "

21And the word of the LORD came to me, saying, 22"Son of man, what *is* this proverb *that* you *people* have about the land of Israel, which says, 'The days are prolonged, and every vision fails'? 23Tell them therefore, 'Thus says the Lord GOD: "I will lay this proverb to rest, and they shall no more use it as a proverb in Israel." ' But say to them, ' "The days are at hand, and the fulfillment of every vision. 24For no more shall there be any false vision or flattering divination within the house of Israel. 25For I *am* the LORD. I speak, and the word which I speak will come to pass; it will no more be postponed; for in your days, O rebellious house, I will say the word and perform it," says the Lord GOD.' "

26Again the word of the LORD came to me, saying, 27"Son of man, look, the house of Israel is saying, 'The vision that he sees *is* for many days *from now,* and he prophesies of times far off.' 28Therefore say to them, 'Thus says the Lord GOD: "None of My words will be postponed any more, but the word which I speak will be done," says the Lord GOD.' "

WOE TO FOOLISH PROPHETS

13 And the word of the LORD came to me, saying, 2"Son of man, prophesy against the prophets of Israel who prophesy, and say to those who prophesy out of their own heart, 'Hear the word of the LORD!' "

3Thus says the Lord GOD: "Woe to the foolish prophets, who follow their own spirit and have seen nothing! 4O Israel, your prophets are like foxes in the deserts. 5You have not gone up into the gaps to build a wall for the house of Israel to stand in battle on the day of the LORD. 6They have envisioned futility and false divination, saying, 'Thus says the LORD!' But the LORD has not sent them; yet they hope that the word may be confirmed. 7Have you not seen a futile vision, and have you not spoken false divination? You say, 'The LORD says,' but I have not spoken."

8Therefore thus says the Lord GOD: "Because you have spoken nonsense and envisioned lies, therefore I *am* indeed against you," says the Lord GOD. 9"My hand will be against the prophets who envision futility and who divine lies; they shall not be in the assembly of My people, nor be written in the record of the house of Israel, nor shall they enter into the land of Israel. Then you shall know that I *am* the Lord GOD.

10"Because, indeed, because they have seduced My people, saying, 'Peace!' when *there is* no peace—and one builds a wall, and they plaster it with untempered *mortar*— 11say to those who plaster *it* with untempered *mortar,* that it will fall. There will be flooding rain, and you, O great hailstones, shall fall; and a stormy wind shall tear *it* down. 12Surely, when the wall has fallen, will it not be said to you, 'Where *is* the mortar with which you plastered *it?* "

13Therefore thus says the Lord GOD: "I will cause a stormy wind to break forth in My fury; and there shall be a flooding rain in My anger, and great hailstones in fury to consume *it.* 14So I will break down the wall you have plastered with untempered *mortar,* and bring it down to the ground, so that its foundation will be uncovered; it will fall, and you shall be consumed in the midst of it. Then you shall know that I *am* the LORD.

15"Thus will I accomplish My wrath on the wall and on those who have plastered it with untempered *mortar;* and I will say to you, 'The wall *is* no *more,* nor those who plastered it, 16*that is,* the prophets of Israel who prophesy concerning Jerusalem, and who see visions of peace for her when *there is* no peace,' " says the Lord GOD.

17"Likewise, son of man, set your face against the daughters of your people, who prophesy out of their own heart; prophesy against them, [18]and say, 'Thus says the Lord GOD: "Woe to the *women* who sew *magic* charms on their sleeves[a] and make veils for the heads of people of every height to hunt souls! Will you hunt the souls of My people, and keep yourselves alive? [19]And will you profane Me among My people for handfuls of barley and for pieces of bread, killing people who should not die, and keeping people alive who should not live, by your lying to My people who listen to lies?"

[20]Therefore thus says the Lord GOD: "Behold, I *am* against your *magic* charms by which you hunt souls there like birds. I will tear them from your arms, and let the souls go, the souls you hunt like birds. [21]I will also tear off your veils and deliver My people out of your hand, and they shall no longer be as prey in your hand. Then you shall know that I *am* the LORD.

[22]"Because with lies you have made the heart of the righteous sad, whom I have not made sad; and you have strengthened the hands of the wicked, so that he does not turn from his wicked way to save his life. [23]Therefore you shall no longer envision futility nor practice divination; for I will deliver My people out of your hand, and you shall know that I *am* the LORD."'"

Idolatry Will Be Punished

14 Now some of the elders of Israel came to me and sat before me. [2]And the word of the LORD came to me, saying, [3]"Son of man, these men have set up their idols in their hearts, and put before them that which causes them to stumble into iniquity. Should I let Myself be inquired of at all by them?

[4]"Therefore speak to them, and say to them, 'Thus says the Lord GOD: "Everyone of the house of Israel who sets up his idols in his heart, and puts before him what causes him to stumble into iniquity, and then comes to the prophet, I the LORD will answer him who comes, according to the multitude of his idols, [5]that I may seize the house of Israel by their heart, because they are all estranged from Me by their idols."'

[6]"Therefore say to the house of Israel, 'Thus says the Lord GOD: "Repent, turn away from your idols, and turn your faces away from all your abominations. [7]For anyone of the house of Israel, or of the strangers who dwell in Israel, who sepa-

rates himself from Me and sets up his idols in his heart and puts before him what causes him to stumble into iniquity, then comes to a prophet to inquire of him concerning Me, I the LORD will answer him by Myself. [8]I will set My face against that man and make him a sign and a proverb, and I will cut him off from the midst of My people. Then you shall know that I *am* the LORD.

[9]"And if the prophet is induced to speak anything, I the LORD have induced that prophet, and I will stretch out My hand against him and destroy him from among My people Israel. [10]And they shall bear their iniquity; the punishment of the prophet shall be the same as the punishment of the one who inquired, [11]that the house of Israel may no longer stray from Me, nor be profaned anymore with all their transgressions, but that they may be My people and I may be their God," says the Lord GOD.'"

Judgment on Persistent Unfaithfulness

[12]The word of the LORD came again to me, saying: [13]"Son of man, when a land sins against Me by persistent unfaithfulness, I will stretch out My hand against it; I will cut off its supply of bread, send famine on it, and cut off man and beast from it. [14]Even *if* these three men, Noah, Daniel, and Job, were in it, they would deliver *only* themselves by their righteousness," says the Lord GOD.

[15]"If I cause wild beasts to pass through the land, and they empty it, and make it so desolate that no man may pass through because of the beasts, [16]*even though* these three men *were* in it, *as* I live," says the Lord GOD, "they would deliver neither sons nor daughters; only they would be delivered, and the land would be desolate.

[17]"Or *if* I bring a sword on that land, and say, 'Sword, go through the land,' and I cut off man and beast from it, [18]*even though* these three men *were* in it, *as* I live," says the Lord GOD, "they would deliver neither sons nor daughters, but only they themselves would be delivered.

[19]"Or *if* I send a pestilence into that land and pour out My fury on it in blood, and cut off from it man and beast, [20]*even though* Noah, Daniel, and

13:18 [a]Literally *over all the joints of My hands;* Vulgate reads *under every elbow;* Septuagint and Targum read *on all elbows of the hands.*

Job *were* in it, *as* I live," says the Lord GOD, "they would deliver neither son nor daughter; they would deliver *only* themselves by their righteousness."

²¹For thus says the Lord GOD: "How much more it shall be when I send My four severe judgments on Jerusalem—the sword and famine and wild beasts and pestilence—to cut off man and beast from it? ²²Yet behold, there shall be left in it a remnant who will be brought out, *both* sons and daughters; surely they will come out to you, and you will see their ways and their doings. Then you will be comforted concerning the disaster that I have brought upon Jerusalem, all that I have brought upon it. ²³And they will comfort you, when you see their ways and their doings; and you shall know that I have done nothing without cause that I have done in it," says the Lord GOD.

The Outcast Vine

15 Then the word of the LORD came to me, saying: ²"Son of man, how is the wood of the vine *better* than any other wood, the vine branch which is among the trees of the forest? ³Is wood taken from it to make any object? Or can *men* make a peg from it to hang any vessel on? ⁴Instead, it is thrown into the fire for fuel; the fire devours both ends of it, and its middle is burned. Is it useful for *any* work? ⁵Indeed, when it was whole, no object could be made from it. How much less will it be useful for *any* work when the fire has devoured it, and it is burned?

⁶"Therefore thus says the Lord GOD: 'Like the wood of the vine among the trees of the forest, which I have given to the fire for fuel, so I will give up the inhabitants of Jerusalem; ⁷and I will set My face against them. They will go out from *one* fire, but *another* fire shall devour them. Then you shall know that I *am* the LORD, when I set My face against them. ⁸Thus I will make the land desolate, because they have persisted in unfaithfulness,' says the Lord GOD."

God's Love for Jerusalem

16 Again the word of the LORD came to me, saying, ²"Son of man, cause Jerusalem to know her abominations, ³and say, 'Thus says the Lord GOD to Jerusalem: "Your birth and your nativity *are* from the land of Canaan; your father *was*

an Amorite and your mother a Hittite. ⁴*As for* your nativity, on the day you were born your navel cord was not cut, nor were you washed in water to cleanse *you;* you were not rubbed with salt nor wrapped in swaddling cloths. ⁵No eye pitied you, to do any of these things for you, to have compassion on you; but you were thrown out into the open field, when you yourself were loathed on the day you were born.

⁶"And when I passed by you and saw you struggling in your own blood, I said to you in your blood, 'Live!' Yes, I said to you in your blood, 'Live!' ⁷I made you thrive like a plant in the field; and you grew, matured, and became very beautiful. *Your* breasts were formed, your hair grew, but you *were* naked and bare.

⁸"When I passed by you again and looked upon you, indeed your time *was* the time of love; so I spread My wing over you and covered your nakedness. Yes, I swore an oath to you and entered into a covenant with you, and you became Mine," says the Lord GOD.

⁹"Then I washed you in water; yes, I thoroughly washed off your blood, and I anointed you with oil. ¹⁰I clothed you in embroidered cloth and gave you sandals of badger skin; I clothed you with fine linen and covered you with silk. ¹¹I adorned you with ornaments, put bracelets on your wrists, and a chain on your neck. ¹²And I put a jewel in your nose, earrings in your ears, and a beautiful crown on your head. ¹³Thus you were adorned with gold and silver, and your clothing *was of* fine linen, silk, and embroidered cloth. You ate *pastry of* fine flour, honey, and oil. You were exceedingly beautiful, and succeeded to royalty. ¹⁴Your fame went out among the nations because of your beauty, for it *was* perfect through My splendor which I had bestowed on you," says the Lord GOD.

Jerusalem's Harlotry

¹⁵"But you trusted in your own beauty, played the harlot because of your fame, and poured out your harlotry on everyone passing by who *would have* it. ¹⁶You took some of your garments and adorned multicolored high places for yourself, and played the harlot on them. *Such* things should not happen, nor be. ¹⁷You have also taken your beautiful jewelry from My gold and My silver,

which I had given you, and made for yourself male images and played the harlot with them. [18]You took your embroidered garments and covered them, and you set My oil and My incense before them. [19]Also My food which I gave you—the pastry of fine flour, oil, and honey *which* I fed you—you set it before them as sweet incense; and *so* it was," says the Lord GOD.

[20]"Moreover you took your sons and your daughters, whom you bore to Me, and these you sacrificed to them to be devoured. *Were* your *acts* of harlotry a small matter, [21]that you have slain My children and offered them up to them by causing them to pass through *the fire?* [22]And in all your abominations and acts of harlotry you did not remember the days of your youth, when you were naked and bare, struggling in your blood.

[23]"Then it was so, after all your wickedness—'Woe, woe to you!' says the Lord GOD— [24]*that* you also built for yourself a shrine, and made a high place for yourself in every street. [25]You built your high places at the head of every road, and made your beauty to be abhorred. You offered yourself to everyone who passed by, and multiplied your acts of harlotry. [26]You also committed harlotry with the Egyptians, your very fleshly neighbors, and increased your acts of harlotry to provoke Me to anger.

[27]"Behold, therefore, I stretched out My hand against you, diminished your allotment, and gave you up to the will of those who hate you, the daughters of the Philistines, who were ashamed of your lewd behavior. [28]You also played the harlot with the Assyrians, because you were insatiable; indeed you played the harlot with them and still were not satisfied. [29]Moreover you multiplied your acts of harlotry as far as the land of the trader, Chaldea; and even then you were not satisfied.

[30]"How degenerate is your heart!" says the Lord GOD, "seeing you do all these *things,* the deeds of a brazen harlot.

JERUSALEM'S ADULTERY

[31]"You erected your shrine at the head of every road, and built your high place in every street. Yet you were not like a harlot, because you scorned payment. [32]*You are* an adulterous wife, *who* takes strangers instead of her husband. [33]Men

make payment to all harlots, but you made your payments to all your lovers, and hired them to come to you from all around for your harlotry. [34]You are the opposite of *other* women in your harlotry, because no one solicited you to be a harlot. In that you gave payment but no payment was given you, therefore you are the opposite."

JERUSALEM'S LOVERS WILL ABUSE HER

[35]"Now then, O harlot, hear the word of the LORD! [36]Thus says the Lord GOD: "Because your filthiness was poured out and your nakedness uncovered in your harlotry with your lovers, and with all your abominable idols, and because of the blood of your children which you gave to them, [37]surely, therefore, I will gather all your lovers with whom you took pleasure, all those you loved, *and* all those you hated; I will gather them from all around against you and will uncover your nakedness to them, that they may see all your nakedness. [38]And I will judge you as women who break wedlock or shed blood are judged; I will bring blood upon you in fury and jealousy. [39]I will also give you into their hand, and they shall throw down your shrines and break down your high places. They shall also strip you of your clothes, take your beautiful jewelry, and leave you naked and bare.

[40]"They shall also bring up an assembly against you, and they shall stone you with stones and thrust you through with their swords. [41]They shall burn your houses with fire, and execute judgments on you in the sight of many women; and I will make you cease playing the harlot, and you shall no longer hire lovers. [42]So I will lay to rest My fury toward you, and My jealousy shall depart from you. I will be quiet, and be angry no more. [43]Because you did not remember the days of your youth, but agitated Me[a] with all these *things,* surely I will also recompense your deeds on *your own* head," says the Lord GOD. "And you shall not commit lewdness in addition to all your abominations.

MORE WICKED THAN SAMARIA AND SODOM

[44]"Indeed everyone who quotes proverbs will use *this* proverb against you: 'Like mother, like

16:43 [a]Following Septuagint, Syriac, Targum, and Vulgate; Masoretic Text reads *were agitated with Me.*

daughter!' ⁴⁵You *are* your mother's daughter, loathing husband and children; and you *are* the sister of your sisters, who loathed their husbands and children; your mother *was* a Hittite and your father an Amorite.

⁴⁶"Your elder sister *is* Samaria, who dwells with her daughters to the north of you; and your younger sister, who dwells to the south of you, *is* Sodom and her daughters. ⁴⁷You did not walk in their ways nor act according to their abominations; but, as *if that were* too little, you became more corrupt than they in all your ways.

⁴⁸"*As* I live," says the Lord GOD, "neither your sister Sodom nor her daughters have done as you and your daughters have done. ⁴⁹Look, this was the iniquity of your sister Sodom: She and her daughter had pride, fullness of food, and abundance of idleness; neither did she strengthen the hand of the poor and needy. ⁵⁰And they were haughty and committed abomination before Me; therefore I took them away as I saw *fit*.ᵃ

⁵¹"Samaria did not commit half of your sins; but you have multiplied your abominations more than they, and have justified your sisters by all the abominations which you have done. ⁵²You who judged your sisters, bear your own shame also, because the sins which you committed were more abominable than theirs; they are more righteous than you. Yes, be disgraced also, and bear your own shame, because you justified your sisters.

⁵³"When I bring back their captives, the captives of Sodom and her daughters, and the captives of Samaria and her daughters, then *I will also bring back* the captives of your captivity among them, ⁵⁴that you may bear your own shame and be disgraced by all that you did when you comforted them. ⁵⁵When your sisters, Sodom and her daughters, return to their former state, and Samaria and her daughters return to their former state, then you and your daughters will return to your former state. ⁵⁶For your sister Sodom was not a byword in your mouth in the days of your pride, ⁵⁷before your wickedness was uncovered. It was like the time of the reproach of the daughters of Syriaᵃ and all *those* around her, and of the daughters of the Philistines, who despise you everywhere. ⁵⁸You have paid for your lewdness and your abominations," says the LORD. ⁵⁹For thus says the Lord GOD: "I will deal with you as you have done, who despised the oath by breaking the covenant.

An Everlasting Covenant

⁶⁰"Nevertheless I will remember My covenant with you in the days of your youth, and I will establish an everlasting covenant with you. ⁶¹Then you will remember your ways and be ashamed, when you receive your older and your younger sisters; for I will give them to you for daughters, but not because of My covenant with you. ⁶²And I will establish My covenant with you. Then you shall know that I *am* the LORD, ⁶³that you may remember and be ashamed, and never open your mouth anymore because of your shame, when I provide you an atonement for all you have done," says the Lord GOD.' "

The Eagles and the Vine

17 And the word of the LORD came to me, saying, ²"Son of man, pose a riddle, and speak a parable to the house of Israel, ³and say, 'Thus says the Lord GOD:

" A great eagle with large wings and long
     pinions,
   Full of feathers of various colors,
   Came to Lebanon
   And took from the cedar the highest
     branch.
⁴He cropped off its topmost young twig
   And carried it to a land of trade;
   He set it in a city of merchants.
⁵Then he took some of the seed of the
     land
   And planted it in a fertile field;
   He placed *it* by abundant waters
   And set it like a willow tree.
⁶And it grew and became a spreading vine of
     low stature;
   Its branches turned toward him,
   But its roots were under it.
   So it became a vine,
   Brought forth branches,
   And put forth shoots.

16:50 ᵃVulgate reads *you saw*; Septuagint reads *he saw*; Targum reads *as was revealed to Me.*   **16:57** ᵃFollowing Masoretic Text, Septuagint, Targum, and Vulgate; many Hebrew manuscripts and Syriac read *Edom.*

[7]"But there was another[a] great eagle with large
    wings and many feathers;
And behold, this vine bent its roots toward
    him,
And stretched its branches toward him,
From the garden terrace where it had been
    planted,
That he might water it.
[8]It was planted in good soil by many waters,
To bring forth branches, bear fruit,
And become a majestic vine." '

[9]"Say, 'Thus says the Lord GOD:

"Will it thrive?
Will he not pull up its roots,
Cut off its fruit,
And leave it to wither?
All of its spring leaves will wither,
And no great power or many people
Will be needed to pluck it up by its roots.
[10]Behold, *it is* planted,
Will it thrive?
Will it not utterly wither when the east wind
    touches it?
It will wither in the garden terrace where it
    grew." ' "

[11]Moreover the word of the LORD came to
me, saying, [12]"Say now to the rebellious house:
'Do you not know what these *things mean?*' Tell
them, 'Indeed the king of Babylon went to
Jerusalem and took its king and princes, and led
them with him to Babylon. [13]And he took the
king's offspring, made a covenant with him, and
put him under oath. He also took away the
mighty of the land, [14]that the kingdom might be
brought low and not lift itself up, *but* that by
keeping his covenant it might stand. [15]But he rebelled against him by sending his ambassadors to
Egypt, that they might give him horses and many
people. Will he prosper? Will he who does such
things escape? Can he break a covenant and still be
delivered?

[16]'*As* I live,' says the Lord GOD, 'surely in the
place *where* the king *dwells* who made him king,
whose oath he despised and whose covenant he
broke—with him in the midst of Babylon he shall
die. [17]Nor will Pharaoh with *his* mighty army and

great company do anything in the war, when they
heap up a siege mound and build a wall to cut off
many persons. [18]Since he despised the oath by
breaking the covenant, and in fact gave his hand
and still did all these *things,* he shall not escape.' "

[19]Therefore thus says the Lord GOD: "*As* I live,
surely My oath which he despised, and My
covenant which he broke, I will recompense on
his own head. [20]I will spread My net over him, and
he shall be taken in My snare. I will bring him to
Babylon and try him there for the treason which
he committed against Me. [21]All his fugitives[a] with
all his troops shall fall by the sword, and those who
remain shall be scattered to every wind; and you
shall know that I, the LORD, have spoken."

ISRAEL EXALTED AT LAST

[22]Thus says the Lord GOD: "I will take also
one of the highest branches of the high cedar and
set *it* out. I will crop off from the topmost of its
young twigs a tender one, and will plant *it* on a
high and prominent mountain. [23]On the mountain height of Israel I will plant it; and it will
bring forth boughs, and bear fruit, and be a majestic cedar. Under it will dwell birds of every
sort; in the shadow of its branches they will dwell.
[24]And all the trees of the field shall know that I,
the LORD, have brought down the high tree and
exalted the low tree, dried up the green tree and
made the dry tree flourish; I, the LORD, have spoken and have done *it.*"

A FALSE PROVERB REFUTED

18 The word of the LORD came to me again,
saying, [2]"What do you mean when you use
this proverb concerning the land of Israel, saying:

'The fathers have eaten sour grapes,
And the children's teeth are set on edge'?

[3]"*As* I live," says the Lord GOD, "you shall no
longer use this proverb in Israel.

[4]"Behold, all souls are Mine;
The soul of the father

17:7 [a]Following Septuagint, Syriac, and Vulgate; Masoretic Text and
Targum read *one*.   17:21 [a]Following Masoretic Text and Vulgate;
many Hebrew manuscripts and Syriac read *choice men;* Targum
reads *mighty men;* Septuagint omits *All his fugitives.*

As well as the soul of the son is Mine;
  The soul who sins shall die.
⁵But if a man is just
  And does what is lawful and right;
⁶If he has not eaten on the mountains,
  Nor lifted up his eyes to the idols of the
      house of Israel,
  Nor defiled his neighbor's wife,
  Nor approached a woman during her
      impurity;
⁷If he has not oppressed anyone,
  But has restored to the debtor his pledge;
  Has robbed no one by violence,
  But has given his bread to the hungry
  And covered the naked with clothing;
⁸If he has not exacted usury
  Nor taken any increase,
  But has withdrawn his hand from iniquity
  And executed true judgment between man
      and man;
⁹*If* he has walked in My statutes
  And kept My judgments faithfully—
  He *is* just;
  He shall surely live!"
Says the Lord GOD.

¹⁰"If he begets a son *who is* a robber
  Or a shedder of blood,
  Who does any of these *things*
¹¹And does none of those *duties,*
  But has eaten on the mountains
  Or defiled his neighbor's wife;
¹²If he has oppressed the poor and needy,
  Robbed by violence,
  Not restored the pledge,
  Lifted his eyes to the idols,
  Or committed abomination;
¹³If he has exacted usury
  Or taken increase—
  Shall he then live?
  He shall not live!
  If he has done any of these abominations,
  He shall surely die;
  His blood shall be upon him.

¹⁴"*If,* however, he begets a son
  Who sees all the sins which his father has
      done,
  And considers but does not do likewise;

¹⁵*Who* has not eaten on the mountains,
  Nor lifted his eyes to the idols of the house of
      Israel,
  Nor defiled his neighbor's wife;
¹⁶Has not oppressed anyone,
  Nor withheld a pledge,
  Nor robbed by violence,
  But has given his bread to the hungry
  And covered the naked with clothing;
¹⁷*Who* has withdrawn his hand from the poorᵃ
  And not received usury or increase,
  But has executed My judgments
  And walked in My statutes—
  He shall not die for the iniquity of his father;
  He shall surely live!

¹⁸"*As for* his father,
  Because he cruelly oppressed,
  Robbed his brother by violence,
  And did what *is* not good among his people,
  Behold, he shall die for his iniquity.

TURN AND LIVE

¹⁹"Yet you say, 'Why should the son not bear the guilt of the father?' Because the son has done what is lawful and right, and has kept all My statutes and observed them, he shall surely live. ²⁰The soul who sins shall die. The son shall not bear the guilt of the father, nor the father bear the guilt of the son. The righteousness of the righteous shall be upon himself, and the wickedness of the wicked shall be upon himself.

²¹"But if a wicked man turns from all his sins which he has committed, keeps all My statutes, and does what is lawful and right, he shall surely live; he shall not die. ²²None of the transgressions which he has committed shall be remembered against him; because of the righteousness which he has done, he shall live. ²³Do I have any pleasure at all that the wicked should die?" says the Lord GOD, "*and* not that he should turn from his ways and live?

²⁴"But when a righteous man turns away from his righteousness and commits iniquity, and does according to all the abominations that the wicked *man* does, shall he live? All the righteousness which he has done shall not be remembered;

18:17 ᵃFollowing Masoretic Text, Targum, and Vulgate; Septuagint reads *iniquity* (compare verse 8).

because of the unfaithfulness of which he is guilty and the sin which he has committed, because of them he shall die.

25"Yet you say, 'The way of the Lord is not fair.' Hear now, O house of Israel, is it not My way which is fair, and your ways which are not fair? 26When a righteous *man* turns away from his righteousness, commits iniquity, and dies in it, it is because of the iniquity which he has done that he dies. 27Again, when a wicked *man* turns away from the wickedness which he committed, and does what is lawful and right, he preserves himself alive. 28Because he considers and turns away from all the transgressions which he committed, he shall surely live; he shall not die. 29Yet the house of Israel says, 'The way of the Lord is not fair.' O house of Israel, is it not My ways which are fair, and your ways which are not fair?

30"Therefore I will judge you, O house of Israel, every one according to his ways," says the Lord GOD. "Repent, and turn from all your transgressions, so that iniquity will not be your ruin. 31Cast away from you all the transgressions which you have committed, and get yourselves a new heart and a new spirit. For why should you die, O house of Israel? 32For I have no pleasure in the death of one who dies," says the Lord GOD. "Therefore turn and live!"

ISRAEL DEGRADED

19 "Moreover take up a lamentation for the princes of Israel, 2and say:

'What *is* your mother? A lioness:
  She lay down among the lions;
  Among the young lions she nourished her
    cubs.
3She brought up one of her cubs,
  And he became a young lion;
  He learned to catch prey,
  And he devoured men.
4The nations also heard of him;
  He was trapped in their pit,
  And they brought him with chains to the
    land of Egypt.

5'When she saw that she waited, *that* her hope
    was lost,

She took another of her cubs *and* made him a
    young lion.
6He roved among the lions,
  And became a young lion;
  He learned to catch prey;
  He devoured men.
7He knew their desolate places,a
  And laid waste their cities;
  The land with its fullness was desolated
  By the noise of his roaring.
8Then the nations set against him from the
    provinces on every side,
  And spread their net over him;
  He was trapped in their pit.
9They put him in a cage with chains,
  And brought him to the king of Babylon;
  They brought him in nets,
  That his voice should no longer be heard on
    the mountains of Israel.

10'Your mother *was* like a vine in your
    bloodline,a
  Planted by the waters,
  Fruitful and full of branches
  Because of many waters.
11She had strong branches for scepters of rulers.
  She towered in stature above the thick
    branches,
  And was seen in her height amid the dense
    foliage.
12But she was plucked up in fury,
  She was cast down to the ground,
  And the east wind dried her fruit.
  Her strong branches were broken and
    withered;
  The fire consumed them.
13And now she *is* planted in the wilderness,
  In a dry and thirsty land.
14Fire has come out from a rod of her branches
  And devoured her fruit,
  So that she has no strong branch— a scepter
    for ruling.' "

This *is* a lamentation, and has become a lamentation.

19:7 aSeptuagint reads *He stood in insolence;* Targum reads *He destroyed its palaces;* Vulgate reads *He learned to make widows.* **19:10** aLiterally *blood,* following Masoretic Text, Syriac, and Vulgate; Septuagint reads *like a flower on a pomegranate tree;* Targum reads *in your likeness.*

The Rebellions of Israel

20 It came to pass in the seventh year, in the fifth *month,* on the tenth *day* of the month, *that* certain of the elders of Israel came to inquire of the LORD, and sat before me. ²Then the word of the LORD came to me, saying, ³"Son of man, speak to the elders of Israel, and say to them, 'Thus says the Lord GOD: "Have you come to inquire of Me? *As* I live," says the Lord GOD, "I will not be inquired of by you." ' ⁴Will you judge them, son of man, will you judge *them?* Then make known to them the abominations of their fathers.

⁵"Say to them, 'Thus says the Lord GOD: "On the day when I chose Israel and raised My hand in an oath to the descendants of the house of Jacob, and made Myself known to them in the land of Egypt, I raised My hand in an oath to them, saying, 'I *am* the LORD your God.' ⁶On that day I raised My hand in an oath to them, to bring them out of the land of Egypt into a land that I had searched out for them, 'flowing with milk and honey,'ª the glory of all lands. ⁷Then I said to them, 'Each of you, throw away the abominations which are before his eyes, and do not defile yourselves with the idols of Egypt. I *am* the LORD your God.' ⁸But they rebelled against Me and would not obey Me. They did not all cast away the abominations which were before their eyes, nor did they forsake the idols of Egypt. Then I said, 'I will pour out My fury on them and fulfill My anger against them in the midst of the land of Egypt.' ⁹But I acted for My name's sake, that it should not be profaned before the Gentiles among whom they *were,* in whose sight I had made Myself known to them, to bring them out of the land of Egypt.

¹⁰"Therefore I made them go out of the land of Egypt and brought them into the wilderness. ¹¹And I gave them My statutes and showed them My judgments, 'which, *if* a man does, he shall live by them.'ª ¹²Moreover I also gave them My Sabbaths, to be a sign between them and Me, that they might know that I *am* the LORD who sanctifies them. ¹³Yet the house of Israel rebelled against Me in the wilderness; they did not walk in My statutes; they despised My judgments, 'which, *if* a man does, he shall live by them';ª and they greatly

defiled My Sabbaths. Then I said I would pour out My fury on them in the wilderness, to consume them. ¹⁴But I acted for My name's sake, that it should not be profaned before the Gentiles, in whose sight I had brought them out. ¹⁵So I also raised My hand in an oath to them in the wilderness, that I would not bring them into the land which I had given *them,* 'flowing with milk and honey,'ª the glory of all lands, ¹⁶because they despised My judgments and did not walk in My statutes, but profaned My Sabbaths; for their heart went after their idols. ¹⁷Nevertheless My eye spared them from destruction. I did not make an end of them in the wilderness.

¹⁸"But I said to their children in the wilderness, 'Do not walk in the statutes of your fathers, nor observe their judgments, nor defile yourselves with their idols. ¹⁹I *am* the LORD your God: Walk in My statutes, keep My judgments, and do them; ²⁰hallow My Sabbaths, and they will be a sign between Me and you, that you may know that I *am* the LORD your God.'

²¹"Notwithstanding, the children rebelled against Me; they did not walk in My statutes, and were not careful to observe My judgments, 'which, *if* a man does, he shall live by them';ª but they profaned My Sabbaths. Then I said I would pour out My fury on them and fulfill My anger against them in the wilderness. ²²Nevertheless I withdrew My hand and acted for My name's sake, that it should not be profaned in the sight of the Gentiles, in whose sight I had brought them out. ²³Also I raised My hand in an oath to those in the wilderness, that I would scatter them among the Gentiles and disperse them throughout the countries, ²⁴because they had not executed My judgments, but had despised My statutes, profaned My Sabbaths, and their eyes were fixed on their fathers' idols.

²⁵"Therefore I also gave them up to statutes *that were* not good, and judgments by which they could not live; ²⁶and I pronounced them unclean because of their ritual gifts, in that they caused all their firstborn to pass through *the fire,* that I might make them desolate and that they might know that I am the LORD." '

²⁷"Therefore, son of man, speak to the house

20:6 ªExodus 3:8   **20:11** ªLeviticus 18:5   **20:13** ªLeviticus 18:5   **20:15** ªExodus 3:8   **20:21** ªLeviticus 18:5

of Israel, and say to them, 'Thus says the Lord GOD: "In this too your fathers have blasphemed Me, by being unfaithful to Me. ²⁸When I brought them into the land *concerning* which I had raised My hand in an oath to give them, and they saw all the high hills and all the thick trees, there they offered their sacrifices and provoked Me with their offerings. There they also sent up their sweet aroma and poured out their drink offerings. ²⁹Then I said to them, 'What *is* this high place to which you go?' So its name is called Bamah^a to this day." ' ³⁰Therefore say to the house of Israel, 'Thus says the Lord GOD: "Are you defiling yourselves in the manner of your fathers, and committing harlotry according to their abominations? ³¹For when you offer your gifts and make your sons pass through the fire, you defile yourselves with all your idols, even to this day. So shall I be inquired of by you, O house of Israel? *As* I live," says the Lord GOD, "I will not be inquired of by you. ³²What you have in your mind shall never be, when you say, 'We will be like the Gentiles, like the families in other countries, serving wood and stone.'

GOD WILL RESTORE ISRAEL

³³"*As* I live," says the Lord GOD, "surely with a mighty hand, with an outstretched arm, and with fury poured out, I will rule over you. ³⁴I will bring you out from the peoples and gather you out of the countries where you are scattered, with a mighty hand, with an outstretched arm, and with fury poured out. ³⁵And I will bring you into the wilderness of the peoples, and there I will plead My case with you face to face. ³⁶Just as I pleaded My case with your fathers in the wilderness of the land of Egypt, so I will plead My case with you," says the Lord GOD. ³⁷"I will make you pass under the rod, and I will bring you into the bond of the covenant; ³⁸I will purge the rebels from among you, and those who transgress against Me; I will bring them out of the country where they dwell, but they shall not enter the land of Israel. Then you will know that I *am* the LORD.

³⁹"As for you, O house of Israel," thus says the Lord GOD: "Go, serve every one of you his idols—and hereafter—if you will not obey Me; but profane My holy name no more with your gifts and your idols. ⁴⁰For on My holy mountain, on the mountain height of Israel," says the Lord GOD, "there all the house of Israel, all of them in the land, shall serve Me; there I will accept them, and there I will require your offerings and the firstfruits of your sacrifices, together with all your holy things. ⁴¹I will accept you as a sweet aroma when I bring you out from the peoples and gather you out of the countries where you have been scattered; and I will be hallowed in you before the Gentiles. ⁴²Then you shall know that I *am* the LORD, when I bring you into the land of Israel, into the country *for* which I raised My hand in an oath to give to your fathers. ⁴³And there you shall remember your ways and all your doings with which you were defiled; and you shall loathe yourselves in your own sight because of all the evils that you have committed. ⁴⁴Then you shall know that I *am* the LORD, when I have dealt with you for My name's sake, not according to your wicked ways nor according to your corrupt doings, O house of Israel," says the Lord GOD.' "

FIRE IN THE FOREST

⁴⁵Furthermore the word of the LORD came to me, saying, ⁴⁶"Son of man, set your face toward the south; preach against the south and prophesy against the forest land, the South,^a ⁴⁷and say to the forest of the South, 'Hear the word of the LORD! Thus says the Lord GOD: "Behold, I will kindle a fire in you, and it shall devour every green tree and every dry tree in you; the blazing flame shall not be quenched, and all faces from the south to the north shall be scorched by it. ⁴⁸All flesh shall see that I, the LORD, have kindled it; it shall not be quenched." ' "

⁴⁹Then I said, "Ah, Lord GOD! They say of me, 'Does he not speak parables?' "

BABYLON, THE SWORD OF GOD

21 And the word of the LORD came to me, saying, ²"Son of man, set your face toward Jerusalem, preach against the holy places, and prophesy against the land of Israel; ³and say to the land of Israel, 'Thus says the LORD: "Behold, I *am* against you, and I will draw My sword out of its

20:29 ^aLiterally *High Place*   **20:46** ^aHebrew *Negev*

sheath and cut off both righteous and wicked from you. ⁴Because I will cut off both righteous and wicked from you, therefore My sword shall go out of its sheath against all flesh from south *to* north, ⁵that all flesh may know that I, the LORD, have drawn My sword out of its sheath; it shall not return anymore." ' ⁶Sigh therefore, son of man, with a breaking heart, and sigh with bitterness before their eyes. ⁷And it shall be when they say to you, 'Why are you sighing?' that you shall answer, 'Because of the news; when it comes, every heart will melt, all hands will be feeble, every spirit will faint, and all knees will be weak *as* water. Behold, it is coming and shall be brought to pass,' says the Lord GOD."

⁸Again the word of the LORD came to me, saying, ⁹"Son of man, prophesy and say, 'Thus says the LORD!' Say:

'A sword, a sword is sharpened
And also polished!
¹⁰Sharpened to make a dreadful slaughter,
Polished to flash like lightning!
Should we then make mirth?
It despises the scepter of My son,
As it does all wood.
¹¹And He has given it to be polished,
That it may be handled;
This sword is sharpened, and it is polished
To be given into the hand of the slayer.'

¹²"Cry and wail, son of man;
For it will be against My people,
Against all the princes of Israel.
Terrors including the sword will be against
My people;
Therefore strike *your* thigh.

¹³"Because *it is* a testing,
And what if *the sword* despises even the
scepter?
The scepter shall be no *more,*"

says the Lord GOD.

¹⁴"You therefore, son of man, prophesy,
And strike *your* hands together.
The third time let the sword do double
damage.

It *is* the sword *that* slays,
The sword that slays the great *men,*
That enters their private chambers.
¹⁵I have set the point of the sword against all
their gates,
That the heart may melt and many may
stumble.
Ah! *It is* made bright;
It is grasped for slaughter:

¹⁶"Swords at the ready!
Thrust right!
Set your blade!
Thrust left—
Wherever your edge is ordered!

¹⁷"I also will beat My fists together,
And I will cause My fury to rest;
I, the LORD, have spoken."

¹⁸The word of the LORD came to me again, saying: ¹⁹"And son of man, appoint for yourself two ways for the sword of the king of Babylon to go; both of them shall go from the same land. Make a sign; put *it* at the head of the road to the city. ²⁰Appoint a road for the sword to go to Rabbah of the Ammonites, and to Judah, into fortified Jerusalem. ²¹For the king of Babylon stands at the parting of the road, at the fork of the two roads, to use divination: he shakes the arrows, he consults the images, he looks at the liver. ²²In his right hand is the divination for Jerusalem: to set up battering rams, to call for a slaughter, to lift the voice with shouting, to set battering rams against the gates, to heap up a *siege* mound, and to build a wall. ²³And it will be to them like a false divination in the eyes of those who have sworn oaths with them; but he will bring their iniquity to remembrance, that they may be taken.

²⁴"Therefore thus says the Lord GOD: 'Because you have made your iniquity to be remembered, in that your transgressions are uncovered, so that in all your doings your sins appear—because you have come to remembrance, you shall be taken in hand.

²⁵'Now to you, O profane, wicked prince of Israel, whose day has come, whose iniquity *shall* end, ²⁶thus says the Lord GOD:

"Remove the turban, and take off the crown;
Nothing *shall remain* the same.
Exalt the humble, and humble the exalted.
27Overthrown, overthrown,
I will make it overthrown!
It shall be no *longer,*
Until He comes whose right it is,
And I will give it *to Him.*" '

A Sword Against the Ammonites

28"And you, son of man, prophesy and say,
'Thus says the Lord GOD concerning the Ammonites and concerning their reproach,' and say:

'A sword, a sword *is* drawn,
Polished for slaughter,
For consuming, for flashing—
29While they see false visions for you,
While they divine a lie to you,
To bring you on the necks of the wicked, the
    slain
Whose day has come,
Whose iniquity *shall* end.

30'Return *it* to its sheath.
I will judge you
In the place where you were created,
In the land of your nativity.
31I will pour out My indignation on you;
I will blow against you with the fire of My
    wrath,
And deliver you into the hands of brutal men
    who are skillful to destroy.
32You shall be fuel for the fire;
Your blood shall be in the midst of the land.
You shall not be remembered,
For I the LORD have spoken.' "

Sins of Jerusalem

22 Moreover the word of the LORD came to me, saying, 2"Now, son of man, will you judge, will you judge the bloody city? Yes, show her all her abominations! 3Then say, 'Thus says the Lord GOD: "The city sheds blood in her own midst, that her time may come; and she makes idols within herself to defile herself. 4You have become guilty by the blood which you have shed, and have defiled yourself with the idols which you have made. You have caused your days to

draw near, and have come to *the end of* your years; therefore I have made you a reproach to the nations, and a mockery to all countries. 5*Those* near and *those* far from you will mock you as infamous *and* full of tumult.

6"Look, the princes of Israel: each one has used his power to shed blood in you. 7In you they have made light of father and mother; in your midst they have oppressed the stranger; in you they have mistreated the fatherless and the widow. 8You have despised My holy things and profaned My Sabbaths. 9In you are men who slander to cause bloodshed; in you are those who eat on the mountains; in your midst they commit lewdness. 10In you men uncover their fathers' nakedness; in you they violate women who are set apart during their impurity. 11One commits abomination with his neighbor's wife; another lewdly defiles his daughter-in-law; and another in you violates his sister, his father's daughter. 12In you they take bribes to shed blood; you take usury and increase; you have made profit from your neighbors by extortion, and have forgotten Me," says the Lord GOD.

13"Behold, therefore, I beat My fists at the dishonest profit which you have made, and at the bloodshed which has been in your midst. 14Can your heart endure, or can your hands remain strong, in the days when I shall deal with you? I, the LORD, have spoken, and will do *it*. 15I will scatter you among the nations, disperse you throughout the countries, and remove your filthiness completely from you. 16You shall defile yourself in the sight of the nations; then you shall know that I *am* the LORD." ' "

Israel in the Furnace

17The word of the LORD came to me, saying, 18"Son of man, the house of Israel has become dross to Me; they *are* all bronze, tin, iron, and lead, in the midst of a furnace; they have become dross from silver. 19Therefore thus says the Lord GOD: 'Because you have all become dross, therefore behold, I will gather you into the midst of Jerusalem. 20*As men* gather silver, bronze, iron, lead, and tin into the midst of a furnace, to blow fire on it, to melt *it;* so I will gather *you* in My anger and in My fury, and I will leave *you there* and melt you. 21Yes, I will gather you and blow on you with the fire of My wrath, and you shall be melted in its midst. [22]As silver is melted in the midst of a furnace, so shall you be melted in its midst; then you shall know that I, the LORD, have poured out My fury on you.' "

ISRAEL'S WICKED LEADERS

[23]And the word of the LORD came to me, saying, [24]"Son of man, say to her: 'You *are* a land that is not cleansed[a] or rained on in the day of indignation.' [25]The conspiracy of her prophets[a] in her midst is like a roaring lion tearing the prey; they have devoured people; they have taken treasure and precious things; they have made many widows in her midst. [26]Her priests have violated My law and profaned My holy things; they have not distinguished between the holy and unholy, nor have they made known *the difference* between the unclean and the clean; and they have hidden their eyes from My Sabbaths, so that I am profaned among them. [27]Her princes in her midst *are* like wolves tearing the prey, to shed blood, to destroy people, and to get dishonest gain. [28]Her prophets plastered them with untempered *mortar,* seeing false visions, and divining lies for them,

saying, 'Thus says the Lord GOD,' when the LORD had not spoken. [29]The people of the land have used oppressions, committed robbery, and mistreated the poor and needy; and they wrongfully oppress the stranger. [30]So I sought for a man among them who would make a wall, and stand in the gap before Me on behalf of the land, that I should not destroy it; but I found no one. [31]Therefore I have poured out My indignation on them; I have consumed them with the fire of My wrath; and I have recompensed their deeds on their own heads," says the Lord GOD.

TWO HARLOT SISTERS

23 The word of the LORD came again to me, saying:

> [2]"Son of man, there were two women,
> The daughters of one mother.
> [3]They committed harlotry in Egypt,
> They committed harlotry in their youth;
> Their breasts were there embraced,

22:24 [a]Following Masoretic Text, Syriac, and Vulgate; Septuagint reads *showered upon.*   **22:25** [a]Following Masoretic Text and Vulgate; Septuagint reads *princes;* Targum reads *scribes.*

LEADERSHIP REALITIES

STAND IN THE GAP   *Ezekiel 22:30*

One hand reaching out to God in intercession, supplication, and worship, and one hand reaching out to others with compassion, love, and a burden: This is the definition of an influencer. Leaders should learn to speak eloquently and to listen intently, but there will be times when those you seek to influence for Christ will have no part of you or of the Lord. It is for these people that the Lord seeks one to *make a hedge* and to *stand in the gap.*

To *make a hedge* is to make a wall, to stand in the way of one making a bad choice. The influencer does more than stand in judgment; he or she puts up a fence with truth of the Scripture and not with opinion.

To *stand in the gap* is to intercede in prayer on behalf of the man who cannot or will not pray himself. We sometimes say, "I wish I could do something for you. All I can do is pray." The Lord makes it clear that the prayer of the intercessor is the greatest single action the leader can undertake. The truth is "I cannot do more than fervently pray." The servant of Christ:

Sees the need;

Accepts the call;

Refuses to quit in the face of indifference.

Their virgin bosom was there pressed.
⁴Their names: Oholah^a the elder and
   Oholibah^b her sister;
They were Mine,
And they bore sons and daughters.
As for their names,
Samaria *is* Oholah, and Jerusalem *is*
   Oholibah.

THE OLDER SISTER, SAMARIA

⁵"Oholah played the harlot even though she
   was Mine;
And she lusted for her lovers, the neighboring
   Assyrians,
  ⁶*Who were* clothed in purple,
Captains and rulers,
All of them desirable young men,
Horsemen riding on horses.
⁷Thus she committed her harlotry with them,
All of them choice men of Assyria;
And with all for whom she lusted,
With all their idols, she defiled herself.
⁸She has never given up her harlotry *brought*
   from Egypt,
For in her youth they had lain with her,
Pressed her virgin bosom,
And poured out their immorality upon her.

⁹"Therefore I have delivered her
Into the hand of her lovers,
Into the hand of the Assyrians,
For whom she lusted.
¹⁰They uncovered her nakedness,
Took away her sons and daughters,
And slew her with the sword;
She became a byword among women,
For they had executed judgment on her.

THE YOUNGER SISTER, JERUSALEM

¹¹"Now although her sister Oholibah saw
this, she became more corrupt in her lust than
she, and in her harlotry more corrupt than her
sister's harlotry.

¹²"She lusted for the neighboring Assyrians,
Captains and rulers,
Clothed most gorgeously,
Horsemen riding on horses,
All of them desirable young men.

¹³Then I saw that she was defiled;
Both *took* the same way.
¹⁴But she increased her harlotry;
She looked at men portrayed on the wall,
Images of Chaldeans portrayed in vermilion,
¹⁵Girded with belts around their waists,
Flowing turbans on their heads,
All of them looking like captains,
In the manner of the Babylonians of Chaldea,
The land of their nativity.
¹⁶As soon as her eyes saw them,
She lusted for them
And sent messengers to them in Chaldea.

¹⁷"Then the Babylonians came to her, into the
   bed of love,
And they defiled her with their immorality;
So she was defiled by them, and alienated
   herself from them.
¹⁸She revealed her harlotry and uncovered her
   nakedness.
Then I alienated Myself from her,
As I had alienated Myself from her sister.

¹⁹"Yet she multiplied her harlotry
In calling to remembrance the days of her
   youth,
When she had played the harlot in the land of
   Egypt.
²⁰For she lusted for her paramours,
Whose flesh *is like* the flesh of donkeys,
And whose issue *is like* the issue of horses.
²¹Thus you called to remembrance the
   lewdness of your youth,
When the Egyptians pressed your bosom
Because of your youthful breasts.

JUDGMENT ON JERUSALEM

²²"Therefore, Oholibah, thus says the Lord
   GOD:

'Behold, I will stir up your lovers against you,
From whom you have alienated yourself,
And I will bring them against you from every
   side:
²³The Babylonians,
All the Chaldeans,

23:4 ^aLiterally *Her Own Tabernacle* ^bLiterally *My Tabernacle Is in Her*

Pekod, Shoa, Koa,
All the Assyrians with them,
All of them desirable young men,
Governors and rulers,
Captains and men of renown,
All of them riding on horses.
²⁴And they shall come against you
With chariots, wagons, and war-horses,
With a horde of people.
They shall array against you
Buckler, shield, and helmet all around.

'I will delegate judgment to them,
And they shall judge you according to their
    judgments.
²⁵I will set My jealousy against you,
And they shall deal furiously with you;
They shall remove your nose and your ears,
And your remnant shall fall by the sword;
They shall take your sons and your
    daughters,
And your remnant shall be devoured by
    fire.
²⁶They shall also strip you of your clothes
And take away your beautiful jewelry.

²⁷'Thus I will make you cease your lewdness
    and your harlotry
Brought from the land of Egypt,
So that you will not lift your eyes to them,
Nor remember Egypt anymore.'

²⁸"For thus says the Lord God: 'Surely I will deliver you into the hand of those you hate, into the hand *of those* from whom you alienated yourself. ²⁹They will deal hatefully with you, take away all you have worked for, and leave you naked and bare. The nakedness of your harlotry shall be uncovered, both your lewdness and your harlotry. ³⁰I will do these *things* to you because you have gone as a harlot after the Gentiles, because you have become defiled by their idols. ³¹You have walked in the way of your sister; therefore I will put her cup in your hand.'

³²"Thus says the Lord God:

'You shall drink of your sister's cup,
The deep and wide one;
You shall be laughed to scorn
And held in derision;
It contains much.
³³You will be filled with drunkenness and
    sorrow,
The cup of horror and desolation,
The cup of your sister Samaria.
³⁴You shall drink and drain it,
You shall break its shards,
And tear at your own breasts;
For I have spoken,'
Says the Lord God.

³⁵"Therefore thus says the Lord God:

'Because you have forgotten Me and cast Me
    behind your back,
Therefore you shall bear the *penalty*
Of your lewdness and your harlotry.' "

BOTH SISTERS JUDGED

³⁶The Lord also said to me: "Son of man, will you judge Oholah and Oholibah? Then declare to them their abominations. ³⁷For they have committed adultery, and blood *is* on their hands. They have committed adultery with their idols, and even *sacrificed* their sons whom they bore to Me, passing them through *the fire,* to devour *them.* ³⁸Moreover they have done this to Me: They have defiled My sanctuary on the same day and profaned My Sabbaths. ³⁹For after they had slain their children for their idols, on the same day they came into My sanctuary to profane it; and indeed thus they have done in the midst of My house.

⁴⁰"Furthermore you sent for men to come from afar, to whom a messenger *was* sent; and there they came. And you washed yourself for them, painted your eyes, and adorned yourself with ornaments. ⁴¹You sat on a stately couch, with a table prepared before it, on which you had set My incense and My oil. ⁴²The sound of a carefree multitude *was* with her, and Sabeans *were* brought from the wilderness with men of the common sort, who put bracelets on their wrists and beautiful crowns on their heads. ⁴³Then I said concerning *her who had grown* old in adulteries, 'Will they commit harlotry with her now, and she *with them?*' ⁴⁴Yet they went in to her, as men go in to a woman who plays the harlot; thus they went in to Oholah and Oholibah, the lewd women.

⁴⁵But righteous men will judge them after the manner of adulteresses, and after the manner of women who shed blood, because they *are* adulteresses, and blood *is* on their hands.

⁴⁶"For thus says the Lord GOD: 'Bring up an assembly against them, give them up to trouble and plunder. ⁴⁷The assembly shall stone them with stones and execute them with their swords; they shall slay their sons and their daughters, and burn their houses with fire. ⁴⁸Thus I will cause lewdness to cease from the land, that all women may be taught not to practice your lewdness. ⁴⁹They shall repay you for your lewdness, and you shall pay for your idolatrous sins. Then you shall know that I *am* the Lord GOD.' "

SYMBOL OF THE COOKING POT

24 Again, in the ninth year, in the tenth month, on the tenth *day* of the month, the word of the LORD came to me, saying, ²"Son of man, write down the name of the day, this very day—the king of Babylon started his siege against Jerusalem this very day. ³And utter a parable to the rebellious house, and say to them, 'Thus says the Lord GOD:

"Put on a pot, set *it* on,
  And also pour water into it.
⁴Gather pieces *of meat* in it,
  Every good piece,
  The thigh and the shoulder.
  Fill *it* with choice cuts;
⁵Take the choice of the flock.
  Also pile *fuel* bones under it,
  Make it boil well,
  And let the cuts simmer in it."

⁶'Therefore thus says the Lord GOD:

"Woe to the bloody city,
  To the pot whose scum *is* in it,
  And whose scum is not gone from it!
  Bring it out piece by piece,
  On which no lot has fallen.
⁷For her blood is in her midst;
  She set it on top of a rock;
  She did not pour it on the ground,
  To cover it with dust.

⁸That it may raise up fury and take vengeance,
  I have set her blood on top of a rock,
  That it may not be covered."

⁹'Therefore thus says the Lord GOD:

"Woe to the bloody city!
  I too will make the pyre great.
¹⁰Heap on the wood,
  Kindle the fire;
  Cook the meat well,
  Mix in the spices,
  And let the cuts be burned up.

¹¹"Then set the pot empty on the coals,
  That it may become hot and its bronze may burn,
  That its filthiness may be melted in it,
  That its scum may be consumed.
¹²She has grown weary with lies,
  And her great scum has not gone from her.
  Let her scum *be* in the fire!
¹³In your filthiness *is* lewdness.
  Because I have cleansed you, and you were not cleansed,
  You will not be cleansed of your filthiness anymore,
  Till I have caused My fury to rest upon you.
¹⁴I, the LORD, have spoken *it;*
  It shall come to pass, and I will do *it;*
  I will not hold back,
  Nor will I spare,
  Nor will I relent;
  According to your ways
  And according to your deeds
  Theyᵃ will judge you,"
  Says the Lord GOD.' "

THE PROPHET'S WIFE DIES

¹⁵Also the word of the LORD came to me, saying, ¹⁶"Son of man, behold, I take away from you the desire of your eyes with one stroke; yet you shall neither mourn nor weep, nor shall your tears run down. ¹⁷Sigh in silence, make no mourning for the dead; bind your turban on your head, and put your sandals on your feet; do not cover *your* lips, and do not eat man's bread *of sorrow.*"

24:14 ᵃSeptuagint, Syriac, Targum, and Vulgate read *I.*

¹⁸So I spoke to the people in the morning, and at evening my wife died; and the next morning I did as I was commanded.

¹⁹And the people said to me, "Will you not tell us what these *things signify* to us, that you behave so?"

²⁰Then I answered them, "The word of the LORD came to me, saying, ²¹"Speak to the house of Israel, "Thus says the Lord GOD: 'Behold, I will profane My sanctuary, your arrogant boast, the desire of your eyes, the delight of your soul; and your sons and daughters whom you left behind shall fall by the sword. ²²And you shall do as I have done; you shall not cover *your* lips nor eat man's bread *of sorrow.* ²³Your turbans shall be on your heads and your sandals on your feet; you shall neither mourn nor weep, but you shall pine away in your iniquities and mourn with one another. ²⁴Thus Ezekiel is a sign to you; according to all that he has done you shall do; and when this comes, you shall know that I *am* the Lord GOD.' "

²⁵"And you, son of man—*will* it not *be* in the day when I take from them their stronghold, their joy and their glory, the desire of their eyes, and that on which they set their minds, their sons and their daughters: ²⁶*that* on that day one who escapes will come to you to let *you* hear *it* with *your* ears? ²⁷On that day your mouth will be opened to him who has escaped; you shall speak and no longer be mute. Thus you will be a sign to them, and they shall know that I *am* the LORD.' "

PROCLAMATION AGAINST AMMON

25 The word of the LORD came to me, saying, ²"Son of man, set your face against the Ammonites, and prophesy against them. ³Say to the Ammonites, 'Hear the word of the Lord GOD! Thus says the Lord GOD: "Because you said, 'Aha!' against My sanctuary when it was profaned, and against the land of Israel when it was desolate, and against the house of Judah when they went into captivity, ⁴indeed, therefore, I will deliver you as a possession to the men of the East, and they shall set their encampments among you and make their dwellings among you; they shall eat your fruit, and they shall drink your milk. ⁵And I will make Rabbah a stable for camels and Ammon a

resting place for flocks. Then you shall know that I *am* the LORD."

⁶For thus says the Lord GOD: "Because you clapped *your* hands, stamped your feet, and rejoiced in heart with all your disdain for the land of Israel, ⁷indeed, therefore, I will stretch out My hand against you, and give you as plunder to the nations; I will cut you off from the peoples, and I will cause you to perish from the countries; I will destroy you, and you shall know that I *am* the LORD."

PROCLAMATION AGAINST MOAB

⁸Thus says the Lord GOD: "Because Moab and Seir say, 'Look! The house of Judah *is* like all the nations,' ⁹therefore, behold, I will clear the territory of Moab of cities, of the cities on its frontier, the glory of the country, Beth Jeshimoth, Baal Meon, and Kirjathaim. ¹⁰To the men of the East I will give it as a possession, together with the Ammonites, that the Ammonites may not be remembered among the nations. ¹¹And I will execute judgments upon Moab, and they shall know that I *am* the LORD."

PROCLAMATION AGAINST EDOM

¹²Thus says the Lord GOD: "Because of what Edom did against the house of Judah by taking vengeance, and has greatly offended by avenging itself on them," ¹³therefore thus says the Lord GOD: "I will also stretch out My hand against Edom, cut off man and beast from it, and make it desolate from Teman; Dedan shall fall by the sword. ¹⁴I will lay My vengeance on Edom by the hand of My people Israel, that they may do in Edom according to My anger and according to My fury; and they shall know My vengeance," says the Lord GOD.

PROCLAMATION AGAINST PHILISTIA

¹⁵'Thus says the Lord GOD: "Because the Philistines dealt vengefully and took vengeance with a spiteful heart, to destroy because of the old hatred," ¹⁶therefore thus says the Lord GOD: "I will stretch out My hand against the Philistines, and I will cut off the Cherethites and destroy the remnant of the seacoast. ¹⁷I will execute great vengeance on them with furious rebukes; and they shall know that I *am* the LORD, when I lay My vengeance upon them." ' "

Proclamation Against Tyre

26 And it came to pass in the eleventh year, on the first *day* of the month, *that* the word of the LORD came to me, saying, 2"Son of man, because Tyre has said against Jerusalem, 'Aha! She is broken who *was* the gateway of the peoples; now she is turned over to me; I shall be filled; she is laid waste.'

3"Therefore thus says the Lord GOD: 'Behold, I *am* against you, O Tyre, and will cause many nations to come up against you, as the sea causes its waves to come up. 4And they shall destroy the walls of Tyre and break down her towers; I will also scrape her dust from her, and make her like the top of a rock. 5It shall be *a place for* spreading nets in the midst of the sea, for I have spoken,' says the Lord GOD; 'it shall become plunder for the nations. 6Also her daughter *villages* which *are* in the fields shall be slain by the sword. Then they shall know that I am the LORD.'

7"For thus says the Lord GOD: 'Behold, I will bring against Tyre from the north Nebuchadnezzar[a] king of Babylon, king of kings, with horses, with chariots, and with horsemen, and an army with many people. 8He will slay with the sword your daughter *villages* in the fields; he will heap up a siege mound against you, build a wall against you, and raise a defense against you. 9He will direct his battering rams against your walls, and with his axes he will break down your towers. 10Because of the abundance of his horses, their dust will cover you; your walls will shake at the noise of the horsemen, the wagons, and the chariots, when he enters your gates, as men enter a city that has been breached. 11With the hooves of his horses he will trample all your streets; he will slay your people by the sword, and your strong pillars will fall to the ground. 12They will plunder your riches and pillage your merchandise; they will break down your walls and destroy your pleasant houses; they will lay your stones, your timber, and your soil in the midst of the water. 13I will put an end to the sound of your songs, and the sound of your harps shall be heard no more. 14I will make you like the top of a rock; you shall be *a place for* spreading nets, and you shall never be rebuilt, for I the LORD have spoken,' says the Lord GOD.

15"Thus says the Lord GOD to Tyre: 'Will the coastlands not shake at the sound of your fall, when the wounded cry, when slaughter is made in the midst of you? 16Then all the princes of the sea will come down from their thrones, lay aside their robes, and take off their embroidered garments; they will clothe themselves with trembling; they will sit on the ground, tremble *every* moment, and be astonished at you. 17And they will take up a lamentation for you, and say to you:

"How you have perished,
O one inhabited by seafaring men,
O renowned city,
Who was strong at sea,
She and her inhabitants,
Who caused their terror *to be* on all her
　　inhabitants!
18Now the coastlands tremble on the day of
　　your fall;
Yes, the coastlands by the sea are troubled at
　　your departure." '

19"For thus says the Lord GOD: 'When I make you a desolate city, like cities that are not inhabited, when I bring the deep upon you, and great waters cover you, 20then I will bring you down with those who descend into the Pit, to the people of old, and I will make you dwell in the lowest part of the earth, in places desolate from antiquity, with those who go down to the Pit, so that you may never be inhabited; and I shall establish glory in the land of the living. 21I will make you a terror, and you *shall be* no *more;* though you are sought for, you will never be found again,' says the Lord GOD."

Lamentation for Tyre

27 The word of the LORD came again to me, saying, 2"Now, son of man, take up a lamentation for Tyre, 3and say to Tyre, 'You who are situated at the entrance of the sea, merchant of the peoples on many coastlands, thus says the Lord GOD:

"O Tyre, you have said,
'I *am* perfect in beauty.'
4Your borders *are* in the midst of the seas.
Your builders have perfected your beauty.

26:7 [a]Hebrew *Nebuchadrezzar,* and so elsewhere in this book

⁵They made all *your* planks of fir trees from
    Senir;
  They took a cedar from Lebanon to make
    you a mast.
⁶Of oaks from Bashan they made your oars;
  The company of Ashurites have inlaid your
    planks
  With ivory from the coasts of Cyprus.ᵃ
⁷Fine embroidered linen from Egypt was what
    you spread for your sail;
  Blue and purple from the coasts of Elishah
    was what covered you.

⁸"Inhabitants of Sidon and Arvad were your
    oarsmen;
  Your wise men, O Tyre, were in you;
  They became your pilots.
⁹Elders of Gebal and its wise men
  Were in you to caulk your seams;
  All the ships of the sea
  And their oarsmen were in you
  To market your merchandise.

¹⁰"Those from Persia, Lydia,ᵃ and Libyaᵇ
  Were in your army as men of war;
  They hung shield and helmet in you;
  They gave splendor to you.
¹¹Men of Arvad with your army *were* on your
    walls *all* around,
  And the men of Gammad were in your
    towers;
  They hung their shields on your walls *all*
    around;
  They made your beauty perfect.

¹²"Tarshish *was* your merchant because of
your many luxury goods. They gave you silver,
iron, tin, and lead for your goods. ¹³Javan, Tubal,
and Meshech *were* your traders. They bartered human lives and vessels of bronze for your merchandise. ¹⁴Those from the house of Togarmah traded
for your wares with horses, steeds, and mules.
¹⁵The men of Dedan *were* your traders; many isles
were the market of your hand. They brought you
ivory tusks and ebony as payment. ¹⁶Syria *was* your
merchant because of the abundance of goods you
made. They gave you for your wares emeralds,
purple, embroidery, fine linen, corals, and rubies.
¹⁷Judah and the land of Israel *were* your traders.

They traded for your merchandise wheat of Minnith, millet, honey, oil, and balm. ¹⁸Damascus *was*
your merchant because of the abundance of goods
you made, because of your many luxury items,
with the wine of Helbon and with white wool.
¹⁹Dan and Javan paid for your wares, traversing
back and forth. Wrought iron, cassia, and cane
were among your merchandise. ²⁰Dedan *was* your
merchant in saddlecloths for riding. ²¹Arabia and
all the princes of Kedar *were* your regular merchants. They traded with you in lambs, rams, and
goats. ²²The merchants of Sheba and Raamah *were*
your merchants. They traded for your wares the
choicest spices, all kinds of precious stones, and
gold. ²³Haran, Canneh, Eden, the merchants of
Sheba, Assyria, *and* Chilmad *were* your merchants.
²⁴These *were* your merchants in choice items—in
purple clothes, in embroidered garments, in chests
of multicolored apparel, in sturdy woven cords,
which were in your marketplace.

²⁵"The ships of Tarshish were carriers of your
    merchandise.
  You were filled and very glorious in the midst
    of the seas.
²⁶Your oarsmen brought you into many waters,
  But the east wind broke you in the midst of
    the seas.

²⁷"Your riches, wares, and merchandise,
  Your mariners and pilots,
  Your caulkers and merchandisers,
  All your men of war who *are* in you,
  And the entire company which *is* in your
    midst,
  Will fall into the midst of the seas on the day
    of your ruin.
²⁸The common-land will shake at the sound of
    the cry of your pilots.

²⁹ "All who handle the oar,
  The mariners,
  All the pilots of the sea
  Will come down from their ships *and* stand
    on the shore.
³⁰They will make their voice heard because of
    you;

27:6 ᵃHebrew *Kittim*, western lands, especially Cyprus **27:10** ᵃHebrew *Lud* ᵇHebrew *Put*

They will cry bitterly and cast dust on their
heads;
They will roll about in ashes;
31They will shave themselves completely bald
because of you,
Gird themselves with sackcloth,
And weep for you
With bitterness of heart *and* bitter wailing.
32In their wailing for you
They will take up a lamentation,
And lament for you:
'What *city is* like Tyre,
Destroyed in the midst of the sea?

33'When your wares went out by sea,
You satisfied many people;
You enriched the kings of the earth
With your many luxury goods and your
merchandise.
34But you are broken by the seas in the depths
of the waters;
Your merchandise and the entire company
will fall in your midst.
35All the inhabitants of the isles will be
astonished at you;
Their kings will be greatly afraid,
And *their* countenance will be troubled.
36The merchants among the peoples will hiss at
you;
You will become a horror, and *be* no more
forever.'"'"

Proclamation Against the King of Tyre

28 The word of the LORD came to me again,
saying, 2"Son of man, say to the prince of
Tyre, 'Thus says the Lord GOD:

"Because your heart *is* lifted up,
And you say, 'I *am* a god,
I sit *in* the seat of gods,
In the midst of the seas,'
Yet you *are* a man, and not a god,
Though you set your heart as the heart of a
god
3(Behold, you *are* wiser than Daniel!
There is no secret that can be hidden from
you!
4With your wisdom and your understanding
You have gained riches for yourself,

And gathered gold and silver into your
treasuries;
5By your great wisdom in trade you have
increased your riches,
And your heart is lifted up because of your
riches),"

6'Therefore thus says the Lord GOD:

"Because you have set your heart as the heart
of a god,
7Behold, therefore, I will bring strangers
against you,
The most terrible of the nations;
And they shall draw their swords against the
beauty of your wisdom,
And defile your splendor.
8They shall throw you down into the Pit,
And you shall die the death of the slain
In the midst of the seas.

9"Will you still say before him who slays you,
'I *am* a god'?
But you *shall be* a man, and not a god,
In the hand of him who slays you.
10You shall die the death of the uncircumcised
By the hand of aliens;
For I have spoken," says the Lord GOD.'"

Lamentation for the King of Tyre

11Moreover the word of the LORD came to
me, saying, 12"Son of man, take up a lamentation
for the king of Tyre, and say to him, 'Thus says the
Lord GOD:

"You *were* the seal of perfection,
Full of wisdom and perfect in beauty.
13You were in Eden, the garden of God;
Every precious stone *was* your covering:
The sardius, topaz, and diamond,
Beryl, onyx, and jasper,
Sapphire, turquoise, and emerald with gold.
The workmanship of your timbrels and pipes
Was prepared for you on the day you *were*
created.

14"You *were* the anointed cherub who covers;
I established you;
You were on the holy mountain of God;

You walked back and forth in the midst of
    fiery stones.
[15]You *were* perfect in your ways from the day
    you were created,
    Till iniquity was found in you.

[16]"By the abundance of your trading
    You became filled with violence within,
    And you sinned;
    Therefore I cast you as a profane thing
    Out of the mountain of God;
    And I destroyed you, O covering cherub,
    From the midst of the fiery stones.

[17]"Your heart was lifted up because of your
    beauty;
    You corrupted your wisdom for the sake of
    your splendor;
    I cast you to the ground,
    I laid you before kings,
    That they might gaze at you.

[18]"You defiled your sanctuaries
    By the multitude of your iniquities,
    By the iniquity of your trading;
    Therefore I brought fire from your midst;
    It devoured you,
    And I turned you to ashes upon the earth
    In the sight of all who saw you.
[19]All who knew you among the peoples are
    astonished at you;
    You have become a horror,
    And *shall be* no more forever." ' "

Proclamation Against Sidon

[20]Then the word of the LORD came to me,
saying, [21]"Son of man, set your face toward Sidon,
and prophesy against her, [22]and say, 'Thus says the
Lord GOD:

"Behold, I *am* against you, O Sidon;
    I will be glorified in your midst;
    And they shall know that I *am* the LORD,
    When I execute judgments in her and am
    hallowed in her.
[23]For I will send pestilence upon her,
    And blood in her streets;
    The wounded shall be judged in her
    midst

    By the sword against her on every side;
    Then they shall know that I *am* the LORD.

[24]"And there shall no longer be a pricking
brier or a painful thorn for the house of Israel
from among all *who are* around them, who despise
them. Then they shall know that I *am* the Lord
GOD."

Israel's Future Blessing

[25]'Thus says the Lord GOD: "When I have
gathered the house of Israel from the peoples
among whom they are scattered, and am hallowed
in them in the sight of the Gentiles, then they
will dwell in their own land which I gave to My
servant Jacob. [26]And they will dwell safely there,
build houses, and plant vineyards; yes, they will
dwell securely, when I execute judgments on all
those around them who despise them. Then they
shall know that I *am* the LORD their God." ' "

Proclamation Against Egypt

29 In the tenth year, in the tenth *month,* on
the twelfth *day* of the month, the word of
the LORD came to me, saying, [2]"Son of man, set
your face against Pharaoh king of Egypt, and
prophesy against him, and against all Egypt.
[3]Speak, and say, 'Thus says the Lord GOD:

"Behold, I *am* against you,
    O Pharaoh king of Egypt,
    O great monster who lies in the midst of his
    rivers,
    Who has said, 'My River[a] *is* my own;
    I have made *it* for myself.'
[4]But I will put hooks in your jaws,
    And cause the fish of your rivers to stick to
    your scales;
    I will bring you up out of the midst of your
    rivers,
    And all the fish in your rivers will stick to
    your scales.
[5]I will leave you in the wilderness,
    You and all the fish of your rivers;
    You shall fall on the open field;
    You shall not be picked up or gathered.[a]
    I have given you as food

29:3 [a]That is, the Nile   **29:5** [a]Following Masoretic Text, Septuagint,
and Vulgate; some Hebrew manuscripts and Targum read *buried.*

To the beasts of the field
And to the birds of the heavens.

6"Then all the inhabitants of Egypt
Shall know that I *am* the LORD,
Because they have been a staff of reed to the
house of Israel.
7When they took hold of you with the hand,
You broke and tore all their shoulders;a
When they leaned on you,
You broke and made all their backs quiver."

8'Therefore thus says the Lord GOD: "Surely I will bring a sword upon you and cut off from you man and beast. 9And the land of Egypt shall become desolate and waste; then they will know that I *am* the LORD, because he said, 'The River *is* mine, and I have made *it*.' 10Indeed, therefore, I *am* against you and against your rivers, and I will make the land of Egypt utterly waste and desolate, from Migdola *to* Syene, as far as the border of Ethiopia. 11Neither foot of man shall pass through it nor foot of beast pass through it, and it shall be uninhabited forty years. 12I will make the land of Egypt desolate in the midst of the countries *that are* desolate; and among the cities *that are* laid waste, her cities shall be desolate forty years; and I will scatter the Egyptians among the nations and disperse them throughout the countries."

13'Yet, thus says the Lord GOD: "At the end of forty years I will gather the Egyptians from the peoples among whom they were scattered. 14I will bring back the captives of Egypt and cause them to return to the land of Pathros, to the land of their origin, and there they shall be a lowly kingdom. 15It shall be the lowliest of kingdoms; it shall never again exalt itself above the nations, for I will diminish them so that they will not rule over the nations anymore. 16No longer shall it be the confidence of the house of Israel, but will remind them of *their* iniquity when they turned to follow them. Then they shall know that I *am* the Lord GOD."'"

Babylonia Will Plunder Egypt

17And it came to pass in the twenty-seventh year, in the first *month*, on the first *day* of the month, *that* the word of the LORD came to me, saying, 18"Son of man, Nebuchadnezzar king of Babylon caused his army to labor strenuously against Tyre; every head *was* made bald, and every shoulder rubbed raw; yet neither he nor his army received wages from Tyre, for the labor which they expended on it. 19Therefore thus says the Lord GOD: 'Surely I will give the land of Egypt to Nebuchadnezzar king of Babylon; he shall take away her wealth, carry off her spoil, and remove her pillage; and that will be the wages for his army. 20I have given him the land of Egypt *for* his labor, because they worked for Me,' says the Lord GOD.

21'In that day I will cause the horn of the house of Israel to spring forth, and I will open your mouth to speak in their midst. Then they shall know that I *am* the LORD.' "

Egypt and Her Allies Will Fall

30 The word of the LORD came to me again, saying, 2"Son of man, prophesy and say, 'Thus says the Lord GOD:

"Wail, 'Woe to the day!'
3For the day *is* near,
Even the day of the LORD *is* near;
It will be a day of clouds, the time of the
Gentiles.
4The sword shall come upon Egypt,
And great anguish shall be in Ethiopia,
When the slain fall in Egypt,
And they take away her wealth,
And her foundations are broken down.

5"Ethiopia, Libya,a Lydia,b all the mingled people, Chub, and the men of the lands who are allied, shall fall with them by the sword."

6'Thus says the LORD:

"Those who uphold Egypt shall fall,
And the pride of her power shall come
down.
From Migdol *to* Syene
Those within her shall fall by the sword,"
Says the Lord GOD.

7"They shall be desolate in the midst of the
desolate countries,

29:7 aFollowing Masoretic Text and Vulgate; Septuagint and Syriac read hand. 29:10 aOr tower 30:5 aHebrew Put bHebrew Lud

And her cities shall be in the midst of the
    cities *that are* laid waste.
[8]Then they will know that I *am* the LORD,
    When I have set a fire in Egypt
    And all her helpers are destroyed.
[9]On that day messengers shall go forth from
    Me in ships
    To make the careless Ethiopians afraid,
    And great anguish shall come upon them,
    As on the day of Egypt;
    For indeed it is coming!"

[10]'Thus says the Lord GOD:

"I will also make a multitude of Egypt to cease
    By the hand of Nebuchadnezzar king of
    Babylon.
[11]He and his people with him, the most terrible
    of the nations,
    Shall be brought to destroy the land;
    They shall draw their swords against Egypt,
    And fill the land with the slain.
[12]I will make the rivers dry,
    And sell the land into the hand of the
    wicked;
    I will make the land waste, and all that is in
    it,
    By the hand of aliens.
    I, the LORD, have spoken."

[13]'Thus says the Lord GOD:

"I will also destroy the idols,
    And cause the images to cease from Noph;[a]
    There shall no longer be princes from the
    land of Egypt;
    I will put fear in the land of Egypt.
[14]I will make Pathros desolate,
    Set fire to Zoan,
    And execute judgments in No.[a]
[15]I will pour My fury on Sin,[a] the strength of
    Egypt;
    I will cut off the multitude of No,
[16]And set a fire in Egypt;
    Sin shall have great pain,
    No shall be split open,
    And Noph *shall be in* distress daily.
[17]The young men of Aven[a] and Pi Beseth shall
    fall by the sword,

And these *cities* shall go into captivity.
[18]At Tehaphnehes[a] the day shall also be
    darkened,[b]
    When I break the yokes of Egypt there.
    And her arrogant strength shall cease in her;
    As for her, a cloud shall cover her,
    And her daughters shall go into captivity.
[19]Thus I will execute judgments on Egypt,
    Then they shall know that I *am* the
    LORD." ' "

PROCLAMATION AGAINST PHARAOH

[20]And it came to pass in the eleventh year, in
the first *month,* on the seventh *day* of the month,
that the word of the LORD came to me, saying,
[21]"Son of man, I have broken the arm of Pharaoh
king of Egypt; and see, it has not been bandaged
for healing, nor a splint put on to bind it, to make
it strong enough to hold a sword. [22]Therefore
thus says the Lord GOD: 'Surely I *am* against
Pharaoh king of Egypt, and will break his arms,
both the strong one and the one that was broken;
and I will make the sword fall out of his hand. [23]I
will scatter the Egyptians among the nations, and
disperse them throughout the countries. [24]I will
strengthen the arms of the king of Babylon and
put My sword in his hand; but I will break
Pharaoh's arms, and he will groan before him
with the groanings of a mortally wounded *man.*
[25]Thus I will strengthen the arms of the king of
Babylon, but the arms of Pharaoh shall fall down;
they shall know that I *am* the LORD, when I put
My sword into the hand of the king of Babylon
and he stretches it out against the land of Egypt.
[26]I will scatter the Egyptians among the nations
and disperse them throughout the countries.
Then they shall know that I *am* the LORD.' "

EGYPT CUT DOWN LIKE A GREAT TREE

31 Now it came to pass in the eleventh year,
in the third *month,* on the first *day* of the
month, *that* the word of the LORD came to me,
saying, [2]"Son of man, say to Pharaoh king of
Egypt and to his multitude:

30:13 [a]That is, ancient Memphis **30:14** [a]That is, ancient Thebes
30:15 [a]That is, ancient Pelusium **30:17** [a]That is, ancient On (Heliopolis) **30:18** [a]Spelled *Tahpanhes* in Jeremiah 43:7 and elsewhere [b]Following many Hebrew manuscripts, Bomberg, Septuagint,
Syriac, Targum, and Vulgate; Masoretic Text reads *refrained.*

'Whom are you like in your greatness?
³Indeed Assyria *was* a cedar in Lebanon,
  With fine branches that shaded the forest,
  And of high stature;
  And its top was among the thick boughs.
⁴The waters made it grow;
  Underground waters gave it height,
  With their rivers running around the place
    where it was planted,
  And sent out rivulets to all the trees of the
    field.

⁵'Therefore its height was exalted above all the
    trees of the field;
  Its boughs were multiplied,
  And its branches became long because of the
    abundance of water,
  As it sent them out.
⁶All the birds of the heavens made their nests
    in its boughs;
  Under its branches all the beasts of the field
    brought forth their young;
  And in its shadow all great nations made their
    home.
⁷'Thus it was beautiful in greatness and in the
    length of its branches,
  Because its roots reached to abundant waters.
⁸The cedars in the garden of God could not
    hide it;
  The fir trees were not like its boughs,
  And the chestnutᵃ trees were not like its
    branches;
  No tree in the garden of God was like it in
    beauty.
⁹I made it beautiful with a multitude of
    branches,
  So that all the trees of Eden envied it,
  That *were* in the garden of God.'

¹⁰"Therefore thus says the Lord God: 'Because you have increased in height, and it set its
top among the thick boughs, and its heart was
lifted up in its height, ¹¹therefore I will deliver it
into the hand of the mighty one of the nations,
and he shall surely deal with it; I have driven it
out for its wickedness. ¹²And aliens, the most terrible of the nations, have cut it down and left it;
its branches have fallen on the mountains and in
all the valleys; its boughs lie broken by all the

rivers of the land; and all the peoples of the earth
have gone from under its shadow and left it.

¹³'On its ruin will remain all the birds of the
    heavens,
  And all the beasts of the field will come to its
    branches—

¹⁴So that no trees by the waters may ever again
exalt themselves for their height, nor set their tops
among the thick boughs, that no tree which
drinks water may ever be high enough to reach
up to them.

  'For they have all been delivered to death,
  To the depths of the earth,
  Among the children of men who go down to
    the Pit.'

¹⁵"Thus says the Lord God: 'In the day when
it went down to hell, I caused mourning. I covered the deep because of it. I restrained its rivers,
and the great waters were held back. I caused
Lebanon to mourn for it, and all the trees of the
field wilted because of it. ¹⁶I made the nations
shake at the sound of its fall, when I cast it down
to hell together with those who descend into the
Pit; and all the trees of Eden, the choice and best
of Lebanon, all that drink water, were comforted
in the depths of the earth. ¹⁷They also went down
to hell with it, with those slain by the sword; and
those who were its *strong* arm dwelt in its shadows
among the nations.

¹⁸'To which of the trees in Eden will you
then be likened in glory and greatness? Yet you
shall be brought down with the trees of Eden to
the depths of the earth; you shall lie in the midst
of the uncircumcised, with *those* slain by the
sword. This *is* Pharaoh and all his multitude,' says
the Lord God."

Lamentation for Pharaoh and Egypt

32 And it came to pass in the twelfth year, in
the twelfth *month,* on the first *day* of the
month, *that* the word of the Lord came to me,
saying, ²"Son of man, take up a lamentation for
Pharaoh king of Egypt, and say to him:

31:8 ᵃHebrew *armon*

'You are like a young lion among the
        nations,
And you *are* like a monster in the seas,
Bursting forth in your rivers,
Troubling the waters with your feet,
And fouling their rivers.

3'Thus says the Lord GOD:

"I will therefore spread My net over you
        with a company of many people,
And they will draw you up in My net.
4Then I will leave you on the land;
I will cast you out on the open fields,
And cause to settle on you all the birds of
        the heavens.
And with you I will fill the beasts of the
        whole earth.
5I will lay your flesh on the mountains,
And fill the valleys with your carcass.

6"I will also water the land with the flow of
        your blood,
Even to the mountains;
And the riverbeds will be full of you.
7When *I* put out your light,
I will cover the heavens, and make its stars
        dark;
I will cover the sun with a cloud,
And the moon shall not give her light.
8All the bright lights of the heavens I will
        make dark over you,
And bring darkness upon your land,"
Says the Lord GOD.

9"I will also trouble the hearts of many peoples, when I bring your destruction among the
nations, into the countries which you have not
known. 10Yes, I will make many peoples astonished at you, and their kings shall be horribly
afraid of you when I brandish My sword before
them; and they shall tremble *every* moment,
every man for his own life, in the day of your
fall.
    11For thus says the Lord GOD: "The sword of
the king of Babylon shall come upon you. 12By
the swords of the mighty warriors, all of them the
most terrible of the nations, I will cause your
multitude to fall.

"They shall plunder the pomp of Egypt,
And all its multitude shall be destroyed.
13Also I will destroy all its animals
From beside its great waters;
The foot of man shall muddy them no more,
Nor shall the hooves of animals muddy them.
14Then I will make their waters clear,
And make their rivers run like oil,"
Says the Lord GOD.

15"When I make the land of Egypt desolate,
And the country is destitute of all that once
        filled it,
When I strike all who dwell in it,
Then they shall know that I *am* the LORD.

16"This *is* the lamentation
With which they shall lament her;
The daughters of the nations shall lament
        her;
They shall lament for her, for Egypt,
And for all her multitude,"
Says the Lord GOD.' "

EGYPT AND OTHERS CONSIGNED TO THE PIT

17It came to pass also in the twelfth year, on
the fifteenth *day* of the month, *that* the word of
the LORD came to me, saying:

18"Son of man, wail over the multitude of
        Egypt,
And cast them down to the depths of the
        earth,
Her and the daughters of the famous nations,
With those who go down to the Pit:
19'Whom do you surpass in beauty?
Go down, be placed with the
        uncircumcised.'

20"They shall fall in the midst of *those* slain by
        the sword;
She is delivered to the sword,
Drawing her and all her multitudes.
21The strong among the mighty
Shall speak to him out of the midst of hell
With those who help him:
'They have gone down,
They lie with the uncircumcised, slain by the
        sword.'

²²"Assyria *is* there, and all her company,
  With their graves all around her,
  All of them slain, fallen by the sword.
 ²³Her graves are set in the recesses of the Pit,
  And her company is all around her grave,
  All of them slain, fallen by the sword,
  Who caused terror in the land of the
    living.

²⁴"There *is* Elam and all her multitude,
  All around her grave,
  All of them slain, fallen by the sword,
  Who have gone down uncircumcised to the
    lower parts of the earth,
  Who caused their terror in the land of the
    living;
  Now they bear their shame with those who
    go down to the Pit.
 ²⁵They have set her bed in the midst of the
    slain,
  With all her multitude,
  With her graves all around it,
  All of them uncircumcised, slain by the
    sword;
  Though their terror was caused
  In the land of the living,
  Yet they bear their shame
  With those who go down to the Pit;
  It was put in the midst of the slain.

²⁶"There *are* Meshech and Tubal and all their
    multitudes,
  With all their graves around it,
  All of them uncircumcised, slain by the
    sword,
  Though they caused their terror in the land
    of the living.
 ²⁷They do not lie with the mighty
  Who are fallen of the uncircumcised,
  Who have gone down to hell with their
    weapons of war;
  They have laid their swords under their
    heads,
  But their iniquities will be on their bones,
  Because of the terror of the mighty in the
    land of the living.
²⁸Yes, you shall be broken in the midst of the
    uncircumcised,
  And lie with *those* slain by the sword.

²⁹"There *is* Edom,
  Her kings and all her princes,
  Who despite their might
  Are laid beside *those* slain by the sword;
  They shall lie with the uncircumcised,
  And with those who go down to the Pit.
³⁰There *are* the princes of the north,
  All of them, and all the Sidonians,
  Who have gone down with the slain
  In shame at the terror which they caused by
    their might;
  They lie uncircumcised with *those* slain by the
    sword,
  And bear their shame with those who go
    down to the Pit.

³¹"Pharaoh will see them
  And be comforted over all his multitude,
  Pharaoh and all his army,
  Slain by the sword,"
  Says the Lord GOD.

³²"For I have caused My terror in the land of
    the living;
  And he shall be placed in the midst of the
    uncircumcised
  With *those* slain by the sword,
  Pharaoh and all his multitude,"
  Says the Lord GOD.

THE WATCHMAN AND HIS MESSAGE

33 Again the word of the LORD came to me,
saying, ²"Son of man, speak to the children of your people, and say to them: 'When I bring the sword upon a land, and the people of the land take a man from their territory and make him their watchman, ³when he sees the sword coming upon the land, if he blows the trumpet and warns the people, ⁴then whoever hears the sound of the trumpet and does not take warning, if the sword comes and takes him away, his blood shall be on his *own* head. ⁵He heard the sound of the trumpet, but did not take warning; his blood shall be upon himself. But he who takes warning will save his life. ⁶But if the watchman sees the sword coming and does not blow the trumpet, and the people are not warned, and the sword comes and takes *any* person from among them, he is taken away in his

iniquity; but his blood I will require at the watchman's hand.'

7"So you, son of man: I have made you a watchman for the house of Israel; therefore you shall hear a word from My mouth and warn them for Me. 8When I say to the wicked, 'O wicked *man,* you shall surely die!' and you do not speak to warn the wicked from his way, that wicked *man* shall die in his iniquity; but his blood I will require at your hand. 9Nevertheless if you warn the wicked to turn from his way, and he does not turn from his way, he shall die in his iniquity; but you have delivered your soul.

10"Therefore you, O son of man, say to the house of Israel: 'Thus you say, "If our transgressions and our sins *lie* upon us, and we pine away in them, how can we then live?" ' 11Say to them: '*As* I live,' says the Lord GOD, 'I have no pleasure in the death of the wicked, but that the wicked turn from his way and live. Turn, turn from your evil ways! For why should you die, O house of Israel?'

THE FAIRNESS OF GOD'S JUDGMENT

12"Therefore you, O son of man, say to the children of your people: 'The righteousness of the righteous man shall not deliver him in the day of his transgression; as for the wickedness of the wicked, he shall not fall because of it in the day that he turns from his wickedness; nor shall the righteous be able to live because of *his righteousness* in the day that he sins.' 13When I say to the righteous *that* he shall surely live, but he trusts in his own righteousness and commits iniquity, none of his righteous works shall be remembered; but because of the iniquity that he has committed, he shall die. 14Again, when I say to the wicked, 'You shall surely die,' if he turns from his sin and does what is lawful and right, 15*if* the wicked restores the pledge, gives back what he has stolen, and walks in the statutes of life without committing iniquity, he shall surely live; he shall not die. 16None of his sins which he has committed shall be remembered against him; he has done what is lawful and right; he shall surely live.

17"Yet the children of your people say, 'The way of the Lord is not fair.' But it is their way which is not fair! 18When the righteous turns from his righteousness and commits iniquity, he shall die because of it. 19But when the wicked turns from his wickedness and does what is lawful and right, he shall live because of it. 20Yet you say, 'The way of the Lord is not fair.' O house of Israel, I will judge every one of you according to his own ways."

THE FALL OF JERUSALEM

21And it came to pass in the twelfth year of our captivity, in the tenth *month,* on the fifth *day* of the month, *that* one who had escaped from Jerusalem came to me and said, "The city has been captured!"

22Now the hand of the LORD had been upon me the evening before the man came who had escaped. And He had opened my mouth; so when he came to me in the morning, my mouth was opened, and I was no longer mute.

THE CAUSE OF JUDAH'S RUIN

23Then the word of the LORD came to me, saying: 24"Son of man, they who inhabit those ruins in the land of Israel are saying, 'Abraham was only one, and he inherited the land. But we *are* many; the land has been given to us as a possession.'

25"Therefore say to them, 'Thus says the Lord GOD: "You eat *meat* with blood, you lift up your eyes toward your idols, and shed blood. Should you then possess the land? 26You rely on your sword, you commit abominations, and you defile one another's wives. Should you then possess the land?" '

27"Say thus to them, 'Thus says the Lord GOD: "*As* I live, surely those who *are* in the ruins shall fall by the sword, and the one who *is* in the open field I will give to the beasts to be devoured, and those who *are* in the strongholds and caves shall die of the pestilence. 28For I will make the land most desolate, her arrogant strength shall cease, and the mountains of Israel shall be so desolate that no one will pass through. 29Then they shall know that I *am* the LORD, when I have made the land most desolate because of all their abominations which they have committed." '

HEARING AND NOT DOING

30"As for you, son of man, the children of your people are talking about you beside the walls and in the doors of the houses; and they speak to one another, everyone saying to his brother, 'Please come and hear what the word is that comes from the LORD.' ³¹So they come to you as people do, they sit before you *as* My people, and they hear your words, but they do not do them; for with their mouth they show much love, *but* their hearts pursue their *own* gain. ³²Indeed you *are* to them as a very lovely song of one who has a pleasant voice and can play well on an instrument; for they hear your words, but they do not do them. ³³And when this comes to pass—surely it will come—then they will know that a prophet has been among them."

IRRESPONSIBLE SHEPHERDS

34And the word of the LORD came to me, saying, ²"Son of man, prophesy against the shepherds of Israel, prophesy and say to them, 'Thus says the Lord GOD to the shepherds: "Woe to the shepherds of Israel who feed themselves! Should not the shepherds feed the flocks? ³You eat the fat and clothe yourselves with the wool; you slaughter the fatlings, *but* you do not feed the flock. ⁴The weak you have not strengthened, nor have you healed those who were sick, nor bound up the broken, nor brought back what was driven away, nor sought what was lost; but with force and cruelty you have ruled them. ⁵So they were scattered because *there was* no shepherd; and they became food for all the beasts of the field when they were scattered. ⁶My sheep wandered through all the mountains, and on every high hill; yes, My flock was scattered over the whole face of the earth, and no one was seeking or searching *for them*."

⁷'Therefore, you shepherds, hear the word of the LORD: ⁸"*As* I live," says the Lord GOD, "surely because My flock became a prey, and My flock became food for every beast of the field, because *there was* no shepherd, nor did My shepherds search for My flock, but the shepherds fed themselves and did not feed My flock"— ⁹therefore, O shepherds, hear the word of the LORD! ¹⁰Thus says the Lord GOD: "Behold, I *am* against the shepherds, and I will require My flock at their hand; I will cause them to cease feeding the sheep, and the shepherds shall feed themselves no more; for I will deliver My flock from their mouths, that they may no longer be food for them."

GOD, THE TRUE SHEPHERD

¹¹"For thus says the Lord GOD: "Indeed I Myself will search for My sheep and seek them out. ¹²As a shepherd seeks out his flock on the day he is among his scattered sheep, so will I seek out My sheep and deliver them from all the places where they were scattered on a cloudy and dark day. ¹³And I will bring them out from the peoples and gather them from the countries, and will bring them to their own land; I will feed them on the mountains of Israel, in the valleys and in all the inhabited places of the country. ¹⁴I will feed them in good pasture, and their fold shall be on the high mountains of Israel. There they shall lie down in a good fold and feed in rich pasture on the mountains of Israel. ¹⁵I will feed My flock, and I will make them lie down," says the Lord GOD. ¹⁶"I will seek what was lost and bring back what was driven away, bind up the broken and strengthen what was sick; but I will destroy the fat and the strong, and feed them in judgment."

¹⁷'And *as for* you, O My flock, thus says the Lord GOD: "Behold, I shall judge between sheep and sheep, between rams and goats. ¹⁸*Is it* too little for you to have eaten up the good pasture, that you must tread down with your feet the residue of your pasture—and to have drunk of the clear waters, that you must foul the residue with your feet? ¹⁹And *as for* My flock, they eat what you have trampled with your feet, and they drink what you have fouled with your feet."

²⁰'Therefore thus says the Lord GOD to them: "Behold, I Myself will judge between the fat and the lean sheep. ²¹Because you have pushed with side and shoulder, butted all the weak ones with your horns, and scattered them abroad, ²²therefore I will save My flock, and they shall no longer be a prey; and I will judge between sheep and sheep. ²³I will establish one shepherd over them, and he shall feed them—My servant David. He shall feed them and be their shepherd. ²⁴And I, the LORD, will be their God, and My servant David a prince among them; I, the LORD, have spoken.

²⁵"I will make a covenant of peace with them, and cause wild beasts to cease from the land; and they will dwell safely in the wilderness

and sleep in the woods. ²⁶I will make them and the places all around My hill a blessing; and I will cause showers to come down in their season; there shall be showers of blessing. ²⁷Then the trees of the field shall yield their fruit, and the earth shall yield her increase. They shall be safe in their land; and they shall know that I *am* the LORD, when I have broken the bands of their yoke and delivered them from the hand of those who enslaved them. ²⁸And they shall no longer be a prey for the nations, nor shall beasts of the land devour them; but they shall dwell safely, and no one shall make *them* afraid. ²⁹I will raise up for them a garden of renown, and they shall no longer be consumed with hunger in the land, nor bear the shame of the Gentiles anymore. ³⁰Thus they shall know that I, the LORD their God, *am* with them, and they, the house of Israel, *are* My people," says the Lord GOD.'

³¹"You are My flock, the flock of My pasture; you *are* men, *and* I *am* your God," says the Lord GOD.

Judgment on Mount Seir

35Moreover the word of the LORD came to me, saying, ²"Son of man, set your face against Mount Seir and prophesy against it, ³and say to it, 'Thus says the Lord GOD:

"Behold, O Mount Seir, I *am* against you;
I will stretch out My hand against you,
And make you most desolate;
⁴I shall lay your cities waste,
And you shall be desolate.
Then you shall know that I *am* the LORD.

⁵"Because you have had an ancient hatred, and have shed *the blood of* the children of Israel by the power of the sword at the time of their calamity, when their iniquity *came to an* end, ⁶therefore, *as* I live," says the Lord GOD, "I will prepare you for blood, and blood shall pursue you; since you have not hated blood, therefore blood shall pursue you. ⁷Thus I will make Mount Seir most desolate, and cut off from it the one who leaves and the one who returns. ⁸And I will fill its mountains with the slain; on your hills and in your valleys and in all your ravines those who are slain by the sword shall fall. ⁹I will make you

perpetually desolate, and your cities shall be uninhabited; then you shall know that I *am* the LORD.

¹⁰"Because you have said, 'These two nations and these two countries shall be mine, and we will possess them,' although the LORD was there, ¹¹therefore, *as* I live," says the Lord GOD, "I will do according to your anger and according to the envy which you showed in your hatred against them; and I will make Myself known among them when I judge you. ¹²Then you shall know that I *am* the LORD. I have heard all your blasphemies which you have spoken against the mountains of Israel, saying, 'They are desolate; they are given to us to consume.' ¹³Thus with your mouth you have boasted against Me and multiplied your words against Me; I have heard *them.*"

¹⁴"Thus says the Lord GOD:"The whole earth will rejoice when I make you desolate. ¹⁵As you rejoiced because the inheritance of the house of Israel was desolate, so I will do to you; you shall be desolate, O Mount Seir, as well as all of Edom—all of it! Then they shall know that I *am* the LORD."'

Blessing on Israel

36"And you, son of man, prophesy to the mountains of Israel, and say, 'O mountains of Israel, hear the word of the LORD! ²Thus says the Lord GOD: "Because the enemy has said of you, 'Aha! The ancient heights have become our possession,' " ' ³therefore prophesy, and say, 'Thus says the Lord GOD:"Because they made *you* desolate and swallowed you up on every side, so that you became the possession of the rest of the nations, and you are taken up by the lips of talkers and slandered by the people"— ⁴therefore, O mountains of Israel, hear the word of the Lord GOD! Thus says the Lord GOD to the mountains, the hills, the rivers, the valleys, the desolate wastes, and the cities that have been forsaken, which became plunder and mockery to the rest of the nations all around— ⁵therefore thus says the Lord GOD: "Surely I have spoken in My burning jealousy against the rest of the nations and against all Edom, who gave My land to themselves as a possession, with wholehearted joy *and* spiteful minds, in order to plunder its open country." '

⁶"Therefore prophesy concerning the land of

Israel, and say to the mountains, the hills, the rivers, and the valleys, 'Thus says the Lord GOD: "Behold, I have spoken in My jealousy and My fury, because you have borne the shame of the nations." ⁷Therefore thus says the Lord GOD: "I have raised My hand in an oath that surely the nations that *are* around you shall bear their own shame. ⁸But you, O mountains of Israel, you shall shoot forth your branches and yield your fruit to My people Israel, for they are about to come. ⁹For indeed I *am* for you, and I will turn to you, and you shall be tilled and sown. ¹⁰I will multiply men upon you, all the house of Israel, all of it; and the cities shall be inhabited and the ruins rebuilt. ¹¹I will multiply upon you man and beast; and they shall increase and bear young; I will make you inhabited as in former times, and do better *for you* than at your beginnings. Then you shall know that I *am* the LORD. ¹²Yes, I will cause men to walk on you, My people Israel; they shall take possession of you, and you shall be their inheritance; no more shall you bereave them *of children*."

¹³"Thus says the Lord GOD: "Because they say to you, 'You devour men and bereave your nation *of children*,' ¹⁴therefore you shall devour men no more, nor bereave your nation anymore," says the Lord GOD. ¹⁵"Nor will I let you hear the taunts of the nations anymore, nor bear the reproach of the peoples anymore, nor shall you cause your nation to stumble anymore," says the Lord GOD.' "

The Renewal of Israel

¹⁶Moreover the word of the LORD came to me, saying: ¹⁷"Son of man, when the house of Israel dwelt in their own land, they defiled it by their own ways and deeds; to Me their way was like the uncleanness of a woman in her customary impurity. ¹⁸Therefore I poured out My fury on them for the blood they had shed on the land, and for their idols *with which* they had defiled it. ¹⁹So I scattered them among the nations, and they were dispersed throughout the countries; I judged them according to their ways and their deeds. ²⁰When they came to the nations, wherever they went, they profaned My holy name—when they said of them, 'These *are* the people of the LORD, *and* yet they have gone out of His land.' ²¹But I had concern for My holy name, which the house

of Israel had profaned among the nations wherever they went.

²²"Therefore say to the house of Israel, 'Thus says the Lord GOD: "I do not do *this* for your sake, O house of Israel, but for My holy name's sake, which you have profaned among the nations wherever you went. ²³And I will sanctify My great name, which has been profaned among the nations, which you have profaned in their midst; and the nations shall know that I *am* the LORD," says the Lord GOD, "when I am hallowed in you before their eyes. ²⁴For I will take you from among the nations, gather you out of all countries, and bring you into your own land. ²⁵Then I will sprinkle clean water on you, and you shall be clean; I will cleanse you from all your filthiness and from all your idols. ²⁶I will give you a new heart and put a new spirit within you; I will take the heart of stone out of your flesh and give you a heart of flesh. ²⁷I will put My Spirit within you and cause you to walk in My statutes, and you will keep My judgments and do *them*. ²⁸Then you shall dwell in the land that I gave to your fathers; you shall be My people, and I will be your God. ²⁹I will deliver you from all your uncleannesses. I will call for the grain and multiply it, and bring no famine upon you. ³⁰And I will multiply the fruit of your trees and the increase of your fields, so that you need never again bear the reproach of famine among the nations. ³¹Then you will remember your evil ways and your deeds that *were* not good; and you will loathe yourselves in your own sight, for your iniquities and your abominations. ³²Not for your sake do I do *this*," says the Lord GOD, "let it be known to you. Be ashamed and confounded for your own ways, O house of Israel!"

³³"Thus says the Lord GOD: "On the day that I cleanse you from all your iniquities, I will also enable *you* to dwell in the cities, and the ruins shall be rebuilt. ³⁴The desolate land shall be tilled instead of lying desolate in the sight of all who pass by. ³⁵So they will say, 'This land that was desolate has become like the garden of Eden; and the wasted, desolate, and ruined cities *are now* fortified *and* inhabited.' ³⁶Then the nations which are left all around you shall know that I, the LORD, have rebuilt the ruined places *and* planted what was desolate. I, the LORD, have spoken *it*, and I will do *it*."

LEADERSHIP ISSUES

GC2: Holy: Others Noticing a Difference

EZEKIEL 36:23

The children of Israel were to live "set apart" in their lifestyle, worship, and relationships in such a way that others around them would notice a difference. So it is to be with Christ's followers.

Recall some of Israel's unique approaches to worship: the tabernacle, the ark of the covenant, and the temple. How were these elements of worship different from the common worship of the sun, of graven images, and of animals? Imagine the children of Israel being asked by a watching world:

- "Why do you worship as you do?"
  "Our God invites us to approach Him in this way."
- "Why do you not eat or drink things that others do?"
  "Our God said it was not best."

After several such testimonies, others would undoubtedly conclude, "Your relationship with your God sure must mean a lot to you!" In a similar way, the Book of Acts records what a watching world noticed about Jesus' disciples: "They realized that [the disciples] had been with Jesus" (Acts 4:13).

No doubt others are observing, watching, and listening to see whether our relationship with Jesus "means a lot to us." Take a moment to consider who might be noticing your life and the differences Christ makes. Then consider this reflection: "I remember _____ noticing that I _____."

Now, pause to pray. First, for the person mentioned above that your life would continue to encourage them toward a deepening commitment to Jesus. Second, the distinction of your life would continue to impress people that you have "been with Jesus."

"Lord, continue to involve me with people like _____ who notice my life; continue to challenge me in sharing a testimony of the difference You make in my life, particularly in my _____." (For example: *choices, attitudes, disciplines*)

GC2
GREAT COMMANDMENT
COMMISSION

³⁷'Thus says the Lord GOD: "I will also let the house of Israel inquire of Me to do this for them: I will increase their men like a flock. ³⁸Like a flock *offered as* holy *sacrifices,* like the flock at Jerusalem on its feast days, so shall the ruined cities be filled with flocks of men. Then they shall know that I *am* the LORD." ' "

THE DRY BONES LIVE

37 The hand of the LORD came upon me and brought me out in the Spirit of the LORD, and set me down in the midst of the valley; and it *was* full of bones. ²Then He caused me to pass by them all around, and behold, *there were* very many in the open valley; and indeed *they were* very dry. ³And He said to me, "Son of man, can these bones live?"

So I answered, "O Lord GOD, You know."

⁴Again He said to me, "Prophesy to these bones, and say to them, 'O dry bones, hear the word of the LORD! ⁵Thus says the Lord GOD to these bones: "Surely I will cause breath to enter into you, and you shall live. ⁶I will put sinews on you and bring flesh upon you, cover you with skin and put breath in you; and you shall live. Then you shall know that I *am* the LORD." ' "

⁷So I prophesied as I was commanded; and as I prophesied, there was a noise, and suddenly a rattling; and the bones came together, bone to bone. ⁸Indeed, as I looked, the sinews and the flesh came upon them, and the skin covered them over; but *there was* no breath in them.

⁹Also He said to me, "Prophesy to the breath, prophesy, son of man, and say to the breath, 'Thus says the Lord GOD: "Come from the four winds, O breath, and breathe on these slain, that they may live." ' " ¹⁰So I prophesied as He commanded me, and breath came into them, and they lived, and stood upon their feet, an exceedingly great army.

¹¹Then He said to me, "Son of man, these bones are the whole house of Israel. They indeed say, 'Our bones are dry, our hope is lost, and we ourselves are cut off!' ¹²Therefore prophesy and say to them, 'Thus says the Lord GOD: "Behold, O My people, I will open your graves and cause you to come up from your graves, and bring you into the land of Israel. ¹³Then you shall know that I *am* the LORD, when I have opened your graves, O My people, and brought you up from your graves. ¹⁴I will put My Spirit in you, and you shall live, and I will place you in your own land. Then you shall know that I, the LORD, have spoken *it* and performed *it,*" says the LORD.' "

ONE KINGDOM, ONE KING

¹⁵Again the word of the LORD came to me, saying, ¹⁶"As for you, son of man, take a stick for yourself and write on it: 'For Judah and for the children of Israel, his companions.' Then take another stick and write on it, 'For Joseph, the stick of Ephraim, and *for* all the house of Israel, his companions.' ¹⁷Then join them one to another for yourself into one stick, and they will become one in your hand.

¹⁸"And when the children of your people speak to you, saying, 'Will you not show us what you *mean* by these?'— ¹⁹say to them, 'Thus says the Lord GOD: "Surely I will take the stick of Joseph, which *is* in the hand of Ephraim, and the tribes of Israel, his companions; and I will join them with it, with the stick of Judah, and make them one stick, and they will be one in My hand." ' ²⁰And the sticks on which you write will be in your hand before their eyes.

²¹"Then say to them, 'Thus says the Lord GOD: "Surely I will take the children of Israel from among the nations, wherever they have gone, and will gather them from every side and bring them into their own land; ²²and I will make them one nation in the land, on the mountains of Israel; and one king shall be king over them all; they shall no longer be two nations, nor shall they ever be divided into two kingdoms again. ²³They shall not defile themselves anymore with their idols, nor with their detestable things, nor with any of their transgressions; but I will deliver them from all their dwelling places in which they have sinned, and will cleanse them. Then they shall be My people, and I will be their God.

²⁴"David My servant *shall be* king over them, and they shall all have one shepherd; they shall also walk in My judgments and observe My statutes, and do them. ²⁵Then they shall dwell in the land that I have given to Jacob My servant, where your fathers dwelt; and they shall dwell there, they, their children, and their children's children, forever; and My servant David *shall be* their

the INFLUENCERS

EZEKIEL: Faithful, In Spite Of . . .

EZEKIEL 24

Ezekiel is one of the most remarkable but neglected characters in Scripture. There is much to learn from the life of this incredible prophet who experienced one of the most difficult days ever recorded. Job might possibly be the only other human in history to have experienced a worse day.

On January 15, 588 BC the Lord gave Ezekiel the terrible news that his hometown of Jerusalem had fallen to the Babylonians. As if things weren't bad enough, the Lord told Ezekiel on that very same day that he would lose his wife, whom the Bible refers to as "the delight of his eyes." Ezekiel wasn't even allowed to mourn! God wanted to use this tragic personal event as a wake up call to Israel.

This sad day became a turning point in Ezekiel's ministry. Prior to this day, he was a prophet of gloom and doom; but the Lord used tragedy to turn Ezekiel into a prophet of hope to the Jewish captives in Babylon. The phrase that best describes the life and times of Ezekiel never actually appears within the pages of the book that bears his name: "In spite of." Ezekiel was faithful to God "in spite of" tragedy. Ezekiel displayed the leadership principle to *rise above* the circumstances of life and allow God to use your life to accomplish His purpose.

prince forever. [26]Moreover I will make a covenant of peace with them, and it shall be an everlasting covenant with them; I will establish them and multiply them, and I will set My sanctuary in their midst forevermore. [27]My tabernacle also shall be with them; indeed I will be their God, and they shall be My people. [28]The nations also will know that I, the LORD, sanctify Israel, when My sanctuary is in their midst forevermore." ' "

GOG AND ALLIES ATTACK ISRAEL

38 Now the word of the LORD came to me, saying, [2]"Son of man, set your face against Gog, of the land of Magog, the prince of Rosh,[a] Meshech, and Tubal, and prophesy against him, [3]and say, 'Thus says the Lord GOD: "Behold, I *am* against you, O Gog, the prince of Rosh, Meshech, and Tubal. [4]I will turn you around, put hooks into your jaws, and lead you out, with all your army, horses, and horsemen, all splendidly clothed, a great company *with* bucklers and shields, all of them handling swords. [5]Persia, Ethiopia,[a] and Libya[b] are with them, all of them *with* shield and helmet; [6]Gomer and all its troops;

the house of Togarmah *from* the far north and all its troops—many people *are* with you.

[7]"Prepare yourself and be ready, you and all your companies that are gathered about you; and be a guard for them. [8]After many days you will be visited. In the latter years you will come into the land of those brought back from the sword *and* gathered from many people on the mountains of Israel, which had long been desolate; they were brought out of the nations, and now all of them dwell safely. [9]You will ascend, coming like a storm, covering the land like a cloud, you and all your troops and many peoples with you."

[10]Thus says the Lord GOD: "On that day it shall come to pass *that* thoughts will arise in your mind, and you will make an evil plan: [11]You will say, 'I will go up against a land of unwalled villages; I will go to a peaceful people, who dwell safely, all of them dwelling without walls, and having neither bars nor gates'— [12]to take plunder and to take booty, to stretch out your hand against the waste places *that are again* inhabited, and

38:2 [a]Targum, Vulgate, and Aquila read *chief prince of* (also verse 3).   **38:5** [a]Hebrew *Cush* [b]Hebrew *Put*

against a people gathered from the nations, who have acquired livestock and goods, who dwell in the midst of the land. [13]Sheba, Dedan, the merchants of Tarshish, and all their young lions will say to you, 'Have you come to take plunder? Have you gathered your army to take booty, to carry away silver and gold, to take away livestock and goods, to take great plunder?' " '

[14]"Therefore, son of man, prophesy and say to Gog, 'Thus says the Lord GOD: "On that day when My people Israel dwell safely, will you not know *it?* [15]Then you will come from your place out of the far north, you and many peoples with you, all of them riding on horses, a great company and a mighty army. [16]You will come up against My people Israel like a cloud, to cover the land. It will be in the latter days that I will bring you against My land, so that the nations may know Me, when I am hallowed in you, O Gog, before their eyes." [17]Thus says the Lord GOD: "Are *you* he of whom I have spoken in former days by My servants the prophets of Israel, who prophesied for years in those days that I would bring you against them?

JUDGMENT ON GOG

[18]"And it will come to pass at the same time, when Gog comes against the land of Israel," says the Lord GOD, "*that* My fury will show in My face. [19]For in My jealousy *and* in the fire of My wrath I have spoken: 'Surely in that day there shall be a great earthquake in the land of Israel, [20]so that the fish of the sea, the birds of the heavens, the beasts of the field, all creeping things that creep on the earth, and all men who *are* on the face of the earth shall shake at My presence. The mountains shall be thrown down, the steep places shall fall, and every wall shall fall to the ground.' [21]I will call for a sword against Gog throughout all My mountains," says the Lord GOD. "Every man's sword will be against his brother. [22]And I will bring him to judgment with pestilence and bloodshed; I will rain down on him, on his troops, and on the many peoples who *are* with him, flooding rain, great hailstones, fire, and brimstone. [23]Thus I will magnify Myself and sanctify Myself, and I will be known in the eyes of many nations. Then they shall know that I *am* the LORD." '

GOG'S ARMIES DESTROYED

39 "And you, son of man, prophesy against Gog, and say, 'Thus says the Lord GOD: "Behold, I *am* against you, O Gog, the prince of Rosh,[a] Meshech, and Tubal; [2]and I will turn you around and lead you on, bringing you up from the far north, and bring you against the mountains of Israel. [3]Then I will knock the bow out of your left hand, and cause the arrows to fall out of your right hand. [4]You shall fall upon the mountains of Israel, you and all your troops and the peoples who *are* with you; I will give you to birds of prey of every sort and *to* the beasts of the field to be devoured. [5]You shall fall on the open field; for I have spoken," says the Lord GOD. [6]"And I will send fire on Magog and on those who live in security in the coastlands. Then they shall know that I *am* the LORD. [7]So I will make My holy name known in the midst of My people Israel, and I will not *let them* profane My holy name anymore. Then the nations shall know that I *am* the LORD, the Holy One in Israel. [8]Surely it is coming, and it shall be done," says the Lord GOD. "This *is* the day of which I have spoken.

[9]"Then those who dwell in the cities of Israel will go out and set on fire and burn the weapons, both the shields and bucklers, the bows and arrows, the javelins and spears; and they will make fires with them for seven years. [10]They will not take wood from the field nor cut down *any* from the forests, because they will make fires with the weapons; and they will plunder those who plundered them, and pillage those who pillaged them," says the Lord GOD.

THE BURIAL OF GOG

[11]"It will come to pass in that day *that* I will give Gog a burial place there in Israel, the valley of those who pass by east of the sea; and it will obstruct travelers, because there they will bury Gog and all his multitude. Therefore they will call *it* the Valley of Hamon Gog.[a] [12]For seven months the house of Israel will be burying them, in order to cleanse the land. [13]Indeed all the people of the land will be burying, and they will gain renown for it on the day that I am glorified," says the Lord

39:1 [a]Targum, Vulgate and Aquila read *chief prince of.* **39:11** [a]Literally *The Multitude of Gog*

GOD. [14]"They will set apart men regularly employed, with the help of a search party,[a] to pass through the land and bury those bodies remaining on the ground, in order to cleanse it. At the end of seven months they will make a search. [15]The search party will pass through the land; and *when anyone* sees a man's bone, he shall set up a marker by it, till the buriers have buried it in the Valley of Hamon Gog. [16]*The* name of *the* city *will* also *be* Hamonah. Thus they shall cleanse the land."'

A Triumphant Festival

[17]"And as for you, son of man, thus says the Lord GOD, 'Speak to every sort of bird and to every beast of the field:

"Assemble yourselves and come;
    Gather together from all sides to My
        sacrificial meal
    Which I am sacrificing for you,
    A great sacrificial meal on the mountains of
        Israel,
    That you may eat flesh and drink blood.
[18]You shall eat the flesh of the mighty,
    Drink the blood of the princes of the earth,
    Of rams and lambs,
    Of goats and bulls,
    All of them fatlings of Bashan.
[19]You shall eat fat till you are full,
    And drink blood till you are drunk,
    At My sacrificial meal
    Which I am sacrificing for you.
[20]You shall be filled at My table
    With horses and riders,
    With mighty men
    And with all the men of war," says the Lord
        GOD.

Israel Restored to the Land

[21]"I will set My glory among the nations; all the nations shall see My judgment which I have executed, and My hand which I have laid on them. [22]So the house of Israel shall know that I *am* the LORD their God from that day forward. [23]The Gentiles shall know that the house of Israel went into captivity for their iniquity; because they were unfaithful to Me, therefore I hid My face from them. I gave them into the hand of their en-

emies, and they all fell by the sword. [24]According to their uncleanness and according to their transgressions I have dealt with them, and hidden My face from them."'

[25]"Therefore thus says the Lord GOD: 'Now I will bring back the captives of Jacob, and have mercy on the whole house of Israel; and I will be jealous for My holy name— [26]after they have borne their shame, and all their unfaithfulness in which they were unfaithful to Me, when they dwelt safely in their *own* land and no one made *them* afraid. [27]When I have brought them back from the peoples and gathered them out of their enemies' lands, and I am hallowed in them in the sight of many nations, [28]then they shall know that I *am* the LORD their God, who sent them into captivity among the nations, but also brought them back to their land, and left none of them captive any longer. [29]And I will not hide My face from them anymore; for I shall have poured out My Spirit on the house of Israel,' says the Lord GOD."

A New City, a New Temple

40 In the twenty-fifth year of our captivity, at the beginning of the year, on the tenth *day* of the month, in the fourteenth year after the city was captured, on the very same day the hand of the LORD was upon me; and He took me there. [2]In the visions of God He took me into the land of Israel and set me on a very high mountain; on it toward the south *was* something like the structure of a city. [3]He took me there, and behold, *there was* a man whose appearance *was* like the appearance of bronze. He had a line of flax and a measuring rod in his hand, and he stood in the gateway.

[4]And the man said to me, "Son of man, look with your eyes and hear with your ears, and fix your mind on everything I show you; for you *were* brought here so that I might show *them* to you. Declare to the house of Israel everything you see." [5]Now there was a wall all around the outside of the temple.[a] In the man's hand was a measuring rod six cubits *long, each being a* cubit and a handbreadth; and he measured the width of the wall structure, one rod; and the height, one rod.

39:14 [a]Literally *those who pass through*   **40:5** [a]Literally *house,* and so elsewhere in this book

The Eastern Gateway of the Temple

⁶Then he went to the gateway which faced east; and he went up its stairs and measured the threshold of the gateway, *which was* one rod wide, and the other threshold *was* one rod wide. ⁷Each gate chamber *was* one rod long and one rod wide; between the gate chambers *was a space of* five cubits; and the threshold of the gateway by the vestibule of the inside gate *was* one rod. ⁸He also measured the vestibule of the inside gate, one rod. ⁹Then he measured the vestibule of the gateway, eight cubits; and the gateposts, two cubits. The vestibule of the gate *was* on the inside. ¹⁰In the eastern gateway *were* three gate chambers on one side and three on the other; the three *were* all the same size; also the gateposts were of the same size on this side and that side.

¹¹He measured the width of the entrance to the gateway, ten cubits; *and* the length of the gate, thirteen cubits. ¹²*There was* a space in front of the gate chambers, one cubit *on this side* and one cubit on that side; the gate chambers *were* six cubits on this side and six cubits on that side. ¹³Then he measured the gateway from the roof of *one* gate chamber to the roof of the other; the width *was* twenty-five cubits, as door faces door. ¹⁴He measured the gateposts, sixty cubits high, and the court all around the gateway *extended* to the gatepost. ¹⁵*From* the front of the entrance gate to the front of the vestibule of the inner gate *was* fifty cubits. ¹⁶*There were* beveled window *frames* in the gate chambers and in their intervening archways on the inside of the gateway all around, and likewise in the vestibules. *There were* windows all around on the inside. And on each gatepost *were* palm trees.

The Outer Court

¹⁷Then he brought me into the outer court; and *there were* chambers and a pavement made all around the court; thirty chambers faced the pavement. ¹⁸The pavement was by the side of the gateways, corresponding to the length of the gateways; *this was* the lower pavement. ¹⁹Then he measured the width from the front of the lower gateway to the front of the inner court exterior, one hundred cubits toward the east and the north.

The Northern Gateway

²⁰On the outer court was also a gateway facing north, and he measured its length and its width. ²¹Its gate chambers, three on this side and three on that side, its gateposts and its archways, had the same measurements as the first gate; its length *was* fifty cubits and its width twenty-five cubits. ²²Its windows and those of its archways, and also its palm trees, *had* the same measurements as the gateway facing east; it was ascended by seven steps, and its archway *was* in front of it. ²³A gate of the inner court was opposite the northern gateway, just as the eastern *gateway;* and he measured from gateway to gateway, one hundred cubits.

The Southern Gateway

²⁴After that he brought me toward the south, and there a gateway was facing south; and he measured its gateposts and archways according to these same measurements. ²⁵*There were* windows in it and in its archways all around like those windows; its length *was* fifty cubits and its width twenty-five cubits. ²⁶Seven steps led up to it, and its archway *was* in front of them; and it had palm trees on its gateposts, one on this side and one on that side. ²⁷*There was* also a gateway on the inner court, facing south; and he measured from gateway to gateway toward the south, one hundred cubits.

Gateways of the Inner Court

²⁸Then he brought me to the inner court through the southern gateway; he measured the southern gateway according to these same measurements. ²⁹Also its gate chambers, its gateposts, and its archways *were* according to these same measurements; *there were* windows in it and in its archways all around; *it was* fifty cubits long and twenty-five cubits wide. ³⁰*There were* archways all around, twenty-five cubits long and five cubits wide. ³¹Its archways faced the outer court, palm trees *were* on its gateposts, and going up to it *were* eight steps.

³²And he brought me into the inner court facing east; he measured the gateway according to these same measurements. ³³Also its gate chambers, its gateposts, and its archways *were* according

to these same measurements; and *there were* windows in it and in its archways all around; *it was* fifty cubits long and twenty-five cubits wide. [34]Its archways faced the outer court, and palm trees *were* on its gateposts on this side and on that side; and going up to it *were* eight steps.

[35]Then he brought me to the north gateway and measured *it* according to these same measurements— [36]also its gate chambers, its gateposts, and its archways. It had windows all around; its length *was* fifty cubits and its width twenty-five cubits. [37]Its gateposts faced the outer court, palm trees *were* on its gateposts on this side and on that side, and going up to it *were* eight steps.

Where Sacrifices Were Prepared

[38]*There was* a chamber and its entrance by the gateposts of the gateway, where they washed the burnt offering. [39]In the vestibule of the gateway *were* two tables on this side and two tables on that side, on which to slay the burnt offering, the sin offering, and the trespass offering. [40]At the outer side of the *vestibule,* as one goes up to the entrance of the northern gateway, *were* two tables; and on the other side of the vestibule of the gateway *were* two tables. [41]Four tables *were* on this side and four tables on that side, by the side of the gateway, eight tables on which they slaughtered *the sacrifices.* [42]*There were* also four tables of hewn stone for the burnt offering, one cubit and a half long, one cubit and a half wide, and one cubit high; on these they laid the instruments with which they slaughtered the burnt offering and the sacrifice. [43]Inside *were* hooks, a handbreadth wide, fastened all around; and the flesh of the sacrifices *was* on the tables.

Chambers for Singers and Priests

[44]Outside the inner gate *were* the chambers for the singers in the inner court, one facing south at the side of the northern gateway, and the other facing north at the side of the southern[a] gateway. [45]Then he said to me, "This chamber which faces south *is* for the priests who have charge of the temple. [46]The chamber which faces north *is* for the priests who have charge of the altar; these *are* the sons of Zadok, from the sons of Levi, who come near the LORD to minister to Him."

Dimensions of the Inner Court and Vestibule

[47]And he measured the court, one hundred cubits long and one hundred cubits wide, foursquare. The altar *was* in front of the temple. [48]Then he brought me to the vestibule of the temple and measured the doorposts of the vestibule, five cubits on this side and five cubits on that side; and the width of the gateway was three cubits on this side and three cubits on that side. [49]The length of the vestibule *was* twenty cubits, and the width eleven cubits; and by the steps which led up to it *there were* pillars by the doorposts, one on this side and another on that side.

Dimensions of the Sanctuary

41 Then he brought me into the sanctuary[a] and measured the doorposts, six cubits wide on one side and six cubits wide on the other side—the width of the tabernacle. [2]The width of the entryway *was* ten cubits, and the side walls of the entrance *were* five cubits on this side and five cubits on the other side; and he measured its length, forty cubits, and its width, twenty cubits.

[3]Also he went inside and measured the doorposts, two cubits; and the entrance, six cubits *high;* and the width of the entrance, seven cubits. [4]He measured the length, twenty cubits; and the width, twenty cubits, beyond the sanctuary; and he said to me, "This *is* the Most Holy *Place.*"

The Side Chambers on the Wall

[5]Next, he measured the wall of the temple, six cubits. The width of each side chamber all around the temple *was* four cubits on every side. [6]The side chambers *were* in three stories, one above the other, thirty chambers in each story; they rested on ledges which *were* for the side chambers all around, that they might be supported, but not fastened to the wall of the temple. [7]As one went up from story to story, the side chambers became wider all around, because their supporting ledges in the wall of the temple ascended like steps; therefore the width of the structure increased as one went up *from* the lowest *story* to the highest by way of the middle one. [8]I also saw an elevation

40:44 [a]Following Septuagint; Masoretic Text and Vulgate read *eastern.* **41:1** [a]Hebrew *heykal,* here the main room of the temple, sometimes called the *holy place* (compare Exodus 26:33)

all around the temple; it was the foundation of the side chambers, a full rod, *that is,* six cubits *high.* ⁹The thickness of the outer wall of the side chambers *was* five cubits, and so also the remaining terrace by the place of the side chambers of the temple. ¹⁰And between *it and* the *wall* chambers was a width of twenty cubits all around the temple on every side. ¹¹The doors of the side chambers opened on the terrace, one door toward the north and another toward the south; and the width of the terrace *was* five cubits all around.

The Building at the Western End

¹²The building that faced the separating courtyard at its western end *was* seventy cubits wide; the wall of the building *was* five cubits thick all around, and its length ninety cubits.

Dimensions and Design of the Temple Area

¹³So he measured the temple, one hundred cubits long; and the separating courtyard with the building and its walls *was* one hundred cubits long; ¹⁴also the width of the eastern face of the temple, including the separating courtyard, *was* one hundred cubits. ¹⁵He measured the length of the building behind it, facing the separating courtyard, with its galleries on the one side and on the other side, one hundred cubits, as well as the inner temple and the porches of the court, ¹⁶their doorposts and the beveled window frames. And the galleries all around their three stories opposite the threshold were paneled with wood from the ground to the windows—the windows were covered— ¹⁷from the space above the door, even to the inner room,ᵃ as well as outside, and on every wall all around, inside and outside, by measure.

¹⁸And *it was* made with cherubim and palm trees, a palm tree between cherub and cherub. *Each* cherub had two faces, ¹⁹so that the face of a man *was* toward a palm tree on one side, and the face of a young lion toward a palm tree on the other side; thus *it was* made throughout the temple all around. ²⁰From the floor to the space above the door, and on the wall of the sanctuary, cherubim and palm trees *were* carved.

²¹The doorposts of the temple *were* square, *as was* the front of the sanctuary; their appearance was similar. ²²The altar *was* of wood, three cubits high, and its length two cubits. Its corners, its length, and its sides *were* of wood; and he said to me, "This *is* the table that *is* before the LORD."

²³The temple and the sanctuary had two doors. ²⁴The doors had two panels *apiece,* two folding panels: two *panels* for one door and two panels for the other *door.* ²⁵Cherubim and palm trees *were* carved on the doors of the temple just as they *were* carved on the walls. A wooden canopy *was* on the front of the vestibule outside. ²⁶*There were* beveled window *frames* and palm trees on one side and on the other, on the sides of the vestibule—also on the side chambers of the temple and on the canopies.

The Chambers for the Priests

42 Then he brought me out into the outer court, by the way toward the north; and he brought me into the chamber which *was* opposite the separating courtyard, and which *was* opposite the building toward the north. ²Facing the length, *which was* one hundred cubits (the width was fifty cubits), was the north door. ³Opposite the inner court of twenty *cubits,* and opposite the pavement of the outer court, *was* gallery against gallery in three *stories.* ⁴In front of the chambers, toward the inside, *was* a walk ten cubits wide, at a distance of one cubit; and their doors faced north. ⁵Now the upper chambers *were* shorter, because the galleries took away *space* from them more than from the lower and middle stories of the building. ⁶For they *were* in three *stories* and did not have pillars like the pillars of the courts; therefore *the upper level* was shortened more than the lower and middle levels from the ground up. ⁷And a wall which *was* outside ran parallel to the chambers, at the front of the chambers, toward the outer court; its length *was* fifty cubits. ⁸The length of the chambers toward the outer court *was* fifty cubits, whereas that facing the temple *was* one hundred cubits. ⁹At the lower chambers *was* the entrance on the east side, as one goes into them from the outer court.

¹⁰Also *there were* chambers in the thickness of the wall of the court toward the east, opposite the separating courtyard and opposite the building. ¹¹*There was* a walk in front of them also, and their appearance *was* like the chambers which *were* to-

41:17 ᵃLiterally *house,* here the Most Holy Place

ward the north; they *were* as long and as wide as the others, and all their exits and entrances *were* according to plan. [12]And corresponding to the doors of the chambers that *were* facing south, as one enters them, *there was* a door in front of the walk, the way directly in front of the wall toward the east.

[13]Then he said to me, "The north chambers *and* the south chambers, which *are* opposite the separating courtyard, *are* the holy chambers where the priests who approach the LORD shall eat the most holy offerings. There they shall lay the most holy offerings—the grain offering, the sin offering, and the trespass offering—for the place *is* holy. [14]When the priests enter them, they shall not go out of the holy *chamber* into the outer court; but there they shall leave their garments in which they minister, for they *are* holy. They shall put on other garments; then they may approach *that* which *is* for the people."

OUTER DIMENSIONS OF THE TEMPLE

[15]Now when he had finished measuring the inner temple, he brought me out through the gateway that faces toward the east, and measured it all around. [16]He measured the east side with the measuring rod,[a] five hundred rods by the measuring rod all around. [17]He measured the north side, five hundred rods by the measuring rod all around. [18]He measured the south side, five hundred rods by the measuring rod. [19]He came around to the west side *and* measured five hundred rods by the measuring rod. [20]He measured it on the four sides; it had a wall all around, five hundred *cubits* long and five hundred wide, to separate the holy areas from the common.

THE TEMPLE, THE LORD'S DWELLING PLACE

43 Afterward he brought me to the gate, the gate that faces toward the east. [2]And behold, the glory of the God of Israel came from the way of the east. His voice *was* like the sound of many waters, and the earth shone with His glory. [3]*It was* like the appearance of the vision which I saw—like the vision which I saw when I[a] came to destroy the city. The visions *were* like the vision which I saw by the River Chebar; and I fell on my face. [4]And the glory of the LORD came into the temple by way of the gate which faces

toward the east. [5]The Spirit lifted me up and brought me into the inner court; and behold, the glory of the LORD filled the temple.

[6]Then I heard *Him* speaking to me from the temple, while a man stood beside me. [7]And He said to me, "Son of man, *this is* the place of My throne and the place of the soles of My feet, where I will dwell in the midst of the children of Israel forever. No more shall the house of Israel defile My holy name, they nor their kings, by their harlotry or with the carcasses of their kings on their high places. [8]When they set their threshold by My threshold, and their doorpost by My doorpost, with a wall between them and Me, they defiled My holy name by the abominations which they committed; therefore I have consumed them in My anger. [9]Now let them put their harlotry and the carcasses of their kings far away from Me, and I will dwell in their midst forever.

[10]"Son of man, describe the temple to the house of Israel, that they may be ashamed of their iniquities; and let them measure the pattern. [11]And if they are ashamed of all that they have done, make known to them the design of the temple and its arrangement, its exits and its entrances, its entire design and all its ordinances, all its forms and all its laws. Write *it* down in their sight, so that they may keep its whole design and all its ordinances, and perform them. [12]This *is* the law of the temple: The whole area surrounding the mountaintop *is* most holy. Behold, this *is* the law of the temple.

DIMENSIONS OF THE ALTAR

[13]"These are the measurements of the altar in cubits (the cubit *is* one cubit and a handbreadth): the base one cubit high and one cubit wide, with a rim all around its edge of one span. This *is* the height of the altar: [14]from the base on the ground to the lower ledge, two cubits; the width of the ledge, one cubit; from the smaller ledge to the larger ledge, four cubits; and the width of the ledge, *one* cubit. [15]The altar hearth *is* four cubits high, with four horns extending upward from the hearth. [16]The altar hearth *is* twelve *cubits* long, twelve wide, square at its four corners; [17]the ledge, fourteen *cubits* long and fourteen wide on its four

42:16 [a]Compare 40:5 **43:3** [a]Some Hebrew manuscripts and Vulgate read *He.*

sides, with a rim of half a cubit around it; its base, one cubit all around; and its steps face toward the east."

CONSECRATING THE ALTAR

[18]And He said to me, "Son of man, thus says the Lord GOD: 'These *are* the ordinances for the altar on the day when it is made, for sacrificing burnt offerings on it, and for sprinkling blood on it. [19]You shall give a young bull for a sin offering to the priests, the Levites, who are of the seed of Zadok, who approach Me to minister to Me,' says the Lord GOD. [20]You shall take some of its blood and put *it* on the four horns of the altar, on the four corners of the ledge, and on the rim around it; thus you shall cleanse it and make atonement for it. [21]Then you shall also take the bull of the sin offering, and burn it in the appointed place of the temple, outside the sanctuary. [22]On the second day you shall offer a kid of the goats without blemish for a sin offering; and they shall cleanse the altar, as they cleansed *it* with the bull. [23]When you have finished cleansing *it,* you shall offer a young bull without blemish, and a ram from the flock without blemish. [24]When you offer them before the LORD, the priests shall throw salt on them, and they will offer them up *as* a burnt offering to the LORD. [25]Every day for seven days you shall prepare a goat *for* a sin offering; they shall also prepare a young bull and a ram from the flock, both without blemish. [26]Seven days they shall make atonement for the altar and purify it, and so consecrate *it*. [27]When these days are over it shall be, on the eighth day and thereafter, that the priests shall offer your burnt offerings and your peace offerings on the altar; and I will accept you,' says the Lord GOD."

THE EAST GATE AND THE PRINCE

44 Then He brought me back to the outer gate of the sanctuary which faces toward the east, but it *was* shut. [2]And the LORD said to me, "This gate shall be shut; it shall not be opened, and no man shall enter by it, because the LORD God of Israel has entered by it; therefore it shall be shut. [3]*As for* the prince, *because* he *is* the prince, he may sit in it to eat bread before the LORD; he shall enter by way of the vestibule of the gateway, and go out the same way."

THOSE ADMITTED TO THE TEMPLE

[4]Also He brought me by way of the north gate to the front of the temple; so I looked, and behold, the glory of the LORD filled the house of the LORD; and I fell on my face. [5]And the LORD said to me, "Son of man, mark well, see with your eyes and hear with your ears, all that I say to you concerning all the ordinances of the house of the LORD and all its laws. Mark well who may enter the house and all who go out from the sanctuary. [6]"Now say to the rebellious, to the house of Israel, 'Thus says the Lord GOD: "O house of Israel, let Us have no more of all your abominations. [7]When you brought in foreigners, uncircumcised in heart and uncircumcised in flesh, to be in My sanctuary to defile it—My house—and when you offered My food, the fat and the blood, then they broke My covenant because of all your abominations. [8]And you have not kept charge of My holy things, but you have set *others* to keep charge of My sanctuary for you." [9]Thus says the Lord GOD: "No foreigner, uncircumcised in heart or uncircumcised in flesh, shall enter My sanctuary, including any foreigner who *is* among the children of Israel.

LAWS GOVERNING PRIESTS

[10]"And the Levites who went far from Me, when Israel went astray, who strayed away from Me after their idols, they shall bear their iniquity. [11]Yet they shall be ministers in My sanctuary, *as* gatekeepers of the house and ministers of the house; they shall slay the burnt offering and the sacrifice for the people, and they shall stand before them to minister to them. [12]Because they ministered to them before their idols and caused the house of Israel to fall into iniquity, therefore I have raised My hand in an oath against them," says the Lord GOD, "that they shall bear their iniquity. [13]And they shall not come near Me to minister to Me as priest, nor come near any of My holy things, nor into the Most Holy *Place;* but they shall bear their shame and their abominations which they have committed. [14]Nevertheless I will make them keep charge of the temple, for all its work, and for all that has to be done in it.

[15]"But the priests, the Levites, the sons of Zadok, who kept charge of My sanctuary when

the children of Israel went astray from Me, they shall come near Me to minister to Me; and they shall stand before Me to offer to Me the fat and the blood," says the Lord GOD. [16]"They shall enter My sanctuary, and they shall come near My table to minister to Me, and they shall keep My charge. [17]And it shall be, whenever they enter the gates of the inner court, that they shall put on linen garments; no wool shall come upon them while they minister within the gates of the inner court or within the house. [18]They shall have linen turbans on their heads and linen trousers on their bodies; they shall not clothe themselves with *anything that causes* sweat. [19]When they go out to the outer court, to the outer court to the people, they shall take off their garments in which they have ministered, leave them in the holy chambers, and put on other garments; and in their holy garments they shall not sanctify the people.

[20]"They shall neither shave their heads, nor let their hair grow long, but they shall keep their hair well trimmed. [21]No priest shall drink wine when he enters the inner court. [22]They shall not take as wife a widow or a divorced woman, but take virgins of the descendants of the house of Israel, or widows of priests.

[23]"And they shall teach My people *the difference* between the holy and the unholy, and cause them to discern between the unclean and the clean. [24]In controversy they shall stand as judges, *and* judge it according to My judgments. They shall keep My laws and My statutes in all My appointed meetings, and they shall hallow My Sabbaths.

[25]"They shall not defile *themselves* by coming near a dead person. Only for father or mother, for son or daughter, for brother or unmarried sister may they defile themselves. [26]After he is cleansed, they shall count seven days for him. [27]And on the day that he goes to the sanctuary to minister in the sanctuary, he must offer his sin offering in the inner court," says the Lord GOD.

[28]"It shall be, in regard to their inheritance, that I *am* their inheritance. You shall give them no possession in Israel, for I *am* their possession. [29]They shall eat the grain offering, the sin offering, and the trespass offering; every dedicated thing in Israel shall be theirs. [30]The best of all firstfruits of any kind, and every sacrifice of any

kind from all your sacrifices, shall be the priest's; also you shall give to the priest the first of your ground meal, to cause a blessing to rest on your house. [31]The priests shall not eat anything, bird or beast, that died naturally or was torn *by wild beasts.*

THE HOLY DISTRICT

45 "Moreover, when you divide the land by lot into inheritance, you shall set apart a district for the LORD, a holy section of the land; its length *shall be* twenty-five thousand *cubits,* and the width ten thousand. It *shall be* holy throughout its territory all around. [2]Of this there shall be a square plot for the sanctuary, five hundred by five hundred *rods,* with fifty cubits around it for an open space. [3]So this is the district you shall measure: twenty-five thousand *cubits* long and ten thousand wide; in it shall be the sanctuary, the Most Holy *Place.* [4]It shall be a holy *section* of the land, belonging to the priests, the ministers of the sanctuary, who come near to minister to the LORD; it shall be a place for their houses and a holy place for the sanctuary. [5]*An area* twenty-five thousand *cubits* long and ten thousand wide shall belong to the Levites, the ministers of the temple; they shall have twenty chambers as a possession.[a]

PROPERTIES OF THE CITY AND THE PRINCE

[6]"You shall appoint as the property of the city *an area* five thousand *cubits* wide and twenty-five thousand long, adjacent to the district of the holy *section;* it shall belong to the whole house of Israel.

[7]"The prince shall have *a section* on one side and the other of the holy district and the city's property; and bordering on the holy district and the city's property, extending westward on the west side and eastward on the east side, the length *shall be* side by side with one of the *tribal* portions, from the west border to the east border. [8]The land shall be his possession in Israel; and My princes shall no more oppress My people, but they shall give *the rest of* the land to the house of Israel, according to their tribes."

LAWS GOVERNING THE PRINCE

[9]"Thus says the Lord GOD: "Enough, O princes of Israel! Remove violence and plundering,

45:5 [a]Following Masoretic Text, Targum, and Vulgate; Septuagint reads *a possession, cities of dwelling.*

execute justice and righteousness, and stop dispossessing My people," says the Lord GOD. ¹⁰"You shall have honest scales, an honest ephah, and an honest bath. ¹¹The ephah and the bath shall be of the same measure, so that the bath contains one-tenth of a homer, and the ephah one-tenth of a homer; their measure shall be according to the homer. ¹²The shekel *shall be* twenty gerahs; twenty shekels, twenty-five shekels, *and* fifteen shekels shall be your mina.

¹³"This *is* the offering which you shall offer: you shall give one-sixth of an ephah from a homer of wheat, and one-sixth of an ephah from a homer of barley. ¹⁴The ordinance concerning oil, the bath of oil, *is* one-tenth of a bath from a kor. *A kor is* a homer or ten baths, for ten baths *are* a homer. ¹⁵And one lamb shall be given from a flock of two hundred, from the rich pastures of Israel. These shall be for grain offerings, burnt offerings, and peace offerings, to make atonement for them," says the Lord GOD. ¹⁶"All the people of the land shall give this offering for the prince in Israel. ¹⁷Then it shall be the prince's part *to give* burnt offerings, grain offerings, and drink offerings, at the feasts, the New Moons, the Sabbaths, and at all the appointed seasons of the house of Israel. He shall prepare the sin offering, the grain offering, the burnt offering, and the peace offerings to make atonement for the house of Israel."

KEEPING THE FEASTS

¹⁸"Thus says the Lord GOD: "In the first *month,* on the first *day* of the month, you shall take a young bull without blemish and cleanse the sanctuary. ¹⁹The priest shall take some of the blood of the sin offering and put *it* on the doorposts of the temple, on the four corners of the ledge of the altar, and on the gateposts of the gate of the inner court. ²⁰And so you shall do on the seventh *day* of the month for everyone who has sinned unintentionally or in ignorance. Thus you shall make atonement for the temple.

²¹"In the first *month,* on the fourteenth day of the month, you shall observe the Passover, a feast of seven days; unleavened bread shall be eaten. ²²And on that day the prince shall prepare for himself and for all the people of the land a bull *for* a sin offering. ²³On the seven days of the feast he shall prepare a burnt offering to the LORD, seven

bulls and seven rams without blemish, daily for seven days, and a kid of the goats daily *for* a sin offering. ²⁴And he shall prepare a grain offering of one ephah for each bull and one ephah for each ram, together with a hin of oil for each ephah.

²⁵"In the seventh *month,* on the fifteenth day of the month, at the feast, he shall do likewise for seven days, according to the sin offering, the burnt offering, the grain offering, and the oil."

THE MANNER OF WORSHIP

46 'Thus says the Lord GOD: "The gateway of the inner court that faces toward the east shall be shut the six working days; but on the Sabbath it shall be opened, and on the day of the New Moon it shall be opened. ²The prince shall enter by way of the vestibule of the gateway from the outside, and stand by the gatepost. The priests shall prepare his burnt offering and his peace offerings. He shall worship at the threshold of the gate. Then he shall go out, but the gate shall not be shut until evening. ³Likewise the people of the land shall worship at the entrance to this gateway before the LORD on the Sabbaths and the New Moons. ⁴The burnt offering that the prince offers to the LORD on the Sabbath day *shall be* six lambs without blemish, and a ram without blemish; ⁵and the grain offering *shall be one* ephah for a ram, and the grain offering for the lambs, as much as he wants to give, as well as a hin of oil with every ephah. ⁶On the day of the New Moon *it shall be* a young bull without blemish, six lambs, and a ram; they shall be without blemish. ⁷He shall prepare a grain offering of an ephah for a bull, an ephah for a ram, as much as he wants to give for the lambs, and a hin of oil with every ephah. ⁸When the prince enters, he shall go in by way of the vestibule of the gateway, and go out the same way.

⁹"But when the people of the land come before the LORD on the appointed feast days, whoever enters by way of the north gate to worship shall go out by way of the south gate; and whoever enters by way of the south gate shall go out by way of the north gate. He shall not return by way of the gate through which he came, but shall go out through the opposite gate. ¹⁰The prince shall then be in their midst. When they go in, he shall go in; and when they go out, he shall go out. ¹¹At the festivals and the appointed feast days the

grain offering shall be an ephah for a bull, an ephah for a ram, as much as he wants to give for the lambs, and a hin of oil with every ephah.

[12]"Now when the prince makes a voluntary burnt offering or voluntary peace offering to the LORD, the gate that faces toward the east shall then be opened for him; and he shall prepare his burnt offering and his peace offerings as he did on the Sabbath day. Then he shall go out, and after he goes out the gate shall be shut.

[13]"You shall daily make a burnt offering to the LORD *of* a lamb of the first year without blemish; you shall prepare it every morning. [14]And you shall prepare a grain offering with it every morning, a sixth of an ephah, and a third of a hin of oil to moisten the fine flour. This grain offering *is* a perpetual ordinance, to be made regularly to the LORD. [15]Thus they shall prepare the lamb, the grain offering, and the oil, *as* a regular burnt offering every morning."

The Prince and Inheritance Laws

[16]'Thus says the Lord GOD: "If the prince gives a gift *of some* of his inheritance to any of his sons, it shall belong to his sons; it is their possession by inheritance. [17]But if he gives a gift of some of his inheritance to one of his servants, it shall be his until the year of liberty, after which it shall return to the prince. But his inheritance shall belong to his sons; it shall become theirs. [18]Moreover the prince shall not take any of the people's inheritance by evicting them from their property; he shall provide an inheritance for his sons from his own property, so that none of My people may be scattered from his property." ' "

How the Offerings Were Prepared

[19]Now he brought me through the entrance, which *was* at the side of the gate, into the holy chambers of the priests which face toward the north; and there a place *was* situated at their extreme western end. [20]And he said to me, "This *is* the place where the priests shall boil the trespass offering and the sin offering, *and* where they shall bake the grain offering, so that they do not bring *them* out into the outer court to sanctify the people."

[21]Then he brought me out into the outer court and caused me to pass by the four corners of the court; and in fact, in every corner of the court *there was another* court. [22]In the four corners of the court *were* enclosed courts, forty *cubits* long and thirty wide; all four corners *were* the same size. [23]*There was* a row *of building stones* all around in them, all around the four of them; and cooking hearths were made under the rows of stones all around. [24]And he said to me, "These *are* the kitchens where the ministers of the temple shall boil the sacrifices of the people."

The Healing Waters and Trees

47 Then he brought me back to the door of the temple; and there was water, flowing from under the threshold of the temple toward the east, for the front of the temple faced east; the water was flowing from under the right side of the temple, south of the altar. [2]He brought me out by way of the north gate, and led me around on the outside to the outer gateway that faces east; and there was water, running out on the right side.

[3]And when the man went out to the east with the line in his hand, he measured one thousand cubits, and he brought me through the waters; the water *came up to my* ankles. [4]Again he measured one thousand and brought me through the waters; the water *came up to my* knees. Again he measured one thousand and brought me through; the water *came up to my* waist. [5]Again he measured one thousand, *and it was* a river that I could not cross; for the water was too deep, water in which one must swim, a river that could not be crossed. [6]He said to me, "Son of man, have you seen *this?*" Then he brought me and returned me to the bank of the river.

[7]When I returned, there, along the bank of the river, *were* very many trees on one side and the other. [8]Then he said to me: "This water flows toward the eastern region, goes down into the valley, and enters the sea. *When it* reaches the sea, *its* waters are healed. [9]And it shall be *that* every living thing that moves, wherever the rivers go, will live. There will be a very great multitude of fish, because these waters go there; for they will be healed, and everything will live wherever the river goes. [10]It shall be *that* fishermen will stand by it from En Gedi to En Eglaim; they will be *places* for spreading their nets. Their fish will be of

the same kinds as the fish of the Great Sea, exceedingly many. [11]But its swamps and marshes will not be healed; they will be given over to salt. [12]Along the bank of the river, on this side and that, will grow all *kinds of* trees used for food; their leaves will not wither, and their fruit will not fail. They will bear fruit every month, because their water flows from the sanctuary. Their fruit will be for food, and their leaves for medicine."

BORDERS OF THE LAND

[13]Thus says the Lord GOD: "These *are* the borders by which you shall divide the land as an inheritance among the twelve tribes of Israel. Joseph *shall have two* portions. [14]You shall inherit it equally with one another; for I raised My hand in an oath to give it to your fathers, and this land shall fall to you as your inheritance.

[15]"This *shall be* the border of the land on the north: from the Great Sea, *by* the road to Hethlon, as one goes to Zedad, [16]Hamath, Berothah, Sibraim (which *is* between the border of Damascus and the border of Hamath), to Hazar Hatticon (which *is* on the border of Hauran). [17]Thus the boundary shall be from the Sea to Hazar Enan, the border of Damascus; and as for the north, northward, it is the border of Hamath. *This is* the north side.

[18]"On the east side you shall mark out the border from between Hauran and Damascus, and between Gilead and the land of Israel, along the Jordan, and along the eastern side of the sea. *This is* the east side.

[19]"The south side, toward the South,[a] *shall be* from Tamar to the waters of Meribah by Kadesh, along the brook to the Great Sea. *This is* the south side, toward the South.

[20]"The west side *shall be* the Great Sea, from the *southern* boundary until one comes to a point opposite Hamath. This *is* the west side.

[21]"Thus you shall divide this land among yourselves according to the tribes of Israel. [22]It shall be that you will divide it by lot as an inheritance for yourselves, and for the strangers who dwell among you and who bear children among you. They shall be to you as native-born among the children of Israel; they shall have an inheritance with you among the tribes of Israel. [23]And it shall be *that* in whatever tribe the stranger

dwells, there you shall give *him* his inheritance," says the Lord GOD.

DIVISION OF THE LAND

48 "Now these *are* the names of the tribes: From the northern border along the road to Hethlon at the entrance of Hamath, to Hazar Enan, the border of Damascus northward, in the direction of Hamath, *there shall be* one *section for* Dan from its east to its west side; [2]by the border of Dan, from the east side to the west, one *section for* Asher; [3]by the border of Asher, from the east side to the west, one *section for* Naphtali; [4]by the border of Naphtali, from the east side to the west, one *section for* Manasseh; [5]by the border of Manasseh, from the east side to the west, one *section for* Ephraim; [6]by the border of Ephraim, from the east side to the west, one *section for* Reuben; [7]by the border of Reuben, from the east side to the west, one *section for* Judah; [8]by the border of Judah, from the east side to the west, shall be the district which you shall set apart, twenty-five thousand *cubits* in width, and *in* length the same as one of the *other* portions, from the east side to the west, with the sanctuary in the center.

[9]"The district that you shall set apart for the LORD *shall be* twenty-five thousand *cubits* in length and ten thousand in width. [10]To these—to the priests—the holy district shall belong: on the north twenty-five thousand *cubits in length,* on the west ten thousand in width, on the east ten thousand in width, and on the south twenty-five thousand in length. The sanctuary of the LORD shall be in the center. [11]*It shall be* for the priests of the sons of Zadok, who are sanctified, who have kept My charge, who did not go astray when the children of Israel went astray, as the Levites went astray. [12]And *this* district of land that is set apart shall be to them a thing most holy by the border of the Levites.

[13]"Opposite the border of the priests, the Levites *shall have an area* twenty-five thousand *cubits* in length and ten thousand in width; its entire length *shall be* twenty-five thousand and its width ten thousand. [14]And they shall not sell or exchange any of it; they may not alienate this best *part* of the land, for *it is* holy to the LORD.

[15]"The five thousand *cubits* in width that re-

47:19 [a]Hebrew *Negev*

main, along the edge of the twenty-five thousand, shall be for general use by the city, for dwellings and common-land; and the city shall be in the center. ¹⁶These *shall be* its measurements: the north side four thousand five hundred *cubits,* the south side four thousand five hundred, the east side four thousand five hundred, and the west side four thousand five hundred. ¹⁷The common-land of the city shall be: to the north two hundred and fifty *cubits,* to the south two hundred and fifty, to the east two hundred and fifty, and to the west two hundred and fifty. ¹⁸The rest of the length, alongside the district of the holy *section, shall be* ten thousand *cubits* to the east and ten thousand to the west. It shall be adjacent to the district of the holy *section,* and its produce shall be food for the workers of the city. ¹⁹The workers of the city, from all the tribes of Israel, shall cultivate it. ²⁰The entire district *shall be* twenty-five thousand *cubits* by twenty-five thousand *cubits,* foursquare. You shall set apart the holy district with the property of the city.

²¹"The rest *shall belong* to the prince, on one side and on the other of the holy district and of the city's property, next to the twenty-five thousand *cubits* of the *holy* district as far as the eastern border, and westward next to the twenty-five thousand as far as the western border, adjacent to the *tribal* portions; *it shall belong* to the prince. It shall be the holy district, and the sanctuary of the temple *shall be* in the center. ²²Moreover, apart from the possession of the Levites and the possession of the city *which are* in the midst of what *belongs* to the prince, *the area* between the border of Judah and the border of Benjamin shall belong to the prince.

²³"As for the rest of the tribes, from the east side to the west, Benjamin *shall have* one *section;* ²⁴by the border of Benjamin, from the east side to the west, Simeon *shall have* one *section;* ²⁵by the border of Simeon, from the east side to the west, Issachar *shall have* one *section;* ²⁶by the border of Issachar, from the east side to the west, Zebulun *shall have* one *section;* ²⁷by the border of Zebulun, from the east side to the west, Gad *shall have* one *section;* ²⁸by the border of Gad, on the south side, toward the South,ᵃ the border shall be from Tamar *to* the waters of Meribah *by* Kadesh, along the brook to the Great Sea. ²⁹This *is* the land which you shall divide by lot as an inheritance among the tribes of Israel, and these *are* their portions," says the Lord GOD.

THE GATES OF THE CITY AND ITS NAME

³⁰"These *are* the exits of the city. On the north side, measuring four thousand five hundred *cubits* ³¹(the gates of the city *shall be* named after the tribes of Israel), the three gates northward: one gate for Reuben, one gate for Judah, and one gate for Levi; ³²on the east side, four thousand five hundred *cubits,* three gates: one gate for Joseph, one gate for Benjamin, and one gate for Dan; ³³on the south side, measuring four thousand five hundred *cubits,* three gates: one gate for Simeon, one gate for Issachar, and one gate for Zebulun; ³⁴on the west side, four thousand five hundred *cubits* with their three gates: one gate for Gad, one gate for Asher, and one gate for Naphtali. ³⁵All the way around *shall be* eighteen thousand *cubits;* and the name of the city from *that* day *shall be:* THE LORD *IS* THERE."ᵃ

48:28 ᵃHebrew *Negev*   **48:35** ᵃHebrew *YHWH Shammah*

IMPACT OF THE BOOK

I   IDEA
: *Courage of conviction will enable you to face the toughest trials and challenges without fear.*

M   MESSAGE
: *It is never easy to swim against the tide, but a courageous leader realizes that the greatest victories usually come after the hardest battles. Even at a young age, Daniel realized the importance of not sacrificing his integrity or giving up on his convictions. He trusted God with the outcome of his life. Even in circumstances where he seemed to have no control, Daniel determined not to sacrifice his walk with the Lord. He determined to pursue excellence, and God was able to use him repeatedly as a witness for Him and as a timeless model of a young leader.*

P   PEOPLE
: *Abed-Nego (Azariah), Belshazzar, Daniel (Belteshazzar), Darius, Meshach (Mishael), Nebuchadnezzar, Shadrach (Hananiah)*

A   AUTHOR
: *Daniel was a contemporary of Jeremiah and Ezekiel. He was taken into exile in Babylon while in his late teens around 605 BC.*

C   CULTURE
: *Daniel was taken captive during the first deportation of exiles in 605 BC. He served the Babylonian king Nebuchadnezzar and later Belshazzar. When Babylon fell to the Medo-Persian Empire in 539 BC, Daniel served Darius the Mede, the new king, who was also known as King Cyrus of Persia. This book can be divided into two major sections: historical narrative recounting Daniel's life and prophetic revelation predicting such events as the fall of Babylon and the coming of the Messiah. This book was originally written in two languages—Hebrew and in Aramaic, which was the international trade language of the day.*

T   TIMELINE
: *c. 530 BC*

KEY SCRIPTURE
MEMORY VERSES
: 2:44; 3:16–18; 6:16; 9:24–27; 12:13

Daniel and His Friends Obey God

1 In the third year of the reign of Jehoiakim king of Judah, Nebuchadnezzar king of Babylon came to Jerusalem and besieged it. [2]And the Lord gave Jehoiakim king of Judah into his hand, with some of the articles of the house of God, which he carried into the land of Shinar to the house of his god; and he brought the articles into the treasure house of his god.

[3]Then the king instructed Ashpenaz, the master of his eunuchs, to bring some of the children of Israel and some of the king's descendants and some of the nobles, [4]young men in whom *there was* no blemish, but good-looking, gifted in all wisdom, possessing knowledge and quick to understand, who *had* ability to serve in the king's palace, and whom they might teach the language and literature of the Chaldeans. [5]And the king appointed for them a daily provision of the king's delicacies and of the wine which he drank, and three years of training for them, so that at the end of *that time* they might serve before the king. [6]Now from among those of the sons of Judah were Daniel, Hananiah, Mishael, and Azariah. [7]To them the chief of the eunuchs gave names: he gave Daniel *the name* Belteshazzar; to Hananiah, Shadrach; to Mishael, Meshach; and to Azariah, Abed-Nego.

[8]But Daniel purposed in his heart that he would not defile himself with the portion of the king's delicacies, nor with the wine which he drank; therefore he requested of the chief of the eunuchs that he might not defile himself. [9]Now God had brought Daniel into the favor and goodwill of the chief of the eunuchs. [10]And the chief of the eunuchs said to Daniel, "I fear my lord the king, who has appointed your food and drink. For why should he see your faces looking worse than the young men who *are* your age? Then you would endanger my head before the king."

[11]So Daniel said to the steward[a] whom the chief of the eunuchs had set over Daniel, Hananiah, Mishael, and Azariah, [12]"Please test your servants for ten days, and let them give us vegetables to eat and water to drink. [13]Then let our appearance be examined before you, and the appearance of the young men who eat the portion of the king's delicacies; and as you see fit, *so* deal with

your servants." [14]So he consented with them in this matter, and tested them ten days.

[15]And at the end of ten days their features appeared better and fatter in flesh than all the young men who ate the portion of the king's delicacies. [16]Thus the steward took away their portion of delicacies and the wine that they were to drink, and gave them vegetables.

[17]As for these four young men, God gave them knowledge and skill in all literature and wisdom; and Daniel had understanding in all visions and dreams.

[18]Now at the end of the days, when the king had said that they should be brought in, the chief of the eunuchs brought them in before Nebuchadnezzar. [19]Then the king interviewed[a] them, and among them all none was found like Daniel, Hananiah, Mishael, and Azariah; therefore they served before the king. [20]And in all matters of wisdom *and* understanding about which the king examined them, he found them ten times better than all the magicians *and* astrologers who *were* in all his realm. [21]Thus Daniel continued until the first year of King Cyrus.

Nebuchadnezzar's Dream

2 Now in the second year of Nebuchadnezzar's reign, Nebuchadnezzar had dreams; and his spirit was *so* troubled that his sleep left him. [2]Then the king gave the command to call the magicians, the astrologers, the sorcerers, and the Chaldeans to tell the king his dreams. So they came and stood before the king. [3]And the king said to them, "I have had a dream, and my spirit is anxious to know the dream."

[4]Then the Chaldeans spoke to the king in Aramaic,[a] "O king, live forever! Tell your servants the dream, and we will give the interpretation."

[5]The king answered and said to the Chaldeans, "My decision is firm: if you do not make known the dream to me, and its interpretation, you shall be cut in pieces, and your houses shall be made an ash heap. [6]However, if you tell the dream and its interpretation, you shall receive from me gifts, rewards, and great honor. Therefore tell me the dream and its interpretation."

1:11 [a]Hebrew *Melzar*, also in verse 16　1:19 [a]Literally *talked with them*　2:4 [a]The original language of Daniel 2:4b through 7:28 is Aramaic.

⁷They answered again and said, "Let the king tell his servants the dream, and we will give its interpretation."

⁸The king answered and said, "I know for certain that you would gain time, because you see that my decision is firm: ⁹if you do not make known the dream to me, *there is only* one decree for you! For you have agreed to speak lying and corrupt words before me till the time has changed. Therefore tell me the dream, and I shall know that you can give me its interpretation."

¹⁰The Chaldeans answered the king, and said, "There is not a man on earth who can tell the king's matter; therefore no king, lord, or ruler has *ever* asked such things of any magician, astrologer, or Chaldean. ¹¹*It is* a difficult thing that the king requests, and there is no other who can tell it to the king except the gods, whose dwelling is not with flesh."

¹²For this reason the king was angry and very furious, and gave the command to destroy all the wise *men* of Babylon. ¹³So the decree went out, and they began killing the wise *men;* and they sought Daniel and his companions, to kill *them.*

God Reveals Nebuchadnezzar's Dream

¹⁴Then with counsel and wisdom Daniel answered Arioch, the captain of the king's guard, who had gone out to kill the wise *men* of Babylon; ¹⁵he answered and said to Arioch the king's captain, "Why is the decree from the king so urgent?" Then Arioch made the decision known to Daniel.

¹⁶So Daniel went in and asked the king to give him time, that he might tell the king the interpretation. ¹⁷Then Daniel went to his house, and made the decision known to Hananiah, Mishael, and Azariah, his companions, ¹⁸that they might seek mercies from the God of heaven concerning this secret, so that Daniel and his companions might not perish with the rest of the wise *men* of Babylon. ¹⁹Then the secret was revealed to Daniel in a night vision. So Daniel blessed the God of heaven.

²⁰Daniel answered and said:

"Blessed be the name of God forever and ever,
 For wisdom and might are His.
²¹And He changes the times and the seasons;

He removes kings and raises up kings;
He gives wisdom to the wise
And knowledge to those who have
 understanding.
²²He reveals deep and secret things;
He knows what *is* in the darkness,
And light dwells with Him.

²³"I thank You and praise You,
 O God of my fathers;
You have given me wisdom and might,
And have now made known to me what we
 asked of You,
For You have made known to us the king's
 demand."

Daniel Explains the Dream

²⁴Therefore Daniel went to Arioch, whom the king had appointed to destroy the wise *men* of Babylon. He went and said thus to him: "Do not destroy the wise *men* of Babylon; take me before the king, and I will tell the king the interpretation."

²⁵Then Arioch quickly brought Daniel before the king, and said thus to him, "I have found a man of the captives[a] of Judah, who will make known to the king the interpretation."

²⁶The king answered and said to Daniel, whose name *was* Belteshazzar, "Are you able to make known to me the dream which I have seen, and its interpretation?"

²⁷Daniel answered in the presence of the king, and said, "The secret which the king has demanded, the wise *men,* the astrologers, the magicians, and the soothsayers cannot declare to the king. ²⁸But there is a God in heaven who reveals secrets, and He has made known to King Nebuchadnezzar what will be in the latter days. Your dream, and the visions of your head upon your bed, were these: ²⁹As for you, O king, thoughts came *to* your *mind while* on your bed, *about* what would come to pass after this; and He who reveals secrets has made known to you what will be. ³⁰But as for me, this secret has not been revealed to me because I have more wisdom than anyone living, but for *our* sakes who make known the interpretation to the king, and that you may know the thoughts of your heart.

2:25 ªLiterally *of the sons of the captivity*

³¹"You, O king, were watching; and behold, a great image! This great image, whose splendor *was* excellent, stood before you; and its form *was* awesome. ³²This image's head *was* of fine gold, its chest and arms of silver, its belly and thighsᵃ of bronze, ³³its legs of iron, its feet partly of iron and partly of clay.ᵃ ³⁴You watched while a stone was cut out without hands, which struck the image on its feet of iron and clay, and broke them in pieces. ³⁵Then the iron, the clay, the bronze, the silver, and the gold were crushed together, and became like chaff from the summer threshing floors; the wind carried them away so that no trace of them was found. And the stone that struck the image became a great mountain and filled the whole earth.

³⁶"This *is* the dream. Now we will tell the interpretation of it before the king. ³⁷You, O king, *are* a king of kings. For the God of heaven has given you a kingdom, power, strength, and glory; ³⁸and wherever the children of men dwell, or the beasts of the field and the birds of the heaven, He has given *them* into your hand, and has made you ruler over them all—you *are* this head of gold. ³⁹But after you shall arise another kingdom inferior to yours; then another, a third kingdom of bronze, which shall rule over all the earth. ⁴⁰And the fourth kingdom shall be as strong as iron, inasmuch as iron breaks in pieces and shatters everything; and like iron that crushes, *that kingdom* will break in pieces and crush all the others. ⁴¹Whereas you saw the feet and toes, partly of potter's clay and partly of iron, the kingdom shall be divided; yet the strength of the iron shall be in it, just as you saw the iron mixed with ceramic clay. ⁴²And *as* the toes of the feet *were* partly of iron and partly of clay, *so* the kingdom shall be partly strong and partly fragile. ⁴³As you saw iron mixed with ceramic clay, they will mingle with the seed of men; but they will not adhere to one another, just as iron does not mix with clay. ⁴⁴And in the days of these kings the God of heaven will set up a kingdom which shall never be destroyed; and the kingdom shall not be left to other people; it shall break in pieces and consume all these kingdoms, and it shall stand forever. ⁴⁵Inasmuch as you saw that the stone was cut out of the mountain without hands, and that it broke in pieces the iron, the bronze, the clay, the silver, and the

gold—the great God has made known to the king what will come to pass after this. The dream is certain, and its interpretation is sure."

DANIEL AND HIS FRIENDS PROMOTED

⁴⁶Then King Nebuchadnezzar fell on his face, prostrate before Daniel, and commanded that they should present an offering and incense to him. ⁴⁷The king answered Daniel, and said, "Truly your God *is* the God of gods, the Lord of kings, and a revealer of secrets, since you could reveal this secret." ⁴⁸Then the king promoted Daniel and gave him many great gifts; and he made him ruler over the whole province of Babylon, and chief administrator over all the wise *men* of Babylon. ⁴⁹Also Daniel petitioned the king, and he set Shadrach, Meshach, and Abed-Nego over the affairs of the province of Babylon; but Daniel *sat* in the gateᵃ of the king.

THE IMAGE OF GOLD

3 Nebuchadnezzar the king made an image of gold, whose height *was* sixty cubits *and* its width six cubits. He set it up in the plain of Dura, in the province of Babylon. ²And King Nebuchadnezzar sent *word* to gather together the satraps, the administrators, the governors, the counselors, the treasurers, the judges, the magistrates, and all the officials of the provinces, to come to the dedication of the image which King Nebuchadnezzar had set up. ³So the satraps, the administrators, the governors, the counselors, the treasurers, the judges, the magistrates, and all the officials of the provinces gathered together for the dedication of the image that King Nebuchadnezzar had set up; and they stood before the image that Nebuchadnezzar had set up. ⁴Then a herald cried aloud: "To you it is commanded, O peoples, nations, and languages, ⁵*that* at the time you hear the sound of the horn, flute, harp, lyre, *and* psaltery, in symphony with all kinds of music, you shall fall down and worship the gold image that King Nebuchadnezzar has set up; ⁶and whoever does not fall down and worship shall be cast immediately into the midst of a burning fiery furnace."

⁷So at that time, when all the people heard the sound of the horn, flute, harp, *and* lyre, in

2:32 ᵃOr *sides*　**2:33** ᵃOr *baked clay,* and so in verses 34, 35, and 42　**2:49** ᵃThat is, the king's court

INSIDE *the* INFLUENCERS

NEBUCHADNEZZAR: Worship Cannot Be Forced

DANIEL 3

If there ever was a megalomaniac, it was Nebuchadnezzar, king of Babylon. History records that he was the most powerful king to rule in the east. Nearly every temple or structure discovered in that part of the world bears the inscription, "Nebuchadnezzar, son of Nabopolassar, king of Babylon." He dominated for 43 years when he ruled Babylon from 605 to 562 BC.

Nebuchadnezzar's giant-sized ego led him to believe he could force worship. In an effort to make the entire nation bow and worship him, he set up a 90 feet tall, golden statue of himself (v. 1–7). Disobedience to the law was punishable by death in the fiery furnace, but that didn't stop the three Hebrew young men from refusing to bow. When their God saved them from the fire, Nebuchadnezzar was forced to proclaim the God of the Hebrews as the Most High God. He enforced a new law demanding that no one in the Babylonian kingdom could say anything against the God of the Hebrews or face being torn apart and their house turned to a pile of ash (v. 29).

The king's arrogance knew no limits. The God of heaven doesn't need or require forced worship. True worship springs forth from a heart of gratitude and awe for the living God.

symphony with all kinds of music, all the people, nations, and languages fell down *and* worshiped the gold image which King Nebuchadnezzar had set up.

DANIEL'S FRIENDS DISOBEY THE KING

⁸Therefore at that time certain Chaldeans came forward and accused the Jews. ⁹They spoke and said to King Nebuchadnezzar, "O king, live forever! ¹⁰You, O king, have made a decree that everyone who hears the sound of the horn, flute, harp, lyre, *and* psaltery, in symphony with all kinds of music, shall fall down and worship the gold image; ¹¹and whoever does not fall down and worship shall be cast into the midst of a burning fiery furnace. ¹²There are certain Jews whom you have set over the affairs of the province of Babylon: Shadrach, Meshach, and Abed-Nego; these men, O king, have not paid due regard to you. They do not serve your gods or worship the gold image which you have set up."

¹³Then Nebuchadnezzar, in rage and fury, gave the command to bring Shadrach, Meshach, and Abed-Nego. So they brought these men before the king. ¹⁴Nebuchadnezzar spoke, saying to them,

"*Is it* true, Shadrach, Meshach, and Abed-Nego, *that* you do not serve my gods or worship the gold image which I have set up? ¹⁵Now if you are ready at the time you hear the sound of the horn, flute, harp, lyre, *and* psaltery, in symphony with all kinds of music, and you fall down and worship the image which I have made, *good!* But if you do not worship, you shall be cast immediately into the midst of a burning fiery furnace. And who *is* the god who will deliver you from my hands?"

¹⁶Shadrach, Meshach, and Abed-Nego answered and said to the king, "O Nebuchadnezzar, we have no need to answer you in this matter. ¹⁷If that *is the case,* our God whom we serve is able to deliver us from the burning fiery furnace, and He will deliver *us* from your hand, O king. ¹⁸But if not, let it be known to you, O king, that we do not serve your gods, nor will we worship the gold image which you have set up."

SAVED IN FIERY TRIAL

¹⁹Then Nebuchadnezzar was full of fury, and the expression on his face changed toward Shadrach, Meshach, and Abed-Nego. He spoke and commanded that they heat the furnace seven

INSIDE *the* INFLUENCERS

SHADRACH, MESHACH, AND ABED-NEGO—Make No Compromise

DANIEL 3:8–18

The pressure to compromise our convictions comes from the agenda of "acceptance;" that is, to accept lifestyles and attitudes that are contrary to the absolute truth in God's Word. In the country of Babylon (modern day Iraq), people faced more than peer pressure. The law demanded worship of a tall idol in the shape of King Nebuchadnezzar. Disobedience to the law meant death.

The young Hebrews refused to worship anything or anyone other than their God. Their accusers turned them in. The three were brought before Nebuchadnezzar, and he offered them a chance to escape the fiery furnace by compromising their faith. Shadrach, Meshach, and Abed-Nego were ready for the king's question and threat, because they had prepared their hearts since childhood. Standing together, their faith gave them the courage to go into the fire, and God's power allowed them to walk back out.

Without hesitation, they informed the king that God would be honored, and they were not willing to waiver. The result was that the pagan king glorified God as the only God "who can deliver like this" (Dan. 3:29).

If you want to be *ready to stand*, you must:

- Actively build your faith by studying the Word of God;
- Decide daily to respond to the pressure of the culture without compromise;
- Be surrounded by like-minded, godly friends who stand strong with you.

times more than it was usually heated. [20]And he commanded certain mighty men of valor who *were* in his army to bind Shadrach, Meshach, and Abed-Nego, *and* cast *them* into the burning fiery furnace. [21]Then these men were bound in their coats, their trousers, their turbans, and their *other* garments, and were cast into the midst of the burning fiery furnace. [22]Therefore, because the king's command was urgent, and the furnace exceedingly hot, the flame of the fire killed those men who took up Shadrach, Meshach, and Abed-Nego. [23]And these three men, Shadrach, Meshach, and Abed-Nego, fell down bound into the midst of the burning fiery furnace.

[24]Then King Nebuchadnezzar was astonished; and he rose in haste *and* spoke, saying to his counselors, "Did we not cast three men bound into the midst of the fire?"

They answered and said to the king, "True, O king."

[25]"Look!" he answered, "I see four men loose,

walking in the midst of the fire; and they are not hurt, and the form of the fourth is like the Son of God."[a]

NEBUCHADNEZZAR PRAISES GOD

[26]Then Nebuchadnezzar went near the mouth of the burning fiery furnace *and* spoke, saying, "Shadrach, Meshach, and Abed-Nego, servants of the Most High God, come out, and come *here*." Then Shadrach, Meshach, and Abed-Nego came from the midst of the fire. [27]And the satraps, administrators, governors, and the king's counselors gathered together, and they saw these men on whose bodies the fire had no power; the hair of their head was not singed nor were their garments affected, and the smell of fire was not on them.

[28]Nebuchadnezzar spoke, saying, "Blessed be the God of Shadrach, Meshach, and Abed-Nego, who sent His Angel[a] and delivered His servants

3:25 [a]Or *a son of the gods*   **3:28** [a]Or *angel*

who trusted in Him, and they have frustrated the king's word, and yielded their bodies, that they should not serve nor worship any god except their own God! [29]Therefore I make a decree that any people, nation, or language which speaks anything amiss against the God of Shadrach, Meshach, and Abed-Nego shall be cut in pieces, and their houses shall be made an ash heap; because there is no other God who can deliver like this."

[30]Then the king promoted Shadrach, Meshach, and Abed-Nego in the province of Babylon.

NEBUCHADNEZZAR'S SECOND DREAM

4 Nebuchadnezzar the king,

To all peoples, nations, and languages that dwell in all the earth:

Peace be multiplied to you.

[2]I thought it good to declare the signs and wonders that the Most High God has worked for me.

[3]How great *are* His signs,
And how mighty His wonders!
His kingdom *is* an everlasting kingdom,
And His dominion *is* from generation to generation.

[4]I, Nebuchadnezzar, was at rest in my house, and flourishing in my palace. [5]I saw a dream which made me afraid, and the thoughts on my bed and the visions of my head troubled me. [6]Therefore I issued a decree to bring in all the wise *men* of Babylon before me, that they might make known to me the interpretation of the dream. [7]Then the magicians, the astrologers, the Chaldeans, and the soothsayers came in, and I told them the dream; but they did not make known to me its interpretation. [8]But at last Daniel came before me (his name *is* Belteshazzar, according to the name of my god; in him *is* the Spirit of the Holy God), and I told the dream before him, *saying:* [9]"Belteshazzar, chief of the magicians, because I know that the Spirit of the Holy God *is* in you, and no

secret troubles you, explain to me the visions of my dream that I have seen, and its interpretation.

[10]"These *were* the visions of my head *while* on my bed:

I was looking, and behold,
A tree in the midst of the earth,
And its height was great.
[11]The tree grew and became strong;
Its height reached to the heavens,
And it could be seen to the ends of all the earth.
[12]Its leaves *were* lovely,
Its fruit abundant,
And in it *was* food for all.
The beasts of the field found shade under it,
The birds of the heavens dwelt in its branches,
And all flesh was fed from it.

[13]"I saw in the visions of my head while on my bed, and there was a watcher, a holy one, coming down from heaven. [14]He cried aloud and said thus:

'Chop down the tree and cut off its branches,
Strip off its leaves and scatter its fruit.
Let the beasts get out from under it,
And the birds from its branches.
[15]Nevertheless leave the stump and roots in the earth,
Bound with a band of iron and bronze,
In the tender grass of the field.
Let it be wet with the dew of heaven,
And *let* him graze with the beasts
On the grass of the earth.
[16]Let his heart be changed from *that of* a man,
Let him be given the heart of a beast,
And let seven times[a] pass over him.

[17]'This decision *is* by the decree of the watchers,
And the sentence by the word of the holy ones,
In order that the living may know

4:16 [a]Possibly *seven years,* and so in verses 23, 25, and 32

That the Most High rules in the kingdom of
　　men,
Gives it to whomever He will,
And sets over it the lowest of men.'

18"This dream I, King Nebuchadnezzar, have
seen. Now you, Belteshazzar, declare its
interpretation, since all the wise *men* of my
kingdom are not able to make known to me
the interpretation; but you *are* able, for the
Spirit of the Holy God *is* in you."

DANIEL EXPLAINS THE SECOND DREAM

19Then Daniel, whose name *was* Belteshazzar,
was astonished for a time, and his thoughts
troubled him. *So* the king spoke, and said,
"Belteshazzar, do not let the dream or its
interpretation trouble you." Belteshazzar
answered and said, "My lord, *may* the dream
concern those who hate you, and its
interpretation concern your enemies!

20"The tree that you saw, which grew and
became strong, whose height reached to the
heavens and which *could be* seen by all the
earth, 21whose leaves *were* lovely and its fruit
abundant, in which *was* food for all, under
which the beasts of the field dwelt, and in
whose branches the birds of the heaven had
their home— 22it *is* you, O king, who have
grown and become strong; for your greatness
has grown and reaches to the heavens, and
your dominion to the end of the earth.

23"And inasmuch as the king saw a watcher, a
holy one, coming down from heaven and
saying, 'Chop down the tree and destroy it,
but leave its stump and roots in the earth,
bound with a band of iron and bronze in the
tender grass of the field; let it be wet with
the dew of heaven, and let him graze with
the beasts of the field, till seven times pass
over him'; 24this is the interpretation, O king,
and this is the decree of the Most High,
which has come upon my lord the king:
25They shall drive you from men, your
dwelling shall be with the beasts of the field,
and they shall make you eat grass like oxen.
They shall wet you with the dew of heaven,

and seven times shall pass over you, till you
know that the Most High rules in the
kingdom of men, and gives it to whomever
He chooses.

26 "And inasmuch as they gave the command to
leave the stump *and* roots of the tree, your
kingdom shall be assured to you, after you
come to know that Heaven rules.
27Therefore, O king, let my advice be
acceptable to you; break off your sins by *being*
righteous, and your iniquities by showing
mercy to *the* poor. Perhaps there may be a
lengthening of your prosperity."

NEBUCHADNEZZAR'S HUMILIATION

28All *this* came upon King Nebuchadnezzar.
29At the end of the twelve months he was
walking about the royal palace of Babylon.
30The king spoke, saying, "Is not this great
Babylon, that I have built for a royal dwelling
by my mighty power and for the honor of
my majesty?"

31While the word *was still* in the king's mouth,
a voice fell from heaven: "King
Nebuchadnezzar, to you it is spoken: the
kingdom has departed from you! 32And they
shall drive you from men, and your dwelling
shall be with the beasts of the field. They shall
make you eat grass like oxen; and seven times
shall pass over you, until you know that the
Most High rules in the kingdom of men, and
gives it to whomever He chooses."

33That very hour the word was fulfilled
concerning Nebuchadnezzar; he was driven
from men and ate grass like oxen; his body
was wet with the dew of heaven till his hair
had grown like eagles' *feathers* and his nails
like birds' *claws.*

NEBUCHADNEZZAR PRAISES GOD

34And at the end of the timea I,
Nebuchadnezzar, lifted my eyes to heaven,
and my understanding returned to me; and I
blessed the Most High and praised and
honored Him who lives forever:

4:34 aLiterally *days*

For His dominion *is* an everlasting dominion,
And His kingdom *is* from generation to
    generation.
³⁵All the inhabitants of the earth *are* reputed as
    nothing;
He does according to His will in the army of
    heaven
And *among* the inhabitants of the earth.
No one can restrain His hand
Or say to Him, "What have You done?"

³⁶At the same time my reason returned to me,
and for the glory of my kingdom, my honor
and splendor returned to me. My counselors
and nobles resorted to me, I was restored to
my kingdom, and excellent majesty was
added to me. ³⁷Now I, Nebuchadnezzar,
praise and extol and honor the King of
heaven, all of whose works *are* truth, and His
ways justice. And those who walk in pride He
is able to put down.

BELSHAZZAR'S FEAST

5 Belshazzar the king made a great feast for a
thousand of his lords, and drank wine in the
presence of the thousand. ²While he tasted the
wine, Belshazzar gave the command to bring
the gold and silver vessels which his father Nebuchadnezzar had taken from the temple which *had
been* in Jerusalem, that the king and his lords, his
wives, and his concubines might drink from them.
³Then they brought the gold vessels that had been
taken from the temple of the house of God which
had been in Jerusalem; and the king and his lords,
his wives, and his concubines drank from them.
⁴They drank wine, and praised the gods of gold
and silver, bronze and iron, wood and stone.

⁵In the same hour the fingers of a man's hand
appeared and wrote opposite the lampstand on the
plaster of the wall of the king's palace; and the
king saw the part of the hand that wrote. ⁶Then
the king's countenance changed, and his thoughts
troubled him, so that the joints of his hips were
loosened and his knees knocked against each
other. ⁷The king cried aloud to bring in the astrologers, the Chaldeans, and the soothsayers. The
king spoke, saying to the wise *men* of Babylon,
"Whoever reads this writing, and tells me its interpretation, shall be clothed with purple and *have* a

chain of gold around his neck; and he shall be the
third ruler in the kingdom." ⁸Now all the king's
wise *men* came, but they could not read the writing, or make known to the king its interpretation.
⁹Then King Belshazzar was greatly troubled, his
countenance was changed, and his lords were astonished.

¹⁰The queen, because of the words of the
king and his lords, came to the banquet hall. The
queen spoke, saying, "O king, live forever! Do not
let your thoughts trouble you, nor let your countenance change. ¹¹There is a man in your kingdom in whom *is* the Spirit of the Holy God. And
in the days of your father, light and understanding
and wisdom, like the wisdom of the gods, were
found in him; and King Nebuchadnezzar your father—your father the king—made him chief of
the magicians, astrologers, Chaldeans, *and* soothsayers. ¹²Inasmuch as an excellent spirit, knowledge, understanding, interpreting dreams, solving
riddles, and explaining enigmas^a were found in
this Daniel, whom the king named Belteshazzar,
now let Daniel be called, and he will give the interpretation."

THE WRITING ON THE WALL EXPLAINED

¹³Then Daniel was brought in before the
king. The king spoke, and said to Daniel, "*Are* you
that Daniel who is one of the captives^a from Judah, whom my father the king brought from Ju-
dah? ¹⁴I have heard of you, that the Spirit of God
is in you, and *that* light and understanding and excellent wisdom are found in you. ¹⁵Now the wise
men, the astrologers, have been brought in before
me, that they should read this writing and make
known to me its interpretation, but they could
not give the interpretation of the thing. ¹⁶And I
have heard of you, that you can give interpretations and explain enigmas. Now if you can read
the writing and make known to me its interpretation, you shall be clothed with purple and *have* a
chain of gold around your neck, and shall be the
third ruler in the kingdom."

¹⁷Then Daniel answered, and said before the
king, "Let your gifts be for yourself, and give your
rewards to another; yet I will read the writing to
the king, and make known to him the interpreta-

5:12 ^aLiterally *untying knots,* and so in verse 16   **5:13** ^aLiterally *of the sons of the captivity*

LEADERSHIP ISSUES

GC2: Humbled by the Lord

DANIEL 4:37

The Book of Daniel clearly contrasts the blessing of humility with the destruction of a prideful life. King Nebuchadnezzar refused to follow Daniel's advice to humbly acknowledge the One, True God. Consequently, the king's pride led to the loss of his kingdom and even his sanity. But by contrast, Daniel, Shadrach, Meshach, and Abed-Nego humbly declared their dependence upon God, hoped for His deliverance and provision—demonstrating remarkable faith in His care (Dan. 3). There's no doubt that these four young men pleased the Lord!

Consider how you might demonstrate your dependence upon God. What changes need to be made in your life—changes that only God can make? In what areas of your own life do you need God's deliverance, provision, and help? In what ways might God want to change you to be more like His Son?

Spend some time reflecting on these questions as you pray a private prayer. Ask the Lord to reveal His hopes and desires for your life and the growth areas in your life. Then share these responses with a friend or small group. Practice your humble demonstration of needing God's help. Begin the process of pleasing the Lord; and be ready for His grace, knowing that you are praying according to His will (1 Thess. 4:1–12).

I need God's help to make me more_____because_____
_____.

Or
I need God's help to make me less_____because_____
_____.

(For example: *I need God's help to make me more courageous at work. I've been called upon to be a witness for Him, and I haven't been able to speak up about my faith.*
Or: I need God's help to make me less critical of my brothers/sisters/mom/dad. I realize that my words have been hurtful to our entire family.)

GC2
GREAT COMMANDMENT
COMMISSION

tion. ¹⁸O king, the Most High God gave Nebuchadnezzar your father a kingdom and majesty, glory and honor. ¹⁹And because of the majesty that He gave him, all peoples, nations, and languages trembled and feared before him. Whomever he wished, he executed; whomever he wished, he kept alive; whomever he wished, he set up; and whomever he wished, he put down. ²⁰But when his heart was lifted up, and his spirit was hardened in pride, he was deposed from his kingly throne, and they took his glory from him. ²¹Then he was driven from the sons of men, his heart was made like the beasts, and his dwelling *was* with the wild donkeys. They fed him with grass like oxen, and his body was wet with the dew of heaven, till he knew that the Most High God rules in the kingdom of men, and appoints over it whomever He chooses.

²²"But you his son, Belshazzar, have not humbled your heart, although you knew all this. ²³And you have lifted yourself up against the Lord of heaven. They have brought the vessels of His house before you, and you and your lords, your wives and your concubines, have drunk wine from them. And you have praised the gods of silver and gold, bronze and iron, wood and stone, which do not see or hear or know; and the God who *holds* your breath in His hand and owns all your ways, you have not glorified. ²⁴Then the fingersᵃ of the hand were sent from Him, and this writing was written.

²⁵"And this is the inscription that was written:

MENE,ᵃ MENE, TEKEL,ᵇ UPHARSIN.ᶜ

²⁶This *is* the interpretation of *each* word. MENE: God has numbered your kingdom, and finished it; ²⁷TEKEL: You have been weighed in the balances, and found wanting; ²⁸PERES: Your kingdom has been divided, and given to the Medes and Persians."ᵃ ²⁹Then Belshazzar gave the command, and they clothed Daniel with purple and *put* a chain of gold around his neck, and made a proclamation concerning him that he should be the third ruler in the kingdom.

Belshazzar's Fall

³⁰That very night Belshazzar, king of the Chaldeans, was slain. ³¹And Darius the Mede received the kingdom, *being* about sixty-two years old.

The Plot Against Daniel

6It pleased Darius to set over the kingdom one hundred and twenty satraps, to be over the whole kingdom; ²and over these, three governors, of whom Daniel *was* one, that the satraps might give account to them, so that the king would suffer no loss. ³Then this Daniel distinguished himself above the governors and satraps, because an excellent spirit *was* in him; and the king gave thought to setting him over the whole realm. ⁴So the governors and satraps sought to find *some* charge against Daniel concerning the kingdom; but they could find no charge or fault, because he *was* faithful; nor was there any error or fault found in him. ⁵Then these men said, "We shall not find any charge against this Daniel unless we find *it* against him concerning the law of his God."

⁶So these governors and satraps thronged before the king, and said thus to him: "King Darius, live forever! ⁷All the governors of the kingdom, the administrators and satraps, the counselors and advisors, have consulted together to establish a royal statute and to make a firm decree, that whoever petitions any god or man for thirty days, except you, O king, shall be cast into the den of lions. ⁸Now, O king, establish the decree and sign the writing, so that it cannot be changed, according to the law of the Medes and Persians, which does not alter." ⁹Therefore King Darius signed the written decree.

Daniel in the Lions' Den

¹⁰Now when Daniel knew that the writing was signed, he went home. And in his upper room, with his windows open toward Jerusalem, he knelt down on his knees three times that day, and prayed and gave thanks before his God, as was his custom since early days.

¹¹Then these men assembled and found Daniel praying and making supplication before his God. ¹²And they went before the king, and spoke concerning the king's decree: "Have you

5:24 ᵃLiterally *palm* **5:25** ᵃLiterally *a mina* (50 shekels) from the verb "to number" ᵇLiterally *a shekel* from the verb "to weigh" ᶜLiterally *and half-shekels* from the verb "to divide" **5:28** ᵃAramaic *Paras,* consonant with *Peres*

INSIDE the INFLUENCERS

DANIEL: *Committed Quiet Time = Excellent Spirit*

DANIEL 6:3–5, 7, 10

In Daniel's time, Babylon was the "it" city of the ancient world. The state religion of Babylon involved big temples filled with large cults worshiping foreign gods of the cities, who were ranked in an order corresponding to the political status of their cities. The multitude of cities and pantheons in Babylonia and the fluctuating political fortunes throughout Babylonian history resulted in a great deal of conflict among the numerous cults.

Young Daniel found himself working and living in Babylon after being kidnapped at the king's request. Far from home and in a different culture, he was in the minority. Scripture says Daniel had "an excellent spirit in him" (v. 3). This defined Daniel's daily routine, his personality, and his morals. Notice the emphasis is on *spirit*, not the mind or body.

- Daniel purposed in his heart that he would not defile himself.
- Daniel kept the traditions of prayer, quiet time, and living a holy life.
- Daniel focused on the Lord and left the world behind.

We know from Scripture that he was good looking, talented, and intelligent (1:4); but did not use any of this to get ahead. Instead he focused on a holy life. The habit of kneeling to pray three times a day, *as was his custom,* gave Daniel an excellent spirit and the strength to live a consistent, godly public life.

---

not signed a decree that every man who petitions any god or man within thirty days, except you, O king, shall be cast into the den of lions?"

The king answered and said, "The thing *is* true, according to the law of the Medes and Persians, which does not alter."

[13]So they answered and said before the king, "That Daniel, who is one of the captives[a] from Judah, does not show due regard for you, O king, or for the decree that you have signed, but makes his petition three times a day."

[14]And the king, when he heard *these* words, was greatly displeased with himself, and set *his* heart on Daniel to deliver him; and he labored till the going down of the sun to deliver him. [15]Then these men approached the king, and said to the king, "Know, O king, that *it is* the law of the Medes and Persians that no decree or statute which the king establishes may be changed."

[16]So the king gave the command, and they brought Daniel and cast *him* into the den of lions. *But* the king spoke, saying to Daniel, "Your God,

whom you serve continually, He will deliver you." [17]Then a stone was brought and laid on the mouth of the den, and the king sealed it with his own signet ring and with the signets of his lords, that the purpose concerning Daniel might not be changed.

DANIEL SAVED FROM THE LIONS

[18]Now the king went to his palace and spent the night fasting; and no musicians[a] were brought before him. Also his sleep went from him. [19]Then the king arose very early in the morning and went in haste to the den of lions. [20]And when he came to the den, he cried out with a lamenting voice to Daniel. The king spoke, saying to Daniel, "Daniel, servant of the living God, has your God, whom you serve continually, been able to deliver you from the lions?"

[21]Then Daniel said to the king, "O king, live forever! [22]My God sent His angel and shut the

6:13 [a]Literally *of the sons of the captivity* **6:18** [a]Exact meaning unknown lions' mouths, so that they have not hurt me, because I was found innocent before Him; and also, O king, I have done no wrong before you."

²³Now the king was exceedingly glad for him, and commanded that they should take Daniel up out of the den. So Daniel was taken up out of the den, and no injury whatever was found on him, because he believed in his God.

Darius Honors God

²⁴And the king gave the command, and they brought those men who had accused Daniel, and they cast *them* into the den of lions—them, their children, and their wives; and the lions overpowered them, and broke all their bones in pieces before they ever came to the bottom of the den.

²⁵Then King Darius wrote:

To all peoples, nations, and languages that dwell in all the earth:

Peace be multiplied to you.

²⁶I make a decree that in every dominion of my kingdom *men must* tremble and fear before the God of Daniel.

For He *is* the living God,
And steadfast forever;
His kingdom *is the one* which shall not be
destroyed,
And His dominion *shall endure* to the end.
²⁷He delivers and rescues,
And He works signs and wonders
In heaven and on earth,
Who has delivered Daniel from the power of
the lions.

²⁸So this Daniel prospered in the reign of Darius and in the reign of Cyrus the Persian.

Vision of the Four Beasts

7 In the first year of Belshazzar king of Babylon, Daniel had a dream and visions of his head *while* on his bed. Then he wrote down the dream, telling the main facts.ᵃ

²Daniel spoke, saying, "I saw in my vision by night, and behold, the four winds of heaven were stirring up the Great Sea. ³And four great beasts came up from the sea, each different from the other. ⁴The first *was* like a lion, and had eagle's wings. I watched till its wings were plucked off; and it was lifted up from the earth and made to stand on two feet like a man, and a man's heart was given to it.

⁵"And suddenly another beast, a second, like a bear. It was raised up on one side, and *had* three ribs in its mouth between its teeth. And they said thus to it: 'Arise, devour much flesh!'

⁶"After this I looked, and there was another, like a leopard, which had on its back four wings of a bird. The beast also had four heads, and dominion was given to it.

⁷"After this I saw in the night visions, and behold, a fourth beast, dreadful and terrible, exceedingly strong. It had huge iron teeth; it was devouring, breaking in pieces, and trampling the residue with its feet. It *was* different from all the beasts that *were* before it, and it had ten horns. ⁸I was considering the horns, and there was another horn, a little one, coming up among them, before whom three of the first horns were plucked out by the roots. And there, in this horn, *were* eyes like the eyes of a man, and a mouth speaking pompous words.

Vision of the Ancient of Days

⁹"I watched till thrones were put in place,
And the Ancient of Days was seated;
His garment *was* white as snow,
And the hair of His head *was* like pure
wool.
His throne *was* a fiery flame,
Its wheels a burning fire;
¹⁰A fiery stream issued
And came forth from before Him.
A thousand thousands ministered to Him;
Ten thousand times ten thousand stood
before Him.
The courtᵃ was seated,
And the books were opened.

¹¹"I watched then because of the sound of the pompous words which the horn was speaking; I watched till the beast was slain, and its body destroyed and given to the burning flame. ¹²As for

7:1 ᵃLiterally *the head* (or *chief*) *of the words*   7:10 ᵃOr *judgment* the rest of the beasts, they had their dominion taken away, yet their lives were prolonged for a season and a time.

13"I was watching in the night visions,
And behold, *One* like the Son of Man,
Coming with the clouds of heaven!
He came to the Ancient of Days,
And they brought Him near before Him.
14Then to Him was given dominion and glory
and a kingdom,
That all peoples, nations, and languages
should serve Him.
His dominion *is* an everlasting dominion,
Which shall not pass away,
And His kingdom *the one*
Which shall not be destroyed.

Daniel's Visions Interpreted

15"I, Daniel, was grieved in my spirit within *my* body, and the visions of my head troubled me. 16I came near to one of those who stood by, and asked him the truth of all this. So he told me and made known to me the interpretation of these things: 17'Those great beasts, which are four, *are* four kings[a] *which* arise out of the earth. 18But the saints of the Most High shall receive the kingdom, and possess the kingdom forever, even forever and ever.'

19"Then I wished to know the truth about the fourth beast, which was different from all the others, exceedingly dreadful, *with* its teeth of iron and its nails of bronze, *which* devoured, broke in pieces, and trampled the residue with its feet; 20and the ten horns that *were* on its head, and the other *horn* which came up, before which three fell, namely, that horn which had eyes and a mouth which spoke pompous words, whose appearance *was* greater than his fellows.

21"I was watching; and the same horn was making war against the saints, and prevailing against them, 22until the Ancient of Days came, and a judgment was made *in favor* of the saints of the Most High, and the time came for the saints to possess the kingdom.

23"Thus he said:

'The fourth beast shall be
A fourth kingdom on earth,

Which shall be different from all *other*
kingdoms,
And shall devour the whole earth,
Trample it and break it in pieces.
24The ten horns *are* ten kings
Who shall arise from this kingdom.
And another shall rise after them;
He shall be different from the first *ones,*
And shall subdue three kings.
25He shall speak *pompous* words against the
Most High,
Shall persecute[a] the saints of the Most High,
And shall intend to change times and law.
Then *the saints* shall be given into his hand
For a time and times and half a time.

26'But the court shall be seated,
And they shall take away his dominion,
To consume and destroy *it* forever.
27Then the kingdom and dominion,
And the greatness of the kingdoms under the
whole heaven,
Shall be given to the people, the saints of the
Most High.
His kingdom *is* an everlasting kingdom,
And all dominions shall serve and obey
Him.'

28"This *is* the end of the account.[a] As for me, Daniel, my thoughts greatly troubled me, and my countenance changed; but I kept the matter in my heart."

Vision of a Ram and a Goat

8 In the third year of the reign of King Belshazzar a vision appeared *to* me—to me, Daniel—after the one that appeared to me the first time. 2I saw in the vision, and it so happened while I was looking, that I *was* in Shushan, the citadel, which *is* in the province of Elam; and I saw in the vision that I was by the River Ulai. 3Then I lifted my eyes and saw, and there, standing beside the river, was a ram which had two horns, and the two horns *were* high; but one *was* higher than the other, and the higher *one* came up last. 4I saw the ram pushing westward, northward, and southward, so that no animal could withstand him; nor *was there any* that

7:17 aRepresenting their kingdoms (compare verse 23)   7:25 aLiterally *wear out*   7:28 aLiterally *the word* could deliver from his hand, but he did according to his will and became great.

⁵And as I was considering, suddenly a male goat came from the west, across the surface of the whole earth, without touching the ground; and the goat *had* a notable horn between his eyes. ⁶Then he came to the ram that had two horns, which I had seen standing beside the river, and ran at him with furious power. ⁷And I saw him confronting the ram; he was moved with rage against him, attacked the ram, and broke his two horns. There was no power in the ram to withstand him, but he cast him down to the ground and trampled him; and there was no one that could deliver the ram from his hand.

⁸Therefore the male goat grew very great; but when he became strong, the large horn was broken, and in place of it four notable ones came up toward the four winds of heaven. ⁹And out of one of them came a little horn which grew exceedingly great toward the south, toward the east, and toward the Glorious *Land*. ¹⁰And it grew up to the host of heaven; and it cast down *some* of the host and *some* of the stars to the ground, and trampled them. ¹¹He even exalted *himself* as high as the Prince of the host; and by him the daily *sacrifices* were taken away, and the place of His sanctuary was cast down. ¹²Because of transgression, an army was given over *to the horn* to oppose the daily *sacrifices;* and he cast truth down to the ground. He did *all this* and prospered.

¹³Then I heard a holy one speaking; and *another* holy one said to that certain *one* who was speaking, "How long *will* the vision *be, concerning* the daily *sacrifices* and the transgression of desolation, the giving of both the sanctuary and the host to be trampled underfoot?"

¹⁴And he said to me, "For two thousand three hundred days;ᵃ then the sanctuary shall be cleansed."

Gabriel Interprets the Vision

¹⁵Then it happened, when I, Daniel, had seen the vision and was seeking the meaning, that suddenly there stood before me one having the appearance of a man. ¹⁶And I heard a man's voice between *the banks of* the Ulai, who called, and said, "Gabriel, make this *man* understand the vi-

sion." ¹⁷So he came near where I stood, and when he came I was afraid and fell on my face; but he said to me, "Understand, son of man, that the vision *refers* to the time of the end."

¹⁸Now, as he was speaking with me, I was in a deep sleep with my face to the ground; but he touched me, and stood me upright. ¹⁹And he said, "Look, I am making known to you what shall happen in the latter time of the indignation; for at the appointed time the end *shall be.* ²⁰The ram which you saw, having the two horns—*they are* the kings of Media and Persia. ²¹And the male goat *is* the kingdomᵃ of Greece. The large horn that *is* between its eyes *is* the first king. ²²As for the broken *horn* and the four that stood up in its place, four kingdoms shall arise out of that nation, but not with its power.

²³"And in the latter time of their kingdom,
   When the transgressors have reached their
      fullness,
   A king shall arise,
   Having fierce features,
   Who understands sinister schemes.
²⁴His power shall be mighty, but not by his
      own power;
   He shall destroy fearfully,
   And shall prosper and thrive;
   He shall destroy the mighty, and *also* the
      holy people.

²⁵"Through his cunning
   He shall cause deceit to prosper under his
      rule;ᵃ
   And he shall exalt *himself* in his heart.
   He shall destroy many in *their* prosperity.
   He shall even rise against the Prince of
      princes;
   But he shall be broken without *human*
      means.ᵇ

²⁶"And the vision of the evenings and
      mornings
   Which was told is true;
   Therefore seal up the vision,
   For *it refers* to many days *in the future.*"

8:14 ᵃLiterally *evening-mornings* **8:21** ᵃLiterally *king,* representing his kingdom (compare 7:17, 23) **8:25** ᵃLiterally *hand* ᵇLiterally *hand*

27And I, Daniel, fainted and was sick for days; afterward I arose and went about the king's business. I was astonished by the vision, but no one understood it.

DANIEL'S PRAYER FOR THE PEOPLE

9 In the first year of Darius the son of Ahasuerus, of the lineage of the Medes, who was made king over the realm of the Chaldeans— 2in the first year of his reign I, Daniel, understood by the books the number of the years *specified* by the word of the LORD through Jeremiah the prophet, that He would accomplish seventy years in the desolations of Jerusalem.

3Then I set my face toward the Lord God to make request by prayer and supplications, with fasting, sackcloth, and ashes. 4And I prayed to the LORD my God, and made confession, and said, "O Lord, great and awesome God, who keeps His covenant and mercy with those who love Him, and with those who keep His commandments, 5we have sinned and committed iniquity, we have done wickedly and rebelled, even by departing from Your precepts and Your judgments. 6Neither have we heeded Your servants the prophets, who spoke in Your name to our kings and our princes, to our fathers and all the people of the land. 7O Lord, righteousness *belongs* to You, but to us shame of face, as *it is* this day—to the men of Judah, to the inhabitants of Jerusalem and all Israel, those near and those far off in all the countries to which You have driven them, because of the unfaithfulness which they have committed against You.

8"O Lord, to us *belongs* shame of face, to our kings, our princes, and our fathers, because we have sinned against You. 9To the Lord our God *belong* mercy and forgiveness, though we have rebelled against Him. 10We have not obeyed the voice of the LORD our God, to walk in His laws, which He set before us by His servants the prophets. 11Yes, all Israel has transgressed Your law, and has departed so as not to obey Your voice; therefore the curse and the oath written in the Law of Moses the servant of God have been poured out on us, because we have sinned against Him. 12And He has confirmed His words, which He spoke against us and against our judges who judged us, by bringing upon us a great disaster; for under the whole heaven such has never been done as what has been done to Jerusalem.

13"As *it is* written in the Law of Moses, all this disaster has come upon us; yet we have not made our prayer before the LORD our God, that we might turn from our iniquities and understand Your truth. 14Therefore the LORD has kept the disaster in mind, and brought it upon us; for the LORD our God *is* righteous in all the works which He does, though we have not obeyed His voice. 15And now, O Lord our God, who brought Your people out of the land of Egypt with a mighty hand, and made Yourself a name, as *it is* this day—we have sinned, we have done wickedly!

16"O Lord, according to all Your righteousness, I pray, let Your anger and Your fury be turned away from Your city Jerusalem, Your holy mountain; because for our sins, and for the iniquities of our fathers, Jerusalem and Your people *are* a reproach to all *those* around us. 17Now therefore, our God, hear the prayer of Your servant, and his supplications, and for the Lord's sake cause Your face to shine on Your sanctuary, which is desolate. 18O my God, incline Your ear and hear; open Your eyes and see our desolations, and the city which is called by Your name; for we do not present our supplications before You because of our righteous deeds, but because of Your great mercies. 19O Lord, hear! O Lord, forgive! O Lord, listen and act! Do not delay for Your own sake, my God, for Your city and Your people are called by Your name."

THE SEVENTY-WEEKS PROPHECY

20Now while I *was* speaking, praying, and confessing my sin and the sin of my people Israel, and presenting my supplication before the LORD my God for the holy mountain of my God, 21yes, while I *was* speaking in prayer, the man Gabriel, whom I had seen in the vision at the beginning, being caused to fly swiftly, reached me about the time of the evening offering. 22And he informed *me,* and talked with me, and said, "O Daniel, I have now come forth to give you skill to understand. 23At the beginning of your supplications the command went out, and I have come to tell *you,* for you *are* greatly beloved; therefore consider the matter, and understand the vision:

24"Seventy weeks[a] are determined
   For your people and for your holy city,
   To finish the transgression,
   To make an end of[b] sins,
   To make reconciliation for iniquity,
   To bring in everlasting righteousness,
   To seal up vision and prophecy,
   And to anoint the Most Holy.

25"Know therefore and understand,
   That from the going forth of the command
   To restore and build Jerusalem
   Until Messiah the Prince,
   There shall be seven weeks and sixty-two
       weeks;
   The street[a] shall be built again, and the wall,[b]
   Even in troublesome times.

26"And after the sixty-two weeks
   Messiah shall be cut off, but not for Himself;
   And the people of the prince who is to come
   Shall destroy the city and the sanctuary.
   The end of it *shall be* with a flood,
   And till the end of the war desolations are
       determined.
27Then he shall confirm a covenant with many
       for one week;
   But in the middle of the week
   He shall bring an end to sacrifice and
       offering.
   And on the wing of abominations shall be
       one who makes desolate,
   Even until the consummation, which is
       determined,
   Is poured out on the desolate."

VISION OF THE GLORIOUS MAN

10 In the third year of Cyrus king of Persia a
message was revealed to Daniel, whose
name was called Belteshazzar. The message *was*
true, but the appointed time *was* long;[a] and he
understood the message, and had understanding
of the vision. 2In those days I, Daniel, was mourning three full weeks. 3I ate no pleasant food, no
meat or wine came into my mouth, nor did I
anoint myself at all, till three whole weeks were
fulfilled.

4Now on the twenty-fourth day of the first
month, as I was by the side of the great river, that
is, the Tigris,[a] 5I lifted my eyes and looked, and
behold, a certain man clothed in linen, whose
waist *was* girded with gold of Uphaz! 6His body
was like beryl, his face like the appearance of
lightning, his eyes like torches of fire, his arms and
feet like burnished bronze in color, and the sound
of his words like the voice of a multitude.

7And I, Daniel, alone saw the vision, for the
men who were with me did not see the vision;
but a great terror fell upon them, so that they fled
to hide themselves. 8Therefore I was left alone
when I saw this great vision, and no strength remained in me; for my vigor was turned to frailty
in me, and I retained no strength. 9Yet I heard the
sound of his words; and while I heard the sound
of his words I was in a deep sleep on my face,
with my face to the ground.

PROPHECIES CONCERNING PERSIA AND GREECE

10Suddenly, a hand touched me, which made
me tremble on my knees and *on* the palms of my
hands. 11And he said to me, "O Daniel, man
greatly beloved, understand the words that I speak
to you, and stand upright, for I have now been
sent to you." While he was speaking this word to
me, I stood trembling.

12Then he said to me, "Do not fear, Daniel,
for from the first day that you set your heart to
understand, and to humble yourself before your
God, your words were heard; and I have come
because of your words. 13But the prince of the
kingdom of Persia withstood me twenty-one
days; and behold, Michael, one of the chief
princes, came to help me, for I had been left alone
there with the kings of Persia. 14Now I have come
to make you understand what will happen to
your people in the latter days, for the vision *refers*
to *many* days yet *to come.*"

15When he had spoken such words to me, I
turned my face toward the ground and became
speechless. 16And suddenly, *one* having the likeness
of the sons[a] of men touched my lips; then I
opened my mouth and spoke, saying to him who
stood before me, "My lord, because of the vision
my sorrows have overwhelmed me, and I have re-

9:24 [a]Literally *sevens,* and so throughout the chapter [b]Following
Qere, Septuagint, Syriac, and Vulgate; Kethib and Theodotion read
To seal up. **9:25** [a]Or *open square* [b]Or *moat* **10:1** [a]Or *and of great
conflict* **10:4** [a]Hebrew *Hiddekel* **10:16** [a]Theodotion and Vulgate
read *the son;* Septuagint reads *a hand.*

tained no strength. [17]For how can this servant of my lord talk with you, my lord? As for me, no strength remains in me now, nor is any breath left in me."

[18]Then again, *the one* having the likeness of a man touched me and strengthened me. [19]And he said, "O man greatly beloved, fear not! Peace *be* to you; be strong, yes, be strong!"

So when he spoke to me I was strengthened, and said, "Let my lord speak, for you have strengthened me."

[20]Then he said, "Do you know why I have come to you? And now I must return to fight with the prince of Persia; and when I have gone forth, indeed the prince of Greece will come. [21]But I will tell you what is noted in the Scripture of Truth. (No one upholds me against these, except Michael your prince.

11 "Also in the first year of Darius the Mede, I, *even* I, stood up to confirm and strengthen him.) [2]And now I will tell you the truth: Behold, three more kings will arise in Persia, and the fourth shall be far richer than *them* all; by his strength, through his riches, he shall stir up all against the realm of Greece. [3]Then a mighty king shall arise, who shall rule with great dominion, and do according to his will. [4]And when he has arisen, his kingdom shall be broken up and divided toward the four winds of heaven, but not among his posterity nor according to his dominion with which he ruled; for his kingdom shall be uprooted, even for others besides these.

Warring Kings of North and South

[5]"Also the king of the South shall become strong, as well as *one* of his princes; and he shall gain power over him and have dominion. His dominion *shall be* a great dominion. [6]And at the end of *some* years they shall join forces, for the daughter of the king of the South shall go to the king of the North to make an agreement; but she shall not retain the power of her authority,[a] and neither he nor his authority[b] shall stand; but she shall be given up, with those who brought her, and with him who begot her, and with him who strengthened her in *those* times. [7]But from a branch of her roots *one* shall arise in his place, who shall come with an army, enter the fortress of the king of the North, and deal with them and

prevail. [8]And he shall also carry their gods captive to Egypt, with their princes[a] *and* their precious articles of silver and gold; and he shall continue *more* years than the king of the North.

[9]"Also *the king of the North* shall come to the kingdom of the king of the South, but shall return to his own land. [10]However his sons shall stir up strife, and assemble a multitude of great forces; and *one* shall certainly come and overwhelm and pass through; then he shall return to his fortress and stir up strife.

[11]"And the king of the South shall be moved with rage, and go out and fight with him, with the king of the North, who shall muster a great multitude; but the multitude shall be given into the hand of his *enemy*. [12]When he has taken away the multitude, his heart will be lifted up; and he will cast down tens of thousands, but he will not prevail. [13]For the king of the North will return and muster a multitude greater than the former, and shall certainly come at the end of some years with a great army and much equipment.

[14]"Now in those times many shall rise up against the king of the South. Also, violent men[a] of your people shall exalt themselves in fulfillment of the vision, but they shall fall. [15]So the king of the North shall come and build a siege mound, and take a fortified city; and the forces[a] of the South shall not withstand *him*. Even his choice troops *shall have* no strength to resist. [16]But he who comes against him shall do according to his own will, and no one shall stand against him. He shall stand in the Glorious Land with destruction in his power.[a]

[17]"He shall also set his face to enter with the strength of his whole kingdom, and upright ones[a] with him; thus shall he do. And he shall give him the daughter of women to destroy it; but she shall not stand *with him,* or be for him. [18]After this he shall turn his face to the coastlands, and shall take many. But a ruler shall bring the reproach against them to an end; and with the reproach removed, he shall turn back on him. [19]Then he shall turn his face toward the fortress of his own land; but he shall stumble and fall, and not be found.

[20]"There shall arise in his place one who

11:6 [a]Literally *arm* [b]Literally *arm* **11:8** [a]Or *molded images* **11:14** [a]Or *robbers,* literally *sons of breakage* **11:15** [a]Literally *arms* **11:16** [a]Literally *hand* **11:17** [a]Or *bring equitable terms* imposes taxes *on* the glorious kingdom; but within a few days he shall be destroyed, but not in anger or in battle. ²¹And in his place shall arise a vile person, to whom they will not give the honor of royalty; but he shall come in peaceably, and seize the kingdom by intrigue. ²²With the force[a] of a flood they shall be swept away from before him and be broken, and also the prince of the covenant. ²³And after the league *is made* with him he shall act deceitfully, for he shall come up and become strong with a small *number of* people. ²⁴He shall enter peaceably, even into the richest places of the province; and he shall do *what* his fathers have not done, nor his forefathers: he shall disperse among them the plunder, spoil, and riches; and he shall devise his plans against the strongholds, but *only* for a time.

²⁵"He shall stir up his power and his courage against the king of the South with a great army. And the king of the South shall be stirred up to battle with a very great and mighty army; but he shall not stand, for they shall devise plans against him. ²⁶Yes, those who eat of the portion of his delicacies shall destroy him; his army shall be swept away, and many shall fall down slain. ²⁷Both these kings' hearts *shall be* bent on evil, and they shall speak lies at the same table; but it shall not prosper, for the end *will* still *be* at the appointed time. ²⁸While returning to his land with great riches, his heart shall be *moved* against the holy covenant; so he shall do *damage* and return to his own land.

The Northern King's Blasphemies

²⁹"At the appointed time he shall return and go toward the south; but it shall not be like the former or the latter. ³⁰For ships from Cyprus[a] shall come against him; therefore he shall be grieved, and return in rage against the holy covenant, and do *damage*.

"So he shall return and show regard for those who forsake the holy covenant. ³¹And forces[a] shall be mustered by him, and they shall defile the sanctuary fortress; then they shall take away the daily *sacrifices,* and place *there* the abomination of desolation. ³²Those who do wickedly against the covenant he shall corrupt with flattery; but the people who know their God shall be strong, and carry out *great exploits.* ³³And those of the people

who understand shall instruct many; yet *for many* days they shall fall by sword and flame, by captivity and plundering. ³⁴Now when they fall, they shall be aided with a little help; but many shall join with them by intrigue. ³⁵And *some* of those of understanding shall fall, to refine them, purify *them,* and make *them* white, *until* the time of the end; because *it is* still for the appointed time.

³⁶"Then the king shall do according to his own will: he shall exalt and magnify himself above every god, shall speak blasphemies against the God of gods, and shall prosper till the wrath has been accomplished; for what has been determined shall be done. ³⁷He shall regard neither the God[a] of his fathers nor the desire of women, nor regard any god; for he shall exalt himself above *them* all. ³⁸But in their place he shall honor a god of fortresses; and a god which his fathers did not know he shall honor with gold and silver, with precious stones and pleasant things. ³⁹Thus he shall act against the strongest fortresses with a foreign god, which he shall acknowledge, *and* advance *its* glory; and he shall cause them to rule over many, and divide the land for gain.

The Northern King's Conquests

⁴⁰"At the time of the end the king of the South shall attack him; and the king of the North shall come against him like a whirlwind, with chariots, horsemen, and with many ships; and he shall enter the countries, overwhelm *them,* and pass through. ⁴¹He shall also enter the Glorious Land, and many *countries* shall be overthrown; but these shall escape from his hand: Edom, Moab, and the prominent people of Ammon. ⁴²He shall stretch out his hand against the countries, and the land of Egypt shall not escape. ⁴³He shall have power over the treasures of gold and silver, and over all the precious things of Egypt; also the Libyans and Ethiopians *shall follow* at his heels. ⁴⁴But news from the east and the north shall trouble him; therefore he shall go out with great fury to destroy and annihilate many. ⁴⁵And he shall plant the tents of his palace between the seas and the glorious holy mountain; yet he shall come to his end, and no one will help him.

11:22 ᵃLiterally *arms* **11:30** ᵃHebrew *Kittim,* western lands, especially Cyprus **11:31** ᵃLiterally *arms* **11:37** ᵃOr *gods*

Prophecy of the End Time

12 "At that time Michael shall stand up,
　　　The great prince who stands *watch* over
　　　　　the sons of your people;
　　And there shall be a time of trouble,
　　Such as never was since there was a nation,
　　Even to that time.
　　And at that time your people shall be
　　　　delivered,
　　Every one who is found written in the book.
²And many of those who sleep in the dust of
　　　the earth shall awake,
　　Some to everlasting life,
　　Some to shame *and* everlasting contempt.
³Those who are wise shall shine
　　Like the brightness of the firmament,
　　And those who turn many to righteousness
　　Like the stars forever and ever.

⁴"But you, Daniel, shut up the words, and seal the book until the time of the end; many shall run to and fro, and knowledge shall increase."

⁵Then I, Daniel, looked; and there stood two others, one on this riverbank and the other on that riverbank. ⁶And *one* said to the man clothed in linen, who *was* above the waters of the river, "How long shall the fulfillment of these wonders *be?*"

⁷Then I heard the man clothed in linen, who *was* above the waters of the river, when he held up his right hand and his left hand to heaven, and swore by Him who lives forever, that *it shall be* for a time, times, and half *a time;* and when the power of the holy people has been completely shattered, all these *things* shall be finished.

⁸Although I heard, I did not understand. Then I said, "My lord, what *shall be* the end of these *things?*"

⁹And he said, "Go *your way,* Daniel, for the words *are* closed up and sealed till the time of the end. ¹⁰Many shall be purified, made white, and refined, but the wicked shall do wickedly; and none of the wicked shall understand, but the wise shall understand.

¹¹"And from the time *that* the daily *sacrifice* is taken away, and the abomination of desolation is set up, *there shall be* one thousand two hundred and ninety days. ¹²Blessed *is* he who waits, and comes to the one thousand three hundred and thirty-five days.

¹³"But you, go *your way* till the end; for you shall rest, and will arise to your inheritance at the end of the days."

IMPACT OF THE BOOK

I **IDEA** | God's people have been like an adulterous woman seeking pleasure in worldly things.

M **MESSAGE** | Hosea's story is one of the most difficult in Scripture. It is true that Gomer—the wife God chose for Hosea—was ungodly, but the marriage relationship was a tangible illustration of God's love for His people. Hosea had to demonstrate love for Gomer despite her unfaithfulness. It may seem unfair, but we ask God to love us in spite of our unfaithfulness to Him. Hosea powerfully demonstrates that a leader must make the decision to answer God's call no matter what the personal cost.

P **PEOPLE** | Gomer, Hosea

A **AUTHOR** | Hosea was the son of Beeri and a native of the northern kingdom. He was a contemporary of Isaiah and Micah. The most remarkable detail of his life concerned his marriage to the harlot Gomer. Hosea's faithfulness to Gomer, despite her many transgressions, serves as a picture of the faithfulness of God despite Israel's continued faithlessness.

C **CULTURE** | Hosea's preaching took place during a time of dire political and spiritual decline in Israel. After Jeroboam II instituted idol worship during his reign (793–743 BC), the people of Israel were unfaithful to God in every way. The kings of Israel sought alliances with foreign kings for political and militaristic reasons, and they fell to the influences of pagan worship practices. It was in this setting that Hosea's call for faithfulness to God rang out. His ministry began in the northern kingdom. After it fell, he ministered and preached to the people of Judah in the southern kingdom.

T **TIMELINE** | c. 715 BC

KEY SCRIPTURE MEMORY VERSES | 3:5; 14:9

1 The word of the LORD that came to Hosea the son of Beeri, in the days of Uzziah, Jotham, Ahaz, *and* Hezekiah, kings of Judah, and in the days of Jeroboam the son of Joash, king of Israel.

THE FAMILY OF HOSEA

²When the LORD began to speak by Hosea, the LORD said to Hosea:

> "Go, take yourself a wife of harlotry
> And children of harlotry,
> For the land has committed great harlotry
> *By departing* from the LORD."

³So he went and took Gomer the daughter of Diblaim, and she conceived and bore him a son. ⁴Then the LORD said to him:

> "Call his name Jezreel,
> For in a little *while*
> I will avenge the bloodshed of Jezreel on the house of Jehu,
> And bring an end to the kingdom of the house of Israel.
> ⁵It shall come to pass in that day
> That I will break the bow of Israel in the Valley of Jezreel."

⁶And she conceived again and bore a daughter. Then *God* said to him:

> "Call her name Lo-Ruhamah,[a]
> For I will no longer have mercy on the house of Israel,
> But I will utterly take them away.[b]
> ⁷Yet I will have mercy on the house of Judah,
> Will save them by the LORD their God,
> And will not save them by bow,
> Nor by sword or battle,
> By horses or horsemen."

⁸Now when she had weaned Lo-Ruhamah, she conceived and bore a son. ⁹Then *God* said:

> "Call his name Lo-Ammi,[a]
> For you *are* not My people,
> And I will not be your *God*.

THE RESTORATION OF ISRAEL

> ¹⁰"Yet the number of the children of Israel
> Shall be as the sand of the sea,
> Which cannot be measured or numbered.
> And it shall come to pass
> In the place where it was said to them,
> 'You *are* not My people,'[a]
> *There* it shall be said to them,
> '*You are* sons of the living God.'
> ¹¹Then the children of Judah and the children of Israel
> Shall be gathered together,
> And appoint for themselves one head;
> And they shall come up out of the land,
> For great *will be* the day of Jezreel!

2 Say to your brethren, 'My people,'[a]
And to your sisters, 'Mercy[b] *is shown*.'

GOD'S UNFAITHFUL PEOPLE

> ²"Bring charges against your mother, bring charges;
> For she *is* not My wife, nor *am* I her Husband!
> Let her put away her harlotries from her sight,
> And her adulteries from between her breasts;
> ³Lest I strip her naked
> And expose her, as in the day she was born,
> And make her like a wilderness,
> And set her like a dry land,
> And slay her with thirst.

> ⁴"I will not have mercy on her children,
> For they *are* the children of harlotry.
> ⁵For their mother has played the harlot;
> She who conceived them has behaved shamefully.
> For she said, 'I will go after my lovers,
> Who give *me* my bread and my water,
> My wool and my linen,
> My oil and my drink.'

> ⁶"Therefore, behold,
> I will hedge up your way with thorns,

1:6 ªLiterally *No-Mercy* ᵇOr *That I may forgive them at all*   **1:9** ªLiterally *Not-My-People*   **1:10** ªHebrew *lo-ammi* (compare verse 9)   **2:1** ªHebrew *Ammi* (compare 1:9, 10) ᵇHebrew *Ruhamah* (compare 1:6)

And wall her in,
So that she cannot find her paths.
⁷She will chase her lovers,
But not overtake them;
Yes, she will seek them, but not find *them.*
Then she will say,
'I will go and return to my first husband,
For then *it was* better for me than now.'
⁸For she did not know
That I gave her grain, new wine, and oil,
And multiplied her silver and gold—
Which they prepared for Baal.

⁹"Therefore I will return and take away
My grain in its time
And My new wine in its season,
And will take back My wool and My
linen,
Given to cover her nakedness.
¹⁰Now I will uncover her lewdness in the sight
of her lovers,
And no one shall deliver her from My
hand.
¹¹I will also cause all her mirth to cease,
Her feast days,
Her New Moons,
Her Sabbaths—
All her appointed feasts.

¹²" And I will destroy her vines and her fig
trees,
Of which she has said,
'These *are* my wages that my lovers have given
me.'
So I will make them a forest,
And the beasts of the field shall eat them.
¹³I will punish her
For the days of the Baals to which she burned
incense.
She decked herself with her earrings and
jewelry,
And went after her lovers;
But Me she forgot," says the LORD.

God's Mercy on His People

¹⁴"Therefore, behold, I will allure her,
Will bring her into the wilderness,
And speak comfort to her.
¹⁵I will give her her vineyards from there,

And the Valley of Achor as a door of hope;
She shall sing there,
As in the days of her youth,
As in the day when she came up from the
land of Egypt.

¹⁶"And it shall be, in that day,"
Says the LORD,
"*That* you will call Me 'My Husband,'ᵃ
And no longer call Me 'My Master,'ᵇ
¹⁷For I will take from her mouth the names of
the Baals,
And they shall be remembered by their name
no more.
¹⁸In that day I will make a covenant for them
With the beasts of the field,
With the birds of the air,
And *with* the creeping things of the
ground.
Bow and sword of battle I will shatter from
the earth,
To make them lie down safely.

¹⁹"I will betroth you to Me forever;
Yes, I will betroth you to Me
In righteousness and justice,
In lovingkindness and mercy;
²⁰I will betroth you to Me in faithfulness,
And you shall know the LORD.

²¹"It shall come to pass in that day
That I will answer," says the LORD;
"I will answer the heavens, ·
And they shall answer the earth.
²²The earth shall answer
With grain,
With new wine,
And with oil;
They shall answer Jezreel.ᵃ
²³Then I will sow her for Myself in the
earth,
And I will have mercy on *her who had* not
obtained mercy;ᵃ
Then I will say to *those who were* not My
people,ᵇ
'You *are* My people!'
And they shall say, '*You are* my God!' "

2:16 ᵃHebrew *Ishi* ᵇHebrew *Baali* **2:22** ᵃLiterally *God Will Sow*
2:23 ᵃHebrew *lo-ruhamah* ᵇHebrew *lo-ammi*

Israel Will Return to God

3 Then the Lord said to me, "Go again, love a woman *who is* loved by a lover[a] and is committing adultery, just like the love of the Lord for the children of Israel, who look to other gods and love *the* raisin cakes *of the pagans.*"

²So I bought her for myself for fifteen *shekels* of silver, and one and one-half homers of barley. ³And I said to her, "You shall stay with me many days; you shall not play the harlot, nor shall you have a man—so, too, *will* I *be* toward you."

⁴For the children of Israel shall abide many days without king or prince, without sacrifice or *sacred* pillar, without ephod or teraphim. ⁵Afterward the children of Israel shall return and seek the Lord their God and David their king. They shall fear the Lord and His goodness in the latter days.

God's Charge Against Israel

4 Hear the word of the Lord,
    You children of Israel,
    For the Lord *brings* a charge against the
        inhabitants of the land:

  "There is no truth or mercy
    Or knowledge of God in the land.
  ²*By* swearing and lying,
    Killing and stealing and committing adultery,
    They break all restraint,
    With bloodshed upon bloodshed.
  ³Therefore the land will mourn;
    And everyone who dwells there will waste
        away
    With the beasts of the field
    And the birds of the air;
    Even the fish of the sea will be taken away.

  ⁴"Now let no man contend, or rebuke another;
    For your people *are* like those who contend
        with the priest.
  ⁵Therefore you shall stumble in the day;
    The prophet also shall stumble with you in
        the night;
    And I will destroy your mother.
  ⁶My people are destroyed for lack of
        knowledge.
    Because you have rejected knowledge,

  I also will reject you from being priest for Me;
    Because you have forgotten the law of your
        God,
    I also will forget your children.

  ⁷"The more they increased,
    The more they sinned against Me;
    I will change[a] their glory[b] into shame.
  ⁸They eat up the sin of My people;
    They set their heart on their iniquity.
  ⁹And it shall be: like people, like priest.
    So I will punish them for their ways,
    And reward them for their deeds.
  ¹⁰For they shall eat, but not have enough;
    They shall commit harlotry, but not increase;
    Because they have ceased obeying the Lord.

The Idolatry of Israel

  ¹¹"Harlotry, wine, and new wine enslave the
        heart.
  ¹²My people ask counsel from their wooden
        idols,
    And their staff informs them.
    For the spirit of harlotry has caused *them* to
        stray,
    And they have played the harlot against their
        God.
  ¹³They offer sacrifices on the mountaintops,
    And burn incense on the hills,
    Under oaks, poplars, and terebinths,
    Because their shade *is* good.
    Therefore your daughters commit harlotry,
    And your brides commit adultery.

  ¹⁴"I will not punish your daughters when they
        commit harlotry,
    Nor your brides when they commit
        adultery;
    For *the men* themselves go apart with harlots,
    And offer sacrifices with a ritual harlot.[a]
    Therefore people *who* do not understand will
        be trampled.

  ¹⁵"Though you, Israel, play the harlot,
    Let not Judah offend.

3:1 [a]Literally *friend* or *husband*   **4:7** [a]Following Masoretic Text, Septuagint, and Vulgate; scribal tradition, Syriac, and Targum read *They will change.* [b]Following Masoretic Text, Septuagint, Syriac, Targum, and Vulgate; scribal tradition reads *My glory.*   **4:14** [a]Compare Deuteronomy 23:18

Do not come up to Gilgal,
Nor go up to Beth Aven,
Nor swear an oath, *saying,* 'As the LORD
lives'—

16"For Israel is stubborn
Like a stubborn calf;
Now the LORD will let them forage
Like a lamb in open country.

17"Ephraim *is* joined to idols,
Let him alone.
18Their drink is rebellion,
They commit harlotry continually.
Her rulers dearlyª love dishonor.
19The wind has wrapped her up in its wings,
And they shall be ashamed because of their
sacrifices.

IMPENDING JUDGMENT ON ISRAEL AND JUDAH

5 "Hear this, O priests!
Take heed, O house of Israel!
Give ear, O house of the king!
For yours *is* the judgment,
Because you have been a snare to Mizpah
And a net spread on Tabor.
2The revolters are deeply involved in slaughter,
Though I rebuke them all.
3I know Ephraim,
And Israel is not hidden from Me;
For now, O Ephraim, you commit harlotry;
Israel is defiled.

4"They do not direct their deeds
Toward turning to their God,
For the spirit of harlotry is in their midst,
And they do not know the LORD.
5The pride of Israel testifies to his face;
Therefore Israel and Ephraim stumble in their
iniquity;
Judah also stumbles with them.

6"With their flocks and herds
They shall go to seek the LORD,
But they will not find *Him;*
He has withdrawn Himself from them.
7They have dealt treacherously with the
LORD,
For they have begotten pagan children.

Now a New Moon shall devour them and
their heritage.

8"Blow the ram's horn in Gibeah,
The trumpet in Ramah!
Cry aloud *at* Beth Aven,
'*Look* behind you, O Benjamin!'
9Ephraim shall be desolate in the day of rebuke;
Among the tribes of Israel I make known
what is sure.

10"The princes of Judah are like those who
remove a landmark;
I will pour out My wrath on them like
water.
11Ephraim is oppressed *and* broken in
judgment,
Because he willingly walked by *human*
precept.
12Therefore I *will be* to Ephraim like a moth,
And to the house of Judah like rottenness.

13"When Ephraim saw his sickness,
And Judah *saw* his wound,
Then Ephraim went to Assyria
And sent to King Jareb;
Yet he cannot cure you,
Nor heal you of your wound.
14For I *will be* like a lion to Ephraim,
And like a young lion to the house of Judah.
I, *even* I, will tear *them* and go away;
I will take *them* away, and no one shall rescue.
15I will return again to My place
Till they acknowledge their offense.
Then they will seek My face;
In their affliction they will earnestly seek
Me."

A CALL TO REPENTANCE

6 Come, and let us return to the LORD;
For He has torn, but He will heal us;
He has stricken, but He will bind us up.
2After two days He will revive us;
On the third day He will raise us up,
That we may live in His sight.
3Let us know,
Let us pursue the knowledge of the LORD.

4:18 ªHebrew is difficult; a Jewish tradition reads *Her rulers shame-fully love,* 'Give!'

His going forth is established as the morning;
He will come to us like the rain,
Like the latter *and* former rain to the earth.

Impenitence of Israel and Judah

4"O Ephraim, what shall I do to you?
O Judah, what shall I do to you?
For your faithfulness is like a morning cloud,
And like the early dew it goes away.
5Therefore I have hewn *them* by the prophets,
I have slain them by the words of My mouth;
And your judgments *are like* light *that* goes
    forth.
6For I desire mercy and not sacrifice,
And the knowledge of God more than burnt
    offerings.

7"But like men[a] they transgressed the
    covenant;
There they dealt treacherously with Me.
8Gilead *is* a city of evildoers
And defiled with blood.
9As bands of robbers lie in wait for a man,
So the company of priests murder on the way
    to Shechem;
Surely they commit lewdness.
10I have seen a horrible thing in the house of
    Israel:
There *is* the harlotry of Ephraim;
Israel is defiled.
11Also, O Judah, a harvest is appointed for you,
When I return the captives of My people.

7 "When I would have healed Israel,
Then the iniquity of Ephraim was uncovered,
And the wickedness of Samaria.
For they have committed fraud;
A thief comes in;
A band of robbers takes spoil outside.
2They do not consider in their hearts
That I remember all their wickedness;
Now their own deeds have surrounded
    them;
They are before My face.
3They make a king glad with their wickedness,
And princes with their lies.

4"They *are* all adulterers.
Like an oven heated by a baker—

He ceases stirring *the fire* after kneading the
    dough,
Until it is leavened.
5In the day of our king
Princes have made *him* sick, inflamed with
    wine;
He stretched out his hand with scoffers.
6They prepare their heart like an oven,
While they lie in wait;
Their baker[a] sleeps all night;
In the morning it burns like a flaming fire.
7They are all hot, like an oven,
And have devoured their judges;
All their kings have fallen.
None among them calls upon Me.

8"Ephraim has mixed himself among the
    peoples;
Ephraim is a cake unturned.
9Aliens have devoured his strength,
But he does not know *it;*
Yes, gray hairs are here and there on him,
Yet he does not know *it.*
10And the pride of Israel testifies to his face,
But they do not return to the LORD their
    God,
Nor seek Him for all this.

Futile Reliance on the Nations

11"Ephraim also is like a silly dove, without
    sense—
They call to Egypt,
They go to Assyria.
12Wherever they go, I will spread My net on
    them;
I will bring them down like birds of the
    air;
I will chastise them
According to what their congregation has
    heard.

13"Woe to them, for they have fled from Me!
Destruction to them,
Because they have transgressed against Me!
Though I redeemed them,
Yet they have spoken lies against Me.

6:7 [a]Or *like Adam*   **7:6** [a]Following Masoretic Text and Vulgate; Syriac and Targum read *Their anger;* Septuagint reads *Ephraim.*

[14]They did not cry out to Me with their heart
When they wailed upon their beds.

"They assemble together for[a] grain and new
wine,
They rebel against Me;[b]
[15]Though I disciplined *and* strengthened their
arms,
Yet they devise evil against Me;
[16]They return, *but* not to the Most High;[a]
They are like a treacherous bow.
Their princes shall fall by the sword
For the cursings of their tongue.
This *shall be* their derision in the land of
Egypt.

THE APOSTASY OF ISRAEL

8 "*Set* the trumpet[a] to your mouth!
He shall come like an eagle against the house
of the LORD,
Because they have transgressed My covenant
And rebelled against My law.
[2]Israel will cry to Me,
'My God, we know You!'
[3]Israel has rejected the good;
The enemy will pursue him.

[4]"They set up kings, but not by Me;
They made princes, but I did not
acknowledge *them.*
From their silver and gold
They made idols for themselves—
That they might be cut off.
[5]Your calf is rejected, O Samaria!
My anger is aroused against them—
How long until they attain to innocence?
[6]For from Israel *is* even this:
A workman made it, and it *is* not God;
But the calf of Samaria shall be broken to
pieces.

[7]"They sow the wind,
And reap the whirlwind.
The stalk has no bud;
It shall never produce meal.
If it should produce,
Aliens would swallow it up.
[8]Israel is swallowed up;
Now they are among the Gentiles

Like a vessel in which *is* no pleasure.
[9]For they have gone up to Assyria,
Like a wild donkey alone by itself;
Ephraim has hired lovers.
[10]Yes, though they have hired among the
nations,
Now I will gather them;
And they shall sorrow a little,[a]
Because of the burden[b] of the king of princes.

[11]"Because Ephraim has made many altars for
sin,
They have become for him altars for
sinning.
[12]I have written for him the great things of My
law,
But they were considered a strange thing.
[13]*For* the sacrifices of My offerings they
sacrifice flesh and eat *it,*
But the LORD does not accept them.
Now He will remember their iniquity and
punish their sins.
They shall return to Egypt.

[14]"For Israel has forgotten his Maker,
And has built temples;[a]
Judah also has multiplied fortified cities;
But I will send fire upon his cities,
And it shall devour his palaces."

JUDGMENT OF ISRAEL'S SIN

9 Do not rejoice, O Israel, with joy like *other*
peoples,
For you have played the harlot against your
God.
You have made love *for* hire on every
threshing floor.
[2]The threshing floor and the winepress
Shall not feed them,
And the new wine shall fail in her.

[3]They shall not dwell in the LORD's land,
But Ephraim shall return to Egypt,
And shall eat unclean *things* in Assyria.

7:14 [a]Following Masoretic Text and Targum; Vulgate reads *thought upon;* Septuagint reads *slashed themselves for* (compare 1 Kings 18:28). [b]Following Masoretic Text, Syriac, and Targum; Septuagint omits *They rebel against Me;* Vulgate reads *They departed from Me.* **7:16** [a]Or *upward* **8:1** [a]Hebrew *shophar,* ram's horn **8:10** [a]Or *begin to diminish* [b]Or *oracle* **8:14** [a]Or *palaces*

⁴They shall not offer wine *offerings* to the
     LORD,
  Nor shall their sacrifices be pleasing to Him.
  It shall be like bread of mourners to them;
  All who eat it shall be defiled.
  For their bread *shall be* for their *own* life;
  It shall not come into the house of the
     LORD.

⁵What will you do in the appointed day,
  And in the day of the feast of the LORD?
⁶For indeed they are gone because of
     destruction.
  Egypt shall gather them up;
  Memphis shall bury them.
  Nettles shall possess their valuables of silver;
  Thorns *shall be* in their tents.

⁷The days of punishment have come;
  The days of recompense have come.
  Israel knows!
  The prophet *is* a fool,
  The spiritual man *is* insane,
  Because of the greatness of your iniquity and
     great enmity.
⁸The watchman of Ephraim *is* with my God;
  But the prophet *is* a fowler'sᵃ snare in all his
     ways—
  Enmity in the house of his God.
⁹They are deeply corrupted,
  As in the days of Gibeah.
  He will remember their iniquity;
  He will punish their sins.

¹⁰"I found Israel
  Like grapes in the wilderness;
  I saw your fathers
  As the firstfruits on the fig tree in its first
     season.
  But they went to Baal Peor,
  And separated themselves *to that* shame;
  They became an abomination like the thing
     they loved.
¹¹*As for* Ephraim, their glory shall fly away like
     a bird—
  No birth, no pregnancy, and no conception!
¹²Though they bring up their children,
  Yet I will bereave them to the last man.
  Yes, woe to them when I depart from them!

¹³Just as I saw Ephraim like Tyre, planted in a
     pleasant place,
  So Ephraim will bring out his children to the
     murderer."

¹⁴Give them, O LORD—
  What will You give?
  Give them a miscarrying womb
  And dry breasts!

¹⁵"All their wickedness *is* in Gilgal,
  For there I hated them.
  Because of the evil of their deeds
  I will drive them from My house;
  I will love them no more.
  All their princes *are* rebellious.
¹⁶Ephraim is stricken,
  Their root is dried up;
  They shall bear no fruit.
  Yes, were they to bear children,
  I would kill the darlings of their womb."

¹⁷My God will cast them away,
  Because they did not obey Him;
  And they shall be wanderers among the
     nations.

ISRAEL'S SIN AND CAPTIVITY

10 Israel empties *his* vine;
     He brings forth fruit for himself.
  According to the multitude of his fruit
  He has increased the altars;
  According to the bounty of his land
  They have embellished *his sacred* pillars.
²Their heart is divided;
  Now they are held guilty.
  He will break down their altars;
  He will ruin their *sacred* pillars.

³For now they say,
  "We have no king,
  Because we did not fear the LORD.
  And as for a king, what would he do for us?"
⁴They have spoken words,
  Swearing falsely in making a covenant.
  Thus judgment springs up like hemlock in
     the furrows of the field.

9:8 ªThat is, one who catches birds in a trap or snare

5The inhabitants of Samaria fear
  Because of the calfa of Beth Aven.
  For its people mourn for it,
  And its priests shriek for it—
  Because its glory has departed from it.
6*The idol* also shall be carried to Assyria
  As a present for King Jareb.
  Ephraim shall receive shame,
  And Israel shall be ashamed of his own
    counsel.

7*As for* Samaria, her king is cut off
  Like a twig on the water.
8Also the high places of Aven, the sin of Israel,
  Shall be destroyed.
  The thorn and thistle shall grow on their
    altars;
  They shall say to the mountains, "Cover us!"
  And to the hills, "Fall on us!"

9"O Israel, you have sinned from the days of
    Gibeah;
  There they stood.
  The battle in Gibeah against the children of
    iniquitya
  Did not overtake them.
10When *it is* My desire, I will chasten them.
  Peoples shall be gathered against them
  When I bind them for their two
    transgressions.a
11Ephraim *is* a trained heifer
  That loves to thresh *grain;*
  But I harnessed her fair neck,
  I will make Ephraim pull *a plow.*
  Judah shall plow;
  Jacob shall break his clods."

12Sow for yourselves righteousness;
  Reap in mercy;
  Break up your fallow ground,
  For *it is* time to seek the LORD,
  Till He comes and rains righteousness on
    you.

13You have plowed wickedness;
  You have reaped iniquity.
  You have eaten the fruit of lies,
  Because you trusted in your own way,
  In the multitude of your mighty men.

14Therefore tumult shall arise among your
    people,
  And all your fortresses shall be plundered
  As Shalman plundered Beth Arbel in the day
    of battle—
  A mother dashed in pieces upon *her* children.
15Thus it shall be done to you, O Bethel,
  Because of your great wickedness.
  At dawn the king of Israel
  Shall be cut off utterly.

GOD'S CONTINUING LOVE FOR ISRAEL

11 "When Israel *was* a child, I loved him,
     And out of Egypt I called My son.
  2*As* they called them,a
  So they went from them;b
  They sacrificed to the Baals,
  And burned incense to carved images.

3"I taught Ephraim to walk,
  Taking them by their arms;a
  But they did not know that I healed them.
4I drew them with gentle cords,a
  With bands of love,
  And I was to them as those who take the
    yoke from their neck.b
  I stooped *and* fed them.

5"He shall not return to the land of Egypt;
  But the Assyrian shall be his king,
  Because they refused to repent.
6And the sword shall slash in his cities,
  Devour his districts,
  And consume *them,*
  Because of their own counsels.
7My people are bent on backsliding from Me.
  Though they call to the Most High,a
  None at all exalt *Him.*

8"How can I give you up, Ephraim?
  How can I hand you over, Israel?

10:5 aLiterally *calves* 10:9 aSo read many Hebrew manuscripts, Septuagint, and Vulgate; Masoretic Text reads *unruliness.* 10:10 aOr *in their two habitations* 11:2 aFollowing Masoretic Text and Vulgate; Septuagint reads *Just as I called them;* Targum interprets as *I sent prophets to a thousand of them.* bFollowing Masoretic Text, Targum, and Vulgate; Septuagint reads *from My face.* 11:3 aSome Hebrew manuscripts, Septuagint, Syriac, and Vulgate read *My arms.* 11:4 aLiterally *cords of a man* bLiterally *jaws* 11:7 aOr *upward*

How can I make you like Admah?
How can I set you like Zeboiim?
My heart churns within Me;
My sympathy is stirred.
⁹I will not execute the fierceness of My anger;
I will not again destroy Ephraim.
For I *am* God, and not man,
The Holy One in your midst;
And I will not come with terror.ᵃ

¹⁰"They shall walk after the Lord.
He will roar like a lion.
When He roars,
Then *His* sons shall come trembling from the
    west;
¹¹They shall come trembling like a bird from
    Egypt,
Like a dove from the land of Assyria.
And I will let them dwell in their houses,"
Says the Lord.

God's Charge Against Ephraim

¹²"Ephraim has encircled Me with lies,
And the house of Israel with deceit;
But Judah still walks with God,
Even with the Holy Oneᵃ *who is* faithful.

12 "Ephraim feeds on the wind,
And pursues the east wind;
He daily increases lies and desolation.
Also they make a covenant with the Assyrians,
And oil is carried to Egypt.

²"The Lord also *brings* a charge against Judah,
And will punish Jacob according to his ways;
According to his deeds He will recompense
    him.
³He took his brother by the heel in the womb,
And in his strength he struggled with God.ᵃ
⁴Yes, he struggled with the Angel and
    prevailed;
He wept, and sought favor from Him.
He found Him *in* Bethel,
And there He spoke to us—
⁵That is, the Lord God of hosts.
The Lord *is* His memorable name.
⁶So you, by *the help of* your God, return;
Observe mercy and justice,
And wait on your God continually.

⁷"A cunning Canaanite!
Deceitful scales *are* in his hand;
He loves to oppress.
⁸And Ephraim said,
'Surely I have become rich,
I have found wealth for myself;
In all my labors
They shall find in me no iniquity that *is* sin.'

⁹"But I *am* the Lord your God,
Ever since the land of Egypt;
I will again make you dwell in tents,
As in the days of the appointed feast.
¹⁰I have also spoken by the prophets,
And have multiplied visions;
I have given symbols through the witness of
    the prophets."

¹¹Though Gilead *has* idols—
Surely they are vanity—
Though they sacrifice bulls in Gilgal,
Indeed their altars *shall be* heaps in the
    furrows of the field.

¹²Jacob fled to the country of Syria;
Israel served for a spouse,
And for a wife he tended *sheep.*
¹³By a prophet the Lord brought Israel out of
    Egypt,
And by a prophet he was preserved.
¹⁴Ephraim provoked *Him* to anger most
    bitterly;
Therefore his Lord will leave the guilt of his
    bloodshed upon him,
And return his reproach upon him.

Relentless Judgment on Israel

13 When Ephraim spoke, trembling,
He exalted *himself* in Israel;
But when he offended through Baal *worship,*
    he died.
²Now they sin more and more,
And have made for themselves molded
    images,
Idols of their silver, according to their skill;
All of it *is* the work of craftsmen.
They say of them,

11:9 ᵃOr *I will not enter a city*   11:12 ᵃOr *holy ones*   12:3 ᵃCompare Genesis 32:28

"Let the men who sacrifice[a] kiss the calves!"
³Therefore they shall be like the morning
cloud
And like the early dew that passes away,
Like chaff blown off from a threshing floor
And like smoke from a chimney.

⁴"Yet I *am* the LORD your God
Ever since the land of Egypt,
And you shall know no God but Me;
For *there is* no savior besides Me.
⁵I knew you in the wilderness,
In the land of great drought.
⁶When they had pasture, they were filled;
They were filled and their heart was exalted;
Therefore they forgot Me.

⁷"So I will be to them like a lion;
Like a leopard by the road I will lurk;
⁸I will meet them like a bear deprived *of her
cubs;*
I will tear open their rib cage,
And there I will devour them like a lion.
The wild beast shall tear them.

⁹"O Israel, you are destroyed,[a]
But your help[b] *is* from Me.
¹⁰I will be your King;[a]
Where *is any other,*
That he may save you in all your cities?
And your judges to whom you said,
'Give me a king and princes'?
¹¹I gave you a king in My anger,
And took *him* away in My wrath.

¹²"The iniquity of Ephraim *is* bound up;
His sin *is* stored up.
¹³The sorrows of a woman in childbirth shall
come upon him.
He *is* an unwise son,
For he should not stay long where children
are born.

¹⁴"I will ransom them from the power of the
grave;[a]
I will redeem them from death.
O Death, I will be your plagues![b]
O Grave,[c] I will be your destruction![d]
Pity is hidden from My eyes."

¹⁵Though he is fruitful among *his* brethren,
An east wind shall come;
The wind of the LORD shall come up from
the wilderness.
Then his spring shall become dry,
And his fountain shall be dried up.
He shall plunder the treasury of every
desirable prize.
¹⁶Samaria is held guilty,[a]
For she has rebelled against her God.
They shall fall by the sword,
Their infants shall be dashed in pieces,
And their women with child ripped open.

ISRAEL RESTORED AT LAST

14 O Israel, return to the LORD your God,
For you have stumbled because of your
iniquity;
²Take words with you,
And return to the LORD.
Say to Him,
"Take away all iniquity;
Receive *us* graciously,
For we will offer the sacrifices[a] of our lips.
³Assyria shall not save us,
We will not ride on horses,
Nor will we say anymore to the work of our
hands, '*You are* our gods.'
For in You the fatherless finds mercy."

⁴"I will heal their backsliding,
I will love them freely,
For My anger has turned away from him.
⁵I will be like the dew to Israel;
He shall grow like the lily,
And lengthen his roots like Lebanon.
⁶His branches shall spread;
His beauty shall be like an olive tree,
And his fragrance like Lebanon.
⁷Those who dwell under his shadow shall
return;
They shall be revived *like* grain,
And grow like a vine.

13:2 [a]*Or those who offer human sacrifice* **13:9** [a]Literally *it* or *he
destroyed you* [b]Literally *in your help* **13:10** [a]Septuagint, Syriac,
Targum, and Vulgate read *Where is your king?* **13:14** [a]*Or Sheol*
[b]Septuagint reads *where is your punishment?* [c]Or *Sheol* [d]Septu-
agint reads *where is your sting?* **13:16** [a]Septuagint reads *shall be
disfigured* **14:2** [a]Literally *bull calves;* Septuagint reads *fruit.*

Their scent[a] *shall be* like the wine of
    Lebanon.

8"Ephraim *shall say,* 'What have I to do
    anymore with idols?'
I have heard and observed him.
I *am* like a green cypress tree;
Your fruit is found in Me."

9Who *is* wise?
    Let him understand these things.
    Who is prudent?
    Let him know them.
For the ways of the LORD *are* right;
The righteous walk in them,
But transgressors stumble in them.

14:7 aLiterally *remembrance*

IMPACT OF THE BOOK

IDEA — *Everyday trials can teach God's people timeless truths and call them back to right living. With the "day of the LORD" approaching, repentance—a true change of mind and direction—should be an urgent priority.*

MESSAGE — *Joel teaches two very important truths about salvation: whoever calls upon the Lord will be saved (2:32), and repentance involves a change of the heart, not merely an external sign like "tearing clothes" (2:12–14). God desires a changed heart; and any good deeds, apart from an internal change, are nothing more than filthy rags. Joel uses the ominous "day of the LORD" five times. It is regarded as a day of terrible judgment, after which the abundant and complete blessings of God are ushered in. Joel is best known for its prophecy concerning the outpouring of the Holy Spirit (Joel 2:28–32). It was fulfilled on the Day of Pentecost (Acts 2:16–21).*

PEOPLE — *Joel*

AUTHOR — *Joel is the son of Pethuel (1:1), his name means "Yahweh Is God," and he served as a priest who was very concerned about fasting and prayer. The repeated references to Jerusalem may mean that he either lived or was born in Jerusalem.*

CULTURE — *A disastrous locust plague wreaked havoc on Judah, deeply impacting the economy and all levels of society. Joel saw this as God's judgment. Judah had slid into spiritual and moral decay with religious practices being nothing more than empty rituals. In this context, Joel warns the people that the locust plague is only the beginning of judgment to come if they did not repent. Joel also reveals God's plans for future judgment and blessings.*

TIMELINE — *unknown, perhaps ninth or fifth century BC*

KEY SCRIPTURE MEMORY VERSES — 1:15; 2:28, 29, 32

1 The word of the LORD that came to Joel the son of Pethuel.

The Land Laid Waste

²Hear this, you elders,
And give ear, all you inhabitants of the land!
Has *anything like* this happened in your days,
Or even in the days of your fathers?
³Tell your children about it,
Let your children *tell* their children,
And their children another generation.

⁴What the chewing locustᵃ left, the swarming
   locust has eaten;
What the swarming locust left, the crawling
   locust has eaten;
And what the crawling locust left, the
   consuming locust has eaten.

⁵Awake, you drunkards, and weep;
And wail, all you drinkers of wine,
Because of the new wine,
For it has been cut off from your mouth.
⁶For a nation has come up against My land,
Strong, and without number;
His teeth *are* the teeth of a lion,
And he has the fangs of a fierce lion.
⁷He has laid waste My vine,
And ruined My fig tree;
He has stripped it bare and thrown *it* away;
Its branches are made white.

⁸Lament like a virgin girded with sackcloth
For the husband of her youth.
⁹The grain offering and the drink offering
Have been cut off from the house of the
   LORD;
The priests mourn, who minister to the
   LORD.
¹⁰The field is wasted,
The land mourns;
For the grain is ruined,
The new wine is dried up,
The oil fails.

¹¹Be ashamed, you farmers,
Wail, you vinedressers,
For the wheat and the barley;
Because the harvest of the field has perished.

¹²The vine has dried up,
And the fig tree has withered;
The pomegranate tree,
The palm tree also,
And the apple tree—
All the trees of the field are withered;
Surely joy has withered away from the sons of
   men.

Mourning for the Land

¹³Gird yourselves and lament, you priests;
Wail, you who minister before the altar;
Come, lie all night in sackcloth,
You who minister to my God;
For the grain offering and the drink
   offering
Are withheld from the house of your God.
¹⁴Consecrate a fast,
Call a sacred assembly;
Gather the elders
And all the inhabitants of the land
Into the house of the LORD your God,
And cry out to the LORD.

¹⁵Alas for the day!
For the day of the LORD *is* at hand;
It shall come as destruction from the
   Almighty.
¹⁶Is not the food cut off before our eyes,
Joy and gladness from the house of our
   God?
¹⁷The seed shrivels under the clods,
Storehouses are in shambles;
Barns are broken down,
For the grain has withered.
¹⁸How the animals groan!
The herds of cattle are restless,
Because they have no pasture;
Even the flocks of sheep suffer punishment.ᵃ

¹⁹O LORD, to You I cry out;
For fire has devoured the open pastures,
And a flame has burned all the trees of the
   field.
²⁰The beasts of the field also cry out to You,
For the water brooks are dried up,
And fire has devoured the open pastures.

1:4 ᵃExact identity of these locusts is unknown.   1:18 ᵃSeptuagint
and Vulgate read *are made desolate.*

THE DAY OF THE LORD

2 Blow the trumpet in Zion,
And sound an alarm in My holy mountain!
Let all the inhabitants of the land tremble;
For the day of the LORD is coming,
For it is at hand:
[2]A day of darkness and gloominess,
A day of clouds and thick darkness,
Like the morning *clouds* spread over the
mountains.
A people *come,* great and strong,
The like of whom has never been;
Nor will there ever be any *such* after them,
Even for many successive generations.

[3]A fire devours before them,
And behind them a flame burns;
The land *is* like the Garden of Eden before
them,
And behind them a desolate wilderness;
Surely nothing shall escape them.
[4]Their appearance is like the appearance of
horses;
And like swift steeds, so they run.
[5]With a noise like chariots
Over mountaintops they leap,
Like the noise of a flaming fire that devours
the stubble,
Like a strong people set in battle array.

[6]Before them the people writhe in pain;
All faces are drained of color.[a]
[7]They run like mighty men,
They climb the wall like men of war;
Every one marches in formation,
And they do not break ranks.
[8]They do not push one another;
Every one marches in his own column.[a]
Though they lunge between the weapons,
They are not cut down.[b]
[9]They run to and fro in the city,
They run on the wall;
They climb into the houses,
They enter at the windows like a thief.

[10]The earth quakes before them,
The heavens tremble;
The sun and moon grow dark,

And the stars diminish their brightness.
[11]The LORD gives voice before His army,
For His camp is very great;
For strong *is the One* who executes His word.
For the day of the LORD *is* great and very
terrible;
Who can endure it?

A CALL TO REPENTANCE

[12]"Now, therefore," says the LORD,
"Turn to Me with all your heart,
With fasting, with weeping, and with
mourning."
[13]So rend your heart, and not your garments;
Return to the LORD your God,
For He *is* gracious and merciful,
Slow to anger, and of great kindness;
And He relents from doing harm.
[14]Who knows *if* He will turn and relent,
And leave a blessing behind Him—
A grain offering and a drink offering
For the LORD your God?

[15]Blow the trumpet in Zion,
Consecrate a fast,
Call a sacred assembly;
[16]Gather the people,
Sanctify the congregation,
Assemble the elders,
Gather the children and nursing babes;
Let the bridegroom go out from his
chamber,
And the bride from her dressing room.
[17]Let the priests, who minister to the LORD,
Weep between the porch and the altar;
Let them say, "Spare Your people, O LORD,
And do not give Your heritage to reproach,
That the nations should rule over them.
Why should they say among the peoples,
'Where *is* their God?' "

THE LAND REFRESHED

[18]Then the LORD will be zealous for His land,
And pity His people.
[19]The LORD will answer and say to His people,
"Behold, I will send you grain and new wine
and oil,

2:6 [a]Septuagint, Targum, and Vulgate read *gather blackness.*
2:8 [a]Literally *his own highway* [b]That is, they are not halted by losses

JOEL: No God but Jehovah

JOEL 2:12, 13

Joel means "Jehovah is God." He was obviously a prophet, speaking on God's behalf during a terrible time for Israel. Joel had the awesome responsibility of proclaiming God's message of judgment to not only those who lived in his lifetime, but also to future generations, even concerning the End Times.

The book gets straight to the issue: Israel received a terrible judgment in the form of locusts, which poured into and devastated the land (1:4). The agricultural devastation was complete.

Joel's message didn't just point out the obvious. He let people know that, as severe and destructive as this judgment was, a greater one was coming. Joel bluntly reported that The day of the Lord would be severe for those who opposed God! In all of this, we have also to see that it is not God's delight to punish or bring terrible circumstances (2:13); but it is His great joy to bless His people, and keep them in relationship with Him (2:14).

The people hearing Joel's message had fallen out of love with Jehovah, the One and Only true God, and they had sold their hearts out to other things. God brought Joel on the scene to remind the people that there really is no other God worthy to be loved or able to love so completely.

And you will be satisfied by them;
I will no longer make you a reproach among
    the nations.

20"But I will remove far from you the northern
    army,
And will drive him away into a barren and
    desolate land,
With his face toward the eastern sea
And his back toward the western sea;
His stench will come up,
And his foul odor will rise,
Because he has done monstrous things."

21Fear not, O land;
Be glad and rejoice,
For the LORD has done marvelous things!
22Do not be afraid, you beasts of the field;
For the open pastures are springing up,
And the tree bears its fruit;
The fig tree and the vine yield their
    strength.
23Be glad then, you children of Zion,
And rejoice in the LORD your God;

For He has given you the former rain
    faithfully,a
And He will cause the rain to come down for
    you—
The former rain,
And the latter rain in the first *month*.
24The threshing floors shall be full of wheat,
And the vats shall overflow with new wine
    and oil.

25"So I will restore to you the years that the
    swarming locust has eaten,
The crawling locust,
The consuming locust,
And the chewing locust,a
My great army which I sent among you.
26You shall eat in plenty and be satisfied,
And praise the name of the LORD your God,
Who has dealt wondrously with you;
And My people shall never be put to shame.
27Then you shall know that I *am* in the midst
    of Israel:
I *am* the LORD your God

2:23 aOr *the teacher of righteousness*   **2:25** aCompare 1:4

LEADERSHIP ISSUES

Go Ahead and Dream

Dreams deliver you from a life of insignificance, immorality, inconsistency, and injustices. To do something great for God, you have to believe that God truly will use you in a way beyond all human possibility. This is not arrogance or boasting but a sure purpose in living and a priority in how you use your time.

- Dream big about how God wants to use you to impact others and don't let money, your past, family history, or your hometown limit you from doing what God wants you to do.
- Dream about what you will do with your life, your career, and your calling.

To see your dreams come true:

- feel more passion to pursue God's will than you do about anything else;
- stay motivated by the chance to influence and impact others;
- mentally and emotionally overrule the "crowd culture" or opinion;
- don't give up even when obstacles come or circumstances change;
- realize that today's actions impact tomorrow's goals.

Leaders who give in to sin or react to circumstances through anger or depression throw their dreams to the wind. Think carefully about whether you want to give up your integrity, reputation, and future dreams for one wrong choice. A leader thinks in the future tense about people, thoughts, or plans. He or she needs to deal with these things ahead of time in order to not be caught "in the moment."

As a leader, focus on the future, rather than dwelling on the difficulty of the present. Believe when one door closes, another will open if you continue in a faithful, hopeful spirit. Every moment of life comes together to prepare you for the future. Focus on establishing habits in your private world—your inner life. You won't have to defend your public world, because your godly habits will speak for themselves.

God gives us the vision before the difficulty, so that when we need inspiration, it is already there. A big dream allows you to see God as the engineer of our circumstances.

And there is no other.
My people shall never be put to shame.

God's Spirit Poured Out

²⁸"And it shall come to pass afterward
That I will pour out My Spirit on all flesh;
Your sons and your daughters shall
     prophesy,
Your old men shall dream dreams,
Your young men shall see visions.
²⁹And also on *My* menservants and on *My*
     maidservants
I will pour out My Spirit in those days.

³⁰"And I will show wonders in the heavens and
     in the earth:
Blood and fire and pillars of smoke.
³¹The sun shall be turned into darkness,
And the moon into blood,
Before the coming of the great and
     awesome day of the LORD.
³²And it shall come to pass
That whoever calls on the name of the
     LORD
Shall be saved.
For in Mount Zion and in Jerusalem there
     shall be deliverance,
As the LORD has said,
Among the remnant whom the LORD calls.

God Judges the Nations

3 "For behold, in those days and at that time,
When I bring back the captives of Judah and
     Jerusalem,
²I will also gather all nations,
And bring them down to the Valley of
     Jehoshaphat;
And I will enter into judgment with them
     there
On account of My people, My heritage
     Israel,
Whom they have scattered among the
     nations;
They have also divided up My land.
³They have cast lots for My people,
Have given a boy *as payment* for a harlot,
And sold a girl for wine, that they may
     drink.

⁴"Indeed, what have you to do with Me,
O Tyre and Sidon, and all the coasts of
     Philistia?
Will you retaliate against Me?
But if you retaliate against Me,
Swiftly and speedily I will return your
     retaliation upon your own head;
⁵Because you have taken My silver and My
     gold,
And have carried into your temples My
     prized possessions.
⁶Also the people of Judah and the people of
     Jerusalem
You have sold to the Greeks,
That you may remove them far from their
     borders.

⁷"Behold, I will raise them
Out of the place to which you have sold
     them,
And will return your retaliation upon your
     own head.
⁸I will sell your sons and your daughters
Into the hand of the people of Judah,
And they will sell them to the Sabeans,ᵃ
To a people far off;
For the LORD has spoken."

⁹Proclaim this among the nations:
"Prepare for war!
Wake up the mighty men,
Let all the men of war draw near,
Let them come up.
¹⁰Beat your plowshares into swords
And your pruning hooks into spears;
Let the weak say, 'I *am* strong.' "
¹¹Assemble and come, all you nations,
And gather together all around.
Cause Your mighty ones to go down there,
O LORD.

¹²"Let the nations be wakened, and come up to
     the Valley of Jehoshaphat;
For there I will sit to judge all the
     surrounding nations.
¹³Put in the sickle, for the harvest is ripe.
Come, go down;

3:8 ᵃLiterally *Shebaites* (compare Isaiah 60:6 and Ezekiel 27:22)

For the winepress is full,
The vats overflow—
For their wickedness *is* great."

14Multitudes, multitudes in the valley of
decision!
For the day of the LORD *is* near in the valley
of decision.
15The sun and moon will grow dark,
And the stars will diminish their brightness.
16The LORD also will roar from Zion,
And utter His voice from Jerusalem;
The heavens and earth will shake;
But the LORD will be a shelter for His
people,
And the strength of the children of Israel.

17"So you shall know that I *am* the LORD your
God,
Dwelling in Zion My holy mountain.
Then Jerusalem shall be holy,
And no aliens shall ever pass through her
again."

GOD BLESSES HIS PEOPLE

18And it will come to pass in that day
That the mountains shall drip with new
wine,
The hills shall flow with milk,
And all the brooks of Judah shall be flooded
with water;
A fountain shall flow from the house of the
LORD
And water the Valley of Acacias.

19"Egypt shall be a desolation,
And Edom a desolate wilderness,
Because of violence *against* the people of
Judah,
For they have shed innocent blood in their
land.
20But Judah shall abide forever,
And Jerusalem from generation to
generation.
21For I will acquit them of the guilt of
bloodshed, whom I had not acquitted;
For the LORD dwells in Zion."

IMPACT OF THE BOOK

I | **IDEA** | *Injustice toward the poor and needy is despicable in the sight of the Lord. Wealth without compassion and responsibility is the same as disregarding His covenant in the eyes of God.*

M | **MESSAGE** | *Believers are called to be "burden bearers" like Amos; and when we behave selfishly and neglect those less fortunate, God's anger is aroused. Selfishness in a leader infects his followers. An effective leader never forgets where he comes from. Amos was the "tender of sycamore fruit" (7:14). His message to all leaders is: lead out of character and righteous justice; two must agree in order to walk together (3:3); leaders must be measured by God's plumb line (7:7–9).*

P | **PEOPLE** | *Amaziah, Amos, Jeroboam II, Uzziah*

A | **AUTHOR** | *The author identifies himself as Amos, a sheepbreeder from Tekoa, a small city in Judah located about ten miles from Jerusalem. Amos left his home in Judah and went to Samaria to preach the word of the Lord. His name literally means "Burden Bearer."*

C | **CULTURE** | *Jeroboam II achieved considerable political and economic stability during his forty-one-year reign. The Book of Amos as a whole seems to imply that there was peace between Israel and Judah because Amos—as a prophet from Judah—was able to preach in Samaria. The nation gave lip service to Yahweh and continued to go through the motions of worship.*

T | **TIMELINE** | *c. 750 BC, two years before the earthquake (1:1) and some thirty years before the fall of Israel.*

KEY SCRIPTURE EMORY VERSES | 3:2; 5:24; 8:11, 12

1 The words of Amos, who was among the sheepbreeders[a] of Tekoa, which he saw concerning Israel in the days of Uzziah king of Judah, and in the days of Jeroboam the son of Joash, king of Israel, two years before the earthquake.

2And he said:

"The LORD roars from Zion,
    And utters His voice from Jerusalem;
    The pastures of the shepherds mourn,
    And the top of Carmel withers."

JUDGMENT ON THE NATIONS

3Thus says the LORD:

"For three transgressions of Damascus, and for
        four,
    I will not turn away its *punishment,*
    Because they have threshed Gilead with
        implements of iron.
4But I will send a fire into the house of
        Hazael,
    Which shall devour the palaces of Ben-
        Hadad.
5I will also break the *gate* bar of Damascus,
    And cut off the inhabitant from the Valley of
        Aven,
    And the one who holds the scepter from
        Beth Eden.
    The people of Syria shall go captive to Kir,"
    Says the LORD.

6Thus says the LORD:

"For three transgressions of Gaza, and for
        four,
    I will not turn away its *punishment,*
    Because they took captive the whole
        captivity
    To deliver *them* up to Edom.
7But I will send a fire upon the wall of Gaza,
    Which shall devour its palaces.
8I will cut off the inhabitant from Ashdod,
    And the one who holds the scepter from
        Ashkelon;
    I will turn My hand against Ekron,
    And the remnant of the Philistines shall
        perish,"
    Says the Lord GOD.

9Thus says the LORD:

"For three transgressions of Tyre, and for four,
    I will not turn away its *punishment,*
    Because they delivered up the whole captivity
        to Edom,
    And did not remember the covenant of
        brotherhood.
10But I will send a fire upon the wall of Tyre,
    Which shall devour its palaces."

11Thus says the LORD:

"For three transgressions of Edom, and for four,
    I will not turn away its *punishment,*
    Because he pursued his brother with the
        sword,
    And cast off all pity;
    His anger tore perpetually,
    And he kept his wrath forever.
12But I will send a fire upon Teman,
    Which shall devour the palaces of Bozrah."

13Thus says the LORD:

"For three transgressions of the people of
        Ammon, and for four,
    I will not turn away its *punishment,*
    Because they ripped open the women with
        child in Gilead,
    That they might enlarge their territory.
14But I will kindle a fire in the wall of Rabbah,
    And it shall devour its palaces,
    Amid shouting in the day of battle,
    And a tempest in the day of the whirlwind.
15Their king shall go into captivity,
    He and his princes together,"
    Says the LORD.

2 Thus says the LORD:

"For three transgressions of Moab, and for
        four,
    I will not turn away its *punishment,*
    Because he burned the bones of the king of
        Edom to lime.
2But I will send a fire upon Moab,

1:1 aCompare 2 Kings 3:4

And it shall devour the palaces of Kerioth;
Moab shall die with tumult,
With shouting *and* trumpet sound.
³And I will cut off the judge from its midst,
And slay all its princes with him,"
Says the LORD.

JUDGMENT ON JUDAH

⁴Thus says the LORD:

"For three transgressions of Judah, and for four,
I will not turn away its *punishment,*
Because they have despised the law of the
    LORD,
And have not kept His commandments.
Their lies lead them astray,
Lies which their fathers followed.
⁵But I will send a fire upon Judah,
And it shall devour the palaces of Jerusalem."

JUDGMENT ON ISRAEL

⁶Thus says the LORD:

"For three transgressions of Israel, and for
    four,
I will not turn away its *punishment,*
Because they sell the righteous for silver,
And the poor for a pair of sandals.
⁷They pant after[a] the dust of the earth *which is*
    on the head of the poor,
And pervert the way of the humble.
A man and his father go in to the *same* girl,
To defile My holy name.
⁸They lie down by every altar on clothes taken
    in pledge,
And drink the wine of the condemned *in* the
    house of their god.

⁹"Yet *it was* I *who* destroyed the Amorite before
    them,
Whose height *was* like the height of the
    cedars,
And he *was as* strong as the oaks;
Yet I destroyed his fruit above
And his roots beneath.
¹⁰Also *it was* I *who* brought you up from the
    land of Egypt,
And led you forty years through the
    wilderness,

To possess the land of the Amorite.
¹¹I raised up some of your sons as prophets,
And some of your young men as Nazirites.
Is it not so, O you children of Israel?"
Says the LORD.

¹²"But you gave the Nazirites wine to drink,
And commanded the prophets saying,
'Do not prophesy!'

¹³"Behold, I am weighed down by you,
As a cart full of sheaves is weighed down.
¹⁴Therefore flight shall perish from the swift,
The strong shall not strengthen his power,
Nor shall the mighty deliver himself;
¹⁵He shall not stand who handles the bow,
The swift of foot shall not escape,
Nor shall he who rides a horse deliver
    himself.
¹⁶The most courageous men of might
Shall flee naked in that day,"
Says the LORD.

AUTHORITY OF THE PROPHET'S MESSAGE

3 Hear this word that the LORD has spoken
against you, O children of Israel, against the
whole family which I brought up from the land
of Egypt, saying:

²"You only have I known of all the families of
    the earth;
Therefore I will punish you for all your
    iniquities."

³Can two walk together, unless they are
    agreed?
⁴Will a lion roar in the forest, when he has no
    prey?
Will a young lion cry out of his den, if he has
    caught nothing?
⁵Will a bird fall into a snare on the earth,
    where there is no trap for it?
Will a snare spring up from the earth, if it has
    caught nothing at all?
⁶If a trumpet is blown in a city, will not the
    people be afraid?
If there is calamity in a city, will not the
    LORD have done *it?*

2:7 ᵃOr *trample on*

⁷Surely the Lord GOD does nothing,
Unless He reveals His secret to His servants
the prophets.
⁸A lion has roared!
Who will not fear?
The Lord GOD has spoken!
Who can but prophesy?

PUNISHMENT OF ISRAEL'S SINS

⁹"Proclaim in the palaces at Ashdod,ᵃ
And in the palaces in the land of Egypt, and
say:
'Assemble on the mountains of Samaria;
See great tumults in her midst,
And the oppressed within her.
¹⁰For they do not know to do right,'
Says the LORD,
'Who store up violence and robbery in their
palaces.'"

¹¹Therefore thus says the Lord GOD:

"An adversary *shall be* all around the land;
He shall sap your strength from you,
And your palaces shall be plundered."

¹²Thus says the LORD:

"As a shepherd takes from the mouth of a lion
Two legs or a piece of an ear,
So shall the children of Israel be taken out
Who dwell in Samaria—
In the corner of a bed and on the edgeᵃ of a
couch!
¹³Hear and testify against the house of Jacob,"
Says the Lord GOD, the God of hosts,
¹⁴"That in the day I punish Israel for their
transgressions,
I will also visit *destruction* on the altars of
Bethel;
And the horns of the altar shall be cut off
And fall to the ground.
¹⁵I will destroy the winter house along with the
summer house;
The houses of ivory shall perish,
And the great houses shall have an end,"
Says the LORD.

4 Hear this word, you cows of Bashan, who *are*
on the mountain of Samaria,
Who oppress the poor,

Who crush the needy,
Who say to your husbands,ᵃ "Bring *wine,* let
us drink!"
²The Lord GOD has sworn by His holiness:
"Behold, the days shall come upon you
When He will take you away with fishhooks,
And your posterity with fishhooks.
³You will go out *through* broken *walls,*
Each one straight ahead of her,
And you will be cast into Harmon,"
Says the LORD.

⁴"Come to Bethel and transgress,
At Gilgal multiply transgression;
Bring your sacrifices every morning,
Your tithes every three days.ᵃ
⁵Offer a sacrifice of thanksgiving with leaven,
Proclaim *and* announce the freewill
offerings;
For this you love,
You children of Israel!"
Says the Lord GOD.

ISRAEL DID NOT ACCEPT CORRECTION

⁶"Also I gave you cleanness of teeth in all your
cities,
And lack of bread in all your places;
Yet you have not returned to Me,"
Says the LORD.

⁷"I also withheld rain from you,
When *there were* still three months to the
harvest.
I made it rain on one city,
I withheld rain from another city.
One part was rained upon,
And where it did not rain the part withered.
⁸So two *or* three cities wandered to another
city to drink water,
But they were not satisfied;
Yet you have not returned to Me,"
Says the LORD.

⁹"I blasted you with blight and mildew.
When your gardens increased,
Your vineyards,

3:9 ᵃFollowing Masoretic Text; Septuagint reads *Assyria.* **3:12** ᵃThe
Hebrew is uncertain. **4:1** ᵃLiterally *their lords* or *their masters*
4:4 ᵃOr *years* (compare Deuteronomy 14:28)

Your fig trees,
And your olive trees,
The locust devoured *them;*
Yet you have not returned to Me,"
Says the LORD.

10"I sent among you a plague after the manner
  of Egypt;
Your young men I killed with a sword,
Along with your captive horses;
I made the stench of your camps come up
  into your nostrils;
Yet you have not returned to Me,"
Says the LORD.

11"I overthrew *some* of you,
As God overthrew Sodom and Gomorrah,
And you were like a firebrand plucked from
  the burning;
Yet you have not returned to Me,"
Says the LORD.

12"Therefore thus will I do to you, O Israel;
Because I will do this to you,
Prepare to meet your God, O Israel!"

13For behold,
He who forms mountains,
And creates the wind,
Who declares to man what his[a] thought *is,*
And makes the morning darkness,
Who treads the high places of the earth—
The LORD God of hosts *is* His name.

A Lament for Israel

5 Hear this word which I take up against you, a
  lamentation, O house of Israel:

2The virgin of Israel has fallen;
She will rise no more.
She lies forsaken on her land;
There is no one to raise her up.

3For thus says the Lord GOD:

"The city that goes out by a thousand
Shall have a hundred left,
And that which goes out by a hundred
Shall have ten left to the house of Israel."

A Call to Repentance

4For thus says the LORD to the house of Israel:

"Seek Me and live;
5But do not seek Bethel,
Nor enter Gilgal,
Nor pass over to Beersheba;
For Gilgal shall surely go into captivity,
And Bethel shall come to nothing.
6Seek the LORD and live,
Lest He break out like fire *in* the house of
  Joseph,
And devour *it,*
With no one to quench *it* in Bethel—
7You who turn justice to wormwood,
And lay righteousness to rest in the earth!"

8He made the Pleiades and Orion;
He turns the shadow of death into morning
And makes the day dark as night;
He calls for the waters of the sea
And pours them out on the face of the earth;
The LORD *is* His name.
9He rains ruin upon the strong,
So that fury comes upon the fortress.

10They hate the one who rebukes in the gate,
And they abhor the one who speaks
  uprightly.
11Therefore, because you tread down the poor
And take grain taxes from him,
Though you have built houses of hewn
  stone,
Yet you shall not dwell in them;
You have planted pleasant vineyards,
But you shall not drink wine from them.
12For I know your manifold transgressions
And your mighty sins:
Afflicting the just *and* taking bribes;
Diverting the poor *from justice* at the gate.
13Therefore the prudent keep silent at that
  time,
For it *is* an evil time.

14Seek good and not evil,
That you may live;

4:13 [a]Or *His*

So the Lord God of hosts will be with you,
As you have spoken.
[15]Hate evil, love good;
Establish justice in the gate.
It may be that the Lord God of hosts
Will be gracious to the remnant of Joseph.

The Day of the Lord

[16]Therefore the Lord God of hosts, the Lord,
says this:

"*There shall be* wailing in all streets,
And they shall say in all the highways,
'Alas! Alas!'
They shall call the farmer to mourning,
And skillful lamenters to wailing.
[17]In all vineyards *there shall be* wailing,
For I will pass through you,"
Says the Lord.

[18]Woe to you who desire the day of the Lord!
For what good *is* the day of the Lord to
you?
It *will be* darkness, and not light.
[19]It *will be* as though a man fled from a lion,
And a bear met him!
Or *as though* he went into the house,
Leaned his hand on the wall,
And a serpent bit him!
[20]*Is* not the day of the Lord darkness, and not
light?
Is it not very dark, with no brightness in it?

[21]"I hate, I despise your feast days,
And I do not savor your sacred assemblies.
[22]Though you offer Me burnt offerings and
your grain offerings,
I will not accept *them,*
Nor will I regard your fattened peace
offerings.
[23]Take away from Me the noise of your songs,
For I will not hear the melody of your
stringed instruments.
[24]But let justice run down like water,
And righteousness like a mighty stream.

[25]"Did you offer Me sacrifices and offerings
In the wilderness forty years, O house of
Israel?

[26]You also carried Sikkuth[a] your king[b]
And Chiun,[c] your idols,
The star of your gods,
Which you made for yourselves.
[27]Therefore I will send you into captivity
beyond Damascus,"
Says the Lord, whose name *is* the God of
hosts.

Warnings to Zion and Samaria

6 Woe to you *who are* at ease in Zion,
And trust in Mount Samaria,
Notable persons in the chief nation,
To whom the house of Israel comes!
[2]Go over to Calneh and see;
And from there go to Hamath the great;
Then go down to Gath of the Philistines.
Are you better than these kingdoms?
Or is their territory greater than your
territory?

[3]*Woe to* you who put far off the day of
doom,
Who cause the seat of violence to come
near;
[4]Who lie on beds of ivory,
Stretch out on your couches,
Eat lambs from the flock
And calves from the midst of the stall;
[5]Who sing idly to the sound of stringed
instruments,
And invent for yourselves musical
instruments like David;
[6]Who drink wine from bowls,
And anoint yourselves with the best
ointments,
But are not grieved for the affliction of
Joseph.
[7]Therefore they shall now go captive as the
first of the captives,
And those who recline at banquets shall be
removed.

[8]The Lord God has sworn by Himself,
The Lord God of hosts says:
"I abhor the pride of Jacob,

5:26 [a]A pagan deity [b]Septuagint and Vulgate read *tabernacle of Moloch.* [c]A pagan deity

And hate his palaces;
Therefore I will deliver up *the* city
And all that is in it."

⁹Then it shall come to pass, that if ten men remain in one house, they shall die. ¹⁰And when a relative *of the dead,* with one who will burn *the bodies,* picks up the bodies[a] to take them out of the house, he will say to one inside the house, "*Are there* any more with you?"

Then someone will say, "None."

And he will say, "Hold your tongue! For we dare not mention the name of the LORD."

¹¹For behold, the LORD gives a command:
He will break the great house into bits,
And the little house into pieces.

¹²Do horses run on rocks?
Does *one* plow *there* with oxen?
Yet you have turned justice into gall,
And the fruit of righteousness into
wormwood,
¹³You who rejoice over Lo Debar,[a]
Who say, "Have we not taken Karnaim[b] for
ourselves
By our own strength?"

¹⁴"But, behold, I will raise up a nation against
you,
O house of Israel,"
Says the LORD God of hosts;
"And they will afflict you from the entrance of
Hamath
To the Valley of the Arabah."

VISION OF THE LOCUSTS

7 Thus the Lord GOD showed me: Behold, He formed locust swarms at the beginning of the late crop; indeed *it was* the late crop after the king's mowings. ²And so it was, when they had finished eating the grass of the land, that I said:

"O Lord GOD, forgive, I pray!
Oh, that Jacob may stand,
For he *is* small!"
³*So* the LORD relented concerning this.
"It shall not be," said the LORD.

VISION OF THE FIRE

⁴Thus the Lord GOD showed me: Behold, the Lord GOD called for conflict by fire, and it consumed the great deep and devoured the territory. ⁵Then I said:

"O Lord GOD, cease, I pray!
Oh, that Jacob may stand,
For he *is* small!"
⁶*So* the LORD relented concerning this.
"This also shall not be," said the Lord GOD.

VISION OF THE PLUMB LINE

⁷Thus He showed me: Behold, the Lord stood on a wall *made* with a plumb line, with a plumb line in His hand. ⁸And the LORD said to me, "Amos, what do you see?"

And I said, "A plumb line."

Then the Lord said:

"Behold, I am setting a plumb line
In the midst of My people Israel;
I will not pass by them anymore.
⁹The high places of Isaac shall be desolate,
And the sanctuaries of Israel shall be laid
waste.
I will rise with the sword against the house
of Jeroboam."

AMAZIAH'S COMPLAINT

¹⁰Then Amaziah the priest of Bethel sent to Jeroboam king of Israel, saying, "Amos has conspired against you in the midst of the house of Israel. The land is not able to bear all his words. ¹¹For thus Amos has said:

'Jeroboam shall die by the sword,
And Israel shall surely be led away captive
From their own land.' "

¹²Then Amaziah said to Amos:

"Go, you seer!
Flee to the land of Judah.
There eat bread,
And there prophesy.

6:10 [a]Literally *bones* **6:13** [a]Literally *Nothing* [b]Literally *Horns,* symbol of strength

INSIDE *the* INFLUENCERS

AMOS: Ordinary in the Hand of The Extraordinary Maker

AMOS 7:14, 15

There was a time when Israel was free and not occupied by enemy nations. This was the time in which Amos lived and ministered. Amos, whose name means "burden" or "burden bearer," would not have been voted most likely to be used by God in Hebrew school. Amos was an average, working Joe, neither rich nor famous. He took care of sheep for a living and had a part-time job picking figs (7:14, 15).

When Amos was alive, the nation experienced great prosperity (2 Kin. 14—15). The rich were getting richer and the poor were being neglected. The people slipped into a dangerous state of self-reliance, so God used a farmer to get their attention and call them back to Himself.

Amos was just an ordinary man, but he was an ordinary man held in the hand of God; and God is the One who adds the "extraordinary" to our lives. Amos never lost sight of the awesome power of God. Understanding God's character was the only motivation he needed to move forward in clarity and power. He proclaimed God's message with God's authority and did not bother to claim recognition for himself. It just wasn't important to him (1:3). Ordinary guy + extraordinary God = Anything is possible.

---

[13]But never again prophesy at Bethel,
For it *is* the king's sanctuary,
And it *is* the royal residence."

[14]Then Amos answered, and said to Amaziah:

"I *was* no prophet,
Nor *was* I a son of a prophet,
But I *was* a sheepbreeder[a]
And a tender of sycamore fruit.
[15]Then the LORD took me as I followed the flock,
And the LORD said to me,
'Go, prophesy to My people Israel.'
[16]Now therefore, hear the word of the LORD:
You say, 'Do not prophesy against Israel,
And do not spout against the house of Isaac.'

[17]"Therefore thus says the LORD:

'Your wife shall be a harlot in the city;
Your sons and daughters shall fall by the sword;

Your land shall be divided by *survey* line;
You shall die in a defiled land;
And Israel shall surely be led away captive
From his own land.' "

VISION OF THE SUMMER FRUIT

8 Thus the Lord GOD showed me: Behold, a basket of summer fruit. [2]And He said, "Amos, what do you see?"
So I said, "A basket of summer fruit."
Then the LORD said to me:

"The end has come upon My people Israel;
I will not pass by them anymore.
[3]And the songs of the temple
Shall be wailing in that day,"
Says the Lord GOD—
"Many dead bodies everywhere,
They shall be thrown out in silence."

[4]Hear this, you who swallow up[a] the needy,
And make the poor of the land fail,

7:14 [a]Compare 2 Kings 3:4 **8:4** [a]Or *trample on* (compare 2:7)

⁵Saying:

"When will the New Moon be past,
  That we may sell grain?
And the Sabbath,
  That we may trade wheat?
Making the ephah small and the shekel large,
  Falsifying the scales by deceit,
⁶That we may buy the poor for silver,
  And the needy for a pair of sandals—
Even sell the bad wheat?"

⁷The LORD has sworn by the pride of
Jacob:
  "Surely I will never forget any of their works.
⁸Shall the land not tremble for this,
  And everyone mourn who dwells in it?
All of it shall swell like the River,ᵃ
Heave and subside
Like the River of Egypt.

⁹"And it shall come to pass in that day," says the
  Lord GOD,
"That I will make the sun go down at noon,
  And I will darken the earth in broad
    daylight;
¹⁰I will turn your feasts into mourning,
  And all your songs into lamentation;
I will bring sackcloth on every waist,
  And baldness on every head;
I will make it like mourning for an only *son,*
  And its end like a bitter day.

¹¹"Behold, the days are coming," says the Lord
  GOD,
"That I will send a famine on the land,
  Not a famine of bread,
  Nor a thirst for water,
But of hearing the words of the LORD.
¹²They shall wander from sea to sea,
  And from north to east;
They shall run to and fro, seeking the word of
  the LORD,
  But shall not find *it.*

¹³"In that day the fair virgins
  And strong young men
  Shall faint from thirst.
¹⁴Those who swear by the sinᵃ of Samaria,

Who say,
'As your god lives, O Dan!'
And, 'As the way of Beersheba lives!'
They shall fall and never rise again."

THE DESTRUCTION OF ISRAEL

9 I saw the Lord standing by the altar, and He
said:
"Strike the doorposts, that the thresholds may
    shake,
And break them on the heads of them all.
I will slay the last of them with the sword.
He who flees from them shall not get away,
And he who escapes from them shall not be
    delivered.

²"Though they dig into hell,ᵃ
  From there My hand shall take them;
Though they climb up to heaven,
  From there I will bring them down;
³And though they hide themselves on top of
    Carmel,
  From there I will search and take them;
Though they hide from My sight at the
    bottom of the sea,
From there I will command the serpent, and
    it shall bite them;
⁴Though they go into captivity before their
    enemies,
  From there I will command the sword,
  And it shall slay them.
I will set My eyes on them for harm and not
    for good."

⁵The Lord GOD of hosts,
  He who touches the earth and it melts,
  And all who dwell there mourn;
All of it shall swell like the River,ᵃ
  And subside like the River of Egypt.
⁶He who builds His layers in the sky,
  And has founded His strata in the earth;
Who calls for the waters of the sea,
  And pours them out on the face of the
    earth—
The LORD *is* His name.

8:8 ᵃThat is, the Nile; some Hebrew manuscripts, Septuagint, Syriac,
Targum, and Vulgate read *River;* Masoretic Text reads *the light.*
8:14 ᵃOr *Ashima,* a Syrian goddess **9:2** ᵃOr *Sheol* **9:5** ᵃThat is,
the Nile

7"*Are* you not like the people of Ethiopia to Me,

O children of Israel?" says the LORD.
"Did I not bring up Israel from the land of Egypt,

The Philistines from Caphtor,

And the Syrians from Kir?

8"Behold, the eyes of the Lord GOD *are* on the sinful kingdom,

And I will destroy it from the face of the earth;

Yet I will not utterly destroy the house of Jacob,"

Says the LORD.

9"For surely I will command,

And will sift the house of Israel among all nations,

As *grain* is sifted in a sieve;

Yet not the smallest grain shall fall to the ground.

10All the sinners of My people shall die by the sword,

Who say, 'The calamity shall not overtake nor confront us.'

ISRAEL WILL BE RESTORED

11"On that day I will raise up

The tabernaclea of David, which has fallen down,

And repair its damages;

I will raise up its ruins,

And rebuild it as in the days of old;

12That they may possess the remnant of Edom,a

And all the Gentiles who are called by My name,"

Says the LORD who does this thing.

13"Behold, the days are coming," says the LORD,

"When the plowman shall overtake the reaper,

And the treader of grapes him who sows seed;

The mountains shall drip with sweet wine,

And all the hills shall flow *with it*.

14I will bring back the captives of My people Israel;

They shall build the waste cities and inhabit *them*;

They shall plant vineyards and drink wine from them;

They shall also make gardens and eat fruit from them.

15I will plant them in their land,

And no longer shall they be pulled up

From the land I have given them,"

Says the LORD your God.

9:11 aLiterally *booth*, figure of a deposed dynasty **9:12** aSeptuagint reads *mankind*.

IMPACT OF THE BOOK

OBADIAH

I IDEA
Your poor decisions will affect generations long after you are gone. The way you judge and treat others will be the way by which you are judged and treated.

M MESSAGE
Obadiah teaches that God cannot stand leaders who abuse their power and take advantage of those weaker than them. In addition, this book, which is the smallest one in the Old Testament, is a tragic testimony to the fact that decisions have consequences. The strife between Isaac's two sons, Jacob and Esau, manifested itself centuries later with their descendants, the Israelites and Edomites. Who knows how history would have been different if the brothers had followed after God instead of taking their destinies into their own hands?

P PEOPLE
Edom's leaders, Obadiah

A AUTHOR
The name "Obadiah" literally means "servant" or "worshiper of the Lord." While he did not give any personal information about himself in his writings, if his ministry occurred between the second and third Babylonian invasions, then he was most likely a contemporary of Jeremiah.

C CULTURE
Obadiah's message was for those who experienced the opposition of the Edomites during their conflict with Nebuchadnezzar, king of Babylon. Obadiah, who ministered during a time of great political upheaval in the sixth century BC, has a two fold message. The first has to do with God's judgment on Edom for participating with those who brought about the downfall of Jerusalem. The second dealt with the hatred between the Israelites and the Edomites, which went all the way back to their respective patriarchs: Jacob and Esau.

T TIMELINE
c. 590 BC

THE COMING JUDGMENT ON EDOM

The vision of Obadiah.

Thus says the Lord GOD concerning Edom
(We have heard a report from the LORD,
And a messenger has been sent among the
    nations, *saying,*
"Arise, and let us rise up against her for
    battle"):

2"Behold, I will make you small among the
    nations;
You shall be greatly despised.
3The pride of your heart has deceived you,
You who dwell in the clefts of the rock,
Whose habitation is high;
You who say in your heart, 'Who will bring
    me down to the ground?'
4Though you ascend *as* high as the eagle,
And though you set your nest among the
    stars,
From there I will bring you down," says the
    LORD.

5"If thieves had come to you,
If robbers by night—
Oh, how you will be cut off!—
Would they not have stolen till they had
    enough?
If grape-gatherers had come to you,
Would they not have left *some* gleanings?

6"Oh, how Esau shall be searched out!
How his hidden treasures shall be
    sought after!
7All the men in your confederacy
Shall force you to the border;
The men at peace with you
Shall deceive you *and* prevail against you.
Those who eat your bread shall lay a trap^a for
    you.
No one is aware of it.

8"Will I not in that day," says the LORD,
"Even destroy the wise *men* from Edom,
And understanding from the mountains of
    Esau?
9Then your mighty men, O Teman, shall be
    dismayed,

To the end that everyone from the mountains
    of Esau
May be cut off by slaughter.

EDOM MISTREATED HIS BROTHER

10"For violence against your brother Jacob,
Shame shall cover you,
And you shall be cut off forever.
11In the day that you stood on the other side—
In the day that strangers carried captive his
    forces,
When foreigners entered his gates
And cast lots for Jerusalem—
Even you *were* as one of them.

12"But you should not have gazed on the day of
    your brother
In the day of his captivity;^a
Nor should you have rejoiced over the
    children of Judah
In the day of their destruction;
Nor should you have spoken proudly
In the day of distress.
13You should not have entered the gate of My
    people
In the day of their calamity.
Indeed, you should not have gazed on their
    affliction
In the day of their calamity,
Nor laid *hands* on their substance
In the day of their calamity.
14You should not have stood at the crossroads
To cut off those among them who escaped;
Nor should you have delivered up those
    among them who remained
In the day of distress.

15"For the day of the LORD upon all the nations
    is near;
As you have done, it shall be done to you;
Your reprisal shall return upon your own
    head.
16For as you drank on My holy mountain,
So shall all the nations drink continually;
Yes, they shall drink, and swallow,
And they shall be as though they had never
    been.

7 ^aOr *wound,* or *plot*   12 ^aLiterally *on the day he became a for-eigner*

the INFLUENCERS

OBADIAH: Faithful Worshiper

Little is known about the author of this book, other than his name *Obadiah*, literally means "worshiper of Yahweh." In Old Testament times, a man's name often defined his character and Obadiah is no exception. Like most Old Testament prophets, he lived in terrible times

Abraham's grandsons, Jacob and Esau had their names changed. Jacob became Israel, and Esau became Edom. Israel's descendents became the nation of Israel as Edom's descendents became the Edomite people. Though the Israelites and the Edomites were related, they were at odds with each other. In Israel's hour of need, the Bible records that Edom did nothing to help; they were completely indifferent to Israel's problems. To make matters worse, Edom betrayed Israel by looting her cities, murdering her survivors, and snitching on citizens who had escaped (1:11–14).

God used Obadiah to respond to Edom's betrayal. God wasn't very happy. Obadiah saw first hand that God took His covenant with His people very seriously. Obadiah was a faithful prophet. He was a "worshiper of Yahweh," and he personally witnessed the faithfulness of the God he served.

Obadiah and all of those who are faithful to God are overcomers because "the kingdom shall be the Lord's" (21). God will sometimes allow His people to experience the consequences for their actions, but He is ready to defend those whom He loves and those who worship Him.

Israel's Final Triumph

[17]"But on Mount Zion there shall be
deliverance,
And there shall be holiness;
The house of Jacob shall possess their
possessions.
[18]The house of Jacob shall be a fire,
And the house of Joseph a flame;
But the house of Esau *shall be* stubble;
They shall kindle them and devour them,
And no survivor shall *remain* of the house of
Esau,"
For the LORD has spoken.

[19]The South[a] shall possess the mountains of
Esau,
And the Lowland shall possess Philistia.
They shall possess the fields of Ephraim
And the fields of Samaria.
Benjamin *shall possess* Gilead.
[20]And the captives of this host of the children
of Israel
Shall possess the land of the Canaanites
As far as Zarephath.
The captives of Jerusalem who are in
Sepharad
Shall possess the cities of the South.[a]
[21]Then saviors[a] shall come to Mount Zion
To judge the mountains of Esau,
And the kingdom shall be the LORD's.

19 [a]Hebrew *Negev*   **20** [a]Hebrew *Negev*   **21** [a]Or *deliverers*

IMPACT OF THE BOOK

I IDEA | *We can never flee the presence of God. He will use even a reluctant leader.*

M MESSAGE | *Motivation is one of the strongest forces in a person's life; why a person does something reveals his character and passions. Jonah's motivations revealed a selfish man. His hatred for the Ninevites overpowered his desire for their salvation. Even though God showed Jonah mercy while he was in the belly of the great fish, Jonah only reluctantly preached God's message to the lost city of Nineveh. God still used him; but because Jonah's motives were not genuine, he missed the real blessing of being able to rejoice in the city's repentance.*

P PEOPLE | *Jonah, King of Nineveh, Sailors*

A AUTHOR | *Jonah, whose name means "dove," is undoubtedly one of the best known of the Twelve Minor Prophets. Apparently, Jonah prophesied under the reign of Jeroboam in Israel. Jonah is the only prophet for the northern kingdom recorded in Scripture in the nearly forty years between the death of Elijah and the ministry of Amos.*

C CULTURE | *The wicked Assyrians were particularly weak between 782 BC and 745 BC. During this time, Assyria was beset with continual conflict with the mountain tribes of Urartu. Their enemies were coming uncomfortably close to Nineveh, the capital city of Assyria. This may explain why they were so ready to accept the preaching of Jonah. The purpose of Jonah's message was to bring the Assyrians to repentance.*

T TIMELINE | *c. 780 BC*

KEY SCRIPTURE
MEMORY VERSES | 2:8, 9; 4:2, 11

Jonah's Disobedience

1 Now the word of the LORD came to Jonah the son of Amittai, saying, ²"Arise, go to Nineveh, that great city, and cry out against it; for their wickedness has come up before Me." ³But Jonah arose to flee to Tarshish from the presence of the LORD. He went down to Joppa, and found a ship going to Tarshish; so he paid the fare, and went down into it, to go with them to Tarshish from the presence of the LORD.

The Storm at Sea

⁴But the LORD sent out a great wind on the sea, and there was a mighty tempest on the sea, so that the ship was about to be broken up.

⁵Then the mariners were afraid; and every man cried out to his god, and threw the cargo that *was* in the ship into the sea, to lighten the load.ᵃ But Jonah had gone down into the lowest parts of the ship, had lain down, and was fast asleep.

⁶So the captain came to him, and said to him, "What do you mean, sleeper? Arise, call on your God; perhaps your God will consider us, so that we may not perish."

⁷And they said to one another, "Come, let us cast lots, that we may know for whose cause this trouble *has come* on us." So they cast lots, and the lot fell on Jonah. ⁸Then they said to him, "Please tell us! For whose cause *is* this trouble upon us? What is your occupation? And where do you come from? What is your country? And of what people are you?"

⁹So he said to them, "I *am* a Hebrew; and I fear the LORD, the God of heaven, who made the sea and the dry *land.*"

Jonah Thrown into the Sea

¹⁰Then the men were exceedingly afraid, and said to him, "Why have you done this?" For the men knew that he fled from the presence of the LORD, because he had told them. ¹¹Then they said to him, "What shall we do to you that the sea may be calm for us?"—for the sea was growing more tempestuous.

¹²And he said to them, "Pick me up and throw me into the sea; then the sea will become calm for you. For I know that this great tempest *is* because of me."

¹³Nevertheless the men rowed hard to return to land, but they could not, for the sea continued to grow more tempestuous against them. ¹⁴Therefore they cried out to the LORD and said, "We pray, O LORD, please do not let us perish for this man's life, and do not charge us with innocent blood; for You, O LORD, have done as it pleased You." ¹⁵So they picked up Jonah and threw him into the sea, and the sea ceased from its raging. ¹⁶Then the men feared the LORD exceedingly, and offered a sacrifice to the LORD and took vows.

Jonah's Prayer and Deliverance

¹⁷Now the LORD had prepared a great fish to swallow Jonah. And Jonah was in the belly of the fish three days and three nights.

2 Then Jonah prayed to the LORD his God from the fish's belly. ²And he said:

"I cried out to the LORD because of my
        affliction,
    And He answered me.

"Out of the belly of Sheol I cried,
    And You heard my voice.
³For You cast me into the deep,
    Into the heart of the seas,
    And the floods surrounded me;
    All Your billows and Your waves passed over
        me.
⁴Then I said, 'I have been cast out of Your
        sight;
    Yet I will look again toward Your holy
        temple.'
⁵The waters surrounded me, *even* to my soul;
    The deep closed around me;
    Weeds were wrapped around my head.
⁶I went down to the moorings of the
        mountains;
    The earth with its bars *closed* behind me
        forever;
    Yet You have brought up my life from the pit,
    O LORD, my God.

⁷"When my soul fainted within me,
    I remembered the LORD;

1:5 ᵃLiterally *from upon them*

the INFLUENCERS

JONAH—The Reluctant Leader

JONAH 1:1–3

Most people focus on whether or not the story of Jonah living three days in a great fish could even be true, and they miss the point. (For the record, there are documented sperm whales and sharks living in the Mediterranean sea that can swallow a person whole.)

Jesus placed his stamp of authenticity on Jonah when he mentioned him by name (Matt.12:39–41; Luke 11:29, 30, 32). The fact that Jonah ran in the opposite direction from Nineveh indicates a great deal about his character. Nineveh was the capital of the large and notoriously violent Assyrian empire. Of course Jonah was intimidated, but that was no excuse to run from God's command. What was the point of running? God is already everywhere, yet we often resist when He requests something that looks impossible or too large or uncomfortable for us. Forfeiting the opportunity to see a nation experience repentance and revival shows racial prejudice, bigotry, and/or selfishness. We must never forget that when we neglect God-given responsibilities, others will be greatly affected.

One big lesson from this reluctant leader is that God's mercy is big enough to give anyone a second chance, when so warranted through repentance. Perhaps this generation will run toward the directives and commands of God so that we will see many enemies and other nations come to repentance. What a day that would be!

And my prayer went *up* to You,
Into Your holy temple.

8"Those who regard worthless idols
Forsake their own Mercy.
9But I will sacrifice to You
With the voice of thanksgiving;
I will pay what I have vowed.
Salvation *is* of the LORD."

10So the LORD spoke to the fish, and it vomited Jonah onto dry *land*.

JONAH PREACHES AT NINEVEH

3 Now the word of the LORD came to Jonah the second time, saying, 2"Arise, go to Nineveh, that great city, and preach to it the message that I tell you." 3So Jonah arose and went to Nineveh, according to the word of the LORD. Now Nineveh was an exceedingly great city, a three-day journey[a] *in extent*. 4And Jonah began to enter the city on the first day's walk. Then he cried out and

said, "Yet forty days, and Nineveh shall be overthrown!"

THE PEOPLE OF NINEVEH BELIEVE

5So the people of Nineveh believed God, proclaimed a fast, and put on sackcloth, from the greatest to the least of them. 6Then word came to the king of Nineveh; and he arose from his throne and laid aside his robe, covered *himself* with sackcloth and sat in ashes. 7And he caused *it* to be proclaimed and published throughout Nineveh by the decree of the king and his nobles, saying,

Let neither man nor beast, herd nor flock, taste anything; do not let them eat, or drink water. 8But let man and beast be covered with sackcloth, and cry mightily to God; yes, let every one turn from his evil way and from the violence that is in his hands. 9Who can tell *if* God will turn and relent,

3:3 aExact meaning unknown

and turn away from His fierce anger,
so that we may not perish?

¹⁰Then God saw their works, that they turned from their evil way; and God relented from the disaster that He had said He would bring upon them, and He did not do it.

4 But it displeased Jonah exceedingly, and he became angry. ²So he prayed to the LORD, and said, "Ah, LORD, was not this what I said when I was still in my country? Therefore I fled previously to Tarshish; for I know that You *are* a gracious and merciful God, slow to anger and abundant in lovingkindness, One who relents from doing harm. ³Therefore now, O LORD, please take my life from me, for *it is* better for me to die than to live!"

⁴Then the LORD said, "*Is it* right for you to be angry?"

⁵So Jonah went out of the city and sat on the east side of the city. There he made himself a shelter and sat under it in the shade, till he might see what would become of the city. ⁶And the LORD God prepared a plantᵃ and made it come up over Jonah, that it might be shade for his head to deliver him from his misery. So Jonah was very grateful for the plant. ⁷But as morning dawned the next day God prepared a worm, and it *so* damaged the plant that it withered. ⁸And it happened, when the sun arose, that God prepared a vehement east wind; and the sun beat on Jonah's head, so that he grew faint. Then he wished death for himself, and said, "*It is* better for me to die than to live."

⁹Then God said to Jonah, "*Is it* right for you to be angry about the plant?"

And he said, "*It is* right for me to be angry, even to death!"

¹⁰But the LORD said, "You have had pity on the plant for which you have not labored, nor made it grow, which came up in a night and perished in a night. ¹¹And should I not pity Nineveh, that great city, in which are more than one hundred and twenty thousand persons who cannot discern between their right hand and their left— and much livestock?"

4:6 ᵃHebrew *kikayon*, exact identity unknown

IMPACT OF THE BOOK

I IDEA

God has shown His people what He requires—"to do justly, to love mercy, and to walk humbly" with Him (6:8).

M MESSAGE

Leaders will never succeed in the long run if they are only look-ing out after their own interests. Healthy leadership benefits everyone, and godly leaders look out for their followers. He closes the book by declaring, "Who is a God like You, pardoning iniquity and passing over the transgressions of the remnant of His heritage?" (7:18).

P PEOPLE

Ahaz, Hezekiah, Jotham, Micah

A AUTHOR

The author identified himself as Micah the Moreshite. His name means "Who Is Like Yahweh?" He was from Moresheth Gath, a small rural village in Judah, 25 miles southwest of Jerusalem. Micah lived within general proximity of Isaiah, which may ex-plain why many of their prophecies overlap.

C CULTURE

Micah challenged the corruption and idolatry of the religious and political leadership in his day. Those leaders had lost all credibility because they were hypocritical and self-serving. The people of Samaria and Jerusalem were engaging in idolatry, and this was the root cause of many of their unjust practices. King Hezekiah tried to bring about moral and spiritual reform in the southern kingdom. His efforts did delay God's judgment for a period of time; but ultimately, his reforms were not complete. Therefore, God declared—through Micah—that He would send Assyria to judge both the northern and southern kingdoms for their sin. Micah witnessed the fall of Samaria in the north and the revival under Hezekiah in the south.

T TIMELINE

c. 700 BC

KEY SCRIPTURE
MEMORY VERSES

5:2; 6:8; 7:18

1 The word of the LORD that came to Micah of Moresheth in the days of Jotham, Ahaz, *and* Hezekiah, kings of Judah, which he saw concerning Samaria and Jerusalem.

THE COMING JUDGMENT ON ISRAEL

²Hear, all you peoples!
Listen, O earth, and all that is in it!
Let the Lord GOD be a witness against you,
The Lord from His holy temple.

³For behold, the LORD is coming out of His
    place;
He will come down
And tread on the high places of the earth.
⁴The mountains will melt under Him,
And the valleys will split
Like wax before the fire,
Like waters poured down a steep place.
⁵All this is for the transgression of Jacob
And for the sins of the house of Israel.
What *is* the transgression of Jacob?
Is it not Samaria?
And what *are* the high places of Judah?
Are they not Jerusalem?

⁶"Therefore I will make Samaria a heap of ruins
    in the field,
Places for planting a vineyard;
I will pour down her stones into the valley,
And I will uncover her foundations.
⁷All her carved images shall be beaten to
    pieces,
And all her pay as a harlot shall be burned
    with the fire;
All her idols I will lay desolate,
For she gathered *it* from the pay of a harlot,
And they shall return to the pay of a
    harlot."

MOURNING FOR ISRAEL AND JUDAH

⁸Therefore I will wail and howl,
I will go stripped and naked;
I will make a wailing like the jackals
And a mourning like the ostriches,
⁹For her wounds *are* incurable.
For it has come to Judah;
It has come to the gate of My people—
To Jerusalem.

¹⁰Tell *it* not in Gath,
Weep not at all;
In Beth Aphrah[a]
Roll yourself in the dust.
¹¹Pass by in naked shame, you inhabitant of
    Shaphir;
The inhabitant of Zaanan[a] does not go out.
Beth Ezel mourns;
Its place to stand is taken away from you.

¹²For the inhabitant of Maroth pined[a] for good,
But disaster came down from the LORD
To the gate of Jerusalem.
¹³O inhabitant of Lachish,
Harness the chariot to the swift steeds
(She *was* the beginning of sin to the daughter
    of Zion),
For the transgressions of Israel were found in
    you.

¹⁴Therefore you shall give presents to
    Moresheth Gath;[a]
The houses of Achzib[b] *shall be* a lie to the
    kings of Israel.
¹⁵I will yet bring an heir to you, O inhabitant
    of Mareshah;[a]
The glory of Israel shall come to Adullam.
¹⁶Make yourself bald and cut off your hair,
Because of your precious children;
Enlarge your baldness like an eagle,
For they shall go from you into captivity.

WOE TO EVILDOERS

2 Woe to those who devise iniquity,
And work out evil on their beds!
At morning light they practice it,
Because it is in the power of their hand.
²They covet fields and take *them* by violence,
Also houses, and seize *them*.
So they oppress a man and his house,
A man and his inheritance.

³Therefore thus says the LORD:

"Behold, against this family I am devising
    disaster,

1:10 [a]Literally *House of Dust*   **1:11** [a]Literally *Going Out*   **1:12** [a]Literally *was sick*   **1:14** [a]Literally *Possession of Gath*   [b]Literally *Lie*   **1:15** [a]Literally *Inheritance*

From which you cannot remove your necks;
Nor shall you walk haughtily,
For this *is* an evil time.
⁴In that day *one* shall take up a proverb against
   you,
And lament with a bitter lamentation, saying:
'We are utterly destroyed!
He has changed the heritage of my people;
How He has removed *it* from me!
To a turncoat He has divided our fields.' "

⁵Therefore you will have no one to determine
   boundariesᵃ by lot
In the assembly of the LORD.

LYING PROPHETS

⁶"Do not prattle," *you say to those* who prophesy.
So they shall not prophesy to you;ᵃ
They shall not return insult for insult.ᵇ
⁷*You who are* named the house of Jacob:
"Is the Spirit of the LORD restricted?
Are these His doings?
Do not My words do good
To him who walks uprightly?

⁸"Lately My people have risen up as an
   enemy—
You pull off the robe with the garment
From those who trust *you,* as they pass by,
Like men returned from war.
⁹The women of My people you cast out
From their pleasant houses;
From their children
You have taken away My glory forever.

¹⁰"Arise and depart,
For this *is* not *your* rest;
Because it is defiled, it shall destroy,
Yes, with utter destruction.
¹¹If a man should walk in a false spirit
And speak a lie, *saying,*
'I will prophesy to you of wine and drink,'
Even he would be the prattler of this people.

ISRAEL RESTORED

¹²"I will surely assemble all of you, O Jacob,
I will surely gather the remnant of Israel;
I will put them together like sheep of the
   fold,ᵃ

Like a flock in the midst of their pasture;
They shall make a loud noise because of *so
   many* people.
¹³The one who breaks open will come up
   before them;
They will break out,
Pass through the gate,
And go out by it;
Their king will pass before them,
With the LORD at their head."

WICKED RULERS AND PROPHETS

3 And I said:

"Hear now, O heads of Jacob,
And you rulers of the house of Israel:
Is it not for you to know justice?
²You who hate good and love evil;
Who strip the skin from My people,ᵃ
And the flesh from their bones;
³Who also eat the flesh of My people,
Flay their skin from them,
Break their bones,
And chop *them* in pieces
Like *meat* for the pot,
Like flesh in the caldron."

⁴Then they will cry to the LORD,
But He will not hear them;
He will even hide His face from them at that
   time,
Because they have been evil in their deeds.

⁵Thus says the LORD concerning the prophets
Who make my people stray;
Who chant "Peace"
While they chew with their teeth,
But who prepare war against him
Who puts nothing into their mouths:
⁶"Therefore you shall have night without
   vision,
And you shall have darkness without
   divination;
The sun shall go down on the prophets,
And the day shall be dark for them.
⁷So the seers shall be ashamed,

2:5 ᵃLiterally *one casting a surveyor's line*   **2:6** ᵃLiterally *to these*
ᵇVulgate reads *He shall not take shame.*   **2:12** ᵃHebrew *Bozrah*
3:2 ᵃLiterally *them*

And the diviners abashed;
Indeed they shall all cover their lips;
For *there is* no answer from God."

⁸But truly I am full of power by the Spirit of
    the LORD,
And of justice and might,
To declare to Jacob his transgression
And to Israel his sin.
⁹Now hear this,
You heads of the house of Jacob
And rulers of the house of Israel,
Who abhor justice
And pervert all equity,
¹⁰Who build up Zion with bloodshed
And Jerusalem with iniquity:
¹¹Her heads judge for a bribe,
Her priests teach for pay,
And her prophets divine for money.
Yet they lean on the LORD, and say,
"Is not the LORD among us?
No harm can come upon us."
¹²Therefore because of you
Zion shall be plowed *like* a field,
Jerusalem shall become heaps of ruins,
And the mountain of the temple[a]
Like the bare hills of the forest.

THE LORD'S REIGN IN ZION

4 Now it shall come to pass in the latter days
    That the mountain of the LORD's house
Shall be established on the top of the
    mountains,
And shall be exalted above the hills;
And peoples shall flow to it.
²Many nations shall come and say,
"Come, and let us go up to the mountain of
    the LORD,
To the house of the God of Jacob;
He will teach us His ways,
And we shall walk in His paths."
For out of Zion the law shall go forth,
And the word of the LORD from Jerusalem.
³He shall judge between many peoples,
And rebuke strong nations afar off;
They shall beat their swords into plowshares,
And their spears into pruning hooks;
Nation shall not lift up sword against nation,
Neither shall they learn war anymore.[a]

⁴But everyone shall sit under his vine and
    under his fig tree,
And no one shall make *them* afraid;
For the mouth of the LORD of hosts has
    spoken.
⁵For all people walk each in the name of his
    god,
But we will walk in the name of the LORD
    our God
Forever and ever.

ZION'S FUTURE TRIUMPH

⁶"In that day," says the LORD,
"I will assemble the lame,
I will gather the outcast
And those whom I have afflicted;
⁷I will make the lame a remnant,
And the outcast a strong nation;
So the LORD will reign over them in Mount
    Zion
From now on, even forever.
⁸And you, O tower of the flock,
The stronghold of the daughter of Zion,
To you shall it come,
Even the former dominion shall come,
The kingdom of the daughter of Jerusalem."

⁹Now why do you cry aloud?
Is there no king in your midst?
Has your counselor perished?
For pangs have seized you like a woman in
    labor.
¹⁰Be in pain, and labor to bring forth,
O daughter of Zion,
Like a woman in birth pangs.
For now you shall go forth from the city,
You shall dwell in the field,
And to Babylon you shall go.
There you shall be delivered;
There the LORD will redeem you
From the hand of your enemies.

¹¹Now also many nations have gathered against
    you,
Who say, "Let her be defiled,
And let our eye look upon Zion."
¹²But they do not know the thoughts of the
    LORD,

3:12 aLiterally *house*   **4:3** aCompare Isaiah 2:2–4

Nor do they understand His counsel;
For He will gather them like sheaves to the
  threshing floor.

¹³"Arise and thresh, O daughter of Zion;
For I will make your horn iron,
And I will make your hooves bronze;
You shall beat in pieces many peoples;
I will consecrate their gain to the LORD,
And their substance to the Lord of the whole
  earth."

5 Now gather yourself in troops,
O daughter of troops;
He has laid siege against us;
They will strike the judge of Israel with a rod
  on the cheek.

THE COMING MESSIAH

²"But you, Bethlehem Ephrathah,
Though you are little among the thousands of
  Judah,
Yet out of you shall come forth to Me
The One to be Ruler in Israel,
Whose goings forth *are* from of old,
From everlasting."

³Therefore He shall give them up,
Until the time *that* she who is in labor has
  given birth;
Then the remnant of His brethren
Shall return to the children of Israel.
⁴And He shall stand and feed *His flock*
In the strength of the LORD,
In the majesty of the name of the LORD His
  God;
And they shall abide,
For now He shall be great
To the ends of the earth;
⁵And this *One* shall be peace.

JUDGMENT ON ISRAEL'S ENEMIES

When the Assyrian comes into our land,
And when he treads in our palaces,
Then we will raise against him
Seven shepherds and eight princely men.
⁶They shall waste with the sword the land of
  Assyria,
And the land of Nimrod at its entrances;

Thus He shall deliver *us* from the Assyrian,
When he comes into our land
And when he treads within our borders.

⁷Then the remnant of Jacob
Shall be in the midst of many peoples,
Like dew from the LORD,
Like showers on the grass,
That tarry for no man
Nor wait for the sons of men.
⁸And the remnant of Jacob
Shall be among the Gentiles,
In the midst of many peoples,
Like a lion among the beasts of the forest,
Like a young lion among flocks of sheep,
Who, if he passes through,
Both treads down and tears in pieces,
And none can deliver.
⁹Your hand shall be lifted against your
  adversaries,
And all your enemies shall be cut off.

¹⁰"And it shall be in that day," says the LORD,
"That I will cut off your horses from your
  midst
And destroy your chariots.
¹¹I will cut off the cities of your land
And throw down all your strongholds.
¹²I will cut off sorceries from your hand,
And you shall have no soothsayers.
¹³Your carved images I will also cut off,
And your *sacred* pillars from your midst;
You shall no more worship the work of your
  hands;
¹⁴I will pluck your wooden images^a from your
  midst;
Thus I will destroy your cities.
¹⁵And I will execute vengeance in anger and
  fury
On the nations that have not heard."^a

GOD PLEADS WITH ISRAEL

6 Hear now what the LORD says:

"Arise, plead your case before the mountains,
And let the hills hear your voice.
²Hear, O you mountains, the LORD's
  complaint,

5:14 ^aHebrew *Asherim,* Canaanite deities   5:15 ^aOr *obeyed*

And you strong foundations of the earth;
For the LORD has a complaint against His
        people,
And He will contend with Israel.

³"O My people, what have I done to you?
And how have I wearied you?
Testify against Me.
⁴For I brought you up from the land of Egypt,
I redeemed you from the house of bondage;
And I sent before you Moses, Aaron, and
        Miriam.
⁵O My people, remember now
What Balak king of Moab counseled,
And what Balaam the son of Beor answered
        him,
From Acacia Groveᵃ to Gilgal,
That you may know the righteousness of the
        LORD."

⁶With what shall I come before the LORD,
And bow myself before the High God?
Shall I come before Him with burnt
        offerings,
With calves a year old?
⁷Will the LORD be pleased with thousands of
        rams,
Ten thousand rivers of oil?
Shall I give my firstborn *for* my transgression,
The fruit of my body *for* the sin of my soul?

⁸He has shown you, O man, what *is* good;
And what does the LORD require of you
But to do justly,
To love mercy,
And to walk humbly with your God?

PUNISHMENT OF ISRAEL'S INJUSTICE

⁹The LORD's voice cries to the city—
Wisdom shall see Your name:

"Hear the rod!
Who has appointed it?
¹⁰Are there yet the treasures of wickedness
In the house of the wicked,
And the short measure *that is* an
        abomination?
¹¹Shall I count pure *those* with the wicked
scales,

And with the bag of deceitful weights?
¹²For her rich men are full of violence,
Her inhabitants have spoken lies,
And their tongue is deceitful in their mouth.

¹³"Therefore I will also make *you* sick by
        striking you,
By making *you* desolate because of your sins.
¹⁴You shall eat, but not be satisfied;
Hungerᵃ *shall be* in your midst.
You may carry *some* away,ᵇ but shall not save
        them;
And what you do rescue I will give over to
        the sword.

¹⁵"You shall sow, but not reap;
You shall tread the olives, but not anoint
        yourselves with oil;
And *make* sweet wine, but not drink wine.
¹⁶For the statutes of Omri are kept;
All the works of Ahab's house *are done;*
And you walk in their counsels,
That I may make you a desolation,
And your inhabitants a hissing.
Therefore you shall bear the reproach of My
        people."ᵃ

SORROW FOR ISRAEL'S SINS

7 Woe is me!
For I am like those who gather summer
        fruits,
Like those who glean vintage grapes;
There is no cluster to eat
Of the first-ripe fruit *which* my soul desires.
²The faithful *man* has perished from the earth,
And *there is* no one upright among men.
They all lie in wait for blood;
Every man hunts his brother with a net.

³That they may successfully do evil with both
        hands—
The prince asks *for gifts,*
The judge *seeks* a bribe,
And the great *man* utters his evil desire;
So they scheme together.
⁴The best of them *is* like a brier;

6:5 ᵃHebrew *Shittim* (compare Numbers 25:1; Joshua 2:1; 3:1)
6:14 ᵃOr *Emptiness* or *Humiliation* ᵇTargum and Vulgate read *You shall take hold.* **6:16** ᵃFollowing Masoretic Text, Targum, and Vulgate; Septuagint reads *of nations.*

INSIDE the INFLUENCERS

MICAH—Requirements of a Leader

MICAH 6:8

Micah's name means, "Who is like the Lord?" He was a contemporary of the major prophet Isaiah, and together they stayed accountable in the midst of great idolatry. The requirements of a leader are summarized in 6:8: "What does the Lord require of you but to do justly, to love mercy, and to walk humbly with your God?" The phrase "high places" is used (1:5) in talking about placing affection on the works of our own hands (5:13). We have become addicted to things acquired through our own success: houses, money, trophies, clothes, cars, etc. The word idolatry refers to anything that is so important to you that it takes priority in your desires over God. It can be people, pleasure, or a possession.

In the middle of his message on judgment, Micah switches gears and adds hope that one day there will be peace on earth and righteousness. In doing so, Micah teaches us that worshiping God is the catalyst for peace. In chapter 5, Micah mentions that the Deliverer would come and that He would be born in Bethlehem (5:2). This righteous prophet was entrusted by God with the honor of writing the prophesy that would lead the wise men to Jesus, thus saving his life from Herod's death order. Leaders who walk humbly and justly will be given such honors. Like Micah, we may not see the grand impact until years after we have gone into eternity.

The most upright *is sharper* than a thorn
　　hedge;
The day of your watchman and your
　　punishment comes;
Now shall be their perplexity.

⁵Do not trust in a friend;
　Do not put your confidence in a companion;
　Guard the doors of your mouth
　From her who lies in your bosom.
⁶For son dishonors father,
　Daughter rises against her mother,
　Daughter-in-law against her mother-in-law;
　A man's enemies *are* the men of his own
　　household.
⁷Therefore I will look to the LORD;
　I will wait for the God of my salvation;
　My God will hear me.

ISRAEL'S CONFESSION AND COMFORT

⁸Do not rejoice over me, my enemy;
　When I fall, I will arise;
　When I sit in darkness,

The LORD *will be* a light to me.
⁹I will bear the indignation of the LORD,
　Because I have sinned against Him,
　Until He pleads my case
　And executes justice for me.
　He will bring me forth to the light;
　I will see His righteousness.
¹⁰Then *she who is* my enemy will see,
　And shame will cover her who said to me,
　"Where is the LORD your God?"
　My eyes will see her;
　Now she will be trampled down
　Like mud in the streets.

¹¹*In* the day when your walls are to be built,
　In that day the decree shall go far and wide.ᵃ
¹²*In* that day theyᵃ shall come to you
　From Assyria and the fortified cities,ᵇ
　From the fortressᶜ to the River,ᵈ
　From sea to sea,

7:11 ᵃOr *the boundary shall be extended* 7:12 ᵃLiterally *he*, collective of the captives ᵇHebrew *arey mazor*, possibly *cities of Egypt* ᶜHebrew *mazor*, possibly *Egypt* ᵈThat is, the Euphrates

And mountain *to* mountain.
¹³Yet the land shall be desolate
Because of those who dwell in it,
And for the fruit of their deeds.

GOD WILL FORGIVE ISRAEL

¹⁴Shepherd Your people with Your staff,
The flock of Your heritage,
Who dwell solitarily *in* a woodland,
In the midst of Carmel;
Let them feed *in* Bashan and Gilead,
As in days of old.

¹⁵"As in the days when you came out of the
    land of Egypt,
I will show them[a] wonders."

¹⁶The nations shall see and be ashamed of all
    their might;
They shall put *their* hand over *their* mouth;
Their ears shall be deaf.
¹⁷They shall lick the dust like a serpent;

They shall crawl from their holes like snakes
    of the earth.
They shall be afraid of the LORD our God,
And shall fear because of You.
¹⁸Who *is* a God like You,
Pardoning iniquity
And passing over the transgression of the
    remnant of His heritage?

He does not retain His anger forever,
Because He delights *in* mercy.
¹⁹He will again have compassion on us,
And will subdue our iniquities.

You will cast all our[a] sins
Into the depths of the sea.
²⁰You will give truth to Jacob
And mercy to Abraham,
Which You have sworn to our fathers
From days of old.

7:15 ᵃLiterally *him,* collective for the captives   **7:19** ᵃLiterally *their*

IMPACT OF THE BOOK

IDEA	*God is patient and merciful; but ultimately, people will reap what they sow if they are unrepentant.*
MESSAGE	*Leaders who do not reproduce fail, in the end, at one of their most important tasks. Jonah's preaching brought revival to the city of Nineveh; but a generation later, God had to send the prophet Nahum back to Nineveh to warn them of impending judgment because of their wickedness. How could that happen? The people did not reproduce their faith; they did not invest in the next generation and failed to pass down God's truth.*
PEOPLE	*King of Nineveh, Nahum*
AUTHOR	*Little is known about Nahum himself. He says that he is an Elkoshite. Arab tradition has identified Elkosh with "Al Qosh," a small village in Iraq, but the exact location is uncertain.*
CULTURE	*Nahum's prophecy must be understood against the backdrop of both Israel's and Judah's painful oppression by Assyria. The northern kingdom of Israel had already succumbed to the power of Assyria in 722 BC. Now Judah was experiencing their cruelty. Although God was the ultimate author of Judah's suffering (as He appointed Assyria to judge Judah for their sin), the cup of His wrath had passed to Nineveh. The capital city of Nineveh seemed impregnable. There were massive and strong walls, mighty towers, and a complete water and food supply. No wonder the Assyrians felt totally secure; but they forgot that when God settles an account, it is settled in full. In 612 BC, Nineveh fell to the Medes and the Babylonians.*
TIMELINE	*c. 650 BC*
KEY SCRIPTURE MEMORY VERSES	1:7

1 The burden[a] against Nineveh. The book of the vision of Nahum the Elkoshite.

God's Wrath on His Enemies

2God *is* jealous, and the LORD avenges;
  The LORD avenges and *is* furious.
  The LORD will take vengeance on His
      adversaries,
  And He reserves *wrath* for His enemies;
3The LORD *is* slow to anger and great in
      power,
  And will not at all acquit *the wicked.*

  The LORD has His way
  In the whirlwind and in the storm,
  And the clouds *are* the dust of His feet.
4He rebukes the sea and makes it dry,
  And dries up all the rivers.
  Bashan and Carmel wither,
  And the flower of Lebanon wilts.
5The mountains quake before Him,
  The hills melt,
  And the earth heaves[a] at His presence,
  Yes, the world and all who dwell in it.

6Who can stand before His indignation?
  And who can endure the fierceness of His
      anger?
  His fury is poured out like fire,
  And the rocks are thrown down by Him.

7The LORD *is* good,
  A stronghold in the day of trouble;
  And He knows those who trust in Him.
8But with an overflowing flood
  He will make an utter end of its place,
  And darkness will pursue His enemies.

9What do you conspire against the LORD?
  He will make an utter end *of it.*
  Affliction will not rise up a second time.
10For while tangled *like* thorns,
  And while drunken *like* drunkards,
  They shall be devoured like stubble fully
      dried.
11From you comes forth *one*
  Who plots evil against the LORD,
  A wicked counselor.

12Thus says the LORD:

"Though *they are* safe, and likewise many,
  Yet in this manner they will be cut down
  When he passes through.
  Though I have afflicted you,
  I will afflict you no more;
13For now I will break off his yoke from you,
  And burst your bonds apart."

14The LORD has given a command concerning
      you:
"Your name shall be perpetuated no longer.
  Out of the house of your gods
  I will cut off the carved image and the
      molded image.
  I will dig your grave,
  For you are vile."

15Behold, on the mountains
  The feet of him who brings good tidings,
  Who proclaims peace!
  O Judah, keep your appointed feasts,
  Perform your vows.
  For the wicked one shall no more pass
      through you;
  He is utterly cut off.

The Destruction of Nineveh

2 He who scatters[a] has come up before your
      face.
  Man the fort!
  Watch the road!
  Strengthen *your* flanks!
  Fortify *your* power mightily.

2For the LORD will restore the excellence of
      Jacob
  Like the excellence of Israel,
  For the emptiers have emptied them out
  And ruined their vine branches.

3The shields of his mighty men *are* made
      red,
  The valiant men *are* in scarlet.
  The chariots *come* with flaming torches

1:1 [a]Or *oracle*   1:5 [a]Targum reads *burns.*   2:1 [a]Vulgate reads *He who destroys.*

INSIDE *the* INFLUENCERS

NAHUM—Every Generation Stands Alone

NAHUM 1:8–13

At first glance this looks like *another* prophet pronouncing judgment. It is important to note that Nahum wrote this book when the Assyrians were at the zenith of power. No one could even imagine the great city of Nineveh falling.

Nahum's message is not only a warning, but it is given to encourage Judah. There was no hope for the Assyrians. Jonah's warning gave them a chance one hundred and fifty years earlier, and their repentance brought a reprieve from God's anger; but the following generations took on the same violent characteristics of their ancestors.

In chapter 1:8–13, Nahum foretells the fall of the city by painting the picture of a destructive flood that sweeps everything away. Subsequently, Nineveh *was* destroyed by a great flood and buried under the mud for almost two thousand years. Huge statues with the body of a lion and the head of man once lined the thriving city, depicting the city's false power and might. In foretelling the city's judgment, Nahum asked the question, "Where is the dwelling of the lions?" (2:11). As a leader, you must remember one of the great lessons of history: every country is only one generation away from either idolatry or atheism.

In the day of his preparation,
And the spears are brandished.[a]
⁴The chariots rage in the streets,
They jostle one another in the broad roads;
They seem like torches,
They run like lightning.

⁵He remembers his nobles;
They stumble in their walk;
They make haste to her walls,
And the defense is prepared.
⁶The gates of the rivers are opened,
And the palace is dissolved.
⁷It is decreed:[a]
She shall be led away captive,
She shall be brought up;
And her maidservants shall lead *her* as with
    the voice of doves,
Beating their breasts.

⁸Though Nineveh of old *was* like a pool of
    water,
Now they flee away.
"Halt! Halt!" *they cry;*
But no one turns back.
⁹Take spoil of silver!

Take spoil of gold!
There is no end of treasure,
Or wealth of every desirable prize.
¹⁰She is empty, desolate, and waste!
The heart melts, and the knees shake;
Much pain *is* in every side,
And all their faces are drained of color.[a]

¹¹Where *is* the dwelling of the lions,
And the feeding place of the young lions,
Where the lion walked, the lioness *and* lion's
    cub,
And no one made *them* afraid?
¹²The lion tore in pieces enough for his cubs,
Killed for his lionesses,
Filled his caves with prey,
And his dens with flesh.

¹³"Behold, I *am* against you," says the LORD
of hosts, "I will burn your[a] chariots in smoke, and
the sword shall devour your young lions; I will cut
off your prey from the earth, and the voice of
your messengers shall be heard no more."

2:3 [a]Literally *the cypresses are shaken;* Septuagint and Syriac read
the horses rush about; Vulgate reads *the drivers are stupefied.*
2:7 [a]Hebrew *Huzzab* 2:10 [a]Compare Joel 2:6 2:13 [a]Literally *her*

The Woe of Nineveh

3 Woe to the bloody city!
It *is* all full of lies *and* robbery.
  Its victim never departs.
²The noise of a whip
  And the noise of rattling wheels,
  Of galloping horses,
  Of clattering chariots!
³Horsemen charge with bright sword and
      glittering spear.
  There is a multitude of slain,
  A great number of bodies,
  Countless corpses—
  They stumble over the corpses—
⁴Because of the multitude of harlotries of the
      seductive harlot,
  The mistress of sorceries,
  Who sells nations through her harlotries,
  And families through her sorceries.

⁵"Behold, I *am* against you," says the LORD of
      hosts;
  "I will lift your skirts over your face,
  I will show the nations your nakedness,
  And the kingdoms your shame.
⁶I will cast abominable filth upon you,
  Make you vile,
  And make you a spectacle.
⁷It shall come to pass *that* all who look upon
      you
  Will flee from you, and say,
  'Nineveh is laid waste!
  Who will bemoan her?'
  Where shall I seek comforters for you?"

⁸Are you better than No Amonᵃ
  That was situated by the River,ᵇ
  That had the waters around her,
  Whose rampart *was* the sea,
  Whose wall *was* the sea?
⁹Ethiopia and Egypt *were* her strength,
  And *it was* boundless;
  Put and Lubim were yourᵃ helpers.
¹⁰Yet she *was* carried away,

  She went into captivity;
  Her young children also were dashed to
      pieces

At the head of every street;
  They cast lots for her honorable men,
  And all her great men were bound in chains.
¹¹You also will be drunk;
  You will be hidden;
  You also will seek refuge from the enemy.

¹²All your strongholds *are* fig trees with ripened
      figs:
  If they are shaken,
  They fall into the mouth of the eater.
¹³Surely, your people in your midst *are* women!
  The gates of your land are wide open for
      your enemies;
  Fire shall devour the bars of your *gates.*

¹⁴Draw your water for the siege!
  Fortify your strongholds!
  Go into the clay and tread the mortar!
  Make strong the brick kiln!
¹⁵There the fire will devour you,
  The sword will cut you off;
  It will eat you up like a locust.

Make yourself many—like the locust!
  Make yourself many— like the *swarming*
      locusts!
¹⁶You have multiplied your merchants more
      than the stars of heaven.
  The locust plunders and flies away.
¹⁷Your commanders *are* like *swarming* locusts,
  And your generals like great grasshoppers,
  Which camp in the hedges on a cold day;
  When the sun rises they flee away,
  And the place where they *are* is not known.

¹⁸Your shepherds slumber, O king of Assyria;
  Your nobles rest *in the dust.*
  Your people are scattered on the mountains,
  And no one gathers them.
¹⁹Your injury *has* no healing,
  Your wound is severe.
  All who hear news of you
  Will clap *their* hands over you,
  For upon whom has not your wickedness
      passed continually?

3:8 ᵃThat is, ancient Thebes; Targum and Vulgate read *populous Alexandria.* ᵇLiterally *rivers,* that is, the Nile and the surrounding canals **3:9** ᵃSeptuagint reads *her.*

IMPACT OF THE BOOK

I IDEA | *God is big enough to handle your tough questions. Once you envision God on His throne, ruling and reigning, you can live by His standard. "The just shall live by his faith" (2:4).*

m MESSAGE | *Habakkuk showed his genuine struggle with his understanding of God. He struggled with why evil seemed to go on for so long without being punished. God's ways will never be completely understood with finite human reasoning, but that does not mean that humans should cease trying to know God. Vision is the single greatest trait a leader can possess, and Habakkuk certainly shows it. He was transformed by this personal vision from a doubter, complainer, and whiner to a proclaimer of truth.*

P PEOPLE | *Habakkuk, Jehoahaz*

A AUTHOR | *Not much is known about Habakkuk outside of his book. His name is unusual and difficult to translate. It is believed to mean "One Who Embraces, Clings To, or Relies Upon His God." The reference to musical notations in chapter 3 seems to suggest that he may have been a Levitical priest.*

C CULTURE | *Overall, Habakkuk ought to be viewed as a spiritual struggle between the prophet and His God. However, the struggle has a historical context. After the fall of Nineveh in 612 BC, the people of Judah experienced a period of relative peace; but when the people began to turn from the Lord, He threatened to use Babylon as His instrument of judgment. In his lifetime, Habakkuk lived to see the prosperity **and** destitution of his people. It moved him to wrestle with God.*

T TIMELINE | *c. 610 BC*

KEY SCRIPTURE
MEMORY VERSES | 2:4; 3:17–19

1 The burden[a] which the prophet Habakkuk saw.

THE PROPHET'S QUESTION

2 O LORD, how long shall I cry,
 And You will not hear?
 Even cry out to You, "Violence!"
 And You will not save.
3 Why do You show me iniquity,
 And cause *me* to see trouble?
 For plundering and violence *are* before me;
 There is strife, and contention arises.
4 Therefore the law is powerless,
 And justice never goes forth.
 For the wicked surround the righteous;
 Therefore perverse judgment proceeds.

THE LORD'S REPLY

5 "Look among the nations and watch—
 Be utterly astounded!
 For *I will* work a work in your days

Which you would not believe, though it were
 told *you*.
6 For indeed I am raising up the Chaldeans,
 A bitter and hasty nation
 Which marches through the breadth of the
 earth,
 To possess dwelling places *that are* not theirs.
7 They are terrible and dreadful;
 Their judgment and their dignity proceed
 from themselves.
8 Their horses also are swifter than leopards,
 And more fierce than evening wolves.
 Their chargers charge ahead;
 Their cavalry comes from afar;
 They fly as the eagle *that* hastens to eat.

9 "They all come for violence;
 Their faces are set *like* the east wind.
 They gather captives like sand.

1:1 [a]Or *oracle*

 the **INFLUENCERS**

HABAKKUK—Transformed by a Vision

HABAKKUK 1—2

Habakkuk is usually called a "minor prophet," which means his ministry had limited impact and responsibility. If anyone should have been disqualified from becoming an impact player it should have been this complaining, critical, negative man described by commentators as the "doubting Thomas of the Old Testament."

Faith Sighs (1:1–4): Habakkuk complained as he questioned God about the violence and corruption of his nation. In verse five, God interrupted him with a truthful picture, which was surprisingly hopeful.

Faith Sees (2:1): He proclaimed, "I will stand my watch . . . to see what He will say to me." That was the heart cry the Lord was waiting on, and He answered:

"The just shall live by his faith," (2:4) not by sight, circumstance, or headlines.

"The earth will be filled with the knowledge of the glory of the LORD as the waters cover the sea" (2:14). God will right all the injustices and end the violence one day, and fill this planet with His glory.

Faith Sings (Hab. 3): Habakkuk was so thunderstruck by God's majesty, he wrote what some call the greatest chapter of praise in Scripture.

You can go from a hopeless, negative individual to a confident leader full of praise when you wait to hear what He will say to you.

¹⁰They scoff at kings,
And princes are scorned by them.
They deride every stronghold,
For they heap up earthen *mounds* and seize it.
¹¹Then *his* mind[a] changes, and he transgresses;
He commits offense,
Ascribing this power to his god."

THE PROPHET'S SECOND QUESTION

¹²Are You not from everlasting,
O LORD my God, my Holy One?
We shall not die.
O LORD, You have appointed them for
    judgment;
O Rock, You have marked them for
    correction.
¹³*You are* of purer eyes than to behold evil,
And cannot look on wickedness.
Why do You look on those who deal
    treacherously,
And hold Your tongue when the wicked
    devours
A *person* more righteous than he?
¹⁴*Why* do You make men like fish of the sea,
Like creeping things *that have* no ruler over
    them?

¹⁵They take up all of them with a hook,
They catch them in their net,
And gather them in their dragnet.
Therefore they rejoice and are glad.
¹⁶Therefore they sacrifice to their net,
And burn incense to their dragnet;
Because by them their share *is* sumptuous
And their food plentiful.
¹⁷Shall they therefore empty their net,
And continue to slay nations without pity?

2 I will stand my watch
And set myself on the rampart,
    And watch to see what He will say to me,
    And what I will answer when I am
    corrected.

THE JUST LIVE BY FAITH

²Then the LORD answered me and said:

"Write the vision
And make *it* plain on tablets,

That he may run who reads it.
³For the vision *is* yet for an appointed time;
But at the end it will speak, and it will
    not lie.
Though it tarries, wait for it;
Because it will surely come,
It will not tarry.

⁴"Behold the proud,
His soul is not upright in him;
But the just shall live by his faith.

WOE TO THE WICKED

⁵"Indeed, because he transgresses by wine,
He is a proud man,
And he does not stay at home.
Because he enlarges his desire as hell,[a]
And he *is* like death, and cannot be satisfied,
He gathers to himself all nations
And heaps up for himself all peoples.

⁶"Will not all these take up a proverb against
    him,
And a taunting riddle against him, and say,
'Woe to him who increases
What is not his—how long?
And to him who loads himself with many
    pledges'?[a]
⁷Will not your creditors[a] rise up suddenly?
Will they not awaken who oppress you?
And you will become their booty.
⁸Because you have plundered many nations,
All the remnant of the people shall plunder
    you,
Because of men's blood
And the violence of the land *and* the city,
And of all who dwell in it.

⁹"Woe to him who covets evil gain for his
    house,
That he may set his nest on high,
That he may be delivered from the power of
    disaster!
¹⁰You give shameful counsel to your house,
Cutting off many peoples,
And sin *against* your soul.

1:11 [a]Literally *spirit* or *wind*   2:5 [a]Or *Sheol*   2:6 [a]Syriac and Vulgate read *thick clay.*   2:7 [a]Literally *those who bite you*

LEADERSHIP
REALITIES

FUELED: LIVE BY INTENTION   *Habakkuk 2:1*

Intentional living is fueled through spiritual intimacy with God. The spiritual experience Habakkuk was seeking was not a church service or a Bible study with friends. He wanted to hear from God personally, and he wanted to improve the condition of his heart. He decided to set himself on the rampart, a quiet place away from the multitudes where he could hear and be heard by his God, and where he could think clearly and deeply.

Prepare your heart for a time with God through these questions: *What will God say? How will I respond? How will I change? What will I answer when I am corrected?*

Living by intention is a result of peaceful, powerful habits. Start now to establish these by turning off the radio, computer, phone, iPod, Internet, and/or TV for at least an hour a day.

- Read through the Psalms and Proverbs.
- Develop the habit of writing in a journal—positive thoughts, words of gratitude, your feelings.
- Plan and organize your goals and time.
- Study, read, and learn new skills.
- Spend time with interesting people, especially mentors.

This time may be quiet, but its results will rock your world as you are empowered and changed, strengthened, and fueled with intention.

---

¹¹For the stone will cry out from the wall,
  And the beam from the timbers will
    answer it.

¹²"Woe to him who builds a town with
    bloodshed,
  Who establishes a city by iniquity!
¹³Behold, *is it* not of the LORD of hosts
  That the peoples labor to feed the fire,ᵃ
  And nations weary themselves in vain?
¹⁴For the earth will be filled
  With the knowledge of the glory of the
    LORD,
  As the waters cover the sea.

¹⁵"Woe to him who gives drink to his neighbor,
  Pressingᵃ *him to* your bottle,
  Even to make *him* drunk,
  That you may look on his nakedness!
¹⁶You are filled with shame instead of glory.
  You also—drink!

And be exposed as uncircumcised!ᵃ
  The cup of the LORD's right hand *will be*
    turned against you,
  And utter shame will be on your glory.
¹⁷For the violence *done to* Lebanon will cover
    you,
  And the plunder of beasts *which* made them
    afraid,
  Because of men's blood
  And the violence of the land *and* the city,
  And of all who dwell in it.

¹⁸"What profit is the image, that its maker
    should carve it,
  The molded image, a teacher of lies,
  That the maker of its mold should trust in it,
  To make mute idols?

2:13 ᵃLiterally *for what satisfies fire,* that is, for what is of no lasting value **2:15** ᵃLiterally *Attaching* or *Joining* **2:16** ᵃDead Sea Scrolls and Septuagint read *And reel!*; Syriac and Vulgate read *And fall fast asleep!*

LEADERSHIP
REALITIES

INTEGRITY—LET YOUR FIRST WORD
BE YOUR BEST WORD   *Habakkuk 2:2*

The result of spiritual intimacy in your personal relationship with God is a life that puts integrity, sincerity, and honesty on public display. In the day of Habakkuk, it was common practice to publish anything of public concern. They did this by engraving tablets of smooth stones or wood in large letters and then hanging the engraving high on a public place to be read. God commanded Habakkuk to put his declaration of faith on public display. He said:

- *Make it plain*—Your words should be easily understood, clear in message, declared by faith, and never double-minded. When you speak the plain truth, you don't have to remember each word for a defense later.

  rab—**plain**—distinct, to make clear, to declare

- *Write it clearly*—so that people can understand it and believe it. Truth and integrity are the primary communication goal, not opinion or popularity.

- *Write it enthusiastically*—so that those who read it will run to tell others. Be known for consistent integrity that motivates and inspires others.

Your first word will be your best word when you carefully choose every thought, motive, and action. Only then can your life be defined by integrity, sincerity, and honesty.

[19] Woe to him who says to wood, 'Awake!'
To silent stone, 'Arise! It shall teach!'
Behold, it is overlaid with gold and silver,
Yet in it there is no breath at all.

[20] "But the LORD is in His holy temple.
Let all the earth keep silence before Him."

THE PROPHET'S PRAYER

3 A prayer of Habakkuk the prophet, on Shigionoth.[a]

[2] O LORD, I have heard Your speech *and* was afraid;
O LORD, revive Your work in the midst of the years!
In the midst of the years make *it* known;
In wrath remember mercy.

[3] God came from Teman,
The Holy One from Mount Paran.   *Selah*

His glory covered the heavens,
And the earth was full of His praise.

[4] *His* brightness was like the light;
He had rays *flashing* from His hand,
And there His power *was* hidden.
[5] Before Him went pestilence,
And fever followed at His feet.

[6] He stood and measured the earth;
He looked and startled the nations.
And the everlasting mountains were scattered,
The perpetual hills bowed.
His ways *are* everlasting.
[7] I saw the tents of Cushan in affliction;
The curtains of the land of Midian trembled.

[8] O LORD, were *You* displeased with the rivers,
Was Your anger against the rivers,
Was Your wrath against the sea,
That You rode on Your horses,
Your chariots of salvation?

3:1 [a] Exact meaning unknown

⁹Your bow was made quite ready;
Oaths were sworn over *Your* arrows.ᵃ   *Selah*

You divided the earth with rivers.
¹⁰The mountains saw You *and* trembled;
The overflowing of the water passed by.
The deep uttered its voice,
And lifted its hands on high.
¹¹The sun and moon stood still in their
    habitation;
At the light of Your arrows they went,
At the shining of Your glittering spear.

¹²You marched through the land in
    indignation;
You trampled the nations in anger.
¹³You went forth for the salvation of Your
    people,
For salvation with Your Anointed.
You struck the head from the house of the
    wicked,
By laying bare from foundation to neck.
                                            Selah

¹⁴You thrust through with his own arrows
The head of his villages.
They came out like a whirlwind to
    scatter me;
Their rejoicing was like feasting on the poor
    in secret.

¹⁵You walked through the sea with Your horses,
Through the heap of great waters.

¹⁶When I heard, my body trembled;
My lips quivered at *the* voice;
Rottenness entered my bones;
And I trembled in myself,
That I might rest in the day of trouble.
When he comes up to the people,
He will invade them with his troops.

A HYMN OF FAITH

¹⁷Though the fig tree may not blossom,
Nor fruit be on the vines;
Though the labor of the olive may fail,
And the fields yield no food;
Though the flock may be cut off from the
    fold,
And there be no herd in the stalls—
¹⁸Yet I will rejoice in the LORD,
I will joy in the God of my salvation.

¹⁹The LORD Godᵃ is my strength;
He will make my feet like deer's *feet*,
And He will make me walk on my high hills.

To the Chief Musician. With my stringed instruments.

3:9 ᵃLiterally *rods* or *tribes* (compare verse 14)   **3:19** ᵃHebrew
YHWH Adonai

ZEPHANIAH

IDEA | *God's people need to be ready for the "day of the Lord" and remain His faithful remnant.*

MESSAGE | *Passion and a plan—these are the qualities that characterized Zephaniah's preaching. He knew that the "day of the Lord" would come, and he grieved that his people would not be ready. He laid out a plan for the people to follow, knowing that all his passionate preaching would not be effective if he did not offer directions for the people.*

PEOPLE | *Josiah, Nebuchadnezzar, Zephaniah*

AUTHOR | *"Zephaniah," meaning "the Lord has hidden," is the only prophet to lay out a lengthy genealogical record. He was the great-great-grandson of one named Hezekiah. Most scholars believe this was the popular king of Judah. If this is correct, then Zephaniah was a member of the royal family. Zephaniah's blatant attacks against the political and religious leaders seem to suggest that he was quite familiar with the elite of his society.*

CULTURE | *Josiah ascended the throne after the wicked reigns of Manasseh (695–642 BC) and Amon (642–640 BC). The moral condition of Judah had been in decline for more than fifty years. Josiah even moved into the territory of the northern kingdom in an attempt to take back some of the land and influence, which had been lost to Assyria. Zephaniah reflected a society that in every aspect had fallen away from the influence of their faith. The main goal of Josiah's reforms was to bring about religious revival in Judah. If Zephaniah preached during Josiah's sweeping reforms, he may have played a major role in helping to bring them about.*

TIMELINE | *625 BC*

KEY SCRIPTURE
MEMORY VERSES | 2:3

1 The word of the LORD which came to Zephaniah the son of Cushi, the son of Gedaliah, the son of Amariah, the son of Hezekiah, in the days of Josiah the son of Amon, king of Judah.

THE GREAT DAY OF THE LORD

2"I will utterly consume everything
  From the face of the land,"
  Says the LORD;
3"I will consume man and beast;
  I will consume the birds of the heavens,
  The fish of the sea,
  And the stumbling blocks[a] along with the
      wicked.
  I will cut off man from the face of the
      land,"
  Says the LORD.

4"I will stretch out My hand against Judah,
  And against all the inhabitants of Jerusalem.
  I will cut off every trace of Baal from this
      place,
  The names of the idolatrous priests[a] with the
      pagan priests—
5Those who worship the host of heaven on
      the housetops;
  Those who worship and swear *oaths* by the
      LORD,
  But who *also* swear by Milcom;[a]
6Those who have turned back from *following*
      the LORD,
  And have not sought the LORD, nor inquired
      of Him."

7Be silent in the presence of the Lord GOD;
  For the day of the LORD *is* at hand,
  For the LORD has prepared a sacrifice;
  He has invited[a] His guests.

8"And it shall be,
  In the day of the LORD's sacrifice,
  That I will punish the princes and the king's
      children,
  And all such as are clothed with foreign
      apparel.
9In the same day I will punish
  All those who leap over the threshold,[a]
  Who fill their masters' houses with violence
      and deceit.

10"And there shall be on that day," says the
      LORD,
  "The sound of a mournful cry from the Fish
      Gate,
  A wailing from the Second Quarter,
  And a loud crashing from the hills.
11Wail, you inhabitants of Maktesh![a]
  For all the merchant people are cut down;
  All those who handle money are cut off.

12"And it shall come to pass at that time
  That I will search Jerusalem with lamps,
  And punish the men
  Who are settled in complacency,[a]
  Who say in their heart,
  'The LORD will not do good,
  Nor will He do evil.'
13Therefore their goods shall become booty,
  And their houses a desolation;
  They shall build houses, but not inhabit *them;*
  They shall plant vineyards, but not drink their
      wine."

14The great day of the LORD *is* near;
  It is near and hastens quickly.
  The noise of the day of the LORD is bitter;
  There the mighty men shall cry out.
15That day *is* a day of wrath,
  A day of trouble and distress,
  A day of devastation and desolation,
  A day of darkness and gloominess,
  A day of clouds and thick darkness,
16A day of trumpet and alarm
  Against the fortified cities
  And against the high towers.

17"I will bring distress upon men,
  And they shall walk like blind men,
  Because they have sinned against the LORD;
  Their blood shall be poured out like dust,
  And their flesh like refuse."

18Neither their silver nor their gold
  Shall be able to deliver them
  In the day of the LORD's wrath;

1:3 [a]Figurative of idols   **1:4** [a]Hebrew *chemarim*   **1:5** [a]Or *Malcam,*
an Ammonite god, also called *Molech* (compare Leviticus 18:21)
1:7 [a]Literally *set apart, consecrated*   **1:9** [a]Compare 1 Samuel 5:5
1:11 [a]Literally *Mortar,* a market district of Jerusalem   **1:12** [a]Literally
on their lees, that is, settled like the dregs of wine

But the whole land shall be devoured
By the fire of His jealousy,
For He will make speedy riddance
Of all those who dwell in the land.

A Call to Repentance

2 Gather yourselves together, yes, gather
together,
O undesirable[a] nation,
²Before the decree is issued,
Or the day passes like chaff,
Before the LORD's fierce anger comes upon
you,
Before the day of the LORD's anger comes
upon you!
³Seek the LORD, all you meek of the earth,
Who have upheld His justice.
Seek righteousness, seek humility.
It may be that you will be hidden
In the day of the LORD's anger.

Judgment on Nations

⁴For Gaza shall be forsaken,
And Ashkelon desolate;
They shall drive out Ashdod at noonday,
And Ekron shall be uprooted.
⁵Woe to the inhabitants of the seacoast,
The nation of the Cherethites!
The word of the LORD *is* against you,
O Canaan, land of the Philistines:
"I will destroy you;
So there shall be no inhabitant."

⁶The seacoast shall be pastures,
With shelters[a] for shepherds and folds for
flocks.
⁷The coast shall be for the remnant of the
house of Judah;
They shall feed *their* flocks there;
In the houses of Ashkelon they shall lie down
at evening.
For the LORD their God will intervene for
them,
And return their captives.

⁸"I have heard the reproach of Moab,
And the insults of the people of Ammon,
With which they have reproached My
people,

And made arrogant threats against their
borders.
⁹Therefore, as I live,"
Says the LORD of hosts, the God of Israel,
"Surely Moab shall be like Sodom,
And the people of Ammon like Gomorrah—
Overrun with weeds and saltpits,
And a perpetual desolation.
The residue of My people shall plunder
them,
And the remnant of My people shall possess
them."

¹⁰This they shall have for their pride,
Because they have reproached and made
arrogant threats
Against the people of the LORD of hosts.
¹¹The LORD *will be* awesome to them,
For He will reduce to nothing all the gods of
the earth;
People shall worship Him,
Each one from his place,
Indeed all the shores of the nations.

¹²"You Ethiopians also,
You shall be slain by My sword."

¹³And He will stretch out His hand against the
north,
Destroy Assyria,
And make Nineveh a desolation,
As dry as the wilderness.
¹⁴The herds shall lie down in her midst,
Every beast of the nation.
Both the pelican and the bittern
Shall lodge on the capitals *of* her *pillars;*
Their voice shall sing in the windows;
Desolation *shall be* at the threshold;
For He will lay bare the cedar work.
¹⁵This is the rejoicing city
That dwelt securely,
That said in her heart,
"I *am it,* and *there is* none besides me."
How has she become a desolation,
A place for beasts to lie down!
Everyone who passes by her
Shall hiss and shake his fist.

2:1 ᵃOr *shameless* **2:6** ᵃLiterally *excavations,* either underground
huts or cisterns

The Wickedness of Jerusalem

3 Woe to her who is rebellious and polluted,
To the oppressing city!
²She has not obeyed *His* voice,
She has not received correction;
She has not trusted in the LORD,
She has not drawn near to her God.

³Her princes in her midst *are* roaring lions;
Her judges *are* evening wolves
That leave not a bone till morning.
⁴Her prophets are insolent, treacherous
people;
Her priests have polluted the sanctuary,
They have done violence to the law.
⁵The LORD *is* righteous in her midst,
He will do no unrighteousness.
Every morning He brings His justice
to light;
He never fails,
But the unjust knows no shame.

⁶"I have cut off nations,
Their fortresses are devastated;
I have made their streets desolate,
With none passing by.
Their cities are destroyed;
There is no one, no inhabitant.
⁷I said, 'Surely you will fear Me,
You will receive instruction'—
So that her dwelling would not be cut off,
Despite everything for which I punished
her.
But they rose early and corrupted all their
deeds.

A Faithful Remnant

⁸"Therefore wait for Me," says the LORD,
"Until the day I rise up for plunder;ᵃ
My determination *is* to gather the nations
To My assembly of kingdoms,
To pour on them My indignation,
All My fierce anger;
All the earth shall be devoured
With the fire of My jealousy.

⁹"For then I will restore to the peoples a pure
language,

That they all may call on the name of the
LORD,
To serve Him with one accord.
¹⁰From beyond the rivers of Ethiopia
My worshipers,
The daughter of My dispersed ones,
Shall bring My offering.
¹¹In that day you shall not be shamed for any
of your deeds
In which you transgress against Me;
For then I will take away from your midst
Those who rejoice in your pride,
And you shall no longer be haughty
In My holy mountain.
¹²I will leave in your midst
A meek and humble people,
And they shall trust in the name of
the LORD.
¹³The remnant of Israel shall do no
unrighteousness
And speak no lies,
Nor shall a deceitful tongue be found in their
mouth;
For they shall feed *their* flocks and lie
down,
And no one shall make *them* afraid."

Joy in God's Faithfulness

¹⁴Sing, O daughter of Zion!
Shout, O Israel!
Be glad and rejoice with all *your* heart,
O daughter of Jerusalem!
¹⁵The LORD has taken away your judgments,
He has cast out your enemy.
The King of Israel, the LORD, *is* in your
midst;
You shall seeᵃ disaster no more.

¹⁶In that day it shall be said to Jerusalem:
"Do not fear;
Zion, let not your hands be weak.
¹⁷The LORD your God in your midst,
The Mighty One, will save;
He will rejoice over you with gladness,

3:8 ᵃSeptuagint and Syriac read *for witness;* Targum reads *for the day of My revelation for judgment;* Vulgate reads *for the day of My resurrection that is to come.* **3:15** ᵃSome Hebrew manuscripts, Septuagint, and Bomberg read *see;* Masoretic Text and Vulgate read *fear.*

LEADERSHIP ISSUES

GC2: Loving the Real God: He Rejoices over You

ZEPHANIAH 3:17 *He will rejoice over you with gladness, He will quiet you with His love, He will rejoice over you with singing.*

Imagine the expression that was on the face of Jesus as you woke up this morning. In your mind's eye, picture His kind, gentle eyes and warm, tender smile. Imagine that as you awoke, God looked down and smiled at you, His precious child. With joy in His heart, He announced, "I am looking forward to sharing the day with you!" (Ps. 139:3).

The real God, who knows you intimately, could not wait to care for you today. The Creator of the universe, who knows every hair upon your head and sees every tear that you cry, cannot wait to show you how much He loves you. The holy God of heaven knows your darkest secrets and deepest failures; yet because of His relationship with you, He longs to show you grace and mercy (Is. 30:18).

What does it do to your heart to consider a God who is acquainted with all your ways and longs to be caringly involved in your life (Ps. 139:3)? How does your heart respond to the amazing truth that God takes great delight in and rejoices over you?

"As I consider the real God, who rejoices over me and looks forward to spending the day with me, my heart is filled with _____."

Pause now and say a prayer that communicates your gratitude, humility, and wonder toward the God who knows you and rejoices over you. Pray with a friend or member of your small group:

"Heavenly Father, I feel _____ as I reflect upon Your heart toward me. Thank You for being the kind of God who _____."

GC2
GREAT COMMANDMENT
COMMISSION

He will quiet *you* with His love,
He will rejoice over you with singing."

18"I will gather those who sorrow over the
    appointed assembly,
Who are among you,
To whom its reproach *is* a burden.
19Behold, at that time
I will deal with all who afflict you;
I will save the lame,

And gather those who were driven out;
I will appoint them for praise and fame
In every land where they were put to shame.
20At that time I will bring you back,
Even at the time I gather you;
For I will give you fame and praise
Among all the peoples of the earth,
When I return your captives before your
    eyes,"
Says the LORD.

IMPACT OF THE BOOK

HAGGAI

I   IDEA
Carefully consider your ways and your priorities. Believers must see if their lives match up to God's call for them.

M   MESSAGE
Lack of accountability is one of the most serious threats to believers and, especially, to leaders. It is so easy to lose sight of the big picture and become complacent when we take our focus off of God. We must have accountability in our lives that encourages us to consider carefully our decisions and practices. Leaders begin with the end in mind and allow their priorities to reflect that their focus is on the prize. The easiest way to be defeated is to be distracted.

P   PEOPLE
Cyrus, Haggai, Joshua, Shealtiel, Zerubbabel

A   AUTHOR
"Haggai," meaning "Feast or Festival," was called a prophet (1:1) and the Lord's messenger (1:13). He ministered for a brief period to encourage the rebuilding of the temple. He was a contemporary of Zechariah, although neither prophet mentions the other.

C   CULTURE
In 538 BC, King Cyrus of Persia allowed any Jewish person in his kingdom to return to Jerusalem to help rebuild the temple. In 537 BC, Zerubbabel journeyed to Jerusalem with the first group of exiles. In 536 BC, the foundation of the temple was laid; but the Israelites faced opposition from their enemies in the surrounding lands. The Jewish remnant became discouraged and left the work God called them to and concentrated on building their own houses. In 520 BC, God sent His prophet Haggai to call His people back to the task.

T   TIMELINE
c. 520 BC

KEY SCRIPTURE
MEMORY VERSES
2:7

The Command to Build God's House

1 In the second year of King Darius, in the sixth month, on the first day of the month, the word of the LORD came by Haggai the prophet to Zerubbabel the son of Shealtiel, governor of Judah, and to Joshua the son of Jehozadak, the high priest, saying, ²"Thus speaks the LORD of hosts, saying: 'This people says, "The time has not come, the time that the LORD's house should be built." ' "

³Then the word of the LORD came by Haggai the prophet, saying, ⁴"*Is it* time for you yourselves to dwell in your paneled houses, and this templeᵃ *to lie* in ruins?" ⁵Now therefore, thus says the LORD of hosts: "Consider your ways!

⁶"You have sown much, and bring in little;
    You eat, but do not have enough;
    You drink, but you are not filled with drink;
    You clothe yourselves, but no one is warm;
    And he who earns wages,
    Earns wages *to put* into a bag with holes."

⁷Thus says the LORD of hosts: "Consider your ways! ⁸Go up to the mountains and bring wood and build the temple, that I may take pleasure in it and be glorified," says the LORD. ⁹"*You* looked for much, but indeed *it came to* little; and when you brought it home, I blew it away. Why?" says the LORD of hosts. "Because of My house that *is in* ruins, while every one of you runs to his own house. ¹⁰Therefore the heavens above you withhold the dew, and the earth withholds its fruit. ¹¹For I called for a drought on the land and the mountains, on the grain and the new wine and the oil, on whatever the ground brings forth, on men and livestock, and on all the labor of *your* hands."

The People's Obedience

¹²Then Zerubbabel the son of Shealtiel, and Joshua the son of Jehozadak, the high priest, with all the remnant of the people, obeyed the voice of the LORD their God, and the words of Haggai the prophet, as the LORD their God had sent him; and the people feared the presence of the LORD. ¹³Then Haggai, the LORD's messenger, spoke the LORD's message to the people, saying, "I *am* with

you, says the LORD." ¹⁴So the LORD stirred up the spirit of Zerubbabel the son of Shealtiel, governor of Judah, and the spirit of Joshua the son of Jehozadak, the high priest, and the spirit of all the remnant of the people; and they came and worked on the house of the LORD of hosts, their God, ¹⁵on the twenty-fourth day of the sixth month, in the second year of King Darius.

The Coming Glory of God's House

2 In the seventh *month,* on the twenty-first of the month, the word of the LORD came by Haggai the prophet, saying: ²"Speak now to Zerubbabel the son of Shealtiel, governor of Judah, and to Joshua the son of Jehozadak, the high priest, and to the remnant of the people, saying: ³'Who is left among you who saw this templeᵃ in its former glory? And how do you see it now? In comparison with it, *is this* not in your eyes as nothing? ⁴Yet now be strong, Zerubbabel,' says the LORD; 'and be strong, Joshua, son of Jehozadak, the high priest; and be strong, all you people of the land,' says the LORD, 'and work; for I *am* with you,' says the LORD of hosts. ⁵'*According to* the word that I covenanted with you when you came out of Egypt, so My Spirit remains among you; do not fear!'

⁶"For thus says the LORD of hosts: 'Once more (it *is* a little while) I will shake heaven and earth, the sea and dry land; ⁷and I will shake all nations, and they shall come to the Desire of All Nations,ᵃ and I will fill this temple with glory,' says the LORD of hosts. ⁸'The silver *is* Mine, and the gold *is* Mine,' says the LORD of hosts. ⁹'The glory of this latter temple shall be greater than the former,' says the LORD of hosts. 'And in this place I will give peace,' says the LORD of hosts."

The People Are Defiled

¹⁰On the twenty-fourth *day* of the ninth *month,* in the second year of Darius, the word of the LORD came by Haggai the prophet, saying, ¹¹"Thus says the LORD of hosts: 'Now, ask the priests *concerning the* law, saying, ¹²'If one carries holy meat in the fold of his garment, and with the edge he touches bread or stew, wine or oil, or any food, will it become holy?' ' "

Then the priests answered and said, "No."

1:4 ᵃLiterally *house,* and so in verse 8   **2:3** ᵃLiterally *house,* and so in verses 7 and 9   **2:7** ᵃOr *the desire of all nations*

¹³And Haggai said, "If *one who is* unclean *because* of a dead body touches any of these, will it be unclean?"

So the priests answered and said, "It shall be unclean."

¹⁴Then Haggai answered and said, " 'So is this people, and so is this nation before Me,' says the LORD, 'and so is every work of their hands; and what they offer there is unclean.

PROMISED BLESSING

¹⁵'And now, carefully consider from this day forward: from before stone was laid upon stone in the temple of the LORD— ¹⁶since those *days,* when *one* came to a heap of twenty ephahs, there were *but* ten; when *one* came to the wine vat to draw out fifty baths from the press, there were *but* twenty. ¹⁷I struck you with blight and mildew and hail in all the labors of your hands; yet you did not *turn* to Me,' says the LORD. ¹⁸'Consider now from this day forward, from the twenty-fourth day of the ninth month, from the day that the foundation of the LORD's temple was laid—consider it: ¹⁹Is the seed still in the barn? As yet the

vine, the fig tree, the pomegranate, and the olive tree have not yielded *fruit. But* from this day I will bless *you.*' "

ZERUBBABEL CHOSEN AS A SIGNET

²⁰And again the word of the LORD came to Haggai on the twenty-fourth day of the month, saying, ²¹"Speak to Zerubbabel, governor of Judah, saying:

'I will shake heaven and earth.
²²I will overthrow the throne of kingdoms;
    I will destroy the strength of the Gentile
        kingdoms.
    I will overthrow the chariots
    And those who ride in them;
    The horses and their riders shall come down,
    Every one by the sword of his brother.

²³'In that day,' says the LORD of hosts, 'I will take you, Zerubbabel My servant, the son of Shealtiel,' says the LORD, 'and will make you like a signet *ring;* for I have chosen you,' says the LORD of hosts.' "

IMPACT OF THE BOOK

ZECHARIAH

IDEA

Never forget the promises God has made to you.

MESSAGE

There is a time for harsh words, but there are also times for comfort and encouragement. Leaders must be discerning and in tune with the voice of God to know which type of word their people need to hear. The people of Israel had become too focused on their lives, and Zechariah was spurring them on to finish the race by reminding them of God's faithful promises.

PEOPLE

Darius, Heldai, Jedaiah, Joshua, Tobijah, Zechariah, Zerubbabel

AUTHOR

The author identifies himself as Zechariah, son of Berechiah, son of Iddo. Iddo was a priest born in Babylon; he returned to Israel in 538–537 BC under the leadership of Zerubbabel and Jeshua (Neh. 12:4). At some point, Zechariah, meaning "Whom Yahweh Remembers," apparently succeeded his grandfather Iddo as head of that priestly family.

CULTURE

Zechariah's ministry began at the time of Judah's return from Babylonian exile known as the postexilic period. The historical circumstances surrounding the ministry of Zechariah are the same as that of Haggai, and Zechariah began preaching about two months after Haggai began his ministry. The overall purpose of Zechariah is to motivate and encourage the people to complete the temple (4:8–10). The eight visions which Zechariah saw also reveal that God was calling His people to return to Him with all their heart. If they did, then His Word would continue to be fulfilled.

TIMELINE

518 BC

**KEY SCRIPTURE
MEMORY VERSES**

9:9

A Call to Repentance

1 In the eighth month of the second year of Darius, the word of the LORD came to Zechariah the son of Berechiah, the son of Iddo the prophet, saying, ²"The LORD has been very angry with your fathers. ³Therefore say to them, 'Thus says the LORD of hosts: "Return to Me," says the LORD of hosts, "and I will return to you," says the LORD of hosts. ⁴"Do not be like your fathers, to whom the former prophets preached, saying, 'Thus says the LORD of hosts: "Turn now from your evil ways and your evil deeds." ' But they did not hear nor heed Me," says the LORD.

⁵"Your fathers, where *are* they?
　And the prophets, do they live forever?
⁶Yet surely My words and My statutes,
　Which I commanded My servants the
　　prophets,
Did they not overtake your fathers?

"So they returned and said:

'Just as the LORD of hosts determined to do to
　us,
According to our ways and according to our
　deeds,
So He has dealt with us.' " ' "

Vision of the Horses

⁷On the twenty-fourth day of the eleventh month, which is the month Shebat, in the second year of Darius, the word of the LORD came to Zechariah the son of Berechiah, the son of Iddo the prophet: ⁸I saw by night, and behold, a man riding on a red horse, and it stood among the myrtle trees in the hollow; and behind him *were* horses: red, sorrel, and white. ⁹Then I said, "My lord, what *are* these?" So the angel who talked with me said to me, "I will show you what they *are.*"

¹⁰And the man who stood among the myrtle trees answered and said, "These *are the ones* whom the LORD has sent to walk to and fro throughout the earth."

¹¹So they answered the Angel of the LORD, who stood among the myrtle trees, and said, "We have walked to and fro throughout the earth, and behold, all the earth is resting quietly."

The Lord Will Comfort Zion

¹²Then the Angel of the LORD answered and said, "O LORD of hosts, how long will You not have mercy on Jerusalem and on the cities of Judah, against which You were angry these seventy years?"

¹³And the LORD answered the angel who talked to me, *with* good *and* comforting words. ¹⁴So the angel who spoke with me said to me, "Proclaim, saying, 'Thus says the LORD of hosts:

"I am zealous for Jerusalem
　And for Zion with great zeal.
¹⁵I am exceedingly angry with the nations at
　　ease;
For I was a little angry,
　And they helped—*but* with evil *intent.*"

¹⁶'Therefore thus says the LORD:

"I am returning to Jerusalem with mercy;
　My house shall be built in it," says the LORD
　　of hosts,
"And a *surveyor's* line shall be stretched out
　　over Jerusalem." '

¹⁷"Again proclaim, saying, 'Thus says the LORD of hosts:

"My cities shall again spread out through
　　prosperity;
The LORD will again comfort Zion,
　And will again choose Jerusalem." ' "

Vision of the Horns

¹⁸Then I raised my eyes and looked, and there *were* four horns. ¹⁹And I said to the angel who talked with me, "What *are* these?"

So he answered me, "These *are* the horns that have scattered Judah, Israel, and Jerusalem."

²⁰Then the LORD showed me four craftsmen. ²¹And I said, "What are these coming to do?"

So he said, "These *are* the horns that scattered Judah, so that no one could lift up his head; but the craftsmenᵃ are coming to terrify them, to cast out the horns of the nations that lifted up *their* horn against the land of Judah to scatter it."

1:21 ᵃLiterally *these*

Vision of the Measuring Line

2 Then I raised my eyes and looked, and behold, a man with a measuring line in his hand. ²So I said, "Where are you going?"

And he said to me, "To measure Jerusalem, to see what *is* its width and what *is* its length."

³And there *was* the angel who talked with me, going out; and another angel was coming out to meet him, ⁴who said to him, "Run, speak to this young man, saying: 'Jerusalem shall be inhabited *as* towns without walls, because of the multitude of men and livestock in it. ⁵For I,' says the LORD, 'will be a wall of fire all around her, and I will be the glory in her midst.' "

Future Joy of Zion and Many Nations

⁶"Up, up! Flee from the land of the north," says the LORD; "for I have spread you abroad like the four winds of heaven," says the LORD. ⁷"Up, Zion! Escape, you who dwell with the daughter of Babylon."

⁸For thus says the LORD of hosts: "He sent Me after glory, to the nations which plunder you; for he who touches you touches the apple of His eye. ⁹For surely I will shake My hand against them, and they shall become spoil for their servants. Then you will know that the LORD of hosts has sent Me.

¹⁰"Sing and rejoice, O daughter of Zion! For behold, I am coming and I will dwell in your midst," says the LORD. ¹¹"Many nations shall be joined to the LORD in that day, and they shall become My people. And I will dwell in your midst. Then you will know that the LORD of hosts has sent Me to you. ¹²And the LORD will take possession of Judah as His inheritance in the Holy Land, and will again choose Jerusalem. ¹³Be silent, all flesh, before the LORD, for He is aroused from His holy habitation!"

Vision of the High Priest

3 Then he showed me Joshua the high priest standing before the Angel of the LORD, and Satan standing at his right hand to oppose him. ²And the LORD said to Satan, "The LORD rebuke you, Satan! The LORD who has chosen Jerusalem

---

INSIDE *the* INFLUENCERS

ZECHARIAH—Teach Vision to Every Generation

ZECHARIAH 2:4

The prophet Zechariah came from a long line of priests and was also a priest himself (Neh. 4:12, 16). As Zechariah 2:4 indicates, he was in ministry, even as a young man. Zechariah's name means "Jehovah remembers," and he played a vital role, along with Haggai in rebuilding the temple, following the return from Exile.

The meaning of his name echoes in his message; that is, *The Lord remembers and keeps His promises*. It is a powerful but simple truth that needs to be taught to each successive generation. It reflects a great lesson of history: We cannot make the same mistakes as our forefathers and expect different results. The prophet also reminds us of the comfort and encouragement that God gives His people.

The book of Zechariah unveils God's plans for the Jews. Jerusalem is at the heart of those plans and is mentioned 39 times in this book. Zechariah 1:14–17 states that Jerusalem will be rebuilt and prosperity will return.

Zechariah recorded the visions that came to him; and like a true priest and prophet, he kept the vision of God's plan and purpose constantly before the people. Zechariah's message is very applicable for us and every generation. We honor God by passing down the message of God's faithfulness to His plan and purpose.

rebuke you! *Is* this not a brand plucked from the fire?"

³Now Joshua was clothed with filthy garments, and was standing before the Angel.

⁴Then He answered and spoke to those who stood before Him, saying, "Take away the filthy garments from him." And to him He said, "See, I have removed your iniquity from you, and I will clothe you with rich robes."

⁵And I said, "Let them put a clean turban on his head."

So they put a clean turban on his head, and they put the clothes on him. And the Angel of the LORD stood by.

THE COMING BRANCH

⁶Then the Angel of the LORD admonished Joshua, saying, ⁷"Thus says the LORD of hosts:

'If you will walk in My ways,
   And if you will keep My command,
   Then you shall also judge My house,
   And likewise have charge of My courts;
   I will give you places to walk
   Among these who stand here.

⁸'Hear, O Joshua, the high priest,
   You and your companions who sit before
      you,
   For they are a wondrous sign;
   For behold, I am bringing forth My Servant
      the BRANCH.
⁹For behold, the stone
   That I have laid before Joshua:
   Upon the stone *are* seven eyes.
   Behold, I will engrave its inscription,'
   Says the LORD of hosts,
   'And I will remove the iniquity of that land in
      one day.
¹⁰In that day,' says the LORD of hosts,
   'Everyone will invite his neighbor
   Under his vine and under his fig tree.'"

VISION OF THE LAMPSTAND AND OLIVE TREES

4 Now the angel who talked with me came back and wakened me, as a man who is wakened out of his sleep. ²And he said to me, "What do you see?"

So I said, "I am looking, and there *is* a lamp-stand of solid gold with a bowl on top of it, and on the *stand* seven lamps with seven pipes to the seven lamps. ³Two olive trees *are* by it, one at the right of the bowl and the other at its left." ⁴So I answered and spoke to the angel who talked with me, saying, "What *are* these, my lord?"

⁵Then the angel who talked with me answered and said to me, "Do you not know what these are?"

And I said, "No, my lord."

⁶So he answered and said to me:

"This *is* the word of the LORD to Zerubbabel:
   'Not by might nor by power, but by My
      Spirit,'
   Says the LORD of hosts.
⁷'Who *are* you, O great mountain?
   Before Zerubbabel *you shall become* a plain!
   And he shall bring forth the capstone
   With shouts of "Grace, grace to it!"'"

⁸Moreover the word of the LORD came to me, saying:

⁹"The hands of Zerubbabel
   Have laid the foundation of this temple;ᵃ
   His hands shall also finish *it*.
   Then you will know
   That the LORD of hosts has sent Me to you.
¹⁰For who has despised the day of small things?
   For these seven rejoice to see
   The plumb line in the hand of Zerubbabel.
   They are the eyes of the LORD,
   Which scan to and fro throughout the whole
      earth."

¹¹Then I answered and said to him, "What *are* these two olive trees—at the right of the lamp-stand and at its left?" ¹²And I further answered and said to him, "What *are these* two olive branches that *drip* into the receptaclesᵃ of the two gold pipes from which the golden *oil* drains?"

¹³Then he answered me and said, "Do you not know what these *are?*"

And I said, "No, my lord."

¹⁴So he said, "These *are* the two anointed ones, who stand beside the Lord of the whole earth."

4:9 ᵃLiterally *house*   **4:12** ᵃLiterally *into the hands of*

VISION OF THE FLYING SCROLL

5 Then I turned and raised my eyes, and saw there a flying scroll.

²And he said to me, "What do you see?"

So I answered, "I see a flying scroll. Its length *is* twenty cubits and its width ten cubits."

³Then he said to me, "This *is* the curse that goes out over the face of the whole earth: 'Every thief shall be expelled,' according *to* this side of *the scroll;* and, 'Every perjurer shall be expelled,' according *to* that side of it."

⁴"I will send out *the curse,*" says the LORD of
  hosts;
 "It shall enter the house of the thief
  And the house of the one who swears falsely
    by My name.
  It shall remain in the midst of his house
  And consume it, with its timber and stones."

VISION OF THE WOMAN IN A BASKET

⁵Then the angel who talked with me came out and said to me, "Lift your eyes now, and see what this *is* that goes forth."

⁶So I asked, "What *is* it?" And he said, "It *is* a basketª that is going forth."

He also said, "This *is* their resemblance throughout the earth: ⁷Here *is* a lead disc lifted up, and this *is* a woman sitting inside the basket"; ⁸then he said, "This *is* Wickedness!" And he thrust her down into the basket, and threw the lead coverª over its mouth. ⁹Then I raised my eyes and looked, and there *were* two women, coming with the wind in their wings; for they had wings like the wings of a stork, and they lifted up the basket between earth and heaven.

¹⁰So I said to the angel who talked with me, "Where are they carrying the basket?"

¹¹And he said to me, "To build a house for it in the land of Shinar;ª when it is ready, *the basket* will be set there on its base."

VISION OF THE FOUR CHARIOTS

6 Then I turned and raised my eyes and looked, and behold, four chariots *were* coming from between two mountains, and the mountains *were* mountains of bronze. ²With the first chariot *were* red horses, with the second chariot black horses,

³with the third chariot white horses, and with the fourth chariot dappled horses—strong *steeds.* ⁴Then I answered and said to the angel who talked with me, "What *are* these, my lord?"

⁵And the angel answered and said to me, "These *are* four spirits of heaven, who go out from *their* station before the Lord of all the earth. ⁶The one with the black horses is going to the north country, the white are going after them, and the dappled are going toward the south country." ⁷Then the strong *steeds* went out, eager to go, that they might walk to and fro throughout the earth. And He said, "Go, walk to and fro throughout the earth." So they walked to and fro throughout the earth. ⁸And He called to me, and spoke to me, saying, "See, those who go toward the north country have given rest to My Spirit in the north country."

THE COMMAND TO CROWN JOSHUA

⁹Then the word of the LORD came to me, saying: ¹⁰"Receive *the gift* from the captives—from Heldai, Tobijah, and Jedaiah, who have come from Babylon—and go the same day and enter the house of Josiah the son of Zephaniah. ¹¹Take the silver and gold, make an elaborate crown, and set *it* on the head of Joshua the son of Jehozadak, the high priest. ¹²Then speak to him, saying, 'Thus says the LORD of hosts, saying:

"Behold, the Man whose name *is* the
    BRANCH!
  From His place He shall branch out,
  And He shall build the temple of the LORD;
  ¹³Yes, He shall build the temple of the LORD.
  He shall bear the glory,
  And shall sit and rule on His throne;
  So He shall be a priest on His throne,
  And the counsel of peace shall be between
    them both." '

¹⁴"Now the elaborate crown shall be for a memorial in the temple of the LORD for Helem,ª Tobijah, Jedaiah, and Hen the son of Zephaniah. ¹⁵Even those from afar shall come and build the

---

5:6 ªHebrew *ephah,* a measuring container, and so elsewhere 5:8 ªLiterally *stone* 5:11 ªThat is, Babylon 6:14 ªFollowing Masoretic Text, Targum, and Vulgate; Syriac reads *for Heldai* (compare verse 10); Septuagint reads *for the patient ones.*

temple of the LORD. Then you shall know that the LORD of hosts has sent Me to you. And *this* shall come to pass if you diligently obey the voice of the LORD your God."

OBEDIENCE BETTER THAN FASTING

7 Now in the fourth year of King Darius it came to pass *that* the word of the LORD came to Zechariah, on the fourth *day* of the ninth month, Chislev, ²when *the people*ᵃ sent Sherezer,ᵇ with Regem-Melech and his men, *to* the house of God,ᶜ to pray before the LORD, ³*and* to ask the priests who *were* in the house of the LORD of hosts, and the prophets, saying, "Should I weep in the fifth month and fast as I have done for so many years?"

⁴Then the word of the LORD of hosts came to me, saying, ⁵"Say to all the people of the land, and to the priests: 'When you fasted and mourned in the fifth and seventh *months* during those seventy years, did you really fast for Me—for Me? ⁶When you eat and when you drink, do you not eat and drink *for yourselves?* ⁷*Should you* not *have obeyed* the words which the LORD proclaimed through the former prophets when Jerusalem and the cities around it were inhabited and prosperous, and the Southᵃ and the Lowland were inhabited?' "

DISOBEDIENCE RESULTED IN CAPTIVITY

⁸Then the word of the LORD came to Zechariah, saying, ⁹"Thus says the LORD of hosts:

'Execute true justice,
Show mercy and compassion
Everyone to his brother.
¹⁰Do not oppress the widow or the fatherless,
The alien or the poor.
Let none of you plan evil in his heart
Against his brother.'

¹¹"But they refused to heed, shrugged their shoulders, and stopped their ears so that they could not hear. ¹²Yes, they made their hearts like flint, refusing to hear the law and the words which the LORD of hosts had sent by His Spirit through the former prophets. Thus great wrath came from the LORD of hosts. ¹³Therefore it happened, *that* just as He proclaimed and they would not hear, so they called out and I would not lis-

ten," says the LORD of hosts. ¹⁴"But I scattered them with a whirlwind among all the nations which they had not known. Thus the land became desolate after them, so that no one passed through or returned; for they made the pleasant land desolate."

JERUSALEM, HOLY CITY OF THE FUTURE

8 Again the word of the LORD of hosts came, saying, ²"Thus says the LORD of hosts:

'I am zealous for Zion with great zeal;
With great fervor I am zealous for her.'

³"Thus says the LORD:

'I will return to Zion,
And dwell in the midst of Jerusalem.
Jerusalem shall be called the City of Truth,
The Mountain of the LORD of hosts,
The Holy Mountain.'

⁴"Thus says the LORD of hosts:

'Old men and old women shall again sit
In the streets of Jerusalem,
Each one with his staff in his hand
Because of great age.
⁵The streets of the city
Shall be full of boys and girls
Playing in its streets.'

⁶"Thus says the LORD of hosts:

'If it is marvelous in the eyes of the remnant of
this people in these days,
Will it also be marvelous in My eyes?'
Says the LORD of hosts.

⁷"Thus says the LORD of hosts:

'Behold, I will save My people from the land
of the east
And from the land of the west;
⁸I will bring them *back,*
And they shall dwell in the midst of
Jerusalem.

7:2 ᵃLiterally *they* (compare verse 5) ᵇOr *Sar-Ezer* ᶜHebrew *Bethel*
7:7 ᵃHebrew *Negev*

They shall be My people
And I will be their God,
In truth and righteousness.'

⁹"Thus says the LORD of hosts:

'Let your hands be strong,
You who have been hearing in these days
These words by the mouth of the prophets,
Who *spoke* in the day the foundation was laid
For the house of the LORD of hosts,
That the temple might be built.
¹⁰For before these days
There were no wages for man nor any hire
      for beast;
There was no peace from the enemy for
      whoever went out or came in;
For I set all men, everyone, against his
      neighbor.

¹¹But now I *will* not *treat* the remnant of this people as in the former days,' says the LORD of hosts.

¹²'For the seed *shall be* prosperous,
The vine shall give its fruit,
The ground shall give her increase,
And the heavens shall give their dew—
I will cause the remnant of this people
To possess all these.
¹³And it shall come to pass
That just as you were a curse among the
      nations,
O house of Judah and house of Israel,
So I will save you, and you shall be a blessing.
Do not fear,
Let your hands be strong.'

¹⁴"For thus says the LORD of hosts:

'Just as I determined to punish you
When your fathers provoked Me to wrath,'
Says the LORD of hosts,
'And I would not relent,
¹⁵So again in these days
I am determined to do good
To Jerusalem and to the house of Judah.
Do not fear.
¹⁶These *are* the things you shall do:

Speak each man the truth to his neighbor;
Give judgment in your gates for truth, justice,
      and peace;
¹⁷Let none of you think evil in your[a] heart
      against your neighbor;
And do not love a false oath.
For all these *are things* that I hate,'
Says the LORD."

¹⁸Then the word of the LORD of hosts came to me, saying, ¹⁹"Thus says the LORD of hosts:

'The fast of the fourth *month,*
The fast of the fifth,
The fast of the seventh,
And the fast of the tenth,
Shall be joy and gladness and cheerful feasts
For the house of Judah.
Therefore love truth and peace.'

²⁰"Thus says the LORD of hosts:

'Peoples shall yet come,
Inhabitants of many cities;
²¹The inhabitants of one *city* shall go to
      another, saying,
"Let us continue to go and pray before the
      LORD,
And seek the LORD of hosts.
I myself will go also."
²²Yes, many peoples and strong nations
Shall come to seek the LORD of hosts in
      Jerusalem,
And to pray before the LORD.'

²³"Thus says the LORD of hosts: 'In those days ten men from every language of the nations shall grasp the sleeve of a Jewish man, saying, "Let us go with you, for we have heard *that* God *is* with you." ' "

ISRAEL DEFENDED AGAINST ENEMIES

9 The burden[a] of the word of the LORD
      Against the land of Hadrach,
      And Damascus its resting place
      (For the eyes of men
      And all the tribes of Israel

8:17 ªLiterally *his*   9:1 ªOr *oracle*

Are on the LORD);
²Also *against* Hamath, *which* borders on it,
And *against* Tyre and Sidon, though they are
    very wise.

³For Tyre built herself a tower,
 Heaped up silver like the dust,
 And gold like the mire of the streets.
⁴Behold, the Lord will cast her out;
 He will destroy her power in the sea,
 And she will be devoured by fire.

⁵Ashkelon shall see *it* and fear;
 Gaza also shall be very sorrowful;
 And Ekron, for He dried up her expectation.
 The king shall perish from Gaza,
 And Ashkelon shall not be inhabited.

⁶"A mixed race shall settle in Ashdod,
 And I will cut off the pride of the Philistines.
 ⁷I will take away the blood from his mouth,
 And the abominations from between his
    teeth.
 But he who remains, even he *shall be* for our
    God,
 And shall be like a leader in Judah,
 And Ekron like a Jebusite.
 ⁸I will camp around My house
 Because of the army,
 Because of him who passes by and him who
    returns.
 No more shall an oppressor pass through
    them,
 For now I have seen with My eyes.

THE COMING KING

⁹"Rejoice greatly, O daughter of Zion!
 Shout, O daughter of Jerusalem!
 Behold, your King is coming to you;
 He *is* just and having salvation,
 Lowly and riding on a donkey,
 A colt, the foal of a donkey.
¹⁰I will cut off the chariot from Ephraim
 And the horse from Jerusalem;
 The battle bow shall be cut off.
 He shall speak peace to the nations;
 His dominion *shall be* 'from sea to sea,
 And from the River to the ends of the
    earth.'ᵃ

GOD WILL SAVE HIS PEOPLE

¹¹"As for you also,
 Because of the blood of your covenant,
 I will set your prisoners free from the
    waterless pit.
¹²Return to the stronghold,
 You prisoners of hope.
 Even today I declare
 That I will restore double to you.
¹³For I have bent Judah, My *bow,*
 Fitted the bow with Ephraim,
 And raised up your sons, O Zion,
 Against your sons, O Greece,
 And made you like the sword of a mighty
    man."

¹⁴Then the LORD will be seen over them,
 And His arrow will go forth like lightning.
 The Lord GOD will blow the trumpet,
 And go with whirlwinds from the south.
¹⁵The LORD of hosts will defend them;
 They shall devour and subdue with
    slingstones.
 They shall drink *and* roar as if with wine;
 They shall be filled *with blood* like basins,
 Like the corners of the altar.
¹⁶The LORD their God will save them in that
    day,
 As the flock of His people.
 For they *shall be like* the jewels of a crown,
 Lifted like a banner over His land—
¹⁷For how great is itsᵃ goodness
 And how great itsᵇ beauty!
 Grain shall make the young men thrive,
 And new wine the young women.

RESTORATION OF JUDAH AND ISRAEL

10 Ask the LORD for rain
 In the time of the latter rain.ᵃ
 The LORD will make flashing clouds;
 He will give them showers of rain,
 Grass in the field for everyone.

²For the idolsᵃ speak delusion;
 The diviners envision lies,
 And tell false dreams;

9:10 ᵃPsalm 72:8   9:17 ᵃOr *His* ᵇOr *His*   10:1 ᵃThat is, spring rain
10:2 ᵃHebrew *teraphim*

They comfort in vain.
Therefore *the people* wend their way like
    sheep;
They are in trouble because *there is* no
    shepherd.

3"My anger is kindled against the shepherds,
  And I will punish the goatherds.
For the LORD of hosts will visit His flock,
The house of Judah,
And will make them as His royal horse in the
    battle.
4From him comes the cornerstone,
From him the tent peg,
From him the battle bow,
From him every ruler^a together.
5They shall be like mighty men,
Who tread down *their enemies*
In the mire of the streets in the battle.
They shall fight because the LORD is with
    them,
And the riders on horses shall be put to
    shame.

6"I will strengthen the house of Judah,
  And I will save the house of Joseph.
I will bring them back,
Because I have mercy on them.
They shall be as though I had not cast them
    aside;
For I *am* the LORD their God,
And I will hear them.
7*Those of* Ephraim shall be like a mighty man,
And their heart shall rejoice as if with wine.
Yes, their children shall see *it* and be glad;
Their heart shall rejoice in the LORD.
8I will whistle for them and gather them,
For I will redeem them;
And they shall increase as they once
    increased.

9"I will sow them among the peoples,
  And they shall remember Me in far
    countries;
They shall live, together with their children,
And they shall return.
10I will also bring them back from the land of
    Egypt,
And gather them from Assyria.

I will bring them into the land of Gilead and
    Lebanon,
Until no *more room* is found for them.
11He shall pass through the sea with affliction,
And strike the waves of the sea:
All the depths of the River^a shall dry up.
Then the pride of Assyria shall be brought
    down,
And the scepter of Egypt shall depart.

12"So I will strengthen them in the LORD,
  And they shall walk up and down in His
    name,"
Says the LORD.

DESOLATION OF ISRAEL

11 Open your doors, O Lebanon,
    That fire may devour your cedars.
2Wail, O cypress, for the cedar has fallen,
Because the mighty *trees* are ruined.
Wail, O oaks of Bashan,
For the thick forest has come down.
3*There is* the sound of wailing shepherds!
For their glory is in ruins.
There is the sound of roaring lions!
For the pride^a of the Jordan is in ruins.

PROPHECY OF THE SHEPHERDS

4Thus says the LORD my God, "Feed the
flock for slaughter, 5whose owners slaughter them
and feel no guilt; those who sell them say, 'Blessed
be the LORD, for I am rich'; and their shepherds
do not pity them. 6For I will no longer pity the
inhabitants of the land," says the LORD. "But indeed I will give everyone into his neighbor's hand
and into the hand of his king. They shall attack
the land, and I will not deliver *them* from their
hand."

7So I fed the flock for slaughter, in particular
the poor of the flock.^a I took for myself two staffs:
the one I called Beauty,^b and the other I called
Bonds;^c and I fed the flock. 8I dismissed the three
shepherds in one month. My soul loathed them,
and their soul also abhorred me. 9Then I said, "I
will not feed you. Let what is dying die, and what

10:4 ^aOr *despot* **10:11** ^aThat is, the Nile **11:3** ^aOr *floodplain,
thicket* **11:7** ^aFollowing Masoretic Text, Targum, and Vulgate; Sep-
tuagint reads *for the Canaanites.* ^bOr *Grace,* and so in verse 10 ^cOr
Unity, and so in verse 14

is perishing perish. Let those that are left eat each other's flesh." ¹⁰And I took my staff, Beauty, and cut it in two, that I might break the covenant which I had made with all the peoples. ¹¹So it was broken on that day. Thus the poorᵃ of the flock, who were watching me, knew that it *was* the word of the LORD. ¹²Then I said to them, "If it is agreeable to you, give *me* my wages; and if not, refrain." So they weighed out for my wages thirty *pieces* of silver.

¹³And the LORD said to me, "Throw it to the potter"—that princely price they set on me. So I took the thirty *pieces* of silver and threw them into the house of the LORD for the potter. ¹⁴Then I cut in two my other staff, Bonds, that I might break the brotherhood between Judah and Israel.

¹⁵And the LORD said to me, "Next, take for yourself the implements of a foolish shepherd. ¹⁶For indeed I will raise up a shepherd in the land *who* will not care for those who are cut off, nor seek the young, nor heal those that are broken, nor feed those that still stand. But he will eat the flesh of the fat and tear their hooves in pieces.

¹⁷"Woe to the worthless shepherd,
    Who leaves the flock!
    A sword *shall be* against his arm
    And against his right eye;
    His arm shall completely wither,
    And his right eye shall be totally blinded."

The Coming Deliverance of Judah

12 The burdenᵃ of the word of the LORD against Israel. Thus says the LORD, who stretches out the heavens, lays the foundation of the earth, and forms the spirit of man within him: ²"Behold, I will make Jerusalem a cup of drunkenness to all the surrounding peoples, when they lay siege against Judah and Jerusalem. ³And it shall happen in that day that I will make Jerusalem a very heavy stone for all peoples; all who would heave it away will surely be cut in pieces, though all nations of the earth are gathered against it. ⁴In that day," says the LORD, "I will strike every horse with confusion, and its rider with madness; I will open My eyes on the house of Judah, and will strike every horse of the peoples with blindness. ⁵And the governors of Judah shall say in their heart, 'The inhabitants of Jerusalem *are* my strength

in the LORD of hosts, their God.' ⁶In that day I will make the governors of Judah like a firepan in the woodpile, and like a fiery torch in the sheaves; they shall devour all the surrounding peoples on the right hand and on the left, but Jerusalem shall be inhabited again in her own place—Jerusalem.

⁷"The LORD will save the tents of Judah first, so that the glory of the house of David and the glory of the inhabitants of Jerusalem shall not become greater than that of Judah. ⁸In that day the LORD will defend the inhabitants of Jerusalem; the one who is feeble among them in that day shall be like David, and the house of David *shall be* like God, like the Angel of the LORD before them. ⁹It shall be in that day *that* I will seek to destroy all the nations that come against Jerusalem.

Mourning for the Pierced One

¹⁰"And I will pour on the house of David and on the inhabitants of Jerusalem the Spirit of grace and supplication; then they will look on Me whom they pierced. Yes, they will mourn for Him as one mourns for *his* only *son,* and grieve for Him as one grieves for a firstborn. ¹¹In that day there shall be a great mourning in Jerusalem, like the mourning at Hadad Rimmon in the plain of Megiddo.ᵃ ¹²And the land shall mourn, every family by itself: the family of the house of David by itself, and their wives by themselves; the family of the house of Nathan by itself, and their wives by themselves; ¹³the family of the house of Levi by itself, and their wives by themselves; the family of Shimei by itself, and their wives by themselves; ¹⁴all the families that remain, every family by itself, and their wives by themselves.

Idolatry Cut Off

13 "In that day a fountain shall be opened for the house of David and for the inhabitants of Jerusalem, for sin and for uncleanness.

²"It shall be in that day," says the LORD of hosts, "*that* I will cut off the names of the idols from the land, and they shall no longer be remembered. I will also cause the prophets and the unclean spirit to depart from the land. ³It shall come to pass *that* if anyone still prophesies, then

11:11 ᵃFollowing Masoretic Text, Targum, and Vulgate; Septuagint reads *the Canaanites.* 12:1 ᵃOr *oracle* 12:11 ᵃHebrew *Megiddon* his father and mother who begot him will say to him, 'You shall not live, because you have spoken lies in the name of the LORD.' And his father and mother who begot him shall thrust him through when he prophesies.

⁴"And it shall be in that day *that* every prophet will be ashamed of his vision when he prophesies; they will not wear a robe of coarse hair to deceive. ⁵But he will say, 'I *am* no prophet, I *am* a farmer; for a man taught me to keep cattle from my youth.' ⁶And *one* will say to him, 'What are these wounds between your arms?'ᵃ Then he will answer, '*Those* with which I was wounded in the house of my friends.'

THE SHEPHERD SAVIOR

⁷"Awake, O sword, against My Shepherd,
   Against the Man who is My Companion,"
Says the LORD of hosts.
"Strike the Shepherd,
   And the sheep will be scattered;
   Then I will turn My hand against the little
      ones.
⁸And it shall come to pass in all the land,"
Says the LORD,
"*That* two-thirds in it shall be cut off *and*
      die,
   But *one*-third shall be left in it:
⁹I will bring the *one*-third through the fire,
   Will refine them as silver is refined,
   And test them as gold is tested.
   They will call on My name,
   And I will answer them.
   I will say, 'This *is* My people';
   And each one will say, 'The LORD *is* my
      God.' "

THE DAY OF THE LORD

14 Behold, the day of the LORD is coming,
   And your spoil will be divided in your
      midst.
²For I will gather all the nations to battle
      against Jerusalem;
   The city shall be taken,
   The houses rifled,
   And the women ravished.
   Half of the city shall go into captivity,
   But the remnant of the people shall not be
      cut off from the city.

³Then the LORD will go forth
   And fight against those nations,
   As He fights in the day of battle.
⁴And in that day His feet will stand on the
      Mount of Olives,
   Which faces Jerusalem on the east.
   And the Mount of Olives shall be split in
      two,
   From east to west,
   Making a very large valley;
   Half of the mountain shall move toward the
      north
   And half of it toward the south.

⁵Then you shall flee *through* My mountain
      valley,
   For the mountain valley shall reach to Azal.
   Yes, you shall flee
   As you fled from the earthquake
   In the days of Uzziah king of Judah.

Thus the LORD my God will come,
   And all the saints with You.ᵃ

⁶It shall come to pass in that day
   That there will be no light;
   The lights will diminish.
⁷It shall be one day
   Which is known to the LORD—
   Neither day nor night.
   But at evening time it shall happen
   That it will be light.

⁸And in that day it shall be
   That living waters shall flow from Jerusalem,
   Half of them toward the eastern sea
   And half of them toward the western sea;
   In both summer and winter it shall occur.
⁹And the LORD shall be King over all the
      earth.
   In that day it shall be—
   "The LORD *is* one,"ᵃ
   And His name one.

¹⁰All the land shall be turned into a plain from Geba to Rimmon south of Jerusalem. *Jerusalem*ᵃ shall be raised up and inhabited in her

13:6 ᵃOr *hands* **14:5** ᵃOr *you;* Septuagint, Targum, and Vulgate read *Him.* **14:9** ᵃCompare Deuteronomy 6:4 **14:10** ᵃLiterally *She*

place from Benjamin's Gate to the place of the First Gate and the Corner Gate, and *from* the Tower of Hananel to the king's winepresses.

[11] *The people* shall dwell in it;
And no longer shall there be utter destruction,
But Jerusalem shall be safely inhabited.

[12] And this shall be the plague with which the LORD will strike all the people who fought against Jerusalem:

Their flesh shall dissolve while they stand on their feet,
Their eyes shall dissolve in their sockets,
And their tongues shall dissolve in their mouths.

[13] It shall come to pass in that day
That a great panic from the LORD will be among them.
Everyone will seize the hand of his neighbor,
And raise his hand against his neighbor's hand;
[14] Judah also will fight at Jerusalem.
And the wealth of all the surrounding nations Shall be gathered together:
Gold, silver, and apparel in great abundance.

[15] Such also shall be the plague
On the horse *and* the mule,
On the camel and the donkey,
And on all the cattle that will be in those camps.
So *shall* this plague *be*.

THE NATIONS WORSHIP THE KING

[16] And it shall come to pass *that* everyone who is left of all the nations which came against Jerusalem shall go up from year to year to worship the King, the LORD of hosts, and to keep the Feast of Tabernacles. [17] And it shall be *that* whichever of the families of the earth do not come up to Jerusalem to worship the King, the LORD of hosts, on them there will be no rain. [18] If the family of Egypt will not come up and enter in, they *shall have* no *rain;* they shall receive the plague with which the LORD strikes the nations who do not come up to keep the Feast of Tabernacles. [19] This shall be the punishment of Egypt and the punishment of all the nations that do not come up to keep the Feast of Tabernacles.

[20] In that day "HOLINESS TO THE LORD" shall be *engraved* on the bells of the horses. The pots in the LORD's house shall be like the bowls before the altar. [21] Yes, every pot in Jerusalem and Judah shall be holiness to the LORD of hosts.[a] Everyone who sacrifices shall come and take them and cook in them. In that day there shall no longer be a Canaanite in the house of the LORD of hosts.

14:21 [a]Or *on every pot* . . . *sha!!* . . . *(engraved)* "HOLINESS TO THE LORD OF HOSTS"

IMPACT OF THE BOOK

MALACHI

IDEA | *God called His people to authentic living according to His covenant laws.*

MESSAGE | *People will never have a vital, life-changing ministry for God if they are willing to compromise His standards in their lives. However, a life that is true and authentic will serve as a bright witness for God. Nothing serves to discredit God more in the eyes of unbelievers than when His people live hypocritical lives. The heart of a leader will be revealed by his actions or words, especially when tested by fire.*

PEOPLE | *Malachi*

AUTHOR | *The Book of Malachi gives no direct information about its author. It is not known for certain whether "Malachi" is a proper name or just a common noun because "Malachi" means "My Messenger." Even though tradition suggests that Ezra could be the author of Malachi, Ezra never referred to himself as a prophet. There is no convincing reason to not accept that a person named Malachi authored this book.*

CULTURE | *The remnant, which had returned from Babylon to Jerusalem, was clearly in a state of spiritual apathy. They were committing the sins that they promised they would avoid when they came back to the land. The people were wondering why God was not blessing them. In Malachi, God clearly explained that He would not reward half-hearted faith.*

TIMELINE | *c. 450 – 420 BC*

KEY SCRIPTURE MEMORY VERSES | 3:1

1
The burden[a] of the word of the LORD to Israel by Malachi.

ISRAEL BELOVED OF GOD

2"I have loved you," says the LORD.
"Yet you say, 'In what way have You loved us?'
Was not Esau Jacob's brother?"
Says the LORD.
"Yet Jacob I have loved;
3But Esau I have hated,
And laid waste his mountains and his
　　heritage
For the jackals of the wilderness."

4Even though Edom has said,
"We have been impoverished,
But we will return and build the desolate
　　places,"

Thus says the LORD of hosts:

"They may build, but I will throw down;
They shall be called the Territory of
　　Wickedness,
And the people against whom the LORD will
　　have indignation forever.
5Your eyes shall see,
And you shall say,
'The LORD is magnified beyond the border of
　　Israel.'

POLLUTED OFFERINGS

6"A son honors *his* father,
And a servant *his* master.
If then I am the Father,
Where *is* My honor?
And if I *am* a Master,
Where *is* My reverence?
Says the LORD of hosts
To you priests who despise My name.
Yet you say, 'In what way have we despised
　　Your name?'

7"You offer defiled food on My altar,
But say,
'In what way have we defiled You?'
By saying,
'The table of the LORD is contemptible.'
8And when you offer the blind as a sacrifice,

Is it not evil?
And when you offer the lame and sick,
Is it not evil?
Offer it then to your governor!
Would he be pleased with you?
Would he accept you favorably?"
Says the LORD of hosts.

9"But now entreat God's favor,
That He may be gracious to us.
While this is being *done* by your hands,
Will He accept you favorably?"
Says the LORD of hosts.
10"Who *is there* even among you who would
　　shut the doors,
So that you would not kindle fire *on* My altar
　　in vain?
I have no pleasure in you,"
Says the LORD of hosts,
"Nor will I accept an offering from your
　　hands.
11For from the rising of the sun, even to its
　　going down,
My name *shall be* great among the Gentiles;
In every place incense *shall be* offered to My
　　name,
And a pure offering;
For My name shall be great among the
　　nations,"
Says the LORD of hosts.

12"But you profane it,
In that you say,
'The table of the LORD[a] is defiled;
And its fruit, its food, *is* contemptible.'
13You also say,
'Oh, what a weariness!'
And you sneer at it,"
Says the LORD of hosts.
"And you bring the stolen, the lame, and the
　　sick;
Thus you bring an offering!
Should I accept this from your hand?"
Says the LORD.
14"But cursed *be* the deceiver
Who has in his flock a male,
And takes a vow,

1:1 [a]Or *oracle*　1:12 [a]Following Bomberg; Masoretic Text reads
Lord.

But sacrifices to the Lord what is
    blemished—
For I *am* a great King,"
Says the LORD of hosts,
"And My name *is to be* feared among the
    nations.

CORRUPT PRIESTS

2 "And now, O priests, this commandment is
    for you.
[2]If you will not hear,
And if you will not take *it* to heart,
To give glory to My name,"
Says the LORD of hosts,
"I will send a curse upon you,
And I will curse your blessings.
Yes, I have cursed them already,
Because you do not take *it* to heart.

[3]"Behold, I will rebuke your descendants
And spread refuse on your faces,
The refuse of your solemn feasts;
And *one* will take you away with it.
[4]Then you shall know that I have sent this
    commandment to you,
That My covenant with Levi may
    continue,"
Says the LORD of hosts.
[5]"My covenant was with him, *one* of life and
    peace,
And I gave them to him *that he might*
    fear *Me;*
So he feared Me
And was reverent before My name.
[6]The law of truth[a] was in his mouth,
And injustice was not found on his lips.
He walked with Me in peace and equity,
And turned many away from iniquity.

[7]"For the lips of a priest should keep
    knowledge,
And *people* should seek the law from his
    mouth;
For he is the messenger of the LORD
    of hosts.
[8]But you have departed from the way;
You have caused many to stumble at the law.
You have corrupted the covenant of Levi,"
Says the LORD of hosts.

[9]"Therefore I also have made you contemptible
    and base
Before all the people,
Because you have not kept My ways
But have shown partiality in the law."

TREACHERY OF INFIDELITY

[10]Have we not all one Father?
Has not one God created us?
Why do we deal treacherously with one
    another
By profaning the covenant of the fathers?
[11]Judah has dealt treacherously,
And an abomination has been committed in
    Israel and in Jerusalem,
For Judah has profaned
The LORD's holy *institution* which He loves:
He has married the daughter of a foreign
    god.
[12]May the LORD cut off from the tents of Jacob
The man who does this, being awake and
    aware,[a]
Yet who brings an offering to the LORD of
    hosts!

[13]And this is the second thing you do:
You cover the altar of the LORD with tears,
With weeping and crying;
So He does not regard the offering anymore,
Nor receive *it* with goodwill from your
    hands.
[14]Yet you say, "For what reason?"
Because the LORD has been witness
Between you and the wife of your youth,
With whom you have dealt treacherously;
Yet she is your companion
And your wife by covenant.
[15]But did He not make *them* one,
Having a remnant of the Spirit?
And why one?
He seeks godly offspring.
Therefore take heed to your spirit,
And let none deal treacherously with the wife
    of his youth.

[16]"For the LORD God of Israel says
That He hates divorce,

2:6 [a]Or *true instruction* 2:12 [a]Talmud and Vulgate read *teacher and student.*

For it covers one's garment with violence,"
Says the LORD of hosts.
"Therefore take heed to your spirit,
That you do not deal treacherously."

[17]You have wearied the LORD with your
                words;
Yet you say,
"In what way have we wearied *Him?*"
In that you say,
"Everyone who does evil
Is good in the sight of the LORD,
And He delights in them,"
Or, "Where *is* the God of justice?"

THE COMING MESSENGER

3 "Behold, I send My messenger,
And he will prepare the way before Me.
And the Lord, whom you seek,
Will suddenly come to His temple,
Even the Messenger of the covenant,
In whom you delight.
Behold, He is coming,"
Says the LORD of hosts.

[2]"But who can endure the day of His coming?
And who can stand when He appears?
For He *is* like a refiner's fire
And like launderers' soap.
[3]He will sit as a refiner and a purifier of silver;
He will purify the sons of Levi,
And purge them as gold and silver,
That they may offer to the LORD
An offering in righteousness.

[4]"Then the offering of Judah and Jerusalem
Will be pleasant to the LORD,
As in the days of old,
As in former years.
[5]And I will come near you for judgment;
I will be a swift witness
Against sorcerers,
Against adulterers,
Against perjurers,
Against those who exploit wage earners and
            widows and orphans,
And against those who turn away an alien—
Because they do not fear Me,"
Says the LORD of hosts.

INSIDE *the* INFLUENCERS

MALACHI—Deliver the Message

Malachi is translated "my messenger." This book was written by a prophet who served in the days of Nehemiah after Israel rebuilt the temple and reinstituted sacrifices. Malachi had the difficult task of writing God's last prophetic words to Israel. After Malachi recorded His words, God remained silent for 400 years. Malachi then became the final book of the Old Testament.

Though it was a time of disillusionment, despair, and skepticism, Malachi thought like a leader: he kept the big picture in mind; he taught others to see from God's perspective; and he resisted defaulting to easy, popular answers.

The people stopped tithing and brought God careless sacrifices. When worship was stale and mechanical, because the priestly leadership was corrupt, Malachi saw their attitudes and reminded the people that God was the same—even if people hoped He would change to meet their standards (3:6).

In this book of remembrance, Malachi describes God's character as fair, true in love, with high expectations for His people. It also records the deeds of the righteous. Malachi taught the people to repent, prophesying of a messenger from God who would prepare the way for the coming Messiah—most believe this to be John the Baptist.

⁶"For I *am* the LORD, I do not change;
Therefore you are not consumed, O sons of
Jacob.
⁷Yet from the days of your fathers
You have gone away from My ordinances
And have not kept *them*.
Return to Me, and I will return to you,"
Says the LORD of hosts.
"But you said,
'In what way shall we return?'

Do Not Rob God

⁸"Will a man rob God?
Yet you have robbed Me!
But you say,
'In what way have we robbed You?'
In tithes and offerings.
⁹You are cursed with a curse,
For you have robbed Me,
Even this whole nation.
¹⁰Bring all the tithes into the storehouse,
That there may be food in My house,
And try Me now in this,"
Says the LORD of hosts,
"If I will not open for you the windows of
heaven
And pour out for you *such* blessing
That *there will* not *be room* enough *to receive it*.

¹¹"And I will rebuke the devourer for your
sakes,
So that he will not destroy the fruit of your
ground,
Nor shall the vine fail to bear fruit for you in
the field,"
Says the LORD of hosts;
¹²And all nations will call you blessed,
For you will be a delightful land,"
Says the LORD of hosts.

The People Complain Harshly

¹³"Your words have been harsh against Me,"
Says the LORD,
"Yet you say,
'What have we spoken against You?'
¹⁴You have said,
'It is useless to serve God;
What profit *is it* that we have kept His
ordinance,

And that we have walked as mourners
Before the LORD of hosts?
¹⁵So now we call the proud blessed,
For those who do wickedness are raised
up;
They even tempt God and go free.' "

A Book of Remembrance

¹⁶Then those who feared the LORD spoke to
one another,
And the LORD listened and heard *them;*
So a book of remembrance was written
before Him
For those who fear the LORD
And who meditate on His name.

¹⁷"They shall be Mine," says the LORD of
hosts,
"On the day that I make them My jewels.ᵃ
And I will spare them
As a man spares his own son who serves
him."
¹⁸Then you shall again discern
Between the righteous and the wicked,
Between one who serves God
And one who does not serve Him.

The Great Day of God

4 "For behold, the day is coming,
Burning like an oven,
And all the proud, yes, all who do wickedly
will be stubble.
And the day which is coming shall burn them
up,"
Says the LORD of hosts,
"That will leave them neither root nor
branch.
²But to you who fear My name
The Sun of Righteousness shall arise
With healing in His wings;
And you shall go out
And grow fat like stall-fed calves.
³You shall trample the wicked,
For they shall be ashes under the soles of your
feet
On the day that I do *this,*"
Says the LORD of hosts.

3:17 ᵃLiterally *special treasure*

[4]"Remember the Law of Moses, My servant,
Which I commanded him in Horeb for all
    Israel,
With the statutes and judgments.
[5]Behold, I will send you Elijah the
    prophet

Before the coming of the great and dreadful
    day of the LORD.
[6]And he will turn
The hearts of the fathers to the children,
And the hearts of the children to their fathers,
Lest I come and strike the earth with a curse."

THE
NEW TESTAMENT

IMPACT OF THE BOOK

MATTHEW

IDEA	*In His birth, life, death, and resurrection, Jesus is the fulfillment of the promised Messiah from the Old Testament Scriptures. He is the chosen one and the promised King; and if we are to enjoy His rule and reign in eternity, we must joyfully submit to His rule and reign in our everyday lives.*
MESSAGE	*The religious leaders of Jesus' day saw Jesus as a threat to their power instead of as the answer to their prayers. Jesus modeled servant leadership, wisdom in the face of persecution, a tireless work ethic, and compassion for the hurting; yet so many of the Jewish people missed the truth. Jesus is the ultimate leader, motivated by a love for people, a desire to serve, and, most of all, a commitment to the mission no matter the cost.*
PEOPLE	*Herod, Jesus, John the Baptist, Pharisees, Pilate, Scribes, Twelve Disciples*
AUTHOR	*"Matthew," whose name means "God's gift," was also known as Levi. A Jew who collected taxes for the hated Romans, Matthew forsook all to be an apostle of Jesus. He fully understood the Jewish and messianic hope, hence the use of phrases "the kingdom of heaven," "our father in heaven," and the frequent use of "the son of David."*
CULTURE	*Matthew's Gospel was written while in Antioch of Syria, a Greek-speaking community with a large Jewish population, and was intended primarily for the Jews. As it traces the entire history of the Jewish people, Matthew's Gospel provides a substantial witness to verify Jesus of Nazareth as the long-awaited Messiah. He quotes the Old Testament sixty times and traces Jesus' genealogy to prove that Jesus is the rightful king of Israel.*
TIMELINE	*c. AD 55–65*
KEY SCRIPTURE MEMORY VERSES	4:4; 5:16; 6:9–13, 16–21, 33, 34; 7:7, 8, 12, 13, 14; 22:37–39; 25:35–40; 28:18–20

THE GENEALOGY OF JESUS CHRIST

1 The book of the genealogy of Jesus Christ, the Son of David, the Son of Abraham:

[2]Abraham begot Isaac, Isaac begot Jacob, and Jacob begot Judah and his brothers. [3]Judah begot Perez and Zerah by Tamar, Perez begot Hezron, and Hezron begot Ram. [4]Ram begot Amminadab, Amminadab begot Nahshon, and Nahshon begot Salmon. [5]Salmon begot Boaz by Rahab, Boaz begot Obed by Ruth, Obed begot Jesse, [6]and Jesse begot David the king.

David the king begot Solomon by her *who had been the wife*[a] of Uriah. [7]Solomon begot Rehoboam, Rehoboam begot Abijah, and Abijah begot Asa.[a] [8]Asa begot Jehoshaphat, Jehoshaphat begot Joram, and Joram begot Uzziah. [9]Uzziah begot Jotham, Jotham begot Ahaz, and Ahaz begot Hezekiah. [10]Hezekiah begot Manasseh, Manasseh begot Amon,[a] and Amon begot Josiah. [11]Josiah begot Jeconiah and his brothers about the time they were carried away to Babylon.

[12]And after they were brought to Babylon, Jeconiah begot Shealtiel, and Shealtiel begot Zerubbabel. [13]Zerubbabel begot Abiud, Abiud begot Eliakim, and Eliakim begot Azor. [14]Azor begot Zadok, Zadok begot Achim, and Achim begot Eliud. [15]Eliud begot Eleazar, Eleazar begot Matthan, and Matthan begot Jacob. [16]And Jacob begot Joseph the husband of Mary, of whom was born Jesus who is called Christ.

[17]So all the generations from Abraham to David *are* fourteen generations, from David until the captivity in Babylon *are* fourteen generations, and from the captivity in Babylon until the Christ *are* fourteen generations.

CHRIST BORN OF MARY

[18]Now the birth of Jesus Christ was as follows: After His mother Mary was betrothed to Joseph, before they came together, she was found with child of the Holy Spirit. [19]Then Joseph her husband, being a just *man,* and not wanting to make her a public example, was minded to put her away secretly. [20]But while he thought about these things, behold, an angel of the Lord appeared to him in a dream, saying, "Joseph, son of David, do not be afraid to take to you Mary your wife, for that which is conceived in her is of the Holy Spirit. [21]And she will bring forth a Son, and you shall call His name JESUS, for He will save His people from their sins."

[22]So all this was done that it might be fulfilled which was spoken by the Lord through the prophet, saying: [23]*"Behold, the virgin shall be with child, and bear a Son, and they shall call His name Immanuel,"*[a] which is translated, "God with us."

[24]Then Joseph, being aroused from sleep, did as the angel of the Lord commanded him and took to him his wife, [25]and did not know her till she had brought forth her firstborn Son.[a] And he called His name JESUS.

WISE MEN FROM THE EAST

2 Now after Jesus was born in Bethlehem of Judea in the days of Herod the king, behold, wise men from the East came to Jerusalem, [2]saying, "Where is He who has been born King of the Jews? For we have seen His star in the East and have come to worship Him."

[3]When Herod the king heard *this,* he was troubled, and all Jerusalem with him. [4]And when he had gathered all the chief priests and scribes of the people together, he inquired of them where the Christ was to be born.

[5]So they said to him, "In Bethlehem of Judea, for thus it is written by the prophet:

[6]*'But you, Bethlehem, in the land of Judah,*
  Are not the least among the rulers of Judah;
  For out of you shall come a Ruler
  Who will shepherd My people Israel.' "[a]

[7]Then Herod, when he had secretly called the wise men, determined from them what time the star appeared. [8]And he sent them to Bethlehem and said, "Go and search carefully for the young Child, and when you have found *Him,* bring back word to me, that I may come and worship Him also."

[9]When they heard the king, they departed; and behold, the star which they had seen in the East went before them, till it came and stood over

---

1:6 [a]Words in italic type have been added for clarity. They are not found in the original Greek. **1:7** [a]NU-Text reads *Asaph.* **1:10** [a]NU-Text reads *Amos.* **1:23** [a]Isaiah 7:14. Words in oblique type in the New Testament are quoted from the Old Testament. **1:25** [a]NU-Text reads *a Son.* **2:6** [a]Micah 5:2

INSIDE *the* INFLUENCERS

WISE MEN (MAGI): Seekers Who Found the Savior

MATTHEW 2:1–12

During the time period of the birth of Christ, the Magi were men skilled in philosophy, medicine, and natural science. They were also mystical, possibly astrologers or at least astronomers, since they were guided by a star and interpreted dreams. They studied the heavens and pondered the One Who made them. It is through these observations that God spoke to them concerning the entry of the King into the world. Some traditions say these men were kings (compare Ps. 72:10 and Is. 49:7); although in later times, they might have been viewed as "magicians."

These "wise" men were from the east, which could mean the regions surrounding Arabia or Mesopotamia. It also means that they were non-Jewish, an interesting first revelation of Jesus' relationship with Gentiles, as noted by Matthew. Respected men from a non-Jewish culture directly disobeyed King Herod—a man known to have a short fuse—in seeking and protecting the Messiah of prophecy. The fact that God chose to reveal this to them at such a crucial moment in history greatly stresses the point that the Christ child came on behalf of the whole world.

While much myth and tradition surrounds these men, one bold reality rises from their lives: *those who wait for, seek after, and sincerely desire to see God will experience Him.*

---

where the young Child was. [10]When they saw the star, they rejoiced with exceedingly great joy. [11]And when they had come into the house, they saw the young Child with Mary His mother, and fell down and worshiped Him. And when they had opened their treasures, they presented gifts to Him: gold, frankincense, and myrrh.

[12]Then, being divinely warned in a dream that they should not return to Herod, they departed for their own country another way.

THE FLIGHT INTO EGYPT

[13]Now when they had departed, behold, an angel of the Lord appeared to Joseph in a dream, saying, "Arise, take the young Child and His mother, flee to Egypt, and stay there until I bring you word; for Herod will seek the young Child to destroy Him."

[14]When he arose, he took the young Child and His mother by night and departed for Egypt, [15]and was there until the death of Herod, that it might be fulfilled which was spoken by the Lord through the prophet, saying, *"Out of Egypt I called My Son."*[a]

MASSACRE OF THE INNOCENTS

[16]Then Herod, when he saw that he was deceived by the wise men, was exceedingly angry; and he sent forth and put to death all the male children who were in Bethlehem and in all its districts, from two years old and under, according to the time which he had determined from the wise men. [17]Then was fulfilled what was spoken by Jeremiah the prophet, saying:

[18]*"A voice was heard in Ramah,*
Lamentation, weeping, and great mourning,
Rachel weeping for her children,
Refusing to be comforted,
Because they are no more."[a]

THE HOME IN NAZARETH

[19]Now when Herod was dead, behold, an angel of the Lord appeared in a dream to Joseph in Egypt, [20]saying, "Arise, take the young Child and His mother, and go to the land of Israel, for those who sought the young Child's life are dead."

2:15 [a]Hosea 11:1 2:18 [a]Jeremiah 31:15

the INFLUENCERS

HEROD THE GREAT—Paranoia and God's Protection

MATTHEW 2

This Herod lived from 74 to 4 BC, and his title as "King of the Jews" was a costly one. He was placed on the throne by the Roman senate, but had to fight for three years to secure the title. This made him suspicious of anyone who might be a threat of any kind, so he murdered wives, stepsons, and even his own son to keep his title. This Herod was known more for his treachery, lust, and greed than for his buildings and administration.

Since he was half Jewish and the son of an Edomite, the Jews saw him as unclean. He built a lavish temple for the Jews to try to win them over. The fact that he was a murderer and idolater who built pagan temples elsewhere infuriated the people, and they saw through his vain efforts.

He lived in fear that a Messiah would come and usurp his throne and power at any moment. When the wise men asked, "Where is He who has been born King of the Jews?" it set off Herod's paranoia. He flew into a rage and ordered all male children two years and under to be put to death in Bethlehem and the surrounding districts. God's protection reigned supreme with a warning by the angel (v. 13) that allowed the family of Jesus to escape.

²¹Then he arose, took the young Child and His mother, and came into the land of Israel. ²²But when he heard that Archelaus was reigning over Judea instead of his father Herod, he was afraid to go there. And being warned by God in a dream, he turned aside into the region of Galilee. ²³And he came and dwelt in a city called Nazareth, that it might be fulfilled which was spoken by the prophets, "He shall be called a Nazarene."

JOHN THE BAPTIST PREPARES THE WAY

3 In those days John the Baptist came preaching in the wilderness of Judea, ²and saying, "Repent, for the kingdom of heaven is at hand!" ³For this is he who was spoken of by the prophet Isaiah, saying:

> "The voice of one crying in the wilderness:
> 'Prepare the way of the Lord;
> Make His paths straight.' "ª

⁴Now John himself was clothed in camel's hair, with a leather belt around his waist; and his food was locusts and wild honey. ⁵Then Jerusalem, all Judea, and all the region around the Jordan went out to him ⁶and were baptized by him in the Jordan, confessing their sins.

⁷But when he saw many of the Pharisees and Sadducees coming to his baptism, he said to them, "Brood of vipers! Who warned you to flee from the wrath to come? ⁸Therefore bear fruits worthy of repentance, ⁹and do not think to say to yourselves, 'We have Abraham as *our* father.' For I say to you that God is able to raise up children to Abraham from these stones. ¹⁰And even now the ax is laid to the root of the trees. Therefore every tree which does not bear good fruit is cut down and thrown into the fire. ¹¹I indeed baptize you with water unto repentance, but He who is coming after me is mightier than I, whose sandals I am not worthy to carry. He will baptize you with the Holy Spirit and fire.ª ¹²His winnowing fan *is* in His hand, and He will thoroughly clean out His threshing floor, and gather His wheat into the barn; but He will burn up the chaff with unquenchable fire."

3:3 ªIsaiah 40:3   **3:11** ªM-Text omits *and fire*.

INSIDE *the* INFLUENCERS

JOSEPH—Purity Is About Personal Sacrifice

MATTHEW 1:24

Joseph was a man God set apart for a purpose. The few words written in Scripture about him speak volumes about his character. He was both a *hearer and doer of God's Word*. Twice during sleep, God spoke to him, requiring immediate obedience and personal sacrifice. Joseph may have had insomnia after those two interventions!

God chose Joseph because He knew that his heart and motives were pure, and that he would respond in obedience rather than panic, anger, or embarrassment. Each time God called, Joseph answered (Matt. 1:24; 2:14).

Joseph took the challenge. God told him to take Mary as his wife—but not to have sexual relations with her until after the baby was born. Joseph's purity was about personal sacrifice. It meant that he had to be patient, make changes, and be willing to serve. He was able to do all those because of his personal intimacy with God.

Matthew Henry said, "The conquest of ourselves, and our own unruly passions, requires more true wisdom, and a more steady, constant, and regular management, than the obtaining of a victory over the forces of an enemy." Joseph was chosen to be the earthly father of the Son of God because he was pure, willing to listen, ready to serve, and ready to make personal sacrifices.

JOHN BAPTIZES JESUS

[13]Then Jesus came from Galilee to John at the Jordan to be baptized by him. [14]And John *tried to* prevent Him, saying, "I need to be baptized by You, and are You coming to me?"

[15]But Jesus answered and said to him, "Permit *it to be so* now, for thus it is fitting for us to fulfill all righteousness." Then he allowed Him.

[16]When He had been baptized, Jesus came up immediately from the water; and behold, the heavens were opened to Him, and He[a] saw the Spirit of God descending like a dove and alighting upon Him. [17]And suddenly a voice *came* from heaven, saying, "This is My beloved Son, in whom I am well pleased."

SATAN TEMPTS JESUS

4 Then Jesus was led up by the Spirit into the wilderness to be tempted by the devil. [2]And when He had fasted forty days and forty nights, afterward He was hungry. [3]Now when the tempter came to Him, he said, "If You are the Son of God, command that these stones become bread."

[4]But He answered and said, "It is written, *'Man shall not live by bread alone, but by every word that proceeds from the mouth of God.'* "[a]

[5]Then the devil took Him up into the holy city, set Him on the pinnacle of the temple, [6]and said to Him, "If You are the Son of God, throw Yourself down. For it is written:

'He shall give His angels charge over you,'

and,

'In their hands they shall bear you up,
Lest you dash your foot against a stone.' "[a]

[7]Jesus said to him, "It is written again, *'You shall not tempt the Lord your God.'* "[a]

[8]Again, the devil took Him up on an exceedingly high mountain, and showed Him all the kingdoms of the world and their glory. [9]And he

3:16 [a]Or *he*   **4:4** [a]Deuteronomy 8:3   **4:6** [a]Psalm 91:11, 12
4:7 [a]Deuteronomy 6:16

INSIDE *the* INFLUENCERS

JOHN THE BAPTIST—Be a Voice, Not an Echo

MATTHEW 3 & JOHN 1, 2

God called John the Baptist before he was even born (Luke 1), to prepare people for Jesus' arrival. As a man, his preaching attracted crowds of common people, soldiers, and business leaders. John's bold testimony of Jesus as the Messiah resulted in Andrew's conversion. Andrew then led his brother Cephas, or Simon Peter, to Christ. They became two of the first disciples of Christ because of John's testimony.

John was not like anyone else. He lived, dressed, and spoke differently; he was a voice *crying in the wilderness,* and never an echo of the current popular culture. This revolutionist gave his life to a purpose bigger than himself. John knew he was to prepare the way for Jesus. A **voice of influence:**

- prepares the way for others to see God work
- doesn't draw attention to self
- has a clear mission
- stays faithful to the purpose.

In prison, John began to doubt his call, and Jesus sent a word of assurance to him. Assured of his purpose, John was ready to die for it. He was beheaded at the request of Herod's step-daughter because he'd spoken out against the sin in Herod's family (Matt. 14:1–12). Until the very end of his life, John faithfully lifted up his voice for Christ.

said to Him, "All these things I will give You if You will fall down and worship me."

[10]Then Jesus said to him, "Away with you,[a] Satan! For it is written, *'You shall worship the Lord your God, and Him only you shall serve.' "*[b]

[11]Then the devil left Him, and behold, angels came and ministered to Him.

JESUS BEGINS HIS GALILEAN MINISTRY

[12]Now when Jesus heard that John had been put in prison, He departed to Galilee. [13]And leaving Nazareth, He came and dwelt in Capernaum, which is by the sea, in the regions of Zebulun and Naphtali, [14]that it might be fulfilled which was spoken by Isaiah the prophet, saying:

[15]*"The land of Zebulun and the land of*
    Naphtali,
  By the way of the sea, beyond the Jordan,
  Galilee of the Gentiles:
[16]*The people who sat in darkness have seen a*
    great light,

And upon those who sat in the region and
    shadow of death
  Light has dawned."[a]

[17]From that time Jesus began to preach and to say, "Repent, for the kingdom of heaven is at hand."

FOUR FISHERMEN CALLED AS DISCIPLES

[18]And Jesus, walking by the Sea of Galilee, saw two brothers, Simon called Peter, and Andrew his brother, casting a net into the sea; for they were fishermen. [19]Then He said to them, "Follow Me, and I will make you fishers of men." [20]They immediately left *their* nets and followed Him.

[21]Going on from there, He saw two other brothers, James *the son* of Zebedee, and John his brother, in the boat with Zebedee their father, mending their nets. He called them, [22]and immediately they left the boat and their father, and followed Him.

4:10 [a]M-Text reads *Get behind Me.* [b]Deuteronomy 6:13
4:16 [a]Isaiah 9:1, 2

LEADERSHIP ISSUES

Extraordinary Leadership

MATTHEW 4:21, 22

Many individuals in the pages of Scripture echo words of hesitancy and excuse when it comes to the call to lead. Moses claimed he was slow of speech and stuttered; Gideon argued with an angel over his lack of ability; Jeremiah claimed to be too young; Saul, who looked the part and was "head and shoulders" over all others, hid from Samuel the prophet; and Jonah ran when asked to lead Nineveh to repentance.

Extraordinary Leadership is not about how to achieve fame or fortune, nor does it excuse us to stay in the shadows and avoid controversy. It is about discovering God's standard of leadership, and this is the direct opposite of what the world proposes. There are two classic examples of individuals who, when they heard the call, saw the opportunity and seized it. Isaiah responded, "Here am I! Send me" (Is. 6:8). The sons of Zebedee willingly dropped their nets on the beach, left their family business, and followed Jesus (Matt. 4:21, 22). That simple act of faith moved them from ordinary to extraordinary.

The Lord shows us in His Word that it *is possible* to achieve the extraordinary *without* seeking worldly position or power; instead, we should desire daily to follow His plan. The end result may be financial success or notoriety, but it could also be serving anonymously in the jungles of a third world country. What makes it extraordinary is that it is planned by a mighty Creator whose heart beats for people, and He uses each of us to touch and influence the lives of others.

The world doesn't need *great* leaders; the world needs great *godly* leaders. The agenda should be God's and not our own. Whatever the call to extraordinary leadership, or wherever the call takes us, be assured that joy will be a great part of the journey; and significance—by God's definition—is within our grasp.

LEAD**ERSHIP**
REAL**ITIES**

FORWARD THINKING   *Matthew 4:1–11*

Immediately following His baptism, Jesus went out into the seclusion of the wilderness where He fasted for forty days and was then tempted by the devil. Although this passage is most often discussed as a time of temptation and testing for Jesus, it was also a time of great blessing. The Father ministered to Him in the difficult days and gave Him sufficient strength and grace for the task. A leader's journey will see a similar sequence of events. It will be accompanied by moments of great exhilaration only to be followed by experiences that exhaust and weaken even the strongest of individuals. The victory is sealed in the wilderness, in a place absent of all that could distract from the calling and communion between the leader and God. It is in these times of temptation that the leader must demonstrate, as Jesus did, *forward thinking;* that is, decisions made with an understanding of one's identity in Christ and ultimate purpose in life.

In all three temptations Jesus never allowed His messianic mission to be negotiated or surrendered.

- He was tempted to devalue His responsibility (vv. 3, 4).
- He was tempted to prove His authority (vv. 5–7).
- He was tempted to compromise His loyalty (vv. 8–10).

Jesus Heals a Great Multitude

²³And Jesus went about all Galilee, teaching in their synagogues, preaching the gospel of the kingdom, and healing all kinds of sickness and all kinds of disease among the people. ²⁴Then His fame went throughout all Syria; and they brought to Him all sick people who were afflicted with various diseases and torments, and those who were demon-possessed, epileptics, and paralytics; and He healed them. ²⁵Great multitudes followed Him—from Galilee, and *from* Decapolis, Jerusalem, Judea, and beyond the Jordan.

The Beatitudes

5And seeing the multitudes, He went up on a mountain, and when He was seated His disciples came to Him. ²Then He opened His mouth and taught them, saying:

³"Blessed *are* the poor in spirit,
  For theirs is the kingdom of heaven.
⁴Blessed *are* those who mourn,
  For they shall be comforted.

⁵Blessed *are* the meek,
  For they shall inherit the earth.
⁶Blessed *are* those who hunger and thirst for righteousness,
  For they shall be filled.
⁷Blessed *are* the merciful,
  For they shall obtain mercy.
⁸Blessed *are* the pure in heart,
  For they shall see God.
⁹Blessed *are* the peacemakers,
  For they shall be called sons of God.
¹⁰Blessed *are* those who are persecuted for righteousness' sake,
  For theirs is the kingdom of heaven.

¹¹"Blessed are you when they revile and persecute you, and say all kinds of evil against you falsely for My sake. ¹²Rejoice and be exceedingly glad, for great *is* your reward in heaven, for so they persecuted the prophets who were before you.

Believers Are Salt and Light

¹³"You are the salt of the earth; but if the salt loses its flavor, how shall it be seasoned? It is then

LEADERSHIP ISSUES

The Power of Comfort

MATTHEW 5:4

When someone is hurting, he or she needs comfort. Comfort is an emotional, heartfelt expression empowered by the Comforter, the Holy Spirit. It is also very simple. If we try to make it complicated, we'll dilute its effectiveness (John 11:35; 2 Cor. 1:2–4). And since comfort is primarily emotional in nature, usually the fewer words spoken, the better. If we say too much, we will inevitably move into explanations, analysis, and feel-good "pep talks," which are typically not helpful.

The "vocabulary" of comfort includes phrases like these:

- "I'm really sorry that you're hurting."
- "It hurts me that you're hurting because I love you and care for you."
- "It saddens me that you felt _____ (embarrassed, rejected, belittled). I know that must have hurt you."

When speaking words of comfort, it's also important that our *tone of voice* be complementary to what is being said. Words of comfort should be spoken gently and with compassion. Becoming a person whose heart is moved to share comfort will help prepare you for healthy, God-honoring relationships.

THROUGH THE GRID	*Thinking Christianly: Ten Foundational Beliefs of a Christian Worldview*

Belief Nine: Social Action (*Matt. 5:13–16*)

The social order of our secular culture should be penetrated by Christian witness. As Christians live out the ethics of Scripture, we are also to be salt and light to a wicked and darkened world that has turned its back on God. We can do so by taking social action. We should oppose racism, greed, and all forms of immorality; and we should help the orphans and the needy around the world (Ex. 20:3–17; Deut. 27:18–26; Ps. 139:13–16; Mic. 6:8; Matt. 5:13–16; Rom. 12—14; 1 Cor. 6:9–20; 7:21–24; Eph. 4:25—5:12; 1 Thess. 4:1–8). *See Through the Grid article on page 1573.*

good for nothing but to be thrown out and trampled underfoot by men.

¹⁴"You are the light of the world. A city that is set on a hill cannot be hidden. ¹⁵Nor do they light a lamp and put it under a basket, but on a lampstand, and it gives light to all *who are* in the house. ¹⁶Let your light so shine before men, that they may see your good works and glorify your Father in heaven.

Christ Fulfills the Law

¹⁷"Do not think that I came to destroy the Law or the Prophets. I did not come to destroy but to fulfill. ¹⁸For assuredly, I say to you, till heaven and earth pass away, one jot or one tittle will by no means pass from the law till all is fulfilled. ¹⁹Whoever therefore breaks one of the least of these commandments, and teaches men so, shall be called least in the kingdom of heaven; but whoever does and teaches *them,* he shall be called great in the kingdom of heaven. ²⁰For I say to you, that unless your righteousness exceeds *the righteousness* of the scribes and Pharisees, you will by no means enter the kingdom of heaven.

Murder Begins in the Heart

²¹"You have heard that it was said to those of old, '*You shall not murder,*ᵃ and whoever murders will be in danger of the judgment.' ²²But I say to you that whoever is angry with his brother without a causeᵃ shall be in danger of the judgment. And whoever says to his brother, 'Raca!' shall be in danger of the council. But whoever says, 'You fool!' shall be in danger of hell fire. ²³Therefore if

you bring your gift to the altar, and there remember that your brother has something against you, ²⁴leave your gift there before the altar, and go your way. First be reconciled to your brother, and then come and offer your gift. ²⁵Agree with your adversary quickly, while you are on the way with him, lest your adversary deliver you to the judge, the judge hand you over to the officer, and you be thrown into prison. ²⁶Assuredly, I say to you, you will by no means get out of there till you have paid the last penny.

Adultery in the Heart

²⁷"You have heard that it was said to those of old,ᵃ '*You shall not commit adultery.*'ᵇ ²⁸But I say to you that whoever looks at a woman to lust for her has already committed adultery with her in his heart. ²⁹If your right eye causes you to sin, pluck it out and cast *it* from you; for it is more profitable for you that one of your members perish, than for your whole body to be cast into hell. ³⁰And if your right hand causes you to sin, cut it off and cast *it* from you; for it is more profitable for you that one of your members perish, than for your whole body to be cast into hell.

Marriage Is Sacred and Binding

³¹"Furthermore it has been said, 'Whoever divorces his wife, let him give her a certificate of divorce.' ³²But I say to you that whoever divorces his wife for any reason except sexual immoralityᵃ

5:21 ᵃExodus 20:13; Deuteronomy 5:17 **5:22** ᵃNU-Text omits *without a cause.* **5:27** ᵃNU-Text and M-Text omit *to those of old.* ᵇExodus 20:14; Deuteronomy 5:18 **5:32** ᵃOr *fornication*

LEADERSHIP ISSUES

GC2: The Light of God's People

MATTHEW 5:14

An important source of God's light, direction, and provision for life is His love as it is demonstrated through His people. Christ reminded us that we are "the light of the world"; and as we love one another, His love is perfected in us. Through our demonstrations of love to one another, we are able to see God more clearly (1 John 4:12). Even the world takes notice when there's something different about our lives (John 13:34, 35).

"Bless the LORD, O my soul, and forget not all His benefits" (Ps. 103:2). Reflect on an occasion when God met a need in your life through another person. Consider a time when God blessed you through another follower of Jesus by involving a family member, friend, or acquaintance in your life. It might have been a time of tragedy or loss, discouragement or disappointment, weariness or loneliness. It might have been a time when you needed wisdom or encouragement, acceptance or care.

I recall a time when God met a need in my life, and He involved (who) by _____.

Share your reflections with a partner or small group. Pause to sense the Lord's pleasure as you actually experience His Word by "forgetting none of His benefits." Thank Him especially that He, at times, brings guidance and blessing through other followers of Jesus.

GC2
GREAT COMMANDMENT
COMMISSION

LEADERSHIP ISSUES

Servanthood

MATTHEW 5:17–20

The more we grow to love Christ, the more we will want to serve Him and to be His hands and feet across the world. Following the Ten Commandments does not keep us in bondage, but instead, liberates us and frees us. We find out that we are freed *from* legalism and cheap grace, and we are freed *for* service to our Creator. As we follow the Ten Commandments, we learn that our proper place is at the feet of Jesus Christ, where we develop our love for Him.

That means that whenever God asks us to do something, our proper response does not consider self, but instead selflessly obeys the calling of God upon our life. God may call one to missions, or to be more active in evangelism, or to become more active in your local church setting. Whatever the calling, we have received grace upon grace from God; and as the Ten Commandments remind us, our lives are not our own. We belong to God, and we conform to the will of God, rather than the other way around.

Thus, we should consider it an awesome privilege to serve our God by following His commands and by living in the will that God has for us. The need in the world is great. Many hundreds of thousands each year die from starvation or from diseases. These people are created by God, too. They are no less important because of their social status; in fact, God loves them as much as God loves us. When we follow the Ten Commandments, we stop thinking selfishly about how we are to use our gain for ourselves. Instead, we follow Christ's example of going to the outsiders, loving them despite their condition, and being a witness for God to their lives. As we obey God, selfishness goes away, and a desire for servanthood begins to form in our lives. When we are at the feet of Jesus, there is no calling for service that is beyond our ability.

causes her to commit adultery; and whoever marries a woman who is divorced commits adultery.

JESUS FORBIDS OATHS

[33]"Again you have heard that it was said to those of old, 'You shall not swear falsely, but shall perform your oaths to the Lord.' [34]But I say to you, do not swear at all: neither by heaven, for it is God's throne; [35]nor by the earth, for it is His footstool; nor by Jerusalem, for it is the city of the great King. [36]Nor shall you swear by your head, because you cannot make one hair white or black. [37]But let your 'Yes' be 'Yes,' and your 'No,' 'No.' For whatever is more than these is from the evil one.

GO THE SECOND MILE

[38]"You have heard that it was said, *'An eye for an eye and a tooth for a tooth.'* [a] [39]But I tell you not to resist an evil person. But whoever slaps you on your right cheek, turn the other to him also. [40]If anyone wants to sue you and take away your tunic, let him have *your* cloak also. [41]And whoever compels you to go one mile, go with him two. [42]Give to him who asks you, and from him who wants to borrow from you do not turn away.

LOVE YOUR ENEMIES

[43]"You have heard that it was said, *'You shall love your neighbor* [a] and hate your enemy.' [44]But I say to you, love your enemies, bless those who curse you, do good to those who hate you, and pray for those who spitefully use you and persecute you,[a] [45]that you may be sons of your Father in heaven; for He makes His sun rise on the evil and on the good, and sends rain on the just and on the unjust. [46]For if you love those who love you, what reward have you? Do not even the tax collectors do the same? [47]And if you greet your brethren[a] only, what do you do more *than others?* Do not even the tax collectors[b] do so? [48]Therefore you shall be perfect, just as your Father in heaven is perfect.

DO GOOD TO PLEASE GOD

6 "Take heed that you do not do your charitable deeds before men, to be seen by them. Otherwise you have no reward from your Father in heaven. [2]Therefore, when you do a charitable deed, do not sound a trumpet before you as the hypocrites do in the synagogues and in the streets, that they may have glory from men. Assuredly, I say to you, they have their reward. [3]But when you do a charitable deed, do not let your left hand know what your right hand is doing, [4]that your charitable deed may be in secret; and your Father who sees in secret will Himself reward you openly.[a]

THE MODEL PRAYER

[5]"And when you pray, you shall not be like the hypocrites. For they love to pray standing in the synagogues and on the corners of the streets, that they may be seen by men. Assuredly, I say to you, they have their reward. [6]But you, when you pray, go into your room, and when you have shut your door, pray to your Father who *is* in the secret *place;* and your Father who sees in secret will reward you openly.[a] [7]And when you pray, do not use vain repetitions as the heathen *do.* For they think that they will be heard for their many words.

[8]"Therefore do not be like them. For your Father knows the things you have need of before you ask Him. [9]In this manner, therefore, pray:

> Our Father in heaven,
> Hallowed be Your name.
> [10]Your kingdom come.
> Your will be done
> On earth as *it is* in heaven.
> [11]Give us this day our daily bread.
> [12]And forgive us our debts,
> As we forgive our debtors.
> [13]And do not lead us into temptation,
> But deliver us from the evil one.
> For Yours is the kingdom and the power and
> the glory forever. Amen.[a]

[14]"For if you forgive men their trespasses, your heavenly Father will also forgive you. [15]But if you do not forgive men their trespasses, neither will your Father forgive your trespasses.

5:38 [a]Exodus 21:24; Leviticus 24:20; Deuteronomy 19:21 **5:43** [a]Compare Leviticus 19:18 **5:44** [a]NU-Text omits three clauses from this verse, leaving, *"But I say to you, love your enemies and pray for those who persecute you."* **5:47** [a]M-Text reads *friends.* [b]NU-Text reads *Gentiles.* **6:4** [a]NU-Text omits *openly.* **6:6** [a]NU-Text omits *openly.* **6:13** [a]NU-Text omits *For Yours* through *Amen.*

LEADERSHIP ISSUES

GC2: Spiritual Formation: From Interruptions to Eternal Impact

MARK 5:33, 34

Jesus was on His way to the home of a synagogue ruler named Jairus. His daughter was ill, and Jairus had come to Jesus to plead for healing for his child. The disciples were no doubt excited about the possibility of winning favor with the synagogue rulers—perhaps this healing would win some favor with the Jews! But on their way to Jairus's house, Jesus stopped to heal a woman in the crowd. While Jesus was still speaking, some men came from the house of Jairus. "Your daughter is dead," they said. "Why trouble the Teacher any further?" (Mark 5:35).

Imagine the disciples' reaction now! "Thanks a lot, lady, you've really messed up our day!" Or maybe, "Jesus, we told you we shouldn't stop!" Is it not our *fear* that underlines our irritated response to interruptions? Am I afraid if I "waste time" with "this person" I'll somehow miss out? Notice with both the woman and with Jairus, Christ's answer is the same: "have *faith*"—just believe!

Jesus' reaction was much different from that of the disciples. Ignoring what Jairus's servants said, Jesus told the synagogue ruler, "Do not be afraid; only believe." And He proceeded to the home of Jairus and found the little girl. He said to her, "Little girl, I say to you, arise" (Mark 5:36, 41).

With these words, even greater blessing and ministry than the disciples could have anticipated takes place at Jairus's house—his daughter, who had died, returns to life!

Like the disciples, we need to learn that stopping to give to those who interrupt us does not mean that we lose out on God's best in our life, ministry, calling, or other pursuits. Rather, such seeming "interruptions" become occasions for eternal impact through which the Spirit transforms us into the likeness of Christ. And being transformed, we then impart Him to others in life-changing ways.

GC2
GREAT COMMANDMENT
COMMISSION

FASTING TO BE SEEN ONLY BY GOD

[16]"Moreover, when you fast, do not be like the hypocrites, with a sad countenance. For they disfigure their faces that they may appear to men to be fasting. Assuredly, I say to you, they have their reward. [17]But you, when you fast, anoint your head and wash your face, [18]so that you do not appear to men to be fasting, but to your Father who *is* in the secret *place;* and your Father who sees in secret will reward you openly.[a]

LAY UP TREASURES IN HEAVEN

[19]"Do not lay up for yourselves treasures on earth, where moth and rust destroy and where thieves break in and steal; [20]but lay up for yourselves treasures in heaven, where neither moth nor rust destroys and where thieves do not break in and steal. [21]For where your treasure is, there your heart will be also.

THE LAMP OF THE BODY

[22]"The lamp of the body is the eye. If therefore your eye is good, your whole body will be full of light. [23]But if your eye is bad, your whole body will be full of darkness. If therefore the light that is in you is darkness, how great *is* that darkness!

YOU CANNOT SERVE GOD AND RICHES

[24]"No one can serve two masters; for either he will hate the one and love the other, or else he will be loyal to the one and despise the other. You cannot serve God and mammon.

DO NOT WORRY

[25]"Therefore I say to you, do not worry about your life, what you will eat or what you will drink; nor about your body, what you will put on. Is not life more than food and the body more than clothing? [26]Look at the birds of the air, for they neither sow nor reap nor gather into barns; yet your heavenly Father feeds them. Are you not of more value than they? [27]Which of you by worrying can add one cubit to his stature?

[28]"So why do you worry about clothing? Consider the lilies of the field, how they grow:

6:18 [a]NU-Text and M-Text omit *openly.*

LEADERSHIP REALITIES

DO FIRST THINGS FIRST   *Matthew 6:33*

In this climactic statement from a portion of the Sermon on the Mount, Jesus simplifies life for all those who follow Him. There is the great temptation to become both overwhelmed and enslaved to certain needs such as food, drink and clothing. But Jesus liberates us from anxieties and calls us back to an eternal daily perspective. *Seek first the kingdom of God and His righteousness* does not mean our basic human needs are not important, but it does instruct us to purge ourselves of any desire that may take its place before our affection for God.

proton—**first**—first in rank, influence, honor

Few truly grasp this great reality and even fewer allow it to be the testimony of their lives. The ability to surrender one's affections and focus on this command of Jesus will serve as a catalyst to have influence beyond what one could possibly imagine. The leader never underestimates the power of doing something well every day. A brief survey of the landscape of Scripture and Christian history will reveal that God has continually used individuals who both understand this principle and live it out in an uncompromising fashion. The life we live will not be judged by how much money or stuff we acquire, but rather by daily doing first things first.

LEADERSHIP ISSUES

Leadership That Matters

MATTHEW 5:41

Attitudes and actions that honor God will result in leadership that matters. In these lessons of biblical principle, we see essential leadership traits.

Focus, Focus, Focus—Focus on goals that are pleasing to God. "I press toward the goal for the prize of the upward call of God in Christ Jesus" (Phil. 3:14). Research shows that just 5 percent of high school seniors will be financially independent at age 65, because they followed clear goals. Take time to consider which goals are important to you. Spiritually, know Christ as your personal Savior and grow in Him. Educationally, never stop learning. Physically, protect your bodies. Vocationally, select a job you love and work at it passionately.

Go the Second Mile—God's plan is that we each have a fulfilling life, and one thing that determines this is our attitude. Student Leadership University teaches the "and then some" philosophy. Rebekah demonstrated this philosophy when she hauled water for both the servant (what was expected) and his camels (and then some). Real achievers meet their obligations and responsibilities, *and then some.* Jesus valued this attitude as well, telling His followers, "And whoever compels you to go one mile, go with him two" (Matt. 5:41). Perfect your own second-mile lifestyle.

Seek Wisdom and Understanding—Search out God's thoughts; allow Him to provide wisdom and understanding as you seek to serve Christ by serving others. "Wisdom is the principal thing; therefore get wisdom. And in all your getting, get understanding" (Prov. 4:7).

Put Christ First, Others Second, and Self Last—Good leadership is living for something greater than self. "Through the proof of this ministry, they glorify God for the obedience of your confession to the gospel of Christ" (2 Cor. 9:13). Follow Christ, serve others, and sacrifice self. Leadership that matters seeks to honor Christ in everything while living life with passion.

they neither toil nor spin; [29]and yet I say to you that even Solomon in all his glory was not arrayed like one of these. [30]Now if God so clothes the grass of the field, which today is, and tomorrow is thrown into the oven, *will He* not much more *clothe* you, O you of little faith?

[31]"Therefore do not worry, saying, 'What shall we eat?' or 'What shall we drink?' or 'What shall we wear?' [32]For after all these things the Gentiles seek. For your heavenly Father knows that you need all these things. [33]But seek first the kingdom of God and His righteousness, and all these things shall be added to you. [34]Therefore do not worry about tomorrow, for tomorrow will worry about its own things. Sufficient for the day *is* its own trouble.

Do Not Judge

7 "Judge not, that you be not judged. [2]For with what judgment you judge, you will be judged; and with the measure you use, it will be measured back to you. [3]And why do you look at the speck in your brother's eye, but do not consider the plank in your own eye? [4]Or how can you say to your brother, 'Let me remove the speck from your eye'; and look, a plank *is* in your own eye? [5]Hypocrite! First remove the plank from your own eye, and then you will see clearly to remove the speck from your brother's eye.

[6]"Do not give what is holy to the dogs; nor cast your pearls before swine, lest they trample them under their feet, and turn and tear you in pieces.

Keep Asking, Seeking, Knocking

[7]"Ask, and it will be given to you; seek, and you will find; knock, and it will be opened to you. [8]For everyone who asks receives, and he who seeks finds, and to him who knocks it will be opened. [9]Or what man is there among you who, if his son asks for bread, will give him a stone? [10]Or if he asks for a fish, will he give him a serpent? [11]If you then, being evil, know how to give good gifts to your children, how much more will your Father who is in heaven give good things to those who ask Him! [12]Therefore, whatever you want men to do to you, do also to them, for this is the Law and the Prophets.

The Narrow Way

[13]"Enter by the narrow gate; for wide *is* the gate and broad *is* the way that leads to destruction, and there are many who go in by it. [14]Because[a] narrow *is* the gate and difficult *is* the way which leads to life, and there are few who find it.

You Will Know Them by Their Fruits

[15]"Beware of false prophets, who come to you in sheep's clothing, but inwardly they are ravenous wolves. [16]You will know them by their fruits. Do men gather grapes from thornbushes or figs from thistles? [17]Even so, every good tree bears good fruit, but a bad tree bears bad fruit. [18]A good tree cannot bear bad fruit, nor *can* a bad tree bear good fruit. [19]Every tree that does not bear good fruit is cut down and thrown into the fire. [20]Therefore by their fruits you will know them.

I Never Knew You

[21]"Not everyone who says to Me, 'Lord, Lord,' shall enter the kingdom of heaven, but he who does the will of My Father in heaven. [22]Many will say to Me in that day, 'Lord, Lord, have we not prophesied in Your name, cast out demons in Your name, and done many wonders in Your name?' [23]And then I will declare to them, 'I never knew you; depart from Me, you who practice lawlessness!'

Build on the Rock

[24]"Therefore whoever hears these sayings of Mine, and does them, I will liken him to a wise man who built his house on the rock: [25]and the rain descended, the floods came, and the winds blew and beat on that house; and it did not fall, for it was founded on the rock.

[26]"But everyone who hears these sayings of Mine, and does not do them, will be like a foolish man who built his house on the sand: [27]and the rain descended, the floods came, and the winds blew and beat on that house; and it fell. And great was its fall."

[28]And so it was, when Jesus had ended these sayings, that the people were astonished at His teaching, [29]for He taught them as one having authority, and not as the scribes.

7:14 [a]NU-Text and M-Text read *How . . . !*

LEADERSHIP ISSUES

GC2: Faith Is Unshakeable

MATTHEW 6:32

Genuine faith is supported by a firm confidence in the Father's love. Mature disciples of Christ follow His leading until they can no longer clearly see the path ahead of them, at which point, genuine faith prompts and empowers them to take the next step. Anxiety, worry, and fear give way to the peace that passes understanding (Phil. 4:7). Upon which foundation does such unshakeable faith rest? It rests upon the simple truth that the heavenly Father knows what we need (Matt. 6:32). Since He knows, and we know that He cares, we can be at peace, believing in faith that He will guide, provide and protect us.

Jesus called out with a loud voice, "'Father, into Your hands I commit My spirit.' Having said this, He breathed His last" (Luke 23:46). Notice Christ's **unshakeable** faith: He displays no anxiety about the circumstance in which He finds Himself, no fears concerning the future, no worries about what others might do.

Which anxieties or worries might you need to be freed from as you experience the Spirit's refining work of faith in you?

I need the Spirit to deepen my faith so that I might be freed from anxiety and worry concerning _____

_____

_____

(For example: *I need the Spirit to deepen my faith so that I might be freed from anxiety and worry concerning what others are thinking about me.*)

After sharing your responses with your partner or small group, pray together a prayer of faith, claiming the simple but profound promise that "your heavenly Father knows" (Matt. 6:32).

As you pray: Trust that He knows. Trust that He cares. Trust that because He cares, you need not be anxious. Trust that, as you ask according to His will, He hears, and that you will have what you request (John 14:14, 15).

GC2
GREAT COMMANDMENT
COMMISSION

Jesus Cleanses a Leper

8 When He had come down from the mountain, great multitudes followed Him. [2]And behold, a leper came and worshiped Him, saying, "Lord, if You are willing, You can make me clean."

[3]Then Jesus put out *His* hand and touched him, saying, "I am willing; be cleansed." Immediately his leprosy was cleansed.

[4]And Jesus said to him, "See that you tell no one; but go your way, show yourself to the priest, and offer the gift that Moses commanded, as a testimony to them."

Jesus Heals a Centurion's Servant

[5]Now when Jesus had entered Capernaum, a centurion came to Him, pleading with Him, [6]saying, "Lord, my servant is lying at home paralyzed, dreadfully tormented."

[7]And Jesus said to him, "I will come and heal him."

[8]The centurion answered and said, "Lord, I am not worthy that You should come under my roof. But only speak a word, and my servant will be healed. [9]For I also am a man under authority, having soldiers under me. And I say to this *one,* 'Go,' and he goes; and to another, 'Come,' and he comes; and to my servant, 'Do this,' and he does *it.*"

[10]When Jesus heard *it,* He marveled, and said to those who followed, "Assuredly, I say to you, I have not found such great faith, not even in Israel! [11]And I say to you that many will come from east and west, and sit down with Abraham, Isaac, and Jacob in the kingdom of heaven. [12]But the sons of the kingdom will be cast out into outer darkness. There will be weeping and gnashing of teeth." [13]Then Jesus said to the centurion, "Go your way; and as you have believed, *so* let it be done for you." And his servant was healed that same hour.

Peter's Mother-in-Law Healed

[14]Now when Jesus had come into Peter's house, He saw his wife's mother lying sick with a fever. [15]So He touched her hand, and the fever left her. And she arose and served them.[a]

Many Healed in the Evening

[16]When evening had come, they brought to Him many who were demon-possessed. And He cast out the spirits with a word, and healed all who were sick, [17]that it might be fulfilled which was spoken by Isaiah the prophet, saying:

> "He Himself took our infirmities
> And bore *our* sicknesses."[a]

The Cost of Discipleship

[18]And when Jesus saw great multitudes about Him, He gave a command to depart to the other side. [19]Then a certain scribe came and said to Him, "Teacher, I will follow You wherever You go."

[20]And Jesus said to him, "Foxes have holes and birds of the air *have* nests, but the Son of Man has nowhere to lay *His* head."

[21]Then another of His disciples said to Him, "Lord, let me first go and bury my father."

[22]But Jesus said to him, "Follow Me, and let the dead bury their own dead."

Wind and Wave Obey Jesus

[23]Now when He got into a boat, His disciples followed Him. [24]And suddenly a great tempest arose on the sea, so that the boat was covered with the waves. But He was asleep. [25]Then His disciples came to *Him* and awoke Him, saying, "Lord, save us! We are perishing!"

[26]But He said to them, "Why are you fearful, O you of little faith?" Then He arose and rebuked the winds and the sea, and there was a great calm. [27]So the men marveled, saying, "Who can this be, that even the winds and the sea obey Him?"

Two Demon-Possessed Men Healed

[28]When He had come to the other side, to the country of the Gergesenes,[a] there met Him two demon-possessed *men,* coming out of the tombs, exceedingly fierce, so that no one could pass that way. [29]And suddenly they cried out, saying, "What have we to do with You, Jesus, You Son of God? Have You come here to torment us before the time?"

[30]Now a good way off from them there was a herd of many swine feeding. [31]So the demons begged Him, saying, "If You cast us out, permit us to go away[a] into the herd of swine."

8:15 [a]NU-Text and M-Text read *Him.*   **8:17** [a]Isaiah 53:4   **8:28** [a]NU-Text reads *Gadarenes.*   **8:31** [a]NU-Text reads *send us.*

³²And He said to them, "Go." So when they had come out, they went into the herd of swine. And suddenly the whole herd of swine ran violently down the steep place into the sea, and perished in the water.

³³Then those who kept *them* fled; and they went away into the city and told everything, including what *had happened* to the demon-possessed *men*. ³⁴And behold, the whole city came out to meet Jesus. And when they saw Him, they begged *Him* to depart from their region.

JESUS FORGIVES AND HEALS A PARALYTIC

9 So He got into a boat, crossed over, and came to His own city. ²Then behold, they brought to Him a paralytic lying on a bed. When Jesus saw their faith, He said to the paralytic, "Son, be of good cheer; your sins are forgiven you."

³And at once some of the scribes said within themselves, "This Man blasphemes!"

⁴But Jesus, knowing their thoughts, said, "Why do you think evil in your hearts? ⁵For which is easier, to say, '*Your* sins are forgiven you,'

or to say, 'Arise and walk'? ⁶But that you may know that the Son of Man has power on earth to forgive sins"—then He said to the paralytic, "Arise, take up your bed, and go to your house."

⁷And he arose and departed to his house.

⁸Now when the multitudes saw *it,* they marveledª and glorified God, who had given such power to men.

MATTHEW THE TAX COLLECTOR

⁹As Jesus passed on from there, He saw a man named Matthew sitting at the tax office. And He said to him, "Follow Me." So he arose and followed Him.

¹⁰Now it happened, as Jesus sat at the table in the house, *that* behold, many tax collectors and sinners came and sat down with Him and His disciples. ¹¹And when the Pharisees saw *it,* they said to His disciples, "Why does your Teacher eat with tax collectors and sinners?"

¹²When Jesus heard *that,* He said to them, "Those who are well have no need of a physician,

9:8 ªNU-Text reads *were afraid.*

INSIDE *the* INFLUENCERS

MATTHEW: The Despised Tax Man Who Became a Disciple

MATTHEW 9:9–13

Matthew, a Galilean Jew also known as Levi (Mark 2:14), intentionally chose to be a tax collector. The Roman government's primary concern with regions they ruled was to gather taxes in a swift, cost effective way. To ensure this, they auctioned tax-collecting jobs to the lowest bidder. A Tax collector typically made money by price-gouging, charging more than the government's requirements, and keeping the extra. Naturally, greed stepped in, and most tax collectors deceived and intimidated people out of their money—which is why they were rich, ostracized, and hated.

Prior to meeting Jesus, Matthew was probably not religious, nor was he welcome in the temple. Although wealthy, Matthew's societal status would have ranked alongside "sinners, prostitutes and Gentiles" (18:17; 21:31, 32; Mark 2:15, 16; Luke 5:30).

His interaction with Jesus shows us a lonely man in need of community who surprised everyone by becoming a believer. That evening Jesus and the disciples had dinner with Matthew and many tax collectors and sinners (9:10). Jesus came to save sinners and to heal the sick, and Matthew's experience is a beautiful portrait of God's grace extending to the unpopular and unloved. After his encounter with Jesus, he is called "Matthew," which means "the gift of God."

but those who are sick. [13]But go and learn what *this* means: *'I desire mercy and not sacrifice.'*[a] For I did not come to call the righteous, but sinners, to repentance."[b]

JESUS IS QUESTIONED ABOUT FASTING

[14]Then the disciples of John came to Him, saying, "Why do we and the Pharisees fast often,[a] but Your disciples do not fast?"

[15]And Jesus said to them, "Can the friends of the bridegroom mourn as long as the bridegroom is with them? But the days will come when the bridegroom will be taken away from them, and then they will fast. [16]No one puts a piece of unshrunk cloth on an old garment; for the patch pulls away from the garment, and the tear is made worse. [17]Nor do they put new wine into old wineskins, or else the wineskins break, the wine is spilled, and the wineskins are ruined. But they put new wine into new wineskins, and both are preserved."

A GIRL RESTORED TO LIFE AND A WOMAN HEALED

[18]While He spoke these things to them, behold, a ruler came and worshiped Him, saying, "My daughter has just died, but come and lay Your hand on her and she will live." [19]So Jesus arose and followed him, and so *did* His disciples.

[20]And suddenly, a woman who had a flow of blood for twelve years came from behind and touched the hem of His garment. [21]For she said to herself, "If only I may touch His garment, I shall be made well." [22]But Jesus turned around, and when He saw her He said, "Be of good cheer, daughter; your faith has made you well." And the woman was made well from that hour.

[23]When Jesus came into the ruler's house, and saw the flute players and the noisy crowd wailing, [24]He said to them, "Make room, for the girl is not dead, but sleeping." And they ridiculed Him. [25]But when the crowd was put outside, He went in and took her by the hand, and the girl arose. [26]And the report of this went out into all that land.

TWO BLIND MEN HEALED

[27]When Jesus departed from there, two blind men followed Him, crying out and saying, "Son of David, have mercy on us!"

[28]And when He had come into the house, the blind men came to Him. And Jesus said to them, "Do you believe that I am able to do this?"

They said to Him, "Yes, Lord."

[29]Then He touched their eyes, saying, "According to your faith let it be to you." [30]And their eyes were opened. And Jesus sternly warned them, saying, "See *that* no one knows *it*." [31]But when they had departed, they spread the news about Him in all that country.

A MUTE MAN SPEAKS

[32]As they went out, behold, they brought to Him a man, mute and demon-possessed. [33]And when the demon was cast out, the mute spoke. And the multitudes marveled, saying, "It was never seen like this in Israel!"

[34]But the Pharisees said, "He casts out demons by the ruler of the demons."

THE COMPASSION OF JESUS

[35]Then Jesus went about all the cities and villages, teaching in their synagogues, preaching the gospel of the kingdom, and healing every sickness and every disease among the people.[a] [36]But when He saw the multitudes, He was moved with compassion for them, because they were weary[a] and scattered, like sheep having no shepherd. [37]Then He said to His disciples, "The harvest truly *is* plentiful, but the laborers *are* few. [38]Therefore pray the Lord of the harvest to send out laborers into His harvest."

THE TWELVE APOSTLES

10 And when He had called His twelve disciples to *Him,* He gave them power *over* unclean spirits, to cast them out, and to heal all kinds of sickness and all kinds of disease. [2]Now the names of the twelve apostles are these: first, Simon, who is called Peter, and Andrew his brother; James the *son* of Zebedee, and John his brother; [3]Philip and Bartholomew; Thomas and Matthew the tax collector; James the *son* of Alphaeus, and Lebbaeus, whose surname was[a] Thaddaeus;

9:13 [a]Hosea 6:6 [b]NU-Text omits *to repentance.* **9:14** [a]NU-Text brackets *often* as disputed. **9:35** [a]NU-Text omits *among the people.* **9:36** [a]NU-Text and M-Text read *harassed.* **10:3** [a]NU-Text omits *Lebbaeus, whose surname was.*

LEADERSHIP
REALITIES

IT TAKES A TEAM TO LAUNCH A DREAM
CALL OF DISCIPLES *Matthew 10:1*

As He began a public ministry, Jesus called out twelve disciples. This is an interesting thought—the Son of God chose a working team! Why? He has all power, all ability, and all knowledge. What could He possibly need a team for? Remember, everything He did is an example to us. In that light, let's examine why a leader chooses to work with a team in order to launch his or her dream.

1. Accountability: Team members expect each other to do what they say and say what they mean.
2. Encouragement: When difficulty, conflict, or discouragement arises, your team can pull together to keep going to the finish.
3. To bless others: Working with others allows you to minister on a greater scale.
4. To give and to gain opportunity: Bringing in individuals who might not otherwise get the chance to accomplish great goals is an important part of a leader's life.
5. For diversity of relationships: Meeting new people teaches a leader to deal with conflict, explore new ideas, and gain wisdom.
6. To allow sharing of ideas and the resulting successes: The Christian life is meant to be shared. Sharing success discourages a false pride and keeps ego in check. The leader rejoices with others and multiplies the motivation to excellence.

[4]Simon the Cananite,[a] and Judas Iscariot, who also betrayed Him.

SENDING OUT THE TWELVE

[5]These twelve Jesus sent out and commanded them, saying: "Do not go into the way of the Gentiles, and do not enter a city of the Samaritans. [6]But go rather to the lost sheep of the house of Israel. [7]And as you go, preach, saying, 'The kingdom of heaven is at hand.' [8]Heal the sick, cleanse the lepers, raise the dead,[a] cast out demons. Freely you have received, freely give. [9]Provide neither gold nor silver nor copper in your money belts, [10]nor bag for your journey, nor two tunics, nor sandals, nor staffs; for a worker is worthy of his food.

[11]"Now whatever city or town you enter, inquire who in it is worthy, and stay there till you go out. [12]And when you go into a household, greet it. [13]If the household is worthy, let your peace come upon it. But if it is not worthy,

let your peace return to you. [14]And whoever will not receive you nor hear your words, when you depart from that house or city, shake off the dust from your feet. [15]Assuredly, I say to you, it will be more tolerable for the land of Sodom and Gomorrah in the day of judgment than for that city!

PERSECUTIONS ARE COMING

[16]"Behold, I send you out as sheep in the midst of wolves. Therefore be wise as serpents and harmless as doves. [17]But beware of men, for they will deliver you up to councils and scourge you in their synagogues. [18]You will be brought before governors and kings for My sake, as a testimony to them and to the Gentiles. [19]But when they deliver you up, do not worry about how or what you should speak. For it will be given to you in that hour what you should speak; [20]for it is not

10:4 [a]NU-Text reads *Cananaean*. **10:8** [a]NU-Text reads *raise the dead, cleanse the lepers;* M-Text omits *raise the dead.*

INSIDE the INFLUENCERS

TWELVE APOSTLES—It Takes a Team

MATTHEW 10:2

When Jesus began His earthly ministry, He called out a team to go with Him. Each of the twelve men, including Judas, gave up jobs and left family and friends because they believed Jesus would change the world. His teachings were brilliant and fascinating; His miracles amazing and wonderful. The crowds grew daily, and people loved Him. Everywhere people talked of Jesus, and they even welcomed Him with a parade of palms crying out "Hosanna! 'Blessed is He who comes in the name of the Lord!'" (John 12:13).

But that was yesterday. Now He speaks again of dying, betrayal, and of going away. Soon He would hang on a cross, beaten, bruised, and suffering. It looked to be the worst day of the disciples' lives. Their hopes and dreams shattered. They felt confused, frightened, disappointed, and even angry. They recalled His words, "A little while, and you will not see Me; and again a little while, and you will see Me" (John 16:16). What did that mean?

Days later, they hid in fear of the Jews. Suddenly, Jesus stood in their midst and said, "Peace to you" (Luke 24:36). Now, they understood that peace is a person. His name is Jesus. These frightened followers became warriors for the Gospel, many dying a martyr's death, and all of them enduring extreme personal sacrifices. For this team, adversity was painfully profitable, and it purified their passion.

you who speak, but the Spirit of your Father who speaks in you.

21"Now brother will deliver up brother to death, and a father *his* child; and children will rise up against parents and cause them to be put to death. 22And you will be hated by all for My name's sake. But he who endures to the end will be saved. 23When they persecute you in this city, flee to another. For assuredly, I say to you, you will not have gone through the cities of Israel before the Son of Man comes.

24"A disciple is not above *his* teacher, nor a servant above his master. 25It is enough for a disciple that he be like his teacher, and a servant like his master. If they have called the master of the house Beelzebub,ᵃ how much more *will they call* those of his household! 26Therefore do not fear them. For there is nothing covered that will not be revealed, and hidden that will not be known.

JESUS TEACHES THE FEAR OF GOD

27"Whatever I tell you in the dark, speak in the light; and what you hear in the ear, preach on the housetops. 28And do not fear those who kill the body but cannot kill the soul. But rather fear Him who is able to destroy both soul and body in hell. 29Are not two sparrows sold for a copper coin? And not one of them falls to the ground apart from your Father's will. 30But the very hairs of your head are all numbered. 31Do not fear therefore; you are of more value than many sparrows.

CONFESS CHRIST BEFORE MEN

32"Therefore whoever confesses Me before men, him I will also confess before My Father who is in heaven. 33But whoever denies Me before men, him I will also deny before My Father who is in heaven.

CHRIST BRINGS DIVISION

34"Do not think that I came to bring peace on earth. I did not come to bring peace but a sword. 35For I have come to *'set a man against his father, a daughter against her mother, and a daughter-in-law against her mother-in-law'*; 36and

10:25 ᵃNU-Text and M-Text read *Beelzebul*.

LEADERSHIP ISSUES

GC2: Spiritual Formation: Jesus' Life and Love Transform Us

MATTHEW 10:8 *Heal the sick, cleanse the lepers, raise the dead, cast out demons. Freely you received, freely give.*

Being a faithful Christ-follower requires that we not only receive of God's glorious riches but that we also share His multifaceted grace with others (Phil. 4:19; 1 Pet. 4:10). We participate in the Spirit's work of making us more like Jesus not just by "freely receiving," but also by "freely giving." This might involve:

- Accepting those who are very different from us, sometimes in spite of their faults and failures (Rom. 15:7)
- Comforting others by just hurting with them—refraining from giving advice, pep talks, or pat assurances that God will "work things out for good." Just as Jesus wept with His friend Mary in the midst of her pain, we can demonstrate tenderness and compassion simply with our presence, a few empathetic words, or tears. (See 2 Cor. 1:3, 4; John 11:35.)
- Giving attention and care to those who inconvenience us, interrupt us, or in some way present themselves as distractions in our path (1 Cor. 12:25, 26)

Pause to minister "to the Lord" (Acts 13:2) by quietly asking Him, "To whom would you send me with Your love?" Just as He set apart Paul and Barnabas, to whom will He send you this week to share His acceptance? His comfort? His attention? Now experience the truth of Isaiah 6:8: "Here am I! Send me."

GC2
GREAT COMMANDMENT
COMMISSION

*'a man's enemies will be those of his own house-hold.'*ª ³⁷He who loves father or mother more than Me is not worthy of Me. And he who loves son or daughter more than Me is not worthy of Me. ³⁸And he who does not take his cross and follow after Me is not worthy of Me. ³⁹He who finds his life will lose it, and he who loses his life for My sake will find it.

A Cup of Cold Water

⁴⁰"He who receives you receives Me, and he who receives Me receives Him who sent Me. ⁴¹He who receives a prophet in the name of a prophet shall receive a prophet's reward. And he who receives a righteous man in the name of a righteous man shall receive a righteous man's reward. ⁴²And whoever gives one of these little ones only a cup of cold *water* in the name of a disciple, assuredly, I say to you, he shall by no means lose his reward."

John the Baptist Sends Messengers to Jesus

11 Now it came to pass, when Jesus finished commanding His twelve disciples, that He departed from there to teach and to preach in their cities.

²And when John had heard in prison about the works of Christ, he sent two ofª his disciples ³and said to Him, "Are You the Coming One, or do we look for another?"

⁴Jesus answered and said to them, "Go and tell John the things which you hear and see: ⁵*The* blind see and *the* lame walk; *the* lepers are cleansed and *the* deaf hear; *the* dead are raised up and *the* poor have the gospel preached to them. ⁶And blessed is he who is not offended because of Me."

⁷As they departed, Jesus began to say to the multitudes concerning John: "What did you go out into the wilderness to see? A reed shaken by the wind? ⁸But what did you go out to see? A man clothed in soft garments? Indeed, those who wear soft *clothing* are in kings' houses. ⁹But what did you go out to see? A prophet? Yes, I say to you, and more than a prophet. ¹⁰For this is *he* of whom it is written:

'*Behold, I send My messenger before Your face,*
Who will prepare Your way before You.'ª

¹¹"Assuredly, I say to you, among those born of women there has not risen one greater than John the Baptist; but he who is least in the kingdom of heaven is greater than he. ¹²And from the days of John the Baptist until now the kingdom of heaven suffers violence, and the violent take it by force. ¹³For all the prophets and the law prophesied until John. ¹⁴And if you are willing to receive *it*, he is Elijah who is to come. ¹⁵He who has ears to hear, let him hear!

¹⁶"But to what shall I liken this generation? It is like children sitting in the marketplaces and calling to their companions, ¹⁷and saying:

'We played the flute for you,
    And you did not dance;
We mourned to you,
    And you did not lament.'

¹⁸For John came neither eating nor drinking, and they say, 'He has a demon.' ¹⁹The Son of Man came eating and drinking, and they say, 'Look, a glutton and a winebibber, a friend of tax collectors and sinners!' But wisdom is justified by her children."ª

Woe to the Impenitent Cities

²⁰Then He began to rebuke the cities in which most of His mighty works had been done, because they did not repent: ²¹"Woe to you, Chorazin! Woe to you, Bethsaida! For if the mighty works which were done in you had been done in Tyre and Sidon, they would have repented long ago in sackcloth and ashes. ²²But I say to you, it will be more tolerable for Tyre and Sidon in the day of judgment than for you. ²³And you, Capernaum, who are exalted to heaven, will beª brought down to Hades; for if the mighty works which were done in you had been done in Sodom, it would have remained until this day. ²⁴But I say to you that it shall be more tolerable for the land of Sodom in the day of judgment than for you."

Jesus Gives True Rest

²⁵At that time Jesus answered and said, "I thank You, Father, Lord of heaven and earth, that

10:36 ªMicah 7:6   **11:2** ªNU-Text reads *by* for *two of.*
11:10 ªMalachi 3:1   **11:19** ªNU-Text reads *works.*   **11:23** ªNU-Text reads *will you be exalted to heaven? No, you will be.*

LEADERSHIP ISSUES

Wise as Serpents

MATTHEW 10:16–20

Jesus' statement to be "as wise as serpents and harmless as doves," can be a little perplexing. We all have a pretty good idea of what it means to be harmless and innocent. Words like "purity" and "integrity" come to mind. That fits our image of Jesus.

However, why did Jesus use the words "wise as serpents"? After all, these words conjure up images of a ruthless, self-serving, or deceitful person who seeks to please self, not to mention the snake in the garden. On the contrary, we know that Jesus cared deeply about people.

What it seems Jesus meant in this passage is: first, we are to bluntly recognize reality for what it is. We live in a fallen, evil, often cruel world. That's reality. We are not to sugarcoat it. We are not to gloss over it. Second, we are to see persecution for what it really is—an opportunity to tell others about Jesus. Verses 18–20 complete the picture. Persecution is not something we should fear, because in reality, persecution is a God-given opportunity to make Jesus the issue. That is God's bottom line.

So the next time you are accused of being "narrow, intolerant, or ignorant," recognize the opportunity God has just given you. Move past the symptom (name calling), to the cause (need for Jesus as Savior). Go directly to God's bottom line. Make Jesus the issue.

You have hidden these things from *the* wise and prudent and have revealed them to babes. ²⁶Even so, Father, for so it seemed good in Your sight. ²⁷All things have been delivered to Me by My Father, and no one knows the Son except the Father. Nor does anyone know the Father except the Son, and *the one* to whom the Son wills to reveal *Him*. ²⁸Come to Me, all *you* who labor and are heavy laden, and I will give you rest. ²⁹Take My yoke upon you and learn from Me, for I am gentle and lowly in heart, and you will find rest for your souls. ³⁰For My yoke *is* easy and My burden is light."

Jesus Is Lord of the Sabbath

12 At that time Jesus went through the grainfields on the Sabbath. And His disciples were hungry, and began to pluck heads of grain and to eat. ²And when the Pharisees saw *it,* they said to Him, "Look, Your disciples are doing what is not lawful to do on the Sabbath!"

³But He said to them, "Have you not read what David did when he was hungry, he and those who were with him: ⁴how he entered the house of God and ate the showbread which was not lawful for him to eat, nor for those who were with him, but only for the priests? ⁵Or have you not read in the law that on the Sabbath the priests in the temple profane the Sabbath, and are blameless? ⁶Yet I say to you that in this place there is *One* greater than the temple. ⁷But if you had known what *this* means, '*I desire mercy and not sacrifice,*'[a] you would not have condemned the guiltless. ⁸For the Son of Man is Lord even[a] of the Sabbath."

Healing on the Sabbath

⁹Now when He had departed from there, He went into their synagogue. ¹⁰And behold, there was a man who had a withered hand. And they asked Him, saying, "Is it lawful to heal on the Sabbath?"—that they might accuse Him.

¹¹Then He said to them, "What man is there among you who has one sheep, and if it falls into a pit on the Sabbath, will not lay hold of it and lift *it* out? ¹²Of how much more value then is a man than a sheep? Therefore it is lawful to do good on the Sabbath." ¹³Then He said to the man, "Stretch out your hand." And he stretched *it* out, and it was restored as whole as the other. ¹⁴Then the

Pharisees went out and plotted against Him, how they might destroy Him.

Behold, My Servant

¹⁵But when Jesus knew *it,* He withdrew from there. And great multitudes[a] followed Him, and He healed them all. ¹⁶Yet He warned them not to make Him known, ¹⁷that it might be fulfilled which was spoken by Isaiah the prophet, saying:

> ¹⁸"*Behold! My Servant whom I have chosen,*
> *My Beloved in whom My soul is well pleased!*
> *I will put My Spirit upon Him,*
> *And He will declare justice to the Gentiles.*
> ¹⁹*He will not quarrel nor cry out,*
> *Nor will anyone hear His voice in the streets.*
> ²⁰*A bruised reed He will not break,*
> *And smoking flax He will not quench,*
> *Till He sends forth justice to victory;*
> ²¹*And in His name Gentiles will trust.*"[a]

A House Divided Cannot Stand

²²Then one was brought to Him who was demon-possessed, blind and mute; and He healed him, so that the blind and[a] mute man both spoke and saw. ²³And all the multitudes were amazed and said, "Could this be the Son of David?"

²⁴Now when the Pharisees heard *it* they said, "This *fellow* does not cast out demons except by Beelzebub,[a] the ruler of the demons."

²⁵But Jesus knew their thoughts, and said to them: "Every kingdom divided against itself is brought to desolation, and every city or house divided against itself will not stand. ²⁶If Satan casts out Satan, he is divided against himself. How then will his kingdom stand? ²⁷And if I cast out demons by Beelzebub, by whom do your sons cast *them* out? Therefore they shall be your judges. ²⁸But if I cast out demons by the Spirit of God, surely the kingdom of God has come upon you. ²⁹Or how can one enter a strong man's house and plunder his goods, unless he first binds the strong man? And then he will plunder his house. ³⁰He who is not with Me is against Me, and he who does not gather with Me scatters abroad.

12:7 [a]Hosea 6:6　**12:8** [a]NU-Text and M-Text omit *even.*　**12:15** [a]NU-Text brackets *multitudes* as disputed.　**12:21** [a]Isaiah 42:1–4　**12:22** [a]NU-Text omits *blind and.*　**12:24** [a]NU-Text and M-Text read *Beelzebul.*

LEADERSHIP ISSUES

GC2: Encountering Jesus: Joining Christ in the Yoke

MATTHEW 11:28

Jesus invites us to come to Him in our weariness. Are you weary of . . .

- the world's ways?
- seeking life fulfillment in what you have acquired, achieved, or accomplished?
- competing demands and ever-changing priorities?
- seeking to live in your own strength?
- trying to love by your own power?

Imagine Jesus standing before you right now, gazing intently at you. Maybe your image is of the resurrected Christ, with nail-pierced hands and feet. But as you look closer, you notice that He is standing in a yoke. One side of the yoke is around His neck, while the other is empty. His eyes are full of compassion as He says, "Take My yoke upon you and learn from Me, for I am gentle and lowly in heart, and you will find rest for your souls" (Matt. 11:29).

Listen as you hear Christ speak to you:

- "I consistently love those around you, but I often do so alone— would you come join me?"
- "I am taking initiative to lovingly sacrifice on behalf of those that you encounter in your daily life, but I often do so without you— would you come join Me?"

This is your invitation to join Him, to partner with the One *who is love* in extending His love to others. Picture yourself rising to join Christ in the yoke. Imagine yourself standing alongside this One who is love.

"Lord Jesus, as I meditate on the wonder that I have been called to join You in this divine purpose, and that I can learn from You how to better love those around me, my heart is filled with _____.

I particularly sense Your call on my life to join You in loving these specific people:

_____."

GC2
GREAT COMMANDMENT
COMMISSION

The Unpardonable Sin

31"Therefore I say to you, every sin and blasphemy will be forgiven men, but the blasphemy *against* the Spirit will not be forgiven men. 32Anyone who speaks a word against the Son of Man, it will be forgiven him; but whoever speaks against the Holy Spirit, it will not be forgiven him, either in this age or in the *age* to come.

A Tree Known by Its Fruit

33"Either make the tree good and its fruit good, or else make the tree bad and its fruit bad; for a tree is known by *its* fruit. 34Brood of vipers! How can you, being evil, speak good things? For out of the abundance of the heart the mouth speaks. 35A good man out of the good treasure of his heart[a] brings forth good things, and an evil man out of the evil treasure brings forth evil things. 36But I say to you that for every idle word men may speak, they will give account of it in the day of judgment. 37For by your words you will be justified, and by your words you will be condemned."

The Scribes and Pharisees Ask for a Sign

38Then some of the scribes and Pharisees answered, saying, "Teacher, we want to see a sign from You."

39But He answered and said to them, "An evil and adulterous generation seeks after a sign, and no sign will be given to it except the sign of the prophet Jonah. 40For as Jonah was three days and three nights in the belly of the great fish, so will the Son of Man be three days and three nights in the heart of the earth. 41The men of Nineveh will rise up in the judgment with this generation and condemn it, because they repented at the preaching of Jonah; and indeed a greater than Jonah *is* here. 42The queen of the South will rise up in the judgment with this generation and condemn it, for she came from the ends of the earth to hear the wisdom of Solomon; and indeed a greater than Solomon *is* here.

An Unclean Spirit Returns

43"When an unclean spirit goes out of a man, he goes through dry places, seeking rest, and finds none. 44Then he says, 'I will return to my house from which I came.' And when he comes, he finds *it* empty, swept, and put in order. 45Then he goes and takes with him seven other spirits more wicked than himself, and they enter and dwell there; and the last *state* of that man is worse than the first. So shall it also be with this wicked generation."

Jesus' Mother and Brothers Send for Him

46While He was still talking to the multitudes, behold, His mother and brothers stood outside, seeking to speak with Him. 47Then one said to Him, "Look, Your mother and Your brothers are standing outside, seeking to speak with You."

48But He answered and said to the one who told Him, "Who is My mother and who are My brothers?" 49And He stretched out His hand toward His disciples and said, "Here are My mother and My brothers! 50For whoever does the will of My Father in heaven is My brother and sister and mother."

The Parable of the Sower

13 On the same day Jesus went out of the house and sat by the sea. 2And great multitudes were gathered together to Him, so that He got into a boat and sat; and the whole multitude stood on the shore.

3Then He spoke many things to them in parables, saying: "Behold, a sower went out to sow. 4And as he sowed, some *seed* fell by the wayside; and the birds came and devoured them. 5Some fell on stony places, where they did not have much earth; and they immediately sprang up because they had no depth of earth. 6But when the sun was up they were scorched, and because they had no root they withered away. 7And some fell among thorns, and the thorns sprang up and choked them. 8But others fell on good ground and yielded a crop: some a hundredfold, some sixty, some thirty. 9He who has ears to hear, let him hear!"

The Purpose of Parables

10And the disciples came and said to Him, "Why do You speak to them in parables?"

11He answered and said to them, "Because it

12:35 aNU-Text and M-Text omit *of his heart*.

LEADERSHIP ISSUES

GC2: Comfort for Those Who Hurt

MATTHEW 5:4

Some people think of mourning as something we need to do only when we suffer a major trauma, but we need to mourn any loss we suffer in our day-to-day living. Sometimes our sin brings mourning or sorrow, but often times, it comes from just living in a pain-filled world.

Many times we're not inclined to admit our disappointment or sadness, because we're not convinced that there will be someone there with us to comfort us. To mourn without being comforted compounds the pain. We need loving, trusting relationships with family, friends, and others so we can vulnerably share our hurts. God often wants to involve a family member or friend to help provide the empathy or sympathy we need.

It takes emotion to heal emotions. Comfort is the prescribed solution for hurt and pain, not instruction, advice, pep talks, or lectures. Here's how some unproductive responses might sound:

Person Needing Comfort—"I lost my part-time job last week."

Responses which do not comfort:
   Advice: "If I were you, I'd get a lawyer!"
   Analysis: "The reason you got fired is . . ."
   Criticism: "There must be something you did to cause them to fire you."
   Complaint: "Man, that reminds me of when I lost my summer job."
   Pep-talk: "Everything will be OK." "Get over it!"
   Neglect: "That's tough . . . so let's get together for some basketball?"
   Comfort: "I'm sorry you lost your job. You probably feel really down. I
      want to pray for you. I promise to stand by you during this time."

Becoming a person who *blesses others with God's comfort* will help prepare you for healthy, God-honoring relationships.

GC2
GREAT COMMANDMENT
COMMISSION

has been given to you to know the mysteries of the kingdom of heaven, but to them it has not been given. ¹²For whoever has, to him more will be given, and he will have abundance; but whoever does not have, even what he has will be taken away from him. ¹³Therefore I speak to them in parables, because seeing they do not see, and hearing they do not hear, nor do they understand. ¹⁴And in them the prophecy of Isaiah is fulfilled, which says:

> 'Hearing you will hear and shall not
> understand,
> And seeing you will see and not perceive;
> ¹⁵For the hearts of this people have grown dull.
> Their ears are hard of hearing,
> And their eyes they have closed,
> Lest they should see with their eyes and hear
> with their ears,
> Lest they should understand with their hearts
> and turn,
> So that I should ᵃ heal them.' ᵇ

¹⁶But blessed are your eyes for they see, and your ears for they hear; ¹⁷for assuredly, I say to you that many prophets and righteous men desired to see what you see, and did not see it, and to hear what you hear, and did not hear it.

The Parable of the Sower Explained

¹⁸"Therefore hear the parable of the sower: ¹⁹When anyone hears the word of the kingdom, and does not understand it, then the wicked one comes and snatches away what was sown in his heart. This is he who received seed by the wayside. ²⁰But he who received the seed on stony places, this is he who hears the word and immediately receives it with joy; ²¹yet he has no root in himself, but endures only for a while. For when tribulation or persecution arises because of the word, immediately he stumbles. ²²Now he who received seed among the thorns is he who hears the word, and the cares of this world and the deceitfulness of riches choke the word, and he becomes unfruitful. ²³But he who received seed on the good ground is he who hears the word and understands it, who indeed bears fruit and produces: some a hundredfold, some sixty, some thirty."

The Parable of the Wheat and the Tares

²⁴Another parable He put forth to them, saying: "The kingdom of heaven is like a man who sowed good seed in his field; ²⁵but while men slept, his enemy came and sowed tares among the wheat and went his way. ²⁶But when the grain had sprouted and produced a crop, then the tares also appeared. ²⁷So the servants of the owner came and said to him, 'Sir, did you not sow good seed in your field? How then does it have tares?' ²⁸He said to them, 'An enemy has done this.' The servants said to him, 'Do you want us then to go and gather them up?' ²⁹But he said, 'No, lest while you gather up the tares you also uproot the wheat with them. ³⁰Let both grow together until the harvest, and at the time of harvest I will say to the reapers, "First gather together the tares and bind them in bundles to burn them, but gather the wheat into my barn." ' "

The Parable of the Mustard Seed

³¹Another parable He put forth to them, saying: "The kingdom of heaven is like a mustard seed, which a man took and sowed in his field, ³²which indeed is the least of all the seeds; but when it is grown it is greater than the herbs and becomes a tree, so that the birds of the air come and nest in its branches."

The Parable of the Leaven

³³Another parable He spoke to them: "The kingdom of heaven is like leaven, which a woman took and hid in three measuresᵃ of meal till it was all leavened."

Prophecy and the Parables

³⁴All these things Jesus spoke to the multitude in parables; and without a parable He did not speak to them, ³⁵that it might be fulfilled which was spoken by the prophet, saying:

> "I will open My mouth in parables;
> I will utter things kept secret from the
> foundation of the world."ᵃ

13:15 ᵃNU-Text and M-Text read would. ᵇIsaiah 6:9, 10 **13:33** ᵃGreek sata, approximately two pecks in all **13:35** ᵃPsalm 78:2

LEADERSHIP ISSUES

GC2: Listen for Needs

MATTHEW 12:34

Sometimes people don't mean what they say; but other times, people mean more than what they say. Learn to listen intently, not only to people's words but also to their hearts. According to Matthew 12:34, when we talk, we're exposing our hearts.

If your best friend says, "I can't do anything right," his or her heart may be saying, "I need you to encourage me. I am feeling insecure." If a classmate says, "I need some down time," he or she might be going through a difficult time, needing someone to listen. When a brother or sister says, "I just want to go to my room," that may mean something hurtful happened at school, and they need your comfort.

Listening is the quickest way to see inside the soul of another human and to discern his or her needs.

The Parable of the Tares Explained

³⁶Then Jesus sent the multitude away and went into the house. And His disciples came to Him, saying, "Explain to us the parable of the tares of the field."

³⁷He answered and said to them: "He who sows the good seed is the Son of Man. ³⁸The field is the world, the good seeds are the sons of the kingdom, but the tares are the sons of the wicked *one.* ³⁹The enemy who sowed them is the devil, the harvest is the end of the age, and the reapers are the angels. ⁴⁰Therefore as the tares are gathered and burned in the fire, so it will be at the end of this age. ⁴¹The Son of Man will send out His angels, and they will gather out of His kingdom all things that offend, and those who practice lawlessness, ⁴²and will cast them into the furnace of fire. There will be wailing and gnashing of teeth. ⁴³Then the righteous will shine forth as the sun in the kingdom of their Father. He who has ears to hear, let him hear!

The Parable of the Hidden Treasure

⁴⁴"Again, the kingdom of heaven is like treasure hidden in a field, which a man found and hid; and for joy over it he goes and sells all that he has and buys that field.

The Parable of the Pearl of Great Price

⁴⁵"Again, the kingdom of heaven is like a merchant seeking beautiful pearls, ⁴⁶who, when he had found one pearl of great price, went and sold all that he had and bought it.

The Parable of the Dragnet

⁴⁷"Again, the kingdom of heaven is like a dragnet that was cast into the sea and gathered some of every kind, ⁴⁸which, when it was full, they drew to shore; and they sat down and gathered the good into vessels, but threw the bad away. ⁴⁹So it will be at the end of the age. The angels will come forth, separate the wicked from among the just, ⁵⁰and cast them into the furnace of fire. There will be wailing and gnashing of teeth."

⁵¹Jesus said to them,^a "Have you understood all these things?"

They said to Him, "Yes, Lord."^b

⁵²Then He said to them, "Therefore every scribe instructed concerning^a the kingdom of heaven is like a householder who brings out of his treasure *things* new and old."

Jesus Rejected at Nazareth

⁵³Now it came to pass, when Jesus had finished these parables, that He departed from there. ⁵⁴When He had come to His own country, He taught them in their synagogue, so that they were astonished and said, "Where did this *Man* get this wisdom and *these* mighty works? ⁵⁵Is this not the carpenter's son? Is not His mother called Mary? And His brothers James, Joses,^a Simon, and Judas? ⁵⁶And His sisters, are they not all with us? Where then did this *Man* get all these things?" ⁵⁷So they were offended at Him.

But Jesus said to them, "A prophet is not without honor except in his own country and in his own house." ⁵⁸Now He did not do many mighty works there because of their unbelief.

John the Baptist Beheaded

14 At that time Herod the tetrarch heard the report about Jesus ²and said to his servants, "This is John the Baptist; he is risen from the dead, and therefore these powers are at work in him." ³For Herod had laid hold of John and bound him, and put *him* in prison for the sake of Herodias, his brother Philip's wife. ⁴Because John had said to him, "It is not lawful for you to have her." ⁵And although he wanted to put him to death, he feared the multitude, because they counted him as a prophet.

⁶But when Herod's birthday was celebrated, the daughter of Herodias danced before them and pleased Herod. ⁷Therefore he promised with an oath to give her whatever she might ask.

⁸So she, having been prompted by her mother, said, "Give me John the Baptist's head here on a platter." ⁹And the king was sorry; nevertheless, because of the oaths and because of those who sat with him, he commanded *it* to be given *to her.* ¹⁰So he sent and had John beheaded in prison. ¹¹And his head was brought on a platter and given to the girl, and she brought *it* to her mother. ¹²Then his

13:51 ^aNU-Text omits *Jesus said to them.* ^bNU-Text omits *Lord.*
13:52 ^aOr *for*   **13:55** ^aNU-Text reads *Joseph.*

LEADERSHIP ISSUES

GC2: Listen Carefully

MATTHEW 13:14

Have you ever been talking to someone, really sharing your heart with them, and they seem distracted? They keeping looking around at other people and they have a far-away look in their eyes. Do your friends or family ever say, "Are you listening to me?"

Healthy relationships are based on good listening skills. Listen to only one person at a time and accompany your listening with direct, focused attention. A great strategy for careful listening might include:

- Eliminate distraction—quiet place, private space.
- Focus on one person—no phone calls, text-messaging, or reading while listening.
- Use eye contact.
- Use appropriate interjections/reflections to affirm your understanding.

GREAT COMMANDMENT
COMMISSION

disciples came and took away the body and buried it, and went and told Jesus.

FEEDING THE FIVE THOUSAND

[13]When Jesus heard *it,* He departed from there by boat to a deserted place by Himself. But when the multitudes heard it, they followed Him on foot from the cities. [14]And when Jesus went out He saw a great multitude; and He was moved with compassion for them, and healed their sick. [15]When it was evening, His disciples came to Him, saying, "This is a deserted place, and the hour is already late. Send the multitudes away, that they may go into the villages and buy themselves food."

[16]But Jesus said to them, "They do not need to go away. You give them something to eat."

[17]And they said to Him, "We have here only five loaves and two fish."

[18]He said, "Bring them here to Me." [19]Then He commanded the multitudes to sit down on the grass. And He took the five loaves and the two fish, and looking up to heaven, He blessed and broke and gave the loaves to the disciples; and the disciples gave to the multitudes. [20]So they all ate and were filled, and they took up twelve baskets full of the fragments that remained. [21]Now those who had eaten were about five thousand men, besides women and children.

JESUS WALKS ON THE SEA

[22]Immediately Jesus made His disciples get into the boat and go before Him to the other side, while He sent the multitudes away. [23]And when He had sent the multitudes away, He went up on the mountain by Himself to pray. Now when evening came, He was alone there. [24]But the boat was now in the middle of the sea,[a] tossed by the waves, for the wind was contrary.

[25]Now in the fourth watch of the night Jesus went to them, walking on the sea. [26]And when the disciples saw Him walking on the sea, they were troubled, saying, "It is a ghost!" And they cried out for fear.

[27]But immediately Jesus spoke to them, saying, "Be of good cheer! It is I; do not be afraid."

[28]And Peter answered Him and said, "Lord, if it is You, command me to come to You on the water."

[29]So He said, "Come." And when Peter had come down out of the boat, he walked on the water to go to Jesus. [30]But when he saw that the wind *was* boisterous,[a] he was afraid; and beginning to sink he cried out, saying, "Lord, save me!"

[31]And immediately Jesus stretched out *His* hand and caught him, and said to him, "O you of little faith, why did you doubt?" [32]And when they got into the boat, the wind ceased.

[33]Then those who were in the boat came and[a] worshiped Him, saying, "Truly You are the Son of God."

MANY TOUCH HIM AND ARE MADE WELL

[34]When they had crossed over, they came to the land of[a] Gennesaret. [35]And when the men of that place recognized Him, they sent out into all that surrounding region, brought to Him all who were sick, [36]and begged Him that they might only touch the hem of His garment. And as many as touched *it* were made perfectly well.

DEFILEMENT COMES FROM WITHIN

15 Then the scribes and Pharisees who were from Jerusalem came to Jesus, saying, [2]"Why do Your disciples transgress the tradition of the elders? For they do not wash their hands when they eat bread."

[3]He answered and said to them, "Why do you also transgress the commandment of God because of your tradition? [4]For God commanded, saying, *'Honor your father and your mother';*[a] and, *'He who curses father or mother, let him be put to death.'*[b] [5]But you say, 'Whoever says to his father or mother, "Whatever profit you might have received from me *is* a gift *to God*"— [6]then he need not honor his father or mother.'[a] Thus you have made the commandment[b] of God of no effect by your tradition. [7]Hypocrites! Well did Isaiah prophesy about you, saying:

> [8]*'These people draw near to Me with their mouth,*
> *And*[a] *honor Me with their lips,*

14:24 [a]NU-Text reads *many furlongs away from the land.*
14:30 [a]NU-Text brackets *that* and *boisterous* as disputed.
14:33 [a]NU-Text omits *came and.* **14:34** [a]NU-Text reads *came to land at.* **15:4** [a]Exodus 20:12; Deuteronomy 5:16 [b]Exodus 21:17
15:6 [a]NU-Text omits *or mother.* [b]NU-Text reads *word.* **15:8** [a]NU-Text omits *draw near to Me with their mouth, And.*

But their heart is far from Me.
[9]*And in vain they worship Me,*
Teaching as doctrines the commandments of
men.' "[a]

[10]When He had called the multitude to *Himself*, He said to them, "Hear and understand: [11]Not what goes into the mouth defiles a man; but what comes out of the mouth, this defiles a man."

[12]Then His disciples came and said to Him, "Do You know that the Pharisees were offended when they heard this saying?"

[13]But He answered and said, "Every plant which My heavenly Father has not planted will be uprooted. [14]Let them alone. They are blind leaders of the blind. And if the blind leads the blind, both will fall into a ditch."

[15]Then Peter answered and said to Him, "Explain this parable to us."

[16]So Jesus said, "Are you also still without understanding? [17]Do you not yet understand that whatever enters the mouth goes into the stomach and is eliminated? [18]But those things which proceed out of the mouth come from the heart, and they defile a man. [19]For out of the heart proceed evil thoughts, murders, adulteries, fornications, thefts, false witness, blasphemies. [20]These are *the things* which defile a man, but to eat with unwashed hands does not defile a man."

A Gentile Shows Her Faith

[21]Then Jesus went out from there and departed to the region of Tyre and Sidon. [22]And behold, a woman of Canaan came from that region and cried out to Him, saying, "Have mercy on me, O Lord, Son of David! My daughter is severely demon-possessed."

[23]But He answered her not a word.

And His disciples came and urged Him, saying, "Send her away, for she cries out after us."

[24]But He answered and said, "I was not sent except to the lost sheep of the house of Israel."

[25]Then she came and worshiped Him, saying, "Lord, help me!"

[26]But He answered and said, "It is not good to take the children's bread and throw *it* to the little dogs."

[27]And she said, "Yes, Lord, yet even the little dogs eat the crumbs which fall from their masters' table."

[28]Then Jesus answered and said to her, "O woman, great *is* your faith! Let it be to you as you desire." And her daughter was healed from that very hour.

Jesus Heals Great Multitudes

[29]Jesus departed from there, skirted the Sea of Galilee, and went up on the mountain and sat down there. [30]Then great multitudes came to Him, having with them *the* lame, blind, mute, maimed, and many others; and they laid them down at Jesus' feet, and He healed them. [31]So the multitude marveled when they saw *the* mute speaking, *the* maimed made whole, *the* lame walking, and *the* blind seeing; and they glorified the God of Israel.

Feeding the Four Thousand

[32]Now Jesus called His disciples to *Himself* and said, "I have compassion on the multitude, because they have now continued with Me three days and have nothing to eat. And I do not want to send them away hungry, lest they faint on the way."

[33]Then His disciples said to Him, "Where could we get enough bread in the wilderness to fill such a great multitude?"

[34]Jesus said to them, "How many loaves do you have?"

And they said, "Seven, and a few little fish."

[35]So He commanded the multitude to sit down on the ground. [36]And He took the seven loaves and the fish and gave thanks, broke *them* and gave *them* to His disciples; and the disciples *gave* to the multitude. [37]So they all ate and were filled, and they took up seven large baskets full of the fragments that were left. [38]Now those who ate were four thousand men, besides women and children. [39]And He sent away the multitude, got into the boat, and came to the region of Magdala.[a]

The Pharisees and Sadducees Seek a Sign

16 Then the Pharisees and Sadducees came, and testing Him asked that He would show them a sign from heaven. [2]He answered and said to them, "When it is evening you say, 'It will be

15:9 [a]Isaiah 29:13   **15:39** [a]NU-Text reads *Magadan.*

LEADERSHIP ISSUES

GC2: Christ's Community: Christ Builds His Church

MATTHEW 16:17 *Flesh and blood has not revealed this to you, but My Father who is in heaven.*

In the New Testament, the word "church" is a translation of the Greek word *ekklesia*. It refers in a general sense to any gathering or assembly of people. It was used in a secular sense for a group of people assembling together for public discussion or business.

Key principles relevant to our understanding of how to live as a community of believers—as Christ's church—include the reality that we have been called out from the world and called to live for Him. The word is actually a combination of the words *ek* (which means "out") and *kaleo* (which means to "call" or "summon"). Literally, then, *ekklesia* refers to the "called-out ones."

The first reference to "Christ's church" in the New Testament has great significance for our understanding of following Christ in community with one another. The Gospel of Matthew records a discussion between Jesus and His disciples where Jesus pointedly asks them, "But who do **you** say that I am?" Peter responds, "You are the Christ, the Son of the living God." How did Peter come to know that Christ was the Son of the living God? It was because the Father revealed this critically important truth to him.

We, too, enter into Christ's family by first having Christ revealed to us: "All things have been delivered to Me by My Father, and no one knows who the Son is except the Father, and who the Father is except the Son, and the one to whom the Son wills to reveal Him" (Luke 10:22).

Pause to reflect on how Christ was revealed to you. Was it through the lives of Christ followers around you? Was it through the testimony of Scripture? Was it through a special, personal encounter with Jesus? These three: the saints, the Scripture, and the Son serve to ground us in our transforming walk as Christ-followers.

GC2
GREAT COMMANDMENT
COMMISSION

fair weather, for the sky is red'; [3]and in the morning, 'It will be foul weather today, for the sky is red and threatening.' Hypocrites![a] You know how to discern the face of the sky, but you cannot *discern* the signs of the times. [4]A wicked and adulterous generation seeks after a sign, and no sign shall be given to it except the sign of the prophet[a] Jonah." And He left them and departed.

THE LEAVEN OF THE PHARISEES AND SADDUCEES

[5]Now when His disciples had come to the other side, they had forgotten to take bread. [6]Then Jesus said to them, "Take heed and beware of the leaven of the Pharisees and the Sadducees."

[7]And they reasoned among themselves, saying, "It is because we have taken no bread."

[8]But Jesus, being aware of it, said to them, "O you of little faith, why do you reason among yourselves because you have brought no bread?[a] [9]Do you not yet understand, or remember the five loaves of the five thousand and how many baskets you took up? [10]Nor the seven loaves of the four thousand and how many large baskets you took up? [11]How is it you do not understand that I did not speak to you concerning bread?—

but to beware of the leaven of the Pharisees and Sadducees." [12]Then they understood that He did not tell *them* to beware of the leaven of bread, but of the doctrine of the Pharisees and Sadducees.

PETER CONFESSES JESUS AS THE CHRIST

[13]When Jesus came into the region of Caesarea Philippi, He asked His disciples, saying, "Who do men say that I, the Son of Man, am?"

[14]So they said, "Some *say* John the Baptist, some Elijah, and others Jeremiah or one of the prophets."

[15]He said to them, "But who do you say that I am?"

[16]Simon Peter answered and said, "You are the Christ, the Son of the living God."

[17]Jesus answered and said to him, "Blessed are you, Simon Bar-Jonah, for flesh and blood has not revealed *this* to you, but My Father who is in heaven. [18]And I also say to you that you are Peter, and on this rock I will build My church, and the gates of Hades shall not prevail against it. [19]And I will give you the keys of the kingdom of heaven,

16:3 [a]NU-Text omits *Hypocrites*. **16:4** [a]NU-Text omits *the prophet*.
16:8 [a]NU-Text reads *you have no bread*.

INSIDE *the* INFLUENCERS

SIMON PETER: A Beautiful Disaster

MATTHEW 16:13–20

Peter has gotten a bad rap, which is inconsistent with his true Bible personality. Instead of focusing on the positives in his life, many are content with a caricature of a big mouth with a foot inserted in it. In reality the Bible is made up of many beautiful disasters, who, at one point or another, failed publicly or privately. These "failures" became the patriarchs, kings, apostles and disciples . . . all beautiful disasters.

During Jesus' ministry, people began discussing opinions of who He really was. Jesus asked Peter, "Who do *you* say that I am?" Peter answered correctly when he stated, "You are the Christ, the Son of the living God." Jesus replied that only God could have revealed that to him and then said, ". . . you are Peter *(which means "rock")*, and on this rock I will build My church, and the gates of Hades shall not prevail against it." It is the first time *church* is used in Scripture. The meaning of this passage has been debated for 1500 years, but it is simple. Jesus told Peter, "You get it! You realize that I am the true Son of the Living God, the Messiah. Welcome to the family!" Jesus proclaimed Peter as the first foundational stone of His church. Many more would also build upon it in the generations that followed.

LEADERSHIP ISSUES

GC2: Christ's Community: Yielded Surrender

MATTHEW 16:18   *On this rock I will build My church.*

As Christ is revealed to each of us by the Holy Spirit, we must yield to Him, just as Peter did through his declaration, "You are the Christ." "Whoever calls on the name of the LORD shall be saved" (Rom. 10:13). To become a part of Christ's community, His church is to be born again through the revealing work of the Holy Spirit and then through yielding our life to Jesus by faith.

In response to the Father's revealing and Peter's yielding, Christ declares, "On this rock I will build My church" (Matt. 16:18).

Here, in the context of this revealing–yielding dynamic, we find the first use of *ekklesia* in the New Testament. Notice that Christ refers to these "called-out ones" as "My" church. There may be other gatherings and assemblies of people, but Jesus is identifying the church as **His** called-out ones.

As Christ's church, we have been *called out* from the world and *called to* live for Him:

- "They are not of the world, just as I am not of the world" (John 17:16).
- Our fellowship together is to provide an environment of mutual encouragement and exhortation, that we might "walk worthy of the calling" we have received (Eph. 4:1).

GC2
GREAT COMMANDMENT
COMMISSION

| **THROUGH THE GRID** | *Making Sense of Your World:* *Definition of Church (Matt. 16:13–20)* |

The term "church" originally stood for an assembly or a congregation of people gathered together for a specific purpose. The root idea revolves around a people who have been "called out." The church's primary identity according to the Bible consists of its being the bride of Christ, as well as the body of Christ. With both of these functions, the church is called to submit to Christ and to remain pure for Christ. Accordingly, one devotes one's allegiance to Christ and removes it from anything else. The body of Christ consists of all of the believers who unite under the headship of Christ.

and whatever you bind on earth will be bound in heaven, and whatever you loose on earth will be loosed[a] in heaven."

[20]Then He commanded His disciples that they should tell no one that He was Jesus the Christ.

JESUS PREDICTS HIS DEATH AND RESURRECTION

[21]From that time Jesus began to show to His disciples that He must go to Jerusalem, and suffer many things from the elders and chief priests and scribes, and be killed, and be raised the third day.

[22]Then Peter took Him aside and began to rebuke Him, saying, "Far be it from You, Lord; this shall not happen to You!"

[23]But He turned and said to Peter, "Get behind Me, Satan! You are an offense to Me, for you are not mindful of the things of God, but the things of men."

TAKE UP THE CROSS AND FOLLOW HIM

[24]Then Jesus said to His disciples, "If anyone desires to come after Me, let him deny himself, and take up his cross, and follow Me. [25]For whoever desires to save his life will lose it, but whoever loses his life for My sake will find it. [26]For what profit is it to a man if he gains the whole world, and loses his own soul? Or what will a man give in exchange for his soul? [27]For the Son of Man will come in the glory of His Father with His angels, and then He will reward each according to his works.

[28]Assuredly, I say to you, there are some standing here who shall not taste death till they see the Son of Man coming in His kingdom."

JESUS TRANSFIGURED ON THE MOUNT

17 Now after six days Jesus took Peter, James, and John his brother, led them up on a high mountain by themselves; [2]and He was transfigured before them. His face shone like the sun, and His clothes became as white as the light. [3]And behold, Moses and Elijah appeared to them, talking with Him. [4]Then Peter answered and said to Jesus, "Lord, it is good for us to be here; if You wish, let us[a] make here three tabernacles: one for You, one for Moses, and one for Elijah."

[5]While he was still speaking, behold, a bright cloud overshadowed them; and suddenly a voice came out of the cloud, saying, "This is My beloved Son, in whom I am well pleased. Hear Him!" [6]And when the disciples heard *it*, they fell on their faces and were greatly afraid. [7]But Jesus came and touched them and said, "Arise, and do not be afraid." [8]When they had lifted up their eyes, they saw no one but Jesus only.

[9]Now as they came down from the mountain, Jesus commanded them, saying, "Tell the vision to no one until the Son of Man is risen from the dead."

[10]And His disciples asked Him, saying, "Why then do the scribes say that Elijah must come first?"

[11]Jesus answered and said to them, "Indeed, Elijah is coming first[a] and will restore all things. [12]But I say to you that Elijah has come already, and they did not know him but did to him whatever they wished. Likewise the Son of Man is also about to suffer at their hands." [13]Then the disciples understood that He spoke to them of John the Baptist.

16:19 [a]Or *will have been bound . . . will have been loosed*
17:4 [a]NU-Text reads *I will.* **17:11** [a]NU-Text omits *first.*

LEADERSHIP ISSUES

Cross-Bearers

MATTHEW 16:24

The modern definition of leadership seems, at first glance, to conflict with Christ's message to His disciples to deny self. Yet, for these men, self-denial became a habit, which ultimately led them to be legendary cross-bearers who impacted the lives of many. They wrote and taught throughout the known world of the glorious truths of God, of intimate knowledge of the Savior, and of eternal truths. They were able to accept significant responsibilities as just, righteous, and humble leaders.

Knowing that living for self can be the leader's greatest obstacle, Jesus set out the demand for self-denial as a prerequisite for joining Him in ministry. Leadership preparation continued with the "taking up" of a personal cross. This call goes beyond the "cross bearing" of a learning difference, economic disadvantage, fractured home life, illness, or betrayal by friends. The disciples knew of the wicked works of Roman General Varus—whose hatred for the Jews was so obvious that he had over two thousand crucified. Each victim carried their own crossbeam to a roadside crucifixion site. Jesus used this real life situation to challenge the disciples to be sold-out under His authority, even to the point of death. It is significant that each person carried their own cross, just as each leader must bear his or her cross by denying the sins, attitudes, or habits that stand in the way of being totally submitted to Christ. This is not self-inflicted pain as some of the pagan gods and ritualistic fanatics demanded of their followers, but it is a sacrificial life joyfully lived.

The disciples had already given up family, wealth, and security. It is easy to think, *Isn't that enough?* The Savior set an amazing precedent: "Follow Me." There is no set of measurement as to what is "enough" to accompany the rule of self-denial, because He intended it as a mind-set for all of life.

As an emerging leader, consider breaking the trend. Get "self" out of the way; sell out totally, and become a passionate cross-bearer.

A Boy Is Healed

¹⁴And when they had come to the multitude, a man came to Him, kneeling down to Him and saying, ¹⁵"Lord, have mercy on my son, for he is an epileptic[a] and suffers severely; for he often falls into the fire and often into the water. ¹⁶So I brought him to Your disciples, but they could not cure him."

¹⁷Then Jesus answered and said, "O faithless and perverse generation, how long shall I be with you? How long shall I bear with you? Bring him here to Me." ¹⁸And Jesus rebuked the demon, and it came out of him; and the child was cured from that very hour.

¹⁹Then the disciples came to Jesus privately and said, "Why could we not cast it out?"

²⁰So Jesus said to them, "Because of your unbelief;[a] for assuredly, I say to you, if you have faith as a mustard seed, you will say to this mountain, 'Move from here to there,' and it will move; and nothing will be impossible for you. ²¹However, this kind does not go out except by prayer and fasting."[a]

Jesus Again Predicts His Death and Resurrection

²²Now while they were staying[a] in Galilee, Jesus said to them, "The Son of Man is about to be betrayed into the hands of men, ²³and they will kill Him, and the third day He will be raised up." And they were exceedingly sorrowful.

Peter and His Master Pay Their Taxes

²⁴When they had come to Capernaum,[a] those who received the *temple* tax came to Peter and said, "Does your Teacher not pay the *temple* tax?"

²⁵He said, "Yes."

And when he had come into the house, Jesus anticipated him, saying, "What do you think, Simon? From whom do the kings of the earth take customs or taxes, from their sons or from strangers?"

²⁶Peter said to Him, "From strangers."

Jesus said to him, "Then the sons are free. ²⁷Nevertheless, lest we offend them, go to the sea, cast in a hook, and take the fish that comes up first. And when you have opened its mouth, you will find a piece of money;[a] take that and give it to them for Me and you."

Who Is the Greatest?

18 At that time the disciples came to Jesus, saying, "Who then is greatest in the kingdom of heaven?"

²Then Jesus called a little child to Him, set him in the midst of them, ³and said, "Assuredly, I say to you, unless you are converted and become as little children, you will by no means enter the kingdom of heaven. ⁴Therefore whoever humbles himself as this little child is the greatest in the kingdom of heaven. ⁵Whoever receives one little child like this in My name receives Me.

Jesus Warns of Offenses

⁶"Whoever causes one of these little ones who believe in Me to sin, it would be better for him if a millstone were hung around his neck, and he were drowned in the depth of the sea. ⁷Woe to the world because of offenses! For offenses must come, but woe to that man by whom the offense comes!

⁸"If your hand or foot causes you to sin, cut it off and cast *it* from you. It is better for you to enter into life lame or maimed, rather than having two hands or two feet, to be cast into the everlasting fire. ⁹And if your eye causes you to sin, pluck it out and cast *it* from you. It is better for you to enter into life with one eye, rather than having two eyes, to be cast into hell fire.

The Parable of the Lost Sheep

¹⁰"Take heed that you do not despise one of these little ones, for I say to you that in heaven their angels always see the face of My Father who is in heaven. ¹¹For the Son of Man has come to save that which was lost.[a]

¹²"What do you think? If a man has a hundred sheep, and one of them goes astray, does he not leave the ninety-nine and go to the mountains to seek the one that is straying? ¹³And if he should find it, assuredly, I say to you, he rejoices more over that *sheep* than over the ninety-nine that did not go astray. ¹⁴Even so it is not the will of your Father who is in heaven that one of these little ones should perish.

17:15 [a]Literally *moonstruck* **17:20** [a]NU-Text reads *little faith.* **17:21** [a]NU-Text omits this verse. **17:22** [a]NU-Text reads *gathering together.* **17:24** [a]NU-Text reads *Capharnaum* (here and elsewhere). **17:27** [a]Greek *stater,* the exact amount to pay the temple tax (didrachma) for two **18:11** [a]NU-Text omits this verse.

LEADERSHIP ISSUES

GC2: Basic Training: Hanging Scripture on Love

MATTHEW 18:6 *Whoever causes one of these little ones who believe in Me to sin, it would be better for him if a millstone were hung around his neck.*

Imagine the scene described in this text. You see a man with a millstone hung around his neck. The stone's weight makes it difficult for the man to walk, and you see him stumbling toward the edge of a boat. You are quite certain that if this man falls into the ocean, the weight of the stone will cause his death. With this scene in your mind's eye, you cannot focus only on the millstone's objective meaning, for to do so would be to miss the relational significance.

Consider the absurdity of reacting to the situation described above by simply asking objective questions about the millstone: "How much does that millstone weigh? How old might it be? Where might that millstone come from?" Limiting our response to such questions would be to miss the critical significance of what we were observing. The significant issue is that the millstone is hanging around a person's neck! To miss where the millstone is hanging is to miss its relevance entirely!

Christ's declaration in Matthew 22:40 reveals that we face a similar challenge as we interpret Scripture. "On these two commandments hang all the Law and the Prophets"; the same word "hang" or "depends" is used here, picturing scripture hanging on the commandments to love. We often observe its objective meaning but miss its relational significance: God's Word "hangs" upon loving Him and loving others. We must find the objective meaning of scripture (What does it say? What does it mean? What does it mean to me?) But we must also find its relational significance (How will this scripture lead me into deepened love of the One who wrote it? And how will it lead me to love others around me?).

GC2
GREAT COMMANDMENT
COMMISSION

Dealing with a Sinning Brother

¹⁵"Moreover if your brother sins against you, go and tell him his fault between you and him alone. If he hears you, you have gained your brother. ¹⁶But if he will not hear, take with you one or two more, that *'by the mouth of two or three witnesses every word may be established.'*ᵃ ¹⁷And if he refuses to hear them, tell *it* to the church. But if he refuses even to hear the church, let him be to you like a heathen and a tax collector.

¹⁸"Assuredly, I say to you, whatever you bind on earth will be bound in heaven, and whatever you loose on earth will be loosed in heaven.

¹⁹"Again I sayᵃ to you that if two of you agree on earth concerning anything that they ask, it will be done for them by My Father in heaven. ²⁰For where two or three are gathered together in My name, I am there in the midst of them."

The Parable of the Unforgiving Servant

²¹Then Peter came to Him and said, "Lord, how often shall my brother sin against me, and I forgive him? Up to seven times?"

²²Jesus said to him, "I do not say to you, up to seven times, but up to seventy times seven. ²³Therefore the kingdom of heaven is like a certain king who wanted to settle accounts with his servants. ²⁴And when he had begun to settle accounts, one was brought to him who owed him ten thousand talents. ²⁵But as he was not able to pay, his master commanded that he be sold, with his wife and children and all that he had, and that payment be made. ²⁶The servant therefore fell down before him, saying, 'Master, have patience with me, and I will pay you all.' ²⁷Then the master of that servant was moved with compassion, released him, and forgave him the debt.

²⁸"But that servant went out and found one of his fellow servants who owed him a hundred denarii; and he laid hands on him and took *him* by the throat, saying, 'Pay me what you owe!' ²⁹So his fellow servant fell down at his feetᵃ and begged him, saying, 'Have patience with me, and I will pay you all.'ᵇ ³⁰And he would not, but went and threw him into prison till he should pay the debt. ³¹So when his fellow servants saw what had been done, they were very grieved, and came and told their master all that had been done. ³²Then his master, after he had called him, said to him, 'You wicked servant! I forgave you all that debt because you begged me. ³³Should you not also have had compassion on your fellow servant, just as I had pity on you?' ³⁴And his master was angry, and delivered him to the torturers until he should pay all that was due to him.

³⁵"So My heavenly Father also will do to you if each of you, from his heart, does not forgive his brother his trespasses."ᵃ

18:16 ᵃDeuteronomy 19:15   **18:19** ᵃNU-Text and M-Text read *Again, assuredly, I say.*   **18:29** ᵃNU-Text omits *at his feet.* ᵇNU-Text and M-Text omit *all.*   **18:35** ᵃNU-Text omits *his trespasses.*

THROUGH THE GRID

Discover God: God Expects Us to Extend Mercy

MATTHEW 18:21, 22   *Then Peter came to Him and said, "Lord, how often shall my brother sin against me, and I forgive him? Up to seven times?" Jesus said to him, "I do not say to you, up to seven times, but up to seventy times seven."*

As recipients of God's mercy, we should serve as examples of God's love by extending the mercy we have received to others. This serves as a powerful testament to how real God's mercy is in our own lives. We can be merciful toward others by forgiving people, by helping those who are in need, by serving others without regard to our own needs, and by loving others even when they least deserve it. As we follow the example of God, we will extend mercy to others and love others unconditionally, with the help of the Holy Spirit.

Marriage and Divorce

19 Now it came to pass, when Jesus had finished these sayings, *that* He departed from Galilee and came to the region of Judea beyond the Jordan. [2]And great multitudes followed Him, and He healed them there.

[3]The Pharisees also came to Him, testing Him, and saying to Him, "Is it lawful for a man to divorce his wife for *just* any reason?"

[4]And He answered and said to them, "Have you not read that He who made[a] *them* at the beginning *'made them male and female,'* [b] [5]and said, *'For this reason a man shall leave his father and mother and be joined to his wife, and the two shall become one flesh'?*[a] [6]So then, they are no longer two but one flesh. Therefore what God has joined together, let not man separate."

[7]They said to Him, "Why then did Moses command to give a certificate of divorce, and to put her away?"

[8]He said to them, "Moses, because of the hardness of your hearts, permitted you to divorce your wives, but from the beginning it was not so. [9]And I say to you, whoever divorces his wife, except for sexual immorality,[a] and marries another, commits adultery; and whoever marries her who is divorced commits adultery."

[10]His disciples said to Him, "If such is the case of the man with *his* wife, it is better not to marry."

Jesus Teaches on Celibacy

[11]But He said to them, "All cannot accept this saying, but only *those* to whom it has been given: [12]For there are eunuchs who were born thus from *their* mother's womb, and there are eunuchs who were made eunuchs by men, and there are eunuchs who have made themselves eunuchs for the kingdom of heaven's sake. He who is able to accept *it,* let him accept *it."*

Jesus Blesses Little Children

[13]Then little children were brought to Him that He might put *His* hands on them and pray, but the disciples rebuked them. [14]But Jesus said, "Let the little children come to Me, and do not forbid them; for of such is the kingdom of heaven." [15]And He laid *His* hands on them and departed from there.

Jesus Counsels the Rich Young Ruler

[16]Now behold, one came and said to Him, "Good[a] Teacher, what good thing shall I do that I may have eternal life?"

[17]So He said to him, "Why do you call Me good?[a] No one *is* good but One, *that is,* God.[b] But if you want to enter into life, keep the commandments."

[18]He said to Him, "Which ones?"

Jesus said, *" 'You shall not murder,' 'You shall not commit adultery,' 'You shall not steal,' 'You shall not bear false witness,'* [19]*'Honor your father and your mother,'*[a] and, *'You shall love your neighbor as yourself.' "*[b]

[20]The young man said to Him, "All these things I have kept from my youth.[a] What do I still lack?"

[21]Jesus said to him, "If you want to be perfect, go, sell what you have and give to the poor, and you will have treasure in heaven; and come, follow Me."

[22]But when the young man heard that saying, he went away sorrowful, for he had great possessions.

With God All Things Are Possible

[23]Then Jesus said to His disciples, "Assuredly, I say to you that it is hard for a rich man to enter the kingdom of heaven. [24]And again I say to you, it is easier for a camel to go through the eye of a needle than for a rich man to enter the kingdom of God."

[25]When His disciples heard *it,* they were greatly astonished, saying, "Who then can be saved?"

[26]But Jesus looked at *them* and said to them, "With men this is impossible, but with God all things are possible."

[27]Then Peter answered and said to Him, "See, we have left all and followed You. Therefore what shall we have?"

[28]So Jesus said to them, "Assuredly I say to you, that in the regeneration, when the Son of

---

19:4 [a]NU-Text reads *created.* [b]Genesis 1:27; 5:2   **19:5** [a]Genesis 2:24   **19:9** [a]Or *fornication*   **19:16** [a]NU-Text omits *Good.*   **19:17** [a]NU-Text reads *Why do you ask Me about what is good?* [b]NU-Text reads *There is One who is good.*   **19:19** [a]Exodus 20:12–16; Deuteronomy 5:16–20 [b]Leviticus 19:18   **19:20** [a]NU-Text omits *from my youth.*

Man sits on the throne of His glory, you who have followed Me will also sit on twelve thrones, judging the twelve tribes of Israel. [29]And everyone who has left houses or brothers or sisters or father or mother or wife[a] or children or lands, for My name's sake, shall receive a hundredfold, and inherit eternal life. [30]But many *who are* first will be last, and the last first.

The Parable of the Workers in the Vineyard

20 "For the kingdom of heaven is like a landowner who went out early in the morning to hire laborers for his vineyard. [2]Now when he had agreed with the laborers for a denarius a day, he sent them into his vineyard. [3]And he went out about the third hour and saw others standing idle in the marketplace, [4]and said to them, 'You also go into the vineyard, and whatever is right I will give you.' So they went. [5]Again he went out about the sixth and the ninth hour, and did likewise. [6]And about the eleventh hour he went out and found others standing idle,[a] and said to them, 'Why have you been standing here idle all day?' [7]They said to him, 'Because no one hired us.' He said to them, 'You also go into the vineyard, and whatever is right you will receive.'[a]

[8]"So when evening had come, the owner of the vineyard said to his steward, 'Call the laborers and give them *their* wages, beginning with the last to the first.' [9]And when those came who *were hired* about the eleventh hour, they each received a denarius. [10]But when the first came, they supposed that they would receive more; and they likewise received each a denarius. [11]And when they had received *it,* they complained against the landowner, [12]saying, 'These last *men* have worked *only* one hour, and you made them equal to us who have borne the burden and the heat of the day.' [13]But he answered one of them and said, 'Friend, I am doing you no wrong. Did you not agree with me for a denarius? [14]Take *what is* yours and go your way. I wish to give to this last man *the same* as to you. [15]Is it not lawful for me to do what I wish with my own things? Or is your eye evil because I am good?' [16]So the last will be first, and the first last. For many are called, but few chosen."[a]

Jesus a Third Time Predicts His Death and Resurrection

[17]Now Jesus, going up to Jerusalem, took the twelve disciples aside on the road and said to them, [18]"Behold, we are going up to Jerusalem, and the Son of Man will be betrayed to the chief priests and to the scribes; and they will condemn Him to death, [19]and deliver Him to the Gentiles to mock and to scourge and to crucify. And the third day He will rise again."

Greatness Is Serving

[20]Then the mother of Zebedee's sons came to Him with her sons, kneeling down and asking something from Him.

[21]And He said to her, "What do you wish?"

She said to Him, "Grant that these two sons of mine may sit, one on Your right hand and the other on the left, in Your kingdom."

[22]But Jesus answered and said, "You do not know what you ask. Are you able to drink the cup that I am about to drink, and be baptized with the baptism that I am baptized with?"[a]

They said to Him, "We are able."

[23]So He said to them, "You will indeed drink My cup, and be baptized with the baptism that I am baptized with;[a] but to sit on My right hand and on My left is not Mine to give, but *it is for those* for whom it is prepared by My Father."

[24]And when the ten heard *it,* they were greatly displeased with the two brothers. [25]But Jesus called them to *Himself* and said, "You know that the rulers of the Gentiles lord it over them, and those who are great exercise authority over them. [26]Yet it shall not be so among you; but whoever desires to become great among you, let him be your servant. [27]And whoever desires to be first among you, let him be your slave— [28]just as the Son of Man did not come to be served, but to serve, and to give His life a ransom for many."

Two Blind Men Receive Their Sight

[29]Now as they went out of Jericho, a great multitude followed Him. [30]And behold, two blind

---

19:29 [a]NU-Text omits *or wife.*   **20:6** [a]NU-Text omits *idle.*
20:7 [a]NU-Text omits the last clause of this verse.   **20:16** [a]NU-Text omits the last sentence of this verse.   **20:22** [a]NU-Text omits *and be baptized with the baptism that I am baptized with.*   **20:23** [a]NU-Text omits *and be baptized with the baptism that I am baptized with.*

men sitting by the road, when they heard that Jesus was passing by, cried out, saying, "Have mercy on us, O Lord, Son of David!"

³¹Then the multitude warned them that they should be quiet; but they cried out all the more, saying, "Have mercy on us, O Lord, Son of David!"

³²So Jesus stood still and called them, and said, "What do you want Me to do for you?"

³³They said to Him, "Lord, that our eyes may be opened." ³⁴So Jesus had compassion and touched their eyes. And immediately their eyes received sight, and they followed Him.

The Triumphal Entry

21 Now when they drew near Jerusalem, and came to Bethphage,ᵃ at the Mount of Olives, then Jesus sent two disciples, ²saying to them, "Go into the village opposite you, and immediately you will find a donkey tied, and a colt with her. Loose *them* and bring *them* to Me. ³And if anyone says anything to you, you shall say, 'The Lord has need of them,' and immediately he will send them."

⁴Allᵃ this was done that it might be fulfilled which was spoken by the prophet, saying:

⁵*"Tell the daughter of Zion,*
'Behold, your King is coming to you,
Lowly, and sitting on a donkey,
*A colt, the foal of a donkey.' "*ᵃ

⁶So the disciples went and did as Jesus commanded them. ⁷They brought the donkey and the colt, laid their clothes on them, and set *Him*ᵃ on them. ⁸And a very great multitude spread their clothes on the road; others cut down branches from the trees and spread *them* on the road. ⁹Then the multitudes who went before and those who followed cried out, saying:

"Hosanna to the Son of David!
'Blessed is He who comes in the name of the
*Lord!'*ᵃ
Hosanna in the highest!"

¹⁰And when He had come into Jerusalem, all the city was moved, saying, "Who is this?"

¹¹So the multitudes said, "This is Jesus, the prophet from Nazareth of Galilee."

Jesus Cleanses the Temple

¹²Then Jesus went into the temple of Godᵃ and drove out all those who bought and sold in the temple, and overturned the tables of the money changers and the seats of those who sold doves. ¹³And He said to them, "It is written, *'My house shall be called a house of prayer,'*ᵃ but you have made it a *'den of thieves.' "*ᵇ

¹⁴Then *the* blind and *the* lame came to Him in the temple, and He healed them. ¹⁵But when the chief priests and scribes saw the wonderful things that He did, and the children crying out in the temple and saying, "Hosanna to the Son of David!" they were indignant ¹⁶and said to Him, "Do You hear what these are saying?"

And Jesus said to them, "Yes. Have you never read,

'Out of the mouth of babes and nursing
infants
You have perfected praise'?" ᵃ

¹⁷Then He left them and went out of the city to Bethany, and He lodged there.

The Fig Tree Withered

¹⁸Now in the morning, as He returned to the city, He was hungry. ¹⁹And seeing a fig tree by the road, He came to it and found nothing on it but leaves, and said to it, "Let no fruit grow on you ever again." Immediately the fig tree withered away.

The Lesson of the Withered Fig Tree

²⁰And when the disciples saw *it,* they marveled, saying, "How did the fig tree wither away so soon?"

²¹So Jesus answered and said to them, "Assuredly, I say to you, if you have faith and do not doubt, you will not only do what was done to the fig tree, but also if you say to this mountain, 'Be removed and be cast into the sea,' it will be done. ²²And whatever things you ask in prayer, believing, you will receive."

21:1 ᵃM-Text reads *Bethsphage.* **21:4** ᵃNU-Text omits *All.* **21:5** ᵃZechariah 9:9 **21:7** ᵃNU-Text reads *and He sat.* **21:9** ᵃPsalm 118:26 **21:12** ᵃNU-Text omits *of God.* **21:13** ᵃIsaiah 56:7 ᵇJeremiah 7:11 **21:16** ᵃPsalm 8:2

JESUS' AUTHORITY QUESTIONED

23Now when He came into the temple, the chief priests and the elders of the people confronted Him as He was teaching, and said, "By what authority are You doing these things? And who gave You this authority?"

24But Jesus answered and said to them, "I also will ask you one thing, which if you tell Me, I likewise will tell you by what authority I do these things: 25The baptism of John—where was it from? From heaven or from men?"

And they reasoned among themselves, saying, "If we say, 'From heaven,' He will say to us, 'Why then did you not believe him?' 26But if we say, 'From men,' we fear the multitude, for all count John as a prophet." 27So they answered Jesus and said, "We do not know."

And He said to them, "Neither will I tell you by what authority I do these things.

THE PARABLE OF THE TWO SONS

28"But what do you think? A man had two sons, and he came to the first and said, 'Son, go, work today in my vineyard.' 29He answered and said, 'I will not,' but afterward he regretted it and went. 30Then he came to the second and said likewise. And he answered and said, 'I go, sir,' but he did not go. 31Which of the two did the will of his father?"

They said to Him, "The first."

Jesus said to them, "Assuredly, I say to you that tax collectors and harlots enter the kingdom of God before you. 32For John came to you in the way of righteousness, and you did not believe him; but tax collectors and harlots believed him; and when you saw it, you did not afterward relent and believe him.

THE PARABLE OF THE WICKED VINEDRESSERS

33"Hear another parable: There was a certain landowner who planted a vineyard and set a hedge around it, dug a winepress in it and built a tower. And he leased it to vinedressers and went into a far country. 34Now when vintage-time drew near, he sent his servants to the vinedressers, that they might receive its fruit. 35And the vinedressers took his servants, beat one, killed one, and stoned another. 36Again he sent other servants,

more than the first, and they did likewise to them. 37Then last of all he sent his son to them, saying, 'They will respect my son.' 38But when the vinedressers saw the son, they said among themselves, 'This is the heir. Come, let us kill him and seize his inheritance.' 39So they took him and cast him out of the vineyard and killed him.

40"Therefore, when the owner of the vineyard comes, what will he do to those vinedressers?"

41They said to Him, "He will destroy those wicked men miserably, and lease his vineyard to other vinedressers who will render to him the fruits in their seasons."

42Jesus said to them, "Have you never read in the Scriptures:

> 'The stone which the builders rejected
> Has become the chief cornerstone.
> This was the LORD's doing,
> And it is marvelous in our eyes'?a

43"Therefore I say to you, the kingdom of God will be taken from you and given to a nation bearing the fruits of it. 44And whoever falls on this stone will be broken; but on whomever it falls, it will grind him to powder."

45Now when the chief priests and Pharisees heard His parables, they perceived that He was speaking of them. 46But when they sought to lay hands on Him, they feared the multitudes, because they took Him for a prophet.

THE PARABLE OF THE WEDDING FEAST

22 And Jesus answered and spoke to them again by parables and said: 2"The kingdom of heaven is like a certain king who arranged a marriage for his son, 3and sent out his servants to call those who were invited to the wedding; and they were not willing to come. 4Again, he sent out other servants, saying, 'Tell those who are invited, "See, I have prepared my dinner; my oxen and fatted cattle are killed, and all things are ready. Come to the wedding." ' 5But they made light of it and went their ways, one to his own farm, another to his business. 6And the rest seized his servants, treated them spitefully, and killed them. 7But

21:42 aPsalm 118:22, 23

LEADERSHIP ISSUES

Bring the Subject Back to God

MATTHEW 22:15–22

Jesus had only one agenda—pointing people toward God. In the process, He employed stories, teaching, miracles, acts of compassion—and sometimes a hammer. After all, Jesus was a carpenter. Matthew 22:15–22 is one of those "hammer" moments.

The religious leaders had come to Jesus and asked Him a question with the intent of trying to "trap" Him. Our first clue that Jesus was about to pull out His hammer is when the text says, "But Jesus perceived their wickedness." If you have ever been confronted by people with evil motives who are trying to "trap" you, then pay attention to Jesus' response.

What were the first words out of Jesus' mouth? "Why do you test Me, you hypocrites!" He pulled out His BIG hammer. He called their bluff in no uncertain terms and seized control. In this age of "tolerance," we would do well to consider Jesus' example.

Keep in mind His ultimate goal was not to humiliate His adversaries, even though that happened. His agenda was always to point people toward God. He simply saw the confrontation as an opportunity.

After answering their question, "Render therefore to Caesar the things that are Caesar's," He closed with the phrase, "and to God to the things that are God's." He always brought the subject back to God.

In this age of "tolerance," sometimes you may find it necessary to pull out your hammer, but make sure your ultimate goal is never to lash out at your adversary. Always drive people back toward God.

when the king heard *about it,* he was furious. And he sent out his armies, destroyed those murderers, and burned up their city. [8]Then he said to his servants, 'The wedding is ready, but those who were invited were not worthy. [9]Therefore go into the highways, and as many as you find, invite to the wedding.' [10]So those servants went out into the highways and gathered together all whom they found, both bad and good. And the wedding *hall* was filled with guests.

[11]"But when the king came in to see the guests, he saw a man there who did not have on a wedding garment. [12]So he said to him, 'Friend, how did you come in here without a wedding garment?' And he was speechless. [13]Then the king said to the servants, 'Bind him hand and foot, take him away, and[a] cast *him* into outer darkness; there will be weeping and gnashing of teeth.'

[14]"For many are called, but few *are* chosen."

The Pharisees: Is It Lawful to Pay Taxes to Caesar?

[15]Then the Pharisees went and plotted how they might entangle Him in *His* talk. [16]And they sent to Him their disciples with the Herodians, saying, "Teacher, we know that You are true, and teach the way of God in truth; nor do You care about anyone, for You do not regard the person of men. [17]Tell us, therefore, what do You think? Is it lawful to pay taxes to Caesar, or not?"

[18]But Jesus perceived their wickedness, and said, "Why do you test Me, *you* hypocrites? [19]Show Me the tax money."

So they brought Him a denarius.

[20]And He said to them, "Whose image and inscription *is* this?"

[21]They said to Him, "Caesar's."

And He said to them, "Render therefore to Caesar the things that are Caesar's, and to God the things that are God's." [22]When they had heard *these words,* they marveled, and left Him and went their way.

The Sadducees: What About the Resurrection?

[23]The same day the Sadducees, who say there is no resurrection, came to Him and asked Him, [24]saying: "Teacher, Moses said that if a man dies, having no children, his brother shall marry his wife and raise up offspring for his brother. [25]Now there were with us seven brothers. The first died

after he had married, and having no offspring, left his wife to his brother. [26]Likewise the second also, and the third, even to the seventh. [27]Last of all the woman died also. [28]Therefore, in the resurrection, whose wife of the seven will she be? For they all had her."

[29]Jesus answered and said to them, "You are mistaken, not knowing the Scriptures nor the power of God. [30]For in the resurrection they neither marry nor are given in marriage, but are like angels of God[a] in heaven. [31]But concerning the resurrection of the dead, have you not read what was spoken to you by God, saying, [32]*I am the God of Abraham, the God of Isaac, and the God of Jacob'?*[a] God is not the God of the dead, but of the living." [33]And when the multitudes heard *this,* they were astonished at His teaching.

The Scribes: Which Is the First Commandment of All?

[34]But when the Pharisees heard that He had silenced the Sadducees, they gathered together. [35]Then one of them, a lawyer, asked *Him a question,* testing Him, and saying, [36]"Teacher, which *is* the great commandment in the law?"

[37]Jesus said to him, " *'You shall love the Lord your God with all your heart, with all your soul, and with all your mind.'*[a] [38]This is *the* first and great commandment. [39]And *the* second *is* like it: *'You shall love your neighbor as yourself.'*[a] [40]On these two commandments hang all the Law and the Prophets."

Jesus: How Can David Call His Descendant Lord?

[41]While the Pharisees were gathered together, Jesus asked them, [42]saying, "What do you think about the Christ? Whose Son is He?"

They said to Him, "*The Son* of David."

[43]He said to them, "How then does David in the Spirit call Him *'Lord,'* saying:

[44]*'The Lord said to my Lord,*
 "Sit at My right hand,
  Till I make Your enemies Your footstool" '?[a]

[45]If David then calls Him *'Lord,'* how is He his Son?" [46]And no one was able to answer Him a

LEADERSHIP ISSUES

GC2: Basic Training: Loving the Lord Our God

MATTHEW 22:37–39 *Jesus said to him, " 'You shall love the LORD your God with all your heart, with all your soul, and with all your mind.' This is the first and great commandment. And the second is like it: 'You shall love your neighbor as yourself.' "*

In order to truly love the Lord with all our heart, soul, mind, and strength, we must first know Him. Although the disciples had been with Jesus day and night for three years, their behavior during Christ's final hours on earth seemed to call into question whether they really knew Him (John 14:9).

As faithful followers of Jesus, we must be sure to grasp who He really is.

Jesus consistently demonstrated that He is God—not only by His miraculous acts and fulfilled prophecies, but also by His words. For example, during that last night with His disciples, Jesus said, "A new commandment I give to you, that you love one another; as I have loved you, that you also love one another" (John 13:34).

The fact that He referred to these words as a "commandment" was revolutionary. Jewish leaders would have issued laws, rituals, and rules, but never "commandments." To claim the power to issue commands was to claim to be God! The Jewish authorities had Jesus put to death primarily because they refused to believe what He consistently tried to demonstrate, through word and deed—that He was and is God. Jesus is literally saying that the God who gave you the Ten Commandments is now giving you number eleven! It's this "real" God whom we must love wholeheartedly, and out of such love will flow His love through us for others.

GC2
GREAT COMMANDMENT
COMMISSION

LEADERSHIP ISSUES

GC2: Hanging Scripture on Love

MATTHEW 22:40

We can say with certainty that part of the early church's success was due to its emphasis on the application of truth. They taught that the truths of God's Word were to be experienced in our attitudes and actions.

The apostle John admonished, "My little children, let us not love in word or in tongue but in deed and in truth" (1 John 3:18). Truth was to be both believed and lived out. The members of the early church learned to demonstrate this identity of love as they became passionately committed to loving Jesus and one another. They lived out Christ's prediction from the Upper Room: "By this all will know that you are My disciples, if you have love for one another" (John 13:35). Paul affirmed this relational purpose of God's Word when he wrote to Timothy, "The purpose of the commandment is love from a pure heart" (1 Tim. 1:5). Finally, Peter affirmed the saints of the 1st century because they had purified themselves by obeying the truth. They believed, behaved rightly, and developed a sincere of the brethren; then Peter encouraged them to do more: "Love one another fervently with a pure heart" (1 Pet. 1:22).

Followers of Jesus must likewise take a firm stand for the truth. We must proclaim that Scripture is the authoritative, absolute truth of God. We must go further because we can have Bible-believing, Bible-teaching churches which are still irrelevant in ministering to the needs of people. If we misapply God's Word by appealing only to the rational mind, hearers of the Word may leave unaffected, pride-filled, or even "turned off" by the truths we hold so dear. When we experience scriptural truth in our relationships with God and others, we put God's love into action. That is what a hurting world needs to see—a model of God's Word in action, a body of believers experiencing God's Book and loving God and one another. That is relevance.

GC2
GREAT COMMANDMENT
COMMISSION

word, nor from that day on did anyone dare question Him anymore.

WOE TO THE SCRIBES AND PHARISEES

23 Then Jesus spoke to the multitudes and to His disciples, [2]saying: "The scribes and the Pharisees sit in Moses' seat. [3]Therefore whatever they tell you to observe,[a] *that* observe and do, but do not do according to their works; for they say, and do not do. [4]For they bind heavy burdens, hard to bear, and lay *them* on men's shoulders; but they *themselves* will not move them with one of their fingers. [5]But all their works they do to be seen by men. They make their phylacteries broad and enlarge the borders of their garments. [6]They love the best places at feasts, the best seats in the synagogues, [7]greetings in the marketplaces, and to be called by men, 'Rabbi, Rabbi.' [8]But you, do not be called 'Rabbi'; for One is your Teacher, the Christ,[a] and you are all brethren. [9]Do not call anyone on earth your father; for One is your Father, He who is in heaven. [10]And do not be called teachers; for One is your Teacher, the Christ. [11]But he who is greatest among you shall be your servant. [12]And whoever exalts himself will be humbled, and he who humbles himself will be exalted.

[13]"But woe to you, scribes and Pharisees, hypocrites! For you shut up the kingdom of heaven against men; for you neither go in *yourselves*, nor do you allow those who are entering to go in. [14]Woe to you, scribes and Pharisees, hypocrites! For you devour widows' houses, and for a pretense make long prayers. Therefore you will receive greater condemnation.[a]

[15]"Woe to you, scribes and Pharisees, hypocrites! For you travel land and sea to win one proselyte, and when he is won, you make him twice as much a son of hell as yourselves.

[16]"Woe to you, blind guides, who say, 'Whoever swears by the temple, it is nothing; but whoever swears by the gold of the temple, he is obliged *to perform it*.' [17]Fools and blind! For which is greater, the gold or the temple that sanctifies[a] the gold? [18]And, 'Whoever swears by the altar, it is nothing; but whoever swears by the gift that is on it, he is obliged *to perform it*.' [19]Fools and blind! For which is greater, the gift or the altar that sanctifies the gift? [20]Therefore he who swears by the altar, swears by it and by all things on it. [21]He who swears by the temple, swears by it and by Him who dwells[a] in it. [22]And he who swears by heaven, swears by the throne of God and by Him who sits on it.

[23]"Woe to you, scribes and Pharisees, hypocrites! For you pay tithe of mint and anise and cummin, and have neglected the weightier *matters* of the law: justice and mercy and faith. These you ought to have done, without leaving the others undone. [24]Blind guides, who strain out a gnat and swallow a camel!

[25]"Woe to you, scribes and Pharisees, hypocrites! For you cleanse the outside of the cup and dish, but inside they are full of extortion and self-indulgence.[a] [26]Blind Pharisee, first cleanse the inside of the cup and dish, that the outside of them may be clean also.

[27]"Woe to you, scribes and Pharisees, hypocrites! For you are like whitewashed tombs which indeed appear beautiful outwardly, but inside are full of dead *men's* bones and all uncleanness. [28]Even so you also outwardly appear righteous to men, but inside you are full of hypocrisy and lawlessness.

[29]"Woe to you, scribes and Pharisees, hypocrites! Because you build the tombs of the prophets and adorn the monuments of the righteous, [30]and say, 'If we had lived in the days of our fathers, we would not have been partakers with them in the blood of the prophets.'

[31]"Therefore you are witnesses against yourselves that you are sons of those who murdered the prophets. [32]Fill up, then, the measure of your fathers' *guilt*. [33]Serpents, brood of vipers! How can you escape the condemnation of hell? [34]Therefore, indeed, I send you prophets, wise men, and scribes: *some* of them you will kill and crucify, and *some* of them you will scourge in your synagogues and persecute from city to city, [35]that on you may come all the righteous blood shed on the earth, from the blood of righteous Abel to the blood of Zechariah, son of Berechiah, whom you murdered between the temple and the altar. [36]Assuredly, I say to you, all these things will come upon this generation.

23:3 [a]NU-Text omits *to observe.*   **23:8** [a]NU-Text omits *the Christ.*
23:14 [a]NU-Text omits this verse.   **23:17** [a]NU-Text reads *sanctified.*
23:21 [a]M-Text reads *dwelt.*   **23:25** [a]M-Text reads *unrighteousness.*

JESUS LAMENTS OVER JERUSALEM

37 "O Jerusalem, Jerusalem, the one who kills the prophets and stones those who are sent to her! How often I wanted to gather your children together, as a hen gathers her chicks under *her* wings, but you were not willing! 38 See! Your house is left to you desolate; 39 for I say to you, you shall see Me no more till you say, *'Blessed is He who comes in the name of the Lord!' "* [a]

JESUS PREDICTS THE DESTRUCTION OF THE TEMPLE

24 Then Jesus went out and departed from the temple, and His disciples came up to show Him the buildings of the temple. 2 And Jesus said to them, "Do you not see all these things? Assuredly, I say to you, not *one* stone shall be left here upon another, that shall not be thrown down."

THE SIGNS OF THE TIMES AND THE END OF THE AGE

3 Now as He sat on the Mount of Olives, the disciples came to Him privately, saying, "Tell us, when will these things be? And what *will be* the sign of Your coming, and of the end of the age?"

4 And Jesus answered and said to them: "Take heed that no one deceives you. 5 For many will come in My name, saying, 'I am the Christ,' and will deceive many. 6 And you will hear of wars and rumors of wars. See that you are not troubled; for all[a] *these things* must come to pass, but the end is not yet. 7 For nation will rise against nation, and kingdom against kingdom. And there will be famines, pestilences,[a] and earthquakes in various places. 8 All these *are* the beginning of sorrows.

9 "Then they will deliver you up to tribulation and kill you, and you will be hated by all nations for My name's sake. 10 And then many will be offended, will betray one another, and will hate one another. 11 Then many false prophets will rise up and deceive many. 12 And because lawlessness will abound, the love of many will grow cold. 13 But he who endures to the end shall be saved. 14 And this gospel of the kingdom will be preached in all the world as a witness to all the nations, and then the end will come.

THE GREAT TRIBULATION

15 "Therefore when you see the *'abomination of desolation,'* [a] spoken of by Daniel the prophet, standing in the holy place" (whoever reads, let him understand), 16 "then let those who are in Judea flee to the mountains. 17 Let him who is on the housetop not go down to take anything out of his house. 18 And let him who is in the field not go back to get his clothes. 19 But woe to those who are pregnant and to those who are nursing babies in those days! 20 And pray that your flight may not be in winter or on the Sabbath. 21 For then there will be great tribulation, such as has not been since the beginning of the world until this time, no, nor ever shall be. 22 And unless those days were shortened, no flesh would be saved; but for the elect's sake those days will be shortened.

23 "Then if anyone says to you, 'Look, here *is* the Christ!' or 'There!' do not believe *it*. 24 For false christs and false prophets will rise and show great signs and wonders to deceive, if possible, even the elect. 25 See, I have told you beforehand.

26 "Therefore if they say to you, 'Look, He is in the desert!' do not go out; or 'Look, *He is* in the inner rooms!' do not believe *it*. 27 For as the lightning comes from the east and flashes to the west, so also will the coming of the Son of Man be. 28 For wherever the carcass is, there the eagles will be gathered together.

THE COMING OF THE SON OF MAN

29 "Immediately after the tribulation of those days the sun will be darkened, and the moon will not give its light; the stars will fall from heaven, and the powers of the heavens will be shaken. 30 Then the sign of the Son of Man will appear in heaven, and then all the tribes of the earth will mourn, and they will see the Son of Man coming on the clouds of heaven with power and great glory. 31 And He will send His angels with a great sound of a trumpet, and they will gather together His elect from the four winds, from one end of heaven to the other.

THE PARABLE OF THE FIG TREE

32 "Now learn this parable from the fig tree: When its branch has already become tender and puts forth leaves, you know that summer *is* near. 33 So you also, when you see all these things, know that it[a] is near—at the doors! 34 Assuredly, I say to

23:39 [a] Psalm 118:26   24:6 [a] NU-Text omits *all.*   24:7 [a] NU-Text omits *pestilences.*   24:15 [a] Daniel 11:31; 12:11   24:33 [a] Or *He* you, this generation will by no means pass away till all these things take place. [35]Heaven and earth will pass away, but My words will by no means pass away.

No One Knows the Day or Hour

[36]"But of that day and hour no one knows, not even the angels of heaven,[a] but My Father only. [37]But as the days of Noah *were,* so also will the coming of the Son of Man be. [38]For as in the days before the flood, they were eating and drinking, marrying and giving in marriage, until the day that Noah entered the ark, [39]and did not know until the flood came and took them all away, so also will the coming of the Son of Man be. [40]Then two *men* will be in the field: one will be taken and the other left. [41]Two *women will be* grinding at the mill: one will be taken and the other left. [42]Watch therefore, for you do not know what hour[a] your Lord is coming. [43]But know this, that if the master of the house had known what hour the thief would come, he would have watched and not allowed his house to be broken into. [44]Therefore you also be ready, for the Son of Man is coming at an hour you do not expect.

The Faithful Servant and the Evil Servant

[45]"Who then is a faithful and wise servant, whom his master made ruler over his household, to give them food in due season? [46]Blessed *is* that servant whom his master, when he comes, will find so doing. [47]Assuredly, I say to you that he will make him ruler over all his goods. [48]But if that evil servant says in his heart, 'My master is delaying his coming,'[a] [49]and begins to beat *his* fellow servants, and to eat and drink with the drunkards, [50]the master of that servant will come on a day when he is not looking for *him* and at an hour that he is not aware of, [51]and will cut him in two and appoint *him* his portion with the hypocrites. There shall be weeping and gnashing of teeth.

The Parable of the Wise and Foolish Virgins

25 "Then the kingdom of heaven shall be likened to ten virgins who took their lamps and went out to meet the bridegroom. [2]Now five of them were wise, and five *were* foolish. [3]Those who *were* foolish took their lamps and took no oil with them, [4]but the wise took oil in

their vessels with their lamps. [5]But while the bridegroom was delayed, they all slumbered and slept.

[6]"And at midnight a cry was *heard:* 'Behold, the bridegroom is coming;[a] go out to meet him!' [7]Then all those virgins arose and trimmed their lamps. [8]And the foolish said to the wise, 'Give us *some* of your oil, for our lamps are going out.' [9]But the wise answered, saying, '*No,* lest there should not be enough for us and you; but go rather to those who sell, and buy for yourselves.' [10]And while they went to buy, the bridegroom came, and those who were ready went in with him to the wedding; and the door was shut.

[11]"Afterward the other virgins came also, saying, 'Lord, Lord, open to us!' [12]But he answered and said, 'Assuredly, I say to you, I do not know you.'

[13]"Watch therefore, for you know neither the day nor the hour[a] in which the Son of Man is coming.

The Parable of the Talents

[14]"For *the kingdom of heaven is* like a man traveling to a far country, *who* called his own servants and delivered his goods to them. [15]And to one he gave five talents, to another two, and to another one, to each according to his own ability; and immediately he went on a journey. [16]Then he who had received the five talents went and traded with them, and made another five talents. [17]And likewise he who *had received* two gained two more also. [18]But he who had received one went and dug in the ground, and hid his lord's money. [19]After a long time the lord of those servants came and settled accounts with them.

[20]"So he who had received five talents came and brought five other talents, saying, 'Lord, you delivered to me five talents; look, I have gained five more talents besides them.' [21]His lord said to him, 'Well *done,* good and faithful servant; you were faithful over a few things, I will make you ruler over many things. Enter into the joy of your lord.' [22]He also who had received two talents came and said, 'Lord, you delivered to me two talents; look, I have gained two more talents besides

---

24:36 [a]NU-Text adds *nor the Son.*　**24:42** [a]NU-Text reads *day.*
24:48 [a]NU-Text omits *his coming.*　**25:6** [a]NU-Text omits *is coming.*
25:13 [a]NU-Text omits the rest of this verse.

LEADERSHIP ISSUES

Live as Though It's the Two-Minute-Drill

MATTHEW 24:36

In every football game, the last two minutes end up being the most important. It is called the "Two-Minute-Drill"; the teams step up the play, increase the passion, and fuel their intensity. When Jesus marched into Jerusalem just days before He was crucified, He had a *now* attitude about His mission and what He was there to accomplish. It wasn't about putting it off any longer—but getting right down to what He had been called to do. Jesus expects us to run the same play and reminds His followers that no one knows the hour of His return, not even the angels in heaven (Matt. 24:36). He closes that warning with "be ready" (24:44).

Scripture tells us that we won't know the day or the hour when the "game" of life is over. We are, essentially, always living in the two-minute-drill. The apostle Paul lived this way when he called the plays for the church at Rome and for all believers throughout the ages. In Romans 13:11 and 12, Paul states, "And do this, knowing the time, that now it is high time to awake out of sleep; for now our salvation is nearer than when we first believed. The night is far spent, the day is at hand." A leader keeps defining and sharpening his or her game; the passion for Christ intensifies—believing with all surety that the day of the Lord is "at hand." The leader works diligently to share the gospel with others and to live every day in a *now* attitude.

LEADERSHIP REALITIES

SERVANTHOOD: THE GATEWAY TO GREATNESS   *Matthew 25:14–30*

The genuine leader is a servant at heart, and the key to increasing opportunity is found in whether we are faithful or unfaithful servants. The talents in this text represent both abilities and opportunities to use unique God-given gifts. Faithful servants understand the keys to leadership. They:

1. **realize their identity in Christ:** If you understand your identity, you will naturally allow that identity to motivate action.
2. **understand and love their Master:** You will live captivated by the goodness of His grace, not motivated by fear of punishment.
3. **value success:** The success of a leader is not based on how much his life produces, but by obedience. Obedience leads to favor with God (vv. 21, 23).
4. **live with a sense of urgency because of the Master's imminent return:** Note that the servants focused on being found faithful. A love for the master and a focus on his return led to a sense of urgency to capture the moments of life.
5. **remain aware that the present moment could be the last opportunity to serve.**

them.' ²³His lord said to him, 'Well *done,* good and faithful servant; you have been faithful over a few things, I will make you ruler over many things. Enter into the joy of your lord.'

²⁴"Then he who had received the one talent came and said, 'Lord, I knew you to be a hard man, reaping where you have not sown, and gathering where you have not scattered seed. ²⁵And I was afraid, and went and hid your talent in the ground. Look, *there* you have *what is* yours.'

²⁶"But his lord answered and said to him, 'You wicked and lazy servant, you knew that I reap where I have not sown, and gather where I have not scattered seed. ²⁷So you ought to have deposited my money with the bankers, and at my coming I would have received back my own with interest. ²⁸So take the talent from him, and give *it* to him who has ten talents.

²⁹'For to everyone who has, more will be given, and he will have abundance; but from him who does not have, even what he has will be taken away. ³⁰And cast the unprofitable servant into the outer darkness. There will be weeping and gnashing of teeth.'

The Son of Man Will Judge the Nations

³¹"When the Son of Man comes in His glory, and all the holy[a] angels with Him, then He will sit on the throne of His glory. ³²All the nations will be gathered before Him, and He will separate them one from another, as a shepherd divides *his* sheep from the goats. ³³And He will set the sheep on His right hand, but the goats on the left. ³⁴Then the King will say to those on His right hand, 'Come, you blessed of My Father, inherit the kingdom prepared for you from the foundation of the world: ³⁵for I was hungry and you gave Me food; I was thirsty and you gave Me drink; I was a stranger and you took Me in; ³⁶I *was* naked and you clothed Me; I was sick and you visited Me; I was in prison and you came to Me.'

³⁷"Then the righteous will answer Him, saying, 'Lord, when did we see You hungry and feed *You,* or thirsty and give *You* drink? ³⁸When did we see You a stranger and take *You* in, or naked and clothe *You?* ³⁹Or when did we see

25:31 [a]NU-Text omits *holy.*

THROUGH THE GRID

Thinking Christianly: Ten Foundational Beliefs of a Christian Worldview

Belief Ten: Judgment (*Matt. 25:31–46*)

History is linear, and it has a beginning and a final goal. God will fulfill all of His purposes at the very end of time, according to the pleasure of His own will and for His own glory. There will be a Day of Judgment, and on that day, God will judge all persons, both living and dead, according to the standards of His holiness. Only believers in God will be redeemed (Matt. 25:31–46; John 14:1–3; Rom. 8:28–39; 14:10; 2 Cor. 5:10; Eph. 1:3–14; Rev. 19:11–21; 20:11–15; 21—22). *See Through the Grid article on page 1574.*

You sick, or in prison, and come to You?' [40]And the King will answer and say to them, 'Assuredly, I say to you, inasmuch as you did *it* to one of the least of these My brethren, you did *it* to Me.'

[41]"Then He will also say to those on the left hand, 'Depart from Me, you cursed, into the everlasting fire prepared for the devil and his angels: [42]for I was hungry and you gave Me no food; I was thirsty and you gave Me no drink; [43]I was a stranger and you did not take Me in, naked and you did not clothe Me, sick and in prison and you did not visit Me.'

[44]"Then they also will answer Him,[a] saying, 'Lord, when did we see You hungry or thirsty or a stranger or naked or sick or in prison, and did not minister to You?' [45]Then He will answer them, saying, 'Assuredly, I say to you, inasmuch as you did not do *it* to one of the least of these, you did not do *it* to Me.' [46]And these will go away into everlasting punishment, but the righteous into eternal life."

The Plot to Kill Jesus

26 Now it came to pass, when Jesus had finished all these sayings, *that* He said to His disciples, [2]"You know that after two days is the Passover, and the Son of Man will be delivered up to be crucified."

[3]Then the chief priests, the scribes,[a] and the elders of the people assembled at the palace of the high priest, who was called Caiaphas, [4]and plotted to take Jesus by trickery and kill *Him*. [5]But they said, "Not during the feast, lest there be an uproar among the people."

The Anointing at Bethany

[6]And when Jesus was in Bethany at the house of Simon the leper, [7]a woman came to Him having an alabaster flask of very costly fragrant oil, and she poured *it* on His head as He sat *at the table.* [8]But when His disciples saw *it,* they were indignant, saying, "Why this waste? [9]For this fragrant oil might have been sold for much and given to *the* poor."

[10]But when Jesus was aware of *it,* He said to them, "Why do you trouble the woman? For she has done a good work for Me. [11]For you have the poor with you always, but Me you do not have always. [12]For in pouring this fragrant oil on My body, she did *it* for My burial. [13]Assuredly, I say to you, wherever this gospel is preached in the whole world, what this woman has done will also be told as a memorial to her."

Judas Agrees to Betray Jesus

[14]Then one of the twelve, called Judas Iscariot, went to the chief priests [15]and said, "What are you willing to give me if I deliver Him to you?" And they counted out to him thirty pieces of silver. [16]So from that time he sought opportunity to betray Him.

Jesus Celebrates Passover with His Disciples

[17]Now on the first *day of the Feast* of the Unleavened Bread the disciples came to Jesus, saying to Him, "Where do You want us to prepare for You to eat the Passover?"

25:44 [a]NU-Text and M-Text omit *Him.*   **26:3** [a]NU-Text omits *the scribes.*

¹⁸And He said, "Go into the city to a certain man, and say to him, 'The Teacher says, "My time is at hand; I will keep the Passover at your house with My disciples." ' "

¹⁹So the disciples did as Jesus had directed them; and they prepared the Passover.

²⁰When evening had come, He sat down with the twelve. ²¹Now as they were eating, He said, "Assuredly, I say to you, one of you will betray Me."

²²And they were exceedingly sorrowful, and each of them began to say to Him, "Lord, is it I?"

²³He answered and said, "He who dipped *his* hand with Me in the dish will betray Me. ²⁴The Son of Man indeed goes just as it is written of Him, but woe to that man by whom the Son of Man is betrayed! It would have been good for that man if he had not been born."

²⁵Then Judas, who was betraying Him, answered and said, "Rabbi, is it I?"

He said to him, "You have said it."

JESUS INSTITUTES THE LORD'S SUPPER

²⁶And as they were eating, Jesus took bread, blessed[a] and broke *it,* and gave *it* to the disciples and said, "Take, eat; this is My body."

²⁷Then He took the cup, and gave thanks, and gave *it* to them, saying, "Drink from it, all of you. ²⁸For this is My blood of the new[a] covenant, which is shed for many for the remission of sins. ²⁹But I say to you, I will not drink of this fruit of the vine from now on until that day when I drink it new with you in My Father's kingdom."

³⁰And when they had sung a hymn, they went out to the Mount of Olives.

JESUS PREDICTS PETER'S DENIAL

³¹Then Jesus said to them, "All of you will be made to stumble because of Me this night, for it is written:

'I will strike the Shepherd,
And the sheep of the flock will be scattered.'[a]

³²But after I have been raised, I will go before you to Galilee."

³³Peter answered and said to Him, "Even if all are made to stumble because of You, I will never be made to stumble."

³⁴Jesus said to him, "Assuredly, I say to you that this night, before the rooster crows, you will deny Me three times."

³⁵Peter said to Him, "Even if I have to die with You, I will not deny You!"

And so said all the disciples.

THE PRAYER IN THE GARDEN

³⁶Then Jesus came with them to a place called Gethsemane, and said to the disciples, "Sit here while I go and pray over there." ³⁷And He took with Him Peter and the two sons of Zebedee, and He began to be sorrowful and deeply distressed. ³⁸Then He said to them, "My soul is exceedingly sorrowful, even to death. Stay here and watch with Me."

³⁹He went a little farther and fell on His face, and prayed, saying, "O My Father, if it is possible, let this cup pass from Me; nevertheless, not as I will, but as You *will.*"

⁴⁰Then He came to the disciples and found them sleeping, and said to Peter, "What! Could you not watch with Me one hour? ⁴¹Watch and pray, lest you enter into temptation. The spirit indeed *is* willing, but the flesh *is* weak."

⁴²Again, a second time, He went away and prayed, saying, "O My Father, if this cup cannot pass away from Me unless[a] I drink it, Your will be done." ⁴³And He came and found them asleep again, for their eyes were heavy.

⁴⁴So He left them, went away again, and prayed the third time, saying the same words. ⁴⁵Then He came to His disciples and said to them, "Are *you* still sleeping and resting? Behold, the hour is at hand, and the Son of Man is being betrayed into the hands of sinners. ⁴⁶Rise, let us be going. See, My betrayer is at hand."

BETRAYAL AND ARREST IN GETHSEMANE

⁴⁷And while He was still speaking, behold, Judas, one of the twelve, with a great multitude with swords and clubs, came from the chief priests and elders of the people.

⁴⁸Now His betrayer had given them a sign, saying, "Whomever I kiss, He is the One; seize

26:26 ᵃM-Text reads *gave thanks for.*　26:28 ᵃNU-Text omits *new.*　26:31 ᵃZechariah 13:7　26:42 ᵃNU-Text reads *if this may not pass away unless.*

LEADERSHIP ISSUES

GC2: Encountering Jesus: Fellowship with His Sufferings

MATTHEW 26:38

The Son of God faces the darkest hour in the history of creation. The One who knew no sin will soon become sin. He has vulnerably sought the prayerful support of Peter, James, and John. These men love the Master dearly. They have left their careers to follow Him. They have walked with Him, sat at His feet, seen His miracles, and heard His teaching. But now they seem oblivious to the Master's need.

He looks down at His dearest friends, who are asleep. Tears, soil, and blood streak His face and stain His cloak. Let yourself sense the pain-filled loneliness and grief of the Savior's heart as He asks, "Could you not watch with Me one hour?" (Matt. 26:40). Imagine the disappointment in His eyes as He returns to His place of agonizing prayer.

Amazingly, the scene plays out again and again. Three times, the Master shares His pain and need with His closest friends; and three times, they let Him down.

Can you care for Him in His sorrow? Can you hurt with Him? Can you feel compassion for the pain He felt when, at His time of greatest need, He was left alone? Ask the Spirit to prompt compassion for Christ within you. Allow your heart to share in the "fellowship of His sufferings" (Phil. 3:10). How might your compassion for Christ prompt your compassion for others? How might it impact your prayer life?

Meditate on Christ's words: "Could you not watch with Me one hour?" (Matt. 26:40). What does it do to your heart to meditate on the saddened Savior? How does it make you feel to hear His plea?

Consider praying this prayer: "Lord Jesus, my heart is touched with
_____ as Your Spirit leads me to encounter You in Your Word."

GC2
GREAT COMMANDMENT
COMMISSION

Him." [49]Immediately he went up to Jesus and said, "Greetings, Rabbi!" and kissed Him.

[50]But Jesus said to him, "Friend, why have you come?"

Then they came and laid hands on Jesus and took Him. [51]And suddenly, one of those *who were* with Jesus stretched out *his* hand and drew his sword, struck the servant of the high priest, and cut off his ear.

[52]But Jesus said to him, "Put your sword in its place, for all who take the sword will perish[a] by the sword. [53]Or do you think that I cannot now pray to My Father, and He will provide Me with more than twelve legions of angels? [54]How then could the Scriptures be fulfilled, that it must happen thus?"

[55]In that hour Jesus said to the multitudes, "Have you come out, as against a robber, with swords and clubs to take Me? I sat daily with you, teaching in the temple, and you did not seize Me. [56]But all this was done that the Scriptures of the prophets might be fulfilled."

Then all the disciples forsook Him and fled.

JESUS FACES THE SANHEDRIN

[57]And those who had laid hold of Jesus led *Him* away to Caiaphas the high priest, where the scribes and the elders were assembled. [58]But Peter followed Him at a distance to the high priest's courtyard. And he went in and sat with the servants to see the end.

[59]Now the chief priests, the elders,[a] and all the council sought false testimony against Jesus to put Him to death, [60]but found none. Even though many false witnesses came forward, they found none.[a] But at last two false witnesses[b] came forward [61]and said, "This *fellow* said, 'I am able to destroy the temple of God and to build it in three days.' "

[62]And the high priest arose and said to Him, "Do You answer nothing? What *is it* these men testify against You?" [63]But Jesus kept silent. And the high priest answered and said to Him, "I put

26:52 [a]M-Text reads *die*. **26:59** [a]NU-Text omits *the elders*. **26:60** [a]NU-Text puts a comma after *but found none*, does not capitalize *Even*, and omits *they found none*. [b]NU-Text omits *false witnesses*.

INSIDE *the* INFLUENCERS

PETER: Great Sincerity Can Be Sincerely Wrong

MATTHEW 26:51–53 & JOHN 18:10, 11

Good intentions cannot erase mistakes. When it's time to act, leaders who are expecting to make a difference must engage not only their hearts, but their heads as well. Does the call for quick action cancel the need to engage the brain as well as the heart? Most certainly not! The apostle Peter faced this very dilemma at a crucial moment, because he was sincere, but sincerely wrong at the same time.

Jesus was going to be arrested in the garden, but as the men stepped forward to seize him, Simon Peter drew his sword and struck the servant of the high priest, cutting off his ear. Peter found himself with blood on his hands because he ignored a leadership principle. Simply put, he reacted to the situation instead of responding like the Savior (Matt. 26:51–53, John 18:10,11).

The story takes an extraordinary twist when Jesus miraculously heals the ear of the injured man and patiently informs Peter of his purpose and destiny on earth. What a response! Jesus' heart was heavy—as He had just spent the entire night praying—but His head was clear as He surrendered Himself to His Father's plan, no matter the cost. Jesus responded appropriately, resulting in salvation for all who would believe.

You under oath by the living God: Tell us if You are the Christ, the Son of God!"

⁶⁴Jesus said to him, "*It is as* you said. Nevertheless, I say to you, hereafter you will see the Son of Man sitting at the right hand of the Power, and coming on the clouds of heaven."

⁶⁵Then the high priest tore his clothes, saying, "He has spoken blasphemy! What further need do we have of witnesses? Look, now you have heard His blasphemy! ⁶⁶What do you think?"

They answered and said, "He is deserving of death."

⁶⁷Then they spat in His face and beat Him; and others struck *Him* with the palms of their hands, ⁶⁸saying, "Prophesy to us, Christ! Who is the one who struck You?"

Peter Denies Jesus, and Weeps Bitterly

⁶⁹Now Peter sat outside in the courtyard. And a servant girl came to him, saying, "You also were with Jesus of Galilee."

⁷⁰But he denied it before *them* all, saying, "I do not know what you are saying."

⁷¹And when he had gone out to the gateway, another *girl* saw him and said to those *who were* there, "This *fellow* also was with Jesus of Nazareth."

⁷²But again he denied with an oath, "I do not know the Man!"

⁷³And a little later those who stood by came up and said to Peter, "Surely you also are *one* of them, for your speech betrays you."

⁷⁴Then he began to curse and swear, *saying,* "I do not know the Man!"

Immediately a rooster crowed. ⁷⁵And Peter remembered the word of Jesus who had said to him, "Before the rooster crows, you will deny Me three times." So he went out and wept bitterly.

Jesus Handed Over to Pontius Pilate

27 When morning came, all the chief priests and elders of the people plotted against Jesus to put Him to death. ²And when they had bound Him, they led Him away and delivered Him to Pontiusᵃ Pilate the governor.

Judas Hangs Himself

³Then Judas, His betrayer, seeing that He had been condemned, was remorseful and brought back the thirty pieces of silver to the chief priests and elders, ⁴saying, "I have sinned by betraying innocent blood."

And they said, "What *is that* to us? You see *to it!*"

⁵Then he threw down the pieces of silver in the temple and departed, and went and hanged himself.

⁶But the chief priests took the silver pieces and said, "It is not lawful to put them into the treasury, because they are the price of blood." ⁷And they consulted together and bought with them the potter's field, to bury strangers in. ⁸Therefore that field has been called the Field of Blood to this day.

⁹Then was fulfilled what was spoken by Jeremiah the prophet, saying, *"And they took the thirty pieces of silver, the value of Him who was priced,* whom they of the children of Israel priced, ¹⁰*and gave them for the potter's field, as the Lord directed me."* ᵃ

Jesus Faces Pilate

¹¹Now Jesus stood before the governor. And the governor asked Him, saying, "Are You the King of the Jews?"

Jesus said to him, "*It is as* you say." ¹²And while He was being accused by the chief priests and elders, He answered nothing.

¹³Then Pilate said to Him, "Do You not hear how many things they testify against You?" ¹⁴But He answered him not one word, so that the governor marveled greatly.

Taking the Place of Barabbas

¹⁵Now at the feast the governor was accustomed to releasing to the multitude one prisoner whom they wished. ¹⁶And at that time they had a notorious prisoner called Barabbas.ᵃ ¹⁷Therefore, when they had gathered together, Pilate said to them, "Whom do you want me to release to you? Barabbas, or Jesus who is called Christ?" ¹⁸For he knew that they had handed Him over because of envy.

¹⁹While he was sitting on the judgment seat, his wife sent to him, saying, "Have nothing to do with that just Man, for I have suffered many things today in a dream because of Him."

27:2 ᵃNU-Text omits *Pontius.* **27:10** ᵃJeremiah 32:6–9
27:16 ᵃNU-Text reads *Jesus Barabbas.*

²⁰But the chief priests and elders persuaded the multitudes that they should ask for Barabbas and destroy Jesus. ²¹The governor answered and said to them, "Which of the two do you want me to release to you?"

They said, "Barabbas!"

²²Pilate said to them, "What then shall I do with Jesus who is called Christ?"

They all said to him, "Let Him be crucified!"

²³Then the governor said, "Why, what evil has He done?"

But they cried out all the more, saying, "Let Him be crucified!"

²⁴When Pilate saw that he could not prevail at all, but rather *that* a tumult was rising, he took water and washed *his* hands before the multitude, saying, "I am innocent of the blood of this just Person.^a You see *to it.*"

²⁵And all the people answered and said, "His blood *be* on us and on our children."

²⁶Then he released Barabbas to them; and when he had scourged Jesus, he delivered *Him* to be crucified.

The Soldiers Mock Jesus

²⁷Then the soldiers of the governor took Jesus into the Praetorium and gathered the whole garrison around Him. ²⁸And they stripped Him and put a scarlet robe on Him. ²⁹When they had twisted a crown of thorns, they put *it* on His head, and a reed in His right hand. And they bowed the knee before Him and mocked Him, saying, "Hail, King of the Jews!" ³⁰Then they spat on Him, and took the reed and struck Him on the head. ³¹And when they had mocked Him, they took the robe off Him, put His *own* clothes on Him, and led Him away to be crucified.

The King on a Cross

³²Now as they came out, they found a man of Cyrene, Simon by name. Him they compelled to bear His cross. ³³And when they had come to a place called Golgotha, that is to say, Place of a Skull, ³⁴they gave Him sour^a wine mingled with gall to drink. But when He had tasted *it,* He would not drink.

³⁵Then they crucified Him, and divided His garments, casting lots,^a that it might be fulfilled which was spoken by the prophet:

"They divided My garments among them,
   And for My clothing they cast lots."^b

³⁶Sitting down, they kept watch over Him there. ³⁷And they put up over His head the accusation written against Him:

THIS IS JESUS
THE KING OF THE JEWS.

³⁸Then two robbers were crucified with Him, one on the right and another on the left.

³⁹And those who passed by blasphemed Him, wagging their heads ⁴⁰and saying, "You who destroy the temple and build *it* in three days, save Yourself! If You are the Son of God, come down from the cross."

⁴¹Likewise the chief priests also, mocking with the scribes and elders,^a said, ⁴²"He saved others; Himself He cannot save. If He is the King of Israel,^a let Him now come down from the cross, and we will believe Him.^b ⁴³He trusted in God; let Him deliver Him now if He will have Him; for He said, 'I am the Son of God.' "

⁴⁴Even the robbers who were crucified with Him reviled Him with the same thing.

Jesus Dies on the Cross

⁴⁵Now from the sixth hour until the ninth hour there was darkness over all the land. ⁴⁶And about the ninth hour Jesus cried out with a loud voice, saying, "Eli, Eli, lama sabachthani?" that is, *"My God, My God, why have You forsaken Me?"* ^a

⁴⁷Some of those who stood there, when they heard *that,* said, "This Man is calling for Elijah!" ⁴⁸Immediately one of them ran and took a sponge, filled *it* with sour wine and put *it* on a reed, and offered it to Him to drink.

⁴⁹The rest said, "Let Him alone; let us see if Elijah will come to save Him."

⁵⁰And Jesus cried out again with a loud voice, and yielded up His spirit.

⁵¹Then, behold, the veil of the temple was torn in two from top to bottom; and the earth

27:24 ^aNU-Text omits *just.* **27:34** ^aNU-Text omits *sour.* **27:35** ^aNU-Text and M-Text omit the rest of this verse. ^bPsalm 22:18 **27:41** ^aM-Text reads *with the scribes, the Pharisees, and the elders.* **27:42** ^aNU-Text reads *He is the King of Israel!* ^bNU-Text and M-Text read *we will believe in Him.* **27:46** ^aPsalm 22:1

quaked, and the rocks were split, [52]and the graves were opened; and many bodies of the saints who had fallen asleep were raised; [53]and coming out of the graves after His resurrection, they went into the holy city and appeared to many.

[54]So when the centurion and those with him, who were guarding Jesus, saw the earthquake and the things that had happened, they feared greatly, saying, "Truly this was the Son of God!"

[55]And many women who followed Jesus from Galilee, ministering to Him, were there looking on from afar, [56]among whom were Mary Magdalene, Mary the mother of James and Joses,[a] and the mother of Zebedee's sons.

Jesus Buried in Joseph's Tomb

[57]Now when evening had come, there came a rich man from Arimathea, named Joseph, who himself had also become a disciple of Jesus. [58]This man went to Pilate and asked for the body of Jesus. Then Pilate commanded the body to be given to him. [59]When Joseph had taken the body, he wrapped it in a clean linen cloth, [60]and laid it in his new tomb which he had hewn out of the rock; and he rolled a large stone against the door of the tomb, and departed. [61]And Mary Magdalene was there, and the other Mary, sitting opposite the tomb.

Pilate Sets a Guard

[62]On the next day, which followed the Day of Preparation, the chief priests and Pharisees gathered together to Pilate, [63]saying, "Sir, we remember, while He was still alive, how that deceiver said, 'After three days I will rise.' [64]Therefore command that the tomb be made secure until the third day, lest His disciples come by night[a] and steal Him *away*, and say to the people, 'He has risen from the dead.' So the last deception will be worse than the first."

[65]Pilate said to them, "You have a guard; go your way, make *it* as secure as you know how." [66]So they went and made the tomb secure, sealing the stone and setting the guard.

27:56 [a]NU-Text reads *Joseph.*   27:64 [a]NU-Text omits *by night.*

 the INFLUENCERS

JOSEPH OF ARIMATHEA

MATTHEW 27:57–61

After Jesus died, a rich man named Joseph approached the Roman governor for permission to give Jesus a better burial than crucified criminals normally received. A burial would also prevent the defilement of the land, in Jewish eyes, which would be caused by leaving the corpse on the cross overnight (Deut. 21:22, 23). Joseph hailed from Arimathea, a town about twenty-two miles northwest of Jerusalem. Joseph had become a follower of Jesus, but he had not yet revealed his loyalties in public (John 19:38) because he also belonged to the Sanhedrin (Mark 15:43). Pilate granted Joseph's request. Joseph put Jesus in his own unused tomb, wrapping him in grave clothes. Joseph must be forever remembered as the man who gave Jesus a tomb, displaying courage and affection toward his Savior. He spoke out on the side of a crucified "criminal," and he braved the possible resentment of Pilate. He even faced the certain hatred of the members in the Sanhedrin.

We know little about this member of the Sanhedrin save his name Joseph, his town Arimathea, that he was rich, a secret disciple, and had not had not agreed to the crucifixion of Jesus. He may have wished that he had made an open profession. But he showed courage when others were cowardly and asked to personally place the body of Jesus in his new tomb.

He Is Risen

28 Now after the Sabbath, as the first *day* of the week began to dawn, Mary Magdalene and the other Mary came to see the tomb. [2]And behold, there was a great earthquake; for an angel of the Lord descended from heaven, and came and rolled back the stone from the door,[a] and sat on it. [3]His countenance was like lightning, and his clothing as white as snow. [4]And the guards shook for fear of him, and became like dead *men*.

[5]But the angel answered and said to the women, "Do not be afraid, for I know that you seek Jesus who was crucified. [6]He is not here; for He is risen, as He said. Come, see the place where the Lord lay. [7]And go quickly and tell His disciples that He is risen from the dead, and indeed He is going before you into Galilee; there you will see Him. Behold, I have told you."

[8]So they went out quickly from the tomb with fear and great joy, and ran to bring His disciples word.

The Women Worship the Risen Lord

[9]And as they went to tell His disciples,[a] behold, Jesus met them, saying, "Rejoice!" So they came and held Him by the feet and worshiped Him. [10]Then Jesus said to them, "Do not be afraid. Go *and* tell My brethren to go to Galilee, and there they will see Me."

The Soldiers Are Bribed

[11]Now while they were going, behold, some of the guard came into the city and reported to the chief priests all the things that had happened. [12]When they had assembled with the elders and consulted together, they gave a large sum of money to the soldiers, [13]saying, "Tell them, 'His disciples came at night and stole Him *away* while we slept.' [14]And if this comes to the governor's ears, we will appease him and make you secure." [15]So they took the money and did as they were

28:2 [a]NU-Text omits *from the door.* **28:9** [a]NU-Text omits the first clause of this verse.

THROUGH THE GRID

Making Sense of Your World: Confronting God in a Biblical Worldview (Matt. 28:18–20)

The clearest source of divine revelation that we have before us today is the Bible, in which the inspired biblical authors wrote the revelation they had received about God. In the Bible, we are also told of God's character, God's nature, and God's plans for the cosmos and for humanity. God is portrayed in the Bible as the sum of all reality, of which human existence is just a mere part. One of the chief characteristics of God is that God is personable, and God relates directly to humankind. In fact, humanity is created *imago dei*—in the very image and likeness of God. Throughout the Bible, we see evidence of God's expressions which take on human forms, such as love, anger, and sorrow. The greatest attribute is that God can relate directly to humanity: the divine relationship with humanity is such that God can communicate with humanity and humanity can communicate with God. God has ordained the details of human existence, and the events that unfold in history are planned events that ultimately demonstrate that God is sovereign and in control of all. No detail escapes God's planning or view. One of the distinguishing characteristics of a biblical worldview is that it has a God who is "triune"—three distinct Persons in one essence: Father, Son, and Holy Spirit are each fully and equally God, yet there is only one God. The Father is the Creator, the Son is God's revelation in Jesus Christ, and the Holy Spirit is the indwelling of God by which God relates to humanity.

LEADERSHIP ISSUES

GC2: Sharing Christ: Partnering Together in the Great Commission

MATTHEW 28:19, 20 *Go therefore and make disciples of all the nations, baptizing them in the name of the Father and of the Son and of the Holy Spirit, teaching them to observe all things that I have commanded you; and lo, I am with you always, even to the end of the age.*

So why has God left us here on the planet after coming to know Christ? He could have taken us directly to heaven, but He did not. He left us here among other things in order that we might "make disciples"—help others to see and follow Jesus.

The word "fellowship" (*koinonia*) refers to caring connectedness within the body of Christ. But it also connotes partnering together for a larger purpose. Our fellowship is intended to transform us in order that we might join together to pursue the eternal purposes of the kingdom, including the undertaking of Christ's Great Commission to make disciples of all nations.

When Jesus said, "Follow Me, and I will make you fishers of men" (Matt. 4:19), what image would have come to the disciples' minds? They would not have pictured an individual trying to catch fish on his own, but rather a crew or team casting nets into the sea together. Imagine trying to carry a large, wet net filled with several hundred pounds of fish. Your resolve to be self-reliant would be broken very quickly! Our only hope of having a major impact for the cause of Christ in the unbelieving world is to function together in *koinonia*, realizing that some of God's glorious riches are in each of God's people. Together, we can cast the net of fellowship in order to see eternal things done for the kingdom.

Take time for prayer about how you might partner together with other believers to see those who are not now following Christ come to experience His life and love.

GREAT COMMANDMENT
COMMISSION

LEADERSHIP
REALITIES

CAMPUS REVOLUTION   *Matthew 28:19, 20*

Campus revolution starts with you—or rather, with Christ *in* you. Personal evangelism naturally happens as the joy of personal salvation and a daily walk with God abundantly floods out to others so that they can also partake and enjoy the fullness of Christ's love. There are four reasons why you might not share your personal faith:

1. **You have never met Christ personally.** You might know *about* Him, but you do not *know Him*. Have you been "born of the spirit"? Are you *in Christ* or only *near Him?*

2. **You have willful sin in your life:** We can grieve (*make sorrowful*) or quench (*put the flame out*) the Holy Spirit of God within us through certain habits or thoughts that we allow to dominate us.

3. **You are *in Christ,* but far from Him.** Because your quiet time is weak, the debris of the culture's media and message has more control in your heart and mind than the Word of God.

4. **You don't know how to share your faith (or *think* you don't know how).** It is a worthy choice to learn how to intelligently discuss world religions or debate the existence of God intellectually. However, the first step is to demonstrate care and concern; and the second to simply tell your own story of how Christ transformed your life.

instructed; and this saying is commonly reported among the Jews until this day.

THE GREAT COMMISSION

[16]Then the eleven disciples went away into Galilee, to the mountain which Jesus had appointed for them. [17]When they saw Him, they worshiped Him; but some doubted.

[18]And Jesus came and spoke to them, saying,

"All authority has been given to Me in heaven and on earth. [19]Go therefore[a] and make disciples of all the nations, baptizing them in the name of the Father and of the Son and of the Holy Spirit, [20]teaching them to observe all things that I have commanded you; and lo, I am with you always, *even* to the end of the age." Amen.[a]

28:19 [a]M-Text omits *therefore.*   **28:20** [a]NU-Text omits *Amen.*

IMPACT OF THE BOOK

MARK

IDEA

Jesus is the greatest example of servant leadership; and the greater the leader, the greater the service. Mark introduces us to the truth that with God all things are possible (10:27).

MESSAGE

Mark focuses on Jesus' earthly ministry and humanity, revealing that Jesus was the perfect Servant of Yahweh. He came to serve others and not be served (10:45); he lived a life of purity, passion, and purpose. Jesus proved that leadership works through compassionate relationships and not from a position of power. He revealed the importance of rest and time alone with His Father, especially when preparing for a life of sacrifice. The Gospel concludes with a world vision for all servants of Christ.

PEOPLE

Chief Priests, Herod, Jesus, John the Baptist, Pharisees, Pilate, Scribes, Twelve Disciples

AUTHOR

John Mark penned this Gospel. John is his Jewish name; Mark is his Roman name. As a young companion, he accompanied Paul and Barnabas to Antioch from Jerusalem (Acts 12:25) and on their first missionary journey (Acts 13:5). John Mark stumbled at one point, abandoned the mission, and caused a schism between Paul and Barnabas. He recovered and Paul said he was "useful to me for ministry" (2 Tim. 4:11). He was also greatly influenced by the sermons of Peter.

CULTURE

Although Matthew and Luke record more events, Mark tends to give more details. His words emphasize more of the things Jesus did rather than what He said. Mark presents Jesus as the master teacher, while presenting all of His humanity: heartfelt compassion (1:41), righteous indignation (3:5), humble submission to the Father's will, and even death (Mark 14:36).

TIMELINE

c. AD 50–60

KEY SCRIPTURE MEMORY VERSES

1:17; 2:17; 7:20–23; 8:34–37; 10:14, 15, 43–45

John the Baptist Prepares the Way

1 The beginning of the gospel of Jesus Christ, the Son of God. [2]As it is written in the Prophets:[a]

> "Behold, I send My messenger before Your
> face,
> Who will prepare Your way before You."[b]

[3]"The voice of one crying in the wilderness:
'Prepare the way of the LORD;
Make His paths straight.' "[a]

[4]John came baptizing in the wilderness and preaching a baptism of repentance for the remission of sins. [5]Then all the land of Judea, and those from Jerusalem, went out to him and were all baptized by him in the Jordan River, confessing their sins.

[6]Now John was clothed with camel's hair and with a leather belt around his waist, and he ate locusts and wild honey. [7]And he preached, saying, "There comes One after me who is mightier than I, whose sandal strap I am not worthy to stoop down and loose. [8]I indeed baptized you with water, but He will baptize you with the Holy Spirit."

John Baptizes Jesus

[9]It came to pass in those days *that* Jesus came from Nazareth of Galilee, and was baptized by John in the Jordan. [10]And immediately, coming up from[a] the water, He saw the heavens parting and the Spirit descending upon Him like a dove. [11]Then a voice came from heaven, "You are My beloved Son, in whom I am well pleased."

Satan Tempts Jesus

[12]Immediately the Spirit drove Him into the wilderness. [13]And He was there in the wilderness forty days, tempted by Satan, and was with the wild beasts; and the angels ministered to Him.

Jesus Begins His Galilean Ministry

[14]Now after John was put in prison, Jesus came to Galilee, preaching the gospel of the kingdom[a] of God, [15]and saying, "The time is fulfilled, and the kingdom of God is at hand. Repent, and believe in the gospel."

Four Fishermen Called as Disciples

[16]And as He walked by the Sea of Galilee, He saw Simon and Andrew his brother casting a net into the sea; for they were fishermen. [17]Then Jesus said to them, "Follow Me, and I will make you become fishers of men." [18]They immediately left their nets and followed Him.

[19]When He had gone a little farther from there, He saw James the *son* of Zebedee, and John his brother, who also *were* in the boat mending their nets. [20]And immediately He called them, and they left their father Zebedee in the boat with the hired servants, and went after Him.

Jesus Casts Out an Unclean Spirit

[21]Then they went into Capernaum, and immediately on the Sabbath He entered the synagogue and taught. [22]And they were astonished at His teaching, for He taught them as one having authority, and not as the scribes.

[23]Now there was a man in their synagogue with an unclean spirit. And he cried out, [24]saying, "Let *us* alone! What have we to do with You, Jesus of Nazareth? Did You come to destroy us? I know who You are—the Holy One of God!"

[25]But Jesus rebuked him, saying, "Be quiet, and come out of him!" [26]And when the unclean spirit had convulsed him and cried out with a loud voice, he came out of him. [27]Then they were all amazed, so that they questioned among themselves, saying, "What is this? What new doctrine *is* this? For with authority[a] He commands even the unclean spirits, and they obey Him." [28]And immediately His fame spread throughout all the region around Galilee.

Peter's Mother-in-Law Healed

[29]Now as soon as they had come out of the synagogue, they entered the house of Simon and Andrew, with James and John. [30]But Simon's wife's mother lay sick with a fever, and they told Him about her at once. [31]So He came and took her by the hand and lifted her up, and immediately the fever left her. And she served them.

1:2 [a]NU-Text reads *Isaiah the prophet.* [b]Malachi 3:1   **1:3** [a]Isaiah 40:3   **1:10** [a]NU-Text reads *out of.*   **1:14** [a]NU-Text omits *of the kingdom.*   **1:27** [a]NU-Text reads *What is this? A new doctrine with authority.*

LEADERSHIP ISSUES

GC2: Following Jesus in Prayer

MARK 1:35

Both the religious leaders of Christ's day and His own followers often misunderstood His priorities. Surely, the disciples thought Jesus would not want to be distracted by children. Yet He rebuked the disciples and welcomed the children with open arms (Mark 10:13–16). Surely, the Pharisees reasoned, a respectable teacher should have nothing to do with tax collectors and sinners; yet Jesus was known as their friend (Matt. 11:19). Throughout His life on earth, Christ displayed countercultural priorities, giving time and attention to people and things that others despised, rejected, or deemed unimportant.

The rationale behind Jesus' behavior becomes perfectly clear when we understand the greater, overarching priority that guided Him: His insistence on hearing from His Father. "I can of Myself do nothing," He declared (John 5:30). The actions that so confounded Pharisees and disciples alike give evidence that Jesus' conduct was not guided by people's opinions, but by His Father's heart. Paradoxically, the God-Man Jesus—the eternally existent One, through whom everything holds together—freely admitted His humble dependence upon His Father, and thus, His need to hear His Father.

Scripture records that Jesus frequently spent time in solitary prayer in order to more clearly hear the Father's voice. While this practice should have served as a model for the disciples, it appears that they sometimes had a different set of priorities. In Mark 1:36 and 37, when they realized Jesus had gotten up early and left the house, they "searched for Him. When they found Him, they said to Him, 'Everyone is looking for You.' " In the disciples' minds, there were more pressing concerns for Jesus to address: crowds to be greeted, lessons to be taught, miracles to be performed.

But Christ's first priority was to hear His Father. So it is for the faithful disciple. Hearing the Father must become our pursuit and passion.

GC2
GREAT COMMANDMENT
COMMISSION

Many Healed After Sabbath Sunset

³²At evening, when the sun had set, they brought to Him all who were sick and those who were demon-possessed. ³³And the whole city was gathered together at the door. ³⁴Then He healed many who were sick with various diseases, and cast out many demons; and He did not allow the demons to speak, because they knew Him.

Preaching in Galilee

³⁵Now in the morning, having risen a long while before daylight, He went out and departed to a solitary place; and there He prayed. ³⁶And Simon and those *who were* with Him searched for Him. ³⁷When they found Him, they said to Him, "Everyone is looking for You."

³⁸But He said to them, "Let us go into the next towns, that I may preach there also, because for this purpose I have come forth."

³⁹And He was preaching in their synagogues throughout all Galilee, and casting out demons.

Jesus Cleanses a Leper

⁴⁰Now a leper came to Him, imploring Him, kneeling down to Him and saying to Him, "If You are willing, You can make me clean."

⁴¹Then Jesus, moved with compassion, stretched out *His* hand and touched him, and said to him, "I am willing; be cleansed." ⁴²As soon as He had spoken, immediately the leprosy left him, and he was cleansed. ⁴³And He strictly warned him and sent him away at once, ⁴⁴and said to him, "See that you say nothing to anyone; but go your way, show yourself to the priest, and offer for your cleansing those things which Moses commanded, as a testimony to them."

⁴⁵However, he went out and began to proclaim *it* freely, and to spread the matter, so that Jesus could no longer openly enter the city, but was outside in deserted places; and they came to Him from every direction.

Jesus Forgives and Heals a Paralytic

2 And again He entered Capernaum after *some* days, and it was heard that He was in the house. ²Immediatelyᵃ many gathered together, so that there was no longer room to receive *them,* not even near the door. And He preached the word to them. ³Then they came to Him, bringing a paralytic who was carried by four *men.* ⁴And when they could not come near Him because of the crowd, they uncovered the roof where He was. So when they had broken through, they let down the bed on which the paralytic was lying.

⁵When Jesus saw their faith, He said to the paralytic, "Son, your sins are forgiven you."

⁶And some of the scribes were sitting there

2:2 ᵃNU-Text omits *Immediately.*

LEADERSHIP REALITIES

PEOPLE MATTER Mark 2:1–12

This text paints a beautiful picture of the leadership reality that *people matter.* Jesus is in Capernaum, at work in their midst, which leads to a response of celebration and praise that becomes contagious to those in the area who have not yet met him. There were phenomenal crowds because people were bringing their friends to the Savior. It was said of Jesus that He was a friend of sinners and tax collectors (Matt. 11:19). Jesus talked to, ate with, and spent time with those who were despised, unworthy and outcasts. It was overwhelmingly obvious throughout His ministry that Jesus genuinely cared about people. He taught in the synagogues, preached the gospel of the kingdom, healed sickness and disease, and was *moved with compassion* (Matt. 9:35, 36) as He met people and walked through cities. The leader must never be consumed or hypnotized by positions, power, or pride, but should always remember that people are infinitely valuable to God. When this is true in your life, then people take priority over tasks on a consistent basis.

and reasoning in their hearts, [7]"Why does this *Man* speak blasphemies like this? Who can forgive sins but God alone?"

[8]But immediately, when Jesus perceived in His spirit that they reasoned thus within themselves, He said to them, "Why do you reason about these things in your hearts? [9]Which is easier, to say to the paralytic, '*Your* sins are forgiven you,' or to say, 'Arise, take up your bed and walk'? [10]But that you may know that the Son of Man has power on earth to forgive sins"—He said to the paralytic, [11]"I say to you, arise, take up your bed, and go to your house." [12]Immediately he arose, took up the bed, and went out in the presence of them all, so that all were amazed and glorified God, saying, "We never saw *anything* like this!"

MATTHEW THE TAX COLLECTOR

[13]Then He went out again by the sea; and all the multitude came to Him, and He taught them. [14]As He passed by, He saw Levi the *son* of Alphaeus sitting at the tax office. And He said to him, "Follow Me." So he arose and followed Him.

[15]Now it happened, as He was dining in *Levi's* house, that many tax collectors and sinners also sat together with Jesus and His disciples; for there were many, and they followed Him. [16]And when the scribes and[a] Pharisees saw Him eating with the tax collectors and sinners, they said to His disciples, "How *is it* that He eats and drinks with tax collectors and sinners?"

[17]When Jesus heard *it,* He said to them, "Those who are well have no need of a physician, but those who are sick. I did not come to call *the* righteous, but sinners, to repentance."[a]

JESUS IS QUESTIONED ABOUT FASTING

[18]The disciples of John and of the Pharisees were fasting. Then they came and said to Him, "Why do the disciples of John and of the Pharisees fast, but Your disciples do not fast?"

[19]And Jesus said to them, "Can the friends of the bridegroom fast while the bridegroom is with them? As long as they have the bridegroom with them they cannot fast. [20]But the days will come when the bridegroom will be taken away from them, and then they will fast in those days. [21]No one sews a piece of unshrunk cloth on an old garment; or else the new piece pulls away from the old, and the tear is made worse. [22]And no one puts new wine into old wineskins; or else the new wine bursts the wineskins, the wine is spilled, and the wineskins are ruined. But new wine must be put into new wineskins."

JESUS IS LORD OF THE SABBATH

[23]Now it happened that He went through the grainfields on the Sabbath; and as they went His disciples began to pluck the heads of grain. [24]And the Pharisees said to Him, "Look, why do they do what is not lawful on the Sabbath?"

[25]But He said to them, "Have you never read what David did when he was in need and hungry, he and those with him: [26]how he went into the house of God *in the days* of Abiathar the high priest, and ate the showbread, which is not lawful to eat except for the priests, and also gave some to those who were with him?"

[27]And He said to them, "The Sabbath was made for man, and not man for the Sabbath. [28]Therefore the Son of Man is also Lord of the Sabbath."

HEALING ON THE SABBATH

3 And He entered the synagogue again, and a man was there who had a withered hand. [2]So they watched Him closely, whether He would heal him on the Sabbath, so that they might accuse Him. [3]And He said to the man who had the withered hand, "Step forward." [4]Then He said to them, "Is it lawful on the Sabbath to do good or to do evil, to save life or to kill?" But they kept silent. [5]And when He had looked around at them with anger, being grieved by the hardness of their hearts, He said to the man, "Stretch out your hand." And he stretched *it* out, and his hand was restored as whole as the other.[a] [6]Then the Pharisees went out and immediately plotted with the Herodians against Him, how they might destroy Him.

A GREAT MULTITUDE FOLLOWS JESUS

[7]But Jesus withdrew with His disciples to the sea. And a great multitude from Galilee followed

---

2:16 [a]NU-Text reads *of the.* **2:17** [a]NU-Text omits *to repentance.* **3:5** [a]NU-Text omits *as whole as the other.*

Him, and from Judea [8]and Jerusalem and Idumea and beyond the Jordan; and those from Tyre and Sidon, a great multitude, when they heard how many things He was doing, came to Him. [9]So He told His disciples that a small boat should be kept ready for Him because of the multitude, lest they should crush Him. [10]For He healed many, so that as many as had afflictions pressed about Him to touch Him. [11]And the unclean spirits, whenever they saw Him, fell down before Him and cried out, saying, "You are the Son of God." [12]But He sternly warned them that they should not make Him known.

THE TWELVE APOSTLES

[13]And He went up on the mountain and called to *Him* those He Himself wanted. And they came to Him. [14]Then He appointed twelve,[a] that they might be with Him and that He might send them out to preach, [15]and to have power to heal sicknesses and[a] to cast out demons: [16]Simon,[a] to whom He gave the name Peter; [17]James the *son* of Zebedee and John the brother of James, to whom He gave the name Boanerges, that is, "Sons of Thunder"; [18]Andrew, Philip, Bartholomew, Matthew, Thomas, James the *son* of Alphaeus, Thaddaeus, Simon the Cananite; [19]and Judas Iscariot, who also betrayed Him. And they went into a house.

A HOUSE DIVIDED CANNOT STAND

[20]Then the multitude came together again, so that they could not so much as eat bread. [21]But when His own people heard *about this,* they went out to lay hold of Him, for they said, "He is out of His mind."

[22]And the scribes who came down from Jerusalem said, "He has Beelzebub," and, "By the ruler of the demons He casts out demons."

[23]So He called them to *Himself* and said to them in parables: "How can Satan cast out Satan? [24]If a kingdom is divided against itself, that kingdom cannot stand. [25]And if a house is divided against itself, that house cannot stand. [26]And if Satan has risen up against himself, and is divided, he cannot stand, but has an end. [27]No one can enter a strong man's house and plunder his goods, unless he first binds the strong man. And then he will plunder his house.

THE UNPARDONABLE SIN

[28]"Assuredly, I say to you, all sins will be forgiven the sons of men, and whatever blasphemies they may utter; [29]but he who blasphemes against the Holy Spirit never has forgiveness, but is subject to eternal condemnation"— [30]because they said, "He has an unclean spirit."

JESUS' MOTHER AND BROTHERS SEND FOR HIM

[31]Then His brothers and His mother came, and standing outside they sent to Him, calling Him. [32]And a multitude was sitting around Him; and they said to Him, "Look, Your mother and Your brothers[a] are outside seeking You."

[33]But He answered them, saying, "Who is My mother, or My brothers?" [34]And He looked around in a circle at those who sat about Him, and said, "Here are My mother and My brothers! [35]For whoever does the will of God is My brother and My sister and mother."

THE PARABLE OF THE SOWER

4 And again He began to teach by the sea. And a great multitude was gathered to Him, so that He got into a boat and sat *in it* on the sea; and the whole multitude was on the land facing the sea. [2]Then He taught them many things by parables, and said to them in His teaching:

[3]"Listen! Behold, a sower went out to sow. [4]And it happened, as he sowed, *that* some *seed* fell by the wayside; and the birds of the air[a] came and devoured it. [5]Some fell on stony ground, where it did not have much earth; and immediately it sprang up because it had no depth of earth. [6]But when the sun was up it was scorched, and because it had no root it withered away. [7]And some *seed* fell among thorns; and the thorns grew up and choked it, and it yielded no crop. [8]But other *seed* fell on good ground and yielded a crop that sprang up, increased and produced: some thirtyfold, some sixty, and some a hundred."

[9]And He said to them,[a] "He who has ears to hear, let him hear!"

3:14 [a]NU-Text adds *whom He also named apostles.* **3:15** [a]NU-Text omits *to heal sicknesses and.* **3:16** [a]NU-Text reads *and He appointed the twelve: Simon. . . .* **3:32** [a]NU-Text and M-Text add *and Your sisters.* **4:4** [a]NU-Text and M-Text omit *of the air.* **4:9** [a]NU-Text and M-Text omit *to them.*

The Purpose of Parables

[10]But when He was alone, those around Him with the twelve asked Him about the parable. [11]And He said to them, "To you it has been given to know the mystery of the kingdom of God; but to those who are outside, all things come in parables, [12]so that

> 'Seeing they may see and not perceive,
> And hearing they may hear and not
>   understand;
> Lest they should turn,
> And *their sins* be forgiven them.' "[a]

The Parable of the Sower Explained

[13]And He said to them, "Do you not understand this parable? How then will you understand all the parables? [14]The sower sows the word. [15]And these are the ones by the wayside where the word is sown. When they hear, Satan comes immediately and takes away the word that was sown in their hearts. [16]These likewise are the ones sown on stony ground who, when they hear the word, immediately receive it with gladness; [17]and they have no root in themselves, and so endure only for a time. Afterward, when tribulation or persecution arises for the word's sake, immediately they stumble. [18]Now these are the ones sown among thorns; *they are* the ones who hear the word, [19]and the cares of this world, the deceitfulness of riches, and the desires for other things entering in choke the word, and it becomes unfruitful. [20]But these are the ones sown on good ground, those who hear the word, accept *it,* and bear fruit: some thirtyfold, some sixty, and some a hundred."

Light Under a Basket

[21]Also He said to them, "Is a lamp brought to be put under a basket or under a bed? Is it not to be set on a lampstand? [22]For there is nothing hidden which will not be revealed, nor has anything been kept secret but that it should come to light. [23]If anyone has ears to hear, let him hear."

[24]Then He said to them, "Take heed what you hear. With the same measure you use, it will be measured to you; and to you who hear, more will be given. [25]For whoever has, to him more

will be given; but whoever does not have, even what he has will be taken away from him."

The Parable of the Growing Seed

[26]And He said, "The kingdom of God is as if a man should scatter seed on the ground, [27]and should sleep by night and rise by day, and the seed should sprout and grow, he himself does not know how. [28]For the earth yields crops by itself: first the blade, then the head, after that the full grain in the head. [29]But when the grain ripens, immediately he puts in the sickle, because the harvest has come."

The Parable of the Mustard Seed

[30]Then He said, "To what shall we liken the kingdom of God? Or with what parable shall we picture it? [31]*It is* like a mustard seed which, when it is sown on the ground, is smaller than all the seeds on earth; [32]but when it is sown, it grows up and becomes greater than all herbs, and shoots out large branches, so that the birds of the air may nest under its shade."

Jesus' Use of Parables

[33]And with many such parables He spoke the word to them as they were able to hear *it.* [34]But without a parable He did not speak to them. And when they were alone, He explained all things to His disciples.

Wind and Wave Obey Jesus

[35]On the same day, when evening had come, He said to them, "Let us cross over to the other side." [36]Now when they had left the multitude, they took Him along in the boat as He was. And other little boats were also with Him. [37]And a great windstorm arose, and the waves beat into the boat, so that it was already filling. [38]But He was in the stern, asleep on a pillow. And they awoke Him and said to Him, "Teacher, do You not care that we are perishing?"

[39]Then He arose and rebuked the wind, and said to the sea, "Peace, be still!" And the wind ceased and there was a great calm. [40]But He said to them, "Why are you so fearful? How *is it* that you have no faith?"[a] [41]And they feared exceedingly,

4:12 [a]Isaiah 6:9, 10   **4:40** [a]NU-Text reads *Have you still no faith?*

LEADERSHIP ISSUES

GC2: Nourished by the Word: Experiencing Scripture

MARK 4:35 *On the same day, when evening had come, He said to them, "Let us cross over to the other side."*

With this declaration, Jesus challenged the disciples to actually experience the parable of the sower (Mark 4:1–20). It's this "experiencing of Scripture" that is life transforming in our walk with Jesus. The sower (Jesus) had just sown the seed (the Word of God) upon the disciples' hearts. How did they respond? As predicted in the parable, the seed was attacked:

- *Satan came to destroy the Word.* A furious squall came up, so Jesus rebuked the wind and said to the waves, "Peace, be still!" (Mark 4:39). Then the wind died down and was completely calm. The word "rebuke" in this text was used by Jesus in other passages to refer to the Evil One (Jude 9).

- *Tribulation came to destroy the Word.* When the storm hit, "the waves beat into the boat, so that it was already filling" (Mark 4:37). In a world of tribulation, the stresses of life can come from many sources: family, friends, jobs, health, church, and ministry. If our hearts are not guarded, the Word can wither within us.

- *Caring for other things choked out the Word.* Jesus' disciples asked Him, "Teacher, do You not care that we are perishing?" (Mark 4:38). The cares of this life can focus our hearts on popularity, material possessions, or other people's success. If our hearts are not guarded, these cares will choke out the Word.

Much like these disciples, which Bible verses have you "heard" recently that you actually need to experience? Consider praying this prayer: "Lord, which Bible verses do I need to experience today?"

GC2
GREAT COMMANDMENT
COMMISSION

and said to one another, "Who can this be, that even the wind and the sea obey Him!"

A Demon-Possessed Man Healed

5 Then they came to the other side of the sea, to the country of the Gadarenes.[a] ²And when He had come out of the boat, immediately there met Him out of the tombs a man with an unclean spirit, ³who had *his* dwelling among the tombs; and no one could bind him,[a] not even with chains, ⁴because he had often been bound with shackles and chains. And the chains had been pulled apart by him, and the shackles broken in pieces; neither could anyone tame him. ⁵And always, night and day, he was in the mountains and in the tombs, crying out and cutting himself with stones.

⁶When he saw Jesus from afar, he ran and worshiped Him. ⁷And he cried out with a loud voice and said, "What have I to do with You, Jesus, Son of the Most High God? I implore You by God that You do not torment me."

⁸For He said to him, "Come out of the man, unclean spirit!" ⁹Then He asked him, "What *is* your name?"

And he answered, saying, "My name *is* Legion; for we are many." ¹⁰Also he begged Him earnestly that He would not send them out of the country.

¹¹Now a large herd of swine was feeding there near the mountains. ¹²So all the demons begged Him, saying, "Send us to the swine, that we may enter them." ¹³And at once Jesus[a] gave them permission. Then the unclean spirits went out and entered the swine (there were about two thousand); and the herd ran violently down the steep place into the sea, and drowned in the sea.

¹⁴So those who fed the swine fled, and they told *it* in the city and in the country. And they went out to see what it was that had happened. ¹⁵Then they came to Jesus, and saw the one *who had been* demon-possessed and had the legion, sitting and clothed and in his right mind. And they were afraid. ¹⁶And those who saw it told them how it happened to him *who had been* demon-possessed, and about the swine. ¹⁷Then they began to plead with Him to depart from their region.

¹⁸And when He got into the boat, he who had been demon-possessed begged Him that he

might be with Him. ¹⁹However, Jesus did not permit him, but said to him, "Go home to your friends, and tell them what great things the Lord has done for you, and how He has had compassion on you." ²⁰And he departed and began to proclaim in Decapolis all that Jesus had done for him; and all marveled.

A Girl Restored to Life and a Woman Healed

²¹Now when Jesus had crossed over again by boat to the other side, a great multitude gathered to Him; and He was by the sea. ²²And behold, one of the rulers of the synagogue came, Jairus by name. And when he saw Him, he fell at His feet ²³and begged Him earnestly, saying, "My little daughter lies at the point of death. Come and lay Your hands on her, that she may be healed, and she will live." ²⁴So *Jesus* went with him, and a great multitude followed Him and thronged Him.

²⁵Now a certain woman had a flow of blood for twelve years, ²⁶and had suffered many things from many physicians. She had spent all that she had and was no better, but rather grew worse. ²⁷When she heard about Jesus, she came behind *Him* in the crowd and touched His garment. ²⁸For she said, "If only I may touch His clothes, I shall be made well."

²⁹Immediately the fountain of her blood was dried up, and she felt in *her* body that she was healed of the affliction. ³⁰And Jesus, immediately knowing in Himself that power had gone out of Him, turned around in the crowd and said, "Who touched My clothes?"

³¹But His disciples said to Him, "You see the multitude thronging You, and You say, 'Who touched Me?'"

³²And He looked around to see her who had done this thing. ³³But the woman, fearing and trembling, knowing what had happened to her, came and fell down before Him and told Him the whole truth. ³⁴And He said to her, "Daughter, your faith has made you well. Go in peace, and be healed of your affliction."

³⁵While He was still speaking, *some* came from the ruler of the synagogue's *house* who said, "Your daughter is dead. Why trouble the Teacher any further?"

5:1 [a]NU-Text reads *Gerasenes.*   **5:3** [a]NU-Text adds *anymore.*
5:13 [a]NU-Text reads *And He gave.*

LEADERSHIP ISSUES

GC2: Sharing Christ: Imparting His Very life

MARK 5:22–24

Notice the significance of Christ and the disciples heading off to minister at the home of a synagogue ruler. Imagine the disciples' excitement: "Finally, a breakthrough with the synagogue officials has come! This is the opportunity we have been waiting for—Jesus will perform a miracle for Jairus, and surely many doors of ministry will open!" And then they are interrupted!

As the crowd pressed against Jesus, a woman in need of healing touched His robe. He asked who had done it, and His disciples said, "You see the multitude thronging You, and You say, 'Who touched Me?'" (Mark 5:31). But Jesus kept looking around to see who had done it (vv. 25–34).

Notice the contrast between Jesus and the disciples. Jesus stops, sensitive to what has happened and wanting to connect with the woman who touched Him. The disciples, in contrast, seem irritated. You can sense their impatience and frustration—their agenda has been interrupted! Undoubtedly, they were thinking, *We need to get to Jairus's house! We may miss this opportunity!*

Pause now to reflect on your own life, calling, ministry, or pursuits. Perhaps you are occasionally interrupted just as you are excitedly heading off to do "important" things. People near you need you!

Who might some of these "interrupting" people be in your life? Family members? Close friends? Coworkers? Small group members? About what might they typically "interrupt" you? Do you ever feel inconvenienced or even irritated by them?

Consider what these people really need—Christ's support, care, and encouragement shared through you. You have freely received His love and life, and you are now being challenged to freely give it to them.

GC2

GREAT COMMANDMENT
COMMISSION

³⁶As soon as Jesus heard the word that was spoken, He said to the ruler of the synagogue, "Do not be afraid; only believe." ³⁷And He permitted no one to follow Him except Peter, James, and John the brother of James. ³⁸Then He came to the house of the ruler of the synagogue, and saw a tumult and those who wept and wailed loudly. ³⁹When He came in, He said to them, "Why make this commotion and weep? The child is not dead, but sleeping."

⁴⁰And they ridiculed Him. But when He had put them all outside, He took the father and the mother of the child, and those *who were* with Him, and entered where the child was lying. ⁴¹Then He took the child by the hand, and said to her, "Talitha, cumi," which is translated, "Little girl, I say to you, arise." ⁴²Immediately the girl arose and walked, for she was twelve years *of age.* And they were overcome with great amazement. ⁴³But He commanded them strictly that no one should know it, and said that *something* should be given her to eat.

JESUS REJECTED AT NAZARETH

6 Then He went out from there and came to His own country, and His disciples followed Him. ²And when the Sabbath had come, He began to teach in the synagogue. And many hearing *Him* were astonished, saying, "Where *did* this Man *get* these things? And what wisdom *is* this which is given to Him, that such mighty works are performed by His hands! ³Is this not the carpenter, the Son of Mary, and brother of James, Joses, Judas, and Simon? And are not His sisters here with us?" So they were offended at Him.

⁴But Jesus said to them, "A prophet is not without honor except in his own country, among his own relatives, and in his own house." ⁵Now He could do no mighty work there, except that He laid His hands on a few sick people and healed *them.* ⁶And He marveled because of their unbelief. Then He went about the villages in a circuit, teaching.

SENDING OUT THE TWELVE

⁷And He called the twelve to *Himself,* and began to send them out two *by* two, and gave them power over unclean spirits. ⁸He commanded them to take nothing for the journey except a staff—no bag, no bread, no copper in *their* money belts— ⁹but to wear sandals, and not to put on two tunics.

¹⁰Also He said to them, "In whatever place you enter a house, stay there till you depart from that place. ¹¹And whoeverᵃ will not receive you nor hear you, when you depart from there, shake off the dust under your feet as a testimony against them.ᵇ Assuredly, I say to you, it will be more tolerable for Sodom and Gomorrah in the day of judgment than for that city!"

¹²So they went out and preached that *people* should repent. ¹³And they cast out many demons, and anointed with oil many who were sick, and healed *them.*

JOHN THE BAPTIST BEHEADED

¹⁴Now King Herod heard *of Him,* for His name had become well known. And he said, "John the Baptist is risen from the dead, and therefore these powers are at work in him."

¹⁵Others said, "It is Elijah."

And others said, "It is the Prophet, orᵃ like one of the prophets."

¹⁶But when Herod heard, he said, "This is John, whom I beheaded; he has been raised from the dead!" ¹⁷For Herod himself had sent and laid hold of John, and bound him in prison for the sake of Herodias, his brother Philip's wife; for he had married her. ¹⁸Because John had said to Herod, "It is not lawful for you to have your brother's wife."

¹⁹Therefore Herodias held it against him and wanted to kill him, but she could not; ²⁰for Herod feared John, knowing that he *was* a just and holy man, and he protected him. And when he heard him, he did many things, and heard him gladly.

²¹Then an opportune day came when Herod on his birthday gave a feast for his nobles, the high officers, and the chief *men* of Galilee. ²²And when Herodias' daughter herself came in and danced, and pleased Herod and those who sat with him, the king said to the girl, "Ask me whatever you want, and I will give *it* to you." ²³He also swore to her, "Whatever you ask me, I will give you, up to half my kingdom."

6:11 ᵃNU-Text reads *whatever place.* ᵇNU-Text omits the rest of this verse. **6:15** ᵃNU-Text and M-Text omit *or.*

²⁴So she went out and said to her mother, "What shall I ask?"

And she said, "The head of John the Baptist!"

²⁵Immediately she came in with haste to the king and asked, saying, "I want you to give me at once the head of John the Baptist on a platter."

²⁶And the king was exceedingly sorry; *yet,* because of the oaths and because of those who sat with him, he did not want to refuse her. ²⁷Immediately the king sent an executioner and commanded his head to be brought. And he went and beheaded him in prison, ²⁸brought his head on a platter, and gave it to the girl; and the girl gave it to her mother. ²⁹When his disciples heard *of it,* they came and took away his corpse and laid it in a tomb.

Feeding the Five Thousand

³⁰Then the apostles gathered to Jesus and told Him all things, both what they had done and what they had taught. ³¹And He said to them, "Come aside by yourselves to a deserted place and rest a while." For there were many coming and going, and they did not even have time to eat. ³²So they departed to a deserted place in the boat by themselves.

³³But the multitudesª saw them departing, and many knew Him and ran there on foot from all the cities. They arrived before them and came together to Him. ³⁴And Jesus, when He came out, saw a great multitude and was moved with compassion for them, because they were like sheep not having a shepherd. So He began to teach them many things. ³⁵When the day was now far spent, His disciples came to Him and said, "This is a deserted place, and already the hour *is* late. ³⁶Send them away, that they may go into the surrounding country and villages and buy themselves bread;ª for they have nothing to eat."

³⁷But He answered and said to them, "You give them something to eat."

And they said to Him, "Shall we go and buy two hundred denarii worth of bread and give them *something* to eat?"

³⁸But He said to them, "How many loaves do you have? Go and see."

And when they found out they said, "Five, and two fish."

³⁹Then He commanded them to make them all sit down in groups on the green grass. ⁴⁰So they sat down in ranks, in hundreds and in fifties. ⁴¹And when He had taken the five loaves and the two fish, He looked up to heaven, blessed and broke the loaves, and gave *them* to His disciples to set before them; and the two fish He divided among *them* all. ⁴²So they all ate and were filled. ⁴³And they took up twelve baskets full of fragments and of the fish. ⁴⁴Now those who had eaten the loaves were aboutª five thousand men.

Jesus Walks on the Sea

⁴⁵Immediately He made His disciples get into the boat and go before Him to the other side, to Bethsaida, while He sent the multitude away. ⁴⁶And when He had sent them away, He departed to the mountain to pray. ⁴⁷Now when evening came, the boat was in the middle of the sea; and He *was* alone on the land. ⁴⁸Then He saw them straining at rowing, for the wind was against them. Now about the fourth watch of the night He came to them, walking on the sea, and would have passed them by. ⁴⁹And when they saw Him walking on the sea, they supposed it was a ghost, and cried out; ⁵⁰for they all saw Him and were troubled. But immediately He talked with them and said to them, "Be of good cheer! It is I; do not be afraid." ⁵¹Then He went up into the boat to them, and the wind ceased. And they were greatly amazed in themselves beyond measure, and marveled. ⁵²For they had not understood about the loaves, because their heart was hardened.

Many Touch Him and Are Made Well

⁵³When they had crossed over, they came to the land of Gennesaret and anchored there. ⁵⁴And when they came out of the boat, immediately the people recognized Him, ⁵⁵ran through that whole surrounding region, and began to carry about on beds those who were sick to wherever they heard He was. ⁵⁶Wherever He entered, into villages, cities, or the country, they laid the sick in the marketplaces, and begged Him that they might just touch the hem of His garment. And as many as touched Him were made well.

6:33 ªNU-Text and M-Text read *they.* **6:36** ªNU-Text reads *something to eat* and omits the rest of this verse. **6:44** ªNU-Text and M-Text omit *about.*

DEFILEMENT COMES FROM WITHIN

7 Then the Pharisees and some of the scribes came together to Him, having come from Jerusalem. [2]Now when[a] they saw some of His disciples eat bread with defiled, that is, with unwashed hands, they found fault. [3]For the Pharisees and all the Jews do not eat unless they wash *their* hands in a special way, holding the tradition of the elders. [4]*When they come* from the marketplace, they do not eat unless they wash. And there are many other things which they have received and hold, *like* the washing of cups, pitchers, copper vessels, and couches.

[5]Then the Pharisees and scribes asked Him, "Why do Your disciples not walk according to the tradition of the elders, but eat bread with unwashed hands?"

[6]He answered and said to them, "Well did Isaiah prophesy of you hypocrites, as it is written:

'This people honors Me with *their* lips,
  But their heart is far from Me.
[7]And in vain they worship Me,
  Teaching *as* doctrines the commandments of
    men.'[a]

[8]For laying aside the commandment of God, you hold the tradition of men[a]—the washing of pitchers and cups, and many other such things you do."

[9]He said to them, "*All too* well you reject the commandment of God, that you may keep your tradition. [10]For Moses said, 'Honor your father and your mother';[a] and, 'He who curses father or mother, let him be put to death.'[b] [11]But you say, 'If a man says to his father or mother, "Whatever profit you might have received from me *is* Corban"—' (that is, a gift *to God*), [12]then you no longer let him do anything for his father or his mother, [13]making the word of God of no effect through your tradition which you have handed down. And many such things you do."

[14]When He had called all the multitude to *Himself*, He said to them, "Hear Me, everyone, and understand: [15]There is nothing that enters a man from outside which can defile him; but the things which come out of him, those are the things that defile a man. [16]If anyone has ears to hear, let him hear!"[a]

[17]When He had entered a house away from the crowd, His disciples asked Him concerning the parable. [18]So He said to them, "Are you thus without understanding also? Do you not perceive that whatever enters a man from outside cannot defile him, [19]because it does not enter his heart but his stomach, and is eliminated, *thus* purifying all foods?"[a] [20]And He said, "What comes out of a man, that defiles a man. [21]For from within, out of the heart of men, proceed evil thoughts, adulteries, fornications, murders, [22]thefts, covetousness, wickedness, deceit, lewdness, an evil eye, blasphemy, pride, foolishness. [23]All these evil things come from within and defile a man."

A GENTILE SHOWS HER FAITH

[24]From there He arose and went to the region of Tyre and Sidon.[a] And He entered a house and wanted no one to know *it*, but He could not be hidden. [25]For a woman whose young daughter had an unclean spirit heard about Him, and she came and fell at His feet. [26]The woman was a Greek, a Syro-Phoenician by birth, and she kept asking Him to cast the demon out of her daughter. [27]But Jesus said to her, "Let the children be filled first, for it is not good to take the children's bread and throw *it* to the little dogs."

[28]And she answered and said to Him, "Yes, Lord, yet even the little dogs under the table eat from the children's crumbs."

[29]Then He said to her, "For this saying go your way; the demon has gone out of your daughter."

[30]And when she had come to her house, she found the demon gone out, and her daughter lying on the bed.

JESUS HEALS A DEAF-MUTE

[31]Again, departing from the region of Tyre and Sidon, He came through the midst of the region of Decapolis to the Sea of Galilee. [32]Then they brought to Him one who was deaf and had an impediment in his speech, and they begged

7:2 [a]NU-Text omits *when* and *they found fault*.   7:7 [a]Isaiah 29:13
7:8 [a]NU-Text omits the rest of this verse.   7:10 [a]Exodus 20:12; Deuteronomy 5:16 [b]Exodus 21:17   7:16 [a]NU-Text omits this verse.
7:19 [a]NU-Text ends quotation with *eliminated*, setting off the final clause as Mark's comment that Jesus has declared all foods clean.
7:24 [a]NU-Text omits *and Sidon*.

Him to put His hand on him. [33]And He took him aside from the multitude, and put His fingers in his ears, and He spat and touched his tongue. [34]Then, looking up to heaven, He sighed, and said to him, "Ephphatha," that is, "Be opened."

[35]Immediately his ears were opened, and the impediment of his tongue was loosed, and he spoke plainly. [36]Then He commanded them that they should tell no one; but the more He commanded them, the more widely they proclaimed *it*. [37]And they were astonished beyond measure, saying, "He has done all things well. He makes both the deaf to hear and the mute to speak."

Feeding the Four Thousand

8 In those days, the multitude being very great and having nothing to eat, Jesus called His disciples *to Him* and said to them, [2]"I have compassion on the multitude, because they have now continued with Me three days and have nothing to eat. [3]And if I send them away hungry to their own houses, they will faint on the way; for some of them have come from afar."

[4]Then His disciples answered Him, "How can one satisfy these people with bread here in the wilderness?"

[5]He asked them, "How many loaves do you have?"

And they said, "Seven."

[6]So He commanded the multitude to sit down on the ground. And He took the seven loaves and gave thanks, broke *them* and gave *them* to His disciples to set before *them;* and they set *them* before the multitude. [7]They also had a few small fish; and having blessed them, He said to set them also before *them*. [8]So they ate and were filled, and they took up seven large baskets of leftover fragments. [9]Now those who had eaten were about four thousand. And He sent them away, [10]immediately got into the boat with His disciples, and came to the region of Dalmanutha.

The Pharisees Seek a Sign

[11]Then the Pharisees came out and began to dispute with Him, seeking from Him a sign from heaven, testing Him. [12]But He sighed deeply in His spirit, and said, "Why does this generation seek a sign? Assuredly, I say to you, no sign shall be given to this generation."

Beware of the Leaven of the Pharisees and Herod

[13]And He left them, and getting into the boat again, departed to the other side. [14]Now the disciples[a] had forgotten to take bread, and they did not have more than one loaf with them in the boat. [15]Then He charged them, saying, "Take heed, beware of the leaven of the Pharisees and the leaven of Herod."

[16]And they reasoned among themselves, saying, "*It is* because we have no bread."

[17]But Jesus, being aware of *it,* said to them, "Why do you reason because you have no bread? Do you not yet perceive nor understand? Is your heart still[a] hardened? [18]Having eyes, do you not see? And having ears, do you not hear? And do you not remember? [19]When I broke the five loaves for the five thousand, how many baskets full of fragments did you take up?"

They said to Him, "Twelve."

[20]"Also, when I broke the seven for the four thousand, how many large baskets full of fragments did you take up?"

And they said, "Seven."

[21]So He said to them, "How *is it* you do not understand?"

A Blind Man Healed at Bethsaida

[22]Then He came to Bethsaida; and they brought a blind man to Him, and begged Him to touch him. [23]So He took the blind man by the hand and led him out of the town. And when He had spit on his eyes and put His hands on him, He asked him if he saw anything.

[24]And he looked up and said, "I see men like trees, walking."

[25]Then He put *His* hands on his eyes again and made him look up. And he was restored and saw everyone clearly. [26]Then He sent him away to his house, saying, "Neither go into the town, nor tell anyone in the town."[a]

Peter Confesses Jesus as the Christ

[27]Now Jesus and His disciples went out to the towns of Caesarea Philippi; and on the road He asked His disciples, saying to them, "Who do men say that I am?"

8:14 [a]NU-Text and M-Text read *they.* **8:17** [a]NU-Text omits *still.*
8:26 [a]NU-Text reads *"Do not even go into the town."*

LEADERSHIP ISSUES

GC2: Becoming a Good Samaritan: Seeing People as People

MARK 8:24

The metaphor in this story of "seeing people as trees" is a useful one in understanding our calling to see people as God sees them. In order to become people who care for others, we must come to see people as people—not as "trees"!

Consider one of the typical things we do with trees. We prune them. If we're not careful, we'll come to think that God has only called us to prune people. Pruning sometimes sounds like: "Hurry up, you're going to be late!" "Wipe that look off your face." "If I've told you once, I've told you a hundred times!" "If you'd just read your Bible more and pray more, you wouldn't get in such a mess." When we see people only as things to be pruned, they continue to be alone (Gen. 2:18). We must see their aloneness in addition to their "sin" or shortcomings. We must come to see people as God sees them, take thought of them, leave where we are, and enter into their lives to be with them.

Those people who answer the call to care for the pain-filled people along the road of life are those that Jesus refers to as "good Samaritans" (Luke 10:30–35). We become equipped to do this as we become people who see people the way God sees them, so we can love them as God loves them. Jesus Christ modeled this sacrificial love by being One who left His heavenly world to enter into ours in order to care for us at our point of greatest need (Phil. 2:5–11).

²⁸So they answered, "John the Baptist; but some *say,* Elijah; and others, one of the prophets."

²⁹He said to them, "But who do you say that I am?"

Peter answered and said to Him, "You are the Christ."

³⁰Then He strictly warned them that they should tell no one about Him.

Jesus Predicts His Death and Resurrection

³¹And He began to teach them that the Son of Man must suffer many things, and be rejected by the elders and chief priests and scribes, and be killed, and after three days rise again. ³²He spoke this word openly. Then Peter took Him aside and began to rebuke Him. ³³But when He had turned around and looked at His disciples, He rebuked Peter, saying, "Get behind Me, Satan! For you are not mindful of the things of God, but the things of men."

Take Up the Cross and Follow Him

³⁴When He had called the people to *Himself,* with His disciples also, He said to them, "Whoever desires to come after Me, let him deny himself, and take up his cross, and follow Me. ³⁵For whoever desires to save his life will lose it, but whoever loses his life for My sake and the gospel's will save it. ³⁶For what will it profit a man if he gains the whole world, and loses his own soul? ³⁷Or what will a man give in exchange for his soul? ³⁸For whoever is ashamed of Me and My words in this adulterous and sinful generation, of him the Son of Man also will be ashamed when He comes in the glory of His Father with the holy angels."

9And He said to them, "Assuredly, I say to you that there are some standing here who will not taste death till they see the kingdom of God present with power."

Jesus Transfigured on the Mount

²Now after six days Jesus took Peter, James, and John, and led them up on a high mountain apart by themselves; and He was transfigured before them. ³His clothes became shining, exceedingly white, like snow, such as no launderer on earth can whiten them. ⁴And Elijah appeared to them with Moses, and they were talking with Je-

sus. ⁵Then Peter answered and said to Jesus, "Rabbi, it is good for us to be here; and let us make three tabernacles: one for You, one for Moses, and one for Elijah"— ⁶because he did not know what to say, for they were greatly afraid.

⁷And a cloud came and overshadowed them; and a voice came out of the cloud, saying, "This is My beloved Son. Hear Him!" ⁸Suddenly, when they had looked around, they saw no one anymore, but only Jesus with themselves.

⁹Now as they came down from the mountain, He commanded them that they should tell no one the things they had seen, till the Son of Man had risen from the dead. ¹⁰So they kept this word to themselves, questioning what the rising from the dead meant.

¹¹And they asked Him, saying, "Why do the scribes say that Elijah must come first?"

¹²Then He answered and told them, "Indeed, Elijah is coming first and restores all things. And how is it written concerning the Son of Man, that He must suffer many things and be treated with contempt? ¹³But I say to you that Elijah has also come, and they did to him whatever they wished, as it is written of him."

A Boy Is Healed

¹⁴And when He came to the disciples, He saw a great multitude around them, and scribes disputing with them. ¹⁵Immediately, when they saw Him, all the people were greatly amazed, and running to *Him,* greeted Him. ¹⁶And He asked the scribes, "What are you discussing with them?"

¹⁷Then one of the crowd answered and said, "Teacher, I brought You my son, who has a mute spirit. ¹⁸And wherever it seizes him, it throws him down; he foams at the mouth, gnashes his teeth, and becomes rigid. So I spoke to Your disciples, that they should cast it out, but they could not."

¹⁹He answered him and said, "O faithless generation, how long shall I be with you? How long shall I bear with you? Bring him to Me." ²⁰Then they brought him to Him. And when he saw Him, immediately the spirit convulsed him, and he fell on the ground and wallowed, foaming at the mouth.

²¹So He asked his father, "How long has this been happening to him?"

And he said, "From childhood. ²²And often

he has thrown him both into the fire and into the water to destroy him. But if You can do anything, have compassion on us and help us."

23Jesus said to him, "If you can believe,a all things *are* possible to him who believes."

24Immediately the father of the child cried out and said with tears, "Lord, I believe; help my unbelief!"

25When Jesus saw that the people came running together, He rebuked the unclean spirit, saying to it, "Deaf and dumb spirit, I command you, come out of him and enter him no more!" 26Then *the spirit* cried out, convulsed him greatly, and came out of him. And he became as one dead, so that many said, "He is dead." 27But Jesus took him by the hand and lifted him up, and he arose.

28And when He had come into the house, His disciples asked Him privately, "Why could we not cast it out?"

29So He said to them, "This kind can come out by nothing but prayer and fasting."a

Jesus Again Predicts His Death and Resurrection

30Then they departed from there and passed through Galilee, and He did not want anyone to know *it*. 31For He taught His disciples and said to them, "The Son of Man is being betrayed into the hands of men, and they will kill Him. And after He is killed, He will rise the third day." 32But they did not understand this saying, and were afraid to ask Him.

Who Is the Greatest?

33Then He came to Capernaum. And when He was in the house He asked them, "What was it you disputed among yourselves on the road?" 34But they kept silent, for on the road they had disputed among themselves who *would be the* greatest. 35And He sat down, called the twelve, and said to them, "If anyone desires to be first, he shall be last of all and servant of all." 36Then He took a little child and set him in the midst of them. And when He had taken him in His arms, He said to them, 37"Whoever receives one of these little children in My name receives Me; and whoever receives Me, receives not Me but Him who sent Me."

Jesus Forbids Sectarianism

38Now John answered Him, saying, "Teacher, we saw someone who does not follow us casting out demons in Your name, and we forbade him because he does not follow us."

39But Jesus said, "Do not forbid him, for no one who works a miracle in My name can soon afterward speak evil of Me. 40For he who is not against us is on oura side. 41For whoever gives you a cup of water to drink in My name, because you belong to Christ, assuredly, I say to you, he will by no means lose his reward.

Jesus Warns of Offenses

42"But whoever causes one of these little ones who believe in Me to stumble, it would be better for him if a millstone were hung around his neck, and he were thrown into the sea. 43If your hand causes you to sin, cut it off. It is better for you to enter into life maimed, rather than having two hands, to go to hell, into the fire that shall never be quenched— 44where

> *Their worm does not die*
> *And the fire is not quenched.'*a

45And if your foot causes you to sin, cut it off. It is better for you to enter life lame, rather than having two feet, to be cast into hell, into the fire that shall never be quenched— 46where

> *Their worm does not die*
> *And the fire is not quenched.'*a

47And if your eye causes you to sin, pluck it out. It is better for you to enter the kingdom of God with one eye, rather than having two eyes, to be cast into hell fire— 48where

> *Their worm does not die*
> *And the fire is not quenched.'*a

Tasteless Salt Is Worthless

49"For everyone will be seasoned with fire,a and every sacrifice will be seasoned with salt.

9:23 aNU-Text reads *"'If You can!' All things. . . ."* **9:29** aNU-Text omits *and fasting.* **9:40** aM-Text reads *against you is on your side.* **9:44** aNU-Text omits this verse. **9:46** aNU-Text omits the last clause of verse 45 and all of verse 46. **9:48** aIsaiah 66:24 **9:49** aNU-Text omits the rest of this verse.

[50]Salt *is* good, but if the salt loses its flavor, how will you season it? Have salt in yourselves, and have peace with one another."

Marriage and Divorce

10 Then He arose from there and came to the region of Judea by the other side of the Jordan. And multitudes gathered to Him again, and as He was accustomed, He taught them again.

[2]The Pharisees came and asked Him, "Is it lawful for a man to divorce *his* wife?" testing Him.

[3]And He answered and said to them, "What did Moses command you?"

[4]They said, "Moses permitted *a man* to write a certificate of divorce, and to dismiss *her.*"

[5]And Jesus answered and said to them, "Because of the hardness of your heart he wrote you this precept. [6]But from the beginning of the creation, God *'made them male and female.'*[a] [7]*'For this reason a man shall leave his father and mother and be joined to his wife,* [8]*and the two shall become one flesh'*;[a] so then they are no longer two, but one flesh. [9]Therefore what God has joined together, let not man separate."

[10]In the house His disciples also asked Him again about the same *matter.* [11]So He said to them, "Whoever divorces his wife and marries another commits adultery against her. [12]And if a woman divorces her husband and marries another, she commits adultery."

Jesus Blesses Little Children

[13]Then they brought little children to Him, that He might touch them; but the disciples rebuked those who brought *them.* [14]But when Jesus saw *it,* He was greatly displeased and said to them, "Let the little children come to Me, and do not forbid them; for of such is the kingdom of God. [15]Assuredly, I say to you, whoever does not receive the kingdom of God as a little child will by no means enter it." [16]And He took them up in His arms, laid *His* hands on them, and blessed them.

Jesus Counsels the Rich Young Ruler

[17]Now as He was going out on the road, one came running, knelt before Him, and asked Him,

"Good Teacher, what shall I do that I may inherit eternal life?"

[18]So Jesus said to him, "Why do you call Me good? No one *is* good but One, *that is,* God. [19]You know the commandments: *'Do not commit adultery,' 'Do not murder,' 'Do not steal,' 'Do not bear false witness,'* 'Do not defraud,' *'Honor your father and your mother.'* "[a]

[20]And he answered and said to Him, "Teacher, all these things I have kept from my youth."

[21]Then Jesus, looking at him, loved him, and said to him, "One thing you lack: Go your way, sell whatever you have and give to the poor, and you will have treasure in heaven; and come, take up the cross, and follow Me."

[22]But he was sad at this word, and went away sorrowful, for he had great possessions.

With God All Things Are Possible

[23]Then Jesus looked around and said to His disciples, "How hard it is for those who have riches to enter the kingdom of God!" [24]And the disciples were astonished at His words. But Jesus answered again and said to them, "Children, how hard it is for those who trust in riches[a] to enter the kingdom of God! [25]It is easier for a camel to go through the eye of a needle than for a rich man to enter the kingdom of God."

[26]And they were greatly astonished, saying among themselves, "Who then can be saved?"

[27]But Jesus looked at them and said, "With men *it is* impossible, but not with God; for with God all things are possible."

[28]Then Peter began to say to Him, "See, we have left all and followed You."

[29]So Jesus answered and said, "Assuredly, I say to you, there is no one who has left house or brothers or sisters or father or mother or wife[a] or children or lands, for My sake and the gospel's, [30]who shall not receive a hundredfold now in this time—houses and brothers and sisters and mothers and children and lands, with persecutions—and in the age to come, eternal life. [31]But many *who are* first will be last, and the last first."

10:6 [a]Genesis 1:27; 5:2 **10:8** [a]Genesis 2:24 **10:19** [a]Exodus 20:12–16; Deuteronomy 5:16–20 **10:24** [a]NU-Text omits *for those who trust in riches.* **10:29** [a]NU-Text omits *or wife.*

LEADERSHIP ISSUES

GC2: Appropriate Affection

MARK 10:16

The need for affection is met by expressing care and closeness through appropriate physical touch and actually saying things like "I care about you." Notice the power of Christ's affection and blessing; there's no record that He taught here. He ministered to the children through the powerful simplicity of a caring touch and words of blessing.

Pause and reflect on these ideas for giving others affection:

- I offer appropriate physical gestures of love and tenderness (hand shake or hug).
- I often tell people "I care about you" or "I love you."
- I welcome people into my life by initiating warm greeting and caring concern.
- I share my heart with others, expressing they are "very dear to me" (1 Thess. 2:8).
- I strive to be careful about how others may or may not wish to receive affection.

Becoming a person who *shares appropriate affection* will help prepare you for healthy, God-honoring relationships.

GC2
GREAT COMMANDMENT
COMMISSION

JESUS A THIRD TIME PREDICTS HIS DEATH AND RESURRECTION

³²Now they were on the road, going up to Jerusalem, and Jesus was going before them; and they were amazed. And as they followed they were afraid. Then He took the twelve aside again and began to tell them the things that would happen to Him: ³³"Behold, we are going up to Jerusalem, and the Son of Man will be betrayed to the chief priests and to the scribes; and they will condemn Him to death and deliver Him to the Gentiles; ³⁴and they will mock Him, and scourge Him, and spit on Him, and kill Him. And the third day He will rise again."

GREATNESS IS SERVING

³⁵Then James and John, the sons of Zebedee, came to Him, saying, "Teacher, we want You to do for us whatever we ask."

³⁶And He said to them, "What do you want Me to do for you?"

³⁷They said to Him, "Grant us that we may sit, one on Your right hand and the other on Your left, in Your glory."

³⁸But Jesus said to them, "You do not know what you ask. Are you able to drink the cup that I drink, and be baptized with the baptism that I am baptized with?"

³⁹They said to Him, "We are able."

So Jesus said to them, "You will indeed drink the cup that I drink, and with the baptism I am baptized with you will be baptized; ⁴⁰but to sit on My right hand and on My left is not Mine to give, but *it is for those* for whom it is prepared."

⁴¹And when the ten heard *it,* they began to be greatly displeased with James and John. ⁴²But Jesus called them to *Himself* and said to them, "You know that those who are considered rulers over the Gentiles lord it over them, and their great ones exercise authority over them. ⁴³Yet it shall not be so among you; but whoever desires to become great among you shall be your servant. ⁴⁴And whoever of you desires to be first shall be slave of all. ⁴⁵For even the Son of Man did not come to be served, but to serve, and to give His life a ransom for many."

JESUS HEALS BLIND BARTIMAEUS

⁴⁶Now they came to Jericho. As He went out of Jericho with His disciples and a great multitude, blind Bartimaeus, the son of Timaeus, sat by the road begging. ⁴⁷And when he heard that it was Jesus of Nazareth, he began to cry out and say, "Jesus, Son of David, have mercy on me!"

⁴⁸Then many warned him to be quiet; but he cried out all the more, "Son of David, have mercy on me!"

⁴⁹So Jesus stood still and commanded him to be called.

Then they called the blind man, saying to him, "Be of good cheer. Rise, He is calling you."

⁵⁰And throwing aside his garment, he rose and came to Jesus.

⁵¹So Jesus answered and said to him, "What do you want Me to do for you?"

The blind man said to Him, "Rabboni, that I may receive my sight."

⁵²Then Jesus said to him, "Go your way; your faith has made you well." And immediately he received his sight and followed Jesus on the road.

THE TRIUMPHAL ENTRY

11 Now when they drew near Jerusalem, to Bethphage[a] and Bethany, at the Mount of Olives, He sent two of His disciples; ²and He said to them, "Go into the village opposite you; and as soon as you have entered it you will find a colt tied, on which no one has sat. Loose it and bring *it.* ³And if anyone says to you, 'Why are you doing this?' say, 'The Lord has need of it,' and immediately he will send it here."

⁴So they went their way, and found the[a] colt tied by the door outside on the street, and they loosed it. ⁵But some of those who stood there said to them, "What are you doing, loosing the colt?"

⁶And they spoke to them just as Jesus had commanded. So they let them go. ⁷Then they brought the colt to Jesus and threw their clothes on it, and He sat on it. ⁸And many spread their clothes on the road, and others cut down leafy branches from the trees and spread *them* on the road. ⁹Then those who went before and those who followed cried out, saying:

"Hosanna!
'Blessed *is* He who comes in the name of the LORD!'[a]

11:1 [a]M-Text reads *Bethsphage.*   **11:4** [a]NU-Text and M-Text read *a.*   **11:9** [a]Psalm 118:26

¹⁰Blessed *is* the kingdom of our father David
That comes in the name of the Lord!^a
Hosanna in the highest!"

¹¹And Jesus went into Jerusalem and into the temple. So when He had looked around at all things, as the hour was already late, He went out to Bethany with the twelve.

The Fig Tree Withered

¹²Now the next day, when they had come out from Bethany, He was hungry. ¹³And seeing from afar a fig tree having leaves, He went to see if perhaps He would find something on it. When He came to it, He found nothing but leaves, for it was not the season for figs. ¹⁴In response Jesus said to it, "Let no one eat fruit from you ever again."

And His disciples heard *it*.

Jesus Cleanses the Temple

¹⁵So they came to Jerusalem. Then Jesus went into the temple and began to drive out those who bought and sold in the temple, and overturned the tables of the money changers and the seats of those who sold doves. ¹⁶And He would not allow anyone to carry wares through the temple. ¹⁷Then He taught, saying to them, "Is it not written, *'My house shall be called a house of prayer for all nations'?*^a But you have made it a *'den of thieves.'*"^b

¹⁸And the scribes and chief priests heard it and sought how they might destroy Him; for they feared Him, because all the people were astonished at His teaching. ¹⁹When evening had come, He went out of the city.

The Lesson of the Withered Fig Tree

²⁰Now in the morning, as they passed by, they saw the fig tree dried up from the roots. ²¹And Peter, remembering, said to Him, "Rabbi, look! The fig tree which You cursed has withered away."

²²So Jesus answered and said to them, "Have faith in God. ²³For assuredly, I say to you, whoever says to this mountain, 'Be removed and be cast into the sea,' and does not doubt in his heart, but believes that those things he says will be done, he will have whatever he says. ²⁴Therefore I say to you, whatever things you ask when you pray, believe that you receive *them,* and you will have *them.*

Forgiveness and Prayer

²⁵"And whenever you stand praying, if you have anything against anyone, forgive him, that your Father in heaven may also forgive you your trespasses. ²⁶But if you do not forgive, neither will your Father in heaven forgive your trespasses."^a

Jesus' Authority Questioned

²⁷Then they came again to Jerusalem. And as He was walking in the temple, the chief priests, the scribes, and the elders came to Him. ²⁸And they said to Him, "By what authority are You doing these things? And who gave You this authority to do these things?"

²⁹But Jesus answered and said to them, "I also will ask you one question; then answer Me, and I will tell you by what authority I do these things: ³⁰The baptism of John—was it from heaven or from men? Answer Me."

³¹And they reasoned among themselves, saying, "If we say, 'From heaven,' He will say, 'Why then did you not believe him?' ³²But if we say, 'From men' "—they feared the people, for all counted John to have been a prophet indeed. ³³So they answered and said to Jesus, "We do not know."

And Jesus answered and said to them, "Neither will I tell you by what authority I do these things."

The Parable of the Wicked Vinedressers

12 Then He began to speak to them in parables: "A man planted a vineyard and set a hedge around *it,* dug *a place for* the wine vat and built a tower. And he leased it to vinedressers and went into a far country. ²Now at vintage-time he sent a servant to the vinedressers, that he might receive some of the fruit of the vineyard from the vinedressers. ³And they took *him* and beat him and sent *him* away empty-handed. ⁴Again he sent them another servant, and at him they threw stones,^a wounded *him* in the head, and sent *him* away shamefully treated. ⁵And again he sent an-

---

11:10 ^aNU-Text omits *in the name of the Lord.*   **11:17** ^aIsaiah 56:7   ^bJeremiah 7:11   **11:26** ^aNU-Text omits this verse.   **12:4** ^aNU-Text omits *and at him they threw stones.*

other, and him they killed; and many others, beating some and killing some. [6]Therefore still having one son, his beloved, he also sent him to them last, saying, 'They will respect my son.' [7]But those vinedressers said among themselves, 'This is the heir. Come, let us kill him, and the inheritance will be ours.' [8]So they took him and killed *him* and cast *him* out of the vineyard.

[9]"Therefore what will the owner of the vineyard do? He will come and destroy the vinedressers, and give the vineyard to others. [10]Have you not even read this Scripture:

> 'The stone which the builders rejected
> Has become the chief cornerstone.
> [11]This was the Lord's doing,
> And it is marvelous in our eyes'? "[a]

[12]And they sought to lay hands on Him, but feared the multitude, for they knew He had spoken the parable against them. So they left Him and went away.

The Pharisees: Is It Lawful to Pay Taxes to Caesar?

[13]Then they sent to Him some of the Pharisees and the Herodians, to catch Him in *His* words. [14]When they had come, they said to Him, "Teacher, we know that You are true, and care about no one; for You do not regard the person of men, but teach the way of God in truth. Is it lawful to pay taxes to Caesar, or not? [15]Shall we pay, or shall we not pay?"

But He, knowing their hypocrisy, said to them, "Why do you test Me? Bring Me a denarius that I may see *it*." [16]So they brought *it*.

And He said to them, "Whose image and inscription *is* this?" They said to Him, "Caesar's."

[17]And Jesus answered and said to them, "Render to Caesar the things that are Caesar's, and to God the things that are God's."

And they marveled at Him.

The Sadducees: What About the Resurrection?

[18]Then *some* Sadducees, who say there is no resurrection, came to Him; and they asked Him, saying: [19]"Teacher, Moses wrote to us that if a man's brother dies, and leaves *his* wife behind, and leaves no children, his brother should take his wife and raise up offspring for his brother. [20]Now

there were seven brothers. The first took a wife; and dying, he left no offspring. [21]And the second took her, and he died; nor did he leave any offspring. And the third likewise. [22]So the seven had her and left no offspring. Last of all the woman died also. [23]Therefore, in the resurrection, when they rise, whose wife will she be? For all seven had her as wife."

[24]Jesus answered and said to them, "Are you not therefore mistaken, because you do not know the Scriptures nor the power of God? [25]For when they rise from the dead, they neither marry nor are given in marriage, but are like angels in heaven. [26]But concerning the dead, that they rise, have you not read in the book of Moses, in the *burning* bush *passage,* how God spoke to him, saying, *'I am the God of Abraham, the God of Isaac, and the God of Jacob'?*[a] [27]He is not the God of the dead, but the God of the living. You are therefore greatly mistaken."

The Scribes: Which Is the First Commandment of All?

[28]Then one of the scribes came, and having heard them reasoning together, perceiving[a] that He had answered them well, asked Him, "Which is the first commandment of all?"

[29]Jesus answered him, "The first of all the commandments *is: 'Hear, O Israel, the LORD our God, the LORD is one.* [30]*And you shall love the LORD your God with all your heart, with all your soul, with all your mind, and with all your strength.'*[a] This *is* the first commandment.[b] [31]And the second, like *it, is* this: *'You shall love your neighbor as yourself.'*[a] There is no other commandment greater than these."

[32]So the scribe said to Him, "Well *said,* Teacher. You have spoken the truth, for there is one God, and there is no other but He. [33]And to love Him with all the heart, with all the understanding, with all the soul,[a] and with all the strength, and to love one's neighbor as oneself, is more than all the whole burnt offerings and sacrifices."

[34]Now when Jesus saw that he answered

12:11 [a]Psalm 118:22, 23   **12:26** [a]Exodus 3:6, 15   **12:28** [a]NU-Text reads *seeing.*   **12:30** [a]Deuteronomy 6:4, 5   [b]NU-Text omits this sentence.   **12:31** [a]Leviticus 19:18   **12:33** [a]NU-Text omits *with all the soul.*

LEADERSHIP ISSUES

GC2: Loving the Real God: See Him as He Truly Is

MARK 12:29 *Jesus answered him, "The first of all the commandments is: 'Hear, O Israel, the LORD our God, the LORD is one.'"*

When Christ gave us the Great Commandment, He actually referenced the Old Testament *Shema*, the Hebrew call to worship. The *Shema* begins with a declaration about the God of the Hebrew people. During Old Testament times, when pagan and idolatrous cultures were the norm and nations frequently worshiped gods of their own making, the first declaration of the Hebrew nation was about the one true God. The Hebrew call to worship clearly defined the One who is worthy of their adoration and loving obedience (Deut. 6:4, 5).

We must also notice that before there was a call to love Him, there was a clear declaration of who He is. In much the same way, before we can truly come to love the Lord our God, we must come to see God as He truly is. Imagine what God's heart was toward you when you woke up this morning: was He upset to see you? Did He even notice you, or could He have been excited? By seeing Him more clearly, we gain greater freedom to truly love Him.

Many of us may have never even considered our view of God. We have believed certain things about Him and have never questioned them or been challenged with an alternative. Take a moment to consider that the key to loving others well is loving the Lord well, and the key to loving the Lord well is seeing Him as He really is.

Pause and pray to know Him better:

"Lord, as I can better come to know You, I want to! Help me see You as You really are so I can love You with all my heart, mind, soul, and strength."

GC2
GREAT COMMANDMENT
COMMISSION

wisely, He said to him, "You are not far from the kingdom of God."

But after that no one dared question Him.

Jesus: How Can David Call His Descendant Lord?

³⁵Then Jesus answered and said, while He taught in the temple, "How *is it* that the scribes say that the Christ is the Son of David? ³⁶For David himself said by the Holy Spirit:

> 'The LORD said to my Lord,
> "Sit at My right hand,
> Till I make Your enemies Your footstool." ' ᵃ

³⁷Therefore David himself calls Him *'Lord'*; how is He *then* his Son?"

And the common people heard Him gladly.

Beware of the Scribes

³⁸Then He said to them in His teaching, "Beware of the scribes, who desire to go around in long robes, *love* greetings in the marketplaces, ³⁹the best seats in the synagogues, and the best places at feasts, ⁴⁰who devour widows' houses, and for a pretense make long prayers. These will receive greater condemnation."

The Widow's Two Mites

⁴¹Now Jesus sat opposite the treasury and saw how the people put money into the treasury. And many *who were* rich put in much. ⁴²Then one poor widow came and threw in two mites,ᵃ which make a quadrans. ⁴³So He called His disciples to *Himself* and said to them, "Assuredly, I say to you that this poor widow has put in more than all those who have given to the treasury; ⁴⁴for they all put in out of their abundance, but she out of her poverty put in all that she had, her whole livelihood."

Jesus Predicts the Destruction of the Temple

13 Then as He went out of the temple, one of His disciples said to Him, "Teacher, see what manner of stones and what buildings *are here!*"

²And Jesus answered and said to him, "Do you see these great buildings? Not *one* stone shall be left upon another, that shall not be thrown down."

The Signs of the Times and the End of the Age

³Now as He sat on the Mount of Olives opposite the temple, Peter, James, John, and Andrew asked Him privately, ⁴"Tell us, when will these things be? And what *will be* the sign when all these things will be fulfilled?"

⁵And Jesus, answering them, began to say: "Take heed that no one deceives you. ⁶For many will come in My name, saying, 'I am *He*,' and will deceive many. ⁷But when you hear of wars and rumors of wars, do not be troubled; for *such things* must happen, but the end *is* not yet. ⁸For nation will rise against nation, and kingdom against kingdom. And there will be earthquakes in various places, and there will be famines and troubles.ᵃ These *are* the beginnings of sorrows.

⁹"But watch out for yourselves, for they will deliver you up to councils, and you will be beaten in the synagogues. You will be broughtᵃ before rulers and kings for My sake, for a testimony to them. ¹⁰And the gospel must first be preached to all the nations. ¹¹But when they arrest *you* and deliver you up, do not worry beforehand, or premeditateᵃ what you will speak. But whatever is given you in that hour, speak that; for it is not you who speak, but the Holy Spirit. ¹²Now brother will betray brother to death, and a father *his* child; and children will rise up against parents and cause them to be put to death. ¹³And you will be hated by all for My name's sake. But he who endures to the end shall be saved.

The Great Tribulation

¹⁴"So when you see the *'abomination of desolation,'* ᵃ spoken of by Daniel the prophet,ᵇ standing where it ought not" (let the reader understand), "then let those who are in Judea flee to the mountains. ¹⁵Let him who is on the housetop not go down into the house, nor enter to take anything out of his house. ¹⁶And let him who is in the field not go back to get his clothes. ¹⁷But woe to those who are pregnant and to those who are nursing babies in those days! ¹⁸And pray that your flight may not be in winter. ¹⁹For *in* those

---

12:36 ᵃPsalm 110:1 **12:42** ᵃGreek *lepta*, very small copper coins worth a fraction of a penny **13:8** ᵃNU-Text omits *and troubles.* **13:9** ᵃNU-Text and M-Text read *will stand.* **13:11** ᵃNU-Text omits *or premeditate.* **13:14** ᵃDaniel 11:31; 12:11 ᵇNU-Text omits *spoken of by Daniel the prophet.*

days there will be tribulation, such as has not been since the beginning of the creation which God created until this time, nor ever shall be. [20]And unless the Lord had shortened those days, no flesh would be saved; but for the elect's sake, whom He chose, He shortened the days.

[21]"Then if anyone says to you, 'Look, here *is* the Christ!' or, 'Look, *He is* there!' do not believe it. [22]For false christs and false prophets will rise and show signs and wonders to deceive, if possible, even the elect. [23]But take heed; see, I have told you all things beforehand.

The Coming of the Son of Man

[24]"But in those days, after that tribulation, the sun will be darkened, and the moon will not give its light; [25]the stars of heaven will fall, and the powers in the heavens will be shaken. [26]Then they will see the Son of Man coming in the clouds with great power and glory. [27]And then He will send His angels, and gather together His elect from the four winds, from the farthest part of earth to the farthest part of heaven.

The Parable of the Fig Tree

[28]"Now learn this parable from the fig tree: When its branch has already become tender, and puts forth leaves, you know that summer is near. [29]So you also, when you see these things happening, know that it[a] is near—at the doors! [30]Assuredly, I say to you, this generation will by no means pass away till all these things take place. [31]Heaven and earth will pass away, but My words will by no means pass away.

No One Knows the Day or Hour

[32]"But of that day and hour no one knows, not even the angels in heaven, nor the Son, but only the Father. [33]Take heed, watch and pray; for you do not know when the time is. [34]*It is* like a man going to a far country, who left his house and gave authority to his servants, and to each his work, and commanded the doorkeeper to watch. [35]Watch therefore, for you do not know when the master of the house is coming—in the evening, at midnight, at the crowing of the rooster, or in the morning— [36]lest, coming suddenly, he find you sleeping. [37]And what I say to you, I say to all: Watch!"

The Plot to Kill Jesus

14 After two days it was the Passover and *the Feast* of Unleavened Bread. And the chief priests and the scribes sought how they might take Him by trickery and put *Him* to death. [2]But they said, "Not during the feast, lest there be an uproar of the people."

The Anointing at Bethany

[3]And being in Bethany at the house of Simon the leper, as He sat at the table, a woman came having an alabaster flask of very costly oil of spikenard. Then she broke the flask and poured *it* on His head. [4]But there were some who were indignant among themselves, and said, "Why was this fragrant oil wasted? [5]For it might have been sold for more than three hundred denarii and given to the poor." And they criticized her sharply.

[6]But Jesus said, "Let her alone. Why do you trouble her? She has done a good work for Me. [7]For you have the poor with you always, and whenever you wish you may do them good; but Me you do not have always. [8]She has done what she could. She has come beforehand to anoint My body for burial. [9]Assuredly, I say to you, wherever this gospel is preached in the whole world, what this woman has done will also be told as a memorial to her."

Judas Agrees to Betray Jesus

[10]Then Judas Iscariot, one of the twelve, went to the chief priests to betray Him to them. [11]And when they heard *it,* they were glad, and promised to give him money. So he sought how he might conveniently betray Him.

Jesus Celebrates the Passover with His Disciples

[12]Now on the first day of Unleavened Bread, when they killed the Passover *lamb,* His disciples said to Him, "Where do You want us to go and prepare, that You may eat the Passover?"

[13]And He sent out two of His disciples and said to them, "Go into the city, and a man will meet you carrying a pitcher of water; follow him. [14]Wherever he goes in, say to the master of the house, 'The Teacher says, "Where is the guest

13:29 [a]Or He

LEADERSHIP ISSUES

What Is Greatness?

MARK 14:3–9

This is the portrayal of a nontraditional leader—a woman who was as ordinary as anybody else and yet who was memorialized by Jesus as an example of greatness in servant leadership. She entered the house and anointed Jesus with an expensive perfume. Despite the criticism, she continued to wash and anoint His feet, and Jesus rewarded her with a memorial of greatness.

First, she recognized she was in God's presence and showed a **SENSITIVE SPIRIT.** Through the writings of the prophets, she was aware of the time in history and responded with uniqueness and extravagance of spirit. Jesus said, "She has come beforehand to anoint My body for burial" (v. 8).

Second, she poured the entire jar of expensive ointment on Christ, an act that displayed a **GENEROUS SPIRIT.** Many in the crowd indignantly commented that the perfume could've been sold for a year's wages, but her choice was applauded by Jesus (vv. 6–8).

Third, she maintained a **DETERMINED SPIRIT.** Despite the accusations and snarling of those who "criticized her sharply" (v. 9), she stayed on track with her mission and focused only on Jesus. Others did not understand it; yet she moved forward in spiritual obedience, even in the face of opposition.

Finally, she showed the most necessary of all leadership qualities, the **SERVANT SPIRIT.** It appears as though she wasn't seeking greatness herself; she knew she was anointing Jesus, the Messiah, who would save the world.

This greatness was rewarded with a place in history. "Wherever this gospel is preached in the whole world, what this woman has done will also be told as a memorial to her." She did not set out for a place in history; she followed her heart to greatness by honoring Christ. This is leadership of the highest caliber.

room in which I may eat the Passover with My disciples?" ' ¹⁵Then he will show you a large upper room, furnished *and* prepared; there make ready for us."

¹⁶So His disciples went out, and came into the city, and found it just as He had said to them; and they prepared the Passover.

¹⁷In the evening He came with the twelve. ¹⁸Now as they sat and ate, Jesus said, "Assuredly, I say to you, one of you who eats with Me will betray Me."

¹⁹And they began to be sorrowful, and to say to Him one by one, "*Is* it I?" And another *said*, "*Is* it I?"ª

²⁰He answered and said to them, "*It is* one of the twelve, who dips with Me in the dish. ²¹The Son of Man indeed goes just as it is written of Him, but woe to that man by whom the Son of Man is betrayed! It would have been good for that man if he had never been born."

Jesus Institutes the Lord's Supper

²²And as they were eating, Jesus took bread, blessed and broke *it,* and gave *it* to them and said, "Take, eat;ª this is My body."

²³Then He took the cup, and when He had given thanks He gave *it* to them, and they all drank from it. ²⁴And He said to them, "This is My blood of the newª covenant, which is shed for many. ²⁵Assuredly, I say to you, I will no longer drink of the fruit of the vine until that day when I drink it new in the kingdom of God."

²⁶And when they had sung a hymn, they went out to the Mount of Olives.

Jesus Predicts Peter's Denial

²⁷Then Jesus said to them, "All of you will be made to stumble because of Me this night,ª for it is written:

'I will strike the Shepherd,
And the sheep will be scattered.'ᵇ

²⁸"But after I have been raised, I will go before you to Galilee."

²⁹Peter said to Him, "Even if all are made to stumble, yet I *will* not *be.*"

³⁰Jesus said to him, "Assuredly, I say to you

that today, *even* this night, before the rooster crows twice, you will deny Me three times."

³¹But he spoke more vehemently, "If I have to die with You, I will not deny You!"

And they all said likewise.

The Prayer in the Garden

³²Then they came to a place which was named Gethsemane; and He said to His disciples, "Sit here while I pray." ³³And He took Peter, James, and John with Him, and He began to be troubled and deeply distressed. ³⁴Then He said to them, "My soul is exceedingly sorrowful, *even* to death. Stay here and watch."

³⁵He went a little farther, and fell on the ground, and prayed that if it were possible, the hour might pass from Him. ³⁶And He said, "Abba, Father, all things *are* possible for You. Take this cup away from Me; nevertheless, not what I will, but what You *will.*"

³⁷Then He came and found them sleeping, and said to Peter, "Simon, are you sleeping? Could you not watch one hour? ³⁸Watch and pray, lest you enter into temptation. The spirit indeed *is* willing, but the flesh *is* weak."

³⁹Again He went away and prayed, and spoke the same words. ⁴⁰And when He returned, He found them asleep again, for their eyes were heavy; and they did not know what to answer Him.

⁴¹Then He came the third time and said to them, "Are you still sleeping and resting? It is enough! The hour has come; behold, the Son of Man is being betrayed into the hands of sinners. ⁴²Rise, let us be going. See, My betrayer is at hand."

Betrayal and Arrest in Gethsemane

⁴³And immediately, while He was still speaking, Judas, one of the twelve, with a great multitude with swords and clubs, came from the chief priests and the scribes and the elders. ⁴⁴Now His betrayer had given them a signal, saying, "Whomever I kiss, He is the One; seize Him and lead *Him* away safely."

⁴⁵As soon as he had come, immediately he

14:19 ªNU-Text omits this sentence. **14:22** ªNU-Text omits *eat.* **14:24** ªNU-Text omits *new.* **14:27** ªNU-Text omits *because of Me this night.* ᵇZechariah 13:7

LEADERSHIP ISSUES

The Power of Personal Relationships

MARK 14:32

When adversity becomes overwhelming, most people find themselves going back and forth between "Doesn't anybody care?" and "Leave me alone!" Well-meaning friends may say, "I know how you feel," but we think, *How come nobody's listening?* The truth is that relationships are essential to getting through adversity. We all know that a genuine relationship with God is the foundation of a successful Christian life, but when we are going through hard times, it helps to be able to talk to someone face-to-face. Our own relational needs are what make us sensitive and aware of the needs of those around us.

Meeting emotional needs through relationships has always been God's plan. In fact, relationships were a vital part of the earthly life of Christ. Jesus began His public ministry by calling twelve disciples, who were also His friends and traveling companions. Jesus knew there would be both joys and disappointments ahead, and He made a choice to surround Himself with genuine friendships. When it was time to face the cross, He celebrated the Lord's Supper in a private room (Luke 22:15), washed His disciples' feet in an intimate teaching time (John 13:14), and asked them to join Him at Gethsemane while He prayed to prepare Himself for the agony on the cross ahead (Mark 14:32). These are significant examples to us from the One we follow.

When we hurt emotionally, it can be difficult to verbalize it. Instead of being honest about our hurt, we sometimes send out confusing signals, hoping our friends and family will interpret them correctly. We do things like slam doors, hide in our rooms, yell out hateful words (that we often don't mean), use offensive language, withdraw from conversation, act out in anger, pretend nothing is wrong, or laugh about serious loss. To acknowledge that we have needs is not an admission of weakness; it's a realization that we are human. We need God, and we need one another. That's the way God made us.

LEADERSHIP ISSUES

The Downward Spiral of a Leader

MARK 14:44–72

After an intimate meal with Jesus, Peter was ready to take on the world. Jesus warned His disciples: "All of you will be made to stumble because of Me this night" (Mark 14:27). The word Jesus used for "stumble" is from the Greek word *skandalon* and pictures bait in a trap. Peter, still on his spiritual and emotional high, protests. He says, "Even if all are made to stumble, yet I will not be" (v. 29). Within just a few hours, he denied Christ privately and publicly on three separate occasions (vv. 53, 54, 66–72).

The anatomy of his spiritual decline is one from which every leader can learn. Although he began with deep, genuine faith and an intimate walk with Christ, overconfidence caused him to assume he could handle this difficult time in his own power and pride. He became spiritually lazy, and he gave up his guard as a man of prayer (vv. 37, 38). Every leader faces the temptation to spend less time in the Word and to rely on his or her strength to stay morally pure. This not only does not work, but we lose joy in our lives as we fight the culture in our own strength. Because we are sinners by nature, we can never let down our guard in the fight against temptation.

Peter's next step in his downward spiral was to react in anger. When adversity came, Peter reacted violently (v. 47). His intimate relationship with Jesus was replaced by following from a distance. Peter had three chances to overcome temptation. First, he only needed enough courage to let one servant girl know that he did know Jesus (vv. 67, 68). Second, he had the chance to tell *a few people* (v. 69). Instead, Peter no longer called Jesus "Lord" but just "this Man" (v. 71). Third, he had time to reconsider his choices, but he failed to do so. He allowed himself to become angry, curse, and swear (v. 71). That he was upset with himself is seen in his weeping after he realized what he had done (v. 72).

Leaders, take note: try to pass the tempter's test on the first go-round, because the second and third tests will be more difficult.

went up to Him and said to Him, "Rabbi,
Rabbi!" and kissed Him.

⁴⁶Then they laid their hands on Him and
took Him. ⁴⁷And one of those who stood by
drew his sword and struck the servant of the high
priest, and cut off his ear.

⁴⁸Then Jesus answered and said to them,
"Have you come out, as against a robber, with
swords and clubs to take Me? ⁴⁹I was daily with
you in the temple teaching, and you did not seize
Me. But the Scriptures must be fulfilled."

⁵⁰Then they all forsook Him and fled.

A Young Man Flees Naked

⁵¹Now a certain young man followed Him,
having a linen cloth thrown around *his* naked
body. And the young men laid hold of him, ⁵²and
he left the linen cloth and fled from them naked.

Jesus Faces the Sanhedrin

⁵³And they led Jesus away to the high priest;
and with him were assembled all the chief priests,
the elders, and the scribes. ⁵⁴But Peter followed
Him at a distance, right into the courtyard of the
high priest. And he sat with the servants and
warmed himself at the fire.

⁵⁵Now the chief priests and all the council
sought testimony against Jesus to put Him to
death, but found none. ⁵⁶For many bore false witness against Him, but their testimonies did not
agree.

⁵⁷Then some rose up and bore false witness
against Him, saying, ⁵⁸"We heard Him say, 'I will
destroy this temple made with hands, and within
three days I will build another made without
hands.' " ⁵⁹But not even then did their testimony
agree.

⁶⁰And the high priest stood up in the midst
and asked Jesus, saying, "Do You answer nothing?
What *is it* these men testify against You?" ⁶¹But
He kept silent and answered nothing.

Again the high priest asked Him, saying to
Him, "Are You the Christ, the Son of the
Blessed?"

⁶²Jesus said, "I am. And you will see the Son
of Man sitting at the right hand of the Power, and
coming with the clouds of heaven."

⁶³Then the high priest tore his clothes and
said, "What further need do we have of witnesses?

⁶⁴You have heard the blasphemy! What do you
think?"

And they all condemned Him to be deserving of death.

⁶⁵Then some began to spit on Him, and to
blindfold Him, and to beat Him, and to say to
Him, "Prophesy!" And the officers struck Him
with the palms of their hands.ᵃ

Peter Denies Jesus, and Weeps

⁶⁶Now as Peter was below in the courtyard,
one of the servant girls of the high priest came.
⁶⁷And when she saw Peter warming himself, she
looked at him and said, "You also were with Jesus
of Nazareth."

⁶⁸But he denied it, saying, "I neither know
nor understand what you are saying." And he
went out on the porch, and a rooster crowed.

⁶⁹And the servant girl saw him again, and began to say to those who stood by, "This is *one* of
them." ⁷⁰But he denied it again.

And a little later those who stood by said to
Peter again, "Surely you are *one* of them; for you
are a Galilean, and your speech shows *it.*"ᵃ

⁷¹Then he began to curse and swear, "I do
not know this Man of whom you speak!"

⁷²A second time *the* rooster crowed. Then Peter called to mind the word that Jesus had said to
him, "Before the rooster crows twice, you will
deny Me three times." And when he thought
about it, he wept.

Jesus Faces Pilate

15 Immediately, in the morning, the chief
priests held a consultation with the elders
and scribes and the whole council; and they
bound Jesus, led *Him* away, and delivered *Him* to
Pilate. ²Then Pilate asked Him, "Are You the King
of the Jews?"

He answered and said to him, "*It is as* you say."

³And the chief priests accused Him of many
things, but He answered nothing. ⁴Then Pilate
asked Him again, saying, "Do You answer nothing? See how many things they testify against
You!"ᵃ ⁵But Jesus still answered nothing, so that
Pilate marveled.

14:65 ᵃNU-Text reads *received Him with slaps.* 14:70 ᵃNU-Text
omits *and your speech shows it.* 15:4 ᵃNU-Text reads *of which
they accuse You.*

Taking the Place of Barabbas

6Now at the feast he was accustomed to releasing one prisoner to them, whomever they requested. 7And there was one named Barabbas, *who was* chained with his fellow rebels; they had committed murder in the rebellion. 8Then the multitude, crying aloud,[a] began to ask *him to do* just as he had always done for them. 9But Pilate answered them, saying, "Do you want me to release to you the King of the Jews?" 10For he knew that the chief priests had handed Him over because of envy.

11But the chief priests stirred up the crowd, so that he should rather release Barabbas to them. 12Pilate answered and said to them again, "What then do you want me to do *with Him* whom you call the King of the Jews?"

13So they cried out again, "Crucify Him!"

14Then Pilate said to them, "Why, what evil has He done?"

But they cried out all the more, "Crucify Him!"

15So Pilate, wanting to gratify the crowd, released Barabbas to them; and he delivered Jesus, after he had scourged *Him,* to be crucified.

The Soldiers Mock Jesus

16Then the soldiers led Him away into the hall called Praetorium, and they called together the whole garrison. 17And they clothed Him with purple; and they twisted a crown of thorns, put it on His *head,* 18and began to salute Him, "Hail, King of the Jews!" 19Then they struck Him on the head with a reed and spat on Him; and bowing the knee, they worshiped Him. 20And when they had mocked Him, they took the purple off Him, put His own clothes on Him, and led Him out to crucify Him.

The King on a Cross

21Then they compelled a certain man, Simon a Cyrenian, the father of Alexander and Rufus, as he was coming out of the country and passing by, to bear His cross. 22And they brought Him to the place Golgotha, which is translated, Place of a Skull. 23Then they gave Him wine mingled with myrrh to drink, but He did not take *it.* 24And when they crucified Him, they divided His garments, casting lots for them *to determine* what every man should take.

25Now it was the third hour, and they crucified Him. 26And the inscription of His accusation was written above:

THE KING OF THE JEWS.

27With Him they also crucified two robbers, one on His right and the other on His left. 28So the Scripture was fulfilled[a] which says, *"And He was numbered with the transgressors."*[b]

29And those who passed by blasphemed Him, wagging their heads and saying, "Aha! *You* who destroy the temple and build *it* in three days, 30save Yourself, and come down from the cross!"

31Likewise the chief priests also, mocking among themselves with the scribes, said, "He saved others; Himself He cannot save. 32Let the Christ, the King of Israel, descend now from the cross, that we may see and believe."[a]

Even those who were crucified with Him reviled Him.

Jesus Dies on the Cross

33Now when the sixth hour had come, there was darkness over the whole land until the ninth hour. 34And at the ninth hour Jesus cried out with a loud voice, saying, "Eloi, Eloi, lama sabachthani?" which is translated, *"My God, My God, why have You forsaken Me?"*[a]

35Some of those who stood by, when they heard *that,* said, "Look, He is calling for Elijah!" 36Then someone ran and filled a sponge full of sour wine, put *it* on a reed, and offered *it* to Him to drink, saying, "Let Him alone; let us see if Elijah will come to take Him down."

37And Jesus cried out with a loud voice, and breathed His last.

38Then the veil of the temple was torn in two from top to bottom. 39So when the centurion, who stood opposite Him, saw that He cried out like this and breathed His last,[a] he said, "Truly this Man was the Son of God!"

40There were also women looking on from afar, among whom were Mary Magdalene, Mary the mother of James the Less and of Joses, and Sa-

15:8 [a]NU-Text reads *going up.*   15:28 [a]Isaiah 53:12   [b]NU-Text omits this verse.   15:32 [a]M-Text reads *believe Him.*   15:34 [a]Psalm 22:1   15:39 [a]NU-Text reads *that He thus breathed His last.*

lome, [41]who also followed Him and ministered to Him when He was in Galilee, and many other women who came up with Him to Jerusalem.

JESUS BURIED IN JOSEPH'S TOMB

[42]Now when evening had come, because it was the Preparation Day, that is, the day before the Sabbath, [43]Joseph of Arimathea, a prominent council member, who was himself waiting for the kingdom of God, coming and taking courage, went in to Pilate and asked for the body of Jesus. [44]Pilate marveled that He was already dead; and summoning the centurion, he asked him if He had been dead for some time. [45]So when he found out from the centurion, he granted the body to Joseph. [46]Then he bought fine linen, took

Him down, and wrapped Him in the linen. And he laid Him in a tomb which had been hewn out of the rock, and rolled a stone against the door of the tomb. [47]And Mary Magdalene and Mary *the mother* of Joses observed where He was laid.

HE IS RISEN

16 Now when the Sabbath was past, Mary Magdalene, Mary *the mother* of James, and Salome bought spices, that they might come and anoint Him. [2]Very early in the morning, on the first *day* of the week, they came to the tomb when the sun had risen. [3]And they said among themselves, "Who will roll away the stone from the door of the tomb for us?" [4]But when they looked up, they saw that the stone had been rolled

THROUGH THE GRID

Thinking Christianly: Different Resurrection Options (Mark 16)

People have traditionally viewed the Resurrection of Jesus Christ in three different ways. Some believe that the Resurrection is actually only a great hoax. That is, the Resurrection never happened and is a fabricated story. Another option is that it is mythology, meaning that the Resurrection is a fictional work. Or the Resurrection could be the supreme event of history, meaning that the Resurrection is fact.

Several theories also exist that attempt to explain the phenomenon of the empty tomb and the post-Resurrection appearances of Jesus. First, there is the swoon theory, which claims that Jesus did not actually die, but just fainted for several days. The spirit theory claims that Jesus never physically returned, but He did return in spirit form. The vision theory claims that His disciples hallucinated and had a vision of Jesus, but that Jesus was not actually resurrected. The legend theory claims that the Resurrection is only a myth that was passed down as folklore. The stolen body theory claims that Jesus' body was stolen from the tomb, explaining the absence of His body. The wrong tomb theory suggests that Jesus' disciples went to the wrong tomb, which was empty, and thus thought Jesus had arisen. The lie theory claims that the disciples made the Resurrection up in order to profit from the story. The mistaken identity theory claims that the disciples didn't actually see Jesus, but they saw someone who looked like Him. The twin theory suggests that Jesus had an identical twin brother, who was the person the disciples saw, not Jesus.

The view of bodily resurrection is the biblical view, which states that Jesus was raised from the dead, historically and bodily, by the supernatural power of God (1 Cor. 15:3). Most of these theories, with the exception of the bodily resurrection view, have many holes and actually do not provide good arguments for why Jesus was not in His tomb or for why there are so many eyewitness accounts of Jesus after His death and resurrection. Only the bodily resurrection view can adequately explain these occurrences.

away—for it was very large. [5]And entering the tomb, they saw a young man clothed in a long white robe sitting on the right side; and they were alarmed.

[6]But he said to them, "Do not be alarmed. You seek Jesus of Nazareth, who was crucified. He is risen! He is not here. See the place where they laid Him. [7]But go, tell His disciples—and Peter—that He is going before you into Galilee; there you will see Him, as He said to you."

[8]So they went out quickly[a] and fled from the tomb, for they trembled and were amazed. And they said nothing to anyone, for they were afraid.

Mary Magdalene Sees the Risen Lord

[9]Now when *He* rose early on the first *day* of the week, He appeared first to Mary Magdalene, out of whom He had cast seven demons. [10]She went and told those who had been with Him, as they mourned and wept. [11]And when they heard that He was alive and had been seen by her, they did not believe.

Jesus Appears to Two Disciples

[12]After that, He appeared in another form to two of them as they walked and went into the country. [13]And they went and told *it* to the rest, *but* they did not believe them either.

The Great Commission

[14]Later He appeared to the eleven as they sat at the table; and He rebuked their unbelief and hardness of heart, because they did not believe those who had seen Him after He had risen. [15]And He said to them, "Go into all the world and preach the gospel to every creature. [16]He who believes and is baptized will be saved; but he who does not believe will be condemned. [17]And these signs will follow those who believe: In My name they will cast out demons; they will speak with new tongues; [18]they[a] will take up serpents; and if they drink anything deadly, it will by no means hurt them; they will lay hands on the sick, and they will recover."

Christ Ascends to God's Right Hand

[19]So then, after the Lord had spoken to them, He was received up into heaven, and sat down at the right hand of God. [20]And they went out and preached everywhere, the Lord working with *them* and confirming the word through the accompanying signs. Amen.[a]

16:8 [a]NU-Text and M-Text omit *quickly.*   **16:18** [a]NU-Text reads *and in their hands they will.*   **16:20** [a]Verses 9–20 are bracketed in NU-Text as not original. They are lacking in Codex Sinaiticus and Codex Vaticanus, although nearly all other manuscripts of Mark contain them.

IMPACT OF THE BOOK

IDEA — *In order to save the world, Jesus chose not to save Himself from the pain and suffering of the cross.*

MESSAGE — *Jesus lived the only perfect life, impacting us two thousand years later. He invested His life into His twelve disciples and other followers by teaching, equipping, and mentoring them so that His legacy would be felt long after His life on earth. Luke highlights Jesus' calm and authoritative responses to difficult and demanding circumstances. Jesus modeled how leaders should respond to challenges, conflicts, and accusations—whether true or false.*

PEOPLE — *Elizabeth, Herod, Jesus, John the Baptist, Joseph, Mary, Mary Magdalene, Pharisees, Pilate, Theophilus, Twelve Disciples, Zacchaeus, Zacharias*

AUTHOR — *Luke was a Gentile doctor who traveled with Paul and the only Gentile writer of the New Testament. Although not an eyewitness to the life of Jesus, his careful investigation of eyewitness accounts enabled him to write the only chronological Gospel account.*

CULTURE — *Luke, concerned with advancing Christianity, used his thoroughness and painstaking attention to detail to assure believers that the events described happened just the way he recorded them. He wove together medical and theological terms. Addressed to "Theophilus," which means "Lover of God," the Gospel of Luke was written for Gentiles. All Jewish customs are explained in great detail, and Greek names are substituted for Hebrew names. The genealogy, traced in reverse order from Matthew's, goes back to Adam to assure his readers that Jesus came to be the Savior of the whole world.*

TIMELINE — c. AD 60–61

KEY SCRIPTURE MEMORY VERSES — 1:37; 2:1–20, 52; 5:31, 32; 11:2–4; 19:10

DEDICATION TO THEOPHILUS

1 Inasmuch as many have taken in hand to set in order a narrative of those things which have been fulfilled[a] among us, [2]just as those who from the beginning were eyewitnesses and ministers of the word delivered them to us, [3]it seemed good to me also, having had perfect understanding of all things from the very first, to write to you an orderly account, most excellent Theophilus, [4]that you may know the certainty of those things in which you were instructed.

JOHN'S BIRTH ANNOUNCED TO ZACHARIAS

[5]There was in the days of Herod, the king of Judea, a certain priest named Zacharias, of the division of Abijah. His wife *was* of the daughters of Aaron, and her name *was* Elizabeth. [6]And they were both righteous before God, walking in all the commandments and ordinances of the Lord blameless. [7]But they had no child, because Elizabeth was barren, and they were both well advanced in years.

[8]So it was, that while he was serving as priest

before God in the order of his division, [9]according to the custom of the priesthood, his lot fell to burn incense when he went into the temple of the Lord. [10]And the whole multitude of the people was praying outside at the hour of incense. [11]Then an angel of the Lord appeared to him, standing on the right side of the altar of incense. [12]And when Zacharias saw *him,* he was troubled, and fear fell upon him.

[13]But the angel said to him, "Do not be afraid, Zacharias, for your prayer is heard; and your wife Elizabeth will bear you a son, and you shall call his name John. [14]And you will have joy and gladness, and many will rejoice at his birth. [15]For he will be great in the sight of the Lord, and shall drink neither wine nor strong drink. He will also be filled with the Holy Spirit, even from his mother's womb. [16]And he will turn many of the children of Israel to the Lord their God. [17]He will also go before Him in the spirit and power of Elijah, *'to turn the hearts of the fathers to the children,'*[a] and the disobedient to the wisdom of the

1:1 [a]Or *are most surely believed*   **1:17** [a]Malachi 4:5, 6

the INFLUENCERS

GABRIEL: Messenger of Peace and Restoration

LUKE 1:11–19; 1:26–29

Gabriel (Dan. 8:16; 9:21; Luke 1:19, 26) is one of only two angels actually mentioned by name in Scripture; the other being Michael (Dan. 10:13, 21; 12:1; Jude 9; Rev. 12:7). From the picture painted in Scripture, Gabriel's job description was to be a messenger. In the first chapter of Luke, Gabriel appeared to two individuals. The first message he delivered was to Zacharias to tell him that his wife Elizabeth would have a son and his name would be John. He said "I am Gabriel, who stands in the presence of God" (Luke 1:19). The second message was delivered to Mary when he told her she would conceive and give birth to Jesus.

Both Zacharias and Mary were frightened when they saw him because angels often brought judgment. After all, the name for the Archangel, "Michael", means *destroyer.* He was the champion of God against evil and the deliverer of his wrath. Gabriel, though, paints a much different picture, for his name means *man of God,* and he was the messenger of peace and restoration. He is a faithful angel who communicated the impossible to humans in a way that enabled them to believe that with God, all things are possible (Matt. 19:26). While both angels are extremely significant, Gabriel's purpose was to foretell the miracles of God and to proclaim the believer's call to faith.

just, to make ready a people prepared for the Lord."

¹⁸And Zacharias said to the angel, "How shall I know this? For I am an old man, and my wife is well advanced in years."

¹⁹And the angel answered and said to him, "I am Gabriel, who stands in the presence of God, and was sent to speak to you and bring you these glad tidings. ²⁰But behold, you will be mute and not able to speak until the day these things take place, because you did not believe my words which will be fulfilled in their own time."

²¹And the people waited for Zacharias, and marveled that he lingered so long in the temple. ²²But when he came out, he could not speak to them; and they perceived that he had seen a vision in the temple, for he beckoned to them and remained speechless.

²³So it was, as soon as the days of his service were completed, that he departed to his own house. ²⁴Now after those days his wife Elizabeth conceived; and she hid herself five months, saying, ²⁵"Thus the Lord has dealt with me, in the days when He looked on *me,* to take away my reproach among people."

CHRIST'S BIRTH ANNOUNCED TO MARY

²⁶Now in the sixth month the angel Gabriel was sent by God to a city of Galilee named Nazareth, ²⁷to a virgin betrothed to a man whose name was Joseph, of the house of David. The virgin's name *was* Mary. ²⁸And having come in, the angel said to her, "Rejoice, highly favored *one,* the Lord *is* with you; blessed *are* you among women!"[a]

²⁹But when she saw *him,*[a] she was troubled at his saying, and considered what manner of greeting this was. ³⁰Then the angel said to her, "Do not be afraid, Mary, for you have found favor with God. ³¹And behold, you will conceive in your womb and bring forth a Son, and shall call His name JESUS. ³²He will be great, and will be called the Son of the Highest; and the Lord God will give Him the throne of His father David. ³³And He will reign over the house of Jacob forever, and of His kingdom there will be no end."

³⁴Then Mary said to the angel, "How can this be, since I do not know a man?"

1:28 ªNU-Text omits *blessed are you among women.*   **1:29** ªNU-Text omits *when she saw him.*

INSIDE *the* INFLUENCERS

MARY: Character Precedes Vision and Greatness

LUKE 1:26, 27

No female in history is more famous than the mother of Jesus. At the time of the angelic announcement, Mary lived in Nazareth of Galilee and was betrothed (engaged) to a carpenter named Joseph. An amazing assignment and calling was placed on this young, common woman living in a remote area of Israel: she was to bring the Messiah into the world. While much can be and has been said concerning Mary, an often overlooked fact rises from the pages of Luke's narrative: before her name is pronounced, she is named as the *virgin* and then identified, "The virgin's name was Mary" (1:27).

She had the purity and character required to carry the Son of God in her womb. Mary testifies to every age that *character precedes vision and greatness*. It is possible to overemphasize Mary's role as a character in the Christmas story, but there cannot be enough emphasis on the *character which defined her*. It is worthy to note that she ran to Elizabeth, an older woman, for counsel, comfort, and fellowship at the urging of the angel (1:35). She will forever be remembered as being chosen to bear the Son of God because of a pure and willing heart. May her words remain as our daily prayer: "*Let it be to me according to your word*" (1:38).

³⁵And the angel answered and said to her, "*The* Holy Spirit will come upon you, and the power of the Highest will overshadow you; therefore, also, that Holy One who is to be born will be called the Son of God. ³⁶Now indeed, Elizabeth your relative has also conceived a son in her old age; and this is now the sixth month for her who was called barren. ³⁷For with God nothing will be impossible."

³⁸Then Mary said, "Behold the maidservant of the Lord! Let it be to me according to your word." And the angel departed from her.

Mary Visits Elizabeth

³⁹Now Mary arose in those days and went into the hill country with haste, to a city of Judah, ⁴⁰and entered the house of Zacharias and greeted Elizabeth. ⁴¹And it happened, when Elizabeth heard the greeting of Mary, that the babe leaped in her womb; and Elizabeth was filled with the Holy Spirit. ⁴²Then she spoke out with a loud voice and said, "Blessed *are* you among women, and blessed *is* the fruit of your womb! ⁴³But why *is* this *granted* to me, that the mother of my Lord should come to me? ⁴⁴For indeed, as soon as the voice of your greeting sounded in my ears, the babe leaped in my womb for joy. ⁴⁵Blessed *is* she who believed, for there will be a fulfillment of those things which were told her from the Lord."

The Song of Mary

⁴⁶And Mary said:

"My soul magnifies the Lord,
⁴⁷And my spirit has rejoiced in God my Savior.
⁴⁸For He has regarded the lowly state of His
　　maidservant;
For behold, henceforth all generations will
　　call me blessed.
⁴⁹For He who is mighty has done great things
　　for me,
And holy *is* His name.
⁵⁰And His mercy *is* on those who fear Him
From generation to generation.
⁵¹He has shown strength with His arm;
He has scattered *the* proud in the imagination
　　of their hearts.
⁵²He has put down the mighty from *their*
　　thrones,

And exalted *the* lowly.
⁵³He has filled *the* hungry with good things,
And *the* rich He has sent away empty.
⁵⁴He has helped His servant Israel,
In remembrance of *His* mercy,
⁵⁵As He spoke to our fathers,
To Abraham and to his seed forever."

⁵⁶And Mary remained with her about three months, and returned to her house.

Birth of John the Baptist

⁵⁷Now Elizabeth's full time came for her to be delivered, and she brought forth a son. ⁵⁸When her neighbors and relatives heard how the Lord had shown great mercy to her, they rejoiced with her.

Circumcision of John the Baptist

⁵⁹So it was, on the eighth day, that they came to circumcise the child; and they would have called him by the name of his father, Zacharias. ⁶⁰His mother answered and said, "No; he shall be called John."

⁶¹But they said to her, "There is no one among your relatives who is called by this name." ⁶²So they made signs to his father—what he would have him called.

⁶³And he asked for a writing tablet, and wrote, saying, "His name is John." So they all marveled. ⁶⁴Immediately his mouth was opened and his tongue *loosed,* and he spoke, praising God. ⁶⁵Then fear came on all who dwelt around them; and all these sayings were discussed throughout all the hill country of Judea. ⁶⁶And all those who heard *them* kept *them* in their hearts, saying, "What kind of child will this be?" And the hand of the Lord was with him.

Zacharias' Prophecy

⁶⁷Now his father Zacharias was filled with the Holy Spirit, and prophesied, saying:

⁶⁸"Blessed *is* the Lord God of Israel,
For He has visited and redeemed His people,
⁶⁹And has raised up a horn of salvation for us
In the house of His servant David,
⁷⁰As He spoke by the mouth of His holy
　　prophets,

Who *have been* since the world began,

[71]That we should be saved from our enemies
And from the hand of all who hate us,

[72]To perform the mercy *promised* to our fathers
And to remember His holy covenant,

[73]The oath which He swore to our father
Abraham:

[74]To grant us that we,
Being delivered from the hand of our
enemies,
Might serve Him without fear,

[75]In holiness and righteousness before Him all
the days of our life.

[76]"And you, child, will be called the prophet of
the Highest;
For you will go before the face of the Lord to
prepare His ways,

[77]To give knowledge of salvation to His people
By the remission of their sins,

[78]Through the tender mercy of our God,
With which the Dayspring from on high has
visited[a] us;

[79]To give light to those who sit in darkness and
the shadow of death,
To guide our feet into the way of peace."

[80]So the child grew and became strong in spirit, and was in the deserts till the day of his manifestation to Israel.

CHRIST BORN OF MARY

2 And it came to pass in those days *that* a decree went out from Caesar Augustus that all the world should be registered. [2]This census first took place while Quirinius was governing Syria. [3]So all went to be registered, everyone to his own city.

[4]Joseph also went up from Galilee, out of the city of Nazareth, into Judea, to the city of David, which is called Bethlehem, because he was of the house and lineage of David, [5]to be registered with Mary, his betrothed wife,[a] who was with child. [6]So it was, that while they were there, the days were completed for her to be delivered. [7]And she brought forth her firstborn Son, and wrapped Him in swaddling cloths, and laid Him in a manger, because there was no room for them in the inn.

GLORY IN THE HIGHEST

[8]Now there were in the same country shepherds living out in the fields, keeping watch over their flock by night. [9]And behold,[a] an angel of the Lord stood before them, and the glory of the Lord shone around them, and they were greatly afraid. [10]Then the angel said to them, "Do not be afraid, for behold, I bring you good tidings of great joy which will be to all people. [11]For there is born to you this day in the city of David a Savior, who is Christ the Lord. [12]And this *will be* the sign to you: You will find a Babe wrapped in swaddling cloths, lying in a manger."

[13]And suddenly there was with the angel a multitude of the heavenly host praising God and saying:

[14]"Glory to God in the highest,
And on earth peace, goodwill toward men!"[a]

[15]So it was, when the angels had gone away from them into heaven, that the shepherds said to one another, "Let us now go to Bethlehem and see this thing that has come to pass, which the Lord has made known to us." [16]And they came with haste and found Mary and Joseph, and the Babe lying in a manger. [17]Now when they had seen *Him,* they made widely[a] known the saying which was told them concerning this Child. [18]And all those who heard *it* marveled at those things which were told them by the shepherds. [19]But Mary kept all these things and pondered *them* in her heart. [20]Then the shepherds returned, glorifying and praising God for all the things that they had heard and seen, as it was told them.

CIRCUMCISION OF JESUS

[21]And when eight days were completed for the circumcision of the Child,[a] His name was called JESUS, the name given by the angel before He was conceived in the womb.

JESUS PRESENTED IN THE TEMPLE

[22]Now when the days of her purification according to the law of Moses were completed,

1:78 [a]NU-Text reads *shall visit.*　**2:5** [a]NU-Text omits *wife.*　**2:9** [a]NU-Text omits *behold.*　**2:14** [a]NU-Text reads *toward men of goodwill.*　**2:17** [a]NU-Text omits *widely.*　**2:21** [a]NU-Text reads *for His circumcision.*

INSIDE *the* INFLUENCERS

JESUS: Small Enough . . . Big Enough

LUKE 2:1–20

In the telling of the miraculous birth of our Lord Jesus, it's easy to miss the details. God came in such a humble, unexpected way. The following meditations on Christmas follow the idea that Christ came to show us that He is indeed big enough, but also that He was small enough:

small enough to be born,
   big enough to have spoken the world into existence;
small enough to enter the "City of Bread,"
   big enough to be the "Bread of Life";
small enough to cry when he was hungry,
   big enough to hear the heart cry of every human;
small enough to be born into a family,
   big enough to welcome all who would come into His family;
small enough to reveal Himself to shepherds close by,
   big enough to draw Magi from afar;
small enough for an old man after a lifetime of waiting,
   big enough for all who are waiting;
small enough to wash feet,
   big enough to lead;
small enough for our sake to become poor,
   big enough that through His poverty we might become rich (2 Cor 8:9);
small enough to live a life free from sin and captivity,
   big enough to bear all the sins of everyone and set His people free;
small enough to need swaddling cloths,
   big enough to one day leave them in the grave;
small enough to become one of us,
   big enough to rescue all of us.

they brought Him to Jerusalem to present *Him* to the Lord ²³(as it is written in the law of the Lord, *"Every male who opens the womb shall be called holy to the LORD"*),ᵃ ²⁴and to offer a sacrifice according to what is said in the law of the Lord, *"A pair of turtledoves or two young pigeons."*ᵃ

SIMEON SEES GOD'S SALVATION

²⁵And behold, there was a man in Jerusalem whose name *was* Simeon, and this man *was* just and devout, waiting for the Consolation of Israel, and the Holy Spirit was upon him. ²⁶And it had been revealed to him by the Holy Spirit that he would not see death before he had seen the Lord's Christ. ²⁷So he came by the Spirit into the tem-

ple. And when the parents brought in the Child Jesus, to do for Him according to the custom of the law, ²⁸he took Him up in his arms and blessed God and said:

²⁹"Lord, now You are letting Your servant depart
      in peace,
   According to Your word;
³⁰For my eyes have seen Your salvation
³¹Which You have prepared before the face of
      all peoples,
³²A light to *bring* revelation to the Gentiles,
   And the glory of Your people Israel."

2:23 ᵃExodus 13:2, 12, 15 2:24 ᵃLeviticus 12:8

the **INFLUENCERS**

ELIZABETH—Leadership Through Mentoring

LUKE 2

Imagine giving birth to John the Baptist. It probably took a lifetime just to get ready. Elizabeth's qualifications are given in one sentence: "righteous before God, walking in all the commandments and ordinances of the Lord blameless" (Luke 1:6). Apparently, that was enough for the Lord to choose her. When the angel came to Mary and foretold the birth of Christ, he also told her about Elizabeth's pregnancy as an encouragement for her to believe that "With God nothing will be impossible" (Luke 1:37). Immediately, Mary rushed to see Elizabeth. She needed a trustworthy person who could understand this leap of faith and who could encourage her. Read through their meeting and then note the role of the mentor displayed in these verses:

- Have a reputation as someone obedient to Scripture, and model that behavior.
- Prepare your heart to listen, not to give advice, not to judge.
- Grieve together; celebrate together.
- Be an encouragement.
- Keep conversations confidential.
- Share Scripture rather than advice.

Mentors encourage people to think about choices by asking questions like, "How will it affect your future? What does the Bible say about that? " The goal is to help people make **the right decision**, not tell them what to do.

³³And Joseph and His motherª marveled at those things which were spoken of Him. ³⁴Then Simeon blessed them, and said to Mary His mother, "Behold, this *Child* is destined for the fall and rising of many in Israel, and for a sign which will be spoken against ³⁵(yes, a sword will pierce through your own soul also), that the thoughts of many hearts may be revealed."

ANNA BEARS WITNESS TO THE REDEEMER

³⁶Now there was one, Anna, a prophetess, the daughter of Phanuel, of the tribe of Asher. She was of a great age, and had lived with a husband seven years from her virginity; ³⁷and this woman *was* a widow of about eighty-four years,ª who did not depart from the temple, but served *God* with fastings and prayers night and day. ³⁸And coming in that instant she gave thanks to the Lord,ª and spoke of Him to all those who looked for redemption in Jerusalem.

THE FAMILY RETURNS TO NAZARETH

³⁹So when they had performed all things according to the law of the Lord, they returned to Galilee, to their *own* city, Nazareth. ⁴⁰And the Child grew and became strong in spirit,ª filled with wisdom; and the grace of God was upon Him.

THE BOY JESUS AMAZES THE SCHOLARS

⁴¹His parents went to Jerusalem every year at the Feast of the Passover. ⁴²And when He was twelve years old, they went up to Jerusalem according to the custom of the feast. ⁴³When they had finished the days, as they returned, the Boy Jesus lingered behind in Jerusalem. And Joseph and His motherª did not know *it;* ⁴⁴but supposing

2:33 ªNU-Text reads *And His father and mother.* **2:37** ªNU-Text reads *a widow until she was eighty-four.* **2:38** ªNU-Text reads *to God.* **2:40** ªNU-Text omits *in spirit.* **2:43** ªNU-Text reads *And His parents.*

INSIDE *the* INFLUENCERS

SIMEON: The Fellowship of Hope

LUKE 2:25–35

Simeon was a just and devout man. He held onto the promise revealed to him by the Holy Spirit, and he had hope because the promise came from the One who always kept His word. This gave rise to a faith that could not be extinguished, no matter how long it took for the promise to be fulfilled.

There were many people looking and waiting for the Messiah; Simeon was part of this fellowship of hope (Mal. 3:1). He was told by the Holy Spirit that he would see the Messiah before he died (v. 26), and he was led by the Holy Spirit to the temple where he met Mary, Joseph, and the Child Jesus (v. 27). By the time he met them, he had probably lived a long life.

After seeing the Messiah, Simeon was able to say, "Lord, now You are letting Your servant depart in peace, according to Your word" (v. 29). This could be paraphrased, "I can die a happy man, knowing I've seen Israel's salvation." Simeon's life revolved around a single purpose: the fulfillment of God's promise.

Simeon also demonstrates what it means to live in the future tense. He knew there was a Savior coming. The Hope of salvation was now in his arms, and he could see with his very eyes the One for whom he had waited all these years.

Him to have been in the company, they went a day's journey, and sought Him among *their* relatives and acquaintances. ⁴⁵So when they did not find Him, they returned to Jerusalem, seeking Him. ⁴⁶Now so it was *that* after three days they found Him in the temple, sitting in the midst of the teachers, both listening to them and asking them questions. ⁴⁷And all who heard Him were astonished at His understanding and answers. ⁴⁸So when they saw Him, they were amazed; and His mother said to Him, "Son, why have You done this to us? Look, Your father and I have sought You anxiously."

⁴⁹And He said to them, "Why did you seek Me? Did you not know that I must be about My Father's business?" ⁵⁰But they did not understand the statement which He spoke to them.

JESUS ADVANCES IN WISDOM AND FAVOR

⁵¹Then He went down with them and came to Nazareth, and was subject to them, but His mother kept all these things in her heart. ⁵²And Jesus increased in wisdom and stature, and in favor with God and men.

JOHN THE BAPTIST PREPARES THE WAY

3 Now in the fifteenth year of the reign of Tiberius Caesar, Pontius Pilate being governor of Judea, Herod being tetrarch of Galilee, his brother Philip tetrarch of Iturea and the region of Trachonitis, and Lysanias tetrarch of Abilene, ²while Annas and Caiaphas were high priests,ᵃ the word of God came to John the son of Zacharias in the wilderness. ³And he went into all the region around the Jordan, preaching a baptism of repentance for the remission of sins, ⁴as it is written in the book of the words of Isaiah the prophet, saying:

> "The voice of one crying in the
>   wilderness:
> 'Prepare the way of the Lord;
>   Make His paths straight.
> ⁵Every valley shall be filled
>   And every mountain and hill brought
>   low;

3:2 ᵃNU-Text and M-Text read *in the high priesthood of Annas and Caiaphas.*

INSIDE *the* INFLUENCERS

ANNA—Live Expecting Something Great

LUKE 2:36–38

This remarkable woman is given only three verses, but that's enough to divulge Anna's leadership secrets. This woman remained faithfully at the temple, studying, praying, fasting, and waiting for God to bring the promised Messiah. That's probably why she was one of the few who recognized Him. She was a prophetess; that is, a woman who studied and declared the Word of God and encouraged others in doing so. Anna, whose Hebrew name means "Grace" didn't predict the future, but she did expect the prophecies to come true; and it was in her daily routine of serving in the temple that she was rewarded with seeing the Messiah in person.

She was a virtuous woman who came to her husband a virgin; and as a widow for 84 years, she faithfully stayed day after day at the temple. She was possibly over 100 years old, still hopeful, and still trusting God. The Scriptures tell us she recognized Jesus "in that instant" and began to give thanks. That so powerful an impact and so special a legacy could be described in three verses tells us that leaders are consistent and ready when the promise appears because they live daily expecting God's promise to come true in their lives and in the world.

> *The crooked places shall be made straight*
> *And the rough ways smooth;*
> [6]*And all flesh shall see the salvation of God.'* "[a]

JOHN PREACHES TO THE PEOPLE

[7]Then he said to the multitudes that came out to be baptized by him, "Brood of vipers! Who warned you to flee from the wrath to come? [8]Therefore bear fruits worthy of repentance, and do not begin to say to yourselves, 'We have Abraham as *our* father.' For I say to you that God is able to raise up children to Abraham from these stones. [9]And even now the ax is laid to the root of the trees. Therefore every tree which does not bear good fruit is cut down and thrown into the fire."

[10]So the people asked him, saying, "What shall we do then?"

[11]He answered and said to them, "He who has two tunics, let him give to him who has none; and he who has food, let him do likewise."

[12]Then tax collectors also came to be baptized, and said to him, "Teacher, what shall we do?"

[13]And he said to them, "Collect no more than what is appointed for you."

[14]Likewise the soldiers asked him, saying, "And what shall we do?"

So he said to them, "Do not intimidate anyone or accuse falsely, and be content with your wages."

[15]Now as the people were in expectation, and all reasoned in their hearts about John, whether he was the Christ *or* not, [16]John answered, saying to all, "I indeed baptize you with water; but One mightier than I is coming, whose sandal strap I am not worthy to loose. He will baptize you with the Holy Spirit and fire. [17]His winnowing fan *is* in His hand, and He will thoroughly clean out His threshing floor, and gather the wheat into His barn; but the chaff He will burn with unquenchable fire."

[18]And with many other exhortations he preached to the people. [19]But Herod the tetrarch, being rebuked by him concerning Herodias, his brother Philip's wife,[a] and for all the evils which Herod had done, [20]also added this, above all, that he shut John up in prison.

JOHN BAPTIZES JESUS

[21]When all the people were baptized, it came to pass that Jesus also was baptized; and while He

3:6 [a]Isaiah 40:3–5   **3:19** [a]NU-Text reads *his brother's wife.*

INSIDE *the* INFLUENCERS

JESUS: Well-Balanced

LUKE 2:52

Jesus accompanied Joseph and Mary, when he was twelve, to Jerusalem for the Passover. Separated by crowds when leaving Jerusalem, they discovered Jesus missing. They returned and found Him teaching in the temple, astonished at His wisdom. Luke 2:52 then packages what would have been His middle school, junior and senior high, and college years into one verse: "And Jesus increased in wisdom and stature, and in favor with God and men." Four developmental dimensions appear in Jesus from childhood to adulthood. He grew in wisdom. Wisdom turns on the discovery light of reality. Life is full of random disconnected data. Wisdom connects the dots, providing context and meaning.

He grew in stature. Jesus took care of himself physically. He modeled for us that our bodies would become the temple of the Holy Spirit. We should live out healthy habits.

He grew in favor with God. The verse turns from His intellectual and physical development to the spiritual. He was in complete fellowship with his heavenly Father in unbroken communication. The spiritual life of Christ as the ideal shows us how we should be living our lives, growing in our relationship and fellowship with God.

Finally, Jesus increased in favor with man. How you get along with people is absolutely important. Jesus was kind. He lived a life of compassion and care, but He never compromised God's standards. Getting along with others in healthy social development rounds out His fourfold growth matrix.

prayed, the heaven was opened. [22]And the Holy Spirit descended in bodily form like a dove upon Him, and a voice came from heaven which said, "You are My beloved Son; in You I am well pleased."

THE GENEALOGY OF JESUS CHRIST

[23]Now Jesus Himself began *His ministry at* about thirty years of age, being (as was supposed) *the* son of Joseph, *the son* of Heli, [24]*the son of* Matthat,[a] *the son* of Levi, *the son* of Melchi, *the son* of Janna, *the son of* Joseph, [25]*the son* of Mattathiah, *the son* of Amos, *the son* of Nahum, *the son* of Esli, *the son* of Naggai, [26]*the son* of Maath, *the son* of Mattathiah, *the son* of Semei, *the son* of Joseph, *the son* of Judah, [27]*the son* of Joannas, *the son* of Rhesa, *the son* of Zerubbabel, *the son* of Shealtiel, *the son* of Neri, [28]*the son* of Melchi, *the son* of Addi, *the son* of Cosam, *the son* of Elmodam, *the son* of Er, [29]*the* son of Jose, *the son* of Eliezer, *the son* of Jorim, *the*

son of Matthat, *the son* of Levi, [30]*the son* of Simeon, *the son* of Judah, *the son* of Joseph, *the son* of Jonan, *the son* of Eliakim, [31]*the son* of Melea, *the son* of Menan, *the son* of Mattathah, *the son* of Nathan, *the son* of David, [32]*the son* of Jesse, *the son* of Obed, *the son* of Boaz, *the son* of Salmon, *the son of* Nahshon, [33]*the son* of Amminadab, *the son* of Ram, *the son* of Hezron, *the son* of Perez, *the son* of Judah, [34]*the son* of Jacob, *the son* of Isaac, *the son of* Abraham, *the son* of Terah, *the son* of Nahor, [35]*the son* of Serug, *the son* of Reu, *the son* of Peleg, *the son* of Eber, *the son* of Shelah, [36]*the son* of Cainan, *the son* of Arphaxad, *the son* of Shem, *the son of* Noah, *the son* of Lamech, [37]*the son* of Methuselah, *the son* of Enoch, *the son* of Jared, *the son* of Maha-

3:24 [a]This and several other names in the genealogy are spelled somewhat differently in the NU-Text. Since the New King James Version uses the Old Testament spelling for persons mentioned in the New Testament, these variations, which come from the Greek, have not been footnoted.

lalel, *the son* of Cainan, [38]*the son* of Enosh, *the son* of Seth, *the son* of Adam, *the son* of God.

SATAN TEMPTS JESUS

4 Then Jesus, being filled with the Holy Spirit, returned from the Jordan and was led by the Spirit into[a] the wilderness, [2]being tempted for forty days by the devil. And in those days He ate nothing, and afterward, when they had ended, He was hungry.

[3]And the devil said to Him, "If You are the Son of God, command this stone to become bread."

[4]But Jesus answered him, saying,[a] "It is written, *'Man shall not live by bread alone, but by every word of God.'* "[b]

[5]Then the devil, taking Him up on a high mountain, showed Him[a] all the kingdoms of the world in a moment of time. [6]And the devil said to Him, "All this authority I will give You, and their glory; for *this* has been delivered to me, and I give it to whomever I wish. [7]Therefore, if You will worship before me, all will be Yours."

[8]And Jesus answered and said to him, "Get behind Me, Satan![a] For[b] it is written, *'You shall worship the Lord your God, and Him only you shall serve.'* "[c]

[9]Then he brought Him to Jerusalem, set Him on the pinnacle of the temple, and said to Him, "If You are the Son of God, throw Yourself down from here. [10]For it is written:

> *'He shall give His angels charge over you,*
> *To keep you,'*

[11]and,

> *'In their hands they shall bear you up,*
> *Lest you dash your foot against a stone.'* "[a]

[12]And Jesus answered and said to him, "It has been said, *'You shall not tempt the Lord your God.'* "[a]

[13]Now when the devil had ended every temptation, he departed from Him until an opportune time.

JESUS BEGINS HIS GALILEAN MINISTRY

[14]Then Jesus returned in the power of the Spirit to Galilee, and news of Him went out through all the surrounding region. [15]And He taught in their synagogues, being glorified by all.

JESUS REJECTED AT NAZARETH

[16]So He came to Nazareth, where He had been brought up. And as His custom was, He went into the synagogue on the Sabbath day, and stood up to read. [17]And He was handed the book of the prophet Isaiah. And when He had opened the book, He found the place where it was written:

> [18]*"The Spirit of the Lord is upon Me,*
> *Because He has anointed Me*
> *To preach the gospel to the poor;*
> *He has sent Me to heal the brokenhearted,*[a]
> *To proclaim liberty to the captives*
> *And recovery of sight to the blind,*
> *To set at liberty those who are oppressed;*
> [19]*To proclaim the acceptable year of the Lord."*[a]

[20]Then He closed the book, and gave *it* back to the attendant and sat down. And the eyes of all who were in the synagogue were fixed on Him. [21]And He began to say to them, "Today this Scripture is fulfilled in your hearing." [22]So all bore witness to Him, and marveled at the gracious words which proceeded out of His mouth. And they said, "Is this not Joseph's son?"

[23]He said to them, "You will surely say this proverb to Me, 'Physician, heal yourself! Whatever we have heard done in Capernaum,[a] do also here in Your country.' " [24]Then He said, "Assuredly, I say to you, no prophet is accepted in his own country. [25]But I tell you truly, many widows were in Israel in the days of Elijah, when the heaven was shut up three years and six months, and there was a great famine throughout all the land; [26]but to none of them was Elijah sent except to Zarephath,[a] *in the region* of Sidon, to a woman *who was* a widow. [27]And many lepers were in Israel in the time of Elisha the prophet, and none of them was cleansed except Naaman the Syrian."

4:1 [a]NU-Text reads *in.*   **4:4** [a]Deuteronomy 8:3   [b]NU-Text omits *but by every word of God.*   **4:5** [a]NU-Text reads *And taking Him up, he showed Him.*   **4:8** [a]NU-Text omits *Get behind Me, Satan.*   [b]NU-Text and M-Text omit *For.*   [c]Deuteronomy 6:13   **4:11** [a]Psalm 91:11, 12   **4:12** [a]Deuteronomy 6:16   **4:18** [a]NU-Text omits *to heal the brokenhearted.*   **4:19** [a]Isaiah 61:1, 2   **4:23** [a]Here and elsewhere the NU-Text spelling is *Capharnaum.*   **4:26** [a]Greek *Sarepta*

LEADERSHIP ISSUES

GC2: Holy: Christ Our Example

LUKE 4:34 *Let us alone! What have we to do with You, Jesus of Nazareth? Did You come to destroy us? I know who You are—the Holy One of God!*

While many in the first century and even in our day miss out on knowing Jesus for who He really is, the demons don't miss out! The forces of evil are very aware of the "Holy One." It is this identity as "the Holy One" that provides the background for His calling that we also be holy.

One particular aspect of His holiness we cannot identify with is Christ's virgin birth (Luke 1:35). Mary being "found with child of the Holy Spirit" meant Christ was set apart from the sinful nature that is ours (Matt. 1:18).

Significant to us is also that He "was in all points tempted as we are, yet without sin" (Heb. 4:15). Christ experienced victory over the tempting powers of sin. We, too, can experience this through the Person and power of the Holy Spirit who indwells the believer. Reflect on His work to set you apart *from* sin. How are you being freed from sin's grip? "Since establishing a personal relationship with Christ, my life has changed particularly as it relates to _____." Celebrate this work of being "set apart."

Next to consider is Christ being set apart *to* the calling God the Father had for Him. Christ did nothing on His own initiative but only those things He *heard* from His Father (John 5:30). We too have been set apart to *hear* Christ:

- as we *listen* in prayer to His still small voice
- as we *sense* His direction through the circumstances of life
- as we are *taught by His Word* to walk in truth
- as we *receive* His counsel, through the wisdom of other followers of Jesus

So how's your "hearing"? It is part of your walk in holiness.

GC2
GREAT COMMANDMENT
COMMISSION

²⁸So all those in the synagogue, when they heard these things, were filled with wrath, ²⁹and rose up and thrust Him out of the city; and they led Him to the brow of the hill on which their city was built, that they might throw Him down over the cliff. ³⁰Then passing through the midst of them, He went His way.

Jesus Casts Out an Unclean Spirit

³¹Then He went down to Capernaum, a city of Galilee, and was teaching them on the Sabbaths. ³²And they were astonished at His teaching, for His word was with authority. ³³Now in the synagogue there was a man who had a spirit of an unclean demon. And he cried out with a loud voice, ³⁴saying, "Let *us* alone! What have we to do with You, Jesus of Nazareth? Did You come to destroy us? I know who You are—the Holy One of God!"

³⁵But Jesus rebuked him, saying, "Be quiet, and come out of him!" And when the demon had thrown him in *their* midst, it came out of him and did not hurt him. ³⁶Then they were all amazed and spoke among themselves, saying, "What a word this *is!* For with authority and power He commands the unclean spirits, and they come out." ³⁷And the report about Him went out into every place in the surrounding region.

Peter's Mother-in-Law Healed

³⁸Now He arose from the synagogue and entered Simon's house. But Simon's wife's mother was sick with a high fever, and they made request of Him concerning her. ³⁹So He stood over her and rebuked the fever, and it left her. And immediately she arose and served them.

Many Healed After Sabbath Sunset

⁴⁰When the sun was setting, all those who had any that were sick with various diseases brought them to Him; and He laid His hands on every one of them and healed them. ⁴¹And demons also came out of many, crying out and saying, "You are the Christ,^a the Son of God!"

And He, rebuking *them,* did not allow them to speak, for they knew that He was the Christ.

Jesus Preaches in Galilee

⁴²Now when it was day, He departed and went into a deserted place. And the crowd sought Him and came to Him, and tried to keep Him from leaving them; ⁴³but He said to them, "I must preach the kingdom of God to the other cities also, because for this purpose I have been sent." ⁴⁴And He was preaching in the synagogues of Galilee.^a

Four Fishermen Called as Disciples

5 So it was, as the multitude pressed about Him to hear the word of God, that He stood by the Lake of Gennesaret, ²and saw two boats standing by the lake; but the fishermen had gone from them and were washing *their* nets. ³Then He got into one of the boats, which was Simon's, and asked him to put out a little from the land. And He sat down and taught the multitudes from the boat.

⁴When He had stopped speaking, He said to Simon, "Launch out into the deep and let down your nets for a catch."

⁵But Simon answered and said to Him, "Master, we have toiled all night and caught nothing; nevertheless at Your word I will let down the net." ⁶And when they had done this, they caught a great number of fish, and their net was breaking. ⁷So they signaled to *their* partners in the other boat to come and help them. And they came and filled both the boats, so that they began to sink. ⁸When Simon Peter saw *it,* he fell down at Jesus' knees, saying, "Depart from me, for I am a sinful man, O Lord!"

⁹For he and all who were with him were astonished at the catch of fish which they had taken; ¹⁰and so also *were* James and John, the sons of Zebedee, who were partners with Simon. And Jesus said to Simon, "Do not be afraid. From now on you will catch men." ¹¹So when they had brought their boats to land, they forsook all and followed Him.

Jesus Cleanses a Leper

¹²And it happened when He was in a certain city, that behold, a man who was full of leprosy saw Jesus; and he fell on *his* face and implored Him, saying, "Lord, if You are willing, You can make me clean."

¹³Then He put out *His* hand and touched him, saying, "I am willing; be cleansed." Immediately the

4:41 ^aNU-Text omits *the Christ.*   **4:44** ^aNU-Text reads *Judea.*

leprosy left him. ¹⁴And He charged him to tell no one, "But go and show yourself to the priest, and make an offering for your cleansing, as a testimony to them, just as Moses commanded."

¹⁵However, the report went around concerning Him all the more; and great multitudes came together to hear, and to be healed by Him of their infirmities. ¹⁶So He Himself *often* withdrew into the wilderness and prayed.

Jesus Forgives and Heals a Paralytic

¹⁷Now it happened on a certain day, as He was teaching, that there were Pharisees and teachers of the law sitting by, who had come out of every town of Galilee, Judea, and Jerusalem. And the power of the Lord was *present* to heal them.ᵃ ¹⁸Then behold, men brought on a bed a man who was paralyzed, whom they sought to bring in and lay before Him. ¹⁹And when they could not find how they might bring him in, because of the crowd, they went up on the housetop and let him down with *his* bed through the tiling into the midst before Jesus.

²⁰When He saw their faith, He said to him, "Man, your sins are forgiven you."

²¹And the scribes and the Pharisees began to reason, saying, "Who is this who speaks blasphemies? Who can forgive sins but God alone?"

²²But when Jesus perceived their thoughts, He answered and said to them, "Why are you reasoning in your hearts? ²³Which is easier, to say, 'Your sins are forgiven you,' or to say, 'Rise up and walk'? ²⁴But that you may know that the Son of Man has power on earth to forgive sins"—He said to the man who was paralyzed, "I say to you, arise, take up your bed, and go to your house."

²⁵Immediately he rose up before them, took up what he had been lying on, and departed to his own house, glorifying God. ²⁶And they were all amazed, and they glorified God and were filled with fear, saying, "We have seen strange things today!"

Matthew the Tax Collector

²⁷After these things He went out and saw a tax collector named Levi, sitting at the tax office. And He said to him, "Follow Me." ²⁸So he left all, rose up, and followed Him.

²⁹Then Levi gave Him a great feast in his own house. And there were a great number of tax collectors and others who sat down with them. ³⁰And their scribes and the Phariseesᵃ complained against His disciples, saying, "Why do You eat and drink with tax collectors and sinners?"

³¹Jesus answered and said to them, "Those who are well have no need of a physician, but those who are sick. ³²I have not come to call *the* righteous, but sinners, to repentance."

Jesus Is Questioned About Fasting

³³Then they said to Him, "Why doᵃ the disciples of John fast often and make prayers, and likewise those of the Pharisees, but Yours eat and drink?"

³⁴And He said to them, "Can you make the friends of the bridegroom fast while the bridegroom is with them? ³⁵But the days will come when the bridegroom will be taken away from them; then they will fast in those days."

³⁶Then He spoke a parable to them: "No one puts a piece from a new garment on an old one;ᵃ otherwise the new makes a tear, and also the piece that was *taken* out of the new does not match the old. ³⁷And no one puts new wine into old wineskins; or else the new wine will burst the wineskins and be spilled, and the wineskins will be ruined. ³⁸But new wine must be put into new wineskins, and both are preserved.ᵃ ³⁹And no one, having drunk old *wine,* immediatelyᵃ desires new; for he says, 'The old is better.' "ᵇ

Jesus Is Lord of the Sabbath

6 Now it happened on the second Sabbath after the firstᵃ that He went through the grainfields. And His disciples plucked the heads of grain and ate *them,* rubbing *them* in *their* hands. ²And some of the Pharisees said to them, "Why are you doing what is not lawful to do on the Sabbath?"

³But Jesus answering them said, "Have you not even read this, what David did when he was hungry, he and those who were with him: ⁴how he went into the house of God, took and ate the

5:17 ᵃNU-Text reads *present with Him to heal.* **5:30** ᵃNU-Text reads *But the Pharisees and their scribes.* **5:33** ᵃNU-Text omits *Why do,* making the verse a statement. **5:36** ᵃNU-Text reads *No one tears a piece from a new garment and puts it on an old one.* **5:38** ᵃNU-Text omits *and both are preserved.* **5:39** ᵃNU-Text omits *immediately.* ᵇNU-Text reads *good.* **6:1** ᵃNU-Text reads *on a Sabbath.*

showbread, and also gave some to those with him, which is not lawful for any but the priests to eat?" [5]And He said to them, "The Son of Man is also Lord of the Sabbath."

HEALING ON THE SABBATH

[6]Now it happened on another Sabbath, also, that He entered the synagogue and taught. And a man was there whose right hand was withered. [7]So the scribes and Pharisees watched Him closely, whether He would heal on the Sabbath, that they might find an accusation against Him. [8]But He knew their thoughts, and said to the man who had the withered hand, "Arise and stand here." And he arose and stood. [9]Then Jesus said to them, "I will ask you one thing: Is it lawful on the Sabbath to do good or to do evil, to save life or to destroy?"[a] [10]And when He had looked around at them all, He said to the man,[a] "Stretch out your hand." And he did so, and his hand was restored as whole as the other.[b] [11]But they were filled with rage, and discussed with one another what they might do to Jesus.

THE TWELVE APOSTLES

[12]Now it came to pass in those days that He went out to the mountain to pray, and continued all night in prayer to God. [13]And when it was day, He called His disciples to *Himself;* and from them He chose twelve whom He also named apostles: [14]Simon, whom He also named Peter, and Andrew his brother; James and John; Philip and Bartholomew; [15]Matthew and Thomas; James the *son* of Alphaeus, and Simon called the Zealot; [16]Judas *the son* of James, and Judas Iscariot who also became a traitor.

JESUS HEALS A GREAT MULTITUDE

[17]And He came down with them and stood on a level place with a crowd of His disciples and a great multitude of people from all Judea and Jerusalem, and from the seacoast of Tyre and Sidon, who came to hear Him and be healed of their diseases, [18]as well as those who were tormented with unclean spirits. And they were healed. [19]And the whole multitude sought to touch Him, for power went out from Him and healed *them* all.

THE BEATITUDES

[20]Then He lifted up His eyes toward His disciples, and said:

"Blessed *are you* poor,
    For yours is the kingdom of God.
[21]Blessed *are you* who hunger now,
    For you shall be filled.
Blessed *are you* who weep now,
    For you shall laugh.
[22]Blessed are you when men hate you,
    And when they exclude you,
    And revile *you,* and cast out your name as evil,
    For the Son of Man's sake.
[23]Rejoice in that day and leap for joy!
    For indeed your reward *is* great in heaven,
    For in like manner their fathers did to the prophets.

JESUS PRONOUNCES WOES

[24]"But woe to you who are rich,
    For you have received your consolation.
[25]Woe to you who are full,
    For you shall hunger.
Woe to you who laugh now,
    For you shall mourn and weep.
[26]Woe to you[a] when all[b] men speak well of you,
    For so did their fathers to the false prophets.

LOVE YOUR ENEMIES

[27]"But I say to you who hear: Love your enemies, do good to those who hate you, [28]bless those who curse you, and pray for those who spitefully use you. [29]To him who strikes you on the *one* cheek, offer the other also. And from him who takes away your cloak, do not withhold *your* tunic either. [30]Give to everyone who asks of you. And from him who takes away your goods do not ask *them* back. [31]And just as you want men to do to you, you also do to them likewise.

[32]"But if you love those who love you, what credit is that to you? For even sinners love those who love them. [33]And if you do good to those

6:9 [a]M-Text reads *to kill.*   6:10 [a]NU-Text and M-Text read *to him.* [b]NU-Text omits *as whole as the other.*   6:26 [a]NU-Text and M-Text omit *to you.* [b]M-Text omits *all.*

who do good to you, what credit is that to you? For even sinners do the same. ³⁴And if you lend *to those* from whom you hope to receive back, what credit is that to you? For even sinners lend to sinners to receive as much back. ³⁵But love your enemies, do good, and lend, hoping for nothing in return; and your reward will be great, and you will be sons of the Most High. For He is kind to the unthankful and evil. ³⁶Therefore be merciful, just as your Father also is merciful.

Do Not Judge

³⁷"Judge not, and you shall not be judged. Condemn not, and you shall not be condemned. Forgive, and you will be forgiven. ³⁸Give, and it will be given to you: good measure, pressed down, shaken together, and running over will be put into your bosom. For with the same measure that you use, it will be measured back to you."

³⁹And He spoke a parable to them: "Can the blind lead the blind? Will they not both fall into the ditch? ⁴⁰A disciple is not above his teacher, but everyone who is perfectly trained will be like his teacher. ⁴¹And why do you look at the speck in your brother's eye, but do not perceive the plank in your own eye? ⁴²Or how can you say to your brother, 'Brother, let me remove the speck that *is* in your eye,' when you yourself do not see the plank that *is* in your own eye? Hypocrite! First remove the plank from your own eye, and then you will see clearly to remove the speck that is in your brother's eye.

A Tree Is Known by Its Fruit

⁴³"For a good tree does not bear bad fruit, nor does a bad tree bear good fruit. ⁴⁴For every tree is known by its own fruit. For *men* do not gather figs from thorns, nor do they gather grapes from a bramble bush. ⁴⁵A good man out of the good treasure of his heart brings forth good; and an evil man out of the evil treasure of his heartᵃ brings forth evil. For out of the abundance of the heart his mouth speaks.

Build on the Rock

⁴⁶"But why do you call Me 'Lord, Lord,' and not do the things which I say? ⁴⁷Whoever comes to Me, and hears My sayings and does them, I will show you whom he is like: ⁴⁸He is like a man

building a house, who dug deep and laid the foundation on the rock. And when the flood arose, the stream beat vehemently against that house, and could not shake it, for it was founded on the rock.ᵃ ⁴⁹But he who heard and did nothing is like a man who built a house on the earth without a foundation, against which the stream beat vehemently; and immediately it fell.ᵃ And the ruin of that house was great."

Jesus Heals a Centurion's Servant

7 Now when He concluded all His sayings in the hearing of the people, He entered Capernaum. ²And a certain centurion's servant, who was dear to him, was sick and ready to die. ³So when he heard about Jesus, he sent elders of the Jews to Him, pleading with Him to come and heal his servant. ⁴And when they came to Jesus, they begged Him earnestly, saying that the one for whom He should do this was deserving, ⁵"for he loves our nation, and has built us a synagogue."

⁶Then Jesus went with them. And when He was already not far from the house, the centurion sent friends to Him, saying to Him, "Lord, do not trouble Yourself, for I am not worthy that You should enter under my roof. ⁷Therefore I did not even think myself worthy to come to You. But say the word, and my servant will be healed. ⁸For I also am a man placed under authority, having soldiers under me. And I say to one, 'Go,' and he goes; and to another, 'Come,' and he comes; and to my servant, 'Do this,' and he does *it*."

⁹When Jesus heard these things, He marveled at him, and turned around and said to the crowd that followed Him, "I say to you, I have not found such great faith, not even in Israel!" ¹⁰And those who were sent, returning to the house, found the servant well who had been sick.ᵃ

Jesus Raises the Son of the Widow of Nain

¹¹Now it happened, the day after, *that* He went into a city called Nain; and many of His disciples went with Him, and a large crowd. ¹²And when He came near the gate of the city, behold, a dead man was being carried out, the only son of his mother; and she was a widow. And a large

6:45 ᵃNU-Text omits *treasure of his heart.* **6:48** ᵃNU-Text reads for it was well built. **6:49** ᵃNU-Text reads *collapsed.* **7:10** ᵃNU-Text omits *who had been sick.*

LEADERSHIP ISSUES

GC2: Spiritual Formation: An Experience with God's Son

LUKE 6:40 *Everyone who is perfectly trained will be like his teacher.*

Imagine Christ standing before you—the only true Teacher (Matt. 23:10), the One who is love (1 John 4:8), the God of all comfort (2 Cor. 1:3, 4), the One who is humble and gentle (Matt. 11:29, 30). Imagine that He invites you to become like Him, to express His life and love, and to extend the light of His presence in a dark world.

Though you may not yet fully know all the transforming work that will be needed in your life, consider yielding in your heart to Christ's invitation. Offer the following prayer with your partner or small group as an expression of the longing of your hearts and your mutual commitment to walk in the light of fellowship:

Lord Jesus, as You see those things in my character, behavior, or attitudes that are distracting to my expression of You to those around me, please bring others into my life to lovingly point them out. Prepare my heart by Your Spirit to receive Your counsel, Your reproof, and Your correction from those whom You send. I want to be changed. I want to be more like You. In Your name, Amen.

GREAT COMMANDMENT
COMMISSION

crowd from the city was with her. ¹³When the Lord saw her, He had compassion on her and said to her, "Do not weep." ¹⁴Then He came and touched the open coffin, and those who carried *him* stood still. And He said, "Young man, I say to you, arise." ¹⁵So he who was dead sat up and began to speak. And He presented him to his mother.

¹⁶Then fear came upon all, and they glorified God, saying, "A great prophet has risen up among us"; and, "God has visited His people." ¹⁷And this report about Him went throughout all Judea and all the surrounding region.

John the Baptist Sends Messengers to Jesus

¹⁸Then the disciples of John reported to him concerning all these things. ¹⁹And John, calling two of his disciples to *him,* sent *them* to Jesus,ᵃ saying, "Are You the Coming One, or do we look for another?"

²⁰When the men had come to Him, they said, "John the Baptist has sent us to You, saying, 'Are You the Coming One, or do we look for another?' " ²¹And that very hour He cured many of infirmities, afflictions, and evil spirits; and to many blind He gave sight.

²²Jesus answered and said to them, "Go and tell John the things you have seen and heard: that *the* blind see, *the* lame walk, *the* lepers are cleansed, *the* deaf hear, *the* dead are raised, *the* poor have the gospel preached to them. ²³And blessed is *he* who is not offended because of Me."

²⁴When the messengers of John had departed, He began to speak to the multitudes concerning John: "What did you go out into the wilderness to see? A reed shaken by the wind? ²⁵But what did you go out to see? A man clothed in soft garments? Indeed those who are gorgeously appareled and live in luxury are in kings' courts. ²⁶But what did you go out to see? A prophet? Yes, I say to you, and more than a prophet. ²⁷This is *he* of whom it is written:

'Behold, I send My messenger before Your face,
Who will prepare Your way before You.'ᵃ

²⁸For I say to you, among those born of women there is not a greater prophet than John the Bap-

tist;ᵃ but he who is least in the kingdom of God is greater than he."

²⁹And when all the people heard *Him,* even the tax collectors justified God, having been baptized with the baptism of John. ³⁰But the Pharisees and lawyers rejected the will of God for themselves, not having been baptized by him.

³¹And the Lord said,ᵃ "To what then shall I liken the men of this generation, and what are they like? ³²They are like children sitting in the marketplace and calling to one another, saying:

'We played the flute for you,
    And you did not dance;
  We mourned to you,
    And you did not weep.'

³³For John the Baptist came neither eating bread nor drinking wine, and you say, 'He has a demon.' ³⁴The Son of Man has come eating and drinking, and you say, 'Look, a glutton and a winebibber, a friend of tax collectors and sinners!' ³⁵But wisdom is justified by all her children."

A Sinful Woman Forgiven

³⁶Then one of the Pharisees asked Him to eat with him. And He went to the Pharisee's house, and sat down to eat. ³⁷And behold, a woman in the city who was a sinner, when she knew that *Jesus* sat at the table in the Pharisee's house, brought an alabaster flask of fragrant oil, ³⁸and stood at His feet behind *Him* weeping; and she began to wash His feet with her tears, and wiped *them* with the hair of her head; and she kissed His feet and anointed *them* with the fragrant oil. ³⁹Now when the Pharisee who had invited Him saw *this,* he spoke to himself, saying, "This Man, if He were a prophet, would know who and what manner of woman *this is* who is touching Him, for she is a sinner."

⁴⁰And Jesus answered and said to him, "Simon, I have something to say to you."

So he said, "Teacher, say it."

⁴¹"There was a certain creditor who had two debtors. One owed five hundred denarii, and the other fifty. ⁴²And when they had nothing with

7:19 ᵃNU-Text reads *the Lord.* 7:27 ᵃMalachi 3:1 7:28 ᵃNU-Text reads *there is none greater than John.* 7:31 ᵃNU-Text and M-Text omit *And the Lord said.*

LEADERSHIP ISSUES

Doubt Is a Natural Thing

LUKE 7:21, 22

When you face difficult circumstances, it can feel like you are processing conflicting or opposite facts: you have put your personal faith in a loving God; but you face real pain, suffering, and discouragement. As a Christ-follower, you are hoping for the "all clear" signal, but instead you hear "storm warnings ahead." It's natural that one might ask, "Is God really who He says He is? Is He able to do anything about my problems? Is He still in control?"

It is natural in the face of stress and hardship to doubt or ask questions. John the Baptist, a mighty prophet called of God to proclaim, or "make way," the ministry of Christ, also had doubts. John's successful ministry was the result of self-denial and an anointing from God. He called for repentance and faced the criticism of many. Jesus called John a great man (Matt. 11:11).

But there came a day when his popularity turned and John the Baptist was put in prison. John, who did not hesitate to give up the comfort of family and home for the honor of proclaiming Christ, was met with a helpless situation. In the face of this adversity, John the Baptist understandably experienced doubt. He sent word from prison through friends to ask Jesus, "Are You the Coming One, or do we look for another?" (Luke 7:19). Merciful Jesus didn't get angry or lose patience with John. He understood and gave this response: "Go and tell John the things you have seen and heard: that the blind see, the lame walk, the lepers are cleansed, the deaf hear, the dead are raised, the poor have the gospel preached to them" (Luke 7:22). Jesus wanted John to focus on the powerful works of God and not on the anger and evil of men.

The leader's secret source of power in times of adversity is to focus on who God is and not on what one feels at the moment.

which to repay, he freely forgave them both. Tell Me, therefore, which of them will love him more?"

⁴³Simon answered and said, "I suppose the *one* whom he forgave more."

And He said to him, "You have rightly judged." ⁴⁴Then He turned to the woman and said to Simon, "Do you see this woman? I entered your house; you gave Me no water for My feet, but she has washed My feet with her tears and wiped *them* with the hair of her head. ⁴⁵You gave Me no kiss, but this woman has not ceased to kiss My feet since the time I came in. ⁴⁶You did not anoint My head with oil, but this woman has anointed My feet with fragrant oil. ⁴⁷Therefore I say to you, her sins, which *are* many, are forgiven, for she loved much. But to whom little is forgiven, *the same* loves little."

⁴⁸Then He said to her, "Your sins are forgiven."

⁴⁹And those who sat at the table with Him began to say to themselves, "Who is this who even forgives sins?"

⁵⁰Then He said to the woman, "Your faith has saved you. Go in peace."

MANY WOMEN MINISTER TO JESUS

8 Now it came to pass, afterward, that He went through every city and village, preaching and bringing the glad tidings of the kingdom of God. And the twelve *were* with Him, ²and certain women who had been healed of evil spirits and infirmities—Mary called Magdalene, out of whom had come seven demons, ³and Joanna the wife of Chuza, Herod's steward, and Susanna, and many others who provided for Him[a] from their substance.

THE PARABLE OF THE SOWER

⁴And when a great multitude had gathered, and they had come to Him from every city, He spoke by a parable: ⁵"A sower went out to sow his seed. And as he sowed, some fell by the wayside; and it was trampled down, and the birds of the air devoured it. ⁶Some fell on rock; and as soon as it sprang up, it withered away because it lacked moisture. ⁷And some fell among thorns, and the thorns sprang up with it and choked it. ⁸But oth-

8:3 ᵃNU-Text and M-Text read *them*.

INSIDE *the* INFLUENCERS

MARY MAGDALENE—From Demons to Devotion

LUKE 8:2

She is "Mary called Magdalene, out of whom had come seven demons." Many stories have been attributed to her, but few are factual. Demon possession is not the same as sin; it was described in Scripture as an affliction. She must have been one of the loneliest, most gossiped about, ignored, and disrespected creatures on the planet. Being demon-possessed was a difficult label to overcome and is not a reputation that is dispelled quickly. She may have been called "the crazy lady," but after Christ touched her, He honored her by allowing her a part of His ministry team (Luke 8:1–3).

Luke and Mark mention her demons, but not in detail. It is only that we might celebrate with her in the goodness and mercy of Christ. The Lord was not ashamed to associate with her; in fact, Luke specifically mentions her by name. She was the last to leave the grave; she was the first to see Him alive after the resurrection. This is the highest esteem and favor that could ever be shown to anyone, much less to a woman who was once possessed by demons. How precious the grace of God. In every moment, whether in life or His death, Jesus wants the world to know that He can use anyone for His glory; anyone can be changed, set free, and victorious in life. It is fitting that this one who had been "set free" would be the first to see the One who died for that freedom.

ers fell on good ground, sprang up, and yielded a crop a hundredfold." When He had said these things He cried, "He who has ears to hear, let him hear!"

The Purpose of Parables

[9]Then His disciples asked Him, saying, "What does this parable mean?"

[10]And He said, "To you it has been given to know the mysteries of the kingdom of God, but to the rest *it is given* in parables, that

'Seeing they may not see,
And hearing they may not understand.'[a]

The Parable of the Sower Explained

[11]"Now the parable is this: The seed is the word of God. [12]Those by the wayside are the ones who hear; then the devil comes and takes away the word out of their hearts, lest they should believe and be saved. [13]But the ones on the rock *are those* who, when they hear, receive the word with joy; and these have no root, who believe for a while and in time of temptation fall away. [14]Now the ones *that* fell among thorns are those who, when they have heard, go out and are choked with cares, riches, and pleasures of life, and bring no fruit to maturity. [15]But the ones *that* fell on the good ground are those who, having heard the word with a noble and good heart, keep *it* and bear fruit with patience.

The Parable of the Revealed Light

[16]"No one, when he has lit a lamp, covers it with a vessel or puts *it* under a bed, but sets *it* on a lampstand, that those who enter may see the light. [17]For nothing is secret that will not be revealed, nor *anything* hidden that will not be known and come to light. [18]Therefore take heed how you hear. For whoever has, to him *more* will be given; and whoever does not have, even what he seems to have will be taken from him."

Jesus' Mother and Brothers Come to Him

[19]Then His mother and brothers came to Him, and could not approach Him because of the crowd. [20]And it was told Him *by some,* who said, "Your mother and Your brothers are standing outside, desiring to see You."

[21]But He answered and said to them, "My mother and My brothers are these who hear the word of God and do it."

Wind and Wave Obey Jesus

[22]Now it happened, on a certain day, that He got into a boat with His disciples. And He said to them, "Let us cross over to the other side of the lake." And they launched out. [23]But as they sailed He fell asleep. And a windstorm came down on the lake, and they were filling *with water,* and were in jeopardy. [24]And they came to Him and awoke Him, saying, "Master, Master, we are perishing!"

Then He arose and rebuked the wind and the raging of the water. And they ceased, and there was a calm. [25]But He said to them, "Where is your faith?"

And they were afraid, and marveled, saying to one another, "Who can this be? For He commands even the winds and water, and they obey Him!"

A Demon-Possessed Man Healed

[26]Then they sailed to the country of the Gadarenes,[a] which is opposite Galilee. [27]And when He stepped out on the land, there met Him a certain man from the city who had demons for a long time. And he wore no clothes,[a] nor did he live in a house but in the tombs. [28]When he saw Jesus, he cried out, fell down before Him, and with a loud voice said, "What have I to do with You, Jesus, Son of the Most High God? I beg You, do not torment me!" [29]For He had commanded the unclean spirit to come out of the man. For it had often seized him, and he was kept under guard, bound with chains and shackles; and he broke the bonds and was driven by the demon into the wilderness.

[30]Jesus asked him, saying, "What is your name?"

And he said, "Legion," because many demons had entered him. [31]And they begged Him that He would not command them to go out into the abyss.

[32]Now a herd of many swine was feeding there on the mountain. So they begged Him that He would permit them to enter them. And He

8:10 [a]Isaiah 6:9   8:26 [a]NU-Text reads *Gerasenes.*   8:27 [a]NU-Text reads *who had demons and for a long time wore no clothes.*

LEADERSHIP ISSUES

GC2: Listen Well

LUKE 8:18

Do you ever feel like no one is listening to you? On the flip side, are you a good listener? Someone has defined listening as "the time I waste listening to you while I plan my next response." For many people, that is sadly true.

Healthy relationships are built on good, wholesome communication; and for that to take place, we must learn the art of listening.

A great strategy is to listen "reflectively." As someone is speaking, pay close enough attention so that when they finish, you can reflect back what you heard them say:

"I understand that you . . . "

"Am I hearing that you . . . "

Then invite feedback or clarifications to make sure you "listened" well.

GC2

GREAT COMMANDMENT
COMMISSION

permitted them. [33]Then the demons went out of the man and entered the swine, and the herd ran violently down the steep place into the lake and drowned.

[34]When those who fed *them* saw what had happened, they fled and told *it* in the city and in the country. [35]Then they went out to see what had happened, and came to Jesus, and found the man from whom the demons had departed, sitting at the feet of Jesus, clothed and in his right mind. And they were afraid. [36]They also who had seen *it* told them by what means he who had been demon-possessed was healed. [37]Then the whole multitude of the surrounding region of the Gadarenes[a] asked Him to depart from them, for they were seized with great fear. And He got into the boat and returned.

[38]Now the man from whom the demons had departed begged Him that he might be with Him. But Jesus sent him away, saying, [39]"Return to your own house, and tell what great things God has done for you." And he went his way and proclaimed throughout the whole city what great things Jesus had done for him.

A Girl Restored to Life and a Woman Healed

[40]So it was, when Jesus returned, that the multitude welcomed Him, for they were all waiting for Him. [41]And behold, there came a man named Jairus, and he was a ruler of the synagogue. And he fell down at Jesus' feet and begged Him to come to his house, [42]for he had an only daughter about twelve years of age, and she was dying.

But as He went, the multitudes thronged Him. [43]Now a woman, having a flow of blood for twelve years, who had spent all her livelihood on physicians and could not be healed by any, [44]came from behind and touched the border of His garment. And immediately her flow of blood stopped.

[45]And Jesus said, "Who touched Me?"

When all denied it, Peter and those with him[a] said, "Master, the multitudes throng and press You, and You say, 'Who touched Me?'"[b]

[46]But Jesus said, "Somebody touched Me, for I perceived power going out from Me." [47]Now when the woman saw that she was not hidden, she came trembling; and falling down before Him, she declared to Him in the presence of all the people the reason she had touched Him and how she was healed immediately.

[48]And He said to her, "Daughter, be of good cheer;[a] your faith has made you well. Go in peace."

[49]While He was still speaking, someone came from the ruler of the synagogue's *house,* saying to him, "Your daughter is dead. Do not trouble the Teacher."[a]

[50]But when Jesus heard *it,* He answered him, saying, "Do not be afraid; only believe, and she will be made well." [51]When He came into the house, He permitted no one to go in[a] except Peter, James, and John,[b] and the father and mother of the girl. [52]Now all wept and mourned for her; but He said, "Do not weep; she is not dead, but sleeping." [53]And they ridiculed Him, knowing that she was dead.

[54]But He put them all outside,[a] took her by the hand and called, saying, "Little girl, arise." [55]Then her spirit returned, and she arose immediately. And He commanded that she be given *something* to eat. [56]And her parents were astonished, but He charged them to tell no one what had happened.

Sending Out the Twelve

9 Then He called His twelve disciples together and gave them power and authority over all demons, and to cure diseases. [2]He sent them to preach the kingdom of God and to heal the sick. [3]And He said to them, "Take nothing for the journey, neither staffs nor bag nor bread nor money; and do not have two tunics apiece.

[4]"Whatever house you enter, stay there, and from there depart. [5]And whoever will not receive you, when you go out of that city, shake off the very dust from your feet as a testimony against them."

[6]So they departed and went through the towns, preaching the gospel and healing everywhere.

Herod Seeks to See Jesus

[7]Now Herod the tetrarch heard of all that was done by Him; and he was perplexed, because it

8:37 [a]NU-Text reads *Gerasenes.* **8:45** [a]NU-Text omits *and those with him.* [b]NU-Text omits *and You say, 'Who touched Me?'* **8:48** [a]NU-Text omits *be of good cheer.* **8:49** [a]NU-Text adds *any-more.* **8:51** [a]NU-Text adds *with Him.* [b]NU-Text and M-Text read *Peter, John, and James.* **8:54** [a]NU-Text omits *put them all outside.*

was said by some that John had risen from the dead, [8]and by some that Elijah had appeared, and by others that one of the old prophets had risen again. [9]Herod said, "John I have beheaded, but who is this of whom I hear such things?" So he sought to see Him.

FEEDING THE FIVE THOUSAND

[10]And the apostles, when they had returned, told Him all that they had done. Then He took them and went aside privately into a deserted place belonging to the city called Bethsaida. [11]But when the multitudes knew *it,* they followed Him; and He received them and spoke to them about the kingdom of God, and healed those who had need of healing. [12]When the day began to wear away, the twelve came and said to Him, "Send the multitude away, that they may go into the surrounding towns and country, and lodge and get provisions; for we are in a deserted place here."

[13]But He said to them, "You give them something to eat."

And they said, "We have no more than five loaves and two fish, unless we go and buy food for all these people." [14]For there were about five thousand men.

Then He said to His disciples, "Make them sit down in groups of fifty." [15]And they did so, and made them all sit down.

[16]Then He took the five loaves and the two fish, and looking up to heaven, He blessed and broke them, and gave *them* to the disciples to set before the multitude. [17]So they all ate and were filled, and twelve baskets of the leftover fragments were taken up by them.

PETER CONFESSES JESUS AS THE CHRIST

[18]And it happened, as He was alone praying, *that* His disciples joined Him, and He asked them, saying, "Who do the crowds say that I am?"

[19]So they answered and said, "John the Baptist, but some *say* Elijah; and others *say* that one of the old prophets has risen again."

[20]He said to them, "But who do you say that I am?"

Peter answered and said, "The Christ of God."

JESUS PREDICTS HIS DEATH AND RESURRECTION

[21]And He strictly warned and commanded them to tell this to no one, [22]saying, "The Son of Man must suffer many things, and be rejected by the elders and chief priests and scribes, and be killed, and be raised the third day."

TAKE UP THE CROSS AND FOLLOW HIM

[23]Then He said to *them* all, "If anyone desires to come after Me, let him deny himself, and take up his cross daily,[a] and follow Me. [24]For whoever desires to save his life will lose it, but whoever loses his life for My sake will save it. [25]For what profit is it to a man if he gains the whole world, and is himself destroyed or lost? [26]For whoever is ashamed of Me and My words, of him the Son of Man will be ashamed when He comes in His *own* glory, and *in His* Father's, and of the holy angels.

[27]But I tell you truly, there are some standing here who shall not taste death till they see the kingdom of God."

JESUS TRANSFIGURED ON THE MOUNT

[28]Now it came to pass, about eight days after these sayings, that He took Peter, John, and James and went up on the mountain to pray. [29]As He prayed, the appearance of His face was altered, and His robe *became* white *and* glistening. [30]And behold, two men talked with Him, who were Moses and Elijah, [31]who appeared in glory and spoke of His decease which He was about to accomplish at Jerusalem. [32]But Peter and those with him were heavy with sleep; and when they were fully awake, they saw His glory and the two men who stood with Him. [33]Then it happened, as they were parting from Him, *that* Peter said to Jesus, "Master, it is good for us to be here; and let us make three tabernacles: one for You, one for Moses, and one for Elijah"—not knowing what he said.

[34]While he was saying this, a cloud came and overshadowed them; and they were fearful as they entered the cloud. [35]And a voice came out of the cloud, saying, "This is My beloved Son.[a] Hear Him!" [36]When the voice had ceased, Jesus was found alone. But they kept quiet, and told no one in those days any of the things they had seen.

9:23 [a]M-Text omits *daily.*   **9:35** [a]NU-Text reads *This is My Son, the Chosen One.*

A Boy Is Healed

[37] Now it happened on the next day, when they had come down from the mountain, that a great multitude met Him. [38] Suddenly a man from the multitude cried out, saying, "Teacher, I implore You, look on my son, for he is my only child. [39] And behold, a spirit seizes him, and he suddenly cries out; it convulses him so that he foams *at the mouth;* and it departs from him with great difficulty, bruising him. [40] So I implored Your disciples to cast it out, but they could not."

[41] Then Jesus answered and said, "O faithless and perverse generation, how long shall I be with you and bear with you? Bring your son here." [42] And as he was still coming, the demon threw him down and convulsed *him.* Then Jesus rebuked the unclean spirit, healed the child, and gave him back to his father.

Jesus Again Predicts His Death

[43] And they were all amazed at the majesty of God.

But while everyone marveled at all the things which Jesus did, He said to His disciples, [44] "Let these words sink down into your ears, for the Son of Man is about to be betrayed into the hands of men." [45] But they did not understand this saying, and it was hidden from them so that they did not perceive it; and they were afraid to ask Him about this saying.

Who Is the Greatest?

[46] Then a dispute arose among them as to which of them would be greatest. [47] And Jesus, perceiving the thought of their heart, took a little child and set him by Him, [48] and said to them, "Whoever receives this little child in My name receives Me; and whoever receives Me receives Him who sent Me. For he who is least among you all will be great."

Jesus Forbids Sectarianism

[49] Now John answered and said, "Master, we saw someone casting out demons in Your name, and we forbade him because he does not follow with us."

[50] But Jesus said to him, "Do not forbid *him,* for he who is not against us[a] is on our[b] side."

A Samaritan Village Rejects the Savior

[51] Now it came to pass, when the time had come for Him to be received up, that He steadfastly set His face to go to Jerusalem, [52] and sent messengers before His face. And as they went, they entered a village of the Samaritans, to prepare for Him. [53] But they did not receive Him, because His face was *set* for the journey to Jerusalem. [54] And when His disciples James and John saw *this,* they said, "Lord, do You want us to command fire to come down from heaven and consume them, just as Elijah did?"[a]

[55] But He turned and rebuked them,[a] and said, "You do not know what manner of spirit you are of. [56] For the Son of Man did not come to destroy men's lives but to save *them.*"[a] And they went to another village.

The Cost of Discipleship

[57] Now it happened as they journeyed on the road, *that* someone said to Him, "Lord, I will follow You wherever You go."

[58] And Jesus said to him, "Foxes have holes and birds of the air *have* nests, but the Son of Man has nowhere to lay *His* head."

[59] Then He said to another, "Follow Me."

But he said, "Lord, let me first go and bury my father."

[60] Jesus said to him, "Let the dead bury their own dead, but you go and preach the kingdom of God."

[61] And another also said, "Lord, I will follow You, but let me first go *and* bid them farewell who are at my house."

[62] But Jesus said to him, "No one, having put his hand to the plow, and looking back, is fit for the kingdom of God."

The Seventy Sent Out

10 After these things the Lord appointed seventy others also,[a] and sent them two by two before His face into every city and place where He Himself was about to go. [2] Then He said to them, "The harvest truly *is* great, but the laborers *are* few; therefore pray the Lord of the harvest to

9:50 [a]NU-Text reads *you.* [b]NU-Text reads *your.*   **9:54** [a]NU-Text omits *just as Elijah did.*   **9:55** [a]NU-Text omits the rest of this verse.   **9:56** [a]NU-Text omits the first sentence of this verse.   **10:1** [a]NU-Text reads *seventy-two others.*

send out laborers into His harvest. ³Go your way; behold, I send you out as lambs among wolves. ⁴Carry neither money bag, knapsack, nor sandals; and greet no one along the road. ⁵But whatever house you enter, first say, 'Peace to this house.' ⁶And if a son of peace is there, your peace will rest on it; if not, it will return to you. ⁷And remain in the same house, eating and drinking such things as they give, for the laborer is worthy of his wages. Do not go from house to house. ⁸Whatever city you enter, and they receive you, eat such things as are set before you. ⁹And heal the sick there, and say to them, 'The kingdom of God has come near to you.' ¹⁰But whatever city you enter, and they do not receive you, go out into its streets and say, ¹¹'The very dust of your city which clings to us[a] we wipe off against you. Nevertheless know this, that the kingdom of God has come near you.' ¹²But[a] I say to you that it will be more tolerable in that Day for Sodom than for that city.

WOE TO THE IMPENITENT CITIES

¹³"Woe to you, Chorazin! Woe to you, Bethsaida! For if the mighty works which were done in you had been done in Tyre and Sidon, they would have repented long ago, sitting in sackcloth and ashes. ¹⁴But it will be more tolerable for Tyre and Sidon at the judgment than for you. ¹⁵And you, Capernaum, who are exalted to heaven, will be brought down to Hades.[a] ¹⁶He who hears you hears Me, he who rejects you rejects Me, and he who rejects Me rejects Him who sent Me."

THE SEVENTY RETURN WITH JOY

¹⁷Then the seventy[a] returned with joy, saying, "Lord, even the demons are subject to us in Your name."

¹⁸And He said to them, "I saw Satan fall like lightning from heaven. ¹⁹Behold, I give you the authority to trample on serpents and scorpions, and over all the power of the enemy, and nothing shall by any means hurt you. ²⁰Nevertheless do not rejoice in this, that the spirits are subject to you, but rather[a] rejoice because your names are written in heaven."

JESUS REJOICES IN THE SPIRIT

²¹In that hour Jesus rejoiced in the Spirit and said, "I thank You, Father, Lord of heaven and

10:11 [a]NU-Text reads *our feet*. **10:12** [a]NU-Text and M-Text omit *But*. **10:15** [a]NU-Text reads *will you be exalted to heaven? You will be thrust down to Hades!* **10:17** [a]NU-Text reads *seventy-two*. **10:20** [a]NU-Text and M-Text omit *rather*.

LEAD**ERSHIP**
REAL**ITIES**

SEE WHAT OTHERS ARE NOT WILLING TO SEE
DO WHAT OTHERS ARE NOT WILLING TO DO *Luke 10:25–37*

The story of the Good Samaritan is one of the most popular and misunderstood of all Bible stories. The most common interpretation is that, like the Samaritan, followers of Jesus should help those in need. The fault behind this is twofold: first, the Good Samaritan isn't just a good guy; he is the Christ-figure, climbing into the ditch of sin and sorrow to rescue humanity. Second, Jesus used this parable to teach His followers to live not just moral lives, but to live transformed lives. *To see what others are not willing to see* is the great litmus test of the genuine ambassador for Christ.

- The lawyer could not see . . . because he treated Jesus like an **opponent** (vv. 25–29).
- The thieves could not see . . . because they treated others like they were **objects** (v. 30).
- The priest and Levite could not see . . . because they treated others like they were **obstacles** (vv. 31, 32).
- The Samaritan, the Christ-figure in the story, had the ability to see . . . because he treated others as an **opportunity** to have compassion (vv. 33–35).

LEADERSHIP ISSUES

GC2: Becoming a Good Samaritan

LUKE 10:28, 29

Hearing Jesus confirm the primary significance of loving God with all your heart, soul, mind, and strength, and loving your neighbor as yourself, the Jewish leader asks, "Who is my neighbor?" The religious leader's question seeks to define limits for the caring he should be expected to do. Isn't there something in each of us that wants to know, "How far does this loving people go? What are the boundaries on this issue of love? What are the limits?"

With that introduction, Jesus begins to paint a picture of what Great Commandment love looks like—defined not by limits, but by its radical and startling power that produces gratitude and glorifies God. Jesus tells what we have come to refer to as the story of the Good Samaritan (Luke 10:30–35).

As we consider this story, we find:

- *The priest saw the man and passed by on the other side.*
- *A Levite saw the man and passed by on the other side.*
- *A Samaritan saw him, took pity on him, and went to him.*

The Samaritan crossed the road! When he noticed the wounded man, he took thought of him and then took initiative to help. He acted out of whom he had become—a person who cares—who takes thought of others. All too often, the ordeal and struggle of people in pain has been made worse by a form of religion that was neither helpful nor relevant.

Jesus reframed the question of the religious leader from one that suggests limits of duty to one that reflects depth of care, grace, and compassion. Rather than "Who is my neighbor?" He asks, who *was* a neighbor? Great Commandment Love is made manifest as we become good neighbors to those God allows us to know—especially those nearest us and those we find in pain along the roads of life. Followers of Jesus live out this calling to be 21st century Good Samaritan Neighbors.

earth, that You have hidden these things from *the* wise and prudent and revealed them to babes. Even so, Father, for so it seemed good in Your sight. ²²All^a things have been delivered to Me by My Father, and no one knows who the Son is except the Father, and who the Father is except the Son, and *the one* to whom the Son wills to reveal *Him*."

²³Then He turned to *His* disciples and said privately, "Blessed *are* the eyes which see the things you see; ²⁴for I tell you that many prophets and kings have desired to see what you see, and have not seen *it,* and to hear what you hear, and have not heard *it.*"

The Parable of the Good Samaritan

²⁵And behold, a certain lawyer stood up and tested Him, saying, "Teacher, what shall I do to inherit eternal life?"

²⁶He said to him, "What is written in the law? What is your reading *of it?*"

²⁷So he answered and said, " *'You shall love the Lord your God with all your heart, with all your soul, with all your strength, and with all your mind,'*^a and *'your neighbor as yourself.' "*^b

²⁸And He said to him, "You have answered rightly; do this and you will live."

²⁹But he, wanting to justify himself, said to Jesus, "And who is my neighbor?"

³⁰Then Jesus answered and said: "A certain *man* went down from Jerusalem to Jericho, and fell among thieves, who stripped him of his clothing, wounded *him,* and departed, leaving *him* half dead. ³¹Now by chance a certain priest came down that road. And when he saw him, he passed by on the other side. ³²Likewise a Levite, when he arrived at the place, came and looked, and passed by on the other side. ³³But a certain Samaritan, as he journeyed, came where he was. And when he saw him, he had compassion. ³⁴So he went to *him* and bandaged his wounds, pouring on oil and wine; and he set him on his own animal, brought him to an inn, and took care of him. ³⁵On the next day, when he departed,^a he took out two denarii, gave *them* to the innkeeper, and said to him, 'Take care of him; and whatever more you spend, when I come

10:22 ^aM-Text reads *And turning to the disciples He said, "All . . .*
10:27 ^aDeuteronomy 6:5 ^bLeviticus 19:18 **10:35** ^aNU-Text omits *when he departed.*

 the INFLUENCERS

MARTHA—Leaders Focus on the Wildly Important

LUKE 10:38–42

Martha gave the classic "It's not fair!" speech. She was tired and stressed, but instead of recognizing the need to rest and prioritize her tasks, she lashed out at Mary. Martha appealed to Jesus, "Don't you care about what I'm going through?" She demanded that Jesus make her sister help her.

Meanwhile, the Son of God, was teaching about heaven. Martha never even noticed that history was being written in her living room. She was so distracted by her personal agenda that she missed the most important thing—the things with eternal value. "To-do" lists aren't immoral, they just aren't as important as Jesus. Jesus quickly **responded** with a teaching point. He said that she was *worried and troubled about many things.* He explained that it is better to focus on first things first, and it should be the *good part.* Literally in the Greek, it is the *best choice*—the wildly important. Jesus told Martha that *best choice* wouldn't be taken from her sister Mary. In other words, it would define her and become her reputation. Martha's heart was for service, but she was a slave to poor priorities. She only had to sit at His feet to reprioritize and choose the best choice.

LEADERSHIP ISSUES

GC2: Sitting at His Feet

LUKE 10:39

Recall Jesus' words of affirmation for His friend, Mary, as she was seated at His feet, listening to His word: "Mary has chosen that good part, which will not be taken away from her" (Luke 10:42). Mary, much like the Samaritan leper of Luke 17, humbly longed to relate to Jesus—the object, author, and perfecter of her faith.

Faithful, maturing followers of Jesus sit humbly at His feet giving careful, deep consideration to Him. But this lifestyle, though empowered by His Spirit, must be chosen. Disciples never "stumble into" maturity. The fulfillment of their life's purpose—the transforming process of encountering Jesus—must be chosen, sought after, and pursued. The psalmist says it like this: "As the deer pants for the water brooks, so pants my soul for You, O God. My soul thirsts for God, for the living God. When shall I come and appear before God?" (Ps. 42:1, 2).

As this thirst develops in us as followers of Jesus, we come to view times of worship, meditation, fellowship, prayer, and study of the Word as privileged opportunities to pursue and encounter Jesus. Through these times, our relationship with Him deepens and a relational history develops. As in any relationship, touching memories and emotional images are etched on our hearts, always ready to be recalled and embraced.

Consider for a moment special memories you have of encountering Jesus: "*I recall the time when*_____."

Pause to give thanks.

Consider also significant images of Jesus you have encountered in scripture as He prays (Heb. 7:25), and as He expresses compassion (John 11:35).

"*A significant image of Jesus I have encountered is when*_____
_____."

GC2
GREAT COMMANDMENT
COMMISSION

again, I will repay you.' 36So which of these three do you think was neighbor to him who fell among the thieves?"

37And he said, "He who showed mercy on him."

Then Jesus said to him, "Go and do likewise."

MARY AND MARTHA WORSHIP AND SERVE

38Now it happened as they went that He entered a certain village; and a certain woman named Martha welcomed Him into her house. 39And she had a sister called Mary, who also sat at Jesus'a feet and heard His word. 40But Martha was distracted with much serving, and she approached Him and said, "Lord, do You not care that my sister has left me to serve alone? Therefore tell her to help me."

41And Jesusa answered and said to her, "Martha, Martha, you are worried and troubled about many things. 42But one thing is needed, and Mary has chosen that good part, which will not be taken away from her."

THE MODEL PRAYER

11 Now it came to pass, as He was praying in a certain place, when He ceased, *that* one of His disciples said to Him, "Lord, teach us to pray, as John also taught his disciples."

2So He said to them, "When you pray, say:

> Our Father in heaven,a
> Hallowed be Your name.
> Your kingdom come.b
> Your will be done
> On earth as *it is* in heaven.

3Give us day by day our daily bread.
4And forgive us our sins,
For we also forgive everyone who is indebted to us.
And do not lead us into temptation,
But deliver us from the evil one."a

10:39 aNU-Text reads *the Lord's.* **10:41** aNU-Text reads *the Lord.* **11:2** aNU-Text omits *Our* and *in heaven.* bNU-Text omits the rest of this verse. **11:4** aNU-Text omits *But deliver us from the evil one.*

INSIDE *the* INFLUENCERS

MARY OF BETHANY—Choose the Better Thing

LUKE 10:38–42

When Martha started complaining to Jesus about her sister Mary, the room could have quickly turned ugly. But when we read this account of Mary, we don't see Mary try to argue. She stayed focused on her Lord and did not even try to defend her actions. Martha was a reactor; Mary was a responder. Responders:

- Look beyond the conflict to the person or situation and what can be done
- Act peacefully
- Accept the opportunity to show love in an emotional situation

When Jesus came to their home, the two sisters greeted Him, probably together at the door. Martha looked into His eyes and saw a tired, hungry man. This she could fix and she set about to do so. Mary looked into those same eyes and might have thought, "He needs someone to listen to Him; someone to believe in Him." She also set about to fulfill her mission. We read that she sat at the feet of Jesus and listened to Him teach. Martha went on a tirade because she wanted help with household chores, but Jesus rebuked her saying, "But one thing is needed, and Mary has chosen that good part, which will not be taken away from her." That's what we are all looking for: The better thing! From this account, we understand that the best effort we can put forth is to listen to others, to believe and encourage them, to focus on the inner person rather than the physical. This "will not be taken away" but will become our legacy, as it did for Mary.

A Friend Comes at Midnight

5And He said to them, "Which of you shall have a friend, and go to him at midnight and say to him, 'Friend, lend me three loaves; 6for a friend of mine has come to me on his journey, and I have nothing to set before him'; 7and he will answer from within and say, 'Do not trouble me; the door is now shut, and my children are with me in bed; I cannot rise and give to you'? 8I say to you, though he will not rise and give to him because he is his friend, yet because of his persistence he will rise and give him as many as he needs.

Keep Asking, Seeking, Knocking

9"So I say to you, ask, and it will be given to you; seek, and you will find; knock, and it will be opened to you. 10For everyone who asks receives, and he who seeks finds, and to him who knocks it will be opened. 11If a son asks for bread[a] from any father among you, will he give him a stone? Or if he asks for a fish, will he give him a serpent instead of a fish? 12Or if he asks for an egg, will he offer him a scorpion? 13If you then, being evil, know how to give good gifts to your children, how much more will your heavenly Father give the Holy Spirit to those who ask Him!"

A House Divided Cannot Stand

14And He was casting out a demon, and it was mute. So it was, when the demon had gone out, that the mute spoke; and the multitudes marveled. 15But some of them said, "He casts out demons by Beelzebub,[a] the ruler of the demons."

16Others, testing Him, sought from Him a sign from heaven. 17But He, knowing their thoughts, said to them: "Every kingdom divided against itself is brought to desolation, and a house divided against a house falls. 18If Satan also is divided against himself, how will his kingdom stand? Because you say I cast out demons by Beelzebub. 19And if I cast out demons by Beelzebub, by whom do your sons cast them out? Therefore they will be your judges. 20But if I cast out demons with the finger of God, surely the kingdom of God has come upon you. 21When a strong man, fully armed, guards his own palace, his goods are in peace. 22But when a stronger than he comes upon him and overcomes him, he takes

from him all his armor in which he trusted, and divides his spoils. 23He who is not with Me is against Me, and he who does not gather with Me scatters.

An Unclean Spirit Returns

24"When an unclean spirit goes out of a man, he goes through dry places, seeking rest; and finding none, he says, 'I will return to my house from which I came.' 25And when he comes, he finds it swept and put in order. 26Then he goes and takes with him seven other spirits more wicked than himself, and they enter and dwell there; and the last state of that man is worse than the first."

Keeping the Word

27And it happened, as He spoke these things, that a certain woman from the crowd raised her voice and said to Him, "Blessed is the womb that bore You, and the breasts which nursed You!"

28But He said, "More than that, blessed are those who hear the word of God and keep it!"

Seeking a Sign

29And while the crowds were thickly gathered together, He began to say, "This is an evil generation. It seeks a sign, and no sign will be given to it except the sign of Jonah the prophet.[a] 30For as Jonah became a sign to the Ninevites, so also the Son of Man will be to this generation. 31The queen of the South will rise up in the judgment with the men of this generation and condemn them, for she came from the ends of the earth to hear the wisdom of Solomon; and indeed a greater than Solomon is here. 32The men of Nineveh will rise up in the judgment with this generation and condemn it, for they repented at the preaching of Jonah; and indeed a greater than Jonah is here.

The Lamp of the Body

33"No one, when he has lit a lamp, puts it in a secret place or under a basket, but on a lampstand, that those who come in may see the light. 34The lamp of the body is the eye. Therefore, when your eye is good, your whole body also is full of light.

11:11 [a]NU-Text omits the words from bread through for in the next sentence. 11:15 [a]NU-Text and M-Text read Beelzebul. 11:29 [a]NU-Text omits the prophet.

But when *your eye* is bad, your body also *is* full of darkness. [35]Therefore take heed that the light which is in you is not darkness. [36]If then your whole body *is* full of light, having no part dark, *the* whole *body* will be full of light, as when the bright shining of a lamp gives you light."

WOE TO THE PHARISEES AND LAWYERS

[37]And as He spoke, a certain Pharisee asked Him to dine with him. So He went in and sat down to eat. [38]When the Pharisee saw *it,* he marveled that He had not first washed before dinner. [39]Then the Lord said to him, "Now you Pharisees make the outside of the cup and dish clean, but your inward part is full of greed and wickedness. [40]Foolish ones! Did not He who made the outside make the inside also? [41]But rather give alms of such things as you have; then indeed all things are clean to you.

[42]"But woe to you Pharisees! For you tithe mint and rue and all manner of herbs, and pass by justice and the love of God. These you ought to have done, without leaving the others undone. [43]Woe to you Pharisees! For you love the best seats in the synagogues and greetings in the marketplaces. [44]Woe to you, scribes and Pharisees, hypocrites![a] For you are like graves which are not seen, and the men who walk over *them* are not aware *of them.*"

[45]Then one of the lawyers answered and said to Him, "Teacher, by saying these things You reproach us also."

[46]And He said, "Woe to you also, lawyers! For you load men with burdens hard to bear, and you yourselves do not touch the burdens with one of your fingers. [47]Woe to you! For you build the tombs of the prophets, and your fathers killed them. [48]In fact, you bear witness that you approve the deeds of your fathers; for they indeed killed them, and you build their tombs. [49]Therefore the wisdom of God also said, 'I will send them prophets and apostles, and *some* of them they will kill and persecute,' [50]that the blood of all the prophets which was shed from the foundation of the world may be required of this generation, [51]from the blood of Abel to the blood of Zechariah who perished between the altar and the temple. Yes, I say to you, it shall be required of this generation.

[52]"Woe to you lawyers! For you have taken away the key of knowledge. You did not enter in yourselves, and those who were entering in you hindered."

[53]And as He said these things to them,[a] the scribes and the Pharisees began to assail *Him* vehemently, and to cross-examine Him about many things, [54]lying in wait for Him, and seeking to catch Him in something He might say, that they might accuse Him.[a]

BEWARE OF HYPOCRISY

12 In the meantime, when an innumerable multitude of people had gathered together, so that they trampled one another, He began to say to His disciples first *of all,* "Beware of the leaven of the Pharisees, which is hypocrisy. [2]For there is nothing covered that will not be revealed, nor hidden that will not be known. [3]Therefore whatever you have spoken in the dark will be heard in the light, and what you have spoken in the ear in inner rooms will be proclaimed on the housetops.

JESUS TEACHES THE FEAR OF GOD

[4]"And I say to you, My friends, do not be afraid of those who kill the body, and after that have no more that they can do. [5]But I will show you whom you should fear: Fear Him who, after He has killed, has power to cast into hell; yes, I say to you, fear Him!

[6]"Are not five sparrows sold for two copper coins?[a] And not one of them is forgotten before God. [7]But the very hairs of your head are all numbered. Do not fear therefore; you are of more value than many sparrows.

CONFESS CHRIST BEFORE MEN

[8]"Also I say to you, whoever confesses Me before men, him the Son of Man also will confess before the angels of God. [9]But he who denies Me before men will be denied before the angels of God.

[10]"And anyone who speaks a word against the Son of Man, it will be forgiven him; but to him

---

11:44 [a]NU-Text omits *scribes and Pharisees, hypocrites.* **11:53** [a]NU-Text reads *And when He left there.* **11:54** [a]NU-Text omits *and seeking* and *that they might accuse Him.* **12:6** [a]Greek *assarion,* a coin of very small value who blasphemes against the Holy Spirit, it will not be forgiven.

¹¹"Now when they bring you to the synagogues and magistrates and authorities, do not worry about how or what you should answer, or what you should say. ¹²For the Holy Spirit will teach you in that very hour what you ought to say."

The Parable of the Rich Fool

¹³Then one from the crowd said to Him, "Teacher, tell my brother to divide the inheritance with me."

¹⁴But He said to him, "Man, who made Me a judge or an arbitrator over you?" ¹⁵And He said to them, "Take heed and beware of covetousness,ᵃ for one's life does not consist in the abundance of the things he possesses."

¹⁶Then He spoke a parable to them, saying: "The ground of a certain rich man yielded plentifully. ¹⁷And he thought within himself, saying, 'What shall I do, since I have no room to store my crops?' ¹⁸So he said, 'I will do this: I will pull down my barns and build greater, and there I will store all my crops and my goods. ¹⁹And I will say to my soul, "Soul, you have many goods laid up for many years; take your ease; eat, drink, and be merry." ' ²⁰But God said to him, 'Fool! This night your soul will be required of you; then whose will those things be which you have provided?'

²¹"So is he who lays up treasure for himself, and is not rich toward God."

Do Not Worry

²²Then He said to His disciples, "Therefore I say to you, do not worry about your life, what you will eat; nor about the body, what you will put on. ²³Life is more than food, and the body is more than clothing. ²⁴Consider the ravens, for they neither sow nor reap, which have neither storehouse nor barn; and God feeds them. Of how much more value are you than the birds? ²⁵And which of you by worrying can add one cubit to his stature? ²⁶If you then are not able to do the least, why are you anxious for the rest? ²⁷Consider the lilies, how they grow: they neither toil nor spin; and yet I say to you, even Solomon in all his glory was not arrayed like one of these. ²⁸If then God so clothes the grass, which today is in the field and tomorrow is thrown into the oven, how much more will He clothe you, O you of little faith?

²⁹"And do not seek what you should eat or what you should drink, nor have an anxious mind. ³⁰For all these things the nations of the world seek after, and your Father knows that you need these things. ³¹But seek the kingdom of God, and all these thingsᵃ shall be added to you.

³²"Do not fear, little flock, for it is your Father's good pleasure to give you the kingdom. ³³Sell what you have and give alms; provide yourselves money bags which do not grow old, a treasure in the heavens that does not fail, where no thief approaches nor moth destroys. ³⁴For where your treasure is, there your heart will be also.

The Faithful Servant and the Evil Servant

³⁵"Let your waist be girded and your lamps burning; ³⁶and you yourselves be like men who wait for their master, when he will return from the wedding, that when he comes and knocks they may open to him immediately. ³⁷Blessed are those servants whom the master, when he comes, will find watching. Assuredly, I say to you that he will gird himself and have them sit down to eat, and will come and serve them. ³⁸And if he should come in the second watch, or come in the third watch, and find them so, blessed are those servants. ³⁹But know this, that if the master of the house had known what hour the thief would come, he would have watched andᵃ not allowed his house to be broken into. ⁴⁰Therefore you also be ready, for the Son of Man is coming at an hour you do not expect."

⁴¹Then Peter said to Him, "Lord, do You speak this parable only to us, or to all people?"

⁴²And the Lord said, "Who then is that faithful and wise steward, whom his master will make ruler over his household, to give them their portion of food in due season? ⁴³Blessed is that servant whom his master will find so doing when he comes. ⁴⁴Truly, I say to you that he will make him ruler over all that he has. ⁴⁵But if that servant says

12:15 ᵃNU-Text reads all covetousness.   **12:31** ᵃNU-Text reads His kingdom, and these things.   **12:39** ᵃNU-Text reads he would not have allowed.

in his heart, 'My master is delaying his coming,' and begins to beat the male and female servants, and to eat and drink and be drunk, [46]the master of that servant will come on a day when he is not looking for *him,* and at an hour when he is not aware, and will cut him in two and appoint *him* his portion with the unbelievers. [47]And that servant who knew his master's will, and did not prepare *himself* or do according to his will, shall be beaten with many *stripes.* [48]But he who did not know, yet committed things deserving of stripes, shall be beaten with few. For everyone to whom much is given, from him much will be required; and to whom much has been committed, of him they will ask the more.

CHRIST BRINGS DIVISION

[49]"I came to send fire on the earth, and how I wish it were already kindled! [50]But I have a baptism to be baptized with, and how distressed I am till it is accomplished! [51]Do *you* suppose that I came to give peace on earth? I tell you, not at all, but rather division. [52]For from now on five in one house will be divided: three against two, and two against three. [53]Father will be divided against son and son against father, mother against daughter and daughter against mother, mother-in-law against her daughter-in-law and daughter-in-law against her mother-in-law."

DISCERN THE TIME

[54]Then He also said to the multitudes, "Whenever you see a cloud rising out of the west, immediately you say, 'A shower is coming'; and so it is. [55]And when *you see* the south wind blow, you say, 'There will be hot weather'; and there is. [56]Hypocrites! You can discern the face of the sky and of the earth, but how *is it* you do not discern this time?

MAKE PEACE WITH YOUR ADVERSARY

[57]"Yes, and why, even of yourselves, do you not judge what is right? [58]When you go with your adversary to the magistrate, make every effort along the way to settle with him, lest he drag you to the judge, the judge deliver you to the officer, and the officer throw you into prison. [59]I tell you, you shall not depart from there till you have paid the very last mite."

REPENT OR PERISH

13 There were present at that season some who told Him about the Galileans whose blood Pilate had mingled with their sacrifices. [2]And Jesus answered and said to them, "Do you suppose that these Galileans were worse sinners than all *other* Galileans, because they suffered such things? [3]I tell you, no; but unless you repent you will all likewise perish. [4]Or those eighteen on whom the tower in Siloam fell and killed them, do you think that they were worse sinners than all *other* men who dwelt in Jerusalem? [5]I tell you, no; but unless you repent you will all likewise perish."

THE PARABLE OF THE BARREN FIG TREE

[6]He also spoke this parable: "A certain *man* had a fig tree planted in his vineyard, and he came seeking fruit on it and found none. [7]Then he said to the keeper of his vineyard, 'Look, for three years I have come seeking fruit on this fig tree and find none. Cut it down; why does it use up the ground?' [8]But he answered and said to him, 'Sir, let it alone this year also, until I dig around it and fertilize *it.* [9]And if it bears fruit, *well.* But if not, after that[a] you can cut it down.' "

A SPIRIT OF INFIRMITY

[10]Now He was teaching in one of the synagogues on the Sabbath. [11]And behold, there was a woman who had a spirit of infirmity eighteen years, and was bent over and could in no way raise *herself* up. [12]But when Jesus saw her, He called *her* to Him and said to her, "Woman, you are loosed from your infirmity." [13]And He laid *His* hands on her, and immediately she was made straight, and glorified God.

[14]But the ruler of the synagogue answered with indignation, because Jesus had healed on the Sabbath; and he said to the crowd, "There are six days on which men ought to work; therefore come and be healed on them, and not on the Sabbath day."

[15]The Lord then answered him and said, "Hypocrite![a] Does not each one of you on the Sabbath loose his ox or donkey from the stall, and lead *it* away to water it? [16]So ought not this

---

13:9 [a]NU-Text reads *And if it bears fruit after that, well. But if not, you can cut it down.*   **13:15** [a]NU-Text and M-Text read *Hypocrites.*

THE CRIPPLED WOMAN—Change Your View of Life

LUKE 13:10–17

On the Sabbath, Jesus was in the synagogue, as was His custom, and saw a woman He called "a descendant of Abraham." This description meant she was a good woman, worthy to be called by this honored name. But she was also bound, not by a physical disease, but a sickness caused by "a spirit." This emotional and spiritual bondage went on for 18 years, crippling her physically: she "was bent over and could in no way raise herself up" (Luke 13:11). Notice that she was in the right place (the synagogue) with the right people (Abraham's descendants), but her body was bound. Even in a place of worship, she was powerless until she met Christ personally.

Jesus called, she responded, and He healed her. She went from staring at the dirt to looking at Him directly. Her sickness became a public display of God's glory and power. Many go through life going to church, being around the things of God, but never trusting Christ for personal salvation. As a result, they see the worst in life until they allow God to give them a new spirit, which opens their eyes to His freedom.

Worshiping together is essential; but personal worship is life-changing.

woman, being a daughter of Abraham, whom Satan has bound—think of it—for eighteen years, be loosed from this bond on the Sabbath?" ¹⁷And when He said these things, all His adversaries were put to shame; and all the multitude rejoiced for all the glorious things that were done by Him.

THE PARABLE OF THE MUSTARD SEED

¹⁸Then He said, "What is the kingdom of God like? And to what shall I compare it? ¹⁹It is like a mustard seed, which a man took and put in his garden; and it grew and became a large^a tree, and the birds of the air nested in its branches."

THE PARABLE OF THE LEAVEN

²⁰And again He said, "To what shall I liken the kingdom of God? ²¹It is like leaven, which a woman took and hid in three measures^a of meal till it was all leavened."

THE NARROW WAY

²²And He went through the cities and villages, teaching, and journeying toward Jerusalem. ²³Then one said to Him, "Lord, are there few who are saved?"

And He said to them, ²⁴"Strive to enter through the narrow gate, for many, I say to you, will seek to enter and will not be able. ²⁵When once the Master of the house has risen up and shut the door, and you begin to stand outside and knock at the door, saying, 'Lord, Lord, open for us,' and He will answer and say to you, 'I do not know you, where you are from,' ²⁶then you will begin to say, 'We ate and drank in Your presence, and You taught in our streets.' ²⁷But He will say, 'I tell you I do not know you, where you are from. Depart from Me, all you workers of iniquity.' ²⁸There will be weeping and gnashing of teeth, when you see Abraham and Isaac and Jacob and all the prophets in the kingdom of God, and yourselves thrust out. ²⁹They will come from the east and the west, from the north and the south, and sit down in the kingdom of God. ³⁰And indeed there are last who will be first, and there are first who will be last."

³¹On that very day^a some Pharisees came, saying to Him, "Get out and depart from here, for Herod wants to kill You."

³²And He said to them, "Go, tell that fox, 'Behold, I cast out demons and perform cures today

13:19 ^{a}NU-Text omits *large.* 13:21 ^{a}Greek *sata*, approximately two pecks in all 13:31 ^{a}NU-Text reads *In that very hour.*

and tomorrow, and the third *day* I shall be perfected.' ³³Nevertheless I must journey today, tomorrow, and the *day* following; for it cannot be that a prophet should perish outside of Jerusalem.

JESUS LAMENTS OVER JERUSALEM

³⁴"O Jerusalem, Jerusalem, the one who kills the prophets and stones those who are sent to her! How often I wanted to gather your children together, as a hen *gathers* her brood under *her* wings, but you were not willing! ³⁵See! Your house is left to you desolate; and assuredly,ᵃ I say to you, you shall not see Me until *the time* comes when you say, *'Blessed is He who comes in the name of the Lord!' "* ᵇ

A MAN WITH DROPSY HEALED ON THE SABBATH

14Now it happened, as He went into the house of one of the rulers of the Pharisees to eat bread on the Sabbath, that they watched Him closely. ²And behold, there was a certain man before Him who had dropsy. ³And Jesus, answering, spoke to the lawyers and Pharisees, saying, "Is it lawful to heal on the Sabbath?"ᵃ

⁴But they kept silent. And He took *him* and healed him, and let him go. ⁵Then He answered them, saying, "Which of you, having a donkeyᵃ or an ox that has fallen into a pit, will not immediately pull him out on the Sabbath day?" ⁶And they could not answer Him regarding these things.

TAKE THE LOWLY PLACE

⁷So He told a parable to those who were invited, when He noted how they chose the best places, saying to them: ⁸"When you are invited by anyone to a wedding feast, do not sit down in the best place, lest one more honorable than you be invited by him; ⁹and he who invited you and him come and say to you, 'Give place to this man,' and then you begin with shame to take the lowest place. ¹⁰But when you are invited, go and sit down in the lowest place, so that when he who invited you comes he may say to you, 'Friend, go up higher.' Then you will have glory in the presence of those who sit at the table with you. ¹¹For whoever exalts himself will be humbled, and he who humbles himself will be exalted."

¹²Then He also said to him who invited Him, "When you give a dinner or a supper, do not ask your friends, your brothers, your relatives, nor rich neighbors, lest they also invite you back, and you be repaid. ¹³But when you give a feast, invite *the* poor, *the* maimed, *the* lame, *the* blind. ¹⁴And you will be blessed, because they cannot repay you; for you shall be repaid at the resurrection of the just."

THE PARABLE OF THE GREAT SUPPER

¹⁵Now when one of those who sat at the table with Him heard these things, he said to Him, "Blessed *is* he who shall eat breadᵃ in the kingdom of God!"

¹⁶Then He said to him, "A certain man gave a great supper and invited many, ¹⁷and sent his servant at supper time to say to those who were invited, 'Come, for all things are now ready.' ¹⁸But they all with one *accord* began to make excuses. The first said to him, 'I have bought a piece of ground, and I must go and see it. I ask you to have me excused.' ¹⁹And another said, 'I have bought five yoke of oxen, and I am going to test them. I ask you to have me excused.' ²⁰Still another said, 'I have married a wife, and therefore I cannot come.' ²¹So that servant came and reported these things to his master. Then the master of the house, being angry, said to his servant, 'Go out quickly into the streets and lanes of the city, and bring in here *the* poor and *the* maimed and *the* lame and *the* blind.' ²²And the servant said, 'Master, it is done as you commanded, and still there is room.' ²³Then the master said to the servant, 'Go out into the highways and hedges, and compel *them* to come in, that my house may be filled. ²⁴For I say to you that none of those men who were invited shall taste my supper.' "

LEAVING ALL TO FOLLOW CHRIST

²⁵Now great multitudes went with Him. And He turned and said to them, ²⁶"If anyone comes to Me and does not hate his father and mother, wife and children, brothers and sisters, yes, and his own life also, he cannot be My disciple. ²⁷And whoever does not bear his cross and come after Me cannot be My disciple. ²⁸For which of you, intending to build a tower, does not sit down first and count the cost, whether he has *enough* to finish

---

13:35 ᵃNU-Text and M-Text omit *assuredly.* ᵇPsalm 118:26
14:3 ᵃNU-Text adds *or not.* **14:5** ᵃNU-Text and M-Text read *son.*
14:15 ᵃM-Text reads *dinner.*

LEADERSHIP REALITIES

FINISH WHAT YOU START   Luke 14:28–33

Here Jesus pulls up a chair and intimately imparts a powerful bit of common sense. As He often does, Jesus uses questions, requiring the hearer to apply the wisdom personally and immediately. He asks you to think about being a **finisher** in life. *"Why get started on a goal, as a leader,"* He asks, *"if you do not plan to finish strong? And why call yourself one of My disciples if you don't plan to follow Me consistently?"* He finishes the lesson with a strong declaration: *"Throw away, let go of, all you have . . . ."*

Forsake—or prepare—make complete?

Some of us might be tempted to reply, "That's easy, I don't have much to give up!" To truly understand what the Lord asks of you, look beyond the physical and material into the emotional and spiritual. The leader is called to *forsake* or "throw away":

- excuses for why you can't finish what you start, live a consistent godly life, and stand strong against the enemy;
- the easy road, the path prepared or ordered by others;
- the way of the crowd.

Finishing strong is about preparation: count the cost, be equipped for battle, and be pointed in the right direction. Walk the road of the future by faith and choose the way of the cross.

---

it— ²⁹lest, after he has laid the foundation, and is not able to finish, all who see *it* begin to mock him, ³⁰saying, 'This man began to build and was not able to finish'? ³¹Or what king, going to make war against another king, does not sit down first and consider whether he is able with ten thousand to meet him who comes against him with twenty thousand? ³²Or else, while the other is still a great way off, he sends a delegation and asks conditions of peace. ³³So likewise, whoever of you does not forsake all that he has cannot be My disciple.

Tasteless Salt Is Worthless

³⁴"Salt *is* good; but if the salt has lost its flavor, how shall it be seasoned? ³⁵It is neither fit for the land nor for the dunghill, *but* men throw it out. He who has ears to hear, let him hear!"

The Parable of the Lost Sheep

15 Then all the tax collectors and the sinners drew near to Him to hear Him. ²And the Pharisees and scribes complained, saying, "This Man receives sinners and eats with them." ³So He spoke this parable to them, saying:

⁴"What man of you, having a hundred sheep, if he loses one of them, does not leave the ninety-nine in the wilderness, and go after the one which is lost until he finds it? ⁵And when he has found *it,* he lays *it* on his shoulders, rejoicing. ⁶And when he comes home, he calls together *his* friends and neighbors, saying to them, 'Rejoice with me, for I have found my sheep which was lost!' ⁷I say to you that likewise there will be more joy in heaven over one sinner who repents than over ninety-nine just persons who need no repentance.

The Parable of the Lost Coin

⁸"Or what woman, having ten silver coins,ᵃ if she loses one coin, does not light a lamp, sweep the house, and search carefully until she finds *it?* ⁹And when she has found *it,* she calls *her* friends

15:8 ªGreek *drachma,* a valuable coin often worn in a ten-piece garland by married women and neighbors together, saying, 'Rejoice with me, for I have found the piece which I lost!' ¹⁰Likewise, I say to you, there is joy in the presence of the angels of God over one sinner who repents."

THE PARABLE OF THE LOST SON

¹¹Then He said: "A certain man had two sons. ¹²And the younger of them said to *his* father, 'Father, give me the portion of goods that falls *to me.*' So he divided to them *his* livelihood. ¹³And not many days after, the younger son gathered all together, journeyed to a far country, and there wasted his possessions with prodigal living. ¹⁴But when he had spent all, there arose a severe famine in that land, and he began to be in want. ¹⁵Then he went and joined himself to a citizen of that country, and he sent him into his fields to feed swine. ¹⁶And he would gladly have filled his stomach with the pods that the swine ate, and no one gave him *anything.*

¹⁷"But when he came to himself, he said, 'How many of my father's hired servants have bread enough and to spare, and I perish with hunger! ¹⁸I will arise and go to my father, and will say to him, "Father, I have sinned against heaven and before you, ¹⁹and I am no longer worthy to be called your son. Make me like one of your hired servants." '

²⁰"And he arose and came to his father. But when he was still a great way off, his father saw him and had compassion, and ran and fell on his neck and kissed him. ²¹And the son said to him, 'Father, I have sinned against heaven and in your sight, and am no longer worthy to be called your son.'

²²"But the father said to his servants, 'Bringᵃ out the best robe and put *it* on him, and put a ring on his hand and sandals on *his* feet. ²³And bring the fatted calf here and kill *it,* and let us eat and be merry; ²⁴for this my son was dead and is alive again; he was lost and is found.' And they began to be merry.

²⁵"Now his older son was in the field. And as he came and drew near to the house, he heard music and dancing. ²⁶So he called one of the servants and asked what these things meant. ²⁷And he said to him, 'Your brother has come, and because he has received him safe and sound, your father has killed the fatted calf.'

²⁸"But he was angry and would not go in. Therefore his father came out and pleaded with him. ²⁹So he answered and said to *his* father, 'Lo, these many years I have been serving you; I never transgressed your commandment at any time; and

15:22 ᵃNU-Text reads *Quickly bring.*

LEADERSHIP REALITIES

RESPONSIBILITY—THE ABILITY TO RESPOND   *Luke 15:20*

This ancient story sounds eerily familiar and hits close to home. To demand and react to a person or situation is sin, because we have within us the **ability to respond** peacefully and in love. Sometimes a person's reaction is not about what's happening in the moment, but is a result of piles of emotion that haven't been dealt with. In this case, we don't know what the emotional trigger was: it could have been a sudden argument or months of unresolved conflict. We do know that the angry reaction caused him to disrespect his father, forsake his family, and offend the treasured values of the day.

When the son finally came to his senses, he went home to seek his father's forgiveness. This patient father was responsible and compassionate while the son was **still** a great way off. He met the son with love and forgiveness instead of anger and judgment. *Reacting* is about **me** and produces more anger. *Responding* is about **the situation** and how to improve it. Anger robs us of a clear view of life, but we are called to see things differently and to believe there is hope in any conflict.

yet you never gave me a young goat, that I might make merry with my friends. ³⁰But as soon as this son of yours came, who has devoured your livelihood with harlots, you killed the fatted calf for him.'

³¹"And he said to him, 'Son, you are always with me, and all that I have is yours. ³²It was right that we should make merry and be glad, for your brother was dead and is alive again, and was lost and is found.' "

THE PARABLE OF THE UNJUST STEWARD

16 He also said to His disciples: "There was a certain rich man who had a steward, and an accusation was brought to him that this man was wasting his goods. ²So he called him and said to him, 'What is this I hear about you? Give an account of your stewardship, for you can no longer be steward.'

³"Then the steward said within himself, 'What shall I do? For my master is taking the stewardship away from me. I cannot dig; I am ashamed to beg. ⁴I have resolved what to do, that when I am put out of the stewardship, they may receive me into their houses.'

⁵"So he called every one of his master's debtors to *him,* and said to the first, 'How much do you owe my master?' ⁶And he said, 'A hundred measuresᵃ of oil.' So he said to him, 'Take your bill, and sit down quickly and write fifty.' ⁷Then he said to another, 'And how much do you owe?' So he said, 'A hundred measuresᵃ of wheat.' And he said to him, 'Take your bill, and write eighty.' ⁸So the master commended the unjust steward because he had dealt shrewdly. For the sons of this world are more shrewd in their generation than the sons of light.

⁹"And I say to you, make friends for yourselves by unrighteous mammon, that when you fail,ᵃ they may receive you into an everlasting home. ¹⁰He who *is* faithful in *what is* least is faithful also in much; and he who is unjust in *what is* least is unjust also in much. ¹¹Therefore if you have not been faithful in the unrighteous mammon, who will commit to your trust the true *riches?* ¹²And if you have not been faithful in what is another man's, who will give you what is your own?

¹³"No servant can serve two masters; for ei-

ther he will hate the one and love the other, or else he will be loyal to the one and despise the other. You cannot serve God and mammon."

THE LAW, THE PROPHETS, AND THE KINGDOM

¹⁴Now the Pharisees, who were lovers of money, also heard all these things, and they derided Him. ¹⁵And He said to them, "You are those who justify yourselves before men, but God knows your hearts. For what is highly esteemed among men is an abomination in the sight of God.

¹⁶"The law and the prophets *were* until John. Since that time the kingdom of God has been preached, and everyone is pressing into it. ¹⁷And it is easier for heaven and earth to pass away than for one tittle of the law to fail.

¹⁸"Whoever divorces his wife and marries another commits adultery; and whoever marries her who is divorced from *her* husband commits adultery.

THE RICH MAN AND LAZARUS

¹⁹"There was a certain rich man who was clothed in purple and fine linen and fared sumptuously every day. ²⁰But there was a certain beggar named Lazarus, full of sores, who was laid at his gate, ²¹desiring to be fed with the crumbs which fellᵃ from the rich man's table. Moreover the dogs came and licked his sores. ²²So it was that the beggar died, and was carried by the angels to Abraham's bosom. The rich man also died and was buried. ²³And being in torments in Hades, he lifted up his eyes and saw Abraham afar off, and Lazarus in his bosom.

²⁴"Then he cried and said, 'Father Abraham, have mercy on me, and send Lazarus that he may dip the tip of his finger in water and cool my tongue; for I am tormented in this flame.' ²⁵But Abraham said, 'Son, remember that in your lifetime you received your good things, and likewise Lazarus evil things; but now he is comforted and you are tormented. ²⁶And besides all this, between us and you there is a great gulf fixed, so that those who want to pass from here to you cannot, nor can those from there pass to us.'

16:6 ᵃGreek *batos,* eight or nine gallons each (Old Testament *bath*) **16:7** ᵃGreek *koros,* ten or twelve bushels each (Old Testament *kor*) **16:9** ᵃNU-Text reads *it fails.*   **16:21** ᵃNU-Text reads *with what fell.*

27"Then he said, 'I beg you therefore, father, that you would send him to my father's house, 28for I have five brothers, that he may testify to them, lest they also come to this place of torment.' 29Abraham said to him, 'They have Moses and the prophets; let them hear them.' 30And he said, 'No, father Abraham; but if one goes to them from the dead, they will repent.' 31But he said to him, 'If they do not hear Moses and the prophets, neither will they be persuaded though one rise from the dead.' "

JESUS WARNS OF OFFENSES

17 Then He said to the disciples, "It is impossible that no offenses should come, but woe to him through whom they do come! 2It would be better for him if a millstone were hung around his neck, and he were thrown into the sea, than that he should offend one of these little ones. 3Take heed to yourselves. If your brother sins against you,a rebuke him; and if he repents, forgive him. 4And if he sins against you seven times in a day, and seven times in a day returns to you,a saying, 'I repent,' you shall forgive him."

FAITH AND DUTY

5And the apostles said to the Lord, "Increase our faith."

6So the Lord said, "If you have faith as a mustard seed, you can say to this mulberry tree, 'Be pulled up by the roots and be planted in the sea,' and it would obey you. 7And which of you, having a servant plowing or tending sheep, will say to him when he has come in from the field, 'Come at once and sit down to eat'? 8But will he not rather say to him, 'Prepare something for my supper, and gird yourself and serve me till I have eaten and drunk, and afterward you will eat and drink'? 9Does he thank that servant because he did the things that were commanded him? I think not.a 10So likewise you, when you have done all those things which you are commanded, say, 'We are unprofitable servants. We have done what was our duty to do.' "

TEN LEPERS CLEANSED

11Now it happened as He went to Jerusalem that He passed through the midst of Samaria and Galilee. 12Then as He entered a certain village, there met Him ten men who were lepers, who stood afar off. 13And they lifted up their voices and said, "Jesus, Master, have mercy on us!"

14So when He saw them, He said to them, "Go, show yourselves to the priests." And so it was that as they went, they were cleansed.

15And one of them, when he saw that he was healed, returned, and with a loud voice glorified God, 16and fell down on his face at His feet, giving Him thanks. And he was a Samaritan.

17So Jesus answered and said, "Were there not ten cleansed? But where are the nine? 18Were there not any found who returned to give glory to God except this foreigner?" 19And He said to him, "Arise, go your way. Your faith has made you well."

THE COMING OF THE KINGDOM

20Now when He was asked by the Pharisees when the kingdom of God would come, He answered them and said, "The kingdom of God does not come with observation; 21nor will they say, 'See here!' or 'See there!'a For indeed, the kingdom of God is within you."

22Then He said to the disciples, "The days will come when you will desire to see one of the days of the Son of Man, and you will not see it. 23And they will say to you, 'Look here!' or 'Look there!'a Do not go after them or follow them. 24For as the lightning that flashes out of one part under heaven shines to the other part under heaven, so also the Son of Man will be in His day. 25But first He must suffer many things and be rejected by this generation. 26And as it was in the days of Noah, so it will be also in the days of the Son of Man: 27They ate, they drank, they married wives, they were given in marriage, until the day that Noah entered the ark, and the flood came and destroyed them all. 28Likewise as it was also in the days of Lot: They ate, they drank, they bought, they sold, they planted, they built; 29but on the day that Lot went out of Sodom it rained fire and brimstone from heaven and destroyed them all. 30Even so will it be in the day when the Son of Man is revealed.

17:3 aNU-Text omits against you.   **17:4** aM-Text omits to you.   **17:9** aNU-Text ends verse with commanded; M-Text omits him.   **17:21** aNU-Text reverses here and there.   **17:23** aNU-Text reverses here and there.

LEADERSHIP ISSUES

GC2: Glorifying Praise

LUKE 17:15

The Samaritan leper in this text experienced a significant transformation: rather than single-mindedly focusing on his own life (including his miraculous healing and his hope for restoration to his family and community), he returned to relate to Jesus—the One who had given those blessings. He threw himself at Jesus' feet and thanked Him (v. 16); and as a result, Christ affirmed him as one who brought glory to God (v. 18). There may be no greater life or ministry objective than this: to bring praise and glory to God (Col. 1:27; Rev. 4:11).

Important in this story is that ten were healed but only one came back to give praise. Christ's words "But where are the nine?" seem to reveal the heart of a saddened Savior; He clearly could have hoped to see all ten before Him in thanksgiving.

Does not Christ continue to bless all of us? Yet how many return to give Him praise? Following Jesus means that very often we are found before Him, giving thanks. When Christ looks around for those He has blessed, you never want Him to ask about you "Where are the others?"

Pause to listen as His Spirit floods your heart with reminders of your own manifold blessings. Allow the Spirit to lead you into a prayer of thanksgiving and praise to the One who is the giver of all good gifts.

GC2
GREAT COMMANDMENT
COMMISSION

[31]"In that day, he who is on the housetop, and his goods *are* in the house, let him not come down to take them away. And likewise the one who is in the field, let him not turn back. [32]Remember Lot's wife. [33]Whoever seeks to save his life will lose it, and whoever loses his life will preserve it. [34]I tell you, in that night there will be two *men* in one bed: the one will be taken and the other will be left. [35]Two *women* will be grinding together: the one will be taken and the other left. [36]Two *men* will be in the field: the one will be taken and the other left."[a]

[37]And they answered and said to Him, "Where, Lord?"

So He said to them, "Wherever the body is, there the eagles will be gathered together."

The Parable of the Persistent Widow

18 Then He spoke a parable to them, that men always ought to pray and not lose heart, [2]saying: "There was in a certain city a judge who did not fear God nor regard man. [3]Now there was a widow in that city; and she came to him, saying, 'Get justice for me from my adversary.' [4]And he would not for a while; but afterward he said within himself, 'Though I do not fear God nor regard man, [5]yet because this widow troubles me I will avenge her, lest by her continual coming she weary me.'"

[6]Then the Lord said, "Hear what the unjust judge said. [7]And shall God not avenge His own elect who cry out day and night to Him, though He bears long with them? [8]I tell you that He will avenge them speedily. Nevertheless, when the Son of Man comes, will He really find faith on the earth?"

The Parable of the Pharisee and the Tax Collector

[9]Also He spoke this parable to some who trusted in themselves that they were righteous, and despised others: [10]"Two men went up to the temple to pray, one a Pharisee and the other a tax collector. [11]The Pharisee stood and prayed thus with himself, 'God, I thank You that I am not like other men—extortioners, unjust, adulterers, or even as this tax collector. [12]I fast twice a week; I give tithes of all that I possess.' [13]And the tax collector, standing afar off, would not so much as raise *his* eyes to heaven, but beat his breast, saying,

'God, be merciful to me a sinner!' [14]I tell you, this man went down to his house justified *rather* than the other; for everyone who exalts himself will be humbled, and he who humbles himself will be exalted."

Jesus Blesses Little Children

[15]Then they also brought infants to Him that He might touch them; but when the disciples saw *it,* they rebuked them. [16]But Jesus called them to *Him* and said, "Let the little children come to Me, and do not forbid them; for of such is the kingdom of God. [17]Assuredly, I say to you, whoever does not receive the kingdom of God as a little child will by no means enter it."

Jesus Counsels the Rich Young Ruler

[18]Now a certain ruler asked Him, saying, "Good Teacher, what shall I do to inherit eternal life?"

[19]So Jesus said to him, "Why do you call Me good? No one *is* good but One, *that is,* God. [20]You know the commandments: 'Do not commit adultery,' 'Do not murder,' 'Do not steal,' 'Do not bear false witness,' 'Honor your father and your mother.'"[a]

[21]And he said, "All these things I have kept from my youth."

[22]So when Jesus heard these things, He said to him, "You still lack one thing. Sell all that you have and distribute to the poor, and you will have treasure in heaven; and come, follow Me."

[23]But when he heard this, he became very sorrowful, for he was very rich.

With God All Things Are Possible

[24]And when Jesus saw that he became very sorrowful, He said, "How hard it is for those who have riches to enter the kingdom of God! [25]For it is easier for a camel to go through the eye of a needle than for a rich man to enter the kingdom of God."

[26]And those who heard it said, "Who then can be saved?"

[27]But He said, "The things which are impossible with men are possible with God."

17:36 [a]NU-Text and M-Text omit verse 36. **18:20** [a]Exodus 20:12–16; Deuteronomy 5:16–20

²⁸Then Peter said, "See, we have left all[a] and followed You."

²⁹So He said to them, "Assuredly, I say to you, there is no one who has left house or parents or brothers or wife or children, for the sake of the kingdom of God, ³⁰who shall not receive many times more in this present time, and in the age to come eternal life."

Jesus a Third Time Predicts His Death and Resurrection

³¹Then He took the twelve aside and said to them, "Behold, we are going up to Jerusalem, and all things that are written by the prophets concerning the Son of Man will be accomplished. ³²For He will be delivered to the Gentiles and will be mocked and insulted and spit upon. ³³They will scourge *Him* and kill Him. And the third day He will rise again."

³⁴But they understood none of these things; this saying was hidden from them, and they did not know the things which were spoken.

A Blind Man Receives His Sight

³⁵Then it happened, as He was coming near Jericho, that a certain blind man sat by the road begging. ³⁶And hearing a multitude passing by, he asked what it meant. ³⁷So they told him that Jesus of Nazareth was passing by. ³⁸And he cried out, saying, "Jesus, Son of David, have mercy on me!"

³⁹Then those who went before warned him that he should be quiet; but he cried out all the more, "Son of David, have mercy on me!"

⁴⁰So Jesus stood still and commanded him to be brought to Him. And when he had come near, He asked him, ⁴¹saying, "What do you want Me to do for you?"

He said, "Lord, that I may receive my sight."

⁴²Then Jesus said to him, "Receive your sight; your faith has made you well." ⁴³And immediately he received his sight, and followed Him, glorifying God. And all the people, when they saw *it,* gave praise to God.

Jesus Comes to Zacchaeus' House

19 Then *Jesus* entered and passed through Jericho. ²Now behold, *there was* a man named Zacchaeus who was a chief tax collector, and he was rich. ³And he sought to see who Jesus

was, but could not because of the crowd, for he was of short stature. ⁴So he ran ahead and climbed up into a sycamore tree to see Him, for He was going to pass that *way.* ⁵And when Jesus came to the place, He looked up and saw him,[a] and said to him, "Zacchaeus, make haste and come down, for today I must stay at your house." ⁶So he made haste and came down, and received Him joyfully. ⁷But when they saw *it,* they all complained, saying, "He has gone to be a guest with a man who is a sinner."

⁸Then Zacchaeus stood and said to the Lord, "Look, Lord, I give half of my goods to the poor; and if I have taken anything from anyone by false accusation, I restore fourfold."

⁹And Jesus said to him, "Today salvation has come to this house, because he also is a son of Abraham; ¹⁰for the Son of Man has come to seek and to save that which was lost."

The Parable of the Minas

¹¹Now as they heard these things, He spoke another parable, because He was near Jerusalem and because they thought the kingdom of God would appear immediately. ¹²Therefore He said: "A certain nobleman went into a far country to receive for himself a kingdom and to return. ¹³So he called ten of his servants, delivered to them ten minas,[a] and said to them, 'Do business till I come.' ¹⁴But his citizens hated him, and sent a delegation after him, saying, 'We will not have this *man* to reign over us.'

¹⁵"And so it was that when he returned, having received the kingdom, he then commanded these servants, to whom he had given the money, to be called to him, that he might know how much every man had gained by trading. ¹⁶Then came the first, saying, 'Master, your mina has earned ten minas.' ¹⁷And he said to him, 'Well *done,* good servant; because you were faithful in a very little, have authority over ten cities.' ¹⁸And the second came, saying, 'Master, your mina has earned five minas.' ¹⁹Likewise he said to him, 'You also be over five cities.'

²⁰"Then another came, saying, 'Master, here is your mina, which I have kept put away in a

18:28 ªNU-Text reads *our own.*   **19:5** ªNU-Text omits *and saw him.*
19:13 ªThe *mina* (Greek *mna,* Hebrew *minah*) was worth about three months' salary.

handkerchief. ²¹For I feared you, because you are an austere man. You collect what you did not deposit, and reap what you did not sow.' ²²And he said to him, 'Out of your own mouth I will judge you, *you* wicked servant. You knew that I was an austere man, collecting what I did not deposit and reaping what I did not sow. ²³Why then did you not put my money in the bank, that at my coming I might have collected it with interest?'

²⁴"And he said to those who stood by, 'Take the mina from him, and give *it* to him who has ten minas.' ²⁵(But they said to him, 'Master, he has ten minas.') ²⁶'For I say to you, that to everyone who has will be given; and from him who does not have, even what he has will be taken away from him. ²⁷But bring here those enemies of mine, who did not want me to reign over them, and slay *them* before me.'"

The Triumphal Entry

²⁸When He had said this, He went on ahead, going up to Jerusalem. ²⁹And it came to pass, when He drew near to Bethphage[a] and Bethany, at the mountain called Olivet, *that* He sent two of His disciples, ³⁰saying, "Go into the village opposite *you,* where as you enter you will find a colt tied, on which no one has ever sat. Loose it and bring *it here.* ³¹And if anyone asks you, 'Why are you loosing *it?*' thus you shall say to him, 'Because the Lord has need of it.'"

³²So those who were sent went their way and found *it* just as He had said to them. ³³But as they were loosing the colt, the owners of it said to them, "Why are you loosing the colt?"

³⁴And they said, "The Lord has need of him." ³⁵Then they brought him to Jesus. And they threw their own clothes on the colt, and they set Jesus on him. ³⁶And as He went, *many* spread their clothes on the road.

³⁷Then, as He was now drawing near the descent of the Mount of Olives, the whole multitude of the disciples began to rejoice and praise God with a loud voice for all the mighty works they had seen, ³⁸saying:

> " 'Blessed is the King who comes in the name of the LORD!'[a]
>
> Peace in heaven and glory in the highest!"

³⁹And some of the Pharisees called to Him from the crowd, "Teacher, rebuke Your disciples."

⁴⁰But He answered and said to them, "I tell you that if these should keep silent, the stones would immediately cry out."

Jesus Weeps over Jerusalem

⁴¹Now as He drew near, He saw the city and wept over it, ⁴²saying, "If you had known, even you, especially in this your day, the things *that make* for your peace! But now they are hidden from your eyes. ⁴³For days will come upon you when your enemies will build an embankment around you, surround you and close you in on every side, ⁴⁴and level you, and your children within you, to the ground; and they will not leave in you one stone upon another, because you did not know the time of your visitation."

Jesus Cleanses the Temple

⁴⁵Then He went into the temple and began to drive out those who bought and sold in it,[a] ⁴⁶saying to them, "It is written, *'My house is*[a] *a house of prayer,'*[b] but you have made it a *'den of thieves.'* "[c]

⁴⁷And He was teaching daily in the temple. But the chief priests, the scribes, and the leaders of the people sought to destroy Him, ⁴⁸and were unable to do anything; for all the people were very attentive to hear Him.

Jesus' Authority Questioned

20 Now it happened on one of those days, as He taught the people in the temple and preached the gospel, *that* the chief priests and the scribes, together with the elders, confronted *Him* ²and spoke to Him, saying, "Tell us, by what authority are You doing these things? Or who is he who gave You this authority?"

³But He answered and said to them, "I also will ask you one thing, and answer Me: ⁴The baptism of John—was it from heaven or from men?"

⁵And they reasoned among themselves, saying, "If we say, 'From heaven,' He will say, 'Why then[a] did you not believe him?' ⁶But if we say,

19:29 [a]M-Text reads *Bethsphage.* 19:38 [a]Psalm 118:26 19:45 [a]NU-Text reads *those who were selling.* 19:46 [a]NU-Text reads *shall be.* [b]Isaiah 56:7 [c]Jeremiah 7:11 20:5 [a]NU-Text and M-Text omit *then.*

LEADERSHIP REALITIES

THE BIG PICTURE   *Luke 19:41–44*

In the final week of the life of our Lord, He spent a considerable amount of time on the Mount of Olives, a limestone ridge that runs parallel to Jerusalem and rises 240 feet above the city. It was on this mount that Jesus stopped, looked over the city, and wept in Matthew 23:37–39 and Luke 19:41–44. It was here that Jesus taught His disciples concerning end times in Matthew 24. It was from this mount that He began to make His triumphal entry into Jerusalem in Luke 19:28–44. And, it was in a garden called Gethsemane on this mount that Jesus prayed "not My will, but Your will be done" just prior to going to the cross in Matthew 26.

With so much significance concerning this mount, one simple fact is often overlooked: that is, from this mount, Jesus saw the big picture, the entire city of Jerusalem. From this vantage point, He had a wide-angled vision of the city, of the people, and of the future. Essential to leadership is the ability to have a "big picture" outlook on life by going to the mount of God in worship and meditation. We learn from Jesus that to see the big picture is to view an entire "city" and not just one "house." One cannot live in isolation: every action and word will impact and influence others.

'From men,' all the people will stone us, for they are persuaded that John was a prophet." [7]So they answered that they did not know where *it was* from.

[8]And Jesus said to them, "Neither will I tell you by what authority I do these things."

The Parable of the Wicked Vinedressers

[9]Then He began to tell the people this parable: "A certain man planted a vineyard, leased it to vinedressers, and went into a far country for a long time. [10]Now at vintage-time he sent a servant to the vinedressers, that they might give him some of the fruit of the vineyard. But the vinedressers beat him and sent *him* away empty-handed. [11]Again he sent another servant; and they beat him also, treated *him* shamefully, and sent *him* away empty-handed. [12]And again he sent a third; and they wounded him also and cast *him* out. [13]"Then the owner of the vineyard said, 'What shall I do? I will send my beloved son. Probably they will respect *him* when they see him.' [14]But when the vinedressers saw him, they reasoned among themselves, saying, 'This is the heir. Come, let us kill him, that the inheritance may be ours.' [15]So they cast him out of the vine-

yard and killed *him*. Therefore what will the owner of the vineyard do to them? [16]He will come and destroy those vinedressers and give the vineyard to others."

And when they heard *it* they said, "Certainly not!"

[17]Then He looked at them and said, "What then is this that is written:

'The stone which the builders rejected
Has become the chief cornerstone'?[a]

[18]Whoever falls on that stone will be broken; but on whomever it falls, it will grind him to powder."

[19]And the chief priests and the scribes that very hour sought to lay hands on Him, but they feared the people[a]—for they knew He had spoken this parable against them.

The Pharisees: Is It Lawful to Pay Taxes to Caesar?

[20]So they watched *Him,* and sent spies who pretended to be righteous, that they might seize on His words, in order to deliver Him to the power and the authority of the governor.

20:17 [a]Psalm 118:22   **20:19** [a]M-Text reads *but they were afraid.*

²¹Then they asked Him, saying, "Teacher, we know that You say and teach rightly, and You do not show personal favoritism, but teach the way of God in truth: ²²Is it lawful for us to pay taxes to Caesar or not?"

²³But He perceived their craftiness, and said to them, "Why do you test Me?ᵃ ²⁴Show Me a denarius. Whose image and inscription does it have?"

They answered and said, "Caesar's."

²⁵And He said to them, "Render therefore to Caesar the things that are Caesar's, and to God the things that are God's."

²⁶But they could not catch Him in His words in the presence of the people. And they marveled at His answer and kept silent.

THE SADDUCEES: WHAT ABOUT THE RESURRECTION?

²⁷Then some of the Sadducees, who deny that there is a resurrection, came to *Him* and asked Him, ²⁸saying: "Teacher, Moses wrote to us *that* if a man's brother dies, having a wife, and he dies without children, his brother should take his wife and raise up offspring for his brother. ²⁹Now there were seven brothers. And the first took a wife, and died without children. ³⁰And the secondᵃ took her as wife, and he died childless. ³¹Then the third took her, and in like manner the seven also; and they left no children,ᵃ and died. ³²Last of all the woman died also. ³³Therefore, in the resurrection, whose wife does she become? For all seven had her as wife."

³⁴Jesus answered and said to them, "The sons of this age marry and are given in marriage. ³⁵But those who are counted worthy to attain that age, and the resurrection from the dead, neither marry nor are given in marriage; ³⁶nor can they die anymore, for they are equal to the angels and are sons of God, being sons of the resurrection. ³⁷But even Moses showed in the *burning* bush *passage* that the dead are raised, when he called the Lord *'the God of Abraham, the God of Isaac, and the God of Jacob.'*ᵃ ³⁸For He is not the God of the dead but of the living, for all live to Him."

³⁹Then some of the scribes answered and said, "Teacher, You have spoken well." ⁴⁰But after that they dared not question Him anymore.

JESUS: HOW CAN DAVID CALL HIS DESCENDANT LORD?

⁴¹And He said to them, "How can they say that the Christ is the Son of David? ⁴²Now David himself said in the Book of Psalms:

'The Lord said to my Lord,
"Sit at My right hand,
⁴³*Till I make Your enemies Your footstool." '*ᵃ

⁴⁴Therefore David calls Him *'Lord';* how is He then his Son?"

BEWARE OF THE SCRIBES

⁴⁵Then, in the hearing of all the people, He said to His disciples, ⁴⁶"Beware of the scribes, who desire to go around in long robes, love greetings in the marketplaces, the best seats in the synagogues, and the best places at feasts, ⁴⁷who devour widows' houses, and for a pretense make long prayers. These will receive greater condemnation."

THE WIDOW'S TWO MITES

21 And He looked up and saw the rich putting their gifts into the treasury, ²and He saw also a certain poor widow putting in two mites. ³So He said, "Truly I say to you that this poor widow has put in more than all; ⁴for all these out of their abundance have put in offerings for God,ᵃ but she out of her poverty put in all the livelihood that she had."

JESUS PREDICTS THE DESTRUCTION OF THE TEMPLE

⁵Then, as some spoke of the temple, how it was adorned with beautiful stones and donations, He said, ⁶"These things which you see—the days will come in which not *one* stone shall be left upon another that shall not be thrown down."

THE SIGNS OF THE TIMES AND THE END OF THE AGE

⁷So they asked Him, saying, "Teacher, but when will these things be? And what sign *will there be* when these things are about to take place?"

20:23 ᵃNU-Text omits *Why do you test Me?*   20:30 ᵃNU-Text ends verse 30 here.   20:31 ᵃNU-Text and M-Text read *the seven also left no children.*   20:37 ᵃExodus 3:6, 15   20:43 ᵃPsalm 110:1   21:4 ᵃNU-Text omits *for God.*

[8]And He said: "Take heed that you not be deceived. For many will come in My name, saying, 'I am *He,*' and, 'The time has drawn near.' Therefore[a] do not go after them. [9]But when you hear of wars and commotions, do not be terrified; for these things must come to pass first, but the end *will* not *come* immediately."

[10]Then He said to them, "Nation will rise against nation, and kingdom against kingdom. [11]And there will be great earthquakes in various places, and famines and pestilences; and there will be fearful sights and great signs from heaven. [12]But before all these things, they will lay their hands on you and persecute *you,* delivering *you* up to the synagogues and prisons. You will be brought before kings and rulers for My name's sake. [13]But it will turn out for you as an occasion for testimony. [14]Therefore settle *it* in your hearts not to meditate beforehand on what you will answer; [15]for I will give you a mouth and wisdom which all your adversaries will not be able to contradict or resist. [16]You will be betrayed even by parents and brothers, relatives and friends; and they will put *some* of you to death. [17]And you will be hated by all for My name's sake. [18]But not a hair of your head shall be lost. [19]By your patience possess your souls.

The Destruction of Jerusalem

[20]"But when you see Jerusalem surrounded by armies, then know that its desolation is near. [21]Then let those who are in Judea flee to the mountains, let those who are in the midst of her depart, and let not those who are in the country enter her. [22]For these are the days of vengeance, that all things which are written may be fulfilled. [23]But woe to those who are pregnant and to those who are nursing babies in those days! For there will be great distress in the land and wrath upon this people. [24]And they will fall by the edge of the sword, and be led away captive into all nations. And Jerusalem will be trampled by Gentiles until the times of the Gentiles are fulfilled.

The Coming of the Son of Man

[25]"And there will be signs in the sun, in the moon, and in the stars; and on the earth distress of nations, with perplexity, the sea and the waves roaring; [26]men's hearts failing them from fear and the expectation of those things which are coming on the earth, for the powers of the heavens will be shaken. [27]Then they will see the Son of Man coming in a cloud with power and great glory. [28]Now when these things begin to happen, look up and lift up your heads, because your redemption draws near."

The Parable of the Fig Tree

[29]Then He spoke to them a parable: "Look at the fig tree, and all the trees. [30]When they are already budding, you see and know for yourselves that summer is now near. [31]So you also, when you see these things happening, know that the kingdom of God is near. [32]Assuredly, I say to you, this generation will by no means pass away till all things take place. [33]Heaven and earth will pass away, but My words will by no means pass away.

The Importance of Watching

[34]"But take heed to yourselves, lest your hearts be weighed down with carousing, drunkenness, and cares of this life, and that Day come on you unexpectedly. [35]For it will come as a snare on all those who dwell on the face of the whole earth. [36]Watch therefore, and pray always that you may be counted worthy[a] to escape all these things that will come to pass, and to stand before the Son of Man."

[37]And in the daytime He was teaching in the temple, but at night He went out and stayed on the mountain called Olivet. [38]Then early in the morning all the people came to Him in the temple to hear Him.

The Plot to Kill Jesus

22 Now the Feast of Unleavened Bread drew near, which is called Passover. [2]And the chief priests and the scribes sought how they might kill Him, for they feared the people.

[3]Then Satan entered Judas, surnamed Iscariot, who was numbered among the twelve. [4]So he went his way and conferred with the chief priests and captains, how he might betray Him to them. [5]And they were glad, and agreed to give him money. [6]So he promised and sought opportunity to betray Him to them in the absence of the multitude.

21:8 [a]NU-Text omits *Therefore.* **21:36** [a]NU-Text reads *may have strength.*

JESUS AND HIS DISCIPLES PREPARE THE PASSOVER

7Then came the Day of Unleavened Bread, when the Passover must be killed. 8And He sent Peter and John, saying, "Go and prepare the Passover for us, that we may eat."

9So they said to Him, "Where do You want us to prepare?"

10And He said to them, "Behold, when you have entered the city, a man will meet you carrying a pitcher of water; follow him into the house which he enters. 11Then you shall say to the master of the house, 'The Teacher says to you, "Where is the guest room where I may eat the Passover with My disciples?" ' 12Then he will show you a large, furnished upper room; there make ready."

13So they went and found it just as He had said to them, and they prepared the Passover.

JESUS INSTITUTES THE LORD'S SUPPER

14When the hour had come, He sat down, and the twelvea apostles with Him. 15Then He said to them, "With *fervent* desire I have desired to eat this Passover with you before I suffer; 16for I say to you, I will no longer eat of it until it is fulfilled in the kingdom of God."

17Then He took the cup, and gave thanks, and said, "Take this and divide *it* among yourselves; 18for I say to you,a I will not drink of the fruit of the vine until the kingdom of God comes."

19And He took bread, gave thanks and broke *it,* and gave *it* to them, saying, "This is My body which is given for you; do this in remembrance of Me."

20Likewise He also *took* the cup after supper, saying, "This cup *is* the new covenant in My blood, which is shed for you. 21But behold, the hand of My betrayer *is* with Me on the table. 22And truly the Son of Man goes as it has been determined, but woe to that man by whom He is betrayed!"

23Then they began to question among themselves, which of them it was who would do this thing.

THE DISCIPLES ARGUE ABOUT GREATNESS

24Now there was also a dispute among them, as to which of them should be considered the greatest. 25And He said to them, "The kings of the Gentiles exercise lordship over them, and those who exercise authority over them are called 'benefactors.' 26But not so *among* you; on the contrary, he who is greatest among you, let him be as the younger, and he who governs as he who serves. 27For who *is* greater, he who sits at the table, or he who serves? *Is* it not he who sits at the table? Yet I am among you as the One who serves.

28"But you are those who have continued with Me in My trials. 29And I bestow upon you a kingdom, just as My Father bestowed *one* upon Me, 30that you may eat and drink at My table in My kingdom, and sit on thrones judging the twelve tribes of Israel."

JESUS PREDICTS PETER'S DENIAL

31And the Lord said,a "Simon, Simon! Indeed, Satan has asked for you, that he may sift *you* as wheat. 32But I have prayed for you, that your faith should not fail; and when you have returned to *Me,* strengthen your brethren."

33But he said to Him, "Lord, I am ready to go with You, both to prison and to death."

34Then He said, "I tell you, Peter, the rooster shall not crow this day before you will deny three times that you know Me."

SUPPLIES FOR THE ROAD

35And He said to them, "When I sent you without money bag, knapsack, and sandals, did you lack anything?"

So they said, "Nothing."

36Then He said to them, "But now, he who has a money bag, let him take *it,* and likewise a knapsack; and he who has no sword, let him sell his garment and buy one. 37For I say to you that this which is written must still be accomplished in Me: *'And He was numbered with the transgressors.'*a For the things concerning Me have an end."

38So they said, "Lord, look, here *are* two swords."

And He said to them, "It is enough."

THE PRAYER IN THE GARDEN

39Coming out, He went to the Mount of Olives, as He was accustomed, and His disciples

22:14 aNU-Text omits *twelve.* **22:18** aNU-Text adds *from now on.*
22:31 aNU-Text omits *And the Lord said.* **22:37** aIsaiah 53:12

LEADERSHIP ISSUES

The Prudent Leader Welcomes Conflict

LUKE 22:24–28

Managing conflict is a big part of the job description of any leader. Jesus modeled for us that conflict must be addressed with an open heart and mind toward resolution. In doing so, we can generate positive change and build stronger relationships.

1. Welcome disagreements. They are a stimulus for change and a corrective for error.

2. Listen carefully. Hear the other person out and repeat what they said in your own words to let them know you've absorbed accurately the meaning of what they said.

3. Keep your cool. Don't blow up; once tempers flare, progress ends. Take a walk, count to 100, or take a break.

4. Focus first on areas of agreement. If you honestly feel that the other person's complaint is in error, look for things you can affirm before launching into your counterarguments. This will help dispel a negative atmosphere and open the door to better communication.

5. When you are wrong, admit it. Leaders who can honestly admit they were wrong are respected and admired.

6. Weigh concerns of and criticism from others honestly, objectively and fairly. After all, these people just might be right.

7. Praise in public; reprimand in private. If you praise one person publicly, you'll make not just one friend but many.

Human nature hasn't changed much in two thousand years. People still compete with each other, jockey for position, and bump their oversized egos against one another as the apostles did. Jesus managed the conflict in His twelve-member organization by facing the issues squarely, bringing the hidden conflicts out into the open, laying down principles for resolving conflict, and modeling a healthy conflict resolution style.

Recognize conflict as an opportunity to teach, to grow, to generate positive change and to build stronger relationships. Use conflict to be a witness in your community.

also followed Him. [40]When He came to the place, He said to them, "Pray that you may not enter into temptation."

[41]And He was withdrawn from them about a stone's throw, and He knelt down and prayed, [42]saying, "Father, if it is Your will, take this cup away from Me; nevertheless not My will, but Yours, be done." [43]Then an angel appeared to Him from heaven, strengthening Him. [44]And being in agony, He prayed more earnestly. Then His sweat became like great drops of blood falling down to the ground.[a]

[45]When He rose up from prayer, and had come to His disciples, He found them sleeping from sorrow. [46]Then He said to them, "Why do you sleep? Rise and pray, lest you enter into temptation."

Betrayal and Arrest in Gethsemane

[47]And while He was still speaking, behold, a multitude; and he who was called Judas, one of the twelve, went before them and drew near to Jesus to kiss Him. [48]But Jesus said to him, "Judas, are you betraying the Son of Man with a kiss?"

[49]When those around Him saw what was going to happen, they said to Him, "Lord, shall we strike with the sword?" [50]And one of them struck the servant of the high priest and cut off his right ear.

[51]But Jesus answered and said, "Permit even this." And He touched his ear and healed him.

[52]Then Jesus said to the chief priests, captains of the temple, and the elders who had come to Him, "Have you come out, as against a robber, with swords and clubs? [53]When I was with you daily in the temple, you did not try to seize Me. But this is your hour, and the power of darkness."

Peter Denies Jesus, and Weeps Bitterly

[54]Having arrested Him, they led *Him* and brought Him into the high priest's house. But Peter followed at a distance. [55]Now when they had kindled a fire in the midst of the courtyard and sat down together, Peter sat among them. [56]And a certain servant girl, seeing him as he sat by the fire, looked intently at him and said, "This man was also with Him."

[57]But he denied Him,[a] saying, "Woman, I do not know Him."

[58]And after a little while another saw him and said, "You also are of them."

But Peter said, "Man, I am not!"

[59]Then after about an hour had passed, another confidently affirmed, saying, "Surely this *fellow* also was with Him, for he is a Galilean."

[60]But Peter said, "Man, I do not know what you are saying!"

Immediately, while he was still speaking, the rooster[a] crowed. [61]And the Lord turned and looked at Peter. Then Peter remembered the word of the Lord, how He had said to him, "Before the rooster crows,[a] you will deny Me three times." [62]So Peter went out and wept bitterly.

Jesus Mocked and Beaten

[63]Now the men who held Jesus mocked Him and beat Him. [64]And having blindfolded Him, they struck Him on the face and asked Him,[a] saying, "Prophesy! Who is the one who struck You?" [65]And many other things they blasphemously spoke against Him.

Jesus Faces the Sanhedrin

[66]As soon as it was day, the elders of the people, both chief priests and scribes, came together and led Him into their council, saying, [67]"If You are the Christ, tell us."

But He said to them, "If I tell you, you will by no means believe. [68]And if I also ask *you*, you will by no means answer Me or let *Me* go.[a] [69]Hereafter the Son of Man will sit on the right hand of the power of God."

[70]Then they all said, "Are You then the Son of God?"

So He said to them, "You *rightly* say that I am."

[71]And they said, "What further testimony do we need? For we have heard it ourselves from His own mouth."

Jesus Handed Over to Pontius Pilate

23 Then the whole multitude of them arose and led Him to Pilate. [2]And they began to accuse Him, saying, "We found this *fellow* pervert-

---

22:44 [a]NU-Text brackets verses 43 and 44 as not in the original text.   22:57 [a]NU-Text reads *denied it.*   22:60 [a]NU-Text and M-Text read *a rooster.*   22:61 [a]NU-Text adds *today.*   22:64 [a]NU-Text reads *And having blindfolded Him, they asked Him.*   22:68 [a]NU-Text omits *also* and *Me or let Me go.*

ing the[a] nation, and forbidding to pay taxes to Caesar, saying that He Himself is Christ, a King."

3Then Pilate asked Him, saying, "Are You the King of the Jews?"

He answered him and said, "*It is as* you say."

4So Pilate said to the chief priests and the crowd, "I find no fault in this Man."

5But they were the more fierce, saying, "He stirs up the people, teaching throughout all Judea, beginning from Galilee to this place."

JESUS FACES HEROD

6When Pilate heard of Galilee,[a] he asked if the Man were a Galilean. 7And as soon as he knew that He belonged to Herod's jurisdiction, he sent Him to Herod, who was also in Jerusalem at that time. 8Now when Herod saw Jesus, he was exceedingly glad; for he had desired for a long *time* to see Him, because he had heard many things about Him, and he hoped to see some miracle done by Him. 9Then he questioned Him with many words, but He answered him nothing. 10And the chief priests and scribes stood and vehemently accused Him. 11Then Herod, with his men of war, treated Him with contempt and mocked *Him,* arrayed Him in a gorgeous robe, and sent Him back to Pilate. 12That very day Pilate and Herod became friends with each other, for previously they had been at enmity with each other.

TAKING THE PLACE OF BARABBAS

13Then Pilate, when he had called together the chief priests, the rulers, and the people, 14said to them, "You have brought this Man to me, as one who misleads the people. And indeed, having examined *Him* in your presence, I have found no fault in this Man concerning those things of which you accuse Him; 15no, neither did Herod, for I sent you back to him;[a] and indeed nothing deserving of death has been done by Him. 16I will therefore chastise Him and release *Him*" 17(for it was necessary for him to release one to them at the feast).[a]

18And they all cried out at once, saying, "Away with this *Man,* and release to us Barabbas"— 19who had been thrown into prison for a certain rebellion made in the city, and for murder.

20Pilate, therefore, wishing to release Jesus,

again called out to them. 21But they shouted, saying, "Crucify *Him,* crucify Him!"

22Then he said to them the third time, "Why, what evil has He done? I have found no reason for death in Him. I will therefore chastise Him and let *Him* go."

23But they were insistent, demanding with loud voices that He be crucified. And the voices of these men and of the chief priests prevailed.[a] 24So Pilate gave sentence that it should be as they requested. 25And he released to them[a] the one they requested, who for rebellion and murder had been thrown into prison; but he delivered Jesus to their will.

THE KING ON A CROSS

26Now as they led Him away, they laid hold of a certain man, Simon a Cyrenian, who was coming from the country, and on him they laid the cross that he might bear *it* after Jesus.

27And a great multitude of the people followed Him, and women who also mourned and lamented Him. 28But Jesus, turning to them, said, "Daughters of Jerusalem, do not weep for Me, but weep for yourselves and for your children. 29For indeed the days are coming in which they will say, 'Blessed *are* the barren, wombs that never bore, and breasts which never nursed!' 30Then they will begin *'to say to the mountains, "Fall on us!" and to the hills, "Cover us!"'*[a] 31For if they do these things in the green wood, what will be done in the dry?"

32There were also two others, criminals, led with Him to be put to death. 33And when they had come to the place called Calvary, there they crucified Him, and the criminals, one on the right hand and the other on the left. 34Then Jesus said, "Father, forgive them, for they do not know what they do."[a]

And they divided His garments and cast lots. 35And the people stood looking on. But even the rulers with them sneered, saying, "He saved others; let Him save Himself if He is the Christ, the chosen of God."

23:2 [a]NU-Text reads *our.*   **23:6** [a]NU-Text omits *of Galilee.*   **23:15** [a]NU-Text reads *for he sent Him back to us.*   **23:17** [a]NU-Text omits verse 17.   **23:23** [a]NU-Text omits *and of the chief priests.*   **23:25** [a]NU-Text and M-Text omit *to them.*   **23:30** [a]Hosea 10:8   **23:34** [a]NU-Text brackets the first sentence as a later addition.

LEADERSHIP ISSUES

GC2: Encountering Jesus: No Greater Love

LUKE 23:33 *And when they had come to the place called Calvary, there they crucified Him, and the criminals, one on the right hand and the other on the left.*

No greater love is there than what we experience from Christ at Calvary. One who has never known sin becomes sin, and He does it for you! (1 Cor. 15:20–22). "God is love" (1 John 4:8); and even at Calvary, in His final hours, Christ startled people with His amazing love:

- Imagine how He must have startled those Roman soldiers—the very ones who had mocked Him, tortured Him, driven the nails into His hands and feet, and gambled for His clothing—as He looked at them and said, "Father, forgive them, for they do not know what they do" (Luke 23:34).

- Consider the thief who was crucified next to Christ. After a lifetime of deception, he must have been startled to hear Jesus' accepting words: "Today you will be with Me in Paradise" (Luke 23:43).

- Recall Jesus looking down from the cross and seeing His mother, Mary, standing with His beloved disciple, John. Once again, Christ displayed His startling, supportive love. Looking ahead to His approaching death, He made provision for His mother by entrusting her into John's care (John 19:26, 27).

- Picture Jesus in agony on the cross. He is prepared to take upon Himself the sins of the world and endure separation from His Father. He will soon cry out in utter abandonment: "My God, My God, why have You forsaken Me?" (Mark 15:34). Yet there He hangs, still startling people with His love.

For whom did He do all this? For whom did He suffer and die? Listen as the Spirit whispers, "He did it for you! If He did not need to die for anyone else, He would have done it just for you!" Allow this wondrous truth to touch you as you quietly whisper the words "He did it for me."

GC2
GREAT COMMANDMENT
COMMISSION

³⁶The soldiers also mocked Him, coming and offering Him sour wine, ³⁷and saying, "If You are the King of the Jews, save Yourself."

³⁸And an inscription also was written over Him in letters of Greek, Latin, and Hebrew:ᵃ

THIS IS THE KING OF THE JEWS.

³⁹Then one of the criminals who were hanged blasphemed Him, saying, "If You are the Christ,ᵃ save Yourself and us."

⁴⁰But the other, answering, rebuked him, saying, "Do you not even fear God, seeing you are under the same condemnation? ⁴¹And we indeed justly, for we receive the due reward of our deeds; but this Man has done nothing wrong." ⁴²Then he said to Jesus, "Lord,ᵃ remember me when You come into Your kingdom."

⁴³And Jesus said to him, "Assuredly, I say to you, today you will be with Me in Paradise."

JESUS DIES ON THE CROSS

⁴⁴Now it wasᵃ about the sixth hour, and there was darkness over all the earth until the ninth hour. ⁴⁵Then the sun was darkened,ᵃ and the veil of the temple was torn in two. ⁴⁶And when Jesus had cried out with a loud voice, He said, "Father, *'into Your hands I commit My spirit.' "*ᵃ Having said this, He breathed His last.

⁴⁷So when the centurion saw what had happened, he glorified God, saying, "Certainly this was a righteous Man!"

⁴⁸And the whole crowd who came together to that sight, seeing what had been done, beat their breasts and returned. ⁴⁹But all His acquaintances, and the women who followed Him from Galilee, stood at a distance, watching these things.

JESUS BURIED IN JOSEPH'S TOMB

⁵⁰Now behold, *there was* a man named Joseph, a council member, a good and just man. ⁵¹He had not consented to their decision and deed. *He was* from Arimathea, a city of the Jews, who himself was also waitingᵃ for the kingdom of God. ⁵²This man went to Pilate and asked for the body of Jesus. ⁵³Then he took it down, wrapped it in linen, and laid it in a tomb *that was* hewn out of the rock, where no one had ever lain before. ⁵⁴That day was the Preparation, and the Sabbath drew near.

⁵⁵And the women who had come with Him from Galilee followed after, and they observed the tomb and how His body was laid. ⁵⁶Then they returned and prepared spices and fragrant oils. And they rested on the Sabbath according to the commandment.

HE IS RISEN

24 Now on the first *day* of the week, very early in the morning, they, and certain *other women* with them,ᵃ came to the tomb bringing the spices which they had prepared. ²But they found the stone rolled away from the tomb. ³Then they went in and did not find the body of the Lord Jesus. ⁴And it happened, as they were greatlyᵃ perplexed about this, that behold, two men stood by them in shining garments. ⁵Then, as they were afraid and bowed *their* faces to the earth, they said to them, "Why do you seek the living among the dead? ⁶He is not here, but is risen! Remember how He spoke to you when He was still in Galilee, ⁷saying, 'The Son of Man must be delivered into the hands of sinful men, and be crucified, and the third day rise again.' "

⁸And they remembered His words. ⁹Then they returned from the tomb and told all these things to the eleven and to all the rest. ¹⁰It was Mary Magdalene, Joanna, Mary *the mother* of James, and the other *women* with them, who told these things to the apostles. ¹¹And their words seemed to them like idle tales, and they did not believe them. ¹²But Peter arose and ran to the tomb; and stooping down, he saw the linen cloths lyingᵃ by themselves; and he departed, marveling to himself at what had happened.

THE ROAD TO EMMAUS

¹³Now behold, two of them were traveling that same day to a village called Emmaus, which was seven milesᵃ from Jerusalem. ¹⁴And they talked together of all these things which had happened. ¹⁵So it was, while they conversed and reasoned, that Jesus Himself drew near and went

23:38 ᵃNU-Text omits *written* and *in letters of Greek, Latin, and Hebrew.* **23:39** ᵃNU-Text reads *Are You not the Christ?* **23:42** ᵃNU-Text reads *And he said, "Jesus, remember me.* **23:44** ᵃNU-Text adds *already.* **23:45** ᵃNU-Text reads *obscured.* **23:46** ᵃPsalm 31:5 **23:51** ᵃNU-Text reads *who was waiting.* **24:1** ᵃNU-Text omits *and certain other women with them.* **24:4** ᵃNU-Text omits *greatly.* **24:12** ᵃNU-Text omits *lying.* **24:13** ᵃLiterally *sixty stadia* with them. [16]But their eyes were restrained, so that they did not know Him.

[17]And He said to them, "What kind of conversation *is* this that you have with one another as you walk and are sad?"[a]

[18]Then the one whose name was Cleopas answered and said to Him, "Are You the only stranger in Jerusalem, and have You not known the things which happened there in these days?"

[19]And He said to them, "What things?"

So they said to Him, "The things concerning Jesus of Nazareth, who was a Prophet mighty in deed and word before God and all the people, [20]and how the chief priests and our rulers delivered Him to be condemned to death, and crucified Him. [21]But we were hoping that it was He who was going to redeem Israel. Indeed, besides all this, today is the third day since these things happened. [22]Yes, and certain women of our company, who arrived at the tomb early, astonished us. [23]When they did not find His body, they came saying that they had also seen a vision of angels who said He was alive. [24]And certain of those *who were* with us went to the tomb and found *it* just as the women had said; but Him they did not see."

[25]Then He said to them, "O foolish ones, and slow of heart to believe in all that the prophets have spoken! [26]Ought not the Christ to have suffered these things and to enter into His glory?" [27]And beginning at Moses and all the Prophets, He expounded to them in all the Scriptures the things concerning Himself.

THE DISCIPLES' EYES OPENED

[28]Then they drew near to the village where they were going, and He indicated that He would have gone farther. [29]But they constrained Him, saying, "Abide with us, for it is toward evening, and the day is far spent." And He went in to stay with them.

[30]Now it came to pass, as He sat at the table with them, that He took bread, blessed and broke *it,* and gave it to them. [31]Then their eyes were opened and they knew Him; and He vanished from their sight.

[32]And they said to one another, "Did not our heart burn within us while He talked with us on the road, and while He opened the Scriptures to

24:17 [a]NU-Text reads *as you walk? And they stood still, looking sad.*

THROUGH THE GRID

Thinking Christianly: Why Should One Believe in Miracles? (Luke 24)

The Bible is filled with miracles. The greatest event of history, the resurrection of Christ, is a miracle. However, in our modern day and age, it seems silly to the average person to consider the reality of miracles. They seem out of place and on the level of magic tricks. Some liberal biblical scholars have attempted to dismiss the reality of miracles by explaining them away by scientific methods. So why should one believe in the reality of miracles?

First, it is prejudicial to eliminate the possibility of miracles before one looks at the evidence. The evidence should form our conclusions, instead of our conclusions shaping the evidence. The fact that every effect has a cause does not mean that every cause is a natural one. If God exists, then miracles are possible. If the Christian God exists, then miracles are definitely possible, if not probable, given God's nature. Without a faith commitment in God, however, one will be unable to see the acts of God, which include the supernatural and the miraculous. Without the basic foundational element of God's existence, one will always search for a naturalistic answer that can explain away the miracles. The life, death, and resurrection of Christ form the greatest evidence for the miraculous. God came into history through the Person of Jesus Christ, in order that we might see and investigate the God who does the supernatural.

LEADERSHIP ISSUES

GC2: Nourished by the Word:
From Knowing Scripture to Experiencing Scripture

LUKE 24:32 *Did not our heart burn within us while He talked with us on the road, and while He opened the Scriptures to us?*

The disciples who walked along the Emmaus Road were certainly familiar with Scripture; they knew the Word of God. We know that these disciples rationally embraced the truths of the Messiah because they made their way to Golgotha during the Passover. They were among the crowd who saw Christ's torture and crucifixion. Yet Scripture tells us that "their eyes were restrained, so that they did not know Him" (Luke 24:16).

It is important to notice that Christ did not leave them in this state of "knowing Scripture" but missing Him. The Gospel recalls that, "Beginning at Moses and all the Prophets, He expounded to them in all the Scriptures the things concerning Himself" (Luke 24:27). As Christ seized the initiative to reveal Himself, transformation took place in the lives of these disciples.

How long has it been since your heart "burned within" as the Spirit revealed the Son through His Word? Perhaps it has been too long. Pause now and ask the Lord to meet you in His Word, bringing revelation and life. Ask Him to join you often and open the Scriptures to you, making them come alive by His Spirit.

us?" ³³So they rose up that very hour and returned to Jerusalem, and found the eleven and those *who were* with them gathered together, ³⁴saying, "The Lord is risen indeed, and has appeared to Simon!" ³⁵And they told about the things *that had happened* on the road, and how He was known to them in the breaking of bread.

JESUS APPEARS TO HIS DISCIPLES

³⁶Now as they said these things, Jesus Himself stood in the midst of them, and said to them, "Peace to you." ³⁷But they were terrified and frightened, and supposed they had seen a spirit. ³⁸And He said to them, "Why are you troubled? And why do doubts arise in your hearts? ³⁹Behold My hands and My feet, that it is I Myself. Handle Me and see, for a spirit does not have flesh and bones as you see I have."

⁴⁰When He had said this, He showed them His hands and His feet.[a] ⁴¹But while they still did not believe for joy, and marveled, He said to them, "Have you any food here?" ⁴²So they gave Him a piece of a broiled fish and some honeycomb.[a] ⁴³And He took *it* and ate in their presence.

THE SCRIPTURES OPENED

⁴⁴Then He said to them, "These *are* the words which I spoke to you while I was still with you, that all things must be fulfilled which were written in the Law of Moses and *the* Prophets and *the* Psalms concerning Me." ⁴⁵And He opened their understanding, that they might comprehend the Scriptures.

⁴⁶Then He said to them, "Thus it is written, and thus it was necessary for the Christ to suffer and to rise[a] from the dead the third day, ⁴⁷and that repentance and remission of sins should be preached in His name to all nations, beginning at Jerusalem. ⁴⁸And you are witnesses of these things. ⁴⁹Behold, I send the Promise of My Father upon you; but tarry in the city of Jerusalem[a] until you are endued with power from on high."

THE ASCENSION

⁵⁰And He led them out as far as Bethany, and He lifted up His hands and blessed them. ⁵¹Now it came to pass, while He blessed them, that He was parted from them and carried up into heaven. ⁵²And they worshiped Him, and returned to Jerusalem with great joy, ⁵³and were continually in the temple praising and[a] blessing God. Amen.[b]

24:40 [a]Some printed New Testaments omit this verse. It is found in nearly all Greek manuscripts. **24:42** [a]NU-Text omits *and some honeycomb.* **24:46** [a]NU-Text reads *written, that the Christ should suffer and rise.* **24:49** [a]NU-Text omits *of Jerusalem.* **24:53** [a]NU-Text omits *praising and.* [b]NU-Text omits *Amen.*

IMPACT OF THE BOOK

JOHN

I IDEA	*You cannot accept Jesus as Savior if you do not also accept Him as Lord over your life. Jesus is God. (See especially John 20:28–31).*
MESSAGE	*Jesus' call to salvation included a call to make Him Lord. Just as He submitted to the will of His Father, we, too, are to submit to Christ. Only then can we truly know how to lead others. Almost half the book is devoted to the Passion (the last week of Jesus' life). How do you respond under pressure or finish well? Look to Jesus who, in His most difficult and trying times, had the clarity, love, and vision to invest in His followers.*
PEOPLE	*Chief Priests, Jesus, John the Baptist, Mary Magdalene, Pharisees, Pilate, Samaritan Woman, Twelve Disciples*
AUTHOR	*John "the beloved disciple" and son of Zebedee wrote from his home in Ephesus. His brother James was also one of Jesus' disciples. They were fishermen in Galilee before the Lord called them. His purpose was to convince people to believe in Christ and experience eternal life.*
CULTURE	*John lived a long life in Ephesus, the largest city in the Roman province of Asia. John included incidents missing from the other Gospels such as Jesus' raising Lazarus from the dead, the seven "I am" statements, and Jesus' meeting with the Samaritan Woman, which shattered racial and religious bigotry. John focuses on the deity of Jesus, yet He willingly humbled Himself to be a servant, highlighted by washing the disciples' feet, and laying down His life to pay the penalty for human sinfulness. John's Gospel was written much later than the other three Gospels. Christianity was now spreading all over the world.*
TIMELINE	*AD 80–90*
KEY SCRIPTURE MEMORY VERSES	1:1–5, 11–14, 29; 3:3, 16; 6:51; 8:12; 10:27–30; 11:25, 26; 13:34, 35; 14:1–6; 15:13; 20:30, 31

The Eternal Word

1 In the beginning was the Word, and the Word was with God, and the Word was God. [2]He was in the beginning with God. [3]All things were made through Him, and without Him nothing was made that was made. [4]In Him was life, and the life was the light of men. [5]And the light shines in the darkness, and the darkness did not comprehend[a] it.

John's Witness: The True Light

[6]There was a man sent from God, whose name *was* John. [7]This man came for a witness, to bear witness of the Light, that all through him might believe. [8]He was not that Light, but *was sent* to bear witness of that Light. [9]That was the true Light which gives light to every man coming into the world.[a]

[10]He was in the world, and the world was made through Him, and the world did not know Him. [11]He came to His own,[a] and His own[b] did not receive Him. [12]But as many as received Him, to them He gave the right to become children of God, to those who believe in His name: [13]who were born, not of blood, nor of the will of the flesh, nor of the will of man, but of God.

The Word Becomes Flesh

[14]And the Word became flesh and dwelt among us, and we beheld His glory, the glory as of the only begotten of the Father, full of grace and truth.

[15]John bore witness of Him and cried out, saying, "This was He of whom I said, 'He who comes after me is preferred before me, for He was before me.' "

[16]And[a] of His fullness we have all received, and grace for grace. [17]For the law was given through Moses, *but* grace and truth came through Jesus Christ. [18]No one has seen God at any time. The only begotten Son,[a] who is in the bosom of the Father, He has declared *Him*.

A Voice in the Wilderness

[19]Now this is the testimony of John, when the Jews sent priests and Levites from Jerusalem to ask him, "Who are you?"

[20]He confessed, and did not deny, but confessed, "I am not the Christ."

[21]And they asked him, "What then? Are you Elijah?"

He said, "I am not."

"Are you the Prophet?"

And he answered, "No."

[22]Then they said to him, "Who are you, that we may give an answer to those who sent us? What do you say about yourself?"

[23]He said: "I *am*

The voice of one crying in the wilderness:
"Make straight the way of the Lord," '[a]

as the prophet Isaiah said."

[24]Now those who were sent were from the Pharisees. [25]And they asked him, saying, "Why

1:5 [a]Or *overcome*   **1:9** [a]Or *That was the true Light which, coming into the world, gives light to every man.*   **1:11** [a]That is, His own things or domain   [b]That is, His own people   **1:16** [a]NU-Text reads *For.*   **1:18** [a]NU-Text reads *only begotten God.*   **1:23** [a]Isaiah 40:3

THROUGH THE GRID

Thinking Christianly: Ten Foundational Beliefs of a Christian Worldview

Belief Five: Jesus Christ (*John 1:1–18*)

Jesus Christ is the eternal Son of God, who is perfect in all His ways. Jesus is at the same time fully God and fully man, providing the bridge between an all-holy and righteous God and sinful humanity. Jesus lived a perfect and sinless life, and He ultimately suffered and died on a cross in order to atone for our sins. Christ died, was buried, and rose from the dead, and He will come again at the end of time (Is. 9:6, 7; Mic. 5:2; John 1:1–18; 8:58; 14:1–9; Acts 1:1–11; 2 Cor. 5:21; Phil. 2:6–11; Col. 1:13–23; 2:9, 10; Heb. 1:1–3; 4:15). *See Through the Grid article on page 1569.*

THROUGH THE GRID

Making Sense of Your World:
The Bible and the World (John 1:10)

The Bible refers to the world in two distinct ways. The first meaning of "the world" includes the cosmos of all created matter. This is the nature that exists all around us. The other meaning of "the world" is the cosmos of the created, personal realm, which includes dealings with the social world of people, cultures, and societies.

---

then do you baptize if you are not the Christ, nor Elijah, nor the Prophet?"

26John answered them, saying, "I baptize with water, but there stands One among you whom you do not know. 27It is He who, coming after me, is preferred before me, whose sandal strap I am not worthy to loose."

28These things were done in Bethabaraa beyond the Jordan, where John was baptizing.

THE LAMB OF GOD

29The next day John saw Jesus coming toward him, and said, "Behold! The Lamb of God who takes away the sin of the world! 30This is He of whom I said, 'After me comes a Man who is preferred before me, for He was before me.' 31I did not know Him; but that He should be revealed to Israel, therefore I came baptizing with water."

32And John bore witness, saying, "I saw the Spirit descending from heaven like a dove, and He remained upon Him. 33I did not know Him, but He who sent me to baptize with water said to me, 'Upon whom you see the Spirit descending, and remaining on Him, this is He who baptizes with the Holy Spirit.' 34And I have seen and testified that this is the Son of God."

THE FIRST DISCIPLES

35Again, the next day, John stood with two of his disciples. 36And looking at Jesus as He walked, he said, "Behold the Lamb of God!"

37The two disciples heard him speak, and they followed Jesus. 38Then Jesus turned, and seeing them following, said to them, "What do you seek?"

They said to Him, "Rabbi" (which is to say, when translated, Teacher), "where are You staying?"

39He said to them, "Come and see." They came and saw where He was staying, and remained with Him that day (now it was about the tenth hour).

40One of the two who heard John *speak,* and followed Him, was Andrew, Simon Peter's brother. 41He first found his own brother Simon, and said to him, "We have found the Messiah" (which is translated, the Christ). 42And he brought him to Jesus.

Now when Jesus looked at him, He said, "You are Simon the son of Jonah.a You shall be called Cephas" (which is translated, A Stone).

PHILIP AND NATHANAEL

43The following day Jesus wanted to go to Galilee, and He found Philip and said to him, "Follow Me." 44Now Philip was from Bethsaida, the city of Andrew and Peter. 45Philip found Nathanael and said to him, "We have found Him of whom Moses in the law, and also the prophets, wrote—Jesus of Nazareth, the son of Joseph."

46And Nathanael said to him, "Can anything good come out of Nazareth?"

Philip said to him, "Come and see."

47Jesus saw Nathanael coming toward Him, and said of him, "Behold, an Israelite indeed, in whom is no deceit!"

48Nathanael said to Him, "How do You know me?"

Jesus answered and said to him, "Before Philip called you, when you were under the fig tree, I saw you."

49Nathanael answered and said to Him, "Rabbi, You are the Son of God! You are the King of Israel!"

50Jesus answered and said to him, "Because I said to you, 'I saw you under the fig tree,' do you believe? You will see greater things than these."

1:28 aNU-Text and M-Text read *Bethany.* **1:42** aNU-Text reads *John.*

INSIDE *the* INFLUENCERS

ANDREW: Keep First Things First

JOHN 1:35–41

In life, many people are defined by the last thing they did, but even more are known for the first thing they did. Leaders can spend a lifetime overcoming a bad beginning. Books are written of lives destroyed by doing the wrong "first things." Leaders not only start by doing the right "first things," but continue to do so.

Andrew was Simon Peter's brother. He was known as a follower of John the Baptist. When John the Baptist pointed out Jesus' true identity, Andrew immediately became a follower. A day spent with Jesus resulted in a life transformed with the knowledge that the Messiah had come (John 1:35–41). Andrew was a leader who got it right.

His first action as a new believer was to find his own brother, Simon Peter, and tell him, "We have found the Messiah" (John 1:41). When the problem of feeding 5,000 people came up, he was the first to bring a solution of faith: "There is a lad here who has five barley loaves and two small fish" (John 6:9).

When foreigners came who wanted to meet Jesus, Andrew set up the meeting (John 12:12). Leaders like Andrew focus on the introduction of Jesus to a lost world as a "first thing" in their lives.

---

⁵¹And He said to him, "Most assuredly, I say to you, hereafter[a] you shall see heaven open, and the angels of God ascending and descending upon the Son of Man."

WATER TURNED TO WINE

2 On the third day there was a wedding in Cana of Galilee, and the mother of Jesus was there. ²Now both Jesus and His disciples were invited to the wedding. ³And when they ran out of wine, the mother of Jesus said to Him, "They have no wine."

⁴Jesus said to her, "Woman, what does your concern have to do with Me? My hour has not yet come."

⁵His mother said to the servants, "Whatever He says to you, do *it*."

⁶Now there were set there six waterpots of stone, according to the manner of purification of the Jews, containing twenty or thirty gallons apiece. ⁷Jesus said to them, "Fill the waterpots with water." And they filled them up to the brim. ⁸And He said to them, "Draw *some* out now, and take *it* to the master of the feast." And they took *it*. ⁹When the master of the feast had tasted the water that was made wine, and did not know where it came from (but the servants who had drawn the water knew), the master of the feast called the bridegroom. ¹⁰And he said to him, "Every man at the beginning sets out the good wine, and when the *guests* have well drunk, then the inferior. You have kept the good wine until now!"

¹¹This beginning of signs Jesus did in Cana of Galilee, and manifested His glory; and His disciples believed in Him.

¹²After this He went down to Capernaum, He, His mother, His brothers, and His disciples; and they did not stay there many days.

JESUS CLEANSES THE TEMPLE

¹³Now the Passover of the Jews was at hand, and Jesus went up to Jerusalem. ¹⁴And He found in the temple those who sold oxen and sheep and doves, and the money changers doing business. ¹⁵When He had made a whip of cords, He drove them all out of the temple, with the sheep and the oxen, and poured out the changers'

1:51 ᵃNU-Text omits *hereafter.*

money and overturned the tables. [16]And He said to those who sold doves, "Take these things away! Do not make My Father's house a house of merchandise!" [17]Then His disciples remembered that it was written, *"Zeal for Your house has eaten[a] Me up."*[b]

[18]So the Jews answered and said to Him, "What sign do You show to us, since You do these things?"

[19]Jesus answered and said to them, "Destroy this temple, and in three days I will raise it up."

[20]Then the Jews said, "It has taken forty-six years to build this temple, and will You raise it up in three days?"

[21]But He was speaking of the temple of His body. [22]Therefore, when He had risen from the dead, His disciples remembered that He had said this to them;[a] and they believed the Scripture and the word which Jesus had said.

The Discerner of Hearts

[23]Now when He was in Jerusalem at the Passover, during the feast, many believed in His name when they saw the signs which He did. [24]But Jesus did not commit Himself to them, because He knew all *men,* [25]and had no need that anyone should testify of man, for He knew what was in man.

The New Birth

3 There was a man of the Pharisees named Nicodemus, a ruler of the Jews. [2]This man came to Jesus by night and said to Him, "Rabbi, we know that You are a teacher come from God; for no one can do these signs that You do unless God is with him."

[3]Jesus answered and said to him, "Most assuredly, I say to you, unless one is born again, he cannot see the kingdom of God."

[4]Nicodemus said to Him, "How can a man be born when he is old? Can he enter a second time into his mother's womb and be born?"

[5]Jesus answered, "Most assuredly, I say to you, unless one is born of water and the Spirit, he cannot enter the kingdom of God. [6]That which is born of the flesh is flesh, and that which is born of the Spirit is spirit. [7]Do not marvel that I said to you, 'You must be born again.' [8]The wind blows where it wishes, and you hear the sound of

it, but cannot tell where it comes from and where it goes. So is everyone who is born of the Spirit."

[9]Nicodemus answered and said to Him, "How can these things be?"

[10]Jesus answered and said to him, "Are you the teacher of Israel, and do not know these things? [11]Most assuredly, I say to you, We speak what We know and testify what We have seen, and you do not receive Our witness. [12]If I have told you earthly things and you do not believe, how will you believe if I tell you heavenly things? [13]No one has ascended to heaven but He who came down from heaven, *that is,* the Son of Man who is in heaven.[a] [14]And as Moses lifted up the serpent in the wilderness, even so must the Son of Man be lifted up, [15]that whoever believes in Him should not perish but[a] have eternal life. [16]For God so loved the world that He gave His only begotten Son, that whoever believes in Him should not perish but have everlasting life. [17]For God did not send His Son into the world to condemn the world, but that the world through Him might be saved.

[18]"He who believes in Him is not condemned; but he who does not believe is condemned already, because he has not believed in the name of the only begotten Son of God. [19]And this is the condemnation, that the light has come into the world, and men loved darkness rather than light, because their deeds were evil. [20]For everyone practicing evil hates the light and does not come to the light, lest his deeds should be exposed. [21]But he who does the truth comes to the light, that his deeds may be clearly seen, that they have been done in God."

John the Baptist Exalts Christ

[22]After these things Jesus and His disciples came into the land of Judea, and there He remained with them and baptized. [23]Now John also was baptizing in Aenon near Salim, because there was much water there. And they came and were baptized. [24]For John had not yet been thrown into prison.

[25]Then there arose a dispute between *some* of

2:17 [a]NU-Text and M-Text read *will eat.* [b]Psalm 69:9　**2:22** [a]NU-Text and M-Text omit *to them.* **3:13** [a]NU-Text omits *who is in heaven.* **3:15** [a]NU-Text omits *not perish but.*

LEADERSHIP ISSUES

GC2: Encountering Jesus: The Startling Love of Jesus

JOHN 3:16 *For God so loved the world that He gave His only begotten Son, that whoever believes in Him should not perish but have everlasting life.*

Possibly the most familiar of all Bible verses is about a God who loves. How startling it is when we begin to imagine the wonder of such love, the miracle of the gift named Jesus!

All across the pages of Scripture we're touched by the uniqueness of the God-Man, Jesus. Christ's words were startling and His miracles amazing, but everything He said and did was meant to call attention to how He loved. Take a moment now to reflect on how Jesus loved people and how He startled them with His love.

Jesus startled lepers by healing their bodies and bringing dignity to their lives, sometimes even touching them in order to heal them (Luke 5:12, 13; 17:11–19).

Christ startled a Samaritan woman when He broke all cultural conventions by asking her for a drink of water. In the midst of her shame and rejection, the Savior entrusted her with a conversation about eternal things (John 4:4–26).

Jesus startled the woman caught in adultery when He knelt down beside her, joining her at the point of her hurt and providing protection for her life. He dispersed her accusers with His words and then offered restoration to her as He lovingly said, "Woman, where are those accusers of yours? Has no one condemned you? . . . Neither do I condemn you; go and sin no more" (John 8:10, 11).

Pause now and ask Jesus to startle you with His love.

GC2
GREAT COMMANDMENT
COMMISSION

John's disciples and the Jews about purification. 26And they came to John and said to him, "Rabbi, He who was with you beyond the Jordan, to whom you have testified—behold, He is baptizing, and all are coming to Him!"

27John answered and said, "A man can receive nothing unless it has been given to him from heaven. 28You yourselves bear me witness, that I said, 'I am not the Christ,' but, 'I have been sent before Him.' 29He who has the bride is the bridegroom; but the friend of the bridegroom, who stands and hears him, rejoices greatly because of the bridegroom's voice. Therefore this joy of mine is fulfilled. 30He must increase, but I *must* decrease. 31He who comes from above is above all; he who is of the earth is earthly and speaks of the earth. He who comes from heaven is above all. 32And what He has seen and heard, that He testifies; and no one receives His testimony. 33He who has received His testimony has certified that God is true. 34For He whom God has sent speaks the words of God, for God does not give the Spirit by measure. 35The Father loves the Son, and has given all things into His hand. 36He who believes in the Son has everlasting life; and he who does not believe the Son shall not see life, but the wrath of God abides on him."

A SAMARITAN WOMAN MEETS HER MESSIAH

4 Therefore, when the Lord knew that the Pharisees had heard that Jesus made and baptized more disciples than John 2(though Jesus Himself did not baptize, but His disciples), 3He left Judea and departed again to Galilee. 4But He needed to go through Samaria.

5So He came to a city of Samaria which is called Sychar, near the plot of ground that Jacob gave to his son Joseph. 6Now Jacob's well was there. Jesus therefore, being wearied from *His* journey, sat thus by the well. It was about the sixth hour.

7A woman of Samaria came to draw water. Jesus said to her, "Give Me a drink." 8For His disciples had gone away into the city to buy food.

9Then the woman of Samaria said to Him, "How is it that You, being a Jew, ask a drink from me, a Samaritan woman?" For Jews have no dealings with Samaritans.

10Jesus answered and said to her, "If you knew the gift of God, and who it is who says to you, 'Give Me a drink,' you would have asked Him, and He would have given you living water."

11The woman said to Him, "Sir, You have nothing to draw with, and the well is deep. Where then do You get that living water? 12Are You greater than our father Jacob, who gave us the well, and drank from it himself, as well as his sons and his livestock?"

13Jesus answered and said to her, "Whoever drinks of this water will thirst again, 14but whoever drinks of the water that I shall give him will never thirst. But the water that I shall give him will become in him a fountain of water springing up into everlasting life."

15The woman said to Him, "Sir, give me this water, that I may not thirst, nor come here to draw."

16Jesus said to her, "Go, call your husband, and come here."

17The woman answered and said, "I have no husband."

Jesus said to her, "You have well said, 'I have no husband,' 18for you have had five husbands, and the one whom you now have is not your husband; in that you spoke truly."

19The woman said to Him, "Sir, I perceive that You are a prophet. 20Our fathers worshiped on this mountain, and you *Jews* say that in Jerusalem is the place where one ought to worship."

21Jesus said to her, "Woman, believe Me, the hour is coming when you will neither on this mountain, nor in Jerusalem, worship the Father. 22You worship what you do not know; we know what we worship, for salvation is of the Jews. 23But the hour is coming, and now is, when the true worshipers will worship the Father in spirit and truth; for the Father is seeking such to worship Him. 24God *is* Spirit, and those who worship Him must worship in spirit and truth."

25The woman said to Him, "I know that Messiah is coming" (who is called Christ). "When He comes, He will tell us all things."

26Jesus said to her, "I who speak to you am *He*."

The Whitened Harvest

²⁷And at this *point* His disciples came, and they marveled that He talked with a woman; yet no one said, "What do You seek?" or, "Why are You talking with her?"

²⁸The woman then left her waterpot, went her way into the city, and said to the men, ²⁹"Come, see a Man who told me all things that I ever did. Could this be the Christ?" ³⁰Then they went out of the city and came to Him.

³¹In the meantime His disciples urged Him, saying, "Rabbi, eat."

³²But He said to them, "I have food to eat of which you do not know."

³³Therefore the disciples said to one another, "Has anyone brought Him *anything* to eat?"

³⁴Jesus said to them, "My food is to do the will of Him who sent Me, and to finish His work. ³⁵Do you not say, 'There are still four months and *then* comes the harvest'? Behold, I say to you, lift up your eyes and look at the fields, for they are already white for harvest! ³⁶And he who reaps receives wages, and gathers fruit for eternal life, that both he who sows and he who reaps may rejoice together. ³⁷For in this the saying is true: 'One sows and another reaps.' ³⁸I sent you to reap that for which you have not labored; others have labored, and you have entered into their labors."

The Savior of the World

³⁹And many of the Samaritans of that city believed in Him because of the word of the woman who testified, "He told me all that I *ever* did." ⁴⁰So when the Samaritans had come to Him, they urged Him to stay with them; and He stayed there two days. ⁴¹And many more believed because of His own word.

⁴²Then they said to the woman, "Now we believe, not because of what you said, for we ourselves have heard *Him* and we know that this is indeed the Christ,ᵃ the Savior of the world."

Welcome at Galilee

⁴³Now after the two days He departed from there and went to Galilee. ⁴⁴For Jesus Himself testified that a prophet has no honor in his own country. ⁴⁵So when He came to Galilee, the Galileans received Him, having seen all the things

He did in Jerusalem at the feast; for they also had gone to the feast.

A Nobleman's Son Healed

⁴⁶So Jesus came again to Cana of Galilee where He had made the water wine. And there was a certain nobleman whose son was sick at Capernaum. ⁴⁷When he heard that Jesus had come out of Judea into Galilee, he went to Him and implored Him to come down and heal his son, for he was at the point of death. ⁴⁸Then Jesus said to him, "Unless you *people* see signs and wonders, you will by no means believe."

⁴⁹The nobleman said to Him, "Sir, come down before my child dies!"

⁵⁰Jesus said to him, "Go your way; your son lives." So the man believed the word that Jesus spoke to him, and he went his way. ⁵¹And as he was now going down, his servants met him and told *him,* saying, "Your son lives!"

⁵²Then he inquired of them the hour when he got better. And they said to him, "Yesterday at the seventh hour the fever left him." ⁵³So the father knew that *it was* at the same hour in which Jesus said to him, "Your son lives." And he himself believed, and his whole household.

⁵⁴This again *is* the second sign Jesus did when He had come out of Judea into Galilee.

A Man Healed at the Pool of Bethesda

5 After this there was a feast of the Jews, and Jesus went up to Jerusalem. ²Now there is in Jerusalem by the Sheep *Gate* a pool, which is called in Hebrew, Bethesda,ᵃ having five porches. ³In these lay a great multitude of sick people, blind, lame, paralyzed, waiting for the moving of the water. ⁴For an angel went down at a certain time into the pool and stirred up the water; then whoever stepped in first, after the stirring of the water, was made well of whatever disease he had.ᵃ ⁵Now a certain man was there who had an infirmity thirty-eight years. ⁶When Jesus saw him lying there, and knew that he already had been *in that condition* a long time, He said to him, "Do you want to be made well?"

⁷The sick man answered Him, "Sir, I have no

4:42 ᵃNU-Text omits *the Christ.*   5:2 ᵃNU-Text reads *Bethzatha.*
5:4 ᵃNU-Text omits *waiting for the moving of the water* at the end of verse 3, and all of verse 4.

LEADERSHIP ISSUES

Come and See What Jesus Did

JOHN 4:29

No one can tell the story of what Christ has done in your life quite like you. The power of a personal testimony is unmatched in evangelism. People may scoff at Scripture and debate doctrine, but no one can deny the life-changing power of Jesus in a person's life.

The Samaritan woman was dramatically changed, and her first thought was to tell everyone to *come see Jesus!* We are to be just that to our world today. Jesus does not need a lawyer to defend Him in today's society, just faithful witnesses of His life-changing power in our personal lives.

A testimony has three very distinct aspects: your life before Christ, how you came to meet Christ, and what Christ is now doing in your life. God can use each of these aspects to draw someone to Himself.

When sharing your personal testimony, study these key ideas to keep you on track: Keep unfamiliar language to a minimum, most people will not understand many terms used in church today. When you use words like "sin," "lost," or other church phrases, take time to define them to your listener; do not assume they understand these key phrases.

Keep your conversation focused on Jesus. Although it is your life story, it was what Christ did that changed your life.

Above all else, practice your testimony to make it fluent and practical. A testimony is designed to be an opening conversation to share how Christ can change the listener's life.

A testimony should always close with an opportunity for response. This can be done with a question like, "Has anything like this ever happened to you?" If the answer is yes, ask the person to elaborate for your encouragement. If the answer is no, there are several great ways to introduce this person to Christ. For more help on being an effective personal evangelist, go to www.sharingthefaith.com.

LEADERSHIP ISSUES

GC2: Humble Dependence

JOHN 5:19

Imagine that you are one of the twelve disciples. You have left everything to follow Jesus, entrusting your life and future to this carpenter from Nazareth. Your hopes are riding on an unclear vision of His plans for a "kingdom." It is becoming increasingly clear that the Jewish leaders are not big fans of His—in fact, they are trying to kill Him, and maybe you too!

Now imagine your reaction as you hear Jesus say: "the Son can do nothing of Himself" (John 5:19). Are you surprised by this declaration of humble dependence? Surely this One whom you are following has some kind of plan, right? Doesn't He enjoy some sense of security about the future? Are you a bit shocked when you hear Him say, in essence, "I just wait around for the Father to show Me what to do"?

Jesus' words, startling though they may be, provide the blueprint for our lives. We are called to express humility through complete dependence upon God. Faithful, maturing disciples who walk intimately with the Spirit are able to declare, as Christ did, "I can of Myself do nothing" (John 5:30).

GC2
GREAT COMMANDMENT
COMMISSION

man to put me into the pool when the water is stirred up; but while I am coming, another steps down before me."

[8]Jesus said to him, "Rise, take up your bed and walk." [9]And immediately the man was made well, took up his bed, and walked.

And that day was the Sabbath. [10]The Jews therefore said to him who was cured, "It is the Sabbath; it is not lawful for you to carry your bed."

[11]He answered them, "He who made me well said to me, 'Take up your bed and walk.' "

[12]Then they asked him, "Who is the Man who said to you, 'Take up your bed and walk'?" [13]But the one who was healed did not know who it was, for Jesus had withdrawn, a multitude being in *that* place. [14]Afterward Jesus found him in the temple, and said to him, "See, you have been made well. Sin no more, lest a worse thing come upon you."

[15]The man departed and told the Jews that it was Jesus who had made him well.

Honor the Father and the Son

[16]For this reason the Jews persecuted Jesus, and sought to kill Him,[a] because He had done these things on the Sabbath. [17]But Jesus answered them, "My Father has been working until now, and I have been working."

[18]Therefore the Jews sought all the more to kill Him, because He not only broke the Sabbath, but also said that God was His Father, making Himself equal with God. [19]Then Jesus answered and said to them, "Most assuredly, I say to you, the Son can do nothing of Himself, but what He sees the Father do; for whatever He does, the Son also does in like manner. [20]For the Father loves the Son, and shows Him all things that He Himself does; and He will show Him greater works than these, that you may marvel. [21]For as the Father raises the dead and gives life to *them,* even so the Son gives life to whom He will. [22]For the Father judges no one, but has committed all judgment to the Son, [23]that all should honor the Son just as they honor the Father. He who does not honor the Son does not honor the Father who sent Him.

Life and Judgment Are Through the Son

[24]"Most assuredly, I say to you, he who hears My word and believes in Him who sent Me has

everlasting life, and shall not come into judgment, but has passed from death into life. [25]Most assuredly, I say to you, the hour is coming, and now is, when the dead will hear the voice of the Son of God; and those who hear will live. [26]For as the Father has life in Himself, so He has granted the Son to have life in Himself, [27]and has given Him authority to execute judgment also, because He is the Son of Man. [28]Do not marvel at this; for the hour is coming in which all who are in the graves will hear His voice [29]and come forth—those who have done good, to the resurrection of life, and those who have done evil, to the resurrection of condemnation. [30]I can of Myself do nothing. As I hear, I judge; and My judgment is righteous, because I do not seek My own will but the will of the Father who sent Me.

The Fourfold Witness

[31]"If I bear witness of Myself, My witness is not true. [32]There is another who bears witness of Me, and I know that the witness which He witnesses of Me is true. [33]You have sent to John, and he has borne witness to the truth. [34]Yet I do not receive testimony from man, but I say these things that you may be saved. [35]He was the burning and shining lamp, and you were willing for a time to rejoice in his light. [36]But I have a greater witness than John's; for the works which the Father has given Me to finish—the very works that I do—bear witness of Me, that the Father has sent Me. [37]And the Father Himself, who sent Me, has testified of Me. You have neither heard His voice at any time, nor seen His form. [38]But you do not have His word abiding in you, because whom He sent, Him you do not believe. [39]You search the Scriptures, for in them you think you have eternal life; and these are they which testify of Me. [40]But you are not willing to come to Me that you may have life.

[41]"I do not receive honor from men. [42]But I know you, that you do not have the love of God in you. [43]I have come in My Father's name, and you do not receive Me; if another comes in his own name, him you will receive. [44]How can you believe, who receive honor from one another, and do not seek the honor that *comes* from the only God? [45]Do not think that I shall accuse you to

5:16 [a]NU-Text omits *and sought to kill Him.*

LEADERSHIP ISSUES

GC2: Sharing Christ: Others-Centered Love

JOHN 5:20 *The Father loves the Son, and shows Him all things that He Himself does.*

God's love is characteristically focused on others. Even the Father "focuses" on loving the Son, and the Son "focuses" on loving the Father. "I have kept My Father's commandments and abide in His love" (John 15:10). To have received this love at your new birth is to have partaken of the divine nature through the renewing work of the Holy Spirit.

This divine "others-centered" nature is birthed in us as we yield to the Holy Spirit in order that we might love as Jesus loved. Consider some of the ways in which Jesus loved those around Him:

- He loved Zaccheaus by accepting him, looking beyond his faults to his needs (Luke 19:1–10).
- He loved the little children with affection, touch, and affirming words (Matt. 19:13–15).
- He loved Mary in her pain with tear-filled eyes of comfort (John 11:35).
- He loved Peter in his failure with promises of prayer and restoration (Luke 22:31, 32).

Just before He went to the cross, Christ gave a new command: that we love one another as He loves us (John 13:34, 35).

Prayerfully reflect on the people in your life as you ask for the Father's promise concerning others-centered love. Pause to consider which of them might benefit from God's acceptance or affection, care or comfort, prayer or promised restoration.

GREAT COMMANDMENT
COMMISSION

the Father; there is *one* who accuses you—Moses, in whom you trust. [46]For if you believed Moses, you would believe Me; for he wrote about Me. [47]But if you do not believe his writings, how will you believe My words?"

FEEDING THE FIVE THOUSAND

6 After these things Jesus went over the Sea of Galilee, which is *the Sea* of Tiberias. [2]Then a great multitude followed Him, because they saw His signs which He performed on those who were diseased. [3]And Jesus went up on the mountain, and there He sat with His disciples.

[4]Now the Passover, a feast of the Jews, was near. [5]Then Jesus lifted up *His* eyes, and seeing a great multitude coming toward Him, He said to Philip, "Where shall we buy bread, that these may eat?" [6]But this He said to test him, for He Himself knew what He would do.

[7]Philip answered Him, "Two hundred denarii worth of bread is not sufficient for them, that every one of them may have a little."

[8]One of His disciples, Andrew, Simon Peter's brother, said to Him, [9]"There is a lad here who has five barley loaves and two small fish, but what are they among so many?"

[10]Then Jesus said, "Make the people sit down." Now there was much grass in the place. So the men sat down, in number about five thousand. [11]And Jesus took the loaves, and when He had given thanks He distributed *them* to the disciples, and the disciples[a] to those sitting down; and likewise of the fish, as much as they wanted. [12]So when they were filled, He said to His disciples, "Gather up the fragments that remain, so that nothing is lost." [13]Therefore they gathered *them* up, and filled twelve baskets with the fragments of the five barley loaves which were left over by those who had eaten. [14]Then those men, when they had seen the sign that Jesus did, said, "This is truly the Prophet who is to come into the world."

JESUS WALKS ON THE SEA

[15]Therefore when Jesus perceived that they were about to come and take Him by force to make Him king, He departed again to the mountain by Himself alone.

[16]Now when evening came, His disciples

went down to the sea, [17]got into the boat, and went over the sea toward Capernaum. And it was already dark, and Jesus had not come to them. [18]Then the sea arose because a great wind was blowing. [19]So when they had rowed about three or four miles,[a] they saw Jesus walking on the sea and drawing near the boat; and they were afraid. [20]But He said to them, "It is I; do not be afraid." [21]Then they willingly received Him into the boat, and immediately the boat was at the land where they were going.

THE BREAD FROM HEAVEN

[22]On the following day, when the people who were standing on the other side of the sea saw that there was no other boat there, except that one which His disciples had entered,[a] and that Jesus had not entered the boat with His disciples, but His disciples had gone away alone— [23]however, other boats came from Tiberias, near the place where they ate bread after the Lord had given thanks— [24]when the people therefore saw that Jesus was not there, nor His disciples, they also got into boats and came to Capernaum, seeking Jesus. [25]And when they found Him on the other side of the sea, they said to Him, "Rabbi, when did You come here?"

[26]Jesus answered them and said, "Most assuredly, I say to you, you seek Me, not because you saw the signs, but because you ate of the loaves and were filled. [27]Do not labor for the food which perishes, but for the food which endures to everlasting life, which the Son of Man will give you, because God the Father has set His seal on Him."

[28]Then they said to Him, "What shall we do, that we may work the works of God?"

[29]Jesus answered and said to them, "This is the work of God, that you believe in Him whom He sent."

[30]Therefore they said to Him, "What sign will You perform then, that we may see it and believe You? What work will You do? [31]Our fathers ate the manna in the desert; as it is written, *'He gave them bread from heaven to eat.'"*[a]

6:11 [a]NU-Text omits *to the disciples, and the disciples.* **6:19** [a]Literally *twenty-five or thirty stadia.* **6:22** [a]NU-Text omits *that* and which *His disciples had entered.* **6:31** [a]Exodus 16:4; Nehemiah 9:15; Psalm 78:24

LEADERSHIP ISSUES

The Heavy Lifting of Leadership

JOHN 6

When Jesus began His ministry, the crowds around Him were huge.
Thousands followed Him, looking for the Messiah, for healing, and for a
place to belong. John 6 reveals the kind of messiah that the people
wanted. They wanted a superhero kind of guy who could do wonders and
fill their bellies at the same time. In fact, the chapter begins by saying,
"Then a great multitude followed Him, because they saw His signs" (v. 2).
The story continues with more crowds beginning to follow Jesus—a generation seeking to fill their bellies and be entertained. Jesus saw through
their motives: "You seek Me, not because you saw the signs, but because
you ate of the loaves and were filled" (v. 26). They were looking for the
sensation of entertainment, and Jesus decided to confront their motives.

The people wanted to speak of a popular and powerful messiah, but He
spoke of Himself as the Messiah who came to save the people from their
sin. He took it a step further when He taught: "He who eats My flesh and
drinks My blood abides in Me, and I in him" (v. 56). The people didn't
like this kind of talk. Feeding the crowds was exciting, and watching the
lame being healed was mind blowing, but this talk of eating flesh and
drinking blood—what was that? Even His disciples said, "This is a hard
saying" (v. 60).

What happens next is one of the most tragic verses in the entire Bible:
"From that time many of His disciples went back and walked with Him
no more" (v. 66). Not only did the *crowd* give up on His "hard saying,"
but some of Jesus' *disciples* left as well.

Leaders are devoted followers who hang in there for the "heavy lifting."
They are not quitters who look for an easy message; they are careful to
examine their motives often. Many are willing to call themselves Christians when the talk is of love and the crowd is social, but there are fewer
who stay devoted when the "hard sayings"—such as criticism and personal sacrifice—come along.

THROUGH THE GRID

Where Have All the Dreamers Gone? Observations from a Biblical Worldview: The Witness of Personal Lives (John 5:32, 33)

Of course, one can study apologetics until one knows all the theories and proofs for the existence of God backward and forward, but the best proof of the validity of Christianity lies in the witness of one's own personal life. Whether one likes it or not, one is constantly being judged by outsiders and non-Christians, who are all yearning to see what's so different and special about the Christian faith. We provide a powerful witness to others when we obediently live our lives under the leadership of God and find innovative ways to love our neighbors and care for nature.

³²Then Jesus said to them, "Most assuredly, I say to you, Moses did not give you the bread from heaven, but My Father gives you the true bread from heaven. ³³For the bread of God is He who comes down from heaven and gives life to the world."

³⁴Then they said to Him, "Lord, give us this bread always."

³⁵And Jesus said to them, "I am the bread of life. He who comes to Me shall never hunger, and he who believes in Me shall never thirst. ³⁶But I said to you that you have seen Me and yet do not believe. ³⁷All that the Father gives Me will come to Me, and the one who comes to Me I will by no means cast out. ³⁸For I have come down from heaven, not to do My own will, but the will of Him who sent Me. ³⁹This is the will of the Father who sent Me, that of all He has given Me I should lose nothing, but should raise it up at the last day. ⁴⁰And this is the will of Him who sent Me, that everyone who sees the Son and believes in Him may have everlasting life; and I will raise him up at the last day."

REJECTED BY HIS OWN

⁴¹The Jews then complained about Him, because He said, "I am the bread which came down from heaven." ⁴²And they said, "Is not this Jesus, the son of Joseph, whose father and mother we know? How is it then that He says, 'I have come down from heaven'?"

⁴³Jesus therefore answered and said to them, "Do not murmur among yourselves. ⁴⁴No one can come to Me unless the Father who sent Me draws him; and I will raise him up at the last day. ⁴⁵It is written in the prophets, '*And they shall all be taught by God.*'ᵃ Therefore everyone who has heard and learnedᵇ from the Father comes to Me. ⁴⁶Not that anyone has seen the Father, except He who is from God; He has seen the Father. ⁴⁷Most assuredly, I say to you, he who believes in Meᵃ has everlasting life. ⁴⁸I am the bread of life. ⁴⁹Your fathers ate the manna in the wilderness, and are dead. ⁵⁰This is the bread which comes down from heaven, that one may eat of it and not die. ⁵¹I am the living bread which came down from heaven. If anyone eats of this bread, he will live forever; and the bread that I shall give is My flesh, which I shall give for the life of the world."

⁵²The Jews therefore quarreled among themselves, saying, "How can this Man give us *His* flesh to eat?"

⁵³Then Jesus said to them, "Most assuredly, I say to you, unless you eat the flesh of the Son of Man and drink His blood, you have no life in you. ⁵⁴Whoever eats My flesh and drinks My blood has eternal life, and I will raise him up at the last day. ⁵⁵For My flesh is food indeed,ᵃ and My blood is drink indeed. ⁵⁶He who eats My flesh and drinks My blood abides in Me, and I in him. ⁵⁷As the living Father sent Me, and I live because of the Father, so he who feeds on Me will live because of Me. ⁵⁸This is the bread which came down from heaven—not as your fathers ate

6:45 ᵃIsaiah 54:13 ᵇM-Text reads *hears and has learned.* **6:47** ᵃNU-Text omits *in Me.* **6:55** ᵃNU-Text reads *true food* and *true drink.*

THROUGH THE GRID

Thinking Christianly:
The Self-Claims of Jesus (John 6:35)

In Scripture, Jesus Himself makes several claims about who He is. He claimed to be the God of Exodus 3:14—the I AM. He again claimed to be God in John 14:9. And He claims that He and God the Father "are one" (John 10:30). In John's Gospel, Jesus makes seven statements that begin with "I am." He states that He is the "Bread of Life" (6:35, 41, 48, 51); the "Light of the World" (8:12); the "Door of the Sheep" (10:7, 9); the "Good Shepherd" (10:11, 14); the "Resurrection and the Life" (11:25); the "Way, the Truth, and the Life" (14:6); and the "True Vine" (15:1, 5).

---

the manna, and are dead. He who eats this bread will live forever."

59These things He said in the synagogue as He taught in Capernaum.

MANY DISCIPLES TURN AWAY

60Therefore many of His disciples, when they heard *this,* said, "This is a hard saying; who can understand it?"

61When Jesus knew in Himself that His disciples complained about this, He said to them, "Does this offend you? 62*What* then if you should see the Son of Man ascend where He was before? 63It is the Spirit who gives life; the flesh profits nothing. The words that I speak to you are spirit, and *they* are life. 64But there are some of you who do not believe." For Jesus knew from the beginning who they were who did not believe, and who would betray Him. 65And He said, "Therefore I have said to you that no one can come to Me unless it has been granted to him by My Father."

66From that *time* many of His disciples went back and walked with Him no more. 67Then Jesus said to the twelve, "Do you also want to go away?"

68But Simon Peter answered Him, "Lord, to whom shall we go? You have the words of eternal life. 69Also we have come to believe and know that You are the Christ, the Son of the living God."[a]

70Jesus answered them, "Did I not choose you, the twelve, and one of you is a devil?" 71He spoke of Judas Iscariot, *the son* of Simon, for it was he who would betray Him, being one of the twelve.

JESUS' BROTHERS DISBELIEVE

7 After these things Jesus walked in Galilee; for He did not want to walk in Judea, because the Jews[a] sought to kill Him. 2Now the Jews' Feast of Tabernacles was at hand. 3His brothers therefore said to Him, "Depart from here and go into Judea, that Your disciples also may see the works that You are doing. 4For no one does anything in secret while he himself seeks to be known openly. If You do these things, show Yourself to the world." 5For even His brothers did not believe in Him.

6Then Jesus said to them, "My time has not yet come, but your time is always ready. 7The world cannot hate you, but it hates Me because I testify of it that its works are evil. 8You go up to this feast. I am not yet[a] going up to this feast, for My time has not yet fully come." 9When He had said these things to them, He remained in Galilee.

THE HEAVENLY SCHOLAR

10But when His brothers had gone up, then He also went up to the feast, not openly, but as it were in secret. 11Then the Jews sought Him at the feast, and said, "Where is He?" 12And there was much complaining among the people concerning Him. Some said, "He is good"; others said, "No, on the contrary, He deceives the people." 13However, no one spoke openly of Him for fear of the Jews.

14Now about the middle of the feast Jesus went up into the temple and taught. 15And the Jews marveled, saying, "How does this Man know letters, having never studied?"

6:69 aNU-Text reads *You are the Holy One of God.*   **7:1** aThat is, the ruling authorities   **7:8** aNU-Text omits *yet.*

[16]Jesus[a] answered them and said, "My doctrine is not Mine, but His who sent Me. [17]If anyone wills to do His will, he shall know concerning the doctrine, whether it is from God or *whether* I speak on My own *authority*. [18]He who speaks from himself seeks his own glory; but He who seeks the glory of the One who sent Him is true, and no unrighteousness is in Him. [19]Did not Moses give you the law, yet none of you keeps the law? Why do you seek to kill Me?"

[20]The people answered and said, "You have a demon. Who is seeking to kill You?"

[21]Jesus answered and said to them, "I did one work, and you all marvel. [22]Moses therefore gave you circumcision (not that it is from Moses, but from the fathers), and you circumcise a man on the Sabbath. [23]If a man receives circumcision on the Sabbath, so that the law of Moses should not be broken, are you angry with Me because I made a man completely well on the Sabbath? [24]Do not judge according to appearance, but judge with righteous judgment."

Could This Be the Christ?

[25]Now some of them from Jerusalem said, "Is this not He whom they seek to kill? [26]But look! He speaks boldly, and they say nothing to Him. Do the rulers know indeed that this is truly[a] the Christ? [27]However, we know where this Man is from; but when the Christ comes, no one knows where He is from."

[28]Then Jesus cried out, as He taught in the temple, saying, "You both know Me, and you know where I am from; and I have not come of Myself, but He who sent Me is true, whom you do not know. [29]But[a] I know Him, for I am from Him, and He sent Me."

[30]Therefore they sought to take Him; but no one laid a hand on Him, because His hour had not yet come. [31]And many of the people believed in Him, and said, "When the Christ comes, will He do more signs than these which this *Man* has done?"

Jesus and the Religious Leaders

[32]The Pharisees heard the crowd murmuring these things concerning Him, and the Pharisees and the chief priests sent officers to take Him. [33]Then Jesus said to them,[a] "I shall be with you a little while longer, and *then* I go to Him who sent Me. [34]You will seek Me and not find *Me,* and where I am you cannot come."

[35]Then the Jews said among themselves, "Where does He intend to go that we shall not find Him? Does He intend to go to the Dispersion among the Greeks and teach the Greeks? [36]What is this thing that He said, 'You will seek Me and not find Me, and where I am you cannot come'?"

The Promise of the Holy Spirit

[37]On the last day, that great *day* of the feast, Jesus stood and cried out, saying, "If anyone thirsts, let him come to Me and drink. [38]He who believes in Me, as the Scripture has said, out of his heart will flow rivers of living water." [39]But this He spoke concerning the Spirit, whom those believing[a] in Him would receive; for the Holy[b] Spirit was not yet *given,* because Jesus was not yet glorified.

Who Is He?

[40]Therefore many[a] from the crowd, when they heard this saying, said, "Truly this is the Prophet." [41]Others said, "This is the Christ."

But some said, "Will the Christ come out of Galilee? [42]Has not the Scripture said that the Christ comes from the seed of David and from the town of Bethlehem, where David was?" [43]So there was a division among the people because of Him. [44]Now some of them wanted to take Him, but no one laid hands on Him.

Rejected by the Authorities

[45]Then the officers came to the chief priests and Pharisees, who said to them, "Why have you not brought Him?"

[46]The officers answered, "No man ever spoke like this Man!"

[47]Then the Pharisees answered them, "Are you also deceived? [48]Have any of the rulers or the Pharisees believed in Him? [49]But this crowd that does not know the law is accursed."

[50]Nicodemus (he who came to Jesus by night,[a] being one of them) said to them, [51]"Does

---

7:16 [a]NU-Text and M-Text read *So Jesus.* **7:26** [a]NU-Text omits *truly.* **7:29** [a]NU-Text and M-Text omit *But.* **7:33** [a]NU-Text and M-Text omit *to them.* **7:39** [a]NU-Text reads *who believed.* [b]NU-Text omits Holy. **7:40** [a]NU-Text reads *some.* **7:50** [a]NU-Text reads *before.*

our law judge a man before it hears him and knows what he is doing?"

⁵²They answered and said to him, "Are you also from Galilee? Search and look, for no prophet has arisenᵃ out of Galilee."

An Adulteress Faces the Light of the World

⁵³And everyone went to his *own* house.ᵃ

8 But Jesus went to the Mount of Olives. ²Now earlyᵃ in the morning He came again into the temple, and all the people came to Him; and He sat down and taught them. ³Then the scribes and Pharisees brought to Him a woman caught in adultery. And when they had set her in the midst, ⁴they said to Him, "Teacher, this woman was caughtᵃ in adultery, in the very act. ⁵Now Moses, in the law, commandedᵃ us that such should be stoned.ᵇ But what do You say?"ᶜ ⁶This they said, testing Him, that they might have *something* of which to accuse Him. But Jesus stooped down and wrote on the ground with *His* finger, as though He did not hear.ᵃ

⁷So when they continued asking Him, He raised Himself upᵃ and said to them, "He who is without sin among you, let him throw a stone at her first." ⁸And again He stooped down and wrote on the ground. ⁹Then those who heard *it,* being convicted by *their* conscience,ᵃ went out one by one, beginning with the oldest *even* to the last. And Jesus was left alone, and the woman standing in the midst. ¹⁰When Jesus had raised Himself up and saw no one but the woman, He said to her,ᵃ "Woman, where are those accusers of yours?ᵇ Has no one condemned you?"

¹¹She said, "No one, Lord."

And Jesus said to her, "Neither do I condemn you; go andᵃ sin no more."

¹²Then Jesus spoke to them again, saying, "I am the light of the world. He who follows Me shall not walk in darkness, but have the light of life."

Jesus Defends His Self-Witness

¹³The Pharisees therefore said to Him, "You bear witness of Yourself; Your witness is not true."

¹⁴Jesus answered and said to them, "Even if I bear witness of Myself, My witness is true, for I know where I came from and where I am going; but you do not know where I come from and

where I am going. ¹⁵You judge according to the flesh; I judge no one. ¹⁶And yet if I do judge, My judgment is true; for I am not alone, but I *am* with the Father who sent Me. ¹⁷It is also written in your law that the testimony of two men is true. ¹⁸I am One who bears witness of Myself, and the Father who sent Me bears witness of Me."

¹⁹Then they said to Him, "Where is Your Father?"

Jesus answered, "You know neither Me nor My Father. If you had known Me, you would have known My Father also."

²⁰These words Jesus spoke in the treasury, as He taught in the temple; and no one laid hands on Him, for His hour had not yet come.

Jesus Predicts His Departure

²¹Then Jesus said to them again, "I am going away, and you will seek Me, and will die in your sin. Where I go you cannot come."

²²So the Jews said, "Will He kill Himself, because He says, 'Where I go you cannot come'?"

²³And He said to them, "You are from beneath; I am from above. You are of this world; I am not of this world. ²⁴Therefore I said to you that you will die in your sins; for if you do not believe that I am *He,* you will die in your sins."

²⁵Then they said to Him, "Who are You?"

And Jesus said to them, "Just what I have been saying to you from the beginning. ²⁶I have many things to say and to judge concerning you, but He who sent Me is true; and I speak to the world those things which I heard from Him."

²⁷They did not understand that He spoke to them of the Father.

²⁸Then Jesus said to them, "When you lift up the Son of Man, then you will know that I am *He,* and *that* I do nothing of Myself; but as My Father taught Me, I speak these things. ²⁹And He who sent Me is with Me. The Father has not left

---

7:52 ᵃNU-Text reads *is to rise.*   **7:53** ᵃThe words *And everyone* through *sin no more* (8:11) are bracketed by NU-Text as not original. They are present in over 900 manuscripts.   **8:2** ᵃM-Text reads *very early.*   **8:4** ᵃM-Text reads *we found this woman.*   **8:5** ᵃM-Text reads *in our law Moses commanded.* ᵇNU-Text and M-Text read *to stone such.* ᶜM-Text adds *about her.*   **8:6** ᵃNU-Text and M-Text omit *as though He did not hear.*   **8:7** ᵃM-Text reads *He looked up.* **8:9** ᵃNU-Text and M-Text omit *being convicted by their conscience.* **8:10** ᵃNU-Text omits *and saw no one but the woman;* M-Text reads *He saw her and said.* ᵇNU-Text and M-Text omit *of yours.* **8:11** ᵃNU-Text and M-Text add *from now on.*

LEADERSHIP ISSUES

GC2: The Light of God's Son

JOHN 8:12

Jesus boldly proclaimed that He is "the light of the world." As we encounter Him and experience His love, we experience one source of God's transforming light (Ps. 36:9; John 12:35).

God the Father is longing for us to pursue Jesus, because He delights in revealing more of Himself to us. Whether through worship, prayer, meditation, and study, or through the mundane happenings of everyday life, Jesus is wanting to be known by you!

Throughout Scripture, we find Christ revealing Himself to others, sometimes when they least expect it. The disciples on the Emmaus Road, for example, thought that they were having a normal conversation with a fellow traveler (albeit a fellow traveler who seemed to be extraordinarily knowledgeable about Old Testament prophecy). However, throughout Jesus' discourse about the scriptural significance of the Messiah, He was gradually revealing Himself—His wisdom, His nature, His loving concern, and finally, His identity (Luke 24:13–32).

- I have recently encountered God's Son, Jesus, by _____

_____

_____

(For example: *I have recently encountered God's Son, Jesus, by picturing Him praying for me, especially during a time when I was feeling very lonely.*)

GC2
GREAT COMMANDMENT
COMMISSION

THROUGH THE GRID

Discover God:
God's Truth Sets Us Free

JOHN 8:31, 32   *If you abide in My word, you are My disciples indeed. And you shall know the truth, and the truth shall make you free.*

God's truth lasts forever, and the power of God's truth is liberating, as it has the ability to set us free from the bonds of sin and death. When we learn to trust God's Word completely, we begin to rely on God for direction and guidance, and we avoid the pitfalls of sin. The world exists in opposition to God's truth as a means of enslavement; but God's truth sets us free from the world, and we are also liberated from the sin and guilt that once bound us. Through God's truth, we can be set free from self-centeredness, from bondage to fear, and from a life of mediocrity and insignificance. God's truth frees us to live a life of holiness in communion with God.

Me alone, for I always do those things that please Him." ³⁰As He spoke these words, many believed in Him.

The Truth Shall Make You Free

³¹Then Jesus said to those Jews who believed Him, "If you abide in My word, you are My disciples indeed. ³²And you shall know the truth, and the truth shall make you free."

³³They answered Him, "We are Abraham's descendants, and have never been in bondage to anyone. How *can* You say, 'You will be made free'?"

³⁴Jesus answered them, "Most assuredly, I say to you, whoever commits sin is a slave of sin. ³⁵And a slave does not abide in the house forever, *but* a son abides forever. ³⁶Therefore if the Son makes you free, you shall be free indeed.

Abraham's Seed and Satan's

³⁷"I know that you are Abraham's descendants, but you seek to kill Me, because My word has no place in you. ³⁸I speak what I have seen with My Father, and you do what you have seen withᵃ your father."

³⁹They answered and said to Him, "Abraham is our father."

Jesus said to them, "If you were Abraham's children, you would do the works of Abraham. ⁴⁰But now you seek to kill Me, a Man who has told you the truth which I heard from God. Abra-

ham did not do this. ⁴¹You do the deeds of your father."

Then they said to Him, "We were not born of fornication; we have one Father—God."

⁴²Jesus said to them, "If God were your Father, you would love Me, for I proceeded forth and came from God; nor have I come of Myself, but He sent Me. ⁴³Why do you not understand My speech? Because you are not able to listen to My word. ⁴⁴You are of *your* father the devil, and the desires of your father you want to do. He was a murderer from the beginning, and does not stand in the truth, because there is no truth in him. When he speaks a lie, he speaks from his own *resources,* for he is a liar and the father of it. ⁴⁵But because I tell the truth, you do not believe Me. ⁴⁶Which of you convicts Me of sin? And if I tell the truth, why do you not believe Me? ⁴⁷He who is of God hears God's words; therefore you do not hear, because you are not of God."

Before Abraham Was, I AM

⁴⁸Then the Jews answered and said to Him, "Do we not say rightly that You are a Samaritan and have a demon?"

⁴⁹Jesus answered, "I do not have a demon; but I honor My Father, and you dishonor Me. ⁵⁰And I do not seek My *own* glory; there is One who seeks and judges. ⁵¹Most assuredly, I say to you, if anyone keeps My word he shall never see death."

8:38 ᵃNU-Text reads *heard from.*

LEADERSHIP ISSUES

GC2: Convictions: Unique Truth

JOHN 8:32 *And you shall know the truth, and the truth shall make you free.*

Truth cannot be subjectively created; truth is and comes from the objective, absolute Person of Christ Himself. As John wrote: "For the law was given through Moses, but grace and truth came through Jesus Christ" (John 1:17).

Truth cannot be relative and change from person to person or from community to community, because Jesus is the incarnation of God, "with whom there is no variation or shadow of turning" (James 1:17). As the Scripture says: "Jesus Christ is the same yesterday, today, and forever" (Heb. 13:8).

All truth cannot be equal because Jesus didn't claim to be "a" truth, one that is equal to all others. His claim was exclusive; He claimed to be the one and only truth, the only way to God. "I am the way, the truth, and the life," He said. "No one comes to the Father except through Me" (John 14:6). Those are not the words of someone who is "one among many," someone who is "equal" to all others; those are the words of One who has no equal.

ISAIAH 45:5, 6 *I am the LORD, and there is no other; there is no God besides Me. I will gird you, though you have not known Me, that they may know from the rising of the sun to its setting that there is none besides Me. I am the LORD, and there is no other.*

Living out our conviction to, at all cost, be pleasing to Jesus means we live a unique and Spirit-led life even as Christ is unique.

GC2

GREAT COMMANDMENT
COMMISSION

⁵²Then the Jews said to Him, "Now we know that You have a demon! Abraham is dead, and the prophets; and You say, 'If anyone keeps My word he shall never taste death.' ⁵³Are You greater than our father Abraham, who is dead? And the prophets are dead. Who do You make Yourself out to be?"

⁵⁴Jesus answered, "If I honor Myself, My honor is nothing. It is My Father who honors Me, of whom you say that He is yourᵃ God. ⁵⁵Yet you have not known Him, but I know Him. And if I say, 'I do not know Him,' I shall be a liar like you; but I do know Him and keep His word. ⁵⁶Your father Abraham rejoiced to see My day, and he saw *it* and was glad."

⁵⁷Then the Jews said to Him, "You are not yet fifty years old, and have You seen Abraham?"

⁵⁸Jesus said to them, "Most assuredly, I say to you, before Abraham was, I AM."

⁵⁹Then they took up stones to throw at Him; but Jesus hid Himself and went out of the temple,ᵃ going through the midst of them, and so passed by.

A Man Born Blind Receives Sight

9 Now as *Jesus* passed by, He saw a man who was blind from birth. ²And His disciples asked Him, saying, "Rabbi, who sinned, this man or his parents, that he was born blind?"

³Jesus answered, "Neither this man nor his parents sinned, but that the works of God should be revealed in him. ⁴Iᵃ must work the works of Him who sent Me while it is day; *the* night is coming when no one can work. ⁵As long as I am in the world, I am the light of the world."

⁶When He had said these things, He spat on the ground and made clay with the saliva; and He anointed the eyes of the blind man with the clay. ⁷And He said to him, "Go, wash in the pool of Siloam" (which is translated, Sent). So he went and washed, and came back seeing.

⁸Therefore the neighbors and those who previously had seen that he was blindᵃ said, "Is not this he who sat and begged?"

⁹Some said, "This is he." Others *said,* "He is like him."ᵃ

He said, "I am *he.*"

¹⁰Therefore they said to him, "How were your eyes opened?"

¹¹He answered and said, "A Man called Jesus made clay and anointed my eyes and said to me, 'Go to the pool ofᵃ Siloam and wash.' So I went and washed, and I received sight."

¹²Then they said to him, "Where is He?"

He said, "I do not know."

The Pharisees Excommunicate the Healed Man

¹³They brought him who formerly was blind to the Pharisees. ¹⁴Now it was a Sabbath when Jesus made the clay and opened his eyes. ¹⁵Then the Pharisees also asked him again how he had received his sight. He said to them, "He put clay on my eyes, and I washed, and I see."

¹⁶Therefore some of the Pharisees said, "This Man is not from God, because He does not keep the Sabbath."

Others said, "How can a man who is a sinner do such signs?" And there was a division among them.

¹⁷They said to the blind man again, "What do you say about Him because He opened your eyes?"

He said, "He is a prophet."

¹⁸But the Jews did not believe concerning him, that he had been blind and received his sight, until they called the parents of him who had received his sight. ¹⁹And they asked them, saying, "Is this your son, who you say was born blind? How then does he now see?"

²⁰His parents answered them and said, "We know that this is our son, and that he was born blind; ²¹but by what means he now sees we do not know, or who opened his eyes we do not know. He is of age; ask him. He will speak for himself." ²²His parents said these *things* because they feared the Jews, for the Jews had agreed already that if anyone confessed *that* He *was* Christ, he would be put out of the synagogue. ²³Therefore his parents said, "He is of age; ask him."

²⁴So they again called the man who was blind, and said to him, "Give God the glory! We know that this Man is a sinner."

²⁵He answered and said, "Whether He is a sinner *or not* I do not know. One thing I know: that though I was blind, now I see."

8:54 ᵃNU-Text and M-Text read *our.*   8:59 ᵃNU-Text omits the rest of this verse.   9:4 ᵃNU-Text reads *We.*   9:8 ᵃNU-Text reads *a beggar.*   9:9 ᵃNU-Text reads *"No, but he is like him."*   9:11 ᵃNU-Text omits *the pool of.*

LEADERSHIP ISSUES

GC2: Becoming a Good Samaritan: Who Sinned?

JOHN 9:2

The entire ninth chapter of John holds many great insights for the follow-ers of Jesus. As Jesus and His disciples are going to Jerusalem, beside the road, they come upon a man blind from birth. The Bible records that Jesus heals the man, subsequently prompting a lot of trouble. The man is called before the religious leaders. His family is brought in to explain what has happened to him. Finally, because he continues to testify that Jesus was re-sponsible for his receiving sight, they throw him out of the synagogue. When Jesus hears about it, He goes out and finds the man and reveals more of Himself to him (John 9:35–39).

Of specific importance to our becoming people who love as Jesus loved is the issue of grace. Surely, He has looked beyond our faults to see our needs (Rom. 5:8; Luke 19:7–10)—but can we do likewise?

One tragic part of the story is that even as Christ's heart is moved with compassion and grace, when the disciples looked at the same man beside the road, they asked who sinned. Was it the man or his parents? Do you see the contrast between the heart of Jesus—moved to minister to needs—and the heart of the disciples wanting to know, "Who sinned?"

Following Jesus and loving as He loves means becoming a person of grace. It means seeing and ministering to needs, such as support, encour-agement, and acceptance, rather than seeing and reacting only to behav-iors. The power for sustaining a ministry to people in need must come from God, and the power to give grace comes from having partaken of God's grace. "For by grace you have been saved through faith" (Eph. 2:8). "But God demonstrates His own love toward us, in that while we were still sinners, Christ died for us" (Rom. 5:8). One of the things that will empower your ministry to hurting people is reflection upon the abundant grace you have received from God, prompting gratitude in your heart. Never get over the wonder that you have been loved, and you'll be con-strained to love others (2 Cor. 5:21).

GC2
GREAT COMMANDMENT
COMMISSION

26Then they said to him again, "What did He do to you? How did He open your eyes?"

27He answered them, "I told you already, and you did not listen. Why do you want to hear *it* again? Do you also want to become His disciples?"

28Then they reviled him and said, "You are His disciple, but we are Moses' disciples. 29We know that God spoke to Moses; *as for* this *fellow,* we do not know where He is from."

30The man answered and said to them, "Why, this is a marvelous thing, that you do not know where He is from; yet He has opened my eyes! 31Now we know that God does not hear sinners; but if anyone is a worshiper of God and does His will, He hears him. 32Since the world began it has been unheard of that anyone opened the eyes of one who was born blind. 33If this Man were not from God, He could do nothing."

34They answered and said to him, "You were completely born in sins, and are you teaching us?" And they cast him out.

True Vision and True Blindness

35Jesus heard that they had cast him out; and when He had found him, He said to him, "Do you believe in the Son of God?"[a]

36He answered and said, "Who is He, Lord, that I may believe in Him?"

37And Jesus said to him, "You have both seen Him and it is He who is talking with you."

38Then he said, "Lord, I believe!" And he worshiped Him.

39And Jesus said, "For judgment I have come into this world, that those who do not see may see, and that those who see may be made blind."

40Then *some* of the Pharisees who were with Him heard these words, and said to Him, "Are we blind also?"

41Jesus said to them, "If you were blind, you would have no sin; but now you say, 'We see.' Therefore your sin remains.

Jesus the True Shepherd

10 "Most assuredly, I say to you, he who does not enter the sheepfold by the door, but climbs up some other way, the same is a thief and a robber. 2But he who enters by the door is the shepherd of the sheep. 3To him the doorkeeper opens, and the sheep hear his voice; and he calls his own sheep by name and leads them out. 4And when he brings out his own sheep, he goes before them; and the sheep follow him, for they know his voice. 5Yet they will by no means follow a stranger, but will flee from him, for they do not know the voice of strangers." 6Jesus used this illustration, but they did not understand the things which He spoke to them.

Jesus the Good Shepherd

7Then Jesus said to them again, "Most assuredly, I say to you, I am the door of the sheep. 8All who *ever* came before Me[a] are thieves and robbers, but the sheep did not hear them. 9I am the door. If anyone enters by Me, he will be saved, and will go in and out and find pasture. 10The thief does not come except to steal, and to kill, and to destroy. I have come that they may have life, and that they may have *it* more abundantly.

11"I am the good shepherd. The good shepherd gives His life for the sheep. 12But a hireling, *he who is* not the shepherd, one who does not own the sheep, sees the wolf coming and leaves the sheep and flees; and the wolf catches the sheep and scatters them. 13The hireling flees because he is a hireling and does not care about the sheep. 14I am the good shepherd; and I know My *sheep,* and am known by My own. 15As the Father knows Me, even so I know the Father; and I lay down My life for the sheep. 16And other sheep I have which are not of this fold; them also I must bring, and they will hear My voice; and there will be one flock *and* one shepherd.

17"Therefore My Father loves Me, because I lay down My life that I may take it again. 18No one takes it from Me, but I lay it down of Myself. I have power to lay it down, and I have power to take it again. This command I have received from My Father."

19Therefore there was a division again among the Jews because of these sayings. 20And many of them said, "He has a demon and is mad. Why do you listen to Him?"

21Others said, "These are not the words of one who has a demon. Can a demon open the eyes of the blind?"

9:35 [a]NU-Text reads *Son of Man.*   **10:8** [a]M-Text omits *before Me.*

LEADERSHIP ISSUES

Finding True Happiness

JOHN 10:10

Our culture advertises the slogan that happiness can be found when we control our own freedom and have things the way we want them to be. As a result, many people live their lives individualistically, without regard to what others have to say about them or what they are doing. Many even formulate their own systems of morality and ethics, and they attempt to find happiness in having the freedom to do whatever they want to do. However, true happiness cannot be found ultimately by following the dictates of our own desires; rather, such behavior can lead to an amoral lifestyle marked by hurt and grief.

True happiness comes when we are at peace with the One who created us. God has set forth rules for humanity. Those rules reveal important truths about God's character and how we are to live in this world. However, happiness does not come by merely adhering to a "to-do" list of divine prescriptions. Rather, true happiness comes when we find a fulfilling and genuine relationship of love with our Creator. This happiness and our love for God, gives us the desire to obey God's commandments and to honor Him with our lives by living obediently.

Successfully finding happiness is rooted in the action of loving God with all our heart, soul, mind, and strength. Only then can we find a personal fulfillment that meets our deepest needs and calms our fears and worries. When we obey God, God gives us the power to serve Him by obeying His other commandments with a joyful and expectant heart. The result is that we develop a fervent desire to serve God with our entire beings, which in turn fuels our desire to follow the Commandments set forth by God. However, it is impossible for us to keep the Ten Commandments perfectly, as we are flawed and fallen human beings.

Thankfully, the mercy, grace, and forgiveness God offers to us enables us to continue striving for obedience. When we obey God fully, and when we love God fully, we find true happiness.

The Shepherd Knows His Sheep

[22]Now it was the Feast of Dedication in Jerusalem, and it was winter. [23]And Jesus walked in the temple, in Solomon's porch. [24]Then the Jews surrounded Him and said to Him, "How long do You keep us in doubt? If You are the Christ, tell us plainly."

[25]Jesus answered them, "I told you, and you do not believe. The works that I do in My Father's name, they bear witness of Me. [26]But you do not believe, because you are not of My sheep, as I said to you.[a] [27]My sheep hear My voice, and I know them, and they follow Me. [28]And I give them eternal life, and they shall never perish; neither shall anyone snatch them out of My hand. [29]My Father, who has given *them* to Me, is greater than all; and no one is able to snatch *them* out of My Father's hand. [30]I and *My* Father are one."

Renewed Efforts to Stone Jesus

[31]Then the Jews took up stones again to stone Him. [32]Jesus answered them, "Many good works I have shown you from My Father. For which of those works do you stone Me?"

[33]The Jews answered Him, saying, "For a good work we do not stone You, but for blasphemy, and because You, being a Man, make Yourself God."

[34]Jesus answered them, "Is it not written in your law, *'I said, "You are gods"'*?[a] [35]If He called them gods, to whom the word of God came (and the Scripture cannot be broken), [36]do you say of Him whom the Father sanctified and sent into the world, 'You are blaspheming,' because I said, 'I am the Son of God'? [37]If I do not do the works of My Father, do not believe Me; [38]but if I do, though you do not believe Me, believe the works, that you may know and believe[a] that the Father *is* in Me, and I in Him." [39]Therefore they sought again to seize Him, but He escaped out of their hand.

The Believers Beyond Jordan

[40]And He went away again beyond the Jordan to the place where John was baptizing at first, and there He stayed. [41]Then many came to Him and said, "John performed no sign, but all the things that John spoke about this Man were true." [42]And many believed in Him there.

The Death of Lazarus

11 Now a certain *man* was sick, Lazarus of Bethany, the town of Mary and her sister Martha. [2]It was *that* Mary who anointed the Lord with fragrant oil and wiped His feet with her hair, whose brother Lazarus was sick. [3]Therefore the sisters sent to Him, saying, "Lord, behold, he whom You love is sick."

[4]When Jesus heard *that,* He said, "This sickness is not unto death, but for the glory of God, that the Son of God may be glorified through it."

[5]Now Jesus loved Martha and her sister and Lazarus. [6]So, when He heard that he was sick, He stayed two more days in the place where He was. [7]Then after this He said to *the* disciples, "Let us go to Judea again."

[8]*The* disciples said to Him, "Rabbi, lately the Jews sought to stone You, and are You going there again?"

[9]Jesus answered, "Are there not twelve hours in the day? If anyone walks in the day, he does not stumble, because he sees the light of this world. [10]But if one walks in the night, he stumbles, because the light is not in him." [11]These things He said, and after that He said to them, "Our friend Lazarus sleeps, but I go that I may wake him up."

[12]Then His disciples said, "Lord, if he sleeps he will get well." [13]However, Jesus spoke of his death, but they thought that He was speaking about taking rest in sleep.

[14]Then Jesus said to them plainly, "Lazarus is dead. [15]And I am glad for your sakes that I was not there, that you may believe. Nevertheless let us go to him."

[16]Then Thomas, who is called the Twin, said to his fellow disciples, "Let us also go, that we may die with Him."

I Am the Resurrection and the Life

[17]So when Jesus came, He found that he had already been in the tomb four days. [18]Now Bethany was near Jerusalem, about two miles[a] away. [19]And many of the Jews had joined the women around Martha and Mary, to comfort them concerning their brother.

[20]Now Martha, as soon as she heard that Jesus

10:26 [a]NU-Text omits *as I said to you.*   **10:34** [a]Psalm 82:6
10:38 [a]NU-Text reads *understand.*   **11:18** [a]Literally *fifteen stadia*

LEADERSHIP ISSUES

GC2: Jesus and His Friends

JOHN 11:5

It's important to remember that Jesus fulfilled all that His Father intended for Him as a single person. Scripture records that as He entered His teen years, He "increased in wisdom and stature, and in favor with God and men" (Luke 2:52). Notice His mental and physical growth, as well as His spiritual. Important also, is that Jesus developed "favor" with others. He was a good student, worker, son, brother, and a good friend!

During His public ministry, the Gospels record several trips to a small village outside Jerusalem called Bethany (Luke 10:38–42; John 12:1–11). There is no apparent religious or political significance to the village, but it was important to Jesus because His three friends lived there! Mary, Martha, and Lazarus appear to be Jesus' "singles group." The Bible records His love for them and refers to "our friend Lazarus" (John 11:11).

As good friends, Jesus is welcomed into their home, meals are taken together, times of significant conversation take place, tears are shed together, and others notice the love between the four friends.

Pause to list some of those in your life with whom you have:

- enjoyed hospitality,
- had meals,
- shared significant conversation,
- shed tears,
- cared for so deeply that others noticed your closeness.

Now thank God for good friendships in your life!

GC2
GREAT COMMANDMENT
COMMISSION

was coming, went and met Him, but Mary was sitting in the house. ²¹Now Martha said to Jesus, "Lord, if You had been here, my brother would not have died. ²²But even now I know that whatever You ask of God, God will give You."

²³Jesus said to her, "Your brother will rise again."

²⁴Martha said to Him, "I know that he will rise again in the resurrection at the last day."

²⁵Jesus said to her, "I am the resurrection and the life. He who believes in Me, though he may die, he shall live. ²⁶And whoever lives and believes in Me shall never die. Do you believe this?"

²⁷She said to Him, "Yes, Lord, I believe that You are the Christ, the Son of God, who is to come into the world."

JESUS AND DEATH, THE LAST ENEMY

²⁸And when she had said these things, she went her way and secretly called Mary her sister, saying, "The Teacher has come and is calling for you." ²⁹As soon as she heard *that,* she arose quickly and came to Him. ³⁰Now Jesus had not yet come into the town, but wasᵃ in the place where Martha met Him. ³¹Then the Jews who were with her in the house, and comforting her, when they saw that Mary rose up quickly and went out, followed her, saying, "She is going to the tomb to weep there."ᵃ

³²Then, when Mary came where Jesus was, and saw Him, she fell down at His feet, saying to Him, "Lord, if You had been here, my brother would not have died."

³³Therefore, when Jesus saw her weeping, and the Jews who came with her weeping, He groaned in the spirit and was troubled. ³⁴And He said, "Where have you laid him?"

They said to Him, "Lord, come and see."

³⁵Jesus wept. ³⁶Then the Jews said, "See how He loved him!"

³⁷And some of them said, "Could not this Man, who opened the eyes of the blind, also have kept this man from dying?"

LAZARUS RAISED FROM THE DEAD

³⁸Then Jesus, again groaning in Himself, came to the tomb. It was a cave, and a stone lay against it. ³⁹Jesus said, "Take away the stone."

Martha, the sister of him who was dead, said

to Him, "Lord, by this time there is a stench, for he has been *dead* four days."

⁴⁰Jesus said to her, "Did I not say to you that if you would believe you would see the glory of God?" ⁴¹Then they took away the stone *from the place* where the dead man was lying.ᵃ And Jesus lifted up *His* eyes and said, "Father, I thank You that You have heard Me. ⁴²And I know that You always hear Me, but because of the people who are standing by I said *this,* that they may believe that You sent Me." ⁴³Now when He had said these things, He cried with a loud voice, "Lazarus, come forth!" ⁴⁴And he who had died came out bound hand and foot with graveclothes, and his face was wrapped with a cloth. Jesus said to them, "Loose him, and let him go."

THE PLOT TO KILL JESUS

⁴⁵Then many of the Jews who had come to Mary, and had seen the things Jesus did, believed in Him. ⁴⁶But some of them went away to the Pharisees and told them the things Jesus did. ⁴⁷Then the chief priests and the Pharisees gathered a council and said, "What shall we do? For this Man works many signs. ⁴⁸If we let Him alone like this, everyone will believe in Him, and the Romans will come and take away both our place and nation."

⁴⁹And one of them, Caiaphas, being high priest that year, said to them, "You know nothing at all, ⁵⁰nor do you consider that it is expedient for usᵃ that one man should die for the people, and not that the whole nation should perish." ⁵¹Now this he did not say on his own *authority;* but being high priest that year he prophesied that Jesus would die for the nation, ⁵²and not for that nation only, but also that He would gather together in one the children of God who were scattered abroad.

⁵³Then, from that day on, they plotted to put Him to death. ⁵⁴Therefore Jesus no longer walked openly among the Jews, but went from there into the country near the wilderness, to a city called Ephraim, and there remained with His disciples.

⁵⁵And the Passover of the Jews was near, and many went from the country up to Jerusalem

---

11:30 ᵃNU-Text adds *still.* **11:31** ᵃNU-Text reads *supposing that she was going to the tomb to weep there.* **11:41** ᵃNU-Text omits *from the place where the dead man was lying.* **11:50** ᵃNU-Text reads *you.*

LEADERSHIP ISSUES

GC2: Weep with Those Who Weep!

JOHN 11:35

We are impressed by two miracles in this chapter: the raising of Lazarus from the dead and the miracle of a God who cries! Imagine "weep with those who weep" (Rom. 12:15) and think that there is "blessing" available when we mourn. The blessing is called comfort (Matt. 5:4).

Jesus was moved deeply within His spirit as He wept with His friend Mary. Comfort flowed through the prompting and power of the Comforter. For us comfort may be as simple as sharing "I'm really sorry that happened." Very often the Holy Spirit's first work is to take captive and resist our common, unhelpful, or unproductive responses. Consider that Jesus could have but didn't give these unhelpful responses:

- **Advice/instruction**
  "Let me tell you how to solve the problem."
  "Maybe next time that happens you should . . . "
- **Logic/reasoning**
  "Let me analyze the situation and tell you why it happened."
  "I think that happened because . . . "
- **Pep talk**
  "You're a winner! You'll make it through these tough times!"
  "I'm sure tomorrow will be a better day."
- **Minimize the incident**
  "Sure it hurt, but there's still a lot going on that's good."
  "Aren't you being overly sensitive?"
- **Spiritualizing**
  "Well, you know that God will work all this out for your good."
  "Joseph's brothers meant evil for him, but God meant it for good."
  "It's good to know that we are more than conquerors through Christ!"

Each response seems to work best *after* we give comfort!

GC2
GREAT COMMANDMENT
COMMISSION

before the Passover, to purify themselves. ⁵⁶Then they sought Jesus, and spoke among themselves as they stood in the temple, "What do you think— that He will not come to the feast?" ⁵⁷Now both the chief priests and the Pharisees had given a command, that if anyone knew where He was, he should report *it,* that they might seize Him.

THE ANOINTING AT BETHANY

12Then, six days before the Passover, Jesus came to Bethany, where Lazarus was who had been dead,ᵃ whom He had raised from the dead. ²There they made Him a supper; and Martha served, but Lazarus was one of those who sat at the table with Him. ³Then Mary took a pound of very costly oil of spikenard, anointed the feet of Jesus, and wiped His feet with her hair. And the house was filled with the fragrance of the oil.

⁴But one of His disciples, Judas Iscariot, Simon's *son,* who would betray Him, said, ⁵"Why was this fragrant oil not sold for three hundred denariiᵃ and given to the poor?" ⁶This he said, not that he cared for the poor, but because he was a thief, and had the money box; and he used to take what was put in it.

⁷But Jesus said, "Let her alone; she has keptᵃ this for the day of My burial. ⁸For the poor you have with you always, but Me you do not have always."

THE PLOT TO KILL LAZARUS

⁹Now a great many of the Jews knew that He was there; and they came, not for Jesus' sake only, but that they might also see Lazarus, whom He had raised from the dead. ¹⁰But the chief priests plotted to put Lazarus to death also, ¹¹because on account of him many of the Jews went away and believed in Jesus.

THE TRIUMPHAL ENTRY

¹²The next day a great multitude that had come to the feast, when they heard that Jesus was coming to Jerusalem, ¹³took branches of palm trees and went out to meet Him, and cried out:

"Hosanna!
 '*Blessed is He who comes in the name of the
     LORD!*'ᵃ
 The King of Israel!"

¹⁴Then Jesus, when He had found a young donkey, sat on it; as it is written:

¹⁵"*Fear not, daughter of Zion;
   Behold, your King is coming,
   Sitting on a donkey's colt.*"ᵃ

¹⁶His disciples did not understand these things at first; but when Jesus was glorified, then they remembered that these things were written about Him and *that* they had done these things to Him. ¹⁷Therefore the people, who were with Him when He called Lazarus out of his tomb and raised him from the dead, bore witness. ¹⁸For this reason the people also met Him, because they heard that He had done this sign. ¹⁹The Pharisees therefore said among themselves, "You see that you are accomplishing nothing. Look, the world has gone after Him!"

THE FRUITFUL GRAIN OF WHEAT

²⁰Now there were certain Greeks among those who came up to worship at the feast. ²¹Then they came to Philip, who was from Bethsaida of Galilee, and asked him, saying, "Sir, we wish to see Jesus." ²²Philip came and told Andrew, and in turn Andrew and Philip told Jesus.

²³But Jesus answered them, saying, "The hour has come that the Son of Man should be glorified. ²⁴Most assuredly, I say to you, unless a grain of wheat falls into the ground and dies, it remains alone; but if it dies, it produces much grain. ²⁵He who loves his life will lose it, and he who hates his life in this world will keep it for eternal life. ²⁶If anyone serves Me, let him follow Me; and where I am, there My servant will be also. If anyone serves Me, him *My* Father will honor.

JESUS PREDICTS HIS DEATH ON THE CROSS

²⁷"Now My soul is troubled, and what shall I say? 'Father, save Me from this hour'? But for this purpose I came to this hour. ²⁸Father, glorify Your name."

Then a voice came from heaven, *saying,* "I have both glorified *it* and will glorify *it* again."

12:1 ᵃNU-Text omits *who had been dead.* **12:5** ᵃAbout one year's wages for a worker **12:7** ᵃNU-Text reads *that she may keep.* **12:13** ᵃPsalm 118:26 **12:15** ᵃZechariah 9:9

LEADERSHIP ISSUES

GC2: Walking in the Light

JOHN 12:35

Each of us has known of family or friends who started out following Jesus, only to be overtaken by the darkness of sin, self or Satan. How do we understand such return to worldliness, coldheartedness, and rebellion? In a simple way, Christ shares this illustration: the darkness is always chasing us, and all we have to do for it to overtake us is to stop walking in God's light!

Then, how are we to understand God's light, and how are we to walk in it? His "light" is made known to us through our conscience and His creation, for sure; but most commonly, He is revealed through His Son, His Scripture, and His Saints (followers of Jesus). To walk in His light involves frequent and recurring encounters with Jesus, Scripture, and other believers.

The Holy Spirit within us is also essential to walking in God's light. It is the Holy Spirit that reveals Jesus to us (John 14:26), brings illumination to Scripture (1 John 2:27), and empowers our fellowship together as Christ's followers (1 Cor. 12:12, 13). How is your walk? Let's be about exercising ourselves!

GC2
GREAT COMMANDMENT
COMMISSION

²⁹Therefore the people who stood by and heard *it* said that it had thundered. Others said, "An angel has spoken to Him."

³⁰Jesus answered and said, "This voice did not come because of Me, but for your sake. ³¹Now is the judgment of this world; now the ruler of this world will be cast out. ³²And I, if I am lifted up from the earth, will draw all *peoples* to Myself." ³³This He said, signifying by what death He would die.

³⁴The people answered Him, "We have heard from the law that the Christ remains forever; and how *can* You say, 'The Son of Man must be lifted up'? Who is this Son of Man?"

³⁵Then Jesus said to them, "A little while longer the light is with you. Walk while you have the light, lest darkness overtake you; he who walks in darkness does not know where he is going. ³⁶While you have the light, believe in the light, that you may become sons of light." These things Jesus spoke, and departed, and was hidden from them.

Who Has Believed Our Report?

³⁷But although He had done so many signs before them, they did not believe in Him, ³⁸that the word of Isaiah the prophet might be fulfilled, which he spoke:

"Lord, who has believed our report?
And to whom has the arm of the LORD been
    revealed?"ᵃ

³⁹Therefore they could not believe, because Isaiah said again:

⁴⁰"He has blinded their eyes and hardened their
    hearts,
Lest they should see with *their* eyes,
Lest they should understand with *their* hearts
    and turn,
So that I should heal them."ᵃ

⁴¹These things Isaiah said whenᵃ he saw His glory and spoke of Him.

Walk in the Light

⁴²Nevertheless even among the rulers many believed in Him, but because of the Pharisees

they did not confess *Him,* lest they should be put out of the synagogue; ⁴³for they loved the praise of men more than the praise of God.

⁴⁴Then Jesus cried out and said, "He who believes in Me, believes not in Me but in Him who sent Me. ⁴⁵And he who sees Me sees Him who sent Me. ⁴⁶I have come *as* a light into the world, that whoever believes in Me should not abide in darkness. ⁴⁷And if anyone hears My words and does not believe,ᵃ I do not judge him; for I did not come to judge the world but to save the world. ⁴⁸He who rejects Me, and does not receive My words, has that which judges him—the word that I have spoken will judge him in the last day. ⁴⁹For I have not spoken on My own *authority;* but the Father who sent Me gave Me a command, what I should say and what I should speak. ⁵⁰And I know that His command is everlasting life. Therefore, whatever I speak, just as the Father has told Me, so I speak."

Jesus Washes the Disciples' Feet

13 Now before the Feast of the Passover, when Jesus knew that His hour had come that He should depart from this world to the Father, having loved His own who were in the world, He loved them to the end.

²And supper being ended,ᵃ the devil having already put it into the heart of Judas Iscariot, Simon's *son,* to betray Him, ³Jesus, knowing that the Father had given all things into His hands, and that He had come from God and was going to God, ⁴rose from supper and laid aside His garments, took a towel and girded Himself. ⁵After that, He poured water into a basin and began to wash the disciples' feet, and to wipe *them* with the towel with which He was girded. ⁶Then He came to Simon Peter. And *Peter* said to Him, "Lord, are You washing my feet?"

⁷Jesus answered and said to him, "What I am doing you do not understand now, but you will know after this."

⁸Peter said to Him, "You shall never wash my feet!"

Jesus answered him, "If I do not wash you, you have no part with Me."

12:38 ᵃIsaiah 53:1   **12:40** ᵃIsaiah 6:10   **12:41** ᵃNU-Text reads *because.*   **12:47** ᵃNU-Text reads *keep them.*   **13:2** ᵃNU-Text reads *And during supper.*

LEADERSHIP ISSUES

Dirty Towels, Clean Hearts

JOHN 13:3–17

In a world where terrorism and crime are routine news stories and distractions abound, it seems unlikely that anyone would notice a message of simple peace and unconditional love. The dilemma of the leader is how to reach a noisy culture with a quiet message; and the answer is found, once again, in the example of Christ.

In the most difficult time of His life, Jesus, the Son of God, met with His disciples to humbly serve as He poured water into a basin, grabbed a towel, and began washing the feet of His disciples (John 13:3–17). As He so often did, He preached a sermon on love without actually talking. They were astounded. These disciples would fight for the chance to reign with Him but not for the towel to serve with Him. He demonstrated leadership in a way they would not forget.

How then shall we lead in such a defining way? By considering the Christ of the cross: the Savior who watched His disciples run as the accusers mocked, beat, and spat upon Him; the One who allowed spikes to pierce His wrists and feet; He who watched the people cheer and the soldiers roll dice for His clothes as He died. And yet, knowing this would happen, only hours earlier, He selflessly communicated one of His final messages by grabbing a towel.

The cross is clearly about commitment. It began with the towel; and then every agonizing step, every blow of a soldier's hand, every mocking word, and the hammered spikes He endured until His death, were proof of that commitment.

As waves of business methodically pound the shores of our personal lives, we must now, more than ever, focus on the cross and what our Lord did just hours before His sacrificial death. Leaders, grab a towel, pour some water, and serve, regardless of the road ahead. If the King has done it, surely we must follow. When our Lord returns, may we have dirty towels in our hands; but surely these will be the measure of the impact of the leadership legacy we lived.

⁹Simon Peter said to Him, "Lord, not my feet only, but also *my* hands and *my* head!"

¹⁰Jesus said to him, "He who is bathed needs only to wash *his* feet, but is completely clean; and you are clean, but not all of you." ¹¹For He knew who would betray Him; therefore He said, "You are not all clean."

¹²So when He had washed their feet, taken His garments, and sat down again, He said to them, "Do you know what I have done to you? ¹³You call Me Teacher and Lord, and you say well, for *so* I am. ¹⁴If I then, *your* Lord and Teacher, have washed your feet, you also ought to wash one another's feet. ¹⁵For I have given you an example, that you should do as I have done to you. ¹⁶Most assuredly, I say to you, a servant is not greater than his master; nor is he who is sent greater than he who sent him. ¹⁷If you know these things, blessed are you if you do them.

Jesus Identifies His Betrayer

¹⁸"I do not speak concerning all of you. I know whom I have chosen; but that the Scripture may be fulfilled, *'He who eats bread with Me*ᵃ *has lifted up his heel against Me.'*ᵇ ¹⁹Now I tell you before it comes, that when it does come to pass, you may believe that I am *He.* ²⁰Most assuredly, I say to you, he who receives whomever I send receives Me; and he who receives Me receives Him who sent Me."

²¹When Jesus had said these things, He was troubled in spirit, and testified and said, "Most assuredly, I say to you, one of you will betray Me." ²²Then the disciples looked at one another, perplexed about whom He spoke.

²³Now there was leaning on Jesus' bosom one of His disciples, whom Jesus loved. ²⁴Simon Peter therefore motioned to him to ask who it was of whom He spoke.

²⁵Then, leaning backᵃ on Jesus' breast, he said to Him, "Lord, who is it?"

²⁶Jesus answered, "It is he to whom I shall give a piece of bread when I have dipped *it.*" And having dipped the bread, He gave *it* to Judas Iscariot, *the son* of Simon. ²⁷Now after the piece of bread, Satan entered him. Then Jesus said to him, "What you do, do quickly." ²⁸But no one at the table knew for what reason He said this to him. ²⁹For some thought, because Judas had the money

box, that Jesus had said to him, "Buy *those things* we need for the feast," or that he should give something to the poor.

³⁰Having received the piece of bread, he then went out immediately. And it was night.

The New Commandment

³¹So, when he had gone out, Jesus said, "Now the Son of Man is glorified, and God is glorified in Him. ³²If God is glorified in Him, God will also glorify Him in Himself, and glorify Him immediately. ³³Little children, I shall be with you a little while longer. You will seek Me; and as I said to the Jews, 'Where I am going, you cannot come,' so now I say to you. ³⁴A new commandment I give to you, that you love one another; as I have loved you, that you also love one another. ³⁵By this all will know that you are My disciples, if you have love for one another."

Jesus Predicts Peter's Denial

³⁶Simon Peter said to Him, "Lord, where are You going?"

Jesus answered him, "Where I am going you cannot follow Me now, but you shall follow Me afterward."

³⁷Peter said to Him, "Lord, why can I not follow You now? I will lay down my life for Your sake."

³⁸Jesus answered him, "Will you lay down your life for My sake? Most assuredly, I say to you, the rooster shall not crow till you have denied Me three times.

The Way, the Truth, and the Life

14 "Let not your heart be troubled; you believe in God, believe also in Me. ²In My Father's house are many mansions;ᵃ if *it were* not *so,* I would have told you. I go to prepare a place for you.ᵇ ³And if I go and prepare a place for you, I will come again and receive you to Myself; that where I am, *there* you may be also. ⁴And where I go you know, and the way you know."

⁵Thomas said to Him, "Lord, we do not

13:18 ᵃNU-Text reads *My bread.* ᵇPsalm 41:9   13:25 ᵃNU-Text and M-Text add *thus.*   14:2 ᵃLiterally *dwellings* ᵇNU-Text adds a word which would cause the text to read either *if it were not so, would I have told you that I go to prepare a place for you?* or *if it were not so I would have told you; for I go to prepare a place for you.*

LEADERSHIP ISSUES

GC2: Basic Training: Loving Yourself as Christ's Beloved

JOHN 13:34 *As I have loved you, that you also love one another.*

With these words, Jesus is both reminding the disciples of His past demonstrations of love and concern for them, as well as foreshadowing His forthcoming display of perfect love at Calvary. Through His sacrifice, and through His continual caring involvement in our lives, Jesus has loved us as well. The more we recognize and receive His love, the more we are able to embrace our true identity as His beloved.

Consider what Scripture reveals about God's love for us:

- God demonstrated His love for us by sending Jesus to die for us while we were still sinners (Rom. 5:8).
- Nothing can separate us from God's love (Rom. 8:38, 39).
- He has poured out His love upon us through the Holy Spirit (Rom. 5:5).
- The love of Christ for us is infinitely great and surpasses knowledge (Eph. 3:18, 19).
- Because of His great love for us, God made us alive with Christ (Eph. 2:4, 5).

We are not simply people who believe Scripture's great doctrines about Christ, nor are we merely people who practice good behavior. Hopefully, we **do** believe right doctrine and practice right behavior, but we must be careful not to think that our identity lies in either of these things.

Our true identity is that we are ones who have been loved by Jesus. We are His beloved.

GC2

GREAT COMMANDMENT
COMMISSION

LEADERSHIP ISSUES

GC2: Spiritual Formation: Encounter Jesus in His Sorrow

JOHN 14:9 *Jesus said to him, "Have I been with you so long, and yet you have not known Me, Philip? He who has seen Me has seen the Father; so how can you say, 'Show us the Father'?"*

Imagine the sadness that must have been in the Savior's heart as He uttered these words. Picture the scene in the Upper Room. Jesus' faithful followers surround Him. Christ has already experienced the painful distraction of the disciples' argument about who was to be the greatest in the kingdom. He has vulnerably shared how His body is about to be broken and His blood is about to be shed, only to be met with the dispute of His closest friends (Luke 22:17–26).

Then, as a testimony of humble servanthood, Christ takes a basin of water and a towel and begins to wash the feet of each disciple. He washes the feet of Peter, James, John, and even Judas (John 13:5–15). He washes the feet of His betrayer, extending love and grace to him one final time. During the Passover meal, Christ turns to Judas and says, "What you do, do quickly" (John 13:27). Judas then departs to complete the terms of his agreement to betray Christ.

As you revisit this familiar story, pause and reflect upon the heart of the Savior. What might Jesus have been feeling as He experienced the dread of crucifixion and the insensitivity of His disciples' response and the anticipation of His imminent betrayal and the departure of His closest friends? What feelings might have been in Christ's heart in the Upper Room? Now imagine that this One who is "a Man of sorrows and acquainted with grief" experiences additional pain as He utters His next words (Is. 53:3). Allow the Holy Spirit to gently lead you to respond to the heart of Jesus as you hear Him say, "Have I been with you so long, and yet you have not known Me?"

Now allow your compassion to prompt your deepened longing to know Him: "Lord Jesus, I want to better know You. I want to know You for who You really are."

GC2
GREAT COMMANDMENT
COMMISSION

THROUGH THE GRID

Thinking Christianly: Four Views of Salvation (John 14:6)

- **Universalism** claims that all people will eventually be saved. God is too loving to send anyone to hell.
- **Pluralism** claims that all the world religions are basically the same, with their particular understanding being true for them. All people will be saved through their own faith.
- **Inclusivism** holds that Christ's work of salvation on the cross is essential and applicable to all—even to those who have never trusted Christ personally.
- **Exclusivism** holds that Christianity is the only way to salvation. All other worldviews are ultimately inadequate, though they may hold partial truths. Only Christianity is sufficient for salvation (John 14:6; Acts 4:12; 1 Tim. 2:5).

know where You are going, and how can we know the way?"

⁶Jesus said to him, "I am the way, the truth, and the life. No one comes to the Father except through Me.

THE FATHER REVEALED

⁷"If you had known Me, you would have known My Father also; and from now on you know Him and have seen Him."

⁸Philip said to Him, "Lord, show us the Father, and it is sufficient for us."

⁹Jesus said to him, "Have I been with you so long, and yet you have not known Me, Philip? He who has seen Me has seen the Father; so how can you say, 'Show us the Father'? ¹⁰Do you not believe that I am in the Father, and the Father in Me? The words that I speak to you I do not speak on My own *authority;* but the Father who dwells in Me does the works. ¹¹Believe Me that I *am* in the Father and the Father in Me, or else believe Me for the sake of the works themselves.

THE ANSWERED PRAYER

¹²"Most assuredly, I say to you, he who believes in Me, the works that I do he will do also; and greater *works* than these he will do, because I go to My Father. ¹³And whatever you ask in My name, that I will do, that the Father may be glorified in the Son. ¹⁴If you ask[a] anything in My name, I will do *it.*

JESUS PROMISES ANOTHER HELPER

¹⁵"If you love Me, keep[a] My commandments. ¹⁶And I will pray the Father, and He will give you another Helper, that He may abide with you forever— ¹⁷the Spirit of truth, whom the world cannot receive, because it neither sees Him nor knows Him; but you know Him, for He dwells with you and will be in you. ¹⁸I will not leave you orphans; I will come to you.

INDWELLING OF THE FATHER AND THE SON

¹⁹"A little while longer and the world will see Me no more, but you will see Me. Because I live, you will live also. ²⁰At that day you will know that I *am* in My Father, and you in Me, and I in you. ²¹He who has My commandments and keeps them, it is he who loves Me. And he who loves Me will be loved by My Father, and I will love him and manifest Myself to him."

²²Judas (not Iscariot) said to Him, "Lord, how is it that You will manifest Yourself to us, and not to the world?"

²³Jesus answered and said to him, "If anyone loves Me, he will keep My word; and My Father will love him, and We will come to him and make Our home with him. ²⁴He who does not love Me does not keep My words; and the word which you hear is not Mine but the Father's who sent Me.

14:14 [a]NU-Text adds *Me.*   **14:15** [a]NU-Text reads *you will keep.*

LEADERSHIP ISSUES

GC2: Convictions: Defining Convictions

JOHN 14:11 *Believe Me that I am in the Father and the Father in Me, or else believe Me for the sake of the works themselves.*

When Jesus invited His disciples to "believe Me for the sake of the works themselves" (John 14:11), He referred not only to the evidences that make believing a rational, reasonable exercise but also to the context of the invitation. He invites us to believe in a person. Believing in Christ and His Word will have a profound and relational meaning in each of our lives.

People can have convictions in misguided and wrong beliefs—as the terrorist attacks of September 11 prove. We must move beyond subjective believing to a conviction in what is objectively true. And those beliefs must be shown to be not only true but also relevant—that is, relationally meaningful to life.

Having convictions, then, can be defined as *"being so thoroughly convinced that Christ and His Word are both objectively true and relationally meaningful that you act on your beliefs regardless of the consequences."*

The expression "WWJD" (What Would Jesus Do) likely had its origin in this idea that to live with God-honoring convictions is to live and love as Jesus would. What's He been doing through you lately?

GC2
GREAT COMMANDMENT
COMMISSION

The Gift of His Peace

25"These things I have spoken to you while being present with you. 26But the Helper, the Holy Spirit, whom the Father will send in My name, He will teach you all things, and bring to your remembrance all things that I said to you. 27Peace I leave with you, My peace I give to you; not as the world gives do I give to you. Let not your heart be troubled, neither let it be afraid. 28You have heard Me say to you, 'I am going away and coming *back* to you.' If you loved Me, you would rejoice because I said,ᵃ 'I am going to the Father,' for My Father is greater than I.

29"And now I have told you before it comes, that when it does come to pass, you may believe. 30I will no longer talk much with you, for the ruler of this world is coming, and he has nothing in Me. 31But that the world may know that I love the Father, and as the Father gave Me commandment, so I do. Arise, let us go from here.

The True Vine

15 "I am the true vine, and My Father is the vinedresser. 2Every branch in Me that does not bear fruit He takes away;ᵃ and every *branch* that bears fruit He prunes, that it may bear more fruit. 3You are already clean because of the word which I have spoken to you. 4Abide in Me, and I in you. As the branch cannot bear fruit of itself, unless it abides in the vine, neither can you, unless you abide in Me.

5"I am the vine, you *are* the branches. He who abides in Me, and I in him, bears much fruit; for without Me you can do nothing. 6If anyone does not abide in Me, he is cast out as a branch and is withered; and they gather them and throw *them* into the fire, and they are burned. 7If you abide in Me, and My words abide in you, you willᵃ ask what you desire, and it shall be done for you. 8By this My Father is glorified, that you bear much fruit; so you will be My disciples.

Love and Joy Perfected

9"As the Father loved Me, I also have loved you; abide in My love. 10If you keep My commandments, you will abide in My love, just as I have kept My Father's commandments and abide in His love.

11"These things I have spoken to you, that My joy may remain in you, and *that* your joy may be full. 12This is My commandment, that you love one another as I have loved you. 13Greater love has no one than this, than to lay down one's life for his friends. 14You are My friends if you do whatever I command you. 15No longer do I call you servants, for a servant does not know what his master is doing; but I have called you friends, for all things that I heard from My Father I have made known to you. 16You did not choose Me, but I chose you and appointed you that you should go and bear fruit, and *that* your fruit should remain, that whatever you ask the Father in My name He may give you. 17These things I command you, that you love one another.

The World's Hatred

18"If the world hates you, you know that it hated Me before *it hated* you. 19If you were of the world, the world would love its own. Yet because you are not of the world, but I chose you out of the world, therefore the world hates you. 20Remember the word that I said to you, 'A servant is not greater than his master.' If they persecuted Me, they will also persecute you. If they kept My word, they will keep yours also. 21But all these things they will do to you for My name's sake, because they do not know Him who sent Me. 22If I had not come and spoken to them, they would have no sin, but now they have no excuse for their sin. 23He who hates Me hates My Father also. 24If I had not done among them the works which no one else did, they would have no sin; but now they have seen and also hated both Me and My Father. 25But *this happened* that the word might be fulfilled which is written in their law, 'They hated Me without a cause.'ᵃ

The Coming Rejection

26"But when the Helper comes, whom I shall send to you from the Father, the Spirit of truth who proceeds from the Father, He will testify of Me. 27And you also will bear witness, because you have been with Me from the beginning.

14:28 ᵃNU-Text omits *I said*.   15:2 ᵃOr *lifts up*   15:7 ᵃNU-Text omits *you will*.   15:25 ᵃPsalm 69:4

LEADERSHIP ISSUES

GC2: Basic Training: Loving Jesus

JOHN 14:15 *If you love Me, you will keep My commandments.*

Some of us view God as an inspecting god. As you read the verse above, you may have imagined a tone of expectation and demand. The words might carry a questioning tone, conveying the sense that there is a test to be passed or a measurement to be taken. You may have even imagined your inspecting god shaking his finger at you as he speaks these words. His stern tone and gestures warn of his constant inspection.

Some of us may view God as disappointed in us. As you read the verse above, you may have heard a voice that seemed full of dissatisfaction. This kind of god might look down at you with arms crossed, shaking his head as he says, "If you really loved me, then you would be able to keep my commandments. In fact, I have known all along that you did not **really** love me, and what you just did proves it!"

Some of us may see God as a distant god. As you read the verse above, the voice you heard may have seemed cold or disinterested. A distant god would speak the verse with halfhearted enthusiasm or great indifference. This kind of god might seem preoccupied with other things or other more important people. You might picture him looking up absent-mindedly and saying, "Oh, if you love me, then you will probably keep my commandments. Thanks for stopping by."

Consider the wonder that this verse may be a promise in a long line of promises! (See John 14:2, 3, 12, 13, and 14.) Could it be when you woke up this morning God was looking down longing for you to love Him, knowing that as you do, you'll then keep His commandments? The real Jesus is not inspecting, disappointed, or distant. He's excited to share in your love!

GC2
GREAT COMMANDMENT
COMMISSION

16

"These things I have spoken to you, that you should not be made to stumble. ²They will put you out of the synagogues; yes, the time is coming that whoever kills you will think that he offers God service. ³And these things they will do to you[a] because they have not known the Father nor Me. ⁴But these things I have told you, that when the[a] time comes, you may remember that I told you of them.

"And these things I did not say to you at the beginning, because I was with you.

The Work of the Holy Spirit

⁵"But now I go away to Him who sent Me, and none of you asks Me, 'Where are You going?' ⁶But because I have said these things to you, sorrow has filled your heart. ⁷Nevertheless I tell you the truth. It is to your advantage that I go away; for if I do not go away, the Helper will not come to you; but if I depart, I will send Him to you. ⁸And when He has come, He will convict the world of sin, and of righteousness, and of judgment: ⁹of sin, because they do not believe in Me; ¹⁰of righteousness, because I go to My Father and you see Me no more; ¹¹of judgment, because the ruler of this world is judged.

¹²"I still have many things to say to you, but you cannot bear *them* now. ¹³However, when He, the Spirit of truth, has come, He will guide you into all truth; for He will not speak on His own *authority,* but whatever He hears He will speak; and He will tell you things to come. ¹⁴He will glorify Me, for He will take of what is Mine and declare *it* to you. ¹⁵All things that the Father has are Mine. Therefore I said that He will take of Mine and declare *it* to you.[a]

Sorrow Will Turn to Joy

¹⁶"A little while, and you will not see Me; and again a little while, and you will see Me, because I go to the Father."

¹⁷Then *some* of His disciples said among themselves, "What is this that He says to us, 'A little while, and you will not see Me; and again a little while, and you will see Me'; and, 'because I go to the Father'?" ¹⁸They said therefore, "What is this that He says, 'A little while'? We do not know what He is saying."

¹⁹Now Jesus knew that they desired to ask Him, and He said to them, "Are you inquiring among yourselves about what I said, 'A little while, and you will not see Me; and again a little while, and you will see Me'? ²⁰Most assuredly, I say to you that you will weep and lament, but the world will rejoice; and you will be sorrowful, but your sorrow will be turned into joy. ²¹A woman, when she is in labor, has sorrow because her hour has come; but as soon as she has given birth to the child, she no longer remembers the anguish, for joy that a human being has been born into the world. ²²Therefore you now have sorrow; but I will see you again and your heart will rejoice, and your joy no one will take from you.

²³"And in that day you will ask Me nothing. Most assuredly, I say to you, whatever you ask the Father in My name He will give you. ²⁴Until now you have asked nothing in My name. Ask, and you will receive, that your joy may be full.

Jesus Christ Has Overcome the World

²⁵"These things I have spoken to you in figurative language; but the time is coming when I will no longer speak to you in figurative language, but I will tell you plainly about the Father. ²⁶In that day you will ask in My name, and I do not say to you that I shall pray the Father for you; ²⁷for the Father Himself loves you, because you have loved Me, and have believed that I came forth from God. ²⁸I came forth from the Father and have come into the world. Again, I leave the world and go to the Father."

²⁹His disciples said to Him, "See, now You are speaking plainly, and using no figure of speech! ³⁰Now we are sure that You know all things, and have no need that anyone should question You. By this we believe that You came forth from God."

³¹Jesus answered them, "Do you now believe? ³²Indeed the hour is coming, yes, has now come, that you will be scattered, each to his own, and will leave Me alone. And yet I am not alone, because the Father is with Me. ³³These things I have spoken to you, that in Me you may have peace. In the world you will[a] have tribulation; but be of good cheer, I have overcome the world."

16:3 [a]NU-Text and M-Text omit *to you.*   **16:4** [a]NU-Text reads *their.*   **16:15** [a]NU-Text and M-Text read *He takes of Mine and will declare it to you.*   **16:33** [a]NU-Text and M-Text omit *will.*

LEADERSHIP ISSUES

The Holy Spirit in Focus

JOHN 14:26

If we are committed to knowing and experiencing God, we must see clearly all that the Bible teaches about the Holy Spirit. Most people see the doctrine of the Spirit as essentially about power, but we must begin with the Person of the Spirit to truly know and experience God.

The Holy Spirit is a Person with a distinct personality, referred to as masculine and never as a genderless "it" (John 14:16, 17, 26). He speaks (Acts 13:2); testifies (John 15:26); intercedes (Rom. 8:26); commands or forbids (Acts 16:6, 7); guides (John 16:13); reacts as a person, and the Holy Spirit has emotion. He may be resisted (Acts 7:51), grieved (Eph. 4:30), lied to and tested (Acts 5:3–9), and blasphemed by man (Mark 3:29, 30). The Christian religion alone has the Holy Spirit. The personal name of the Holy Spirit is unknown; the title "Holy Spirit" is a designation or what He is. This silence in the Scripture is very significant; He withholds His own name that the name of the Lord Jesus Christ may be exalted.

He is coequal to God, coeternal, and coexistent. Both the Old and New Testament identify Him as God. He is called God explicitly (Acts 5:3, 4; 1 Cor. 3:16; 2 Cor. 3:17). He possesses the divine attributes of being omnipotent (Luke 1:35), omniscient (1 Cor. 2:10), omnipresent (Ps. 139:7–10), and everlasting (Heb. 9:14). The Holy Spirit was a part of creation (Gen. 1:1, 2) and performs the works of God: regeneration (John 3:3, 5–8), resurrection (Rom. 8:11), and transformation (Rom. 8:10).

Once clearly focused on the personhood of the Holy Spirit, we can experience His power. The ministry of the Holy Spirit in us as believers allows us to represent the Lord Jesus on this earth. It is by His power that we become witnesses and give true testimony to the resurrection of the Lord Jesus (Acts 1:8; 4:33). Paul prayed that the Romans "may abound in hope by the power of the Holy Spirit" (Rom. 15:13). Only the Holy Spirit is designated as our Helper (John 14:26) who strengthens us (Phil. 4:13).

JESUS PRAYS FOR HIMSELF

17 Jesus spoke these words, lifted up His eyes to heaven, and said: "Father, the hour has come. Glorify Your Son, that Your Son also may glorify You, ²as You have given Him authority over all flesh, that He should[a] give eternal life to as many as You have given Him. ³And this is eternal life, that they may know You, the only true God, and Jesus Christ whom You have sent. ⁴I have glorified You on the earth. I have finished the work which You have given Me to do. ⁵And now, O Father, glorify Me together with Yourself, with the glory which I had with You before the world was.

JESUS PRAYS FOR HIS DISCIPLES

⁶"I have manifested Your name to the men whom You have given Me out of the world. They were Yours, You gave them to Me, and they have kept Your word. ⁷Now they have known that all things which You have given Me are from You. ⁸For I have given to them the words which You have given Me; and they have received *them,* and have known surely that I came forth from You; and they have believed that You sent Me.

⁹"I pray for them. I do not pray for the world but for those whom You have given Me, for they are Yours. ¹⁰And all Mine are Yours, and Yours are Mine, and I am glorified in them. ¹¹Now I am no longer in the world, but these are in the world, and I come to You. Holy Father, keep through Your name those whom You have given Me,[a] that they may be one as We *are.* ¹²While I was with them in the world,[a] I kept them in Your name. Those whom You gave Me I have kept;[b] and none of them is lost except the son of perdition, that the Scripture might be fulfilled. ¹³But now I come to You, and these things I speak in the world, that they may have My joy fulfilled in themselves. ¹⁴I have given them Your word; and the world has hated them because they are not of the world, just as I am not of the world. ¹⁵I do not pray that You should take them out of the world, but that You should keep them from the evil one. ¹⁶They are not of the world, just as I am not of the world. ¹⁷Sanctify them by Your truth. Your word is truth. ¹⁸As You sent Me into the world, I also have sent them into the world. ¹⁹And for

their sakes I sanctify Myself, that they also may be sanctified by the truth.

JESUS PRAYS FOR ALL BELIEVERS

²⁰"I do not pray for these alone, but also for those who will[a] believe in Me through their word; ²¹that they all may be one, as You, Father, *are* in Me, and I in You; that they also may be one in Us, that the world may believe that You sent Me. ²²And the glory which You gave Me I have given them, that they may be one just as We are one: ²³I in them, and You in Me; that they may be made perfect in one, and that the world may know that You have sent Me, and have loved them as You have loved Me.

²⁴"Father, I desire that they also whom You gave Me may be with Me where I am, that they may behold My glory which You have given Me; for You loved Me before the foundation of the world. ²⁵O righteous Father! The world has not known You, but I have known You; and these have known that You sent Me. ²⁶And I have declared to them Your name, and will declare *it,* that the love with which You loved Me may be in them, and I in them."

BETRAYAL AND ARREST IN GETHSEMANE

18 When Jesus had spoken these words, He went out with His disciples over the Brook Kidron, where there was a garden, which He and His disciples entered. ²And Judas, who betrayed Him, also knew the place; for Jesus often met there with His disciples. ³Then Judas, having received a detachment *of troops,* and officers from the chief priests and Pharisees, came there with lanterns, torches, and weapons. ⁴Jesus therefore, knowing all things that would come upon Him, went forward and said to them, "Whom are you seeking?"

⁵They answered Him, "Jesus of Nazareth."

Jesus said to them, "I am *He.*" And Judas, who betrayed Him, also stood with them. ⁶Now when He said to them, "I am *He,*" they drew back and fell to the ground.

17:2 [a]M-Text reads *shall.* **17:11** [a]NU-Text and M-Text read *keep them through Your name which You have given Me.* **17:12** [a]NU-Text omits *in the world.* [b]NU-Text reads *in Your name which You gave Me. And I guarded them;* (or *it;*). **17:20** [a]NU-Text and M-Text omit *will.*

LEADERSHIP ISSUES

GC2: Encountering Jesus: Running with Compassion

LUKE 15:20 *And he arose and came to his father.*

This familiar story of the "prodigal son" is really about the loving father. And on another level it's really about you; you're the prodigal, and it's Christ who comes to seek and to save you! (Luke 19:10)

Meditate on the Scripture as you imagine that Christ is waiting for you to return home. When He sees you in the distance, He is moved with compassion in spite of your selfishness, pride, condemnation, and sin—and He **runs** toward you. He leaps quickly, anxiously off the front porch because He cannot wait to see you. He embraces you, kisses you, and whispers in your ear. He does not offer lectures or criticism. There is no rebuke or scorn. His voice is filled with compassion as He embraces you. There's a ring, a robe, and the announcement of a party. The real God welcomes you with outstretched arms, ready to embrace you and excited to love you!

Let God fill your heart with gratitude for the grace that you have received, just like the prodigal in this story. Ask Him to bring you back often to a time of fresh reflection upon the grace of the embracing Christ. Pray that He would fill you with wonder and gratitude for His care that would compel you to love those around you.

Spend the next few moments praying with a friend or small group. You might offer a prayer of gratitude and then one of calling. Your prayers might sound like these:

- of gratitude—"Fill my heart, Holy Spirit, with the wonder of an embracing, celebrating Christ; may my joy and gratitude for being so loved empower my love of others."

- of calling—"I sense Your calling, heavenly Father, to love others around me with this same caring initiative. Make my heart especially sensitive to passing on Your love to my _____." (For example: *friend, family member, fellow student, or coworker*)

GC2
GREAT COMMANDMENT
COMMISSION

LEADERSHIP REALITIES

FEEL YOUR MUSCLE, NOT YOUR PULSE   *John 18:10, 11*

It was a highly charged, emotional moment. The soldiers came to drag Jesus away—to shame, humiliate, and kill Him. Peter reacted with anger and cut off the high priest's servant's ear, but Jesus stood by ready to respond. While Peter saw danger and betrayal, Jesus understood that God was calling Him to obedience and courage.

When you feel your muscle, you feel the result of days, months, and years of exercise, nutrition, and sleep. You have gotten out of it what you have put into it. Your pulse, on the other hand, can race and sleep, go from 0 to 100 in a matter of seconds, or drop so low that you can't raise your head up, all based on the emotion and circumstances of the moment.

Like Peter, we often allow emotion and drama in the heat of the moment to make decisions for us. Decisions should not be based on whether we feel good or bad, but on God's will for our lives. What *cup* is He calling you to drink?

> *pothvrion*—**cup**—metaphor: one's lot or experience, whether joyous or adverse, and divine appointments, whether favorable or unfavorable, are likened to a cup that God presents one to drink: so of prosperity and adversity

Stay true to God's Word, even when tempted by emotion to do otherwise. Remember that emotion is not the lead dog in choices, but God's Word is sure for all the ages.

---

[7]Then He asked them again, "Whom are you seeking?"

And they said, "Jesus of Nazareth."

[8]Jesus answered, "I have told you that I am *He*. Therefore, if you seek Me, let these go their way," [9]that the saying might be fulfilled which He spoke, "Of those whom You gave Me I have lost none."

[10]Then Simon Peter, having a sword, drew it and struck the high priest's servant, and cut off his right ear. The servant's name was Malchus.

[11]So Jesus said to Peter, "Put your sword into the sheath. Shall I not drink the cup which My Father has given Me?"

BEFORE THE HIGH PRIEST

[12]Then the detachment *of troops* and the captain and the officers of the Jews arrested Jesus and bound Him. [13]And they led Him away to Annas first, for he was the father-in-law of Caiaphas who was high priest that year. [14]Now it was Caiaphas who advised the Jews that it was expedient that one man should die for the people.

PETER DENIES JESUS

[15]And Simon Peter followed Jesus, and so *did* another[a] disciple. Now that disciple was known to the high priest, and went with Jesus into the courtyard of the high priest. [16]But Peter stood at the door outside. Then the other disciple, who was known to the high priest, went out and spoke to her who kept the door, and brought Peter in. [17]Then the servant girl who kept the door said to Peter, "You are not also *one* of this Man's disciples, are you?"

He said, "I am not."

[18]Now the servants and officers who had made a fire of coals stood there, for it was cold, and they warmed themselves. And Peter stood with them and warmed himself.

JESUS QUESTIONED BY THE HIGH PRIEST

[19]The high priest then asked Jesus about His disciples and His doctrine.

[20]Jesus answered him, "I spoke openly to the

18:15 [a]M-Text reads *the other*.

LEADERSHIP ISSUES

Accountability Is Not an Option

JOHN 15:15

Neither Paul nor Timothy traveled alone in the Book of Acts. These two had a part in changing the world, just as leaders desire to do, and they chose accountability. If these men, used of God and powerful in anointing, needed partners in the gospel, how can we even begin to think we can do it alone? Jesus also showed the power of accountability when He began His earthly ministry by first choosing a team to whom He would be accountable. This was the kind of open accountability Jesus had with His disciples: "No longer do I call you servants, for a servant does not know what his master is doing; but I have called you friends, for all things that I heard from My Father I have made known to you" (John 15:15).

From these examples leaders learn that an accountability friendship is not a casual suggestion; it is an absolute imperative and a trusted, intimate friendship. The accountability partner cancels out the opportunity to cover up emotional problems, sin, or temptation, and to pretend all is OK when it's not; they give permission to get in one another's faces to ask the hard questions: "What about your quiet time? How are you handling temptation?" These remind you that life is about influence, purpose, and significance. They remind you of God's call to lead and what you have to do to stay faithful. In order for other influencers to pray sincerely for you, they need to know your deepest fears and your highest dreams. You can sing in church next to someone for a year, share stories and tears, but never help each other live with victory and strength.

Your accountability partners should be people with whom you are committed to sharing deepest part of yourself. Pray about a person of the same gender who could be that for you, and ask God to arrange this relationship. Consider making your parents part of your accountability team and in so doing show commitment to their authority. This honors and pleases God and gives you the opportunity to live a consistent life without secrets or regrets.

world. I always taught in synagogues and in the temple, where the Jews always meet,ᵃ and in secret I have said nothing. ²¹Why do you ask Me? Ask those who have heard Me what I said to them. Indeed they know what I said."

²²And when He had said these things, one of the officers who stood by struck Jesus with the palm of his hand, saying, "Do You answer the high priest like that?"

²³Jesus answered him, "If I have spoken evil, bear witness of the evil; but if well, why do you strike Me?"

²⁴Then Annas sent Him bound to Caiaphas the high priest.

Peter Denies Twice More

²⁵Now Simon Peter stood and warmed himself. Therefore they said to him, "You are not also *one* of His disciples, are you?"

He denied *it* and said, "I am not!"

²⁶One of the servants of the high priest, a relative *of him* whose ear Peter cut off, said, "Did I not see you in the garden with Him?" ²⁷Peter then denied again; and immediately a rooster crowed.

In Pilate's Court

²⁸Then they led Jesus from Caiaphas to the Praetorium, and it was early morning. But they themselves did not go into the Praetorium, lest they should be defiled, but that they might eat the Passover. ²⁹Pilate then went out to them and said, "What accusation do you bring against this Man?"

³⁰They answered and said to him, "If He were not an evildoer, we would not have delivered Him up to you."

³¹Then Pilate said to them, "You take Him and judge Him according to your law."

Therefore the Jews said to him, "It is not lawful for us to put anyone to death," ³²that the saying of Jesus might be fulfilled which He spoke, signifying by what death He would die.

³³Then Pilate entered the Praetorium again, called Jesus, and said to Him, "Are You the King of the Jews?"

³⁴Jesus answered him, "Are you speaking for yourself about this, or did others tell you this concerning Me?"

³⁵Pilate answered, "Am I a Jew? Your own nation and the chief priests have delivered You to me. What have You done?"

³⁶Jesus answered, "My kingdom is not of this world. If My kingdom were of this world, My servants would fight, so that I should not be delivered to the Jews; but now My kingdom is not from here."

³⁷Pilate therefore said to Him, "Are You a king then?"

Jesus answered, "You say *rightly* that I am a king. For this cause I was born, and for this cause I have come into the world, that I should bear witness to the truth. Everyone who is of the truth hears My voice."

³⁸Pilate said to Him, "What is truth?" And when he had said this, he went out again to the Jews, and said to them, "I find no fault in Him at all.

Taking the Place of Barabbas

³⁹"But you have a custom that I should release someone to you at the Passover. Do you therefore want me to release to you the King of the Jews?"

⁴⁰Then they all cried again, saying, "Not this Man, but Barabbas!" Now Barabbas was a robber.

The Soldiers Mock Jesus

19 So then Pilate took Jesus and scourged *Him.* ²And the soldiers twisted a crown of thorns and put *it* on His head, and they put on Him a purple robe. ³Then they said,ᵃ "Hail, King of the Jews!" And they struck Him with their hands.

⁴Pilate then went out again, and said to them, "Behold, I am bringing Him out to you, that you may know that I find no fault in Him."

Pilate's Decision

⁵Then Jesus came out, wearing the crown of thorns and the purple robe. And *Pilate* said to them, "Behold the Man!"

⁶Therefore, when the chief priests and officers saw Him, they cried out, saying, "Crucify *Him,* crucify *Him!* "

Pilate said to them, "You take Him and crucify *Him,* for I find no fault in Him."

18:20 ᵃNU-Text reads *where all the Jews meet.* 19:3 ᵃNU-Text reads *And they came up to Him and said.*

LEADERSHIP ISSUES

GC2: He Calls Me Friend

JOHN 15:15

It will no doubt seem strange, but friendship with God is foundational to our being a good friend to others! The startling possibility that you and I (the created) can relate closely, even intimately, with the Creator is hard to grasp; but it's true. The Bible says Moses spoke with God as with a friend, and Abraham is referred to as "a friend of God" (Ex. 33:11; James 2:23). In the New Testament, as we encounter the God-Man Jesus, this possibility of friendship seems closer, more possible.

The apostle James reminds us that our "friendship with the world" will hinder our friendship with the Lord (James 4:4). God, in fact, is a "jealous" friend—knowing that our friendship with the world will bring pain, while our intimacy with Him brings blessings.

True friendship, which is learned in our relationship with the Lord, brings blessings:

- Friends deeply know one another—He knows you, and you make a priority of knowing Him (Jer. 1:5; Phil. 3:8).
- Friends initiate care for one another—He meets needs, speaks with you, and stays committed to you (Pss. 37:25; 85:8; 139:3; Phil. 4:19). You listen to what He says, try not to grieve Him, and celebrate His goodness toward you (1 Sam. 3:9; Ps. 100:2; Eph. 4:30).
- Friends vulnerably trust one another—In the Scripture, Christ shares His joys, hurts, and hopes (John 15:11, 18; 17:5). You share with Him your joys, hurts, and hopes (Jer. 33:3; Rom. 8:26).

GC2
GREAT COMMANDMENT
COMMISSION

INSIDE *the* INFLUENCERS

PILATE—Denial Is Not the Same As Innocence

Pilate was appointed governor of Judea by Emperor Tiberius from AD 26 until AD 36. He will be forever remembered as an ineffective leader who failed to assume responsibility when he said, "I am innocent of the blood of this just Person" (Matt. 27:24), even as he had the power to release Jesus. On that Thursday evening after Jesus and his disciples ate the Passover meal, known as the Last Supper, they made their way up the Mount of Olives to a place of solitude called the Garden of Gethsemane. It was there that he prayed until the early morning hours and was betrayed with a kiss.

The council of the Sanhedrin wanted Jesus dead, but they weren't authorized to deliver the death sentence, so they went to Pilate. He succumbed to mob psychology to try to retain his power, but ultimately lost it anyway. Pilate made several mistakes: he assumed the crowd would be rational and free Jesus, instead of a criminal. He also ignored his wife's warnings, his own conscience, and the evidence. He was in denial of the Truth when it was staring him right in the face.

Under Caligula, Pilate was exiled where legend claims that he spent years washing his hands in a water basin while proclaiming his innocence, until he committed suicide in about AD 38.

[7]The Jews answered him, "We have a law, and according to our[a] law He ought to die, because He made Himself the Son of God."

[8]Therefore, when Pilate heard that saying, he was the more afraid, [9]and went again into the Praetorium, and said to Jesus, "Where are You from?" But Jesus gave him no answer.

[10]Then Pilate said to Him, "Are You not speaking to me? Do You not know that I have power to crucify You, and power to release You?"

[11]Jesus answered, "You could have no power at all against Me unless it had been given you from above. Therefore the one who delivered Me to you has the greater sin."

[12]From then on Pilate sought to release Him, but the Jews cried out, saying, "If you let this Man go, you are not Caesar's friend. Whoever makes himself a king speaks against Caesar."

[13]When Pilate therefore heard that saying, he brought Jesus out and sat down in the judgment seat in a place that is called The Pavement, but in Hebrew, Gabbatha. [14]Now it was the Preparation Day of the Passover, and about the sixth hour. And he said to the Jews, "Behold your King!"

[15]But they cried out, "Away with *Him,* away with *Him!* Crucify Him!"

Pilate said to them, "Shall I crucify your King?"

The chief priests answered, "We have no king but Caesar!"

[16]Then he delivered Him to them to be crucified. Then they took Jesus and led *Him* away.[a]

The King on a Cross

[17]And He, bearing His cross, went out to a place called *the Place* of a Skull, which is called in Hebrew, Golgotha, [18]where they crucified Him, and two others with Him, one on either side, and Jesus in the center. [19]Now Pilate wrote a title and put *it* on the cross. And the writing was:

> JESUS OF NAZARETH,
> THE KING OF THE JEWS.

[20]Then many of the Jews read this title, for the place where Jesus was crucified was near the city; and it was written in Hebrew, Greek, *and* Latin.

[21]Therefore the chief priests of the Jews said

19:7 [a]NU-Text reads *the law.*   **19:16** [a]NU-Text omits *and led Him away.*

LEADERSHIP ISSUES

GC2: Hurt Is Inevitable

JOHN 16:33

It's not a matter of *if* we're going to be hurt, but rather *when,* and what are we going to do about it? Hurt can come from many sources: circumstances (illness, accidents); family members (parents, siblings, grandparents); friends; teachers; coaches; enemies. It seems ironic, but sometimes those closest to us can hurt us more frequently and more deeply than others can. This is because we are around them more often, and our hopes for those close to us are heightened. Hurt also takes many forms. Synonyms for hurt or trouble in this world might include phrases such as:

I was *disappointed* that my classmate didn't finish his part of our project.

I was *embarrassed* when I tripped and fell in front of my classmates.

I was *offended* at the racist remark that was made.

I felt *betrayed* when my friend spoke against me.

I was *frustrated* when my car wouldn't start.

I felt *abandoned* when my dad left the rest of us.

I felt *sad* on the first anniversary of my mother's death.

Incredibly, we have a great High Priest who can sympathize with our pain (Heb. 4:15), while being reminded of His own:

• Rejected in His family and His hometown—Mark 3:20, 21; 6:2–4
• Called demon-possessed by the Pharisees—John 10:20
• Insulted by His disciples—Matthew 26:6–9
• Disappointed by Philip—John 14:6–9
• Offended in the Upper Room at the Last Supper—Luke 22:24
• Unsupported in the Garden of Gethsemane—Mark 14:32–40
• Embarrassed on the cross—John 19:23
• Mocked, cursed, or blasphemed—Luke 23:36, 39

GC2

GREAT COMMANDMENT
COMMISSION

INSIDE *the* INFLUENCERS

MARY—Courage to Keep Believing

JOHN 19:23

She watched as her son hung between life and death on the cross, and the prophecy of Simeon in the temple became a reality: "a sword will pierce through your own soul" (Luke 2:35). The emotions flooded her heart: the fear of the future; the loneliness of Bethlehem; the joy of birth; the pain of watching Him leave home; the joy of His miracles; the pain of the angry crowd and the beatings; the peace of trusting God; and then the pain of watching Him die. And now, could Mary even dare to believe He would rise again? She wasn't at the grave; perhaps it was more than she could bear. But the angel said, "Do not be afraid," and her son, Jesus, taught, "Let not your heart be troubled; you believe in God, believe also in Me" (John 14:1).

Believing was all this mother could do now. The rest was out of her hands. She knew this day would come because Jesus spoke of His death often. He would have to bear the sins of the world, and she could do nothing to help with that. "It's not fair!" probably crossed her mind more than once. What we see about Mary is not that she was chosen to carry the baby Jesus, but that she was chosen to love Him, support Him, and mother Him. The courage it took to be by His side through the good and bad was something that only a woman of deep, passionate faith could have.

to Pilate, "Do not write, 'The King of the Jews,' but, 'He said, "I am the King of the Jews."'"

²²Pilate answered, "What I have written, I have written."

²³Then the soldiers, when they had crucified Jesus, took His garments and made four parts, to each soldier a part, and also the tunic. Now the tunic was without seam, woven from the top in one piece. ²⁴They said therefore among themselves, "Let us not tear it, but cast lots for it, whose it shall be," that the Scripture might be fulfilled which says:

"They divided My garments among them,
And for My clothing they cast lots."[a]

Therefore the soldiers did these things.

BEHOLD YOUR MOTHER

²⁵Now there stood by the cross of Jesus His mother, and His mother's sister, Mary the *wife* of Clopas, and Mary Magdalene. ²⁶When Jesus therefore saw His mother, and the disciple whom He loved standing by, He said to His mother,

"Woman, behold your son!" ²⁷Then He said to the disciple, "Behold your mother!" And from that hour that disciple took her to his own *home.*

IT IS FINISHED

²⁸After this, Jesus, knowing[a] that all things were now accomplished, that the Scripture might be fulfilled, said, "I thirst!" ²⁹Now a vessel full of sour wine was sitting there; and they filled a sponge with sour wine, put *it* on hyssop, and put *it* to His mouth. ³⁰So when Jesus had received the sour wine, He said, "It is finished!" And bowing His head, He gave up His spirit.

JESUS' SIDE IS PIERCED

³¹Therefore, because it was the Preparation *Day,* that the bodies should not remain on the cross on the Sabbath (for that Sabbath was a high day), the Jews asked Pilate that their legs might be broken, and *that* they might be taken away. ³²Then the soldiers came and broke the legs of the first and of the other who was crucified with Him. ³³But when they came to Jesus and saw that He

19:24 [a]Psalm 22:18   19:28 [a]M-Text reads *seeing.*

LEADERSHIP ISSUES

GC2: Unity: Christ's Prayer for Unity

JOHN 17:20, 21 *I do not pray for these alone, but also for those who will believe in Me through their word; that they all may be one, as You, Father, are in Me, and I in You; that they also may be one in Us, that the world may believe that You sent Me.*

Imagine this most sacred time in the Upper Room in Jerusalem. The Passover meal is finished. The Servant Christ has washed the feet of each disciple, and the betrayer has departed to complete his betrayal of the Messiah. Christ will soon be arrested, crucified, and buried; and three days later He will rise from the dead.

It's during these final moments together that Christ and His now eleven disciples must complete preparations for His death and for their leadership of the early church. Christ will provide instruction, encouragement, and hope in this "Upper Room Discourse," culminating in His longest recorded prayer (John 13—17.) It is during this John 17 prayer that we also see the personal relevance to our lives. Verse 20 records that this prayer is not just for these eleven disciples but also "for those who will believe in Me through their word." Imagine all the multitudes down through the ages who have put their trust in Christ because of the testimony of these eleven!

Are you not one of His disciples? If not, pause quietly even now to invite Him into your life: "Lord Jesus, thanks for loving me, praying for me, and desiring a relationship with me. I need You to forgive me and change me as You come into my life to make me part of Your family. Thank You for doing so even now; by faith I receive You as my Savior and Lord."

Now to each of us who belong to Christ, He has declared a critical ingredient in our lives as we follow Him: that we would live in oneness—without division, strife, jealousy, or pride—being diligent to mutually care for, yield to, and love one another (1 Cor. 12:24–27; Eph. 5:21; Gal. 5:13). And it will have divine results: "that the world may believe!" (John 17:21).

GC2
GREAT COMMANDMENT
COMMISSION

THROUGH THE GRID

Sharing Christ:
From Skepticism to Service

JOHN 19:38   *After this, Joseph of Arimathea, being a disciple of Jesus, but secretly, for fear of the Jews, asked Pilate that he might take away the body of Jesus; and Pilate gave him permission. So he came and took the body of Jesus.*

Nicodemus probably would not have been voted "most likely to believe" based on his earlier encounter with Jesus (John 3:1–21). This Pharisee may have felt fearful, insecure, concerned about his future, or embarrassed as he waited until dark to approach the Savior (v. 2). Within the safety of darkness, Nicodemus's questions exposed the uncertainties and misunderstandings of his heart. Christ patiently addressed the leader's questions, revealing His desire to bring change to this man's heart and life.

Something about this encounter with Christ piqued the curiosity of Nicodemus. We do not hear about his immediate conversion, but we do read of Nicodemus after Christ's death. We cannot be sure how often Nicodemus listened to the Master as He spoke to the crowds. We do not know how often he may have witnessed the miracles of Christ or sensed the Messiah's compassion. We do know, however, that these encounters likely occurred, because Nicodemus's life was transformed.

The same man, who had been afraid to go to Jesus during the light of day, was involved in asking permission to bury Jesus' body. Nicodemus and Joseph of Arimathea took the body away, prepared it for burial, and laid Jesus in the tomb (John 19:38–42). The one who had approached Christ in secrecy was now apparently willing to be identified with Him.

Pause now and consider any uncertainties or questions in your own heart. Have you, like Nicodemus, been afraid to boldly identify yourself with Christ? Have you been fearful, embarrassed, reluctant, skeptical, or insecure? Ask the Holy Spirit to empower you with the same power that transformed the life of Nicodemus. Ask Him to make the changes inside of you that prompted the bold steps of this religious leader. May the Spirit lead you to serve the Savior in courageous ways!

was already dead, they did not break His legs. [34]But one of the soldiers pierced His side with a spear, and immediately blood and water came out. [35]And he who has seen has testified, and his testimony is true; and he knows that he is telling the truth, so that you may believe. [36]For these things were done that the Scripture should be fulfilled, *"Not one of His bones shall be broken."*[a] [37]And again another Scripture says, *"They shall look on Him whom they pierced."*[a]

JESUS BURIED IN JOSEPH'S TOMB

[38]After this, Joseph of Arimathea, being a disciple of Jesus, but secretly, for fear of the Jews, asked Pilate that he might take away the body of Jesus; and Pilate gave *him* permission. So he came and took the body of Jesus. [39]And Nicodemus, who at first came to Jesus by night, also came,

19:36 [a]Exodus 12:46; Numbers 9:12; Psalm 34:20   **19:37** [a]Zechariah 12:10

LEADERSHIP ISSUES

GC2: Convictions: Truth Is a Person

JOHN 18:38   *Pilate said to Him, "What is truth?" And when he had said this, he went out again to the Jews, and said to them, "I find no fault in Him at all."*

Imagine for a moment that you are in that hall with Pilate and his prisoner. Imagine the words of the governor's question echoing off the marbled walls of that great hall. Imagine the expression of Pilate's face as he poses the question, scornful at first, then turning serious when the answer does not quickly come.

Seconds tick by. Still the prisoner and the governor study each other. Imagine the governor's thoughts: *Who is this Man? Why does He gaze at me so?* And the prisoner's thoughts: *Have I not just told you? I came to bring truth to the world. Pilate, you are looking at the answer to your own question: I am the truth* (John 14:6).

Pilate was not just *discussing* the truth in his Jerusalem palace the day he met Jesus; he was literally *looking* at it. Truth was standing before him, clothed in human flesh! Jesus Christ is the very embodiment and essence of absolute moral and spiritual truth itself. "And the Word became flesh and dwelt among us, and we beheld His glory, the glory as of the only begotten of the Father, full of grace and truth" (John 1:14).

Moral and spiritual truth isn't so much a concept as it is a person. It isn't so much something we believe as it is someone we relate to. Moral and spiritual truth has flesh. And, thus, truth is not just conceptual; it is intrinsically relational. Truth is a person!

To develop God-honoring convictions is to relate intimately to Jesus, the One who is truth.

GC2
GREAT COMMANDMENT
COMMISSION

bringing a mixture of myrrh and aloes, about a hundred pounds. ⁴⁰Then they took the body of Jesus, and bound it in strips of linen with the spices, as the custom of the Jews is to bury. ⁴¹Now in the place where He was crucified there was a garden, and in the garden a new tomb in which no one had yet been laid. ⁴²So there they laid Jesus, because of the Jews' Preparation *Day,* for the tomb was nearby.

THE EMPTY TOMB

20 Now the first *day* of the week Mary Magdalene went to the tomb early, while it was still dark, and saw *that* the stone had been taken away from the tomb. ²Then she ran and came to Simon Peter, and to the other disciple, whom Jesus loved, and said to them, "They have taken away the Lord out of the tomb, and we do not know where they have laid Him."

³Peter therefore went out, and the other disciple, and were going to the tomb. ⁴So they both ran together, and the other disciple outran Peter and came to the tomb first. ⁵And he, stooping down and looking in, saw the linen cloths lying *there;* yet he did not go in. ⁶Then Simon Peter came, following him, and went into the tomb; and he saw the linen cloths lying *there,* ⁷and the handkerchief that had been around His head, not lying with the linen cloths, but folded together in a place by itself. ⁸Then the other disciple, who came to the tomb first, went in also; and he saw and believed. ⁹For as yet they did not know the Scripture, that He must rise again from the dead. ¹⁰Then the disciples went away again to their own homes.

MARY MAGDALENE SEES THE RISEN LORD

¹¹But Mary stood outside by the tomb weeping, and as she wept she stooped down *and looked* into the tomb. ¹²And she saw two angels in white sitting, one at the head and the other at the feet, where the body of Jesus had lain. ¹³Then they said to her, "Woman, why are you weeping?"

She said to them, "Because they have taken away my Lord, and I do not know where they have laid Him."

¹⁴Now when she had said this, she turned around and saw Jesus standing *there,* and did not know that it was Jesus. ¹⁵Jesus said to her,

"Woman, why are you weeping? Whom are you seeking?"

She, supposing Him to be the gardener, said to Him, "Sir, if You have carried Him away, tell me where You have laid Him, and I will take Him away."

¹⁶Jesus said to her, "Mary!"

She turned and said to Him,ᵃ "Rabboni!" (which is to say, Teacher).

¹⁷Jesus said to her, "Do not cling to Me, for I have not yet ascended to My Father; but go to My brethren and say to them, 'I am ascending to My Father and your Father, and *to* My God and your God.' "

¹⁸Mary Magdalene came and told the disciples that she had seen the Lord,ᵃ and *that* He had spoken these things to her.

THE APOSTLES COMMISSIONED

¹⁹Then, the same day at evening, being the first *day* of the week, when the doors were shut where the disciples were assembled,ᵃ for fear of the Jews, Jesus came and stood in the midst, and said to them, "Peace *be* with you." ²⁰When He had said this, He showed them *His* hands and His side. Then the disciples were glad when they saw the Lord.

²¹So Jesus said to them again, "Peace to you! As the Father has sent Me, I also send you." ²²And when He had said this, He breathed on *them,* and said to them, "Receive the Holy Spirit. ²³If you forgive the sins of any, they are forgiven them; if you retain the *sins* of any, they are retained."

SEEING AND BELIEVING

²⁴Now Thomas, called the Twin, one of the twelve, was not with them when Jesus came. ²⁵The other disciples therefore said to him, "We have seen the Lord."

So he said to them, "Unless I see in His hands the print of the nails, and put my finger into the print of the nails, and put my hand into His side, I will not believe."

²⁶And after eight days His disciples were again inside, and Thomas with them. Jesus came, the doors being shut, and stood in the midst, and said, "Peace to you!" ²⁷Then He said to Thomas,

20:16 ᵃNU-Text adds *in Hebrew.*   20:18 ᵃNU-Text reads *disciples, "I have seen the Lord," . . .*   20:19 ᵃNU-Text omits *assembled.*

LEADERSHIP ISSUES

Restoration of Leadership Is Good News

JOHN 21:4–6, 9–12

Like most leaders, once Peter had time to think about what he had done, he was sad and began to suffer the consequences of his choice—spiritual emptiness and discouragement. Unfortunately, when he stopped following Jesus, he led others to do the same. He went from fisherman to "fisher of men" and back again. There is a happy ending to this poor choice, however. Jesus forgave Peter and restored him to intimacy through a personal encounter. The disciples may have been angry, refused to talk to Peter, and some probably gossiped about him; but that is not the case with Jesus.

Jesus came and found Peter. The God we love and serve, the One who desires so intensely to be with us, comes to us even when we have sinned. Jesus wanted to be restored to Peter, just as Peter wanted to be restored to Him. Jesus showed His power by providing a huge catch of fish, but He showed personal love by serving Him a personally cooked breakfast. He could have spoken the breakfast into existence; but the Scripture specifically says He cooked it, once again demonstrating His personal involvement in our lives.

Peter's life was reclaimed for godly influence by the unconditional love of God. He takes our sinful choices, uses them for His glory, writes a story for others to learn from, and leaves them for future generations to remember. God used the denial in Peter's life, to completely transform and embolden him in a way that he might have never known before. That doesn't make his mistake OK, but it does show the power of Christ to redeem a wrong choice. We can know that Peter's repentance was real and not a show because his behavior changed, and once again, he became a fisher of men. He finished his ministry with persecution and crucifixion; he became a martyr for Christ—a sharp contrast to the earlier betrayal.

THROUGH THE GRID

*Thinking Christianly: Specific
Evidences for the Resurrection
of Jesus (John 20)*

There are several specific pieces of evidence that attest to the historical and bodily resurrection of Jesus from the dead:

- Naturalistic theories fail to explain away the event and have been disproved or rejected.
- The arguments from subjective and personal experiences by Christians around the globe throughout history also attest to the pragmatic power of the living Christ.
- Christianity would not be such a strong religion if it were not true—Jesus' resurrection gave birth to Christianity; and from its earliest days, the church held the Resurrection as central.
- The Jews who believed in Christ changed the Sabbath day from Saturday to Sunday (the day Christ was resurrected).
- The first witnesses of the risen Jesus were women, though the witness of women was generally invalidated by their social status in that time.
- There was a radical change to the disciples, who held new power, new courage, and were faithful to Christ and His message until death.
- The moral character of the eyewitnesses suggests that they would not have lied about witnessing such an appearance.
- Of course, the tomb is empty, and there is no body of Jesus to be found anywhere. Jesus had numerous and various post-Resurrection appearances. Also, it is unlikely that a group of people would all share the same hallucination.
- The multitude of fulfilled Old Testament prophecies points to the reality of Christ's resurrection (Gen. 49:10; 2 Sam. 7:12; Ps. 22; Is. 7:14; 52:13—53:12; Mic. 5:2).
- The Jewish leaders could not disprove the message.
- Two skeptics were converted: James and Paul.
- Then, there are the accepted character and claims of Jesus, in which He claimed to be God; and He claimed that He would rise (John 5:58; 10:30; 14:9).
- The articles of clothing left in the tomb also testify to the risen nature of Jesus (John 20:5).
- The Resurrection was something that was very unexpected, and it would be a far-fetched claim to make if not true.
- And finally, eyewitness documents record the facts of the Resurrection.

These evidences provide a solid foundational ground for establishing the reality of the historical event of Jesus' death and consequent resurrection from the dead. The Christian hope hinges on the Resurrection, in which God defeats death and makes redemption available to all.

"Reach your finger here, and look at My hands; and reach your hand *here,* and put *it* into My side. Do not be unbelieving, but believing."

28And Thomas answered and said to Him, "My Lord and my God!"

29Jesus said to him, "Thomas,ᵃ because you have seen Me, you have believed. Blessed *are* those who have not seen and *yet* have believed."

THAT YOU MAY BELIEVE

30And truly Jesus did many other signs in the presence of His disciples, which are not written in this book; 31but these are written that you may believe that Jesus is the Christ, the Son of God, and that believing you may have life in His name.

BREAKFAST BY THE SEA

21 After these things Jesus showed Himself again to the disciples at the Sea of Tiberias, and in this way He showed *Himself:* 2Simon Peter, Thomas called the Twin, Nathanael of Cana in Galilee, the *sons* of Zebedee, and two others of His disciples were together. 3Simon Peter said to them, "I am going fishing."

They said to him, "We are going with you also." They went out and immediatelyᵃ got into the boat, and that night they caught nothing. 4But when the morning had now come, Jesus stood on the shore; yet the disciples did not know that it was Jesus. 5Then Jesus said to them, "Children, have you any food?"

They answered Him, "No."

6And He said to them, "Cast the net on the right side of the boat, and you will find *some.*" So they cast, and now they were not able to draw it in because of the multitude of fish.

7Therefore that disciple whom Jesus loved said to Peter, "It is the Lord!" Now when Simon Peter heard that it was the Lord, he put on *his* outer garment (for he had removed it), and plunged into the sea. 8But the other disciples came in the little boat (for they were not far from land, but about two hundred cubits), dragging the net with fish. 9Then, as soon as they had come to land, they saw a fire of coals there, and fish laid on it, and bread. 10Jesus said to them, "Bring some of the fish which you have just caught."

11Simon Peter went up and dragged the net to land, full of large fish, one hundred and fifty-

three; and although there were so many, the net was not broken. 12Jesus said to them, "Come *and* eat breakfast." Yet none of the disciples dared ask Him, "Who are You?"—knowing that it was the Lord. 13Jesus then came and took the bread and gave it to them, and likewise the fish.

14This *is* now the third time Jesus showed Himself to His disciples after He was raised from the dead.

JESUS RESTORES PETER

15So when they had eaten breakfast, Jesus said to Simon Peter, "Simon, *son* of Jonah,ᵃ do you love Me more than these?"

He said to Him, "Yes, Lord; You know that I love You."

He said to him, "Feed My lambs."

16He said to him again a second time, "Simon, *son* of Jonah,ᵃ do you love Me?"

He said to Him, "Yes, Lord; You know that I love You."

He said to him, "Tend My sheep."

17He said to him the third time, "Simon, *son* of Jonah,ᵃ do you love Me?" Peter was grieved because He said to him the third time, "Do you love Me?"

And he said to Him, "Lord, You know all things; You know that I love You."

Jesus said to him, "Feed My sheep. 18Most assuredly, I say to you, when you were younger, you girded yourself and walked where you wished; but when you are old, you will stretch out your hands, and another will gird you and carry *you* where you do not wish." 19This He spoke, signifying by what death he would glorify God. And when He had spoken this, He said to him, "Follow Me."

THE BELOVED DISCIPLE AND HIS BOOK

20Then Peter, turning around, saw the disciple whom Jesus loved following, who also had leaned on His breast at the supper, and said, "Lord, who is the one who betrays You?" 21Peter, seeing him, said to Jesus, "But Lord, what *about* this man?"

22Jesus said to him, "If I will that he remain till I come, what *is that* to you? You follow Me."

20:29 ᵃNU-Text and M-Text omit *Thomas.* **21:3** ᵃNU-Text omits *immediately.* **21:15** ᵃNU-Text reads *John.* **21:16** ᵃNU-Text reads *John.* **21:17** ᵃNU-Text reads *John.*

[23]Then this saying went out among the brethren that this disciple would not die. Yet Jesus did not say to him that he would not die, but, "If I will that he remain till I come, what *is that* to you?"

[24]This is the disciple who testifies of these things, and wrote these things; and we know that his testimony is true.

[25]And there are also many other things that Jesus did, which if they were written one by one, I suppose that even the world itself could not contain the books that would be written. Amen.

IMPACT OF THE BOOK

A C T S

I   **IDEA**

Christianity spreads by the work of the Holy Spirit through the devoted and faithful followers of Jesus.

M   **MESSAGE**

The early church spread because the leaders were committed to living the teachings of Christ, sharing them with others, and teaching others how to share the teachings. They were multiplying rapidly. However, they were careful in choosing leaders, knowing that a bad or sinful leader could have disastrous results. The Holy Spirit led and energized these followers causing brokenness and boldness. Luke tells of the struggles that the leaders had with division over what to do with Gentiles and their reluctance to leave Jerusalem.

P   **PEOPLE**

Agrippa, Apollos, Aquila, Barnabas, Festus, Luke, Lydia, Paul, Peter, Philip, Silas, Stephen, Timothy

A   **AUTHOR**

Luke, the physician and author of the Gospel of Luke, was an eyewitness to the missionary thrust of the early church and was especially familiar with Paul's journeys to the major cities dotting the coasts and islands of the Mediterranean and Aegean Seas.

C   **CULTURE**

Acts was a sequel to the Gospel of Luke. During the first century, the two books likely circulated as a two-volume set. Early in the second century, the two works separated, and Luke became identified with the other three Gospels. The Book of Acts extends Luke's carefully investigated narrative of the life and teachings of Jesus to include the early church's history. Acts is also addressed to Theophilus. The identity of Theophilus remains a mystery; he could have been a new convert in need of full knowledge concerning the origins of Christianity, or he could have been an interested Greek whom Luke hoped to convert to Christ.

T   **TIMELINE**

c. AD 59–61

KEY SCRIPTURE MEMORY VERSES

1:8; 2:42–47; 4:12; 17:11

PROLOGUE

1 The former account I made, O Theophilus, of all that Jesus began both to do and teach, [2]until the day in which He was taken up, after He through the Holy Spirit had given commandments to the apostles whom He had chosen, [3]to whom He also presented Himself alive after His suffering by many infallible proofs, being seen by them during forty days and speaking of the things pertaining to the kingdom of God.

THE HOLY SPIRIT PROMISED

[4]And being assembled together with *them,* He commanded them not to depart from Jerusalem, but to wait for the Promise of the Father, "which," *He said,* "you have heard from Me; [5]for John truly baptized with water, but you shall be baptized with the Holy Spirit not many days from now." [6]Therefore, when they had come together, they asked Him, saying, "Lord, will You at this time restore the kingdom to Israel?" [7]And He said to them, "It is not for you to know times or seasons which the Father has put in His own authority. [8]But you shall receive power when the Holy Spirit has come upon you; and you shall be witnesses to Me[a] in Jerusalem, and in all Judea and Samaria, and to the end of the earth."

JESUS ASCENDS TO HEAVEN

[9]Now when He had spoken these things, while they watched, He was taken up, and a cloud received Him out of their sight. [10]And while they looked steadfastly toward heaven as He went up, behold, two men stood by them in white apparel, [11]who also said, "Men of Galilee, why do you stand gazing up into heaven? This *same* Jesus, who was taken up from you into heaven, will so come in like manner as you saw Him go into heaven."

THE UPPER ROOM PRAYER MEETING

[12]Then they returned to Jerusalem from the mount called Olivet, which is near Jerusalem, a Sabbath day's journey. [13]And when they had entered, they went up into the upper room where they were staying: Peter, James, John, and Andrew; Philip and Thomas; Bartholomew and Matthew; James *the son* of Alphaeus and Simon the Zealot; and Judas *the son* of James. [14]These all continued with one accord in prayer and supplication,[a] with the women and Mary the mother of Jesus, and with His brothers.

MATTHIAS CHOSEN

[15]And in those days Peter stood up in the midst of the disciples[a] (altogether the number of names was about a hundred and twenty), and said, [16]"Men *and* brethren, this Scripture had to be fulfilled, which the Holy Spirit spoke before by the mouth of David concerning Judas, who became a guide to those who arrested Jesus; [17]for he was numbered with us and obtained a part in this ministry."

[18](Now this man purchased a field with the wages of iniquity; and falling headlong, he burst open in the middle and all his entrails gushed out. [19]And it became known to all those dwelling in Jerusalem; so that field is called in their own language, Akel Dama, that is, Field of Blood.)

[20]"For it is written in the Book of Psalms:

> 'Let his dwelling place be desolate,
> And let no one live in it';[a]

and,

1:8 [a]NU-Text reads *My witnesses.*   1:14 [a]NU-Text omits *and supplication.*   1:15 [a]NU-Text reads *brethren.*   1:20 [a]Psalm 69:25

THROUGH THE GRID

Making Sense of Your World:
Humanity as God's Agents (Acts 1:16)

God inspired the biblical authors to write the Scriptures through the Holy Spirit, who guided the authors to produce the Scripture that God desired to produce in order to communicate with humanity through the agents. Of course, human beings are imperfect agents; but with the help of the Holy Spirit, these human limitations were overcome to preserve Scripture.

LEADERSHIP ISSUES

GC2: Sharing Christ: Empowered to Be a Witness

ACTS 1:8   *You shall be witnesses to Me.*

Living out a passionate love for God and gratefully embracing our identity as the "beloved of God" will flow outwardly in our love of others, specifically as we share His Good News in the power of the Holy Spirit. What is our Good News?

- Love comes from God, and "God is love" (1 John 4:7, 8).
- God is intimately acquainted (caringly involved) with all our ways (Ps. 139:3).
- God longs to show us grace and rises to share with us compassion (Is. 30:18)
- God in Christ has made complete provision for our sin that keeps us alone—separated from God and others around us (Rom. 3:23; 6:23).
- His abundant life can be ours both now and for eternity (John 10:10).
- "Whoever calls on the name of the LORD shall be saved" (Rom. 10:13).

As you consider sharing the Good News of Christ's love with those around you, offer the following prayer in closing:

"Jesus, I need You. I receive Your forgiveness and Your love. I receive Your care and acceptance of me. I give to You my life, my future, my all. Thank You for loving me, forgiving me, and changing me. I yield to Your Spirit within me. Change me so that I may express You to others around me. In Your name, Amen."

GC2
GREAT COMMANDMENT
COMMISSION

'Let[b] *another take his office.'*[c]

[21]"Therefore, of these men who have accompanied us all the time that the Lord Jesus went in and out among us, [22]beginning from the baptism of John to that day when He was taken up from us, one of these must become a witness with us of His resurrection."

[23]And they proposed two: Joseph called Barsabas, who was surnamed Justus, and Matthias. [24]And they prayed and said, "You, O Lord, who know the hearts of all, show which of these two You have chosen [25]to take part in this ministry and apostleship from which Judas by transgression fell, that he might go to his own place." [26]And they cast their lots, and the lot fell on Matthias. And he was numbered with the eleven apostles.

COMING OF THE HOLY SPIRIT

2 When the Day of Pentecost had fully come, they were all with one accord[a] in one place. [2]And suddenly there came a sound from heaven, as of a rushing mighty wind, and it filled the whole house where they were sitting. [3]Then there appeared to them divided tongues, as of fire, and *one* sat upon each of them. [4]And they were all filled with the Holy Spirit and began to speak with other tongues, as the Spirit gave them utterance.

THE CROWD'S RESPONSE

[5]And there were dwelling in Jerusalem Jews, devout men, from every nation under heaven. [6]And when this sound occurred, the multitude came together, and were confused, because everyone heard them speak in his own language. [7]Then they were all amazed and marveled, saying to one another, "Look, are not all these who speak Galileans? [8]And how *is it that* we hear, each in our own language in which we were born? [9]Parthians and Medes and Elamites, those dwelling in Mesopotamia, Judea and Cappadocia, Pontus and Asia, [10]Phrygia and Pamphylia, Egypt and the parts of Libya adjoining Cyrene, visitors from Rome, both Jews and proselytes, [11]Cretans and Arabs—we hear them speaking in our own tongues the wonderful works of God." [12]So they

were all amazed and perplexed, saying to one another, "Whatever could this mean?"

[13]Others mocking said, "They are full of new wine."

PETER'S SERMON

[14]But Peter, standing up with the eleven, raised his voice and said to them, "Men of Judea and all who dwell in Jerusalem, let this be known to you, and heed my words. [15]For these are not drunk, as you suppose, since it is *only* the third hour of the day. [16]But this is what was spoken by the prophet Joel:

[17] *'And it shall come to pass in the last days, says*
　　 God,
　　　 That I will pour out of My Spirit on all flesh;
　　　 Your sons and your daughters shall prophesy,
　　　 Your young men shall see visions,
　　　 Your old men shall dream dreams.
[18] *And on My menservants and on My*
　　　 maidservants
　　　 I will pour out My Spirit in those days;
　　　 And they shall prophesy.
[19] *I will show wonders in heaven above*
　　　 And signs in the earth beneath:
　　　 Blood and fire and vapor of smoke.
[20] *The sun shall be turned into darkness,*
　　　 And the moon into blood,
　　　 Before the coming of the great and awesome
　　　　 day of the LORD.
[21] *And it shall come to pass*
　　　 That whoever calls on the name of the LORD
　　　 Shall be saved.'[a]

[22]"Men of Israel, hear these words: Jesus of Nazareth, a Man attested by God to you by miracles, wonders, and signs which God did through Him in your midst, as you yourselves also know— [23]Him, being delivered by the determined purpose and foreknowledge of God, you have taken[a] by lawless hands, have crucified, and put to death; [24]whom God raised up, having loosed the pains of death, because it was not possible that He should be held by it. [25]For David says concerning Him:

1:20 [b]Psalm 109:8　[c]Greek *episkopen*, position of overseer
2:1 [a]NU-Text reads *together.*　**2:21** [a]Joel 2:28–32　**2:23** [a]NU-Text omits *have taken.*

'I foresaw the Lord always before my face,
For He is at my right hand, that I may not be
   shaken.
²⁶*Therefore my heart rejoiced, and my tongue*
   was glad;
Moreover my flesh also will rest in hope.
²⁷*For You will not leave my soul in Hades,*
Nor will You allow Your Holy One to see
   corruption.
²⁸*You have made known to me the ways of*
   life;
You will make me full of joy in Your
   *presence.'*ᵃ

²⁹"Men *and* brethren, let *me* speak freely to you of the patriarch David, that he is both dead and buried, and his tomb is with us to this day. ³⁰Therefore, being a prophet, and knowing that God had sworn with an oath to him that of the fruit of his body, according to the flesh, He would raise up the Christ to sit on his throne,ᵃ ³¹he, foreseeing this, spoke concerning the resurrection of the Christ, that His soul was not left in Hades, nor did His flesh see corruption. ³²This Jesus God has raised up, of which we are all witnesses. ³³Therefore being exalted to the right hand of God, and having received from the Father the promise of the Holy Spirit, He poured out this which you now see and hear. ³⁴"For David did not ascend into the heavens, but he says himself:

The Lord said to my Lord,
"Sit at My right hand,
³⁵*Till I make Your enemies Your footstool."'*ᵃ

³⁶"Therefore let all the house of Israel know assuredly that God has made this Jesus, whom you crucified, both Lord and Christ."

³⁷Now when they heard *this,* they were cut to the heart, and said to Peter and the rest of the apostles, "Men *and* brethren, what shall we do?" ³⁸Then Peter said to them, "Repent, and let every one of you be baptized in the name of Jesus Christ for the remission of sins; and you shall receive the gift of the Holy Spirit. ³⁹For the promise is to you and to your children, and to all who are afar off, as many as the Lord our God will call."

A Vital Church Grows

⁴⁰And with many other words he testified and exhorted them, saying, "Be saved from this perverse generation." ⁴¹Then those who gladlyᵃ received his word were baptized; and that day about three thousand souls were added *to them.* ⁴²And they continued steadfastly in the apostles' doctrine and fellowship, in the breaking of bread, and in prayers. ⁴³Then fear came upon every soul, and many wonders and signs were done through the apostles. ⁴⁴Now all who believed were together, and had all things in common, ⁴⁵and sold their possessions and goods, and divided them among all, as anyone had need.

⁴⁶So continuing daily with one accord in the temple, and breaking bread from house to house, they ate their food with gladness and simplicity of heart, ⁴⁷praising God and having favor with all the people. And the Lord added to the churchᵃ daily those who were being saved.

A Lame Man Healed

3 Now Peter and John went up together to the temple at the hour of prayer, the ninth *hour.* ²And a certain man lame from his mother's womb was carried, whom they laid daily at the gate of the temple which is called Beautiful, to ask alms from those who entered the temple; ³who, seeing Peter and John about to go into the temple, asked for alms. ⁴And fixing his eyes on him, with John, Peter said, "Look at us." ⁵So he gave them his attention, expecting to receive something from them. ⁶Then Peter said, "Silver and gold I do not have, but what I do have I give you: In the name of Jesus Christ of Nazareth, rise up and walk." ⁷And he took him by the right hand and lifted *him* up, and immediately his feet and ankle bones received strength. ⁸So he, leaping up, stood and walked and entered the temple with them— walking, leaping, and praising God. ⁹And all the people saw him walking and praising God. ¹⁰Then they knew that it was he who sat begging alms at the Beautiful Gate of the temple; and they were filled with wonder and amazement at what had happened to him.

2:28 ᵃPsalm 16:8–11   **2:30** ᵃNU-Text omits *according to the flesh, He would raise up the Christ* and completes the verse with *He would seat one on his throne.*   **2:35** ᵃPsalm 110:1   **2:41** ᵃNU-Text omits *gladly.*   **2:47** ᵃNU-Text omits *to the church.*

LEADERSHIP ISSUES

Ministry Outside the Gate

ACTS 3

Peter and John arrived for prayer and entered through the "gate of the temple which is called Beautiful." The entryway was lined with those who were sick, disabled, poor, or in need. They knew the "religious" leaders would walk by and possibly give money. For some religious leaders, it was a place to be seen as compassionate.

One particular day, Peter stopped and spoke to one man. Perhaps he was in a blur of activity, rushing to events and places. The early church was growing, and there was much to do. As Peter passed through the sick, hurting, and needy people on the way to synagogue, he heard only one voice in the crowd.

As a leader, try to hear that one voice God is calling you to touch in the midst of the hurry and noise. The quiet whispers from the Holy Spirit urge us to listen. Peter and John, in tune with the Holy Spirit, stopped and responded in obedience. The beggar asked for a small token, but they give him more—the hope and healing of Christ. Peter and John's obedience to the Spirit caused a great stirring among the crowds. Peter seized the moment and began to speak of the glorified Servant Jesus.

This true account urges leaders to listen for the whisper of the Spirit and to be ready to respond in anticipation of the opportunity to glorify God. Each time we hear the whisper but do not answer, we give up an opportunity to speak in His name.

Often, we are so busy going to the "place of prayer" that we miss the ministry outside the "gate." It could be in the neighborhood, on the drive to school, or at lunch where many lonely people sit waiting. We sometimes need reminding that the "church" is not just a place, an institution, a program, a logo, or any one person alone. The Holy Spirit doesn't need a building in which to speak. We are the church, and He waits for us to listen and respond so He can do His work through us anywhere.

Preaching in Solomon's Portico

[11]Now as the lame man who was healed held on to Peter and John, all the people ran together to them in the porch which is called Solomon's, greatly amazed. [12]So when Peter saw *it*, he responded to the people: "Men of Israel, why do you marvel at this? Or why look so intently at us, as though by our own power or godliness we had made this man walk? [13]The God of Abraham, Isaac, and Jacob, the God of our fathers, glorified His Servant Jesus, whom you delivered up and denied in the presence of Pilate, when he was determined to let *Him* go. [14]But you denied the Holy One and the Just, and asked for a murderer to be granted to you, [15]and killed the Prince of life, whom God raised from the dead, of which we are witnesses. [16]And His name, through faith in His name, has made this man strong, whom you see and know. Yes, the faith which *comes* through Him has given him this perfect soundness in the presence of you all.

[17]"Yet now, brethren, I know that you did *it* in ignorance, as *did* also your rulers. [18]But those things which God foretold by the mouth of all His prophets, that the Christ would suffer, He has thus fulfilled. [19]Repent therefore and be converted, that your sins may be blotted out, so that times of refreshing may come from the presence of the Lord, [20]and that He may send Jesus Christ, who was preached to you before,[a] [21]whom heaven must receive until the times of restoration of all things, which God has spoken by the mouth of all His holy prophets since the world began. [22]For Moses truly said to the fathers, 'The Lord your God will raise up for you a Prophet like me from your brethren. Him you shall hear in all things, whatever He says to you. [23]And it shall be that every soul who will not hear that Prophet shall be utterly destroyed from among the people.'[a] [24]Yes, and all the prophets, from Samuel and those who follow, as many as have spoken, have also foretold[a] these days. [25]You are sons of the prophets, and of the covenant which God made with our fathers, saying to Abraham, 'And in your seed all the families of the earth shall be blessed.'[a] [26]To you first, God, having raised up His Servant Jesus, sent Him to bless you, in turning away every one *of you* from your iniquities."

Peter and John Arrested

4 Now as they spoke to the people, the priests, the captain of the temple, and the Sadducees came upon them, [2]being greatly disturbed that they taught the people and preached in Jesus the resurrection from the dead. [3]And they laid hands on them, and put *them* in custody until the next day, for it was already evening. [4]However, many of those who heard the word believed; and the number of the men came to be about five thousand.

Addressing the Sanhedrin

[5]And it came to pass, on the next day, that their rulers, elders, and scribes, [6]as well as Annas the high priest, Caiaphas, John, and Alexander, and as many as were of the family of the high priest, were gathered together at Jerusalem. [7]And when they had set them in the midst, they asked, "By what power or by what name have you done this?"

[8]Then Peter, filled with the Holy Spirit, said to them, "Rulers of the people and elders of Israel: [9]If we this day are judged for a good deed *done* to a helpless man, by what means he has been made well, [10]let it be known to you all, and to all the people of Israel, that by the name of Jesus Christ of Nazareth, whom you crucified, whom God raised from the dead, by Him this man stands here before you whole. [11]This is the *'stone which was rejected by you builders, which has become the chief cornerstone.'*[a] [12]Nor is there salvation in any other, for there is no other name under heaven given among men by which we must be saved."

The Name of Jesus Forbidden

[13]Now when they saw the boldness of Peter and John, and perceived that they were uneducated and untrained men, they marveled. And they realized that they had been with Jesus. [14]And seeing the man who had been healed standing with them, they could say nothing against it. [15]But when they had commanded them to go aside out of the council, they conferred among themselves, [16]saying, "What shall we do to these

3:20 [a]NU-Text and M-Text read *Christ Jesus, who was ordained for you before.* **3:23** [a]Deuteronomy 18:15, 18, 19 **3:24** [a]NU-Text and M-Text read *proclaimed.* **3:25** [a]Genesis 22:18; 26:4; 28:14 **4:11** [a]Psalm 118:22

THROUGH THE GRID
*Thinking Christianly:
Four Sources of Authority*

Everyone draws from four sources of authority:

1. Reason: How I think
2. Experience: How I feel
3. Tradition: How it's always been done
4. Scripture: God's Word, our ultimate authority

---

men? For, indeed, that a notable miracle has been done through them *is* evident to all who dwell in Jerusalem, and we cannot deny it. [17]But so that it spreads no further among the people, let us severely threaten them, that from now on they speak to no man in this name."

[18]So they called them and commanded them not to speak at all nor teach in the name of Jesus. [19]But Peter and John answered and said to them, "Whether it is right in the sight of God to listen to you more than to God, you judge. [20]For we cannot but speak the things which we have seen and heard." [21]So when they had further threatened them, they let them go, finding no way of punishing them, because of the people, since they all glorified God for what had been done. [22]For the man was over forty years old on whom this miracle of healing had been performed.

PRAYER FOR BOLDNESS

[23]And being let go, they went to their own *companions* and reported all that the chief priests and elders had said to them. [24]So when they heard that, they raised their voice to God with one accord and said: "Lord, You *are* God, who made heaven and earth and the sea, and all that is in them, [25]who by the mouth of Your servant David[a] have said:

'Why did the nations rage,
  And the people plot vain things?
[26]The kings of the earth took their stand,
  And the rulers were gathered together
  Against the LORD and against His Christ.'[a]

[27]"For truly against Your holy Servant Jesus, whom You anointed, both Herod and Pontius Pi-

late, with the Gentiles and the people of Israel, were gathered together [28]to do whatever Your hand and Your purpose determined before to be done. [29]Now, Lord, look on their threats, and grant to Your servants that with all boldness they may speak Your word, [30]by stretching out Your hand to heal, and that signs and wonders may be done through the name of Your holy Servant Jesus."

[31]And when they had prayed, the place where they were assembled together was shaken; and they were all filled with the Holy Spirit, and they spoke the word of God with boldness.

SHARING IN ALL THINGS

[32]Now the multitude of those who believed were of one heart and one soul; neither did anyone say that any of the things he possessed was his own, but they had all things in common. [33]And with great power the apostles gave witness to the resurrection of the Lord Jesus. And great grace was upon them all. [34]Nor was there anyone among them who lacked; for all who were possessors of lands or houses sold them, and brought the proceeds of the things that were sold, [35]and laid *them* at the apostles' feet; and they distributed to each as anyone had need.

[36]And Joses,[a] who was also named Barnabas by the apostles (which is translated Son of Encouragement), a Levite of the country of Cyprus, [37]having land, sold *it*, and brought the money and laid *it* at the apostles' feet.

4:25 [a]NU-Text reads *who through the Holy Spirit, by the mouth of our father, Your servant David.* **4:26** [a]Psalm 2:1, 2 **4:36** [a]NU-Text reads *Joseph.*

LEADERSHIP ISSUES

Evangelism Through Prayer

ACTS 4:29–31

Our primary tool in effective witnessing is prayer. All power comes through prayer. When we pray, we are trusting God to draw men to Himself. The early Christians knew this. In Acts 4:29–31, we see that their prayers were not about their own problems; rather, they prayed for boldness and power, so they would not fail in proclaiming Christ. In verse 31, God answered their prayers by allowing them to speak the gospel with boldness so that none could stand against them.

We must understand the power to change lives is not ours. It doesn't matter how polished our presentation of the gospel is, how authentic our lifestyle is, or how much knowledge we have about the Bible. The power to boldly proclaim Christ and see lives changed comes from the Spirit of God who opens people's hearts to hear the message of Christ (John 6:44). We have the privilege of being coworkers with God in building His kingdom. Our job in this process is to pray for non-Christians and to be obedient to the Spirit when He opens doors to share our faith. In regard to non-Christians, pray that:

- God draws them to Himself (John 6:44);
- They will seek to know God (Deut. 4:29);
- They will believe the Scriptures (1 Thess. 2:13);
- Satan is bound from blinding them to the truth (Matt. 13:19);
- The Holy Spirit will work in them (John 16:8–13);
- God will send, if not you, someone to lead them to Christ (Matt. 9:37, 38);
- They will believe Christ is the Savior (John 1:12);
- They will turn from their sin (Acts 17:30, 31);
- They will confess Christ as Lord (Rom. 10:9, 10);
- They will surrender all to follow Him (Phil. 3:7, 8).

LEADERSHIP
REALITIES

COMMUNITY: IF YOU GO, WE ALL GO
ACTS 4:32–37

The New Testament church is about a cooperative spirit. Without a group of other Christians to sharpen and challenge on a consistent basis, the follower of God is prone to drift. The Book of Acts paints a portrait of the early life of the church and provides certain characteristics of community. One cannot help but get the sense the early church believed "as one goes, we all go." The leader is able to understand this principle and to demonstrate to the group that each person's role is essential to the health and success of that cooperation. The leader who is not attached to a community of other believers will become an unspiritual Christian. This text teaches four common denominators to community:

miva—**agree**—"one" heart and soul

- There was unity of mind and heart because each was governed by the Holy Spirit (v. 32).
- The atmosphere was absent from any sense of entitlements (v. 32).
- There was great power when proclaiming the gospel of Christ (v. 33).
- There was an intense responsibility that all physical needs were met (vv. 34–37).

LYING TO THE HOLY SPIRIT

5 But a certain man named Ananias, with Sapphira his wife, sold a possession. ²And he kept back *part* of the proceeds, his wife also being aware *of it,* and brought a certain part and laid *it* at the apostles' feet. ³But Peter said, "Ananias, why has Satan filled your heart to lie to the Holy Spirit and keep back *part* of the price of the land for yourself? ⁴While it remained, was it not your own? And after it was sold, was it not in your own control? Why have you conceived this thing in your heart? You have not lied to men but to God."

⁵Then Ananias, hearing these words, fell down and breathed his last. So great fear came upon all those who heard these things. ⁶And the young men arose and wrapped him up, carried *him* out, and buried *him.*

⁷Now it was about three hours later when his wife came in, not knowing what had happened. ⁸And Peter answered her, "Tell me whether you sold the land for so much?"

She said, "Yes, for so much."

⁹Then Peter said to her, "How is it that you have agreed together to test the Spirit of the Lord? Look, the feet of those who have buried your husband *are* at the door, and they will carry you out." ¹⁰Then immediately she fell down at his feet and breathed her last. And the young men came in and found her dead, and carrying *her* out, buried *her* by her husband. ¹¹So great fear came upon all the church and upon all who heard these things.

CONTINUING POWER IN THE CHURCH

¹²And through the hands of the apostles many signs and wonders were done among the people. And they were all with one accord in Solomon's Porch. ¹³Yet none of the rest dared join them, but the people esteemed them highly. ¹⁴And believers were increasingly added to the Lord, multitudes of both men and women, ¹⁵so that they brought the sick out into the streets and laid *them* on beds and couches, that at least the shadow of Peter passing by might fall on some of them. ¹⁶Also a multitude gathered from the surrounding cities to Jerusalem, bringing sick people and those who were tormented by unclean spirits, and they were all healed.

LEADERSHIP ISSUES

GC2: Unity: First-Century Unity

ACTS 4:32

In fulfillment of Christ's prayer for unity, the first-century world was turned "upside down" (Acts 17:6) by faithful followers of Jesus as they lived out their "oneness" of heart and soul (John 17:20, 21). Unity among Christ's followers doesn't just happen; it must be pursued and protected even as first-century followers did.

The first-century believers were of one mind and continually devoted themselves to prayer (Acts 1:14). Frequent and fervent prayer together seems to melt away differences. Conflicts, divisions, and strife take place on a human or "horizontal" level, but unity is founded upon mutual, humble dependence as together we "vertically" encounter the same Christ in prayer. Think of those with whom you have prayed; list some of them, and then reflect on how prayer drew you closer together.

The first-century church made hospitality a habit. "So continuing daily with one accord in the temple, and breaking bread from house to house, they ate their food with gladness and simplicity of heart, praising God and having favor with all the people. And the Lord added to the church daily those who were being saved" (Acts 2:46, 47). Consider now the friends you've shared your home and meals with. Reflect on how sharing "from house to house" breaks down barriers and promotes unity.

The first-century church emphasized corporate worship. "Praising God" together might include "structured" times of worship at church or in a small group with more informal times of rejoicing "with those who rejoice" (Rom. 12:15). Consider friends with whom you have praised God and reflect on how this mutual focus on Christ prompts unity and how a glad, praise-filled heart encourages oneness.

Who might you add to your prayer times? Mealtimes from house to house? Praise times? Reach out, expand your circle of unity—turn your part of the world upside down for Jesus.

GC2

GREAT COMMANDMENT
COMMISSION

INSIDE *the* INFLUENCERS

BARNABAS: Leader and Encourager

ACTS 4:36–37

The Holy Spirit led Dr. Luke, author of Acts, to follow this description of Barnabas with the story of Ananias and Sapphira. What a contrast! Barnabas, whose real name was Joseph, was called "The Encourager," but Ananias and Sapphira were selfish and deceitful. A study of Paul's letters reveals that Barnabas lived his life to serve the Lord, and to encourage others.

Barnabas was able to embrace ministry because he didn't live for his ego. From Acts 9 when Barnabas and Paul are first associated with each other through the first half of Acts 13, when Luke writes about Barnabas and Paul, he lists Barnabas first. After this, however, Barnabas takes on more of a supporting role as an encourager and mentor to the apostle Paul.

Barnabas first acted as a mentor to Paul, who went on to rock the entire world. He also mentored his cousin John-Mark, who would later serve as an encourager to Paul as Barnabas himself had done (2 Tim. 4:11). Barnabas was faithful to serve the Lord whether he led from out in front of the group or by being an encouragement to others. His life is a great example of how influence multiplies when we help others to be successful and don't concern ourselves with who gets the credit.

IMPRISONED APOSTLES FREED

17Then the high priest rose up, and all those who *were* with him (which is the sect of the Sadducees), and they were filled with indignation, 18and laid their hands on the apostles and put them in the common prison. 19But at night an angel of the Lord opened the prison doors and brought them out, and said, 20"Go, stand in the temple and speak to the people all the words of this life."

21And when they heard *that,* they entered the temple early in the morning and taught. But the high priest and those with him came and called the council together, with all the elders of the children of Israel, and sent to the prison to have them brought.

APOSTLES ON TRIAL AGAIN

22But when the officers came and did not find them in the prison, they returned and reported, 23saying, "Indeed we found the prison shut securely, and the guards standing outside[a] before the doors; but when we opened them, we

found no one inside!" 24Now when the high priest,[a] the captain of the temple, and the chief priests heard these things, they wondered what the outcome would be. 25So one came and told them, saying,[a] "Look, the men whom you put in prison are standing in the temple and teaching the people!"

26Then the captain went with the officers and brought them without violence, for they feared the people, lest they should be stoned. 27And when they had brought them, they set *them* before the council. And the high priest asked them, 28saying, "Did we not strictly command you not to teach in this name? And look, you have filled Jerusalem with your doctrine, and intend to bring this Man's blood on us!"

29But Peter and the *other* apostles answered and said: "We ought to obey God rather than men. 30The God of our fathers raised up Jesus whom you murdered by hanging on a tree. 31Him God has exalted to His right hand *to be* Prince

5:23 [a]NU-Text and M-Text omit *outside.*   5:24 [a]NU-Text omits *the high priest.*   5:25 [a]NU-Text and M-Text omit *saying.*

INSIDE *the* INFLUENCERS

ANANIAS AND SAPPHIRA: Clouds without Rain

ACTS 5

Ananias, which means "God is gracious," and Sapphira, which means "beautiful," clearly demonstrated that names don't always reflect character. It was written that the early church was "in one accord" in giving, in providing for others, and in worship. People sacrificially sold their belongings to share with others. Unfortunately, Ananias and Sapphira brought hypocrisy and selfishness to this atmosphere of unity and sacrifice. Seeing the love the members held for one another, this couple wanted to fit in without giving up. Their sin was hypocrisy, and God would not tolerate this, "Peter said, 'You have not lied to men but to God'" (v. 4). The sin was not in keeping the money, but in lying about it. Both husband and wife dropped dead on the spot the moment each lied, and "great fear came upon all the church and upon all who heard these things" (5:11). This case of divine judgment is reminiscent of Joshua 7 in which Achan tried to hide sin from God, and was killed. God calls each of us to give and respond to the Holy Spirit in truth; this is our personal worship and gift of sacrifice. We grieve the Holy Spirit and give Satan the opportunity to work in the church when we live as hypocrites.

and Savior, to give repentance to Israel and forgiveness of sins. ³²And we are His witnesses to these things, and *so* also *is* the Holy Spirit whom God has given to those who obey Him."

GAMALIEL'S ADVICE

³³When they heard *this,* they were furious and plotted to kill them. ³⁴Then one in the council stood up, a Pharisee named Gamaliel, a teacher of the law held in respect by all the people, and commanded them to put the apostles outside for a little while. ³⁵And he said to them: "Men of Israel, take heed to yourselves what you intend to do regarding these men. ³⁶For some time ago Theudas rose up, claiming to be somebody. A number of men, about four hundred, joined him. He was slain, and all who obeyed him were scattered and came to nothing. ³⁷After this man, Judas of Galilee rose up in the days of the census, and drew away many people after him. He also perished, and all who obeyed him were dispersed. ³⁸And now I say to you, keep away from these men and let them alone; for if this plan or this work is of men, it will come to nothing; ³⁹but if it is of God, you cannot overthrow it—lest you even be found to fight against God."

⁴⁰And they agreed with him, and when they

had called for the apostles and beaten *them,* they commanded that they should not speak in the name of Jesus, and let them go. ⁴¹So they departed from the presence of the council, rejoicing that they were counted worthy to suffer shame for His[a] name. ⁴²And daily in the temple, and in every house, they did not cease teaching and preaching Jesus *as* the Christ.

SEVEN CHOSEN TO SERVE

6 Now in those days, when *the number of* the disciples was multiplying, there arose a complaint against the Hebrews by the Hellenists,[a] because their widows were neglected in the daily distribution. ²Then the twelve summoned the multitude of the disciples and said, "It is not desirable that we should leave the word of God and serve tables. ³Therefore, brethren, seek out from among you seven men of *good* reputation, full of the Holy Spirit and wisdom, whom we may appoint over this business; ⁴but we will give ourselves continually to prayer and to the ministry of the word."

⁵And the saying pleased the whole multitude. And they chose Stephen, a man full of faith and the Holy Spirit, and Philip, Prochorus, Nicanor,

5:41 ªNU-Text reads *the name;* M-Text reads *the name of Jesus.*
6:1 ªThat is, Greek-speaking Jews

Timon, Parmenas, and Nicolas, a proselyte from Antioch, [6]whom they set before the apostles; and when they had prayed, they laid hands on them.

[7]Then the word of God spread, and the number of the disciples multiplied greatly in Jerusalem, and a great many of the priests were obedient to the faith.

Stephen Accused of Blasphemy

[8]And Stephen, full of faith[a] and power, did great wonders and signs among the people. [9]Then there arose some from what is called the Synagogue of the Freedmen (Cyrenians, Alexandrians, and those from Cilicia and Asia), disputing with Stephen. [10]And they were not able to resist the wisdom and the Spirit by which he spoke. [11]Then they secretly induced men to say, "We have heard him speak blasphemous words against Moses and God." [12]And they stirred up the people, the elders, and the scribes; and they came upon *him,* seized him, and brought *him* to the council. [13]They also set up false witnesses who said, "This man does not cease to speak blasphemous[a] words against this holy place and the law; [14]for we have heard him say that this Jesus of Nazareth will destroy this place and change the customs which Moses delivered to us." [15]And all who sat in the council, looking steadfastly at him, saw his face as the face of an angel.

Stephen's Address: The Call of Abraham

7 Then the high priest said, "Are these things so?"

[2]And he said, "Brethren and fathers, listen: The God of glory appeared to our father Abraham when he was in Mesopotamia, before he dwelt in Haran, [3]and said to him, *'Get out of your country and from your relatives, and come to a land that I will show you.'* [a] [4]Then he came out of the land of the Chaldeans and dwelt in Haran. And from there, when his father was dead, He moved him to this land in which you now dwell. [5]And *God* gave him no inheritance in it, not even *enough* to set his foot on. But even when *Abraham* had no child, He promised to give it to him for a possession, and to his descendants after him. [6]But God spoke in this way: that his descendants would dwell in a foreign land, and that they would bring them into bondage and oppress *them* four hundred years.

[7]*'And the nation to whom they will be in bondage I will judge,'* [a] said God, *'and after that they shall come out and serve Me in this place.'* [b] [8]Then He gave him the covenant of circumcision; and so *Abraham* begot Isaac and circumcised him on the eighth day; and Isaac *begot* Jacob, and Jacob *begot* the twelve patriarchs.

The Patriarchs in Egypt

[9]"And the patriarchs, becoming envious, sold Joseph into Egypt. But God was with him [10]and delivered him out of all his troubles, and gave him favor and wisdom in the presence of Pharaoh, king of Egypt; and he made him governor over Egypt and all his house. [11]Now a famine and great trouble came over all the land of Egypt and Canaan, and our fathers found no sustenance. [12]But when Jacob heard that there was grain in Egypt, he sent out our fathers first. [13]And the second *time* Joseph was made known to his brothers, and Joseph's family became known to the Pharaoh. [14]Then Joseph sent and called his father Jacob and all his relatives to *him,* seventy-five[a] people. [15]So Jacob went down to Egypt; and he died, he and our fathers. [16]And they were carried back to Shechem and laid in the tomb that Abraham bought for a sum of money from the sons of Hamor, *the father* of Shechem.

God Delivers Israel by Moses

[17]"But when the time of the promise drew near which God had sworn to Abraham, the people grew and multiplied in Egypt [18]till another king arose who did not know Joseph. [19]This man dealt treacherously with our people, and oppressed our forefathers, making them expose their babies, so that they might not live. [20]At this time Moses was born, and was well pleasing to God; and he was brought up in his father's house for three months. [21]But when he was set out, Pharaoh's daughter took him away and brought him up as her own son. [22]And Moses was learned in all the wisdom of the Egyptians, and was mighty in words and deeds.

[23]"Now when he was forty years old, it came into his heart to visit his brethren, the children of

6:8 [a]NU-Text reads *grace.* **6:13** [a]NU-Text omits *blasphemous.* **7:3** [a]Genesis 12:1 **7:7** [a]Genesis 15:14 [b]Exodus 3:12 **7:14** [a]Or *seventy* (compare Exodus 1:5)

Israel. ²⁴And seeing one of *them* suffer wrong, he defended and avenged him who was oppressed, and struck down the Egyptian. ²⁵For he supposed that his brethren would have understood that God would deliver them by his hand, but they did not understand. ²⁶And the next day he appeared to *two of* them as they were fighting, and *tried to* reconcile them, saying, 'Men, you are brethren; why do you wrong one another?' ²⁷But he who did his neighbor wrong pushed him away, saying, *'Who made you a ruler and a judge over us? ²⁸Do you want to kill me as you did the Egyptian yesterday?'*ᵃ ²⁹Then, at this saying, Moses fled and became a dweller in the land of Midian, where he had two sons.

³⁰"And when forty years had passed, an Angel of the Lordᵃ appeared to him in a flame of fire in a bush, in the wilderness of Mount Sinai. ³¹When Moses saw *it*, he marveled at the sight; and as he drew near to observe, the voice of the Lord came to him, ³²*saying, 'I am the God of your fathers—the God of Abraham, the God of Isaac, and the God of Jacob.'*ᵃ And Moses trembled and dared not look. ³³*Then the Lord said to him, "Take your sandals off your feet, for the place where you stand is holy ground. ³⁴I have surely seen the oppression of My people who are in Egypt; I have heard their groaning and have come down to deliver them. And now come, I will send you to Egypt."* ᵃ

³⁵"This Moses whom they rejected, saying, *'Who made you a ruler and a judge?'*ᵃ is the one God sent *to be* a ruler and a deliverer by the hand of the Angel who appeared to him in the bush. ³⁶He brought them out, after he had shown wonders and signs in the land of Egypt, and in the Red Sea, and in the wilderness forty years.

Israel Rebels Against God

³⁷"This is that Moses who said to the children of Israel,ᵃ *'The Lord your God will raise up for you a Prophet like me from your brethren. Him you shall hear.'*ᵇ

³⁸"This is he who was in the congregation in the wilderness with the Angel who spoke to him on Mount Sinai, and *with* our fathers, the one who received the living oracles to give to us, ³⁹whom our fathers would not obey, but rejected. And in their hearts they turned back to Egypt,

⁴⁰saying to Aaron, *'Make us gods to go before us; as for this Moses who brought us out of the land of Egypt, we do not know what has become of him.'*ᵃ ⁴¹And they made a calf in those days, offered sacrifices to the idol, and rejoiced in the works of their own hands. ⁴²Then God turned and gave them up to worship the host of heaven, as it is written in the book of the Prophets:

> *'Did you offer Me slaughtered animals and*
> *   sacrifices during forty years in the*
> *   wilderness,*
> *   O house of Israel?*
> ⁴³*You also took up the tabernacle of Moloch,*
> *   And the star of your god Remphan,*
> *   Images which you made to worship;*
> *   And I will carry you away beyond Babylon.'*ᵃ

God's True Tabernacle

⁴⁴"Our fathers had the tabernacle of witness in the wilderness, as He appointed, instructing Moses to make it according to the pattern that he had seen, ⁴⁵which our fathers, having received it in turn, also brought with Joshua into the land possessed by the Gentiles, whom God drove out before the face of our fathers until the days of David, ⁴⁶who found favor before God and asked to find a dwelling for the God of Jacob. ⁴⁷But Solomon built Him a house.

⁴⁸"However, the Most High does not dwell in temples made with hands, as the prophet says:

> ⁴⁹*'Heaven is My throne,*
> *   And earth is My footstool.*
> *   What house will you build for Me? says the*
> *   Lord,*
> *   Or what is the place of My rest?*
> ⁵⁰*Has My hand not made all these things?'*ᵃ

Israel Resists the Holy Spirit

⁵¹" *You* stiff-necked and uncircumcised in heart and ears! You always resist the Holy Spirit; as your fathers *did*, so *do* you. ⁵²Which of the prophets did your fathers not persecute? And

7:28 ᵃExodus 2:14 **7:30** ᵃNU-Text omits *of the Lord.* **7:32** ᵃExodus 3:6, 15 **7:34** ᵃExodus 3:5, 7, 8, 10 **7:35** ᵃExodus 2:14 **7:37** ᵃDeuteronomy 18:15 ᵇNU-Text and M-Text omit *Him you shall hear.* **7:40** ᵃExodus 32:1, 23 **7:43** ᵃAmos 5:25–27 **7:50** ᵃIsaiah 66:1, 2

LEADERSHIP ISSUES

Can I Get a Witness?

ACTS 7:59, 60

When pressure mounted on the early church, persecution began, and Stephen became the first martyr. We know that Saul, the persecutor of Christians who became the apostle Paul, was there approving of the stoning (Acts 7:57, 58). Stephen cried as His Savior Jesus had, "Lord, do not charge them with this sin" (v. 60).

Notice the words translated *martureo* (verb) and *marturion* (noun). Although we think of a martyr as someone who died for the faith, the Greek word for martyr means "a witness," and it referred to someone who gave testimony to things they had experienced through words and actions. Peter declared that he spoke of things he saw and heard (Acts 4:20). Many early believers died because of their commitment to Christ, leading to the use of "martyr" to describe such faithful witnesses. For many early Christians, it was better to die than to stop testifying about Christ. Many believers today do not attempt to share their faith because they have "gotten over" their salvation. It is no longer an amazing wonder; it has become a ritual of words. The early believers did not—indeed they could not—get past the radical transformation they experienced through the gospel.

In fact, they were not only known as witnesses, but they were proclaimers. The verb form of *kerusso* means "to proclaim in the manner of a herald." It implies the declaration of an event. The verb form is found sixty-one times in the New Testament. While not always referring to proclaiming the gospel, often it is used in that regard. In fact, at times *kerusso* and *evangelizomai* are based as synonyms, as in Romans 10:14, 15. On twelve occasions the expression *kerussein to euaggelion*, "preach the gospel," is found in the New Testament, showing the close relation between the terms. The noun *kerygma* is found eight times in the New Testament. It means "the proclamation."

It was with this type of fervor that the passionate early church leaders devoted themselves. Whether they lived or died, the goal was to preach Christ and Him crucified.

they killed those who foretold the coming of the Just One, of whom you now have become the betrayers and murderers, ⁵³who have received the law by the direction of angels and have not kept *it*."

STEPHEN THE MARTYR

⁵⁴When they heard these things they were cut to the heart, and they gnashed at him with *their* teeth. ⁵⁵But he, being full of the Holy Spirit, gazed into heaven and saw the glory of God, and Jesus standing at the right hand of God, ⁵⁶and said, "Look! I see the heavens opened and the Son of Man standing at the right hand of God!"

⁵⁷Then they cried out with a loud voice, stopped their ears, and ran at him with one accord; ⁵⁸and they cast *him* out of the city and stoned *him*. And the witnesses laid down their clothes at the feet of a young man named Saul. ⁵⁹And they stoned Stephen as he was calling on *God* and saying, "Lord Jesus, receive my spirit." ⁶⁰Then he knelt down and cried out with a loud voice, "Lord, do not charge them with this sin." And when he had said this, he fell asleep.

SAUL PERSECUTES THE CHURCH

8 Now Saul was consenting to his death.
At that time a great persecution arose against the church which was at Jerusalem; and they were all scattered throughout the regions of Judea and Samaria, except the apostles. ²And devout men carried Stephen *to his burial,* and made great lamentation over him.

³As for Saul, he made havoc of the church, entering every house, and dragging off men and women, committing *them* to prison.

CHRIST IS PREACHED IN SAMARIA

⁴Therefore those who were scattered went everywhere preaching the word. ⁵Then Philip went down to theᵃ city of Samaria and preached Christ to them. ⁶And the multitudes with one accord heeded the things spoken by Philip, hearing and seeing the miracles which he did. ⁷For unclean spirits, crying with a loud voice, came out of many who were possessed; and many who were paralyzed and lame were healed. ⁸And there was great joy in that city.

THE SORCERER'S PROFESSION OF FAITH

⁹But there was a certain man called Simon, who previously practiced sorcery in the city and astonished the people of Samaria, claiming that he was someone great, ¹⁰to whom they all gave heed, from the least to the greatest, saying, "This man is the great power of God." ¹¹And they heeded him because he had astonished them with his sorceries for a long time. ¹²But when they believed Philip as he preached the things concerning the kingdom of God and the name of Jesus Christ, both men and women were baptized. ¹³Then Simon himself also believed; and when he was baptized he continued with Philip, and was amazed, seeing the miracles and signs which were done.

THE SORCERER'S SIN

¹⁴Now when the apostles who were at Jerusalem heard that Samaria had received the word of God, they sent Peter and John to them, ¹⁵who, when they had come down, prayed for them that they might receive the Holy Spirit. ¹⁶For as yet He had fallen upon none of them. They had only been baptized in the name of the Lord Jesus. ¹⁷Then they laid hands on them, and they received the Holy Spirit.

¹⁸And when Simon saw that through the laying on of the apostles' hands the Holy Spirit was given, he offered them money, ¹⁹saying, "Give me this power also, that anyone on whom I lay hands may receive the Holy Spirit."

²⁰But Peter said to him, "Your money perish with you, because you thought that the gift of God could be purchased with money! ²¹You have neither part nor portion in this matter, for your heart is not right in the sight of God. ²²Repent therefore of this your wickedness, and pray God if perhaps the thought of your heart may be forgiven you. ²³For I see that you are poisoned by bitterness and bound by iniquity."

²⁴Then Simon answered and said, "Pray to the Lord for me, that none of the things which you have spoken may come upon me."

²⁵So when they had testified and preached the word of the Lord, they returned to Jerusalem, preaching the gospel in many villages of the Samaritans.

8:5 ᵃOr *a*

CHRIST IS PREACHED TO AN ETHIOPIAN

²⁶Now an angel of the Lord spoke to Philip, saying, "Arise and go toward the south along the road which goes down from Jerusalem to Gaza." This is desert. ²⁷So he arose and went. And behold, a man of Ethiopia, a eunuch of great authority under Candace the queen of the Ethiopians, who had charge of all her treasury, and had come to Jerusalem to worship, ²⁸was returning. And sitting in his chariot, he was reading Isaiah the prophet. ²⁹Then the Spirit said to Philip, "Go near and overtake this chariot."

³⁰So Philip ran to him, and heard him reading the prophet Isaiah, and said, "Do you understand what you are reading?"

³¹And he said, "How can I, unless someone guides me?" And he asked Philip to come up and sit with him. ³²The place in the Scripture which he read was this:

"He was led as a sheep to the slaughter;
And as a lamb before its shearer is silent,
So He opened not His mouth.

³³*In His humiliation His justice was taken*
    away,
And who will declare His generation?
*For His life is taken from the earth."*ᵃ

³⁴So the eunuch answered Philip and said, "I ask you, of whom does the prophet say this, of himself or of some other man?" ³⁵Then Philip opened his mouth, and beginning at this Scripture, preached Jesus to him. ³⁶Now as they went down the road, they came to some water. And the eunuch said, "See, *here is* water. What hinders me from being baptized?"

³⁷Then Philip said, "If you believe with all your heart, you may."

And he answered and said, "I believe that Jesus Christ is the Son of God."ᵃ

³⁸So he commanded the chariot to stand still. And both Philip and the eunuch went down into the water, and he baptized him. ³⁹Now when they came up out of the water, the Spirit of the Lord

8:33 ᵃIsaiah 53:7, 8   8:37 ᵃNU-Text and M-Text omit this verse. It is found in Western texts, including the Latin tradition.

INSIDE the INFLUENCERS

PHILIP: The Heart of an Evangelist

ACTS 8:4–40

Philip is often referred to in Scripture as an evangelist. He was originally selected as one of the seven deacons (along with Stephen) in the Jerusalem church to deal with the church's social issues. After Stephen's murder, Philip didn't waste any time carrying the gospel to the world outside of Israel (8:4, 5).

When persecution hit the young church, Philip followed Jesus' command and took the good news of Jesus to the scorned city of Samaria. Scripture tells us Philip preached "the kingdom of God and the name of Jesus Christ" in Samaria (8:12).

Philip preached his way back to Jerusalem. God filled him with a desire to go the desert and witness to a man from Ethiopia. There he found the man reading a prophecy about Jesus. Philip took advantage of this opportunity, and Scripture says that he "preached Jesus to him" (8:35).

Philip spent his life pointing others to Christ. He wanted to make a big deal about Jesus; he was a man marked by the gospel. It so defined him that he was known by all he came in contact with as "the evangelist." For him there was no other message. It was Jesus Christ or nothing at all.

caught Philip away, so that the eunuch saw him no more; and he went on his way rejoicing. [40]But Philip was found at Azotus. And passing through, he preached in all the cities till he came to Caesarea.

THE DAMASCUS ROAD: SAUL CONVERTED

9 Then Saul, still breathing threats and murder against the disciples of the Lord, went to the high priest [2]and asked letters from him to the synagogues of Damascus, so that if he found any who were of the Way, whether men or women, he might bring them bound to Jerusalem.

[3]As he journeyed he came near Damascus, and suddenly a light shone around him from heaven. [4]Then he fell to the ground, and heard a voice saying to him, "Saul, Saul, why are you persecuting Me?"

[5]And he said, "Who are You, Lord?"

Then the Lord said, "I am Jesus, whom you are persecuting.[a] It is hard for you to kick against the goads."

[6]So he, trembling and astonished, said, "Lord, what do You want me to do?"

Then the Lord said to him, "Arise and go into the city, and you will be told what you must do."

[7]And the men who journeyed with him stood speechless, hearing a voice but seeing no one. [8]Then Saul arose from the ground, and when his eyes were opened he saw no one. But they led him by the hand and brought him into Damascus. [9]And he was three days without sight, and neither ate nor drank.

ANANIAS BAPTIZES SAUL

[10]Now there was a certain disciple at Damascus named Ananias; and to him the Lord said in a vision, "Ananias."

And he said, "Here I am, Lord."

[11]So the Lord said to him, "Arise and go to the street called Straight, and inquire at the house of Judas for one called Saul of Tarsus, for behold, he is praying. [12]And in a vision he has seen a man named Ananias coming in and putting his hand on him, so that he might receive his sight."

[13]Then Ananias answered, "Lord, I have heard

9:5 [a]NU-Text and M-Text omit the last sentence of verse 5 and begin verse 6 with *But arise and go.*

INSIDE the INFLUENCERS

SAUL WHO BECAME PAUL: Drastic Call, Dramatic Ministry

ACTS 9:1–5

Saul was raised in Tarsus, a town known for its school of philosophy. He was educated by the great Pharisee Gamaliel. In Tarsus, Saul would have been influenced by Greek philosophy, Roman economics, and Jewish religion. He was no doubt a man of influence and culture with a pedigree for success.

Saul chased down the Jesus-followers who fled to Damascus, probably hoping to guarantee his place at the table of the Sanhedrin. Judaism did not teach hate, but he was zealous.

Coming face to face with the God of the universe on his way to Damascus was not part of Saul's plan. A flash of light, a fall to the ground, and the voice of God all led him to the most painful, yet amazing discovery of his life. Jesus Christ was God. This hurt because it meant Saul had attacked the very God he desired to serve. He remembered watching in agreement as an innocent and godly man, Stephen, died at the hands of a bloodthirsty mob (7:58). He was so wrong. Jesus, however, had been so right. Saul, who became Paul, was later used to change the entire world with the love of Christ, just the way he had been changed.

from many about this man, how much harm he has done to Your saints in Jerusalem. ¹⁴And here he has authority from the chief priests to bind all who call on Your name."

¹⁵But the Lord said to him, "Go, for he is a chosen vessel of Mine to bear My name before Gentiles, kings, and the children of Israel. ¹⁶For I will show him how many things he must suffer for My name's sake."

¹⁷And Ananias went his way and entered the house; and laying his hands on him he said, "Brother Saul, the Lord Jesus,ᵃ who appeared to you on the road as you came, has sent me that you may receive your sight and be filled with the Holy Spirit." ¹⁸Immediately there fell from his eyes *something* like scales, and he received his sight at once; and he arose and was baptized.

¹⁹So when he had received food, he was strengthened. Then Saul spent some days with the disciples at Damascus.

Saul Preaches Christ

²⁰Immediately he preached the Christᵃ in the synagogues, that He is the Son of God.

²¹Then all who heard were amazed, and said, "Is this not he who destroyed those who called on this name in Jerusalem, and has come here for that purpose, so that he might bring them bound to the chief priests?"

²²But Saul increased all the more in strength, and confounded the Jews who dwelt in Damascus, proving that this *Jesus* is the Christ.

Saul Escapes Death

²³Now after many days were past, the Jews plotted to kill him. ²⁴But their plot became known to Saul. And they watched the gates day and night, to kill him. ²⁵Then the disciples took him by night and let *him* down through the wall in a large basket.

Saul at Jerusalem

²⁶And when Saul had come to Jerusalem, he tried to join the disciples; but they were all afraid of him, and did not believe that he was a disciple. ²⁷But Barnabas took him and brought *him* to the apostles. And he declared to them how he had seen the Lord on the road, and that He had spoken to him, and how he had preached boldly at

Damascus in the name of Jesus. ²⁸So he was with them at Jerusalem, coming in and going out. ²⁹And he spoke boldly in the name of the Lord Jesus and disputed against the Hellenists, but they attempted to kill him. ³⁰When the brethren found out, they brought him down to Caesarea and sent him out to Tarsus.

The Church Prospers

³¹Then the churchesᵃ throughout all Judea, Galilee, and Samaria had peace and were edified. And walking in the fear of the Lord and in the comfort of the Holy Spirit, they were multiplied.

Aeneas Healed

³²Now it came to pass, as Peter went through all *parts of the country,* that he also came down to the saints who dwelt in Lydda. ³³There he found a certain man named Aeneas, who had been bedridden eight years and was paralyzed. ³⁴And Peter said to him, "Aeneas, Jesus the Christ heals you. Arise and make your bed." Then he arose immediately. ³⁵So all who dwelt at Lydda and Sharon saw him and turned to the Lord.

Dorcas Restored to Life

³⁶At Joppa there was a certain disciple named Tabitha, which is translated Dorcas. This woman was full of good works and charitable deeds which she did. ³⁷But it happened in those days that she became sick and died. When they had washed her, they laid *her* in an upper room. ³⁸And since Lydda was near Joppa, and the disciples had heard that Peter was there, they sent two men to him, imploring *him* not to delay in coming to them. ³⁹Then Peter arose and went with them. When he had come, they brought *him* to the upper room. And all the widows stood by him weeping, showing the tunics and garments which Dorcas had made while she was with them. ⁴⁰But Peter put them all out, and knelt down and prayed. And turning to the body he said, "Tabitha, arise." And she opened her eyes, and when she saw Peter she sat up. ⁴¹Then he gave her *his* hand and lifted her up; and when he had called the saints and widows, he presented her alive. ⁴²And it became known throughout all Joppa, and many

9:17 ᵃM-Text omits *Jesus.* **9:20** ᵃNU-Text reads *Jesus.* **9:31** ᵃNU-Text reads *church . . . was edified.*

believed on the Lord. ⁴³So it was that he stayed many days in Joppa with Simon, a tanner.

CORNELIUS SENDS A DELEGATION

10 There was a certain man in Caesarea called Cornelius, a centurion of what was called the Italian Regiment, ²a devout *man* and one who feared God with all his household, who gave alms generously to the people, and prayed to God always. ³About the ninth hour of the day he saw clearly in a vision an angel of God coming in and saying to him, "Cornelius!"

⁴And when he observed him, he was afraid, and said, "What is it, lord?"

So he said to him, "Your prayers and your alms have come up for a memorial before God. ⁵Now send men to Joppa, and send for Simon whose surname is Peter. ⁶He is lodging with Simon, a tanner, whose house is by the sea.ᵃ He will tell you what you must do." ⁷And when the angel who spoke to him had departed, Cornelius called two of his household servants and a devout soldier from among those who waited on him continually. ⁸So when he had explained all *these* things to them, he sent them to Joppa.

PETER'S VISION

⁹The next day, as they went on their journey and drew near the city, Peter went up on the housetop to pray, about the sixth hour. ¹⁰Then he became very hungry and wanted to eat; but while they made ready, he fell into a trance ¹¹and saw heaven opened and an object like a great sheet bound at the four corners, descending to him and let down to the earth. ¹²In it were all kinds of four-footed animals of the earth, wild beasts, creeping things, and birds of the air. ¹³And a voice came to him, "Rise, Peter; kill and eat."

¹⁴But Peter said, "Not so, Lord! For I have never eaten anything common or unclean."

¹⁵And a voice *spoke* to him again the second time, "What God has cleansed you must not call common." ¹⁶This was done three times. And the object was taken up into heaven again.

SUMMONED TO CAESAREA

¹⁷Now while Peter wondered within himself what this vision which he had seen meant, behold, the men who had been sent from Cornelius

had made inquiry for Simon's house, and stood before the gate. ¹⁸And they called and asked whether Simon, whose surname was Peter, was lodging there.

¹⁹While Peter thought about the vision, the Spirit said to him, "Behold, three men are seeking you. ²⁰Arise therefore, go down and go with them, doubting nothing; for I have sent them."

²¹Then Peter went down to the men who had been sent to him from Cornelius,ᵃ and said, "Yes, I am he whom you seek. For what reason have you come?"

²²And they said, "Cornelius *the* centurion, a just man, one who fears God and has a good reputation among all the nation of the Jews, was divinely instructed by a holy angel to summon you to his house, and to hear words from you." ²³Then he invited them in and lodged *them*.

On the next day Peter went away with them, and some brethren from Joppa accompanied him.

PETER MEETS CORNELIUS

²⁴And the following day they entered Caesarea. Now Cornelius was waiting for them, and had called together his relatives and close friends. ²⁵As Peter was coming in, Cornelius met him and fell down at his feet and worshiped *him*. ²⁶But Peter lifted him up, saying, "Stand up; I myself am also a man." ²⁷And as he talked with him, he went in and found many who had come together. ²⁸Then he said to them, "You know how unlawful it is for a Jewish man to keep company with or go to one of another nation. But God has shown me that I should not call any man common or unclean. ²⁹Therefore I came without objection as soon as I was sent for. I ask, then, for what reason have you sent for me?"

³⁰So Cornelius said, "Four days ago I was fasting until this hour; and at the ninth hourᵃ I prayed in my house, and behold, a man stood before me in bright clothing, ³¹and said, 'Cornelius, your prayer has been heard, and your alms are remembered in the sight of God. ³²Send therefore to Joppa and call Simon here, whose surname is Peter. He is lodging in the house of Simon, a tan-

---

10:6 ᵃNU-Text and M-Text omit the last sentence of this verse. **10:21** ᵃNU-Text and M-Text omit *who had been sent to him from Cornelius*. **10:30** ᵃNU-Text reads *Four days ago to this hour, at the ninth hour.*

ner, by the sea.ª When he comes, he will speak to you.' ³³So I sent to you immediately, and you have done well to come. Now therefore, we are all present before God, to hear all the things commanded you by God."

Preaching to Cornelius' Household

³⁴Then Peter opened *his* mouth and said: "In truth I perceive that God shows no partiality. ³⁵But in every nation whoever fears Him and works righteousness is accepted by Him. ³⁶The word which *God* sent to the children of Israel, preaching peace through Jesus Christ—He is Lord of all— ³⁷that word you know, which was proclaimed throughout all Judea, and began from Galilee after the baptism which John preached: ³⁸how God anointed Jesus of Nazareth with the Holy Spirit and with power, who went about doing good and healing all who were oppressed by the devil, for God was with Him. ³⁹And we are witnesses of all things which He did both in the land of the Jews and in Jerusalem, whom theyª killed by hanging on a tree. ⁴⁰Him God raised up on the third day, and showed Him openly, ⁴¹not to all the people, but to witnesses chosen before by God, *even* to us who ate and drank with Him after He arose from the dead. ⁴²And He commanded us to preach to the people, and to testify that it is He who was ordained by God *to be* Judge of the living and the dead. ⁴³To Him all the prophets witness that, through His name, whoever believes in Him will receive remission of sins."

The Holy Spirit Falls on the Gentiles

⁴⁴While Peter was still speaking these words, the Holy Spirit fell upon all those who heard the word. ⁴⁵And those of the circumcision who believed were astonished, as many as came with Peter, because the gift of the Holy Spirit had been poured out on the Gentiles also. ⁴⁶For they heard them speak with tongues and magnify God.

Then Peter answered, ⁴⁷"Can anyone forbid water, that these should not be baptized who have received the Holy Spirit just as we *have?*" ⁴⁸And he commanded them to be baptized in the name of the Lord. Then they asked him to stay a few days.

Peter Defends God's Grace

11 Now the apostles and brethren who were in Judea heard that the Gentiles had also received the word of God. ²And when Peter came up to Jerusalem, those of the circumcision contended with him, ³saying, "You went in to uncircumcised men and ate with them!"

⁴But Peter explained *it* to them in order from the beginning, saying: ⁵"I was in the city of Joppa praying; and in a trance I saw a vision, an object descending like a great sheet, let down from heaven by four corners; and it came to me. ⁶When I observed it intently and considered, I saw fourfooted animals of the earth, wild beasts, creeping things, and birds of the air. ⁷And I heard a voice saying to me, 'Rise, Peter; kill and eat.' ⁸But I said, 'Not so, Lord! For nothing common or unclean has at any time entered my mouth.' ⁹But the voice answered me again from heaven, 'What God has cleansed you must not call common.' ¹⁰Now this was done three times, and all were drawn up again into heaven. ¹¹At that very moment, three men stood before the house where I was, having been sent to me from Caesarea. ¹²Then the Spirit told me to go with them, doubting nothing. Moreover these six brethren accompanied me, and we entered the man's house. ¹³And he told us how he had seen an angel standing in his house, who said to him, 'Send men to Joppa, and call for Simon whose surname is Peter, ¹⁴who will tell you words by which you and all your household will be saved.' ¹⁵And as I began to speak, the Holy Spirit fell upon them, as upon us at the beginning. ¹⁶Then I remembered the word of the Lord, how He said, 'John indeed baptized with water, but you shall be baptized with the Holy Spirit.' ¹⁷If therefore God gave them the same gift as *He gave* us when we believed on the Lord Jesus Christ, who was I that I could withstand God?"

¹⁸When they heard these things they became silent; and they glorified God, saying, "Then God has also granted to the Gentiles repentance to life."

Barnabas and Saul at Antioch

¹⁹Now those who were scattered after the persecution that arose over Stephen traveled as far

10:32 ªNU-Text omits the last sentence of this verse.   **10:39** ªNU-Text and M-Text add *also.*

as Phoenicia, Cyprus, and Antioch, preaching the word to no one but the Jews only. 20But some of them were men from Cyprus and Cyrene, who, when they had come to Antioch, spoke to the Hellenists, preaching the Lord Jesus. 21And the hand of the Lord was with them, and a great number believed and turned to the Lord.

22Then news of these things came to the ears of the church in Jerusalem, and they sent out Barnabas to go as far as Antioch. 23When he came and had seen the grace of God, he was glad, and encouraged them all that with purpose of heart they should continue with the Lord. 24For he was a good man, full of the Holy Spirit and of faith. And a great many people were added to the Lord.

25Then Barnabas departed for Tarsus to seek Saul. 26And when he had found him, he brought him to Antioch. So it was that for a whole year they assembled with the church and taught a great many people. And the disciples were first called Christians in Antioch.

Relief to Judea

27And in these days prophets came from Jerusalem to Antioch. 28Then one of them, named Agabus, stood up and showed by the Spirit that there was going to be a great famine throughout all the world, which also happened in the days of Claudius Caesar. 29Then the disciples, each according to his ability, determined to send relief to the brethren dwelling in Judea. 30This they also did, and sent it to the elders by the hands of Barnabas and Saul.

Herod's Violence to the Church

12 Now about that time Herod the king stretched out his hand to harass some from the church. 2Then he killed James the brother of John with the sword. 3And because he saw that it pleased the Jews, he proceeded further to seize Peter also. Now it was during the Days of Unleavened Bread. 4So when he had arrested him, he put him in prison, and delivered him to four squads of soldiers to keep him, intending to bring him before the people after Passover.

Peter Freed from Prison

5Peter was therefore kept in prison, but constanta prayer was offered to God for him by the church. 6And when Herod was about to bring him out, that night Peter was sleeping, bound with two chains between two soldiers; and the guards before the door were keeping the prison. 7Now behold, an angel of the Lord stood by him, and a light shone in the prison; and he struck Peter on the side and raised him up, saying, "Arise quickly!" And his chains fell off his hands. 8Then the angel said to him, "Gird yourself and tie on your sandals"; and so he did. And he said to him, "Put on your garment and follow me." 9So he went out and followed him, and did not know that what was done by the angel was real, but thought he was seeing a vision. 10When they were past the first and the second guard posts, they came to the iron gate that leads to the city, which opened to them of its own accord; and they went out and went down one street, and immediately the angel departed from him.

11And when Peter had come to himself, he said, "Now I know for certain that the Lord has sent His angel, and has delivered me from the hand of Herod and from all the expectation of the Jewish people."

12So, when he had considered this, he came to the house of Mary, the mother of John whose surname was Mark, where many were gathered together praying. 13And as Peter knocked at the door of the gate, a girl named Rhoda came to answer. 14When she recognized Peter's voice, because of her gladness she did not open the gate, but ran in and announced that Peter stood before the gate. 15But they said to her, "You are beside yourself!" Yet she kept insisting that it was so. So they said, "It is his angel."

16Now Peter continued knocking; and when they opened the door and saw him, they were astonished. 17But motioning to them with his hand to keep silent, he declared to them how the Lord had brought him out of the prison. And he said, "Go, tell these things to James and to the brethren." And he departed and went to another place.

18Then, as soon as it was day, there was no small stir among the soldiers about what had become of Peter. 19But when Herod had searched for him and not found him, he examined the guards and commanded that they should be put to death.

12:5 aNU-Text reads constantly (or earnestly).

And he went down from Judea to Caesarea, and stayed *there*.

HEROD'S VIOLENT DEATH

20Now Herod had been very angry with the people of Tyre and Sidon; but they came to him with one accord, and having made Blastus the king's personal aide their friend, they asked for peace, because their country was supplied with food by the king's *country*.

21So on a set day Herod, arrayed in royal apparel, sat on his throne and gave an oration to them. 22And the people kept shouting, "The voice of a god and not of a man!" 23Then immediately an angel of the Lord struck him, because he did not give glory to God. And he was eaten by worms and died.

24But the word of God grew and multiplied.

BARNABAS AND SAUL APPOINTED

25And Barnabas and Saul returned from[a] Jerusalem when they had fulfilled *their* ministry,

and they also took with them John whose surname was Mark.

13 Now in the church that was at Antioch there were certain prophets and teachers: Barnabas, Simeon who was called Niger, Lucius of Cyrene, Manaen who had been brought up with Herod the tetrarch, and Saul. 2As they ministered to the Lord and fasted, the Holy Spirit said, "Now separate to Me Barnabas and Saul for the work to which I have called them." 3Then, having fasted and prayed, and laid hands on them, they sent *them* away.

PREACHING IN CYPRUS

4So, being sent out by the Holy Spirit, they went down to Seleucia, and from there they sailed to Cyprus. 5And when they arrived in Salamis, they preached the word of God in the synagogues of the Jews. They also had John as *their* assistant.

6Now when they had gone through the

12:25 [a]NU-Text and M-Text read *to*.

INSIDE the INFLUENCERS

JOHN MARK: Galvanized by Encouragement

John Mark was the younger cousin of Barnabas, the man known as The Encourager (Col. 4:10). It is believed the apostle Peter led Mark to faith in Christ when Mark was still young (1 Pet. 5:13).

Mark traveled with Barnabas and the apostle Paul as an assistant, or minister in training (Acts 12:25, 13:5). For one reason or another, Mark decided that traveling with Paul and Barnabas was too much. When Paul and Barnabas were moving forward in their mission, Mark headed back to Jerusalem (Acts 13:13).

Although Mark abandoned Barnabas and Paul, Barnabas wanted to give Mark another chance. He and Paul disagreed over this, but to Barnabas it was a matter of principle (Acts 15:36–39). Barnabas took Mark and they went on to Cyprus together. Barnabas probably used this opportunity to teach his younger cousin what it meant to persevere in the faith. Mark became galvanized by encouragement.

Mark was a changed man. Never again does Scripture show him running from difficulty. When Paul was imprisoned for the first time in Rome, Mark was with him (Col. 4:10, Philem. 1:24). When persecution of the church spread and Peter sought to prepare the church, Mark was by his side (1 Pet. 5:13). When Paul faced another prison term and certain death, who was it that he requested? Mark, of course. He was called in from Ephesus where he was ministering alongside Timothy (2 Tim. 4:11).

island[a] to Paphos, they found a certain sorcerer, a false prophet, a Jew whose name *was* Bar-Jesus, [7]who was with the proconsul, Sergius Paulus, an intelligent man. This man called for Barnabas and Saul and sought to hear the word of God. [8]But Elymas the sorcerer (for so his name is translated) withstood them, seeking to turn the proconsul away from the faith. [9]Then Saul, who also *is called* Paul, filled with the Holy Spirit, looked intently at him [10]and said, "O full of all deceit and all fraud, *you* son of the devil, *you* enemy of all righteousness, will you not cease perverting the straight ways of the Lord? [11]And now, indeed, the hand of the Lord *is* upon you, and you shall be blind, not seeing the sun for a time."

And immediately a dark mist fell on him, and he went around seeking someone to lead him by the hand. [12]Then the proconsul believed, when he saw what had been done, being astonished at the teaching of the Lord.

AT ANTIOCH IN PISIDIA

[13]Now when Paul and his party set sail from Paphos, they came to Perga in Pamphylia; and John, departing from them, returned to Jerusalem. [14]But when they departed from Perga, they came to Antioch in Pisidia, and went into the synagogue on the Sabbath day and sat down. [15]And after the reading of the Law and the Prophets, the rulers of the synagogue sent to them, saying, "Men *and* brethren, if you have any word of exhortation for the people, say on."

[16]Then Paul stood up, and motioning with *his* hand said, "Men of Israel, and you who fear God, listen: [17]The God of this people Israel[a] chose our fathers, and exalted the people when they dwelt as strangers in the land of Egypt, and with an uplifted arm He brought them out of it. [18]Now for a time of about forty years He put up with their ways in the wilderness. [19]And when He had destroyed seven nations in the land of Canaan, He distributed their land to them by allotment.

[20]"After that He gave *them* judges for about four hundred and fifty years, until Samuel the prophet. [21]And afterward they asked for a king; so God gave them Saul the son of Kish, a man of the tribe of Benjamin, for forty years. [22]And when He had removed him, He raised up for them David as king, to whom also He gave testimony and said, '*I have found David[a] the son* of Jesse, *a man after My own heart, who will do all My will.*'[b] [23]From this man's seed, according to *the* promise, God raised up for Israel a Savior—Jesus—[a] [24]after John had first preached, before His coming, the baptism of repentance to all the people of Israel. [25]And as John was finishing his course, he said, 'Who do you think I am? I am not *He.* But behold, there comes One after me, the sandals of whose feet I am not worthy to loose.'

[26]"Men *and* brethren, sons of the family of Abraham, and those among you who fear God, to you the word of this salvation has been sent. [27]For those who dwell in Jerusalem, and their rulers, because they did not know Him, nor even the voices of the Prophets which are read every Sabbath, have fulfilled *them* in condemning *Him.* [28]And though they found no cause for death *in Him,* they asked Pilate that He should be put to death. [29]Now when they had fulfilled all that was written concerning Him, they took *Him* down from the tree and laid *Him* in a tomb. [30]But God raised Him from the dead. [31]He was seen for many days by those who came up with Him from Galilee to Jerusalem, who are His witnesses to the people. [32]And we declare to you glad tidings—that promise which was made to the fathers. [33]God has fulfilled this for us their children, in that He has raised up Jesus. As it is also written in the second Psalm:

'You are My Son,
    Today I have begotten You.'[a]

[34]And that He raised Him from the dead, no more to return to corruption, He has spoken thus:

'I will give you the sure mercies of David.'[a]

[35]Therefore He also says in another *Psalm:*

'You will not allow Your Holy One to see
    corruption.'[a]

13:6 [a]NU-Text reads *the whole island.*   **13:17** [a]M-Text omits *Israel.*   **13:22** [a]Psalm 89:20 [b]1 Samuel 13:14   **13:23** [a]M-Text reads *for Israel salvation.*   **13:33** [a]Psalm 2:7   **13:34** [a]Isaiah 55:3   **13:35** [a]Psalm 16:10

36"For David, after he had served his own generation by the will of God, fell asleep, was buried with his fathers, and saw corruption; 37but He whom God raised up saw no corruption. 38Therefore let it be known to you, brethren, that through this Man is preached to you the forgiveness of sins; 39and by Him everyone who believes is justified from all things from which you could not be justified by the law of Moses. 40Beware therefore, lest what has been spoken in the prophets come upon you:

41*'Behold, you despisers,*
Marvel and perish!
For I work a work in your days,
A work which you will by no means believe,
*Though one were to declare it to you.' "*a

Blessing and Conflict at Antioch

42So when the Jews went out of the synagogue,a the Gentiles begged that these words might be preached to them the next Sabbath. 43Now when the congregation had broken up, many of the Jews and devout proselytes followed Paul and Barnabas, who, speaking to them, persuaded them to continue in the grace of God.

44On the next Sabbath almost the whole city came together to hear the word of God. 45But when the Jews saw the multitudes, they were filled with envy; and contradicting and blaspheming, they opposed the things spoken by Paul. 46Then Paul and Barnabas grew bold and said, "It was necessary that the word of God should be spoken to you first; but since you reject it, and judge yourselves unworthy of everlasting life, behold, we turn to the Gentiles. 47For so the Lord has commanded us:

'I have set you as a light to the Gentiles,
That you should be for salvation to the ends
*of the earth.' "*a

48Now when the Gentiles heard this, they were glad and glorified the word of the Lord. And as many as had been appointed to eternal life believed.

49And the word of the Lord was being spread throughout all the region. 50But the Jews stirred up the devout and prominent women and the chief men of the city, raised up persecution against Paul and Barnabas, and expelled them from their region. 51But they shook off the dust from their feet against them, and came to Iconium. 52And the disciples were filled with joy and with the Holy Spirit.

At Iconium

14 Now it happened in Iconium that they went together to the synagogue of the Jews, and so spoke that a great multitude both of the Jews and of the Greeks believed. 2But the unbelieving Jews stirred up the Gentiles and poisoned their minds against the brethren. 3Therefore they stayed there a long time, speaking boldly in the Lord, who was bearing witness to the word of His grace, granting signs and wonders to be done by their hands.

4But the multitude of the city was divided: part sided with the Jews, and part with the apostles. 5And when a violent attempt was made by both the Gentiles and Jews, with their rulers, to abuse and stone them, 6they became aware of it and fled to Lystra and Derbe, cities of Lycaonia, and to the surrounding region. 7And they were preaching the gospel there.

Idolatry at Lystra

8And in Lystra a certain man without strength in his feet was sitting, a cripple from his mother's womb, who had never walked. 9*This* man heard Paul speaking. Paul, observing him intently and seeing that he had faith to be healed, 10said with a loud voice, "Stand up straight on your feet!" And he leaped and walked. 11Now when the people saw what Paul had done, they raised their voices, saying in the Lycaonian *language,* "The gods have come down to us in the likeness of men!" 12And Barnabas they called Zeus, and Paul, Hermes, because he was the chief speaker. 13Then the priest of Zeus, whose temple was in front of their city, brought oxen and garlands to the gates, intending to sacrifice with the multitudes.

14But when the apostles Barnabas and Paul heard this, they tore their clothes and ran in among the multitude, crying out 15and saying,

13:41 aHabakkuk 1:5   **13:42** aOr *And when they went out of the synagogue of the Jews;* NU-Text reads *And when they went out, they begged.*   **13:47** aIsaiah 49:6

"Men, why are you doing these things? We also are men with the same nature as you, and preach to you that you should turn from these useless things to the living God, who made the heaven, the earth, the sea, and all things that are in them, 16who in bygone generations allowed all nations to walk in their own ways. 17Nevertheless He did not leave Himself without witness, in that He did good, gave us rain from heaven and fruitful seasons, filling our hearts with food and gladness." 18And with these sayings they could scarcely restrain the multitudes from sacrificing to them.

Stoning, Escape to Derbe

19Then Jews from Antioch and Iconium came there; and having persuaded the multitudes, they stoned Paul *and* dragged *him* out of the city, supposing him to be dead. 20However, when the disciples gathered around him, he rose up and went into the city. And the next day he departed with Barnabas to Derbe.

Strengthening the Converts

21And when they had preached the gospel to that city and made many disciples, they returned to Lystra, Iconium, and Antioch, 22strengthening the souls of the disciples, exhorting *them* to continue in the faith, and *saying,* "We must through many tribulations enter the kingdom of God." 23So when they had appointed elders in every church, and prayed with fasting, they commended them to the Lord in whom they had believed. 24And after they had passed through Pisidia, they came to Pamphylia. 25Now when they had preached the word in Perga, they went down to Attalia. 26From there they sailed to Antioch, where they had been commended to the grace of God for the work which they had completed.

27Now when they had come and gathered the church together, they reported all that God had done with them, and that He had opened the door of faith to the Gentiles. 28So they stayed there a long time with the disciples.

Conflict over Circumcision

15 And certain *men* came down from Judea and taught the brethren, "Unless you are circumcised according to the custom of Moses, you cannot be saved." 2Therefore, when Paul and

Barnabas had no small dissension and dispute with them, they determined that Paul and Barnabas and certain others of them should go up to Jerusalem, to the apostles and elders, about this question.

3So, being sent on their way by the church, they passed through Phoenicia and Samaria, describing the conversion of the Gentiles; and they caused great joy to all the brethren. 4And when they had come to Jerusalem, they were received by the church and the apostles and the elders; and they reported all things that God had done with them. 5But some of the sect of the Pharisees who believed rose up, saying, "It is necessary to circumcise them, and to command *them* to keep the law of Moses."

The Jerusalem Council

6Now the apostles and elders came together to consider this matter. 7And when there had been much dispute, Peter rose up *and* said to them: "Men *and* brethren, you know that a good while ago God chose among us, that by my mouth the Gentiles should hear the word of the gospel and believe. 8So God, who knows the heart, acknowledged them by giving them the Holy Spirit, just as *He did* to us, 9and made no distinction between us and them, purifying their hearts by faith. 10Now therefore, why do you test God by putting a yoke on the neck of the disciples which neither our fathers nor we were able to bear? 11But we believe that through the grace of the Lord Jesus Christ[a] we shall be saved in the same manner as they."

12Then all the multitude kept silent and listened to Barnabas and Paul declaring how many miracles and wonders God had worked through them among the Gentiles. 13And after they had become silent, James answered, saying, "Men *and* brethren, listen to me: 14Simon has declared how God at the first visited the Gentiles to take out of them a people for His name. 15And with this the words of the prophets agree, just as it is written:

16'After this I will return
    And will rebuild the tabernacle of David,
        which has fallen down;

15:11 [a]NU-Text and M-Text omit *Christ.*

THROUGH THE GRID

Written by the Hand of God:
The Importance of Grace

ACTS 15:11   *But we believe that through the grace of the Lord Jesus Christ we shall be saved.*

It is because of grace that we receive what we do not earn—eternal salvation. Grace is one of the cornerstones of biblical theology, and the Ten Commandments serve to point humanity toward that grace. We are all deeply in need of God's grace; but no one deserves anything from God, as we are all fallen and sinful creatures.

Obeying the Ten Commandments verifies that they cannot be kept perfectly, as we have all broken some of the Commandments in our lives. However, it is because of grace that all is not lost. Even though we are all fallen and do not deserve to receive anything good from God, He freely gives the gift of salvation to all who accept Him in the Person of Jesus Christ (Eph. 2:8, 9). Grace is important because without it, we would not be able to merit our own salvation, and we would be destined for an eternity apart from God.

When we obey the Ten Commandments, we do so through the grace given to us, empowering us to serve others and to be faithful witnesses to the world. However, no one is capable of obeying God's Law in one's own strength. But, through the grace given in the Holy Spirit, we are able to lead productive and obedient lives. God's grace as exhibited through the Holy Spirit enables us to live the Christian life and to be pleasing to God. In no way can we be acceptable to God on our own merits and strengths. Thus, the source of the Christian's power and strength lies in the grace of God as well as in the empowerment by the Holy Spirit—not in exertions of willpower or self-effort. It is only through grace that we can accomplish anything at all. Without grace, we would be powerless and lost. May we thank God for His innumerable gifts of grace to us each and every day. Our response to God in gratitude is to obey God with all of our beings.

I will rebuild its ruins,
   And I will set it up;
17 So that the rest of mankind may seek the
      LORD,
   Even all the Gentiles who are called by My
      name,
   Says the LORD who does all these things.'ᵃ

18"Known to God from eternity are all His works.ᵃ 19Therefore I judge that we should not trouble those from among the Gentiles who are turning to God, 20but that we write to them to abstain from things polluted by idols, *from* sexual immorality,ᵃ *from* things strangled, and *from* blood.

21For Moses has had throughout many generations those who preach him in every city, being read in the synagogues every Sabbath."

THE JERUSALEM DECREE

22Then it pleased the apostles and elders, with the whole church, to send chosen men of their own company to Antioch with Paul and Barnabas, *namely,* Judas who was also named Barsabas,ᵃ and Silas, leading men among the brethren.

15:17 ᵃAmos 9:11, 12   **15:18** ᵃNU-Text (combining with verse 17) reads *Says the Lord, who makes these things known from eternity (of old).*   **15:20** ᵃOr *fornication*   **15:22** ᵃNU-Text and M-Text read *Barsabbas.*

²³They wrote this, *letter* by them:

The apostles, the elders, and the brethren,

To the brethren who are of the Gentiles in Antioch, Syria, and Cilicia:

Greetings.

²⁴Since we have heard that some who went out from us have troubled you with words, unsettling your souls, saying, "*You must* be circumcised and keep the law"ᵃ—to whom we gave no *such* commandment—²⁵it seemed good to us, being assembled with one accord, to send chosen men to you with our beloved Barnabas and Paul, ²⁶men who have risked their lives for the name of our Lord Jesus Christ. ²⁷We have therefore sent Judas and Silas, who will also report the same things by word of mouth. ²⁸For it seemed good to the Holy Spirit, and to us,

to lay upon you no greater burden than these necessary things: ²⁹that you abstain from things offered to idols, from blood, from things strangled, and from sexual immorality.ᵃ If you keep yourselves from these, you will do well.

Farewell.

CONTINUING MINISTRY IN SYRIA

³⁰So when they were sent off, they came to Antioch; and when they had gathered the multitude together, they delivered the letter. ³¹When they had read it, they rejoiced over its encouragement. ³²Now Judas and Silas, themselves being prophets also, exhorted and strengthened the brethren with many words. ³³And after they had stayed *there* for a time, they were sent back with greetings from the brethren to the apostles.ᵃ

15:24 ᵃNU-Text omits *saying, "You must be circumcised and keep the law."* **15:29** ᵃOr *fornication* **15:33** ᵃNU-Text reads *to those who had sent them.*

INSIDE *the* INFLUENCERS

SILAS: Marked By Faithfulness

ACTS 15:40

When Paul was gearing up for his second missionary journey, he and Barnabas had a "sharp disagreement." Paul wouldn't allow Mark on the trip because he wasn't dependable. Barnabas was loyal to his cousin Mark, and so he and Paul parted ways. This is where Silas came on the scene.

Paul selected Silas to go with him. He must have had a good reputation for Paul to choose him at this point in his ministry. The two were about to face intense persecution, but Silas proved to be a man of consistent faith.

In Philippi, Paul and Silas were imprisoned for preaching Jesus. The two men began singing songs of praise in the middle of the night, and the prison doors flung open, their chains were broken, and the jailer came to believe in Jesus when Paul and Silas assured him that none of the prisoners had escaped. Revival broke out in prison! Paul's joy on what appeared to be an awful day probably had a lot to do with the presence and encouragement of Silas.

Silas's faithfulness secured for him a significant part in the furthering of the Gospel. When Peter writes his letter to those believers who have been scattered and persecuted by the strong arm of Rome, the Lord entrusted Silas, the "faithful brother" to deliver its contents (1 Pet. 5:12).

³⁴However, it seemed good to Silas to remain there.ᵃ ³⁵Paul and Barnabas also remained in Antioch, teaching and preaching the word of the Lord, with many others also.

DIVISION OVER JOHN MARK

³⁶Then after some days Paul said to Barnabas, "Let us now go back and visit our brethren in every city where we have preached the word of the Lord, *and see* how they are doing." ³⁷Now Barnabas was determined to take with them John called Mark. ³⁸But Paul insisted that they should not take with them the one who had departed from them in Pamphylia, and had not gone with them to the work. ³⁹Then the contention became so sharp that they parted from one another. And so Barnabas took Mark and sailed to Cyprus; ⁴⁰but Paul chose Silas and departed, being commended by the brethren to the grace of God. ⁴¹And he went through Syria and Cilicia, strengthening the churches.

TIMOTHY JOINS PAUL AND SILAS

16 Then he came to Derbe and Lystra. And behold, a certain disciple was there, named Timothy, *the* son of a certain Jewish woman who believed, but his father *was* Greek. ²He was well spoken of by the brethren who were at Lystra and Iconium. ³Paul wanted to have him go on with him. And he took *him* and circumcised him because of the Jews who were in that region, for they all knew that his father was Greek. ⁴And as they went through the cities, they delivered to them the decrees to keep, which were determined by the apostles and elders at Jerusalem. ⁵So the churches were strengthened in the faith, and increased in number daily.

THE MACEDONIAN CALL

⁶Now when they had gone through Phrygia and the region of Galatia, they were forbidden by

15:34 ᵃNU-Text and M-Text omit this verse.

---

 the **INFLUENCERS**

TIMOTHY—Small Start—Big Opportunities

2 TIMOTHY 1:1–7

Timothy grew up hearing about the things of God from his Jewish mother and grandmother. His Greek father's faith is not mentioned. Timothy may have been shy or fearful. We read that Paul assured him, "God has not given us a spirit of fear" (v. 7). Timothy was a believer; the apostle Paul calls him "a true son in the faith" (1 Tim. 1:2).

Paul's ministry deeply impressed Timothy. He was not deterred from the ministry by the stoning and beatings Paul endured. Therefore, Timothy is called a *disciple,* one whose life was marked by discipline and the willingness to learn. His reputation preceded him as a young man upon which Paul could depend (Acts 16:1, 2).

Young Timothy was given many responsibilities by the apostle Paul as Paul traveled and was later imprisoned. Paul sent two helpers, one of whom was Timothy, to Macedonia in his place. His faithfulness earned him the incredible opportunities to both lead and teach in the early Christian church. Paul told the Corinthians, "I have sent Timothy to you, who is my beloved and faithful son in the Lord, who will remind you of my ways in Christ, as I teach everywhere in every church" (1 Cor. 4:17).

Timothy showed himself trustworthy through a servant-hearted friendship to Paul, and Paul trusted Timothy to serve alongside him in Christian history.

the Holy Spirit to preach the word in Asia. ⁷After they had come to Mysia, they tried to go into Bithynia, but the Spiritᵃ did not permit them. ⁸So passing by Mysia, they came down to Troas. ⁹And a vision appeared to Paul in the night. A man of Macedonia stood and pleaded with him, saying, "Come over to Macedonia and help us." ¹⁰Now after he had seen the vision, immediately we sought to go to Macedonia, concluding that the Lord had called us to preach the gospel to them.

Lydia Baptized at Philippi

¹¹Therefore, sailing from Troas, we ran a straight course to Samothrace, and the next *day* came to Neapolis, ¹²and from there to Philippi, which is the foremost city of that part of Macedonia, a colony. And we were staying in that city for some days. ¹³And on the Sabbath day we went out of the city to the riverside, where prayer was customarily made; and we sat down and spoke to the women who met *there.* ¹⁴Now a certain woman named Lydia heard *us.* She was a seller of purple from the city of Thyatira, who worshiped God. The Lord opened her heart to heed the things spoken by Paul. ¹⁵And when she and her household were baptized, she begged *us,* saying, "If you have judged me to be faithful to the Lord, come to my house and stay." So she persuaded us.

Paul and Silas Imprisoned

¹⁶Now it happened, as we went to prayer, that a certain slave girl possessed with a spirit of divination met us, who brought her masters much profit by fortune-telling. ¹⁷This girl followed Paul and us, and cried out, saying, "These men are the servants of the Most High God, who proclaim to us the way of salvation." ¹⁸And this she did for many days.

But Paul, greatly annoyed, turned and said to the spirit, "I command you in the name of Jesus Christ to come out of her." And he came out that very hour. ¹⁹But when her masters saw that their

16:7 ᵃNU-Text adds *of Jesus.*

---

 the **INFLUENCERS**

LYDIA—An Open Heart

ACTS 16

One particular trip took Paul to Macedonia, a colony called Philippi where he met a "seller of purple" cloth named Lydia by the riverside where she worshiped God. When Lydia heard Paul's message of genuine salvation, she understood that knowing **about** God is not the same as **knowing** God. Scripture says, "The Lord opened her heart to heed the things spoken by Paul" (16:14).

As a wealthy businesswoman, Lydia's friendship with these Christian strangers, Paul in particular, could have been risky. However, the risk was worth the result. The change in Lydia was immediate and genuine. She identified herself publicly as a Christian through baptism, shared her faith with her household, and opened her home as the first church of Philippi at risk of her own life and livelihood.

Lydia took the *grace of God* and began a revolution. She denied social and cultural laws by having a house church, where Jew and Greek sat together; slaves and masters worshiped side by side; and men and women worshiped together.

This was the first church in Europe. About ten years after he led Lydia to Christ, Paul wrote to the Philippian church: "To all the saints in Christ Jesus who are in Philippi, . . ." Her open heart helped to plant a healthy, vibrant church that funded Paul's ministry on many occasions, as written about in the Scriptures.

hope of profit was gone, they seized Paul and Silas and dragged *them* into the marketplace to the authorities.

20And they brought them to the magistrates, and said, "These men, being Jews, exceedingly trouble our city; 21and they teach customs which are not lawful for us, being Romans, to receive or observe." 22Then the multitude rose up together against them; and the magistrates tore off their clothes and commanded *them* to be beaten with rods. 23And when they had laid many stripes on them, they threw *them* into prison, commanding the jailer to keep them securely. 24Having received such a charge, he put them into the inner prison and fastened their feet in the stocks.

The Philippian Jailer Saved

25But at midnight Paul and Silas were praying and singing hymns to God, and the prisoners were listening to them. 26Suddenly there was a great earthquake, so that the foundations of the prison were shaken; and immediately all the doors were opened and everyone's chains were loosed. 27And the keeper of the prison, awaking from sleep and seeing the prison doors open, supposing the prisoners had fled, drew his sword and was about to kill himself. 28But Paul called with a loud voice, saying, "Do yourself no harm, for we are all here."

29Then he called for a light, ran in, and fell down trembling before Paul and Silas. 30And he brought them out and said, "Sirs, what must I do to be saved?"

31So they said, "Believe on the Lord Jesus Christ, and you will be saved, you and your household." 32Then they spoke the word of the Lord to him and to all who were in his house. 33And he took them the same hour of the night and washed *their* stripes. And immediately he and all his *family* were baptized. 34Now when he had brought them into his house, he set food before them; and he rejoiced, having believed in God with all his household.

Paul Refuses to Depart Secretly

35And when it was day, the magistrates sent the officers, saying, "Let those men go."

36So the keeper of the prison reported these words to Paul, saying, "The magistrates have sent to let you go. Now therefore depart, and go in peace."

37But Paul said to them, "They have beaten us openly, uncondemned Romans, *and* have thrown *us* into prison. And now do they put us out secretly? No indeed! Let them come themselves and get us out."

38And the officers told these words to the magistrates, and they were afraid when they heard that they were Romans. 39Then they came and pleaded with them and brought *them* out, and asked *them* to depart from the city. 40So they went out of the prison and entered *the house of* Lydia; and when they had seen the brethren, they encouraged them and departed.

Preaching Christ at Thessalonica

17 Now when they had passed through Amphipolis and Apollonia, they came to Thessalonica, where there was a synagogue of the Jews. 2Then Paul, as his custom was, went in to them, and for three Sabbaths reasoned with them from the Scriptures, 3explaining and demonstrating that the Christ had to suffer and rise again from the dead, and *saying,* "This Jesus whom I preach to you is the Christ." 4And some of them were persuaded; and a great multitude of the devout Greeks, and not a few of the leading women, joined Paul and Silas.

Assault on Jason's House

5But the Jews who were not persuaded, becoming envious,a took some of the evil men from the marketplace, and gathering a mob, set all the city in an uproar and attacked the house of Jason, and sought to bring them out to the people. 6But when they did not find them, they dragged Jason and some brethren to the rulers of the city, crying out, "These who have turned the world upside down have come here too. 7Jason has harbored them, and these are all acting contrary to the decrees of Caesar, saying there is another king— Jesus." 8And they troubled the crowd and the rulers of the city when they heard these things. 9So when they had taken security from Jason and the rest, they let them go.

17:5 aNU-Text omits *who were not persuaded;* M-Text omits *becoming envious.*

LEADERSHIP
REALITIES

FLEXIBILITY: LEARN TO ROLL WITH THE PUNCHES   *Acts 17*

In these days of constant change and global news, life is anything but predictable for this generation. The leader prepares and plans to reach goals, but must also be prepared for interruptions and disappointments and difficult situations. It is in these moments of stress and surprise that the leader has to demonstrate the Christlike attitude of flexibility. The ability to be flexible provides a journey of more insight than that of actually arriving at the destination. Paul most likely understood this better than anyone:

Thessalonica: On a great high of success, he hears that the Jews are infuriated by the conversions to Christianity and have caused uproar in the city. Forced to retreat, Paul escapes the city by night.

Berea: He had much victory in presenting the gospel only to have the Jews from Thessalonica follow him there. The crowds were stirred up in such a way that he had to escape under cover of darkness once again.

Athens: Paul took note of the idols and studied the culture in great detail. Given the chance to stand on the Areopagus and give a testimony of the gospel, he was greeted with sneers but others wanted to hear more.

Opportunities are seldom perfect, but when one is flexible, as Paul was, they can be doors that lead to a greater privilege and a resulting testimony of strength, courage, and faith for generations to come.

MINISTERING AT BEREA

[10]Then the brethren immediately sent Paul and Silas away by night to Berea. When they arrived, they went into the synagogue of the Jews. [11]These were more fair-minded than those in Thessalonica, in that they received the word with all readiness, and searched the Scriptures daily *to find out* whether these things were so. [12]Therefore many of them believed, and also not a few of the Greeks, prominent women as well as men. [13]But when the Jews from Thessalonica learned that the word of God was preached by Paul at Berea, they came there also and stirred up the crowds. [14]Then immediately the brethren sent Paul away, to go to the sea; but both Silas and Timothy remained there. [15]So those who conducted Paul brought him to Athens; and receiving a command for Silas and Timothy to come to him with all speed, they departed.

THE PHILOSOPHERS AT ATHENS

[16]Now while Paul waited for them at Athens, his spirit was provoked within him when he saw that the city was given over to idols. [17]Therefore he reasoned in the synagogue with the Jews and with the *Gentile* worshipers, and in the marketplace daily with those who happened to be there. [18]Then[a] certain Epicurean and Stoic philosophers encountered him. And some said, "What does this babbler want to say?"

Others said, "He seems to be a proclaimer of foreign gods," because he preached to them Jesus and the resurrection.

[19]And they took him and brought him to the Areopagus, saying, "May we know what this new doctrine *is* of which you speak? [20]For you are bringing some strange things to our ears. There-

17:18 [a]NU-Text and M-Text add *also.*

INSIDE *the* INFLUENCERS

PAUL: Influence on the Mountain Begins with Faithfulness in the Streets

ACTS 17

It is often said that when Paul preached in a city, it either saw a revival or a rebellion. Chapter 17 provides examples of both. In Thessalonica Paul and his missionary team caused an uproar. A mob formed and demanded justice because they "turned the world upside down." Paul and Silas escaped under cover of darkness. In Berea, following their modus operandi of preaching in the synagogues and then the streets, Paul and Silas were well received by the "more fair-minded" citizens (v. 11). The Thessalonians came to Berea to stir up crowds against Paul, who fled alone to Athens.

Athens was known for culture, education and idolatry. One ancient philosopher said there were more idols in the city than people. It was a crossroads of many different types of beliefs. Paul made a conscious decision to communicate the Gospel in that culture. He was provoked to immediate action (vv. 16, 17) and saw opportunity in opposition (vv. 17, 18). Paul chose to "cowboy up" rather than cower from the moment and the message (vv. 22, 23). His influence expanded because of consistent obedience (vv. 19, 20) and the measure of his success was determined only by his faithfulness to the message (vv. 24–34).

---

fore we want to know what these things mean." 21For all the Athenians and the foreigners who were there spent their time in nothing else but either to tell or to hear some new thing.

Addressing the Areopagus

22Then Paul stood in the midst of the Areopagus and said, "Men of Athens, I perceive that in all things you are very religious; 23for as I was passing through and considering the objects of your worship, I even found an altar with this inscription:

TO THE UNKNOWN GOD.

Therefore, the One whom you worship without knowing, Him I proclaim to you: 24God, who made the world and everything in it, since He is Lord of heaven and earth, does not dwell in temples made with hands. 25Nor is He worshiped with men's hands, as though He needed anything, since He gives to all life, breath, and all things. 26And He has made from one blood[a] every nation of men to dwell on all the face of

the earth, and has determined their preappointed times and the boundaries of their dwellings, 27so that they should seek the Lord, in the hope that they might grope for Him and find Him, though He is not far from each one of us; 28for in Him we live and move and have our being, as also some of your own poets have said, 'For we are also His offspring.' 29Therefore, since we are the offspring of God, we ought not to think that the Divine Nature is like gold or silver or stone, something shaped by art and man's devising. 30Truly, these times of ignorance God overlooked, but now commands all men everywhere to repent, 31because He has appointed a day on which He will judge the world in righteousness by the Man whom He has ordained. He has given assurance of this to all by raising Him from the dead."

32And when they heard of the resurrection of the dead, some mocked, while others said, "We will hear you again on this *matter*." 33So Paul departed from among them. 34However, some men joined him and believed, among them Dionysius

17:26 [a]NU-Text omits *blood*.

LEADERSHIP ISSUES

React or Reframe

ACTS 17:16–34

In any situation, we can respond in one of three ways; we can roll over, react, or reframe. Reframing is always the most difficult. It requires self-control, thought, and creativity. Here we see Paul reframe the issue. In verse 16, Paul is "provoked within him" by the widespread idolatry in Athens. Instead of reacting (condemning idol worship), he figured out a way to use the situation as a platform for making Jesus the issue—reframing.

In verse 22, he begins his comments by finding common ground with his audience. Employing one of their own icons, an altar "To an Unknown God," he points them toward Jesus. He used the platform by giving new meaning to something that was already familiar to them.

Three very important things occurred in this story. First, Paul did not condemn pagans for behaving like pagans, which would have caused them to react defensively. Second, Paul reframed the agenda, putting himself in the "driver's seat." Third, because he clearly defined the issue, some people understood and responded positively.

Today our culture has a far better grasp of what the church stands against than of what we stand for. What do you think might happen if Christians adopted Paul's approach to all the divisive symptomatic social issues of our day from abortion to homosexuality? Sure, it would take some self-control, thought, and creativity; but that is why God gave us intellect. We can continue to react defensively to symptoms, or we can use the symptoms in order to make God the focus by reframing.

the Areopagite, a woman named Damaris, and others with them.

MINISTERING AT CORINTH

18 After these things Paul departed from Athens and went to Corinth. [2]And he found a certain Jew named Aquila, born in Pontus, who had recently come from Italy with his wife Priscilla (because Claudius had commanded all the Jews to depart from Rome); and he came to them. [3]So, because he was of the same trade, he stayed with them and worked; for by occupation they were tentmakers. [4]And he reasoned in the synagogue every Sabbath, and persuaded both Jews and Greeks.

[5]When Silas and Timothy had come from Macedonia, Paul was compelled by the Spirit, and testified to the Jews *that* Jesus *is* the Christ. [6]But when they opposed him and blasphemed, he shook *his* garments and said to them, "Your blood *be* upon your *own* heads; I *am* clean. From now on I will go to the Gentiles." [7]And he departed from there and entered the house of a certain *man* named Justus,[a] *one* who worshiped God, whose house was next door to the synagogue. [8]Then Crispus, the ruler of the synagogue, believed on the Lord with all his household. And many of the Corinthians, hearing, believed and were baptized.

[9]Now the Lord spoke to Paul in the night by a vision, "Do not be afraid, but speak, and do not keep silent; [10]for I am with you, and no one will attack you to hurt you; for I have many people in this city." [11]And he continued *there* a year and six months, teaching the word of God among them.

[12]When Gallio was proconsul of Achaia, the Jews with one accord rose up against Paul and brought him to the judgment seat, [13]saying, "This *fellow* persuades men to worship God contrary to the law."

[14]And when Paul was about to open *his* mouth, Gallio said to the Jews, "If it were a matter of wrongdoing or wicked crimes, O Jews, there would be reason why I should bear with you. [15]But if it is a question of words and names and your own law, look *to it* yourselves; for I do not want to be a judge of such *matters.*" [16]And he drove them from the judgment seat. [17]Then all the Greeks[a] took Sosthenes, the ruler of the syna-

gogue, and beat *him* before the judgment seat. But Gallio took no notice of these things.

PAUL RETURNS TO ANTIOCH

[18]So Paul still remained a good while. Then he took leave of the brethren and sailed for Syria, and Priscilla and Aquila *were* with him. He had *his* hair cut off at Cenchrea, for he had taken a vow. [19]And he came to Ephesus, and left them there; but he himself entered the synagogue and reasoned with the Jews. [20]When they asked *him* to stay a longer time with them, he did not consent, [21]but took leave of them, saying, "I must by all means keep this coming feast in Jerusalem;[a] but I will return again to you, God willing." And he sailed from Ephesus.

[22]And when he had landed at Caesarea, and gone up and greeted the church, he went down to Antioch. [23]After he had spent some time *there,* he departed and went over the region of Galatia and Phrygia in order, strengthening all the disciples.

MINISTRY OF APOLLOS

[24]Now a certain Jew named Apollos, born at Alexandria, an eloquent man *and* mighty in the Scriptures, came to Ephesus. [25]This man had been instructed in the way of the Lord; and being fervent in spirit, he spoke and taught accurately the things of the Lord, though he knew only the baptism of John. [26]So he began to speak boldly in the synagogue. When Aquila and Priscilla heard him, they took him aside and explained to him the way of God more accurately. [27]And when he desired to cross to Achaia, the brethren wrote, exhorting the disciples to receive him; and when he arrived, he greatly helped those who had believed through grace; [28]for he vigorously refuted the Jews publicly, showing from the Scriptures that Jesus is the Christ.

PAUL AT EPHESUS

19 And it happened, while Apollos was at Corinth, that Paul, having passed through the upper regions, came to Ephesus. And finding some disciples [2]he said to them, "Did you receive the Holy Spirit when you believed?"

18:7 [a]NU-Text reads *Titius Justus.*   **18:17** [a]NU-Text reads *they all.*
18:21 [a]NU-Text omits *I must* through *Jerusalem.*

So they said to him, "We have not so much as heard whether there is a Holy Spirit."

³And he said to them, "Into what then were you baptized?"

So they said, "Into John's baptism."

⁴Then Paul said, "John indeed baptized with a baptism of repentance, saying to the people that they should believe on Him who would come after him, that is, on Christ Jesus."

⁵When they heard *this,* they were baptized in the name of the Lord Jesus. ⁶And when Paul had laid hands on them, the Holy Spirit came upon them, and they spoke with tongues and prophesied. ⁷Now the men were about twelve in all.

⁸And he went into the synagogue and spoke boldly for three months, reasoning and persuading concerning the things of the kingdom of God. ⁹But when some were hardened and did not believe, but spoke evil of the Way before the multitude, he departed from them and withdrew the disciples, reasoning daily in the school of Tyrannus. ¹⁰And this continued for two years, so that all who dwelt in Asia heard the word of the Lord Jesus, both Jews and Greeks.

MIRACLES GLORIFY CHRIST

¹¹Now God worked unusual miracles by the hands of Paul, ¹²so that even handkerchiefs or aprons were brought from his body to the sick, and the diseases left them and the evil spirits went out of them. ¹³Then some of the itinerant Jewish exorcists took it upon themselves to call the name of the Lord Jesus over those who had evil spirits, saying, "We[a] exorcise you by the Jesus whom Paul preaches." ¹⁴Also there were seven sons of Sceva, a Jewish chief priest, who did so.

¹⁵And the evil spirit answered and said, "Jesus I know, and Paul I know; but who are you?"

¹⁶Then the man in whom the evil spirit was leaped on them, overpowered[a] them, and prevailed against them,[b] so that they fled out of that house naked and wounded. ¹⁷This became known both to all Jews and Greeks dwelling in Ephesus; and fear fell on them all, and the name of the Lord Jesus was magnified. ¹⁸And many who had believed came confessing and telling their deeds. ¹⁹Also, many of those who had practiced magic brought their books together and burned *them* in the sight of all. And they counted up the value of them, and *it* totaled fifty thousand *pieces* of silver. ²⁰So the word of the Lord grew mightily and prevailed.

THE RIOT AT EPHESUS

²¹When these things were accomplished, Paul purposed in the Spirit, when he had passed through Macedonia and Achaia, to go to Jerusalem, saying, "After I have been there, I must also see Rome." ²²So he sent into Macedonia two of those who ministered to him, Timothy and Erastus, but he himself stayed in Asia for a time.

²³And about that time there arose a great commotion about the Way. ²⁴For a certain man named Demetrius, a silversmith, who made silver shrines of Diana,[a] brought no small profit to the craftsmen. ²⁵He called them together with the workers of similar occupation, and said: "Men, you know that we have our prosperity by this trade. ²⁶Moreover you see and hear that not only at Ephesus, but throughout almost all Asia, this Paul has persuaded and turned away many people, saying that they are not gods which are made with hands. ²⁷So not only is this trade of ours in danger of falling into disrepute, but also the temple of the great goddess Diana may be despised and her magnificence destroyed,[a] whom all Asia and the world worship."

²⁸Now when they heard *this,* they were full of wrath and cried out, saying, "Great *is* Diana of the Ephesians!" ²⁹So the whole city was filled with confusion, and rushed into the theater with one accord, having seized Gaius and Aristarchus, Macedonians, Paul's travel companions. ³⁰And when Paul wanted to go in to the people, the disciples would not allow him. ³¹Then some of the officials of Asia, who were his friends, sent to him pleading that he would not venture into the theater. ³²Some therefore cried one thing and some another, for the assembly was confused, and most of them did not know why they had come together. ³³And they drew Alexander out of the multitude, the Jews putting him forward. And Alexander motioned with his hand, and wanted to make his defense to the people. ³⁴But when they found out that he was a Jew, all with one

19:13 [a]NU-Text reads *I.* **19:16** [a]M-Text reads *and they overpowered.* [b]NU-Text reads *both of them.* **19:24** [a]Greek *Artemis* **19:27** [a]NU-Text reads *she be deposed from her magnificence.*

voice cried out for about two hours, "Great *is* Diana of the Ephesians!"

[35]And when the city clerk had quieted the crowd, he said: "Men of Ephesus, what man is there who does not know that the city of the Ephesians is temple guardian of the great goddess Diana, and of the *image* which fell down from Zeus? [36]Therefore, since these things cannot be denied, you ought to be quiet and do nothing rashly. [37]For you have brought these men here who are neither robbers of temples nor blasphemers of your[a] goddess. [38]Therefore, if Demetrius and his fellow craftsmen have a case against anyone, the courts are open and there are proconsuls. Let them bring charges against one another. [39]But if you have any other inquiry to make, it shall be determined in the lawful assembly. [40]For we are in danger of being called in question for today's uproar, there being no reason which we may give to account for this disorderly gathering." [41]And when he had said these things, he dismissed the assembly.

Journeys in Greece

20 After the uproar had ceased, Paul called the disciples to *himself*, embraced *them*, and departed to go to Macedonia. [2]Now when he had gone over that region and encouraged them with many words, he came to Greece [3]and stayed three months. And when the Jews plotted against him as he was about to sail to Syria, he decided to return through Macedonia. [4]And Sopater of Berea accompanied him to Asia—also Aristarchus and Secundus of the Thessalonians, and Gaius of Derbe, and Timothy, and Tychicus and Trophimus of Asia. [5]These men, going ahead, waited for us at Troas. [6]But we sailed away from Philippi after the Days of Unleavened Bread, and in five days joined them at Troas, where we stayed seven days.

Ministering at Troas

[7]Now on the first *day* of the week, when the disciples came together to break bread, Paul, ready to depart the next day, spoke to them and continued his message until midnight. [8]There were many lamps in the upper room where they[a] were gathered together. [9]And in a window sat a certain young man named Eutychus, who was sinking into a deep sleep. He was overcome by sleep; and

as Paul continued speaking, he fell down from the third story and was taken up dead. [10]But Paul went down, fell on him, and embracing *him* said, "Do not trouble yourselves, for his life is in him." [11]Now when he had come up, had broken bread and eaten, and talked a long while, even till daybreak, he departed. [12]And they brought the young man in alive, and they were not a little comforted.

From Troas to Miletus

[13]Then we went ahead to the ship and sailed to Assos, there intending to take Paul on board; for so he had given orders, intending himself to go on foot. [14]And when he met us at Assos, we took him on board and came to Mitylene. [15]We sailed from there, and the next *day* came opposite Chios. The following *day* we arrived at Samos and stayed at Trogyllium. The next *day* we came to Miletus. [16]For Paul had decided to sail past Ephesus, so that he would not have to spend time in Asia; for he was hurrying to be at Jerusalem, if possible, on the Day of Pentecost.

The Ephesian Elders Exhorted

[17]From Miletus he sent to Ephesus and called for the elders of the church. [18]And when they had come to him, he said to them: "You know, from the first day that I came to Asia, in what manner I always lived among you, [19]serving the Lord with all humility, with many tears and trials which happened to me by the plotting of the Jews; [20]how I kept back nothing that was helpful, but proclaimed it to you, and taught you publicly and from house to house, [21]testifying to Jews, and also to Greeks, repentance toward God and faith toward our Lord Jesus Christ. [22]And see, now I go bound in the spirit to Jerusalem, not knowing the things that will happen to me there, [23]except that the Holy Spirit testifies in every city, saying that chains and tribulations await me. [24]But none of these things move me; nor do I count my life dear to myself,[a] so that I may finish my race with joy, and the ministry which I received from the Lord Jesus, to testify to the gospel of the grace of God.

[25]"And indeed, now I know that you all, among whom I have gone preaching the kingdom

19:37 [a]NU-Text reads *our.*   **20:8** [a]NU-Text and M-Text read *we.*
20:24 [a]NU-Text reads *But I do not count my life of any value or dear to myself.*

LEADERSHIP ISSUES

Bound in the Spirit

ACTS 20:19–31

The apostle Paul is a man who has no equal. Driven by discipline and humility, he is an example of excellence to every leader. Paul told Timothy to discipline himself for the purpose of godliness (1 Tim. 4:7). The word for discipline in this verse is the Greek word translated as "gymnasium," indicating that the same dedication needed for a healthy body is to be applied to spiritual health.

Paul reminded the Ephesians that for three years he served continuously with humility, tears, and trials (Acts 20:19). Paul was not bragging; he was stating the purity of his motives and asking them to review the public record. For three years, they watched as he served without coveting silver, gold, or apparel (v. 33).

For many leaders, the greatest temptation is the desire for status, but a significant part of serving God is avoiding those things that pull us away from Him. We start out asking, "Why me, Lord?" surprised that God has chosen to use us. But as we become experienced, educated, and inflated, we are more tempted to say, "Why *not* me, Lord?" wondering why we were overlooked for this or that.

Paul went on to remind them further of his heart and the tears he shed on their behalf. This man had no room for pride. He showed openly an emotional and passionate leadership that was devoted only to preaching the Good News and caring for the early church (vv. 19, 31). So devoted was this apostle that he claimed to be "bound in the spirit"; that is, he went forward out of a direct command and commitment to obedience to the One who led Him. That he had no plans of his own is evident in his words "not knowing the things that will happen to me there" (v. 22). Leaders would do well to follow such an eloquent example in defining their own passion and drive. Paul was not concerned about whether his hearers would accept or reject him. Leaders can only overcome the rejection that may come with evangelism if they are infused with a passion for God.

of God, will see my face no more. ²⁶Therefore I testify to you this day that I *am* innocent of the blood of all *men*. ²⁷For I have not shunned to declare to you the whole counsel of God. ²⁸Therefore take heed to yourselves and to all the flock, among which the Holy Spirit has made you overseers, to shepherd the church of God^a which He purchased with His own blood. ²⁹For I know this, that after my departure savage wolves will come in among you, not sparing the flock. ³⁰Also from among yourselves men will rise up, speaking perverse things, to draw away the disciples after themselves. ³¹Therefore watch, and remember that for three years I did not cease to warn everyone night and day with tears.

³²"So now, brethren, I commend you to God and to the word of His grace, which is able to build you up and give you an inheritance among all those who are sanctified. ³³I have coveted no one's silver or gold or apparel. ³⁴Yes,^a you yourselves know that these hands have provided for my necessities, and for those who were with me. ³⁵I have shown you in every way, by laboring like this, that you must support the weak. And remember the words of the Lord Jesus, that He said, 'It is more blessed to give than to receive.' "

³⁶And when he had said these things, he knelt down and prayed with them all. ³⁷Then they all wept freely, and fell on Paul's neck and kissed him, ³⁸sorrowing most of all for the words which he spoke, that they would see his face no more. And they accompanied him to the ship.

Warnings on the Journey to Jerusalem

21 Now it came to pass, that when we had departed from them and set sail, running a straight course we came to Cos, the following *day* to Rhodes, and from there to Patara. ²And finding a ship sailing over to Phoenicia, we went aboard and set sail. ³When we had sighted Cyprus, we passed it on the left, sailed to Syria, and landed at Tyre; for there the ship was to unload her cargo. ⁴And finding disciples,^a we stayed there seven days. They told Paul through the Spirit not to go up to Jerusalem. ⁵When we had come to the end of those days, we departed and went on our way; and they all accompanied us, with wives and children, till *we were* out of the city. And we knelt down on the shore and prayed. ⁶When we had

taken our leave of one another, we boarded the ship, and they returned home.

⁷And when we had finished *our* voyage from Tyre, we came to Ptolemais, greeted the brethren, and stayed with them one day. ⁸On the next *day* we who were Paul's companions^a departed and came to Caesarea, and entered the house of Philip the evangelist, who was *one* of the seven, and stayed with him. ⁹Now this man had four virgin daughters who prophesied. ¹⁰And as we stayed many days, a certain prophet named Agabus came down from Judea. ¹¹When he had come to us, he took Paul's belt, bound his *own* hands and feet, and said, "Thus says the Holy Spirit, 'So shall the Jews at Jerusalem bind the man who owns this belt, and deliver *him* into the hands of the Gentiles.' "

¹²Now when we heard these things, both we and those from that place pleaded with him not to go up to Jerusalem. ¹³Then Paul answered, "What do you mean by weeping and breaking my heart? For I am ready not only to be bound, but also to die at Jerusalem for the name of the Lord Jesus."

¹⁴So when he would not be persuaded, we ceased, saying, "The will of the Lord be done."

Paul Urged to Make Peace

¹⁵And after those days we packed and went up to Jerusalem. ¹⁶Also some of the disciples from Caesarea went with us and brought with them a certain Mnason of Cyprus, an early disciple, with whom we were to lodge.

¹⁷And when we had come to Jerusalem, the brethren received us gladly. ¹⁸On the following *day* Paul went in with us to James, and all the elders were present. ¹⁹When he had greeted them, he told in detail those things which God had done among the Gentiles through his ministry. ²⁰And when they heard *it,* they glorified the Lord. And they said to him, "You see, brother, how many myriads of Jews there are who have believed, and they are all zealous for the law; ²¹but they have been informed about you that you teach all the Jews who are among the Gentiles to forsake Moses, saying that they ought not to circumcise

LEADERSHIP ISSUES

Too Good to Keep

ACTS 20:20, 21

You will never overcome the rejection that comes with evangelism apart from a passion for God. Leaders genuinely impact society when their passion extends to sharing the gospel with others.

The basic word for "evangelism" in the New Testament is the term transliterated into the English as "evangel" (noun) or "evangelize" (verb). The verb form is seen several ways. The term *euangelizo* means: "I communicate good news." Think of other words that begin with *eu*, meaning "good": *eulogy*—a good word spoken of someone at a funeral; *eureka*— a good discovery; *euphoria*—a good feeling. The main part of the word "evangelism" contains the English term "angel," a messenger. So to evangelize is to tell a good message. In the New Testament, the term implies a good message, as in a victory.

While some people might attempt to make us feel as though evangelism imposes on the privacy of others, let us never forget we are telling the Good News: that Jesus has conquered sin, death, and the grave. This verb form is found thirty-three times in the New Testament and is common in the Gospel of Luke, the Acts, and Paul's epistles (Luke 4:18; 1 Cor. 1:17).

The noun form is *euangelion* and is found seventy-six times in the New Testament. It can be translated "gospel," "good news," or "evangel." It emphasizes a specific message: Jesus died and rose again (1 Cor. 15:1). Paul summarized the gospel with Jesus' death, burial, and resurrection. Two essential issues eventually confront every person: sin and death. On the cross, Jesus dealt with the sin problem; in the empty tomb, He defeated death. This is truly good news leaders should be sharing!

Another interesting use of this term is the expression *evangelistes*. It is found three times in the New Testament and is translated "evangelist." Philip is called evangelist (Acts 21:8). Jesus gave some to be evangelists (note, distinct from "evangelism" in the same way the "messenger" is distinct from the "message"), and it is one of the spiritual gifts (Eph. 4:11). Paul exhorted all ministers to do "the work of an evangelist" (2 Tim. 4:5). Evangelism is the telling of a specific, victorious message about what Jesus has done, and is doing, in your life.

their children nor to walk according to the customs. ²²What then? The assembly must certainly meet, for they will[a] hear that you have come. ²³Therefore do what we tell you: We have four men who have taken a vow. ²⁴Take them and be purified with them, and pay their expenses so that they may shave *their* heads, and that all may know that those things of which they were informed concerning you are nothing, but *that* you yourself also walk orderly and keep the law. ²⁵But concerning the Gentiles who believe, we have written *and* decided that they should observe no such thing, except[a] that they should keep themselves from *things* offered to idols, from blood, from things strangled, and from sexual immorality."

Arrested in the Temple

²⁶Then Paul took the men, and the next day, having been purified with them, entered the temple to announce the expiration of the days of purification, at which time an offering should be made for each one of them.

²⁷Now when the seven days were almost ended, the Jews from Asia, seeing him in the temple, stirred up the whole crowd and laid hands on him, ²⁸crying out, "Men of Israel, help! This is the man who teaches all *men* everywhere against the people, the law, and this place; and furthermore he also brought Greeks into the temple and has defiled this holy place." ²⁹(For they had previously[a] seen Trophimus the Ephesian with him in the city, whom they supposed that Paul had brought into the temple.)

³⁰And all the city was disturbed; and the people ran together, seized Paul, and dragged him out of the temple; and immediately the doors were shut. ³¹Now as they were seeking to kill him, news came to the commander of the garrison that all Jerusalem was in an uproar. ³²He immediately took soldiers and centurions, and ran down to them. And when they saw the commander and the soldiers, they stopped beating Paul. ³³Then the commander came near and took him, and commanded *him* to be bound with two chains; and he asked who he was and what he had done. ³⁴And some among the multitude cried one thing and some another.

So when he could not ascertain the truth because of the tumult, he commanded him to be

taken into the barracks. ³⁵When he reached the stairs, he had to be carried by the soldiers because of the violence of the mob. ³⁶For the multitude of the people followed after, crying out, "Away with him!"

Addressing the Jerusalem Mob

³⁷Then as Paul was about to be led into the barracks, he said to the commander, "May I speak to you?"

He replied, "Can you speak Greek? ³⁸Are you not the Egyptian who some time ago stirred up a rebellion and led the four thousand assassins out into the wilderness?"

³⁹But Paul said, "I am a Jew from Tarsus, in Cilicia, a citizen of no mean city; and I implore you, permit me to speak to the people."

⁴⁰So when he had given him permission, Paul stood on the stairs and motioned with his hand to the people. And when there was a great silence, he spoke to *them* in the Hebrew language, saying,

22 "Brethren and fathers, hear my defense before you now." ²And when they heard that he spoke to them in the Hebrew language, they kept all the more silent.

Then he said: ³"I am indeed a Jew, born in Tarsus of Cilicia, but brought up in this city at the feet of Gamaliel, taught according to the strictness of our fathers' law, and was zealous toward God as you all are today. ⁴I persecuted this Way to the death, binding and delivering into prisons both men and women, ⁵as also the high priest bears me witness, and all the council of the elders, from whom I also received letters to the brethren, and went to Damascus to bring in chains even those who were there to Jerusalem to be punished.

⁶"Now it happened, as I journeyed and came near Damascus at about noon, suddenly a great light from heaven shone around me. ⁷And I fell to the ground and heard a voice saying to me, 'Saul, Saul, why are you persecuting Me?' ⁸So I answered, 'Who are You, Lord?' And He said to me, 'I am Jesus of Nazareth, whom you are persecuting.'

⁹"And those who were with me indeed saw the light and were afraid,[a] but they did not hear

---

21:22 [a]NU-Text reads *What then is to be done? They will certainly.* **21:25** [a]NU-Text omits *that they should observe no such thing, except.* **21:29** [a]M-Text omits *previously.* **22:9** [a]NU-Text omits *and were afraid.*

LEADERSHIP ISSUES

GC2: Give to Others

ACTS 20:35

Significant from the life of Jesus is that His life focus was on giving, not receiving! In His giving, though, He received (Acts 26:23; Phil. 2:5–11). Luke 6:38 presents a simple but profound reinforcement of this truth, "Give, and it will be given to you." The "it" in this verse refers to whatever you "give." If you give forgiveness, you'll receive forgiveness. If you judge others, you'll be judged yourself. If you give love, you'll receive love (Matt. 6:14; 7:1; 1 John 4:7). The same truth is stated in Galatians 6:7, "for whatever a man sows, that he will also reap."

Now, let's apply this verse to unmet needs in your life, which will at times inevitably occur—friends, family, and other Christians will let you down. Is your need for comfort being neglected? Then call upon God as the "God of all comfort who comforts us" and then begin giving comfort to others (2 Cor. 1:2–4). Is no one encouraging you? Instead of sulking about it, begin to encourage others. Whatever it is that you need, receive from God, and then give it to others who have needs! By giving to others, you'll not only be able to experience the promise of Luke 6:38, but you'll enjoy the blessing and joy of living and loving as Jesus does!

Becoming a person who *gives to others* from God's unlimited supply will help prepare you for healthy, God-honoring relationships.

GC2
GREAT COMMANDMENT
COMMISSION

the voice of Him who spoke to me. [10]So I said, 'What shall I do, Lord?' And the Lord said to me, 'Arise and go into Damascus, and there you will be told all things which are appointed for you to do.' [11]And since I could not see for the glory of that light, being led by the hand of those who were with me, I came into Damascus.

[12]"Then a certain Ananias, a devout man according to the law, having a good testimony with all the Jews who dwelt *there,* [13]came to me; and he stood and said to me, 'Brother Saul, receive your sight.' And at that same hour I looked up at him. [14]Then he said, 'The God of our fathers has chosen you that you should know His will, and see the Just One, and hear the voice of His mouth. [15]For you will be His witness to all men of what you have seen and heard. [16]And now why are you waiting? Arise and be baptized, and wash away your sins, calling on the name of the Lord.'

[17]"Now it happened, when I returned to Jerusalem and was praying in the temple, that I was in a trance [18]and saw Him saying to me, 'Make haste and get out of Jerusalem quickly, for they will not receive your testimony concerning Me.' [19]So I said, 'Lord, they know that in every synagogue I imprisoned and beat those who believe on You. [20]And when the blood of Your martyr Stephen was shed, I also was standing by consenting to his death,[a] and guarding the clothes of those who were killing him.' [21]Then He said to me, 'Depart, for I will send you far from here to the Gentiles.' "

Paul's Roman Citizenship

[22]And they listened to him until this word, and *then* they raised their voices and said, "Away with such a *fellow* from the earth, for he is not fit to live!" [23]Then, as they cried out and tore off *their* clothes and threw dust into the air, [24]the commander ordered him to be brought into the barracks, and said that he should be examined under scourging, so that he might know why they shouted so against him. [25]And as they bound him with thongs, Paul said to the centurion who stood by, "Is it lawful for you to scourge a man who is a Roman, and uncondemned?"

[26]When the centurion heard *that,* he went and told the commander, saying, "Take care what you do, for this man is a Roman."

[27]Then the commander came and said to him, "Tell me, are you a Roman?"

He said, "Yes."

[28]The commander answered, "With a large sum I obtained this citizenship."

And Paul said, "But I was born *a citizen."*

[29]Then immediately those who were about to examine him withdrew from him; and the commander was also afraid after he found out that he was a Roman, and because he had bound him.

The Sanhedrin Divided

[30]The next day, because he wanted to know for certain why he was accused by the Jews, he released him from *his* bonds, and commanded the chief priests and all their council to appear, and brought Paul down and set him before them.

23 Then Paul, looking earnestly at the council, said, "Men *and* brethren, I have lived in all good conscience before God until this day." [2]And the high priest Ananias commanded those who stood by him to strike him on the mouth. [3]Then Paul said to him, "God will strike you, *you* whitewashed wall! For you sit to judge me according to the law, and do you command me to be struck contrary to the law?"

[4]And those who stood by said, "Do you revile God's high priest?"

[5]Then Paul said, "I did not know, brethren, that he was the high priest; for it is written, *'You shall not speak evil of a ruler of your people.' "*[a]

[6]But when Paul perceived that one part were Sadducees and the other Pharisees, he cried out in the council, "Men *and* brethren, I am a Pharisee, the son of a Pharisee; concerning the hope and resurrection of the dead I am being judged!"

[7]And when he had said this, a dissension arose between the Pharisees and the Sadducees; and the assembly was divided. [8]For Sadducees say that there is no resurrection—and no angel or spirit; but the Pharisees confess both. [9]Then there arose a loud outcry. And the scribes of the Pharisees' party arose and protested, saying, "We find no evil in this man; but if a spirit or an angel has spoken to him, let us not fight against God."[a]

22:20 [a]NU-Text omits *to his death.* **23:5** [a]Exodus 22:28 **23:9** [a]NU-Text omits last clause and reads *what if a spirit or an angel has spoken to him?*

[10]Now when there arose a great dissension, the commander, fearing lest Paul might be pulled to pieces by them, commanded the soldiers to go down and take him by force from among them, and bring him into the barracks.

The Plot Against Paul

[11]But the following night the Lord stood by him and said, "Be of good cheer, Paul; for as you have testified for Me in Jerusalem, so you must also bear witness at Rome."

[12]And when it was day, some of the Jews banded together and bound themselves under an oath, saying that they would neither eat nor drink till they had killed Paul. [13]Now there were more than forty who had formed this conspiracy. [14]They came to the chief priests and elders, and said, "We have bound ourselves under a great oath that we will eat nothing until we have killed Paul. [15]Now you, therefore, together with the council, suggest to the commander that he be brought down to you tomorrow,[a] as though you were going to make further inquiries concerning him; but we are ready to kill him before he comes near."

[16]So when Paul's sister's son heard of their ambush, he went and entered the barracks and told Paul. [17]Then Paul called one of the centurions to him and said, "Take this young man to the commander, for he has something to tell him." [18]So he took him and brought him to the commander and said, "Paul the prisoner called me to him and asked me to bring this young man to you. He has something to say to you."

[19]Then the commander took him by the hand, went aside, and asked privately, "What is it that you have to tell me?"

[20]And he said, "The Jews have agreed to ask that you bring Paul down to the council tomorrow, as though they were going to inquire more fully about him. [21]But do not yield to them, for more than forty of them lie in wait for him, men who have bound themselves by an oath that they will neither eat nor drink till they have killed him; and now they are ready, waiting for the promise from you."

[22]So the commander let the young man depart, and commanded him, "Tell no one that you have revealed these things to me."

Sent to Felix

[23]And he called for two centurions, saying, "Prepare two hundred soldiers, seventy horsemen, and two hundred spearmen to go to Caesarea at the third hour of the night; [24]and provide mounts to set Paul on, and bring him safely to Felix the governor." [25]He wrote a letter in the following manner:

[26]Claudius Lysias,

To the most excellent governor Felix:

Greetings.

[27]This man was seized by the Jews and was about to be killed by them. Coming with the troops I rescued him, having learned that he was a Roman. [28]And when I wanted to know the reason they accused him, I brought him before their council. [29]I found out that he was accused concerning questions of their law, but had nothing charged against him deserving of death or chains. [30]And when it was told me that the Jews lay in wait for the man,[a] I sent him immediately to you, and also commanded his accusers to state before you the charges against him.

Farewell.

[31]Then the soldiers, as they were commanded, took Paul and brought him by night to Antipatris. [32]The next day they left the horsemen to go on with him, and returned to the barracks. [33]When they came to Caesarea and had delivered the letter to the governor, they also presented Paul to him. [34]And when the governor had read it, he asked what province he was from. And when he understood that he was from Cilicia, [35]he said, "I will hear you when your accusers also have come." And he commanded him to be kept in Herod's Praetorium.

23:15 [a]NU-Text omits *tomorrow.*   **23:30** [a]NU-Text reads *there would be a plot against the man.*

ACCUSED OF SEDITION

24 Now after five days Ananias the high priest came down with the elders and a certain orator *named* Tertullus. These gave evidence to the governor against Paul.

2And when he was called upon, Tertullus began his accusation, saying: "Seeing that through you we enjoy great peace, and prosperity is being brought to this nation by your foresight, 3we accept *it* always and in all places, most noble Felix, with all thankfulness. 4Nevertheless, not to be tedious to you any further, I beg you to hear, by your courtesy, a few words from us. 5For we have found this man a plague, a creator of dissension among all the Jews throughout the world, and a ringleader of the sect of the Nazarenes. 6He even tried to profane the temple, and we seized him,ª and wanted to judge him according to our law. 7But the commander Lysias came by and with great violence took *him* out of our hands, 8commanding his accusers to come to you. By examining him yourself you may ascertain all these things of which we accuse him." 9And the Jews also assented,ª maintaining that these things were so.

THE DEFENSE BEFORE FELIX

10Then Paul, after the governor had nodded to him to speak, answered: "Inasmuch as I know that you have been for many years a judge of this nation, I do the more cheerfully answer for myself, 11because you may ascertain that it is no more than twelve days since I went up to Jerusalem to worship. 12And they neither found me in the temple disputing with anyone nor inciting the crowd, either in the synagogues or in the city. 13Nor can they prove the things of which they now accuse me. 14But this I confess to you, that according to the Way which they call a sect, so I worship the God of my fathers, believing all things which are written in the Law and in the Prophets. 15I have hope in God, which they themselves also accept, that there will be a resurrection of *the* dead,ª both of *the* just and *the* unjust. 16This *being* so, I myself always strive to have a conscience without offense toward God and men.

17"Now after many years I came to bring alms and offerings to my nation, 18in the midst of

which some Jews from Asia found me purified in the temple, neither with a mob nor with tumult. 19They ought to have been here before you to object if they had anything against me. 20Or else let those who are *here* themselves say if they found any wrongdoingª in me while I stood before the council, 21unless *it is* for this one statement which I cried out, standing among them, 'Concerning the resurrection of the dead I am being judged by you this day.'"

FELIX PROCRASTINATES

22But when Felix heard these things, having more accurate knowledge of *the* Way, he adjourned the proceedings and said, "When Lysias the commander comes down, I will make a decision on your case." 23So he commanded the centurion to keep Paul and to let *him* have liberty, and told him not to forbid any of his friends to provide for or visit him.

24And after some days, when Felix came with his wife Drusilla, who was Jewish, he sent for Paul and heard him concerning the faith in Christ. 25Now as he reasoned about righteousness, self-control, and the judgment to come, Felix was afraid and answered, "Go away for now; when I have a convenient time I will call for you." 26Meanwhile he also hoped that money would be given him by Paul, that he might release him.ª Therefore he sent for him more often and conversed with him.

27But after two years Porcius Festus succeeded Felix; and Felix, wanting to do the Jews a favor, left Paul bound.

PAUL APPEALS TO CAESAR

25 Now when Festus had come to the province, after three days he went up from Caesarea to Jerusalem. 2Then the high priestª and the chief men of the Jews informed him against Paul; and they petitioned him, 3asking a favor against him, that he would summon him to Jerusalem—while *they* lay in ambush along the road to kill him. 4But Festus answered that Paul

24:6 ªNU-Text ends the sentence here and omits the rest of verse 6, all of verse 7, and the first clause of verse 8. **24:9** ªNU-Text and M-Text read *joined the attack.* **24:15** ªNU-Text omits *of the dead.* **24:20** ªNU-Text and M-Text read *say what wrongdoing they found.* **24:26** ªNU-Text omits *that he might release him.* **25:2** ªNU-Text reads *chief priests.*

should be kept at Caesarea, and that he himself was going *there* shortly. [5]"Therefore," he said, "let those who have authority among you go down with *me* and accuse this man, to see if there is any fault in him."

[6]And when he had remained among them more than ten days, he went down to Caesarea. And the next day, sitting on the judgment seat, he commanded Paul to be brought. [7]When he had come, the Jews who had come down from Jerusalem stood about and laid many serious complaints against Paul, which they could not prove, [8]while he answered for himself, "Neither against the law of the Jews, nor against the temple, nor against Caesar have I offended in anything at all."

[9]But Festus, wanting to do the Jews a favor, answered Paul and said, "Are you willing to go up to Jerusalem and there be judged before me concerning these things?"

[10]So Paul said, "I stand at Caesar's judgment seat, where I ought to be judged. To the Jews I have done no wrong, as you very well know. [11]For if I am an offender, or have committed anything deserving of death, I do not object to dying; but if there is nothing in these things of which these men accuse me, no one can deliver me to them. I appeal to Caesar."

[12]Then Festus, when he had conferred with the council, answered, "You have appealed to Caesar? To Caesar you shall go!"

PAUL BEFORE AGRIPPA

[13]And after some days King Agrippa and Bernice came to Caesarea to greet Festus. [14]When they had been there many days, Festus laid Paul's case before the king, saying: "There is a certain man left a prisoner by Felix, [15]about whom the chief priests and the elders of the Jews informed *me*, when I was in Jerusalem, asking for a judgment against him. [16]To them I answered, 'It is not the custom of the Romans to deliver any man to destruction[a] before the accused meets the accusers face to face, and has opportunity to answer for himself concerning the charge against him.' [17]Therefore when they had come together, without any delay, the next day I sat on the judgment seat and commanded the man to be brought in. [18]When the accusers stood up, they brought no

accusation against him of such things as I supposed, [19]but had some questions against him about their own religion and about a certain Jesus, who had died, whom Paul affirmed to be alive. [20]And because I was uncertain of such questions, I asked whether he was willing to go to Jerusalem and there be judged concerning these matters. [21]But when Paul appealed to be reserved for the decision of Augustus, I commanded him to be kept till I could send him to Caesar."

[22]Then Agrippa said to Festus, "I also would like to hear the man myself."

"Tomorrow," he said, "you shall hear him."

[23]So the next day, when Agrippa and Bernice had come with great pomp, and had entered the auditorium with the commanders and the prominent men of the city, at Festus' command Paul was brought in. [24]And Festus said: "King Agrippa and all the men who are here present with us, you see this man about whom the whole assembly of the Jews petitioned me, both at Jerusalem and here, crying out that he was not fit to live any longer. [25]But when I found that he had committed nothing deserving of death, and that he himself had appealed to Augustus, I decided to send him. [26]I have nothing certain to write to my lord concerning him. Therefore I have brought him out before you, and especially before you, King Agrippa, so that after the examination has taken place I may have something to write. [27]For it seems to me unreasonable to send a prisoner and not to specify the charges against him."

PAUL'S EARLY LIFE

26 Then Agrippa said to Paul, "You are permitted to speak for yourself."

So Paul stretched out his hand and answered for himself: [2]"I think myself happy, King Agrippa, because today I shall answer for myself before you concerning all the things of which I am accused by the Jews, [3]especially because you are expert in all customs and questions which have to do with the Jews. Therefore I beg you to hear me patiently. [4]"My manner of life from my youth, which was spent from the beginning among my own nation at Jerusalem, all the Jews know. [5]They knew me from the first, if they were willing to testify,

25:16 [a]NU-Text omits *to destruction*, although it is implied.

that according to the strictest sect of our religion I lived a Pharisee. ⁶And now I stand and am judged for the hope of the promise made by God to our fathers. ⁷To this *promise* our twelve tribes, earnestly serving *God* night and day, hope to attain. For this hope's sake, King Agrippa, I am accused by the Jews. ⁸Why should it be thought incredible by you that God raises the dead?

⁹"Indeed, I myself thought I must do many things contrary to the name of Jesus of Nazareth. ¹⁰This I also did in Jerusalem, and many of the saints I shut up in prison, having received authority from the chief priests; and when they were put to death, I cast my vote against *them*. ¹¹And I punished them often in every synagogue and compelled *them* to blaspheme; and being exceedingly enraged against them, I persecuted *them* even to foreign cities.

PAUL RECOUNTS HIS CONVERSION

¹²"While thus occupied, as I journeyed to Damascus with authority and commission from the chief priests, ¹³at midday, O king, along the road I saw a light from heaven, brighter than the sun, shining around me and those who journeyed with me. ¹⁴And when we all had fallen to the ground, I heard a voice speaking to me and saying in the Hebrew language, 'Saul, Saul, why are you persecuting Me? *It is* hard for you to kick against the goads.' ¹⁵So I said, 'Who are You, Lord?' And He said, 'I am Jesus, whom you are persecuting. ¹⁶But rise and stand on your feet; for I have appeared to you for this purpose, to make you a minister and a witness both of the things which you have seen and of the things which I will yet reveal to you. ¹⁷I will deliver you from the *Jewish* people, as well as *from* the Gentiles, to whom I now[a] send you, ¹⁸to open their eyes, *in order* to turn *them* from darkness to light, and *from* the power of Satan to God, that they may receive forgiveness of sins and an inheritance among those who are sanctified by faith in Me.'

26:17 [a]NU-Text and M-Text omit *now*.

 the INFLUENCERS

KING AGRIPPA—Almost Isn't Good Enough

ACTS 26

Paul, the apostle, bound in chains, spoke about Jesus with confidence. Across from him is King Agrippa, the great grandson of Herod the Great (Acts 12:1) surrounded by servants, royal guards, and pageantry. Paul was on trial for his life, but he spoke only of Agrippa's need to know the Savior.

After Paul's brilliant, penetrating message, Agrippa said, "You almost persuade me to become a Christian!" Some believe that the king's words were sarcastic, but when one examines the passion and content of Paul's message, it is probable that he was truly convicted by the Holy Spirit.

Paul presented a *personal testimony of salvation,* the greatest weapon of any believer. He omitted opinion and spoke the powerful Word of God, which the Bible calls "sharper than any two-edged sword . . . a discerner of the thoughts and intents of the heart" (Heb. 4:12). Paul exalted Christ as he boldly proclaimed the truth.

Paul's words, his lifestyle, and the Holy Spirit's power spoke to Agrippa, and he was "almost persuaded." Festus and Bernice stood nearby. Festus feared that he might lose power and standing if Agrippa were to side with Paul. History reveals that all three soon lost their power and position anyway.

Paul's Post-Conversion Life

19"Therefore, King Agrippa, I was not disobedient to the heavenly vision, 20but declared first to those in Damascus and in Jerusalem, and throughout all the region of Judea, and *then* to the Gentiles, that they should repent, turn to God, and do works befitting repentance. 21For these reasons the Jews seized me in the temple and tried to kill *me*. 22Therefore, having obtained help from God, to this day I stand, witnessing both to small and great, saying no other things than those which the prophets and Moses said would come— 23that the Christ would suffer, that He would be the first to rise from the dead, and would proclaim light to the *Jewish* people and to the Gentiles."

Agrippa Parries Paul's Challenge

24Now as he thus made his defense, Festus said with a loud voice, "Paul, you are beside yourself! Much learning is driving you mad!"

25But he said, "I am not mad, most noble Festus, but speak the words of truth and reason. 26For the king, before whom I also speak freely, knows these things; for I am convinced that none of these things escapes his attention, since this thing was not done in a corner. 27King Agrippa, do you believe the prophets? I know that you do believe."

28Then Agrippa said to Paul, "You almost persuade me to become a Christian."

29And Paul said, "I would to God that not only you, but also all who hear me today, might become both almost and altogether such as I am, except for these chains."

30When he had said these things, the king stood up, as well as the governor and Bernice and those who sat with them; 31and when they had gone aside, they talked among themselves, saying, "This man is doing nothing deserving of death or chains."

32Then Agrippa said to Festus, "This man might have been set free if he had not appealed to Caesar."

The Voyage to Rome Begins

27 And when it was decided that we should sail to Italy, they delivered Paul and some other prisoners to *one* named Julius, a centurion of the Augustan Regiment. 2So, entering a ship of Adramyttium, we put to sea, meaning to sail along the coasts of Asia. Aristarchus, a Macedonian of Thessalonica, was with us. 3And the next *day* we landed at Sidon. And Julius treated Paul kindly and gave *him* liberty to go to his friends and receive care. 4When we had put to sea from there, we sailed under *the shelter of* Cyprus, because the winds were contrary. 5And when we had sailed over the sea which is off Cilicia and Pamphylia, we came to Myra, *a city* of Lycia. 6There the centurion found an Alexandrian ship sailing to Italy, and he put us on board.

7When we had sailed slowly many days, and arrived with difficulty off Cnidus, the wind not permitting us to proceed, we sailed under *the shelter of* Crete off Salmone. 8Passing it with difficulty, we came to a place called Fair Havens, near the city *of* Lasea.

Paul's Warning Ignored

9Now when much time had been spent, and sailing was now dangerous because the Fast was already over, Paul advised them, 10saying, "Men, I perceive that this voyage will end with disaster and much loss, not only of the cargo and ship, but also our lives." 11Nevertheless the centurion was more persuaded by the helmsman and the owner of the ship than by the things spoken by Paul. 12And because the harbor was not suitable to winter in, the majority advised to set sail from there also, if by any means they could reach Phoenix, a harbor of Crete opening toward the southwest and northwest, *and* winter *there.*

In the Tempest

13When the south wind blew softly, supposing that they had obtained *their* desire, putting out to sea, they sailed close by Crete. 14But not long after, a tempestuous head wind arose, called Euroclydon.[a] 15So when the ship was caught, and could not head into the wind, we let her drive. 16And running under *the shelter of* an island called Clauda,[a] we secured the skiff with difficulty. 17When they had taken it on board, they used cables to undergird the ship; and fearing lest they should run aground on the Syrtis[a] *Sands*, they

27:14 aNU-Text reads *Euraquilon*. **27:16** aNU-Text reads *Cauda*. **27:17** aM-Text reads *Syrtes*.

struck sail and so were driven. ¹⁸And because we were exceedingly tempest-tossed, the next *day* they lightened the ship. ¹⁹On the third *day* we threw the ship's tackle overboard with our own hands. ²⁰Now when neither sun nor stars appeared for many days, and no small tempest beat on *us*, all hope that we would be saved was finally given up.

²¹But after long abstinence from food, then Paul stood in the midst of them and said, "Men, you should have listened to me, and not have sailed from Crete and incurred this disaster and loss. ²²And now I urge you to take heart, for there will be no loss of life among you, but only of the ship. ²³For there stood by me this night an angel of the God to whom I belong and whom I serve, ²⁴saying, 'Do not be afraid, Paul; you must be brought before Caesar; and indeed God has granted you all those who sail with you.' ²⁵Therefore take heart, men, for I believe God that it will be just as it was told me. ²⁶However, we must run aground on a certain island."

²⁷Now when the fourteenth night had come, as we were driven up and down in the Adriatic *Sea*, about midnight the sailors sensed that they were drawing near some land. ²⁸And they took soundings and found *it* to be twenty fathoms; and when they had gone a little farther, they took soundings again and found *it* to be fifteen fathoms. ²⁹Then, fearing lest we should run aground on the rocks, they dropped four anchors from the stern, and prayed for day to come. ³⁰And as the sailors were seeking to escape from the ship, when they had let down the skiff into the sea, under pretense of putting out anchors from the prow, ³¹Paul said to the centurion and the soldiers, "Unless these men stay in the ship, you cannot be saved." ³²Then the soldiers cut away the ropes of the skiff and let it fall off.

³³And as day was about to dawn, Paul implored *them* all to take food, saying, "Today is the fourteenth day you have waited and continued without food, and eaten nothing. ³⁴Therefore I urge you to take nourishment, for this is for your survival, since not a hair will fall from the head of any of you." ³⁵And when he had said these things, he took bread and gave thanks to God in the presence of them all; and when he had broken *it* he began to eat. ³⁶Then they were all encouraged,

and also took food themselves. ³⁷And in all we were two hundred and seventy-six persons on the ship. ³⁸So when they had eaten enough, they lightened the ship and threw out the wheat into the sea.

SHIPWRECKED ON MALTA

³⁹When it was day, they did not recognize the land; but they observed a bay with a beach, onto which they planned to run the ship if possible. ⁴⁰And they let go the anchors and left *them* in the sea, meanwhile loosing the rudder ropes; and they hoisted the mainsail to the wind and made for shore. ⁴¹But striking a place where two seas met, they ran the ship aground; and the prow stuck fast and remained immovable, but the stern was being broken up by the violence of the waves.

⁴²And the soldiers' plan was to kill the prisoners, lest any of them should swim away and escape. ⁴³But the centurion, wanting to save Paul, kept them from *their* purpose, and commanded that those who could swim should jump *overboard* first and get to land, ⁴⁴and the rest, some on boards and some on *parts* of the ship. And so it was that they all escaped safely to land.

PAUL'S MINISTRY ON MALTA

28 Now when they had escaped, they then found out that the island was called Malta. ²And the natives showed us unusual kindness; for they kindled a fire and made us all welcome, because of the rain that was falling and because of the cold. ³But when Paul had gathered a bundle of sticks and laid *them* on the fire, a viper came out because of the heat, and fastened on his hand. ⁴So when the natives saw the creature hanging from his hand, they said to one another, "No doubt this man is a murderer, whom, though he has escaped the sea, yet justice does not allow to live." ⁵But he shook off the creature into the fire and suffered no harm. ⁶However, they were expecting that he would swell up or suddenly fall down dead. But after they had looked for a long time and saw no harm come to him, they changed their minds and said that he was a god.

⁷In that region there was an estate of the leading citizen of the island, whose name was Publius, who received us and entertained us courteously

for three days. [8]And it happened that the father of Publius lay sick of a fever and dysentery. Paul went in to him and prayed, and he laid his hands on him and healed him. [9]So when this was done, the rest of those on the island who had diseases also came and were healed. [10]They also honored us in many ways; and when we departed, they provided such things as were necessary.

ARRIVAL AT ROME

[11]After three months we sailed in an Alexandrian ship whose figurehead was the Twin Brothers, which had wintered at the island. [12]And landing at Syracuse, we stayed three days. [13]From there we circled round and reached Rhegium. And after one day the south wind blew; and the next day we came to Puteoli, [14]where we found brethren, and were invited to stay with them seven days. And so we went toward Rome. [15]And from there, when the brethren heard about us, they came to meet us as far as Appii Forum and Three Inns. When Paul saw them, he thanked God and took courage.

[16]Now when we came to Rome, the centurion delivered the prisoners to the captain of the guard; but Paul was permitted to dwell by himself with the soldier who guarded him.

PAUL'S MINISTRY AT ROME

[17]And it came to pass after three days that Paul called the leaders of the Jews together. So when they had come together, he said to them: "Men *and* brethren, though I have done nothing against our people or the customs of our fathers, yet I was delivered as a prisoner from Jerusalem into the hands of the Romans, [18]who, when they had examined me, wanted to let *me* go, because there was no cause for putting me to death. [19]But when the Jews[a] spoke against *it*, I was compelled to appeal to Caesar, not that I had anything of which to accuse my nation. [20]For this reason therefore I have called for you, to see *you* and speak with *you*, because for the hope of Israel I am bound with this chain."

[21]Then they said to him, "We neither received letters from Judea concerning you, nor have any of the brethren who came reported or spoken any evil of you. [22]But we desire to hear from you what you think; for concerning this sect, we know that it is spoken against everywhere."

[23]So when they had appointed him a day, many came to him at *his* lodging, to whom he explained and solemnly testified of the kingdom of God, persuading them concerning Jesus from both the Law of Moses and the Prophets, from morning till evening. [24]And some were persuaded by the things which were spoken, and some disbelieved. [25]So when they did not agree among themselves, they departed after Paul had said one word: "The Holy Spirit spoke rightly through Isaiah the prophet to our[a] fathers, [26]saying,

'Go to this people and say:
"Hearing you will hear, and shall not
   understand;
   And seeing you will see, and not perceive;
[28]For the hearts of this people have grown dull.
   Their ears are hard of hearing,
   And their eyes they have closed,
   Lest they should see with *their* eyes and hear
      with *their* ears,
   Lest they should understand with *their* hearts
      and turn,
   So that I should heal them." '[a]

[28]"Therefore let it be known to you that the salvation of God has been sent to the Gentiles, and they will hear it!" [29]And when he had said these words, the Jews departed and had a great dispute among themselves.[a]

[30]Then Paul dwelt two whole years in his own rented house, and received all who came to him, [31]preaching the kingdom of God and teaching the things which concern the Lord Jesus Christ with all confidence, no one forbidding him.

28:19 [a]That is, the ruling authorities **28:25** [a]NU-Text reads *your.*
28:27 [a]Isaiah 6:9, 10 **28:29** [a]NU-Text omits this verse.

IMPACT OF THE BOOK

I IDEA

Romans reveals the human dilemma and God's remedy for the question: "How can a person have a right relationship with God?"

M MESSAGE

Right belief leads to right practice. Paul realized that the early Christians needed a systematic explanation of their faith to guide their walk.

P PEOPLE

Aquila, Paul, Phoebe, Priscilla (see Rom. 16 for a list of names)

A AUTHOR

Paul, originally named Saul, was a Jew from the tribe of Benjamin. Well educated and trained under Gamaliel, Paul later became one of the fiercest persecutors of Christians until his conversion on the way to Damascus. After receiving Christ, he spent his life planting churches and serving as a special apostle to the Gentiles. Romans was probably written in Corinth—at the home of a wealthy Christian business man named Gaius—during Paul's three-month stay on his third missionary journey (Acts 20:3).

C CULTURE

Paul completed his third missionary journey to the East and turned his eyes to the West, to Spain. He changed his missionary base from Antioch to Rome. Paul wrote Romans to introduce himself, prepare the church for his visit, and to secure the prayers and support of the Roman believers for his Spanish mission. He presents his message and theological position, explains his doctrine to the church, and applies it to the practical, daily lives of Christians. The believers probably heard the witness of merchants and travelers who came to Rome. Jewish converts may have started the church, which had a strong Jewish minority. Predominantly Gentile when it received Paul's letter, he knew they needed to be grounded in the faith and sound in doctrine.

T TIMELINE

c. AD 57

KEY SCRIPTURE
MEMORY VERSES

1:16–23; 3:10, 11, 23; 5:8; 6:23; 8:28–30; 10:9, 10; 11:33; 12:1, 2, 21

ROMANS

GREETING

1 Paul, a bondservant of Jesus Christ, called *to be* an apostle, separated to the gospel of God [2]which He promised before through His prophets in the Holy Scriptures, [3]concerning His Son Jesus Christ our Lord, who was born of the seed of David according to the flesh, [4]*and* declared *to be* the Son of God with power according to the Spirit of holiness, by the resurrection from the dead. [5]Through Him we have received grace and apostleship for obedience to the faith among all nations for His name, [6]among whom you also are the called of Jesus Christ;

[7]To all who are in Rome, beloved of God, called *to be* saints:

Grace to you and peace from God our Father and the Lord Jesus Christ.

DESIRE TO VISIT ROME

[8]First, I thank my God through Jesus Christ for you all, that your faith is spoken of throughout the whole world. [9]For God is my witness, whom I serve with my spirit in the gospel of His Son, that without ceasing I make mention of you always in my prayers, [10]making request if, by some means, now at last I may find a way in the will of God to come to you. [11]For I long to see you, that I may impart to you some spiritual gift, so that you may be established— [12]that is, that I may be encouraged together with you by the mutual faith both of you and me.

[13]Now I do not want you to be unaware, brethren, that I often planned to come to you (but was hindered until now), that I might have some fruit among you also, just as among the other Gentiles. [14]I am a debtor both to Greeks and to barbarians, both to wise and to unwise. [15]So, as much as is in me, *I am* ready to preach the gospel to you who are in Rome also.

THE JUST LIVE BY FAITH

[16]For I am not ashamed of the gospel of Christ,[a] for it is the power of God to salvation for everyone who believes, for the Jew first and also for the Greek. [17]For in it the righteousness of God is revealed from faith to faith; as it is written, *"The just shall live by faith."*[a]

GOD'S WRATH ON UNRIGHTEOUSNESS

[18]For the wrath of God is revealed from heaven against all ungodliness and unrighteousness of men, who suppress the truth in unrighteousness, [19]because what may be known of

1:16 [a]NU-Text omits *of Christ.*   **1:17** [a]Habakkuk 2:4

LEADERSHIP REALITIES

IT'S NOT HOW YOU START; IT'S HOW YOU FINISH *Romans 1:5; 16:26*

The apostle Paul uses a phrase to bookend this important letter: *obedience to the faith*. Not only are the words of the Bible inspired by the Holy Spirit, but the order of the writer's thoughts is also inspired. There is a profound message Paul is attempting to communicate to those who would seriously study this book.

First, his desire was that *obedience to the faith* would define his ministry; that at the end of the day he would be known as a man who was faithful to the message of God. Second, this phrase is the biblical definition of success. While there are many qualities that can serve as a gauge for success, only obedience to God can define it. Third, there is a liberating reality being communicated by using this phrase both at the beginning and end of this letter. That message is that though one may not have had an *obedience to the faith* in the beginning (as in Paul's life) each of us can have an *obedience to the faith* finish. Success is to daily say "yes" to choosing God's best.

God is manifest in them, for God has shown *it* to them. ²⁰For since the creation of the world His invisible *attributes* are clearly seen, being understood by the things that are made, *even* His eternal power and Godhead, so that they are without excuse, ²¹because, although they knew God, they did not glorify *Him* as God, nor were thankful, but became futile in their thoughts, and their foolish hearts were darkened. ²²Professing to be wise, they became fools, ²³and changed the glory of the incorruptible God into an image made like corruptible man—and birds and four-footed animals and creeping things.

²⁴Therefore God also gave them up to uncleanness, in the lusts of their hearts, to dishonor their bodies among themselves, ²⁵who exchanged the truth of God for the lie, and worshiped and served the creature rather than the Creator, who is blessed forever. Amen.

²⁶For this reason God gave them up to vile passions. For even their women exchanged the natural use for what is against nature. ²⁷Likewise also the men, leaving the natural use of the woman, burned in their lust for one another, men with men committing what is shameful, and receiving in themselves the penalty of their error which was due.

²⁸And even as they did not like to retain God in *their* knowledge, God gave them over to a debased mind, to do those things which are not fitting; ²⁹being filled with all unrighteousness, sexual immorality,ᵃ wickedness, covetousness, maliciousness; full of envy, murder, strife, deceit, evil-mindedness; *they are* whisperers, ³⁰backbiters, haters of God, violent, proud, boasters, inventors of evil things, disobedient to parents, ³¹undiscerning, untrustworthy, unloving, unforgiving,ᵃ unmerciful; ³²who, knowing the righteous judgment of God, that those who practice such things are deserving of death, not only do the same but also approve of those who practice them.

God's Righteous Judgment

2 Therefore you are inexcusable, O man, whoever you are who judge, for in whatever you judge another you condemn yourself; for you who judge practice the same things. ²But we know that the judgment of God is according to truth against those who practice such things. ³And

do you think this, O man, you who judge those practicing such things, and doing the same, that you will escape the judgment of God? ⁴Or do you despise the riches of His goodness, forbearance, and longsuffering, not knowing that the goodness of God leads you to repentance? ⁵But in accordance with your hardness and your impenitent heart you are treasuring up for yourself wrath in the day of wrath and revelation of the righteous judgment of God, ⁶who *"will render to each one according to his deeds"*:ᵃ ⁷eternal life to those who by patient continuance in doing good seek for glory, honor, and immortality; ⁸but to those who are self-seeking and do not obey the truth, but obey unrighteousness—indignation and wrath, ⁹tribulation and anguish, on every soul of man who does evil, of the Jew first and also of the Greek; ¹⁰but glory, honor, and peace to everyone who works what is good, to the Jew first and also to the Greek. ¹¹For there is no partiality with God.

¹²For as many as have sinned without law will also perish without law, and as many as have sinned in the law will be judged by the law ¹³(for not the hearers of the law *are* just in the sight of God, but the doers of the law will be justified; ¹⁴for when Gentiles, who do not have the law, by nature do the things in the law, these, although not having the law, are a law to themselves, ¹⁵who show the work of the law written in their hearts, their conscience also bearing witness, and between themselves *their* thoughts accusing or else excusing *them*) ¹⁶in the day when God will judge the secrets of men by Jesus Christ, according to my gospel.

The Jews Guilty as the Gentiles

¹⁷Indeedᵃ you are called a Jew, and rest on the law, and make your boast in God, ¹⁸and know *His* will, and approve the things that are excellent, being instructed out of the law, ¹⁹and are confident that you yourself are a guide to the blind, a light to those who are in darkness, ²⁰an instructor of the foolish, a teacher of babes, having the form of knowledge and truth in the law. ²¹You, therefore, who teach another, do you not teach yourself? You who preach that a man should not steal, do

1:29 ᵃNU-Text omits *sexual immorality.*   **1:31** ᵃNU-Text omits *unforgiving.*   **2:6** ᵃPsalm 62:12; Proverbs 24:12   **2:17** ᵃNU-Text reads *But if.*

you steal? 22You who say, "Do not commit adultery," do you commit adultery? You who abhor idols, do you rob temples? 23You who make your boast in the law, do you dishonor God through breaking the law? 24For *"the name of God is blasphemed among the Gentiles because of you,"*a as it is written.

Circumcision of No Avail

25For circumcision is indeed profitable if you keep the law; but if you are a breaker of the law, your circumcision has become uncircumcision. 26Therefore, if an uncircumcised man keeps the righteous requirements of the law, will not his uncircumcision be counted as circumcision? 27And will not the physically uncircumcised, if he fulfills the law, judge you who, *even* with *your* written *code* and circumcision, *are* a transgressor of the law? 28For he is not a Jew who *is one* outwardly, nor *is* circumcision that which *is* outward in the flesh; 29but *he is* a Jew who *is one* inwardly; and circumcision *is that* of the heart, in the Spirit, not in the letter; whose praise *is* not from men but from God.

God's Judgment Defended

3 What advantage then has the Jew, or what *is* the profit of circumcision? 2Much in every way! Chiefly because to them were committed the oracles of God. 3For what if some did not believe? Will their unbelief make the faithfulness of God without effect? 4Certainly not! Indeed, let God be true but every man a liar. As it is written:

"That You may be justified in Your words,
*And may overcome when You are judged."*a

5But if our unrighteousness demonstrates the righteousness of God, what shall we say? *Is* God unjust who inflicts wrath? (I speak as a man.) 6Certainly not! For then how will God judge the world?

7For if the truth of God has increased through my lie to His glory, why am I also still judged as a sinner? 8And *why* not *say,* "Let us do evil that good may come"?—as we are slanderously reported and as some affirm that we say. Their condemnation is just.

All Have Sinned

9What then? Are we better *than they?* Not at all. For we have previously charged both Jews and Greeks that they are all under sin.

10As it is written:

"There is none righteous, no, not one;
11*There is none who understands;*
There is none who seeks after God.
12*They have all turned aside;*
They have together become unprofitable;
*There is none who does good, no, not one."*a
13*"Their throat is an open tomb;*
With their tongues they have practiced
*deceit";*a
*"The poison of asps is under their lips";*b
14*"Whose mouth is full of cursing and*
*bitterness."*a
15*"Their feet are swift to shed blood;*
16*Destruction and misery are in their ways;*
17*And the way of peace they have not known."*a
18*"There is no fear of God before their eyes."*a

19Now we know that whatever the law says, it says to those who are under the law, that every mouth may be stopped, and all the world may become guilty before God. 20Therefore by the deeds of the law no flesh will be justified in His sight, for by the law *is* the knowledge of sin.

God's Righteousness Through Faith

21But now the righteousness of God apart from the law is revealed, being witnessed by the Law and the Prophets, 22even the righteousness of God, through faith in Jesus Christ, to all and on alla who believe. For there is no difference; 23for all have sinned and fall short of the glory of God, 24being justified freely by His grace through the redemption that is in Christ Jesus, 25whom God set forth *as* a propitiation by His blood, through faith, to demonstrate His righteousness, because in His forbearance God had passed over the sins that were previously committed, 26to demonstrate at the present time His righteousness, that He might

2:24 aIsaiah 52:5; Ezekiel 36:22 **3:4** aPsalm 51:4 **3:12** aPsalms 14:1–3; 53:1–3; Ecclesiastes 7:20 **3:13** aPsalm 5:9 bPsalm 140:3 **3:14** aPsalm 10:7 **3:17** aIsaiah 59:7, 8 **3:18** aPsalm 36:1 **3:22** aNU-Text omits *and on all.*

THROUGH THE GRID

Written by the Hand of God: God's Law Leads to Grace in Christ

ROMANS 3:20 *Therefore by the deeds of the law no flesh will be justified in His sight, for by the law is the knowledge of sin.*

The more we experience the grace and mercy of God, the more clearly the Commandments of God are inscribed upon our hearts and minds. The Ten Commandments serve the great purpose of guiding us to God's grace, upon the recognition that all of us fall short and are ultimately unable to merit any good. Yet God's grace gives to us that which we do not deserve. The Ten Commandments help bring the promises of the Old Testament to fulfillment in the New Testament. The Law is not the be-all and end-all of Christian identity; rather, the purpose of the Law is to serve as a guide that ultimately points us to Christ. The Law was originally given to Israel to ensure that the gift of the gospel that was promised to us in Abraham would belong to all believers through the faithful obedience of Jesus Christ.

Another function of the Ten Commandments is that they help us continue living the Christian life. The Ten Commandments have shown people that they are sinful and in need of God's grace, demonstrated through Christ. This is not to say that one can earn one's salvation by obeying the Ten Commandments; but rather, the Commandments themselves point us to the necessity and to the adequacy of Christ. Our failure to keep the Ten Commandments demonstrates clearly how much we need God's grace. Thus, the Ten Commandments enable us to experience grace because God's grace is designed for sinners. Law and grace are intertwined in a beautiful way.

The Ten Commandments also provide a powerful revelation of God, as we see the nature of God reflected in the Commandments. As we follow them, we are led to a deeper respect and awe for God. Then, in response to the Commandments, as we follow the Law, our individual growth in God can be seen. Ultimately, we as believers are led to grace as we observe the Law of God.

be just and the justifier of the one who has faith in Jesus.

BOASTING EXCLUDED

27Where *is* boasting then? It is excluded. By what law? Of works? No, but by the law of faith. 28Therefore we conclude that a man is justified by faith apart from the deeds of the law. 29Or *is He* the God of the Jews only? *Is He* not also the God of the Gentiles? Yes, of the Gentiles also, 30since *there is* one God who will justify the circumcised by faith and the uncircumcised through faith. 31Do

we then make void the law through faith? Certainly not! On the contrary, we establish the law.

ABRAHAM JUSTIFIED BY FAITH

4 What then shall we say that Abraham our father has found according to the flesh?a 2For if Abraham was justified by works, he has *something* to boast about, but not before God. 3For what does the Scripture say? *"Abraham believed God, and it was accounted to him for righteousness."*a

4:1 aOr *Abraham our (fore)father according to the flesh has found?*
4:3 aGenesis 15:6

THROUGH THE GRID

Making Sense of Your World:
Transcendentalism

Transcendentalism encompasses the worldview that ultimate reality consists of the spiritual energy that comprises our world. For transcendentalists, each individual connects with a sense of the spiritual and finds God all around us and in all matter. Under transcendentalism, we have several similar views, including pantheism, animism, panpsychism, panentheism, and polytheism. This encompasses religious views such as Hinduism, Buddhism, Taoism, Confucianism, Christian Science, and new ageism. There is some variety among the different views, but overall transcendentalism attempts to locate itself in a middle ground between naturalism and narrow views of some theists. The transcendental worldview situates itself in many different forms, and the list of these transcendental expressions is not easily exhausted.

⁴Now to him who works, the wages are not counted as grace but as debt.

DAVID CELEBRATES THE SAME TRUTH

⁵But to him who does not work but believes on Him who justifies the ungodly, his faith is accounted for righteousness, ⁶just as David also describes the blessedness of the man to whom God imputes righteousness apart from works:

⁷"Blessed *are those* whose lawless deeds are
      forgiven,
   And whose sins are covered;
⁸Blessed *is the* man to whom the LORD shall
      not impute sin."ᵃ

ABRAHAM JUSTIFIED BEFORE CIRCUMCISION

⁹*Does* this blessedness then *come* upon the circumcised *only*, or upon the uncircumcised also? For we say that faith was accounted to Abraham for righteousness. ¹⁰How then was it accounted? While he was circumcised, or uncircumcised? Not while circumcised, but while uncircumcised. ¹¹And he received the sign of circumcision, a seal of the righteousness of the faith which *he had while still* uncircumcised, that he might be the father of all those who believe, though they are uncircumcised, that righteousness might be imputed to them also, ¹²and the father of circumcision to those who not only *are* of the circumcision, but who also walk in the steps of the faith which our father Abraham *had while still* uncircumcised.

THE PROMISE GRANTED THROUGH FAITH

¹³For the promise that he would be the heir of the world *was* not to Abraham or to his seed through the law, but through the righteousness of faith. ¹⁴For if those who are of the law *are* heirs, faith is made void and the promise made of no effect, ¹⁵because the law brings about wrath; for where there is no law *there is* no transgression.

¹⁶Therefore *it is* of faith that *it might be* according to grace, so that the promise might be sure to all the seed, not only to those who are of the law, but also to those who are of the faith of Abraham, who is the father of us all ¹⁷(as it is written, "I have made *you* a father of many nations"ᵃ) in the presence of Him whom he believed—God, who gives life to the dead and calls those things which do not exist as though they did; ¹⁸who, contrary to hope, in hope believed, so that he became the father of many nations, according to what was spoken, "So shall your descendants be." ᵃ ¹⁹And not being weak in faith, he did not consider his own body, already dead (since he was about a hundred years old), and the deadness of Sarah's womb. ²⁰He did not waver at the promise of God through unbelief, but was strengthened in faith, giving glory to God, ²¹and being fully convinced that what He had promised He was also able to perform. ²²And therefore *"it was accounted to him for righteousness."* ᵃ

²³Now it was not written for his sake alone

4:8 ᵃPsalm 32:1, 2   **4:17** ᵃGenesis 17:5   **4:18** ᵃGenesis 15:5
4:22 ᵃGenesis 15:6

LEADERSHIP ISSUES

GC2: Good News: God Accepts You Unconditionally

ROMANS 5:8 *But God demonstrates His own love toward us, in that while we were still sinners, Christ died for us.*

Christ's divine passion to relate to you and enter your world isn't based on anything you have done or could do in the future. It is purely the result of God's grace (Eph. 2:8). It was extended to you while you were gripped by death; a sinner by birth and an enemy of God (Rom. 5:8–12). Regardless of all you have done—or haven't done—He offers grace. God accepts you completely; and in spite of your sin, He provides a way back to Him.

The revelation of Christ—the gospel story—is about turning the paradise lost of Genesis into the paradise regained of Revelation, even though none of us deserves it (see Christ's first sermon from Is. 61:1 and Luke 4:18, 19). It is about abolishing your death sentence even though you have done nothing to warrant eternal life in relationship with God. "In Him was life," John said, "and the life was the light of men" (John 1:4). Yet the basis of receiving such life is nothing we can do; it is strictly a gift from God. The good news of the gospel story is about Christ, who took the initiative and entered our world when we were helpless, unable to even ask for help, and showed us grace—favor that was not merited at all (Phil. 2:8–11).

that it was imputed to him, 24but also for us. It shall be imputed to us who believe in Him who raised up Jesus our Lord from the dead, 25who was delivered up because of our offenses, and was raised because of our justification.

FAITH TRIUMPHS IN TROUBLE

5 Therefore, having been justified by faith, we havea peace with God through our Lord Jesus Christ, 2through whom also we have access by faith into this grace in which we stand, and rejoice in hope of the glory of God. 3And not only *that,* but we also glory in tribulations, knowing that tribulation produces perseverance; 4and perseverance, character; and character, hope. 5Now hope does not disappoint, because the love of God has been poured out in our hearts by the Holy Spirit who was given to us.

CHRIST IN OUR PLACE

6For when we were still without strength, in due time Christ died for the ungodly. 7For scarcely for a righteous man will one die; yet perhaps for a good man someone would even dare to die. 8But God demonstrates His own love toward us, in that while we were still sinners, Christ died for us. 9Much more then, having now been justified by His blood, we shall be saved from wrath through Him. 10For if when we were enemies we were reconciled to God through the death of His Son, much more, having been reconciled, we shall be saved by His life. 11And not only *that,* but we also rejoice in God through our Lord Jesus Christ, through whom we have now received the reconciliation.

DEATH IN ADAM, LIFE IN CHRIST

12Therefore, just as through one man sin entered the world, and death through sin, and thus death spread to all men, because all sinned— 13(For until the law sin was in the world, but sin is not imputed when there is no law. 14Nevertheless death reigned from Adam to Moses, even over those who had not sinned according to the likeness of the transgression of Adam, who is a type of Him who was to come. 15But the free gift *is* not like the offense. For if by the one man's offense many died, much more the grace of God and the gift by the grace of the one Man, Jesus

Christ, abounded to many. 16And the gift *is* not like *that which came* through the one who sinned. For the judgment *which came* from one *offense resulted* in condemnation, but the free gift *which came* from many offenses *resulted* in justification. 17For if by the one man's offense death reigned through the one, much more those who receive abundance of grace and of the gift of righteousness will reign in life through the One, Jesus Christ.)

18Therefore, as through one man's offense *judgment came* to all men, resulting in condemnation, even so through one Man's righteous act *the free gift came* to all men, resulting in justification of life. 19For as by one man's disobedience many were made sinners, so also by one Man's obedience many will be made righteous.

20Moreover the law entered that the offense might abound. But where sin abounded, grace abounded much more, 21so that as sin reigned in death, even so grace might reign through righteousness to eternal life through Jesus Christ our Lord.

DEAD TO SIN, ALIVE TO GOD

6 What shall we say then? Shall we continue in sin that grace may abound? 2Certainly not! How shall we who died to sin live any longer in it? 3Or do you not know that as many of us as were baptized into Christ Jesus were baptized into His death? 4Therefore we were buried with Him through baptism into death, that just as Christ was raised from the dead by the glory of the Father, even so we also should walk in newness of life.

5For if we have been united together in the likeness of His death, certainly we also shall be *in the likeness* of *His* resurrection, 6knowing this, that our old man was crucified with *Him,* that the body of sin might be done away with, that we should no longer be slaves of sin. 7For he who has died has been freed from sin. 8Now if we died with Christ, we believe that we shall also live with Him, 9knowing that Christ, having been raised from the dead, dies no more. Death no longer has dominion over Him. 10For *the death* that He died, He died to sin once for all; but *the life* that He lives, He lives to God. 11Likewise you also, reckon

5:1 aAnother ancient reading is, *let us have peace.*

LEADERSHIP ISSUES

GC2: Good News: God Makes His Move

ROMANS 5:17 *For if by the one man's offense death reigned through the one, much more those who receive abundance of grace and of the gift of righteousness will reign in life through the One, Jesus Christ.*

Imagine God as He watches in grief and sadness while you are born into the very world where He and Adam once walked in perfect relationship (Gen. 3:8, 9). He longs to relate to you as intimately as He once did to Adam and Eve. He wants to take pleasure in you. He wants to see in your eyes the delight that only His life and love can bring you. But that's not possible because you have been dead to Him, separated from the life that is found in Him, from the moment you were born (Eph. 2:1–3). Not only that, but God has been watching from the very first moments of your life as you follow in Adam and Eve's footsteps, becoming His enemy by re-peatedly and selfishly choosing your own sinful ways instead of His holy ways.

So God makes His move. He takes the initiative (Luke 19:10; Eph. 2:4–7). You are the one who desperately needs Him, but you didn't seek Him out. You are the one who should have been crying out for help, saying, "Please, God, do something; I can't live without You, please help." Yet the all-sufficient Lord, who has no needs but "gives to all life, breath, and all things" (Acts 17:25) wants *you.* He wants to relate to you—to enjoy and delight and take pleasure in a personal relationship with you.

Pause to reflect on 1 Peter 1:3–5 as Peter gives thanks, praise, and blessings to the God and Father of our Lord Jesus Christ; now spend time sharing with the Lord your thanks, praise, and blessings.

GC2

GREAT COMMANDMENT
COMMISSION

yourselves to be dead indeed to sin, but alive to God in Christ Jesus our Lord.

[12]Therefore do not let sin reign in your mortal body, that you should obey it in its lusts. [13]And do not present your members *as* instruments of unrighteousness to sin, but present yourselves to God as being alive from the dead, and your members *as* instruments of righteousness to God. [14]For sin shall not have dominion over you, for you are not under law but under grace.

FROM SLAVES OF SIN TO SLAVES OF GOD

[15]What then? Shall we sin because we are not under law but under grace? Certainly not! [16]Do you not know that to whom you present yourselves slaves to obey, you are that one's slaves whom you obey, whether of sin *leading* to death, or of obedience *leading* to righteousness? [17]But God be thanked that *though* you were slaves of sin, yet you obeyed from the heart that form of doctrine to which you were delivered. [18]And having been set free from sin, you became slaves of righteousness. [19]I speak in human *terms* because of the weakness of your flesh. For just as you presented your members *as* slaves of uncleanness, and of lawlessness *leading* to *more* lawlessness, so now present your members *as* slaves *of* righteousness for holiness.

[20]For when you were slaves of sin, you were free in regard to righteousness. [21]What fruit did you have then in the things of which you are now ashamed? For the end of those things *is* death. [22]But now having been set free from sin, and having become slaves of God, you have your fruit to holiness, and the end, everlasting life. [23]For the wages of sin *is* death, but the gift of God *is* eternal life in Christ Jesus our Lord.

FREED FROM THE LAW

7Or do you not know, brethren (for I speak to those who know the law), that the law has dominion over a man as long as he lives? [2]For the woman who has a husband is bound by the law to *her* husband as long as he lives. But if the husband dies, she is released from the law of *her* husband. [3]So then if, while *her* husband lives, she marries another man, she will be called an adulteress; but if her husband dies, she is free from that law, so that she is no adulteress, though she has

married another man. [4]Therefore, my brethren, you also have become dead to the law through the body of Christ, that you may be married to another—to Him who was raised from the dead, that we should bear fruit to God. [5]For when we were in the flesh, the sinful passions which were aroused by the law were at work in our members to bear fruit to death. [6]But now we have been delivered from the law, having died to what we were held by, so that we should serve in the newness of the Spirit and not *in* the oldness of the letter.

SIN'S ADVANTAGE IN THE LAW

[7]What shall we say then? *Is* the law sin? Certainly not! On the contrary, I would not have known sin except through the law. For I would not have known covetousness unless the law had said, *"You shall not covet."*[a] [8]But sin, taking opportunity by the commandment, produced in me all *manner of* evil desire. For apart from the law sin *was* dead. [9]I was alive once without the law, but when the commandment came, sin revived and I died. [10]And the commandment, which *was* to *bring* life, I found to *bring* death. [11]For sin, taking occasion by the commandment, deceived me, and by it killed *me.* [12]Therefore the law *is* holy, and the commandment holy and just and good.

LAW CANNOT SAVE FROM SIN

[13]Has then what is good become death to me? Certainly not! But sin, that it might appear sin, was producing death in me through what is good, so that sin through the commandment might become exceedingly sinful. [14]For we know that the law is spiritual, but I am carnal, sold under sin. [15]For what I am doing, I do not understand. For what I will to do, that I do not practice; but what I hate, that I do. [16]If, then, I do what I will not to do, I agree with the law that *it* is good. [17]But now, *it is* no longer I who do it, but sin that dwells in me. [18]For I know that in me (that is, in my flesh) nothing good dwells; for to will is present with me, but *how* to perform what is good I do not find. [19]For the good that I will *to do,* I do not do; but the evil I will not *to do,* that I practice. [20]Now if I do what I will not *to do,* it is no longer I who do it, but sin that dwells in me.

7:7 [a]Exodus 20:17; Deuteronomy 5:21

²¹I find then a law, that evil is present with me, the one who wills to do good. ²²For I delight in the law of God according to the inward man. ²³But I see another law in my members, warring against the law of my mind, and bringing me into captivity to the law of sin which is in my members. ²⁴O wretched man that I am! Who will deliver me from this body of death? ²⁵I thank God—through Jesus Christ our Lord!

So then, with the mind I myself serve the law of God, but with the flesh the law of sin.

Free from Indwelling Sin

8 There is therefore now no condemnation to those who are in Christ Jesus,ᵃ who do not walk according to the flesh, but according to the Spirit. ²For the law of the Spirit of life in Christ Jesus has made me free from the law of sin and death. ³For what the law could not do in that it was weak through the flesh, God *did* by sending His own Son in the likeness of sinful flesh, on account of sin: He condemned sin in the flesh, ⁴that the righteous requirement of the law might be fulfilled in us who do not walk according to the flesh but according to the Spirit. ⁵For those who live according to the flesh set their minds on the things of the flesh, but those *who live* according to the Spirit, the things of the Spirit. ⁶For to be carnally minded *is* death, but to be spiritually minded *is* life and peace. ⁷Because the carnal mind *is* enmity against God; for it is not subject to the law of God, nor indeed can be. ⁸So then, those who are in the flesh cannot please God.

⁹But you are not in the flesh but in the Spirit, if indeed the Spirit of God dwells in you. Now if anyone does not have the Spirit of Christ, he is not His. ¹⁰And if Christ *is* in you, the body *is* dead because of sin, but the Spirit *is* life because of righteousness. ¹¹But if the Spirit of Him who raised Jesus from the dead dwells in you, He who raised Christ from the dead will also give life to your mortal bodies through His Spirit who dwells in you.

Sonship Through the Spirit

¹²Therefore, brethren, we are debtors—not to the flesh, to live according to the flesh. ¹³For if you live according to the flesh you will die; but if by the Spirit you put to death the deeds of the body, you will live. ¹⁴For as many as are led by the Spirit of God, these are sons of God. ¹⁵For you did not receive the spirit of bondage again to fear, but you received the Spirit of adoption by whom we cry out, "Abba, Father." ¹⁶The Spirit Himself bears witness with our spirit that we are children of God, ¹⁷and if children, then heirs—heirs of God and joint heirs with Christ, if indeed we suffer with *Him,* that we may also be glorified together.

From Suffering to Glory

¹⁸For I consider that the sufferings of this present time are not worthy *to be compared* with the glory which shall be revealed in us. ¹⁹For the earnest expectation of the creation eagerly waits for the revealing of the sons of God. ²⁰For the creation was subjected to futility, not willingly, but because of Him who subjected *it* in hope; ²¹because the creation itself also will be delivered from

8:1 ᵃNU-Text omits the rest of this verse.

THROUGH THE GRID

Making Sense of Your World:
Family in the Bible (Rom. 8:16, 17)

The Bible is filled with metaphors regarding the family. In fact, God's own identity as a triune being is tied up in family terminology—God the Father and Jesus the Son—and those who are born again become children of God who are adopted into the divine family. As such, we are beloved sons and daughters. The church is also commonly referred to as the bride of Christ, with Christ as the Bridegroom (Rev. 18:23; 19:7). God intended familial structures to provide the human relationships that would mirror humanity's relationship with the divine. Through these biblical illustrations, we begin to see the way God intended human families to be.

THROUGH THE GRID

Discover God:
God Directs Our Lives

ROMANS 8:28   *And we know that all things work together for good to those who love God, to those who are the called according to His purpose.*

With all the chaos in the world and the trouble in our lives, sometimes we can wonder who is in control of everything. Part of God's sovereignty allows us to rest securely in the fact that God is indeed in control of everything—from the inner workings of the universe down to the smallest details of our lives. When things seem to go wrong, we should not think that God has abandoned us or feel discouraged; rather, we should rest in God's sovereign power to work out His will in accordance with His own divine plan for the universe, the world, and our lives. In God's sovereign will, there is no room for "luck," but everything works itself out according to the divine plan. Why, then, does God allow bad things to happen to good people? Why is there evil and suffering in the world? Sometimes God allows these things to happen in order to draw our attention to God and to allow us to redirect our focus away from our present situation toward our eternal future. God always works things out for His good purpose, will, and plan because God alone is sovereign.

the bondage of corruption into the glorious liberty of the children of God. [22]For we know that the whole creation groans and labors with birth pangs together until now. [23]Not only *that,* but we also who have the firstfruits of the Spirit, even we ourselves groan within ourselves, eagerly waiting for the adoption, the redemption of our body. [24]For we were saved in this hope, but hope that is seen is not hope; for why does one still hope for what he sees? [25]But if we hope for what we do not see, we eagerly wait for *it* with perseverance.

[26]Likewise the Spirit also helps in our weaknesses. For we do not know what we should pray for as we ought, but the Spirit Himself makes intercession for us[a] with groanings which cannot be uttered. [27]Now He who searches the hearts knows what the mind of the Spirit *is,* because He makes intercession for the saints according to *the will of* God.

[28]And we know that all things work together for good to those who love God, to those who are the called according to *His* purpose. [29]For whom He foreknew, He also predestined *to be* conformed to the image of His Son, that He might be the firstborn among many brethren. [30]Moreover whom He predestined, these He also

called; whom He called, these He also justified; and whom He justified, these He also glorified.

GOD'S EVERLASTING LOVE

[31]What then shall we say to these things? If God *is* for us, who *can be* against us? [32]He who did not spare His own Son, but delivered Him up for us all, how shall He not with Him also freely give us all things? [33]Who shall bring a charge against God's elect? *It is* God who justifies. [34]Who *is* he who condemns? *It is* Christ who died, and furthermore *is* also risen, who is even at the right hand of God, who also makes intercession for us. [35]Who shall separate us from the love of Christ? *Shall* tribulation, or distress, or persecution, or famine, or nakedness, or peril, or sword? [36]As it is written:

> "For Your sake we are killed all day long;
>   We are accounted as sheep for the
>   slaughter."[a]

[37]Yet in all these things we are more than conquerors through Him who loved us. [38]For I

8:26 [a]NU-Text omits *for us.*   8:36 [a]Psalm 44:22

| THROUGH THE GRID | *Thinking Christianly: Why Do Bad Things Happen, Especially to Good People? (Rom. 8:28–30)* |

This question is one of the toughest facing Christianity, as it deals with the problem of theodicy, or the justice of God. The problem is as stated: If God is all-good, God is opposed to evil. And if God is all-powerful, God can prevent evil from happening. However, there exists seemingly no end to the evil, injustice, pain, and suffering that is in our world. We have natural disasters that happen quite frequently, diseases are rampant on the earth, and all people die. Why would an all-good and all-powerful God allow these things instead of preventing them? There are several possible responses to the issue.

Some would deduce from the existence of evil that there is no God at all. Others believe that God might exist, but perhaps God is not all-good or all-powerful. But even in the asking of these questions we have demonstrated a sense of morality, of right and wrong. Animals do not have such feelings. Did human beings develop this sense of right and wrong through an accident of evolution? Or, perhaps, are these senses evidence and a reflection of our being made in the very image of a good and just God? There are several possible answers to the problem of theodicy.

1. The **free will argument** states that God made humanity with free will, so people always have the choice of choosing good or evil. This posture partially accounts for the existence of evil, since free beings can make bad choices.

2. The **soul building argument** holds that God desires to develop our character to be like His own. Thus, we must go through necessary evils of this world in order to gain a dependence on God.

3. The **theological and eschatological argument** holds that although all things are not good, God causes all things to work together for good for those who love Him (Rom. 8:28–30). In the end, God will end evil and suffering and usher in a new reality. The Cross teaches us that God has defeated evil decisively and will do away with evil completely in eternity.

am persuaded that neither death nor life, nor angels nor principalities nor powers, nor things present nor things to come, [39]nor height nor depth, nor any other created thing, shall be able to separate us from the love of God which is in Christ Jesus our Lord.

ISRAEL'S REJECTION OF CHRIST

9 I tell the truth in Christ, I am not lying, my conscience also bearing me witness in the Holy Spirit, [2]that I have great sorrow and continual grief in my heart. [3]For I could wish that I myself were accursed from Christ for my brethren,

my countrymen[a] according to the flesh, [4]who are Israelites, to whom *pertain* the adoption, the glory, the covenants, the giving of the law, the service *of God,* and the promises; [5]of whom *are* the fathers and from whom, according to the flesh, Christ *came,* who is over all, *the* eternally blessed God. Amen.

ISRAEL'S REJECTION AND GOD'S PURPOSE

[6]But it is not that the word of God has taken no effect. For they *are* not all Israel who *are* of

9:3 [a]Or *relatives*

THROUGH THE GRID

Encountering Jesus:
Christ Prays for You!

ROMANS 8:33, 34 *Who shall bring a charge against God's elect? It is God who justifies.*
Who is he who condemns? It is Christ who died, and furthermore is also risen, who is even
at the right hand of God, who also makes intercession for us.

Picture yourself walking into a courtroom—an intimidating place for most of
us. As you enter—alone, uncertain of why you are even there—your anxiety
is real. As you move further into the room, you begin to notice the faces of
those who have in times past accused you. Perhaps they are acquaintances who have criticized or judged you. Maybe they are people from your
past who rejected, neglected, or abused you. Perhaps they are those
whose love and acceptance was always contingent upon your performance. Your anxiety turns to fear, your self-doubt to self-condemnation. You
are alone with your accusers.

Now imagine that into the courtroom walks Jesus Christ. Whatever image
you have of Christ—in robes, sandals, maybe with nail-pierced hands and
feet—meditate on Jesus joining you in the courtroom. He does not take a
place behind the courtroom bench as a judge (though He has every right
to), but instead He walks right up beside you. He puts His arm around you
and gently bows with you to your knees (Luke 22:32; Heb. 7:25).

Kneeling beside you is the only One who has the right to bring any charge
against you. But as you listen to His soft words, you realize that He is not
accusing you—He is interceding for you! He is praying for the burdens of
your heart—requesting provision, speaking blessing over your relationships, and most importantly, asking that you might experience freedom
from condemnation (Rom. 8:1).

Now allow your heart to give Jesus thanks that He prays for you!

Israel, ⁷nor *are they* all children because they are
the seed of Abraham; but, *"In Isaac your seed shall
be called."* ᵃ ⁸That is, those who *are* the children
of the flesh, these *are* not the children of God; but
the children of the promise are counted as the
seed. ⁹For this *is* the word of promise: *"At this
time I will come and Sarah shall have a son."* ᵃ

¹⁰And not only *this,* but when Rebecca also
had conceived by one man, *even* by our father Isaac
¹¹(for *the children* not yet being born, nor having
done any good or evil, that the purpose of God
according to election might stand, not of works
but of Him who calls), ¹²it was said to her, *"The
older shall serve the younger."* ᵃ ¹³As it is written,
"Jacob I have loved, but Esau I have hated." ᵃ

ISRAEL'S REJECTION AND GOD'S JUSTICE

¹⁴What shall we say then? *Is there* unrighteousness with God? Certainly not! ¹⁵For
He says to Moses, *"I will have mercy on
whomever I will have mercy, and I will have
compassion on whomever I will have compassion."* ᵃ ¹⁶So then *it is* not of him who wills, nor
of him who runs, but of God who shows mercy.
¹⁷For the Scripture says to the Pharaoh, *"For
this very purpose I have raised you up, that I
may show My power in you, and that My name
may be declared in all the earth."* ᵃ ¹⁸Therefore

9:7 ᵃGenesis 21:12   **9:9** ᵃGenesis 18:10, 14   **9:12** ᵃGenesis 25:23
9:13 ᵃMalachi 1:2, 3   **9:15** ᵃExodus 33:19   **9:17** ᵃExodus 9:16

He has mercy on whom He wills, and whom He wills He hardens.

¹⁹You will say to me then, "Why does He still find fault? For who has resisted His will?" ²⁰But indeed, O man, who are you to reply against God? Will the thing formed say to him who formed *it*, "Why have you made me like this?" ²¹Does not the potter have power over the clay, from the same lump to make one vessel for honor and another for dishonor?

²²*What* if God, wanting to show *His* wrath and to make His power known, endured with much longsuffering the vessels of wrath prepared for destruction, ²³and that He might make known the riches of His glory on the vessels of mercy, which He had prepared beforehand for glory, ²⁴even us whom He called, not of the Jews only, but also of the Gentiles?

²⁵As He says also in Hosea:

> "I will call them My people, who were not My
>   people,
> And her beloved, who was not beloved."ᵃ
> ²⁶"And it shall come to pass in the place where it
>   was said to them,
> 'You are not My people,'
> There they shall be called sons of the living
>   God."ᵃ

²⁷Isaiah also cries out concerning Israel:ᵃ

> "Though the number of the children of Israel
>   be as the sand of the sea,
> The remnant will be saved.
> ²⁸For He will finish the work and cut *it* short in
>   righteousness,
> Because the LORD will make a short work
>   upon the earth."ᵃ

²⁹And as Isaiah said before:

> "Unless the LORD of Sabaothᵃ had left us a seed,
> We would have become like Sodom,
> And we would have been made like
>   Gomorrah."ᵇ

PRESENT CONDITION OF ISRAEL

³⁰What shall we say then? That Gentiles, who did not pursue righteousness, have attained to

righteousness, even the righteousness of faith; ³¹but Israel, pursuing the law of righteousness, has not attained to the law of righteousness.ᵃ ³²Why? Because *they did* not *seek it* by faith, but as it were, by the works of the law.ᵃ For they stumbled at that stumbling stone. ³³As it is written:

> "Behold, I lay in Zion a stumbling stone and
>   rock of offense,
> And whoever believes on Him will not be put
>   to shame."ᵃ

ISRAEL NEEDS THE GOSPEL

10 Brethren, my heart's desire and prayer to God for Israelᵃ is that they may be saved. ²For I bear them witness that they have a zeal for God, but not according to knowledge. ³For they being ignorant of God's righteousness, and seeking to establish their own righteousness, have not submitted to the righteousness of God. ⁴For Christ *is* the end of the law for righteousness to everyone who believes.

⁵For Moses writes about the righteousness which is of the law, *"The man who does those things shall live by them."* ᵃ ⁶But the righteousness of faith speaks in this way, *"Do not say in your heart, 'Who will ascend into heaven?'"*ᵃ (that is, to bring Christ down *from above*) ⁷or, *"Who will descend into the abyss?'"*ᵃ (that is, to bring Christ up from the dead). ⁸But what does it say? *"The word is near you, in your mouth and in your heart"*ᵃ (that is, the word of faith which we preach): ⁹that if you confess with your mouth the Lord Jesus and believe in your heart that God has raised Him from the dead, you will be saved. ¹⁰For with the heart one believes unto righteousness, and with the mouth confession is made unto salvation. ¹¹For the Scripture says, *"Whoever believes on Him will not be put to shame."*ᵃ ¹²For there is no distinction between Jew and Greek, for the same Lord over all is rich to all who call upon Him. ¹³For *"whoever calls on the name of the Lord shall be saved."*ᵃ

9:25 ᵃHosea 2:23   **9:26** ᵃHosea 1:10   **9:27** ᵃIsaiah 10:22, 23   **9:28** ᵃNU-Text reads *For the LORD will finish the work and cut it short upon the earth.*   **9:29** ᵃLiterally, in Hebrew, *Hosts* ᵇIsaiah 1:9   **9:31** ᵃNU-Text omits *of righteousness.*   **9:32** ᵃNU-Text reads *by works.*   **9:33** ᵃIsaiah 8:14; 28:16   **10:1** ᵃNU-Text reads *them.*   **10:5** ᵃLeviticus 18:5   **10:6** ᵃDeuteronomy 30:12   **10:7** ᵃDeuteronomy 30:13   **10:8** ᵃDeuteronomy 30:14   **10:11** ᵃIsaiah 28:16   **10:13** ᵃJoel 2:32

LEADERSHIP ISSUES

GC2: Faith Restored

ROMANS 10:17

Faithful followers of Jesus embrace the importance of growing in faith. To be Christlike is to be faith-filled, just as God and His Word encourage and empower our deepened trust in a Person named Jesus! At humankind's fall into sin, Satan undermined faith: "You will not surely die," the serpent said (Gen. 3:4). Adam and Eve's faith was attacked as God's truth was questioned. Faith comes through hearing and accepting God at the point of His Word, and it is threatened when His Word is devalued, ignored, or denied.

Prior to the Fall, God's provision of air, food, water, and relationships (just to name a few of His blessings) simply served as a reminder to Adam and Eve that God was the appropriate object of their faith and that they should keep their eyes and hearts fixed on Him. When Eve, however, gave heed to the serpent and questioned the truth of what God had said, her faith (and Adam's in turn) was weakened. The restoration of expectant faith to the lives of His people has been on God's heart ever since. "The life which I now live in the flesh I live by faith in the Son of God" (Gal. 2:20). The object of our faith is Jesus. Time in His Word exercises the muscles of our faith (1 Pet. 2:2).

GC2
GREAT COMMANDMENT
COMMISSION

Israel Rejects the Gospel

[14]How then shall they call on Him in whom they have not believed? And how shall they believe in Him of whom they have not heard? And how shall they hear without a preacher? [15]And how shall they preach unless they are sent? As it is written:

> "How beautiful are the feet of those who
>   preach the gospel of peace,[a]
> Who bring glad tidings of good things!"[b]

[16]But they have not all obeyed the gospel. For Isaiah says, *"Lord, who has believed our report?"*[a] [17]So then faith *comes* by hearing, and hearing by the word of God.

[18]But I say, have they not heard? Yes indeed:

> "Their sound has gone out to all the earth,
> And their words to the ends of the world."[a]

[19]But I say, did Israel not know? First Moses says:

> "I will provoke you to jealousy by those who are
>   not a nation,
> I will move you to anger by a foolish nation."[a]

[20]But Isaiah is very bold and says:

> "I was found by those who did not seek Me;
> I was made manifest to those who did not ask
>   for Me."[a]

[21]But to Israel he says:

> "All day long I have stretched out My hands
> To a disobedient and contrary people."[a]

Israel's Rejection Not Total

11 I say then, has God cast away His people? Certainly not! For I also am an Israelite, of the seed of Abraham, of the tribe of Benjamin. [2]God has not cast away His people whom He foreknew. Or do you not know what the Scripture says of Elijah, how he pleads with God against Israel, saying, [3]*"LORD, they have killed Your prophets and torn down Your altars, and I*

alone am left, and they seek my life"?[a] [4]But what does the divine response say to him? *"I have reserved for Myself seven thousand men who have not bowed the knee to Baal."*[a] [5]Even so then, at this present time there is a remnant according to the election of grace. [6]And if by grace, then *it is* no longer of works; otherwise grace is no longer grace.[a] But if *it is* of works, it is no longer grace; otherwise work is no longer work.

[7]What then? Israel has not obtained what it seeks; but the elect have obtained it, and the rest were blinded. [8]Just as it is written:

> "God has given them a spirit of stupor,
> Eyes that they should not see
> And ears that they should not hear,
> To this very day."[a]

[9]And David says:

> "Let their table become a snare and a trap,
> A stumbling block and a recompense to them.
> [10]Let their eyes be darkened, so that they do
>   not see,
> And bow down their back always."[a]

Israel's Rejection Not Final

[11]I say then, have they stumbled that they should fall? Certainly not! But through their fall, to provoke them to jealousy, salvation *has come* to the Gentiles. [12]Now if their fall *is* riches for the world, and their failure riches for the Gentiles, how much more their fullness!

[13]For I speak to you Gentiles; inasmuch as I am an apostle to the Gentiles, I magnify my ministry, [14]if by any means I may provoke to jealousy *those who are* my flesh and save some of them. [15]For if their being cast away *is* the reconciling of the world, what *will* their acceptance *be* but life from the dead?

[16]For if the firstfruit *is* holy, the lump *is* also *holy;* and if the root *is* holy, so *are* the branches. [17]And if some of the branches were broken off,

10:15 [a]NU-Text omits *preach the gospel of peace, Who.* [b]Isaiah 52:7; Nahum 1:15   **10:16** [a]Isaiah 53:1   **10:18** [a]Psalm 19:4   **10:19** [a]Deuteronomy 32:21   **10:20** [a]Isaiah 65:1   **10:21** [a]Isaiah 65:2   **11:3** [a]1 Kings 19:10, 14   **11:4** [a]1 Kings 19:18   **11:6** [a]NU-Text omits the rest of this verse.   **11:8** [a]Deuteronomy 29:4; Isaiah 29:10   **11:10** [a]Psalm 69:22, 23

THROUGH THE GRID

Written by the Hand of God:
Legalism

ROMANS 11:6 *And if by grace, then it is no longer of works; otherwise grace is no longer grace. But if it is of works, it is no longer grace; otherwise work is no longer work.*

Two extremes offer themselves whenever one follows the Ten Commandments: *cheap grace* and *legalism*. Both offer specific temptations, but both are unbiblical.

Cheap grace is taking advantage of the grace of God. It happens when people ask for forgiveness but do not actually change their behavior or take responsibility for their own spiritual formation. Certainly, we have forgiveness and reconciliation in Jesus Christ; but God also demands discipline and order, and He expects conformance to His will. Many who fall into the trap of cheap grace do not honor God with their lives, and they tend to view God as a mere convenience—God is there for them when they mess up, but they never make an effort to conform to His will. When we take all of the goods of God's grace and do not change, that is cheap grace. Grace is not cheap; it is costly. The price for forgiveness was death on a cross, and our response is to submit to Christ and obey the God who has given grace abundantly to us.

Legalism, on the other hand, is the meticulous adherence to the law as a way of gaining God's acceptance. Those who are only concerned about keeping the law have missed the point about God. God desires a personal relationship with us, and legalism kills the romance between God and us. Legalism places human tradition above God's Word, hinders our vision of God, and denies the power of Christ's work on the cross. Legalism stems from selfish pride—the desire to say, "I did this!" or "I earned this!" However, legalism ignores the fact that we are all completely fallen and in need of grace. Legalism can also produce rivalry, deception, and contempt—the "I'm holier than you" attitude.

To avoid these extremes, we must walk by faith in Jesus Christ, who offers us freedom, not bondage, through the grace that is available in Him.

and you, being a wild olive tree, were grafted in among them, and with them became a partaker of the root and fatness of the olive tree, [18]do not boast against the branches. But if you do boast, *remember that* you do not support the root, but the root *supports* you.

[19]You will say then, "Branches were broken off that I might be grafted in." [20]Well *said*. Because of unbelief they were broken off, and you stand by faith. Do not be haughty, but fear. [21]For if God did not spare the natural branches, He may not spare you either. [22]Therefore consider the goodness and severity of God: on those who fell, severity; but toward you, goodness,[a] if you continue in *His* goodness. Otherwise you also will be cut off. [23]And they also, if they do not continue in unbelief, will be grafted in, for God is able to graft them in again. [24]For if you were cut out of the olive tree which is wild by nature, and were grafted contrary to nature into a cultivated olive

11:22 [a]NU-Text adds *of God.*

tree, how much more will these, who *are* natural *branches,* be grafted into their own olive tree?

²⁵For I do not desire, brethren, that you should be ignorant of this mystery, lest you should be wise in your own opinion, that blindness in part has happened to Israel until the fullness of the Gentiles has come in. ²⁶And so all Israel will be saved,ᵃ as it is written:

> "The Deliverer will come out of Zion,
> And He will turn away ungodliness from
>   Jacob;
> ²⁷For this *is* My covenant with them,
> When I take away their sins."ᵃ

²⁸Concerning the gospel *they are* enemies for your sake, but concerning the election *they are* beloved for the sake of the fathers. ²⁹For the gifts and the calling of God *are* irrevocable. ³⁰For as you were once disobedient to God, yet have now obtained mercy through their disobedience, ³¹even so these also have now been disobedient, that through the mercy shown you they also may obtain mercy. ³²For God has committed them all to disobedience, that He might have mercy on all.

³³Oh, the depth of the riches both of the wisdom and knowledge of God! How unsearchable *are* His judgments and His ways past finding out!

> ³⁴*"For who has known the mind of the LORD?*
>   *Or who has become His counselor?"*ᵃ
> ³⁵*"Or who has first given to Him*
>   *And it shall be repaid to him?"*ᵃ

³⁶For of Him and through Him and to Him *are* all things, to whom *be* glory forever. Amen.

LIVING SACRIFICES TO GOD

12 I beseech you therefore, brethren, by the mercies of God, that you present your bodies a living sacrifice, holy, acceptable to God, *which is* your reasonable service. ²And do not be conformed to this world, but be transformed by the renewing of your mind, that you may prove what *is* that good and acceptable and perfect will of God.

SERVE GOD WITH SPIRITUAL GIFTS

³For I say, through the grace given to me, to everyone who is among you, not to think *of himself* more highly than he ought to think, but to think soberly, as God has dealt to each one a

11:26 ᵃOr *delivered*   **11:27** ᵃIsaiah 59:20, 21   **11:34** ᵃIsaiah 40:13; Jeremiah 23:18   **11:35** ᵃJob 41.11

LEAD**ERSHIP**
REAL**ITIES**

TIME MANAGEMENT: THE VALUE OF A MOMENT   *Romans 12:1*

In what is possibly the most important letter Paul wrote, he appealed to the reader to make an offering of his/her life in such a way that it could be called a *living sacrifice*.

zavw—**living**—to enjoy real life

When the word "sacrifice" was read aloud to the house church in Rome, many listeners remembered the sacrificial system of Mosaic Law in which an animal was born and bred for the one moment when it would be placed as an offering before a priest. Its lifeblood was drained, placing humankind's sins on a "system of credit" that would one day be paid in full by the True Sacrifice, the blood of Christ. Knowing the impact of this word picture, Paul exhorts the reader not to consider sacrifice as death but as a way to live. To live as a sacrifice is to live as if the present moment in life could be one's last. Time management is more about capturing the moments of life as an act of worship than managing them. It is to live with an attitude of intentionality, to proactively capture the present in order to experience a blessed future.

LEADERSHIP ISSUES

GC2: Holy: You As a Living and Holy Sacrifice

ROMANS 12:1 *I beseech you therefore, brethren, by the mercies of God, that you present your bodies a living sacrifice, holy, acceptable to God, which is your reasonable service.*

In this passage, Paul makes appeal to the "reasonableness" of our commitment to holiness, being set apart *to* and *for* Christ. He draws upon the extensive presentation in the previous eleven chapters of all that God in Christ has done for us. Remembering Christ's words in the Gospel, "freely you have received, freely give" (Matt. 10:8), Paul recounts all we have freely received in Christ:

- being made right as a gift by His grace (Rom. 3:24)
- peace with God through Jesus (Rom. 5:1)
- unmerited redemption (Rom. 5:8)
- ability to walk in newness of life (Rom. 6:4)
- freedom from condemnation because we are in Christ (Rom. 8:1)

It is the wonder of such free and indescribable gifts that prompts offering ourselves freely to the Lord's service in the world. Pause to thank Him that His purity and holiness have benefited you! Recall with gratitude the incarnate life, the sacrificial death, and the glorious resurrection of the Lord Jesus Christ. Imagine now in your heart the suffering Savior on a cross giving His life. "Why did He do it?" you ask. Because only a perfect, holy sacrifice can pay the price of sin, providing access to intimacy with God.

But just as important is the question: "For whom did He do it?" Consider this thought: if you were the only one who needed a Savior, Christ would have gone to Calvary just for you.

Picture Christ on the cross—despised and rejected, sorrowed and alone—this One who never sinned yet took upon Himself our sin so that we might present ourselves as a living sacrifice to God (2 Cor. 5:21). Allow God's Spirit to stir gratitude in your heart as you consider the words: "He did it for me!"

GC2
GREAT COMMANDMENT
COMMISSION

LEADERSHIP
REALITIES

AUTHENTICITY: MIRROR OR MASQUERADE *Romans 12:2*

syschēmatizō—**conformed**—to put on a mask and attend a party or masquerade. It is to act in such a way as to misrepresent one's true inner nature.

metamorphoō—**transformed**—one's outward actions represent an inner change in the essential nature of a person

The question must be asked of every Christian leader: "Does my life mirror the Christ within me, or is it a masquerade on display to the world around me?" The authentic leader does not "put on" false pretenses. He or she is transparent, seeking to mirror the very character of Christ in everything, and open to change if so prompted by the Holy Spirit. This daily process of experiencing Scripture *transforms* the mind and heart through a deeper understanding of what it means to be *in* Christ.

> *Read* the Word.
> *Believe* the Word.
> *Obey* the Word.

Each of us has to choose between *conforming* to the culture and being *transformed* by the Holy Spirit. One mirrors the world and one mirrors the spirit of Christ. One pretends to be a lover of Christ and one presents an authentic life, one of the most important and attractive characteristics of a leader.

---

measure of faith. ⁴For as we have many members in one body, but all the members do not have the same function, ⁵so we, *being* many, are one body in Christ, and individually members of one another. ⁶Having then gifts differing according to the grace that is given to us, *let us use them:* if prophecy, *let us prophesy* in proportion to our faith; ⁷or ministry, *let us use it* in *our* ministering; he who teaches, in teaching; ⁸he who exhorts, in exhortation; he who gives, with liberality; he who leads, with diligence; he who shows mercy, with cheerfulness.

BEHAVE LIKE A CHRISTIAN

⁹*Let* love *be* without hypocrisy. Abhor what is evil. Cling to what is good. ¹⁰*Be* kindly affectionate to one another with brotherly love, in honor giving preference to one another; ¹¹not lagging in diligence, fervent in spirit, serving the Lord; ¹²rejoicing in hope, patient in tribulation, continuing

steadfastly in prayer; ¹³distributing to the needs of the saints, given to hospitality.

¹⁴Bless those who persecute you; bless and do not curse. ¹⁵Rejoice with those who rejoice, and weep with those who weep. ¹⁶Be of the same mind toward one another. Do not set your mind on high things, but associate with the humble. Do not be wise in your own opinion.

¹⁷Repay no one evil for evil. Have regard for good things in the sight of all men. ¹⁸If it is possible, as much as depends on you, live peaceably with all men. ¹⁹Beloved, do not avenge yourselves, but *rather* give place to wrath; for it is written, *"Vengeance is Mine, I will repay,"*ᵃ says the Lord. ²⁰Therefore

> *"If your enemy is hungry, feed him;*
> *If he is thirsty, give him a drink;*

12:19 ᵃDeuteronomy 32:35

LEADERSHIP ISSUES

Renew Your Mind

ROMANS 12:2

Each of us faces a barrage of distraction and suggestion on a daily basis. If these are allowed to remain in the mind, they are then given the power to suggest a lifestyle of counterfeit PEACE.

Pressure: There are two main types of pressure that work on the mind of a leader. The first is outer pressure or the crush of what the culture is promoting at the moment through constant media and message. Second, there is inner pressure such as restlessness, boredom, and emotion.

Escape: Escape is a coping tool when responsibilities and demands feel like more than you can handle. Sometimes we "check out" mentally, putting the mind in a neutral state, which makes us easy prey to destructive messages.

Availability: It's no secret that destructive substances and behaviors are readily available anytime. The offers for casual sex and "friends with benefits" are way too easy to receive and accept. When Jesus met the woman at the well, instead of being tempted by her loose moral lifestyle, He changed the conversation to spiritual things. Begin to formulate a plan on how you can do the same.

Curiosity: The natural response to popular and available vices is *"maybe I should try it once."* When you program your mind, curiosity is not a serious factor, only a fleeting one. Choices bring long-lasting consequences. Leaders who focus their minds on the goal of adventures with God are not willing to settle for second-rate experiments.

Emptiness: The first four mind-altering factors are why many of us get into trouble, but emptiness is the reason some stay there. All of us were born with a God-shaped vacuum in our hearts. We can either fill it on purpose with righteousness, or it will fill itself with unrighteousness.

God's promise is that you can be "transformed," and the result will be "good and acceptable and the perfect will of God." A radical, powerful life is one that steps away from the ideals, methods, and goals of those who do not follow Christ; instead, it steps toward the peace of God.

LEADERSHIP
REALITIES

LEADERSHIP IS BUILT ON RELATIONSHIPS   *Romans 12:15*

Leadership is built on relationships, and it begins at the feet of Jesus in a relationship with Him. With this foundation, the leader gains the ability to cultivate healthy bonds with others. Surprisingly, the ability to build lasting relationships is often the most neglected of all leadership skills. Thus, Paul makes two suggestions that are essential to having Christlike, lasting relationships:

- *Rejoice with others' successes.* It is important that we are proactive in celebrating others' successes. Don't give in when you're tempted to be jealous of the successes of others. Their achievement is not your failure. It is God who shows favor, and it is God who grants success to His children. All good things come from Him.

- *Share tears with others' sorrows:* True friends do not hurt from a distance by offering up a token "I'm praying for you." They crawl into the ditch of despair and down into the depths of sorrow alongside hurting friends and help to lift them to peace. Genuine friends close the distance and move from hurting *for* to hurting *with.*

For in so doing you will heap coals of fire on his head."[a]

[21]Do not be overcome by evil, but overcome evil with good.

SUBMIT TO GOVERNMENT

13 Let every soul be subject to the governing authorities. For there is no authority except from God, and the authorities that exist are appointed by God. [2]Therefore whoever resists the authority resists the ordinance of God, and those who resist will bring judgment on themselves. [3]For rulers are not a terror to good works, but to evil. Do you want to be unafraid of the authority? Do what is good, and you will have praise from the same. [4]For he is God's minister to you for good. But if you do evil, be afraid; for he does not bear the sword in vain; for he is God's minister, an avenger to *execute* wrath on him who practices evil. [5]Therefore *you* must be subject, not only because of wrath but also for conscience' sake. [6]For because of this you also pay taxes, for they are God's ministers attending continually to this very thing. [7]Render therefore to all their due: taxes to whom taxes *are due,* customs to whom customs, fear to whom fear, honor to whom honor.

LOVE YOUR NEIGHBOR

[8]Owe no one anything except to love one another, for he who loves another has fulfilled the law. [9]For the commandments, *"You shall not commit adultery," "You shall not murder," "You shall not steal," "You shall not bear false witness,"*[a] *"You shall not covet,"*[b] and if *there is* any other commandment, are *all* summed up in this saying, namely, *"You shall love your neighbor as yourself."*[c] [10]Love does no harm to a neighbor; therefore love *is* the fulfillment of the law.

PUT ON CHRIST

[11]And *do* this, knowing the time, that now *it is* high time to awake out of sleep; for now our salvation *is* nearer than when we *first* believed. [12]The night is far spent, the day is at hand. Therefore let us cast off the works of darkness, and let us put on the armor of light. [13]Let us walk properly, as in the day, not in revelry and drunkenness, not in lewdness and lust, not in strife and envy. [14]But put on the Lord Jesus Christ, and make no provision for the flesh, to *fulfill its* lusts.

12:20 [a]Proverbs 25:21, 22   **13:9** [a]NU-Text omits *"You shall not bear false witness."* [b]Exodus 20:13–15, 17; Deuteronomy 5:17–19, 21 [c]Leviticus 19:18

LEADERSHIP ISSUES

Making Good Decisions

ROMANS 12:2

The first bad decision was made in the Garden of Eden. Adam and Eve were given many good options, but they chose the only bad choice, about which they were warned (Gen. 2:17). Placed in a garden with every need met, every delight available, and all potential within their grasp, they still were deceived into thinking that God was holding out on them.

People have not changed these thousands of years later. Rebellion and distraction win out, and choices are made that have a lifetime of consequences. Like Adam and Eve, we think God is holding good things back from us, when just the opposite is true. We are told that the Father desires the best for us (Luke 11:13); and when we renew the mind from evil suggestion, we "prove what is that good and acceptable and perfect will of God."

The will of God is:

1. understood through trust and surrender: "Trust in the LORD with all your heart, and lean not on your own understanding" (Prov. 3:5).
2. received by faith: "But without faith it is impossible to please Him" (Heb. 11:6).
3. directed by His Word: Although God knows the future, He may reveal only enough of the path ahead for the next step. When the road looks dark, go back to Psalm 119:105: "Your word is a lamp to my feet and a light to my path."
4. proven through unity of the Trinity of God:
   God the Father—What does He say? His will never contradicts His Word.
   God the Son—What did Jesus do? Is Christ Himself giving you the choice before you, or is it coming from elsewhere?
   God the Spirit—There should be a great peace about the choice.

All three Persons of the Godhead must be united, never divided. Scripture can be twisted and misapplied to satisfy a decision. Choices may seem OK but not exactly right; the emotions can dismiss God's Word as "not relevant to the situation." It is only when the Trinity of God supports your decision that you can say, "Good decision. I am walking in His will."

LEADERSHIP ISSUES

GC2: Emotion Meets Emotion

ROMANS 12:15

How are we to respond to people's emotional expression? If they express
positive emotions, we should rejoice with them; if they express painful
emotions, we should mourn with them. It is a simple but powerful truth.
It is also significant that human emotion can be categorized as either
"positive" or "painful."

- Positive emotions might include joy, gratitude, security, encouragement, happiness, etc.
- Painful emotions might include fear, anger, hurt, guilt, shame, loneliness, etc.

Healthy, God-honoring relationships are ones where we become secure in
experiencing Romans 12:15. Consider the examples below, and look for
opportunities to experience the verse this week.

Emotion	meets	Emotion
I felt very excited today. I fin-ished the project I was work-ing on.		I'm glad you did; I'm excited for you.
I got really angry today be-cause someone at school took advantage of me.		I really regret that happened.
I felt embarrassed when I was the last one chosen for the baseball team.		I know that really hurt; I'm sorry it happened.
I was so happy to have lunch with a friend I haven't seen in years.		I'm glad that worked out for you; I'm sure you enjoyed the time.

GC2
GREAT COMMANDMENT
COMMISSION

THROUGH THE GRID	*Thinking Christianly: Ten Foundational Beliefs of a Christian Worldview*

Belief Eight: Government and Society (*Rom. 13:1–7*)

Human society, government, nations, and cultures were created by God for the good of humanity. However, all societies are marred by sin and are thus limited in authority. Christians should espouse to make the will of God supreme, not only in our own lives but also in government and society (Ex. 20:3–17; Prov. 14:34; Matt. 22:21; Acts 5:29; Rom. 13:1–7). *See Through the Grid article on page 1572.*

THE LAW OF LIBERTY

14 Receive one who is weak in the faith, *but* not to disputes over doubtful things. ²For one believes he may eat all things, but he who is weak eats *only* vegetables. ³Let not him who eats despise him who does not eat, and let not him who does not eat judge him who eats; for God has received him. ⁴Who are you to judge another's servant? To his own master he stands or falls. Indeed, he will be made to stand, for God is able to make him stand.

⁵One person esteems *one* day above another; another esteems every day *alike.* Let each be fully convinced in his own mind. ⁶He who observes the day, observes *it* to the Lord;ᵃ and he who does not observe the day, to the Lord he does not observe *it.* He who eats, eats to the Lord, for he gives God thanks; and he who does not eat, to the Lord he does not eat, and gives God thanks. ⁷For none of us lives to himself, and no one dies to himself. ⁸For if we live, we live to the Lord; and if we die, we die to the Lord. Therefore, whether we live or die, we are the Lord's. ⁹For to this end Christ died and roseᵃ and lived again, that He might be Lord of both the dead and the living. ¹⁰But why do you judge your brother? Or why do you show contempt for your brother? For we shall all stand before the judgment seat of Christ.ᵃ ¹¹For it is written:

"As I live, says the LORD,
Every knee shall bow to Me,
And every tongue shall confess to God."ᵃ

¹²So then each of us shall give account of himself to God. ¹³Therefore let us not judge one

another anymore, but rather resolve this, not to put a stumbling block or a cause to fall in *our* brother's way.

THE LAW OF LOVE

¹⁴I know and am convinced by the Lord Jesus that *there is* nothing unclean of itself; but to him who considers anything to be unclean, to him *it is* unclean. ¹⁵Yet if your brother is grieved because of *your* food, you are no longer walking in love. Do not destroy with your food the one for whom Christ died. ¹⁶Therefore do not let your good be spoken of as evil; ¹⁷for the kingdom of God is not eating and drinking, but righteousness and peace and joy in the Holy Spirit. ¹⁸For he who serves Christ in these thingsᵃ *is* acceptable to God and approved by men.

¹⁹Therefore let us pursue the things *which make* for peace and the things by which one may edify another. ²⁰Do not destroy the work of God for the sake of food. All things indeed *are* pure, but *it is* evil for the man who eats with offense. ²¹*It is* good neither to eat meat nor drink wine nor *do anything* by which your brother stumbles or is offended or is made weak.ᵃ ²²Do you have faith?ᵃ Have *it* to yourself before God. Happy *is* he who does not condemn himself in what he approves. ²³But he who doubts is condemned if he eats, because *he does* not *eat* from faith; for whatever *is* not from faith is sin.ᵃ

14:6 ᵃNU-Text omits the rest of this sentence.   **14:9** ᵃNU-Text omits *and rose.*   **14:10** ᵃNU-Text reads *of God.*   **14:11** ᵃIsaiah 45:23   **14:18** ᵃNU-Text reads *this.*   **14:21** ᵃNU-Text omits *or is offended or is made weak.*   **14:22** ᵃNU-Text reads *The faith which you have—have.*   **14:23** ᵃM-Text puts Romans 16:25–27 here.

LEADERSHIP ISSUES

GC2: Providing Security (Peace)

ROMANS 12:18

The need for security is met when we establish and maintain harmony and peace in relationships. We have freedom from anxiety and from the fear of rejections and lack of provision.

"Be of the same mind toward one another," (Rom. 12:16).

During His earthly ministry, Jesus offered security to those who were close to Him; and He lived in peace with all by continually meeting physical, relational, and spiritual needs. At times, He even performed miracles to meet physical needs such as the need for food (Mark 6:30–45).

How does God meet this need for us? God meets our need for security in that He has promised never to leave or forsake us (Josh. 1:5; Matt. 28:20; Heb. 13:5). He gives reassurance concerning our need for food, clothing, and shelter (Matt. 6:25–32); and He has gone to prepare a place for us, promising to come again that we might be with Him (John 14:1–3).

Pause and reflect on these ideas for giving others security:

- The people to whom I am closest never have to wonder where our relationship stands. I am open and transparent in sharing my heart, care, and concern.
- I proactively attempt to maintain health in all my relationships. If a relationship is strained, I try to reconcile it quickly with forgiveness, confession, and care as appropriate.
- I am even-tempered and not prone to moodiness or outbursts of anger; there is consistency in how I relate to people, freeing them from fear.
- I make decisions based on the well-being of those for whom I love and care, not just my own well-being.
- I am self-controlled . . . others around me sense my peaceful trust in God, providing a "safe" place for us to relate.

GC2
GREAT COMMANDMENT
COMMISSION

LEADERSHIP ISSUES

Authority Is About Order

ROMANS 13:1

Authority

Authority can be defined as the legitimate right to exercise power, set rules, and give orders. One of the greatest challenges leaders face is dealing with the issue of authority. Many people have a hard time being under it, and leaders often have a difficult time exercising authority effectively. The Bible informs and directs us when it comes to this important issue.

Authority comes from God.

The Bible makes it clear that God is *sovereign*. He created everything and everyone in the universe, and He is absolutely in control of everything that happens. It logically follows that all authority belongs to Him (Matt. 28:18), and all human authority comes from Him (Rom. 13:1).

Authority can be abused.

Although authority is supposed to help us, sometimes people abuse their positions of authority. Unfit parents abuse their kids, tyrannical governments abuse their people, and immoral church leaders abuse their members. That is why authority has limits of legitimacy. If a person in authority tries to get us to violate God's Word, we must always obey God first (Acts 4:19).

Authority has important purposes.

While authority can be abused, authority properly exercised fulfills an important role in our lives. Authority is there to provide for our needs and to protect us from making foolish decisions. Because God is the One who has placed people in authority over us, our response to our authorities is actually a response to God. Even when we don't understand why those in authority do what they do, we are encouraged by the Scriptures to submit to them and to trust that God has ultimate authority.

Five "spheres" of authority.

The Bible teaches us that God has set up five different "spheres," or categories, of authority to help order our lives. The Bible, the family, the church, the government, and employers are all biblically recognized systems of authority. God is very concerned that we learn to respond to authority appropriately because it reflects the way we respond to God.

Bearing Others' Burdens

15 We then who are strong ought to bear with the scruples of the weak, and not to please ourselves. ²Let each of us please *his* neighbor for *his* good, leading to edification. ³For even Christ did not please Himself; but as it is written, *"The reproaches of those who reproached You fell on Me."*[a] ⁴For whatever things were written before were written for our learning, that we through the patience and comfort of the Scriptures might have hope. ⁵Now may the God of patience and comfort grant you to be like-minded toward one another, according to Christ Jesus, ⁶that you may with one mind *and* one mouth glorify the God and Father of our Lord Jesus Christ.

Glorify God Together

⁷Therefore receive one another, just as Christ also received us,[a] to the glory of God. ⁸Now I say that Jesus Christ has become a servant to the circumcision for the truth of God, to confirm the promises *made* to the fathers, ⁹and that the Gentiles might glorify God for *His* mercy, as it is written:

> *"For this reason I will confess to You among the Gentiles,*
> *And sing to Your name."*[a]

¹⁰And again he says:

> *"Rejoice, O Gentiles, with His people!"*[a]

¹¹And again:

> *"Praise the LORD, all you Gentiles!*
> *Laud Him, all you peoples!"*[a]

¹²And again, Isaiah says:

> *"There shall be a root of Jesse;*
> *And He who shall rise to reign over the Gentiles,*
> *In Him the Gentiles shall hope."*[a]

¹³Now may the God of hope fill you with all joy and peace in believing, that you may abound in hope by the power of the Holy Spirit.

From Jerusalem to Illyricum

¹⁴Now I myself am confident concerning you, my brethren, that you also are full of goodness, filled with all knowledge, able also to admonish one another.[a] ¹⁵Nevertheless, brethren, I have written more boldly to you on *some* points, as reminding you, because of the grace given to me by God, ¹⁶that I might be a minister of Jesus Christ to the Gentiles, ministering the gospel of God, that the offering of the Gentiles might be acceptable, sanctified by the Holy Spirit. ¹⁷Therefore I have reason to glory in Christ Jesus in the things *which pertain* to God. ¹⁸For I will not dare to speak of any of those things which Christ has not accomplished through me, in word and deed, to make the Gentiles obedient— ¹⁹in mighty signs and wonders, by the power of the Spirit of God, so that from Jerusalem and round about to Illyricum I have fully preached the gospel of Christ. ²⁰And so I have made it my aim to preach the gospel, not where Christ was named, lest I should build on another man's foundation, ²¹but as it is written:

> *"To whom He was not announced, they shall see;*
> *And those who have not heard shall understand."*[a]

Plan to Visit Rome

²²For this reason I also have been much hindered from coming to you. ²³But now no longer having a place in these parts, and having a great desire these many years to come to you, ²⁴whenever I journey to Spain, I shall come to you.[a] For I hope to see you on my journey, and to be helped on my way there by you, if first I may enjoy your *company* for a while. ²⁵But now I am going to Jerusalem to minister to the saints. ²⁶For it pleased those from Macedonia and Achaia to make a certain contribution for the poor among the saints who are in Jerusalem. ²⁷It pleased them indeed, and they are their debtors. For if the Gentiles have been partakers of their spiritual things,

---

15:3 [a]Psalm 69:9   **15:7** [a]NU-Text and M-Text read *you*.
15:9 [a]2 Samuel 22:50; Psalm 18:49   **15:10** [a]Deuteronomy 32:43
15:11 [a]Psalm 117:1   **15:12** [a]Isaiah 11:10   **15:14** [a]M-Text reads *others*.   **15:21** [a]Isaiah 52:15   **15:24** [a]NU-Text omits *I shall come to you* (and joins *Spain* with the next sentence).

LEADERSHIP ISSUES

GC2: Becoming a Good Samaritan: The Encouragement of Scripture

ROMANS 15:4

Followers of Jesus are to be equipped in the Word "for every good work" (2 Tim. 3:16, 17). The Word guards us from sin, guides our way and equips us for loving and serving others (see Ps. 119:9, 11, 105). Recalling specific times of being encouraged in the Word both encourages us and gives us confidence in sharing the Word with others.

We have all had times in life when God has shown up with a specific Bible truth that has encouraged our hearts and brought hope. Think now about that time when you went through a loss, a health issue, a broken relationship, a struggle to discern God's will—and God encouraged you through a Scripture in the Bible. Recall a time when you were hurt, sad, confused, or disappointed and God encouraged you with a verse out of His Book, the Bible. You may not remember its "address" right now—you can check book, chapter, and verse later. Complete the sentence below. It will give you a taste of the importance of being encouraged in the Word that you might encourage others.

I remember a time when _____

and God encouraged me with the truth from the Scriptures that

basically says _____.

Take time now with one or two others in your group to share testimonies of how God's Word offered you encouragement and hope at a time of need. Then express your gratitude to God through a time of praying together, asking Him to open your eyes to others around you who need to encounter God at the point of His Word.

GC2
GREAT COMMANDMENT
COMMISSION

LEADERSHIP ISSUES

GC2: Giving Others "Acceptance"

ROMANS 15:7

Acceptance can be defined as receiving another person willingly and unconditionally, especially when the other person might be "different," irritating, or even offensive; being willing to love another in spite of their faults.

How has God "given first" to our need for acceptance? Jesus met our ultimate need for acceptance in that "while we were still sinners, Christ died for us" (Rom. 5:8). He looked beyond our faults and met our needs. During His earthly ministry, Jesus accepted people regardless of background, race, or condition: the Samaritan woman (John 4:4–27); the thief on the cross (Luke 23:39–43);); the Gentile Centurion (Luke 7:1–12); and the woman caught in adultery (John 8:1–11). He helped people overcome failures (Peter's denial, John 21:15–19); He loved all people unconditionally and forgave freely, even from the cross (Luke 23:34).

Becoming a good friend who "gives first" *by accepting others*, will prepare you for healthy, God-honoring relationships.

Pause and reflect on these ideas for giving others acceptance:

- I go out of my way to welcome people who may look, believe, live, or act differently than I do.
- When I'm in a group of people, I try to spot anyone who may feel uneasy or alone, and I initiate conversation and try to make him or her feel welcome.
- I generally "look beyond people's faults" and minister to their needs.
- I accept people, not just when they're "up" but also when they're "down."
- When someone "blows it," "messes up," or offends me, I'm quick to forgive them.

GC2
GREAT COMMANDMENT
COMMISSION

their duty is also to minister to them in material things. [28]Therefore, when I have performed this and have sealed to them this fruit, I shall go by way of you to Spain. [29]But I know that when I come to you, I shall come in the fullness of the blessing of the gospel[a] of Christ.

[30]Now I beg you, brethren, through the Lord Jesus Christ, and through the love of the Spirit, that you strive together with me in prayers to God for me, [31]that I may be delivered from those in Judea who do not believe, and that my service for Jerusalem may be acceptable to the saints, [32]that I may come to you with joy by the will of God, and may be refreshed together with you. [33]Now the God of peace be with you all. Amen.

SISTER PHOEBE COMMENDED

16 I commend to you Phoebe our sister, who is a servant of the church in Cenchrea, [2]that you may receive her in the Lord in a manner worthy of the saints, and assist her in whatever business she has need of you; for indeed she has been a helper of many and of myself also.

GREETING ROMAN SAINTS

[3]Greet Priscilla and Aquila, my fellow workers in Christ Jesus, [4]who risked their own necks for my life, to whom not only I give thanks, but also all the churches of the Gentiles. [5]Likewise greet the church that is in their house.

Greet my beloved Epaenetus, who is the first-fruits of Achaia[a] to Christ. [6]Greet Mary, who labored much for us. [7]Greet Andronicus and Junia, my countrymen and my fellow prisoners, who are of note among the apostles, who also were in Christ before me.

[8]Greet Amplias, my beloved in the Lord. [9]Greet Urbanus, our fellow worker in Christ, and Stachys, my beloved. [10]Greet Apelles, approved in Christ. Greet those who are of the household of Aristobulus. [11]Greet Herodion, my countryman.[a] Greet those who are of the household of Narcissus who are in the Lord.

[12]Greet Tryphena and Tryphosa, who have labored in the Lord. Greet the beloved Persis, who labored much in the Lord. [13]Greet Rufus, chosen in the Lord, and his mother and mine. [14]Greet

Asyncritus, Phlegon, Hermas, Patrobas, Hermes, and the brethren who are with them. [15]Greet Philologus and Julia, Nereus and his sister, and Olympas, and all the saints who are with them.

[16]Greet one another with a holy kiss. The[a] churches of Christ greet you.

AVOID DIVISIVE PERSONS

[17]Now I urge you, brethren, note those who cause divisions and offenses, contrary to the doctrine which you learned, and avoid them. [18]For those who are such do not serve our Lord Jesus[a] Christ, but their own belly, and by smooth words and flattering speech deceive the hearts of the simple. [19]For your obedience has become known to all. Therefore I am glad on your behalf; but I want you to be wise in what is good, and simple concerning evil. [20]And the God of peace will crush Satan under your feet shortly.

The grace of our Lord Jesus Christ be with you. Amen.

GREETINGS FROM PAUL'S FRIENDS

[21]Timothy, my fellow worker, and Lucius, Jason, and Sosipater, my countrymen, greet you.

[22]I, Tertius, who wrote this epistle, greet you in the Lord.

[23]Gaius, my host and the host of the whole church, greets you. Erastus, the treasurer of the city, greets you, and Quartus, a brother. [24]The grace of our Lord Jesus Christ be with you all. Amen.[a]

BENEDICTION

[25]Now to Him who is able to establish you according to my gospel and the preaching of Jesus Christ, according to the revelation of the mystery kept secret since the world began [26]but now made manifest, and by the prophetic Scriptures made known to all nations, according to the commandment of the everlasting God, for obedience to the faith— [27]to God, alone wise, be glory through Jesus Christ forever. Amen.[a]

15:29 [a]NU-Text omits of the gospel. **16:5** [a]NU-Text reads Asia.
16:11 [a]Or relative **16:16** [a]NU-Text reads All the churches.
16:18 [a]NU-Text and M-Text omit Jesus. **16:24** [a]NU-Text omits this verse. **16:27** [a]M-Text puts Romans 16:25–27 after Romans 14:23.

IMPACT OF THE BOOK

IDEA

Love is the highest virtue which should motivate each Christian to seek purity and unity.

MESSAGE

People will know Christians by their love; it is a testimony of the countercultural aspect of the Gospel that says other people are more important than you. Paul demonstrated strong spiritual leadership by correcting evils in the church and answering questions about the faith, which were causing great confusion. He courageously dealt with confrontation, criticism, and division by speaking the truth in love, focusing on God's sacrificial, agape love.

PEOPLE

Apollos, Aquila, Crispus, Priscilla, Stephanas, Timothy

AUTHOR

The apostle Paul spent much time with the church at Corinth. Paul wrote the Corinthians several strong letters, diligently teaching doctrine and carefully explaining Christian behavior.

CULTURE

On Paul's second missionary journey to Corinth, he built a strong friendship with fellow tentmakers, a Jewish couple named Aquila and Priscilla. Paul evangelized and preached in the Jewish synagogues for about a year and a half. As the political capital of Greece, Corinth was a seat of commerce and intellectual life with a reputation for luxury, sexual immorality, and even sacred prostitution. Its acropolis was used for defense and for pagan worship; the temple to Aphrodite, located in Acrocorinth enticed many locals and foreigners. The church faced hardships while protecting itself and reaching out to the world; however, its ministry effectively demonstrated the power of God. The culture of Corinth (1 Cor. 6:9–11) shows the power of God to cleanse and make brand-new.

TIMELINE

c. AD 55

KEY SCRIPTURE
MEMORY VERSES

1:9; 2:14—3:3; 3:11–17; 6:19, 20; 10:12, 13; 11:23–26; 12:13, 27; 13:1–13; 15:1–4, 55–57

GREETING

1 Paul, called *to be* an apostle of Jesus Christ through the will of God, and Sosthenes *our* brother,

²To the church of God which is at Corinth, to those who are sanctified in Christ Jesus, called *to be* saints, with all who in every place call on the name of Jesus Christ our Lord, both theirs and ours:

³Grace to you and peace from God our Father and the Lord Jesus Christ.

SPIRITUAL GIFTS AT CORINTH

⁴I thank my God always concerning you for the grace of God which was given to you by Christ Jesus, ⁵that you were enriched in everything by Him in all utterance and all knowledge, ⁶even as the testimony of Christ was confirmed in you, ⁷so that you come short in no gift, eagerly waiting for the revelation of our Lord Jesus Christ, ⁸who will also confirm you to the end, *that you may be* blameless in the day of our Lord Jesus Christ. ⁹God *is* faithful, by whom you were called into the fellowship of His Son, Jesus Christ our Lord.

SECTARIANISM IS SIN

¹⁰Now I plead with you, brethren, by the name of our Lord Jesus Christ, that you all speak the same thing, and *that* there be no divisions among you, but *that* you be perfectly joined together in the same mind and in the same judgment. ¹¹For it has been declared to me concerning you, my brethren, by those of Chloe's *household*, that there are contentions among you. ¹²Now I say this, that each of you says, "I am of Paul," or "I am of Apollos," or "I am of Cephas," or "I am of Christ." ¹³Is Christ divided? Was Paul crucified for you? Or were you baptized in the name of Paul? ¹⁴I thank God that I baptized none of you except Crispus and Gaius, ¹⁵lest anyone should say that I had baptized in my own name. ¹⁶Yes, I also baptized the household of Stephanas. Besides, I do not know whether I baptized any other. ¹⁷For Christ did not send me to baptize,

but to preach the gospel, not with wisdom of words, lest the cross of Christ should be made of no effect.

CHRIST THE POWER AND WISDOM OF GOD

¹⁸For the message of the cross is foolishness to those who are perishing, but to us who are being saved it is the power of God. ¹⁹For it is written:

> "I will destroy the wisdom of the wise,
> And bring to nothing the understanding of
>   the prudent."ᵃ

²⁰Where *is* the wise? Where *is* the scribe? Where *is* the disputer of this age? Has not God made foolish the wisdom of this world? ²¹For since, in the wisdom of God, the world through wisdom did not know God, it pleased God through the foolishness of the message preached to save those who believe. ²²For Jews request a sign, and Greeks seek after wisdom; ²³but we preach Christ crucified, to the Jews a stumbling block and to the Greeksᵃ foolishness, ²⁴but to those who are called, both Jews and Greeks, Christ the power of God and the wisdom of God. ²⁵Because the foolishness of God is wiser than men, and the weakness of God is stronger than men.

GLORY ONLY IN THE LORD

²⁶For you see your calling, brethren, that not many wise according to the flesh, not many mighty, not many noble, *are called*. ²⁷But God has chosen the foolish things of the world to put to shame the wise, and God has chosen the weak things of the world to put to shame the things which are mighty; ²⁸and the base things of the world and the things which are despised God has chosen, and the things which are not, to bring to nothing the things that are, ²⁹that no flesh should glory in His presence. ³⁰But of Him you are in Christ Jesus, who became for us wisdom from God—and righteousness and sanctification and redemption— ³¹that, as it is written, *"He who glories, let him glory in the Lᴏʀᴅ."* ᵃ

1:19 ᵃIsaiah 29:14   **1:23** ᵃNU-Text reads *Gentiles.*   **1:31** ᵃJeremiah 9:24

CHRIST CRUCIFIED

2 And I, brethren, when I came to you, did not come with excellence of speech or of wisdom declaring to you the testimony[a] of God. [2]For I determined not to know anything among you except Jesus Christ and Him crucified. [3]I was with you in weakness, in fear, and in much trembling. [4]And my speech and my preaching *were* not with persuasive words of human[a] wisdom, but in demonstration of the Spirit and of power, [5]that your faith should not be in the wisdom of men but in the power of God.

SPIRITUAL WISDOM

[6]However, we speak wisdom among those who are mature, yet not the wisdom of this age, nor of the rulers of this age, who are coming to nothing. [7]But we speak the wisdom of God in a mystery, the hidden *wisdom* which God ordained before the ages for our glory, [8]which none of the rulers of this age knew; for had they known, they would not have crucified the Lord of glory.

[9]But as it is written:

"Eye has not seen, nor ear heard,
Nor have entered into the heart of man
The things which God has prepared for those
who love Him."[a]

[10]But God has revealed *them* to us through His Spirit. For the Spirit searches all things, yes, the deep things of God. [11]For what man knows the things of a man except the spirit of the man which is in him? Even so no one knows the things of God except the Spirit of God. [12]Now we have received, not the spirit of the world, but the Spirit who is from God, that we might know the things that have been freely given to us by God.

[13]These things we also speak, not in words which man's wisdom teaches but which the Holy[a] Spirit teaches, comparing spiritual things with spiritual. [14]But the natural man does not receive the things of the Spirit of God, for they are foolishness to him; nor can he know *them,* because they are spiritually discerned. [15]But he who is spiritual judges all things, yet he himself is *rightly* judged by no one. [16]For *"who has known the mind of the LORD that he may instruct Him?"*[a] But we have the mind of Christ.

SECTARIANISM IS CARNAL

3 And I, brethren, could not speak to you as to spiritual *people* but as to carnal, as to babes in Christ. [2]I fed you with milk and not with solid food; for until now you were not able *to receive it,* and even now you are still not able; [3]for you are still carnal. For where *there are* envy, strife, and divisions among you, are you not carnal and behaving like *mere* men? [4]For when one says, "I am of Paul," and another, "I *am* of Apollos," are you not carnal?

WATERING, WORKING, WARNING

[5]Who then is Paul, and who *is* Apollos, but ministers through whom you believed, as the Lord gave to each one? [6]I planted, Apollos watered, but God gave the increase. [7]So then neither he who plants is anything, nor he who waters, but God who gives the increase. [8]Now he who plants and he who waters are one, and each one will receive his own reward according to his own labor.

[9]For we are God's fellow workers; you are God's field, *you are* God's building. [10]According to the grace of God which was given to me, as a wise master builder I have laid the foundation, and another builds on it. But let each one take heed how he builds on it. [11]For no other foundation can anyone lay than that which is laid, which is Jesus Christ. [12]Now if anyone builds on this foundation *with* gold, silver, precious stones, wood, hay, straw, [13]each one's work will become clear; for the Day will declare it, because it will be revealed by fire; and the fire will test each one's work, of what sort it is. [14]If anyone's work which he has built on *it* endures, he will receive a reward. [15]If anyone's work is burned, he will suffer loss; but he himself will be saved, yet so as through fire.

[16]Do you not know that you are the temple of God and *that* the Spirit of God dwells in you? [17]If anyone defiles the temple of God, God will destroy him. For the temple of God is holy, which *temple* you are.

2:1 [a]NU-Text reads *mystery.*   **2:4** [a]NU-Text omits *human.*
2:9 [a]Isaiah 64:4   **2:13** [a]NU-Text omits *Holy.*   **2:16** [a]Isaiah 40:13

AVOID WORLDLY WISDOM

[18]Let no one deceive himself. If anyone among you seems to be wise in this age, let him become a fool that he may become wise. [19]For the wisdom of this world is foolishness with God. For it is written, *"He catches the wise in their own craftiness"*;[a] [20]and again, *"The* LORD *knows the thoughts of the wise, that they are futile."*[a] [21]Therefore let no one boast in men. For all things are yours: [22]whether Paul or Apollos or Cephas, or the world or life or death, or things present or things to come—all are yours. [23]And you *are* Christ's, and Christ *is* God's.

STEWARDS OF THE MYSTERIES OF GOD

4 Let a man so consider us, as servants of Christ and stewards of the mysteries of God. [2]Moreover it is required in stewards that one be found faithful. [3]But with me it is a very small thing that I should be judged by you or by a human court.[a] In fact, I do not even judge myself. [4]For I know of nothing against myself, yet I am not justified by this; but He who judges me is the Lord. [5]Therefore judge nothing before the time, until the Lord comes, who will both bring to light the hidden things of darkness and reveal the counsels of the hearts. Then each one's praise will come from God.

FOOLS FOR CHRIST'S SAKE

[6]Now these things, brethren, I have figuratively transferred to myself and Apollos for your sakes, that you may learn in us not to think beyond what is written, that none of you may be puffed up on behalf of one against the other. [7]For who makes you differ *from another*? And what do you have that you did not receive? Now if you did indeed receive *it*, why do you boast as if you had not received *it*?

[8]You are already full! You are already rich! You have reigned as kings without us—and indeed I could wish you did reign, that we also might reign with you! [9]For I think that God has displayed us, the apostles, last, as men condemned to death; for we have been made a spectacle to the world, both to angels and to men. [10]We *are* fools for Christ's sake, but you *are* wise in Christ! We *are* weak, but you *are* strong! You *are* distinguished,

but we *are* dishonored! [11]To the present hour we both hunger and thirst, and we are poorly clothed, and beaten, and homeless. [12]And we labor, working with our own hands. Being reviled, we bless; being persecuted, we endure; [13]being defamed, we entreat. We have been made as the filth of the world, the offscouring of all things until now.

PAUL'S PATERNAL CARE

[14]I do not write these things to shame you, but as my beloved children I warn *you*. [15]For though you might have ten thousand instructors in Christ, yet *you do* not *have* many fathers; for in Christ Jesus I have begotten you through the gospel. [16]Therefore I urge you, imitate me. [17]For this reason I have sent Timothy to you, who is my beloved and faithful son in the Lord, who will remind you of my ways in Christ, as I teach everywhere in every church.

[18]Now some are puffed up, as though I were not coming to you. [19]But I will come to you shortly, if the Lord wills, and I will know, not the word of those who are puffed up, but the power. [20]For the kingdom of God *is* not in word but in power. [21]What do you want? Shall I come to you with a rod, or in love and a spirit of gentleness?

IMMORALITY DEFILES THE CHURCH

5 It is actually reported *that there is* sexual immorality among you, and such sexual immorality as is not even named[a] among the Gentiles—that a man has his father's wife! [2]And you are puffed up, and have not rather mourned, that he who has done this deed might be taken away from among you. [3]For I indeed, as absent in body but present in spirit, have already judged (as though I were present) him who has so done this deed. [4]In the name of our Lord Jesus Christ, when you are gathered together, along with my spirit, with the power of our Lord Jesus Christ, [5]deliver such a one to Satan for the destruction of the flesh, that his spirit may be saved in the day of the Lord Jesus.[a]

[6]Your glorying *is* not good. Do you not know that a little leaven leavens the whole lump? [7]Therefore purge out the old leaven, that you may be a new lump, since you truly are unleavened.

3:19 [a]Job 5:13 **3:20** [a]Psalm 94:11 **4:3** [a]Literally *day* **5:1** [a]NU-Text omits *named.* **5:5** [a]NU-Text omits *Jesus.*

For indeed Christ, our Passover, was sacrificed for us.[a] [8]Therefore let us keep the feast, not with old leaven, nor with the leaven of malice and wickedness, but with the unleavened *bread* of sincerity and truth.

IMMORALITY MUST BE JUDGED

[9]I wrote to you in my epistle not to keep company with sexually immoral people. [10]Yet *I* certainly *did* not *mean* with the sexually immoral people of this world, or with the covetous, or extortioners, or idolaters, since then you would need to go out of the world. [11]But now I have written to you not to keep company with anyone named a brother, who is sexually immoral, or covetous, or an idolater, or a reviler, or a drunkard, or an extortioner—not even to eat with such a person.

[12]For what *have I to do* with judging those also who are outside? Do you not judge those who are inside? [13]But those who are outside God judges. Therefore *"put away from yourselves the evil person."*[a]

DO NOT SUE THE BRETHREN

6Dare any of you, having a matter against another, go to law before the unrighteous, and not before the saints? [2]Do you not know that the saints will judge the world? And if the world will be judged by you, are you unworthy to judge the smallest matters? [3]Do you not know that we shall judge angels? How much more, things that pertain to this life? [4]If then you have judgments concerning things pertaining to this life, do you appoint those who are least esteemed by the church to judge? [5]I say this to your shame. Is it so, that there is not a wise man among you, not even one, who will be able to judge between his brethren? [6]But brother goes to law against brother, and that before unbelievers!

[7]Now therefore, it is already an utter failure for you that you go to law against one another. Why do you not rather accept wrong? Why do you not rather *let yourselves* be cheated? [8]No, you yourselves do wrong and cheat, and *you do* these things *to your* brethren! [9]Do you not know that the unrighteous will not inherit the kingdom of God? Do not be deceived. Neither fornicators, nor idolaters, nor adulterers, nor homosexuals,[a] nor sodomites, [10]nor thieves, nor covetous, nor drunkards, nor revilers, nor extortioners will inherit the kingdom of God. [11]And such were some of you. But you were washed, but you were sanctified, but you were justified in the name of the Lord Jesus and by the Spirit of our God.

5:7 [a]NU-Text omits *for us.*   **5:13** [a]Deuteronomy 17:7; 19:19; 22:21, 24; 24:7   **6:9** [a]That is, catamites

---

THROUGH THE GRID

Thinking Christianly: God's Guidelines for the Gray Areas of Life (1 Cor. 6:12—11:1)

When in doubt whether a particular action we are about to undertake is OK or not, we must turn to Scripture as our ultimate source of authority on what to do. God gives us several guidelines in Scripture. We must ask ourselves these guiding questions:

- Will the action I'm about to undertake edify myself? That is, will it build me up and help me succeed? (1 Cor. 6:12)
- Will this action enslave my soul? (1 Cor. 6:12)
- Can it addict me or put me in emotional/psychological bondage? (1 Cor. 6:12)
- Will this action exalt the Savior? (1 Cor. 6:13; 10:31)
- Will this action encourage other saints? (1 Cor. 8:13)
- Will it be a potential stumbling block to others? (Rom. 14:13)
- Will this action evangelize sinners? (1 Cor. 9:19, 22; 10:32, 33)
- Will this action be an example of my Savior? (1 Cor. 11:1)

GLORIFY GOD IN BODY AND SPIRIT

[12]All things are lawful for me, but all things are not helpful. All things are lawful for me, but I will not be brought under the power of any. [13]Foods for the stomach and the stomach for foods, but God will destroy both it and them. Now the body is not for sexual immorality but for the Lord, and the Lord for the body. [14]And God both raised up the Lord and will also raise us up by His power.

[15]Do you not know that your bodies are members of Christ? Shall I then take the members of Christ and make them members of a harlot? Certainly not! [16]Or do you not know that he who is joined to a harlot is one body with her? For "the two," He says, "shall become one flesh."[a] [17]But he who is joined to the Lord is one spirit with Him.

[18]Flee sexual immorality. Every sin that a man does is outside the body, but he who commits sexual immorality sins against his own body. [19]Or do you not know that your body is the temple of the Holy Spirit who is in you, whom you have from God, and you are not your own? [20]For you were bought at a price; therefore glo-rify God in your body[a] and in your spirit, which are God's.

PRINCIPLES OF MARRIAGE

7 Now concerning the things of which you wrote to me:

It is good for a man not to touch a woman. [2]Nevertheless, because of sexual immorality, let each man have his own wife, and let each woman have her own husband. [3]Let the husband render to his wife the affection due her, and likewise also the wife to her husband. [4]The wife does not have authority over her own body, but the husband does. And likewise the husband does not have authority over his own body, but the wife does. [5]Do not deprive one another except with consent for a time, that you may give yourselves to fasting and prayer; and come together again so that Satan does not tempt you because of your lack of self-control. [6]But I say this as a concession, not as a commandment. [7]For I wish that all men were even as I myself. But each one has his own gift from God, one in this manner and another in that.

[8]But I say to the unmarried and to the wid-

6:16 [a]Genesis 2:24   6:20 [a]NU-Text ends the verse at body.

THROUGH THE GRID

Making Sense of Your World:
Redemption (1 Cor. 6:20)

Fortunately for us, all is not lost. God has made a provision for our fallen condition and our depravity by sending Jesus Christ to die on the cross for our sins. A biblical world-view not only acknowledges that we as human beings are fallen but also that the only way we can be redeemed is through faith in Jesus Christ, who obediently took our place of punishment and enabled our redemption. This finds its root in the mercy, grace, and goodness of a God who loved humanity deeply. The death of Christ is the means by which the judgment of everyone's sin was accomplished, so that when any person responds in faith toward the offer of forgiveness that is offered by God through Christ, one becomes a child of God and is granted eternal life in heaven. Certainly, the need for redemption is a global need, as people around the world remain fallen without remedy. Humanity remains sinful at its core; and as a result of sin, evil, suffering, pain, death, and injustices continue to plague the world. It is only through the salvation offered through Jesus Christ that one can find peace and purpose in the midst of a world that is completely fallen. Only through Christ can one find transformation and redemption. Of course, when one is redeemed, it does not mean that we become perfect; rather, we enter into a process of transformation and sanctification that only ends at the end of time.

THROUGH THE GRID

Thinking Christianly:
The Purpose of Sex (1 Cor. 7:2–5)

God created sex for humanity to enjoy within the correct prescribed context of marriage. The purposes of sex include the following: procreation (Gen. 1:28; 4:1), partnership (Gen. 2:24; 24:67), pleasure (Prov. 5:15–19; Song of Solomon), and protection (Prov. 5:20; 1 Cor. 6:18; 7:2–5). These are the original purposes for which God intended sex, and these are the reasons God endowed each human being with a sense of sexuality. Outside of these purposes, sex can have very harmful results. Sex should ultimately build our relationship with our spouse as something both can enjoy as God's gift.

ows: It is good for them if they remain even as I am; ⁹but if they cannot exercise self-control, let them marry. For it is better to marry than to burn *with passion.*

Keep Your Marriage Vows

¹⁰Now to the married I command, *yet* not I but the Lord: A wife is not to depart from *her* husband. ¹¹But even if she does depart, let her remain unmarried or be reconciled to *her* husband. And a husband is not to divorce *his* wife.

¹²But to the rest I, not the Lord, say: If any brother has a wife who does not believe, and she is willing to live with him, let him not divorce her. ¹³And a woman who has a husband who does not believe, if he is willing to live with her, let her not divorce him. ¹⁴For the unbelieving husband is sanctified by the wife, and the unbelieving wife is sanctified by the husband; otherwise your children would be unclean, but now they are holy. ¹⁵But if the unbeliever departs, let him depart; a brother or a sister is not under bondage in such *cases.* But God has called us to peace. ¹⁶For how do you know, O wife, whether you will save *your* husband? Or how do you know, O husband, whether you will save *your* wife?

Live as You Are Called

¹⁷But as God has distributed to each one, as the Lord has called each one, so let him walk. And so I ordain in all the churches. ¹⁸Was anyone called while circumcised? Let him not become uncircumcised. Was anyone called while uncircumcised? Let him not be circumcised. ¹⁹Circumcision is nothing and uncircumcision is nothing, but keeping the commandments of God *is what matters.*

²⁰Let each one remain in the same calling in which he was called. ²¹Were you called *while* a slave? Do not be concerned about it; but if you can be made free, rather use *it.* ²²For he who is called in the Lord *while* a slave is the Lord's freedman. Likewise he who is called *while* free is Christ's slave. ²³You were bought at a price; do not become slaves of men. ²⁴Brethren, let each one remain with God in that *state* in which he was called.

To the Unmarried and Widows

²⁵Now concerning virgins: I have no commandment from the Lord; yet I give judgment as one whom the Lord in His mercy has made trustworthy. ²⁶I suppose therefore that this is good because of the present distress—that *it is* good for a man to remain as he is: ²⁷Are you bound to a wife? Do not seek to be loosed. Are you loosed from a wife? Do not seek a wife. ²⁸But even if you do marry, you have not sinned; and if a virgin marries, she has not sinned. Nevertheless such will have trouble in the flesh, but I would spare you.

²⁹But this I say, brethren, the time *is* short, so that from now on even those who have wives should be as though they had none, ³⁰those who weep as though they did not weep, those who rejoice as though they did not rejoice, those who buy as though they did not possess, ³¹and those who use this world as not misusing *it.* For the form of this world is passing away.

³²But I want you to be without care. He who is unmarried cares for the things of the Lord—how he may please the Lord. ³³But he who is married cares about the things of the world—how he may please *his* wife. ³⁴There is[a] a difference

7:34 [a]M-Text adds *also.*

between a wife and a virgin. The unmarried woman cares about the things of the Lord, that she may be holy both in body and in spirit. But she who is married cares about the things of the world—how she may please *her* husband. [35]And this I say for your own profit, not that I may put a leash on you, but for what is proper, and that you may serve the Lord without distraction.

[36]But if any man thinks he is behaving improperly toward his virgin, if she is past the flower of youth, and thus it must be, let him do what he wishes. He does not sin; let them marry. [37]Nevertheless he who stands steadfast in his heart, having no necessity, but has power over his own will, and has so determined in his heart that he will keep his virgin,[a] does well. [38]So then he who gives *her*[a] in marriage does well, but he who does not give *her* in marriage does better.

[39]A wife is bound by law as long as her husband lives; but if her husband dies, she is at liberty to be married to whom she wishes, only in the Lord. [40]But she is happier if she remains as she is, according to my judgment—and I think I also have the Spirit of God.

Be Sensitive to Conscience

8 Now concerning things offered to idols: We know that we all have knowledge. Knowledge puffs up, but love edifies. [2]And if anyone thinks that he knows anything, he knows nothing yet as he ought to know. [3]But if anyone loves God, this one is known by Him.

[4]Therefore concerning the eating of things offered to idols, we know that an idol *is* nothing in the world, and that *there is* no other God but one. [5]For even if there are so-called gods, whether in heaven or on earth (as there are many gods and many lords), [6]yet for us *there is* one God, the Father, of whom *are* all things, and we for Him; and one Lord Jesus Christ, through whom *are* all things, and through whom we *live.*

[7]However, *there is* not in everyone that knowledge; for some, with consciousness of the idol, until now eat *it* as a thing offered to an idol; and their conscience, being weak, is defiled. [8]But food does not commend us to God; for neither if we eat are we the better, nor if we do not eat are we the worse.

[9]But beware lest somehow this liberty of yours become a stumbling block to those who are weak. [10]For if anyone sees you who have knowledge eating in an idol's temple, will not the conscience of him who is weak be emboldened to eat those things offered to idols? [11]And because of your knowledge shall the weak brother perish, for whom Christ died? [12]But when you thus sin against the brethren, and wound their weak conscience, you sin against Christ. [13]Therefore, if food makes my brother stumble, I will never again eat meat, lest I make my brother stumble.

A Pattern of Self-Denial

9 Am I not an apostle? Am I not free? Have I not seen Jesus Christ our Lord? Are you not my work in the Lord? [2]If I am not an apostle to others, yet doubtless I am to you. For you are the seal of my apostleship in the Lord.

[3]My defense to those who examine me is this: [4]Do we have no right to eat and drink? [5]Do we have no right to take along a believing wife, as *do* also the other apostles, the brothers of the Lord, and Cephas? [6]Or *is it* only Barnabas and I *who* have no right to refrain from working? [7]Who ever goes to war at his own expense? Who plants a vineyard and does not eat of its fruit? Or who tends a flock and does not drink of the milk of the flock?

[8]Do I say these things as a *mere* man? Or does not the law say the same also? [9]For it is written in the law of Moses, *"You shall not muzzle an ox while it treads out the grain."*[a] Is it oxen God is concerned about? [10]Or does He say *it* altogether for our sakes? For our sakes, no doubt, *this* is written, that he who plows should plow in hope, and he who threshes in hope should be partaker of his hope. [11]If we have sown spiritual things for you, *is it* a great thing if we reap your material things? [12]If others are partakers of *this* right over you, *are* we not even more?

Nevertheless we have not used this right, but endure all things lest we hinder the gospel of Christ. [13]Do you not know that those who minister the holy things eat *of the things* of the temple, and those who serve at the altar partake of *the offerings of* the altar? [14]Even so the Lord has commanded that those who preach the gospel should live from the gospel.

7:37 [a]Or *virgin daughter* **7:38** [a]NU-Text reads *his own virgin.*
9:9 [a]Deuteronomy 25:4

THROUGH THE GRID

Where Have All the Dreamers Gone?
Observations from a Biblical
Worldview: "All Things to All Men"
(1 Cor. 9:19–23)

One famous refrain from the apostle Paul's epistles is his encouragement to his followers to be "all things to all men," meaning that Christians should attempt to reach out to their neighbors in a way that is culturally relevant and understandable to others (1 Cor. 9:22). One of the great things about Scriptures is that it is relevant for all people at all times. The challenge is communicating its message in a way that its hearers and readers can understand. Yet Christians must be careful not to completely assimilate to culture, for risk of losing their Christian identity.

15But I have used none of these things, nor have I written these things that it should be done so to me; for it *would be* better for me to die than that anyone should make my boasting void. 16For if I preach the gospel, I have nothing to boast of, for necessity is laid upon me; yes, woe is me if I do not preach the gospel! 17For if I do this willingly, I have a reward; but if against my will, I have been entrusted with a stewardship. 18What is my reward then? That when I preach the gospel, I may present the gospel of Christ^a without charge, that I may not abuse my authority in the gospel.

Serving All Men

19For though I am free from all *men,* I have made myself a servant to all, that I might win the more; 20and to the Jews I became as a Jew, that I might win Jews; to those *who are* under the law, as under the law,^a that I might win those *who are* under the law; 21to those *who are* without law, as without law (not being without law toward God,^a but under law toward Christ^b), that I might win those *who are* without law; 22to the weak I became as^a weak, that I might win the weak. I have become all things to all *men,* that I might by all means save some. 23Now this I do for the gospel's sake, that I may be partaker of it with *you.*

Striving for a Crown

24Do you not know that those who run in a race all run, but one receives the prize? Run in such a way that you may obtain *it.* 25And everyone who competes *for the prize* is temperate in all

things. Now they *do it* to obtain a perishable crown, but we *for* an imperishable *crown.* 26Therefore I run thus: not with uncertainty. Thus I fight: not as *one who* beats the air. 27But I discipline my body and bring *it* into subjection, lest, when I have preached to others, I myself should become disqualified.

Old Testament Examples

10 Moreover, brethren, I do not want you to be unaware that all our fathers were under the cloud, all passed through the sea, 2all were baptized into Moses in the cloud and in the sea, 3all ate the same spiritual food, 4and all drank the same spiritual drink. For they drank of that spiritual Rock that followed them, and that Rock was Christ. 5But with most of them God was not well pleased, for *their bodies* were scattered in the wilderness.

6Now these things became our examples, to the intent that we should not lust after evil things as they also lusted. 7And do not become idolaters as *were* some of them. As it is written, *"The people sat down to eat and drink, and rose up to play."*^a 8Nor let us commit sexual immorality, as some of them did, and in one day twenty-three thousand fell; 9nor let us tempt Christ, as some of them also tempted, and were destroyed by serpents; 10nor complain, as some of them also complained, and were destroyed by the destroyer. 11Now all^a these things happened to them as examples, and they

9:18 ^aNU-Text omits *of Christ.* **9:20** ^aNU-Text adds *though not being myself under the law.* **9:21** ^aNU-Text reads *God's law.* ^bNU-Text reads *Christ's law.* **9:22** ^aNU-Text omits *as.* **10:7** ^aExodus 32:6 **10:11** ^aNU-Text omits *all.*

were written for our admonition, upon whom the ends of the ages have come.

¹²Therefore let him who thinks he stands take heed lest he fall. ¹³No temptation has overtaken you except such as is common to man; but God *is* faithful, who will not allow you to be tempted beyond what you are able, but with the temptation will also make the way of escape, that you may be able to bear *it*.

FLEE FROM IDOLATRY

¹⁴Therefore, my beloved, flee from idolatry. ¹⁵I speak as to wise men; judge for yourselves what I say. ¹⁶The cup of blessing which we bless, is it not the communion of the blood of Christ? The bread which we break, is it not the communion of the body of Christ? ¹⁷For we, *though* many, are one bread *and* one body; for we all partake of that one bread.

¹⁸Observe Israel after the flesh: Are not those who eat of the sacrifices partakers of the altar? ¹⁹What am I saying then? That an idol is anything, or what is offered to idols is anything? ²⁰Rather, that the things which the Gentiles sacrifice they sacrifice to demons and not to God, and I do not want you to have fellowship with demons. ²¹You cannot drink the cup of the Lord and the cup of demons; you cannot partake of the Lord's table and of the table of demons. ²²Or do we provoke the Lord to jealousy? Are we stronger than He?

ALL TO THE GLORY OF GOD

²³All things are lawful for me,ᵃ but not all things are helpful; all things are lawful for me,ᵇ but not all things edify. ²⁴Let no one seek his own, but each one the other's *well-being*.

²⁵Eat whatever is sold in the meat market, asking no questions for conscience' sake; ²⁶for *"the earth is the LORD's, and all its fullness."*ᵃ

²⁷If any of those who do not believe invites you *to dinner,* and you desire to go, eat whatever is set before you, asking no question for conscience' sake. ²⁸But if anyone says to you, "This was offered to idols," do not eat it for the sake of the one who told you, and for conscience' sake;ᵃ for *"the earth is the LORD's, and all its fullness."*ᵇ

²⁹"Conscience," I say, not your own, but that of the other. For why is my liberty judged by an-

other *man's* conscience? ³⁰But if I partake with thanks, why am I evil spoken of for *the food* over which I give thanks?

³¹Therefore, whether you eat or drink, or whatever you do, do all to the glory of God. ³²Give no offense, either to the Jews or to the Greeks or to the church of God, ³³just as I also please all *men* in all *things,* not seeking my own profit, but the *profit* of many, that they may be saved.

11 Imitate me, just as I also *imitate* Christ.

HEAD COVERINGS

²Now I praise you, brethren, that you remember me in all things and keep the traditions just as I delivered *them* to you. ³But I want you to know that the head of every man is Christ, the head of woman *is* man, and the head of Christ *is* God. ⁴Every man praying or prophesying, having *his* head covered, dishonors his head. ⁵But every woman who prays or prophesies with *her* head uncovered dishonors her head, for that is one and the same as if her head were shaved. ⁶For if a woman is not covered, let her also be shorn. But if it is shameful for a woman to be shorn or shaved, let her be covered. ⁷For a man indeed ought not to cover *his* head, since he is the image and glory of God; but woman is the glory of man. ⁸For man is not from woman, but woman from man. ⁹Nor was man created for the woman, but woman for the man. ¹⁰For this reason the woman ought to have *a symbol of* authority on *her* head, because of the angels. ¹¹Nevertheless, neither *is* man independent of woman, nor woman independent of man, in the Lord. ¹²For as woman *came* from man, even so man also *comes* through woman; but all things are from God.

¹³Judge among yourselves. Is it proper for a woman to pray to God with her head uncovered? ¹⁴Does not even nature itself teach you that if a man has long hair, it is a dishonor to him? ¹⁵But if a woman has long hair, it is a glory to her; for *her* hair is given to herᵃ for a covering. ¹⁶But if anyone seems to be contentious, we have no such custom, nor *do* the churches of God.

10:23 ᵃNU-Text omits *for me.*   ᵇNU-Text omits *for me.*
10:26 ᵃPsalm 24:1   **10:28** ᵃNU-Text omits the rest of this verse.
ᵇPsalm 24:1   **11:15** ᵃM-Text omits *to her.*

LEADERSHIP ISSUES

GC2: Giving Others "Appreciation"

1 CORINTHIANS 11:2
"Now I praise you, brethren, that you remember me in all things."

The need for appreciation is met through expressing thanks, praise, or commendation, particularly recognizing someone's accomplishments or efforts. During His earthly ministry, Jesus frequently voiced appreciation to individuals: the Canaanite woman (Matt. 15:28), Mary of Bethany (Mark 14:6), a centurion (Luke 7:9), and John the Baptist (Luke 7:28). God has also promised to appreciate those who are faithful (Luke 6:35; Eph. 6:8; 2 Tim. 4:8).

The Corinthian church was full of problems. They were split with factions (1 Cor. 1:10–13; 3:3). They tolerated immorality in their midst and were proud of it (1 Cor. 5:1, 2). They were prosecuting lawsuits against each other in pagan courts (1 Cor. 6:1–11). Yet, in the midst of writing to ad-monish and correct them, the apostle Paul found specific things they were doing well for which to commend them (1 Cor. 11:2).

The Holy Spirit knew that they needed some appreciation in the midst of all the correction! Seeing something good in others' lives, and then appre-ciating them for it, is a powerful way to live and love as Jesus did!

Pause and reflect on these ideas for giving others appreciation:

- I commend others for doing well or putting forth effort.
- I write notes or send messages thanking others for what they do for me.
- I notice special times in people's lives when they should be com-mended (athletic accomplishments, godly choices, big projects com-pleted, etc.).
- I focus on what people do that's right, rather than on what they do that's wrong.
- I've learned how others close to me prefer to receive appreciation: pub-lic vs. private, written vs. verbal, and I make giving to them a priority.

GC2
GREAT COMMANDMENT
COMMISSION

Conduct at the Lord's Supper

[17]Now in giving these instructions I do not praise *you,* since you come together not for the better but for the worse. [18]For first of all, when you come together as a church, I hear that there are divisions among you, and in part I believe it. [19]For there must also be factions among you, that those who are approved may be recognized among you. [20]Therefore when you come together in one place, it is not to eat the Lord's Supper. [21]For in eating, each one takes his own supper ahead of *others;* and one is hungry and another is drunk. [22]What! Do you not have houses to eat and drink in? Or do you despise the church of God and shame those who have nothing? What shall I say to you? Shall I praise you in this? I do not praise *you.*

Institution of the Lord's Supper

[23]For I received from the Lord that which I also delivered to you: that the Lord Jesus on the *same* night in which He was betrayed took bread; [24]and when He had given thanks, He broke *it* and said, "Take, eat;[a] this is My body which is broken[b] for you; do this in remembrance of Me." [25]In the same manner *He* also *took* the cup after supper, saying, "This cup is the new covenant in My blood. This do, as often as you drink *it,* in remembrance of Me."

[26]For as often as you eat this bread and drink this cup, you proclaim the Lord's death till He comes.

Examine Yourself

[27]Therefore whoever eats this bread or drinks *this* cup of the Lord in an unworthy manner will be guilty of the body and blood[a] of the Lord. [28]But let a man examine himself, and so let him eat of the bread and drink of the cup. [29]For he who eats and drinks in an unworthy manner[a] eats and drinks judgment to himself, not discerning the Lord's[b] body. [30]For this reason many *are* weak and sick among you, and many sleep. [31]For if we would judge ourselves, we would not be judged. [32]But when we are judged, we are chastened by the Lord, that we may not be condemned with the world.

[33]Therefore, my brethren, when you come together to eat, wait for one another. [34]But if anyone is hungry, let him eat at home, lest you come together for judgment. And the rest I will set in order when I come.

Spiritual Gifts: Unity in Diversity

12 Now concerning spiritual *gifts,* brethren, I do not want you to be ignorant: [2]You know that[a] you were Gentiles, carried away to these dumb idols, however you were led. [3]Therefore I make known to you that no one speaking by the Spirit of God calls Jesus accursed, and no one can say that Jesus is Lord except by the Holy Spirit.

[4]There are diversities of gifts, but the same Spirit. [5]There are differences of ministries, but the same Lord. [6]And there are diversities of activities, but it is the same God who works all in all. [7]But the manifestation of the Spirit is given to each one for the profit *of all:* [8]for to one is given the word of wisdom through the Spirit, to another the word of knowledge through the same Spirit, [9]to another faith by the same Spirit, to another gifts of healings by the same[a] Spirit, [10]to another the working of miracles, to another prophecy, to another discerning of spirits, to another *different* kinds of tongues, to another the interpretation of tongues. [11]But one and the same Spirit works all these things, distributing to each one individually as He wills.

Unity and Diversity in One Body

[12]For as the body is one and has many members, but all the members of that one body, being many, are one body, so also *is* Christ. [13]For by one Spirit we were all baptized into one body—whether Jews or Greeks, whether slaves or free—and have all been made to drink into[a] one Spirit. [14]For in fact the body is not one member but many.

[15]If the foot should say, "Because I am not a hand, I am not of the body," is it therefore not of the body? [16]And if the ear should say, "Because I am not an eye, I am not of the body," is it therefore not of the body? [17]If the whole body *were* an

11:24 [a]NU-Text omits *Take, eat.* [b]NU-Text omits *broken.* **11:27** [a]NU-Text and M-Text read *the blood.* **11:29** [a]NU-Text omits *in an unworthy manner.* [b]NU-Text omits *Lord's.* **12:2** [a]NU-Text and M-Text add *when.* **12:9** [a]NU-Text reads *one.* **12:13** [a]NU-Text omits *into.*

LEADERSHIP ISSUES

GC2: Who Am I? Uniquely Gifted

1 CORINTHIANS 12:6, 7 *And there are diversities of activities, but it is the same God who works all in all. But the manifestation of the Spirit is given to each one for the profit of all.*

God wants to unleash His love and power through the special, one-of-a-kind child of God that you are. No one else can do it as you can. His Holy Spirit is the means by which each of us loves and relates to Him. His Holy Spirit is the means by which we are to love and relate to each other. God redeemed us for His purpose, so we could have a loving, personalized relationship with our Father and then express His love within God's family and beyond to those who don't know Him.

Who are you? You are God's child chosen to love Him and others as only you can. Receiving Jesus as your Lord and Savior made you part of His family as the Holy Spirit came to live inside you (1 Cor. 12:12, 13).

We all intuitively realize we are originals. Our personal identification is distinctly ours. Our fingerprints are unique, our retina scans are distinct, and our faces and bodies are all slightly different. But it may be challenging to understand the distinctiveness with which God created us and what gifts the Holy Spirit has distributed to us.

God has chosen special gifts just for you to express His love for others in a special way. Are you aware of those gifts? Consider reviewing Romans 12:3–8 and other scriptures as you notice special Holy Spirit gifts like prophecy, serving, teaching, exhortation, giving, and mercy.

Pause to thank God for the Holy Spirit in your life; then ask Him to lead you in knowing and sharing your unique gifts.

GC2
GREAT COMMANDMENT
COMMISSION

eye, where *would be* the hearing? If the whole *were* hearing, where *would be* the smelling? [18]But now God has set the members, each one of them, in the body just as He pleased. [19]And if they were all one member, where *would* the body *be?*

[20]But now indeed *there are* many members, yet one body. [21]And the eye cannot say to the hand, "I have no need of you"; nor again the head to the feet, "I have no need of you." [22]No, much rather, those members of the body which seem to be weaker are necessary. [23]And those *members* of the body which we think to be less honorable, on these we bestow greater honor; and our unpresentable *parts* have greater modesty, [24]but our presentable *parts* have no need. But God composed the body, having given greater honor to that *part* which lacks it, [25]that there should be no schism in the body, but *that* the members should have the same care for one another. [26]And if one member suffers, all the members suffer with *it;* or if one member is honored, all the members rejoice with *it.*

[27]Now you are the body of Christ, and members individually. [28]And God has appointed these in the church: first apostles, second prophets, third teachers, after that miracles, then gifts of healings, helps, administrations, varieties of tongues. [29]*Are* all apostles? *Are* all prophets? *Are* all teachers? *Are* all workers of miracles? [30]Do all have gifts of healings? Do all speak with tongues? Do all interpret? [31]But earnestly desire the best[a] gifts. And yet I show you a more excellent way.

The Greatest Gift

13 Though I speak with the tongues of men and of angels, but have not love, I have become sounding brass or a clanging cymbal. [2]And though I have *the gift of* prophecy, and understand all mysteries and all knowledge, and though I have all faith, so that I could remove mountains, but have not love, I am nothing. [3]And though I bestow all my goods to feed *the poor,* and though I give my body to be burned,[a] but have not love, it profits me nothing.

[4]Love suffers long *and* is kind; love does not envy; love does not parade itself, is not puffed up; [5]does not behave rudely, does not seek its own, is not provoked, thinks no evil; [6]does not rejoice in iniquity, but rejoices in the truth; [7]bears all things,

believes all things, hopes all things, endures all things.

[8]Love never fails. But whether *there are* prophecies, they will fail; whether *there are* tongues, they will cease; whether *there is* knowledge, it will vanish away. [9]For we know in part and we prophesy in part. [10]But when that which is perfect has come, then that which is in part will be done away.

[11]When I was a child, I spoke as a child, I understood as a child, I thought as a child; but when I became a man, I put away childish things. [12]For now we see in a mirror, dimly, but then face to face. Now I know in part, but then I shall know just as I also am known.

[13]And now abide faith, hope, love, these three; but the greatest of these *is* love.

Prophecy and Tongues

14 Pursue love, and desire spiritual *gifts,* but especially that you may prophesy. [2]For he who speaks in a tongue does not speak to men but to God, for no one understands *him;* however, in the spirit he speaks mysteries. [3]But he who prophesies speaks edification and exhortation and comfort to men. [4]He who speaks in a tongue edifies himself, but he who prophesies edifies the church. [5]I wish you all spoke with tongues, but even more that you prophesied; for[a] he who prophesies *is* greater than he who speaks with tongues, unless indeed he interprets, that the church may receive edification.

Tongues Must Be Interpreted

[6]But now, brethren, if I come to you speaking with tongues, what shall I profit you unless I speak to you either by revelation, by knowledge, by prophesying, or by teaching? [7]Even things without life, whether flute or harp, when they make a sound, unless they make a distinction in the sounds, how will it be known what is piped or played? [8]For if the trumpet makes an uncertain sound, who will prepare for battle? [9]So likewise you, unless you utter by the tongue words easy to understand, how will it be known what is spoken? For you will be speaking into the air. [10]There are, it may be, so many kinds of languages

12:31 [a]NU-Text reads *greater*. 13:3 [a]NU-Text reads *so I may boast.*
14:5 [a]NU-Text reads *and.*

LEADERSHIP ISSUES

GC2: Giving Others Attention/Care

1 CORINTHIANS 12:25

The need for attention is met by conveying appropriate interest, concern, and care for another person. We meet people's need for attention when we take thought of them, particularly when we enter into their "world." Just as Christ left heaven to enter our world, so also we give first to others in our care for them.

During His earthly ministry, Jesus didn't just spend time with the masses but gave individual attention to people such as Zacchaeus (Luke 19:1–10), Nicodemus (John 3:1–16), the Samaritan woman (John 4:7–30), and the disciples. How does God meet our need for attention? Jesus met our need for attention by leaving His world (heaven) and entering into our world. He became like us so that we could know Him and have a personal relationship with Him (Phil. 2:5–11).

God continues to give us attention as we pray; in that, we receive His individual, undivided, and unlimited attention. Furthermore, He knew us in our mother's womb (Ps. 139:13); He knows our thoughts (Ps. 139:2), counts the number of hairs on our head (Luke 12:7), and promises to provide for our every need (Matt. 6:25–34).

Pause and reflect on these ideas for giving others attention:

- I spend time finding out about another's struggles, joys, and dreams.
- I try to enter into another's physical world; I try to visit their activities, school, and home.
- I try to enter into another's emotional world. When I come in contact with people, I try to discern their emotional state, gain understanding, and then show care to them.
- I'm a good listener, giving good eye contact, appropriate feedback, and seeking to hear fully before I respond.
- I enjoy spending time with people, doing what they enjoy doing.

GC2
GREAT COMMANDMENT
COMMISSION

LEADERSHIP ISSUES

GC2: Put Away Childish Things

1 CORINTHIANS 13:11

Following Jesus into Christlikeness involves growing up and putting away childish things.

- Childish justifying must be replaced by personal accountability (Rom. 14:12).
  —Do you get defensive or start justifying your actions when you make mistakes?
- Childish overtalking is to be superseded by increased listening— first to God, then to others (James 1:19).
  —Could you benefit from talking less and listening more?
- Childish self-preoccupation should give way to living out God's "others-centered" love (Phil. 2:3, 4).
  —Has "giving first" to others become a life priority for you?

*Search me, O Lord, for **childish things** that distract me from hearing You. Free me from rationalizing my behavior, blaming others, from idle chatter and self-focus. Free me to practice personal responsibility before You and others. Speak now; Your servant is listening.*

GC2

GREAT COMMANDMENT
COMMISSION

in the world, and none of them *is* without significance. [11]Therefore, if I do not know the meaning of the language, I shall be a foreigner to him who speaks, and he who speaks *will be* a foreigner to me. [12]Even so you, since you are zealous for spiritual *gifts, let it be* for the edification of the church *that* you seek to excel.

[13]Therefore let him who speaks in a tongue pray that he may interpret. [14]For if I pray in a tongue, my spirit prays, but my understanding is unfruitful. [15]What is *the conclusion* then? I will pray with the spirit, and I will also pray with the understanding. I will sing with the spirit, and I will also sing with the understanding. [16]Otherwise, if you bless with the spirit, how will he who occupies the place of the uninformed say "Amen" at your giving of thanks, since he does not understand what you say? [17]For you indeed give thanks well, but the other is not edified.

[18]I thank my God I speak with tongues more than you all; [19]yet in the church I would rather speak five words with my understanding, that I may teach others also, than ten thousand words in a tongue.

Tongues a Sign to Unbelievers

[20]Brethren, do not be children in understanding; however, in malice be babes, but in understanding be mature.

[21]In the law it is written:

> "With *men of other tongues and other lips*
> *I will speak to this people;*
> *And yet, for all that, they will not hear Me,"*[a]

says the Lord.

[22]Therefore tongues are for a sign, not to those who believe but to unbelievers; but prophesying is not for unbelievers but for those who believe. [23]Therefore if the whole church comes together in one place, and all speak with tongues, and there come in *those who are* uninformed or unbelievers, will they not say that you are out of your mind? [24]But if all prophesy, and an unbeliever or an uninformed person comes in, he is convinced by all, he is convicted by all. [25]And thus[a] the secrets of his heart are revealed; and so, falling down on *his* face, he will worship God and report that God is truly among you.

Order in Church Meetings

[26]How is it then, brethren? Whenever you come together, each of you has a psalm, has a teaching, has a tongue, has a revelation, has an interpretation. Let all things be done for edification. [27]If anyone speaks in a tongue, *let there be* two or at the most three, *each* in turn, and let one interpret. [28]But if there is no interpreter, let him keep silent in church, and let him speak to himself and to God. [29]Let two or three prophets speak, and let the others judge. [30]But if *anything* is revealed to another who sits by, let the first keep silent. [31]For you can all prophesy one by one, that all may learn and all may be encouraged. [32]And the spirits of the prophets are subject to the prophets. [33]For God is not *the author* of confusion but of peace, as in all the churches of the saints.

[34]Let your[a] women keep silent in the churches, for they are not permitted to speak; but *they are* to be submissive, as the law also says. [35]And if they want to learn something, let them ask their own husbands at home; for it is shameful for women to speak in church.

[36]Or did the word of God come *originally* from you? Or *was it* you only that it reached? [37]If anyone thinks himself to be a prophet or spiritual, let him acknowledge that the things which I write to you are the commandments of the Lord. [38]But if anyone is ignorant, let him be ignorant.[a]

[39]Therefore, brethren, desire earnestly to prophesy, and do not forbid to speak with tongues. [40]Let all things be done decently and in order.

The Risen Christ, Faith's Reality

15 Moreover, brethren, I declare to you the gospel which I preached to you, which also you received and in which you stand, [2]by which also you are saved, if you hold fast that word which I preached to you—unless you believed in vain.

[3]For I delivered to you first of all that which I also received: that Christ died for our sins according to the Scriptures, [4]and that He was buried, and that He rose again the third day according to the Scriptures, [5]and that He was seen by Cephas,

14:21 [a]Isaiah 28:11, 12 14:25 [a]NU-Text omits *And thus.*
14:34 [a]NU-Text omits *your.* 14:38 [a]NU-Text reads *if anyone does not recognize this, he is not recognized.*

then by the twelve. [6]After that He was seen by over five hundred brethren at once, of whom the greater part remain to the present, but some have fallen asleep. [7]After that He was seen by James, then by all the apostles. [8]Then last of all He was seen by me also, as by one born out of due time.

[9]For I am the least of the apostles, who am not worthy to be called an apostle, because I persecuted the church of God. [10]But by the grace of God I am what I am, and His grace toward me was not in vain; but I labored more abundantly than they all, yet not I, but the grace of God *which was* with me. [11]Therefore, whether *it was* I or they, so we preach and so you believed.

THE RISEN CHRIST, OUR HOPE

[12]Now if Christ is preached that He has been raised from the dead, how do some among you say that there is no resurrection of the dead? [13]But if there is no resurrection of the dead, then Christ is not risen. [14]And if Christ is not risen, then our preaching *is* empty and your faith *is* also empty. [15]Yes, and we are found false witnesses of God, because we have testified of God that He raised up Christ, whom He did not raise up—if in fact the dead do not rise. [16]For if the dead do not rise, then Christ is not risen. [17]And if Christ is not risen, your faith *is* futile; you are still in your sins! [18]Then also those who have fallen asleep in Christ have perished. [19]If in this life only we have hope in Christ, we are of all men the most pitiable.

THE LAST ENEMY DESTROYED

[20]But now Christ is risen from the dead, *and* has become the firstfruits of those who have fallen asleep. [21]For since by man *came* death, by Man also *came* the resurrection of the dead. [22]For as in Adam all die, even so in Christ all shall be made alive. [23]But each one in his own order: Christ the firstfruits, afterward those *who are* Christ's at His coming. [24]Then *comes* the end, when He delivers the kingdom to God the Father, when He puts an end to all rule and all authority and power. [25]For He must reign till He has put all enemies under His feet. [26]The last enemy *that* will be destroyed *is* death. [27]For *"He has put all things under His feet."*[a] But when He says "all things are put under *Him*," *it is* evident that He who put all things under Him is excepted.

[28]Now when all things are made subject to Him, then the Son Himself will also be subject to Him who put all things under Him, that God may be all in all.

EFFECTS OF DENYING THE RESURRECTION

[29]Otherwise, what will they do who are baptized for the dead, if the dead do not rise at all? Why then are they baptized for the dead? [30]And why do we stand in jeopardy every hour? [31]I affirm, by the boasting in you which I have in Christ Jesus our Lord, I die daily. [32]If, in the manner of men, I have fought with beasts at Ephesus, what advantage *is it* to me? If *the* dead do not rise, *"Let us eat and drink, for tomorrow we die!"*[a]

[33]Do not be deceived: "Evil company corrupts good habits." [34]Awake to righteousness, and do not sin; for some do not have the knowledge of God. I speak *this* to your shame.

A GLORIOUS BODY

[35]But someone will say, "How are the dead raised up? And with what body do they come?" [36]Foolish one, what you sow is not made alive unless it dies. [37]And what you sow, you do not sow that body that shall be, but mere grain—perhaps wheat or some other *grain*. [38]But God gives it a body as He pleases, and to each seed its own body. [39]All flesh *is* not the same flesh, but *there is* one *kind of* flesh[a] of men, another flesh of animals, another of fish, *and* another of birds.

[40]*There are* also celestial bodies and terrestrial bodies; but the glory of the celestial *is* one, and the *glory* of the terrestrial *is* another. [41]*There is* one glory of the sun, another glory of the moon, and another glory of the stars; for *one* star differs from *another* star in glory.

[42]So also *is* the resurrection of the dead. *The body* is sown in corruption, it is raised in incorruption. [43]It is sown in dishonor, it is raised in glory. It is sown in weakness, it is raised in power. [44]It is sown a natural body, it is raised a spiritual body. There is a natural body, and there is a spiritual body. [45]And so it is written, *"The first man Adam became a living being."*[a] The last Adam *became* a life-giving spirit.

15:27 [a]Psalm 8:6   **15:32** [a]Isaiah 22:13   **15:39** [a]NU-Text and M-Text omit *of flesh.*   **15:45** [a]Genesis 2:7

LEADERSHIP ISSUES

GC2: Faith in the New Testament

1 CORINTHIANS 15:45

Jesus, the "last Adam," lived out the perfect faith that the first Adam lost. Adam and Eve's taking of forbidden fruit tainted all humankind with self-centered perspectives. We mistakenly believe the lie that: "If no one else is looking out for me, then I'd better!" But what if the truth is that God in Christ is looking out for every detail of life?

As recounted in the Gospels, Christ consistently demonstrated confidence in God's power and provision. One clear example of the Son's faith in the Father is found in the account of the resurrection of Lazarus (John 11:1–44). After assuring Mary and Martha that their brother would live again, Jesus paused in the midst of the crowd and publicly thanked God for the miracle of Lazarus's resurrection—before it had even occurred (vv. 41, 42)! Expectant faith in the Father was a constant theme in Christ's life, ministry, and miracles. Even as He drew His last breath, Jesus demonstrated faith by committing His spirit to the Father's care (Luke 23:46).

The perfect faith that Jesus modeled inspired His followers to exercise expectant faith as well. Following Christ's ascension and the coming of the Holy Spirit, the disciples' faith, which had been tried greatly following the Crucifixion, continued to grow and strengthen. Soon, the disciples began to perform miracles of healing and deliverance just as Jesus had (Acts 4:29–31). The remainder of the New Testament bears witness to the power of the faith that comes through knowing Christ (Rom. 5:1; Gal. 3:11; Eph. 2:8, 9; Heb. 12:2).

Faith-filled followers of Jesus live confidently in the knowledge of God's attentive and personal care, expectant of Him to provide and guide, bringing forth all good things (James 1:17).

GC2
GREAT COMMANDMENT
COMMISSION

[46]However, the spiritual is not first, but the natural, and afterward the spiritual. [47]The first man *was* of the earth, *made* of dust; the second Man *is* the Lord[a] from heaven. [48]As *was* the *man* of dust, so also *are* those *who are made* of dust; and as *is* the heavenly *Man*, so also *are* those *who are* heavenly. [49]And as we have borne the image of the *man* of dust, we shall also bear[a] the image of the heavenly *Man*.

OUR FINAL VICTORY

[50]Now this I say, brethren, that flesh and blood cannot inherit the kingdom of God; nor does corruption inherit incorruption. [51]Behold, I tell you a mystery: We shall not all sleep, but we shall all be changed— [52]in a moment, in the twinkling of an eye, at the last trumpet. For the trumpet will sound, and the dead will be raised incorruptible, and we shall be changed. [53]For this corruptible must put on incorruption, and this mortal *must* put on immortality. [54]So when this corruptible has put on incorruption, and this mortal has put on immortality, then shall be brought to pass the saying that is written: *"Death is swallowed up in victory."*[a]

[55]*"O Death, where is your sting?*[a]
O Hades, where is your victory?"[b]

[56]The sting of death *is* sin, and the strength of sin *is* the law. [57]But thanks *be* to God, who gives us the victory through our Lord Jesus Christ.

[58]Therefore, my beloved brethren, be steadfast, immovable, always abounding in the work of the Lord, knowing that your labor is not in vain in the Lord.

COLLECTION FOR THE SAINTS

16 Now concerning the collection for the saints, as I have given orders to the churches of Galatia, so you must do also: [2]On the first *day* of the week let each one of you lay something aside, storing up as he may prosper, that there be no collections when I come. [3]And when I come, whomever you approve by *your* letters I will send to bear your gift to Jerusalem. [4]But if it is fitting that I go also, they will go with me.

PERSONAL PLANS

[5]Now I will come to you when I pass through Macedonia (for I am passing through

Macedonia). [6]And it may be that I will remain, or even spend the winter with you, that you may send me on my journey, wherever I go. [7]For I do not wish to see you now on the way; but I hope to stay a while with you, if the Lord permits.

[8]But I will tarry in Ephesus until Pentecost. [9]For a great and effective door has opened to me, and *there are* many adversaries.

[10]And if Timothy comes, see that he may be with you without fear; for he does the work of the Lord, as I also *do.* [11]Therefore let no one despise him. But send him on his journey in peace, that he may come to me; for I am waiting for him with the brethren.

[12]Now concerning *our* brother Apollos, I strongly urged him to come to you with the brethren, but he was quite unwilling to come at this time; however, he will come when he has a convenient time.

FINAL EXHORTATIONS

[13]Watch, stand fast in the faith, be brave, be strong. [14]Let all *that* you *do* be done with love.

[15]I urge you, brethren—you know the household of Stephanas, that it is the firstfruits of Achaia, and *that* they have devoted themselves to the ministry of the saints— [16]that you also submit to such, and to everyone who works and labors with *us.*

[17]I am glad about the coming of Stephanas, Fortunatus, and Achaicus, for what was lacking on your part they supplied. [18]For they refreshed my spirit and yours. Therefore acknowledge such men.

GREETINGS AND A SOLEMN FAREWELL

[19]The churches of Asia greet you. Aquila and Priscilla greet you heartily in the Lord, with the church that is in their house. [20]All the brethren greet you.

Greet one another with a holy kiss.

[21]The salutation with my own hand—Paul's.

[22]If anyone does not love the Lord Jesus Christ, let him be accursed.[a] O Lord, come![b]

[23]The grace of our Lord Jesus Christ *be* with you. [24]My love *be* with you all in Christ Jesus. Amen.

15:47 [a]NU-Text omits *the Lord.* **15:49** [a]M-Text reads *let us also bear.* **15:54** [a]Isaiah 25:8 **15:55** [a]Hosea 13:14 [b]NU-Text reads *O Death, where is your victory? O Death, where is your sting?* **16:22** [a]Greek *anathema* [b]Aramaic *Maranatha*

IMPACT OF THE BOOK

I   IDEA   *God's truth is worthy of our strongest defense.*

M   MESSAGE   *Paul stood his ground in the face of opposition and critics. He did not flee but remained firm, knowing that not only his testimony, but also his preaching concerning Christ, was at stake. Paul reveals his deepest feelings and motives as he casts a vision for the church's future ministry. He demonstrates great leadership by connecting with the people and sharing his own struggles with his "thorn in the flesh."*

P   PEOPLE   *False Teachers, Paul, Timothy, Titus*

A   AUTHOR   *Paul is the undisputed author of this epistle, which contains many characteristics of his style. He wrote with a familiarity of the people, including many references and much autobiographical information. Paul and Timothy had a close relationship. Paul mentored Timothy, respected him, and involved this younger man in ministry. He invited Timothy to become his helper, sending him on missionary journeys.*

C   CULTURE   *Paul diligently mentored and led the Corinthians. The church was sometimes very responsive; sometimes they were very hostile. Much growth came as a result of Paul's efforts; but at times, they regressed in their attitudes and behavior. Paul's authority and apostleship were challenged. He addressed this lack of respect for authority in his last letter and then met with Titus. His good report must have been a great encouragement to Paul. However, a small fraction still opposed the apostle. Paul followed this letter with a personal visit, which appears to have been successful.*

T   TIMELINE   *c. AD 56*

KEY SCRIPTURE
MEMORY VERSES   4:7–12, 16–18; 5:10, 17–21; 11:13; 12:9, 10

SECOND CORINTHIANS

1 Paul, an apostle of Jesus Christ by the will of God, and Timothy *our* brother,

To the church of God which is at Corinth, with all the saints who are in all Achaia:

²Grace to you and peace from God our Father and the Lord Jesus Christ.

COMFORT IN SUFFERING

³Blessed *be* the God and Father of our Lord Jesus Christ, the Father of mercies and God of all comfort, ⁴who comforts us in all our tribulation, that we may be able to comfort those who are in any trouble, with the comfort with which we ourselves are comforted by God. ⁵For as the sufferings of Christ abound in us, so our consolation also abounds through Christ. ⁶Now if we are afflicted, *it is* for your consolation and salvation, which is effective for enduring the same sufferings which we also suffer. Or if we are comforted, *it is* for your consolation and salvation. ⁷And our hope for you *is* steadfast, because we know that as you are partakers of the sufferings, so also *you will partake* of the consolation.

DELIVERED FROM SUFFERING

⁸For we do not want you to be ignorant, brethren, of our trouble which came to us in Asia: that we were burdened beyond measure, above strength, so that we despaired even of life. ⁹Yes, we had the sentence of death in ourselves, that we should not trust in ourselves but in God who raises the dead, ¹⁰who delivered us from so great a death, and doesᵃ deliver us; in whom we trust that He will still deliver *us,* ¹¹you also helping together in prayer for us, that thanks may be given by many persons on ourᵃ behalf for the gift *granted* to us through many.

PAUL'S SINCERITY

¹²For our boasting is this: the testimony of our conscience that we conducted ourselves in the world in simplicity and godly sincerity, not with fleshly wisdom but by the grace of God, and more abundantly toward you. ¹³For we are not writing any other things to you than what you read or understand. Now I trust you will understand, even to the end ¹⁴(as also you have understood us in part), that we are your boast as you also *are* ours, in the day of the Lord Jesus.

SPARING THE CHURCH

¹⁵And in this confidence I intended to come to you before, that you might have a second benefit— ¹⁶to pass by way of you to Macedonia, to come again from Macedonia to you, and be helped by you on my way to Judea. ¹⁷Therefore, when I was planning this, did I do it lightly? Or the things I plan, do I plan according to the flesh, that with me there should be Yes, Yes, and No, No? ¹⁸But *as* God *is* faithful, our word to you was not Yes and No. ¹⁹For the Son of God, Jesus Christ, who was preached among you by us—by me, Silvanus, and Timothy—was not Yes and No, but in Him was Yes. ²⁰For all the promises of God in Him *are* Yes, and in Him Amen, to the glory of God through us. ²¹Now He who establishes us with you in Christ and has anointed us *is* God, ²²who also has sealed us and given us the Spirit in our hearts as a guarantee.

²³Moreover I call God as witness against my soul, that to spare you I came no more to Corinth. ²⁴Not that we have dominion over your faith, but are fellow workers for your joy; for by faith you stand.

2 But I determined this within myself, that I would not come again to you in sorrow. ²For if I make you sorrowful, then who is he who makes me glad but the one who is made sorrowful by me?

FORGIVE THE OFFENDER

³And I wrote this very thing to you, lest, when I came, I should have sorrow over those from whom I ought to have joy, having confidence in you all that my joy is *the joy* of you all. ⁴For out of much affliction and anguish of heart I wrote to you, with many tears, not that you should be grieved, but that you might know the love which I have so abundantly for you.

⁵But if anyone has caused grief, he has not grieved me, but all of you to some extent—not to be too severe. ⁶This punishment which *was inflicted* by the majority *is* sufficient for such a man,

1:10 ᵃNU-Text reads *shall.*   1:11 ᵃM-Text reads *your behalf.*

LEADERSHIP ISSUES

GC2: Giving Others Comfort

2 CORINTHIANS 1:3, 4

The need for comfort is met by responding to a hurting person with appropriate words, feelings, and physical touch. Comfort involves feeling and expressing sadness for another person's grief and pain. We are admonished to "weep with those who weep" (Rom. 12:15); and we are assured, "Blessed are those who mourn, for they shall be comforted" (Matt. 5:4).

Jesus comforted people throughout His earthly ministry, often identifying with the hurt in others, so much that He wept with them (John 11:35) or for them (Luke 19:41). Even on the eve of His death, He comforted His disciples as He sensed their sorrow and anxiety (John 14:1, 18; 16:33).

How does God meet our need for comfort? We can be assured that God will comfort us in our distress, because He is "the God and Father of our Lord Jesus Christ, the Father of mercies and God of all comfort," (2 Cor. 1:3). He sends the Holy Spirit to comfort us. The Holy Spirit is often referred to as the "Comforter" or "Helper" (John 14:16, 26; 15:26; 16:7). In the New Testament, the Greek word for comfort (and the word used to describe the Holy Spirit's ministry to us) is *parakaleo*, which means, "to come to one's side, to one's aid."

Pause and reflect on these ideas for giving others comfort:

- I am sensitive to notice when people are hurting, anxious, frustrated, or emotionally down.
- I have developed an appropriate "comforting vocabulary" and communicate my care and concern for hurting people.
- I have learned how to sense God's compassion for others and enter into their emotional pain.
- I know how to respond to hurting people with a gentle touch and affirming words.
- When people are hurting, instead of giving them advice, or exhortation, I express my feelings of sadness and hurt for them.

GC2
GREAT COMMANDMENT
COMMISSION

⁷so that, on the contrary, you *ought* rather to forgive and comfort *him,* lest perhaps such a one be swallowed up with too much sorrow. ⁸Therefore I urge you to reaffirm *your* love to him. ⁹For to this end I also wrote, that I might put you to the test, whether you are obedient in all things. ¹⁰Now whom you forgive anything, I also *forgive.* For if indeed I have forgiven anything, I have forgiven that oneᵃ for your sakes in the presence of Christ, ¹¹lest Satan should take advantage of us; for we are not ignorant of his devices.

TRIUMPH IN CHRIST

¹²Furthermore, when I came to Troas to *preach* Christ's gospel, and a door was opened to me by the Lord, ¹³I had no rest in my spirit, because I did not find Titus my brother; but taking my leave of them, I departed for Macedonia.

¹⁴Now thanks *be* to God who always leads us in triumph in Christ, and through us diffuses the fragrance of His knowledge in every place. ¹⁵For we are to God the fragrance of Christ among those who are being saved and among those who are perishing. ¹⁶To the one *we are* the aroma of death *leading* to death, and to the other the aroma of life *leading* to life. And who *is* sufficient for these things? ¹⁷For we are not, as so many,ᵃ peddling the word of God; but as of sincerity, but as from God, we speak in the sight of God in Christ.

CHRIST'S EPISTLE

3 Do we begin again to commend ourselves? Or do we need, as some *others,* epistles of commendation to you or *letters* of commendation from you? ²You are our epistle written in our hearts, known and read by all men; ³clearly you are an epistle of Christ, ministered by us, written not with ink but by the Spirit of the living God, not on tablets of stone but on tablets of flesh, *that is,* of the heart.

THE SPIRIT, NOT THE LETTER

⁴And we have such trust through Christ toward God. ⁵Not that we are sufficient of ourselves to think of anything as *being* from ourselves, but our sufficiency *is* from God, ⁶who also made us sufficient as ministers of the new covenant, not of the letter but of the Spirit;ᵃ for the letter kills, but the Spirit gives life.

GLORY OF THE NEW COVENANT

⁷But if the ministry of death, written *and* engraved on stones, was glorious, so that the children of Israel could not look steadily at the face of Moses because of the glory of his countenance, which *glory* was passing away, ⁸how will the ministry of the Spirit not be more glorious? ⁹For if the ministry of condemnation *had* glory, the ministry of righteousness exceeds much more in glory. ¹⁰For even what was made glorious had no glory in this respect, because of the glory that excels. ¹¹For if what is passing away *was* glorious, what remains *is* much more glorious.

¹²Therefore, since we have such hope, we use great boldness of speech— ¹³unlike Moses, *who* put a veil over his face so that the children of Israel could not look steadily at the end of what was passing away. ¹⁴But their minds were blinded. For until this day the same veil remains unlifted in the reading of the Old Testament, because the *veil* is taken away in Christ. ¹⁵But even to this day, when Moses is read, a veil lies on their heart. ¹⁶Nevertheless when one turns to the Lord, the veil is taken away. ¹⁷Now the Lord is the Spirit; and where the Spirit of the Lord *is,* there *is* liberty. ¹⁸But we all, with unveiled face, beholding as in a mirror the glory of the Lord, are being transformed into the same image from glory to glory, just as by the Spirit of the Lord.

THE LIGHT OF CHRIST'S GOSPEL

4 Therefore, since we have this ministry, as we have received mercy, we do not lose heart. ²But we have renounced the hidden things of shame, not walking in craftiness nor handling the word of God deceitfully, but by manifestation of the truth commending ourselves to every man's conscience in the sight of God. ³But even if our gospel is veiled, it is veiled to those who are perishing, ⁴whose minds the god of this age has blinded, who do not believe, lest the light of the gospel of the glory of Christ, who is the image of God, should shine on them. ⁵For we do not preach ourselves, but Christ Jesus the Lord, and ourselves your bondservants for Jesus' sake. ⁶For it is the God who commanded light to shine out of darkness, who

2:10 ᵃNU-Text reads *For indeed, what I have forgiven, if I have forgiven anything, I did it.* 2:17 ᵃM-Text reads *the rest.* 3:6 ᵃOr *spirit*

LEADERSHIP ISSUES

GC2: Sharing Christ: Imparting the Gospel

2 CORINTHIANS 3:2 *You are our epistle written in our hearts, known and read by all men.*

Only as our "walk" matches our "talk" will we have an effective, contagious witness for Christ.

As we impart His life and love **in spite of people's faults and failures,** we give witness to a Christ who accepts us, who demonstrated His love by dying for us "while we were still sinners" (Rom. 5:8).

As we impart His life and love **through supportive involvement, caring concern, and practical help,** we give witness to a Christ who bears burdens. "Bear one another's burdens, and so fulfill the law of Christ" (Gal. 6:2).

As we impart His life and love **through compassion and comfort** when others are hurting, disappointed, or sorrowful, we give witness to a Christ who was "despised and rejected by men, a Man of sorrows and acquainted with grief" (Is. 53:3); who wept for His friend, Mary (John 11:35); and who is often moved with compassion.

Consider *who* in the "traffic patterns" of your life could benefit from *His* life imparted through you!

GC2
GREAT COMMANDMENT
COMMISSION

has shone in our hearts to *give* the light of the knowledge of the glory of God in the face of Jesus Christ.

Cast Down but Unconquered

[7]But we have this treasure in earthen vessels, that the excellence of the power may be of God and not of us. [8]*We are* hard-pressed on every side, yet not crushed; *we are* perplexed, but not in despair; [9]persecuted, but not forsaken; struck down, but not destroyed— [10]always carrying about in the body the dying of the Lord Jesus, that the life of Jesus also may be manifested in our body. [11]For we who live are always delivered to death for Jesus' sake, that the life of Jesus also may be manifested in our mortal flesh. [12]So then death is working in us, but life in you.

[13]And since we have the same spirit of faith, according to what is written, *"I believed and therefore I spoke,"*[a] we also believe and therefore speak, [14]knowing that He who raised up the Lord Jesus will also raise us up with Jesus, and will present *us* with you. [15]For all things *are* for your sakes, that grace, having spread through the many, may cause thanksgiving to abound to the glory of God.

Seeing the Invisible

[16]Therefore we do not lose heart. Even though our outward man is perishing, yet the inward *man* is being renewed day by day. [17]For our light affliction, which is but for a moment, is working for us a far more exceeding *and* eternal weight of glory, [18]while we do not look at the things which are seen, but at the things which are not seen. For the things which are seen *are* temporary, but the things which are not seen *are* eternal.

Assurance of the Resurrection

5 For we know that if our earthly house, *this* tent, is destroyed, we have a building from God, a house not made with hands, eternal in the heavens. [2]For in this we groan, earnestly desiring to be clothed with our habitation which is from heaven, [3]if indeed, having been clothed, we shall not be found naked. [4]For we who are in *this* tent groan, being burdened, not because we want to be unclothed, but further clothed, that mortality may be

swallowed up by life. [5]Now He who has prepared us for this very thing *is* God, who also has given us the Spirit as a guarantee.

[6]So *we are* always confident, knowing that while we are at home in the body we are absent from the Lord. [7]For we walk by faith, not by sight. [8]We are confident, yes, well pleased rather to be absent from the body and to be present with the Lord.

The Judgment Seat of Christ

[9]Therefore we make it our aim, whether present or absent, to be well pleasing to Him. [10]For we must all appear before the judgment seat of Christ, that each one may receive the things *done* in the body, according to what he has done, whether good or bad. [11]Knowing, therefore, the terror of the Lord, we persuade men; but we are well known to God, and I also trust are well known in your consciences.

Be Reconciled to God

[12]For we do not commend ourselves again to you, but give you opportunity to boast on our behalf, that you may have *an answer* for those who boast in appearance and not in heart. [13]For if we are beside ourselves, *it is* for God; or if we are of sound mind, *it is* for you. [14]For the love of Christ compels us, because we judge thus: that if One died for all, then all died; [15]and He died for all, that those who live should live no longer for themselves, but for Him who died for them and rose again.

[16]Therefore, from now on, we regard no one according to the flesh. Even though we have known Christ according to the flesh, yet now we know *Him thus* no longer. [17]Therefore, if anyone *is* in Christ, *he is* a new creation; old things have passed away; behold, all things have become new. [18]Now all things *are* of God, who has reconciled us to Himself through Jesus Christ, and has given us the ministry of reconciliation, [19]that is, that God was in Christ reconciling the world to Himself, not imputing their trespasses to them, and has committed to us the word of reconciliation.

[20]Now then, we are ambassadors for Christ, as though God were pleading through us: we implore *you* on Christ's behalf, be reconciled to

4:13 [a]Psalm 116:10

LEADERSHIP ISSUES

New Creation in Christ: Identity Theft

2 CORINTHIANS 5:17

Many of us are the victims of abandonment, betrayal, and hurt. These feelings may have been caused by childhood or just everyday life, from those close to us or those we barely know. The hurt they leave behind is real and affects how we think, what our relationships are like, and how we live in the future.

If we aren't careful, that hurt can take us from being *victims* to being *villains*. We deal with our pain by hurting others with actions or with words; we replace good choices with risky behavior and an "I don't care" attitude. It's important to remember your hurt is very real. Talk to a trusted friend or counselor about how to start your journey to healing.

When we are too embarrassed to get help, or when we just simply choose to stay in an unhealthy state of mind, we allow sin to rule our lives. We become a *volunteer*, rather than a victim. The underlying issue is our lack of confidence in God to be able to heal us and a fear of facing the pain.

When you accept Christ as your Savior, you become "in Christ" (2 Cor. 5:15–17). He is no longer just an outward god that you know about; He is the Savior of your soul who lives within you. Because of this, you receive a new life, the power to live it successfully, and the ability to influence and impact others. The life we want to live is one of triumph over the pain of the past, whether it was years ago or yesterday. We must make a conscious, definite choice to accept it by faith.

A leader understands that the failures and mistakes of the past have been used throughout history to show the unconditional love of God, the depth of His forgiveness, and the power of new life in Christ. To believe anything less is to discount the gift of Christ's death on the cross—a gift so complete that we need nothing more.

LEAD**ERSHIP**
REAL**ITIES**

IDENTITY: CONFESSIONS OF A LIFE
EN CHRISTOS 2 Corinthians 5:17–21

The phrase "in Christ" (*en Christos*) utilizes two of the greatest words one could use to describe life. Eternity's destination and all of life's motivations hinge on the significance they bear. "In Christ" is the wondrous reality that we as believers have been brought into His presence and given His grace, and on this the leader's thoughts should focus both night and day. Paul uses this saying, or something very close to it, almost 170 times in his New Testament letters. It has been called his "magnificent obsession," and it should also be ours as leaders. Paul is communicating with these two words that the identity and actions are never to be separated for one who is "in Christ." This leads to certain confessions that serve as common denominators and must be true in the life of every leader:

- The reality of a life *in Christ* is that I am a new creation (v. 17).
- The reason for a life being *in Christ* is that I am unconditionally and intimately loved by God (vv. 18–21).
- The result of a life *in Christ* is that I am motivated to lead in the ministry of reconciliation, helping to reestablish relationships with God and with people (vv. 18–21).

God. ²¹For He made Him who knew no sin *to be* sin for us, that we might become the righteousness of God in Him.

MARKS OF THE MINISTRY

6 We then, *as* workers together *with Him* also plead with *you* not to receive the grace of God in vain. ²For He says:

> "In an acceptable time I have heard you,
> And in the day of salvation I have helped
> you."ᵃ

Behold, now *is* the accepted time; behold, now *is* the day of salvation.

³We give no offense in anything, that our ministry may not be blamed. ⁴But in all *things* we commend ourselves as ministers of God: in much patience, in tribulations, in needs, in distresses, ⁵in stripes, in imprisonments, in tumults, in labors, in sleeplessness, in fastings; ⁶by purity, by knowledge, by longsuffering, by kindness, by the Holy Spirit, by sincere love, ⁷by the word of truth, by the power of God, by the armor of righteousness on the right hand and on the left,

⁸by honor and dishonor, by evil report and good report; as deceivers, and *yet* true; ⁹as unknown, and *yet* well known; as dying, and behold we live; as chastened, and *yet* not killed; ¹⁰as sorrowful, yet always rejoicing; as poor, yet making many rich; as having nothing, and *yet* possessing all things.

BE HOLY

¹¹O Corinthians! We have spoken openly to you, our heart is wide open. ¹²You are not restricted by us, but you are restricted by your *own* affections. ¹³Now in return for the same (I speak as to children), you also be open.

¹⁴Do not be unequally yoked together with unbelievers. For what fellowship has righteousness with lawlessness? And what communion has light with darkness? ¹⁵And what accord has Christ with Belial? Or what part has a believer with an unbeliever? ¹⁶And what agreement has the temple of God with idols? For youᵃ are the temple of the living God. As God has said:

6:2 ᵃIsaiah 49:8   **6:16** ᵃNU-Text reads *we.*

"I will dwell in them
And walk among them.
I will be their God,
And they shall be My people."[b]

[17]Therefore

"Come out from among them
And be separate, says the Lord.
Do not touch what is unclean,
And I will receive you."[a]
[18]*"I will be a Father to you,*
And you shall be My sons and daughters,
Says the Lord *Almighty."*[a]

7 Therefore, having these promises, beloved, let us cleanse ourselves from all filthiness of the flesh and spirit, perfecting holiness in the fear of God.

The Corinthians' Repentance

[2]Open *your hearts* to us. We have wronged no one, we have corrupted no one, we have cheated no one. [3]I do not say *this* to condemn; for I have said before that you are in our hearts, to die together and to live together. [4]Great *is* my boldness of speech toward you, great *is* my boasting on your behalf. I am filled with comfort. I am exceedingly joyful in all our tribulation.

[5]For indeed, when we came to Macedonia, our bodies had no rest, but we were troubled on every side. Outside *were* conflicts, inside *were* fears. [6]Nevertheless God, who comforts the downcast, comforted us by the coming of Titus, [7]and not only by his coming, but also by the consolation with which he was comforted in you, when he told us of your earnest desire, your mourning, your zeal for me, so that I rejoiced even more.

[8]For even if I made you sorry with my letter, I do not regret it; though I did regret it. For I perceive that the same epistle made you sorry, though only for a while. [9]Now I rejoice, not that you were made sorry, but that your sorrow led to repentance. For you were made sorry in a godly manner, that you might suffer loss from us in nothing. [10]For godly sorrow produces repentance *leading* to salvation, not to be regretted; but the sorrow of the world produces death. [11]For observe this very thing, that you sorrowed in a godly manner: What diligence it produced in you, *what* clearing *of yourselves, what* indignation, *what* fear, *what* vehement desire, *what* zeal, *what* vindication! In all *things* you proved yourselves to be clear in this matter. [12]Therefore, although I wrote to you, I *did* not *do it* for the sake of him who had done the wrong, nor for the sake of him who suffered wrong, but that our care for you in the sight of God might appear to you.

The Joy of Titus

[13]Therefore we have been comforted in your comfort. And we rejoiced exceedingly more for the joy of Titus, because his spirit has been refreshed by you all. [14]For if in anything I have boasted to him about you, I am not ashamed. But as we spoke all things to you in truth, even so our boasting to Titus was found true. [15]And his affections are greater for you as he remembers the obedience of you all, how with fear and trembling you received him. [16]Therefore I rejoice that I have confidence in you in everything.

Excel in Giving

8 Moreover, brethren, we make known to you the grace of God bestowed on the churches of Macedonia: [2]that in a great trial of affliction the abundance of their joy and their deep poverty abounded in the riches of their liberality. [3]For I bear witness that according to *their* ability, yes, and beyond *their* ability, *they were* freely willing, [4]imploring us with much urgency that we would receive[a] the gift and the fellowship of the ministering to the saints. [5]And not *only* as we had hoped, but they first gave themselves to the Lord, and *then* to us by the will of God. [6]So we urged Titus, that as he had begun, so he would also complete this grace in you as well. [7]But as you abound in everything—in faith, in speech, in knowledge, in all diligence, and in your love for us—*see* that you abound in this grace also.

Christ Our Pattern

[8]I speak not by commandment, but I am testing the sincerity of your love by the diligence of others. [9]For you know the grace of our Lord Jesus

6:16 [b]Leviticus 26:12; Jeremiah 32:38; Ezekiel 37:27   6:17 [a]Isaiah 52:11; Ezekiel 20:34, 41   6:18 [a]2 Samuel 7:14   8:4 [a]NU-Text and M-Text omit *that we would receive,* thus changing text to *urgency for the favor and fellowship. . . .*

LEADERSHIP ISSUES

GC2: Basic Training: The Dread of Displeasing God

2 CORINTHIANS 7:1

Think back to when you developed your first "best friend" or even your first boyfriend or girlfriend. You might recall having a dread of displeasing the one you cared about—at all costs, you wanted to please that person. On a human level, you had a "healthy" fear of letting him or her down.

With this backdrop of an admittedly human analogy, let us reconsider our understanding of what it means to possess the "fear of the LORD," which "is the beginning of wisdom" (Prov. 9:10). This "fear" is not just an anxious concern that we will suffer dreadful consequences for our disobedience. That is a very childlike understanding of the situation. Out of love, parents prescribe "consequences" for wrong behavior, and children comply in order to avoid the consequences. But as maturity comes, a trusting love for the parents begins to motivate compliance.

So it is to be with Christ's disciples. A dread of painful consequences may motivate short-term compliance, but it will not motivate our whole-hearted participation in the journey toward Christlikeness. Scripture addresses the limitation of this "dread of consequences" as the aging apostle John states, "There is no fear in love," and then declares, "because fear involves torment. But he who fears has not been made perfect in love" (1 John 4:18).

Would God, who graced us with His infinite, unmerited, loving favor when He saved us, now seek to motivate our walk with Him through fear of consequences? Would not such fear simply cause us to seek to perfect by works that which was begun by grace, thus undermining the wonder of our worth as joint heirs with Christ and replacing it with performance-based worth? (Gal. 3:1–3).

Pause in prayer to affirm your love for the Lord and your deep desire to please Him.

GC2
GREAT COMMANDMENT
COMMISSION

Christ, that though He was rich, yet for your sakes He became poor, that you through His poverty might become rich.

[10]And in this I give advice: It is to your advantage not only to be doing what you began and were desiring to do a year ago; [11]but now you also must complete the doing *of it;* that as *there was a* readiness to desire *it,* so *there* also *may be* a completion out of what *you* have. [12]For if there is first a willing mind, *it is* accepted according to what one has, *and* not according to what he does not have.

[13]For *I do* not *mean* that others should be eased and you burdened; [14]but by an equality, *that* now at this time your abundance *may supply* their lack, that their abundance also may *supply* your lack—that there may be equality. [15]As it is written, *"He who* gathered much had nothing left over, and he who gathered little had no lack."* [a]

COLLECTION FOR THE JUDEAN SAINTS

[16]But thanks *be* to God who puts[a] the same earnest care for you into the heart of Titus. [17]For he not only accepted the exhortation, but being more diligent, he went to you of his own accord. [18]And we have sent with him the brother whose praise *is* in the gospel throughout all the churches, [19]and not only *that,* but who was also chosen by the churches to travel with us with this gift, which is administered by us to the glory of the Lord Himself and *to show* your ready mind, [20]avoiding this: that anyone should blame us in this lavish gift which is administered by us— [21]providing honorable things, not only in the sight of the Lord, but also in the sight of men.

[22]And we have sent with them our brother whom we have often proved diligent in many things, but now much more diligent, because of the great confidence which *we have* in you. [23]If *anyone inquires* about Titus, *he is* my partner and fellow worker concerning you. Or if our brethren *are inquired about, they are* messengers of the churches, the glory of Christ. [24]Therefore show to them, and[a] before the churches, the proof of your love and of our boasting on your behalf.

ADMINISTERING THE GIFT

9 Now concerning the ministering to the saints, it is superfluous for me to write to you; [2]for I know your willingness, about which I boast of

you to the Macedonians, that Achaia was ready a year ago; and your zeal has stirred up the majority. [3]Yet I have sent the brethren, lest our boasting of you should be in vain in this respect, that, as I said, you may be ready; [4]lest if *some* Macedonians come with me and find you unprepared, we (not to mention you!) should be ashamed of this confident boasting.[a] [5]Therefore I thought it necessary to exhort the brethren to go to you ahead of time, and prepare your generous gift beforehand, which *you had* previously promised, that it may be ready as *a matter of* generosity and not as a grudging obligation.

THE CHEERFUL GIVER

[6]But this *I say:* He who sows sparingly will also reap sparingly, and he who sows bountifully will also reap bountifully. [7]So let each one *give* as he purposes in his heart, not grudgingly or of necessity; for God loves a cheerful giver. [8]And God *is* able to make all grace abound toward you, that you, always having all sufficiency in all *things,* may have an abundance for every good work. [9]As it is written:

> *"He has dispersed abroad,*
> *He has given to the poor;*
> *His righteousness endures forever."*[a]

[10]Now may[a] He who supplies seed to the sower, and bread for food, supply and multiply the seed you have *sown* and increase the fruits of your righteousness, [11]while *you are* enriched in everything for all liberality, which causes thanksgiving through us to God. [12]For the administration of this service not only supplies the needs of the saints, but also is abounding through many thanksgivings to God, [13]while, through the proof of this ministry, they glorify God for the obedience of your confession to the gospel of Christ, and for *your* liberal sharing with them and all *men,* [14]and by their prayer for you, who long for you because of the exceeding grace of God in you. [15]Thanks *be* to God for His indescribable gift!

8:15 [a]Exodus 16:18   **8:16** [a]NU-Text reads *has put.*   **8:24** [a]NU-Text and M-Text omit *and.*   **9:4** [a]NU-Text reads *this confidence.*
9:9 [a]Psalm 112:9   **9:10** [a]NU-Text reads *Now He who supplies . . . will supply. . . .*

LEADERSHIP ISSUES

GC2: Christ's Community: Enjoying Community

2 CORINTHIANS 9:8 *And God is able to make all grace abound toward you, that you, always having all sufficiency in all things, may have an abundance for every good work.*

Consider for a moment the abundant grace of God of which Paul speaks in this passage. God's grace—His unmerited favor—has, at times, been expressed toward you as:

- acceptance when you have failed (Rom. 15:7).
- encouragement when you were down (1 Thess. 5:11).
- support when you have struggled (Gal. 6:2).

Then pause to ask God, *"How could I better express Your grace to others?"* Ask Him specifically about how better to express acceptance, encouragement, and support. Listen—be still. Allow God's Spirit to reveal who needs to receive His glorious grace through you. Then complete the following sentences:

I could better express God's abundant grace as I take initiative to give

- *acceptance to* _____.
- *encouragement to* _____.
- *support to* _____.

GC2
GREAT COMMANDMENT
COMMISSION

THE SPIRITUAL WAR

10 Now I, Paul, myself am pleading with you by the meekness and gentleness of Christ—who in presence *am* lowly among you, but being absent am bold toward you. ²But I beg *you* that when I am present I may not be bold with that confidence by which I intend to be bold against some, who think of us as if we walked according to the flesh. ³For though we walk in the flesh, we do not war according to the flesh. ⁴For the weapons of our warfare *are* not carnal but mighty in God for pulling down strongholds, ⁵casting down arguments and every high thing that exalts itself against the knowledge of God, bringing every thought into captivity to the obedience of Christ, ⁶and being ready to punish all disobedience when your obedience is fulfilled.

REALITY OF PAUL'S AUTHORITY

⁷Do you look at things according to the outward appearance? If anyone is convinced in himself that he is Christ's, let him again consider this in himself, that just as he *is* Christ's, even so we *are* Christ's.ᵃ ⁸For even if I should boast somewhat more about our authority, which the Lord gave usᵃ for edification and not for your destruction, I shall not be ashamed— ⁹lest I seem to terrify you by letters. ¹⁰"For *his* letters," they say, "*are* weighty and powerful, but *his* bodily presence *is* weak, and *his* speech contemptible." ¹¹Let such a person consider this, that what we are in word by letters when we are absent, such *we will* also *be* in deed when we are present.

LIMITS OF PAUL'S AUTHORITY

¹²For we dare not class ourselves or compare ourselves with those who commend themselves. But they, measuring themselves by themselves, and comparing themselves among themselves, are not wise. ¹³We, however, will not boast beyond measure, but within the limits of the sphere which God appointed us—a sphere which especially includes you. ¹⁴For we are not overextending ourselves (as though *our authority* did not extend to you), for it was to you that we came with the gospel of Christ; ¹⁵not boasting of things beyond measure, *that is,* in other men's labors, but having hope, *that* as your faith is increased, we

shall be greatly enlarged by you in our sphere, ¹⁶to preach the gospel in the *regions* beyond you, *and* not to boast in another man's sphere of accomplishment.

¹⁷But *"he who glories, let him glory in the LORD."*ᵃ ¹⁸For not he who commends himself is approved, but whom the Lord commends.

CONCERN FOR THEIR FAITHFULNESS

11 Oh, that you would bear with me in a little folly—and indeed you do bear with me. ²For I am jealous for you with godly jealousy. For I have betrothed you to one husband, that I may present *you as* a chaste virgin to Christ. ³But I fear, lest somehow, as the serpent deceived Eve by his craftiness, so your minds may be corrupted from the simplicityᵃ that is in Christ. ⁴For if he who comes preaches another Jesus whom we have not preached, or *if* you receive a different spirit which you have not received, or a different gospel which you have not accepted—you may well put up with it!

PAUL AND FALSE APOSTLES

⁵For I consider that I am not at all inferior to the most eminent apostles. ⁶Even though *I am* untrained in speech, yet *I am* not in knowledge. But we have been thoroughly manifestedᵃ among you in all things.

⁷Did I commit sin in humbling myself that you might be exalted, because I preached the gospel of God to you free of charge? ⁸I robbed other churches, taking wages *from them* to minister to you. ⁹And when I was present with you, and in need, I was a burden to no one, for what I lacked the brethren who came from Macedonia supplied. And in everything I kept myself from being burdensome to you, and so I will keep *myself.* ¹⁰As the truth of Christ is in me, no one shall stop me from this boasting in the regions of Achaia. ¹¹Why? Because I do not love you? God knows!

¹²But what I do, I will also continue to do, that I may cut off the opportunity from those who desire an opportunity to be regarded just as we are in the things of which they boast. ¹³For

10:7 ᵃNU-Text reads *even as we are.*   **10:8** ᵃNU-Text omits *us.*   **10:17** ᵃJeremiah 9:24   **11:3** ᵃNU-Text adds *and purity.*   **11:6** ᵃNU-Text omits *been.*

THROUGH THE GRID

Christ's Community:
Relevant vs. Irrelevant

2 CORINTHIANS 11:3   *But I fear, lest somehow, as the serpent deceived Eve by his crafti-ness, so your minds may be corrupted from the simplicity that is in Christ.*

Is it possible that our culture no longer sees Christ's church as relevant to its needs because we have lost touch with the very heart of who we are? Could it be that the Holy Spirit is drawing us back to our true identity as fol-lowers of Christ?

Fundamentally, the gospel promise of new life is about a Person; it is about the One who lived and died and rose again on our behalf. It is for this rea-son that the foundations of our faith must be relational. Jesus lived and died so that we might have life eternal with Him. He has now equipped us to live out the wonder of this relationship as His light in a darkened world.

Is it possible that in the complexity of our lives and ministries, we have been led astray from our sincere and pure devotion to Christ? Is it possible that God would say of us that we have made the journey so complex and, as a result, so irrelevant that the Spirit of God is shaking things up in order to bring us back to the core of our faith? (Heb. 12:27).

Pause to celebrate that the "core" of our faith is a Person named Jesus!

such *are* false apostles, deceitful workers, trans-forming themselves into apostles of Christ. [14]And no wonder! For Satan himself transforms himself into an angel of light. [15]Therefore *it is* no great thing if his ministers also transform themselves into ministers of righteousness, whose end will be according to their works.

Reluctant Boasting

[16]I say again, let no one think me a fool. If otherwise, at least receive me as a fool, that I also may boast a little. [17]What I speak, I speak not ac-cording to the Lord, but as it were, foolishly, in this confidence of boasting. [18]Seeing that many boast according to the flesh, I also will boast. [19]For you put up with fools gladly, since you *yourselves* are wise! [20]For you put up with it if one brings you into bondage, if one devours *you,* if one takes *from you,* if one exalts himself, if one strikes you on the face. [21]To *our* shame I say that we were too weak for that! But in whatever anyone is bold—I speak foolishly—I am bold also.

Suffering for Christ

[22]Are they Hebrews? So *am* I. Are they Is-raelites? So *am* I. Are they the seed of Abraham? So *am* I. [23]Are they ministers of Christ?—I speak as a fool—I *am* more: in labors more abundant, in stripes above measure, in prisons more frequently, in deaths often. [24]From the Jews five times I re-ceived forty *stripes* minus one. [25]Three times I was beaten with rods; once I was stoned; three times I was shipwrecked; a night and a day I have been in the deep; [26]*in* journeys often, *in* perils of waters, *in* perils of robbers, *in* perils of *my own* countrymen, *in* perils of the Gentiles, *in* perils in the city, *in* perils in the wilderness, *in* perils in the sea, *in* per-ils among false brethren; [27]in weariness and toil, in sleeplessness often, in hunger and thirst, in fastings often, in cold and nakedness— [28]besides the other things, what comes upon me daily: my deep con-cern for all the churches. [29]Who is weak, and I am not weak? Who is made to stumble, and I do not burn *with indignation?*

³⁰If I must boast, I will boast in the things which concern my infirmity. ³¹The God and Father of our Lord Jesus Christ, who is blessed forever, knows that I am not lying. ³²In Damascus the governor, under Aretas the king, was guarding the city of the Damascenes with a garrison, desiring to arrest me; ³³but I was let down in a basket through a window in the wall, and escaped from his hands.

The Vision of Paradise

12It is doubtless[a] not profitable for me to boast. I will come to visions and revelations of the Lord: ²I know a man in Christ who fourteen years ago—whether in the body I do not know, or whether out of the body I do not know, God knows—such a one was caught up to the third heaven. ³And I know such a man—whether in the body or out of the body I do not know, God knows— ⁴how he was caught up into Paradise and heard inexpressible words, which it is not lawful for a man to utter. ⁵Of such a one I will boast; yet of myself I will not boast, except in my infirmities. ⁶For though I might desire to boast, I will not be a fool; for I will speak the truth. But I refrain, lest anyone should think of me above what he sees me *to be* or hears from me.

The Thorn in the Flesh

⁷And lest I should be exalted above measure by the abundance of the revelations, a thorn in the flesh was given to me, a messenger of Satan to buffet me, lest I be exalted above measure. ⁸Concerning this thing I pleaded with the Lord three times that it might depart from me. ⁹And He said to me, "My grace is sufficient for you, for My strength is made perfect in weakness." Therefore most gladly I will rather boast in my infirmities, that the power of Christ may rest upon me. ¹⁰Therefore I take pleasure in infirmities, in reproaches, in needs, in persecutions, in distresses, for Christ's sake. For when I am weak, then I am strong.

Signs of an Apostle

¹¹I have become a fool in boasting;[a] you have compelled me. For I ought to have been commended by you; for in nothing was I behind the most eminent apostles, though I am nothing.

¹²Truly the signs of an apostle were accomplished among you with all perseverance, in signs and wonders and mighty deeds. ¹³For what is it in which you were inferior to other churches, except that I myself was not burdensome to you? Forgive me this wrong!

Love for the Church

¹⁴Now *for* the third time I am ready to come to you. And I will not be burdensome to you; for I do not seek yours, but you. For the children ought not to lay up for the parents, but the parents for the children. ¹⁵And I will very gladly spend and be spent for your souls; though the more abundantly I love you, the less I am loved.

¹⁶But be that *as it may,* I did not burden you. Nevertheless, being crafty, I caught you by cunning! ¹⁷Did I take advantage of you by any of those whom I sent to you? ¹⁸I urged Titus, and sent our brother with *him.* Did Titus take advantage of you? Did we not walk in the same spirit? Did *we* not *walk* in the same steps?

¹⁹Again, do you think[a] that we excuse ourselves to you? We speak before God in Christ. But *we do* all things, beloved, for your edification. ²⁰For I fear lest, when I come, I shall not find you such as I wish, and *that* I shall be found by you such as you do not wish; lest *there be* contentions, jealousies, outbursts of wrath, selfish ambitions, backbitings, whisperings, conceits, tumults; ²¹lest, when I come again, my God will humble me among you, and I shall mourn for many who have sinned before and have not repented of the uncleanness, fornication, and lewdness which they have practiced.

Coming with Authority

13This *will be* the third *time* I am coming to you. *"By the mouth of two or three witnesses every word shall be established."*[a] ²I have told you before, and foretell as if I were present the second time, and now being absent I write[a] to those who have sinned before, and to all the rest, that if I come again I will not spare— ³since you seek a proof of Christ speaking in me, who is not

12:1 ªNU-Text reads *necessary, though not profitable, to boast.* **12:11** ªNU-Text omits *in boasting.* **12:19** ªNU-Text reads *You have been thinking for a long time.* . . . **13:1** ªDeuteronomy 19:15 **13:2** ªNU-Text omits *I write.*

weak toward you, but mighty in you. ⁴For though He was crucified in weakness, yet He lives by the power of God. For we also are weak in Him, but we shall live with Him by the power of God toward you.

⁵Examine yourselves *as to* whether you are in the faith. Test yourselves. Do you not know yourselves, that Jesus Christ is in you?—unless indeed you are disqualified. ⁶But I trust that you will know that we are not disqualified.

PAUL PREFERS GENTLENESS

⁷Now I[a] pray to God that you do no evil, not that we should appear approved, but that you should do what is honorable, though we may seem disqualified. ⁸For we can do nothing against the truth, but for the truth. ⁹For we are glad when we are weak and you are strong. And this also we pray, that you may be made complete. ¹⁰Therefore I write these things being absent, lest being present I should use sharpness, according to the authority which the Lord has given me for edification and not for destruction.

GREETINGS AND BENEDICTION

¹¹Finally, brethren, farewell. Become complete. Be of good comfort, be of one mind, live in peace; and the God of love and peace will be with you.

¹²Greet one another with a holy kiss.

¹³All the saints greet you.

¹⁴The grace of the Lord Jesus Christ, and the love of God, and the communion of the Holy Spirit *be* with you all. Amen.

13:7 [a]NU-Text reads *we.*

IMPACT OF THE BOOK

GALATIANS

IDEA

Any gospel different from the one Christ preached is a false gospel.

MESSAGE

Good leaders do not run from a confrontation nor are they quick to run into a fight. They pick battles wisely, as Paul did, knowing that if someone was perverting the truth of the gospel, then he had to make a stand. God is still looking for men and women who will not be afraid to stand boldly for the truth.

PEOPLE

Abraham, Hagar, Isaac, Ishmael, Judaizers, Paul, Sarah

AUTHOR

Paul wrote to the Galatians because he was concerned that they were deserting the gospel he had preached to them—turning to another gospel (1:6, 7)

CULTURE

A group commonly referred to as the "Judaizers" were presenting a gospel based on works of the Law, and Paul decried this "different gospel" as no gospel at all (1:7). This group was spreading a dangerous teaching that Gentiles must first become Jewish proselytes and submit to all the Mosaic Law before they could become Christians (1:7; 4:17, 21; 5:2–12; 6:12,13). Shocked by the Galatians' openness to this dangerous heresy, Paul wrote this letter to defend justification by faith and to warn these churches of the dire consequences of abandoning the essential doctrine he had faithfully taught them. The letter was addressed to the churches that Paul founded in the southern area of Galatia—Antioch, Iconium, Lystra, and Derbe (Acts 13:14–14:23)—during his first missionary journey. Evidently, the Galatians were quick-tempered, impulsive, and fickle—one day showing Paul great reverence and respect, the next wanting him dead (Gal. 4:13–16).

TIMELINE

c. AD 51–55

KEY SCRIPTURE MEMORY VERSES

2:16, 20, 21; 5:16, 22, 23; 6:7–9

GREETING

1 Paul, an apostle (not from men nor through man, but through Jesus Christ and God the Father who raised Him from the dead), [2]and all the brethren who are with me,

To the churches of Galatia:

[3]Grace to you and peace from God the Father and our Lord Jesus Christ, [4]who gave Himself for our sins, that He might deliver us from this present evil age, according to the will of our God and Father, [5]to whom be glory forever and ever. Amen.

ONLY ONE GOSPEL

[6]I marvel that you are turning away so soon from Him who called you in the grace of Christ, to a different gospel, [7]which is not another; but there are some who trouble you and want to pervert the gospel of Christ. [8]But even if we, or an angel from heaven, preach any other gospel to you than what we have preached to you, let him be accursed. [9]As we have said before, so now I say again, if anyone preaches any other gospel to you than what you have received, let him be accursed.

[10]For do I now persuade men, or God? Or do I seek to please men? For if I still pleased men, I would not be a bondservant of Christ.

CALL TO APOSTLESHIP

[11]But I make known to you, brethren, that the gospel which was preached by me is not according to man. [12]For I neither received it from man, nor was I taught it, but it came through the revelation of Jesus Christ.

[13]For you have heard of my former conduct in Judaism, how I persecuted the church of God beyond measure and tried to destroy it. [14]And I advanced in Judaism beyond many of my contemporaries in my own nation, being more exceedingly zealous for the traditions of my fathers.

[15]But when it pleased God, who separated me from my mother's womb and called me through His grace, [16]to reveal His Son in me, that I might preach Him among the Gentiles, I did not immediately confer with flesh and blood, [17]nor did I go up to Jerusalem to those who were apostles before

me; but I went to Arabia, and returned again to Damascus.

CONTACTS AT JERUSALEM

[18]Then after three years I went up to Jerusalem to see Peter,[a] and remained with him fifteen days. [19]But I saw none of the other apostles except James, the Lord's brother. [20](Now concerning the things which I write to you, indeed, before God, I do not lie.)

[21]Afterward I went into the regions of Syria and Cilicia. [22]And I was unknown by face to the churches of Judea which were in Christ. [23]But they were hearing only, "He who formerly persecuted us now preaches the faith which he once tried to destroy." [24]And they glorified God in me.

DEFENDING THE GOSPEL

2 Then after fourteen years I went up again to Jerusalem with Barnabas, and also took Titus with me. [2]And I went up by revelation, and communicated to them that gospel which I preach among the Gentiles, but privately to those who were of reputation, lest by any means I might run, or had run, in vain. [3]Yet not even Titus who was with me, being a Greek, was compelled to be circumcised. [4]And this occurred because of false brethren secretly brought in (who came in by stealth to spy out our liberty which we have in Christ Jesus, that they might bring us into bondage), [5]to whom we did not yield submission even for an hour, that the truth of the gospel might continue with you.

[6]But from those who seemed to be something—whatever they were, it makes no difference to me; God shows personal favoritism to no man—for those who seemed to be something added nothing to me. [7]But on the contrary, when they saw that the gospel for the uncircumcised had been committed to me, as the gospel for the circumcised was to Peter [8](for He who worked effectively in Peter for the apostleship to the circumcised also worked effectively in me toward the Gentiles), [9]and when James, Cephas, and John, who seemed to be pillars, perceived the grace that had been given to me, they gave me and Barnabas the right hand of fellowship, that we should go to the Gentiles and they to the circumcised. [10]They

1:18 [a]NU-Text reads Cephas.

LEADERSHIP ISSUES

GC2: Good News: Jesus and Close Relationship

GALATIANS 2:20 *I have been crucified with Christ; it is no longer I who live, but Christ lives in me; and the life which I now live in the flesh I live by faith in the Son of God, who loved me and gave Himself for me.*

Through the good news of the gospel, God made it possible for His followers to experience a real relationship with God in Christ. By becoming human and by dying, rising from the dead, and ascending into heaven again, God made all the affection, acceptance, and affirmation of Jesus available to us every moment of our lives through the constant, indwelling presence of the Comforter, His Holy Spirit. "Now hope does not disappoint, because the love of God has been poured out in our hearts by the Holy Spirit who was given to us" (Rom. 5:5; see also John 16:7–15).

That is how Jesus delivers on His promise to His first disciples and to His followers today: "I am with you always, even to the end of the age" (Matt. 28:20). Through the indwelling presence of the Holy Spirit, Jesus is available to us anywhere, anytime, and all the time.

Jesus Christ is not some distant historical figure who lived two thousand years ago. He's not a mythic hero who died on a cross. He is as real as your heartbeat, as relevant as your closest friends, and as "right now" as the latest e-mail or instant message. He is able to literally take up residence within you by His Holy Spirit. He so deeply wants to connect with us and others in our lives that He enters our very being to become one with us. Now that's a close relationship! (John 17:20, 21).

desired only that we should remember the poor, the very thing which I also was eager to do.

No Return to the Law

[11]Now when Peter[a] had come to Antioch, I withstood him to his face, because he was to be blamed; [12]for before certain men came from James, he would eat with the Gentiles; but when they came, he withdrew and separated himself, fearing those who were of the circumcision. [13]And the rest of the Jews also played the hypocrite with him, so that even Barnabas was carried away with their hypocrisy.

[14]But when I saw that they were not straightforward about the truth of the gospel, I said to Peter before *them* all, "If you, being a Jew, live in the manner of Gentiles and not as the Jews, why do you[a] compel Gentiles to live as Jews?[b] [15]We *who are* Jews by nature, and not sinners of the Gentiles, [16]knowing that a man is not justified by the works of the law but by faith in Jesus Christ, even we have believed in Christ Jesus, that we might be justified by faith in Christ and not by the works of the law; for by the works of the law no flesh shall be justified.

[17]"But if, while we seek to be justified by Christ, we ourselves also are found sinners, *is* Christ therefore a minister of sin? Certainly not! [18]For if I build again those things which I destroyed, I make myself a transgressor. [19]For I through the law died to the law that I might live to God. [20]I have been crucified with Christ; it is no longer I who live, but Christ lives in me; and the *life* which I now live in the flesh I live by faith in the Son of God, who loved me and gave Himself for me. [21]I do not set aside the grace of God; for if righteousness *comes* through the law, then Christ died in vain."

Justification by Faith

3 O foolish Galatians! Who has bewitched you that you should not obey the truth,[a] before whose eyes Jesus Christ was clearly portrayed among you[b] as crucified? [2]This only I want to learn from you: Did you receive the Spirit by the works of the law, or by the hearing of faith? [3]Are you so foolish? Having begun in the Spirit, are you now being made perfect by the flesh? [4]Have you suffered so many things in vain—if indeed *it was* in vain?

[5]Therefore He who supplies the Spirit to you and works miracles among you, *does He do it* by the works of the law, or by the hearing of faith?— [6]just as Abraham *"believed God, and it was accounted to him for righteousness."*[a] [7]Therefore know that *only* those who are of faith are sons of Abraham. [8]And the Scripture, foreseeing that God would justify the Gentiles by faith, preached the gospel to Abraham beforehand, *saying, "In you all the nations shall be blessed."*[a] [9]So then those who *are* of faith are blessed with believing Abraham.

The Law Brings a Curse

[10]For as many as are of the works of the law are under the curse; for it is written, *"Cursed is everyone who does not continue in all things which are written in the book of the law, to do them."*[a] [11]But that no one is justified by the law in the sight of God *is* evident, for *"the just shall live by faith."* [a] [12]Yet the law is not of faith, but *"the man who does them shall live by them."*[a]

[13]Christ has redeemed us from the curse of the law, having become a curse for us (for it is written, *"Cursed is everyone who hangs on a tree"*[a]), [14]that the blessing of Abraham might come upon the Gentiles in Christ Jesus, that we might receive the promise of the Spirit through faith.

The Changeless Promise

[15]Brethren, I speak in the manner of men: Though *it is* only a man's covenant, yet *if it is* confirmed, no one annuls or adds to it. [16]Now to Abraham and his Seed were the promises made. He does not say, "And to seeds," as of many, but of one, *"And to your Seed,"*[a] who is Christ. [17]And this I say, *that* the law, which was four hundred and thirty years later, cannot annul the covenant that was confirmed before by God in Christ,[a] that it should make the promise of no effect. [18]For if the inheritance *is* of the law, *it is* no longer of promise; but God gave *it* to Abraham by promise.

2:11 [a]NU-Text reads *Cephas.* 2:14 [a]NU-Text reads *how can you.* [b]Some interpreters stop the quotation here. 3:1 [a]NU-Text omits *that you should not obey the truth.* [b]NU-Text omits *among you.* 3:6 [a]Genesis 15:6 3:8 [a]Genesis 12:3; 18:18; 22:18; 26:4; 28:14 3:10 [a]Deuteronomy 27:26 3:11 [a]Habakkuk 2:4 3:12 [a]Leviticus 18:5 3:13 [a]Deuteronomy 21:23 3:16 [a]Genesis 12:7; 13:15; 24:7 3:17 [a]NU-Text omits *in Christ.*

LEADERSHIP ISSUES

GC2: Faith Is Sacrificial

GALATIANS 3:11

The "shock" of Galatians 3:11's few words has drawn many great saints into a deepened intimacy with Jesus. No amount of rule-keeping or good works can gain eternal life for us—only the simplicity of faith in a Person named Jesus (Titus 3:5)! Key to this reality is: Jesus, through His sacrificial love, has ALREADY done all that needs be done!

In stark contrast to the first Adam's selfish taking, the Second Adam, Jesus, willingly laid down His life for others. He believed by faith that the Father would bring forth unimaginable good through His sacrifice; so it is with faith-filled followers of Jesus. Confident that their heavenly Father is thinking of and caring for them, maturing disciples are free to think of and care for others. The temptation to take greedily is replaced by the desire to give graciously. The self-centered life gives way to one in which the Holy Spirit often whispers, "It's not about you—it's about Him! And Jesus wants it to be about 'them'!"

"Them?"—Who are they in your life? Who needs to experience His life and love through you?

Recall that in the final hours of His earthly life, as Jewish leaders plotted His death, Jesus Christ, well aware of His true identity, calling, and destiny, focused His attention on those nearest Him. He sacrificially took on the role of the lowest servant and washed their feet (John 13:4, 5). What sacrifices might others need from you? Who might you be able to serve as you grow in mature faith?

As my confidence in God's care and provision grows, I will be freed to sacrificially serve _____ *by* _____
_____ .

(For example: *As my confidence in God's care and provision grows, I will be freed to sacrificially serve my family by helping to clean around the house; those less fortunate through our youth missions ministry; younger students in personal discipleship.*)

GC2
GREAT COMMANDMENT
COMMISSION

PURPOSE OF THE LAW

[19]What purpose then *does* the law *serve?* It was added because of transgressions, till the Seed should come to whom the promise was made; *and it was* appointed through angels by the hand of a mediator. [20]Now a mediator does not *mediate* for one *only,* but God is one.

[21]*Is* the law then against the promises of God? Certainly not! For if there had been a law given which could have given life, truly righteousness would have been by the law. [22]But the Scripture has confined all under sin, that the promise by faith in Jesus Christ might be given to those who believe. [23]But before faith came, we were kept under guard by the law, kept for the faith which would afterward be revealed. [24]Therefore the law was our tutor *to bring us* to Christ, that we might be justified by faith. [25]But after faith has come, we are no longer under a tutor.

SONS AND HEIRS

[26]For you are all sons of God through faith in Christ Jesus. [27]For as many of you as were baptized into Christ have put on Christ. [28]There is neither Jew nor Greek, there is neither slave nor free, there is neither male nor female; for you are all one in Christ Jesus. [29]And if you *are* Christ's, then you are Abraham's seed, and heirs according to the promise.

4 Now I say *that* the heir, as long as he is a child, does not differ at all from a slave, though he is master of all, [2]but is under guardians and stewards until the time appointed by the father. [3]Even so we, when we were children, were in bondage under the elements of the world. [4]But when the fullness of the time had come, God sent forth His Son, born[a] of a woman, born under the law, [5]to redeem those who were under the law, that we might receive the adoption as sons.

[6]And because you are sons, God has sent forth the Spirit of His Son into your hearts, crying out, "Abba, Father!" [7]Therefore you are no longer a slave but a son, and if a son, then an heir of[a] God through Christ.

FEARS FOR THE CHURCH

[8]But then, indeed, when you did not know God, you served those which by nature are not gods. [9]But now after you have known God, or rather are known by God, how *is it that* you turn again to the weak and beggarly elements, to which you desire again to be in bondage? [10]You observe days and months and seasons and years. [11]I am afraid for you, lest I have labored for you in vain.

[12]Brethren, I urge you to become like me, for I *became* like you. You have not injured me at all. [13]You know that because of physical infirmity I preached the gospel to you at the first. [14]And my trial which was in my flesh you did not despise or reject, but you received me as an angel of God, *even* as Christ Jesus. [15]What[a] then was the blessing you *enjoyed?* For I bear you witness that, if possible, you would have plucked out your own eyes and given them to me. [16]Have I therefore become your enemy because I tell you the truth?

[17]They zealously court you, *but* for no good; yes, they want to exclude you, that you may be zealous for them. [18]But it is good to be zealous in a good thing always, and not only when I am present with you. [19]My little children, for whom I labor in birth again until Christ is formed in you, [20]I would like to be present with you now and to change my tone; for I have doubts about you.

TWO COVENANTS

[21]Tell me, you who desire to be under the law, do you not hear the law? [22]For it is written that Abraham had two sons: the one by a bondwoman, the other by a freewoman. [23]But he *who was* of the bondwoman was born according to the flesh, and he of the freewoman through promise, [24]which things are symbolic. For these are the[a] two covenants: the one from Mount Sinai which gives birth to bondage, which is Hagar— [25]for this Hagar is Mount Sinai in Arabia, and corresponds to Jerusalem which now is, and is in bondage with her children— [26]but the Jerusalem above is free, which is the mother of us all. [27]For it is written:

> "Rejoice, O barren,
> You who do not bear!
> Break forth and shout,

4:4 [a]Or *made*   **4:7** [a]NU-Text reads *through God* and omits *through Christ.*   **4:15** [a]NU-Text reads *Where.*   **4:24** [a]NU-Text and M-Text omit *the.*

LEADERSHIP ISSUES

GC2: Becoming a Good Samaritan: Free to Love

GALATIANS 5:13

Imagine people studying the familiar principle God gave us in John 8:32, which says, "And you shall know the truth, and the truth shall make you free." What if we then ask, "Free to what?" We often find Christians convinced that truth will set them free, but they haven't thought about the purpose of that freedom. Week after week people leave church convinced that God's Word is true and it really will set you free, but they haven't yet discovered the purpose of truth setting them free. They know that truth can set them free from some bad or disturbing things, but once set free, they lack clarity about God's purpose for their freedom. God's answer can be found in Galatians 5:13. The purpose of being set free by God's truth is that we might love and serve better!

It is important to sense that God is using His truth to set us free for the purpose of love. His purpose is expressed through us as we lovingly convey compassion to people around us. We are free to be moved by the Holy Spirit to feel and communicate His compassionate heart toward other people (see Matt. 9:36–38). Think of the impact of this work of God in us to an unbelieving world. Recall the account of Jesus coming to be with Mary and Martha after their brother had died. Jesus saw Mary weeping and was moved to hurt with Mary—"Jesus wept" (John 11:35). The next verse says that the unbelieving Jews noticed that and said, "See how He loved him!" Later in that chapter, we see that many of those Jews came to believe in Christ. In a world where love is growing cold, people will be startled by the fact that we care. God's compassion ministered through us will affect them as it did those unbelieving Jews—"See how He loved him!" Oh, that it might be said of us!

GC2
GREAT COMMANDMENT
COMMISSION

You who are not in labor!
For the desolate has many more children
Than she who has a husband."[a]

[28]Now we, brethren, as Isaac *was,* are children of promise. [29]But, as he who was born according to the flesh then persecuted him *who was born* according to the Spirit, even so *it is* now. [30]Nevertheless what does the Scripture say? *"Cast out the bondwoman and her son, for the son of the bondwoman shall not be heir with the son of the freewoman."*[a] [31]So then, brethren, we are not children of the bondwoman but of the free.

CHRISTIAN LIBERTY

5 Stand fast therefore in the liberty by which Christ has made us free,[a] and do not be entangled again with a yoke of bondage. [2]Indeed I, Paul, say to you that if you become circumcised, Christ will profit you nothing. [3]And I testify again to every man who becomes circumcised that he is a debtor to keep the whole law. [4]You have become estranged from Christ, you who *attempt to* be justified by law; you have fallen from grace. [5]For we

4:27 [a]Isaiah 54:1   4:30 [a]Genesis 21:10   5:1 [a]NU-Text reads *For freedom Christ has made us free; stand fast therefore.*

THROUGH THE GRID

Written by the Hand of God: The Principle of Sowing and Reaping

GALATIANS 6:7   *Do not be deceived, God is not mocked; for whatever a man sows, that he will also reap.*

Spiritual laws are just as binding as physical ones, but we forget this when we break God's commands. People may try to disregard the consequences of their sin or ignore the rules set by their authorities, but this demonstrates that they have misunderstood the purpose of the Ten Commandments, as they produce liberation, not bondage. The Ten Commandments are the standard God uses to judge our lives.

Whenever we sow good habits, we reap good results. But if we sow bad habits, we reap brokenness and spiritual harm. We will reap what we sow—this rule of cause and effect is especially true spiritually. In order to reap a spiritual harvest, we must see our own behavior from God's perspective, and we must acknowledge that God knows and sees everything. Sin is sin, no matter how you cut it. God abhors sin, and to think that we can sin without God noticing dishonors God and His omniscience. Our decisions in life are serious, because they carry serious consequences. Reaping a spiritual harvest also involves looking forward to the final judgment. To deny this is to deny the accountability that we should have.

Another way we can reap what we sow is to sow godly relationships with other people. The more we sow godly behavior, the more others will see us as a witness to the God of the universe. We must sow and invest in relationships with other people by going out and witnessing, in obedience to God's command to make disciples. The more we sow in evangelism, the more we reap. Remember that when we evangelize others, we are presenting God's offering to them—an eternity with Him! The investments we make in relationships may not pay off in the immediate moment, but you never know how and when the Holy Spirit will move in their lives and use what you have said for God's glory, drawing them to Himself.

LEADERSHIP ISSUES

GC2: Providing Support

GALATIANS 6:2

The need for support can be met by coming alongside someone who is struggling with a problem and providing appropriate assistance. During His earthly ministry, Jesus invited the multitudes: "Come to Me, all you who labor and are heavy laden, and I will give you rest" (Matt. 11:28). He provided physical, emotional, and spiritual support for people who were struggling. Often, His miracles of healing and provision provided tangible support.

How has God met our need for support? He met our ultimate need for support by anticipating the great burden that we could not bear ourselves (the penalty for our sins). God also committed His personal resources (His Son Jesus) to do whatever it took to bear our burdens. He was tempted in all ways and suffered in all ways. The Holy Spirit is given to us as the "Paraclete"—the "One called alongside" who will teach (John 16:12–15), encourage (Acts 9:31), comfort (John 14:16), assure (Rom. 8:16), guide (Rom. 8:14), and intercede (Rom. 8:26) for us.

Pause and reflect on these ideas for giving others support:

- I often get involved in helping others when they are in need.
- I often ask others "How can I help?"
- I often attend school activities, recitals, sports activities, family activities, etc., just to show my care for someone.
- I often use personal resources to help "bless" others.
- I willingly defer my plans, agenda, and schedule in order to be available for others.

Becoming a person who *gives support* will help prepare you for healthy, God-honoring relationships.

through the Spirit eagerly wait for the hope of righteousness by faith. [6]For in Christ Jesus neither circumcision nor uncircumcision avails anything, but faith working through love.

LOVE FULFILLS THE LAW

[7]You ran well. Who hindered you from obeying the truth? [8]This persuasion does not *come* from Him who calls you. [9]A little leaven leavens the whole lump. [10]I have confidence in you, in the Lord, that you will have no other mind; but he who troubles you shall bear his judgment, whoever he is.

[11]And I, brethren, if I still preach circumcision, why do I still suffer persecution? Then the offense of the cross has ceased. [12]I could wish that those who trouble you would even cut themselves off!

[13]For you, brethren, have been called to liberty; only do not *use* liberty as an opportunity for the flesh, but through love serve one another. [14]For all the law is fulfilled in one word, *even* in this: *"You shall love your neighbor as yourself."*[a]

[15]But if you bite and devour one another, beware lest you be consumed by one another!

WALKING IN THE SPIRIT

[16]I say then: Walk in the Spirit, and you shall not fulfill the lust of the flesh. [17]For the flesh lusts against the Spirit, and the Spirit against the flesh; and these are contrary to one another, so that you do not do the things that you wish. [18]But if you are led by the Spirit, you are not under the law.

[19]Now the works of the flesh are evident, which are: adultery,[a] fornication, uncleanness, lewdness, [20]idolatry, sorcery, hatred, contentions, jealousies, outbursts of wrath, selfish ambitions, dissensions, heresies, [21]envy, murders,[a] drunkenness, revelries, and the like; of which I tell you beforehand, just as I also told *you* in time past, that those who practice such things will not inherit the kingdom of God.

[22]But the fruit of the Spirit is love, joy, peace, longsuffering, kindness, goodness, faithfulness,

5:14 [a]Leviticus 19:18 **5:19** [a]NU-Text omits *adultery.* **5:21** [a]NU-Text omits *murders.*

LEADERSHIP REALITIES

THE LAW OF THE HARVEST *Galatians 6:7–10*

Some critics of the Bible say that it's too difficult for the average person to understand. That may be the case for certain prophetic passages, but not in this case. Two plain but powerful truths are evident:

1. Don't even think about getting away with deceit or halfheartedness.
2. What you put into life is what you get out.

The law of the harvest tells the farmer that if he plants seed corn, he will harvest corn. If he plants an apple seed, he will get an apple tree. Likewise, habits planted in youth take root and bear fruit into adult years.

Don't fool yourself or try to mock God; you can't live any way you want now and think, *Later, when I am an adult, I'll become a leader. I'll choose a life of excellence then.*

Choose in your youth not to plant seeds of shortcuts, halfheartedness, and procrastination. Plant the seed of virtue now; and allow enough time for the seeds to germinate, to make their own living plants, to grow strong, and to produce fruit.

The seed of moral excellence gives life to every choice and action in life. It bears the fruit of integrity, consistency, commitment, and loyalty.

²³gentleness, self-control. Against such there is no law. ²⁴And those *who are* Christ's have crucified the flesh with its passions and desires. ²⁵If we live in the Spirit, let us also walk in the Spirit. ²⁶Let us not become conceited, provoking one another, envying one another.

Bear and Share the Burdens

6Brethren, if a man is overtaken in any trespass, you who *are* spiritual restore such a one in a spirit of gentleness, considering yourself lest you also be tempted. ²Bear one another's burdens, and so fulfill the law of Christ. ³For if anyone thinks himself to be something, when he is nothing, he deceives himself. ⁴But let each one examine his own work, and then he will have rejoicing in himself alone, and not in another. ⁵For each one shall bear his own load.

Be Generous and Do Good

⁶Let him who is taught the word share in all good things with him who teaches.

⁷Do not be deceived, God is not mocked; for whatever a man sows, that he will also reap. ⁸For he who sows to his flesh will of the flesh reap corruption, but he who sows to the Spirit will of the Spirit reap everlasting life. ⁹And let us not grow weary while doing good, for in due season we shall reap if we do not lose heart. ¹⁰Therefore, as we have opportunity, let us do good to all, especially to those who are of the household of faith.

Glory Only in the Cross

¹¹See with what large letters I have written to you with my own hand! ¹²As many as desire to make a good showing in the flesh, these *would* compel you to be circumcised, only that they may not suffer persecution for the cross of Christ. ¹³For not even those who are circumcised keep the law, but they desire to have you circumcised that they may boast in your flesh. ¹⁴But God forbid that I should boast except in the cross of our Lord Jesus Christ, by whomᵃ the world has been crucified to me, and I to the world. ¹⁵For in Christ Jesus neither circumcision nor uncircumcision avails anything, but a new creation.

Blessing and a Plea

¹⁶And as many as walk according to this rule, peace and mercy *be* upon them, and upon the Israel of God.

¹⁷From now on let no one trouble me, for I bear in my body the marks of the Lord Jesus.

¹⁸Brethren, the grace of our Lord Jesus Christ *be* with your spirit. Amen.

6:14 ᵃOr *by which* (the cross)

IMPACT OF THE BOOK

EPHESIANS

I   IDEA | *In its diversity, the church is to be the greatest picture of unity. Believers should have an obviously different perspective because of our position in Christ—sitting in "heavenly places" (3:10).*

M   MESSAGE | *Good leaders know how to cultivate unity in diversity by empowering people to use their unique gifts and talents to build up the body of Christ. Each individual body part is crucial to the health and the performance of the entire body. This book shows the balance between doctrine and duty. What God has done for us is laid out in chapters 1—3, and what we should do for God is laid out in chapters 4—6. Leaders should be greatly encouraged by Ephesians 6: everything for spiritual warfare is provided for us, but it must be "taken up" and "put on."*

P   PEOPLE | *Paul, Timothy, Tychicus*

A   AUTHOR | *Paul intended this epistle to circulate among churches; it was first sent to the Ephesian church in Asia Minor.*

C   CULTURE | *Ephesus was a very influential city located on the eastern portion of the Aegean Sea, modern day Turkey. It boasted the world-renowned Temple of Diana (or "Artemis" in Greek mythology) and was steeped in paganism and temple prostitution. Paul spent time and effort working with these believers, who influenced the world for Christ. He went with Aquila and Priscilla, to the city on his second missionary journey. On his third journey, he spent three years with them. They understood the persecution he faced and the importance of the gospel message. This epistle holds some of Paul's greatest theology, coupled with practical truths for living.*

T   TIMELINE | *c. AD 60—62*

KEY SCRIPTURE MEMORY VERSES | 1:3–5, 11–14; 2:8–10; 4:11, 12, 26, 27, 29–32; 5:8, 18, 22–33; 6:1, 12–17

GREETING

1 Paul, an apostle of Jesus Christ by the will of God,

To the saints who are in Ephesus, and faithful in Christ Jesus:

²Grace to you and peace from God our Father and the Lord Jesus Christ.

REDEMPTION IN CHRIST

³Blessed *be* the God and Father of our Lord Jesus Christ, who has blessed us with every spiritual blessing in the heavenly *places* in Christ, ⁴just as He chose us in Him before the foundation of the world, that we should be holy and without blame before Him in love, ⁵having predestined us to adoption as sons by Jesus Christ to Himself, according to the good pleasure of His will, ⁶to the praise of the glory of His grace, by which He made us accepted in the Beloved.

⁷In Him we have redemption through His blood, the forgiveness of sins, according to the riches of His grace ⁸which He made to abound toward us in all wisdom and prudence, ⁹having made known to us the mystery of His will, according to His good pleasure which He purposed in Himself, ¹⁰that in the dispensation of the fullness of the times He might gather together in one all things in Christ, both[a] which are in heaven and which are on earth—in Him. ¹¹In Him also we have obtained an inheritance, being predestined according to the purpose of Him who works all things according to the counsel of His will, ¹²that we who first trusted in Christ should be to the praise of His glory.

¹³In Him you also *trusted,* after you heard the word of truth, the gospel of your salvation; in whom also, having believed, you were sealed with the Holy Spirit of promise, ¹⁴who[a] is the guarantee of our inheritance until the redemption of the purchased possession, to the praise of His glory.

PRAYER FOR SPIRITUAL WISDOM

¹⁵Therefore I also, after I heard of your faith in the Lord Jesus and your love for all the saints, ¹⁶do not cease to give thanks for you, making mention of you in my prayers: ¹⁷that the God of our Lord Jesus Christ, the Father of glory, may

give to you the spirit of wisdom and revelation in the knowledge of Him, ¹⁸the eyes of your understanding[a] being enlightened; that you may know what is the hope of His calling, what are the riches of the glory of His inheritance in the saints, ¹⁹and what *is* the exceeding greatness of His power toward us who believe, according to the working of His mighty power ²⁰which He worked in Christ when He raised Him from the dead and seated *Him* at His right hand in the heavenly *places,* ²¹far above all principality and power and might and dominion, and every name that is named, not only in this age but also in that which is to come.

²²And He put all *things* under His feet, and gave Him *to be* head over all *things* to the church, ²³which is His body, the fullness of Him who fills all in all.

BY GRACE THROUGH FAITH

2 And you *He made alive,* who were dead in trespasses and sins, ²in which you once walked according to the course of this world, according to the prince of the power of the air, the spirit who now works in the sons of disobedience, ³among whom also we all once conducted ourselves in the lusts of our flesh, fulfilling the desires of the flesh and of the mind, and were by nature children of wrath, just as the others.

⁴But God, who is rich in mercy, because of His great love with which He loved us, ⁵even when we were dead in trespasses, made us alive together with Christ (by grace you have been saved), ⁶and raised *us* up together, and made *us* sit together in the heavenly *places* in Christ Jesus, ⁷that in the ages to come He might show the exceeding riches of His grace in *His* kindness toward us in Christ Jesus. ⁸For by grace you have been saved through faith, and that not of yourselves; *it is* the gift of God, ⁹not of works, lest anyone should boast. ¹⁰For we are His workmanship, created in Christ Jesus for good works, which God prepared beforehand that we should walk in them.

BROUGHT NEAR BY HIS BLOOD

¹¹Therefore remember that you, once Gentiles in the flesh—who are called Uncircumcision

1:10 ᵃNU-Text and M-Text omit *both.* **1:14** ᵃNU-Text reads *which.*
1:18 ᵃNU-Text and M-Text read *hearts.*

LEADERSHIP ISSUES

GC2: Gratitude for His Grace

EPHESIANS 1:6

Gratitude and praise come natural to Christ's followers who focus often on His grace, His underserved love, and His unmerited favor (Eph. 2:8, 9; 1 Pet. 4:10).

Imagine taking a blank sheet of paper with a line down the middle. On the left side of the paper, you make a list of all the things you've done this week that prompted God to love you *more*; on the right side of the paper, you make a list of all the things you've done this week that caused God to love you *less*. Now before you start frantically writing, your paper should remain blank; that's GRACE!

Pause to reflect upon your experience of the glory of God's grace, recently or in the past. Be still before the Lord, and ask His Spirit to stir up remembrances, perhaps of times when:

- He unexpectedly provided for you.
- He accepted you in the midst of a failure.
- He healed your physical or emotional pain.
- He restored a broken relationship.

Complete the following sentence:

I give thanks and praise to God for the grace He gave me when _____

_____

_____

_____

Share your completed sentence with a friend or small group. Then pray together, and express further thanks and praise to God.

GC2

GREAT COMMANDMENT
COMMISSION

THROUGH THE GRID

Belief Six: Salvation By Grace Alone Through Faith Alone in Christ Alone (*Eph. 2:1–10*)

Salvation is God's work accomplished in us by God's grace alone, through faith alone, in the Lord Jesus Christ alone. Christ's death on the cross allowed all humanity to be redeemed, since all of humanity exists as fallen and sinful. Christ died as our penal substitution and was raised victorious over death in His resurrection (Is. 52:13—53:12; Mark 10:45; Rom. 3:21–26; 1 Cor. 15:1–11; 2 Cor. 5:17–21; Gal. 3:13, 14; Eph. 2:1–10; 1 John 2:1, 2; 4:10). *See Through the Grid article on page 1570.*

by what is called the Circumcision made in the flesh by hands— [12]that at that time you were without Christ, being aliens from the commonwealth of Israel and strangers from the covenants of promise, having no hope and without God in the world. [13]But now in Christ Jesus you who once were far off have been brought near by the blood of Christ.

CHRIST OUR PEACE

[14]For He Himself is our peace, who has made both one, and has broken down the middle wall of separation, [15]having abolished in His flesh the enmity, *that is,* the law of commandments *contained* in ordinances, so as to create in Himself one new man *from* the two, *thus* making peace, [16]and that He might reconcile them both to God in one body through the cross, thereby putting to death the enmity. [17]And He came and preached peace to you who were afar off and to those who were near. [18]For through Him we both have access by one Spirit to the Father.

CHRIST OUR CORNERSTONE

[19]Now, therefore, you are no longer strangers and foreigners, but fellow citizens with the saints and members of the household of God, [20]having been built on the foundation of the apostles and prophets, Jesus Christ Himself being the chief corner*stone,* [21]in whom the

---

THROUGH THE GRID

EPHESIANS 2:4, 5 *But God, who is rich in mercy, because of His great love with which He loved us, even when we were dead in trespasses, made us alive together with Christ (by grace you have been saved).*

We have seen that God is a judge; but God is characterized as merciful, even in His judgments. In God's goodness, our Merciful Judge has become our Gracious Savior. God not only forgives our sins but always acts in abundance of mercy, which we have for all of our lives. God's mercy brings us peace and forgiveness, and it enables us to have grace in our interaction with others as well. God's mercy means God has compassion for us, and it is even evident in God's discipline. God displays His mercy through us, as others can see the mercy of God through the ways in which we are merciful to others. As a result, we should never lose the awe and the appreciation of what God has done for us.

THROUGH THE GRID
Making Sense of Your World: Forces Changing the Church (Eph. 2:11–22)

There are at least three major forces at work in society that have garnered a significant impact on the way in which the church operates and is identified. Relativism, privatization, and individualism have all impacted the dynamics of how the church operates. Relativism has entered the church and claimed that there are not absolutes of truth or of morals. Privatization has also changed the church dynamic by perpetuating the view that one as an individual has a right to keep a private life that is no business of the church's. And individualism also pervades the church, detracting away from dependence on Christ as the "chief cornerstone" (Eph. 2:20).

whole building, being fitted together, grows into a holy temple in the Lord, 22in whom you also are being built together for a dwelling place of God in the Spirit.

The Mystery Revealed

3 For this reason I, Paul, the prisoner of Christ Jesus for you Gentiles— 2if indeed you have heard of the dispensation of the grace of God which was given to me for you, 3how that by revelation He made known to me the mystery (as I have briefly written already, 4by which, when you read, you may understand my knowledge in the mystery of Christ), 5which in other ages was not made known to the sons of men, as it has now been revealed by the Spirit to His holy apostles and prophets: 6that the Gentiles should be fellow heirs, of the same body, and partakers of His

LEADERSHIP REALITIES

FEED YOUR FAITH ON TRUTH *Ephesians 3:20, 21*

The apostle Paul was a leader who possessed a mission that kept him motivated. He demonstrated passion and discipline. He reveals the source of his faith here, a multi-tiered truth, miraculous in magnitude. In the original Greek, this verse can be written as:

First, God is able to do **all that we ask Him to do.**

Second, God is able to do all that we dare not ask but **merely imagine!**

Third, He can do **more** than this!

Fourth, He can do **far more** than this!

Fifth, He can do **very far more** than this!

He then reveals the depth of his gratitude and praise by this Doxology: *Therefore to the One who does not need to overexert Himself in order to fulfill our desires, but can do it with ease.* The phrase "to all generations" is then reinforced with the addition of *forever and ever.* The absolute power in these words is unshakable, unchangeable, and unmatched by any other. This praise refers to the flow of moments from the past to the present and on to the future, continuing on and on without ever coming to an end. As you apply yourself with passion and purity to the wonderful future in front of you, feed your faith these powerful truths.

LEADERSHIP ISSUES

GC2: Unity: Christ the Cornerstone

EPHESIANS 2:19, 20 *Now, therefore, you are no longer strangers and foreigners, but the foundation of the apostles and prophets, Jesus Christ Himself being the chief cornerstone.*

A building of any type is no more solid and stable than its foundation, and so it is with Christ's church. Our unity is found not in total agreement or conformity but in a Person! With Him as the cornerstone—the Eternal One who is the same yesterday, today, and forever—His body, the church, is secure and safe. God has always had a people. Even in the darkest hours of the Dark Ages, the worst hours of Nazism, Communism, or racism, God has always had those who embraced Christ the Cornerstone.

Paul rightly reminds the church at Corinth, a church torn by divisions, conflicts, strife, and sin, that his concern for them was that they had been led astray from the simplicity and purity of devotion to Christ (2 Cor. 11:3). Their unity, as well as ours, relates to our proximity to Christ. When we stay close to Him, Christian brothers "dwell together in unity" (Ps. 133:1), but drifting away from Him causes inevitable division.

Key to our unity in Christ is the Holy Spirit's work of humility within each of us. Just as Christ humbled Himself even to the point of death, so also are we to regard one another as more important than ourselves (Phil. 2:5–8). Consider taking initiative to "give first" to a friend in Christ. Maybe send a text message of encouragement, a surprising gift, or offer of assistance in some way. It is this journey in humility to become a "giving first" person just as Christ "gave first" that will fulfill Paul's prayer for our unity that we be "like-minded, having the same love, being of one accord, of one mind" (Phil. 2:2).

GC2
GREAT COMMANDMENT
COMMISSION

INSIDE *the* INFLUENCERS

THE GOD WHO IS ABLE

EPHESIANS 3:20

Paul praises the God "who is able to do exceedingly abundantly above all that we ask or think" (Eph. 3:20). God isn't just worthy of praise; He's all-powerful. As stated in the previous Leadership Realities, the original Greek paints this picture:

- God is able to do anything **we ask Him to do.**
- Second, God is able to do anything we *dare not ask* but **merely imagine!**
- Third, God can do **more** than this!
- Fourth, God can do **far more** than this!
- Fifth, He God can do **very far more** than this!

Paul then reveals his gratitude and praise to the One Who does not need to over-exert Himself in order to fulfill our desires, but can do it with ease. "To all generations" is then reinforced with *forever and ever.* This means all moments from the past, present and future, never coming to an end.

There are three "*Now to Him who is able*" passages in the New Testament: Eph. 3:20; Jude 1:24—*to keep you from stumbling*; and Rom. 16:25—*to establish you* (to stabilize). The power in these words is unshakable, unchangeable, and unequaled. As you apply yourself with passion to the future before you, feed your faith with these truths—as did Paul and Jude.

promise in Christ through the gospel, [7]of which I became a minister according to the gift of the grace of God given to me by the effective working of His power.

PURPOSE OF THE MYSTERY

[8]To me, who am less than the least of all the saints, this grace was given, that I should preach among the Gentiles the unsearchable riches of Christ, [9]and to make all see what *is* the fellowship[a] of the mystery, which from the beginning of the ages has been hidden in God who created all things through Jesus Christ;[b] [10]to the intent that now the manifold wisdom of God might be made known by the church to the principalities and powers in the heavenly *places,* [11]according to the eternal purpose which He accomplished in Christ Jesus our Lord, [12]in whom we have boldness and access with confidence through faith in Him. [13]Therefore I ask that you do not lose heart at my tribulations for you, which is your glory.

APPRECIATION OF THE MYSTERY

[14]For this reason I bow my knees to the Father of our Lord Jesus Christ,[a] [15]from whom the whole family in heaven and earth is named, [16]that He would grant you, according to the riches of His glory, to be strengthened with might through His Spirit in the inner man, [17]that Christ may dwell in your hearts through faith; that you, being rooted and grounded in love, [18]may be able to comprehend with all the saints what *is* the width and length and depth and height— [19]to know the love of Christ which passes knowledge; that you may be filled with all the fullness of God.

[20]Now to Him who is able to do exceedingly abundantly above all that we ask or think, according to the power that works in us, [21]to Him *be* glory in the church by Christ Jesus to all generations, forever and ever. Amen.

3:9 [a]NU-Text and M-Text read *stewardship (dispensation).* [b]NU-Text omits *through Jesus Christ.* **3:14** [a]NU-Text omits *of our Lord Jesus Christ.*

LEADERSHIP ISSUES

A Worthy Walk

EPHESIANS 4:1

ETHICS has its origin in the Greek and means *moral precepts, rules of conduct and values.* Do not be squeezed in to the mold of those in society and culture who lecture that there are no moral absolutes. We know there is a higher, nobler, unchanging path that God has set forth. Aristotle had it right with what he called "settled habits" of right living. The Ten Commandments and the Sermon on the Mount admonish us to learn the absolutes of virtue and to lean on God for His strength to live up to those standards. Character counts today as much as ever before. Be an action person who feels personally responsible for making any changes in this world that are within your power. Do what is right when no one is looking.

EDUCATION fuels us to heights beyond what we can achieve on our own power. If the focus of your studies centers on getting a degree, you have missed the power of learning. Educate your mind, soul and spirit, and especially your attitude. Aim at going all the way to the top of the mountain in your education, both in the classroom and out. Leaders are learners; leaders are readers, and education prepares you for the road ahead.

"The man who graduates today and stops learning tomorrow is uneducated the day after." (Newton D. Baker)

The individual who fails to plan for the electrifying changes that appear in the immediate future may become in danger of being unemployable." (Dr. Tim LaHaye)

"Great educators have always known that learning is not something you do only in the classroom or under supervision." (Bill Gates)

ENDURANCE: Be known as a finisher and not one who fizzles out. Emotions can steal the show, and they profoundly affect our mental and physical responses. Mentally and spiritually tough people learn how to harness their emotions to create optimal performance. Crystallize your goals. Then, with supreme confidence, determination and disregard for obstacles and other people's criticism carry out your plan.

"Character is doing what is right long after the emotion of the moment of decision has past." (Stephen Covey)

THROUGH THE GRID

Making Sense of Your World: Church as God Intended (Eph. 4:15, 16)

God intended for the church to play an integral role in the development of a biblical worldview, not only as a community of believers who can and should "sharpen each other" as "iron sharpens iron" (Prov. 27:17); but also as a community in which God can demonstrate reconciliation, restoration, as well as accountability.

WALK IN UNITY

4 I, therefore, the prisoner of the Lord, beseech you to walk worthy of the calling with which you were called, [2]with all lowliness and gentleness, with longsuffering, bearing with one another in love, [3]endeavoring to keep the unity of the Spirit in the bond of peace. [4]*There is* one body and one Spirit, just as you were called in one hope of your calling; [5]one Lord, one faith, one baptism; [6]one God and Father of all, who *is* above all, and through all, and in you[a] all.

SPIRITUAL GIFTS

[7]But to each one of us grace was given according to the measure of Christ's gift. [8]Therefore He says:

"When He ascended on high,
He led captivity captive,
And gave gifts to men."[a]

[9](Now this, *"He ascended"*—what does it mean but that He also first[a] descended into the lower

parts of the earth? [10]He who descended is also the One who ascended far above all the heavens, that He might fill all things.)

[11]And He Himself gave some *to be* apostles, some prophets, some evangelists, and some pastors and teachers, [12]for the equipping of the saints for the work of ministry, for the edifying of the body of Christ, [13]till we all come to the unity of the faith and of the knowledge of the Son of God, to a perfect man, to the measure of the stature of the fullness of Christ; [14]that we should no longer be children, tossed to and fro and carried about with every wind of doctrine, by the trickery of men, in the cunning craftiness of deceitful plotting, [15]but, speaking the truth in love, may grow up in all things into Him who is the head—Christ— [16]from whom the whole body, joined and knit together by what every joint supplies, according to the effective working by which every part does its share, causes growth of the body for the edifying of itself in love.

4:6 [a]NU-Text omits *you;* M-Text reads *us.*   **4:8** [a]Psalm 68:18
4:9 [a]NU-Text omits *first.*

THROUGH THE GRID

Discover God:
God Helps Us Live Righteously

EPHESIANS 4:21–24 *You have heard Him and have been taught by Him, as the truth is in Jesus: that you put off, concerning your former conduct, the old man which grows corrupt according to the deceitful lusts, and be renewed in the spirit of your mind, and that you put on the new man which was created according to God, in true righteousness and holiness.*

We are to be righteous as God is righteous, and we can do so by the power of the Holy Spirit. As we submit our will and our entire selves to God, God empowers us to live righteously in the blessings of His grace. We must strive to live up to the standards of God's righteousness and put aside our old selves and our worldly desires in order to fully follow after God.

LEADERSHIP ISSUES

GC2: Who Am I? A Unique Part of the Body

EPHESIANS 4:4–6 *There is one body and one Spirit, just as you were called in one hope of your calling; one Lord, one faith, one baptism; one God and Father of all, who is above all, and through all, and in you all.*

When God infused you with His life and made you His child, He uniquely crafted you as part of His family for a relational purpose. As sons and daughters, we have been made part of the family of faith, even as Abraham entered by faith (Gal. 3:29; Heb. 11:8–10). It's this family of faith that is often referred to in Scripture as the "body of Christ."

God intends you to use your unique God-given characteristics to relate not only to Him but to others as well. "For as we have many members in one body," Paul said, "but all the members do not have the same function, so we, being many, are one body in Christ, and individually members of one another" (Rom. 12:4, 5).

There will never be another you. God has specially gifted you to fill a role and a purpose that no one else can fill. Each of us inwardly wants to know our place in this world. God has crafted you specifically for that place that you and only you can fill. You are a child of God by means of a new birth, having unique characteristics with which to love and live for God in a way that only you are empowered to do. You belong to Christ's body, God's family. That family needs you because there will never be another who can fill that place as you can.

And God wants to exercise His love and life in and through you in a unique and original fashion. Yes, He wants all of us to love each other, but He wants you to do that in the unique and original fashion in which He has crafted the one-of-a-kind you (John 13:34, 35).

GC2
GREAT COMMANDMENT
COMMISSION

LEADERSHIP ISSUES

GC2: Giving Approval (Blessing)

EPHESIANS 4:29

The need for approval is met by building up or affirming other people and acknowledging the importance of your relationship. Approval also involves noticing and affirming positive character qualities—affirming people for who they are, not just for what they do. A powerful example of approval occurred at Jesus' baptism. God the Father said, "You are My beloved Son, in whom I am well pleased" (Mark 1:11). He affirmed the fact of their relationship ("You are My Son") and that it was important ("My beloved Son").

During His earthly ministry, Jesus frequently expressed approval to various people. He affirmed: a generous widow (Mark 12:41–44), Peter (Matt. 16:13–19), a devoted Mary of Bethany (John 12:2–9), and a grateful leper (Luke 17:11–19).

Pause and reflect on these ideas for giving others approval:

- I am able to view people through God's eyes—to separate *who* they are (valuable, important and significant) from what they *do* (sometimes good, sometimes bad).

- I look beyond a person's "surface" issues and caringly affirm their character, heart, and spiritual maturity.

- I am quick to commend people when they have done something that is good and honorable.

- I am particularly careful to affirm those to whom I am close (family, siblings, close friends, mentors), giving specific focus on the character qualities (diligence, sensitivity, honesty) that are a blessing to me or others.

- I go out of my way to tell others how blessed I am to be in relationship with them (friend, father, mother, sibling, mentor, brother or sister in Christ).

GC2
GREAT COMMANDMENT
COMMISSION

THE NEW MAN

[17]This I say, therefore, and testify in the Lord, that you should no longer walk as the rest of[a] the Gentiles walk, in the futility of their mind, [18]having their understanding darkened, being alienated from the life of God, because of the ignorance that is in them, because of the blindness of their heart; [19]who, being past feeling, have given themselves over to lewdness, to work all uncleanness with greediness.

[20]But you have not so learned Christ, [21]if indeed you have heard Him and have been taught by Him, as the truth is in Jesus: [22]that you put off, concerning your former conduct, the old man which grows corrupt according to the deceitful lusts, [23]and be renewed in the spirit of your mind, [24]and that you put on the new man which was created according to God, in true righteousness and holiness.

DO NOT GRIEVE THE SPIRIT

[25]Therefore, putting away lying, *"Let each one of you speak truth with his neighbor,"*[a] for we are members of one another. [26]*"Be angry, and do not sin"*:[a] do not let the sun go down on your wrath, [27]nor give place to the devil. [28]Let him who stole steal no longer, but rather let him labor, working with *his* hands what is good, that he may have something to give him who has need. [29]Let no corrupt word proceed out of your mouth, but what is good for necessary edification, that it may impart grace to the hearers. [30]And do not grieve the Holy Spirit of God, by whom you were sealed for the day of redemption. [31]Let all bitterness, wrath, anger, clamor, and evil speaking be put away from you, with all malice. [32]And be kind to one another, tenderhearted, forgiving one another, even as God in Christ forgave you.

WALK IN LOVE

5 Therefore be imitators of God as dear children. [2]And walk in love, as Christ also has loved us and given Himself for us, an offering and a sacrifice to God for a sweet-smelling aroma.

[3]But fornication and all uncleanness or covetousness, let it not even be named among you, as is fitting for saints; [4]neither filthiness, nor foolish talking, nor coarse jesting, which are not fitting, but rather giving of thanks. [5]For this you know,[a] that no fornicator, unclean person, nor covetous man, who is an idolater, has any inheritance in the kingdom of Christ and God. [6]Let no one deceive you with empty words, for because of these things the wrath of God comes upon the sons of disobedience. [7]Therefore do not be partakers with them.

WALK IN LIGHT

[8]For you were once darkness, but now *you are* light in the Lord. Walk as children of light [9](for the fruit of the Spirit[a] *is* in all goodness, righteousness, and truth), [10]finding out what is acceptable to the Lord. [11]And have no fellowship with the unfruitful works of darkness, but rather expose *them.* [12]For it is shameful even to speak of those things which are done by them in secret. [13]But all things that are exposed are made manifest by the light, for whatever makes manifest is light. [14]Therefore He says:

"Awake, you who sleep,
　Arise from the dead,
　And Christ will give you light."

WALK IN WISDOM

[15]See then that you walk circumspectly, not as fools but as wise, [16]redeeming the time, because the days are evil.

[17]Therefore do not be unwise, but understand what the will of the Lord *is.* [18]And do not be drunk with wine, in which is dissipation; but be filled with the Spirit, [19]speaking to one another in psalms and hymns and spiritual songs, singing and making melody in your heart to the Lord, [20]giving thanks always for all things to God the Father in the name of our Lord Jesus Christ, [21]submitting to one another in the fear of God.[a]

MARRIAGE—CHRIST AND THE CHURCH

[22]Wives, submit to your own husbands, as to the Lord. [23]For the husband is head of the wife, as also Christ is head of the church; and He is the Savior of the body. [24]Therefore, just as the church

4:17 [a]NU-Text omits *the rest of.* **4:25** [a]Zechariah 8:16
4:26 [a]Psalm 4:4 **5:5** [a]NU-Text reads *For know this.* **5:9** [a]NU-Text reads *light.* **5:21** [a]NU-Text reads *Christ.*

LEADERSHIP ISSUES

GC2: Forgiving Others

EPHESIANS 4:31, 32

Forgiveness is a choice—empowered by God's spirit—not primarily a feeling. The question is not "Do you feel like forgiving?" but "Will you?" Forgiveness is a conscious decision on our part to release the debt of our offender and let go of our anger and bitterness (Matt. 6:12).

Forgiveness is actually for our benefit. Anger and bitterness are like infections in our heart. If the infection is not "cleaned out" our heart will not heal. In fact, infection may spread and come out in other hurtful behavior—sarcasm, a quick temper, or "passive aggressive" behaviors—which could be intentionally ignoring others, putting off what we know to do, or avoiding certain people. When we forgive, we are cooperating with God's process of cleansing our heart so that it can heal. Thus, for our own sakes, we should forgive—even if our offender doesn't ask for our forgiveness, even if our offender's behavior hasn't changed, or even if we don't "feel like" forgiving. Our example for this type of forgiveness is Christ who, even when no one had asked or had changed their behaviors, still cried out from the cross: "Father forgive them" (Luke 23:34).

Additionally, forgiveness is a matter of stewardship. We forgive because we have been forgiven (Matt. 18:21–35; Eph. 4:32; Col. 3:13). It's often helpful to thoroughly explore how we've hurt others, to experience the sorrow of our guilt, and the gratitude for God's forgiveness. This gratitude for our own sins being forgiven, empowers us to forgive others. When forgiving others seems hard, pause to meditate on how much Christ has forgiven you!

Becoming a person who *forgives* will help prepare you for healthy, God-honoring relationships.

GC2
GREAT COMMANDMENT
COMMISSION

THROUGH THE GRID	*Thinking Christianly: Ten Foundational Beliefs of a Christian Worldview*

Belief Seven: The Family (*Eph. 5:21—6:4*)

The family is God's gracious gift to humanity, designed to be a source of our protection, our growth, our pleasure, and our partnership. God has granted sexuality to every member of humanity. One's sexuality is to be used only within the covenant of marriage between a male and a female. Sex was designed for intimacy, pleasure, and the gift of children (Gen. 2:18–25; Ex. 20:12; Ps. 127; 128; Prov. 5:15–20; 31:10–31; 1 Cor. 6:18–20; 7:1–16; Eph. 5:21—6:4; Col. 3:18–21; Heb. 13:4; 1 Pet. 3:1–7). *See Through the Grid article on page 1571.*

is subject to Christ, so *let* the wives *be* to their own husbands in everything.

²⁵Husbands, love your wives, just as Christ also loved the church and gave Himself for her, ²⁶that He might sanctify and cleanse her with the washing of water by the word, ²⁷that He might present her to Himself a glorious church, not having spot or wrinkle or any such thing, but that she should be holy and without blemish. ²⁸So husbands ought to love their own wives as their own bodies; he who loves his wife loves himself. ²⁹For no one ever hated his own flesh, but nour-

ishes and cherishes it, just as the Lord *does* the church. ³⁰For we are members of His body,ª of His flesh and of His bones. ³¹*"For this reason a man shall leave his father and mother and be joined to his wife, and the two shall become one flesh."*ª ³²This is a great mystery, but I speak concerning Christ and the church. ³³Nevertheless let each one of you in particular so love his own wife as himself, and let the wife *see* that she respects *her* husband.

5:30 ªNU-Text omits the rest of this verse. **5:31** ªGenesis 2:24

LEADERSHIP REALITIES

BATTLE FOR THE FAMILY *Ephesians 6:1, 2*

Satan is described as a "roaring lion," and you should know that this beast uses his roar to separate youth from the protection of their parents. He knows that if a teen runs ahead or falls behind the protection and care of the family, then that teen becomes easy prey. God's plan is that the family nurtures, encourages, protects, and cares for each other. When the family breaks down, so does God's protection for you. Satan knows this, and he delights in family conflicts. Don't help him by making casual decisions or breaking trust with your parents.

First Samuel 15:23 warns, "Rebellion is as the sin of witchcraft, and stubbornness is as iniquity and idolatry." Alcohol and other drug use, anger and direct disobedience escalates conflict and a lack of trust. The result is often a breakdown of parent-child, spouse, and sibling relationships. *Honor your parents* by putting them in your heart, letting them walk beside you, and following them cheerfully as they walk in front of you. *Honor* begets *honor.* If you honor your parents, they will honor you as well.

timavw—**honor**—fix the value, for the value of something belonging to one's self, to revere

LEADERSHIP ISSUES

GC2: The Marriage Testimony

EPHESIANS 5:31, 32

It's not likely on your radar screen yet; but for most of us, marriage is in our future. King Solomon presided over a powerful and wealthy kingdom; but when it came time to pray, he prayed, "Give me wisdom and knowledge" (2 Chr. 1:10). Knowing that marriage may be in your future, "wisdom and knowledge," beginning *NOW*, would be helpful!

Developing healthy, relational skills in your friendships *now* will be great wisdom for life. Learning to "give first," speak the truth in love, confess, forgive, offer comfort, and listen well, will be just a few of the biblical principles—if lived out in your friendships—will pay lifelong dividends (Acts 20:35; Rom. 12:14; Eph. 4:15, 31, 32; James 1:9; 5:16).

If God does have marriage in your future, the same Book that helped shape healthy friendships can be counted on to guide and bless your marriage. It also provides insight that you'll one day be challenged to:

- "leave father and mother"—meaning more than get a job and have your own place. Be secure in your identity as God's beloved so you're free to
- "cleave and become one" with a spouse, noticing that
- the bond formed in "becoming one" in body, soul, and spirit is to remain pure for the covenant relationship of marriage.

As God may one day have marriage in mind, you will also want to understand more fully the "mystery" Paul speaks about as he portrays marriage as a picture of how much Christ loves His church. Pause to pray that if marriage is in your future, yours would be a great testimony of Christ's love to the watching world.

LEADERSHIP REALITIES

DRESS FOR SUCCESS   *Ephesians 6:11–13*

This adversary *cannot* read our minds, but he *can* influence our thoughts; and a battle for your choices awaits you every day. The key to victory in the invisible war with Satan and his demons is found in the armor of God described in Ephesians 6. We are to *put on* this divinely crafted and bestowed clothing in order to make the fiery darts of the evil totally useless.

Every soldier in ancient times was to *gird his loins* at all times so that he could be ready at a moment's notice for action. A robe that was not girded or belted indicated a soldier who was not ready to fight. As your waist is the center of your body, so the belt of truth is central to preparation for spiritual battle. The quickest way to slay the enemy was to go directly for a stab in the heart. It would have been foolish for a Roman soldier to engage a physical enemy without a breastplate. To face the enemy of our souls without the covering of the *breastplate of righteousness* is just as foolish and carries more hazardous consequences. Without it, we are not only weak, but we leave ourselves helpless in the invisible spiritual war.

Children and Parents

6 Children, obey your parents in the Lord, for this is right. 2*"Honor your father and mother,"* which is the first commandment with promise: 3*"that it may be well with you and you may live long on the earth."*[a]

4And you, fathers, do not provoke your children to wrath, but bring them up in the training and admonition of the Lord.

Bondservants and Masters

5Bondservants, be obedient to those who are your masters according to the flesh, with fear and trembling, in sincerity of heart, as to Christ; 6not with eyeservice, as men-pleasers, but as bondservants of Christ, doing the will of God from the heart, 7with goodwill doing service, as to the Lord, and not to men, 8knowing that whatever good anyone does, he will receive the same from the Lord, whether *he is* a slave or free.

9And you, masters, do the same things to them, giving up threatening, knowing that your own Master also[a] is in heaven, and there is no partiality with Him.

The Whole Armor of God

10Finally, my brethren, be strong in the Lord and in the power of His might. 11Put on the whole armor of God, that you may be able to stand against the wiles of the devil. 12For we do not wrestle against flesh and blood, but against principalities, against powers, against the rulers of the darkness of this age,[a] against spiritual *hosts* of wickedness in the heavenly *places.* 13Therefore take up the whole armor of God, that you may be able to withstand in the evil day, and having done all, to stand.

14Stand therefore, having girded your waist with truth, having put on the breastplate of righteousness, 15and having shod your feet with the preparation of the gospel of peace; 16above all, taking the shield of faith with which you will be able to quench all the fiery darts of the wicked one. 17And take the helmet of salvation, and the sword of the Spirit, which is the word of God; 18praying always with all prayer and supplication in the Spirit, being watchful to this end with all perseverance and supplication for all the saints— 19and for me, that utterance may be given to me, that I may open my mouth boldly to make known the mystery of the gospel, 20for which I am an ambassador in chains; that in it I may speak boldly, as I ought to speak.

6:3 aDeuteronomy 5:16   **6:9** aNU-Text reads *He who is both their Master and yours.*   **6:12** aNU-Text reads *rulers of this darkness.*

A Gracious Greeting

[21]But that you also may know my affairs *and* how I am doing, Tychicus, a beloved brother and faithful minister in the Lord, will make all things known to you; [22]whom I have sent to you for this very purpose, that you may know our affairs, and *that* he may comfort your hearts.

[23]Peace to the brethren, and love with faith, from God the Father and the Lord Jesus Christ. [24]Grace *be* with all those who love our Lord Jesus Christ in sincerity. Amen.

IMPACT OF THE BOOK

I IDEA

Your attitude determines your altitude, and your attitude is either one of your greatest strengths or one of your greatest weaknesses (Phil. 4:1–9).

M MESSAGE

Paul demonstrates leadership lessons by focusing on his mission even while in prison. That courageous attitude proved to be contagious. Supernatural joy is available to the believer in spite of circumstances. Each morning you can choose to be happy or sad, joyful or pessimistic. Only you have control over your attitude. Paul exhorts believers to have the same attitude as Christ's—one of humility, sacrifice, and obedience.

P PEOPLE

Epaphroditus, Euodia, Paul, Syntyche, Timothy

A AUTHOR

Paul wrote this epistle to the Philippian church, which he established during his second missionary journey.

C CULTURE

At the time of his writing, Paul was facing an upcoming trial and was uncertain of the outcome: life or death. He thought he would be released and would revisit Philippi. Paul had a certain measure of freedom: he was able to write letters, welcome friends, and receive gifts. The city of Philippi was named after King Philip of Macedonia, who was father to Alexander the Great. Philippi was founded in 350 BC and made a Roman colony in 42 BC. Augustus granted this unusual privilege when the citizens preferred Roman rule over the Greek hardships. When the Roman soldiers threatened to lay down their weapons and return home because of not being paid, the citizens of Philippi took all the salt of the city—which was a form of monetary compensation—and presented it to the Roman soldiers, giving us the phrase a person is "worth their salt."

T TIMELINE

c. AD 61

KEY SCRIPTURE
MEMORY VERSES

1:6, 21; 2:3–11; 3:14; 4:4, 8, 13

Greeting

1 Paul and Timothy, bondservants of Jesus Christ,

To all the saints in Christ Jesus who are in Philippi, with the bishops[a] and deacons:

²Grace to you and peace from God our Father and the Lord Jesus Christ.

Thankfulness and Prayer

³I thank my God upon every remembrance of you, ⁴always in every prayer of mine making request for you all with joy, ⁵for your fellowship in the gospel from the first day until now, ⁶being confident of this very thing, that He who has begun a good work in you will complete *it* until the day of Jesus Christ; ⁷just as it is right for me to think this of you all, because I have you in my heart, inasmuch as both in my chains and in the defense and confirmation of the gospel, you all are partakers with me of grace. ⁸For God is my witness, how greatly I long for you all with the affection of Jesus Christ.

⁹And this I pray, that your love may abound still more and more in knowledge and all discernment, ¹⁰that you may approve the things that are excellent, that you may be sincere and without offense till the day of Christ, ¹¹being filled with the fruits of righteousness which *are* by Jesus Christ, to the glory and praise of God.

Christ Is Preached

¹²But I want you to know, brethren, that the things *which happened* to me have actually turned out for the furtherance of the gospel, ¹³so that it has become evident to the whole palace guard, and to all the rest, that my chains are in Christ; ¹⁴and most of the brethren in the Lord, having become confident by my chains, are much more bold to speak the word without fear.

¹⁵Some indeed preach Christ even from envy

1:1 ªLiterally *overseers*

INSIDE the INFLUENCERS

BONDSERVANT OF CHRIST—Called to Serve

PHILIPPIANS 1:1

When Paul wrote to the church at Philippi, he addressed the letter from "Paul and Timothy, bondservants of Jesus Christ." The word *bondservant* is from the Greek "*to bind*" and wasn't a flattering term. It represented the lowest class, but to these Christians, it was a privileged title.

A *bondservant* could be bound to slavery by birth. Paul wanted the church to know that he has been born again into a spiritual bondage to serve Christ, which he holds as an honor and a joy. The union between servant and master was permanent, only broken by death, just as you can be joined to Jesus forever. *Bondservant* means one whose will is swallowed up in the will of another. Paul and Timothy yielded themselves to the will of God in all things. Paul and Timothy delighted in being bondservants for their Lord. Jude also referred to himself as a bondservant, which seems a strange title for a half-brother to use.

These people referred to Jesus as *Lord,* and wanted all to know that they willingly yielded to Him. The Greek word translated Lord (*despotes*) means "master," and refers to one who holds power over the affairs and the life of a person. Primarily, it emphasizes His sovereignty, an important characteristic better demonstrated to others through *serving* than simply *teaching.*

and strife, and some also from goodwill: [16]The former[a] preach Christ from selfish ambition, not sincerely, supposing to add affliction to my chains; [17]but the latter out of love, knowing that I am appointed for the defense of the gospel. [18]What then? Only *that* in every way, whether in pretense or in truth, Christ is preached; and in this I rejoice, yes, and will rejoice.

To Live Is Christ

[19]For I know that this will turn out for my deliverance through your prayer and the supply of the Spirit of Jesus Christ, [20]according to my earnest expectation and hope that in nothing I shall be ashamed, but with all boldness, as always, so now also Christ will be magnified in my body, whether by life or by death. [21]For to me, to live *is* Christ, and to die *is* gain. [22]But if *I* live on in the flesh, this *will mean* fruit from *my* labor; yet what I shall choose I cannot tell. [23]For[a] I am hard-pressed between the two, having a desire to depart and be with Christ, *which is* far better. [24]Nevertheless to remain in the flesh *is* more needful for you. [25]And being confident of this, I know that I shall remain and continue with you all for your progress and joy of faith, [26]that your rejoicing for me may be more abundant in Jesus Christ by my coming to you again.

Striving and Suffering for Christ

[27]Only let your conduct be worthy of the gospel of Christ, so that whether I come and see you or am absent, I may hear of your affairs, that you stand fast in one spirit, with one mind striving together for the faith of the gospel, [28]and not in any way terrified by your adversaries, which is to them a proof of perdition, but to you of salvation,[a] and that from God. [29]For to you it has been granted on behalf of Christ, not only to believe in Him, but also to suffer for His sake, [30]having the same conflict which you saw in me and now hear *is* in me.

Unity Through Humility

2 Therefore if *there is* any consolation in Christ, if any comfort of love, if any fellowship of the Spirit, if any affection and mercy, [2]fulfill my joy by being like-minded, having the same love, *being* of one accord, of one mind. [3]*Let* nothing *be done*

1:16 aNU-Text reverses the contents of verses 16 and 17. **1:23** aNU-Text and M-Text read *But.* **1:28** aNU-Text reads *of your salvation.*

THROUGH THE GRID

Where Have All the Dreamers Gone? Observations from a Biblical Worldview: Sense and Sensuality (Phil. 2:2–5)

Most Christians have adopted a passive approach to encountering entertainment, where they simply allow themselves to sit back, watch, and enjoy. However, the more we sit idly and passively by, the more that culture has an opportunity to form and shape our worldview. One of the effects of the TV culture is that the more we view images, the more we become desensitized to what the images mean and represent. Certainly, TV's entertainment can be used to positively affect how we think and live; however, many shows present harmful worldviews and messages. As a developing Christian leader, one should seek to fill one's mind with as much good and positive as possible, as well as those things that edify our relationship with God and enhance our relationships with nature and with other people. Reading good books can influence a young developing mind, and one can learn timeless truths just from reading a few minutes every day. As we develop a Christian mind, we must learn to separate the wheat from the chaff in terms of entertainment. In order to help yourself and others develop a Christian worldview, we must promote things that build character, starting with our homes and families. We cannot allow the dregs of the entertainment industry to infiltrate our precious minds.

through selfish ambition or conceit, but in lowliness of mind let each esteem others better than himself. [4]Let each of you look out not only for his own interests, but also for the interests of others.

THE HUMBLED AND EXALTED CHRIST

[5]Let this mind be in you which was also in Christ Jesus, [6]who, being in the form of God, did not consider it robbery to be equal with God, [7]but made Himself of no reputation, taking the form of a bondservant, *and* coming in the likeness of men. [8]And being found in appearance as a man, He humbled Himself and became obedient to *the point of* death, even the death of the cross. [9]Therefore God also has highly exalted Him and given Him the name which is above every name, [10]that at the name of Jesus every knee should bow, of those in heaven, and of those on earth, and of those under the earth, [11]and *that* every tongue should confess that Jesus Christ *is* Lord, to the glory of God the Father.

LIGHT BEARERS

[12]Therefore, my beloved, as you have always obeyed, not as in my presence only, but now much more in my absence, work out your own salvation with fear and trembling; [13]for it is God who works in you both to will and to do for *His* good pleasure.

[14]Do all things without complaining and disputing, [15]that you may become blameless and harmless, children of God without fault in the midst of a crooked and perverse generation, among whom you shine as lights in the world, [16]holding fast the word of life, so that I may re-

joice in the day of Christ that I have not run in vain or labored in vain.

[17]Yes, and if I am being poured out *as a drink offering* on the sacrifice and service of your faith, I am glad and rejoice with you all. [18]For the same reason you also be glad and rejoice with me.

TIMOTHY COMMENDED

[19]But I trust in the Lord Jesus to send Timothy to you shortly, that I also may be encouraged when I know your state. [20]For I have no one likeminded, who will sincerely care for your state. [21]For all seek their own, not the things which are of Christ Jesus. [22]But you know his proven character, that as a son with *his* father he served with me in the gospel. [23]Therefore I hope to send him at once, as soon as I see how it goes with me. [24]But I trust in the Lord that I myself shall also come shortly.

EPAPHRODITUS PRAISED

[25]Yet I considered it necessary to send to you Epaphroditus, my brother, fellow worker, and fellow soldier, but your messenger and the one who ministered to my need; [26]since he was longing for you all, and was distressed because you had heard that he was sick. [27]For indeed he was sick almost unto death; but God had mercy on him, and not only on him but on me also, lest I should have sorrow upon sorrow. [28]Therefore I sent him the more eagerly, that when you see him again you may rejoice, and I may be less sorrowful. [29]Receive him therefore in the Lord with all gladness, and hold such men in esteem; [30]because for the work of Christ he came close to death, not

THROUGH THE GRID

Making Sense of Your World: Christianity's Exclusivist Claims— Jesus' Followers (Phil. 2:9–11)

Not only did Jesus lay down the claims for Himself as the only true way to God and to eternal salvation, but we also hear this claim being made by His followers as well. The apostles preached this message with force, and there are many scriptural examples of teachings that point to Christian exclusivity. Peter claimed that salvation does not come through any other than Jesus and also that God has not provided for any salvation but through the Person of Jesus (Acts 4:12). Paul also urged his followers to believe in the name of the Lord Jesus to be saved (Phil. 2:9–11).

LEADERSHIP ISSUES

Humility Is a Choice

PHILIPPIANS 2

God values humility.

The Bible constantly affirms that God's people, particularly His leaders, must be humble. The highest praise of Moses is that he was the most humble man on the face of the earth (Num. 12:3). The humility of Hezekiah impressed God so much that God actually extended the length of Hezekiah's life (2 Chr. 32:26). Even the wicked King Ahab was spared from God's punishment because he chose to humble himself before God (1 Kin. 21:29). Humility, however, is not just for Old Testament kings. Humility is a virtue for leaders in the New Testament as well.

Jesus modeled humility.

The humility of Jesus Christ is the most remarkable aspect of His human character. Jesus was born in a barn in Bethlehem, raised in the small town of Nazareth, and conducted His ministry in the obscure region of Galilee. He was hated, mocked, and falsely accused by the political and religious leaders of His day; He was executed in public like a common criminal. Some might hear His story and think of Jesus as a victim of unfortunate circumstances and mean people, but the Bible says in Philippians 2 that Jesus made a choice to humble Himself. He made a decision to leave heaven, to become a man, and to allow Himself to become a sacrifice for the sins of the world. Jesus is the supreme example of a humble leader.

Humility is a choice.

Throughout Scripture, Christians are encouraged to make the choice to be humble. In the Old Testament, God promises that if His people will humble themselves, pray, turn from their wicked ways, and seek Him, He will hear, heal, and forgive (2 Chr. 7:14). In the New Testament Jesus said that greatness in His kingdom requires childlike humility (Matt. 18:4). Leaders have influence over people, so pride is a HUGE temptation for *every* leader. Pride has to be resisted—it is there, whether we want it to be or not. Humility, though, requires a choice and an effort on our part. Pride comes naturally. You can be prideful *by accident*, but you can only be humble *on purpose*. Humility is a choice.

LEADERSHIP ISSUES

GC2: Unity: Unity for a Purpose

PHILIPPIANS 2:15, 16

We live in a world filled with crises. The Bible shows us what our world will look like just before Christ returns. We might even describe these characteristics as symptoms of the irrelevance in our culture. In a world of irrelevance, people will . . .

- be lovers of self, focusing on their own plans, needs, and desires;
- be lovers of money, giving priority to what they can acquire;
- be boastful and arrogant;
- be unloving, irreconcilable, and prone to gossip;
- be lovers of pleasure;
- display only a form of godliness;
- indulge the flesh;
- become self-willed;
- speak arrogant words;
- be enticed by fleshly lusts and sensuality and will become entangled in the world's defilements (2 Tim. 3:1–5; 2 Pet. 2:10–18).

Prayerfully and humbly look at this list again. Which of these characteristics do you struggle with? Which of these symptoms of irrelevance is true for you?

"I sometimes struggle with _____."
(For example: "*I sometimes struggle with selfishness when faced with the needs and demands of my family and friends.*" Or "*I sometimes struggle to give loving responses. My boss tells me that I can be harsh and critical when I interact with customers.*")

Consider humbly sharing these struggles and praying for one another that your mutual commitment to live "differently" in a crisis-filled world will draw you together.

GC2
GREAT COMMANDMENT
COMMISSION

regarding his life, to supply what was lacking in your service toward me.

ALL FOR CHRIST

3 Finally, my brethren, rejoice in the Lord. For me to write the same things to you *is* not tedious, but for you *it is* safe. [2]Beware of dogs, beware of evil workers, beware of the mutilation! [3]For we are the circumcision, who worship God in the Spirit,[a] rejoice in Christ Jesus, and have no confidence in the flesh, [4]though I also might have confidence in the flesh. If anyone else thinks he may have confidence in the flesh, I more so: [5]circumcised the eighth day, of the stock of Israel, *of* the tribe of Benjamin, a Hebrew of the Hebrews; concerning the law, a Pharisee; [6]concerning zeal, persecuting the church; concerning the righteousness which is in the law, blameless.

[7]But what things were gain to me, these I have counted loss for Christ. [8]Yet indeed I also count all things loss for the excellence of the knowledge of Christ Jesus my Lord, for whom I have suffered the loss of all things, and count them as rubbish, that I may gain Christ [9]and be found in Him, not having my own righteousness, which *is* from the law, but that which *is* through faith in Christ, the righteousness which is from God by faith; [10]that I may know Him and the power of His resurrection, and the fellowship of His sufferings, being conformed to His death, [11]if, by any means, I may attain to the resurrection from the dead.

PRESSING TOWARD THE GOAL

[12]Not that I have already attained, or am already perfected; but I press on, that I may lay hold

3:3 [a]NU-Text and M-Text read *who worship in the Spirit of God.*

LEADERSHIP REALITIES

CONSISTENCY—THE RIGHT TO INFLUENCE　*Philippians 4:8*

Where do you live emotionally and spiritually on a daily basis, and who or what lives in you? We are called to *meditate on,* or *consistently think about,* truth. Only then can we earn the right to influence others.

　　　logivzomai—**meditate**—to reckon, count, compute, calculate, count over

Consistently think about *whatever is* . . .

- *True*—that which will not let you down or vary with opinion
- *Noble*—that which has the dignity of holiness upon it
- *Just and pure*—that which is morally undefiled, meaning it is fit to be brought into the presence of God and used in His service
- *Lovely*—that which calls forth love, encouragement, health, and well-being
- *Of good report*—it is positive and beneficial for people and for God to hear
- *Virtue*—is morally excellent

A focus on absolute truth prevents you from being tossed about by despair or discouragement. Just as you can preset music or bookmark a Web site, you can *set your mind.* Leaders stay consistently positive and look for new possibilities in life. As a result, people listen, watch, and are positively influenced.

The influential leader is one whose life is consistently believable because of the words, attitudes, and actions he or she presents daily.

LEADERSHIP ISSUES

Shake Off the Dust: Identify Theft

PHILIPPIANS 3:13, 14

There are four myths about the past that will rob you of the powerful, peaceful identity Christ intends for you as His child.

Myth #1: "My past is a mess. I have nothing to live for."

Truth: God provides you with a **new purpose in life** (2 Cor. 5:15). When you no longer live for yourself, you leave behind the bitterness, hurt, and the grip of the past. Christ rose from the dead; and when He did, He proclaimed His victory over death, sin, and the pain of the past. The leader will choose to put the past behind, change the negative past attitude, and walk in a hopeful future.

Remembering the mistakes of his past, Paul writes "forgetting those things which are behind and reaching forward to those things which are ahead" (Phil. 3:13).

Myth #2: "I can't help it. It's not my fault. You don't know what I went through."

Truth: In Christ, you are "a **new creation**" (2 Cor. 5:15), *so stop making excuses.* Some people use the past as an excuse to continue making bad choices. They hope their excuses will lessen their feeling of guilt, but instead the guilt continues to build.

It is true that we are deeply affected by both the successes and failures of our lives, but there comes a time when we must grow up emotionally. You are commanded to love as He loves you—unconditionally.

Myth #3: "I've made too many mistakes. I won't ever be anything but a failure."

Truth: In Christ, you are the owner of a **new potential**. This transformation is the main thing that distinguishes being a Christian from any other religion. Your future does not depend on what you *think* you can achieve or even on what others think about you. The Genesis story tells us that God made man out of the dust of the earth just because He wanted to. He can also make you a brand-new creation just because He loves you. *It isn't about trying harder.* You must allow God to do for you what you cannot do for yourself.

of that for which Christ Jesus has also laid hold of me. [13]Brethren, I do not count myself to have apprehended; but one thing *I do,* forgetting those things which are behind and reaching forward to those things which are ahead, [14]I press toward the goal for the prize of the upward call of God in Christ Jesus.

[15]Therefore let us, as many as are mature, have this mind; and if in anything you think otherwise, God will reveal even this to you. [16]Nevertheless, to *the degree* that we have already attained, let us walk by the same rule,[a] let us be of the same mind.

Our Citizenship in Heaven

[17]Brethren, join in following my example, and note those who so walk, as you have us for a pattern. [18]For many walk, of whom I have told you often, and now tell you even weeping, *that they are* the enemies of the cross of Christ: [19]whose end *is* destruction, whose god *is their* belly, and *whose* glory *is* in their shame—who set their mind on earthly things. [20]For our citizenship is in heaven, from which we also eagerly wait for the Savior, the Lord Jesus Christ, [21]who will transform our lowly body that it may be conformed to His glorious body, according to the working by which He is able even to subdue all things to Himself.

4 Therefore, my beloved and longed-for brethren, my joy and crown, so stand fast in the Lord, beloved.

Be United, Joyful, and in Prayer

[2]I implore Euodia and I implore Syntyche to be of the same mind in the Lord. [3]And[a] I urge you also, true companion, help these women who

3:16 [a]NU-Text omits *rule* and the rest of the verse. **4:3** [a]NU-Text and M-Text read *Yes.*

LEADERSHIP REALITIES

MAKE YOUR FIRST THOUGHT POSITIVE *Philippians 4:8, 9*

The wrong thoughts lead to the wrong attitudes, and these in turn lead to the wrong actions. The leader who allows his first thoughts to be negative pollutes his own life and the lives of others. Here Paul sums up his letter to the Philippians by calling them to capture the content of their thoughts with two explicit commands: first "meditate" or "think" and second to "practice." Paul provides a list of virtues that should fill the Christians thoughts and thus lead to *practice* Christlike actions:

Whatever is:

- **true** (*alēthēs*): virtuous character and great stability.
- **honorable** (*semnos*): attractive because of its sense of dignity and integrity and so invites and inspires reverence.
- **right** or **just** (*dikaios*): admirable or worthy first of God and then of others.
- **pure** (*hagnos*): stainless, more than just that which refrains from impurities but rather that which seeks to be exhaustively pure.
- **lovely** (*prosphilēs*): calls forth love, the Christian mind must be centered on winsome characteristics so that for him to see is to love.
- **of good report** or **commendable** (*euphēmos*): suitable for God to hear.
- Whatever possesses **virtue** or **excellence** (*aretē*): rises above and reflects a characteristic of God such as the beauty of a painting, the courage of a soldier, or a simple kind act.
- **praiseworthy** (*epainos*): deserves to be praised.

LEADERSHIP ISSUES

GC2: Loving the Real God: A Need-Meeting God

PHILIPPIANS 4:19 *And my God shall supply all your need according to His riches in glory by Christ Jesus.*

It is noteworthy that Paul's expression, "my God" is rare in the New Testament. It is almost as if Paul, by using the phrase "my God," is bragging on his God. He seems to be excited to declare that his God is a God who meets needs. Perhaps he is saying:

- If you have a "sin-inspecting god" who is always trying to catch you doing something wrong, I am sad for you, because my God—the real God—is seeking to meet your needs!
- If you have a "disappointed god" who is constantly communicating that He is disappointed with you, I am sad for you, because my God is longing to meet your needs!
- If you have a "distant god" who does not even seem to notice you, I am sad for you, because my God notices and cares for even the birds and the flowers—and much more so for you!

Pause to celebrate the real God who, across the pages of Scripture and in countless lives like Paul's and yours, has been revealed as a need-meeting God!

Take time to "forget not all His benefits" (Ps. 103:2). "I remember God meeting me at my point of need when He _____."

Now "serve the LORD with gladness" (Ps. 100:2). "Lord, I'm especially grateful to You as a need-meeting God when I remember _____; I thank You and praise You for taking such initiative to love me."

GC2

GREAT COMMANDMENT
COMMISSION

labored with me in the gospel, with Clement also, and the rest of my fellow workers, whose names *are* in the Book of Life.

⁴Rejoice in the Lord always. Again I will say, rejoice!

⁵Let your gentleness be known to all men. The Lord *is* at hand.

⁶Be anxious for nothing, but in everything by prayer and supplication, with thanksgiving, let your requests be made known to God; ⁷and the peace of God, which surpasses all understanding, will guard your hearts and minds through Christ Jesus.

MEDITATE ON THESE THINGS

⁸Finally, brethren, whatever things are true, whatever things *are* noble, whatever things *are* just, whatever things *are* pure, whatever things *are* lovely, whatever things *are* of good report, if *there is* any virtue and if *there is* anything praiseworthy—meditate on these things. ⁹The things which you learned and received and heard and saw in me, these do, and the God of peace will be with you.

PHILIPPIAN GENEROSITY

¹⁰But I rejoiced in the Lord greatly that now at last your care for me has flourished again; though you surely did care, but you lacked opportunity. ¹¹Not that I speak in regard to need, for I have learned in whatever state I am, to be content: ¹²I know how to be abased, and I know how to abound. Everywhere and in all things I have learned both to be full and to be hungry, both to abound and to suffer need. ¹³I can do all things through Christ[a] who strengthens me.

¹⁴Nevertheless you have done well that you shared in my distress. ¹⁵Now you Philippians know also that in the beginning of the gospel, when I departed from Macedonia, no church shared with me concerning giving and receiving but you only. ¹⁶For even in Thessalonica you sent *aid* once and again for my necessities. ¹⁷Not that I seek the gift, but I seek the fruit that abounds to your account. ¹⁸Indeed I have all and abound. I am full, having received from Epaphroditus the things *sent* from you, a sweet-smelling aroma, an

4:13 [a]NU-Text reads *Him who.*

LEADERSHIP REALITIES

SWALLOW THE BIG FROG *Philippians 4:13, 14*

At a time when life comes at you with alarming speed, every leader must be able to prioritize and select tasks based on what is both urgent and important. It is well said that for many the most difficult part of a task is to begin. The thing which you know you must do, want to do, and need to do can become dreadful in your mind when procrastination takes over. "Swallow the big frog first" has become a popular cultural term for tackling an urgent or difficult assignment at the beginning of the day, while you have the most available energy and time. The reasoning is that if you swallow a live frog and still live, the rest of the day will be easy! Paul understood this principle and gave us the *"this one thing I do"* mentality.

1. **Clarify**—Ask yourself, Is this task in line with my mission and purpose? Should this task be done today? Is this a responsible use of time and energy?

2. **Change the way you think**—Instead of looking at the task as an obstacle, think of it as an opportunity to move toward a larger goal, to overcome procrastination, and to build peaceful habits.

3. **Commit to it**—Begin the practice of discipline to begin in a timely manner and to finish with excellence. If you need to, swallow it one bite at a time instead of all at once by cutting up the project into manageable pieces.

acceptable sacrifice, well pleasing to God. ¹⁹And my God shall supply all your need according to His riches in glory by Christ Jesus. ²⁰Now to our God and Father *be* glory forever and ever. Amen.

GREETING AND BLESSING

²¹Greet every saint in Christ Jesus. The brethren who are with me greet you. ²²All the saints greet you, but especially those who are of Caesar's household.

²³The grace of our Lord Jesus Christ be with you all.ᵃ Amen.

4:23 ᵃNU-Text reads *your spirit.*

IMPACT OF THE BOOK

COLOSSIANS

IDEA | Jesus Christ is the Lord of the universe and the Head of the church; forgiveness of sins is available only through Him.

MESSAGE | Paul admonishes the church at Colosse that the Christ he preached is the only true God; the very heart of the gospel is wrapped up in the identity of Christ. He presents Jesus as the wonderful Savior and Lord, creator, maker of all things, and excellent (Col. 1:12–17). Paul's prayer for the Colossians (and all leaders) is that we will be filled with His wisdom and that we will walk worthy of the Lord (Col. 1:9, 10).

PEOPLE | Aristarchus, Barnabas, Epaphras, False Teachers, Justus, Paul, Timothy, Tychicus

AUTHOR | Evidence suggests that Paul had not visited Colosse when he wrote this letter (Col. 2:1), even though he was certainly acquainted with individuals from the church. Colossians 1:1 and 7 tell us that Timothy and Ephaphras had preached there and established the church during Paul's third missionary journey.

CULTURE | Colosse, at the base of Mount Cadmus, was about 120 miles east of Ephesus in the Lycus River Valley. Historical records are few regarding this fairly insignificant Roman city. Colosse was overshadowed by the larger, more affluent city of Laodicea, only eleven miles to its northwest. Colosse did benefit from a textile industry and from its strategic location on a major trade route from the Aegean coast to the center of Asia Minor and on to Syria and further east. Evidence suggests a significant Jewish population existed in the area surrounding Colosse and probably in the city as well.

TIMELINE | c. AD 61

KEY SCRIPTURE MEMORY VERSES | 1:9, 10, 28, 29; 2:8, 9; 3:1, 2, 16, 17, 23

GREETING

1 Paul, an apostle of Jesus Christ by the will of God, and Timothy our brother,

²To the saints and faithful brethren in Christ *who are* in Colosse:

Grace to you and peace from God our Father and the Lord Jesus Christ.ᵃ

THEIR FAITH IN CHRIST

³We give thanks to the God and Father of our Lord Jesus Christ, praying always for you, ⁴since we heard of your faith in Christ Jesus and of your love for all the saints; ⁵because of the hope which is laid up for you in heaven, of which you heard before in the word of the truth of the gospel, ⁶which has come to you, as *it has* also in all the world, and is bringing forth fruit,ᵃ as *it is* also among you since the day you heard and knew the grace of God in truth; ⁷as you also learned from Epaphras, our dear fellow servant, who is a faithful minister of Christ on your behalf, ⁸who also declared to us your love in the Spirit.

PREEMINENCE OF CHRIST

⁹For this reason we also, since the day we heard it, do not cease to pray for you, and to ask that you may be filled with the knowledge of His will in all wisdom and spiritual understanding; ¹⁰that you may walk worthy of the Lord, fully pleasing *Him,* being fruitful in every good work and increasing in the knowledge of God; ¹¹strengthened with all might, according to His glorious power, for all patience and longsuffering with joy; ¹²giving thanks to the Father who has qualified us to be partakers of the inheritance of the saints in the light. ¹³He has delivered us from the power of darkness and conveyed *us* into the kingdom of the Son of His love, ¹⁴in whom we have redemption through His blood,ᵃ the forgiveness of sins.

¹⁵He is the image of the invisible God, the firstborn over all creation. ¹⁶For by Him all things were created that are in heaven and that are on earth, visible and invisible, whether thrones or

1:2 ᵃNU-Text omits *and the Lord Jesus Christ.* **1:6** ᵃNU-Text and M-Text add *and growing.* **1:14** ᵃNU-Text and M-Text omit *through His blood.*

THROUGH THE GRID

Discover God:
God Is Present Everywhere

COLOSSIANS 1:17, 18 *And He is before all things, and in Him all things consist. And He is the head of the body, the church, who is the beginning, the firstborn from the dead, that in all things He may have the preeminence.*

God is present everywhere at the same time, in the fullest sense. God fills the heavens and the earth with His presence of being; and thus, God is always and immediately present with the entirety of creation. This attribute is called *God's omnipresence*—the extent of God's being everywhere at all times in the fullest sense. Nothing in the entire universe can contain God, whose Spirit transcends all of creation but at the same time is in all of creation. Wherever you are, God is right there, right now, and always there. God's infinite presence is that which sustains the vast universe, that which reveals God's presence to humanity, and that which allows humanity to live consciously *coram deo*—in the very presence of God. There are several important characteristics of God's presence: it affects every person, can be revealed to humanity in special times and places, is made manifest through Jesus Christ, and resides within every believer. In response to God's omnipresence, our response as believers should be to practice the presence of God, keeping Him in mind in whatever we do and wherever we go.

LEADERSHIP ISSUES

Praying Scripture

COLOSSIANS 1:9–11

Paul teaches us to pray for ourselves and for others:

"Do not cease to pray" (v. 9)—A powerful prayer life begins with consistency. Make this a wildly important part of your day, and keep a journal to go back to for rejoicing.

"You may be filled" (v. 9)—Enjoy the value of simple pleasures, appreciate family and friends, and guard against wastefulness of time or money.

"With the knowledge of His will" (v. 9)—In the Greek, Paul says be "headed in the right direction." Seek to know God's perfect will for your life.

"In all wisdom" (v. 9)—Establish effective study habits; pray for good memory and guidance in dealing skillfully with learning differences. Memorize Scripture for wisdom in all choices.

"Spiritual understanding" (v. 9)—Pray for genuine faith in Christ, that the truth and teachings of Scripture will permeate and rule your life.

"That you may walk worthy of the Lord" (v. 10)—Pray for responsibility, the understanding of right and wrong, and the ability to overcome temptation.

"Fully pleasing Him" (v. 10)—Pray for a place of service in your church; be a "time-tither" by giving 10 percent of your time with a right motive.

"Being fruitful in every good work" (v. 10)—Pray not just to be successful but to want to give of yourself and to enjoy what you do.

"Increasing in the knowledge of God" (v. 10)—Learn about the character of God, and your life will be empowered and transformed.

"Strengthened with all might" (v. 11)—Pray to be strong in your choices and not be tempted to compromise.

"For all patience" (v. 11)—Pray for patience with people, particularly with those over you in authority. Pray for the skills to get along with difficult people and to deal with the unlovely without irritation, bitterness, or retaliation.

"Longsuffering with joy" (v. 11)—In the Greek, this phrase evokes pictures of turning burdens into glory—of a prayer for consistent self-restraint and even-temperedness with joy.

LEADERSHIP ISSUES

GC2: Unity: Christ the Head of the Church

COLOSSIANS 1:18 *And He is the head of the body, the church, who is the beginning, the firstborn from the dead, that in all things He may have the preeminence.*

As the body of Christ, the church is to relate in oneness to Christ as the Head (Eph. 4:15; Col. 2:19). Just as our physical body works together in unity as our brain gives direction, so it is to be with Christ's body.

Our unity of fellowship flows from common submission (yielding) to Christ as our Head, with each member of the body exercising specific gifts and ministries as He sovereignly wills (1 Cor. 12:4–7). True fellowship leads to recognition that, though it may be in some ways "organized," the church as Christ's body is a living, relational organism, not merely an organization.

As the temple of God, the church is also portrayed in Scripture as God's building, with Christ as the cornerstone (1 Cor. 3:9–17; 1 Tim. 3:15; 1 Pet. 2:4–8). Clearly seen in this picture is that each "stone" in the building truly needs the others.

Our fellowship together in mutually caring for one another is to give evidence of God's glory and purity, realizing that we have become the temple for the indwelling of the Holy Spirit (1 Cor. 6:19).

dominions or principalities or powers. All things were created through Him and for Him. [17]And He is before all things, and in Him all things consist. [18]And He is the head of the body, the church, who is the beginning, the firstborn from the dead, that in all things He may have the preeminence.

RECONCILED IN CHRIST

[19]For it pleased *the Father that* in Him all the fullness should dwell, [20]and by Him to reconcile all things to Himself, by Him, whether things on earth or things in heaven, having made peace through the blood of His cross.

[21]And you, who once were alienated and enemies in your mind by wicked works, yet now He has reconciled [22]in the body of His flesh through death, to present you holy, and blameless, and above reproach in His sight— [23]if indeed you continue in the faith, grounded and steadfast, and are not moved away from the hope of the gospel which you heard, which was preached to every creature under heaven, of which I, Paul, became a minister.

SACRIFICIAL SERVICE FOR CHRIST

[24]I now rejoice in my sufferings for you, and fill up in my flesh what is lacking in the afflictions of Christ, for the sake of His body, which is the church, [25]of which I became a minister according to the stewardship from God which was given to me for you, to fulfill the word of God, [26]the mystery which has been hidden from ages and from generations, but now has been revealed to His saints. [27]To them God willed to make known what are the riches of the glory of this mystery among the Gentiles: which[a] is Christ in you, the hope of glory. [28]Him we preach, warning every man and teaching every man in all wisdom, that we may present every man perfect in Christ Jesus. [29]To this *end* I also labor, striving according to His working which works in me mightily.

NOT PHILOSOPHY BUT CHRIST

2 For I want you to know what a great conflict I have for you and those in Laodicea, and *for* as many as have not seen my face in the flesh, [2]that their hearts may be encouraged, being knit together in love, and *attaining* to all riches of the full assurance of understanding, to the knowledge of the mystery of God, both of the Father and[a] of Christ, [3]in whom are hidden all the treasures of wisdom and knowledge.

[4]Now this I say lest anyone should deceive you with persuasive words. [5]For though I am absent in the flesh, yet I am with you in spirit, rejoicing to see your *good* order and the steadfastness of your faith in Christ.

[6]As you therefore have received Christ Jesus the Lord, so walk in Him, [7]rooted and built up in Him and established in the faith, as you have been taught, abounding in it[a] with thanksgiving.

[8]Beware lest anyone cheat you through philosophy and empty deceit, according to the tradition of men, according to the basic principles of the world, and not according to Christ. [9]For in Him dwells all the fullness of the Godhead bodily; [10]and you are complete in Him, who is the head of all principality and power.

NOT LEGALISM BUT CHRIST

[11]In Him you were also circumcised with the circumcision made without hands, by putting off the body of the sins[a] of the flesh, by the circumcision of Christ, [12]buried with Him in baptism, in which you also were raised with *Him* through faith in the working of God, who raised Him from the dead. [13]And you, being dead in your trespasses and the uncircumcision of your flesh, He has made alive together with Him, having forgiven you all trespasses, [14]having wiped out the handwriting of requirements that was against us, which was contrary to us. And He has taken it out of the way, having nailed it to the cross. [15]Having disarmed principalities and powers, He made a public spectacle of them, triumphing over them in it.

[16]So let no one judge you in food or in drink, or regarding a festival or a new moon or sabbaths, [17]which are a shadow of things to come, but the substance is of Christ. [18]Let no one cheat you of your reward, taking delight in *false* humility and worship of angels, intruding into those things which he has not[a] seen, vainly puffed up by his fleshly mind, [19]and not holding fast to the

---

1:27 [a]M-Text reads *who*. **2:2** [a]NU-Text omits *both of the Father and*. **2:7** [a]NU-Text omits *in it*. **2:11** [a]NU-Text omits *of the sins*. **2:18** [a]NU-Text omits *not*.

LEADERSHIP ISSUES

GC2: Following Jesus

COLOSSIANS 2:6

Discipleship involves Jesus "revealing" the way and our following or "yielding" to Him. Think about how God revealed Jesus to you to bring you to salvation. Did He reveal Christ through Scripture? Did He reveal Christ through the testimony of changed lives in those around you? Did He meet you and reveal Himself to you directly? How did you "hear" Him?

Christ was revealed to me for who He really is through _____

_____

_____ .

(For example: *Christ was revealed to me for who He really is through the gentle and gracious example of my grandfather.*)

My yielding to Him involved _____

_____

_____ .

(For example: *My yielding to Him involved a life transformation in which I stopped rebelling and began pursuing Him.*)

Take the time to share with one another the encounter with Christ that brought you into His kingdom. Then rejoice together "to the praise of the glory of His grace" (Eph. 1:6).

Close by reflecting on Colossians 2:6: "As you therefore have received Christ Jesus the Lord"—by God's revealing Himself and your yielding— continue to follow Jesus in this same way. Have a time of group prayer, praising God for the grace that brought you to salvation and asking Him for more revelation to which you might yield.

Heavenly Father, thank You for revealing Your Son to me. Praise You for the grace that has brought countless blessings to me as I have followed You. Please continue to reveal Yourself to me, as I continue to yield myself to You. In Jesus' name, Amen.

GC2

GREAT COMMANDMENT
COMMISSION

Head, from whom all the body, nourished and knit together by joints and ligaments, grows with the increase *that is* from God.

20Therefore,ª if you died with Christ from the basic principles of the world, why, as *though* living in the world, do you subject yourselves to regulations— 21"Do not touch, do not taste, do not handle," 22which all concern things which perish with the using—according to the commandments and doctrines of men? 23These things indeed have an appearance of wisdom in self-imposed religion, *false* humility, and neglect of the body, *but are* of no value against the indulgence of the flesh.

Not Carnality but Christ

3 If then you were raised with Christ, seek those things which are above, where Christ is, sitting at the right hand of God. 2Set your mind on things above, not on things on the earth. 3For you died, and your life is hidden with Christ in God. 4When Christ *who is* our life appears, then you also will appear with Him in glory.

5Therefore put to death your members which are on the earth: fornication, uncleanness, passion, evil desire, and covetousness, which is idolatry. 6Because of these things the wrath of God is coming upon the sons of disobedience, 7in which you yourselves once walked when you lived in them.

8But now you yourselves are to put off all these: anger, wrath, malice, blasphemy, filthy language out of your mouth. 9Do not lie to one another, since you have put off the old man with his deeds, 10and have put on the new *man* who is renewed in knowledge according to the image of Him who created him, 11where there is neither Greek nor Jew, circumcised nor uncircumcised, barbarian, Scythian, slave *nor* free, but Christ *is* all and in all.

Character of the New Man

12Therefore, as *the* elect of God, holy and beloved, put on tender mercies, kindness, humility, meekness, longsuffering; 13bearing with one another, and forgiving one another, if anyone has a complaint against another; even as Christ forgave you, so you also *must do.* 14But above all these things put on love, which is the bond of perfection. 15And let the peace of God rule in your hearts, to which also you were called in one body; and be thankful. 16Let the word of Christ dwell in you richly in all wisdom, teaching and admonishing one another in psalms and hymns and spiritual songs, singing with grace in your hearts to the Lord. 17And whatever you do in word or deed, *do*

2:20 ªNU-Text and M-Text omit *Therefore.*

LEADERSHIP REALITIES

EXCELLENCE *Colossians 3:1, 2*

Translated from the Latin, *excellence* is literally "to rise above." It is the standard set in heaven for us. In this sweeping current of change, we are all deeply affected by our carnal selves, circumstances, the crowd, and criticism. The effective leader must be steadfast in the goal of excellence in all things and no longer be bound by old habits, family traits, or personality. We cannot use our mistakes or the actions of others as an excuse for our inability to live strong and true. Christ most certainly can make us into godly, peaceful leaders. When we receive Christ as personal Savior, we no longer live according to the carnal self. Instead, we value others and ourselves in a new way. We are commanded to love ourselves as He loves us—unconditionally, without regard to past mistakes. We are commanded to live by His power. When we get this, a fresh wind fills our sails and a new start energizes in our hearts. Life is no longer about excuses and blame: "It's not my fault. My _____ (friend, parent, teacher, boss—fill in the blank) made me." Instead, you are committed to *rise above* life with an attitude of excellence.

all in the name of the Lord Jesus, giving thanks to God the Father through Him.

THE CHRISTIAN HOME

[18]Wives, submit to your own husbands, as is fitting in the Lord.

[19]Husbands, love your wives and do not be bitter toward them.

[20]Children, obey your parents in all things, for this is well pleasing to the Lord.

[21]Fathers, do not provoke your children, lest they become discouraged.

[22]Bondservants, obey in all things your masters according to the flesh, not with eyeservice, as men-pleasers, but in sincerity of heart, fearing God. [23]And whatever you do, do it heartily, as to the Lord and not to men, [24]knowing that from the Lord you will receive the reward of the inheritance; for[a] you serve the Lord Christ. [25]But he who does wrong will be repaid for what he has done, and there is no partiality.

4 Masters, give your bondservants what is just and fair, knowing that you also have a Master in heaven.

CHRISTIAN GRACES

[2]Continue earnestly in prayer, being vigilant in it with thanksgiving; [3]meanwhile praying also for us, that God would open to us a door for the word, to speak the mystery of Christ, for which I am also in chains, [4]that I may make it manifest, as I ought to speak.

[5]Walk in wisdom toward those *who are* outside, redeeming the time. [6]*Let* your speech always *be* with grace, seasoned with salt, that you may know how you ought to answer each one.

FINAL GREETINGS

[7]Tychicus, a beloved brother, faithful minister, and fellow servant in the Lord, will tell you all the news about me. [8]I am sending him to you for this very purpose, that he[a] may know your circumstances and comfort your hearts, [9]with Onesimus, a faithful and beloved brother, who is *one* of you. They will make known to you all things which *are happening* here.

[10]Aristarchus my fellow prisoner greets you, with Mark the cousin of Barnabas (about whom you received instructions: if he comes to you, welcome him), [11]and Jesus who is called Justus. These *are my* only fellow workers for the kingdom of God who are of the circumcision; they have proved to be a comfort to me.

[12]Epaphras, who is *one* of you, a bondservant of Christ, greets you, always laboring fervently for you in prayers, that you may stand perfect and complete[a] in all the will of God. [13]For I bear him witness that he has a great zeal[a] for you, and those who are in Laodicea, and those in Hierapolis. [14]Luke the beloved physician and Demas greet you. [15]Greet the brethren who are in Laodicea, and Nymphas and the church that *is* in his[a] house.

CLOSING EXHORTATIONS AND BLESSING

[16]Now when this epistle is read among you, see that it is read also in the church of the Laodiceans, and that you likewise read the *epistle* from Laodicea. [17]And say to Archippus, "Take heed to the ministry which you have received in the Lord, that you may fulfill it."

[18]This salutation by my own hand—Paul. Remember my chains. Grace *be* with you. Amen.

3:24 [a]NU-Text omits *for.* **4:8** [a]NU-Text reads *you may know our circumstances and he may.* **4:12** [a]NU-Text reads *fully assured.* **4:13** [a]NU-Text reads *concern.* **4:15** [a]NU-Text reads *Nympha . . . her house.*

IMPACT OF THE BOOK

I	IDEA	*The second coming of Jesus is the true hope of all humankind; it should be the source of motivation and comfort.*
m,	MESSAGE	*As Christians you will face hardships, but you must keep your focus on Christ. He alone is our salvation. The sufferings of this present life are bearable knowing that we will one day be united with our Savior and loved ones in the faith. Paul challenged, corrected, and comforted the Thessalonians like a parent.*
P	PEOPLE	*Paul, Silas, Silvanus, Timothy*
A	AUTHOR	*The apostle Paul, the principal author, used plural pronouns throughout most of the letter, referring to Timothy and Silvanus (Silas) who also contributed. When Paul left Thessalonica and Berea because of persecution, he went to Athens, sent word to Silas and Timothy to come to the city quickly, and immediately sent them to the church in Thessalonica.*
C	CULTURE	*Located on the Egnatian Way, Thessalonica, the self-governing capital of Macedonia and seat of Roman power, was situated at the intersection of river trade routes. The climate was ideal for crops, rain was abundant, forests provided timber for construction, and the rivers provided fish. Consequently, Thessalonica was not only the largest city but also a very strategic one from which to advance the gospel throughout the Roman Empire. The city's religious climate was diverse and included Judaism, the imperial cult, Greek gods Cabirus and Dionysus, along with Egyptian gods. Resident Jews had established a synagogue there. Religious affiliation was not private; it had far-reaching civic and social implications. Paul established this church during his second missionary journey recorded in Acts 17:1–9.*
T	TIMELINE	*c. AD 50*
	KEY SCRIPTURE MEMORY VERSES	2:8, 12; 4:13–18; 5:9, 10, 15–19

FIRST THESSALONIANS

GREETING

1 Paul, Silvanus, and Timothy,

To the church of the Thessalonians in God the Father and the Lord Jesus Christ:

Grace to you and peace from God our Father and the Lord Jesus Christ.[a]

THEIR GOOD EXAMPLE

[2]We give thanks to God always for you all, making mention of you in our prayers, [3]remembering without ceasing your work of faith, labor of love, and patience of hope in our Lord Jesus Christ in the sight of our God and Father, [4]knowing, beloved brethren, your election by God. [5]For our gospel did not come to you in word only, but also in power, and in the Holy Spirit and in much assurance, as you know what kind of men we were among you for your sake.

[6]And you became followers of us and of the Lord, having received the word in much affliction, with joy of the Holy Spirit, [7]so that you became examples to all in Macedonia and Achaia who believe. [8]For from you the word of the Lord has sounded forth, not only in Macedonia and Achaia, but also in every place. Your faith toward God has gone out, so that we do not need to say anything. [9]For they themselves declare concerning us what manner of entry we had to you, and how you turned to God from idols to serve the living and true God, [10]and to wait for His Son from heaven, whom He raised from the dead, *even* Jesus who delivers us from the wrath to come.

PAUL'S CONDUCT

2 For you yourselves know, brethren, that our coming to you was not in vain. [2]But even[a] after we had suffered before and were spitefully treated at Philippi, as you know, we were bold in our God to speak to you the gospel of God in much conflict. [3]For our exhortation *did* not *come* from error or uncleanness, nor *was it* in deceit.

[4]But as we have been approved by God to be entrusted with the gospel, even so we speak, not as pleasing men, but God who tests our hearts. [5]For neither at any time did we use flattering

words, as you know, nor a cloak for covetousness—God *is* witness. [6]Nor did we seek glory from men, either from you or from others, when we might have made demands as apostles of Christ. [7]But we were gentle among you, just as a nursing *mother* cherishes her own children. [8]So, affectionately longing for you, we were well pleased to impart to you not only the gospel of God, but also our own lives, because you had become dear to us. [9]For you remember, brethren, our labor and toil; for laboring night and day, that we might not be a burden to any of you, we preached to you the gospel of God.

[10]You *are* witnesses, and God *also,* how devoutly and justly and blamelessly we behaved ourselves among you who believe; [11]as you know how we exhorted, and comforted, and charged[a] every one of you, as a father *does* his own children, [12]that you would walk worthy of God who calls you into His own kingdom and glory.

THEIR CONVERSION

[13]For this reason we also thank God without ceasing, because when you received the word of God which you heard from us, you welcomed *it* not *as* the word of men, but as it is in truth, the word of God, which also effectively works in you who believe. [14]For you, brethren, became imitators of the churches of God which are in Judea in Christ Jesus. For you also suffered the same things from your own countrymen, just as they *did* from the Judeans, [15]who killed both the Lord Jesus and their own prophets, and have persecuted us; and they do not please God and are contrary to all men, [16]forbidding us to speak to the Gentiles that they may be saved, so as always to fill up *the measure of* their sins; but wrath has come upon them to the uttermost.

LONGING TO SEE THEM

[17]But we, brethren, having been taken away from you for a short time in presence, not in heart, endeavored more eagerly to see your face with great desire. [18]Therefore we wanted to come to you—even I, Paul, time and again—but Satan hindered us. [19]For what *is* our hope, or joy, or

1:1 [a]NU-Text omits *from God our Father and the Lord Jesus Christ.*
2:2 [a]NU-Text and M-Text omit *even.* 2:11 [a]NU-Text and M-Text read *implored.*

LEADERSHIP ISSUES

GC2: Who Am I? Sharing God's Life and Love

1 THESSALONIANS 2:8 *So, affectionately longing for you, we were well pleased to impart to you not only the gospel of God, but also our own lives, because you had become dear to us.*

When you and I reach out and relationally connect with someone, the Spirit of Christ actually ministers through us to that person, so that we are not just offering our own care and concern; we become a conduit of God's care. God has positioned each of us, as a member of His family, to express His love and acceptance as no one else can. Who are you? You are a unique expression of His life and love!

What that means in practical terms is that if another of Christ's followers—for any reason—feels disconnected and alone, God intends for other members of the body to provide that missing connection and remove that person's aloneness. If someone is hurting, the rest of the body can bring comfort and healing among the members, so that all the members care for each other equally. If one part suffers, all the parts suffer with it; and if one part is honored, all the parts are glad (1 Cor. 12:25, 26).

When you as a unique child of God demonstrate a sacrificial love to others, you are allowing them to experience a sampling of God's love. When you encounter someone who feels lonely and discouraged and you make yourself available to them, or when you say, "I identify with you and understand what you're going through," you are not only saying that they are valuable to you—you are also ministering God's love, availability, and understanding to them.

Additionally, as Christ's followers love one another well, others who do not yet know Christ see the difference He makes—and are drawn to Him (John 13:35).

GC2
GREAT COMMANDMENT
COMMISSION

crown of rejoicing? *Is it* not even you in the presence of our Lord Jesus Christ at His coming? [20]For you are our glory and joy.

CONCERN FOR THEIR FAITH

3 Therefore, when we could no longer endure it, we thought it good to be left in Athens alone, [2]and sent Timothy, our brother and minister of God, and our fellow laborer in the gospel of Christ, to establish you and encourage you concerning your faith, [3]that no one should be shaken by these afflictions; for you yourselves know that we are appointed to this. [4]For, in fact, we told you before when we were with you that we would suffer tribulation, just as it happened, and you know. [5]For this reason, when I could no longer endure it, I sent to know your faith, lest by some means the tempter had tempted you, and our labor might be in vain.

ENCOURAGED BY TIMOTHY

[6]But now that Timothy has come to us from you, and brought us good news of your faith and love, and that you always have good remembrance of us, greatly desiring to see us, as we also *to see* you— [7]therefore, brethren, in all our affliction and distress we were comforted concerning you by your faith. [8]For now we live, if you stand fast in the Lord.

[9]For what thanks can we render to God for you, for all the joy with which we rejoice for your sake before our God, [10]night and day praying exceedingly that we may see your face and perfect what is lacking in your faith?

PRAYER FOR THE CHURCH

[11]Now may our God and Father Himself, and our Lord Jesus Christ, direct our way to you. [12]And may the Lord make you increase and abound in love to one another and to all, just as we *do* to you, [13]so that He may establish your hearts blameless in holiness before our God and Father at the coming of our Lord Jesus Christ with all His saints.

PLEA FOR PURITY

4 Finally then, brethren, we urge and exhort in the Lord Jesus that you should abound more and more, just as you received from us how you ought to walk and to please God; [2]for you know what commandments we gave you through the Lord Jesus.

[3]For this is the will of God, your sanctification: that you should abstain from sexual immorality; [4]that each of you should know how to possess his own vessel in sanctification and honor, [5]not in passion of lust, like the Gentiles who do not know God; [6]that no one should take advantage of and defraud his brother in this matter, because the Lord *is* the avenger of all such, as we also forewarned you and testified. [7]For God did not call us to uncleanness, but in holiness. [8]Therefore he who rejects *this* does not reject man, but God, who has also given[a] us His Holy Spirit.

A BROTHERLY AND ORDERLY LIFE

[9]But concerning brotherly love you have no need that I should write to you, for you yourselves are taught by God to love one another; [10]and indeed you do so toward all the brethren who are in all Macedonia. But we urge you, brethren, that you increase more and more; [11]that you also aspire to lead a quiet life, to mind your own business, and to work with your own hands, as we commanded you, [12]that you may walk properly toward those who are outside, and *that* you may lack nothing.

THE COMFORT OF CHRIST'S COMING

[13]But I do not want you to be ignorant, brethren, concerning those who have fallen asleep, lest you sorrow as others who have no hope. [14]For if we believe that Jesus died and rose again, even so God will bring with Him those who sleep in Jesus.[a]

[15]For this we say to you by the word of the Lord, that we who are alive *and* remain until the coming of the Lord will by no means precede those who are asleep. [16]For the Lord Himself will descend from heaven with a shout, with the voice of an archangel, and with the trumpet of God. And the dead in Christ will rise first. [17]Then we who are alive *and* remain shall be caught up together with them in the clouds to meet the Lord in the air. And thus we shall always be with the

4:8 [a]NU-Text reads *who also gives.* **4:14** [a]Or *those who through Jesus sleep*

LEADERSHIP ISSUES

GC2: Spiritual Formation: Transformed in Fellowship

1 THESSALONIANS 5:5 *You are all sons of light and sons of the day. We are not of the night nor of darkness.*

At different times, Jesus declared to the disciples both, "I am the light of the world" (John 8:12) and "You are the light of the world" (Matt. 5:14). Undoubtedly the disciples found this paradox confusing. Maybe at some point, in an attempt to clear up the matter, they may have asked Him, "Master, are **You** the light of the world, or are **we** the light of the world?" Perhaps Jesus responded, "Yes!"

We, Christ's followers, have the privilege and calling to reveal God's light. This is a key way by which we express the life of Christ that dwells within us to others. Some of the acceptance that people who are failing need, you have within you! Some of the comfort that pain-filled people need, you have within you! Some of the support that struggling people need, you have within you!

Encountering God's light in one another is a significant aspect of the process of spiritual formation—becoming like Jesus. As we encounter God in and through other believers, we are transformed. This is why genuine fellowship is not optional; it is a necessary requirement for the spiritual transformation of every believer!

Pause to consider specific believers in your life: family, friends, and leaders who have passed along His light to you. They have accepted, comforted, supported, and loved you. Now experience Philippians 1:3 as you give thanks for every remembrance of them.

GC2
GREAT COMMANDMENT
COMMISSION

THROUGH THE GRID   *Discover God: God Is Faithful*

1 THESSALONIANS 5:24 *He who calls you is faithful, who also will do it.*

In the Old Testament, God's faithfulness is a central aspect that describes God's actions and relationships with humanity time and time again. God always keeps His word and always upholds His promises. God's love, grace, and mercy toward us never go away because God remains faithful to us, whether we deserve it or not. We can say with certainty that God's faithfulness is new every morning and available to us at every moment of the day and night. We can rely on God's faithfulness—God never forgets a promise He has made, and He will bring everything to completion in His good will. God is reliable, trustworthy, and faithful because God cannot be otherwise.

Lord. [18]Therefore comfort one another with these words.

THE DAY OF THE LORD

5 But concerning the times and the seasons, brethren, you have no need that I should write to you. [2]For you yourselves know perfectly that the day of the Lord so comes as a thief in the night. [3]For when they say, "Peace and safety!" then sudden destruction comes upon them, as labor pains upon a pregnant woman. And they shall not escape. [4]But you, brethren, are not in darkness, so that this Day should overtake you as a thief. [5]You are all sons of light and sons of the day. We are not of the night nor of darkness. [6]Therefore let us not sleep, as others *do,* but let us watch and be sober. [7]For those who sleep, sleep at night, and those who get drunk are drunk at night. [8]But let us who are of the day be sober, putting on the breastplate of faith and love, and *as* a helmet the hope of salvation. [9]For God did not appoint us to wrath, but to obtain salvation through our Lord Jesus Christ, [10]who died for us, that whether we wake or sleep, we should live together with Him.

[11]Therefore comfort each other and edify one another, just as you also are doing.

VARIOUS EXHORTATIONS

[12]And we urge you, brethren, to recognize those who labor among you, and are over you in the Lord and admonish you, [13]and to esteem them very highly in love for their work's sake. Be at peace among yourselves.

[14]Now we exhort you, brethren, warn those who are unruly, comfort the fainthearted, uphold the weak, be patient with all. [15]See that no one renders evil for evil to anyone, but always pursue what is good both for yourselves and for all.

[16]Rejoice always, [17]pray without ceasing, [18]in everything give thanks; for this is the will of God in Christ Jesus for you.

[19]Do not quench the Spirit. [20]Do not despise prophecies. [21]Test all things; hold fast what is good. [22]Abstain from every form of evil.

BLESSING AND ADMONITION

[23]Now may the God of peace Himself sanctify you completely; and may your whole spirit, soul, and body be preserved blameless at the coming of our Lord Jesus Christ. [24]He who calls you *is* faithful, who also will do *it.*

[25]Brethren, pray for us.

[26]Greet all the brethren with a holy kiss.

[27]I charge you by the Lord that this epistle be read to all the holy[a] brethren.

[28]The grace of our Lord Jesus Christ *be* with you. Amen.

5:27 [a]NU-Text omits *holy.*

GREETING

1 Paul, Silvanus, and Timothy,

To the church of the Thessalonians in God our Father and the Lord Jesus Christ:

²Grace to you and peace from God our Father and the Lord Jesus Christ.

GOD'S FINAL JUDGMENT AND GLORY

³We are bound to thank God always for you, brethren, as it is fitting, because your faith grows exceedingly, and the love of every one of you all abounds toward each other, ⁴so that we ourselves boast of you among the churches of God for your patience and faith in all your persecutions and tribulations that you endure, ⁵*which is* manifest evidence of the righteous judgment of God, that you may be counted worthy of the kingdom of God, for which you also suffer; ⁶since *it is* a righteous thing with God to repay with tribulation those who trouble you, ⁷and to *give* you who are troubled rest with us when the Lord Jesus is revealed from heaven with His mighty angels, ⁸in flaming fire taking vengeance on those who do not know God, and on those who do not obey the gospel of our Lord Jesus Christ. ⁹These shall be punished with everlasting destruction from the presence of the Lord and from the glory of His power, ¹⁰when He comes, in that Day, to be glorified in His saints and to be admired among all those who believe,ᵃ because our testimony among you was believed.

¹¹Therefore we also pray always for you that our God would count you worthy of *this* calling, and fulfill all the good pleasure of *His* goodness and the work of faith with power, ¹²that the name of our Lord Jesus Christ may be glorified in you, and you in Him, according to the grace of our God and the Lord Jesus Christ.

THE GREAT APOSTASY

2 Now, brethren, concerning the coming of our Lord Jesus Christ and our gathering together to Him, we ask you, ²not to be soon shaken in mind or troubled, either by spirit or by word or by letter, as if from us, as though the day of Christᵃ had come. ³Let no one deceive you by any means; for

that Day will not come unless the falling away comes first, and the man of sinᵃ is revealed, the son of perdition, ⁴who opposes and exalts himself above all that is called God or that is worshiped, so that he sits as Godᵃ in the temple of God, showing himself that he is God.

⁵Do you not remember that when I was still with you I told you these things? ⁶And now you know what is restraining, that he may be revealed in his own time. ⁷For the mystery of lawlessness is already at work; only Heᵃ who now restrains *will do so* until Heᵇ is taken out of the way. ⁸And then the lawless one will be revealed, whom the Lord will consume with the breath of His mouth and destroy with the brightness of His coming. ⁹The coming of the *lawless one* is according to the working of Satan, with all power, signs, and lying wonders, ¹⁰and with all unrighteous deception among those who perish, because they did not receive the love of the truth, that they might be saved. ¹¹And for this reason God will send them strong delusion, that they should believe the lie, ¹²that they all may be condemned who did not believe the truth but had pleasure in unrighteousness.

STAND FAST

¹³But we are bound to give thanks to God always for you, brethren beloved by the Lord, because God from the beginning chose you for salvation through sanctification by the Spirit and belief in the truth, ¹⁴to which He called you by our gospel, for the obtaining of the glory of our Lord Jesus Christ. ¹⁵Therefore, brethren, stand fast and hold the traditions which you were taught, whether by word or our epistle.

¹⁶Now may our Lord Jesus Christ Himself, and our God and Father, who has loved us and given *us* everlasting consolation and good hope by grace, ¹⁷comfort your hearts and establish you in every good word and work.

PRAY FOR US

3 Finally, brethren, pray for us, that the word of the Lord may run *swiftly* and be glorified, just as *it is* with you, ²and that we may be delivered

1:10 ᵃNU-Text and M-Text read *have believed.* 2:2 ᵃNU-Text reads *the Lord.* 2:3 ᵃNU-Text reads *lawlessness.* 2:4 ᵃNU-Text omits *as God.* 2:7 ᵃOr he ᵇOr he

IMPACT OF THE BOOK

I   **IDEA**   *Believers must never be idle, allowing winds of false teachings to distract them from serving Christ.*

M   **MESSAGE**   *Good leaders cultivate compassion for their followers and intuition regarding their needs. The young Thessalonian church faced great persecution and was being easily distracted by false beliefs; Paul knew he needed to lovingly correct their beliefs and at the same time to encourage them in the face of persecution. Like good parents, good leaders learn to chastise and to encourage with wisdom.*

P   **PEOPLE**   *Paul, Silvanus, Timothy*

A   **AUTHOR**   *Paul wrote his second letter to the Thessalonians shortly after his first letter, and most likely from Corinth where he stayed for eighteen months during his second missionary journey.*

C   **CULTURE**   *Since their arrival in Thessalonica, Paul, Silvanus, and Timothy were the cause of civil unrest (Acts 17:1–9). After spending at least three weeks and perhaps up to six months in Thessalonica, persecution forced Paul, Silvanus, and Timothy to flee. From Athens, Paul sent Timothy back to check on his beloved spiritual sons and daughters. Timothy met Paul in Corinth with his report. The believers in Thessalonica falsely believed that the "day of Christ" (2:2) had come. Many members quit their jobs to await the second coming of Christ. Paul wrote to them to correct this false belief.*

T   **TIMELINE**   *c. AD 50–51*

KEY SCRIPTURE MEMORY VERSES   3:3

SECOND THESSALONIANS

from unreasonable and wicked men; for not all have faith.

3But the Lord is faithful, who will establish you and guard *you* from the evil one. 4And we have confidence in the Lord concerning you, both that you do and will do the things we command you.

5Now may the Lord direct your hearts into the love of God and into the patience of Christ.

WARNING AGAINST IDLENESS

6But we command you, brethren, in the name of our Lord Jesus Christ, that you withdraw from every brother who walks disorderly and not according to the tradition which he* received from us. 7For you yourselves know how you ought to follow us, for we were not disorderly among you; 8nor did we eat anyone's bread free of charge, but worked with labor and toil night and day, that we might not be a burden to any of you, 9not because we do not have authority, but to make ourselves an example of how you should follow us.

10For even when we were with you, we commanded you this: If anyone will not work, neither

shall he eat. 11For we hear that there are some who walk among you in a disorderly manner, not working at all, but are busybodies. 12Now those who are such we command and exhort through our Lord Jesus Christ that they work in quietness and eat their own bread.

13But *as for you*, brethren, do not grow weary *in* doing good. 14And if anyone does not obey our word in this epistle, note that person and do not keep company with him, that he may be ashamed. 15Yet do not count *him* as an enemy, but admonish *him* as a brother.

BENEDICTION

16Now may the Lord of peace Himself give you peace always in every way. The Lord *be* with you all.

17The salutation of Paul with my own hand, which is a sign in every epistle; so I write.

18The grace of our Lord Jesus Christ *be* with you all. Amen.

3:6 NU-Text and M-Text read *they.*

FIRST TIMOTHY

IDEA

Never let anyone look down on you because of your youth. A "novice" means newly planted or not tested, but one can be a disciplined and trusted servant leader even at a young age.

MESSAGE

Leaders must hold themselves to higher standards as they are examples to other believers in their speech, acts, love, and spirit. One's ability to influence is in direct proportion to one's integrity. A leader can inspire and inform from a distance but can only influence and impact by being up close and personal.

PEOPLE

Alexander, Hymenaeus, Paul, Timothy

AUTHOR

First Timothy is one of two letters Paul wrote to his disciple and son in the faith. These letters, together with a third written to his disciple Titus, are commonly called the Pastoral Epistles since they gave instruction and encouragement to two young men in pastoral roles. Since Paul refers to Timothy as "a true son in the faith," he possibly led Timothy to personal faith in Christ.

CULTURE

Timothy was from Lystra, a city in southern Asia Minor. Timothy's mother and grandmother, who were Jewish, taught him the Scriptures from an early age. He was highly esteemed by the church leaders in Lystra. During Paul's second visit there, he asked Timothy to join him. In order to avoid potential conflicts with Jews, who knew Timothy's father was a Gentile, Paul circumcised him. Later, traveling with Paul and as Paul's representative to various churches, his purpose was to bring doctrinal clarity, set up organizational stability, and to lovingly train up the believers in righteous living.

TIMELINE c. AD 63

KEY SCRIPTURE 1:15, 18, 19; 2:5; 3:1–15; 4:8, 12; 5:22; 6:7, 10
MEMORY VERSES

Greeting

1 Paul, an apostle of Jesus Christ, by the commandment of God our Savior and the Lord Jesus Christ, our hope,

²To Timothy, a true son in the faith:

Grace, mercy, *and* peace from God our Father and Jesus Christ our Lord.

No Other Doctrine

³As I urged you when I went into Macedonia—remain in Ephesus that you may charge some that they teach no other doctrine, ⁴nor give heed to fables and endless genealogies, which cause disputes rather than godly edification which is in faith. ⁵Now the purpose of the commandment is love from a pure heart, *from* a good conscience, and *from* sincere faith, ⁶from which some, having strayed, have turned aside to idle talk, ⁷desiring to be teachers of the law, understanding neither what they say nor the things which they affirm.

⁸But we know that the law *is* good if one uses it lawfully, ⁹knowing this: that the law is not made for a righteous person, but for *the* lawless and insubordinate, for *the* ungodly and for sinners, for *the* unholy and profane, for murderers of fathers and murderers of mothers, for manslayers, ¹⁰for fornicators, for sodomites, for kidnappers, for liars, for perjurers, and if there is any other thing that is contrary to sound doctrine, ¹¹according to the glorious gospel of the blessed God which was committed to my trust.

Glory to God for His Grace

¹²And I thank Christ Jesus our Lord who has enabled me, because He counted me faithful, putting *me* into the ministry, ¹³although I was formerly a blasphemer, a persecutor, and an insolent man; but I obtained mercy because I did *it* ignorantly in unbelief. ¹⁴And the grace of our Lord was exceedingly abundant, with faith and love which are in Christ Jesus. ¹⁵This *is* a faithful saying and worthy of all acceptance, that Christ Jesus came into the world to save sinners, of whom I am chief. ¹⁶However, for this reason I obtained mercy, that in me first Jesus Christ might show all

longsuffering, as a pattern to those who are going to believe on Him for everlasting life. ¹⁷Now to the King eternal, immortal, invisible, to God who alone is wise,[a] *be* honor and glory forever and ever. Amen.

Fight the Good Fight

¹⁸This charge I commit to you, son Timothy, according to the prophecies previously made concerning you, that by them you may wage the good warfare, ¹⁹having faith and a good conscience, which some having rejected, concerning the faith have suffered shipwreck, ²⁰of whom are Hymenaeus and Alexander, whom I delivered to Satan that they may learn not to blaspheme.

Pray for All Men

2 Therefore I exhort first of all that supplications, prayers, intercessions, *and* giving of thanks be made for all men, ²for kings and all who are in authority, that we may lead a quiet and peaceable life in all godliness and reverence. ³For this *is* good and acceptable in the sight of God our Savior, ⁴who desires all men to be saved and to come to the knowledge of the truth. ⁵For *there is* one God and one Mediator between God and men, *the* Man Christ Jesus, ⁶who gave Himself a ransom for all, to be testified in due time, ⁷for which I was appointed a preacher and an apostle—I am speaking the truth in Christ[a] *and* not lying—a teacher of the Gentiles in faith and truth.

Men and Women in the Church

⁸I desire therefore that the men pray everywhere, lifting up holy hands, without wrath and doubting; ⁹in like manner also, that the women adorn themselves in modest apparel, with propriety and moderation, not with braided hair or gold or pearls or costly clothing, ¹⁰but, which is proper for women professing godliness, with good works. ¹¹Let a woman learn in silence with all submission. ¹²And I do not permit a woman to teach or to have authority over a man, but to be in silence. ¹³For Adam was formed first, then Eve. ¹⁴And Adam was not deceived, but the woman being deceived, fell into transgression. ¹⁵Nevertheless she will be saved in childbearing if they

---

1:17 [a]NU-Text reads *to the only God.*   **2:7** [a]NU-Text omits *in Christ.*

THROUGH THE GRID

Thinking Christianly: Six Points of Divergence Between Christianity and Other Religions (1 Tim. 2:5)

1. The Christian God is personal, and He is the Father! Most religions have a more impersonal view of God.
2. Christ is Savior. All the other religions merely offer great teachers, such as Mohammed and Buddha.
3. All people are valued greatly according to a Christian anthropology. Human beings are image bearers of God. Other religions place much less value on personhood and the individual's relation to God.
4. A Christian philosophy of history is linear and has an ultimate meaning and purpose. The Eastern religions have a cyclical view of history.
5. Christian salvation is by grace through faith in Christ. Virtually all other religions offer salvation by works.
6. Christian eschatology is based on the hope of the bodily resurrection. Other religions offer immortality of the soul, reincarnation, or nirvana. The body is basically deemed evil or inferior in those systems.

continue in faith, love, and holiness, with self-control.

QUALIFICATIONS OF OVERSEERS

3 This *is* a faithful saying: If a man desires the position of a bishop,[a] he desires a good work. [2]A bishop then must be blameless, the husband of one wife, temperate, sober-minded, of good behavior, hospitable, able to teach; [3]not given to wine, not violent, not greedy for money,[a] but gentle, not quarrelsome, not covetous; [4]one who rules his own house well, having *his* children in submission with all reverence [5](for if a man does not know how to rule his own house, how will he take care of the church of God?); [6]not a novice, lest being puffed up with pride he fall into the *same* condemnation as the devil. [7]Moreover he must have a good testimony among those who are outside, lest he fall into reproach and the snare of the devil.

QUALIFICATIONS OF DEACONS

[8]Likewise deacons *must be* reverent, not double-tongued, not given to much wine, not greedy for money, [9]holding the mystery of the faith with a pure conscience. [10]But let these also first be tested; then let them serve as deacons, being *found*

blameless. [11]Likewise, *their* wives *must be* reverent, not slanderers, temperate, faithful in all things. [12]Let deacons be the husbands of one wife, ruling *their* children and their own houses well. [13]For those who have served well as deacons obtain for themselves a good standing and great boldness in the faith which is in Christ Jesus.

THE GREAT MYSTERY

[14]These things I write to you, though I hope to come to you shortly; [15]but if I am delayed, *I write* so that you may know how you ought to conduct yourself in the house of God, which is the church of the living God, the pillar and ground of the truth. [16]And without controversy great is the mystery of godliness:

God[a] was manifested in the flesh,
Justified in the Spirit,
Seen by angels,
Preached among the Gentiles,
Believed on in the world,
Received up in glory.

3:1 [a]Literally *overseer* **3:3** [a]NU-Text omits *not greedy for money.*
3:16 [a]NU-Text reads *Who.*

| THROUGH THE GRID | *Making Sense of Your World:*
Inerrancy of the Canon (1 Tim. 3:16) |

Since we can be confident that the Scripture we have is the Word of God to humanity, we must ask about the content of the Scripture: Is Scripture reliable and dependable? Is it accurate? Biblical scholars refer to the term "inerrancy" to denote the degree to which a Scripture is trustworthy. Because the Scriptures were divinely inspired, we must trust the process by which the texts were written and believe the canon is inerrant and without fault in all of its contents and teachings. This is what sets the Bible over and above any other book or authoritative source. We have the direct Word of God for humanity, and it is inerrant in content. The purpose for inspiration was to direct the thoughts of the human authors, since they were fallible and errant beings, as well as to render them incapable of producing error. This is not to say that they lost their individuality and their unique ways of writing. The Holy Spirit did not dictate the text word for word, but rather guided the writers as they wrote and kept them from error in their writings. The authority of the Bible rests firmly in the Person and the claims of Jesus Christ. Jesus believed that Scripture was given by God, that it was authoritative, and that it was inerrant. Inerrancy is stated both explicitly and implicitly by Christ. We can rest assured as readers of the Scripture today that the Bible we hold in our hands has been thoroughly preserved by the Holy Spirit and is relevant to us.

THE GREAT APOSTASY

4 Now the Spirit expressly says that in latter times some will depart from the faith, giving heed to deceiving spirits and doctrines of demons, ²speaking lies in hypocrisy, having their own conscience seared with a hot iron, ³forbidding to marry, *and commanding* to abstain from foods which God created to be received with thanksgiving by those who believe and know the truth. ⁴For every creature of God *is* good, and nothing is to be refused if it is received with thanksgiving; ⁵for it is sanctified by the word of God and prayer.

A GOOD SERVANT OF JESUS CHRIST

⁶If you instruct the brethren in these things, you will be a good minister of Jesus Christ, nourished in the words of faith and of the good doctrine which you have carefully followed. ⁷But reject profane and old wives' fables, and exercise yourself toward godliness. ⁸For bodily exercise profits a little, but godliness is profitable for all things, having promise of the life that now is and of that which is to come. ⁹This *is* a faithful saying and worthy of all acceptance. ¹⁰For to this *end* we both labor and suffer reproach,ᵃ because we trust

in the living God, who is *the* Savior of all men, especially of those who believe. ¹¹These things command and teach.

TAKE HEED TO YOUR MINISTRY

¹²Let no one despise your youth, but be an example to the believers in word, in conduct, in love, in spirit,ᵃ in faith, in purity. ¹³Till I come, give attention to reading, to exhortation, to doctrine. ¹⁴Do not neglect the gift that is in you, which was given to you by prophecy with the laying on of the hands of the eldership. ¹⁵Meditate on these things; give yourself entirely to them, that your progress may be evident to all. ¹⁶Take heed to yourself and to the doctrine. Continue in them, for in doing this you will save both yourself and those who hear you.

TREATMENT OF CHURCH MEMBERS

5 Do not rebuke an older man, but exhort *him* as a father, younger men as brothers, ²older women as mothers, younger women as sisters, with all purity.

4:10 ᵃNU-Text reads *we labor and strive.* **4:12** ᵃNU-Text omits *in spirit.*

HONOR TRUE WIDOWS

[3]Honor widows who are really widows. [4]But if any widow has children or grandchildren, let them first learn to show piety at home and to repay their parents; for this is good and[a] acceptable before God. [5]Now she who is really a widow, and left alone, trusts in God and continues in supplications and prayers night and day. [6]But she who lives in pleasure is dead while she lives. [7]And these things command, that they may be blameless. [8]But if anyone does not provide for his own, and especially for those of his household, he has denied the faith and is worse than an unbeliever.

[9]Do not let a widow under sixty years old be taken into the number, *and not unless* she has been the wife of one man, [10]well reported for good works: if she has brought up children, if she has lodged strangers, if she has washed the saints' feet, if she has relieved the afflicted, if she has diligently followed every good work.

[11]But refuse *the* younger widows; for when they have begun to grow wanton against Christ, they desire to marry, [12]having condemnation because they have cast off their first faith. [13]And besides they learn *to be* idle, wandering about from house to house, and not only idle but also gossips and busybodies, saying things which they ought not. [14]Therefore I desire that *the* younger *widows* marry, bear children, manage the house, give no opportunity to the adversary to speak reproachfully. [15]For some have already turned aside after Satan. [16]If any believing man or[a] woman has widows, let them relieve them, and do not let the church be burdened, that it may relieve those who are really widows.

HONOR THE ELDERS

[17]Let the elders who rule well be counted worthy of double honor, especially those who labor in the word and doctrine. [18]For the Scripture says, *"You shall not muzzle an ox while it treads out the grain,"*[a] and, "The laborer *is* worthy of his wages."[b] [19]Do not receive an accusation against an elder except from two or three witnesses. [20]Those who are sinning rebuke in the presence of all, that the rest also may fear.

[21]I charge *you* before God and the Lord Jesus Christ and the elect angels that you observe these things without prejudice, doing nothing with partiality. [22]Do not lay hands on anyone hastily, nor share in other people's sins; keep yourself pure.

[23]No longer drink only water, but use a little wine for your stomach's sake and your frequent infirmities.

[24]Some men's sins are clearly evident, preceding *them* to judgment, but those of some *men* follow later. [25]Likewise, the good works *of some* are clearly evident, and those that are otherwise cannot be hidden.

HONOR MASTERS

6 Let as many bondservants as are under the yoke count their own masters worthy of all honor, so that the name of God and *His* doctrine may not be blasphemed. [2]And those who have believing masters, let them not despise *them* because they are brethren, but rather serve *them* because those who are benefited are believers and beloved. Teach and exhort these things.

ERROR AND GREED

[3]If anyone teaches otherwise and does not consent to wholesome words, *even* the words of our Lord Jesus Christ, and to the doctrine which accords with godliness, [4]he is proud, knowing nothing, but is obsessed with disputes and arguments over words, from which come envy, strife, reviling, evil suspicions, [5]useless wranglings[a] of men of corrupt minds and destitute of the truth, who suppose that godliness is a *means of* gain. From such withdraw yourself.[b]

[6]Now godliness with contentment is great gain. [7]For we brought nothing into *this* world, *and it is* certain[a] we can carry nothing out. [8]And having food and clothing, with these we shall be content. [9]But those who desire to be rich fall into temptation and a snare, and *into* many foolish and harmful lusts which drown men in destruction and perdition. [10]For the love of money is a root of all *kinds of* evil, for which some have strayed from the faith in their greediness, and pierced themselves through with many sorrows.

The Good Confession

[11]But you, O man of God, flee these things and pursue righteousness, godliness, faith, love, patience, gentleness. [12]Fight the good fight of faith, lay hold on eternal life, to which you were also called and have confessed the good confession in the presence of many witnesses. [13]I urge you in the sight of God who gives life to all things, and *before* Christ Jesus who witnessed the good confession before Pontius Pilate, [14]that you keep *this* commandment without spot, blameless until our Lord Jesus Christ's appearing, [15]which He will manifest in His own time, *He who is* the blessed and only Potentate, the King of kings and Lord of lords, [16]who alone has immortality, dwelling in unapproachable light, whom no man has seen or can see, to whom *be* honor and everlasting power. Amen.

Instructions to the Rich

[17]Command those who are rich in this present age not to be haughty, nor to trust in uncertain riches but in the living God, who gives us richly all things to enjoy. [18]*Let them* do good, that they be rich in good works, ready to give, willing to share, [19]storing up for themselves a good foundation for the time to come, that they may lay hold on eternal life.

Guard the Faith

[20]O Timothy! Guard what was committed to your trust, avoiding the profane *and* idle babblings and contradictions of what is falsely called knowledge— [21]by professing it some have strayed concerning the faith.

Grace *be* with you. Amen.

IMPACT OF THE BOOK

SECOND TIMOTHY

IDEA		*Christians must be committed to the message of truth that has been entrusted to them. Effective leaders must re-mind themselves of their heritage, their calling, and their gifts. By stirring up those gifts, the leader will be able to demonstrate courage, perseverance, and sound doctrine, even in the last days.*
MESSAGE		*Great leaders know their strengths and their weaknesses, and they learn to lead based on their own unique gifts. Timothy would never be a Paul, nor was he as tough as Titus; but God had especially equipped Timothy with the gifts of power, love, and a sound mind (2 Tim. 1:7). Love allowed him to be accessible and to connect with those around him. A sound mind is not divided by fear, but it has a clear vision of what needs to be done and how.*
PEOPLE		*Alexander, Carpus, Crescens, Demas, John Mark, Luke, Paul, Timothy, Titus*
AUTHOR		*Paul wrote this letter from a cold, damp dungeon, bound in chains in a Roman prison where he awaited a second judicial hearing. He was virtually alone, and he urged Timothy to come see him before his execution. This epistle was his final instruction, his last will and testament to the one person he wanted with him in the final hours.*
CULTURE		*Timothy received this very personal letter in Ephesus where he served the church, founded by Paul, which was infiltrated by false teachers. The culture in Ephesus is revealed by studying the activities of Paul's opponents: a group of itinerant Jewish Christians promoting strict ascetic practices and teaching that the resurrection "is already past," a false doctrine not mentioned in the previous letter. Paul, impris-oned, admonishes Timothy to swim against the tide of apostasy and to stay true to the inspired scriptures (2 Tim. 3:10–17).*
TIMELINE		*c. AD 66*
KEY SCRIPTURE MEMORY VERSES		2:2, 15, 22; 3:14–17; 4:1, 2, 7, 8

GREETING

1 Paul, an apostle of Jesus Christ[a] by the will of God, according to the promise of life which is in Christ Jesus,

[2]To Timothy, a beloved son:

Grace, mercy, *and* peace from God the Father and Christ Jesus our Lord.

TIMOTHY'S FAITH AND HERITAGE

[3]I thank God, whom I serve with a pure conscience, as *my* forefathers *did,* as without ceasing I remember you in my prayers night and day, [4]greatly desiring to see you, being mindful of your tears, that I may be filled with joy, [5]when I call to remembrance the genuine faith that is in you, which dwelt first in your grandmother Lois and your mother Eunice, and I am persuaded is in you also. [6]Therefore I remind you to stir up the gift of God which is in you through the laying on of my hands. [7]For God has not given us a spirit of fear, but of power and of love and of a sound mind.

NOT ASHAMED OF THE GOSPEL

[8]Therefore do not be ashamed of the testimony of our Lord, nor of me His prisoner, but share with me in the sufferings for the gospel according to the power of God, [9]who has saved us and called *us* with a holy calling, not according to our works, but according to His own purpose and grace which was given to us in Christ Jesus before time began, [10]but has now been revealed by the appearing of our Savior Jesus Christ, *who* has abolished death and brought life and immortality to light through the gospel, [11]to which I was appointed a preacher, an apostle, and a teacher of the Gentiles.[a] [12]For this reason I also suffer these things; nevertheless I am not ashamed, for I know whom I have believed and am persuaded that He is able to keep what I have committed to Him until that Day.

BE LOYAL TO THE FAITH

[13]Hold fast the pattern of sound words which you have heard from me, in faith and love which are in Christ Jesus. [14]That good thing which was committed to you, keep by the Holy Spirit who dwells in us.

[15]This you know, that all those in Asia have turned away from me, among whom are Phygellus and Hermogenes. [16]The Lord grant mercy to

1:1 [a]NU-Text and M-Text read *Christ Jesus.* 1:11 [a]NU-Text omits *of the Gentiles.*

LEADERSHIP REALITIES

ATTITUDE: A SUPERNATURAL GIFT OR A GOOD SUGGESTION *2 Timothy 1:6–12*

Attitude is the most significant daily decision of leadership. The last letter the apostle Paul wrote was addressed to a young man he mentored named Timothy. In the opening words, he provides a twofold insight about attitude that could easily be overlooked: it is both a holy calling and a gift from God. Because of this, leaders must make a daily decision to stir up the gift of God within them. The key to comprehending this principle is in understanding the manner in which Paul uses the word "spirit" (*pneuma*) in verse 7. Here it does not refer to the Holy Spirit but rather to characteristics or attitudes that find their **source** in the Holy Spirit. The attitudes that should be reflected in the leader's life are as follows:

- *Dynamis:* **power**—the ability to operate with strength of character and moral authority allowing the leader to rise above any situation that may occur in life.
- *Agapē:* **love**—genuine love not only for God but for those the leader influences.
- *Sōphronismos:* **self-control**—the ability to master one's moods, control one's desires, and never be held hostage by feelings and circumstances.

LEADERSHIP ISSUES

Identity Theft

2 TIMOTHY 1:12–14

Followers of Christ were first called *Christians* in Acts 11:26 because of what they believed, how they behaved, and to whom they belonged. Their identity was sure and strong. Jesus warned us that Satan would try to rob the leader of his or her integrity and testimony as a Christ-follower. "The thief does not come except to steal, and to kill, and to destroy." (John 10:10).

Forces at work in our culture want to rob the identity of Christians. Instead of a pure, peaceful identity as a child of God, they want us to appear confused, weak-willed, spiritually impotent, and emotionally unhealthy. There is a form of identity theft taking place among Christian students. In record numbers, people are simply walking away from what they once believed, and they are assuming the spiritual identity of the "crowd" or the popular culture around them. Second Timothy 1:12–14 tells us to "hold fast the pattern of sound words." By doing this, we can find the power to both establish and continue in the identity of a Christ-follower.

There are identity thieves at the door of every heart. They wait for the chance to rob our genuine joy, peace, and confidence from Christ. They try to replace it with the counterfeit and temporary offerings of the present culture. Leaders must guard against the thieves of:

- alcohol and other drugs,
- the past,
- sexual experiences and experiments,
- self-sabotage,
- the agenda of the culture,
- the rationalization of bad choices,
- settling for "good enough" instead excellence,
- measuring lifestyle by the culture instead of by absolute truth.

It is the responsibility of every leader to live in such a way that identity in Christ will be clear and significant. The wisdom to live skillfully cannot be found in a dictionary or in an on-line search. Only through earnest study of the Scriptures (God's personal message to the world) will one find understanding, strength, and passion for real life.

the household of Onesiphorus, for he often refreshed me, and was not ashamed of my chain; [17]but when he arrived in Rome, he sought me out very zealously and found *me*. [18]The Lord grant to him that he may find mercy from the Lord in that Day—and you know very well how many ways he ministered *to me*[a] at Ephesus.

BE STRONG IN GRACE

2 You therefore, my son, be strong in the grace that is in Christ Jesus. [2]And the things that you have heard from me among many witnesses, commit these to faithful men who will be able to teach others also. [3]You therefore must endure[a] hardship as a good soldier of Jesus Christ. [4]No one engaged in warfare entangles himself with the affairs of *this* life, that he may please him who enlisted him as a soldier. [5]And also if anyone competes in athletics, he is not crowned unless he competes according to the rules. [6]The hardworking farmer must be first to partake of the crops. [7]Consider what I say, and may[a] the Lord give you understanding in all things.

[8]Remember that Jesus Christ, of the seed of David, was raised from the dead according to my gospel, [9]for which I suffer trouble as an evildoer, *even* to the point of chains; but the word of God is not chained. [10]Therefore I endure all things for the sake of the elect, that they also may obtain the salvation which is in Christ Jesus with eternal glory.

[11]*This is* a faithful saying:

For if we died with *Him,*
　　We shall also live with *Him.*
[12]If we endure,
　　We shall also reign with *Him.*
If we deny *Him,*
　　He also will deny us.
[13]If we are faithless,
　　He remains faithful;
　　He cannot deny Himself.

APPROVED AND DISAPPROVED WORKERS

[14]Remind *them* of these things, charging *them* before the Lord not to strive about words to no profit, to the ruin of the hearers. [15]Be diligent to present yourself approved to God, a worker who does not need to be ashamed, rightly dividing the word of truth. [16]But shun profane *and* idle babblings, for they will increase to more ungodliness. [17]And their message will spread like cancer. Hymenaeus and Philetus are of this sort, [18]who have strayed concerning the truth, saying that the resurrection is already past; and they overthrow the faith of some. [19]Nevertheless the solid foundation of God stands, having this seal: "The Lord knows those who are His," and, "Let everyone who names the name of Christ[a] depart from iniquity."

[20]But in a great house there are not only vessels of gold and silver, but also of wood and clay, some for honor and some for dishonor. [21]Therefore if anyone cleanses himself from the latter, he will be a vessel for honor, sanctified and useful for the Master, prepared for every good work. [22]Flee also youthful lusts; but pursue righteousness, faith, love, peace with those who call on the Lord out of a pure heart. [23]But avoid foolish and ignorant disputes, knowing that they generate strife. [24]And a servant of the Lord must not quarrel but be gentle to all, able to teach, patient, [25]in humility correcting those who are in opposition, if God perhaps will grant them repentance, so that they may know the truth, [26]and *that* they may come to their senses *and escape* the snare of the devil, having been taken captive by him to *do* his will.

PERILOUS TIMES AND PERILOUS MEN

3 But know this, that in the last days perilous times will come: [2]For men will be lovers of themselves, lovers of money, boasters, proud, blasphemers, disobedient to parents, unthankful, unholy, [3]unloving, unforgiving, slanderers, without self-control, brutal, despisers of good, [4]traitors, headstrong, haughty, lovers of pleasure rather than lovers of God, [5]having a form of godliness but denying its power. And from such people turn away! [6]For of this sort are those who creep into households and make captives of gullible women loaded down with sins, led away by various lusts, [7]always learning and never able to come to the knowledge of the truth. [8]Now as Jannes and Jambres resisted Moses, so do these also resist the truth: men of corrupt minds, disapproved concerning

---

1:18 [a]*To me* is from the Vulgate and a few Greek manuscripts. **2:3** [a]NU-Text reads *You must share.* **2:7** [a]NU-Text reads *the Lord will give you.* **2:19** [a]NU-Text and M-Text read *the Lord.*

LEADERSHIP ISSUES

GC2: Who to "Hang With"

2 TIMOTHY 2:22

The apostle Paul is being a good friend to young Timothy as he passes on wisdom from life experience. Paul has seen the pain of "youthful lusts" as it destroyed lives, fellowship, and witness (1 Cor. 5:1, 2; 6:15–20).

Therefore Paul's counsel is to flee immorality just as Joseph fled from the temptation of Potiphar's wife (Gen. 39:12). Immorality of thought, action, and habit brings reproach upon our body as the "temple of the Holy Spirit." It selfishly wounds others, and it scars our conscience concerning God's plan for future relationships.

Significantly, Paul couples his counsel to "flee" with wisdom concerning friendship. Who is it that we "hang with"? Where are we to find our close friends? Paul's counsel is clear: "with those who call on the Lord out of a pure heart" (2 Tim. 2:22).

Do your close friends know the Lord in an intimate personal way? Do they "call" on Him for wisdom and direction? Are they able to come before Him in prayer and worship with a pure heart? They're not perfect, but they are pure in heart because of His forgiveness and cleansing.

Pause to thank God for making you this kind of friend and for blessing you with those like-minded. Now, together as friends, you are ready to pursue Him, to know Him, and to make Him known!

LEADERSHIP ISSUES

Why Do Bad Things Happen to Me?

JOHN 16:33

In John 16:33, Jesus didn't say, "If you have tribulation" or, "You might have tribulation." No, He told His disciples, "You will have tribulation." It's a given—everyone who lives in this world will experience tribulation, or hard times, at some point in life.

As Christians, we have an even higher likelihood of experiencing difficulty in this world. Concerning this, the apostle Paul wrote, "All who desire to live godly in Christ Jesus will suffer persecution" (2 Tim. 3:12). We go against the grain, and that can make life rough sometimes. "All" is a little word, but it has a big meaning. There are no exceptions: every person who follows Christ in this world will experience tribulation, suffering, and persecution at some point in life. Why would one person, who is loved by God, be exempt from adversity when another is not? The Lord Jesus was not exempt; in fact, He faced the worst adversity.

A false view of God causes us to feel that anytime adversity occurs, it is the result of something we did. That outlook implies that the world revolves around one individual's life and that God is an angry judge standing by ready to pour out judgment upon that person. The truth is, God hates sin, but loves every sinner intensely. The judgment for our sin was already poured out on Jesus.

Every adversity is not about an individual's sin. Jesus' disciples assumed that a man's blindness was because of sin. They asked Jesus, "Rabbi, who sinned, this man or his parents, that he was born blind?" (John 9:2). Listen carefully to what Jesus answered because this wisdom will carry you through every adversity of your life: "Neither this man nor his parents sinned, but that the works of God should be revealed in him" (John 9:3). Adversity is the opportunity to see God at work. When a person looks at adversity from his or her own point of view, a pity-party is sure to follow. These parties are not usually well attended, and the result is depression. However, a leader who walks confidently through life looks at difficulty from God's point of view; he or she sees it not as an obstacle but as an opportunity for God to work.

LEADERSHIP ISSUES

GC2: Convictions: The Power Behind the Bible

2 TIMOTHY 3:16, 17   *All Scripture is given by inspiration of God, and is profitable for doctrine, for reproof, for correction, for instruction in righteousness, that the man of God may be complete, thoroughly equipped for every good work.*

All the teachings of Scripture—whether in the form of an instruction, parable, admonition, precept, ordinance, or command—are intended to show us the right way. And when God's Word says, "Follow this way," "Avoid those places," "Abstain from those actions," or "Embrace those thoughts," it is not trying to restrict us or bully us.

God always has our best interests at heart, and His work is intended to protect us and provide for us. The convictions He leads us in through His Word are "for our good," just as Moses instructed the nation of Israel: "Keep the commandments of the LORD and His statutes which I command you today for your good" (Deut. 10:13).

To be "instructed in righteousness" is to be "raised" or "matured" through our intimate relationship with God. Being honest brings blessings because God is true. Staying sexually pure brings blessing because God is just. God's commands for us to act in certain ways flow out of who He is and how He Himself acts. His ways simply reflect who He is—perfectly right—and that way of living brings blessing.

But the fundamental purpose of the Bible goes even deeper than providing us with rules and guidelines that can bless our lives. The authority and power of Scripture to protect us and provide for us derive from the Author of the Book—God Himself. God is the power behind the Book.

Pause and ask God to lead you often in Scripture that will deepen your love for Him!

GREAT COMMANDMENT
COMMISSION

| **THROUGH THE GRID** | *Thinking Christianly: Ten Foundational Beliefs of a Christian Worldview* |

Belief Two: Revelation (*2 Tim. 3:16, 17*)

God has revealed Himself in nature and in Scripture and supremely in His Son, Jesus Christ. The Bible is God's revelation to us, which is infallible and inerrant. It truthfully reveals knowledge to us about God, the world, and humanity. The Bible is the ultimate authority for faith and life (Ps. 19; 119; Matt. 5:17, 18; John 10:35; Rom. 1:18–20; 2 Tim. 3:16, 17; 2 Pet. 1:20, 21). *See Through the Grid article on page 1566.*

the faith; [9]but they will progress no further, for their folly will be manifest to all, as theirs also was.

The Man of God and the Word of God

[10]But you have carefully followed my doctrine, manner of life, purpose, faith, longsuffering, love, perseverance, [11]persecutions, afflictions, which happened to me at Antioch, at Iconium, at Lystra—what persecutions I endured. And out of *them* all the Lord delivered me. [12]Yes, and all who desire to live godly in Christ Jesus will suffer persecution. [13]But evil men and impostors will grow worse and worse, deceiving and being deceived. [14]But you must continue in the things which you have learned and been assured of, knowing from whom you have learned *them,* [15]and that from childhood you have known the Holy Scriptures, which are able to make you wise for salvation through faith which is in Christ Jesus.

[16]All Scripture *is* given by inspiration of God, and *is* profitable for doctrine, for reproof, for correction, for instruction in righteousness, [17]that the man of God may be complete, thoroughly equipped for every good work.

Preach the Word

4 I charge *you* therefore before God and the Lord Jesus Christ, who will judge the living and the dead at[a] His appearing and His kingdom: [2]Preach the word! Be ready in season *and* out of season. Convince, rebuke, exhort, with all longsuffering and teaching. [3]For the time will come when they will not endure sound doctrine, but according to their own desires, *because* they have itching ears, they will heap up for themselves teachers; [4]and they will turn *their* ears away from the truth, and be turned aside to fables. [5]But you be watchful in

all things, endure afflictions, do the work of an evangelist, fulfill your ministry.

Paul's Valedictory

[6]For I am already being poured out as a drink offering, and the time of my departure is at hand. [7]I have fought the good fight, I have finished the race, I have kept the faith. [8]Finally, there is laid up for me the crown of righteousness, which the Lord, the righteous Judge, will give to me on that Day, and not to me only but also to all who have loved His appearing.

The Abandoned Apostle

[9]Be diligent to come to me quickly; [10]for Demas has forsaken me, having loved this present world, and has departed for Thessalonica—Crescens for Galatia, Titus for Dalmatia. [11]Only Luke is with me. Get Mark and bring him with you, for he is useful to me for ministry. [12]And Tychicus I have sent to Ephesus. [13]Bring the cloak that I left with Carpus at Troas when you come—and the books, especially the parchments.

[14]Alexander the coppersmith did me much harm. May the Lord repay him according to his works. [15]You also must beware of him, for he has greatly resisted our words.

[16]At my first defense no one stood with me, but all forsook me. May it not be charged against them.

The Lord Is Faithful

[17]But the Lord stood with me and strengthened me, so that the message might be preached fully through me, and *that* all the Gentiles might

4:1 [a]NU-Text omits *therefore* and reads *and by* for *at.*

LEADERSHIP ISSUES

Paul's Last Will and Testament

2 TIMOTHY 4:6

Paul, writing his last letter to Timothy, a sort of Last Will and Testament, gives him specific instructions concerning his ministry and how to carry on the work. Paul expected to die (2 Tim. 4:6) and wanted to make sure he gave Timothy some parting advice, in case they never saw each other again. One can imagine Timothy reading this letter by candlelight as the tears flowed down his face, remembering all the incredible things God had taught him through Paul's life and ministry.

Paul's counsel and mentoring of Timothy has at least six components.

1. Paul tells him not to be timid (2 Tim. 1:7). He has the power of the Spirit to strengthen him, the love of the Father to motivate him, and the sound judgment of Jesus to guide him.

2. Paul said not to be ashamed (2 Tim. 1:8). The Apostle warned Timothy not to be ashamed of Jesus Christ, the one who saved him, or Paul, the one who discipled him, or of the suffering that would surely come.

3. Timothy was charged with keeping the faith (2 Tim. 1:13, 14). He was cautioned not to change anything Paul had taught him and to guard the information like priceless treasure.

4. Paul exhorts Timothy to run away from "youthful lusts" (2 Tim. 2:22). He wanted to make sure that Timothy did not give in to the desire for power, fame, fortune, or worldly satisfaction of any kind.

5. Paul admonished him to hold firmly to his convictions (2 Tim. 3:14). So many had fallen away that the Apostle wanted to make sure Timothy did not.

6. Paul sums up the letter by commanding Timothy to preach the Word (2 Tim. 4:2). Timothy was to identify sin through reproof, confront sin through rebuke, and change behavior through exhortation by the preaching of God's Word.

The closing phrases of Paul's letter provide an epitaph that all believers should want on their tombstones. He tells Timothy with confidence that he has "fought the good fight," "finished the course," and "kept the faith" (2 Tim. 4:7).

LEADERSHIP ISSUES

GC2: Spiritual Formation: Exercise in Godliness

1 TIMOTHY 4:7 *But reject profane and old wives' fables, and exercise yourself toward godliness.*

Walking as a follower of Jesus requires that we continually grow in godliness. We must spiritually train ourselves to hear the Lord's direction for our lives and then yield in faith as God reveals Himself through His Son, His Word, and His people.

This walk in the light of God's Son, His Word, and with His followers not only keeps us from being overtaken by darkness (John 12:35), but also transforms us into the image of Jesus. Through every relationship, situation, triumph, and tragedy in our lives, the Spirit is at work to conform us to the likeness of Christ.

A story is told of Michelangelo unveiling a beautiful sculpture that depicted angelic glory. When asked how he could capture such splendor and divine mystery in his work, the artist responded simply, "From the block of common and flawed marble, I chip away everything that doesn't look like an angel!"

It is this very work that the Spirit does in us as we encounter the divine reality of God's Word, embrace life-changing intimacy with His Son, and experience the wonder of His love through His followers.

God the Father seems to look deep within us, looking past both sin and self to see the glory of Christ within us! The Holy Spirit begins His active work of creating Christ's likeness. Everything in us that does not look like Christ is chipped away—such is the mystery of spiritual transformation.

GC2
GREAT COMMANDMENT
COMMISSION

LEADERSHIP ISSUES

Paul's Last Imprisonment

2 TIMOTHY 1:16

Located at the northeastern slope of the Capitoline Hill at the edge of the Roman Forum there are two small superimposed churches built on top of the dungeon where, according to tradition, the apostle Paul spent his last days before execution. The dungeon was originally constructed around the early 3rd century BC as a cistern to collect the water that came up through the spring. It was used as a prison from at least the 1st century BC forward and consisted of an upper and lower chamber.

To enter, one must walk down a flight of stairs from the street level. Walking into the upper level of the prison reveals a hole in the floor about 2½ feet in diameter with an iron grate over it, the only entrance or exit to the lower chamber at the time of its use. Prisoners were put through the hole into the lower chamber to await execution. However, many were so neglected that death resulted from the harsh conditions. Walking down another flight of recently constructed stairs, one enters the cold, dark, and damp dungeon where Paul wrote his second letter to Timothy. It is no wonder that he asked Timothy to "bring the cloak" and "come before winter" (2 Tim. 4:13, 21). There is an altar in the lower chamber honoring the apostle Peter, who, according to tradition, also spent his last days before execution there. The upside-down cross on the front of the altar honors the traditional claim that Peter was crucified upside down.

Paul had been in prison in Rome earlier (Acts 28:16–31), but it was very different this time. He was deserted by those in Asia, except Onesiphorus and Luke, for fear of persecution (2 Tim. 1:16; 4:11). Emperor Nero declared it illegal to be a Christian. Paul expected execution (2 Tim. 4:6), and tradition again tells us that he was beheaded on the Ostian Road, a few miles outside the city. The greatest preacher of all time fought a good fight, finished the course, and kept the faith.

hear. Also I was delivered out of the mouth of the lion. [18]And the Lord will deliver me from every evil work and preserve *me* for His heavenly kingdom. To Him *be* glory forever and ever. Amen!

Come Before Winter

[19]Greet Prisca and Aquila, and the household of Onesiphorus. [20]Erastus stayed in Corinth, but Trophimus I have left in Miletus sick.

[21]Do your utmost to come before winter.

Eubulus greets you, as well as Pudens, Linus, Claudia, and all the brethren.

Farewell

[22]The Lord Jesus Christ[a] be with your spirit. Grace be with you. Amen.

4:22 [a]NU-Text omits *Jesus Christ.*

IMPACT OF THE BOOK

TITUS

I IDEA *Sound doctrine is the necessary foundation for the Christian life.*

M MESSAGE *Every believer needs a mentor and a model in their life. Believers must invest in younger believers, teaching them correct doctrine and tools for right living. Just as Paul mentored Titus, he called Titus to invest in those younger than him in the faith. Titus displayed mental, spiritual, and physical toughness. Paul knew him as a man who could be trusted to get things done.*

P PEOPLE *Apollos, Paul, Titus, Zenas*

A AUTHOR *Paul wrote this letter to Titus, his young protégé—true son in the faith (Titus 1:4). Although Titus is not identified as a pastor, Paul deals with practical and timely issues that would have been foremost in the minds of congregants and church leaders. Titus was Paul's prime example of "good" and "lasting fruit" among the Gentiles.*

C CULTURE *Crete is one of the larger islands in the Mediterranean; and according to Greek legend, Minos, the son of Zeus, became king of Crete. His reign has been documented in history. Extensive archaeological excavations with fascinating evidence of this earlier civilization can be found in the ancient Minoan Palace. The Cretans were overwhelmingly stereotyped by ancient writers as immoral, rude, and part of a barbarous culture. Paul's reference to an earlier visit to Crete would suggest that he established a church, leaving Titus to organize and disciple the new believers. A Greek by ethnic heritage, Titus chose to remain uncircumcised, perhaps as a testimony to the power of the gospel for Gentiles as well as for Jews.*

T TIMELINE *c. AD 63*

KEY SCRIPTURE MEMORY VERSES 1:6–9; 3:4–8

GREETING

1 Paul, a bondservant of God and an apostle of Jesus Christ, according to the faith of God's elect and the acknowledgment of the truth which accords with godliness, ²in hope of eternal life which God, who cannot lie, promised before time began, ³but has in due time manifested His word through preaching, which was committed to me according to the commandment of God our Savior;

⁴To Titus, a true son in *our* common faith:

Grace, mercy, *and* peace from God the Father and the Lord Jesus Christᵃ our Savior.

QUALIFIED ELDERS

⁵For this reason I left you in Crete, that you should set in order the things that are lacking, and appoint elders in every city as I commanded you— ⁶if a man is blameless, the husband of one wife, having faithful children not accused of dissipation or insubordination. ⁷For a bishopᵃ must be blameless, as a steward of God, not self-willed, not quick-tempered, not given to wine, not violent, not greedy for money, ⁸but hospitable, a lover of what is good, sober-minded, just, holy, self-controlled, ⁹holding fast the faithful word as he has been taught, that he may be able, by sound doctrine, both to exhort and convict those who contradict.

THE ELDERS' TASK

¹⁰For there are many insubordinate, both idle talkers and deceivers, especially those of the circumcision, ¹¹whose mouths must be stopped, who subvert whole households, teaching things which they ought not, for the sake of dishonest gain. ¹²One of them, a prophet of their own, said, "Cretans *are* always liars, evil beasts, lazy gluttons." ¹³This testimony is true. Therefore rebuke them sharply, that they may be sound in the faith, ¹⁴not giving heed to Jewish fables and commandments of men who turn from the truth. ¹⁵To the pure all things are pure, but to those who are defiled and unbelieving nothing is pure; but even their mind and conscience are defiled. ¹⁶They profess to

1:4 ᵃNU-Text reads *and Christ Jesus.*   1:7 ᵃLiterally *overseer*

---

 the INFLUENCERS

TITUS: The Ministry of Example

TITUS 1:4–9

Titus lived at an exciting time in history. He lived in the years immediately following the life and death of Jesus Christ. It is likely that his heroes growing up were men like Peter, Stephen, John, and the apostle Paul. It must have been incredible to consider the great apostle to the gentiles a mentor.

Titus was Greek and didn't have the spiritual heritage his friend Timothy had. When Titus accepted Jesus Christ as his personal Savior, he became a rock-solid, dependable man of faith and action.

Titus's greatest ministry was his example. He was an example of things which had never been done before! In Galatians 2, Paul took him before the Jerusalem leaders, where a man insisted that gentile converts be circumcised, but Paul introduced Titus as an example of how a gentile convert did not need to become a slave to the law to be saved.

Paul trusted him when he sent Titus to the Corinthians as his representative, to oversee a collection for the poor in Jerusalem (2 Cor. 8:16–24). Titus was then left on the island of Crete to organize and train leadership (1:4–9). He appointed men who were godly and of rock-solid character—men like himself. Titus was a leader of leaders.

know God, but in works they deny *Him,* being abominable, disobedient, and disqualified for every good work.

QUALITIES OF A SOUND CHURCH

2 But as for you, speak the things which are proper for sound doctrine: ²that the older men be sober, reverent, temperate, sound in faith, in love, in patience; ³the older women likewise, that they be reverent in behavior, not slanderers, not given to much wine, teachers of good things— ⁴that they admonish the young women to love their husbands, to love their children, ⁵to be discreet, chaste, homemakers, good, obedient to their own husbands, that the word of God may not be blasphemed.

⁶Likewise, exhort the young men to be soberminded, ⁷in all things showing yourself *to be* a pattern of good works; in doctrine *showing* integrity, reverence, incorruptibility,ª ⁸sound speech that cannot be condemned, that one who is an opponent may be ashamed, having nothing evil to say of you.ª

⁹*Exhort* bondservants to be obedient to their own masters, to be well pleasing in all *things,* not answering back, ¹⁰not pilfering, but showing all good fidelity, that they may adorn the doctrine of God our Savior in all things.

TRAINED BY SAVING GRACE

¹¹For the grace of God that brings salvation has appeared to all men, ¹²teaching us that, denying ungodliness and worldly lusts, we should live soberly, righteously, and godly in the present age, ¹³looking for the blessed hope and glorious appearing of our great God and Savior Jesus Christ, ¹⁴who gave Himself for us, that He might redeem us from every lawless deed and purify for Himself *His* own special people, zealous for good works.

¹⁵Speak these things, exhort, and rebuke with all authority. Let no one despise you.

GRACES OF THE HEIRS OF GRACE

3 Remind them to be subject to rulers and authorities, to obey, to be ready for every good work, ²to speak evil of no one, to be peaceable,

gentle, showing all humility to all men. ³For we ourselves were also once foolish, disobedient, deceived, serving various lusts and pleasures, living in malice and envy, hateful and hating one another. ⁴But when the kindness and the love of God our Savior toward man appeared, ⁵not by works of righteousness which we have done, but according to His mercy He saved us, through the washing of regeneration and renewing of the Holy Spirit, ⁶whom He poured out on us abundantly through Jesus Christ our Savior, ⁷that having been justified by His grace we should become heirs according to the hope of eternal life.

⁸This is a faithful saying, and these things I want you to affirm constantly, that those who have believed in God should be careful to maintain good works. These things are good and profitable to men.

AVOID DISSENSION

⁹But avoid foolish disputes, genealogies, contentions, and strivings about the law; for they are unprofitable and useless. ¹⁰Reject a divisive man after the first and second admonition, ¹¹knowing that such a person is warped and sinning, being self-condemned.

FINAL MESSAGES

¹²When I send Artemas to you, or Tychicus, be diligent to come to me at Nicopolis, for I have decided to spend the winter there. ¹³Send Zenas the lawyer and Apollos on their journey with haste, that they may lack nothing. ¹⁴And let our *people* also learn to maintain good works, to *meet* urgent needs, that they may not be unfruitful.

FAREWELL

¹⁵All who *are* with me greet you. Greet those who love us in the faith.

Grace *be* with you all. Amen.

2:7 ªNU-Text omits *incorruptibility.*   **2:8** ªNU-Text and M-Text read *us.*

IMPACT OF THE BOOK

PHILEMON

I IDEA
How you treat the lowliest of brothers is a testimony of your walk with the Lord. The ability to forgive speaks volumes about our relationship to Jesus and how much we've been forgiven.

M MESSAGE
A valuable leadership lesson can be learned by studying Paul's use of tact and courtesy as he calls for Christian maturity in handling a difficult situation. All believers, regardless of race, gender, social status, or economic background, are to be treated with love and respect. This thought echoes Christ's words: "By this all will know that you are My disciples, if you have love for one another" (John 13:35). He used his relationships and his apostolic authority to extend the kingdom and to benefit others. Paul demonstrated a great leadership principle: reconciliation shows Christ's love.

P PEOPLE
Apphia, Archippus, Onesimus, Paul, Philemon, Timothy

A AUTHOR
The Book of Philemon—together with Ephesians, Philippians, and Colossians—is among Paul's Prison Epistles.

C CULTURE
Philemon was a businessman who, because of his faith, allowed the church to meet in his home. Paul wrote this letter to encourage Philemon to accept Onesimus—the runaway slave who had robbed from Philemon—as "a beloved brother." Onesimus demonstrated true repentance and was led to Christ by Paul while in prison. This story reveals much about the culture of the day, because Onesimus could have been scourged, mutilated, or even crucified under Roman law. Paul's plea for mercy, grace, and brotherhood struck a blow at the heart of slavery.

T TIMELINE
c. AD 61

KEY SCRIPTURE MEMORY VERSES
4–6

GREETING

Paul, a prisoner of Christ Jesus, and Timothy *our* brother,

To Philemon our beloved *friend* and fellow laborer, [2]to the beloved[a] Apphia, Archippus our fellow soldier, and to the church in your house:

[3]Grace to you and peace from God our Father and the Lord Jesus Christ.

PHILEMON'S LOVE AND FAITH

[4]I thank my God, making mention of you always in my prayers, [5]hearing of your love and faith which you have toward the Lord Jesus and toward all the saints, [6]that the sharing of your faith may become effective by the acknowledgment of every good thing which is in you[a] in Christ Jesus. [7]For we have[a] great joy[b] and consolation in your love, because the hearts of the saints have been refreshed by you, brother.

THE PLEA FOR ONESIMUS

[8]Therefore, though I might be very bold in Christ to command you what is fitting, [9]yet for love's sake I rather appeal *to you*—being such a one as Paul, the aged, and now also a prisoner of Jesus Christ— [10]I appeal to you for my son Onesimus, whom I have begotten *while* in my chains, [11]who once was unprofitable to you, but now is profitable to you and to me.

[12]I am sending him back.[a] You therefore receive him, that is, my own heart, [13]whom I wished to keep with me, that on your behalf he might minister to me in my chains for the gospel. [14]But without your consent I wanted to do nothing, that your good deed might not be by compulsion, as it were, but voluntary.

[15]For perhaps he departed for a while for this *purpose,* that you might receive him forever, [16]no longer as a slave but more than a slave—a beloved brother, especially to me but how much more to you, both in the flesh and in the Lord.

PHILEMON'S OBEDIENCE ENCOURAGED

[17]If then you count me as a partner, receive him as *you would* me. [18]But if he has wronged you or owes anything, put that on my account. [19]I, Paul, am writing with my own hand. I will repay—not to mention to you that you owe me even your own self besides. [20]Yes, brother, let me

2 [a]NU-Text reads *to our sister Apphia.*   6 [a]NU-Text and M-Text read *us.*   7 [a]NU-Text reads *had.* [b]M-Text reads *thanksgiving.*   12 [a]NU-Text reads *back to you in person, that is, my own heart.*

INSIDE *the* INFLUENCERS

ONESIMUS

PHILEMON 1

Onesimus, whose name means *useful*, was a slave in the house of Philemon. It appears that Onesimus robbed Philemon and then ran away. He kept running until one day his path collided with Paul in prison. Paul refers to Onesimus as one "whom I have begotten while in my chains" (v. 10), meaning that he led the young man to salvation in prison.

Paul writes the words that were hopefully ointment to Philemon's wounded heart: "Perhaps he departed for a while for this purpose, that you might receive him forever" (1:15). In fact, the verse may be saying even more. Notice that Paul says that Onesimus departed for a while for a purpose. In the grammar of the original language the first part of the sentence is closely connected to the last part. It is a purpose statement in which Paul may be suggesting that God may have even *intended* to use the "departing" for His glory. The Scriptures offer hope that *every* life can be reclaimed to the glory of God. Paul wanted Philemon to accept Onesimus "no longer as a slave, but . . . a beloved brother."

INSIDE *the* INFLUENCERS

PHILEMON—Live What You Teach

PHILEMON 17, 18

Philemon, to whom Paul addresses this letter, lived in the town of Colosse. He was a wealthy Christian businessman who allowed the church to meet in his home. From the way Paul praises Philemon in the opening verses of the book, we can surmise that he was a committed Christian with a servant's heart. Paul describes him as a beloved friend and fellow laborer (v. 1), who loved God and people (v. 5), shared his faith publicly (v. 6), and refreshed people by caring for them (v. 7).

It was estimated that slaves comprised more than 60 percent of the Roman population, so the environment of any ancient city under Roman rule was tense. Tradition says Philemon took on a slave who was perhaps abandoned or left for dead. This boy, Onesimus, robbed Philemon and ran away.

Onesimus landed in a prison in Rome with the Apostle Paul, who led him to salvation in Christ Jesus. Onesimus was released, and Paul wrote Philemon compelling him to forgive Onesimus and take him back. Knowing Philemon was shamed, wronged, and probably angry, Paul appealed to him—asking him to treat Onesimus as he would treat Paul (v. 17, 18).

Paul had confidence that Philemon would not only accept him back, but that he would do more than that (v. 21). This is a story urging all of us to put mistakes and shame behind us and extend forgiveness to those who have made mistakes that may have wronged us.

have joy from you in the Lord; refresh my heart in the Lord.

²¹Having confidence in your obedience, I write to you, knowing that you will do even more than I say. ²²But, meanwhile, also prepare a guest room for me, for I trust that through your prayers I shall be granted to you.

FAREWELL

²³Epaphras, my fellow prisoner in Christ Jesus, greets you, ²⁴as do Mark, Aristarchus, Demas, Luke, my fellow laborers.

²⁵The grace of our Lord Jesus Christ *be* with your spirit. Amen.

IMPACT OF THE BOOK

HEBREWS

I | IDEA

Jesus is the Christ, and the new covenant is "superior" to the old covenant under Judaism. We can run the race with endurance and victory motivated by Jesus—the author and finisher of our faith—and by the great cloud of witnesses of those who ran before us.

M | MESSAGE

By becoming a man, Jesus bridged the chasm created by sin so men and women could enter into a relationship with God. He sits at God's right hand waiting to intercede for believers. Leaders must possess self-discipline in order to lead others. We must hold fast to the truth of the gospel we have heard.

P | PEOPLE

Jesus, Joshua, Melchizedek, Moses, Old Testament Saints

A | AUTHOR

Scholars propose that Paul, Luke, Apollos, Barnabas, or Silvanus penned this letter. The author of the only anonymous epistle in the New Testament knows a great deal about Judaism. Perhaps Paul did not sign his name because of the suspicion and hatred from the Jews. Paul does refer to himself as a "Hebrew of the Hebrews" and a "Pharisee" (Phil. 3:5). The reference to "my chains" (10:34), as well as his reference to Timothy (13:23), and the salutation "grace" (13:25) all sound very Paul-like.

C | CULTURE

The Book of Hebrews was written to Jewish men and women— Hebrew people—who recognized and believed that Jesus was the Messiah. The author calls for his readers to hold fast to that confession, don't succumb to the pressures of the Judaizers' arguements about the prophets, angels, and Moses being greater than Jesus, even if they use the Old Testament to bolster their argument. The author then demonstrates the superiority of Jesus on all accounts, using Old Testament texts to prove the point.

T | TIMELINE

c. AD 66

KEY SCRIPTURE MEMORY VERSES

1:1, 2; 2:18; 4:12, 14–16; 9:27; 10:24, 25; 11:1, 6; 12:1–3, 11; 13:5, 8, 17

GOD'S SUPREME REVELATION

1 God, who at various times and in various ways spoke in time past to the fathers by the prophets, [2]has in these last days spoken to us by *His* Son, whom He has appointed heir of all things, through whom also He made the worlds; [3]who being the brightness of *His* glory and the express image of His person, and upholding all things by the word of His power, when He had by Himself[a] purged our[b] sins, sat down at the right hand of the Majesty on high, [4]having become so much better than the angels, as He has by inheritance obtained a more excellent name than they.

THE SON EXALTED ABOVE ANGELS

[5]For to which of the angels did He ever say:

> "You are My Son,
> Today I have begotten You"?[a]

And again:

> "I will be to Him a Father,
> And He shall be to Me a Son"?[b]

[6]But when He again brings the firstborn into the world, He says:

> "Let all the angels of God worship Him."[a]

[7]And of the angels He says:

> "Who makes His angels spirits
> And His ministers a flame of fire."[a]

[8]But to the Son *He says:*

> "Your throne, O God, *is* forever and ever;
> A scepter of righteousness *is* the scepter of
> Your kingdom.
> [9]You have loved righteousness and hated
> lawlessness;
> Therefore God, Your God, has anointed You
> With the oil of gladness more than Your
> companions."[a]

[10]And:

> "You, LORD, in the beginning laid the
> foundation of the earth,
> And the heavens are the work of Your hands.
> [11]They will perish, but You remain;
> And they will all grow old like a garment;
> [12]Like a cloak You will fold them up,
> And they will be changed.
> But You are the same,
> And Your years will not fail."[a]

[13]But to which of the angels has He ever said:

> "Sit at My right hand,
> Till I make Your enemies Your footstool"?[a]

[14]Are they not all ministering spirits sent forth to minister for those who will inherit salvation?

1:3 [a]NU-Text omits *by Himself.* [b]NU-Text omits *our.* **1:5** [a]Psalm 2:7 [b]2 Samuel 7:14 **1:6** [a]Deuteronomy 32:43 (Septuagint, Dead Sea Scrolls); Psalm 97:7 **1:7** [a]Psalm 104:4 **1:9** [a]Psalm 45:6, 7 **1:12** [a]Psalm 102:25–27 **1:13** [a]Psalm 110:1

THROUGH THE GRID
Making Sense of Your World: The Biblical Worldview of Jesus (Heb. 1:1–4)

The Scriptures show us that Jesus Christ is the ultimate revelation of God to humanity—Jesus is God made man, for the purpose of connecting with humanity and of providing the atonement for humanity's sins. So if we examine what Jesus believed, we are receiving the beliefs that God would have us to receive, since Jesus was, in fact, fully God and fully human. Jesus confronted error with truth, and what Jesus says is the final word that settles all issues for Christians, including those about Scripture. Questions we have regarding Scripture's authority, extent, authenticity, and integrity can be answered by looking to the example of Christ's beliefs. His views should be our own.

THROUGH THE GRID

Discover God:
God Never Changes

HEBREWS 1:11, 12 *They will perish, but You remain; and they will all grow old like a garment; like a cloak You will fold them up, and they will be changed. But You are the same, and Your years will not fail.*

Although many things in life will change, God always stays the same. In fact, God has been the same since the beginning of time; and thus, God is the one constant that we can count on while everything around us remains subject to change. The unchanging nature of God can be described as *God's immutability*—the inability of God to ever change. We can depend on God because we can know that He will never change and will always remain faithful to us. God does not grow or change, and God's Word remains the same throughout the ages. Amidst the challenges of life, how comforting it is to know that we can always rely on the unchanging and perfect nature of God!

Do Not Neglect Salvation

2 Therefore we must give the more earnest heed to the things we have heard, lest we drift away. ²For if the word spoken through angels proved steadfast, and every transgression and disobedience received a just reward, ³how shall we escape if we neglect so great a salvation, which at the first began to be spoken by the Lord, and was confirmed to us by those who heard *Him,* ⁴God also bearing witness both with signs and wonders, with various miracles, and gifts of the Holy Spirit, according to His own will?

The Son Made Lower than Angels

⁵For He has not put the world to come, of which we speak, in subjection to angels. ⁶But one testified in a certain place, saying:

"What is man that You are mindful of him,
Or the son of man that You take care of him?
⁷You have made him a little lower than the angels;
You have crowned him with glory and honor,ᵃ
And set him over the works of Your hands.
⁸You have put all things in subjection under his feet."ᵃ

For in that He put all in subjection under him, He left nothing *that is* not put under him. But now we do not yet see all things put under him. ⁹But we see Jesus, who was made a little lower than the angels, for the suffering of death crowned with glory and honor, that He, by the grace of God, might taste death for everyone.

Bringing Many Sons to Glory

¹⁰For it was fitting for Him, for whom *are* all things and by whom *are* all things, in bringing many sons to glory, to make the captain of their salvation perfect through sufferings. ¹¹For both He who sanctifies and those who are being sanctified *are* all of one, for which reason He is not ashamed to call them brethren, ¹²saying:

"I will declare Your name to My brethren;
In the midst of the assembly I will sing praise to You."ᵃ

¹³And again:

"I will put My trust in Him."ᵃ

And again:

"Here am I and the children whom God has given Me."ᵇ

2:7 ᵃNU-Text and M-Text omit the rest of verse 7.   2:8 ᵃPsalm 8:4–6
2:12 ᵃPsalm 22:22   2:13 ᵃ2 Samuel 22:3; Isaiah 8:17   ᵇIsaiah 8:18

¹⁴Inasmuch then as the children have partaken of flesh and blood, He Himself likewise shared in the same, that through death He might destroy him who had the power of death, that is, the devil, ¹⁵and release those who through fear of death were all their lifetime subject to bondage. ¹⁶For indeed He does not give aid to angels, but He does give aid to the seed of Abraham. ¹⁷Therefore, in all things He had to be made like *His* brethren, that He might be a merciful and faithful High Priest in things *pertaining* to God, to make propitiation for the sins of the people. ¹⁸For in that He Himself has suffered, being tempted, He is able to aid those who are tempted.

The Son Was Faithful

3 Therefore, holy brethren, partakers of the heavenly calling, consider the Apostle and High Priest of our confession, Christ Jesus, ²who was faithful to Him who appointed Him, as Moses also *was faithful* in all His house. ³For this One has been counted worthy of more glory than Moses, inasmuch as He who built the house has more honor than the house. ⁴For every house is built by someone, but He who built all things *is* God. ⁵And Moses indeed *was* faithful in all His house as a servant, for a testimony of those things which would be spoken *afterward,* ⁶but Christ as a Son over His own house, whose house we are if we hold fast the confidence and the rejoicing of the hope firm to the end.ᵃ

Be Faithful

⁷Therefore, as the Holy Spirit says:

"Today, if you will hear His voice,
⁸Do not harden your hearts as in the rebellion,
In the day of trial in the wilderness,
⁹Where your fathers tested Me, tried Me,
And saw My works forty years.
¹⁰Therefore I was angry with that generation,
And said, 'They always go astray in *their* heart,
And they have not known My ways.'
¹¹So I swore in My wrath,
'They shall not enter My rest.' "ᵃ

¹²Beware, brethren, lest there be in any of you an evil heart of unbelief in departing from the living God; ¹³but exhort one another daily, while it is called *"Today,"* lest any of you be hardened through the deceitfulness of sin. ¹⁴For we have become partakers of Christ if we hold the beginning of our confidence steadfast to the end, ¹⁵while it is said:

"Today, if you will hear His voice,
Do not harden your hearts as in the rebellion."ᵃ

Failure of the Wilderness Wanderers

¹⁶For who, having heard, rebelled? Indeed, *was it* not all who came out of Egypt, *led* by Moses? ¹⁷Now with whom was He angry forty years? *Was it* not with those who sinned, whose corpses fell in the wilderness? ¹⁸And to whom did He swear that they would not enter His rest, but to those who did not obey? ¹⁹So we see that they could not enter in because of unbelief.

The Promise of Rest

4 Therefore, since a promise remains of entering His rest, let us fear lest any of you seem to have come short of it. ²For indeed the gospel was preached to us as well as to them; but the word which they heard did not profit them,ᵃ not being mixed with faith in those who heard *it.* ³For we who have believed do enter that rest, as He has said:

"So I swore in My wrath,
'They shall not enter My rest,' "ᵃ

although the works were finished from the foundation of the world. ⁴For He has spoken in a certain place of the seventh *day* in this way: "And God rested on the seventh day from all His works";ᵃ ⁵and again in this *place:* "They shall not enter My rest."ᵃ

⁶Since therefore it remains that some *must* enter it, and those to whom it was first preached did not enter because of disobedience, ⁷again He designates a certain day, saying in David, *"Today,"* after such a long time, as it has been said:

3:6 ᵃNU-Text omits *firm to the end.*   **3:11** ᵃPsalm 95:7–11
3:15 ᵃPsalm 95:7, 8   **4:2** ᵃNU-Text and M-Text read *profit them, since they were not united by faith with those who heeded it.*
4:3 ᵃPsalm 95:11   **4:4** ᵃGenesis 2:2   **4:5** ᵃPsalm 95:11

LEADERSHIP ISSUES

GC2: Nourished by the Word: The Word Alive

HEBREWS 4:12   *For the word of God is living and powerful.*

What is the evidence that God's Word is truly "living" in my life? What does it look like for the Spirit of God to take the Word of God and empower our experience of it?

Through the "alive" Word of God, the Holy Spirit wants to reveal right beliefs and encourage right living—but there's more! Taking this journey into a deepened, loving relationship with the God who wrote the Scriptures is an experience because any relationship must be experienced. It involves more than knowledge and dutiful compliance. Our journey in loving the Lord will change our lives in relevant, meaningful ways. Here are some of the benefits of taking this journey toward a more intimate relationship with the God of the Bible:

- You will live life with an expectancy of actually encountering Him—the One who wrote the Book!
- You will experience freedom like never before. Your Christian life will move beyond duties and obligations, from "*got* tos" to "*get* tos." You will be compelled by the love of Christ (2 Cor. 5:14).
- You will be empowered to actually live out what you believe. You will find that this power comes not from right doctrine or a code of conduct, but from a Person.
- You will express humility instead of pride. Your heart will not be able to get over the wonder of how the Creator of the universe meets you in His Word.
- You will demonstrate vulnerability instead of judgment. You will be excited to share what God's Word is doing in you rather than pointing out the failures of others.

GREAT COMMANDMENT
COMMISSION

*"Today, if you will hear His voice,
Do not harden your hearts."* ª

⁸For if Joshua had given them rest, then He would not afterward have spoken of another day. ⁹There remains therefore a rest for the people of God. ¹⁰For he who has entered His rest has himself also ceased from his works as God *did* from His.

The Word Discovers Our Condition

¹¹Let us therefore be diligent to enter that rest, lest anyone fall according to the same example of disobedience. ¹²For the word of God *is* living and powerful, and sharper than any two-edged sword, piercing even to the division of soul and spirit, and of joints and marrow, and is a discerner of the thoughts and intents of the heart. ¹³And there is no creature hidden from His sight, but all things *are* naked and open to the eyes of Him to whom we *must give* account.

Our Compassionate High Priest

¹⁴Seeing then that we have a great High Priest who has passed through the heavens, Jesus the Son of God, let us hold fast *our* confession. ¹⁵For we do not have a High Priest who cannot sympathize with our weaknesses, but was in all *points* tempted as *we are, yet* without sin. ¹⁶Let us therefore come boldly to the throne of grace, that we may obtain mercy and find grace to help in time of need.

Qualifications for High Priesthood

5 For every high priest taken from among men is appointed for men in things *pertaining* to God, that he may offer both gifts and sacrifices for sins. ²He can have compassion on those who are ignorant and going astray, since he himself is also subject to weakness. ³Because of this he is required as for the people, so also for himself, to offer *sacrifices* for sins. ⁴And no man takes this honor to himself, but he who is called by God, just as Aaron *was.*

A Priest Forever

⁵So also Christ did not glorify Himself to become High Priest, but *it was* He who said to Him:

*"You are My Son,
Today I have begotten You."* ª

⁶As *He* also says in another *place:*

*"You are a priest forever
According to the order of Melchizedek";* ª

⁷who, in the days of His flesh, when He had offered up prayers and supplications, with vehement cries and tears to Him who was able to save Him from death, and was heard because of His godly fear, ⁸though He was a Son, *yet* He learned obedience by the things which He suffered. ⁹And having been perfected, He became the author of eternal salvation to all who obey Him, ¹⁰called by God as High Priest *"according to the order of Melchizedek,"* ¹¹of whom we have much to say, and hard to explain, since you have become dull of hearing.

Spiritual Immaturity

¹²For though by this time you ought to be teachers, you need *someone* to teach you again the first principles of the oracles of God; and you have come to need milk and not solid food. ¹³For everyone who partakes *only* of milk *is* unskilled in the word of righteousness, for he is a babe. ¹⁴But solid food belongs to those who are of full age, *that is,* those who by reason of use have their senses exercised to discern both good and evil.

The Peril of Not Progressing

6 Therefore, leaving the discussion of the elementary *principles* of Christ, let us go on to perfection, not laying again the foundation of repentance from dead works and of faith toward God, ²of the doctrine of baptisms, of laying on of hands, of resurrection of the dead, and of eternal judgment. ³And this we willª do if God permits.

⁴For *it is* impossible for those who were once enlightened, and have tasted the heavenly gift, and have become partakers of the Holy Spirit, ⁵and have tasted the good word of God and the powers of the age to come, ⁶if they fall away,ª to renew them again to repentance, since they crucify again

---

4:7 ªPsalm 95:7, 8   **5:5** ªPsalm 2:7   **5:6** ªPsalm 110:4
6:3 ªM-Text reads *let us do.*   **6:6** ªOr *and have fallen away*

LEADERSHIP ISSUES

GC2: Loving the Real God: Jesus Understands

HEBREWS 4:15 *For we do not have a High Priest who cannot sympathize with our weaknesses, but was in all points tempted as we are, yet without sin.*

There is nothing you have experienced that God in Christ on some level does not understand firsthand! He, like you, has experienced:

- rejection—by His own people (Luke 4:14–30; Mark 6:1–6)
- abandonment—by His own disciples (Mark 14:43–50, 66–72)
- misunderstanding—by His own followers (Mark 8:14–21)
- ridicule—at His own trial (Matt. 27:11–14, 22–31)
- betrayal—by a close friend (Matt. 26:47–50; 27:1–10)
- criticism—by the religious leaders of His day (Luke 20:17–20; 22:1–6)

But that is not all. He has also experienced human achievement and victories. He knows what it is like to feel loved and accepted. He knows the joy of completing a job well done (John 17:4). He has also known the joy of fulfilling His Father's will and the victory of conquering what no one has ever conquered: death. "While he was still speaking, behold, a bright cloud overshadowed them; and suddenly a voice came out of the cloud, saying, "This is My beloved Son, in whom I am well pleased. Hear Him!" (Matt. 17:5).

Jesus has experienced all the ups—and downs—of human existence. He's "been there, done that," just like you. Jesus understands!

GC2
GREAT COMMANDMENT
COMMISSION

for themselves the Son of God, and put *Him* to an open shame.

[7]For the earth which drinks in the rain that often comes upon it, and bears herbs useful for those by whom it is cultivated, receives blessing from God; [8]but if it bears thorns and briers, *it is* rejected and near to being cursed, whose end *is* to be burned.

A Better Estimate

[9]But, beloved, we are confident of better things concerning you, yes, things that accompany salvation, though we speak in this manner. [10]For God *is* not unjust to forget your work and labor of[a] love which you have shown toward His name, *in that* you have ministered to the saints, and do minister. [11]And we desire that each one of you show the same diligence to the full assurance of hope until the end, [12]that you do not become sluggish, but imitate those who through faith and patience inherit the promises.

God's Infallible Purpose in Christ

[13]For when God made a promise to Abraham, because He could swear by no one greater, He swore by Himself, [14]saying, *"Surely blessing I will bless you, and multiplying I will multiply you."*[a] [15]And so, after he had patiently endured, he obtained the promise. [16]For men indeed swear by the greater, and an oath for confirmation *is* for them an end of all dispute. [17]Thus God, determining to show more abundantly to the heirs of promise the immutability of His counsel, confirmed *it* by an oath, [18]that by two immutable things, in which it *is* impossible for God to lie, we might[a] have strong consolation, who have fled for refuge to lay hold of the hope set before *us.*

[19]This *hope* we have as an anchor of the soul, both sure and steadfast, and which enters the *Presence* behind the veil, [20]where the forerunner has entered for us, *even* Jesus, having become High Priest forever according to the order of Melchizedek.

The King of Righteousness

[7]For this Melchizedek, king of Salem, priest of the Most High God, who met Abraham returning from the slaughter of the kings and blessed him, [2]to whom also Abraham gave a tenth part of all, first being translated "king of righteousness," and then also king of Salem, meaning "king of peace," [3]without father, without mother, without genealogy, having neither beginning of days nor end of life, but made like the Son of God, remains a priest continually.

[4]Now consider how great this man *was,* to whom even the patriarch Abraham gave a tenth of the spoils. [5]And indeed those who are of the sons of Levi, who receive the priesthood, have a commandment to receive tithes from the people according to the law, that is, from their brethren, though they have come from the loins of Abraham; [6]but he whose genealogy is not derived from them received tithes from Abraham and blessed him who had the promises. [7]Now beyond all contradiction the lesser is blessed by the better. [8]Here mortal men receive tithes, but there he *receives them,* of whom it is witnessed that he lives. [9]Even Levi, who receives tithes, paid tithes through Abraham, so to speak, [10]for he was still in the loins of his father when Melchizedek met him.

Need for a New Priesthood

[11]Therefore, if perfection were through the Levitical priesthood (for under it the people received the law), what further need *was there* that another priest should rise according to the order of Melchizedek, and not be called according to the order of Aaron? [12]For the priesthood being changed, of necessity there is also a change of the law. [13]For He of whom these things are spoken belongs to another tribe, from which no man has officiated at the altar.

[14]For *it is* evident that our Lord arose from Judah, of which tribe Moses spoke nothing concerning priesthood.[a] [15]And it is yet far more evident if, in the likeness of Melchizedek, there arises another priest [16]who has come, not according to the law of a fleshly commandment, but according to the power of an endless life. [17]For He testifies:[a]

*"You are a priest forever
According to the order of Melchizedek."*[b]

6:10 [a]NU-Text omits *labor of.* 6:14 [a]Genesis 22:17 6:18 [a]M-Text omits *might.* 7:14 [a]NU-Text reads *priests.* 7:17 [a]NU-Text reads *it is testified.* [b]Psalm 110:4

[18]For on the one hand there is an annulling of the former commandment because of its weakness and unprofitableness, [19]for the law made nothing perfect; on the other hand, *there is the* bringing in of a better hope, through which we draw near to God.

GREATNESS OF THE NEW PRIEST

[20]And inasmuch as *He was* not *made priest* without an oath [21](for they have become priests without an oath, but He with an oath by Him who said to Him:

"The LORD has sworn
And will not relent,
'You are a priest forever[a]
According to the order of Melchizedek' "),[b]

[22]by so much more Jesus has become a surety of a better covenant.

[23]Also there were many priests, because they were prevented by death from continuing. [24]But He, because He continues forever, has an unchangeable priesthood. [25]Therefore He is also able to save to the uttermost those who come to God through Him, since He always lives to make intercession for them.

[26]For such a High Priest was fitting for us, *who is* holy, harmless, undefiled, separate from sinners, and has become higher than the heavens; [27]who does not need daily, as those high priests, to offer up sacrifices, first for His own sins and then for the people's, for this He did once for all when He offered up Himself. [28]For the law appoints as high priests men who have weakness, but the word of the oath, which came after the law, *appoints* the Son who has been perfected forever.

THE NEW PRIESTLY SERVICE

8 Now *this is* the main point of the things we are saying: We have such a High Priest, who is seated at the right hand of the throne of the Majesty in the heavens, [2]a Minister of the sanctuary and of the true tabernacle which the Lord erected, and not man.

[3]For every high priest is appointed to offer both gifts and sacrifices. Therefore *it is* necessary that this One also have something to offer. [4]For if He were on earth, He would not be a priest, since there are priests who offer the gifts according to the law; [5]who serve the copy and shadow of the heavenly things, as Moses was divinely instructed when he was about to make the tabernacle. For He said, *"See that you make all things according to the pattern shown you on the mountain."*[a] [6]But now He has obtained a more excellent ministry, inasmuch as He is also Mediator of a better covenant, which was established on better promises.

A NEW COVENANT

[7]For if that first *covenant* had been faultless, then no place would have been sought for a second. [8]Because finding fault with them, He says: *"Behold, the days are coming, says the LORD, when I will make a new covenant with the house of Israel and with the house of Judah—* [9]*not according to the covenant that I made with their fathers in the day when I took them by the hand to lead them out of the land of Egypt; because they did not continue in My covenant, and I disregarded them, says the LORD.* [10]*For this is the covenant that I will make with the house of Israel after those days, says the Lord: I will put My laws in their mind and write them on their hearts; and I will be their God, and they shall be My people.* [11]*None of them shall teach his neighbor, and none his brother, saying, 'Know the Lord,' for all shall know Me, from the least of them to the greatest of them.* [12]*For I will be merciful to their unrighteousness, and their sins and their lawless deeds*[a] *I will remember no more."*[b]

[13]In that He says, *"A new covenant,"* He has made the first obsolete. Now what is becoming obsolete and growing old is ready to vanish away.

THE EARTHLY SANCTUARY

9 Then indeed, even the first *covenant* had ordinances of divine service and the earthly sanctuary. [2]For a tabernacle was prepared: the first *part,* in which *was* the lampstand, the table, and the showbread, which is called the sanctuary; [3]and behind the second veil, the part of the tabernacle which is called the Holiest of All, [4]which had the golden censer and the ark of the covenant over-

7:21 [a]NU-Text ends the quotation here. [b]Psalm 110:4   **8:5** [a]Exodus 25:40   **8:12** [a]NU-Text omits *and their lawless deeds.* [b]Jeremiah 31:31–34 laid on all sides with gold, in which *were* the golden pot that had the manna, Aaron's rod that budded, and the tablets of the covenant; [5]and above it were the cherubim of glory overshadowing the mercy seat. Of these things we cannot now speak in detail.

LIMITATIONS OF THE EARTHLY SERVICE

[6]Now when these things had been thus prepared, the priests always went into the first part of the tabernacle, performing the services. [7]But into the second part the high priest *went* alone once a year, not without blood, which he offered for himself and *for* the people's sins *committed* in ignorance; [8]the Holy Spirit indicating this, that the way into the Holiest of All was not yet made manifest while the first tabernacle was still standing. [9]It *was* symbolic for the present time in which both gifts and sacrifices are offered which cannot make him who performed the service perfect in regard to the conscience— [10]*concerned* only with foods and drinks, various washings, and fleshly ordinances imposed until the time of reformation.

THE HEAVENLY SANCTUARY

[11]But Christ came *as* High Priest of the good things to come,[a] with the greater and more perfect tabernacle not made with hands, that is, not of this creation. [12]Not with the blood of goats and calves, but with His own blood He entered the Most Holy Place once for all, having obtained eternal redemption. [13]For if the blood of bulls and goats and the ashes of a heifer, sprinkling the unclean, sanctifies for the purifying of the flesh, [14]how much more shall the blood of Christ, who through the eternal Spirit offered Himself without spot to God, cleanse your conscience from dead works to serve the living God? [15]And for this reason He is the Mediator of the new covenant, by means of death, for the redemption of the transgressions under the first covenant, that those who are called may receive the promise of the eternal inheritance.

THE MEDIATOR'S DEATH NECESSARY

[16]For where there *is* a testament, there must also of necessity be the death of the testator. [17]For a testament *is* in force after men are dead, since it has no power at all while the testator lives. [18]Therefore not even the first *covenant* was dedicated without blood. [19]For when Moses had spoken every precept to all the people according to the law, he took the blood of calves and goats, with water, scarlet wool, and hyssop, and sprinkled both the book itself and all the people, [20]saying, *"This is the blood of the covenant which God has commanded you."*[a] [21]Then likewise he sprinkled with blood both the tabernacle and all the vessels of the ministry. [22]And according to the law almost all things are purified with blood, and without shedding of blood there is no remission.

GREATNESS OF CHRIST'S SACRIFICE

[23]Therefore *it was* necessary that the copies of the things in the heavens should be purified with these, but the heavenly things themselves with better sacrifices than these. [24]For Christ has not entered the holy places made with hands, *which are* copies of the true, but into heaven itself, now to appear in the presence of God for us; [25]not that He should offer Himself often, as the high priest enters the Most Holy Place every year with blood of another— [26]He then would have had to suffer often since the foundation of the world; but now, once at the end of the ages, He has appeared to put away sin by the sacrifice of Himself. [27]And as it is appointed for men to die once, but after this the judgment, [28]so Christ was offered once to bear the sins of many. To those who eagerly wait for Him He will appear a second time, apart from sin, for salvation.

ANIMAL SACRIFICES INSUFFICIENT

10 For the law, having a shadow of the good things to come, *and* not the very image of the things, can never with these same sacrifices, which they offer continually year by year, make those who approach perfect. [2]For then would they not have ceased to be offered? For the worshipers, once purified, would have had no more consciousness of sins. [3]But in those *sacrifices there is* a reminder of sins every year. [4]For *it is* not possible that the blood of bulls and goats could take away sins.

9:11 [a]NU-Text reads *that have come.*   **9:20** [a]Exodus 24:8

Christ's Death Fulfills God's Will

[5]Therefore, when He came into the world, He said:

"Sacrifice and offering You did not desire,
But a body You have prepared for Me.
[6]In burnt offerings and sacrifices for sin
You had no pleasure.
[7]Then I said, 'Behold, I have come—
In the volume of the book it is written of Me—
To do Your will, O God.' "[a]

[8]Previously saying, "Sacrifice and offering, burnt offerings, and offerings for sin You did not desire, nor had pleasure in them" (which are offered according to the law), [9]then He said, "Behold, I have come to do Your will, O God."[a] He takes away the first that He may establish the second. [10]By that will we have been sanctified through the offering of the body of Jesus Christ once for all.

Christ's Death Perfects the Sanctified

[11]And every priest stands ministering daily and offering repeatedly the same sacrifices, which can never take away sins. [12]But this Man, after He had offered one sacrifice for sins forever, sat down at the right hand of God, [13]from that time waiting till His enemies are made His footstool. [14]For by one offering He has perfected forever those who are being sanctified.

[15]But the Holy Spirit also witnesses to us; for after He had said before,

[16]"This is the covenant that I will make with them after those days, says the Lord: I will put My laws into their hearts, and in their minds I will write them,"[a] [17]then He adds, "Their sins and their lawless deeds I will remember no more."[a] [18]Now where there is remission of these, there is no longer an offering for sin.

Hold Fast Your Confession

[19]Therefore, brethren, having boldness to enter the Holiest by the blood of Jesus, [20]by a new and living way which He consecrated for us, through the veil, that is, His flesh, [21]and having a High Priest over the house of God, [22]let us draw near with a true heart in full assurance of faith, having our hearts sprinkled from an evil conscience and our bodies washed with pure water. [23]Let us hold fast the confession of our hope without wavering, for He who promised is faithful. [24]And let us consider one another in order to stir up love and good works, [25]not forsaking the assembling of ourselves together, as is the manner of some, but exhorting one another, and so much the more as you see the Day approaching.

The Just Live by Faith

[26]For if we sin willfully after we have received the knowledge of the truth, there no longer remains a sacrifice for sins, [27]but a certain fearful expectation of judgment, and fiery indignation which will devour the adversaries. [28]Anyone who has rejected Moses' law dies without mercy on the testimony of two or three witnesses. [29]Of how much worse punishment, do you suppose, will he be thought worthy who has trampled the Son of God underfoot, counted the blood of the covenant by which he was sanctified a common thing, and insulted the Spirit of grace? [30]For we know Him who said, "Vengeance is Mine, I will repay,"[a] says the Lord.[b] And again, "The Lord will judge His people."[c] [31]It is a fearful thing to fall into the hands of the living God.

[32]But recall the former days in which, after you were illuminated, you endured a great struggle with sufferings: [33]partly while you were made a spectacle both by reproaches and tribulations, and partly while you became companions of those who were so treated; [34]for you had compassion on me[a] in my chains, and joyfully accepted the plundering of your goods, knowing that you have a better and an enduring possession for yourselves in heaven.[b] [35]Therefore do not cast away your confidence, which has great reward. [36]For you have need of endurance, so that after you have done the will of God, you may receive the promise:

10:7 [a]Psalm 40:6–8 **10:9** [a]NU-Text and M-Text omit O God. **10:16** [a]Jeremiah 31:33 **10:17** [a]Jeremiah 31:34 **10:30** [a]Deuteronomy 32:35 [b]NU-Text omits says the Lord. [c]Deuteronomy 32:36 **10:34** [a]NU-Text reads the prisoners instead of me in my chains. [b]NU-Text omits in heaven.

[37] *"For yet a little while,*
  And He[a] who is coming will come and will
    not tarry.
[38] *Now the[a] just shall live by faith;*
  But if anyone draws back,
  My soul has no pleasure in him."[b]

[39] But we are not of those who draw back to perdition, but of those who believe to the saving of the soul.

By Faith We Understand

11 Now faith is the substance of things hoped for, the evidence of things not seen. [2]For by it the elders obtained a *good* testimony.

[3] By faith we understand that the worlds were framed by the word of God, so that the things which are seen were not made of things which are visible.

Faith at the Dawn of History

[4] By faith Abel offered to God a more excellent sacrifice than Cain, through which he obtained witness that he was righteous, God testifying of his gifts; and through it he being dead still speaks.

[5] By faith Enoch was taken away so that he did not see death, *"and was not found, because God had taken him";[a]* for before he was taken he had this testimony, that he pleased God. [6]But without faith *it is* impossible to please *Him,* for he who comes to God must believe that He is, and *that* He is a rewarder of those who diligently seek Him.

[7] By faith Noah, being divinely warned of things not yet seen, moved with godly fear, pre-

pared an ark for the saving of his household, by which he condemned the world and became heir of the righteousness which is according to faith.

Faithful Abraham

[8] By faith Abraham obeyed when he was called to go out to the place which he would receive as an inheritance. And he went out, not knowing where he was going. [9]By faith he dwelt in the land of promise as *in* a foreign country, dwelling in tents with Isaac and Jacob, the heirs with him of the same promise; [10]for he waited for the city which has foundations, whose builder and maker *is* God.

[11] By faith Sarah herself also received strength to conceive seed, and she bore a child[a] when she was past the age, because she judged Him faithful who had promised. [12]Therefore from one man, and him as good as dead, were born *as many* as the stars of the sky in multitude—innumerable as the sand which is by the seashore.

The Heavenly Hope

[13] These all died in faith, not having received the promises, but having seen them afar off were assured of them,[a] embraced *them* and confessed that they were strangers and pilgrims on the earth. [14]For those who say such things declare plainly that they seek a homeland. [15]And truly if they had called to mind that *country* from which they had come out, they would have had opportunity to

10:37 [a]Or *that which* **10:38** [a]NU-Text reads *My just one.*
[b]Habakkuk 2:3, 4 **11:5** [a]Genesis 5:24 **11:11** [a]NU-Text omits *she bore a child.* **11:13** [a]NU-Text and M-Text omit *were assured of them.*

THROUGH THE GRID

Making Sense of Your World:
Confronting Nature (Heb. 11:3)

As we live our lives, we also confront all the other elements in the universe, including nature and how the world works. The way in which we view our relation to nature also forms part of our worldview; if we view humanity and nature as partners, then we will act accordingly by taking care of nature and our environment. Conversely, if we view nature as something to be taken for granted, we will act in ways that abuse and destroy the natural resources around us. Understanding our relation to nature informs our worldview by allowing us to catch a glimpse of the world around us and our responsibility to it.

LEADERSHIP ISSUES

GC2: Faith in the Old Testament

HEBREWS 11:1, 2

Beginning almost immediately after the Fall, the Father began to nurture the damaged faith of His children. Though Adam and Eve's descendants never experienced the perfect faith that their ancestors originally enjoyed in the Garden, many of them, nonetheless, brought pleasure to their Creator by demonstrating faith. It was by faith that Abel offered a sacrifice pleasing to God, Enoch walked with God, Noah built the ark, and Abraham followed God toward an unknown destination (Heb. 11:4–8). Throughout the Old Testament, obedient followers of God exhibited faith in the face of difficult circumstances. This is how it is to be with faith-filled followers of Jesus.

Of course, the Old Testament is also full of instances in which people failed to demonstrate faith in God's provision: Sarah laughed at God's promise of a son (Gen. 18:10–12), the children of Israel feared that God would let them die in the wilderness (Ex. 14:10–12), the ten spies insisted that they could not possess the land of Canaan (Num. 13:26–33), and Jonah ran from the Lord rather than trusting His instructions (Jon. 1:1–3). In order for humankind to experience more mature faith, they would first have to encounter the One who modeled perfect faith, even God's Son Jesus.

Pause to celebrate that you have encountered Jesus, just as personally as He instructed Noah, called Moses, and guided Abraham and Sarah. Now ask Him in prayer to deepen your trust in Him—that your faith might bring Him pleasure (Heb. 11:6).

GC2
GREAT COMMANDMENT
COMMISSION

return. ¹⁶But now they desire a better, that is, a heavenly *country*. Therefore God is not ashamed to be called their God, for He has prepared a city for them.

The Faith of the Patriarchs

¹⁷By faith Abraham, when he was tested, offered up Isaac, and he who had received the promises offered up his only begotten *son,* ¹⁸of whom it was said, *"In Isaac your seed shall be called,"*ᵃ ¹⁹concluding that God *was* able to raise *him* up, even from the dead, from which he also received him in a figurative sense.

²⁰By faith Isaac blessed Jacob and Esau concerning things to come.

²¹By faith Jacob, when he was dying, blessed each of the sons of Joseph, and worshiped, *leaning* on the top of his staff.

²²By faith Joseph, when he was dying, made mention of the departure of the children of Israel, and gave instructions concerning his bones.

The Faith of Moses

²³By faith Moses, when he was born, was hidden three months by his parents, because they saw *he was* a beautiful child; and they were not afraid of the king's command.

²⁴By faith Moses, when he became of age, refused to be called the son of Pharaoh's daughter, ²⁵choosing rather to suffer affliction with the people of God than to enjoy the passing pleasures of sin, ²⁶esteeming the reproach of Christ greater riches than the treasures inᵃ Egypt; for he looked to the reward.

²⁷By faith he forsook Egypt, not fearing the wrath of the king; for he endured as seeing Him who is invisible. ²⁸By faith he kept the Passover and the sprinkling of blood, lest he who destroyed the firstborn should touch them.

²⁹By faith they passed through the Red Sea as by dry *land, whereas* the Egyptians, attempting to do so, were drowned.

By Faith They Overcame

³⁰By faith the walls of Jericho fell down after they were encircled for seven days. ³¹By faith the harlot Rahab did not perish with those who did not believe, when she had received the spies with peace.

³²And what more shall I say? For the time would fail me to tell of Gideon and Barak and Samson and Jephthah, also *of* David and Samuel and the prophets: ³³who through faith subdued kingdoms, worked righteousness, obtained promises, stopped the mouths of lions, ³⁴quenched the violence of fire, escaped the edge of the sword, out of weakness were made strong, became valiant in battle, turned to flight the armies of the aliens. ³⁵Women received their dead raised to life again.

Others were tortured, not accepting deliverance, that they might obtain a better resurrection. ³⁶Still others had trial of mockings and scourgings, yes, and of chains and imprisonment. ³⁷They were stoned, they were sawn in two, were tempted,ᵃ were slain with the sword. They wandered about in sheepskins and goatskins, being destitute, afflicted, tormented— ³⁸of whom the world was not worthy. They wandered in deserts and mountains, *in* dens and caves of the earth.

³⁹And all these, having obtained a good testimony through faith, did not receive the promise, ⁴⁰God having provided something better for us, that they should not be made perfect apart from us.

The Race of Faith

12 Therefore we also, since we are surrounded by so great a cloud of witnesses, let us lay aside every weight, and the sin which so easily ensnares *us,* and let us run with endurance the race that is set before us, ²looking unto Jesus, the author and finisher of *our* faith, who for the joy that was set before Him endured the cross, despising the shame, and has sat down at the right hand of the throne of God.

The Discipline of God

³For consider Him who endured such hostility from sinners against Himself, lest you become weary and discouraged in your souls. ⁴You have not yet resisted to bloodshed, striving against sin. ⁵And you have forgotten the exhortation which speaks to you as to sons:

11:18 ᵃGenesis 21:12   **11:26** ᵃNU-Text and M-Text read *of.*
11:37 ᵃNU-Text omits *were tempted.*

LEADERSHIP ISSUES

GC2: Christ's Community: Followers of Christ Journey Together!

HEBREWS 12:1 *Let us run with endurance the race that is set before us.*

Scripture speaks of "us" running the race. Following Jesus is not a solo sprint, but a team relay, with each of us at times being encouraged toward "love and good works" by one another (Heb. 10:24).

Years ago, during the U.S. Special Olympics, TV viewers were brought to tears during the 100-yard dash. When the starter's gun sounded, the runners, most of whom had Down Syndrome, took off down the track. About midway through the race, one young boy stumbled and fell, sprawling on the track.

As the crowds present and the millions who were viewing the scene on TV looked on in sympathy, they were given an unforgettable lesson in the power of fellowship by the other runners: One by one, they stopped running and went back to the fallen boy. Helping him to his feet, the crowd of runners headed off again toward the finish line, crossing it together arm-in-arm.

Pause to consider two questions:

- First, a celebration: Who, in your life, has "come back" to support and encourage you to finish well? Pray a prayer of thanksgiving.
- Second, a calling: Who, in the traffic patterns of your life, might God want you to notice, seek out, and encourage with His love? Pray a prayer of yielding to this call.

GC2
GREAT COMMANDMENT
COMMISSION

"My son, do not despise the chastening of the
LORD,
Nor be discouraged when you are rebuked by
Him;
⁶*For whom the LORD loves He chastens,*
*And scourges every son whom He receives."*ᵃ

⁷Ifᵃ you endure chastening, God deals with
you as with sons; for what son is there whom a
father does not chasten? ⁸But if you are without
chastening, of which all have become partakers,
then you are illegitimate and not sons. ⁹Further-
more, we have had human fathers who corrected
us, and we paid *them* respect. Shall we not much
more readily be in subjection to the Father of
spirits and live? ¹⁰For they indeed for a few days
chastened *us* as seemed *best* to them, but He for
our profit, that *we* may be partakers of His holiness. ¹¹Now no chastening seems to be joyful for
the present, but painful; nevertheless, afterward it
yields the peaceable fruit of righteousness to those
who have been trained by it.

RENEW YOUR SPIRITUAL VITALITY

¹²Therefore strengthen the hands which hang
down, and the feeble knees, ¹³and make straight
paths for your feet, so that what is lame may not
be dislocated, but rather be healed.

¹⁴Pursue peace with all *people,* and holiness,
without which no one will see the Lord: ¹⁵look-
ing carefully lest anyone fall short of the grace of
God; lest any root of bitterness springing up cause
trouble, and by this many become defiled; ¹⁶lest
there *be* any fornicator or profane person like
Esau, who for one morsel of food sold his
birthright. ¹⁷For you know that afterward, when
he wanted to inherit the blessing, he was rejected,
for he found no place for repentance, though he
sought it diligently with tears.

THE GLORIOUS COMPANY

¹⁸For you have not come to the mountain
thatᵃ may be touched and that burned with fire,
and to blackness and darknessᵇ and tempest, ¹⁹and
the sound of a trumpet and the voice of words, so
that those who heard *it* begged that the word
should not be spoken to them anymore. ²⁰(For
they could not endure what was commanded:
"And if so much as a beast touches the mountain,

*it shall be stoned*ᵃ *or shot with an arrow."*ᵇ ²¹And
so terrifying was the sight *that* Moses said, *"I am*
exceedingly afraid and trembling."ᵃ)

²²But you have come to Mount Zion and to
the city of the living God, the heavenly Jerusalem,
to an innumerable company of angels, ²³to the
general assembly and church of the firstborn *who*
are registered in heaven, to God the Judge of all,
to the spirits of just men made perfect, ²⁴to Jesus
the Mediator of the new covenant, and to the
blood of sprinkling that speaks better things than
that of Abel.

HEAR THE HEAVENLY VOICE

²⁵See that you do not refuse Him who speaks.
For if they did not escape who refused Him who
spoke on earth, much more *shall we not escape* if
we turn away from Him who *speaks* from heaven,
²⁶whose voice then shook the earth; but now He
has promised, saying, *"Yet once more I shake*ᵃ *not*
*only the earth, but also heaven."*ᵇ ²⁷Now this,
"Yet once more," indicates the removal of those
things that are being shaken, as of things that are
made, that the things which cannot be shaken
may remain.

²⁸Therefore, since we are receiving a kingdom
which cannot be shaken, let us have grace, by
which we mayᵃ serve God acceptably with reverence and godly fear. ²⁹For our God *is* a consuming fire.

CONCLUDING MORAL DIRECTIONS

13 Let brotherly love continue. ²Do not forget
to entertain strangers, for by so *doing* some
have unwittingly entertained angels. ³Remember
the prisoners as if chained with them—those who
are mistreated—since you yourselves are in the
body also.

⁴Marriage *is* honorable among all, and the
bed undefiled; but fornicators and adulterers God
will judge.

⁵*Let your* conduct *be* without covetousness; *be*
content with such things as you have. For He

12:6 ᵃProverbs 3:11, 12 **12:7** ᵃNU-Text and M-Text read *It is for*
discipline that you endure; God . . . . **12:18** ᵃNU-Text reads *to that*
which. ᵇNU-Text reads *gloom.* **12:20** ᵃNU-Text and M-Text omit
the rest of this verse. ᵇExodus 19:12, 13 **12:21** ᵃDeuteronomy
9:19 **12:26** ᵃNU-Text reads *will shake.* ᵇHaggai 2:6 **12:28** ᵃM-Text
omits *may.*

THROUGH THE GRID

*Making Sense of Your World:
Marriage (Heb. 13:4)*

Marriage is in serious trouble; and in recent days, the divorce court gavels are louder than the wedding bells. The divorce rate is higher than it has ever been, and traditional roles in marriage have all but been demolished. The roles of the husband and the wife have become so blurred that it is difficult to define any role with certainty.

Himself has said, *"I will never leave you nor forsake you."*[a] [6]So we may boldly say:

*"The LORD is my helper;
I will not fear.
What can man do to me?"*[a]

CONCLUDING RELIGIOUS DIRECTIONS

[7]Remember those who rule over you, who have spoken the word of God to you, whose faith follow, considering the outcome of *their* conduct. [8]Jesus Christ *is* the same yesterday, today, and forever. [9]Do not be carried about[a] with various and strange doctrines. For *it is* good that the heart be established by grace, not with foods which have not profited those who have been occupied with them.

[10]We have an altar from which those who serve the tabernacle have no right to eat. [11]For the bodies of those animals, whose blood is brought into the sanctuary by the high priest for sin, are burned outside the camp. [12]Therefore Jesus also, that He might sanctify the people with His own blood, suffered outside the gate. [13]Therefore let us go forth to Him, outside the camp, bearing His reproach. [14]For here we have no continuing city, but we seek the one to come. [15]Therefore by Him let us continually offer the sacrifice of praise to God, that is, the fruit of *our* lips, giving thanks to His name. [16]But do not forget to do good and to share, for with such sacrifices God is well pleased.

[17]Obey those who rule over you, and be submissive, for they watch out for your souls, as those who must give account. Let them do so with joy and not with grief, for that would be unprofitable for you.

PRAYER REQUESTED

[18]Pray for us; for we are confident that we have a good conscience, in all things desiring to live honorably. [19]But I especially urge *you* to do this, that I may be restored to you the sooner.

BENEDICTION, FINAL EXHORTATION, FAREWELL

[20]Now may the God of peace who brought up our Lord Jesus from the dead, that great Shepherd of the sheep, through the blood of the everlasting covenant, [21]make you complete in every good work to do His will, working in you[a] what is well pleasing in His sight, through Jesus Christ, to whom *be* glory forever and ever. Amen.

[22]And I appeal to you, brethren, bear with the word of exhortation, for I have written to you in few words. [23]Know that *our* brother Timothy has been set free, with whom I shall see you if he comes shortly.

[24]Greet all those who rule over you, and all the saints. Those from Italy greet you.

[25]Grace *be* with you all. Amen.

13:5 [a]Deuteronomy 31:6, 8; Joshua 1:5   **13:6** [a]Psalm 118:6
13:9 [a]NU-Text and M-Text read *away.*   **13:21** [a]NU-Text and M-Text read *us.*

IMPACT OF THE BOOK

I IDEA	*Faith and hearing must be translated into obedience and action.*
M MESSAGE	*Good works will not save you, but a saved person's life will show good works as daily evidence of genuine faith—when our words and actions collide. The leadership premise is very plain: we must be willing to humble ourselves and serve others. God will exalt us in His time.*
P PEOPLE	*James, Job, Rahab*
A AUTHOR	*James, the Lord's half brother, is the author of this book. His authorship has been disputed because four men named James are mentioned in the New Testament. During Jesus' earthly ministry, His brother James was bitterly opposed to the Lord, but he converted following His resurrection (1 Cor. 15:7). He became a man of prayer and the leader of the Jerusalem church. Tradition says James earned the nickname "old camel knees" because of his lengthy prayer life. Secular history says that he was slain by Jews in AD 62.*
C CULTURE	*James wrote the letter to strengthen and encourage the faith of persecuted and oppressed Jewish Christians. He addressed social and ethical aspects of the gospel, not just doctrinal matters. He knew that the believers were struggling with how their faith should impact their daily lives. The culture demanded less talk and more action; James encouraged his readers to display love, Christlike attitudes and speech, and perseverance during trials.*
T TIMELINE	*c. AD 45*
KEY SCRIPTURE MEMORY VERSES	1:2, 3, 5, 13–15, 17, 22, 27; 2:14–17, 26; 3:1, 5; 4:7, 8, 10, 17; 5:12, 16

GREETING TO THE TWELVE TRIBES

1 James, a bondservant of God and of the Lord Jesus Christ,

To the twelve tribes which are scattered abroad:

Greetings.

PROFITING FROM TRIALS

²My brethren, count it all joy when you fall into various trials, ³knowing that the testing of your faith produces patience. ⁴But let patience have *its* perfect work, that you may be perfect and complete, lacking nothing. ⁵If any of you lacks wisdom, let him ask of God, who gives to all liberally and without reproach, and it will be given to him. ⁶But let him ask in faith, with no doubting, for he who doubts is like a wave of the sea driven and tossed by the wind. ⁷For let not that man suppose that he will receive anything from the Lord; ⁸*he is* a double-minded man, unstable in all his ways.

THE PERSPECTIVE OF RICH AND POOR

⁹Let the lowly brother glory in his exaltation, ¹⁰but the rich in his humiliation, because as a flower of the field he will pass away. ¹¹For no sooner has the sun risen with a burning heat than it withers the grass; its flower falls, and its beautiful appearance perishes. So the rich man also will fade away in his pursuits.

LOVING GOD UNDER TRIALS

¹²Blessed *is* the man who endures temptation; for when he has been approved, he will receive the crown of life which the Lord has promised to those who love Him. ¹³Let no one say when he is tempted, "I am tempted by God"; for God cannot be tempted by evil, nor does He Himself tempt anyone. ¹⁴But each one is tempted when he is drawn away by his own desires and enticed. ¹⁵Then, when desire has conceived, it gives birth to sin; and sin, when it is full-grown, brings forth death.

INSIDE *the* INFLUENCERS

JAMES: A Servant's Perspective

JAMES 1:1

James, who wrote the Book of James, was the half brother of Jesus Christ. His mother and his father were Mary and Joseph. Jesus was the oldest of Mary's children, but certainly not the last. The Bible lists James, Joseph, Simon, and Judas as sons of Mary and Joseph (Matt. 13:55), and apparently they had daughters as well. (Mark 6:3)

James did not come to faith in Christ at an early age. Scripture paints a picture of a young man who resented his older brother (John 7:3–5). It probably wasn't an easy thing to grow up in a house alongside the Son of God, who just so happens to be your older brother!

At some point, James became a believer and committed follower. After the death of Christ, James became a recognized leader in the church. (Acts 15). He traded in his antagonistic attitude for the attitude of a servant. When James opened his letter to the church he could have boastfully referred to himself as "James, The Brother of Christ." Instead, he chooses to only identify himself as a "bondservant," literally one bound to another for service (James 1:1). What humility! James went from seeing Jesus as his crazy brother to recognizing that He is his Lord and Savior. He went from seeing himself as a younger brother who had the right to criticize, to a slave privileged to serve! James experienced an incredible change in perspective, because of his incredible change in heart.

LEADERSHIP ISSUES

Sexual Experimentation: "L.S.D."

JAMES 1:14, 15

Remember this about sexual experimentation: *no one can make you do it.* You have a built-in compass that says, "Don't." You might feel like everyone is doing it; but when the consequences come down, you will have to deal with them alone. The choice to be sexually active before marriage crosses the line of everything you believe as a Christian. Sexual experimentation is the same as playing with fire—it will burn you and scar you for life.

The apostle James describes a kind of LSD that isn't chemical, but just as deadly. It is the progression of **L**ust to **S**in to **D**eath (James 1:14, 15). These verses banish any chance of blaming Satan or anyone else. The "enticing" comes about through our own desires, which cause us to be baited, hooked, and dragged away.

Second Timothy 2:22 says, "Flee also youthful lusts; but pursue righteousness, faith, love, peace with those who call on the Lord out of a pure heart."

1. **Flee.** Run away from the situation—literally, "escape" in the Greek. Forget about debating if it's wrong or not that bad. Leave it behind altogether.
2. **Pursue.** In the Latin, this word is *prosequi* (from *pro-,* forward and *sequi,* to follow). The future-tense thinker does not fall into the moment of temptation; instead, he or she actively, energetically moves forward in life to follow righteousness, faith, love, and peace.

What the culture labels as harmless sexual fantasy actually drives the mind and then causes the body to crave the action of sin. We are drawn away from God's perfect plan, from the protection of the Holy Spirit, and from the moral compass that lives within our heart. Notice that the desire is already there. Giving in is all that has to happen to bring death to good habits, positive thoughts, and godliness.

Don't play the game of calling yourself a "technical virgin" while you experiment sexually. God looks on the heart and doesn't play the game of "How far is too far?"

LEADERSHIP ISSUES

GC2: Grateful Simplicity

JAMES 1:17

In our day, have we not been subjected to the same subtle attack as Adam and Eve in Genesis 3:1–7 somehow believing a lie that God is "holding out" on us? Does gratefulness for the simplicity and purity of Christ's love empower us, or have we bought into the lie that we have needs for which God is not committed to provide? (2 Cor. 11:3).

Do we at times make following Jesus so complex that we miss Jesus? Have we missed out on the grateful simplicity that the Christian life is primarily about loving Jesus? (John 14:15).

What is it that prompts our witness, encourages our service, and enlists our commitment? Is it merely a sense of our duty to live up to others' expectations? Is it a sense of obligation, a feeling that we must somehow "pay God back" in some measure for the forgiveness and love we have received?

May it never be! The maturing disciple's heart will be prompted often by the Holy Spirit to consider anew the wonder of being loved by God, the privilege of laboring with the Creator, and the awesome truth that we get to relate intimately with Christ (Ps. 139:3; 2 Cor. 5:14).

GC2
GREAT COMMANDMENT
COMMISSION

What is meant by the term "evil"? By this we mean the moral and natural evil that occurs in the world. Moral evil is when bad choices are made that create evil and suffering or injustice in our world (James 1:13–15). Natural evil includes things like natural disasters or diseases and even death—things that a human agency doesn't necessarily cause (Job).

16Do not be deceived, my beloved brethren. 17Every good gift and every perfect gift is from above, and comes down from the Father of lights, with whom there is no variation or shadow of turning. 18Of His own will He brought us forth by the word of truth, that we might be a kind of firstfruits of His creatures.

QUALITIES NEEDED IN TRIALS

19So then,a my beloved brethren, let every man be swift to hear, slow to speak, slow to wrath; 20for the wrath of man does not produce the righteousness of God.

DOERS—NOT HEARERS ONLY

21Therefore lay aside all filthiness and overflow of wickedness, and receive with meekness the implanted word, which is able to save your souls.

22But be doers of the word, and not hearers only, deceiving yourselves. 23For if anyone is a

1:19 aNU-Text reads *Know this* or *This you know.*

LEADERSHIP REALITIES

EXECUTION   *James 1:22–24*

The exciting life of a *doer* sharply contrasts with that of the person who is a *hearer* only. Maybe you have been one of those people—sitting in church, listening to the sermon, singing the songs, closing your eyes during the prayer, and maybe even putting in an offering, and then thinking, *Hey, I've done what I am supposed to, and now I'm done.* Not so fast! The *hearer only* "observes himself, goes away, and immediately forgets" what God has revealed in His Word about making changes and moving forward. He may have been in the room when the Scripture was read, but he is oblivious to the smudge marks of the human heart and neglects the call of the Holy Spirit.

This mirror of the Word shows us two views: *who we are* and *who we can be* for Christ. The **doer** remembers both views and is ready to respond.

Doers are set apart from all the rest. They:

Depend on the power of God to provide.
Overcome obstacles, limitations, and habits.
Execute dreams.
Risk failure.

A sermon is not truly *heard* unless it moves you to *do.*

LEADERSHIP ISSUES

GC2: Listen More

JAMES 1:19

It's been said that a picture is worth a thousand words, but some people still prefer the one thousand words. Do you talk too much and listen too little? The next time you visit with your family, friends, or others, keep track of how much time you talk and how much time you listen.

You might say, "My friends or family won't talk. If I don't talk, we will have a silent relationship." Share that you really enjoy hearing from him/her, and then ask some questions to "prime the pump."

Healthy relationships are built on good listening skills. A great strategy to promote communication is to ask "open-ended questions":

- "What was the best part of your day?"
- "Of all the places you have ever visited, what is your favorite?"

GC2
GREAT COMMANDMENT
COMMISSION

THROUGH THE GRID

Nourished by the Word:
Rehanging the Mirror
of God's Word

JAMES 1:23, 24 *For if anyone is a hearer of the word and not a doer, he is like a man observing his natural face in a mirror; for he observes himself, goes away, and immediately forgets what kind of man he was.*

Imagine that God's Word is like a mirror that hangs on a wall in our home. We can look into this mirror and see how closely we resemble Jesus. We can gaze into the glass and see a reflection of God's glory as the Spirit works to transform us into the likeness of Christ (2 Cor. 3:18).

Just as the mirrors in our home hang from nails, God's "mirror" (the Bible) must hang upon something as well. In dramatic fashion, while answering a question concerning which commandment was greatest, Christ revealed that God's Word actually hangs upon two commandments: "Love the LORD your God with all your heart, with all your soul, and with all your mind. . . . "Love your neighbor as yourself. On these two commandments hang all the Law and the Prophets" (Matt. 22:37–40).

Christ said that all of Scripture "hangs," "depends," or "must be considered in relation to" the way we love God and one another. Every book of the Bible, every command, and every scriptural principle hangs on the "nails" of loving God and loving one another. We are to consistently ask of the Lord, "How does this Scripture lead me into a deepening love for You? And more caring love for others?"

hearer of the word and not a doer, he is like a man observing his natural face in a mirror; 24for he observes himself, goes away, and immediately forgets what kind of man he was. 25But he who looks into the perfect law of liberty and continues *in it,* and is not a forgetful hearer but a doer of the work, this one will be blessed in what he does.

26If anyone among youª thinks he is religious, and does not bridle his tongue but deceives his own heart, this one's religion *is* useless. 27Pure and undefiled religion before God and the Father is this: to visit orphans and widows in their trouble, *and* to keep oneself unspotted from the world.

BEWARE OF PERSONAL FAVORITISM

2 My brethren, do not hold the faith of our Lord Jesus Christ, *the Lord* of glory, with partiality. 2For if there should come into your assembly a man with gold rings, in fine apparel, and there should also come in a poor man in filthy clothes,

3and you pay attention to the one wearing the fine clothes and say to him, "You sit here in a good place," and say to the poor man, "You stand there," or, "Sit here at my footstool," 4have you not shown partiality among yourselves, and become judges with evil thoughts?

5Listen, my beloved brethren: Has God not chosen the poor of this world *to be* rich in faith and heirs of the kingdom which He promised to those who love Him? 6But you have dishonored the poor man. Do not the rich oppress you and drag you into the courts? 7Do they not blaspheme that noble name by which you are called?

8If you really fulfill *the* royal law according to the Scripture, *"You shall love your neighbor as yourself,"*ª you do well; 9but if you show partiality, you commit sin, and are convicted by the law as transgressors. 10For whoever shall keep the whole law, and yet stumble in one *point,* he is

1:26 ªNU-Text omits *among you.*   2:8 ªLeviticus 19:18

LEADERSHIP ISSUES

GC2: Listen and Remember

JAMES 1:25

We often may do a decent job of listening, but when we leave the conversation, we soon forget what was said. We fall prey to the "out of sight, out of mind" syndrome. If your best friend or "significant" person shares with you his or her fears about a particular issue, what will be your long-term response to this shared information?

To listen with remembrance means the information shared will stay in the forefront of your mind, and you will be particularly sensitive to your friend in that area. In other words, what you heard will eventually affect *your* behavior. What you heard may need to be added to your regular prayer list or what you heard may need to translate into action and "giving" on your part. This sometimes requires that you write things down so as not to forget them.

One of the golden rules of relationships is to listen to others, just as you would have them listen to you. Why not try asking a close friend to give you feedback on how you can be a better listener? Pray first, don't be defensive, and then listen.

GC2
GREAT COMMANDMENT
COMMISSION

THROUGH THE GRID

Where Have All the Dreamers Gone?
Observations from a Biblical
Worldview: Spirituality vs. Religion
(James 1:27)

More and more, people are being drawn toward being "spiritual" rather than religious. When asked if she held religious beliefs, one girl replied: "I'm more spiritual than religious." This implies that there is a growing trend of transcendentalism prevailing in our culture, where people are attempting to be spiritual—that is, an agent of their own religion—rather than conform to the rules of any organized religion. This is called "individuation"—the desire to make everything conform to one's own wishes and preferences. This "bar code" faith puts personal choice at the top of the list, relegating anything with other standards or rules to the undesirable category.

guilty of all. [11]For He who said, *"Do not commit adultery,"*[a] also said, *"Do not murder."*[b] Now if you do not commit adultery, but you do murder, you have become a transgressor of the law. [12]So speak and so do as those who will be judged by the law of liberty. [13]For judgment is without mercy to the one who has shown no mercy. Mercy triumphs over judgment.

Faith Without Works Is Dead

[14]What *does it* profit, my brethren, if someone says he has faith but does not have works? Can faith save him? [15]If a brother or sister is naked and destitute of daily food, [16]and one of you says to them, "Depart in peace, be warmed and filled," but you do not give them the things which are needed for the body, what *does it* profit? [17]Thus also faith by itself, if it does not have works, is dead.

[18]But someone will say, "You have faith, and I have works." Show me your faith without your[a] works, and I will show you my faith by my[b] works. [19]You believe that there is one God. You do well. Even the demons believe—and tremble! [20]But do you want to know, O foolish man, that faith without works is dead?[a] [21]Was not Abraham our father justified by works when he offered Isaac his son on the altar? [22]Do you see that faith was working together with his works, and by works faith was made perfect? [23]And the Scripture was fulfilled which says, *"Abraham believed God, and it was accounted to him for righteous-*

ness."[a] And he was called the friend of God. [24]You see then that a man is justified by works, and not by faith only.

[25]Likewise, was not Rahab the harlot also justified by works when she received the messengers and sent *them* out another way?

[26]For as the body without the spirit is dead, so faith without works is dead also.

The Untamable Tongue

3 My brethren, let not many of you become teachers, knowing that we shall receive a stricter judgment. [2]For we all stumble in many things. If anyone does not stumble in word, he *is* a perfect man, able also to bridle the whole body. [3]Indeed,[a] we put bits in horses' mouths that they may obey us, and we turn their whole body. [4]Look also at ships: although they are so large and are driven by fierce winds, they are turned by a very small rudder wherever the pilot desires. [5]Even so the tongue is a little member and boasts great things.

See how great a forest a little fire kindles! [6]And the tongue *is* a fire, a world of iniquity. The tongue is so set among our members that it defiles the whole body, and sets on fire the course of nature; and it is set on fire by hell. [7]For every kind of beast and bird, of reptile and creature of the sea, is tamed and has been tamed by mankind.

2:11 [a]Exodus 20:14; Deuteronomy 5:18 [b]Exodus 20:13; Deuteronomy 5:17   **2:18** [a]NU-Text omits *your.* [b]NU-Text omits *my.*   **2:20** [a]NU-Text reads *useless.*   **2:23** [a]Genesis 15:6   **3:3** [a]NU-Text reads *Now if.*

LEADERSHIP ISSUES

GC2: Grace for the Humble

JAMES 4:6

God promises in the Book of James, to resist the proud, but give grace to the humble (James 4:6). Peter furthers the thought by saying, "Therefore humble yourselves under the mighty hand of God, that He may exalt you in due time" (1 Pet. 5:6). Humility, then, must certainly be at the top of God's desires for our lives. But what exactly is it?

Humility is an attitude and a response of our heart. It is a response of vulnerability, a ready declaration of neediness before God and hope in His provision. It is this hope that becomes the substance of our faith. These elements are linked in succession: admitting our neediness and demonstrating our own humility. Only then can we begin to hope for God's provision. As we hope for His provision, we exercise faith; and without faith, it is impossible to please God (Heb. 11:6).

[8]But no man can tame the tongue. *It is* an unruly evil, full of deadly poison. [9]With it we bless our God and Father, and with it we curse men, who have been made in the similitude of God. [10]Out of the same mouth proceed blessing and cursing. My brethren, these things ought not to be so. [11]Does a spring send forth fresh *water* and bitter from the same opening? [12]Can a fig tree, my brethren, bear olives, or a grapevine bear figs? Thus no spring yields both salt water and fresh.[a]

Heavenly Versus Demonic Wisdom

[13]Who *is* wise and understanding among you? Let him show by good conduct *that* his works *are done* in the meekness of wisdom. [14]But if you have bitter envy and self-seeking in your hearts, do not boast and lie against the truth. [15]This wisdom does not descend from above, but *is* earthly, sensual, demonic. [16]For where envy and self-seeking *exist,* confusion and every evil thing *are* there. [17]But the wisdom that is from above is first pure, then peaceable, gentle, willing to yield, full of mercy and good fruits, without partiality and without hypocrisy. [18]Now the fruit of righteousness is sown in peace by those who make peace.

Pride Promotes Strife

4 Where do wars and fights *come* from among you? Do *they* not *come* from your *desires for* pleasure that war in your members? [2]You lust and do not have. You murder and covet and cannot obtain. You fight and war. Yet[a] you do not have because you do not ask. [3]You ask and do not receive, because you ask amiss, that you may spend *it* on your pleasures. [4]Adulterers and[a] adulteresses! Do you not know that friendship with the world is enmity with God? Whoever therefore wants to be a friend of the world makes himself an enemy of God. [5]Or do you think that the Scripture says in vain, "The Spirit who dwells in us yearns jealously"?

[6]But He gives more grace. Therefore He says:

"God resists the proud,
But gives grace to the humble."[a]

Humility Cures Worldliness

[7]Therefore submit to God. Resist the devil and he will flee from you. [8]Draw near to God and He will draw near to you. Cleanse *your* hands, *you* sinners; and purify *your* hearts, *you* double-minded. [9]Lament and mourn and weep! Let your laughter be turned to mourning and *your* joy to gloom. [10]Humble yourselves in the sight of the Lord, and He will lift you up.

Do Not Judge a Brother

[11]Do not speak evil of one another, brethren. He who speaks evil of a brother and judges his brother, speaks evil of the law and judges the law. But if you judge the law, you are not a doer of the law but a judge. [12]There is one Lawgiver,[a] who is able to save and to destroy. Who[b] are you to judge another?[c]

Do Not Boast About Tomorrow

[13]Come now, you who say, "Today or tomorrow we will[a] go to such and such a city, spend a year there, buy and sell, and make a profit"; [14]whereas you do not know what *will happen* tomorrow. For what *is* your life? It is even a vapor that appears for a little time and then vanishes away. [15]Instead you *ought* to say, "If the Lord wills, we shall live and do this or that." [16]But now you boast in your arrogance. All such boasting is evil. [17]Therefore, to him who knows to do good and does not do *it,* to him it is sin.

Rich Oppressors Will Be Judged

5 Come now, *you* rich, weep and howl for your miseries that are coming upon *you!* [2]Your riches are corrupted, and your garments are moth-eaten. [3]Your gold and silver are corroded, and their corrosion will be a witness against you and will eat your flesh like fire. You have heaped up treasure in the last days. [4]Indeed the wages of the laborers who mowed your fields, which you kept back by fraud, cry out; and the cries of the reapers have reached the ears of the Lord of Sabaoth.[a] [5]You have lived on the earth in pleasure and luxury; you have fattened your hearts as[a] in a day of slaughter. [6]You have condemned, you have murdered the just; he does not resist you.

3:12 [a]NU-Text reads *Neither can a salty spring produce fresh water.* **4:2** [a]NU-Text and M-Text omit *Yet.* **4:4** [a]NU-Text omits *Adulterers and.* **4:6** [a]Proverbs 3:34 **4:12** [a]NU-Text adds *and Judge.* [b]NU-Text and M-Text read *But who.* [c]NU-Text reads *a neighbor.* **4:13** [a]M-Text reads *let us.* **5:4** [a]Literally, in Hebrew, *Hosts* **5:5** [a]NU-Text omits *as.*

LEADERSHIP ISSUES

GC2: Confessing Your Wrongs

JAMES 5:16A

Admitting our wrongs to those we've hurt is a great exercise in humility; it also requires the special empowerment of God's Spirit. An appropriate confession, whether to God or another person, will include *being specific, saying you were wrong,* and *not offering excuses or rationalizations.*

- Be Specific: which of these two statements is more humbling and truthful?

  ___ "If I've offended you or hurt you in any way, I'm sorry."

  ___ "I was very selfish and insensitive when I _____ (specifically name how you acted selfishly or insensitively). That was wrong of me." (For example, you might say, *"I've been selfish in not doing my part around the house,"* or *"I was not sensitive to you in my critical comments."*)

- Admit wrong: Use the words *"I was wrong,"* instead of "I'm sorry," because to simply say "I'm sorry" might only mean, "I'm sorry I got caught," or "I'm sorry we can't get along." *To say, "I was wrong" is a more truthful admission of guilt.*

- Don't offer excuses, explanations, or rationalizations.

  ___ No references like: "If you had not done ____, then I would not have ____."

  ___ "I didn't mean to, but you ____."

- Putting it all together:

  ___ I was selfish/insensitive(etc.), when I _____; I was wrong; will you please forgive me?"

Becoming a person who *humbly confesses when wrong,* will help prepare you for healthy, God-honoring relationships.

GC2
GREAT COMMANDMENT
COMMISSION

Be Patient and Persevering

⁷Therefore be patient, brethren, until the coming of the Lord. See *how* the farmer waits for the precious fruit of the earth, waiting patiently for it until it receives the early and latter rain. ⁸You also be patient. Establish your hearts, for the coming of the Lord is at hand.

⁹Do not grumble against one another, brethren, lest you be condemned.ᵃ Behold, the Judge is standing at the door! ¹⁰My brethren, take the prophets, who spoke in the name of the Lord, as an example of suffering and patience. ¹¹Indeed we count them blessed who endure. You have heard of the perseverance of Job and seen the end *intended by* the Lord—that the Lord is very compassionate and merciful.

¹²But above all, my brethren, do not swear, either by heaven or by earth or with any other oath. But let your "Yes" be "Yes," and *your* "No," "No," lest you fall into judgment.ᵃ

Meeting Specific Needs

¹³Is anyone among you suffering? Let him pray. Is anyone cheerful? Let him sing psalms. ¹⁴Is anyone among you sick? Let him call for the elders of the church, and let them pray over him, anointing him with oil in the name of the Lord. ¹⁵And the prayer of faith will save the sick, and the Lord will raise him up. And if he has committed sins, he will be forgiven. ¹⁶Confess *your* trespassesᵃ to one another, and pray for one another, that you may be healed. The effective, fervent prayer of a righteous man avails much. ¹⁷Elijah was a man with a nature like ours, and he prayed earnestly that it would not rain; and it did not rain on the land for three years and six months. ¹⁸And he prayed again, and the heaven gave rain, and the earth produced its fruit.

Bring Back the Erring One

¹⁹Brethren, if anyone among you wanders from the truth, and someone turns him back, ²⁰let him know that he who turns a sinner from the error of his way will save a soulᵃ from death and cover a multitude of sins.

5:9 ᵃNU-Text and M-Text read *judged.*   **5:12** ᵃM-Text reads *hypocrisy.*   **5:16** ᵃNU-Text reads *Therefore confess your sins.*   **5:20** ᵃNU-Text reads *his soul.*

IMPACT OF THE BOOK

I IDEA *Christ is a believer's sure hope in light of present suf-ferings. Peter's warm tone and practical advice make this beloved epistle one that encourages believers to remain steadfast in their faith. He expresses the affirmation and the for-giveness that he himself received.*

M MESSAGE *Sometimes God allows trials and persecution to refine and strengthen His children's faith, just as fire is used to purify metal. Leaders must expect persecution and opposition. A leader must have a faith that has endured trials and that will not be easily shaken.*

P PEOPLE *Peter*

A AUTHOR *Peter was the son of Jonah and the older brother of Andrew—another of Christ's disciples. Peter was a fisherman on the shores of the Sea of Galilee. Peter was also married (Mark 1:30, 31). Among the twelve disciples, Peter was considered to be one of the men closest to Jesus. Christian tradition holds he was martyred in Rome between AD 64 and 67, crucified upside down.*

C CULTURE *First Peter was written to believers who were experiencing perse-cution because of their faith in Jesus Christ. It was written from Babylon (1 Pet. 5:13). These believers lived where they were considered aliens, strangers, or pilgrims in a pagan cul-ture with practices foreign to them. Peter exhorted these believ-ers to stand strong in their faith by giving glory to God through their Christlike behavior toward their persecutors.*

T TIMELINE *AD 64*

KEY SCRIPTURE MEMORY VERSES 1:14–16; 2:9, 24; 3:15; 4:10; 5:6, 7; 5:8

FIRST PETER

GREETING TO THE ELECT PILGRIMS

1 Peter, an apostle of Jesus Christ,

To the pilgrims of the Dispersion in Pontus, Galatia, Cappadocia, Asia, and Bithynia, [2]elect according to the foreknowledge of God the Father, in sanctification of the Spirit, for obedience and sprinkling of the blood of Jesus Christ:

Grace to you and peace be multiplied.

A HEAVENLY INHERITANCE

[3]Blessed *be* the God and Father of our Lord Jesus Christ, who according to His abundant mercy has begotten us again to a living hope through the resurrection of Jesus Christ from the dead, [4]to an inheritance incorruptible and undefiled and that does not fade away, reserved in heaven for you, [5]who are kept by the power of God through faith for salvation ready to be revealed in the last time.

[6]In this you greatly rejoice, though now for a little while, if need be, you have been grieved by various trials, [7]that the genuineness of your faith, *being* much more precious than gold that perishes, though it is tested by fire, may be found to praise, honor, and glory at the revelation of Jesus Christ, [8]whom having not seen[a] you love. Though now you do not see *Him,* yet believing, you rejoice with joy inexpressible and full of glory, [9]receiving the end of your faith—the salvation of *your* souls.

[10]Of this salvation the prophets have inquired and searched carefully, who prophesied of the grace *that would come* to you, [11]searching what, or what manner of time, the Spirit of Christ who was in them was indicating when He testified beforehand the sufferings of Christ and the glories that would follow. [12]To them it was revealed that, not to themselves, but to us[a] they were ministering the things which now have been reported to you through those who have preached the gospel to you by the Holy Spirit sent from heaven— things which angels desire to look into.

LIVING BEFORE GOD OUR FATHER

[13]Therefore gird up the loins of your mind, be sober, and rest *your* hope fully upon the grace that is to be brought to you at the revelation of Jesus Christ; [14]as obedient children, not conforming yourselves to the former lusts, *as* in your ignorance; [15]but as He who called you *is* holy, you also be holy in all *your* conduct, [16]because it is written, *"Be holy, for I am holy."*[a]

[17]And if you call on the Father, who without partiality judges according to each one's work, conduct yourselves throughout the time of your stay *here* in fear; [18]knowing that you were not redeemed with corruptible things, *like* silver or gold, from your aimless conduct *received* by tradition from your fathers, [19]but with the precious blood of Christ, as of a lamb without blemish and without spot. [20]He indeed was foreordained before the foundation of the world, but was manifest in these last times for you [21]who through

1:8 [a]M-Text reads *known.* **1:12** [a]NU-Text and M-Text read *you.* **1:16** [a]Leviticus 11:44, 45; 19:2; 20:7

THROUGH THE GRID

Discover God: God Gives Us the Power to Become Holy

1 PETER 1:15 *But as He who called you is holy, you also be holy in all your conduct.*

Just as God is characterized by holiness, so we too must be characterized as people of holiness. God gives us the power to live holy lives, and to do so, we must yield to the power of the Holy Spirit and allow Him to work in our lives. Our response to God involves turning away from evil and embracing integrity and holiness. Thankfully, this is not the basis of our salvation, but a response, as Christ has come to take away the sins of the world. Through the power of the Holy Spirit, we can live a holy life that is pleasing to God and allows for fellowship with God.

Him believe in God, who raised Him from the dead and gave Him glory, so that your faith and hope are in God.

THE ENDURING WORD

[22]Since you have purified your souls in obeying the truth through the Spirit[a] in sincere love of the brethren, love one another fervently with a pure heart, [23]having been born again, not of corruptible seed but incorruptible, through the word of God which lives and abides forever,[a] [24]because

> "All flesh is as grass,
> And all the glory of man[a] as the flower of the grass.
> The grass withers,
> And its flower falls away,
> [25]But the word of the LORD endures forever."[a]

Now this is the word which by the gospel was preached to you.

2 Therefore, laying aside all malice, all deceit, hypocrisy, envy, and all evil speaking, [2]as new-born babes, desire the pure milk of the word, that you may grow thereby,[a] [3]if indeed you have tasted that the Lord is gracious.

THE CHOSEN STONE AND HIS CHOSEN PEOPLE

[4]Coming to Him as to a living stone, rejected indeed by men, but chosen by God and precious, [5]you also, as living stones, are being built up a spiritual house, a holy priesthood, to offer up spiritual sacrifices acceptable to God through Jesus Christ. [6]Therefore it is also contained in the Scripture,

> "Behold, I lay in Zion
> A chief cornerstone, elect, precious,
> And he who believes on Him will by no means be put to shame."[a]

[7]Therefore, to you who believe, He is precious; but to those who are disobedient,[a]

1:22 [a]NU-Text omits *through the Spirit.* **1:23** [a]NU-Text omits *forever.* **1:24** [a]NU-Text reads *all its glory.* **1:25** [a]Isaiah 40:6–8 **2:2** [a]NU-Text adds *up to salvation.* **2:6** [a]Isaiah 28:16 **2:7** [a]NU-Text reads *to those who disbelieve.*

THROUGH THE GRID

Making Sense of Your World:
The Mission of the Church (1 Pet. 2:9)

God has designed the church to fulfill three fundamental goals: intimacy with God, community with believers, and mission to the world. Each local or individual church must respond to their calling by developing a community of believers. This community should be bonding together, worshiping God, striving to develop knowledge of and intimacy with God, actively doing the work of missions by reaching out to the world, and letting others know the Good News of the gospel of Christ. Worship of God helps facilitate an intimacy with God, whereby the church can express its outward devotion to God, serving God in spirit and in truth. Worship also includes the teaching role of the church, where God is honored as God's people are instructed by the Word. Through teaching, believers are equipped with a biblical worldview and are prepared to handle the spiritual challenges that may arise. They can be edified through the teaching of the church, and they can develop a stronger biblical worldview. Community with believers is an integral part of the church as each church carries on the rites of the Christian community, joining together with the larger body of Christ as they perform the sacraments of Christian worship and service. God intended for individuals to practice Christian charity and giving as they attempt to live out the oneness of the body of Christ. The mission aspect of the church fulfills Christ's command to make disciples of all nations. The church works to tell others about God and to work toward unity with other churches.

LEADERSHIP ISSUES

GC2: Nourished by the Word: Living As He Lived

1 PETER 2:2 *As newborn babes, desire the pure milk of the word, that you may grow thereby.*

Disciples grow in maturity as the Word of God nourishes them. Satan sought to tempt Christ in the desert, but Christ overcame him by continuing to walk in the light of the Word of God (Matt. 4:1–11). His declarations speak to the power and necessity of being nourished by the Word: "Man shall not live by bread alone, but by every word that proceeds from the mouth of God" (v. 4). As we live out the divine calling to express and extend God's presence in a dark world, we must take full advantage of every opportunity to encounter God in His Word and to experience its nourishing benefits and blessings.

- As we **hear** the Word taught, preached, and shared, our faith will be strengthened: "Faith comes by hearing" God's Word (Rom. 10:17).
- As we **read** the Word, we will be blessed: "Blessed is he who reads . . . the words of this prophecy" (Rev. 1:3).
- As we **study** the Word, we will be approved by God as "a worker who . . . rightly [divides] the word of truth" (2 Tim. 2:15).
- As we **memorize** the Word, we will be less vulnerable to sin: "Your word I have hidden in my heart, that I might not sin against You" (Ps. 119:11).
- As we **meditate** upon the Word, our yielding to it will increase: "This Book of the Law shall not depart from your mouth, but you shall meditate in it day and night, that you may observe to do according to all that is written in it" (Josh. 1:8). Meditation upon the Word will also encourage spiritual prosperity, health, and fruitfulness (Ps. 1:1–3).

Reflect on how many of these five ways of being nourished by the Word have become life disciplines for you. Which might you want to increase?

GC2
GREAT COMMANDMENT
COMMISSION

THROUGH THE GRID

Making Sense of Your World: The View from Above (1 Pet. 2:22–24)

Since God is the Creator of the universe and of humanity, the way we view ourselves is intrinsically linked with how we view God. Our view of the self must begin with our view of God. The more we know about the One who created us, the more we are able to know God's creation, including ourselves. But the beginning point is God—knowing God's character and His revelation helps us to develop our own self-view. A biblical self-view acknowledges that we are originally good but have been corrupted by sin. Only in Christ can we be restored and redeemed.

*"The stone which the builders rejected
Has become the chief cornerstone,"*[b]

[8]and

*"A stone of stumbling
And a rock of offense."*[a]

They stumble, being disobedient to the word, to which they also were appointed.

[9]But you *are* a chosen generation, a royal priesthood, a holy nation, His own special people, that you may proclaim the praises of Him who called you out of darkness into His marvelous light; [10]who once *were* not a people but *are* now the people of God, who had not obtained mercy but now have obtained mercy.

LIVING BEFORE THE WORLD

[11]Beloved, I beg *you* as sojourners and pilgrims, abstain from fleshly lusts which war against the soul, [12]having your conduct honorable among the Gentiles, that when they speak against you as evildoers, they may, by *your* good works which they observe, glorify God in the day of visitation.

SUBMISSION TO GOVERNMENT

[13]Therefore submit yourselves to every ordinance of man for the Lord's sake, whether to the king as supreme, [14]or to governors, as to those who are sent by him for the punishment of evildoers and *for the* praise of those who do good. [15]For this is the will of God, that by doing good you may put to silence the ignorance of foolish men— [16]as free, yet not using liberty as a cloak for vice, but as bondservants of God. [17]Honor all

people. Love the brotherhood. Fear God. Honor the king.

SUBMISSION TO MASTERS

[18]Servants, *be* submissive to *your* masters with all fear, not only to the good and gentle, but also to the harsh. [19]For this *is* commendable, if because of conscience toward God one endures grief, suffering wrongfully. [20]For what credit *is it* if, when you are beaten for your faults, you take it patiently? But when you do good and suffer, if you take it patiently, this *is* commendable before God. [21]For to this you were called, because Christ also suffered for us,[a] leaving us[b] an example, that you should follow His steps:

[22]*"Who committed no sin,
Nor was deceit found in His mouth",*[a]

[23]who, when He was reviled, did not revile in return; when He suffered, He did not threaten, but committed *Himself* to Him who judges righteously; [24]who Himself bore our sins in His own body on the tree, that we, having died to sins, might live for righteousness—by whose stripes you were healed. [25]For you were like sheep going astray, but have now returned to the Shepherd and Overseer[a] of your souls.

SUBMISSION TO HUSBANDS

3 Wives, likewise, *be* submissive to your own husbands, that even if some do not obey the word, they, without a word, may be won by the conduct

2:7 [b]Psalm 118:22   2:8 [a]Isaiah 8:14   2:21 [a]NU-Text reads *you.*
[b]NU-Text and M-Text read *you.*   2:22 [a]Isaiah 53:9   2:25 [a]Greek *Episkopos*

LEADERSHIP ISSUES

GC2: Showing Respect

1 PETER 2:17

The need for respect is met by valuing, honoring, and regarding others highly and by treating them as important. "Be kindly affectionate to one another with brotherly love, in honor giving preference to one another" (Rom. 12:10).

During His earthly ministry, Jesus ignored all the social prejudices of His society by showing respect to tax collectors, Samaritans, the poor, lepers, and women. Even though all had sinned, He valued them as people, "created in God's image" (Gen. 1:26). He treated all people as having infinite value, regardless of their status.

How has God shown respect for us? God considered us of such great worth that He sacrificed His only Son so we might be redeemed (2 Cor. 5:21). Furthermore, He respects our individuality and our choices; He will not force our obedience. He longs for us to love Him, but He will not force us.

Pause and reflect on these ideas for giving others respect:

- Before making a decision, I solicit input from those whose lives will be impacted by the decision.
- I have a high regard for other people's ideas, opinions, and perspectives even though they may differ from mine.
- I treat other people's property, personal belongings, and privacy as I would like mine to be treated.
- I treat everyone with dignity and courtesy regardless of their race, lifestyle, or socioeconomic status.
- I'm careful to be on time to school, work, appointments, and meetings.

Becoming a person who *shows respect* will help prepare you for healthy, God-honoring relationships.

GC2
GREAT COMMANDMENT
COMMISSION

LEADERSHIP ISSUES

The Woman of Virtue

1 PETER 3:3, 4

The early church historian, Tertullian, wrote of the complaints that women who converted to Christianity began to dress too modestly. They changed their behavior so that they were known as homemakers, and they were virtuous in their conduct. They were "different."

Peter gives women the honor of being able to offer to God a precious and personal gift. He speaks of pure conversation and inner beauty; this hidden person of the heart is an "incorruptible" beauty. It is important that we not read this passage as a command not to wear makeup, jewelry, or nice clothing. More importantly, it says that those outward trappings must not be what draws others to you, nor must they become the focus of your beauty.

Peter goes on to say that a gentle and quiet spirit are "very precious" to God. Imagine being dear to the heart of God. Truly this is a major privilege, which should not be taken lightly. Some have tried to use this verse to say that women should not teach, speak publicly, or be in leadership, but this view disregards the fact that God has chosen many women as leaders and influencers throughout history. Just think about some of the women from the Bible—women like the judge and prophetess Deborah and like Queen Esther.

Christ chose to come to earth through a woman. Jesus showed Himself first to a woman after His resurrection. Women such as Martha and Mary cared for Jesus and were His personal friends. Lydia began a church in her home and financed the ministry for Paul on many occasions.

This passage involves both power and privilege. A gentle and quiet spirit is to be favored, and pure conversation is a jewel to be worn. To be gentle and quiet is to exhibit a peaceful, encouraging spirit. The goal is godliness—not popularity—although the end result is respect, friendship, and a reputation for being Christlike.

The woman of virtue thinks first how she can offer herself as a precious gift to God; and second, she considers how she wants to present herself as a living sacrifice in her daily walk. Women who want to be influencers must begin with the hidden person.

of their wives, [2]when they observe your chaste conduct *accompanied* by fear. [3]Do not let your adornment be *merely* outward—arranging the hair, wearing gold, or putting on *fine* apparel— [4]rather *let it be* the hidden person of the heart, with the incorruptible *beauty* of a gentle and quiet spirit, which is very precious in the sight of God. [5]For in this manner, in former times, the holy women who trusted in God also adorned themselves, being submissive to their own husbands, [6]as Sarah obeyed Abraham, calling him lord, whose daughters you are if you do good and are not afraid with any terror.

A Word to Husbands

[7]Husbands, likewise, dwell with *them* with understanding, giving honor to the wife, as to the weaker vessel, and as *being* heirs together of the grace of life, that your prayers may not be hindered.

Called to Blessing

[8]Finally, all *of you be* of one mind, having compassion for one another; love as brothers, *be* tenderhearted, *be* courteous;[a] [9]not returning evil for evil or reviling for reviling, but on the contrary blessing, knowing that you were called to this, that you may inherit a blessing. [10]For

> "He who would love life
> And see good days,
> Let him refrain his tongue from evil,
> And his lips from speaking deceit.
> [11]Let him turn away from evil and do good;
> Let him seek peace and pursue it.
> [12]For the eyes of the LORD are on the righteous,
> And His ears are open to their prayers;
> But the face of the LORD is against those who
> do evil."[a]

Suffering for Right and Wrong

[13]And who *is* he who will harm you if you become followers of what is good? [14]But even if you should suffer for righteousness' sake, *you are* blessed. *"And do not be afraid of their threats, nor be troubled."*[a] [15]But sanctify the Lord God[a] in your hearts, and always *be* ready to *give* a defense to everyone who asks you a reason for the hope that is in you, with meekness and fear; [16]having a

good conscience, that when they defame you as evildoers, those who revile your good conduct in Christ may be ashamed. [17]For *it is* better, if it is the will of God, to suffer for doing good than for doing evil.

Christ's Suffering and Ours

[18]For Christ also suffered once for sins, the just for the unjust, that He might bring us[a] to God, being put to death in the flesh but made alive by the Spirit, [19]by whom also He went and preached to the spirits in prison, [20]who formerly were disobedient, when once the Divine longsuffering waited[a] in the days of Noah, while *the* ark was being prepared, in which a few, that is, eight souls, were saved through water. [21]There is also an antitype which now saves us—baptism (not the removal of the filth of the flesh, but the answer of a good conscience toward God), through the resurrection of Jesus Christ, [22]who has gone into heaven and is at the right hand of God, angels and authorities and powers having been made subject to Him.

4 Therefore, since Christ suffered for us[a] in the flesh, arm yourselves also with the same mind, for he who has suffered in the flesh has ceased from sin, [2]that he no longer should live the rest of *his* time in the flesh for the lusts of men, but for the will of God. [3]For we *have spent* enough of our past lifetime[a] in doing the will of the Gentiles— when we walked in lewdness, lusts, drunkenness, revelries, drinking parties, and abominable idolatries. [4]In regard to these, they think it strange that you do not run with *them* in the same flood of dissipation, speaking evil of *you*. [5]They will give an account to Him who is ready to judge the living and the dead. [6]For this reason the gospel was preached also to those who are dead, that they might be judged according to men in the flesh, but live according to God in the spirit.

Serving for God's Glory

[7]But the end of all things is at hand; therefore be serious and watchful in your prayers. [8]And

---

3:8 [a]NU-Text reads *humble.*   **3:12** [a]Psalm 34:12–16   **3:14** [a]Isaiah 8:12   **3:15** [a]NU-Text reads *Christ as Lord.*   **3:18** [a]NU-Text and M-Text read *you.*   **3:20** [a]NU-Text and M-Text read *when the long-suffering of God waited patiently.*   **4:1** [a]NU-Text omits *for us.*   **4:3** [a]NU-Text reads *time.*

LEADERSHIP ISSUES

GC2: Giving First: Listening for Others' Needs

1 PETER 4:10B

Imagine our "need-meeting" God (Phil. 4:19) giving to each of His followers a many sided diamond called "grace" and each side represents a relational need He has met in our life. One side is called *acceptance,* one is *appreciation, attention, comfort* and *encouragement.* These are five of the relational needs God has met in your life, and He challenges you to share with others. It's important to become a person who "gives first" to others needs.

What constitutes a valid need? What is the difference between a genuine need and a personal "want"? A valid need is something that God has specifically met in our lives and then encourages us to give to others. The fact that God has met a particular need means that it must be all right to need it! For instance, Romans 15:7 says, *"Receive one another, just as Christ also received us."* The fact that Christ has accepted us (and instructs us to accept others) means it's all right to need acceptance. He comforts us (2 Cor. 1:3, 4) and encourages us to comfort others; that indicates comfort is a legitimate human need.

Even though it may seem that we "need" these things, they are actually "wants." People sometimes express needs through what they say. If we are familiar with these needs, we can "listen" for needs being expressed. Below are some phrases you might hear from others. Write down the relational need that possibly is being expressed.

Five possible needs are: acceptance, appreciation, attention, comfort and encouragement

"You're always so busy." _____

"Look what I did!" _____

"I just can't do this." _____

"I've had a really bad day." _____

"I wish my feet weren't so big." _____

Focus on "giving" to those around you, as Christ has given to you! (Matt. 9:17).

GC2

GREAT COMMANDMENT
COMMISSION

above all things have fervent love for one another, for *"love will cover a multitude of sins."*[a] [9]*Be* hospitable to one another without grumbling. [10]As each one has received a gift, minister it to one another, as good stewards of the manifold grace of God. [11]If anyone speaks, *let him speak* as the oracles of God. If anyone ministers, *let him do it* as with the ability which God supplies, that in all things God may be glorified through Jesus Christ, to whom belong the glory and the dominion forever and ever. Amen.

SUFFERING FOR GOD'S GLORY

[12]Beloved, do not think it strange concerning the fiery trial which is to try you, as though some strange thing happened to you; [13]but rejoice to the extent that you partake of Christ's sufferings, that when His glory is revealed, you may also be glad with exceeding joy. [14]If you are reproached for the name of Christ, blessed *are you,* for the Spirit of glory and of God rests upon you.[a] On their part He is blasphemed, but on your part He is glorified. [15]But let none of you suffer as a murderer, a thief, an evildoer, or as a busybody in other people's matters. [16]Yet if *anyone suffers* as a Christian, let him not be ashamed, but let him glorify God in this matter.[a]

[17]For the time *has come* for judgment to begin at the house of God; and if *it begins* with us first, what will *be* the end of those who do not obey the gospel of God? [18]Now

> *"If the righteous one is scarcely saved,*
> *Where will the ungodly and the sinner*
> *appear?"*[a]

[19]Therefore let those who suffer according to the will of God commit their souls *to Him* in doing good, as to a faithful Creator.

SHEPHERD THE FLOCK

5 The elders who are among you I exhort, I who am a fellow elder and a witness of the sufferings of Christ, and also a partaker of the glory that will be revealed: [2]Shepherd the flock of God which is among you, serving as overseers, not by compulsion but willingly,[a] not for dishonest gain but eagerly; [3]nor as being lords over those entrusted to you, but being examples to the flock; [4]and when the Chief Shepherd appears, you will receive the crown of glory that does not fade away.

4:8 [a]Proverbs 10:12   **4:14** [a]NU-Text omits the rest of this verse.   **4:16** [a]NU-Text reads *name.*   **4:18** [a]Proverbs 11:31   **5:2** [a]NU-Text adds *according to God.*

LEADERSHIP REALITIES

BATTLE FOR THE MIND   *1 Peter 5:8*

Peter is probably describing the lions used to kill Christians in Roman arenas under the reign of Nero. The fierce beasts put on a show for thousands of spectators who came to watch the roaring lions tear bodies from limb to limb in a disgusting and torturous event. This graphic but true reference gives us a clear mental picture of Satan's violent and insatiable thirst for prey.

"Be sober" literally means to have a sound and healthy mind, to guard with a wall. It is to "watch, and be mindful." In other words, *pay attention to what you allow into your mind!* "Be vigilant" refers to one who is morally alert. As John Wesley noted, "It is as if he [Peter] had said, Awake, and keep awake. Sleep no more."

Sleepwalking through life is the surest way to lose the battle. What Peter is saying to us is that making a one-time stand against alcohol, drugs, and immoral sexual behaviors is not enough. You have to stay on guard, awake, ready to do battle every day of the journey. There is no vaccination against substance abuse because the struggle is presented to you in a different way and by different people all through life.

LEADERSHIP ISSUES

Roaring Lion Versus Leader

1 PETER 5:8

As stated in the previous Leadership Realities, the apostle Peter warns that Satan attacks from all sides, threatening the body, soul, mind, and spirit. Peter may have thought of the lions used for sport under the reign of Nero. The fierce beasts put on a show for thousands of spectators who came to watch as the roaring lions tore Christians limb from limb in a disgusting and torturous event. This graphic reference paints a clear picture of Satan's violent and insatiable thirst for prey. He is our adversary—that is, one who contends with and opposes us—and he wars against young leaders in three main arenas:

Battle for the Mind: "Be sober" literally means to have a sound and healthy mind, to guard with a wall. It is to "watch, and be mindful." In other words, *pay attention to what you allow into your mind.* When a person uses alcohol and other drugs, he or she opens the gate to psychiatric problems such as depression, anxiety, oppositional defiant disorder, and antisocial personality disorder.

Battle for the Body: "Be vigilant" refers to one who is morally alert. Sleepwalking through life is the surest way to lose the battle. What Peter is saying to us is that making a one-time stand against alcohol, drugs, and immoral sexual behavior is not enough. You have to stay on guard, awake, ready to do battle every day of the journey.

Battle for the Family: Satan is out to destroy the family through any means possible. Alcohol and other drug use escalate conflict and lack of trust in the home. It can lead to the breakdown of parent-child, spouse to spouse, and sibling relationships.

Satan is your enemy, and he will slander and accuse you to cause conflict in your family in an effort to tear it apart. Don't help him by making casual decisions or breaking trust with your parents. If a young person runs ahead or falls behind the protection and care of the family, then that person becomes easy prey. God's plan is that the family nurtures, encourages, and cares for each other. When the family breaks down, so does God's protection for you. Satan knows this, and he delights in family conflicts.

Submit to God, Resist the Devil

[5]Likewise you younger people, submit yourselves to *your* elders. Yes, all of *you* be submissive to one another, and be clothed with humility, for

> *"God resists the proud,*
> *But gives grace to the humble."*[a]

[6]Therefore humble yourselves under the mighty hand of God, that He may exalt you in due time, [7]casting all your care upon Him, for He cares for you.

[8]Be sober, be vigilant; because[a] your adversary the devil walks about like a roaring lion, seeking whom he may devour. [9]Resist him, steadfast in the faith, knowing that the same sufferings are experienced by your brotherhood in the world. [10]But may[a] the God of all grace, who called us[b] to His eternal glory by Christ Jesus, after you have suffered a while, perfect, establish, strengthen, and settle *you*. [11]To Him *be* the glory and the dominion forever and ever. Amen.

Farewell and Peace

[12]By Silvanus, our faithful brother as I consider him, I have written to you briefly, exhorting and testifying that this is the true grace of God in which you stand.

[13]She who is in Babylon, elect together with *you*, greets you; and *so does* Mark my son. [14]Greet one another with a kiss of love.

Peace to you all who are in Christ Jesus. Amen.

5:5 [a]Proverbs 3:34   **5:8** [a]NU-Text and M-Text omit *because*.
5:10 [a]NU-Text reads *But the God of all grace . . . will perfect, establish, strengthen, and settle you.* [b]NU-Text and M-Text read *you.*

IMPACT OF THE BOOK

I | **IDEA**
God's truths are timeless. Since God will make all things new, we are urged to live godly lives, giving heed to all the truths in the Scriptures.

M | **MESSAGE**
Believers, living in a time when the fundamentals of the Christian faith are questioned, ridiculed, and dismissed, must continue to engage in a spiritual battle waged against the truth of God's Word. Recognizing and making preparations for these attacks—by living in a worthy manner and continuing to grow in the knowledge of Jesus Christ—is the leadership principle.

P | **PEOPLE**
False Teachers, Peter

A | **AUTHOR**
Peter was probably addressing the churches in Asia Minor identified in his first letter: Galatia, Cappadocia, Asia, and Bithynia. The author claims to have written the same group of churches before (2 Pet. 3:1), which confirms he is Peter.

C | **CULTURE**
Second Peter is both an exhortation and a farewell speech. The fervency and urgency of Peter's words suggest the probability of his impending death. Peter seized the opportunity to encourage fellow believers and to warn them of serious attacks that would be made against their faith from the false teachers. He exhorted his readers not to neglect growing in their faith and remain alert to erroneous teaching. The knowledge that believers are to attain is based solely on the word of God (1:19). Such knowledge originates with God and not with human beings.

T | **TIMELINE**
c. AD 67

KEY SCRIPTURE
MEMORY VERSES
1:16, 20, 21; 3:8–11

GREETING THE FAITHFUL

1 Simon Peter, a bondservant and apostle of Jesus Christ,

To those who have obtained like precious faith with us by the righteousness of our God and Savior Jesus Christ:

[2]Grace and peace be multiplied to you in the knowledge of God and of Jesus our Lord, [3]as His divine power has given to us all things that *pertain* to life and godliness, through the knowledge of Him who called us by glory and virtue, [4]by which have been given to us exceedingly great and precious promises, that through these you may be partakers of the divine nature, having escaped the corruption *that is* in the world through lust.

FRUITFUL GROWTH IN THE FAITH

[5]But also for this very reason, giving all diligence, add to your faith virtue, to virtue knowl-

edge, [6]to knowledge self-control, to self-control perseverance, to perseverance godliness, [7]to godliness brotherly kindness, and to brotherly kindness love. [8]For if these things are yours and abound, you will be neither barren nor unfruitful in the knowledge of our Lord Jesus Christ. [9]For he who lacks these things is shortsighted, even to blindness, and has forgotten that he was cleansed from his old sins.

[10]Therefore, brethren, be even more diligent to make your call and election sure, for if you do these things you will never stumble; [11]for so an entrance will be supplied to you abundantly into the everlasting kingdom of our Lord and Savior Jesus Christ.

PETER'S APPROACHING DEATH

[12]For this reason I will not be negligent to remind you always of these things, though you know and are established in the present truth. [13]Yes, I think it is right, as long as I am in this tent, to stir you up by reminding *you,* [14]knowing

---

THROUGH THE GRID

Where Have All the Dreamers Gone?
Observations from a Biblical
Worldview: Christianity and Morality
(2 Pet. 1:5–8)

The real issues surrounding morality today are in actuality probing the question of God's existence and God's authority in the world today. Many have attempted to separate God from morality, arguing that moral behavior is possible without having to acknowledge God and the biblical worldview. In response, Christians must turn the focus back to the issue of God's existence. If there is no God, then there is no system of morality and accountability. However, if the God of Christianity exists, then humanity is held to the moral expectations presented in Scripture. A biblical worldview indeed affirms that morality does not come from us but from God; therefore, we must acknowledge the existence of God as the very basis for morality and living morally in the world. Christians must be raised and trained in the biblical worldview that acknowledges morality and seeks to develop the biblical sense of morality within each believer.

Ultimately, character does matter, even more than the occupations we hold. Developing character and integrity is at the heart of the biblical worldview; and those who are developing a Christian mindset must also focus on these aspects of personal development, with the ultimate goal of becoming like Christ in the process of true Christian discipleship. What we do is an extension of who we are because our actions reflect our true nature and character. As we develop, we must keep in mind that God is sovereign and that God's grace is sufficient for us.

that shortly I *must* put off my tent, just as our Lord Jesus Christ showed me. [15]Moreover I will be careful to ensure that you always have a reminder of these things after my decease.

The Trustworthy Prophetic Word

[16]For we did not follow cunningly devised fables when we made known to you the power and coming of our Lord Jesus Christ, but were eyewitnesses of His majesty. [17]For He received from God the Father honor and glory when such a voice came to Him from the Excellent Glory: "This is My beloved Son, in whom I am well pleased." [18]And we heard this voice which came from heaven when we were with Him on the holy mountain.

[19]And so we have the prophetic word confirmed,[a] which you do well to heed as a light that shines in a dark place, until the day dawns and the morning star rises in your hearts; [20]knowing this first, that no prophecy of Scripture is of any private interpretation,[a] [21]for prophecy never came by the will of man, but holy men of God[a] spoke *as they were* moved by the Holy Spirit.

Destructive Doctrines

2 But there were also false prophets among the people, even as there will be false teachers among you, who will secretly bring in destructive heresies, even denying the Lord who bought them, *and* bring on themselves swift destruction. [2]And many will follow their destructive ways, because of whom the way of truth will be blasphemed. [3]By covetousness they will exploit you with deceptive words; for a long time their judgment has not been idle, and their destruction does[a] not slumber.

Doom of False Teachers

[4]For if God did not spare the angels who sinned, but cast *them* down to hell and delivered *them* into chains of darkness, to be reserved for judgment; [5]and did not spare the ancient world, but saved Noah, *one of* eight *people,* a preacher of righteousness, bringing in the flood on the world of the ungodly; [6]and turning the cities of Sodom and Gomorrah into ashes, condemned *them* to destruction, making *them* an example to those who afterward would live ungodly; [7]and delivered righteous Lot, *who was* oppressed by the filthy conduct of the wicked [8](for that righteous man, dwelling among them, tormented *his* righteous soul from day to day by seeing and hearing *their* lawless deeds)— [9]*then* the Lord knows how to deliver the godly out of temptations and to reserve the unjust under punishment for the day of judgment, [10]and especially those who walk according to the flesh in the lust of uncleanness and despise authority. *They are* presumptuous, self-willed. They are not afraid to speak evil of dignitaries, [11]whereas angels, who are greater in power and might, do not bring a reviling accusation against them before the Lord.

Depravity of False Teachers

[12]But these, like natural brute beasts made to be caught and destroyed, speak evil of the things they do not understand, and will utterly perish in their own corruption, [13]*and* will receive the wages of unrighteousness, *as* those who count it pleasure to carouse in the daytime. *They are* spots and blemishes, carousing in their own deceptions while they feast with you, [14]having eyes full of adultery and

1:19 [a]Or *We also have the more sure prophetic word.* **1:20** [a]Or *origin* **1:21** [a]NU-Text reads *but men spoke from God.* **2:3** [a]M-Text reads *will not.*

THROUGH THE GRID

Making Sense of Your World: A Biblical Worldview (2 Pet. 1:21)

A biblical worldview follows the conservative, evangelical understanding of the Bible, and it views the books of the Bible as divinely inspired writings that make up our Old and New Testaments. The basic assumption of a biblical worldview is that God is a living and personal God who reveals Himself through revelation, scripture, and Christ.

that cannot cease from sin, enticing unstable souls. They have a heart trained in covetous practices, *and are* accursed children. [15]They have forsaken the right way and gone astray, following the way of Balaam the *son* of Beor, who loved the wages of unrighteousness; [16]but he was rebuked for his iniquity: a dumb donkey speaking with a man's voice restrained the madness of the prophet.

[17]These are wells without water, clouds[a] carried by a tempest, for whom is reserved the blackness of darkness forever.[b]

DECEPTIONS OF FALSE TEACHERS

[18]For when they speak great swelling *words* of emptiness, they allure through the lusts of the flesh, through lewdness, the ones who have actually escaped[a] from those who live in error. [19]While they promise them liberty, they themselves are slaves of corruption; for by whom a person is overcome, by him also he is brought into bondage. [20]For if, after they have escaped the pollutions of the world through the knowledge of the Lord and Savior Jesus Christ, they are again entangled in them and overcome, the latter end is worse for them than the beginning. [21]For it would have been better for them not to have known the way of righteousness, than having known *it*, to turn from the holy commandment delivered to them. [22]But it has happened to them according to the true proverb: *"A dog returns to his own vomit,"*[a] and, "a sow, having washed, to her wallowing in the mire."

GOD'S PROMISE IS NOT SLACK

3 Beloved, I now write to you this second epistle (in *both of* which I stir up your pure minds by way of reminder), [2]that you may be mindful of the words which were spoken before by the holy prophets, and of the commandment of us,[a] the apostles of the Lord and Savior, [3]knowing this first: that scoffers will come in the last days, walking according to their own lusts, [4]and saying, "Where is the promise of His coming? For since the fathers fell asleep, all things continue as *they were* from the beginning of creation." [5]For this they willfully forget: that by the word of God the heavens were of old, and the earth standing out of water and in the water, [6]by which the world *that* then existed perished, being flooded with water. [7]But the heavens and the earth *which* are now preserved by the same word, are reserved for fire until the day of judgment and perdition of ungodly men.

[8]But, beloved, do not forget this one thing, that with the Lord one day *is* as a thousand years, and a thousand years as one day. [9]The Lord is not slack concerning *His* promise, as some count slackness, but is longsuffering toward us,[a] not willing that any should perish but that all should come to repentance.

2:17 [a]NU-Text reads *and mists.* [b]NU-Text omits *forever.* **2:18** [a]NU-Text reads *are barely escaping.* **2:22** [a]Proverbs 26:11 **3:2** [a]NU-Text and M-Text read *commandment of the apostles of your Lord and Savior* or *commandment of your apostles of the Lord and Savior.* **3:9** [a]NU-Text reads *you.*

THROUGH THE GRID
Discover God:
God's Justice Works for Our Good

2 PETER 3:9 *The Lord is not slack concerning His promise, as some count slackness, but is longsuffering toward us, not willing that any should perish but that all should come to repentance.*

Although God is just, God delays bringing justice about in order to extend His mercy to as many people as possible. God knows when injustice happens; and though things may not be fixed instantly, God is working slowly and patiently to bring about justice. In the end, Christ will judge the words we have spoken, the deeds we have done, our motives, and our faithfulness. In the meantime, we must trust God's perfect justice, because God is the perfect judge who administers justice through perfect holiness, truth, and righteousness.

THE DAY OF THE LORD

[10]But the day of the Lord will come as a thief in the night, in which the heavens will pass away with a great noise, and the elements will melt with fervent heat; both the earth and the works that are in it will be burned up.[a] [11]Therefore, since all these things will be dissolved, what manner *of persons* ought you to be in holy conduct and godliness, [12]looking for and hastening the coming of the day of God, because of which the heavens will be dissolved, being on fire, and the elements will melt with fervent heat? [13]Nevertheless we, according to His promise, look for new heavens and a new earth in which righteousness dwells.

BE STEADFAST

[14]Therefore, beloved, looking forward to these things, be diligent to be found by Him in peace, without spot and blameless; [15]and consider *that* the longsuffering of our Lord *is* salvation—as also our beloved brother Paul, according to the wisdom given to him, has written to you, [16]as also in all his epistles, speaking in them of these things, in which are some things hard to understand, which untaught and unstable *people* twist to their own destruction, as *they do* also the rest of the Scriptures.

[17]You therefore, beloved, since you know *this* beforehand, beware lest you also fall from your own steadfastness, being led away with the error of the wicked; [18]but grow in the grace and knowledge of our Lord and Savior Jesus Christ.

To Him *be* the glory both now and forever. Amen.

3:10 [a]NU-Text reads *laid bare* (literally *found*).

IMPACT OF THE BOOK

I IDEA

You cannot separate right belief in your heart from righteous conduct in your lifestyle. We must love and accept one another as a sign of God's ownership and of our salvation (1 John 3:18, 19).

M MESSAGE

Any doctrine that takes away from, or adds to, who Christ is or what He did, must be rejected as false. God's full revelation concerning Christ is proclaimed in the Scriptures, and any departure from this is false. A true leader must be very confident. John was confident; he was an eyewitness to the life, death, and resurrection of Jesus (1 John 1:1–4).

P PEOPLE

John (the Beloved)

A AUTHOR

The name of the author is not mentioned, however, there is external and internal evidence to support John—the son of Zebedee, brother of James, and the beloved disciple—as the author.

C CULTURE

First John was written to protect the fellowship of believers from the heretical doctrines of false teachers, who claimed that the historical Jesus was not the Christ. This form of heresy likely became known as Gnosticism, a set of beliefs that began prior to the expansion of Christianity. Gnostics believed they had superior knowledge. John addresses it when he uses "to know" or "assurance" thirty-eight times. Cerinthus, a false teacher from Ephesus, taught that Jesus was a mere man upon whom God's Spirit came at His baptism. Some people left the church and then returned to disrupt its fellowship (2:19). They refused to recognize Jesus Christ as the God-Man He claimed to be.

T TIMELINE

c. AD 80–90

KEY SCRIPTURE MEMORY VERSES

1:9; 2:15–17; 3:1–3, 16; 4:7, 8, 10, 11, 19; 5:11–13

What Was Heard, Seen, and Touched

1 That which was from the beginning, which we have heard, which we have seen with our eyes, which we have looked upon, and our hands have handled, concerning the Word of life— ²the life was manifested, and we have seen, and bear witness, and declare to you that eternal life which was with the Father and was manifested to us— ³that which we have seen and heard we declare to you, that you also may have fellowship with us; and truly our fellowship *is* with the Father and with His Son Jesus Christ. ⁴And these things we write to you that your[a] joy may be full.

Fellowship with Him and One Another

⁵This is the message which we have heard from Him and declare to you, that God is light and in Him is no darkness at all. ⁶If we say that we have fellowship with Him, and walk in darkness, we lie and do not practice the truth. ⁷But if we walk in the light as He is in the light, we have fellowship with one another, and the blood of Jesus Christ His Son cleanses us from all sin.

⁸If we say that we have no sin, we deceive ourselves, and the truth is not in us. ⁹If we confess our sins, He is faithful and just to forgive us *our* sins and to cleanse us from all unrighteousness. ¹⁰If we say that we have not sinned, we make Him a liar, and His word is not in us.

2 My little children, these things I write to you, so that you may not sin. And if anyone sins, we have an Advocate with the Father, Jesus Christ the righteous. ²And He Himself is the propitiation for our sins, and not for ours only but also for the whole world.

The Test of Knowing Him

³Now by this we know that we know Him, if we keep His commandments. ⁴He who says, "I know Him," and does not keep His commandments, is a liar, and the truth is not in him. ⁵But whoever keeps His word, truly the love of God is perfected in him. By this we know that we are in Him. ⁶He who says he abides in Him ought himself also to walk just as He walked.

⁷Brethren,[a] I write no new commandment to you, but an old commandment which you have had from the beginning. The old commandment is the word which you heard from the beginning.[b] ⁸Again, a new commandment I write to you, which thing is true in Him and in you, because the darkness is passing away, and the true light is already shining.

⁹He who says he is in the light, and hates his brother, is in darkness until now. ¹⁰He who loves his brother abides in the light, and there is no cause for stumbling in him. ¹¹But he who hates his brother is in darkness and walks in darkness, and does not know where he is going, because the darkness has blinded his eyes.

Their Spiritual State

¹²I write to you, little children,
Because your sins are forgiven you for His name's sake.
¹³I write to you, fathers,
Because you have known Him *who is* from the beginning.
I write to you, young men,
Because you have overcome the wicked one.
I write to you, little children,
Because you have known the Father.
¹⁴I have written to you, fathers,
Because you have known Him *who is* from the beginning.
I have written to you, young men,
Because you are strong, and the word of God abides in you,
And you have overcome the wicked one.

Do Not Love the World

¹⁵Do not love the world or the things in the world. If anyone loves the world, the love of the Father is not in him. ¹⁶For all that *is* in the world—the lust of the flesh, the lust of the eyes, and the pride of life—is not of the Father but is of the world. ¹⁷And the world is passing away, and the lust of it; but he who does the will of God abides forever.

Deceptions of the Last Hour

¹⁸Little children, it is the last hour; and as you have heard that the[a] Antichrist is coming, even now many antichrists have come, by which we

1:4 [a]NU-Text and M-Text read *our*.   2:7 [a]NU-Text reads *Beloved*. [b]NU-Text omits *from the beginning*.   2:18 [a]NU-Text omits *the*.

know that it is the last hour. ¹⁹They went out from us, but they were not of us; for if they had been of us, they would have continued with us; but *they went out* that they might be made manifest, that none of them were of us.

²⁰But you have an anointing from the Holy One, and you know all things.ᵃ ²¹I have not written to you because you do not know the truth, but because you know it, and that no lie is of the truth.

²²Who is a liar but he who denies that Jesus is the Christ? He is antichrist who denies the Father and the Son. ²³Whoever denies the Son does not have the Father either; he who acknowledges the Son has the Father also.

LET TRUTH ABIDE IN YOU

²⁴Therefore let that abide in you which you heard from the beginning. If what you heard from the beginning abides in you, you also will abide in the Son and in the Father. ²⁵And this is the promise that He has promised us—eternal life.

²⁶These things I have written to you concerning those who *try to* deceive you. ²⁷But the anointing which you have received from Him abides in you, and you do not need that anyone teach you; but as the same anointing teaches you concerning all things, and is true, and is not a lie, and just as it has taught you, you willᵃ abide in Him.

THE CHILDREN OF GOD

²⁸And now, little children, abide in Him, that whenᵃ He appears, we may have confidence and not be ashamed before Him at His coming. ²⁹If you know that He is righteous, you know that everyone who practices righteousness is born of Him.

2:20 ᵃNU-Text reads *you all know.*   **2:27** ᵃNU-Text reads *you abide.*
2:28 ᵃNU-Text reads *if.*

THROUGH THE GRID

Discover God:
God Knows Everything

1 JOHN 3:20   *God is greater than our heart, and knows all things.*

It is said that "the more you know, the more you know that you can't know everything." Cultural experts estimate that the amount of knowledge in the world is doubling at an incredible rate—almost every seven months! With all that knowledge, it is impossible for us as finite human beings to come close to knowing more than mere fractions of all the available knowledge. But the One who does know all is Creator God, who not only knows everything but is also the source of all knowledge—and the reason we can have knowledge as human beings. This characteristic of God is called *God's omniscience*—the ability of God to know all because God is the source of all knowledge. God knows absolutely everything that can be known. We as finite human beings can never know in this existence all there is to know about God, because God is infinite. However, God knows all there is to know about God, and only God knows everything there is to know about creation—namely, because God created it. But God is also concerned with the details of our lives. God knows everything that has happened in the past, everything that is happening now, and everything that ever will happen in the future. We can rest assured that God is the One who holds the future, even in the midst of the world's biggest and worst problems. We can worship God as a response by acknowledging His omniscience and allowing His all-knowing Spirit to speak to us and guide us in our actions.

LEADERSHIP ISSUES

GC2: Created Needy—But Why?

1 JOHN 3:17, 18

It's obvious that we have needs, but why? Why did God create us with a need for sleep? Why do we need air? And why do we all need comfort, attention, and security? He is sovereign; He could have created us not needing anything! Do these needs represent flaws in God's design? Did He create imperfect creatures? God's Word gives us several reasons why He created us with needs.

- Our needs encourage us to depend ultimately upon God, looking beyond ourselves to Him for our needs to be met (Phil. 4:19).

- Our needs encourage us to be interdependent with each other (1 Cor. 12:21, 27). Because we all have needs, we need each other! If we didn't have needs, we'd be like computerized robots on an assembly line—doing our own thing with no regard for others. Jesus often expressed His needs to His disciples, most dramatically at the time of His greatest trial: "My soul is exceedingly sorrowful, even to death. Stay here and watch with Me," (Matt. 26:38).

- Acknowledging our needs challenges us to both receive and give. It's difficult to give others what we have not received. When we acknowledge our needs and receive from others, we are then free to experience the joy of giving (Matt. 10:8).

Needs are an essential aspect of healthy, close relationships! Tragically, it's possible to "hydroplane" through life and never share the joys of intimacy with another human being. Unfortunately, that's exactly where many people live—in a world of superficial, unfulfilling relationships—but God's plan is that we become deeply connected to one another. Instead of our relationships being distant, formal, removed, and superficial, they can be personal, deep, affectionate, and warm. They can be intimate!—but how? When people lovingly draw upon God's unlimited resources to meet one another's needs, the result is intimacy.

GC2
GREAT COMMANDMENT
COMMISSION

3 Behold what manner of love the Father has bestowed on us, that we should be called children of God![a] Therefore the world does not know us,[b] because it did not know Him. [2]Beloved, now we are children of God; and it has not yet been revealed what we shall be, but we know that when He is revealed, we shall be like Him, for we shall see Him as He is. [3]And everyone who has this hope in Him purifies himself, just as He is pure.

Sin and the Child of God

[4]Whoever commits sin also commits lawlessness, and sin is lawlessness. [5]And you know that He was manifested to take away our sins, and in Him there is no sin. [6]Whoever abides in Him does not sin. Whoever sins has neither seen Him nor known Him.

[7]Little children, let no one deceive you. He who practices righteousness is righteous, just as He is righteous. [8]He who sins is of the devil, for the devil has sinned from the beginning. For this purpose the Son of God was manifested, that He might destroy the works of the devil. [9]Whoever has been born of God does not sin, for His seed remains in him; and he cannot sin, because he has been born of God.

The Imperative of Love

[10]In this the children of God and the children of the devil are manifest: Whoever does not practice righteousness is not of God, nor *is* he who does not love his brother. [11]For this is the message that you heard from the beginning, that we should love one another, [12]not as Cain *who* was of the wicked one and murdered his brother. And why did he murder him? Because his works were evil and his brother's righteous.

[13]Do not marvel, my brethren, if the world hates you. [14]We know that we have passed from death to life, because we love the brethren. He who does not love *his* brother[a] abides in death. [15]Whoever hates his brother is a murderer, and you know that no murderer has eternal life abiding in him.

The Outworking of Love

[16]By this we know love, because He laid down His life for us. And we also ought to lay down *our* lives for the brethren. [17]But whoever has this world's goods, and sees his brother in need, and shuts up his heart from him, how does the love of God abide in him?

[18]My little children, let us not love in word or in tongue, but in deed and in truth. [19]And by this we know[a] that we are of the truth, and shall assure our hearts before Him. [20]For if our heart condemns us, God is greater than our heart, and knows all things. [21]Beloved, if our heart does not condemn us, we have confidence toward God. [22]And whatever we ask we receive from Him, because we keep His commandments and do those things that are pleasing in His sight. [23]And this is

3:1 [a]NU-Text adds *And we are.* [b]M-Text reads *you.* **3:14** [a]NU-Text omits *his brother.* **3:19** [a]NU-Text reads *we shall know.*

THROUGH THE GRID   *God Is Love*

1 JOHN 4:8 *God is love.*

We have seen the extent of God's abilities through creation, and we have seen how God's righteousness, holiness, and justice establish the basis for humanity and humanity's response toward God. But the central characteristic describing God as a being who relates to others is God's love for humanity. God's love is the reason for His creation, and it affects all of God's other attributes. God's love extends to all humanity, and it never changes or expires. In fact, God loved us to such a great extent that He met our deepest need through the atoning sacrifice and faithfulness of Jesus Christ—a matter of eternal significance.

LEADERSHIP ISSUES

GC2: Good News: Declaring Your Worth

1 JOHN 4:10 *In this is love, not that we loved God, but that He loved us and sent His Son to be the propitiation for our sins.*

If you were to wear a price tag indicating your worth to God, it would read: "Jesus!" The truth of the Incarnation—Jesus becoming the God-Man—reveals that God so desires a relationship with you that He made the ultimate sacrifice . . . for you. God loves you and longs to relate to you. He proved it by becoming human Himself and laying down His life for you.

An interesting story from the Gospels recalls the disciples being challenged over paying taxes. Referring to a Roman coin, Christ asked the disciples, "Whose image and inscription is this?"

"Caesar's," they responded.

"Render therefore to Caesar the things that are Caesar's, and to God the things that are God's" (Matt. 22:15–22).

Critical to the story is this principle: the one whose image the coin bears has a right to declare its worth and to collect taxes! The same is true today: governments that print money declare what the money is worth in terms of one-dollar bills, five-dollar bills, etc. But on a personal note the question is this: "Whose image do *you* bear?" (Gen. 1:26). It's God's image, even though it's marred by sin; and since you bear His image, He has the right to declare your worth, and He did so at Calvary. You're worth the gift of Jesus! Now "render" or yield yourself to Him!

Pause to celebrate the gift of Jesus, just for you. Prayerfully declare your submission to Him.

GC2
GREAT COMMANDMENT
COMMISSION

His commandment: that we should believe on the name of His Son Jesus Christ and love one another, as He gave us[a] commandment.

THE SPIRIT OF TRUTH AND THE SPIRIT OF ERROR

24Now he who keeps His commandments abides in Him, and He in him. And by this we know that He abides in us, by the Spirit whom He has given us.

4 Beloved, do not believe every spirit, but test the spirits, whether they are of God; because many false prophets have gone out into the world. 2By this you know the Spirit of God: Every spirit that confesses that Jesus Christ has come in the flesh is of God, 3and every spirit that does not confess that[a] Jesus Christ has come in the flesh is not of God. And this is the *spirit* of the Antichrist, which you have heard was coming, and is now already in the world.

4You are of God, little children, and have overcome them, because He who is in you is greater than he who is in the world. 5They are of the world. Therefore they speak *as* of the world, and the world hears them. 6We are of God. He who knows God hears us; he who is not of God does not hear us. By this we know the spirit of truth and the spirit of error.

KNOWING GOD THROUGH LOVE

7Beloved, let us love one another, for love is of God; and everyone who loves is born of God and knows God. 8He who does not love does not know God, for God is love. 9In this the love of God was manifested toward us, that God has sent His only begotten Son into the world, that we might live through Him. 10In this is love, not that we loved God, but that He loved us and sent His Son *to be* the propitiation for our sins. 11Beloved, if God so loved us, we also ought to love one another.

SEEING GOD THROUGH LOVE

12No one has seen God at any time. If we love one another, God abides in us, and His love has been perfected in us. 13By this we know that we abide in Him, and He in us, because He has given us of His Spirit. 14And we have seen and testify that the Father has sent the Son *as* Savior of the world. 15Whoever confesses that Jesus is the Son of God, God abides in him, and he in God. 16And we have known and believed the love that God has for us. God is love, and he who abides in love abides in God, and God in him.

THE CONSUMMATION OF LOVE

17Love has been perfected among us in this: that we may have boldness in the day of judgment; because as He is, so are we in this world. 18There is no fear in love; but perfect love casts out fear, because fear involves torment. But he

3:23 aM-Text omits *us.* **4:3** aNU-Text omits *that* and *Christ has come in the flesh.*

THROUGH THE GRID

Discover God:
God Helps Us Spread His Love

1 JOHN 4:16 *And we have known and believed the love that God has for us. God is love, and he who abides in love abides in God, and God in him.*

Because God first loved us, we are also to extend that love back to God and then to our neighbors, ourselves, and our enemies as well. Christian charity and love are key characteristics for those who are disciples of Christ; and using God's undeserved and unearned love as an example, we are to model and enact that love to all those around us, no matter the circumstances. Part of loving God involves telling others about God and the newness of life in which we live. The Good News we have received is meant to be shared widely with all of humanity. The love by which we live can usher in forgiveness and reconciliation.

LEADERSHIP ISSUES

GC2: Who Am I? Discovering Your Uniqueness

1 JOHN 4:12 *No one has seen God at any time. If we love one another, God abides in us, and His love has been perfected in us.*

God has placed deep within you a natural bent; they are your talents, gifts, and unique interests. He wants you to use them within His and your family as only you can. Do you know what your bent is? (Prov. 22:6).

God has given you built-in preferences: things like how you are energized, how you process information, how you make decisions. These things make up your distinct personality. Do you know your personality traits? God's love is to be distinctly expressed through this distinct personality, as only you can express it. As you uniquely express His life and love, others around you experience Him; they see Him in you!

God has instilled within you certain passions: things you feel strongly about, things you're fervently interested in, things that give you a special sense of joy when you talk about them or pursue them. Can you specifically identify your God-given passions in life? Those passions direct you to whom, where, and what God wants you to love in life . . . as only you can.

Understanding that we are God's children who have a special place in His body doesn't mean that unbelievers don't have talents or natural gifts. It also doesn't mean that they can't come to understand themselves and their uniqueness to varying degrees. What it does mean, however, is that unless and until people come to know God as their Father through Christ, they will never understand their ultimate fulfillment and true place in this world as God designed. The true thrill of forming a relationship with God through Christ is that you discover you really are God's child, chosen to love Him and others as only you can.

Pause to consider: Who are the people around me that I'm uniquely called to love? How has God uniquely prepared me to express His love to them?

GC2

GREAT COMMANDMENT
COMMISSION

LEADERSHIP ISSUES

Deadly Distractions

1 JOHN 5:4

John summarizes the issue of victorious leadership perfectly: "For whatever is born of God overcomes the world. And this is the victory that has overcome the world—our faith" (1 John 5:4). Scripture challenges and encourages Christ-followers not to be defeated by the "world." This challenge is even more prevalent when you accept the responsibilities of leadership.

Every leader described in Scripture wrestles with distractions and varying degrees of defeat. John categorizes Deadly Distractions as "all that is in the world—the lust of the flesh, the lust of the eyes, and the pride of life" (1 John 2:16). The first two focus on an unhealthy desire for appeasing the body (sex, food, drugs, etc.) or possessions (cars, clothes, cash, etc.). The latter represents boastful pride, which is simply an overconfident or arrogant attitude.

It is essential to understand that the more responsibility a leader accepts, the greater the intensity of these distractions. In order to develop as an authentic Christian leader, you must learn to recognize which of the three Deadly Distractions personally entices you. As you move into organizational leadership, you will often hear statements like "we're only as strong as our weakest link," suggesting that either a person or process needs to be strengthened. This principle applies tenfold in your personal development. Do not be deceived; every leader *will* face *all that is in the world* in various forms, on a daily basis.

Preparation involves the practice of meditation, which has unfortunately been discarded by most as "eastern mysticism." The word "meditation" occurs eighteen times in the NKJV, the last being just after Paul says, "Let no one despise your youth, but be an example to the believers in word, in conduct, in love, in spirit, in faith, in purity"(1 Tim. 4:12). Verse 15 commands us to "meditate on these things." This exercise requires that a person seek the heart of God and allow it to become one's own heart. Meditation allows us to recognize the Deadly Distraction we face as the weakest link, to be honest about it, and to adopt a more focused approach to keeping His commandments. Through this, we find victory over sin and peace in Christ.

who fears has not been made perfect in love. [19]We love Him[a] because He first loved us.

Obedience by Faith

[20]If someone says, "I love God," and hates his brother, he is a liar; for he who does not love his brother whom he has seen, how can[a] he love God whom he has not seen? [21]And this commandment we have from Him: that he who loves God *must* love his brother also.

5 Whoever believes that Jesus is the Christ is born of God, and everyone who loves Him who begot also loves him who is begotten of Him. [2]By this we know that we love the children of God, when we love God and keep His commandments. [3]For this is the love of God, that we keep His commandments. And His commandments are not burdensome. [4]For whatever is born of God overcomes the world. And this is the victory that has overcome the world—our[a] faith. [5]Who is he who overcomes the world, but he who believes that Jesus is the Son of God?

The Certainty of God's Witness

[6]This is He who came by water and blood— Jesus Christ; not only by water, but by water and blood. And it is the Spirit who bears witness, because the Spirit is truth. [7]For there are three that bear witness in heaven: the Father, the Word, and the Holy Spirit; and these three are one. [8]And there are three that bear witness on earth:[a] the Spirit, the water, and the blood; and these three agree as one.

[9]If we receive the witness of men, the witness of God is greater; for this is the witness of God which[a] He has testified of His Son. [10]He who believes in the Son of God has the witness in himself; he who does not believe God has made Him a liar, because he has not believed the testimony that God has given of His Son. [11]And this is the testimony: that God has given us eternal life, and this life is in His Son. [12]He who has the Son has life; he who does not have the Son of God does not have life. [13]These things I have written to you who believe in the name of the Son of God, that you may know that you have eternal life,[a] and that you may *continue to* believe in the name of the Son of God.

Confidence and Compassion in Prayer

[14]Now this is the confidence that we have in Him, that if we ask anything according to His will, He hears us. [15]And if we know that He hears us, whatever we ask, we know that we have the petitions that we have asked of Him.

[16]If anyone sees his brother sinning a sin *which does* not *lead* to death, he will ask, and He will give him life for those who commit sin not *leading* to death. There is sin *leading* to death. I do not say that he should pray about that. [17]All unrighteousness is sin, and there is sin not *leading* to death.

Knowing the True—Rejecting the False

[18]We know that whoever is born of God does not sin; but he who has been born of God keeps himself,[a] and the wicked one does not touch him.

[19]We know that we are of God, and the whole world lies *under the sway of* the wicked one.

[20]And we know that the Son of God has come and has given us an understanding, that we may know Him who is true; and we are in Him who is true, in His Son Jesus Christ. This is the true God and eternal life.

[21]Little children, keep yourselves from idols. Amen.

4:19 [a]NU-Text omits *Him*.   **4:20** [a]NU-Text reads *he cannot*.   **5:4** [a]M-Text reads *your*.   **5:8** [a]NU-Text and M-Text omit the words from *in heaven* (verse 7) through *on earth* (verse 8). Only four or five very late manuscripts contain these words in Greek.   **5:9** [a]NU-Text reads *God, that*.   **5:13** [a]NU-Text omits the rest of this verse.   **5:18** [a]NU-Text reads *him*.

IMPACT OF THE BOOK

IDEA

God calls His followers to remain faithful to the true gospel.

MESSAGE

What a person values reveals a lot about his character. Godly leaders treasure truth more than anything else. Truth sets people free; error brings them into bondage.

PEOPLE

Elect lady, John

AUTHOR

Unlike 1 John, 2 John's author does identify himself, referring to himself as "The Elder," suggesting one in a position of authority and influence. The fact that John would have written these letters in his senior years, from a position of influence in the church, supports this.

CULTURE

John, ministering to churches throughout Asia Minor, probably wrote from Ephesus to encourage the believers to continue to grow in their love for one another, to remain in the truth, and to avoid welcoming the heretics into their homes. The letter was written "to the elect lady and her children" (v. 1). The church was typically personified in a feminine manner in the New Testament, yet some believe the recipients included an actual woman in history. The content, however, seems more directed to a group of people—such as a church—possibly the same church to whom the first letter was written.

TIMELINE

c. AD 80—90

KEY SCRIPTURE MEMORY VERSES

6

GREETING THE ELECT LADY

The Elder,

To the elect lady and her children, whom I love in truth, and not only I, but also all those who have known the truth, [2]because of the truth which abides in us and will be with us forever:

[3]Grace, mercy, *and* peace will be with you[a] from God the Father and from the Lord Jesus Christ, the Son of the Father, in truth and love.

WALK IN CHRIST'S COMMANDMENTS

[4]I rejoiced greatly that I have found *some* of your children walking in truth, as we received commandment from the Father. [5]And now I plead with you, lady, not as though I wrote a new commandment to you, but that which we have had from the beginning: that we love one another. [6]This is love, that we walk according to His commandments. This is the commandment, that as you have heard from the beginning, you should walk in it.

BEWARE OF ANTICHRIST DECEIVERS

[7]For many deceivers have gone out into the world who do not confess Jesus Christ *as* coming in the flesh. This is a deceiver and an antichrist. [8]Look to yourselves, that we[a] do not lose those things we worked for, but *that* we[b] may receive a full reward.

[9]Whoever transgresses[a] and does not abide in the doctrine of Christ does not have God. He who abides in the doctrine of Christ has both the Father and the Son. [10]If anyone comes to you and does not bring this doctrine, do not receive him into your house nor greet him; [11]for he who greets him shares in his evil deeds.

JOHN'S FAREWELL GREETING

[12]Having many things to write to you, I did not wish *to do so* with paper and ink; but I hope to come to you and speak face to face, that our joy may be full.

[13]The children of your elect sister greet you. Amen.

3 [a]NU-Text and M-Text read *us*.   **8** [a]NU-Text reads *you*.   [b]NU-Text reads *you*.   **9** [a]NU-Text reads *goes ahead*.

IMPACT OF THE BOOK

I	**IDEA**	*Christians put the needs of others before their own.*
M	**MESSAGE**	*Diotrephes had to be first in everything; he stands in stark contrast to Christ who humbled Himself and suffered for the sins of others. John tells his readers not to imitate evil but to imitate good, and Christ is the ultimate example of goodness.*
P	**PEOPLE**	*Demetrius, Diotrephes, Gaius, John*
A	**AUTHOR**	*Like 2 John, 3 John's author identifies himself as "The Elder." John wrote this letter after receiving a report about the ministry and hospitality of his friend Gaius—who had questions about how to exercise hospitality.*
C	**CULTURE**	*Tradition says John lived in Ephesus and worked from his residence there in ministries among the churches in Asia Minor. One of the differences from 2 John is that this letter of encouragement was explicitly written to a person, John's "beloved" friend Gaius (v. 1). Gaius, a common name during this time, is mentioned three other times in Scripture (Acts 19:29; 20:4; Rom. 16:23). Yet it is highly unlikely that any of these other men knew John. Also mentioned is Diotrephes, who was causing trouble and who thus received a rebuke for being inhospitable. Demetrius, who received a commendation from John, was probably the bearer of the letter.*
T	**TIMELINE**	*c. AD 80–90*
	KEY SCRIPTURE MEMORY VERSES	4; 11

THIRD JOHN

GREETING TO GAIUS

The Elder,

To the beloved Gaius, whom I love in truth:

[2]Beloved, I pray that you may prosper in all things and be in health, just as your soul prospers. [3]For I rejoiced greatly when brethren came and testified of the truth *that is* in you, just as you walk in the truth. [4]I have no greater joy than to hear that my children walk in truth.[a]

GAIUS COMMENDED FOR GENEROSITY

[5]Beloved, you do faithfully whatever you do for the brethren and[a] for strangers, [6]who have borne witness of your love before the church. *If* you send them forward on their journey in a manner worthy of God, you will do well, [7]because they went forth for His name's sake, taking nothing from the Gentiles. [8]We therefore ought to receive[a] such, that we may become fellow workers for the truth.

DIOTREPHES AND DEMETRIUS

[9]I wrote to the church, but Diotrephes, who loves to have the preeminence among them, does not receive us. [10]Therefore, if I come, I will call to mind his deeds which he does, prating against us with malicious words. And not content with that, he himself does not receive the brethren, and forbids those who wish to, putting *them* out of the church.

[11]Beloved, do not imitate what is evil, but what is good. He who does good is of God, but[a] he who does evil has not seen God.

[12]Demetrius has a *good* testimony from all, and from the truth itself. And we also bear witness, and you know that our testimony is true.

FAREWELL GREETING

[13]I had many things to write, but I do not wish to write to you with pen and ink; [14]but I hope to see you shortly, and we shall speak face to face.

Peace to you. Our friends greet you. Greet the friends by name.

4 [a]NU-Text reads *the truth.* **5** [a]NU-Text adds *especially.* **8** [a]NU-Text reads *support.* **11** [a]NU-Text and M-Text omit *but.*

LEADERSHIP ISSUES

Portraits of Leadership

Though 3 John is the smallest book in the Bible we need not underestimate the gravity of what is communicated, especially about leadership. For in fourteen short verses John paints three portraits of leadership, each accentuating the witness of that character.

• **Gaius (vv. 1–8):** *A Portrait of Generosity*
The first character John illuminates is the one to whom he gives the most attention. In fact, the majority of the letter is dedicated to emphasizing the Christ-like characteristics in two of the three persons' lives discussed. It is important for the leader to always keep in mind: *How beautiful are the feet of those who preach the gospel of peace, who bring glad tidings of good things!* (Rom. 10:15). Gaius was probably a convert of John's ministry (v. 4) for John writes to him from the perspective as a spiritual father or authority. John's joyous approval of Gaius spills off the page with encouragement concerning his:

  • Reputation of faithfulness (v. 3)
  • Hospitality towards other Christians (v. 5)
  • Focus on authentic Christian community (vv. 6–8)

• **Diotrephes (vv. 9, 10):** *A Portrait of Sinful Pride*
Pride is a poison in the life of so many leaders. The philosophy or standard modus operandi of pride is, "do whatever it takes to be number one." Diotrephes elevated himself (v. 9) by speaking wickedness against John and his fellow missionaries (v. 10). A life that revolves around self sees everyone else as property not persons. Diotrephes' pride led him to be a destructor of community, leaving behind a legacy no bigger than his own carnality.

• **Demetrius (vv. 11, 12):** *A Portrait of a Life Worth Imitating*
Our third character is introduced with a charge to imitate that which is good. John then provides an example of what "good" looks like in Demetrius. There are three qualities that can be extracted concerning his witness:

  • He is well spoken of by those around him (v. 12)
  • He is a witness of the heavenly authority above him (v. 12)
  • He is a supported by earthly leadership close to him (vv. 11, 12)

IMPACT OF THE BOOK

I   **IDEA**   *Leaders must guard their people against spiritual error.*

M   **MESSAGE**   *Creativity, visual examples, and positive and negative encouragement serve to clarify and illustrate spiritual truths, and they are valuable tools in the hands of a gifted leader.*

P   **PEOPLE**   *Enoch, False Teachers, Jude*

A   **AUTHOR**   *Probably writing to Jewish believers in the region of Asia Minor, Jude identified himself as the "brother" of James and the "bondservant" of Jesus, denoting a marked change in the way Jude related to his half brother Jesus. By the time he wrote this epistle, Jude had quite a different relationship with Jesus than his fraternal relationship to Him before the cross (Matt. 13:55; Mark 6:3). The humility exhibited in the title "bondservant" sets the stage for the rest of Jude's letter.*

C   **CULTURE**   *Jude did not specify the church or churches to which he was writing, but his main concern was the dangerous influence of false teachers who had apparently infiltrated a particular congregation. The letter doesn't identify these false teachers, but Jude's characterization of their beliefs and practices reflects heretical ideas that emerged during the first century as the gospel spread throughout Asia Minor. Jude targeted at least two particularly deceptive heresies: antinomianism—casting off moral restraint in the name of freedom, and spiritual elitism—claims to spiritual authority on the basis of ecstatic visions and private spiritual experience.*

T   **TIMELINE**   *c. AD 65–80*

KEY SCRIPTURE   3; 24, 25
MEMORY VERSES

GREETING TO THE CALLED

Jude, a bondservant of Jesus Christ, and brother of James,

To those who are called, sanctified[a] by God the Father, and preserved in Jesus Christ:

²Mercy, peace, and love be multiplied to you.

CONTEND FOR THE FAITH

³Beloved, while I was very diligent to write to you concerning our common salvation, I found it necessary to write to you exhorting you to contend earnestly for the faith which was once for all delivered to the saints. ⁴For certain men have crept in unnoticed, who long ago were marked out for this condemnation, ungodly men, who turn the grace of our God into lewdness and deny the only Lord God[a] and our Lord Jesus Christ.

OLD AND NEW APOSTATES

⁵But I want to remind you, though you once knew this, that the Lord, having saved the people out of the land of Egypt, afterward destroyed those who did not believe. ⁶And the angels who did not keep their proper domain, but left their own abode, He has reserved in everlasting chains under darkness for the judgment of the great day; ⁷as Sodom and Gomorrah, and the cities around them in a similar manner to these, having given themselves over to sexual immorality and gone after strange flesh, are set forth as an example, suffering the vengeance of eternal fire.

⁸Likewise also these dreamers defile the flesh, reject authority, and speak evil of dignitaries. ⁹Yet Michael the archangel, in contending with the devil, when he disputed about the body of Moses, dared not bring against him a reviling accusation, but said, "The Lord rebuke you!" ¹⁰But these

1 ªNU-Text reads *beloved.* 4 ªNU-Text omits *God.*

INSIDE the INFLUENCERS

JUDE—Earnestly Fight for the Faith

JUDE 1:3

Jesus' half-brother Jude became a believer after the resurrection. Because false teachers were circulating bad theology, he was compelled to alert and awaken believers. He may have come to the party late, but he came with passion. He exhorts the church to "contend earnestly for the faith which was once for all delivered to the saints" (1:3).

Contend earnestly stems from a Greek verb from which our English word *agony* is derived. It speaks of athletes contending in a grueling contest, of a serious effort, or of two soldiers fighting to the finish. You have to adjust the intensity of your effort to match the intensity of your opposition.

The inspired truth of God the New Testament calls *the faith* refers to Christianity itself, its history, and its life-giving salvation. It is the story of Jesus, the Person and the work of God.

The phrase *once for all* emphatically says that no better faith will arrive in the future. This one true faith is given to us for safekeeping.

Jude warns believers of the dangers of those who *creep in unnoticed* to distort the truth. His advice: build yourselves up in this faith, pray in the Holy Spirit, stay in the love of God, look to the mercy of Jesus Christ for eternal life (vv. 20, 21).

speak evil of whatever they do not know; and whatever they know naturally, like brute beasts, in these things they corrupt themselves. [11]Woe to them! For they have gone in the way of Cain, have run greedily in the error of Balaam for profit, and perished in the rebellion of Korah.

APOSTATES DEPRAVED AND DOOMED

[12]These are spots in your love feasts, while they feast with you without fear, serving *only* themselves. *They are* clouds without water, carried about[a] by the winds; late autumn trees without fruit, twice dead, pulled up by the roots; [13]raging waves of the sea, foaming up their own shame; wandering stars for whom is reserved the blackness of darkness forever.

[14]Now Enoch, the seventh from Adam, prophesied about these men also, saying, "Behold, the Lord comes with ten thousands of His saints, [15]to execute judgment on all, to convict all who are ungodly among them of all their ungodly deeds which they have committed in an ungodly way, and of all the harsh things which ungodly sinners have spoken against Him."

APOSTATES PREDICTED

[16]These are grumblers, complainers, walking according to their own lusts; and they mouth great swelling *words,* flattering people to gain advantage. [17]But you, beloved, remember the words which were spoken before by the apostles of our Lord Jesus Christ: [18]how they told you that there would be mockers in the last time who would walk according to their own ungodly lusts. [19]These are sensual persons, who cause divisions, not having the Spirit.

MAINTAIN YOUR LIFE WITH GOD

[20]But you, beloved, building yourselves up on your most holy faith, praying in the Holy Spirit, [21]keep yourselves in the love of God, looking for the mercy of our Lord Jesus Christ unto eternal life.

[22]And on some have compassion, making a distinction;[a] [23]but others save with fear, pulling *them* out of the fire,[a] hating even the garment defiled by the flesh.

GLORY TO GOD

[24]Now to Him who is able to keep you[a] from
    stumbling,
  And to present *you* faultless
  Before the presence of His glory with
    exceeding joy,
[25]To God our Savior,[a]
  Who alone is wise,[b]
  Be glory and majesty,
  Dominion and power,[c]
  Both now and forever.
  Amen.

---

12 [a]NU-Text and M-Text read *along.*   **22** [a]NU-Text reads *who are doubting* (or *making distinctions*).   **23** [a]NU-Text adds *and on some have mercy with fear* and omits *with fear* in first clause.   **24** [a]M-Text reads *them.*   **25** [a]NU-Text reads *To the only God our Savior.* [b]NU-Text omits *Who . . . is wise* and adds *Through Jesus Christ our Lord.* [c]NU-Text adds *Before all time.*

IMPACT OF THE BOOK

REVELATION

IDEA | *Believers should not despair because the final victory belongs to Jesus. Revelation is the unveiling of Jesus.*

MESSAGE | *Revelation is to be interpreted as an apocalyptic prophecy referring primarily to the end times, yet it speaks to the problems and needs of the first-century churches as well. Its truths are equally binding and applicable to hearers at any point in history until the end of the age. From the description given in chapter 1, to the sight of Him sitting on the throne in judgment at the close, there is none like Jesus in all of history.*

PEOPLE | *Angels, Dragon, Jesus, John, Seven Churches, the Two Witnesses*

AUTHOR | *The writer of Revelation identified himself as "His servant John" (1:1) and the "brother and companion" (1:9) of the believing readers. He was a man of authority in the churches, well acquainted with the conditions in which the people lived. Traditionally, the author of Revelation has been identified as the apostle John, who also wrote the Gospel of John, 1 John, 2 John, and 3 John in the New Testament.*

CULTURE | *The immediate recipients of this book were seven churches of Asia Minor located in: Ephesus, Smyrna, Pergamum, Thyatira, Sardis, Philadelphia, and Laodicea. The seven churches were located on an ancient postal route of the Asian mainland. The choice of seven individual churches is a purposeful literary device pointing toward the universal application of the directives. The problems they faced then have emerged in congregations throughout various cultures and ages. Revelation was then distributed throughout the region for the edification of all the churches.*

TIMELINE | *c. AD 95*

KEY SCRIPTURE MEMORY VERSES | 1:8; 3:20; 4:11; 19:11–15; 20:11–15; 22:18, 19

INTRODUCTION AND BENEDICTION

1 The Revelation of Jesus Christ, which God gave Him to show His servants—things which must shortly take place. And He sent and signified *it* by His angel to His servant John, ²who bore witness to the word of God, and to the testimony of Jesus Christ, to all things that he saw. ³Blessed *is* he who reads and those who hear the words of this prophecy, and keep those things which are written in it; for the time *is* near.

GREETING THE SEVEN CHURCHES

⁴John, to the seven churches which are in Asia:

Grace to you and peace from Him who is and who was and who is to come, and from the seven Spirits who are before His throne, ⁵and from Jesus Christ, the faithful witness, the first-born from the dead, and the ruler over the kings of the earth.

To Him who loved us and washedª us from our sins in His own blood, ⁶and has made us kingsª and priests to His God and Father, to Him *be* glory and dominion forever and ever. Amen.

⁷Behold, He is coming with clouds, and every eye will see Him, even they who pierced Him. And all the tribes of the earth will mourn because of Him. Even so, Amen.

⁸"I am the Alpha and the Omega, *the* Beginning and *the* End,"ª says the Lord,ᵇ "who is and who was and who is to come, the Almighty."

VISION OF THE SON OF MAN

⁹I, John, bothª your brother and companion in the tribulation and kingdom and patience of Jesus Christ, was on the island that is called Patmos for the word of God and for the testimony of Jesus Christ. ¹⁰I was in the Spirit on the Lord's Day, and I heard behind me a loud voice, as of a trumpet, ¹¹saying, "I am the Alpha and the Omega, the First and the Last,"ª and, "What you see, write in a book and send *it* to the seven churches which are in Asia:ᵇ to Ephesus, to Smyrna, to Pergamos, to Thyatira, to Sardis, to Philadelphia, and to Laodicea."

¹²Then I turned to see the voice that spoke with me. And having turned I saw seven golden lampstands, ¹³and in the midst of the seven lampstands *One* like the Son of Man, clothed with a garment down to the feet and girded about the chest with a golden band. ¹⁴His head and hair *were* white like wool, as white as snow, and His eyes like a flame of fire; ¹⁵His feet *were* like fine brass, as if refined in a furnace, and His voice as the sound of many waters; ¹⁶He had in His right hand seven stars, out of His mouth went a sharp two-edged sword, and His countenance *was* like the sun shining in its strength. ¹⁷And when I saw Him, I fell at His feet as dead. But He laid His right hand on me, saying to me,ª "Do not be afraid; I am the First and the Last. ¹⁸I *am* He who lives, and was dead, and behold, I am alive forevermore. Amen. And I have the keys of Hades and of Death. ¹⁹Writeª the things which you have seen, and the things which are, and the things which will take place after this. ²⁰The mystery of the seven stars which you saw in My right hand, and the seven golden lampstands: The seven stars are the angels of the seven churches, and the seven lampstands which you sawª are the seven churches.

THE LOVELESS CHURCH

2 "To the angel of the church of Ephesus write,
'These things says He who holds the seven stars in His right hand, who walks in the midst of the seven golden lampstands: ²"I know your works, your labor, your patience, and that you cannot bear those who are evil. And you have tested those who say they are apostles and are not, and have found them liars; ³and you have persevered and have patience, and have labored for My name's sake and have not become weary. ⁴Nevertheless I have *this* against you, that you have left your first love. ⁵Remember therefore from where you have fallen; repent and do the first works, or else I will come to you quickly and remove your lampstand from its place—unless you repent. ⁶But this you have, that you hate the deeds of the Nicolaitans, which I also hate.

1:5 ªNU-Text reads *loves us and freed;* M-Text reads *loves us and washed.* **1:6** ªNU-Text and M-Text read *a kingdom.* **1:8** ªNU-Text and M-Text omit *the Beginning and the End.* ᵇNU-Text and M-Text add *God.* **1:9** ªNU-Text and M-Text omit *both.* **1:11** ªNU-Text and M-Text omit *I am* through third *and.* ᵇNU-Text and M-Text omit *which are in Asia.* **1:17** ªNU-Text and M-Text omit *to me.* **1:19** ªNU-Text and M-Text read *Therefore, write.* **1:20** ªNU-Text and M-Text omit *which you saw.*

LEADERSHIP ISSUES

GC2: Worthy Is the Lamb

REVELATION 1:18

Consider what would be missing in your life if Christ had not been resurrected, if the Alpha and Omega did not hold the keys! You have much to be grateful for, and John's writings in Revelation remind us that as followers of Jesus we're destined for an eternity of thanksgiving for the Lamb who was slain (Rev. 6:9–14).

Pause to consider these blessings:

- Because Christ died and rose, we can live **in union with Him,** drawing on His strength, wisdom, and love: "It is no longer I who live, but Christ lives in me" (Gal. 2:20).

- Because Christ died and rose, we can live **for Him,** dedicating ourselves to the pursuit of His will and the advancement of His kingdom: "And He died for all, that those who live should no longer live for themselves, but for Him who died for them and rose again" (2 Cor. 5:15).

- Because Christ died and rose, we can live **as His representatives,** extending His presence into the world by the power of His Spirit: "We are ambassadors for Christ, as though God were pleading through us" (2 Cor. 5:20).

- Because Christ died and rose, we can live **to glorify Him,** responding with gratefulness and wonder to the grace given to us: "Do you not know . . . you are not your own? For you were bought at a price; therefore glorify God in your body" (1 Cor. 6:19, 20).

Now celebrate with a glad heart as you join the angels of heaven in declaring: "Worthy is the Lamb who was slain" (Rev. 5:12).

GC2
GREAT COMMANDMENT
COMMISSION

7"He who has an ear, let him hear what the Spirit says to the churches. To him who overcomes I will give to eat from the tree of life, which is in the midst of the Paradise of God." '

The Persecuted Church

8"And to the angel of the church in Smyrna write,

'These things says the First and the Last, who was dead, and came to life: 9"I know your works, tribulation, and poverty (but you are rich); and *I know* the blasphemy of those who say they are Jews and are not, but *are* a synagogue of Satan. 10Do not fear any of those things which you are about to suffer. Indeed, the devil is about to throw *some* of you into prison, that you may be tested, and you will have tribulation ten days. Be faithful until death, and I will give you the crown of life.

11"He who has an ear, let him hear what the Spirit says to the churches. He who overcomes shall not be hurt by the second death." '

The Compromising Church

12"And to the angel of the church in Pergamos write,

'These things says He who has the sharp two-edged sword: 13"I know your works, and where you dwell, where Satan's throne *is*. And you hold fast to My name, and did not deny My faith even in the days in which Antipas *was* My faithful martyr, who was killed among you, where Satan dwells. 14But I have a few things against you, because you have there those who hold the doctrine of Balaam, who taught Balak to put a stumbling block before the children of Israel, to eat things sacrificed to idols, and to commit sexual immorality. 15Thus you also have those who hold the doctrine of the Nicolaitans, which thing I hate.ᵃ 16Repent, or else I will come to you quickly and will fight against them with the sword of My mouth.

17"He who has an ear, let him hear what the Spirit says to the churches. To him who overcomes I will give some of the hidden manna to eat. And I will give him a white stone, and on the stone a new name written which no one knows except him who receives *it*." '

The Corrupt Church

18"And to the angel of the church in Thyatira write,

'These things says the Son of God, who has eyes like a flame of fire, and His feet like fine brass: 19"I know your works, love, service, faith,ᵃ and your patience; and *as* for your works, the last *are* more than the first. 20Nevertheless I have a few things against you, because you allowᵃ that womanᵇ Jezebel, who calls herself a prophetess, to teach and seducᵉ My servants to commit sexual immorality and eat things sacrificed to idols. 21And I gave her time to repent of her sexual immorality, and she did not repent.ᵃ 22Indeed I will cast her into a sickbed, and those who commit adultery with her into great tribulation, unless they repent of theirᵃ deeds. 23I will kill her children with death, and all the churches shall know that I am He who searches the minds and hearts. And I will give to each one of you according to your works.

24"Now to you I say, andᵃ to the rest in Thyatira, as many as do not have this doctrine, who have not known the depths of Satan, as they say, I willᵇ put on you no other burden. 25But hold fast what you have till I come. 26And he who overcomes, and keeps My works until the end, to him I will give power over the nations—

27'He shall rule them with a rod of iron;
    They shall be dashed to pieces like the
        potter's vessels'ᵃ—

as I also have received from My Father; 28and I will give him the morning star.

29"He who has an ear, let him hear what the Spirit says to the churches." '

The Dead Church

3 "And to the angel of the church in Sardis write,

'These things says He who has the seven Spirits of God and the seven stars: "I know your works, that you have a name that you are alive, but you are dead. 2Be watchful, and strengthen the things

2:15 ᵃNU-Text and M-Text read *likewise* for *which thing I hate.* **2:19** ᵃNU-Text and M-Text read *faith, service.* **2:20** ᵃNU-Text and M-Text read *I have against you that you tolerate.* ᵇM-Text reads *your wife Jezebel.* ᶜNU-Text and M-Text read *and teaches and seduces.* **2:21** ᵃNU-Text and M-Text read *time to repent, and she does not want to repent of her sexual immorality.* **2:22** ᵃNU-Text and M-Text read *her.* **2:24** ᵃNU-Text and M-Text omit *and.* ᵇNU-Text and M-Text omit *will.* **2:27** ᵃPsalm 2:9

which remain, that are ready to die, for I have not found your works perfect before God.[a] [3]Remember therefore how you have received and heard; hold fast and repent. Therefore if you will not watch, I will come upon you as a thief, and you will not know what hour I will come upon you. [4]You[a] have a few names even in Sardis who have not defiled their garments; and they shall walk with Me in white, for they are worthy. [5]He who overcomes shall be clothed in white garments, and I will not blot out his name from the Book of Life; but I will confess his name before My Father and before His angels.

[6]"He who has an ear, let him hear what the Spirit says to the churches." '

The Faithful Church

[7]"And to the angel of the church in Philadelphia write,

'These things says He who is holy, He who is true, *"He who has the key of David, He who opens and no one shuts, and shuts and no one opens"*:[a] [8]"I know your works. See, I have set before you an open door, and no one can shut it;[a] for you have a little strength, have kept My word, and have not denied My name. [9]Indeed I will make *those* of the synagogue of Satan, who say they are Jews and are not, but lie—indeed I will make them come and worship before your feet, and to know that I have loved you. [10]Because you have kept My command to persevere, I also will keep you from the hour of trial which shall come upon the whole world, to test those who dwell on the earth. [11]Behold,[a] I am coming quickly! Hold fast what you have, that no one may take your crown. [12]He who overcomes, I will make him a pillar in the temple of My God, and he shall go out no more. I will write on him the name of My God and the name of the city of My God, the New Jerusalem, which comes down out of heaven from My God. And *I will write on him* My new name.

[13]"He who has an ear, let him hear what the Spirit says to the churches." '

The Lukewarm Church

[14]"And to the angel of the church of the Laodiceans[a] write,

'These things says the Amen, the Faithful and True Witness, the Beginning of the creation of God: [15]"I know your works, that you are neither cold nor hot. I could wish you were cold or hot. [16]So then, because you are lukewarm, and neither cold nor hot,[a] I will vomit you out of My mouth. [17]Because you say, 'I am rich, have become wealthy, and have need of nothing'—and do not know that you are wretched, miserable, poor, blind, and naked— [18]I counsel you to buy from Me gold refined in the fire, that you may be rich; and white garments, that you may be clothed, *that* the shame of your nakedness may not be revealed; and anoint your eyes with eye salve, that you may see. [19]As many as I love, I rebuke and chasten. Therefore be zealous and repent. [20]Behold, I stand at the door and knock. If anyone hears My voice and opens the door, I will come in to him and dine with him, and he with Me. [21]To him who overcomes I will grant to sit with Me on My throne, as I also overcame and sat down with My Father on His throne.

[22]"He who has an ear, let him hear what the Spirit says to the churches." ' "

The Throne Room of Heaven

4 After these things I looked, and behold, a door *standing* open in heaven. And the first voice which I heard *was* like a trumpet speaking with me, saying, "Come up here, and I will show you things which must take place after this."

[2]Immediately I was in the Spirit; and behold, a throne set in heaven, and *One* sat on the throne. [3]And He who sat there was[a] like a jasper and a sardius stone in appearance; and *there was* a rainbow around the throne, in appearance like an emerald. [4]Around the throne *were* twenty-four thrones, and on the thrones I saw twenty-four elders sitting, clothed in white robes; and they had crowns[a] of gold on their heads. [5]And from the throne proceeded lightnings, thunderings, and voices.[a] Seven lamps of fire *were* burning before the throne, which are the[b] seven Spirits of God.

3:2 [a]NU-Text and M-Text read *My God.* **3:4** [a]NU-Text and M-Text read *Nevertheless you have a few names in Sardis.* **3:7** [a]Isaiah 22:22 **3:8** [a]NU-Text and M-Text read *which no one can shut.* **3:11** [a]NU-Text and M-Text omit *Behold.* **3:14** [a]NU-Text and M-Text read *in Laodicea.* **3:16** [a]NU-Text and M-Text read *hot nor cold.* **4:3** [a]M-Text omits *And He who sat there was* (which makes the description in verse 3 modify the throne rather than God). **4:4** [a]NU-Text and M-Text read *robes, with crowns.* **4:5** [a]NU-Text and M-Text read *voices, and thunderings.* [b]M-Text omits *the.*

THROUGH THE GRID
Discover God: God Is Sovereign

REVELATION 4:11 *You are worthy, O Lord, to receive glory and honor and power; for You created all things, and by Your will they exist and were created.*

Because God alone created the universe, is all-powerful, and is all-knowing, only God has a rulership that is supreme, paramount, and absolute. God can do anything that needs to be done. God brings everything into being, according with His plans. God is the One who determines the course of the world's events, and it is God who allows people to come into worldly power and allows plans to unfold. God works supernaturally in the world and accomplishes His purposes for all of creation. There are several ways in which God reigns: through omniscient wisdom, through righteousness, and by revealing His goodness, which we can always count on. By focusing on God's sovereignty, we remove the focus from ourselves and place it on God. We begin to realize that God controls the universe and is the only One who can fill our lives with joy, meaning, and purpose.

⁶Before the throne *there was*ᵃ a sea of glass, like crystal. And in the midst of the throne, and around the throne, *were* four living creatures full of eyes in front and in back. ⁷The first living creature *was* like a lion, the second living creature like a calf, the third living creature had a face like a man, and the fourth living creature *was* like a flying eagle. ⁸*The* four living creatures, each having six wings, were full of eyes around and within. And they do not rest day or night, saying:

"Holy, holy, holy,ᵃ
Lord God Almighty,
Who was and is and is to come!"

⁹Whenever the living creatures give glory and honor and thanks to Him who sits on the throne, who lives forever and ever, ¹⁰the twenty-four elders fall down before Him who sits on the throne and worship Him who lives forever and ever, and cast their crowns before the throne, saying:

¹¹"You are worthy, O Lord,ᵃ
To receive glory and honor and power;
For You created all things,
And by Your will they existᵇ and were created."

THE LAMB TAKES THE SCROLL

5 And I saw in the right *hand* of Him who sat on the throne a scroll written inside and on the back, sealed with seven seals. ²Then I saw a strong angel proclaiming with a loud voice, "Who is worthy to open the scroll and to loose its seals?" ³And no one in heaven or on the earth or under the earth was able to open the scroll, or to look at it.

⁴So I wept much, because no one was found worthy to open and readᵃ the scroll, or to look at it. ⁵But one of the elders said to me, "Do not weep. Behold, the Lion of the tribe of Judah, the Root of David, has prevailed to open the scroll and to looseᵃ its seven seals."

⁶And I looked, and behold,ᵃ in the midst of the throne and of the four living creatures, and in the midst of the elders, stood a Lamb as though it had been slain, having seven horns and seven eyes, which are the seven Spirits of God sent out into all the earth. ⁷Then He came and took the scroll out of the right hand of Him who sat on the throne.

4:6 ᵃNU-Text and M-Text add *something like.*   4:8 ᵃM-Text has *holy nine times.*   4:11 ᵃNU-Text and M-Text read *our Lord and God.* ᵇNU-Text and M-Text read *existed.*   5:4 ᵃNU-Text and M-Text omit *and read.*   5:5 ᵃNU-Text and M-Text omit *to loose.*   5:6 ᵃNU-Text and M-Text read *I saw in the midst . . . a Lamb standing.*

WORTHY IS THE LAMB

[8]Now when He had taken the scroll, the four living creatures and the twenty-four elders fell down before the Lamb, each having a harp, and golden bowls full of incense, which are the prayers of the saints. [9]And they sang a new song, saying:

"You are worthy to take the scroll,
  And to open its seals;
For You were slain,
  And have redeemed us to God by Your blood
  Out of every tribe and tongue and people
    and nation,
[10]And have made us[a] kings[b] and priests to our
    God;
  And we[c] shall reign on the earth."

[11]Then I looked, and I heard the voice of many angels around the throne, the living creatures, and the elders; and the number of them was ten thousand times ten thousand, and thousands of thousands, [12]saying with a loud voice:

"Worthy is the Lamb who was slain
  To receive power and riches and wisdom,
  And strength and honor and glory and
    blessing!"

[13]And every creature which is in heaven and on the earth and under the earth and such as are in the sea, and all that are in them, I heard saying:

"Blessing and honor and glory and power
  Be to Him who sits on the throne,
  And to the Lamb, forever and ever!"[a]

[14]Then the four living creatures said, "Amen!" And the twenty-four[a] elders fell down and worshiped Him who lives forever and ever.[b]

FIRST SEAL: THE CONQUEROR

6 Now I saw when the Lamb opened one of the seals;[a] and I heard one of the four living creatures saying with a voice like thunder, "Come and see." [2]And I looked, and behold, a white horse. He who sat on it had a bow; and a crown was given to him, and he went out conquering and to conquer.

SECOND SEAL: CONFLICT ON EARTH

[3]When He opened the second seal, I heard the second living creature saying, "Come and see."[a] [4]Another horse, fiery red, went out. And it was granted to the one who sat on it to take peace from the earth, and that *people* should kill one another; and there was given to him a great sword.

THIRD SEAL: SCARCITY ON EARTH

[5]When He opened the third seal, I heard the third living creature say, "Come and see." So I looked, and behold, a black horse, and he who sat on it had a pair of scales in his hand. [6]And I heard a voice in the midst of the four living creatures saying, "A quart[a] of wheat for a denarius,[b] and three quarts of barley for a denarius; and do not harm the oil and the wine."

FOURTH SEAL: WIDESPREAD DEATH ON EARTH

[7]When He opened the fourth seal, I heard the voice of the fourth living creature saying, "Come and see." [8]So I looked, and behold, a pale horse. And the name of him who sat on it was Death, and Hades followed with him. And power was given to them over a fourth of the earth, to kill with sword, with hunger, with death, and by the beasts of the earth.

FIFTH SEAL: THE CRY OF THE MARTYRS

[9]When He opened the fifth seal, I saw under the altar the souls of those who had been slain for the word of God and for the testimony which they held. [10]And they cried with a loud voice, saying, "How long, O Lord, holy and true, until You judge and avenge our blood on those who dwell on the earth?" [11]Then a white robe was given to each of them; and it was said to them that they should rest a little while longer, until both *the number of* their fellow servants and their brethren, who would be killed as they *were,* was completed.

5:10 [a]NU-Text and M-Text read *them.* [b]NU-Text reads *a kingdom.* [c]NU-Text and M-Text read *they.* **5:13** [a]M-Text adds *Amen.* **5:14** [a]NU-Text and M-Text omit *twenty-four.* [b]NU-Text and M-Text omit *Him who lives forever and ever.* **6:1** [a]NU-Text and M-Text read *seven seals.* **6:3** [a]NU-Text and M-Text omit *and see.* **6:6** [a]Greek *choinix;* that is, approximately one quart [b]This was approximately one day's wage for a worker.

Sixth Seal: Cosmic Disturbances

[12]I looked when He opened the sixth seal, and behold,[a] there was a great earthquake; and the sun became black as sackcloth of hair, and the moon[b] became like blood. [13]And the stars of heaven fell to the earth, as a fig tree drops its late figs when it is shaken by a mighty wind. [14]Then the sky receded as a scroll when it is rolled up, and every mountain and island was moved out of its place. [15]And the kings of the earth, the great men, the rich men, the commanders,[a] the mighty men, every slave and every free man, hid themselves in the caves and in the rocks of the mountains, [16]and said to the mountains and rocks, "Fall on us and hide us from the face of Him who sits on the throne and from the wrath of the Lamb! [17]For the great day of His wrath has come, and who is able to stand?"

The Sealed of Israel

7 After these things I saw four angels standing at the four corners of the earth, holding the four winds of the earth, that the wind should not blow on the earth, on the sea, or on any tree. [2]Then I saw another angel ascending from the east, having the seal of the living God. And he cried with a loud voice to the four angels to whom it was granted to harm the earth and the sea, [3]saying, "Do not harm the earth, the sea, or the trees till we have sealed the servants of our God on their foreheads." [4]And I heard the number of those who were sealed. One hundred *and* forty-four thousand of all the tribes of the children of Israel *were* sealed:

[5]of the tribe of Judah twelve thousand *were* sealed;[a]
of the tribe of Reuben twelve thousand *were* sealed;
of the tribe of Gad twelve thousand *were* sealed;
[6]of the tribe of Asher twelve thousand *were* sealed;
of the tribe of Naphtali twelve thousand *were* sealed;
of the tribe of Manasseh twelve thousand *were* sealed;
[7]of the tribe of Simeon twelve thousand *were* sealed;

of the tribe of Levi twelve thousand *were* sealed;
of the tribe of Issachar twelve thousand *were* sealed;
[8]of the tribe of Zebulun twelve thousand *were* sealed;
of the tribe of Joseph twelve thousand *were* sealed;
of the tribe of Benjamin twelve thousand *were* sealed.

A Multitude from the Great Tribulation

[9]After these things I looked, and behold, a great multitude which no one could number, of all nations, tribes, peoples, and tongues, standing before the throne and before the Lamb, clothed with white robes, with palm branches in their hands, [10]and crying out with a loud voice, saying, "Salvation *belongs* to our God who sits on the throne, and to the Lamb!" [11]All the angels stood around the throne and the elders and the four living creatures, and fell on their faces before the throne and worshiped God, [12]saying:

"Amen! Blessing and glory and wisdom,
  Thanksgiving and honor and power and might,
  Be to our God forever and ever.
  Amen."

[13]Then one of the elders answered, saying to me, "Who are these arrayed in white robes, and where did they come from?"

[14]And I said to him, "Sir,[a] you know."

So he said to me, "These are the ones who come out of the great tribulation, and washed their robes and made them white in the blood of the Lamb. [15]Therefore they are before the throne of God, and serve Him day and night in His temple. And He who sits on the throne will dwell among them. [16]They shall neither hunger anymore nor thirst anymore; the sun shall not strike them, nor any heat; [17]for the Lamb who is in the midst of the throne will shepherd them and lead

---

6:12 [a]NU-Text and M-Text omit *behold.* [b]NU-Text and M-Text read *the whole moon.*   **6:15** [a]NU-Text and M-Text read *the commanders, the rich men.*   **7:5** [a]In NU-Text and M-Text *were sealed* is stated only in verses 5a and 8c; the words are understood in the remainder of the passage.   **7:14** [a]NU-Text and M-Text read *My lord.*

them to living fountains of waters.[a] And God will wipe away every tear from their eyes."

SEVENTH SEAL: PRELUDE TO THE SEVEN TRUMPETS

8 When He opened the seventh seal, there was silence in heaven for about half an hour. [2]And I saw the seven angels who stand before God, and to them were given seven trumpets. [3]Then another angel, having a golden censer, came and stood at the altar. He was given much incense, that he should offer *it* with the prayers of all the saints upon the golden altar which was before the throne. [4]And the smoke of the incense, with the prayers of the saints, ascended before God from the angel's hand. [5]Then the angel took the censer, filled it with fire from the altar, and threw *it* to the earth. And there were noises, thunderings, lightnings, and an earthquake.

[6]So the seven angels who had the seven trumpets prepared themselves to sound.

FIRST TRUMPET: VEGETATION STRUCK

[7]The first angel sounded: And hail and fire followed, mingled with blood, and they were thrown to the earth.[a] And a third of the trees were burned up, and all green grass was burned up.

SECOND TRUMPET: THE SEAS STRUCK

[8]Then the second angel sounded: And *something* like a great mountain burning with fire was thrown into the sea, and a third of the sea became blood. [9]And a third of the living creatures in the sea died, and a third of the ships were destroyed.

THIRD TRUMPET: THE WATERS STRUCK

[10]Then the third angel sounded: And a great star fell from heaven, burning like a torch, and it fell on a third of the rivers and on the springs of water. [11]The name of the star is Wormwood. A third of the waters became wormwood, and many men died from the water, because it was made bitter.

FOURTH TRUMPET: THE HEAVENS STRUCK

[12]Then the fourth angel sounded: And a third of the sun was struck, a third of the moon, and a third of the stars, so that a third of them were darkened. A third of the day did not shine, and likewise the night.

[13]And I looked, and I heard an angel[a] flying through the midst of heaven, saying with a loud voice, "Woe, woe, woe to the inhabitants of the earth, because of the remaining blasts of the trumpet of the three angels who are about to sound!"

FIFTH TRUMPET: THE LOCUSTS FROM THE BOTTOMLESS PIT

9 Then the fifth angel sounded: And I saw a star fallen from heaven to the earth. To him was given the key to the bottomless pit. [2]And he opened the bottomless pit, and smoke arose out of the pit like the smoke of a great furnace. So the sun and the air were darkened because of the smoke of the pit. [3]Then out of the smoke locusts came upon the earth. And to them was given power, as the scorpions of the earth have power. [4]They were commanded not to harm the grass of the earth, or any green thing, or any tree, but only those men who do not have the seal of God on their foreheads. [5]And they were not given *authority* to kill them, but to torment them *for* five months. Their torment *was* like the torment of a scorpion when it strikes a man. [6]In those days men will seek death and will not find it; they will desire to die, and death will flee from them.

[7]The shape of the locusts was like horses prepared for battle. On their heads were crowns of something like gold, and their faces *were* like the faces of men. [8]They had hair like women's hair, and their teeth were like lions' *teeth.* [9]And they had breastplates like breastplates of iron, and the sound of their wings *was* like the sound of chariots with many horses running into battle. [10]They had tails like scorpions, and there were stings in their tails. Their power *was* to hurt men five months. [11]And they had as king over them the angel of the bottomless pit, whose name in Hebrew *is* Abaddon, but in Greek he has the name Apollyon.

[12]One woe is past. Behold, still two more woes are coming after these things.

SIXTH TRUMPET: THE ANGELS FROM THE EUPHRATES

[13]Then the sixth angel sounded: And I heard a voice from the four horns of the golden altar

7:17 [a]NU-Text and M-Text read *to fountains of the waters of life.*
8:7 [a]NU-Text and M-Text add *and a third of the earth was burned up.*
8:13 [a]NU-Text and M-Text read *eagle.*

which is before God, [14]saying to the sixth angel who had the trumpet, "Release the four angels who are bound at the great river Euphrates." [15]So the four angels, who had been prepared for the hour and day and month and year, were released to kill a third of mankind. [16]Now the number of the army of the horsemen *was* two hundred million; I heard the number of them. [17]And thus I saw the horses in the vision: those who sat on them had breastplates of fiery red, hyacinth blue, and sulfur yellow; and the heads of the horses *were* like the heads of lions; and out of their mouths came fire, smoke, and brimstone. [18]By these three *plagues* a third of mankind was killed—by the fire and the smoke and the brimstone which came out of their mouths. [19]For their power[a] is in their mouth and in their tails; for their tails *are* like serpents, having heads; and with them they do harm.

[20]But the rest of mankind, who were not killed by these plagues, did not repent of the works of their hands, that they should not worship demons, and idols of gold, silver, brass, stone, and wood, which can neither see nor hear nor walk. [21]And they did not repent of their murders or their sorceries[a] or their sexual immorality or their thefts.

THE MIGHTY ANGEL WITH THE LITTLE BOOK

10 I saw still another mighty angel coming down from heaven, clothed with a cloud. And a rainbow *was* on his head, his face *was* like the sun, and his feet like pillars of fire. [2]He had a little book open in his hand. And he set his right foot on the sea and *his* left *foot* on the land, [3]and cried with a loud voice, as *when* a lion roars. When he cried out, seven thunders uttered their voices. [4]Now when the seven thunders uttered their voices,[a] I was about to write; but I heard a voice from heaven saying to me,[b] "Seal up the things which the seven thunders uttered, and do not write them."

[5]The angel whom I saw standing on the sea and on the land raised up his hand[a] to heaven [6]and swore by Him who lives forever and ever, who created heaven and the things that are in it, the earth and the things that are in it, and the sea and the things that are in it, that there should be delay no longer, [7]but in the days of the sounding

of the seventh angel, when he is about to sound, the mystery of God would be finished, as He declared to His servants the prophets.

JOHN EATS THE LITTLE BOOK

[8]Then the voice which I heard from heaven spoke to me again and said, "Go, take the little book which is open in the hand of the angel who stands on the sea and on the earth."

[9]So I went to the angel and said to him, "Give me the little book."

And he said to me, "Take and eat it; and it will make your stomach bitter, but it will be as sweet as honey in your mouth."

[10]Then I took the little book out of the angel's hand and ate it, and it was as sweet as honey in my mouth. But when I had eaten it, my stomach became bitter. [11]And he[a] said to me, "You must prophesy again about many peoples, nations, tongues, and kings."

THE TWO WITNESSES

11 Then I was given a reed like a measuring rod. And the angel stood,[a] saying, "Rise and measure the temple of God, the altar, and those who worship there. [2]But leave out the court which is outside the temple, and do not measure it, for it has been given to the Gentiles. And they will tread the holy city underfoot *for* forty-two months. [3]And I will give *power* to my two witnesses, and they will prophesy one thousand two hundred and sixty days, clothed in sackcloth."

[4]These are the two olive trees and the two lampstands standing before the God[a] of the earth. [5]And if anyone wants to harm them, fire proceeds from their mouth and devours their enemies. And if anyone wants to harm them, he must be killed in this manner. [6]These have power to shut heaven, so that no rain falls in the days of their prophecy; and they have power over waters to turn them to blood, and to strike the earth with all plagues, as often as they desire.

9:19 [a]NU-Text and M-Text read *the power of the horses.*   **9:21** [a]NU-Text and M-Text read *drugs.*   **10:4** [a]NU-Text and M-Text read *sounded.* [b]NU-Text and M-Text read *to me.*   **10:5** [a]NU-Text and M-Text read *right hand.*   **10:11** [a]NU-Text and M-Text read *they.*   **11:1** [a]NU-Text and M-Text omit *And the angel stood.*   **11:4** [a]NU-Text and M-Text read *Lord.*

THE WITNESSES KILLED

[7]When they finish their testimony, the beast that ascends out of the bottomless pit will make war against them, overcome them, and kill them. [8]And their dead bodies *will lie* in the street of the great city which spiritually is called Sodom and Egypt, where also our[a] Lord was crucified. [9]Then *those* from the peoples, tribes, tongues, and nations will see their dead bodies three-and-a-half days, and not allow[a] their dead bodies to be put into graves. [10]And those who dwell on the earth will rejoice over them, make merry, and send gifts to one another, because these two prophets tormented those who dwell on the earth.

THE WITNESSES RESURRECTED

[11]Now after the three-and-a-half days the breath of life from God entered them, and they stood on their feet, and great fear fell on those who saw them. [12]And they[a] heard a loud voice from heaven saying to them, "Come up here." And they ascended to heaven in a cloud, and their enemies saw them. [13]In the same hour there was a great earthquake, and a tenth of the city fell. In the earthquake seven thousand people were killed, and the rest were afraid and gave glory to the God of heaven.

[14]The second woe is past. Behold, the third woe is coming quickly.

SEVENTH TRUMPET: THE KINGDOM PROCLAIMED

[15]Then the seventh angel sounded: And there were loud voices in heaven, saying, "The kingdoms[a] of this world have become *the kingdoms* of our Lord and of His Christ, and He shall reign forever and ever!" [16]And the twenty-four elders who sat before God on their thrones fell on their faces and worshiped God, [17]saying:

"We give You thanks, O Lord God Almighty,
    The One who is and who was and who is to
        come,[a]
    Because You have taken Your great power and
        reigned.
[18]The nations were angry, and Your wrath has
        come,
    And the time of the dead, that they should
        be judged,

And that You should reward Your servants the
        prophets and the saints,
    And those who fear Your name, small and
        great,
    And should destroy those who destroy the
        earth."

[19]Then the temple of God was opened in heaven, and the ark of His covenant[a] was seen in His temple. And there were lightnings, noises, thunderings, an earthquake, and great hail.

THE WOMAN, THE CHILD, AND THE DRAGON

12 Now a great sign appeared in heaven: a woman clothed with the sun, with the moon under her feet, and on her head a garland of twelve stars. [2]Then being with child, she cried out in labor and in pain to give birth.

[3]And another sign appeared in heaven: behold, a great, fiery red dragon having seven heads and ten horns, and seven diadems on his heads. [4]His tail drew a third of the stars of heaven and threw them to the earth. And the dragon stood before the woman who was ready to give birth, to devour her Child as soon as it was born. [5]She bore a male Child who was to rule all nations with a rod of iron. And her Child was caught up to God and His throne. [6]Then the woman fled into the wilderness, where she has a place prepared by God, that they should feed her there one thousand two hundred and sixty days.

SATAN THROWN OUT OF HEAVEN

[7]And war broke out in heaven: Michael and his angels fought with the dragon; and the dragon and his angels fought, [8]but they did not prevail, nor was a place found for them[a] in heaven any longer. [9]So the great dragon was cast out, that serpent of old, called the Devil and Satan, who deceives the whole world; he was cast to the earth, and his angels were cast out with him.

[10]Then I heard a loud voice saying in heaven, "Now salvation, and strength, and the kingdom of

11:8 [a]NU-Text and M-Text read *their.*   11:9 [a]NU-Text and M-Text read *nations see . . . and will not allow.*   11:12 [a]M-Text reads *I.*   11:15 [a]NU-Text and M-Text read *kingdom . . . has become.*   11:17 [a]NU-Text and M-Text omit *and who is to come.*   11:19 [a]M-Text reads *the covenant of the Lord.*   12:8 [a]M-Text reads *him.*

our God, and the power of His Christ have come, for the accuser of our brethren, who accused them before our God day and night, has been cast down. [11]And they overcame him by the blood of the Lamb and by the word of their testimony, and they did not love their lives to the death. [12]Therefore rejoice, O heavens, and you who dwell in them! Woe to the inhabitants of the earth and the sea! For the devil has come down to you, having great wrath, because he knows that he has a short time."

The Woman Persecuted

[13]Now when the dragon saw that he had been cast to the earth, he persecuted the woman who gave birth to the male *Child.* [14]But the woman was given two wings of a great eagle, that she might fly into the wilderness to her place, where she is nourished for a time and times and half a time, from the presence of the serpent. [15]So the serpent spewed water out of his mouth like a flood after the woman, that he might cause her to be carried away by the flood. [16]But the earth helped the woman, and the earth opened its mouth and swallowed up the flood which the dragon had spewed out of his mouth. [17]And the dragon was enraged with the woman, and he went to make war with the rest of her offspring, who keep the commandments of God and have the testimony of Jesus Christ.[a]

The Beast from the Sea

13 Then I[a] stood on the sand of the sea. And I saw a beast rising up out of the sea, having seven heads and ten horns,[b] and on his horns ten crowns, and on his heads a blasphemous name. [2]Now the beast which I saw was like a leopard, his feet were like *the feet of* a bear, and his mouth like the mouth of a lion. The dragon gave him his power, his throne, and great authority. [3]And I saw one of his heads as if it had been mortally wounded, and his deadly wound was healed. And all the world marveled and followed the beast. [4]So they worshiped the dragon who gave authority to the beast; and they worshiped the beast, saying, "Who *is* like the beast? Who is able to make war with him?"

[5]And he was given a mouth speaking great things and blasphemies, and he was given au-

thority to continue[a] for forty-two months. [6]Then he opened his mouth in blasphemy against God, to blaspheme His name, His tabernacle, and those who dwell in heaven. [7]It was granted to him to make war with the saints and to overcome them. And authority was given him over every tribe,[a] tongue, and nation. [8]All who dwell on the earth will worship him, whose names have not been written in the Book of Life of the Lamb slain from the foundation of the world.

[9]If anyone has an ear, let him hear. [10]He who leads into captivity shall go into captivity; he who kills with the sword must be killed with the sword. Here is the patience and the faith of the saints.

The Beast from the Earth

[11]Then I saw another beast coming up out of the earth, and he had two horns like a lamb and spoke like a dragon. [12]And he exercises all the authority of the first beast in his presence, and causes the earth and those who dwell in it to worship the first beast, whose deadly wound was healed. [13]He performs great signs, so that he even makes fire come down from heaven on the earth in the sight of men. [14]And he deceives those[a] who dwell on the earth by those signs which he was granted to do in the sight of the beast, telling those who dwell on the earth to make an image to the beast who was wounded by the sword and lived. [15]He was granted *power* to give breath to the image of the beast, that the image of the beast should both speak and cause as many as would not worship the image of the beast to be killed. [16]He causes all, both small and great, rich and poor, free and slave, to receive a mark on their right hand or on their foreheads, [17]and that no one may buy or sell except one who has the mark or[a] the name of the beast, or the number of his name.

[18]Here is wisdom. Let him who has understanding calculate the number of the beast, for it is the number of a man: His number *is* 666.

12:17 [a]NU-Text and M-Text omit *Christ.* **13:1** [a]NU-Text reads *he.* [b]NU-Text and M-Text read *ten horns and seven heads.* **13:5** [a]M-Text reads *make war.* **13:7** [a]NU-Text and M-Text add *and people.* **13:14** [a]M-Text reads *my own people.* **13:17** [a]NU-Text and M-Text omit *or.*

The Lamb and the 144,000

14 Then I looked, and behold, a[a] Lamb standing on Mount Zion, and with Him one hundred *and* forty-four thousand, having[b] His Father's name written on their foreheads. [2]And I heard a voice from heaven, like the voice of many waters, and like the voice of loud thunder. And I heard the sound of harpists playing their harps. [3]They sang as it were a new song before the throne, before the four living creatures, and the elders; and no one could learn that song except the hundred *and* forty-four thousand who were redeemed from the earth. [4]These are the ones who were not defiled with women, for they are virgins. These are the ones who follow the Lamb wherever He goes. These were redeemed[a] from *among* men, *being* firstfruits to God and to the Lamb. [5]And in their mouth was found no deceit,[a] for they are without fault before the throne of God.[b]

The Proclamations of Three Angels

[6]Then I saw another angel flying in the midst of heaven, having the everlasting gospel to preach to those who dwell on the earth—to every nation, tribe, tongue, and people— [7]saying with a loud voice, "Fear God and give glory to Him, for the hour of His judgment has come; and worship Him who made heaven and earth, the sea and springs of water."

[8]And another angel followed, saying, "Babylon[a] is fallen, is fallen, that great city, because she has made all nations drink of the wine of the wrath of her fornication."

[9]Then a third angel followed them, saying with a loud voice, "If anyone worships the beast and his image, and receives *his* mark on his forehead or on his hand, [10]he himself shall also drink of the wine of the wrath of God, which is poured out full strength into the cup of His indignation. He shall be tormented with fire and brimstone in the presence of the holy angels and in the presence of the Lamb. [11]And the smoke of their torment ascends forever and ever; and they have no rest day or night, who worship the beast and his image, and whoever receives the mark of his name."

[12]Here is the patience of the saints; here *are* those[a] who keep the commandments of God and the faith of Jesus.

[13]Then I heard a voice from heaven saying to me,[a] "Write: 'Blessed *are* the dead who die in the Lord from now on.' "

"Yes," says the Spirit, "that they may rest from their labors, and their works follow them."

Reaping the Earth's Harvest

[14]Then I looked, and behold, a white cloud, and on the cloud sat *One* like the Son of Man, having on His head a golden crown, and in His hand a sharp sickle. [15]And another angel came out of the temple, crying with a loud voice to Him who sat on the cloud, "Thrust in Your sickle and reap, for the time has come for You[a] to reap, for the harvest of the earth is ripe." [16]So He who sat on the cloud thrust in His sickle on the earth, and the earth was reaped.

Reaping the Grapes of Wrath

[17]Then another angel came out of the temple which is in heaven, he also having a sharp sickle. [18]And another angel came out from the altar, who had power over fire, and he cried with a loud cry to him who had the sharp sickle, saying, "Thrust in your sharp sickle and gather the clusters of the vine of the earth, for her grapes are fully ripe." [19]So the angel thrust his sickle into the earth and gathered the vine of the earth, and threw *it* into the great winepress of the wrath of God. [20]And the winepress was trampled outside the city, and blood came out of the winepress, up to the horses' bridles, for one thousand six hundred furlongs.

Prelude to the Bowl Judgments

15 Then I saw another sign in heaven, great and marvelous: seven angels having seven last plagues, for in them the wrath of God is complete.

[2]And I saw *something* like a sea of glass mingled with fire, and those who have the victory over the beast, over his image and over his mark[a]

14:1 [a]NU-Text and M-Text read *the*. [b]NU-Text and M-Text add *His name and*. **14:4** [a]M-Text adds *by Jesus*. **14:5** [a]NU-Text and M-Text read *falsehood*. [b]NU-Text and M-Text omit *before the throne of God*. **14:8** [a]NU-Text reads *Babylon the great is fallen,* is fallen, which has made; M-Text reads *Babylon the great is fallen. She has made*. **14:12** [a]NU-Text and M-Text omit *here are those*. **14:13** [a]NU-Text and M-Text omit *to me*. **14:15** [a]NU-Text and M-Text omit *for You*. **15:2** [a]NU-Text and M-Text omit *over his mark*.

and over the number of his name, standing on the sea of glass, having harps of God. ³They sing the song of Moses, the servant of God, and the song of the Lamb, saying:

"Great and marvelous *are* Your works,
　Lord God Almighty!
Just and true *are* Your ways,
　O King of the saints!ᵃ
⁴Who shall not fear You, O Lord, and glorify
　　Your name?
For *You* alone *are* holy.
For all nations shall come and worship before
　　You,
For Your judgments have been manifested."

⁵After these things I looked, and behold,ᵃ the temple of the tabernacle of the testimony in heaven was opened. ⁶And out of the temple came the seven angels having the seven plagues, clothed in pure bright linen, and having their chests girded with golden bands. ⁷Then one of the four living creatures gave to the seven angels seven golden bowls full of the wrath of God who lives forever and ever. ⁸The temple was filled with smoke from the glory of God and from His power, and no one was able to enter the temple till the seven plagues of the seven angels were completed.

16 Then I heard a loud voice from the temple saying to the seven angels, "Go and pour out the bowlsᵃ of the wrath of God on the earth."

First Bowl: Loathsome Sores

²So the first went and poured out his bowl upon the earth, and a foul and loathsome sore came upon the men who had the mark of the beast and those who worshiped his image.

Second Bowl: The Sea Turns to Blood

³Then the second angel poured out his bowl on the sea, and it became blood as of a dead *man;* and every living creature in the sea died.

Third Bowl: The Waters Turn to Blood

⁴Then the third angel poured out his bowl on the rivers and springs of water, and they became blood. ⁵And I heard the angel of the waters saying:

"You are righteous, O Lord,ᵃ
The One who is and who was and who is to
　　be,ᵇ
Because You have judged these things.
⁶For they have shed the blood of saints and
　　prophets,
And You have given them blood to drink.
Forᵃ it is their just due."

⁷And I heard another fromᵃ the altar saying, "Even so, Lord God Almighty, true and righteous *are* Your judgments."

Fourth Bowl: Men Are Scorched

⁸Then the fourth angel poured out his bowl on the sun, and power was given to him to scorch men with fire. ⁹And men were scorched with great heat, and they blasphemed the name of God who has power over these plagues; and they did not repent and give Him glory.

Fifth Bowl: Darkness and Pain

¹⁰Then the fifth angel poured out his bowl on the throne of the beast, and his kingdom became full of darkness; and they gnawed their tongues because of the pain. ¹¹They blasphemed the God of heaven because of their pains and their sores, and did not repent of their deeds.

Sixth Bowl: Euphrates Dried Up

¹²Then the sixth angel poured out his bowl on the great river Euphrates, and its water was dried up, so that the way of the kings from the east might be prepared. ¹³And I saw three unclean spirits like frogs *coming* out of the mouth of the dragon, out of the mouth of the beast, and out of the mouth of the false prophet. ¹⁴For they are spirits of demons, performing signs, *which* go out to the kings of the earth andᵃ of the whole world, to gather them to the battle of that great day of God Almighty.

15:3 ᵃNU-Text and M-Text read *nations.* 15:5 ᵃNU-Text and M-Text omit *behold.* 16:1 ᵃNU-Text and M-Text read *seven bowls.* 16:5 ᵃNU-Text and M-Text omit *O Lord.* ᵇNU-Text and M-Text read *who was, the Holy One.* 16:6 ᵃNU-Text and M-Text omit *For.* 16:7 ᵃNU-Text and M-Text omit *another from.* 16:14 ᵃNU-Text and M-Text omit *of the earth and.*

[15]"Behold, I am coming as a thief. Blessed *is* he who watches, and keeps his garments, lest he walk naked and they see his shame."

[16]And they gathered them together to the place called in Hebrew, Armageddon.[a]

Seventh Bowl: The Earth Utterly Shaken

[17]Then the seventh angel poured out his bowl into the air, and a loud voice came out of the temple of heaven, from the throne, saying, "It is done!" [18]And there were noises and thunderings and lightnings; and there was a great earthquake, such a mighty and great earthquake as had not occurred since men were on the earth. [19]Now the great city was divided into three parts, and the cities of the nations fell. And great Babylon was remembered before God, to give her the cup of the wine of the fierceness of His wrath. [20]Then every island fled away, and the mountains were not found. [21]And great hail from heaven fell upon men, *each hailstone* about the weight of a talent. Men blasphemed God because of the plague of the hail, since that plague was exceedingly great.

The Scarlet Woman and the Scarlet Beast

17 Then one of the seven angels who had the seven bowls came and talked with me, saying to me,[a] "Come, I will show you the judgment of the great harlot who sits on many waters, [2]with whom the kings of the earth committed fornication, and the inhabitants of the earth were made drunk with the wine of her fornication."

[3]So he carried me away in the Spirit into the wilderness. And I saw a woman sitting on a scarlet beast *which was* full of names of blasphemy, having seven heads and ten horns. [4]The woman was arrayed in purple and scarlet, and adorned with gold and precious stones and pearls, having in her hand a golden cup full of abominations and the filthiness of her fornication.[a] [5]And on her forehead a name *was* written:

MYSTERY, BABYLON THE GREAT,
THE MOTHER OF HARLOTS AND
OF THE ABOMINATIONS
OF THE EARTH.

[6]I saw the woman, drunk with the blood of the saints and with the blood of the martyrs of Jesus. And when I saw her, I marveled with great amazement.

The Meaning of the Woman and the Beast

[7]But the angel said to me, "Why did you marvel? I will tell you the mystery of the woman and of the beast that carries her, which has the seven heads and the ten horns. [8]The beast that you saw was, and is not, and will ascend out of the bottomless pit and go to perdition. And those who dwell on the earth will marvel, whose names are not written in the Book of Life from the foundation of the world, when they see the beast that was, and is not, and yet is.[a]

[9]"Here *is* the mind which has wisdom: The seven heads are seven mountains on which the woman sits. [10]There are also seven kings. Five have fallen, one is, *and* the other has not yet come. And when he comes, he must continue a short time. [11]The beast that was, and is not, is himself also the eighth, and is of the seven, and is going to perdition.

[12]"The ten horns which you saw are ten kings who have received no kingdom as yet, but they receive authority for one hour as kings with the beast. [13]These are of one mind, and they will give their power and authority to the beast. [14]These will make war with the Lamb, and the Lamb will overcome them, for He is Lord of lords and King of kings; and those *who are* with Him *are* called, chosen, and faithful."

[15]Then he said to me, "The waters which you saw, where the harlot sits, are peoples, multitudes, nations, and tongues. [16]And the ten horns which you saw on[a] the beast, these will hate the harlot, make her desolate and naked, eat her flesh and burn her with fire. [17]For God has put it into their hearts to fulfill His purpose, to be of one mind, and to give their kingdom to the beast, until the words of God are fulfilled. [18]And the woman whom you saw is that great city which reigns over the kings of the earth."

16:16 [a]M-Text reads *Megiddo.* **17:1** [a]NU-Text and M-Text omit *to me.* **17:4** [a]M-Text reads *the filthiness of the fornication of the earth.* **17:8** [a]NU-Text and M-Text read *and shall be present.* **17:16** [a]NU-Text and M-Text read *saw, and the beast.*

The Fall of Babylon the Great

18 After these things I saw another angel coming down from heaven, having great authority, and the earth was illuminated with his glory. ²And he cried mightily[a] with a loud voice, saying, "Babylon the great is fallen, is fallen, and has become a dwelling place of demons, a prison for every foul spirit, and a cage for every unclean and hated bird! ³For all the nations have drunk of the wine of the wrath of her fornication, the kings of the earth have committed fornication with her, and the merchants of the earth have become rich through the abundance of her luxury."

⁴And I heard another voice from heaven saying, "Come out of her, my people, lest you share in her sins, and lest you receive of her plagues. ⁵For her sins have reached[a] to heaven, and God has remembered her iniquities. ⁶Render to her just as she rendered to you,[a] and repay her double according to her works; in the cup which she has mixed, mix double for her. ⁷In the measure that she glorified herself and lived luxuriously, in the same measure give her torment and sorrow; for she says in her heart, 'I sit *as* queen, and am no widow, and will not see sorrow.' ⁸Therefore her plagues will come in one day—death and mourning and famine. And she will be utterly burned with fire, for strong *is* the Lord God who judges[a] her.

The World Mourns Babylon's Fall

⁹"The kings of the earth who committed fornication and lived luxuriously with her will weep and lament for her, when they see the smoke of her burning, ¹⁰standing at a distance for fear of her torment, saying, 'Alas, alas, that great city Babylon, that mighty city! For in one hour your judgment has come.'

¹¹"And the merchants of the earth will weep and mourn over her, for no one buys their merchandise anymore: ¹²merchandise of gold and silver, precious stones and pearls, fine linen and purple, silk and scarlet, every kind of citron wood, every kind of object of ivory, every kind of object of most precious wood, bronze, iron, and marble; ¹³and cinnamon and incense, fragrant oil and frankincense, wine and oil, fine

flour and wheat, cattle and sheep, horses and chariots, and bodies and souls of men. ¹⁴The fruit that your soul longed for has gone from you, and all the things which are rich and splendid have gone from you,[a] and you shall find them no more at all. ¹⁵The merchants of these things, who became rich by her, will stand at a distance for fear of her torment, weeping and wailing, ¹⁶and saying, 'Alas, alas, that great city that was clothed in fine linen, purple, and scarlet, and adorned with gold and precious stones and pearls! ¹⁷For in one hour such great riches came to nothing.' Every shipmaster, all who travel by ship, sailors, and as many as trade on the sea, stood at a distance ¹⁸and cried out when they saw the smoke of her burning, saying, 'What *is* like this great city?'

¹⁹"They threw dust on their heads and cried out, weeping and wailing, and saying, 'Alas, alas, that great city, in which all who had ships on the sea became rich by her wealth! For in one hour she is made desolate.'

²⁰"Rejoice over her, O heaven, and *you* holy apostles[a] and prophets, for God has avenged you on her!"

Finality of Babylon's Fall

²¹Then a mighty angel took up a stone like a great millstone and threw *it* into the sea, saying, "Thus with violence the great city Babylon shall be thrown down, and shall not be found anymore. ²²The sound of harpists, musicians, flutists, and trumpeters shall not be heard in you anymore. No craftsman of any craft shall be found in you anymore, and the sound of a millstone shall not be heard in you anymore. ²³The light of a lamp shall not shine in you anymore, and the voice of bridegroom and bride shall not be heard in you anymore. For your merchants were the great men of the earth, for by your sorcery all the nations were deceived. ²⁴And in her was found the blood of prophets and saints, and of all who were slain on the earth."

18:2 ªNU-Text and M-Text omit *mightily* 18:5 ªNU-Text and M-Text read *have been heaped up* 18:6 ªNU-Text omit *to you* 18:8 ªNU-Text and M-Text read *has judged* 18:14 ªNU-Text and M-Text read *been lost to you* 18:20 ªNU-Text and M-Text read *saints and apostles*

HEAVEN EXULTS OVER BABYLON

19After these things I heard[a] a loud voice of a great multitude in heaven, saying, "Alleluia! Salvation and glory and honor and power *belong* to the Lord[b] our God! [2]For true and righteous *are* His judgments, because He has judged the great harlot who corrupted the earth with her fornication; and He has avenged on her the blood of His servants *shed* by her." [3]Again they said, "Alleluia! Her smoke rises up forever and ever!" [4]And the twenty-four elders and the four living creatures fell down and worshiped God who sat on the throne, saying, "Amen! Alleluia!" [5]Then a voice came from the throne, saying, "Praise our God, all you His servants and those who fear Him, both[a] small and great!"

[6]And I heard, as it were, the voice of a great multitude, as the sound of many waters and as the sound of mighty thunderings, saying, "Alleluia! For the[a] Lord God Omnipotent reigns! [7]Let us be glad and rejoice and give Him glory, for the marriage of the Lamb has come, and His wife has made herself ready." [8]And to her it was granted to be arrayed in fine linen, clean and bright, for the fine linen is the righteous acts of the saints.

[9]Then he said to me, "Write: 'Blessed *are* those who are called to the marriage supper of the Lamb!' " And he said to me, "These are the true sayings of God." [10]And I fell at his feet to worship him. But he said to me, "See *that you do* not *do that!* I am your fellow servant, and of your brethren who have the testimony of Jesus. Worship God! For the testimony of Jesus is the spirit of prophecy."

CHRIST ON A WHITE HORSE

[11]Now I saw heaven opened, and behold, a white horse. And He who sat on him *was* called Faithful and True, and in righteousness He judges and makes war. [12]His eyes *were* like a flame of fire, and on His head *were* many crowns. He had[a] a name written that no one knew except Himself. [13]He *was* clothed with a robe dipped in blood, and His name is called The Word of God. [14]And the armies in heaven, clothed in fine linen, white and clean,[a] followed Him on white horses. [15]Now out of His mouth goes a sharp[a] sword, that with it He should strike the nations. And He Himself will rule them with a rod of iron. He Himself treads the winepress of the fierceness and wrath of Almighty God. [16]And He has on *His* robe and on His thigh a name written:

KING OF KINGS AND
LORD OF LORDS.

THE BEAST AND HIS ARMIES DEFEATED

[17]Then I saw an angel standing in the sun; and he cried with a loud voice, saying to all the birds that fly in the midst of heaven, "Come and gather together for the supper of the great God,[a] [18]that you may eat the flesh of kings, the flesh of captains, the flesh of mighty men, the flesh of horses and of those who sit on them, and the flesh of all *people,* free[a] and slave, both small and great."

[19]And I saw the beast, the kings of the earth, and their armies, gathered together to make war against Him who sat on the horse and against His army. [20]Then the beast was captured, and with him the false prophet who worked signs in his presence, by which he deceived those who received the mark of the beast and those who worshiped his image. These two were cast alive into the lake of fire burning with brimstone. [21]And the rest were killed with the sword which proceeded from the mouth of Him who sat on the horse. And all the birds were filled with their flesh.

SATAN BOUND 1000 YEARS

20Then I saw an angel coming down from heaven, having the key to the bottomless pit and a great chain in his hand. [2]He laid hold of the dragon, that serpent of old, who is *the* Devil and Satan, and bound him for a thousand years; [3]and he cast him into the bottomless pit, and shut him up, and set a seal on him, so that he should deceive the nations no more till the thousand years were finished. But after these things he must be released for a little while.

19:1 [a]NU-Text and M-Text add *something like.* [b]NU-Text and M-Text omit *the Lord.* **19:5** [a]NU-Text and M-Text omit *both.* **19:6** [a]NU-Text and M-Text read *our.* **19:12** [a]M-Text adds *names written, and.* **19:14** [a]NU-Text and M-Text read *pure white linen.* **19:15** [a]M-Text adds *two-edged.* **19:17** [a]NU-Text and M-Text read *the great supper of God.* **19:18** [a]NU-Text and M-Text read *both free.*

LEADERSHIP ISSUES

GC2: Christ's Community: Christ Builds His Church

REVELATION 19:7, 8 *For the marriage of the Lamb has come, and His wife has made herself ready. And to her it was granted to be arrayed in fine linen.*

As the "bride of Christ," the church awaits the coming of the Bridegroom, ever faithful and watchful. Our fellowship together empowers our worshipful expectancy, courageous witness, and worthy walk as we await the coming of Jesus.

What a privilege to be part of His church, His "called-out ones," His body, His temple, His bride! Take a moment and give thanks to Him for this wondrous blessing of our connection with Him and with each other!

Lord Jesus,
Thank You for placing us into Your body, the church. Thank You for connecting us through the Holy Spirit with Yourself and with each other. I want to participate as a fully functioning member of Christ's body, using my gifts, talents, and skills for Your glory and for the building up of Your body. Enable me to cooperate with You fully in Your work of conforming me to the image of Christ as I seek to walk by the power of Your Spirit in the light of Your people. In Your Name, Amen.

GC2
GREAT COMMANDMENT
COMMISSION

The Saints Reign with Christ 1000 Years

[4]And I saw thrones, and they sat on them, and judgment was committed to them. Then I *saw* the souls of those who had been beheaded for their witness to Jesus and for the word of God, who had not worshiped the beast or his image, and had not received *his* mark on their foreheads or on their hands. And they lived and reigned with Christ for a[a] thousand years. [5]But the rest of the dead did not live again until the thousand years were finished. This *is* the first resurrection. [6]Blessed and holy *is* he who has part in the first resurrection. Over such the second death has no power, but they shall be priests of God and of Christ, and shall reign with Him a thousand years.

Satanic Rebellion Crushed

[7]Now when the thousand years have expired, Satan will be released from his prison [8]and will go out to deceive the nations which are in the four corners of the earth, Gog and Magog, to gather them together to battle, whose number *is* as the sand of the sea. [9]They went up on the breadth of the earth and surrounded the camp of the saints and the beloved city. And fire came down from God out of heaven and devoured them. [10]The devil, who deceived them, was cast into the lake of fire and brimstone where[a] the beast and the false prophet *are*. And they will be tormented day and night forever and ever.

The Great White Throne Judgment

[11]Then I saw a great white throne and Him who sat on it, from whose face the earth and the heaven fled away. And there was found no place for them. [12]And I saw the dead, small and great, standing before God,[a] and books were opened. And another book was opened, which is *the Book* of Life. And the dead were judged according to their works, by the things which were written in the books. [13]The sea gave up the dead who were in it, and Death and Hades delivered up the dead who were in them. And they were judged, each one according to his works. [14]Then Death and Hades were cast into the lake of fire. This is the second death.[a] [15]And anyone not found written in the Book of Life was cast into the lake of fire.

All Things Made New

21 Now I saw a new heaven and a new earth, for the first heaven and the first earth had passed away. Also there was no more sea. [2]Then I, John,[a] saw the holy city, New Jerusalem, coming down out of heaven from God, prepared as a bride adorned for her husband. [3]And I heard a loud voice from heaven saying, "Behold, the tabernacle of God *is* with men, and He will dwell with them, and they shall be His people. God Himself will be with them *and be* their God. [4]And God will wipe away every tear from their eyes; there shall be no more death, nor sorrow, nor crying. There shall be no more pain, for the former things have passed away."

[5]Then He who sat on the throne said, "Behold, I make all things new." And He said to me,[a] "Write, for these words are true and faithful."

[6]And He said to me, "It is done![a] I am the Alpha and the Omega, the Beginning and the End. I will give of the fountain of the water of life freely to him who thirsts. [7]He who overcomes shall inherit all things,[a] and I will be his God and he shall be My son. [8]But the cowardly, unbelieving,[a] abominable, murderers, sexually immoral, sorcerers, idolaters, and all liars shall have their part in the lake which burns with fire and brimstone, which is the second death."

The New Jerusalem

[9]Then one of the seven angels who had the seven bowls filled with the seven last plagues came to me[a] and talked with me, saying, "Come, I will show you the bride, the Lamb's wife."[b] [10]And he carried me away in the Spirit to a great and high mountain, and showed me the great city, the holy[a] Jerusalem, descending out of heaven from God, [11]having the glory of God. Her light *was* like a most precious stone, like a jasper stone, clear as crystal. [12]Also she had a great and high wall with twelve gates, and twelve angels at the gates, and

---

20:4 [a]M-Text reads *the*.   **20:10** [a]NU-Text and M-Text add *also*.   **20:12** [a]NU-Text and M-Text read *the throne*.   **20:14** [a]NU-Text and M-Text add *the lake of fire*.   **21:2** [a]NU-Text and M-Text omit *John*.   **21:5** [a]NU-Text and M-Text omit *to me*.   **21:6** [a]M-Text omits *It is done*.   **21:7** [a]M-Text reads *overcomes, I shall give him these things*.   **21:8** [a]M-Text adds *and sinners*.   **21:9** [a]NU-Text and M-Text omit *to me*.   [b]M-Text reads *I will show you the woman, the Lamb's bride*.   **21:10** [a]NU-Text and M-Text omit *the great* and read *the holy city, Jerusalem*.

THROUGH THE GRID

Where Have All the Dreamers Gone?
Observations from a Biblical
Worldview: Temporary Suffering
(Rev. 21:4)

The suffering of this world, along with the evil in the world, will one day be done away with at the eschaton ushered in by God. Until then, we are left to trust that God's plans for our lives have purpose and meaning, as God's ways are higher than our own. When suffering comes, we are able to relate to our neighbor by affirming the common realities of finite human existence. This provides opportunities for new friendships, for coming to appreciate people, and for relating to others in the way that God has ordained human relationships to work. In the midst of our interactions, we discover that what unites humanity is stronger than what divides it.

Suffering allows us to come to the stark realization that we are ultimately not in control of our own lives. Suffering reminds Christians of the fallenness of the world we live in and the tragic realities of human existence because we, and all of nature, are marred by the devastating effects of sin. This should affirm the worldview of the Christian that humanity is in need of redemption, which is available through Christ. Only God can renew, restore, and redeem humanity; and God has graciously provided redemption through Christ. The opportunities we have in the midst of suffering to communicate to a watching world the promises of redemption can indeed make a huge difference in the lives of other people, as our response serves as a witness and a testimony of our faith in a sovereign and good God.

names written on them, which are *the names* of the twelve tribes of the children of Israel: [13]three gates on the east, three gates on the north, three gates on the south, and three gates on the west.

[14]Now the wall of the city had twelve foundations, and on them were the names[a] of the twelve apostles of the Lamb. [15]And he who talked with me had a gold reed to measure the city, its gates, and its wall. [16]The city is laid out as a square; its length is as great as its breadth. And he measured the city with the reed: twelve thousand furlongs. Its length, breadth, and height are equal. [17]Then he measured its wall: one hundred *and* forty-four cubits, *according* to the measure of a man, that is, of an angel. [18]The construction of its wall was *of* jasper; and the city *was* pure gold, like clear glass. [19]The foundations of the wall of the city *were* adorned with all kinds of precious stones: the first foundation *was* jasper, the second sapphire, the third chalcedony, the fourth emerald, [20]the fifth sardonyx, the sixth sardius, the seventh

chrysolite, the eighth beryl, the ninth topaz, the tenth chrysoprase, the eleventh jacinth, and the twelfth amethyst. [21]The twelve gates *were* twelve pearls: each individual gate was of one pearl. And the street of the city *was* pure gold, like transparent glass.

The Glory of the New Jerusalem

[22]But I saw no temple in it, for the Lord God Almighty and the Lamb are its temple. [23]The city had no need of the sun or of the moon to shine in it,[a] for the glory[b] of God illuminated it. The Lamb *is* its light. [24]And the nations of those who are saved[a] shall walk in its light, and the kings of the earth bring their glory and honor into it.[b] [25]Its gates shall not be shut at all by day (there shall be no night there). [26]And they shall bring

21:14 [a]NU-Text and M-Text read *twelve names.*   **21:23** [a]NU-Text and M-Text omit *in it.* [b]M-Text reads *the very glory.*   **21:24** [a]NU-Text and M-Text omit *of those who are saved.* [b]M-Text reads *the glory and honor of the nations to Him.*

THROUGH THE GRID
Making Sense of Your World:
The Eschaton (Rev. 21; 22)

It is true that at the end of time, God will usher in a new heaven and a new earth, removing our current world with all sin and its consequences. However, we are still to care for the earth, since to neglect the earth is to act selfishly in opposition to a biblical worldview that calls for us as human beings and agents of God's creation to preserve and to protect the world around us. By remaining inactive, we think only of ourselves; but by working to address the environmental concerns of today, we work to provide a better environmental future for our children and neighbors.

the glory and the honor of the nations into it.[a] [27]But there shall by no means enter it anything that defiles, or causes[a] an abomination or a lie, but only those who are written in the Lamb's Book of Life.

THE RIVER OF LIFE

22And he showed me a pure[a] river of water of life, clear as crystal, proceeding from the throne of God and of the Lamb. [2]In the middle of its street, and on either side of the river, *was* the tree of life, which bore twelve fruits, each *tree* yielding its fruit every month. The leaves of the tree *were* for the healing of the nations. [3]And there shall be no more curse, but the throne of God and of the Lamb shall be in it, and His servants shall serve Him. [4]They shall see His face, and His name *shall be* on their foreheads. [5]There shall be no night there: They need no lamp nor light of the sun, for the Lord God gives them light. And they shall reign forever and ever.

THE TIME IS NEAR

[6]Then he said to me, "These words *are* faithful and true." And the Lord God of the holy[a] prophets sent His angel to show His servants the things which must shortly take place.

[7]"Behold, I am coming quickly! Blessed *is* he who keeps the words of the prophecy of this book."

[8]Now I, John, saw and heard[a] these things. And when I heard and saw, I fell down to worship before the feet of the angel who showed me these things.

[9]Then he said to me, "See *that you do* not *do that.* For[a] I am your fellow servant, and of your

brethren the prophets, and of those who keep the words of this book. Worship God." [10]And he said to me, "Do not seal the words of the prophecy of this book, for the time is at hand. [11]He who is unjust, let him be unjust still; he who is filthy, let him be filthy still; he who is righteous, let him be righteous[a] still; he who is holy, let him be holy still."

JESUS TESTIFIES TO THE CHURCHES

[12]"And behold, I am coming quickly, and My reward *is* with Me, to give to every one according to his work. [13]I am the Alpha and the Omega, *the* Beginning and *the* End, the First and the Last."[a]

[14]Blessed *are* those who do His commandments,[a] that they may have the right to the tree of life, and may enter through the gates into the city. [15]But[a] outside *are* dogs and sorcerers and sexually immoral and murderers and idolaters, and whoever loves and practices a lie.

[16]"I, Jesus, have sent My angel to testify to you these things in the churches. I am the Root and the Offspring of David, the Bright and Morning Star."

[17]And the Spirit and the bride say, "Come!" And let him who hears say, "Come!" And let him who thirsts come. Whoever desires, let him take the water of life freely.

21:26 [a]M-Text adds *that they may enter in.* **21:27** [a]NU-Text and M-Text read *anything profane, nor one who causes.* **22:1** [a]NU-Text and M-Text omit *pure.* **22:6** [a]NU-Text and M-Text read *spirits of the prophets.* **22:8** [a]NU-Text and M-Text read *am the one who heard and saw.* **22:9** [a]NU-Text and M-Text omit *For.* **22:11** [a]NU-Text and M-Text read *do right.* **22:13** [a]NU-Text and M-Text read the *First and the Last, the Beginning and the End.* **22:14** [a]NU-Text reads *wash their robes.* **22:15** [a]NU-Text and M-Text omit *But.*

THROUGH THE GRID
How Our Bible Came to Us

A Warning

[18]For[a] I testify to everyone who hears the words of the prophecy of this book: If anyone adds to these things, God will add[b] to him the plagues that are written in this book; [19]and if anyone takes away from the words of the book of this prophecy, God shall take away[a] his part from the Book[b] of Life, from the holy city, and *from the* things which are written in this book.

I Am Coming Quickly

[20]He who testifies to these things says, "Surely I am coming quickly."

Amen. Even so, come, Lord Jesus!

[21]The grace of our Lord Jesus Christ *be* with you all.[a] Amen.

22:18 [a]NU-Text and M-Text omit *For.* [b]M-Text reads *may God add.*
22:19 [a]M-Text reads *may God take away.* [b]NU-Text and M-Text read *tree of life.*   22:21 [a]NU-Text reads *with all;* M-Text reads *with all the saints.*

THROUGH THE GRID

Thinking Christianly:
Ten Foundational Beliefs of a
Christian Worldview

Belief One: God (*Deut. 6:4–6*)

A Christian worldview begins with the belief in God. The nature, character, and essence of God are revealed to humanity through Scripture, God's special revelation to humankind. Christians believe that only one God exists and that the God of Christianity is the true God who exhibits the characteristics of being all-powerful, all-knowing, and all-present. The Christian God is not limited in power; rather, He is the Sovereign Controller over all of the happenings in the universe. Because God knows all, there is nothing that goes unnoticed by God. This is a foundational claim of Christianity since everything else in developing a Christian worldview revolves around this understanding of God. God has existed before all of time and creation from eternity past as an uncreated being. That is, God is self-existent and is not dependent upon any other being or entity. God's attributes include being righteous, holy, and redemptive. God is the very definition of righteousness, since in God there is no wrong or impurity. In God, we have the perfect example of purity and perfection. God is holy and set apart from the rest of creation. God is also eternal, in that for God there was no beginning, and there will be no end. God is infinite and eternal, and thus, supersedes all human understanding.

We can only know about God through revelation, and thankfully, God has revealed Himself to us through nature, through Scripture, and through Jesus Christ. God exists as a three-Persons-in-one being: Father, Son, and Holy Spirit. Although distinct Persons, they are one God; and they act together as one, which demonstrates the relational aspect of God. One of the key characteristics of the Christian God that sets Him apart from the gods of other religions is that God is personal and relational. These beliefs of God are foundational to the Christian worldview and also demonstrate the extensive power and majesty of the one true God. It is on this belief of God that the other characteristics and worldview principles rest.

THROUGH THE GRID

Thinking Christianly:
Ten Foundational Beliefs of a
Christian Worldview

Belief Two: Revelation (*2 Tim. 3:16, 17*)

God has graciously given to humanity the revelation of Himself. Without revelation, there would be no way of learning about or knowing God. God has chosen to reveal Himself primarily in three ways: through the Bible, through nature and the world around us, and through Jesus Christ. We as human beings can learn about God through His revelation to us.

The Bible contains much information about God, and it is a trustworthy source to learn about God because it is infallible and inerrant. That is, it cannot contain any errors or mistakes because it is God's Word to us. Since God is perfect and free from error, God's message to us reflects His character and is also infallible and inerrant. The Word of God is inspired by God, meaning that God breathed His message and His life into the Bible. Thus, the Bible is referred to as the living Word. It is literally God's Word to us.

Nature and the world around us also reveal much about our God. Looking around, it is not difficult to see how everything in nature is so intricately designed and has its own place. God reveals Himself through nature, as it reveals the glory, majesty, splendor, and goodness of God. God cherishes all of creation, and a casual survey of nature with its intricate details demonstrates that there must be a God who placed all of it there and who designed every little detail. Nature also testifies that God has a plan and purpose for our lives as well.

Jesus Christ is the clearest revelation of God, since Jesus was fully God and fully man, making Him the only 200 percent being ever to exist. Through Jesus, we can see the nature and character of God the Father. The Person of Jesus Christ shows us the love of God, as well as the mercy and grace of God. It is only through Christ that one can be saved, but this is due to the very mercy and forgiveness that God extends to us through Jesus Christ. The forms of revelation we have point us to God and encourage us to know more about the One who formed us and who had us in mind before the beginning of time.

THROUGH THE GRID

Belief Three: Creation (*Gen. 1; 2*)

Creation and the evidence we have in the world of nature and beauty are great witnesses to the creative power of God. God created the universe out of nothing. There was no preexisting matter, since God was all there was before the creation of time. God's creation demonstrates divine design, as every little detail of the cosmos is ordered before God. The power of God's Word revolves around creation. When God spoke something, it came into existence. The creation of the world displays the very glory of God, as we see His handiwork throughout all of creation.

Humanity was the crowning point of creation, as we are special beings made in the image of God. Just as we can witness the extreme intricacy of details in all of creation, God has designed us carefully with a plan, purpose, and meaning. Although all things were originally created good, the Fall and the entering of sin into the world corrupted nature. Brokenness and hurt ensued after the Fall, and nature fell equally victim to the consequences of human sin.

God will redeem all of creation at the end of time, ushering in a new heaven and a new earth, where creation will once again be perfect. Until then, God has not abandoned creation; rather, He remains intimately involved with what He has made. God did not just abandon the universe to run on its own: He knows, sees, and hears all of the cries, groans, and pains, as well as the joys, of His creation. The fact that God created the universe and humanity demonstrates the great power of our God, as well as the beginning point of human existence. Nothing can have its being outside of or apart from God, as God is the author of all life and of all that exists in the universe.

When we look into nature and the rest of creation, our response should be to give praise, honor, and glory to God for all of His wonderful and mighty works. We owe our very being and existence to God, and thankfully, it is not one that is futile or useless; rather, it is endowed with meaning and purpose.

THROUGH THE GRID

Belief Four: Human Beings (*Gen. 1:26–31*)

Humanity was created by God as the highlight of creation. We are set apart from everything else God created because we are created in God's very image and likeness. God's creation of human beings in His image shows the great potential with which God endows each member of humanity, as well as the responsibility we are to bear.

Human beings are to be God's representatives on earth, as we were created to have a protective dominion over the rest of creation, as well as to make sure that creation is taken care of. Since we bear God's image, we are all responsible for valuing the rest of humanity and preserving the rest of creation.

Although human beings were initially created good and perfect, humankind eventually fell into sin, damaging the relationship between humanity and God and between humanity and the world. Unlike other worldviews, the Christian worldview acknowledges that humanity is evil and sinful and in need of redemption. Other worldviews accentuate the positive elements of humanity, as should be done; but they do not mention the fundamental need human beings have of salvation from sin and from their fallen condition. Only through the Person of Jesus Christ is redemption made available to humanity, through the graciousness and mercy of Creator God. Human beings bring glory to God when we worship Him, when we treat others with Christian love, and when we take care of the world around us. Human beings are the only members of creation with whom God desires to have a personal relationship, since we are created as special and in God's image. However, our relationship with God has been damaged by sin, for all of humanity has sinned and fallen short of the perfect standard of our Creator. Our destiny as human beings is to find fulfillment in our Creator by acknowledging our sinfulness and accepting the grace of God through Christ. Only through Christ can we have true salvation and obtain the relationship with God we were all meant to have.

THROUGH THE GRID

Belief Five: Jesus Christ (*John 1:1–18*)

Jesus Christ is the eternal Son of God, who was born of the virgin Mary, lived a perfect life, and then suffered and died for the sins of humanity. Jesus was at the same time both fully God and fully human. This was the only way that God could provide humanity with a means of salvation—a perfect sacrifice had to be made to atone for the sins of humanity.

Christ was God's gift to humanity, in that we would not have a way to God without Christ. Christ makes the claim that He is the way, the truth, and the life. That is, the only way to God and to salvation is through Christ. He also is the truth of all existence since He is God. And Christ is the only way to finding a meaningful and fulfilled existence—He is life itself, as His resurrection from the dead demonstrates to humanity. It was only through the complete faithfulness and obedience of Christ that we are able to be redeemed, as it was Christ's horrible death on the cross that made redemption available to us.

Christ did indeed die, and He was indeed buried. The miraculous event that shatters all of time and history revolves around His resurrection from the dead on the third day. It is chiefly the resurrection of Christ that sets Christianity apart from other religions with great leaders. The founders of all the other major world religions are dead and buried; however, it is only Christ who has broken the barriers of death and has come back to life. After Christ's resurrection, He ascended to sit at the place of authority at God's throne.

One day Christ will return again at the end of time to gather His own to Himself. Assurance of eternal life lies only in Jesus Christ, who provided the miraculous gift of grace and redemption. When we acknowledge our sinfulness and accept Jesus as the Lord of our lives, He saves us from our sin and from eternity away from God. The goal of Christians is to live according to the very ways of Christ.

THROUGH THE GRID

Thinking Christianly:
Ten Foundational Beliefs of a
Christian Worldview

Belief Six: Salvation By Grace Alone Through Faith Alone in Christ Alone *(Eph. 2:1–10)*

Human beings exist as fallen and sinful creatures, as the Fall of humankind made us all sinners by nature. We sin by choice as well, and in doing so, we demonstrate that we are unable to achieve perfection—God's holy standard for salvation. All of our best efforts fail at being perfect, and since God requires perfection, we are unable to merit our own salvation. However, God saw humanity in its deepest moment of need and acted out of love by giving us what we do not deserve—a way out of our condition of fallenness. This demonstrates the great and bold grace of God, who did not have to provide for humanity, yet He did.

The only way that we can have redemption is through faith in God's Son, the Lord Jesus Christ. God sent Christ to earth to be the sacrifice for all of humanity's sin, so Christ obeyed by living a perfect life, as both fully God and fully man, and then obediently emptying Himself for the benefit of humanity with death on the cross. Jesus demonstrated that He was God's Son by obeying God perfectly, dying on the cross, and then being raised up from the dead on the third day. In this manner, Christ proved that He had conquered death and that He indeed was the true Son of God.

With these acts, God graciously made available to humanity the redemption that was so desperately needed. All humanity has to do to accept God's gracious and free offer of redemption from sin is to put one's faith completely in the Lord Jesus Christ. God's offer of salvation to us is thus by God's grace alone, through faith alone, in Jesus Christ alone. Many other offers of salvation or enlightenment are extended in today's world. But only God can bring true fulfillment, happiness, and redemption. Each day, believers must remain thankful for the audacious grace of God who dared to love humanity, even when humanity was unlovable.

THROUGH THE GRID

Belief Seven: The Family (*Eph. 5:21—6:4*)

The erosion of the institution of the family may be the greatest tragedy of the last century. No longer are traditional family structures in place, and no longer do families value being together. More and more, the trend of individualism has affected the family, such that parents now spend more time than ever pursuing jobs, wealth, and new possessions, taking them away from their home and the relationships that are to be nurtured within. Children also have less desire than ever to be at home, since the parents aren't home, which has contributed to a number of moral, ethical, and security problems in regard to the children.

The family today has become sort of an "anything goes" type of environment; and as the divorce rate continues to skyrocket, the family continues to fall apart. Many relationships are now often based on convenience. A quick look at pop culture demonstrates that the importance of marriage has become generally disregarded, with relationships only lasting a few years.

Homosexual unions are now becoming more and more accepted and will continue to be the single greatest moral issue the church will have to face. This has thrown God's plan of the family into disarray, as homes, families, relationships, and children are all deeply and hurtfully affected.

The family is God's gift to humanity; and as such, the family is to be structured as God desires. In the Bible, the order of the home is laid out; as husbands are to love their wives as Christ loves the church, wives are to submit in genuine relationship to their husbands; parents are to care for their children, and children are to honor and obey their parents.

The gift of sexuality God gave us was to be enjoyed within the context of marriage between a man and his wife. However, with adultery, marital infidelity, and homosexuality becoming commonplace, humanity has destroyed God's gift by using it whenever and however they please. Sex was designed for a couple to become closer to each other, for our human pleasure, and for the incredible gift of children.

THROUGH THE GRID

Thinking Christianly:
Ten Foundational Beliefs of a
Christian Worldview

Belief Eight: Government and Society (*Rom. 13:1–7*)

Governments exist in order to provide structure and support for the people whom they govern. In the United States, our process of government creates laws; and then it entrusts people to make sure those laws are followed and not broken. However, the desire for power and prestige make it increasingly difficult for those who enter politics to walk a moral and ethical pathway. Yet this is the risk with any democratic system. It is tempting to want to have control over the governance of a state, but to whom much is given, much is also required.

God created government for the good of humanity, as God saw that it would help to provide the needed protection, structure, and balance that is needed by a depraved and fallen humanity. However, as we can see with regimes and governments gone bad, once someone gets a taste of power, they often do not wish to relinquish that power, as totalitarian regimes have demonstrated.

Governments are not infallible because they are also marred by sin. Therefore, the ultimate authority they have is limited, and they are not able to control their states with perfection. Since God created the institutions of government, society, and nation, they are also in need of redemption. As Christians engage their culture, their government, and their world, they must aim to make God's will supreme in not only their own actions but also in the actions and behaviors of the state.

Christians are also in the unique position of having to be allegiant to both God and to one's country. However, if the government is wrong, then Christians must obey and follow God and what God says. As many social issues are being debated, Christians must take a stand for what God says is true, not the values or morals handed down by secular society and government. This issue will likely remain in the forefront as Christians seek to honor God by their political actions and choices.

THROUGH THE GRID

Belief Nine: Social Action (*Matt. 5:13–16*)

Christians must endeavor to live unselfishly in relation to the world by becoming Christian servants in the world today. The tendency has been to keep our faith a private affair—we restrict our definition of Christian activity to reading the Bible, praying, and attending church services. However, this largely misses the point of a Christian's relationship with God. The Bible instructs us to love God with all of our beings and to love our neighbor as we love ourselves. We must seek to redefine the concept of neighbor. No longer is it just the person who lives next door to you, but it is literally all of humanity, as we all share our finitude in flesh and blood, and we all share our creation in the image and likeness of God.

Social action must be enacted by Christians. The Book of James states that "pure and undefiled religion" consists of helping the widowed and the orphaned (1:27). We live in a world with so many needs. Hundreds of thousands die from starvation every year and some in the very cities we live in. Hundreds in each city remain homeless. Although the slogan "What Would Jesus Do?" has been popular in American culture, few have lived out its ethical implications. Certainly, we cannot provide for all the need in the world, but we must do our part to be the hands and feet of Jesus Christ, reaching out to the world in its moments of need. Most believers never think to actually provide for others though; and when we see people in need, the first reaction is to remove ourselves from an uncomfortable situation. It is important to remember that Jesus fellowshipped among the outcasts, the rejects, the physically sick and ill, and those who had been told that they were worthless to society. These were the people Jesus loved. Social action makes our participation in Jesus' mission possible; we can donate to good charities, engage in feeding the hungry, and actively work against homelessness and other social issues that plague our world. We must not be like the Pharisees, but we must instead be like Jesus, who extended open arms to all.

THROUGH THE GRID

Belief Ten: Judgment (*Matt. 25:31–46*)

God created time and history. It began with the creation of the world, and it will end with the Final Judgment in the last days. God has ordained the last days as a final point of separation between all that is perfect and all that is fallen. Because believers are redeemed, they are secure on the Day of Judgment—Christ's atoning sacrifice enables Christians to be at peace and at one with God. Certainly, this is due to no merit of Christian individuals; salvation comes only through the grace of God, by placing one's faith in Jesus Christ and giving to Him lordship over one's entire life.

This world is finite, fallen, and temporal. It will one day end. Believers must be prepared for the final judgment. Thus, every moment must be made to count. The salvation of others may be at stake; and we must make our best efforts to reach out to them in friendly, relational ways that glorify God at all times.

In the Final Judgment, those who have received the free gift of God's salvation will be separated from those who have not received God's gracious gift. There are no exemptions to whom God judges; all will be judged on that day, according first to whether they have accepted Christ, then according to how they have lived their lives. What will your legacy be on that final Day of Judgment? Those who do not believe that the Final Judgment is coming are entitled to their belief; however, it either will happen, or it will not happen. The coming judgment is in the end not the final motivation for preparing one's life and setting it apart for service to God. If we truly have turned our lives over to God, then God is the master and ruler of all we say and do. But more than that, we should come to love God with our entire beings. The motivation for living a Christian life is not to be saved from hell; it is to make every moment with the Lord count.

WHAT YOU WANT TO KNOW, BUT DON'T KNOW WHO TO ASK

1. How Do I Stop Being Angry?

Anger is a natural human emotion; it is the Creator's way of empowering us to ward off our perception of an attack or threat to our well-being. However, the Bible says, "Be angry, and do not sin" (Ps. 4:4). Notice the directive to "be angry." There is good anger, which causes us to set things right and to declare truth. Bad anger is reactive and gives birth to more anger. Work actively at processing your anger so it no longer controls you.

A—Acknowledge that you are angry. This important first step is an honest look at why you are angry and who you are angry at.

N—Note who and what the anger is about.
You are angry at your mom, dad, sister, brother, etc., for doing or saying _____.
You are angry at your friends for leaving you out or letting you down.
You are angry at parents for fighting about family issues.
You are angry because you failed in a certain area of your life.

G—Get to the deeper emotions.
I think I am feeling _____ (hurt, disappointment, embarrassment, rejection, loneliness, insecurity, anxiety) as well as feeling angry.

E—Express your feelings to a parent, counselor, or friend.
I really wish that my brother/sister, mother/father had not done _____; it really hurt.
I am sad that my friends let me down/hurt my feelings.
I am upset that our family is fractured. I feel afraid/abandoned/lonely/angry.

R—Respond wisely, and pray it through.
Dear God, thank You for beginning to heal the painful emotions in my heart. I admit that I am angry about _____. I am choosing to forgive _____ today because You have forgiven me. I choose to let go of my anger, and I pray that You would continue to heal me, in Jesus' name.

2. Are Satan and Demons Real?

YES! Satan was cast out of heaven for desiring to be mightier than God, and his angelic followers were cast out with him (Ezek. 28:12–19; Rev. 12:4). His name was "Lucifer, son of the morning" (Is. 14:12–15). He is:

- "the accuser of our brethren" (Rev. 12:10);
- a "murderer" and "liar" (John 8:44);
- "your adversary" (1 Pet. 5:8);
- "the lawless one" (2 Thess. 2:9).

Paul wants believers to know that our battle is against "spiritual hosts of wickedness" and not with flesh and blood (Eph. 6:12). These are spiteful, wicked demons whose intellect exceeds that of any human.

Satan cannot directly overtake a believer physically (a Christian cannot be possessed), but he can definitely influence our thoughts. If we open the door to him, he will gladly whisper into the "ear" of the mind suggesting things. All along he makes it seem as if the thoughts are our own. We cannot explain how such communication takes place any more than we can explain how the physical synapses of the brain fire information, but such mind-to-mind communication does take place.

The devil tempted Judas to betray his Master (Luke 22:3–6; John 13:2), seduced Ananias and Sapphira to lie to Peter (Acts 5:1–11), and incited David to take a census (1 Chr. 21:1–7). Paul clarified any doubts when he instructed: "take up the whole armor of God, that you may be able to withstand in the evil day" (Eph. 6:13).

Without the spiritual armor listed by Paul in Ephesians 6, we are pawns in the devil's game. However, with it, we have been assured of complete victory in our spiritual lives. Believers need not fear him, but they must be careful not to "give place to the devil" (Eph. 4:27). Though it may appear that Satan and his demons have great influence in the world, we know the outcome: "The devil, who deceived them, was cast into the lake of fire and brimstone where the beast and the false prophet are. And they will be tormented day and night forever and ever" (Rev. 20:10).

3. Are There Any Exceptions to Allow for an Abortion?

Abortion focuses on the right of the *mother*, not the *child*. A staggering 93 percent of abortions are performed as a means of birth control. Only 7 percent of women cited so-called "hard cases" (e.g., rape, incest, or some health concern with either the baby or the mother) as the primary reason they were seeking an abortion. ("Abortion in the United States: Statistics," National Right to Life. http://www.nrlc.org/abortion/facts/abortionstats2.html; accessed 21 July 2005).

The taking of human life can only be defended when it is the only way to protect another human life—namely, in the case that a mother will die if her pregnancy continues. This is an extremely rare circumstance in a medically advanced country like the United States.

4. Can a Person Stop Being "Gay"?

Popular culture may say no, but Scripture and the authentic stories of countless thousands of former homosexuals tell us otherwise. Remind those who debate you: "With God nothing will be impossible" (Luke 1:37).

God *can* change a person's heart toward sin, but it is not up to us to dictate *how* or *when* a person gives up a homosexual lifestyle. The Holy Spirit is powerful; and while salvation is received in a moment of surrender and prayer, the healing journey to wholeness takes time because the emotional issues attached to it must be addressed and processed in God's strength. As Christians, we are to pray for and care for others with the same patience and love that God exhibits on our behalf. It is our privilege to walk patiently alongside those on the journey to wholeness with prayer and encouragement.

One thing we can do is offer the hope found in the words of the apostle Paul. He anticipated and answered the question of whether a person can find freedom from homosexual behavior in his letter to the Corinthians: "*Such were some of you.* But you were washed, but you were sanctified, but you were justified in the name of the Lord Jesus and by the Spirit of our God" (1 Cor. 6:11).

There were Christians in Corinth who had been transformed and delivered from sexual perversion by accepting Jesus Christ as their Lord and Savior. Salvation changed homosexual behavior two thousand years ago, and it has that power still. *God's love is strong, His Word is true, and His Spirit is life transforming.*

For more great testimonies of people who have experienced freedom from the homosexual lifestyle, go to www.exodus.to.

5. Can Christians Be Possessed or Inhabited by Demons?

Demons cannot possess believers unless the demon first binds the *strong man* who occupies the believer—namely, Christ Himself—and no demon is powerful enough to bind Jesus. If our house (body/soul) is Christ's home, then the devil finds no place to dwell in us. Jesus explains that those who are not occupied by the Holy Spirit are subject to the possibility of being inhabited by demons (Matt. 12:43–45).

The teaching of Scripture is that Christians cannot be controlled against their wills through demonic inhabitation. The principle is foolproof. If you are a Christ-follower, the King Himself dwells in you (John 14:23). Rest assured with this statement: "You are of God, little children, and have overcome them, because He who is in you is greater than he who is in the world" (1 John 4:4). To deny the truth of these scriptures because of someone's alleged experiences or stories is to greatly overestimate the power and realm of Satan.

6. Can the Devil Make Me Sin?

Satan can work to tempt you, but he cannot force you to act upon that temptation. Do not give Satan glory that he does not deserve. The Bible says, "Each one is tempted when he is drawn away by his own desires and enticed. Then, when desire has conceived, it gives birth to sin" (James 1:14, 15).

Jesus spoke of *temptation* and not *demonization* as the means by which Satan entices us. He specifically taught the disciples to pray for victory (Matt. 6:13). Jesus taught that the heart of man, not demon possession, is responsible for evil acts (Matt. 15:19).

It is not the rule of Satan that a believer need be concerned with; it is the rule of one's own heart that must receive our full attention. No Christian can be indwelled by Satan, but we are forewarned to "be sober, be vigilant" (1 Pet. 5:8). Satan is like a roaring lion, but the length of his leash is determined by the believer's trust in the Lord to keep him or her from temptation.

Satan wants nothing more than to destroy your testimony and to disrupt your fellowship with God. He cannot have you, but he will do whatever he can to keep you from bringing others to Christ. Paul urges us to "put on the whole armor of God" (Eph. 6:11). To understand spiritual warfare and to overcome temptation, the Christian must focus on the power of God rather than on the schemes of the devil.

7. What's Morally Wrong with Human Cloning?

Scientists now understand the basic building blocks of life at the earliest stages of human development and at certain levels have the power to create and manipulate human fetal development. The eventual result of this work may be the cloning of human life, a process of reproducing a human offspring with genetic material from only one adult, rather than half the material from each parent. A clone is made by emptying all of the genetic material from a mother's egg and then inserting material from an adult's cell into the egg. Then an electric spark is applied that stimulates the egg to begin the division process. After a period of four to five days of cell division and growth, the cloned egg-embryo can be implanted in the uterus of a prospective mother-to-be, where it will continue to grow and develop in utero until birth (*reproductive cloning*); or used for research and destroyed (*therapeutic cloning*).

When a woman's egg is fertilized by a man's sperm, it is called *conception,* and the resulting child will have attributes and genetic material from both mother and father. In the *cloning* process, the newborn clone baby will be the virtual genetic identical twin of the adult cell donor only.

Reproductive cloning is an ethical nightmare and an extremely dangerous process, with most clones (nonhuman) dying or being destroyed before maturation because of horrendous and often fatal developmental abnormalities. This raises the ugly possibility that horrifically deformed clone babies with agonizingly painful and debilitating birth defects may someday soon be created in cloning clinics. Adult cell donors may claim the clones are their property rather than their children. They may keep them as a source for spare parts, such as replacement kidneys or other vital organs because there would be no risk of organ rejection since the "donor" would genetically be the same as the one receiving the transplant. It can lead to the further exploitation of women, as their eggs become a commodity in the marketplace.

Therapeutic cloning sounds beneficial, but it is immoral because the embryo is created to be killed. Harvesting of embryonic stem cells for research likewise carries the same potential to become a vast business of cloning to kill for profit. It involves women selling their eggs to use in the mass production of human clone embryos, which are dismembered for research purposes.

No matter how much science advances, it will never be able to: *create out of nothing as God did* (Gen. 2:7); *create out of love* (1 John 4:19); *be intimately involved with the life of a child* (Ps. 139:15, 16).

Christ-followers must never follow the slippery slope of "reason alone," but measure every choice by the unchanging Word of God. Human cloning has no moral foundation in Scripture.

8. Could I Be the Cause of My Parents' Divorce?

The feeling of guilt you experience after a divorce in your family is normal. A parent's leaving should not be interpreted as happening because of something you did or a lack of love for you, but rather as an indication of difficulty in coping with things as they are in the home. He or she believes that leaving is necessary, but that does not mean it is right. People's attitudes toward each other change; and in their frustration and anger, it may unintentionally pass to you, or they may say hurtful things.

Consider the heartache your parents are experiencing, and commit to pray for them on a daily basis by asking God to meet the needs of their lives. Perhaps one of the greatest ways to encourage your parents' relationship is to live in harmony with them. Be respectful and caring; live a Spirit-filled life so that your life will have a positive effect. Be responsible in your spending and choices.

If remarriage has occurred, then the possibility of reconciliation is in the past. Live in the future, and give the step-parent relationship time to develop. In a single-parent home, give all the support and encouragement you can to this parent, knowing they are probably lonely, carrying a great load of financial stress, and sacrificing self to ensure that the family is cared for. Decide to live without complaining, arguing (Phil. 2:14), and the things you don't really *need*.

During this difficult time, draw close to God, and He will draw close to you (James 4:8). Ask God to help you love and understand, and especially to forgive. There are many causes for divorce, but fully understand that you are not one of them. Strengthen relationships with other relatives to feel the security of family. Establish a prayer-partner relationship for support, and talk openly with a Christian who can counsel you. You can find peace in God's great love for you during this time of turmoil (Rom. 8:38, 39).

9. Do We Obey God's Laws or Man's Laws When They Conflict?

As citizens of heaven through faith in Christ, our ultimate allegiance is to Jesus and His kingdom. This can feel confusing in the light of conflicting government or cultural agendas. This conflict was also evident in Jesus' day, and the leaders asked Him what to do. He gave them a simple answer: "Render therefore to Caesar the things that are Caesar's, and to God the things that are God's" (Luke 20:25). As Christians, even though our ultimate loyalty is to our heavenly Father, we live on the earth and have to obey the laws of our nation. Our testimony for Christ includes being good citizens by following the divinely given responsibilities and duties of earthly government "for conscience' sake" (Rom. 13:5). God has ordained government to punish and restrict evildoers and to reward and protect moral behavior.

The question: *Where do I draw the line between God's law and the government's law?*

The answer: *Render . . . honor to whom honor is due.* Christians are commanded to support the civil state unless and until government requires Christians to support or do evil in direct contradiction to their ultimate allegiance to their heavenly Father. Right now, the United States' laws *allow* us to do things that are in direct contradiction to God's Word, but *do not require* us to do so. Do you understand the difference?

If the government were to require Christians to do that which their conscience tells them is evil, then Christians have a responsibility to conscientiously object, to nonviolently refuse to comply, and to agree to suffer the legal consequences of disobedience.

Christian leaders are to be involved in both government and nongovernment efforts to right wrongs and alleviate suffering. People of faith brought their faith convictions to bear on the public policy issues of the day, and thereby brought about the nineteenth-century abolition of slavery and Civil Rights Revolution in the twentieth century. We should be informed about the issues confronting our society and vote in elections; obey the law; fulfill our civil obligations; pay our taxes; and pray for those in authority (1 Tim. 2:1, 2).

10. Is Genetic Engineering Really Possible?

As a result of the federally funded project known as the Human Genome Project (HGP), we have now mapped the sequence of the three billion base pairs of DNA that together complete the human genetic blueprint, known as a "genome." Scientists know which genes control hair and eye color, skin pigmentation, height, allergies, intelligence, and athletic aptitude. The medical community is optimistic that developments in this area will lead to the eventual successful treatment of conditions such as Alzheimer's, cancer, cystic fibrosis, diabetes, Down syndrome in utero, muscular dystrophy, and other diseases.

At first glance, these advancements seem positive; but we must never allow science to disregard the sanctity of the human embryo. Our ability to identify and diagnose ailments continues to exceed our ability to treat them. With genetic mapping, expectant parents may be advised to terminate their pregnancy (abortion) and "try again" if a potential birth defect is discovered. It appears the practice of genetic engineering will lead some to "play God." The Christ-follower must always choose *truth over logic* (Rom. 1:25) and effectively lead others to do so in spite of popular culture and reasoning.

11. How Do You Know God's Will?

To read clear biblical principles for daily walking in the will of God and being led to a specific decision, see Ephesians 3:

- Live by eternal purpose, not in the temporary (v. 11).
- Substitute self-confidence for God-confidence (v. 12).
- Bow your knee before God; this honors Him and will give birth to humility, inner strength, and dedication to God's will (v. 14).
- Strengthen yourself through His Spirit during private devotional times (v. 16).
- Live by faith and not by reason (v. 17).
- Check your motives and your foundation often. Both should be to love as Christ loved (v. 17).
- Focus on the power of Christ and its availability to you. Think about it often, and thank Him for it (vv. 19, 20).

His power and the answer will be there when you need them.

12. How Can I Pray with Power?

Approach in Surrender—The powerful and effective prayer of faith must be approached with complete surrender to the authority and will of God.

Anchored in Scripture—Anchoring prayer to Scripture keeps us from floating into selfishness, pride, arrogance and control. The will of God and the Word of God never contradict each other. Praying Scripture allows our faith to be guided by absolute truth.

Ask Specifically—The focus of prayer is not the miraculous, but the dispelling of darkness by the revealing of the light of God. Our needs take on new meaning when they are considered in the bigger picture of releasing light into the darkness of every situation and allowing the glory of God to be seen.

Anticipate the Solution—Answered prayer may not be immediately recognized, and effective prayer does not take place in an instant. Jesus speaks with certainty that the prayer will be answered without giving specifics as to when or how. Begin by asking in faith; but continue to believe whether you see the answer or not; whether the answer is as you expected or not.

Aggressively Stand—Prayer was the foundation of Jesus' aggressive stand against the darkness. As we pray specifically, the "Light of the World" dispels the darkness. If you pray in the will and Word of God, you will be strengthened to keep believing.

Jesus prayed that diseases would be healed and that the dead would be raised, and they were. The focus of His prayer was that the glory of God would be seen (John 9). In the process, the influence of the enemy would be destroyed in the lives of people (Matt. 21:21, 22). That is our ultimate goal.

13. If Wine Is in the Bible, Why Is It Wrong to Drink?

The media portrays drinking alcohol as an instant party and as many students' favorite pastime. These snapshots are not good representatives of the statistics of the day, and they don't reflect the words of Scripture. Before we can look at biblical principle, we have to note that modern alcoholic beverages are higher in alcoholic content than those used in the ancient world. The wine of the Bible was a grape juice-like syrup mixed at a ratio of two parts wine to three parts water and had little alcoholic content, depending on whether or not it was fresh. The wine of ancient times had beneficial uses as an *antiseptic* and as *medicine*: The Good Samaritan (Luke 10:34) poured oil and *wine* on the man's wounds; Paul advised young Timothy to "use a little wine for your stomach's sake and your frequent infirmities" (1 Tim. 5:23).

Christ's first miracle was turning the water into wine, but it does not fit that Jesus would use His first miracle to cause drunkenness. Jesus spoke of the "fruit of the vine" at the Last Supper (Luke 22:18), but this cup was unfermented just as the bread was unleavened. He refused wine as a painkiller on the cross (Mark 15:23) because He was determined to die as an act of His conscious will.

Ancient secular sources report that intoxication was a great social disgrace. Drunkenness is presented as sin throughout the Old and New Testaments (Gen. 9:20, 21; 19:34, 35; Rom. 13:13; 1 Cor. 6:9, 10; Gal. 5:19–21; 1 Pet. 4:3).

Proverbs 23:29–35 paints a vivid picture, which directly contradicts the picture the media paints: "Who has woe, who has sorrow, who has contentions? Those who linger long at the wine, . . . it bites like a serpent" (vv. 29, 30, 32). The drinker's senses are out of his control (vv. 34, 35). The big push in media is to "drink responsibly." That is an oxymoron if ever there was one. Statistics show that alcohol is a leading cause of divorce, rape, murder, assault, incest, abuse, and deadly auto accidents.

Most students will say, "I don't get drunk; I just drink socially." Any intelligent decision about "social drinking" by a Christ-follower must be preceded by studying the law of love. Paul urged us not to live just for ourselves, but to strengthen others (Rom. 15:1; 1 Cor. 8:9; 10:23, 24).

The "strong" Christian will have little difficulty in making the choice: to live in love, to be filled with the Spirit (Eph. 5:18), and to present the body as a living sacrifice

(Rom. 12:1, 2). If you already have a problem with alcohol, seek counsel. Jesus is the Savior who delivers us from our sin habits.

14. Is Homosexuality Really Wrong?

The Christ-follower never looks to the culture for answers to moral or spiritual questions, but he or she chooses the Word of God as the only and final authority. In the case of homosexuality, both the Old and New Testaments speak clearly and unequivocally that homosexual *behavior* is sinful and contrary to God's plan for human beings, just as any sexual behavior outside of a God-ordained, biblical marriage is contrary to God's plans and desires.

- God judged the wicked cities of Sodom and Gomorrah because of sexual perversions (Gen. 19:1–11).
- "You shall not lie with a male as with a woman. It is an *abomination*" (Lev. 18:22; 20:13). *Abomination* is the Hebrew *tow`ebah*, meaning "a disgusting thing."
- "God gave them up to *vile* passions" (Rom. 1:26, 27). *Vile* is the Greek word *ajtimiva,* meaning "dishonor, disgrace."
- "Do you not know that the unrighteous will not inherit the kingdom of God? Do not be deceived. Neither fornicators, nor idolaters, nor adulterers, nor homosexuals, nor sodomites" (1 Cor. 6:9).
- Paul says that for men to have sex with men and women to have sex with women is unnatural, or "against nature," and "shameful" (Rom. 1:21–32).

Often you will hear people distort Scripture in an attempt to justify "gay" behavior. They may say that the apostle Paul's instruction to the Corinthians is a reference to temple prostitution and not to individuals in the homosexual lifestyle. They claim that a loving, monogamous gay relationship is not condemned in Scripture. Not true. Writing to the Christians in Corinth, a first-century city noted for widespread homosexual behavior, Paul declares that among the "unrighteous" are the "effeminate" and the "abusers of themselves with mankind."

- *Effeminate* (*malakos*) refers to the "passive partner in a homosexual relationship."
- *Abusers of themselves* (*arsenokoitai*) refers to the "active member" in such a relationship.

Paul attacks this modern-day argument with a detailed description of homosexual conduct.

Many homosexual rights groups have attempted to distort or discount these Scriptures, but the Bible speaks clearly about the subject. God's Word condemns homosexual and lesbian behavior and is not in need of interpretation concerning it. No matter what you may or may not feel, it's ridiculous to say that your feelings are more important than God's Word.

15. Is Mercy Killing Fair, or Is It Death on Demand?

Euthanasia and assisted-suicide advocates continue to push their agenda throughout the world to make death-on-demand acceptable and legal. Those of us who believe in God's supreme control and creative design of all people are horrified when we hear about killing the elderly instead of waiting for God's timing of natural death or when we hear of the disposing of babies who don't "measure up."

Our convenience-driven culture has created a specific language of "mercy killing," which is supposed to act in defense of the poor victims who should have "the right to die" and "death with dignity." *Euthanasia* could easily be translated *disposable;* it focuses on the convenience of society, not the rights of the elderly or handicapped. Contrast this to the deep, intense, unconditional love of God. He loves every life without regard to circumstance, need, ability, or handicap; and He sees potential in every new life.

Whenever euthanasia issues are discussed, a critical distinction must be made between *active measures* that are taken to shorten life as opposed to *not taking extraordinary or heroic measures* to prolong life when death is imminent.

- Active measures to shorten life would be lethal injection, lethal medical overdose, or other more violent means of actively killing another human being.
- Not taking extraordinary measures to prolong the life of a terminally ill individual is a decision made by the patient or the family in consultation with their physician. They understand that death is imminent and they wish for no more extraordinary measures to be taken to prolong life. Giving comatose patients food and water through a feeding tube is not an "extraordinary measure."

People, who are infirm, mentally challenged, or physically handicapped, are created by God in His own image. They are equally valuable to Him, and thus, they must be to us (Ex. 4:11; Lev. 19:14). *The idea that an individual has a "right to die" is totally at odds with the Christian belief that we are under God's authority* (1 Cor. 6:19, 20). God is the giver and sustainer of life. Human beings must not seek to usurp God's authority over life and death.

16. Is Suicide a Sin?

God's description of His creation was "very good" (Gen. 1:31). Jesus came that you might have a life of abundance (John 10:10). Suicide is the rejection of the joy and goodness that God created. Eternal life is based on our personal relationship with God, not on the manner in which we die. If you have a friend or loved one who has committed suicide, do not let that last irrational act be the one on which you dwell. The wonderful memories should not be forgotten. Some people are not able to cope with the pressures of life; and we need to respond in love, rather than with condemnation.

There are many reasons why students consider suicide:

- Problems—hopelessness prevails because of family conflict, relationship problems, loneliness, failure, etc.
- To "get even"—the offended may use suicide as revenge, hoping to leave the survivors with guilt.
- To gain attention—hoping for a failed attempt at suicide so that people lavish attention on them afterward.
- To join deceased loved ones—particularly in the case of a parent or other close relative or relationship who died.
- To avoid consequences—the inability to make good choices, stop using drugs, facing punishment by law, or an illegitimate pregnancy.
- To pledge love—in the case of a broken relationship, it is a statement of "I can't live without you."

Suicide is the murder of oneself, but God does forgive the sin. Most who attempt suicide do not really want to die; they want direction. If you are or a friend is having thoughts of suicide, seek the counsel of parents, pastor, youth worker, or counselor. We all face pressure, and you should not be afraid or ashamed to seek help. Jesus told Paul in a time of great distress, "My grace is sufficient for you, for My strength is made perfect in weakness" (2 Cor. 12:9). That same promise is yours; He will walk with you in any difficulty, darkness, or distress.

17. Is Temptation the Same as Sin?

It is not uncommon to experience sexual temptation because all of us have a sin nature (Rom. 3:23). You can be tempted to think lustful thoughts, but you choose whether or not you will dwell on them and, ultimately, act on them. God does not condemn you for impure sexual urges, attractions, or temptations—whether homosexual or heterosexual. These come from our sinful nature just like the temptation to tell a lie, hide a fault to avoid punishment, or give in to selfish desires. Add to this the culture's attempt at normalizing sexual perversion and experimentation, and you will find your mind naturally affected by it all (1 Cor. 10:31).

The Bible clearly denounces immoral heterosexual and homosexual *conduct*. Lustful thoughts, both heterosexual and homosexual, become sinful behavior when you allow them to remain in your thought processes and continue to *consider* them. Jesus said, "But I say to you that whoever looks at a woman to lust for her has already committed adultery with her in his heart" (Matt. 5:27, 28).

It has been said that you cannot stop a bird from landing on your head, but you can surely keep it from building a nest there! Fleeting, unwelcome thoughts that you quickly and prayerfully dismiss are not the same as lustful thoughts that you keep in your mind and develop in your heart. Sexual attraction is normal, and the influence of these attractions is a powerful force; but every believer has been given power over the sinful nature so that the constant suggestion and information need not degenerate into impure, sinful behavior. A repeated *choice* becomes a *habit*; and a repeated *habit* becomes a *lifestyle*, whether positive or negative, righteous or unrighteous.

18. Is the Theory of Evolution Based on Fact?

There are fundamentally only two explanations for the existence of humankind and their environs: either all was supernaturally created (Gen. 1; 2), or it is the accidental, evolutionary product of a mechanistic and impersonal universe.

Being made in the image of God (Gen. 1:26) is a spiritual endowment that gave man the power of choice with moral, emotional, and spiritual capabilities. Adam had special self-awareness, which allowed him to think, dream, reflect, and react in a unique way because he was made in the image and likeness of God.

FACTS:
- Humans are distinct from beasts. In blood, in bone, in flesh, in cells, in mind, in soul, in spirit, humans are unique.
- Only humans have a thumb, which enables them to handle tools and instruments.
- Humans walk erect. No anthropoid does so.
- Humans have a mentality superior to that of animals (Gen. 1:28).
- Every need of the human body can be met in creation (Gen 1:29).
- If we were one degree closer to the sun, the planet would burn; one degree further and it would freeze (Is. 40:22).
- The human body is able to heal itself and contains life in its blood (Lev. 17:13, 14).

THEORY:
- Darwin taught that a speck (cell) of protoplasm somehow came into being and that human beings evolved through innumerable transitional forms, although there are no fossil remains of transitional forms or "links" between species of animal life.
- Some scientists believe that poisonous gases were "possibly" hit by lightning, or an explosion "possibly" formed our oceans; then an amino acid resulted that evolved into a tiny cell that was invisible to the naked eye. From that single cell, millions of years later, the plant and animal world evolved.

That theory takes much more faith than to believe that creation is God-breathed from nothing. To believe the theory of evolution is similar to believing that an explosion of a print shop resulted in *Webster's Dictionary*! God asks these scientific theorists: "Where were you when I laid the foundations of the earth?" (Job 38:4).

19. Is There a Specific Way to Pray?

Prayer is the privilege of the Christ-follower. Sincerity and faith are the requirements, and it can be helpful to use a guideline like this one: A—C—T—S

A doration—God is worthy of our praise. Begin each day with worship of His character (Ps. 138).

C onfession—Though Christ has completely forgiven every sin in both our past and future by His death on the cross, we still must ask His forgiveness in order to keep our relationship growing in love. Confession is to agree with God about a particular sin and to ask God to help you feel as much hatred for sin as He does. Then and only then can you forsake the sin that holds you (Ps. 51).

T hanksgiving—This is the part of your prayer time in which you can thank God for His blessings, for the answers to prayer you have received, and for all that is in your future by His hand. A grateful heart is one that is blessed again and again (Ps. 103).

S upplication—Supplication is the act of requesting. You will ask for physical and material needs; but above all, there is need for spiritual power. There must also be prayer for the unbeliever and the wayward Christ-follower. Pray for, and claim by name, the spiritual transformation of those you are concerned about (Ps. 5).

20. Is There Any Sin That Can't Be Forgiven?

There is only one sin that Jesus says will *not be forgiven;* that is, the blasphemy against the Holy Spirit (Matt. 12:31, 32). It refers to the sin of defiant hostility toward God—decisively and finally rejecting the testimony of the Holy Spirit regarding the Person and work of Jesus Christ.

Our speech is the expression of what is in our hearts. Rather than admitting Christ's miracles were wrought by divine power, the Pharisees ascribed them to power from Satan (Mark 3:30). They denied the testimony of the Holy Spirit concerning Jesus. Jesus responded that all the sins of people can be forgiven, with this one fearful exception. This severe warning was addressed to highly regarded religious leaders, proving that no one is exempt from this sin of free will. Any who witness evidence of the Lord's power and deny finally that it is from the One True God exhibit a condition of the heart beyond divine illumination; they are, therefore, hopeless.

If you or someone you know is fearful that the unpardonable sin has already been committed, keep this in mind: As long as the Spirit still convicts a person's heart, he or she can still be forgiven. The unpardonable sin is *final* rejection of the truth concerning Jesus Christ. It is within the power of every person to accept Him or to deny Him once and for all. Have you rejected Christ in your own life? Then you must, without delay, accept the truth about Christ, humble yourself, turn from your sin, and personally receive Christ as your Lord and Savior.

21. Is There a Biblical "Just War"?

Just War theory was never intended to justify war, per se. Instead the theory seeks to bring war under the rules of justice as understood by Christians; and seeks to ensure that war, if and when it does occur, has limits and boundaries that at least limit its barbarity. There is a commonly accepted list of seven criteria for a "just war posited by Just War theory" based on biblical principles.

Just cause: Armed conflict is only permissible when necessary to resist and repel aggression and to defend those victimized by it. This does not mean that a country must wait to be attacked. In the modern world of technology, if a country has compelling evidence that an enemy is preparing to attack (marshalling its forces, positioning its planes and ships to attack), that government need not necessarily wait for an enemy attack before defending itself by the use of force.

Just intent: The only acceptable motive for armed conflict must be to secure justice for all involved. Conquest, subjugation, revenge, or economic benefits are unacceptable, insufficient, and illegitimate motives for going to war. The commandment "You shall not murder" (Ex. 20:13) remains God's law. However, there is a vast difference between murder and defending your family, your country, and your freedom.

Last resort: Resort to armed force can only be morally acceptable when all other reasonable avenues of resolving the conflict in question have been rejected or have failed.

Legitimate authority: Only the civil magistrate has the authority to use lethal force (Rom. 13:2–4). For Americans, the duly constituted authority is the government of the United States. However reassuring or helpful a United Nation's Security Council or General Assembly vote may be, the only way in which the American government authorizes military action is by a declaration of war or a joint resolution of U.S. Congress.

Limited goals: If the purpose of the resort to armed conflict is to resist aggression, to defend the innocent, to restore peace and to secure justice, then total annihilation of the enemy is never acceptable. Also, unless one's survival or freedom is in danger, Just War theory decrees that warfare is unacceptable unless the stated goals for the war have a reasonable chance of being achieved (Prov. 24:11).

Proportionality: Does the good gained by armed conflict justify the cost of injuries and loss of lives? Will the human cost of the armed conflict to both sides be proportionate to the stated objectives and goals? At what point is the good gained by warfare outweighed by the human costs expended in achieving it?

Noncombatant immunity: A war can only be just if it disqualifies noncombatants as legitimate military targets and seeks to minimize inadvertent civilian casualties. Making war on civilians is never justified.

Most Christians have agreed over the centuries that we have an obligation to defend people who are being victimized, and to participate in a government's defense of those victims, through war, if the war meets Just War's causes, intents, goals, and restrictions.

22. What about the "Morning-After Pill"?

One of the greatest dangers of the morning-after pill may be the temptation for women to keep taking it without regard to the number of babies who are killed because it seems to have no physical consequence. The morning-after pill works by blocking the implantation of a tiny embryo in the uterine wall after conception. In such a case, an abortion occurs because a life has been conceived but medically prevented from continued development. Many women reason that if the pregnancy is never medically pronounced, then it never existed, but this is self-deception. Pretending and denying do not make it so. If you have to terminate a pregnancy to prevent the baby from growing, then it was real and the baby was aborted. Scripture passages plainly reveal that from the moment of conception, God is fashioning a new and wonderfully unique individual.

23. What Is the Christ-Follower's "Philosophy of Life"?

All human beings face the tri-dilemma of life: *Who am I? Why am I here? Where am I headed?* The answers are often labeled as one's *philosophy of life*. For the Christ-follower, it is called a *biblical worldview.*

Our worldview is the perspective through which we look at people, cultural issues, and our responsibilities; it affects how we process decisions and what we believe about important issues. It is the baseline we use for interpreting our reality and establishing priorities.

In an effort to resolve these probing, universal questions, our culture bombards us with various views, opinions, and belief systems that sometimes seem to answer these questions. But all too often, these multiple views and philosophies collide with the truths plainly taught throughout the pages of the Bible. As followers of Jesus Christ, it is our privilege and our responsibility to *know what we believe and why* (2 Tim. 1:12; 1 Pet. 3:15).

24. What's Wrong with One Look at Pornography?—It's Legal!

Pornography is widely available. Whether you look for it or not, pornography, which indicates human depravity, is now easily and privately accessible online with 12 percent of all Web sites offering pornographic content. Studies indicate that 90 percent of 8- to 16-year-olds with Internet access have viewed porn online. The average age of first exposure to Internet pornography is 11 years old, with the largest consumers of Internet pornography being 35- to 49-year-olds.

God created sex to be holy, not dirty; it's to be private and intimate, not flaunted and publicly discussed (Gen. 2:18, 24, 25; Matt. 19:5, 6). Pornography perverts and distorts all of the God-given purposes for sexual intimacy. Instead, it feeds the lust of the flesh and the lust of the eyes (1 John 2:16) as it encourages self-gratification.

Pornography is able to be destructive because *sex is powerful,* both to bless as defined by God and to destroy as distorted by pornography. Even though TV sitcoms and dramas may suggest the use of pornography is a "normal pastime," it has been well documented to be *addictive,* and, therefore, destructively influential on one's lifestyle and thought process. Some who have become addicted adopt deviant and violent sexual lifestyles as they act upon their pornography-fed fantasies.

The most serious offense of the person who watches pornography is to give up the role of gatekeeper in your own life and allow this spiritual and emotional toxic waste to poison a life that God intended to be incredible and joyful. Don't contaminate your heart and soul with this filth; walk away from it, and make the choice to not look back. If you think you might be addicted or that you have crossed the line in your heart or actions, seek counseling immediately, knowing that *the truth will set you free* (John 8:32). God's plan for you is to be filled with His Spirit, His love (Eph. 3:17–19). Christians know that the *full love of Christ* cannot coexist with pornography and that just being "legal" doesn't make pornography moral.

25. What Can I Do for My Pregnant Friend or One Who Has Already Had an Abortion?

Twenty-two times the Scripture speaks of God's *truth* and *mercy* in the same verse. When we stand on truth, we must not neglect to show the mercy of God. Christ died for your friend's sin, and He is willing to forgive and restore.

L isten—we speak the loudest by listening (Eccl. 3:7). Listen intently. Encourage her to go to her parents first, then to a youth pastor or counselor.

I nvest—love in her life and the baby's life (Prov. 3:3). Go with her to a pregnancy center for the support she needs, and take the time to pray with her and visit her in this time of need.

F ocus—on her problem with patience (Prov. 14:29). Show your genuine love and compassion by not judging and by supporting her emotionally, as you are able. Stop all gossipers when you are around by reminding them not to "throw stones."

E nsure—that she knows the Lord (Matt. 11:28, 29). Do not condone the sin, but do let her know of the mercy and forgiveness of Christ. Be sure she understands salvation and give her the opportunity to know Jesus as her Savior and Lord. Bring her Scriptures reflecting God's love and forgiveness in writing so that she can look at them again and again, and also bring her books to read that will be spiritually helpful to her in her situation.

26. What Is Meant by "Separation of Church and State"?

The principle of the separation of church and state was never intended to mean the separation of religiously informed moral values from the nation's laws and public policy. In fact, the phrase "separation of church and state" is not in the U.S. Constitution. As a practical matter, all governments must legislate morality in order to fulfill their God-ordained mandate to punish evildoers and reward those who do right (Rom. 13).

God expects Christians to hold their government accountable to its purpose of punishing evil and protecting society. When Christians seek to make murder, theft, rape, and racism illegal, they are not so much trying to impose their *morality* on the state as they are using the government to keep such perpetrators from imposing their *immorality* on their victims. This is not only the right of Christian citizens, but it is their responsibility and obligation.

When Christians seek to pass legislation protecting unborn children from being aborted by their mothers, they are not so much trying to impose their values on pregnant mothers as they are seeking to keep such mothers from imposing their immoral values on their unborn children, resulting in the death of these children.

A total separation of morality and politics is as harmful to moral values and public virtue as a complete dominance of a church by the state (or the state by the church) would be to all personal and religious freedom. The U.S. Constitution provides for a healthy balance in which the institutions of the church and state are kept separate, but individual citizens have the right to bring their religiously informed values to the debate on laws and public policies.

27. Should Christians Serve in the Military?

As God calls you to stand on behalf of those in danger around the world, pray about your response and choices, which could include serving as a soldier, sailor, airman, chaplain, medic, or medical assistant. An alternative to military service would be to work with any one of the numerous civilian humanitarian organizations or to serve as a missionary volunteer in ravaged areas.

You can also make a difference by committing to a regular prayer time for those in the armed forces, writing to and encouraging those in the armed forces, and regularly praying for the president and those in decision-making positions.

If we see others being brutalized and victimized, we have an obligation to defend the innocent. God tells us that He will hold us accountable if we don't "deliver those who are drawn toward death, and hold back those stumbling to the slaughter" (Prov. 24:11).

If our nation were being attacked, we would want our neighbors to defend our families, our communities, and innocent civilians. As Christians, we should want for all people the least possible amount of violence necessary to restore peace and achieve justice for the greatest number of people.

Jesus' teaching that we should turn the other cheek (Matt. 5:39) refers to a personal decision not to defend oneself and is an entirely different ethical decision than the decision to defend one's neighbors when their lives are threatened by violent assault. Once the governmental authority has endorsed the use of armed force, each Christian must make an individual decision, whether or not to participate in a particular war. Christians cannot abdicate their personal moral responsibility to the state, but our ultimate allegiance is to the Lord (Luke 20:25). The decision to participate in a particular armed conflict is not a liberal or a conservative political decision, but a right or wrong moral decision. Christians must work for peace, contend for peace, and seek to avert warfare if at all possible.

28. How Did Our Society Get So Debased in Its Ethics?

Human sinfulness: It began when Adam and Eve rebelled against God's law. This rebellion led to humankind's first murder. Cain decided that his brother's life was disposable. He killed him, buried him, and went about his business (Gen. 4:8–10).

The Supreme Court's 1973 *Roe v. Wade* decision to legalize abortion: This decision has brutalized society's understanding of the unique value of each human life. A country cannot stand by while babies are legally aborted (as they have been for more than three decades) without devaluing the societal attitude toward human life.

The culture's increasing disregard for the truth of God's Word:

- *God forbids murder* (Ex. 20:13).
- *God hates murder of the innocent* (Prov. 6:16, 17).
- *God created all human beings in His image and gave them value* (Gen. 5:1).
- *People who are infirm, mentally challenged, or physically handicapped are created by God in His own image and are equally valuable to Him; and thus, they must be to us* (Ex. 4:11; Lev. 19:14).
- *People are to show merciful care for the suffering and the weak* (Matt. 25:40).
- *We are to accept God's will for both life and death* (Luke 22:42).

29. Do Christians Oppose Stem-Cell Research?

The truth is that Christians are genuinely enthusiastic about the prospect of *adult* stem-cell research and its potential therapies to bring unheard of relief to millions of suffering people. However, we reject the immoral practice of *embryonic* stem-cell research, which causes the death of unborn babies.

As a student leader, you need to know the difference and take the lead to help others understand it, as well. There is a major distinction between *embryonic* stem cells and *adult* stem cells:

- Currently, *embryonic stem cells* can only be obtained by destroying a human life.
- *Adult stem cells* can be obtained from a person without causing harm. In contrast to embryonic stem-cell retrieval, adult stem-cell retrieval from the human body does not require the death of the person. Stem cells may be safely obtained from myriad sources, as diverse as the umbilical cord blood harvested after a baby's birth or even a person's nasal passages.

30. Is There Such a Thing as a "Technical Virgin"?

This commonality of vaguely defined sexual boundaries has helped to bring about a new pastime of sexual experimentation. The new criteria for "virginity" says that mutual genital stimulation to orgasm and oral sex are OK because those activities aren't really "sex." Those promoting this view are deluding themselves; if the activity involves a sex organ, then it is sex.

Sex was not a casual afterthought by God. It was divinely planned to be powerful and, therefore, has its own set of rules. God's intention was for this human experience to be exercised only within the nurturing confines of holy matrimony.

God intends for one man and one woman to find completion in each other through physical intimacy as they experience unity (Gen. 2:24, 25); intimate knowledge (Gen. 4:1); procreation (Gen. 1:28); delight and joy (Prov. 5:19); relaxation and satisfaction (Song 2:8–17; 4:1–16); and avoidance of sexual temptation (1 Cor. 7:2–5). Sexual experimentation may seem harmless, and it may be viewed as normal by the current culture; but that doesn't make it right.

"Technical virgins," male and female, find themselves trying to delete memories of non-intercourse and sexually related experiences from their emotional "hard drives." As they prepare to marry the one to whom they want to give their whole selves, they are fully aware that they have already given some of themselves away.

Christ-followers should ask themselves: "Am I content to live by a mere technicality?" Do we take what God says, mix in some of the culture, and come up with self-rule in sexual matters? This is what the people to whom Jesus spoke were inclined to do, and He called them on it (Matt. 5:27, 28). Jesus let them know that *physical adultery* and *adultery in the heart* were one and the same.

31. How Does a Christian Deal with Constant Temptation?

The Lord will never leave you powerless in any situation (1 Cor. 10:31). You might not be able to stop the temptations from pouring in, but you can so fill your mind and heart with God-honoring thoughts that the temptations will be overtaken and forced out. Follow Philippians 4:8. It's a prescription for spiritual and emotional health. Meditate, or think on, *whatever things are:*

True: The truth of God's Word concerning human sexuality and other important choices will never let you down. The "feel-good" lie of the culture promises satisfaction, but cannot provide it.

Noble: This is "that which has the dignity of holiness on it." The seriousness of this definition makes it easy for you to discern if a thought or action is *noble.*

Just: The Christian chooses responsibility over pleasure, serving God over satisfying self.

Pure: *Pure* thoughts are morally undefiled thoughts. Focus your thoughts and prayers on what you would be happy, and not ashamed, to present to God.

Lovely: The Greek word is *prosphiles,* and it might be paraphrased as "that which calls forth love."

Of good report: These are the inner thoughts that form the outward reputation.

Of virtue: In your studies, relationships, and daily thought life, settle for nothing less than excellence. This leaves no room for "degrees" of immoral thought or halfhearted commitment.

Praiseworthy: God's character of forgiveness, mercy, holiness, His deep abiding love for you, and the blessings of your life are worth thinking about.

When you set a habit of focusing your mind on what is *true, noble, just, pure, lovely, of good report, virtuous,* and *praiseworthy,* then you crowd out temptation. You are drawn toward the plan of God for your life and repelled by the thought of going against it. A God-focused thought life takes the destructive power out of temptation.

32. How about Those Who Haven't Heard of Jesus?

What about people who have never heard the name of Jesus before? Are they equally responsible for accepting Him? Is salvation just for those who have heard?

Dr. Bill Brown, renowned apologist, states:

> This is a very common question in relation to the issue of pluralism. Because
> we live in a world in which cultural pluralism is the norm, it has led to cul-
> tural and social tolerance. The Christian doctrine of salvation through Jesus
> Christ only is an example of the exclusive intolerance of Christianity—not a
> popular thing in a world that calls for tolerance. Because of its nature, a plu-
> ralistic society cannot tolerate intolerance. Of course, this raises the question
> of God's justice: Would a just and fair God exclude people from salvation just
> because they had not encountered the name of Christ? As far as biblical re-
> sponses go, there are several modes of thought: Universal Light, Designated
> Light, Existing Light, Greater Light, and Later Light. According to the Uni-
> versal Light view, all people will eventually be saved, as Jesus enlightens each
> person from the inside. The Designated Light view holds that God has desig-
> nated those who will be saved and has also designated those who will not be
> saved. The Existing Light view holds that those who respond positively to
> the light can be saved without further light—through revelation in creation
> and conscience. The Greater Light view holds that those who respond to the
> light they have will be given greater light. And finally, the Later Light view
> holds that God will allow those who have never heard of Christ a chance to
> hear the gospel and accept Christ.

What does all that mean? First, Christ-followers should remember the nature and
mercy of the God of the Bible: He is "not willing that any should perish but that all
should come to repentance" (2 Pet. 3:9). Second, it is plainly stated that every individual who inhabits this earth has been given the light by the Creator—both the light of
creation and the light of a conscience.

Therefore, when an individual responds and obeys the light that has been given to
him or her, God out of mercy gives more light. The apostle Paul declares: "And He
has made from one blood every nation of men to dwell on all the face of the earth,
and has determined their preappointed times and the boundaries of their dwellings, so
that they should seek the Lord, in the hope that they might grope for Him and find
Him, though He is not far from each one of us" (Acts 17:26, 27).

Jesus Himself declared, "I am the way, the truth, and the life. No one comes to the
Father except through Me" (John 14:6). As devoted followers of Jesus, we must trust
in His statements. We also know that He validated His claim by His undeniable resurrection from the dead. All other religious leaders have died, and they are still dead and
buried. Acts 4:12 declares: "Nor is there salvation in any other, for there is no other
name under heaven given among men by which we must be saved."

33. What Do I Say to a "Gay" Friend?

Christians are called upon to love and act in a redemptive manner toward people who are in a homosexual or lesbian lifestyle, but we are not to condone or accept their sexual conduct, which is clearly condemned by Scripture. How can we do this? We love the sinner but not the sin.

Pray. Ask God for a compassionate heart to share His love rather than condemn. Ask God to remove the sin in your own life, and be ready to share a testimony of God's forgiveness.

Begin with compassion. Understand that many of those in this lifestyle are blinded to the truth. Many homosexuals honestly feel they have no choice in the matter. Many young people who find themselves enmeshed in homosexuality have been molested and abused sexually by homosexuals or pedophiles. By showing genuine unconditional love, you can show the truth of God's Word and allow the Holy Spirit to do the transforming work that only He can do.

Know your stuff. Don't use phrases such as "My friend/parent/church says it's wrong." "I hear it in church." "Everyone knows it." Have clear, easily understood scriptures memorized and marked in your Bible to show to others.

Stay true to God's Word. Even when tempted to go with your emotions, remember that emotion is not the "lead dog" in life's choices. God's everlasting Word is what should lead you.

Look for ways to love people. Love those who, by their actions, make it especially difficult to love them. Write a note or send an e-mail offering to pray for their needs, encourage them, and always share personal spiritual blessings.

Don't try to go along out of curiosity, even on a dare. You don't have to experience homosexuality to help him or her. Invite him/her to church activities and secular, fun events that are neutral in the area of sexual behavior.

34. What Does the Bible Say about Masturbation?

There are no verses in the Bible that use the word "masturbation." However, we are given many biblical principles by which to judge ourselves. In adolescence, new hormonal activity begins, which produces sexual desires and tensions. The sex drive is one of the strongest desires you will ever experience, and it is the beginning of learning self-control throughout your life. While masturbation may offer temporary relief, it is not the answer to this new stage of life.

Study God's divine plan for sex in the light of your spiritual growth and development as a young adult. Consider that masturbation may increase your sexual drive, and this desire will be difficult enough to cope with and control without increasing the desire outside of the marriage relationship.

Compulsive masturbation often leads to sexual fantasy, which is a dangerous gateway to open up in a young mind. Use of pornographic materials is a common next step as the mind explores the pleasures of sex leading to an unnatural and unhealthy view of what God meant as blessed. It can be more than a bad habit; it may be a cover-up for insecurity, unhappiness, loneliness, anger, or a lack of direction in life. The compulsion leads to withdrawal and low self-esteem, causing the person to miss out on healthy relationships.

Temptation is inevitable. If sexual desire is overwhelming to you, change your social habits and reading materials; get into sports activities and vigorous physical exertion; set new goals and develop hobbies and interests. Healthy friendships and family relationships are essential, as is a guarded mind and spiritual growth.

Wisely seek out a qualified Christian—parent, pastor, counselor, teacher—and talk this out. The guilt you may feel becomes a negative cycle causing you to withdraw and leads to more loneliness and often more masturbation. Exchange your thoughts of how sex is portrayed in the media for the beautiful and honorable portrayal found in God's Word. "Be transformed by the renewing of your mind" (Rom. 12:2). Ask yourself, "Is the lifestyle I have chosen moving me toward being an emotionally healthy, and spiritually empowered Christ-follower?"

35. What Do I Do if I Am Pregnant?

- *Know that you are carrying in your body a baby who was crafted by God's own hands.* Your baby may be an accident to you, but he or she is not an accident to God.
- *Remember that God's love for you and your baby is unchangeable.* His complete forgiveness covers any sin. God offers you the power to face life, to complete your decision, and to live a wonderful future.
- *Go to your parents; they are God's protection and authority in your life.* They love you, and they will be there for you. If you honestly cannot go to your parents alone, contact your youth minister or pastor.
- *Remember that abortion is not birth control,* but God's mercy is ready to walk alongside you.
- *Contact a Christian pregnancy center* that will help you with counseling, Bible study, parenting advice, and physical needs for you and your baby. Take your parents with you for counseling as you consider the options: to keep the baby or to give the baby up for adoption.

36. What Is a "Call to the Ministry"?

All Christ-followers are called to be "on mission"; and whatever occupation we choose, we must make our lives count for Him. What can be confusing is knowing whether you are called to serve in *full-time* ministry. Every call will be unique because God's plan for you is personal. Know that He wants you to do His will more than you want to do it, and He will provide clear guidance (Ps. 32:8) through spiritual gifts (1 Cor. 12:8–10, 28–30) and by encouraging certain feelings within you. The word translated "work" in Philippians 2:12 and 13 comes from the Greek word *energo,* which is where our word "energy" comes from. God will energize you to find and do His will and will give you the *desire* to minister with your gifts.

- Character is given prominence over talent in the list of ministry qualifications (1 Tim. 3:1–7).
- Take a spiritual gifts test, a personality profile, and a personal talent inventory (Matt. 25:14–30). What do you like to do?
- Begin now to faithfully use the talents you have (Matt. 25:23).
- Make a list of vocations that utilize your talents and skills, but be open to new possibilities. A call to ministry is not confined to preaching.
- Talk to those already in ministry and ask for wisdom (1 Sam. 3:7–19).
- Develop a prayer life of faith (Prov. 3:5, 6). One cannot know the mind of God without being filled with the Spirit through prayer and study of His Word.
- Don't grieve the Holy Spirit of God, for it is He who will guide you into all truth (John 16:13) and teach you all things (John 14:26).
- Willingness to sacrifice self and serve others precedes the call "to minister"— literally, *to serve.*
- Live with the goal of daily virtue and excellence. You can only plan for tomorrow what you are willing to do for God today.
- Know that before God calls you to a position, He calls you to Himself in worship.
- Peace does not precede a decision to obey the Lord; it is the product of (comes after) obeying His voice and guidance.

37. When Does Human Life Begin?

The debate in our culture and in our government roars on as to when life begins. Science tells us that when the male's sperm combines with the female's egg within the fallopian tube, the miracle of life begins. Almost all the distinctive traits, including the baby's gender, are determined at the moment of conception. The talents and traits that make us different from our biological siblings are decided at that moment. Reason and culture tell us that if a pregnancy is unwanted, it can be labeled as a "fetus" rather than a "baby."

The most important absolute truth that you must know if you are to accurately and clearly explain that life begins at conception is this: ***The Bible makes no distinction between the humanity and personhood of the unborn and the born.***

- The Greek word used for "babe" to describe the unborn child in the womb of Elizabeth is *brephos* (Luke 1:44).
- The same word is used to describe the baby Jesus, born in the manger (Luke 2:16).

- *Brephos* is used in speaking of Timothy as a "child" learning the Scriptures (2 Tim. 3:15).
- The final word belongs to the One who created life. Only He really knows, and He is talking:
- *God's involvement in an individual's human conception begins in the womb* (Is. 44:24).
- *God ordains a unique life purpose while a human is in the womb* (Jer. 1:5).
- *Each unborn child is uniquely and carefully formed by God* (Ps. 139:13).
- *With detailed preparation, planning, and participation, God gives the unborn child specific personal attributes* (Ps. 139:16).
- *God's personal involvement in a person's life begins in the womb* (Luke 1:15).

38. Why Is It Important to Go to Church?

The New Testament word translated "church" referred to an assembly of people "called out" from their homes to the gathering place for discussion; it was used of Christians who came together for public worship and teaching. The word is used many times in the New Testament to describe both the church throughout the ages and a local congregation meeting regularly for worship. See, for example, the epistles written to believers in Corinth, Galatia, Philippi, and Ephesus.

Believers love the church because Jesus loves it and gave Himself for it (Eph. 5:25), founded the church and calls it His (Matt. 16:18), and is the Head of the church (Col. 1:18). Believers are committed to the local church because of its purpose as Christ's appointed instrument for fulfilling the Great Commission through preaching, teaching, discipling, baptizing, and ministering (Matt. 28:19, 20). Paul went from city to city preaching the gospel of Christ and founded churches in those cities to carry on the work. The church is "the pillar and ground of the truth" (1 Tim. 3:15) and a place where hearts and resources are shared (Acts 4:32). The church is a place where Christians join with others to worship, to gain encouragement, to serve, and to be faithful. It is not to be forsaken (Heb. 10:25).

Finally, to be a Christ-follower is to walk in His example: "And as His custom was, He went into the synagogue on the Sabbath day" (Luke 4:16). Not everyone who belongs to a church is a true Christ-follower; but every believer should belong to a visible, New Testament-believing congregation called a church.

24/7 COUNSELOR:TOPICAL INDEX

Topic	Key Scriptures	Related Article Page Numbers
Abortion	Gen. 1:26–28; Ex. 21:22–25; Ps. 139; Prov. 31:8, 9; Is. 49:1–5; Jer. 1:4, 5; Luke 1:15	102, 1576, 1590, 1597
Anger	Ps. 30:5; Matt. 5:22; Rom. 12:19; Eph. 4:26	18, 1198, 1261, 1575
Anxiety	Ps. 55:22; John 14:27; 16:33; Rom. 8:28; Phil. 4:6, 7	1078
Attitude	Ps. 23; 25:9; 149:4; Prov. 14:13; 23:7; Matt. 5:3–11; 18:3, 4; 23:12; John 15:9–11; Gal. 5:22; Phil. 4:11–13; Heb. 12:2; James 1:2–5; 4:10; 1 Pet. 1:6–8	40, 98, 640, 943, 1076, 1101, 1112, 1116, 1308, 1413, 1429, 1459, 1502
Boredom	Ps. 42:1, 2; Prov. 6:6–11; Matt. 5:3, 6	1348
Calling	Ex. 3:4–20; Is. 6:1–8; Jer. 1:4–10; Matt. 4:18–22	75, 93, 291, 621, 994, 1072, 1163, 1260, 1459, 1597
Character	Ps. 78:72; 84:11; Is. 32:17; Matt. 5:6; Rom. 3:3–5; Col. 15:33	591, 695, 717, 1065, 1163, 1413, 1416
Comfort	Ps. 34:18; 55:22; Nah. 1:7; Matt. 28:22	1069, 1245, 1318
Communication	Prov. 15:1; Matt. 12:36, 37; Eph. 4:15, 25, 29, 31, 32; Col. 4:6	1182, 1498